NATIONAL SECURITY LAW

Aspen Casebook Series

NATIONAL SECURITY LAW

Seventh Edition

Stephen Dycus
Professor of Law
Vermont Law School

William C. Banks
Board of Advisors Distinguished Professor Emeritus
Syracuse University College of Law

Peter Raven-Hansen
Glen Earl Weston Research Professor of Law Emeritus
George Washington University School of Law

Stephen I. Vladeck
A. Dalton Cross Professor in Law
University of Texas School of Law

Wolters Kluwer

Published by Wolters Kluwer in New York.

Wolters Kluwer Legal & Regulatory U.S. serves customers worldwide with CCH, Aspen Publishers, and Kluwer Law International products. (www.WKLegaledu.com)

To contact Customer Service, e-mail customer.service@wolterskluwer.com, call 1-800-234-1660, fax 1-800-901-9075, or mail correspondence to:

Wolters Kluwer
Attn: Order Department
PO Box 990
Frederick, MD 21705

Printed in the United States of America.

1 2 3 4 5 6 7 8 9 0

ISBN 978-1-5438-0679-3

Library of Congress Cataloging-in-Publication Data

Names: Dycus, Stephen, author. | Banks, William C., author. | Raven-Hansen, Peter, 1946- author. | Vladeck, Stephen I., author.
Title: National security law / Stephen Dycus, Professor of Law, Vermont Law School; William C. Banks, Director, Institute for National Security and Counterterrorism (INSCT), Board of Advisors Distinguished Professor, Syracuse University; Peter Raven-Hansen, Glen Earl Weston Research Professor of Law Emeritus, George Washington University; Stephen I. Vladeck, A. Dalton Cross Professor of Law, University of Texas School of Law.
Description: Seventh edition. | New York : Wolters Kluwer, [2020] | Series: Aspen casebook series | Includes index. | Summary: “Casebook for courses on National Security Law” — Provided by publisher.
Identifiers: LCCN 2020005289 (print) | LCCN 2020005290 (ebook) | ISBN 9781543806793 (hardcover) | ISBN 9781543821000 (epub)
Subjects: LCSH: National security — Law and legislation — United States. | LCGFT: Casebooks (Law)
Classification: LCC KF4651 .N377 2020 (print) | LCC KF4651 (ebook) | DDC 343.73/01 — dc23
LC record available at https://lccn.loc.gov/2020005289
LC ebook record available at https://lccn.loc.gov/2020005290

About Wolters Kluwer Legal & Regulatory U.S.

Wolters Kluwer Legal & Regulatory U.S. delivers expert content and solutions in the areas of law, corporate compliance, health compliance, reimbursement, and legal education. Its practical solutions help customers successfully navigate the demands of a changing environment to drive their daily activities, enhance decision quality and inspire confident outcomes.

Serving customers worldwide, its legal and regulatory portfolio includes products under the Aspen Publishers, CCH Incorporated, Kluwer Law International, ftwilliam.com and MediRegs names. They are regarded as exceptional and trusted resources for general legal and practice-specific knowledge, compliance and risk management, dynamic workflow solutions, and expert commentary.

To our teachers

SUMMARY OF CONTENTS

CONTENTS

PREFACE

Even after 30 years and six earlier editions, we find that preparing a new edition of this casebook is just as challenging and as rewarding as ever. Recent judicial rulings, legislative initiatives, and executive reforms — or the lack thereof — have refined our understanding of structures, processes, and institutions for national security and counterterrorism. They have also raised critically important new questions. So have the emergence of new threats and breathtaking advances in technology. And the election of President Donald Trump has brought dramatic changes in executive branch decisionmaking. All of these developments, furthermore, have come with unprecedented speed. Some of the materials presented here became available just days before this new book went to press.

In this edition we debut a chapter on nuclear war. While the threat posed by nuclear weapons is not new, global dynamics and the Trump administration's decision to withdraw from existing nuclear agreements has prompted us to call attention to the many legal challenges in preventing nuclear war. At the same time, the pace of change in cyber capabilities — for the good guys and the bad guys — has prompted major revisions to the cyber operations chapter. Apparent Russian preparations to attack critical U.S. infrastructure raise new legal questions about evolving U.S. cyber security efforts, including Defense Department plans to "defend forward" to stop malicious cyber intrusions outside existing armed conflicts. In a similar vein, new technologies to detect security threats and to evade detection have required important revisions and updates to the intelligence chapters.

Meanwhile, separation of powers disputes in national security law have become headline news. In this edition we present a detailed treatment of the Trump administration travel bans, the outcome of which turned in part on interpretation of the Immigration and Nationality Act, and in part on the Supreme Court's view of the judicial role in disputes purporting to implicate national security. We have also developed a powerful case study and extended treatment of the congressional defense appropriations powers alongside President Trump's determination to build a wall along our southern border based in part on his constitutional and statutory emergency powers. Last but certainly not least, congressional investigations of Russian interference in the 2016 elections and beyond have generated unprecedented clashes, described here, between the Executive and House of Representatives over access to information that may be critical for national security.

In this new edition we have refined our Framework chapters in an effort to make them easier to navigate. Thus, for the first time, we have omitted *The Steel Seizure Case* (although we will leave our lengthy edit of it on the casebook's website for those who can't let go) in favor of shorter excerpts in the chapters on presidential and congressional powers. We have expanded the discussion of emergency and appropriations powers to keep abreast of current events, and we have substituted a new case on justiciability to streamline the chapter on courts.

The continuing rapid growth of the field underscores one of the main challenges to teaching and learning national security law. The original sources included here — judicial opinions, statutes, executive orders, and the like — often lack clarity or coherence, and they typically raise as many questions as they answer. We nevertheless rely on such materials because they are the stock in trade of lawyers working in the field and of political decision makers. They reflect the state of the law, such as it is, and they illustrate the law's very dynamic character.

A mastery of this subject necessarily requires considerable patience and devotion. In this edition of the casebook we have redoubled our efforts to guide students and faculty alike in their study. Even a book as up to date as this one is, however, unavoidably incomplete. Courts continue to write opinions at a rapid clip, new sausage is being made (if at a somewhat slower pace) up on the Hill, and officials in the defense and intelligence communities scramble to respond to a bewildering variety of new security threats. Constant attention to these developments is essential.

We therefore urge our students to read a national newspaper every day, and in most classes a discussion of current events lends a special sense of urgency to our assigned readings. Further updates are provided by annual published supplements to this casebook and by additional edited original materials that will be made available to teachers on the book's web site throughout each year.

Perhaps because of the importance of the subject matter, hardly any course in the curriculum is likely to provoke stronger feelings or more spirited debate. In our classrooms we encourage that debate, while at the same time demanding respect for everyone's opinions. So in this casebook we have tried to fuel that debate by fairly presenting both sides of the most contentious issues. We also have repeatedly stressed the strong interdependence of law and policy, and of the critical role of politics in shaping and implementing law. We have opinions, too, however, and we dare not hope that we have always been politically or ideologically neutral. We only wish to emphasize that national security is too important to be left to either "conservative" or "liberal" characterizations. Good legal analysis and the nation's future security depend on a careful consideration of all points of view.

In spite of — and perhaps because of — its inherent difficulty and political sensitivity, we believe that teaching and learning National Security Law will be more fun and more rewarding than ever in the years to come. And we hope that this book contributes to the indispensable work that lawyers do in keeping this nation safe and free. As always, we welcome your feedback and suggestions.

Stephen Dycus
William C. Banks
Peter Raven-Hansen
Stephen I. Vladeck

December 2019

ACKNOWLEDGMENTS

Stephen Dycus owes a special debt of gratitude to Alan B. Sherr and the late Reverend William Sloane Coffin Jr., whose independent, nearly simultaneous suggestions provided the genesis for this book. I am also especially grateful to my wife Elizabeth for her many sacrifices during its preparation. Thanks are due to Dean Jesse H. Choper and the faculty at Boalt Hall and to the late William A. Brockett for their hospitality during a sabbatical leave, to Colonel Dennis R. Hunt and the faculty of the Law Department at the U.S. Military Academy, West Point, and to my colleagues at Vermont Law School. I also want to recognize the contributions of a long succession of bright, energetic research assistants, now too numerous to list here individually. Finally, I am grateful for the opportunity to undertake this work with four wonderful coauthors, who have become best friends in the process.

William Banks dedicates this edition to the memory of Brady Howell, a former National Security Law student and victim of the September 11 attack on the Pentagon. Thanks to the law and graduate students at Syracuse who have helped test drive many of these materials over the years, through successive editions. Thanks as well to a group of fine research assistants who supported my work on this and earlier editions, most recently Jake Saracino. The best part of this project has always been working with the finest co-authors and best friends any of us could ask for. We continue the good fortune of having Steve Vladeck on our team, and all of us know that Steve Dycus makes everything we write a little better. Thanks, too, to my wife, Cheryl, whose patience and encouragement has been so important.

Peter Raven-Hansen thanks George Washington University Law School students Christine Chen and Kristianna Anderson, and their many able and careful predecessors, for invaluable research and editorial assistance. Thank you, too, to my friends and co-authors for keeping this project fun and challenging (and to Steve Vladeck for raising our average national security IQ by double digits). Special thanks and respect to our commander in chief, Steve Dycus, who led this time from multiple locations. Without him, there would be no book, let alone seven editions. Finally, thank you, as always, to my wife Winnie for enduring (but encouraging) yet another edition.

Steve Vladeck thanks his co-authors, colleagues, and friends, Bill Banks, Steve Dycus, and Peter Raven-Hansen, for their camaraderie, collegiality, tutelage, and patience — and for providing a model of scholarly engagement and pedagogical thoughtfulness to which we all can and should aspire. He also thanks Ward Farnsworth, Dean of the University of Texas School of Law, for his unwavering support; his research assistants, especially Rachael Jensen, University of Texas School of Law

Class of 2020; and, most importantly, his family — Karen, Madeleine, Sydney, and Roxy — for everything that can't be put into words.

This work would not have been started and could not have been completed without the efforts of our esteemed original co-author, Arthur Berney. Arthur thinks and writes with piercing clarity. He has provided inspiration and moral leadership for the book. He is kind to a fault, yet stubborn when it comes to speaking the truth. In the Preface to the First Edition he wrote, "I did what little I could" to promote understanding of the work of lawyers as peacemakers. He was far too modest. We remain enormously grateful to Arthur for his original contributions and for his continuing friendship.

Together, the authors deeply appreciate the support and encouragement of the staff at Little, Brown and Wolters Kluwer, especially our longtime Editor and Publisher Carol McGeehan, our former Senior Managing Editor John Devins, our current Managing Editor for Legal Education Jeff Slutzky, and our marvelous Production Editor, Patrick Cline and Copy Editor, Renee Cote.

The authors also gratefully acknowledge permission to reprint excerpts or to reproduce images from the following:

Abrams, Floyd. Telegram from John Mitchell.

Carroll Publishing. Chart on organization of the intelligence community (2005). Reprinted by permission of Carroll Publishing.

Curator, Supreme Court of the United States. Image of Justice Jackson.

Getty Images. *Vietnam Veterans Memorial Wall, Washington, DC.* Photo by Joe Guetzloff.com.

Inglesby, Thomas, Rita Grossman & Tara O'Toole, *A Plague on Your City: Observations from TOPOFF,* 32 Clinical Infectious Diseases 436 (2001). Copyright © 2001 by The University of Chicago Press. Reprinted by permission of the authors and Oxford University Press.

Ken Heinen. *Associate Justice Lewis F. Powell Jr.* Copyright © 1986 by Ken Heinen.

National Archives and Records Administration. *Japanese-American heads of families line up for relocation, San Francisco, 1942.*

National Security Archive. Image of Elvis Presley and President Nixon.

Steven Starr, Lynn Eden & Theodore A. Postol, *What Would Happen If an 800-Kiloton Nuclear Warhead Detonated Above Midtown Manhattan?,* Bull. Atomic Scientists, Feb. 25, 2015. Copyright © 2015 by the Bulletin of the Atomic Scientists.

EDITORS' NOTE

In general we have adhered to the rules for citation of authority followed by most lawyers and courts. They are set out in *The Bluebook: A Uniform System of Citation* (20th ed. 2015). For reasons of economy we have omitted without notation many citations within excerpted materials, and we have removed almost all parallel citations. We have, on the other hand, sought to provide citations that will enable readers to locate and review original sources. We have included URLs for many materials available online, but not for those easily located by a Google search.

To make it easier to refer back to materials where they were originally published, we have preserved original footnote numbers in all excerpted materials. Editors' footnotes are numbered consecutively throughout each chapter. Additions to quoted or excerpted materials are enclosed in brackets.

NATIONAL SECURITY LAW

Introduction

The law spoke too softly to be heard amidst the din of arms.

Plutarch, Lives: Caius Marius[1]

A. PURPOSES

There is no field of legal study more critical to the well-being of our people or our republic than National Security Law. In an ever more dangerous world, an inadequate national defense would jeopardize our lives and ideals. Yet measures taken in the name of national security sometimes pose comparable threats to those same ideals of liberty and justice. This irony has not escaped the attention of the Supreme Court:

> [T]his concept of "national defense" cannot be deemed an end in itself, justifying any exercise of legislative power designed to promote such a goal. Implicit in the term "national defense" is the notion of defending those values and ideals which set this Nation apart. For almost two centuries, our country has taken singular pride in the democratic ideals enshrined in its Constitution.... It would indeed be ironic if, in the name of national defense, we would sanction the subversion of one of those liberties... which make the defense of the Nation worthwhile. [*United States v. Robel*, 389 U.S. 258, 264 (1968).]

President Ronald Reagan described the goal of national defense this way: "The primary objective of U.S.... security policy is to protect the integrity of our democratic institutions... embodied in the Declaration of Independence and the Constitution." National Security Decision Directive 238, *Basic National Security Strategy*, Sept. 2, 1986, http://www.reagan.utexas.edu/archives/reference/Scanned%20NSDDS/NSDD238.pdf. The delicate balance of liberty and security must be appraised and learned, and learned again, by each generation of students and teachers. One purpose of this book is to study that balance.

---

1. John Langhorne & William Langhorne, trans. (n.d.).

It might appear that national security issues have taken center stage in our national life only since the 9/11 terrorist attacks. In fact, they have held that position periodically throughout our history. In the first 75 years of the Republic, the federal courts unhesitatingly, though infrequently, grappled with core issues of national defense — the existence, legality, and scope of war and military authority. Congress and the Executive closely debated questions of war power and foreign policy, not just because they were conscious of setting precedent, but also because each assumed an independent constitutional duty to consider the legality of executive conduct. No one called the resulting body of law — articulated in relatively few judicial opinions and laid bare in a larger number of congressional debates — "national security law." The makers of this law simply applied their evolving understanding of the constitutional framework and their ordinary legal skills to the problems of security as these presented themselves.

Seven major wars in a little more than a century (including the first one ever lost — or at least not won — by American forces), the prolonged tension of the Cold War, the specter of a nuclear holocaust, the unstable post — Cold War world, and the rise of transnational terrorism at home and abroad have changed the way we approach national security law. Today, the lines between foreign and domestic issues of national security, and even between peace and war, have seriously eroded: every foreign affairs issue has domestic ramifications, and the country lives in a seemingly permanent state of war. In 2012, the National Intelligence Council issued a report titled *Global Trends 2030: An Alternative World* (Dec. 2012). It describes megatrends and tectonic geopolitical shifts that the Council believes may shape our increasingly fraught national security affairs. It also warns us to be on the lookout for potential "black swans" — outlier events outside the scope of traditional planning that might cause massive disruptions to American society.

This state of affairs has empowered and perhaps emboldened the Commander in Chief — the President — to stake out national security as executive domain. Justice Stewart noted as much when he said executive power "in the two related fields of national defense and international relations[,] . . . largely unchecked by the Legislative and Judicial branches, has been pressed to the very hilt since the advent of the nuclear missile age." *New York Times Co. v. United States,* 403 U.S. 713, 727 (1971) (Stewart, J., concurring). A second purpose of our study is therefore to examine the constitutional distribution of decision-making authority among the branches of government in our democracy. This has become even more important amidst concerns that an aggressive executive branch is challenging the informal understandings that have historically shaped that distribution.

Despite these developments, or perhaps because of them, the judiciary's ability and responsibility to answer questions involving national security claims has grown increasingly unpredictable, even for some questions that it squarely addressed earlier in our nation's history. In some contemporary contexts, courts seem willing to tackle fundamental questions of national security law; in others, they seem all too content to stay their hand. Congress, too, with but few exceptions, has tended to shy away from serious debate of the same questions in recent years. Ironically, it has sometimes done so by asserting that such questions are for the courts, not for Congress, to resolve. More often, it has simply avoided the questions by acquiescing in executive conduct, even while criticizing that conduct publicly. If it is true, as Justice Black said, that "[t]he word 'security' is a broad, vague generality," *id.* at 719 (Black, J., concurring), it nonetheless has today assumed a talismanic quality that often mesmerizes the courts into inaction, quiets congressional debate, and sometimes persuades the executive to think of national security as an end in itself.

Another major purpose of this book is to demonstrate that national security is no talisman.

> [T]he concept of military necessity is seductively broad, and has a dangerous plasticity. Because they invariably have the visage of overriding importance, there is always a temptation to invoke security "necessities" to justify an encroachment upon civil liberties. For that reason, the military-security argument must be approached with a healthy skepticism. . . . [*Brown v. Glines*, 444 U.S. 348, 369 (1980) (Brennan, J., dissenting).]

We hope to encourage that skepticism by using ordinary legal skills to help find answers to questions about national security. Not all answers, of course; not always comforting answers either, because security concerns are always factors that weigh in legal analysis.

Relatively few of these answers are to be found in reported judicial opinions addressing national security. Such opinions are "rare, episodic, and afford little precedential value for subsequent cases," given their typically narrow and contextually limited holdings. *Dames & Moore v. Regan*, 453 U.S. 654, 661 (1981). We do try to demonstrate, however, that legal analysis is important and sometimes decisive outside of the courtroom and appellate opinions, and that legal questions of national security do not lose their urgency just because courts will not answer them. Legal analysis figures prominently in dialogues both within and between the political branches. In that nonjudicial setting, they are not so much answered authoritatively as temporarily negotiated. But legal analysis, with an appreciation for the constitutional framework of our system, is crucial in formulating the negotiating positions, defining terms of the dialogue, and memorializing the bargains that are struck.

The failure of courts to give authoritative answers to many questions of national security law suggests to some that public opinion is what ultimately counts in this field.

> In the absence of governmental checks and balances present in other areas of our national life, the only effective restraint upon executive policy and power in the areas of national defense and international affairs may lie in an enlightened citizenry — in an informed and critical public opinion which alone can here protect the values of democratic government. [*N.Y. Times*, 403 U.S. at 728 (Stewart, J., concurring).]

Another facet of our study is therefore to explore the law governing access to the information that would enlighten citizens (and their representatives in Congress) about matters of national security. Again, ordinary legal skills and analysis, here applied by a sometimes less reluctant judiciary, are critical in weighing rights of access against the need to protect truly sensitive information.

Finally, we intend to demonstrate not only that legal skills and analysis *can* be brought to bear on questions of national security, but that they *should* be. Our unabashed purpose here is to stimulate wider thought about the appropriate legal framework for national security decisions. Ultimately, the study of national security law is simply the study of how we can simultaneously protect both our security and the rule of law, mindful of the age-old admonition that "[d]angerous precedents occur in dangerous times," when it becomes the law's responsibility "calmly to poise the scales of justice, unmoved by the arm of power, undisturbed by the clamor of the multitude." *United States v. Bollman,* 24 F. Cas. 1189, 1192 (C.C.D.D.C. 1807) (No. 14,622) (Cranch, C.J., dissenting).

B. ORGANIZATION

In Part I we establish a legal framework for the study of particular national security subjects in later chapters. Starting with the text of the U.S. Constitution, we see that two centuries of interpretation have lent meaning to the often cryptic language of the founding document, but that questions still outnumber answers. We systematically examine the role that each branch of the government plays in national security matters. Separate chapters address the creation and application of international law to domestic national security law, the extraterritorial application of our law, and the content of international laws concerning resort to war and the conduct of war.

Part II of the book explores our use of force abroad. Beginning with a case study of the Vietnam War, this part of the book then successively considers collective self-defense, unilateral self-defense, targeted killings, peace operations and humanitarian interventions, cyber operations, and nuclear war. Part III deals with intelligence operations, intelligence collection, electronic surveillance, and screening for security, related subjects that sometimes bring the President and Congress into conflict, but that, especially after the 2013 disclosures of controversial NSA surveillance programs by Edward Snowden, drive home the oft-intractable tension between security and privacy. Part IV addresses the detention of terrorist suspects, while Part V concerns the rules for interrogation of suspects in custody. In Part VI we consider criminal prosecution of terrorists in civilian and military courts. Part VII analyzes plans for responding to another major terrorist attack on the U.S. homeland and the domestic role of the military more generally. Finally, Part VIII addresses access to and protection of national security information, including the classification system, public access to such information by statute and other means, "leaks," and censorship.

Our hope is to provide you with a well-rounded, albeit far from comprehensive, introduction to this very dynamic field. For even after more than two centuries of experience, the field of national security law is still evolving rapidly. Patterns for controlling the nation's defense apparatus change from one presidential administration to the next, and sometimes *within* a single administration, while some of the most fundamental questions about allocation of authority remain unanswered. There are nevertheless some constant analytic approaches and underlying principles in the field. We believe that mastery of these will provide the knowledge, skills, and experience you need to play a role in the future development and refinement of U.S. national security law and policy.

PART I FRAMEWORK

2

Providing for the "Common Defence": The Original Understanding

The purpose of this chapter is to plumb the original understanding of the Constitution's allocation of national security powers. Because the text alone furnishes an incomplete record, our search for the Framers' intent requires a brief review of English history and European political theory that probably influenced the Framers, the American experience with government prior to the Constitution, records of the 1787 Convention, and the subsequent ratification debates. *See* Louis Fisher, *Presidential War Power* 1-16 (2d ed. 2004). We nevertheless begin with the text, as we must in any quest for the meaning of a written constitution.

A. THE CONSTITUTIONAL TEXT

Read the excerpts from Articles I-IV of the Constitution found in the Appendix. Try to suppress what you know about our nation's history since 1787. What are your first impressions? How is the responsibility to "provide for the common defence" allocated among the three branches of government?

Judging simply by the proportion of words, the extensive national security powers given Congress in Article I appear to overwhelm the meager listing for the President in Article II. Article I gives Congress authority to "declare War, grant Letters of Marque and Reprisal, and make Rules concerning Captures on Land and Water," which indicates some legislative role in the commitment of American armed forces to combat. Congress also is empowered to "raise and support" the armed forces (and must reappropriate funds for them at least every two years) and to "make Rules for the Government and Regulation of the land and naval Forces." In addition, Congress is authorized to "regulate Commerce with foreign Nations," to provide for the militia and for calling it forth "to execute the Laws of the Union, suppress

Insurrections, and repel Invasions," and "to make all Laws which shall be necessary and proper" for executing any power conferred by the Constitution. Other provisions, particularly the one for impeachment of the President, also suggest legislative dominance. Congress escapes subservience to the Executive by the guarantee of meeting "at least once in every Year," by the grant of immunity from arrest during a legislative session and from questioning in any other place about any speech or debate, and by the assignment to each House of control over its membership.

By contrast, the President is provided only one obvious national security power by being designated the "Commander in Chief." Moreover, the President is directed to command the armed forces only when they are "called into the actual Service of the United States." National security powers may be allocated to the President as part of the mandate to "take Care that the Laws be faithfully executed." The other Article II grants that may concern national security seem modest in comparison to powers conferred upon Congress: to appoint and receive ambassadors and ministers, to appoint other executive officers, and to make treaties (powers that are each shared with the Senate).

We now know that the judiciary may have a role in resolving disputes between the other two branches. However, aside from the reference in Article III, section 3, to the crime of treason, and the more general reference in Article III, section 2 to federal jurisdiction over all cases arising under the Constitution or other federal laws, there is no indication in the constitutional text that the judiciary is to be involved in decisions about the national defense.

Yet both the executive and the courts have played powerful roles in providing for our national security over the last two centuries. How can this history be reconciled with the language of the Constitution? Closer examination of the text reveals the potential for the allocation of national security powers actually reflected in our history. It also demonstrates the futility of trying to divine the Framers' intent from the text alone.

First, Articles I and II assign overlapping functions. For example, the President becomes a legislator of sorts when recommending to Congress "such measures as he shall judge necessary and expedient" and when vetoing bills and resolutions, subject to a two-thirds override by each chamber of Congress. Further, although Congress may tax to "provide for the common Defence" and direct how monies are spent, the President may argue that the "take Care" Clause permits him to act alone in an emergency, using unappropriated or otherwise obligated funds from the Treasury. Similarly, because the President is required to give Congress information "from time to time," he must have been expected to obtain information of interest to Congress. He may obtain the opinion in writing of the principal officer in each of the executive departments, including the Department of Defense, concerning that department's duties. Finally, while the declaration of war is textually committed to Congress, the Commander-in-Chief power could be read to enable the President to use the military to defend against an attack on the United States. Because Article I, section 10, allows a state to "engage in War" if "actually invaded, or in such imminent Danger as will not admit of delay," it seems reasonable to claim as much power for the President if the nation is attacked, when consultation with Congress is not possible or practical.

Second, the text itself is anything but precise. Many of its words are general, not self-defining, and are capable of supporting multiple meanings. Consider the power to "declare War." While the language clearly allocates control over some important aspects of national security decision making to Congress, the text does not say what constitutes a "war" or, for that matter, what it means to "declare" one. Does "war" include small-scale skirmishes, purposefully limited in duration? Does the "Marque and Reprisal" power instead cover these limited hostilities? Or should "Marque and Reprisal" be thought of as an anachronism, referring to long-abandoned state-sponsored private battles with pirates? Should "to declare" be read to give Congress merely a right to recognize an existing state of war? Or is that language intended to confer the general control over initiating war? Or something in between these polar extremes? What about uses of the military that do not create or perpetuate a state of war? To what extent does the clause giving Congress the power to "make Rules concerning Captures on Land and Water" enable Congress to control detention of persons and property during wartime? And what is the meaning of the text that empowers Congress "[t]o make Rules for the Government and Regulation" of the military? There is similar textual uncertainty about the reach of congressional fiscal powers. May Congress exercise its appropriation powers to limit executive powers? To what extent must Congress provide basic operating funds for the Executive? May funding be conditioned on compliance with congressional wishes?

Concerning presidential authority, there is also vagueness in the language of Article II, most notably the Commander-in-Chief Clause. A narrow reading of that provision indicates no policy-making authority and relegates the President to the status of first general. A broad reading of Article II, on the other hand, combined with a restrictive reading of Article I — the Declaration, Marque and Reprisal, and Rules and Regulation Clauses — would expand the Commander-in-Chief power to include all military actions not unequivocally given to Congress. A similar range of constructions may be afforded the "take Care" language, the power to "receive Ambassadors and other public Ministers," and the statement in Article II, section 1, vesting "[t]he executive Power" in the President. Because the parallel Article I language vests in Congress "[a]ll legislative Powers herein granted," the omission of the words "herein granted" from the text of Article II could be construed to allow the President to do virtually anything "executive" in nature, so long as such action is not assigned exclusively to Congress by explicit Article I language. *See* Alexander Hamilton, *Pacificus No. 1*, Gazette of the United States (Philadelphia), June 29, 1793, *reprinted in* 15 *The Papers of Alexander Hamilton* 33-43 (Harold C. Syrett ed., 1969).

Third, the text fails altogether to prescribe or allocate power over some important areas of national security. For example, while Article I, section 9, forbids suspending the privilege of the writ of habeas corpus "unless when in Cases of Rebellion or Invasion the public Safety may require it," the text does not say who possesses the power to suspend the writ or to assess when the prescribed conditions are satisfied. In addition, the meager text is by itself inadequate for deciding the scope and locus of authority for deploying American troops abroad or in defense of the homeland, contracting for private or foreign fighting forces, engaging in covert paramilitary actions (or, for that matter, any intelligence activities), interdicting convoys, engaging in airlifts or blockades, or threatening or promising to do any of the above.

May Congress delegate power to the President? In part because there is no explicit rule in the text forbidding congressional delegations to the executive, such delegations have been routinely upheld. But how far may Congress go in delegating its own powers? May the power to declare war be delegated, or would such a wholesale transfer violate the Constitution? The text itself provides little guidance, although the structure of the Constitution may be read to forbid such a sweeping delegation. When Congress merely remains silent while the President takes some national security initiative committed by the Constitution to Congress, is the President acting legally? The answer depends on the construction given to the vague text, since the Constitution fails to describe the effect of legislative inaction. What if the President acts unilaterally in an area not explicitly prescribed or allocated by the Constitution to any branch?

All these uncertainties provoke spirited debates at both ends of Pennsylvania Avenue and among academics. Most national security disputes are resolved in the political process. But when persuasion fails, and the political process will not yield a clear or generally acceptable answer, these disputes end up in court, where the Framers arguably meant for them to be resolved.

Fortunately, the three branches have usually cooperated in making and carrying out national security policy. The practical need for effective administration provides an incentive for Congress to nurture executive branch cooperation. Further, the President's participation in the legislative process is textually assured through his powers to call Congress into special session, to recommend legislation, to provide information about the state of the Union, and to veto any legislative measure. At the same time, any tendency of the President to seek autonomy in the wording of ambiguous text is confined by some explicit and crucial grants to Congress — appropriations and declaration of war to name just two.

Thus, the original understanding of the allocation of national security powers cannot be derived solely from the text of the Constitution. We must broaden our search and consider what is likely to have influenced the delegates to the Philadelphia Convention: British history and European political theory, as well as seminal American events such as the Revolutionary War and earlier efforts at self-government. While the effect of these influences cannot be measured precisely in the Constitution or in the views of any single delegate, it is generally accepted that a combination of theory and practical experience weighed heavily in the plan for a new government.

B. PRE-CONSTITUTIONAL HISTORY AND POLITICAL THEORY IN EUROPE

Many of the Philadelphia delegates were well read in history and political philosophy — from ancient Greece and Rome to contemporary Continental Europe. As erstwhile Englishmen, however, the Framers turned to English ideas and experiences above all others.

It is nonetheless difficult to calculate the British influence on the Constitution and on its national security provisions in particular. The allocation of war-making and foreign affairs powers fluctuated widely in England between the fifteenth and eighteenth centuries, and the unwritten British constitution simply reflected rather than guided these changes.

In general, the Crown dominated all foreign and military affairs until the seventeenth century, when Parliament began successfully to assert its constitutional claims to power. John Locke described the early "royal prerogative" expansively:

> Where the Legislative and Executive Power are in distinct hands, . . . there the good of the Society requires, that several things should be left to the discretion of him, that has the Executive Power. For the Legislators not being able to foresee, and provide, by Laws, for all, that may be useful to the Community, the Executor of the Laws, having the power in

his hands, has by the common Law of Nature, a right to make use of it, for the good of the Society, in many Cases, where the municipal Law has given no direction, till the Legislative can conveniently be Assembled to provide for it....

This Power to act according to discretion, for the publick good, without the prescription of the Law, and sometimes even against it, *is* that which is called *Prerogative.* For since in some Governments the Law-making Power is not always in being, and is usually too numerous, and so too slow, for the dispatch requisite to Execution ... there is a latitude left to the Executive power, to do many things of choice, which the Laws do not prescribe....

The old Question will be asked in this matter of *Prerogative,* But *who shall be Judge* when this Power is made a right use of? I Answer: Between an Executive Power in being, with such a Prerogative, and a Legislative that depends upon his will for their convening, there can be no *Judge on Earth:* As there can be none, between the Legislative, and the People, should either the Executive, or the Legislative, when they have got the Power in their hands, design, or go about to enslave, or destroy them. The People have no other remedy in this, as in all other cases where they have no Judge on Earth, but to *appeal to Heaven.* [John Locke, *Two Treatises of Government* 392-393, 397 (Peter Laslett ed., 1967).]

Thus, before the seventeenth-century surge in parliamentary strength, the "prerogative" powers of the Crown permitted it to exercise unilaterally, among other things, most national security powers — declaring wars, issuing letters of marque and reprisal, making treaties and appointments, and raising armies and navies. The prerogative powers were generally accepted as being free from limitation by Parliament or the courts.

From the mid-seventeenth century onward, Parliament and the Crown alternately dominated decision making about national security matters. When Parliament asserted itself it often relied on its control of the purse and its ability to obtain information from the executive. The Parliament taxed for military programs, controlled the raising and keeping of standing armies in times of peace, and successfully placed restrictive conditions on military appropriations. If the Crown ignored legislation restricting a foreign affairs initiative, the Parliament could and on occasion did resort to impeachment, dismissal, or execution. On the other hand, if Parliament was uncooperative, the Crown might secure funding for its ventures from local governments or by borrowing, and it could dismiss Parliament for any reason — if Parliament had not acted first. Further, secret initiatives were sometimes undertaken, and information was often withheld from Parliament under a claim of executive discretion.

In addition to their legacy of shifting royal and parliamentary powers, which had so affected war-making and foreign affairs, the British brought with them theoretical principles central to their own constitutional development that greatly influenced the Americans. The most important intellectual contribution was the idea of separation of powers. The theory of separation assigned different powers to different institutions and persons in government in order to forestall tyranny, to promote the government's legitimacy, and to make government more efficient. John Locke, writing between 1679 and 1683, relied on his theory of separation to advance the argument for the Whig view of government. His ideas significantly influenced constitutional development in England and in America.

In all Cases, whilst the Government subsists, *the Legislative is the Supream Power.* For what can give Laws to another, must needs be superiour to him....

But because the Laws, that are at once, and in a short time made, have a constant and lasting force, and need a *perpetual Execution,* or an attendance thereunto: Therefore 'tis

> necessary there should be a *Power always in being*, which should see to the *Execution* of the Laws that are made, and remain in force. And thus the *Legislative* and *Executive Power* come often to be separated.
>
> There is another *Power* in every Commonwealth, which one may call *natural*, because it is that which answers to the Power every Man naturally had before he entered into Society. For though in a Commonwealth the Members of it are distinct Persons still in reference to one another, and as such are governed by the Laws of Society; yet in reference to the rest of Mankind, they make one Body, which is, as every Member of it before was, still in the State of Nature with the rest of Mankind. Hence it is, that the Controversies that happen between any Man of the Society with those that are out of it, are managed by the publick; and an injury done to a Member of their Body, engages the whole in the reparation of it. So that under this Consideration, the whole Community is one Body in the State of Nature, in respect of all other States or Persons out of its Community.
>
> This therefore contains the Power of War and Peace, Leagues and Alliances, and all the Transactions, with all Persons and Communities without the Commonwealth, and may be called *Federative*, if any one pleases. So the thing be understood, I am indifferent to the Name.
>
> These two Powers, *Executive* and *Federative*, though they be really distinct in themselves, yet one comprehending the *Execution* of the Municipal Laws of the Society *within* its self, upon all that are parts of it; the other the management of the *security and interest of the publick without*, with all those that it may receive benefit or damage from, yet they are always almost united. And though this *federative Power* in the well or ill management of it be of great moment to the Commonwealth, yet it is much less capable to be directed by antecedent, standing, positive Laws, than the *Executive;* and so must necessarily be left to the Prudence and Wisdom of those whose hands it is in, to be managed for the publick good. For the *Laws* that concern Subjects one amongst another, being to direct their actions, may well enough *precede* them. But what is to be done in reference to *Foreigners*, depending much upon their actions, and the variation of designs and interests, must be *left* in great part *to* the *Prudence* of those who have this Power committed to them, to be managed by the best of their Skill, for the advantage of the Commonwealth.
>
> Though, as I said, the *Executive* and *Federative Power* of every Community be really distinct in themselves, yet they are hardly to be separated, and placed, at the same time, in the hands of distinct Persons. For both of them requiring the force of the Society for their exercise, it is almost impracticable to place the Force of the Commonwealth in distinct, and not subordinate hands; or that the *Executive* and *Federative Power* should be *placed* in Persons that might act separately, whereby the Force of the Publick would be under different Commands: which would be apt sometime or other to cause disorder and ruine. [Locke, *supra*, at 382-386.]

The judicial power was born as the third real power in England when Parliament assured the independence of the judges from the King's previously unfettered control over their removal. Yet the judges still were viewed as executive officers while in office. It was Montesquieu in his *Spirit of Laws*, published in 1748, who provided the theoretical challenge to the distinct federative power of the executive described by Locke. Montesquieu's theory subdivided the federative and the law enforcement powers of the executive, treated the judiciary as a distinct branch, and offered the tripartite separation that is reflected in the American Constitution. For Montesquieu, the preservation of liberty required such a separation:

> When the legislative and executive powers are united in the same person, or in the same body of magistracy, there can be no liberty; because apprehensions may arise, lest the same monarch or senate should enact tyrannical laws, to execute them in a tyrannical manner.

> Again, there is no liberty, if the power of judging be not separated from the legislative and executive powers. Were it joined with the legislative, the life and liberty of the subject would be exposed to arbitrary control; for the judge would be then the legislator. Were it joined to the executive power, the judge might behave with all the violence of an oppressor. [Charles Louis de Secondat, Baron de Montesquieu, *The Spirit of Laws* 202 (David Wallace Carrithers ed., 1977).]

The problem with the separation of powers theory, however, was that it failed to account for the real class conflicts and overlapping authority that actually characterized the British system. A second theory, that of mixed government, helped to harmonize theory and practice. According to mixed government theory, balance in government could be maintained by mixing classes and institutions of society — kings, lords, and commoners — and combining various primary forms of government, namely monarchy, aristocracy, and democracy. A systematic attempt at creating "counterpoisal pressures . . . might keep the system stable and healthy." Bernard Bailyn, *The Origins of American Politics* 20 (1970). Thus, separated branches would share all the government's powers, checking against abuses by any single group in society or in government. For example, broad prerogative powers did not necessarily always belong to the King unchecked by the Parliament. The King or his ministers could be criticized or even impeached for their misuse of power. Moreover, either branch could initiate or exercise a prerogative power.

Locke recognized the importance of balancing and mixing powers when he conceded that many things must be left to executive discretion, subject to nullification or modification by legislation. For Locke, both separation of powers and mixed government served to make the King subject to the representative Parliament. Thus, assuming that both the separation and mixed government theories of Locke and Montesquieu influenced the U.S. Constitution, the ambiguities of the American text might be quite intentional reflections of the essential fluidity of these concepts.

General theories of government were not the only European notions to influence the text of the Constitution. The Framers' views of war and peace, in their declared and undeclared forms, seem to be derived especially from Grotius, Pufendorf, Vattel, and Burlamaqui, scholars of the law of nations. Charles A. Lofgren, *War-Making Under the Constitution: The Original Understanding*, 81 Yale L.J. 672, 689-697 (1972). For Grotius, declared wars were "perfect," involving committed nations in opposition. Undeclared wars were "imperfect," and occurred in situations where the sovereign authorized private reprisals aimed at claiming property held by subjects of another sovereign. Hugo Grotius, *The Rights of Wars and Peace* 538-549 (Jean Barbeyrac trans., 1738) (1625). Burlamaqui argued that imperfect war and reprisals were often one and the same, but that a sovereign might itself engage in reprisals using its own forces:

> A perfect war is that, which entirely interrupts the tranquillity of the state, and lays a foundation for all possible acts of hostility. An imperfect war, on the contrary, is that, which does not entirely interrupt the peace, but only in certain particulars, the public tranquillity being in other respects undisturbed.
>
> This last species of war is generally called reprisals, of the nature which we shall here give some account. By reprisals then we mean that imperfect kind of war, or those acts of hostility, which sovereigns exercise against each other, or, with their consent, their subjects, by seizing the persons or effects of the subjects of a foreign commonwealth, that

> refuseth to do us justice. . . . [II Jean Jacques Burlamaqui, *The Principles of Natural and Political Law* 180 (Thomas Nugent trans., 5th ed. 1807), cited with approval in *Miller v. The Resolution,* 2 U.S. (2 Dall.) 1, 21 (Ct. App. in Cases of Capture 1781).]

There was no consensus among the theorists about whether a declaration was necessary to initiate war, though no one argued that a declaration was required to wage a defensive war. Before the American Revolution, however, when such "declarations" were made, they were usually only formal, largely ceremonial announcements. Lofgren, *supra,* at 691-693.

Contemporaneous writings indicate that "a nation might 'declare' war, not only by a formal announcement, but also by an act of hostility." Michael D. Ramsey, *Textualism and War Powers,* 69 U. Chi. L. Rev. 1543, 1590 (2002). For example, Locke wrote, "The State of War is a State of Enmity and Destruction; And therefore declaring by Word or Action, not a passionate or hasty, but a sedate settled Design, upon another Man's life, puts him in a State of War with him against whom he has declared such an intention." Locke, *supra,* at 278. According to Professor Ramsey, Locke, Blackstone, and other international law scholars used "declare" to mean "an action (taking up arms) that itself makes a statement." Launching an attack could constitute "declaring" war. Ramsey, *supra,* at 1636.

War making without a formal declaration was common in the eighteenth century, some of it under the collective noses of the soon-to-be American convention delegates. Between 1754 and 1756 the undeclared beginnings of the Seven Years War between Britain and France occurred mostly on American soil, and Americans were exposed to the undeclared war between Britain and France during the Revolutionary War.

The long-standing European practice of state-sanctioned private reprisals to satisfy private claims during peacetime all but disappeared during the first half of the eighteenth century. Yet sovereign states continued to press their own claims by reprisal, either through use of public forces or private ships, or by the issuance of letters of marque and reprisal. Indeed, recent English history known to the Americans included examples of state reprisals that resulted in general war.

This history underscores the importance of the Declaration and the Marque and Reprisal Clauses in the U.S. Constitution. The Framers knew from the European experience that war might be limited or complete, that limited hostilities were often authorized through letters of marque and reprisal, and that minor skirmishes or even major ones could begin by "Word or Action," as Locke put it. Lofgren, *supra,* at 693-697.

C. THE AMERICAN EXPERIENCE PRIOR TO 1787

These British and European influences may have seemed secondary to the Framers compared with the lessons learned firsthand from state, colonial, and national governments prior to the Philadelphia Convention in 1787. Before the Revolution, the mood in the colonies was notoriously antiexecutive. While the structures of colonial governments varied, all but Connecticut and Rhode Island formally placed most of the important powers in their governors, including command of the military, a veto of legislation, authority to raise and spend funds on certain projects, and discretion to delay enforcement of legislation until approved in England. The colonial governors were mostly British agents and were widely disliked in the colonies, even though the colonists' complaints often were traceable to the actions of Parliament. Yet despite the theoretical preeminence of the governors, the legislatures dominated colonial government through fiscal initiatives, investigations, and various other measures, and they effectively controlled the governors, even in the exercise of war and foreign affairs powers.

After the Revolution, constitutional theories of separation and mixed government seem to have been ignored, as seven of the eight state governments formed between 1776 and 1778 adopted constitutions that subordinated the executive to the legislature. A second wave of state constitution-making, however, including in New York, Massachusetts, and New Hampshire, provided relatively greater authority for the governors. The new state legislatures responded early and often to popular local issues, sometimes restricting interstate commerce and undermining national stability. Eventually, as disorder and instability increased, many began to feel that a stronger national government was needed.

Again, early experiences with a national government had been marked by a pervasive antiexecutive mood. Beginning with the First Continental Congress in 1774, the national legislature was used by the states as a national executive, at first to conduct the Revolutionary War and later to manage other fiscal and national security tasks. But while Congress sought to carry out its policies through committees, boards, and appointed agents, it soon became apparent that the exigencies of the war were beyond the legislature's capacity to manage. Broad powers had to be delegated to the Board of War and to General George Washington. Nevertheless, Washington and other military leaders were often forced to choose between acting on the basis of ambiguous grants of authority or referring questions to Congress for decisions. This arrangement proved to be extremely inefficient.

> The subordination of the military to civilian control was a central axiom of the [English constitutional theory] that had led the colonists into rebellion. But broad agreement on this principle hardly provided Congress with useful guidelines for determining how direct and close its supervision of the army should be.... From 1775 to 1781, Congress was intimately concerned with the organization and administration of the army. It established rules of war and discipline, pay scales, terms of enlistment, and detailed regulations governing the procurement of supplies and provisions by the quartermaster and commissary departments; it also seemed to be regularly beset with the incessant complaints — sometimes petty, sometimes substantive, but never forgotten — of its officer corps. [Jack N. Rakove, *The Beginning of National Politics: An Interpretive History of the Continental Congress* 196-197 (1979).]

Congressional direction of the war even threatened the loyalty of its soldiers:

> Loyalty to the Congress was constantly strained but it never snapped; every soldier and officer may have cursed Congress fifty times for every word of praise, and most may have thought their hardships stemmed as much from congressional indifference, ineptness, and corruption as from unavoidable difficulties; but discontent rarely threatened to erupt into mutiny. [Forrest McDonald, *E Pluribus Unum: The Formation of the American Republic 1776-1790*, at 12 (1965).]

The Continental Congress's cumbersome executive structures and its inability to raise money for the national government led many influential Americans, including Washington and Hamilton, to urge a strengthened national executive.

One consequence of the Revolutionary War was the emergence of a decidedly American view concerning standing armies. On the one hand, the war served to remind the 1787 Convention delegates that a regular standing army was needed to enable the nation to defend itself against another nation. As Alexander Hamilton later argued, the part-time militia was not an adequate substitute for a regular army:

> These garrisons must either be furnished by occasional detachments from the militia, or by permanent corps in the pay of the government. The first is impracticable; and if practicable, would be pernicious. The militia would not long, if at all, submit to be dragged from their occupations and families to perform that most disagreeable duty in times of profound peace. And if they could be prevailed upon or compelled to do it, the increased expense of a frequent rotation of service, and the loss of labor and disconcertion of the industrious pursuits of individuals, would form conclusive objections to the scheme. It would be as burdensome and injurious to the public as ruinous to private citizens. [*The Federalist No. 24*, at 161 (Alexander Hamilton) (Clinton Rossiter ed., 1961).]

On the other hand, the Americans knew that a standing army could be dangerous if not adequately controlled. They had come to deplore the use of the British army to enforce unpopular policies. The post–Revolutionary War solution, then, was to place responsibility for control of the military in the hands of the legislature. Legislative dominance of the military could be accomplished, it was first thought, by strict control over appropriations. The state assemblies controlled the governors' use of the military by imposing conditions on supply bills and even by specifying the conduct of military operations.

D. THE FRAMERS' VIEW

The adoption of the Articles of Confederation in 1781 did little to satisfy the demand for a stronger executive. First, the states retained sovereignty except to the extent that powers were "expressly" granted to the United States. Second, while Congress was given significant powers, including "the sole and exclusive right and power of determining on peace and war," the national government had no enforcement power and no independent executive. The business of governing thus continued much as it had before, with increasing delegations over foreign and military affairs to agents such as General Washington. As the national debt grew and the states threatened the national economy by disrupting commerce, issuing paper money, and refusing to do their part in funding the national government, the national government proved unable to maintain order in the fragile Union. By early 1787 the Continental Congress could no longer ignore the demand for change.

Congress called upon the states to send delegates to a convention for the purpose of reforming the government of the Union. The 55 delegates representing all states except Rhode Island ranged from 81-year old Benjamin Franklin to John Dickinson, who had refused to sign the Declaration of Independence. Most of the delegates had served in the Continental Congress, and most were wealthy. So much a part of the American elite were the delegates that Thomas Jefferson, who was in Paris and did not attend, called the convention "really an assembly of demi-gods." Max Farrand, *The Framing of the Constitution of the United States* 39 (1913).

Widespread demand for a stronger executive forced the Philadelphia delegates to confront basic structural questions: Should the executive be one person or many? Should there be an executive veto? How should the executive be selected, and should the executive serve more than one term? An even bigger issue was how to resolve the federalism question. The federalists wanted a stronger executive than did the states' righters, later known as antifederalists. Compared to these questions, the nature and scope of specific powers for the executive, especially in relation to those of Congress, were peripheral issues in 1787. Indeed, most of the attention given by the Framers and ratifying conventions to issues of national security was directed toward national survival and state responsibilities, state incitements of other states and Indians, and state diplomatic activity.

1. The Convention

Unfortunately, records of deliberations at the Constitutional Convention are few and are unreliable. The meetings themselves were secret, and the Convention Journal recorded only formal motions and votes. Many delegates took notes. The most extensive of these were James Madison's, though his were revised 30 years after the Convention. The various sources are compiled in the four-volume Max Farrand, *The Records of the Federal Convention of 1787* (rev. ed. 1937) (hereinafter *Records*).

There was a general consensus among Convention delegates about the need for a strengthened national government. They approved the so-called Virginia Plan, drafted by Madison, to give Congress the rights vested in it by the earlier Articles of Confederation. 3 *Records, supra,* at 593. They also agreed in principle to a single executive who would have explicit powers of execution and a conditional veto over legislation. It was clear from the start that the delegates wanted to create an executive who would be more than a mere agent of the legislature. They rejected the New Jersey Plan, which would have provided for a relatively weak, plural, single-term executive, removable by a majority of the states, yet having the power "to direct all military operations." *Id.* at 611-613.

After additional debate the delegates instructed a Committee on Detail to prepare a draft Constitution. The resulting draft vested "The Executive Power of the United States . . . in a . . . President," who would be "Commander in Chief of the Army and Navy of the United States, and of the Militia of the several States." Congress was given the power to "make war," to appropriate funds, and "to call for the aid of the militia, in order to execute the laws of the Union, enforce treaties, suppress insurrections, and repel invasions." 2 *Records, supra,* at 167-172.

In the ensuing Convention debates on the draft, James Wilson of Pennsylvania opposed granting the House sole power to initiate revenue bills. Wilson's arguments and Edmund Randolph's prevailing response indicate a general understanding that the appropriations power would be employed to control the military. *Id.* at 273-274, 279.

Charles Pinckney of South Carolina complained that requiring the whole Congress to declare war would be cumbersome:

> Mr. Pinckney. . . . Its proceedings were too slow. It wd. meet but once a year. The Hs. of Reps. would be too numerous for such deliberations. The Senate would be the best depositary, being more acquainted with foreign affairs, and most capable of proper resolutions. If the States are equally represented in Senate, so as to give no advantage to large States, the power will notwithstanding be safe, as the small have their all at stake in such

> cases as well as the large States. It would be singular for one authority to make war, and another peace.
>
> Mr. Butler. The Objections agst the Legislature lie in a great degree agst the Senate. He was for vesting the power in the President, who will have all the requisite qualities, and will not make war but when the Nation will support it.
>
> Mr. M(adison) and Mr. Gerry moved to insert "*declare,*" striking out "*make*" war; leaving to the Executive the power to repel sudden attacks.
>
> Mr. Sharman thought it stood very well. The Executive shd. be able to repel and not to commence war. "Make" better than "declare" the latter narrowing the power too much.
>
> Mr. Gerry never expected to hear in a republic a motion to empower the Executive alone to declare war.
>
> Mr. Elseworth. there is a material difference between the cases of making war, and making peace. It shd. be more easy to get out of war, than into it. War also is a simple and overt declaration. peace attended with intricate & secret negociations.
>
> Mr. Mason was agst giving the power of war to the Executive, because not (safely) to be trusted with it; or to the Senate, because not so constructed as to be entitled to it. He was for clogging rather than facilitating war; but for facilitating peace. He preferred "*declare*" to "*make.*" [*Id.* at 318-319.]

In support of Madison's motion, Rufus King of Massachusetts argued "that 'make' war might be understood to 'conduct' it which was an Executive function." *Id.* at 319.

Eventually, Pinckney's motion to vest the war power solely in the Senate was overwhelmingly rejected and Madison's motion was approved. The Journal records and Madison's notes unfortunately report inconsistent tallies on the two votes taken on Madison's motion, one before and one after King's speech, making it impossible to be certain about the meaning of the change. Madison and Gerry probably wanted the President to be able to respond to "sudden attacks" without a declaration of war, which some delegates thought was intended by the original language. Others, including King, wanted to be certain it was understood that the conduct of a war after its initiation was for the executive. No better consensus from the debate can be safely stated, although nothing in the change suggests an intention to allow the President to "make" war without a declaration. *See* Abraham D. Sofaer, *War, Foreign Affairs and Constitutional Power: The Origins* 31-32 (1976). Even Hamilton, ardent advocate of a strong executive, favored limiting the executive in war making and would have given the Senate the declaration power, leaving to the President the "direction of war when authorized or begun," 1 *Records, supra,* at 292, though he knew that many contemporary wars were not technically declared. Lofgren, *supra,* at 680.

Viewing the larger debate and the process of drafting the Constitution does help place the war powers allocation question in some perspective. First, the draft presented to the Convention by the Committee on Detail assigned the power "to make war" to Congress, though the point had scarcely been debated. The same Committee named the President as Commander in Chief without any record of controversy. The President was to be first general, but was not to initiate hostilities. As for military action short of declared war, the Committee on Detail did not include in the list of powers given to the new legislature the power to issue letters of marque and reprisal, which the old Congress enjoyed under the Articles. At Pinckney's request such language was added and approved without discussion. 2 *Records, supra,* at 324, 326. We cannot ascertain from the Convention records whether this action was meant to ensure congressional primacy over undeclared hostilities. However, the contemporaneous understanding about the use of letters of marque and reprisal suggests that purpose.

Pinckney's motion to vest the war power in the Senate included granting to the Senate the power "to make treaties." 3 *Records, supra,* at 427. As in the debate on the War Declaration Clause, Madison and others eventually cautioned against unfettered Senate power over treaties. After floor discussion, in which Madison urged a role for the President out of fear of parochialism in the Senate, a committee was formed, which reported the following language: "The president, by and with the advice and consent of the Senate, shall have power to make treaties. . . . But no treaty shall be binding without the consent of two-thirds of the members present." 2 *Records, supra,* at 495. James Wilson proposed adding "and House of Representatives" after the word "Senate," on grounds that treaties should be fully sanctioned as laws if they were to operate as laws. Following objections from Robert Sherman and others that the secrecy that would necessarily attend some treaty negotiations made referral to the House impractical, Wilson's motion was defeated. *Id.* at 538. Among several other failed amendments was a proposal by Madison to permit the Senate alone to make peace treaties. Madison argued that the President "would necessarily derive so much power and importance from a state of war that he might be tempted, if authorized, to impede a treaty of peace." *Id.* at 540.

While the treaty-making powers were being shaped, the eventual Supremacy Clause was drafted to make "all treaties made and ratified under the authority of the United States," along with laws enacted by the Congress, "the supreme law." *Id.* at 28. Supported by Madison's admonition that federal dominance in foreign relations was necessary "to the efficacy and security of the general government," *id.* at 27, the Supremacy Clause became a part of the Constitution, along with the provision in Article I, section 10, restricting states from entering into treaties or entering into any "agreement or compact" with a foreign nation without the consent of Congress. Complaints from those who feared the loss of state sovereignty and from others who feared that omission of the House of Representatives from the treaty-making process could lead to abuse of the power, did not sway the delegates. Nor did the Framers prescribe any limits on the subject matter of treaties, or supply a rule for resolving a conflict between a treaty and the Constitution or the laws.

Meanwhile, the delegates were gradually constructing an executive branch that would be unitary and independent and vested with considerable authority. In keeping with their general interest in balancing the powers of government, the President's selection, vested in the Congress by the Committee on Detail, became an election by state electors for an unrestricted number of four-year terms. The President was also given a conditional veto over legislation. Once the independence of the office was established, the delegates broadened the grounds for impeachment by the legislature to provide a check in the other direction. But they voted down proposals to allow Congress to define the content of "executive power," and no general argument was advanced against Congress's ability to delegate powers to the executive. Sofaer, *supra,* at 36-38, 56. In the end, the delegates themselves did little to define the executive.

2. Ratification

There remained the difficult task of persuading the state ratifying conventions to approve the new Constitution. The ensuing debates in the states, like those in Philadelphia, scarcely addressed the question of how and by which institution the new government would initiate war. Indeed, the Confederation government already had the war-making power, and the question of initiating war was eclipsed by the more immediately volatile issues of federal, state, or civilian-military sovereignty. At the same time, there was debate about supporting an existing war through taxation, about control of the military, and about the use of standing armies.

Despite the limited debates on war-making powers, there is indirect evidence from the ratification period that reveals more clearly how the war-making provisions were understood. Because the Philadelphia debates were secret, the ratifiers themselves had to rely on the words of the Constitution and on the propaganda of the time to establish the meaning of the document.

The Federalist Papers, written by Madison, Hamilton, and Jay to promote ratification, indicate that the new war declaration clause was practically the same as the earlier Articles' grant to Congress of "determining on" war. In *The Federalist No. 41*, Madison wrote: "The existing confederation establishes this power in the most ample form." *The Federalist No. 41*, at 256 (James Madison) (Clinton Rossiter ed., 1961). Delegate Wilson made the same point at the Pennsylvania convention. He rejected the notion of a unilateral presidential power over war-making, remarking that the new "system will not hurry us into war.... It will not be in the power of a single man, or a single body of men, to involve us in such distress; for the important power of declaring war is vested in the legislature at large." 1 *Debates in the Several State Conventions on the Adoption of the Federal Constitution* 528 (Jonathan Elliot ed., 1888) (hereinafter *Elliot's Debates*).

There is similar evidence that the Commander-in-Chief power was viewed narrowly. In *The Federalist No. 69*, Hamilton compared the Commander in Chief's prerogative to that of the British Crown, finding the former "much inferior."

> It would amount to nothing more than the supreme command and direction of the military... while that of the British King extends to the *declaring* of war, and to the *raising and regulating* of fleets and armies — all which by the Constitution under consideration, would appertain to the legislature. [*The Federalist No. 69*, at 418 (Alexander Hamilton) (Clinton Rossiter ed., 1961).]

The fact that the authors of the Federalist Papers described the assignment of war powers in such terms suggests that they believed this view would be well received in the states.

Madison insisted in general argument that pure separation of the nation's powers was neither desirable nor intended by the theorists. Instead, mixed powers and checks and balances were essential:

> Ambition must be made to counteract ambition.... But what is government itself but the greatest of all reflections on human nature? If men were angels, no government would be necessary. If angels were to govern men, neither external nor internal controls on government would be necessary. In framing a government which is to be administered by men over men, the great difficulty lies in this: you must first enable the government to control the governed; and in the next place oblige it to control itself. A dependence on the people is, no doubt, the primary control on the government; but experience has taught mankind the necessity of auxiliary precautions. [*The Federalist No. 51*, at 322 (James Madison) (Clinton Rossiter ed., 1961).]

For Madison, the balance was completed by having a dominant bicameral legislature and a partial veto in the executive. The House retained the original appropriations power, while the Senate had a special role in treaties and appointments. Similarly, the strong and independent President would be able to prevent legislative tyranny. Thus, separation ensured independence while it divided responsibilities along functional lines.

To be sure, there were arguments during this period that a stronger executive would promote governmental efficiency and dispatch. For example, it might have been inferred from the proposed government's ability to raise and support armed forces, and thereby to deter a surprise attack on the United States, that the President was empowered to respond to such a sudden attack. However, the arguments based on efficiency and dispatch were not made in connection with initiating war. *See, e.g.*, *The Federalist No. 64*, at 12-13 (John Jay) (Clinton Rossiter ed., 1961) (discussing the treaty power).

During the South Carolina debate on the Constitution, convention delegate Major Pierce Butler explained that, while the initial proposal to vest the treaty power solely in the Senate was defeated as "inimical to the genious of a republic, by destroying the necessary balance," a motion to give the power to the President was overcome as "throwing into his hands the influence of a monarch, having an opportunity of involving his country in a war whenever he wished. . . ." 4 *Elliot's Debates, supra*, at 262-263. Only when it was suggested that the House of Representatives join the Senate in approving treaties was it noted that "negotiations always required the greatest secrecy, which could not be expected in a large body." *Id.*

Throughout the ratification process, the objective of the federalists was to defend the entire proposed national government, not one branch of it at the expense of another. For example, Hamilton argued that the two-year limit on military appropriations would prevent the legislature from giving the executive power to build a large standing army. But his objective was to persuade ratifiers to support the proposed new government, not to aggrandize legislative power. In addition, to the extent that the vagueness in describing the President's powers caused fears among the ratifiers, they were substantially mollified by the comforting, though unspoken, assumption that Washington would become the first President, and that he would never abuse his powers.

The ratification debates tend to confirm that the "declare" language could not fairly be read to limit Congress to formal war-initiation. No ratifier argued that the President has unilateral power to engage in hostilities without congressional approval in the absence of a sudden attack. Undeclared wars were thought to be possible, but it is not altogether clear under what circumstances and by whom they could be initiated. *See* Lofgren, *supra*, at 694-700.

New Hampshire became the necessary ninth state to ratify the Constitution in June 1788, and the new government officially commenced in March 1789. In that year, Jefferson wrote to Madison that "[w]e have already given in example one effectual check to the Dog of War by transferring the power of letting him loose from the Executive to the Legislative body, from those who are to spend to those who are to pay." 15 *The Papers of Thomas Jefferson* 397 (Julian P. Boyd ed., 1958).

Still, careful analysis of the original understanding leaves much unsettled. No provision or argument was made against legislative delegations of military matters to the executive; nor were the required indicia of a valid delegation spelled out. Similarly, there is no evidence that Congress was barred from authorizing hostilities without a declaration of war. The President's authority to "repel sudden attacks" was not clarified; nor was there any indication of what constitutes an attack, or when an attack should be considered imminent. Yet *The Federalist* strongly suggests that the textual uncertainties and overlaps in function and power were intended as an integral part of the overall design. Sofaer, *supra*, at 58-59.

Notes and Questions

1. *The Preamble.* Does the language of the Preamble to the Constitution help to describe the locus or scope of authority for keeping the nation secure? Suppose that some government action demonstrably harmed the "common defence," or threatened to do so. Could the Preamble be invoked to stop it?

2. *Textual Conflicts and Silences in the National Security Constitution.* Can you say exactly which provisions of Articles I and II might bring the President and Congress into conflict in providing for the national security, and why?

Various national defense issues are not addressed at all in the text of the Constitution. For example, may the President solicit the financial support of foreign countries for military initiatives not authorized by Congress? May the Congress authorize and appropriate funds for the purchase of military hardware and then restrict its use by the President? May the courts direct the President to disclose sensitive information about foreign affairs to Congress? How should such questions be resolved?

3. *Antiexecutive Sentiments.* Are you clear on the reasons for the strong antiexecutive sentiment in America before the 1787 Constitutional Convention? Can you see any of that sentiment reflected in the text of the Constitution or in the ratification debates? Do you see evidence of it in political debates today about national security issues?

4. *A Merely "Juridical" War Power?* Professor John Yoo maintains that the Declaration Clause reflects the Framers' understanding of eighteenth-century practice that a declaration of war is not required to authorize combat. Instead, he argues, a declaration simply reflects Congress's "judgment of a current status of relations, not an authorization of war." John C. Yoo, *The Continuation of Politics by Other Means: The Original Understanding of War Powers*, 84 Cal. L. Rev. 167, 248 (1996). According to Professor Yoo, in this role Congress performs a judicial function rather than its typical enactment of positive law. *Id.* at 248-249. How would you respond to Professor Yoo's assessment?

Professor Yoo argues further that the Constitution permits the President to initiate wars unless Congress acts through an appropriations restriction or impeachment to stop him. *Id.* at 174. He finds partial support for his conclusion in Article I, section 10, which states, "No State shall . . . engage in war." Thus, "if the Framers intended to require congressional consent before war, they . . . were perfectly capable of making their wishes known. . . . Had the Framers intended to prohibit the President from initiating wars, they easily could have incorporated a Section 10 analogue into Article II." *Id.* at 255. What are the strengths and weaknesses of this argument?

Professor Yoo rests his argument partly on the claim that the Framers adopted a strong executive model from England. But this claim makes two assumptions: first, that they *adopted* rather than *rejected* the English model; and second, that the English model best known to the Framers *was* strongly executive. In fact, the King's power had been substantially carved back in the period closest to the framing. *See* Ryan Patrick Alford, *Not Even Wrong: The Use of British Constitutional History to Defend the Vesting Clause Thesis* (Oct. 27, 2012), https://ssrn.com/abstract=2167760 or http://dx.doi.org/10.2139/ssrn.2167760 ("[T]he revolutionary generation understood that British constitutional theory had abandoned any conception of a separation of powers during the eighteenth century, as the new theory of the supremacy of Parliament had been a key point of contention between the United Kingdom and the American Colonists during the pre-revolutionary crisis. There simply was no independent executive power in the British constitution of 1787, as every Patriot knew.").

5. Tactical War Powers. There is ample evidence that the legislature was not meant to make tactical military decisions once war was initiated. But where exactly does the legislature's responsibility stop? Just how much autonomy should the President enjoy as Commander in Chief? If the Framers had addressed these questions, what basic political values would have shaped their debate?

6. An Obsolete War Power? "That was then; this is now," the saying goes. Why should we care what the Framers intended? Of what relevance today is the "original understanding" of the Constitution when, from a distance of two centuries, we have to decide whether the President can unilaterally send American warships into the Persian Gulf, or whether Congress can limit the President's ability to use nuclear weapons first, or whether the courts can help decide either question?

PROVIDING FOR THE "COMMON DEFENCE" — THE ORIGINAL UNDERSTANDING: SUMMARY OF BASIC PRINCIPLES

- The constitutional text divides war powers between Congress and the President (quantitatively assigning the greater number to Congress), leaving the courts to decide federal questions. However, the text is ambiguous and omits important national security powers, including, for example, powers to repel attacks, collect intelligence, and safeguard national security secrets.

- Pre-constitutional history and political theory differentiated between a broad royal prerogative to exercise national security powers (especially abroad) and legislative power to make domestic laws and provide funds for government.

- The American colonial experience taught the Framers of the Constitution to be suspicious of a broad executive prerogative and of a standing army, and that the legislature should control funds for national security, but also that legislative (committee) command of troops in the field — as opposed to unified command — was inefficient and impractical.

- The Framers therefore assigned Congress the power to Declare War (formerly a royal prerogative), as well as to issue letters of marque and reprisal, but made the President the Commander in Chief. Notes of the Constitutional

Convention — though not the constitutional text itself — suggest that this designation included some power to repel sudden attacks.

- It is likely that the Framers understood "Declare" to mean either an official announcement of a commitment to war or an act of war, suggesting that the Declare War Clause vests in Congress the power to authorize war either by formal declaration or by a statute authorizing the President to order an act of war.

- Some scholars have argued, however, that the Declare War Clause vests Congress only with the juridical power to determine legal status or relations in war, leaving to the President the power to decide on war subject only to Congress's power to control or deny funding the war.

3

The President's National Security Powers

The constitutional text offers little help in tracing the President's national security powers. These powers are nebulously vested in broad and opaque phrases like "executive Power," "take Care that the Laws be faithfully executed," and "Commander in Chief," or secreted between the lines by implication or practical necessity. Building on this spare text, theorists and Presidents have reached sharply contrasting conclusions about the scope of presidential authority.

President Theodore Roosevelt espoused by words and by example the "stewardship" theory of presidential power. "[The President is] a steward of the people bound actively and affirmatively to do all he could for the people. [It is] not only his right but his duty to do anything that the needs of the Nation demand, unless such action [is] forbidden by the Constitution or by the law." Theodore Roosevelt, *Autobiography* 372 (1914). Alexander Hamilton drew support for the same theory from the difference between Article I's opening sentence, conferring only "[a]ll legislative Powers *herein granted*" (emphasis supplied), and Article II's opening sentence, vesting the President with "[t]he executive Power," without the "herein" qualifier. 7 *The Works of Alexander Hamilton* 80 (John C. Hamilton ed., 1851).

By contrast, former President (and, at the time of his writing, Chief Justice) William H. Taft asserted that "[t]he true view of the Executive function is . . . that the President can exercise no power which cannot be fairly and reasonably traced to some specific grant of power or justly implied and included within such express grant as proper and necessary to its exercise." William H. Taft, *Our Chief Magistrate and His Powers* 139-140 (1925). This view did not leave the President bereft of power, of course, because Congress could delegate it to him by statute.

And that's the wrinkle in trying to consider the President's national security powers in isolation: there's almost always some relevant statute (or so the President's creative lawyers will say) that either delegates authority to him, so that he need not rest alone or at all on his independent Article II powers, or, more rarely, constrains him. As Justice Jackson famously observed in *Youngstown Sheet & Tube Co. v. Sawyer*

(*The Steel Seizure Case*), 343 U.S. 579, 635 (1952) (Jackson, J., concurring), "Presidential powers are not fixed but fluctuate, depending upon their disjunction or conjunction with those of Congress."

This chapter begins, like Justice Jackson, with "a somewhat oversimplified grouping of practical situations in which a President may doubt, or others may challenge, his powers, and by distinguishing roughly the legal consequences of this factor of relativity." *Id.* We use three foreign relations cases to reflect that grouping and to describe the President's foreign relations power. We then consider two other functional categories of presidential national security power, Commander-in-Chief (war) powers and emergency powers, before concluding with a summary of basic principles.

A. THE SPECTRUM OF PRESIDENTIAL POWER

During the Korean War, labor unrest in the steel industry threatened the supply of armaments for the troops in the field. When Congress spurned his requests for legislative intervention, President Harry S. Truman invoked his constitutional power as President and Commander in Chief to order the Secretary of Commerce to seize the steel plants temporarily. The plant owners challenged the constitutionality of his order in court. In *The Steel Seizure Case*, Justice Black's pithy opinion for the Court asserted that "the President's power to see that the laws are faithfully executed refutes the idea that he is to be a lawmaker." 343 U.S. at 587. As no statute gave him the authority to seize private property, the seizure was unlawful.

Justice Jackson, concurring, took a more nuanced view of executive power, befitting one who had served the President as both Solicitor General and Attorney General before mounting the bench. He described three groupings of presidential powers, each depending on its relationship to those of Congress.

> 1. When the President acts pursuant to an express or implied authorization of Congress, his authority is at its maximum, for it includes all that he possesses in his own right plus all that Congress can delegate. In these circumstances, and in these only, may he be said (for what it may be worth) to personify the federal sovereignty. If his act is held unconstitutional under these circumstances, it usually means that the federal government as an undivided whole lacks power. A seizure executed by the President pursuant to an act of Congress would be supported by the strongest of presumptions and the widest latitude of judicial interpretation, and the burden of persuasion would rest heavily upon any who might attack it.

Associate Justice Robert H. Jackson

Photograph by Harris Ewing. Collection of the Supreme Court of the United States

> 2. When the President acts in absence of either a congressional grant or denial of authority, he can only rely upon his own independent powers, but there is a zone of twilight in which he and Congress may have concurrent authority, or in which its distribution is uncertain. Therefore, congressional inertia, indifference or quiescence may sometimes, at least as a practical matter, enable, if not invite, measures on independent presidential responsibility. In this area, any actual test of power is likely to depend on the imperatives of events and contemporary imponderables rather than on abstract theories of law.
>
> 3. When the President takes measures incompatible with the expressed or implied will of Congress, his power is at its lowest ebb, for then he can rely only upon his own constitutional powers minus any constitutional powers of Congress over the matter. Courts can sustain exclusive presidential control in such a case only by disabling the Congress from acting upon the subject. Presidential claim to a power at once so conclusive and preclusive must be scrutinized with caution, for what is at stake is the equilibrium established by our constitutional system. [343 U.S. at 637-638 (Jackson, J., concurring).]

Although his groupings were more descriptive than analytic, and while many exercises of presidential power do fall "not neatly in one of the three pigeonholes, but rather at some point along a spectrum running from explicit congressional authorization to explicit congressional prohibition," *Dames & Moore v. Regan*, 453 U.S. 654, 669 (1981), they provide a useful organizing device for studying presidential power.

1. When the President Acts Pursuant to Delegated Authority in Foreign Relations

In 1892, the Supreme Court declared, "That Congress cannot delegate legislative power to the President is a principle universally recognized as vital to the integrity and maintenance of the system of government ordained by the Constitution." *Field v. Clark*, 143 U.S. 649, 692 (1892). The principle was called the *nondelegation doctrine* and has never been repudiated by the Court.

However, as early as 1813, the Court declined to apply any such doctrine literally. In *The Brig Aurora*, 11 U.S. (7 Cranch) 382, 384 (1813), the Court upheld a statute that delegated power to the President to lift an embargo on European trade if he found that the Europeans had "ceased to violate the neutral commerce of the United States." The Court reasoned that by enacting the statute, Congress had itself made the law, conditioned on the President's finding of facts. In *Field v. Clark*, the Court upheld a statute that delegated power to the President to impose tariffs whenever he was "satisfied" of a need for them. 143 U.S. at 691-692.

Subsequently, reasoning partly from "governmental necessity," the Court suggested that as long as a statute delegating legislative power contains an "intelligible principle" to guide the delegate's discretion it can withstand a nondelegation attack. *J.W. Hampton, Jr. & Co. v. United States*, 276 U.S. 394, 409-410 (1928). In only two cases has the Supreme Court applied the nondelegation doctrine to strike down statutory delegations of power to the Executive: *Schechter Poultry Corp. v. United States*, 295 U.S. 495 (1935), and *Panama Refining Co. v. Ryan*, 293 U.S. 388 (1935). The Court has not done so since 1935, and it has repeatedly stated that the intelligible-principle/general policy standards for lawful delegations "are not demanding." *Gundy v. United States*, 139 S. Ct. 2116, 2129 (2019) (plurality opinion). "[W]e have 'almost never felt qualified to second-guess Congress regarding the permissible degree of policy judgment that can be left to those executing or applying the law.'" *Whitman v. Am.*

Trucking Ass'ns, 531 U.S. 457, 474-475 (2001) (internal citations omitted). In 2019, four Justices suggested that the Court may soon revisit the scope of the doctrine. *See Gundy*, 139 S. Ct. at 2131 (Alito, J., concurring in the judgment); *id.* at 2133-2142 (Gorsuch, J., dissenting). For the moment, though, the deferential doctrinal understanding remains intact.

The legality of the President's exercise of delegated authority therefore turns on whether:

- Congress may delegate the specific authority to the Executive,
- the delegating statute contains standards for the exercise of the delegated discretion,
- the Executive follows the standards, and
- the exercise of delegated authority otherwise violates the Constitution.

Justice Jackson's first group of presidential powers involves situations in which "the President acts pursuant to an express or implied authorization of Congress," and "his authority is [therefore] at its maximum. . . . " 343 U.S. at 635 (Jackson, J., concurring). In these situations, the President purports to act on authority delegated by Congress. One scholar reports that in 50 cases purporting to apply Justice Jackson's framework, *none* falling into this category has found the President's action unconstitutional, or "even suggested that such an outcome was possible." Edward T. Swaine, *The Political Economy of Youngstown*, 83 S. Cal. L. Rev. 263, 311 (2010).

Reading *United States v. Curtiss-Wright Export Corp.*

In the 1930s, Paraguay and Bolivia went to war over the Chaco region that lay between them, thought to contain valuable oil reserves. To prevent American arms from fuelling the fight (which eventually caused 100,000 deaths), Congress passed a joint resolution delegating to the President the power to prohibit arms sales there if he made certain findings, and making it a felony to violate the President's prohibition. When Curtiss-Wright was indicted for conspiring to sell machine guns in violation of the Joint Resolution and of the President's ensuing proclamation, it argued that the Resolution violated the nondelegation doctrine by leaving the decision to prohibit arms sales to the essentially unfettered discretion of the President.

- What standards, if any, did the Joint Resolution provide for the President's decision?
- Would those standards have sufficed to overcome a nondelegation challenge to the Joint Resolution had it merely delegated some domestic power to the President (say, to regulate overtime hours of workers in the Curtiss-Wright plants)?
- If not, how was the actual delegation of power in the Joint Resolution different? What functional difference did the kind of delegated power make?
- What, exactly, is the holding of the case? Was the Court's discussion of the "plenary and exclusive power of the President" necessary to the result?

United States v. Curtiss-Wright Export Corp.

United States Supreme Court, 1936
299 U.S. 304

Mr. Justice SUTHERLAND delivered the opinion of the Court. On January 27, 1936, an indictment was returned in the court below, the first count of which charges that appellees, beginning with the 29th day of May, 1934, conspired to sell in the United States certain arms of war, namely, fifteen machine guns, to Bolivia, a country then engaged in armed conflict in the Chaco, in violation of the Joint Resolution of Congress approved May 28, 1934, and the provisions of a proclamation issued on the same day by the President of the United States pursuant to authority conferred by §1 of the resolution. In pursuance of the conspiracy, the commission of certain overt acts was alleged, details of which need not be stated. The Joint Resolution follows:

> *Resolved by the Senate and House of Representatives of the United States of America in Congress assembled,* That if the President finds that the prohibition of the sale of arms and munitions of war in the United States to those countries now engaged in armed conflict in the Chaco may contribute to the reestablishment of peace between those countries, and if after consultation with the governments of other American Republics and with their cooperation, as well as that of such other governments as he may deem necessary, he makes proclamation to that effect, it shall be unlawful to sell, except under such limitations and exceptions as the President prescribes, any arms or munitions of war in any place in the United States to the countries now engaged in that armed conflict, or to any person, company, or association acting in the interest of either country, until otherwise ordered by the President or by Congress.
>
> Sec. 2. Whoever sells any arms or munitions of war in violation of section 1 shall, on conviction, be punished by a fine not exceeding $10,000 or by imprisonment not exceeding two years, or both.

The President's proclamation, after reciting the terms of the Joint Resolution, declares:

> Now, therefore, I, Franklin D. Roosevelt, President of the United States of America, acting under and by virtue of the authority conferred in me by the said joint resolution of Congress, do hereby declare and proclaim that I have found that the prohibition of the sale of arms and munitions of war in the United States to those countries now engaged in armed conflict in the Chaco may contribute to the reestablishment of peace between those countries, and that I have consulted with the governments of other American Republics and have been assured of the cooperation of such governments as I have deemed necessary as contemplated by the said joint resolution; and I do hereby admonish all citizens of the United States and every person to abstain from every violation of the provisions of the Joint Resolution above set forth, hereby made applicable to Bolivia and Paraguay, and I do hereby warn them that all violations of such provisions will be rigorously prosecuted.
>
> And I do hereby enjoin upon all officers of the United States charged with the execution of the laws thereof, the utmost diligence in preventing violations of the said joint resolution and this my proclamation issued thereunder, and in bringing to trial and punishment any offenders against the same.
>
> And I do hereby delegate to the Secretary of State the power of prescribing exceptions and limitations to the application of the said joint resolution of May 28, 1934, as made effective by this my proclamation issued thereunder....

It is contended that by the Joint Resolution, the going into effect and continued operation of the resolution was conditioned (a) upon the President's judgment as to its beneficial effect upon the reestablishment of peace between the countries engaged in armed conflict in the Chaco; (b) upon the making of a proclamation, which was left to his unfettered discretion, thus constituting an attempted substitution of the President's will for that of Congress; (c) upon the making of a proclamation putting an end to the operation of the resolution, which again was left to the President's unfettered discretion; and (d) further, that the extent of its operation in particular cases was subject to limitation and exception by the President, controlled by no standard. In each of these particulars, appellees urge that Congress abdicated its essential functions and delegated them to the Executive.

Whether, if the Joint Resolution had related solely to internal affairs it would be open to the challenge that it constituted an unlawful delegation of legislative power to the Executive, we find it unnecessary to determine. The whole aim of the resolution is to affect a situation entirely external to the United States, and falling within the category of foreign affairs. The determination which we are called to make, therefore, is whether the Joint Resolution, as applied to that situation, is vulnerable to attack under the rule that forbids a delegation of the lawmaking power. In other words, assuming (but not deciding) that the challenged delegation, if it were confined to internal affairs, would be invalid, may it nevertheless be sustained on the ground that its exclusive aim is to afford a remedy for a hurtful condition within foreign territory?

It will contribute to the elucidation of the question if we first consider the differences between the powers of the federal government in respect of foreign or external affairs and those in respect of domestic or internal affairs. That there are differences between them, and that these differences are fundamental, may not be doubted.

The two classes of powers are different, both in respect of their origin and their nature. The broad statement that the federal government can exercise no powers except those specifically enumerated in the Constitution, and such implied powers as are necessary and proper to carry into effect the enumerated powers, is categorically true only in respect of our internal affairs. In that field, the primary purpose of the Constitution was to carve from the general mass of legislative powers *then possessed by the states* such portions as it was thought desirable to vest in the federal government, leaving those not included in the enumeration still in the states. *Carter v. Carter Coal Co.*, 298 U.S. 238, 294. That this doctrine applies only to powers which the states had, is self evident. And since the states severally never possessed international powers, such powers could not have been carved from the mass of state powers but obviously were transmitted to the United States from some other source. During the colonial period, those powers were possessed exclusively by and were entirely under the control of the Crown. By the Declaration of Independence, "the Representatives of the United States of America" declared the United (not the several) Colonies to be free and independent states, and as such to have "full Power to levy War, conclude Peace, contract Alliances, establish Commerce and to do all other Acts and Things which Independent States may of right do."

As a result of the separation from Great Britain by the colonies acting as a unit, the powers of external sovereignty passed from the Crown not to the colonies severally, but to the colonies in their collective and corporate capacity as the United States of America. Even before the Declaration, the colonies were a unit in foreign affairs, acting through a common agency — namely the Continental Congress, composed of delegates from the thirteen colonies. That agency exercised the powers of war and peace, raised an army, created a navy, and finally adopted the Declaration of Independence. Rulers come and go; governments end and forms of government change; but sovereignty survives. A political society cannot endure without a supreme will somewhere. Sovereignty is never held in suspense. When, therefore, the external sovereignty of Great Britain in respect of the colonies ceased, it immediately passed to the union. *See Penhallow v. Doane*, 3 Dall. 54, 80-81. That fact was given practical application almost at once. The treaty of peace, made on September 3, 1783, was concluded between his Britannic Majesty and the "United States of America."

The Union existed before the Constitution, which was ordained and established among other things to form "a more perfect Union." Prior to that event, it is clear that the Union, declared by the Articles of Confederation to be "perpetual," was the sole possessor of external sovereignty and in the Union it remained without change save in so far as the Constitution in express terms qualified its exercise. The Framer's Convention was called and exerted its powers upon the irrefutable postulate that though the states were several their people in respect of foreign affairs were one. . . .

It results that the investment of the federal government with the powers of external sovereignty did not depend upon the affirmative grants of the Constitution. The powers to declare and wage war, to conclude peace, to make treaties, to maintain diplomatic relations with other sovereignties, if they had never been mentioned in the Constitution, would have vested in the federal government as necessary concomitants of nationality. Neither the Constitution nor the laws passed in pursuance of it have any force in foreign territory unless in respect of our own citizens; and operations of the nation in such territory must be governed by treaties, international understandings and compacts, and the principles of international law. As a member of the family of nations, the right and power of the United States in that field are equal to the right and power of the other members of the international family. Otherwise, the United States is not completely sovereign. The power to acquire territory by discovery and occupation, the power to expel undesirable aliens, the power to make such international agreements as do not constitute treaties in the constitutional sense, none of which is expressly affirmed by the Constitution, nevertheless exist as inherently inseparable from the conception of nationality. This the court recognized, and [in each of seven cases cited] found the warrant for its conclusions not in the provisions of the Constitution, but in the law of nations. . . .

Not only, as we have shown, is the federal power over external affairs in origin and essential character different from that over internal affairs, but participation in the exercise of the power is significantly limited. In this vast external realm, with its important, complicated, delicate and manifold problems, the President alone has the power to speak or listen as a representative of the nation. He *makes* treaties with the advice and consent of the Senate; but he alone negotiates. Into the field of negotiation the Senate cannot intrude; and Congress itself is powerless to invade it. As Marshall said in his great argument of March 7, 1800, in the House of Representatives, "the President is the sole organ of the nation in its external relations, and its sole representative with foreign nations." Annals, 6th Cong., col. 613. The Senate Committee on Foreign Relations at a very early day in our history (February 15, 1816), reported to the Senate, among other things, as follows:

> The President is the constitutional representative of the United States with regard to foreign nations. He manages our concerns with foreign nations and must necessarily be most competent to determine when, how, and upon what subjects negotiation may be urged with the greatest prospect of success. For his conduct he is responsible to the

> Constitution. The committee considers this responsibility the surest pledge for the faithful discharge of his duty. They think the interference of the Senate in the direction of foreign negotiations calculated to diminish that responsibility and thereby to impair the best security for the national safety. The nature of transactions with foreign nations, moreover, requires caution and unity of design, and their success frequently depends on secrecy and dispatch. U.S. Senate, Reports, Committee on Foreign Relations, vol. 8, p. 24.

It is important to bear in mind that we are here dealing not alone with an authority vested in the President by an exertion of legislative power, but with such an authority plus the very delicate, plenary and exclusive power of the President as the sole organ of the federal government in the field of international relations — a power which does not require as a basis for its exercise an act of Congress, but which, of course, like every other governmental power, must be exercised in subordination to the applicable provisions of the Constitution. It is quite apparent that if, in the maintenance of our international relations, embarrassment — perhaps serious embarrassment — is to be avoided and success for our aims achieved, congressional legislation which is to be made effective through negotiation and inquiry within the international field must often accord to the President a degree of discretion and freedom from statutory restriction which would not be admissible were domestic affairs alone involved. Moreover, he, not Congress, has the better opportunity of knowing the conditions which prevail in foreign countries, and especially is this true in time of war. He has his confidential sources of information. He has his agents in the form of diplomatic, consular and other officials. Secrecy in respect of information gathered by them may be highly necessary, and the premature disclosure of it productive of harmful results. Indeed, so clearly is this true that the first President refused to accede to a request to lay before the House of Representatives the instructions, correspondence, and documents relating to the negotiation of the Jay treaty — a refusal the wisdom of which was recognized by the House itself and has never since been doubted. In his reply to the request, President Washington said:

> The nature of foreign negotiations requires caution, and their success must often depend on secrecy; and even when brought to a conclusion a full disclosure of all the measures, demands, or eventual concessions which may have been proposed or contemplated would be extremely impolitic; for this might have a pernicious influence on future negotiations, or produce immediate inconveniences, perhaps danger and mischief, in relation to other powers. The necessity of such caution and secrecy was one cogent reason for vesting the power of making treaties in the President, with the advice and consent of the Senate, the principle on which that body was formed confining it to a small number of members. To admit, then, a right in the House of Representatives to demand and to have as a matter of course all the papers respecting a negotiation with a foreign power would be to establish a dangerous precedent.

The marked difference between foreign affairs and domestic affairs in this respect is recognized by both houses of Congress in the very form of their requisitions for information from the executive departments. In the case of every department except the Department of State, the resolution *directs* the official to furnish the information. In the case of the State Department, dealing with foreign affairs, the President is *requested* to furnish the information "if not incompatible with the public interest." A statement that to furnish the information is not compatible with the public interest rarely, if ever, is questioned.

When the President is to be authorized by legislation to act in respect of a matter intended to affect a situation in foreign territory, the legislator properly bears in mind the important consideration that the form of the President's action — or, indeed, whether he shall act at all — may well depend, among other things, upon the nature of the confidential information which he has or may thereafter receive, or upon the effect which his action may have upon our foreign relations. This consideration, in connection with what we have already said on the subject, discloses the unwisdom of requiring Congress in this field of governmental power to lay down narrowly definite standards by which the President is to be governed. . . .

In the light of the foregoing observations, it is evident that this court should not be in haste to apply a general rule which will have the effect of condemning legislation like that under review as constituting an unlawful delegation of legislative power. The principles which justify such legislation find overwhelming support in the unbroken legislative practice which has prevailed almost from the inception of the national government to the present day. . . .

. . . A legislative practice such as we have here, evidenced not by only occasional instances, but marked by the movement of a steady stream for a century and a half of time, goes a long way in the direction of proving the presence of unassailable ground for the constitutionality of the practice, to be found in the origin and history of the power involved, or in its nature, or in both combined. . . .

Mr. Justice McReynolds does not agree. . . .

Mr. Justice Stone took no part in the consideration or decision of this case.

Notes and Questions

1. Standardless Delegation? From your other courses, you may have become accustomed to thinking that statutes provide extensive details about the powers they delegate and the conditions and limitations to which those powers are subject. But statutory standards are not always either detailed or clearly enumerated. (Consider, for example, statutes delegating regulatory powers to the Environmental Protection Agency, the Department of Labor, or the Food and Drug Administration.) Why not? How and why is delegation to the President of authority in domestic affairs limited?

The Joint Resolution in *Curtiss-Wright* contains several standards for the President's exercise of the delegated authority, as well as a limitation. The issue was not so much whether it was standardless as it was whether the standards it contained were sufficient to reflect some congressional policy decision, or were instead merely "an attempted substitution of the President's will for that of Congress." What answer did the Court say it would have given if the Resolution had "related solely to internal affairs," and why?

2. Presidential Law. How did President Roosevelt exercise the authority that Congress delegated to him by the Joint Resolution? He issued a *proclamation* making the necessary findings on which Congress conditioned his authority, ordering subordinates to enforce the now-activated criminal law, and sub-delegating to the Secretary of State the task of prescribing exceptions and limitations.

More often, the President issues an *executive order*. Presidential national security law also may take the form of a National Security Decision Directive (NSDD), National Security Directive (NSD), Presidential Decision Directive (PDD), National Security Presidential Directive (NSPD), Presidential Policy Directive, or Presidential Study Directive (the labels vary from administration to administration), or perhaps a Military Order. One survey of presidential laws identifies no fewer than 14 different labels that Presidents have used. Harold C. Relyea, *Presidential Directives: Background and Overview* (Cong. Res. Serv. 98-611 GOV), Nov. 26, 2008.

One difference is that executive orders and proclamations must be published in the *Federal Register*, 44 U.S.C. §1505 (2018), while national security directives need not be. In fact, only 247 of at least 1,042 presidential directives issued through the National Security Council (NSC) between 1961 and 1988 were publicly released for either congressional or public scrutiny. Gen. Accounting Off., *National Security: The Use of Presidential Directives to Make and Implement U.S. Policy* 2 (Dec. 1988). At times, however, the Department of Justice has reportedly taken the view that even executive orders can be rescinded or modified without public notice. *See* Dakota Rudesill, *Coming to Terms with Secret Law*, 7 Harv. Nat'l Security J. 241, 291 (2015).

Another difference is that executive orders are usually sent to the U.S. Attorney General "for his consideration as to both form and legality," 1 C.F.R. §19.2(b) (2018), while national security directives are not. No published regulation provides criteria for the legal vetting of such directives, but some national security directives are reviewed by the State Department's Legal Adviser, the White House Counsel, the legal adviser to the National Security Adviser, or lawyers in the Department of Defense.

Typically an executive order cites its promulgating authority in its preamble. Most such orders invoke delegated legislative authority and carry the same force and effect as statutes. *See generally* Peter Raven-Hansen, *Making Agencies Follow Orders: Judicial Review of Agency Violations of Executive Order 12,291*, 1983 Duke L.J. 285, 297-301. Most others are either executive housekeeping orders directed solely at the internal workings of the executive branch or purported exercises of independent constitutional lawmaking authority in the President.

3. Agency Regulations. Presidential "law" may also take the form of regulations promulgated by presidential subordinates in the executive branch or in the "independent" agencies. Usually, but not always, these regulations, or "legislative rules" in the administrative lawyer's jargon, are promulgated as exercises of legislative authority delegated directly to the subordinates. The Supreme Court has declared that so "long as [a] regulation remains in force the Executive Branch is bound by it, and indeed the United States as the sovereign composed of the three branches is bound to respect and enforce it." *United States v. Nixon*, 418 U.S. 683, 696 (1974).

4. Practical Differences Between Foreign and Domestic Powers and Their Shared Limitation. Curtiss-Wright found that the Joint Resolution related to "a situation entirely external to the United States." Was the situation "entirely external"?

What are the practical differences between the federal government's foreign or external powers and its domestic or internal powers? Consider, for example, the government's ability to forecast when and how the powers will come into play, the speed with which they may need to be exercised, the need for flexibility once they have been exercised, their immediate impact on our daily lives, their long-term impact on our daily lives, their relationship to state powers, and the need for secrecy. Do you agree that these considerations, as a practical matter, may justify broader and less precise delegations from Congress to the President of authority for foreign affairs than those appropriate for delegations of authority for domestic matters?

Would *Curtiss-Wright* have come out the same way if the Court had applied criteria for delegations of authority in domestic affairs? If so, why did the Court not decide on that narrower ground?

Whatever their differences, the government's foreign and domestic powers share a common limitation: even Justice Sutherland concluded his "sole organ" statement by declaring that this power must, "like every other governmental power, . . . be exercised in subordination to the applicable provisions of the Constitution."

5. *Broader Constitutional or Extra-Constitutional Foreign Relations Powers?* Do the same kinds of practical considerations require that we recognize broader *constitutional* powers in the President in foreign than in domestic affairs? Can such broad foreign affairs powers be inferred from the spare text of Article II? Are such powers inherent in the constitutional office of the presidency, or have they been created by executive custom in which Congress has acquiesced? However created, are they limited? If so, how?

Do the same considerations, reinforced by history, require that we recognize *extra-constitutional* powers in the President in foreign affairs, as Justice Sutherland argues? Is his theory consistent with the historical account of the framing of the Constitution set out in Chapter 2, or with the itemization of foreign affairs powers vested in Congress by Article I, section 8? Does Sutherland's theory necessarily dictate the primacy of the President in foreign affairs or instead the sovereignty of the federal government as a whole? Does it follow from his theory that the Constitution has no application outside our borders?

6. *The "Sole Organ" Claim.* Sutherland quotes then-Congressman, later Chief Justice, John Marshall for the proposition that "[t]he President is the sole organ of the nation in its external relations, and its sole representative with foreign nations." 299 U.S. at 319. This language seems to go beyond a simple affirmation of delegated authority, to hint at an independent Article II authority in foreign affairs.

But does it logically follow from the fact that the President is the sole organ for *communicating* U.S. foreign policy (typically through subordinates like ambassadors and the Secretary of State) that he is also solely responsible for the *formulation* of foreign policy? Or does Marshall's language suggest only that the President is the nation's sole spokesperson and agent for communicating and executing foreign policy made by Congress or by him and the Congress together? One answer is suggested by the rest of John Marshall's statement from which Sutherland quoted. Marshall was defending President John Adams's extradition of a British subject to England pursuant to the Jay Treaty of 1795. He observed:

> The treaty, which is a law, enjoins the performance of a particular object. The person who is to perform this object is marked out by the Constitution, since the person is named who conducts the foreign intercourse, and is to take care that the laws be faithfully executed. The means by which it is to be performed, the force of the nation, are in the hands of this person. . . . Congress, unquestionably, may prescribe the mode, and Congress may devolve on others the whole execution of the contract; but, till this be done, it seems the duty of the Executive department to execute the contract by any means it possesses. [10 *Annals of Cong.* 613-614.]

7. *Holding or Dictum?* What did the Court in *Curtiss-Wright* hold and what is the rationale for the holding? Is the discussion of the President's "plenary and exclusive" foreign affairs power dictum or is it a necessary first principle supporting the holding?

Does it matter more than three-quarters of a century later? Sometimes a memorable phrase, especially one that may escape close examination at the time because it seems not central to the result, can take on a life of its own, almost transcending the case in which it first appeared. Sutherland's statement has been cited countless times by both the courts and the President's lawyers — usually with little analysis of its origin — to support assertions of presidential authority. *See* Louis Fisher, *The Staying Power of Erroneous Dicta: From* Curtiss-Wright *to* Zivotofsky, 31 Const. Comment. 149 (2016). The most persuasive way to counter such assertions now may be not to fault the reasoning of *Curtiss-Wright,* but to point instead to the role assigned to Congress in a particular action under review, the collaborative character of the action, and the precise terms of any relevant statutory delegation.

2. When the President Acts in the "Zone of Twilight" in Foreign Relations

Justice Jackson's second category was a nebulous "zone of twilight in which [the President] and Congress may have concurrent authority, or in which its distribution is uncertain," and where therefore "congressional inertia, indifference or quiescence may sometimes, at least as a practical matter, enable, if not invite, measures on independent presidential responsibility." A recurring example here, when Congress has largely remained silent, is the President's deployment of military forces abroad without express congressional approval.

Justice Jackson did not elaborate, but Justice Frankfurter, concurring, explained:

> The Constitution is a framework for Government. Therefore the way the framework has consistently operated fairly establishes that it has operated according to its true nature. Deeply embedded traditional ways of conducting government cannot supplant the Constitution or legislation, but they give meaning to the words of a text or supply them. It is an inadmissibly narrow conception of American constitutional law to confine it to the words of the Constitution and to disregard the gloss which life has written upon them. In short, a systematic, unbroken, executive practice, long pursued to the knowledge of the Congress and never before questioned, engaged in by presidents who have also sworn to uphold the Constitution, making as it were such exercise of power part of the structure of our Government, may be treated as a gloss on "executive Power" vested in the President by §1 of Art. II. . . . [343 U.S. at 610-611 (Frankfurter, J., concurring).]

Congress's knowing acquiescence in an executive practice acts as a kind of tacit approval for the Executive's exercise of what could be called a "customary authority." Of course, Congress can always reclaim and exercise its constitutional authority, moving the executive practice into Jackson's first or third category.

In *United States v. Midwest Oil Co.*, 236 U.S. 459 (1919), the Supreme Court found customary authority in 252 instances over 80 years in which the President had temporarily barred public entry on certain public lands. But in *The Steel Seizure Case,* Justice Frankfurter found "[n]o remotely comparable practice . . . [of] executive seizure of property at a time when this country is not at war, in the only constitutional way in which it can be at war." 343 U.S. at 611 (Frankfurter, J., concurring). Although Presidents had seized private property before President Truman's takeover of the steel plants, some of these seizures occurred during declared wars, and others were made pursuant to express statutory authority. Justice Frankfurter found just three that were comparable.

> [I]t suffices to say that these three isolated instances do not add up, either in number, scope, duration or contemporaneous legal justification, to the kind of executive construction of the Constitution revealed in the *Midwest Oil* case. Nor do they come to us sanctioned by long-continued acquiescence of Congress giving decisive weight in a construction by the Executive of its powers. [*Id.* at 613.]

In determining whether customary authority has been created by executive practice, one scholar suggests consideration of the following factors: the consistency, frequency, duration, "density" (the number of times an act is repeated over the course of its duration), continuity, and normalcy (nonattribution to presidential or congressional personality aberrations or unique historical circumstances) of the executive practice, congressional notice of the practice, and meaningful congressional acquiescence. Michael J. Glennon, *The Use of Custom in Resolving Separation of Powers Disputes,* 64 B.U. L. Rev. 109, 128-138 (1984). Acquiescence, in turn, depends on the absence of objection, the institutional opportunity to object, the utility of objection (none for a *fait accompli*), and noninterference with protected freedoms (tantamount to a rule of clear statement for acquiescence in executive practices restricting individual freedoms). *Id.* at 139-144.

Reading *Dames & Moore v. Regan*

In 1979, Iranian "students" took 52 American diplomatic personnel hostage after seizing the U.S. embassy in Tehran. (The dramatic escape of a few with the help of the Canadian Embassy and a CIA agent is recounted in the movie *Argo*.) President Carter responded by declaring a national emergency and issuing an executive order blocking the removal or transfer of Iranian assets, and nullifying attachments of those assets in suits against Iran. More than a year later, the United States and Iran reached an agreement (the Algiers Accords) for release of the hostages in return for the termination of legal proceedings against Iran in U.S. courts, the nullification of all attachments and judgments therein, and the remission of all claims to binding international arbitration, among other provisions.

Meanwhile, Dames & Moore, an engineering and construction firm, had obtained summary judgment on a contract claim against Iran, only to see its pre-judgment attachments vacated *and* its claim suspended pursuant to the President's order. It then sought to prevent enforcement of the executive order and attendant regulations on the ground that they were unlawful.

- The President relied on the International Emergency Economic Powers Act (IEEPA). Why didn't the IEEPA provision described in footnote 2 expressly authorize *all* the challenged actions with respect to Dames & Moore?

- The Hostage Act seemed to supply an alternative statutory authority for the challenged actions. Can you say how? Why did the Court reject this argument?
- If neither of the foregoing statutes did the job, how were they still relevant to the legality of the challenged actions?
- What are the ingredients of the authority that the Court found? In answering this question, recall Justice Frankfurter's description of customary authority in *The Steel Seizure Case*. How was the custom of claims settlement different from the custom of plant seizure?
- Has the President now obtained plenary claims settlement authority by something like adverse possession? If not plenary, then how is the authority limited?

Dames & Moore v. Regan

United States Supreme Court, 1981
453 U.S. 654

Justice Rehnquist delivered the opinion of the Court. . . . On November 4, 1979, the American Embassy in Tehran was seized and our diplomatic personnel were captured and held hostage. In response to that crisis, President Carter, acting pursuant to the International Emergency Economic Powers Act, 50 U.S.C. §§1701-1706 (1976 ed., Supp. III) (hereinafter IEEPA), declared a national emergency on November 14, 1979,[1] and blocked the removal or transfer of [Iranian assets]. Exec. Order No. 12170, 3 C.F.R. 457 (1980), note following 50 U.S.C. §1701 (1976 ed., Supp. III).[2] . . .

[Pursuant to the Order, the Secretary of the Treasury promulgated regulations nullifying attachments of Iranian assets on or after November 14, 1979, unless licensed by the Treasury Department. The Department subsequently licensed pre-judgment attachments in judicial proceedings against Iran. Dames & Moore sued Iranian defendants for breach of contract and obtained a pre-judgment attachment of Iranian assets.

Thereafter, the American hostages were released pursuant to an agreement obligating the United States to terminate all legal proceedings in U.S. courts involving

---

1. Title 50 U.S.C. §1701(a) (1976 ed., Supp. III) states that the President's authority under the Act "may be exercised to deal with any unusual and extraordinary threat, which has its source in whole or substantial part outside the United States, to the national security, foreign policy, or economy of the United States, if the President declares a national emergency with respect to such threat." Petitioner does not challenge President Carter's declaration of a national emergency.

2. Title 50 U.S.C. §1702(a)(1)(B) (1976 ed., Supp. III) empowers the President to investigate, regulate, direct and compel, nullify, void, prevent or prohibit, any acquisition, holding, withholding, use, transfer, withdrawal, transportation, importation or exportation of, or dealing in, or exercising any right, power, or privilege with respect to, or transactions involving, any property in which any foreign country or a national thereof has any interest. . . .

claims of U.S. nationals against Iran, to nullify all attachments and judgments therein, to terminate such claims through binding arbitration, and to transfer U.S.-held Iranian assets to foreign banks for the satisfaction of any arbitration awards rendered against Iran. President Carter issued a series of executive orders implementing this agreement and "nullif[ying]" all non-Iranian interests in Iranian assets acquired after his initial blocking order. President Reagan subsequently ratified the Carter orders.

Meanwhile, Dames & Moore was granted summary judgment on its claim against the Iranian defendants, but the district court vacated all pre-judgment attachments and stayed further proceedings in light of the executive orders discussed above. Dames & Moore then filed an action in the district court to prevent enforcement of the executive orders and Treasury Department regulations implementing the agreement with Iran on the grounds that they were beyond the statutory and constitutional powers of the Executive.]

Although we have in the past found and do today find Justice Jackson's classification [in *The Steel Seizure Case*, 343 U.S. at 635-638] of executive actions into three general categories analytically useful, we should be mindful of Justice Holmes' admonition, quoted by Justice Frankfurter in [that case at 343 U.S. 597] that "[t]he great ordinances of the Constitution do not establish and divide fields of black and white." *Springer v. Philippine Islands*, 277 U.S. 189, 209 (1928) (dissenting opinion). Justice Jackson himself recognized that his three categories represented "a somewhat over-simplified grouping," and it is doubtless the case that executive action in any particular instance falls, not neatly in one of three pigeonholes, but rather at some point along a spectrum running from explicit congressional authorization to explicit congressional prohibition. This is particularly true as respects cases such as the one before us, involving responses to international crises the nature of which Congress can hardly have been expected to anticipate in any detail.

In nullifying post-November 14, 1979, attachments and directing those persons holding blocked Iranian funds and securities to transfer them to the Federal Reserve Bank of New York for ultimate transfer to Iran, President Carter cited five sources of express or inherent power. The Government, however, has principally relied on §203 of the IEEPA as authorization for these actions. [The Court concluded that this statute expressly authorized the nullification of the attachments and the transfer of assets.] . . .

. . . [T]here remains the question of the President's authority to suspend claims pending in American courts. Such claims have, of course, an existence apart from the attachments which accompanied them. In terminating these claims through Executive Order No. 12294 the President purported to act under authority of both the IEEPA and 22 U.S.C. §1732, the so-called "Hostage Act."

We conclude that although the IEEPA authorized the nullification of the attachments, it cannot be read to authorize the suspension of the claims. The claims of American citizens against Iran are not in themselves transactions involving Iranian property or efforts to exercise any rights with respect to such property. An in personam lawsuit, although it might eventually be reduced to judgment and that judgment might be executed upon, is an effort to establish liability and fix damages and does not focus on any particular property within the jurisdiction. The terms of the IEEPA therefore do not authorize the President to suspend claims in American courts. This is the view of all the courts which have considered the question.

The Hostage Act, passed in 1868, provides:

> Whenever it is made known to the President that any citizen of the United States has been unjustly deprived of his liberty by or under the authority of any foreign government, it shall be the duty of the President forthwith to demand of that government the reasons of such imprisonment; and if it appears to be wrongful and in violation of the rights of American citizenship, the President shall forthwith demand the release of such citizen, and if the release so demanded is unreasonably delayed or refused, the President shall use such means, not amounting to acts of war, as he may think necessary and proper to obtain or effectuate the release; and all the facts and proceedings relative thereto shall as soon as practicable be communicated by the President to Congress. Rev. Stat. §2001, 22 U.S.C. §1732.

We are reluctant to conclude that this provision constitutes specific authorization to the President to suspend claims in American courts. Although the broad language of the Hostage Act suggests it may cover this case, there are several difficulties with such a view. The legislative history indicates that the Act was passed in response to a situation unlike the recent Iranian crisis. Congress in 1868 was concerned with the activity of certain countries refusing to recognize the citizenship of naturalized Americans traveling abroad, and repatriating such citizens against their will. These countries were not interested in returning the citizens in exchange for any sort of ransom. This also explains the reference in the Act to imprisonment "in violation of the rights of American citizenship." Although the Iranian hostage-taking violated international law and common decency, the hostages were not seized out of any refusal to recognize their American citizenship — they were seized precisely *because* of their American citizenship. The legislative history is also somewhat ambiguous on the question whether Congress contemplated Presidential action such as that involved here or rather simply reprisals directed against the offending foreign country and *its* citizens.

Concluding that neither the IEEPA nor the Hostage Act constitutes specific authorization of the President's action suspending claims, however, is not to say that these statutory provisions are entirely irrelevant to the question of the validity of the President's action. We think both statutes highly relevant in the looser sense of indicating congressional acceptance of a broad scope for executive action in circumstances such as those presented in this case. . . . [T]he IEEPA delegates broad authority to the President to act in times of national emergency with respect to property of a foreign country. The Hostage Act similarly indicates congressional willingness that the President have broad discretion when responding to the hostile acts of foreign sovereigns. . . .

Although we have declined to conclude that the IEEPA or the Hostage Act directly authorizes the President's suspension of claims for the reasons noted, we cannot ignore the general tenor of Congress's legislation in this area in trying to determine whether the President is acting alone or at least with the acceptance of Congress. As we have noted, Congress cannot anticipate and legislate with regard to every possible action the President may find it necessary to take or every possible situation in which he might act. Such failure of Congress specifically to delegate authority does not, "especially . . . in the areas of foreign policy and national security," imply "congressional disapproval" of action taken by the Executive. *Haig v. Agee*, [453 U.S. 280 (1981)], at 291. On the contrary, the enactment of legislation closely related to the question of the President's authority in a particular case which evinces legislative intent to accord the President broad discretion may be considered to "invite" "measures on independent presidential responsibility," *Youngstown*, 343 U.S. at 637 (Jackson, J., concurring). At least this is so where there is no contrary indication of legislative intent and when, as here, there is a history of congressional acquiescence in conduct of the sort engaged in by the President. It is to that history which we now turn.

Not infrequently in affairs between nations, outstanding claims by nationals of one country against the government of another country are "sources of friction" between the two sovereigns. *United States v. Pink*, 315 U.S. 203, 225 (1942). To resolve these difficulties, nations have often entered into agreements settling the claims of their respective nationals. As one treatise writer puts it, international agreements settling claims by nationals of one state against the government of another "are established international practice reflecting traditional international theory." L. Henkin, *Foreign Affairs and the Constitution* 262 (1972). Consistent with that principle, the United States has repeatedly exercised its sovereign authority to settle the claims of its nationals against foreign countries. Though those settlements have sometimes been made by treaty, there has also been a longstanding practice of settling such claims by executive agreement without the advice and consent of the Senate.[8] . . . It is clear that the practice of settling claims continues today. Since 1952, the President has entered into at least 10 binding settlements with foreign nations, including an $80 million settlement with the People's Republic of China.

Crucial to our decision today is the conclusion that Congress has implicitly approved the practice of claim settlement by executive agreement. This is best demonstrated by Congress' enactment of the International Claims Settlement Act of 1949, 22 U.S.C. §1621 et seq. (1976 ed. and Supp. IV). The Act had two purposes: (1) to allocate to United States nationals funds received in the course of an executive claims settlement with Yugoslavia, and (2) to provide a procedure whereby funds resulting from future settlements could be distributed. To achieve these ends Congress created the International Claims Commission, now the Foreign Claims Settlement Commission, and gave it jurisdiction to make final and binding decisions with respect to claims by United States nationals against settlement funds. By creating a procedure to implement future settlement agreements, Congress placed its stamp of approval on such agreements. Indeed, the legislative history of the Act observed that the United States was seeking settlements with countries other than Yugoslavia and that the bill contemplated settlements of a similar nature in the future.

Over the years Congress has frequently amended the International Claims Settlement Act to provide for particular problems arising out of settlement agreements, thus demonstrating Congress' continuing acceptance of the President's claim settlement authority. . . . As with legislation involving other executive agreements, Congress did not question the fact of the settlement or the power of the President to have concluded it. . . . Finally, the legislative history of the IEEPA further reveals that Congress has accepted the authority of the Executive to enter into settlement agreements. Though the IEEPA was enacted to provide for some limitation on the President's

8. At least since the case of the "Wilmington Packet" in 1799, Presidents have exercised the power to settle claims of United States nationals by executive agreement. In fact, during the period of 1817-1917, "no fewer than eighty executive agreements were entered into by the United States looking toward the liquidation of claims of its citizens." W. McClure, *International Executive Agreements* 53 (1941).

emergency powers, Congress stressed that "[n]othing in this act is intended . . . to interfere with the authority of the President to [block assets], or to impede the settlement of claims of U.S. citizens against foreign countries." S. Rep. No. 95-466, p. 6 (1977), U.S. Code Cong. & Admin. News, 1977, pp. 4540, 4544; 50 U.S.C. §1706(a)(1) (1976 ed., Supp. III).[10]

In addition to congressional acquiescence in the President's power to settle claims, prior cases of this Court have also recognized that the President does have some measure of power to enter into executive agreements without obtaining the advice and consent of the Senate. In *United States v. Pink*, 315 U.S. 203 (1942), for example, the Court upheld the validity of the Litvinov Assignment, which was part of an Executive Agreement whereby the Soviet Union assigned to the United States amounts owed to it by American nationals so that outstanding claims of other American nationals could be paid. The Court explained that the resolution of such claims was integrally connected with normalizing United States' relations with a foreign state:

> Power to remove such obstacles to full recognition as settlement of claims of our nationals . . . certainly is a modest implied power of the President. . . . No such obstacle can be placed in the way of rehabilitation of relations between this country and another nation, unless the historic conception of the powers and responsibilities . . . is to be drastically revised. *Id.* at 229-230. . . .

Just as importantly, Congress has not disapproved of the action taken here. Though Congress has held hearings on the Iranian Agreement itself, Congress has not enacted legislation, or even passed a resolution, indicating its displeasure with the Agreement. Quite the contrary, the relevant Senate Committee has stated that the establishment of the Tribunal is "of vital importance to the United States." S. Rep. No. 97-71, p. 5 (1981).[13] We are thus clearly not confronted with a situation in which Congress has in some way resisted the exercise of Presidential authority.

Finally, we re-emphasize the narrowness of our decision. We do not decide that the President possesses plenary power to settle claims, even as against foreign governmental entities. As the Court of Appeals for the First Circuit stressed, "[t]he sheer magnitude of such a power, considered against the background of the diversity and complexity of modern international trade, cautions against any broader construction of authority than is necessary." *Chas. T. Main Intl., Inc. v. Khuzestan Water & Power Authority,* 651 F.2d [800 (1st Cir. 1980)], at 814. But where, as here, the settlement

---

10. Indeed, Congress has consistently failed to object to this longstanding practice of claim settlement by executive agreement, even when it has had an opportunity to do so. In 1972, Congress entertained legislation relating to congressional oversight of such agreements. But Congress took only limited action, requiring that the text of significant executive agreements be transmitted to Congress. 1 U.S.C. §112b. In *Haig v. Agee*, 453 U.S. 280, we noted that "[d]espite the longstanding and officially promulgated view that the Executive has the power to withhold passports for reasons of national security and foreign policy, Congress in 1978, 'though it once again enacted legislation relating to passports, left completely untouched the broad rule-making authority granted in the earlier Act.'" *Ante*, at 301, quoting *Zemel v. Rusk*, 381 U.S. 1, 12 (1965). Likewise in this case, Congress, though legislating in the area, has left "untouched" the authority of the President to enter into settlement agreements. . . .

13. Contrast congressional reaction to the Iranian Agreements with congressional reaction to a 1973 Executive Agreement with Czechoslovakia. There the President sought to settle over $105 million in claims against Czechoslovakia for $20.5 million. Congress quickly demonstrated its displeasure by enacting legislation requiring that the Agreement be renegotiated. Though Congress has shown itself capable of objecting to executive agreements, it has rarely done so and has not done so in this case.

of claims has been determined to be a necessary incident to the resolution of a major foreign policy dispute between our country and another, and where, as here, we can conclude that Congress acquiesced in the President's action, we are not prepared to say that the President lacks the power to settle such claims. . . .

The judgment of the District Court is accordingly affirmed. . . .

[The opinions of Justice STEVENS, concurring in part, and Justice POWELL, concurring in part and dissenting in part, are omitted.]

Notes and Questions

1. *Why No Express Statutory Authority?* The IEEPA addresses rights in "any *property in which any foreign country or a national thereof* has any interest." 50 U.S.C. §1702(a)(1)(B) (2018) (emphasis added). Thus, it authorized the nullification of attachments of Iranian property. The contract claim of Dames & Moore, a U.S. company, by contrast, was not *property of a foreign country or national*, so IEEPA did not authorize its suspension.

The Hostage Act delegated to the President the power to "use such means, not amounting to acts of war, as he may think necessary and proper to obtain or effectuate the release" of American hostages. The Court, viewing the legislative history of the Act, concluded that it was aimed at obtaining the release of naturalized Americans seized *despite*, and not *because of*, their American citizenship. But do you think the statutory text was clear enough to make it unnecessary to seek interpretation by review of the history? Can you argue, for example, that the suspension of Dames & Moore's claims in favor of international arbitration in return for the release of hostages was one of "such means" authorized by the statute?

2. *"General Tenor" Legislation?* According to the Court, the fact that neither the IEEPA nor the Hostage Act provided express authority did not mean that these acts were entirely irrelevant to the validity of the suspension. In the Court's view, "the enactment of legislation closely related to the question of the President's authority in a particular case . . . evinces legislative intent to accord the President broad discretion [which] may be considered to 'invite' 'measures on independent presidential responsibility'" (quoting Justice Jackson). Is this a fair reading of Congress's intent? Is it possible that by enacting measures such as the International Claims Settlement Act, which addressed claims against Yugoslavia, Congress intended to "occupy the field" of such settlements, and to approve them only selectively? Or can Congress's failure specifically to delegate the authority asserted in this case be explained or excused by the fact that "foreign policy and national security" were implicated?

3. *The Significance of Congressional Silence.* The Court attached considerable importance to the fact that Congress had "not disapproved of the action taken here," although it also had not specifically approved that action. What, if any, is the significance of such congressional silence? Did Congress fail to delegate such authority because it wished to deny it to the President, because Congress thought he had such authority already, or because it wanted to leave the question to the courts to decide as a matter of federal common or constitutional law? Justice Scalia once argued that it is "impossible to assert with any degree of assurance that congressional failure to act

represents (1) approval of the status quo, as opposed to (2) inability to agree upon how to alter the status quo, (3) unawareness of the status quo, (4) indifference to the status quo, or even (5) political cowardice." *Johnson v. Transp. Agency,* 480 U.S. 616, 672 (1987) (Scalia, J., dissenting). Can you guess which of these possibilities explains Congress's silence in this case?

4. Independent Executive Authority? The hostage release agreement with Iran was an executive agreement rather than a treaty. Although the Constitution refers to agreements between states and foreign powers in Article I, section 10, it prescribes no procedure for their making by the national government. However, Presidents have long assumed the sole power to make them. As noted in *Dames & Moore,* the practice of settling claims by executive agreement is long-standing. In *United States v. Belmont,* 301 U.S. 324, 330-331 (1937), Justice Sutherland, writing for the Court, upheld such an agreement incident to the recognition of the Soviet Union as well "within the competence of the President," citing his view of the President as "sole organ" of the nation in foreign relations. Does *Dames & Moore* support an inherent power in the President to make executive agreements?

The Court was careful to "re-emphasize the narrowness of [its] decision." How was it limited? Was the authority it found for the claims settlement (especially the suspension of claims) an Article I or an Article II authority? In other words, did the President's power in this case fall into Justice Jackson's first or second category, or somewhere in between?

5. Practice or Just Policy? Dames & Moore found that Presidents had engaged in a long *practice* of claims settlement. That is, they had actually settled numerous claims over a lengthy period. But suppose the executive branch had merely *declared as policy* that it had the authority to negotiate claims settlements, without actually executing that policy very often? Would a consistent *claim* of authority, as opposed to an actual practice, be sufficient to establish customary authority by congressional acquiescence?

The Supreme Court so held in *Haig v. Agee,* 453 U.S. 280 (1981), in which a former CIA agent challenged the President's authority to revoke his passport on national security grounds. (Agee had disclosed the names of other CIA agents stationed abroad, placing them in peril.) "Although a pattern of actual enforcement is one indicator of Executive policy, it suffices that the Executive has 'openly asserted' the power at issue." *Id.* at 303. The Court noted that the Executive had long and consistently asserted the power of passport revocation, that no statute prohibited it, that Congress had delegated to the Executive the power to make rules and regulations regarding the issuance of passports, and that Congress had re-enacted general passport authority, leaving that rule-making authority intact, notwithstanding the Executive's publication of regulations regarding revocation of passports. *Id.* at 298-299.

3. When the President Takes Measures Incompatible with the Expressed or Implied Will of Congress in Foreign Relations

Justice Jackson's third group of presidential powers consists of those that the President asserts in conflict with the express or implied will of Congress. Although the Supreme Court has decided many cases in which the President or the executive branch was charged with violating statutory commands, it has decided only a few in which it was argued that the President was constitutionally empowered to violate a statute, none involving national security per se (unless you categorize *The Steel Seizure Case* as such a case).[1] In *Public Citizen v. U.S. Dep't of Justice,* 491 U.S. 440 (1989), Justice Kennedy's concurring opinion asserted that these cases fall into two groups, each representing a different analytical approach:

> In some of our more recent cases involving the powers and prerogatives of the President, we have employed something of a balancing approach, asking whether the statute at issue prevents the President "'from accomplishing [his] constitutionally assigned functions,'" 487 U.S. 654, 695 (1988), quoting *Nixon v. Administrator of General Services,* 433 U.S. 425, 443 (1977), and whether the extent of the intrusion on the President's powers "is justified by an overriding need to promote objectives within the constitutional authority of Congress." *Ibid.* In each of these cases, the power at issue was not explicitly assigned by the text of the Constitution to be within the sole province of the President, but rather was thought to be encompassed within the general grant to the President of the "executive Power." U.S. Const., Art. II, §1, cl. 1. . . .
>
> In a line of cases of equal weight and authority, however, where the Constitution by explicit text commits the power at issue to the exclusive control of the President, we have refused to tolerate *any* intrusion by the Legislative Branch. For example, the Constitution confers upon the President the "Power to grant Reprieves and Pardons for Offenses against the United States, except in Cases of Impeachment." U.S. Const., Art. II, §2, cl. 1. In *United States v. Klein,* 13 Wall. 128 (1872), the Court considered a federal statute that allowed citizens who had remained loyal to the Union during the Civil War to recover compensation for property abandoned to Union troops during the War. At issue was the validity of a provision in the statute that barred the admission of a Presidential pardon in such actions as proof of loyalty. Although this provision did not impose direct restrictions on the President's power to pardon, the Court held that the Congress could not in any manner limit the full legal effect of the President's power. As we said there: "[I]t is clear that the legislature cannot change the effect of . . . a pardon any more than the executive can change a law." *Id.,* at 148. . . .
>
> The justification for our refusal to apply a balancing test in these cases, though not always made explicit, is clear enough. Where a power has been committed to a particular Branch of the Government in the text of the Constitution, the balance already has been struck by the Constitution itself. It is improper for this Court to arrogate to itself the power to adjust a balance settled by the explicit terms of the Constitution. . . . [*Id.* at 484-487 (Kennedy, J., concurring in the judgment).]

Under either test, a President's action will be declared unlawful or a statute will be declared unconstitutional.

1. In *Hamdan v. Rumsfeld,* 548 U.S. 557 (2006), the petitioner argued that his trial by military commission violated several statutes, as well as the Geneva Conventions. A majority of the Court agreed, citing to Justice Jackson's discussion of the three categories of disputes in explaining why the President "may not disregard limitations that Congress has, in proper exercise of its own war powers, placed on his powers." *Id.* at 593 n.23. But the Court added the caveat that "[t]he government does not argue otherwise." *Id.*

Reading *Zivotofsky ex rel. Zivotofsky v. Kerry (Zivotofsky II)*

The recognition of foreign governments and foreign claims of sovereignty is an important part of the nation's foreign relations. Such claims have been made by the winners, for example, after the power shifts caused by a civil war or an international conflict. Which branch of our government has the power to recognize such claims?

In *Zivotofsky II,* the executive branch had not recognized any country as having sovereignty over Jerusalem, thus avoiding taking a position on one aspect of a long-standing Israeli-Palestinian controversy. But Congress passed a statute entitled "United States Policy with Respect to Jerusalem as the Capital of Israel," seeking to override State Department policy by allowing U.S. citizens born in Jerusalem to list their place of birth on their passports as "Israel." The State Department's refusal to comply with this act posed a rare dispute in Justice Jackson's third category of presidential power.

- Does the President have the constitutional power to recognize foreign governments? If so, what provision of the Constitution vests that power in him?
- Why isn't a conclusion that the President has the recognition power sufficient to decide the case? If Congress shares that power, what are the practical consequences if the two political branches disagree about recognizing a state?
- If the President has the exclusive power to recognize a foreign state, is Congress powerless in cases in which it disagrees about recognition? The Court asserts that the President's recognition determination is "part of a political process." What is that process?
- What mode of separation of powers analysis does the Court employ to decide the case?

Zivotofsky ex rel. Zivotofsky v. Kerry (*Zivotofsky II*)

United States Supreme Court, 2015
135 S. Ct. 2076

Justice KENNEDY delivered the opinion of the Court. . . . The Court addresses two questions to resolve the interbranch dispute now before it. First, it must determine whether the President has the exclusive power to grant formal recognition to a foreign sovereign. Second, if he has that power, the Court must determine whether Congress can command the President and his Secretary of State to issue a formal statement that contradicts the earlier recognition. . . .

I

A . . .

The President's position on Jerusalem is reflected in State Department policy regarding passports and consular reports of birth abroad. Understanding that passports will be construed as reflections of American policy, the State Department's

Foreign Affairs Manual instructs its employees, in general, to record the place of birth on a passport as the "country [having] present sovereignty over the actual area of birth." Dept. of State, 7 Foreign Affairs Manual (FAM) §1383.4 (1987). If a citizen objects to the country listed as sovereign by the State Department, he or she may list the city or town of birth rather than the country. See *id.*, §1383.6. The FAM, however, does not allow citizens to list a sovereign that conflicts with Executive Branch policy. See generally *id.*, §1383. Because the United States does not recognize any country as having sovereignty over Jerusalem, the FAM instructs employees to record the place of birth for citizens born there as "Jerusalem." *Id.*, §1383.5-6 (emphasis deleted).

In 2002, Congress passed the Act at issue here, the Foreign Relations Authorization Act, Fiscal Year 2003, 116 Stat. 1350. Section 214 of the Act is titled "United States Policy with Respect to Jerusalem as the Capital of Israel." The subsection that lies at the heart of this case, §214(d), addresses passports. That subsection seeks to override the FAM by allowing citizens born in Jerusalem to list their place of birth as "Israel." Titled "Record of Place of Birth as Israel for Passport Purposes," §214(d) states "[f]or purposes of the registration of birth, certification of nationality, or issuance of a passport of a United States citizen born in the city of Jerusalem, the Secretary shall, upon the request of the citizen or the citizen's legal guardian, record the place of birth as Israel."

When he signed the Act into law, President George W. Bush issued a statement declaring his position that §214 would, "if construed as mandatory rather than advisory, impermissibly interfere with the President's constitutional authority to formulate the position of the United States, speak for the Nation in international affairs, and determine the terms on which recognition is given to foreign states." Statement on Signing the Foreign Relations Authorization Act, Fiscal Year 2003, *Public Papers of the Presidents*, George W. Bush, Vol. 2, Sept. 30, 2002, p. 1698 (2005). The President concluded, "U.S. policy regarding Jerusalem has not changed." *Ibid.*...

II...

In this case the Secretary contends that §214(d) infringes on the President's exclusive recognition power by "requiring the President to contradict his recognition position regarding Jerusalem in official communications with foreign sovereigns." In so doing the Secretary acknowledges the President's power is "at its lowest ebb." *Youngstown* [*Sheet & Tube Co. v. Sawyer*, 343 U.S. 579 (1952)], at 637. Because the President's refusal to implement §214(d) falls into Justice Jackson's third category, his claim must be "scrutinized with caution," and he may rely solely on powers the Constitution grants to him alone. *Id.*, at 638....

A

Recognition is a "formal acknowledgement" that a particular "entity possesses the qualifications for statehood" or "that a particular regime is the effective government of a state." *Restatement (Third) of Foreign Relations Law of the United States* §203, Comment *a*, p. 84 (1986). It may also involve the determination of a state's territorial bounds. See 2 M. Whiteman, *Digest of International Law* §1, p. 1 (1963) (*Whiteman*) ("[S]tates may recognize or decline to recognize territory as belonging to, or under the sovereignty of, or having been acquired or lost by, other states"). Recognition is often effected by an express "written or oral declaration." 1 J. Moore, *Digest of International Law* §27, p. 73 (1906) (*Moore*). It may also be implied — for example, by concluding a bilateral treaty or by sending or receiving diplomatic agents.

Legal consequences follow formal recognition. Recognized sovereigns may sue in United States courts, and may benefit from sovereign immunity when they are sued. The actions of a recognized sovereign committed within its own territory also receive deference in domestic courts under the act of state doctrine. Recognition at international law, furthermore, is a precondition of regular diplomatic relations. Recognition is thus "useful, even necessary," to the existence of a state.

Despite the importance of the recognition power in foreign relations, the Constitution does not use the term "recognition," either in Article II or elsewhere. The Secretary asserts that the President exercises the recognition power based on the Reception Clause, which directs that the President "shall receive Ambassadors and other public Ministers." Art. II, §3. As Zivotofsky notes, the Reception Clause received little attention at the Constitutional Convention. . . .

At the time of the founding, however, prominent international scholars suggested that receiving an ambassador was tantamount to recognizing the sovereignty of the sending state. It is a logical and proper inference, then, that a Clause directing the President alone to receive ambassadors would be understood to acknowledge his power to recognize other nations. . . .

The inference that the President exercises the recognition power is further supported by his additional Article II powers. It is for the President, "by and with the Advice and Consent of the Senate," to "make Treaties, provided two thirds of the Senators present concur." Art. II, §2, cl. 2. In addition, "he shall nominate, and by and with the Advice and Consent of the Senate, shall appoint Ambassadors" as well as "other public Ministers and Consuls." *Ibid.*

As a matter of constitutional structure, these additional powers give the President control over recognition decisions. At international law, recognition may be effected by different means, but each means is dependent upon Presidential power. In addition to receiving an ambassador, recognition may occur on "the conclusion of a bilateral treaty," or the "formal initiation of diplomatic relations," including the dispatch of an ambassador. The President has the sole power to negotiate treaties, and the Senate may not conclude . . . a treaty without Presidential action. The President, too, nominates the Nation's ambassadors and dispatches other diplomatic agents. Congress may not send an ambassador without his involvement. Beyond that, the President himself has the power to open diplomatic channels simply by engaging in direct diplomacy with foreign heads of state and their ministers. The Constitution thus assigns the President means to effect recognition on his own initiative. Congress, by contrast, has no constitutional power that would enable it to initiate diplomatic relations with a foreign nation. Because these specific Clauses confer the recognition power on the President, the Court need not consider whether or to what extent the Vesting Clause, which provides that the "executive Power" shall be vested in the President, provides further support for the President's action here. Art. II, §1, cl. 1.

The text and structure of the Constitution grant the President the power to recognize foreign nations and governments. The question then becomes whether that power is exclusive. The various ways in which the President may unilaterally effect recognition — and the lack of any similar power vested in Congress — suggest that it is. So, too, do functional considerations. Put simply, the Nation must have a single policy regarding which governments are legitimate in the eyes of the United States and which are not. Foreign countries need to know, before entering into diplomatic relations or commerce with the United States, whether their ambassadors will be received; whether their officials will be immune from suit in federal court; and whether they may initiate lawsuits here to vindicate their rights. These assurances cannot be equivocal.

Recognition is a topic on which the Nation must "'speak . . . with one voice.'" *American Ins. Assn. v. Garamendi,* 539 U.S. 396, 424 (2003) (quoting *Crosby v. National Foreign Trade Council,* 530 U.S. 363 (2000)). That voice must be the President's. Between the two political branches, only the Executive has the characteristic of unity at all times. And with unity comes the ability to exercise, to a greater degree, "[d]ecision, activity, secrecy, and dispatch." *The Federalist No. 70,* p. 424 (A. Hamilton). The President is capable, in ways Congress is not, of engaging in the delicate and often secret diplomatic contacts that may lead to a decision on recognition. See, *e.g., United States v. Pink,* 315 U.S. 203, 229 (1942). He is also better positioned to take the decisive, unequivocal action necessary to recognize other states at international law. 1 *Oppenheim's International Law* §50, p. 169 (R. Jennings & A. Watts eds., 9th ed. 1992) (act of recognition must "leave no doubt as to the intention to grant it"). These qualities explain why the Framers listed the traditional avenues of recognition — receiving ambassadors, making treaties, and sending ambassadors — as among the President's Article II powers. . . .

It remains true, of course, that many decisions affecting foreign relations — including decisions that may determine the course of our relations with recognized countries — require congressional action. . . .

In foreign affairs, as in the domestic realm, the Constitution "enjoins upon its branches separateness but interdependence, autonomy but reciprocity." *Youngstown,* 343 U.S., at 635 (Jackson, J., concurring). Although the President alone effects the formal act of recognition, Congress' powers, and its central role in making laws, give it substantial authority regarding many of the policy determinations that precede and follow the act of recognition itself. If Congress disagrees with the President's recognition policy, there may be consequences. Formal recognition may seem a hollow act if it is not accompanied by the dispatch of an ambassador, the easing of trade restrictions, and the conclusion of treaties. And those decisions require action by the Senate or the whole Congress.

In practice, then, the President's recognition determination is just one part of a political process that may require Congress to make laws. The President's exclusive recognition power encompasses the authority to acknowledge, in a formal sense, the legitimacy of other states and governments, including their territorial bounds. Albeit limited, the exclusive recognition power is essential to the conduct of Presidential duties. The formal act of recognition is an executive power that Congress may not qualify. If the President is to be effective in negotiations over a formal recognition determination, it must be evident to his counterparts abroad that he speaks for the Nation on that precise question.

A clear rule that the formal power to recognize a foreign government subsists in the President therefore serves a necessary purpose in diplomatic relations. All this, of course, underscores that Congress has an important role in other aspects of foreign policy, and the President may be bound by any number of laws Congress enacts. In this way ambition counters ambition, ensuring that the democratic will of the people is observed and respected in foreign affairs as in the domestic realm. *See The Federalist No. 51*, p. 322 (J. Madison).

B

The Secretary now urges the Court to define the executive power over foreign relations in even broader terms. He contends that under the Court's precedent the President has "exclusive authority to conduct diplomatic relations," along with "the bulk of foreign-affairs powers." In support of his submission that the President has broad, undefined powers over foreign affairs, the Secretary quotes *United States v. Curtiss-Wright Export Corp.*, which described the President as "the sole organ of the federal government in the field of international relations." 299 U.S. [304 (1936)], at 320. This Court declines to acknowledge that unbounded power. A formulation broader than the rule that the President alone determines what nations to formally recognize as legitimate — and that he consequently controls his statements on matters of recognition — presents different issues and is unnecessary to the resolution of this case.

The *Curtiss-Wright* case does not extend so far as the Secretary suggests. . . .

. . . [Its] description of the President's exclusive power was not necessary to the holding of *Curtiss-Wright* — which, after all, dealt with congressionally authorized action, not a unilateral Presidential determination. Indeed, *Curtiss-Wright* did not hold that the President is free from Congress' lawmaking power in the field of international relations. The President does have a unique role in communicating with foreign governments, as then-Congressman John Marshall acknowledged. *See* 10 *Annals of Cong.* 613 (1800) (cited in *Curtiss-Wright, supra,* at 319). But whether the realm is foreign or domestic, it is still the Legislative Branch, not the Executive Branch, that makes the law.

In a world that is ever more compressed and interdependent, it is essential the congressional role in foreign affairs be understood and respected. For it is Congress that makes laws, and in countless ways its laws will and should shape the Nation's course. The Executive is not free from the ordinary controls and checks of Congress merely because foreign affairs are at issue. It is not for the President alone to determine the whole content of the Nation's foreign policy.

That said, judicial precedent and historical practice teach that it is for the President alone to make the specific decision of what foreign power he will recognize as legitimate, both for the Nation as a whole and for the purpose of making his own position clear within the context of recognition in discussions and negotiations with foreign nations. Recognition is an act with immediate and powerful significance for international relations, so the President's position must be clear. Congress cannot require him to contradict his own statement regarding a determination of formal recognition. . . .

Having examined the Constitution's text and this Court's precedent, it is appropriate to turn to accepted understandings and practice. In separation-of-powers cases this Court has often "put significant weight upon historical practice." *NLRB v. Noel Canning*, 573 U.S. ____, ____ (2014) (slip op., at 6) (emphasis deleted). . . .

This history confirms the Court's conclusion in the instant case that the power to recognize or decline to recognize a foreign state and its territorial bounds resides in the President alone. . . .

III

As the power to recognize foreign states resides in the President alone, the question becomes whether §214(d) infringes on the Executive's consistent decision to withhold recognition with respect to Jerusalem. See *Nixon v. Administrator of General Services,* 433 U.S. 425, 443 (1977) (action unlawful when it "prevents the Executive Branch from accomplishing its constitutionally assigned functions")....

If the power over recognition is to mean anything, it must mean that the President not only makes the initial, formal recognition determination but also that he may maintain that determination in his and his agent's statements. This conclusion is a matter of both common sense and necessity. If Congress could command the President to state a recognition position inconsistent with his own, Congress could override the President's recognition determination....

As Justice Jackson wrote in *Youngstown,* when a Presidential power is "exclusive," it "disabl[es] the Congress from acting upon the subject." 343 U.S., at 637-638 (concurring opinion). Here, the subject is quite narrow: The Executive's exclusive power extends no further than his formal recognition determination. But as to that determination, Congress may not enact a law that directly contradicts it. This is not to say Congress may not express its disagreement with the President in myriad ways. For example, it may enact an embargo, decline to confirm an ambassador, or even declare war. But none of these acts would alter the President's recognition decision.

If Congress may not pass a law, speaking in its own voice, that effects formal recognition, then it follows that it may not force the President himself to contradict his earlier statement. That congressional command would not only prevent the Nation from speaking with one voice but also prevent the Executive itself from doing so in conducting foreign relations.

Although the statement required by §214(d) would not itself constitute a formal act of recognition, it is a mandate that the Executive contradict his prior recognition determination in an official document issued by the Secretary of State. As a result, it is unconstitutional....

...From the face of §214, from the legislative history, and from its reception, it is clear that Congress wanted to express its displeasure with the President's policy by, among other things, commanding the Executive to contradict his own, earlier stated position on Jerusalem. This Congress may not do....

The judgment of the Court of Appeals for the District of Columbia Circuit is

Affirmed.

[The opinions of Justice BREYER, concurring, and Justice THOMAS, concurring in the judgment in part and dissenting in part, are omitted.]

Chief Justice ROBERTS, with whom Justice ALITO joins, dissenting. Today's decision is a first: Never before has this Court accepted a President's direct defiance of an Act of Congress in the field of foreign affairs. We have instead stressed that the President's power reaches "its lowest ebb" when he contravenes the express will of Congress, "for what is at stake is the equilibrium established by our constitutional system." *Youngstown Sheet & Tube Co. v. Sawyer,* 343 U.S. 579, 637-638 (1952) (Jackson, J., concurring)....

. . . [A]lthough the President has authority over recognition, I am not convinced that the Constitution provides the "conclusive and preclusive" power required to justify defiance of an express legislative mandate. *Youngstown,* 343 U.S., at 638 (Jackson, J., concurring). As the leading scholar on this issue has concluded, the "text, original understanding, post-ratification history, and structure of the Constitution do not support the . . . expansive claim that this executive power is plenary." Reinstein, Is the President's Recognition Power Exclusive? 86 Temp. L. Rev. 1, 60 (2013).

But even if the President does have exclusive recognition power, he still cannot prevail in this case, because the statute at issue *does not implicate recognition.* The relevant provision, §214(d), simply gives an American citizen born in Jerusalem the option to designate his place of birth as Israel "[f]or purposes of" passports and other documents. Foreign Relations Authorization Act, Fiscal Year 2003, 116 Stat. 1366. The State Department itself has explained that "identification" — not recognition — "is the principal reason that U.S. passports require 'place of birth.'" Congress has not disputed the Executive's assurances that §214(d) does not alter the longstanding United States position on Jerusalem. And the annals of diplomatic history record no examples of official recognition accomplished via optional passport designation. . . .

I respectfully dissent.

Justice SCALIA, with whom THE CHIEF JUSTICE and Justice ALITO join, dissenting. Before this country declared independence, the law of England entrusted the King with the exclusive care of his kingdom's foreign affairs. The royal prerogative included the "sole power of sending ambassadors to foreign states, and receiving them at home," the sole authority to "make treaties, leagues, and alliances with foreign states and princes," "the sole prerogative of making war and peace," and the "sole power of raising and regulating fleets and armies." 1 W. Blackstone, *Commentaries* *253, *257, *262. The People of the United States had other ideas when they organized our Government. They considered a sound structure of balanced powers essential to the preservation of just government, and international relations formed no exception to that principle. . . .

. . . The Constitution contemplates that the political branches will make policy about the territorial claims of foreign nations the same way they make policy about other international matters: The President will exercise his powers on the basis of his views, Congress its powers on the basis of its views. That is just what has happened here.

I

Before turning to Presidential power under Article II, I think it well to establish the statute's basis in congressional power under Article I. Congress's power to "establish an uniform Rule of Naturalization," Art. I, §8, cl. 4, enables it to grant American citizenship to someone born abroad. The naturalization power also enables Congress to furnish the people it makes citizens with papers verifying their citizenship — say a consular report of birth abroad (which certifies citizenship of an American born outside the United States) or a passport (which certifies citizenship for purposes of international travel). . . .

One would think that if Congress may grant Zivotofsky a passport and a birth report, it may also require these papers to record his birthplace as "Israel." . . .

II

The Court holds that the Constitution makes the President alone responsible for recognition and that §214(d) invades this exclusive power. I agree that the Constitution *empowers* the President to extend recognition on behalf of the United States, but I find it a much harder question whether it makes that power exclusive. The Court tells us that "the weight of historical evidence" supports exclusive executive authority over "the formal determination of recognition." But even with its attention confined to formal recognition, the Court is forced to admit that "history is not all on one side." . . . Fortunately, I have no need to confront these matters today — nor does the Court — because §214(d) plainly does not concern recognition. . . .

. . . Section 214(d) does not require the Secretary to make a formal declaration about Israel's sovereignty over Jerusalem. And nobody suggests that international custom infers acceptance of sovereignty from the birthplace designation on a passport or birth report, as it does from bilateral treaties or exchanges of ambassadors. Recognition would preclude the United States (as a matter of international law) from later contesting Israeli sovereignty over Jerusalem. But making a notation in a passport or birth report does not encumber the Republic with any international obligations. It leaves the Nation free (so far as international law is concerned) to change its mind in the future. That would be true even if the statute required *all* passports to list "Israel." But in fact it requires only those passports to list "Israel" for which the citizen (or his guardian) *requests* "Israel"; all the rest, under the Secretary's policy, list "Jerusalem." It is utterly impossible for this deference to private requests to constitute an act that unequivocally manifests an intention to grant recognition. . . .

IV . . .

In the end, the Court's decision does not rest on text or history or precedent. It instead comes down to "functional considerations" — principally the Court's perception that the Nation "must speak with one voice" about the status of Jerusalem. *Ante,* at 11 (ellipsis and internal quotation marks omitted). The vices of this mode of analysis go beyond mere lack of footing in the Constitution. Functionalism of the sort the Court practices today will *systematically* favor the unitary President over the plural Congress in disputes involving foreign affairs. It is possible that this approach will make for more effective foreign policy, perhaps as effective as that of a monarchy. It is certain that, in the long run, it will erode the structure of separated powers that the People established for the protection of their liberty. . . .

I dissent.

Notes and Questions

1. *The Implied Recognition Power.* The Constitution does not have a Recognition Clause. What then is the source of a power to recognize foreign states? In which clause or clauses of Article II is it found?

2. *The Exclusive Recognition Power?* It is one thing to hold that the President has an implied constitutional power of recognition, and quite another to hold that it is exclusive. Which Justices hold that it is exclusive and why? What does "exclusive" mean in this context? The controversy described in *Zivotofsky* is a longstanding one that continues. Congress passed the Jerusalem Embassy Act of 1995, Pub. L. No. 104-45, 109 Stat. 398 (1995), without the President's signature, purporting to recognize Jerusalem as the capital of the State of Israel. But it allowed the President to waive application of the law every six months on "national security" grounds, something every President did until 2017, when President Trump recognized Jerusalem as Israel's capital. The U.S. Embassy then relocated to Jerusalem on May 14, 2018.

If the executive power is exclusive, but Congress now disagrees with the Executive, what powers does Congress have to give expression or effect to that disagreement? In other words, what are the checks and balances on recognition?

3. *Diplomatic Communications.* Had Congress tried to exercise a recognition power by enacting §214? If not, what was the constitutional problem with the provision? Is there a difference between the policy of recognition and a statement about the passport holder's identity? Why can't Congress just require a statement about identity to be made in a passport?

4. *Is Curtiss-Wright Wrong? Curtiss-Wright* described the President as "the sole organ of the federal government in the field of international relations." 299 U.S. at 320. The *Zivotofsky II* Court called that statement a dictum — "not necessary to the holding." Was the *Zivotofsky II* Court's characterization of *Curtiss-Wright* also a dictum?

Did *Curtiss-Wright* survive *Zivotofsky II*? What is *Curtiss-Wright*'s precedential weight today?

5. *Dodging the Question: The Doctrine of Avoidance.* Striking down executive action in Justice Jackson's category 3, or upholding that action by finding that Congress lacks constitutional power on the subject, is such an extreme outcome that neither political branch may risk pressing its claim. The President often avoids a dispute by straining to construe statutes, or to construe executive practice and any congressional response, to find implied statutory authority or customary authority. *See* Trevor W. Morrison, *Constitutional Avoidance in the Executive Branch*, 106 Colum. L. Rev. 1189 (2006). Moreover, according to one scholar,

> (1) the president's reluctance to risk review at Justice Jackson's "lowest ebb" will tend to discourage seeking congressional authorization at all; (2) the sufficiency within the framework of implied legislative authorization [e.g., its acceptance of either explicit or implied legislative authorization] diminishes the president's incentive to seek explicit authorization; (3) the president will seek to defuse any adverse expressions of congressional will with interpretive techniques [e.g., reading a statute narrowly to avoid a constitutional question, disfavoring "implied repeal," or insisting on a "clear statement"] that may confound the framework; and (4) attributing categorical significance to congressional action (or inaction) tends to substitute judicial for congressional judgment [i.e., it empowers the courts]. [Swaine, *supra*, at 273.]

Category 3 conflicts therefore rarely reach the courts or prompt judicial resolution.

B. THE COMMANDER IN CHIEF'S WAR POWERS

The President's war powers are nowhere spelled out in the Constitution; they must inhere in the Commander in Chief Clause and the judicial and executive glosses on it. First, we consider in this part of the chapter the President's power to defend the nation against attack or insurrection — what we will call "the defensive war power." Second, we address "customary war powers" the President may have acquired by consistent practice with congressional acquiescence, said to be evidenced by more than 300 uses of armed force in our history. Third, we analyze what many consider to be the "core" command authority inherent in the title Commander in Chief and statutory limits on that authority. We will return to each of these issues several times in the following chapters.

1. Defensive War Power

Reading *The Prize Cases*

Barely a week after the bombardment of Fort Sumter marked the start of the Civil War, while Congress was not in session, President Lincoln ordered a naval blockade of the states in "insurrection." He directed U.S. naval vessels to intercept blockade-runners, warn them, and then capture and sell them for prize money if they tried again. The owners of several prize ships then sued, challenging the legality of the blockade.

- Was the country at war? To what law does the Court look for an answer?
- What constitutional text or framing history would you cite for the proposition that the President has inherent constitutional authority to defend the nation against an attack?
- The Court notes two possible statutory authorities for the blockade. How did they apply? Is the resulting decision one of statutory or constitutional law?
- What authority does the President acquire if we are at war? What is its scope?

The Prize Cases

United States Supreme Court, 1863
67 U.S. (2 Black) 635

Mr. Justice Grier. . . . [At the beginning of the Civil War, during a congressional recess, President Lincoln issued a proclamation by which he

> deemed it advisable to set on foot a blockade of the ports within [certain of the Confederate states], in pursuance of the laws of the United States and of the law of nations. . . . If, therefore, with a view to violate such blockade, a vessel shall approach or shall attempt to leave either of said ports, she will be duly warned by the commander of one of the blockading vessels, who will endorse on her register the fact and date of such warning, and if the same vessel shall again attempt to enter or leave the blockaded port, she will be

captured and sent to the nearest convenient port for such proceedings against her and her cargo, as prize, as may be deemed advisable. [Proclamation of a Blockade (Apr. 19, 1861), *in* 4 *Collected Works of Abraham Lincoln* 339 (Roy P. Basler ed., 1953).]

The owners of vessels that were captured as prizes during the blockade brought this action challenging the legality of the President's proclamation.]

... Had the President a right to institute a blockade of ports in possession of persons in armed rebellion against the Government, on the principles of international law, as known and acknowledged among civilized States? ...

The right of prize and capture has its origin in the "*jus belli,*" and is governed and adjudged under the law of nations. To legitimate the capture of a neutral vessel or property on the high seas, a war must exist *de facto,* and the neutral must have a knowledge or notice of the intention of one of the parties belligerent to use this mode of coercion against a port, city, or territory, in possession of the other.

Let us enquire whether, at the time this blockade was instituted, a state of war existed which would justify a resort to these means of subduing the hostile force.

War has been well defined to be, "That state in which a nation prosecutes its right by force." ...

By the Constitution, Congress alone has the power to declare a national or foreign war. It cannot declare war against a State, or any number of States, by virtue of any clause in the Constitution. The Constitution confers on the President the whole Executive power. He is bound to take care that the laws be faithfully executed. He is Commander-in-Chief of the Army and Navy of the United States, and of the militia of the several States when called into the actual service of the United States. He has no power to initiate or declare a war either against a foreign nation or a domestic State. But by the Acts of Congress of February 28th, 1795, and 3d of March, 1807, he is authorized to call out the militia and use the military and naval forces of the United States in case of invasion by foreign nations, and to suppress insurrection against the government of a State or of the United States.

If a war be made by invasion of a foreign nation, the President is not only authorized but bound to resist force by force. He does not initiate the war, but is bound to accept the challenge without waiting for any special legislative authority. And whether the hostile party be a foreign invader, or States organized in rebellion, it is none the less a war, although the declaration of it be "*unilateral.*" Lord Stowell (1 Dodson, 247) observes, "It is not the less a war on *that account,* for war may exist without a declaration on either side. It is so laid down by the best writers on the law of nations. A declaration of war by one country only, is not a mere challenge to be accepted or refused at pleasure by the other." ...

This greatest of civil wars was not gradually developed by popular commotion, tumultuous assemblies, or local unorganized insurrections. However long may have been its previous conception, it nevertheless sprung forth suddenly from the parent brain, a Minerva in the full panoply of *war.* The President was bound to meet it in the shape it presented itself, without waiting for Congress to baptize it with a name; and no name given to it by him or them could change the fact. ...

Whether the President in fulfilling his duties, as Commander-in-Chief, in suppressing an insurrection, has met with such armed hostile resistance, and a civil war of such alarming proportions as will compel him to accord to them the character of belligerents, is a question to be decided *by him,* and this Court must be governed by the decisions and acts of the political department of the Government to which this power was entrusted. "He must determine what degree of force the crisis demands." The proclamation of blockade is itself official and conclusive evidence to the Court that a state of war existed which demanded and authorized a recourse to such a measure, under the circumstances peculiar to the case. . . .

If it were necessary to the technical existence of a war, that it should have a legislative sanction, we find it in almost every act passed at the extraordinary session of the Legislature of 1861, which was wholly employed in enacting laws to enable the Government to prosecute the war with vigor and efficiency. And finally, in 1861, we find Congress "*ex majore cautela*" [out of caution] and in anticipation of such astute objections, passing an act "approving, legalizing, and making valid all the acts, proclamations, and orders of the President, &c., as if they had been *issued and done under the previous express authority* and direction of the Congress of the United States."

Without admitting that such an act was necessary under the circumstances, it is plain that if the President had in any manner assumed powers which it was necessary should have the authority or sanction of Congress, that on the well known principle of law, "*omnis ratihabitio retrotrahitur et mandato equiparatur*" [ratifications relate back and are the equivalent of prior authority], this ratification has operated to perfectly cure the defect. . . .

On this first question therefore we are of the opinion that the President had a right, *jure belli*, to institute a blockade of ports in possession of the States in rebellion, which neutrals are bound to regard. . . .

Mr. Justice NELSON, dissenting [in an opinion in which Chief Justice TANEY and Justices CATRON and CLIFFORD concurred]. . . . It is not to be denied . . . that if a civil war existed between that portion of the people in organized insurrection to overthrow this Government at the time this vessel and cargo were seized, and if she was guilty of a violation of the blockade, she would be lawful prize of war. But before this insurrection against the established Government can be dealt with on the footing of a civil war, within the meaning of the law of nations and the Constitution of the United States, and which will draw after it belligerent rights, it must be recognized or declared by the war-making power of the Government. No power short of this can change the legal status of the Government or the relations of its citizens from that of peace to a state of war, or bring into existence all those duties and obligations of neutral third parties growing out of a state of war. The war power of the Government must be exercised before this changed condition of the Government and people and of neutral third parties can be admitted. There is no difference in this respect between a civil or a public war. . . .

. . . [W]e find . . . that to constitute a civil war in the sense in which we are speaking, before it can exist, in contemplation of law, it must be recognized or declared by the sovereign power of the State, and which sovereign power by our Constitution is lodged in the Congress of the United States — civil war, therefore, under our system of government, can exist only by an act of Congress, which requires the assent of two of the great departments of the Government, the Executive and Legislative. . . .

. . . But we are asked, what would become of the peace and integrity of the Union in case of an insurrection at home or invasion from abroad if this power could not be exercised by the President in the recess of Congress, and until that body could be assembled?

The framers of the Constitution fully comprehended this question, and provided for the contingency. Indeed, it would have been surprising if they had not, as a rebellion had occurred in the State of Massachusetts while the Convention was in session, and which had become so general that it was quelled only by calling upon the military power of the State. The Constitution declares that Congress shall have power "to provide for calling forth the militia to execute the laws of the Union, suppress insurrections, and repel invasions." Another clause, "that the President shall be Commander-in-chief of the Army and Navy of the United States, and of the Militia of the several States when called into the actual service of the United States;" and, again: "He shall take care that the laws shall be faithfully executed." Congress passed laws on this subject in 1792 and 1795. 1 United States Laws, pp. 264, 424. [It also passed a law on the subject in 1807. Act of Mar. 3, 1807, ch. 39, 2 Stat. 443.] . . .

The Acts of 1795 and 1807 did not, and could not under the Constitution, confer on the President the power of declaring war against a State of this Union, or of deciding that war existed, and upon that ground authorize the capture and confiscation of the property of every citizen of the State whenever it was found on the waters. The laws of war, whether the war be civil or *inter gentes,* as we have seen, convert every citizen of the hostile State into a public enemy, and treat him accordingly, whatever may have been his previous conduct. This great power over the business and property of the citizen is reserved to the legislative department by the express words of the Constitution. It cannot be delegated or surrendered to the Executive. Congress alone can determine whether war exists or should be declared; and until they have acted, no citizen of the State can be punished in his person or property, unless he has committed some offence against a law of Congress passed before the act was committed, which made it a crime, and defined the punishment. The penalty of confiscation for the acts of others with which he had no concern cannot lawfully be inflicted. . . .

. . . [C]onsequently, . . . the President had no power to set on foot a blockade under the law of nations, and . . . the capture of the vessel and cargo in this case, and in all cases before us in which the capture occurred before the 13th of July, 1861 [the date on which Congress first authorized a naval blockade of the Confederacy], for breach of blockade, or as enemies' property, are illegal and void, and . . . the decrees of condemnation should be reversed and the vessel and cargo restored.

Notes and Questions

1. De Facto War? When the President proclaimed a blockade against the South in April 1861, Congress had not declared war (nor would it), nor had it passed what we today call an authorization for the use of military force (AUMF); indeed, Congress was in recess. But war is not just made *by* the United States; it may also be made *on* the United States. "It is not the less a war on *that account,*" the *Prize Cases* Court said, "for war may exist without a declaration of war on either side." What counted was the use of force against the United States. That rebellious states rather than a foreign invader fired the first shots made no practical difference: an attack by either can create a war *de facto.* But why did the Court take such pains to define "war"? And why was it important to determine the existence of a war?

Wars preceded the Constitution, and an international law of war (partly as reflected in learned treatises) had evolved to deal with their legality. What role, if any, did "principles of international law" play in the Court's decision?

On September 12, 2001, President George W. Bush declared that the terrorist attacks on the World Trade Center and the Pentagon were "acts of war." *Remarks by the President in Photo Opportunity with the National Security Team,* Sept. 12, 2001, *at* http://georgewbush-whitehouse.archives.gov/news/releases/2001/09/20010912-4.html. Did the circumstances that day or since fit the *Prize Cases* Court's definition of "war"?

2. *Inherent Defensive War Power?* Both the majority and the dissenters discussed the allocation of domestic war powers under the Constitution. Apart from any congressional authorization, where does the Court find constitutional authority for the President to use force in erecting the blockade? If not in the text of the Constitution, can that authority be found in the history of the framing of the Declare War Clause?

Is there any danger that a President might create the conditions said to warrant a military response? Abraham Lincoln offered this warning about the President's invocation of his "repel attack" authority to fight the undeclared Mexican War of 1846:

> Allow the President to invade a neighboring nation, whenever he shall deem it necessary to repel an invasion and you allow him to do so, whenever he may choose to say he deems it necessary for such purpose, and you allow him to make war at pleasure. Study to see if you can fix any limit to his power in this respect, after you have given him so much as you propose. [2 Abraham Lincoln, *The Writings of Abraham Lincoln* 51 (Arthur Brooks Lapsley ed., 1906).]

Do you think President Lincoln's caution was justified in the middle of the nineteenth century? Is it warranted today?

3. *Statutory Authority for the Blockade?* The Court cited two statutes as authority for the blockade. One of them, the Calling Forth Act of 1795, gave the President the power to call forth the militia "as he may judge necessary" to repel an invasion by a "foreign nation or Indian tribe" or in case of "insurrection in any state." 1 Stat. 424. In *Martin v. Mott,* 25 U.S. (12 Wheat.) 19, 29 (1827), the Court found the President to be "the sole and exclusive judge whether the exigency has arisen" that would justify invocation of the statute, and it implied the unsuitability of such a determination for judicial review. "Whenever a statute gives a discretionary power to any person, to be exercised by him upon his own opinion of certain facts," the Court explained, "it is a sound rule of construction, that the statute constitutes him the sole and exclusive judge of the existence of those facts." *Id.* at 31-32. The other statute cited by the *Prize Cases* Court authorized the President to deploy federal forces in the same circumstances in which the earlier statute authorized the calling forth of the militia. 2 Stat. 443 (1807).

Into which of Justice Jackson's three categories of presidential power did *The Prize Cases* fall? Given these statutes, was it necessary to the decision in *The Prize Cases* to find that the President has inherent constitutional authority to respond to an attack? Was this holding or dictum?

The dissenters in *The Prize Cases* did not contest the proposition that a civil war places the nation *in extremis.* Why then did they find the blockade unlawful?

4. *The Scope of the Defensive War Power.* The Court asserted that the President is "not only authorized but bound to resist force by force," and that the question of how much force was needed was for him, not the courts, to decide. This might suggest

that there is no limit on his defensive war power. But does the power to repel attacks extend equally to large attacks, which threaten the survival of the nation, and to small ones, which do not? To attacks on U.S. military forces? To attacks on U.S. interests abroad?

Does the power extend to mere threats of attack? If so, how great and how imminent must such a threat be?

Does the repel attack power have temporal limits? Does the claim of national self-defense erode over time, as the threat of continuing or renewed attack recedes? What if a President fighting a defensive war runs out of money?

Is the President's repel attack power exclusive, or may Congress regulate its exercise? Can you describe legislation that would do that?

2. Customary War Power

Although we have formally declared war only 11 times in our history, we have used armed force abroad hundreds of times, sometimes covertly. Congress has not expressly approved most of these uses. *See* Barbara Salazar Torreon, *Instances of Use of United States Armed Forces Abroad, 1798-2018* (Cong. Res. Serv. R42738), Dec. 28, 2018; *see also Presidential Power to Use Armed Forces Abroad Without Statutory Authorization,* 4a Op. Off. Legal Counsel 185, 187 (1980) ("We believe that the substantive constitutional limits on the exercise of these inherent powers by the President are, at any particular time, a function of historical practice and the political relationship between the President and Congress."). Does this history indicate that the President may use armed force whenever he thinks it necessary to protect national security?

That argument was made to support the legality of U.S. participation in the Vietnam War. The Legal Adviser to the State Department inferred from 125 prior congressionally unauthorized uses of armed force abroad that the President has the "power to deploy American forces abroad and commit them to military operations when [he] deems such action necessary to maintain the security and defense of the United States." Leonard C. Meeker, *The Legality of United States Participation in the Defense of Viet-Nam,* 75 Yale L.J. 1085, 1100-1101 (1966). One scholar has concluded that

> this historical development of our institutions has settled the legitimacy of "inherent" presidential power to commit the armed forces to hostilities. A practice so deeply embedded in our governmental structure should be treated as decisive of the constitutional issue. History and practice are not here being appealed to in order to freeze forever the scope of a constitutional guarantee framed in terms of individual liberty; rather, this issue deals with the distribution of political power between the legislative and executive branches. Matters of this character are, in the words of Chief Justice Marshall, best left "to the practice of government." [Henry P. Monaghan, *Presidential War-Making,* 50 B.U. L. Rev. 19, 31 (Special Issue 1970).]

Or does history suggest a narrower claim of presidential war power: that he has acquired *some* customary war powers with congressional acquiescence? Professors Wormuth and Firmage argue that the particulars matter, and that after the history is disaggregated, the pieces do not reassemble into a general inherent war power in the President. *See* Francis D. Wormuth & Edwin B. Firmage, *To Chain the Dog of War: The War Power of Congress in History and Law* 145-151 (2d ed. 1989). Thus, more than 70 U.S. military interventions to protect U.S. citizens abroad, many known to

Congress and none disapproved by statute, may offer evidence that the President has acquired a customary power for "protective intervention" for the limited purpose of protecting Americans abroad from violence. But they do not add up to a power to engage massive U.S. military forces in Korea or Vietnam for a multi-year period to protect or shore up a foreign ally, or a power to use force for "humanitarian intervention" to protect non-U.S. persons. In fact, the vast majority of historical uses of military force abroad without prior congressional approval were small-scale, defensive deployments for which Presidents rarely claimed inherent constitutional authority.

Notes and Questions

1. *Usage and Denials of Authority.* If usage is significant, should the relevant list include instances in which the Congress *refused* presidential requests for delegations of authority to use force abroad or *denied funding* for the continued use of force abroad? *See* Wormuth & Firmage, *supra,* at ch. 5 (discussing such instances). Do such instances refute the claim that usage consists of an unbroken line of precedents for unilateral presidential military initiatives?

2. *Usage and Necessity.* Alexander Hamilton wrote in *The Federalist No. 23* that it was undesirable to impose "constitutional shackles" on "the power to which the care of [the safety of the nation] is committed," because "it is impossible to foresee or define the extent and variety of national exigencies, or the correspondent extent and variety of means that may be necessary to satisfy them." *The Federalist No. 23,* at 153 (Clinton Rossiter ed., 1961). James Madison also noted in *The Federalist No. 41* that

> [t]he means of security can only be regulated by the means and the danger of attack. They will, in fact, be ever determined by these rules and no others. It is in vain to oppose constitutional barriers to the impulse of self-preservation. It is worse than in vain; because it places in the Constitution itself necessary usurpations of power; every precedent of which is a germ of unnecessary and multiplied repetitions. [*Id.* at 257.]

Both observations, however, go only to the necessity of a flexible war power in the government at large, without specifying a branch. Indeed, both Hamilton and Madison made their comments in defense of the *congressional* power to raise armies. Nevertheless, they gave clear expression to the view that war powers are necessarily adaptive, depending on variable and unforeseeable threats to the national security. From this premise, it is a small step to find the shape of presidential war powers in usage: the accumulation of presidential military initiatives since 1789.

Does the very diversity of usage prove that Madison was right in warning that the "means of security" will be governed only by the rule of necessity "and no others"? Doesn't the President alone have the practical capacity to respond to that rule? In short, isn't unpredictability inherent in the nature of the problem, justifying allocation of war powers to the branch that is able to respond most quickly and flexibly?

On the other hand, does the rule of necessity operate with equal force in all instances? If the nation is not itself put at risk and there is time to consider a response to foreign threats, *should* the President be empowered to fashion that response without first going to Congress?

3. *Customary Law Redux.* Upon what constitutional theory does a historically based claim of inherent presidential power to commit troops to hostilities rest? If the theory is customary law by congressional acquiescence, aren't the particular circumstances of each military initiative relevant to the constitutional theory? And does it matter whether a use of force was a "quick strike military mission" or secret?

4. *Negotiated War Powers.* Professor Monaghan's theory, broadly stated, is that exercise of the war power is negotiated between the political branches. If he's right, what is the point of studying legal limits on war powers? Isn't whatever the political branches agree to then constitutional per se, and doesn't the President hold all the cards in the negotiations? How do constitutional claims, international law doctrines, and past military precedents fit into the next negotiation? *See generally* David J. Barron & Martin S. Lederman, *The Commander in Chief at the Lowest Ebb — Framing the Problem, Doctrine, and Original Understanding,* 121 Harv. L. Rev. 689, 724-725 (2008) (arguing that the "politics is law" model of war powers "seriously underestimates the role of traditional constitutional analysis — especially historical exegesis — in war powers disputation outside the context of litigation. . . . The interdepartmental struggle for war powers supremacy itself, in other words, is precisely about the rules of engagement."); Abram Chayes, *The Cuban Missile Crisis* 6-7 (1974) (suggesting that law affects the decisional process by acting as a constraint, supplying justification or legitimation, and providing organizational structures, procedures, and forums).

5. *Jackson's Category 3 Again.* If the President has acquired customary war power by congressional acquiescence, does it follow that Congress cannot take it away? Whether or not history establishes that the President may order the use of armed force abroad without prior statutory authority, may he do so after Congress acts to limit that use?

3. "Core" Presidential War Power and Statutory Limits

The majority in *The Prize Cases* asserted that when the nation is attacked, the President "must determine what degree of force the crisis demands." In another Civil War era decision, Chief Justice Chase declared in a concurring opinion that Congress's war power

> necessarily extends to all legislation essential to the prosecution of war with vigor and success, *except such as interferes with the command of the forces and the conduct of campaigns. That power and duty belong to the President as commander-in-chief.* Both these powers are derived from the Constitution, but neither is defined by that instrument. Their extent must be determined by their nature, and by the principles of our institutions. [*Ex parte Milligan,* 71 U.S. (4 Wall.) 2, 139 (1866) (Chase, C.J., concurring) (emphasis added).]

Do these statements suggest that the President's authority as Commander in Chief contains some "core" command authority that is not shared with Congress and is beyond its statutory reach? Could Congress, for example, make someone *else* Commander in Chief of the armed forces? *See, e.g.,* Command of the Army Act, 14 Stat. 485, 486-487 (1867).

Reading *Little v. Barreme*

Although France had been a crucial ally and creditor in the Revolutionary War, after the French Revolution in 1789 the United States refused to pay its debts to France, and it declared neutrality in the war between France and Great Britain. In retaliation, French warships then began preying on American commerce, starting what is known as the Quasi-War (or Naval War) with France. In 1799, Congress passed an act that embargoed U.S. trade with France and authorized U.S. naval vessels to intercept suspected U.S. ships that were sailing to French ports in violation of the embargo. Acting under President Adams' orders (conveyed through his Secretary of the Navy), Captain Little, commanding the U.S. frigate *Boston*, stopped the *Flying-Fish*, which he suspected of flying false Danish colors, then had it condemned for prize money. The owners then sued for recovery of their vessel and damages from Little.

- What precisely did the act authorize the President to instruct his naval commanders to do?
- If Congress had simply authorized an embargo, without further detail, what, according to Chief Justice Marshall, could the President then have instructed his commanders to do? Why did President Adams' orders not adhere strictly to the terms of the statute?
- Captain Little was just following the President's orders. Why was he personally liable?
- In *Dames & Moore*, Congress had delegated broad claims settlement authority to the President, but not the precise authority that President Carter claimed. Yet the Court upheld his action. In *Little*, Congress had delegated authority to enforce the embargo against France, just not the precise authority asserted by the President. Yet the Court declared that Captain Little's action was unlawful. Why the different outcomes? Are the cases consistent?

Little v. Barreme

United States Supreme Court, 1804
6 U.S. (2 Cranch) 170

MARSHALL, Chief Justice, now delivered the opinion of the Court.... During the hostilities between the United States and France, an act for the suspension of all intercourse between the two nations was annually passed. That under which the *Flying-Fish* was condemned, declared every vessel, owned, hired, or employed wholly or in part by an American, which should be employed in any traffic or commerce with or for any person resident within the jurisdiction or under the authority of the French republic, to be forfeited together with her cargo; the one half to accrue to the United States, and the other to any person or persons, citizens of the United States, who will inform and prosecute for the same.

The 5th section of this act authorizes the President of the United States, to instruct the commanders of armed vessels, "to stop and examine any ship or vessel of the United States on the high sea, which there may be reason to suspect to be engaged in any traffic or commerce contrary to the true tenor of the act, and if upon examination it should appear that such ship or vessel is bound or sailing *to* any port or place within the territory of the French republic or her dependencies, it is rendered lawful to seize such vessel, and send her into the United States for adjudication."

[By this authority, a U.S. frigate commanded by Captain Little intercepted and captured an ostensibly Danish vessel named the *Flying-Fish* as it was returning *from* a French port. The ship's owners subsequently sued Captain Little for trespass.]

It is by no means clear that the President of the United States, whose high duty it is to "take care that the laws be faithfully executed," and who is commander in chief of the armies and navies of the United States, might not, without any special authority for that purpose, in the then existing state of things, have empowered the officers commanding the armed vessels of the United States, to seize and send into port for adjudication, American vessels which were forfeited by being engaged in this illicit commerce. But when it is observed that the . . . 5th section [of the act] gives a special authority to seize on the high seas, and limits that authority to the seizure of vessels bound or sailing *to* a French port, the legislature seem to have prescribed that the manner in which this law shall be carried into execution was to exclude a seizure of any vessel not bound *to* a French port. Of consequence, however strong the circumstances might be, which induced Captain Little to suspect the *Flying-Fish* to be an American vessel, they could not excuse the detention of her, since he would not have been authorised to detain her had she been really American.

It was so obvious, that if only vessels sailing to a French port could be seized on the high seas, that the law would be very often evaded, that this act of congress appears to have received a different construction from the executive of the United States; a construction much better calculated to give it effect.

A copy of his act was transmitted by the secretary of the navy to the captains of the armed vessels, who were ordered to consider the 5th section as a part of their instructions. The same letter contained the following clause.

> A proper discharge of the important duties enjoined on you, arising out of this act, will require the exercise of a sound and an impartial judgment. You are not only to do all that in you lies, to prevent all intercourse, whether direct or circuitous, between the ports of the *United States* and those of *France* or her dependencies, where the vessels *are apparently as well as really American,* and protected by *American* papers only, but you are to be vigilant that vessels or cargoes really *American,* but covered by *Danish* or other foreign papers, and bound *to* or *from French* ports, do not escape you.

These orders, given by the executive under the construction of the act of congress made by the department to which its execution was assigned, enjoin the seizure of American vessels sailing from a French port. Is the officer who obeys them liable for damages sustained by this misconstruction of the act, or will his orders excuse him? If his instructions afford him no protection, then the law must take its course, and he must pay such damages as are legally awarded against him; if they excuse an act not otherwise excusable, it would then be necessary to inquire whether this is a case in which the probable cause which existed to induce a suspicion that the vessel was American, would excuse the captor from damages when the vessel appeared in fact to be neutral.

I confess the first bias of my mind was very strong in favor of the opinion that though the instructions of the executive could not give a right, they might yet excuse from damages. I was very much inclined to think that a distinction ought to be taken between acts of civil and those of military officers; and between proceedings within the body of the country and those on the high seas. That implicit obedience which military men usually pay to the orders of their superiors, which indeed is indispensably necessary to every military system, appeared to me strongly to imply the principle that those orders, if not to perform a prohibited act, ought to justify the person whose general duty it is to obey them, and who is placed by the laws of his country in a situation which in general requires that he should obey them. I was strongly inclined to think that where, in consequence of orders from the legitimate authority, a vessel is seized with pure intention, the claim of the injured party for damages would be against that government from which the orders proceeded, and would be a proper subject for negotiation. But I have been convinced that I was mistaken, and I have receded from this first opinion. I acquiesce in that of my brethren, which is, that the instructions cannot change the nature of the transaction, or legalize an act which without those instructions would have been a plain trespass. . . .

Captain Little then must be answerable in damages to the owner of this neutral vessel. . . .

Notes and Questions

1. *Ascertaining the Will of Congress (Again).* Chief Justice Marshall suggested that if Congress had simply authorized an embargo, the President would have had broad authority to enforce it, including ordering the stopping of U.S. vessels sailing either to or from French ports. In fact, he reasoned that stopping all U.S. commerce with France would make better sense than just stopping ships headed for France.

The trouble was that the authority *expressly delegated* by Congress was more limited. Commerce either goes to France or comes from France — specifying one seemed to exclude the other: the "5th section gives a special authority to seize on the high seas, and limits that authority to the seizure of vessels bound or sailing *to* a French port."

How was *Dames & Moore* different? In the IEEPA Congress approved actions directed at foreign property. Why did it not implicitly disapprove actions directed at U.S. property (claims against Iran)? Is the difference to be found in the history of claims settlement authority, with the Court construing statutes that affect claims settlement narrowly to avoid limiting customary authority? There was no comparable history of embargo enforcement requiring the Court to read the 1799 act narrowly.

2. *Precedential Value.* What is the precedential value of *Little*? Does the case really address the scope of the Commander in Chief's powers or of Congress's power to control the conduct of war? *Compare* Abraham D. Sofaer, *War, Foreign Affairs and Constitutional Power: The Origins* 163 (1976) (*Little* "rests on the notion . . . that declared war involved a delegation to the executive and all citizens of general authority to commit hostilities against the enemy, while the conduct of undeclared or 'imperfect' war was limited to those actions authorized by Congress."), *with* John C. Yoo, *The Continuation of Politics by Other Means: The Original Understanding of War*

Powers, 84 Cal. L. Rev. 167, 294-295 n.584 (1996) (*Little* never reached the issue of "the President's inherent constitutional authority to order captures going beyond Congress's commands"), *and* J. Gregory Sidak, *The Quasi War Cases — And Their Relevance to Whether "Letters of Marque and Reprisal" Constrain Presidential War Powers*, 28 Harv. J.L. & Pub. Pol'y 465, 492 (2005) ("[The] negative implication [of Chief Justice Marshall's statements in *Little*] was that congressional silence leaves the President free to act."). Can *Little* be distinguished from other cases on the ground that the Constitution provides Congress with express authority to make rules for capture? *See* U.S. Const. art. I, §8, cl. 11. Even more narrowly, does *Little* address just the liability of military subordinates asserting the "I was only following orders" defense?

Or does *Little* stand for the intermediate proposition that when Congress has prescribed the manner in which its authorization for the use of armed force is to be executed, its prescription "occupies the field" and is binding even on the President? *See, e.g., Youngstown Sheet & Tube Co. v. Sawyer*, 343 U.S. 579, 660-662 (1952) (Clark, J., concurring in the judgment).

3. "Core" Presidential War Powers. One possible interpretation of the Framers' intent is that designation of the President as Commander in Chief merely placed him at the top of the military chain of command, making him First General and Admiral — essentially the top military commander, but without independent war policy-making authority. At least as late as 1850, the Supreme Court clearly took this position. A unanimous Court held that the military occupation of a Mexican port by order of the President during the congressionally declared Mexican War did not annex it to the United States. *Fleming v. Page*, 50 U.S. (9 How.) 603 (1850). It reasoned that the President's

> duty and power are purely military. As commander in chief, he is authorized to direct the movements of the naval and military forces *placed by law at his command*, and to employ them in the manner he may deem most effectual to harass and conquer and subdue the enemy. He may invade the hostile country, and subject it to the sovereignty and authority of the United States. But his conquests do not enlarge the boundaries of this Union, *nor extend the operation of our institutions and laws beyond the limits assigned to them by the legislative power.* [*Id.* at 615 (emphasis added).]

While *Fleming* assigns a relatively narrow command authority to the President, subject to limits set by Congress, the assertion in *The Prize Cases* and the passage from *Milligan* quoted in the introduction to this section have anchored a broader view of that power. That view is that the President, as Commander in Chief, has inherent and *preclusive* authority to command the military in authorized armed conflicts — variously called the authority to conduct campaigns, to command the troops on the battlefield, and to decide on tactics. By "preclusive," adherents of this theory of presidential war powers mean that these "core" war powers cannot be interfered with or limited by statute; that exercises of core command authority fall into Justice Jackson's category 3, in which "[c]ourts sustain exclusive Presidential control . . . only by disabling the Congress from acting upon the subject." *The Steel Seizure Case*, 343 U.S. 579, 637-638 (1952) (Jackson, J., concurring). For example, an infamous 2002 Office of Legal Counsel memorandum on torture argued that

> Congress can no more interfere with the President's conduct of the interrogation of enemy combatants than it can dictate strategic or tactical decisions on the battlefield. Just as statutes that order the President to conduct warfare in a certain manner or for specific

> goals would be unconstitutional, so too are laws that seek to prevent the President from gaining the intelligence he believes necessary to prevent attacks upon the United States. [Memorandum from Jay S. Bybee, Assistant Att'y Gen., Off. of Legal Counsel, to Alberto R. Gonzales, Counsel to the President (Aug. 1, 2002), in *The Torture Papers: The Road to Abu Ghraib* 172, 207 (Karen J. Greenberg & Joshua L. Dratel eds., 2005).]

Does the case law we have read support this argument? The constitutional understanding? Interestingly, the United States argued to the Court in *The Prize Cases* that

> [t]he function to use the army and navy being in the President, the mode of using them, within the rules of civilized warfare, and *subject to established laws of Congress*, must be subject to his discretion as a necessary incident to the use, *in the absence of any act of Congress controlling him.* [Brief for the United States and Captors at 22, *The Prize Cases*, 67 U.S. (2 Black) 635, in 3 *Landmark Briefs and Arguments of the Supreme Court of the United States: Constitutional Law* 495 (Philip B. Kurland & Gerhard Casper eds., 1978) (emphases added).]

4. Tactical Command Authority. Consider this summary of the President's powers as Commander in Chief in time of war:

> The President, not Congress, makes all day-to-day tactical decisions in the combat deployment of armed forces. Indeed, even when it ends a use of force by cutting off funds, Congress cannot constitutionally interfere with the Commander in Chief's tactical decisions for the safe withdrawal of the armed forces. But as powerful as the command authority is, the framers still intended that the Commander in Chief "would amount to nothing more than the supreme command and direction of the military and naval forces, as first General and Admiral of the Confederacy . . . ," as Alexander Hamilton explained in The Federalist Papers. By making the President the Commander in Chief in Article II, the framers addressed what they recognized as a defect in the conduct of the Revolutionary War. They did not compromise their insistence in Article I on collective judgment in the decision for war.
>
> Nor did they give the Commander in Chief any constitutional right to ignore the terms of a congressional authorization for the use of force. When Congress gives the President the authority to conduct war, he or she must conduct it within that authority, just as the President must follow any law that is constitutionally made. [*Deciding to Use Force Abroad: War Powers in a System of Checks and Balances* 15 (The Constitution Project, Peter Raven-Hansen rptr., 2005).]

Can you say what distinguishes uses of force that are tactical from those that are strategic? Do you think congressional constraints have the same force when the President is fighting a defensive war thrust upon us by attack as when he is fighting one authorized by Congress? Put another way, are you clear about precisely which Commander-in-Chief powers are preclusive?

5. Begging the Question of Core Presidential War Powers? Recent scholarship asserts that the widely held view that Congress cannot intrude on the core command powers of the President — like the "day-to-day tactical decisions in the combat deployment" or for "safe withdrawal" mentioned above — begs the question: what *are* the core powers? An exhaustive review of historical evidence and case law found that

> there is surprisingly little Founding-era evidence supporting the notion that the conduct of military campaigns is beyond legislative control and a fair amount of evidence that affirmatively undermines it. Instead, the text and evidence of original understanding provide

> substantial support only for the recognition of some version of a very different sort of preclusive power of the Commander in Chief — namely, a prerogative of superintendence when it comes to the military chain of command itself. That is, the President must to some considerable extent retain control over the vast reservoirs of military discretion that exist in every armed conflict, even when bounded by important statutory limitations; and thus Congress may not assign such ultimate decisionmaking discretion to anyone else (including subordinate military officers). [Barron & Lederman, *supra*, at 696.]

Although this "prerogative of superintendence" importantly protects civilian command of the armed forces, Barron and Lederman found little evidence that it includes substantive war powers that are beyond the reach of statute. Indeed, they conclude, even historical practice shows that

> a repeated, though not unbroken, deferential executive branch stance . . . appears to be premised on the assumption that the constitutional plan requires the nation's chief commander to guard his supervisory powers over the military chain of command jealously, to be willing to act in times of exigency if Congress is not available for consultation, and to use the very powerful weapon of the veto to forestall unacceptable limits proposed in the midst of military conflict — but that otherwise, the Constitution compels the Commander in Chief to comply with legislative restrictions. . . .
>
> . . . [F]or more than a century, there has been a working, dynamic practice within the political departments in which neither the Executive nor the legislature acted as if the Constitution prohibited congressional regulation [of the President's exercise of war powers]. [David J. Barron & Martin S. Lederman, *The Commander in Chief at the Lowest Ebb — A Constitutional History*, 121 Harv. L. Rev. 941, 949, 1108 (2008).]

On the other hand, recognizing that the "law of presidential power is often made through accretion" — in part, what we have called customary authority — this scholarship also suggests that recent claims of preclusive war power in the "War on Terror" may "subtly but increasingly influence future Executives to eschew the harder work of accepting legislative constraints as legitimate and actively working to make them tolerable by building public support for modifications." *Id.* at 1111. As we turn to such claims in the following chapters, consider the degree to which presidential power may, in fact, have grown by "accretion."

C. THE PRESIDENT'S EMERGENCY POWERS

The Constitution contains four references to emergencies, none of which expressly vests independent emergency power in the President. For example, while a person in detention may file a petition in court for a writ of habeas corpus, requiring his jailor to show a legal basis for his detention, the Suspension Clause provides that "the privilege of the writ of habeas corpus shall not be suspended, unless when in cases of rebellion or invasion the public safety may require it." U.S. Const., art. I, §9, cl. 2. Thus, the privilege of the writ may be suspended in such an emergency, leaving the government free to detain persons without the check of judicial review. But this Clause appears in Article I, listing (and limiting) Congress's powers, not in Article II.[2]

---

2. As we shall see in Chapter 27, it is disputed whether the President may unilaterally suspend or authorize suspension of the writ (as President Lincoln did during the Civil War). The Clause does not expressly provide an answer.

The Calling Forth Clause authorizes Congress to "provide for calling forth the militia to execute the laws of the Union, suppress insurrections and repel invasions." *Id.* art. I, §8, cl. 15. The President can "call forth," but first Congress must first give him that power.

Two other provisions address emergencies within individual states. Article I, §10, cl. 3 provides that a state may not engage in war "unless actually invaded, or in such imminent danger as will not admit of delay." Article IV, §4, provides that the United States shall protect a state against "domestic Violence" "on Application of [its] Legislature, or of the Executive (when the Legislature cannot be convened)." These provisions thus anticipate emergencies from invasion or domestic violence, but empower the threatened state or its executive, in the first instance, to act to meet the threat or request federal assistance. Since these provisions show that the Framers anticipated emergencies and knew textually how to empower the states or their executives to respond, it is telling that they nowhere expressly gave any analogous independent power to the federal executive.

Nevertheless, the President's lawyers argued for an emergency power to seize private property in *The Steel Seizure Case.* Justice Jackson responded:

> The appeal . . . that we declare the existence of inherent powers *ex necessitate* to meet an emergency asks us to do what many think would be wise, although it is something the forefathers omitted. They knew what emergencies were, knew the pressures they engender for authoritative action, knew, too, how they afford a ready pretext for usurpation. We may also suspect that they suspected that emergency powers would tend to kindle emergencies. Aside from suspension of the privilege of the writ of habeas corpus in time of rebellion or invasion, when the public safety may require it, they made no express provision for exercise of extraordinary authority because of a crisis. I do not think we rightfully may so amend their work, and, if we could, I am not convinced it would be wise to do so, although many modern nations have forthrightly recognized that war and economic crisis may upset the normal balance between liberty and authority. . . .
>
> In the practical working of our government we already have evolved a technique within the framework of the Constitution by which normal executive powers may be considerably expanded to meet an emergency. Congress may and has granted extraordinary authorities which lie dormant in normal times but may be called into play by the Executive in war or upon proclamation of a national emergency. . . .
>
> In view of the ease, expedition and safety with which Congress can grant and has granted large emergency powers, certainly ample to embrace this crisis, I am quite unimpressed with the argument that we should affirm possession of them without statute. Such power either has no beginning or it has no end. If it exists, it need submit to no legal restraint. I am not alarmed that it would plunge us straightway into dictatorship, but it is at least a step in that wrong direction. [343 U.S. at 649-653 (Jackson, J., concurring).]

See also id. at 603-604 (Frankfurter, J., concurring) ("Absence of authority in the President to deal with a crisis does not imply want of power in the Government.").

In fact, Congress has enacted more than 120 standby emergency statutes that permit the President to act in ways that would be impermissible in the absence of a crisis. *See* Brennan Ctr. for Justice, *A Guide to Emergency Powers and Their Use,* Dec. 5, 2018, https://www.brennancenter.org/analysis/emergency-powers); Jennifer K. Elsea & Matthew C. Weed, *Declarations of War and Authorization for the Use of Military Force: Historical Background and Legal Implications* (Cong. Res. Serv. RL31133), Apr. 18, 2014, at 43-75;

see generally Elizabeth Goitein, *What the President Could Do If He Declares a State of Emergency*, The Atlantic, Jan./Feb. 2019.

During the Vietnam War, President Nixon relied on one of these emergency statutes, the Feed and Forage Act of 1861, 41 U.S.C. §6301 (2018) (originally intended to provide fodder for cavalry horses), to finance the secret invasion of Cambodia. Nixon based his action on national emergencies that had been previously declared (one as early as 1933) and never revoked. When Congress learned of this use of emergency authority, in 1976 it passed the National Emergencies Act, 50 U.S.C. §§1601-1651 (2018), cancelling all existing national emergencies. The Act provides:

> (a) With respect to Acts of Congress authorizing the exercise, during the period of a national emergency, of any special or extraordinary power, the President is authorized to declare such national emergency. Such proclamation shall immediately be transmitted to the Congress and published in the Federal Register.
>
> (b) Any provisions of law conferring powers and authorities to be exercised during a national emergency shall be effective and remain in effect (1) only when the President (in accordance with subsection (a) of this section), specifically declares a national emergency, and (2) only in accordance with this chapter. . . . [*Id.* §1621.]

If a President now wishes to activate standby legislation, she must declare a new national emergency, indicate the statutory authority she intends to exercise, and notify Congress. *Id.* §§1621(a), 1631, 1641. *See* L. Elaine Halchin, *National Emergency Powers* (Cong. Res. Serv. 98-505 GOV), Aug. 5, 2019. As reported in August 2019, 31 of 53 declared national emergencies were still in effect. *Id.* at 12.

What is the emergency declared by the following proclamation and what authorities did it activate?

Presidential Proclamation No. 9844, Declaring a National Emergency Concerning the Southern Border of the United States

84 Fed. Reg. 4949 (Feb. 15, 2019)

A Proclamation

The current situation at the southern border presents a border security and humanitarian crisis that threatens core national security interests and constitutes a national emergency. The southern border is a major entry point for criminals, gang members, and illicit narcotics. The problem of large-scale unlawful migration through the southern border is long-standing, and despite the executive branch's exercise of existing statutory authorities, the situation has worsened in certain respects in recent years. In particular, recent years have seen sharp increases in the number of family units entering and seeking entry to the United States and an inability to provide detention space for many of these aliens while their removal proceedings are pending. If not detained, such aliens are often released into the country and are often difficult to remove from the United States because they fail to appear for hearings, do not comply with orders of removal, or are otherwise difficult to locate. In response to the directive in my April 4, 2018, memorandum and subsequent requests for support by the Secretary of Homeland Security, the Department of Defense has provided support and resources to the Department of Homeland Security at the southern border. Because of the gravity of the current emergency situation, it is necessary for the Armed Forces to provide additional support to address the crisis.

NOW, THEREFORE, I, DONALD J. TRUMP, by the authority vested in me by the Constitution and the laws of the United States of America, including sections 201 and 301 of the National Emergencies Act (50 U.S.C. 1601 et seq.), hereby declare that a national emergency exists at the southern border of the United States, and that section 12302 of title 10, United States Code, is invoked and made available, according to its terms, to the Secretaries of the military departments concerned, subject to the direction of the Secretary of Defense in the case of the Secretaries of the Army, Navy, and Air Force. To provide additional authority to the Department of Defense to support the Federal Government's response to the emergency at the southern border, I hereby declare that this emergency requires use of the Armed Forces and, in accordance with section 301 of the National Emergencies Act (50 U.S.C. 1631), that the construction authority provided in section 2808 of title 10, United States Code, is invoked and made available, according to its terms, to the Secretary of Defense and, at the discretion of the Secretary of Defense, to the Secretaries of the military departments. I hereby direct as follows:

Section 1. The Secretary of Defense, or the Secretary of each relevant military department, as appropriate and consistent with applicable law, shall order as many units or members of the Ready Reserve to active duty as the Secretary concerned, in the Secretary's discretion, determines to be appropriate to assist and support the activities of the Secretary of Homeland Security at the southern border.

Sec. 2. The Secretary of Defense, the Secretary of the Interior, the Secretary of Homeland Security, and, subject to the discretion of the Secretary of Defense, the Secretaries of the military departments, shall take all appropriate actions, consistent with applicable law, to use or support the use of the authorities herein invoked, including, if necessary, the transfer and acceptance of jurisdiction over border lands. . . .

IN WITNESS WHEREOF, I have hereunto set my hand this fifteenth day of February, in the year of our Lord two thousand nineteen, and of the Independence of the United States of America the two hundred and forty-third.

Donald J. Trump

Notes and Questions

a. The National Emergencies Act and Standby Emergency Legislation

1. *First Step: Declaring a National Emergency.* Soon after the 9/11 terrorist attacks, President George W. Bush issued Proclamation No. 7463, 66 Fed. Reg. 48,199 (Sept. 14, 2001), declaring that the 9/11 attacks created a national emergency. Given the loss of life and chaos they created, the continuing threat that possible unknown associates of the perpetrators posed, and the continuing nationwide ground stop of air traffic, it seems self-evident that the nation was experiencing an emergency.

But when do less dramatic circumstances justify proclamation of a national emergency? The National Emergencies Act does not define a national emergency. According to one commentator, "[t]he test for when a national emergency exists is completely subjective — anything the President says is a national emergency is a national emergency." Glenn E. Fuller, Note, *The National Emergency Dilemma: Balancing the Executive's Crisis Powers and the Need for Accountability,* 52 S. Cal. L. Rev. 1453, 1458 (1979). Another commentator asserts:

> There are perhaps at least four aspects of an emergency condition. The first is its temporal character: an emergency is sudden, unforeseen, and of unknown duration. The second is its potential gravity: an emergency is dangerous and threatening to life and well-being. The third, in terms of governmental role and authority, is the matter of perception: who discerns this phenomenon? The Constitution may be guiding on this question, but not always conclusive. Fourth, there is the element of response: By definition, an emergency requires immediate action, but is, as well, unanticipated and, therefore . . . cannot always be "dealt with according to rule." [Halchin, *supra,* at 3-4 (citations omitted).]

Should Congress try to define the term? Can you suggest suitable language?

In the absence of a statutory definition of emergency, can you say how and by whom a presidential declaration of a national emergency could be challenged? Is insufficient evidence a basis for a court to reject the determination of emergency, if a case comes properly before it? Are courts equipped to second-guess such a claim by the President? Is Congress better equipped? If Congress disagrees, how should it respond?

2. *A National Emergency at the Border?* Does the national emergency declared by President Trump in Proclamation No. 9844 meet the four-part standard suggested above? The Proclamation cites as one basis for the declaration of emergency national security risks posed by the inflow of "criminals, gang members, and illicit narcotics" across the border. But the evidence shows that aliens in the United States commit crime at a lower rate than U.S. citizens, and that most drug-smuggling takes place primarily at legal ports of entry, not at the rest of the border. *See, e.g.,* Gina Martinez & Abigail Abrams, *Trump Repeated Many of His Old Claims About the Border to Justify the State of Emergency. Here Are the Facts,* Time, Feb. 15, 2019, http://time.com/5530506/Donald-trump-emergency-border-fact-check/.

Can you say that Congress concurred in the determination that an emergency existed by appropriating some money for border barriers, even if less than the President requested?

3. The Second Step: Invoking Standby Statutory Authority. Proclamation No. 9844, standing alone, confers no power. The power of a declared national emergency comes from the statutes that it invokes. Thus, the invocation of national emergency authority is essentially a two-step process: first, the President declares an emergency in accordance with the requirements of the National Emergencies Act, and then he uses the authority provided by and in accordance with the standby statutes that he identifies (assuming that he does not rely solely on a claim of independent emergency authority).

President Trump invokes two standby statutes in the Proclamation. We defer analysis of them, and related authorities, until the following chapter.

4. IEEPA. In 1917, during World War I, Congress passed the Trading with the Enemy Act, which gives the President authority to regulate a variety of domestic and international economic transactions in wartime. The Act was amended in 1933 to make it applicable during peacetime national emergencies as well. *See* 50 U.S.C. App. §§1-44 (2018), as amended. It has been invoked by a succession of Presidents to take extraordinary foreign and domestic executive actions.

The International Emergency Economic Powers Act (IEEPA), 50 U.S.C. §§1701-1708 (2018), was enacted in 1977 to curb perceived presidential abuses of authority under the Trading with the Enemy Act. It was invoked by President Carter and analyzed by the Supreme Court in *Dames & Moore*, which we encountered earlier in this chapter. Without disturbing the President's wartime authority under earlier legislation, the IEEPA gives the President the same peacetime emergency economic powers as previously, but those powers may only be exercised following a new national emergency declaration. After that declaration, the President is authorized to prohibit "any transactions in foreign exchange, transfers of credit or payments between, by, through, or to any banking institution, to the extent that such transfers or payments involve any interest of any foreign country or a national thereof, or the importing or exporting of currency or securities," as well as to freeze and block certain property in which a foreign national as an interest. 50 U.S.C. §1702(a)(1).

In addition to its use in the Iran hostage crisis, the IEEPA has been invoked by Presidents to limit trade with South Africa, Libya, Panama, Iraq, Haiti, and the Balkans, and to block assets of designated terrorists and other foreign nationals whose actions threaten interests of the United States or its allies, as well as to restrict activities that threaten the further proliferation of nuclear, chemical, and biological weapons. Executive orders declaring national emergencies and invoking the IEEPA are set out in the United States Code following the text of the statute.

5. IEEPA Emergencies Under the Trump Administration. In May 2019, President Donald J. Trump declared a national emergency (the fifth of his presidency) by Executive Order No. 13,873, *Securing the Information and Communications Technology and Services Supply Chain*, 84 Fed. Reg. 22,689 (May 15, 2019). The order invoked his authority under IEEPA to impose sanctions on certain technology suppliers, and it tasked the Secretary of Commerce to come up with plans to implement the sanctions within 150 days (suggesting to some a tension between the declared emergency and the five-month runway). *See* Andrew Boyle, *An Emergency or Business as Usual? Huawei and Trump's Emergency Powers*, Just Security, May 24, 2019.

Commentators saw the order as targeting a particular Chinese technology firm, Huawei, as part of a U.S. trade war with China. Note that the IEEPA standard for sanctions is "any unusual and extraordinary threat, which has its source in whole or substantial part outside the United States, to the national security, foreign policy, or economy of the United States, if the President declares a national emergency with respect to such threat." 50 U.S.C. §1701(a). Is the use of IEEPA "as leverage in a trade war" with China an "abuse of the intent of emergency powers," as some have charged? *See* Boyle, *supra.*

In August 2019, President Trump tweeted, "Our great American companies are hereby ordered to immediately start looking for an alternative to China, including bringing your companies HOME and making your products in the USA." Jeanne Whalen, Abha Bhattarai & Reed Albergotti, *Trump "Hereby" Orders U.S. Business Out of China. Can He Do That?*, Wash. Post., Aug. 24, 2019. When the media quoted scholars who were skeptical of his authority, he responded — by tweet again — "For all of the Fake News Reporters that don't have a clue as to what the law is relative to Presidential powers, China, etc., try looking at the Emergency Economic Powers Act of 1977. Case closed!" *Id.*

Is it closed? Consider the standard set out above. What does the President have to find to invoke his IEEPA powers? One commentator argues that "Trump's escalation of a self-initiated trade war with China and inability to cut whatever deal might be necessary to end it are hardly the type of threat described by IEEPA's text." Joshua Geltzer, *Blame Trump, Not the U.S. Code, for His Abuse of Emergency Authority,* Just Security, Aug. 26, 2019. Is that conclusion consistent with IEEPA's language? Does it depend on the kinds of threats for which Presidents have previously invoked their IEEPA authority? A law firm that advises U.S. companies doing business in China cautiously concludes, "Given the broad authority provided by IEEPA, President Trump's threat to prohibit U.S. companies from doing business with China has a serious basis." Paul/Weiss (Client Memorandum), *Does President Trump Have Authority to Force U.S. Companies to Leave China?*, Aug. 26, 2019.

The "threat" argument relies on §1701(a) of IEEPA. Can you make a different argument based on §1702(a)(1)(A)?

> At the times and to the extent specified in section 1701 of this title, the President may, under such regulations as he may prescribe, by means of instructions, licenses, or otherwise — (A) investigate, regulate, or prohibit — (i) any transactions in foreign exchange, (ii) transfers of credit or payments between, by, through, or to any banking institution, to the extent that such transfers or payments involve any interest of any foreign country or a national thereof . . . by any person, or with respect to any property, subject to the jurisdiction of the United States. [50 U.S.C. §1702(a)(1)(A).]

Does this authority (or §1702(a)(1)(B), quoted by *Dames & Moore, supra* p. 38 n.2) authorize the President to order companies that are already in China to pull out? Does it authorize him to order U.S. companies not to invest in operations in China in the future?

6. *Terminating Emergencies.* The National Emergencies Act originally provided that a declared national emergency terminates either by concurrent resolution or when the President proclaims the termination. After the Supreme Court invalidated legislative vetoes in *INS v. Chadha,* 462 U.S. 919 (1983), Congress changed the termination requirement to a joint resolution — requiring presentment to the President. 50 U.S.C. §1622. A declared emergency also terminates automatically after one year, unless the President extends it by notice to Congress and publication in the *Federal*

Register. Id. §1622(d). Congress also imposed a duty on itself to meet every six months after an emergency has been declared "to consider a vote on a joint resolution to determine whether that emergency shall be terminated." *Id.* §1622(b). It has never met specifically for this purpose in the more than 40 years since the Act became law.

In March 2019, Congress passed a joint resolution to terminate the national emergency President Trump declared at the southern border. But President Trump vetoed the resolution. The House then voted 248-181 to override the veto, falling short of the two-thirds supermajority needed for override. Thus, once the President declares a national emergency, he can continue it indefinitely as long as more than one-third of *either* house agrees with him. Should Congress amend the National Emergencies Act to preserve a greater role for itself in exigent circumstances? *See* Steve Vladeck, *Will Trump Use a National Emergency to End the Shutdown? Either Way, Congress Must Revisit the National Emergencies Act,* NBC News THINK, Jan. 24, 2019, https://www.nbcnews.com/think/opinion/will-trump-use-national-emergency-end-shutdown-either-way-congress-ncna962556.

Sometimes the implementation of statutory authority activated by the declaration of a national emergency requires the expenditure of taxpayer dollars. Proclamation No. 9844 explicitly invokes 10 U.S.C. §2808 (2018), which allows the reallocation of funds previously appropriated for the Defense Department, presumably for construction of President Trump's promised "Border Wall," for which he had tried and failed to get funded through the regular appropriations process. Might the national emergency thus be effectively terminated by legislation cutting off funding? See *infra* p. 106 (the Appropriations Power).

b. Independent Executive Emergency Authority?

1. The Steel Seizure Case and Independent Executive Emergency Authority. Although in *The Steel Seizure Case* Justice Jackson looked to Congress to provide for emergencies, Congress cannot anticipate every one. There may be emergencies calling for immediate action for which Congress has enacted no standby statutory authority and for which it has no time to act. Justice Jackson himself dropped a footnote to his jeremiad against executive emergency power asserting that he would "exclude, as in a very limited category by itself, the establishment of martial law," that is, the exercise of power by military commanders when civil authority breaks down. 343 U.S. at 650 n.19 (Jackson, J., concurring). Justice Burton, concurring in the opinion and the judgment of the Court, emphasized that

> [t]he present situation is not comparable to that of an imminent invasion or threatened attack. We do not face the issue of what might be the President's constitutional power to meet such catastrophic situations. Nor is it claimed that the current seizure is in the nature of a military command addressed by the President, as Commander in Chief, to a mobilized nation waging, or imminently threatened with, total war. [*Id.* at 659 (Burton, J., concurring).]

Justice Clark, concurring in the judgment, added,

> I conclude that where Congress has laid down specific procedures to deal with the type of crisis confronting the President, he must follow those procedures in meeting the crisis; but that in the absence of such action by Congress, the President's independent

power to act depends upon the gravity of the situation confronting the nation. [*Id.* at 662 (Clark, J., concurring in the judgment).]

Finally, the three dissenters stressed that "[t]he Constitution was itself 'adopted in a period of grave emergency. . . . While emergency does not create power, emergency may furnish the occasion for the exercise of power.'" 343 U.S. at 703-704 (Vinson, C.J., dissenting) (quoting *Home Building & Loan Ass'n v. Blaisdell,* 290 U.S. 398, 425-426 (1934)). In their view, the Korean War furnished that occasion, when President Truman seized private property "to save the situation until Congress could act." *Id.* at 704.

Do you think *The Steel Seizure Case* ruled out independent executive power in future emergencies? If not, under what conditions can such power be exercised?

2. *Independent Constitutional Authority for Proclamation No. 9844?* Although in issuing Proclamation No. 9844 President Trump in part invoked the authority purportedly vested in him by the Constitution (like other Presidents who have declared emergencies), the Administration disavowed reliance on independent constitutional authority for the Proclamation, invoking instead statutory authorities. *Sierra Club v. Trump,* 379 F. Supp. 3d 883, 909 (N.D. Cal. 2019) ("The Government is not relying on independent Article II authority to undertake border construction; rather, the actions alleged are being undertaken pursuant to express statutory authority."). As these statutory authorities deeply implicate Congress's appropriations power, they are discussed *infra* p. 106.

3. *In re Neagle: Executive Power to Protect the Government?* In 1889, David Neagle, a federal marshal appointed to protect U.S. Supreme Court Justice Stephen Field while he sat on circuit, shot and killed a man who tried to attack the Justice with a large Bowie knife. California authorities arrested both Marshal Neagle *and Justice Field.* Field, but not Neagle, was quickly released on a writ of habeas corpus. A federal statute provided that the writ was available to one "in custody for an act done or omitted in pursuance of a law of the United States." *In re Neagle,* 135 U.S. 1, 41 (1890) (quoting the statute). Was Marshal Neagle held in custody for an act done in pursuance of a law of the United States?

While the Court found no statute expressly authorizing a federal marshal to protect a Supreme Court Justice, it asserted that it would be lamentable if there were "no means of protecting the judges, in the conscientious and faithful discharge of their duties, from the malice and hatred of those upon whom their judgments may operate unfavorably." *Id.* at 59. "In the view we take of the Constitution of the United States, any obligation fairly and properly inferable from that instrument, or any duty of the marshal to be derived from the general scope of his duties under the laws of the United States, is a 'law'" within the meaning of the habeas statute. *Id.* Specifically, the Court said, that obligation may be found in the Take Care Clause, under which the executive duty includes "the rights, duties and obligations growing out of the constitution itself, our international relations, and all the protection implied by the nature of the government under the constitution?" *Id.* at 64.

> We cannot doubt the power of the president to take measures for the protection of a judge of one of the courts of the United States who, while in the discharge of the duties of his office, is threatened with a personal attack which may probably result in his death, and

> we think it clear that where this protection is to be afforded through the civil power, the Department of Justice is the proper one to set in motion the necessary means of protection. [*Id.* at 67.]

The Court thus rejected the claim that the President was powerless when "no such law has been passed by Congress." The power of government self-protection (like the power of national self-defense), said the Court, is implied by the very "nature of the government under the Constitution." *Id.* at 64.

An alternative basis for the majority opinion, however, was a statute vesting U.S. marshals with the same powers to keep the peace as those possessed by local sheriffs. *Id.* at 68. But the majority opinion mentioned this statute only in passing, and only after concluding that the President had independent constitutional power to take measures to protect a federal judge. Was the Court's constitutional analysis holding or dictum?

Surprisingly, given the fact that the case involved a threat to the life of a fellow Justice, the two dissenters emphasized that while Article II imposes a duty on the President to take care that the laws be faithfully executed, "it is not his duty to make laws or a law of the United States." *Id.* at 83 (Lamar, J., dissenting). If the Justices needed protection, they argued, Congress "was perfectly able to pass such laws as it should deem expedient in reference to such matter." *Id.*

4. Neagle and Rescue Abroad. The *Neagle* Court described with approval a historical incident in which an American naval captain threatened force to obtain the release of an applicant for U.S. citizenship, a Hungarian named Martin Koszta, who was imprisoned by Austria. Unlike Marshal Neagle, the naval captain apparently acted against the instructions of the President and the Secretary of the Navy. *See* Wormuth & Firmage, *supra*, at 152 ("[H]is action was illegal when undertaken but was later ratified by congressional commendation."). By approving this incident, is *Neagle* authority for military rescue operations without prior congressional authorization? How do you think the Hostage Act of 1868, set forth at casebook p. 40, affects any such authority?

5. Neagle and Emergencies at Home. Is *Neagle* authority for the domestic use of troops without prior congressional authorization? In 1895, five years after *Neagle*, the President sued to enjoin the Pullman Strike on the ground that it threatened transportation of the mails. The Court upheld an injunction, despite the absence of any statutory authority for such a suit, stating that

> [t]he entire strength of the nation may be used to enforce in any part of the land the full and free exercise of all national powers and security of all rights entrusted by the Constitution to its care. The strong arm of the national government may be put forth to brush away all obstructions to the freedom of interstate commerce or the transportation of the mails. If the emergency arises, the army of the Nation, and all its militia, are at the service of the Nation to compel obedience to its laws. . . .
>
> . . . [I]t is more to the praise than to the blame of the government, that, instead of determining for itself questions of right or wrong on the part of these petitioners and their associates and enforcing that determination by the club of the policeman and the bayonet of the soldier, it submitted all those questions to the peaceful determination of judicial tribunals. . . . [*In re Debs*, 158 U.S. 564, 582-583 (1895).]

Both *Debs* and *The Steel Seizure Case* involved presidential actions allegedly necessary to protect against the effects of labor strikes. Is *Debs* good law after *The Steel Seizure Case*? Is *Neagle*? Can the three decisions be reconciled?

6. *The Limits of Independent Emergency Power.* Consider the Court's statement in *Home Building & Loan Ass'n v. Blaisdell*, 290 U.S. 398, 425-426 (1934):

> Emergency does not increase granted power or remove or diminish the restrictions imposed upon power granted or reserved. The Constitution was adopted in a period of grave emergency. Its grants of power to the Federal Government and its limitations of the powers of the States were determined in the light of emergency, and they are not altered by emergency. What power was thus granted and what limitations were thus imposed are questions which have always been, and always will be, the subject of close examination under our constitutional system.

In *Reid v. Covert*, 354 U.S. 1, 5-6 (1957) (plurality opinion), a four-Justice plurality of the Court added, "The United States is entirely a creature of the Constitution. Its power and authority have no other source. It can only act in accordance with all the limitations imposed by the Constitution." But if emergency power can be found within the Constitution, does it necessarily follow that such power may be exercised by the President acting alone? The dissenters in *The Steel Seizure Case* thought so:

> The Framers knew, as we should know in these times of peril, that there is real danger in Executive weakness. There is no cause to fear Executive tyranny so long as the laws of Congress are being faithfully executed. Certainly there is no basis for fear of dictatorship when the Executive acts, as he did in this case, only to save the situation until Congress could act. [343 U.S. at 704 (Vinson, C.J., dissenting).]

If the independent executive power described in *Neagle* and *Debs* is not unlimited, what is its scope? Can Congress limit any such executive power by statute? If it exists only during emergencies, how are "emergencies" to be defined? What emergency was presented in *Debs* that could not have been addressed by legislation? Was the emergency in *Neagle* more acute?

7. *Lincoln's Extra-Constitutional Claims.* Consider President Lincoln's justification for his unilateral issuance of the Emancipation Proclamation:

> [M]y oath to preserve the constitution to the best of my ability, imposed upon me the duty of preserving, by every indispensable means, that government — that nation — of which the constitution was the organic law. Was it possible to lose the nation, and yet preserve the constitution? By general law life and limb must be protected; yet often a limb must be amputated to save a life; but a life is never wisely given to save a limb. I felt that measures, otherwise unconstitutional, might become lawful, by becoming indispensable to the preservation of the constitution, through the preservation of the nation. [Letter to Albert G. Hodges (Apr. 4, 1864), in 7 *Collected Works of Abraham Lincoln* 281 (Roy P. Basler ed., 1953).]

Did Lincoln claim constitutional authority for the Proclamation? If his authority is extra-constitutional, what is its source? If there is some emergency power of self-preservation in the government, does it necessarily follow that it is vested in the

President when Congress can act? Note that the Confiscation Act had already freed all slaves put to hostile use by the Confederate forces. Act of Aug. 6, 1861, ch. 60, 12 Stat. 319; *see also* Act of July 17, 1862, ch. 195, 12 Stat. 589.

THE PRESIDENT'S NATIONAL SECURITY POWERS: SUMMARY OF BASIC PRINCIPLES

- In *Zivotofsky II*, the Supreme Court held for the first time that the President has an exclusive implied power that trumps inconsistent legislation. At the same time, it recognized that the President's recognition determination is part of a political process that may require Congress to make laws.

- While the President thus recognizes foreign states, negotiates treaties, receives ambassadors, collects and analyzes foreign intelligence, conducts foreign relations, and, as a practical matter, usually takes the initiative in making foreign policy, no constitutional text vests him with any *general* "plenary and exclusive" foreign affairs power. The Supreme Court's description of such a power of the President ("as the sole organ of the federal government in the field of international relations") in *Curtiss-Wright* was dictum and does not mean that the President is free from Congress's lawmaking power in the field of international relations.

- The President's practical advantages and experience in exercising foreign affairs powers, however, coupled with Congress's disadvantages, may often require broad and generously construed delegations of statutory authority to him, and concede the initiative to him when Congress has not acted.

- The same factors may help support finding customary authority derived from repeated executive actions in foreign affairs, such as the claims settlement in *Dames & Moore* or, arguably, repeated but limited uses of armed force abroad to rescue Americans.

- The framing of the Declare War Clause ("leaving to the Executive the power to repel sudden attacks," according to Madison's notes), the practical necessity to defend against attacks, and the Commander in Chief Clause all suggest that the President has an inherent power to fight what we have called defensive war.

- But the defensive war power may be subject to legal limits imposed by Congress, as well as temporal limits that depend on the duration of a threat or attack and the availability of funding. These limits are disputed, mainly unaddressed by case law, and subject to inter-branch negotiation.

- The Commander in Chief Clause at a minimum vests the President with the unitary civilian command of the armed forces. It is also understood to give the Commander in Chief control of day-to-day tactical military operations in authorized conflicts or defensive war, subject to the terms of any authorization from Congress. But which operations fall within the Commander in Chief's command authority, and whether command authority is beyond the reach of statute, are disputed and mainly unaddressed by case law.

- The President has inherent constitutional authority to order measures to protect government officers and functions, at least from imminent or ongoing attack, when Congress has not occupied the field by applicable legislation.
- When the President declares a national emergency, he may then exercise a variety of standby statutory authorities. The definition of a national emergency, however, like the existence of independent presidential emergency powers, is uncertain.

4

Congress's National Security Powers

Congress, unlike the President, is expressly vested by the Constitution with a host of specific foreign affairs and war powers. Apart from the declaration of war power, however, these powers are rarely considered in isolation. The courts typically review national security legislation from the perspective of the aggregate of congressional war powers.

In this chapter we begin with a brief study of the power to authorize war, then address the delegation of national security powers. Following an in-depth look at national security appropriations, we conclude with an analysis of substantive and procedural limits on Congress's national security powers.

A. CONGRESSIONAL AUTHORIZATIONS FOR WAR

John Locke wrote that a nation could "declare" war "by Word or Action." John Locke, *Two Treatises of Government* 278 (Peter Laslett ed., 1967). A nation could declare war, he wrote, "by Word" by issuing a formal declaration of war. It could declare war by "Action" by engaging in an act of war. In our system, of course, Congress may not engage in an act of war, but it can authorize the Executive to do so. Yet on a number of occasions the Executive has engaged in war without congressional authorization. For a partial listing of each kind of war, see *U.S. Periods of War and Dates of Recent Conflicts* (Cong. Res. Serv. RS21405), Dec. 14, 2018.

The following materials provide an example of each method of "declaring" war: a formal declaration of war, an early statutory authorization for war (prior authorizations for the use of military force were directed at Native Americans and pirates), and a modern Authorization for the Use of Military Force (AUMF). Consider how they differ in scope and whether they exhaust the ways in which Congress may authorize war.

1. Formal Declaration of War

Joint Resolution Declaring That a State of War Exists Between the Government of Germany and the Government and the People of the United States and Making Provisions to Prosecute the Same

Pub. L. No. 77-331, 55 Stat. 796 (1941)

Whereas the Government of Germany has formally declared war against the Government and the people of the United States of America: Therefore be it

Resolved by the Senate and House of Representatives of the United States of America in Congress assembled, That the state of war between the United States and the Government of Germany which has thus been thrust upon the United States is hereby formally declared; and the President is hereby authorized and directed to employ the entire naval and military forces of the United States and the resources of the Government to carry on war against the Government of Germany; and, to bring the conflict to a successful termination, all of the resources of the country are hereby pledged by the Congress of the United States.

Notes and Questions

1. Formally Declaring a State of War. A formal declaration may be used to start a war. As the declaration against Germany in World War II shows, a declaration may also recognize that we are already in a "state of war" by virtue of an attack. Each of the 11 formal declarations in five separate wars (the War of 1812, the 1846 War with Mexico, the Spanish-American War, and the two World Wars) recites that a state of war "exists" between the United States and the enemy state. All of the twentieth-century declarations say that the enemy state initiated the hostilities, and every declaration grants sweeping authority to the President. *See generally* Jennifer K. Elsea & Matthew C. Weed, *Declarations of War and Authorizations for the Use of Military Force: Historical Background and Legal Implications* (Cong. Res. Serv. RL31133), Apr. 18, 2014.

Increasing state sensitivity to public diplomacy and world opinion, however, as well as the decline of opportunities for the lawful use of force occasioned by the proliferation of treaties and the evolution of customary international law, have long made declarations of war impolitic. The last declaration of war by the United States was against Rumania in 1942. Thus, "declarations of war may have become anachronistic in contemporary international law." *Id.* at 23.

In fact, there is evidence that formal declarations were already largely obsolete in 1787, by which date the concept of "defensive war" had taken such firm root in the law of nations that it was widely understood that war could be started without the formality of declaration. *See, e.g., The Federalist No. 25,* at 165 (Alexander Hamilton) (Clinton Rossiter ed., 1961) ("[T]he ceremony of a formal denunciation of war has of late fallen into disuse."). In this light, is it likely that the Framers intended to vest Congress only with an already increasingly anachronistic formal declaration power and no other constitutional means to choose war?

2. The Legal Domino Effects of War. A declaration of war by Congress gives notice to neutrals of the existence of hostilities and of the identity of the belligerents, and it activates certain rights and obligations of neutrals and belligerents alike, a requirement of international law noted in *The Prize Cases.* It also triggers approximately 33 standby statutory authorities that would not otherwise be available to the President. *See generally* Elsea & Weed, *supra,* at 43-48. For example, under the Alien Enemy Act, 50 U.S.C. §21 (2018), "[w]henever there is a declared war between the United States and any foreign nation or government," citizens of the "hostile nation or government" who are at least 14 years old and not naturalized are subject to summary arrest, internment, and deportation when the President so proclaims. The Trading with the Enemy Act, 50 U.S.C. App. §§2, 5(b) (2018), enables the President to regulate or prohibit commerce with any foreign state or its citizens after "Congress has declared war or . . . the existence of a state of war." And the President may authorize electronic surveillance, physical searches, and the use of pen registers and trap and trace devices to acquire foreign intelligence without a court order for up to 15 days "following a declaration of war" by Congress. 50 U.S.C. §§1811, 1829, 1844 (2018).

More than 100 other standby authorities are available even without a declaration of war, during a "time of war" or "when war is imminent." *See generally* Elsea & Weed, *supra,* at 49-68. These authorize the President to take land for military purposes; commandeer private production lines for war manufacturing; take control of private transportation for war transport; and sequester, hold, and dispose of enemy property, among other powers.

3. Is Congress's War-Declaring Role Strictly Juridical? In light of the legal domino effects of a declaration of war, some scholars have argued that a declaration is strictly a juridical pronouncement to trigger legal consequences and is not needed by the President to use force. *See* John C. Yoo, *The Continuation of Politics by Other Means: The Original Understanding of War Powers,* 84 Cal. L. Rev. 167 (1996). According to this theory, the President manages international relations and, when diplomacy fails, decides unilaterally whether to use military force. *Id.* at 291. Congress only enters into the equation to raise and supply troops or to provide an after-the-fact "appropriations check" on disfavored military adventures by the President. In short, "the Framers created a framework designed to encourage presidential initiative in war. Congress was given a role in war-making decisions not by the Declare War Clause, but by its powers over funding and impeachment. The courts were given no role at all." *Id.* at 170. Does this theory square with what we learned in Chapter 2 about the history of the framing of the Constitution?

4. Declaring War on Terrorists? Formal declarations of war have always named belligerents that were sovereign states. Following the September 11, 2001, terrorist attacks on the World Trade Center and the Pentagon, however, a newspaper columnist wrote, and some members of Congress reportedly agreed, that "Congress . . . should immediately declare war. It does not have to name a country. It can declare war against those who carried out [the] attack." Robert Kagan, Opinion, *We Must*

Fight This War, Wash. Post, Sept. 12, 2001. May Congress declare war on a group of people? May it declare war without naming any enemy at all? Supposing Congress could declare war against a group of terrorists, why didn't it do so in 2001?

2. Authorizing War by Statute

Reading *Bas v. Tingy*

As relations between France and the United States deteriorated between 1798 and 1800, Congress enacted a succession of measures approving naval actions against France. (We considered one such measure in *Little v. Barreme*, see Chapter 3.) Initially, it authorized U.S. armed vessels to capture French vessels that had "committed depredations" on U.S.-owned vessels or that were found "hovering" off U.S. coasts for that purpose. Act of May 28, 1798, ch. 48, 1 Stat. 561. When this measure did not adequately protect U.S. shipping, Congress next authorized merchant vessels to defend themselves against "any search, restraint or seizure" by ships operating under French colors. Act of June 25, 1798, ch. 60, 1 Stat. 572. Three days later, Congress passed another act that provided for the judicial condemnation of captured vessels and for the return of recaptured U.S. vessels to their owners for a salvage payment of one-eighth of the full value. Act of June 28, 1798, ch. 62, 1 Stat. 574. The next year Congress passed a set of rules and regulations for its infant navy. This act provided in part:

> That for the ships or goods belonging to the citizens of the United States, or to the citizens or subjects of any nation, in amity with the United States, if retaken from the *enemy*... the owners are to allow... one half [of the whole value for salvage].... [Act of Mar. 2, 1799, ch. 24, §7, 1 Stat. 709, 716 (emphasis added).]

On April 21, 1799, Captain Tingy, commander of the public armed ship *Ganges*, recaptured the *Eliza*, which belonged to John Bas and had been captured by a French privateer on the high seas on March 31, 1799. Tingy sought one-half the value of the *Eliza*, as provided by the 1799 act. But Bas argued that the act only applied to vessels retaken from the "enemy," and that France was not an enemy. On appeal to the Supreme Court, the Justices delivered their opinions seriatim. The opinion of Justice Moore in favor of affirmance is omitted.

- Congress had not formally declared war on France. How then did France become an "enemy"?
- Justice Washington asserted that a declaration of war creates a "perfect war." What is a perfect war? How was the "imperfect war" with France different? "Perfect" and "imperfect" sound anachronistic today; what synonyms do the opinions suggest?
- The Court was not called upon to decide precisely the scope of the President's powers to fight a war authorized but not formally declared by Congress. What do the opinions nevertheless suggest as an answer, and why?

Bas v. Tingy

United States Supreme Court, 1800
4 U.S. (4 Dall.) 37

WASHINGTON, Justice. . . . 1st. [The 1798 Act] relates to re-captures from *the French,* and [the 1799 Act] relates to re-captures from *the enemy;* and, it is said, that "the enemy" is not descriptive of France, or of her armed vessels, according to the correct and technical understanding of the word.

The decision of this question must depend upon another; which is, whether, at the time of passing the act of congress of the 2d of March 1799, there subsisted a state of war between the two nations? It may, I believe, be safely laid down, that every contention by force between two nations, in external matters, under the authority of their respective governments, is not only war, but public war. If it be declared in form, it is called *solemn,* and is of the perfect kind; because one whole nation is at war with another whole nation; and *all* the members of the nation declaring war, are authorised to commit hostilities against all the members of the other, in every place, and under every circumstance. In such a war all the members act under a general authority, and all the rights and consequences of war attach to their condition.

But hostilities may subsist between two nations more confined in its nature and extent; being limited as to places, persons, and things; and this is more properly termed *imperfect war,* because not solemn, and because those who are authorised to commit hostilities, act under special authority, and can go no farther than to the extent of their commission. Still, however, it is *public war,* because it is an external contention by force, between some of the members of the two nations, authorised by the legitimate powers. It is a war between the two nations, though all the members are not authorised to commit hostilities such as in a solemn war, where the government restrain the general power.

Now, if this be the true definition of war, let us see what was the situation of the United States in relation to France. In March 1799, congress had raised an army; stopped all intercourse with France; dissolved our treaty; built and equipt ships of war; and commissioned private armed ships; enjoining the former, and authorising the latter, to defend themselves against the armed ships of France, to attack them on the high seas, to subdue and take them as prize, and to re-capture armed vessels found in their possession. Here, then, let me ask, what were the technical characters of an American and French armed vessel, combating on the high seas, with a view the one to subdue the other, and to make prize of his property? They certainly were not friends, because there was a contention by force; nor were they private enemies, because the contention was external, and authorised by the legitimate authority of the two governments. If they were not our enemies, I know not what constitutes an enemy.

2d. But, secondly, it is said, that a war of the imperfect kind, is more properly called acts of hostility, or reprizal, and that congress did not mean to consider the hostility subsisting between France and the United States, as constituting a state of war.

In support of this position, it has been observed, that in no law prior to March 1799, is France styled our enemy, nor are we said to be at war. This is true; but neither of these things were necessary to be done: because as to France, she was sufficiently described by the title of the French republic; and as to America, the degree of hostility meant to be carried on, was sufficiently described without declaring war, or declaring that we were at war. Such a declaration by congress, might have constituted a perfect state of war, which was not intended by the government. . . .

...[T]herefore, in my opinion, the decree of the Circuit Court ought to be affirmed.

CHASE, Justice.... Congress is empowered to declare a general war, or congress may wage a limited war; limited in place, in objects, and in time. If a general war is declared, its extent and operations are only restricted and regulated by the *jus belli*, forming a part of the law of nations; but if a partial war is waged, its extent and operation depend on our municipal laws.

What, then, is the nature of the contest subsisting between America and France? In my judgment, it is a limited, partial, war. Congress has not declared war in general terms; but congress has authorized hostilities on the high seas by certain persons in certain cases. There is no authority given to commit hostilities on land; to capture unarmed French vessels, nor even to capture French armed vessels lying in a French port; and the authority is not given, indiscriminately, to every citizen of America, against every citizen of France; but only to citizens appointed by commissions, or exposed to immediate outrage and violence. So far it is, unquestionably, a partial war; but, nevertheless, it is a public war, on account of the public authority from which it emanates.

There are four acts, authorised by our government, that are demonstrative of a state of war. A belligerent power has a right, by the law of nations, to search a neutral vessel; and, upon suspicion of a violation of her neutral obligations, to seize and carry her into port for further examination. But by the acts of congress, an American vessel is authorised: 1st. To resist the search of a French public vessel: 2d. To capture any vessel that should attempt, by force, to compel submission to a search: 3d. To re-capture any American vessel seized by a French vessel; and 4th. To capture any French armed vessel wherever found on the high seas. This suspension of the law of nations, this right of capture and re-capture, can only be authorized by an act of the government, which is, in itself, an act of hostility. But still it is a restrained, or limited, hostility; and there are, undoubtedly, many rights attached to a general war, which do not attach to this modification of the powers of defence and aggression....

The acts of congress have been analyzed to show, that a war is not openly denounced against France, and that France is no where expressly called the enemy of America: but this only proves the circumspection and prudence of the legislature. Considering our national prepossessions in favour of the French republic, congress had an arduous task to perform, even in preparing for necessary defence, and just retaliation. As the temper of the people rose, however, in resentment of accumulated wrongs, the language and the measures of the government became more and more energetic and indignant; though hitherto the popular feeling may not have been *ripe* for a solemn declaration of war; and an active and powerful opposition in our public councils, has postponed, if not prevented that decisive event, which many thought would have best suited the interest, as well as the honour of the United States. The progress of our contest with France, indeed, resembles much the progress of our revolutionary contest; in which, watching the current of public sentiment, the patriots of that day proceeded, step by step, from the supplicatory language of petitions for a redress of grievances, to the bold and noble declaration of national independence.

Having, then, no hesitation in pronouncing, that a partial war exists between America and France, and that France was an enemy, within the meaning of the act of March 1799, my voice must be given for affirming the decree of the Circuit Court.

PATERSON, Justice. As the case appears on the record, and has been accurately stated by the counsel, and by the judges, who have delivered their opinions, it is not necessary to recapitulate the facts. My opinion shall be expressed in a few words. The United States and the French republic are in a qualified state of hostility. An imperfect war, or a war, as to certain objects, and to a certain extent, exists between the two nations; and this modified warfare is authorized by the constitutional authority of our country. It is a war *quoad hoc* [to this extent]. As far as congress tolerated and authorized the war on our part, so far may we proceed in hostile operations. It is a maritime war; a war at sea as to certain purposes. The national armed vessels of France attack and capture the national armed vessels of the United States; and the national armed vessels of the United States are expressly authorized and directed to attack, subdue, and take, the national armed vessels of France, and also to recapture American vessels. It is therefore a public war between the two nations, qualified, on our part, in the manner prescribed by the constitutional organ of our country. In such a state of things, it is scarcely necessary to add, that the term "enemy," applies; it is the appropriate expression, to be limited in its signification, import, and use, by the qualified nature and operation of the war on our part. The word enemy proceeds the full length of the war, and no farther. . . .

By the COURT: Let the decree of the Circuit Court be affirmed.

Notes and Questions

1. *Authorizing War Without Expressly Declaring It.* Congress authorized the use of force against French naval vessels in a succession of gradually escalating statutes. None formally declared war, but each unmistakably singled out France as the enemy. Less than a year after *Bas,* the Court was again called upon to decide rights of salvage during the so-called Quasi-War with France. Writing for the Court, Chief Justice Marshall concluded that "[t]he whole powers of war being, by the constitution of the United States, vested in congress, the acts of that body can alone be resorted to as our guides in this enquiry." *Talbot v. Seeman,* 5 U.S. (1 Cranch) 1, 28 (1801). The Court unanimously found that Congress had authorized "partial hostilities" against France. Recall that the Court later considered another of these statutes in *Little v. Barreme,* 6 U.S. (2 Cranch) 170 (1804). In none of these opinions did the Supreme Court express any doubt that Congress could constitutionally authorize "imperfect" war by statute.

2. *Perfect vs. Imperfect War.* A formal declaration of war, Justice Bushrod Washington wrote in *Bas v. Tingy,* creates a "perfect" war, placing "one whole nation . . . at war with another whole nation; and *all* the members of the nation declaring war, are authorised to commit hostilities against all the members of the other, in every place, and under every circumstance." A more modern term might be *total war.* Most of our declarations of war are consistent with the suggested scope by expressly empowering the President to use all of the armed forces and resources of government to prosecute the war.

An "imperfect" war, by contrast, "is limited as to places, persons, and things." A more modern term might be *limited war.* As its names suggest, the Naval War or Quasi-War with France was limited both by place (U.S. coastal waters, high seas), persons (under the statute construed in *Little,* vessels traveling *to* France), and things (naval forces and armed merchant vessels). AUMFs have historically authorized only limited wars, sometimes subject to specific area or use limitations.

3. *Congressional Limits?* Some have argued that the President has plenary power to conduct a constitutionally authorized war, and that congressional efforts to control the use of weapons or the movement of troops are therefore unconstitutional. Is this view consistent with *Bas*? With *Little v. Barreme*? Although *Bas* did not pose the question whether a President must abide by the limits of an AUMF, the Justices' reasoning and dicta surely so suggested. Moreover, the Court so held in *Little* four years later.

Is there any constitutional difference between defining the scope of a limited war in the initial authorization and doing so during the war? Is there a constitutional ratchet that prevents Congress from modifying or rescinding an authorization for war, once granted? If not, what is the difference between such a modification and a statute directing the conduct of the war — for example, by ordering Platoon A to attack Hill B? What about a legislative command *not* to attack Hill B? Might the answer turn on the location of Hill B?

4. *War Without Congressional Authorization?* Do the dicta in *Bas* tell us anything about whether the President may conduct war without congressional authorization? *Compare* J. Gregory Sidak, *The Quasi-War Cases — and Their Relevance to Whether "Letters of Marque and Reprisal" Constrain Presidential War Powers*, 28 Harv. J.L. & Pub. Pol'y 465, 482, 486 (2005) (asserting that the answer is "no," because the cases do not address "how the Constitution divides between Congress and the President the power to commit the nation to waging a limited war"), *with Campbell v. Clinton*, 203 F.3d 19, 30 n.7 (D.C. Cir. 2000) (Randolph, J., concurring in the judgment) (citing *Little* for the proposition that executive power in war "was constrained by an absence of legislation"), *and id.* at 38 (Tatel, J., concurring) (citing *Talbot* for the proposition that Congress possesses the "whole powers of war").

Authorization for Use of Military Force

Pub. L. No. 107-40, 115 Stat. 224 (Sept. 18, 2001)

Whereas, on September 11, 2001, acts of treacherous violence were committed against the United States and its citizens; and

Whereas, such acts render it both necessary and appropriate that the United States exercise its rights to self-defense and to protect United States citizens both at home and abroad; and

Whereas, in light of the threat to the national security and foreign policy of the United States posed by these grave acts of violence; and

Whereas, such acts continue to pose an unusual and extraordinary threat to the national security and foreign policy of the United States; and

Whereas, the President has authority under the Constitution to take action to deter and prevent acts of international terrorism against the United States: Now, therefore, be it

Resolved by the Senate and House of Representatives of the United States of America in Congress assembled . . .

SEC. 2. AUTHORIZATION FOR USE OF UNITED STATES ARMED FORCES.

(a) In General. — That the President is authorized to use all necessary and appropriate force against those nations, organizations, or persons he determines planned, authorized, committed, or aided the terrorist attacks that occurred on September 11, 2001, or harbored such organizations or persons, in order to prevent any future acts of international terrorism against the United States by such nations, organizations or persons.

(b) War Powers Resolution Requirements —

(1) Specific Statutory Authorization. — Consistent with section 8(a)(1) of the War Powers Resolution, the Congress declares that this section is intended to constitute specific statutory authorization within the meaning of section 5(b) of the War Powers Resolution.

(2) Applicability of Other Requirements. — Nothing in this resolution supercedes any requirement of the War Powers Resolution.

Notes and Questions

1. *Authorizing War on Terrorists?* President Bush signed the 9/11 AUMF into law on September 18, 2001 — and it remains on the books today. Are there any important differences between this law and a formal declaration of war? Between it and the form of authorization found in *Bas v. Tingy*? Do these different forms of legislative authority affect U.S. relations with other nations differently? Do they affect the domestic powers of the President, or the legal "dominos" discussed above?

2. *Scope of the Authorized War Power.* Can you discern from the text of the 9/11 AUMF any limits on the President's authority to use military force? Could she, for example, deploy any number of troops equipped with any kind of weaponry to fight anywhere in the world for an unlimited period? If not, how is she otherwise constrained? See *infra* pp. 322-323

3. *Impliedly Authorizing War by Statute.* How explicit must a statute be that authorizes the use of force? In *Orlando v. Laird*, 443 F.2d 1039 (2d Cir. 1971), the court inferred congressional authorization for the Vietnam War in part from military appropriations and selective service statutes. It did not cite *Bas v. Tingy*. If Congress may impliedly authorize war by appropriating money for it, is there any constitutional or practical limit on the form of war authorization?

3. Limiting War Power? The War Powers Resolution

The War Powers Resolution (WPR), enacted in the fall of 1973, was a direct legislative response to the Vietnam War. Congress hoped the measure would establish a consensual interbranch procedure that would prevent the President alone or both political branches together from taking the country to war by stealth or inadvertence in the future. But any hope of consent or cooperation was dashed when President Nixon vetoed the bill, and Congress overrode his veto. No President has conceded the constitutionality of the WPR — or, many would say, fully complied with it — and its legal and practical effects today are unclear.

Reading the War Powers Resolution

- When, according to the WPR, may the President constitutionally use U.S. armed forces troops in hostilities? Upon what constitutional understandings or historical practices do these uses rest?
- When must the President consult with Congress concerning the deployment of U.S. armed forces into hostilities? When must she report concerning such a deployment?
- Is the "hostilities" criterion for various activities in the WPR any more or less clear or practically useful than the term "war" in the Constitution?
- The WPR describes a requirement for congressional action within 60 days. When does this "60-day clock" start running? Does the WPR authorize the deployment of U.S. armed forces in the interim?
- If the WPR's rules of interpretation (§8) had been in force when *Orlando v. Laird* was decided, how, if at all, might it have affected the court's reasoning?
- What provisions of the WPR did President Nixon find unconstitutional and why? Given that his veto was overridden, and that Congress has never rescinded or modified the WPR, what advice concerning compliance with the WPR would you give a President today?

War Powers Resolution

50 U.S.C. §§1541-1548 (2018)

SECTION 2 [§1541]. PURPOSE AND POLICY

(a) It is the purpose of this chapter to fulfill the intent of the framers of the Constitution of the United States and insure that the collective judgment of both the Congress and the President will apply to the introduction of United States Armed Forces into hostilities, or into situations where imminent involvement in hostilities is clearly indicated by the circumstances, and to the continued use of such forces in hostilities or in such situations.

(b) Under article I, section 8, of the Constitution, it is specifically provided that the Congress shall have the power to make all laws necessary and proper for carrying into execution, not only its own powers but also all other powers vested by the Constitution in the Government of the United States, or in any department or officer thereof.

(c) The constitutional powers of the President as Commander-in-Chief to introduce United States Armed Forces into hostilities, or into situations where imminent involvement in hostilities is clearly indicated by the circumstances, are exercised only pursuant to (1) a declaration of war, (2) specific statutory authorization, or (3) a national emergency created by attack upon the United States, its territories or possessions, or its armed forces.

SECTION 3 [§1542]. CONSULTATION

The President in every possible instance shall consult with Congress before introducing United States Armed Forces into hostilities or into situations where imminent involvement in hostilities is clearly indicated by the circumstances, and after every such introduction shall consult regularly with the Congress until United States Armed Forces are no longer engaged in hostilities or have been removed from such situations.

SECTION 4 [§1543]. REPORTING REQUIREMENT

(a) In the absence of a declaration of war, in any case in which United States Armed Forces are introduced—

(1) into hostilities or into situations where imminent involvement in hostilities is clearly indicated by the circumstances;

(2) into the territory, airspace or waters of a foreign nation, while equipped for combat, except for deployments which relate solely to supply, replacement, repair, or training of such forces; or

(3) in numbers which substantially enlarge United States Armed Forces equipped for combat already located in a foreign nation;

the President shall submit within 48 hours to the Speaker of the House of Representatives and to the President pro tempore of the Senate a report, in writing, setting forth

(A) the circumstances necessitating the introduction of United States Armed Forces;

(B) the constitutional and legislative authority under which such introduction took place; and

(C) the estimated scope and duration of the hostilities or involvement.

(b) The President shall provide such other information as the Congress may request in the fulfillment of its constitutional responsibilities with respect to committing the Nation to war and to the use of United States Armed Forces abroad.

(c) Whenever United States Armed Forces are introduced into hostilities or into any situation described in subsection (a) of this section, the President shall, so long as such Armed Forces continue to be engaged in such hostilities or situation, report to the Congress periodically on the status of such hostilities or situation . . . , but in no event . . . less often than once every six months.

SECTION 5 [§1544]. CONGRESSIONAL ACTION . . .

(b) Within sixty calendar days after a report is submitted or is required to be submitted pursuant to section 1543(a)(1) of this title, whichever is earlier, the President shall terminate any use of United States Armed Forces with respect to which such report was submitted (or required to be submitted), unless the Congress (1) has declared war or has enacted a specific authorization for such use of United States Armed Forces, (2) has extended by law such sixty-day period, or (3) is physically unable to meet as a result of an armed attack upon the United States. Such sixty-day period shall be extended for not more than an additional thirty days if the President determines and certifies to the Congress in writing that unavoidable military necessity respecting the safety of United States Armed Forces requires the continued use of such Armed Forces in the course of bringing about a prompt removal of such forces. . . .

SECTION 8 [§1547]. INTERPRETATION OF JOINT RESOLUTION

(a) Authority to introduce United States Armed Forces into hostilities or into situations wherein involvement in hostilities is clearly indicated by the circumstances shall not be inferred—

(1) from any provision of law (whether or not in effect before November 7, 1973), including any provision contained in any Appropriation Act, unless such provision specifically authorizes the introduction of United States Armed Forces into hostilities or into such situations and states that it is intended to constitute specific statutory authorization within the meaning of this chapter; or

(2) from any treaty heretofore or hereafter ratified unless such treaty is implemented by legislation specifically authorizing the introduction of United States Armed Forces into hostilities or into such situations and stating that it is intended to constitute specific statutory authorization within the meaning of this chapter. . . .

(c) For purposes of this chapter, the term "introduction of United States Armed Forces" includes the assignment of members of such Armed Forces to command, coordinate, participate in the movement of, or accompany the regular or irregular military forces of any foreign country or government when such military forces are engaged, or there exists an imminent threat that such forces will become engaged, in hostilities.

(d) Nothing in this chapter—

(1) is intended to alter the constitutional authority of the Congress or of the President, or the provisions of existing treaties; or

(2) shall be construed as granting any authority to the President with respect to the introduction of United States Armed Forces into hostilities or into situations wherein involvement in hostilities is clearly indicated by the circumstances which authority he would not have had in the absence of this chapter.

Richard M. Nixon, Veto of the War Powers Resolution

1 Pub. Papers 893 (Oct. 24, 1973)

To the House of Representatives:

I hereby return without my approval House Joint Resolution 542—the War Powers Resolution. While I am in accord with the desire of the Congress to assert its proper role in the conduct of our foreign affairs, the restrictions which this resolution would impose upon the authority of the President are both unconstitutional and dangerous to the best interests of our Nation. . . .

CLEARLY UNCONSTITUTIONAL

House Joint Resolution 542 would attempt to take away, by a mere legislative act, authorities which the President has properly exercised under the Constitution for almost 200 years. One of its provisions would automatically cut off certain authorities after sixty days unless the Congress extended them. . . .

. . . The only way in which the constitutional powers of a branch of the Government can be altered is by amending the Constitution — and any attempt to make such alterations by legislation alone is clearly without force.

UNDERMINING OUR FOREIGN POLICY

. . . I am also deeply disturbed by the practical consequences of this resolution. For it would seriously undermine this Nation's ability to act decisively and convincingly in times of international crisis. As a result, the confidence of our allies in our ability to assist them could be diminished and the respect of our adversaries for our deterrent posture could decline. A permanent and substantial element of unpredictability would be injected into the world's assessment of American behavior, further increasing the likelihood of miscalculation and war. . . .

While all the specific consequences of House Joint Resolution 542 cannot yet be predicted, it is clear that it would undercut the ability of the United States to act as an effective influence for peace. For example, the provision automatically cutting off certain authorities after 60 days unless they are extended by the Congress could work to prolong or intensify a crisis. Until the Congress suspended the deadline, there would be at least a chance of United States withdrawal and an adversary would be tempted therefore to postpone serious negotiations until the 60 days were up. Only after the Congress acted would there be a strong incentive for an adversary to negotiate. In addition, the very existence of a deadline could lead to an escalation of hostilities in order to achieve certain objectives before the 60 days expired.

The measure would jeopardize our role as a force for peace in other ways as well. It would, for example, strike from the President's hand a wide range of important peace-keeping tools by eliminating his ability to exercise quiet diplomacy backed by subtle shifts in our military deployments. It would also cast into doubt authorities which Presidents have used to undertake certain humanitarian relief missions in conflict areas, to protect fishing boats from seizure, to deal with ship or aircraft hijackings, and to respond to threats of attack. Not the least of the adverse consequences of this resolution would be the prohibition contained in section 8 against fulfilling our obligations under the NATO treaty as ratified by the Senate. Finally, since the bill is somewhat vague as to when the 60 day rule would apply, it could lead to extreme confusion and dangerous disagreements concerning the prerogatives of the two branches, seriously damaging our ability to respond to international crises.

FAILURE TO REQUIRE POSITIVE CONGRESSIONAL ACTION

I am particularly disturbed by the fact that certain of the President's constitutional powers as Commander in Chief of the Armed Forces would terminate automatically under this resolution 60 days after they were invoked. No overt Congressional action would be required to cut off these powers — they would disappear automatically unless the Congress extended them. In effect, the Congress is here attempting to increase its policymaking role through a provision which requires it to take absolutely no action at all.

In my view, the proper way for the Congress to make known its will on such foreign policy questions is through a positive action, with full debate on the merits of the issue and with each member taking the responsibility of casting a yes or no vote after considering those merits. The authorization and appropriations process represents one of the ways in which such influence can be exercised. I do not, however, believe that the Congress can responsibly contribute its considered, collective judgment on such grave questions without full debate and without a yes or no vote. Yet this is precisely what the joint resolution would allow. It would give every future Congress the ability to handcuff every future President merely by doing nothing and sitting still. In my view, one cannot become a responsible partner unless one is prepared to take responsible action.

STRENGTHENING COOPERATION BETWEEN THE CONGRESS AND THE EXECUTIVE BRANCHES

The responsible and effective exercise of the war powers requires the fullest cooperation between the Congress and the Executive and the prudent fulfillment by each branch of its constitutional responsibilities. House Joint Resolution 542 includes certain constructive measures which would foster this process by enhancing the flow of information from the executive branch to the Congress. Section 3, for example, calls for consultation with the Congress before and during the involvement of the United States forces in hostilities abroad. This provision is consistent with the desire of this Administration for regularized consultations with the Congress in an even wider range of circumstances. . . .

Richard Nixon
The White House

Notes and Questions

a. The Recital of Presidential War Powers

1. *The Listing of Presidential War Powers.* One of the most controversial parts of the WPR is the purportedly comprehensive list in §2(c) of the President's constitutional powers to introduce U.S. troops into actual or imminent hostilities. Is the list of powers complete, or is it, as some critics insist, vastly under-inclusive? Should it also include military responses to imminent threats of attack on the United States? How about rescues of Americans in peril abroad, low-level deployments for regional peacekeeping, actions in defense of freedom of navigation, humanitarian interventions, defensive quarantines (e.g., as in the Cuban missile crisis), non-combat deployments

of military advisers, protection of American embassies and legations, suppression of civil disorder in the United States, and deployments of military forces to implement cease-fires, armistices, and treaties?

Could *any* list be complete? If not, can you think of any other way to frame the list that is not under-inclusive?

2. *The Power of Congress to Define the President's War Powers.* If the list of presidential war powers is incomplete, is the WPR unconstitutional? What bearing does WPR §8(d)(1) have on your answer? Does Congress have any authority to define the inherent constitutional powers of the President?

3. *The WPR and Acquiescence.* Critics of the WPR argue that it unconstitutionally attempts to overturn 200 years of history, during which the President established his claim to war-making authority by usage. Defenders point out, instead, that past congressional acquiescence in executive war powers at most establishes that the President may exercise them "*if Congress does not try to stop him.* If Congress *does* try to stop him, then by definition it is no longer acquiescing." Stephen L. Carter, *The Constitutionality of the War Powers Resolution,* 70 Va. L. Rev. 101, 124 (1984). Within the framework of the Constitution, they insist, Congress surely may retrieve any authority tacitly delegated by it to the Executive, and that is precisely what the WPR does. If the defenders are correct, what is the effect of the WPR on claims of usage prior to 1973?

b. Consultation

1. *Why Consult?* Should the President be required to seek the advice of members of Congress before deploying U.S. troops in operations short of war? After all, as the Supreme Court noted in *United States v. Curtiss-Wright Export Corp.*, the President has "the better opportunity of knowing the conditions which prevail in foreign countries," he has agents and confidential sources of information abroad, and he may need to act quickly or in secret. Critics of the WPR point out that members of Congress may be parochial, partisan, poorly informed, or preoccupied with re-election — in other words, collectively unwise about national security and foreign affairs. Indeed, involving them may effectively amount only to involving their staffs, with a substantially increased risk of leaks that could compromise national security. *See, e.g.*, Robert F. Turner, *Repealing the War Powers Resolution* 110 (1991). On the other hand, some members of Congress have far more experience and a much more sophisticated understanding of national security and foreign affairs than some Presidents, who have had no prior experience in national office or even in *any* public office.

How, if at all, do the reasons for and against consultation bear on the constitutionality of the WPR? The Senate Foreign Relations Committee's answer, in part, was that the Framers vested the war power in Congress "not primarily because they felt confident that the legislature would necessarily exercise it more wisely but because they expected the legislature to exercise it more *sparingly* than it had been exercised by the Crown, or would be likely to be exercised by the President as successor to the Crown." S. Rep. No. 93-220, at 86 (1973) (emphasis in original).

2. *Consult When?* When does the WPR require the President to consult with Congress before introducing U.S. armed forces? If consultation is required "before" sending U.S. troops into harm's way, how long before? What is the significance of the term "in every possible instance"? Might the answers to these questions affect the definition of "consult" in a given case?

3. *Consult with Whom?* Is WPR §3 satisfied by consultation with a few selected members of Congress? With the relevant congressional leadership? With the leadership plus the members of relevant committees? With the entire Congress? What are the practical problems attending each alternative?

4. *Consult How?* The House report on the WPR expressly rejected

> the notion that consultation should be synonymous with merely being informed. Rather, consultation in this provision means that a decision is pending on a problem and that Members of Congress are being asked by the President for their advice and opinions and, in appropriate circumstances, their approval of action contemplated. Furthermore, for consultation to be meaningful, the President must himself participate and all information relevant to the situation must be made available. [H.R. Rep. No. 93-287, at 6-7 (1973).]

Former Secretary of State Cyrus Vance has written that "consultation" means not only advance transmittal of all relevant information to the congressional leadership in sufficient time "to permit a reasonable opportunity to absorb the information, consider its implications, and form a judgment before irrevocable decisions are made by the President," but also "that the congressional leadership should have a real opportunity to communicate its views to the President or at least to his closest advisors." Cyrus R. Vance, *Striking the Balance: Congress and the President Under the War Powers Resolution*, 133 U. Pa. L. Rev. 79, 87-91 (1984).

Does the WPR require advance consultation about exercises of independent presidential war-making authority? If it does, is such a requirement constitutional?

c. Triggers and the Reporting Requirements

1. *The Textual Triggers.* What are the triggers for the reporting requirement in WPR §4(a), and what is their purpose? Why is the 60-day clock provision in WPR §5(b) activated only by reporting or the requirement to report under §4(a)(1)?

2. *The Definition of "Hostilities."* Can you say precisely when §4(a)(1) requires reporting to congressional leaders? The House Report explained:

> In addition to a situation in which fighting actually has begun, *hostilities* also encompasses a state of confrontation in which no shots have been fired but where there is a clear and present danger of armed conflict. "*Imminent hostilities*" denotes a situation in which there is a clear potential either for such a state of confrontation or for actual armed conflict. [H.R. Rep. No. 93-287, at 7 (1973).]

What is a "clear potential" for a "clear and present danger"? What does WPR §8(c) add?

In a 2011 statement before Congress, State Department Legal Adviser Harold H. Koh noted that

> as virtually every lawyer recognizes, the operative term "hostilities" is an ambiguous standard, which is nowhere defined in the statute. Nor has this standard ever been defined by the courts or by Congress in any subsequent war powers legislation. . . . Members of Congress understood that the term was vague, but specifically declined to give it more concrete meaning, in part to avoid unduly hampering future Presidents by making the Resolution a "one size fits all" straitjacket that would operate mechanically, without regard to particular circumstances. [*Libya and War Powers: Hearing Before the S. Comm. on Foreign Relations,* 112th Cong., at 4-5 (2011).]

Koh went on to argue that application of the term "must be addressed in light of a long history of military actions abroad, without guidance from the courts. . . . [W]hether a particular set of facts constitutes 'hostilities' for purposes of the Resolution has been determined more by interbranch practice than by a narrow parsing of dictionary definitions." *Id.* at 5. If the mission of U.S. troops is limited in time or extent, he indicated, the risk of harm to those troops is small, the potential for escalation is minimal, and the violence is relatively modest, withdrawal after 60 days is not required.

Do you have a clear sense of how to apply the statutory term "hostilities" in a given case? Can you think of a rhetorical trigger for consultation, reporting, and withdrawal that would more likely satisfy the aims of the WPR?

3. The Content of WPR Reports. If the President wanted to evade the 60-day clock without openly defying the WPR reporting requirement, what could he do? Of 168 WPR reports submitted by Presidents through March 2017, only one — the 1975 deployment of U.S. forces to rescue the crew of the *SS Mayaguez* taken hostage in Cambodia — specifically cited §4(a)(1). *See* Matthew C. Weed, *The War Powers Resolution: Concepts and Practice* (Cong. Res. Serv. R42699), Mar. 8, 2019. Instead, the reports have been calculatingly vague about the statutory authority to which they relate: "consistent with the War Powers Resolution," or "taking note of Section 4" of the WPR or "[b]ecause of my desire that Congress be informed on this matter and consistent with the reporting provisions of the War Powers Resolution." *See* Richard F. Grimmett, *War Powers Resolution: Presidential Compliance* (Cong. Res. Serv. RL33532), Sept. 25, 2012. What is the significance of a WPR report's description of the legal authority for a deployment?

WPR reports are also typically short on details about military operations or about circumstances that prompted the deployment of U.S. forces in the first place. How much information should such reports provide to Congress?

d. The 60-Day Clock

1. A Self-Executing Clock? WPR §5(b) establishes a 60-day (plus 30-day extension) limit on the commitment of troops without congressional authorization. What happens if the President refuses to file a §4(a)(1) report or files under the wrong provision? The court in *Crockett v. Reagan,* 558 F. Supp. 893 (D.D.C. 1982), *aff'd,* 720 F.2d 1355 (D.C. Cir. 1983), faced this question when a small number of U.S. troops were deployed as "advisors" in El Salvador during the Reagan administration. The court declined to answer, ruling that the case presented a political question. Congress had to pull a "second trigger" by declaring that a report is "required to be submitted" before the 60-day clock would begin running. "[A] case could arise with facts less elusive than these," said the court, citing the Vietnam War as an illustration. But it concluded that when a smaller number of American troops had been deployed as alleged military advisors without suffering casualties, "the subtleties of fact finding" were best left to Congress. *Id.* at 898-899.

Can you describe the "subtleties of fact finding" that counselled judicial restraint? Is it possible that any member of Congress was unaware of the WPR's 60-day clock provision? Can you think of other reasons for a court's reluctance to intervene?

2. *Constitutionality of the 60-Day Clock.* Why did President Nixon oppose WPR §5(b)? Does this provision not simply place the burden squarely on the President to convince Congress of the wisdom of continued deployment of troops in hostilities? Recalling the debate on war powers in the Philadelphia Convention, do you think the Framers intended to place the burden instead on Congress to affirmatively halt an ongoing deployment not previously approved? If so, should it require a simple majority vote in Congress to pull the troops out, or will a two-thirds vote in each house be needed (in order to overcome a presidential veto)?

What practical impact could §5(b) have on the President's decision to arm U.S. forces? On the degree to which a President might escalate U.S. involvement? On the safety with which a required withdrawal of troops could be carried out? Are these practical consequences the product of the WPR alone or of any reading of the Constitution that requires congressional approval for nondefensive hostilities abroad?

3. *A 60-Day Free Pass?* Many in the media and even some members of Congress believe — mistakenly — that the WPR gives the President a 60- (or 90-) day free pass to use armed force abroad. Does §5(b) have that effect? How does §8(d) address this question?

Although some might quarrel about triggering events, except for the Operation Allied Force bombing campaign against the Federal Republic of Yugoslavia in 1999, no combat operation has ever "run the sixty-day clock" without either a report, at least purported statutory authorization, or an argument that the clock was never triggered in the first place. *See* Geoffrey S. Corn, *Clinton, Kosovo, and the Final Destruction of the War Powers Resolution*, 42 Wm. & Mary L. Rev. 1149, 1154 (2001); Weed, *supra*, at 42 (reporting that the Obama administration delivered a letter to Congress on the 60th day of an operation in Libya, declaring that the United States had transferred responsibility to NATO forces and was thereafter only fulfilling a "supporting" role, and then delivered another letter on the 86th day, denying that forces had been introduced into "hostilities"). Does this history prove that the WPR has *become* a "free pass"?

e. The Concurrent Resolution

The WPR was a *joint resolution*, which must be presented to the President before becoming law. A *concurrent resolution* is not presented to the President for his signature and, according to *Immigration & Naturalization Service v. Chadha*, 462 U.S. 919 (1983), is therefore not law. See *infra* p. 324. Is WPR §5(c), which authorizes Congress by concurrent resolution to direct the removal of troops engaged in hostilities abroad, still constitutional after *Chadha*? Or is such a resolution a constitutional expression of congressional disapproval in the "twilight zone," where the President and Congress may have concurrent authority, and where the exercise of independent presidential authority may depend in part on Congress's failure to express its will? See Justice Jackson's concurring opinion in *The Steel Seizure Case*, 343 U.S. 579, 637 (1952) (Jackson, J., concurring).

f. The Rule of Construction

1. *Inferences of Authorization from Other Statutes.* WPR §8(a)(1) supplies a rule of construction intended to prevent inferences of authority for the use of armed forces from legislation that fails to invoke the WPR. Suppose that Congress passed and the President signed into law a supplemental appropriation providing $2 billion for "the use and support of U.S. armed forces to protect citizens of Yemen from military and paramilitary aggression." How, if at all, would the rule of construction apply if the measure failed to include a specific reference to the WPR? Would the WPR control by telling us how to interpret the later intent of Congress? Or would the last-in-time rule allow the appropriations measure to override the earlier WPR restriction?

2. *Inferences of Authorization from Treaties.* WPR §8(a)(2) prohibits the inference of authorization from treaties such as the Southeast Asia Collective Defense Treaty (SEATO). Does it make all mutual defense treaties non-self-executing, regardless of their language? Does it prevent deployment of U.S. armed forces in U.N. operations without a specific authorization from Congress?

B. DELEGATIONS AND APPROPRIATIONS FOR NATIONAL SECURITY

In *Curtiss-Wright*, the Supreme Court held that Congress could, partly for reasons of practical necessity, delegate more loosely in foreign affairs than in domestic affairs. May it also delegate more loosely in domestic affairs if the legislation implicates national security? In *Lichter v. United States*, 334 U.S. 742 (1948), the Court rejected a nondelegation challenge to a wartime statute permitting the government to recapture excess war profits from defense contractors. It quoted from a speech by former Justice (and future Chief Justice) Charles Evans Hughes on constitutional war powers:

> The power to wage war is the power to wage war successfully. . . .
>
> . . . [I]t may be said that the power has been expressly given to Congress to prosecute war, and to pass all laws which shall be necessary and proper for carrying that power into execution. That power explicitly conferred and absolutely essential to the safety of the Nation is not destroyed or impaired by any later provision of the Constitution or by any one of the amendments. These may all be construed so as to avoid making the constitution self-destructive, so as to preserve the rights of the citizen from unwarrantable attack, while assuring beyond all hazard the common defence and the perpetuity of our liberties. These rest upon the preservation of the nation.

> It has been said that the Constitution marches. That is, there are constantly new applications of unchanged powers, and it is ascertained that in novel and complex situations, the old grants contain, in their general words and true significance, needed and adequate authority. So, also, we have a fighting Constitution. [*Id.* at 780-782.]

The Court then concluded,

> The war powers of Congress and the President are only those which are to be derived from the Constitution but, in the light of the language just quoted, the primary implication of a war power is that it shall be an effective power to wage the war successfully. Thus, while the constitutional structure and controls of our Government are our guides equally in war and in peace, they must be read with the realistic purposes of the entire instrument fully in mind. [*Id.* at 782.]

In a variety of cases the Supreme Court has approved the exercise of the defense appropriations power and related congressional war powers to

> control the price of every commodity bought and sold within the national boundaries; to fix the amount of rent to be charged for every room, home, or building and this even though to an individual landlord there may be less than a fair return; to construct extensive systems of public works; to operate railroads; to prohibit the sale of liquor; to restrict freedom of speech in a manner that would be unwarranted in time of peace; to ration and allocate the distribution of every commodity important to the war effort; to restrict the personal freedom of American citizens by curfew orders and the designation of areas of exclusion; and, finally, to demand of every citizen that he serve in the armed forces of the nation. [*Spaulding v. Douglas Aircraft Co.*, 154 F.2d 419, 422-423 (9th Cir. 1946) (citations omitted).]

These powers may continue even after the cessation of hostilities. The Court has recognized that the congressional war power "is not limited to victories in the field. . . . It carries with it inherently the power to guard against the immediate renewal of the conflict, and to remedy the evils which have arisen from its rise and progress." *Stewart v. Kahn*, 78 U.S. (11 Wall.) 493, 507 (1871).

Reading *Greene v. McElroy*

William L. Greene, an aeronautical engineer employed by a private defense contractor, was fired when his security clearance (giving him necessary access to classified defense contract information) was revoked. Afterward, he was unable to find another job as an aeronautical engineer in the defense industry. He sued the government, arguing that the action of the Department of Defense, barring him from access to classified information on the basis of statements by confidential informants whom he could not confront, was not authorized by either Congress or the President, and that it deprived him of "liberty" and "property" without "due process of law" in contravention of the Fifth Amendment.

- Had Congress expressly authorized the summary hearing procedures by which Greene's clearance was revoked?

- Alternatively, had Congress impliedly authorized those procedures either by the Procurement Act of 1947 or by ratifying — or at least acquiescing in — them in various authorization or appropriation acts? If not, why not?
- How would you state the rule of construction that the Court applied to decide *Greene*?
- Did the Court hold that the President lacks inherent power to create the hearing procedures used against Greene? Or that the procedures violated the Due Process Clause?
- What is the holding of the case?

Greene v. McElroy

United States Supreme Court, 1959
360 U.S. 474

Mr. Chief Justice WARREN delivered the opinion of the Court. . . . The issue, as we see it, is whether the Department of Defense has been authorized to create an industrial security clearance program under which affected persons may lose their jobs and may be restrained in following their chosen professions on the basis of fact determinations concerning their fitness for clearance made in proceedings in which they are denied the traditional procedural safeguards of confrontation and cross-examination. . . .

The first proffered statute is the National Security Act of 1947, as amended, 5 U.S.C. §171 et seq. That Act created the Department of Defense and gave to the Secretary of Defense and the Secretaries of the armed services the authority to administer their departments. Nowhere in the Act, or its amendments, is there found specific authority to create a clearance program similar to the one now in effect.

Another Act cited by respondents is the Armed Service Procurement Act of 1947, as amended. It provides in 10 U.S.C. §2304 that:

> (a) Purchases of and contracts for property or services covered by this chapter shall be made by formal advertising. However, the head of an agency may negotiate such a purchase or contract, if— . . .
>
> (12) the purchase or contract is for property or services whose procurement he determines should not be publicly disclosed because of their character, ingredients, or components.

It further provides in 10 U.S.C. §2306:

> (a) The cost-plus-a-percentage-of-cost system of contracting may not be used. Subject to this limitation and subject to subsections (b)-(e), the head of an agency may, in negotiating contracts under section 2304 of this title, make any kind of contract that he considers will promote the best interests of the United States.

Respondents argue that these statutes, together with 18 U.S.C. §798, which makes it a crime willfully and knowingly to communicate to unauthorized persons information concerning cryptographic or intelligence activities, and 50 U.S.C. §783(b), which makes it a crime for an officer or employee of the United States to communicate classified information to agents of foreign governments or officers and members of "Communist organizations," reflect a recognition by Congress of the existence of military secrets and the necessity of keeping those secrets inviolate.

Although these statutes make it apparent that Congress recognizes the existence of military secrets, they hardly constitute an authorization to create an elaborate clearance program which embodies procedures traditionally believed to be inadequate to protect affected persons.[29]

Lastly, the Government urges that if we refuse to adopt its "inferred" authorization reasoning, nevertheless, congressional ratification is apparent by the continued appropriation of funds to finance aspects of the program fashioned by the Department of Defense. Respondents refer us to Hearings before the House Committee on Appropriations on Department of Defense Appropriations for 1956, 84th Cong., 1st Sess. 774-781. At those hearings, the Committee was asked to approve the appropriation of funds to finance a program under which reimbursement for lost wages would be made to employees of government contractors who were temporarily denied, but later granted, security clearance. Apparently, such reimbursements had been made prior to that time out of general appropriations. Although a specific appropriation was eventually made for this purpose, it could not conceivably constitute a ratification of the hearing procedures, for the procedures were in no way involved in the special reimbursement program.

Respondents' argument on delegation resolves itself into the following: The President, in general terms, has authorized the Department of Defense to create procedures to restrict the dissemination of classified information and has apparently acquiesced in the elaborate program established by the Secretary of Defense even where application of the program results in restraints on traditional freedoms without the use of long-required procedural protections. Similarly, Congress, although it has not enacted specific legislation relating to clearance procedures to be utilized for industrial workers, has acquiesced in the existing Department of Defense program and has ratified it by specifically appropriating funds to finance one aspect of it.

If acquiescence or implied ratification were enough to show delegation of authority to take actions within the area of questionable constitutionality, we might agree with respondents that delegation has been shown here. In many circumstances, where the Government's freedom to act is clear, and the Congress or the President has provided general standards of action and has acquiesced in administrative interpretation, delegation may be inferred. Thus, even in the absence of specific delegation, we have no difficulty in finding, as we do, that the Department of Defense has been authorized to fashion and apply an industrial clearance program which affords affected persons the safeguards of confrontation and cross-examination. But this case does not present that situation. We deal here with substantial restraints on employment opportunities of numerous persons imposed in a manner which is in conflict with our long-accepted notions of fair procedures. Before we are asked to judge whether, in the context of security clearance cases, a person may be deprived of the right to follow his chosen

---

29. As far as appears, the most substantial official notice which Congress had of the non-confrontation procedures used in screening industrial workers was embodied in S. Doc. No. 40, 84th Cong., 1st Sess., a 354-page compilation of laws, executive orders, and regulations relating to internal security, printed at the request of a single Senator, which reproduced, among other documents and without specific comment, the Industrial Personnel Security Review Regulation [which established the summary hearing procedures by which Greene's security clearance was revoked].

profession without full hearings where accusers may be confronted, it must be made clear that the President or Congress, within their respective constitutional powers, specifically has decided that the imposed procedures are necessary and warranted and has authorized their use. Such decisions cannot be assumed by acquiescence or nonaction. *Kent v. Dulles*, 357 U.S. 116; *Peters v. Hobby*, 349 U.S. 331; *Ex parte Endo*, 323 U.S. 283, 301-302. They must be made explicitly not only to assure that individuals are not deprived of cherished rights under procedures not actually authorized, but also because explicit action, especially in areas of doubtful constitutionality, requires careful and purposeful consideration by those responsible for enacting and implementing our laws. Without explicit action by lawmakers, decisions of great constitutional import and effect would be relegated by default to administrators who, under our system of government, are not endowed with authority to decide them.

Where administrative action has raised serious constitutional problems, the Court has assumed that Congress or the President intended to afford those affected by the action the traditional safeguards of due process. These cases reflect the Court's concern that traditional forms of fair procedure not be restricted by implication or without the most explicit action by the Nation's lawmakers, even in areas where it is possible that the Constitution presents no inhibition.

In the instant case, petitioner's work opportunities have been severely limited on the basis of a fact determination rendered after a hearing which failed to comport with our traditional ideas of fair procedure. The type of hearing was the product of administrative decision not explicitly authorized by either Congress or the President. Whether those procedures under the circumstances comport with the Constitution we do not decide. Nor do we decide whether the President has inherent authority to create such a program, whether congressional action is necessary, or what the limits on executive or legislative authority may be. We decide only that in the absence of explicit authorization from either the President or Congress the respondents were not empowered to deprive petitioner of his job in a proceeding in which he was not afforded the safeguards of confrontation and cross-examination.

Accordingly, the judgment is reversed and the case is remanded to the district court for proceedings not inconsistent herewith. . . .

Mr. Justice Frankfurter, Mr. Justice Harlan and Mr. Justice Whittaker concur in the judgment on the ground that it has not been shown that either Congress or the President authorized the procedures whereby petitioner's security clearance was revoked, intimating no views as to the validity of those procedures.

[The opinions of Justices Harlan, concurring specially, and Clark, dissenting, are omitted.]

Notes and Questions

a. Delegations of National Security Authority

1. Comparing Lichter and Greene. Lichter tested the authority of the federal government to limit the wartime profits of defense contractors. *Greene* tested the authority of the federal government to revoke a security clearance without "traditional procedural safeguards of confrontation and cross-examination." The earlier case concluded that under the Constitution the war power must be "an effective power to wage the war successfully." *Lichter* concerned government actions during World War II, while *Greene* concerned actions at the height of the Cold War. Why did the government prevail in the one case but not the other? What is the holding of *Greene*?

Congress's approval of the President's actions in *Lichter* was fairly clear, although the legislation challenged in that case granted very broad discretion to the President. If no statute expressly authorized the security clearance procedures tested in *Greene*, hadn't Congress at least impliedly authorized or acquiesced in them? Recall and apply the requirements for implied authorization by congressional acquiescence to the facts of *Greene*.

2. *The Clear Statement Rule.* In *Greene* the Court concluded that before it will judge the constitutionality of a procedure that "is in conflict with our long-accepted notions of fair practices, . . . it must be made clear that the President or Congress, within their respective constitutional powers, specifically has decided that the imposed procedures are necessary and warranted and has authorized their use." What is the practical purpose of this "clear statement rule"? Does it apply to all administrative actions, or just some? Which kinds?

The Court's willingness to find specific congressional approval of presidential actions in cases implicating national security has shifted over time. Consistent with its ruling in *Greene*, in *Kent v. Dulles*, 357 U.S. 116 (1958), the Court declined to find statutory authority for the Secretary of State to restrict the right of travel protected by the Fifth Amendment absent explicit delegation from Congress. But nearly a quarter century later, in *Haig v. Agee*, 453 U.S. 280 (1981), it inferred authority to restrict the right of travel from congressional acquiescence in a previously announced but unexercised State Department policy.

3. *The Delegability of the War Power.* In *Lichter*, the Supreme Court decided that Congress could delegate to the President the power to curtail "excess profits" by defense contractors during the Second World War. In *Greene*, the Court acknowledged that Congress could empower the Defense Department to fashion and apply a security clearance program. Is Congress's ability to delegate war power to the President unlimited, provided the delegation is done with sufficient clarity?

Might Congress even delegate the power to declare war? Does the impracticality of antecedent standard-setting for a declaration of war suggest that Congress has no choice? Or does it suggest just the opposite: that it may not delegate so extensively? Consider the following argument advanced during the height of the Vietnam War after Congress had, by the Gulf of Tonkin Resolution, allegedly delegated war-making power to the President:

> [S]pecific contingencies which give sense and shape to the general doctrine permitting limited delegations of legislative power in other areas of congressional responsibility are already provided for in respect to war, *so far as it was felt safe to do so.* Thus, it was contemplated and made possible that peacetime armies might be raised under presidential discretion though this might even increase the risk of war. Similarly, an interim executive capacity to respond to outright emergencies, authorizing the president to resist invasion or repel an attack when war might be thrust upon the nation too quickly for Congress to convene to authorize even such limited defensive measures, was provided. Additionally,

> executive discretion to make command decisions of tactics and strategy within the express war declaration by Congress was conceded. Further confidence was also reposed of necessity in the President in recognizing that the congressional power would be exercised or not substantially depending upon the information and advice the President would provide in his emergency message of exigent circumstances asking for *their* decision to initiate hostilities, sustain present emergency defensive war actions he had taken, enlarge upon them, or, by doing nothing, require that our extraterritorial forces be immediately disengaged and withdrawn. Finally, although there might have been much to be said for a different view (so to make going to war especially grave and therefore desirably difficult to accomplish), the Constitution does not require that the declaration of war be an all or nothing response. . . .
>
> But precisely because of these various provisions and accommodations, it is even more clearly the case that there is no standing room left for a theory which would transfer to the executive the power to authorize war on his own initiation. [William Van Alstyne, *Congress, the President, and the Power to Declare War: A Requiem for Vietnam*, 121 U. Pa. L. Rev. 1, 17-18 (1972).]

Can Professor Van Alstyne's argument be squared with *Lichter*?

In *Skinner v. Mid-Am. Pipeline Co.*, 490 U.S. 212 (1989), the Court declared:

> We discern nothing in this placement of the Taxing clause that would distinguish Congress' power to tax from its other enumerated powers — such as its commerce power, its power to "*raise and support Armies*," its power to borrow money, or *its power to "make Rules for the government"* — in terms of the scope and degree of discretionary authority that Congress may delegate to the Executive in order that the President may "take Care that the Laws be faithfully executed." [*Id.* at 220-221 (emphasis added).]

Indeed, the Court has never expressly held any Article I power to be nondelegable. Does this cast doubt on Professor Van Alstyne's analysis?

b. Implied Authorization by Defense Appropriation

1. Appropriation as Implied Authorization. Greene suggests that in some instances appropriations might be regarded as a form of congressional ratification of executive practice. But *Greene* also cites *Ex parte Endo*, 323 U.S. 283 (1944), in which the Court applied an especially strong version of the clear statement rule to appropriations. There it found no congressional intent to authorize the continued internment of loyal Japanese Americans during World War II. An "appropriation must plainly show a purpose to bestow the precise authority which is claimed. We can hardly deduce such a purpose here where a lump appropriation was made for the overall [internment] program . . . and no sums were earmarked for the single phase of the total program which is here involved." *Id.* at 303 n.24.

2. Appropriations as "Back-Door Law." Congress has traditionally distinguished *authorizations* — statutes delegating authority to the executive branch — from *appropriations* — statutes that fund the execution of delegated authority. The former have generally emanated from congressional committees with jurisdiction to oversee the relevant government function or executive agency, while the latter usually come out of the appropriations committees.

Some scholars and a few judges have seized upon this distinction to raise doubts of the legal effect of "mere" appropriations. But the text of Article I makes no distinction. As the product of the Article I legislative process, appropriations are as much legislation as authorizations. Moreover, appropriations "are not only legislative specifications of money *amounts,* but also legislative specifications of the *powers, activities,* and *purposes*—what we may call, simply, 'objects'—for which the appropriated funds may be used." Kate Stith, *Congress' Power of the Purse,* 97 Yale L.J. 1343, 1352 (1988). Both chambers recognize the legislative nature of appropriations by requiring explanation or identification of appropriations bills that change "existing law." *See* House R. XXI, cl. 2(c); Senate R. XVI, cl. 1.

Nevertheless, the incidental nature of many appropriations measures and the often summary deliberation that attends them properly makes courts more hesitant to infer authority from such "back-door legislation" than from other kinds of legislation, as *Greene* suggests. *Compare Tenn. Valley Auth. v. Hill,* 437 U.S. 153, 174-188 (1978) (holding that the doctrine pursuant to which repeals by implication are disfavored applies with special force to repeals by appropriations), *with United States v. Dickerson,* 310 U.S. 554 (1940) (finding repeal by an appropriations rider after exhaustive analysis of its legislative history). Moreover, because most appropriations are for a specific term, the purposes for which they are enacted and the limitations they impose are also time-limited and generally not subject to variation, absent statutory exceptions. "Court interpretations of limitation riders as amendments to previously enacted legislation, therefore, are inherently unreliable; they may be accurate one day, inaccurate the next, and irrelevant at the end of the fiscal year." *See* Neal Devins, *Regulation of Government Agencies Through Limitations Riders,* 1987 Duke L.J. 456, 458.

c. Wielding the Appropriations Power

The Appropriations Clause

U.S. Const. art. I, §9, cl. 7

"No Money shall be drawn from the Treasury, but in Consequence of Appropriations made by Law. . . . "

In its power struggles with the King, the English Parliament successfully used its approval or denial of "bills of supply" to bargain for greater legislative powers and to discourage his military adventures. Colonialists in America took note and used their power of the purse (most colonies were self-financing) to control the scope and conduct of colonial military operations and to thwart British-appointed governors. William C. Banks & Peter Raven-Hansen, *National Security Law and the Power of the Purse* 11-26 (1994).

The Framers were well aware of these power struggles, and of the importance of keeping a legislative hand on the purse strings, especially for military operations that were otherwise hard, if not impossible, to control. *Id.* at 27-32. They therefore built the power of the purse directly into the Constitution in framing the Appropriations Clause. U.S. Const., art. I, §9, cl. 7; *see also* 31 U.S.C. §1301 (2018) ("Appropriations shall be applied only to the objects for which the appropriations were made except as otherwise provided by law."); Anti-Deficiency Act, 31 U.S.C. §1341(a)(1)(A) (2018) (prohibiting expenditures or obligations in excess of appropriations).

As we noted in Chapter 2, the Framers also deliberately vested Congress with detailed defense appropriations powers and simultaneously limited the duration of any blank check that Congress might draw to support a standing army to two years. While the power of Congress generally to appropriate monies for national security may be implied from the Common Defense Clause, U.S. Const., art. I, §8, cl. 1, appropriations for the Army (subject to that time limit) and Navy are separately and expressly authorized in clause 12 of the same section.

Appropriations are not just checks to be drawn on the Treasury.

> [They] may be conceived of as lump-sum grants with "strings" attached. These strings, or conditions of expenditure, constitute legislative prescriptions that bind the operating arm of the government. Occasionally, conditions may be stated in an appropriations statute itself. For instance, an appropriations act may provide that "[n]o part of any appropriation contained in this Act shall be used . . . for publicity or propaganda purposes. . . ." Alternatively, the appropriations act may require that the recipient agency allocate the amount appropriated among certain activities or in accordance with certain conditions. Often, the appropriations act explicitly incorporates other legislation, notably substantive legislation creating particular federal agencies or programs or granting particular agency powers. Moreover, all appropriations legislation effectively incorporates the prescriptions of statutes of general applicability. [Stith, *supra,* at 1353.]

Usually, express limitations in appropriations acts pertain to the particular appropriated funds, but Congress has also used an appropriations "rider" to limit the Executive in ways unrelated to the use or purpose of the appropriation measure in which it appears. The Constitution, after all, contains no rule restricting any piece of legislation to a single subject.[1]

Government costs money, and the executive branch depends on appropriations for all that it does. Appropriations are therefore a particularly strong tool for legislative control.

> [A]ppropriations oversight is effective precisely because the statutory controls are so direct, unambiguous, and virtually self-enforcing. While agencies are able to bend the more ambiguous language of authorizing legislation to their own purposes, the dollar figures in appropriations bills represent commands which cannot be bent or ignored except at extreme peril to agency officials. [S. Comm. on Governmental Operations, 95th Cong., *Study of Federal Regulation: Congressional Oversight of Regulatory Agencies* 31 (Comm. Print 1977).][2]

Thus, in *Spaulding v. Douglas Aircraft Co.*, 60 F. Supp. 985 (S.D. Cal. 1945), *aff'd*, 154 F.2d 419 (9th Cir. 1946), the court emphasized, "The purpose of the appropriations, the terms and conditions under which said appropriations were made, is a matter

---

1. Each house has imposed a limited version of such a rule on itself, restricting the use of riders to modify substantive legislation, *see* Senate R. XVI(4); House R. XXI(2), but a violation of the rule merely makes the rider subject to procedural objection within the Congress, and does not invalidate it as law.

2. Another reason for their effectiveness is that sponsors of limitations can sometimes avoid the jurisdiction of hostile committees by inserting the limitations as riders into appropriations bills. They can also make it difficult for the President to veto the limitations by embedding them in needed appropriations bills, especially omnibus bills that provide for funding of many different programs.

solely in the hands of Congress and it is the plain and explicit duty of the executive branch . . . to comply with the same." *Id.* at 988.

In practice, the appropriations power has often been softened, especially for defense operations. Congress has made lump sum appropriations that leave administrators substantial discretion over the expenditure of the funds, funded contingency funds with similar discretion, and enacted standby emergency spending authority for war or national emergency. *See* Banks & Raven-Hansen, *supra,* at 71-73. Informal agreements between agencies and congressional committees have also evolved for "reprogramming," a practice that apparently originated through a World War II "gentlemen's agreement" that permitted the War Department to shift funds from one purpose to another within an appropriation to meet wartime exigencies with the approval of the military appropriations subcommittee. It evolved into a procedure by which an agency is permitted to use "funds in an account . . . for different purposes than those contemplated when the funds were appropriated," if the new use is within the general purpose of the appropriation and not otherwise prohibited by statute and is reported to (and sometimes subject to approval by) one or more congressional committees — requirements sometimes triggered only when the reprogrammed funds exceed certain thresholds. *Id.*

In contrast to reprogramming, budget transfer shifts funds *between* appropriations. Budget transfer is prohibited without statutory authority. 31 U.S.C. §1532 (2018) ("An amount available under any law may be withdrawn from one appropriation account and credited to another . . . only when authorized by law."); *see* Banks & Raven-Hansen, *supra,* at 77; Sam Wice, *Why the Transfer of Funds to Build the Wall Is Likely Illegal,* Notice & Comment (Mar. 29, 2019), https://yalejreg.com/nc/why-the-transfer-of-funds-to-build-the-wall-is-likely-illegal/. After the funding scandal known as the Iran-Contra Affair in the Reagan administration, Congress limited reprogramming and transfers to "higher priority items based on unforeseen military requirements" and prohibited either practice when the item for which reprogramming or transfer is requested "is an item for which Congress has denied funds." *See* 10 U.S.C. §2214 (2018).

Reading *Sierra Club v. Trump*

The appropriations power was put to the test by the Trump administration's proposed plan for funding construction of the Border Wall, after Congress declined to appropriate the full funding that he had requested. President Trump declared a national emergency by issuing Proclamation No. 9844 (reproduced *supra* p. 70), invoking standby statutory authority under 10 U.S.C. §2808 (2018), by which the Administration could reprogram funds from military construction appropriations. That statute provides:

> (a) In the event of a declaration of war or the declaration by the President of a national emergency in accordance with the National Emergencies Act (50 U.S.C. 1601 et seq.) that requires use of the armed forces, the Secretary of Defense, without regard to any other provision of law, may undertake military construction projects, and may authorize the Secretaries of the military departments to undertake military construction projects, not otherwise authorized by law that are necessary to support such use of the armed forces. Such projects

> may be undertaken only within the total amount of funds that have been appropriated for military construction, including funds appropriated for family housing, that have not been obligated.

Separately, the Administration sought to transfer other funds to augment the total needed for construction of the Border Wall. These transfers did not depend on the declaration of national emergency. The Department of Homeland Security (DHS) requested Department of Defense (DOD) "assistance" under 10 U.S.C. §284 (2018) to block drug-smuggling corridors along the southern border. Section 284 authorizes the Secretary of Defense to provide support on request for "the counterdrug activities or activities to counter transnational organized crime of any other department or agency of the Federal Government." *Id.* §284(a). Such support may include "[c]onstruction of roads and *fences* and installation of lighting to block drug smuggling corridors across international boundaries of the United States." *Id.* §284(b)(7) (emphasis added). DOD then invoked the following provision of the Department of Defense and Labor, Health and Human Services, and Education Appropriations Act, 2019 and Continuing Appropriations Act, 2019, Pub. L. No. 115-245, 132 Stat. 2981 (2018), to transfer $2.5 billion in funds, originally appropriated for military personnel costs, to meet DHS's request by constructing border barriers based on its §284 authority:

> Upon determination by the Secretary of Defense that such action is necessary in the national interest, he may, with the approval of the Office of Management and Budget, transfer not to exceed $4,000,000,000 of working capital funds of the Department of Defense or funds made available in this Act to the Department of Defense for military functions (except military construction) between such appropriations or funds or any subdivision thereof, to be merged with and to be available for the same purposes, and for the same time period, as the appropriation or fund to which transferred: *Provided*, That such authority to transfer may not be used unless for higher priority items, based on unforeseen military requirements, than those for which originally appropriated and in no case where the item for which funds are requested has been denied by the Congress. . . . [*Id.* §8005, 132 Stat. at 2999.]

Numerous lawsuits were filed to block that construction, including the following suit by the Sierra Club and others, invoking not just statutory requirements that the plaintiffs alleged were not met, but also the Appropriations Clause and the separation of powers.

- The Administration had not yet decided to use any of the construction funds provided by §2808 at the time of the suit and so informed the court. Does this case address or even need to address his *emergency* spending authority?
- The government argued that *DHS*'s request for support was "unforeseen." Why did the court disagree?
- Section 8005 authority cannot be used for an "item" for which Congress has denied funds. §8005. *See also* 10 U.S.C. §2214(b)(2). *Had* Congress denied the use of funds for §284 "counterdrug activities"? Is that the right "item"?

- Government lawyers asserted that Congress had not passed any law specifically prohibiting the use of reprogrammed funds for Border Wall construction. Why wasn't the "If they wanted to prevent it, they could just say so" argument a winner? If it were correct, how would you describe the resulting appropriations power?
- The dissent pointed out that the district court decision relied entirely on the construction of statutory authority. Why, then, did the majority reach the constitutional claim?

Sierra Club v. Trump

United States Court of Appeals, Ninth Circuit, 2019
929 F.3d 670
stay granted, 140 S. Ct. 1 (2019) (mem.)

CLIFTON and FRIEDLAND, Circuit Judges: This emergency proceeding arises from a challenge to a decision by the President and certain of his cabinet members (collectively, "Defendants") to "reprogram" funds appropriated by Congress to the Department of Defense ("DoD") for Army personnel needs and to redirect those funds toward building a barrier along portions of our country's southern border. . . .

The Sierra Club and the Southern Border Communities Coalition (collectively, "Plaintiffs") sued Defendants to enjoin the reprogramming and the funds' expenditure. They argued that the requirements of section 8005 had not been satisfied and that the use of the funds to build a border barrier was accordingly unsupported by any congressional appropriation and thus unconstitutional. A federal district court agreed with Plaintiffs and enjoined Defendants from using reprogrammed funds to construct a border barrier. [*Sierra Club v. Trump*, 379 F. Supp. 3d 883 (N.D. Cal. 2019) (issuing preliminary injunction); Order Granting in Part and Denying in Part Plaintiffs' Motion for Partial Summary Judgment, *Sierra Club v. Trump*, No. 19-cv-00892-HSG, 2019 WL 2715422, at *2 (N.D. Cal. June 28, 2019) (issuing permanent injunction).] Defendants now move for an emergency stay of the district court's injunction. . . .

I. FACTUAL & PROCEDURAL BACKGROUND

President Trump has made numerous requests to Congress for funding for construction of a barrier on the U.S.-Mexico border. In his proposed budget for Fiscal Year 2018, for example, the President requested $2.6 billion for border security, including "funding to plan, design, and construct a physical wall along the southern border." Congress partially obliged, allocating in the 2018 Consolidated Appropriations Act $1.571 billion for border fencing, "border barrier planning and design," and the "acquisition and deployment of border security technology." Consolidated Appropriations Act, 2018, Pub. L. No. 115-141, div. F, tit. II, §230(a), 132 Stat. 348, 616 (2018). Throughout 2018, House and Senate lawmakers introduced numerous bills that would have authorized or appropriated additional billions for border barrier construction. . . . Lawmakers spent countless hours considering these various proposals, but none ultimately passed.

The situation reached an impasse in December 2018. During negotiations with Congress over an appropriations bill to fund various parts of the federal government for the remainder of the fiscal year, the President announced his unequivocal position that "any measure that funds the government must include border security." He declared that he would not sign any funding bill that did not allocate substantial funding for a physical barrier on the U.S.-Mexico border. The President also stated that he was willing to declare a national emergency and use other mechanisms to get the money he desired if Congress refused to allocate it. On December 20, 2018, the House of Representatives passed a continuing resolution that allocated $5.7 billion in border barrier funding. H.R. 695, 115th Cong. §141 (2018) ("[T]here is appropriated for 'U.S. Customs and Border Protection — Procurement, Construction, and Improvements' $5,710,357,000 for fiscal year 2019."). But the Senate rejected the bill. The President could not reach an agreement with lawmakers on whether the spending bill would include border barrier funding, triggering what would become the nation's longest partial government shutdown. . . .

After 35 days, the government shutdown ended without an agreement providing increased border barrier funding. Congress passed and the President signed a stopgap spending measure to reopen for three weeks the parts of the Government that had been shut down. H.R.J. Res. 28, 116th Cong. (2019). But the President made clear that he still intended to build a border barrier, with or without funding from Congress. As the Acting White House Chief of Staff explained, the President was prepared to both reprogram money and declare a national emergency to obtain a total sum "well north of $5.7 billion."

Congress passed the Consolidated Appropriations Act of 2019 ("CAA") on February 14, 2019, which included the Department of Homeland Security Appropriations Act for Fiscal Year 2019. Pub. L. No. 116-6, div. A, 133 Stat. 13 (2019). The CAA appropriated only $1.375 billion of the $5.7 billion the President had sought in border barrier funding and specified that the $1.375 billion was "for the construction of primary pedestrian fencing . . . in the Rio Grande Valley Sector." *Id.* §230(a)(1), 133 Stat. at 28. . . .

The President signed the CAA into law the following day. He concurrently issued a proclamation under the National Emergencies Act, 50 U.S.C. §§1601-1651, "declar[ing] that a national emergency exists at the southern border of the United States." Proclamation No. 9844, 84 Fed. Reg. 4949 (Feb. 15, 2019) ("Proclamation No. 9844") [*supra* p. 70]. . . .

An accompanying White House Fact Sheet explained that the President was "using his legal authority to take Executive action to secure additional resources" to build a border barrier. It continued: "Including funding in Homeland Security appropriations, the Administration has so far identified up to $8.1 billion that will be available to build the border wall once a national emergency is declared and additional funds have been reprogrammed." *Id.* The fact sheet specifically identified three funding sources: (1) "[a]bout $601 million from the Treasury Forfeiture Fund," 31 U.S.C. §9705(a); (2) "[u]p to $2.5 billion under the Department of Defense [reprogrammed] funds transferred [to DHS] for Support for Counterdrug Activities" pursuant to 10 U.S.C. §284 ("section 284"); and (3) "[u]p to $3.6 billion reallocated from [DoD] military construction projects under the President's declaration of a national emergency" pursuant to 10 U.S.C. §2808 ("section 2808"), which provides that the Secretary of Defense may authorize military construction projects whenever the President declares a national emergency that requires use of the armed forces. *Id.*

The House and Senate adopted a joint resolution terminating the President's declaration of a national emergency pursuant to Congress's authority under 50 U.S.C. §1622(a)(1). H.R.J. Res. 46, 116th Cong. (2019). The President vetoed the joint resolution, and a vote in the House to override the veto fell short of the required two-thirds majority, 165 Cong. Rec. H2799, H2814-15 (2019).

Almost immediately, executive branch agencies began to use the funds identified in Proclamation 9844 for border barrier construction.[3] ... [O]n February 25, DHS submitted a request to DoD for assistance, pursuant to section 284, with construction of fences, roads, and lighting within eleven drug-smuggling corridors identified by DHS along the border. In response to that request, on March 25, the Acting Secretary of Defense, Patrick Shanahan, approved the transfer of up to $1 billion in funds from DoD to DHS for the three highest priority drug-smuggling corridors: the Yuma Sector Project 1 and Yuma Sector Project 2 in Arizona, and the El Paso Sector Project 1 in New Mexico.

To fund the approved projects, Shanahan invoked section 8005 of the Department of Defense Appropriations Act of 2019 and section 1001 of the John S. McCain National Defense Authorization Act ("NDAA") for Fiscal Year 2019 [Pub. L. 115-232, §1001, 132 Stat. 1636, 1945 (2018)] to "reprogram" approximately $1 billion from Army personnel funds to the counter-narcotics support budget, which Shanahan asserted then made those funds available for transfer to DHS pursuant to section 284. . . .

A memo from Shanahan asserted that the statutory requirements for reprogramming under section 8005 had been met: that the items to be funded were a higher priority than the Army personnel funds; that the need to provide support for the Yuma and El Paso Projects was "an unforeseen military requirement not known at the time of the FY 2019 budget request"; and that support for construction of the border barrier in these areas "ha[d] not been denied by Congress." Specifically, DoD concluded that "Army personnel funds were available for transfer because expenditures for service member pay and compensation, retirements benefits, food, and moving expenses through the end of fiscal year 2019 [would] be lower than originally budgeted." As required by section 8005, Shanahan also formally notified Congress of the reprogramming authorization, explaining that the reprogrammed funds were "required" so that DoD could provide DHS the support it requested under section 284.[6]

The next day, both the House Committee on Armed Services and the House Committee on Appropriations formally disapproved of DoD's section 8005 reprogramming. The Armed Services Committee wrote in a letter to DoD that it "denie[d] this [reprogramming] request," and that the committee "[did] not approve the proposed use of Department of Defense funds to construct additional

---

[3. In fact, the agencies had only begun using the §284 and §8005 authorities — which were not identified in the Proclamation — and not the §2808 authority, which was identified. — Eds.]

6. DoD had previously adhered to a "gentlemen's agreement" with Congress where it sought approval from the relevant committees *before* reprogramming funds, rather than simply notifying them after the decision had been finalized.

physical barriers and roads or install lighting in the vicinity of the United States border." The Appropriations committee similarly denied the reprogramming request.

Officials at DoD and DHS pressed forward with reprogramming-enabled border barrier construction plans [and awarded construction contracts]. . . .

. . . On May 9, Shanahan invoked section 8005 and section 1001 of the NDAA again — along with related reprogramming provisions, section 9002 of the Department of Defense Appropriations Act of 2019 and section 1512 of the NDAA[7] — to authorize an additional $1.5 billion in reprogramming to fund four more projects. . . . Around the same time, the President indicated that he expected to approve additional projects using funds authorized by the national emergency declaration pursuant to section 2808, although no concrete action has been taken in that regard. . . .

III. JUSTICIABILITY

Defendants have not argued that jurisdiction over this action is lacking. Nor have they asserted that Plaintiffs' challenge to the section 8005 reprogramming presents a nonjusticiable "political question." They have contended, however, that "[t]he real separation-of-powers concern is the district court's intrusion into the budgeting process," which "is between the Legislative and Executive Branches — not the judiciary." We consider, therefore, whether it is appropriate for the courts to entertain Plaintiffs' action in the first place. We conclude that it is. . . .

The current action does not ask us to decide whether the projects for which Defendants seek to reprogram funds are worthy or whether, as a policy judgment, funds should be spent on them. Instead, we are asked whether the reprogramming of funds is consistent with the Appropriations Clause and section 8005. That "is a familiar judicial exercise." [*Zivotofsky ex rel. Zivotofsky v. Clinton*, 566 U.S. 189, 196 (2012)]. . . .

IV. STAY STANDARDS

We decide whether to issue a stay by considering four factors, reiterated by the Supreme Court in *Nken v. Holder*, 556 U.S. 418 (2009):

> (1) whether the stay applicant has made a strong showing that he is likely to succeed on the merits; (2) whether the applicant will be irreparably injured absent a stay; (3) whether issuance of the stay will substantially injure the other parties interested in the proceeding; and (4) where the public interest lies.

Id. at 434 (quoting *Hilton v. Braunskill*, 481 U.S. 770, 776 (1987)). The first two factors "are the most critical," and we only reach the last two "[o]nce an applicant satisfies the first two factors." *Id.* at 434-35. . . .

---

7. . . . Because it is uncontested that all of these reprogramming provisions are subject to section 8005's requirements, we refer to these requirements collectively by reference to section 8005.

V. LIKELIHOOD OF SUCCESS ON THE MERITS . . .

A. Plaintiffs' Constitutional Claim

The Constitution's Appropriations Clause provides that "No Money shall be drawn from the Treasury, but in Consequence of Appropriations made by Law." U.S. Const. art. I, §9, cl. 7. In addition to safeguarding "the public treasure, the common fund of all," and providing "a most useful and salutary check upon . . . corrupt influence and public peculation," it ensures that the "the executive [does not] possess an unbounded power over the public purse of the nation." 3 Joseph Story, *Commentaries on the Constitution of the United States* §1342 (Boston, Hilliard, Gray & Co. ed. 1833).

This approach to the power of the purse comported with the Founders' "declared purpose of separating and dividing the powers of government," namely "to 'diffus[e] power the better to secure liberty.'" *Bowsher v. Synar,* 478 U.S. 714, 721 (1986) (alteration in original) (quoting *Youngstown Sheet & Tube Co. v. Sawyer,* 343 U.S. 579, 635 (1952) (Jackson, J., concurring)); *see also INS v. Chadha,* 462 U.S. 919, 949-50 (1983) (collecting sources and explaining the Founders' belief in "the need to divide and disperse power in order to protect liberty"). In response to critiques that his proposed Constitution would dangerously concentrate power in a single central government, James Madison argued that the risk of abuse of such power was low because "the sword and purse are not to be given to the same member" of the government. 3 *Debates in the Several State Conventions on the Adoption of the Federal Constitution* 393 (Jonathan Elliot ed., 2d ed. 1836). Instead, Madison explained that "[t]he purse is in the hands of the representatives of the people," who "have the appropriation of all moneys." *Id.*

Plaintiffs' principal legal theory is that Defendants seek to spend funds for a different purpose than that for which Congress appropriated them, thereby violating the Appropriations Clause. Defendants' defense to this claim is that, through section 8005, Congress allowed Defendants to make this reallocation. If Defendants were correct that section 8005 allowed this spending reallocation, Plaintiffs' claim would fail, because the spending would be consistent with Congress's appropriation legislation. If section 8005 does not authorize the reallocation, however, then Defendants are acting outside of any statutory appropriation and are therefore spending funds contrary to Congress's appropriations decisions. We believe Plaintiffs are correct that there is no statutory appropriation for the expenditures that are the subject of the injunction. Reprogramming and spending those funds therefore violates the Appropriations Clause.

1. Section 8005's Meaning

Defendants argue that they are likely to prevail on appeal because Congress has authorized DoD to reprogram funds, the planned use of funds is consistent with that reprogramming authorization, and this spending is therefore authorized by an appropriation from Congress as the Appropriations Clause requires. We disagree. DoD's proposed expenditures are not authorized by the applicable reprogramming statute. They therefore are not "in Consequence of Appropriations made by Law." U.S. Const. art. I, §9, cl. 7.

At bottom, this constitutional issue turns on a question of statutory interpretation. Section 8005 of the Department of Defense Appropriations Act of 2019 provides that the Secretary of Defense may reprogram funds for certain military functions other than those for which they were initially appropriated, but it limits the Secretary's ability to do so to a narrow set of circumstances. Pub. L. No. 115-245, §8005, 132 Stat. 2981, 2999 (2018). Transferred funds must address "higher priority items, based on unforeseen military requirements, than those for which originally appropriated." *Id.* And "in no case" may the Secretary use the funds "where the item for which reprogramming is requested has been denied by the Congress." *Id.* We conclude, as Plaintiffs argue, that those requirements are not satisfied.

i. "Unforeseen"

Plaintiffs argue that the President's repeated and unsuccessful requests for more border barrier funding make the request here obviously not unforeseen. Defendants assert in response, without citation, that "[a]n expenditure is 'unforeseen' . . . if DoD was not aware of the specific need when it made its budgeting requests." Defendants contend that DoD could not have foreseen the "need to provide support" to DHS for border barrier construction in the relevant sectors when it made its budget requests for 2019, before DHS's own budget was even finalized.

Defendants mistakenly focus on the assertion that DoD "could not have anticipated that DHS would request specific support for roads, fences, and lighting." Even assuming that is true, the fact remains that DHS came to DoD for funds because Congress refused to grant DHS itself those funds. And when properly viewed as applying to the broader "requirement" of a border wall, not to DHS's specific need to turn to an entity other than Congress for funds, it is not credible that DoD did not foresee this requirement. The long history of the President's efforts to build a border barrier and of Congress's refusing to appropriate the funds he requested makes it implausible that this need was unforeseen.

ii. "Denied by the Congress"

Even if there could be doubt about how to interpret "unforeseen," it is clear that Congress denied this request. Because each of section 8005's conditions must be satisfied for DoD's reprogramming and spending to be constitutionally permissible, this conclusion alone undermines Defendants' likelihood of success on the merits on appeal.

Defendants urge that "an 'item for which funds are requested'" refers to "a *particular* budget item" for section 8005 purposes, so "Congress's decisions with respect to DHS's more general request for border-wall funding [are] irrelevant." But this interpretation, which would require that a specific funding request be explicitly rejected by Congress, is not compatible with the plain text of section 8005. First, the statute refers to "item[s] . . . denied by the Congress," not to *funding requests* denied by the Congress, suggesting that the inquiry centers on what DoD wishes to spend the funds on, not on the form in which Congress considered whether to permit such spending. Second, Defendants give the term "denied" a meaning other than its "ordinary, contemporary, and common" one. *United States v. Iverson*, 162 F.3d 1015, 1022 (9th Cir. 1998). In common usage, a general denial of something requested can, and in this case does, encompass more specific or narrower forms of that request. To illustrate, if someone offered a new job asks her potential future employer for a larger compensation package than was included in the job offer and the request is denied, she has been denied a five percent higher salary even if her request did not specifically ask for that amount.

As the district court noted, Defendants' reading of section 8005 also would produce the perverse result that DoD could, by declining to present Congress with a particular line item to deny, reprogram funds for a purpose that Congress refused to grant another agency elsewhere in the budgeting process.[18] In other words, it would simply invite creative repackaging. But putting a gift in different wrapping paper does not change the gift. Identifying the request to Congress as having come previously from DHS instead of from DoD does not change what funding was requested for: a wall along the southern border.

Construing section 8005 with an eye towards the ordinary and common-sense meaning of "denied," real-world events in the months and years leading up to the 2019 appropriations bills leave no doubt that Congress considered and denied appropriations for the border barrier construction projects that DoD now seeks to finance using its section 8005 authority. Long before the emergency declaration and DoD's reprogramming at issue here, the President made plain his desire to construct a border barrier, requesting $5.7 billion from Congress to do so. Throughout 2018, Congress considered multiple bills that would have supported construction of such a barrier; it passed none of them.

That DoD never specifically requested from Congress the specific sums at issue here for the specific purpose of counterdrug funding at the southern border (and that Congress therefore never had cause to deny that specific request) is of no moment. The amount to be appropriated for a border barrier occupied center stage of the budgeting process for months, culminating in a prolonged government shutdown that both the Legislative and Executive Branches clearly understood as hinging on whether Congress would accede to the President's request for $5.7 billion to build a border barrier.

In sum, Congress considered the "item" at issue here — a physical barrier along the entire southern border, including in the Yuma, El Paso, Tucson, and El Centro sectors — and decided in a transparent process subject to great public scrutiny to appropriate less than the total amount the President had sought for that item. To call that anything but a "denial" is not credible. . . .

2. Defendants' Interpretation and Agency Deference . . .

. . . The two documents in the record that appear to contain DoD's analysis of the section 8005 requirements — the official reprogramming action and a related memorandum to DoD's comptroller — are entirely conclusory. The reprogramming action merely parrots the statute without analysis:

> This reprogramming action provides funding in support of higher priority items, based on unforeseen military requirements, than those for which originally appropriated; and is determined to be necessary in the national interest. It meets all administrative and legal requirements, and none of the items has previously been denied by the Congress.

18. That result would hardly comport with Congress's stated desire in drafting the language currently in section 8005 "to tighten congressional control of the reprogramming process." H.R. Rep. No. 93-662, at 16 (1973).

The memorandum contains little more, stating that "[t]he need to provide support . . . was . . . not known at the time of the [Fiscal Year] 2019 budget request" and that Congress had not denied funding for the items. . . .

* * *

Without section 8005's statutory authorization to reprogram funds for section 284 security measures, no congressional action permits Defendants to use those funds to construct border barriers. "The President's power . . . must stem either from an act of Congress or from the Constitution itself. There is no statute that expressly authorizes the President to [act] as he did here. Nor is there any act of Congress to which our attention has been directed from which such a power can fairly be implied." *Youngstown,* 343 U.S. at 585. Defendants' attempt to reprogram and spend these funds therefore violates the Appropriations Clause and intrudes on Congress's exclusive power of the purse, for it would cause funds to be "drawn from the Treasury" not "in Consequence of Appropriations made by Law." U.S. Const. art. I, §9, cl. 7.

B. Whether Plaintiffs Have a Cause of Action . . .

Defendants argue that none of the foregoing analysis matters because Plaintiffs lack a cause of action to challenge the reprogramming of funds at issue here. We disagree. Plaintiffs may bring their challenge through an equitable action to enjoin unconstitutional official conduct, or under the judicial review provisions of the Administrative Procedure Act ("APA"), 5 U.S.C. §701 *et seq.*, as a challenge to a final agency decision that is alleged to violate the Constitution, or both. Either way, Plaintiffs have an avenue for seeking relief. . . .

The Supreme Court has "long held that federal courts may in some circumstances grant injunctive relief against" federal officials violating federal law. *Armstrong v. Exceptional Child Ctr., Inc.*, 135 S. Ct. 1378, 1384 (2015); *see also Corr. Servs. Corp. v. Malesko,* 534 U.S. 61, 74 (2001) ("[I]njunctive relief has long been recognized as the proper means for preventing entities from acting unconstitutionally."). "The ability to sue to enjoin unconstitutional actions by state and federal officers is the creation of courts of equity, and reflects a long history of judicial review of illegal executive action, tracing back to England." *Armstrong,* 135 S. Ct. at 1384. . . .

Plaintiffs' claim is also cognizable under the APA. The APA provides for judicial review of "[a]gency action made reviewable by statute and final agency action for which there is no other adequate remedy in a court." 5 U.S.C. §704. Here, Plaintiffs have a cause of action under the APA as long as there has been final agency action, and as long as Congress has not limited review of such actions through other statutes or committed them to agency discretion. Neither of these bars to APA relief is present here. *See* 5 U.S.C. §§701(a), 704, 706. . . .

VI. THE REMAINING STAY FACTORS . . .

Defendants have discussed . . . three remaining factors together in terms of the "equitable balance of harms." There is logic in that, so we will do the same, considering the respective impacts on Defendants, Plaintiffs and others interested in the proceedings, and the general public.

The primary harm cited by Defendants if a stay is not granted is that a "delay in the construction of border fencing pending appeal will create irreparable harm" because "deadly drugs [will] flow into this country in the interim." They argue that CBP has recorded over 4,000 "drug-related events" between border crossings in the El Paso, El Centro, Tucson, and Yuma Sectors in Fiscal Year 2018 and cites CBP's seizure of thousands of pounds of marijuana and lesser amounts of other illegal substances, including cocaine, heroin, methamphetamine, and fentanyl.

We do not question in the slightest the scourge that is illegal drug trafficking and the public interest in combatting it. Our circuit includes several border states, and our courts deal with no small number of cases involving illegal drugs crossing those states' borders.

Defendants have not actually spoken to the more relevant questions, however. What will be the impact of building the barriers they propose? Even more to the point, what would be the impact of delaying the construction of those barriers? If these specific leaks are plugged, will the drugs flow through somewhere else? We do not know, but the evidence before us does not support a conclusion that enjoining the construction of the proposed barriers until this appeal is fully resolved will have a significant impact.

To begin with, the statistics cited by Defendants describe drug trafficking that CBP has detected with existing barriers and law enforcement efforts. They do not tell us how much gets through undetected or what additional amounts would be stopped by the proposed barriers.

As Plaintiffs point out, according to the Drug Enforcement Administration's most recent assessment, the "majority of the [heroin] flow is through [privately operated vehicles] entering the United States at legal ports of entry, followed by tractor-trailers, where the heroin is co-mingled with legal goods." Only "a small percentage of all heroin seized by [CBP] along the land border was between Ports of Entry." Fentanyl transiting the southern border is likewise most commonly smuggled in "multi-kilogram loads" in vehicles crossing at legal ports of entry. Defendants have not disputed these assessments.

That does not lead to a conclusion that leaks should not be plugged. It does suggest, however, that Defendants' claim that failing to stay the injunction pending appeal will cause significant irreparable harm is supported by much less than meets the eye. Congress could have appropriated funds to construct these barriers if it concluded that the expenditure was in the public interest, but it did not.

For similar reasons, we are unmoved by Defendants' contention that "the injunction threatens to permanently deprive DoD of its authorization to use the funds at issue to complete" the selected projects, including "approximately $1.1 billion it has transferred for these projects but has not yet obligated via construction contracts," because "the funding will likely lapse during the appeal's pendency." A lapse in funding does not mean that the money will disappear from the Treasury. The country will still have that money. It could be spent in the future, including through appropriations enacted by Congress for the next fiscal year. The lapse simply means that Defendants' effort to justify spending those funds based on the appropriations act for the current fiscal year and the authority to reprogram funds under section 8005 may be thwarted.

Defendants' identification of this lapse as a factor that should tip the balance of harms in their favor actually serves instead to illustrate the underlying weakness in their position. Defendants' rush to spend this money is necessarily driven by their understanding that Congress did not appropriate requested funding for these purposes in the current budget and their expectation that Congress will not authorize that spending in the next fiscal year, either. The effort by Defendants to spend this money is not consistent with Congress's power over the purse or with the tacit assessment by Congress that the spending would not be in the public interest. . . .

Moving to the impacts on the Plaintiffs, Defendants denigrate those impacts as limited to "aesthetic and recreational injuries." . . . Defendants have elected not to dispute that Plaintiffs' interests are sufficiently substantial to support Article III standing. Environmental injuries have been held sufficient in many cases to support injunctions blocking substantial government projects. The Supreme Court has observed that "[e]nvironmental injury, by its nature, can seldom be adequately remedied by money damages and is often permanent or at least of long duration, *i.e.*, irreparable. If such injury is sufficiently likely, therefore, the balance of harms will usually favor the issuance of an injunction to protect the environment." *Amoco Prod. Co. v. Village of Gambell*, 480 U.S. 531, 545 (1987).

As to the public interest, we conclude that the public interest weighs forcefully against issuing a stay. The Constitution assigns to Congress the power of the purse. Under the Appropriations Clause, it is Congress that is to make decisions regarding how to spend taxpayer dollars. As we have explained, the Appropriations Clause serves as a check by requiring that "not a dollar of [money in the Treasury] can be used in the payment of any thing not thus previously sanctioned" by Congress, as "[a]ny other course would give to the fiscal officers a most dangerous discretion." *Reeside v. Walker*, 52 U.S. 272, 291 (1850). In the words of then-Judge Kavanaugh, the Appropriations Clause is

> a bulwark of the Constitution's separation of powers among the three branches of the National Government. It is particularly important as a restraint on Executive Branch officers: If not for the Appropriations Clause, the executive would possess an unbounded power over the public purse of the nation; and might apply all its monied resources at his pleasure.

U.S. Dep't of Navy v. Fed. Labor Relations Auth., 665 F.3d 1339, 1347 (D.C. Cir. 2012) (Kavanaugh, J.) (quotation marks omitted). The Clause prevents the Executive Branch from "even inadvertently obligating the Government to pay money without statutory authority." *Id.* The public interest in ensuring protection of this separation of powers is foundational and requires little elaboration.

Similarly, when Congress chooses how to address a problem, "[i]t is quite impossible . . . to find secreted in the interstices of legislation the very grant of power which Congress consciously withheld," as doing so is "not merely to disregard in a particular instance the clear will of Congress," but "to disrespect the whole legislative process and the constitutional division of authority between President and Congress." *Youngstown*, 343 U.S. at 609 (1952) (Frankfurter, J., concurring). Congress did not appropriate money to build the border barriers Defendants seek to build here. Congress presumably decided such construction at this time was not in the public interest. It is not for us to reach a different conclusion.

The public interest and the balance of hardships do not support granting the motion to stay.

VII. CONCLUSION

In his concurrence in *Youngstown,* Justice Jackson made eloquent comments that seem equally apt today:

> The essence of our free Government is "leave to live by no man's leave, underneath the law" — to be governed by those impersonal forces which we call law. Our Government is fashioned to fulfill this concept so far as humanly possible. The Executive, except for recommendation and veto, has no legislative power. The executive action we have here originates in the individual will of the President and represents an exercise of authority without law. . . . With all its defects, delays and inconveniences, men have discovered no technique for long preserving free government except that the Executive be under the law, and that the law be made by parliamentary deliberations.
>
> Such institutions may be destined to pass away. But it is the duty of the Court to be last, not first, to give them up.

343 U.S. at 654-55 (Jackson, J., concurring).

Heeding Justice Jackson's words, we deny Defendants' motion for a stay.

N.R. SMITH, Circuit Judge, dissenting: . . . Because Defendants have satisfied their burden to obtain the requested relief when Plaintiffs' claim is properly cast as a statutory issue, the majority should grant Defendants' motion to stay the permanent injunction until the matter is finally determined on appeal. . . .

I. DEFENDANTS ARE LIKELY TO SUCCEED ON THE MERITS

The district court granted a permanent injunction in Plaintiffs' favor based on a purported statutory claim under the DoD Appropriations Act for Fiscal Year 2019, Pub. L. No. 115-245, §§8005, 9002, 132 Stat. 2981, 2999. The district court analyzed only whether Defendants exceeded their statutory authority under §8005, without discussing whether they also separately violated any constitutional provision. Nevertheless, the majority views Plaintiffs' claim as, "at its core, one alleging a constitutional violation." As discussed below, viewing Plaintiffs' claim as alleging a statutory violation is the proper approach.

When their claim is properly viewed as alleging a statutory violation, Plaintiffs have no mechanism to challenge Defendants' actions. Plaintiffs have neither an implied statutory cause of action under §8005, nor an equitable cause of action. Nor do Plaintiffs have a cause of action to challenge the DoD's §8005 reprogramming under the Administrative Procedure Act (APA), as they fall outside of the zone of interests for such a claim. Consequently, Defendants have made a strong showing that they are likely to succeed on the merits of their appeal. . . .

Notes and Questions

1. The Stay. The dissent avoided the constitutional problem by another route. It found that the plaintiffs likely lacked a cause of action to challenge the funding plan. We explore the availability of causes of action in Chapter 5. In *Trump v. Sierra Club,* 140 S. Ct. 1 (2019) (mem.), the Supreme Court granted a stay:

> The application for stay presented to Justice Kagan and by her referred to the Court is granted. Among the reasons is that the Government has made a sufficient showing at this stage that the plaintiffs have no cause of action to obtain review of the Acting Secretary's compliance with Section 8005. The District Court's June 28, 2019 order granting a permanent injunction is stayed pending disposition of the Government's appeal in the United States Court of Appeals for the Ninth Circuit and disposition of the Government's petition for a writ of certiorari, if such writ is timely sought. Should the petition for a writ of certiorari be denied, this stay shall terminate automatically. In the event the petition for a writ of certiorari is granted, the stay shall terminate when the Court enters its judgment. *Id.* at 1.

In other words, the Court suggested that it might not reach the merits because the plaintiffs might not have either an equitable cause of action or a cause of action under the Administrative Procedure Act. The government was therefore permitted to go forward with construction, pending the Court's final decision.

If there is no cause of action, however, does that present another constitutional problem? If so, what is it?

2. Sections 284 and 8005: Diverting Funds for "Drug Interdiction." Note that the court described as "reprogramming" what appears instead to be transferring funds between appropriations, which is subject to §8005. What are the standards set out in §§284 and 8005 for the diversion of appropriated funds? Given the Proclamation's stated concern about "illicit narcotics" at the southern border and §284(a)'s authorization for the construction of "fences" to block cross-border drug-smuggling, why did the court rule that plaintiffs had shown a likelihood of success on their claim that it was unlawful for DOD to transfer funds for drug interdiction?

Recall the §8005 limitation on transfers for an item that has been "denied" by Congress. What is the relevant "item" involved in the Administration's funding plan? Did Congress "deny" it? *See generally* Michael McCord, *Power Struggle over the Wall: Presidential Emergency Powers vs. Congressional Power of the Purse,* Just Security, Feb. 21, 2019 (concluding, "If I had been directed, when I was Chief Financial Officer of the Department of Defense, to implement the bulk of this plan that lies within the purview of the Department of Defense, I don't believe that I would have concluded it was legal and appropriate to do so or that I would have received legal clearance from the Department's General Counsel.").

3. Avoiding the Question. The district court had explained that its refusal to read §8005 to permit funding for the Border Wall avoided "a serious constitutional problem under the Constitution's separation of powers principles." What is that problem? Did the court of appeals avoid it as well? If not, why not?

4. Section 2808: It's the Statute, Stupid. Subsequent to the Supreme Court's stay of the district court's injunction in *Sierra Club,* the Administration started using its §2808 authority to fund construction of the Border Wall. This standby authority is dependent on the declaration of national emergency. If you represented plaintiffs challenging this funding, would you attack the *bona fides* of the emergency? If so, what judicially manageable standard would you say is available?

Look again at §2808. What requirements does it impose on funding? *See* McCord, *supra* (questioning the meaning of "military construction project"); *cf.* Michael

J. Vassalotti & Brendan W. McGarry, *Military Construction Funding in the Event of a National Emergency* (Cong. Res. Serv.), Jan. 11, 2019 (listing prior projects).

Measuring the legality of executive action by statutory standards is what the courts do every day. The cry of emergency is mesmerizing and counsels cautious deference, but an "emergency" is no more a talisman than "national security." It does not relieve courts of the duty to construe standby statutes invoked by the President. Does it affect the duty of courts to judge the application of those statutes to particular facts?

5. *The Specific Controls the General?* In early 2019, Congress passed the Consolidated Appropriations Act (CAA), Pub. L. No. 116-6, 133 Stat. 13. The CAA provided $1.375 billion for "the construction of primary pedestrian fencing" in "the Rio Grande Valley Sector," *id.*, div. A, §230(a)(1), 133 Stat. at 28, but added that none of the funds appropriated by the Act may be used "for the construction of pedestrian fencing" in any other areas along the border. *Id.* §231. Another part of the CAA provided:

> None of the funds made available in this or any other appropriations Act may be used to increase, eliminate, or reduce funding for a program, project, or activity as proposed in the President's budget request for a fiscal year until such proposed change is subsequently enacted in an appropriation Act, or unless such change is made pursuant to the reprogramming or transfer provisions of this or any other appropriations Act. [*Id.*, div. D, §739, 133 Stat. at 197.]

Did this specific appropriation for "pedestrian fencing" in one sector of the border foreclose the Administration's reliance on §§284, 2808, or 8005 funding for construction elsewhere?

In *El Paso County v. Trump*, 408 F. Supp. 3d 840 (W.D. Tex. 2019), the court said yes. It held that

> the CAA specifically appropriates $1.375 billion for border-wall expenditures and requires those expenditures to be made on "construction . . . in the Rio Grande Valley Sector" alone. CAA §§230, 231. Defendants' funding plan, by contrast, will transfer $6.1 billion of funds appropriated for other more general purposes — military construction, under §2808, and counterdrug activities, under §284. Their plan therefore flouts the cardinal principle that a specific statute controls a general one and violates the CAA. [*Id.* at 857.]

In fact, the court found, "CAA §739 *expressly forbids* Defendants' funding plan." *Id.* at 859 (emphasis added), insofar as the plan sought to increase funding for an item that had already been proposed in the President's budget request, but not yet approved by appropriation. No appropriation act provided reprogramming or transfer authority to trigger §739's exceptions. The court therefore held Proclamation No. 9844 (*supra* p. 70), invoking §2808 authority, to be unlawful.

Was the Proclamation the right target or did the court over-reach? Should it, instead, have centered its finding on the Administration's *use* of funds pursuant to its funding plan? Does it matter whether it declares that the Proclamation is unlawful or that the use of the funds is unlawful?

6. *Absolute Power?* The district court quoted with approval the proposition that Congress's control over federal expenditures is "absolute." Do you agree?

C. LIMITATIONS ON CONGRESSIONAL WAR POWERS

1. The Nondelegation Principle

We have seen that Congress's power to delegate national security powers to the executive branch is, at least theoretically, constrained by the "nondelegation principle." That principle requires Congress to make fundamental legislative judgments by including "intelligible principles" in any statutory delegation, so that executive discretion can be channeled and, on judicial review, measured. *Lichter* and *Curtiss-Wright* showed, however, that if the nondelegation principle ever had any teeth, they hardly leave marks on national security and foreign relations delegations.

This could change. In *Gundy v. United States*, 139 S. Ct. 2216 (2019), a four-Justice plurality held that a statute delegating authority to the Attorney General to issue regulations under 34 U.S.C. §20913 (requiring registration of sex offenders) did not violate the nondelegation doctrine. But the Chief Justice and Justices Gorsuch and Thomas dissented, while Justice Kavanaugh took no part. Perhaps because the Court would otherwise have been divided 4-4, Justice Alito filed a lukewarm concurrence in the judgment: "If a majority of this Court were willing to reconsider the approach we have taken for the past 84 years, I would support that effort. But because a majority is not willing to do that, it would be freakish to single out the provision at issue here for special treatment." *Id.* at 2131 (Alito, J., concurring in the judgment).

2. The *Lovett* Principle

The nondelegation principle is just one example of a broader substantive constraint: that a statutory delegation not violate any provision of the Constitution. *Lovett v. United States*, 66 F. Supp. 142 (Ct. Cl. 1945), *aff'd on other grounds*, 328 U.S. 303 (1946), provides an illustration. There Congress had enacted a rider to the Wartime Urgent Deficiency Appropriation of 1943, which forbade the executive branch to disburse salaries to certain identified "subversive" employees unless they were reappointed with the advice and consent of the Senate. Because the House would not approve any appropriation without this provision, the Senate agreed to it. The President reluctantly signed the bill into law, asserting that the rider was unconstitutional. When affected employees sued the United States in the Court of Claims for their salaries, the court ruled in favor of the employees on contract grounds. But Judge Whitaker, concurring, found that the provision violated the Bill of Attainder Clause of the Constitution, U.S. Const. art. I, §9, cl. 3, by inflicting punishment without a judicial trial. 66 F. Supp. at 148 (Whitaker, J., concurring). He asserted that even an exercise of the appropriation power "is subject to the limitation that it must not be exercised in a way that would nullify another provision of the Constitution." *Id.* Judge Madden acknowledged that Congress has the absolute power to withhold appropriations, but not the lawful authority.

> I do not think, therefore, that the power of the purse may be constitutionally exercised to produce an unconstitutional result such as taking of a citizen's liberty or property without due process of law, a conviction and punishment of a citizen for wholly innocent conduct, or a trespass upon the constitutional functions of another branch of the Government. [*Id.* at 152 (Madden, J., concurring in the result).]

The Supreme Court affirmed the judgment for the employees on the ground that the rider constituted an unconstitutional bill of attainder. 328 U.S. at 313-315. "The fact that the punishment is inflicted through the instrumentality of an Act specifically cutting off the pay of certain named individuals found guilty of disloyalty, makes it no less galling or effective than if it had been done by an Act which designated the conduct as criminal." *Id.* at 316.

Lovett does not stand alone. *See, e.g., Blitz v. Donovan,* 538 F. Supp. 1119 (D.D.C. 1982) (an appropriations provision that denies funds to persons who advocate the overthrow of the government violates the First Amendment); *United States v. Robel,* 389 U.S. 258, 263-264 (1967) ("'[E]ven the war power does not remove constitutional limitations safeguarding individual liberties.'" (quoting *Home Bldg. & Loan Ass'n v. Blaisdell,* 290 U.S. 398, 426 (1934))). Presumably what we call the *Lovett* principle applies with equal force to legislation enacted under Congress's necessary and proper lawmaking authority and is not confined just to appropriations measures.

3. The *Chadha* Principle

The *Lovett* line of cases highlights the *substantive* constitutional limitation on the congressional national security power. Almost as important are the *procedural* limitations established by Article I. In *Immigration & Naturalization Service v. Chadha,* 462 U.S. 919, 952, 958 (1983), the Supreme Court held that to take legislative action — "action that had the purpose and effect of altering the legal rights, duties and relations of persons . . . outside the legislative branch" — Congress must act "in conformity with the express procedures of the Constitution's prescription for legislative action: passage by a majority of both Houses and presentment to the President." Accordingly, the Court struck down a statutory provision for a "one-house veto" by which Congress reserved to either House the power to veto by resolution an exercise of delegated authority by the Attorney General that would have changed the legal status of an alien.

Shortly after *Chadha,* the Court summarily affirmed a decision striking down a two-House veto by concurrent resolution (requiring both Houses to veto an executive action, but omitting presentment of the veto resolution to the President). *See U.S. Senate v. Federal Trade Comm'n,* 463 U.S. 1216 (1983) (mem.).

Before *Chadha,* legislative vetoes had been an increasingly popular device for legislative control of executive action, inserted into nearly 200 statutes, including the War Powers Resolution, various Department of Defense appropriation and authorization acts, the International Security Assistance and Arms Control Act of 1976, and the National Emergencies Act.

Notes and Questions

1. Lovett or Lichter? Can the *Lovett* limitation be squared with *Lichter*'s approval of the assertion that the congressional war power "is not destroyed or impaired by any later provision of the Constitution or by any one of the amendments"? *Lichter,* 334 U.S. at 781. One answer — or dodge — may be to read an appropriations rider or other statutory limitation narrowly to avoid impairing the executive war power. This principle of avoidance is reflected in the canon of statutory construction that "[w]hen the validity of an act of the Congress is drawn in question, and even if a serious doubt of constitutionality is raised, it is a cardinal principle that this Court will first ascertain whether a construction of the statute is fairly possible by which the question may be avoided." *Crowell v. Benson*, 285 U.S. 22, 62 (1932). Why didn't this canon apply in *Lovett*?

2. Lovett and War Powers. Does *Lovett* also support the proposition that Congress may not use its national security powers to "micro-manage" the conduct of war or foreign policy? Various judicial dicta assert that "Congress cannot direct the conduct of campaigns," *Ex parte Milligan*, 71 U.S. (4 Wall.) 2, 139 (1866) (Chase, C.J., concurring), and that "Congress can not in the disguise of 'rules for the government' of the Army impair the authority of the President as commander in chief." *Swaim v. United States*, 28 Ct. Cl. 173, 221 (1893) (dictum), *aff'd*, 165 U.S. 553 (1897); *see also The Steel Seizure Case*, 343 U.S. 579, 644 (1952) (Jackson, J., concurring) ("Congress cannot deprive the President of the command of the army and navy," although "only Congress can provide him an army and navy to command").

The Minority Report of the Iran-Contra Committees described its objection to the use of appropriations limitations to manage foreign policy in these terms:

> Congress may not use its control over appropriations, including salaries, to prevent the executive or the judiciary from fulfilling Constitutionally mandated obligations. . . .
>
> Congress does not have to create a State Department or an intelligence agency. Once such departments are created, however, the Congress may not prevent the President from using his executive branch employees from serving as the country's "eyes and ears" in foreign policy. Even if Congress refuses to fund such departments, it may not prevent the President from doing what he can without funds to act as the nation's "sole organ" in foreign affairs. . . .
>
> What Congress grants by statute may be taken away by statute. But Congress may not ask the President to give up a power he gets from the Constitution, as opposed to one he gets from Congress, as a condition for getting something, whether money or some other good or power from Congress. [*Report of the Congressional Committees Investigating the Iran-Contra Affair, The Minority Report*, H.R. Rep. No. 100-433, S. Rep. No. 100-216, at 476 (1987).]

Is there any difference between the constitutional commands discussed in *Lovett* and its companion cases and the "Constitutionally mandated obligations" to which the *Minority Report* refers?

3. Lovett and Appropriations Limitations. On rare occasions, the Supreme Court has struck down legislation for intruding impermissibly on the President's inherent constitutional authority. *See, e.g., Myers v. United States*, 272 U.S. 52 (1926) (statute requiring Senate consent to removal of a purely executive officer); *Ex parte Garland*, 71 U.S. (4 Wall.) 333 (1867) (statute limiting the effect of a presidential pardon). Until 1988, however, no federal court had ever struck down an appropriations limitation on the President's exercise of national security powers. In *Nat'l Federation of Fed. Employees v. United States*, 688 F. Supp. 671 (D.D.C. 1988), *vacated and remanded sub nom. Am. Foreign Service Ass'n v. Garfinkel*, 490 U.S. 153 (1989), a district court held unconstitutional an appropriations limitation on portions of an executive order regulating disclosure of national security information to Congress by executive branch employees. The court found that Congress's "tug on the purse strings" intruded dramatically and unconstitutionally on the President's constitutionally imposed duty, as

Commander in Chief and chief executive, to oversee national security information. *Id.* at 685. The court noted that the congressional limitation "is merely an appropriations measure by which no substantive rights or causes of action are created. By such a measure, Congress cannot accomplish that which by direct legislative action would be beyond its constitutional authority." *Id.* at 684 n.17. Was the court right in suggesting that "mere" appropriations measures may not create or presumably limit rights?

The Supreme Court subsequently vacated and remanded, chastising the district court for reaching the constitutional question before exhausting nonconstitutional grounds for decision. 490 U.S. at 161.

4. *A Presidential Spending Power?* May the President transfer funds from other appropriations in disregard of their otherwise valid limitations? Logic may suggest an affirmative answer, but the Appropriations Clause seems to provide the opposite answer: "No money shall be drawn from the Treasury, but in Consequence of Appropriations made by law. . . ." U.S. Const. art. I, §9, cl. 7. When Congress refuses to appropriate for the President's independent constitutional functions, her only constitutional options are seemingly political — to seek the electoral replacement of the recalcitrant Congress or to violate appropriations laws and the Constitution, hoping for congressional ratification after the fact and risking her own replacement or, worse, impeachment.

Yet in this matter, too, custom has overtaken formalism, and the Executive has from time to time transferred some funds between accounts without explicit appropriations authority but with apparent congressional acquiescence. *See* Louis Fisher, *Presidential Spending Power* 99-122 (1975). For example, during the Vietnam War, President Nixon financed a military "incursion" into Cambodia by transferring funds from foreign assistance accounts. *Id.* at 107.

5. *Other Legislative Controls.* Congress, of course, has a variety of devices for legislative control besides direct, real-time regulations and limits on appropriations. These include durational limits on authorizations ("sunset" provisions), joint resolutions of approval or disapproval (requiring presentment, unlike concurrent resolutions), and report-and-wait rules that require reporting to Congress for some specified period before executive action becomes legally effective. Congress can also set a "fast track" for legislation in response to certain uses of delegated power. Are these constitutional after *Chadha*? Why or why not? *See Chadha,* 462 U.S. at 955 n.19 ("Beyond the obvious fact that Congress ultimately controls administrative agencies in the legislation that creates them, other means of control, such as durational limits on authorizations and formal reporting requirements, lie well within Congress' constitutional power.").

CONGRESS'S NATIONAL SECURITY POWERS: SUMMARY OF BASIC PRINCIPLES

- Congress may authorize the use of armed force by declaring war or by enacting an authorization for the use of military force (AUMF). Because the Constitution does not prescribe the form of AUMFs, some courts have inferred congressional authorization for the use of force from defense appropriation acts and related legislation that does not expressly authorize force.

- Historically, declarations of war have authorized "perfect" or total war, while AUMFs have authorized "imperfect" or limited war, limiting the use of force by area, weapon, or enemy. Early Supreme Court authority suggests that the President must abide by those limits, but also hints that he has some core constitutional command authority with which Congress may not interfere.

- A declaration of war, AUMF, or simply a "state of war" can activate standby statutory authorities authorizing the President to take a broad range of actions that she could not take in peacetime without further legislation.

- Congress has broad constitutional power to delegate national security authorities to the Executive, and the Court has asserted that wartime delegations should be construed to vest authority to wage war successfully. But the Court has also applied a clear statement rule to claims of national security authority that would restrict traditional constitutional rights.

- Defense appropriations can both specify purposes for which funds are appropriated and limit the uses to which they can be put. The British Parliament, American colonial legislatures, and then Congress all historically used funding measures to control national security initiatives by their executives.

- The Appropriations Clause forbids drawing money from the Treasury except pursuant to an appropriation. While it is not trumped by a declaration of emergency, the standby statutory authorities that a declaration triggers may themselves authorize spending from existing appropriations, and the Department of Defense enjoys some statutory authority to transfer and reprogram appropriated funds as well.

- Notwithstanding the permissible breadth of statutory delegations of national security authority to the Executive, they are constrained by the *Greene* rule of clear statement, the nondelegation principle (requiring intelligible principles enforceable by judicial review), the *Lovett* principle that congressional legislative power — even the powerful appropriation power — cannot override express constitutional limits, and the *Chadha* principle that Congress must act in conformity with the full Article I legislative process for its actions to have the force of law.

5

The Courts' National Security Powers

Almost two centuries ago, a visitor to this country had this to say about the way we govern ourselves: "Scarcely any political question arises in the United States that is not resolved, sooner or later, into a judicial question." Alexis de Tocqueville, 1 *Democracy in America* 280 (Phillips Bradley ed., Vintage Books 1945) (1835). This chapter shows that in cases involving national security, many courts have turned his observation upside down by refusing to hear seemingly judicial questions on grounds that they present "political questions." Or they appear to have gone out of their way to refuse to hear such cases because plaintiffs lack standing to sue, or because the controversies are not yet "ripe" for hearing. Even where courts have jurisdiction, in many cases they have deferred broadly to the political branches in matters that implicate national security, or they have declined to find that a plaintiff has an implied private right of action for damages, or they have held that the defendant is immune from liability because the law was not clearly established at the time of the allegedly unlawful act. In still other cases they have excluded critical evidence from trials — or prevented trials altogether — on the ground that the evidence might be helpful to our enemies.

This chapter is about the role that courts play in the resolution of national security disputes. The starting point is Article III of the Constitution, which establishes the limits of federal judicial power and authorizes Congress to create lower federal courts to exercise some or all of that power. We first examine the text briefly, then recall that an important job of courts is to "say what the law is." *Marbury v. Madison,* 5 U.S. (1 Cranch) 137, 177 (1803). But this places the federal courts in a position to define their own role, subject to limits that Article III and Congress set. We therefore proceed to explore the self-defining role of the federal courts and the various impediments they have erected to justiciability. Next, we briefly consider two substantive obstacles to plaintiffs' national security claims: the availability of any right of action and the affirmative defense of qualified immunity. The chapter concludes with a review of an additional barrier to justiciability based on the law of evidence: the state secrets privilege.

A. THE FEDERAL JUDICIAL POWER GENERALLY

Records of the 1787 Philadelphia Convention tell us little about the Framers' original intent regarding the federal courts' responsibility for national security. We necessarily begin instead with the text of Article III, which states generally that the judicial power is "vested in one supreme Court, and in such inferior Courts as the Congress may from time to time ordain and establish." The language suggests an independent judiciary designed to interpret the laws and decide cases. *See generally The Federalist Nos. 22, 78, 80* (Clinton Rossiter ed., 1961). The federal judicial power includes all cases "arising under this Constitution, the Laws of the United States, and Treaties made," and controversies "between a State, or the Citizens thereof, and foreign States, Citizens, or Subjects." The Supreme Court is also given original jurisdiction over "all Cases affecting Ambassadors, other public Ministers and Consuls," while it is granted appellate jurisdiction over other types of cases, subject to Congress's power to make "Exceptions, and . . . Regulations." Congress has conferred general federal question jurisdiction on the lower federal courts since 1875. *See* 28 U.S.C. §1331 (2018). Thus, struggles over national security prerogatives — at least if they pose questions arising under federal law, the Constitution, or treaties (and possibly other international law) — seem to meet both constitutional and statutory jurisdictional requirements for resolution in the federal courts today.

B. A SELF-DEFINING ROLE FOR COURTS: THE JUSTICIABILITY DOCTRINES

We saw in the last two chapters that courts have often been called on to decide important national security law questions and have decided them. Illustrative are *The Steel Seizure Case, Little v. Barreme, Bas v. Tingy,* and *The Prize Cases.* Recall Justice Jackson's admonition, in *The Steel Seizure Case,* that in preserving the institutions of free government, "it is the duty of the Court to be last, not first, to give them up." 343 U.S. 579, 655 (1952) (Jackson, J., concurring).

We can see the same determination to "say what the law is" in more recent litigation involving the so-called global war on terrorism. In one prominent case, for example, American citizen Yaser Hamdi, who allegedly was captured on the battlefield in Afghanistan, challenged his designation by the President as an "enemy combatant" and his indefinite military detention without judicial process. The government argued that the courts should not question the Commander in Chief's decision during wartime. In *Hamdi v. Rumsfeld,* 316 F.3d 450 (4th Cir. 2003), the court conceded that "Article III contains nothing analogous to the specific powers of war carefully enumerated in Articles I and II." *Id.* at 463. Nonetheless, important countervailing interests persuaded the court to review Hamdi's detention:

> The duty of the judicial branch to protect our individual freedoms does not simply cease whenever military forces are committed by the political branches to armed conflict. The Founders "foresaw that troublous times would arise, when rulers and people would . . . seek by sharp and decisive measures to accomplish ends deemed just and proper; and that the principles of constitutional liberty would be in peril, unless established by irrepealable law." *Ex parte Milligan,* 71 U.S. (4 Wall.) 2, 120 (1866). While that recognition does not

> dispose of this case, it does indicate one thing: The detention of United States citizens must be subject to judicial review. [316 F.3d at 464.]

More recently still, in a case challenging the legality of the first Trump administration travel ban, the government took the position that "the President's decisions about immigration policy, particularly when motivated by national security concerns, are *unreviewable*, even if those actions potentially contravene constitutional rights and protections." *Washington v. Trump*, 847 F.3d 1151, 1161 (9th Cir. 2017). The court rejected that assertion:

> There is no precedent to support this claimed unreviewability, which runs contrary to the fundamental structure of our constitutional democracy. *See Boumediene v. Bush*, 553 U.S. 723, 765 (2008) (rejecting the idea that, even by congressional statute, Congress and the Executive could eliminate federal court habeas jurisdiction over enemy combatants, because the "political branches" lack "the power to switch the Constitution on or off at will"). Within our system, it is the role of the judiciary to interpret the law, a duty that will sometimes require the "[r]esolution of litigation challenging the constitutional authority of one of the three branches." *Zivotofsky ex rel. Zivotofsky v. Clinton*, 566 U.S. 189, 196 (2012) (quoting *INS v. Chadha*, 462 U.S. 919, 943 (1983)). . . .
>
> It would indeed be ironic if, in the name of national defense, we would sanction the subversion of one of those liberties . . . which makes the defense of the Nation worthwhile."); *Zemel v. Rusk*, 381 U.S. 1, 17 (1965) ("[S]imply because a statute deals with foreign relations [does not mean that] it can grant the Executive totally unrestricted freedom of choice."). . . . [847 F.3d at 1161-1163.]

Courts have nevertheless tended to defer to the political branches and avoid the resolution of national security disputes in what may be an increasing number of cases. First, courts have insisted that plaintiffs have a personal stake in the outcome of cases brought before them for resolution. The *standing* requirement has both textual roots in the case-or-controversy language of Article III and a prudential root in the courts' self-limitation.

Second, the federal courts have been keenly aware of their own practical limitations in deciding such disputes. Thus, in a case involving a court's de novo review of classified documents withheld from a Freedom of Information Act requester, the court declared, "In view of the knowledge, experience and positions held by the three [government] affiants regarding military secrets, military planning and national security, their affidavits were entitled to 'the utmost deference.'" *Taylor v. Dep't of the Army*, 684 F.2d 99, 109 (D.C. Cir. 1982). This deference also stems in part from the courts' concern about their proper function in our constitutional system of government. Both of these judicial concerns — competence and constitutional function — are reflected in the judicial invocation of the *political question doctrine* to dismiss some national security disputes.

Third, the need for a clear conflict and a concrete record of underlying facts — and sometimes the hope that with the passage of time the political branches might resolve a dispute on their own — have prompted courts to invoke the *ripeness doctrine*, by which courts sometimes defer hearing a case on the grounds that it is simply not yet ready for judicial review.

These three nonjusticiability doctrines are addressed below. They may seem frustrating to a lawyer who thinks that national security law disputes should, like others, be resolved "neutrally" by the "least dangerous branch," as Hamilton described the judiciary. *The Federalist No. 78*, at 465 (Alexander Hamilton) (Clinton Rossiter ed., 1961). We must remember, however, that when pressed in a national security emergency, even that branch may make decisions based on contemporary political realities rather than on neutral principles of law. *Korematsu v. United States*, 323 U.S. 214 (1944), upholding the exclusion of persons of Japanese ancestry (including U.S. citizens) from West Coast military areas out of deference to "military judgment" during World War II, is a tragic example.

1. Standing to Sue

Reading *Smith v. Obama*

The Plaintiff, Nathan Michael Smith, was deployed to Kuwait on an intelligence mission in Operation Inherent Resolve, the military campaign against the Islamic State of Iraq and the Levant (ISIL) initiated by the United States and its allies in 2014. He sought a declaration that the Operation was unlawful because Congress had not authorized it.

- Suppose he disagreed strongly with sending U.S. forces to the Middle East. Is that an "injury" sufficient to confer standing? If not, why not?
- Suppose he feared an ISIL attack on the intelligence installation in Kuwait where he was working. Is that fear a sufficient injury to confer standing? If not, do you have to be physically or emotionally injured to be able to challenge the legality of the deployment that put you in harm's way?
- He also asserted that he might have to disobey unlawful orders, and his oath to defend the Constitution, as a result of the deployment. Does *Little v. Barreme* (*supra* p. 63) impose such a duty on military officers?
- If the plaintiff lacks standing to assert his challenge, would *any* U.S. service member deployed in Operation Inherent Resolve have standing? Who and why?

Smith v. Obama

United States District Court, District of Columbia, 2016
217 F. Supp. 3d 283, *vacated as moot sub nom.*
Smith v. Trump, 731 F. App'x 8 (D.C. Cir. 2018)

Colleen Kollar-Kotelly, United States District Judge. Plaintiff is a U.S. Army Captain who was deployed, until recently, to the Kuwait headquarters of the Combined Joint Task Force-Operation Inherent Resolve. . . . Plaintiff acknowledges that whether military action has been duly authorized is generally a question "Congress is supposed to answer," but complains that Congress is "AWOL." Plaintiff also claims that the Take Care Clause requires President Obama to publish a "sustained legal justification" for Operation Inherent Resolve to enable Plaintiff to determine for himself whether this military action is consistent with his oath to preserve and protect the Constitution.

Before the Court is Defendant's Motion to Dismiss. Defendant argues that this Court lacks jurisdiction over Plaintiff's claims for a number of reasons. Specifically, Defendant argues that (1) Plaintiff's claims raise non-justiciable political questions, (2) Plaintiff lacks standing. . . .

I. BACKGROUND

A. Operation Inherent Resolve

On September 10, 2014, President Obama announced to the American people that America would "lead a broad coalition to roll back" the "terrorist threat" posed by ISIL. The President announced that the United States would "degrade and ultimately destroy ISIL through a comprehensive and sustained counterterrorism strategy," which included "a systematic campaign of airstrikes," increased "support to forces fighting these terrorists on the ground," counterterrorism strategies, and humanitarian assistance. The President stated that he had "secured bipartisan support for this approach here at home," and that although he had "the authority to address the threat from ISIL," he "welcome[d] congressional support for this effort in order to show the world that Americans are united in confronting this danger." The Department of Defense later designated this effort "Operation Inherent Resolve."

Following his address, on September 23, 2014, the President sent a letter to Congress reiterating that he had "ordered implementation of a new comprehensive and sustained counterterrorism strategy to degrade, and ultimately defeat, ISIL." In this letter, President Obama explained the military actions he had ordered, and stated that:

> I have directed these actions, which are in the national security and foreign policy interests of the United States, pursuant to my constitutional and statutory authority as Commander in Chief (including the authority to carry out Public Law 107-40 and Public Law 107-243) and as Chief Executive, as well as my constitutional and statutory authority to conduct the foreign relations of the United States.
>
> I am providing this report as part of my efforts to keep the Congress fully informed, consistent with the War Powers Resolution (Public Law 93-148). I appreciate the support of the Congress in this action.

Public Law 107-40 and Public Law 107-243, referenced by the President, were passed by Congress in 2001 and 2002, and each constitute[s] specific authorization for the use of military force. First, in response to the terrorist attacks of September 11, 2001, Congress passed a Joint Resolution to "authorize the use of United States Armed Forces against those responsible for the recent attacks launched against the United States." Authorization for Use of Military Force, Pub. L. No. 107-40, 115 Stat. 224 (2001) ("2001 AUMF"). The 2001 AUMF states that "the President is authorized to use all necessary and appropriate force against those nations, organizations, or persons he determines planned, authorized, committed, or aided the terrorist attacks that occurred on September 11, 2001, or harbored such organizations or persons, in order to prevent any future acts of international terrorism against the United States by such nations, organizations or persons." Pub. L. No. 107-40, §2(a). It also states that "[c]onsistent with section 8(a)(1) of the War Powers Resolution, the Congress declares that this section is intended to constitute specific statutory authorization within the meaning of section 5(b) of the War Powers Resolution." Pub. L. No. 107-40, §2(b)(1).

Second, in 2002 Congress passed a Joint Resolution authorizing the President "to use the Armed Forces of the United States as he determines to be necessary and appropriate in order to . . . defend the national security of the United States against the continuing threat posed by Iraq." Authorization for Use of Military Force against Iraq Resolution of 2002, Pub. L. No. 107-243, §3(a)(1), 116 Stat. 1498 (2002) ("2002 AUMF"). The 2002 AUMF also states that "[c]onsistent with section 8(a)(1) of the War Powers Resolution, the Congress declares that this section is intended to constitute specific statutory authorization within the meaning of section 5(b) of the War Powers Resolution." Pub. L. No. 107-243, §3(c)(1).

. . . [I]n a speech . . . at an annual meeting of the American Society of International Law on April 10, 2015 . . . [Stephen W. Preston, the General Counsel of the Department of Defense] explained that ISIL was an appropriate target under the 2001 AUMF because the group had long fought the United States alongside al Qaeda, which was responsible for the September 11th attacks. Preston stated that ISIL had previously been known as al Qaeda in Iraq after its leader, Abu Musab al-Zarqawi, had pledged his allegiance to Osama bin Laden in 2004. . . . He went on to explain that:

> The recent split between ISIL and current al-Qa'ida leadership does not remove ISIL from coverage under the 2001 AUMF, because ISIL continues to wage the conflict against the United States that it entered into when, in 2004, it joined bin Laden's al-Qa'ida organization in its conflict against the United States. . . . ISIL continues to denounce the United States as its enemy and to target U.S. citizens and interests. . . .

Preston also explained that "[t]he President's authority to fight ISIL is further reinforced by the" 2002 AUMF because "[a]lthough the threat posed by Saddam Hussein's regime in Iraq was the primary focus of the 2002 AUMF, the statute, in accordance with its express goals, has always been understood to authorize the use of force for the related purposes of helping to establish a stable, democratic Iraq and addressing terrorist threats emanating from Iraq." . . .

III. DISCUSSION . . .

A. Standing . . .

"Standing to sue is a doctrine rooted in the traditional understanding of a case or controversy." *Spokeo, Inc. v. Robins*, ____ U.S. ____, 136 S. Ct. 1540, 1547 (2016), *as revised* (May 24, 2016). To establish standing, Plaintiff bears the burden of demonstrating that he "(1) suffered an injury in fact, (2) that is fairly traceable to the challenged conduct of the defendant, and (3) that is likely to be redressed by a favorable judicial decision." *Id.* (citing *Lujan v. Defs. of Wildlife*, 504 U.S. 555, 560-61 (1992)). . . . The Court notes that the standing inquiry is "especially rigorous when reaching the merits of the dispute would force [the Court] to decide whether an action taken by one of the other two branches of the Federal Government was unconstitutional." *Raines v. Byrd*, 521 U.S. 811, 819-20 (1997). . . .

As a starting point, Plaintiff's bare disagreement with, or simple uncertainty about the legality of, President Obama's decision to take military action against ISIL does not constitute an injury in fact. Such disagreement or uncertainty presents no "concrete" harm, nor is it "particularized" because it does not affect Plaintiff in any individual or particular way. It is well-established that "a bare assertion that the government is engaging in illegal or unconstitutional activity does not allege injury sufficient to confer standing." *Haitian Refugee Ctr. v. Gracey*, 809 F.2d 794, 799 (D.C. Cir. 1987). In other words, "the psychological consequence presumably produced by observation of conduct with which one disagrees," is not an injury in fact. *Valley Forge Christian Coll. v. Ams. United for Separation of Church & State, Inc.*, 454 U.S. 464, 485 (1982). From this baseline, it is Plaintiff's burden to clearly allege some additional concrete, particularized harm that the alleged violations caused or threaten to cause him.

. . . Plaintiff does not allege the traditional types of injuries one might expect a service person challenging the legality of military action to allege. Plaintiff *does not* allege that he suffers any injury in the form of physical or emotional harms, or the risk thereof, associated with deployment to a theatre of combat. He also *does not* allege that he has been involuntarily forced to participate in a military action in violation of his own constitutional rights or liberties. And he *does not* allege that he has any moral or philosophical objections to the military action against ISIL. Indeed, Plaintiff has no qualms about participating in a fight against ISIL, and his lawsuit does not seek to relieve him of his obligation to do so. . . .

Instead, the Court discerns two different types of harms for which Plaintiff seeks relief. First, Plaintiff alleges that he "suffers legal injury because, to provide support for an illegal war, he must violate his oath to 'preserve, protect, and defend the Constitution of the United States.'" In addition, Plaintiff alleges that he is at risk of being punished for disobeying legally-given orders. . . .

1. Little v. Barreme Does Not Require Plaintiff to Disobey Orders

First, Plaintiff seeks to base his standing on the Supreme Court case *Little v. Barreme*, 6 U.S. (2 Cranch) 170 (1804) [*supra* p. 63]. Plaintiff argues that this case stands for the proposition that "military officers must disobey orders that are beyond the legal authorization of their commander-in-chief." Plaintiff reads too much into *Little*. . . .

As the Supreme Court has since explained, *Little* stands for the proposition that "a federal official [is] protected for action tortious under state law only if his acts were authorized by controlling federal law." *Butz v. Economou*, 438 U.S. 478, 490 (1978). *Little* does not stand for the proposition, as Plaintiff argues, that military personnel have a *duty to disobey* orders they believe are beyond Congressional authorization. There is a significant difference between a holding that Presidential authorization for an act beyond Congressional authority does not *immunize* military personnel from tort liability under state law, and a holding that military personnel *must disobey* orders that they believe are beyond such authority. Plaintiff points the Court to no authority that has interpreted *Little* to stand for the latter proposition, and the Court has found none.

To the contrary, it appears well-settled in the post-*Little* era that there is no right, let alone a duty, to disobey military orders simply because one questions the Congressional authorization of the broader military effort. *See U.S. ex rel. New v. Rumsfeld*, 448 F.3d 403, 411 (D.C. Cir. 2006) (in the context of challenging a military order that plaintiff alleged was given in violation of the United Nations Participation Act, holding that "nothing gives a soldier 'authority for a self-help remedy of disobedience'") (quoting *United States v. New*, 55 M.J. 95, 108 (C.A.A.F. 2001)); *United States v. Huet-Vaughn*, 43 M.J. 105, 114 (C.A.A.F. 1995) ("... The so-called 'Nuremberg defense' applies only to individual acts committed in wartime; it does not apply to the Government's decision to wage war."); *see also New*, 55 M.J. at 109 ("The duty to disobey an unlawful order applies only to a positive act that constitutes a crime that is so manifestly beyond the legal power or discretion of the commander as to admit of no rational doubt of their unlawfulness.") (quoting *Huet-Vaughn*, 43 M.J. at 114).

Nor does the oath Plaintiff was required to swear as an officer in the Army change this outcome. The modern oath for officers requires the officer to swear to "support and defend the Constitution." 5 U.S.C. §3331.... An oath to "support" the Constitution does not "involve[ ] nebulous, undefined responsibilities for action in some hypothetical situations," but has instead "been interpreted to mean simply a commitment to abide by our constitutional system." *Cole v. Richardson*, 405 U.S. 676, 684 (1972). Although, as discussed below, such an oath may require Plaintiff to refrain from violating the Constitution, Plaintiff offers no real support for the extremely expansive and apparently novel interpretation of the officer's oath that would require disobedience of military orders based on an officer's legal interpretation of whether Congress had properly authorized the broader military effort. Beyond the fact that there is no legal support for such a proposition, the Court finds persuasive Defendant's argument regarding the obvious and problematic practical consequences such an interpretation would have on military effectiveness. Namely, that it would leave "individual service members to decide which orders to follow based on their individual assessment of" whether the order falls within prior Congressional authorizations for the use of military force.

Because neither *Little* nor Plaintiff's oath can plausibly be read to *require* Plaintiff to disobey his orders, Plaintiff was not forced to experience or risk concrete and particularized harms associated with wrongful disobedience, such as court-martial or dishonorable discharge.... The risk of military punishment for disobedience, therefore, does not give Plaintiff standing.

2. Plaintiff Does Not Have Standing Under the "Oath of Office" Cases

Plaintiff also seeks to base his standing on "oath of office" cases [chiefly *Board of Education of Central School District No. 1 v. Allen*, 392 U.S. 236 (1968)]. These cases generally stand for the proposition that an official who has taken an oath to support the Constitution has standing to challenge a government action if he or she is then forced to choose between violating the Constitution and facing concrete harm....

... Plaintiff in this case alleges that President Obama has violated a statute, the War Powers Resolution, by not seeking Congressional authorization for military actions against ISIL, and violated the Take Care Clause of the Constitution by failing to publish an explanation of the legal justifications for these actions....

... However, even assuming that Plaintiff is correct that the President violated the War Powers Resolution, it does not follow that any act Plaintiff himself was asked to take as an intelligence officer in that Operation would itself be unconstitutional.... [T]he alleged violation of the War Powers Resolution in this case is based solely on the alleged actions, or lack thereof, of President Obama, not

Plaintiff. The same is true with regard to the alleged violation of the Take Care Clause. . . . Even accepting his allegations as true, he is not himself being ordered to violate the Constitution, and therefore his oath. . . .

3. Plaintiff Does Not Allege Physical or Individual Liberty-Based Injuries

Finally, the Court rejects Plaintiff's argument that the "decisions in cases brought by service members challenging the Vietnam War further confirm [Plaintiff's] standing." To be sure, such cases do stand for the proposition that service men and women ordered into a war that they contend is illegal may have standing to challenge that war, and the Court finds the reasoning of those cases logical and persuasive. *See Berk v. Laird*, 429 F.2d 302 (2d Cir. 1970); *Massachusetts v. Laird*, 451 F.2d 26 (1st Cir. 1971). The Court does not question as a general matter the apparent assumption of certain courts that service members may be appropriate parties to challenge the legality of military action that they claim endangers them.

These cases do not, however, address the novel legal injury put forth by Plaintiff. In the cases referred to by Plaintiff, plaintiff-service members claimed that they were being forced to fight in violation of their constitutional rights, and the injuries that they alleged were the deprivation of liberty and the risk of injury or death. *See Berk*, 429 F.2d at 304 (soldier ordered to dispatch to Vietnam alleging violations of his constitutional rights could bring suit challenging legality of war where "the complaint can be construed as putting in controversy his future earning capacity, which serious injury or even death might diminish by an amount exceeding $10,000"); *Massachusetts v. Laird*, 451 F.2d at 28 (soldiers serving in Southeast Asia had standing to challenge Vietnam War where "[t]hey allege[d] that their forced service in an undeclared war is a deprivation of liberty in violation of the due process clause of the Fifth Amendment"). . . .

In sum, the Court concludes that the "injuries" upon which Plaintiff grounds his claim do not constitute "injury in fact" as required to support Article III standing. . . . The Court draws no conclusions as to the standing of a service member ordered into a war he or she believes is unlawful where the soldier's claim is based on his own constitutional rights, individual liberties, physical or emotional well-being, or other injuries. This case simply does not present those questions. . . .

Notes and Questions

1. Injury in Fact. The court emphasizes that injury sufficient to confer standing must be "concrete" and "particularized." It does not explain why. But one reason is that such injury is easier to discern than a vague psychological unhappiness. More broadly, the more concrete and particularized the injury, the greater the plaintiff's incentive to present a sharp "case or controversy" to which Article III generally refers, helping ensure that the court is being asked to decide a real dispute and not to issue an advisory opinion. Erwin Chemerinsky, *Federal Jurisdiction* §2.3.2 (6th ed. 2012). The Supreme Court has emphasized that the doctrine of standing is "an essential and unchanging part of the case-or-controversy requirement of Article III," *Lujan v. Defenders of Wildlife*, 504 U.S. 555, 559 (1992), which "defines with respect to the

Judicial Branch the idea of separation of powers on which the Federal Government is founded." *Allen v. Wright*, 468 U.S. 737, 750 (1984).

In addition, any more expansive interpretation of injury would expand judicial power. *See United States v. Richardson*, 418 U.S. 166, 188 (1974) ("Relaxation of standing requirements is directly related to the expansion of judicial power."). Insistence on concrete and particularized injury is therefore partly an exercise in judicial self-restraint in the interests of the separation of powers.

The law of standing thus has both constitutional and prudential components. Unlike the Article III requirements, however, the prudential limits may be modified or abrogated by Congress. *Warth v. Seldin*, 422 U.S. 490, 501 (1975).

2. *Past, Current, or Imminent Injury?* Reasoning that waiting for an actual injury might be too late for some claims, courts have uniformly held that the injury-in-fact requirement for standing can be satisfied by "actual *or* imminent injury." *Monsanto Co. v. Geertson Seed Farms*, 561 U.S. 139, 149 (2010) (emphasis added). In *Clapper v. Amnesty International USA*, 568 U.S. 398 (2013), human rights workers, labor union leaders, and journalists sought an injunction against secret, warrantless electronic surveillance of them, claiming violations of their First and Fourth Amendment rights. Because the plaintiffs were unable to obtain or present evidence that they were actually targeted for surveillance, however, the Supreme Court ruled that any injuries were too speculative to confer standing. Instead, they had to show that their imminent injury was "certainly pending." *Id.* at 401.

In the *Smith* decision, the court acknowledged case law that upheld the standing of service members deployed in the Vietnam War to challenge the war's legality. How were they different from Captain Smith? Was the mere risk of being shot in Vietnam an injury that was "certainly pending"?

What about a plaintiff who alleges that he is on a U.S. "kill list" for targeted killing as a terrorist? In *Zaidan v. Trump*, 317 F. Supp. 3d 8 (D.D.C. 2018), a foreign journalist alleged that the Trump administration had included him (on the basis of metadata from his communications, writings, social media postings, and travel) on SKYNET, a classified list of potential terrorists, and that he was therefore probably on the "kill list" for targeted killing as well. The court held that

> [w]hile it is possible that there is a correlation between a list like SKYNET and the Kill List, the Court finds no allegations in the Complaint that raise that possibility above mere speculation. Accordingly, the Court finds Mr. Zaidan has failed to allege a plausible injury-in-fact and therefore has no standing to sue." [*Id.* at 19.]

But a second journalist alleged that he had actually experienced five "near-miss" aerial attacks in Syria, including one at his place of work, one on his vehicle, and one using a Hellfire missile of the kind launched by U.S. drones. Unsurprisingly, the court found that his allegation that he was on a U.S. kill list was not just sheer speculation, and rather dryly observed, "Since the Complaint alleges that Mr. Kareem was on the U.S. Kill List in 2016 but was not killed, it posits that his danger continues to the present time." *Id.* at 20 n.3.

Smith v. Obama was dismissed as moot and the district court's order was vacated when Capt. Smith was honorably discharged from the Army in May 2018, ending any possible interest he might have had in the "controversy" that he claimed gave him standing to sue. *Smith v. Trump*, 731 F. App'x 8 (D.C. Cir. 2018).

3. Causation and Redressability. Although the Supreme Court has held that the causation and redressability requirements for standing are separate, they are often treated together "as if they were a single test: Did the defendant cause the harm such that it can be concluded that limiting the defendant will remedy the injury?" Chemerinsky, *supra*, §2.3.1. Suppose, for example, that an American who had been injured in Yemen by a Saudi air raid sued the President and other executive branch defendants for supplying military aid to the Saudi Air Force in violation of a statutory ban on military assistance to Saudi Arabia. Even if he sufficiently asserted a concrete and particularized injury, a court might well rule that it was not caused by the defendants and not redressable by an injunction, because the Saudis could continue their air campaign in Yemen without U.S. aid.

4. Citizen Standing. Would a concerned citizen have standing to bring a lawsuit seeking to enjoin a prospective military operation by the United States? In *Pietsch v. Bush*, 755 F. Supp. 62 (E.D.N.Y. 1991), a citizen sought a court order preventing hostilities between the United States and Iraq before the 1991 Gulf War. In concluding that Pietsch was not injured in fact, the court distinguished the interest of a concerned citizen from that of members of Congress (who "plainly have an interest in protecting their right to vote in matters entrusted to their respective chambers by the Constitution"), or a member of the armed forces deployed to the potential combat area. According to the court, Pietsch's claim that he was being made "an accessory to murder against his will," a compulsion causing him emotional distress, was "too abstract" to meet Article III requirements. *Id.* at 65-66. Indeed, with one equivocal exception, *see Flast v. Cohen*, 392 U.S. 83 (1968) (recognizing the standing of taxpayers to bring certain types of claims that government spending violates the Establishment Clause), the Supreme Court has generally rejected "citizen" or "taxpayer" standing even where no one would otherwise have standing to enforce the Constitution. *See, e.g., Richardson*, 418 U.S. 166.

5. Congressional Standing. Members of Congress have often turned to the courts and sought relief for alleged harm to them in their official roles, or, put another way, to protect what they see as interests central to Congress. In 1997, however, the Supreme Court ruled that legislators may sue in their institutional capacity only when their vote has been "completely nullified" by an allegedly unlawful action. *Raines v. Byrd*, 521 U.S. 811, 829 (1997). In *Raines*, four Senators and two Representatives challenged the constitutionality of the Line-Item Veto Act (which the Supreme Court later invalidated in *Clinton v. City of New York*, 524 U.S. 417 (1998)), arguing that, because the President could excise individual appropriations under the Act, their votes on appropriations bills would be "less 'effective' than before, and that the 'meaning' and 'integrity' of their vote has changed." 521 U.S. at 825.

According to Chief Justice Rehnquist's opinion for the Court, the plaintiffs' nay votes on the line-item veto bill "were given full effect. They simply lost. . . ." *Id.* at 824. The disgruntled members' votes in the future were not "completely nullified" by the Line-Item Veto Act because a majority "may repeal the Act or exempt appropriations bills from its reach." *Id.* at 829.

Raines was essentially a suit by members of Congress against Congress itself. The Court did not indicate whether standing for members of Congress in a suit for allegedly unlawful action by the Executive would be similarly limited.

In one pre-*Raines* case, 53 House members and one Senator sought to prevent President George H.W. Bush from ordering a massive military attack against Iraq (to initiate the 1991 Gulf War) without a formal declaration of war or express congressional authorization. *Dellums v. Bush,* 752 F. Supp. 1141 (D.D.C. 1990). The court concluded that the plaintiffs had stated a "legally-cognizable injury," because "members of Congress plainly have an interest in protecting their right to vote on matters entrusted to their respective chambers by the Constitution," in this instance a right "guaranteed by the War Clause of the Constitution." *Id.* at 1147.

Two years after the *Raines* decision, 31 members of the House of Representatives sued President Clinton seeking a declaration that the use of U.S. forces against the Federal Republic of Yugoslavia was unlawful under the Constitution and the War Powers Resolution. *Campbell v. Clinton,* 52 F. Supp. 2d 34 (D.D.C. 1999), *aff'd,* 203 F.3d 19 (D.C. Cir. 2000). The lawsuit was filed after the President announced the commencement of NATO air and cruise missile attacks on Serbian targets on March 24, 1999, and after House votes on April 28 defeating a declaration of war (427-2), defeating an authorization of the air strikes (213-213), defeating a resolution ordering an immediate end to U.S. participation in the NATO operation (290-139), and approving a restriction on Defense Department appropriations for the deployment of U.S. ground troops in Yugoslavia without specific authorization. On May 20, however, Congress approved a supplemental appropriations bill for the conflict in Yugoslavia.

The plaintiffs sought to distinguish *Raines* by arguing that President Clinton's unilateral commitment of the United States to the air strikes "completely nullified" their votes against authorizing the military operation. They further asserted that while Congress voted down an authorization for the air strikes and a declaration of war, President Clinton ignored the votes and carried on as if Congress had authorized his actions.

A D.C. Circuit panel ruled, however, that the nullification standard of *Raines* is not met "whenever the government does something Congress voted against," that is, voted not to approve. 203 F.3d at 22. Instead, the court construed *Raines* to require that the plaintiffs have "no legislative remedy." *Id.* at 23. In this case, the court pointed out, Congress could have passed a prohibition on the use of U.S. forces in the Yugoslavia campaign. Similarly, Congress could have restricted appropriations for the same end, or it could have sought to impeach the President. Citing *Raines,* it denied the plaintiffs' "standing as congressmen because they possessed political tools with which to remedy their purported injury." *Id.* at 24.

Concurring in the judgment, Judge Randolph added that the plaintiffs' votes "were not for naught." *Id.* at 31 (Randolph, J., concurring in the judgment). The defeat of the declaration of war deprived the President of the authority to expand hostilities against Yugoslavia, and the defeat of the authorization resolution denied the President the right to say that he was prosecuting the bombing campaign with the House's approval.

If the *Raines* nullification standard was indeed properly applicable in *Campbell,* did the court apply it properly? Can you now say confidently when a member of Congress will have standing to challenge an action of the President as violating either the Constitution or a statute?

2. The Political Question Doctrine

Consider the following hypotheticals. John Henry has been nominated by the President to the Supreme Court and confirmed by the Senate. The Secretary of State has signed and sealed Henry's commission to the office, pursuant to a federal statute that also provides that a U.S. marshal shall deliver the commission to Henry. But the U.S. marshal refuses. Henry sues for a writ of mandamus (like an injunction ordering a public official to do his duty), compelling the marshal to deliver the commission.

Now assume, instead, that Henry was not nominated to the Court by the President, but is convinced that he should have been. He sues for a writ of mandamus compelling the President to nominate him to the Supreme Court.

How are these cases different? In the first case, a federal statute sets a standard for deciding whether the defendant marshal has acted lawfully. A court could decide whether the marshal has violated the statute and, if it finds that he has and that it has mandamus jurisdiction, could issue a writ ordering the marshal to do his statutory duty. In the second case, neither a federal statute nor the Constitution supplies any standard for deciding whom the President should nominate to the Supreme Court. Article II, section 2, merely declares that "he shall nominate, and by and with the Advice and Consent of the Senate, shall appoint . . . Judges of the supreme Court. . . ." It doesn't say who they have to be, whether they need a law degree, whether they must be male or female, Catholic or Jewish, old or young, white or black. The Constitution leaves the selection to the President, in his or her discretion, subject to the check of Senate confirmation. Whether the President should nominate Henry or someone else is a "political question" and not a question for the courts.

As Chief Justice John Marshall explained in *Marbury v. Madison*, 5 U.S. (1 Cranch) 137 (1803), on related (though not the same) facts:

> By the constitution of the United States, the President is invested with certain important political powers, in the exercise of which he is to use his own discretion, and is accountable only to his country in his political character, and to his own conscience. To aid him in the performance of these duties, he is authorized to appoint certain officers, who act by his authority and in conformity with his orders. In such cases, their acts are his acts; and whatever opinion may be entertained of the manner in which executive discretion may be used, still there exists, and can exist, no power to control that discretion. The subjects are political. They respect the nation, not individual rights, and being entrusted to the executive, the decision of the executive is conclusive. [*Id.* at 165-166.]

The selection of nominees to the Supreme Court is similarly a political question, "in the exercise of which [the President] is to use his own discretion, and is accountable only to his country in his political character," and is not for the courts to decide.

The Supreme Court subsequently invoked what became known as the political question doctrine in a number of cases, without providing any consistent or fully reasoned explanation. In *Baker v. Carr*, 369 U.S. 186 (1962), however, it inventoried factors from the prior cases in a paragraph that later courts have treated as a test for invoking the doctrine:

> It is apparent that several formulations which vary slightly according to the settings in which the questions arise may describe a political question, although each has one or more elements which identify it as essentially a function of the separation of powers. Prominent on the surface of any case held to involve a political question is found a textually demonstrable constitutional commitment of the issue to a coordinate political department; or a lack of judicially discoverable and manageable standards for resolving it; or the impossibility of deciding without an initial policy determination of a kind clearly for nonjudicial discretion; or the impossibility of a court's undertaking independent resolution without expressing lack of the respect due coordinate branches of government; or

> an unusual need for unquestioning adherence to a political decision already made; or the potentiality of embarrassment from multifarious pronouncements by various departments on one question.
>
> Unless one of these formulations is inextricable from the case at bar, there should be no dismissal for non-justiciability on the ground of a political question's presence. [*Id.* at 217.]

Although *Baker* identified six different factors, in practice most analyses of the political question doctrine rise and fall on the first two. *See Zivotofsky ex rel. Zivotofsky v. Clinton* (*Zivotofsky I*), 566 U.S. 189, 207 (2012) (Sotomayor, J., concurring) ("[I]t will be the rare case in which *Baker*'s final factors alone render a case nonjusticiable.").

Reading *Smith v. Obama*

Recall the facts and legal challenge posed by this case, *supra* p. 132.

- Look again at Smith's claims. What exactly is the legal question that they present?
- Smith argues that Operation Inherent Resolve is not authorized by the 2001 and 2002 AUMFs. Does the court have a judicially manageable standard for deciding whether it is?
- The court acknowledges that resolution of the case would require *interpretation* of these AUMFs. Is the difficulty in doing so a good reason for the court to refuse to decide?
- Or is the court more concerned about *applying* the AUMFs? How is that different from interpreting them? If the difficulty lies in applying relevant facts to statutory standards, is it harder for a court to find national security facts than other facts?
- Suppose the President sends Special Forces to combat drug gangs in Central America, asserting without evidence that the gangs harbor or have assistance from some members of Al Qaeda. If someone has standing to challenge the legality of that deployment, should the court dismiss that challenge on political question grounds?

Smith v. Obama

United States District Court, District of Columbia, 2016
217 F. Supp. 3d 283, *vacated as moot sub nom.*
Smith v. Trump, 731 F. App'x 8 (D.C. Cir. 2018)

[The first part of this opinion appears at p. 132.]

COLLEEN KOLLAR-KOTELLY, United States District Judge. . . .

B. The Political Question Doctrine

. . . Plaintiff's claims are premised on the notion that Congress has not previously authorized the use of force against ISIL. Defendant disputes this. Resolving this dispute would require the Court to determine whether the legal authorizations for the use of military force relied on by President Obama — the 2001 and 2002 AUMFs — in fact authorize the use of force against ISIL. With regard to the 2001 AUMF, the Court would have to determine whether the President is correct that ISIL is among "those nations, organizations, or persons" that "planned, authorized, committed, or aided the terrorist attacks that occurred on September 11, 2001, or harbored such organizations or persons," and that Operation Inherent Resolve represents "necessary and appropriate force" against that group. Pub. L. No. 107-40, §2(a). With regard to the 2002 AUMF, the Court would have to determine whether the President is correct that operations against ISIL are "necessary and appropriate in order to . . . defend the national security of the United States against the continuing threat posed by Iraq." Pub. L. No. 107-243, §3(a)(1). For the reasons set out below, the Court finds that these are political questions under the first two *Baker* [*v. Carr*, 369 U.S. 186 (1962)] factors: the issues raised are primarily ones committed to the political branches of government, and the Court lacks judicially manageable standards, and is otherwise ill-equipped, to resolve them.

There can be "no doubt that decision-making in the fields of foreign policy and national security is textually committed to the political branches of government." *Schneider* [*v. Kissinger*, 412 F.3d 190 (2005)] at 194; *see also Gilligan* [*v. Morgan*, 413 U.S. 1 (1973)] at 10 ("It would be difficult to think of a clearer example of the type of governmental action that was intended by the Constitution to be left to the political branches . . . [than the] complex, subtle, and professional decisions as to the . . . control of a military force. . . ."); *Luftig v. McNamara*, 373 F.2d 664, 665-66 (D.C. Cir. 1967) ("The fundamental division of authority and power established by the Constitution precludes judges from overseeing the conduct of foreign policy or the use and disposition of military power; these matters are plainly the exclusive province of Congress and the Executive.").

Questions of statutory construction and interpretation, however, are committed to the Judiciary, and Plaintiff argues that this is a "garden-variety statutory construction case," that presents "straightforward problems of statutory interpretation." . . .

. . . The questions posed in this case go significantly beyond interpreting statutes and determining whether they are constitutional. Plaintiff asks the Court to second-guess the Executive's *application* of these statutes to specific facts on the ground in an ongoing combat mission halfway around the world. For example, the Court is not asked simply to "interpret" the 2001 AUMF, or to determine its constitutionality. It is asked to determine whether the President is correct that ISIL, as it exists today, is an appropriate target under that resolution based on the nature and extent of ISIL's relationship and connections with the terrorist organization that the President has determined was responsible for the September 11, 2001 attacks. The Court would also have to go further than simply "interpreting" the 2002 AUMF. It would have to determine whether the President is correct that the ongoing military action against ISIL is in fact "necessary and appropriate in order to . . . defend the national security of the United States against the continuing threat posed by Iraq." Pub. L. No. 107-243, §3(a)(1).

The reality, then, is more nuanced than Plaintiff suggests. Plaintiff's claims raise mixed questions of both discretionary military judgment *and* statutory interpretation. . . . [U]nder the particular facts of this case, the Court determines that dismissal under that doctrine is in fact warranted for three reasons.

First, certain aspects of the questions posed by this case are indisputably and completely committed to the political branches of government. Both the 2001 and

2002 AUMFs authorize only that force that the President determines is "necessary and appropriate." Pub. L. No. 107-40, §2(a); Pub. L. No. 107-243, §3(a)(1). The necessity and appropriateness of military action is precisely the type of discretionary military determination that is committed to the political branches and which the Court has no judicially manageable standards to adjudicate.

Second, whatever factual questions are raised by Plaintiff's claims are not of the type that the Court is well-equipped to resolve. Instead, the particular questions presented in this case "require judicial inquiry into sensitive military matters" about which "[t]he Court lacks the resources and expertise (which are accessible to the Congress) to resolve disputed questions of fact concerning." *Crockett v. Reagan*, 558 F. Supp. 893, 898 (D.D.C. 1982), *aff'd*, 720 F.2d 1355 (D.C. Cir. 1983) (dismissing claim that the President violated the War Powers Resolution under the political question doctrine, holding that "[t]he subtleties of factfinding in this situation should be left to the political branches"); *Crockett v. Reagan*, 720 F.2d 1355, 1356 (D.C. Cir. 1983) (affirming the trial court's reasoning in dismissing the case because it "did not have the resources or expertise to resolve the particular factual disputes involved in this case").

. . . The President and Department of Defense officials apparently believe that ISIL is connected with al Qaeda and that, despite public rifts, some allegiances between the groups persist and ISIL continues to pursue the same mission today as it did before allegedly splintering from al Qaeda. Plaintiff disputes these factual assertions, relying on an affidavit from scholars of Islamic Law that argue that as of today, the groups are in fact sufficiently distinct, and potentially even antagonistic, that they can no longer be viewed as the same terrorist organization. Resolving this dispute would require inquiries into sensitive military determinations, presumably made based on intelligence collected on the ground in a live theatre of combat, and potentially changing and developing on an ongoing basis. *See Al-Aulaqi v. Obama*, 727 F. Supp. 2d 1, 45 (D.D.C. 2010) ("The difficulty that U.S. courts would encounter if they were tasked with 'ascertaining the "facts" of military decisions exercised thousands of miles from the forum, lies at the heart of the determination whether the question [posed] is a "political" one.'") (quoting *DaCosta v. Laird*, 471 F.2d 1146, 1148 (2d Cir. 1973)).

Finally, an additional factor makes judicial intervention particularly inappropriate on the specific facts of this case. Unlike the situation presented in *Zivotofsky* [*ex rel. Zivotofsky v. Clinton* (*Zivotofsky I*), 566 U.S. 189 (2012)], the Court in this case is not presented with a dispute between the two political branches regarding the challenged action. In fact, Congress has repeatedly provided funding for the effort against ISIL. . . .

This lack of conflict is relevant to the *justiciability* of Plaintiff's claims under the political question doctrine because judicial intervention into military affairs is particularly inappropriate when the two political branches to whom war-making powers are committed are not in dispute as to the military action at issue. . . .

. . . Congress is vested with considerable power to restrain the President in the conduct of military operations. *See Schneider*, 412 F.3d at 198 ("If the executive in fact has exceeded his appropriate role in the constitutional scheme, Congress enjoys a broad range of authorities with which to exercise restraint and balance," including withholding funding); *Massachusetts v. Laird*, 451 F.2d at 34 ("When the executive takes a strong hand, Congress has no lack of corrective power."); *Ange v. Bush*, 752 F. Supp. 509, 514 (D.D.C. 1990) ("Congress possesses ample powers under the

Constitution to prevent Presidential overreaching, should Congress choose to exercise them."). Such powers may not always be sufficient, and judicial intervention may be necessary when they fail. But in this case, where these powers have not been exercised and there does not appear to be any disagreement between the two political branches as to the legality of a live military operation, the Court finds it inappropriate to inject itself into these affairs. In sum, the Court finds that dismissal under the political question doctrine is appropriate. . . .

Notes and Questions

1. A Political Case? The relevant justiciability doctrine is called "the political *question* doctrine" for a reason. "The doctrine of which we treat is one of 'political questions,' not one of 'political cases,'" the Supreme Court said in *Baker v. Carr.* 369 U.S. at 217. To successfully invoke the doctrine it is therefore not enough to assert simply that a case touches on, or even centrally involves, highly political judgments about foreign or military affairs. It depends on the question — the legal issue — posed by the claims or defenses in the case.

The key to determining whether the political question doctrine applies is thus to identify the question that the case poses. Many of the judicial decisions we have read up to this point — notably *The Steel Seizure Case, Curtiss-Wright, Dames & Moore, Little v. Barreme, Bas v. Tingy*, and *Greene v. McElroy* — have presented national security law disputes involving discretionary decisions by the elected branches. Yet the courts decided those cases on the merits. Why did the court in each of them reach the merits instead of dismissing on political question grounds? (Hint: Identify the question posed and consider whether the law supplied a judicially manageable standard for deciding that question.)

For the same reason, neither immigration, foreign policy, nor national security is a talisman protecting a government policy from judicial review, as the court made clear in *Washington v. Trump, supra.* The key, again, is the legal question the case presents. This is not to say that on questions raised by these subjects the government may not be entitled to deference, but the degree of deference itself depends on the question and is not necessarily a trump card for the government.

2. What Was the Question in Smith? If Smith had framed his challenge as whether the United States should use military force in Iraq, there would seem to be little doubt that it would pose a political question. The Constitution assigns the decision to declare war to Congress, and arguably leaves the President the decision to use military force in self-defense. These are quintessentially policy judgments for which there is no judicially manageable standard. But was this the question Smith raised? Or was it whether Congress had already made the decision by enacting the AUMFs? That may still be a hard question, but it's not the same question. It's no longer strictly a policy question, and the AUMFs themselves now provide a standard.

In the 1999 suit by 31 members of the House of Representatives challenging President Clinton's air strikes against Yugoslavia without congressional authorization, the judges disagreed on the application of the political question doctrine. Judge Silberman maintained that "no one" could challenge the President's actions, because of a lack of "judicially discoverable and manageable standards," and because "the War Powers

Clause claim implicates the political question doctrine." *Campbell v. Clinton*, 203 F.3d at 24-25 (Silberman, J., concurring). Judge Tatel opined that "[w]hether the military activity in Yugoslavia amounted to 'war' within the meaning of the Declare War Clause . . . is no more standardless than any other question regarding the constitutionality of government action. . . . Courts have proven no less capable of developing standards to resolve war power challenges [than Fourth or First Amendment actions]." *Id.* at 40 (Tatel, J., concurring). Should the "lack of standards" rationale carry more weight in war powers disputes than it does in individual rights litigation?

3. Textual Commitment? Baker v. Carr identified "a textually demonstrable constitutional commitment of the issue to a coordinate political department" as a factor for invoking the doctrine to dismiss a case. The constitutional text appears to assign to Congress the decision to decide on "war" with Iraq. One court, hearing challenge to the invasion of Iraq, took a different view:

> In the present case, there is an explicit textual commitment of the war powers not to *one* of the political branches, but to *both.* The various provisions of the Constitution do not grant the war power exclusively to either the legislative or the executive branch. The powers granted to both branches, however, enable those branches to resolve the dispute themselves. Meddling by the judicial branch in determining the allocation of constitutional powers where the text of the Constitution appears ambiguous as to the allocation of those powers "extends judicial power beyond the limits inherent in the constitutional scheme for dividing federal power." [*Ange v. Bush*, 752 F. Supp. 509, 514 (D.D.C. 1990).]

Do you agree? Should courts decide "ambiguous" questions of the allocation of power between branches? *See, e.g., Zivotofsky I*, 566 U.S. at 201 ("This is what courts do."). If they won't, who will?

4. Fact-Finding Difficulties? Should the size or scope of a military operation affect a court's willingness to adjudicate its legality? Is the difficulty in deciding about a smaller military operation one of judicially discoverable and manageable standards, or of judicial resources and expertise? *See Dellums v. Bush*, 752 F. Supp. 1141, 1145 (D.D.C. 1990) (suggesting that if "the issue is factually close or ambiguous or fraught with intricate technical military and diplomatic baggage," courts might "defer to the political branches to determine whether or not particular hostilities might qualify as a 'war.' However, [when 380,000 American troops are deployed for an offensive military attack] . . . the forces involved are of such magnitude and significance as to present no serious claim that a war would not ensue if they became engaged in combat, and it is therefore clear that congressional approval is required if Congress desires to become involved.").

5. Relationship of Standing to Merits and Political Question. In theory, the focus in deciding standing is on the fitness of a particular plaintiff to present a case adverse to the defendant, not on the merits of the substantive issues presented in the complaint. A dismissal on standing grounds may simply mean that the wrong plaintiff initiated the action, not that the merits may not be adjudicated in a suit by a different plaintiff.

But a dismissal on political question grounds means that the claim is not justiciable. There is no "right" plaintiff; any plaintiff who presents the same claim will face dismissal on political question grounds. The standing doctrine thus is a narrower and less radical basis for dismissal of a lawsuit than the political question doctrine.

6. Political Questions and Individual Rights. The cases above generally involve interbranch disputes over the constitutional allocation of war powers. Do challenges to military conduct on individual rights grounds raise similar — or at least comparable — justiciability concerns? Is resolution of these disputes textually committed to another branch of government? If not, do they present judicially unmanageable standards?

In the *Zaidan* case discussed above, a U.S. citizen journalist inferred from five "near-miss" aerial attacks on him in Syria that he was wrongfully included on a U.S. "kill list." He claimed, *inter alia,* that his listing violated procedures set forth in a presidential policy guidance for listing terrorist targets. The court ruled that his challenge was barred by the political question doctrine, because the guidance provided "no test or standard that must be satisfied before the government may add an individual (known or unknown) to the Kill List; it only specifies the steps and processes that the relevant defense agencies must complete." 317 F. Supp. 3d at 25. While agreeing that the claimed violations of an executive order, a statute prohibiting war crimes, and the 2001 AUMF "appear at first blush to present 'pure[] legal issues,'" the court went on to conclude, cryptically, that "the process of determining whether Defendants exceeded their authority or violated any of the statutes referenced in the Complaint would require the Court to make a finding on the propriety of the alleged action, which is prohibited by the political question doctrine." *Id.* at 26. But isn't every question of legal authority or prohibition one of the "propriety" of the challenged action?

The court found itself on more comfortable ground in assessing the justiciability of the plaintiff's due process claim — that his alleged placement on the kill list denied him an opportunity to be heard.

> Due process is not merely an old and dusty procedural obligation required by Robert's Rules. Instead, it is a living, breathing concept that protects U.S. persons from overreaching government action even, perhaps, on an occasion of war. . . .
>
> . . . Mr. Kareem does not seek a ruling that a strike by the U.S. military was mistaken or improper. He seeks his birthright instead: a timely assertion of his due process rights under the Constitution to be heard before he might be included on the Kill List and his First Amendment rights to free speech before he might be targeted for lethal action due to his profession. [*Id.* at 27-28.]

His constitutional claims therefore presented justiciable constitutional questions that "are the bread and butter of the federal judiciary." *Id.* at 29.

7. Should the Status of the Defendant Matter? In *Al Shimari v. CACI Premier Technology, Inc.*, 840 F.3d 147 (4th Cir. 2016), the Court of Appeals held that claims arising out of a private military contractor's alleged abuses of U.S. military detainees while operating a prison in Iraq did not necessarily present a political question. The distinction on which *Al Shimari* turned was whether the plaintiffs' claims were that the defendants acted unlawfully, and not just tortiously. *See id.* at 158. Is there a meaningful distinction for purposes of the political question doctrine between the two kinds of claims?

Al Shimari was a suit against a private military contractor, and not against the military itself. Should that matter for purposes of the political question doctrine? Why or why not? *See, e.g., Harris v. Kellogg Brown & Root Servs., Inc.*, 724 F.3d 458, 465 (3d Cir. 2013) ("Defense contractors do not have independent constitutional authority and are not coordinate branches of government to which we owe deference."). Do tort suits against private military contractors in state courts raise the same questions? *See, e.g., Am. K-9 Detection Servs., LLC v. Freeman*, 556 S.W.3d 246 (Tex. 2018) (applying the federal political question doctrine to bar a state-law tort suit against a private military contractor arising out of a dog bite).

3. Ripeness

Smith v. Obama rested dismissal partly on the grounds that it could "discern no impasse or conflict between the political branches on the question of whether ISIL is an appropriate target under the AUMFs cited by the President as authority for Operation Inherent Resolve." 217 F. Supp. 3d at 302. Although the court gave this as an additional reason to invoke the political question doctrine, it also fits under the alternative rubric of ripeness. The ripeness doctrine allows the judiciary to avoid present adjudication of a dispute by determining that future events may affect its shape or even its existence. The doctrine maintains that "federal courts . . . do not render advisory opinions. For adjudication of constitutional issues 'concrete legal issues, presented in actual cases, not abstractions' are requisite." *United Pub. Workers v. Mitchell*, 330 U.S. 75, 89 (1947) (internal citations omitted). Concerning claims that the President's actions lack needed congressional approval, or that the President is acting contrary to a congressional mandate, Justice Powell, concurring in *Goldwater v. Carter*, 444 U.S. 996 (1979) (mem.), put it this way: "The Judicial Branch should not decide issues affecting the allocation of power between the President and Congress until the political branches reach a constitutional impasse." *Id.* at 997 (Powell, J., concurring).

In October 2002 Congress authorized the President to "use the Armed Forces of the United States as he determines to be necessary and appropriate in order to (1) defend the national security of the United States against the continuing threat posed by Iraq; and (2) enforce all relevant United Nations Security Council resolutions regarding Iraq." Authorization for Use of Military Force Against Iraq Resolution of 2002, Pub. L. No. 107-243, §3(a), 116 Stat. 1498, 1501. In February 2003, active-duty members of the military, parents of military personnel, and members of Congress sued to enjoin the President from initiating a war against Iraq. *Doe v. Bush*, 323 F.3d 133 (1st Cir. 2003). The plaintiffs argued that "Congress and the President are in collision — that the President is about to act in violation of the October Resolution" — and that "Congress and the President are in collusion — that Congress has handed over to the President its exclusive power to declare war." *Id.* at 134. The court responded:

> Ripeness doctrine involves more than simply the timing of the case. It mixes various mutually reinforcing constitutional and prudential considerations. One such consideration is the need "to prevent the courts, through avoidance of premature adjudication, from entangling themselves in abstract disagreements." Another is to avoid unnecessary constitutional decisions. A third is the recognition that, by waiting until a case is fully developed before deciding it, courts benefit from a focus sharpened by particular facts. The case before us raises all three of these concerns. [*Id.* at 138.]

Ruling that the lawsuit was not ripe, the court said it was unable to determine that the President would disregard conditions attached to the statutory authorization: "In the present posture of this case, we do not know whether there will ever be an actual confrontation between the Legislative and Executive Branches." *Id.* at 139 (quoting from *Goldwater, supra*). Regarding the allegation of collusion, the court emphasized the "shared nature of the powers in question here," declaring that "courts are rightly hesitant to second-guess the form or means by which the coequal political branches choose to exercise their textually committed constitutional powers." *Id.* at 142, 144.

Do you agree with the *Doe* court that the case failed to "clearly raise[] the specter of undermining the constitutional structure"? *Id.* at 135. Can you articulate a test for determining when a national security activity so undermines the constitutional structure that courts ought to intervene?

The court's decision was announced on March 13, 2003. The war was launched seven days later. Would the plaintiffs have obtained a ruling on the merits if the court had delayed its decision by a few days?

C. SUBSTANTIVE HURDLES: *BIVENS* AND QUALIFIED IMMUNITY

1. A Cause of Action?

Even if she survives the justiciability barriers to suit described above, a plaintiff must still state a claim that would entitle her to relief. That is, she must assert a legally cognizable theory of recovery supported by plausible allegations — a cause of action, in the traditional terminology.

Sometimes Congress has created an express claim or cause of action by statute. Examples include the Antiterrorism Act, 18 U.S.C. §2333 (2018) (creating a civil damages claim for U.S. nationals injured by reason of an act of international terrorism); the Torture Victim Protection Act, Pub. L. No. 102-256, 106 Stat. 73 (1992) (codified at 28 U.S.C. §1350 note (2018)) (creating a civil damages claim for victims of torture or extrajudicial killing); and the Foreign Intelligence Surveillance Act (FISA), 50 U.S.C. §1810 (2018) (creating a civil claim for individuals who are "aggrieved" by certain unlawful searches under FISA). It has also provided federal jurisdiction for at least some customary international law claims against aliens. Alien Tort Statute, 28 U.S.C. §1350 (2018). *See Sosa v. Alvarez-Machain*, 542 U.S. 692 (2004).

Congress has also provided for other claims against the federal government that may implicate national security. For example, the Administrative Procedure Act (APA) provides that "[a] person suffering legal wrong because of agency action, or adversely affected or aggrieved by agency action within the meaning of a relevant statute, is entitled to judicial review thereof." 5 U.S.C. §702 (2018). APA review, however, is generally limited to "final" agency actions, and it does not apply to military commissions or "military authority exercised in the field in time of war or in occupied territory." *Id.* §701(b)(1)(G).

In addition to these statutory remedies, plaintiffs who seek relief for an injury caused by federal government action in violation of a constitutional right may assert an implied right of action — that is, a cause of action that the courts infer from a constitutional or statutory right on the theory that where there is a right, there should be a remedy. Although the existence of such a cause of action for injunctive relief against ongoing government action is well established, the ability to obtain *damages* for constitutional violations that have ceased is much murkier. In *Bivens v. Six Unknown Named Agents of Fed. Bureau of Narcotics*, 403 U.S. 388 (1971), the Supreme Court inferred a cause of action for damages against federal narcotics agents who allegedly violated the plaintiff's Fourth Amendment rights by an illegal search. The Court declared:

> Of course, the Fourth Amendment does not in so many words provide for its enforcement by an award of money damages for the consequences of its violation. But "it is . . . well settled that where legal rights have been invaded, and a federal statute provides for a general right to sue for such invasion, federal courts may use any available remedy to make good the wrong done." *Bell v. Hood*, 327 U.S. [678,] 684 [(1946)] (footnote omitted). The present case involves no special factors counseling hesitation in the absence of affirmative action by Congress. [403 U.S. at 396.]

Subsequently, courts inferred private claims under the First, Fifth, and Eighth Amendments, as well. *See* Chemerinsky, *supra*, §9.1.2.

More recently, however, the Supreme Court has made clear that expanding the *Bivens* remedy is now "disfavored." *Ashcroft v. Iqbal*, 556 U.S. 662, 675 (2009). It has "consistently refused to extend *Bivens* to any new context or new category of defendants." *Corr. Servs. Corp. v. Malesko*, 534 U.S. 61, 68 (2001). Even when the context is not entirely new, the Court has repeatedly relied upon the caveats identified in *Bivens*—where Congress has provided an alternative remedy or where there are "special factors counseling hesitation"—to decline to recognize new *Bivens* remedies. For example, the Court has held the special nature of military command and discipline is a factor counseling hesitation in inferring a *Bivens* remedy. *Chappel v. Wallace*, 462 U.S. 296, 300 (1983) ("Civilian courts must, at the very least, hesitate long before entertaining a suit which asks the court to tamper with the established relationship between enlisted military personnel and their superior officers; that relationship is at the heart of the necessarily unique structure of the military establishment.").

In *Ziglar v. Abbasi*, 137 S. Ct. 1843 (2017), a case arising out of the post-September 11 immigration "roundup" of young men of Muslim and/or Arab descent in and around New York City, a 4-2 majority of the Supreme Court expressed serious skepticism that *Bivens* claims for damages will *ever* be appropriate in the context of national security. As Justice Kennedy explained,

> National-security policy is the prerogative of the Congress and President. *See* U.S. Const. Art. I, §8; Art. II, §1, §2. Judicial inquiry into the national-security realm raises "concerns for the separation of powers in trenching on matters committed to the other branches." *Christopher v. Harbury*, 536 U.S. 403, 417 (2002). *These concerns are even more pronounced when the judicial inquiry comes in the context of a claim seeking money damages rather than a claim seeking injunctive or other equitable relief.* The risk of personal damages liability is more likely to cause an official to second-guess difficult but necessary decisions concerning national-security policy. [137 S. Ct. at 1861 (emphasis added).]

One important consequence of *Ziglar* is that the denial of a cause of action for damages is fatal to a claim for any *retrospective* judicial relief whatever, even for the most egregious and clearly established constitutional violations. But won't such a holding confer a form of "absolute" immunity on federal government officers who never have to fear damages liability for constitutional violations in national security litigation (if not more generally)?

Can you argue that we should prefer retrospective relief over prospective relief in national security cases, given the difficulty, both factually and legally, of fully ascertaining the validity of government action as it is ongoing? This was the argument with which Justice Breyer closed his dissent:

> [T]here may well be a particular need for *Bivens* remedies when security-related Government actions are at issue. History tells us of far too many instances where the Executive or Legislative Branch took actions during time of war that, on later examination, turned out unnecessarily and unreasonably to have deprived American citizens of basic constitutional rights. . . .
>
> . . . Complaints seeking [prospective] relief typically come during the emergency itself, when emotions are strong, when courts may have too little or inaccurate information, and when courts may well prove particularly reluctant to interfere with even the least well-founded Executive Branch activity. . . .
>
> A damages action, however, is typically brought after the emergency is over, after emotions have cooled, and at a time when more factual information is available. In such circumstances, courts have more time to exercise such judicial virtues as calm reflection and dispassionate application of the law to the facts. . . . I should think that the wisdom of permitting courts to consider *Bivens* actions, later granting monetary compensation to those wronged at the time, would follow *a fortiori*. [*Id.* at 1884 (Breyer, J., dissenting).]

The *Ziglar* Court went out of its way to reaffirm the viability of claims in a factual context similar to *Bivens*. *See id.* at 1856 ("[T]his opinion is not intended to cast doubt on the continued force, or even the necessity, of *Bivens* in the search-and-seizure context in which it arose."). But the Court then emphasized that the relevant contextual question to ask in *Bivens* cases is whether "the case is different in a meaningful way from previous *Bivens* cases decided by *this* Court." *Id.* at 1859 (emphasis added). Given that the Supreme Court has only expressly affirmed *Bivens* claims in three circumstances, the context inquiry is likely to cabin the expansion of *Bivens*—especially in settings, such as challenges to national security or counterterrorism policies (or the enforcement thereof), in which it has not previously thrived.

For example, in *Hernandez v. Mesa* (*Hernández II*), 885 F.3d 811 (5th Cir. 2018) (en banc), *cert. granted*, 139 S. Ct. 2636 (2019), the plaintiffs were parents of a 15-year old boy who was shot and killed in Mexico by a U.S. Customs and Border Patrol agent standing on U.S. soil. Their *Bivens* action for violation of their son's Fourth and Fifth Amendment rights turned crucially on whether those rights extended extraterritorially to an alien on foreign soil. Rejecting the plaintiffs' argument that their claims were just "rogue cop" claims analogous to *Bivens*, the court of appeals said:

> Pursuant to [*Ziglar v.*] *Abbasi*, the cross-border shooting at issue here must present a "new context" for a *Bivens* claim. Because Hernandez was a Mexican citizen with no ties to this country, and his death occurred on Mexican soil, the very existence of any "constitutional" right benefitting him raises novel and disputed issues. There has been no direct judicial guidance concerning the extraterritorial scope of the Constitution and its potential application to foreign citizens on foreign soil. [*Id.* at 816-817.]

If the contextual difference alone did not require dismissal of the claim, then numerous "special factors counseling hesitation" did: it involved national security at the border, risked interference in foreign affairs and diplomacy with Mexico, and implicated a subject in which Congress had frequently legislated (immigration and border security), without enacting a private remedy for damages. *Id.* at 818-821. Furthermore, the "novelty and uncertain scope of an extraterritorial *Bivens* remedy [also] counsel hesitation." *Id.* at 822; *see also Vanderklok v. United States*, 868 F.3d 189 (3d Cir. 2017) (refusing to recognize a *Bivens* cause of action against TSA screeners).

On similar facts, however, the Ninth Circuit came out the other way. *Rodriguez v. Swartz*, 899 F.3d 719, 748 (9th Cir. 2018), *petition for cert. filed*, No. 18-309 (U.S. Sept. 11, 2018). It acknowledged that the case presented a new context for *Bivens*, but disagreed with *Hernández II*'s hesitation, because

> this case is not about searches and seizures broadly speaking. Neither is it about warrants or overseas operations. It is about the unreasonable use of deadly force by a federal agent on American soil. Under those limited circumstances, there are no practical obstacles to extending the Fourth Amendment. Applying the Constitution in this case would simply say that American officers must not shoot innocent, non-threatening people for no reason. [*Id.* at 731.]

The court then held that "despite our reluctance to extend *Bivens*, we do so here: no other adequate remedy is available, there is no reason to infer that Congress deliberately chose to withhold a remedy, and the asserted special factors either do not apply or counsel in favor of extending *Bivens*." *Id.* at 748. It reasoned that the case was not about policy, does not implicate national security ("no one suggests that national security involves shooting people who are just walking down a street in Mexico"), and had no "problematic" foreign policy implications ("To the contrary: it would threaten international relations if we declined to extend a cause of action, because it would mean American courts could not give a remedy for a gross violation of Mexican sovereignty."). *Id.* at 744-747.

Which analysis, that of the Fifth Circuit or the Ninth Circuit, do you find more convincing? The Supreme Court heard arguments in *Hernández II* on November 12, 2019, and a decision was pending at this writing.

2. Qualified Immunity

Even if a plaintiff is found to have a cause of action for damages under *Bivens* or a federal statute, recovery may be barred by the affirmative defense of qualified immunity. In *Harlow v. Fitzgerald*, 457 U.S. 800 (1982), the Supreme Court held that

> government officials performing discretionary functions generally are shielded from liability for civil damages insofar as their conduct does not violate clearly established statutory or constitutional rights of which a reasonable person would have known. . . . On summary judgment, the judge appropriately may determine, not only the currently applicable law, but whether that law was clearly established at the time an action occurred. If the law at that time was not clearly established, an official could not reasonably be expected to anticipate subsequent legal developments, nor could he fairly be said to "know" that the law forbade conduct not previously identified as unlawful. Until this threshold immunity question is resolved, discovery should not be allowed. If the law was clearly established, the immunity defense ordinarily should fail, since a reasonably competent public official should know the law governing his conduct. [*Id.* at 818-819.]

Thus, although a district court had found that José Padilla, a U.S. citizen who was detained and allegedly tortured in military custody after 9/11, had stated a *Bivens* claim against former Deputy Assistant Attorney General John Yoo for advising on the legality of coercive interrogation, and that Padilla had alleged violations of clearly established constitutional and statutory rights, the Court of Appeals reversed.

> We assume without deciding that Padilla's alleged treatment rose to the level of torture. That it was torture was not, however, "beyond debate" in 2001-03. There was at that time considerable debate, both in and out of government, over the definition of torture as applied to specific interrogation techniques. In light of that debate, as well as the judicial decisions discussed above, we cannot say that any reasonable official in 2001-03 would have known that the specific interrogation techniques allegedly employed against Padilla, however appalling, necessarily amounted to torture. Thus, although we hold that the unconstitutionality of torturing an American citizen was beyond debate in 2001-03, it was not clearly established at that time that the treatment Padilla alleges he was subjected to amounted to torture. [*Padilla v. Yoo*, 678 F.3d 748, 767-768 (9th Cir. 2012).]

As should be clear from *Harlow*, qualified immunity defenses present courts with two questions: (1) was the defendant's conduct *actually* unlawful (the "legality" question); and (2) was the illegality of the defendant's conduct "clearly established" at the time it occurred (the "liability" question). Critically, though, if courts resolve the liability question in the defendant's favor (as in *Padilla*), the Supreme Court has held that they do not have to answer the legality question — and can therefore avoid setting a precedent that *would* "clearly establish" the law going forward. *See Pearson v. Callahan*, 555 U.S. 223 (2009) (overruling *Saucier v. Katz*, 533 U.S. 194 (2001), which had required courts to answer both questions). Thus, in *Padilla*, the Ninth Circuit not only held that "it was not clearly established [when Padilla was allegedly abused] that the treatment Padilla alleges he was subjected to amounted to torture," 678 F.3d at 768, it also held that it did not need to decide (and thereby "clearly establish") whether that treatment was actually unlawful. *See id.* at 768 n.16. In light of that holding, what would stop a future government official from pursuing the exact same course of conduct in a future case like *Padilla*?

In *Hernandez v. United States* (*Hernández I*), 785 F.3d 117 (5th Cir. 2015) (en banc) (per curiam), the plaintiffs sued a U.S. Customs and Border Protection officer for shooting from U.S. soil into Mexico, killing their son. The full court of appeals affirmed dismissal of a Fifth Amendment claim on the ground that it was not clearly established at the time of the shooting "whether the general prohibition of excessive force applies where the person injured by a U.S. official standing on U.S. soil is an alien who had no significant voluntary connection to, and was not in, the United States when the incident occurred." *Id.* at 120. The Supreme Court vacated and remanded sub nom. *Hernandez v. Mesa*, 137 S. Ct. 2003 (2017) (per curiam), finding in part that the court of appeals erred because at the time of the shooting, the defendant did not know the boy's nationality or the extent of his connections to the United States. "The qualified immunity analysis . . . is limited to 'the facts that were knowable to the defendant officers' at the time they engaged in the conduct in question. Facts an officer learns after the incident ends — whether those facts would support granting immunity or denying it — are not relevant." *Id.* at 2007 (citation omitted). As noted above, the en banc Fifth Circuit ultimately refused to infer a *Bivens* remedy and affirmed dismissal of the complaint on remand. *Hernández II*, 885 F.3d 811.

D. EVIDENTIARY HURDLES: THE STATE SECRETS PRIVILEGE

An early draft of the Federal Rules of Evidence included this provision:

Rule 509. Secrets of State and Other Official Information

> (a) Definitions. (1) Secret of state. A "secret of state" is a governmental secret relating to the national defense or the international relations of the United States. . . .
>
> (b) General rule of privilege. The government has a privilege to refuse to give evidence and to prevent any person from giving evidence upon a showing of reasonable likelihood of danger that the evidence will disclose a secret of state or official information, as defined in this rule.

26 Charles Alan Wright & Kenneth W. Graham, *Federal Practice and Procedure* 415-416 (1992). Rule 509 was never enacted, leaving recognition of a "state secrets privilege" to judicial application as common law. Some of this law long preceded September 11 and the "war on terror," but there were relatively few cases before then. The most important Supreme Court cases involving the protection of national security secrets in civil litigation — *Totten v. United States*, 92 U.S. 105 (1875), and *United States v. Reynolds*, 345 U.S. 1 (1953) — and the two lines of case law they spawned are discussed in the following opinion.

Reading *El-Masri v. United States*

Khaled El-Masri, a German citizen of Lebanese descent, was subjected to "extraordinary rendition" when he was captured in Macedonia and secretly transferred by CIA operatives and defense contractors to a U.S. detention facility in Afghanistan. There, he alleged, he was subjected to prolonged arbitrary detention, torture, and cruel, inhuman, or degrading treatment in violation of federal and international laws. After U.S. authorities determined that his capture was a case of mistaken identity, they released him. El-Masri then sued the former Director of the CIA and others for damages. The U.S. government, however, asserted that his claims necessarily implicated state secrets and asked the court to dismiss his lawsuit on the ground that it could not be tried without revealing those secrets.

- How did the government invoke the state secrets privilege? (Note who must swear the declarations supporting the privilege.)
- Is the privilege of common law or constitutional origin?
- What standard does the court employ to decide whether information that would be revealed qualifies for the privilege? By what procedures does it apply the standard?
- Since the general facts of the CIA's extraordinary rendition program had already been disclosed to the media (and even admitted by the President), how could information about El-Masri's rendition be a state *secret*?
- If information qualifies for the privilege, may a court still order its disclosure? If not, what alternatives should a court consider? How can a case ever proceed after a court has upheld the privilege?

- Did dismissal of El-Masri's claims necessarily deny him *any* remedy for a grievous wrong? Where else could he possibly find relief? Did the dismissal mean that the court abdicated any role as a check on the Executive? The court says "no," but why not, and what role did it still play?

El-Masri v. United States

United States Court of Appeals, Fourth Circuit, 2007
479 F.3d 296

King, Circuit Judge....

I.

A....

On March 8, 2006, the United States filed a Statement of Interest in the underlying proceedings, pursuant to 28 U.S.C. §517, and interposed a claim of the state secrets privilege. The then Director of the CIA, Porter Goss, submitted two sworn declarations to the district court in support of the state secrets privilege claim. The first declaration was unclassified, and explained in general terms the reasons for the United States' assertion of privilege. The other declaration was classified; it detailed the information that the United States sought to protect, explained why further court proceedings would unreasonably risk that information's disclosure, and spelled out why such disclosure would be detrimental to the national security (the "Classified Declaration")....

II.

El-Masri maintains on appeal that the district court misapplied the state secrets doctrine in dismissing his Complaint without requiring any responsive pleadings from the defendants or permitting any discovery to be conducted. Importantly, El-Masri does not contend that the state secrets privilege has no role in these proceedings. To the contrary, he acknowledges that at least some information important to his claims is likely to be privileged, and thus beyond his reach. But he challenges the court's determination that state secrets are so central to this matter that any attempt at further litigation would threaten their disclosure. As explained below, we conclude that the district court correctly assessed the centrality of state secrets in this dispute. We therefore affirm its Order and the dismissal of El-Masri's Complaint.

A.

1.

Under the state secrets doctrine, the United States may prevent the disclosure of information in a judicial proceeding if "there is a reasonable danger" that such disclosure "will expose military matters which, in the interest of national security, should not be divulged." *United States v. Reynolds,* 345 U.S. 1, 10 (1953). *Reynolds,* the Supreme Court's leading decision on the state secrets privilege, established the doctrine in its modern form. There, an Air Force B-29 bomber had crashed during testing of secret electronic equipment, killing three civilian observers who were on board. Their widows sued the United States under the Federal Tort Claims Act, and they sought discovery of certain Air Force documents relating to the crash. The Air Force refused to disclose the documents and filed a formal "Claim of Privilege," contending that the plane had been on "a highly secret mission of the Air Force," and that disclosure of the requested materials would "seriously hamper[ ] national security, flying safety and the development of highly technical and secret military equipment." *Id.* at 4-5.

The Court sustained the Air Force's refusal to disclose the documents sought by the plaintiffs, concluding that the officials involved had properly invoked the "privilege against revealing military secrets." 345 U.S. at 6-7. This state secrets privilege, the Court observed, was "well established in the law of evidence." *Id.*. . . The *Reynolds* Court also reviewed a long line of decisions, both American and English, that had recognized and refined a privilege for state secrets. These included *Totten v. United States,* where, in 1875, the Supreme Court affirmed the dismissal of an action for breach of a secret espionage contract, concluding that "public policy forbids the maintenance of any suit in a court of justice, the trial of which would inevitably lead to the disclosure of matters which the law itself regards as confidential, and respecting which it will not allow the confidence to be violated." 92 U.S. 105, 107 (1875).

Although the state secrets privilege was developed at common law, it performs a function of constitutional significance, because it allows the executive branch to protect information whose secrecy is necessary to its military and foreign-affairs responsibilities. *Reynolds* itself suggested that the state secrets doctrine allowed the Court to avoid the constitutional conflict that might have arisen had the judiciary demanded that the Executive disclose highly sensitive military secrets. In *United States v. Nixon,* the Court further articulated the doctrine's constitutional dimension, observing that the state secrets privilege provides exceptionally strong protection because it concerns "areas of Art. II duties [in which] the courts have traditionally shown the utmost deference to Presidential responsibilities." 418 U.S. 683, 710 (1974). The *Nixon* Court went on to recognize that, to the extent an executive claim of privilege "relates to the effective discharge of a President's powers, it is constitutionally based." *Id.* at 711. Significantly, the Executive's constitutional authority is at its broadest in the realm of military and foreign affairs. The Court accordingly has indicated that the judiciary's role as a check on presidential action in foreign affairs is limited. Moreover, both the Supreme Court and this Court have recognized that the Executive's constitutional mandate encompasses the authority to protect national security information. *See Dep't of the Navy v. Egan,* 484 U.S. 518, 527 (1988) (observing that "authority to protect [national security] information falls on the President as head of the Executive Branch and as Commander in Chief"); *United States v. Marchetti,* 466 F.2d 1309, 1315 (4th Cir. 1972) ("Gathering intelligence information and the other activities of the [CIA], including clandestine affairs against other nations, are all within the President's constitutional responsibility for the security of the Nation as the Chief Executive and as Commander in Chief of our Armed forces."). The state secrets privilege that the United States has interposed in this civil proceeding thus has a firm foundation in the Constitution, in addition to its basis in the common law of evidence.

2.

A court faced with a state secrets privilege question is obliged to resolve the matter by use of a three-part analysis. At the outset, the court must ascertain that the procedural requirements for invoking the state secrets privilege have been satisfied. Second, the court must decide whether the information sought to be protected qualifies as privileged under the state secrets doctrine. Finally, if the subject information is determined to be privileged, the ultimate question to be resolved is how the matter should proceed in light of the successful privilege claim.

a.

The procedural requirements for invoking the state secrets privilege are set forth in *Reynolds*, which derived them largely from prior decisions on the subject. First, the state secrets privilege must be asserted by the United States. *See* 345 U.S. at 7. It "belongs to the Government and . . . can neither be claimed nor waived by a private party." *Id.* Second, "[t]here must be a formal claim of privilege, lodged by the head of the department which has control over the matter." *Id.* at 7-8. Third, the department head's formal privilege claim may be made only "after actual personal consideration by that officer." *Id.* at 8. *Reynolds* emphasized that the state secrets privilege "is not to be lightly invoked," and the foregoing constraints on its assertion give practical effect to that principle. *Id.* at 7.

b.

After a court has confirmed that the *Reynolds* procedural prerequisites are satisfied, it must determine whether the information that the United States seeks to shield is a state secret, and thus privileged from disclosure. This inquiry is a difficult one, for it pits the judiciary's search for truth against the Executive's duty to maintain the nation's security. The *Reynolds* Court recognized this tension, observing that "[j]udicial control over the evidence in a case cannot be abdicated to the caprice of executive officers" — no matter how great the interest in national security — but that the President's ability to preserve state secrets likewise cannot be placed entirely at the mercy of the courts. 345 U.S. at 9-10. Moreover, a court evaluating a claim of privilege must "do so without forcing a disclosure of the very thing the privilege is designed to protect."

The *Reynolds* Court balanced those concerns by leaving the judiciary firmly in control of deciding whether an executive assertion of the state secrets privilege is valid, but subject to a standard mandating restraint in the exercise of its authority. A court is obliged to honor the Executive's assertion of the privilege if it is satisfied, "from all the circumstances of the case, that there is a reasonable danger that compulsion of the evidence will expose military matters which, in the interest of national security, should not be divulged." *Reynolds*, 345 U.S. at 10. In assessing the risk that such a disclosure might pose to national security, a court is obliged to accord the "utmost deference" to the responsibilities of the executive branch. *Nixon,* 418 U.S. at 710. Such deference is appropriate not only for constitutional reasons, but also practical ones: the Executive and the intelligence agencies under his control occupy a position superior to that of the courts in evaluating the consequences of a release of sensitive information. In the related context of confidentiality classification decisions, we have observed that "[t]he courts, of course, are ill-equipped to become sufficiently steeped in foreign intelligence matters to serve effectively in the review of secrecy classifications in that area." *United States v. Marchetti,* 466 F.2d 1309, 1318 (4th Cir. 1972). The executive branch's expertise in predicting the potential consequences of intelligence disclosures is particularly important given the sophisticated nature of modern intelligence analysis, in which "[t]he significance of one item of information may frequently depend upon knowledge of many other items of information," and "[w]hat may seem trivial to the uninformed, may appear of great moment to one who has a broad view of the scene and may put the questioned item of information in its proper context." *Id.* In the same vein, in those situations where the state secrets privilege has been invoked because disclosure risks impairing our foreign relations, the President's assessment of the diplomatic situation is entitled to great weight.

The Executive bears the burden of satisfying a reviewing court that the *Reynolds* reasonable-danger standard is met. A court considering the Executive's assertion of the state secrets privilege, however, must take care not to "forc[e] a disclosure of the very thing the privilege is designed to protect" by demanding more information than is necessary. *Reynolds,* 345 U.S. at 8. Frequently, the explanation of the department head who has lodged the formal privilege claim, provided in an affidavit or personal declaration, is sufficient to carry the Executive's burden. In some situations, a court may conduct an in camera examination of the actual information sought to be protected, in order to ascertain that the criteria set forth in *Reynolds* are fulfilled. The degree to which such a reviewing court should probe depends in part on the importance of the assertedly privileged information to the position of the party seeking it. "Where there is a strong showing of necessity, the claim of privilege should not be lightly accepted. . . ." *Id.* On the other hand, "even the most compelling necessity cannot overcome the claim of privilege if the court is ultimately satisfied that military secrets are at stake." *Id.* Indeed, in certain circumstances a court may conclude that an explanation by the Executive of why a question cannot be answered would itself create an unacceptable danger of injurious disclosure. In such a situation, a court is obliged to accept the executive branch's claim of privilege without further demand.

After information has been determined to be privileged under the state secrets doctrine, it is absolutely protected from disclosure — even for the purpose of in camera examination by the court. On this point, *Reynolds* could not be more specific: "When . . . the occasion for the privilege is appropriate, . . . the court should not jeopardize the security which the privilege is meant to protect by insisting upon an examination of the evidence, even by the judge alone, in chambers." 345 U.S. at 10. Moreover, no attempt is made to balance the need for secrecy of the privileged information against a party's need for the information's disclosure; a court's determination that a piece of evidence is a privileged state secret removes it from the proceedings entirely.

c.

The effect of a successful interposition of the state secrets privilege by the United States will vary from case to case. If a proceeding involving state secrets can be fairly litigated without resort to the privileged information, it may continue. But if "'the circumstances make clear that sensitive military secrets will be so central to the subject matter of the litigation that any attempt to proceed will threaten disclosure of the privileged matters,' dismissal is the proper remedy." *Sterling* [*v. Tenet,* 416 F.3d 338, 348 (4th Cir. 2005)] (quoting *DTM Research, LLC v. AT & T Corp.*, 245 F.3d 327, 334 (4th Cir.

2001)). The Supreme Court has recognized that some matters are so pervaded by state secrets as to be incapable of judicial resolution once the privilege has been invoked. *See Totten,* 92 U.S. at 107; *Reynolds,* 345 U.S. at 11 n.26. . . . [I]n *Reynolds,* while concluding that dismissal was unnecessary because the privileged information was peripheral to the plaintiffs' action, the Court made clear that where state secrets form the very subject matter of a court proceeding, as in *Totten,* dismissal at the pleading stage — "without ever reaching the question of evidence" — is appropriate. *See* 345 U.S. at 11 n.26. . . .

B.

1. . . .

a.

The heart of El-Masri's appeal is his assertion that the facts essential to his Complaint have largely been made public, either in statements by United States officials or in reports by media outlets and foreign governmental entities. He maintains that the subject of this action is simply "a rendition and its consequences," and that its critical facts — the CIA's operation of a rendition program targeted at terrorism suspects, plus the tactics employed therein — have been so widely discussed that litigation concerning them could do no harm to national security. As a result, El-Masri contends that the district court should have allowed his case to move forward with discovery, perhaps with special procedures imposed to protect sensitive information.

El-Masri's contention in that regard, however, misapprehends the nature of our assessment of a dismissal on state secrets grounds. The controlling inquiry is not whether the general subject matter of an action can be described without resort to state secrets. Rather, we must ascertain whether an action can be *litigated* without threatening the disclosure of such state secrets. Thus, for purposes of the state secrets analysis, the "central facts" and "very subject matter" of an action are those facts that are essential to prosecuting the action or defending against it.

El-Masri is therefore incorrect in contending that the central facts of this proceeding are his allegations that he was detained and interrogated under abusive conditions, or that the CIA conducted the rendition program that has been acknowledged by United States officials. Facts such as those furnish the general terms in which El-Masri has related his story to the press, but advancing a case in the court of public opinion, against the United States at large, is an undertaking quite different from prevailing against specific defendants in a court of law. If El-Masri's civil action were to proceed, the facts central to its resolution would be the roles, if any, that the defendants played in the events he alleges. To establish a prima facie case, he would be obliged to produce admissible evidence not only that he was detained and interrogated, but that the defendants were involved in his detention and interrogation in a manner that renders them personally liable to him. Such a showing could be made only with evidence that exposes how the CIA organizes, staffs, and supervises its most sensitive intelligence operations. With regard to Director Tenet, for example, El-Masri would be obliged to show in detail how the head of the CIA participates in such operations, and how information concerning their progress is relayed to him. With respect to the defendant corporations and their unnamed employees, El-Masri would have to demonstrate the existence and details of CIA espionage contracts, an endeavor practically indistinguishable from that categorically barred by *Totten* and *Tenet v. Doe. See Totten v. United States,* 92 U.S. 105,

107 (1875) (establishing absolute bar to enforcement of confidential agreements to conduct espionage, on ground that "public policy forbids the maintenance of any suit in a court of justice, the trial of which would inevitably lead to the disclosure of matters which the law itself regards as confidential"); *Tenet v. Doe,* 544 U.S. 1, 10-11 (2005) (reaffirming *Totten* in unanimous decision). Even marshalling the evidence necessary to make the requisite showings would implicate privileged state secrets, because El-Masri would need to rely on witnesses whose identities, and evidence the very existence of which, must remain confidential in the interest of national security. *See Sterling,* [416 F.3d] at 347 ("[T]he very methods by which evidence would be gathered in this case are themselves problematic.").

b.

Furthermore, if El-Masri were somehow able to make out a prima facie case despite the unavailability of state secrets, the defendants could not properly defend themselves without using privileged evidence. The main avenues of defense available in this matter are to show that El-Masri was not subject to the treatment that he alleges; that, if he was subject to such treatment, the defendants were not involved in it; or that, if they were involved, the nature of their involvement does not give rise to liability. Any of those three showings would require disclosure of information regarding the means and methods by which the CIA gathers intelligence. If, for example, the truth is that El-Masri was detained by the CIA but his description of his treatment is inaccurate, that fact could be established only by disclosure of the actual circumstances of his detention, and its proof would require testimony by the personnel involved. Or, if El-Masri was in fact detained as he describes, but the operation was conducted by some governmental entity other than the CIA, or another government entirely, that information would be privileged. Alternatively, if the CIA detained El-Masri, but did so without Director Tenet's active involvement, effective proof thereof would require a detailed explanation of how CIA operations are supervised. Similarly, although an individual CIA officer might demonstrate his lack of involvement in a given operation by disclosing that he was actually performing some other function at the time in question, establishing his alibi would likely require him to reveal privileged information.

Moreover, proof of the involvement — or lack thereof — of particular CIA officers in a given operation would provide significant information on how the CIA makes its personnel assignments. Similar concerns would attach to evidence produced in defense of the corporate defendants and their unnamed employees. And, like El-Masri's prima facie case, any of the possible defenses suggested above would require the production of witnesses whose identities are confidential and evidence the very existence of which is a state secret. We do not, of course, mean to suggest that any of these hypothetical defenses represents the true state of affairs in this matter, but they illustrate that virtually any conceivable response to El-Masri's allegations would disclose privileged information....

C....

Contrary to El-Masri's assertion, the state secrets doctrine does not represent a surrender of judicial control over access to the courts. As we have explained, it is the court, not the Executive, that determines whether the state secrets privilege has been properly invoked. In order to successfully claim the state secrets privilege, the Executive must satisfy the court that disclosure of the information sought to be protected would expose matters that, in the interest of national security, ought to remain secret. Similarly, in order to win dismissal of an action on state secrets grounds, the Executive must persuade the court that state secrets are so central to the action that it cannot be fairly litigated without threatening their disclosure. The state secrets privilege cannot be successfully interposed, nor can it lead to dismissal of an action, based merely on the Executive's assertion that the pertinent standard has been met.

In this matter, the reasons for the United States' claim of the state secrets privilege and its motion to dismiss were explained largely in the Classified Declaration, which sets forth in detail the nature of the information that the Executive seeks to protect and explains why its disclosure would be detrimental to national security. We have reviewed the Classified Declaration, as did the district court, and the extensive information it contains is crucial to our decision in this matter. El-Masri's contention that his Complaint was dismissed based on the Executive's "unilateral assert[ion] of a need for secrecy" is entirely unfounded. It is no doubt frustrating to El-Masri that many of the specific reasons for the dismissal of his Complaint are classified. An inherent feature of the state secrets privilege, however, is that the party against whom it is asserted will often not be privy to the information that the Executive seeks to protect. That El-Masri is unfamiliar with the Classified Declaration's explanation for the privilege claim does not imply, as he would have it, that no such explanation was required, or that the district court's ruling was simply an unthinking ratification of a conclusory demand by the executive branch.

We also reject El-Masri's view that we are obliged to jettison procedural restrictions — including the law of privilege — that might impede our ability to act as a check on the Executive. Indeed, El-Masri's position in that regard fundamentally misunderstands the nature of our relationship to the executive branch. El-Masri envisions a judiciary that possesses a roving writ to ferret out and strike down executive excess. Article III, however, assigns the courts a more modest role: we simply decide cases and controversies. Thus, when an executive officer's liability for official action can be established in a properly conducted judicial proceeding, we will not hesitate to enter judgment accordingly. But we would be guilty of excess in our own right if we were to disregard settled legal principles in order to reach the merits of an executive action that would not otherwise be before us — especially when the challenged action pertains to military or foreign policy. We decline to follow such a course, and thus reject El-Masri's invitation to rule that the state secrets doctrine can be brushed aside on the ground that the President's foreign policy has gotten out of line. . . .

Affirmed.

Notes and Questions

1. *Invoking the State Secrets Privilege.* Because application of the privilege may have the draconian effect of ending a case or making it impossible to prove or to defend, the privilege must be asserted in writing by a senior government official who has personally examined the allegedly privileged material. In this case, the then-Director of

the CIA filed a declaration so stating, in two forms — one classified for the court's eyes only, and one redacted and unclassified for El-Masri and the public. In the Obama administration, a proposed invocation of the privilege was also reviewed by the "State Secrets Review Committee," composed of senior Department of Justice officials, who make a recommendation to the Deputy Attorney General. *See* Memorandum from the Attorney General for Heads of Executive Departments and Agencies, *Policies and Procedures Governing Invocation of the State Secrets Privilege* (Sept. 23, 2009), http://www.justice.gov/opa/documents/state-secret-privileges.pdf.

2. *Criteria for Invocation.* The common law standard is whether there is "a reasonable danger" that disclosure will expose military secrets that, in the interests of national security, should not be disclosed (whether or not the secret thereby shields unlawful government action). How could a court second-guess the sworn declaration of an agency head and make a contrary appraisal of the "interests of national security," interests that, according to the *El-Masri* court, ordinarily compel "utmost [judicial] deference"?

Do you think such extreme deference is always justified? In a case involving a warrantless wiretap of an alleged domestic terrorist, the Supreme Court observed, "We cannot accept the Government's argument that internal security matters are too subtle and complex for judicial evaluation. Courts regularly deal with the most difficult issues of our society. There is no reason to believe that federal judges will be insensitive to or uncomprehending of the issues involved in domestic security cases." *United States v. U.S. Dist. Ct.* (*Keith*), 407 U.S. 297, 320-321 (1972).

Might even a deferential application of the "reasonable danger" test flush out phony invocations of the privilege made to conceal wrongdoing or to prevent agency embarrassment? *See Mohamed v. Holder*, No. 1:11-cv-50 (AJT/TRJ), 2014 WL 11516538 (E.D. Va. Oct. 30, 2014) (finding that information presented by government was insufficient to meet the test in challenge to the plaintiff's listing on the No-Fly list, but also finding that the parties did not need allegedly secret evidence to present or defend against claims).

3. *United States v. Reynolds: A Cautionary Tale?* The Supreme Court's landmark 1953 decision in *Reynolds* grew out of the crash in 1948 of a B-29 bomber. Surviving family members of three civilian engineers who perished brought suit for damages under the Federal Tort Claims Act. When they sought access through discovery to the official accident report, the Supreme Court accepted without question the Air Force's assertion that disclosure of the report would "seriously hamper[] national security." 345 U.S. at 5. The Court refused even to order in camera review of the report. Yet when the report was declassified many years later, it was found to contain nothing that could apparently have been helpful to the nation's enemies, but instead to show pilot error, a failure to carry out special safety orders, and a history of maintenance problems with the B-29.

Despite this showing of apparent government misconduct, the Supreme Court denied without comment a motion for leave to file a petition for a writ of error *coram nobis* on June 23, 2003. *In re Herring*, 539 U.S. 940 (2003) (mem.). When the *Reynolds* survivors filed a new action in the federal district court where the case had been heard 54 years earlier, they were again denied relief because they were unable to show that government officials in 1953 had committed intentional fraud on the court. *Herring v. United States*, 424 F.3d 384 (3d Cir. 2005), *cert. denied*, 547 U.S. 1123 (2006).

Do you think these developments should affect the way courts consider state secrets privilege claims?

4. Consequences of Recognizing the State Secrets Privilege. Once the government has properly invoked the state secrets privilege, how should a court proceed? Disclosing the state secrets is not an option: "[A] court's determination that a piece of evidence is a privileged state secret removes it from the proceedings entirely." *El-Masri,* 479 F.3d at 306. A litigant will be denied discovery of information deemed subject to the privilege or denied the ability to introduce it into evidence. The litigant's need for the information or its relevance to the case at hand has no bearing on its discovery or admissibility once the court has determined that the information is privileged. (Note that a party may already possess the contested information but be barred from using it.)

Such a denial may not affect the eventual outcome of the case. After all, it is not a ruling on the use of *all* evidence in a case, it applies only to the "piece [or pieces] of evidence" that the court held privileged. But the privileged evidence may be the only evidence that would avoid summary judgment for the defendant, or that would enable a defendant to defend itself. It also may prevent a plaintiff from showing that she has an individual interest that entitles her to standing to sue. In *Halkin v. Helms,* 690 F.2d 977 (D.C. Cir. 1982), for example, the plaintiffs were unable to obtain records that might have shown that they were individually targeted by illegal FBI, CIA, Secret Service, and NSA surveillance of U.S. citizens opposed to the Vietnam War. What was the effect of the unavailability of the privileged evidence on El-Masri's ability to prove his claim and on the defendants' ability to defend themselves?

5. The Need for Secure Adjudication. Is *El-Masri*'s dismissal at the pleading stage, before the defendants were even required to answer, fair or necessary? Can you imagine how, in other circumstances, upholding a state secrets privilege might *not* require dismissal of the action? In *In re United States,* 872 F.2d 472, 477 (D.C. Cir. 1989), the court declared, "Dismissal of a suit, and the consequent denial of a forum without giving the plaintiff her day in court . . . is indeed draconian." The court ordered instead that the case "be tried to the bench, a circumstance that will reduce the threat of unauthorized disclosure of confidential material." *Id.* at 478. Other courts have sought to avoid the harsh effect of outright dismissal by employing a special master, *Loral Corp. v. McDonnell Douglas Corp.,* 558 F.2d 1130 (2d Cir. 1977); imposing protective orders, *In re Under Seal,* 945 F.2d 1285 (4th Cir. 1992); or even conducting a secret trial, *Halpern v. United States,* 258 F.2d 36 (2d Cir. 1958). A special court, organized along the lines of the Foreign Intelligence Surveillance Court (see *infra* p. 624), might also be created to deal with these difficult cases. Can you think of other ways to try such cases without undue risk? Should the *El-Masri* court have considered one of these alternatives?

6. Totten Bar vs. Reynolds Privilege. How is the "*Totten* bar" different from the state secrets privilege? As a categorical bar, *Totten* applies at the front of a lawsuit, as soon as the court is able to identify its subject matter as "inherently secret." It does not turn on a proffer-by-proffer evaluation of the evidence. The state secrets privilege, on the other hand, like other evidentiary privileges, has until recently been invoked as evidence is sought or offered during the course of litigation. Insofar as its application turns on specific evidence, it would ordinarily be inappropriate to invoke in a motion to dismiss, before an answer is filed, discovery has been taken, and any specific evidence has been sought or offered. Do you think the *El-Masri* court improperly conflated the two?

THE COURTS' NATIONAL SECURITY POWERS: SUMMARY OF PRINCIPLES

- Article III extends the judicial power to all cases arising under the Constitutions, the laws of the United States, and treaties, and Congress has by statute vested such "federal question" jurisdiction in the lower federal courts. Neither Article III nor the federal question statute exempts "national security cases."

- Article III standing is rooted partly in the constitutional case or controversy requirement and partly in judicial prudence. It requires (1) a concrete, particularized, and actual or certainly imminent injury, (2) fairly traceable to the challenged action, and (3) redressable by a favorable ruling. A ruling that the plaintiff lacks standing requires dismissal of that plaintiff's claims, but the standing doctrine is plaintiff-specific, not claim-specific; it would not necessarily preclude a differently situated plaintiff.

- The political question doctrine may be invoked to dismiss a claim. Although the Supreme Court has never defined a political question, it has identified its elements, including especially a textual commitment of the question to one or both of the political branches and the lack of a judicially manageable standard for resolving it. The doctrine is question-specific, and the threshold inquiry is always, what is the question? A finding that the question is a political question requires dismissal of any claim posing the question, whoever the claimant is.

- Merely concerned citizen plaintiffs who bring "good government" complaints cannot ordinarily meet the injury-in-fact requirement. Nor can members of Congress who complain of the executive branch's violation of law unless the illegal action "completely nullifies" their votes, a standard that is not met just because the Executive does something that Congress voted against.

- The ripeness doctrine is a prudential doctrine by which the courts avoid deciding claims before the political branches reach an impasse, in the hope that interbranch political negotiation and compromise will moot the claims.

- Although courts have awarded damages for constitutional violations under *Bivens* in the absence of statutory authority, implied causes of action are disfavored in new contexts or where special factors counsel hesitation. Courts have been especially reluctant to recognize such claims when they involve national security issues.

- Government defendants may enjoy qualified immunity from liability if the law they are accused of violating was not "clearly established" at the time of an alleged violation. By ruling for defendants on this ground, however, courts have avoided having to clearly establish the relevant law to guide government officials and courts in the future.
- If, on a formally asserted claim of the state secrets privilege, the government can show that there is a reasonable danger that discovery of information or its introduction into evidence at trial would jeopardize national security, the court must uphold the privilege. The court may then dismiss the suit if the plaintiff cannot establish a prima facie case or standing, or if the defendant cannot defend itself, without the privileged evidence.
- A case may be dismissed before trial if a trial poses too great a risk that state secrets would be exposed.

PART II

INTERNATIONAL LAW AND "OUR LAW"

6

The Domestic Effect of International Law

Charging a grand jury in a 1793 national security case, our first Chief Justice declared that "the laws of the United States admit of being classed under the three heads of descriptions. 1st. All treaties made under the authority of the United States. 2d. The laws of nations. 3dly. The constitution, and statutes of the United States." *Trial of Gideon Henfield* (C.C.D. Pa. 1793) (charge to the grand jury by Jay, C.J.), *reprinted in* Francis Wharton, *State Trials of the United States During the Administrations of Washington and Adams* 49, 52-53 (1849). John Jay thus indicated that at least some international agreements and customary international laws are part of our domestic law.

But which ones? And what is their effect in U.S. law? A thorough study of the framework of national security law must necessarily consider these questions, because so many national security actions implicate international law. This chapter provides an introduction to the making and interpretation of treaties and executive agreements under U.S. law, and the effect of such instruments and of customary international law on (and as) domestic national security law.

The Supremacy Clause declares that "all Treaties made, or which shall be made, under the Authority of the United States, shall be the supreme Law of the Land. . . ." U.S. Const. art. VI, cl. 2. But this provision fails to explain the effect of a treaty that requires domestic legislation for its execution or that is inconsistent with a statute, let alone the effect of executive agreements or customary international law.

In this chapter we begin by looking briefly at the treaty-making process and how treaties are interpreted under our law, then do the same for executive agreements. We next consider the domestic legal effect of treaties and executive agreements. After that, we address the statutory incorporation of international law into our own law. Finally, we analyze the domestic legal effect of customary international law that has not been expressly codified as our own law.

A. THE MAKING AND INTERPRETATION OF TREATIES[1]

Under international law, a treaty is "an international agreement governed by international law and concluded in written form between one or more States and one or more international organizations or between international organizations . . . whatever its particular designation." Vienna Convention on the Law of Treaties between States and International Organizations art. 2(1)(a), Mar. 21, 1986, 25 I.L.M. 543. In other words, it does not have to be designated a "treaty"; it could be called a convention, pact, protocol, accord, or agreement.

But under our Constitution, "treaties" for purposes of the Supremacy Clause are only those international agreements approved by a two-thirds vote of the Senate. U.S. Const. art. II, §2. However, the President is not constitutionally required to make international agreements by such treaties alone; he can also enter into what is termed an "executive agreement" with another state or states.

In the usual case, the executive branch negotiates an international agreement with a foreign state. If the agreement is to serve as a treaty under the Constitution, the President then transmits the agreement and any documents it considers to be integral parts of the treaty to the Senate for approval. Under Senate rules, the proposed treaty is referred to the Senate Foreign Relations Committee, which typically holds hearings on it. At the hearings, the Department of State ordinarily will send a witness to provide the Administration's view of the meaning and importance of the treaty.

If the Committee reports the treaty out favorably, the full Senate will vote on it. The Senate may approve it by a vote of at least two-thirds of the Senators present — with or without conditions ("understandings" concerning its meaning, or "reservations," or "amendments," which condition consent on amendment or limitation of the substantive obligations the treaty imposes) — or disapprove it.

Approval by the Senate is not "ratification." It is the President who ratifies an approved treaty by transmitting instruments of ratification to the treaty partners. If the Senate conditions its approval, the President communicates the conditions to the treaty partners in the instruments of ratification exchanged with them. Once these have been exchanged and any conditions satisfied, the President proclaims that the treaty is in force or will come into force according to its terms (for example, when some prescribed number of states have ratified it).

Notes and Questions

1. Negotiations — A Presidential Monopoly? The making of a treaty starts with the states parties' negotiation of its terms. Does the Senate have any role to play in the negotiations? According to one scholar, from the Framers' use of the phrase "Advice and Consent" to describe the Senate's constitutional role and from other evidence, "it is fair to say that the original understanding of the treaty Power

---

1. This brief account of the treaty process is based upon Cong. Research Serv., *Treaties and Other International Agreements: The Role of the United States Senate, A Study Prepared for the S. Comm. on Foreign Relations,* 106th Cong. 25-28 (Comm. Print 2001) (hereinafter *CRS Treaty Study*); *Relevance of Senate Ratification History to Treaty Interpretation,* 11 Op. O.L.C. 28 (1987); and Phillip R. Trimble, *International Law: United States Foreign Relations Law* 109-191 (2002).

envisioned Senate participation prior to the negotiation and conclusion of treaties." Trimble, *supra,* at 116.

What are the pros and cons of involving the Senate in treaty negotiations? This was John Jay's answer:

> It seldom happens in the negotiation of treaties, of whatever nature, but that perfect *secrecy* and immediate *dispatch* are sometimes requisite. These are cases where the most useful intelligence may be obtained, if the persons possessing it can be relieved from apprehensions of discovery. . . . [T]here doubtless are many . . . who would rely on the secrecy of the President, but who would not confide in that of the Senate, and still less in that of a large popular Assembly. The [constitutional] convention have done well, therefore, in so disposing of the power of making treaties that although the President must, in forming them, act by the advice and consent of the Senate, yet he will be able to manage the business of intelligence in such manner as prudence may suggest. [*The Federalist No. 64,* at 392-393 (John Jay) (Clinton Rossiter ed., 1961).]

By the end of the Washington administration, it became the President's custom merely to inform the Senate of proposed negotiations when it consented to his appointment of the negotiator and to submit to the Senate a copy of instructions to the negotiator only with the completed treaty. *See* Ralston Hayden, *The Senate and Treaties, 1789-1817,* at 105-106 (1920). Since then, the President has usually dominated the negotiating process and has typically consulted the Senate only after completing negotiations, when formally submitting the negotiated treaty to it for approval. *CRS Treaty Study, supra,* at 87.

Given this background, may the Senate alone or the Congress direct the President (or his delegate, the Secretary of State) to, say, "initiate negotiations as soon as possible for the development of bilateral or multilateral agreements with other nations" for the protection of sea turtles? *See* Pub. L. No. 101-162, §609(a)(1), 103 Stat. 988, 1037 (1989). In an opinion refusing an injunction to order the President to comply with such a statutory mandate, the court ruled that it

> has not and cannot lawfully order the Executive to comply with the terms of a statute that impinges upon power exclusively granted to the Executive Branch under the Constitution. . . . Because "the Constitution plainly grants the President the initiative in matters directly involved in the conduct of diplomatic" affairs, we cannot enforce the statute. [*Earth Island Inst. v. Christopher,* 6 F.3d 648, 653 (9th Cir. 1993) (internal citation omitted).]

Compare United States v. Curtiss-Wright Export Corp., 299 U.S. 304, 319 (1936) (dictum) (the President "alone negotiates. Into the field of negotiation the Senate cannot intrude; and Congress itself is powerless to invade it."), *with* Louis Fisher, *Congressional Participation in the Treaty Process,* 137 U. Pa. L. Rev. 1511, 1512 (1989) (asserting that a presidential monopoly of treaty negotiation is an "historical myth").

2. Consent. After a treaty has been negotiated and signed or initialed, it is submitted to the Senate for "advice and consent." *See generally CRS Treaty Study, supra,* at 87-93. Should the President also be required to submit the full negotiating record to the Senate Foreign Relations Committee to aid in its consideration of the treaty? Should Committee hearings on the treaty be conducted in public? What implications, if any, do your answers have for subsequent interpretation of a treaty?

3. To What Treaty Did the Senate Consent? An uncontroversial paraphrase of the Treaty Clause is that the President may make a treaty if the Senate has consented to it. A necessary corollary of this proposition is that "the President can only make the treaty to which the Senate consented; he cannot make a treaty other than the one to which the Senate consented." *The ABM Treaty and the Constitution: Joint Hearings Before the S. Comm. on Foreign Relations and S. Comm. on the Judiciary*, 100th Cong. 318 (1987) (hereinafter *ABM Treaty Hearings*) (statement of Professor Louis Henkin). But to what does the Senate consent and how do we divine that consent?

The Reagan administration claimed that "the Executive is, as a matter of domestic law, required to adhere to the interpretation of a treaty authoritatively shared with, and clearly intended, generally understood and relied upon by the Senate at the time of its advice and consent to ratification." Letter from White House Counsel Arthur B. Culvahouse to Senator Richard G. Lugar (Mar. 17, 1988), *reprinted in The INF Treaty*, S. Exec. Rep. No. 100-15, at 443 (1988). The Office of Legal Counsel (OLC) has opined:

> The weight to be given to an interpretative statement made by an Executive Branch official to the Senate during the ratification process will likely depend upon such factors as the formality of the statement, the identity and position of the Executive Branch official making the statement, the level of attention and interest focused on the meaning of the relevant treaty provision, and the consistency with which members of the Executive Branch adhered at the time to the view of the treaty provision reflected in the statement. [*Relevance of Senate Ratification History*, *supra*, 11 Op. O.L.C. at 37.]

In response to these claims by the Reagan administration, then-Senator Joseph Biden introduced Senate Resolution 167, which purported to set forth "constitutional principles" governing treaty interpretation. The resolution provided that "the meaning [of a treaty] is to be determined in light of what the Senate understands the treaty to mean when it gives its advice and consent." *The ABM Treaty Interpretation Resolution*, S. Rep. No. 100-164, at 117 (1987). That understanding, the resolution stated, is manifested by what the Senate formally expressed and also by "Senate approval or acceptance of, or Senate acquiescence in, interpretations of the treaty by the executive branch communicated to the Senate," but never "by matter of which it is not aware," *id.*, such as secret negotiations not communicated to it. The supporters of the Biden resolution also argued that "[i]mplicit understandings represent informal — but equally significant — legislative history," including hearings, committee reports, and floor debates. *The INF Treaty*, *supra*, at 439.

The so-called Biden Condition even provided that the Senate's unenacted "acquiescence" in executive branch interpretations was controlling. According to the OLC, however, absent explicit "conditions, the Senate does not participate in setting the terms of the agreement between the [treaty] parties, and therefore statements made by Senators, whether individually in hearings and debates or collectively in committee reports, should be accorded little weight unless confirmed by the Executive." 11 Op. O.L.C. at 34. Since the Senate knows how to formalize its interpretations in amendments and reservations, why should we look past such explicit conditions?

4. The Importance of the Negotiating Record. A negotiating record is an ill-defined and uneven collection of plenary statements read and exchanged by the negotiators, draft treaty texts prepared in the negotiations, and often numerous "memoranda of conversations" written after the fact by individual negotiators to summarize discussions. *See* David A. Koplow, *Constitutional Bait and Switch: Executive Reinterpretation of Arms Control Treaties,* 137 U. Pa. L. Rev. 1353, 1385-1386 (1989); *see also* Michael J. Glennon, *Constitutional Diplomacy* 139 (1991) (asserting that the "*negotiating record* is a term of art used to describe an *agreed* negotiating record, since it is only the joint intent of the parties that has significance under international law").

The Reagan administration contended that when a treaty is ambiguous, the Executive may resort to a secret negotiating record to resolve the ambiguity, even though the record has not been disclosed to the Senate. Supporters of the Biden Condition disagreed, asserting that legislative history unknown to the Senate "could not, logically, be part of the 'meeting of the minds' between the President and the Senate extant on the date of Senate consent." *The INF Treaty, supra,* at 439. Thus, according to Professor Laurence Tribe,

> the President cannot present one treaty to the Senate, accompanied by various formal submittals, obtain the consent of the Senate to that treaty based in part on those submittals, and then unveil a hitherto secret record of negotiations or understandings — either internal to the executive branch or between the executive and the foreign signatory to the treaty — to defend an interpretation of the treaty inconsistent with what the Senate had been led to believe it was accepting. [*ABM Treaty Hearings, supra,* at 417-418.]

If the Administration intends to resolve treaty ambiguities using a secret negotiating record, how would you, as Chief Counsel to the Senate Foreign Relations Committee, advise the Committee to proceed in hearings on submitted treaties?

5. Interpretative Deference to the Executive? The Supreme Court has stated that "[w]hile courts interpret treaties for themselves, the meaning given them by the departments of government particularly charged with their negotiation and enforcement is given great weight." *Kolovrat v. Oregon,* 366 U.S. 187, 194 (1961). In urging that the 1949 Geneva Conventions did not apply to the U.S. conflict in Afghanistan in 2002, Attorney General John Ashcroft advised President George W. Bush that "when a President determines that a treaty does not apply, his determination is fully discretionary and will not be reviewed by the federal courts." Letter of Att'y General John Ashcroft to President George W. Bush (Feb. 1, 2002), *available at* https://nsarchive2.gwu.edu/torturingdemocracy/documents/20020201.pdf. Is this advice consistent with the weight suggested by the Supreme Court? Or the role assigned to the courts by Article III?

6. Terminating Treaties. In *Goldwater v. Carter,* 617 F.2d 697 (D.C. Cir.) (per curiam), *vacated and remanded,* 444 U.S. 996 (1979) (mem.), Senator Barry Goldwater challenged the constitutionality of President Jimmy Carter's unilateral termination of a U.S. Mutual Defense Treaty with Taiwan. The Court of Appeals sided with the President, rejecting the argument that treaties must be terminated in the same way they are approved — with the advice and consent of the Senate — noting, *inter alia*, that the President's comparable unilateral power to remove ambassadors appointed with Senate approval had never been questioned. The Supreme Court subsequently vacated the opinion on justiciability grounds, leaving the question of termination authority unsettled.

The President has terminated other treaties unilaterally from time to time. This history is described in *Restatement (Fourth) of Foreign Relations Law of the United States* §313 rptrs. note 3 (Am. Law Inst. 2018). What sort of history would demonstrate constitutional power in the President to terminate treaties? See *supra* p. 36, describing a theory of constitutional customary law based on congressional acquiescence. According to one scholar, "[t]reaty termination is an especially rich example of how governmental practices can inform and even define the Constitution's separation of powers." Curtis A. Bradley, *Treaty Termination and Historical Gloss*, 92 Tex. L. Rev. 773 (2014).

In 2002, 32 members of the House of Representatives challenged the President's unilateral withdrawal from the 1972 Treaty on the Limitation of Anti-Ballistic Missile Systems (ABM Treaty), May 26, 1972, U.S.-U.S.S.R., 23 U.S.T. 3435. *Kucinich v. Bush*, 236 F. Supp. 2d 1 (D.D.C. 2002). Despite the enormous strategic significance of the withdrawal, the court dismissed the case on grounds that the congressional plaintiffs lacked standing to sue, citing *Raines v. Byrd*, 521 U.S. 811 (1987), analyzed *supra* p. 139. It also held that the case presented a nonjusticiable political question, citing *Goldwater*.

More recently, in 2019, President Trump formally announced that the United States was withdrawing from the Treaty on the Elimination of Intermediate-Range and Shorter-Range Missiles (INF Treaty), Dec. 8, 1987, U.S.-U.S.S.R., 27 I.L.M. 84, signed by Ronald Reagan and Mikhail Gorbachev. Who would have standing to maintain a challenge to this treaty termination? How would you argue that Senate approval was required?

B. EXECUTIVE AND OTHER AGREEMENTS

Reading *Dames & Moore v. Regan*

In this case, the plaintiff challenged executive action nullifying its prejudgment attachment of Iranian assets, which the President ordered pursuant to an agreement with Iran. The executive agreement required the United States to terminate U.S. legal proceedings involving claims against Iran in return for the release of Iranian-held American hostages. The claims would be settled instead by international arbitration.

- What kind of agreement was it?
- What constitutional text or practice authorizes the making of such agreements?
- How is such an agreement different from a treaty? Note that international and domestic law may give different answers to this question.

Dames & Moore v. Regan

United States Supreme Court, 1981
453 U.S. 654

[The opinion is set forth *supra* p. 38.]

Notes and Questions

1. *The Death(?) of Article II Treaties and the Explosion in Executive Agreements.* The international agreement involved in *Dames & Moore* was clearly not a treaty: not only does the Court never call it a treaty, but the Senate had never formally approved it. It was, instead, an agreement made by the Executive acting alone. In the half-century before World War II, executive agreements outnumbered treaties by a factor of only two to one. In the next 60 years, the discrepancy rose to almost 12 to 1. By the 1980s, the United States was entering into 300-400 executive agreements per year, compared to 8-26 treaties per year. *CRS Treaty Study, supra,* at 39-40. The agreements cover such diverse national security subjects as collective security, arms control and disarmament, status of U.S. forces stationed abroad, extradition, human rights, cease-fires, armistices and peace terms, military cooperation, and presumably intelligence collection and sharing.

As the number of executive agreements has increased, the number of treaties has decreased. President George W. Bush submitted more than 100 treaties to the Senate during his two terms (about the historical average from 1930 to 1999). President Obama submitted 38 during his two terms. President Trump submitted one during his first two years in office (a treaty amending an earlier fisheries agreement). One reason for the decrease may be an administration's prioritization of treaties. Another may be more mundane: much of the work of treaty-making has been completed since World War II. *See* Curtis Bradley, Oona Hathaway & Jack Goldsmith, *The Death of Article II Treaties?*, Lawfare, Dec. 13, 2018.

A more important reason may be that Presidents are increasingly substituting executive agreements for treaties. Why would they do that?

2. *Types of Executive Agreements.* Executive agreements can be categorized by the source of domestic legal authority. *See CRS Treaty Study, supra,* at 76-95; *Restatement (Third) of Foreign Relations Law of the United States* §303 (Am. Law Inst. 1987). The first category consists of *congressional-executive agreements.* Congress either expressly enacts such agreements or, more commonly, delegates the authority to make them to the President. We saw in Chapter 3 that the courts have routinely sustained such delegations. *See, e.g., Field v. Clark,* 143 U.S. 649 (1892) (sustaining a foreign affairs delegation under which reciprocal trade agreements were made by the Executive).

The second category consists of *agreements made pursuant to treaty,* either by express authorization or by reasonable inference. Although the legal authority for treaty agreements has not been fully explored in the cases, in *Wilson v. Girard,* 354 U.S. 524, 528-529 (1957), the Supreme Court suggested that the Senate's approval of a treaty impliedly authorized the agreements necessary to carry it out.

The 1981 Algiers Accords, which provided for the release of U.S. hostages held by Iran and the resolution of certain claims against Iran, fell into a third, more controversial category of executive agreements: *sole executive agreements.* What constitutional authority would you cite for that type of agreement? *See United States v. Belmont,* 301 U.S. 324, 330-331 (1937) (citing the President's role as sole organ of foreign relations in finding an executive agreement "within [his] competence"). Sole executive agreements are legally most controversial because neither the Senate nor the House clearly approves their making. But they were historically relatively rare and typically confined to routine matters like exchanging information, holding consultations, and facilitating specific kinds of cooperation. Trimble, *supra* p. 170, at 115. The Court in *Dames & Moore* determined that Congress had acquiesced in a number of sole executive claims adjustment agreements comparable to the Algiers Accords, placing them somewhere between the first and third categories described here.

3. Executive Agreements and the Constitutional Text. The Constitution expressly mentions treaties and describes the procedure for their making as well as their force and effect. Does the Constitution identify any other kind of international agreement? *See Ntakirutimana v. Reno,* 184 F.3d 419, 426 (5th Cir. 1999) (endorsing the assertion that the Constitution apparently contemplates other kinds of international agreements). What textual constitutional arguments can you make for and against the constitutionality of executive agreements in general? *See* U.S. Const. art. I, §10, cl. 3. One scholar argues that sole executive "agreements were clearly part of Crown prerogative and the eighteenth century concept of executive power. Not having been removed from the executive, like participation in the treaty power [given partly to the Senate], they fall comfortably within the Vesting Clause." Trimble, *supra,* at 132.

4. The Interchangeability of Sole Executive Agreements and Treaties. Are there some putative sole executive agreements for which the treaty process is constitutionally required? If not, what becomes of the Treaty Clause? If so, what differentiates permissible sole executive agreements from agreements for which the treaty process is required? Professor Louis Henkin suggests that "[o]ne is compelled to conclude that there are agreements which the President can make on his sole authority and others which he can make only with the consent of the Senate, but neither Justice Sutherland nor any one else has told us which are which." Louis Henkin, *Foreign Affairs and the Constitution* 179 (1972). Do you think the President has constitutional authority to make a sole executive agreement that would require the United States to use military force to protect an ally against attack? If so, would the agreement also provide domestic authority for such use of force?

5. The Interchangeability of Congressional-Executive Agreements and Treaties. Congressional-executive agreements require approval by a simple majority of each House, while treaties require approval by a supermajority of the Senate. Consequently, some multilateral or bilateral national security undertakings that could obtain the requisite approval as congressional-executive agreements might fail as treaties. Are there some putative congressional-executive agreements for which the treaty process is constitutionally required? If so, how can they be identified?

The State Department lists the following "considerations for selecting among constitutionally authorized procedures": degree of commitment or risk involved, intent to override state laws, need for subsequent legislation, past practice for similar agreements, congressional preference, degree of formality desired, proposed duration, need for prompt conclusion, and general international practice. *Treaties and Other International Agreements,* in 2 *Foreign Affairs Manual* ch. 700 (rev. Feb. 25, 1985), reprinted in *CRS Treaty Study, supra* p. 170, at 301.

6. International Effects of Executive Agreements. Under international law, a treaty is any international agreement between states that is governed by international law. An executive agreement that the parties intend to be "governed by international law" is therefore legally binding under the customary international law principle *pacta sunt servanda* ("all agreements must be kept").

But what about an executive agreement that the parties do not intend to be *legally* binding? Sometimes once called a "gentleman's agreement" in a less politically correct age, it has been defined as "an agreement between two or more nations in which the parties intend to establish commitments *of an exclusively political or moral nature.*" Duncan B. Hollis & Joshua J. Newcomer, *"Political" Commitments and the Constitution,* 49 Va. J. Int'l L. 507, 517 (2009) (emphasis added); *see* Transmittal of the Treaty with the U.S.S.R. on the Reduction and Limitation of Strategic Offensive Arms (START Treaty), Nov. 25, 1991, S. Treaty Doc. No. 102-20, at 1086 ("A 'political' undertaking is not governed by international law. . . . Until and unless a party extricates itself from its 'political undertaking,' which it may do without legal penalty, it has given a promise to honor that commitment, and the other Party has every reason to be concerned about compliance with such undertakings. If a Party contravenes a political commitment, it will be subject to an appropriate political response.").

Examples abound: the Atlantic Charter, which was a basis for the Allied Powers' coordination in World War II; the Shanghai Communique, which helped establish modern relations with China; the Helsinki Accords, which created an institutional forum for conducting dialogues during the Cold War on human rights and other subjects; the Algiers Accords, which resulted in Iran's release of American hostages; and, in 2015, the Joint Comprehensive Plan of Action (JCPOA or Iran Nuclear Deal), negotiated with Iran by the United States and its allies to lift sanctions against Iran in return for a curtailment (or slowdown) of Iran's development of a nuclear weapon capability. *See* Hollis & Newcomer, *supra,* at 510. Recall that *Dames & Moore, supra* p. 38, indicates not only that the President can unilaterally make such non-binding political commitments based upon long-standing and consistent executive practice with notice to Congress, but also that such commitments have binding domestic legal effect. Of course, that such a gentleman's agreement may be constitutional does not necessarily make it wise. *See* David S. Jonas & Dyllan M. Taxman, *JCP-No-Way: A Critique of the Iran Nuclear Deal as a Non-Legally Binding Political Commitment,* 9 J. Nat'l Security L. & Pol'y 589 (2018) (so arguing).

7. Breaking a "Gentlemen's Agreement." While the United States and other nations were negotiating with Iran about the latter's nuclear weapons program, 47 Republican Senators wrote to Iranian leaders that the signatories would "consider any agreement regarding your nuclear-weapons program that is not approved by the Congress as nothing more than an executive agreement between President Obama and Ayatollah Khameni" that could be abrogated by the next President "with the stroke of a pen." Open letter from Tom Cotton et al. to the Leaders of the Islamic Republic of

Iran (Mar. 9, 2015), *available at* https://www.cotton.senate.gov/?p=press_release&id=120. Some read the letter as implying that the President was constitutionally obliged to obtain either Senate or bicameral approval for any deal with Iran. Were they correct? What other reading is consistent with customary practice?

Iran's Foreign Minister responded, "I wish to enlighten the authors that if the next administration revokes any agreement with the stroke of a pen, as they boast, it will have simply committed a blatant violation of international law." Was he right? *See* Debra Cassens Weiss, *Did GOP Authors of Iran Letter Get International Law Wrong?*, ABA J., Mar. 11, 2015.

In spite of Senator Cotton's warning, President Obama on behalf of the United States, and the other four permanent members of the U.N. Security Council — Russia, China, France, and the United Kingdom — plus Germany and the European Union, approved the Joint Comprehensive Plan of Action (JCPOA) with Iran on July 14, 2015. In the JCPOA the United States and its allies agreed to lift sanctions against Iran in return for a curtailment (or slowdown) of Iran's development of a nuclear weapon capability. Was the agreement internationally binding on the parties? If not, did it have any practical effect at all? What would have been the legal consequences if Iran were found to have continued developing nuclear weapons in derogation of such a commitment?

On May 8, 2018, President Trump used his "stroke of the pen" to sign a presidential memorandum withdrawing the United States from the JCPOA and reimposing U.S. sanctions on Iran. Donald J. Trump, *Ceasing U.S. Participation in the JCPOA and Taking Additional Action to Counter Iran's Malign Influence and Deny Iran All Paths to a Nuclear Weapon* (May 8, 2018). *See generally* Kenneth Katzman, Paul K. Kerr & Valerie Heithusen, *U.S. Decision to Cease Implementing the Iran Nuclear Agreement* (Cong. Res. Serv. R44942), May 9, 2018. Because both Administrations treated the JCPOA as a nonbinding political commitment relying only on "voluntary measures," rather than as a binding international agreement, the withdrawal was arguably lawful as a matter of domestic law. *See* Stephen P. Mulligan, *Withdrawal from the Iran Nuclear Deal: Legal Authorities and Implications* 1-2 (Cong. Res. Serv. LSB10134, May 17, 2018); Jimmy Chalk, *Can President-Elect Trump "Dismantle" the JCPOA? It's Complicated*, Lawfare, Nov. 17, 2016 (JCPOA "is no more binding on the parties than a handshake").

But the JCPOA was "endorsed" by U.N. Security Council Resolution 2231, S.C. Res. 2231, U.N. Doc. S/RES/2231 (July 20, 2015), which "calls on member states" to take actions to support the implementation of the agreement. Did the Security Council resolution create a treaty-based obligation of the United States to implement JCPOA? Or is "calls on" merely a hortatory, nonbinding expression? See *infra* pp. 242, 247.

8. The Case-Zablocki Act: A Congressional Limit on Agreements. Congress has long worried about erosion of the treaty power in light of the increasing number of executive agreements. In 1961, Congress enacted the Arms Control and Disarmament Act, which provides that "no action shall be taken under this or any other law that will obligate the United States to disarm or to reduce or to limit the Armed Forces or armaments of the United States, except pursuant to the treaty making power of the President under the Constitution or unless authorized by further affirmative legislation by the Congress of the United States." Pub. L. No. 87-297, §33, 75 Stat. 631, 634 (codified as amended at 22 U.S.C. §2573(b) (2018)). Is this provision constitutional in all its applications?

Nine years later Congress enacted the broader Case-Zablocki Act, requiring the President to make a timely submission to Congress of "the text of any international agreement (including the text of any oral international agreement, which agreement shall be reduced to writing) other than a treaty." Pub. L. No. 92-404, 86 Stat. 619 (1972) (codified as amended at 1 U.S.C. §112b(a) (2018)). The Act provides that the President may submit classified agreements to the Senate Committee on Foreign Relations and the House Committee on International Affairs with an injunction of secrecy. Does the Act validate sole executive agreements by implication? Presidents Nixon, Ford, and Carter made secret agreements regarding South Vietnam, the Sinai, and disarmament, respectively, which they labeled "arrangements" or "accords" to avoid reporting. Does such labeling avoid the Case-Zablocki Act?

C. THE DOMESTIC LEGAL EFFECT OF TREATIES AND EXECUTIVE AGREEMENTS

The Supremacy Clause clearly elevates treaties as the Supreme Law of the Land over state laws. U.S. Const. art. VI, cl. 2. Less clearly, it has been periodically interpreted to give executive agreements that same status, either as a form of "treaty" or as "laws of the United States." But this means only that treaties and executive agreements are supreme over state law, not that they are necessarily equal to one another. William C. Banks, *Treaties and Treaty Power*, in *Oxford Companion to the Supreme Court of the United States* 878 (Kermit L. Hall ed., 1992). The Supremacy Clause also fails to indicate expressly whether a statute or a treaty takes precedence when the two are inconsistent.

Reading *Reid v. Covert*

The United States often enters into status-of-forces executive agreements (SOFAs) with foreign countries in which U.S. armed forces are stationed. The agreements discussed in *Reid* provided that U.S. military dependents could be tried by U.S. courts-martial without a jury trial for certain crimes committed abroad.

Mrs. Covert killed her husband, a U.S. Air Force sergeant, at an airbase in England. Pursuant to a "status-of-forces" executive agreement with that country, she was tried and convicted by U.S. court-martial without a jury trial under the Uniform Code of Military Justice (UCMJ). In a petition for a writ of habeas corpus, she attacked her conviction on the grounds that it violated her Fifth and Sixth Amendment rights to be tried by a jury after indictment by a grand jury. The district court granted the petition, and this appeal followed. Mrs. Covert's appeal was consolidated with a like appeal by Mrs. Smith, who had been tried and convicted for a similar offense in similar fashion in Japan.

- What constitutional rights did the executive agreements apparently violate?
- What two reasons did the Court give for concluding that the executive agreements were subordinate to the defendants' constitutional rights?

Reid v. Covert

United States Supreme Court, 1957
354 U.S. 1

Mr. Justice BLACK announced the judgment of the Court and delivered an opinion, in which THE CHIEF JUSTICE, Mr. Justice DOUGLAS, and Mr. Justice BRENNAN join. . . .

I.

[The four-Justice plurality first held that the Fifth and Sixth Amendments protect American citizens abroad.]

II.

At the time of Mrs. Covert's alleged offense, an executive agreement was in effect between the United States and Great Britain which permitted United States military courts to exercise exclusive jurisdiction over offenses committed in Great Britain by American servicemen or their dependents. For its part, the United States agreed that these military courts would be willing and able to try and to punish all offenses against the laws of Great Britain by such persons. In all material respects, the same situation existed in Japan when Mrs. Smith killed her husband. Even though a court-martial does not give an accused trial by jury and other Bill of Rights protections, the Government contends that Art. 2(11) of U.C.M.J., insofar as it provides for the military trial of dependents accompanying the armed forces in Great Britain and Japan, can be sustained as legislation which is necessary and proper to carry out the United States' obligations under the international agreements made with those countries. The obvious and decisive answer to this, of course, is that no agreement with a foreign nation can confer power on the Congress, or on any other branch of Government, which is free from the restraints of the Constitution.

Article VI, the Supremacy Clause of the Constitution, declares:

> This Constitution, and the Laws of the United States which shall be made in Pursuance thereof; and all Treaties made, or which shall be made, under the Authority of the United States, shall be the supreme Law of the Land; . . .

There is nothing in this language which intimates that treaties and laws enacted pursuant to them do not have to comply with the provisions of the Constitution. Nor is there anything in the debates which accompanied the drafting and ratification of the Constitution which even suggests such a result. These debates as well as the history that surrounds the adoption of the treaty provision in Article VI make it clear that the reason treaties were not limited to those made in "pursuance" of the Constitution was so that agreements made by the United States under the Articles of Confederation, including the important peace treaties which concluded the Revolutionary War, would remain in effect. It would be manifestly contrary to the objectives of those who created the Constitution, as well as those who were responsible for the Bill of Rights — let alone alien to our entire constitutional history and tradition — to construe Article VI as permitting the United

States to exercise power under an international agreement without observing constitutional prohibitions. In effect, such construction would permit amendment of that document in a manner not sanctioned by Article V. The prohibitions of the Constitution were designed to apply to all branches of the National Government and they cannot be nullified by the Executive or by the Executive and the Senate combined.

There is nothing new or unique about what we say here. This Court has regularly and uniformly recognized the supremacy of the Constitution over a treaty.[33] For example, in *Geofroy v. Riggs*, 133 U.S. 258, 267, it declared:

> The treaty power, as expressed in the Constitution, is in terms unlimited except by those restraints which are found in that instrument against the action of the government or of its departments, and those arising from the nature of the government itself and of that of the States. It would not be contended that it extends so far as to authorize what the Constitution forbids, or a change in the character of the government or in that of one of the States, or a cession of any portion of the territory of the latter, without its consent.

This Court has also repeatedly taken the position that an Act of Congress, which must comply with the Constitution, is on a full parity with a treaty, and that when a statute which is subsequent in time is inconsistent with a treaty, the statute to the extent of conflict renders the treaty null.[34] It would be completely anomalous to say that a treaty need not comply with the Constitution when such an agreement can be overridden by a statute that must conform to that instrument....

In summary, we conclude that the Constitution in its entirety applied to the trials of Mrs. Smith and Mrs. Covert. Since their court-martial did not meet the requirements of Art. III, §2, or the Fifth and Sixth Amendments we are compelled to determine if there is anything *within* the Constitution which authorizes the military trial of dependents accompanying the armed forces overseas....

[The opinions of Justices HARLAN and FRANKFURTER, concurring in the result, and Justice CLARK, dissenting, are omitted here. Justice WHITTAKER took no part in the consideration or decision of the case.]

[Other parts of this decision are reproduced *infra* p. 210

---

33. We recognize that executive agreements are involved here but it cannot be contended that such an agreement rises to greater stature than a treaty.

34. In *Whitney v. Robertson*, 124 U.S. 190, 194, the Court stated: "By the Constitution a treaty is placed on the same footing, and made of like obligation, with an act of legislation. Both are declared by that instrument to be the supreme law of the land, and no superior efficacy is given to either over the other.... [I]f the two are inconsistent, the one last in date will control the other...."

Reading *Committee of U.S. Citizens Living in Nicaragua v. Reagan*

In 1986, the International Court of Justice (ICJ) ruled that U.S. support for paramilitary activities against the government of Nicaragua violated both an international treaty and customary international law. *Military and Paramilitary Activities in and Against Nicaragua* (Nicar. v. U.S.), 1986 I.C.J. 14 (June 27) (*infra* p. 249). Despite this ruling, Congress continued appropriating funds for such support.

The plaintiffs, organizations and individuals, then sued to enjoin the ongoing U.S. funding, relying in part on U.N. Charter Art. 94, which provides that each member of the United Nations "undertakes to comply with the decision of the [ICJ] in any case to which it is a party." The U.S. Senate consented to the U.N. Charter, a multilateral treaty, in 1946.

- The appropriation of funds for the paramilitary activities was made by a statute. Assuming that the statute was inconsistent with the obligation imposed by the U.N. Charter provision, why did the statute trump the treaty? By the court's reasoning, could a treaty ever trump a statute?
- But *was* the statute inconsistent with the obligation imposed by the Charter? What rule of construction does the court seemingly use to explore this question? Why does it apply this (implicit) rule of construction?
- If the statute does trump the Charter obligation, does it make the treaty obligation null and void?
- The Court concludes by asserting that even if the appropriation did violate the Charter obligation, the plaintiffs cannot enforce the latter. Why not? When, if ever, can a private litigant enforce a treaty obligation?

Committee of U.S. Citizens Living in Nicaragua v. Reagan

United States Court of Appeals, D.C. Circuit, 1988
859 F.2d 929

MIKVA, Circuit Judge: . . .

B. Appellants Have No Basis in Domestic Law for Enforcing the ICJ Judgment

1. The Status of International Law in the United States' Domestic Legal Order

Appellants argue that the United States' decision to disregard the ICJ judgment . . . violate[s] part of a United States treaty, namely Article 94 of the U.N. Charter. That article provides that "[e]ach Member of the United Nations undertakes to comply with the decision of the International Court of Justice in any case to which it is a party." . . .

For purposes of the present lawsuit, the key question is not simply whether the United States has violated any . . . legal norms but whether such violations can be remedied by an American court or whether they can only be redressed on an international level. In short, do violations of international law have domestic legal consequences? The answer largely depends on what form the "violation" takes. Here, the alleged violation is the law that Congress enacted and that the President signed, appropriating funds for the Contras. When our government's two political branches, acting together, contravene an international legal norm, does this court have any authority to remedy the violation? The answer is "no" if the type of international obligation that Congress and the President violate is either a treaty or a rule of customary international law....

2. The Effect of Subsequent Statutes upon Prior Inconsistent Treaties

Although appellants' complaint alleges that Congress' funding of the Contras violates Article 94 of the U.N. Charter, appellants seem to concede here that such a claim is unavailing. They acknowledge, as they must, that "[o]rdinarily, treaty obligations may be overridden by subsequent inconsistent statutes."...

In the *Head Money Cases,* 112 U.S. 580 (1884), shipping companies protested payment of a tax on immigrants they had transported to America, arguing that the tax violated treaties of friendship with the immigrants' nations of origin. The Court held that, even if the statute requiring the tax was inconsistent with prior treaties, it necessarily displaced any conflicting treaty provisions for purposes of domestic law.

> A treaty, then, is a law of the land as an act of Congress is, whenever its provisions prescribe a rule by which the rights of the private citizen or subject may be determined....
>
> But even [so]...there is nothing in [a treaty] which makes it irrepealable or unchangeable. The Constitution gives it no superiority over an act of Congress in this respect, which may be repealed or modified by an act of a later date....
>
> In short, we are of the opinion that, so far as a treaty made by the United States with any foreign nation can become the subject of judicial cognizance in the courts of this country, it is subject to such acts as Congress may pass for its enforcement, modification, or repeal. [*Id.* at 598-599.]

No American court has wavered from this view in the subsequent century. Indeed, in a comparatively recent case, our court reaffirmed the principle that treaties and statutes enjoy equal status and therefore that inconsistencies between the two must be resolved in favor of the *lex posterior.* In *Diggs v. Shultz,* 470 F.2d 461 (D.C. Cir. 1972), *cert. denied,* 411 U.S. 931 (1973), this court reviewed a claim by citizens of what was then Southern Rhodesia, assailing the United States' failure to abide by U.N. Security Council Resolution 232. That resolution directed U.N. members to impose a trade embargo against Rhodesia. The court found that America's contravention of Resolution 232 was required by Congress' adoption of the so-called Byrd Amendment "whose purpose and effect...was to detach this country from the U.N. boycott of Southern Rhodesia in blatant disregard of our treaty undertakings." *Id.* at 466. "Under our constitutional scheme," the court concluded, "Congress can denounce treaties if it sees fit to do so, and there is nothing the other branches of government can do about it... [; thus] the complaint [states] no tenable claim in law." *Id.* at 466-467.

These precedents dispose of any claim by appellants that the United States has violated its treaty obligation under Article 94. It is true, of course, that the facts here differ somewhat from the situation in *Diggs.* Congress has not clearly repudiated the requirement in Article 94 that every nation comply with an ICJ decision "in any case to which it is a party." U.N. Charter, art. 94. Rather, our government asserts that it never consented to ICJ jurisdiction in cases like the Nicaragua dispute. Thus, Congress may well believe that its support for the Contras, while contravening the ICJ judgment, does not violate its treaty obligation under Article 94. And, unless Congress makes clear its intent to abrogate a treaty, a court will not lightly infer such intent but will strive to harmonize the conflicting enactments.

At this stage of the present case, however, the key question is not whether Congress intended to abrogate Article 94. Since appellants *allege* that Congress has breached Article 94, we must determine whether such a claim could ever prevail. The claim could succeed only if appellants could prove that a prior treaty — the U.N. Charter — preempts a subsequent statute, namely the legislation that funds the Contras. It is precisely that argument that the precedents of the Supreme Court and of this court foreclose. We therefore hold that appellants' claims based on treaty violations must fail.

Our conclusion, of course, speaks not at all to whether the United States has upheld its treaty obligations under international law. As the Supreme Court said in the *Head Money Cases*, a treaty "depends for the enforcement of its provisions on the interest and honor of the governments which are parties to it. If these fail, its infraction becomes the subject of international negotiations and reclamations . . . [but] with all this the judicial courts have nothing to do and can give no redress." 112 U.S. at 598. This conclusion reflects the United States' adoption of a partly "dualist" — rather than strictly "monist" — view of international and domestic law. "[D]ualists view international law as a discrete legal system [which] . . . operates wholly on an inter-nation plane." Louis Henkin, *The Constitution and United States Sovereignty: A Century of Chinese Exclusion and Its Progeny*, 100 Harv. L. Rev. 853, 864 (1987) (hereinafter Henkin, *United States Sovereignty*).

It is uncertain whether either our republican form of government or our Constitution's supremacy clause requires this subordination of treaties to inconsistent domestic statutes. Nevertheless, the "[Supreme] Court's jurisprudence about treaties inevitably reflects certain assumptions about the relation between international law and United States law." Henkin, *United States Sovereignty*, 100 Harv. L. Rev. at 870. Given that dualist jurisprudence, we cannot find — as a matter of *domestic* law — that congressional enactments violate prior treaties.

Finally, we note that even if Congress' breach of a treaty were cognizable in domestic court, appellants would lack standing to rectify the particular breach that they allege here. Article 94 of the U.N. Charter simply does not confer rights on private individuals. Treaty clauses must confer such rights in order for individuals to assert a claim "arising under" them. See U.S. Const. art. III, §2, cl. 1; 28 U.S.C. §1331 (1982). Whether a treaty clause does create such enforcement rights is often described as part of the larger question of whether that clause is "self-executing."

This court has noted that, in "determining whether a treaty is self-executing" in the sense of its creating private enforcement rights, "courts look to the intent of the signatory parties as manifested by the language of the instrument." *Diggs v. Richardson*, 555 F.2d 848, 851 (D.C. Cir. 1976). The court in *Diggs v. Richardson* concluded that the U.N. Security Council Resolution that plaintiffs sought to enforce (which barred commercial relations between U.N. members and Namibia) was "not addressed to the judicial branch of our government." *Id.* The resolution's provisions did not "by their terms confer rights upon individual citizens [but] call[ed] upon governments to take certain actions." *Id.* Applying the same test to Article 94 of the U.N. Charter, we reach a similar conclusion.

The second paragraph of Article 94 provides that,

> [i]f any party to a case fails to perform the obligations incumbent upon it under a judgment rendered by the [ICJ], the other party may have recourse to the Security Council, which may, if it deems necessary, make recommendations or decide upon measures to be taken to give effect to the judgment. [U.N. Charter art. 94, ¶2.]

Because only nations can be parties before the ICJ, appellants are not "parties" within the meaning of this paragraph. Clearly, this clause does not contemplate that individuals having no relationship to the ICJ case should enjoy a private right to enforce the ICJ's decision. Our interpretation of Article 94 is buttressed by a related provision in the Statute of the ICJ, which is incorporated by reference in the U.N. Charter. See U.N. Charter art. 92. The Statute provides that "[t]he decision of the Court has no binding force except between the parties and in respect of th[e] particular case." Taken together, these Charter clauses make clear that the purpose of establishing the ICJ was to resolve disputes between national governments. We find in these clauses no intent to vest citizens who reside in a U.N. member nation with authority to enforce an ICJ decision against their own government. . . .

Notes and Questions

1. *The Supremacy Clause.* The Supremacy Clause declares treaties to be the supreme law of the land, but says the same of "Laws of the United States." It thus arguably assigns the same legal effect to treaties and statutes. If a particular international agreement is the legal equivalent of a statute, then why, according to the *Committee of U.S. Citizens* decision, can it be modified or superseded by statute — and vice-versa? *See Restatement (Fourth) of Foreign Relations Law* §309.

The Supremacy Clause also declares the Constitution to be supreme law, apparently placing it on the same plane with treaties. How, then, could a constitutional provision trump a treaty? The plurality reasoned in *Reid* that if it did not, then a treaty could amend the Constitution, which would supplant the Article V amendment process. 354 U.S. at 17. Moreover, said the Court, if the rule were otherwise, a treaty could trump the Constitution, whereas an equally "supreme" statute could not, as only statutes made "in Pursuance" of the Constitution qualify — an anomaly avoided by the Constitution-trumps-all principle. *Id.* at 18.

The status-of-force agreements in *Reid* were not treaties, but Justice Black's opinion reasoned that "it cannot be contended that such an agreement rises to greater stature than a treaty." *Id.* at 17 n.33. Hence they could not trump the constitutional right to a jury trial after indictment by a grand jury.

2. *The "Charming Betsy" Rule of Avoiding Conflict with International Law.* Did the appropriation for the Contra rebels in Nicaragua nullify the 1986 ICJ decision and the U.N. Charter provision requiring compliance with that decision? Clearly, as a matter of international law, the answer is no. The United States still had the same *international law* obligations after the appropriation statute was enacted. Continued U.S. support pursuant to the congressional appropriation violated international law, even though its acts were perfectly lawful under *domestic law.* As the court pointed out in *Committee of U.S. Citizens,* the United States recognizes two distinct, possibly conflicting, bodies of law covering the same subject. This is the principle of "dualism."

U.S. courts have long sought to avoid such conflicts by employing the *Charming Betsy* rule of construction: "an Act of Congress ought never to be construed to violate the law of nations if any other possible construction remains. . . ." *Murray v. The Schooner Charming Betsy,* 6 U.S. (2 Cranch) 64, 118 (1804); *see also Restatement (Third), supra,* §114 ("Where fairly possible, a United States statute is to be construed so as not to conflict with international law or with an international agreement of the United States."). Will a conflict exist if Congress did not intend to create one? *See id.* §115(1)(a) (yes, if the provisions "cannot be fairly reconciled").

3. Self-Executing and Non-Self-Executing Treaties. Committee of U.S. Citizens quotes *The Head Money Cases,* 112 U.S. 580, 598-599 (1884), for the proposition that a treaty is the legal equivalent of a statute "whenever its provisions prescribe a rule by which the rights of the private citizen or subject may be determined." If it operates in this fashion, it is said to be "self-executing," and it can usually be affirmatively invoked by a private, civil litigant. Chief Justice John Marshall explained in an earlier decision that "[o]ur constitution declares a treaty to be the law of the land. It is, consequently, to be regarded in courts of justice as equivalent to an act of the legislature, *whenever it operates of itself, without the aid of any legislative provision.*" *Foster v. Neilson,* 27 U.S. (2 Pet.) 253, 314 (1829) (emphasis added).

On the other hand, Marshall declared, "when the terms of the stipulation import a contract, when either of the parties engages to perform a particular act, the treaty addresses itself to the political, not the judicial department; and the legislature must execute the contract before it can become the rule for the Court." *Id.* As *Committee of U.S. Citizens* shows, private litigants are usually held either to lack standing or to have failed to state a cause of action, or both, to enforce such *non-self-executing* international agreements. Courts often reason that private rights are merely "derivative" through their states, and that private parties therefore lack standing to invoke international agreements as either swords or shields in the absence of a protest by the signatory state itself. *See, e.g., Matta-Ballesteros v. Henman,* 896 F.2d 255, 259 (7th Cir. 1990).

Whether a treaty or a provision thereof is "self-executing" or not is significant not only for deciding its enforceability in U.S. courts without the need for independent action by the legislature or Executive. It may also bear on whether the treaty authorizes the President to act alone, without further legislation. Indeed, some have argued that making a treaty non-self-executing is "[t]he normal way to accommodate the interests of the House or Congress as a whole during the exercise of the Treaty Power." Trimble, *supra* p. 170, at 178. A non-self-executing treaty would remain the law of the land even though not enforceable in the courts; the executive and legislative branches would still have the duty to carry it out in good faith, but "[t]heir accountability is political, not judicial." *Id.* at 163. Such a treaty would also still establish an international duty that the United States would breach by failing in due course to execute it. *See Restatement (Fourth)* §310(3) ("Whether a treaty provision is self-executing does not affect the obligation of the United States to comply with it under international law").

How did the court in *Committee of U.S. Citizens* decide whether or not U.N. Charter Article 94 is self-executing? Did the court need to address the issue of self-execution in order to resolve the case before it?

4. Subject Matter Limitations on Self-Executing Treaties? Are there some subjects on which self-executing treaties cannot operate because they fall within the exclusive legislative power of Congress? *See Edwards v. Carter,* 580 F.2d 1055, 1059 (D.C. Cir. 1978) (asserting that the Revenue Bill and Appropriations Clauses, U.S. Const. art. I, §7, cl. 1, & §9, cl. 7, respectively, "operate to limit the treaty power because the language of these provisions clearly precludes any method of appropriating money or raising taxes other than through the enactment of laws by the full Congress") (dictum).

Many collective defense treaties to which the United States is a party provide that, in the event of an armed attack on a treaty partner, each partner will "act to meet the common danger in accordance with its constitutional processes," or words to that effect. Is such a provision self-executing? If it were, would it be constitutional? *See Restatement (Fourth)* §310(3) (asserting that an international agreement of the United States is non-self-executing "if implementing legislation is constitutionally required").

5. Domestic Force and Effect of Executive Agreements. The Supremacy Clause explicitly equates "treaties" with laws of the United States. Do executive agreements have the same domestic legal effect as treaties? In *United States v. Pink,* 315 U.S. 203, 230 (1942), the Supreme Court declared that a treaty is the law of the land, and that "international compacts and agreements . . . have a similar dignity." While case law suggests that *congressional-executive* agreements and agreements made pursuant to treaties have the same domestic legal effect as constitutional treaties, it is less clear about the effect of *sole executive* agreements. *See CRS Treaty Study, supra* p. 170, at 65-68.

In *United States v. Guy W. Capps, Inc.,* 204 F.2d 655, 659-660 (4th Cir. 1953), *aff'd on other grounds,* 348 U.S. 296 (1955), the court held that a sole executive agreement concerning import limitations does not supersede a prior statute, citing Congress's express authority to regulate foreign commerce. U.S. Const. art. I, §8, cl. 3; *see also Seery v. United States,* 127 F. Supp. 601 (Ct. Cl. 1955) (asserting that it "would indeed be incongruous if the Executive Department alone, without even the limited participation by Congress which is present when a treaty is ratified, could not only nullify . . . [an Act of Congress], but, by nullifying that Act . . . , destroy the Constitutional right of a citizen."). By one view, sole executive agreements should only be permitted "to override preexisting legal rights . . . when the President has independent authority to do so," as he has to recognize foreign governments, to pardon a foreign national, or to conduct peaceful military exercises with a foreign power. Bradford R. Clark, *Domesticating Sole Executive Agreements,* 93 Va. L. Rev. 1573, 1577, 1660 (2007).

D. STATUTORY INCORPORATION OF INTERNATIONAL LAW

The Law of Nations Clause expressly gives Congress the power to "define and punish . . . Offences against the Law of Nations." U.S. Const. art. I, §8, cl. 10. Some say the Clause makes all customary international law self-executing against the U.S. government, while others argue just the opposite. *See* J. Andrew Kent, *Congress's Under-Appreciated Power to Define and Punish Offenses Against the Law of Nations,* 85 Tex. L. Rev. 843, 848 (2007).

Congress has frequently legislated to codify both international conventional and customary law. For example, the War Crimes Act criminalizes certain conduct — including torture, rape, and hostage-taking — committed in war by or against U.S. nationals or members of the U.S. Armed Forces, asserting that this conduct "constitutes a grave breach of common Article 3" of the 1949 Geneva Conventions. *See* 18 U.S.C. §2441(c)(3), (d)(1) (2018). The Genocide Convention Implementation Act of 1987 implements a non-self-executing treaty to which the United States is a party. *See* 18 U.S.C. §§1091-1093 (2018), implementing the Convention on the Prevention and Punishment of the Crime of Genocide, Dec. 9, 1948, S. Treaty Doc. No. 81-15; *see also* 8 U.S.C. §§2340-2340A (2018), implementing the Convention Against Torture and Other Cruel, Inhuman or Degrading Treatment or Punishment, Dec. 10, 1984, S. Treaty Doc. No. 100-20.

Other statutes codify international law more generically. The piracy statute provides for the capture and forfeiture of vessels used for, and the punishment of those who commit, acts of "piracy as defined by the law of nations." 18 U.S.C. §1651 (2018); 33 U.S.C. §§384-385 (2018); *see also* 10 U.S.C. §821 (2018) (authorizing the use of military commissions to the extent permitted by statute or the "law of war"); 22 U.S.C. §462 (2018) (authorizing the President to use military force to detain foreign vessels at American ports when permitted "by the law of nations or the treaties of the United States"); 22 U.S.C. §§5604-5605 (2018) (authorizing the President to impose sanctions on foreign countries that use chemical or biological weapons "in violation of international law").

E. THE DOMESTIC LEGAL EFFECT OF CUSTOMARY INTERNATIONAL LAW AND *JUS COGENS*

International law norms are established not only by treaties and executive agreements, but also by custom.

> "Customary international law results from a general and consistent practice of states followed by them from a sense of legal obligation." Restatement (Third) of Foreign Relations Law §102(2) (1987) (hereinafter "*Restatement*"). Thus, customary international law is continually evolving. At a crucial stage of that process, "[w]ithin the relevant states, the will has to be formed that the rule will become law if the relevant number of states who share this will is reached." Meijers, *How Is International Law Made?*, 9 Netherlands Y.B. Intl. L. 3, 5 (1978). As to what constitutes the necessary number of "relevant states," the ICJ has said that "State practice . . . should have been both extensive and virtually uniform in the sense of the provision invoked." *The North Sea Continental Shelf Case (Judgment)*, 1969 I.C.J. 12, 43. Finally, in order for such a customary norm of international law to become a peremptory norm, there must be a further recognition by "the international community . . . *as a whole* [that this is] a norm from which no derogation is permitted." Vienna Convention art. 53 (emphasis added). [*Comm. of U.S. Citizens Living in Nicaragua v. Reagan*, 859 F.2d 929, 940 (D.C. Cir. 1988).]

The formation of such norms is explored further in Chapter 8. Whether customary norms are cognizable by U.S. courts as part of domestic law is currently the subject of an extremely contentious debate.

Reading *Al-Bihani v. Obama*

Al-Bihani was captured in Afghanistan during combat between the Taliban and U.S.-led Coalition Forces. He challenged his subsequent detention at Guantánamo Bay partly on the grounds that it violated customary international laws of armed conflict.

- Judge Brown argues that incorporation arguments are "an aggrandizement of the judicial role." How do they aggrandize that role?

- According to then-Judge Kavanaugh's analysis, what could Congress have done to incorporate limits from the law of armed conflict into the AUMF, if it had so desired?
- Why does Judge Williams refer to the use of customary international law as an interpretative tool (through the medium of the *Charming Betsy* rule) as the "weaker" use of international law? Why do both Judges Brown and Kavanaugh reject even this use of customary international law?
- The judges who concurred in denial of rehearing en banc held that the incorporation controversy made no difference to the outcome, thus summarily dismissing the lengthy concurring opinions as dicta. Why do you suppose they did so?

Al-Bihani v. Obama

United States Court of Appeals, D.C. Circuit, 2010
619 F.3d 1

[Ghaleb Nassar Al-Bihani was a cook for a Taliban brigade in combat with U.S.-led Coalition Forces in Afghanistan. He was captured and detained in the U.S. detention facility at Guantánamo Bay based on the government's claim of legal authority to detain anyone who was part of or who supported Taliban or Al Qaeda forces or associated forces in hostilities against the United States or its coalition partners. Al-Bihani petitioned for habeas corpus, and then appealed denial of his petition, partly on the theory that detaining him for just "support[ing]" the Taliban violates international law. A panel of the Court of Appeals rejected this argument, asserting that "[t]here is no indication in the AUMF [authorizing combat against Al Qaeda and the Taliban, see *supra* p. 88] that Congress intended the international laws of war to act as extra-textual limiting principles for the President's war powers under the AUMF." *Al-Bihani v. Obama,* 590 F.3d 866, 871 (D.C. Cir. 2010). Unless such laws have been "implemented domestically," it reasoned, international laws of war "are not a source of authority for U.S. Courts." *Id.* Judge Stephen Williams concurred only in part in the panel decision, stating that because the AUMF clearly authorized Al-Bihani's detention, there was no need for the panel to pronounce "dictum" about the role of law-of-war limitations in limning the President's authority, which went beyond even the government's arguments in the case.

The following decision denying Al-Bihani's petition for rehearing en banc highlighted the debate and prompted a 44-page article-length statement by then-Judge Kavanaugh, concurring in the denial, and a partial rebuttal by Judge Williams. Note that the first statement is signed by every judge then in active service on the D.C. Circuit except the judges who formed the majority on the original panel. Excerpts follow.]

SENTELLE, Chief Judge, and GINSBURG, HENDERSON, ROGERS, TATEL, GARLAND, and GRIFFITH, Circuit Judges, concurring in the denial of rehearing en banc: We decline to en banc this case to determine the role of international law-of-war principles in interpreting the AUMF because, as the various opinions issued in the case indicate, the panel's discussion of that question is not necessary to the disposition of the merits.

BROWN, Circuit Judge, concurring in the denial of rehearing en banc: . . . The idea that international norms hang over domestic law as a corrective force to be implemented by courts is not only alien to our caselaw, but an aggrandizement of the judicial role beyond the Constitution's conception of the separation of powers. *See United States v. Yunis,* 924 F.2d 1086, 1091 (D.C. Cir. 1991) ("[T]he role of judges . . . is to enforce the Constitution, laws, and treaties of the United States, not to conform the law of the land to norms of customary international law."). That aggrandizement is clear in the more extreme scholarly opinions calling for courts to ignore congressional intent in favor of international norms. And it is only slightly better disguised in the superficially restrained claims that Congress intends to conform its actions with global ideals, and that a clear statement is required if courts are to be prevented from reading international law into statutory text. Traditional clear statement rules are justified on the basis of preserving statutes against possible nullification by a constitutional value, keeping both Congress and the judiciary within their constitutional capacities. However, a demand that Congress clearly enunciate the inapplicability of international norms is not premised on any constitutional value; nothing in the Constitution compels the domestic incorporation of international law. Instead, what such a demand protects is a *policy* preference, imputing to Congress a general posture toward international restrictions and erecting the highest interpretive hurdle to the legitimate prerogative of Congress to legislate apart from them. This is a restrained search for legislative "intent" only in the most Orwellian sense — one that grants judges license to usurp the legislative role and dictate to Congress what it is supposed to think. . . .

. . . I am unaware of *any* federal judicial opinion — and Judge Williams cites none — that has ever before characterized international discourse as a traditional tool of statutory interpretation on par with legislative history, usage in other domestic statutes and cases, or dictionary definitions. The varied process by which international law is made — through treaty, tribunal decision, and the constant churn of state practice and *opinio juris* — shares few, if any, of the qualities that give the traditional sources of interpretation their authority. Courts turn to legislative history because it comes from the mouths of legislators and therefore arguably sheds light on their intentions and understandings. Courts examine the usage of terms in other statutes and judicial decisions because our law is a closed and coherent system that strives for internal consistency. And courts consult dictionaries for the same reason most people do: our law, like the rest of our society, is dependent on language's technical meaning among American English speakers. On none of these grounds can the use of international law be justified. . . .

There is no indication that the AUMF placed any international legal limits on the President's discretion to prosecute the war and, in light of the challenge our nation faced after September 11, 2001, that makes eminent sense. Confronted with a shadowy, non-traditional foe that succeeded in bringing a war to our doorstep by asymmetric means, it was (and still is) unclear how international law applies in all respects to this new context. The prospect is very real that some tradeoffs traditionally struck by the laws of war no longer make sense. That Congress wished the President to retain the discretion to recalibrate the military's strategy and tactics in light of circumstances not contemplated by our international obligations is therefore sensible, and reflects the traditional sovereign prerogative to violate international law or terminate international agreements.

The only way a court could reach the opposite conclusion is to go beyond the AUMF's text, freeing it — as Judge Williams suggests — to appeal to an international meta-narrative, one activated whenever a legal issue touches on matters that strike the judge as transnational in flavor. Judges act prudently when they consciously forego opportunities for policymaking. Therefore, ignoring the text and plain meaning of a statute to privilege a more creative interpretation is the antithesis of prudence. And, in a time of war, it has the inconvenient effect of upending more than a century of our jurisprudence based on an understanding as old as the Republic: that the "conduct of foreign relations of our government is committed by the Constitution to the executive and legislative . . . departments," not to the judiciary. *Oetjen v. Cent. Leather Co.*, 246 U.S. 297, 302 (1918).

The only proper judicial role in this case is the truly modest route taken by the panel opinion in *Al-Bihani.* We read [the AUMF words] "necessary and appropriate" in its traditional sense, taking Congress at its word that the President is to have wide discretion. This is a modest course because the President retains the leeway to implement his authority as broadly or narrowly as he believes appropriate — consistent with international law or not — and the legislature, in turn, may add whatever limits or constraints it deems wise as the war progresses. This ensures that wartime decisions will be informed by the expertise of the political branches, stated in a clear fashion, and that the decisionmakers will be accountable to the electorate.

None of those benefits accrue if the conduct of the military is subject to judicial correction based on norms of international discourse. Such an approach would place ultimate control of the war in the one branch insulated from both the battlefield and the ballot box. That would add further illegitimacy to the unpredictable and ad hoc rules judges would draw from the primordial stew of treaties, state practice, tribunal decisions, scholarly opinion, and foreign law that swirls beyond our borders. It is no comfort to the military to say, as Judge Williams does, that courts will only apply international rules they deem to possess the qualities of serious reason, evenhandedness, and practicality. Those are not judicially manageable standards. Those are buzzwords, the pleasing sound of which nearly lulls the mind into missing the vision of judicial supremacy at the heart of Judge Williams' opinion.

KAVANAUGH, Circuit Judge, concurring in the denial of rehearing en banc: . . . Al-Bihani's invocation of international law raises two fundamental questions. First, are international-law norms automatically part of domestic U.S. law? Second, even if international-law norms are not automatically part of domestic U.S. law, does the 2001 AUMF incorporate international-law principles as judicially enforceable limits on the President's wartime authority under the AUMF? The answer to both questions is no.

First, international-law norms are not domestic U.S. law in the absence of action by the political branches to codify those norms. Congress and the President can and often do incorporate international-law principles into domestic U.S. law by way of a statute (or executive regulations issued pursuant to statutory authority) or a self-executing treaty. When that happens, the relevant international-law principles become part of the domestic U.S. law that federal courts must enforce, assuming there is a cognizable cause of action and the prerequisites for federal jurisdiction are satisfied. But in light of the Supreme Court's 1938 decision in *Erie Railroad Co. v. Tompkins,* 304 U.S. 64 (1938), which established that there is no federal general common law, international-law norms are not enforceable in federal courts unless the political branches have incorporated the norms into domestic U.S. law. None of the international-law norms cited by Al-Bihani has been so incorporated into domestic U.S. law.

Second, the 2001 AUMF does not expressly or impliedly incorporate judicially enforceable international-law limits on the President's direction of the war against al

Qaeda and the Taliban. In authorizing the President to employ force, the AUMF authorizes the President to command the U.S. military to kill, capture, and detain the enemy, as Commanders in Chief traditionally have done in waging wars throughout American history. Congress enacted the AUMF with knowledge that the U.S. Constitution and other federal statutes would limit the President's conduct of the war. But neither the AUMF's text nor contemporaneous statements by Members of Congress suggest that Congress intended to impose judicially enforceable *international-law* limits on the President's authority under the AUMF. . . .

Before proceeding to the analysis of these issues, I emphasize three overarching points about the position advanced in this separate opinion.

First, this opinion recognizes and reinforces the traditional roles of Congress, the President, and the Judiciary in national-security-related matters — roles enduringly articulated in Justice Jackson's separate opinion in *Youngstown Sheet & Tube Co. v. Sawyer,* 343 U.S. 579 (1952). Courts enforce constitutionally permissible constraints imposed *by Congress* on the President's war powers. So, too, courts enforce judicially manageable limits imposed *by the U.S. Constitution* on the President's war powers. But courts may not interfere with the President's exercise of war powers based on international-law norms that the political branches have not seen fit to enact into domestic U.S. law.

Second, the limited authority of *the Judiciary* to rely on international law to restrict the American war effort does not imply that *the political branches* should ignore or disregard international-law norms. The principles of the international laws of war (and of international law more generally) deserve the respect of the United States. Violating international-law norms and breaching international obligations may trigger serious consequences, such as subjecting the United States to sanctions, undermining U.S. standing in the world community, or encouraging retaliation against U.S. personnel abroad. . . .

But in our constitutional system of separated powers, it is for Congress and the President — not the courts — to determine in the first instance whether and how the United States will meet its international obligations. When Congress and the President have chosen not to incorporate international-law norms into domestic U.S. law, bedrock principles of judicial restraint and separation of powers counsel that courts respect that decision.

Third, consistent with that constitutional division of authority, Congress has enacted a significant body of legislation to prohibit certain wartime actions by the Executive and military that contravene American values. . . .

. . . [W]hen Congress authorized war in 2001, it did so knowing that domestic U.S. law already prohibited a variety of improper wartime conduct. Judge Williams' worrisome hypotheticals are thus already taken care of — by the domestic U.S. laws of war — and do not support his suggestion that the AUMF incorporates international-law norms. . . .

I . . .

B . . .

To be sure, there was a time when U.S. courts stated that customary international law was "part of our law" so that "where there is no treaty, and no controlling executive or legislative act or judicial decision, resort must be had to the customs and usages of civilized nations; and, as evidence of these, to the works of jurists and commentators." *The Paquete Habana,* 175 U.S. 677, 700 (1900). But that oft-quoted statement reflected the notion, common in the early years of the Nation but now discredited, that international law was part of the general common law that federal courts could apply.

But as decided by the Supreme Court in its landmark *Erie* decision in 1938, the view that federal courts may ascertain and enforce international-law norms as part of the general common law is fundamentally inconsistent with a proper understanding of the role of the Federal Judiciary in our constitutional system. In *Erie,* the Supreme Court famously held that there is no general common law enforceable by federal courts. *Erie,* 304 U.S. at 78. The Court said that "law in the sense in which courts speak of it today does not exist without some definite authority behind it." *Id.* at 79 (quotation omitted).

Erie means that, in our constitutional system of separated powers, federal courts may not enforce law that lacks a domestic sovereign source. *Erie* "requires federal courts to identify the sovereign source for every rule of decision," and the "appropriate 'sovereigns' under the U.S. Constitution are the federal government and the states." [Curtis A. Bradley & Jack L. Goldsmith, *Customary International Law,* 110 Harv. L. Rev. 815, 852 (1997).] . . .

II . . .

. . . [T]he *Charming Betsy* canon of statutory construction does not authorize courts to read international-law limitations into the authority granted to the President by the AUMF. . . .

To sum up on *Charming Betsy*: The canon exists to the extent it supports applying the presumption against extraterritorial application of federal statutes. Beyond that, after *Erie* and particularly after *Sosa* [*v. Alvarez-Machain,* 542 U.S. 692, 724 (2004)]. . . , it is not appropriate for courts to use the *Charming Betsy* canon to alter interpretation of federal statutes to conform them to norms found in non-self-executing treaties and customary international law, which Congress has not chosen to incorporate into domestic U.S. law. In the alternative, even if one disagrees with that broader proposition and concludes that use of the *Charming Betsy* canon is appropriate in some such cases, it should not be invoked against the Executive Branch, which has the authority to weigh international-law considerations when interpreting the scope of ambiguous statutes. And even if one also disagrees with that, it is not appropriate for courts to narrow a congressional authorization of war based on international-law norms that are not part of domestic U.S. law. . . .

WILLIAMS, Senior Circuit Judge: . . . Judge Kavanaugh, I think, fails to adequately distinguish between treatment of international law norms as "judicially enforceable limits" on Presidential authority, or as "domestic U.S. law," and use of such norms as a "basis for courts to alter their interpretation of federal statutes." By "alter their interpretation," I take Judge Kavanaugh to mean . . . for a court to allow international law to persuade it to adopt a *narrower* interpretation of the President's authority than it would otherwise have chosen. I will assume that Judge Kavanaugh is correct as to the impropriety of the stronger use of international law (treating it as "domestic law"), but I believe him incorrect on the weaker (allowing it to affect a court's statutory interpretation).

Courts use a wide range of information outside the words of a statute to find those words' meaning. This reflects the simple truth that the question of a word's meaning is an empirical one: what have persons in the relevant community actually meant when using the words that appear in a statute? Among the most obvious outside sources to resolve that question are legislative history, usage in other laws and in judicial decisions, and dictionaries. Courts use all three incessantly. Dictionaries, of course, are only scholars' claims as to how people have historically used the words in question. Because military conflict is commonly an international phenomenon, words relating to such conflict are used in international discourse, of which international law is a subset. That international law has a normative element is nothing special; virtually all laws do — yet laws represent widely known public uses of language that legislatures often repackage in novel combinations and contexts. It would be an odd member of Congress who supposed that in authorizing the use of military force he was embracing uses equivalent to *all* such uses that have ever occurred: think Nanking 1937-38; Katyn 1940; Lidice 1942; My Lai 1968. More generally, it seems improbable that in authorizing the use of all "necessary and appropriate force" Congress could have contemplated employment of methods clearly and unequivocally condemned by international law.

Judge Kavanaugh agrees with that conclusion, but argues that we infer such limits on Congress's grant of power simply from penalties or prohibitions in *domestic* law. He is surely correct that this is *one* source for finding limits on an authorization of military force, but that does not make it the only legitimate source of such limits. In some circumstances, Judge Kavanaugh's "domestic U.S. law of war" may have relatively little to say on a question that international practice has addressed for centuries. It obviously seemed so to the Supreme Court in *Hamdi v. Rumsfeld*, 542 U.S. 507, 518-21 (2004), where the plurality looked to international norms on the question of whom the President may detain pursuant to the AUMF, and for how long.

Before *Erie R.R. Co. v. Tompkins*, 304 U.S. 64 (1938), U.S. courts undoubtedly used international law to help resolve cases. It appears to have been uncontroversial for international law to serve not only as a species of federal general common law, binding absent contrary domestic law, but also as a source of interpretive guidance regarding statutes passed by Congress, see, e.g., *Brown v. United States*, 8 Cranch 110, 124-28 (1814) (Marshall, C.J.) (interpreting the domestic legal effects of a U.S. declaration of war in part by reference to international norms, along with constitutional principles and domestic statutes). To dispute that commonsensical understanding, after all, requires defending the unlikely view that international law — unlike other known binding laws — offered no useful information whatsoever regarding the meaning of new laws on similar subjects. In Judge Kavanaugh's view, *Erie* effectively proscribed use of international law as "enforceable" U.S. law. But that landmark case left intact the pre-existing alternative role of international law as a store of information regarding the sense of words Congress enacts into laws governing international matters — a role that never depended on international law's being a form of federal general common law (which *Erie* famously banished). *Erie* hardly requires that every last source of information regarding the meaning of words in statutes be an enacted law; if it does, federal courts have been disobeying its command for more than seven decades.

Even Judge Kavanaugh appears to acknowledge that international law may in some circumstances properly shape a court's interpretation of a federal statute. If I understand him correctly, though, he accepts reliance on international law to *expand* the meaning of a statutory grant of executive authority but never to *contract* it (the benchmark being the reading the court would otherwise have reached). Use of international law as a one-way ratchet seems to me illogical. As Curtis Bradley and Jack Goldsmith put it in *Congressional Authorization and the War on Terrorism*, if the international laws of war "can inform the powers that Congress has implicitly granted to the President in the AUMF, they logically can inform the boundaries of such powers." 118 Harv. L. Rev. 2047, 2094 (2005). To whatever extent the international laws of war shed light on what the AUMF lets the President do, they shed light in all directions, not just one. If international law supports finding a grant of the "X" power (a power that by hypothesis the court would not otherwise have found), it must support some inquiry into what "X" means. . . .

Reading *Al Shimari v. CACI Premier Technology, Inc.*

The U.S. detention of Iraqis at Abu Ghraib prison notoriously made headlines when pictures of abused detainees leaked to the press. In the following case, some detainees sued the U.S. military contractor involved in administration of the prison for their mistreatment, including torture, and the contractor impleaded the United States. The United States claimed that it enjoyed sovereign immunity from suit, but the plaintiffs argued that peremptory customary international law — *jus cogens* — trumped any immunity.

- What was the relevant *jus cogens* law? How was it made? How is it different from "ordinary" customary international law?
- Assuming that the relevant *jus cogens* principle bars torture, does it also give the victim a judicial remedy? If not, by what authority did the court entertain that remedy?
- The district court cited the 1900 Supreme Court opinion in *The Paquete Habana* for the proposition that "[i]nternational law is part of our law," and the 1804 Supreme Court opinion in *Murray v. Schooner Charming Betsy* for the proposition that acts of Congress "ought never to be construed to violate the law of nations if any other construction remains" (an avoidance principle of statutory construction analogous to the constitutional avoidance principle that U.S. courts also follow). See *supra* p. 185. But does anything more than the age of these opinions support incorporation of *jus cogens*? What theoretical justification did the district court offer?
- Statutes are enacted by legislatures. Federal common law is declared by elected or appointed U.S. judges. How is incorporating such law into our own law consistent with our representative democracy?

Al Shimari v. CACI Premier Technology, Inc.

United States District Court, Eastern District of Virginia, 2019
368 F. Supp. 3d 935

Leonie M. Brinkema, United States District Judge. . . .

I. BACKGROUND

This civil action arises out of the alleged torture; cruel, inhuman, or degrading treatment ("CIDT"); and war crimes inflicted on plaintiffs . . . by members of the United States military and CACI employees while plaintiffs were detained at the Abu Ghraib prison. . . . For the purposes of the present motions, it is sufficient to understand that plaintiffs, all of whom are Iraqi citizens who were detained at Abu Ghraib for a significant period of time, allege that they suffered severe mistreatment at the hands of military personnel and CACI employees. As summarized in the [Court's prior] Memorandum Opinion:

> Over the course of six weeks, Al-Ejaili was subjected to repeated stress positions, including at least one that made him vomit black liquid; sexually-related humiliation; disruptive sleeping patterns and long periods of being kept naked or without food or water; and multiple instances of being threatened with dogs. The approximately ten to twelve times he was interrogated involved systematic beatings, including to the head, and being doused with hot and cold liquids. Al-Zuba'e was subjected to sexual assault and threats of rape; being left in a cold shower until he was unable to stand; dog bites and repeated beatings, including with sticks and to the genitals; repeated stress positions, including at least one that lasted an entire day and resulted in his urinating and defecating on himself; and threats that his family would be brought to Abu Ghraib. Al Shimari was subjected to systematic beatings, including on his head and genitals, with a baton and rifle, and some where he was hit against the wall; multiple stress positions, including one where he was forced to kneel on sharp stones, causing lasting damage to his legs; being threatened with dogs; a cold shower similar to Al-Zuba'e's, being doused with water, and being kept in a dark cell and with loud music nearby; threats of being shot and having his wife brought to Abu Ghraib; electric shocks; being dragged around the prison by a rope tied around his neck; and having fingers inserted into his rectum.

Mem. Op. [Dkt. No. 678] 31-32. Plaintiffs allege that as a result of this treatment, they have suffered "severe and lasting physical and mental damage." *Id.* at 33. . . .

[Plaintiffs sued CACI under the Alien Tort Statute (ATS), 28 U.S.C. §1350, for engaging in, conspiring to engage in, and aiding and abetting torture; CIDT; and war crimes, all in violation of international law. CACI filed a third-party complaint against the United States, alleging that U.S. military personnel, and not CACI personnel, were ultimately responsible for directing the interrogations of the plaintiffs and mistreating the plaintiffs. The United States then moved to dismiss on the grounds that all of CACI's claims against it are barred by sovereign immunity.]

II. UNITED STATES' MOTION TO DISMISS . . .

C. Sovereign Immunity and *Jus Cogens* Violations

CACI . . . argues that the government has waived sovereign immunity for violations of *jus cogens* norms — that is, those peremptory international law norms from which states may not derogate. This question appears to be one of first impression, not just in this district or circuit but nationally. Accordingly, before the question presented may be addressed, it is necessary to examine the history and development of sovereign immunity doctrine and *jus cogens* norms to contextualize the current dispute.

1. Development of Sovereign Immunity Doctrine

[The Court explored the "murky origins" of the doctrine and acknowledged "the binding nature of the determinations by the Supreme Court and the Fourth Circuit that the federal government may not be sued in tort without its consent," as well as "the academic and judicial criticism of the path the United States has taken."]

2. Jus Cogens Norms

a. Development of *Jus Cogens* Norms

Jus cogens norms are defined as those "peremptory norms" that "are nonderogable and enjoy the highest status within international law." *Comm. of U.S. Citizens Living in Nicar. v. Reagan*, 859 F.2d 929, 940 (D.C. Cir. 1988); *see also* Vienna Convention on the Law of Treaties art. 53, May 23, 1969, 1155 U.N.T.S. 331 ("Vienna Convention") (defining a *jus cogens* norm as "a norm accepted and recognized by the international community of States as a whole as a norm from which no derogation is permitted and which can be modified only by a subsequent norm of general international law having the same character"). Such norms come first from "customary international law," which is a body of law that "results from a general and consistent practice of states followed by them from a sense of legal obligation." *Comm. of U.S. Citizens*, 859 F.2d at 940. . . . After a norm has been incorporated into customary international law, it may become a *jus cogens*, or peremptory, norm if there is "a further recognition by the international community as a whole that this is a norm from which no derogation is permitted." *Id.* (alterations, internal quotation marks, and citation omitted). Once a norm has achieved the status of *jus cogens*, it assumes a place at the top of the hierarchy of international norms, such that no state is permitted to derogate from the norm and any treaty or other agreement is void if it conflicts with the norm. *See* Vienna Convention art. 53; *Comm. of U.S. Citizens*, 859 F.2d at 940.

The development of the concept of *jus cogens* norms has proceeded as the "status of individuals under international law has undergone a fundamental change" since World War II, such that "individuals are now said to possess substantive international rights vis-a-vis states." [Adam C. Belsky et al., Comment, *Implied Waiver Under the FSIA: A Proposed Exception to Immunity for Violations of Peremptory Norms of International Law*, 77 Calif. L. Rev. 365, 393 (1989).] This change has corresponded with a shift in the emphasis of international law from "the formal structure of the relationships between States and the delimitation of their jurisdiction to the development of substantive rules on matters of common concern vital to the growth of an international community and to the individual well-being of the citizens of its member States." *Id.* at 392-93 (quoting Wilfred Jenks, *The Common Law of Mankind* 17 (1958)). As a result, the "irreducible element" of international law has become "the sovereignty of the individual, not the sovereignty of states." *Id.* at 393.

Against this backdrop, *jus cogens* norms have developed as an expression of the international community's recognition that all states are obligated, in their capacity as states, to respect certain fundamental rights of individuals. Although the exact content of the set of *jus cogens* norms is debatable, it is clear that certain "fundamental human rights law[s]," such as those that "prohibit[ ] genocide, slavery, murder, torture," and similarly universally condemned practices, have achieved the status of *jus cogens. Comm. of U.S. Citizens,* 859 F.2d at 941. In particular, "[t]orture is widely recognized as contravening *jus cogens,*" and "[a]ll major human rights agreements and instruments contain a prohibition against torture" that "is non-derogable." Karen Parker & Lyn Beth Neylon, *Jus Cogens: Compelling the Law of Human Rights,* 12 Hastings Int'l & Comp. L. Rev. 411, 437-38 (1989)....

3. Jus Cogens and Domestic Sovereign Immunity...

a. Rights and Remedies

Jus cogens norms not only carry with them an obligation on the part of states to respect the norms but also confer an unquestionable right on each individual to be free from states violating those norms. This right, which is created by international law, is binding on the federal government and enforceable in the federal courts, and the basic axiom that where there is a right, there must be a remedy leads to the conclusion that the government has waived its sovereign immunity with respect to alleged *jus cogens* violations.

The basic principle that international law is incorporated into American law and is binding on the federal government and enforceable by American courts is as old as the Republic itself. In 1796, the Supreme Court "held that the United States had been bound to receive the law of nations upon declaring its independence," which meant that "the United States was required" to recognize international norms when those norms were recognized by all other nations. David F. Klein, Comment, *A Theory for the Application of the Customary International Law of Human Rights by Domestic Courts,* 13 Yale J. Int'l L. 332, 338 (1988) (citing *Ware v. Hylton,* 3 U.S. (3 Dall.) 199 (1796)); *see also* Jules Lobel, *The Limits of Constitutional Power: Conflicts Between Foreign Policy and International Law,* 71 Va. L. Rev. 1071, 1084 (1985) ("The early American leadership believed that the attainment of independence obligated the United States to receive and to follow the law of nations."). Indeed, at the time of the Founding, American law was expected to conform to the dictates of international law. "Early federal court cases also suggested that laws or executive actions in violation of international law were void," Lobel, *supra,* at 1087, and at least one state court permitted the indictment of a defendant for a violation of the law of nations, finding that law to be, "in its full extent,... part of the law of th[e] State," *Respublica v. De Longchamps,* 1 U.S. (1 Dall.) 111, 116 (Pa. Ct. Oyer & Terminer 1784). In a similar vein, the Supreme Court held in 1804 that an "act of Congress ought never to be construed to violate the law of nations if any other possible construction remains, and consequently can never be construed to violate neutral rights, or to affect neutral commerce, further than is warranted by the law of nations as understood in this country." *Murray v. Schooner Charming Betsy*, 6 U.S. (2 Cranch) 64, 118 (1804).

In the last two centuries, the principle that "federal common law incorporates international law" has become a "settled proposition." *Kadic v. Karadzic*, 70 F.3d 232, 246 (2d Cir. 1995). Over that time, "Supreme Court decisions, executive statements, and scholarly commentary have . . . considered customary international law to be the law of the land." Lobel, *supra*, at 1072; *see also The Paquete Habana*, 175 U.S. 677, 700 (1900) ("International law is part of our law, and must be ascertained and administered by the courts of justice of appropriate jurisdiction, as often as questions of right depending upon it are duly presented for their determination."). Moreover, because the "Constitution does not freeze international law to its state of development [as of] 1789," as international law has evolved to incorporate *jus cogens* norms, so too has federal common law. Belsky *et al.*, *supra*, at 398; *see also Sosa* [*v. Alvarez-Machain*, 542 U.S. 692, 724 (2004)] (holding that the ATS is a jurisdictional statute "creating no new causes of action" but that the common law "provide[s] a cause of action for . . . certain torts in violation of the law of nations"). Accordingly, there is today a federal common law right derived from international law that entitles individuals not to be the victims of *jus cogens* violations.

Once it is determined that *jus cogens* violations infringe on federal rights, it becomes clear that there must be a remedy available to the victims. Indeed, the "ancient legal maxim" *ubi jus, ibi remedium*—"[w]here there is a right, there should be a remedy"—is as "basic and universally embraced" today as it was two hundred years ago. Akhil Reed Amar, *Of Sovereignty and Federalism*, 96 Yale L.J. 1425, 1485-86 (1987). As Chief Justice Marshall famously stated in *Marbury v. Madison*, "The government of the United States has been emphatically termed a government of laws, and not of men. It will certainly cease to deserve this high appellation, if the laws furnish no remedy for the violation of a vested legal right." 5 U.S. (1 Cranch) at 163. In fact, not only did the early Supreme Court embrace this principle, but it was also endorsed by many state constitutions and in *The Federalist Papers*. Since that time, the principle has been incorporated into the basic fabric of American law. Accordingly, by joining the community of nations and accepting the law of nations, the federal government has impliedly waived any right to claim sovereign immunity with respect to *jus cogens* violations when sued for such violations in an American court. . . .

c. Hierarchy of Norms

The place of *jus cogens* norms at the top of the hierarchy of international law norms and their status as obligatory and overriding principles that invalidate any contradictory state acts, as well as their development from the ashes of World War II, provide an additional reason that the United States does not have sovereign immunity here.

Jus cogens norms "enjoy the highest status within international law," and their supremacy "extends over all rules of international law." *Siderman de Blake* [*v. Republic of Argentina*, 965 F.2d 699, 715-716 (9th Cir. 1992)] (internal quotation marks and citation omitted). Accordingly, these norms "prevail over and invalidate international agreements and other rules of international law in conflict with them." *Id.* (internal quotation marks and citation omitted). As one specific example, it is unquestionable that *jus cogens* norms "limit the scope of treaties, such that a treaty concluded in violation of a *jus cogens* norm [i]s null and void." Belsky *et al., supra,* at 390. Because the concept that a sovereign may claim immunity from suit "itself is a principle of international law," *Siderman de Blake,* 965 F.2d at 718, the peremptory status of *jus cogens* norms means that when sovereign immunity and *jus cogens* norms conflict, the sovereign immunity principle must give way. *See id.* (concluding that as "a matter of international law, [this] argument carries much force"). In this case, the two norms conflict because the *jus cogens* norms in question inherently include not only a rule prohibiting states from torturing individuals but also necessarily a rule requiring an effective means to redress that violation. Without such a remedial principle, the prohibitory norm itself would be toothless and, given the recognized importance of ensuring adherence to *jus cogens* norms, any interpretation defanging the norm would impermissibly "undo what [the international community] has done" in implementing the norm. *King v. Burwell,* ___ U.S. ___, 135 S. Ct. 2480, 2496 (2015). So interpreted, any *jus cogens* norm must prevail over and invalidate any principle allowing the assertion of sovereign immunity in response to claims of *jus cogens* violations.

Moreover, the circumstances surrounding the development of the concept of peremptory norms — ones that can bind all states even without their explicit consent and even with regard to domestic conduct — provide additional force to the conclusion that sovereign immunity must give way in the face of violations of such norms. The concept of such binding norms arose in the wake of World War II and the Nuremberg trials. Before the atrocities committed by Nazi Germany, "a state's treatment of its own citizens was considered immune from the dictates of international law." *Princz* [*v. Federal Republic of Germany,* 26 F.3d 1166, 1182 (D.C. Cir. 1994)] (Wald, J., dissenting). The Nuremberg trials, in which German officials were prosecuted for crimes against humanity, including crimes against German citizens, "permanently eroded any notion that the mantle of sovereign immunity could serve to cloak an act that constitutes a 'crime against humanity,' even if that act is confined within the borders of a single sovereign state." *Id.* . . . The principle at the heart of the Nuremberg trials, and the concomitant acceptance of the existence of certain peremptory norms, is simple and persuasive: there are some acts that are, as a matter of morality and reason, fundamentally wrong such that no state may authorize their commission nor immunize those involved in such acts from liability. This principle compels the conclusion that just as a government official is unable to cloak himself in the mantle of sovereign immunity to avoid prosecution when he commits a *jus cogens* violation, so too is a government unable to immunize itself from civil liability for such violations. And indeed, not only has the United States accepted the principles advanced at Nuremberg, it actually

> led the way in these developments and must therefore accept domestically these legal limitations on national sovereignty. As Justice Jackson, the United States prosecutor at Nuremberg, stated, "[i]f certain acts in violation of treaties are crimes, they are crimes whether the United States does them or whether Germany does them, and we are not prepared to lay down a rule of criminal conduct against others which we would not be willing to have invoked against us." A complete deference by United States courts to executive orders or congressional acts irrespective of international law implications would be simply inconsistent with the spirit and rationale of Nuremberg.

Lobel, *supra,* at 1074 (alteration in original) (footnotes omitted). Accordingly, both by participating in the Nuremberg trials and the parallel development of peremptory norms of international law and by continuing to recognize the existence of such peremptory norms, the United States has waived its sovereign immunity for any claims arising from the violations of such norms.

d. Consent Through Membership in the Community of Nations

The United States has also consented to suit with respect to *jus cogens* violations by holding itself out as a member of the international community because the respect and enforcement of *jus cogens* norms are fundamental to the existence of a functioning community of nations. *Jus cogens* norms have been developed not only to safeguard the rights of individuals but also to provide an obligatory framework for ordering the relations of states because, as in any community, the "absolute protection" of "certain norms and values" is necessary for the "public order of the international community." Belsky *et al., supra,* at 387. . . .

Accordingly, by holding itself out as a member of the international community, the United States has impliedly waived its sovereign immunity for *jus cogens* violations because the continued deployment of such immunity would be fundamentally inconsistent with any desire to maintain an international legal order.

e. The Character of Sovereign Acts

The United States also may not claim immunity for *jus cogens* violations because when government agents commit such violations, their actions are not sovereign in nature. Under international law, *jus cogens* norms are "by definition nonderogable," which means that the "rise of *jus cogens* norms limits state sovereignty in the sense that the general will of the international community of states, and other actors, will take precedence over the individual wills of states to order their relations." *Princz* [*v. Federal Republic of Germany,* 26 F.3d 1166, 1182 (D.C. Cir. 1994)] (Wald, J., dissenting) (internal quotation marks and citation omitted). As such, when "a state thumbs its nose at such a norm, in effect overriding the collective will of the entire international community, the state cannot be performing a sovereign act entitled to immunity" because such an act is fundamentally inconsistent with the obligations of every state. *Id.* . . .

This conclusion is reinforced by the nature of sovereignty in the American system. Since the Founding, Americans have recognized that "indivisible, final, and unlimited authority," *i.e.,* sovereignty, rests in the People, not the government. *See* Amar, *supra,* at 1435-37. Accordingly, when speaking of the "government as sovereign," the Founders "mean[t] sovereign in a necessarily limited sense" because "[b]y definition, government's sovereignty was bounded" to "its sphere of delegated power." *See id.* at 1437. Therefore, the federal government may only exercise power that has been legitimately delegated to it by the People. . . .

Putting these two conclusions together: the federal government may immunize itself from liability for *jus cogens* violations only if the acts of authorizing or engaging in such violations fall within the sphere of authority that has been legitimately delegated by the People. Under the principles of international law discussed in this section, the People as sovereign are bound by the nonderogability of *jus cogens* norms, which means that the People may not legitimately delegate to the government the power to engage in *jus cogens* violations. Accordingly, the federal government, bounded by its status as a limited government of delegated powers, has no sovereign power to immunize itself from liability for such violations.

For these reasons, the United States does not retain sovereign immunity for violations of *jus cogens* norms of international law. . . .

Notes and Questions

a. The Making and Incorporation of Customary International Law

1. *The Making of Customary International Law.* How is customary international law made? How is *jus cogens* different from "ordinary" customary international law? How does the process for making customary international law compare to the process for making U.S. domestic common law? *See* Henkin, *supra* p. 184, at 878-886. To the U.S. process for establishing constitutional custom?

2. *Incorporating Customary International Law as a Rule of Decision.* As the *Al Shimari* court remarked, the Supreme Court's holding in *The Paquete Habana* that "international law is part of our law" had until recently become almost hornbook law, as reflected in the *Restatement (Third)* §111 cmt. d ("customary international law, while not mentioned explicitly in the Supremacy Clause, [is] also federal law. . . . Customary international law is considered to be like common law in the United States, but it is federal law."). Proponents of incorporation have argued that incorporation falls squarely within what the Supreme Court has called an "enclave" of federal common lawmaking authority for matters dealing with foreign relations. *See* Michael P. Van Alstine, *Federal Common Law in an Age of Treaties,* 89 Cornell L. Rev. 892 (2004) (citing *Banco Nacional De Cuba v. Sabbatino,* 376 U.S. 398, 426-427 (1964)).

But Judge Brown and then-Judge Kavanaugh argued that customary international law lacks democratic legitimacy: it is made by the practice of states (including some that are not democracies), not by a vote of the people or their representatives, let alone by a vote of the American people or their representatives. *See* Trimble, *supra* p. 170, at 708-709, 713-714, 716-725 (arguing that courts lack the institutional capacity to participate fully in the development of customary international law, and that application of that law by U.S. courts is illegitimate because it is irreconcilable with American political tradition). Of course, U.S. common law is not made by the people either, but at least it is made by the decisions of judges who are either appointed by elected officials or directly elected.

What was Judge Brinkema's answer in *Al Shimari* to this counter-majoritarian critique of incorporation?

3. *Customary International Law and Federal Common Law.* The Alien Tort Statute (ATS), 28 U.S.C. §1350 (2018), provides that "district courts shall have original jurisdiction of any civil action by an alien for a tort only, committed in violation of the law of nations or a treaty of the United States." When alien Humberto Alvarez-Machain asserted a claim under the ATS for arbitrary arrest and detention, the Supreme Court held that the First Congress (the ATS was enacted in 1789) had in mind just a narrow

range of claims for offenses against ambassadors, violations of safe conduct, and actions arising out of prize captures and piracy. While the majority did not close the door completely to recognizing new claims for torts in violation of the law of nations, it held that any such claim had to "rest on a norm of international character accepted by the civilized world and defined with a specificity comparable" to these historically recognized claims. *Sosa v. Alvarez-Machain*, 542 U.S. 692, 725 (2004). Alvarez-Machain's claim did not meet this exacting standard.

The Court explained that a central reason for this crabbed view of international law claims was the early-twentieth-century rejection in the United States of the jurisprudential concept that common law was a "transcendental body of law outside of any particular State," in favor of the positivist view that "law is not so much found or discovered as it was either made or created." *Id.* This shift was driven in part by another: the denial in *Erie R.R. Co. v. Tompkins*, 304 U.S. 64 (1938), of the existence of "general federal common law," accompanied by a substantial shrinking of the federal courts' common lawmaking power. Both developments point to an increasing skepticism by U.S. courts about incorporating customary *international* customary law into federal common law.

4. Incorporation in the New Supreme Court? Then-Judge Kavanaugh's views have taken on added significance now that he has joined the Supreme Court. But he is hardly alone there. Consider these comments by Justice Alito:

> You might wonder, for example, if the First Congress considered a "violation of the law of nations" to be a violation of, and thus "arise under," federal law. But that does not seem likely. At the founding, the law of nations was considered a distinct "system of rules, deducible by natural reason, and established by universal consent among the civilized inhabitants of the world," 4 *Blackstone* 66. While this Court has called international law "part of our law," *The Paquete Habana*, 175 U.S. 677, 700 (1900), and a component of the "law of the land," *The Nereide*, 9 Cranch 388, 423 (1815), that simply meant international law was no different than the law of torts or contracts — it was "part of the so-called general common law," but not part of federal law. The text of the Constitution appears to recognize just this distinction. Article I speaks of "Offences against the Law of Nations," while both Article III and Article VI's Supremacy Clause, which defines the scope of pre-emptive federal law, omit that phrase while referring to the "Laws of the United States." Congress may act to bring provisions of international law into federal law, but they cannot find their way there on their own. "The law of nations is not embodied in any provision of the Constitution, nor in any treaty, act of Congress, or any authority, or commission derived from the United States." *Caperton v. Bowyer*, 14 Wall. 216, 228 (1872). [*Jesner v. Arab Bank, PLC*, 138 S. Ct. 1386, 1416 (2018) (Alito, J., concurring in part).]

On the other hand, apparently Justice Kavanaugh's view of the significance of foreign law may depend on the issue. *See* Adam Liptak, *Conservatives, Often Wary of Foreign Law, Embrace It in Census Case*, N.Y. Times, Apr. 29, 2019 (quoting Justice Kavanaugh as commenting during oral argument on the legality of including a question about citizenship in the census questionnaire: "The United Nations recommends that countries ask a citizenship question on the census. . . . And a number of other countries do it. Spain, Germany, Canada, Australia, Ireland, Mexico ask a citizenship question. It's a very common question internationally."). Does his reasoning for rejecting foreign law, as reflected in *Al-Bihani*, support any subject-matter distinction?

5. *Interpretative Incorporation?* The 2001 AUMF authorizes the President to use all "necessary and appropriate force." Al-Bihani could argue that Congress intended the measure of "necessary and appropriate" to be supplied, at least in part, by the customary law of armed conflict, thus incorporating it into the authorization. Alternatively, he could argue that the AUMF should be construed narrowly to avoid a conflict with this customary international law. Judge Williams would call the first theory the stronger use of international law, and the second, the weaker. Why? Which leaves a court with broader interpretative discretion? The weaker use of international law has been called "interpretative incorporation." *See* Bart M.J. Szewczyk, *Customary International Law and Statutory Interpretation: An Empirical Analysis of Federal Court Decisions*, 82 Geo. Wash. L. Rev. 1118 (2014) (showing that judges use international custom across a diverse range of fields, but proposing that courts only interpret statutes in a manner that is consistent with custom that is "clear and accepted").

Why do Judge Brown and then-Judge Kavanaugh object to interpretative incorporation? Both stress that courts should look only to the express statutory text for limits on the President's detention authority. But the text authorizes only "necessary *and appropriate*" action (emphasis added). Does it go beyond the text to interpret "appropriate" consistently with the customary international law of war? Suppose there is no text, as was arguably the case in *Al Shimari*. Did the district court "aggrandize" itself by weighing the common law of sovereign immunity against the universal ban on torture?

Judges Brown and Kavanaugh argue that *limits* on presidential powers are described only by the *text* of a statute authorizing him to act. But may the same statute be interpreted in describing the *scope* of the President's powers by incorporating customary international law? That is what the Supreme Court did in *Hamdi v. Rumsfeld*, 542 U.S. 507 (2004), when a four-Justice plurality, joined by Justice Thomas, decided that the AUMF, which is silent on the issue of prisoners, includes the authority to detain "enemy combatants" as an aspect of the customary international law of armed conflict. See *infra* p. 837. Judge Brown explained the difference in approach this way:

> The *Hamdi* plurality forecast a restrained process that "meddles little, if at all, in the strategy or conduct of war, inquiring only into the appropriateness of continuing to detain an individual claimed to have taken up arms against the United States." 542 U.S. 507, 535 (2004). It seems farfetched that "inquiring only into the appropriateness" of detention should be freighted with the awesome power of deciding which international constraints to enforce *against* the President. [*Al Bihani*, 619 F.3d at 5 (Brown, J., concurring in the denial of rehearing en banc) (emphasis added).]

And according to then-Judge Kavanaugh, "*Hamdi* is not properly read as applying *Charming Betsy* or imposing international-law *limits* on the scope of the President's authority under the AUMF." 619 F.3d at 44 (Kavanaugh, J., concurring in the denial of rehearing en banc) (emphasis added). What, if anything, do their explanations reveal about their understanding of the separation of powers?

6. *Changing Perspectives on International Law.* At the start of this chapter, we quoted Chief Justice Jay's charge to a jury that "the laws of the United States admit of being classed under the three heads of descriptions," treaties, statutes, and "the law of nations." Is any of the concurring opinions in *Al-Bihani* consistent with this charge?

One explanation for the Framers' apparent greater tolerance for accepting the law of nations as part of our law is practical necessity. The fledgling United States of America, without either a standing army or a navy in the beginning, and surrounded by hostile Native Americans, the British (with whom we had just had a war and were to have another in 1812), the French (with whom we would fight the naval Quasi-War), and the Spanish (with whom we eventually went to war a century later), looked to the law of nations as a kind of *security*—a possible limit on acts against us. More than 200 years later, many say that a robust United States of America, with the world's largest economy and largest military (and the third largest population), no longer needs the law of nations, which is now, irritatingly, often deployed to try to *limit* us.

Might this American exceptionalist view account for hostility to incorporation in our age? If so, is it likely to be a lasting foundation for rejecting "unexecuted" international law? Should it take into account the claim that there are certain moral precepts that are universal—like the prohibition of torture invoked in *Al Shimari*? Is it relevant to the incorporation debate that the Declaration of Independence not only started by declaring certain "truths to be self-evident," but also stated that "a decent respect to the opinions of mankind" required them to be declared? Or is what might be called an "internationalist" view both unrealistic and unnecessary, insofar as the United States can formally and democratically incorporate such international laws as are still necessary or desirable?

b. "Controlling" Executive and Legislative Acts and Judicial Decisions

1. Controlling Legislative Acts and Customary Law. As the Supreme Court said in *Charming Betsy*, our laws should be construed, where fairly possible, to avoid violating customary, no less than conventional, international law. 6 U.S. (2 Cranch) at 118. But if reconciliation proves impossible, which prevails? If the conflict cannot be fairly avoided and customary international law is incorporated into our federal common law, does it necessarily follow that Congress can override it by statute? Did the Supreme Court's reference in *The Paquete Habana* to a "*controlling*... legislative act" (emphasis added) imply that there are some non-controlling statutes that do not override at least ordinary customary international law? What is the implication of the last-in-time rule, *supra* p. 181 n.34, for the domestic effect of customary international law?

2. Controlling Judicial Decisions and Customary Law. The dictum in *The Paquete Habana* also suggests that controlling *judicial* decisions can override customary international law. By what theory?

3. Controlling Executive Acts and Customary Law. The most controversial implication of the *Paquete Habana* dictum is that a controlling executive act may also override customary international law. That implication is that, as a practical matter, the President enjoys discretion to refuse incorporation of such law.

Consider, first, arguments *against* the "override" proposition. Can you make one based on the *Charming Betsy* rule of avoidance? If you recast this rule as a presumption of congressional intent that the United States abide by international law, what is the implication for presidential power under Justice Jackson's typology, *supra* p. 26?

Another argument against the executive power to override customary international law flows from its asserted incorporation into the federal common law.

> Federal common law is binding on every executive branch official, including the President. Congress can by statute create a different rule, however, because federal common law is interstitial; it fills in gaps between the statutes and gives way when an inconsistent law is enacted. Consequently, with congressional authorization, the Chief Executive can disregard any norm of customary international law. But in the face of congressional silence, he is required to respect a clearly defined and widely accepted norm of customary international law. [Michael J. Glennon, *Can the President Do No Wrong?*, 80 Am. J. Int'l L. 923 (1986).]

Consider also the potential consequences of a U.S. violation of international law. Do they suggest any practical allocation of the power to violate among the three branches? *See* Michael J. Glennon, *Raising the Paquete Habana: Is Violation of Customary International Law by the Executive Unconstitutional?*, 80 Nw. U. L. Rev. 321, 360-361 (1985).

THE DOMESTIC EFFECT OF INTERNATIONAL LAW: SUMMARY OF BASIC PRINCIPLES

- The President negotiates a treaty and submits it to the Senate for advice and consent. The Senate may consent to a treaty with or without conditions.

- A treaty carries the interpretation that the Administration authoritatively provided to the Senate and that the Senate understood and relied upon when it gave its consent. But there is no consensus about which administration statements are authoritative or about how the Senate's understanding is determined when the plain words of a treaty are ambiguous. Courts are the final interpreters of treaties, but they give substantial deference to interpretations provided by the executive branch.

- International agreements may also be made by executive agreement without the advice and consent of the Senate. Congressional-executive agreements are made pursuant to delegated statutory authority. Treaty agreements are made pursuant to a treaty to which the Senate has consented. Sole executive agreements are made on the President's independent authority with or without congressional acquiescence. Some executive agreements are nonbinding under international law because they simply express moral or political commitments.

- A treaty has the same domestic force and effect of law as a statute, but both are subject to provisions of the Constitution. When a treaty and a statute conflict, the one enacted later in time controls. The Supreme Court has declared that treaties and executive agreements have the "same dignity," but it has not expressly held that a sole executive agreement may trump an inconsistent statute.

- When a statute violates a treaty, the treaty still has the force and effect of *international law* under the dualist U.S. legal system. Under the *Charming*

Betsy rule of construction, courts must read U.S. statutes to avoid a conflict with international law, if such a reading is possible.

- A self-executing treaty creates rights and duties without the need for implementing legislation, and is usually privately enforceable in U.S. courts, while a non-self-executing treaty must be implemented by statute. There is no consensus about which is which, or even about whether there is any applicable presumption that a treaty is either.

- Customary international law is made by the consistent practice of states motivated by their sense of legal obligation. The traditional historical view that such law is part of our federal common law is today sharply contested as counter-majoritarian and therefore lacking in democratic legitimacy. Regardless, for domestic purposes most customary international law may be trumped by statute or, more controversially, by executive action or judicial opinion.

- A customary international law rule becomes a *jus cogens*, or peremptory, norm when the international community recognizes that it is a norm from which no derogation is permitted, such as prohibitions against slavery, genocide, and torture. A few cases suggest that *jus cogens* is incorporated into our law, but such incorporation has been hotly disputed.

The Extraterritorial Reach of U.S. Law

The preceding chapter explored some of the ways in which international law reaches into our own. This chapter explores the converse: the extent to which our laws reach abroad. When may a person assert constitutional rights against U.S. government actions abroad, and which rights? The answers to these questions may depend in part upon that person's status — citizen or not. Limits on U.S. government actions abroad also may depend on U.S. statutes intended to regulate those actions, as well as on the jurisdiction or willingness of U.S. courts to enforce either constitutional or statutory limits.

We begin by considering the extraterritorial reach of constitutional protections for individual rights, and introduce the distinction between U.S. persons and others that runs through U.S. national security law. We then address the extraterritorial effect of U.S. statutes and the international law principles of extraterritorial jurisdiction.

A. EXTRATERRITORIAL REACH OF CONSTITUTIONAL RIGHTS

Reading *Reid v. Covert*

This case addresses the important questions of whether and to what extent the Constitution applies to protect a citizen abroad. Mrs. Covert was tried without a jury by a U.S. military court for killing her husband, a U.S. Air Force sergeant, in England. Did Article III, §2, the Fifth Amendment, and the Sixth Amendment apply to Mrs. Covert's trial, or are they strictly applicable inside the United States?

- Why, according to the plurality opinion, do these constitutional provisions apply abroad? In Justice Black's view, what other provisions would apply outside the United States? How, for example, might the Fourth Amendment warrant requirement apply to a surreptitious search by U.S. agents of an American citizen's hotel room in Moscow?
- Justice Harlan concurs only in the result, providing the fifth vote. Why does he concur? What is his theory of constitutional extraterritoriality? Would he require a warrant for the search in the preceding hypothetical?
- Suppose Mrs. Covert was a British subject married to an American serviceman, and a treaty permitted her trial by an American military court. Would the constitutional provisions at issue in *Reid* then apply?

Reid v. Covert

United States Supreme Court, 1957
354 U.S. 1

[The facts and a portion of the opinion in this case are set out *supra* p. 180.]

Mr. Justice BLACK announced the opinion of the Court and delivered an opinion, in which THE CHIEF JUSTICE, Mr. Justice DOUGLAS, and Mr. Justice BRENNAN join.... At the beginning we reject the idea that when the United States acts against citizens abroad it can do so free of the Bill of Rights. The United States is entirely a creature of the Constitution. Its power and authority have no other source. It can only act in accordance with all the limitations imposed by the Constitution. When the Government reaches out to punish a citizen who is abroad, the shield which the Bill of Rights and other parts of the Constitution provide to protect his life and liberty should not be stripped away just because he happens to be in another land....

The rights and liberties which citizens of our country enjoy are not protected by custom and tradition alone, they have been jealously preserved from the encroachments of Government by express provisions of our written Constitution.

Among those provisions, Art. III, §2 and the Fifth and Sixth Amendments are directly relevant to these cases. Article III, §2 lays down the rule that:

> "The Trial of all Crimes, except in Cases of Impeachment, shall be by Jury; and such Trial shall be held in the State where the said Crimes shall have been committed; but when not committed within any State, the Trial shall be at such Place or Places as the Congress may by Law have directed."

The Fifth Amendment declares:

> "No person shall be held to answer for a capital, or otherwise infamous crime, unless on a presentment or indictment of a Grand Jury, except in cases arising in the land or naval forces, or in the Militia, when in actual service in time of War or public danger...."

And the Sixth Amendment provides:

> "In all criminal prosecutions, the accused shall enjoy the right to a speedy and public trial, by an impartial jury of the State and district wherein the crime shall have been committed. . . ."

The language of Art. III, §2 manifests that constitutional protections for the individual were designed to restrict the United States Government when it acts outside of this country, as well as here at home. After declaring that all criminal trials must be by jury, the section states that when a crime is "not committed within any State, the Trial shall be at such Place or Places as the Congress may by Law have directed." If this language is permitted to have its obvious meaning, §2 is applicable to criminal trials outside of the States as a group without regard to where the offense is committed or the trial held. From the very first Congress, federal statutes have implemented the provisions of §2 by providing for trial of murder and other crimes committed outside the jurisdiction of any State "in the district where the offender is apprehended, or into which he may first be brought." The Fifth and Sixth Amendments, like Art. III, §2, are also all inclusive with their sweeping references to "no person" and to "all criminal prosecutions."

This Court and other federal courts have held or asserted that various constitutional limitations apply to the Government when it acts outside the continental United States. While it has been suggested that only those constitutional rights which are "fundamental" protect Americans abroad, we can find no warrant, in logic or otherwise, for picking and choosing among the remarkable collection of "Thou shalt nots" which were explicitly fastened on all departments and agencies of the Federal Government by the Constitution and its Amendments. Moreover, in view of our heritage and the history of the adoption of the Constitution and the Bill of Rights, it seems peculiarly anomalous to say that trial before a civilian judge and by an independent jury picked from the common citizenry is not a fundamental right. . . .

Trial by jury in a court of law and in accordance with traditional modes of procedure after an indictment by grand jury has served and remains one of our most vital barriers to governmental arbitrariness. These elemental procedural safeguards were embedded in our Constitution to secure their inviolateness and sanctity against the passing demands of expediency or convenience. . . .

The [holding in *In re Ross,* 140 U.S. 453 (1891)] that the Constitution has no applicability abroad has long since been directly repudiated by numerous cases. That approach is obviously erroneous if the United States Government, which has no power except that granted by the Constitution, can and does try citizens for crimes committed abroad. . . . At best, the *Ross* case should be left as a relic from a different era.

[Last term the Court] relied on the "*Insular Cases*" to support its conclusion that Article III and the Fifth and Sixth Amendments were not applicable to the trial of Mrs. Smith and Mrs. Covert.[22] We believe that reliance was misplaced. The "*Insular Cases,*" which arose at the turn of the [twentieth] century, involved territories which had only recently been conquered or acquired by the United States. These territories, governed and regulated by Congress under Art. IV, §3, had entirely different cultures and customs from those of this country. . . .

---

22. *Downes v. Bidwell,* 182 U.S. 244; *Territory of Hawaii v. Mankichi,* 190 U.S. 197; *Dorr v. United States,* 195 U.S. 138; *Balzac v. Porto Rico,* 258 U.S. 298.

...Moreover, it is our judgment that neither the cases nor their reasoning should be given any further expansion. The concept that the Bill of Rights and other constitutional protections against arbitrary government are inoperative when they become inconvenient or when expediency dictates otherwise is a very dangerous doctrine and if allowed to flourish would destroy the benefit of a written Constitution and undermine the basis of our government. If our foreign commitments become of such nature that the Government can no longer satisfactorily operate within the bounds laid down by the Constitution, that instrument can be amended by the method which it prescribes. But we have no authority, or inclination, to read exceptions into it which are not there....

Mr. Justice HARLAN, concurring in the result.... I do not think that it can be said that these safeguards of the Constitution are never operative without the United States, regardless of the particular circumstances. On the other hand, I cannot agree with the suggestion that every provision of the Constitution must always be deemed automatically applicable to American citizens in every part of the world. For *Ross* and the *Insular Cases* do stand for an important proposition, one which seems to me a wise and necessary gloss on our Constitution. The proposition is, of course, not that the Constitution "does not apply" overseas, but that there are provisions in the Constitution which do not *necessarily* apply in all circumstances in every foreign place.... In other words, what *Ross* and the *Insular Cases* hold is that the particular local setting, the practical necessities, and the possible alternatives are relevant to a question of judgment, namely, whether jury trial should be deemed a necessary condition of the exercise of Congress' power to provide for the trial of Americans overseas....

...And so I agree with my brother Frankfurter that, in view of *Ross* and the *Insular Cases,* we have before us a question analogous, ultimately, to issues of due process; one can say, in fact, that the question of which specific safeguards of the Constitution are appropriately to be applied in a particular context overseas can be reduced to the issue of what process is "due" a defendant in the particular circumstances of a particular case.

On this basis, I cannot agree with the sweeping proposition that a full Article III trial, with indictment and trial by jury, is required in every case for the trial of a civilian dependent of a serviceman overseas. The Government, it seems to me, has made an impressive showing that at least for the run-of-the-mill offenses committed by dependents overseas, such a requirement would be as impractical and anomalous as it would have been to require jury trial for Balzac in Porto Rico....

So far as capital cases are concerned, I think they stand on quite a different footing than other offenses. In such cases the law is especially sensitive to demands for that procedural fairness which inheres in a civilian trial where the judge and trier of fact are not responsive to the command of the convening authority. I do not concede that whatever process is "due" an offender faced with a fine or a prison sentence necessarily satisfies the requirements of the Constitution in a capital case.... The number of such cases would appear to be so negligible that the practical problems of affording the defendant a civilian trial would not present insuperable problems.

On this narrow ground I concur in the result in these cases.

[The opinions of FRANKFURTER, J., concurring in the judgment, and of CLARK, J., dissenting, are omitted.]

Reading *United States v. Verdugo-Urquidez*

U.S. agents searched Verdugo-Urquidez's property in Mexico without a warrant. He moved to suppress the resulting evidence on the ground that the search violated the Fourth Amendment. His case differed from *Reid* in two key respects: he was an alien, not a citizen like Mrs. Covert, and the constitutional provision at issue was different from the ones in *Reid*.

- Why did the Court conclude that the Fourth Amendment did not protect Verdugo-Urquidez from a search in Mexico? When, according to the Court, would the Fourth Amendment ever apply to protect an alien abroad?
- Does the Court's reasoning also mean that the Fifth Amendment would not apply to protect an alien abroad?
- Justice Kennedy concurs on different reasoning. What is his theory of the extraterritorial effect of the Constitution? How would it apply to the extraterritorial reach of the Fourth Amendment?
- Verdugo-Urquidez was tried in a federal court in the United States. Suppose the court refused to allow him to be represented by a lawyer, to see the evidence against him, or to have a jury trial. Is the majority opinion authority for denial of these constitutional rights? If not, why not?

United States v. Verdugo-Urquidez

United States Supreme Court, 1990
494 U.S. 259

Chief Justice REHNQUIST delivered the opinion of the Court. The question presented by this case is whether the Fourth Amendment applies to the search and seizure by United States agents of property that is owned by a nonresident alien and located in a foreign country. We hold that it does not. . . .

[Respondent René Martin Verdugo-Urquidez was a citizen and resident of Mexico who was apprehended by Mexican police and delivered to U.S. border authorities in response to a U.S. warrant for his arrest on drug-smuggling charges. Following his arrest, and while he was incarcerated in the United States, DEA agents searched Verdugo-Urquidez's property in Mexico with the approval of Mexican authorities, but without a U.S. warrant, and seized certain documents that were subsequently offered as evidence against him. The defendant sought to have that evidence excluded.]

The Fourth Amendment provides:

> "The right of the people to be secure in their persons, houses, papers, and effects, against unreasonable searches and seizures, shall not be violated, and no Warrants shall issue, but upon probable cause, supported by Oath or affirmation, and particularly describing the place to be searched, and the persons or things to be seized."

That text, by contrast with the Fifth and Sixth Amendments, extends its reach only to "the people." Contrary to the suggestion of *amici curiae* that the Framers used this phrase "simply to avoid [an] awkward rhetorical redundancy," "the people" seems to have been a term of art employed in select parts of the Constitution. The Preamble declares that the Constitution is ordained and established by "the People of the United States." The Second Amendment protects "the right of the people to keep and bear Arms," and the Ninth and Tenth Amendments provide that certain rights and powers are retained by and reserved to "the people." See also U.S. Const., Amdt. 1 ("Congress shall make no law . . . abridging . . . *the right of the people* peaceably to assemble") (emphasis added); Art. I, §2, cl. 1 ("The House of Representatives shall be composed of Members chosen every second Year *by the People of the several States*") (emphasis added). While this textual exegesis is by no means conclusive, it suggests that "the people" protected by the Fourth Amendment, and by the First and Second Amendments, and to whom rights and powers are reserved in the Ninth and Tenth Amendments, refers to a class of persons who are part of a national community or who have otherwise developed sufficient connection with this country to be considered part of that community. The language of these Amendments contrasts with the words "person" and "accused" used in the Fifth and Sixth Amendments regulating procedure in criminal cases.

What we know of the history of the drafting of the Fourth Amendment also suggests that its purpose was to restrict searches and seizures which might be conducted by the United States in domestic matters. . . . The available historical data show, therefore, that the purpose of the Fourth Amendment was to protect the people of the United States against arbitrary action by their own Government; it was never suggested that the provision was intended to restrain the actions of the Federal Government against aliens outside of the United States territory.

There is likewise no indication that the Fourth Amendment was understood by contemporaries of the Framers to apply to activities of the United States directed against aliens in foreign territory or in international waters. Only seven years after the ratification of the Amendment, French interference with American commercial vessels engaged in neutral trade triggered what came to be known as the "undeclared war" with France. In an Act to "protect the Commerce of the United States" in 1798, Congress authorized President Adams to "instruct the commanders of the public armed vessels which are, or which shall be employed in the service of the United States, to subdue, seize and take any armed French vessel, which shall be found within the jurisdictional limits of the United States, or elsewhere, on the high seas." §1 of An Act Further to Protect the Commerce of the United States, ch. 68, 1 Stat. 578. . . . Some commanders were held liable by this Court for unlawful seizures because their actions were beyond the scope of the congressional grant of authority, *see, e.g., Little v. Barreme*, 2 Cranch 170, 177-178 (1804); *cf. Talbot v. Seeman*, 1 Cranch 1, 31 (1801) (seizure of neutral ship lawful where American captain had probable cause to believe vessel was French), but it was never suggested that the Fourth Amendment restrained the authority of congress or of United States agents to conduct operations such as this.

The global view taken by the Court of Appeals of the application of the Constitution is also contrary to this Court's decisions in the *Insular Cases*, which held that not every constitutional provision applies to governmental activity even where the United States has sovereign power. In *Dorr* [*v. United States*, 195 U.S. 138 (1904)], we declared the general rule that in an unincorporated territory — one not clearly destined for statehood — Congress was not required to adopt "a system of laws which shall include the right of trial by jury, and that *the Constitution does not, without legislation and of its own force, carry such right to territory so situated.*" 195 U.S. at 149 (emphasis added). Only "fundamental" constitutional rights are guaranteed to inhabitants of those territories.... [C]ertainly, it is not open to us in light of the *Insular Cases* to endorse the view that every constitutional provision applies wherever the United States Government exercises its power.

Indeed, we have rejected the claim that aliens are entitled to Fifth Amendment rights outside the sovereign territory of the United States. In *Johnson v. Eisentrager*, 339 U.S. 763 (1950), the Court held that enemy aliens arrested in China and imprisoned in Germany after World War II could not obtain writs of habeas corpus in our federal courts on the ground that their convictions for war crimes had violated the Fifth Amendment and other constitutional provisions. The *Eisentrager* opinion acknowledged that in some cases constitutional provisions extend beyond the citizenry; "[t]he alien... has been accorded a generous and ascending scale of rights as he increases his identity with our society." *Id.*, at 770. But our rejection of extraterritorial application of the Fifth Amendment was emphatic:

> "Such extraterritorial application of organic law would have been so significant an innovation in the practice of governments that, if intended or apprehended, it could scarcely have failed to excite contemporary comment. Not one word can be cited. No decision of this Court supports such a view. *Cf. Downes v. Bidwell*, 182 U.S. 244 [(1901)]. None of the learned commentators on our Constitution has even hinted at it. The practice of every modern government is opposed to it." *Id.*, at 784.

If such is true of the Fifth Amendment, which speaks in the relatively universal term of "person," it would seem even more true with respect to the Fourth Amendment, which applies only to "the people."

To support his all-encompassing view of the Fourth Amendment, respondent points to language from the plurality opinion in *Reid v. Covert*, 354 U.S. 1 (1957).... Four Justices "reject[ed] the idea that when the United States acts *against citizens* abroad it can do so free of the Bill of Rights." *Id.*, at 5 (emphasis added). The plurality went on to say:

> "The United States is entirely a creature of the Constitution. Its power and authority have no other source. It can only act in accordance with all the limitations imposed by the Constitution. When the Government reaches out to punish a citizen who is abroad, the shield which the Bill of Rights and other parts of the Constitution provide to protect his life and liberty should not be stripped away just because he happens to be in another land." *Id.*, at 5-6 (emphasis added; footnote omitted).

Respondent urges that we interpret this discussion to mean that federal officials are constrained by the Fourth Amendment wherever and against whomever they act. But the holding of *Reid* stands for no such sweeping proposition: it decided that United States citizens stationed abroad could invoke the protection of the Fifth and Sixth Amendments. The concurring opinions by Justices Frankfurter and Harlan in *Reid* resolved the case on much narrower grounds than the plurality and declined even to hold that United States citizens were entitled to the full range of constitutional protections in all overseas criminal prosecutions. *See id.*, at 75 (Harlan, J., concurring in result) ("I agree with my brother Frankfurter that... we have before us a question analogous, ultimately, to issues of due process; one can say, in fact, that the question of which specific safeguards of the Constitution are appropriately to be applied in a particular context overseas can be reduced to the issue of what process is 'due' a defendant in the particular circumstances of a particular case"). Since respondent is not a United States citizen, he can derive no comfort from the *Reid* holding.

Verdugo-Urquidez also relies on a series of cases in which we have held that aliens enjoy certain constitutional rights. *See, e.g., Plyler v. Doe*, 457 U.S. 202, 211-212 (1982) (illegal aliens protected by Equal Protection Clause); *Kwong Hai Chew v. Colding*, 344 U.S. 590, 596 (1953) (resident alien is a "person" within the meaning of the Fifth Amendment); *Bridges v. Wixon*, 326 U.S. 135, 148 (1945) (resident aliens have First Amendment rights); *Russian Volunteer Fleet v. United States*, 282 U.S. 481 (1931) (Just Compensation Clause of Fifth Amendment); *Wong Wing v. United States*, 163 U.S. 228, 238 (1896) (resident aliens entitled to Fifth and Sixth Amendment rights); *Yick Wo v. Hopkins*, 118 U.S. 356, 369 (1886) (Fourteenth Amendment protects resident aliens). These cases, however, establish only that aliens receive constitutional protections when they have come within the territory of the United States and developed substantial connections with this country. Respondent is an alien who has had no previous significant voluntary connection with the United States, so these cases avail him not....

Not only are history and case law against respondent, but as pointed out in *Johnson v. Eisentrager*, 339 U.S. 763 (1950), the result of accepting his claim would have significant and deleterious consequences for the United States in conducting activities beyond its boundaries. The rule adopted by the Court of Appeals would apply not only to law enforcement operations abroad, but also to other foreign policy operations which might result in "searches or seizures." The United States frequently employs armed forces outside this country — over 200 times in our history — for the protection of American citizens or national security. Congressional Research Service, *Instances of Use of United States Armed Forces Abroad, 1798-1989* (E. Collier ed. 1989). Application of the Fourth Amendment to those circumstances could significantly disrupt the ability of the political branches to respond to foreign situations involving our national interest. Were respondent to prevail, aliens with no attachment to this country might well bring actions for damages to remedy claimed violations of the Fourth Amendment in foreign countries or in international waters. *See Bivens v. Six Unknown Federal Narcotics Agents*, 403 U.S. 388 (1971).... The Members of the Executive and Legislative Branches are sworn to uphold the Constitution, and they presumably desire to follow its commands. But the Court of Appeals' global view of its applicability would plunge them into a sea of uncertainty as to what might be reasonable in the way of searches and seizures conducted abroad. Indeed, the Court of Appeals held that absent exigent circumstances, United States agents could not effect a "search or seizure" for law enforcement purposes in a foreign country without first obtaining a warrant — which would be a dead letter outside the United States — from a magistrate in this country. Even if no warrant were required, American agents would have to articulate specific facts giving them probable cause to undertake a search or seizure if they wished to comply with the Fourth Amendment as conceived by the Court of Appeals....

For better or for worse, we live in a world of nation-states in which our Government must be able to "function effectively in the company of sovereign nations." *Perez v. Brownell*, 356 U.S. 44, 57 (1958). Some who violate our laws may live outside our borders under a regime quite different from that which obtains in this country.

Situations threatening to important American interests may arise halfway around the globe, situations which in the view of the political branches of our Government require an American response with armed force. If there are to be restrictions on searches and seizures which occur incident to such American action, they must be imposed by the political branches through diplomatic understanding, treaty, or legislation.

The judgment of the Court of Appeals is accordingly

Reversed.

Justice Kennedy, concurring. . . . I take it to be correct, as the plurality opinion in *Reid v. Covert* sets forth, that the Government may act only as the Constitution authorizes, whether the actions in question are foreign or domestic. *See* 354 U.S., at 6. But this principle is only a first step in resolving this case. The question before us then becomes what constitutional standards apply when the Government acts, in reference to an alien, within its sphere of foreign operations. . . . [Various cases], as well as *United States v. Curtiss-Wright Export Corp.*, 299 U.S. 304, 318 (1936), stand for the proposition that we must interpret constitutional protections in light of the undoubted power of the United States to take actions to assert its legitimate power and authority abroad. Justice Harlan made this observation in his opinion concurring in the judgment in Reid v. Covert:

> "I cannot agree with the suggestion that every provision of the Constitution must always be deemed automatically applicable to American citizens in every part of the world. For *Ross* and the *Insular Cases* do stand for an important proposition, one which seems to me a wise and necessary gloss on our Constitution. The proposition is, of course, not that the Constitution 'does not apply' overseas, but that there are provisions in the Constitution which do not *necessarily* apply in all circumstances in every foreign place. In other words, it seems to me that the basic teaching of *Ross* and the *Insular Cases* is that there is no rigid and abstract rule that Congress, as a condition precedent to exercising power over Americans overseas, must exercise it subject to all the guarantees of the Constitution, no matter what the conditions and considerations are that would make adherence to a specific guarantee altogether impracticable and anomalous." 354 U.S., at 74.

The conditions and considerations of this case would make adherence to the Fourth Amendment's warrant requirement impracticable and anomalous. . . . The absence of local judges or magistrates available to issue warrants, the differing and perhaps unascertainable conceptions of reasonableness and privacy that prevail abroad, and the need to cooperate with foreign officials all indicate that the Fourth Amendment's warrant requirement should not apply in Mexico as it does in this country. For this reason, in addition to the other persuasive justifications stated by the Court, I agree that no violation of the Fourth Amendment has occurred in the case before us. The rights of a citizen, as to whom the United States has continuing obligations, are not presented by this case.

I do not mean to imply, and the Court has not decided, that persons in the position of the respondent have no constitutional protection. The United States is prosecuting a foreign national in a court established under Article III, and all of the trial proceedings are governed by the Constitution. All would agree, for instance, that the dictates of the Due Process Clause of the Fifth Amendment protect the defendant. Indeed, as Justice Harlan put it, "the question of which specific safeguards ... are appropriately to be applied in a particular context ... can be reduced to the issue of what process is 'due' a defendant in the particular circumstances of a particular case." *Reid, supra,* at 75. Nothing approaching a violation of due process has occurred in this case.

[The opinion of Justice STEVENS, concurring in the judgment on the ground that, although the Fourth Amendment applied, the search was reasonable, is omitted.]

Justice BRENNAN, with whom Justice MARSHALL joins, dissenting.... The Court today creates an antilogy: the Constitution authorizes our Government to enforce our criminal laws abroad, but when Government agents exercise this authority, the Fourth Amendment does not travel with them. This cannot be. At the very least, the Fourth Amendment is an unavoidable correlative of the Government's power to enforce the criminal law....

... When we tell the world that we expect all people, wherever they may be, to abide by our laws, we cannot in the same breath tell the world that our law enforcement officers need not do the same. Because we cannot expect others to respect our laws until we respect our Constitution, I respectfully dissent.

Justice BLACKMUN, dissenting. I cannot accept the Court of Appeals' conclusion, echoed in some portions of Justice Brennan's dissent, that the Fourth Amendment governs every action by an American official that can be characterized as a search or seizure. American agents acting abroad generally do not purport to exercise sovereign authority over the foreign nationals with whom they come in contact. The relationship between these agents and foreign nationals is therefore fundamentally different from the relationship between United States officials and individuals residing within this country.

I am inclined to agree with Justice Brennan, however, that when a foreign national is held accountable for purported violations of United States criminal laws, he has effectively been treated as one of "the governed" and therefore is entitled to Fourth Amendment protections. Although the Government's exercise of *power* abroad does not ordinarily implicate the Fourth Amendment, the enforcement of domestic criminal law seems to me to be the paradigmatic exercise of sovereignty over those who are compelled to obey. In any event, as Justice Stevens notes, respondent was lawfully (though involuntarily) within this country at the time the search occurred. Under these circumstances I believe that respondent is entitled to invoke protections of the Fourth Amendment. I agree with the Government, however, that an American magistrate's lack of power to authorize a search abroad renders the Warrant Clause inapplicable to the search of a noncitizen's residence outside this country.

The Fourth Amendment nevertheless requires that the search be "reasonable." And when the purpose of a search is the procurement of evidence for a criminal prosecution, we have consistently held that the search, to be reasonable, must be based upon probable cause. Neither the District Court nor the Court of Appeals addressed the issue of probable cause, and I do not believe that a reliable determination could be made on the basis of the record before us. I therefore would vacate the judgment of the Court of Appeals and remand the case for further proceedings.

Notes and Questions

1. *All Constitutional Rights?* In *Reid,* Justice Black took a characteristically (for him) black and white view of the Constitution's extraterritoriality: the government "can only act in accordance with all the limitations imposed by the Constitution," whether it acts at home or "reaches out to punish a citizen who is abroad." Constitutional rights cannot be sliced and diced, because there is no basis "for picking and choosing" among them to identify some sub-set that is more fundamental than others. The implications of Black's absolutist position and later developments are analyzed in Kal Raustiala, *Does the Constitution Follow the Flag? The Evolution of Territoriality in American Law* (2009).

2. *Some Constitutional Rights?* Justice Black's sweeping statement seems to suggest that the government would need a warrant to search a U.S. citizen's hotel room in Moscow, at least for criminal evidence. But a warrant might be impractical in such a case. Our government would not likely ask for one from a Russian court, and if it did, their laws for issuing warrants (if any) might bear little resemblance to ours. Our agents could seek a warrant from a U.S. court, but only if the court had the authority to issue warrants for searches outside its jurisdiction. Moreover, issuance of such a warrant might unduly delay a search if, for example, it required a complicated translation of an affidavit in support of probable cause.

Justice Harlan's reasoning could allow for consideration of such practicalities. He argued that some "provisions of the Constitution . . . do not *necessarily* apply in all circumstances in every foreign place." *Reid,* 354 U.S. at 74 (Harlan, J., concurring in the result). Whether they apply, he wrote, depends on "the particular local setting, the practical necessities, and the possible alternatives." *Id.* at 75. He thought it would be "impractical and anomalous" to require trial by jury for "run-of-the-mill" offenses. Yet he indicated that capital cases are different, not just because they are more sensitive to demands for fairness, but also because there would probably be so few of them (located abroad) that the practical problems were surmountable.

Is Justice Harlan's theory of conditional applicability based in the Constitution? If not, what is its source? Is it "very dangerous," as Justice Black warns? How is that theory reflected in Justice Kennedy's concurring opinion in *Verdugo-Urquidez*? Does it provide an answer to the *Verdugo-Urquidez* majority's worry that application of the Fourth Amendment abroad would plunge government officials into a "sea of uncertainty"?

3. *Citizens vs. Noncitizens.* How did the citizenship of the defendants affect the outcomes in *Reid* and *Verdugo-Urquidez*? Chief Justice Rehnquist pointed out in *Verdugo-Urquidez* that noncitizens inside this country generally enjoy the same constitutional protections that U.S. citizens do, although there may be some newfound exceptions, as discussed in Chapter 31, *infra.* Can the largely equal treatment of citizens and noncitizens inside the United States be reconciled with his "textual exegesis" of the various Amendments — distinguishing between "persons" and "the people" — to make them apply differently to citizens and aliens abroad?

The majority in *Verdugo-Urquidez* indicated that in drafting the Fourth Amendment "it was never suggested that the provision was intended to restrain the actions of the Federal Government against aliens outside of the United States territory." 494 U.S. at 266. The Court also found no evidence that the Framers intended for the Amendment to constrain wartime military operations against enemies. Does it follow logically that the Framers therefore intended that the Fourth Amendment *not* apply to aliens abroad? Should we assume that they considered the matter at all? Can you think of any reason why the Framers might have wanted to guarantee freedom from unreasonable searches abroad to citizens but not aliens? *See generally* J. Andrew Kent, *A Textual and Historical Case Against a Global Constitution*, 95 Geo. L.J. 463, 465 (2007) (arguing that "noncitizens outside the United States are to be protected only by diplomacy, treaties, the law of nations . . . and nonconstitutional policy choices of the political branches").

4. *Sufficient Connection.* The *Verdugo-Urquidez* Court declared that the Fourth Amendment is inapplicable to aliens abroad who lack a "substantial" or "significant voluntary" or "sufficient connection" with the United States. Can this limitation be found in the text of the Constitution?

What is a "sufficient connection"? The Court said only that Verdugo-Urquidez had no "previous significant voluntary connection" that would entitle him to the protection of the Fourth Amendment, even though he was issued a green card in 1970 that he insisted was still valid, and even though the government claimed that he had engaged in trade (drug-trafficking) within the United States. Subsequent lower court decisions are inconsistent. *Compare United States v. Defreitas*, 701 F. Supp. 2d 297 (E.D.N.Y. 2010) (alleged conspiracy to commit terrorist attack in the United States not a sufficient "voluntary connection"), *with Martinez-Aguero v. Gonzalez*, 459 F.3d 618 (5th Cir. 2006) (regular and lawful entry into the United States sufficient). The resulting ambiguity makes it difficult for U.S. officials engaged in overseas surveillance of aliens to know how to proceed. The differentiation among aliens also means that disparate standards may apply to codefendants engaged in the same conduct and subjected to the same search. What kind of connection did Justice Blackmun, dissenting, say made the Fourth Amendment applicable to Verdugo-Urquidez? And will a federal officer always know in advance whether a noncitizen he is searching or seizing on foreign soil does or does not have sufficient connections to trigger constitutional protection? *Cf. Hernandez v. Mesa*, 137 S. Ct. 2003 (2017) (per curiam) (holding that an officer was not entitled to qualified immunity where he did not know the nationality of an individual against whom he used lethal force, and would not have been entitled to qualified immunity had the individual been a U.S. citizen).

Should courts draw a bright line? If so, what should it be? *Compare* Randall K. Miller, *The Limits of U.S. International Law Enforcement After Verdugo-Urquidez: Resurrecting Rochin*, 58 U. Pitt. L. Rev. 867, 885 n.88 (1997) (drawing the line at the border, thus denying Fourth Amendment protections to all aliens searched abroad, regardless of their connection to the United States), *with* Douglas I. Koff, *Post-Verdugo-Urquidez: The Sufficient Connection Test — Substantially Ambiguous, Substantially Unworkable*, 25 Colum. Hum. Rts. L. Rev. 435, 485 (1994) (extending Fourth Amendment protections to all persons except nonresident enemy aliens searched incident to a military confrontation). Is it possible that a better line would differentiate between *searches* (which raise all of the practical concerns flagged above) and *seizures* (which implicate a greater deprivation of liberty)?

5. "U.S. Persons." The distinction that *Verdugo-Urquidez* draws between citizens and sufficiently connected noncitizens, on one hand, and all other noncitizens, on the other, runs through U.S. national security law. For example, the Foreign Intelligence Surveillance Act, 50 U.S.C. §§1801-1885c (2018), defines "United States person" in relevant part as "a citizen of the United States [or] an alien lawfully admitted for permanent residence." *Id.* §1801(i). It then establishes more stringent requirements for surveillance of U.S. persons than of non-U.S. persons. *Id.* §§1801(b), 1805(a).

An executive order governing the intelligence community adopts the same definition. Exec. Order No. 12,333, *United States Intelligence Activities,* §3.5(k), 46 Fed. Reg. 59,941 (Dec. 4, 1981), as amended. It also imposes more stringent requirements for collection of foreign intelligence that targets U.S. persons abroad than for collection against non-U.S. persons. For example, physical surveillance of a U.S. person abroad is forbidden, "except to obtain significant information that cannot reasonably be acquired by other means." *Id.* §2.4(d).

Are these statutory and executive exceptions to the Fourth Amendment warrant requirement consistent with the Supreme Court's holding in *Reid v. Covert*? Can these categorical distinctions between U.S. citizens and certain noncitizens be squared with the "sufficient connection" criterion articulated in *Verdugo-Urquidez*?

6. Application of the Fifth Amendment to Aliens Abroad? The *Verdugo-Urquidez* majority stated that in *Johnson v. Eisentrager,* a 1950 habeas corpus case brought by German nationals convicted by a U.S. military commission and imprisoned abroad, "our rejection of extraterritorial application of the Fifth Amendment was emphatic." 494 U.S. at 269. But that rejection was also deeply conditional. In the course of rejecting the petitioners' challenge to the jurisdiction of the military commission that tried and convicted them, the *Eisentrager* Court noted that "[i]f the Fifth Amendment confers its rights on all the world . . . the same must be true of the companion civil-rights Amendments, for none of them is limited by its express terms, territorially or as to persons." 339 U.S. at 784. It then concluded that the Constitution does not confer such rights on "an alien enemy engaged in the hostile service of a government at war with the United States." *Id.* at 785. But the "disabilities this country lays upon the alien who becomes also an enemy are imposed temporarily as an incident of war and not as an incident of alienage." *Id.* at 772.

In a 2008 case involving petitions for habeas corpus brought by noncitizen "enemy combatants" held at a U.S. prison in Guantánamo Bay (over which Cuba retains *de jure* sovereignty), the Supreme Court distinguished *Eisentrager. Boumediene v. Bush,* 553 U.S. 723 (2008) (*infra* pp. 850, 864). Justice Kennedy wrote the opinion for the majority, declaring that

> if the Government's reading of *Eisentrager* were correct, the opinion would have marked not only a change in, but a complete repudiation of, the *Insular Cases*' (and later *Reid*'s) functional approach to questions of extraterritoriality. We cannot accept the Government's view. Nothing in *Eisentrager* says that *de jure* sovereignty is or has ever been the only relevant consideration in determining the geographic reach of the Constitution or of habeas corpus. Were that the case, there would be considerable tension between *Eisentrager,* on the one hand, and the *Insular Cases* and *Reid,* on the other. Our cases need not be read to conflict in this manner. A constricted reading of *Eisentrager* overlooks what we see as a common thread uniting the *Insular Cases, Eisentrager,* and *Reid*: the idea that

> questions of extraterritoriality turn on objective factors and practical concerns, not formalism. [*Id.* at 726-727.]

So saying, the Court applied a functional test for whether the right to petition for habeas should extend to noncitizens detained at the Guantánamo Bay prison. The Court concluded that the Guantánamo prisoners *could* apply for a writ of habeas corpus, although it expressly withheld any opinion about their substantive rights. Justice Scalia, dissenting, warned that the decision paved the way for "the extraterritorial reach of other constitutional protections as well." *Id.* at 850.

We leave the deeper exploration of habeas corpus and the *Eisentrager* and *Boumediene* decisions to a later chapter. But insofar as they raise the question of the future extraterritorial application of *other* constitutional rights, that question divided the en banc Fifth Circuit Court of Appeals in the following 2015 decision.

Reading *Hernandez v. United States*

A 15-year old Mexican boy was shot and killed while he was playing in a cement culvert separating the United States from Mexico. The fatal shot across the international border was fired by a U.S. Customs and Border Protection agent, Jesus Mesa Jr., standing on U.S. soil. The boy's parents brought an action against Mesa and other defendants, alleging violations of the Fourth Amendment's ban on unreasonable seizures and the Fifth Amendment's Due Process Clause. Like Verdugo-Urquidez, the boy had no substantial connection to the United States (unless it was the shot fired from the United States that killed him). Mesa argued that he was immune from liability because aliens had no clearly established constitutional right in these circumstances. Sitting en banc, the Ninth Circuit agreed that no such right was "clearly" established, but it divided over whether there was any Fifth Amendment right at all in light of *Verdugo-Urquidez* and *Eisentrager*.

- *Boumediene* used a functional three-part test to decide whether the right to petition for habeas extended to prisoners at Guantánamo. Why did Judge Jones refuse to apply that test to the Hernandez Fifth Amendment claim? If she is right, what constitutional rights extend abroad to an alien who lacks any substantial connection to the United States?
- Judge Prado applied the *Boumediene* three-part test to conclude that the Fifth Amendment right to due process did extend to Hernandez (though he agreed that this was not clearly established at the time of the shooting). What support, if any, did he draw from prior Supreme Court precedent for this approach?
- Judge Dennis ultimately concluded that the Fifth Amendment did extend to the circumstances of this case. Did he apply Judge Jones' "formalist" approach or Judge Prado's "functionalist" approach to decide the question of extraterritoriality?
- Wasn't the fatal bullet a connection to the United States that was as substantial as a connection can be, in view of the tragic result? Why isn't this case decided by *Verdugo-Urquidez*?

Hernandez v. United States (*Hernández I*)

United States Court of Appeals, Fifth Circuit, 2015
785 F.3d 117,
vacated sub nom. Hernandez v. Mesa, 137 S. Ct. 2003 (2017),
aff'd on remand, 885 F.3d 811 (5th Cir. 2018) (en banc),
cert. granted, 139 S. Ct. 2636 (2019) (mem.)

PER CURIAM: We rehear this matter en banc, *see Hernandez v. United States,* 771 F.3d 818 (5th Cir. 2014) (per curiam) (on petitions for rehearing en banc), to resolve whether, under facts unique to this or any other circuit, the individual defendants in these consolidated appeals are entitled to qualified immunity. Unanimously concluding that the plaintiffs fail to allege a violation of the Fourth Amendment, and that the Fifth Amendment right asserted by the plaintiffs was not clearly established at the time of the complained-of incident, we affirm the judgment of dismissal. . . .

EDITH H. JONES, Circuit Judge, joined by SMITH, CLEMENT, and OWEN, Circuit Judges, concurring: The court has unfortunately taken the path of least resistance. We hold unanimously that Agent Mesa has qualified immunity from this suit for a Fifth Amendment substantive due process violation because he did not violate any clearly established rights flowing from that Amendment. *Pearson v. Callahan,* 555 U.S. 223, 236 (2009). This compromise simply delays the day of reckoning until another appellate panel revisits non-citizen tort claims for excessive force resting on extraterritorial application of the United States Constitution. Ongoing incursions across our national borders and our nation's applications of force abroad ensure that other lawsuits will be pursued. We should discourage this litigation before it takes root.

Because it is clear that United States constitutional rights do not extend to aliens who (a) lack any connection to the United States and (b) are injured on foreign soil, I would also resolve this appeal on the first prong of qualified immunity analysis. *See id.* at 236 ("In some cases, a discussion of why the relevant facts do not violate clearly established law may make it apparent that in fact the relevant facts do not make out a constitutional violation at all."). . . .

III. THE NON-EXTRATERRITORIALITY OF THE FIFTH AMENDMENT[6]

After agreeing that [*United States v. Verdugo-Urquidez,* 494 U.S. 259 (1990),] forecloses the plaintiffs' Fourth Amendment claim, this court should have been quick to conclude that their alternate Fifth Amendment claim is equally thwarted by *Johnson v. Eisentrager.* 339 U.S. 763 (1950). The Supreme Court held in *Johnson,* and has reiterated since then, that as a general matter aliens outside the sovereign territory of the United States are not entitled to Fifth Amendment rights. *Id.* at 782-85. *Verdugo-Urquidez* described *Johnson* as unambiguously "reject[ing] the claim that aliens are entitled to Fifth Amendment rights outside the sovereign territory of the United

---

6. The plaintiffs argue without conviction that because Agent Mesa's conduct occurred solely on U.S. soil, this case does not require extraterritorial application of the Constitution. In both *Verdugo-Urquidez* and *Sosa* [*v. Alvarez-Machain,* 542 U.S. 692 (2004)], however, the Supreme Court treated the cases as involving extraterritorial violations despite the presence of actions on American soil that preceded the foreign incidents. This case is no different. Indeed, the hoary principle of *lex loci delicti* ("law of the place of injury") historically required the application of the law at the place where the last act causing injury (here, the bullet hitting Hernandez) occurred.

States." *Verdugo-Urquidez,* 494 U.S. at 269. . . . This court is not at liberty to "underrule" Supreme Court decisions when the Court has explicitly failed to overrule its own precedents. Consequently, the plaintiffs' substantive due process claim is barred by these precedents.

The plaintiffs' implicit position is that *Johnson* was *de facto* overruled by *Boumediene* [*v. Bush,* 553 U.S. 723 (2008)], and [that] *Johnson*'s refusal to apply the Fifth Amendment extraterritorially was replaced by the three-part test inaugurated in *Boumediene.*[7] . . .

. . . *Boumediene* was expressly limited to holding that the Suspension Clause, art. I, §9, cl. 2 of the Constitution, applies to enemy combatants detained in the Guantanamo Bay, Cuba, military facility. *Boumediene,* 553 U.S. at 771. . . . The Court also held that the concerns regarding separation of powers "have particular bearing upon the Suspension Clause question in the cases now before us, for the writ of habeas corpus is itself an indispensable mechanism for monitoring the separation of powers." *Id.* at 765. . . .

Boumediene fashioned a test that it claimed to derive from past decisions that considered the extraterritorial reach of other constitutional provisions. The Court concluded that *de jure* sovereignty does not alone determine the extraterritorial reach of the Constitution; instead, "questions of extraterritoriality turn on objective factors and practical concerns, not formalism." *Id.* at 764. But the Court ultimately held its three-factor test relevant "in determining the reach *of the Suspension Clause*. . . ." *Id.* at 766 (emphasis added). Moreover, the Court disclaimed any intention to overrule the holdings of *Johnson* or *Verdugo-Urquidez. Id.* at 795.

Given that *Boumediene* applied its three-factor test to a different constitutional provision than those with which we are confronted, and that it did not overrule the controlling precedents, it bears repeating: this court may not step ahead of the Supreme Court to hold *Johnson* (or *Verdugo-Urquidez*) no longer binding. Thus, this is not a case where no "clearly established law" articulates the plaintiffs' rights to exterritorial application of the Fifth Amendment. Following *Boumediene,* there is no law at all supporting their position, and thus no Fifth Amendment claim exists. . . .

For all these reasons, the plaintiffs plainly have no cognizable constitutional claim against Agent Mesa. . . .

JAMES L. DENNIS, Circuit Judge, concurring in part and concurring in the judgment: I join the en banc court's opinion in its entirety except as to its reason for denying Appellants' Fourth Amendment claim, with which I agree in result. I also join the concurring opinion of Judge Prado, except to the extent that it adopts the en banc court's reason for denying this claim. . . . I am inclined to agree . . . with those who have suggested that the *Verdugo-Urquidez* view cannot be squared with the Court's later holding in *Boumediene v. Bush,* 553 U.S. 723 (2008), that "questions of extraterritoriality turn on objective factors, and practical concerns, not formalism." *Id.* at 764.

The Mexican government has indicated that our adjudication of the Appellants' claims, whether under the Fourth or Fifth Amendment, in this particular case would not cause any friction with its sovereign interests. However, it appears that our judicial entanglement with extraterritorial Fourth Amendment excessive-force claims would

7. That test requires courts to examine "(1) the citizenship and status of the detainee and the adequacy of the process through which that status determination was made; (2) the nature of the sites where apprehension and then detention took place; and (3) the practical obstacles inherent in resolving the prisoner's entitlement to the writ." *Boumediene,* 553 U.S. at 766.

be likely to involve impracticable and anomalous factors. For these reasons, I agree with the opinion of the court in declining to apply the Fourth Amendment to adjudicate the Appellants' claims but I do so out of concern for pragmatic and political questions rather than on a formal classification of the litigants involved.

EDWARD C. PRADO, Circuit Judge, concurring: I agree with the en banc court's holding that the constitutional rights asserted by 15-year-old Sergio Hernández and his family were not clearly established in 2010, when Agent Mesa fired his fatal shots across the international border. However, I am compelled to write separately in response to Judge Jones's concurring opinion, which, in my view, sets forth an oversimplified and flawed analysis of the Fifth Amendment and the Supreme Court's extraterritoriality precedents. . . .

II. THE EXTRATERRITORIALITY OF THE FIFTH AMENDMENT

Judge Jones's concurrence paints our extraterritoriality case law in broad strokes, with a palette of black and white. The state of the law, as the concurrence views it, permits no gray.[3] According to the concurrence, the Constitution cannot apply extraterritorially to the facts of this case because the Supreme Court has held, generally, that the Fourth and Fifth Amendments do not apply to noncitizens with no significant voluntary connection to the United States. Citing *Eisentrager* and *Verdugo-Urquidez,* the concurrence asserts that the Supreme Court has foreclosed the question before our Court. This uncomplicated view of extraterritoriality fails to exhibit due regard for the Court's watershed opinion in *Boumediene,* which not only authoritatively interpreted these earlier cases but also announced the bedrock standards for determining the extraterritorial reach of *the Constitution* — not just the writ of habeas corpus. Applying these standards, I would hold the Fifth Amendment applicable to the particular facts alleged by Hernández.

In *Boumediene,* the Court provided its clearest and most definitive articulation of the principles governing the application of constitutional provisions abroad. Although the Court was tasked with deciding the narrow question of whether aliens designated enemy combatants and detained at Guantanamo Bay had the constitutional privilege of habeas corpus, Justice Kennedy wrote a lengthy opinion for the Court that grappled with the foundations of extraterritoriality. . . . [T]he Court read beyond the bare holdings of these cases and concluded that they shared a common thread: "the idea that questions of extraterritoriality turn on objective factors and practical concerns, not formalism." *Id.* at 764. Based on these considerations, the

---

3. The absolutism of the concurrence's analytical framework is epitomized by its phrasing of the constitutional issue in this case: "United States constitutional rights do not extend to aliens who (a) lack any connection to the United States and (b) are injured on foreign soil." All nuance is lost, and only one conclusion follows from the question presented. But there is no question that Hernández had *some* connection to the United States, even if not the "significant voluntary connection" required to invoke the protections of the Fourth Amendment under *Verdugo-Urquidez,* 494 U.S. at 271, by virtue of the acts of Agent Mesa that originated in the United States and had their effect in Mexico. Likewise, it is misguided to focus exclusively on Hernández's location within Mexico when the bullets Agent Mesa fired from United States soil found their target. This is not a case involving a drone strike, an act of war on a distant battlefield, or law-enforcement conduct occurring entirely within another nation's territory; it is a fatal shooting by small-arms fire in which the short distance separating those involved was bisected by an international border. These distinct facts cast doubt on the concurrence's simplistic framework and belie its warning that this case implicates "our nation's applications of force abroad."

Court identified at least three factors that were relevant in determining the reach of the Suspension Clause: (1) the citizenship and status of the detainee and the quality of the process underlying this finding; (2) the nature of the sites where the apprehension and detention occurred; and (3) the practical obstacles inherent in determining the detainee's entitlement to the writ. *Id.* at 766. After analyzing these factors, the Court held that the Suspension Clause "has full effect at Guantanamo Bay." *Id.* at 771.

This holding may have been limited to the Suspension Clause, but the Court's reasoning was decidedly not so constricted. Justice Kennedy's opinion drew from the analysis of numerous rights in numerous contexts *other than habeas, id.* at 755-64, framing its review of the case law as a survey of the Court's discussions of "*the Constitution's* extraterritorial application," *id.* at 755 (emphasis added). More importantly, when the Court rejected the Government's proffered reading of *Eisentrager*— the case that Judge Jones's concurrence cites as facially foreclosing Hernández's Fifth Amendment claim — it announced in no uncertain terms that "[n]othing in *Eisentrager* says that *de jure* sovereignty is or has ever been the only relevant consideration in determining the geographic reach of *the Constitution* or of habeas corpus." *Id.* at 764 (emphasis added).

Boumediene, and its functionality-focused reading of the Court's previous extraterritoriality decisions, is instructive here. Confronted with a novel extraterritoriality question, we must apply the only appropriate analytical framework the Court has given us: the *Boumediene* factors. Adapted to the present context, three objective factors and practical concerns are relevant to our extraterritoriality determination: (1) the citizenship and status of the claimant, (2) the nature of the location where the constitutional violation occurred, and (3) the practical obstacles inherent in enforcing the claimed right. *Cf. id.* at 766-71. The relevant practical obstacles include the consequences for U.S. actions abroad, the substantive rules that would govern the claim, and the likelihood that a favorable ruling would lead to friction with another country's government. As the panel majority's original opinion explained, the *Boumediene* factors, coupled with an analysis of the operation, text, and history of the Fifth Amendment, militate in favor of the extraterritorial application of substantive due process protections on these facts.

In sum, were we to reach the constitutional merits, I would hold, as the vacated panel majority's opinion did, that a noncitizen situated immediately beyond our nation's borders may invoke the protection of the Fifth Amendment against the arbitrary use of lethal small-arms force by a U.S. government official standing on U.S. soil. To hold otherwise would enshrine an unsustainably strict, territorial approach to constitutional rights — one the Supreme Court rejected in *Boumediene*. . . .

I respectfully concur in the en banc opinion.

[Concurring opinions of CATHARINA HAYNES, Circuit Judge, joined by SOUTHWICK and HIGGINSON, Circuit Judges, and of JAMES E. GRAVES, JR., Circuit Judge, are omitted.]

Notes and Questions

1. The Question Deferred: No Cause of Action. In a per curiam opinion, the Supreme Court vacated and remanded in *Hernández I,* finding in part that whether the plaintiffs had stated a *Bivens* claim was, in the first instance, a question for the court of appeals and "antecedent" to the "sensitive" and potentially "far-reaching" Fourth Amendment question. *Hernández I*, 137 S. Ct. 2003. Dissenting, Justices Breyer and Ginsburg would have reached that question, relying on *Boumediene*'s functional test to find that Hernandez was protected by the Fourth Amendment on the unique facts of his case. Justice Thomas dissented on the grounds that *Bivens* should be confined to its "precise circumstances," not met here.

On remand, the Fifth Circuit in *Hernández II* once again sidestepped the merits question, holding en banc that the plaintiffs had failed to state a *Bivens* claim. 885 F.3d 811 (5th Cir. 2018) (en banc). The Court again granted certiorari, but only on the *Bivens* question, and it heard argument on November 12, 2019.

2. *Eisentrager's Legacy? Eisentrager* rejected a claim that the Fifth Amendment barred the military commission trial of the plaintiff German nationals imprisoned abroad in 1950. Forty years later, *Verdugo-Urquidez* read the earlier case much more broadly as categorically refusing the protection of the Fifth Amendment to any alien abroad.

Because *Boumediene* in 2008 dealt exclusively with rights under the Suspension Clause, Judge Jones concluded that it left prior precedents — including *Verdugo*'s sweeping reading of *Eisentrager* — in place in every other respect. Her "formalist" interpretation thus would reach a categorical result for all aliens, regardless of the circumstances. But did the *Verdugo-Urquidez* Court's reading of *Eisentrager* furnish a binding precedent for application of the Fifth Amendment abroad?

Judge Jones also reasoned that habeas corpus rights are arguably different from rights under the Bill of Rights, in part because the right to petition a court to decide the legality of one's detention is an instrument of the separation of powers; it subjects the Executive to a measure of judicial supervision. Do courts not, however, perform the same function in enforcing provisions of the Bill of Rights?

3. *Functionalism: Practical Necessities in the Circumstances.* Judge Prado reads *Boumediene* differently — as a sea change in extraterritorial application of the Constitution, or perhaps more accurately, a belated triumph of the Harlan and Kennedy concurrences in *Reid* and *Verdugo-Urquidez*, respectively. (Justice Kennedy wrote the opinion for the Court in *Boumediene.*) While we defer until a later chapter an analysis of the three-factor test the Court used in *Boumediene*, it should already be apparent that it is eminently pragmatic, and, indeed, even expressly addresses "the practical obstacles inherent in resolving the prisoner's entitlement to the writ." *See* Prado opinion, *supra*, n.7 (quoting the factors).

Of course, by such a functional test, constitutional provisions "do not *necessarily* apply in all circumstances in every foreign place." *Reid*, 354 U.S. at 74 (Harlan, J., concurring in the result). Judge Dennis believed that *Boumediene* even superseded *Verdugo-Urquidez*'s analysis of the extraterritorial application of the *Fourth* Amendment, although he refused to extend the Fourth Amendment in *Hernandez* owing to unstated "pragmatic and political questions."

4. *Border Shootings. Hernández* does not stand alone. In *Rodriguez v. Swartz*, 899 F.3d 719 (9th Cir. 2018), *petition for cert. filed*, No. 18-309 (U.S. Sept. 11, 2018), the plaintiffs also brought a civil action for damages against a Border Patrol officer who shot and killed their son across the border. *See generally* Mark Binelli, *The Killing of a Mexican 16-Year-Old Raises Troubling Questions About the United States Border Patrol*, N.Y. Times (Mag.), Mar. 6, 2016, at 36 (describing the shooting of José Rodriquez, and

reporting that the defendant Border Patrol officer in the civil lawsuit was indicted for second-degree murder for shooting Rodriguez — the first Border Patrol officer to be prosecuted for a cross-border shooting). In 2018, a U.S. jury found the officer who shot Rodriguez not guilty of second-degree murder, but deadlocked on lesser counts of manslaughter. Rory Carroll, *Border Patrol Agent Found Not Guilty of Murder in Mexican Teen's 2012 Death,* The Guardian, Apr. 24, 2018.

The Ninth Circuit affirmed a district court ruling in the civil suit, finding that the plaintiffs stated a *Bivens* cause of action and that the shooting, as pleaded, violated clearly established law, precluding a defense of qualified immunity. The court reasoned that

> unlike the American agents in *Verdugo-Urquidez,* who acted on Mexican soil, [defendant] Swartz acted on American soil. Just as Mexican law controls what people do there, American law controls what people do here. *Verdugo-Urquidez* simply did not address the conduct of American agents on American soil. Also, the agents in *Verdugo-Urquidez* knew that they were searching a Mexican citizen's property in Mexico, but Swartz could not have known whether J.A. [the victim] was an American citizen or not. [899 F.3d at 731.]

The Fifth Circuit focused on the location and constitutional rights of the victim of the shooting, while the Ninth Circuit looked also to the location of and the constitutional limits on the shooter. Which is right? *Is Verdugo-Urquidez* meaningfully distinguishable?

B. EXTRATERRITORIAL EFFECT OF U.S. STATUTES

Reading *Kiobel v. Royal Dutch Petroleum Co.*

Kiobel is a "foreign-cubed" case: (1) foreign plaintiffs sued (2) foreign defendants for (3) acts committed in a foreign place. They brought the case under the Alien Tort Statute (ATS), 28 U.S.C. §1350 (2018), which permits aliens to sue in U.S. federal courts for torts committed in violation of the law of nations (customary international law) or a U.S. treaty. The lower courts dismissed on the ground that the statute did not confer jurisdiction over claims against corporations, because corporations could not be liable under international law. But the Supreme Court directed the parties to brief a very different and broader threshold question: whether the ATS has extraterritorial application.

- What is the applicable canon of statutory construction? What is its purpose?
- The ATS does not expressly state that it has extraterritorial application. Why isn't this enough to require dismissal of the claims? If the presumption against extraterritoriality can be overcome by implication, why doesn't the provision of relief for aliens under the ATS imply a congressional intent that it apply extraterritorially? What is Justice Alito's answer?
- Historically, the ATS reached claims for injuries from piracy arising on the high seas. Why doesn't that fact rebut the presumption against extraterritoriality?
- Does *Kiobel* bar all ATS claims if the acts giving rise to the claims took place abroad? If not, which claims survive?

Kiobel v. Royal Dutch Petroleum Co.

United States Supreme Court, 2013
569 U.S. 108

Chief Justice Roberts delivered the opinion of the Court. . . . [Plaintiffs were Nigerian nationals who claimed that Dutch, British, and Nigerian corporations had aided and abetted the Nigerian government in attacking them in Nigeria for protesting the environmental effects of the defendants' practices there. They filed claims in district court under the Alien Tort Statute (ATS), which provides, in full, that "[t]he district courts shall have original jurisdiction of any civil action by an alien for a tort only, committed in violation of the law of nations or a treaty of the United States." 28 U.S.C. §1350 (2012).

The district court dismissed their complaint in part, and the Second Circuit then dismissed the entire complaint, reasoning that the law of nations does not recognize corporate liability. The Supreme Court granted certiorari, and after oral argument it directed the parties to brief this additional question: "Whether and under what circumstances the [ATS] allows courts to recognize a cause of action for violations of the law of nations occurring within the territory of a sovereign other than the United States."]

II . . .

The question here is not whether petitioners have stated a proper claim under the ATS, but whether a claim may reach conduct occurring in the territory of a foreign sovereign. Respondents contend that claims under the ATS do not, relying primarily on a canon of statutory interpretation known as the presumption against extraterritorial application. That canon provides that "[w]hen a statute gives no clear indication of an extraterritorial application, it has none," *Morrison v. National Australia Bank Ltd.*, 561 U.S. ____, ____ (2010), and reflects the "presumption that United States law governs domestically but does not rule the world," *Microsoft Corp. v. AT & T Corp.*, 550 U.S. 437, 454 (2007).

This presumption "serves to protect against unintended clashes between our laws and those of other nations which could result in international discord." *EEOC v. Arabian American Oil Co.*, 499 U.S. 244, 248 (1991) (*Aramco*). As this Court has explained:

> "For us to run interference in . . . a delicate field of international relations there must be present the affirmative intention of the Congress clearly expressed. It alone has the facilities necessary to make fairly such an important policy decision where the possibilities of international discord are so evident and retaliative action so certain." *Benz v. Compania Naviera Hidalgo, S.A.*, 353 U.S. 138 (1957). The presumption against extraterritorial application helps ensure that the Judiciary does not erroneously adopt an interpretation of U.S. law that carries foreign policy consequences not clearly intended by the political branches.

We typically apply the presumption to discern whether an Act of Congress regulating conduct applies abroad. See, *e.g.*, *Aramco*, *supra*, at 246 ("These cases present the issue whether Title VII applies extraterritorially to regulate the employment practices of United States employers who employ United States citizens abroad"); *Morrison*, *supra*, at ____ (noting that the question of extraterritorial application was a "merits question," not a question of jurisdiction). The ATS, on the other hand, is "strictly jurisdictional." *Sosa* [*v. Alvarez-Machain,* 542 U.S. 692 (2004)], at 713. It does not directly regulate conduct or afford relief. It instead allows federal courts to recognize certain causes of action based on sufficiently definite norms of international law. But we think the principles underlying the canon of interpretation similarly constrain courts considering causes of action that may be brought under the ATS.

Indeed, the danger of unwarranted judicial interference in the conduct of foreign policy is magnified in the context of the ATS, because the question is not what Congress has done but instead what courts may do. This Court in *Sosa* repeatedly stressed the need for judicial caution in considering which claims could be brought under the ATS, in light of foreign policy concerns. As the Court explained, "the potential [foreign policy] implications . . . of recognizing . . . causes [under the ATS] should make courts particularly wary of impinging on the discretion of the Legislative and Executive Branches in managing foreign affairs." *Id.,* at 727; see also *id.,* at 727-728 ("Since many attempts by federal courts to craft remedies for the violation of new norms of international law would raise risks of adverse foreign policy consequences, they should be undertaken, if at all, with great caution"); *id.,* at 727 ("[T]he possible collateral consequences of making international rules privately actionable argue for judicial caution"). These concerns, which are implicated in any case arising under the ATS, are all the more pressing when the question is whether a cause of action under the ATS reaches conduct within the territory of another sovereign. . . .

The principles underlying the presumption against extraterritoriality thus constrain courts exercising their power under the ATS.

III

Petitioners contend that even if the presumption applies, the text, history, and purposes of the ATS rebut it for causes of action brought under that statute. It is true that Congress, even in a jurisdictional provision, can indicate that it intends federal law to apply to conduct occurring abroad. See, *e.g.,* 18 U.S.C. §1091(e) (2006 ed., Supp. V) (providing jurisdiction over the offense of genocide "regardless of where the offense is committed" if the alleged offender is, among other things, "present in the United States"). But to rebut the presumption, the ATS would need to evince a "clear indication of extraterritoriality." *Morrison,* 561 U.S., at ____. It does not.

To begin, nothing in the text of the statute suggests that Congress intended causes of action recognized under it to have extraterritorial reach. The ATS covers actions by aliens for violations of the law of nations, but that does not imply extraterritorial reach — such violations affecting aliens can occur either within or outside the United States. Nor does the fact that the text reaches "*any* civil action" suggest application to torts committed abroad; it is well established that generic terms like "any" or "every" do not rebut the presumption against extraterritoriality. . . .

Nor does the historical background against which the ATS was enacted overcome the presumption against application to conduct in the territory of another sovereign. See *Morrison, supra,* at ____ (noting that "[a]ssuredly context can be consulted" in determining whether a cause of action applies abroad). We explained in *Sosa* that when Congress passed the ATS, "three principal offenses against the law of nations" had been identified by Blackstone: violation of safe conducts, infringement of the rights of ambassadors, and piracy. 542 U.S., at 723, 724; see 4

W. Blackstone, Commentaries on the Laws of England 68 (1769). The first two offenses have no necessary extraterritorial application. Indeed, Blackstone — in describing them — did so in terms of conduct occurring within the forum nation.

Two notorious episodes involving violations of the law of nations occurred in the United States shortly before passage of the ATS. Each concerned the rights of ambassadors, and each involved conduct within the Union. . . . The two cases in which the ATS was invoked shortly after its passage also concerned conduct within the territory of the United States. See *Bolchos,* 3 F. Cas. 810 (wrongful seizure of slaves from a vessel while in port in the United States); *Moxon,* 17 F. Cas. 942 (wrongful seizure in United States territorial waters).

These prominent contemporary examples — immediately before and after passage of the ATS — provide no support for the proposition that Congress expected causes of action to be brought under the statute for violations of the law of nations occurring abroad.

The third example of a violation of the law of nations familiar to the Congress that enacted the ATS was piracy. Piracy typically occurs on the high seas, beyond the territorial jurisdiction of the United States or any other country. This Court has generally treated the high seas the same as foreign soil for purposes of the presumption against extraterritorial application. Petitioners contend that because Congress surely intended the ATS to provide jurisdiction for actions against pirates, it necessarily anticipated the statute would apply to conduct occurring abroad.

Applying U.S. law to pirates, however, does not typically impose the sovereign will of the United States onto conduct occurring within the territorial jurisdiction of another sovereign, and therefore carries less direct foreign policy consequences. Pirates were fair game wherever found, by any nation, because they generally did not operate within any jurisdiction. We do not think that the existence of a cause of action against them is a sufficient basis for concluding that other causes of action under the ATS reach conduct that does occur within the territory of another sovereign; pirates may well be a category unto themselves. See *Morrison,* 561 U.S., at ___ ("[W]hen a statute provides for some extraterritorial application, the presumption against extraterritoriality operates to limit that provision to its terms"). . . .

Finally, there is no indication that the ATS was passed to make the United States a uniquely hospitable forum for the enforcement of international norms. As Justice Story put it, "No nation has ever yet pretended to be the custos morum of the whole world. . . ." *United States v. The La Jeune Eugenie,* 26 F. Cas. 832, 847 (No. 15,551) (C.C. Mass. 1822). It is implausible to suppose that the First Congress wanted their fledgling Republic — struggling to receive international recognition — to be the first. Indeed, the parties offer no evidence that any nation, meek or mighty, presumed to do such a thing.

The United States was, however, embarrassed by its potential inability to provide judicial relief to foreign officials injured in the United States. Such offenses against ambassadors violated the law of nations, "and if not adequately redressed could rise to an issue of war." *Sosa,* 542 U.S., at 715. The ATS ensured that the United States could provide a forum for adjudicating such incidents. Nothing about this historical context suggests that Congress also intended federal common law under the ATS to provide a cause of action for conduct occurring in the territory of another sovereign.

Indeed, far from avoiding diplomatic strife, providing such a cause of action could have generated it. Recent experience bears this out. See *Doe v. Exxon Mobil Corp.,* 654 F.3d 11, 77-78 (C.A.D.C. 2011) (Kavanaugh, J., dissenting in part) (listing recent objections to extraterritorial applications of the ATS by Canada, Germany, Indonesia, Papua New Guinea, South Africa, Switzerland, and the United Kingdom). Moreover, accepting petitioners' view would imply that other nations, also applying the law of nations, could hale our citizens into their courts for alleged violations of the law of nations occurring in the United States, or anywhere else in the world. The presumption against extraterritoriality guards against our courts triggering such serious foreign policy consequences, and instead defers such decisions, quite appropriately, to the political branches.

We therefore conclude that the presumption against extraterritoriality applies to claims under the ATS, and that nothing in the statute rebuts that presumption. "[T]here is no clear indication of extraterritoriality here," *Morrison,* 561 U.S., at _____, and petitioners' case seeking relief for violations of the law of nations occurring outside the United States is barred.

IV

On these facts, all the relevant conduct took place outside the United States. And even where the claims touch and concern the territory of the United States, they must do so with sufficient force to displace the presumption against extraterritorial application. Corporations are often present in many countries, and it would reach too far to say that mere corporate presence suffices. If Congress were to determine otherwise, a statute more specific than the ATS would be required.

The judgment of the Court of Appeals is affirmed.

It is so ordered.

Justice KENNEDY, concurring. The opinion for the Court is careful to leave open a number of significant questions regarding the reach and interpretation of the Alien Tort Statute. In my view that is a proper disposition. Many serious concerns with respect to human rights abuses committed abroad have been addressed by Congress in statutes such as the Torture Victim Protection Act of 1991 (TVPA), 106 Stat. 73, note following 28 U.S.C. §1350, and that class of cases will be determined in the future according to the detailed statutory scheme Congress has enacted. Other cases may arise with allegations of serious violations of international law principles protecting persons, cases covered neither by the TVPA nor by the reasoning and holding of today's case; and in those disputes the proper implementation of the presumption against extraterritorial application may require some further elaboration and explanation.

Justice ALITO, with whom Justice THOMAS joins, concurring. I concur in the judgment and join the opinion of the Court as far as it goes. Specifically, I agree that when Alien Tort Statute (ATS) "claims touch and concern the territory of the United States, they must do so with sufficient force to displace the presumption against extraterritorial application." *Ante,* at 14. This formulation obviously leaves much unanswered, and perhaps there is wisdom in the Court's preference for this narrow approach. I write separately to set out the broader standard that leads me to the conclusion that this case falls within the scope of the presumption.

In *Morrison v. National Australia Bank Ltd.,* 561 U.S. _____ (2010), we explained that "the presumption against extraterritorial application would be a craven watchdog indeed if it retreated to its kennel whenever *some* domestic activity is involved in the case." *Id.,* at ___. We also reiterated that a cause of action falls outside the scope of the presumption — and thus is not barred by the presumption — only if the event or relationship that was "the 'focus' of congressional concern" under the relevant statute takes place within the United States. *Ibid.* (quoting *EEOC v. Arabian American Oil Co.,* 499 U.S. 244, 255 (1991)). For example, because "the focus of the [Securities] Exchange Act [of 1934] is not upon the place where the deception originated, but upon purchases and sales of securities in the United States," we held in *Morrison* that §10(b) of the Exchange Act applies "only" to "transactions in securities listed on domestic exchanges, and domestic transactions in other securities." 561 U.S., at ___.

The Court's decision in *Sosa v. Alvarez-Machain,* 542 U.S. 692 (2004), makes clear that when the ATS was enacted, "congressional concern" was "'focus[ed],'" *Morrison, supra,* at ___, on the "three principal offenses against the law of nations" that had been identified by Blackstone: violation of safe conducts, infringement of the rights of ambassadors, and piracy, *Sosa,* 542 U.S., at 723-724. . . . As a result, a putative ATS cause of action will fall within the scope of the presumption against extraterritoriality — and will therefore be barred — unless the domestic conduct is sufficient to violate an international law norm that satisfies *Sosa*'s requirements of definiteness and acceptance among civilized nations.

Justice Breyer, with whom Justice Ginsburg, Justice Sotomayor and Justice Kagan join, concurring in the judgment. I agree with the Court's conclusion but not with its reasoning. . . .

I . . .

B

In my view the majority's effort to answer the question by referring to the "presumption against extraterritoriality" does not work well. That presumption "rests on the perception that Congress ordinarily legislates with respect to domestic, not foreign matters." *Morrison v. National Australia Bank Ltd.,* 561 U.S. ___, ___ (2010). The ATS, however, was enacted with "foreign matters" in mind. The statute's text refers explicitly to "alien[s]," "treat[ies]," and "the law of nations." 28 U.S.C. §1350. The statute's purpose was to address "violations of the law of nations, admitting of a judicial remedy and at the same time threatening serious consequences in international affairs." *Sosa,* 542 U.S., at 715. And at least one of the three kinds of activities that we found to fall within the statute's scope, namely piracy, *ibid.,* normally takes place abroad.

The majority cannot wish this piracy example away by emphasizing that piracy takes place on the high seas. That is because the robbery and murder that make up piracy do not normally take place in the water; they take place on a ship. And a ship is like land, in that it falls within the jurisdiction of the nation whose flag it flies. . . .

The majority nonetheless tries to find a distinction between piracy at sea and similar cases on land. . . . But, as I have just pointed out, "[a]pplying U.S. law to pirates" *does* typically involve applying our law to acts taking place within the jurisdiction of another sovereign. Nor can the majority's words "territorial jurisdiction" sensibly distinguish land from sea for purposes of isolating adverse foreign policy risks, as the

Barbary Pirates, the War of 1812, the sinking of the *Lusitania,* and the Lockerbie bombing make all too clear.

The majority also writes, "Pirates were fair game wherever found, by any nation, because they generally did not operate within any jurisdiction." *Ibid.* I very much agree that pirates were fair game "wherever found." Indeed, that is the point. That is why we asked, in *Sosa,* who are today's pirates? Certainly today's pirates include torturers and perpetrators of genocide. And today, like the pirates of old, they are "fair game" where they are found. Like those pirates, they are "common enemies of all mankind and all nations have an equal interest in their apprehension and punishment." 1 Restatement §404 Reporters' Note 1, p. 256 (quoting *In re Demjanjuk,* 612 F. Supp. 544, 556 (N.D. Ohio 1985) (internal quotation marks omitted)). See *Sosa, supra,* at 732. And just as a nation that harbored pirates provoked the concern of other nations in past centuries, so harboring "common enemies of all man-kind" provokes similar concerns today. . . .

II

In applying the ATS to acts "occurring within the territory of a[nother] sovereign," I would assume that Congress intended the statute's jurisdictional reach to match the statute's underlying substantive grasp. That grasp, defined by the statute's purposes set forth in *Sosa,* includes compensation for those injured by piracy and its modern-day equivalents, at least where allowing such compensation avoids "serious" negative international "consequences" for the United States. 542 U.S., at 715. And just as we have looked to established international substantive norms to help determine the statute's substantive reach, *id.,* at 729, so we should look to international jurisdictional norms to help determine the statute's jurisdictional scope.

The Restatement (Third) of Foreign Relations Law is helpful. Section 402 recognizes that, subject to §403's "reasonableness" requirement, a nation may apply its law (for example, federal common law, see 542 U.S., at 729-730) not only (1) to "conduct" that "takes place [or to persons or things] within its territory" but also (2) to the "activities, interests, status, or relations of its nationals outside as well as within its territory," (3) to "conduct outside its territory that has or is intended to have substantial effect within its territory," and (4) to certain foreign "conduct outside its territory . . . that is directed against the security of the state or against a limited class of other state interests." In addition, §404 of the Restatement explains that a "state has jurisdiction to define and prescribe punishment for certain offenses recognized by the community of nations as of universal concern, such as piracy, slave trade," and analogous behavior.

Considering these jurisdictional norms in light of both the ATS's basic purpose (to provide compensation for those injured by today's pirates) and *Sosa*'s basic caution (to avoid international friction), I believe that the statute provides jurisdiction where (1) the alleged tort occurs on American soil, (2) the defendant is an American national, or (3) the defendant's conduct substantially and adversely affects an important American national interest, and that includes a distinct interest in preventing the United States from becoming a safe harbor (free of civil as well as criminal liability) for a torturer or other common enemy of mankind.

I would interpret the statute as providing jurisdiction only where distinct American interests are at issue. Doing so reflects the fact that Congress adopted the present statute at a time when, as Justice Story put it, "No nation ha[d] ever yet pretended to be the custos morum of the whole world." *United States v. La Jeune Eugenie,* 26 F. Cas. 832, 847 (C.C.D. Mass. 1822) (No. 15,551). That restriction also should help to minimize international friction. Further limiting principles such as exhaustion, *forum non conveniens,* and comity would do the same. So would a practice of courts giving weight to the views of the Executive Branch. See *Sosa,* 542 U.S., at 733, n.21; *id.,* at 761 (opinion of Breyer, J.)....

III

Applying these jurisdictional principles to this case, however, I agree with the Court that jurisdiction does not lie. The defendants are two foreign corporations. Their shares, like those of many foreign corporations, are traded on the New York Stock Exchange. Their only presence in the United States consists of an office in New York City (actually owned by a separate but affiliated company) that helps to explain their business to potential investors. The plaintiffs are not United States nationals but nationals of other nations. The conduct at issue took place abroad. And the plaintiffs allege, not that the defendants directly engaged in acts of torture, genocide, or the equivalent, but that they helped others (who are not American nationals) to do so.

Under these circumstances, even if the New York office were a sufficient basis for asserting general jurisdiction, it would be farfetched to believe, based solely upon the defendants' minimal and indirect American presence, that this legal action helps to vindicate a distinct American interest, such as in not providing a safe harbor for an "enemy of all mankind." Thus I agree with the Court that here it would "reach too far to say" that such "mere corporate presence suffices."

I consequently join the Court's judgment but not its opinion.

Notes and Questions

1. The Presumption Against Extraterritoriality. This canon of statutory construction was originally based on a desire to avoid unintended conflicts between our law and foreign laws. In *EEOC v. Arabian American Oil Co.* (*Aramco*), 499 U.S. 244, 248 (1991), for example, the Court declared that the presumption "helps ensure that the Judiciary does not erroneously adopt an interpretation of U.S. law that carries foreign policy consequences not clearly intended by the political branches." (The *Aramco* Court neglected, however, to indicate how enforcement of the 1964 Civil Rights Act's prohibition of discrimination based on race, religion, and national origin by a U.S. company employing a U.S. citizen in Saudi Arabia might offend the host country.) The Court went much farther in 2010, concluding that the presumption

> rests on the perception that Congress ordinarily legislates with respect to domestic, not foreign matters. Thus, "unless there is the affirmative intention of the Congress clearly expressed" to give a statute extraterritorial effect, "we must presume it is primarily concerned with domestic conditions." The canon or presumption applies regardless of whether there is a risk of conflict between the American statute and a foreign law. When a statute gives no clear indication of an extraterritorial application, it has none. [*Morrison v. Nat'l Austr. Bank Ltd.*, 561 U.S. 247, 255 (2010) (citation omitted).]

The plaintiffs in *Kiobel* alleged that the defendant corporations aided and abetted the Nigerian military and police in beating, raping, killing, and arresting Ogoni villagers who protested the environmental impacts of oil exploration and production in the Niger delta. Judicial relief under the ATS clearly would have complicated U.S. diplomatic relations with Nigeria. But if a defendant cannot show at least a potential conflict with another nation's laws, should the presumption against extraterritoriality apply? In today's globally interconnected economy, is it true that "Congress ordinarily legislates with respect to domestic, not foreign matters"? More generally, should the presumption apply to statutes — like the ATS — that expressly incorporate the "law of nations" and/or "treat[ies] of the United States"?

2. Does the Presumption Against Extraterritoriality Count Against Inferring a Bivens Remedy? In *Hernández II,* the court of appeals considered whether a presumption against the extraterritorial application of *statutes* also militated against recognizing a *Bivens* remedy for an alleged constitutional violation occurring on foreign soil. Noting first that "the novelty and uncertain scope" of an extraterritorial remedy was a special factor counseling hesitation, it found that the presumption against territoriality reinforced such hesitation.

> Even when a statute's substantive provisions do apply extraterritorially, a court must "separately apply the presumption against extraterritoriality" when it determines whether to provide a private right of action for damages. By extension, even if the Constitution applies extraterritorially, a court should hesitate to provide an extraterritorial damages remedy with "potential for international friction beyond that presented by merely applying U.S. substantive law to that foreign conduct." [885 F.3d at 822-823 (internal citation omitted).]

The court agreed with then-Judge Kavanaugh's reasoning that "[i]t would be grossly anomalous . . . to apply *Bivens* extraterritorially when we would not apply an identical statutory cause of action for constitutional torts extraterritorially." *Id.* at 823 (quoting *Meshal v. Higgenbotham*, 804 F.3d 417, 430 (D.C. Cir. 2015) (Kavanaugh, J., concurring)).

But insofar as the presumption is based upon a desire to avoid international discord and the assumption that Congress "generally legislates with domestic concerns in mind," *RJR Nabisco v. European Cmty.*, 136 S. Ct. 2090, 2100 (2016), does it have any bearing on the extent to which the *Constitution* should be enforceable against U.S. government officers? *See Meshal*, 804 F.3d at 441 (Pillard, J., dissenting) ("[T]hat presumption has no relevance to . . . *Bivens* claims to enforce constitutional provisions that all agree apply abroad, especially given that the very genesis of *Bivens* lies in the acknowledged inactivity of Congress.").

Moreover, the plaintiffs in *Hernández* were foreign nationals urging their son's entitlement to constitutional rights outside the United States. In contrast, the plaintiff in *Meshal* was a U.S. citizen who claimed that he had been imprisoned and tortured by FBI agents abroad. Arguably, a citizen's constitutional rights travel with him or her abroad (even if they do not always apply abroad in the same way they do at home). Should the presumption against extraterritoriality apply differently to *Bivens* claims asserted by noncitizens than to *Bivens* claims asserted by citizens? If the constitutional *right* that the plaintiff invokes is indisputably extraterritorial, should that make a difference to the extraterritoriality of the *Bivens* remedy?

3. Congress's Power to Enact Extraterritorial Legislation. The presumption against extraterritoriality does not address Congress's power to legislate. "This principle represents a canon of construction, or a presumption about a statute's meaning, rather than a limit upon Congress's power to legislate." *Morrison,* 561 U.S. at 255. At least for domestic law purposes, as we have seen, not only do statutes trump inconsistent international law, but Congress has express constitutional authority to "Define and punish . . . Offences against the Law of Nations." The presumption aims at avoiding *unintended* clashes between our law and foreign laws, not *intended* clashes.

4. Rebutting the Presumption. The presumption may be rebutted by express language in a statute asserting its extraterritorial reach. For example, the statute that criminalizes knowing or intentional material support of a U.S.-designated foreign terrorist organization (like Hamas or Al Qaeda) reads, "There is extraterritorial Federal jurisdiction over an offense under this section." 18 U.S.C. §2339B(d)(2) (2018). A related statute provides a civil cause of action for American victims of "acts of international terrorism," 18 U.S.C. §2333(a) (2018), defining such acts in part as activities that would be criminal under our law and "occur primarily outside the territorial jurisdiction of the United States, or transcend national boundaries in terms of the means by which they are accomplished. . . ." 18 U.S.C. §2331(1)(C) (2018); *see Weiss v. Nat'l Westminster Bank PLC,* 768 F.3d 202, 207 n.5 (2d Cir. 2014) ("Congress clearly expressed its intention for §2333(a) to apply extraterritorially by focusing on 'international terrorism' and defining it to include exclusively activities that 'occur primarily outside the territorial jurisdiction of the United States.'"). In other cases, Congress's intent is not nearly so clear — and *Morrison* and *Kiobel* appear to place a heavy thumb on the scale against extraterritorial application.

5. Life for the ATS After Kiobel? *Kiobel* threw a fragile lifeline to ATS plaintiffs in its penultimate paragraph: "[E]ven where the claims touch and concern the territory of the United States, they must do so with sufficient force to displace the presumption against extraterritorial application."

In one important early case clarifying *Kiobel*'s scope, a Fourth Circuit panel ruled that claims brought against private military contractors by noncitizens detained and allegedly tortured at the Abu Ghraib prison in Iraq could go forward notwithstanding *Kiobel. See Al Shimari v. CACI Premier Tech., Inc.,* 758 F.3d 516 (4th Cir. 2014). The court identified six grounds in *Al Shimari* on which *Kiobel* could be distinguished: (1) "the plaintiffs' claims allege acts of torture committed by United States citizens who were employed by an American corporation, CACI, which has corporate headquarters located in Fairfax County, Virginia"; (2) "[t]he alleged torture occurred at a military facility operated by United States government personnel"; (3) "the employees who allegedly participated in the acts of torture were hired by CACI in the United States to fulfill the terms of a contract that CACI executed with the United States Department of the Interior"; (4) "[t]he contract between CACI and the Department of the Interior was issued by a government office in Arizona, and CACI was authorized to collect payments by mailing invoices to government accounting offices in Colorado"; (5) "[u]nder the terms of the contract, CACI interrogators were required to obtain security clearances from the United States Department of Defense"; and (6) "[t]he plaintiffs also allege that CACI's managers located in the United States were aware of reports of misconduct abroad, attempted to 'cover up' the misconduct, and 'implicitly, if not expressly, encouraged' it." *Id.* at 528-529. Do these distinctions suggest that foreign-squared cases (in which the defendant is American, for example), by definition "touch and concern"?

In *Cardona v. Chiquita Brands Int'l, Inc.*, 760 F.3d 1185 (11th Cir. 2014), the Eleventh Circuit denied recovery to foreign plaintiffs who sued an American corporation under the ATS for conduct in the United States that supported terrorist attacks abroad which injured the plaintiffs. Chiquita was alleged to have orchestrated its financial support for FARC — a U.S.-designated Foreign Terrorist Organization in Colombia — from its headquarters in the United States. According to the *Cardona* court,

> [*Kiobel*] noted that "even where the claims touch and concern the territory of the United States, they must do so with sufficient force to displace the presumption against extraterritorial application." Plaintiff-appellants attempt to anchor ATS jurisdiction in the nature of the defendants as United States corporations. Corporate defendants in *Kiobel* were not United States corporations, but were present in the United States. The Supreme Court declared that "[c]orporations are often present in many countries, and it would reach too far to say that mere corporate presence suffices." The distinction between the corporations does not lead us to any indication of a congressional intent to make the statute apply to extraterritorial torts. As the Supreme Court said in *Kiobel*, "[i]f Congress were to determine otherwise, a statute more specific than the ATS would be required." There is no other statute. There is no jurisdiction. [*Id.* at 1189.]

Can you articulate criteria for distinguishing between cases that "touch and concern" the United States "sufficiently" to avoid the presumption against extraterritoriality, and those that do not? The significance of the "touch and concern" test may have been diminished by the Court's subsequent ruling in *Jesner v. Arab Bank, PLC*, 138 S. Ct. 1386 (2018), which forecloses ATS claims against foreign corporate defendants.

6. *Extraterritoriality Under International Law.* In *Kiobel*, Justice Breyer looked "to international norms to help determine the statute's jurisdictional scope." While Congress may disregard such norms, another familiar canon of statutory construction is that "an Act of Congress ought never to be construed to violate the law of nations if any other possible construction remains." *Murray v. The Schooner Charming Betsy*, 6 U.S. (2 Cranch) 64, 118 (1804).

One important international law question in construing a statute is whether Congress had jurisdiction to prescribe regulations for a particular extraterritorial activity.

> Under international law, the primary basis of jurisdiction is the "subjective territorial principle," under which "a state has jurisdiction to prescribe law with respect to . . . conduct that, wholly or in substantial part, takes place within its territory." *Restatement (Third) of the Foreign Relations Law of the United States* §402(1)(a) (1987). International law recognizes five other principles of jurisdiction by which a state may reach conduct *outside* its territory: (1) the objective territorial principle; (2) the protective principle; (3) the nationality principle; (4) the passive personality principle; and (5) the universality principle. The objective territoriality principle provides that a state has jurisdiction to prescribe law with respect to "conduct outside its territory that has or is intended to have substantial effect within its territory." *Restatement* §402(1)(c). The protective principle provides that a state has jurisdiction to prescribe law with respect to "certain conduct outside its territory *by persons not its nationals* that is directed against *the security of the state* or against a limited class of other state interests." *Id.* §402(3) (emphasis added). The nationality principle provides that a state has jurisdiction to prescribe law with respect to "the activities, interests, status, or relations of its nationals outside as well as within its territory." *Id.* §402(2). The passive

personality principle provides that "a state may apply law — particularly criminal law — to an act committed outside its territory by a person not its national where the victim of the act was its national." *Id.* §402, cmt. g. The universality principle provides that, "[a] state has jurisdiction to define and prescribe punishment for certain offenses recognized by the community of nations as of universal concern, such as piracy, slave trade, attacks on or hijacking of aircraft, genocide, war crimes, and perhaps *certain acts of terrorism*," regardless of the locus of their occurrence. *Id.* §404 (emphasis added). Because Congress has the power to override international law if it so chooses, *Restatement* §402, cmt. I., none of these five principles places ultimate limits on Congress's power to reach extraterritorial conduct. At the same time, however, "[i]n determining whether a statute applies extraterritorially, [courts] presume that Congress does not intend to violate principles of international law . . . [and] in the absence of an explicit Congressional directive, courts do not give extraterritorial effect to any statute that violates principles of international law." *United States v. Vasquez-Velasco*, 15 F.3d 833, 839 (9th Cir. 1994) (citing *McCulloch v. Sociedad Nacional de Marineros de Honduras*, 372 U.S. 10, 21-22 (1963)). Hence, courts that find that a given statute applies extraterritorially typically pause to note that this finding is consistent with one or more of the five principles of extraterritorial jurisdiction under international law. [*United States v. Bin Laden*, 92 F. Supp. 2d 189, 195-196 (S.D.N.Y. 2000) (citation omitted).]

In *Bin Laden*, the government prosecuted foreign defendants for bombing U.S. embassies in Kenya and Tanzania and killing U.S. nationals, as well as foreigners. The extraterritorial effect of one statute applied in that case, 18 U.S.C. §2332(b) (2018), which criminalizes conspiracy to kill U.S. nationals, is clearly consistent with the protective principle. A different statute applied in *Bin Laden*, 18 U.S.C. §930(c) (2018), which criminalizes killing "in the course of an attack on a Federal facility," also has extraterritorial effect under this principle irrespective of the nationality of the attackers, inasmuch as some such facilities lie outside the United States.

The defendant argued that applying this statute extraterritorially was not consistent with the principle of universal jurisdiction, because that principle does not encompass terrorist attacks on non-diplomatic personnel. The court rejected this argument, recognizing that the universality principle "is increasingly accepted for certain acts of terrorism." 92 F. Supp. 2d at 222.

Would a finding of extraterritorial jurisdiction in *Kiobel* have been consistent with any of these five international law principles?

7. *Reasonableness in International Law.* A finding of congressional jurisdiction to prescribe is just the beginning of an inquiry into the consistency of a statute with international law. As Justice Breyer noted, that law also requires more broadly that any application of the principle be "reasonable." According to the *Restatement (Third) of Foreign Relations Law*, criteria for determining reasonableness include:

(a) the link of the activity to the territory of the regulating state, i.e., the extent to which the activity takes place within the territory, or has substantial, direct, and foreseeable effect upon or in the territory;

(b) the connections, such as nationality, residence, or economic activity, between the regulating state and the person principally responsible for the activity to be regulated, or between that state and those whom the regulation is designed to protect;

(c) the character of the activity to be regulated, the importance of regulation to the regulating state, the extent to which other states regulate such activities, and the degree to which the desirability of such regulation is generally accepted;

(d) the existence of justified expectations that might be protected or hurt by the regulation;

(e) the importance of the regulation to the international political, legal, or economic system;

(f) the extent to which the regulation is consistent with the traditions of the international system;

(g) the extent to which another state may have an interest in regulating the activity; and

(h) the likelihood of conflict with regulation by another state. [*Restatement* §403(2).]

The *Bin Laden* court had no problem holding that the exercise of criminal jurisdiction over those accused of the embassy bombings was reasonable in light of these factors. 92 F. Supp. 2d at 222-224. Assuming that extraterritoriality of the ATS in *Kiobel* was consistent with some principle of jurisdiction to prescribe, would it also have been reasonable?

THE EXTRATERRITORIAL REACH OF U.S. LAW: SUMMARY OF BASIC PRINCIPLES

- The Constitution applies abroad to protect citizens, and also to protect aliens who have a substantial connection to the United States, although what constitutes a "substantial connection" is unclear.

- Constitutional protections do not, however, necessarily apply in every particular circumstance in every foreign place, even to a citizen or qualifying alien. The scope of their application may depend on pragmatic and political concerns, although the Supreme Court has so held only with respect to the right to petition for a writ of habeas corpus.

- There is a presumption against extraterritorial application of a statute. This presumption is a canon of statutory construction, not a limit on congressional legislative power.

- The presumption may be rebutted by express statutory language asserting extraterritorial effect. It also may be rebutted by implication from the text, context, and purpose of a statute, or, more narrowly, according to Justices Alito and Thomas, from the "focus of the statute."

- Although a statute may trump international law for domestic purposes, and Congress is free to give extraterritorial effect to a law even in violation of international norms, our laws are construed to avoid conflict with such norms if possible.

- Under international law, Congress may prescribe regulations for activities abroad if the regulations satisfy one of five principles reflecting the legitimate sovereign interests of the United States. If they are consistent with one or more of these principles, they also must be reasonable in the circumstances.

The Right to Wage War (*jus ad bellum*)

On June 26, 1945, world leaders gathered in San Francisco to sign the Charter of the United Nations. The agony of the world's greatest armed conflict was fresh in their minds. The fighting in Europe had just ended, but the U.S. atomic bombings of Hiroshima and Nagasaki, as well as a peace treaty with Japan, still lay in the future. This searing experience inspired a declaration that the first purpose of the newly formed organization was

> [t]o maintain international peace and security, and to that end: to take effective control measures for the prevention and removal of threats to the peace, and for the suppression of acts of aggression or other breaches of the peace, and to bring about by peaceful means, and in conformity with the principles of justice and international law, adjustment or settlement of international disputes or situations which might lead to a breach of the peace. [U.N. Charter art. 1, para. 1.]

The U.N. Charter is only the latest in a long series of efforts to avoid the bane of war, extending at least as far back as Biblical times. In between, theologians and jurists from St. Augustine to Hugo Grotius, among many others, developed a theory of a "just war." In 1919, in the wake of World War I, Article 10 of the Covenant of the League of Nations called for states to "respect and preserve as against external aggression the territorial integrity and political independence of all Members of the League." Then, in the General Treaty for the Renunciation of War as an Instrument of National Policy (Kellogg-Briand Pact), Aug. 27, 1928, 94 L.N.T.S. 57, the parties declared that they "condemn recourse to war for the solution to international controversies," and agreed that settlement of disputes "shall never be sought except by pacific means." *See generally* Ian Brownlie, *International Law and the Use of Force by States* 3-111 (1963); Yoram Dinstein, *War, Aggression and Self-Defence* 65-89 (6th ed. 2017).

The tragic history of the world shows, however, that these efforts to preserve the peace have so far achieved only limited success. Yet they have profoundly affected the development of a part of the international law of armed conflict that we refer to as *jus ad bellum*— Latin for "the right to wage war." That law was codified to some degree by the U.N. Charter in 1945, and it has since been shaped by the Charter, as we will see in this chapter.

A related, parallel body of law, *jus in bello,* is concerned with the conduct of war once it has begun. Also referred to as the law of war, the law of armed conflict, or international humanitarian law, its purpose is to limit the suffering of combatants and noncombatants alike to what is necessary to achieve the legitimate political goals of a conflict. Principles of *jus in bello* are introduced in the next chapter.

We begin this chapter with a look at some of the main structural elements of the modern *jus ad bellum,* as spelled out in the U.N. Charter. Then we review a historic 1986 World Court decision, the *Nicaragua* case, that supplies content not only to the law of the Charter, but also to customary norms that both inspired and are inspired by the Charter. The principles introduced and analyzed here play a central role in the relations of the United States with the rest of the world, and they strongly inform much of national security law, as we see in later chapters.

A. LAW REGARDING RESORT TO THE USE OF FORCE: THE BASIC ELEMENTS

1. The United Nations Charter: Making War to Preserve or Restore Peace

The Preamble to the United Nations Charter expresses a determination "to save succeeding generations from the scourge of war." To that end, Article 2(4) of the Charter forbids the "threat or use of force against the territorial integrity or political independence of any state." But the signers of the Charter were students of history, and they understood that conflicts would erupt into violence in the future. They therefore adopted two carefully tailored, narrow exceptions to this foundational prohibition. These exceptions, found in Chapter VII of the Charter, are designed to ward off breaches of the peace or to restore peace if fighting breaks out.

One exception concerns the Security Council, to which the Charter gives "primary responsibility for the maintenance of international peace and security." Art. 24(1). The Security Council is a political body with five permanent members (China, France, Russia, the United Kingdom, and the United States), each of which has veto power, and ten non-permanent, elected members. Acting entirely on its own initiative, the Security Council may approve the use of force when it determines the existence of a threat to the peace, a breach of the peace, or an act of aggression. Member states have agreed in Article 25 to "accept and carry out the decisions of the Security Council."

The other recognized exception to the Article 2(4) ban on the use of force allows one nation to defend itself from an armed attack by another, or to come to the aid of another state that is attacked — at least for a time. But the Security Council also has an important role to play in the exercise of this "inherent right of individual or collective self-defense."

Charter of the United Nations

June 26, 1945, 59 Stat. 1031, T.S. No. 993

CHAPTER I. PURPOSES AND PRINCIPLES . . .

Article 2 . . .

3. All Members shall settle their international disputes by peaceful means in such a manner that international peace and security, and justice, are not endangered.

4. All Members shall refrain in their international relations from the threat or use of force against the territorial integrity or political independence of any state, or in any other manner inconsistent with the Purposes of the United Nations.

5. All Members shall give the United Nations every assistance in any action it takes in accordance with the present Charter, and shall refrain from giving assistance to any state against which the United Nations is taking preventive or enforcement action. . . .

7. Nothing contained in the present Charter shall authorize the United Nations to intervene in matters which are essentially within the domestic jurisdiction of any state. . . .

CHAPTER V. THE SECURITY COUNCIL . . .

Article 25 . . .

The Members of the United Nations agree to accept and carry out the decisions of the Security Council in accordance with the present Charter. . . .

CHAPTER VII. ACTION WITH RESPECT TO THREATS TO THE PEACE, BREACHES OF THE PEACE, AND ACTS OF AGGRESSION

Article 39

The Security Council shall determine the existence of any threat to the peace, breach of the peace, or act of aggression and shall make recommendations, or decide what measures shall be taken in accordance with Articles 41 and 42, to maintain and restore international peace and security.

Article 40

In order to prevent an aggravation of the situation, the Security Council may, before making the recommendations or deciding upon the measures provided for in Article 39, call upon the parties concerned to comply with such provisional measures as it deems necessary or desirable. Such provisional measures shall be without prejudice to the rights, claims, or position of the parties concerned. The Security Council shall duly take account of failure to comply with such provisional measures.

Article 41

The Security Council may decide what measures not involving the use of armed force are to be employed to give effect to its decisions, and it may call upon the Members of the United Nations to apply such measures. These may include complete or partial interruption of economic relations and of rail, sea, air, postal, telegraphic, radio, and other means of communication, and the severance of diplomatic relations.

Article 42

Should the Security Council consider that measures provided for in Article 41 would be inadequate or have proved to be inadequate, it may take such action by air, sea, or land forces as may be necessary to maintain or restore international peace and security. Such actions may include demonstrations, blockade, and other operations by air, sea, or land forces of Members of the United Nations.

Article 43

1. All Members of the United Nations, in order to contribute to the maintenance of international peace and security, undertake to make available to the Security Council, on its call and in accordance with a special agreement or agreements, armed forces, assistance, and facilities, including rights of passage, necessary for the purpose of maintaining international peace and security.

2. Such agreement or agreements shall govern the numbers and types of forces, their degree of readiness and general location, and the nature of the facilities and assistance to be provided.

3. The agreement or agreements shall be negotiated as soon as possible on the initiative of the Security Council. They shall be concluded between the Security Council and Members or between the Security Council and groups of Members and shall be subject to ratification by the signatory states in accordance with their respective constitutional processes. . . .

Article 51

Nothing in the present charter shall impair the inherent right of individual and collective self-defense if an armed attack occurs against a Member of the United Nations, until the Security Council has taken measures necessary to maintain international peace and security. Measures taken by Members in the exercise of this right of self-defense shall be immediately reported to the Security Council and shall not in any way affect the authority and responsibility of the Security Council under the present Charter to take at any time such action as it deems necessary in order to maintain or restore international peace and security. . . .

Notes and Questions

1. *The Need for Security Council Approval.* Recognizing the provisions of Chapter VII of the U.N. Charter as exceptional, can you describe the sequence of events required by Articles 39 to 42 in order to authorize the use of military force?

The Security Council has invoked Chapter VII, in whole or in part, to approve the use of force a number of times, including the Korean War, the 1991 Persian Gulf War, and the post-9/11 war in Afghanistan. It has also authorized a number of military deployments for humanitarian purposes, among them missions in Somalia in 1992 and Libya in 2011.

Do you think an individual state or group of states might sometimes find it extremely inconvenient, even dangerous, to have to persuade the U.N. Security Council to authorize the use of force (and persuade all of the permanent members not to veto it)? Can you imagine why every member state agreed to abide by these provisions? Comparing the U.N. Charter to the U.S. Constitution, one scholar offers this explanation: "By adopting the Constitution, 'the people' sacrificed aspects of their liberty to advance their collective wellbeing and security. By adopting the U.N. Charter, states did exactly the same thing." John Dehn, *When Constitutional Rules May No Longer Be Law: A Response to Goldsmith and Glennon*, Lawfare, May 14, 2018.

States have occasionally resorted to the use of force without clear Security Council approval, and without invoking their Article 51 right of self-defense. Examples include NATO's bombing of the Federal Republic of Yugoslavia in 1999, the 2003 invasion of Iraq by the United States and its coalition partners, and more recently the U.S. military intervention in Syria in the fight against the Islamic State. Does this breakdown in the Charter's collective security mechanism mean it should be abandoned?

2. *Article 42: Actions "It May Take."* Since the signing of the U.N. Charter in 1945, not a single Article 43 agreement has been signed.

> The tensions of the Cold War soon eclipsed efforts to negotiate any special agreements, leaving the Security Council dependent on the willingness of member states to provide troops on an ad hoc basis. Moreover, with the notable exception of Korea, superpower disagreement essentially barred the United Nations from authorizing collective military action in response to acts of aggression — until the Persian Gulf War following Iraq's invasion of Kuwait in August 1990. Instead, during the Cold War, the United Nations developed a more limited capacity for responding to conflict, namely, consensual deployment of "peacekeeping" forces to perform tasks such as monitoring ceasefires and observing the demobilization of opposing forces. [Jane E. Stromseth, *Rethinking War Powers: Congress, the President, and the United Nations*, 81 Geo. L.J. 597, 598-599 (1993).]

The Security Council has come to rely instead on voluntary contributions of forces by member states in response to "recommendations" or "authorizations" under Article 39 — or more generally under Chapter VII.

Until 1990 the Security Council had determined the existence of a breach of the peace on only three occasions — the Korean War in 1950, the Falkland Islands War in 1982, and the Iran-Iraq War in 1987 — and threats to the peace another three times. And it had approved the use of force in response only once, in Korea, when the Soviets were boycotting the Security Council, and then only to "recommend" that member states assist South Korea in repelling the attack from the North. (Excluded from consideration here is approval of numerous so-called "peacekeeping" deployments, analyzed in Chapter 16.) Yet even since 1990, when the Security Council approved the use of force to expel Saddam Hussein's Iraqi troops from Kuwait (see *infra* Chapter 11), the exercise or threat of a veto by one of the permanent members, often for reasons having nothing to do with collective security, has largely continued to prevent the Security Council from playing the peacemaking role envisioned for it by the signers of the U.N. Charter.

3. Individual and Collective Self-Defense. The use of force is permissible without Security Council approval, at least for a time, as an exercise of every state's inherent right of individual or collective self-defense, as set forth in Article 51. Some commentators argue that Article 51 was meant to replace traditional self-help measures, providing for an immediate response to aggression until — but only until — the Security Council has had time to act. *See* Thomas M. Franck & Faiza Patel, *UN Police Action in Lieu of War: "The Old Order Changeth,"* 85 Am. J. Int'l L. 63, 64 (1991). Others maintain that Article 51 simply restates the right of individual and collective self-defense that is inherent in sovereignty, and that this right remains intact until the Security Council has dealt *successfully* with an international conflict. Eugene V. Rostow, *Until What? Enforcement Action or Collective Self-Defense?,* 85 Am. J. Int'l L. 506, 511 (1991). Can you see practical difficulties with each claimed meaning?

Article 51 conditions the use of force in self-defense without Security Council approval on the existence of an "armed attack," whereas under Article 39 the Security Council may authorize the use of force if it determines the existence of "any threat to the peace, breach of the peace, or act of aggression," a potentially much lower standard. What accounts for the difference?

2. The Role of the United States Under Chapter VII

In 1945, during debate on the United Nations Charter, some Senators argued for a reservation to the Charter that would have allowed Congress to approve or reject each use of American armed forces under an Article 43 special agreement. Otherwise, they insisted, the Charter represented an unconstitutional delegation of war-making authority to the U.N. Security Council. But two-thirds of the Senate were persuaded to approve the Charter without reservation, partly on grounds that (1) Congress would have an opportunity to approve the terms of any special agreement, and (2) the United States could veto any Security Council resolution invoking the special agreement. *See* Stromseth, *supra,* at 604-612.

Within months of ratification of the Charter, however, Congress undertook to spell out more clearly the respective roles of the executive and legislative branches in fulfilling U.S. obligations under Chapter VII. The United Nations Participation Act, 22 U.S.C. §§287-287*l* (2018), instructs U.S. representatives at the United Nations to vote in accordance with instructions from the President, and it directs the President to report any Security Council enforcement actions to the Congress. It also authorizes the President to implement any economic sanctions approved by the Security Council. Concerning the deployment of U.S. military forces pursuant to a resolution of the Security Council under Article 42, the Act provides as follows:

United Nations Participation Act

22 U.S.C. §§287 to 287*l* (2018)

§287d. USE OF ARMED FORCES; LIMITATIONS

The President is authorized to negotiate a special agreement or agreements with the Security Council which shall be subject to the approval of the Congress by appropriate Act or joint resolution, providing for the numbers and types of armed forces, their degree of readiness and general location, and the nature of facilities and assistance, including rights of passage, to be made available to the Security Council on its call for the purpose of maintaining international peace and security in accordance with article 43 of said Charter. The President shall not be deemed to require the authorization of the Congress to make available to the Security Council on its call in order to take action under article 42 of said Charter and pursuant to such special agreement or agreements the armed forces, facilities, or assistance provided for therein: *Provided*, That, except as authorized in section 287d-1 of this title [referring to noncombatant assistance to the United Nations, see *infra* p. 473], nothing herein contained shall be construed as an authorization to the President by the Congress to make available to the Security Council for such purpose armed forces, facilities, or assistance in addition to the forces, facilities, and assistance provided for in such special agreement or agreements.

Notes and Questions

1. *The U.N. Charter as U.S. Law?* Article 2(5) of the United Nations Charter provides that "[a]ll Members shall give the United Nations every assistance in any action it takes in accordance with the present Charter." Article 25 provides that "Members of the United Nations agree to accept and carry out the decisions of the Security Council." Articles 48 and 49 contain similar commitments. As a treaty approved by the Senate, the U.N. Charter is part of the "Law of the Land" under Article VI of the U.S. Constitution. Is the President not therefore empowered — indeed obliged — to "execute" the terms of the Charter, just as he would any other law under the Take Care Clause, by enforcing resolutions of the Security Council? How do you think the Framers of the Constitution would have answered? One leading scholar responded this way: "The President and the Senate cannot use the treaty procedure to strip the House of Representatives of its prerogatives over the use of military force." Louis Fisher, *Sidestepping Congress: Presidents Acting Under the U.N. and NATO*, 47 Case W. Res. L. Rev. 1237, 1256 (1997).

2. *Effect of the United Nations Participation Act.* What is the effect, if any, of the United Nations Participation Act on the President's domestic authority to send U.S. military forces into battle pursuant to a Security Council mandate, but without the approval of Congress? What does the timing of its passage suggest? Would your

answer be affected by the provisions of the Charter under which the Security Council purported to act? According to one commentator, "the President could not, by an affirmative vote in the Security Council, confer upon himself power to use armed force that he would not otherwise possess. The text of the UNPA [United Nations Participation Act] makes that clear, as does a review of its legislative history." Glennon, *supra*, 85 Am. J. Int'l L. at 78.

3. Categorizing Uses of U.S. Troops. During debate on approval of the U.N. Charter, the Senate was persuaded that special agreement forces would be used only in a "police action" of such limited scope and duration that it would not constitute a "war" in either an international or constitutional sense. Secretary of State John Foster Dulles testified that Congress's war powers would not be implicated if "we are talking about a little bit of force to be used as a police demonstration.... [But] if this is going to be a large volume of force which is going to put a big drain on the resources of the United States or commit us to great and costly adventures, then the Congress ought to have a voice in this matter." *The Charter of the United Nations: Hearings Before the Senate Committee on Foreign Relations*, 79th Cong. 655 (1945), *quoted in* Stromseth, *supra*, at 609. Can this explanation be squared with the text of the Constitution or with your understanding of the Framers' intent?

Others argued that a police action would not be war for constitutional purposes because small-scale forces had historically been deployed by U.S. Presidents without congressional authorization "to protect American citizens abroad, to prevent an invasion of the territory, or to suppress insurrection." Memorandum by John W. Davis, Phillip C. Jessup & Quincy Wright, *reprinted in* 91 Cong. Rec. 8065, 8066 (1945). Do such deployments furnish a precedent for U.N.-mounted police actions?

Can you define "police action"? If your answer is that it is "not a war," are you prepared to say what a "war" is? Is the Supreme Court's definition of war in *The Prize Cases*, 67 U.S. (2 Black) 635, 666 (1863), *supra* p. 55 ("that state in which a nation prosecutes its right by force"), hopelessly outdated for this purpose? However the terms are defined, would Congress need to be consulted if a conflict in which U.S. forces were deployed escalated from "police action" to "war"? If the labels are important, who should be able to make an authoritative pronouncement about the character of a particular conflict?

B. CONTENT OF *JUS AD BELLUM*

Reading the *Nicaragua* Case

After the fall of President Anastasio Somoza Debayle in Nicaragua in July 1979, a junta led by the Frente Sandinista de Liberacion Nacional (the "Sandinistas") took over the government. Opponents of the new regime, mainly former supporters of Somoza, in particular ex-members of the National Guard, formed themselves into irregular military forces known as the Contras and began an armed opposition.

In 1981, partly in response to reports that the Sandinistas were supplying arms and other logistical support to guerrillas in El Salvador, the Reagan administration began covert aid to the Contras. This aid was later publicly acknowledged in official statements by the President and high United States officials, and in a 1983 budget resolution Congress provided funds for U.S. intelligence agencies to support "directly or indirectly, military or paramilitary operations in Nicaragua."

In 1984 Nicaragua filed an application with the International Court of Justice (ICJ or World Court) asserting that the United States was engaged in aggression against it, in violation of Article 2(4) of the United Nations Charter, other treaty obligations, and customary international norms. Specifically, it alleged (1) that U.S. forces had carried out direct armed attacks against Nicaragua by air, land, and sea; and (2) that the United States had recruited, trained, armed, equipped, financed, and directed paramilitary actions in and against Nicaragua by the Contras. Nicaragua sought an order from the Court to stop the aggression and pay compensation.

Because the United States had expressly withheld consent to the Court's jurisdiction over "disputes arising under a multilateral treaty" like the Charter, absent conditions not met in the principal case, the Court relied on customary international law instead of the Charter in the following opinion.

The opinion is very long and complex, and we have edited it extensively here, occasionally summarizing detailed explanations. We have also inserted section headings in outline form, lacking in the original, to help keep the issues straight. Among the issues, consider these:

- How are provisions of the U.N. Charter and customary international law norms related, and how have they influenced each other?
- How are the technical terms "armed attack," "use of force," and "intervention" distinguished?
- What are the content and legal effect of these terms under the U.N. Charter and as customary norms?
- How are these terms applied to the actions of the United States and Nicaragua, respectively?

Military and Paramilitary Activities in and against Nicaragua (Nicaragua v. United States of America)

International Court of Justice, 1986
1986 I.C.J. 14

[I. ESTABLISHED FACTS]

[A. U.S. Direct Attacks]

80. . . . [T]he Court finds it established that, on a date in late 1983 or early 1984, the President of the United States authorized a United States government agency to lay mines in Nicaraguan ports; that in early 1984 mines were laid in or close to [two such] ports . . . by persons in the pay and acting on the instructions of that agency, under the supervision and with the logistic support of United States agents. . . .

86.... [T]he Court finds [that in late 1983 and early 1984 direct attacks were carried out against Nicaraguan ports, oil storage facilities, and a naval base].... The general pattern followed by these attacks appears to the Court... to have been as follows. A "mother ship" was supplied (apparently leased) by the CIA.... Speedboats, guns and ammunition were supplied by the United States administration, and the actual attacks were carried out by [either U.S. military personnel or unidentified Latin American nationals, paid by, and acting on the direct instructions of, United States military or intelligence personnel].... Helicopters piloted by Nicaraguans and others piloted by United States nationals were also involved on some occasions.... The imputability to the United States of these attacks appears therefore to the Court to be established.

[B. U.S. Support for the Contras]

108.... [T]he Court has not been able to satisfy itself that the respondent State "created" the contra force in Nicaragua.... Nor does the evidence warrant a finding that the United States gave "direct and critical combat support," at least if that form of words is taken to mean that this support was tantamount to direct intervention by the United States combat forces, or that all contra operations reflected strategy and tactics wholly devised by the United States. On the other hand, the Court holds it established that the United States authorities largely financed, trained, equipped, armed and organized the [contras].

109. What the Court has to determine at this point is whether or not the relationship of the contras to the United States Government was so much one of dependence on the one side and control on the other that it would be right to equate the contras, for legal purposes, with an organ of the United States Government, or as acting on behalf of that Government.... [D]espite the heavy subsid[i]es and other support provided to them by the United States, there is no clear evidence of the United States having actually exercised such a degree of control in all fields as to justify treating the contras as acting on its behalf.

110.... The Court... is a fortiori unable to determine that the contra force may be equated for legal purposes with the forces of the United States. This conclusion, however, does not of course suffice to resolve the entire question of the responsibility incurred by the United States through its assistance to the contras.

111.... [T]he contra force has, at least at one period, been so dependent on the United States that it could not conduct its crucial or most significant military and paramilitary activities without the multi-faceted support of the United States. This finding is fundamental in the present case.... [A] degree of control by the United States Government, as described above, is inherent in the position in which the contra force finds itself in relation to that Government....

[C. U.S. Defense of El Salvador]

127.... [I]f Nicaragua has been giving support to the armed opposition in El Salvador, and if this constitutes an armed attack on El Salvador and the other appropriate conditions are met, collective self-defence could be legally invoked by the United States....

160.... [T]he Court is satisfied that, between July 1979, the date of the fall of the Somoza regime in Nicaragua, and the early months of 1981, an intermittent flow of arms was routed via the territory of Nicaragua to the armed opposition in El Salvador. On the other hand, the evidence is insufficient to satisfy the Court that, since the early months of 1981, assistance has continued to reach the Salvadorian armed opposition from the territory of Nicaragua on any significant scale, or that the Government of Nicaragua was responsible for any flow of arms at either period. . . .

[II. APPLICABLE LAW]

[A. U.N. Charter vs. Customary International Law]

173. . . . The United States contends that the only general and customary international law on which Nicaragua can base its claims is that of the Charter: in particular, the Court could not, it is said, consider the lawfulness of an alleged use of armed force without referring to the "principal source of the relevant international law," namely, Article 2, paragraph 4, of the United Nations Charter. In brief, in a more general sense "the provisions of the United Nations Charter relevant here subsume and supervene related principles of customary and general international law." The United States concludes that "since the multilateral treaty reservation bars adjudication of claims based on those treaties, it bars all of Nicaragua's claims." . . .

176. . . . [T]he United Nations Charter . . . itself refers to pre-existing customary international law; this reference to customary law is contained in the actual text of Article 51, which mentions the "inherent right" (in the French text the "droit naturel") of individual or collective self-defence, which "nothing in the present Charter shall impair" and which applies in the event of an armed attack. The Court therefore finds that Article 51 of the Charter is only meaningful on the basis that there is a "natural" or "inherent" right of self-defence, and it is hard to see how this can be other than of a customary nature, even if its present content has been confirmed and influenced by the Charter. Moreover the Charter, having itself recognized the existence of this right, does not go on to regulate directly all aspects of its content. For example, it does not contain any specific rule whereby self-defence would warrant only measures which are proportional to the armed attack and necessary to respond to it, a rule well established in customary international law. Moreover, a definition of the "armed attack" which, if found to exist, authorizes the exercise of the "inherent right" of self-defence, is not provided in the Charter, and is not part of treaty law. It cannot therefore be held that Article 51 is a provision which "subsumes and supervenes" customary international law. It rather demonstrates that in the field in question, the importance of which for the present dispute need hardly be stressed, customary international law continues to exist alongside treaty law. The areas governed by the two sources of law thus do not overlap exactly, and the rules do not have the same content. This could also be demonstrated for other subjects, in particular for the principle of non-intervention. . . .

181. . . . [T]he Charter gave expression in this field to principles already present in customary international law, and that law has in the subsequent four decades developed under the influence of the Charter, to such an extent that a number of rules contained in the Charter have acquired a status independent of it. The essential consideration is that both the Charter and the customary international law flow from a common fundamental principle outlawing the use of force in international relations. . . .

[B. Content of Customary International Law]

[1. Prohibition on the Threat or Use of Force]

183. In view of this conclusion, the Court has next to consider what are the rules of customary international law applicable to the present dispute. For this purpose, it has to direct its attention to the practice and opinio juris of States; as the Court recently observed,

> It is of course axiomatic that the material of customary international law is to be looked for primarily in the actual practice and opinio juris of States, even though multilateral conventions may have an important role to play in recording and defining rules deriving from custom, or indeed in developing them. (*Continental Shelf (Libyan Arab Jamahiriya/Malta)*, I.C.J. Reports 1985, pp. 29-30, para. 27.)

In this respect the Court must not lose sight of the Charter of the United Nations . . . , notwithstanding the operation of the multilateral treaty reservation. Although the Court has no jurisdiction to determine whether the conduct of the United States constitutes a breach of [that] convention[], it can and must take [it] into account in ascertaining the content of the customary international law which the United States is also alleged to have infringed. . . .

186. It is not to be expected that in the practice of States the application of the rules in question should have been perfect, in the sense that States should have refrained, with complete consistency, from the use of force or from intervention in each other's internal affairs. The Court does not consider that, for a rule to be established as customary, the corresponding practice must be in absolutely rigorous conformity with the rule. In order to deduce the existence of customary rules, the Court deems it sufficient that the conduct of States should, in general, be consistent with such rules, and that instances of State conduct inconsistent with a given rule should generally have been treated as breaches of that rule, not as indications of the recognition of a new rule. If a State acts in a way prima facie incompatible with a recognized rule, but defends its conduct by appealing to exceptions or justifications contained within the rule itself, then whether or not the State's conduct is in fact justifiable on that basis, the significance of that attitude is to confirm rather than to weaken the rule. . . .

188. . . . The Parties . . . both take the view that the fundamental principle in this area is expressed in the terms employed in Article 2, paragraph 4, of the United Nations Charter. They therefore accept a treaty-law obligation to refrain in their international relations from the threat or use of force against the territorial integrity or political independence of any State, or in any other manner inconsistent with the purposes of the United Nations. The Court has however to be satisfied that there exists in customary international law an opinio juris as to the binding character of such abstention. This opinio juris may, though with all due caution, be deduced from, inter alia, the attitude of the Parties and the attitude of States towards certain General Assembly resolutions. . . . [T]he attitude referred to expresses an opinio juris respecting such rule (or set of rules), to be thenceforth treated separately from the provisions . . . of the Charter. . . .

190. . . . The United States, in its Counter-Memorial on the questions of jurisdiction and admissibility, found it material to quote the views of scholars that this principle [barring the use of force] is a "universal norm," a "universal international law," a "universally recognized principle of international law," and a "principle of jus cogens." . . .

[2. Exception to the Prohibition for Self-Defense]

193. The general rule prohibiting force allows for certain exceptions.... [I]n the language of Article 51 of the United Nations Charter, the inherent right (or "droit naturel") which any State possesses in the event of an armed attack, covers both collective and individual self-defence. Thus, the Charter itself testifies to the existence of the right of collective self-defence in customary international law....

194. With regard to the characteristics governing the right of self-defence, since the Parties consider the existence of this right to be established as a matter of customary international law, they have concentrated on the conditions governing its use.... The Parties also agree in holding that whether the response to the attack is lawful depends on observance of the criteria of the necessity and the proportionality of the measures taken in self-defence....

195. In the case of individual self-defence, the exercise of this right is subject to the State concerned having been the victim of an armed attack. Reliance on collective self-defence of course does not remove the need for this. There appears now to be general agreement on the nature of the acts which can be treated as constituting armed attacks.... [I]n customary law, the prohibition of armed attacks may apply to the sending by a State of armed bands to the territory of another State, if such an operation, because of its scale and effects, would have been classified as an armed attack rather than as a mere frontier incident had it been carried out by regular armed forces. But the Court does not believe that the concept of "armed attack" includes... assistance to rebels in the form of the provision of weapons or logistical or other support. Such assistance may be regarded as a threat or use of force, or amount to intervention in the internal or external affairs of other States. It is also clear that it is the State which is the victim of an armed attack which must form and declare the view that it has been so attacked. There is no rule in customary international law permitting another State to exercise the right of collective self-defence on the basis of its own assessment of the situation....

199.... [T]he Court finds that in customary international law... there is no rule permitting the exercise of collective self-defence in the absence of a request by the State which regards itself as the victim of an armed attack....

200.... Article 51 of the United Nations Charter requires that measures taken by States in exercise of this right of self-defence must be "immediately reported" to the Security Council.... Whatever influence the Charter may have had on customary international law in these matters, it is clear that in customary international law it is not a condition of the lawfulness of the use of force in self-defence that a procedure so closely dependent on the content of a treaty commitment and of the institutions established by it, should have been followed. On the other hand, if self-defence is advanced as a justification for measures which would otherwise be in breach both of the principle of customary international law and of that contained in the Charter, it is to be expected that the conditions of the Charter should be respected. Thus for the purpose of enquiry into the customary law position, the absence of a report may be one of the factors indicating whether the State in question was itself convinced that it was acting in self-defence....

[3. Intervention]

202. The principle of non-intervention involves the right of every sovereign State to conduct its affairs without outside interference; though examples of trespass against this principle are not infrequent, the Court considers that it is part and parcel of customary international law.... Expressions of an opinio juris regarding the existence of the principle of non-intervention in customary international law are numerous and not difficult to find.... The existence in the opinio juris of States of the principle of non-intervention is backed by established and substantial practice....

205. ... [T]he principle of non-intervention ... forbids all States or groups of States to intervene directly or indirectly in internal or external affairs of other States. A prohibited intervention must accordingly be one bearing on matters in which each State is permitted, by the principle of State sovereignty, to decide freely. One of these is the choice of a political, economic, social and cultural system, and the formulation of foreign policy. Intervention is wrongful when it uses methods of coercion in regard to such choices, which must remain free ones. The element of coercion, which defines, and indeed forms the very essence of, prohibited intervention, is particularly obvious in the case of an intervention which uses force, either in the direct form of military action, or in the indirect form of support for subversive or terrorist armed activities within another State....

206. ... [The Court must nevertheless consider whether there exists] a kind of general right for States to intervene, directly or indirectly, with or without armed force, in support of an internal opposition in another State, whose cause appeared particularly worthy by reason of the political and moral values with which it was identified....

209. The Court ... finds that no such general right of intervention, in support of an opposition within another State, exists in contemporary international law. The Court concludes that acts constituting a breach of the customary principle of non-intervention will also, if they directly or indirectly involve the use of force, constitute a breach of the principle of non-use of force in international relations.

210. ... [I]f one State acts towards another State in breach of the principle of non-intervention, may a third State lawfully take such action by way of countermeasures against the first State as would otherwise constitute an intervention in its internal affairs? A right to act in this way in the case of intervention would be analogous to the right of collective self-defence in the case of an armed attack, but both the act which gives rise to the reaction, and that reaction itself, would in principle be less grave. Since the Court is here dealing with a dispute in which a wrongful use of force is alleged, it has primarily to consider whether a State has a right to respond to intervention with intervention going so far as to justify a use of force in reaction to measures which do not constitute an armed attack but may nevertheless involve a use of force....

211. ... [F]or one State to use force against another, on the ground that that State has committed a wrongful act of force against a third State, is regarded as lawful, by way of exception, only when the wrongful act provoking the response was an armed attack. Thus the lawfulness of the use of force by a State in response to a wrongful act of which it has not itself been the victim is not admitted when this wrongful act is not an armed attack. In the view of the Court, under international law in force today — whether customary international law or that of the United Nations system — States do not have a right of "collective" armed response to acts which do not constitute an "armed attack." ...

[4. Respect for State Sovereignty]

212. The Court should now mention the principle of respect for State sovereignty, which in international law is of course closely linked with the principles of the prohibition of the use of force and of non-intervention. The basic legal concept of State sovereignty in customary international law, expressed in, inter alia, Article 2, paragraph 1, of the United Nations Charter ["The Organization is based on the principle of the sovereign equality of all its Members."], extends to the internal waters and territorial sea of every State and to the air space above its territory. . . .

[III. APPLICATION OF LAW TO THE FACTS]

[A. Direct and Indirect Uses of Force]

227. . . . For the most part, the complaints by Nicaragua are of the actual use of force against it by the United States. Of the acts which the Court has found imputable to the Government of the United States, the following are relevant in this respect:

— the laying of mines in Nicaraguan internal or territorial waters in early 1984;
— certain attacks on Nicaraguan ports, oil installations and a naval base.

These activities constitute infringements of the principle of the prohibition of the use of force, defined earlier, unless they are justified by circumstances which exclude their unlawfulness. . . .

228. . . . As to the claim that United States activities in relation to the contras constitute a breach of the customary international law principle of the non-use of force, the Court finds that, subject to the question whether the action of the United States might be justified as an exercise of the right of self-defence, the United States has committed a prima facie violation of that principle by its assistance to the contras in Nicaragua, by "organizing or encouraging the organization of irregular forces or armed bands . . . for incursion into the territory of another State," and "participating in acts of civil strife . . . in another State," in the terms of General Assembly resolution 2625 (XXV) [U.N. Doc. A/2625 (Oct. 24, 1970)]. According to that resolution, participation of this kind is contrary to the principle of the prohibition of the use of force when the acts of civil strife referred to "involve a threat or use of force." In the view of the Court, while the arming and training of the contras can certainly be said to involve the threat or use of force against Nicaragua, this is not necessarily so in respect of all the assistance given by the United States Government. In particular, the Court considers that the mere supply of funds to the contras, while undoubtedly an act of intervention in the internal affairs of Nicaragua . . . does not in itself amount to a use of force.

[B. Collective Self-Defense]

229. The Court must thus consider whether, as the Respondent claims, the acts in question of the United States are justified by the exercise of its right of collective self-defence against an armed attack. . . . For the Court to conclude that the United States was lawfully exercising its right of collective self-defence, it must first find that Nicaragua engaged in an armed attack against El Salvador. . . .

230. . . . Even assuming that the supply of arms to the opposition in El Salvador could be treated as imputable to the Government of Nicaragua, to justify invocation of the right of collective self-defence in customary international law, it would have to be equated with an armed attack by Nicaragua on El Salvador. As stated above, the Court is unable to consider that, in customary international law, the provision of arms to the opposition in another State constitutes an armed attack on that State. . . .

237. Since the Court has found that the condition sine qua non required for the exercise of the right of collective self-defence by the United States is not fulfilled in this case, the appraisal of the United States activities in relation to the criteria of necessity and proportionality takes on a different significance. As a result of this conclusion of the Court, even if the United States activities in question had been carried on in strict compliance with the canons of necessity and proportionality, they would not thereby become lawful. If however they were not, this may constitute an additional ground of wrongfulness. . . . [The Court then concluded that U.S. activities in and against Nicaragua failed to satisfy the criterion of "necessity," because they began and continued long after significant Nicaraguan assistance to the armed opposition in El Salvador had ended. It also found that the mining of the Nicaraguan ports and the attacks on ports and oil installations were not "proportional" to the aid received by the Salvadorian armed opposition from Nicaragua.]

238. Accordingly, the Court concludes that the plea of collective self-defence against an alleged armed attack on El Salvador . . . advanced by the United States to justify its conduct toward Nicaragua, cannot be upheld; and accordingly that the United States has violated the principle prohibiting recourse to the threat or use of force by the acts listed in paragraph 227 above, and by its assistance to the contras to the extent that this assistance "involve[s] a threat or use of force" (paragraph 228 above). . . .

[C. Intervention]

241. . . . It appears to the Court to be clearly established . . . that the United States intended, by its support of the contras, to coerce the Government of Nicaragua in respect of matters in which each State is permitted, by the principle of State sovereignty, to decide freely. . . . The Court considers that in international law, if one State, with a view to the coercion of another State, supports and assists armed bands in that State whose purpose is to overthrow the government of that State, that amounts to an intervention by the one State in the internal affairs of the other, whether or not the political objective of the State giving such support and assistance is equally far reaching. . . .

242. The Court therefore finds that the support given by the United States, up to the end of September 1984, to the military and paramilitary activities of the contras in Nicaragua, by financial support, training, supply of weapons, intelligence and logistic support, constitutes a clear breach of the principle of non-intervention. . . .

249. . . . While an armed attack would give rise to an entitlement to collective self-defence, a use of force of a lesser degree of gravity cannot, as the Court has already observed, produce any entitlement to take collective counter-measures involving the use of force. The acts of which Nicaragua is accused, even assuming them to have been established and imputable to that State, could only have justified proportionate counter-measures on the part of the State which had been the victim of these acts, namely El Salvador. . . . They could not justify counter-measures taken by a third State, the United States, and particularly could not justify intervention involving the use of force. . . .

[D. Respect for State Sovereignty]

251. The effects of the principle of respect for territorial sovereignty inevitably overlap with those of the principles of the prohibition of the use of force and of non-intervention. Thus the assistance to the contras, as well as the direct attacks on Nicaraguan ports, oil installations, etc. . . . not only amount to an unlawful use of force, but also constitute infringements of the territorial sovereignty of Nicaragua, and incursions into its territorial and internal waters. Similarly, the mining operations in the Nicaraguan ports not only constitute breaches of the principle of the non-use of force, but also affect Nicaragua's sovereignty over certain maritime expanses. . . .

252. These violations cannot be justified either by collective self-defence, for which, as the Court has recognized, the necessary circumstances are lacking, nor by any right of the United States to take counter-measures involving the use of force in the event of intervention by Nicaragua in El Salvador, since no such right exists under the applicable international law. . . .

263. The finding of the United States Congress also expressed the view that the Nicaraguan Government had taken "significant steps towards establishing a totalitarian Communist dictatorship." However the regime in Nicaragua be defined, adherence by a State to any particular doctrine does not constitute a violation of customary international law; to hold otherwise would make nonsense of the fundamental principle of State sovereignty, on which the whole of international law rests, and the freedom of choice of the political, social, economic and cultural system of a State. Consequently, Nicaragua's domestic policy options, even assuming that they correspond to the description given of them by the Congress finding, cannot justify on the legal plane the various actions of the Respondent complained of. The Court cannot contemplate the creation of a new rule opening up a right of intervention by one State against another on the ground that the latter has opted for some particular ideology or political system. . . .

[The enumeration of votes by individual judges, and separate and dissenting opinions of various judges, are omitted.]

Notes and Questions

1. The Political Decision to Support the Contras. The Reagan administration's military involvement in Central America was part of a larger campaign to thwart the spread of communism in the Western Hemisphere. Support for the Contras reflected a commitment to a friendly regime in El Salvador and opposition to a new Nicaraguan government thought to be allied with Cuba. We cannot be certain what influence, if any, U.S. obligations under the U.N. Charter had on the Administration's decision making, or whether anyone imagined that Nicaragua would seek relief in the World Court. We think it notable, however, that the United States sought to avoid accountability by concealing its actions from public view for a time. For sometimes sharply contrasting views of these developments, compare Theodore Draper, *A Very Thin Line: The Iran-Contra Affairs* 15-50, 558-579 (1991), with John Norton Moore, *The Secret War in Central America: Sandinista Assault on World Order* 5-73 (1987).

2. *Effect of the Nicaragua Case.* The World Court's decision in the *Nicaragua* case is legally binding only on the parties before the Court. But it is widely regarded as an authoritative statement of current law. How likely is it that it will dissuade states from resorting to force in resolving future disputes? What politically viable legal reforms can you suggest that would further deter aggression?

3. *World Court vs. Security Council.* In contesting the subject-matter jurisdiction of the Court at an earlier stage in the proceedings, the United States argued that questions about the unlawful use of force were committed exclusively to the political organs of the United Nations, in particular to the Security Council, and that the Court's involvement would improperly interfere with an exercise of the inherent right of individual and collective self-defense under Article 51. It noted further that only a few days before filing an application with the Court, Nicaragua had submitted a draft resolution containing the same allegations to the Security Council, and that the resolution had not been adopted.

The Court responded that the "Council has functions of a political nature assigned to it, whereas the Court exercises purely judicial functions. Both organs can therefore perform their separate but complementary functions with respect to the same events.... [The Court] was not asked to say that the Security Council was wrong in its decision." 1984 I.C.J. 392, 435-436 (Nov. 26).

Recall that Article 25 of the Charter requires member states to follow the dictates of the Security Council. Each state coming within the jurisdiction of the World Court also "undertakes to comply" with its decisions, which may be enforced by the Security Council. Art. 94. Do the two bodies — the Court and the Security Council — differ in their competence to address the issues raised in the *Nicaragua* case? Should we worry that the two might someday come into conflict? What would be the practical effect of a contrary ruling?

4. *Treaty Law vs. Customary International Law.* The refusal of the United States to submit to the jurisdiction of the Court in a dispute involving a multilateral treaty obligation reflects one of the most hallowed aspects of sovereignty in our international system: a state may not be compelled to do anything it has not voluntarily agreed to do. Did the United States argue that the U.N. Charter codified existing customary international norms, or that the norms are the product of international agreement in the Charter? Are the two really different? Does it matter?

5. *Formation of Customary International Law.* The formation of customary international law "results from a general and consistent practice of states followed by them from a sense of legal obligation." *Restatement (Third) of Foreign Relations Law* §102(2) (1987). Regarding the consistency of state practice, in another case the Court remarked, "State practice... should have been both extensive and virtually uniform in the sense of the provision invoked." *North Sea Continental Shelf* (Fed. Rep. Ger. v. Den., Neth.), Judgment, 1969 I.C.J. 12, 43 (Feb. 20). Unfortunately,

history is replete with examples, many of them very recent, of states resorting to violence without the approval of the U.N. Security Council and for reasons having nothing to do with self-defense. How then did the *Nicaragua* Court determine that the practice of states was sufficiently consistent to form a customary norm prohibiting the use of force? Do you think the degree of consistency required in this case might be different from that in the formation of a customary norm concerned with, say, welcoming ceremonies for visiting heads of state? Should it be different?

The development of customary international law also requires state practice to be based on a sense of legal obligation, or *opinio juris*. Where does the Court find expressions of that sense of legal obligation independent of the requirements of the Charter? What, if any, was the effect of its characterization of the prohibition on the use of force as peremptory law — *jus cogens*?

6. *Scope of the Prohibition of the Use of Force.* In a 2005 case the World Court called the prohibition on the use of force "a cornerstone of the United Nations Charter." *Armed Activities on the Territory of the Congo* (Dem. Rep. Congo v. Uganda), 2005 I.C.J. 168, 223 (Dec. 19). There is general agreement that a substantial, direct, armed attack by one state's regular military forces against another state violates the customary prohibition on the use of force, just as it does Article 2(4), unless it is excused by one of the two recognized exceptions to the prohibition. But there is less certainty about the precise scope of the prohibition when it comes to less flagrant hostile actions.

The *Nicaragua* Court found that the United States violated the prohibition when U.S. government personnel mined harbors and carried out aerial strikes against ports, a military base, and oil installations in Nicaragua. ¶227. It also did so by "organizing or encouraging the organization of irregular forces or armed bands . . . for incursion into the territory of another State," and "participating in acts of civil strife . . . in another State" that involved a threat or use of force. ¶228. But while "arming and training" the Contras violated the prohibition, financing them did not.

Can you tell from the opinion what kinds of assistance for rebel groups are forbidden? Why did the Court exclude financial support alone?

Since 1945, states have repeatedly tested the limits of Article 2(4) by asserting the right to use force to: (1) defend against organized groups of non-state actors, like Al Qaeda; (2) prevent an attack that has not yet been completed or perhaps even initiated; (3) stop violations of human rights; and (4) protect their nationals. These assertions are explored in the chapters that follow. Because they are often accepted as legitimate, if not strictly legal, they may be thought to have effectively altered the practical meaning of Article 2(4). But can you describe problems in defining and applying each such possible further exception to the prohibition on the use of force? *See* Ashley Deeks, *Commentary: Multi-Part Tests in the Jus ad Bellum*, 53 Hous. L. Rev. 1035 (2016); Matthew C. Waxman, *Regulating Resort to Force: Form and Substance of the UN Charter Regime*, 24 Eur. J. Int'l L. 151 (2013) (analyzing tension between form and strict compliance).

In 2014, Russian troops invaded and occupied the Ukrainian territory of Crimea. Russia claimed that it acted to protect a threatened minority of its citizens there, many of whom had only recently been issued Russian passports, and that it was invited in by the then–Prime Minister of Ukraine. The takeover was completed without a shot being fired. In the absence of any violence, did the Russian action violate Article 2(4)? *See* Ashley Deeks, *Russian Forces in Ukraine: A Sketch of the International Law Issues*, Lawfare, Mar. 2, 2014 (apparently an "unjustifiable armed attack on Ukraine"). Because Russia would veto any sanctions by the U.N. Security Council, is international law meaningless in this context? *See* Peter Spiro, *Ukraine, International Law, and the Perfect Compliance Fallacy*, Opinio Juris, Mar. 2, 2014 (no).

7. *The Threat of Force.* The Court has described the relationship between "threat" and "use" in Article 2(4) this way: "[I]f the use of force itself in a given case is illegal — for whatever reason — the threat to use such force will likewise be illegal." *Legality of the Threat or Use of Nuclear Weapons*, Advisory Opinion, 1996 I.C.J. 226, ¶47 (July 8). But might a threat to use force actually help to keep the peace? That is the theory behind, for example, the policy of nuclear deterrence. *See* James A. Green & Francis Grimal, *The Threat of Force as an Action in Self-Defense under International Law*, 44 Vand. J. Transnat'l L. 285 (2011) (examining the legality of threats made in self-defense). Still, threats of force may themselves be highly undesirable. Can you say how? *See* Romana Sadurska, *Threats of Force*, 82 Am. J. Int'l L. 239, 247 (1988) (arguing that in practice states apply different criteria to determine the legality of threats, and describing reliance on threats as "a precarious game").

8. *Self-Defense.* Because of the U.S. multilateral treaty reservation, the *Nicaragua* Court was asked to identify not only a customary general ban on the use of force in international relations, but also customary exceptions to that ban. Where did it find a customary exception for self-defense?

The threat or use of force in self-defense can only be justified, under either Article 51 or customary law, by the existence of an "armed attack," an especially serious violation of the prohibition on the use of force. The term "armed attack" includes not only direct, substantially destructive uses of military force, but also the "sending by a State of armed bands to the territory of another State, if such an operation, because of its scale and effects, would have been classified as an armed attack . . . had it been carried out by regular armed forces." ¶195. It does not include "assistance to rebels in the form of the provision of weapons or logistical or other support," although such assistance may amount to a prohibited threat or use of force. *Id.* Why do you suppose the threshold for self-help has been set so high?

The right of self-defense is also generally agreed to be qualified by a requirement that it be based on "a necessity of self-defense, instant, overwhelming, leaving no choice of means, no moment for deliberation." Secretary of State Daniel Webster penned this formula in connection with an 1837 dispute between the United States and Great Britain — the *Caroline* affair. 6 *The Works of Daniel Webster* 261 (1851). Along with the criterion of necessity, the Court notes the additional requirement of proportionality. *See* ¶¶194, 237. What purpose is served by each of these criteria?

In another case the Court declared that the burden of proving facts showing the existence of an armed attack rests on the state claiming to act in self-defense. *Oil Platforms (Iran v. United States)*, 2003 I.C.J. 161, 189 (Nov. 6). Why place the burden there?

Why did the Court insist that before one state comes to the aid of another as an act of collective self-defense, the second state must (a) declare that it has come under attack and (b) request assistance? Even with these safeguards, of course, one can see a potential for collusion between assisting and assisted states to create a pretext for aggression against a third state. How could this potential be reduced?

Article 51 provides that any exercise of the inherent right of self-defense "shall be immediately reported to the Security Council." What is the purpose of this requirement? How does it bear on the outcome of the *Nicaragua* case?

Only illegal uses of force amounting to armed attacks can justify forceful responses in self-defense. What recourse is available to victims of lesser uses of force?

9. Non-Intervention. What is the principle of non-intervention? Why does the Court address it, instead of disposing of the case solely on the basis of the customary norm prohibiting the use of force? Can you say what forms of coercion are forbidden by this principle? How about promises of financial aid or threats to withhold such aid? Trade sanctions? Did Russia violate the principle when it interfered in the 2016 U.S. presidential election? *See* Ido Kilovaty, *Doxfare: Politically Motivated Leaks and the Future of the Norm on Non-Intervention in the Era of Weaponized Information*, 9 Harv. Nat'l Security J. 146 (2018) (criticizing the standard of coercion as vague and outdated).

Might an intervention in support of an internal opposition ever be permissible? What about intervention against a state with a corrupt, tyrannical, non-democratic government? Suppose the state were engaged in genocide against some of its own people? Whether intervention is permitted on purely humanitarian grounds is currently subject to vigorous debate. See Chapter 16.

What if military intervention is invited by one of several factions within a state, when none of the factions can establish a clearly legitimate claim to leadership of the government? U.S. military involvement in Vietnam from 1954-1975 (see Chapter 10), in Grenada in 1983, and in Panama in 1989 might be characterized this way. So might military intervention by Saudi Arabia, aided by the United States, in the civil war that began in Yemen in 2014. *See* Clare Duncan, *The Conflict in Yemen: A Primer*, Lawfare, Nov. 28, 2017.

If one state commits a prohibited intervention against another, but not an armed attack, what sorts of countermeasures are permissible? Why should a third state not be entitled to employ forceful "countermeasures" to assist the first state, by way of analogy to the inherent right of collective self-defense?

10. Respect for Sovereignty. What is protected by the principle of respect for state sovereignty? How is this principle related to the customary prohibition on the use of force and to the principle of non-intervention?

11. Aggression as a Crime. At the end of World War II, the tribunal established to punish Nazi war criminals described the initiation of a war of aggression as "not only an international crime; it is the supreme international crime differing only from other war crimes in that it contains within itself the accumulated evil of the whole." *International Military Tribunal (Nuremberg)*, Judgment, 1 I.M.T. 171, 186 (Oct. 1, 1946). U.N. General Assembly Resolution 3314, G.A. Res. 3314 (XXIX), Annex art. 5(2) (Dec. 14, 1974), also states that a "war of aggression is a crime against international peace. Aggression gives rise to international responsibility."

The Rome Statute of the International Criminal Court, July 17, 1998, 2187 U.N.T.S. 90, as amended, describes a process for determining and punishing the crime of "planning, preparation, initiation or execution, by a person in a position effectively to exercise control over or to direct the political or military action of a State, of an act of aggression which, by its character, gravity and scale, constitutes a manifest violation of the Charter of the United Nations." *Id.* art. 8 *bis* (1). "Aggression" is defined to include the invasion, bombardment, or blockade by one state's armed forces of the territory of another state, annexation of another state's territory, an attack on another state's armed forces, and the sending or sponsorship of "armed bands, groups, irregulars or mercenaries" to perform any of these acts. *Id.* art. 8 *bis* (2). For the purpose of this treaty it does not, however, include the threat of force.

The practical effect of this provision is uncertain, as it remains unclear what "character, gravity and scale" of aggressive act constitutes a "manifest violation" of the U.N. Charter. And without a referral from the U.N. Security Council, the jurisdiction of the Court extends only to states parties that use armed force against other states parties, *id.*, and then only to states that have ratified the aggression provision, some 35 in early 2018. *See* Alex Whiting, *Crime of Aggression Activated at the ICC; Does It Matter?*, Just Security, Dec. 19, 2017; Harold Hongju Koh & Todd F. Buchwald, *The Crime of Aggression: The United States Perspective*, Faculty Scholarship Series Paper 5006 (2015), http://digitalcommons.law.yale.edu/fss_papers/5006.

12. U.S. Self-Protection from ICC Prosecution. In order to avoid possible prosecution of senior U.S. government officials or members of the U.S. armed forces by the ICC for war crimes, the United States has refused to become a party to the treaty that established it. Moreover, in 2002 Congress enacted the American Servicemembers' Protection Act, 22 U.S.C. §§7421-7433 (2018), which forbids U.S. cooperation with the ICC, including extradition to the Court of persons accused of war crimes. *Id.* §7423. The 2002 statute also bars the deployment of U.S. troops on peacekeeping or peace enforcement missions authorized by the U.N. Security Council without assurances from the Security Council or the ICC that they will not be liable to prosecution. *Id.* §§7422, 7424. In addition, it authorizes the President to use "all means necessary and appropriate" to free U.S. military personnel, government officials, or anyone working on behalf of the government who is held by or at the request of the ICC. *Id.* §7427(a). When the ICC's Chief Counsel, a Gambian lawyer, sought to investigate possible war crimes in Afghanistan, the United States cancelled her visa, and the Court shut down her investigation. *See* Mike Corder, *Judges Reject Afghanistan Probe; Cite Lack of Cooperation*, AP, Apr. 12, 2019. Do you think this U.S. opposition will make aggression more or less likely in the future?

THE RIGHT TO WAGE WAR: SUMMARY OF BASIC PRINCIPLES

- Any threat or use of force in international relations must conform to the provisions of the United Nations Charter. Those provisions reflect and are influenced by a parallel body of customary international law norms, and vice versa.
- The U.N. Charter is generally regarded as not providing domestic authority for U.S. troop deployments. And since 1945, Congress has been reluctant to give open-ended approval for such deployments on United Nations missions.

- The International Court of Justice may rule on the legality of armed conflicts when the states involved have submitted to the jurisdiction of the Court, and parties are bound to abide by its rulings, which may be enforced by the Security Council.

- Both the Charter and customary international law permit the use of force in only two circumstances: unilateral or collective self-defense in response to an armed attack, and collective action with the approval of the U.N. Security Council. But states have often used force in situations that do not strictly comply with these limits, suggesting an evolving flexibility in the rules.

- Direct, substantial attacks by one state's regular military forces against another state will violate the prohibition on the use of force. So will arming and training paramilitary forces to engage in civil strife in another state, if that support produces a sufficient measure of dependency and control. Financing of such forces alone, however, is not a violation.

- Force may be used in self-defense, in the absence of Security Council approval, only in response to an armed attack. If one state "sends" paramilitary forces into another state, it may be guilty of an armed attack if the scale and effects of the invasion are sufficiently great. But not if it merely furnishes weapons and other support to rebels there.

- Legitimate uses of force in self-defense must be necessary (no time for deliberation and no reasonable alternative) and proportional (no nuclear weapons in response to a minor border incursion), and they may continue only until the U.N. Security Council has "taken measures necessary to maintain international peace and security."

- States may not use coercion to intervene in matters that other sovereign states must be free to choose, including political, economic, social, and cultural systems, and the formulation of foreign policy. Whether intervention is permitted on purely humanitarian grounds is subject to vigorous current debate.

- Uses of force falling short of an armed attack may be met by proportionate countermeasures by the victim state, but collective armed responses are not permitted.

9

International Humanitarian Law (*jus in bello*)

The international law concerning the right to wage war, or *jus ad bellum*, examined in the last chapter, is aimed at deterring the use of armed force by states against each other. It is also supposed to regulate the use of force by states against terrorists and other non-state actors. A related, parallel body of law, *jus in bello*, is concerned with the conduct of war once it has begun. Also referred to as international humanitarian law (IHL) or the law of armed conflict (LOAC),[1] its purpose is to limit the suffering of combatants and noncombatants alike to what is necessary to achieve the legitimate political goals of a conflict.

Several framework principles constitute IHL, including requirements that any use of military force be based on:

- *necessity* (only measures that are actually necessary to accomplish a legitimate military purpose and not otherwise prohibited by IHL),
- *distinction* (distinguishing carefully between military targets and civilians in order to protect the latter),
- *proportionality* (forbidding any use of force that causes incidental civilian casualties that are disproportionate to the military advantage from the operation), and
- *humanity* (avoidance of unnecessary suffering).

The International Court of Justice summarized the key principles of IHL in a 1996 advisory opinion:

> 78. The Cardinal principles . . . constituting the fabric of humanitarian law are the following. The first is aimed at the protection of the civilian population and civilian objects

1. We use the term "international humanitarian law" (IHL) here because of its international currency and its growing use in academic discourse. The terms "law of armed conflict" and "laws of war" are synonymous.

> and establishes the distinction between combatants and non-combatants; States must never make civilians the object of attack and must consequently never use weapons that are incapable of distinguishing between civilian and military targets. [Second], it is prohibited to cause unnecessary suffering to combatants: it is accordingly prohibited to use weapons causing them such harm or uselessly aggravating their suffering. In application of that second principle, States do not have unlimited freedom of choice of means in the weapons they use. [*Legality of the Threat or Use of Nuclear Weapons, Advisory Opinion,* 1996 I.C.J. 226, 257 (July 8).]

IHL has been extensively codified, most prominently in a series of Hague Conventions, which address permissible targets and weaponry, and Geneva Conventions, which are concerned with the treatment of prisoners and other noncombatants and the conduct of occupying forces. It is also expressed in conventions that deal with poison gas, anti-personnel land mines, blinding lasers, the protection of cultural objects, and other matters relating to the effects of war. IHL norms are found, as well, in a robust, rapidly evolving body of customary international law.

IHL is a subset of international law, partially incorporated into U.S. law. Another subset of international law, international human rights law (HRL), applies in peacetime and, some would say, during armed conflicts as well. Traditionally, the view of the United States is that, during armed conflicts, the more general HRL gives way to the more specific IHL and its *jus in bello* principles. U.S. Army, *Operational Law Handbook* 51-52 (2018).

The extensive provisions of the Geneva Conventions of 1949 apply only to armed conflicts of an international (interstate) character, not to non-international armed conflicts (including at least some insurrections), except for baseline, general humanitarian protections for victims of all armed conflicts found in Common Article 3. Two Additional Protocols to the Geneva Conventions, adopted 28 years later, seek to extend the basic Geneva principles to a wider range of conflicts, and to describe emerging customs and new principles. Additional Protocol I (AP I) is concerned with international armed conflicts, while Additional Protocol II (AP II) is applicable to non-international armed conflicts, but neither has been ratified by the United States.[2] Nevertheless, the United States follows some of their principles as customary international law.

The existing law leaves much to be desired. Because armed conflicts today frequently involve violent clashes between states and non-state actors — terrorists, insurgents, guerrilla groups, even pirates — the Geneva Conventions and their Protocols often fail to provide clear guidance for belligerents. *See* John B. Bellinger III & Vijay M. Padmanabhan, *Detention Operations in Contemporary Conflicts: Four Challenges for the Geneva Conventions and Other Existing Law,* 105 Am. J. Int'l L. 201, 205-213 (2011). Even when the Conventions apply to such conflicts, they may not adapt easily to the weaponry, tactics, and personnel employed in modern irregular warfare.

Some argue that HRL, supplemented by domestic laws, should govern all such conflicts. But the relationship of these laws to IHL is complex, and the patchwork of rules that would result from this approach might be more bewildering than helpful. *Id.* at 209-212. As things now stand, states and lawyers struggle to apply IHL to these conflicts, and state militaries may in practice simply treat all armed conflicts the same.

---

2. A third Additional Protocol, adopted in 2005, adds a third distinctive emblem — the red crystal — to the two previously established (the red cross and the red crescent) for denoting those performing humanitarian services during wartime.

See Michael N. Schmitt, *Targeting and International Humanitarian Law in Afghanistan*, 85 Int'l L. Stud. 307, 308 (2009) (IHL norms in international and non-international armed conflicts "have become nearly indistinguishable").

This chapter offers an introduction to IHL—just enough to understand the basics and the significance of *jus in bello* for national security law. Our broader objective here is to lay the foundation for a more extensive application of IHL principles when we consider targeted killings, detention and interrogation of terrorist suspects, and military commissions in later chapters.

A. AUTHORITIES FOR *JUS IN BELLO*

1. When Does IHL Apply?

The United States deploys armed forces in a wide range of settings, including humanitarian relief, peacekeeping, and counterterrorism operations. Because IHL applies only during an armed conflict, an important threshold question is whether a particular military operation *is* an "armed conflict."

As we have seen, the application of domestic law authorities often turns on whether the United States is "at war." Early in the twentieth century, Article 2 of the Hague Convention stated that its Regulations on the Laws and Customs of War on Land applied "in case of war." But after several instances during World War II and other conflicts in which states argued that certain military operations did not involve "war" or that war was not "declared," the drafters of the four 1949 Geneva Conventions determined to clarify and strengthen the threshold requirements in the following provision that appears in each Convention:

Common Article 2

... [T]he present Convention shall apply to all cases of declared war or of any other armed conflict which may arise between two or more of the High Contracting Parties, even if the state of war is not recognized by one of them.

The Convention shall also apply to all of cases of partial or total occupation of the territory of a High Contracting Party, even if said occupation meets with no armed resistance....

The drafters' commentary on the Conventions explains that, instead of a formal declaration or recognition of the existence of a state of war, the "occurrence of *de facto* hostilities is sufficient" to trigger the application of the Conventions. The commentary elaborates on what is meant by "armed conflict":

> The substitution of this much more general expression for the word "war" was deliberate. It is possible to argue almost endlessly about the legal definition of "war." A... State can always maintain that it is not making war, but merely engaging in a police action, or acting in legitimate self-defence. The expression "armed conflict" makes such arguments less easy. Any difference arising between two States and leading to the intervention of

> members of the armed forces is an armed conflict within the meaning of Article 2, even if one of the Parties denies the existence of a state of war. It makes no difference how long the conflict lasts, how much slaughter takes place. [Int'l Comm. of the Red Cross, *Commentary: IV Geneva Convention Relative to the Protection of Civilian Persons in Time of War* 20 (Oscar M. Uhler et al. eds., 1958).]

Aside from violent confrontations between or among states, many conflicts today involve fighting between a state and non-state entities, or among non-state groups, for power or territory inside a state. The drafters of the 1949 Conventions also determined to codify a much more modest set of protections for those involved in what came to be called non-international armed conflicts:

Common Article 3

In the case of armed conflict not of an international character occurring in the territory of one of the High Contracting Parties, each party to the conflict shall be bound to apply, as a minimum, the following provisions:

> 1. Persons taking no active part in the hostilities, including members of armed forces who have laid down their arms and those placed hors de combat by sickness, wounds, detention, or any other cause, shall in all circumstances be treated humanely, without any adverse distinction founded on race, colour, religion or faith, sex, birth or wealth, or any other similar criteria.
>
> To this end the following acts are and shall remain prohibited at any time and in any place whatsoever with respect to the above-mentioned persons:
>
> (a) Violence to life and person, in particular murder of all kinds, mutilation, cruel treatment and torture;
>
> (b) Taking of hostages;
>
> (c) Outrages upon personal dignity, in particular, humiliating and degrading treatment;
>
> (d) The passing of sentences and the carrying out of executions without previous judgment pronounced by a regularly constituted court affording all the judicial guarantees which are recognized as indispensable by civilized peoples. . . .

Common Article 3 is a sort of mini-convention that operates entirely independently of the rest of the Conventions. It was negotiated and regarded in 1949 as applicable mainly in civil wars and colonial conflicts. Unlike Common Article 2, it was very controversial, with opponents arguing that extension of the full protections of the Conventions (including POW status for captives) would allow rebels and "common brigands" to represent their crimes as "acts of war" in order to escape punishment for them, and to seek release as soon as order was restored. Terrorists apparently were not considered in drafting Common Article 3, although its provision for "judgment . . . by a regularly constituted court" would in any case allow for their trial. This history is spelled out in detail at Int'l Comm. of the Red Cross, *Convention (III) Relative to the Treatment of Prisoners of War. Geneva, 12 August 1949. Commentary of 1960* (n.d.), at

28-44, *available at* https://ihl-databases.icrc.org/applic/ihl/ihl.nsf/Comment.xsp?action=openDocument&documentId=466097D7A301F8C4C12563CD00424E2B.

Notes and Questions

1. *The Either/Or of the Geneva Conventions.* Under the 1949 Geneva Conventions, every "armed conflict" is either international (Common Article 2) or non-international (Common Article 3). How are the protections offered by the two articles different? Are you persuaded that changing the threshold requirement for their application from a state of "war" to "armed conflict" was wise? What law applies if the "armed conflict" threshold is not crossed?

2. *Defining Armed Conflict.* What should be the criteria for deciding the existence of an "armed conflict"? The Geneva Conventions make it clear that it is not up to the states parties to say whether or not an armed conflict exists. Who decides, then? Recall that as early as *The Prize Cases, supra* p. 55, our Supreme Court did not require a declaration as a prerequisite to the existence of general or civil war. Even earlier decisions of the Court, including *Little v. Barreme,* 6 U.S. (2 Cranch) 170 (1804), and *Bas v. Tingy,* 4 U.S. (4 Dall.) 37 (1800), recognized the existence of an imperfect war without a formal declaration.

In the context of attempts to try perpetrators of war crimes, crimes against humanity, and genocide during the conflict in the former Yugoslavia in the early 1990s, the International Criminal Tribunal for the former Yugoslavia (ICTY) found that

> an armed conflict exists whenever there is a resort to armed force between States or protracted armed violence between governmental authorities and organized armed groups or between such groups within a State. [IHL] . . . extends beyond the cessation of hostilities until a general conclusion of peace is reached; or, in the case of internal conflicts, a peaceful settlement is achieved. Until that moment, [IHL] continues to apply in the whole territory of the warring States or, in the case of internal conflicts, the whole territory under the control of a party, whether or not actual combat takes place there. [*Prosecutor v. Tadic,* Case No. IT-94-1-I, Decision on Defence Motion for Interlocutory Appeal on Jurisdiction, ¶70 (Int'l Crim. Trib. for the Former Yugoslavia Oct. 2, 1995).]

Can you now say what an armed conflict is?

2. IHL for the Victims of War — The 1949 Geneva Conventions

Reading the Geneva Conventions

There are four separate 1949 Geneva Conventions. The Convention for the Amelioration of the Condition of the Wounded and Sick in Armed Forces in the Field (Geneva I) and the Convention for the Amelioration of the Condition of Wounded, Sick and Shipwrecked Members of the Armed Forces at Sea (Geneva II) provide similar protections for, respectively, land and seaborne forces. Several provisions of Geneva III and Geneva IV, excerpted below, contain central components of contemporary *in bello* safeguards. Note that Common Articles 1-3 are identical throughout the four Conventions.

Provisions of Geneva III and IV and Additional Protocol I set out below fall roughly into three categories: (1) those stating broad ideals or describing procedural requirements, (2) those regulating the means for waging warfare, and (3) those dealing in greater detail with the treatment of prisoners. See if you can place each provision into one of these categories, recognizing that there may be some overlap in a few instances.

Geneva Convention Relative to the Treatment of Prisoners of War, August 12, 1949 (Geneva III)

T.I.A.S. No. 3362, 75 U.N.T.S. 135

Article 1

The High Contracting Parties undertake to respect and to ensure respect for the present Convention in all circumstances.

Article 2 [*see supra* p. 267]

Article 3 [*see supra* p. 268]

Article 4

A. Prisoners of war, in the sense of the present Convention, are persons belonging to one of the following categories, who have fallen into the power of the enemy:

1. Members of the armed forces of a Party to the conflict as well as members of militias or volunteer corps forming part of such armed forces.

2. Members of other militias and members of other volunteer corps, including those of organized resistance movements, belonging to a Party to the conflict and operating in or outside their own territory, even if this territory is occupied, provided that such militias or volunteer corps, including such organized resistance movements, fulfil the following conditions:

(a) That of being commanded by a person responsible for his subordinates;

(b) That of having a fixed distinctive sign recognizable at a distance;

(c) That of carrying arms openly;

(d) That of conducting their operations in accordance with the laws and customs of war.

3. Members of regular armed forces who profess allegiance to a government or an authority not recognized by the Detaining Power.

4. Persons who accompany the armed forces without actually being members thereof, such as civilian members of military aircraft crews, war correspondents, supply contractors, members of labour units or of services responsible for the welfare of the armed forces, provided that they have received

authorization from the armed forces which they accompany, who shall provide them for that purpose with an identity card similar to the annexed model.

5. Members of crews, including masters, pilots and apprentices, of the merchant marine and the crews of civil aircraft of the Parties to the conflict, who do not benefit by more favourable treatment under any other provisions of international law.

6. Inhabitants of a non-occupied territory, who on the approach of the enemy spontaneously take up arms to resist the invading forces, without having had time to form themselves into regular armed units, provided they carry arms openly and respect the laws and customs of war. . . .

Article 5

The present Convention shall apply to the persons referred to in Article 4 from the time they fall into the power of the enemy and until their final release and repatriation.

Should any doubt arise as to whether persons, having committed a belligerent act and having fallen into the hands of the enemy, belong to any of the categories enumerated in Article 4, such persons shall enjoy the protection of the present Convention until such time as their status has been determined by a competent tribunal. . . .

Article 17

Every prisoner of war, when questioned on the subject, is bound to give only his surname, first names and rank, date of birth, and army, regimental, personal or serial number, or failing this, equivalent information.

If he wilfully infringes this rule, he may render himself liable to a restriction of the privileges accorded to his rank or status. . . .

[Most of the remaining provisions of Geneva III spell out conditions of confinement of prisoners of war, including rights to health care, exercise, mail, food, and the right to be released at the end of a conflict.]

Article 87

Prisoners of war may not be sentenced by the military authorities and courts of the Detaining Power to any penalties except those provided for in respect of members of the armed forces of the said Power who have committed the same acts.

When fixing the penalty, the courts or authorities of the Detaining Power shall take into consideration, to the widest extent possible, the fact that the accused, not being a national of the Detaining Power, is not bound to it by any duty of allegiance, and that he is in its power as the result of circumstances independent of his own will. . . .

Collective punishment for individual acts, corporal punishments, imprisonment in premises without daylight and, in general, any form of torture or cruelty, are forbidden. . . .

Geneva Convention Relative to the Protection of Civilian Persons in Time of War, August 12, 1949 (Geneva IV)

T.I.A.S. No. 3362, 75 U.N.T.S. 287

Article 4

Persons protected by the Convention are those who, at a given moment and in any manner whatsoever, find themselves, in case of a conflict or occupation, in the hands of a Party to the conflict or Occupying Power of which they are not nationals.

Nationals of a State which is not bound by the Convention are not protected by it. Nationals of a neutral State who find themselves in the territory of a belligerent State, and nationals of a co-belligerent State, shall not be regarded as protected persons while the State of which they are nationals has normal diplomatic representation in the State in whose hands they are. . . .

Article 5

Where, in the territory of a Party to the conflict, the latter is satisfied that an individual protected person is definitely suspected of or engaged in activities hostile to the security of the State, such individual person shall not be entitled to claim such rights and privileges under the present Convention as would, if exercised in the favour of such individual person, be prejudicial to the security of such State.

Where in occupied territory an individual protected person is detained as a spy or saboteur, or as a person under definite suspicion of activity hostile to the security of the Occupying Power, such person shall, in those cases where absolute military security so requires, be regarded as having forfeited rights of communication under the present Convention.

In each case, such persons shall nevertheless be treated with humanity, and in case of trial, shall not be deprived of the rights of fair and regular trial prescribed by the present Convention. They shall also be granted the full rights and privileges of a protected person under the present Convention at the earliest date consistent with the security of the State or Occupying Power, as the case may be. . . .

Article 31

No physical or moral coercion shall be exercised against protected persons, in particular to obtain information from them or from third parties. . . .

Article 49

Individual or mass forcible transfers, as well as deportations of protected persons from occupied territory to the territory of the Occupying Power or to that of any other country, occupied or not, are prohibited, regardless of their motive.

Nevertheless, the Occupying Power may undertake total or partial evacuation of a given area if the security of the population or imperative military reasons do demand. Such evacuations may not involve the displacement of protected persons outside the bounds of the occupied territory except when for material reasons it is impossible to avoid such displacement. Persons thus evacuated shall be transferred back to their homes as soon as hostilities in the area in question have ceased. . . .

Article 146

The High Contracting Parties undertake to enact any legislation necessary to provide effective penal sanctions for persons committing, or ordering to be committed, any of the grave breaches of the present Convention defined in the following Article.

Each High Contracting Party shall be under the obligation to search for persons alleged to have committed, or to have ordered to be committed, such grave breaches, and shall bring such persons, regardless of their nationality, before its own courts. It may also, if it prefers, and in accordance with the provisions of its own legislation, hand such persons over for trial to another High Contracting Party concerned, provided such High Contracting Party has made out a *prima facie* case.

Each High Contracting Party shall take measures necessary for the suppression of all acts contrary to the provisions of the present Convention other than the grave breaches defined in the following Article.

In all circumstances, the accused persons shall benefit by safeguards of proper trial and defence, which shall not be less favourable than those provided by Article 105 and those following of the Geneva Convention relative to the Treatment of Prisoners of War of August 12, 1949.

Article 147

Grave breaches to which the preceding Article relates shall be those involving any of the following acts, if committed against persons or property protected by the present Convention: wilful killing, torture or inhuman treatment, including biological experiments, wilfully causing great suffering or serious injury to body or health, unlawful deportation or transfer or unlawful confinement of a protected person, compelling a protected person to serve in the forces of a hostile Power, or wilfully depriving a protected person of the rights of fair and regular trial prescribed in the present Convention, taking of hostages and extensive destruction and appropriation of property, not justified by military necessity and carried out unlawfully and wantonly. . . .

---

3. IHL Revised: The Geneva Protocols Additional

After the Korean War, the world's wars began to evolve from large, state-against-state conflicts involving competing armies into smaller, more episodic conflicts, often involving states fighting non-state entities, such as insurgents, guerrillas, revolutionaries, or terrorists. At the same time, a growing body of human rights law called into question certain international humanitarian law assumptions. In 1977, with the encouragement of national liberation groups, and despite strong opposition from the United States and some of its allies, delegates from a majority of states approved significant amendments to the Geneva Conventions. The Protocols supplement rather than replace the Conventions. Protocol I, excerpted below, covers international armed conflicts — defined more broadly than before — and it effectively codifies the *in bello* regulation of the battlefield. Protocol II, not included here, expands upon the protections in Common Article 3 for individuals in armed conflicts that are not of an international (inter-state) character.

As noted above, the United States has not ratified either Protocol I (AP I) or Protocol II (AP II) to the Geneva Conventions. In AP I, the United States particularly objected to detailed rules about discrimination during attacks, a prohibition on reprisals that could deter IHL violations, modifications to prisoner-of-war (POW) categories, and changes in the definition of international armed conflicts to include indigenous armed struggles against colonial or racist regimes. However, in 1987 the Deputy Legal Adviser to the Department of State indicated that the United States recognizes nearly two-thirds of the articles in Protocol I as customary international law. Theodore Meron, W. Hays Parks, Michael J. Matheson, Hans-Peter Gasser, Burrus M. Carnahan & Waldemar Solf, Am. Soc'y of Int'l Law, *Customary Law and Additional Protocol I to the Geneva Conventions for Protection of War Victims: Future Directions in Light of the U.S. Decision Not to Ratify* 28 (1987). This recognition is indicated by annotations to some of the provisions below. Almost 20 years later, Matheson affirmed his earlier position. Michael J. Matheson, *Continuity and Change in the Law of War: 1975-2005: Detainees and POWs*, 38 Geo. Wash. Int'l L. Rev. 543 (2006).

In March 2011, President Obama announced that he would urge the Senate to ratify AP II, and that the United States would apply Article 75 of AP I (set out below) to individuals detained in international armed conflicts. Office of the Press Secretary, The White House, *Fact Sheet: New Actions on Guantanamo and Detainee Policy*, Mar. 7, 2011. The Department of Defense *Law of War Manual* (June 2015, updated Dec. 2016), affirms that U.S. military practices are consistent with AP II, and that the United States "intend[s] to contribute to the crystallization of the principles contained in Article 75 as rules of customary international law applicable in international armed conflict." *Id.* at 512.

Protocol Additional to the Geneva Conventions of August 12, 1949, and Relating to the Protection of Victims of International Armed Conflicts, June 8, 1977 (Additional Protocol I)

1125 U.N.T.S. 3, 16 I.L.M. 1391

PART I — GENERAL PROVISIONS

Article 1 — General principles and scope of application

1. The High Contracting Parties undertake to respect and to ensure respect for this Protocol in all circumstances.

2. In cases not covered by this Protocol or by other international agreements, civilians and combatants remain under the protection and authority of the principles of international law derived from established custom, from the principles of humanity and from the dictates of public conscience.

3. This Protocol, which supplements the Geneva Conventions of 12 August 1949 for the protection of war victims, shall apply in the situations referred to in Article 2 common to those Conventions.

4. The situations referred to in the preceding paragraph include armed conflicts in which peoples are fighting against colonial domination and alien occupation and against racist regimes in the exercise of their right of self-determination,

as enshrined in the Charter of the United Nations and the Declaration on Principles of International Law concerning Friendly Relations and Co-operation among States in accordance with the Charter of the United Nations. . . .

PART III — METHODS AND MEANS OF WARFARE, COMBATANT AND PRISONER-OF-WAR STATUS

Article 35 — Basic rules[3]

1. In any armed conflict, the right of the Parties to the conflict to choose methods or means of warfare is not unlimited.

2. It is prohibited to employ weapons, projectiles and material and methods of warfare of a nature to cause superfluous injury or unnecessary suffering.

3. It is prohibited to employ methods or means of warfare which are intended, or may be expected, to cause widespread, long-term and severe damage to the natural environment. . . .

Article 41 — Safeguard of an enemy *hors de combat*

1. A person who is recognized or who, in the circumstances should be recognized to be *hors de combat* shall not be made the object of attack.

2. A person is *hors de combat* if:

(a) he is in the power of an adverse Party;

(b) he clearly expresses an intention to surrender; or

(c) he has been rendered unconscious or is otherwise incapacitated by wounds or sickness, and therefore is incapable of defending himself;

provided that in any of these cases he abstains from any hostile act and does not attempt to escape.

3. When persons entitled to protection as prisoners of war have fallen into the power of an adverse Party under unusual conditions of combat which prevent their evacuation as provided for in Part III, Section I, of the Third Convention, they shall be released and all feasible precautions shall be taken to ensure their safety. . . .

Article 43 — Armed forces

1. The armed forces of a Party to a conflict consist of all organized armed forces, groups and units which are under a command responsible to that Party for the conduct of its subordinates, even if that Party is represented by a government or an authority not recognized by an adverse Party. Such armed forces shall be subject to an internal disciplinary system which, inter alia, shall enforce compliance with the rules of international law applicable in armed conflict.

2. Members of the armed forces of a Party to a conflict (other than medical personnel and chaplains covered by Article 33 of the Third Convention) are combatants, that is to say, they have the right to participate directly in hostilities.

[3. Recognized as customary international law by the United States. — Eds.]

3. Whenever a Party to a conflict incorporates a paramilitary or armed law enforcement agency into its armed forces it shall so notify the other Parties to the conflict.

Article 44 — Combatants and prisoners of war

1. Any combatant, as defined in Article 43, who falls into the power of an adverse Party shall be a prisoner of war.

2. While all combatants are obliged to comply with the rules of international law applicable in armed conflict, violations of these rules shall not deprive a combatant of his right to be a combatant or, if he falls into the power of an adverse Party, of his right to be a prisoner of war, except as provided in paragraphs 3 and 4.

3. In order to promote the protection of the civilian population from the effects of hostilities, combatants are obliged to distinguish themselves from the civilian population while they are engaged in an attack or in a military operation preparatory to an attack. Recognizing, however, that there are situations in armed conflicts where, owing to the nature of the hostilities an armed combatant cannot so distinguish himself, he shall retain his status as a combatant, provided that, in such situations, he carries his arms openly:

(a) during each military engagement, and

(b) during such time as he is visible to the adversary while he is engaged in a military deployment preceding the launching of an attack in which he is to participate.

Acts which comply with the requirements of this paragraph shall not be considered as perfidious within the meaning of Article 37, paragraph 1(c).

4. A combatant who falls into the power of an adverse Party while failing to meet the requirements set forth in the second sentence of paragraph 3 shall forfeit his right to be a prisoner of war, but he shall, nevertheless, be given protections equivalent in all respects to those accorded to prisoners of war by the Third Convention and by this Protocol. This protection includes protections equivalent to those accorded to prisoners of war by the Third Convention in the case where such a person is tried and punished for any offences he has committed.

5. Any combatant who falls into the power of an adverse Party while not engaged in an attack or in a military operation preparatory to an attack shall not forfeit his rights to be a combatant and a prisoner of war by virtue of his prior activities.

6. This Article is without prejudice to the right of any person to be a prisoner of war pursuant to Article 4 of the Third Convention.

7. This Article is not intended to change the generally accepted practice of States with respect to the wearing of the uniform by combatants assigned to the regular, uniformed armed units of a Party to the conflict. . . .

Article 45 — Protection of persons who have taken part in hostilities

1. A person who takes part in hostilities and falls into the power of an adverse Party shall be presumed to be a prisoner of war, and therefore shall be protected by the Third Convention, if he claims the status of prisoner of war, or if he appears to be entitled to such status, or if the Party on which he depends claims such status on his behalf by notification to the detaining Power or to the Protecting Power.

Should any doubt arise as to whether any such person is entitled to the status of prisoner of war, he shall continue to have such status and, therefore, to be protected by the Third Convention and this Protocol until such time as his status has been determined by a competent tribunal.

2. If a person who has fallen into the power of an adverse Party is not held as a prisoner of war and is to be tried by that Party for an offence arising out of the hostilities, he shall have the right to assert his entitlement to prisoner-of-war status before a judicial tribunal and to have that question adjudicated. Whenever possible under the applicable procedure, this adjudication shall occur before the trial for the offence. The representatives of the Protecting Power shall be entitled to attend the proceedings in which that question is adjudicated, unless, exceptionally, the proceedings are held in camera in the interest of State security. In such a case the detaining Power shall advise the Protecting Power accordingly.

3. Any person who has taken part in hostilities, who is not entitled to prisoner-of-war status and who does not benefit from more favourable treatment in accordance with the Fourth Convention shall have the right at all times to the protection of Article 75 of this Protocol. In occupied territory, any such person, unless he is held as a spy, shall also be entitled, notwithstanding Article 5 of the Fourth Convention, to his rights of communication under that Convention. . . .

PART IV — CIVILIAN POPULATION

Article 48 — Basic rule

In order to ensure respect for and protection of the civilian population and civilian objects, the Parties to the conflict shall at all times distinguish between the civilian population and combatants and between civilian objects and military objectives and accordingly shall direct their operations only against military objectives.

Article 49 — Definition of attacks and scope of application

1. "Attacks" means acts of violence against the adversary, whether in offence or in defence.

2. The provisions of this Protocol with respect to attacks apply to all attacks in whatever territory conducted, including the national territory belonging to a Party to the conflict but under the control of an adverse Party.

3. The provisions of this section apply to any land, air or sea warfare which may affect the civilian population, individual civilians or civilian objects on land. They further apply to all attacks from the sea or from the air against objectives on land but do not otherwise affect the rules of international law applicable in armed conflict at sea or in the air.

4. The provisions of this section are additional to the rules concerning humanitarian protection contained in the Fourth Convention, particularly in Part II thereof, and in other international agreements binding upon the High Contracting Parties, as well as to other rules of international law relating to the protection of civilians and civilian objects on land, at sea or in the air against the effects of hostilities.

Article 50 — Definition of civilians and civilian population

1. A civilian is any person who does not belong to one of the categories of persons referred to in Article 4(A) (1), (2), (3) and (6) of the Third Convention and in Article 43 of this Protocol. In case of doubt whether a person is a civilian, that person shall be considered to be a civilian.

2. The civilian population comprises all persons who are civilians.

3. The presence within the civilian population of individuals who do not come within the definition of civilians does not deprive the population of its civilian character.

Article 51 — Protection of the civilian population[4]

1. The civilian population and individual civilians shall enjoy general protection against dangers arising from military operations. To give effect to this protection, the following rules, which are additional to other applicable rules of international law, shall be observed in all circumstances.

2. The civilian population as such, as well as individual civilians, shall not be the object of attack. Acts or threats of violence the primary purpose of which is to spread terror among the civilian population are prohibited.

3. Civilians shall enjoy the protection afforded by this Section, unless and for such time as they take a direct part in hostilities.

4. Indiscriminate attacks are prohibited. Indiscriminate attacks are:

(a) those which are not directed at a specific military objective;

(b) those which employ a method or means of combat which cannot be directed at a specific military objective; or

(c) those which employ a method or means of combat the effects of which cannot be limited as required by this Protocol;

and consequently, in each such case, are of a nature to strike military objectives and civilians or civilian objects without distinction.

5. Among others, the following types of attacks are to be considered as indiscriminate:

(a) an attack by bombardment by any methods or means which treats as a single military objective a number of clearly separated and distinct military objectives located in a city, town, village or other area containing a similar concentration of civilians or civilian objects; and

(b) an attack which may be expected to cause incidental loss of civilian life, injury to civilians, damage to civilian objects, or a combination thereof, which would be excessive in relation to the concrete and direct military advantage anticipated.

6. Attacks against the civilian population or civilians by way of reprisals are prohibited.

7. The presence or movements of the civilian population or individual civilians shall not be used to render certain points or areas immune from military operations, in particular in attempts to shield military objectives from attacks or to shield, favour or impede military operations. The Parties to the conflict shall not direct the

[4. Recognized in part as customary law by the United States. — Eds.]

movement of the civilian population or individual civilians in order to attempt to shield military objectives from attacks or to shield military operations.

8. Any violation of these prohibitions shall not release the Parties to the conflict from their legal obligations with respect to the civilian population and civilians, including the obligation to take the precautionary measures provided for in Article 57. . . .

Article 57 — Precautions in attack[5]

1. In the conduct of military operations, constant care shall be taken to spare the civilian population, civilians and civilian objects.

2. With respect to attacks, the following precautions shall be taken:

(a) those who plan or decide upon an attack shall:

(i) do everything feasible to verify that the objectives to be attacked are neither civilians nor civilian objects and are not subject to special protection but are military objectives within the meaning of paragraph 2 of Article 52 and that it is not prohibited by the provisions of this Protocol to attack them;

(ii) take all feasible precautions in the choice of means and methods of attack with a view to avoiding, and in any event to minimizing, incidental loss of civilian life, injury to civilians and damage to civilian objects;

(iii) refrain from deciding to launch any attack which may be expected to cause incidental loss of civilian life, injury to civilians, damage to civilian objects, or a combination thereof, which would be excessive in relation to the concrete and direct military advantage anticipated;

(b) an attack shall be cancelled or suspended if it becomes apparent that the objective is not a military one or is subject to special protection or that the attack may be expected to cause incidental loss of civilian life, injury to civilians, damage to civilian objects, or a combination thereof, which would be excessive in relation to the concrete and direct military advantage anticipated;

(c) effective advance warning shall be given of attacks which may affect the civilian population, unless circumstances do not permit.

3. When a choice is possible between several military objectives for obtaining a similar military advantage, the objective to be selected shall be that the attack on which may be expected to cause the least danger to civilian lives and to civilian objects.

4. In the conduct of military operations at sea or in the air, each Party to the conflict shall, in conformity with its rights and duties under the rules of international law applicable in armed conflict, take all reasonable precautions to avoid losses of civilian lives and damage to civilian objects.

5. No provision of this article may be construed as authorizing any attacks against the civilian population, civilians or civilian objects. . . .

Article 75 — Fundamental guarantees[6]

1. In so far as they are affected by a situation referred to in Article 1 of this Protocol, persons who are in the power of a Party to the conflict and who do not

[5. Recognized as customary law by the United States. — Eds.]

[6. Recognized as customary law by the United States. — Eds.]

benefit from more favourable treatment under the Conventions or under this Protocol shall be treated humanely in all circumstances and shall enjoy, as a minimum, the protection provided by this Article without any adverse distinction based upon race, colour, sex, language, religion or belief, political or other opinion, national or social origin, wealth, birth or other status, or on any other similar criteria. Each Party shall respect the person, honour, convictions and religious practices of all such persons.

2. The following acts are and shall remain prohibited at any time and in any place whatsoever, whether committed by civilian or by military agents:

(a) violence to the life, health, or physical or mental well-being of persons, in particular:

(i) murder;

(ii) torture of all kinds, whether physical or mental;

(iii) corporal punishment; and

(iv) mutilation;

(b) outrages upon personal dignity, in particular humiliating and degrading treatment, enforced prostitution and any form of indecent assault;

(c) the taking of hostages;

(d) collective punishments; and

(e) threats to commit any of the foregoing acts.

3. Any person arrested, detained or interned for actions related to the armed conflict shall be informed promptly, in a language he understands, of the reasons why these measures have been taken. Except in cases of arrest or detention for penal offences, such persons shall be released with the minimum delay possible and in any event as soon as the circumstances justifying the arrest, detention or internment have ceased to exist.

4. No sentence may be passed and no penalty may be executed on a person found guilty of a penal offence related to the armed conflict except pursuant to a conviction pronounced by an impartial and regularly constituted court respecting the generally recognized principles of regular judicial procedure, which include the following:

(a) the procedure shall provide for an accused to be informed without delay of the particulars of the offence alleged against him and shall afford the accused before and during his trial all necessary rights and means of defence;

(b) no one shall be convicted of an offence except on the basis of individual penal responsibility;

(c) no one shall be accused or convicted of a criminal offence on account of any act or omission which did not constitute a criminal offence under the national or international law to which he was subject at the time when it was committed; nor shall a heavier penalty be imposed than that which was applicable at the time when the criminal offence was committed; if, after the commission of the offence, provision is made by law for the imposition of a lighter penalty, the offender shall benefit thereby;

(d) anyone charged with an offence is presumed innocent until proved guilty according to law;

(e) anyone charged with an offence shall have the right to be tried in his presence;

(f) no one shall be compelled to testify against himself or to confess guilt;

(g) anyone charged with an offence shall have the right to examine, or have examined, the witnesses against him and to obtain the attendance and examination of witnesses on his behalf under the same conditions as witnesses against him;

(h) no one shall be prosecuted or punished by the same Party for an offence in respect of which a final judgement acquitting or convicting that person has been previously pronounced under the same law and judicial procedure;

(i) anyone prosecuted for an offence shall have the right to have the judgement pronounced publicly; and

(j) a convicted person shall be advised on conviction of his judicial and other remedies and of the time-limits within which they may be exercised. . . .

6. Persons who are arrested, detained or interned for reasons related to the armed conflict shall enjoy the protection provided by this Article until their final release, repatriation or re-establishment, even after the end of the armed conflict.

7. In order to avoid any doubt concerning the prosecution and trial of persons accused of war crimes or crimes against humanity, the following principles shall apply:

(a) persons who are accused of such crimes should be submitted for the purpose of prosecution and trial in accordance with the applicable rules of international law; and

(b) any such persons who do not benefit from more favourable treatment under the Conventions or this Protocol shall be accorded the treatment provided by this Article, whether or not the crimes of which they are accused constitute grave breaches of the Conventions or of this Protocol.

8. No provision of this Article may be construed as limiting or infringing any other more favourable provision granting greater protection, under any applicable rules of international law, to persons covered by paragraph 1. . . .

Article 85 — Repression of breaches of this Protocol[7]

1. The provisions of the Conventions relating to the repression of breaches and grave breaches, supplemented by this Section, shall apply to the repression of breaches and grave breaches of this Protocol.

2. Acts described as grave breaches in the Conventions are grave breaches of this Protocol if committed against persons in the power of an adverse Party protected by Articles 44, 45 and 73 of this Protocol, or against the wounded, sick and shipwrecked of the adverse Party who are protected by this Protocol, or against those medical or religious personnel, medical units or medical transports which are under the control of the adverse Party and are protected by this Protocol.

3. In addition to the grave breaches defined in Article 11, the following acts shall be regarded as grave breaches of this Protocol, when committed wilfully, in violation of the relevant provisions of this Protocol, and causing death or serious injury to body or health:

(a) making the civilian population or individual civilians the object of attack;

(b) launching an indiscriminate attack affecting the civilian population or civilian objects in the knowledge that such attack will cause excessive loss of life,

[7. Recognized as customary law by the United States. — Eds.]

injury to civilians or damage to civilian objects, as defined in Article 57, paragraph 2(a)(iii);

(c) launching an attack against works or installations containing dangerous forces in the knowledge that such attack will cause excessive loss of life, injury to civilians or damage to civilian objects, as defined in Article 57, paragraph 2(a)(iii);

(d) making non-defended localities and demilitarized zones the object of attack;

(e) making a person the object of attack in the knowledge that he is *hors de combat*;

(f) the perfidious use, in violation of Article 37, of the distinctive emblem of the red cross, red crescent or red lion and sun or of other protective signs recognized by the Conventions or this Protocol.

4. In addition to the grave breaches defined in the preceding paragraphs and in the Conventions, the following shall be regarded as grave breaches of this Protocol, when committed wilfully and in violation of the Conventions or the Protocol:

(a) the transfer by the occupying Power of parts of its own civilian population into the territory it occupies, or the deportation or transfer of all or parts of the population of the occupied territory within or outside this territory, in violation of Article 49 of the Fourth Convention;

(b) unjustifiable delay in the repatriation of prisoners of war or civilians;

(c) practices of apartheid and other inhuman and degrading practices involving outrages upon personal dignity, based on racial discrimination;

(d) making the clearly-recognized historic monuments, works of art or places of worship which constitute the cultural or spiritual heritage of peoples and to which special protection has been given by special arrangement, for example, within the framework of a competent international organization, the object of attack, causing as a result extensive destruction thereof, where there is no evidence of the violation by the adverse Party of Article 53, subparagraph (b), and when such historic monuments, works of art and places of worship are not located in the immediate proximity of military objectives;

(e) depriving a person protected by the Conventions or referred to in paragraph 2 of this Article of the rights of fair and regular trial.

5. Without prejudice to the application of the Conventions and of this Protocol, grave breaches of these instruments shall be regarded as war crimes.

Article 86 — Failure to act[8]

1. The High Contracting Parties and the Parties to the conflict shall repress grave breaches, and take measures necessary to suppress all other breaches, of the Conventions or of this Protocol which result from a failure to act when under a duty to do so.

2. The fact that a breach of the Conventions or of this Protocol was committed by a subordinate does not absolve his superiors from penal disciplinary responsibility, as the case may be, if they knew, or had information which should have enabled them to conclude in the circumstances at the time, that he was committing or was

[8. Recognized as customary law by the United States. — Eds.]

going to commit such a breach and if they did not take all feasible measures within their power to prevent or repress the breach. . . .

---

4. The International Criminal Court

After World War II, the U.N. Security Council approved the establishment of several ad hoc special tribunals to prosecute violations of the laws of war. An example is the International Criminal Tribunal for the former Yugoslavia (ICTY), established by S.C. Res. 827, U.N. Doc. S/RES/827 (May 25, 1993), which deals with genocide, war crimes, and crimes against humanity committed during the conflicts in the Balkans during the 1990s. *See* UN/ICTY, *About the ICTY* (n.d.), http://www.icty.org/en. Nevertheless, a continuing determination to provide a permanent forum for international criminal prosecution of the worst offenders of *in bello* rules came to fruition in 1998, with adoption of a treaty creating the International Criminal Court. Its central provision conferring jurisdiction over war crimes incorporates some provisions of the Geneva Conventions, as well as uncodified customary IHL norms.

Rome Statute of the International Criminal Court

2187 U.N.T.S. 90, July 17, 1998

ARTICLE 8: WAR CRIMES

1. The Court shall have jurisdiction in respect of war crimes in particular when committed as part of a plan or policy or as part of a large-scale commission of such crimes.

2. For the purpose of this Statute, "war crimes" means:

(a) Grave breaches of the Geneva Conventions of 12 August 1949, namely, any of the following acts against persons or property protected under the provisions of the relevant Geneva Convention:

(i) Wilful killing;

(ii) Torture or inhuman treatment, including biological experiments;

(iii) Wilfully causing great suffering, or serious injury to body or health;

(iv) Extensive destruction and appropriation of property, not justified by military necessity and carried out unlawfully and wantonly;

(v) Compelling a prisoner of war or other protected person to serve in the forces of a hostile Power;

(vi) Wilfully depriving a prisoner of war or other protected person of the rights of fair and regular trial;

(vii) Unlawful deportation or transfer or unlawful confinement;

(viii) Taking of hostages.

(b) Other serious violations of the laws and customs applicable in international armed conflict, within the established framework of international law, namely, any of the following acts:

(i) Intentionally directing attacks against the civilian population as such or against individual civilians not taking direct part in hostilities;

(ii) Intentionally directing attacks against civilian objects, that is, objects which are not military objectives;

(iii) Intentionally directing attacks against personnel, installations, material, units or vehicles involved in a humanitarian assistance or peacekeeping mission in accordance with the Charter of the United Nations, as long as they are entitled to the protection given to civilians or civilian objects under the international law of armed conflict;

(iv) Intentionally launching an attack in the knowledge that such attack will cause incidental loss of life or injury to civilians or damage to civilian objects or widespread, long-term and severe damage to the natural environment which would be clearly excessive in relation to the concrete and direct overall military advantage anticipated;

(v) Attacking or bombarding, by whatever means, towns, villages, dwellings or buildings which are undefended and which are not military objectives; . . .

(xiv) Declaring abolished, suspended or inadmissible in a court of law the rights and actions of the nationals of the hostile party; . . .

(xxi) Committing outrages upon personal dignity, in particular humiliating and degrading treatment;. . . .

(c) In the case of an armed conflict not of an international character, serious violations of article 3 common to the four Geneva Conventions of 12 August 1949, namely, any of the following acts committed against persons taking no active part in the hostilities, including members of armed forces who have laid down their arms and those placed hors de combat by sickness, wounds, detention or any other cause:

(i) Violence to life and person, in particular murder of all kinds, mutilation, cruel treatment and torture;

(ii) Committing outrages upon personal dignity, in particular humiliating and degrading treatment;

(iii) Taking of hostages;

(iv) The passing of sentences and the carrying out of executions without previous judgement pronounced by a regularly constituted court, affording all judicial guarantees which are generally recognized as indispensable.

(d) Paragraph 2(c) applies to armed conflicts not of an international character and thus does not apply to situations of internal disturbances and tensions, such as riots, isolated and sporadic acts of violence or other acts of a similar nature.

(e) Other serious violations of the laws and customs applicable in armed conflicts not of an international character, within the established framework of international law, namely, any of the following acts:

(i) Intentionally directing attacks against the civilian population as such or against individual civilians not taking direct part in hostilities; . . .

(f) Paragraph 2(e) applies to armed conflicts not of an international character and thus does not apply to situations of internal disturbances and tensions, such as riots, isolated and sporadic acts of violence or other acts of a similar nature. It applies to armed conflicts that take place in the territory of a State when there is protracted armed conflict between governmental authorities and organized armed groups or between such groups.

3. Nothing in paragraph 2(c) and (e) shall affect the responsibility of a Government to maintain or re-establish law and order in the State or to defend the unity and territorial integrity of the State, by all legitimate means.

Notes and Questions

1. Architecture and Stature of the Geneva Conventions. Every nation in the world has ratified the four 1949 Geneva Conventions. Like earlier Geneva Conventions, the over-arching purpose of the 1949 Conventions is to protect the victims of armed conflict, including the wounded, prisoners of war, and civilians. The regulation of battlefield tactics is left to other treaties, such as the 1907 Hague Regulation IV, and to customary law. Can you see the basic orientation of the Conventions toward protection of the victims of war in the provisions of Geneva III and IV excerpted above?

2. Grave Breaches. Each of the four Geneva Conventions requires the enactment of domestic legislation to punish grave breaches. *See, e.g.*, Geneva IV, art. 146. Exactly what constitutes a "grave breach"? What is the difference between a grave breach and a war crime, and where would you expect to find a list of war crimes? What are the scope and content of each state's obligation to seek redress for grave breaches? *See id.* art. 147.

What domestic criminal provisions would you expect to find in U.S. laws that reflect the obligations of Geneva IV? Consider, for example, the Torture Act, 18 U.S.C. §§2340-2340A (2018), assessed *infra* pp. 980-988 What do you suppose is the measure of compliance with Article 146?

In the United States, the Uniform Code of Military Justice (UCMJ) has since 1950 provided one mechanism for trying our own soldiers for alleged grave breaches. U.S. soldiers and other U.S. nationals may now also be tried for grave breaches in civilian court pursuant to the War Crimes Act of 1996, 18 U.S.C. §2441 (2018), and U.S. soldiers and anyone "employed by or accompanying the Armed Forces outside the United States" may be so tried under the Military Extraterritorial Jurisdiction Act, 18 U.S.C. §§3261-3267 (2018). See *infra* p. 1020. Historically, enemy soldiers have been tried for grave breaches before military commissions comprised of "juries" of military officers. See *infra* Chapter 36.

What is the jurisdiction of the International Criminal Court (ICC)? Could it try alleged grave breaches? What about war crimes? Genocide? Crimes against humanity?

3. Jus in Bello as Custom and the Protocols. The 1949 Geneva Conventions did not address issues of targeting, including the core principles of distinction, military necessity, unnecessary suffering, and proportionality. Yet those principles were part of customary law and were, to some extent, codified separately in the Hague and other treaties. What difference does it make whether IHL is customary or enshrined in a treaty provision? Can you figure out why the United States has recognized some of the AP I provisions as customary law but not others? Why not sign on lock, stock, and barrel?

Reviewing the excerpted provisions of AP I, which ones articulate the principles of distinction, necessity, unnecessary suffering, and proportionality? See if you can extract from those articles a workable set of rules to guide soldiers in the field.

4. Are the Geneva Conventions Obsolete? Fresh from the horrors of World War II, the delegates to the 1949 conference in Geneva were determined to codify an extensive set of protections for the victims of state-on-state wars. They were not thinking about terrorism, insurgencies, guerrilla movements, or armed revolutions. The 1977 Additional Protocols made only modest progress toward explicitly addressing such asymmetric warfare.

Even before the September 11 attacks, however, it was clear that conflicts between states and non-state entities were becoming increasingly common. In 2002, then–White House Counsel Alberto Gonzales wrote that the war on terrorism "renders obsolete Geneva's strict limitations on questioning of enemy prisoners and renders quaint some of its provisions." Memorandum from Alberto R. Gonzales to the President, *Decision re Application of the Geneva Convention on Prisoners of War to the Conflict with Al Qaeda and the Taliban* (Jan. 25, 2002). Do you agree?

From the perspective of the United States, an important expression of the role of IHL as U.S. law is set forth in the Defense Department's *Law of War Manual* (June 2015, updated Dec. 2016) (providing the first comprehensive compilation of U.S. understandings of the treaties and state practice that make up IHL).

5. The United States and the ICC. The United States is not a signatory to the Rome Statute of the International Criminal Court. The Trump administration struck a hostile posture toward the ICC in 2018 after ICC prosecutor Fatou Bensouda sought authorization from the Court to open an investigation into crimes connected with the armed conflict in Afghanistan. In March 2019 Secretary of State Mike Pompeo announced that the United States will deny or revoke visas to ICC staff who may be seeking to investigate U.S. involvement in potentially criminal conduct in Afghanistan. Secretary Pompeo stated that "[w]e are determined to protect the American and allied military and civilian personnel from living in fear of unjust prosecution for actions taken to defend our great nation." Carol Morello, *U.S. Will Not Give Visas to Employees of the International Criminal Court*, Wash. Post, Mar. 15, 2019. Soon thereafter, a Pre-Trial Chamber of the ICC rejected the prosecutor's request. Paras Shah, *U.S. Imposes Visa Ban on International Criminal Court Prosecutor*, Lawfare, Apr. 13, 2019. Has the United States thus created a measure of immunity for its military personnel from punishment for war crimes?

B. APPLYING IHL — CONFLICT CLASSIFICATION AND COMBATANT IMMUNITY

Reading *United States v. Hamidullin*

Irek Hamidullin, a reported defector from the Russian Army, was taken into custody by Afghan and U.S. forces in Afghanistan in 2009 after he led a group of Taliban and Haqqani Network insurgents in an attack on an Afghan Border Police post. He was detained in Afghanistan and eventually was indicted in federal district court in 2014 and charged with multiple counts, including providing material support to terrorism and use of a weapon of mass destruction. He was found guilty of all charges in 2015 and given multiple life sentences. Hamidullin moved to overturn his conviction and argued that he was entitled to POW status and its concomitant combatant immunity for committing hostilities as a combatant in an armed conflict. Consider these questions:

- What evidence persuaded the court that there was an armed conflict in Afghanistan at the time of Hamidullin's capture?
- Why did the court find that the ongoing armed conflict in Afghanistan at the time of Hamidullin's capture failed to trigger the protections of Common Article 2 of Geneva III?
- Why did Hamidullin seek classification as a POW?
- Why was Hamidullin unsuccessful in claiming that Article 4 of Geneva III and "common law" (customary international law) entitled him to combatant immunity and POW status as a member of an armed group?
- Why wasn't Hamidullin entitled to an Article 5 "competent tribunal" to determine his status?

United States v. Hamidullin

United States Court of Appeals, Fourth Circuit, 2018
888 F.3d 62, *cert. denied*, 139 S. Ct. 1165 (2019)

Before Wilkinson, King, and Floyd, Circuit Judges.

Floyd, Circuit Judge: . . . Irek Hamidullin is a former Russian Army officer affiliated with the Taliban and Haqqani Network. He was captured by the Afghan Border Police and American soldiers in the Khost province of Afghanistan in 2009 after he planned and participated in an attack on an Afghan Border Police post at Camp Leyza. He was taken into U.S. custody and held in U.S. facilities in Afghanistan. He was later indicted in the Eastern District of Virginia for acts associated with the attack. . . .

Prior to trial, Hamidullin moved for dismissal . . . on the grounds that he qualified for combatant immunity pursuant to the Third Geneva Convention and common law. . . .

The district court . . . denied Hamidullin's motion to dismiss. The district court assumed without deciding that in 2009, when the alleged acts took place, the conflict in Afghanistan was an international armed conflict and determined that Hamidullin was not a lawful combatant because neither the Taliban nor the Haqqani Network fell within any of the categories of lawful combatants listed in Article 4 of the Third Geneva Convention. Thus, the district court concluded that, as a matter of law, Hamidullin was not entitled to combatant immunity under the Third Geneva Convention or common law and precluded him from presenting this defense at trial. . . .

In August 2015, Hamidullin was convicted by a jury on all charges and sentenced to multiple life sentences. On appeal, Hamidullin argues that the district court erred in . . . holding that his prosecution was not barred by the doctrine of combatant immunity, as articulated by the Third Geneva Convention and common law. . . .

II.

. . . Combatant immunity is rooted in the customary international law of war and "forbids prosecution of soldiers for their lawful belligerent acts committed during the course of armed conflicts against legitimate military targets." *United States v. Lindh,* 212 F. Supp. 2d 541, 553 (E.D. Va. 2002). Instead, "[b]elligerent acts committed in armed conflict by enemy members of the armed forces may be punished as crimes under a belligerent's municipal law only to the extent that they violate international humanitarian law or are unrelated to the armed conflict." *Id.* In order to invoke combatant immunity, a combatant must also be lawful, as described below. *Ex parte Quirin,* 317 U.S. 1, 31 (1942) ("Lawful combatants are subject to capture and detention as prisoners of war by opposing military forces. Unlawful combatants are likewise subject to capture and detention, but in addition they are subject to trial and punishment by military tribunals for acts which render their belligerency unlawful.").

The current doctrine of combatant immunity is codified in the Third Geneva Convention. . . .

Article 2 of each of the Geneva Conventions renders the full protections of the Conventions, including combatant immunity, applicable only in international armed conflicts between signatories of the Conventions. Third Geneva Convention, art. 2 [*supra* p. 267]. If Article 2 is applicable, then the Third Geneva Convention provides that lawful combatants who are captured in such a conflict are considered prisoners of war (POWs). The categories of combatants qualifying as lawful are listed in Article 4 of the Convention [*supra* p. 270]. . . . Under the Convention, POWs are granted combatant immunity. If there is doubt as to whether a captured combatant is a lawful combatant and thus entitled to POW status, Article 5 of the Convention requires that the captured person be treated as a POW until their status is determined by a "competent tribunal." *Id.* art. 5 [*supra* p. 271]. The text of the Convention is silent as to what qualifies as a competent tribunal.

When a conflict is not an international conflict between Geneva Convention signatories, at least one article of the Geneva Conventions still applies. Article 3 of each Convention provides that in an "armed conflict not of an international character occurring in the territory of one of the High Contracting Parties, each Party to the conflict shall be bound to apply, as a minimum," certain provisions, including protecting "[p]ersons taking no active part in the hostilities," and refraining from "the passing of sentences and the carrying out of executions without previous judgment pronounced by a regularly constituted court affording all the judicial guarantees which are recognized as indispensable by civilized peoples." *Id.* art. 3; *see also Hamdan v. Rumsfeld,* 548 U.S. 557, 629-30 (2006). Thus, Article 3 allows for combatants captured during non-international conflicts to face trial and judgment for their actions as long as they are tried in the opposing force's country's "regularly constituted court." *Id.*; *see also* 1 Int'l Comm. of Red Cross (ICRC), *Customary International Humanitarian Law* 354-55 (2005) (stating that pursuant to Article 3 of the Third Geneva Convention, captured combatants can be sentenced in a "regularly constituted court" that is "established and organised in accordance with the laws and procedures already in force in a country.").

The Supreme Court has determined that Article 2 of the Third Geneva Convention applies when a conflict "involve[s] a clash between nations," whereas Article 3 "affords some minimal protection, falling short of full protection under the

Conventions, to individuals associated with neither a signatory nor even a nonsignatory 'Power' who are involved in a conflict." *See Hamdan*, 548 U.S. at 628-29 (discussing the conflict in Afghanistan between the U.S. and al-Qaeda and applying Article 3). *See also* ICRC, *Commentary on the Additional Protocols to the Geneva Conventions of 12 August 1949* 1350-51 (1987) (discussing the Conventions' distinction between international and non-international conflicts and explaining that "in a non-international armed conflict the legal status of the parties involved in the struggle is fundamentally unequal. Insurgents (usually part of the population), fight against the government in power").

Here, Hamidullin claims that he cannot be tried in a United States criminal court because he is a POW entitled to combatant immunity under the Third Geneva Convention. We now turn to that inquiry.

III. . . .

A. . . .

The conflict in Afghanistan began in 2001 as an international armed conflict arising between two or more Third Geneva Convention signatories — it was a conflict between the United States and its coalition partners on one side, and the Taliban-controlled Afghan government on the other. Shortly thereafter, in 2002, the Taliban lost control of the government and was replaced by a government led by Hamid Karzai. The United States and its coalition partners remained in Afghanistan at the request of this new government, assisting it in combating the continued Taliban insurgency. Thus, by 2009, the conflict in Afghanistan had shifted from an international armed conflict between the United States and the Taliban-run Afghan government to a non-international armed conflict against unlawful Taliban insurgents. . . .

The International Committee of the Red Cross and the executive branch of the United States government have reached this same conclusion. Common sense agrees. If the conflict in Afghanistan was originally an international armed conflict occurring between two "High Contracting Parties" — the United States and the Afghan government — the conflict cannot remain international when the conflict between the recognized Afghan government and the United States has ceased. . . .

. . . [B]ecause we conclude that the conflict in Afghanistan was non-international at the time of Hamidullin's offense, the protections of Article 3 of the Convention apply. Under Article 3, however, there is no provision entitling combatants captured during non-international conflicts to POW status or the resulting combatant immunity. Therefore, there is no process by which Hamidullin is entitled to a determination of whether he is a POW, as no POW status exists under Article 3, and, consequently, combatant immunity cannot be granted.

Pursuant to Article 3, Hamidullin can be sentenced in a "regularly constituted court" that is "established and organised in accordance with the laws and procedures already in force in a country." 1 ICRC, *Customary Int'l Humanitarian Law* 355 (2005) (interpreting Third Geneva Convention, art. 3). A U.S. federal district court is one such court. Thus, the district court had jurisdiction to adjudicate Hamidullin's case. . . .

IV. . . .

A.

To be entitled to combatant immunity, the Third Geneva Convention requires that a combatant (1) be captured during an international armed conflict, Third Geneva Convention, art. 2, and (2) be a lawful combatant—in other words, the combatant must belong to one of the Article 4 categories defining POW's, *id.* art. 4. Article 4 lists six categories of lawful combatants, but only two categories, Article 4(A)(2) and (A)(3), are relevant here. Article 4(A)(2) provides that members of militias belonging to a party to the conflict are lawful combatants entitled to POW status so long as they are commanded by a person responsible for subordinates, carry a "fixed distinctive sign," carry arms openly, and operate in accordance with the laws of war. *Id.* art. 4(A)(2). Article 4(A)(3) provides that "[m]embers of regular armed forces who profess allegiance to a government or an authority not recognized by the Detaining Power" are likewise POWs. *Id.* art. 4(A)(3).

Below, the district court assumed, without deciding, that the conflict in Afghanistan in 2009 was international and determined that neither the Taliban nor the Haqqani Network fit into an Article 4 category. It held that the Taliban and Haqqani Network most closely resembled a "militia" or "organized resistance movement" as described in Article 4(A)(2), but that neither organization fulfilled the criteria of Article (4)(2). Specifically, the district court found that neither organization has a fixed, distinctive sign recognizable at a distance, carries arms openly, or conducts operations in accordance with the laws and customs of war.

Hamidullin . . . contends he is entitled to POW status under Article 4(A)(3), which covers "[m]embers of regular armed forces who profess allegiance to a government or an authority not recognized by the Detaining Power." *Id.* art. 4(A)(3). Unlike the criteria for militia in Article 4(A)(2), Article 4(A)(3) contains no conditions that groups must fulfill in order to be entitled to POW status; membership in a regular armed force expressing allegiance to a government not recognized by the detaining power is the only enumerated requirement. Hamidullin contends that because the Third Geneva Convention does not expressly incorporate the Article 4(A)(2) criteria into Article 4(A)(3), he is entitled to POW status regardless of whether the Taliban satisfies the Article 4(A)(2) criteria.

The difficulty with Hamidullin's argument is that, as discussed above, we hold that the conflict in Afghanistan was not an international armed conflict. As a result, irrespective of whether Taliban fighters are entitled to POW status pursuant to Article 4(A)(3), Hamidullin is not entitled to combatant immunity because the protections of Article 3 (governing non-international conflicts), rather than Article 2 (governing international conflicts), apply. Article 3 only requires that Hamidullin be tried "by a regularly constituted court, affording all the judicial guarantees which are recognized as indispensable by civilized peoples." Third Geneva Convention, art. 3. The U.S. federal district courts are "established and organised in accordance with the laws and procedures already in force" in the United States. *See* 1 ICRC, *Customary International Humanitarian Law* 355 (2005); 18 U.S.C. §3231. Accordingly, the district court did not err in determining that Hamidullin was properly tried in a regularly constituted American court.

B.

In the alternative, Hamidullin argues that even if he does not qualify for combatant immunity under the Third Geneva Convention, he is eligible for common law combatant immunity as an enemy soldier fighting for a rival sovereign. . . .

The Third Geneva Convention is the governing articulation of lawful combatant status. The principles reflected in the common law decisions cited by Hamidullin were refined and collected in 20th century efforts to codify the international law of war that resulted in the Third Geneva Convention. Just as a statute preempts common law when Congress speaks directly to the question, a self-executing treaty like the Third Geneva Convention would similarly preempt common law if the treaty speaks directly to the question. The Third Geneva Convention explicitly defines the category of individuals entitled to POW status, and concomitantly, combatant immunity. Third Geneva Convention, art. 4. As such, the Third Geneva Convention's definition of lawful and unlawful combatants is conclusive.

Moreover, Hamidullin's broad framing of common law combatant immunity would extend immunity far beyond the Third Geneva Convention, to every person acting on behalf of an organization that claims sovereignty. For example, it could supply a claim of immunity to terrorists operating on behalf of the Islamic State, which itself claims sovereignty. We decline to broaden the scope of combatant immunity beyond the carefully constructed framework of the Geneva Convention. . . .

Affirmed.

WILKINSON, Circuit Judge, concurring. [omitted]

KING, Circuit Judge, dissenting: . . . In my view, these circumstances demand a clear statement from the Executive Branch on whether Hamidullin should be accorded POW status and, if not, an explanation as to why not. Contrary to the Government, the Executive has not already rendered Article 2 and Article 4 determinations to which we can or should defer. Yet I agree with the Government insofar as it contends the Third Convention questions are initially for the Executive, not the courts. Consequently, I would remand this matter for the limited purpose of the Executive's consideration and explanation of Hamidullin's POW status. . . . Perhaps . . . the President would pronounce that the war against the Taliban was not an Article 2 international armed conflict at the time of Hamidullin's capture in late 2009. Or perhaps the President would endorse the 2002 Presidential Statement's categorical Article 4 ruling and proclaim its continuing applicability. Or perhaps the President would elect to bestow POW protections upon Hamidullin, regardless of Article 2 and Article 4, in an effort to obtain reciprocal treatment of U.S. forces. Whatever the Executive would decide, we would have the opportunity for an informed and appropriate review upon this matter's return to our Court. . . .

Notes and Questions

1. *Classifying the Conflict. Hamidullin* provides an important review of conflict classification in IHL. As Common Article 2 of the Geneva Conventions makes clear, an

international armed conflict is a conflict between two or more states, even if a state of war is not recognized by one of them. Under Common Article 3, armed conflicts can also be "not of an international character" under IHL — not between states. The Special Rapporteur for the Human Rights Committee of the United Nations explained:

> The tests for the existence of a non-international armed conflict are not as categorical as those for international armed conflict. This recognizes the fact that there may be various types of non-international armed conflicts. The applicable test may also depend on whether a State is party to Additional Protocol II to the Geneva Conventions. Under treaty and customary international law, the elements which would point to the existence of a non-international armed conflict against a non-state armed group are:
>
> (i) The non-state armed group must be identifiable as such, based on criteria that are objective and verifiable. This is necessary for IHL to apply meaningfully, and so that States may comply with their obligation to distinguish between lawful targets and civilians. The criteria include:
>
> - Minimal level of organization. . . . (GC Art. 3; AP II).
> - Capability of the group to apply the Geneva Conventions (i.e., adequate command structure, and separation of military and political command) (GC Art. 3; AP II).
> - Engagement of the group in collective, armed, anti-government action (GC Art. 3).
> - For a conflict involving a State, the State uses its regular military forces against the group (GC Art. 3).
> - Admission of the conflict against the group to the agenda of the UN Security Council or the General Assembly (GC Art. 3).
>
> (ii) There must be a minimal threshold of intensity and duration. The threshold of violence is higher than required for the existence of an international armed conflict. To meet the minimum threshold, violence must be:
>
> - "Beyond the level of intensity of internal disturbances and tensions, such as riots, isolated and sporadic acts of violence and other acts of a similar nature" (AP II).
> - "[P]rotracted armed violence" among non-state armed groups or between a non-state armed group and a State;
> - If an isolated incident, the incident itself should be of a high degree of intensity, with a high level of organization on the part of the non-state armed group;
>
> (iii) The territorial confines can be:
>
> - Restricted to the territory of a State and between the State's own armed forces and the non-state group (AP II); or
> - A transnational conflict, i.e., one that crosses State borders (GC Art. 3). This does not mean, however, that there is no territorial nexus requirement.
>
> [Report of the Special Rapporteur on Extrajudicial, Summary or Arbitrary Executions (Philip Alston), *Addendum: Study on Targeted Killings*, at 17-18, U.N. Doc. A/HRC/14/24/Add.6 (May 28, 2010).]

In short, non-international armed conflict is a conflict between identifiable groups, above some minimal level of intensity and duration, with some territorial nexus either in the territory of a state or across borders. Applying these criteria, was the war in Afghanistan such a conflict in 2009, at the time of Hamidullin's capture?

Applying the Special Rapporteur's analysis, is the United States engaged in an armed conflict with the Islamic State (ISIS)? With Al Qaeda, the Taliban, and associated forces outside of Iraq and Afghanistan? How important are the duration and intensity of the violent contacts between the United States and each group? What about the closeness of ties among the groups?

If the United States is not engaged in an armed conflict, are law enforcement methods the only lawful methods for countering those groups?

2. Why Was Hamidullin Not a POW? The district court found that at the time of Hamidullin's capture the conflict in Afghanistan was international, yet the court still denied Hamidullin's combatant immunity claim. Why? Are you persuaded that Hamidullin's membership in an armed group — the Taliban and/or Haqqani Network — was not sufficient to entitle him to POW status? If instead the Fourth Circuit correctly labeled the conflict in 2009 as non-international, was its discussion of Article 4 dictum, or was there any plausible legal basis for recognizing combatant immunity and POW status for Hamidullin? If not, what law governs his detention and trial?

3. Conflicts Involving Non-State Actors. Common Article 3 clearly applies to armed conflicts involving a state and non-state parties. But which non-state parties? Does it apply when a state is fighting a non-state entity outside the state's territory? *See Hamdan v. Rumsfeld*, 548 U.S. 557 (2006) (yes). The ICRC commentary on the Geneva Conventions suggests that Common Article 3 applies when, among other criteria, a non-state group "possesses an organized military force, and authority responsible for its acts, acting within a determinate territory and having the means of respecting and ensuring respect for the Convention." *Commentary: IV Geneva Convention, supra* p. 267, at 35. Is this definition broad enough to reach transnational terrorist groups, like Al Qaeda, that conduct terrorist attacks in a number of different countries? Does it apply to members of less well-organized splinter groups or even lone-wolf terrorists who purport to act on behalf of such organizations?

4. Counterterrorism. Do counterterrorism military operations fall within the definition of armed conflict? Does IHL govern such operations? If not, what law does?

Whether or not IHL governs or even applies to counterterrorism military operations, human rights law (HRL) may apply. The extent to which the United States considers counterterrorism military operations governed in any way by HRL, however, remains unclear. Although the United States has not ratified some human rights treaties, the U.S. military apparently considers itself bound by at least some customary HRL. *See* Ryan Goodman, *Human Rights Law and U.S. Military Operations in Foreign Countries: The Prohibition on Arbitrary Deprivation of Life*, Just Security, Feb. 19, 2019.

5. Distinction. Many feel that the principle of distinction is the most important *jus in bello* rule. An ICRC study begins its list of customary norms this way: "Rule 1. The parties to the conflict must at all times distinguish between civilians and combatants. . . . Attacks must not be directed against civilians." Jean-Marie Henckaerts, *Study on Customary International Humanitarian Law: A Contribution to the Understanding and Respect for the Rule of Law in Armed Conflict*, 87 Int'l Rev. Red Cross 175, 198 (Mar. 2005).

Distinction was not mentioned as such in the Geneva Conventions until the Additional Protocols were adopted in 1977. Now AP I art. 48 provides that "the Parties to the conflict shall at all times distinguish between the civilian population and combatants and between civilian objects and military objects and accordingly shall direct their operations only against military objectives." Civilian objects are subject to the same principle. *Id.* art. 52.

How would you translate AP I art. 48 into operational rules? If terrorist forces purposefully wear civilian clothing, with no insignias or other identifying features, how will U.S. commanders or pilots in the air know who their lawful targets are?

6. *Military Necessity.* If distinction is the most humanitarian principle in IHL, military necessity is "the principle that justifies the use of all measures needed to defeat the enemy as quickly and efficiently as possible that are not prohibited by the law of war." *Department of Defense Law of War Manual, supra* p. 274, at 52. Which Geneva Convention provisions reflect the principle of military necessity? How should legal advisers give the concept practical meaning?

7. *Unnecessary Suffering.* AP I art. 35 makes it clear that any weapons or "methods of warfare of a nature to cause superfluous injury or unnecessary suffering" are forbidden. How would you define the key terms "of a nature," "superfluous injury," and "unnecessary suffering"? How is the principle of unnecessary suffering different from the principle of distinction? Does the use of cluster munitions violate either principle? Anti-personnel land mines? How about a Hellfire laser-guided missile launched from a drone?

8. *Proportionality.* Review AP I arts. 51.5(b) and 57.2(b), *supra.* The focus is clearly on civilians, not combatants. Paragraph 2.4.1.2 of the *Department of Defense Law of War Manual, supra,* at 61, states that "incidental" harm to "the civilian population and civilian objects" from an attack must not be "excessive in relation to the military advantage anticipated to be gained." *Id.*

How do these provisions differ? What do you suppose is the measure of "excessive" harm to civilians? Why do you think the drafters of each measure employed such open-ended terms? Can you draft a rule that would be more helpful in planning a military operation?

Do proportionality requirements apply in non-international armed conflicts? How does the principle of proportionality differ from the principles of distinction and unnecessary suffering?

Twice in 2016 the Obama administration revised the *Department of Defense Law of War Manual, supra,* to better protect civilians in combat. July 2016 revisions were focused on protecting journalists working in battlefield areas. December 2016 changes tightened rules for when it is lawful to fire on a military target where civilians, including human shields and civilian workers at weapons factories, are nearby. The changes are reflected largely in the discussion of the principle of proportionality. While the original version of the *Manual* suggested that commanders could exclude entire categories of civilians when analyzing proportionality before targeting— including human shields, civilians accompanying an enemy force, and civilians working at munitions factories— the revisions make clear that commanders must take these groups into account in assessing the anticipated harm to civilians. *See* Charlie Savage, *To Protect Civilians, Pentagon Tightens Rules on Combat,* N.Y. Times, Dec. 14, 2016. Do you agree that these changes to the *Manual* were warranted? Can you think of other precautions that should be explicitly factored into a proportionality analysis?

9. War Crimes. What, according to the Rome Statute of the International Criminal Court, must be shown to prove a war crime? How are the requirements for international and non-international armed conflicts different? What is the difference between war crimes and grave breaches?

Because no definition can capture all possible violations of IHL, there is no fixed catalog of offenses. May civilians commit war crimes? How about members of organized armed groups? ISIS, Taliban, or Al Qaeda members? Where would prosecutions against such persons be brought? Should a greater effort be made to try to define all war crimes?

In May 2019, the *New York Times* reported that President Trump was preparing to issue pardons to military servicemembers for misconduct during military operations, including in completed and ongoing military justice cases in the court-martial pipeline. Dave Phillips, *Trump May Be Preparing Pardons for Servicemen Accused of War Crimes*, N.Y. Times, May 18, 2019. In response, a former Army JAG officer opined that "[p]ardons, particularly pardons of service members who haven't yet been court-martialed, undermine the military justice system for which the President, as commander in chief, is responsible." Chris Jenks, *Sticking It to Yourself: Preemptive Pardons for Battlefield Crimes Undercut Military Justice and Military Effectiveness*, Just Security, May 20, 2019. While not disputing that the President has the legal authority to issue the pardons, Jenks argued that their issuance "would denigrate everyone in the United States military who is committed to a fair and effective military justice system." *Id.* Why might the President want to issue such pardons?

INTERNATIONAL HUMANITARIAN LAW: SUMMARY OF BASIC PRINCIPLES

- International humanitarian law (IHL) has evolved alongside domestic and other international law to govern the conduct of states and individuals during armed conflicts and to limit the suffering caused by war.
- The threshold question of when IHL applies is complicated when states carry out military operations against non-state terrorist and insurgent groups. The difficulty lies chiefly in determining whether an "armed conflict" is underway, and in distinguishing combatants from non-combatants.
- Different IHL rules apply to international and non-international conflicts. The distinction is important in determining the level and detail of protections afforded civilians and limits on military operations.
- The United States is committed to following IHL, including many of the provisions of the Geneva Protocols.
- The core principles of distinction, military necessity, proportionality, and unnecessary suffering are reflected in the Geneva Conventions and Protocols, and in customary law. Their application in individual cases, such as the Palestinian intifada, requires careful analysis of the particular facts.

PART III USING FORCE ABROAD

How We Go to War: Lessons from Vietnam

This chapter is the first of seven in which we rehearse the lessons of the preceding framework chapters, then apply those lessons to the use of military force abroad. We begin with a case study of the Vietnam War, focusing especially on issues of domestic legal authority and separation of powers. The chapters that follow explore more deeply the right to go to war (*jus ad bellum*) in international law, emphasizing the role of the United Nations in helping to avoid armed conflicts or restore peace. They are concerned with self-defense, collective security, targeted killings, cyber warfare, nuclear war, and the use of force for humanitarian purposes.

In this chapter we explore both the process for going to war and the difficulty of ending it. We begin with a brief history of the Vietnam War, arguments for its legality, and how these arguments fared in courts. We then take up legislative efforts to limit the scope of the war once it was underway. Finally, we analyze the end game, especially an appropriations measure designed to bring the war to a close.

A. GOING TO WAR IN VIETNAM

The Vietnam War was — and remains, even after half a century — extremely controversial. You must not underestimate the complexity of the legal and political issues surrounding it, nor the depth of feeling in those it touched. Much of what appears here was not known to the American people until long after the events described, and was not known even to members of Congress charged by the Constitution with initiating and supporting the continuation of war.

1. How the War Began: A Very Brief History[1]

At the end of World War II, Vietnam, like its neighbors Laos and Cambodia, resumed its colonial status as a part of French Indochina. Even before the Japanese withdrew, however, the Viet Minh, a coalition of nationalist groups led by Ho Chi Minh, declared an independent Democratic Republic of Vietnam with its headquarters in Hanoi. The French refused to recognize this indigenous government, and repeated appeals by Ho Chi Minh during 1945-1946 for U.S. assistance were ignored. France then became locked in a guerilla war that continued for more than seven years, with the Viet Minh receiving critical support from the Communist Chinese beginning in 1950.

Alarmed at the prospect of a Communist takeover in Vietnam, the U.S. government provided escalating economic and military aid to the French — from $10 million in 1950 to $1.1 billion in 1954 — and even drew up contingency plans for U.S. military intervention that included the use of atomic weapons. After the disastrous defeat of French forces at Dienbienphu in May 1954, the Geneva Accords established a cease-fire and a demilitarized zone along the 17th parallel, dividing the country into two — North Vietnam and South Vietnam. They also called for reunification of the two parts following elections in 1956. But U.S. leaders, fearing a Communist electoral victory, began secret paramilitary operations and psychological warfare against the North, and sent military aid to the newly formed South Vietnamese government of President Ngo Dinh Diem, all in violation of the Geneva Accords. The elections were never held.

Meanwhile, the United States signed the Southeast Asia Collective Defense Treaty (SEATO Treaty) and persuaded other SEATO members to extend the treaty's protection to South Vietnam, which was not a signatory. The treaty called for each signer to "act to meet the common danger" posed by an attack on any area covered by the treaty.

As the United States assumed an ever larger role in South Vietnamese affairs, widespread corruption and nepotism in the Diem regime, the failure of land reform, imprisonment of political opponents, and forced resettlements helped to create an estranged populace and pave the way for a growing insurgency in the South led by the Viet Cong. Hanoi then began to take control of Viet Cong operations in 1959 and infiltrate its own forces into the South in violation of the Geneva Accords. In July 1959, two American servicemen in uniform (the first of many) were killed by guerillas at Bien Hoa. At about the same time, troops from the North invaded Laos and began construction of the Ho Chi Minh Trail, which was used to transport personnel and equipment into the heart of South Vietnam.

---

1. This account is drawn from a variety of original and secondary sources, among them *The Pentagon Papers: The Defense Department History of United States Decision-making on Vietnam* (Mike Gravel ed., 1971) (4 vols.); S. Comm. on Foreign Relations, *Hearings on the Causes, Origins, and Lessons of the Vietnam War*, 92d Cong. (1972); and a multivolume report prepared by the Congressional Research Service for the Senate Committee on Foreign Relations, *The U.S. Government and the Vietnam War: Part I, 1945-1961*, and *Part II, 1961-1964*, S. Prt. No. 98-185 (1984); *Part III, January-July 1965*, S. Prt. No. 100-163 (1988).

From S. Comm. on Foreign Relations, *The U.S. Government and the Vietnam War (Part I)*, S. Prt. No. 98-185, at XIII (1984).

In 1961, President Kennedy secretly dispatched 400 Special Forces troops and 100 other military advisors to the South, again clearly violating the Geneva Accords. He also approved clandestine attacks on North Vietnamese and Laotian targets using U.S.-trained South Vietnamese forces. Kennedy was persuaded, like Presidents Truman and Eisenhower before him, that the fall of South Vietnam would quickly result in the Communist domination of all Southeast Asia — the so-called "domino" theory. Late the same year, he sent additional support forces, including helicopters and other airlift equipment, naval patrols, and intelligence units. By the end of 1962 there were 11,000 U.S. troops in South Vietnam, and within another year the number had grown to 16,000.

Despite this assistance, control of the South Vietnamese countryside slipped more and more from the hands of the Saigon government. After President Kennedy's assassination in November 1963, President Johnson authorized stepped-up clandestine commando raids against northern rail and highway targets and the bombardment of North Vietnamese coastal installations by PT boats. Elaborate secret plans were drawn up for even greater U.S. military involvement, including full-scale bombing of the North in an effort to cut off support for the Viet Cong. In the early summer of 1964, the President's advisors even drafted a standby congressional resolution intended to be the equivalent of a declaration of war, while the deteriorating military situation in the South and in neighboring Laos was largely concealed from Congress and the public. Privately, President Johnson called the war "the biggest damn mess I ever saw," lamenting that "I don't think it's worth fighting for, and I don't think we can get out."[2]

On July 30, 1964, South Vietnamese commandos directed by General William Westmoreland, the U.S. commander in Saigon, launched raids against two North Vietnamese islands in the Gulf of Tonkin. Three days later, on August 2, several North Vietnamese PT boats attacked the U.S. destroyer *Maddox*, which was on an intelligence-gathering mission in the Gulf. One PT boat was sunk by gunfire from the *Maddox*, while two others were damaged by U.S. aircraft from a nearby carrier. The next day, the *Maddox* was ordered back into the Gulf accompanied by the destroyer *C. Turner Joy* at the same time that South Vietnamese naval forces were attacking additional targets in the North. The day after that, on August 4, North Vietnamese torpedo boats reportedly attacked both U.S. destroyers in what came to be called the "Tonkin Gulf incident." There were no confirmed visual sightings of any North Vietnamese craft, however, and it is now clear that there was no second attack.[3]

Without waiting for confirmation, the President briefed congressional leaders on the supposed incident and described his plan for a military response. He apparently neglected to tell them about U.S. involvement in potentially provocative clandestine actions against the North. Before the day was over, U.S. forces launched retaliatory raids against targets selected months earlier — four North Vietnamese PT boat bases and an oil depot holding about 10 percent of the North's petroleum supply.

Just before midnight on August 4, President Johnson went on television to describe these events to the nation, calling the U.S. response "limited and fitting." "We still seek no wider war," he declared.[4] With a presidential election just 90 days away, the President apparently was eager to appear firmly anti-Communist but not

---

2. *Tapes Show Johnson Saw Vietnam War as Pointless in 1964*, N.Y. Times, Feb. 15, 1997.

3. A study by a National Security Agency (NSA) historian released in late 2005, supported by now-declassified signals intelligence reports, indicates that there was no attack on U.S. ships in the Tonkin Gulf on August 4, 1964, and that evidence pointing to an attack was "deliberately skewed" by NSA officials. *See* National Security Archive, *Tonkin Gulf Intelligence "Skewed" According to Official History and Intercepts*, Dec. 1, 2005, *at* http://www.gwu.edu/~nsarchiv/NSAEBB/NSAEBB132/press20051201.htm (with links to relevant documents).

4. 2 Pub. Papers 927, 927 (Aug. 4, 1964).

reckless. According to one observer, "the Gulf of Tonkin affair presented itself as the perfect vehicle for Johnson to ride from August through election day."[5]

The next day, August 5, the resolution prepared earlier in the summer by the Johnson administration was introduced in Congress by Senator J. William Fulbright and Representative Thomas E. Morgan. In the ensuing brief debate, the Administration acknowledged the U.S.-directed raids on July 30 (but not those on August 3), while it disavowed any connection between the raids and the movements of the *Maddox*. The Tonkin Gulf Resolution, as it is now known, was passed on August 7, 1964, with only two dissenting votes in the Senate and none in the House. The resolution provided in part:

Tonkin Gulf Resolution

Pub. L. No. 88-408, 78 Stat. 384 (1964)

Whereas naval units of the Communist regime in Vietnam, in violation of the principles of the Charter of the United Nations and of international law, have deliberately and repeatedly attacked United States naval vessels lawfully present in international waters, and have thereby created a serious threat to international peace; and

Whereas these attacks are part of a deliberate and systematic campaign of aggression that the Communist regime in North Vietnam has been waging against its neighbors and the nations joined with them in the collective defense of their freedom; and

Whereas the United States is assisting the peoples of southeast Asia to protect their freedom and has no territorial, military or political ambitions in the area, but desires only that these peoples should be left in peace to work out their own destinies in their own way: Now, therefore, be it

Resolved... That the Congress approves and supports the determination of the President, as Commander in Chief, to take all necessary measures to repel any armed attack against the forces of the United States and to prevent further aggression.

Sec. 2.... Consonant with the Constitution of the United States and the Charter of the United Nations and in accordance with its obligations under the Southeast Asia Collective Defense Treaty, the United States is, therefore, prepared, as the President determines, to take all necessary steps, including the use of armed force, to assist any member or protocol state of the Southeast Asia Collective Defense Treaty requesting assistance in defense of its freedom.

Sec. 3. This resolution shall expire when the President shall determine that the peace and security of the area is reasonably assured... except that it may be terminated earlier by concurrent resolution of the Congress.

---

5. Gordon M. Goldstein, *Lessons in Disaster: McGeorge Bundy and the Path to War in Vietnam* 133 (2008).

It is surely no accident that the resolution was drawn in such broad terms. President Johnson is said to have remarked that it was "like grandma's nightshirt — it covered everything."[6]

As the U.S. military commitment in Vietnam expanded in the months that followed, members of the public and Congress, especially Senator Fulbright, began to grow uneasy about the apparent lack of clear military and political objectives there. On April 7, 1965, President Johnson offered this rationale in a speech at Johns Hopkins University:

> Why are we in South Viet-Nam? We are there because we have a promise to keep. Since 1954 every American President has offered support to the people of South Viet-Nam. We have helped to build, and we have helped to defend. Thus, over many years, we have made a national pledge to help South Viet-Nam defend its independence. And I intend to keep that promise. To dishonor that pledge, to abandon this small and brave nation to its enemies, and to the terror that must follow, would be an unforgivable wrong.
>
> We are also there to strengthen world order. Around the globe from Berlin to Thailand are people whose well-being rests in part on the belief that they can count on us if they are attacked. To leave Viet-Nam to its fate would be to shake the confidence of all these people in the value of an American commitment and in the value of America's word. The result would be increased unrest and instability, and even wider war.
>
> We are also there because there are great stakes in the balance. Let no one think for a moment that retreat from Viet-Nam would bring an end to conflict. The battle would be renewed in one country and then another. The central lesson of our time is that the appetite of aggression is never satisfied. . . .
>
> In recent months attacks on South Viet-Nam were stepped up. Thus, it became necessary for us to increase our response and to make attacks by air. This is not a change of purpose. It is a change in what we believe that purpose requires.
>
> We do this in order to slow down aggression. We do this to increase the confidence of the brave people of South Viet-Nam who have bravely borne this brutal battle for so many years with so many casualties. And we do this to convince the leaders of North Viet-Nam — and all who seek to share their conquest — of a simple fact: We will not be defeated. We will not grow tired. We will not withdraw, either openly or under the cloak of a meaningless agreement. . . . [Lyndon B. Johnson, *Peace Without Conquest,* Address at Johns Hopkins University, 1 Pub. Papers 394, 395-396 (Apr. 7, 1965) (emphases omitted).]

The day before his April 7 address, the President approved an 18,000-20,000 man increase in U.S. forces in the South. More important, he ordered Marine battalions to leave their coastal enclaves for the first time and go on the offensive against Communist forces. But he kept his orders secret to avoid the appearance of a change in policy.

In May, the President asked for and Congress approved a $700 million supplemental appropriation to help finance the expanding war effort. Pub. L. No. 89-18, 79 Stat. 109 (1965). General Westmoreland then requested large increases in ground forces to carry out a new search-and-destroy strategy against a rapid buildup in Viet Cong recruitment and infiltration of troops from North Vietnam. Westmoreland's requests were not made public, but by the end of 1965 there were 184,000 U.S. troops in Vietnam, most of them supplied by a draft. Approval was given for another 207,000 troops during 1966, and by early 1968 U.S. combat forces there totaled 510,000.

---

6. Stanley Karnow, *Vietnam: A History* 374 (1983).

It was not enough. Then-Defense Secretary Robert S. McNamara lamented much later that the United States had undertaken "a guerrilla war with conventional military tactics against a foe willing to absorb enormous casualties in a country without the fundamental political stability necessary to conduct effective military and pacification operations. It could not be done, and it was not done."[7]

A major turning point in the war came on January 31, 1968, during the Lunar New Year holiday, when Viet Cong and North Vietnamese forces launched the so-called "Tet offensive" against more than 100 cities and bases and the U.S. embassy in Saigon. The massive scale and ferocity of the attacks caused Pentagon planners to rethink their goals and strategies. More important, images of the combat in television news reports back in the United States focused public attention more closely on the conflict, raising for the first time the specter of defeat. *See* Joel Achenbach, *Did the News Media, Led by Walter Cronkite, Lose the War in Vietnam?*, Wash. Post, May 25, 2018.

President Johnson relieved General Westmoreland of his command not long after, then announced a cutback in the bombing of the North. A short time later, North Vietnam agreed to peace talks in Paris. But the negotiations would continue for four more very bloody years before bearing fruit.

Not until 1971 was it disclosed that a succession of Presidents had withheld from Congress and the American people a great deal of information about the deepening U.S. military involvement in Vietnam. In that year the *New York Times* and the *Washington Post* published parts of a leaked 7,000-page top-secret Pentagon history of the Vietnam conflict, the so-called *Pentagon Papers*, covering the period from 1945 to 1968. Among other details, it revealed U.S. complicity in the overthrow of South Vietnamese President Ngo Dinh Diem in 1963, White House planning for a wider war in the months before the Tonkin Gulf incident, and the careful cultivation of public opinion for support of an expanded conflict. (The leaking of the *Pentagon Papers* — and government efforts to prevent their publication — are recounted in Chapter 41.)

2. Legal Foundations for the Commitment of U.S. Forces

Reading the Meeker Memo — The Johnson Administration's Legal Brief for the War

In 1966, the Legal Adviser to the Department of State, Leonard C. Meeker, issued a memorandum defending the legality of U.S. military actions in Vietnam. Consider these questions, among others, in reviewing the memorandum:

- Meeker argues that the President has broad, inherent power under Article II to deploy U.S. military forces abroad. Does he?
- Meeker cites 125 instances in which the President ordered the use of force abroad "without congressional authorization." Based on your understanding of the separation of powers and the categories of presidential action identified by Justice Jackson, can you identify his argument here? Do the historical precedents he cites support his argument?

7. Robert S. McNamara, *In Retrospect: The Tragedy and Lessons of Vietnam* 212 (1995).

- What is Meeker's "treaty argument," and how does it rest on the language of the SEATO Treaty? Is this argument consistent with what you know of the Treaty Clause and the Declare War Clauses and their history?
- What language in the Gulf of Tonkin Resolution authorized U.S. military actions in Vietnam? Did it satisfy the Constitution's requirements for commitment of the nation to war?

Leonard C. Meeker, The Legality of United States Participation in the Defense of Viet Nam

54 Dep't St. Bull. 474 (Mar. 4, 1966), *reprinted in* 75 Yale L.J. 1085 (1966)

IV. THE PRESIDENT HAS FULL AUTHORITY TO COMMIT UNITED STATES FORCES IN THE COLLECTIVE DEFENSE OF SOUTH VIET NAM

There can be no question in present circumstances of the President's authority to commit United States forces to the defense of South Viet Nam. The grant of authority to the President in article II of the Constitution extends to the actions of the United States currently undertaken in Viet Nam. In fact, however, it is unnecessary to determine whether this grant standing alone is sufficient to authorize the actions taken in Viet Nam. These actions rest not only on the exercise of Presidential powers under article II but on the SEATO treaty—a treaty advised and consented to by the Senate—and on actions of the Congress, particularly the joint resolution of August 10, 1964....

A. The President's Power under Article II of the Constitution Extends to the Actions Currently Undertaken in Viet Nam

Under the Constitution, the President, in addition to being Chief Executive, is Commander in Chief of the Army and Navy. He holds the prime responsibility for the conduct of United States foreign relations. These duties carry very broad powers, including the power to deploy American forces abroad and commit them to military operations when the President deems such action necessary to maintain the security and defense of the United States....

In 1787 the world was a far larger place, and the framers probably had in mind attacks upon the United States. In the 20th century, the world has grown much smaller. An attack on a country far from our shores can impinge directly on the nation's security. In the SEATO treaty, for example, it is formally declared that an armed attack against Viet Nam would endanger the peace and safety of the United States.

Since the Constitution was adopted there have been at least 125 instances in which the President has ordered the armed forces to take action or maintain positions abroad without obtaining prior congressional authorization, starting with the "undeclared war" with France (1798-1800). For example, President Truman ordered 250,000 troops to Korea during the Korean War of the early 1950's. President Eisenhower dispatched 14,000 troops to Lebanon in 1958.

The Constitution leaves to the President the judgment to determine whether the circumstances of a particular armed attack are so urgent and the potential consequences so threatening to the security of the United States that he should act without formally consulting the Congress.

B. The Southeast Asia Collective Defense Treaty Authorizes the President's Actions

Under article VI of the United States Constitution, "all Treaties made, or which shall be made, under the Authority of the United States, shall be the supreme Law of the Land." Article IV, paragraph 1, of the SEATO treaty establishes as a matter of law that a Communist armed attack against South Viet Nam endangers the peace and safety of the United States. In this same provision the United States has undertaken a commitment in the SEATO treaty to "act to meet the common danger in accordance with its constitutional processes" in the event of such an attack.

Under our Constitution it is the President who must decide when an armed attack has occurred. He has also the constitutional responsibility for determining what measures of defense are required when the peace and safety of the United States are endangered. If he considers that deployment of U.S. forces to South Viet Nam is required, and that military measures against the source of Communist aggression in North Viet Nam are necessary, he is constitutionally empowered to take those measures....

C. The Joint Resolution of Congress of August 10, 1964, Authorizes United States Participation in the Collective Defense of South Viet Nam...

Following the North Vietnamese attacks in the Gulf of Tonkin against United States destroyers, Congress adopted, by a Senate vote of 88-2 and a House vote of 416-0, a joint resolution containing a series of important declarations and provisions of law.

Section 1 resolved that "the Congress approves and supports the determination of the President, as Commander in Chief, to take all necessary measures to repel any armed attack against the forces of the United States and to prevent further aggression." Thus, the Congress gave its sanction to specific actions by the President to repel attacks against United States naval vessels in the Gulf of Tonkin and elsewhere in the western Pacific. Congress further approved the taking of "all necessary measures... to prevent further aggression." This authorization extended to those measures the President might consider necessary to ward off further attacks and to prevent further aggression by North Viet Nam in Southeast Asia....

Section 2... constitutes an authorization to the President, in his discretion, to act — using armed force if he determines that is required — to assist South Viet-Nam at its request in defense of its freedom. The identification of South Viet-Nam through the reference to "protocol state" in this section is unmistakable, and the grant of authority "as the President determines" is unequivocal....

Congressional realization of the scope of authority being conferred by the joint resolution is shown by the legislative history of the measure as a whole. The following exchange between Senators Cooper and Fulbright is illuminating:

Mr. Cooper [John Sherman Cooper]: ... The Senator will remember that the SEATO Treaty, in article IV, provides that in the event an armed attack is made upon a party to the Southeast Asia Collective Defense Treaty, or upon one of the protocol states such as South Vietnam, the parties to the treaty, one of whom is the United States, would then take such action as might be appropriate, after resorting to their constitutional processes. I assume that would mean, in the case of the United States, that Congress would be asked to grant the authority to act.

Does the Senator consider that in enacting this resolution we are satisfying that requirement of article IV of the Southeast Asia Collective Defense Treaty? In other words, are we now giving the President advance authority to take whatever action he may deem necessary respecting South Vietnam and its defense or with respect to the defense of any other country included in the treaty?

Mr. Fulbright: I think that is correct.

Mr. Cooper: Then, looking ahead, if the President decided that it was necessary to use such force as could lead into war, we will give the authority by this resolution?

Mr. Fulbright: That is the way I would interpret it. If a situation later developed in which we thought the approval should be withdrawn it could be withdrawn by concurrent resolution.

The August 1964 joint resolution continues in force today [1966]. Section [3] of the resolution provides that it shall expire "when the President shall determine that the peace and security of the area is reasonably assured by international conditions created by action of the United Nations or otherwise, except that it may be terminated earlier by concurrent resolution of the Congress." The President has made no such determination, nor has Congress terminated the joint resolution.

Instead, Congress in May 1965 approved an appropriation of $700 million to meet the expense of mounting military requirements in Viet Nam. (Public Law 89-18, 79 Stat. 109.) The President's message asking for this appropriation stated that this was "not a routine appropriation. For each Member of Congress who supports this request is also voting to persist in our efforts to halt Communist aggression in South Vietnam." The appropriation act constitutes a clear congressional endorsement and approval of the actions taken by the President.

On March 1, 1966, the Congress continued to express its support of the President's policy by approving a $4.8 billion supplemental military authorization by votes of 392-4 and 93-2. An amendment that would have limited the President's authority to commit forces to Viet Nam was rejected in the Senate by a vote of 94-2.

D. No Declaration of War by the Congress Is Required to Authorize United States Participation in the Collective Defense of South Viet Nam

No declaration of war is needed to authorize American actions in Viet Nam. As shown in the preceding sections, the President has ample authority to order the participation of United States armed forces in the defense of South Viet Nam.

Over a very long period in our history, practice and precedent have confirmed the constitutional authority to engage United States forces in hostilities without a declaration of war. This history extends from the undeclared war with France and the war against the Barbary pirates at the end of the 18th century to the Korean war of 1950-53.

James Madison, one of the leading framers of the Constitution, and Presidents John Adams and Jefferson all construed the Constitution, in their official actions during the early years of the Republic, as authorizing the United States to employ its armed forces abroad in hostilities in the absence of any congressional declaration of war. Their views and actions constitute highly persuasive evidence as to the meaning and effect of the Constitution. History has accepted the interpretation that was placed on the Constitution by the early Presidents and Congresses in regard to the lawfulness of hostilities without a declaration of war. The instances of such action in our history are numerous.

In the Korean conflict, where large-scale hostilities were conducted with an American troop participation of a quarter of a million men, no declaration of war was made by the Congress. The President acted on the basis of his constitutional responsibilities. While the Security Council, under a treaty of this country — the United Nations Charter — recommended assistance to the Republic of Korea against the Communist armed attack, the United States had no treaty commitment at that time obligating us to join in the defense of South Korea. In the case of South Viet Nam we have the obligation of the SEATO treaty and clear expressions of congressional support. If the President could act in Korea without a declaration of war, *a fortiori* he is empowered to do so now in Viet Nam.

It may be suggested that a declaration of war is the only available constitutional process by which congressional support can be made effective for the use of United States armed forces in combat abroad. But the Constitution does not insist on any rigid formalism. It gives Congress a choice of ways in which to exercise its powers. In the case of Viet Nam the Congress has supported the determination of the President by the Senate's approval of the SEATO treaty, the adoption of the joint resolution of August 10, 1964, and the enactment of the necessary authorizations and appropriations. . . .

Notes and Questions

1. *Inherent Presidential Authority?* Leonard Meeker described the President's foreign relations powers in very broad terms, insisting that the Article II designation as Executive and Commander in Chief enabled the President to commit American forces to military operations "when the President deems such actions necessary to maintain the security and defense of the United States." Can you briefly marshal, from your earlier reading, arguments for and against such an expansive reading of the President's powers?

2. *Changing Circumstances and War-Making Authority.* As Mr. Meeker pointed out, strategic considerations in defending the nation in the 1960s were quite different from those that faced the Framers two centuries earlier. Did they require, however, an interpretation of the Constitution that gave greater independence to the President than in the past? Professor Velvel argued that the President's war powers had instead diminished:

> [I]n the world of today and tomorrow, even small wars can cause a chain of events which could bring mass destruction to the human race. . . . Such wars have a way of escalating, as has the struggle in Vietnam. They thus carry with them the ultimate risk of nuclear war. If the nation is to run this risk, the decision to do so should be as widely dispersed as the Constitution permits — the decision should be made by 535 federal legislators rather than a tiny handful of executive officials. [Lawrence R. Velvel, *The War in Viet Nam: Unconstitutional, Justiciable, and Jurisdictionally Attackable,* 16 U. Kan. L. Rev. 449, 470-471 (1968).]

How would you compare Professor Velvel's assumptions about the strategic implications of American involvement in Southeast Asia with those of Mr. Meeker?

With the ongoing threat of international terrorism, advances in modern weaponry, and innovations in technology, the world today seems smaller still. How should a court respond to these developments in interpreting the President's Article II powers?

3. The Power to Repel Sudden Attacks. Is there any doubt that North Vietnamese military operations in South Vietnam created a "state of war" as that term was defined in *The Prize Cases, supra* p. 55? Did the President have the authority as Commander in Chief to treat an attack on an ally or on U.S. military forces abroad as if it were an attack on the United States?

4. Usage and Presidential War Making. Recall Justice Frankfurter's argument, in *The Steel Seizure Case,* that "a systematic, unbroken, executive practice, long pursued to the knowledge of the Congress and never before questioned . . . may be treated as a gloss on 'executive Power' vested in the President." *Supra* p. 36. The spare language of Article II was said by Mr. Meeker to be augmented by usage. He recalled 125 earlier instances when troops were deployed by the President without the approval of Congress. But Professor Moore observed that while these incidents represent "a substantial gloss which experience has placed on the Constitution," most of them involved short commitments and few losses; the ones that did not were highly controversial, such as the Korean War and the Mexican War of 1846. John Norton Moore, *Law and the Indo-China War* 542-543 (1972).

5. Authorization by Treaty? The SEATO Treaty provided in part:

> Each Party recognizes that aggression by means of armed attack in the treaty area against any of the Parties or against any State or territory which the Parties by unanimous agreement may hereafter designate, would endanger its own peace and safety, and agrees that it will in that event act to meet the common danger in accordance with its constitutional processes. [Southeast Asia Collective Defense Treaty art. 4, ¶1, Sept. 28, 1954, 6 U.S.T. 81, 83, 209 U.N.T.S. 28, 30.]

The treaty was, as Mr. Meeker pointed out, the "supreme Law of the Land," according to Article VI of the Constitution. Was the President therefore obliged as part of his Article II duties to "faithfully execute" the treaty as law by sending U.S. troops and equipment to Southeast Asia? Professor Van Alstyne argued that the SEATO Treaty was not self-executing — that it depended upon further congressional action for its implementation. William Van Alstyne, *Congress, the President, and the Power to Declare War: A Requiem for Vietnam,* 121 U. Pa. L. Rev. 1, 14 (1972) (arguing that the treaty was merely "an international contractual obligation — obliging Congress to make the declaration of war if it intends to fulfill the treaty commitment").

Could the treaty itself be taken to satisfy U.S. "constitutional processes" — to authorize presidential action without additional debate and approval? Recall that the Framers rejected a proposal by Charles Pinckney to give the Senate alone the power to commit the nation to a state of war. See *supra* p. 17. Did Mr. Meeker not seek to achieve the same result indirectly, since the power to enter into treaties is given in Article II, section 2, to the President, with the advice and consent of two-thirds of the Senators present but without the concurrence of the House of Representatives?

6. Tonkin Gulf Resolution as a Declaration of War? Undersecretary of State Nicholas Katzenbach called the Tonkin Gulf Resolution "not a declaration of war" but "the functional equivalent" of such a declaration. *U.S. Commitments to Foreign Powers: Hearings Before the S. Comm. on Foreign Relations on S. Res. No. 151*, 90th Cong. 82, 145 (1967). Congress has since styled similar legislation as an "Authorization for the Use of Military Force," often called by its acronym, "AUMF." Can you suggest why Congress did not formally declare war if it intended to authorize hostilities on such a large scale?

7. Scope of the Tonkin Gulf Resolution. If you had been sitting in Congress in 1964 when the Tonkin Gulf Resolution came up for a vote, would you have voted for it? If so, would you have intended to vest the President with the broad powers claimed by him? Was the language of the resolution sufficient to authorize the bombing of North Vietnam and the introduction of several hundred thousand American ground troops into the South, perhaps even the use of nuclear weapons to halt the spread of Communism in Southeast Asia, as some military leaders recommended?

Are any doubts about the scope of the resolution dispelled by Mr. Meeker's reference to the debate between Senators Fulbright and Cooper at the time of passage? Other exchanges during consideration of the measure indicate a very different understanding. Five years later it was recalled:

> The prevailing attitude was not so much that Congress was granting or acknowledging the executive's authority to take certain actions but that it was expressing unity and support for the President in a moment of national crisis and, therefore, that the exact words in which it expressed those sentiments were not of primary importance.
>
> . . . Although the language of the resolution lends itself to the interpretation that Congress was consenting in advance to a full-scale war in Asia should the President think it necessary, that was not the expectation of Congress at the time. In adopting the resolution Congress was closer to believing that it was helping to *prevent* a large-scale war by taking a firm stand than it was laying the legal basis for the conduct of such a war. [S. Comm. on Foreign Relations, S. Rep. No. 91-129, at 22-23 (1969).]

But does the Committee's statement reflect more than just congressional sour grapes? What should we make of the fact that the Committee then failed to take decisive action to repudiate the President's interpretation of the resolution?

Referring not only to the Tonkin Gulf Resolution but also to the appropriations and draft legislation that followed it, Professor Ely argued that Congress did approve U.S. military activities in Vietnam, although it "invariably did so with enormous ambiguity. . . . [Congress] lacks the will and/or courage to stop the President from involving us in military ventures, but at the same time has no wish to be held accountable for the wars he gets us into." John Hart Ely, *The American War in Indochina, Part I: The (Troubled) Constitutionality of the War They Told Us About*, 42 Stan. L. Rev. 876, 922 (1990). Professor Ely wanted to devise a "bright-line test of authorization as a way of forcing our representatives in Congress to take a clear stand, up front, on questions of war and peace." *Id.* at 924. Do you think a bright-line test would be a good idea? Can you articulate such a test?

8. Delegating War Power. Assuming that Congress is empowered to delegate at least some of its war powers to the President, is it a legal problem, a practical problem, or both, that in the Gulf of Tonkin Resolution the delegation is described in very broad terms? Is any risk of executive overreaching minimized by Congress's ability to modify or repeal its authorization at any subsequent time?

9. Collective Self-Defense and International Law. Did U.S. involvement in the Vietnam conflict violate either the U.N. Charter's prohibition on the use of force or customary international norms? In a portion of Mr. Meeker's opinion omitted here, he argued that the Republic of Viet Nam (R.V.N.) was subjected to armed attack by Communist North Vietnam, and that the United States was engaged in a lawful collective defense of its ally. The R.V.N. certainly declared publicly that it was the victim of an armed attack, and it requested the military assistance of the United States—prerequisites to collective self-defense noted by the World Court in the *Nicaragua* case, *supra* p. 249.

Some critics of the war contended, however, that the R.V.N. was not a separate sovereign state, and that Vietnam was embroiled in a civil, rather than an international war, making foreign intervention impermissible. The 1954 Geneva Accords, they noted, declared that the cease-fire line along the 17th parallel was "not in any way [to] be interpreted as constituting a political or territorial boundary." The Accords also called for elections and unification of the country in 1956. Yet when Mr. Meeker wrote his opinion, the Saigon and Hanoi governments had functioned as separate political and ideological entities for more than a decade, and each had been recognized by a number of other nations.

Supposing U.S. intervention to be justified as an act of collective self-defense, it was also circumscribed by Article 51 of the U.N. Charter, which permits such acts only "until the Security Council has taken measures necessary to maintain international peace and security," and requires such acts to be "immediately reported" to the Security Council. Why didn't the United States seek Security Council approval of its intervention? How long do you think the intervention could legitimately continue without such approval?

10. Legal Opinion or Advocacy? More than four decades after Mr. Meeker, the State Department's Legal Adviser, wrote the memorandum set out above, he offered this observation:

> I know you understand the situation in which we found ourselves when asked to write the 1966 memorandum. It had to be, and indeed was intended to be, an advocate's piece. Senator Joseph Sill Clark, of Pennsylvania, observed sympathetically three years later when I was being questioned by the Senate Foreign Relations Committee, "As lawyers we have all had the experience of being given a bad brief to argue; we just do the best we can with it." An unbiased memorandum meant to be objective would naturally have been different—giving both sides of the arguments about Presidential power and recognizing that justification of U.S. actions under international law was open to much dispute.
>
> Back in the 1960s we in the Office of the Legal Adviser spent much time on the necessity of constructing the Viet Nam memorandum. What we cared about a good deal more was trying to assure that U.S. conduct in the Viet Nam war be compatible with the requirements of the Geneva Conventions, and making the case to Secretary of State Dean Rusk that the U.S. should seek at once a cease-fire in place to stop the hostilities. It should be

said that he always gave us a fair hearing. He simply disagreed, for reasons we understood, and the up-shot was a failure of our efforts.

Today the American public and the rest of the world are confronted with a U.S. Administration that acts on the principle of unilateral decision and with disregard of treaty and other international obligations. I continue to hope that change for the better lies ahead. As Thomas Hardy is reported to have said, "if way to the Better there be, it exacts a full look at the Worst." [Letter from Leonard Meeker to Stephen Dycus (Mar. 25, 2007).]

Do you think most readers in 1966 would have regarded the memorandum as merely an "advocate's piece"? Who, in any event, was the Legal Adviser's client?

11. Shared Responsibility for the War? Why do you suppose that several presidential administrations withheld so much information about the war from Congress and the public? Of course, Congress might have voted the same way if it had been fully briefed on U.S. activities in the Tonkin Gulf or told about Administration plans for possible escalation of the war effort. We can never know for sure.

Should the withholding of such information have affected the force of the Tonkin Gulf Resolution as law? Senator Fulbright, who sponsored the resolution in the Senate, later ruefully offered this analysis: "Now in contract law, a contract induced by fraud or mistake is voidable. Perhaps some analogous doctrine in constitutional law should apply when statutory authority is given a president on the basis of fraudulent or mistaken representations." J. William Fulbright, *Foreword,* in Michael J. Glennon, *Constitutional Diplomacy,* at xiii (1990). Is Senator Fulbright's analogy fair or useful? What might Congress have done to better inform itself about what was going on? See Chapter 40.

3. Testing the Legitimacy of the War in Court

Reading *Orlando v. Laird*

United States involvement in the military conflict in Southeast Asia was challenged in court by a number of plaintiffs on various grounds. All but a few of the suits were dismissed on the ground that the plaintiffs lacked standing to sue or that the issues presented to the court were political and therefore nonjusticiable. In the decision that follows, consider especially these issues:

- Why did the plaintiffs have standing to bring this claim?
- What role did the court give itself in the process of deciding to go to war?
- Why was a formal declaration of war not required before sending U.S. troops into battle?
- To what extent must Congress collaborate in the decision to use military force abroad, and what forms may its approval take?
- Which aspects of the controversy did the court find to be nonjusticiable, and why?

Orlando v. Laird

United States Court of Appeals, Second Circuit, 1971
443 F.2d 1039, *cert. denied*, 404 U.S. 869 (1971)

ANDERSON, J. Shortly after receiving orders to report for transfer to Vietnam, Pfc. Malcolm A. Berk and Sp. E5 Salvatore Orlando, enlistees in the United States Army, commenced separate actions in June, 1970, seeking to enjoin the Secretary of Defense, the Secretary of the Army and the commanding officers, who signed their deployment orders, from enforcing them. The plaintiffs-appellants contended that these executive officers exceeded their constitutional authority by ordering them to participate in a war not properly authorized by Congress.

... [I]n *Berk v. Laird*, 429 F.2d 302 (2nd Cir. 1970) ... [w]e held that the war declaring power of Congress, enumerated in Article I, section 8, of the Constitution, contains a "discoverable standard calling for *some* mutual participation by Congress," and directed that Berk be given an opportunity "to provide a method for resolving the question of when specified joint legislative-executive action is sufficient to authorize various levels of military activity," and thereby escape application of the political question doctrine to his claim that congressional participation has been in this instance, insufficient....

It is the appellants' position that the sufficiency of congressional authorization is a matter within judicial competence because that question can be resolved by "judicially discoverable and manageable standards" dictated by the congressional power "to declare War." *See Baker v. Carr*, 369 U.S. 186 (1962); *Powell v. McCormack*, 395 U.S. 486 (1969). They interpret the constitutional provision to require an express and explicit congressional authorization of the Vietnam hostilities though not necessarily in the words, "We declare that the United States of America is at war with North Vietnam." In support of this construction they point out that the original intent of the clause was to place responsibility for the initiation of war upon the body most responsive to popular will and argue that historical developments have not altered the need for significant congressional participation in such commitments of national resources. They further assert that, without a requirement of express and explicit congressional authorization, developments committing the nation to war, as a *fait accompli*, became the inevitable adjuncts of presidential direction of foreign policy, and, because military appropriations and other war-implementing enactments lack an explicit authorization of particular hostilities, they cannot, as a matter of law, be considered sufficient.

Alternatively, appellants would have this court find that, because the President requested accelerating defense appropriations and extensions of the conscription laws after the war was well under way, Congress was, in effect, placed in a straitjacket and could not freely decide whether or not to enact this legislation, but rather was compelled to do so. For this reason appellants claim that such enactments cannot, as a factual matter, be considered sufficient congressional approval or ratification.

The Government on the other hand takes the position that the suits concern a non-justiciable political question; that the military action in South Vietnam was authorized by Congress in the [Tonkin Gulf Resolution] considered in connection with the SEATO Treaty; and that the military action was authorized and ratified by congressional appropriations expressly designated for use in support of the military operations in Vietnam.

We held in the first *Berk* opinion that the constitutional delegation of the war-declaring power to the Congress contains a discoverable and manageable standard imposing on the Congress a duty of mutual participation in the prosecution of war.

Judicial scrutiny of that duty, therefore, is not foreclosed by the political question doctrine. *Baker v. Carr, supra; Powell v. McCormack, supra.* As we see it, the test is whether there is any action by the Congress sufficient to authorize or ratify the military activity in question. The evidentiary materials produced at the hearings in the district court clearly disclose that this test is satisfied.

The Congress and the Executive have taken mutual and joint action in the prosecution and support of military operations in Southeast Asia from the beginning of those operations. The Tonkin Gulf Resolution, enacted August 10, 1964 (repealed December 31, 1970) was passed at the request of President Johnson and, though occasioned by specific naval incidents in the Gulf of Tonkin, was expressed in broad language which clearly showed the state of mind of the Congress and its intention fully to implement and support the military and naval actions taken by and planned to be taken by the President at that time in Southeast Asia, and as might be required in the future "to prevent further aggression." Congress has ratified the executive's initiatives by appropriating billions of dollars to carry out military operations in Southeast Asia[2] and by extending the Military Selective Service Act with full knowledge that persons conscripted under that Act had been, and would continue to be, sent to Vietnam. Moreover, it specifically conscripted manpower to fill "the substantial induction calls necessitated by the current Vietnam buildup."[3]

There is, therefore, no lack of clear evidence to support a conclusion that there was an abundance of continuing mutual participation in the prosecution of the war. Both branches collaborated in the endeavor, and neither could long maintain such a war without the concurrence and cooperation of the other.

Although appellants do not contend that Congress can exercise its war-declaring power only through a formal declaration, they argue that congressional authorization cannot, as a matter of law, be inferred from military appropriations or other war-implementing legislation that does not contain an express and explicit authorization for the making of war by the President. Putting aside for a moment the explicit authorization of the Tonkin Gulf Resolution, we disagree with appellants' interpretation of the declaration clause for neither the language nor the purpose underlying that provision prohibits an inference of the fact of authorization from such legislative action as we have in this instance. The framers' intent to vest the war power in Congress is in no way defeated by permitting an inference of authorization from legislative action furnishing the manpower and materials of war for the protracted military operation in Southeast Asia.

---

2. In response to the demands of the military operations the executive during the 1960s ordered more and more men and material into the war zone; and congressional appropriations have been commensurate with each new level of fighting. Until 1965, defense appropriations had not earmarked funds for Vietnam. In May of that year President Johnson asked Congress for an emergency supplemental appropriation "to provide our forces [then numbering 35,000] with the best and most modern supplies and equipment." 111 Cong. Rec. 9283 (May 4, 1965). Congress appropriated $700 million for use "upon determination by the President that such action is necessary in connection with military activities in Southeast Asia." Pub. L. 89-18, 79 Stat. 109 (1965). Appropriation acts in each subsequent year explicitly authorized expenditures for men and material sent to Vietnam. The 1967 appropriations act, for example, declared Congress' "firm intention to provide all necessary support for members of the Armed Forces of the United States fighting in Vietnam" and supported "the efforts being made by the President of the United States . . . to prevent an expansion of the war in Vietnam and to bring that conflict to an end through a negotiated settlement. . . ." Pub. L. 90-5, 81 Stat. 5 (1967). . . .

3. In H. Rep. No. 267, 90th Cong., 1st Sess. 38 (1967), in addition to extending the conscription mechanism, Congress continued a suspension of the permanent ceiling on the active duty strength of the Armed Forces, fixed at 2 million men, and replaced it with a secondary ceiling of 5 million. . . .

The choice, for example, between an explicit declaration on the one hand and a resolution and war-implementing legislation, on the other, as the medium for expression of congressional consent involves "the exercise of a discretion demonstrably committed to the . . . legislature," *Baker v. Carr, supra* at 211, and therefore, invokes the political question doctrine.

Such a choice involves an important area of decision making in which, through mutual influence and reciprocal action between the President and the Congress, policies governing the relationship between this country and other parts of the world are formulated in the best interests of the United States. If there can be nothing more than minor military operations conducted under any circumstances, short of an express and explicit declaration of war by Congress, then extended military operations could not be conducted even though both the Congress and the President were agreed that they were necessary and were also agreed that a formal declaration of war would place the nation in a posture in its international relations which would be against its best interests. For the judicial branch to enunciate and enforce such a standard would be not only extremely unwise but also would constitute a deep invasion of the political question domain. As the Government says, ". . . decisions regarding the form and substance of congressional enactments authorizing hostilities are determined by highly complex considerations of diplomacy, foreign policy and military strategy inappropriate to judicial inquiry." It would, indeed, destroy the flexibility of action which the executive and legislative branches must have in dealing with other sovereigns. What has been said and done by both the President and the Congress in their collaborative conduct of the military operations in Vietnam implies a consensus on the advisability of *not* making a formal declaration of war because it would be contrary to the interests of the United States to do so. The making of a policy decision of that kind is clearly within the constitutional domain of those two branches and is just as clearly not within the competency or power of the judiciary.

Beyond determining that there has been *some* mutual participation between the Congress and the President, which unquestionably exists here, with action by the Congress sufficient to authorize or ratify the military activity at issue, it is clear that the constitutional propriety of the means by which Congress has chosen to ratify and approve the protracted military operations in Southeast Asia is a political question. The form which congressional authorization should take is one of policy, committed to the discretion of the Congress and outside the power and competency of the judiciary, because there are no intelligible and objectively manageable standards by which to judge such actions. *Baker v. Carr, supra,* 369 U.S. at 217; *Powell v. McCormack, supra,* 395 U.S. at 518. . . .

[The concurring opinion of KAUFMAN, J., is omitted.]

Notes and Questions

1. Standing to Sue? The plaintiffs in *Orlando* asserted direct injury in fact from their deployment to a war zone. Despite some uncertainty early on, it seems to have been settled that military personnel with orders for duty in Vietnam had standing to test the legitimacy of the war. *See, e.g., Berk v. Laird,* 429 F.2d 302, 306 (2d Cir. 1970).

In *Massachusetts v. Laird,* 451 F.2d 26 (1st Cir. 1971), the Commonwealth asserted standing based on its interest as a sovereign state and as *parens patriae* on behalf of its residents. The court failed to rule on this issue, but it expressed doubt about the status of the Commonwealth as protector of the rights of its citizens, since the "federal government is the ultimate *parens patriae* of every American citizen." *Id.* at 29.

Standing for members of Congress who brought suit challenging the legitimacy of the war was recognized in one case, *Mitchell v. Laird,* 488 F.2d 611, 613-614 (D.C. Cir. 1973), but denied in another, *Holtzman v. Schlesinger,* 484 F.2d 1307, 1315 (2d Cir. 1973). More recent refinements in the law of standing for members of Congress are described *supra* pp. 139-140.

2. The "Threshold Constitutional Duty" of Collaboration. In *Orlando*'s companion case, *Berk v. Laird,* 429 F.2d 302, 304 (2d Cir. 1970), the government insisted that "the President's authority as Commander in Chief, in the absence of a declared war, is co-extensive with his broad and unitary power in the field of foreign affairs," citing *Curtiss-Wright.* The *Berk* court rejected this contention because "the congressional power to 'declare' a war would be reduced to an antique formality, leaving no executive 'duty' to follow constitutional steps which can be judicially identified." *Id.* at 305.

The *Berk* court went on to say, "Since orders to fight must be issued in accordance with proper authorization from both branches under some circumstances, executive officers are under a threshold constitutional 'duty [that] can be judicially identified and its breach judicially determined.'" *Id.* (quoting *Baker v. Carr,* 369 U.S. 186, 198 (1962)). Can you describe the "threshold constitutional duty" that the courts must be prepared to identify, in order to avoid dismissal under the political question doctrine? Can you say under what "circumstances" proper authorization from both political branches would *not* be required to fight?

3. The Adequacy of Collaboration. What is the source of the *Orlando* court's "mutual participation" standard for prosecution of the war? What is the source of the court's test for determining when there has been "sufficient" mutual participation? Do you see an element of circularity in the test? Does that circularity make this case look "political" and therefore nonjusticiable?

If the standard of "some mutual participation" is discoverable by the courts, will the "highly complex considerations of diplomacy, foreign policy and military strategy" be compromised less than if a single clear act — a declaration of war — were required?

4. Different Approaches to Collaboration. In *Massachusetts v. Laird, supra,* on facts substantially identical to those in *Orlando,* the court focused on the first decisional factor in *Baker v. Carr, supra* — "whether there is a 'textually demonstrable commitment of the issue to a coordinate political department' of government." 451 F.2d at 31.

> [T]he war power of the country is an amalgam of powers, some distinct and others less sharply limned. In certain respects, the executive and the Congress may act independently. The Congress may without executive cooperation declare war, thus triggering treaty obligations and domestic emergency powers. The executive may without Congressional participation repel attack, perhaps catapulting the country into a major conflict. But beyond these independent powers, each of which has its own rationale, the Constitutional scheme envisages the joint participation of the Congress and the executive in determining the scale and duration of hostilities. . . .

> As to the power to conduct undeclared hostilities beyond emergency defense, then, we are inclined to believe that the Constitution, in giving some essential powers to Congress and others to the executive, committed the matter to both branches, whose joint concord precludes the judiciary from measuring a specific executive action against any specific clause in isolation. In arriving at this conclusion we are aware that while we have addressed the problem of justiciability in the light of the textual commitment criterion, we have also addressed the merits of the constitutional issue. [*Id.* at 31-33.]

The court found the requisite joint concord in Congress's appropriation of billions of dollars over a number of years to support the war effort. In short, *Massachusetts v. Laird* found a constitutional requirement for collaboration between the political branches in a "textually demonstrable commitment" to those two branches, while the *Orlando* court found it in a judicially "discoverable and manageable standard" in the Declaration Clause.

With the tests in *Orlando* and *Massachusetts v. Laird* compare this suggested alternative:

> Congressional authorization need not be by formal declaration of war. . . . A joint resolution, signed by the President, is the most tenable method of authorizing the use of force today. To be meaningful, the resolution should be passed only after Congress is aware of the basic elements of the situation, and has had reasonable time to consider their implications. The resolution should not, as a rule, be a blank check leaving the place, purpose and duration of hostilities to the President's sole discretion. To be realistic, however, the resolution must leave the Executive wide discretion to respond to changing circumstances. [W. Taylor Reveley III, *Presidential War-Making: Constitutional Prerogative or Usurpation?*, 55 Va. L. Rev. 1243, 1289-1290 (1969).]

Is Reveley's test constitutionally sound? How difficult would it be for the court to apply in a given case? Would the test be satisfied by the Tonkin Gulf Resolution or the subsequent appropriations and selective service legislation or both?

5. Collaboration by Appropriation. An important aspect of Congress's collaboration, according to both the First and Second Circuits, was that it approved the expenditure of very large sums of money for the conduct of the war. Is the courts' analysis consistent with *Greene v. McElroy, supra* p. 101? Could the appropriations be said to have ratified the Executive's actions? Did they meet the requirements for congressional acquiescence? See *supra* pp. 36-44; *see also* John Hart Ely, *War and Responsibility: Constitutional Lessons of Vietnam and Its Aftermath* 27-30 (1993).

6. The Importance of Being First. What is the practical political importance of the plaintiffs' "straitjacket" argument that after the President put U.S. resources and honor on the line, Congress was hard put to pull them back? Should that argument have affected the court's judgment about compliance with the Declare War Clause in Article I? Do you think Congress felt so constrained when it voted for the Gulf of Tonkin Resolution?

7. The Political Importance of the Political Question Doctrine. Invocation of the political question doctrine in many of the Vietnam cases caused great consternation among some commentators. For example, "If the judiciary, the organ of government most fundamentally committed to the vindication of constitutional principle, decides it cannot play its accustomed role in the Vietnam controversy, our basic institutional alternative to lawlessness is lost." Warren F. Schwartz & Wayne McCormack, *The Justiciability of Legal Objections to the American Military Effort in Vietnam*, 46 Tex. L. Rev. 1033, 1036 (1968). Professor Moore, on the other hand, while noting the importance of judicial candor in abstaining in these cases, cautioned against what he called an oversimplification of difficulties inherent in the judicial resolution of such major claims. Moore, *supra* p. 310, at 573.

The nation's highest court maintained sphinx-like silence on the justiciability of the Vietnam War cases. Dissenting from the refusal even to hear *Massachusetts v. Laird*, Justice Douglas complained, "The question of an unconstitutional war is neither academic nor 'political.' This case has raised the question in an adversary setting. It should be settled here and now." 400 U.S. 886, 900 (1970) (Douglas, J., dissenting from denial of leave to file a bill of complaint). Only in *Atlee v. Richardson*, 411 U.S. 911 (1973) (mem.), did the Court affirm (without opinion) a lower court ruling that a test of the constitutionality of the war presented a nonjusticiable political question. Can you guess why the Court decided not even to hear arguments in any of these cases? *See* Rodric B. Schoen, *A Strange Silence: Vietnam and the Supreme Court*, 33 Washburn L.J. 275 (1994).

8. Challenges Based on International Law. What result, on a motion to dismiss, if Orlando had asserted that his orders to Vietnam were unlawful because the United States was waging an aggressive war in violation of international law? In *United States v. Sisson*, 294 F. Supp. 515 (D. Mass. 1968), the court refused to rule on such an assertion, calling the case political and therefore nonjusticiable on grounds that the court (especially a court of the state accused of the violation) was "incapable of eliciting the facts during a war." *Id.* at 517-518; *see also United States v. Berrigan*, 283 F. Supp. 336 (D. Md. 1968), *aff'd*, 417 F.2d 1009 (4th Cir. 1969).

Vietnam Veterans Memorial Wall, Washington, DC.

Getty Images. Photo by Joe Guetzloff.com.

More recently, however, in *Committee of U.S. Citizens Living in Nicaragua v. Reagan*, 859 F.2d 929 (D.C. Cir. 1988), *supra* p. 182, the court indicated that if Congress adopted a foreign policy that violated a peremptory norm of international law, "that policy might well be subject to challenge in domestic court." *Id.* at 941. The court mentioned as examples of such norms the prohibitions on slavery, torture, summary execution, and genocide. And in *Nicaragua v. United States*, 1986 I.C.J. 14, the World Court declared that "the prohibition of the use of force . . . constitutes a conspicuous example of a rule in international law having the character of *jus cogens*." *Id.* at 100 [¶190].

Taking an altogether different tack, an even more recent decision by a different D.C. Circuit panel included the remarkable and much remarked-upon statement that "[t]he international laws of war as a whole have not been implemented domestically by Congress and are therefore not a source of authority for U.S. courts." *Al-Bihani v. Obama*, 590 F.3d 866, 871 (D.C. Cir. 2010). For more on the debate that this assertion provoked, see *infra* p. 915.

B. LIMITING THE SCOPE OF THE VIETNAM WAR

Following the Tet offensive in early 1968, public controversy over U.S. involvement in Indochina grew dramatically. Antiwar demonstrations at the Democratic National Convention in Chicago that year turned violent when police and National Guard troops clashed with protesters, while military intelligence units infiltrated dissident groups for the stated purpose of preventing domestic disorder. Massive demonstrations in cities around the country followed later in the year. Vice President Hubert Humphrey became the Democratic Party nominee for President, first supporting and then renouncing the Johnson administration's policies in Southeast Asia, but not in time to save his candidacy, leaving Richard Nixon to win the election in November by a narrow margin.

During the 1968 election campaign, candidate Nixon pledged to bring the Vietnam War to an end as quickly as possible. President Nixon described his progress in fulfilling that promise in a speech to the nation on April 7, 1971:

> When I left Washington in January of 1961 after serving 8 years as Vice President under President Eisenhower, there were no American combat forces in Vietnam. No Americans had died in combat in Vietnam.
>
> When I returned to Washington as President 8 years later, there were 540,000 American troops in Vietnam. Thirty-one thousand had died there. Three hundred Americans were being lost every week and there was no comprehensive plan to end the United States involvement in the war.
>
> . . . In June of 1969, I announced a withdrawal of 25,000 men; in September, 40,000; December, 50,000; April of 1970, 150,000. By the first of next month, May 1, I will have brought home more than 265,000 Americans — almost half of the troops in Vietnam when I took office. [Richard M. Nixon, Address to the Nation on the Situation in Southeast Asia, 1 Pub. Papers 522, 523 (Apr. 7, 1971).]

The President then announced that he would pull out an additional 100,000 American troops before the end of 1971. *Id.* at 524.

The pace of withdrawal was not quick enough for many. Questions about the moral basis for the war multiplied with the revelation that U.S. troops had massacred 347 civilians in the village of My Lai in 1968. Pressure for ending the war reached a crescendo with the publication of the *Pentagon Papers* in June 1971.

Key to President Nixon's plans for winding down the war was a process called "Vietnamization." It was hoped that after U.S. troops were withdrawn, U.S. political objectives in Vietnam still might be achieved if only South Vietnamese forces were better able to defend themselves, so in 1969 large quantities of modern military supplies were shipped to the Saigon government for that purpose.

Meanwhile, President Nixon decided to launch air strikes across the Cambodian border against a massing of North Vietnamese troops there. The extension of U.S. might into new territory was necessary, he reasoned, to ensure the safety of U.S. forces in South Vietnam and to signal his resolve to the North Vietnamese. But the bombing was kept secret from the American people, from all but a few members of Congress, and even from many in the Pentagon. Then on April 30, 1970, President Nixon announced to the nation that 20,000 U.S. and South Vietnamese troops supported by U.S. aircraft had attacked Viet Cong and North Vietnamese bases inside Cambodia.

The President's announcement caused a spasm of protest in this country. Demonstrators at Kent State University were met by National Guard troops called out by the Ohio governor, and in the ensuing clash four students were shot and killed. In the days following, hundreds of other universities were forced by student and faculty strikes to close down, and 100,000 protestors marched on government buildings in Washington.

The Senate, but not the House, then passed the Cooper-Church Amendment to the Foreign Military Sales Act. *See* S. Rep. No. 91-865, at 15 (1970), *reprinted in* 1970 U.S.C.C.A.N. 6054, 6069. It would have prohibited expenditures from any source for "retaining United States forces in Cambodia" or "conducting any combat activity in the air above Cambodia in support of Cambodian forces." Then, in January 1971, Congress passed and the President agreed to the following amendment to the Supplemental Foreign Assistance Authorization of 1971:

> In line with the expressed intention of the President . . . , none of the funds authorized or appropriated pursuant to this or any other Act may be used to finance the introduction of United States ground combat troops into Cambodia, or to provide United States advisers to or for Cambodian military forces in Cambodia. [Pub. L. No. 91-652, §7, 85 Stat. 1942, 1943 (1971).]

Much earlier, in 1961, President Kennedy had sent a small covert U.S. force to Laos in an effort to contain a Communist Pathet Lao insurgency there supported by North Vietnam. Following a second Geneva Agreement the following year, which called for withdrawal of foreign troops, the United States withdrew its uniformed military personnel, but it continued to support a "secret" army of some 70,000 Hmong tribesmen and as many as 21,000 Thai "volunteers." This large force was financed, trained, supplied, transported, and sometimes accompanied into battle by CIA operatives, many of whom were former U.S. Army Green Berets. In addition, between 1967 and 1972, U.S. military units based in South Vietnam apparently crossed the border more than 1,000 times to fight in Laos.

In June 1964, the United States began bombing operations in northern Laos to support the "secret" army and to try to interrupt the Ho Chi Minh Trail in the Laotian panhandle. By the time the attacks stopped nine years later, U.S. planes had dropped between 1.6 and 2 million tons of bombs in Laos, more than were released over Germany and Japan during all of World War II. Congress and the American public were kept in substantial ignorance of these developments.

Anxious about increasing U.S. military involvement in Southeast Asia and skeptical about President Nixon's assurances to the contrary, Congress passed this amendment to the Department of Defense Appropriation Act, 1970: "In line with the expressed intention of the President of the United States, none of the funds appropriated by this Act shall be used to finance the introduction of American ground combat troops into Laos or Thailand." Pub. L. No. 91-171, §643, 83 Stat. 469, 487 (1969).

In February 1971, President Nixon, observing the strict language of the amendment, approved the invasion of northern Laos by a 30,000-troop South Vietnamese force supported by U.S. helicopters and bombers. This attempt to cut off troops and matériel from the Ho Chi Minh Trail ended in failure, and there was the predictable outcry that the war had been expanded without authorization from Congress.

Notes and Questions

1. Mutual Participation in a Secret War? What was the source of the President's authority to extend U.S. military might into Cambodia and Laos? Can it be found in the language of the Gulf of Tonkin Resolution? Did other congressional acts constitute "some mutual participation" or "joint concord" between the political branches to authorize these incursions without full knowledge on the part of Congress?

2. Inherent Tactical Authority? Did the President's Article II powers alone furnish the needed authority? Assistant Attorney General William Rehnquist, then the head of the Office of Legal Counsel, offered this legal rationale for the introduction of U.S. ground forces into Cambodia:

> The President's determination to authorize incursion into these Cambodian border areas is precisely the sort of tactical decision traditionally confided to the Commander-in-Chief in the conduct of armed conflict. . . . Faced with a substantial troop commitment to such hostilities made by the previous Chief Executive, and approved by successive Congresses, President Nixon had an obligation as Commander-in-Chief of the Armed Forces to take what steps he deemed necessary to assure their safety in the field. . . . It is a decision made during the course of an armed conflict already commenced as to how that conflict will be conducted, rather than a determination that some new and previously unauthorized military venture will be taken. [William H. Rehnquist, *The Constitutional Issues — Administration Position*, 45 N.Y.U. L. Rev. 628, 638-639 (1970).]

Do you agree with Rehnquist's analysis? Does it contain a standard for distinguishing between tactical decisions and those that need advance approval from Congress?

3. Area and Use Limitations. May Congress properly approve the induction of troops and the purchase of military supplies, then restrict the President's use of those forces in certain areas? Could it limit the President's use of some weaponry? Congress has occasionally adopted such limitations — for example, in the Selective Service Act of 1940, Pub. L. No. 76-783, 54 Stat. 885 (1940), which prohibited the assignment of U.S. conscripts to duty outside the Western Hemisphere, except in U.S. possessions. Do the Supreme Court's early decisions in *Little v. Barreme*, 6 U.S. (2 Cranch) 170 (1804), *supra* p. 63, and *Bas v. Tingy*, 4 U.S. (4 Dall.) 37 (1800), *supra* p. 85, suggest answers?

Military leaders repeatedly urged Presidents Kennedy and Johnson to authorize the use of nuclear weapons in Vietnam, even though such use was thought to present the risk that China would be drawn into the conflict. Might Congress have barred such use? See *infra* pp. 457-464.

4. Border "Incursions" and International Law. Were U.S. and South Vietnamese military activities in Laos and Cambodia permissible defensive measures incident to the defense of South Vietnam according to international law principles? Or did they represent naked aggression against the territories of two neutral sovereign states?

On the one hand, Cambodia was accused of violating its duty as a neutral to expel Viet Cong and North Vietnamese forces operating from its territory, although as a practical matter it hardly seemed capable of doing so. On the other hand, Cambodia was said to be justified by Article 51 of the U.N. Charter in requesting U.S. assistance to defend against attack from those same forces. For their part, North Vietnam and the Viet Cong were charged with violating Cambodian and Laotian neutrality and with ignoring the requirements of the second Geneva Agreement concerning withdrawal of foreign troops from Laos. These violations, as well as the need to defend South Vietnamese territory, were said to justify the actions in question.

C. ENDING THE VIETNAM WAR

In 1971, Senator Fulbright opened hearings to consider various proposed measures to end the Vietnam War with this statement: "Under our system Congress, and especially the Senate, shares responsibility with the President for making our Nation's foreign policy. This war, however, started and continues as a Presidential war in which the Congress, since the fraudulent Gulf of Tonkin episode, has not played a significant role." *Legislative Proposals Relating to the War in Southeast Asia: Hearings Before the S. Comm. on Foreign Relations*, 92d Cong. 21 (Comm. Print 1971). But it turned out to be much easier to unleash Jefferson's metaphorical "dog of war" than to get it back into its kennel.

1. Repeal of the Gulf of Tonkin Resolution

Several months earlier, spurred by public dissent and frustrated by President Nixon's decision to invade Cambodia, Congress had voted to repeal the Gulf of Tonkin Resolution by a single sentence attached to an unrelated measure. Pub. L. No. 91-672, §12, 84 Stat. 2053, 2055 (1971). In another case challenging the President's orders for deployment to Vietnam, an Army draftee argued that the repeal eliminated the congressional "mutual participation" on which the *Orlando* court based its finding of presidential authority. *DaCosta v. Laird* (*DaCosta I*), 448 F.2d 1368 (2d Cir. 1971). The *DaCosta I* court concluded, however, that "there was sufficient legislative action in extending the Selective Service Act and in appropriating billions of dollars to carry on military and naval operations in Vietnam to ratify and approve the measures taken by the Executive, even in the absence of the Gulf of Tonkin Resolution." *Id.* at 1369. Calling the case political and therefore nonjusticiable, the court went on to declare, "It was not the intent of Congress in passing the repeal amendment to bring all military operations in Vietnam to an abrupt halt. The Executive was then endeavoring to unwind the conflict as rapidly as it was feasible to do so." *Id.* at 1369.

Notes and Questions

1. *Unwinding the Conflict?* How did the court know that it was not the intent of Congress to halt all military operations immediately when it repealed the Gulf of Tonkin Resolution?

Why did Congress not express its intentions more clearly? The court in *DaCosta I* seemed to characterize the repealer simply as a kind of legislative housekeeping, although Congress has rarely been so fastidious. *Compare* Van Alstyne, *supra* p. 310, 121 U. Pa. L. Rev. at 20-21, 27-28 (authority for war revoked), *with* Ely, *War and Responsibility, supra* p. 318, at 33 ("just more of Congress's playing Pontius Pilate").

How did the court know that the Executive was endeavoring to unwind the conflict as rapidly as possible? Was it because the President publicly said so? Should the court have decided a case of such moment simply on the assurance of one of the parties to the controversy? What if it could have been demonstrated that the President's statement did not reveal the whole truth, or even that he had deliberately lied? Do you think the court would then have been willing to declare the war effort unconstitutional, since the legitimacy of the war depended on "joint concord" or "some mutual participation" between the President and Congress?

2. *The Straightjacket Redux.* Unlike the *DaCosta I* court, the court in *Mitchell v. Laird*, 488 F.2d 611 (D.C. Cir. 1973), refused to characterize other legislation as "approval or ratification of a war already being waged at the direction of the President alone." *Id.* at 615.

> This court cannot be unmindful of what every schoolboy knows: that in voting to appropriate money or to draft men a Congressman is not necessarily approving of the continuation of a war no matter how specifically the appropriation or draft act refers to that war. A Congressman wholly opposed to the war's commencement and continuation might vote for the military appropriations and for the draft measures because he was unwilling to abandon without support men already fighting. An honorable, decent, compassionate act of aiding those already in peril is no proof of consent to the actions that placed and continued them in that dangerous posture. We should not construe votes cast in pity and piety as though they were votes freely given to express consent. [*Id.*]

Does the *Mitchell* court's theory help to explain why Congress continued to pour troops and matériel into the war effort year after year? Does the phenomenon described by the court raise doubts about the feasibility of inferring congressional authorization or ratification from "mere" appropriations?

2. Winding Up to Wind Down

Like the war itself, peace talks that began in Paris in 1968 seemed to drag on interminably as first one side and then the other hoped to gain some advantage at the bargaining table from success on the battlefield. In February 1970, direct, secret talks began between National Security Adviser Henry Kissinger and North Vietnamese envoy Le Duc Tho, but those negotiations, too, moved slowly. At the end of March 1972, North Vietnamese regulars and the Viet Cong launched a new coordinated offensive in the South. Only 6,000 Americans remaining in the country were equipped for combat, while more than a million South Vietnamese were under arms. President Nixon decided that the only way to conclude peace talks on favorable terms was to finally cut off the flow of war matériel from the Soviet Union and China to North Vietnam — not by a diplomatic initiative but by forcibly closing the northern seaports. To that end, in May the President ordered the mining of the ports and harbors of North Vietnam and the continuation of air and naval strikes against military targets north of the 17th parallel.

The expanded use of force produced yet another challenge in court. The plaintiff argued that "the President's conduct has so altered the course of hostilities in Vietnam as to make the war as it is currently pursued different from the war . . . held in *Orlando* and *DaCosta* [*I*] to have been constitutionally ratified and authorized by Congress." *DaCosta v. Laird* (*DaCosta III*), 471 F.2d 1146, 1154 (2d Cir. 1973). The court again dismissed the suit on political question grounds, this time citing a lack of discoverable and manageable judicial standards:

> Judges, deficient in military knowledge, lacking vital information upon which to assess the nature of battlefield decisions, and sitting thousands of miles from the field of action, cannot reasonably or appropriately determine whether a specific military operation constitutes an "escalation" of the war or is merely a new tactical approach within a continuing strategic plan. [*Id.* at 1155.]

In the late fall of 1971, following the publication of the *Pentagon Papers,* Congress passed and the President signed a defense appropriations measure, to which was attached the Mansfield Amendment, named after its Senate sponsor. It provided, in part:

> It is hereby declared to be the policy of the United States to terminate at the earliest possible date all military operations of the United States in Indochina, and to provide for the prompt and orderly withdrawal of all United States military forces at a date certain, subject to the release of all American prisoners of war held by the government of North Vietnam and forces allied with such Government and an accounting for all Americans missing in action who have been held by or known to such Government or such forces. . . . [Pub. L. No. 92-156, §601(a), 85 Stat. 423, 430 (1971).]

The failure of Congress to employ more forceful language merely reflected the contentious political climate in the country at the time.

3. Cutting Off Funding for the War

In the summer of 1972 Le Duc Tho met again in Paris with Dr. Kissinger. When their negotiations broke down, President Nixon ordered yet another round of bombing in the North, and in late December U.S. B-52s and other aircraft dropped 40,000 tons of bombs on the area between Hanoi and Haiphong. Then on January 27, 1973, a formal peace agreement was signed in Paris. The last U.S. troops left South Vietnam on March 29, 1973, and the last U.S. prisoners of war were allegedly released in Hanoi on April 1.

Meanwhile, when an effort to end fighting between the Khmer Rouge and Cambodian government ended in failure early in the same year, U.S. forces began saturation bombing of Communist positions there. But a majority in Congress had finally had enough, and on May 31 it approved a bill containing the following amendment by Senator Thomas Eagleton:

> None of the funds herein appropriated under this Act or heretofore appropriated under any other Act may be expended to support directly or indirectly combat activities in, over

or from off the shores of Cambodia or in or over Laos by United States forces. [29 Cong. Q. Almanac 95, 102 (1973).]

President Nixon vetoed the bill on June 27, complaining that it would interfere with chances for a negotiated settlement in Cambodia, and the House failed to override his veto. Then at the end of June, in a compromise, Congress approved and the President signed a measure to end all further U.S. military involvement in Southeast Asia:

Joint Resolution Making Continuing Appropriations for Fiscal Year 1974

Pub. L. No. 93-52, §108, 87 Stat. 130, 134 (1973)

Notwithstanding any other provision of law, on or after August 15, 1973, no funds herein or heretofore appropriated may be obligated or expended to finance directly or indirectly combat activities by United States military forces in or over or from off the shores of North Vietnam, South Vietnam, Laos or Cambodia.

On July 25, a federal district court issued an unprecedented injunction ordering the President and military personnel to stop combat operations in Cambodia, after finding that those operations were not authorized by Congress. *Holtzman v. Schlesinger*, 361 F. Supp. 553 (E.D.N.Y. 1973). The court also remarked that "[t]he bombing of Cambodia in July 1973 is not 'the sort of tactical decision traditionally confided to the Commander-in-Chief in the conduct of armed conflict,' as once described by then Assistant Attorney General Rehnquist." *Id.* at 563.

Two weeks after that, the court of appeals (which had stayed the injunction pending appeal) reversed: "While we as men may well agonize and bewail the horror of this or any war, the sharing of Presidential and Congressional responsibility particularly at this juncture is a bluntly political and not a judicial question." 484 F.2d 1307, 1311 (2d Cir. 1973). Concerning the joint resolution set forth above, the court offered this observation: "Assuming arguendo that the military and diplomatic issues were manageable and that we were obliged to find some participation by Congress, we cannot see how this provision does not support the proposition that the Congress has approved the Cambodian bombing. The statute is facially clear. . . . " *Id.* at 1313.

The congressional plaintiff, Elizabeth Holtzman, argued that "since the Constitution entrusts the power to declare war to a majority of the Congress, the veto exercised makes it possible for the President to thwart the will of Congress by holding one-third plus one of the members of either House." *Id.* at 1313-1314. The court responded:

> We cannot agree that the Congress was "coerced" by the President's veto. There was unquestionably a Congressional impasse resulting from the desire of a majority of Congress to stop bombing immediately and the desire of the President that his discretion be unfettered by an arbitrarily selected date. Instead of an acute constitutional confrontation, . . . an "agreement" was reached. . . .

> While the Constitution vests the war declaring authority in the Congress, the Founding Fathers also conferred the veto power upon the President. (Art. I, §7, cl. 2). The suggestion that the veto power is impotent with respect to an authority vested solely in Congress by the Constitution is unsupported by any citation of authority and is hardly persuasive. [*Id.* at 1314.]

Notes and Questions

1. *Vetoing Peace?* Is there any reason to suspect that the presidential veto process described in Article I, section 7, of the Constitution does not apply to congressional war making, as it does to other congressional acts? Should it matter that a particular act of Congress could be viewed not as war making, but as peacemaking — that it might take two-thirds of Congress to stop a war already begun? Should the appellate court have been influenced by remarks during the Philadelphia Convention of George Mason, who was "for clogging rather than facilitating war; but for facilitating peace," and of Oliver Ellsworth, that "[i]t shld. be more easy to get out of war, than into it" (*supra* p. 18)?

2. *Judicial Realpolitik? Holtzman v. Schlesinger* was heard in a highly charged political atmosphere, exacerbated by an unusually public battle between Justices Thurgood Marshall and William O. Douglas over whether the district court's injunction should be stayed pending the government's appeal. *See Schlesinger v. Holtzman,* 414 U.S. 1321 (Marshall, Circuit Justice 1973). Newspaper headlines were filled with the story of secret bombings, and the threat of impeachment proceedings was in the air. Although the Executive protested that Congress had no right to fetter its use of force, the Secretary of State submitted an affidavit to the court committing the government to a termination of the bombing on August 15, only seven days after the *Holtzman* case was decided on the merits by the Second Circuit. Do you think these circumstances influenced the court's decision? Should they have?

U.S. bombing in Cambodia was halted on August 14, 1973, in accordance with the congressional mandate. In spite of the ceasefire prescribed in the Paris peace agreement, forces on both sides moved quickly to consolidate their holdings in the South, but by the summer of 1974 Viet Cong and North Vietnamese troops had recaptured all of the ground they had lost earlier. U.S. support for the Saigon regime was reduced sharply after President Nixon resigned in August 1974, while the North Vietnamese poured new troops and supplies into the South for a climactic assault. Finally, Communist troops entered Saigon on April 30, 1975, bringing the war to an end.

When it was all over, 58,220 U.S. servicemembers had lost their lives in the war, and more than 150,000 were wounded. Vietnam estimated that 1.1 million North Vietnamese and Viet Cong fighters died, and that as many as 2 million civilians on both sides perished.

The American people were — and remain today — deeply divided about the war. Many were disillusioned about the failure of five Presidents to reveal the enormous scope of the U.S. military commitment in Southeast Asia. The public's aversion to a new involvement in protracted armed conflict is sometimes called the "Vietnam Syndrome." It also affected many members of Congress. In 1973, Congress sought to reclaim its war-making authority by enactment of the War Powers Resolution over President Nixon's veto. See *supra* pp. 89-99. The Vietnam War has also had a profound, lasting influence on thinking about U.S. war-making policy, as we will see in the chapters ahead.

HOW WE GO TO WAR: LESSONS FROM VIETNAM SUMMARY OF BASIC PRINCIPLES

- A major commitment of U.S. armed forces to a conflict abroad does not require a formal declaration of war, but it does require "some mutual participation" by the two political branches in the decision to do so.

- Courts in the Vietnam-era cases generally were willing to rule on the constitutional sufficiency of the collaboration between the political branches.

- The adequacy of the *form* of that collaboration, however, which included the Tonkin Gulf Resolution, measures to extend the draft, and appropriations, was a nonjusticiable political question.

- Statutory authorizations for the use of force may be cast in very broad terms, such as "all necessary measures," leaving in doubt Congress's intentions regarding the magnitude, geographical scope, duration, or weaponry to be used in a conflict.

- The constitutionality of such broad delegations of authority has not been tested in court.

- The scope of Congress's authority to limit a President's conduct of a war underway have not yet been clearly established.

- Whether, as a matter of international law, the United States was justified in its military actions in Southeast Asia depends in part upon whether those actions are characterized as an act of collective self-defense under Article 51 of the U.N. Charter or as intervention in a civil war without U.N. Security Council approval.

Collective Use of Force

The transcendent purpose of the United Nations Charter is to make war less likely or, if war breaks out, to end it as quickly as possible. It seeks to do so primarily by expressing the signing states' shared commitment to "refrain in their international relations from the threat or use of force against the territorial integrity or political independence of any state." U.N. Charter art. 2(4).

The signers of the Charter were acutely aware, however, that peace was a work in progress. They knew that some institutional mechanism was needed to abate the threat or use of force, and to help restore order if armed conflict erupted. They also recognized that military force might be necessary to preserve or bring about peace. They understood, as well, that a decision to employ force ought to be undertaken deliberately and only as a last resort, and that the resulting violence would likely be more limited and purposeful if it required the agreement of many nations acting together. Thus, Articles 39-43 of the Charter spell out standards and procedures for the use of force under the authority of the United Nations, as we saw in Chapter 8.

Nevertheless, the U.N. Charter would not have been signed without an understanding that in some instances states should not have to wait for the deliberative mechanism spelled out in Article 39 of the Charter to respond militarily to an emerging threat or an act of aggression. Accordingly, Article 51 preserves the universally recognized right of every state, or of states collaboratively, to act in self-defense.

In this chapter we consider the application of these provisions in three large-scale conflicts in which the United States played a leading role — the Korean War, the 1991 Persian Gulf War, and the war in Afghanistan against Al Qaeda and the Taliban. We also introduce the North Atlantic Treaty Organization (NATO) as an example of a regional organization operating under the auspices of the Security Council. Each of these case studies raises important questions of legitimacy under international as well as domestic law. All three offer important lessons about the interactions of these two sources of law, and about the correlative roles of the President, Congress, and U.S. courts in deciding to use military force abroad.

A. THE KOREAN "POLICE ACTION"[1]

1. The Outbreak of War

In 1943, while Korea was still occupied by the Japanese, President Roosevelt, Prime Minister Churchill, and Generalissimo Chiang Kai-shek announced in the Cairo Declaration that Korea would "in due course" be free and independent. Two years later, at the Potsdam Conference in July 1945, it was agreed that at war's end the United States would occupy the Korean peninsula south of the 38th parallel, while the Soviets would take over the area north to Korea's border with China. United Nations — sponsored efforts to establish a unified democratic government soon broke down, leaving the two major powers to sponsor their own politically sympathetic governments led, respectively, by Syngman Rhee in the South and Kim Il Sung in the North. Each one eventually claimed to represent all of Korea.

Early on the morning of Sunday, June 25, 1950 (local time), without any warning, North Korean forces launched a massive invasion of the South. A 500-man U.S. military assistance group was stationed in South Korea at the time. Later the same day, a U.S.-sponsored resolution of the U.N. Security Council called on North Korea to stop its aggression and asked member states to "render every assistance to the United Nations in the execution of this resolution." S.C. Res. 82, U.N. Doc. S/INF/4/Rev. 1 (1950). The Soviet Union, which presumably would have vetoed the resolution, was boycotting the Security Council at the time to protest Nationalist Chinese representation of China at the United Nations. The vote was 9-0 in favor of the resolution, with one abstention.

2. The President's Response

Before the day ended, President Truman ordered U.S. air and naval forces to assist in the evacuation of American dependents and noncombatants from Korea. The next day, June 26, as the military situation quickly deteriorated, the President directed U.S. forces, including warplanes, to provide support for South Korean troops. He announced his decision to the American people the day after that. Later on June 27, the U.N. Security Council adopted a second resolution in which it "recommended" that member states "furnish such assistance to the Republic of Korea as may be necessary to repel the armed attack and to restore international peace and security in the area." S.C. Res. 83, U.N. Doc. S/INF/4/Rev. 1 (1950).

Although Congress was in session at the time of the North Korean invasion, President Truman waited until June 27 to brief congressional leaders on the conflict — after he had ordered U.S. forces into combat. On June 29 and 30, the President approved U.S. air strikes against North Korea and directed the deployment of U.S. ground combat forces. But he elected not to ask Congress to approve any of these actions, fearing

1. Background for this study was drawn in part from Max Hastings, *The Korean War* (1987); Burton I. Kaufman, *The Korean War: Challenge in Crisis, Credibility, and Command* (1986); Callum A. MacDonald, *Korea: The War Before Vietnam* (1986); Glenn D. Paige, *The Korean Decision, June 24-30, 1950* (1968); David Rees, *Korea: The Limited War* (1964); James L. Stokesbury, *A Short History of the Korean War* (1988); Jane E. Stromseth, *Rethinking War Powers: Congress, the President, and the United Nations*, 81 Geo. L.J. 597, 621-640 (1993); A. Kenneth Pye, *The Legal Status of the Korean Hostilities*, 45 Geo. L.J. 45 (1956); and Dean Acheson, *Review of U.N. and U.S. Action to Restore Peace*, 23 Dep't St. Bull. 43 (1950).

that an extended public debate might weaken the American effort to blunt this first major Communist aggression in the Far East.

Almost every member of Congress publicly supported the substance of the President's decision to act promptly to repel the North Korean attack. Still, some worried about Congress's exclusion from the process of deciding to enter the conflict. Responding to that concern, a July 3 State Department memorandum declared:

> The President, as Commander in Chief of the Armed Forces of the United States, has full control over the use thereof. He also has authority to conduct the foreign relations of the United States. Since the beginning of United States history, he has, upon numerous occasions, utilized these powers in sending armed forces abroad. The preservation of the United Nations for the maintenance of peace is a cardinal interest of the United States. Both traditional international law and Article 39 of the United Nations Charter and the resolution pursuant thereto authorize the United States to repel the armed aggression against the Republic of Korea. [*Authority of the President to Repel the Attack in Korea,* 23 Dep't St. Bull. 173, 173 (1950).]

The memorandum called North Korean defiance of the Security Council resolutions "a threat to the peace and security of the United States and to the security of United States forces in the Pacific." *Id.* at 177. The memorandum also cited 85 earlier instances in which Presidents had used military force abroad without a declaration of war. The President's supporters referred to the Korean conflict as a "police action" rather than a war, to suggest that congressional approval was not required.

Despite some members' misgivings, in the days and weeks that followed the invasion, Congress tacitly approved President Truman's actions. On June 27, it voted overwhelmingly to approve an extension of the draft, a matter on which it had been sharply divided earlier. Congress also lifted the ceiling on the size of the armed forces, and it increased taxes to help pay for the war. In early September it gave the President extensive new powers to manage the wartime economy in the Defense Production Act of 1950, 64 Stat. 798, codified as amended at 50 U.S.C. §§4501-4568 (2018), stating, for example, that the President is authorized to "allocate materials, services, and facilities in such manner . . . as he shall deem necessary or appropriate to promote the national defense." *Id.* §4511(a).

The first U.S. ground forces arrived in Korea on July 1. One week later, the Security Council adopted a third resolution placing all forces defending South Korea under the unified command of the United States. The fighting ended three years later where it had started, with a cease-fire along the 38th parallel. The United States had suffered 33,629 killed and more than 100,000 wounded. Some 50,000 South Korean troops were killed. The exact extent of North Korean losses is still unknown.

Notes and Questions

1. *Source of the President's Domestic Authority?* If you had written the July 3, 1950 State Department memorandum excerpted above, what authority would you have cited for the President's claim to have "full control" over the use of the armed forces? Could you argue that Congress lacked authority to *stop* him from sending U.S. troops to Korea?

2. *A Role for Congress or the Courts?* What is the significance of President Truman's decision not to ask Congress for its approval of his actions, even retrospectively? How, if at all, was the President's domestic authority affected by the United Nations Participation Act, *supra* p. 247?

Did subsequent legislation extending the draft and financing the war effort cure any constitutional deficiency? Is there any doubt in your mind that there was "some mutual participation" between the President and Congress, as that term was used in *Orlando v. Laird, supra* p. 314? If the War Powers Resolution of 1973 (*supra* p. 90) had been in effect, how might it have affected domestic legal authority for the conflict?

3. *A Paradigm Shift?* The Korean conflict was different from the later one in Indochina in several ways that might bear on the legality of President Truman's actions. Can you say how? Consider the relevant treaties, legislation, and the scope and duration of the hostilities.

In 1966, early in the Vietnam War, the State Department Legal Adviser cited the Korean War as precedent for the President's exercise of inherent Article II power to send U.S. forces into battle without first getting Congress's approval. See *supra* p. 306. Professor Moore called it "a poor precedent." John Norton Moore, *Law and the Indo-China War* 557 (1972). The Korean War was cited again in 1990 by members of the first Bush administration, who argued that the President did not need Congress's approval for offensive military action in the Persian Gulf War.

What is the value of Korea as a precedent for the unilateral executive use of force? What effect, if any, do you think enactment of the 1973 War Powers Resolution had on this precedent?

4. *The U.N. Security Council's Role.* Note the exceptions in Chapter VII of the U.N. Charter to the general prohibition in Article 2(4) of the threat or use of force by one state against another, *supra* pp. 243-244. Which provisions do you think authorized the U.N. Security Council resolutions responding to the North Korean invasion?

The June 27, 1950 Security Council resolution "recommended" that member states furnish military assistance to South Korea. Why do you suppose the resolution took the form of a recommendation rather than an authorization or directive? Do you think the choice of words had any legal significance? Does it matter, for purposes of international law, that President Truman ordered U.S. military forces into action *before* the Security Council adopted its June 27 resolution?

What did the Security Council authorize when, in Resolution 83, it recommended that member states "furnish such assistance to the Republic of Korea as may be necessary to repel the armed attack and to restore international peace and security in the area"? Did it mean, for example, that forces coming to the aid of South Korea could push north of the 38th parallel?

5. *Collective Self-Defense?* Did President Truman get the international law authority he needed from Article 51, which approves acts of collective self-defense "until the Security Council has taken measures necessary to maintain international peace and security"? Might Article 51 have provided justification for President Truman's deployment of troops to Korea even *after* the June 27 Security Council resolution?

B. THE 1991 PERSIAN GULF WAR[2]

1. The Invasion of Kuwait

CIA map of Kuwait

In 1990, Iraq boasted the world's second-largest oil reserves and fourth-largest army, which had been battle-tested in a multiyear war with Iran. Iraq and Kuwait had long disputed drilling rights to large oil fields that lie near their common border. Asserting that Kuwait was extracting oil from fields that lay partly in Iraq, that Kuwait was not paying its fair share of the costs of defending the area from Iran, and that some Kuwaiti territory belonged to Iraq, Iraq invaded Kuwait on August 2, 1990. More than 100,000 Iraqi troops quickly occupied Kuwait and detained many foreigners, including some 2,500 Americans. Eventually, the Iraqi troop level in the Kuwait theater reached 450,000, substantially more than were needed to garrison Kuwait, posing a serious threat to the adjacent kingdom of Saudi Arabia, a long-time U.S. ally in the Middle East.

2. Operation Desert Shield

"For forty years after the United Nations authorized the use of force in Korea, Cold War tensions rendered the collective security machinery of the U.N. Charter largely unusable. On August 2, 1990, however, . . . the Security Council took united action." Stromseth, *supra* p. 330, 81 Geo. L.J. at 640. Acting expressly under Articles 39 and 40, the Security Council adopted a resolution declaring a breach of international peace and security, condemning the invasion, and demanding Iraq's immediate and unconditional withdrawal. S.C. Res. 660, U.N. Doc. S/RES/660 (Aug. 2, 1990). Four days later, the Security Council imposed a trade embargo on Iraq. S.C. Res. 661, U.N. Doc. S/RES/661 (Aug. 6, 1990). Over the next several months, additional resolutions declared the purported Iraqi annexation of Kuwait null and void, demanded release of third-state nationals, approved a maritime blockade, and cut off air transport in and out of Iraq and Kuwait.

Determined not to appease Saddam Hussein, who was Iraq's military leader, President George H.W. Bush acted quickly to enforce the embargo imposed by Resolution

---

2. This study is drawn in part from Rick Atkinson, *Crusade* (1993); Bob Woodward, *The Commanders* (1991); Lawrence Freedman & Efraim Karsh, *The Gulf Conflict, 1990-1991: Diplomacy and War in the New World Order* (1993); *Gulf War Legal and Diplomatic Documents*, 13 Hous. J. Int'l L. 281 (1991); and *Iraqi Symposium*, 15 S. Ill. U. L.J. 411 (1991).

661. He also dispatched elements of the 82nd Airborne Division and the U.S. Air Force to Saudi Arabia on August 8, commencing what became known as Operation Desert Shield. Although he asserted that the mission of the U.S. forces was "wholly defensive," he declared that the United States sought "the immediate and unconditional withdrawal of all Iraqi forces from Kuwait," restoration of the legitimate Kuwaiti government, security in the Gulf, and protection of Americans in Kuwait.

Congress was in recess at the time, and the President did not call it back. On August 10, however, he sent a letter to the Speaker of the House and the President Pro Tempore of the Senate "in accordance with my desire that Congress be fully informed and consistent with the War Powers Resolution." The letter stated that he had dispatched U.S. forces "equipped for combat" to respond to the Iraqi "threat" along the Kuwaiti-Saudi Arabian border, "pursuant to my constitutional authority to conduct our foreign relations and as Commander in Chief." He added that he did "not believe that involvement in hostilities is imminent." 26 Weekly Comp. Pres. Docs. 1225, 1225 (Aug. 9, 1990).

On August 28, President Bush briefed selected members of Congress at the White House about Operation Desert Shield. By that time, U.S. military operations in Saudi Arabia had expanded, as American commanders nervously eyed the growing number of Iraqi troops poised at the Saudi border and expressed open concern about the consequences if they crossed.

On October 1, the House of Representatives passed a simple resolution condemning Iraq, reaffirming the objectives asserted by President Bush, affirming its support for the Security Council resolutions, and noting the requirements of the War Powers Resolution. The House also expressed support for

> the President's emphasis on diplomatic efforts, international sanctions, and negotiations under the auspices of the United Nations to achieve the United States objectives. . . . The United States shall continue to emphasize the use of diplomatic and other nonmilitary means in order to achieve those objectives and policies, while maintaining credible United States and multinational deterrent military force. [H.R. Res. 658, §3, 101st Cong. (1990).]

Representative Dante Fascell, Chairman of the House Foreign Affairs Committee, explained that the House resolution was "not a declaration of war," but was intended "to show that the Congress has acted affirmatively." 136 Cong. Rec. H8441 (daily ed., Oct. 1, 1990). The Senate passed its own resolution the following day, "strongly approv[ing] the leadership of the President," and supporting

> continued action by the President in accordance with the decisions of the United Nations Security Council and in accordance with United States constitutional and statutory processes, including authorization and appropriation of funds by the Congress, to deter Iraqi aggression and to protect American lives and vital interests in the region. [S. Res. 147, 101st Cong. (1990).]

Neither resolution was voted on by both Houses.

On October 1, however, Congress did approve supplemental appropriations for Operation Desert Shield, including lines for "military personnel" and "operation and maintenance," without further detail. Pub. L. No. 101-403, 104 Stat. 867 (1990). Five weeks later, on November 5, Congress passed the Iraq Sanctions Act of 1990. Pub. L. No. 101-513, §586A, 104 Stat. 1979, 2047-2048 (1990), declaring its support for "the actions that have been taken by the President in response to . . . [the] invasion," requiring continued consultation with Congress, and approving economic and trade sanctions against Iraq, although it failed to mention the War Powers Resolution.

3. The Buildup

United States and Saudi forces were augmented by troops from other U.N. members who were persuaded (chiefly by U.S. diplomatic efforts) to join the "coalition." United States naval forces patrolled the Persian Gulf, intercepting vessels bound to or from Iraq and Kuwait, in order to enforce the trade embargo. By early November, President Bush had deployed approximately 230,000 U.S. armed forces in Saudi Arabia and the Persian Gulf. Although Iraq had by that time released Americans and other foreigners it had earlier detained, and the threat of further invasion had apparently receded, on November 8 the Administration announced its intention to deploy an additional 150,000 U.S. troops to provide the United States and its allies with what President Bush called an "adequate offensive military option" to oust Iraq from Kuwait. The decision reportedly was made a week earlier, on October 30, but not made public until after the mid-term congressional elections. Secretary of Defense Richard Cheney also rationalized the buildup by emphasizing the coalition forces' ability "to conduct offensive military operations."

On November 29, in a vote widely attributed to the diplomatic efforts of the Bush administration, the Security Council passed the following resolution:

United Nations Security Council Resolution 678

U.N. Doc. S/RES/678 (Nov. 29, 1990)

The Security Council. . .

Noting that, despite all efforts by the United Nations, Iraq refuses to comply with its obligations to implement resolution 660 (1990) and [ten] subsequent relevant resolutions, in flagrant contempt of the Security Council, . . .

Determined to secure full compliance with its decisions,

Acting under Chapter VII of the Charter,

1. *Demands* that Iraq comply fully with resolution 660 (1990) and all subsequent relevant resolutions and decides, while maintaining all its decisions, to allow Iraq one final opportunity, as a pause of good will, to do so;

2. *Authorizes* Member States cooperating with the Government of Kuwait, unless Iraq on or before 15 January 1991 fully implements, as set forth in paragraph 1 above, the above-mentioned resolutions, to use all necessary means to uphold and implement resolution 660 (1990) and all subsequent relevant resolutions and to restore international peace and security in the area;

3. *Requests* all States to provide appropriate support for the actions undertaken in pursuance of paragraph 2 of this resolution. . . .

In short, Resolution 678 established a deadline for Iraqi compliance with Resolution 660 and "all subsequent relevant resolutions," and authorized the use of "all necessary means" to enforce those resolutions thereafter.

During this period, the President did not request any authorization for the use of force from Congress. Asked at a press conference on January 9, 1991, whether he thought he needed such authorization, he replied, "I don't think I need it. . . . I feel that I have the authority to fully implement the United Nations resolutions." 27 Weekly Comp. Pres. Docs. 23, 25 (Jan. 14, 1991). The following year President Bush remarked, "I didn't have to get permission from some old goat in the United States Congress to kick Saddam Hussein out of Kuwait." 28 Weekly Comp. Pres. Docs. 1119, 1120-1121 (June 29, 1992).

4. Operation Desert Storm

Notwithstanding his repeated insistence that he already possessed all the authority he needed to send U.S. troops into battle against Saddam Hussein, in early January the President sent the following letter to congressional leaders:

Letter to Congressional Leaders on the Persian Gulf Crisis

27 Weekly Comp. Pres. Doc. 17 (Jan. 8, 1991)

Dear Mr. Speaker:

The current situation in the Persian Gulf, brought about by Iraq's unprovoked invasion and subsequent brutal occupation of Kuwait, threatens vital U.S. interests. The situation also threatens the peace. It would, however, greatly enhance the chances for peace if Congress were now to go on record supporting the position adopted by the UN Security Council on twelve separate occasions. Such an action would underline that the United States stands with the international community and on the side of law and decency; it also would help dispel any belief that may exist in the minds of Iraq's leaders that the United States lacks the necessary unity to act decisively in response to Iraq's continued aggression against Kuwait. . . .

I therefore request that the House of Representatives and the Senate adopt a Resolution stating that Congress supports the use of all necessary means to implement UN Security Council Resolution 678. Such action would send the clearest possible message to Saddam Hussein that he must withdraw without condition or delay from Kuwait. Anything less would only encourage Iraqi intransigence; anything else would risk detracting from the international coalition arrayed against Iraq's aggression.

Mr. Speaker, I am determined to do whatever is necessary to protect America's security. I ask Congress to join with me in this task. I can think of no better way than for Congress to express its support for the President at this critical time. This truly is the last best chance for peace.

Sincerely,
George Bush

After a dramatic debate four days later, Congress responded by passing the following joint resolution, by a vote of 52-47 in the Senate and 250-183 in the House:

Authorization for Use of Military Force Against Iraq

Pub. L. No. 102-1, 105 Stat. 3 (Jan. 14, 1991)

Joint Resolution to authorize the use of United States Armed Forces pursuant to United Nations Security Council Resolution 678. . . .

Resolved by the Senate and House of Representatives of the United States of America in Congress assembled, . . .

SECTION 2. AUTHORIZATION FOR USE OF UNITED STATES ARMED FORCES

(a) **Authorization.** The President is authorized, subject to subsection (b), to use United States Armed Forces pursuant to United Nations Security Council Resolution 678 (1990) in order to achieve implementation of Security Council Resolutions 660, 661, 662, 664, 665, 666, 667, 669, 670, 674, and 677.

(b) **Requirement for Determination That Use of Military Force Is Necessary.** Before exercising the authority granted in subsection (a), the President shall make available to the Speaker of the House of Representatives and the President pro tempore of the Senate his determination that—

(1) the United States has used all appropriate diplomatic and other peaceful means to obtain compliance by Iraq with the United Nations Security Council resolutions cited in subsection (a); and

(2) that those efforts have not been and would not be successful in obtaining such compliance.

(c) **War Powers Resolution Requirements.**—

(1) Specific Statutory Authorization.—Consistent with section 8(a)(1) of the War Powers Resolution, the Congress declares that this section is intended to constitute specific statutory authorization within the meaning of section 5(b) of the War Powers Resolution. . . .

On January 16, 1991, President Bush reported to Congress that the United Nations had exhausted diplomatic and other peaceful means of obtaining Iraqi compliance with the Security Council's resolutions. The next day, at 2:38 A.M. local time, Army Apache helicopters carrying rockets, missiles, and extra fuel tanks commenced Operation Desert Storm by hitting Iraqi radar sites to help clear the way for more massive attacks by a coalition of forces representing 34 nations, led by the United States. For the next six weeks, coalition aircraft bombed Iraqi military targets and infrastructure, then on February 24 coalition ground forces launched an attack into southern Iraq and Kuwait. By February 26, Iraqi forces were fleeing Kuwait City under fire, and the city was liberated the next day. On February 28, President Bush ordered a halt in the fighting. The war officially ended a month later with Iraqi acceptance of cease-fire terms in U.N. Security Council Resolution 687, U.N. Doc. S/RES/687 (Apr. 3, 1991).

Notes and Questions

1. Role of the U.N. Security Council. U.N. Security Council Resolution 660, adopted on the day Iraqi forces invaded Kuwait, relied expressly on the authority of Articles 39 and 40 of the Charter. All the subsequent resolutions dealing with the crisis either were silent on the source of their authority or simply claimed to be based on Chapter VII, rather than on a specific article. What provisions of the Charter authorized each resolution?

Would the coalition forces led by the United States have been justified, as a matter of international law, in using force to evict Saddam Hussein from Kuwait without any action on the part of the Security Council? By one view, "the military operations of the Coalition in 1991 were a manifestation of collective self-defense," and not dependent on Security Council approval. Thus, "there was technically no need for the specific mandate of Resolution 678 to legally validate the launching of the strikes against Iraq. Article 51 *per se* ought to have sufficed." Yoram Dinstein, *War, Aggression and Self-Defence* 325 (6th ed. 2017). If so, why did the Security Council get involved?

Could Resolution 678 have been interpreted to authorize coalition forces to fight all the way to Baghdad, in order to remove the Saddam Hussein regime? Or perhaps beyond?

2. Domestic Authority for Operation Desert Shield. Upon what domestic authority did President Bush deploy U.S. military forces equipped for combat to the Gulf beginning on August 8, 1990? Did the President's report to congressional leaders two days later start the 60-day clock ticking under War Powers Resolution §5(b) (*supra* p. 91)? Do you think the President complied with the War Powers Resolution? What domestic authorization, if any, did either congressional actions or the U.N. Security Council resolutions give the President for Operation Desert Shield during the fall of 1990?

3. Domestic Authority for Operation Desert Storm. Did President Bush have constitutional authority to launch Operation Desert Storm without congressional approval, as he contended? Consider not only the President's inherent war powers, but also the effect, if any, of various U.N. Security Council resolutions.

Why do you suppose President Bush, after maintaining so emphatically that he needed no congressional approval to order U.S. troops into battle in Iraq, finally decided to send Congress the January 8, 1991, letter set out above? What exactly did the letter request?

Did the President get what he asked for? Did the joint resolution passed on January 12, 1991, give President Bush the authority to annihilate the Iraqi Republican Guards? To carpet-bomb Baghdad? Did that authority change after the Iraqis were driven out of Kuwait?

C. AFGHANISTAN

1. The U.S. Response to 9/11 in Afghanistan

In the immediate aftermath of the terrorist attacks on September 11, 2001, the United States reached out to other nations around the globe for assistance in gathering intelligence about terrorist suspects, apprehending persons believed to be connected with the attacks, freezing their financial assets, and mounting a military response against Al Qaeda in Afghanistan. It also asked for help from international organizations.

On the evening of the 11th, the NATO Council announced:

> The NATO nations unanimously condemn these barbaric acts committed against a NATO member state. The mindless slaughter of so many innocent civilians is an unacceptable act of violence without precedent in the modern era. It underscores the urgency of intensifying the battle against terrorism, a battle that the NATO countries — indeed all civilised nations — must win. All Allies stand united in their determination to combat this scourge. [NATO Press Release PR/CP (2001) 122, Sept. 12, 2001.]

The next day, the U.N. Security Council passed a resolution calling on "all States to work together urgently to bring to justice the perpetrators, organizers, and sponsors of these terrorist attacks." S.C. Res. 1368, U.N. Doc. S/RES/1368 (Sept. 12, 2001). In both Resolution 1368 and Resolution 1373, U.N. Doc. S/RES 1373 (Sept. 28, 2001), which likewise condemned the 9/11 attacks, the Security Council expressly recognized "the inherent right of individual or collective self-defence in accordance with the Charter."

Three days after the attack, Congress passed the joint resolution set forth *supra* p. 88, authorizing the President to

> use all necessary and appropriate force against those nations, organizations, or persons he determines planned, authorized, committed, or aided the terrorist attacks that occurred on September 11, 2001, or harbored such organizations or persons, in order to prevent any future acts of international terrorism against the United States by such nations, organizations or persons. [Authorization for Use of Military Force, Pub. L. No. 107-40, §2(a), 115 Stat. 224, 224 (2001).]

This AUMF has subsequently been invoked as authority for a variety of national security-related U.S. government activities in Afghanistan and elsewhere, only some of which involved the use of military force.

On September 20, the United States issued an ultimatum to the Taliban-led government of Afghanistan to turn over Al Qaeda leaders. When its ultimatum was rejected, the United States wrote to the Security Council on October 7, 2001, to say that it had clear and compelling evidence that Al Qaeda played a central role in the 9/11 attacks. Furthermore, it said, in the exercise of its Article 51 right of self-defense to prevent and deter further attacks, it was initiating military action — Operation Enduring Freedom (OEF) — against Al Qaeda terrorist training camps

Afghanistan CIA Map

Courtesy worldatlas.com.

and Taliban military bases in Afghanistan. Letter from the Permanent Representative of the United States of America to the President of the Security Council, Oct. 7, 2001, 40 I.L.M. 1281 (2001). The letter presumably satisfied Article 51's requirement to report immediately to the Security Council any resort to self-defense. Operation Enduring Freedom eventually drew support from 70 nations.

2. The United Nations' Role

Two years before the terrorist attacks of 9/11, the Security Council determined that the Taliban's provision of sanctuary and training for terrorists inside Afghanistan, as well as its refusal to turn over Osama bin Laden and others for criminal prosecution, posed a threat to international peace and security. It directed member states to bar most Taliban air traffic and to freeze all Taliban financial resources. S.C. Res. 1267, U.N. Doc. S/RES 1267 (Oct. 15, 1999). In December 2000, the Security Council expanded its injunction to halt all non-humanitarian flights in or out of Afghanistan and cut off shipments of arms into the country. S.C. Res. 1333, U.N. Doc. S/RES 1333 (Dec. 19, 2000). Unfortunately, these measures failed to dislodge bin Laden.

By early December 2001, however, the Taliban had been routed from Afghanistan by U.S. and indigenous Afghan forces. The Security Council endorsed the Agreement on Provisional Arrangements in Afghanistan Pending the Re-establishment of Permanent Government Institutions (Bonn Agreement), Dec. 5, 2001, *available at* http://www.afghangovernment.com/AfghanAgreementBonn.htm, to create a new interim government in Kabul led by Hamid Karzai. S.C. Res. 1383, U.N. Doc. S/RES 1383 (Dec. 6, 2001).

Independent of the OEF military deployment led by the United States, the Security Council then authorized the creation of an International Security Assistance Force (ISAF) in Afghanistan, with responsibility for supporting the interim Afghan government in and around Kabul. S.C. Res. 1386, U.N. Doc. S/RES 1386 (Dec. 20, 2001). ISAF's mission was security and stabilization — to disarm the insurgents, train the Afghan police and military, establish the rule of law, help with elections, and combat drug production and trafficking — while that of OEF was counterterrorism. There was, however, significant geographical and functional overlap. The Security Council resolution "call[ed] upon" member states to contribute personnel and equipment to ISAF, which was organized and led initially by Great Britain, then by a succession of other states, until it was taken over by NATO in August 2003. ISAF's mandate was later extended to cover all of Afghanistan. S.C. Res. 1510, U.N. Doc. S/RES 1510 (Oct. 13, 2003). At its height, ISAF included more than 130,000 troops from 51 countries, a large majority of them from the United States. *See* NATO/OTAN, *ISAF's Mission in Afghanistan (2001-2014)* (updated Sept. 1, 2015), http://www.nato.int/cps/en/natohq/topics_69366.htm.

The Security Council also approved a number of non-military measures in an effort to restore and preserve the peace in Afghanistan. In January 2002, for example, it directed U.N. member states to freeze all financial assets of Osama bin Laden and various members of Al Qaeda and the Taliban, to block international travel by these individuals, and to prevent their acquisition of weapons. S.C. Res. 1390, U.N. Doc. S/RES 1390 (Jan. 28, 2002). The following March, the Security Council endorsed the establishment of the United Nations Assistance Mission in Afghanistan (UNAMA), whose job is to coordinate international donor activity in the recovery and reconstruction of the country. S.C. Res. 1401, U.N. Doc. S/RES 1401 (Mar. 28, 2002); S.C. Res. 2210, U.N. Doc. S/RES 2210 (Mar. 16, 2015) (extending UNAMA's mandate). *See* Rhoda Margesson, *United Nations Assistance Mission in Afghanistan: Background and Policy Issues* (Cong. Res. Serv. R40747), Dec. 27, 2010. Other resolutions have dealt variously with human rights (especially the rights of women and children), the rule of law, elections, corruption, and the drug trade.

The U.N. Secretary General delivers an extensive report to the Security Council every three months on conditions in Afghanistan, most recently at this writing U.N. Secretary-General, *The Situation in Afghanistan and Its Implications for International Peace and Security*, U.N. Doc. A/74/582-S/2019/935 (Dec. 10, 2019).

3. A New Role for NATO

The North Atlantic Treaty Organization (NATO) was created in 1949 by the North Atlantic Treaty, Apr. 4, 1949, 63 Stat. 2241, 34 U.N.T.S. 243. It originally consisted of five European states, plus Canada and the United States. Greece and Turkey joined two years later. NATO's original mission was the defense of Western Europe against the Soviet Union. Since the end of the Cold War, NATO has grown to include 29 states, a number of them former Soviet bloc countries.

The signers of the U.N. Charter anticipated the creation of regional organizations like NATO. Article 52(1) provides:

> Nothing in the present Charter precludes the existence of regional arrangements or agencies for dealing with such matters relating to the maintenance of international peace and security as are appropriate for regional action, provided that such arrangements or agencies and their activities are consistent with the Purposes and Principles of the United Nations.

Article 53(1) goes on to state that the Security Council may use regional agencies to enforce its resolutions, but that "no enforcement action shall be taken under regional arrangements or by regional agencies without the authorization of the Security Council."

Because NATO's goals are relatively limited, its founding document is much shorter and simpler than the U.N. Charter. Its governing body, the NATO Council, based in Brussels, makes decisions by consensus. Unlike the Security Council, NATO has a military command structure, headed as of mid-2019 by a U.S. general. Like the Security Council, however, it has no military force of its own, but depends on contributions of troops and matériel from member states.[3]

The day after the 9/11 terrorist attacks on the World Trade Center and the Pentagon, the NATO Council decided that if "this attack was directed from abroad against the United States, it shall be regarded as an action covered by Article 5 of the [North Atlantic] Treaty, which states that an armed attack against one or more of the Allies in Europe or North America shall be considered an attack against them

---

3. A number of other regional alliances around the world have also been organized to address breaches or threatened breaches of the peace. For example, in the Western Hemisphere the Organization of American States was used to enforce a quarantine of Cuba during the missile crisis there in 1962 and to send peacekeeping forces into the Dominican Republic in 1965. The Organization of Eastern Caribbean States was said to have requested the U.S. invasion of Grenada in 1983. Elsewhere, the Organization of African Unity has deployed peacekeeping forces a number of times, including in the Darfur region of Sudan.

all." NATO Press Release (2001) 124, Sept. 12, 2001. On October 2, the Council determined that the attack had come from abroad.

Article 5 goes on to say that when one or more member states comes under attack, each of the other states,

> in exercise of the right of individual or collective self-defence recognised by Article 51 of the Charter of the United Nations, will assist the Party or Parties so attacked by taking forthwith, individually and in concert with the other Parties, such action as it deems necessary, including the use of armed force, to restore and maintain the security of the North Atlantic area.

Each NATO member state thus had to decide for itself whether to come to the aid of the United States. Some immediately did so by contributing forces to OEF.

On August 11, 2003, NATO became directly involved as an institution by taking command of ISAF. This was NATO's first-ever deployment of forces outside of Europe. Subsequently, NATO member states all contributed personnel to ISAF, although not all were combat-equipped or permitted by their governments to engage in combat, and there was persistent disagreement about the scope of ISAF's mission. NATO's role in Afghanistan is described in Catherine Dale, *War in Afghanistan: Strategy, Operations, and Issues for Congress* (Cong. Res. Serv. R40156), Mar. 9, 2011; and Vincent Morelli & Paul Belkin, *NATO in Afghanistan: A Test of the Transatlantic Alliance* (Cong. Res. Serv. RL33627), Dec. 3, 2009.

In various resolutions the Security Council declared its appreciation and support for OEF and for NATO's leadership of ISAF. It even declared that OEF "operates . . . in accordance with the applicable rules of international law." S.C. Res. 1943, U.N. Doc. S/RES/1943 (Oct. 13, 2010). Yet the Security Council never expressly authorized OEF. Neither did it explicitly approve NATO's institutional role as leader of ISAF, despite the requirement in Article 53(1) for authorization of enforcement actions by regional organizations.

4. A Plan for Transition to Peace

At its peak in 2012, the number of U.S. military personnel deployed in Afghanistan reached about 100,000, and forces from other states numbered around 39,000. By early 2019, those numbers were down to about 14,000 and 8,600, respectively. More than 2,400 U.S. troops had lost their lives there, while other states suffered more than 1,100 deaths.

In 2010, the Afghan government, NATO, and ISAF foreign ministers agreed on a plan for a "phased transition" in which Afghans would gradually "take full responsibility for security, governance and development." The inauguration of President Ashraf Ghani in September 2014, and the establishment of a Government of National Unity, marked the first-ever democratic transition of power in Afghanistan.

At the beginning of 2015, ISAF officially ended, and a smaller force, renamed Resolute Support, shifted from a combat mission to one of training, advising, and assisting Afghan security forces. *See* NATO/OTAN, *Resolute Support Mission in Afghanistan* (updated July 18, 2018), https://www.nato.int/cps/en/natohq/topics_113694.htm?selectedLocale=en. Similarly, Operation Enduring Freedom ended on December 28, 2014, when it was replaced by Operation Freedom's Sentinel (OFS). About 2,000 OFS troops were assigned to combat against Al Qaeda and other terrorist groups, while most other U.S. forces are deployed with Resolute Support.

By mid-2019, the end of the longest running war in American history was nowhere in sight. While peace talks continued sporadically, the Taliban gradually reclaimed control of districts around Afghanistan, fighters aligned with the Islamic State began to gain a foothold there, and civilian casualties reached record levels. *See* Thomas Gibbons-Neff, *U.S. Special Forces Battle Against ISIS Turns to Containment, and Concern*, N.Y. Times, June 15, 2019. Joint Chiefs Chair Gen. Joseph Dunford Jr. testified before Congress, "I think we will need to maintain a counterterrorism presence as long as an insurgency continues in Afghanistan." *U.S. Will Need Forces in Afghanistan Until No Insurgency Left: Dunford*, Reuters, May 8, 2019. The Trump administration, however, has limited information about the state of the fighting in quarterly reports from DOD's Special Inspector General for Afghanistan Reconstruction. Merrit Kennedy, *The U.S. Public Will No Longer Have a Key Data Point About Afghanistan War*, NPR, May 1, 2019. Meanwhile, legislation introduced in 2019 would require withdrawal of all U.S. troops from Afghanistan within one year, and would repeal the 2001 AUMF. AFGHAN Service Act, S.J. Res. 12, 116th Cong. (2019).

U.S. and NATO involvement in Afghanistan are outlined in Kenneth Katzman & Clayton Thomas, *Afghanistan: Post-Taliban Governance, Security, and U.S. Policy* (Cong. Res. Serv. RL30588), Dec. 13, 2017.

Notes and Questions

1. *The President's Domestic Authority.* What domestic authority was President George W. Bush exercising when he ordered the launch of Operation Enduring Freedom on October 7, 2001? Did the Authorization for Use of Military Force (AUMF), enacted three weeks earlier on September 18, provide authority to invade Afghanistan? Can you tell from the language of the measure precisely what Congress intended to authorize the President to do, with how many troops and what kind of weaponry, where, and for how long? How did it differ in scope from the 1964 Tonkin Gulf Resolution, *supra* p. 303?

2. *9/11 as Armed Attack?* Any exercise of the inherent right of individual and collective self-defense under Article 51 must be premised on the existence of a significant "armed attack," as we learned in the *Nicaragua* case, *supra* p. 249. Otherwise, the use of force must be approved by the Security Council. Article 51 says nothing, however, about the source of an attack. If the attack comes from another sovereign state, as it did when Iraq invaded Kuwait in 1990, military force may be used against the attacking state. But on 9/11 the attack came from a non-state entity, Al Qaeda. Does such an attack justify a military response, or is a criminal prosecution of Al Qaeda members the only permissible recourse?

Should the answer turn on the size or destructive effect of the terrorist action? How do you think the World Court would answer this question, based on its decision in the *Nicaragua* case?

3. *Criteria for Self-Defense.* The World Court has declared that any use of force in self-defense must be necessary and proportional. See *supra* p. 253. The following

criteria were articulated by Daniel Webster in the mid-nineteenth-century *Caroline* affair: a violent response to an attack must reflect "a necessity of self-defense, instant, overwhelming, leaving no choice of means, no moment for deliberation." See *supra* p. 260. More recently, a former legal adviser to the British government has asserted that

> [w]hether an armed attack may be regarded as "imminent" will fall to be assessed by reference to all relevant circumstances, including (a) the nature and immediacy of the threat, (b) the probability of an attack, (c) whether the anticipated attack is part of a concerted pattern of continuing armed activity, (d) the likely scale of the attack and the injury, loss, or damage likely to result therefrom in the absence of mitigating action, and (e) the likelihood that there will be other opportunities to undertake effective action in self-defense that may be expected to cause less serious collateral injury, loss, or damage. [Daniel Bethlehem, *Self-Defense Against an Imminent or Actual Armed Attack by Nonstate Actors*, 106 Am. J. Int'l L. 770, 775-776 (2012).]

Were these criteria satisfied when the United States launched OEF?

4. *Attacking the Terrorists Where They Live.* Following the terrorist attacks of 9/11, in order to abate the threat of another attack it clearly was reasonably necessary to deny Al Qaeda the safe haven from which it operated, that is, to use force to kill, capture, or displace its members wherever they could be found. If the de facto Taliban government of Afghanistan had consented to U.S. military actions inside its borders to root out Al Qaeda, of course, Operation Enduring Freedom could not have violated either Afghanistan's sovereignty or the Article 2(4) ban on the use of force. But that consent was not forthcoming. Without such an invitation from the Taliban, did OEF violate international law?

Non-state terrorist attackers like Al Qaeda may be based in a failed state, like Somalia, or in one where the government is not in full control of its territory, like Yemen. The state from which an attack is launched may be a willing host—perhaps because its political goals are aligned with the non-state entity. Or the host state may actually sponsor the attacker. But should it matter whether the non-state attacker was controlled by, sponsored by, merely tolerated by, or even known to the host state?

A partial answer was provided by the World Court in 1949, when it declared that it is "every State's obligation not to allow knowingly its territory to be used for acts contrary to the rights of other States." *Corfu Channel*, Merits (U.K. v. Alb.), 1949 I.C.J. 4, 22 (Apr. 9). More broadly, there is general agreement that a state coming under attack from non-state terrorists may use force against the terrorists if they are located in another state that is "unwilling or unable" to stop their cross-border predations. *See* Dinstein, *supra* p. 338, at 293-294. The "unwilling or unable" test has been invoked by Russia in attacking Chechen rebels in Georgia, by Israel in attacking Hezbollah and PLO targets inside Lebanon, and by Turkey in attacking Kurdish forces in Iraq.

If the threat from non-state terrorists is ongoing, logic dictates that the victim state be allowed to mount an immediate preemptive counterstrike wherever the terrorists may be found. If the nature (or perhaps the location) of the threat cannot be established with sufficient clarity, however, the host state must be given a reasonable opportunity to abate it. But should the victim state be required to provide notice to the host state, or assess the host state's ability to respond, before mounting its own forceful response? How long must the victim state wait to act?

In Afghanistan it appeared that the Taliban government was not only a knowing, willing host to Al Qaeda, but was also controlled by Al Qaeda to some degree, rather than the other way around. According to one observer, "the Taliban, Afghanistan's de facto government, developed such close links to the known terrorist organization al Qaeda that it became responsible for the acts of al Qaeda." Mary Ellen O'Connell, *Lawful Self-Defense to Terrorism,* 63 U. Pitt. L. Rev. 889, 901 (2002). Was the OEF thus entitled to remove the Taliban from its control of the Afghan government?

5. *Duration of the Response.* The inherent right of self-defense presumably continues as long as the threat of another armed attack persists. Article 51 permits the use of force in self-defense "until the Security Council has taken measures necessary to maintain international peace and security." As of mid-2019, international peace and security clearly had not been fully restored in Afghanistan. Moreover, the terrorist threat that was said to justify the exercise of self-defense in the first place was still very significant. To make matters worse, the threat has metastasized, as off-shoots of Al Qaeda have sprung up in Yemen, Iraq, East Africa, and elsewhere, and as the Islamic State has gained a foothold in Afghanistan. How long will the United States and its partners be justified in using force to abate this threat?

In late 2019, the *Washington Post* reported hundreds of interviews by the Special Inspector General for Afghanistan Reconstruction, as well as other documents, indicating that "[y]ear after year, U.S. officials failed to tell the public the truth about the war in Afghanistan." Craig Whitlock, Leslie Shapiro & Armand Emamdjomeh, *A Secret History of the War,* Wash. Post, Dec. 9, 2019. According to its findings, moreover, "U.S. and allied officials admitted the mission had no clear strategy and poorly defined objectives," and "[t]he United States wasted vast sums of money trying to remake Afghanistan and bred corruption in the process." *Id.* Do these revelations have any bearing on the legitimacy, under either international or domestic law, of continued U.S. military involvement in Afghanistan?

6. *The Roles of International Organizations.* According to one authority,

> there is a stark difference between the exercise of collective self-defense and an enforcement undertaking stemming from Article 53(1). . . . When exercising collective self-defense, NATO does not require the advance authorization of the Security Council; contrarily, when functioning as a regional organization under Article 53(1), it is imperative for NATO to seek first the authorization of the Council. [Dinstein, *supra* p. 338, at 362.]

Once the Security Council has approved the use of force, however, as it did when it authorized the *creation* of ISAF, can we distinguish between self-defense under Article 51 and an enforcement action by a regional organization under Article 53(1)? Does the distinction have any legal significance?

7. *Comparing the Conflicts.* How do the conflicts in Korea, Kuwait, and Afghanistan compare in terms of

(a) Contemporary economic and geopolitical conditions?
(b) Contemporary U.S. domestic politics?

(c) The magnitude of the violence and destruction resulting from the initial outbreak of hostilities?

(d) The legal character of the entity initiating the conflict — whether the entity was a sovereign state, a non-state actor, or some combination of the two?

(e) The responses of international organizations?

(f) The responses of individual states, including the United States?

(g) The geographical scope of the battlefield?

(h) The duration of the conflict?

How, if at all, did these facts influence the legal rights and obligations of the parties in each of these conflicts?

COLLECTIVE USE OF FORCE: SUMMARY OF PRINCIPLES

- The President may send U.S. troops into battle without congressional approval, at least for a time, as an exercise of her inherent power to repel attacks on the United States. However, there is no consensus about precisely what constitutes such an attack.

- In the absence of such an attack, most scholars — and a few lower court opinions — agree that the President's domestic authority to use force abroad depends on some form of congressional approval. In Korea, arguments that such approval could be found in scores of earlier unapproved deployments, and in Congress's acquiescence in those deployments, seem to be refuted by the unprecedented scale and duration of the conflict there. Similar arguments following the Iraqi invasion of Kuwait may be cast in doubt by the passage of the War Powers Resolution in 1973.

- U.N. Security Council resolutions approving the use of force in the three conflicts analyzed here used the term "recommends" or "authorizes," rather than "orders" or "directs." The obligation of member states to carry out such resolutions is uncertain.

- Aside from Security Council resolutions, the use of force in each of the three conflicts was an exercise of each state's inherent right of individual and collective self-defense under Article 51, at least until the Security Council acted, and possibly beyond, until peace and security were effectively restored.

- A state may use force in self-defense against non-state-sponsored terrorists in another state if the host state is unwilling or unable to abate the threat they pose, although the precise meaning of this condition is unclear. Any such use of force must be discriminating and proportional.

12

Unilateral Use of Force

Since the United Nations Charter was ratified in 1945, the United States has sent its armed forces into hostilities with the approval of the U.N. Security Council a number of times. In the largest and most violent of these commitments — in Korea, Kuwait, and Afghanistan — the Security Council said it was acting to halt breaches of or threats to international peace and security, as we saw in the last chapter. Each time, however, the United States clearly would have been justified in acting on its own, at least for a while, as an exercise of its inherent right of individual and collective self-defense under Article 51.

On other occasions U.S. troops have been sent into battle without Security Council approval — in Vietnam, Grenada, Panama, Iraq, and elsewhere. Each of these deployments was also said by the United States to be justified as an act of self-defense. *See* Barbara Salazar Torreon & Sofia Plagakis, *Instances of Use of United States Armed Forces Abroad, 1798-2019* (Cong. Res. Serv. R42738), July 17, 2019. Whether each one met the criteria in Article 51 for resort to military force is a matter of vigorous debate. One of the goals of this chapter is therefore to determine as nearly as possible just what Article 51 requires.

U.S. involvement in belligerent acts without Security Council approval also raises questions about domestic authority — the power of the President to act without congressional approval. One theory is that the President may rely on his inherent repel-attack authority not only to resist direct aggression against the United States, but also to abate threats to U.S. interests or to rescue U.S. citizens abroad. Another is that it is supported by customary usage with congressional acquiescence. The broadest theory of all is simply that the President's constitutional authority to use force abroad is subject only to Congress's spending power and its power to decide the juridical consequences of using force. In this chapter we seek new insight into these issues, as well.

We rehearse these questions here in the context of several historical events, including conflicts between the United States and Libya during the 1980s, and the war in Iraq that began in 2003. We also examine continuing U.S. military actions in Syria and Iraq to combat the Islamic State, and (as of this writing) a threatened war with Iran. Finally, we briefly explore the right of the United States (and other states) to act alone in rescuing citizens in peril abroad.

A. SELF-DEFENSE AND REPRISAL

Article 51 of the U.N. Charter describes an "inherent right of individual and collective self-defense if an armed attack occurs." Most authorities agree, however, that a targeted state need not wait until an armed attack is completed before employing force to protect itself. A practical, flexible reading of the term "armed attack" suggests instead that a forceful response is also justified once an attack has moved beyond the planning stage, and the plan is being implemented. The target state may then engage in what we call here "anticipatory self-defense." *See* Mary Ellen O'Connell, *Lawful Self-Defense to Terrorism*, 63 U. Pitt. L. Rev. 889, 894 (2002) ("[W]here one state is in the process of launching an attack on another, self-defense may begin. There must be a plan for the attack, and the plan must be in the course of implementation."); Yoram Dinstein, *War, Aggression and Self-Defence* 228 (6th ed. 2017) ("[T]he right to self-defence can be invoked in response to an armed attack at an incipient stage, as soon as it becomes evident to the victim State (on the basis of hard intelligence available at the time) that the attack is actually in the process of being mounted. There is no need to wait for the bombs to fall. . . ."). The trouble, as always, comes in the details, both in deciding precisely the point in time at which a growing threat warrants a resort to force, and in determining what force to use and how.

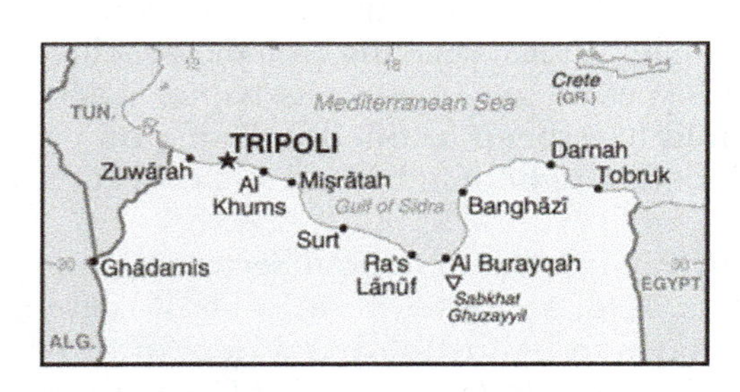

Libya CIA Map

Courtesy of worldatlas.com.

The difficulty can be seen in a series of incidents from 1981-1986, when U.S. naval forces, asserting freedom of navigation in international waters, repeatedly crossed what Libyan leader Muammar el-Qaddafi called a "line of death" across the entrance to the Gulf of Sidra, a body of water that extends roughly 90 to 150 miles north of the Libyan coast and measures about 275 miles across. The United States has generally refused to recognize any claims of territorial waters running more than 12 miles offshore.

In early April 1986, a terrorist bomb exploded in a Berlin nightclub, killing a U.S. soldier and injuring 64 other Americans. Administration officials immediately linked the Libyan People's Bureau in East Berlin to the bombing. News quickly spread that the United States was planning a retaliatory raid using carrier-based aircraft and F-111s based in Britain. The response came on April 14, with U.S. planes dropping bombs on Libyan coastal targets, suspected terrorist training facilities, and Qaddafi's residential compound.

Although Congress was in session at the time, President Reagan contacted congressional leaders just three hours before the first bombs fell. That evening he announced to the American people in a televised address:

> I warned Colonel Qaddafi we would hold his regime accountable for any new terrorist attacks launched against American citizens. More recently, I made it clear we would respond as soon as we determined conclusively who was responsible for such attacks. . . .
>
> This monstrous brutality is but the latest act in Colonel Qaddafi's reign of terror. The evidence is now conclusive that the terrorist bombing of La Belle discotheque was planned and executed under the direct orders of the Libyan regime. . . .
>
> . . . When our citizens are abused or attacked anywhere in the world, on the direct orders of a hostile regime, we will respond, so long as I'm in this Oval Office. Self-defense is not only our right, it is our duty. It is the purpose behind the mission undertaken tonight — a mission fully consistent with Article 51 of the United Nations Charter.
>
> We believe that this pre-emptive action against his terrorist installations will not only diminish Colonel Qaddafi's capacity to export terror — it will provide him with incentives and reasons to alter his criminal behavior. [Address by President Reagan on Libya (Apr. 14, 1986).]

Responding to criticism from members of Congress that the President had failed to engage in the advance consultation required by §3 of the War Powers Resolution, *supra* p. 91, the State Department Legal Adviser insisted that

> extensive consultations occurred with congressional leaders. They were advised of the President's intention after the operational deployments had commenced, but hours before military action occurred. This satisfied the resolution's requirement that consultation occur "before" the "introduction" of troops into hostilities or a situation of imminent hostilities. Congressional leaders had ample opportunity to convey their views to the President before any irrevocable actions were taken (in fact, no one who was consulted objected to the actions undertaken). [Abraham D. Sofaer, *The War Powers Resolution and Antiterrorist Operations* (Apr. 29, 1986).]

He went on to declare that Congress had effectively given its approval in advance by voting appropriations for "the creation and maintenance of the forces whose function, at least in part, is to defend Americans from terrorism through the measured use of force." *Id.*

Notes and Questions

1. Freedom of Navigation. As a general principle, freedom of navigation and overflight of international waters is a well-established customary international norm. This right of passage has been codified and clarified to some extent by the United Nations Convention on the Law of the Sea, Dec. 10, 1982, 1833 U.N.T.S. 397. While the United States is not yet a party, it regards the convention as an accurate reflection of customary norms. Nevertheless, some states object to certain of its terms regarding maritime boundaries and conditions of passage.

Since 1979, the Defense Department's Freedom of Navigation program has repeatedly conducted exercises like those in the Gulf of Sidra to dispute what it regards as "excessive maritime claims," for example in the Straits of Gibraltar, Hormuz, and Malacca. During FY 2018, the U.S. Navy challenged such claims by 26 riparian states. *See* Dep't of Defense, *Annual Freedom of Navigation Report: Fiscal Year 2018*, Dec. 31, 2018, *at* http://policy.defense.gov/OUSDPOffices/FON.aspx.

Establishing freedom of navigation is one, but not the only, purpose of these minatory (saber-rattling) exercises. They are also intended to demonstrate national strength and resolve. They are often classified, however, to avoid international political friction. To what extent may Congress be said to have tacitly approved by acquiescence this tactic for pursuing U.S. foreign policy interests? Is congressional approval needed?

Navigation by U.S. naval forces in parts of the South China Sea claimed by China recently has evoked threats of a violent response. Do minatory exercises violate the ban in Article 2(4) of the U.N. Charter on the "threat or use of force against the territorial integrity" of another state? If so, is the riparian state or the one asserting freedom of navigation guilty of a violation? How could violence be averted?

2. *Anticipatory Self-Defense?* Was the April 14, 1986 U.S. attack on Libya an appropriate act of self-defense under Article 51 in response to a plan of armed attack "in the course of implementation"? According to one scholar, "[u]nilateralism sits uncomfortably in a multilateral world. At the most general level, unilateral determinations can evoke concern that one state has taken on the role of judge, jury and policeman." Ruth Wedgwood, *The Enforcement of Security Council Resolution 687: The Threat of Force Against Iraq's Weapons of Mass Destruction*, 92 Am. J. Int'l L. 724, 726 (1998). Should a state that invokes its right of anticipatory self-defense be required to explain its factual predicate for doing so? Can you think of a way to avoid the perception that a purported act of anticipatory self-defense is really just naked aggression?

Any use of military force, including a justifiable act of anticipatory self-defense, must be necessary, discriminating, and proportional. *See supra* pp. 265, 293-294. Did the U.S. response to the Berlin nightclub bombing satisfy these criteria?

3. *Reprisal?* Or was it a punitive act of retaliation — a reprisal? In the view of one eminent scholar, "few propositions about international law have enjoyed more support than the proposition that, under the Charter of the United Nations, the use of force by way of reprisals is illegal." Derek Bowett, *Reprisals Involving Recourse to Armed Force*, 66 Am. J. Int'l L. 1, 1 (1972); *see also* Ian Brownlie, *International Law and the Use of Force by States* 281 (1963). Professor Bowett goes on to point out that

> reprisals are punitive in character: they seek to impose reparation for the harm done, or to compel a satisfactory settlement of the dispute created by the initial illegal act, or to compel the delinquent state to abide by the law in the future. But, coming after the event and when the harm has already been inflicted, reprisals cannot be characterized as a means of protection. [Bowett, *supra*, at 3.]

Bowett's emphatic declaration does not, however, reflect a uniform practice of states. Many examples can be cited of states' taking matters into their own hands. *See* William V. O'Brien, *Reprisals, Deterrence and Self-Defense in Counterterror Operations*, 30 Va. J. Int'l L. 421, 475-476 (1990) ("The distinction between actions taken in self-defense and actions taken to punish antecedent armed attacks as a self-help sanction of the law is unrealistic, given the lack of Security Council enforcement of the U.N. jus ad bellum legal regime and the competing . . . practices in the contemporary international system.").

Bowett points out that the difference between illegal reprisal and legal self-defense lies chiefly in the motives of the responding state. Even with a public explanation, of course, it may be exceptionally difficult to discern a responding state's true motives, especially given the possible influence of domestic politics on the decision to use force.

Was the legitimacy of the U.S. bombing raid diminished by the fact that it occurred nine days after the nightclub bombing? Or might the delay be excused by the difficulty in attribution of responsibility for the terrorist attack in Berlin, or by the need for reflection to decide on a proper response?

4. A Role for Congress? The State Department Legal Adviser argued that the "need for swiftness and secrecy" justified delaying notice to congressional leaders until just hours before the 1986 attack on Tripoli. One purpose of the consultation requirement in WPR §3 is to improve the quality of executive branch decision making by seeking outside advice. Could that purpose have been served by the President's briefings? Were members of Congress really given time to convey their disapproval — indeed, even to decide whether they approved or not?

B. PREEMPTIVE SELF-DEFENSE

While there is general agreement that force may be used in self-defense once an armed attack has actually gotten underway, but before the bombs begin to fall, many authorities believe that force may not be employed in response to a mere threat, however great. This despite the fact that Article 2(4) prohibits threats to use force.

> [S]elf-defence consonant with Article 51 . . . comes in reaction to the use of force by the other Party. When a country feels menaced by the threat of an armed attack, all that it is free to do — pursuant to the Charter of the United Nations — is make the necessary military preparations for repulsing the anticipated attack should it materialize, as well as bring the matter forthwith to the attention of the Security Council (hoping that the latter will take collective security measures on a preemptive basis). . . . [T]he option of a preventive use of inter-State force is excluded by Article 51. [Dinstein, *supra*, at 228.]

In September 2002, however, just weeks before a congressional vote on authority for war against Iraq, the White House announced for the first time as a public policy "the option of preemptive actions to counter a sufficient threat to our national security." Without referring to Article 51, it explained the policy this way:

> For centuries, international law recognized that nations need not suffer an attack before they can lawfully take action to defend themselves against forces that present an imminent danger of attack. Legal scholars and international jurists often conditioned the legitimacy of preemption on the existence of an imminent threat — most often a visible mobilization of armies, navies, and air forces preparing to attack.
>
> We must adapt the concept of imminent threat to the capabilities and objectives of today's adversaries. Rogue states and terrorists do not seek to attack us using conventional means. They know such attacks would fail. Instead, they rely on acts of terror and, potentially, the use of weapons of mass destruction — weapons that can be easily concealed, delivered covertly, and used without warning. . . .
>
> . . . The greater the threat, the greater is the risk of inaction — and the more compelling the case for taking anticipatory action to defend ourselves, even if uncertainty remains as to the time and place of the enemy's attack. To forestall or prevent such hostile acts by our adversaries, the United States will, if necessary, act preemptively. [*National Security Strategy of the United States of America* 15 (Sept. 2002), *available at* https://georgewbush-whitehouse.archives.gov/nsc/nss/2002/.]

Controversy over the legitimacy of preemptive resort to self-defense is based on this very practical problem:

> As one moves from an actual armed attack as the requisite threshold of reactive self-defense, to the palpable and imminent threat of attack, which is the threshold of anticipatory self-defense, and from there to the conjectural and contingent threat of the mere possibility of an attack at some future time, which is the threshold of preemptive self-defense, the self-assigned interpretive latitude of the unilateralist becomes wider, yet the nature and quantum of evidence that can satisfy the burden of proof resting on the unilateralist becomes less and less defined and is often, by the very nature of the exercise, extrapolative and speculative. . . . [U]ltimately the central issue is assessment by the risk-averse security specialists of one international actor of the intentions of another actor. . . . [O]ne actor's self-perceived good faith conviction will often look like serious or hysterical misjudgment to some actors and like either cynical or self-deluded, naked aggression to others. [W. Michael Reisman & Andrea Armstrong, *The Past and Future of the Claim of Preemptive Self-Defense,* 100 Am. J. Int'l L. 525, 526 (2006).]

See also Jules Lobel, *Preventive War and the Lessons of History,* 67 U. Pitt. L. Rev. 307 (2006) (offering evidence that preventive wars are often "unnecessary and disastrous").

1. Planning for Another War in Iraq

The Persian Gulf War of 1991, analyzed in the last chapter, ended with a formal cease-fire when Iraq accepted the terms of U.N. Security Council Resolution 687, U.N. Doc. S/RES/687 (Apr. 3, 1991). Iraq agreed that it would allow a U.N. Special Commission (UNSCOM) to destroy and remove all of its chemical and biological weapons, as well as longer-range missiles, together with any facilities for research, development, and production of such weapons. *Id.* ¶¶8, 9. *See United Nations Special Commission (UNSCOM)* (n.d.), *at* http://www.un.org/Depts/unscom/General/basicfacts.html. A similar commitment was made concerning nuclear weapons, to be carried out by the Director General of the International Atomic Energy Agency (IAEA) with the assistance of UNSCOM. S.C. Res. 687, ¶¶9(b)(iii), 12, 13. Iraq also promised not to develop or acquire any such weapons in the future and to submit to monitoring to assure compliance. *Id.* ¶¶10, 12. In addition, it agreed that it would "not commit or support any act of international terrorism or allow any organization directed towards commission of such acts to operate within its territory." *Id.* ¶32.

CIA map of Iraq

During the next seven years, UNSCOM destroyed large quantities of chemical weapons and precursors, chemical and biological weapons facilities, and missile components. But Iraq violated its obligations repeatedly by interfering with UNSCOM inspectors and by failing to disclose information about its weapons programs. *See UNSCOM: Chronology of Main Events,* Dec. 1999, *at* http://www.un.org/Depts/unscom/Chronology/chronologyframe.htm.

In August 1998, Congress adopted a measure declaring that Iraq was in "material and unacceptable breach" of various U.N. Security Council resolutions and urging the President to "take appropriate action, in accordance with the Constitution and relevant laws of the United States, to bring Iraq into compliance with its international obligations." Pub. L. No. 105-235, §1, 112 Stat. 1538, 1541 (1998). Two months later, in response to Saddam Hussein's threat to terminate weapons-monitoring activities of the IAEA and UNSCOM, Congress passed the Iraq Liberation Act of 1998, Pub. L. No. 105-338, 112 Stat. 3178. Included was a "sense of Congress" provision declaring, "It should be the policy of the United States to support efforts to remove the regime headed by Saddam Hussein from power in Iraq and to promote the emergence of a democratic government to replace that regime." *Id.* §3, 112 Stat. at 3179.

Matters finally came to a head on October 31, 1998, when Iraq formally ended all cooperation with UNSCOM. Six weeks later, UNSCOM withdrew its staff from Iraq.

Members of the George W. Bush administration began in early 2001 to plan for "regime change" in Iraq. They provided support for Iraqi opposition groups, and they leaked information about a supposed Iraqi nuclear weapons program that was discredited by Energy Department officials. Defense Secretary Donald Rumsfeld wrote in July, "If Saddam's regime were ousted, we would have a much-improved position in the region and elsewhere." Joyce Battle, *The Iraq War — Part I: The U.S. Prepares for Conflict, 2001,* Sept. 22, 2010, *at* http://www.gwu.edu/~nsarchiv/NSAEBB/NSAEBB326/index.htm.

Immediately after 9/11, President Bush pushed hard to identify a link between Saddam Hussein and the terrorist attacks on the World Trade Center and the Pentagon. Within days he asked for plans for an attack on Iraq. Then in the late summer of 2002, the Bush administration launched a campaign to generate public support for an invasion, describing Iraq as a threat to the United States. Vice President Dick Cheney declared on August 26, for example, "Simply stated, there is no doubt that Saddam Hussein now has weapons of mass destruction." *In Cheney's Words: The Administration Case for Removing Saddam Hussein,* N.Y. Times, Aug. 27, 2002. National Security Adviser Condoleezza Rice warned, "We don't want the smoking gun to be a mushroom cloud." *Top Bush Officials Push Case Against Saddam,* CNN.com, Sept. 8, 2002. And in a speech to the United Nations General Assembly President Bush stated,

> Saddam Hussein's regime is a grave and gathering danger. To suggest otherwise is to hope against the evidence. To assume this regime's good faith is to bet the lives of millions and the peace of the world in a reckless gamble. And this is a risk we must not take. [President's Remarks at the United Nations General Assembly (Sept. 12, 2002).]

In October 2002, the CIA released a top-secret National Intelligence Estimate (NIE), *Iraq's Continuing Programs for Weapons of Mass Destruction,* to members of Congress. An unclassified summary declared that "Iraq has continued its weapons of mass destruction (WMD) programs in defiance of UN resolutions and restrictions. Baghdad has chemical and biological weapons as well as missiles with ranges in excess of UN restrictions; if left unchecked, it probably will have a nuclear weapon during this decade." Director of Central Intelligence, *Iraq's Weapons of Mass Destruction Programs*

(Oct. 2002), *available at* http://nsarchive.gwu.edu/NSAEBB/NSAEBB129/nie_first%20release.pdf. Much of the information in the NIE turned out to be wrong.

2. Authority for a New War in Iraq?

Shortly after the release of the NIE, and just three weeks before the mid-term congressional elections in 2002, Congress approved the invasion of Iraq.

Authorization for Use of Military Force Against Iraq Resolution of 2002

Pub. L. No. 107-243, 116 Stat. 1498 (Oct. 16, 2002)

Whereas Iraq both poses a continuing threat to the national security of the United States and international peace and security in the Persian Gulf region and remains in material and unacceptable breach of its international obligations by, among other things, continuing to possess and develop a significant chemical and biological weapons capability, actively seeking a nuclear weapons capability, and supporting and harboring terrorist organizations;...

Whereas members of al Qaida, an organization bearing responsibility for attacks on the United States, its citizens, and interests, including the attacks that occurred on September 11, 2001, are known to be in Iraq;

Whereas Iraq continues to aid and harbor other international terrorist organizations, including organizations that threaten the lives and safety of United States citizens;...

Whereas Iraq's demonstrated capability and willingness to use weapons of mass destruction, the risk that the current Iraqi regime will either employ those weapons to launch a surprise attack against the United States or its Armed Forces or provide them to international terrorists who would do so, and the extreme magnitude of harm that would result to the United States and its citizens from such an attack, combine to justify action by the United States to defend itself;...

Whereas it is in the national security interests of the United States to restore international peace and security to the Persian Gulf region: Now, therefore, be it

Resolved by the Senate and House of Representatives of the United States of America in Congress assembled...

SEC. 3. AUTHORIZATION FOR USE OF UNITED STATES ARMED FORCES

(a) Authorization — The President is authorized to use the Armed Forces of the United States as he determines to be necessary and appropriate in order to —

(1) defend the national security of the United States against the continuing threat posed by Iraq; and

(2) enforce all relevant United Nations Security Council resolutions regarding Iraq.

(b) Presidential Determination — In connection with the exercise of the authority granted in subsection (a) to use force the President shall, prior to such exercise or as soon thereafter as may be feasible, but no later than 48 hours after exercising such authority, make available to the Speaker of the House of Representatives and the President pro tempore of the Senate his determination that —

(1) reliance by the United States on further diplomatic or other peaceful means alone either (A) will not adequately protect the national security of the United States against the continuing threat posed by Iraq or (B) is not likely to lead to enforcement of all relevant United Nations Security Council resolutions regarding Iraq; and

(2) acting pursuant to this joint resolution is consistent with the United States and other countries continuing to take the necessary actions against international terrorist and terrorist organizations, including those nations, organizations, or persons who planned, authorized, committed or aided the terrorist attacks that occurred on September 11, 2001. . . .

The Bush administration also worked hard to obtain a resolution from the U.N. Security Council approving an invasion of Iraq — one at least as clear as Resolution 678, which on November 29, 1990, authorized the expulsion of Iraqi forces from Kuwait. See *supra* p. 335. On November 8, 2002, the Security Council adopted the following resolution:

United Nations Security Council Resolution 1441

U.N. Doc. S/RES/1441 (Nov. 8, 2002)

The Security Council. . .

Recognizing the threat Iraq's non-compliance with Council resolutions and proliferation of weapons of mass destruction and long-range missiles poses to international peace and security. . .

Recalling that in its resolution 687 (1991) the Council declared that a ceasefire would be based on acceptance by Iraq of the provisions of that resolution, including the obligations on Iraq contained therein. . .

Acting under Chapter VII of the Charter of the United Nations,

1. *Decides* that Iraq has been and remains in material breach of its obligations under relevant resolutions, including resolution 687 (1991), in particular through Iraq's failure to cooperate with United Nations inspectors and the IAEA. . . ;

2. *Decides*, while acknowledging paragraph 1 above, to afford Iraq, by this resolution, a final opportunity to comply with its disarmament obligations under relevant resolutions of the Council; and accordingly decides to set up an enhanced inspection regime with the aim of bringing to full and verified completion the disarmament process established by resolution 687 (1991) . . . ;

3. *Decides* that. . . the Government of Iraq shall provide to [U.N. weapons inspectors] and the Council, not later than 30 days from the date of this

> resolution, a currently accurate, full, and complete declaration of all aspects of its programmes to develop chemical, biological, and nuclear weapons, ballistic missiles, and other delivery systems . . .
>
> 12. *Decides* to convene immediately upon receipt of a report [of noncompliance by Iraq with this resolution], in order to consider the situation and the need for full compliance with all of the relevant Council resolutions in order to secure international peace and security;
>
> 13. *Recalls*, in that context, that the Council has repeatedly warned Iraq that it will face serious consequences as a result of its continued violations of its obligations. . . .

On December 7, 2002, Iraq submitted a 12,000-page declaration stating that it had no weapons of mass destruction. But the declaration was deemed inadequate by the head of a new U.N. inspection team, Hans Blix, and others. Saddam Hussein later told FBI interrogators he worried that full disclosure might make him appear weak and invite attack from Iran. *See* Scott Shane, *Iraqi Dictator Told of Fearing Iran More Than He Did U.S.*, N.Y. Times, July 3, 2009. Meanwhile, U.N. weapons inspectors had resumed their search for weapons of mass destruction (WMD) in Iraq on November 27, 2002. *See* Sean D. Murphy, *Use of Military Force to Disarm Iraq*, 97 Am. J. Int'l L. 419, 419-421 (2003). Aside from some intermediate range missiles, however, which were destroyed, no such weapons were found before inspectors were forced to leave on March 17, 2003, in the face of the impending U.S.-led military invasion.

On the home front, President Bush and members of his administration continued to press the case for war. In his State of the Union address, the President declared, "Saddam Hussein has gone to elaborate lengths, spent enormous sums, taken great risks to build and keep weapons of mass destruction." *State of the Union Address*, Jan. 28, 2003. "If Saddam Hussein does not fully disarm," he continued, "for the safety of our people and for the peace of the world, we will lead a coalition to disarm him." *Id.*

On February 5, 2003, Secretary of State Colin Powell delivered an address to the U.N. Security Council, punctuated by photographic exhibits, insisting, "There can be no doubt that Saddam Hussein has biological weapons and the capability to rapidly produce more, many more. . . . If biological weapons seem too terrible to contemplate, chemical weapons are equally chilling." *Powell's Address, Presenting "Deeply Troubling" Evidence on Iraq*, N.Y. Times, Feb. 6, 2003. Powell added, "These are not assertions. What we're giving you are facts and conclusions based on solid evidence." *Id.* Nevertheless, faced with opposition from France, Germany, and Russia, the United States was unable to procure a more forceful resolution than the one set out above. Members of a U.S.-led coalition asserted, however, that even without waiting for the inspection process to be completed and without further action by the Security Council, Resolution 1441 had cleared the way for coalition forces to "take their own steps" to secure Iraq's disarmament.

On March 18, 2003, President Bush sent the "determination" required by §3(b) of the October 16, 2002, joint resolution to congressional leaders. The next day, Operation Iraqi Freedom was launched with missile and aircraft attacks on Iraqi targets. The President addressed the nation in these words: "My fellow citizens, at this hour, American and coalition forces are in the early stages of military operations to disarm Iraq, to free its people, and to defend the world from grave danger." *President Bush Addresses the Nation,* Mar. 19, 2003. "Our nation enters this conflict reluctantly—yet, our purpose is sure," he declared. "The people of the United States and our friends and allies will not live at the mercy of an outlaw regime that threatens the peace with weapons of mass murder. We will meet that threat now... so that we do not have to meet it later with armies of firefighters and police and doctors on the streets of our cities." *Id.*

Less than a month later, with 135,000 U.S. troops deployed in Iraq, the last stronghold of forces loyal to Saddam Hussein was captured. On May 1, 2003, President Bush, standing in front of a banner proclaiming "Mission Accomplished," declared that "[m]ajor combat operations in Iraq have ended." *President Bush Announces Major Combat Operations in Iraq Have Ended* (May 1, 2003).

Notes and Questions

1. *War Without the 2002 Joint Resolution?* Prior to Congress's approval of the October 16, 2002 joint resolution, some maintained that the President already had the domestic authority needed to send troops into battle. Could the President have taken the country to war solely on the strength of his implied "repel attack" authority, based on the asserted imminence and gravity of an Iraqi threat?

Did the President already have Congress's approval to go to war? Could he have relied, for example, on the 1991 Authorization for Use of Military Force Against Iraq, *supra* p. 337? Would such reliance have been dependent on the continued viability of U.N. Security Council Resolution 678, *supra* p. 335? Did either the Iraq Liberation Act of 1998 or Pub. L. No. 105-235, described *supra* p. 353, provide the needed authority? What about the Authorization for Use of Military Force (AUMF) approved by Congress three days after the September 11, 2001 terrorist attack, *supra* p. 88?

2. *Security Council Approval?* The United States asserted that if Security Council approval was needed to make war with Iraq in 2003, it came from the 1990 resolution authorizing the expulsion of Iraqi forces from Kuwait. On March 27, 2003, for example, the U.S. Permanent Representative to the United Nations, John Negroponte, declared that

> Resolution 687 (1991) imposed a series of obligations on Iraq that were the conditions of the ceasefire. It has long been recognized and understood that a material breach of those obligations removes the basis of the ceasefire and revives the authority to use force under resolution 678 (1990). Resolution 1441 (2002) explicitly found Iraq in continuing material breach. In view of Iraq's additional material breaches, the basis for the existing ceasefire has been removed and the use of force is authorized under resolution 678 (1990). [U.N. SCOR, 58th Sess., 4726th mtg. at 25, U.N. Doc. S/PV.4726 (Resumption 1).]

Coming at the question of legality from a different direction, one scholar claims, "A cease-fire, as an instrument which merely suspends hostilities without terminating the war, does not extinguish the right of collective self-defense that remains legally intact for the duration of the war." Dinstein, *supra,* at 326-327. But does it seem likely that in 1990 (or 1991) the Security Council intended to approve military action more than a decade hence under circumstances impossible to predict? *See* Sean D. Murphy,

Assessing the Legality of Invading Iraq, 92 Geo. L.J. 173 (2004) (arguing, based on an extensive analysis of the various Security Council resolutions, that they did not authorize war in 2003).

In the alternative, the United States argued that if contemporaneous Security Council approval was required to make the invasion comply with international law, Resolution 1441 satisfied that requirement. According to the State Department Legal Adviser at the time,

> Just last November, in resolution 1441, the Council unanimously decided that Iraq has been and remains in material breach of its obligation. 1441 then gave Iraq a "final opportunity" to comply, but stated specifically that violations of the obligations, including the obligation to cooperate fully, under 1441 would constitute a further material breach. Iraq has clearly committed such violations and, accordingly, the authority to use force to address Iraq's material breaches is clear. [William H. Taft IV, Remarks Before National Association of Attorneys General (Mar. 20, 2003), *at* http://usinfo.org/wf-archive/2003/030321/epf515.htm.]

Many disagreed with his assessment. In the view of one expert, for example,

> While a full public account of the understandings among Security Council members regarding Resolution 1441 has yet to be disclosed, the text of Resolution 1441 can fairly be read as an agreement to disagree over whether an additional Security Council resolution authorizing force was needed in the event of Iraqi noncompliance. [Jane E. Stromseth, *Law and Force After Iraq: A Transitional Moment,* 97 Am. J. Int'l L. 628, 630 (2003).]

Do you think Resolution 1441 left it to individual states to determine Iraqi compliance with the Security Council's various resolutions, or to decide how to respond to any perceived violations?

3. Preemptive War. The President did not "explicitly characterize his military action as an implementation of the expansive concept of preemptive use of military force against rogue states with WMD." Richard F. Grimmett, *U.S. Use of Preemptive Military Force* 6 (Cong. Res. Serv. RS21311), Apr. 11, 2003. It was nevertheless viewed that way by many.

If the preemptive use of force can somehow be reconciled with the Article 51 requirement of an "armed attack," was the threat against the United States in March 2003 grave enough to justify Operation Iraqi Freedom? Is your answer affected by the U.N. Security Council's refusal to explicitly authorize the invasion of Iraq? By the fact that no weapons of mass destruction or significant terrorist connections were ever found?

3. Justifications for the War

The preamble to the October 16, 2002 joint resolution set out above declared that the United States faced a threat posed by a "significant" Iraqi chemical, biological, and nuclear weapons capability, by the risk that the Iraqi regime would "employ those weapons to launch a surprise attack against the United States or its Armed Forces," and by "the extreme gravity of harm that would result to the United States and its citizens from such an attack." After coalition forces invaded Iraq, however, no chemical, biological, or nuclear weapons were ever found. A detailed account of the fruitless search for WMD appears in *Comprehensive Report of the Special Advisor to the DCI on Iraq's WMD (Duelfer Report)*, Sept. 30, 2004, *available at* https://www.cia.gov/library/reports/general-reports-1/iraq_wmd_2004/index.html.

Concerning the ongoing threat of terrorism, President Bush asserted before the war that "Saddam Hussein aids and protects terrorists, including members of al Qaeda." State of the Union Address, *supra*. The independent 9/11 Commission, however, found "no evidence [of] a collaborative operational relationship" between Iraq and al Qaeda. National Commission on Terrorist Attacks Upon the United States, *The 9/11 Commission Report* 66 (2004). The Senate Select Committee on Intelligence found no "established formal relationship" between the two. *Report on the U.S. Intelligence Community's Prewar Intelligence Assessments on Iraq*, July 7, 2004, at 346. The Senate committee also cited a CIA assessment that there was "no evidence proving Iraqi complicity or assistance in an al-Qaida attack." *Id.* at 347.

How could the factual predicate for the war have been so totally, tragically wrong? According to the Senate Intelligence Committee, most of the information available in the CIA's October 2002 *National Intelligence Estimate* concerning Iraq's WMD program was either "overstated" or "not supported by" the underlying intelligence reporting. *Id.* at 14. *See also* Commission on the Intelligence Capabilities of the United States Regarding Weapons of Mass Destruction (Silberman/Robb Commission), *Report to the President of the United States* (Mar. 31, 2005). An Iraqi exile appropriately code-named Curveball apparently provided fabricated information about Iraqi mobile bioweapons labs. And a key piece of intelligence about asserted Iraqi training of Al Qaeda members in the use of WMD reportedly came from Ibn al-Shaykh al-Libi, who was captured in Pakistan, then "rendered" to Egypt, where he says he was tortured to compel statements that he later recanted. Both of these sources were widely discredited within the intelligence community, yet the information they supplied found its way into speeches given by the President and others.

New concerns were raised in 2005 by the account of a meeting of top British officials, including Prime Minister Tony Blair, some three months before Congress voted to authorize the use of force in Iraq. The head of the British Secret Intelligence Service (MI6), just returned from talks with Director of Central Intelligence George Tenet and other Washington officials, reported that "[m]ilitary action was now seen as inevitable. Bush wanted to remove Saddam, through military action, justified by the conjunction of terrorism and WMD. But the intelligence and facts were being fixed around the policy." Memorandum from Matthew Rycroft to David Manning, *Iraq: Prime Minister's Meeting, 23 July*, July 23, 2002, *reprinted in The Secret Downing Street Memo*, Sunday Times (London), May 1, 2005; *see also* Mark Danner, *The Secret Way to War*, N.Y. Rev. Books, June 9, 2005, at 70.

President Bush reacted angrily to charges from some in Congress that his administration's use of that intelligence was deliberately misleading. "It is irresponsible," he countered, "for Democrats to now claim that we misled them and the American people. Leaders in my administration and members of the United States Congress from both political parties looked at the same intelligence on Iraq, and reached the same conclusion: Saddam Hussein was a threat." *President Delivers Remarks at Elmendorf AFB on War on Terror*, Nov. 14, 2005.

A final Senate Intelligence Committee study surely failed to satisfy either the President or his critics. "Statements by the President, Vice President, Secretary of State and the National Security Advisor regarding a possible Iraqi nuclear weapons program," it said, "were generally substantiated by intelligence community estimates, but did not convey the substantial disagreements that existed in the intelligence community." *Report on Whether Public Statements Regarding Iraq by U.S. Government Officials Were Substantiated by Intelligence Information,* S. Rep. No. 110-345, at 15 (2008). It reached similar conclusions about other purported weapons programs and about links to terrorists.

Notes and Questions

1. *War Based on False Premises?* How important do you suppose the perceived WMD threat was in justifying the war? The terrorist connection? Did the fact that both of these factual predicates for the war were false affect the legal authority conferred by the 2002 joint resolution? Did it matter how the mistakes arose? Compare the debate about the Tonkin Gulf Resolution, *supra* p. 303. Senator Fulbright, one of the 1964 resolution's sponsors, later remarked, "I was hoodwinked." *Quoted in* John Hart Ely, *The American War in Indochina, Part I: The (Troubled) Constitutionality of the War They Told Us About,* 42 Stan. L. Rev. 877, 889 (1990).

2. *What Members of Congress Knew and When They Knew It.* Do you think members of Congress had access to the same intelligence that the President did when they voted to authorize the use of force in Iraq? What bearing, if any, does your answer have on the legitimacy of the October 16 resolution?

3. *Continuing Authority for the War?* The invasion of Iraq toppled Saddam Hussein, and the United States and its coalition allies occupied Iraq as its government was re-assembled. But an active insurgency delayed withdrawal. By the end of 2011, more than 4,400 U.S. military personnel had been killed in Iraq, and some 32,000 had been wounded. Perhaps 100,000 Iraqis, some say more, had also died, the majority at the hands of other Iraqis; many of the Iraqi dead were civilians. If the reasons for military action changed over time, was the President's mandate under the October 16, 2002 joint resolution still good? Was the continued deployment merely a tactical decision properly entrusted to the President? Was the earlier mandate extended by Congress's recurring votes of appropriations for the war? Or should the President have sought new authority from Congress?

4. *War Without End?* In August 2005, President Bush declared:

> An immediate withdrawal of our troops in Iraq, or the broader Middle East, as some have called for, would only embolden the terrorists and create a staging ground to launch more attacks against America and free nations. So long as I'm the President, we will stay, we will fight, and we will win the war on terror. [*President Addresses Military Families, Discusses War on Terror* (Aug. 24, 2005).]

Congress nevertheless passed an appropriations measure in 2007 calling for the withdrawal of U.S. forces from Iraq by the end of March 2008, leaving behind only enough troops to protect U.S. citizens and diplomatic facilities, train and equip Iraqi security forces, and engage in "targeted special actions limited in duration and scope to killing or capturing members of al-Qaeda and other terrorist organizations with global reach." H.R. 1591, 110th Cong. §1904(c), (e) (2007). But the bill was vetoed by President Bush, who complained that it infringed on his powers as Commander in Chief. 43 Weekly Comp. Pres. Doc. 560, 560 (May 7, 2007). Did it?

Should Congress attach a fixed time limit to any authorization for the use of force, so that the President must return to Congress at intervals for approval to continue fighting? *See* Stephen I. Vladeck, *Ludecke's Lengthening Shadow: The Disturbing Prospect of War Without End*, 2 J. Nat'l Security L. & Pol'y 53 (2006) (so recommending). Can you think of a constitutional objection to such a requirement? A practical objection? Recall the critique of the "sixty-day clock" in the War Powers Resolution, *supra* p. 97.

C. ADDRESSING NEW THREATS: SYRIA, THE ISLAMIC STATE, AND IRAN

Wars that began in Afghanistan in 2001 and Iraq in 2003 have changed in character over time. But armed conflict and its attendant horrors continue across the region and beyond. Once again, lawyers have been involved in ongoing efforts to assure the lawfulness of the conflicts, as well as in the search for peaceful solutions.

1. Syria and the Islamic State

The civil war in Syria that started in 2011 was still underway at this writing in 2019, although government forces under President Bashar al-Assad had recaptured most of the territory lost earlier to Syrian rebels and Islamic State (ISIS or ISIL) fighters. The conflict there was enormously complicated by fighting among various interest groups that failed to unite in their opposition to the Assad regime, and it produced millions of internal and external refugees. A 2015 report described the situation this way:

> [Rebel] forces are formidable, but, as a whole, the anti-Asad movement has lacked unity of purpose, central command, and coordinated support. Various opposition groups have, depending on the circumstances, cooperated and competed. . . . [S]ignificant elements of the opposition [have] clashed with one another. . . .
>
> As fighting continues, Syrian civilians continue to suffer in what U.S. Director of National Intelligence James Clapper described in early 2014 as an "apocalyptic disaster." U.N. sources report that since March 2011, the conflict has driven more than four million Syrians into neighboring countries as refugees (out of a total population of more than 22 million). At the end of 2014, an estimated 12.2 million people inside Syria, more than half the population, were in need of humanitarian assistance, of which more than 7.6 million were internally displaced. . . . [Christopher M. Blanchard, Carla E. Humud & Mary Beth D. Nikitin, *Armed Conflict in Syria: Overview and U.S. Response* 1-2 (Cong. Res. Serv. RL33487), July 15, 2015.]

CIA map of Syria

In the resulting chaos, the Islamic State established a firm foothold for a time, threatening neighboring Iraq and Turkey, and it remains a threat today.

> The Islamic State (IS, aka the Islamic State of Iraq and the Levant, ISIL/ISIS, or the Arabic acronym *Da'esh*) is a transnational Sunni Islamist insurgent and terrorist group that controlled large areas of Iraq and Syria from 2014 through 2017. [An "insurgent" is one fighting an organized government who is not part of an organized revolution.] The group attracted a network of global supporters and its leader, Abu Bakr al Baghdadi, received pledges of affiliation from groups in several other countries. A series of terrorist attacks attributed to the group or to individuals it has inspired have claimed hundreds of lives on four continents since November 2015, including in the United States.
>
> While U.S. and allied forces in 2017 and 2018 successfully liberated most of the territory formerly held by the group in Syria and Iraq, IS leadership remains at large and IS fighters appear to be evolving into an insurgent force. The group's international affiliates continue to operate, and individuals inspired by the group continue to attempt attacks in Europe and elsewhere. The stabilization of areas recovered from the group in Iraq and Syria remains an ongoing challenge, and a U.S. military spokesperson for the counter-IS campaign warned in August 2018 that, "We cannot emphasize enough that the threat of losing the gains we have made is real, especially if we are not able to give the people a viable alternative to the ISIS problem." . . .
>
> The U.S. military continues to conduct operations against the group in Iraq, Syria, and Afghanistan, while monitoring and occasionally striking its affiliates and personnel elsewhere. . . .
>
> Interrelated conflicts and political crises in Iraq, Syria, and other countries where the Islamic State operates complicate efforts to address and durably eliminate the threats posed by the group. Military operations may reduce the numbers of IS fighters and liberate IS-held territory, but the underlying political disputes and development challenges that the Islamic State has exploited may create ongoing openings for the group if governance and reconstruction needs go unmet. [Christopher M. Blanchard & Carla E. Humud, *The Islamic State and U.S. Policy,* at ii (Con. Res. Serv. R43612), Sept. 25, 2018.]

U.S. and allied air and ground forces have thus been drawn into the conflict in Syria, as have the Turkish and Israeli militaries. Syria's ally Russia has also sent its air force and ground troops into the battle, while Iran has provided support for its surrogates fighting on the side of the Saddam regime. In 2019, an end to the fighting was nowhere in sight.

Notes and Questions

1. *Individual and Collective Self-Defense?* On September 23, 2014, the United States reported to the United Nations that Iraq was "facing a serious threat of continuing attacks from ISIL coming out of safe havens in Syria," and that Iraq had asked the United States to "lead international efforts to strike ISIL sites and military strongholds in Syria in order to end the continuing attacks" against it. Letter from Samantha J. Power, U.S. Permanent Representative to the United Nations, to Ban Ki-moon, Secretary-General of the United Nations (Sept. 23, 2014). The U.S. letter went on declare:

> States must be able to defend themselves, in accordance with the inherent right of individual and collective self-defense, as reflected in Article 51 of the UN Charter, when, as is the

> case here, the government of the State where the threat is located is unwilling or unable to prevent the use of its territory for such attacks. . . . Accordingly, the United States has initiated necessary and proportionate military actions in Syria in order to eliminate the ongoing ISIL threat to Iraq. . . . [*Id.*]

The letter apparently was intended to satisfy the Article 51 requirement that states exercising their right of self-defense provide notice to the Security Council. Did it also convincingly address the criteria for acting in self-defense, as set forth in the *Nicaragua* case, *supra* p. 249? If U.S. intrusions into Syria did not violate Article 2(4) of the Charter, how long could they legally continue without doing so?

2. The U.N. Security Council Gets Involved. In late 2015, the Security Council adopted a resolution determining that

> by its violent extremist ideology, its terrorist acts, its continued gross systematic and widespread attacks directed against civilians, abuses of human rights and violations of international humanitarian law, including those driven on religious or ethnic ground, its eradication of cultural heritage and trafficking of cultural property, but also its control over significant parts and natural resources across Iraq and Syria and its recruitment and training of foreign terrorist fighters whose threat affects all regions and Member States, even those far from conflict zones, the Islamic State in Iraq and the Levant (ISIL, also known as Da'esh), constitutes a global and unprecedented threat to international peace and security. . . . [S.C. Res. 2249, U.N. Doc. S/RES/2249 (Nov. 20, 2015).]

It also described the Al-Nusrah Front (ANF) and other groups associated with Al Qaeda as "a threat to international peace and security." Then, without invoking the authority of any particular article of the U.N. Charter, it

> *[c]all[ed] upon* Member States that have the capacity to do so to take all necessary measures, in compliance with international law, . . . on the territory under the control of ISIL also known as Da'esh, in Syria and Iraq, to redouble and coordinate their efforts to prevent and suppress terrorist acts committed specifically by ISIL also known as Da'esh as well as ANF, . . . and to eradicate the safe haven they have established over significant parts of Iraq and Syria. [*Id.*]

Did this resolution authorize the United States and its allies to conduct air strikes in Syria and deploy ground forces there? How, if at all, did it affect the authority asserted by the United States to act in collective self-defense under Article 51? Why do you suppose that Russia, Syria's staunchest ally, failed to veto the resolution?

3. U.S. Assistance to the Syrian Opposition. In 2014, Congress approved the provision of training, equipment, supplies, and other forms of assistance to "appropriately vetted elements of the Syrian opposition" for the purposes of

> (1) Defending the Syrian people from attacks by the Islamic State of Iraq and the Levant (ISIL), and securing territory controlled by the Syrian opposition.
>
> (2) Protecting the United States, its friends and allies, and the Syrian people from the threats posed by terrorists in Syria.
>
> (3) Promoting the conditions for a negotiated settlement to end the conflict in Syria. [National Defense Authorization Act for Fiscal Year 2015, Pub. L. No. 113-291, §1209(a), 128 Stat. 3292, 3541 (2014).]

The "vetting" of recipients was supposed to take into account their associations with terrorist groups, the government of Syria, or the government of Iran, as well as their commitment to promoting respect for human rights and the rule of law. Meanwhile, the Obama administration repeatedly insisted that the Assad regime step down.

Did U.S. support for selected rebel forces in Syria violate U.N. Charter Article 2(4)? Was it an intervention barred by customary international law?

4. Deployment of U.S. Military Forces in Syria. In September 2014, President Obama ordered U.S. air strikes against ISIS forces in Syria and Iraq, as well as the deployment of additional U.S. troops on the ground in Iraq. The President claimed that he was acting "pursuant to my constitutional and statutory authority as Commander in Chief (including the authority to carry out Public Law 107-40 [2001 AUMF] and Public Law 107-243 [2002 Iraq War resolution]) and as Chief Executive, as well as my constitutional and statutory authority to conduct the foreign relations of the United States." Letter from the President to the Speaker of the House of Representatives and the President Pro Tempore of the Senate (Sept. 23, 2014); *see also* White House, *Report on the Legal and Policy Frameworks Guiding the United States' Use of Military Force and Related National Security Operations* 3-7, 16 (Dec. 2016) (also claiming support from congressional appropriations).

Following the precedent set by the Obama administration, U.S. aircraft have continued to conduct strikes against ISIS targets inside Syria since President Trump took office. These actions are reported regularly on the website of the Defense Department's Central Command, http://www.centcom.mil/MEDIA/PRESS-RELEASES/.

U.S. ground troops were first deployed inside Syria in 2015. They were said to be engaged in training, advice, and support for Kurdish and Arab fighters attacking ISIS. Their numbers grew to some 2,000 by the end of 2017, and about 1,000 remained there in mid-2019. *See* Carla E. Humud, Christopher M. Blanchard & Mary Beth D. Nikitin, *Armed Conflict in Syria: Overview and U.S. Response* 1 (Cong. Res. Serv. RL33487), Mar. 25, 2019.

Did either the 2001 AUMF or the Iraq AUMF provide domestic authority for these U.S. actions? Did the WPR require the withdrawal of U.S. forces when explicit congressional approval was not forthcoming?

Both the Obama and Trump administrations claimed that U.S. operations in Syria have complied with international law. If that claim was justified initially, is it still justified, now that ISIS forces have been expelled from their strongholds throughout Syria?

5. Russia Gets Involved. In September 2015, Russia began to deploy its own combat aircraft and ground troops in Syria, and to carry out air strikes against Syrian rebels opposed to the Assad regime. Its direct involvement raised the potential for conflict with U.S. forces there.

In May 2017, U.S. warplanes attacked a pro-Assad military convoy as it approached a base in southern Syria where American and British personnel were training and advising Syrian rebels battling the Islamic State. According to U.S. officials, the purpose of the strike was to protect coalition forces, not to directly attack the Assad regime. *See* Eric Schmitt & Anne Barnard, *U.S. Warplanes in Syria Hit Pro-Government Militia Convoy*, N.Y. Times, May 18, 2017. But both Syria and Russia condemned the strike as an illegal act of aggression, asserting that the United States had no right either to establish a base inside Syria or to defend it without Syrian permission. *See* Anne Barnard, *Russia and Syria Denounce U.S. Airstrike on Pro-Assad Militia,* N.Y. Times, May 19, 2017.

The following month, a U.S. fighter jet shot down a Syrian warplane that the United States claimed was attacking Syrian Democratic Forces, which fought both ISIS and Syrian government forces. In response, Russia suspended the use of a U.S. hotline designed to avoid inadvertent clashes, and it threatened to shoot down any U.S. aircraft flying over Syria west of the Euphrates River. Michael R. Gordon & Ivan Nechepurenko, *Russia Warns U.S. After Downing of Syrian Warplane,* N.Y. Times, June 19, 2017.

Could Russia lawfully invoke Article 51 to strike U.S. military forces in the region or even the U.S. homeland as an act of collective self-defense on behalf of Syria?

6. Specific Statutory Authority? Apparently dissatisfied with the statutory authorities cited immediately above, President Obama repeatedly asked for new legislation approving the U.S. military actions already underway in Syria and Iraq. A group of scholars recommended that if such new enabling legislation were passed, it should:

- be ISIL-specific and mission-specific
- include geographic limits
- include a sunset clause
- ensure that U.S. uses of force are consistent with international law
- require greater transparency and congressional oversight.

Rosa Brooks et al., *Principles to Guide Congressional Authorization of the Continued Use of Force Against ISIL,* Nov. 10, 2014, http://justsecurity.org/wp-content/uploads/2014/11/ISIS-AUMF-Statement-FINAL.pdf. Can you explain the probable reasoning behind each recommendation, based on your understanding of history and the law?

A number of bills in Congress have been designed to clarify the President's authority and to exercise greater congressional oversight and control over his use of military force against terrorists, but by late 2019 none had been enacted. Here is an example:

S.J. Res. 59

115th Congress, 2d Session
Apr. 16, 2018

JOINT RESOLUTION . . .

Sec. 3. Authorization for use of United States Armed Forces.

(a) In general. — The President is authorized to use all necessary and appropriate force against

(1) the Taliban, al Qaeda, and the Islamic State in Iraq and Syria (ISIS); and

(2) associated forces designated pursuant to section 5.

(b) War Powers Resolution. —

(1) Specific Statutory Authorization. — Consistent with section 8(a)(1) of the War Powers Resolution (50 U.S.C. 1547(a)(1)), Congress declares that this section is intended to constitute specific statutory authorization within the meaning of section 5(b) of the War Powers Resolution (50 U.S.C. 1544(b)). . . .

Sec. 4. Quadrennial review of the authorization for use of military force.

(a) Presidential submission. — On January 20, 2022, and again every 4 years thereafter, the President shall submit to Congress a report regarding the use of military force pursuant to this joint resolution, which shall include a proposal to repeal, modify, or leave in place this joint resolution. . . .

Sec. 5. Congressional oversight.

(a) Associated forces. —

(1) Existing Associated Forces. — The following organizations, persons, or forces are designated associated forces covered by the authorization for use of military force provided by section 3(a) of this joint resolution:

(A) Al Qaeda in the Arabian Peninsula.

(B) Al Shabaab.

(C) Al Qaeda in Syria (including Al Nusrah Front).

(D) The Haqqani Network.

(E) Al Qaeda in the Islamic Mahgreb (AQIM).

(2) Designation. — . . . [T]he President shall designate all organizations, persons, or forces other than those listed in paragraph (1) that the President has determined are associated forces covered by the authorization for use of military force provided by section 3(a) of this joint resolution by submitting to the appropriate congressional committees and leadership a report listing all such associated forces. . . .

(5) Congressional Review. — [providing for expedited consideration of a resolution to remove additional associated forces designated by the President]. . . .

(b) Geography. —

(1) in General. —

(A) Initial List. — Not later than 30 calendar days after the date of the enactment of this joint resolution, the President shall submit to the appropriate congressional committees and leadership a report detailing all foreign countries in which the United States is using military force pursuant to this joint resolution, including a detailed description of the military objectives and the organizations, persons, or forces targeted.

(B) New Foreign Countries. — Not later than 48 hours after the use of military force in a new foreign country pursuant to this joint resolution, the President shall submit an updated report required by this paragraph and consult with the appropriate congressional committees and leadership. Authorization for use of military force pursuant to this joint resolution in a new foreign country is contingent upon the reporting to Congress pursuant to this paragraph.

(C) New Foreign Country Defined. — In this resolution, the term "new foreign country" means a foreign country other than Afghanistan, Iraq, Syria, Somalia, Yemen, or Libya not previously reported to Congress pursuant to this paragraph.

(2) Congressional Review. — [providing for expedited consideration of a resolution to rescind authority for the use of force in a new foreign country]. . . .

Sec. 6. Repeal of 2001 Authorization for Use of Military Force and uninterrupted authority.

(a) Repeal. — The Authorization for Use of Military Force (Public Law 107-40; 115 Stat. 224; 50 U.S.C. 1541 note) is hereby repealed. . . .

(b) Uninterrupted authority. — This joint resolution provides uninterrupted authority for ongoing military operations conducted pursuant to the Authorization for Use of Military Force (Public Law 107-40; 115 Stat. 224; 50 U.S.C. 1541 note) as of the date of the enactment of this joint resolution. . . .

Sec. 7. Repeal of 2002 Authorization for Use of Military Force.

The Authorization for Use of Military Force Against Iraq Resolution of 2002 (Public Law 107-243; 116 Stat. 1498; 50 U.S.C. 1541 note) is hereby repealed. . . .

Does S.J. Res. 59 follow the scholars' recommendations for such legislation outlined above?

One of the bipartisan bill's sponsors insisted that it did not expand the President's war-making authority. Tim Kaine, Opinion, *Congress Must Take Away Trump's Unlimited Authority to Wage War*, Wash. Post, Apr. 29, 2018. An opponent argued that the measure would give "nearly unlimited power to this or any President to be at war anywhere, anytime and against anyone." Sen. Rand Paul, Letter to Colleagues, Apr. 18, 2018. Who was right?

What amendments to the resolution would you have recommended? Why do you suppose it was not enacted?

In July 2019, the Trump administration outlined its objections to any such legislation: "[A]ny new AUMF must have no sunset provision, no geographic limitation, and no repeal before replacement. . . . It is also essential that any new legislation not undermine the President's Constitutional authority to defend the nation against threats or attacks." *Reviewing Authorities for the Use of Military Force: Hearing Before the S. Comm. on Foreign Relations*, 116th Cong. (2019) (statement of Marik String, State Dep't Acting Legal Adviser). Do you understand the reasoning behind each of these objections? Would S.J. Res. 59 have undermined the President's constitutional authority?

2. Iran[1]

Relations between the United States and Iran have long been complicated and difficult. After Iranian Prime Minister Mohammed Mossadegh sought to nationalize his country's oil industry, he was overthrown in a 1953 coup organized by the CIA and Britain's MI-6. Then in 1979, in the midst of the Iranian Revolution that expelled Shah Mohammad Reza Pahlavi, militants stormed the U.S. embassy in Tehran and held 52 Americans hostage for 444 days (until a few minutes after President Ronald Reagan's inauguration in January 1981). Formal diplomatic relations between Iran and the United States were severed in 1980 and have not been restored. Nevertheless, the United States secretly sold weapons to Iran during the 1980s for use in its war against Iraq, while at the same time supplying intelligence and other assistance to Iraq. The United States established an embargo on trading with Iran in 1995.

More recently, Iran has sought to develop nuclear weapons, in violation of its obligations under the Nuclear Non-Proliferation Treaty (see *infra* p. 445). A 2015 agreement

---

1. The following account is drawn from contemporary news sources.

between Iran and the five permanent members of the U.N. Security, plus Germany and the European Union — the Joint Comprehensive Plan of Action (JCPOA) — froze this development, in return for the lifting of some trade restrictions. But in 2018, the Trump administration withdrew from the agreement and re-imposed punitive economic sanctions aimed, it said, at halting Iran's development of new missile systems, curtailing its support of terrorists and proxies, and stopping its mistreatment of U.S. citizens. According to some critics, however, the real purpose of these actions was to promote regime change in Iran.

CIA map of Iran

Meanwhile, Iran has provided support to Shia militants attacking U.S. targets in Iraq and Syria, as well as to surrogate Hezbollah militants fighting on behalf of the Assad regime in Syria. These same Hezbollah forces, along with the Palestinian extremist group Hamas, also supported by Iran, threaten the security of U.S. ally Israel. And Iran-backed Houthi rebels in Yemen threaten Saudi Arabia, another U.S. ally.

Tensions between the two nations increased dramatically in 2019. After a meeting with Israeli Prime Minister Benjamin Netanyahu in February, U.S. Secretary of State Mike Pompeo declared, "You can't achieve stability in the Middle East without confronting Iran." *See* David Brennan, *Mike Pompeo Pushes for Iran Confrontation at Middle East Peace Conference*, Newsweek, Feb. 19, 2019. In May, the United States deployed naval warships, bombers, and missile batteries to the Persian Gulf region to counter unspecified threats to U.S. forces and U.S. "interests," and it sent additional ground troops there. Then when Iranian Revolutionary Guards attacked oil tankers near the Strait of Hormuz, Secretary Pompeo called the attacks "a clear threat to international peace and security." David E. Sanger & Edward Wong, *After Placing Blame for Attacks, Trump Faces Difficult Choices on Confronting Iran*, N.Y. Times, June 14, 2019.

In late June 2019, an Iranian surface-to-air missile shot down an unpiloted U.S. surveillance drone (whether over international waters was sharply disputed). President Trump authorized a retaliatory military strike against three targets in Iran, then canceled the operation minutes before it could be launched, calling the predicted loss of 150 lives in Iran "not proportionate to shooting down an unmanned drone." *See* David E. Sanger, David D. Kirkpatrick & Isabel Kershner, *Trump Threatens "Obliteration" of Iran, as Sanctions Dispute Escalates*, N.Y. Times, June 25, 2019. But a few days later the President tweeted, "Any attack by Iran on anything American will be met with great and overwhelming force. In some areas, overwhelming will mean obliteration." *Id.*

Then in July, the United States deployed additional troops in Saudi Arabia, while Iran seized a British tanker in the Strait of Hormuz in retaliation for Britain's seizure in the Strait of Gibraltar of an Iranian tanker apparently bound for Syria in violation of EU sanctions. As tensions mounted, many worried that an accident or miscalculation might lead to an all-out armed conflict. For a cautionary geopolitical analysis, see Steven Simon & Jonathan Stevenson, *Iran: The Case Against War*, N.Y. Rev. Books, Aug. 15, 2019.

Notes and Questions

1. Domestic Authority for a New War? In April 2019, the U.S. Secretary of State declared, without offering proof, that "there is no doubt there is a connection" between Al Qaeda and Iran, suggesting that the United States might engage in a conflict with Iran without seeking Congress's approval, perhaps relying instead on authority supplied by the 2001 AUMF. *See* Catie Edmondson & Edward Wong, *Pompeo Is Warned Against Sidestepping Congress for Conflict with Iran,* N.Y. Times, Apr. 10, 2019; *see also* Testimony of Marik String, *supra* ("We have sufficient statutory and Constitutional authorities to protect the national security interests of the United States.").

Could the President constitutionally order an attack on Iran without further approval from Congress? *See* Tom Udall & Richard J. Durbin, Opinion, *Trump Is Barreling Toward War with Iran. Congress Must Act to Stop Him,* Wash. Post, Mar. 5, 2019 (arguing no); Brian Egan & Tess Bridgeman, *Top Experts' Backgrounder: Military Action Against Iran and US Domestic Law,* Just Security, June 21, 2019 (answer may depend in part on the existence of an important "national interest," whether the engagement constitutes a "war," compliance with international law, and the potential for escalation).

Legislation introduced in Congress in 2019 provided that "[n]o funds may be used for kinetic military operations in or against Iran except pursuant to an Act or joint resolution of Congress specifically authorizing such use," although the limitation would not apply to operations in response to "an imminent threat to the United States," to "repel a sudden attack on the United States, its territories or possessions, or its Armed Forces," or to "rescue or remove United States citizens or personnel." Prevention of Unconstitutional War with Iran Act of 2019, S. 1039, H.R. 2354, 116th Cong. §3. Another bill declared that neither the 2001 AUMF nor the 2002 law approving the use of force in Iraq "may be construed to provide authorization for the use of military force against Iran." AUMF Clarification Act, H.R. 2829, 116th Cong. §4 (2019). Would either measure unconstitutionally restrict the President's options as Commander in Chief?

2. Compliance with International Law? Under what circumstances, if any, could the United States justify its use of military force against Iran without violating international law? Could it mount an all-out attack on Iran without U.N. Security Council approval? *See* Oona Hathaway, *Bolton's Stated Predicate for War with Iran Doesn't Work,* Just Security, May 31, 2019 (no, asserting that Iran does not exercise "effective control" over its proxy forces in the region, and that Iran's support for those forces is not an "armed attack," citing the *Nicaragua* case, *supra* p. 249).

D. RESCUE

In November 1979, Iranian militants stormed the American Embassy in Teheran and took 52 U.S. citizens hostage. The following April, after diplomatic initiatives failed to gain their release, President Carter ordered a daring military operation that sent helicopters and transport aircraft into the Iranian desert to bring them home. The mission ended in failure, with the death of eight U.S. troops and loss of equipment. Details are set forth in Letter of President Jimmy Carter to the Speaker of the

House and President Pro Tempore of the Senate, 1 Pub. Papers 777 (Apr. 26, 1980). The President claimed international law authority for his actions in Article 51 of the U.N. Charter. He also asserted that Section 8(d)(1) of the War Powers Resolution, *supra* p. 92, "expressly recognized" his constitutional authority to act. *Id.*

This was only one of many claims over the years of unilateral presidential authority to use military force to protect Americans or their property abroad. Such authority was asserted, for example, when troops were deployed to China in 1900 during the Boxer Rebellion, to Nicaragua in 1912 during a revolution there, to the Dominican Republic in 1965, to Grenada in 1983, and to Somalia in 1993. *See* Dep't of Justice Off. of Legal Counsel, *Authority to Order Targeted Airstrikes Against the Islamic State of Iraq and the Levant* 18 (Dec. 30, 2014).

Historical practice aside, the case cited most often as establishing the President's authority to rescue is a pre–Civil War case that did not involve rescue at all.

Reading *Durand v. Hollins*

In 1852, U.S. investors sought to corner the business of conducting travelers headed for the California Gold Rush over the Central American isthmus. The eastern terminus of their route was Greytown in Nicaragua. Following the killing of a local citizen by an American sea-captain, a Greytown mob threatened the U.S. minister to Nicaragua and hit him with a bottle. The U.S. Secretary of the Navy, acting on orders from President Franklin Pierce, then sent Commander George Hollins of the USS *Cyane* to Greytown to obtain redress for damages to property of the American owners and an apology for the attack on the minister. When Greytown authorities refused his demands, Hollins shelled the town and then burned what was left to the ground. *See* Matthew Waxman, *Remembering the Bombardment of Greytown*, Lawfare, July 19, 2019. An American owner of property destroyed in the attack sued Hollins for damages. Hollins asserted in his defense that he was merely following orders.

- What, precisely, is the holding of *Durand v. Hollins*?
- Why do you think *Durand* is cited so often as authority for presidential authority to rescue Americans abroad?
- Might the decision be cited as precedent for other unilateral presidential uses of military force?

Durand v. Hollins

United States Circuit Court, Southern District of New York, 1860
8 F. Cas. 111 (No. 4186)

NELSON, Circuit Justice. The principal ground of objection to the pleas, as a defence of the action, is, that . . . the president . . . had [no] authority to give the orders relied on to the defendant, and hence, that they afford no ground of justification.

As the executive head of the nation, the president is made the only legitimate organ of the general government, to open and carry on correspondence or negotiations with foreign nations, in matters concerning the interests of the country or of its citizens. It is to him, also, the citizens abroad must look for protection of person and of property, and for the faithful execution of the laws existing and intended for their protection. For this purpose, the whole executive power of the country is placed in his hands, under the constitution, and the laws passed in pursuance thereof; and different departments of government have been organized, through which this power may be most conveniently executed, whether by negotiation or by force. . . .

Now, as it respects the interposition of the executive abroad, for the protection of the lives or property of the citizen, the duty must, of necessity, rest in the discretion of the president. Acts of lawless violence, or of threatened violence to the citizen or his property, cannot be anticipated and provided for; and the protection, to be effectual or of any avail, may, not unfrequently, require the most prompt and decided action. Under our system of government, the citizen abroad is as much entitled to protection as the citizen at home. The great object and duty of government is the protection of the lives, liberty, and property of the people composing it, whether abroad or at home; and any government failing in the accomplishment of the object, or the performance of the duty, is not worth preserving.

I have said, that the interposition of the president abroad, for the protection of the citizen, must necessarily rest in his discretion; and it is quite clear that, in all cases where a public act or order rests in executive discretion neither he nor his authorized agent is personally civilly responsible for the consequences. As was observed by Chief Justice Marshall, in *Marbury v. Madison*, 1 Cranch [5 U.S.] 165: "By the constitution of the United States, the president is invested with certain important political powers, in the exercise of which he is to use his own discretion, and is accountable only to his country in his political character, and to his own conscience. To aid him in the performance of these duties, he is authorized to appoint certain officers, who act by his authority, and in conformity with his orders. In such cases, their acts are his acts, and, whatever opinion may be entertained of the manner in which executive discretion may be used, still there exists, and can exist, no power to control that discretion. The subjects are political. They respect the nation, not individual rights, and, being intrusted to the executive, the decision of the executive is conclusive." This is a sound principle, and governs the present case. The question whether it was the duty of the president to interpose for the protection of the citizens at Greytown against an irresponsible and marauding community that had established itself there, was a public political question, in which the government, as well as the citizens whose interests were involved, was concerned, and which belonged to the executive to determine; and his decision is final and conclusive, and justified the defendant in the execution of his orders given through the secretary of the navy.

Judgment for defendant.

Notes and Questions

1. *The President's Domestic Authority to Rescue.* The Constitution is silent on the rescue of Americans in peril abroad, and Congress has not expressly approved the use of military force to effect such rescues. It is widely believed, however, that the President not only has the authority to rescue, but also that he is obligated to use it.

Some believe that authority to rescue is an aspect of the President's inherent repel-attack power. Yet there is no evidence that the Framers considered this issue.

In addition to *Durand v. Hollins*, the Supreme Court's decision in *In re Neagle*, 135 U.S. 1 (1890), analyzed *supra* p. 76, is often viewed as a precedent for the use of military force to rescue an American. There the Court cited with approval the action of a U.S. sloop of war in 1853 to rescue one Martin Koszta, a Hungarian who had applied for U.S. citizenship, from his Austrian captors. But *Neagle* concerned the attempted assassination in California of a Supreme Court Justice. Does either case actually furnish a precedent for the claimed presidential authority, or are the references merely dicta? If they do provide authority for the President to rescue Americans abroad, do they also suggest any limits to that authority?

As a political matter, is any relevant law likely to influence a President's decision to attempt a rescue? Does law really have any practical value in this context?

One observer believes that the real motivation for the attack on Greytown was not protection of American property, but removal of the town itself as an obstacle to the business of U.S. investors. *See* Will Soper, *Can an Amateur Historian Rewrite History?*, History News Network, Oct. 23, 2018. If true, would that alter the value of *Durand v. Hollins* as a precedent?

Might *Durand* be read even more broadly to authorize military force in other contexts? *See* Waxman, *supra* (speculating that it might be invoked to justify a U.S. attack on Iran).

2. *Congressional Limits on the Rescue Power?* The use of military force to rescue might have unintended and highly undesirable consequences, perhaps by provoking wider violence. This concern lay in part behind Congress's passage in 1868 of the Hostage Act, 22 U.S.C. §1732 (2018), set forth *supra* p. 40. The Act provides that "the President shall use such means, not amounting to acts of war and not otherwise prohibited by law, as he may think necessary and proper to obtain or effectuate the release" of persons held wrongfully and "in violation of the rights of American citizenship." Is the statute's express *approval* of presidential efforts to rescue using "means, not amounting to acts of war" also a constitutionally permissible *restriction* on the President's use of military force? How might Chief Justice John Marshall, author of the Supreme Court's decision in *Little v. Barreme*, *supra* p. 63, have answered?

Section 2(c) of the War Powers Resolution, *supra* p. 90, declares that the President may introduce U.S. troops into hostilities only pursuant to a declared war, specific statutory authorization, or "a national emergency created by attack upon the United States, its territories or possessions, or its armed forces." But it is silent concerning attacks on private citizens or their property, let alone their rescue. Does it therefore unconstitutionally intrude on the President's rescue power? Or is it instead merely a permissible *regulation* of the exercise of that power?

3. *International Law of Rescue.* Iran complained that the failed U.S. hostage rescue effort in 1980 was an act of naked aggression, in violation of Article 2(4) of the U.N. Charter. But when the United States subsequently sought an order from the World Court for the release of the hostages and reparations, the Court referred to the seizure of the hostages as an "armed attack" on the United States, one of the preconditions under Article 51 for the use of force in response. *Case Concerning United States Diplomatic and Consular Staff in Tehran*, 1980 I.C.J. 3, 29, 42 (May 24, 1980). The ICJ opinion was punctuated, however, by references to the fact that the American

hostages were diplomatic personnel. We cannot be sure the Court would have reacted the same way if the hostages had been tourists or journalists, and expert opinion is divided on this point. *See* Dinstein, *supra*, at 219-221, 275-279.

UNILATERAL USE OF FORCE: SUMMARY OF PRINCIPLES

- It is generally agreed that under Article 51 of the U.N. Charter a state may use force in "anticipatory" self-defense once an armed attack is underway but before it is completed.

- Most authorities believe that the use of force in response to a mere threat, however great, is not justified, although the George W. Bush administration asserted such a right of "preemptive" self-defense in advance of the 2003 U.S. invasion of Iraq.

- Because terrorists attack soft civilian targets without warning, some have argued that the only effective defense against a terrorist attack is to attack the terrorists even before they can begin to implement their plan of attack. But there is no consensus about the factual predicates for such use of force.

- A state exercising its inherent right of self-defense should be prepared not only to report its use of force to the Security Council, as required by Article 51, but also to describe the circumstances that justified that use.

- Reprisals — the use of force simply to punish an attacker — are forbidden, unless they are also designed to prevent another attack. Distinguishing between deterrence and revenge, however, may be very difficult.

- The political character of the U.N. Security Council, and the permanent membership on it of contending super-powers, have seriously limited that body's ability to prevent or limit breaches of the peace in Iraq, Syria, and elsewhere.

- As a matter of domestic law, the geographical scope of the President's repel-attack power is uncertain. The U.S. armed forces nevertheless may always use force anywhere to defend themselves against an unjustified attack.

- Mutual participation by Congress in a decision to go to war, as the Framers intended, requires a shared understanding of the reasons for war. If those reasons change over time, the President may need to secure new congressional approval to continue fighting.

- Under international law, a state may use force to rescue its nationals held hostage abroad if their capture amounted to an armed attack, pursuant to Article 51. Otherwise, authority for rescue is uncertain.

- Domestic authority for rescue of Americans in peril abroad is widely assumed, although its source is uncertain. The President's historical use of force to protect or rescue U.S. citizens suggests congressional acquiescence in that use. And *Durand v. Hollins* indicates judicial recognition of the rescue power.

- Congress sought to limit the use of force in rescues when it passed the Hostage Act of 1868. But the Act's coverage and constitutionality are uncertain.

Targeting Terrorists

"Targeted killing" was not a term of art in law prior to the 9/11 attacks. It has been used with increasing frequency since then to refer to U.S. attacks by unmanned aerial vehicles (UAVs) or "drones" on alleged terrorist targets. But it may also refer to attacks by other means on selected individuals. A U.N. Special Rapporteur for Human Rights asserts:

> The common element in all these contexts is that lethal force is intentionally and deliberately used, with a degree of pre-meditation, against an individual or individuals specifically identified in advance by the perpetrator. In a targeted killing, the specific goal of the operation is to use lethal force. This distinguishes targeted killings from unintentional, accidental, or reckless killings, or killings made without conscious choice. It also distinguishes them from law enforcement operations, e.g., against a suspected suicide bomber. Under such circumstances, it may be legal for law enforcement personnel to shoot to kill based on the imminence of the threat, but the goal of the operation, from its inception, should not be to kill. [Special Rapporteur on Extrajudicial, Summary or Arbitrary Executions, Philip Alston, *Addendum: Study on Targeted Killings* at 5, U.N. Doc. A/HRC/14/24/Add.6 (May 28, 2010).]

In this chapter, we begin with brief accounts of several U.S. targeted killing operations. The legality of each operation depends in part on the legal paradigm under which it is analyzed and on how it was conducted. We next apply the paradigm of international human rights law (HRL) to these operations, then shift to the paradigm of international humanitarian law (IHL). Finally, we consider the targeting of U.S. citizens and an executive ban on "assassination."

A. TARGETED KILLING BY THE UNITED STATES AFTER 9/11[1]

In October 2001, on the first night of the campaign against Al Qaeda and the Taliban authorized by Congress after the September 11 attacks, the Predator, a

1. This report is drawn from William C. Banks, *The Predator* (Maxwell Sch. of Citizenship & Pub. Affairs, Syracuse Univ., CS 0603-32, 2003); Zachary Donnenfeld, *Drone Strikes a Growing Threat to African*

27-foot-long, unmanned aerial vehicle with a 49-foot wingspan deployed over southern Afghanistan, apparently identified Taliban leader Mullah Mohammed Omar in a convoy of cars fleeing Kabul. Following its agreement with military commanders, the CIA operators sought approval from the United States Central Command in Tampa to remotely launch a Hellfire missile from the Predator at Omar, who by then had sought cover in a building with an estimated 100 guards. General Tommy Franks reportedly declined to give approval based upon on-the-spot advice of his military lawyer. Other reports suggest that, in light of the number of possible casualties, he sought approval from the President, who personally approved the strike. But the resulting delay apparently allowed Omar to escape.

In February 2002, another Predator filmed a very tall man being greeted effusively by villagers. Osama bin Laden was said to be about six feet five inches tall. The order was quickly given to fire, but by that time the group had disbanded, and the Predator captured another image of a tall man and two others emerging from a wooded area. The Hellfire was launched, killing all three. Journalists later reported that they were locals who had been scavenging for wood. Bin Laden was not among them.

On November 3, 2002, video feeds from television cameras on a Predator flying slowly 10,000-15,000 feet above Marib Province in Yemen showed an RV speeding through the desert. A joint Yemeni and American intelligence team had for days been tracing cell phone calls by an Al Qaeda leader named Qaed Salim Sinan al-Harethi, and it determined that he was in the car. Al-Harethi was a prime suspect in the 2000 suicide bombing of the USS *Cole*, which had killed 17 U.S. sailors. Using a joystick to control the Predator remotely, a U.S. operator fired a Hellfire missile from the plane, striking the RV dead center and killing all five of its passengers. Yemeni security officials later took the bodies to a hospital in Yemen's capital, where U.S. officials obtained DNA samples. They confirmed that the Predator attack had "taken out" al-Harethi. They also identified one of the other victims as Kamal Derwish, a U.S. citizen who grew up near Buffalo and who reportedly recruited American Muslims for training in Al Qaeda camps.

After months of careful intelligence gathering and extensive planning, on May 1, 2011, 79 American special forces personnel in four helicopters descended on a walled compound in Abbottabad, Pakistan, and, near the end of a 40-minute firefight, shot and killed Osama bin Laden. President Obama settled on a commando raid rather than a drone strike to avoid incidental civilian casualties in a residential area and to permit verification of bin Laden's identity once he was captured or killed. When the Navy SEALs located bin Laden on the top floor of the dwelling, he reportedly resisted arrest and was shot in the head. He was not armed at the time, however. Several couriers and a woman were also killed, but others in the compound (reportedly including one of bin Laden's wives) were uninjured, and apparently no damage was caused outside the compound.

On September 30, 2011, missiles from one or more pilotless U.S. drones struck the vehicle Anwar al-Aulaqi was riding in and killed him and at least three others.

Civilians (Inst. for Security Studies, Feb. 27, 2019); Kristen Eichensehr, *On the Offensive: Assassination Policy Under International Law*, 25 Harv. Int'l Rev. 1 (2003); Seymour Hersh, *Manhunt*, New Yorker, Dec. 23, 2002, at 66, 74; Eblen Kaplan, *Targeted Killings* (Council on Foreign Rel., Mar. 2, 2006); Mark Mazzetti, Helene Cooper & Peter Baker, *Behind the Hunt for Bin Laden*, N.Y. Times, May 2, 2011; Jack Searle & Jessica Perkiss, *Drone Wars: The Full Data* (Jan. 1, 2017), *available at* https://www.thebureauinvestigates.com/stories/2017-01-01/drone-wars-the-full-data; Scott Shane, Mark Mazzetti & Robert F. Worth, *Secret Assault on Terrorism Widens on Two Continents*, N.Y. Times, Aug. 14, 2010; Michael D. Shear, *White House Corrects Bin Laden Narrative*, N.Y. Times, May 3, 2011; *U.S. Airstrikes in the Long War* (FDD's Long War Journal 2017), *available at* https://www.longwarjournal.org/us-airstrikes-in-the-long-war; White House, *Report on the Legal and Policy Frameworks Guiding the United States' Use of Military Force and Related National Security Operations* (Dec. 2016).

Al-Aulaqi was a U.S. citizen who served as a propagandist for Al Qaeda in the Arabian Peninsula (AQAP). Subsequently, President Obama explained:

> For the record, I do not believe it would be constitutional for the government to target and kill any U.S. citizen — with a drone, or a shotgun — without due process. Nor should any President deploy armed drones over U.S. soil.
>
> But when a U.S. citizen goes abroad to wage war against America — and is actively plotting to kill U.S. citizens; and when neither the United States, nor our partners are in a position to capture him before he carries out a plot — his citizenship should no more serve as a shield than a sniper shooting down on an innocent crowd should be protected from a swat team. . . .
>
> . . . I would have detained and prosecuted Awlaki if we captured him before he carried out a plot. But we couldn't. And as President, I would have been derelict in my duty had I not authorized the strike that took out Awlaki. [Remarks by the President at the National Defense University (May 23, 2013).]

A separate U.S. drone strike inadvertently killed al-Aulaqi's son and at least six others two weeks later in a mission that did not kill its intended target.

Since then, UAVs have reportedly been used hundreds of times to fire on targets in Afghanistan, Iraq, Libya, Pakistan, Somalia, and Yemen. In addition to Osama bin Laden, multiple senior Taliban, Al Qaeda, ISIS operatives, and al-Shabab militants have been killed in such attacks. But some number of innocent civilians have also been killed, sometimes deliberately as unavoidable collateral damage and sometimes simply by mistake.

The following table shows comparative numbers of strikes across three administrations from data compiled by non-governmental organizations.

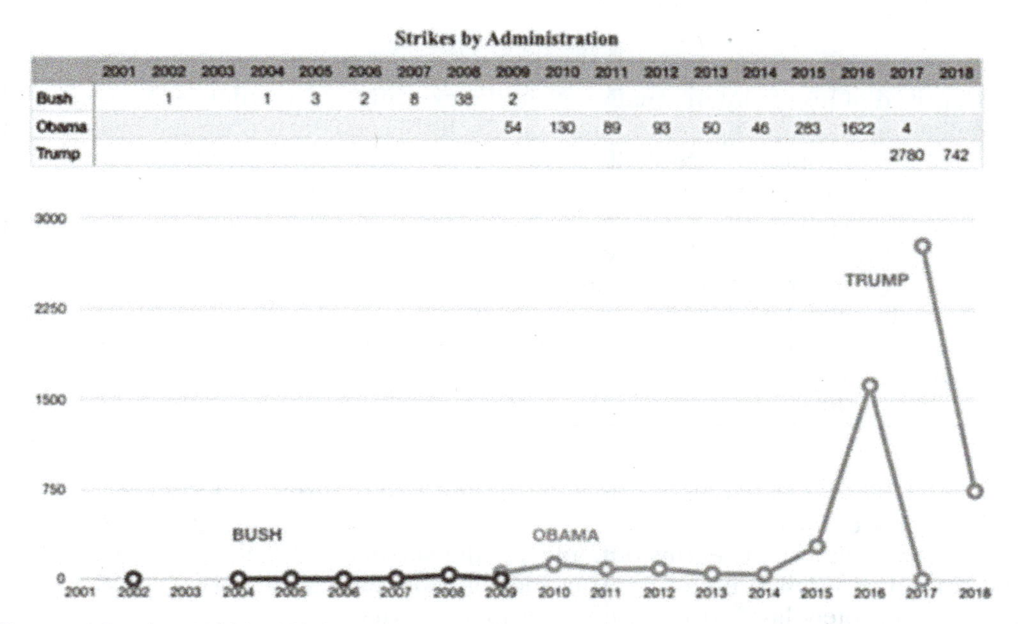

Strikes by Administration

	2001	2002	2003	2004	2005	2006	2007	2008	2009	2010	2011	2012	2013	2014	2015	2016	2017	2018
Bush		1		1	3	2	8	38	2									
Obama									54	130	89	93	50	46	283	1622	4	
Trump																	2780	742

Prepared October 2018 by Kristianna Anderson from data compiled by Bureau of Investigative Journalism, https://www.thebureauinvestigates.com/projects/drone-war, and Foundation for the Defense of Democracies' Long War Journal, https://www.longwarjournal.org/us-airstrikes-in-the-long-war.

B. TARGETED KILLING AND HUMAN RIGHTS LAW (HRL)

Human rights law — international law that constrains governments in their treatment of civilians during peacetime — generally requires some kind of judicial procedure before anyone is executed (hence, the oft-stated concern about "*extrajudicial* killing or imprisonment"). The law enforcement model under human rights law rests on a presumption of innocence, a preference for arrest and detention by due process, and an insistence on credible evidence and fair trial before judicial punishment. *See generally* David Kretzmer, *Targeted Killing of Suspected Terrorists: Extra-Judicial Executions or Legitimate Means of Defence?*, 16 Eur. J. Int'l L. 171 (2005).

Article 6 of the International Covenant on Civil and Political Rights (ICCPR), Mar. 23, 1976, 999 U.N.T.S. 171, provides: "Every human being has the inherent right to life. This right shall be protected by law. No one shall be arbitrarily deprived of his life." This language resembles the text of the Fifth Amendment to the United States Constitution, which states: "No person shall . . . be deprived of life, liberty, or property, without due process of law. . . ." The European Convention on Human Rights is similar:

Convention for the Protection of Human Rights and Fundamental Freedoms

Nov. 4, 1950, 213 U.N.T.S. 222

ARTICLE 2 — RIGHT TO LIFE

1. Everyone's right to life shall be protected by law. No one shall be deprived of his life intentionally save in the execution of a sentence of a court following his conviction of a crime for which this penalty is provided by law.

2. Deprivation of life shall not be regarded as inflicted in contravention of this Article when it results from the use of force which is no more than absolutely necessary:

(a) in defence of any person from unlawful violence;

(b) in order to effect a lawful arrest or to prevent the escape of a person lawfully detained;

(c) in action lawfully taken for the purpose of quelling a riot or insurrection.

The United Nations Basic Principles on the Use of Force and Firearms by Law Enforcement Officials (Sept. 7, 1990), *available at* http://www2.ohchr.org/english/law/pdf/firearms.pdf, address the subject in detail. Article 9 provides that "intentional lethal use of firearms may only be made when strictly unavoidable in order to protect life." Article 10 further provides that

> law enforcement officials shall identify themselves as such and shall give a clear warning of their intent to use firearms, with sufficient time for the warnings to be observed, unless to

> do so would unduly place the law enforcement officials at risk or would create a risk of death or serious harm to other persons, or would be clearly inappropriate or pointless in the circumstances of the incident.

In effect, the imminence of the threat provides the evidence needed to justify the use of lethal force and obviates any need to prove the target's intention. Kretzmer, *supra*, at 182. But unless the strict requirements of imminence and necessity through unavailability of other means are satisfied, the use of lethal force by law enforcement officers or, except in armed conflict, military personnel would deny a suspected terrorist basic due process, "preventing the target from contesting the determination that he or she is a terrorist, and imposing a unilateral death penalty." Vincent-Joel Proulx, *If the Hat Fits, Wear It, If the Turban Fits, Run for Your Life: Reflections on the Indefinite Detention and Targeted Killing of Suspected Terrorists*, 56 Hastings L.J. 801, 889 (2005). Thus, "the very purpose of international human rights is defeated, whether through the violation of the right to a fair trial, the absolute circumvention of the right to liberty, or the disregard of the inherent right to life." *Id.* at 889-890.

Case Study: The Gibraltar Killings

Authorities in the United Kingdom learned that Daniel McCann, Sean Savage, and Mairead Farrell of the Provisional IRA (PIRA) were planning to detonate a car bomb at a changing of the guard ceremony in Gibraltar on March 8, 1988, using a radio-controlled detonation device. On March 6, 1988, the suspects were allowed to enter Gibraltar and were clandestinely followed by soldiers in the Special Air Service (SAS) who wore plain clothes and carried concealed weapons. When the suspects parked a car and began to walk away, the soldiers, fearing that the suspects were going to detonate a car bomb, shot and killed all three. The suspects, it turned out, were unarmed and had no detonation device, but one had keys to a parked car in which were found keys to another car containing 64 kilograms of Semtex explosives, around which were packed 200 rounds of ammunition.

Relatives of the deceased IRA members filed a complaint alleging that the killings violated Article 2 of the European Convention, in an action that eventually reached the European Court of Human Rights in *McCann v. United Kingdom*, 21 E.H.R.R. 97 (1995). The case raised these questions, among others:

- Were the killings "in defence of any person from unlawful violence"? Should it matter whether such violence was ongoing, imminent, likely, or merely possible?
- The suspects were identified at the Spanish border, but allowed to cross. Since they could have been stopped at the border, was *any* subsequent use of force therefore "no more than absolutely necessary"? Does it matter that the suspects could lawfully have been arrested at the border or merely turned away?
- The SAS are soldiers trained to kill as a first resort. Law enforcement officers, by contrast, are trained to kill only as last resort; when they use force,

it is the minimum force needed to prevent unlawful violence or effect an arrest, usually preceded by a warning or even a warning shot, as the United Nations Basic Principles suggest. Does the very fact that the SAS, rather than civilian law enforcement officers, were put on the suspects' trail violate human rights law?

Notes and Questions

1. Preventing Violence. Under human rights law, the predicate for the lawful extrajudicial killing of someone outside of armed conflict is that the killing is to defend persons from unlawful violence, to effect an arrest or prevent an escape, or to quell a riot or insurrection. The Provisional IRA had previously committed a series of bombings, including some using remotely detonated car bombs. In these circumstances, it was perhaps no surprise that the European Court unanimously held,

> The Court accepts that the soldiers honestly believed, in the light of the information that they had been given, . . . that it was necessary to shoot the suspects in order to prevent them from detonating a bomb and causing serious loss of life. The actions which they took, in obedience to superior orders, were thus perceived by them as absolutely necessary in order to safeguard innocent lives. [*McCann*, ¶200.]

It mattered not that the soldiers honestly held a belief that turned out to be mistaken, namely, that the suspects had a bomb in the car they had just parked.

2. No More than Absolutely Necessary? Even if the SAS soldiers did not individually commit a human rights violation, the Court had to determine "whether the anti-terrorist operation as a whole was controlled and organized in a manner which respected the requirements of Article 2. . . ." *Id.* ¶201. A bare majority of the Court (10-9) answered no.

First, the majority found that the suspects might have been arrested or at least turned away at the border, perhaps rendering a subsequent use of lethal force unnecessary. But suppose there was insufficient evidence to arrest and hold them. Might the PIRA, alerted then to the fact that the suspects were on the government's radar, have simply sent in a different team of bombers?

Second, the majority questioned whether the SAS soldiers had been trained to "assess whether the use of firearms to wound their targets may have been warranted. . . . Their reflex action in this vital respect lacks the degree of caution in the use of firearms to be expected from law enforcement personnel in a democratic society. . . ." *Id.* ¶212. But the dissenters noted that the Gibraltar police had expressly requested military assistance, given the gravity of the car bomb threat and a previous discovery of radio-controlled detonators and explosives collected by PIRA operatives in other countries.

> Troops trained in a counter-terrorist role and to operate successfully in small groups would clearly be a suitable choice to meet the threat of an IRA active service unit at large

> in a densely populated area such as Gibraltar, where there would be an imperative need to limit as far as possible the risk of accidental harm to passers-by. [*Id.* ¶10 (joint dissenting opinion).]

The majority of the Court concluded,

> having regard to the decision not to prevent the suspects from travelling into Gibraltar, to the failure of the authorities to make sufficient allowances for the possibility that their intelligence assessments might, in some respects at least, be erroneous and to the automatic recourse to lethal force when the soldiers opened fire, the Court is not persuaded that the killing of the three terrorists constituted the use of force which was no more than absolutely necessary in defence of persons from unlawful violence within the meaning of Article 2 para. 2(a) of the Convention. [*Id.* ¶213 (majority opinion).]

The dissenters disagreed.

> [W]e are satisfied that no failings have been shown in the organisation and control of the operation by the authorities which could justify a conclusion that force was used against the suspects disproportionately to the purpose of defending innocent persons from unlawful violence. [*Id.* ¶25 (joint dissenting opinion).]

Who was right? If you side with the dissenters, why do you think the vote was so close? Is one answer that human rights law is inherently cautious and erects a powerful presumption against extrajudicial deprivation of life?

3. Were the Predator Attacks in Pakistan and Yemen Extrajudicial Killings? Applying HRL, the U.N. Special Rapporteur to the Commission on Human Rights expressed the opinion that the 2002 U.S. "attack in Yemen [killing al-Harethi] constitutes a clear case of extrajudicial killing." U.N. Econ. & Soc. Council, *Civil and Political Rights, Including the Questions of Disappearances and Summary Executions, Submitted to Comm'n on Human Rights,* U.N. Doc. E/CN.4/2003/3 (Jan. 13, 2003). The Swedish Foreign Minister reached a similar conclusion, calling the attack "a summary execution that violates human rights. Terrorists must be treated according to international law. Otherwise, any country can start executing those whom they consider terrorists." *Quoted in* Hersh, *supra* p. 376 n.1, at 4.

Do you agree? Does it matter legally whether the targeted killing is in the border region of Pakistan, in remote provinces of Yemen, in Somalia — or in Germany? Note that although Yemeni officials apparently cooperated in the targeted killing of al-Harethi, they had previously failed to apprehend him and may have been reluctant to do so because of a perceived debt owed to Osama bin Laden, who had assisted the Yemeni president in putting down a separatist movement in 1994. Should the availability of "normal judicial channels" make a difference in the law enforcement analysis? Should it matter legally that one of the persons traveling with al-Harethi in 2002 in Yemen was a U.S. citizen?

4. Human Rights Law in Times of War or Armed Conflict? If the incident that gave rise to the *McCann* litigation had occurred in Northern Ireland in the 1970s, or in Afghanistan in 2010, with the UK personnel deployed as part of the NATO force there, would HRL apply?

The European view is that HRL always applies, even alongside IHL on the battlefield. Marco Sassoli & Laura M. Olson, *The Relationship Between Human Rights and Humanitarian Law Where It Matters: Admissible Killing and Internment of Fighters in Non-International Armed Conflicts,* 90 Int'l Rev. Red Cross 599, 603 (Sept. 2008). Thus, the International Court of Justice and other international courts have applied HRL in armed-conflict settings. *See Legality of the Threat or Use of Nuclear Weapons, Advisory Opinion,* 1996 I.C.J. 226 (July 8). Indeed, there is a growing tendency to apply HRL in armed conflicts, expanding the protections otherwise available to civilians and disarmed combatants.

By contrast, historically the United States took the position that during armed conflicts HRL gives way to IHL and its *jus in bello* principles. Thus, in the event of a conflict between HRL and IHL on the battlefield, the traditional U.S. view has been that the *in bello* rules are *lex specialis,* trumping the *lex generalis* of HRL. *Operational Law Handbook* 40 (Marie Anderson & Emily Zukauskas eds., 2008). However, in a 2011 report to the U.N. Human Rights Committee, the State Department noted that HRL and IHL "are in many respects complementary and mutually reinforcing. . . . Determining the international law rule that applies to a particular action taken by a government in the context of an armed conflict is a fact-specific determination, which cannot be easily generalized, and raises especially complex issues in the context of non-international armed conflicts. . . ." U.S. Dep't of State, *Fourth Periodic Report of the United States of America to the United Nations Committee on Human Rights Concerning the International Covenant on Civil and Political Rights* ¶507 (Dec. 30, 2011), https://2009-2017.state.gov/j/drl/rls/179781.htm#iii.

What difference does it make? That is, how do the requirements of HRL and IHL for lethal uses of force relevantly differ?

C. TARGETED KILLING AND INTERNATIONAL HUMANITARIAN LAW (IHL)

Reading *Public Committee Against Torture in Israel v. Israel*

The Second Intifada began in February 2000. Palestinian groups carried out terrorist attacks against civilian targets in Israel, including restaurants and shopping centers. Over a five-year period, thousands of Israelis and Palestinians were killed or injured in the attacks. In response, the Israeli military initiated preventive strikes against suspected individual Palestinian terrorists. In carrying out these strikes, approximately 150 civilians were killed. The Public Committee Against Torture in Israel petitioned the High Court of Justice in Israel to declare the preventive strike policy unlawful. In reading the Court's response, consider especially these questions:

- Did the Court determine the legality of Israel's preventive strike policy?
- Was Israel engaged in an "armed conflict"?
- How did the Court distinguish among combatants, unlawful combatants, and civilians? What were the practical consequences of the distinctions?
- How did the Court apply the basic IHL principles of necessity, distinction, and proportionality?

Public Committee Against Torture in Israel v. Israel

Supreme Court of Israel, sitting as the High Court of Justice, 2006
46 I.L.M. 375

President (Emeritus) A. BARAK: The Government of Israel employs a policy of preventative strikes which cause the death of terrorists in Judea, Samaria, or the Gaza Strip. It fatally strikes these terrorists, who plan, launch, or commit terrorist attacks in Israel and in the area of Judea, Samaria, and the Gaza Strip, against both civilians and soldiers. These strikes at times also harm innocent civilians. Does the State thus act illegally? That is the question posed before us.

1. FACTUAL BACKGROUND

In February 2000, the second *intifada* began. A massive assault of terrorism was directed against the State of Israel, and against Israelis, merely because they are Israelis. This assault of terrorism differentiates neither between combatants and civilians, nor between women, men, and children. The terrorist attacks take place both in the territory of Judea, Samaria, and the Gaza Strip, and within the borders of the State of Israel. They are directed against civilian centers, shopping centers and markets, coffee houses and restaurants. Over the last five years, thousands of acts of terrorism have been committed against Israel. In the attacks, more than one thousand Israeli citizens have been killed. Thousands of Israeli citizens have been wounded. Thousands of Palestinians have been killed and wounded during this period as well.

2. In its war against terrorism, the State of Israel employs various means. As part of the security activity intended to confront the terrorist attacks, the State employs what it calls "the policy of targeted frustration" of terrorism. Under this policy, the security forces act in order to kill members of terrorist organizations involved in the planning, launching, or execution of terrorist attacks against Israel. During the second *intifada*, such preventative strikes have been performed across Judea, Samaria, and the Gaza Strip. According to the data relayed by petitioners, since the commencement of these acts, and up until the end of 2005, close to three hundred members of terrorist organizations have been killed by them. More than thirty targeted killing attempts have failed. Approximately one hundred and fifty civilians who were proximate to the location of the targeted persons have been killed during those acts. Hundreds of others have been wounded. The policy of targeted killings is the focus of this petition. . . .

5. THE GENERAL NORMATIVE FRAMEWORK

A. International Armed Conflict

16. The general, principled starting point is that between Israel and the various terrorist organizations active in Judea, Samaria, and the Gaza Strip (hereinafter "the area") a continuous situation of armed conflict has existed since the first *intifada*. . . .

23. . . . Are terrorist organizations and their members combatants, in regard[] to their rights in the armed conflict? Are they civilians taking an active part in the armed conflict? Are they possibly neither combatants nor civilians? What, then, is the status of those terrorists?

B. Combatants

24. What makes a person a combatant? This category includes, of course, the armed forces. It also includes people who fulfill the following conditions: [see Geneva Convention III, art. 4].... In one case, I wrote:

> The Lebanese detainees are not to be seen as prisoners of war. It is sufficient, in order to reach that conclusion, that they do not fulfill the provisions of article 4a(2)(d) of The Third Geneva Convention, which provides that one of the conditions which must be fulfilled in order to fit the definition of "a prisoner of war" is "that of conducting their operations in accordance with the laws and customs of war." The organizations to which the Lebanese detainees belonged are terrorist organizations acting contrary to the laws and customs of war. Thus, for example, these organizations intentionally harm civilians, and shoot from within the civilian population, which serves them as a shield. Each of these is an act contrary to international law. Indeed, Israel's constant stance throughout the years has been to view the various organizations, like the Hizbollah, as organizations to which The Third Geneva Convention does not apply. We found no cause to intervene in that stance.

25. The terrorists and their organizations, with which the State of Israel has an armed conflict of international character, do not fall into the category of combatants. They do not belong to the armed forces, and they do not belong to units to which international law grants status similar to that of combatants. Indeed, the terrorists and the organizations which send them to carry out attacks are unlawful combatants. They do not enjoy the status of prisoners of war. They can be tried for their participation in hostilities, judged, and punished. The Chief Justice of the Supreme Court of the United States, Stone C.J. discussed that, writing:

> By universal agreement and practice, the law of war draws a distinction between the armed forces and the peaceful population of belligerent nations and also between those who are lawful and unlawful combatants. Lawful combatants are subject to capture and detention as prisoners of war by opposing military forces. Unlawful combatant are likewise subject to capture and detention, but in addition they are subject to trial and punishment by military tribunals for acts which render their belligerency unlawful (*Ex parte Quirin*, 317 U.S. 1, 30 (1942); see also *Hamdi v. Rumsfeld*, 542 U.S. 507 (2004)).

... Needless to say, unlawful combatants are not beyond the law. They are not "outlaws." God created them as well in his image; their human dignity as well is to be honored; they as well enjoy and are entitled to protection, even if most minimal, by customary international law. That is certainly the case when they are in detention or brought to justice (see §75 of The First Protocol, which reflects customary international law). Does it follow that in Israel's conduct of combat against the terrorist organizations, Israel is not entitled to harm them, and Israel is not entitled to kill them even if they are planning, launching, or committing terrorist attacks? If they were seen as (legal) combatants, the answer would of course be that Israel is entitled to harm them. Just as it is permissible to harm a soldier of an enemy country, so can terrorists be harmed. Accordingly, they would also enjoy the status of prisoners of war, and the rest of the protections granted to legal combatants. However, as we have seen, the terrorists acting against Israel are not combatants according to the definition of that term in international law; they are not entitled to the status of prisoners of war; they can be put on trial for their membership in terrorist organizations and for their operations against the army. Are they seen as civilians under the law? It is to the examination of that question which we now turn.

C. Civilians

26. Customary international law regarding armed conflicts protects "civilians" from harm as a result of the hostilities. . . . From that follows also the duty to do everything possible to minimize collateral damage to the civilian population during the attacks on "combatants." Against the background of that protection granted to "civilians," the question what constitutes a "civilian" for the purposes of that law arises. The approach of customary international law is that "civilians" are those who are not "combatants" (see §50(1) of The First Protocol). In the *Blaskic* case, the International Criminal Tribunal for the former Yugoslavia ruled that civilians are—

> Persons who are not, or no longer, members of the armed forces.

That definition is "negative" in nature. It defines the concept of "civilian" as the opposite of "combatant." It thus views unlawful combatants—who, as we have seen, are not "combatants"—as civilians. Does that mean that the unlawful combatants are entitled to the same protection to which civilians who are not unlawful combatants are entitled? The answer is, no. Customary international law regarding armed conflicts determines that a civilian taking a direct part in the hostilities does not, at such time, enjoy the protection granted to a civilian who is not taking a direct part in the hostilities (see §51(3) of The First Protocol). The result is that an unlawful combatant is not a combatant, rather a "civilian." However, he is a civilian who is not protected from attack as long as he is taking a direct part in the hostilities. . . .

D. A Third Category: Unlawful Combatants?

27. In the oral and written arguments before us, the State asked us to recognize a third category of persons, that of unlawful combatants. These are people who take active and continuous part in an armed conflict, and therefore should be treated as combatants, in the sense that they are legitimate targets of attack, and they do not enjoy the protections granted to civilians. However, they are not entitled to the rights and privileges of combatants, since they do not differentiate themselves from the civilian population, and since they do not obey the laws of war. Thus, for example, they are not entitled to the status of prisoners of war. The State's position is that the terrorists who participate in the armed conflict between Israel and the terrorist organizations fall under this category of unlawful combatants.

28. . . . We shall take no stance regarding the question whether it is desirable to recognize this third category. The question before us is not one of desirable law, rather one of existing law. In our opinion, as far as existing law goes, the data before us are not sufficient to recognize this third category. . . .

6. CIVILIANS WHO ARE UNLAWFUL COMBATANTS

A. The Basic Principle: Civilians Taking a Direct Part in Hostilities Are Not Protected at Such Time They Are Doing So

29. Civilians enjoy comprehensive protection of their lives, liberty, and property. "The protection of the lives of the civilian population is a central value in humanitarian law." "The right to life and bodily integrity is the basic right standing at the center of the humanitarian law intended to protect the local population." As opposed to combatants, whom one can harm due to their status as combatants, civilians are not to be harmed, due to their status as civilians. A provision in this spirit is determined in article 51(2) of The First Protocol, which constitutes customary international law. . . .

B. The Source of the Basic Principle and its Customary Character

30. The basic principle is that the civilians taking a direct part in hostilities are not protected from attack upon them at such time as they are doing so. This principle is manifest in §51(3) of The First Protocol. . . .

As is well known, Israel is not party to The First Protocol. Thus, it clearly was not enacted in domestic Israeli legislation. Does the basic principle express customary international law? The position of The Red Cross is that it is a principle of customary international law. That position is acceptable to us. . . . In military manuals of many states, including England, France, Holland, Australia, Italy, Canada, Germany, the United States (Air Force), and New Zealand, the provision has been copied verbatim, or by adopting its essence, according to which civilians are not to be attacked, unless they are taking a (direct) part in the hostilities. The legal literature sees that provision as an expression of customary international law. . . .

C. The Essence of the Basic Principle. . . .

32. . . . [T]he basic principle is that the civilian population, and single civilians, are protected from the dangers of military activity and are not targets for attack. That protection is granted to civilians "unless and for such time as they take a direct part in hostilities" (§51(3) of The First Protocol). That provision is composed of three main parts. The first part is the requirement that civilians take part in "hostilities"; the second part is the requirement that civilians take a "direct" part in hostilities; the third part is the provision by which civilians are not protected from attack "for such time" as they take a direct part in hostilities. We shall discuss each of those parts separately.

D. The First Part: "Taking . . . Part in Hostilities"

33. Civilians lose the protection of customary international law dealing with hostilities of international character if they "take . . . part in hostilities." What is the meaning of that provision? The accepted view is that "hostilities" are acts which by nature and objective are intended to cause damage to the army. Thus determines *Commentary on the Additional Protocols*, published by the Red Cross in 1987:

> Hostile acts should be understood to be acts which by their nature and purpose are intended to cause actual harm to the personnel and equipment of the armed forces.

. . . It seems that acts which by nature and objective are intended to cause damage to civilians should be added to that definition. According to the accepted definition, a civilian is taking part in hostilities when using weapons in an armed conflict, while gathering intelligence, or while preparing himself for the hostilities. Regarding taking part in hostilities, there is no condition that the civilian use his weapon, nor is [there] a condition that he bear arms (openly or concealed). It is possible to take part in hostilities without using weapons at all. *Commentary on the Additional Protocols* discussed that issue:

> It seems that the word "hostilities" covers not only the time that the civilian actually makes use of a weapon, but also, for example, the time that he is carrying it, as well as situations in which he undertakes hostile acts without using a weapon.

As we have seen, that approach is not limited merely to the issue of "hostilities" toward the army or the state. It applies also to hostilities against the civilian population of the state.

E. Second Part: "Takes a Direct Part"

34. Civilians lose the protection against military attack, granted to them by customary international law dealing with international armed conflict (as adopted in The First Protocol, §51(3)), if "they take a direct part in hostilities." That provision differentiates between civilians taking a direct part in hostilities (from whom the protection from attack is removed) and civilians taking an indirect part in hostilities (who continue to enjoy protection from attack). What is that differentiation? A similar provision appears in Common Article 3 of The Geneva Conventions, which uses the wording "active part in hostilities." The judgment of the International Criminal Tribunal for Rwanda determined that these two terms are of identical content. What is that content? It seems accepted in the international literature that an agreed upon definition of the term "direct" in the context under discussion does not exist.

In that state of affairs, and without a comprehensive and agreed upon customary standard, there is no escaping going case by case, while narrowing the area of disagreement.... On this issue, the following passage from *Commentary on the Additional Protocols* is worth quoting:

> Undoubtedly there is room here for some margin of judgment: to restrict this concept to combat and active military operations would be too narrow, while extending it to the entire war effort would be too broad, as in modern warfare the whole population participates in the war effort to some extent, albeit indirectly.

Indeed, a civilian bearing arms (openly or concealed) who is on his way to the place where he will use them against the army, at such place, or on his way back from it, is a civilian taking "an active part" in the hostilities. However, a civilian who generally supports the hostilities against the army is not taking a direct part in the hostilities. Similarly, a civilian who sells food or medicine to unlawful combatants is also taking an indirect part in the hostilities. The third report of the Inter-American Commission on Human Rights states:

> Civilians whose activities merely support the adverse party's war or military effort or otherwise only indirectly participate in hostilities cannot on these grounds alone be considered combatants. This is because indirect participation, such as selling goods to one or more of the armed parties, expressing sympathy for the cause of one of the parties or, even more clearly, failing to act to prevent an incursion by one of the armed parties, does not involve acts of violence which pose an immediate threat of actual harm to the adverse party.

And what is the law in the space between these two extremes? On the one hand, the desire to protect innocent civilians leads, in the hard cases, to a narrow interpretation of the term "direct" part in hostilities. Professor Cassese writes:

> The rationale behind the prohibition against targeting a civilian who does not take a direct part in hostilities, despite his possible (previous or future) involvement in fighting, is linked to the need to avoid killing innocent civilians.

On the other hand, it can be said that the desire to protect combatants and the desire to protect innocent civilians lead[ ], in the hard cases, to a wide interpretation of the "direct" character of the hostilities, as thus civilians are encouraged to stay away from the hostilities to the extent possible. Schmitt writes:

> Gray areas should be interpreted liberally, i.e., in favor of finding direct participation. One of the seminal purposes of the law is to make possible a clear distinction between civilians and combatants. Suggesting that civilians retain their immunity even when they are intricately involved in a conflict is to engender disrespect for the law by combatants endangered by their activities. Moreover, a liberal approach creates an incentive for civilians to remain as distant from the conflict as possible — in doing so they can better avoid being charged with participation in the conflict and are less liable to being directly targeted.

35. Against the background of these considerations, the following cases should also be included in the definition of taking a "direct part" in hostilities: a person who collects intelligence on the army, whether on issues regarding the hostilities or beyond those issues; a person who transports unlawful combatants to or from the place where the hostilities are taking place; a person who operates weapons which unlawful combatants use, or supervises their operation, or provides service to them, be the distance from the battlefield as it may. All those persons are performing the function of combatants. The function determines the directness of the part taken in the hostilities. However, a person who sells food or medicine to an unlawful combatant is not taking a direct part, rather an indirect part in the hostilities. The same is the case regarding a person who aids the unlawful combatants by general strategic analysis, and grants them logistical, general support, including monetary aid. The same is the case regarding a person who distributes propaganda supporting those unlawful combatants. If such persons are injured, the State is likely not to be liable for it, if it falls into the framework of collateral or incidental damage. . . .

36. What is the law regarding civilians serving as a "human shield" for terrorists taking a direct part in the hostilities? Certainly, if they are doing so because they were forced to do so by terrorists, those innocent civilians are not to be seen as taking a direct part in the hostilities. They themselves are victims of terrorism. However, if they do so of their own free will, out of support for the terrorist organization, they should be seen as persons taking a direct part in the hostilities.

37. We have seen that a civilian causing harm to the army is taking "a direct part" in hostilities. What says the law about those who enlist him to take a direct part in the hostilities, and those who send him to commit hostilities? Is there a difference between his direct commanders and those responsible for them? Is the "direct" part taken only by the last terrorist in the chain of command, or by the entire chain? In our opinion, the "direct" character of the part taken should not be narrowed merely to the person committing the physical act of attack. Those who have sent him, as well, take "a direct part." The same goes for the person who decided upon the act, and the person who planned it. It is not to be said about them that they are taking an indirect part in the hostilities. Their contribution is direct (and active).

F. The Third Part: "For Such Time"

38. Article 51(3) of The First Protocol states that civilians enjoy protection from the dangers stemming from military acts, and that they are not targets for attack, unless "and for such time" as they are taking a direct part in hostilities. The provisions of article 51(3) of The First Protocol present a time requirement. A civilian taking a part in hostilities loses the protection from attack "for such time" as he is taking part in those hostilities. If "such time" has passed — the protection granted to the civilian returns. . . .

39. As regarding the scope of the wording "takes a direct part" in hostilities, so too regarding the scope of the wording "and for such time" there is no consensus in the international literature. Indeed, both these concepts are close to each other. However, they are not identical. With no consensus regarding the interpretation of the wording "for such time," there is no choice but to proceed from case to case. Again, it is helpful to examine the extreme cases. On the one hand, a civilian taking a direct part in hostilities one single time, or sporadically, who later detaches himself from that activity, is a civilian who, starting from the time he detached himself from that activity, is entitled to protection from attack. He is not to be attacked for the hostilities which he committed in the past. On the other hand, a civilian who has joined a terrorist organization which has become his "home," and in the framework of his role in that organization he commits a chain of hostilities, with short periods of rest between them, loses his immunity from attack "for such time" as he is committing the chain of acts. Indeed, regarding such a civilian, the rest between hostilities is nothing other than preparation for the next hostility.

40. These examples point out the dilemma which the "for such time" requirement presents before us. On the one hand, a civilian who took a direct part in hostilities once, or sporadically, but detached himself from them (entirely, or for a long period) is not to be harmed. On the other hand, the "revolving door" phenomenon, by which each terrorist has "horns of the altar" (1 Kings 1:50) to grasp or a "city of refuge" (Numbers 35:11) to flee to, to which he turns in order to rest and prepare while they grant him immunity from attack, is to be avoided. In the wide area between those two possibilities, one finds the "gray" cases, about which customary international law has not yet crystallized. There is thus no escaping examination of each and every case. In that context, the following four things should be said: first, well based information is needed before categorizing a civilian as falling into one of the discussed categories. Innocent civilians are not to be harmed. Information which has been most thoroughly verified is needed regarding the identity and activity of the civilian who is allegedly taking part in the hostilities. Cassese rightly stated that —

> [I]f a belligerent were allowed to fire at enemy civilians simply suspected of somehow planning or conspiring to plan military attacks, or of having planned or directed hostile actions, the basic foundations of international humanitarian law would be seriously undermined. The basic distinction between civilians and combatants would be called into question and the whole body of law relating to armed conflict would eventually be eroded.

The burden of proof on the attacking army is heavy. In the case of doubt, careful verification is needed before an attack is made. Henckaerts & Doswald-Beck made this point:

> [W]hen there is a situation of doubt, a careful assessment has to be made under the conditions and restraints governing a particular situation as to whether there are sufficient indications to warrant an attack. One cannot automatically attack anyone who might appear dubious.

Second, a civilian taking a direct part in hostilities cannot be attacked at such time as he is doing so, if a less harmful means can be employed. In our domestic law, that rule is called for by the principle of proportionality. Indeed, among the military means, one must choose the means whose harm to the human rights of the harmed person is smallest. Thus, if a terrorist taking a direct part in hostilities can be arrested, interrogated, and tried, those are the means which should be employed. Trial is preferable to use of force. A rule-of-law state employs, to the extent possible, procedures of law and not procedures of force. . . .

. . . Third, after an attack on a civilian suspected of taking an active part, at such time, in hostilities, a thorough investigation regarding the precision of the identification of the target and the circumstances of the attack upon him is to be performed (retroactively). That investigation must be independent. In appropriate cases it is appropriate to pay compensation as a result of harm caused to an innocent civilian. Last, if the harm is not only to a civilian directly participating in the hostilities, rather also to innocent civilians nearby, the harm to them is collateral damage. That damage must withstand the proportionality test. We shall now proceed to the examination of that question.

7. PROPORTIONALITY . . .

B. Proportionality in an International Armed Conflict

42. The principle of proportionality is a substantial part of international law regarding armed conflict (compare §51(5)(b) and 57 of The First Protocol). That law is of customary character. The principle of proportionality arises when the military operation is directed toward combatants and military objectives, or against civilians at such time as they are taking a direct part in hostilities, yet civilians are also harmed. The rule is that the harm to innocent civilians caused by collateral damage during combat operations must be proportionate. Civilians might be harmed due to their presence inside of a military target, such as civilians working in an army base; civilians might be harmed when they live or work in, or pass by, military targets; at times, due to a mistake, civilians are harmed even if they are far from military targets; at times civilians are forced to serve as "human shields" from attack upon a military target, and they are harmed as a result. In all those situations, and in other similar ones, the rule is that the harm to the innocent civilians must fulfill, inter alia, the requirements of the principle of proportionality. . . .

44. The requirement of proportionality in the laws of armed conflict focuses primarily upon what our constitutional law calls proportionality "stricto senso," that is, the requirement that there be a proper proportionate relationship between the military objective and the civilian damage. However, the laws of armed conflict include additional components. . . .

C. Proper Proportion between Benefit and Damage

45. The proportionality test determines that attack upon innocent civilians is not permitted if the collateral damage caused to them is not proportionate to the military advantage (in protecting combatants and civilians). In other words, attack is proportionate if the benefit stemming from the attainment of the proper military objective is proportionate to the damage caused to innocent civilians harmed by it. That is a values based test. It is based upon a balancing between conflicting values and interests. It is accepted in the national law of various countries. It constitutes a central normative test for examining the activity of the government in general, and of the military specifically, in Israel. In one case I stated:

> Basically, this subtest carries on its shoulders the constitutional view that the ends do not justify the means. It is a manifestation of the idea that there is a barrier of values which democracy cannot surpass, even if the purpose whose attainment is being attempted is worthy....

46. That aspect of proportionality is not required regarding harm to a combatant, or to a civilian taking a direct part in the hostilities at such time as the harm is caused. Indeed, a civilian taking part in hostilities is endangering his life, and he might — like a combatant — be the objective of a fatal attack. That killing is permitted. However, that proportionality is required in any case in which an innocent civilian is harmed. Thus, the requirements of proportionality stricto senso must be fulfilled in a case in which the harm to the terrorist carries with it collateral damage caused to nearby innocent civilians. The proportionality rule applies in regards to harm to those innocent civilians (see §51(5)(b) of The First Protocol). The rule is that combatants and terrorists are not to be harmed if the damage expected to be caused to nearby innocent civilians is not proportionate to the military advantage in harming the combatants and terrorists. Performing that balance is difficult. Here as well, one must proceed case by case, while narrowing the area of disagreement. Take the usual case of a combatant, or of a terrorist sniper shooting at soldiers or civilians from his porch. Shooting at him is proportionate even if as a result, an innocent civilian neighbor or passerby is harmed. That is not the case if the building is bombed from the air and scores of its residents and passersby are harmed. The hard cases are those which are in the space between the extreme examples. There, a meticulous examination of every case is required; it is required that the military advantage be direct and anticipated (see §57(2)(iii) of The First Protocol). Indeed, in international law, as in internal law, the ends do not justify the means....

IMPLEMENTATION OF THE GENERAL PRINCIPLES IN THIS CASE

60.... The examination of the "targeted killing" — and in our terms, the preventative strike causing the deaths of terrorists, and at times also of innocent civilians — has shown that the question of the legality of the preventative strike according to customary international law is complex. The result of that examination is not that such strikes are always permissible or that they are always forbidden. The approach of customary international law applying to armed conflicts of an international nature is that civilians are protected from attacks by the army. However, that protection does not exist regarding those civilians "for such time as they take a direct part in hostilities" (§51(3) of The First

Protocol). Harming such civilians, even if the result is death, is permitted, on the condition that there is no other less harmful means, and on the condition that innocent civilians nearby are not harmed. Harm to the latter must be proportionate. That proportionality is determined according to a values based test, intended to balance between the military advantage and the civilian damage. As we have seen, we cannot determine that a preventative strike is always legal, just as we cannot determine that it is always illegal. All depends upon the question whether the standards of customary international law regarding international armed conflict allow that preventative strike or not.

CONCLUSION

61. The State of Israel is fighting against severe terrorism, which plagues it from the area. The means at Israel's disposal are limited. The State determined that preventative strikes upon terrorists in the area which cause their deaths are a necessary means from the military standpoint. These strikes at times cause harm and even death to innocent civilians. These preventative strikes, with all the military importance they entail, must be made within the framework of the law. The saying "when the cannons roar, the muses are silent" is well known. A similar idea was expressed by Cicero, who said: "during war, the laws are silent" (silent enim legis inter arma). Those sayings are regrettable. They reflect neither the existing law nor the desirable law. It is when the cannons roar that we especially need the laws. Every struggle of the state — against terrorism or any other enemy — is conducted according to rules and law. There is always law which the state must comply with. There are no "black holes." In this case, the law was determined by customary international law regarding conflicts of an international character. Indeed, the State's struggle against terrorism is not conducted "outside" of the law. It is conducted "inside" the law, with tools that the law places at the disposal of democratic states. . . .

U.S. Policy Standards and Procedures for the Use of Force in Counterterrorism Operations Outside the United States and Areas of Active Hostilities[2]

May 22, 2013

available at https://fas.org/irp/offdocs/ppd/ppg-fs.pdf

. . . [T]he President has approved, and senior members of the Executive Branch have briefed to the Congress, written policy standards and procedures that formalize and strengthen the Administration's rigorous process for reviewing and approving

[2. The *U.S. Policy Standards* excerpted here are a summary of a Presidential Policy Guidance, *Procedures for Approving Direct Action Against Terrorist Targets Located Outside the United States and Areas of Active Hostilities* (May 22, 2013). A partially redacted version of the Guidance was released by the Obama administration in March 2016. It is available at https://www.aclu.org/sites/default/files/field_document/presidential_policy_guidance.pdf. The Presidential Policy Guidance is generally consistent with the *U.S. Policy Standards*, but the Guidance clarifies that so-called "signature strikes" are not always directed against persons whose identity is unknown; they may also be directed at military targets such as improvised explosive devices and explosives storage facilities. *Id.* §4.A, at 15. — Eds.]

operations to capture or employ lethal force against terrorist targets outside the United States and outside areas of active hostilities. Additionally, the President has decided to share, in this document, certain key elements of these standards and procedures with the American people so that they can make informed judgments and hold the Executive Branch accountable. . . .

Preference for Capture

The policy of the United States is not to use lethal force when it is feasible to capture a terrorist suspect, because capturing a terrorist offers the best opportunity to gather meaningful intelligence and to mitigate and disrupt terrorist plots. Capture operations are conducted only against suspects who may lawfully be captured or otherwise taken into custody by the United States and only when the operation can be conducted in accordance with all applicable law and consistent with our obligations to other sovereign states.

Standards for the Use of Lethal Force

Any decision to use force abroad — even when our adversaries are terrorists dedicated to killing American citizens — is a significant one. Lethal force will not be proposed or pursued as punishment or as a substitute for prosecuting a terrorist suspect in a civilian court or a military commission. Lethal force will be used only to prevent or stop attacks against U.S. persons, and even then, only when capture is not feasible and no other reasonable alternatives exist to address the threat effectively. In particular, lethal force will be used outside areas of active hostilities only when the following preconditions are met:

First, there must be a legal basis for using lethal force, whether it is against a senior operational leader of a terrorist organization or the forces that organization is using or intends to use to conduct terrorist attacks.

Second, the United States will use lethal force only against a target that poses a continuing, imminent threat to U.S. persons. It is simply not the case that all terrorists pose a continuing, imminent threat to U.S. persons; if a terrorist does not pose such a threat, the United States will not use lethal force.

Third, the following criteria must be met before lethal action may be taken:

1) Near certainty that the terrorist target is present;
2) Near certainty that non-combatants[1] will not be injured or killed;
3) An assessment that capture is not feasible at the time of the operation;
4) An assessment that the relevant governmental authorities in the country where action is contemplated cannot or will not effectively address the threat to U.S. persons; and
5) An assessment that no other reasonable alternatives exist to effectively address the threat to U.S. persons.

---

1. Non-combatants are individuals who may not be made the object of attack under applicable international law. The term "non-combatant" does not include an individual who is part of a belligerent party to an armed conflict, an individual who is taking a direct part in hostilities, or an individual who is targetable in the exercise of national self-defense. Males of military age may be non-combatants; it is not the case that all military-aged males in the vicinity of a target are deemed to be combatants.

Finally, whenever the United States uses force in foreign territories, international legal principles, including respect for sovereignty and the law of armed conflict, impose important constraints on the ability of the United States to act unilaterally — and on the way in which the United States can use force. The United States respects national sovereignty and international law.

U.S. Government Coordination and Review

Decisions to capture or otherwise use force against individual terrorists outside the United States and areas of active hostilities are made at the most senior levels of the U.S. Government, informed by departments and agencies with relevant expertise and institutional roles. Senior national security officials — including the deputies and heads of key departments and agencies — will consider proposals to make sure that our policy standards are met, and attorneys — including the senior lawyers of key departments and agencies — will review and determine the legality of proposals.

These decisions will be informed by a broad analysis of an intended target's current and past role in plots threatening U.S. persons; relevant intelligence information the individual could provide; and the potential impact of the operation on ongoing terrorism plotting, on the capabilities of terrorist organizations, on U.S. foreign relations, and on U.S. intelligence collection. Such analysis will inform consideration of whether the individual meets both the legal and policy standards for the operation.

Other Key Elements

U.S. Persons. If the United States considers an operation against a terrorist identified as a U.S. person, the Department of Justice will conduct an additional legal analysis to ensure that such action may be conducted against the individual consistent with the Constitution and laws of the United States.

Reservation of Authority. These new standards and procedures do not limit the President's authority to take action in extraordinary circumstances when doing so is both lawful and necessary to protect the United States or its allies.

Congressional Notification. Since entering office, the President has made certain that the appropriate Members of Congress have been kept fully informed about our counterterrorism operations. Consistent with this strong and continuing commitment to congressional oversight, appropriate Members of the Congress will be regularly provided with updates identifying any individuals against whom lethal force has been approved. In addition, the appropriate committees of Congress will be notified whenever a counterterrorism operation covered by these standards and procedures has been conducted.

Notes and Questions

1. *Classifying the Conflict.* Recall that the Geneva Conventions apply only to "armed conflicts," and that different parts of those Conventions apply depending upon whether a conflict is between two or more states, even if a state of war is not recognized by one of them, or is "not of an international character" — not between states. See *supra* pp. 267-269.

Was the Second Intifada an armed conflict under international law? If so, what kind? Is the United States engaged in a non-international armed conflict with the Islamic State (ISIS) or Al Qaeda? What difference, if any, does it make?

2. *"Outside Areas of Active Hostilities."* The 2013 *U.S. Policy Standards* applied to uses of force in counterterrorism operations that were conducted in a foreign country outside "areas of active hostilities." In 2017, President Trump reportedly declared parts of Somalia an "area of active hostilities," thus exempting them from the 2013 *U.S. Policy Standards*. This change permitted the U.S. military to strike suspected Somali Al-Shabab fighters based strictly on their combatant status, instead of the threat they pose to Americans. *See* Charlie Savage & Eric Schmidt, *Trump Eases Combat Rules in Somalia Intended to Protect Civilians*, N.Y. Times, Mar. 30, 2017. A strike under the new rules on an Al-Shabab training camp in Somalia in March 2017 reportedly killed more than 150 people described by U.S. officials as newly minted Al-Shabab fighters attending a graduation ceremony. Charlie Savage, Helene Cooper & Eric Schmidt, *U.S. Strikes Shabab, Likely a First Since Trump Relaxed Rules for Somalia*, N.Y. Times, June 11, 2017. Did the United States effectively alter the legitimacy of its actions under IHL by recharacterizing the geographical scope of its conflict with Al-Shabab?

3. *Targeting Based on Status.* In an armed conflict, persons may be targeted based on their status rather than just on their conduct. On what basis did the Israeli Supreme Court determine the status of the terrorist organizations and their members? Does Article 4 of the Third Geneva Convention (*supra* p. 270) answer the question? Is the netherworld between combatants and civilians unregulated by IHL? Should IHL regulate this third category of "unlawful combatants"?

The Obama administration asserted that

> an individual who is formally or functionally a member of an armed group against which the United States is engaged in an armed conflict is generally targetable. Determining that someone is a "functional" member of an armed group may include looking to, among other things, the extent to which that person performs functions for the benefit of the group that are analogous to those traditionally performed by members of a country's armed forces; whether that person is carrying out or giving orders to others within the group; and whether that person has undertaken certain acts that reliably connote meaningful integration into the group. [*Report on the Legal and Policy Frameworks*, *supra* p. 376 n.1, at 19.]

Is this targeting based on status (group affiliation), conduct, or both? Was Anwar al-Aulaqi (*supra* pp. 376-377) targetable under these criteria? Do they comply with international humanitarian law?

4. *Targeting Based on Conduct.* The U.N. Special Rapporteur for Human Rights offered the following perspective on targeting civilians who directly participate in hostilities:

> There are three key controversies over DPH [direct participation in hostilities]. First, there is dispute over the kind of conduct that constitutes "direct participation" and makes an individual subject to attack. Second, there is disagreement over the extent to which "membership" in an organized armed group may be used as a factor in determining whether a person is directly participating in hostilities. Third, there is controversy over how long direct participation lasts.

It is not easy to arrive at a definition of direct participation that protects civilians and at the same time does not "reward" an enemy that may fail to distinguish between civilians and lawful military targets, that may deliberately hide among civilian populations and put them at risk, or that may force civilians to engage in hostilities. The key, however, is to recognize that regardless of the enemy's tactics, in order to protect the vast majority of civilians, direct participation may only include conduct close to that of a fighter, or conduct that directly supports combat. More attenuated acts, such as providing financial support, advocacy, or other non-combat aid, does not constitute direct participation.

Some types of conduct have long been understood to constitute direct participation, such as civilians who shoot at State forces or commit acts of violence in the context of hostilities that would cause death or injury to civilians. Other conduct has traditionally been excluded from direct participation, even if it supports the general war effort; such conduct includes political advocacy, supplying food or shelter, or economic support and propaganda (all also protected under other human rights standards). Even if these activities ultimately impact hostilities, they are not considered "direct participation." But there is a middle ground, such as for the proverbial "farmer by day, fighter by night," that has remained unclear and subject to uncertainty.

In 2009, the ICRC issued its Interpretive Guidance on DPH, which provides a useful starting point for discussion. In non-international armed conflict, according to the ICRC Guidance, civilians who participate directly in hostilities and are members of an armed group who have a "continuous combat function" may be targeted at all times and in all places. With respect to the temporal duration of DPH for all other civilians, the ICRC Guidance takes the view that direct participation for civilians is limited to each single act: the earliest point of direct participation would be the concrete preparatory measures for that specific act (e.g., loading bombs onto a plane), and participation terminates when the activity ends.

Under the ICRC's Guidance, each specific act by the civilian must meet three cumulative requirements to constitute DPH:

> (i) There must be a "threshold of harm" that is objectively likely to result from the act, either by adversely impacting the military operations or capacity of the opposing party, or by causing the loss of life or property of protected civilian persons or objects; and
>
> (ii) The act must cause the expected harm directly, in one step, for example, as an integral part of a specific and coordinated combat operation (as opposed to harm caused in unspecified future operations); and
>
> (iii) The act must have a "belligerent nexus" — i.e., it must be specifically designed to support the military operations of one party to the detriment of another.

[*Addendum: Study on Targeted Killings, supra* p. 375, at 19-20.]

Article 51 of Additional Protocol I of the Geneva Conventions, *supra* p. 278, declares that "civilians shall enjoy general protection against dangers arising from military operations . . . unless and for such time as they take a direct part in hostilities." What does it mean to end a civilian's protection from attack "for such time" as she directly participates in hostilities? Must she take part in specific hostile acts, or would hostile intent suffice? Is a bomb maker or military accountant taking "direct part"? A driver? A chef? Does the civilian who takes direct part regain her immunity when she goes home at night?

How do the criteria suggested by the Special Rapporteur and the ICRC differ from those employed by the Israeli Supreme Court? Does the "continuous combat function" designator provide needed flexibility or unbridled discretion for the targeting personnel?

Was Anwar al-Aulaqi (*supra* pp. 376-377) taking a direct part in hostilities against the United States?

5. *Self-Defense?* If the United States is not engaged in an armed conflict in Pakistan or Yemen, is the only lawful means for countering terrorist groups there the use of law enforcement methods subject to HRL? Consider one scholar's answer:

> In circumstances where the targeted strike takes place within the context of an armed conflict, the law of armed conflict will determine the legality of any lethal targeting. . . . However, in many cases in which a state uses force against a non-state actor outside its own territory, it will be in the context of counterterrorism as self-defense, outside of any armed conflict. In the absence of an armed conflict, international human rights law and the principles governing the use of force in law enforcement will govern. . . .
>
> . . . During armed conflict, the LOAC authorizes the use of force as a first resort against those identified as the enemy, whether insurgents, terrorists or the armed forces of another state. In contrast, human rights law, which would be the dominant legal framework in areas where there is no armed conflict, authorizes the use of force only as a last resort. . . . The former permits targeting of individuals based on their status as members of a hostile force; the latter — human rights law — permits lethal force against individuals only on the basis of their conduct posing a direct threat at that time. The LOAC also accepts the incidental loss of civilian lives as collateral damage, within the bounds of the principle of proportionality; human rights law contemplates no such casualties. These contrasts can literally mean the difference between life and death in many situations. [Laurie R. Blank, *Targeted Strikes: The Consequences of Blurring the Armed Conflict and Self-Defense Justifications*, 38 Wm. Mitchell L. Rev. 1655, 1667, 1681-1682 (2012).]

Which paradigm — IHL (LOAC) or HRL — is reflected by the *U.S. Policy Standards*? Do the *U.S. Policy Standards* actually blend IHL and HRL principles to create a new paradigm, at least for "senior operational leaders of terrorist organizations"? Or do they keep them separate by their geographical specificity (within or "outside . . . areas of active hostilities"). If they suggest a new blended paradigm, do they violate or change IHL or HRL?

6. *Relaxation of Combat Rules.* On President Trump's visit to the CIA on his first full day in office,

> when the agency's head of drone operations explained that the CIA had developed special munitions to limit civilian casualties, the president seemed unimpressed. Watching a previously recorded strike in which the agency held off on firing until the target had wandered away from a house with his family inside, Trump asked, "Why did you wait?" one participant in the meeting recalled. [Greg Jaffe, *For Trump and His Generals, "Victory" Has Different Meanings*, Wash. Post, Apr. 5, 2018.]

Why *did* the drone operator wait? Can you articulate a legal rationale for the answer?

Later in 2017, the Trump administration reportedly considered a more general relaxation of the Obama administration's *Policy Standards.* Charlie Savage & Eric Schmidt, *Trump Poised to Drop Some Limits on Drone Strikes and Commando Raids*, N.Y. Times, Sept. 21, 2017. *See generally* Robert Chesney, *President Trump Ponders Changes to the Lethal Force Policy Constraints: What You Need to Know*, Lawfare, Sept. 17, 2017. The proposed standards would water down the "continuing, imminent threat" criterion to more clearly allow attacks on foot-soldiers, and narrow the requirement for top-level approval in some cases, in order to speed up decision making for attacks. *Id.* Would these changes violate HRL?

7. Congressional Oversight? The Secretary of Defense must notify the congressional armed services committees in writing of any "sensitive military operation" within 48 hours following such an operation. 10 U.S.C. §130f(a) (2018). A sensitive military operation is

> (A) a lethal operation or capture operation conducted by the armed forces or conducted by a foreign partner in coordination with the armed forces that targets a specific individual or individuals; or
>
> (B) an operation conducted by the armed forces in self-defense or in defense of foreign partners, including during a cooperative operation. [*Id.* §130f(d)(1).]

But it does not include operations in Afghanistan, Syria, or Iraq. *Id.* §130f(d)(2). Would this notification requirement apply to a lethal operation in Nigeria by a Nigerian military unit against suspected members of the militant Islamist group Boko Haram, if U.S. military authorities provide reconnaissance for the operation? How do you think this notification requirement might influence the use of targeted killings by the U.S. military?

8. Killing Bin Laden. Was the killing of Osama bin Laden by U.S. special forces lawful under HRL? *See* Nils Melzer, *Targeted Killing in International Law* 423 (2008) (targeted killing must have a legal basis in domestic law, be preventive rather than punitive, have protection of human life from unlawful attack by the target as its exclusive purpose, "be absolutely necessary in qualitative, quantitative and temporal terms for the achievement of this purpose," and "be the undesired outcome of an operation planned and conducted to minimize resource to lethal force"). Apparently, bin Laden was not armed when he was shot. Would that fact make the operation unlawful from an HRL perspective? Is it important that the Navy SEALs feared that bin Laden might have prepared for the threat of capture by rigging himself as a "human IED" (improvised explosive device)?

Alternatively, was the killing lawful under IHL? Review the *in bello* rules applied by the Israeli Supreme Court. *See also* Melzer, *supra*, at 426-427 (during armed conflict, a targeted killing must be "likely to contribute effectively to the achievement of a concrete and direct military advantage without there being an equivalent non-lethal alternative," and abide by principles of distinction and proportionality and any other precautionary measures required by IHL). If there was no armed conflict in Abbottabad, Pakistan, where bin Laden was killed, was the killing lawful as an act of national self-defense? If so, how? *See* Thomas Darnstadt, *Was Bin Laden's Killing Legal?*, Spiegel Online, May 3, 2011, *at* http://www.spiegel.de/international/world/0,1518,druck-760358,00.html (suggesting that it is not clear that, at the time of his death, bin Laden commanded an organization that was conducting an armed conflict in or from Pakistan).

For an inside look at how four Obama administration lawyers actually handled the legal questions posed here, see Charlie Savage, *How 4 Federal Lawyers Paved the Way to Kill Osama bin Laden*, N.Y. Times, Oct. 28, 2015.

9. Costs and Benefits of Targeted Killing. In 2013, President Obama asserted that drone strikes have been effective.

> Don't take my word for it. In the intelligence gathered at bin Laden's compound, we found that he wrote, "we could lose the reserves to the enemy's air strikes. We cannot fight air strikes with explosives." Other communications from al Qaeda operatives confirm this as well. Dozens of highly skilled al Qaeda commanders, trainers, bomb makers, and operatives have been taken off the battlefield. Plots have been disrupted that would have targeted international aviation, U.S. transit systems, European cities and our troops in Afghanistan. Simply put, these strikes have saved lives. [Remarks by the President at the National Defense University (May 23, 2013).]

Targeted killing of the leaders of a terrorist group can change the group's organizational behavior. Elimination of its leaders may cause confusion and disarray; successors may become paranoid and secretive, impeding their ability to communicate with members; and members may become fearful about communicating even with one another. The terrorists may spend more and more of their time protecting themselves, with correspondingly less time to attack others. *See, e.g.*, Daniel Byman, *Do Targeted Killings Work?*, For. Aff., Mar./Apr. 2006, at 95, 102-104 (reporting significant drop-off in Israeli civilian deaths from terrorist attacks, "partly because Israel's targeted killings have shattered Palestinian terrorist groups and made it difficult for them to conduct effective operations"); Gal Luft, *The Logic of Israel's Targeted Killing*, 10 Middle East Q. 1 (Winter 2003). Lives are saved by attacks averted. In addition, the targeted killing of a suspected terrorist may cause fewer casualties (and lower costs) among counterterrorist forces than seeking to arrest him in hostile territory, let alone invading to destroy his group. Eichensehr, *supra* p. 376 n.1, at 4. Furthermore, extradition and prosecution may not be viable alternatives to the use of force when terrorists take refuge in failed or sympathetic states. Finally, targeted killing satisfies domestic demands for the government to "do something" after a society has suffered terrorist attacks. *See* Byman, *supra*, at 102. Can you identify other benefits from targeted killing?

On the other hand, targeted killings carry significant costs as well. Terrorist groups adjust to decapitation; their decentralization largely negates the disruptive effect by creating many, or no, leaders. Successful targeted killing requires a heavy investment in real-time continuing intelligence and surveillance, as well as rapid response capability. Byman, *supra*, at 100 (quoting a former Israeli intelligence director as saying, "When a Palestinian child draws a picture of the sky, he doesn't draw it without a helicopter"). Even a successful killing may create a martyr for the terrorists, and perversely help them to recruit others, and it will often prompt retaliation. Finally, as the discussion of international law should suggest and the tense relationship between the United States and Pakistan after U.S. targeted killings inside Pakistani territory proves, targeted killing carries serious diplomatic costs, not just for negotiations to end the terrorism or to coordinate allies in the counterterrorist effort, but also for diplomatic efforts to condemn targeted killing by other states. Can you think of other costs of targeted killing? Should we include a moral cost in the calculus?

How would you balance costs and benefits of targeted killings by the United States in Afghanistan? In Northern Pakistan? In Yemen?

D. U.S. LAW AND THE TARGETING OF U.S. CITIZENS

Anwar al-Aulaqi was a U.S. citizen. His killing by a U.S. drone in 2011 thus implicated not only IHL, but also domestic U.S. law. An executive order prohibits U.S. officials from engaging in "assassination." More relevantly, various U.S. criminal statutes may apply to killings abroad, and U.S. persons abroad are entitled to due process when the U.S. government deprives them of life. The executive order ban is set out below, followed by Department of Justice memoranda defending the legality of al-Aulaqi's targeted killing.

Executive Order No. 12,333

46 Fed. Reg. 59,941 (Dec. 4, 1981)

2.11 Prohibition on Assassination. No person employed by or acting on behalf of the United States Government shall engage in, or conspire to engage in, assassination.

2.12 Indirect Participation. No agency of the Intelligence Community shall participate in or request any person to undertake activities forbidden by this Order. . . .

Department of Justice, White Paper: Lawfulness of a Lethal Operation Directed Against a U.S. Citizen Who Is a Senior Operational Leader of Al-Qa'ida or an Associated Force

Draft, Nov. 8, 2011

available at www.fas.org/irp/eprint/doj-lethal.pdf

This white paper sets forth a legal framework for considering the circumstances in which the U.S. government could use lethal force in a foreign country outside the area of active hostilities against a U.S. citizen who is a senior operational leader of al-Qa'ida or an associated force[1] of al-Qa'ida — that is, an al-Qa'ida leader actively engaged in planning operations to kill Americans. The paper does not attempt to determine the minimum requirements necessary to render such an operation lawful; nor does it assess what might be required to render a lethal operation against a U.S. citizen lawful in other circumstances, including an operation against enemy forces on a traditional battlefield or an operation against a U.S. citizen who is not a senior operational leader of such forces. . . .

I. . . .

[The paper argues that the conflict with al Qa'ida is a non-international armed conflict authorized by the 2001 AUMF and by the national right of self-

1. An associated force of al-Qa'ida includes a group that would qualify as a co-belligerent under the laws of war.

defense, and that the President could therefore order the use of necessary and appropriate force against a senior operational leader of al-Qa'ida or its associated forces like AQAP.]

II.

The Department assumes that the rights afforded by Fifth Amendment's Due Process Clause, as well as the Fourth Amendment, attach to a U.S. citizen even while he is abroad. *See Reid v. Covert*, 354 U.S. 1, 5-6 (1957) (plurality opinion); *United States v. Verdugo-Urquidez*, 494 U.S. 259, 269-70 (1990); *see also In re Terrorist Bombings of U.S. Embassies in East Africa*, 552 F.3d 157, 170 n.7 (2d Cir. 2008). The U.S. citizenship of a leader of al-Qa'ida or its associated forces, however, does not give that person constitutional immunity from attack. . . .

A.

The Due Process Clause would not prohibit a lethal operation of the sort contemplated here. In *Hamdi*, a plurality of the Supreme Court used the *Mathews v. Eldridge* balancing test to analyze the Fifth Amendment due process rights of a U.S. citizen who had been captured on the battlefield in Afghanistan and detained in the United States, and who wished to challenge the government's assertion that he was part of enemy forces. The Court explained that the "process due in any given instance is determined by weighing 'the private interest that will be affected by the official action' against the Government's asserted interest, 'including the function involved' and the burdens the Government would face in providing greater process." *Hamdi*, 542 U.S. at 529 (plurality opinion) (quoting *Mathews v. Eldridge*, 424 U.S. 319, 335 (1976)). The due process balancing analysis applied to determine the Fifth Amendment rights of a U.S. citizen with respect to law-of-war detention supplies the framework for assessing the process due a U.S. citizen who is a senior operational leader of an enemy force planning violent attacks against Americans before he is subjected to lethal targeting.

In the circumstances considered here, the interests on both sides would be weighty. *See Hamdi*, 542 U.S. at 529 (plurality opinion) ("It is beyond question that substantial interests lie on both sides of the scale in this case."). An individual's interest in avoiding erroneous deprivation of his life is "uniquely compelling." *See Ake v. Oklahoma*, 470 U.S. 68, 178 (1985). No private interest is more substantial. At the same time, the government's interest in waging war, protecting its citizens, and removing the threat posed by members of enemy forces is also compelling. *Cf. Hamdi*, 542 U.S. at 531 (plurality opinion) ("On the other side of the scale are the weighty and sensitive governmental interests in ensuring that those who have in fact fought with the enemy during a war do not return to battle against the United States."). As the *Hamdi* plurality observed, in the "circumstances of war," "the risk of erroneous deprivation of a citizen's liberty in the absence of sufficient process . . . is very real," *id.* at 530 (plurality opinion), and, of course, the risk of an erroneous deprivation of a citizen's life is even more significant. But, "the realities of combat" render certain uses of force "necessary and appropriate," including force against U.S. citizens who have joined enemy forces in the armed conflict against the United States and whose activities pose an imminent threat of violent attack against the United States — and "due process analysis need not blink at those realities." *id.* at 531 (plurality opinion).

These same realities must also be considered in assessing "the burdens the Government would face in providing greater process" to a member of enemy forces. *Id.* at 529, 531 (plurality opinion).

In view of these interests and practical considerations, the United States would be able to use lethal force against a U.S. citizen, who is located outside the United States and is an operational leader continually planning attacks against U.S. persons and interests, in at least the following circumstances: (1) where an informed, high-level official of the U.S. government has determined that the targeted individual poses an imminent threat of violent attack against the United States; (2) where a capture operation would be infeasible — and where those conducting the operation continue to monitor whether capture becomes feasible; and (3) where such an operation would be conducted consistent with applicable law of war principles. In these circumstances, the "realities" of the conflict and the weight of the government's interest in protecting its citizens from an imminent attack are such that the Constitution would not require the government to provide further process to such a U.S. citizen before using lethal force. *Cf. Hamdi*, 542 U.S. at 535 (plurality opinion) (noting that the Court "accord[s] the greatest respect and consideration to the judgments of military authorities in matters relating to the actual prosecution of war, and... the scope of that discretion necessarily is wide").

Certain aspects of this legal framework require additional explication. *First*, the condition that an operational leader present an "imminent" threat of violent attack against the United States does not require the United States to have clear evidence that a specific attack on U.S. persons and interests will take place in the immediate future. Given the nature of, for example, the terrorist attacks on September 11, in which civilian airliners were hijacked to strike the World Trade Center and the Pentagon, this definition of imminence, which would require the United States to refrain from action until preparations for an attack are concluded, would not allow the United States sufficient time to defend itself. The defensive options available to the United States may be reduced or eliminated if al-Qa'ida operatives disappear and cannot be found when the time of their attack approaches. Consequently, with respect to al-Qa'ida leaders who are continually planning attacks, the United States is likely to have only a limited window of opportunity within which to defend Americans in a manner that has both a high likelihood of success and sufficiently reduces the probabilities of civilian causalities. Furthermore, a "terrorist 'war' does not consist of a massive attack across an international border, nor does it consist of one isolated incident that occurs and is then past. It is a drawn out, patient, sporadic pattern of attacks. It is very difficult to know when or where the next incident will occur." Gregory M. Travalio, *Terrorism, International Law, and the Use of Military Force*, 18 Wis. Int'l L.J. 145, 173 (2000). Delaying action against individuals continually planning to kill Americans until some theoretical end stage of the planning for a particular plot would create an unacceptably high risk that the action would fail and that American casualties would result.

By its nature, therefore, the threat posed by al-Qa'ida and its associated forces demands a broader concept of imminence in judging when a person continually planning terror attacks presents an imminent threat, making the use of force appropriate. In this context, imminence must incorporate considerations of the relevant window of opportunity, the possibility of reducing collateral damage to civilians, and the likelihood of heading off future disastrous attacks on Americans. Thus, a decision maker determining whether an al-Qa'ida operational leader presents an imminent threat of violent attack against the United States must take into account that certain members of al-Qa'ida (including any potential target of lethal force) are continually plotting attacks against the United States; that al-Qa'ida would engage in such attacks regularly to the extent it were able to do so; that the U.S. government may not be aware of all al-Qa'ida plots as they are developing and thus cannot be confident that none is about to occur; and that, in light of these predicates, the nation may have a limited window of opportunity within which to strike in a manner that both has a high likelihood of success and reduces the probability of American casualties.

With this understanding, a high-level official could conclude, for example, that an individual poses an "imminent threat" of violent attack against the United States where he is an operational leader of al-Qa'ida or an associated force and is personally and continually involved in planning terrorist attacks against the United States. Moreover, where the al-Qa'ida member in question has recently been involved in activities posing an imminent threat of violent attack against the United States, and there is no evidence suggesting that he has renounced or abandoned such activities, that member's involvement in al-Qa'ida's continuing terrorist campaign against the United States would support the conclusion that the member poses an imminent threat.

Second, regarding the feasibility of capture, capture would not be feasible if it could not be physically effectuated during the relevant window of opportunity or if the relevant country were to decline to consent to a capture operation. Other factors such as undue risk to U.S. personnel conducting a potential capture operation also could be relevant. Feasibility would be a highly fact-specific and potentially time-sensitive inquiry.

Third, it is a premise here that any such lethal operation by the United States would comply with the four fundamental law-of-war principles governing the use of force: necessity, distinction, proportionality, and humanity (the avoidance of unnecessary suffering). For example, it would not be consistent with those principles to continue an operation if anticipated civilian casualties would be excessive in relation to the anticipated military advantage. An operation consistent with the laws of war could not violate the prohibitions against treachery and perfidy, which address a breach of confidence by the assailant. These prohibitions do not, however, categorically forbid the use of stealth or surprise, nor forbid attacks on identified individual soldiers or officers. And the Department is not aware of any other law-of-war grounds precluding use of such tactics. Relatedly, "there is no prohibition under the laws of war on the use of technologically advanced weapons systems in armed conflict — such as pilotless aircraft or so-called smart bombs — as long as they are employed in conformity with applicable laws of war." 2010 Koh ASIL Speech. Further, under this framework, the United States would also be required to accept a surrender if it were feasible to do so....

III....

A....

[The *White Paper* invokes the "public authority" justification for killing a U.S. citizen in the circumstances, by which it is assumed that Congress did not intend to criminalize conduct by public officials in the legitimate exercise of their otherwise lawful authority, even if it did criminalize the same conduct when undertaken by persons not acting pursuant to public authority.]

C. . . .

The United States is currently in the midst of a congressionally authorized armed conflict with al-Qa'ida and associated forces, and may act in national self-defense to protect U.S. persons and interests who are under continual threat of violent attack by certain al-Q'aida operatives planning operations against them. The public authority justification would apply to a lethal operation of the kind discussed in this paper if it were conducted in accord with applicable law of war principles. As one legal commentator has explained, "if a soldier intentionally kills an enemy combatant in time of war and within the rules of warfare, he is not guilty of murder," whereas, for example, if that soldier intentionally kills a prisoner of war — a violation of the laws of war — "then he commits murder." 2 LaFave, *Substantive Criminal Law* §10.2(c), at 136. . . .

The fact that an operation may target a U.S. citizen does not alter this conclusion. . . .

. . . Such an operation would not violate the assassination ban in Executive Order No. 12333. Section 2.11 of Executive Order No. 12333 provides that "[n]o person employed by or acting on behalf of the United States Government shall engage in, or conspire to engage in, assassination." 46 Fed. Reg. 59,941, 59, 952 (Dec. 4, 1981). A lawful killing in self-defense is not an assassination. In the Department's view, a lethal operation conducted against a U.S. citizen whose conduct poses an imminent threat of violent attack against the United States would be a legitimate act of national self-defense that would not violate the assassination ban. Similarly, the use of lethal force, consistent with the laws of war, against an individual who is a legitimate military target would be lawful and would not violate the assassination ban.

IV.

The War Crimes Act, 18 U.S.C. §2441 (2006) makes it a federal crime for a member of the Armed Forces or a national of the United States to "commit[] a war crime." *Id.* §2441(a). The only potentially applicable provision of section 2441 to operations of the type discussed herein makes it a war crime to commit a "grave breach" of Common Article 3 of the Geneva Conventions when that breach is committed "in the context of and in association with an armed conflict not of an international character." *Id.* §2441(c)(3). As defined by the statute, a "grave breach" of Common Article 3 includes "[m]urder," described in pertinent part as "[t]he act of a person who intentionally kills, or conspires or attempts to kill . . . one or more persons taking no active part in the hostilities, including those placed out of combat by sickness, wounds, detention, or any other cause." *Id.* §2441(d)(1)(D).

Whatever might be the outer bounds of this category of covered persons, Common Article 3 does not alter the fundamental law of war principle concerning a belligerent party's right in an armed conflict to target individuals who are part of an enemy's armed forces or eliminate a nation's authority to take legitimate action in national self-defense. The language of Common Article 3 "makes clear that members of such armed forces [of both the state and non-state parties to the conflict] . . . are considered as 'taking no active part in the hostilities' only once they have disengaged from their fighting function ('have laid down their arms') or are placed *hors de combat*; mere suspension of combat is insufficient." International Committee of the Red Cross, *Interpretive Guidance on the Notion of Direct Participation in Hostilities Under International Humanitarian Law* 28 (2009). An operation against a senior operational leader of al-Qa'ida or its associated forces who poses an imminent threat of violent attack against the United States would target a person who is taking "an active part in hostilities" and therefore would not constitute a "grave breach" of Common Article 3....

The 2011 Department of Justice White Paper was based in substantial part on a 2010 memorandum by the Office of Legal Counsel. In 2014, a court ordered disclosure of a partially redacted version of the 2010 memorandum pursuant to a Freedom of Information Act request. *See N.Y. Times Co. v. Dep't of Justice*, 756 F.3d 100, 124-151 (2d Cir. 2014). Portions of the earlier memorandum are reproduced below.

U.S. Dep't of Justice, Office of Legal Counsel, Applicability of Federal Criminal Laws and the Constitution to Contemplated Lethal Operations Against Shaykh Anwar al-Aulaqi

July 16, 2010

available at https://www.justice.gov/olc/olc-foia-electronic-reading-room

[Redacted] ...

III. ...

A. ...

Based upon the facts represented to us, ... the target of the contemplated operation has engaged in conduct as part of that organization that brings him within the scope of the AUMF. High-level government officials have concluded, on the basis of al-Aulaqi's activities in Yemen, that al-Aulaqi is a leader of AQAP whose activities in Yemen pose a "continued and imminent threat" of violence to United States persons and interests. Indeed, the facts represented to us indicate that al-Aulaqi has been involved, through his operational and leadership roles within AQAP, in an abortive attack within the United States and continues to plot attacks intended to kill Americans from his base of operations in Yemen. The contemplated DoD operation, therefore, would be carried out against someone who is within the core of individuals against whom Congress has authorized the use of necessary and appropriate force....

Here, unlike in *Hamdan* [*v. Rumsfeld*, 548 U.S. 557 (2006)], the contemplated DoD operation would occur in Yemen, a location that is far from the most active theater of combat between the United States and al-Qaida. That does not affect our conclusion, however, that the combination of facts present here would make the DoD operation in Yemen part of the non-international armed conflict with al-Qaida. To be sure, *Hamdan* did not directly address the geographic scope of the noninternational armed conflict between the United States and al-Qaida that the Court recognized, other than to implicitly hold that it extended to Afghanistan, where Hamdan was apprehended. *See* 548 U.S. at 566; *see also id.* at 641-42 (Kennedy, J., concurring in part) (referring to Common Article 3 as "applicable to our Nation's armed conflict with al Qaeda in Afghanistan"). The Court did, however, specifically reject the argument that non-international armed conflicts are necessarily limited to internal conflicts. The Common Article 3 term "conflict not of an international character," the Court explained, bears its "literal meaning" — namely, that it is a conflict that "does not involve a clash between nations." *Id.* at 630 (majority opinion). . . .

For present purposes, in applying the more context-specific approach to determining whether an operation would take place within the scope of a particular armed conflict, it is sufficient that the facts as they have been represented to us here, in combination, support the judgment that DoD's operation in Yemen would be conducted as part of the non-international armed conflict between the United States and al-Qaida. Specifically, DoD proposes to target a leader of AQAP, an organized enemy force that is either a component of al-Qaida or that is a co-belligerent of that central party to the conflict and engaged in hostilities against the United States as part of the same comprehensive armed conflict, in league with the principal enemy. Moreover, DoD would conduct the operation in Yemen, where, according to the facts related to us, AQAP has a significant and organized presence, and from which AQAP is conducting terrorist training in an organized manner and has executed and is planning to execute attacks against the United States. Finally, the targeted individual himself, on behalf of that force, is continuously planning attacks from that Yemeni base of operations against the United States, as the conflict with al-Qaida continues. Taken together, these facts support the conclusion that the DoD operation would be part of the non-international armed conflict the Court recognized in *Hamdan*. . . .

DoD represents that it would conduct its operation against al-Aulaqi in compliance with these fundamental law-of-war norms. *See* Chairman of the Joint Chiefs of Staff, Instruction 5810.01D, *Implementation of the DoD Law of War Program* ¶14.a, at 1 (Apr. 30, 2010) ("It is DOD policy that . . . [m]embers of the DOD Components comply with the law of war during all armed conflicts, however such conflicts are characterized, and in all other military operations."). In particular, the targeted nature of the operation would help to ensure that it would comply with the principle of distinction, and DoD has represented to us that it would make every effort to minimize civilian casualties and that the officer who launches the ordnance would be required to abort a strike if he or she concludes that civilian casualties will be disproportionate or that such a strike will in any other respect violate the laws of war. *See DoD May 18 Memorandum for OLC,* at 1 ("Any official in the chain of command has the authority and duty to abort" a strike "if he or she concludes that civilian casualties will be disproportionate or that such a strike will otherwise violate the laws of war."). . . .

In light of all these circumstances, we believe DoD's contemplated operation against al-Aulaqi would comply with international law, including the laws of war applicable to this armed conflict, and would fall within Congress's authorization to use "necessary and appropriate force" against al-Qaida. In consequence, the operation should be understood to constitute the lawful conduct of war and thus to be encompassed by the public authority justification. Accordingly, the contemplated attack, if conducted by DoD in the manner described, would not result in an "unlawful" killing and thus would not violate section 1119(b).

B.

We next consider whether the CIA's contemplated operation against al-Aulaqi in Yemen would be covered by the public authority justification. . . .

Specifically, we understand that the CIA, like DoD, would carry out the attack against an operational leader of an enemy force, as part of the United States's ongoing non-international armed conflict with al-Qaida.

[Redacted] the CIA [redacted] would conduct the operation in a manner that accords with the rules of international humanitarian law governing this armed conflict, and in circumstances [redacted].[44] . . .

Accordingly, we conclude that, just as the combination of circumstances present here supports the judgment that the public authority justification would apply to the contemplated operation by the armed forces, the combination of circumstances also supports the judgment that the CIA's operation, too, would be encompassed by that justification. The CIA's contemplated operation, therefore, would not result in an "unlawful" killing under section 1111 and thus would not violate section 1119. . . .

Please let us know if we can be of further assistance.

Notes and Questions

1. Origins of the Assassination Ban. In 1976, a congressional committee found evidence of CIA involvement in assassination plots against foreign leaders (including President Ngo Dinh Diem of South Vietnam, who was murdered in a coup, and General René Schneider of Chile, who died in a kidnapping attempt), but it

---

44. [Redacted] If the killing by a member of the armed forces would comply with the law of war and otherwise be lawful, actions of CIA officials facilitating that killing should also not be unlawful. *See, e.g., Shoot Down Opinion* at 165 n.33 ("[O]ne cannot be prosecuted for aiding and abetting the commission of an act that is not itself a crime.") (citing *Shuttlesworth v. City of Birmingham*, 373 U.S. 262 (1963)).

Nor would the fact that CIA personnel would be involved in the operation itself cause the operation to violate the laws of war. It is true that CIA personnel, by virtue of their not being part of the armed forces, would not enjoy the immunity from prosecution under the domestic law of the countries in which they act for their conduct in targeting and killing enemy forces in compliance with the laws of war — an immunity that the armed forces enjoy by virtue of their status. *See Report of the Special Rapporteur* ¶71, at 22; *see also* Dinstein, *Conduct of Hostilities*, at 31. Nevertheless, lethal activities conducted in accord with the laws of war, and undertaken in the course of lawfully authorized hostilities, do not violate *the laws of war* by virtue of the fact that they are carried out in part by government actors who are not entitled to the combatant's privilege. The contrary view "arises . . . from a fundamental confusion between acts punishable under international law and acts with respect to which international law affords no protection." Richard R. Baxter, *So-Called "Unprivileged Belligerency": Spies, Guerillas, and Saboteurs*, 28 Brit. Y.B. Int'l L. 323, 342 (1951). [redacted] Statements in the Supreme Court's decision in *Ex parte Quirin*, 317 U.S. 1 (1942), are sometimes cited for the contrary view. *See, e.g., id.* at 36 n.12 (suggesting that passing through enemy lines in order to commit "any hostile act" while not in uniform "renders the offender liable to trial for violation of the laws of war"); *id.* at 31 (enemies who come secretly through the lines for purposes of waging war by destruction of life or property "without uniform" not only are "generally not to be entitled to the status of prisoners of war," but also "to be offenders against the law of war subject to trial and punishment by military tribunals"). Because the Court in *Quirin* focused on conduct taken behind enemy lines, it is not clear whether the Court in these passages intended to refer only to conduct that would constitute perfidy or treachery. To the extent the Court meant to suggest more broadly that any hostile acts performed by unprivileged belligerents are for that reason violations of the laws of war, the authorities the Court cited (the Lieber Code and Colonel Winthrop's military law treatise) do not provide clear support. . . .

was unable to determine whether such involvement had been approved by senior officials. *See* Select Comm. to Study Governmental Operations with Respect to Intelligence Activities (Church Comm.), *Alleged Assassination Plots Involving Foreign Leaders,* S. Rep. No. 94-465 (1975) (*Church Comm. Report*). The CIA acknowledged, however, that it subsequently made payments to the Schneider kidnappers. *See* Central Intelligence Agency, *CIA Activities in Chile,* Sept. 18, 2000, *at* https://www.cia.gov/cia/reports/chile/index.html#15.

Responding to this history, the Church Committee in 1976 proposed to criminalize the assassination or attempted assassination of "any foreign official because of such official's political views, actions, or statements, while such official is outside the United States." *Church Comm. Report, supra,* at App. A. "Foreign official" was defined as "Chief of State or the political equivalent . . . of a foreign government . . . or of a foreign political group, party, military force, movement or other association with which the United States is not at war pursuant to a declaration of war or against which the United States Armed Forces have not been introduced into hostilities or situations pursuant to the provisions of the War Powers Resolution." *Id.*

President Ford headed off such legislation, however, by adopting Executive Order No. 11,905, 41 Fed. Reg. 7703 (Feb. 19, 1976), prohibiting U.S. employees from engaging in "political assassination." In 1978, President Carter dropped the modifier "political," and President Reagan thereafter retained Carter's language as sections 2.11 and 2.12 in the still-current Executive Order No. 12,333, set out above.

2. Murder vs. Assassination. When is murder not assassination? A seminal legal analysis for the Department of the Army explains:

> While assassination generally is regarded as an act of murder for political reasons, its victims are not necessarily limited to persons of public office or prominence. The murder of a private person, if carried out for political purposes, may constitute an act of assassination. For example, the 1978 "poisoned-tip umbrella" killing of Bulgarian defector Georgi Markov by Bulgarian State Security agents on the streets of London falls into the category of an act of murder carried out for political purposes, and constitutes an assassination. In contrast, the murder of Leon Klinghoffer, a private citizen, by the terrorist Abu el Abbas during the 1985 hijacking of the Italian cruise ship *Achille Lauro,* though an act of murder for political purposes, would not constitute an assassination. The distinction lies not merely in the purpose of the act and/or its intended victim, but also under certain circumstances in its covert nature.[1] Finally, the killings of Martin Luther King and Presidents Abraham Lincoln, James A. Garfield, William McKinley and John F. Kennedy generally are regarded as assassination because each involved the murder of a public figure or national leader for political purposes accomplished through a surprise attack. [W. Hays Parks, *Memorandum of Law: Executive Order 12,333 and Assassination,* Dep't of the Army Pamphlet 27-50-204, *reprinted in* Army Law. 4 (Dec. 1989).]

1. *Covert operations* are defined as "operations which are planned and executed so as to conceal the identity of or permit plausible denial by the sponsor. They differ from clandestine operations in that emphasis is placed on concealment of identity of [the] sponsor rather than on concealment of the operation." In contrast, low visibility operations are . . . undertaken with the knowledge that the action and or sponsorship of the operation may preclude plausible denial by the initiating power. JCS Pub. 1, *Dictionary of Military and Associated Terms* (1 June 1987).

3. Was Al-Aulaqi Assassinated? The same Army memorandum asserts:

> In wartime the role of the military includes the legalized killing (as opposed to murder) of the enemy, whether lawful combatants or unprivileged belligerents, and may include in either category civilians who take part in the hostilities.
>
> The term *assassination* when applied to wartime military activities against enemy combatants or military objectives does not preclude acts of violence involving the element of surprise. Combatants are liable to attack at any time or place, regardless of their activity when attacked. [*Id.*]

A Legal Adviser to the Department of State subsequently argued that "the use of lawful weapons systems — consistent with the applicable laws of war — for precision targeting of specific high-level belligerent leaders when acting in self-defense or during an armed conflict is not unlawful, and hence does not constitute 'assassination'" under the executive order. Harold Koh, *The Obama Administration and International Law*, Remarks to the Annual Meeting of the American Society of International Law (Mar. 25, 2010), *available at* http://www.state.gov/s/l/releases/remarks/139119.htm.

Was al-Aulaqi a "high-level belligerent leader"? Would it make any difference whether he had carried arms and planned operations, or was just a senior propagandist? Would the executive order have barred the killing of Saddam Hussein, leader of Iraq, in 1991 during the first Gulf War, or in 2003, during the invasion of Iraq? *See* Stuart Taylor Jr., *Should We Just Kill Saddam?*, Legal Times, Feb. 4, 1991.

4. Force and Effect of the Assassination Ban. Since the President issued the executive order banning assassination, why can't he order the CIA or DOD to ignore it in conducting an operation to which it seemingly applies? *See* Memorandum from Acting Ass't Attorney General Randolph D. Moss to the President, *Legal Effectiveness of a Presidential Directive as Compared to an Executive Order*, Jan. 29, 2000 (concluding that presidential directives — and, by implication, findings — can have the same substantive legal effect as an executive order, and that any such presidential decision, however it is memorialized, remains effective upon a change in administration and until subsequent presidential action is taken).

5. The Process Due. To reduce "the risk of erroneous deprivation of a citizen's life" under the *Mathews v. Eldridge* due process balancing test, what *additional* procedures or standards has the United States adopted for the targeted killing of U.S. citizens beyond those for targeting non-U.S. citizens? Do they apply to all targeted killings of citizens anywhere? If not, why not? How do the final procedures and standards compare to those required by IHL? What additional requirement did the Israeli Supreme Court apply to killings by the IDF?

Alberto R. Gonzales was counsel to President George W. Bush and later his Attorney General during the immediate post-9/11 targeted killings by the United States. He later argued that the process due U.S. citizen targets should include some opportunity for an advocate for the target to challenge the target's listing before a neutral decision maker, presumably before an attack is undertaken. Alberto R. Gonzales, *Drones: The Power to Kill*, 82 Geo. Wash. L. Rev. 1, 4, 52-58 (2013). Do you think that would be a good idea? Who should be the decision maker? What standard of decision does the 2011 DOJ White Paper suggest? If you have concerns about *ex ante* review, what about after-the-fact review, perhaps through a suit for damages?

In *Zaidan v. Trump*, 317 F. Supp. 3d 8 (D.D.C. 2018), the court held justiciable a due process claim by a U.S. citizen that he was entitled to be heard before being added to a U.S. "kill list," but also found that his claim that his listing violated the Trump administration's policy standards was barred by the political question doctrine. The district court subsequently dismissed the suit on the ground that it was barred by the state secrets privilege. *See Kareem v. Haspel*, No. 17-581, 2019 WL 4645155 (D.D.C. Sept. 24, 2019).

6. *Due Process and Judicial Review.* Is the U.S. Constitution's requirement of due process a requirement of *judicial* process, either before or after a targeted killing of a U.S. citizen? Consider the following remarks of then-Attorney General Holder in a 2012 speech:

> Some have argued that the President is required to get permission from a federal court before taking action against a United States citizen who is a senior operational leader of al Qaeda or associated forces. This is simply not accurate. "Due process" and "judicial process" are not one and the same, particularly when it comes to national security. The Constitution guarantees due process, not judicial process.
>
> The conduct and management of national security operations are core functions of the Executive Branch, as courts have recognized throughout our history. Military and civilian officials must often make real-time decisions that balance the need to act, the existence of alternative options, the possibility of collateral damage, and other judgments — all of which depend on expertise and immediate access to information that only the Executive Branch may possess in real time. The Constitution's guarantee of due process is ironclad, and it is essential — but, as a recent court decision makes clear, it does not require judicial approval before the President may use force abroad against a senior operational leader of a foreign terrorist organization with which the United States is at war — even if that individual happens to be a U.S. citizen.
>
> That is not to say that the Executive Branch has — or should ever have — the ability to target any such individuals without robust oversight. Which is why, in keeping with the law and our constitutional system of checks and balances, the Executive Branch regularly informs the appropriate members of Congress about our counterterrorism activities, including the legal framework, and would of course follow the same practice where lethal force is used against United States citizens. [Att'y Gen. Eric Holder, Speech at Northwestern University School of Law (Mar. 5, 2012).]

Do you agree with Attorney General Holder's analysis regarding the role of judicial review (or lack thereof)? How does it square with *Hamdi v. Rumsfeld*, 542 U.S. 507 (2004), *infra* p. 887, in which six Justices held that a U.S. citizen detained as an enemy combatant has a due process right to a meaningful opportunity to rebut the factual basis for his detention before a neutral decision maker? Is there a distinction between military detention and targeted killing? If not, what process is due someone targeted for killing?

7. *Who May Conduct a Targeted Killing?* Assuming the existence of an armed conflict, may targeted killings lawfully be committed by agents of a state who are not members of its armed forces? Consider the views of the U.N. Special Rapporteur for Human Rights:

> Under IHL, civilians, including intelligence agents, are not prohibited from participating in hostilities. Rather, the consequence of participation is two-fold. First, because

> they are "directly participating in hostilities" by conducting targeted killings, intelligence personnel may themselves be targeted and killed. Second, intelligence personnel do not have immunity from prosecution under domestic law for their conduct. They are thus unlike State armed forces which would generally be immune from prosecution for the same conduct (assuming they complied with IHL requirements). Thus, CIA personnel could be prosecuted for murder under the domestic law of any country in which they conduct targeted drone killings, and could also be prosecuted for violations of applicable US law.
>
> It is important to note that if a targeted killing violates IHL (by, for example, targeting civilians who were not "directly participating in hostilities"), then regardless of who conducts it — intelligence personnel or State armed forces — the author, as well as those who authorized it, can be prosecuted for war crimes.
>
> Additionally, unlike a State's armed forces, its intelligence agents do not generally operate within a framework which places appropriate emphasis upon ensuring compliance with IHL, rendering violations more likely and causing a higher risk of prosecution both for war crimes and for violations of the laws of the State in which any killing occurs. To the extent a State uses intelligence agents for targeted killing to shield its operations from IHL and human rights law transparency and accountability requirements, it could also incur State responsibility for violating those requirements. [*Study on Targeted Killings*, *supra* p. 375, at 22.]

Does it make sense legally to authorize the CIA to engage in targeted killings but not to immunize them from prosecution? In the ongoing counterterrorism campaign against Al Qaeda, the Taliban, and associated groups, who would prosecute CIA or contract personnel for war crimes? Do you think that the CIA could earn immunity from prosecution by demonstrating that its agents are trained in IHL? That they or contract personnel are subject to accountability mechanisms that approximate a chain of command? How did the Department of Justice answer these questions? *See* Charles Kels, *Contractors in the "Kill Chain"? At the Nexus of LOAC and Procurement Law*, Lawfare, Jan. 24, 2016 ("[I]ndividuals acting on behalf of the government (whether military, civil service, or contractor) should be adequately apprised of the legal authority for their actions and the extent of their protections. This is especially true in the case of lethal force, which is the most serious activity that any government can authorize or conduct.").

TARGETING TERRORISTS: SUMMARY OF BASIC PRINCIPLES

- Outside of armed conflict or a judicial process, human rights law (HRL), in relevant part, forbids a governmental killing unless the government uses no more force than absolutely necessary as a last resort to defend a person from imminent unlawful violence. The right to use lethal force thus turns on the conduct, not the status, of the target.
- An international armed conflict is a conflict between states, whether or not one of them recognizes a state of war, and a non-international armed conflict is a conflict between a state and an identifiable group, or between identifiable groups, exceeding a minimal level of intensity and duration, with a territorial nexus to a state or across borders.

- The United States takes the view that in armed conflicts international humanitarian law (IHL) (also called the law of armed conflict or LOAC) supplants HRL.

- In an armed conflict lethal force may be used against combatants, civilians for as long as they take a direct part in hostilities, and other civilians incidental to a lawful military attack (collateral damage). The use of force must be necessary to achieve legitimate military objectives and proportionate (e.g., the incidental loss of civilian lives must be justified by the legitimate military benefit of the attack), but it is not restricted to defense against imminent attack.

- During the Obama administration, the United States took the view that national self-defense also justifies the use of lethal force even outside an area of active hostilities (or armed conflict), but it has declared that it will use such force only when (1) a terrorist target poses a continuing, imminent threat to U.S. persons, (2) capture and other non-lethal alternatives are not feasible, (3) the state where the target is located is unwilling or unable to address the threat, and (4) there is near certainty that the target is present and that non-combatants (other than those taking a direct part in hostilities) will not be injured or killed.

- The Trump administration has reportedly lowered the "continuing, imminent threat" standard to permit targeting individuals based on their combatant status alone, and has streamlined the strike approval process.

- Executive Order No. 12,333's ban on assassination does not apply to the targeted killing of combatants or civilians taking a direct part in hostilities in armed conflict or to targeted killing in self-defense.

- The Fifth Amendment affords a U.S. citizen due process before the government deprives him of life both at home and abroad, but the United States takes the view that these standards, as implemented by a reportedly deliberate inter-agency executive process in which the President personally approves additions to a "kill list," with periodic notice to congressional committees, is all the process that U.S. citizens are due. No U.S. court has yet ruled on what process is due a targeted U.S. citizen, although the Supreme Court has ruled on the process due a U.S. citizen who is detained by the military.

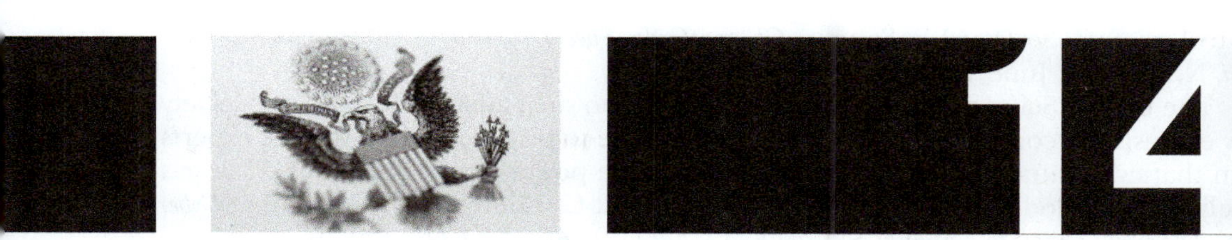

Cyber Operations

The global interconnectedness provided by our linked digital networks brings enormous societal and personal benefits, but it also places new weapons in the hands of states and non-state actors, including terrorists. What are the national security threats in (and arising out of) cyberspace?

> [T]here are only three things you can do to a computer: steal its data, misuse credentials, and hijack resources. Unfortunately, our dependence on information systems means that a skilled actor could wreak a lot of damage by doing any one of those. Stolen data can reveal the strategic plans of a country or undermine the competitiveness of an entire industry. Stolen credentials can give the ability to change or destroy code and data, changing payrolls or opening up dams, as well as the ability to cover tracks. Hijacking resources can prevent a company from reaching customers or deny an army the ability to communicate. [P.W. Singer & Allan Friedman, *Cybersecurity and Cyberwar: What Everyone Needs to Know* 39 (2013).]

By "cyber operations," we refer generally to the use of cyber capabilities to achieve objectives in or through the use of cyberspace. *See Tallinn Manual on the International Law Applicable to Cyber Warfare* 24 (Michael N. Schmitt ed., 2013) (hereinafter *Tallinn Manual*). "Cyber exploitation" is the use of cyber operations to obtain otherwise confidential information, and is usually conducted clandestinely so that the targeted computer user never knows of the intrusion. *See* Herbert S. Lin, *Offensive Cyber Operations and the Use of Force*, 4 J. Nat'l Security L. & Pol'y 63 (2010).

But cyber operations may also involve more destructive cyber attacks intended to "alter, disrupt, deceive, degrade, or destroy adversary computer systems or networks or the information and (or) programs resident in or transiting these systems or networks." *Id.* at 63. Military networks, weapons systems, and defense research can be remotely disabled, damaged, or destroyed. For example, the Stuxnet attack on the computers that run Iran's nuclear enrichment program was part of a larger "Olympic Games" campaign of cyber operations begun in 2006 during the George W. Bush administration by the United States, and perhaps Israel. The malware it planted impaired and significantly delayed the Iranian program by disrupting the program's control systems. *See* David E. Sanger, *Obama Order Sped Up Wave of Cyberattacks Against Iran*, N.Y. Times, June 1, 2012.

The United States may be especially vulnerable to such attacks. Because our society now entrusts the control of much of its infrastructure to private, online systems, experts warn that cyber attackers could derail trains, initiate power blackouts, cause oil or gas pipelines to explode, or ground aircraft. Richard A. Clarke & Robert K. Knake, *Cyber War: The Next Threat to National Security and What to Do About It* 64-68 (2010).

Whether large or small, cyber attacks are proliferating, at least in part because the means are becoming cheaper and easier to acquire and use. *See* Joel Brenner, *America the Vulnerable: Inside the New Threat Matrix of Digital Espionage, Crime, and Warfare* 154 (2011). Particularly when targeted at powerful adversaries like the United States, cyber intrusions are also a favored weapon of asymmetric warfare, by which weaker adversaries can exploit vulnerabilities of a foe that is much stronger in conventional terms. The asymmetric attackers are helped by the fact that they may be able to mask their identity and location, at least temporarily, and thereby avoid immediate attribution for — and response to — the attacks. Moreover, even when it is possible to correctly trace an attack back to its roots, there may be strong reasons to keep identification of the perpetrator secret — leaving the impression that the perpetrator was never identified.

Applying conventional legal principles to cyber operations is particularly challenging. International and domestic law frameworks to protect national and international security were established long before cyber technology was even envisioned, much less realized. In this chapter we address that challenge, first seeking to apply the concepts of "war," "armed attack," and "use of force" to cyber operations that may have no kinetic effects, similarly attempting to apply international humanitarian law to such operations, and then exploring domestic legal authority for the use of cyber weapons. At the end of the chapter, we consider the growing importance of a digital "war of ideas."

A. ASSESSING THE RISK OF CYBER WARFARE

Whistling in the Dark: A Vision of Things to Come?

Imagine that the lights just went out. Why? There's no way to find out, because the Internet is down, and we can't turn on cable news to find out what's going on, as we did on 9/11. Neither is it possible to know when power will be restored.

Before you head home, you might want to grab a bottle of water and use the restroom, because wherever you're going, the plumbing probably won't work without electricity. Unfortunately, you can't call ahead to say you'll be late, because your cell phone doesn't work. Incidentally, you should drive slowly, as there won't be any more gas to fill your car until the lights come back on. And stop at the nearest grocery store for supplies, before shelves are stripped bare.

Now suppose the lights stay out for a week. Let's hope you don't break a leg or have a heart attack or need some medicine. If you still have food and water, you'd better also have a self-defense plan, because your neighbors will want you to share.

What if power is not restored for a month? You'd better hope for mild weather, since you will have neither heating nor air conditioning. Meanwhile, let's hope that an enemy doesn't take this opportunity to attack, because the Defense Department depends almost entirely on civilian power at its bases around the country.

Now try to imagine a blackout that covers the entire country for a year. This may seem not very likely, but it's certainly not implausible. Most Americans probably would not survive that long without electricity. Those who did would surely experience a total breakdown of civil society and the rule of law, and the United States might not exist as a nation.

Some experts believe that a cyber attack on the U.S. electric grid is one of the two greatest, immediate existential threats to the nation.[1] (The other is nuclear war, addressed in the next chapter.) The power grid is the one element of our critical infrastructure on which most of the others depend — including water, transportation, and communication.[2] And our defense and intelligence agencies would quickly be paralyzed without it. The grid is thus an extremely attractive potential target for enemies.

It is hardly surprising, therefore, that Russia and perhaps other states have hacked into public utilities around the country and implanted malware in computerized control systems that might someday be activated to shut down the grid.[3] According to an official at the cyber security firm Symantec, the Russians now "have the ability to shut the power off. All that's missing is some political motivation."[4] Presumably, we have done the same in Russia. These hacks are made possible by the connection of the grids to the Internet — or at least by our near-total dependence on computer systems to generate and control the distribution of electricity.[5]

One might expect the nation to have adopted heroic measures to eliminate or at least minimize this extreme vulnerability. Those measures could include requirements for the mostly privately owned electric infrastructure to employ state-of-the-art computer hardware, software, and operating practices to ward off cyber attacks.

---

1. *See Protecting the Electric Grid from the Potential Threats of Solar Storms and Electromagnetic Pulse: Hearing Before the S. Comm. on Homeland Sec. & Gov't Aff.* 61, 114th Cong. (2015) (statement of R. James Woolsey, former Director of Central Intelligence, reporting one estimate that "9 of 10 Americans could die from starvation and societal collapse from a nationwide blackout lasting one year").

2. *See* Dep't of Energy, *Strategic Transformer Reserve: Report to Congress* 1 (Mar. 2017) ("[E]lectricity is an essential part of public health and safety and national security . . . a 'lifeline' function.").

3. *See* Dep't of Homeland Security, U.S. Computer Emergency Readiness Team, *Alert (TA18-074A): Russian Government Cyber Activity Targeting Energy and Other Critical Infrastructure Sectors* (Mar. 15, 2018), https://www.us-cert.gov/ncas/alerts/TA18-074A; Jim Finkle, *U.S. Warns Businesses of Hacking Campaign Against Nuclear, Energy Firms,* Reuters, June 30, 2017.

4. Nicole Perlroth & David E. Sanger, *Cyberattacks Put Russian Fingers on the Switch at Power Plants, U.S. Says,* N.Y. Times, Mar. 15, 2018.

5. *See* Richard J. Campbell, *Cybersecurity Issues for the Bulk Power System* (Cong. Res. Serv. R43989), June 10, 2015; Nat'l Research Council, *Terrorism and the Electric Power Delivery System* (2012).

They could also include verifiable agreements with potential enemies to forgo such attacks. What we have done instead, however, is left protection of the grid largely to the voluntary efforts of its private owners, developed and deployed ever more refined cyber weapons, and threatened retaliation using those weapons.

The electric grid is not the only potential target of a cyber attack, of course. What all this means for us near-term is that we must develop enforceable rules to reduce the threats, building on existing laws and procedures that may require considerable tailoring to address rapidly evolving new digital weaponry.

B. APPLYING INTERNATIONAL LAW TO CYBER OPERATIONS

1. Cyber Operations and *Jus ad Bellum*

In 2011, the Obama administration asserted that "[t]he development of norms for state conduct in cyberspace does not require a reinvention of customary international law, nor does it render existing international norms obsolete. Long-standing international norms guiding state behavior — in times of peace and conflict — also apply in cyberspace." The White House, *International Strategy for Cyberspace: Prosperity, Security, and Openness in a Networked World* 9 (2011). The World Court declared in 1996 that provisions of the U.N. Charter relating to the threat or use of force "do not refer to specific weapons. They apply to any use of force, regardless of the weapons employed." *Legality of the Threat or Use of Nuclear Weapons, Advisory Opinion,* 1996 I.C.J. 226, ¶39 (July 8).

Still, cyber weapons and their potential effects are unique in many respects. How do existing norms apply to them? What additional rules might be required to meet the objectives of the U.N. Charter and customary international law? The U.S. Defense Department sought to provide at least some answers in its 2015 *Law of War Manual.*

Department of Defense, Law of War Manual — Chapter 16, Cyber Operations

pp. 1013-1019, June 2015 (updated Dec. 2016)

16.2 APPLICATION OF THE LAW OF WAR TO CYBER OPERATIONS . . .

16.2.1 Application of Specific Law of War Rules to Cyber Operations. Specific law of war rules may be applicable to cyber operations, even though these rules were developed long before cyber operations were possible.

The law of war affirmatively anticipates technological innovation and contemplates that its existing rules will apply to such innovation, including cyber operations.[8] Law of war rules may apply to new technologies because the rules often are not framed in terms of specific technological means. For example, the rules on

8. Harold Hongju Koh, Legal Adviser, Department of State, *International Law in Cyberspace: Remarks as Prepared for Delivery to the USCYBERCOM Inter-Agency Legal Conference* (Sept. 18, 2012), *reprinted in* 54 Harv. Int'l L.J. Online 3 (2012). [The Koh remarks are cited as authoritative throughout this chapter of the *Manual.* — Eds.]

conducting attacks do not depend on what type of weapon is used to conduct the attack. Thus, cyber operations may be subject to a variety of law of war rules depending on the rule and the nature of the cyber operation. For example, if the physical consequences of a cyber attack constitute the kind of physical damage that would be caused by dropping a bomb or firing a missile, that cyber attack would equally be subject to the same rules that apply to attacks using bombs or missiles. . . .

16.2.2 Application of Law of War Principles as a General Guide to Cyber Operations. When no specific rule applies, the principles of the law of war form the general guide for conduct during war, including conduct during cyber operations. For example, under the principle of humanity, suffering, injury, or destruction unnecessary to accomplish a legitimate military purpose must be avoided in cyber operations. . . .

16.3 CYBER OPERATIONS AND *JUS AD BELLUM* . . .

16.3.1 Prohibition on Cyber Operations That Constitute Illegal Uses of Force Under Article 2(4) of the Charter of the United Nations. . . . Cyber operations may in certain circumstances constitute uses of force within the meaning of Article 2(4) of the Charter of the United Nations and customary international law. For example, if cyber operations cause effects that, if caused by traditional physical means, would be regarded as a use of force under *jus ad bellum,* then such cyber operations would likely also be regarded as a use of force. Such operations may include cyber operations that: (1) trigger a nuclear plant meltdown; (2) open a dam above a populated area, causing destruction; or (3) disable air traffic control services, resulting in airplane crashes. Similarly, cyber operations that cripple a military's logistics systems, and thus its ability to conduct and sustain military operations, might also be considered a use of force under *jus ad bellum.* Other factors, besides the effects of the cyber operation, may also be relevant to whether the cyber operation constitutes a use of force under *jus ad bellum.*[22] . . .

16.3.2 Peacetime Intelligence and Counterintelligence Activities. . . . [T]he question of the legality of peacetime intelligence and counterintelligence activities must be considered on a case-by-case basis. Generally, to the extent that cyber operations resemble traditional intelligence and counter-intelligence activities, such as unauthorized intrusions into computer networks solely to acquire information, then such cyber operations would likely be treated similarly under international law. The United States conducts such activities via cyberspace, and such operations are governed by long-standing and well-established considerations, including the possibility that those operations could be interpreted as a hostile act.

16.3.3 Responding to Hostile or Malicious Cyber Operations. A State's inherent right of self-defense, recognized in Article 51 of the Charter of the United Nations, may be triggered by cyber operations that amount to an armed attack or imminent threat thereof. As a matter of national policy, the United States has expressed the view

---

22. [Koh, *supra,* at 4] ("In assessing whether an event constituted a use of force in or through cyberspace, we must evaluate factors including the context of the event, the actor perpetrating the action (recognizing challenging issues of attribution in cyberspace), the target and location, effects and intent, among other possible issues.").

that when warranted, it will respond to hostile acts in cyberspace as it would to any other threat to the country.

Measures taken in the exercise of the right of national self-defense in response to an armed attack must be reported immediately to the U.N. Security Council in accordance with Article 51 of the Charter of the United Nations.

16.3.3.1 Use of Force Versus Armed Attack. The United States has long taken the position that the inherent right of self-defense potentially applies against any illegal use of force. Thus, any cyber operation that constitutes an illegal use of force against a State potentially gives rise to a right to take necessary and proportionate action in self-defense.

16.3.3.2 No Legal Requirement for a Cyber Response to a Cyber Attack. There is no legal requirement that the response in self-defense to a cyber armed attack take the form of a cyber action, as long as the response meets the requirements of necessity and proportionality.

16.3.3.3 Responses to Hostile or Malicious Cyber Acts That Do Not Constitute Uses of Force. Although cyber operations that do not constitute uses of force under jus ad bellum would not permit injured States to use force in self-defense, those injured States may be justified in taking necessary and appropriate actions in response that do not constitute a use of force. Such actions might include, for example, a diplomatic protest, an economic embargo, or other acts of retorsion.

16.3.3.4 Attribution and Self-Defense Against Cyber Operations. Attribution may pose a difficult factual question in responding to hostile or malicious cyber operations because adversaries may be able to hide or disguise their activities or identities in cyberspace more easily than in the case of other types of operations.

A State's right to take necessary and proportionate action in self-defense in response to an armed attack originating through cyberspace applies whether the attack is attributed to another State or to a non-State actor.

16.3.3.5 Authorities Under U.S. Law to Respond to Hostile Cyber Acts. Decisions about whether to invoke a State's inherent right of self-defense would be made at the national level because they involve the State's rights and responsibilities under international law. For example, in the United States, such decisions would generally be made by the President.

The Standing Rules of Engagement for U.S. forces have addressed the authority of the U.S. armed forces to take action in self-defense in response to hostile acts or hostile intent, including such acts perpetrated in or through cyberspace.

16.4 CYBER OPERATIONS AND THE LAW OF NEUTRALITY

. . . [U]nder the law of neutrality, belligerent States are bound to respect the sovereign rights of neutral States. Because of the interconnected nature of cyberspace, cyber operations targeting networked information infrastructures in one State may create effects in another State that is not a party to the armed conflict.

16.4.1 Cyber Operations That Use Communications Infrastructure in Neutral States. . . . The use of communications infrastructure in neutral States may be implicated under the general rule that neutral territory may not serve as a base of operations for one belligerent against another. In particular, belligerent States are prohibited from erecting on the territory of a neutral State any apparatus for the purpose of communicating with belligerent forces on land or sea, or from using any installation of this kind established by them before the armed conflict on the territory of a neutral State for purely military purposes, and which has not been opened for the service of public messages.

However, merely relaying information through neutral communications infrastructure (provided that the facilities are made available impartially) generally would not constitute a violation of the law of neutrality that belligerent States would have an obligation to refrain from and that a neutral State would have an obligation to prevent. . . .

Notes and Questions

1. When Is a Cyber Operation a Use of Force? Whether an action is a use of force under international law depends on its scope, duration, and intensity. David E. Graham, *Cyber Threats and the Law of War*, 4 J. Nat'l Security L. & Pol'y 87, 90 (2010). Under what circumstances should a cyber attack qualify as a use of force that would violate Article 2(4) of the U.N. Charter? Could it ever amount to an armed attack that could trigger the inherent right of self-defense under Article 51? Why would the United States treat a use of force and armed attack as legally indistinguishable in the cyber domain?

The *Law of War Manual* adopts an "effects test" to answer this question by considering whether the effect of a cyber attack would be regarded as a use of force under *jus ad bellum* if it had been brought about instead by kinetic means. *See* Michael N. Schmitt, *International Law in Cyberspace: The Koh Speech and Tallinn Manual Juxtaposed*, 54 Harv. Int'l L.J. Online 13, 26-28 (2012) (cyber operations directed against civilian computer systems only constitute armed attacks if their consequences are similar to those caused by kinetic attacks). The examples it gives are all easy. In each, a cyber attack actually causes serious physical damage similar to that which would result from a missile attack. But a cyber attack on a state's banking and financial institutions that cripples the economy could also qualify. Graham, *supra*, at 91. Indeed, in some cases, cyber attacks might achieve results unlike anything that kinetic attacks previously have, yet qualify as uses of force or armed attacks because of the character or scope of the damages they cause.

When Iran allegedly mined foreign-flagged tankers in international waters and shot down a U.S. Navy Global Hawk unmanned surveillance drone in the summer of 2019, the Trump administration came very close to ordering air strikes targeting Iranian military infrastructure. After those responsive strikes were called off, media reports asserted that the United States instead carried out a significant cyber operation against Iran. Robert Chesney, *The Legal Context for CYBERCOM's Reported Operations Against Iran*, Lawfare, June 24, 2019. The U.S. cyber operation was reportedly intended to disable Iranian missile and rocket launch systems and the forces that had mined the tankers. Julian E. Barnes & Thomas Gibbons-Neff, *U.S. Carried Out Cyberattacks on Iran*, N.Y. Times, June 22, 2019. If these U.S. cyber operations had no kinetic effect, did they violate international law?

2. Other Cyber Intrusions. In the modern era, electronic espionage has assumed an outsized role, augmenting and significantly supplanting the more traditional spies in trench coats and slouch hats. Many states employ computer hackers to eavesdrop on (or simply steal) the secrets of other states. Such intrusions are not ordinarily considered acts of war, even though they may gather information in preparation for war, and even though human spies caught in the target state may be shot for their efforts.

The DOD *Law of War Manual* distinguishes between cyber attacks that are uses of force and cyber exploitation. How does it treat them differently, and why? What does it mean by asserting that cyber operations "solely to acquire information" should be treated like "traditional intelligence and counter-intelligence activities" under international law?

What if one state plants malware in the systems of another state that could be destructive if activated, but does not then activate it? *See* Lin, *supra*, at 76 ("Because an existing vulnerability can be used for cyber attacks (which can be a use of force) or cyberexploitation, the answer is not clear."). An attack that disabled widespread portions of the U.S. power grid for an extended period of time, utilizing malware secretly implanted in advance, might be immensely deadly and destructive. Does the severity of this threat, as well as the difficulty in combating it, affect your assessment of the legality of the Russian hacks into U.S. grid control systems?

What if the shoe were on the other foot? In 2019 the *New York Times* reported that the United States is "stepping up digital incursions into Russia's electric power grid," apparently to warn Russia against conducting further hostile cyber operations against U.S. critical infrastructure. David E. Sanger & Nicole Perloth, *U.S. Escalates Online Attacks on Russia's Power Grid,* N.Y. Times, June 15, 2019. President Trump authorized these offensive cyber operations in classified National Security Presidential Memorandum 13 in 2018, apparently giving DOD's Cyber Command authority to launch them without additional presidential approval. *Id.* Congress confirmed such authority in the John S. McCain National Defense Authorization Act (NDAA) for Fiscal Year 2019, Pub. L. No. 115-232, §1632(2), 132 Stat. 1636, 2123 (2018) (codified at 10 U.S.C. §394(a) (2018)), which authorized the Secretary of Defense to approve "clandestine military activities or operations in cyberspace, to defend the United States and its allies."

International law experts generally agree that a remotely conducted cyber operation attributed to a state is a violation of the victim state's sovereignty if damage or relatively permanent loss of functionality occurs. Michael Schmitt, *U.S. Cyber Command, Russia, and Critical Infrastructure: What Norms and Laws Apply?,* Just Security, June 18, 2019. If these intrusions cause no actual harm and are conducted while the United States and Russia are at peace, do they nonetheless violate peacetime international law norms? *See id.* (no consensus view on this question).

3. Cyber Counterattacks. If a cyber operation qualifies as a use of force, what may the victim state do in self-defense? May it respond in kind? May it use kinetic force? If so, how much? Does the DOD *Law of War Manual* answer these questions?

The historical requirements for self-defense are necessity (no practical peaceful alternative) and proportionality (no more force than required to defeat the ongoing attack or deter an imminent attack). See Chapter 8. "Thus, if an armed attack by a non-State actor exposes and takes advantage of a particular vulnerability in a State's cyber defenses that can then be repaired to deny further cyber incursions, such bolstering of defenses might be a sufficient non-forceful alternative, making the use of force unlawful." Laurie R. Blank, *International Law and Cyber Threats from Non-State Actors,* 89 Int'l L. Studies 406, 418 (2013).

Assuming a destructive cyber attack on a state's financial institutions, what response would be necessary and proportionate? Does the *Law of War Manual* address these questions?

Considering the gravity and unpredictability of the ongoing threat to the U.S. electric grid described earlier, would the United States be justified in ordering an immediate preemptive strike, either cyber or kinetic, on the Russian operatives controlling the threatening malware — that is, before the malware can be activated?

In May 2017, the Pentagon adopted a policy of attacking enemy nuclear missiles before they can be launched, including the use of "non-kinetic" means to disable launch controls, guidance systems, or supply chains. Dep't of Defense, *Declaratory Policy, Concept of Operations, and Employment Guidelines for Left-of-Launch Capability* (May 10, 2017), https://fas.org/man/eprint/left.pdf. "Non-kinetic" means is presumably a reference to cyber operations. *See* Spencer Ackerman, *Revealed: Pentagon Push to Hack Nuke Missiles Before They Launch*, Daily Beast, May 22, 2018. The policy is apparently meant to bolster largely unreliable ballistic missile defense systems. According to the DOD policy, a decision to conduct a pre-conflict, left-of-launch operation would only be made "at the highest levels of the U.S. Government." *Declaratory Policy, supra*, at 1. Such an operation would be a legal act of individual or collective self-defense under the U.N. Charter, the policy declares, because it would only be conducted if a missile attack were "imminent." *Id.* at 2. A determination of "imminence" would be based on

> the amount of time available to take action to counter the threat, including whether there is substantial danger of missing a limited window of opportunity to prevent widespread harm. Other important circumstances to be considered may include the nature and immediacy of the threat; the probability of an attack; whether the anticipated attack is part of a concerted pattern of continuing armed activity; the likely scale of the attack and the injury, loss, or damage likely to result from the attack in the absence of mitigating action; and the likelihood that there will be other opportunities to undertake effective action in self-defense that may be expected to cause less serious collateral, loss, or damage. [*Id.*]

Whether or not a left-of-launch cyber operation would constitute a use of force, would application of these criteria justify the operation as an act of self-defense in compliance with Article 51 of the Charter? Would it meet the requirements for self-defense articulated in the *Caroline* affair: "a necessity of self-defense, instant, overwhelming, leaving no choice of means, no moment for deliberation"? See *supra* p. 260.

4. "Lesser" Cyber Attacks and Sovereignty. In general, every state retains legal and regulatory control over the cyber infrastructure located on its territory, regardless of ownership. Schmitt, *International Law in Cyberspace, supra*, at 31. Uninvited invasion of that infrastructure from abroad thus can be a breach of the territorial state's sovereignty.

For example, in 2014 a malicious cyber attack reportedly was unleashed by North Korea against Sony Pictures as the company prepared to release a comedy film involving a fictional assassination of the North Korean "supreme leader" Kim Jong-un. The cyber operation involved the acquisition and release of sensitive information from Sony systems, the destruction of company data, and physical damage to Sony's computers. Whether or not the North Korean operation constituted an illegal use of force or armed attack, it breached U.S. sovereignty. If in fact the attack was conducted by North Korea, it may therefore be considered an "internationally wrongful act" under customary international law, entitling the injured state (but not the injured company) to engage in "countermeasures." *See* Int'l Law Comm'n, *Draft Articles on Responsibility of States for Internationally Wrongful Acts,* arts. 22, 49-54 (2001).

> Countermeasures are actions by an injured State that breach obligations owed to the "responsible" State (the one initially violating its legal obligations) in order to persuade the latter to return to a state of lawfulness. Thus, if the cyber operation against Sony is attributable to North Korea and breached U.S. sovereignty, the United States could have responded with countermeasures, such as a "hack back" against North Korean cyber assets. . . . [T]hey are only available against States and the prevailing view is that a countermeasure may not rise to the level of a use of force. [Michael Schmitt, *International Law and Cyber Attacks: Sony v. North Korea,* Just Security, Dec. 17, 2014.]

Does the *Law of War Manual* address "lesser" cyber attacks that do not amount to a use of force but still violate sovereignty? If so, does it set any standard for countermeasures?

5. Attribution. Tracing the source of a cyber attack remains one the most vexing technological and legal issues. A skillful, determined attacker may route an attack through the infrastructure of many nations before it finally reaches its target, making it extremely difficult (and time-consuming) for the victim state to identify the attacker. Similarly, attacks may come simultaneously from many computers — perhaps thousands — in many different places, called botnets, using software implanted in them in advance and triggered remotely by a signal from the individual who planned the attack.

A key element in any nation's deterrence strategy is a credible declaration that any attack will be met with a swift and terrible retaliation. The U.S. Defense Department's *Cyber Strategy* (Apr. 2015) addresses this challenge, perhaps optimistically, this way:

> Attribution is a fundamental part of an effective cyber deterrence strategy as anonymity enables malicious cyber activity by state and non-state groups. On matters of intelligence, attribution, and warning, DoD and the intelligence community have invested significantly in all source collection, analysis, and dissemination capabilities, all of which reduce the anonymity of state and non-state actor activity in cyberspace. Intelligence and attribution capabilities help to unmask an actor's cyber persona, identify the attack's point of origin, and determine tactics, techniques, and procedures. Attribution enables the Defense Department or other agencies to conduct response and denial operations against an incoming cyberattack. [*Id.* at 11-12.]

But at least some states may lack the technical know-how to make good on this retaliatory threat if they cannot be sure where to direct their response. Still others, including the United States and other states with sophisticated cyber capabilities, may not wish to reveal particular capabilities either to the public or to the attackers, only further contributing to indeterminacy, or at least a sense thereof. *See* William C. Banks, *The Bumpy Road to a Meaningful International Law of Cyber Attribution,* 113 Am. J. Int'l L. Unbound 191 (2019).

6. Cyber Attacks from Non-State Actors. The *Tallinn Manual* declares that "[a] State shall not *knowingly* allow the cyber infrastructure located in its territory or under its exclusive governmental control to be used for acts that adversely and unlawfully affect other states." *Tallinn Manual, supra,* Rule 5 (emphasis added). According to Professor

Schmitt, a state has a duty to take "feasible" measures to end cyber attacks it *knows about* that are launched from within its territory against other states. Schmitt, *International Law in Cyberspace, supra,* at 33. But how can a government discharge this responsibility when most of its cyber infrastructure is privately held, as it is in the United States? What must a state do in order to *become* aware of the cyber operations of a terrorist group or other non-state actor? What is its obligation then to curtail those operations?

Under what circumstances would a state have "imputed responsibility" (Graham, *supra,* at 93) to a victim state for cyber attacks carried out by a terrorist organization operating within its territory? The *Tallinn Manual* provides that before responsibility attaches, a state must have "effective control" over non-state actors within its borders. Drawing on ICJ decisions, such as the *Nicaragua* case, *supra* p. 249, the *Manual* concludes that, for a state to be held *responsible* for a cyber operation by a resident non-state actor, the state must have instructed or directed or controlled the operation. Mere encouragement or expressions of support for the actions of the non-state actor would not cross the "effective control" threshold. *Tallinn Manual,* Rule 6, cmt. 11. Would a state be responsible for cyber operations conducted by non-state terrorists if the state provided cyber target data to the group? Provided the malware needed to carry out the operations? *See* Schmitt, *International Law in Cyberspace, supra,* at 36 (yes).

Col. Graham suggests that each state has a "duty" to:

- enact stringent criminal laws against the commission of international cyber attacks from within national boundaries.
- conduct meaningful, detailed investigations into cyber attacks.
- prosecute those who have engaged in these attacks.
- cooperate with the victim states' own investigations and prosecutions of those responsible for the attacks. [Graham, *supra,* at 94.]

Will a state from which non-state actors launch cyber operations be responsible for the results if it fails to discharge this duty?

What does state responsibility mean in this context? May a victim state or its residents collect damages for injuries inflicted by terrorists in the host state? *See* Michael N. Schmitt, *Cyber Operations and the Jus Ad Bellum Revisited,* 56 Vill. L. Rev. 569, 581 (2011) (yes). May the victim state legitimately mount a defensive counterattack against the host state using either cyber or kinetic weapons? *See id.* at 582 (only non-forceful countermeasures are permitted unless the original intrusion constitutes a use of force or armed attack).

7. *The Tallinn Manuals.* Following rioting by ethnic Russians in Estonia in 2007, cyber attacks widely attributed to Russian government institutions shut down Estonian government offices, banks, and news services for several weeks. One product of the episode was the creation of the NATO Cooperative Cyber Defence Center of Excellence (CCDCOE), located in Tallinn. International experts based there published the *Tallinn Manual* cited above in 2013, describing international law norms for warfare in cyberspace, commenting on the bases for the norms, and setting forth differences of opinion among the experts. A second project, the *Tallinn Manual 2.0 on the International Law Applicable to Cyber Operations* (Michael N. Schmitt & Liis Vihul eds., 2017), provides commentaries and a distillation of customary international law applicable to both wartime and peacetime cyber operations.

2. Cyber Operations and *Jus in Bello*

The International Court of Justice has not been asked specifically to opine on the legality of cyber weapons under international humanitarian law. But in 1996 it declared emphatically that IHL applies to all conflicts, regardless of the circumstances or the weaponry:

> "'[T]he right of belligerents to adopt means of injuring the enemy is not unlimited' as stated in Article 22 of the 1907 Hague Regulations relating to the laws and customs of war on land. . . ."
>
> The cardinal principles contained in the texts constituting the fabric of humanitarian law are the following. The first is aimed at the protection of the civilian population and civilian objects and establishes the distinction between combatants and non-combatants; States must never make civilians the object of attack and must consequently never use weapons that are incapable of distinguishing between civilian and military targets. According to the second principle, it is prohibited to cause unnecessary suffering to combatants: it is accordingly prohibited to use weapons causing them such harm or uselessly aggravating their suffering. In application of that second principle, States do not have unlimited freedom of choice of means in the weapons they use. [*Legality of the Threat or Use of Nuclear Weapons, Advisory Opinion,* 1996 I.C.J. 226, ¶¶77, 78 (July 8).]

The same principles are reflected in conventional law.

Protocol Additional to the Geneva Conventions of August 12, 1949, and Relating to the Protection of Victims of International Armed Conflicts, June 8, 1977 (Protocol I)

1125 U.N.T.S. 3, 16 I.L.M. 1391

Article 1 — General Principles and Scope of Application . . .

2. In cases not covered by this Protocol or by other international agreements, civilians and combatants remain under the protection and authority of the principles of international law derived from established custom, from the principles of humanity and from the dictates of public conscience.

Article 36 — New Weapons

In the study, development, acquisition or adoption of a new weapon, means or method of warfare, a High Contracting Party is under an obligation to determine whether its employment would, in some or all circumstances, be prohibited by this Protocol or any other rule of international law applicable to the High Contracting Party.

[Articles 48-51 and 57, also relevant here, are set forth *supra* pp. 277-279.]

The United States has embraced these principles in its own rules for cyber operations.

Department of Defense, Law of War Manual — Chapter 16, Cyber Operations

pp. 1020-1026, June 2015

16.5 CYBER OPERATIONS AND *JUS IN BELLO*...

16.5.1 Cyber Operations That Constitute "Attacks" for the Purpose of Applying Rules on Conducting Attacks. If a cyber operation constitutes an attack, then the law of war rules on conducting attacks must be applied to those cyber operations. For example, such operations must comport with the requirements of distinction and proportionality.

For example, a cyber attack that would destroy enemy computer systems could not be directed against ostensibly civilian infrastructure, such as computer systems belonging to stock exchanges, banking systems, and universities, unless those computer systems met the test for being a military objective under the circumstances. A cyber operation that would not constitute an attack, but would nonetheless seize or destroy enemy property, would have to be imperatively demanded by the necessities of war.

16.5.1.1 Assessing Incidental Injury or Damage during Cyber Operations. The principle of proportionality prohibits attacks in which the expected loss of life or injury to civilians, and damage to civilian objects incidental to the attack, would be excessive in relation to the concrete and direct military advantage expected to be gained.

For example, in applying this proportionality rule to cyber operations, it might be important to assess the potential effects of a cyber attack on computers that are not military objectives, such as private, civilian computers that hold no military significance, but that may be networked to computers that are valid military objectives.

In assessing incidental injury or damage during cyber operations, it may be important to consider that remote harms and lesser forms of harm, such as mere inconveniences or temporary disruptions, need not be considered in assessing whether an attack is prohibited by the principle of proportionality. For example, a minor, brief disruption of internet services to civilians that results incidentally from a cyber attack against a military objective generally would not need to be considered in a proportionality analysis. In addition, the economic harms in the belligerent State resulting from such disruptions, such as civilian businesses in the belligerent State being unable to conduct e-commerce, generally would not need to be considered in a proportionality analysis....

16.5.3 Duty to Take Feasible Precautions and Cyber Operations. Parties to a conflict must take feasible precautions to reduce the risk of incidental harm to the civilian population and other protected persons and objects. Parties to the conflict that employ cyber operations should take precautions to minimize the harm of their cyber activities on civilian infrastructure and users.

The obligation to take feasible precautions may be of greater relevance in cyber operations than other law of war rules because this obligation applies to a broader set of activities than those to which other law of war rules apply. For example, the obligation to take feasible precautions to reduce the risk of incidental harm would apply to a party conducting an attack even if the attack would not be prohibited by the principle of proportionality. In addition, the obligation to take feasible precautions applies even if a party is not conducting an attack because the obligation also applies to a party that is subject to attack.

16.5.3.1 Cyber Tools as Potential Measures to Reduce the Risk of Harm to Civilians or Civilian Objects. In some cases, cyber operations that result in non-kinetic or reversible effects can offer options that help minimize unnecessary harm to civilians. In this regard, cyber capabilities may in some circumstances be preferable, as a matter of policy, to kinetic weapons because their effects may be reversible, and they may hold the potential to accomplish military goals without any destructive kinetic effect at all.

As with other precautions, the decision of which weapon to use will be subject to many practical considerations, including effectiveness, cost, and "fragility," i.e., the possibility that once used an adversary may be able to devise defenses that will render a cyber tool ineffective in the future. Thus, as with special kinetic weapons, such as precision-guided munitions that have the potential to produce less incidental damage than other kinetic weapons, cyber capabilities usually will not be the only type of weapon that is legally permitted. . . .

16.6 LEGAL REVIEW OF WEAPONS THAT EMPLOY CYBER CAPABILITIES

DoD policy requires the legal review of the acquisition of weapons or weapon systems. This policy would include the review of weapons that employ cyber capabilities to ensure that they are not *per se* prohibited by the law of war. . . .

Although which issues may warrant legal analysis would depend on the characteristics of the weapon being assessed, a legal review of the acquisition or procurement of a weapon that employs cyber capabilities likely would assess whether the weapon is inherently indiscriminate. For example, a destructive computer virus that was programmed to spread and destroy uncontrollably within civilian internet systems would be prohibited as an inherently indiscriminate weapon.

Notes and Questions

1. Distinction in Cyber Operations. Applying the principle of distinction in cyber operations is tricky, and the law is unsettled. Distinction prohibits attacks against protected persons and objects, restricts how attacks may be conducted, and limits the incidental harm that may be caused to civilians and civilian objects during an attack. *See* Additional Protocol I, Part IV, *supra* pp. 277-283. Although it is widely agreed that cyber operations that cause injury or death to persons or damage or destruction to objects should be subject to the same restrictions as kinetic attacks, there is not yet consensus on whether or under what circumstances cyber operations that cause no physical damage qualify as attacks that violate the requirement of distinction. *See* Schmitt, *International Law in Cyberspace, supra*, at 26.

How should distinction apply in cyber operations? Should it prohibit attacks on, say, oil-production facilities in a country that finances its war through oil exports? To denial of service attacks on military communications networks or civilian air traffic control?

Complicating compliance with the requirement of distinction in the cyber domain, computers that are legitimate targets of cyber attack may be connected via the Internet or local networks to others that are protected from attack, such as those that operate civilian public utilities or serve hospitals. An otherwise legitimate cyber attack may thus have an unexpected and unintended, destructive ripple effect that extends far beyond the legitimate target. What must an attacking state do to avoid injuries to such connected parties that are both unintended and excessive in relation to the military value of the effect on its intended target?

2. Proportionality in Cyber Operations. As in kinetic conflicts, proportionality in cyber operations requires a comparison of military advantage and collateral harm. *See* Additional Protocol I, *supra,* arts. 51(5)(b), 57(2)(a)(iii). Would cyber operations that caused inconveniences, stress, or fear violate the requirement of proportionality? What about delays in services or communications, or the loss of data? *See* Schmitt, *International Law in Cyberspace, supra,* at 27-28 (noting that a majority of the *Tallinn Manual* experts concluded that only civilian death, injury, damage, or destruction typically bear on the proportionality analysis, but that indirect effects must be taken into account where there are foreseeable collateral effects on civilian systems).

How does the typical networking of computers, both legitimate targets of cyber attack and others, affect the determination of proportionality in an attack? The *Tallinn Manual* provides that "[a] cyber attack that may be expected to cause incidental loss of civilian life, injury to civilians, damage to civilian objects, or a combination thereof, which would be excessive in relation to the concrete and direct military advantage anticipated is prohibited." *Tallinn Manual,* Rule 51. Can you see the challenges in applying this rule to cyber operations in practice?

3. Discrimination in Responding to a Cyber Attack. When a state comes under cyber attack, it may be exceptionally difficult, as noted above, either to determine the source of the attack or to know how that source might be networked with computer systems that would not be legitimate targets of countermeasures. How should this indeterminacy affect a victim state's calculation of its compliance with the requirement of discrimination when it uses a cyber weapon in self-defense against a suspected state attacker? Can you draft a rule to describe its responsibility? *See Tallinn Manual,* Rules 52-58 (describing the types of harm to civilians and civilian objects that constitute collateral damage and thus implicate the principles of distinction and proportionality).

C. APPLYING DOMESTIC LAW TO CYBER OPERATIONS

Apart from the challenges of fitting conflict in the cyber domain into a legal architecture developed in response to centuries of kinetic warfare, it is easy to see how and why international law is in many ways at the forefront of the emerging national security law for cyber operations. After all, digital interconnectedness transcends national boundaries. As in every other national security law paradigm, however, domestic law may be critically important in establishing the scope and limits of our own government's authority to respond to hostile cyber intrusions, initiate offensive cyber operations, and otherwise act in ways that could impact the rights and interests of U.S. persons and businesses.

In considering the relevant domestic law, the framing questions are similar to those asked in international law: Has there been an attack that triggers the defensive war power of the Commander in Chief? If so, what are the scope and limits of the repel power? If not, what measures may legally be taken to respond to a hostile cyber intrusion, and who may order them? When may cyber weapons be used offensively, and who is permitted to make that judgment? To what extent may privately owned entities conduct their own cyber operations against attackers? What are the individual rights implications of increasing cyber operations?

In 2018, the U.S. government suggested some answers, but also raised new questions, in the *National Cyber Strategy of the United States of America* (Sept. 2018), https://www.whitehouse.gov/wp-content/uploads/2018/09/National-Cyber-Strategy.pdf, and a related Defense Department document, excerpted below.

Dep't of Defense, Summary: Department of Defense Cyber Strategy 2018

Sept. 18, 2018

https://media.defense.gov/2018/Sep/18/2002041658/-1/-1/1/cyber_strategy_summary_final.pdf

We are engaged in a long-term strategic competition with China and Russia. These States have expanded that competition to include persistent campaigns in and through cyberspace that *pose long-term strategic risk to the Nation as well as to our allies and partners.* China is eroding U.S. military overmatch and the Nation's economic vitality by persistently exfiltrating sensitive information from U.S. public and private sector institutions. Russia has used cyber-enabled information operations to influence our population and challenge our democratic processes. Other actors, such as North Korea and Iran, have similarly employed malicious cyber activities to harm U.S. citizens and threaten U.S. interests. Globally, the scope and pace of malicious cyber activity continue to rise. The United States' growing dependence on the cyberspace domain for nearly every essential civilian and military function makes this an urgent and unacceptable risk to the Nation.

The Department must take *action in cyberspace during day-to-day competition* to preserve U.S. military advantages and to defend U.S. interests. Our *focus will be on the States* that can pose strategic threats to U.S. prosperity and security, particularly China and Russia. We will *conduct cyberspace operations to collect intelligence and prepare military cyber capabilities* to be used in the event of crisis or conflict. We will *defend forward* to disrupt or halt malicious cyber activity at its source, including activity that falls below the level of armed conflict. We will *strengthen the security and resilience* of networks and systems that contribute to current and future U.S. military advantages. We will collaborate with our *interagency, industry, and international partners* to advance our mutual interests.

During wartime, U.S. cyber forces will be prepared to operate alongside our air, land, sea, and space forces to target adversary weaknesses, offset adversary strengths, and amplify the effectiveness of other elements of the Joint Force. Adversary militaries are increasingly reliant on the same type of computer and network technologies that have become central to Joint Force warfighting. The Department will exploit this reliance to gain military advantage. The Joint Force will employ *offensive cyber capabilities* and *innovative concepts* that allow for the use of cyberspace operations *across the full spectrum of conflict*. . . .

Notes and Questions

1. "Defending Forward." DOD's *Cyber Strategy 2018* declares, "We will *defend forward* to disrupt or halt malicious cyber activity at its source, including activity that falls below the level of armed conflict." *Id.* at 1. The term "defend forward" is not defined in the document, but it suggests an intention to engage in anticipatory or perhaps even preemptive self-defense by striking apparently threatening cyber targets. And the reference to "activity that falls below the level of armed conflict" suggests a cyber threat that would, if carried out, not cause loss of life or extensive property damage. *See* Dave Weinstein, *The Pentagon's New Cyber Strategy: Defend Forward,* Lawfare, Sept. 21, 2018. Clearly, this policy statement is meant to deter potential attackers from engaging in activities that could possibly be perceived as threatening. But may the United States legitimately mount a preemptive cyber attack against an enemy? Can you describe legal limits on its ability to do so?

The *Cyber Strategy* also states that DOD will place a priority on "deterring malicious cyber activities that constitute a use of force against the United States, our allies, or our partners. Should deterrence fail, the Joint Force stands ready to employ the full range of military capabilities in response," presumably including kinetic weapons. *Cyber Strategy 2018,* at 4. Does U.N. Charter Article 51 permit the United States to employ cyber weapons in collective self-defense in aid of another state? If so, under what circumstances?

Might the U.S. policy of deterrence by "defending forward" to hold a potential enemy's defenses and assets at risk be mistaken by that enemy as preparation-of-the-battlefield, that is, the beginning of an actual attack? If so, would the strategic instability created by such a policy affect its legality under the U.N. Charter? *See* Robert Chesney, *The 2018 DOD Cyber Strategy: Understanding "Defense Forward" in Light of the NDAA and PPD-20 Changes,* Lawfare, Sept. 25, 2018.

2. DOD Capabilities. Another 2018 DOD publication offers some insight into U.S. military capabilities in cyberspace, and into related legal concerns. Jt. Chiefs of Staff, *Cyber Operations* (Jt. Pub. 3-12) (June 8, 2018), describes the organization and operation of various military efforts to dominate the cyber environment on and off the battlefield, including protection of civilian critical infrastructure. Included are countermeasures

> that, by the employment of devices and/or techniques, [have] as [their] objective the impairment of the operational effectiveness of enemy activity. . . . As in the physical domains, countermeasure actions can be taken either internal or external to the defended terrain and can be used preemptively or reactively. [*Id.* at II-7.]

The Joint Chiefs publication nevertheless acknowledges the ongoing difficulty of attribution:

> The nature of cyberspace, government policies, and laws, both domestic and international, presents challenges to determining the exact origin of cyberspace threats. The ability to hide the sponsor and/or the threat behind a particular malicious effect in cyberspace makes it difficult to determine how, when, and where to respond. The design of the Internet lends itself to anonymity and, combined with applications intended to

> hide the identity of users, attribution will continue to be a challenge for the foreseeable future. [*Id.* at I-12.]

According to the Joint Chiefs, "[s]ince each CO [cyberspace operation] mission has unique legal considerations, the applicable legal framework depends on the nature of the activities to be conducted. . . . It is essential [that] commanders, planners, and operators consult with legal counsel during planning and execution of CO." *Id.* at III-11. If you were a JAG officer, what information would you need in order to confidently offer advice about the legality of a proposed operation?

3. Statutory Authority for Cyber Operations. In the FY2019 NDAA, cited above, Congress included this declaration:

> It shall be the policy of the United States, with respect to matters pertaining to cyberspace, cybersecurity, and cyber warfare, that the United States should employ all instruments of national power, including the use of offensive cyber capabilities, to deter if possible, and respond to when necessary, all cyber attacks or other malicious cyber activities of foreign powers that target United States interests with the intent to—
>
> (1) cause casualties among United States persons or persons of United States allies;
>
> (2) significantly disrupt the normal functioning of United States democratic society or government (including attacks against critical infrastructure that could damage systems used to provide key services to the public or government);
>
> (3) threaten the command and control of the Armed Forces, the freedom of maneuver of the Armed Forces, or the industrial base or other infrastructure on which the United States Armed Forces rely to defend United States interests and commitments; or
>
> (4) achieve an effect, whether individually or in aggregate, comparable to an armed attack or imperil a vital interest of the United States. [FY2019 NDAA §1636(a), 132 Stat. at 2126 (codified at 10 U.S.C. §394 note).]

To implement this policy, the NDAA affirms that the Secretary of Defense, "when appropriately authorized to do so," shall conduct "military cyber activities or operations in cyberspace, including clandestine military activities or operations in cyberspace, to defend the United States and its allies." *Id.* §1632(2) (codified at 10 U.S.C. §394(a)). Does this language confer upon the President or the Secretary any authority they did not already possess? Can you say what circumstances would trigger this authority?

The NDAA provides particular authority for cyber operations against four potential enemy states:

> In the event that the National Command Authority determines that the Russian Federation, People's Republic of China, Democratic People's Republic of Korea, or Islamic Republic of Iran is conducting an active, systematic, and ongoing campaign of attacks against the Government or people of the United States in cyberspace, including attempting to influence American elections and democratic political processes, the National Command Authority may authorize the Secretary of Defense, acting through the Commander of the United States Cyber Command, to take appropriate and proportional action in foreign cyberspace to disrupt, defeat, and deter such attacks. [*Id.* §1642(a)(1) (codified at 10 U.S.C. §394 note).]

"National Command Authority" means the President and the Defense Secretary. One commentator views this provision as a possible "mini-cyber AUMF" that allows pre-delegation of authority for cyber operations against the named states. Robert Chesney, *The Law of Military Cyber Operations and the New NDAA*, Lawfare, July 26, 2018. Within a few days of signing the NDAA, President Trump reportedly issued a classified order (National Security Presidential Memorandum 13) delegating authority to the Secretary of Defense to conduct cyber operations and revoking an earlier, still-classified order by President Obama (PPD-20) that required extensive interagency discussions and coordination before the military could conduct such operations. Ellen Nakashima, *Trump Gives the Military More Latitude to Use Offensive Cyber Tools Against Adversaries*, Wash. Post, Aug. 16, 2018. But given the potentially enormous strategic consequences, may Congress constitutionally delegate such authority to the President? May the President constitutionally redelegate it to the Secretary of Defense?

Would you say that this NDAA provision provides sufficient legal authority for the June 2019 U.S. cyber operations targeting Iranian rocket and missile launch capabilities and the Iranian group reportedly responsible for mining tankers in the Persian Gulf, discussed *supra* p. 419? *See* Chesney, *Legal Context, supra*.

4. Congressional Oversight. A 2017 measure requires notice to the Armed Services Committees within 48 hours following the "use as a weapon of any cyber capability," but not including a "covert action." 10 U.S.C. §396(a)(2), (c)(2) (2018). A covert action is one that is meant to "influence political, economic, or military conditions abroad, where it intended that the role of the United States Government will not be apparent or acknowledged publicly," that is, plausibly deniable. 50 U.S.C. §3093(e) (2018). But it does not include "traditional . . . military activities." *Id.* §3093(e)(2). See *infra* p. 561.

Section 1632(3) of the 2019 NDAA, 10 U.S.C. §394(c), however, declares that a "clandestine military activity or operation in cyberspace shall be considered a traditional military activity" for the purposes of §3093(e)(2), meaning that neither a specific written finding by the President nor prompt reporting to the congressional Intelligence Committees otherwise required for covert actions is necessary. A clandestine operation is one approved by the President or the Secretary that is conducted in secret and "will not be apparent or acknowledged publicly." *Id.* §1632(3), 10 U.S.C. §394(f)(1)(A).

As a practical matter, military cyber operations will rarely be conducted openly in real time, making them both clandestine and covert, according to the statutory definitions. Has Congress thus effectively surrendered any real-time oversight of such operations? In any case, do you think the President should held accountable for such operations by a requirement of a written finding? When, if ever, would the American people learn about such cyber operations?

If the U.S. military is guided in its use of cyber weapons by the same rules that govern kinetic operations, may it employ kinetic weaponry to respond to a cyber attack? The Defense Department's most recent *Nuclear Posture Review* (Feb. 2018) declares that the United States might use nuclear weapons first in "extreme circumstances" such as "significant non-nuclear strategic attacks." *Id.* at 21. Such attacks might target "U.S., allied, or partner civilian population or infrastructure," or U.S. or allied nuclear forces. *Id.* The term "cyber attack" is not used in the *Review*, but it is widely believed that the quoted language is designed to deter an enemy's use of cyber weapons to, say, disable the U.S. power grid. Does the President possess the authority to order the first use of nuclear weapons in such circumstances? Is your answer affected by the likelihood that such use would precipitate a retaliatory nuclear counterstrike by the enemy, or even an all-out nuclear war? Does this likelihood suggest the need for explicit congressional approval for such use?

5. *A Role for Private Industry?* It is widely believed that a number of private companies have hacked back against foreign attackers in recent years. Could Sony Pictures legally have hacked back against its attacker? The Computer Fraud and Abuse Act, 18 U.S.C. §1030 (2018), criminalizes "the transmission of a program, information, code, or command, and as a result of such conduct, intentionally causes damage to . . . a computer . . . which is used in or affecting interstate or foreign commerce or communication, including a computer located outside the United States." *Id.* §1030(a)(5)(A), (e)(2)(B). Even cyber attackers in North Korea appear to be protected by this statute. Might Sony have escaped criminal liability by pleading self-defense?

Legislation pending at this writing would amend the Computer Fraud and Abuse Act by authorizing a private entity to hack back against an attacker in order to "disrupt continued unauthorized activity against the defender's own network," but only after the entity notifies the FBI, and the FBI acknowledges receipt of the notice. Active Cyber Defense Certainty (AC/DC) Act, H.R. 3270, 116th Cong., §§4-5 (2019). *See* Robert Chesney, *Hackback Is Back: Assessing the Active Cyber Defense Certainty Act,* Lawfare, June 14, 2019.

But is it wise to allow or perhaps even encourage private companies to hack back? Can you see a danger that a company, lacking the resources available to the government, might accidentally hack the wrong computer? That its action might mistakenly be interpreted as an official act of the U.S. government?

Evolving U.S. policy stresses communication and cooperation among all parties affected by a cyber threat or attack. The Cybersecurity Information Sharing Act of 2015 (CISA), 6 U.S.C. §§1501-1510 (2018), authorizes, but does not require, the government to share data about cyber threats and defensive measures with private industry, and vice-versa. *Id.* §§1502-1504. DHS says it will "increase access to and collaboration regarding cybersecurity information" among critical infrastructure stakeholders. U.S. Dep't of Homeland Security, *Cybersecurity Strategy* 13 (May 15, 2018). To do that it will encourage *voluntary* reporting of cyber threats and attacks to national authorities and potential victims. *Id.* at 20. But such reporting is not required. Why do you suppose reporting of cyber threats or attacks is not compulsory?

Outside of government, some 40 global technology and security companies — including Cisco, Dell, Facebook, Microsoft, and Symantec — have signed a pact agreeing to "protect all our users and customers from cyberattacks . . . whether criminal or geopolitical." *Cybersecurity Tech Accord: Protecting Users and Customers Everywhere* (Apr. 17, 2018), https://cybertechaccord.org/accord/; *see also* David E. Sanger, *Tech Firms Sign "Digital Geneva Accord" Not to Aid Governments in Cyberwar,* N.Y. Times, Apr. 17, 2018. The signers have also pledged that they would collaborate in "threat sharing" and would encourage civilian efforts to "respond to . . . cyberattacks." *Cybersecurity Tech Accord, supra.* Nevertheless, they have agreed that they would "not help governments launch cyberattacks against innocent citizens and enterprises from anywhere." *Id.* Do you think the signers will be able to distinguish between government attacks against "innocent" parties and attacks against not so innocent ones? Or have they effectively agreed not to share any information about cyber threats with the government? What do you think motivated the companies to withhold assistance to the government?

D. CYBER WAR OF IDEAS

Information warfare — that is, the secret use of information to deceive and influence an enemy — is nothing new. Its employment as a tactical device in armed conflict is documented in the Bible. Elisha, for example, saved the city of Dothan by misdirecting the Syrian army to Samaria. 2 *Kings* 6:18-20. The United States and other countries have also covertly spread lies and exposed embarrassing truths in an effort to achieve political goals unattainable on the battlefield. *See* Ishaan Tharoor, *The Long History of the U.S. Interfering with Elections Elsewhere*, Wash. Post, Oct. 13, 2016 (providing examples).

The development of the Internet and the rapid emergence of electronic social media, like Facebook, have connected the world's people in entirely new ways. They have also created new opportunities for military and intelligence services to target one another's populations with information designed to change hearts and minds. The result is not truth that sets us free, but data without provenance and with a corrupt purpose. The 2016 U.S. presidential election provided a spectacular example.

In the weeks preceding the election, WikiLeaks released thousands of e-mails hacked from the Democratic National Committee (DNC) and Hillary Clinton campaign officials. The release was designed to embarrass the Democrats, disrupt the Clinton presidential campaign, and benefit the campaign of candidate Donald Trump. Only after the election did the Obama administration officially attribute the hacking and releases to the Russian government, and announce sanctions against Russia. *See* David E. Sanger, *Obama Strikes Back at Russia for Election Hacking*, N.Y. Times, Dec. 29, 2016. The Director of National Intelligence concluded that Russia had conducted a large-scale cyber operation on the orders of President Vladimir Putin with the intention of "undermin[ing] public faith in the US democratic process." Off. of the Dir. of Nat'l Intelligence, *Assessing Russian Activities and Intentions in Recent US Elections: The Analytic Process and Cyber Incident Attribution*, at ii (Jan. 6, 2017).

We have since learned that the Russian interference went far beyond hacking e-mails to a broader military strategy known as "active measures" — weaponization of information to achieve strategic goals, including weakening the United States and the West. As early as 2014, an associate of President Putin set up an Internet troll farm to generate fake social media posts, and Russian operatives traveled to the United States to gather intelligence on our domestic political process. Russia then invested heavily in social media influence operations in the run-up to the 2016 presidential election.

The Senate Intelligence Committee subsequently conducted its own bipartisan investigation into Russian interference in the 2016 election. Its initial, unclassified report concluded that the earlier Intelligence Community assessment was "a sound intelligence product," and that the Russians had made even more extensive efforts to "sow discord, undermine democratic institutions, and interfere in U.S. elections" than those identified by the IC. S. Select Comm. on Intelligence, *The Intelligence Community Assessment: Assessing Russian Activities and Intentions in Recent U.S. Elections*, July 3, 2018, https://www.burr.senate.gov/imo/media/doc/SSCI%20ICA%20ASSESSMENT_FINALJULY3.pdf.

According to Special Counsel Robert Mueller's February 2018 indictment of three Russian companies and 13 individuals on charges including conspiracy to defraud the United States, wire fraud, and identity theft, the goal of the Russian effort was to "spread distrust towards the candidates and the political system in general." Indictment, *United States v. Internet Research Agency LLC*, No. 18-32 (D.D.C. Feb. 16, 2018), https://www.justice.gov/file/1035477/download; *see also* Devlin Barrett, Sari Horwitz & Rosalind S. Helderman, *Russian Troll Farm, 13 Suspects Indicted in 2016 Election Interference*, Wash. Post, Feb. 16, 2018. The indictment charges that Russians stole the identities of U.S. citizens and posed as political activists, while trolls attempted to sow discord by spreading inflammatory messages on social media on the issues of immigration, religion, gun rights, and race. Their efforts targeted swing states, like Florida, Virginia, and Colorado, where they sought to suppress minority voter turnout and promote the candidacies of Donald Trump, Bernie Sanders, and Jill Stein, while disparaging candidate Hillary Clinton. Facebook estimated that fraudulent Russian posts reached 126 million of its American users. *See* Scott Shane & Mark Mazzetti, *Inside a 3-Year Russian Campaign to Influence U.S. Voters*, N.Y. Times, Feb. 16, 2018.

Russian efforts are described in even greater detail in Volume I of the Mueller Report, U.S. Dep't of Justice, *Report on the Investigation into Russian Interference in the 2016 Presidential Election* 14-35 (Mar. 2019). Whether and to what extent these Russian activities succeeded in influencing American voters and perhaps altering the outcome of the election is, at this writing, unknown.

The *Tallinn Manual 2.0, supra*, indicates that "cyber means that are coercive in nature may not be used to alter or suborn modification of another State's governmental or social structure." *Id.* at 315, Rule 10. Such acts violate the customary international law norm forbidding intervention in "matters in which each State is permitted, by the principle of State sovereignty, to decide freely." *Military and Paramilitary Activities in and Against Nicaragua* (Nicar. v. U.S.), 1986 I.C.J. 14, 108 (June 27) (*supra* p. 249). If the Russian campaign to subvert U.S. elections was and remains broader and deeper than mere hacks of campaign documents, does it constitute an unlawful act of intervention? Are there legal differences between spreading misinformation, hacking, and altering electronic voting equipment? Does the fact that the United States has historically engaged in similar influence operations in foreign countries affect the lawfulness of the Russian operation?

If the Russian campaign was or is an illegal intervention, is the United States justified in employing otherwise unlawful responsive countermeasures? If so, what sort? *See* Michael N. Schmitt & Liis Vihul, *Respect for Sovereignty in Cyberspace*, 95 Tex. L. Rev. 1639, 1640-1642 (2017). On the day of the 2018 midterm elections in the United States, Cyber Command carried out an operation to block access to a Russian troll factory, the Internet Research Agency. The operation was characterized by U.S. officials as the first ever offensive cyber operation against Russia designed to thwart attempts to interfere with U.S. elections. Ellen Nakashima, *U.S. Cyber Command Operation Disrupted Internet Access of Russian Troll Factory on Day of 2018 Midterms*, Wash. Post, Feb. 27, 2019. Was the U.S. operation lawful?

CYBER OPERATIONS: SUMMARY OF BASIC PRINCIPLES

- There is a growing consensus that basic principles of international law governing state behavior in times of armed conflict as well as in peacetime apply to cyber operations. Interpreting those principles in light of the differences between kinetic and cyber attacks is an international law work in progress.

- The United States has collected its understandings of the legal basis for the military's use of cyber operations in the Defense Department's 2015 *Law of War Manual.*

- The most important criterion in assessing whether a cyber intrusion triggers *jus ad bellum* norms or IHL is its practical, and perhaps its physical, impact. The "use of force" and "armed attack" thresholds for triggering a lawful defensive response apply in the cyber domain as they do in kinetic warfare.

- The IHL principles of distinction and proportionality apply to cyber operations, but their application is unsettled due to the difficulties in predicting and assessing harm to civilians in the cyber domain.

- Below the threshold of a use of force or armed attack, a cyber operation may breach a state's sovereignty and may justify countermeasures by the victim state not rising to the level of a use of force.

- As in kinetic warfare, a neutral state is responsible for cyber operations conducted from within its sovereign territory or transiting its territory only if it is aware of the operations and is capable of exercising "effective control" over the operations.

- Domestic national security law may apply in the cyber domain largely the same way that it applies to kinetic warfare. But because cyber operations may not cause any physical destruction or injury, and because they may have to be carried out with great speed and secrecy, the President's unilateral authority to order them may be greater than his unilateral authority to order kinetic operations.

- Congress's proper constitutional role in deciding to conduct offensive cyber operations is uncertain, even though such operations may have enormous implications for U.S. foreign policy. But Congress has not yet tried to play a meaningful role.

Nuclear War

> The destructive power of nuclear weapons cannot be contained in either space or time. They have the potential to destroy all civilization and the entire ecosystem of the planet.[1]

The only uses of nuclear weapons in war to date came in 1945, when the U.S. bombings of Hiroshima and Nagasaki killed some 200,000 people, mostly civilians. Two parallel, often conflicting, developments followed. Scientists have labored since then to make these weapons vastly more powerful and accurate, while military strategists have created plans for their strategic and tactical use. At the same time, lawyers, politicians, and diplomats have sought to reduce the threat they pose, or even to eliminate them entirely. In this chapter, we are mainly concerned with the second development.

In a 1996 World Court advisory opinion on the legality of the threat or use of nuclear weapons, one judge called clarification of the question facing the Court the "most important of legal issues ever to face the global community."[2] But three-quarters of a century after the bomb's first use, the legal issue remains largely unresolved because exceptionally difficult political, strategic, diplomatic, psychological, and moral questions surrounding its use also have yet to be answered. No clearer or perhaps more complex example exists of the interdependence of law and policy.

We begin with a brief description of nuclear weapons and their delivery systems, then examine policies to deter their use, or to use them if deterrence fails. An analysis of relevant international law follows, including treaties, the World Court advisory opinion referred to above, and a recent U.N. treaty designed to ban nuclear weapons altogether. Finally, we consider domestic law concerned with the command and control of these weapons.

---

1. *Legality of the Threat or Use of Nuclear Weapons*, Advisory Opinion, 1996 I.C.J. 226, ¶35 (July 8).

2. *Id.* at 450 (Weeramantry, J., dissenting).

A. THE NATURE AND EFFECTS OF NUCLEAR WEAPONS

1. One City, One Bomb

Steven Starr, Lynn Eden & Theodore A. Postol, What Would Happen If an 800-Kiloton Nuclear Warhead Detonated Above Midtown Manhattan?

Bull. of the Atomic Scientists, Feb. 25, 2015

Russian intercontinental ballistic missiles are believed to carry a total of approximately 1,000 strategic nuclear warheads that can hit the US less than 30 minutes after being launched. Of this total, about 700 warheads are rated at 800 kilotons; that is, each has the explosive power of 800,000 tons of TNT. What follows is a description of the consequences of the detonation of a single such warhead over midtown Manhattan, in the heart of New York City.

The initial fireball. The warhead would probably be detonated slightly more than a mile above the city, to maximize the damage created by its blast wave. Within a few tenths of millionths of a second after detonation, the center of the warhead would reach a temperature of roughly 200 million degrees Fahrenheit (about 100 million degrees Celsius), or about four to five times the temperature at the center of the sun.

A ball of superheated air would form, initially expanding outward at millions of miles per hour. It would act like a fast-moving piston on the surrounding air, compressing it at the edge of the fireball and creating a shockwave of vast size and power....

On a clear day with average weather conditions, the enormous heat and light from the fireball would almost instantly ignite fires over a total area of about 100 square miles.

Hurricane of fire. Within seconds after the detonation, fires set within a few miles of the fireball would burn violently. These fires would force gigantic masses of heated air to rise, drawing cooler air from surrounding areas toward the center of the fire zone from all directions.

...Within tens of minutes of the detonation, fires from near and far would join to form a single, gigantic fire....

The mass fire, or firestorm, would quickly increase in intensity, heating enormous volumes of air that would rise at speeds approaching 300 miles per hour. This chimney effect would pull cool air from outside the fire zone towards the center of the fire at speeds of hundreds of miles per hour.... At the edge of the fire zone, the winds would be powerful enough to uproot trees three feet in diameter and suck people from outside the fire into it....

Ground zero: Midtown Manhattan. The fireball would vaporize the structures directly below it and produce an immense blast wave and high-speed winds, crushing even heavily built concrete structures within a couple miles of ground zero. The blast would tear apart high-rise buildings and expose their contents to the solar temperatures; it would spread fires by exposing ignitable surfaces, releasing flammable materials, and dispersing burning materials.

At the Empire State Building, Grand Central Station, the Chrysler Building, and St. Patrick's Cathedral, about one half to three quarters of a mile from ground zero, light from the fireball would melt asphalt in the streets, burn paint off walls, and melt metal surfaces within a half second of the detonation. Roughly one second later, the blast wave and 750-mile-per-hour winds would arrive, flattening buildings and tossing burning cars into the air like leaves in a windstorm. Throughout Midtown, the interiors of vehicles and buildings in line of sight of the fireball would explode into flames.

Slightly more than a mile from ground zero are the neighborhoods of Chelsea, Midtown East, and Lenox Hill, as well as the United Nations; at this distance, for a split second the fireball would shine 10,000 times brighter than a desert sun at noon. All combustible materials illuminated by the fireball would spew fire and black smoke. . . .

At this distance from the fireball, it would take about four seconds for the blast wave to arrive. As it passed over, the blast wave would engulf all structures and crush them; it would generate ferocious winds of 400 to 500 miles per hour that would persist for a few seconds. . . .

Two miles from ground zero, the Metropolitan Museum of Art, with all its magnificent historical treasures, would be obliterated. Two and half miles from ground zero, in Lower Manhattan, the East Village, and Stuyvesant Town, . . . thermal radiation would melt and warp aluminum surfaces, ignite the tires of autos, and turn exposed skin to charcoal, before the blast wave arrived and ripped apart the buildings. . . .

No survivors. Within tens of minutes, everything within approximately five to seven miles of Midtown Manhattan would be engulfed by a gigantic firestorm. The fire zone would cover a total area of 90 to 152 square miles (230 to 389 square kilometers). The firestorm would rage for three to six hours. . . .

Those who tried to escape through the streets would have been incinerated by the hurricane-force winds filled with firebrands and flames. Even those able to find shelter in the lower-level sub-basements of massive buildings would likely suffocate from fire-generated gases or be cooked alive as their shelters heated to oven-like conditions.

The fire would extinguish all life and destroy almost everything else. Tens of miles downwind of the area of immediate destruction, radioactive fallout would begin to arrive within a few hours of the detonation. . . .

This horrifying story unfortunately does not describe nearly all of the likely effects of a nuclear attack on a major U.S. city.[3] Many individuals in the vicinity would die from blunt force trauma or be killed or sickened by ionizing radiation from gamma rays and neutrons. Survivors in outlying areas would find treatment for burns and other injuries largely unavailable, as health care facilities would be overwhelmed. Radiation from fallout would kill or sicken many more downwind. Communications and electric power over a wide area would be non-existent, as an electromagnetic pulse (EMP) generated by the nuclear explosion would have destroyed virtually all unshielded electronic devices. Infrastructure dependent on electricity, including

3. For an extensive description of such effects, based on atmospheric testing of nuclear weapons and the bombings of Hiroshima and Nagasaki, see *The Effects of Nuclear Weapons* (Samuel Glasstone & Philip J. Dolan, eds.) (3d ed. 1977), http://fissilematerials.org/library/gla77.pdf.

transportation and water systems, would be disabled. In the ensuing panic, martial law would almost certainly be declared.

This nightmare scenario also fails to address the likelihood that New York City would not be the only target of a Russian attack, and that U.S. forces would respond in kind with a nuclear attack on one or more Russian targets, implementing our long-standing but, in these circumstances, failed policy of deterrence.

Any such exchange could, in turn, threaten the existence of all civilized life on Earth. One recent scientific study indicates that the detonation of as few as four nuclear weapons like the one described above might loft enough black carbon particles into the atmosphere to significantly lower temperatures and rainfall worldwide for years, resulting in the deaths by starvation of perhaps a billion people. *See* Adam J. Liska et al., *Nuclear Weapons in a Changing Climate: Probability, Increasing Risks, and Perception*, Environment, July 6, 2017. The economic and geopolitical implications of such a development are difficult to imagine.

Is this all just fevered speculation, the stuff of apocalyptic novels? Or does it describe a substantial ongoing risk? Is any such risk now inevitable — or perhaps even acceptable — in a world bristling with nuclear weapons and increasingly sophisticated delivery systems?

2. Current Nuclear Arsenals

As of early 2019, the world's nuclear arsenals include around 13,890 weapons. Most of these are held by the United States and Russia. The rest, fewer than 10 percent, are owned by Britain, France, China, Israel, India, Pakistan, and North Korea. They can be delivered to their targets by land- or submarine-based ballistic missiles, bombers, cruise missiles, or artillery shells. A small number of U.S. nuclear weapons are deployed at bases in Belgium, Germany, Italy, Netherlands, and Turkey.

Some 9,330 warheads are in military stockpiles. Roughly 3,600 are deployed with operational forces, and at least 1,800 of these are on high alert and ready for use on short notice. The remainder are retired and scheduled for disassembly. *See* Hans M. Kristensen & Matt Korda, Fed'n Am. Scientists, *Status of World Nuclear Forces* (May 2019), https://fas.org/issues/nuclear-weapons/status-world-nuclear-forces/ (containing regularly updated estimates of nuclear forces and their deployment). In 2019, the Pentagon stopped publishing official information about U.S. nuclear arsenals. *See Pentagon Blocks Declassification of 2018 Nuclear Stockpile*, Secrecy News, Apr. 10, 2019.

Trident II D5 missile

U.S. Navy

Efforts to reduce the threat posed by growing nuclear arsenals were complicated enormously by the deployment of multiple independently targetable reentry vehicles (MIRVs) beginning in the 1970s. Thus, as many as ten warheads, each of which might be directed to a different target, may be placed atop a single ICBM, making them much harder to defend against. *See* Dakota S. Rudesill, *MIRVs Matter: Banning Hydra-Headed Missiles in a New Start II Treaty*, 54 Stan. J. Int'l L. 83, 86 (2018) (describing land-based MIRVed missiles as "the most destabilizing strategic (i.e., long-range) nuclear forces: . . . at once the most deadly nuclear forces and the most attractive targets").

Following U.S. withdrawal from the ABM Treaty in 2002 (see below), the George W. Bush administration began deployment of a missile defense system in Alaska and California, ostensibly to counter a growing threat from North Korean ICBMs equipped with nuclear warheads. But after nearly two decades of development, the system has managed to intercept and destroy incoming missiles in carefully controlled tests only about 50 percent of the time. *See* Laura Grego & David Wright, *Broken Shield*, Sci. Am., June 2019, at 62. Other missile defense systems are designed to disable short- and intermediate-range enemy ballistic missiles. They are based on ships and on land in East Asia, as well as in Poland and Romania, where they are supposedly poised to knock down still-nonexistent Iranian nuclear missiles aimed at European targets. *See* Arms Control Ass'n, *Current U.S. Missile Defense Programs at a Glance* (Aug. 2019).

Russia recently announced its development of two new, hard-to-counter nuclear delivery systems: a stealthy nuclear-propelled underwater drone guided by artificial intelligence that could navigate into any harbor in the world, and a "hypersonic" missile capable of speeds up to Mach 8 that would be nearly impossible to intercept. *See* Amie Ferris-Rotman, *Putin Warns New Weapons Will Point Toward U.S. If Missiles Are Deployed in Europe*, Wash. Post, Feb. 20, 2019. Meanwhile, the United States is developing its own hypersonic missiles.

3. Modernization

In the 1968 Nuclear Non-Proliferation Treaty (see below), the major nuclear states pledged to work toward total nuclear disarmament. Instead, U.S. and Soviet arsenals grew rapidly during the Cold War to include tens of thousands of warheads. Those numbers have since been reduced dramatically, but the reductions now appear to have stalled, and a new arms race may be underway. Both nuclear superpowers are currently engaged in programs to "modernize" their forces — replacing aging delivery systems, designing and installing new warheads, and upgrading command and control systems.

The Trump administration's plan for modernization is outlined in Dep't of Defense, *Nuclear Posture Review* (Feb. 2018). It includes a new "low-yield" submarine-launched ballistic missile (SLBM) and a new submarine-launched cruise missile (SLCM), as well as a new strategic bomber and a new class of ballistic missile submarine. Some 400 Minuteman III ICBMs will be replaced by a new land-based missile, and weapons production facilities will be reopened. The Congressional Budget Office has estimated that completion of the plan over 30 years will cost $1.2 trillion in inflation-adjusted dollars.

Plans are also underway to dramatically expand U.S. missile defense systems, with space-based sensors, airborne lasers, and new defenses against enemy cruise missiles. *See* Dep't of Defense, *2019 Missile Defense Review* (Feb. 2019).

4. U.S. Nuclear Policy

The keystone of U.S. nuclear policy is "a flexible, tailored nuclear deterrent strategy"—a credible commitment to respond in kind to any use of nuclear weapons against the United States, its allies, or its military forces. *Nuclear Posture Review, supra*, at II. "Our goal is to convince adversaries they have nothing to gain and everything to lose from the use of nuclear weapons." *Id.* A policy of "extended deterrence" promises to use U.S. nuclear forces to repel non-nuclear aggression against allies, as well. *Id.* at VIII. Money is also a concern: "Maintaining an effective nuclear deterrent is much less expensive than fighting a war that we were unable to deter." *Id.* at III. If deterrence fails, however, "the United States will strive to end any conflict at the lowest level of damage possible and on the best achievable terms for the United States, allies, and partners." *Id.* at VIII.

The United States says it is "committed to arms control efforts that advance U.S., allied, and partner security; are verifiable and enforceable; and include partners that comply responsibly with their obligations." But it expresses doubt that progress is possible in the face of continuing Russian non-compliance. *Id.* at XVII.

Early in the Cold War, U.S. nuclear strategy called for deliberately targeting Soviet cities, in order to demoralize the enemy, as well as to destroy its military-industrial and economic base. Later plans specified pre-selected urban-industrial targets throughout the Soviet Union and China. Then, as deterrence began to dominate strategic thinking, the United States adopted a retaliatory plan of graduated nuclear escalation, with the real-time selection of specific targets and weapons, although urban centers remained on the target list. *See* Theodore T. Richard, *Nuclear Weapons Targeting: The Evolution of Law and U.S. Policy*, 224 Mil. L. Rev. 862 (2016). Today, U.S. policy states that any use of nuclear weapons must comply with fundamental principles of the law of war, and that "[t]he United States will not intentionally target civilian populations or civilian objects." Dep't of Defense, *Report on Nuclear Employment Strategy of the United States Specified in Section 491 of 10 U.S.C.*, at 5 (June 19, 2013); *see also* Dep't of Defense, *Joint Targeting* (Jt. Pub. 3-60) (Jan. 31, 2013). In fact, in 1945 the United States claimed to target Hiroshima because it was a supply and logistics center for the Japanese military and home of its southern defense command, and Nagaski because it was a major industrial center for manufacturing munitions and building ships. But in both cities, the population was primarily civilian—overwhelmingly so in Nagasaki. With this history, can you say what "not intentionally target civilian populations" means?

B. INTERNATIONAL LAW OF NUCLEAR WEAPONS

1. Arms Control Treaties

Once the Soviet Union tested its first atomic weapon in 1949, limits on the further development and deployment of such weapons became the subject of intense international negotiations that continue to this day. These efforts were prompted in part by expressions of concern from scientists, many of whom worked on the Manhattan Project during World War II, and by massive public protests, including a demonstration by one million people in New York City in 1982.

According to their proponents, arms control treaties may serve not only to limit the development of these weapons, they may also make war less likely by providing insights into potential enemies' strategic capabilities and planning, and by building confidence among wary adversaries. Nevertheless, they are opposed by many who argue that the United States should not surrender its strategic flexibility or risk cheating by treaty partners.

The results to date are outlined in Amy F. Woolf, Mary Beth D. Nikitin & Paul K. Kerr, *Arms Control and Nonproliferation: A Catalog of Treaties and Agreements* (Cong. Res. Serv. RL33865), Mar. 18, 2019. For explainers and links to texts for each treaty, see Arms Control Ass'n, *Treaties and Agreements* (n.d.), https://www.armscontrol.org/treaties; and U.S. Dep't of State, *Treaties and Agreements* (n.d.), https://web.archive.org/web/20190515123953/https://www.state.gov/t/isn/c18882.htm (removed from the official State Dep't website in 2019). A very brief summary follows.

a. Limits on Testing

Early on it was recognized that one way to slow the quickening arms race was to stop the testing of nuclear weapons, since no nation would be likely to deploy a new weapon without first testing it. A comprehensive test ban was formally discussed by President Eisenhower and Soviet Premier Khrushchev in 1958. The idea of a total ban was not popular with U.S. strategic planners, however, as the United States enjoyed a technological edge in nuclear weapons and sought to exploit the economic and political advantages these weapons offered, compared with conventional weapons, in providing for the defense of Western European allies.

Since then, treaties between the United States and the Soviet Union (now Russia) have barred all tests larger than those larger than those equal to 150 kilotons of TNT. The Comprehensive Test Ban Treaty (CTBT), 35 I.L.M. 1439 (opened for signature Sept. 24, 1996), would forbid all nuclear explosions and allow on-site inspections of suspected violations. By early 2019, 168 nations had ratified the treaty. Yet while President Clinton was the first world leader to sign it, it was rejected by the Senate in 1999 on a vote of 51-48. Five other nuclear states also have either not signed or not ratified the treaty, preventing its entry into force thus far. The United States nevertheless participates in the International Monitoring System (IMS) established pursuant to the treaty, with more than 330 monitoring stations worldwide to collect seismic, airborne radionuclide, acoustic, and hydroacoustic data. Recent underground nuclear tests by North Korea were detected by more than 90 of these stations.

In 2012, a National Academies report concluded that, while "surprise by clandestine nuclear weapons activity cannot be prevented with absolute certainty with or without the CTBT," the development of a new type of strategic weapon "would require the adversary to test at levels detectable by adequately resourced U.S. national technical means and a completed IMS network." Nat'l Research Council, *The Comprehensive Nuclear Test Ban Treaty — Technical Issues for the United States* 12-13 (2012). The report also found that "the United States has the technical capabilities to maintain a safe, secure, and reliable stockpile of nuclear weapons into the foreseeable future without nuclear-explosion testing." *Id.* at 119. Despite these assurances, however, the Trump administration announced in 2018 that while it would continue to support the CTBT monitoring program, it would not seek ratification of the treaty, and it reserved the right to resume testing. *Nuclear Posture Review, supra,* at 72.

b. Limits on Delivery Systems and Warheads

In a succession of treaties beginning in 1972, the United States and the Soviet Union (and subsequently Russia) agreed to freeze the numbers of launchers and warheads, then to dramatically reduce those numbers. The most recent of these is the 2010 New START Treaty, which limits each side's deployed strategic warheads to 1,550; its deployed ICBMs, SLBMs, and nuclear-capable heavy bombers to 700; and its deployed and non-deployed ICBM and SLBM launchers and heavy bombers to 800. New START, which includes an extensive monitoring and verification regime, is set to expire by its terms in February 2021. *See* Amy F. Woolf, *The New START Treaty: Central Limits and Key Provisions* (Cong. Res. Serv. R41219), May 30, 2019. At the time of this writing in 2019, the Trump administration has not indicated whether it would pursue an extension of New START or seek further weapons limitations, *id.* at 41-44, and some argue that the treaty should be allowed to expire. *See, e.g.*, Michaela Dodge, *New START Sunk by Old Problem — Russian Cheating,* Heritage Found., May 29, 2019.

The 1987 Intermediate-Range Nuclear Forces (INF) Treaty was the first to eliminate an entire class of weapons — ballistic missiles and ground-launched cruise missiles with a range between 300 and 3,400 miles. Aimed especially at Soviet missiles that threatened NATO allies, and at U.S. missiles based in Europe, it included an intrusive verification regime. This bilateral treaty did not, however, include China, which has recently developed its own INF forces. In August 2019, responding to Russia's development of a new ground-launched SSC-8 cruise missile of INF range, the Trump administration withdrew from the INF Treaty. Two weeks later, the United States tested its own new missile that would have violated the treaty. *See Pentagon Conducts 1st Test of Previously Banned Missile,* N.Y. Times, Aug. 19, 2019, Many fear that abandonment of the INF Treaty marks the beginning of a new nuclear arms race. *See* Steven Erlanger, *Erosion of Nuclear Deals Puts World on Brink of New Arms Race,* N.Y. Times, Aug. 9, 2019.

In 1991, Presidents George H.W. Bush and Mikhail Gorbachev announced unilateral, but reciprocal, initiatives to eliminate most of the thousands of tactical or "non-strategic" nuclear weapons from their arsenals, including land mines, depth charges, artillery shells, and short-range missiles. *See* Arms Control Ass'n, *The Presidential Nuclear Initiatives (PNIs) on Tactical Nuclear Weapons at a Glance* (updated July 2017), https://www.armscontrol.org/factsheets/pniglance. The precise numbers and locations of such weapons remaining today are unknown, however, as no agreement has been reached for monitoring compliance. *See* Dakota S. Rudesill, *Regulating Tactical Nuclear Weapons,* 102 Geo. L.J. 99, 99 (2013) (arguing that "all nuclear weapons have 'strategic' (that is, major) significance," and that "tactical nuclear weapons ultimately ought to be regulated via [a] new treaty").

c. Limits on Missile Defenses

Following the deployment of crude missile defense systems by both the Soviet Union and the United States in the early 1970s, it became clear that they could be overwhelmed by larger numbers of much cheaper, proven offensive missiles, especially those outfitted with MIRVs. In 1972, the two states agreed in the Anti-Ballistic Missile (ABM) Treaty to limit defensive missiles to 100 each around a single site — Moscow and ICBM silos in North Dakota.

Then in 1983, President Ronald Reagan announced a research program called Strategic Defense Initiative (SDI) — dubbed "Star Wars" by detractors. Critics worried about the destabilizing effect of a U.S. ability to conduct a first strike on Soviet nuclear forces without fear of retaliation. In 2002, President George W. Bush withdrew from the ABM Treaty in order, purportedly, to develop and deploy new ABM missiles to counter threats from still-nonexistent North Korean ICBMs tipped with nuclear warheads. Long-range ABM interceptors are now deployed in Alaska and California, although repeated tests have raised serious questions about their efficacy. Since then, China, which had long relied on a "minimum deterrent" force of some two dozen strategic nuclear weapons, has fielded at least 100 more, some with multiple warheads, to ensure that it could successfully counter a possible U.S. first strike.

d. Other Measures

Several agreements, formal and informal, are aimed at building confidence and lowering tensions between nuclear adversaries, and at reducing the risk of accidents. These include the 1992 Open Skies Treaty, permitting overflight inspections of each party's territory, and a 2000 Pre- and Post-Launch Notification System (hotline) for launches of ballistic missiles and space craft.

The Nuclear Non-Proliferation Treaty (NPT) was signed in 1968 and ratified by all but three nuclear nations — Israel, India, and Pakistan (North Korea withdrew from the treaty in 2003). It provides that no nation that does not already possess nuclear weapons will develop or acquire them. Under the treaty, the International Atomic Energy Agency monitors nuclear programs in non-nuclear weapons states to make sure they remain peaceful. A particular objective of the treaty today is to prevent nuclear weapons or materials from falling into the hands of terrorists. Article VI of the NPT declares that the nuclear states will "pursue negotiations in good faith on effective measures relating to cessation of the nuclear arms race at an early date and to nuclear disarmament, and on a treaty on general and complete disarmament under strict and effective international control." While the United States insists that it continues to support the goals of the NPT, however, it offers no indication of how it intends to pursue "complete disarmament." *Nuclear Posture Review, supra,* at 69-72.

Another effort to halt the spread of nuclear weapons involves treaties that create nuclear weapons-free zones in the Antarctic, Latin America, the South Pacific, Southeast Asia, Central Asia, Africa, the ocean floor, and outer space.

In 2015, the five permanent members of the U.N. Security Council, plus Germany, entered into an agreement with Iran that halted that nation's development of nuclear weapons, in return for the lifting of related economic sanctions. The Joint Comprehensive Plan of Action (JCPOA) would have sharply reduced Iran's enrichment of uranium for 10-15 years, and it provided intrusive monitoring of compliance by the International Atomic Energy Agency (IAEA). Three years later, however, President Trump withdrew the United States from the agreement, calling it "one of the worst and most one-sided transactions the United States has ever entered into," and complaining that it failed to curtail Iran's development of new missiles or its support for paramilitary proxies in the region. White House, *President Donald J. Trump Is Ending United States Participation in an Unacceptable Iran Deal,* May 8, 2018. Even though Iran was in compliance with the agreement at the time, it soon resumed its enrichment efforts.

2. The International Court of Justice's Advisory Opinion

Reading the *Nuclear Weapons* Opinion

In the following case the International Court of Justice (ICJ) was asked to provide authoritative answers to questions about the legality of nuclear weapons. One judge described it as a matter of "global interest unparalleled in the annals of this Court." The Court received briefs from 35 states and petitions bearing more than 3 million signatures. The United States submitted a statement arguing, for reasons set out below, that the Court should decline to render an opinion. The advisory opinion remains today the Court's only direct statement on the subject.

- The ICJ's decision even to consider this case was and still is extremely controversial. What does that decision say about the Court's proper function in the world's legal order?
- Bedrock international law principles of sovereignty and humanitarian law dominate the Court's opinion, especially its analyses of self-defense and deterrence. How are the two principles related?
- Critical questions about risk also pervade the opinion. Could the Court convincingly dispose of the case without resolving them?
- After reading the advisory opinion, can you confidently describe the existing international law regarding nuclear weapons?

Legality of the Threat or Use of Nuclear Weapons

International Court of Justice, July 8, 1996
1996 I.C.J. 226

THE COURT . . . gives the following Advisory Opinion:

1. The question upon which the advisory opinion of the Court has been requested is set forth in resolution 49/75 K adopted by the General Assembly of the United Nations . . . [as follows]: "Is the threat or use of nuclear weapons in any circumstance permitted under international law?" . . .

11. . . . The Charter provides in Article 96, paragraph 1, that: "The General Assembly or the Security Council may request the International Court of Justice to give an advisory opinion on any legal question." . . .

13. . . . The fact that this question also has political aspects, as, in the nature of things, is the case with so many questions which arise in international life, does not suffice to deprive it of its character as a "legal question" and to "deprive the Court of a competence expressly conferred on it by its Statute" (I.C.J. Reports 1973, p. 172, para. 14)....

..."Indeed, in situations in which political considerations are prominent it may be particularly necessary for an international organization to obtain an advisory opinion from the Court as to the legal principles applicable with respect to the matter under debate..." (I.C.J. Reports 1980; p. 87, para. 33.)...

15. Most of the reasons adduced in these proceedings in order to persuade the Court that in the exercise of its discretionary power it should decline to render the opinion requested by General Assembly resolution 49/75K were summarized in the following statement made by one State in the written proceedings: "The question presented is vague and abstract, addressing complex issues which are the subject of consideration among interested States and within other bodies of the United Nations which have an express mandate to address these matters. An opinion by the Court in regard to the question presented would provide no practical assistance to the General Assembly in carrying out its functions under the Charter. Such an opinion has the potential of undermining progress already made or being made on this sensitive subject and, therefore, is contrary to the interests of the United Nations Organization." (United States of America, Written Statement, pp. 1-2; cf. pp. 3-7, II.)

In contending that the question put to the Court is vague and abstract, some States appeared to mean by this that there exists no specific dispute on the subject-matter of the question.... The purpose of the advisory function is not to settle — at least directly — disputes between States, but to offer legal advice to the organs and institutions requesting the opinion. The fact that the question put to the Court does not relate to a specific dispute should consequently not lead the Court to decline to give the opinion requested....

29. The Court recognizes that the environment is under daily threat and that the use of nuclear weapons could constitute a catastrophe for the environment. The Court also recognizes that the environment is not an abstraction but represents the living space, the quality of life and the very health of human beings, including generations unborn. The existence of the general obligation of States to ensure that activities within their jurisdiction and control respect the environment of other States or of areas beyond national control is now part of the corpus of international law relating to the environment.

30. However, the Court... does not consider that the treaties in question could have intended to deprive a State of the exercise of its right of self-defence under international law because of its obligations to protect the environment. Nonetheless, States must take environmental considerations into account when assessing what is necessary and proportionate in the pursuit of legitimate military objectives....

34. In the light of the foregoing the Court concludes that the most directly relevant applicable law governing the question of which it was seised, is that relating to the use of force enshrined in the United Nations Charter and the law applicable in armed conflict which regulates the conduct of hostilities, together with any specific treaties on nuclear weapons that the Court might determine to be relevant.

35. In applying this law to the present case, the Court cannot however fail to take into account certain unique characteristics of nuclear weapons.

The Court... notes that nuclear weapons are explosive devices whose energy results from the fusion or fission of the atom. By its very nature, that process, in nuclear weapons as they exist today, releases not only immense quantities of heat and energy, but also powerful and prolonged radiation. According to the material before the Court, the first two causes of damage are vastly more powerful than the damage caused by other weapons, while the phenomenon of radiation is said to be peculiar to nuclear weapons. These characteristics render the nuclear weapon potentially catastrophic. The destructive power of nuclear weapons cannot be contained in either space or time. They have the potential to destroy all civilization and the entire ecosystem of the planet.

The radiation released by a nuclear explosion would affect health, agriculture, natural resources and demography over a very wide area. Further, the use of nuclear weapons would be a serious danger to future generations. Ionizing radiation has the potential to damage the future environment, food and marine ecosystem, and to cause genetic defects and illness in future generations. . . .

39. . . . The Charter neither expressly prohibits, nor permits, the use of any specific weapon, including nuclear weapons. . . .

41. The submission of the exercise of the right of self-defence to the conditions of necessity and proportionality is a rule of customary international law. As the Court stated in the case concerning *Military and Paramilitary Activities in and against Nicaragua (Nicaragua v. United States of America)*: there is a "specific rule whereby self-defence would warrant only measures which are proportional to the armed attack and necessary to respond to it, a rule well established in customary international law" (I.C.J. Reports 1986, p. 94, para. 176). This dual condition applies equally to Article 51 of the Charter, whatever the means of force employed.

42. The proportionality principle may thus not in itself exclude the use of nuclear weapons in self-defence in all circumstances. But at the same time, a use of force that is proportionate under the law of self-defence, must, in order to be lawful, also meet the requirements of the law applicable in armed conflict which comprise in particular the principles and rules of humanitarian law.

43. Certain States have in their written and oral pleadings suggested that in the case of nuclear weapons, the condition of proportionality must be evaluated in the light of still further factors. They contend that the very nature of nuclear weapons, and the high probability of an escalation of nuclear exchanges, mean that there is an extremely strong risk of devastation. The risk factor is said to negate the possibility of the condition of proportionality being complied with. The Court does not find it necessary to embark upon the quantification of such risks; nor does it need to enquire into the question whether tactical nuclear weapons exist which are sufficiently precise to limit those risks: it suffices for the Court to note that the very nature of all nuclear weapons and the profound risks associated therewith are further considerations to be borne in mind by States believing they can exercise a nuclear response in self-defence in accordance with the requirements of proportionality. . . .

47. In order to lessen or eliminate the risk of unlawful attack, States sometimes signal that they possess certain weapons to use in self-defence against any State violating their territorial integrity or political independence. Whether a signalled intention to use force if certain events occur is or is not a "threat" within Article 2, paragraph 4, of the Charter depends upon various factors. If the envisaged use of force is itself unlawful, the stated readiness to use it would be a threat prohibited under Article 2, paragraph 4. . . . [I]f the use of force itself in a given case is illegal — for whatever reason — the threat to use such force will likewise be illegal. . . .

65. States which hold the view that the use of nuclear weapons is illegal have endeavoured to demonstrate the existence of a customary rule prohibiting this use.

They refer to a consistent practice of non-utilization of nuclear weapons by States since 1945 and they would see in that practice the expression of an *opinio juris* on the part of those who possess such weapons.

66. Some other States, which assert the legality of the threat and use of nuclear weapons in certain circumstances, invoked the doctrine and practice of deterrence in support of their argument. They recall that they have always, in concert with certain other States, reserved the right to use those weapons in the exercise of the right to self-defence against an armed attack threatening their vital security interests. In their view, if nuclear weapons have not been used since 1945, it is not on account of an existing or nascent custom but merely because circumstances that might justify their use have fortunately not arisen.

67. The Court does not intend to pronounce here upon the practice known as the "policy of deterrence." It notes that it is a fact that a number of States adhered to that practice during the greater part of the Cold War and continue to adhere to it. Furthermore, the members of the international community are profoundly divided on the matter of whether non-recourse to nuclear weapons over the past 50 years constitutes the expression of an *opinio juris*. Under these circumstances the Court does not consider itself able to find that there is such an *opinio juris*.

68. According to certain States, the important series of General Assembly resolutions, beginning with resolution 1653 (XVI) of 24 November 1961, that deal with nuclear weapons and that affirm, with consistent regularity, the illegality of nuclear weapons, signify the existence of a rule of international customary law which prohibits recourse to those weapons. According to other States, however, the resolutions in question have no binding character on their own account and are not declaratory of any customary rule of prohibition of nuclear weapons; some of these States have also pointed out that this series of resolutions not only did not meet with the approval of all of the nuclear-weapon States but of many other States as well. . . .

71. . . . [A]lthough those resolutions are a clear sign of deep concern regarding the problem of nuclear weapons, they still fall short of establishing the existence of an *opinio juris* on the illegality of the use of such weapons. . . .

73. . . . The emergence, as *lex lata* ["the law as it exists"], of a customary rule specifically prohibiting the use of nuclear weapons as such is hampered by the continuing tensions between the nascent *opinio juris* on the one hand, and the still strong adherence to the practice of deterrence on the other. . . .

75. A large number of customary rules have[, however,] been developed by the practice of States and are an integral part of the international law relevant to the question posed. The "laws and customs of war" — as they were traditionally called — . . . [are] known today as international humanitarian law. . . .

79. It is undoubtedly because a great many rules of humanitarian law applicable in armed conflict are so fundamental to the respect of the human person and "elementary considerations of humanity" as the Court put it in its Judgment of 9 April 1949 in the *Corfu Channel* case (*I.C.J. Reports 1949*, p. 22), that the Hague and Geneva Conventions have enjoyed a broad accession. Further these fundamental rules are to be observed by all States whether or not they have ratified the conventions that contain them, because they constitute intransgressible principles of international customary law. . . .

91. According to one point of view, the fact that recourse to nuclear weapons is subject to and regulated by the law of armed conflict does not necessarily mean that such recourse is as such prohibited. As one State put it to the Court: "Assuming that a State's use of nuclear weapons meets the requirements of self-defence, it must then be considered whether it conforms to the fundamental principles of the law of armed conflict regulating the conduct of hostilities" (United Kingdom, Written Statement, p. 40, para. 3.44).... "The reality... is that nuclear weapons might be used in a wide variety of circumstances with very different results in terms of likely civilian casualties. In some cases, such as the use of a low yield nuclear weapon against warships on the High Seas or troops in sparsely populated areas, it is possible to envisage a nuclear attack which caused comparatively few civilian casualties. It is by no means the case that every use of nuclear weapons against a military objective would inevitably cause very great collateral civilian casualties." (*Ibid.*, p. 53, para. 3.70; *see also* United States of America, CR 95/34, pp. 89-90.)

92. Another view holds that recourse to nuclear weapons could never be compatible with the principles and rules of humanitarian law and is therefore prohibited. In the event of their use, nuclear weapons would in all circumstances be unable to draw any distinction between the civilian population and combatants, or between civilian objects and military objectives, and their effects, largely uncontrollable, could not be restricted, either in time or in space, to lawful military targets. Such weapons would kill and destroy in a necessarily indiscriminate manner, on account of the blast, heat and radiation occasioned by the nuclear explosion and the effects induced; and the number of casualties which would ensue would be enormous. The use of nuclear weapons would therefore be prohibited in any circumstance, notwithstanding the absence of any explicit conventional prohibition.

93. A similar view has been expressed with respect to the effects of the principle of neutrality. Like the principles and rules of humanitarian law, that principle has therefore been considered by some to rule out the use of a weapon the effects of which simply cannot be contained within the territories of the contending States.

94. The Court would observe that none of the States advocating the legality of the use of nuclear weapons under certain circumstances, including the "clean" use of smaller, low yield, tactical nuclear weapons, has indicated what, supposing such limited use were feasible, would be the precise circumstances justifying such use; nor whether such limited use would not tend to escalate into the all-out use of high yield nuclear weapons. This being so, the Court does not consider that it has a sufficient basis for a determination on the validity of this view.

95. Nor can the Court make a determination on the validity of the view that the recourse to nuclear weapons would be illegal in any circumstance owing to their inherent and total incompatibility with the law applicable in armed conflict. Certainly, as the Court has already indicated, the principles and rules of law applicable in armed conflict—at the heart of which is the overriding consideration of humanity—make the conduct of armed hostilities subject to a number of strict requirements. Thus, methods and means of warfare, which would preclude any distinction between civilian and military targets, or which would result in unnecessary suffering to combatants, are prohibited. In view of the unique characteristics of nuclear weapons, to which the Court has referred above, the use of such weapons in fact seems scarcely reconcilable with respect for such requirements. Nevertheless, the Court considers that it does not have sufficient elements to enable it to conclude with certainty that the use of nuclear weapons would necessarily be at variance with the principles and rules of law applicable in armed conflict in any circumstance....

97. Accordingly, in view of the present state of international law viewed as a whole, as examined above by the Court, and of the elements of fact at its disposal, the Court is led to observe that it cannot reach a definitive conclusion as to the legality or illegality of the use of nuclear weapons by a State in an extreme circumstance of self-defence, in which its very survival would be at stake....

105. The Court, ... *Replies* in the following manner to the question put by the General Assembly:

A. Unanimously, There is in neither customary nor conventional international law any specific authorization of the threat or use of nuclear weapons;

B. By eleven votes to three, There is in neither customary nor conventional international law any comprehensive and universal prohibition of the threat or use of nuclear weapons as such;

C. Unanimously, A threat or use of force by means of nuclear weapons that is contrary to Article 2, paragraph 4, of the United Nations Charter and that fails to meet all the requirements of Article 51, is unlawful;

D. Unanimously, A threat or use of nuclear weapons should also be compatible with the requirements of the international law applicable in armed conflict, particularly those of the principles and rules of international humanitarian law, as well as with specific obligations under treaties and other undertakings which expressly deal with nuclear weapons;

E. By seven votes to seven, by the President's casting vote, It follows from the above-mentioned requirements that the threat or use of nuclear weapons would generally be contrary to the rules of international law applicable in armed conflict, and in particular the principles and rules of humanitarian law;

However, in view of the current state of international law, and of the elements of fact at its disposal, the Court cannot conclude definitively whether the threat or use of nuclear weapons would be lawful or unlawful in an extreme circumstance of self-defence, in which the very survival of a State would be at stake;

F. Unanimously, There exists an obligation to pursue in good faith and bring to a conclusion negotiations leading to nuclear disarmament in all its aspects under strict and effective international control....

Dissenting Opinion of VICE-PRESIDENT SCHWEBEL.... The ... Court's ultimate, paramount — and sharply controverted — conclusion in the case, narrowly adopted by the President's casting vote [is]: "However, in view of the current state of international law, and of the elements of fact at its disposal, the Court cannot conclude definitively whether the threat or use of nuclear weapons would be lawful or unlawful in an extreme circumstance of self-defence, in which the very survival of a State would be at stake."

This is an astounding conclusion to be reached by the International Court of Justice. Despite the fact that its Statute "forms an integral part" of the United Nations Charter, and despite the comprehensive and categorical terms of Article 2, paragraph 4, and Article 51 of that Charter, the Court concludes on the supreme issue of the threat or use of force of our age that it has no opinion. In "an extreme circumstance of self-defence, in which the very survival of a State would be at stake," the Court finds that international law and hence the Court have nothing to say. After many months of agonizing appraisal of the law, the Court discovers that there is none. When it comes to the supreme interests of State, the Court discards the legal progress of the twentieth century, puts aside the provisions of the Charter of the United Nations of which it is "the principal judicial organ," and proclaims, in terms redolent of *Realpolitik,* its ambivalence about the most important provisions of modern international law. If this was to be its ultimate holding, the Court would have done better to have drawn on its undoubted discretion not to render an opinion at all. . . .

. . . [F]ar from justifying the Court's inconclusiveness, contemporary events rather demonstrate the legality of the threat or use of nuclear weapons in extraordinary circumstances. . . .

[Separate declarations and opinions of other judges are omitted.]

Notes and Questions

1. *The Role of the Court.* Why did the nuclear states, led by the United States, argue that the ICJ should decline to render an advisory opinion in this case? Do you think the Court acted beyond either its legal authority or its practical competence in doing so? *Compare* (State Dep't Principal Deputy Legal Adviser) Michael J. Matheson, *The Opinions of the International Court of Justice on the Threat or Use of Nuclear Weapons,* 91 Am. J. Int'l L. 417, 420-421 (1997) (rehearsing arguments for abstention), *with* Richard A. Falk, *Nuclear Weapons, International Law and the World Court: A Historic Encounter,* 91 Am. J. Int'l L. 64, 73 (1997) (approving the Court's "taking on such a politically sensitive and geopolitically risky request from the General Assembly").

2. *Nuclear Threat to the Environment.* The Court found certain environmental protection treaties relevant in this case. Why weren't they controlling? How are environmental law and the law of armed conflict nevertheless related? *See* Stephen Dycus, *Nuclear War: Still the Gravest Threat to the Environment,* 25 Vt. L. Rev. 753, 756-766 (2001).

The Court noted that the blast and radiation from nuclear weapons uniquely "have the potential to destroy all civilization and the entire ecosystem of the planet." ¶35. But only Judge Weeramantry, in a lengthy dissenting opinion, referred explicitly to the threat of a nuclear winter, which appears to represent an even greater danger to all of humanity. 1996 I.C.J. at 456-457 (Weeramantry, J., dissenting). Supposing the Court did consider this additional threat, can you write a paragraph for the Court explaining its likely response?

3. *Law of Armed Conflict.* The Court made much of the international law requirements of necessity, distinction, and proportionality in the use of any weapon, including a nuclear one, even for self-defense. And toward the end of its opinion, the Court declared, "In view of the unique characteristics of nuclear weapons . . . the use of such weapons in fact seems scarcely reconcilable" with humanitarian law principles of distinction and unnecessary suffering. ¶95. Yet in the end it could not "conclude with certainty that the use of nuclear weapons would necessarily be at variance with the principles and rules of law applicable in armed conflict in any circumstance." *Id.* Why was the Court unable to reach a conclusion on this critically important point?

Did the Court effectively leave it to states to determine whether any contemplated use of a nuclear weapon will conform to these principles? Did the Court give states enough guidance to allow them to do so?

4. Tactical Nuclear Weapons. Nuclear states argued that the "use of a low yield nuclear weapon against warships on the High Seas or troops in sparsely populated areas" might avoid a violation of humanitarian law. ¶91. Yet "none of the States advocating the legality of the use of nuclear weapons under certain circumstances, including the 'clean' use of smaller, low yield, tactical nuclear weapons, . . . indicated what, supposing such limited use were feasible, would be the precise circumstances justifying such use." ¶94. The Court also noted that those states could not say "whether such limited use would not tend to escalate into the all-out use of high yield nuclear weapons." *Id.* Should the Court have required proof of "precise circumstances" and quantification of the risk of escalation before ruling that the use of such weapons would not invariably be illegal?

5. A Customary Norm? Given the consistent practice of states in refraining from the use of nuclear weapons for half a century, why did the Court conclude that no customary norms exist barring either the policy of deterrence or the use of nuclear weapons in all circumstances? How would you compare the Court's earlier decision in the *Nicaragua* case (*supra* p. 249)?

What would it take for such a norm to emerge? With the approval over time of various conventions, including prohibitions of specific types of weapons, that are "fundamental to the respect of the human person and 'elementary considerations of humanity,'" the Court noted the emergence of "intransgressible principles of international customary law" that must be "observed by all States whether or not they have ratified the conventions that contain them." ¶79. If all but two or three states ratified and came into compliance with a treaty banning such weapons, would the Court rule differently?

According to the U.S. Defense Department, "[t]he United States has not accepted a treaty rule that prohibits the use of nuclear weapons *per se*, and thus nuclear weapons are lawful weapons for the United States." *Law of War Manual, supra*, at ¶6.18. Did the Court effectively conclude that whatever is not expressly forbidden to a state is therefore permitted?

6. Right to Survival. The Court concluded that it could not "reach a definitive conclusion as to the legality or illegality of the use of nuclear weapons by a State in an extreme circumstance of self-defence, in which its very survival would be at stake." ¶97. In such an extreme circumstance, could the threatened state ignore humanitarian law? *See* Matheson, *supra*, at 430 ("[I]t has never been supposed that a state that is losing a war has the right to disregard the rules of armed conflict to the extent necessary to avoid defeat.").

Who decides whether a state's very survival is at stake? Could Israel, for example, use nuclear weapons to counter what it viewed as an existential threat posed by Hezbollah or Hamas?

If one state declares that invasion by another state using conventional forces threatens its continued existence, may a third state legally use nuclear weapons to try to stop the invasion? *See* Matheson, *supra*, at 431 (yes). Might the United States have used nuclear weapons to evict Iraqi forces from Kuwait in 1991?

7. *"The International Law We Have."* The badly splintered advisory opinion was widely criticized by those on both sides of the question facing the Court, not least for its failure to come to a firm conclusion on the current state of the law. Do you think the opinion has had any practical effect? *See* Falk, *supra*, at 74 ("There is little likelihood in the near future that the decision will have any discernible impact on the behavior of nuclear weapons states."). Is there any way to enforce the Court's pronouncements regarding targeting or the first use of nuclear weapons?

3. A Treaty Banning Nuclear Weapons

Shortly after taking office in 2009, President Obama committed the United States to work for the abolition of nuclear weapons.

> Today, the Cold War has disappeared but thousands of those weapons have not. In a strange turn of history, the threat of global nuclear war has gone down, but the risk of a nuclear attack has gone up. More nations have acquired these weapons. Testing has continued. Black market trade in nuclear secrets and nuclear materials abound[s]. The technology to build a bomb has spread. Terrorists are determined to buy, build or steal one....
>
> Some argue that the spread of these weapons cannot be stopped, cannot be checked — that we are destined to live in a world where more nations and more people possess the ultimate tools of destruction. Such fatalism is a deadly adversary, for if we believe that the spread of nuclear weapons is inevitable, then in some way we are admitting to ourselves that the use of nuclear weapons is inevitable.
>
> ...[T]oday, I state clearly and with conviction America's commitment to seek the peace and security of a world without nuclear weapons. [Barack Obama, President of the United States, Speech in Prague, Czech Republic (Apr. 5, 2009).]

Whether or to what extent that U.S. commitment continues today is unclear. But the United Nations expressed its own commitment in 2017 in the following treaty.

Treaty on the Prohibition of Nuclear Weapons

opened for signature Sept. 20, 2017, U.N. Doc. A/CONF.229/2017/8

Article 1. Prohibitions

1. Each State Party undertakes never under any circumstances to:

(a) Develop, test, produce, manufacture, otherwise acquire, possess or stockpile nuclear weapons or other nuclear explosive devices;

(b) Transfer to any recipient whatsoever nuclear weapons or other nuclear explosive devices or control over such weapons or explosive devices directly or indirectly;

(c) Receive the transfer of or control over nuclear weapons or other nuclear explosive devices directly or indirectly;

(d) Use or threaten to use nuclear weapons or other nuclear explosive devices;...

(g) Allow any stationing, installation or deployment of any nuclear weapons or other nuclear explosive devices in its territory or at any place under its jurisdiction or control....

Article 4. Towards the total elimination of nuclear weapons . . .

2. . . . [E]ach State Party that owns, possesses or controls nuclear weapons or other nuclear explosive devices shall immediately remove them from operational status, and destroy them as soon as possible but not later than a deadline to be determined by the first meeting of States Parties, in accordance with a legally binding, time-bound plan for the verified and irreversible elimination of that State Party's nuclear-weapon programme, including the elimination or irreversible conversion of all nuclear-weapons-related facilities. . . .

3. A State Party to which paragraph 2 above applies shall conclude a safeguards agreement with the International Atomic Energy Agency sufficient to provide credible assurance of the non-diversion of declared nuclear material from peaceful nuclear activities and of the absence of undeclared nuclear material or activities in the State as a whole. . . .

6. The States Parties shall designate a competent international authority or authorities to negotiate and verify the irreversible elimination of nuclear-weapons programmes. . . .

Article 16. Reservations

The Articles of this Treaty shall not be subject to reservations.

Article 17. Duration and withdrawal

1. This Treaty shall be of unlimited duration.

2. Each State Party shall, in exercising its national sovereignty, have the right to withdraw from this Treaty if it decides that extraordinary events related to the subject matter of the Treaty have jeopardized the supreme interests of its country. . . .

3. Such withdrawal shall only take effect 12 months after . . . notification of withdrawal. . . . If, however, on the expiry of that 12-month period, the withdrawing State Party is a party to an armed conflict, the State Party shall continue to be bound by the obligations of this Treaty and of any additional protocols until it is no longer party to an armed conflict. . . .

Omitted here is a lengthy preamble describing nuclear weapons as "abhorrent to the principles of humanity and the dictates of public conscience." The treaty was approved by the U.N. General Assembly when 122 states voted in favor of it. As of mid-2019, 70 states had signed the treaty, and 26 of the 50 needed to bring it into force had ratified or acceded to it. None of the current nuclear states, however, had signed.

Notes and Questions

1. *Treaty as Political Theater?* The U.N. treaty has been very controversial, and many have questioned its practical importance, especially given the refusal of nuclear

states even to participate in its negotiation. The President of the International Committee of the Red Cross acknowledged that

> adopting a treaty to prohibit nuclear weapons will not make them immediately disappear. But it will reinforce the stigma against their use, support commitments to nuclear risk reduction, and be a disincentive for proliferation. It will be a concrete step towards fulfilling existing commitments for nuclear disarmament, notably those of Article VI of the Non-Proliferation Treaty. [ICRC, *Bringing the Era of Nuclear Weapons to an End in the Name of Humanity*, Mar. 27, 2017.]

According to another observer,

> The basic intent is to codify the norms of nonuse and nonpossession of nuclear weapons in light of the humanitarian consequences of nuclear explosions and to contribute to the eventual achievement of the global abolition of the weapons. Issues related to elimination of nuclear weapons will largely be left to later negotiations, within or outside the treaty framework.... [John Burroughs, *Key Issues in Negotiations for a Nuclear Weapons Prohibition Treaty*, Arms Control Today, June 2017.]

What, if anything, do these observations suggest about the treaty's legal significance?

2. Treaty as Opinio Juris? Immediately following the signing of the treaty, the United States declared that

> France, the United Kingdom and the United States have not taken part in the negotiation of the treaty on the prohibition of nuclear weapons. We do not intend to sign, ratify or ever become party to it. Therefore, there will be no change in the legal obligations on our countries with respect to nuclear weapons. For example, we would not accept any claim that this treaty reflects or in any way contributes to the development of customary international law. [U.S. Mission to the United Nations, *Joint Press Statement*, July 7, 2017, https://usun.state.gov/remarks/7892.]

Why do you suppose these states professed their opposition to the treaty in such absolute, unrelenting terms? Could such a statement prevent the emergence of a customary norm barring the threat or use of nuclear weapons if all but the three named states ratified the treaty?

3. Objections to the Treaty. The U.S. joint statement cited above called accession to the treaty "incompatible with the policy of nuclear deterrence, which has been essential to keeping the peace in Europe and North Asia for over 70 years." *Id.* While it is true that nuclear weapons have not been used in anger since 1945, does it necessarily follow that the deterrence policy is responsible for such forbearance? Has the policy prevented non-nuclear armed conflicts?

A U.S. State Department spokesman complained that the treaty could not ensure verification of the elimination of nuclear weapons, calling IAEA inspections "outdated," and decrying reliance on a yet-to-be-identified "competent international authority or authorities to negotiate and verify" compliance. Christopher Ashley Ford, Ass't Sec'y of State, *The Treaty on the Prohibition of Nuclear Weapons: A Well-Intentioned*

Mistake, Remarks at the University of Iceland (Oct. 30, 2018). Can you think of ways to ensure verification without amending the treaty?

Treaty critics also objected that it could divide Western allies when unity was essential to ward off threats from potential nuclear adversaries. *See, e.g.*, Matthew Harries, *The Real Problem with a Nuclear Ban Treaty*, Carnegie Endowment for Int'l Peace, Mar. 15, 2017 (warning that the treaty could disrupt the NATO alliance). *But see* Bernadette Stadler & Suzanne Claeys, Ctr. for Strategic & Int'l Studies, *Bad Idea: Ignoring the Treaty on the Prohibition of Nuclear Weapons*, Dec. 6, 2018 ("By refusing to meaningfully engage with the treaty, the United States and other nuclear states continue to drive a wedge between nuclear and non-nuclear states and impede significant progress in nonproliferation and disarmament."). What provision of the treaty might have a divisive effect? Can you argue that that effect might nevertheless promote the abolition of nuclear weapons?

In 2018, Russia and China joined the United States, the United Kingdom, and France in opposing the treaty, arguing that it risks undermining the NPT. *P5 Joint Statement on the Treaty on the Non-Proliferation of Nuclear Weapons*, Oct. 24, 2018 ("We firmly believe that the best way to achieve a world without nuclear weapons is through a gradual process that takes into account the international security environment."). How do you suppose the World Court would respond to their argument?

The ban treaty has been criticized, as well, for lacking any mechanism for enforcement of its provisions. Can you formulate an answer to this criticism?

One expert suggests a more deliberate approach, utilizing non-binding commitments to build confidence while reducing weapons inventories, in advance of an abolition treaty. *See* David A. Koplow, *What Would Zero Look Like? A Treaty for the Abolition of Nuclear Weapons*, 45 Geo. J. Int'l L. 683 (2014).

4. Duration? One observer complains that the withdrawal provision in Article 17(1) is an acknowledgment that "nothing in law or morality or human wellbeing takes precedence over [the] exercise of sovereign rights." Richard Falk, *Challenging Nuclearism: The Nuclear Ban Treaty Assessed*, Global Res., July 17, 2017.

> [N]ational security continues to take precedence over international law, even with respect to genocidal weaponry of mass destruction with regional and global implications such as the danger of nuclear winter. As such the obligation[s] undertaken by parties to the [treaty] are reversible in ways that are not present in multilateral conventions outlawing genocide, apartheid, and torture. [*Id.*]

How could you answer his complaint?

C. DOMESTIC LAW OF NUCLEAR WEAPONS

"Button, Button, Who's Got the Button?" is a children's game. It is also the name of a 1980 performance-art work depicting the end of the world, with the subtitle "A Dream of Nuclear War."

In 1974, President Richard Nixon remarked to reporters, "I can go back into my office and pick up the telephone and in 25 minutes 70 million people will be dead." The President reportedly was drinking heavily, as the House conducted hearings on his impeachment. Alarmed, the Secretary of Defense instructed the Joint Chiefs that any such "emergency order" from the President should first go through him or the Secretary of State. *See* Lisbeth Gronlund, David Wright & Steve Fetter, *How to Limit Presidential Authority to Order the Use of Nuclear Weapons*, Bull. of Atomic Scientists, Jan. 23, 2018.

Of course, neither cabinet secretary possessed the authority to countermand a launch order from the Commander in Chief, and it is widely believed that the President's power to direct the use of nuclear weapons is absolute, at least within the executive branch. *See* Amy F. Woolf, *Defense Primer: Command and Control of Nuclear Forces* (Cong. Res. Serv. IF10521), Dec. 11, 2018. It is not clear, however, that Congress lacks the authority to regulate the President's use of those weapons. Nevertheless, according to one of us, "Congress has surely been in equal measure uninterested, uninformed and unduly dependent on the Executive in the control and planning of nuclear war." Peter Raven-Hansen, *Nuclear War Powers*, 83 Am. J. Int'l L. 786, 795 (1989).

In this section we consider who has the button, and we examine possible domestic legal constraints on its use in different circumstances.

1. A Bolt from the Blue

In a practical sense, the President's constitutional authority to use nuclear weapons is necessarily defined in part by the nature of those weapons and their delivery systems, as well as by the policy of deterrence. One aspect of that policy rests on a promise to retaliate in kind promptly against an enemy nuclear attack. The prospect of a U.S. nuclear counterstrike is supposed to dissuade an enemy from using a nuclear weapon first. The President's ability to launch U.S. nuclear weapons immediately on *warning* of an impending enemy attack might also save those weapons from destruction or prevent a decapitating strike on the U.S. leadership, thus preserving the capacity of the United States to carry out its retaliatory threat. And the credibility of the policy depends on a commitment to execute it without delay.

The time for the President's response to notice of an incoming enemy attack might be less than ten minutes. The procedure is outlined in Woolf, *supra*; *see also* Bruce G. Blair, *Strengthening Checks on Presidential Nuclear Launch Authority*, Arms Control Today, Jan./Feb. 2018. The President might therefore have to decide whether and how to respond on the basis of very limited information and without the benefit of real-time counsel from experts in either political branch. She would need to determine the authenticity of the attack warning, then choose targets for a U.S. nuclear response that hopefully would not provoke an all-out nuclear exchange, which would be suicidal. Her orders to launch would then have to be carried out immediately by officers in the relevant military chain of command. *See* Blair, *supra* (suggesting that "[r]eactions from the bottom to the top of the chain of command to an apparent attack are driven by checklists and virtually preordained").

The U.S. launch-on-warning, use-it-or-lose-it policy has produced a number of close calls, when a technical glitch, human error, or diplomatic misjudgment might have triggered an accidental nuclear war. False alarms were produced, for example, by the moon rising over Norway, a bear climbing a perimeter fence at a Minnesota defense installation, a faulty computer chip, a solar storm, and, more than once, computer operators incorrectly reading training programs as depicting real attacks. *See* Union of Concerned Scientists, *Close Calls with Nuclear Weapons* (Apr. 2015), http://www.ucsusa.org/weaponsincidents.

Notes and Questions

1. Rumors of War. In 2017, in the midst of U.S. efforts to thwart North Korea's development of nuclear weapons and delivery systems, President Donald Trump told reporters that "North Korea best not make any more threats to the United States. They will be met with fire and the fury like the world has never seen." *See* Noah Bierman, *Trump Warns North Korea of "Fire and Fury,"* L.A. Times, Apr. 8, 2017. His remark was widely understood as a threat to use nuclear weapons against the DPRK. Does the President have domestic authority to make such threats, whether or not she is legally empowered to make good on those threats?

2. Repelling a Nuclear Attack? In 1787, the Framers understood that a surprise attack on the United States might leave the President as Commander in Chief too little time to seek Congress's approval before ordering a military response to effectively repel that attack. They agreed that the President should be able to use military force immediately in that case. Recall the Supreme Court's conclusion in *The Prize Cases,* 67 U.S. (2 Black) 635, 670 (1863), that in such an emergency, "[h]e must determine what degree of force the crisis demands." Thus, it is generally assumed that the President acting alone may order the launch of a nuclear weapon in the exercise of her inherent repel-attack power to ward off a nuclear attack (or an imminently threatened attack) on the United States.

The Framers could hardly have imagined either an enemy attack or a President's response having such speed or destructive potential, however, much less an attack against which it was impossible to defend. But U.S. ballistic missile defenses have worked successfully in trials no more than half the time, and they have never been tested under actual combat conditions. Furthermore, the BMD system is incapable of countering enemy cruise missiles or weapons delivered by enemy aircraft or submarines. If deterrence fails, the only defensive purpose of U.S. strategic nuclear weapons would be to destroy any unexpended enemy weapons in order to prevent a follow-on attack. Is the President's inherent repel-attack power similarly limited? If so, does she have the authority to order a launch on warning of an enemy nuclear attack?

Presumably, the Framers also never thought that the President might order the use of military force based on news of an enemy attack that might not actually be true, or that the U.S. response might cause more damage to the homeland than the enemy attack would—for example, by prompting an all-out nuclear exchange, or by precipitating a nuclear winter. Can you fashion an argument that the President's constitutional repel-attack power may be exercised using nuclear weapons only when she can be certain that an enemy nuclear attack is actually underway? When that response would not itself pose an existential threat to the nation? Might criteria for various responses be agreed upon in advance of a crisis? Can you articulate such criteria?

3. Pre-delegation of Launch Authority? An attack on the United States might come so quickly that the President would not have time to respond before she was killed or disabled in the attack. Or such an attack might interrupt communications with forces in the field. Anticipating such an event, Presidents during the Cold War reportedly gave advance approval to launch officers for nuclear strikes against specified targets under certain circumstances. *See* Raven-Hansen, *supra,* at 786-787 (suggesting that half of U.S. strategic nuclear weapons could be fired without the President's participation); William Burr, *First Declassification of Eisenhower's Instructions to Commanders Predelegating Nuclear Weapons Use, 1959-1960,* Nat'l Security Archive, May 18, 2001, http://nsarchive.gwu.edu/NSAEBB/NSAEBB45/. The extent of such pre-delegation today is unknown.

The President is authorized by statute to delegate any functions vested in him by law. 3 U.S.C. §§301-302 (2018). But given the strategic implications of any use of nuclear weapons, does pre-delegation of launch authority raise any constitutional concerns? Any practical risks?

Would a U.S. launch-on-warning policy unconstitutionally pre-delegate that authority by effectively allowing computers to make critical, real-time decisions? How could such a policy be challenged? *See Johnson v. Weinberger,* No. CV 86-3334-SW (N.D. Cal. Apr. 29, 1987), *aff'd,* 851 F.2d 233 (9th Cir. 1988) (dismissing such a challenge on political question and standing grounds, respectively).

2. First Use

At least in principle, as noted above, the President is authorized to use nuclear weapons *second,* in response to an attack on the United States. *See* Raven-Hansen, *supra,* at 788. The United States has long maintained, however, that it is prepared to use nuclear weapons *first* in defense of its NATO and other allies against a conventional attack. "To help preserve deterrence and the assurance of allies and partners, the United States has never adopted a 'no first use' policy and, given the contemporary threat environment, such a policy is not justified today." *Nuclear Posture Review, supra,* at 22.

Congress has never clearly authorized first use, however. And a conventional or even nuclear attack on a U.S. ally, or an attack on the U.S. homeland using conventional weaponry, would not present the President with the use-it-or-lose-it dilemma described above. Neither would such an attack necessarily pose an immediate existential threat to the United States. The President presumably would have an opportunity to communicate with an attacker, gather critical data from the field, assess the strategic and humanitarian implications of various possible U.S. responses, and seek the advice and possibly approval of other individuals. A more relaxed decision-making process might thus reduce the risk of a nuclear war based on accident, equipment failure, misinformation, or misjudgment.

At least one kind of non-nuclear attack could nevertheless threaten the continued existence of the United States — a cyber attack that succeeded in shutting down the nation's electric transmission grid for an extended period. See *supra* p. 414. Accordingly, the most recent U.S. nuclear policy statement makes it clear that such an attack could provoke a nuclear response.

> The United States would only consider the employment of nuclear weapons in extreme circumstances to defend the vital interests of the United States, its allies, and partners. Extreme circumstances could include significant non-nuclear strategic attacks. Significant non-nuclear strategic attacks include, but are not limited to, attacks on the U.S., allied, or partner civilian population or infrastructure. . . . [*Id.* at 21.]

Yet because first use could have profound strategic implications, some doubt that the President possesses that authority.

> The decision to "go nuclear" in a conventional war "is a political decision of the highest order," as President Lyndon Johnson said, not a tactical choice of weapons. As such, it is not an inherent component of the commander in chief's command authority or a technical byproduct of military expertise, but precisely the ultimate national life-or-death decision that the Framers intended Congress to make when time permits. [Raven-Hansen, *supra*, at 790.]

Others assert that even if the President is entitled unilaterally to use nuclear weapons first, Congress may regulate that use. Consider the following legislative proposals to impose such regulation.

The Policy of the United States Regarding the No-First-Use of Nuclear Weapons

H.R. 921, S. 272, 116th Cong. (2019)

Sec. 1. Policy on no-first-use of nuclear weapons.

It is the policy of the United States to not use nuclear weapons first.

Restricting First Use of Nuclear Weapons Act of 2019

H.R. 669, S. 200, 116th Cong. (2019)

Sec. 2. Findings and declaration of policy.

(a) Findings. — . . .

(5) By any definition of war, a first-use nuclear strike from the United States would constitute a major act of war.

(6) A first-use nuclear strike conducted absent a declaration of war by Congress would violate the Constitution. . . .

Sec. 3. Prohibition on conduct of first-use nuclear strikes.

(a) Prohibition. — Notwithstanding any other provision of law, the President may not use the Armed Forces of the United States to conduct a first-use nuclear strike unless such strike is conducted pursuant to a declaration of war by Congress that expressly authorizes such strike.

(b) First-Use nuclear strike defined. — In this section, the term "first-use nuclear strike" means an attack using nuclear weapons against an enemy that is conducted without the President determining that the enemy has first launched a nuclear strike against the United States or an ally of the United States.

Notes and Questions

1. Strategic vs. Tactical? Current U.S. policy contemplates the use of small tactical or "non-strategic" nuclear weapons to halt an enemy attack using conventional forces — large enough to stop the attack, yet small enough to avoid provoking a nuclear response. As of early 2018, the only such weapons in the U.S. arsenal were a few hundred gravity bombs delivered by aircraft. *Nuclear Posture Review, supra,* at 48. But plans were underway to fit low-yield nuclear warheads to submarine-launched ballistic missiles and sea-launched cruise missiles. *Id.* at 54-55. Criteria for their use apparently had not been set, however, in order to preserve flexibility for the President in responding to unpredictable developments, and in order to complicate an enemy's planning. *See generally* Amy F. Woolf, *Nonstrategic Nuclear Weapons* (Cong. Res. Serv. RL32572), Sept. 6, 2019.

In principle, of course, tactical decisions about the use of military force are left entirely to the President as Commander in Chief. But in 2018 Defense Secretary James Mattis told Congress, "I don't think there's any such thing as a tactical nuclear weapon. Any nuclear weapon used any time is a strategic game changer." *See* Paul Sonne, *Mattis: Plans for New U.S. Nuclear Weapon Could Be Bargaining Chip with Russia,* Wash. Post, Feb. 6, 2018. Does uncertainty about the probable consequences suggest either a practical need or a constitutional requirement of approval in advance by Congress?

2. Congressional Approval of First Use? The Atomic Energy Act provides that "[t]he President from time to time may direct the [Atomic Energy] Commission . . . to deliver such quantities of special nuclear material or atomic weapons to the Department of Defense for such use as he deems necessary in the interest of national defense. . . ." 42 U.S.C. §2121(b) (2018). Does this statutory language give the President unfettered discretion in the use of nuclear weapons? Can you argue that it violates the non-delegation doctrine? See *supra* pp. 27-33, 99-105.

Congress has not provided clearer authorization for any use of nuclear weapons. Nor has it ever distinguished between the first use of such weapons and their maintenance as a deterrent against enemy attack. Nevertheless, as one observer points out, "Congress has been on notice of presidential claims to nuclear war powers, and of our first-use policy in particular, for so long and with so many opportunities to disapprove during at least the annual defense appropriations cycle, that it must be deemed to have acquiesced by now." Raven-Hansen, *supra,* at 791. By one estimate, between 1940 and 1996, Congress approved the expenditure of some $5.5 trillion on nuclear weapons programs, nearly 11 percent of all federal spending. Stephen I. Schwartz, *Atomic Audit: The Costs and Consequences of U.S. Nuclear Weapons Since 1940,* at 3 (1998).

If Congress has tacitly approved first use, can it now rescind or restrict that approval? If so, how? Would H.R. 921, set forth above, do that?

3. Congress's Power to Regulate First Use? May Congress provide the Commander in Chief with weapons of war, then restrict her use of them? In *The Steel Seizure Case,* Justice Jackson famously noted:

> While Congress cannot deprive the President of the command of the army and navy, only Congress can provide him an army or navy to command. It is also empowered to make

> rules for the "Government and Regulation of land and naval Forces," by which it may to some unknown extent impinge upon even command functions. [343 U.S. 579, 644 (1952) (Jackson, J., concurring).]

Without referring specifically to either the Government and Regulation Clause or the distinction between strategic and tactical goals, the Court in *Little v. Barreme*, 6 U.S. (2 Cranch) 170 (1804), *supra* p. 63, held that the President may not exceed war-making authority explicitly prescribed by Congress. *See also Bas v. Tingy*, 4 U.S. (4 Dall.) 37, 40 (1800) (Washington, J.) (in an undeclared war, "those who are authorised to commit hostilities . . . can go no farther than to the extent of their commission"), *supra* p. 85. Do these early precedents help describe the scope of Congress's power to constrain the use of particular weapons?

H.R. 669, set forth above, would bar any first use unless Congress had approved a declaration of war explicitly authorizing such use. If enacted into law, would it be constitutional?

Would Congress be on firmer ground constitutionally or politically if it enacted legislation declaring that the President may not expend any appropriated funds to launch nuclear weapons first? *See* Stephen P. Mulligan, Cong. Res. Serv., *Legislation Limiting the President's Power to Use Nuclear Weapons: Separation of Powers Implications* 8–9 (Nov. 23, 2017) (concluding that "Congress likely has the authority to limit the President's ability to use nuclear weapons by prohibiting the use of appropriated funds for such weapons' development and maintenance," but noting uncertainty about Congress's ability to limit their use once deployed).

4. Requiring Approval of Other Officials? According to one former government insider, the President would not make the decision to use nuclear weapons entirely on his own. "The system for decision is designed to ensure that the President consults with the National Security Council and his other senior civilian and military advisers, and I would expect that to occur in every case where the use of nuclear weapons is contemplated." *Hearing on Authority to Order the Use of Nuclear Weapons Before the S. Comm. on Foreign Relations*, 115th Cong. (2017) (statement of Brian P. McKeon). The President is not legally obliged to consult with anyone, however, and a President's launch order would go directly to officers at the bottom of the chain of command. Blair, *supra*.

Some have recommended that the President be *required* to secure not only the *advice* but also the *approval* of other officials before ordering the first use of nuclear weapons. One proposal would require the President to secure the approval of a committee of 16 congressional leaders before using nuclear weapons first. *See* William C. Banks, *First Use of Nuclear Weapons: The Constitutional Role of a Congressional Leadership Committee*, 13 J. Legis. 1 (1986) (arguing that because committee approval would delegate power to the President, it would not involve a withdrawal of congressional authority barred by *Immigration & Naturalization Serv. v. Chadha*, 462 U.S. 919 (1983) (see *supra* p. 124), but would broadly serve separation-of-powers goals).

A different proposal calls for the agreement of the next two people in the presidential chain of succession, normally the Vice President and Speaker of the House. Gronlund, Wright & Fetter, *supra*. In addition to helping the President assess the strategic implications of such a move, these two individuals would be in a position to "assess the president's state of mind and could veto the launch order if they judged the president to be mentally unstable or otherwise unfit to give such an order." *Id.*

And their involvement would lend political legitimacy, democratic input, and independence to the decision-making process. *Id.*

Others propose requiring *written certification* from the Attorney General that a first-use launch order is legal and from the Secretary of Defense that the order is valid. Richard K. Betts & Matthew C. Waxman, *The President and the Bomb: Reforming the Nuclear Lunch Process,* Foreign Aff., Mar./Apr. 2018, at 119. These prerequisites could, they say, reduce the risk of a false order resulting from a "wayward president," a computer malfunction, a cyber hacker, or an "unhinged military aide in charge of the football." *Id.* at 122.

Can you say how any of these requirements of consultation and approval could be enforced?

5. *Executing the Launch Order.* According to one head of the U.S. Strategic Command, he would resist an illegal order to use nuclear weapons. Daniella Diaz, *Top General Says He'd Push Back Against "Illegal" Nuclear Strike Order,* CNN, Nov. 20, 2017. But how should the legality of a launch order be determined?

Every military officer has a duty to follow legitimate orders, but also "must refuse to comply with clearly illegal orders to commit law of war violations." *Law of War Manual, supra,* at ¶18.3.2. The generally accepted standard is that an officer must disobey an order that "a man of ordinary sense and understanding would, under the circumstances, know to be unlawful." *United States v. Calley,* 48 C.M.R. 19, 27 (1973). However, "subordinates are not required to screen the orders of superiors for questionable points of legality, and may, absent specific knowledge to the contrary, presume that orders have been lawfully issued." *Law of War Manual, supra,* ¶5.10.2.4.

If a launch officer knows that a nuclear missile is aimed at a city, may she — or must she — legally refuse to push the button when ordered to do so? *Compare* Anthony J. Colangelo, *The Duty to Disobey Illegal Nuclear Strike Orders,* 9 Harv. Nat'l Security J. 84 (2018) (arguing that while a subordinate must ordinarily judge the legality of an order based on specific contextual information, a nuclear attack near any civilian population would almost surely be "manifestly illegal"), *with* Charlie Dunlap, *The Danger of Tampering with America's Nuclear Command and Control System,* Lawfire, Nov. 22, 2017, https://sites.duke.edu/lawfire/2017/11/22/the-danger-of-tampering-with-americas-nuclear-command-and-control-system/ (arguing that "in rapidly developing situations where even momentary hesitation can mean death and defeat, the inference of legality is essential. . . . We must avoid doing anything that would remotely suggest to any opponent that he has any chance of success against our nuclear deterrent."). If you were a launch officer, how would you respond?

NUCLEAR WAR: SUMMARY OF BASIC PRINCIPLES

- A number of treaties and informal agreements have limited the testing and deployment of nuclear weapons and of defenses against such weapons. A recent U.N. treaty, not yet in force, would abolish them.

- In its 1996 advisory opinion, the International Court of Justice concluded that while the threat or use of nuclear weapons would "generally" be illegal, it could not say whether such threat or use would be unlawful "in an extreme circumstance of self-defence, in which the very survival of a State would be at stake."
- The Court considered each state's inherent right of self-defense superior to treaty obligations to protect the environment in wartime.
- The Court insisted that while "[t]he destructive power of nuclear weapons cannot be contained in either space or time," any use of them must comply with international humanitarian law.
- No statute explicitly confers authority on the President to use nuclear weapons, although decades of funding for those weapons, as well as the U.S. policy of deterrence, suggest that Congress has acquiesced in such use.
- Although the President may have inherent repel-attack power to use nuclear weapons, it may be difficult to determine when such use would be defensive rather than simply retaliatory.
- The constitutional power of Congress to regulate the President's use of nuclear weapons is a matter of ongoing debate.

16

Humanitarian and Peace Operations

Congress has declared that "prompt United States assistance to alleviate human suffering caused by natural and manmade disasters is an important expression of the humanitarian concern and tradition of the people of the United States." 22 U.S.C. §2292(a) (2018). Disaster relief may also serve U.S. strategic needs by restoring stability and fostering good will in the affected areas.

U.S. military forces have often played a key role in providing humanitarian assistance abroad, because they uniquely possess the transport capacity, personnel, and equipment to respond quickly where needed. When monsoon-triggered floods submerged almost one-fifth of Pakistan in 2010, for example, U.S. military fixed-wing aircraft and helicopters, as well as ground forces, delivered 25 million pounds of food, water, and other relief supplies to victims, built bridges, rescued thousands of people, and evacuated many more. Also in 2010, some 22,000 U.S. servicemembers ferried supplies, provided medical assistance, and performed engineering and construction work in Haiti after a devastating earthquake. DOD personnel typically work with other federal agencies (such as the U.S. Agency for International Development), indigenous militaries, international organizations (such as the United Nations), nongovernmental organizations (such as the International Committee of the Red Cross), and contractors. They are always prepared to defend themselves if necessary, but hostilities are rarely expected and seldom encountered.

U.S. military forces also conduct missions abroad in which engagement in armed conflict is not the objective, or at least is not the primary objective, but when violence may be more likely. Some of these are concerned with establishing or preserving peace or stability, usually under the auspices of the U.N. Security Council or NATO.

In principle, "peacekeeping" forces are deployed in "transition situations where a state lacks capacity to manage affairs to assure domestic or international tranquility, yet the use of force in the traditional sense of armed conflict is not contemplated." George K. Walker, *United States National Security Law and United Nations Peacekeeping or Peacemaking Operations*, 29 Wake Forest L. Rev. 435, 445-446 (1994). Such deployments often come at the end of armed hostilities and usually involve the use of unarmed or lightly armed personnel to police or "observe" cease-fires or armistices with the consent of the parties involved. Unfortunately, U.S. troops deployed on these missions may meet armed opposition from remnants of defeated armies or groups, or from insurgents.

"Peacemaking" interventions, "where the use of force in the traditional sense of armed conflict may be employed to restore tranquility," *id.* at 446, pose greater risks. These involve the deployment of armed forces into hostilities with the mission of using force to halt or limit the fighting, usually without the consent of all the contending parties.

Some U.S. military missions abroad are both humanitarian and strategic, as in deployments to stop a government from engaging in genocide or ethnic cleansing of its own people, when the internal conflict threatens to spill across national borders. These may present the greatest risk of violence.

A U.S. Navy sailor carries a young earthquake victim bound for a hospital ship in Port-au-Prince, Haiti, Jan. 23, 2010.

DOD photo by Jim Garamone.

Toward the end of the twentieth century a new threat emerged that portends human suffering and conflict on a scale unprecedented in human history—climate change. This development will profoundly influence efforts to defend the United States. It also will almost surely prompt the United States to send military forces abroad more often than previously to furnish humanitarian assistance. According to the Director of National Intelligence,

> The United States will probably have to manage the impact of global human security challenges, such as . . . climate change. . . .
>
> . . . Climate hazards such as extreme weather, higher temperatures, droughts, floods, wildfires, storms, sea level rise, soil degradation, and acidifying oceans are intensifying,

> threatening infrastructure, health, and water and food security . . . [and] increasing the risk of social unrest, migration, and interstate tension. [Daniel R. Coats, *Worldwide Threat Assessment of the US Intelligence Community* 21-23 (Jan. 29, 2019).]

DOD has described the effects of climate change as "threat multipliers that will aggravate stressors abroad such as poverty, environmental degradation, political instability, and social tensions — conditions that can enable terrorist activity and other forms of violence." Dep't of Defense, *Quadrennial Defense Review 2014*, at 8 (Mar. 4, 2014);[1] *see also* 2 U.S. Global Change Res. Program, *Fourth National Climate Assessment* 59 (2018) ("[C]hanges in climate increase risks to our national security by affecting factors that can exacerbate conflict."); *Climate Change Recognized as "Threat Multiplier," UN Security Council Debates Its Impact on Peace*, UN News, Jan. 25, 2019. For example, climate change is widely blamed for a severe five-year drought in Syria that contributed to "massive agriculture failures and population displacements" and helped precipitate the ongoing civil war there. Dep't of Defense, *Response to Congressional Inquiry on National Security Implications of Climate-Related Risks and a Changing Climate* 4 (July 23, 2015).

In this chapter we consider various uses of U.S. military forces abroad in which combat is not the primary purpose. We first examine existing international and domestic authorities for such operations, then apply these authorities to two recent humanitarian interventions, one invited and the other uninvited.

A. AUTHORITY FOR PEACEFUL DEPLOYMENTS

1. International Authorities

Many U.S. noncombat military operations are carried out in conjunction with the United Nations or regional organizations. Since 1948, the U.N. Security Council has launched numerous humanitarian, peacekeeping, and stabilization missions. In mid-2019, some 89,000 troops and non-military personnel from 93 countries were deployed in 14 such missions around the world. *See United Nations Peacekeeping: Where We Operate* (n.d.), *at* https://peacekeeping.un.org/en/where-we-operate.

The U.N. Charter includes no express provision for the use of military forces in humanitarian or other kinds of noncombat missions. Chapter VI, entitled Peaceful Settlement of Disputes, nevertheless declares that

> [t]he Security Council may investigate any dispute, or any situation which might lead to international friction or give rise to a dispute, in order to determine whether the continuance of the dispute or situation is likely to endanger the maintenance of international peace and security. [U.N. Charter art. 34.]

Chapter VII of the Charter authorizes the Security Council to determine the existence of breaches or threats to the peace, and to "decide what measures shall be taken," including "such action by air, sea, or land forces as may be necessary to

---

1. The congressionally mandated public *Quadrennial Defense Review* was replaced in 2018 by a classified *National Defense Strategy*, the public summary of which fails to mention climate change. Dep't of Defense, *Summary of the 2018 National Defense Strategy of the United States of America* (n.d.).

maintain or restore international peace and security." *Id.* arts. 39, 42. See *supra* p. 243. "Dag Hammarskjöld, the second U.N. Secretary-General, referred to [peacekeeping] as belonging to 'Chapter Six and a Half' of the Charter, placing it between traditional methods of resolving disputes peacefully, such as negotiation and mediation under Chapter VI, and more forceful action as authorized under Chapter VII." U.N. Info. Serv., *60 Years of United Nations Peacekeeping* (updated Oct. 4, 2019), *at* http://www.unis.unvienna.org/unis/en/60yearsPK/.

According to the U.N. Secretariat, the Security Council authorizes the deployment of peacekeepers only when three principles are satisfied:

> **Consent of the parties.** United Nations peacekeeping operations are deployed with the consent of the main parties to the conflict. This requires a commitment by the parties to a political process and their acceptance of a peacekeeping operation mandated to support that process.... In the absence of such consent, a United Nations peacekeeping operation risks becoming a party to the conflict; and being drawn towards enforcement action, and away from its intrinsic role of keeping the peace....
>
> **Impartiality.** United Nations peacekeeping operations must implement their mandate without favour or prejudice to any party. Impartiality is crucial to maintaining the consent and cooperation of the main parties, but should not be confused with neutrality or inactivity. United Nations peacekeepers should be impartial in their dealings with the parties to the conflict, but not neutral in the execution of their mandate....
>
> **Non-use of force except in self-defense and defense of the mandate.**... The environments into which United Nations peacekeeping operations are deployed are often characterized by the presence of militias, criminal gangs, and other spoilers who may actively seek to undermine the peace process or pose a threat to the civilian population. In such situations, the Security Council has given United Nations peacekeeping operations "robust" mandates authorizing them to "use all necessary means" to deter forceful attempts to disrupt the political process, protect civilians under imminent threat of physical attack, and/or assist the national authorities in maintaining law and order....
>
> Although on the ground they may sometimes appear similar, robust peacekeeping should not be confused with peace enforcement, as envisaged under Chapter VII of the Charter. Robust peacekeeping involves the use of force at the tactical level with the authorization of the Security Council and consent of the host nation and/or the main parties to the conflict. By contrast, peace enforcement does not require the consent of the main parties and may involve the use of military force at the strategic or international level, which is normally prohibited for Member States under Article 2(4) of the Charter, unless authorized by the Security Council.
>
> A United Nations peacekeeping operation should only use force as a measure of last resort, when other methods of persuasion have been exhausted.... [*United Nations Peacekeeping Operations: Principles and Guidelines* 31-35 (2008), https://www.un.org/ruleoflaw/blog/document/united-nations-peacekeeping-operations-principles-and-guidelines-the-capstone-doctrine/.]

Notes and Questions

1. Authority for Peace Operations. Are humanitarian and other deployments of military forces on noncombat missions authorized by Chapter VI or Chapter VII of the U.N. Charter? Both? Neither? If not undertaken on U.N. auspices, are they illegal?

2. *The Importance of Labels.* What is the difference between "peacekeeping" and "peace enforcement" operations? Of what legal significance, if any, is the nomenclature? Who is entitled to designate a given operation as one or the other?

3. *Consent of the Parties.* Why is it important that the "main parties" to a conflict consent to the introduction of peacekeeping forces? Who are the main parties? What if the territory into which troops would be introduced has no functioning government?

2. Domestic Authorities

As of mid-2019, some 35 U.S. troops, police, and experts were serving in seven humanitarian or peacekeeping operations under the auspices of the U.N. Security Council. They were deployed in the Central African Republic, Mali, Haiti, the Democratic Republic of the Congo, Libya, South Sudan, and Jerusalem. A much larger number of U.S. armed forces were deployed on other noncombat missions around the globe. For example, some 450 U.S. soldiers were serving as part of the Multinational Force and Observers (MFO) in the Sinai, established in 1981 by an agreement between Israel, Egypt, and the United States to help keep the peace following the Egypt-Israel Peace Treaty of 1979.

The United States has adopted the following criteria for lending its troops to peace operations under either Chapter VI or Chapter VII:

> A. Participation advances U.S. interests and both the unique and general risks to American personnel have been weighed and are considered acceptable.
> B. Funds, personnel, and other resources are available for U.S. participation.
> C. U.S. participation is necessary for the success of the mission or to persuade other nations or organizations to participate.
> D. The role of U.S. forces is tied to clear objectives and an endpoint for U.S. participation can be identified.
> E. There is domestic political and congressional support for U.S. participation, or such support can be marshalled.
> F. Command and control arrangements governing the participation of American and foreign forces are acceptable to the U.S. [Presidential Decision Directive/PDD-25, *U.S. Policy on Reforming Multilateral Peace Operations*, at Annex II, May 3, 1994, https://fas.org/irp/offdocs/pdd25.htm.]

Significant U.S. involvement in Chapter VII peace enforcement operations additionally requires the commitment of "sufficient forces to achieve our clearly defined political and military objectives," and a "clear intention of decisively achieving these objectives." *Id.*

At least some U.S. peace operations have been ordered pursuant to one or more of the following statutory authorities:

International Disaster Assistance

22 U.S.C. §2292 (2018)

(b) General authority. Subject to the limitations in section 2292a of this title [relating to appropriations], and notwithstanding any other provision of this chapter or any other Act, the President is authorized to furnish assistance to any foreign country, international organization, or private voluntary organization, on such terms and conditions as he may determine, for international disaster relief and rehabilitation, including assistance relating to disaster preparedness, and to the prediction of, and contingency planning for, natural disasters abroad. . . .

Humanitarian and Other Assistance

10 U.S.C. §§401-409 (2018)

§401. Humanitarian and Civic Assistance Provided in Conjunction with Military Operations

(a) (1) Under regulations prescribed by the Secretary of Defense, the Secretary of a military department may carry out humanitarian and civic assistance activities in conjunction with authorized military operations of the armed forces in a country if the Secretary concerned determines that the activities will promote —

(A) the security interests of both the United States and the country in which the activities are to be carried out. . . .

(e) In this section, the term "humanitarian and civic assistance" means any of the following:

(1) Medical, surgical, dental, and veterinary care provided in areas of a country that are rural or are underserved by medical, surgical, dental, and veterinary professionals, respectively, including education, training, and technical assistance related to the care provided.

(2) Construction of rudimentary surface transportation systems.

(3) Well drilling and construction of basic sanitation facilities.

(4) Rudimentary construction and repair of public facilities.

§404. Foreign Disaster Assistance

(a) In general. — The President may direct the Secretary of Defense to provide disaster assistance outside the United States to respond to manmade or natural disasters when necessary to prevent loss of lives or serious harm to the environment.

(b) Forms of assistance. — Assistance provided under this section may include transportation, supplies, services, and equipment.

(c) Notification required. — Not later than 48 hours after the commencement of disaster assistance activities to provide assistance under this section, the President shall transmit to Congress a report containing notification of the assistance provided, and proposed to be provided, under this section and a description of so much of the following as is then available:

(1) The manmade or natural disaster for which disaster assistance is necessary.

(2) The threat to human lives or the environment presented by the disaster.

(3) The United States military personnel and material resources that are involved or expected to be involved.

(4) The disaster assistance that is being provided or is expected to be provided by other nations or public or private relief organizations.

(5) The anticipated duration of the disaster assistance activities. . . .

Detail of Personnel to International Organizations

22 U.S.C. §2388 (2018)

Whenever the President determines it to be consistent with and in furtherance of the purposes of this chapter [relating to foreign assistance], the head of any agency of the United States Government is authorized to detail, assign, or otherwise make available to any international organization any officer or employee of his agency to serve with, or as a member of, the international staff of such organization, or to render any technical, scientific, or professional advice or service to, or in cooperation with, such organization.

United Nations Participation Act

22 U.S.C. §§287-287*l* (2018)

§287d-1. Noncombatant Assistance to United Nations

(a) Armed forces details; supplies and equipment; obligation of funds; procurement and replacement of requested items. Notwithstanding the provisions of any other law, the President, upon the request by the United Nations for cooperative action, and to the extent that he finds that it is consistent with the national interest to comply with such request, may authorize, in support of such activities of the United Nations as are specifically directed to the peaceful settlement of disputes and not involving the employment of armed forces contemplated by chapter VII of the United Nations Charter —

(1) the detail to the United Nations, under such terms and conditions as the President shall determine, of personnel of the armed forces of the United States to serve as observers, guards, or in any non-combatant capacity, but in no event shall more than a total of one thousand of such personnel be so detailed at any one time. . . .

Also relevant is 10 U.S.C. §2561(a)(1) (2018), which allows the Defense Department to use funds appropriated for humanitarian assistance for "transportation of humanitarian relief and for other humanitarian purposes worldwide."

Notes and Questions

1. *Making Peace, Not War?* Does either a humanitarian or a peace operation involve the war power? If not, does Congress have to approve it? May Congress restrict such operations? If the critical test is whether a particular deployment "threatens war," who should make that determination?

Should it make any difference whether the government (if there is one) of the country to which troops are deployed invites their intervention? Can an invited intervention be a war?

2. *U.S. Involvement in Peace Operations.* The U.N. Security Council has always requested — never ordered — contributions of troops by individual member states to humanitarian and other peace operations. Contributions of U.S. military forces are therefore always voluntary. *United Nations Peacekeeping Operations: Principles and Guidelines, supra,* at 52. Given the expense and danger, not to mention possible diplomatic complications, why would the United States ever want to commit its personnel to such an operation?

What is the significance of the policy that U.S. participation be "tied to clear objectives" and have an identifiable "endpoint"? Who must approve the objectives? How should "domestic political and congressional support" be determined?

3. *The Importance of Labels, Redux.* The primary purpose of any humanitarian mission is to "alleviate human suffering." 22 U.S.C. §2292(a). U.S. troops are deployed on "peacekeeping" or "stability" missions when there is a peace to keep, but that peace is threatened. "Peacemaking," by contrast, involves the restoration of peace, employing force if necessary. Is it important to characterize a mission initially as one or another of these? Who should be able to make an authoritative pronouncement about the character of a particular mission?

Consider the following definitions provided by the Defense Department:

> [S]tabilization. A political endeavor involving an integrated civilian-military process to create conditions where locally legitimate authorities and systems can peaceably manage conflict and prevent a resurgence of violence. [DOD Instr. 3000.05, *Stabilization,* Dec. 13, 2018, at 15.]
>
> FDR [Foreign Disaster Relief]. Assistance that can be used immediately to alleviate the suffering of foreign disaster victims. Normally, it includes services and commodities as well as the rescue and evacuation of victims; the provision and transportation of food, water, clothing, medicines, beds, and bedding, temporary shelter, the furnishing of medical equipment, medical and technical personnel; and making repairs to essential services. [DOD Dir. 5100.46, *Foreign Disaster Relief,* July 6, 2012, at 10.]
>
> PKO [Peacekeeping Operations] consist of military support to diplomatic, informational, and economic efforts to establish or maintain peace in areas of potential or actual conflict. [Dep't of Defense, Jt. Pub. 3-07.3, *Peace Operations,* Mar. 1, 2018, at III-1.]
>
> PO [Peace Operations] encompass multiagency and multinational crisis response and limited contingency operations involving all instruments of national power with military missions to contain conflict, redress the peace, and shape the environment to support

> reconciliation and rebuilding and facilitate the transition to legitimate governance. PO include peacekeeping, peace enforcement, peacemaking, peace building, and conflict prevention efforts. [Dep't of Defense, Jt. Pub. 3-29, *Foreign Humanitarian Assistance,* May 14, 2019, at I-10.]

Can you relate each of these definitions to the statutory authorities set out above? What, if any, is their legal significance?

4. *Congressional Authority for Humanitarian or Peace Operations.* Should Congress provide its own definitions for the terms "disaster," "humanitarian," and "civic assistance"? How about "peacekeeping," "peacemaking," and "stability"?

In a given instance it may be necessary to act promptly, perhaps before there is time to seek the approval of Congress for a particular deployment. Should Congress give its approval in advance for such deployments? If so, how much flexibility should the President be given? What is the effect of the language "notwithstanding any other provision of this chapter or any other Act" in 22 U.S.C. §2292(b)? To what extent do you think Congress may constitutionally delegate or withhold such authority?

What if a purely humanitarian mission cannot prudently be carried out without the support of troops equipped for combat? Do these statutes authorize the deployment of such supporting forces? If so, might the President have to comply with the consultation, reporting, and other requirements of the War Powers Resolution, *supra* p. 90?

5. *Mission Creep or Mission Shift.* Suppose a mission begins peacefully, then turns violent. Under what circumstances, if any, must the President then seek congressional approval to stay and fight — to do more than simply use whatever force is necessary to safely withdraw the troops? Does the onset of hostilities trigger a requirement for the President to consult, report, or take any other action under the War Powers Resolution?

B. CROSSING THE MOGADISHU LINE: GOOD INTENTIONS GONE TERRIBLY WRONG

In 1991, Somalia plunged into a civil war among rival clans. The war not only directly threatened the population, it also disrupted food production and transportation in the midst of an extended drought and resulting famine. Over the next two years, some 350,000 Somalis would die from hunger and civil strife, and more than a million others would flee into refugee camps.

Alarmed at the heavy loss of life and the associated threat to international peace and security, the U.N. Security Council adopted a series of resolutions beginning in January 1992 that urged the clans to cease hostilities, installed an arms embargo, and approved the dispatch of a small contingent of member state troops to help restore government institutions and provide security for humanitarian relief operations.

Congress got involved in April 1992 by passing the Horn of Africa Recovery and Food Security Act, Pub. L. No. 102-274, 106 Stat. 115 (1992), expressing the "sense of the Congress" that the President should, *inter alia,* "ensure, to the maximum extent possible and in conjunction with other donors, that emergency humanitarian assistance is being made available to those in need." *Id.* §3(b)(3). Four months later, U.S. planes began helping airlift humanitarian relief supplies to Somalia. Subsequently, Congress authorized the transfer of funds from Defense Department appropriations to meet "unexpected and urgent" budget shortfalls for "international peacekeeping activities of the United Nations." National Defense Authorization Act for Fiscal Year 1993, Pub. L. No. 102-484, §1342, 106 Stat. 2315, 2556 (1992).

In December 1992, as clan militias continued to imperil relief workers and intercept relief convoys, the Security Council condemned ongoing "violations of international humanitarian law" in Somalia. It called for the deployment of 3,500 U.N. personnel there to coordinate humanitarian relief and to provide a secure environment for relief operations, and, pursuant to Chapter VII, authorized member states to use "all necessary means" to achieve these ends. S.C. Res. 794, U.N. Doc. S/RES/794 (Dec. 3, 1992).

President George H.W. Bush responded the next day by ordering U.S. military forces to secure the airfield and port facility of Mogadishu and to provide a secure environment for the relief effort. The troops were deployed on December 8 and 9, and the President reported the deployment to Congress two days later. Within a month, 28,000 U.S. troops were deployed in and off the shores of Somalia in Operation Restore Hope.

Asked by the Attorney General to describe the legal authority for the deployment, the Office of Legal Counsel declared that

> the President's role under our Constitution as Commander in Chief and Chief Executive vests him with the constitutional authority to order United States troops abroad to further national interests such as protecting the lives of Americans overseas. Accordingly, where, as here, United States government personnel and private citizens are participating in a lawful relief effort in a foreign nation, we conclude that the President may commit United States troops to protect those involved in the relief effort. In addition, we believe that long-standing precedent supports the use of the Armed Forces to protect Somalians and other foreign nationals in Somalia. We also believe that the President, in determining to commit the Armed Forces to this operation, may lawfully look to the importance to the national interests of the United States of upholding the recent United Nations resolutions regarding Somalia. Finally, we note that Congress has expressed its tacit approval for the President's exercise of his constitutional authority in this matter. [Timothy E. Flanigan, *Authority to Use United States Military Forces in Somalia,* 16 Op. O.L.C. 6, 8-9 (1992).]

The OLC opinion went on to recall the more than "200 times in our history" when the President sent troops abroad "for the protection of American citizens or national security." It cited as precedents the deployment of U.S. forces in Korea in June 1950, as well as judicial support for the President's actions in *Durand v. Hollins,* 8 F. Cas. 111 (C.C.S.D.N.Y. 1860) (No. 4186), and *In re Neagle,* 135 U.S. 1, 64 (1890). 16 Op. O.L.C. at 9-12.

In his letter to Congress, President Bush wrote, "We do not intend that U.S. Armed Forces deployed to Somalia become involved in hostilities. Nonetheless, these forces are equipped and ready to take such measures as may be needed to accomplish their humanitarian mission and defend themselves, if necessary." Letter to Congressional Leaders on the Situation in Somalia (Dec. 10, 1992), 28 Weekly Comp. Pres.

Doc. 2338, 2339 (Dec. 14, 1992). But despite the best-laid plans, the U.S. mission in Somalia was destined to go terribly wrong.

The United States turned over command of the U.N. operation in May 1993, although it continued to support U.N. efforts by providing approximately 3,000 U.S. logistics and other support personnel. In addition, approximately 1,100 U.S. troops remained in the area as part of a Quick Reaction Force (QRF) for emergency operations under the operational control of U.S. commanders.

On June 5, 1993, forces of Somali warlord Mohammed Farah Hassan Aidid ambushed a U.N. convoy, killing 24 Pakistani troops and injuring three U.S. soldiers. The following day, the Security Council adopted Resolution 837, which authorized troops furnished by member states to take "all necessary measures against all those responsible" for the attack and to secure "their arrest and detention for prosecution, trial, and punishment." S.C. Res. 837, U.N. Doc. S/RES/837 (June 6, 1993). On June 10, 1993, President Clinton reported these events to Congress and reaffirmed the deployment of U.S. armed forces to Somalia to accomplish their humanitarian mission "and to defend themselves."

Approximately one week later, elements of the QRF launched air and ground strikes against Aidid's headquarters in a search for Aidid. This phase of the operations concluded in a bloody firefight with Aidid's forces on October 3-4, 1993, in which 17 U.S. soldiers were killed and 84 were wounded. The name of a popular book and movie, *Black Hawk Down,* is based on the destruction of two U.S. helicopters during the attack. The press subsequently popularized the phrase "crossing the Mogadishu line" to describe a change in mission from peacekeeping to peacemaking.

President Clinton then reported to Congress that he would withdraw the troops by March 31, 1994. *Report on Military Operations in Somalia — Message from the President,* 139 Cong. Rec. H7796 (daily ed., Oct. 13, 1993). Congress, now leery about U.S. military involvement in the Horn of Africa, responded by authorizing appropriations for U.S. forces in Somalia only through the same date. Department of Defense Appropriations Act, 1994, Pub. L. No. 103-139, §8151(b)(2)(B), 107 Stat. 1418, 1476-1477 (1993). Beyond that date, it authorized the obligation of funds for forces "sufficient only to protect American diplomatic facilities and American citizens, and noncombat personnel to advise the United Nations commander in Somalia," and to protect themselves. *Id.*

More generally, Congress expressed its sense that no funds appropriated by the act should be used in "international peacekeeping or peace-enforcement operations" under the authority of Chapters VI or VII of the U.N. Charter or of a U.N. Security Council Resolution, or in "any significant . . . peacekeeping, or peace-enforcement operations," unless the President consulted with Congress prior to the operation, whenever possible, regarding the goals, mission, cost, funding, and anticipated duration and scope of the operation. *Id.* §8153(1)(a), 107 Stat. at 1477. Three weeks later, Congress directed the President to submit detailed reports about operations in Somalia, and it expressed the sense that he "should by November 15, 1993, seek and receive Congressional authorization in order for the deployment of United States Forces to Somalia to continue." National Defense Authorization Act for Fiscal Year 1994, Pub. L. No. 103-160, §1512(b)(3)-(4), 107 Stat. 1547, 1841 (1993). Early the following year, on February 26, 1994, all U.S. forces were withdrawn from Somalia.

Notes and Questions

1. *Domestic Authority for the Somalia Mission?* By what domestic authority, if any, did President George H.W. Bush initially deploy U.S. armed forces in Somalia? If there was statutory authority for the initial deployment of U.S. forces, did it also authorize subsequent deployments and mission changes? If the troops were lawfully deployed at the outset, did the President need any further authority to order them to find warlord Aidid? To put it differently, is "mission creep" inherently within the tactical discretion of the Commander in Chief?

2. *Characterizing the Mission.* Does it matter whether the deployment in Somalia was primarily for humanitarian purposes, or whether its goal was either peacekeeping or peacemaking? Is there a meaningful distinction among these missions? Consider this response:

> When U.S. troops intervened in December 1992 to stop theft of food, they disrupted the political economy and stepped deep into the muck of Somali politics. By reestablishing some order, the U.S. operation inevitably affected the direction of Somali politics and became nation-building because the most basic component of nation-building is an end to anarchy. The current conventional wisdom that draws the distinctions between different types of intervention and stresses the desire to avoid nation-building may be analytically attractive, but it is not particularly helpful. How could anyone believe that landing 30,000 troops in a country was anything but a gross interference in its politics? The Mogadishu line was crossed as soon as troops were sent in. [Walter Clarke & Jeffrey Herbst, *Somalia and the Future of Humanitarian Intervention*, Foreign Aff., Mar./Apr. 1996, at 70, 74.]

If Clarke and Herbst are right, what implication, if any, does their conclusion carry for the President's authority to order a humanitarian intervention into a politically unstable area?

3. *Operation Restore Hope and the War Powers Resolution.* Did the deployments of U.S. armed forces in Somalia satisfy the War Powers Resolution, *supra* p. 90? Is 22 U.S.C. §287d-1, part of the U.N. Participation Act, *supra* p. 473, pertinent to this question?

C. HUMANITARIAN INTERVENTION IN LIBYA — 2011

The U.S. military deployment in Somalia in 1992 was carried out with the invitation of — or at least without the objection of — the Somali government, such as it was. U.S. intentions were purely humanitarian, and early on there was no expectation that U.S. troops would engage in any fighting. Even when violence erupted, there was never any concern that the U.S. military presence in the Horn of Africa might violate the sovereignty of Somalia or basic principles of international law.

The U.S. use of military force in Libya in 2011 was very different. It presented a much clearer case of the kind of humanitarian intervention defined by one scholar as "the threat or use of force by a state, group of states, or international organization primarily for the purpose of protecting the nationals of the target state from widespread deprivations of internationally recognized human rights." Sean Murphy, *Humanitarian Intervention: The United Nations in an Evolving World* 11-12 (1996). In Libya, the very purpose of the intervention by the United States and other states was to protect Libyan citizens from their own government, which was engaged in a concerted campaign to deny them basic human rights, including the right to life. Thus, the target state was very much opposed to the intervention.

There is widespread skepticism that a single state or group of states, or even a regional organization like NATO, may legally use force on humanitarian grounds in the absence of approval by the U.N. Security Council. In the *Nicaragua* case, *supra* p. 249, for example, the World Court declared that "while the United States might form its own appraisal of the situation as to respect for human rights in Nicaragua, the use of force could not be the appropriate method to monitor or ensure such respect." *Id.* ¶268. NATO air attacks against Serbian forces engaged in shocking atrocities against ethnic Albanians in Kosovo in the spring of 1999 were criticized as a violation of U.N. Charter Article 2(4), although carried out with the best of intentions. *See, e.g.*, Louis Henkin, *Kosovo and the Law of "Humanitarian Intervention,"* 93 Am. J. Int'l L. 824 (1999). According to one view, "only the Security Council is empowered to take forcible action against a State which is in breach of its international undertakings to respect human rights." Yoram Dinstein, *War, Aggression and Self-Defence* 76 (6th ed. 2017). The Genocide Convention also declares that states parties "may call upon the competent organs of the United Nations to take such action . . . as they consider appropriate for the prevention and suppression of acts of genocide." Convention on the Prevention and Punishment of the Crime of Genocide art. VIII, Dec. 9, 1948, 78 U.N.T.S. 277, 282.

But even authorization by the Security Council for intervention in a purely internal conflict is illegal, some say, as well as unwise. The Charter makes no clear provision for such actions, although the United Nations is variously concerned with the protection and promotion of human rights and the rule of law. More important, according to critics, is the seeming inconsistency with Article 2(7) of the Charter, which states,

> Nothing contained in the present Charter shall authorize the United Nations to intervene in matters which are essentially within the domestic jurisdiction of any state or shall require the Members to submit such matters to settlement under the present Charter; but this principle shall not prejudice the application of enforcement measures under Chapter VII.

The World Court has declared, moreover, that

> the principle of non-intervention . . . forbids all States or groups of States to intervene directly or indirectly in internal or external affairs of other States . . . bearing on matters in which each State is permitted, by the principle of State sovereignty, to decide freely. One of these is the choice of a political, economic, social and cultural system, and the formulation of foreign policy. [*Nicaragua*, ¶205, *supra* p. 254.]

No "general right of intervention, in support of an opposition within another State, exists in contemporary international law," the Court said, even when the cause espoused by that opposition "appear[s] particularly worthy by reason of the political and moral values with which it [i]s identified." *Id.* ¶¶206, 209; *see* Murphy, *supra*, at 290-294 (rehearsing arguments on both sides).

If a right of humanitarian intervention is recognized, moreover, problems abound in the enforcement of that right. With but few exceptions — genocide being one — there is no consensus among states about which human rights are inviolable, or which ones rise to a level of importance that excuses interference from foreign states. Equally troublesome is the question of who should be entitled to make an authoritative determination that such rights are being violated. Who is entitled to decide that a particular remedy — peaceful or forceful — is justified in a given case? All of these difficulties are present in the case study that follows.

The story of the U.S. military mission in Libya in 2011 began with the 2010 Arab Spring uprising in Tunisia, Libya's neighbor to the west, demanding democratic reforms in that country. Weeks of massive, widely televised street protests followed in Egypt in early 2011, forcing the resignation of Egyptian President Hosni Mubarak. Meanwhile, demonstrators took to the streets in Jordan, Yemen, Algeria, Syria, Bahrain, Saudi Arabia, Libya, Iraq, and non-Arab Iran. Protestors were often brutally suppressed by government forces.

In Libya, beginning in mid-February 2011, hundreds of demonstrators were killed by police, military forces, and mercenary soldiers loyal to Colonel Muammar el-Qaddafi, who had ruled that country with an iron hand for more than 40 years. Protesters nevertheless managed to seize control of Benghazi, Libya's second largest city, and other areas in the East. Western media accounts and images of government atrocities raised grave concerns in Europe and North America, and produced calls for measures to stop Qaddafi's slaughter of his own people. Moreover, there was widespread support for democratic reform in Libya, especially given Qaddafi's long and well-documented history of sponsoring international terrorism.

A number of states, including the United States, immediately took non-forceful steps to put pressure on Qaddafi to stop the violence. For example, citing the "extreme measures against the people of Libya" taken by Muammar Qadhafi, his government, and close associates, President Obama issued Executive Order No. 13,566, *Blocking Property and Prohibiting Certain Transactions Related to Libya*, 76 Fed. Reg. 11,315 (Feb. 25, 2011). The order froze their assets and blocked their transactions in the United States. Libyan assets in the United States were estimated to be worth about $30 billion.

The United Nations Security Council got involved the next day, when it adopted Resolution 1970, condemning the "violence and use of force against civilians," deploring the "gross and systematic violation of human rights," and calling on the Libyan government to "respect the freedoms of peaceful assembly and of expression, including freedom of the media." S.C. Res. 1970, U.N. Doc. S/RES/1970 (Feb. 26, 2011). At the same time, it declared its "strong commitment to the sovereignty, independence, territorial integrity and national unity of the Libyan Arab Jamahiriya." *Id.* Then, acting under "Chapter VII of the Charter of the United Nations, and taking measures under its Article 41," the Security Council "decided" that:

> 9. . . . all Member States shall immediately take the necessary measures to prevent the direct or indirect supply, sale or transfer to the Libyan Arab Jamahiriya . . . of arms and related materiel of all types, including weapons and ammunition, military vehicles and

> equipment, paramilitary equipment, and spare parts for the aforementioned, and technical assistance, training, financial or other assistance, related to military activities....
>
> 15. ... all Member States shall take the necessary measures to prevent the entry into or transit through their territories of individuals listed in Annex I of this resolution or designated [by a committee established for that purpose by the resolution]....
>
> 17. ... all Member States shall freeze without delay all funds, other financial assets and economic resources which are on their territories, which are owned or controlled, directly or indirectly, by the individuals or entities listed in Annex II of this resolution or designated by [the committee referred to above].... [*Id.*]

The travel ban applied to Qaddafi, certain members of his family, and several high Libyan government officials. The asset freeze applied to Qaddafi and to several of his sons and a daughter. Unfortunately, these measures only seemed to strengthen Qaddafi's resolve to hold on to power.

As the country descended toward all-out civil war, the Libyan government turned its considerable military power against the protestors. "We will come house by house, room by room," Qaddafi declared. "We will have no mercy and no pity." Dan Bilefsky & Mark Landler, *Military Action Against Qaddafi Is Backed by U.N.*, N.Y. Times, Mar. 18, 2011. Many outside Libya described a moral imperative to intervene quickly to stop the slaughter of innocents, citing the tragic consequences of delay in responding to earlier internal conflicts in Bosnia, Rwanda, and Darfur.

An intense debate erupted within the Obama administration and in Congress about how the United States should respond to these developments. Some argued that the United States should immediately provide military assistance to the Libyan rebels. Others urged caution, stressing that no action should be taken without clearly articulated goals and an exit strategy. Still others insisted that no important U.S. interests would be served by any involvement. In the midst of this debate, the Senate approved a measure on March 1

> strongly condemn[ing] the gross and systematic violations of human rights in Libya, including violent attacks on protesters demanding democratic reforms;... urg[ing] the United Nations Security Council to take such further action as may be necessary to protect civilians in Libya from attack, including the possible imposition of a no-fly zone over Libyan territory;... [and] support[ing] an orderly, irreversible transition to a legitimate democratic government in Libya. [S. Res. 85, 112th Cong. (2011).]

But the Senate bill was not acted on by the House. Other measures introduced in Congress called for the U.S. military to establish a no-fly zone in Libya — to prevent Qaddafi from attacking rebel forces from the air — and for the recognition of a new government there, while still others expressed the sense of Congress that the President should obtain specific statutory authorization for the use of U.S. armed forces in Libya. Another sought to cut off any funding for such use. None of these measures were approved by both houses of Congress.

As the fighting continued, and rebel fighters began to be overmatched by Qaddafi forces, the Security Council, with Russia, China, India, and Brazil abstaining, then approved the following additional resolution:

United Nations Security Council Resolution 1973

U.N. Doc. S/RES/1973 (Mar. 17, 2011)

The Security Council, . . .

Deploring the failure of the Libyan authorities to comply with resolution 1970 (2011),

Expressing grave concern at the deteriorating situation, the escalation of violence, and the heavy civilian casualties, . . .

Condemning the gross and systematic violation of human rights, including arbitrary detentions, enforced disappearances, torture and summary executions, . . .

Acting under Chapter VII of the Charter of the United Nations,

1. *Demands* the immediate establishment of a cease-fire and a complete end to violence and all attacks against, and abuses of, civilians; . . .

4. *Authorizes* Member States that have notified the Secretary-General, acting nationally or through regional organizations or arrangements, and acting in cooperation with the Secretary-General, to take all necessary measures . . . to protect civilians and civilian populated areas under threat of attack in the Libyan Arab Jamahiriya, including Benghazi, while excluding a foreign occupation force of any form on any part of Libyan territory, . . .

6. *Decides* to establish a ban on all flights in the airspace of the Libyan Arab Jamahiriya in order to help protect civilians;

7. *Decides further* that the ban imposed by paragraph 6 shall not apply to flights whose sole purpose is humanitarian, such as delivering or facilitating the delivery of assistance, including medical supplies, food, humanitarian workers and related assistance, or evacuating foreign nationals . . .

8. *Authorizes* Member States . . . acting nationally or through regional organizations or arrangements, to take all necessary measures to enforce compliance with the ban on flights imposed by paragraph 6 above, as necessary . . .

29. *Decides* to remain actively seized of the matter.

Questions immediately arose about precisely what the Security Council resolution authorized, how it would be implemented, and by whom. Two days later, on March 19, President Obama reported to Congress that he had ordered

> strikes against Libyan air defense systems and military airfields for the purposes of preparing a no-fly zone. These strikes will be limited in their nature, duration, and scope. Their purpose is to support an international coalition as it takes all necessary measures to enforce the terms of U.N. Security Council Resolution 1973. These limited U.S. actions will set the stage for further action by other coalition partners.
>
> The United States has not deployed ground forces into Libya. . . .
>
> . . . I have directed these actions, which are in the national security and foreign policy interests of the United States, pursuant to my constitutional authority to conduct U.S. foreign relations and as Commander in Chief and Chief Executive. [Letter from the

President to the Speaker of the House of Representatives and the President Pro Tempore of the Senate (Mar. 21, 2011).]

The President described the report as "part of my efforts to keep the Congress fully informed, consistent with the War Powers Resolution." *Id.* Separately, he stressed that Great Britain, France, and Arab states would take the lead in implementing the resolution. He and other Administration officials also insisted that the goal of U.S. involvement was not to remove Colonel Qaddafi from power.

Over the next several days, U.S. forces launched a large number of Tomahawk cruise missiles at Libyan air defenses, to enable U.S., British, and French aircraft to enforce the no-fly zone prescribed in Resolution 1973. These same aircraft also began attacking Qaddafi's tanks and heavy artillery, expanding the no-fly zone into a no-drive zone, ostensibly in support of the broader humanitarian mission authorized by the Security Council. On March 27, NATO agreed to take on the entire military operation in Libya under Security Council Resolution 1973, with the United States handing over to its NATO allies all but support functions — supplies, aerial refueling, intelligence, and the like.

During the summer, as rebels expanded their control of the country, they organized the National Transitional Council, which was widely recognized as the new legitimate government of Libya. In September the Security Council lifted the no-fly zone and unfroze Libyan assets, and it established a United Nations Support Mission in Libya (UNSMIL) to help restore security and order. S.C. Res. 2009, U.N. Doc. S/RES/2009 (Sept. 16, 2011). On October 20, Qaddafi was captured and killed in his hometown of Sirte. Then on October 27, the Security Council voted to terminate its approval of the use of force in Libya, S.C. Res. 2016, U.N. Doc. S/RES/2016, and the NATO mission there ended several days later.

Unfortunately, the bloodshed was to continue in Libya, as several rival groups — Islamist and anti-Islamist, including some linked to Al Qaeda or the Islamic State — competed for power and territory. In September 2019, the Security Council expressed "grave concern over ongoing hostilities in and around Tripoli, and the targeting of civilian infrastructure, [and] concern over the exploitation of the conflict by terrorist and violent extremist groups," and it ordered UNSMIL to continue working to promote the formation of a stable national government. S.C. Res. 2486, U.N. Doc. S/RES/2486 (Sept. 12, 2019).

Notes and Questions

1. The President's Authority? In his report to Congress on March 19, 2011, President Obama claimed that he had directed U.S. military intervention in Libya "pursuant to my constitutional authority to conduct U.S. foreign relations and as Commander in Chief and Chief Executive." In a similar vein, the Justice Department's Office of Legal Counsel issued an opinion on April 1 concluding that "President Obama could rely on his constitutional power to safeguard the national interest by directing the anticipated military operations in Libya . . . without prior congressional authorization." Off. of Legal Counsel, *Authority to Use Military Force in Libya*, 2011 WL 1459998, at *14 (Apr. 1, 2011). It stressed that two national interests in particular — "preserving regional stability and supporting the UNSC's credibility and effectiveness — provided a sufficient basis for the President's exercise of his constitutional authority to order the use of military force." Moreover, the opinion argued, the deployment in Libya was "limited in nature, scope, and duration," and "the risk of substantial casualties for U.S. forces would be low." The conflict was not a "'war' within the meaning of the Declaration of War Clause," furthermore, because it did not concern a "prolonged and substantial military engagement[] . . . involving exposure of U.S. military personnel to significant risk over a substantial period." *Id.* at *8-10. Are you convinced that specific congressional approval was not needed?

2. *The Scope of Security Council Resolution 1973.* Did the authorization in U.N. Security Council Resolution 1973 to protect "civilians and civilian populated areas" include the defense of Libyan rebels seeking to overthrow the Qaddafi regime? Did it permit an alliance with the rebels?

What military actions were authorized by the term "all necessary measures"? In addition to a no-fly zone, did it approve air strikes on Qaddafi ground forces? Could member states have introduced ground troops to fight alongside Libyan rebels?

3. *Grounds for Humanitarian Intervention?* Should the conflict in Libya be regarded as a civil war — a matter to be settled internally, for better or for worse? If so, could Resolution 1973 be squared with the principle of non-intervention in Article 2(7), set forth *supra* p. 479? With what the World Court declared in the *Nicaragua* case about customary international law concerning interventions on humanitarian grounds, *supra* p. 479?

Are you clear about which basic human rights the intervening states sought to vindicate? Are these rights so important that they justify what would otherwise be considered an inexcusable violation of Libya's sovereignty? One possible answer is that the justification turns partly on possible effects of the conflict outside Libya's borders — for example, the creation of large numbers of refugees, who might threaten the peace and stability of neighboring states.

The 2011 intervention in Libya was celebrated by some as based on the emergent principle of a "responsibility to protect," or R2P, according to which individual state sovereignty must give way to each state's obligation to refrain from human rights violations against its own people, and a correlative right of all other states to intervene to prevent those violations. *See* Monica Hakimi, *Toward a Legal Theory on the Responsibility to Protect*, 39 Yale J. Int'l L. 247 (2014). Recognized in a limited form by the U.N. General Assembly in 2005, the principle was also endorsed publicly by the Obama administration. If you think such a right should exist to prevent, say, genocide or crimes against humanity, should it apply equally to other human rights violations? Taking into account the strong reluctance of some states, like China (a permanent member of the U.N. Security Council), to permit interference in their internal affairs, can you describe a politically acceptable arrangement to regulate the implementation of R2P?

4. *Authority for "Regime Change"?* Was Resolution 1973 authority for "regime change" in Libya? Many believed that the humanitarian goals of the resolution could not be achieved unless Qaddafi were forced to step down. If the resolution could be read to have that practical effect, did it exceed the scope of the Security Council's

authority under the U.N. Charter? If not, what are the implications for the concept of sovereignty, always the touchstone of international relations?

5. *NATO's Role.* What was the legal basis for NATO's military involvement in Libya? If, as a regional organization, it needed the approval of the U.N. Security Council under Article 53(1), see *supra* p. 341, did it get it?

6. *Unilateral Humanitarian Intervention.* Two years after the intervention in Libya sanctioned by NATO and the U.N. Security Council, President Obama threatened a U.S. military response when Syrian President Bashar al Assad used chemical weapons against Syrian civilians early in that nation's civil war. Another four years later, President Trump made good on that threat. On April 4, 2017, Syrian forces conducted an attack against a target in northern Syria using chemical weapons — possibly sarin gas — killing dozens of civilians. In response, President Trump ordered the bombardment two days later of Syria's Shayrat Airfield using 59 Tomahawk cruise missiles launched from U.S. warships in the Mediterranean. *See* Michael R. Gordon, Helene Cooper & Michael D. Shear, *Dozens of U.S. Missiles Hit Air Base in Syria,* N.Y. Times, Apr. 6, 2017. The following year, after another Syrian poison gas attack killed more than 40 people, this time probably with chlorine, U.S. and allied forces carried out a much larger strike on three Syrian chemical weapons facilities using both cruise missiles and piloted aircraft, a move immediately condemned by Syria's ally Russia. *See* Helene Cooper, Thomas Gibbons-Neff & Ben Hubbard, *U.S., Britain and France Strike Syria over Suspected Chemical Weapons Attack,* N.Y. Times, Apr. 13, 2018.

Just as President Obama's authority to use force in Libya had been supported by an opinion from the OLC, so, too, President Trump's authority was supported by a lengthy OLC opinion asserting that no prior approval from Congress was needed. Off. of Legal Counsel, *April 2018 Airstrikes Against Syrian Chemical-Weapons Facilities* (May 31, 2018). Like the opinion six years earlier, it concluded that the U.S. strikes did not constitute a "war" requiring congressional approval, because they did not involve "prolonged and substantial military engagements" or "exposure of U.S. military personnel to significant risk over a substantial period," and because escalation was "unlikely." *Id.* at 18-22; *see* Charlie Savage, *Legal Memo Says Trump Has Wide Power to Attack,* N.Y. Times, June 2, 2018. Can you reconcile OLC's criteria with what you know about Congress's role in going to war? Do the criteria furnish helpful guidance for future Presidents in deciding when to seek congressional approval for the use of force? In conjunction with the uses of force that they approved, do they support a customary authority of the President to use force abroad in certain circumstances? If so, what is the scope of the emerging customary authority?

Without approval from the U.N. Security Council, did the U.S. attacks violate international law? They were criticized by some as unconstitutional and a violation of U.N. Charter Article 2(4). *See, e.g.,* Marty Lederman, *Why the Strikes Against Syria Probably Violate the U.N. Charter and (Therefore) the U.S. Constitution,* Just Security, Apr. 6, 2017; Jack Goldsmith & Oona Hathaway, *Bad Legal Arguments for the Syria Strikes,* Just Security, Apr. 14, 2018 (arguing that "there is no apparent domestic or international legal authority for the strikes"). According to others, however, they were excused as an act of humanitarian intervention in exercise of every nation's responsibility to protect innocent civilians. *See, e.g.,* Harold Hongju Koh, *Not Illegal: But Now the Hard Part Begins,* Just Security, Apr. 7, 2017. Who do you think was right?

HUMANITARIAN AND PEACE OPERATIONS: SUMMARY OF BASIC PRINCIPLES

- The United States has often sent troops abroad to provide relief in natural disasters, as well as to serve in peacekeeping missions authorized by the U.N. Security Council, when engagement in hostilities was not expected.
- Legal authority for such deployments depends to some uncertain degree on their characterization as humanitarian, peacekeeping, or peacemaking. But the character of a deployment, and therefore the legal justification for it, may change before a mission is completed.
- Domestic authority for humanitarian or peace missions may be found in one or more of a series of statutes delegating broad, ill-defined powers to the President.
- If troops are deployed at the invitation of the state where they will serve, international law principles limiting the use of force are not implicated.
- If foreign troops are not invited in, their introduction will violate U.N. Charter Article 2(4) or the customary prohibition against intervention, unless their deployment is: (1) approved by the U.N. Security Council, acting under Chapter VI or VII to abate threats or breaches of the peace; or (2) justified by the very controversial responsibility to protect (R2P).
- Troops properly deployed on peaceful missions may always use necessary force to defend themselves.
- Presidents Obama and Trump both unilaterally used force abroad for humanitarian objectives on the rationale that each use of force was of limited nature, scope, and duration, and unlikely to escalate or to pose a substantial risk of U.S. casualties. It is possible that, in the future, Presidents will cite these instances as precedent for a customary authority of the President to use force in similar circumstances.

PART IV

INTELLIGENCE OPERATIONS AND COLLECTION

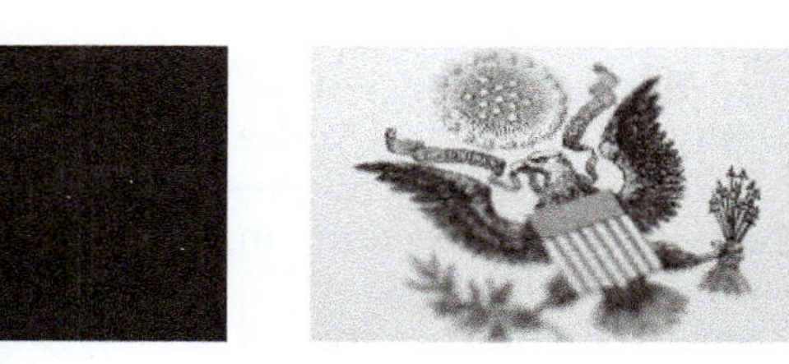

17

Introducing Intelligence

The intelligence community is really two communities with distinctly different roles in protecting national security. This dual character has been the source of much confusion. Both roles are sometimes played by a single government agency, sometimes acting under the same statutory authority. The two roles are usually unrelated, although one may sometimes support the other.

One role of the intelligence community is the collection, analysis, and dissemination of information about threats to national security. The end of the Cold War and the emergence of asymmetric attacks on the United States have presented unprecedented challenges in this regard. Instead of a single-minded focus on the Soviet Union, intelligence agents now must keep tabs on a wide range of potential enemies across the globe, including both states and potentially lethal non-state actors that are intent on doing harm to the United States. With the introduction of new technology, the cloak-and-dagger excitement of spy novels has given way somewhat to a tedious, mechanical sifting through masses of electronic data. Information is now easier to come by, harder to digest, and less trustworthy. Meanwhile, counterespionage efforts have become much more sophisticated. All these collection activities have raised new concerns about constitutional guarantees of privacy, free expression, and free association.

The other major role of the intelligence community is the conduct of covert actions. For most of our post-World War II history, the CIA (and occasionally other agencies) carried out such actions against the former Soviet Union or perceived communist threats around the world — in Southeast Asia, the Middle East, Latin America, and the Caribbean. U.S. agents secretly generated propaganda and took part in political actions in an effort to influence other governments. They helped to overthrow governments in, for example, Iran, Guatemala, and Chile. They were even involved in political assassinations, and they employed unsavory individuals and groups who were later revealed to be engaged in drug-trafficking and human rights abuses. Increasingly today, covert actions seek to disrupt terrorist groups and ward off their planned attacks, to foil narcotics shipments, and to thwart financial transactions of black market weapons traders. In the post-9/11 era, the CIA has also conducted covert operations aimed at killing terrorists, including, by many accounts, a number of unacknowledged drone attacks. In doing so, according to a former CIA lawyer, "CIA officers break the law [in other countries] around the world every day." A. John Radsan, Remarks at a Conference at Duke University (Apr. 15, 2011). The CIA lawyer was referring to committing espionage abroad, and as we'll see such activities are authorized by our laws, although our agents may be subject to prosecution in those countries.

Revelations about secret aspects of the Vietnam War and related disruptions of domestic protest groups, along with congressional investigations into intelligence excesses around the world through the early 1970s, began an intelligence reform process that truly took root only after the exposure of the Iran-Contra Affair (the secret and arguably illegal financial support of a dissident paramilitary group in Nicaragua with funds diverted from weapons sales to Iran by members of the Reagan administration) and the collapse of the Soviet Union. Congress has enacted a number of measures designed to give it a much larger oversight role than previously in both intelligence collection and covert actions, while the Executive has generally resisted these legislative initiatives, preferring to act independently. The unauthorized disclosures of classified intelligence programs by National Security Agency contractor Edward Snowden in 2013 prompted additional executive branch reforms and promises of greater transparency. Congress continues to debate legislative reforms. The courts, meanwhile, have become involved in the resulting disputes between the two political branches only rarely and reluctantly.

In this chapter, we lay the foundation for a later systematic consideration of the rules and techniques for intelligence collection and covert action by considering what the intelligence community does and how it does it. We begin by introducing the intelligence cycle, then survey briefly the range of intelligence collection disciplines and their evolution from 1947 to the present. Finally, we briefly consider several types of covert action.

A. THE INTELLIGENCE CYCLE

Select Committee to Study Governmental Operations with Respect to Intelligence Activities (Church Committee), Foreign and Military Intelligence

S. Rep. No. 94-755, bk. I, at 17-19 (1976)

In theory at least [intelligence] operations can be described in simple terms by the following cycle:

— Those who use intelligence, the "consumers," indicate the kind of information needed.

— These needs are translated into concrete "requirements" by senior intelligence managers.

— The requirements are used to allocate resources to the "collectors" and serve to guide their efforts.

— The collectors obtain the required information or "raw intelligence."

— The "raw intelligence" is collated and turned into "finished intelligence" by the "analysts."

— The finished intelligence is distributed to the consumer and the intelligence managers who state new needs, define new requirements, and make necessary adjustments in the intelligence programs to improve effectiveness and efficiency.

In reality, this pattern is barely recognizable.

There are many different consumers, from the President to the weapons designer. Their needs can conflict. Consumers rarely take the time to define their intelligence needs and even if they do so there is no effective and systematic mechanism for translating them into intelligence requirements.

Therefore, intelligence requirements reflect what intelligence managers think the consumers need, and equally important, what they think their organizations can produce. Since there are many managers and little central control, each is relatively free to set his own requirements.

Resources therefore tend to be allocated according to the priorities and concerns of the various intelligence bureaucracies. Most intelligence collection operations are part of other organizations — the Department of Defense, the Department of State — and so their requirements and their consumers are often the first to be served.

Collecting intelligence is not an automatic process. There are many different kinds of intelligence, from a radar return to an indiscreet remark, and the problems in acquiring it vary greatly. Information that is wanted may not be available, or years may be required to develop an agency or a technical device to get it. Meanwhile intelligence agencies collect what they can.

In the world of bureaucracy, budgets, programs, procurement, and managers, the needs of the analyst can be lost in the shuffle. There has been an explosion in the volume and quality of raw intelligence but no equivalent increase in the capacity of analytical capabilities. As a result, "raw" intelligence increasingly dominates "finished" intelligence; analysts find themselves on a treadmill where it is difficult to do more than summarize and put in context the intelligence flowing in. There is little time or reward for the task of providing insight.

In the end the consumer, particularly at the highest levels of the government, finds that his most important questions are not only unanswered, but sometimes not even addressed.

To some extent, all this is in the nature of things. Many questions cannot be answered. The world of intelligence is dominated by uncertainty and chance, and those in the intelligence bureaucracy, as elsewhere in the Government, try to defend themselves against uncertainties in ways which militate against efficient management and accountability.

Beyond this is the fact that the organizations of the intelligence community must operate in peace but be prepared for war. This has an enormous impact on the kind of intelligence that is sought, the way resources are allocated, and the way the intelligence community is organized and managed.

The assertion by the Church Committee that "there is no effective and systematic mechanism for translating [consumer needs] into intelligence requirements" is no longer strictly true. Particularly in the years since the 9/11 attacks, the Intelligence Community has become a process-rich enterprise. *See* Off. of the Dir. of Nat'l

Intelligence, *Intelligence Community Directive 204, National Intelligence Priorities Framework* (Jan. 2, 2015), https://www.hsdl.org/?view&did=761901.

The Idealized Intelligence Cycle

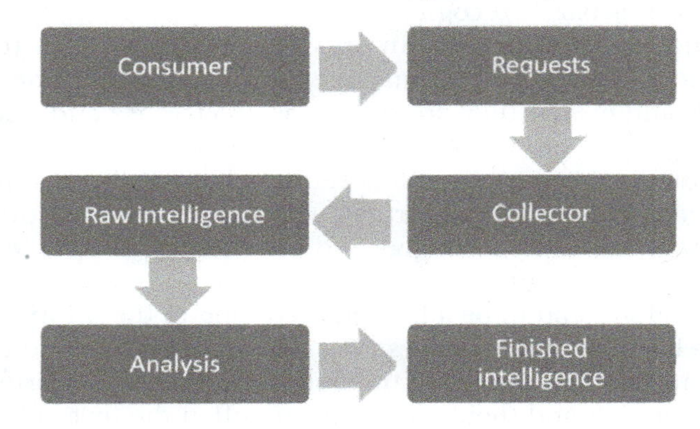

Notes and Questions

1. Setting Requirements. Intelligence serves policymakers and helps to shape policy. That policy in turn determines the need for additional intelligence and guides intelligence operations. There is, however, no formal mechanism for translating policy into intelligence requirements. Who should set intelligence objectives? How should those objectives be communicated to intelligence officials, following what kind of process?

2. Collection. Technical means, as opposed to human sources, offer tremendous advantages in collecting large volumes of information. Technical collection is, however, very expensive. Human intelligence is cheaper and may be more narrowly focused. How should these collection tradeoffs be made, and by whom? If the mass of data collected through technical means cannot realistically be processed and analyzed, how should collection priorities be modified?

3. Analysis, Delivery, and Consumption. Some intelligence products are widely known — the President's Daily Briefings (PDBs), for example, and National Intelligence Estimates (NIEs). Other analytical products are discussed in this and the following chapters. How do you suppose it is decided which material collected is important enough to report, in whatever form? Who should receive intelligence reports — in the executive branch and in Congress? How rapidly should the information be provided, in how much detail, and in what form?

4. Changing Requirements. The Cold War and a preoccupation with the Soviet Union dominated the intelligence agenda until the fall of the Berlin Wall in 1989. From 1989 until the September 11 terrorist attacks in 2001, there was no comparably focused intelligence mission. 9/11 provided a mission. The dominant role and most important legal questions concerning intelligence collection now revolve around countering the ongoing threat of terrorism, along with evolving nuclear proliferation and cyberspace threats.

B. HOW IS INTELLIGENCE COLLECTED? — THE "INTS"

Intelligence collection is done by people — human intelligence or espionage (HUMINT) — and by machines — geospatial intelligence (GEOINT), signals intelligence (SIGINT), imagery intelligence (IMINT), and measurement and signatures intelligence (MASINT). Different collection techniques may be used in pursuit of the same intelligence in order to learn from the shared perspectives they offer — "all-source intelligence." To some extent, each INT also compensates for gaps in coverage by others. Except for open-source intelligence (OSINT), however, each of the INTs has a largely self-contained vertical flow of information, from collection to delivery. This tendency toward under-coordinated "stovepipes" may make sharing of collected information within and among members of the intelligence community more difficult.

Marshall Curtis Erwin, Intelligence Issues for Congress

Cong. Res. Serv. RL33539, at 15-17, Apr. 23, 2013

THE "INTS": INTELLIGENCE DISCIPLINES

The intelligence community has been built around major agencies responsible for specific intelligence collection systems known as disciplines. Three major intelligence disciplines or "INTs" — signals intelligence (*sigint*), imagery intelligence (*imint*), and human intelligence (*humint*) — provide the most important information for analysts and absorb the bulk of the intelligence budget. Sigint collection is the responsibility of NSA at Fort Meade, MD. Sigint operations are classified, but there is little doubt that the need for intelligence on a growing variety of nations and groups that are increasingly using sophisticated and rapidly changing encryption systems requires a far different sigint effort than the one prevailing during the Cold War. Since the late 1990s a process of change in NSA's culture and methods of operations has been initiated, a change required by the need to target terrorist groups and affected by the proliferation of communications technologies and inexpensive encryption systems. . . .

National Security Agency Headquarters, Ft. Meade, Maryland.

A second major intelligence discipline, imagery or *imint*, is also facing profound changes. Imagery is collected in essentially three ways: by satellites, manned aircraft, and unmanned aerial vehicles (UAVs). The satellite program that covered the Soviet Union and acquired highly accurate intelligence concerning submarines, missiles, bombers, and other military targets is perhaps the greatest achievement of the U.S. intelligence community — it served as a foundation for defense planning and strategic planning that led to the end of the Cold War. In today's environment, there is a greater number of collection targets than existed during the Cold War and more satellites are required, especially those that can be maneuvered to collect information about a variety of targets. At the same time, the availability of high-quality commercial satellite imagery and its widespread use by federal agencies has raised questions about the extent to which coverage from the private sector can meet the requirements of intelligence agencies. High altitude UAVs such as the Global Hawk may also provide surveillance capabilities that overlap those of satellites.

The National Imagery and Mapping Agency (NIMA) was established in 1996 to manage imagery processing and dissemination previously undertaken by a number of separate agencies. NIMA was renamed the National Geospatial-Intelligence Agency (NGA) by the FY2004 Defense Authorization Act, Pub. L. No. 108-136, §921(a), 117 Stat. 1392, 1568 (2003). The goal of NGA is, according to the agency, to use imagery and other geospatial information "to describe, assess, and visually depict physical features and geographically referenced activities on the Earth."

Intelligence from human contacts — *humint* — is the oldest intelligence discipline and the one that is most often written about in the media. The CIA is the primary collector of humint, but the Defense Department also has responsibilities filled by defense attachés at embassies around the world and by other agents working on behalf of theater commanders. Many observers have argued that inadequate humint has been a systemic problem and contributed to the inability to gain prior knowledge of the 9/11 plots. In part, these criticisms reflect the changing nature of the international environment. During the Cold War, principal targets of U.S. humint collection were foreign government officials and military leaders. Intelligence agency officials working under cover as diplomats could approach potential contacts at receptions or in the context of routine embassy business. Today, however, the need is to seek information from clandestine terrorist groups or narcotics traffickers who do not appear at embassy social gatherings. Humint from such sources can be especially important as there may be little evidence of activities or intentions that can be gathered from imagery, and their communications may be carefully limited.

Placing U.S. intelligence officials in foreign countries under "nonofficial cover" (NOC) in businesses or other private capacities is possible, but it presents significant challenges to U.S. agencies. Administrative mechanisms are vastly more complicated than they are for officials formally attached to an embassy; special arrangements have to be made for pay, allowances, retirement, and healthcare. The responsibilities of operatives under nonofficial cover to the parent intelligence agency have to be reconciled with those to private employers, and there is an unavoidable potential for conflicts of interest or even corruption. Any involvement with terrorist groups or smugglers has a potential for major embarrassment to the U.S. government and, of course, physical danger to those immediately involved. . . .

Other "INTs"

A fourth INT, measurement and signatures analysis — *masint* — has received greater emphasis in recent years. A highly technical discipline, masint involves the application of complicated analytical refinements to information collected by sigint and imint sensors. It also includes spectral imaging by which the identities and characteristics of objects can be identified on the basis of their reflection and absorption of light. Masint is undertaken by DIA [the Defense Intelligence Agency] and other DOD agencies. A key problem has been retaining personnel with expertise in masint systems who are offered more remunerative positions in private industry.

Another category of information, open source information — *osint* (newspapers, periodicals, pamphlets, books, radio, television, and Internet websites) — is increasingly important given requirements for information about many regions and topics (instead of the former concentration on political and military issues affecting a few countries). At the same time, requirements for translation, dissemination, and systematic analysis have increased, given the multitude of different areas and the volume of materials. Many observers believe that intelligence agencies should be more aggressive in using osint; some believe that the availability of osint may even reduce the need for certain collection efforts. The availability of osint also raises questions regarding the need for intelligence agencies to undertake collection, analysis, and dissemination of information that could be directly obtained by user agencies. The Intelligence Reform and Terrorism Prevention Act of 2004, Pub. L. No. 108-458, §1052, 118 Stat. 3638, 3683, expressed the sense of Congress that there should be an open source intelligence center to coordinate the collection, analysis, production, and dissemination of open source intelligence to other intelligence agencies. An Open Source Center was subsequently established, although it has been managed by CIA personnel.

National Research Council, Bulk Collection of Signals Intelligence: Technical Options

pp. 27-34 (2015)

2.1 A CONCEPTUAL MODEL OF THE SIGNALS INTELLIGENCE PROCESS . . .

2.1.1 Collection

Signals are derived from many sources, but the specific steps taken to winnow large data streams to those that are manageable and potentially productive are the same regardless of the source. . . . The first three steps in the SIGINT model, taken together, are what the committee [Committee on Responding to Section 5(d) of Presidential Policy Directive 28: The Feasibility of Software to Provide Alternatives to Bulk Signals Intelligence Collection] informally calls *collection*:

- *Extract.* The first step is to obtain the signal from a source, convert it into a digital stream, and parse the stream to extract the kind of information being sought, such as an email message or the digital audio of a telephone call. Extraction interprets layers of communications and Internet protocols, such as Optical Transport Network (OTN), Synchronous Digital Hierarchy (SDH), Ethernet, Internet Protocol (IP), Transmission Control Protocol

(TCP), Simple Mail Transport Protocol (SMTP), or Hypertext Transport Protocol (HTTP). In cases where business records are sought, this step extracts and reformats relevant SIGINT data from a business record format used by the business.

- *Filter.* This step selects, from all the items extracted, items of interest that should be retained. It is sometimes controlled by a "discriminant," which the IC agency running the collection provides to describe in precise terms the properties of an item that should be retained. For example, a discriminant might specify "all telephone calls from 301-555-1212 to Somalia," "all telephone calls from France to Yemen," or "all search-engine queries containing the word 'sarin.'" If there is no discriminant, then all extracted items are retained.
- *Store.* Retained items are stored in a database operated by the U.S. Government. This is the point at which collection is deemed in this model to occur for the retained data. By contrast, the previous steps are fleeting, with data processed in near real-time (keeping data only for short periods of time — minutes to hours — for technical reasons) as fast as it is supplied, with all but the items to be retained discarded. Items collected from separate sources are usually combined into a modest number of large databases to facilitate searching and analysis.

In modem communication systems, traffic from many sources and destinations is aggregated into a single channel. For example, the radio signals to and from a base station serving all mobile phones in a cell are all on the same radio channels, and all of the IP packets between two routers may be carried on the same fiber. With rare exceptions, there is no single physical access point comparable to the central office connection of a landline telephone at which to observe only the items of interest and nothing more. Reflecting this reality, the committee's definition of "collection" says that SIGINT data is collected only when it is stored, *not* when it is extracted. Put another way, every piece of data that passes by a potential monitoring point must be machine-filtered as part of the extraction process to determine whether it is potentially relevant or can be thrown away without further examination.

The committee notes that there are at least two differing conceptions of privacy with respect to when data is acquired. One view asserts that a violation of privacy occurs when the electronic signal is first captured, irrespective of what happens to the signal after that point. Another view asserts that processing the signal only to determine if it is irrelevant does not compromise privacy rights in any way, even if that signal is held for a non-zero period of time. In a technological environment in which different communications streams are mixed together on the same physical channel, picking out the sought-after communication stream *requires* the latter approach. Further, note that the committee has made a technical judgment about a useful definition of collection while remaining silent about what does or does not constitute an appropriate definition of privacy.

The committee also uses "collection" as a term to describe only *government* retention of data. If non-government actors acquire information from or about various parties in some legal manner but the government does not have access to that information, the government is not engaging in collection as a result of the actions of those parties. In contrast, if the government gains access to that information through technical or legal means and stores some or all of it for government use, it is reasonable to consider this collection. . . .

TABLE 2.1 Hypothetical Call Detail Records as They Might Appear in a Signals Intelligence Database

Caller	Called	Call Start Time	Call Duration
1-617-555-0131	1-703-555-0198	2014:10:3:15:45:10	3:41
1-703-555-0198	1-703-555-0013	2014:10:3:15:49:10	1:10
1-415-555-0103	963 99 2210403	2014:10:3:16:01:43	73:43
1-603-555-0141	1-603-555-0152	2014:10:3:22:10:03	3:01
1-617-555-0183	1-413-555-0137	2014:10:3:22:33:48	7:03
1-802-555-0141	1-802-555-0108	2014:10:3:22:41:17	3:02

NOTE: In this hypothetical example of call detail records as they might appear in a signals intelligence database, the call shown in the first line might be relaying a message through an intermediary at 1-703-555-0198. The call on the third line is to an international number, which might belong to a foreign national or a U.S. person. The call in the fourth line was probably ordering a pizza, since a directory of telephone numbers reveals that the called number is a pizza shop.

2.1.2 Analysis

Intelligence collection results in large databases holding records that are expected to have intelligence value. (Table 2.1 provides a hypothetical example of records in such a database.) In counterterrorism investigations, an analyst generally starts with a "seed," an identifier of a communications endpoint that has been obtained in the course of intelligence gathering and is deemed relevant to a possible threat. The analyst uses the seed identifier to formulate one or more queries of the databases to seek more information, e.g., identifiers for other parties communicating with the seed. The analyst may also query for communications content, if it exists or can be obtained. Thus analysts can build a pattern of a seed's connections to other parties and/or to other data that provide a richer and fuller picture of that party's role within a larger enterprise, such as a terrorist organization. Other databases may be consulted as well. In this way, analysts can build a network that depicts how parties of interest relate to one another and characterize the activities of each of the parties in a network or more formally structured enterprise.

Analysts use a variety of software tools as they work with SIGINT data. They may use tools to formulate queries or display the results. They may set up "standing queries" (which need special approval) that run each day to report new events associated with their active targets. Using results of queries of the data, they build a record of data and evidence for investigations in a "working store," a set of digital files separate from the SIGINT databases.

2.1.3 Dissemination

The last step in the SIGINT process is dissemination. SIGINT analysts will routinely disseminate the results of their work to others, both inside and outside the IC. For example, NSA analysts working on a specific terrorism investigation might disseminate their findings to other analysts and collectors who are working on related issues or directly to policy makers who may choose to take action based on the SIGINT.

Like the initial collection, SIGINT dissemination is governed by various laws and regulations designed to protect the sources and methods involved in the collection as well as the privacy and civil liberties of the subjects of the collection, especially if the intelligence involves U.S. persons. Specifically to the latter, and pursuant to U.S. Signals Intelligence Directive (USSID) 18,[6] such reports will normally cloak the identity of U.S. persons until a reader of the report specifically asks for the identity to be disclosed and provides a valid reason for the release, such as initiating a further investigation. This process is designed to ensure that both the requesting agency and NSA, as the disseminator of the information, can verify that disclosing this sensitive information is appropriate and necessary to understand the foreign intelligence value of the report.

2.2 BULK AND TARGETED COLLECTION . . .

Bulk collection results in a database in which a significant portion of the data pertains to identifiers not relevant to current targets. Such items usually refer to parties that have not been, are not now, and will not become subjects of interest. Moreover, they are not closely linked to anyone of that sort: knowing to whom these parties talk will not help locate threats or develop more information about threats. Bulk collection occurs because it is usually impossible to determine at the time of filtering and collection that a party will have no intelligence value. Although the amount of information retained from bulk collection is often large, and often larger than the amount of information retained from targeted collection, it is not their size that makes them "bulk." Rather, it is the (larger) proportion of extra data beyond currently known targets that defines them.

Targeted collection tries to reduce, insofar as possible, items about parties with no past, present, or future intelligence value. This is achieved by using discriminants that narrowly select relevant items to store. For example, if the email address hardcase45@example.com was obtained from a terrorist's smart phone when he was arrested, using a discriminant to instruct the filter to save only "email to or from hardcase45@example.com" would result in a targeted collection. Some or many of the people communicating with this person might turn out to have no intelligence value, but the collection is far more selective than, say, collecting all email to or from anyone with an email address served by aol.com. A discriminant could be a top-level

---

6. National Security Agency, "United States Signals Intelligence Directive USSID SP0018, (U) Legal Compliance and U.S. Persons Minimization Procedures," Issue Date January 25, 2011, approved for release on November 13, 2013, referred to as USSID 18, http://www.dni.gov/files/documents/1118/CLEANEDFinalUSSIDSP0018.pdf.

Internet domain, a country code (e.g., .cn for China, .fr for France), a date on which communication occurred, a device type, and so on. A discriminant could even refer to the content in a communication, such as "all email with the word 'nuclear' in it." Note that if a discriminant is broadly crafted, the filter may retain such a large proportion of data on people of no intelligence value that the collection cannot be called "targeted." . . .

The fundamental trade-off . . . is between more intrusive information collection that may yield extremely valuable information about threats unknown at the time of collection and less intrusive information collection that may miss information about dangerous threats.

Bulk and targeted collection can apply to many different kinds of communication modalities — telephone, email, instant message, and so on. Various web-based applications such as electronic banking or online shopping that allow users to exchange information electronically are among these modalities, even if they are not usually thought of as means for communication, per se. . . .

Notes and Questions

1. *Redundancy.* Recall that one aim of intelligence collection is redundancy: send as many INTs as possible to pursue the same issue, resulting in all-source intelligence. Can you see the value in this purposeful overkill? Do you see particular strengths or weaknesses in any of the INTs that would cause you to emphasize or reduce its role in collection?

2. *Wheat vs. Chaff.* Technical collection systems are like vacuum cleaners. They sweep up lots of information, only some of which may be useful for intelligence purposes. Billions of telephones generate more billions of calls every day, not counting the countless text messages, tweets, and other means of interactive communication. The National Security Agency (NSA) records 650 million events each day (apart from its metadata program, reviewed in Chapter 22), and it produces 10,000 daily reports, relying on key-word searches of collected data. Mark M. Lowenthal, *Intelligence: From Secrets to Policy* 97 (7th ed. 2017). Can you see downside risks in relying on these technical systems?

C. COVERT ACTIONS

Covert action is a means to implement policy and is intended to influence people and events without revealing the source, or perhaps even the existence, of the influence. Although covert action had its heyday as an instrument of the broad-based Cold War struggle against the Soviet Union, current and future threats continue to provide situations where it may be the preferred means of achieving policy objectives.

Since its coming of age as an instrument of U.S. policy after World War II, covert action has taken various forms, from barely more intrusive than diplomacy to large-scale military operations. What they all have in common is an intent that the hand of the United States be invisible — that the operation be "plausibly deniable." By contrast, *clandestine military operations* (for example, secret killing of enemy sentries) are initially secret for operational reasons, but are not intended to remain secret after the operations are concluded.

At one extreme, *propaganda* is a covert action to spread information or misinformation that has been generated by the United States with some policy objective in mind. For example, the CIA might pay foreign journalists to write stories favorable to a U.S. position or critical of a foreign government. Or the stories might start rumors of local government unrest or economic troubles that could spur citizens to act against their government. Propaganda operations can produce *blowback*—as when a false story planted by the CIA is reported by media in the United States. With worldwide digitization of the news and the 24-hour news cycle, some blowback is nearly inevitable, creating a dilemma for government officials in deciding whether to respond to a false story.

Political action often complements propaganda by inserting an intelligence operation into the politics of another nation. Money may be spent to support friends or to work against foes, or locals may be hired to disrupt political rallies or jam publications. A variant, *economic action*, works to cause economic hardship in a targeted nation. Some techniques might use propaganda to spread false rumors about prices or food stocks, for example. More aggressive measures might attempt to destroy crops or inject counterfeit currency into a targeted nation's money supply. Economic sanctions are, of course, another form of such action, but they are public and typically administered by the Department of the Treasury, not the core intelligence community.

Farther along an intrusiveness scale, *sabotage* deliberately destroys property or facilities in a targeted nation. Sabotage may, for example, accompany economic action. Or it may be used to thwart the development of an enemy's new weapons system. In one instance U.S. efforts to stop or slow down Iran's nuclear development program reportedly included damaging equipment and replacement parts by engaging in cyber sabotage—the Stuxnet malware—to affect computers and destroy centrifuges that were instrumental in the Iranian nuclear program. Indeed, cyberspace methods can deliver all of the covert action types described above. Because such actions are covert, of course, important questions about their legality may be difficult to answer. And if they are kept secret even from Congress, they may prove impossible to regulate or monitor.

The United States has also participated in *coups d'etat*, overthrowing the governments of other nations either directly or through surrogates. In Iran in 1953 and Guatemala in 1954, for example, such coups succeeded in toppling the national governments. In Chile, the United States undertook a range of covert actions in the early 1970s designed to weaken the democratically elected Chilean government, before Chileans perpetrated a coup of their own, apparently without direct U.S. support.

Some of these coups involved *assassinations* (or at least planned assassinations) of government officials or political leaders. A covert action could also entail an assassination without a coup.

Finally, *paramilitary operations* involve secret military aid and training for surrogate fighters who advance U.S. policy objectives. Because paramilitary operations involve unattributed uses of force, they have always been controversial. Such actions take a variety of forms:

> At one extreme, paramilitary operations have been tantamount to full-scale wars—"covert" only in the sense that the United States wanted to be able to deny that it was

> directly involved. Witness the "secret war" in Laos, an unadmitted war on the cheap, with CIA paramilitary specialists providing the advice and Laotian hill tribesmen doing the fighting. . . . Like earlier CIA paramilitary campaigns in Korea, Laos was part of an open American war; if the campaigns were meant to be secret, neither the war nor its purposes were.
>
> At the other end of the spectrum, some paramilitary operations have amounted to little more than the clandestine transfer of a few weapons or of small amounts of training—for instance, for "palace guards" to protect friendly heads of state who would prefer not to be widely known as protected by the United States. . . .
>
> All these paramilitary operations involved the same elements: money and weaponry for groups and movements the United States was supporting, plus clandestine ways to transfer both, plus CIA officers and others to provide training and advice. The weaponry was "sterile"—that is, not easy to identify as coming from the United States. . . .
>
> To backstop these paramilitary operations, the CIA has developed networks of air carriers, some CIA "fronts," and some contractors to move arms and supplies—if not secretly, then at least as less visibly "American." [Gregory F. Treverton, *Covert Action: The Limits of American Intervention in the Postwar World* 26-27 (1987).]

The law distinguishes paramilitary operations from those conducted by U.S. military *special operations forces (SOF)*. The United States has a Special Operations Command (SOCOM), comprised of uniformed military personnel conducting combat missions not performed by regular military units. Special forces may operate secretly, and the United States may deny their missions, but members of the uniformed military do not normally conduct what U.S. law calls "covert action." We say "normally" because Special Forces personnel may engage in covert action, or may cooperate with the CIA in a covert action. In fact, there is an ongoing debate in the United States about whether the CIA or DOD should be responsible for paramilitary operations—sometimes called the "Title 10/Title 50 debate"—because 10 U.S.C. generally governs uses of military force, while 50 U.S.C. generally governs covert actions by the intelligence community. We will examine elements of the debate in Chapter 19.

In the years after the 9/11 attacks, the CIA also assumed a growing role in a shadow war against Al Qaeda, ISIS, and their allies in countries distant from the recognized battlefields in Afghanistan and Iraq. In an increasingly stepped-up campaign against Al Qaeda early in the Obama administration, the CIA increasingly became "a paramilitary organization as much as a spying agency." Scott Shane, Mark Mazzetti & Robert F. Worth, *Secret Assault on Terrorism Widens on Two Continents*, N.Y. Times, Aug. 15, 2010. The CIA activities have not been publicly acknowledged, and many of its paramilitary and other intelligence operations have been outsourced to private contractors, whose accountability remains in question. *Id.*

Two other forms of covert action deserve mention here. *Targeted killings*, addressed in some detail in Chapter 13, may or may not be carried out covertly, depending on whether they are conducted by the CIA or the military. If they are conducted by the military, they may not follow the usual legal procedures for covert actions. Another variant of covert action is *extraordinary rendition*, described briefly in Chapter 33. These secret actions involve seizing a person abroad and transporting him to another country for detention in U.S. custody, or sending him to a different state, where he may be subject to coercive interrogation that U.S. officials are forbidden to conduct.

Notes and Questions

1. *Covert vs. Secret.* Most intelligence operations abroad are conducted secretly. So, sometimes, are military operations to prepare the battlefield, scout the enemy, or operate behind enemy lines. Are these latter military actions therefore covert actions? If not, what distinguishes them from covert actions?

2. *"Routine" Espionage vs. Covert Operations.* Although the discovery and arrest of a foreign spy may occasionally spark a protest, there is a broad understanding among governments that they will spy on one another. Covert actions, on the other hand, may more often cause outrage, which is one reason that governments try to make them plausibly deniable. Why the outrage? What often makes them more controversial than "mere" espionage?

Even the population of a state that conducts covert actions may share such outrage. Why? What risks might plausible deniability of such actions pose in a democratic state?

INTRODUCING INTELLIGENCE: SUMMARY OF BASIC PRINCIPLES

- Intelligence operations consist of collecting and analyzing intelligence, and of conducting covert actions abroad with plausible deniability — that is, in such a manner that, if the action is exposed, the state that carried it out can credibly deny involvement.

- The intelligence cycle is an idealized depiction of intelligence collection. The needs of intelligence consumers (typically senior officers of the executive branch or military officers) are translated into intelligence requirements by senior intelligence managers, who task collectors to fulfill them. The collectors acquire raw intelligence, which is processed into finished intelligence by analysts and then distributed to consumers.

- Intelligence can be characterized in part by how it is collected. It includes human intelligence (HUMINT) (collected in part by espionage), geospatial intelligence (GEOINT), signals intelligence (SIGINT) (collected in part by electronic surveillance of telephone, radio, and Internet communications), imagery intelligence (IMINT) (collected in part by satellite surveillance), measurement and signatures intelligence (MASINT), and open-source intelligence (OSINT). Because most agencies in the intelligence community are tasked with collecting only some kinds of intelligence, the community is often said to be "stovepiped," with each agency operating as a distinct stovepipe for collection.

- SIGINT has achieved growing significance with the rapid expansion of electronic communications and the corresponding increase (thus far) in electronic surveillance capabilities. The huge volume of electronic communications requires extraction of signals, filtering (often by "discriminants," such as word searches and their analogs), and storage as part of the collection process, followed by analysis by both computers and human beings. SIGINT presents a tradeoff between more intrusive collection in bulk (beyond currently identified targets) for possible future targeted analysis, and less intrusive targeted collection, which may miss intelligence whose value will only be known at some future time.

- Covert actions range from propaganda, political action, economic action, sabotage, coups, and assassination, to paramilitary operations and proxy wars. What they have in common is the objective of influencing political, economic, or military conditions abroad, and the expectation of plausible deniability. While a successful covert action is therefore at least partly secret, not every secret operation is covert. Thus, clandestine military operations are normally secret only until they are underway or concluded, and not intended to remain secret.

The Intelligence Community: Organization and Authority

This chapter addresses the organization of — and legal authorities for — the intelligence community. Here we explore both statutory and executive authorities, then review two rogue intelligence community operations that influenced subsequent reforms. After that, we focus on the intelligence budget and management problems inside the intelligence community. How is the intelligence budget created, managed, and shared with citizens? How is electronic surveillance managed and overseen? What legal arrangements help ensure that the collection and dissemination of that information do not threaten personal freedoms? Finally, we consider problems of coordinating and sharing intelligence.

A. AUTHORITY FOR INTELLIGENCE ACTIVITIES

1. Statutory Authorities

General George Washington employed a cadre of spies and saboteurs during the Revolutionary War, the most famous of whom was Nathan Hale. Indeed, his intelligence agents played an important role in winning U.S. independence. Likewise, President Abraham Lincoln relied heavily on secret intelligence collection during the Civil War. One of his agents reportedly served as a housemaid for Confederate President Jefferson Davis. Until World War II, intelligence was chiefly the responsibility of the military services (augmented by the FBI domestically). Caught by surprise when the Japanese bombed Pearl Harbor, wartime intelligence slowly developed a civilian capacity in the Office of Strategic Services (OSS), and, by war's end, the Central Intelligence Group (CIG). *See* Tim Weiner, *Legacy of Ashes: The History of the CIA* 3-19 (2007). But at the end of the war, there still was no coherent national intelligence service and no statutory authority for one.

That changed in 1947 with the passage of legislation that, now much amended, still forms the charter for both the defense and intelligence communities. National Security Act of 1947, Pub. L. No. 80-253, 61 Stat. 495 (codified as amended in scattered sections of 10 & 50 U.S.C.).

The September 11, 2001, attacks on the World Trade Center and the Pentagon prompted numerous critiques of what some regarded as massive failures of intelligence. *See, e.g.*, S. Select Comm. on Intelligence & H. Permanent Select Comm. on Intelligence, *Joint Inquiry into Intelligence Community Activities Before and After the Terrorist Attacks of September 11, 2001*, S. Rep. No. 107-351, H.R. Rep. No. 107-792 (2002); Nat'l Comm'n on Terrorist Attacks Upon the United States, *The 9/11 Commission Report* (2004).

The two congressional intelligence committees and the 9/11 Commission found that inadequate organization and management of the intelligence community prevented the head of the CIA, then designated as Director of Central Intelligence (DCI), from ensuring that information about the hijackers' plans was shared with various agency analysts, who could have "connected the dots" and uncovered the plot in advance. *9/11 Commission Report, supra,* at 400. The 9/11 Commission also noted that limited legal authority forced the DCI to "direct agencies without controlling them." *Id.* at 357. The commission pointed out that, especially for intelligence elements within the Department of Defense (DOD), the DCI "does not receive an appropriation for their activities, and therefore does not control their purse strings." *Id.* Similarly, the congressional joint inquiry found that even after DCI George J. Tenet ordered the intelligence community to give the Osama bin Laden network its highest priority, his words had little effect beyond the CIA. *Joint Inquiry, supra,* at 236.

Meanwhile, the Bush administration's case for the 2003 Iraq war relied heavily on intelligence-based assertions that the Saddam Hussein regime had stockpiles of weapons of mass destruction (WMD) that would imminently be used against the United States and its allies. After President Bush declared an end to major combat operations in Iraq and investigators cleared the battlefield rubble, no WMD were found. In 2005, a presidentially appointed commission found "that the Intelligence Community was dead wrong in almost all of its pre-war judgments about Iraq's weapons of mass destruction." Comm'n on the Intelligence Capabilities of the United States Regarding Weapons of Mass Destruction (Silberman/Robb Commission), *Report to the President of the United States* (transmittal letter) (Mar. 31, 2005). The commission found an "inability to collect good information," "serious errors in analyzing" the information collected, and a failure to distinguish assumptions from evidence in its analysis. *Id.*

The intelligence failures of September 11 and in Iraq appeared to many observers as symptomatic of a larger struggle by our nation's intelligence agencies to confront the post-Cold War environment. Instead of focusing on the Soviet Union as the dominant threat, as it had since the origins of the CIA in 1947, the intelligence community now faced dozens of high-priority targets that included not only states but also highly diffuse transnational terrorism, insurgents, crime, and weapons proliferation networks. Worse yet, advances in technology and potential dual uses of goods made detection of weapons and facilities harder and made their concealment easier.

In its July 2004 report, the 9/11 Commission recommended several changes in the structure of the intelligence community:

- unifying strategic intelligence and operational planning against Islamist terrorists across the foreign-domestic divide with a National Counterterrorism Center;
- unifying the intelligence community with a new National Intelligence Director;

- unifying the many participants in the counterterrorism effort and their knowledge in a network-based information-sharing system that transcends traditional governmental boundaries;
- unifying and strengthening congressional oversight to improve quality and accountability; and
- strengthening the FBI and homeland defenders. [*9/11 Commission Report, supra,* at 399-400.]

Partly in response to the recommendations of the 9/11 Commission, in December 2004 Congress approved the most extensive reorganization of the U.S. intelligence community in more than half a century. *See* Intelligence Reform and Terrorism Prevention Act of 2004 (IRTPA), Pub. L. No. 108-458, 118 Stat. 3638. (Unless otherwise noted, references hereinafter are to sections of the National Security Act of 1947 as amended by IRTPA and as currently codified.)

The 2004 Act responded — at least in part — to those who sought the creation of a cabinet-level intelligence czar. The Act created the position of Director of National Intelligence (DNI), appointed by the President and confirmed by the Senate, and subject to the "authority, direction, and control of the President." 50 U.S.C. §3023(b) (2018). The DNI replaces the DCI as "head of the intelligence community" and serves as principal advisor to the President, National Security Council, and Homeland Security Council "for intelligence matters related to the national security." *Id.* §3023(b)(1), (2). The DNI also oversees and directs implementation of the National Intelligence Program. *Id.* §3023(b)(3). The DNI may not simultaneously serve as Director of the CIA or as head of any other component of the intelligence community. *Id.* §3023(c).

a. The DNI

The National Security Act describes the authority of the DNI and of the CIA only in the most general terms. Regarding the DNI, the Act provides:

50 U.S.C. §3024. Responsibilities and Authorities of the Director of National Intelligence

(a) Provision of intelligence

(1) The Director of National Intelligence shall be responsible for ensuring that national intelligence is provided —

(A) to the President;

(B) to the heads of departments and agencies of the executive branch;

(C) to the Chairman of the Joint Chiefs of Staff and senior military commanders;

(D) to the Senate and House of Representatives and the committees thereof; and

(E) to such other persons as the Director of National Intelligence determines to be appropriate.

(2) Such national intelligence should be timely, objective, independent of political considerations, and based upon all sources available to the intelligence community and other appropriate entities.

(b) Access to intelligence. Unless otherwise directed by the President, the Director of National Intelligence shall have access to all national intelligence and intelligence related to the national security which is collected by any Federal department, agency, or other entity, except as otherwise provided by law or, as appropriate, under guidelines agreed upon by the Attorney General and the Director of National Intelligence. . . .

(f) Tasking and other authorities

(1)(A) The Director of National Intelligence shall—

(i) establish objectives, priorities, and guidance for the intelligence community to ensure timely and effective collection, processing, analysis, and dissemination (including access by users to collected data consistent with applicable law and, as appropriate, the guidelines referred to in subsection (b) and analytic products generated by or within the intelligence community) of national intelligence;

(ii) determine requirements and priorities for, and manage and direct the tasking of, collection, analysis, production, and dissemination of national intelligence by elements of the intelligence community, including—

(I) approving requirements (including those requirements responding to needs provided by consumers) for collection and analysis; and

(II) resolving conflicts in collection requirements and in the tasking of national collection assets of the elements of the intelligence community; and

(iii) provide advisory tasking to intelligence elements of those agencies and departments not within the National Intelligence Program. [See *infra* p. 530.] . . .

(4) The Director of National Intelligence shall ensure compliance with the Constitution and laws of the United States by the Central Intelligence Agency and shall ensure such compliance by other elements of the intelligence community through the host executive departments that manage the programs and activities that are part of the National Intelligence Program. . . .

(6) The Director of National Intelligence shall establish requirements and priorities for foreign intelligence information to be collected under the Foreign Intelligence Surveillance Act of 1978 (50 U.S.C. 1801 et seq.), and provide assistance to the Attorney General to ensure that information derived from electronic surveillance or physical searches under that Act is disseminated so it may be used efficiently and effectively for national intelligence purposes, except that the Director shall have no authority to direct or undertake electronic surveillance or physical search operations pursuant to that Act unless authorized by statute or Executive order. . . .

(8) The Director of National Intelligence shall perform such other functions as the President may direct. . . .

(h) Analysis. To ensure the most accurate analysis of intelligence is derived from all sources to support national security needs, the Director of National Intelligence shall—

(1) implement policies and procedures—

(A) to encourage sound analytic methods and tradecraft throughout the elements of the intelligence community;

(B) to ensure that analysis is based upon all sources available; and

(C) to ensure that the elements of the intelligence community regularly conduct competitive analysis of analytic products, whether such products are produced by or disseminated to such elements; . . .

(i) Protection of intelligence sources and methods

(1) The Director of National Intelligence shall protect intelligence sources and methods from unauthorized disclosure. . . .

b. The CIA

Concerning the Central Intelligence Agency, the National Security Act provides:

50 U.S.C. §3036. Director of the Central Intelligence Agency

(a) Director of Central Intelligence Agency. There is a Director of the Central Intelligence Agency who shall be appointed by the President, by and with the advice and consent of the Senate.

(b) Supervision. The Director of the Central Intelligence Agency shall report to the Director of National Intelligence regarding the activities of the Central Intelligence Agency.

(c) Duties. The Director of the Central Intelligence Agency shall —

(1) serve as the head of the Central Intelligence Agency; and

(2) carry out the responsibilities specified in subsection (d).

(d) Responsibilities. The Director of the Central Intelligence Agency shall —

(1) collect intelligence through human sources and by other appropriate means, except that the Director of the Central Intelligence Agency shall have no police, subpoena, or law enforcement powers or internal security functions;

(2) correlate and evaluate intelligence related to the national security and provide appropriate dissemination of such intelligence;

(3) provide overall direction for and coordination of the collection of national intelligence outside the United States through human sources by elements of the intelligence community authorized to undertake such collection and, in coordination with other departments, agencies, or elements of the United States Government which are authorized to undertake such collection, ensure that the most effective use is made of resources and that appropriate account is taken of the risks to the United States and those involved in such collection; and

(4) perform such other functions and duties related to intelligence affecting the national security as the President or the Director of National Intelligence may direct. . . .

c. The FBI

The National Security Act did not address the authority of the FBI, which preceded it. The Attorney General is expressly vested with "primary investigative responsibility for all Federal crimes of terrorism." 18 U.S.C. §2332b(f) (2018). The FBI, in contrast, has scant statutory authority to carry out its mission. Lacking a legislative charter, the FBI operates on the basis of the Attorney General's authority found in 28 U.S.C. §533 (2018) to appoint officials:

(1) to detect and prosecute crimes against the United States;

(2) to assist in the protection of the person of the President; and . . .

(4) to conduct such other investigations regarding official matters under the control of the Department of Justice and the Department of State as may be directed by the Attorney General.

The FBI also draws investigative authority from statutes authorizing specific methods or purposes for collection, such as the Foreign Intelligence Surveillance Act (FISA), analyzed in Chapter 21.

d. The NSA

The NSA is the largest agency within the intelligence community. It is devoted to communications security and to collecting and disseminating signals intelligence (SIGINT). In October 1952, President Truman signed a secret directive to create the NSA in order to provide an effective structure for coordinating SIGINT activities for civilian and military consumers. Richard A. Best Jr., *The National Security Agency: Issues for Congress* (Cong. Res. Serv. RL30740), Jan. 16, 2001; *see* Jeffrey T. Richelson,

The U.S. Intelligence Community 32 (7th ed. 2016). Apart from annual appropriations for the NSA based on secret briefings about SIGINT activities before the appropriations committees, the first major legislation dealing with NSA was the National Security Agency Act of 1959, Pub. L. No. 86-36, 73 Stat. 63. It authorized the Secretary of Defense to "establish such positions, and to appoint . . . such officers and employees, in the National Security Agency, as may be necessary to carry out the functions of such agency." *Id.* §2, 73 Stat. at 63.

Until it was revealed that U.S. intelligence agencies were spying on domestic groups opposed to the Vietnam War, there was little interest in the NSA among members of Congress or the public, and little knowledge about the secretive agency. In response to these revelations, in 1975 the Senate created the Select Committee to Study Governmental Operations with Respect to Intelligence Activities (later known as the Church Committee after its Chair, Senator Frank Church of Idaho). During the Church Committee hearings in 1976, NSA Director Lieutenant General Lew Allen Jr. provided the first open-session congressional testimony about NSA SIGINT activities and the NSA practice of establishing "watch lists," discussed in *Halkin v. Helms*, 690 F.2d 977 (D.C. Cir. 1982), *infra* p. 514. Although the Church Committee and its House counterpart, known as the Pike Committee, acknowledged the continuing importance of NSA's foreign intelligence collection activities, both committees also recommended specific authorizing legislation for NSA that would have included strict limits on monitoring the communications of U.S. citizens. *See* Church Committee, *Final Report of the Select Comm. to Study Governmental Operations with Respect to Intelligence Activities*, S. Rep. No. 94-755, bk. I, at 464 (1976), *available at* http://www.intelligence.senate.gov/churchcommittee.html; *Recommendations of the Final Report of the House Select Comm. on Intelligence*, H.R. Rep. No. 94-833, at 3 (1976). The congressional initiative toward a "legislative charter" for the intelligence agencies was slowed when President Ford issued a broad executive order for management of the intelligence community in 1976, Exec. Order 11,905, 41 Fed. Reg. 7707 (Feb. 18, 1976), and the initiative died in the 1979-1980 congressional session amidst partisan disputes, when the Soviet invasion of Afghanistan caught the United States by surprise and provoked new efforts to invigorate intelligence capabilities.

Congress did, however, enact the Privacy Act in 1974, limiting the collection, retention, and dissemination of personal information about U.S. citizens, and the Foreign Intelligence Surveillance Act (FISA) in 1978, authorizing and regulating electronic surveillance in the United States to obtain foreign intelligence. Because the NSA conducts electronic surveillance, both measures became an important part of the NSA's regulatory framework. We address FISA in detail in Chapters 21 and 22.

In 1992, the National Security Act of 1947 was amended to state that

> the Secretary of Defense shall ensure . . . through the National Security Agency (except as otherwise directed by the President or the National Security Council), the continued operation of an effective unified organization for the conduct of signals intelligence activities and shall ensure that the product is disseminated in a timely manner to authorized recipients. [Intelligence Authorization Act for Fiscal Year 1993, Pub. L. No. 102-496, §706, 106 Stat. 3180, 3194-3195 (1992) (codified as amended at 50 U.S.C. §3038(b)(1) (2018).]

The power of NSA computers to collect massive amounts of SIGINT data is staggering. NSA "employs more mathematicians than any other organization in the world and [its facilities contain] the densest concentration of computer power on the planet." Patrick Radden Keefe, *Chatter: Dispatches from the Secret World of Global Eavesdropping* 8 (2005). It uses sophisticated key-word searching and other techniques (such as data mining and data analytics) to cull and analyze large quantities of electronic data before output is delivered to other agencies. Its technical capacity actually far outstrips the human capacity to evaluate or use all the information it collects.

The Agency does not act upon the intelligence it collects. Instead, NSA passes that intelligence to various civilian and military agencies and officials. In its communications security role, NSA uses its SIGINT capabilities to detect espionage and other intelligence activities directed against the United States. For example, throughout much of the Cold War, NSA conducted a program code-named VENONA that used signal intercepts to detect Soviet espionage in the United States. VENONA helped identify Alger Hiss, Julius Rosenberg, Klaus Fuchs, and others who served as Soviet agents. *See* Robert L. Benson, *The Venona Story* (Nat'l Security Agency/Cent. Security Serv.) (n.d.), https://www.nsa.gov/Portals/70/documents/about/cryptologic-heritage/historical-figures-publications/coldwar/venona_story.pdf.

e. The National Security Council

The National Security Council (NSC) was created in the 1947 Act "to advise the President with respect to the integration of domestic, foreign, and military policies relating to the national security." 50 U.S.C. §3021(a) (2018). Its original statutory members were the President, the Vice President, the Secretary of State, and the Secretary of Defense. The Secretary of Energy was added as a statutory member in 2007. Other cabinet members and executive officials have been authorized by Congress to attend and participate in NSC meetings, subject to the President's direction (e.g., the Chairman of the Joint Chiefs of Staff and the Director of National Intelligence), or have simply been invited by Presidents to attend. *See* Cody M. Brown, *The National Security Council: A Legal History of the President's Most Powerful Advisers* 71-72 (2008).

The statutory functions of the NSC include the following:

> Consistent with the direction of the President, the functions of the Council shall be to —
>
> (1) advise the President with respect to the integration of domestic, foreign, and military policies relating to the national security so as to enable the Armed Forces and the other departments and agencies of the United States Government to cooperate more effectively in matters involving the national security;
>
> (2) assess and appraise the objectives, commitments, and risks of the United States in relation to the actual and potential military power of the United States, and make recommendations thereon to the President;
>
> (3) make recommendations to the President concerning policies on matters of common interest to the departments and agencies of the United States Government concerned with the national security; and
>
> (4) coordinate without assuming operational authority, the United States Government response to malign foreign influence operations and campaigns. [50 U.S.C. §3021(b).]

Originally, the 1947 Act authorized an executive secretariat to serve as staff to the NSC. In 1953, however, President Eisenhower created the position of Assistant to the President for National Security Affairs, now known as National Security Adviser, pursuant to a statute that authorizes the appointment of "employees in the White House

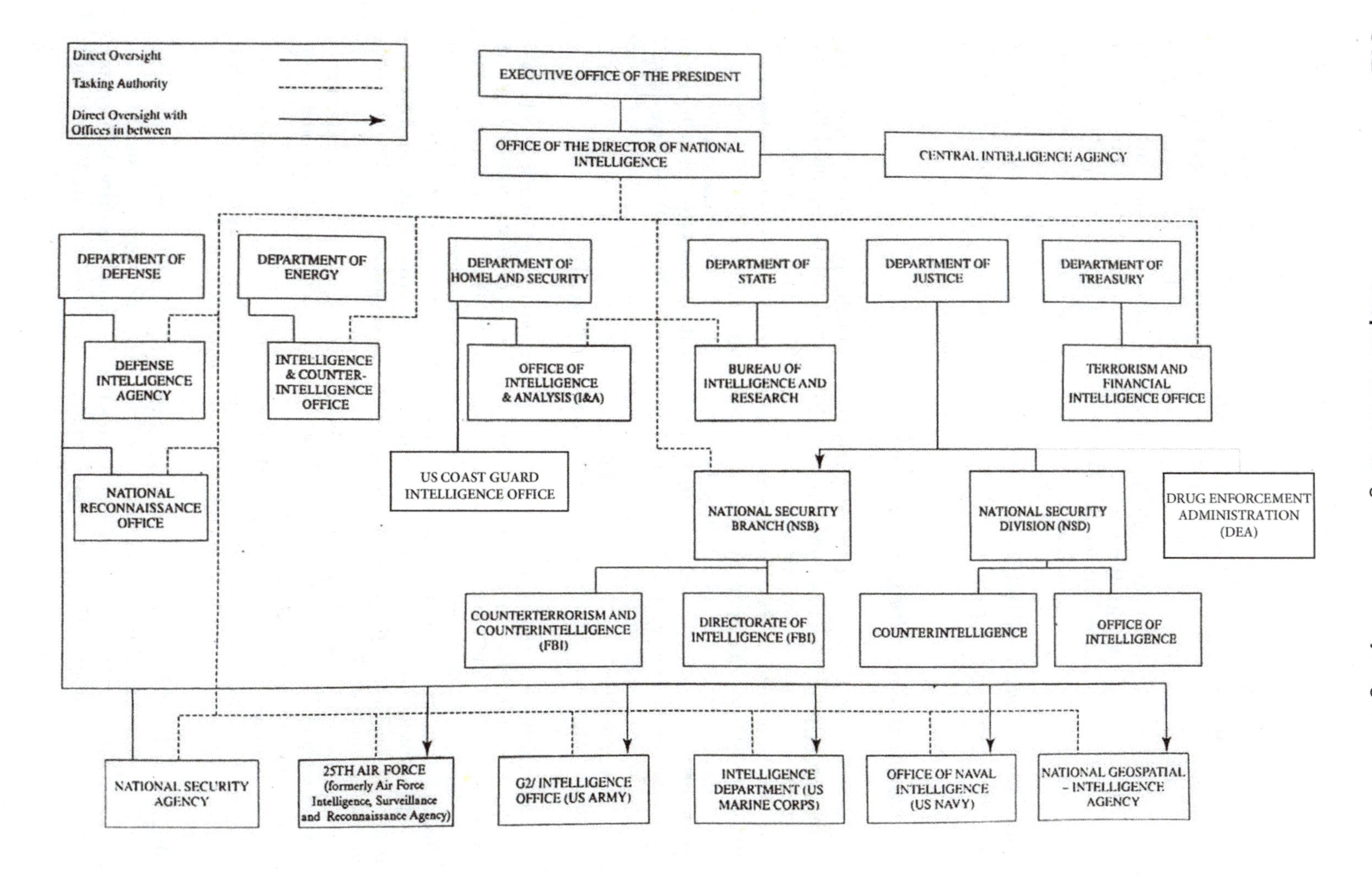

Adapted from Carroll Publishing, Bethesda, Md. (2005), used by permission.

Office." 3 U.S.C. §105(a)(1) (2018). This individual supervises the NSC staff and briefs the President on national security affairs. Nevertheless, the National Security Adviser's role has varied widely since then.

Every President since Truman has personalized the organization of the NSC and its staff and functions. President Trump signed *National Security Presidential Memorandum 4, Organization of the National Security Council, the Homeland Security Council, and Subcommittees*, 82 Fed. Reg. 16,881 (Apr. 6, 2017), which includes the Chair of the Joint Chiefs of Staff, DNI, and CIA Director as regular attendees of NSC meetings. The Homeland Security Council (HSC) and component committees are subordinate to the National Security Adviser.

Notes and Questions

1. *Why a Statute?* During World War II, intelligence collection abroad (and some at home) was carried out largely by military services, the Army and Navy. Some covert operations were directed by an agency called the Office of Strategic Services. When the war ended, the Administration debated whether to continue these practices based on executive authority or to seek statutory approval for them. Why would President Truman have sought legislative authority for intelligence operations? What impact did passage of the National Security Act of 1947 have on claims of inherent executive power to conduct such operations?

2. *The CIA's Duties.* What does it mean to say that "the Director of the Central Intelligence Agency shall . . . have no police, subpoena, or law enforcement powers or internal security functions"? 50 U.S.C. §3036(d)(1). To what extent may the CIA act within the United States? How are CIA authorities different when operating abroad?

3. *Authority to Create the NSA?* Did the President possess constitutional authority in 1952 to create an agency to collect SIGINT for foreign intelligence purposes? To collect SIGINT in the United States? The National Security Act of 1947 created a Secretary of Defense and states that "[u]nder the direction of the President and subject to the provisions of this Act he shall . . . [e]stablish general policies and programs for the National Military Establishment and for all the departments and agencies therein." Pub. L. No. 80-253, §202(a)(1), 61 Stat. 495, 500. Does the 1947 Act, the 1959 National Security Agency Act, or the 1992 amendment to the 1947 Act authorize the activities of the NSA?

4. *Who Makes Intelligence Policy?* It is clear from the 1947 Act that the NSC was created neither to make national security decisions nor to carry them out. The same may be said of the later-created National Security Adviser. In practice, however, both the NSC staff and the National Security Adviser have occasionally engaged in operations, although these instances may be aberrations. Consider this assessment of the evolving role of the NSC:

> Since passage of the original National Security Act of 1947, Congress has left unchanged the fundamental purpose, function, and duties of the NSC. Each President has made an independent determination of the type of NSC that would best serve the nation. But over time, it is clear that the NSC has evolved from a limited advisory council to a vast network of interagency

> groups that are deeply involved in integrating national security policy development, oversight of implementation, and crisis management. This evolution has not been the result of congressional action, but rather presidential determination, rooted in the increasingly complex task of managing and optimizing U.S. national security. [Brown, *supra*, at 81.]

It is equally clear from the 1947 Act that the CIA was not meant to make intelligence policy, especially given the requirement that the CIA act at the direction of the NSC. However, the CIA has on occasion been the driving force in intelligence operations policymaking, notwithstanding the 1947 Act. If the NSC and the CIA are strictly confined to executive roles, who *does* establish intelligence policy?

5. Military Intelligence. The role for military intelligence agencies was not clearly spelled out in the 1947 Act:

> The 1947 Act provided no explicit charter for military intelligence. The charter and mission of military intelligence activities [were] established either by executive orders . . . or various National Security Council directives. These National Security Council Intelligence Directives (NSCIDs) were the principal means of establishing the roles and functions of all the various entities in the intelligence community. They composed the so-called "secret charter" for the CIA. However, most of them also permitted "departmental" intelligence activities, and in this way also provided the executive charter for the intelligence activities of the State Department and the Pentagon. However, the intelligence activities of the Department of Defense remained with the military rather than with the new Defense Department civilians. [Church Comm., *supra*, bk. I, at 21.]

The military regularly collected intelligence for its own operations long before the enactment of the National Security Act.

f. Rogue Operations

As you review what may seem to you to be increasingly arcane and perhaps restrictive statutory limits on an intelligence community whose work is essential to our security, it is easy to wonder if those limits go too far. It is therefore instructive to look briefly at two rogue operations — one by the CIA and one by the FBI — before turning to later-promulgated executive authorities, in order to appreciate the continuing tension between the necessary secrecy of what the intelligence community does and the risk that individual intelligence officers or whole agencies will imperil the very liberties they are charged with protecting. Consider the following episodes from our recent history.

Halkin v. Helms

United States Court of Appeals, District of Columbia Circuit, 1982
690 F.2d 977

MacKinnon, J. . . . Operation CHAOS, was an intelligence-gathering activity conducted by the CIA originally at the request of President Johnson which sought to determine the extent to which foreign governments or political organizations exerted influence on or provided support to domestic critics of the government's Vietnam policies. . . .

Over the course of several years, Operation CHAOS produced six reports for the White House and some thirty-four reports for cabinet-level officials, dealing with the subject of foreign influence on the domestic antiwar movement. In the normal course of its operations, CHAOS also produced a steady stream of reports to the FBI and other agencies detailing the results of its various intelligence activities with respect to the antiwar movement....

... [B]eginning in late 1969, the CHAOS office developed its own network of informants for the purposes of infiltrating various foreign antiwar groups located in foreign countries that might have had ties to domestic antiwar activity. Although the principal focus of such infiltration was foreign groups, it is now known that informants destined for such assignments were directed to infiltrate antiwar circles within the United States for the purpose of gaining knowledge of their operations and credibility as antiwar activists. In the course of these preliminary associations, CHAOS agents apparently supplied information on the activities of domestic antiwar groups, and this information was placed in the general CHAOS data base.

... Operation CHAOS made use of the facilities of other ongoing CIA surveillance programs. These included: (1) the CIA letter-opening program, which was directed at letters passing between the United States and the Soviet Union, and involved the examination of correspondence to and from individuals or organizations placed on a "watchlist"; (2) the Domestic Contact Service, a CIA office which solicits foreign intelligence information overtly from willing sources within the United States; (3) the CIA's "Project 2," which was directed at the infiltration of foreign intelligence targets by agents posing as dissident sympathizers and which, like CHAOS, had placed agents within domestic radical organizations for the purposes of training and establishment of dissident credentials; (4) the CIA's Project MERRIMAC, operated by the Office of Security, which was designed to infiltrate domestic antiwar and radical organizations thought to pose a threat to the security of CIA property and personnel; and (5) Project RESISTANCE, also a creature of the Office of Security, which gathered information on domestic groups without any actual infiltration.

From its inception, CHAOS also regularly received information from the FBI on that agency's investigations of the domestic antiwar movement....

In addition to the surveillance activities carried out under the aegis of Operation CHAOS, plaintiffs complained of the CIA's practice of obtaining the contents of international communications (telephone, telegraph and radio transmissions) by submitting subjects' names on "watchlists" to the National Security Agency (NSA). NSA possesses the technology to scan the mass of signals transmitted through various communications systems and then to select out by computer those messages in which certain words or phrases occur. It is thereby possible for that agency to acquire all communications over a monitored system in which, for example, a person's name is mentioned. Between 1967 and 1973, the FBI, the Secret Service, and military intelligence agencies, as well as the CIA, submitted the names of domestic individuals and organizations on watchlists to NSA, and ultimately acquired through NSA the international communications of over a thousand American citizens....

[Despite these findings, the court upheld the government's assertion of the state secrets privilege to prevent discovery that would have enabled any individual plaintiff to show that she was directly injured by the CIA's activities. Thus, the suit for damages and injunctive relief for violations of the Bill of Rights and the National Security Act of 1947 was dismissed, because the plaintiffs could not establish standing to sue.]

Select Committee to Study Governmental Operations with Respect to Intelligence Activities (Church Committee), Intelligence Activities and the Rights of Americans

S. Rep. No. 94-755, bk. II, at 86-89 (1976)

The FBI's initiation of COINTELPRO operations against the Ku Klux Klan, "Black Nationalists" and the "New Left" brought to bear upon a wide range of domestic groups the techniques previously developed to combat Communists and persons who happened to associate with them.

The start of each program coincided with significant national events. The Klan program followed the widely-publicized disappearance in 1964 of three civil rights workers in Mississippi. The "Black Nationalist" program was authorized in the aftermath of the Newark and Detroit riots in 1967. The "New Left" program developed shortly after student disruption of the Columbia University campus in the spring of 1968. While the initiating memoranda approved by Director Hoover do not refer to these specific events, it is clear that they shaped the context for the Bureau's decisions.

These programs were not directed at obtaining evidence for use in possible criminal prosecutions arising out of those events. Rather, they were secret programs—"under no circumstances" to be "made known outside the Bureau"—which used unlawful or improper acts to "disrupt" or "neutralize" the activities of groups and individuals targeted on the basis of imprecise criteria.

(1) *Klan and "White Hate" COINTELPRO.*—The expansion of Klan investigations, in response to pressure from President Johnson and Attorney General Kennedy, was accompanied by an internal Bureau decision to shift their supervision from the General Investigative Division to the Domestic Intelligence Division. One internal FBI argument for the transfer was that the Intelligence Division was "in a position to launch a disruptive counterintelligence program" against the Klan with the "same effectiveness" it had against the Communist Party.

Accordingly, in September 1964 a directive was sent to seventeen field offices instituting a COINTELPRO against the Klan and what the FBI considered to be other "White Hate" organizations (e.g., American Nazi Party, National States Rights Party) "to expose, disrupt, and otherwise neutralize" the activities of the groups, "their leaders, and adherents."

During the 1964-1971 period, when the program was in operation, 287 proposals for COINTELPRO actions against Klan and "White Hate" groups were authorized by FBI headquarters. Covert techniques used in this COINTELPRO included creating new Klan chapters to be controlled by Bureau informants and sending an anonymous letter designed to break up a marriage.

(2) *"Black Nationalist" COINTELPRO.*—The stated strategy of the "Black Nationalist" COINTELPRO instituted in 1967 was "to expose, disrupt, misdirect, discredit, or otherwise neutralize" such groups and their "leadership, spokesmen, members, and supporters." The larger objectives were to "counter" their "propensity for violence" and to "frustrate" their efforts to "consolidate their forces" or to "recruit new or youthful adherents." Field offices were instructed to exploit conflicts within and between groups; to use news media contacts to ridicule and otherwise discredit groups; to prevent "rabble rousers" from spreading their "philosophy" publicly; and to gather information on the "unsavory backgrounds" of group leaders.

In March 1968, the program was expanded from twenty-three to forty-one field offices and the following long-range goals were set forth:

(1) prevent the "coalition of militant black nationalist groups";
(2) prevent the rise of a "messiah" who could "unify and electrify" the movement, naming specifically Dr. Martin Luther King, Jr., Stokely Carmichael, and Elijah Muhammed;
(3) prevent violence by pinpointing "potential troublemakers" and "neutralizing" them before they "exercise their potential for violence";
(4) prevent groups and leaders from gaining "respectability" by discrediting them to the "responsible" Negro community, the "responsible" white community, "liberals" with "vestiges of sympathy" for militant black nationalists and "Negro radicals"; and
(5) "prevent these groups from recruiting young people."

After the Black Panther Party emerged as a group of national stature, FBI field offices were instructed to develop "imaginative and hard-hitting counterintelligence measures aimed at crippling the BPP." Particular attention was to be given to aggravating conflicts between the Black Panthers and rival groups in a number of cities where such conflict had already taken on the character of "gang warfare with attendant threats of murder and reprisals."

During 1967-1971, FBI headquarters approved 379 proposals for COINTELPRO actions against "black nationalists." These operations utilized dangerous and unsavory techniques which gave rise to the risk of death and often disregarded the personal rights and dignity of the victims.

(3) *"New Left" COINTELPRO.* — The most vaguely defined and haphazard of the COINTELPRO operations was that initiated against the "New Left" in May 1968. It was justified to the FBI Director by his subordinates on the basis of the following considerations:

> The nation was "undergoing an era of disruption and violence" which was "caused to a large extent" by individuals "generally connected with the New Left."
>
> Some of these "activists" were urging "revolution" and calling for "the defeat of the United States in Vietnam."
>
> The problem was not just that they committed "unlawful acts," but also that they "falsely" alleged police brutality, and that they "scurrilously attacked the Director and the Bureau" in an attempt to "hamper" FBI investigations and to "drive us off the college campuses."

Consequently, the COINTELPRO was intended to "expose, disrupt, and otherwise neutralize" the activities of "this group" and "persons connected with it." The lack of any clear definition of "New Left" meant, as an FBI supervisor testified, that "legitimate" and nonviolent antiwar groups were targeted because they were "lending aid and comfort" to more disruptive groups.

Further directives issued soon after initiation of the program urged field offices to "vigorously and enthusiastically" explore "every avenue of possible embarrassment" of New Left adherents. Agents were instructed to gather information on the "immorality" and the "scurrilous and depraved" behavior, "habits, and living conditions" of the members of targeted groups. This message was reiterated several months later, when the offices were taken to task for their failure to remain alert for and seek specific data depicting the "depraved nature and moral looseness of the New Left" and to "use this material in a vigorous and enthusiastic approach to neutralizing them."

In July 1968, the field offices were further prodded by FBI headquarters to:

(1) prepare leaflets using "the most obnoxious pictures" of New Left leaders at various universities;
(2) instigate "personal conflicts or animosities" between New Left leaders;
(3) create the impression that leaders are "informants for the Bureau or other law enforcement agencies" (the "snitch jacket" technique);
(4) send articles from student or "underground" newspapers which show "depravity" ("use of narcotics and free sex") of New Left leaders to university officials, donors, legislators, and parents;
(5) have members arrested on marijuana charges;
(6) send anonymous letters about a student's activities to parents, neighbors, and the parents' employers;
(7) send anonymous letters about New Left faculty members (signed "A Concerned Alumni" or "A Concerned Taxpayer") to university officials, legislators, Board of Regents, and the press;
(8) use "cooperative press contacts";
(9) exploit the "hostility" between New Left and Old Left groups;
(10) disrupt New Left coffee houses near military bases which are attempting to "influence members of the Armed forces";
(11) use cartoons, photographs, and anonymous letters to "ridicule" the New Left;
(12) use "misinformation" to "confuse and disrupt" New Left activities, such as by notifying members that events have been cancelled.

During the period 1968-1971, 291 COINTELPRO actions against the "New Left" were approved by headquarters. Particular emphasis was placed upon preventing the targeted individuals from public speaking or teaching and providing "misinformation" to confuse demonstrators.

Notes and Questions

1. Authority for Operation CHAOS? From the very start, Congress mandated that the CIA "shall have no police, subpoena, or law enforcement powers or internal security functions." 50 U.S.C. §3036(d)(1). Having just completed a worldwide conflict with a Nazi dictatorship in which the Gestapo (an acronym for "Geheime Staatspolizei" or "Secret State Police") had played a horrific role, Congress was determined that the CIA direct its collection efforts abroad and not engage in any internal policing.

Did the CIA violate this mandate in Operation CHAOS? Look again at the relevant provisions of the National Security Act of 1947, as amended. On one hand, what arguments could you make for the CIA from 50 U.S.C. §3024(i) (directing the DNI to protect intelligence sources and methods), or 50 U.S.C. §3036(d)(3) (directing collection of intelligence outside the United States)? On the other hand, what is the impact of the denial of "internal security" functions in 50 U.S.C. §3036(d)(1)? Could Operation CHAOS lawfully target Americans if the CIA or FBI suspected them of links to foreign powers? If you believe the operation exceeded statutory limits, does the Constitution supply the needed authority?

2. *Watch Lists.* If the *Halkin* court had reached the merits, how should it have ruled on the plaintiffs' complaints concerning the NSA's use of watch lists? Watch lists were developed by identifying individual names, subjects, locations, and the like within a mass of communications to separate useful intelligence from background "noise." Watch lists were thus precursors to contemporary data-mining techniques, including those at issue in the post-9/11 NSA domestic eavesdropping program discussed in Chapter 22, *infra.*

3. *Suing the FBI over COINTELPRO.* The provision of the National Security Act of 1947 that barred CIA involvement in domestic security and law enforcement made sense in part because the United States already had an internal federal police agency, the FBI, which was located within the Department of Justice and ultimately answerable to the nation's chief law enforcement officer, the Attorney General. The internal federal police were therefore embedded in a culture of law and law enforcement, and for that reason presumably sensitized to civil rights and liberties in general, and the rigid requirements of criminal justice in particular. Did the FBI protect those rights and liberties in the COINTELPRO operation?

In 1976, several Washington, D.C. area residents who had been politically active in anti-war and civil rights protests in the 1960s and early 1970s brought suit against the FBI and District of Columbia officials for alleged violations of constitutional rights related to the COINTELPRO program. In *Hobson v. Wilson,* 737 F.2d 1 (D.C. Cir. 1984), the plaintiffs prevailed against most of the defendants. As the Court of Appeals concluded, "Government action, taken with the intent to disrupt or destroy lawful organizations, or to deter membership in those groups, is absolutely unconstitutional." *Id.* at 29. What likely explains the different outcomes in *Halkin* and *Hobson*? Do you think the outcome would have been different in either case if the target had been suspected agents of the Islamic State? The Democratic National Committee?

4. *Avoiding CHAOS and COINTELPRO?* What statutory reforms, if any, to the intelligence authorities you have read would have prevented Operation CHAOS and COINTELPRO? What executive regulations could the President issue to do so?

2. Presidential Authority

As noted above, in 1975 the Senate created the Church Committee to ascertain "the extent, if any, to which illegal, improper, or unethical activities were engaged in by any agency of the Federal Government." S. Res. 21, 94th Cong. (1975). Its report included an ambitious legislative proposal for a charter to regulate activities of the intelligence community. Partly to preempt such legislation, President Ford responded to the Church Committee report by promulgating Executive Order No. 11,905, 41

Fed. Reg. 7707 (Feb. 18, 1976). The order created an Operations Advisory Group (OAG) with roughly the same membership recommended by the Church Committee. The OAG was charged with making a recommendation for each "special activity" and forwarding it, along with any dissents, to the President. An Intelligence Oversight Board (IOB) was also created to review "activities that raise questions of legality or propriety." In addition, the order prohibited government employees from participating in assassinations.

The Ford order was followed by a similar one from President Carter, although the Carter order also required the Director of the CIA to keep the congressional intelligence committees "fully and currently" informed of ongoing or "significant anticipated" activities. Exec. Order No. 12,036, 43 Fed. Reg. 3675 (Jan. 24, 1978).

In 1981, President Reagan issued yet another order that, as amended, continues to set out presidential direction for intelligence operations and collection today. Executive Order No. 12,333 (referred to by intelligence professionals as "twelve-triple-three") remains the most-nearly comprehensive regulatory framework for U.S. intelligence activities today. Developing a solid understanding of the order and what it does will pay dividends as you learn about other intelligence authorities in the chapters that follow.

Reading Executive Order No. 12,333

This order is the executive charter for intelligence collection. Read it carefully, as it will be invoked frequently in subsequent chapters.

- Turn first to the definitions in §3.5. Who is in the "intelligence community" (IC)? What is "foreign intelligence"? Who is a "U.S. person"? Why did the order bother to define U.S. persons? What is "covert action"?
- Now consider Part 1. How are intelligence activities distributed among the members of the IC? Compare the statutory authorities to the chart on p. 512. Who is in charge of the IC? Is the organizational structure enshrined in the order conducive to effective intelligence functions? To the oversight of intelligence activities?
- Many of the intelligence activities assigned to specific agencies are subject to rules and procedures approved by other entities, such as the Attorney General or heads of different agencies. But the order establishes various baselines for intelligence collection activities in Part 2. What are the baseline principles?
- Section 2.5 gives the Attorney General authority to approve intelligence techniques "for which a warrant would be required if undertaken for law enforcement purposes." What is the legal and practical significance of this delegation of authority from the President to the Attorney General?
- Where and against whom can the collection techniques described in §2.5 be used? Is the Attorney General's approval required for collection of intelligence abroad from non-U.S. persons? If not, why not?
- Does the Order authorize any member of the IC to violate U.S. law? Could it?

Executive Order No. 12,333
United States Intelligence Activities

46 Fed. Reg. 59,941 (Dec. 4, 1981)
(as amended by Executive Order Nos. 13,284 (2003),
13,355 (2004), and 13,470 (2008))

Timely, accurate, and insightful information about the activities, capabilities, plans, and intentions of foreign powers, organizations, and persons and their agents, is essential to the national security of the United States. All reasonable and lawful means must be used to ensure that the United States will receive the best intelligence available. For that purpose, by virtue of the authority vested in me by the Constitution and the laws of the United States of America, including the National Security Act of 1947 (Act), as amended, and as President of the United States of America, in order to provide for the effective conduct of United States intelligence activities and the protection of constitutional rights, it is hereby ordered as follows:

PART 1. GOALS, DIRECTIONS, DUTIES, AND RESPONSIBILITIES WITH RESPECT TO UNITED STATES INTELLIGENCE EFFORTS

1.1 ***Goals.*** The United States intelligence effort shall provide the President, the National Security Council, and the Homeland Security Council with the necessary information on which to base decisions concerning the development and conduct of foreign, defense, and economic policies, and the protection of United States national interests from foreign security threats. All departments and agencies shall cooperate fully to fulfill this goal.

(a) All means, consistent with applicable Federal law and this order, and with full consideration of the rights of United States persons, shall be used to obtain reliable intelligence information to protect the United States and its interests. . . .

(g) All departments and agencies have a responsibility to prepare and to provide intelligence in a manner that allows the full and free exchange of information, consistent with applicable law and presidential guidance.

1.2 ***The National Security Council.***

(a) *Purpose.* The National Security Council (NSC) shall act as the highest ranking executive branch entity that provides support to the President for review of, guidance for, and direction to the conduct of all foreign intelligence, counterintelligence, and covert action, and attendant policies and programs.

(b) *Covert Action and Other Sensitive Intelligence Operations.* The NSC shall consider and submit to the President a policy recommendation, including all dissents, on each proposed covert action and conduct a periodic review of ongoing covert action activities, including an evaluation of the effectiveness and consistency with current national policy of such activities and consistency with applicable legal requirements. The NSC shall perform such other functions related to covert action as the President may direct, but shall not undertake the conduct of covert actions. The NSC shall also review proposals for other sensitive intelligence operations.

1.3 ***Director of National Intelligence.*** Subject to the authority, direction, and control of the President, the Director of National Intelligence (Director) shall serve as the head of the Intelligence Community, act as the principal adviser to the President, to the NSC, and to the Homeland Security Council for intelligence matters related to national security, and shall oversee and direct the implementation of the National Intelligence Program and execution of the National Intelligence Program budget.... In addition, the Director shall ... take into account the views of the heads of departments containing an element of the Intelligence Community and of the Director of the Central Intelligence Agency.

> (a) Except as otherwise directed by the President or prohibited by law, the Director shall have access to all information and intelligence described in section 1.5(a) of this order....
>
> (b) In addition to fulfilling the obligations and responsibilities prescribed by the Act, the Director:
>
> > (1) Shall establish objectives, priorities, and guidance for the Intelligence Community to ensure timely and effective collection, processing, analysis, and dissemination of intelligence, of whatever nature and from whatever source derived; ...
> >
> > (3) Shall oversee and provide advice to the President and the NSC with respect to all ongoing and proposed covert action programs;
> >
> > (4) In regard to the establishment and conduct of intelligence arrangements and agreements with foreign governments and international organizations:
> >
> > > (A) May enter into intelligence and counterintelligence arrangements and agreements with foreign governments and international organizations; ...
> >
> > (6) Shall establish common security and access standards for managing and handling intelligence systems, information, and products, with special emphasis on facilitating:
> >
> > > (A) The fullest and most prompt access to and dissemination of information and intelligence practicable, assigning the highest priority to detecting, preventing, preempting, and disrupting terrorist threats and activities against the United States, its interests, and allies; ...
> >
> > (7) Shall ensure that appropriate departments and agencies have access to intelligence and receive the support needed to perform independent analysis;
> >
> > (8) Shall protect, and ensure that programs are developed to protect, intelligence sources, methods, and activities from unauthorized disclosure;
> >
> > (9) Shall, after consultation with the heads of affected departments and agencies, establish guidelines for Intelligence Community elements for:
> >
> > > (A) Classification and declassification of all intelligence and intelligence-related information classified under the authority of the Director or the authority of the head of a department or Intelligence Community element; ...
> >
> > (14) Shall have ultimate responsibility for production and dissemination of intelligence produced by the Intelligence Community and authority to levy analytic tasks on intelligence production organizations within the Intelligence Community ...
> >
> > (16) Shall ensure the timely exploitation and dissemination of data gathered by national intelligence collection means, and ensure that the resulting intelligence is disseminated immediately to appropriate government elements, including military commands;
> >
> > (17) Shall determine requirements and priorities for, and manage and direct the tasking, collection, analysis, production, and dissemination of, national

intelligence by elements of the Intelligence Community, including approving requirements for collection and analysis and resolving conflicts in collection requirements and in the tasking of national collection assets of Intelligence Community elements (except when otherwise directed by the President or when the Secretary of Defense exercises collection tasking authority under plans and arrangements approved by the Secretary of Defense and the Director); . . .

(20) Shall ensure, through appropriate policies and procedures, the deconfliction, coordination, and integration of all intelligence activities conducted by an Intelligence Community element or funded by the National Intelligence Program. In accordance with these policies and procedures:

(A) The Director of the Federal Bureau of Investigation shall coordinate the clandestine collection of foreign intelligence collected through human sources or through human-enabled means and counterintelligence activities inside the United States;

(B) The Director of the Central Intelligence Agency shall coordinate the clandestine collection of foreign intelligence collected through human sources or through human-enabled means and counterintelligence activities outside the United States;

(C) All policies and procedures for the coordination of counterintelligence activities and the clandestine collection of foreign intelligence inside the United States shall be subject to the approval of the Attorney General; and

(D) All policies and procedures developed under this section shall be coordinated with the heads of affected departments and Intelligence Community elements; . . .

(c) The Director's exercise of authorities in the Act and this order shall not abrogate the statutory or other responsibilities of the heads of departments of the United States Government or the Director of the Central Intelligence Agency. . . .

1.4. ***The Intelligence Community.*** Consistent with applicable Federal law and with the other provisions of this order, and under the leadership of the Director, as specified in such law and this order, the Intelligence Community shall:

(a) Collect and provide information needed by the President and, in the performance of executive functions, the Vice President, the NSC, the Homeland Security Council, the Chairman of the Joint Chiefs of Staff, senior military commanders, and other executive branch officials and, as appropriate, the Congress of the United States;

(b) In accordance with priorities set by the President, collect information concerning, and conduct activities to protect against, international terrorism, proliferation of weapons of mass destruction, intelligence activities directed against the United States, international criminal drug activities, and other hostile activities directed against the United States by foreign powers, organizations, persons, and their agents;

(c) Analyze, produce, and disseminate intelligence; . . .

(f) Protect the security of intelligence related activities, information, installations, property, and employees by appropriate means, including such investigations of applicants, employees, contractors, and other persons with similar associations with the Intelligence Community elements as are necessary; . . .

(i) Perform such other functions and duties related to intelligence activities as the President may direct.

1.5. ***Duties and Responsibilities of the Heads of Executive Branch Departments and Agencies.*** The heads of all departments and agencies shall:

(a) Provide the Director access to all information and intelligence relevant to the national security or that otherwise is required for the performance of the Director's duties . . . except such information excluded by law, by the President, or by the Attorney General acting under this order at the direction of the President. . . .

(h) Inform the Attorney General, either directly or through the Federal Bureau of Investigation, and the Director of clandestine collection of foreign intelligence and counterintelligence activities inside the United States not coordinated with the Federal Bureau of Investigation. . . .

1.6. ***Heads of Elements of the Intelligence Community.*** The heads of elements of the Intelligence Community shall:

(a) Provide the Director access to all information and intelligence relevant to the national security or that otherwise is required for the performance of the Director's duties . . .

(b) Report to the Attorney General possible violations of Federal criminal laws by employees and of specified Federal criminal laws by any other person . . .

(c) Report to the Intelligence Oversight Board, consistent with Executive Order 13462 of February 29, 2008, and provide copies of all such reports to the Director, concerning any intelligence activities of their elements that they have reason to believe may be unlawful or contrary to executive order or presidential directive;

(d) Protect intelligence and intelligence sources, methods, and activities from unauthorized disclosure in accordance with guidance from the Director;

(e) Facilitate, as appropriate, the sharing of information or intelligence, as directed by law or the President, to State, local, tribal, and private sector entities;

(f) Disseminate information or intelligence to foreign governments and international organizations under intelligence or counterintelligence arrangements or agreements established in accordance with section 1.3(b)(4) of this order; . . .

(h) Ensure that the inspectors general, general counsels, and agency officials responsible for privacy or civil liberties protection for their respective organizations have access to any information or intelligence necessary to perform their official duties.

1.7. ***Intelligence Community Elements.*** Each element of the Intelligence Community shall have the duties and responsibilities specified below, in addition to those specified by law or elsewhere in this order. . . .

(a) *The Central Intelligence Agency.* The Director of the Central Intelligence Agency shall:

(1) Collect (including through clandestine means), analyze, produce, and disseminate foreign intelligence and counterintelligence;

(2) Conduct counterintelligence activities without assuming or performing any internal security functions within the United States;

(3) Conduct administrative and technical support activities within and outside the United States as necessary for cover and proprietary arrangements;

(4) Conduct covert action activities approved by the President. No agency except the Central Intelligence Agency (or the Armed Forces of the United States in time of war declared by the Congress or during any period covered by

a report from the President to the Congress consistent with the War Powers Resolution, Public Law 93-148) may conduct any covert action activity unless the President determines that another agency is more likely to achieve a particular objective;

(5) Conduct foreign intelligence liaison relationships with intelligence or security services of foreign governments or international organizations consistent with section 1.3(b)(4) of this order;...

(7) Perform such other functions and duties related to intelligence as the Director may direct....

(c) *The National Security Agency.* The Director of the National Security Agency shall:

(1) Collect (including through clandestine means), process, analyze, produce, and disseminate signals intelligence information and data for foreign intelligence and counterintelligence purposes to support national and departmental missions;

(2) Establish and operate an effective unified organization for signals intelligence activities, except for the delegation of operational control over certain operations that are conducted through other elements of the Intelligence Community. No other department or agency may engage in signals intelligence activities except pursuant to a delegation by the Secretary of Defense, after coordination with the Director;...

(5) Provide signals intelligence support for national and departmental requirements and for the conduct of military operations;...

(f) *The Intelligence and Counterintelligence Elements of the Army, Navy, Air Force, and Marine Corps.* The Commanders and heads of the intelligence and counterintelligence elements of the Army, Navy, Air Force, and Marine Corps shall:

(1) Collect (including through clandestine means), produce, analyze, and disseminate defense and defense-related intelligence and counterintelligence to support departmental requirements, and, as appropriate, national requirements;

(2) Conduct counterintelligence activities;...

(g) *Intelligence Elements of the Federal Bureau of Investigation.* Under the supervision of the Attorney General and pursuant to such regulations as the Attorney General may establish, the intelligence elements of the Federal Bureau of Investigation shall:

(1) Collect (including through clandestine means), analyze, produce, and disseminate foreign intelligence and counterintelligence to support national and departmental missions, in accordance with procedural guidelines approved by the Attorney General, after consultation with the Director;

(2) Conduct counterintelligence activities; and

(3) Conduct foreign intelligence and counterintelligence liaison relationships with intelligence, security, and law enforcement services of foreign governments or international organizations in accordance with sections 1.3(b)(4) and 1.7(a)(6) of this order....

(i) *The Bureau of Intelligence and Research, Department of State; the Office of Intelligence and Analysis, Department of the Treasury; the Office of National Security Intelligence, Drug Enforcement Administration; the Office of Intelligence and Analysis, Department of Homeland Security; and the Office of Intelligence and Counterintelligence, Department of Energy.* [These entities] shall:

(1) Collect (overtly or through publicly available sources), analyze, produce, and disseminate information, intelligence, and counterintelligence to support national and departmental missions;...

(j) *The Office of the Director of National Intelligence.* The Director shall collect (overtly or through publicly available sources), analyze, produce, and disseminate information, intelligence, and counterintelligence to support the missions of the Office of the Director of National Intelligence, including the National Counterterrorism Center, and to support other national missions....

1.10. ***The Department of Defense.*** The Secretary of Defense shall:

(a) Collect (including through clandestine means), analyze, produce, and disseminate information and intelligence...

(b) Collect (including through clandestine means), analyze, produce, and disseminate defense and defense related intelligence and counterintelligence, as required for execution of the Secretary's responsibilities;

(c) Conduct programs and missions necessary to fulfill national, departmental, and tactical intelligence requirements;

(d) Conduct counterintelligence activities in support of Department of Defense components and coordinate counterintelligence activities in accordance with section 1.3(b)(20) and (21) of this order;

(e) Act, in coordination with the Director, as the executive agent of the United States Government for signals intelligence activities....

PART 2. CONDUCT OF INTELLIGENCE ACTIVITIES...

2.2. ***Purpose.***... Set forth below are certain general principles that, in addition to and consistent with applicable laws, are intended to achieve the proper balance between the acquisition of essential information and protection of individual interests. Nothing in this Order shall be construed to apply to or interfere with any authorized civil or criminal law enforcement responsibility of any department or agency.

2.3. ***Collection of Information.*** Elements of the Intelligence Community are authorized to collect, retain, or disseminate information concerning United States persons only in accordance with procedures established by the head of the Intelligence Community element concerned... and approved by the Attorney General... after consultation with the Director. Those procedures shall permit collection, retention, and dissemination of the following types of information:...

(b) Information constituting foreign intelligence or counterintelligence, including such information concerning corporations or other commercial organizations. Collection within the United States of foreign intelligence not otherwise obtainable shall be undertaken by the Federal Bureau of Investigation (FBI) or, when significant foreign intelligence is sought, by other authorized elements of the Intelligence Community, provided that no foreign intelligence collection by such elements may be undertaken for the purpose of acquiring information concerning the domestic activities of United States persons;

(c) Information obtained in the course of a lawful foreign intelligence, counterintelligence, international drug or international terrorism investigation;

(d) Information needed to protect the safety of any persons or organizations, including those who are targets, victims, or hostages of international terrorist organizations;

(e) Information needed to protect foreign intelligence or counterintelligence sources, methods, and activities from unauthorized disclosure. Collection within the United States shall be undertaken by the FBI except that other elements of the Intelligence Community may also collect any such information concerning present or former employees, present or former intelligence element contractors or their present or former employees, or applicants for such employment or contracting. . . .

In addition, elements of the Intelligence Community may disseminate information to each appropriate element within the Intelligence Community for purposes of allowing the recipient element to determine whether the information is relevant to its responsibilities and can be retained by it, except that information derived from signals intelligence may only be disseminated or made available to Intelligence Community elements in accordance with procedures established by the Director in coordination with the Secretary of Defense and approved by the Attorney General.

2.4. *Collection Techniques.* Elements of the Intelligence Community shall use the least intrusive collection techniques feasible within the United States or directed against United States persons abroad. Elements of the Intelligence Community are not authorized to use such techniques as electronic surveillance, unconsented physical search, mail surveillance, physical surveillance, or monitoring devices unless they are in accordance with procedures established by the head of the Intelligence Community element concerned or the head of a department containing such element and approved by the Attorney General, after consultation with the Director. Such procedures shall protect constitutional and other legal rights and limit use of such information to lawful governmental purposes. These procedures shall not authorize:

(a) The Central Intelligence Agency (CIA) to engage in electronic surveillance within the United States except for the purpose of training, testing, or conducting countermeasures to hostile electronic surveillance;

(b) Unconsented physical searches in the United States by elements of the Intelligence Community other than the FBI, except for:

(1) Searches by counterintelligence elements of the military services directed against military personnel within the United States or abroad for intelligence purposes, when authorized by a military commander empowered to approve physical searches for law enforcement purposes, based upon a finding of probable cause to believe that such persons are acting as agents of foreign powers; and

(2) Searches by CIA of personal property of non-United States persons lawfully in its possession;

(c) Physical surveillance of a United States person in the United States by elements of the Intelligence Community other than the FBI, except for:

(1) Physical surveillance of present or former employees, present or former intelligence element contractors or their present or former employees, or applicants for any such employment or contracting; and

(2) Physical surveillance of a military person employed by a non-intelligence element of a military service; and

(d) Physical surveillance of a United States person abroad to collect foreign intelligence, except to obtain significant information that cannot reasonably be acquired by other means.

2.5. ***Attorney General Approval.*** The Attorney General hereby is delegated the power to approve the use for intelligence purposes, within the United States or against a United States person abroad, of any technique for which a warrant would be required if undertaken for law enforcement purposes, provided that such techniques shall not be undertaken unless the Attorney General has determined in each case that there is probable cause to believe that the technique is directed against a foreign power or an agent of a foreign power. The authority delegated pursuant to this paragraph, including the authority to approve the use of electronic surveillance as defined in the Foreign Intelligence Surveillance Act of 1978, as amended, shall be exercised in accordance with that Act.

2.6. ***Assistance to Law Enforcement and Other Civil Authorities.*** Elements of the Intelligence Community are authorized to:...

(b) Unless otherwise precluded by law or this Order, participate in law enforcement activities to investigate or prevent clandestine intelligence activities by foreign powers, or international terrorist or narcotics activities....

2.7. ***Contracting.*** Elements of the Intelligence Community are authorized to enter into contracts or arrangements for the provision of goods or services with private companies or institutions in the United States and need not reveal the sponsorship of such contracts or arrangements for authorized intelligence purposes. Contracts or arrangements with academic institutions may be undertaken only with the consent of appropriate officials of the institution.

2.8. ***Consistency with Other Laws.*** Nothing in this Order shall be construed to authorize any activity in violation of the Constitution or statutes of the United States.

2.9. ***Undisclosed Participation in Organizations Within the United States.*** No one acting on behalf of elements of the Intelligence Community may join or otherwise participate in any organization in the United States on behalf of any element of the Intelligence Community without disclosing such person's intelligence affiliation to appropriate officials of the organization, except in accordance with procedures established by the head of the Intelligence Community element concerned or the head of a department containing such element and approved by the Attorney General, after consultation with the Director. Such participation shall be authorized only if it is essential to achieving lawful purposes as determined by the Intelligence Community element head or designee. No such participation may be undertaken for the purpose of influencing the activity of the organization or its members except in cases where:

(a) The participation is undertaken on behalf of the FBI in the course of a lawful investigation; or

(b) The organization concerned is composed primarily of individuals who are not United States persons and is reasonably believed to be acting on behalf of a foreign power....

2.11. ***Prohibition on Assassination.*** No person employed by or acting on behalf of the United States Government shall engage in, or conspire to engage in, assassination.

2.12. ***Indirect Participation.*** No element of the Intelligence Community shall participate in or request any person to undertake activities forbidden by this Order.

2.13. ***Limitation on Covert Action.*** No covert action may be conducted which is intended to influence United States political processes, public opinion, policies, or media.

PART 3. GENERAL PROVISIONS

3.1. ***Congressional Oversight.*** The duties and responsibilities of the Director and the heads of other departments, agencies, elements, and entities engaged in intelligence activities to cooperate with the Congress in the conduct of its responsibilities for oversight of intelligence activities shall be implemented in accordance with applicable law, including title V of the [National Security Act of 1947, as amended]. The requirements of applicable law, including title V of the [National Security Act of 1947, as amended], shall apply to all covert action activities as defined in this Order. . . .

3.5. ***Definitions.*** For the purposes of this Order, the following terms shall have these meanings:

(a) *Counterintelligence* means information gathered and activities conducted to identify, deceive, exploit, disrupt, or protect against espionage, other intelligence activities, sabotage, or assassinations conducted for or on behalf of foreign powers, organizations, or persons, or their agents, or international terrorist organizations or activities.

(b) *Covert action* means an activity or activities of the United States Government to influence political, economic, or military conditions abroad, where it is intended that the role of the United States Government will not be apparent or acknowledged publicly, but does not include:

(1) Activities the primary purpose of which is to acquire intelligence, traditional counterintelligence activities, traditional activities to improve or maintain the operational security of United States Government programs, or administrative activities;

(2) Traditional diplomatic or military activities or routine support to such activities;

(3) Traditional law enforcement activities conducted by United States Government law enforcement agencies or routine support to such activities; or

(4) Activities to provide routine support to the overt activities (other than activities described in paragraph (1), (2), or (3)) of other United States Government agencies abroad.

(c) *Electronic surveillance* means acquisition of a nonpublic communication by electronic means without the consent of a person who is a party to an electronic communication or, in the case of a nonelectronic communication, without the consent of a person who is visibly present at the place of communication, but not including the use of radio direction-finding equipment solely to determine the location of a transmitter. . . .

(e) *Foreign intelligence* means information relating to the capabilities, intentions, or activities of foreign governments or elements thereof, foreign organizations, foreign persons, or international terrorists.

(f) *Intelligence* includes foreign intelligence and counterintelligence.

(g) *Intelligence activities* means all activities that elements of the Intelligence Community are authorized to conduct pursuant to this order.

(h) *Intelligence Community* and *elements of the Intelligence Community* refers to:

(1) The Office of the Director of National Intelligence;

(2) The Central Intelligence Agency;

(3) The National Security Agency;

(4) The Defense Intelligence Agency;

(5) The National Geospatial-Intelligence Agency;

(6) The National Reconnaissance Office;

(7) The other offices within the Department of Defense for the collection of specialized national foreign intelligence through reconnaissance programs;

(8) The intelligence and counterintelligence elements of the Army, the Navy, the Air Force, and the Marine Corps;

(9) The intelligence elements of the Federal Bureau of Investigation;

(10) The Office of National Security Intelligence of the Drug Enforcement Administration;

(11) The Office of Intelligence and Counterintelligence of the Department of Energy;

(12) The Bureau of Intelligence and Research of the Department of State;

(13) The Office of Intelligence and Analysis of the Department of the Treasury;

(14) The Office of Intelligence and Analysis of the Department of Homeland Security;

(15) The intelligence and counterintelligence elements of the Coast Guard; and

(16) Such other elements of any department or agency as may be designated by the President, or designated jointly by the Director and the head of the department or agency concerned, as an element of the Intelligence Community.

(i) *National Intelligence* and *Intelligence Related to National Security* means all intelligence, regardless of the source from which derived and including information gathered within or outside the United States, that pertains, as determined consistent with any guidance issued by the President, or that is determined for the purpose of access to information by the Director in accordance with section 1.3(a)(1) of this order, to pertain to more than one United States Government agency; and that involves threats to the United States, its people, property, or interests; the development, proliferation, or use of weapons of mass destruction; or any other matter bearing on United States national or homeland security.

(j) *The National Intelligence Program* means all programs, projects, and activities of the Intelligence Community, as well as any other programs of the Intelligence Community designated jointly by the Director and the head of a United States department or agency or by the President. Such term does not include programs, projects, or activities of the military departments to acquire intelligence solely for the planning and conduct of tactical military operations by United States Armed Forces.

(k) *United States person* means a United States citizen, an alien known by the intelligence element concerned to be a permanent resident alien, an unincorporated association substantially composed of United States citizens or permanent resident aliens, or a corporation incorporated in the United States, except for a corporation directed and controlled by a foreign government or governments. . . .

Notes and Questions

a. Authority for the Order

1. *The President's Claim of Authority.* The preamble to Executive Order No. 12,333 is directed at intelligence information and its importance to the national security. Preambular language typically sets forth the presumed authority for the prescriptions that follow. Precisely what constitutional or statutory authority empowered the President to promulgate this executive order?

2. *Executive Order or Legislation?* The order provides for at least some of what intelligence legislation might regulate, with this difference: the President arguably may change or waive self-imposed limitations on intelligence activities. Does it really matter whether regulations for intelligence activities take the form of legislation rather than an executive order?

b. Deciding on Intelligence Operations

1. *Who Initiates and Who Approves?* According to the executive order, which official or entity must approve an intelligence operation? Which officials or entities may originate proposals for covert action?

2. *Role of the NSC.* Consider the role of the NSC, as described in §1.2. As the "highest executive branch entity" involved in various intelligence activities, the NSC appears to be the primary link between the intelligence community and the President in deciding on intelligence policy and individual operations. According to the executive order, how does the NSC obtain the information it needs to fulfill its statutory role? Is NSC review of covert operations limited to the policies or criteria that inform decisions about individual operations, or is each proposal subject to the NSC review process? Does the NSC role include the conduct of covert operations?

3. *Role of the DNI.* Section 1.3 of the order makes the DNI the "head" of the "Intelligence Community," a term defined at §3.5(h). Can you say how the "head" of the "community" is like or unlike the Secretary of a cabinet-level department, such as Homeland Security or Justice?

4. *Collection Assignments.* Sections 1.3(b)(20) and 2.3 of the order assign collection responsibilities. How are collections inside and outside the United States treated differently?

5. *Military Intelligence Activities.* Which official approves intelligence collection by military agencies? What do you suppose constitute the "programs and missions" that

the Secretary of Defense may conduct in meeting intelligence requirements? Does the executive order provide adequate legal authority to carry out those activities?

c. The Internal Executive Branch Process for Approving Intelligence Operations

1. Sorting Out the Players and Their Roles. Can you describe the respective roles of the DNI, Director of the Central Intelligence Agency, the NSC, National Security Adviser, and Attorney General, as well as their relationships to each other and to the President and NSC? What duties are assigned exclusively to the CIA? *See* §1.7(a). You may wish to consult the organization chart on p. 512, *supra.*

Can you tell who is now in charge of operational controls? How do you think the assignments of responsibility in the executive order affect the speed with which decisions are made about intelligence operations? The quality of those decisions?

2. The Role of Lawyers. The Ford and Carter executive orders, unlike the later Reagan order, formally included the Justice Department in the covert action decision-making process. What role, if any, does the amended order assign to the Attorney General in approving covert actions? What other provisions does the order make for lawyers to participate in the intelligence activities it addresses? Does their participation really matter if the President is free to ignore their advice?

3. President's Intelligence Advisory Board (PIAB). The President's Intelligence Advisory Board (PIAB) is maintained within the Executive Office of the President and is charged to

> assess the quality, quantity, and adequacy of intelligence collection, of analysis and estimates, and of counterintelligence and other intelligence activities, assess the adequacy of management, personnel and organization in the intelligence community, and review the performance of all agencies of the Federal Government that are engaged in the collection, evaluation, or production of intelligence or the execution of intelligence policy and report the results of such assessments or reviews [to the President and DNI and heads of concerned departments]. [Exec. Order No. 13,462, §4(a), 73 Fed. Reg. 11,805, 11,806 (Feb. 29, 2008), *as amended by* Exec. Order No. 13,516, 74 Fed. Reg. 56,521 (Nov. 2, 2009).]

The PIAB's several members (up to 16) serve at the pleasure of the President and are appointed from among citizens outside of government. It is specifically charged with making appropriate recommendations for actions to improve and enhance the performance of the intelligence efforts of the United States.

President George W. Bush removed and President Obama restored a requirement that the PIAB alert the Attorney General whenever it learns of "intelligence activities that involve possible violations of Federal criminal laws." Exec. Order No. 13,516, §1(d). The Obama order also restored a requirement that the DNI and other agencies "provide such information and assistance as the PIAB and IOB [Intelligence Oversight Board] determine [are] needed to perform their functions." *Id.* §1(e). Can you imagine reasons for these changes?

d. Conducting Intelligence Operations

1. Assigning Functions Among Agencies. How can the intelligence functions of the various agencies addressed in §§1.7 and 1.10 of the executive order be distinguished? Why do you suppose their responsibilities are assigned as they are? Do you see any grounds for possible confusion or conflict?

2. Executive Order No. 12,333 and the National Security Act of 1947. Compare §§1.7(a) and 2.3(b) to the National Security Act of 1947. Do you see any significant differences in the "such other functions and duties" authorizations in the Act and the executive order? How may the CIA "conduct counterintelligence activities" without performing any "internal security functions" within the United States? What do you suppose constitutes "foreign intelligence information not otherwise obtainable," and how may the CIA or NSA collect "significant" foreign intelligence within the United States without violating the proscription against collecting information on the domestic activities of United States persons? Executive Order No. 12,333 also anticipates that the CIA will "collect . . . foreign intelligence and counterintelligence," although counterintelligence activities may not involve "any internal security functions within the United States." *Id.* §1.7(a)(1) and (2). Yet it goes on to declare that "[e]lements of the intelligence community," presumably including the CIA, may "participate in law enforcement activities to investigate or prevent clandestine intelligence activities by foreign powers, or international terrorist or narcotics activities." *Id.* §2.6(b). Can you reconcile these authorities with the "no police . . . or internal security" proviso in the 1947 Act?

3. Investigatory Authorizations Under Executive Order No. 12,333. What constitutes a "lawful" FBI investigation within the meaning of Executive Order No. 12,333? What are the likely elements of a probable cause determination under §2.5? Review §2.4. Under what circumstances may the FBI engage in physical surveillance of a U.S. person abroad?

4. Attorney General and FBI Guidelines. Relying on relatively scant statutory authority and Executive Order No. 12,333, the Attorney General and the FBI have promulgated detailed guidelines for the conduct of FBI investigations. *See, e.g.*, Fed. Bureau of Investigation, U.S. Dep't of Justice, *Domestic Investigations and Operations Guide* (2011); Office of the Attorney Gen., U.S. Dep't of Justice, *The Attorney General's Guidelines for Domestic FBI Operations* (2011) (hereinafter *2011 Guidelines*); *The Attorney General's Guidelines for National Security Investigations and Foreign Intelligence Collection* (Oct. 31, 2003). *See generally* Emily Berman, *Regulating Domestic Intelligence Collection*, 71 Wash. & Lee L. Rev. 3, 8 (2014) ("This broad discretion, democracy deficit, and absence of counterweight to the FBI's prevention goal means that — despite the privacy and liberty implications of the FBI's activities — the responsibility of striking a balance between security needs and other important interests is left almost entirely to the Attorney General and the FBI itself."). Unlike the CIA or any other intelligence collector, the FBI therefore operates under the direction of the nation's highest law enforcement officer and within a culture of law enforcement.

5. Predicated Investigations. For the FBI, predicated investigations are generally based on "allegations, reports, facts or circumstances indicative of possible criminal or national security-threatening activity, or the potential for acquiring information responsive to foreign intelligence requirements . . . [where] supervisory approval must be obtained." *2011 Guidelines, supra,* §II, at 18. Does the Constitution require some predicate activity before the FBI may launch an investigation? Would you infer such a requirement from statutes, or from Executive Order No. 12,333? What is the value of supervisory approval in predicated investigations?

6. *Infiltration.* When is CIA or FBI infiltration of domestic organizations permitted by Executive Order No. 12,333? On the basis of what information will the "agency head or designee" determine that infiltration is "essential to achieving lawful purposes"? If infiltration is authorized outside the limits of the order, what redress would be available to aggrieved persons?

7. *Assessments vs. Investigations.* Prior to the opening of a formal investigation, FBI "assessments" may be undertaken without any predicate suspicion or threat. According to the 2011 *Domestic Investigations and Operations Guide,* the basis for opening an assessment "cannot be arbitrary or groundless speculation," but the standard is "difficult to define." §5.1. What is the value of an assessment? Does the FBI have statutory authority to conduct one?

8. *Restrictions on Collection.* What kind of information may be collected by members of the intelligence community? Does it include information about, say, drug smuggling? Industrial espionage? The order distinguishes among collection techniques by kind, location, and target. We examine these techniques in detail in later chapters, but here consider *why* the order treats them differently.

How and why is collection against U.S. persons more restricted than against others?

Why do you think collection inside the United States is generally limited to the FBI? What purpose is served by a requirement that the Attorney General approve collections for "intelligence purposes" inside the United States or against U.S. persons abroad when a judicial warrant would be needed if undertaken for law enforcement purposes? Why must the Attorney General find probable cause to believe that the target is a foreign power or agent of a foreign power?

9. *Political Impacts.* Why does §2.13 of the executive order prohibit covert actions intended to influence U.S. "political processes, public opinion, policies, or media"? Should the order address such influence if it is unintended — commonly referred to as "blowback"?

e. Overseeing Intelligence Operation Decisions

1. *Making a Record.* Does the executive order require that intelligence operation decisions be made in writing? What considerations would enter into deciding whether to impose such a requirement within the executive branch? If such decisions are made in writing, should or must the writing be done before the operation is carried out?

2. *Reporting to Congress.* Section 3.1 of the order refers to oversight legislation that Congress has from time to time amended in response to its concerns about executive

self-regulation. (Current intelligence oversight legislation is found in the Intelligence Oversight Act, Fiscal Year 1991, Pub. L. No. 102-88, §§601-603, 105 Stat. 429, 441-445 (codified as amended at 50 U.S.C. §§3091-3094, considered *infra* p. 557).) What intelligence activities does the order say must be reported to Congress? Do such requirements apply to the NSC or its staff?

Over time, an informal system of congressional oversight has also developed regarding certain particularly sensitive *non-covert action intelligence* (mostly collection) activities. So-called "Gang of Four" notifications of such activities are given to the chairs and ranking members of the two congressional intelligence committees, when "the intelligence community believes a particular intelligence activity to be of such sensitivity that a restricted notification is warranted in order to reduce the risk of disclosure, inadvertent or otherwise." Marshal Curtis Erwin, *"Gang of Four" Congressional Intelligence Notifications* (Cong. Res. Serv. R40698), Apr. 16, 2013. Other non-covert action activities are generally briefed to the full committees.

3. Intelligence Oversight Board (IOB). The Intelligence Oversight Board, referred to in §1.6(c) of the executive order, is a standing committee of the PIAB. As reconfigured most recently by President Obama, the functions of the IOB include informing the President of intelligence activities that the IOB believes "may be unlawful or contrary to Executive Order or presidential directive," notifying the Attorney General whenever it learns of "intelligence activities that involve possible violations of Federal criminal laws," and reviewing and assessing "the effectiveness, efficiency, and sufficiency of the processes by which the DNI and the heads of departments concerned perform their respective functions." Exec. Order No. 13,516, *supra*, §6(b), (c). Will the IOB provide an effective check on violations of either statutory or executive order restrictions?

4. Rogue Operations Redux. Would either Operation CHAOS or Operation COINTELPRO be lawful under amended Executive Order 12,333?

B. FUNDING AND MANAGING THE INTELLIGENCE COMMUNITY

An old inside-the-beltway adage says to "follow the money" if you want to find out where the power lies. According to Executive Order No. 12,333, the National Intelligence Program (NIP) includes all programs conducted by the intelligence community, other than programs to acquire intelligence "solely for the planning and conduct of tactical military operations by the United States Armed Forces." Exec. Order No. 12,333, *supra*, §3.5(j). The latter programs, plans, and activities of the military departments constitute the Military Intelligence Program (MIP). The National Security Act of 1947, as amended, provides that the DNI must "develop and determine" the annual consolidated NIP budget. 50 U.S.C. §3024(c)(1)(B). Under the statute, the DNI also directs the allocation of appropriations through the heads of departments containing agencies or organizations within the intelligence community and through the Director of the CIA. *Id.* §3024(c)(5)(A). (Component intelligence agencies and lines of reporting are shown in the chart on p. 512.)

But while the DNI's budget authority extends over much of the intelligence community, the DNI has no such authority over the Military Intelligence Program. *Id.* §3024(c)(3)(A). The DNI's direct budgetary authority thus does not include vast parts of the DOD budget, so DOD largely escapes the organizational structure and control mechanisms created by the reform legislation. Despite the DNI's lack of control over the DOD intelligence budget, after consultation with the Secretary of Defense, the DNI must ensure that National Intelligence Program budgets for components of the intelligence community within DOD are adequate for the intelligence needs of DOD, including the intelligence needs of the military service branches. *Id.* §3024(p). Within the Office of the Director of National Intelligence (ODNI), a National Intelligence Council (NIC), composed of senior analysts and other experts appointed by the DNI, is charged with producing national intelligence estimates, evaluating intelligence collection and production, and otherwise assisting the DNI. *Id.* §3027(b), (c).

The DNI oversees the statutory National Counterterrorism Center (NCTC), created in 2004 by IRTPA, and any other national intelligence centers determined necessary by the Director. *Id.* §3056. The Director of the NCTC is a Senate-confirmed presidential appointee who reports to the DNI generally but to the President specifically on the planning and implementation of joint counterterrorism operations.

IRTPA also created the Privacy and Civil Liberties Oversight Board (PCLOB), whose members are appointed by the President. IRTPA §1061, 118 Stat. at 3684-3688 (as amended by Pub. L. No. 110-53, §801, 121 Stat. 266, 352-358 (2007)). The PCLOB is charged with ensuring that privacy and civil liberties concerns are appropriately considered in the implementation of policies designed to protect against terrorism. It provides oversight of regulations and policies, advises the President and agencies in the executive branch, and reports to Congress. The Board is given access to any executive branch information, but the Director of National Intelligence and/or the Attorney General may decline to enforce that access. §1061(d)(2), 121 Stat. at 3685-3686. PCLOB was actively involved in assessing a wide range of intelligence activities uncovered by the 2013 leaks of classified information by Edward Snowden and the resulting declassification of materials by ODNI. These developments are examined in Chapter 24.

Notes and Questions

1. *The DNI and the Intelligence Community.* According to IRTPA §1073, the "intelligence community," now headed by the DNI, consists of all the entities depicted in the chart on p. 512, except the President and the six listed cabinet departments. Given this definition, despite the incomplete budgetary authority now vested in the DNI, is the DNI effectively a "Secretary of Intelligence"? If not, how does the new post fall short of the Secretary model? Does IRTPA, provisions of which are reflected in the excerpt of the National Security Act of 1947 on p. 507, give the ODNI the authority it needs to be effective? May the DNI hire or fire agency heads? Does IRTPA tell the CIA or other agencies within the National Intelligence Program what to do?

2. *Military Intelligence.* If the NIP does not include military intelligence collected solely in support of tactical military operations, can you say which military intelligence activities are subject to IRTPA? Reading the pertinent provisions of Executive Order No. 12,333 (§§1.3, 1.4, 1.5, 1.7, 1.10, and 3.5) alongside IRTPA, can you stitch

together a complete picture of how military intelligence is controlled? What would you need to know to complete the picture?

3. The Budget and Its Control. In October 2010, DNI James R. Clapper reported that the Fiscal Year 2010 budget figure for the NIP was $53.1 billion. For the first time, General Clapper also disclosed the budget total for the Military Intelligence Program (MIP) — $27 billion for FY2010. Off. of the Dir. of Nat'l Intelligence, News Release (Oct. 28, 2010), *at* http://www.fas.org/irp/news/2010/10/dni102810.pdf. Within the NIP budget, about three-fourths of the total is for various DOD agencies, most for NSA and the National Reconnaissance Office (NRO). The rest is shared among the CIA, the FBI, and other agencies. Media Conference Call with the Director of National Intelligence Mr. Dennis C. Blair (Sept. 15, 2009), http://www.fas.org/irp/news/2009/09/dni091509-m.pdf. In Fiscal Year 2018, $81.5 billion was appropriated for U.S. intelligence in the NIP and MIP. Office of the Director of National Intelligence, *U.S. Intelligence Community Budget*, Nov. 2, 2018.

Although intelligence budgets continue to be developed in various individual agencies, the DNI has discretion under IRTPA to reject or revise items or programs and to direct that funds be spent or withheld. 50 U.S.C. §3024(c)(5)(A). Can you see how this budget and spending authority makes the DNI the final decision maker in the various agencies implementing the NIP?

4. The NCTC. The National Counterterrorism Center is the "primary organization in the USG for analyzing and integrating *all* intelligence possessed or acquired by the USG pertaining to terrorism and CT except intelligence pertaining exclusively to domestic terrorism)." It also serves as a "shared knowledge bank on known and suspected terrorists and international terror groups," providing "USG agencies with the terrorism intelligence analysis and other information they need to fulfill their missions." *About the National Counterterrorism Center*, http://www.nctc.gov/overview.html; *see* Richard A. Best Jr., *The National Counterterrorism Center (NCTC) — Responsibilities and Potential Congressional Concerns* (Cong. Res. Serv. R41022), Dec. 19, 2011.

The Fort Hood attack by Major Nidal Hassan in November 2009 and the Abdulmutallab "underwear bomber" incident on December 25, 2009, prompted substantial criticisms of inadequate intelligence analysis by NCTC and other agencies, and served as reminders that NCTC lacks legal authority to require the cooperation of other agencies and departments in its efforts to integrate intelligence. What reforms would make the NCTC more effective?

5. The National Intelligence Strategy. In 2019, DNI Daniel R. Coats issued *The National Intelligence Strategy of the United States of America* (2019). Seven "mission objectives" identified in the *Strategy* are strategic intelligence, anticipatory intelligence, current operations intelligence, cyber threat intelligence, counterterrorism, counter proliferation, and counterintelligence and security. *Id.* In a news release, Coats stated that "[t]his strategy is based on the core principle of seeking the truth and speaking the truth to our policymakers and the American people in order to protect our country." Press Release, Director of Nat'l Intelligence, *DNI Coats Unveils 2019 National Intelligence Strategy* (Jan. 22, 2019). He also declared that "[t]ransparency will be our hallmark. . . . Transparency will make us stronger. It is the right thing to do, across the board." *Id.* In the chapters that follow, we consider prospects for meeting those objectives.

6. *Historical and Contemporary Transparency in the Intelligence Community.* There has been a considerable increase in transparency by agencies in the intelligence community in recent years, most of it since the 2013 leak of secret surveillance and other intelligence information by Edward Snowden. See *infra* pp. 676, 736. The CIA, for example, has posted its CREST (CIA Records Research Tool) database of more than 11 million pages of historical CIA records that have been declassified and approved for public release here: https://www.cia.gov/library/readingroom/collection/crest-25-year-program-archive.

Meanwhile, in 2015 the Office of the Director of National Intelligence released *Principles of Intelligence Transparency for the Intelligence Community* (n.d.), https://www.dni.gov/index.php/ic-legal-reference-book/the-principles-of-intelligence-transparency-for-the-ic. The principles do not change legal requirements, but are "intended to facilitate IC decisions on making information publicly available." The same posting links to the *Intelligence Community Legal Reference Book* (Dec. 2016), https://www.dni.gov/index.php/who-we-are/organizations/ogc/ogc-related-menus/ogc-related-content/ic-legal-reference-book, a 1,000-plus page compilation of laws, regulations, and background materials concerning intelligence. ODNI also hosts *IC on the Record* (ICOTR), https://icontherecord.tumblr.com, an online platform to provide officially released information about the IC; the *ICOTR Transparency Tracker,* https://www.dni.gov/files/CLPT/documents/ICOTR-Transparency-Tracker.pdf, a spreadsheet index of online intelligence materials; *Intelligence.gov,* https://www.intel.gov/, a digital entry point to all agencies of the intelligence community; and *Intel Vault,* https://www.intel.gov/intel-vault, designed for members of the public to explore repositories of officially released information about the IC.

C. COORDINATION AND SHARING OF INTELLIGENCE

Some of the September 11 hijackers lived openly in the United States when their names or names of their close associates were on intelligence "watch lists." The watch list information was not shared in a timely fashion among federal agencies, which might have been able to detect the hijackers' plot before it was implemented. Because intelligence about would-be terrorists might be obtained by the FBI, CIA, NSA, State Department, or agencies inside the Defense Department, or by a state or local law enforcement agency, the challenges of sharing intelligence are staggering. Moreover, the FBI, long embedded in its role as the federal government's chief law enforcement agency, has struggled to reshape its mission to incorporate a vigorous counterterrorism component. How should information classified by one agency be shared with another agency? How should a federal agency share with a state or local agency? How can information be shared in a secure way without jeopardizing the privacy interests of those identified in the intelligence?

Some coordination is required by Executive Order No. 12,333, and ODNI provides guidance to federal, state, and local agencies on sharing information. *See Information Sharing Environment* (updated regularly), *at* http://www.ise.gov/. The FBI leads and coordinates foreign intelligence and counterintelligence activities in the United States, and the CIA, Department of Defense, and military intelligence entities must coordinate with the FBI. Exec. Order No. 12,333 §§1.8(a), 1.11(d), 1.14, 1.12(d)(1). Outside the United States, all the intelligence agencies are required to coordinate with the CIA. *Id.* §§1.8(d), 1.11, 1.12. In practice, coordination has sometimes been difficult to achieve.

It was implicitly determined by Congress in the National Security Act of 1947 that the already functioning FBI would continue to serve as the nation's domestic security agency. At the same time, it was understood early on that the "internal security" prohibition in the 1947 Act would not forbid the CIA from coordinating or collecting *foreign* intelligence information in the United States. However, there was nothing in the Act to provide for CIA and FBI coordination, and no rules to say when the CIA could play a counterintelligence role in the United States. In theory, law enforcement and intelligence collection roles, activities, and methods had been legally and functionally separated to protect the integrity of their tasks and to protect the civil liberties of those targeted for investigation by the government. Thus, the 1947 Act "cut the man down the middle . . . between domestic and foreign counterespionage." Mark Riebling, *Wedge: The Secret War Between the FBI and CIA* 78 (1994).

While the FBI has expanded its extraterritorial role to acquire information about transnational threats, the CIA and agencies inside the Departments of Homeland Security and Defense have also stepped up their efforts in support of counterterrorism. Intelligence gathering for counterterrorism must anticipate threats before they are carried out, while law enforcement typically reacts after the event. However, because terrorism and international crime pose national security threats that transcend both national borders *and* the borders between law enforcement and intelligence collection, coordination and cooperation are required among intelligence agencies and between the intelligence and law enforcement arms of the FBI.

As amended in 1996, the National Security Act permits agencies of the intelligence community, upon the request of a law enforcement agency, to "collect information outside the United States about individuals who are not United States persons." 50 U.S.C. §3039a. Executive Order No. 12,333 establishes a legal presumption that agencies of the intelligence community may "participate in law enforcement activities to investigate or prevent clandestine intelligence activities by foreign powers, or international terrorist or narcotics activities," unless "otherwise precluded by law or this Order." Exec. Order No. 12,333, §2.6(b). The order also explicitly charges the DNI with developing guidelines for sharing of intelligence information by members of the intelligence community, subject to approval by the Attorney General. *Id.* §1.3(a)(2). The DNI also "shall ensure, through appropriate policies and procedures, the deconfliction, coordination, and integration of all intelligence activities conducted by an Intelligence Community element or funded by the National Intelligence Program." *Id.* §1.3(b)(20).

A USA Patriot Act provision authorizes a greater degree of interagency cooperation and sharing of information than was permitted previously. The Act permits, "[n]otwithstanding any other provision of law . . . foreign intelligence or counterintelligence . . . information obtained as part of a criminal investigation to be disclosed to any Federal law enforcement, intelligence, protective, immigration, national defense, or national security official in order to assist the official receiving that information in the performance of his official duties." Pub. L. No. 107-56, §203(d)(1), 115 Stat. 272, 281 (2001) (codified as amended at 50 U.S.C. §3365). The same discretion is given for the sharing of grand jury information. *Id.* §203(a)(1), 115 Stat. 278-279 (codified as amended at 18 U.S.C. app. §6(e)(3)(c)).

Notes and Questions

1. Intelligence Reform and the FBI. The restructuring accomplished by Congress in IRTPA and later was "intended to break down old walls between foreign and domestic intelligence activities." Douglas Jehl, *Bush to Create New Unit in F.B.I. for Intelligence,* N.Y. Times, June 30, 2005. Do you see any downside risk in tearing down the wall between foreign and domestic intelligence? In lowering the historic barrier between the FBI and the CIA?

2. Fusion Centers. Almost every adult American has seen a movie or TV show in which FBI or other federal security officials are at loggerheads with local law enforcement officials, and no one is "sharing." In part to address this problem, the federal government created more than 70 "fusion centers" after 9/11, under the auspices of the Departments of Homeland Security and Justice, to facilitate intelligence sharing between federal and state and local law enforcement agencies. Congress defined a fusion center as "a collaborative effort of 2 or more Federal, State, local, or tribal government agencies that combines resources, expertise, or information with the goal of maximizing the ability of such agencies to detect, prevent, investigate, apprehend, and respond to criminal or terrorist activity." Implementing Recommendations of the 9/11 Commission Act of 2007, Pub. L. No. 110-53, §511, 121 Stat. 317, 322-324 (codified at 6 U.S.C. §124h (2018)). The centers are maintained by state and local agencies with federal funding.

Fusion centers prepare and share "Suspicious Activity Reports" (SARs) based on the following standard: "[o]bserved behavior reasonably indicative of pre-operational planning associated with terrorism or other criminal activity." *See Gill v. U.S. Dep't of Justice,* 913 F.3d 1179, 1183 (9th Cir. 2019). In one recent case, a court rejected a challenge to the standard as arbitrary and capricious, when an SAR was based on an individual's "potential access to a 'flight simulator type of game,' his conversion to Islam, and his 'pious demeanor.'" *Id.*

> As originally conceived in October 2007, SARs involved "tips and leads" information, that is, an "uncorroborated report or information that alleges or indicates some form of possible criminal activity." Tips and leads required only "mere suspicion," a lower standard than the reasonable suspicion required for criminal intelligence data.... [A] somewhat stricter standard [was subsequently implemented] — "reasonably indicative" — albeit one still less demanding than the reasonable suspicion standard. Given the lower reasonably indicative standard . . . some SARs do not rise to the level of criminal intelligence. This lower threshold underscores the purpose of [SARs]: to determine whether to engage in "follow-up information gathering" about potential terrorist activity, not necessarily to determine whether a crime has occurred. [*Id.* at 1188.]

Should the standard be higher? Does the answer depend in part on what the fusion centers or their participants do with the SARs?

Unfortunately, these centers reportedly have not always targeted their collection efforts appropriately and have not often produced actionable intelligence. A 2012 Senate study found that "the fusion centers often produced irrelevant, useless or inappropriate intelligence reporting to DHS, and many produced no intelligence reporting whatsoever." U.S. Senate Permanent Subcomm. on Investigations, *Federal Support for and Involvement in State and Local Fusion Centers* 2 (Oct. 3, 2012).

THE INTELLIGENCE COMMUNITY: ORGANIZATION AND AUTHORITY: SUMMARY OF BASIC PRINCIPLES

- The post–WWII structure of the U.S. national security community was initially set by the National Security Act of 1947, which created the National Security Council and the Central Intelligence Agency, but which left military intelligence services untouched.

- The 1947 Act, as amended, charges the CIA with collection abroad and "such other functions and duties related to intelligence affecting the national security as the President . . . may direct." But the CIA was denied authority for "police, subpoena, or law enforcement powers or internal security functions," leaving these by default to the Federal Bureau of Investigation at the federal level, and to state and local police.

- After the Church Committee in 1976 exposed abuses by various members of the intelligence community, President Gerald Ford issued a comprehensive executive order regulating that community in order to preempt proposed statutory reform and regulation. That order evolved into Executive Order No. 12,333, issued by President Ronald Reagan, which, as amended, is still one cornerstone of intelligence law.

- The intelligence community today is made up of various agencies, as described in Executive Order No. 12,333, §3.5(h), and partly depicted in the organization chart on p. 512. Those agencies engage in the collection, analysis, and dissemination of intelligence, and in the conduct of both covert and overt kinetic activities.

- Executive Order No. 12,333 assigns responsibility for intelligence activities among members of the intelligence community, regulates their conduct, and places special limits on operations in the United States or aimed at "U.S. persons" abroad.

- Since 1947, both Congress and the Executive have adopted a variety of oversight measures to create greater accountability for intelligence activities.

- The Intelligence Reform and Terrorism Prevention Act of 2004 created the Director of National Intelligence as a cabinet-level czar of the intelligence community, with some budgetary authority over the National Intelligence Program (but not over most of the military budget), and a statutory National Counterterrorism Center in the ODNI, among other components.

- Executive Order No. 12,333 remains important as a gap-filler, supplying limits on agency intelligence activities where statutory rules do not apply or are ambiguous.

19

Covert Operations

Beginning with George Washington, virtually every President has deployed special agents to spy on and secretly engage in other activities against foreign countries on behalf of the United States. Every nation engages in clandestine espionage, of course, and spying is for the most part unregulated by either international or domestic laws. But "other activities" — covert actions — have been more controversial and more often the subject of legal regulation, at least in the post-World War II years in the United States.

These covert operations, and sometimes even secret wars, have their own particular legal authorities. This chapter provides brief case-study examples of covert operations other than intelligence collection, and it explores attempts to regulate them. In the process, it poses difficult questions about balancing security against the checks and balances supplied by the separation of powers.

We begin with a look at congressional controls on secret private military and foreign policy initiatives. Then we trace the evolution of congressional oversight of covert actions — from World War II through the Cold War and the Vietnam era to the Iran-Contra Affair — and the oversight reforms that resulted. At the end of the chapter we consider the military's role in secret warfare, as well as the employment of foreign surrogates and private contractors.

A. CURTAILING PRIVATE ACTIONS

While Congress was silent and perhaps uninformed of the President's earliest uses of covert agents, it quickly asserted control of military and other foreign adventures by private Americans. To augment the nation's fledging Navy, it issued letters of marque and reprisal to authorize privateers to attack enemy shipping, especially during the War of 1812. But it also acted early on to prohibit other independent military initiatives by passing the Neutrality Act in 1794. Five years later it passed the Logan Act of 1799, 18 U.S.C. §953 (2018), in an effort to stop private meddling in U.S. foreign affairs.

The Neutrality Act

18 U.S.C. §960 (2018)

Whoever, within the United States, knowingly begins or sets on foot or provides or prepares a means for or furnishes the money for, or takes part in, any military or naval expedition or enterprise to be carried on from thence against the territory or dominion of any foreign prince or state, or of any colony, district, or people with whom the United States is at peace, shall be fined under this title or imprisoned not more than three years, or both.

"One of the aims of the Neutrality Act was to protect the sovereignty of the United States by keeping United States citizens aloof from the intrigues of foreign government," one scholar notes. Jules Lobel, *The Rise and Decline of the Neutrality Act: Sovereign and Congressional War Powers in United States Foreign Policy,* 24 Harv. Int'l L.J. 1, 24 (1983). More important, "[b]y outlawing private warfare, the Act would insure that national policy would be made by the government acting through Congress, and not by the acts of individuals." *Id.* at 25.

The courts have had few occasions to consider the application of the Neutrality Act in modern times. One recent case, however, involved a failed coup attempt against the government of Cambodia. *United States v. Chhun,* 513 F. Supp. 2d 1179 (C.D. Cal. 2007), *aff'd,* 744 F.3d 1110 (9th Cir. 2014). There the court ruled that as a matter of fact, not law, the United States is "at peace" unless it is "involved in a declared war or active military operations against a foreign nation." *Id.* at 1184; *see also United States v. Jack,* 257 F.R.D. 221, 231 (E.D. Cal. 2009) ("active military operations" may be "open and notorious" or covert).

In a similar vein, the Logan Act criminalizes unauthorized efforts by any U.S. citizen who "directly or indirectly commences or carries on any correspondence or intercourse with any foreign government or of any officer or agent thereof, in relation to any disputes or controversies with the United States. . . ." 18 U.S.C. §953.

The Logan Act has been "used as a political tool to threaten citizens engaged in private diplomacy and to solidify the President's foreign relations power." Christiaan Highsmith, *The Liberty-Speech Framework: Resolving the Tension Between Foreign Affairs Power and First Amendment Freedoms,* 88 B.U. L. Rev. 745, 753 (2008). Persons accused by political opponents of having violated the Logan Act include former Senator George McGovern, the Reverend Jesse Jackson, and activist Jane Fonda for their private trips as self-declared unofficial envoys of the United States; then-Speaker of the House Nancy Pelosi for travel to Syria and dialog with Syrian officials; and 47 Republican senators who sent a letter to the Iranian government regarding President Obama's attempts to complete a nuclear weapons agreement between Iran and six major powers. *See* Steve Vladeck, *The Iran Letter and the Logan Act,* Lawfare, Mar. 10, 2015. However, no one has ever been prosecuted for violating the Logan Act (the only indictment under the statute came in 1803), and an attempt to invoke it today would raise serious First and Fifth Amendment problems.

Those difficulties notwithstanding, a potential violation of the statute was apparently one of the concerns that led then-Acting Attorney General Sally Yates to warn the Trump administration in early 2017 about then-National Security Adviser Michael

Flynn — a warning that may have helped to force Flynn's resignation. *See* Adam Entous, Ellen Nakashima & Philip Rucker, *Justice Department Warned White House That Flynn Could Be Vulnerable to Russian Blackmail, Officials Say,* Wash. Post, Feb. 13, 2017. Indeed, when Flynn pleaded guilty on December 1, 2017, to making false statements to federal investigators, two prominent scholars concluded that he almost certainly admitted to violating the Logan Act, as well. *See* Daniel Hemel & Eric Posner, *Why the Trump Team Should Fear the Logan Act,* N.Y. Times, Dec. 4, 2017. Do these developments suggest that the Logan Act is not such a dead letter, after all? That it is useful at least as a means through which government investigators and prosecutors can obtain leverage over potential witnesses? Something else?

In the controversial report by the House Intelligence Committee summarizing its investigation into Russian interference in the 2016 presidential election, Republican members recommended repealing the Logan Act altogether. *See* H. Perm. Select Comm. on Intelligence, *Report on Russian Active Measures* 124 (Mar. 22, 2018). Would that be wise?

Notes and Questions

1. *The Problem with Private Foreign Initiatives?* Why should Congress care about non-government uses of force against foreign governments or about private efforts to intercede in disputes between the United States and other nations? Should any such concerns be allayed by the clear identification of private initiatives as clearly private?

2. *Problems in Applying the Laws?* If you were defending someone charged with violating either the Neutrality Act or the Logan Act, can you describe First and Fifth Amendment challenges you would raise on behalf of your client?

3. *A Problem of Selective Prosecution?* Can you guess why the two statutes described here have been invoked so rarely? On June 9, 2016, several individuals associated with the Trump presidential campaign met secretly with representatives of the Russian government to discuss the easing of U.S. sanctions against Russian officials. U.S. Dep't of Justice, *Report on the Investigation into Russian Interference in the 2016 Presidential Election* (Mueller Report) 110-120 (Mar. 2019). Should that private initiative be prosecuted as a violation of the Logan Act?

B. EARLY CIA COVERT OPERATIONS

The CIA traces its origins to an executive order, issued by President Roosevelt in 1941, establishing the Office of Coordination and Information in the White House. Eleven months later, OCI became the Office of Strategic Services, and OSS undertook both clandestine intelligence collection and covert action throughout the Second World War.

In 1945, President Truman disbanded OSS and in its place established the National Intelligence Authority and the Central Intelligence Group by a presidential directive. He authorized the CIG to plan, develop and coordinate "such other functions and duties related to intelligence affecting the national security as the President . . . may from time to time direct," an instruction later interpreted by some to include covert actions. Robert Borosage, *Para-Legal Authority and Its Perils*, 40 Law & Contemp. Probs. 166, 173-174 (1976).

In the National Security Act of 1947, Congress established the Central Intelligence Agency to replace the CIG and manage all of the nation's intelligence operations. Pub. L. No. 80-253, §102, 61 Stat. 495, 497-499 (codified as amended at 50 U.S.C. §§3035-3037 (2018)), set forth in part *supra* p. 508. Like the earlier directive establishing the CIG, the National Security Act of 1947 includes language that authorizes the CIA to "perform such other functions and duties related to intelligence affecting the national security as the President . . . may direct." 50 U.S.C. §3036(d)(4). This provision was originally referred to as "the fifth function" because of its original numbering in the National Security Act and the ambiguity surrounding the actual operations it authorized. CIA Special Counsel Rogovin argued that the fifth function permitted the CIA "to conduct a broad range of operational assignments," including what are today called covert actions. *U.S. Intelligence Agencies and Activities: Risks and Control of Foreign Intelligence: Hearings Before the H. Select Comm. on Intelligence*, 94th Cong., pt. 5, 1729, 1734-1735 (1976) (statement of Mitchell Rogovin, Special Counsel to the Director of Central Intelligence). Others disagreed, asserting that the fifth function included only intelligence collection, citing the absence from the legislative history of explicit references to covert or paramilitary actions. *See, e.g.*, Borosage, *supra*, at 175-177. *See generally* Church Committee, *Final Report of the Select Committee to Study Governmental Operations with Respect to Intelligence Activities*, S. Rep. No. 94-755, bk. I, at 131-135 (1976), *available at* http://www.intelligence.senate.gov/churchcommittee.html.

As the CIA's resort to covert operations grew more frequent, attempts to harmonize its use with public policy were halting and controversial. Alex Whiting, Ctr. for Nat'l Security Studies (CNSS), *Covert Operations and the Democratic Process: The Implications of the Iran/Contra Affair* 9 (1987) (hereinafter *CNSS*). Many officials argued that a range of covert activities seemed to be at odds with American principles. A 1954 report on CIA activities reflected this view:

> It is now clear that we are facing an implacable enemy whose avowed objective is world domination by whatever means and at whatever cost. There are no rules in such a game. Hitherto acceptable norms of human conduct do not apply. If the U.S. is to survive, long-standing American concepts of "fair play" must be reconsidered. We must develop effective espionage and counterespionage services and must learn to subvert, sabotage, and destroy our enemies by more clever, more sophisticated, and more effective methods than those used against us. It may become necessary that the American people be made acquainted with, understand and support this fundamentally repugnant philosophy. [*Quoted in Church Comm., supra*, bk. I, at 50.]

These concerns seemed to be borne out by secret CIA operations in Cuba beginning in the Kennedy administration.

Case Study: Covert Operations in Cuba

In 1959, Fidel Castro seized power in Cuba after a guerrilla war, and soon provided the Soviet Union with a military footprint just 90 miles from the United States. By 1960, fearing that Castro's communism might spread through Latin America, President Dwight Eisenhower ordered the CIA to come up with a covert plan for getting rid of Castro. The plan approved by the President authorized the CIA to unify and strengthen the opposition to Castro outside of Cuba, build a guerrilla army inside Cuba, carry out a propaganda campaign against Castro, and train a paramilitary force outside of Cuba that could lead an invasion.

Although the paramilitary force numbered only about 1,000 persons by early 1961, CIA Director Allen Dulles told a congressional oversight panel that he expected an invasion by the exile force to spark a general uprising on the island. Newly inaugurated President Kennedy went ahead with the Bay of Pigs invasion on April 15, 1961. The invaders were pinned down on the beach, and, to maintain the deniability of its part in the operation, the United States declined to provide air cover. Within two days the fighting ended, after Cuban forces killed 114 of the exiles and took 1,189 prisoners.

Between the Bay of Pigs invasion in 1961 and the reestablishment of diplomatic relations between the United States and Cuba in 2015, the CIA and other U.S. agencies engaged in a wide range of covert actions in Cuba. The CIA attempted to assassinate Castro in far-fetched schemes, including placing an exploding seashell where he went snorkeling and recruiting a mistress to poison his drinks. (The failure of such efforts led some wags to suggest that the CIA adopt the motto, "Killing Castro for Fifty Years.") Throughout the Cold War, the United States also used covert economic destabilization actions in an effort to undermine the Castro government.

Even after the end of the Cold War and well into the Obama presidency, the U.S. Agency for International Development (USAID) sponsored a series of covert programs in Cuba that came to light along with the normalization of news coverage. Among the USAID programs was a "Cuban Twitter" platform, another sending Latin American young people to Cuba to set up front organizations such as an HIV/AIDS workshop, and one involving secret recruiting of Cuban rappers to mobilize young audiences against the government.

Notes and Questions

1. *Covert Actions in Cuba.* Consider the range of covert operations carried out by the CIA in Cuba in light of the requirements of the Constitution, the Neutrality Act, the National Security Act, and Executive Order No. 12,333. Can you say which operations were clearly lawful or unlawful under U.S. law? What additional information would you need to decide the lawfulness of individual operations?

2. *Covert Policies vs. Overt Principles.* In an effort to harmonize covert and public policies, it has been suggested that covert operations form some part of a larger overt program. *CNSS, supra,* at 9. Even more broadly, "consistency with American principles" has been suggested as a test for covert operations, requiring that both the aims and methods of particular operations be capable of winning public support if the operations were overt. *Id.* Would the CIA actions in Cuba have met this test? Would

political assassinations? Efforts to subvert democratic governments? Support for internal security forces that engage in the systematic violation of human rights?

If there are to be "occasional circumstances in which strikes must be covert and/ or unacknowledged," how and by whom would those occasional circumstances be determined? Would such a policy be lawful?

3. Secrecy and Inherent Power. Arguments that the President may unilaterally engage the nation in covert intelligence operations, including paramilitary warfare, typically rely on the perceived need for secrecy. *See* Statement of Mitchell Rogovin, *supra,* at 1731-1733. Is there an inherent executive power to act secretly? *See In re Sealed Case,* 310 F.3d 717, 742 (FISA Ct. Rev. 2002) (presuming that the President has inherent authority to conduct warrantless surveillance to obtain foreign intelligence information). Does either the Declare War Clause or the Marque and Reprisal Clause represent a check on that power?

4. Secrecy and Delegated Power. Recall the theories of congressional acquiescence and executive usage from Chapters 3-4 Can Congress be said to have tacitly approved the Executive's covert actions in Cuba?

C. CIA OPERATIONS AND CONGRESSIONAL OVERSIGHT

The justification for covert operations shifted sharply between the immediate post-war years and the early 1970s, from containing international communism to serving more broadly as an instrument of U.S. foreign policy. With the shift came growing efforts by Congress to play a meaningful role in regulating those operations.

1. From the Cold War Through Vietnam

> For the first thirty years of its existence the agency's relationship with Congress was very informal indeed. In essence, the DCI and his close colleagues dealt personally and informally with the chairmen of the important and relevant Senate and House committees . . . and other senators and congressmen who were "friends" or who had significant political influence in areas important to the agency in Washington. This worked because the agency was trusted, its directors were respected, and it was seen as being America's principal defense against the subterranean machinations of world communism. . . .
>
> The reluctance of the legislators to press the CIA for information about operations . . . was entirely understandable. . . . They preferred to be able to plead ignorance of specific information so that they would not find themselves compromised politically. CIA officials were content with this arrangement; they made it clear that they would provide the information asked of them, and if it was not asked, so be it. For over twenty-five years the system worked. [John Ranelagh, *The Agency: The Rise and Decline of the CIA* 281-285 (1988).]

This all changed with congressional hearings into intelligence activities at home and abroad during the Vietnam War era. In particular, the Church Committee reports detailed CIA actions that seemed to betray not only U.S. public policy but also fundamental American values. They disclosed, for example, covert actions in Chile during the 1960s and early 1970s, outlined below.

Central Intelligence Agency, CIA Activities in Chile

Sept. 18, 2000

https://www.cia.gov/library/reports/general-reports-1/chile/

In the 1960s and the early 1970s, as part of the US Government policy to try to influence events in Chile, the CIA undertook specific covert action projects in Chile.... The overwhelming objective — firmly rooted in the policy of the period — was to discredit Marxist-leaning political leaders, especially Dr. Salvador Allende, and to strengthen and encourage their civilian and military opponents to prevent them from assuming power.

Overview of Covert Actions. At the direction of the White House and interagency policy coordination committees, CIA undertook... sustained propaganda efforts, including financial support for major news media, against Allende and other Marxists. Political action projects supported selected parties before and after the 1964 elections and after Allende's 1970 election....

Support for Coup in 1970.... CIA sought to instigate a coup to prevent Allende from taking office after he won a plurality in the 4 September election and before, as Constitutionally required because he did not win an absolute majority, the Chilean Congress reaffirmed his victory. CIA was working with three different groups of plotters. All three groups made it clear that any coup would require the kidnapping of Army Commander Rene Schneider, who felt deeply that the Constitution required that the Army allow Allende to assume power. CIA agreed with that assessment. Although CIA provided weapons to one of the groups, we have found no information that the plotters' or CIA's intention was for the general to be killed. Contact with one group of plotters was dropped early on because of its extremist tendencies. CIA provided tear gas, submachine-guns and ammunition to the second group. The third group attempted to kidnap Schneider, mortally wounding him in the attack. CIA had previously encouraged this group to launch a coup but withdrew support four days before the attack because, in CIA's assessment, the group could not carry it out successfully.

Awareness of Coup Plotting in 1973. Although CIA did not instigate the coup that ended Allende's government on 11 September 1973, it was aware of coup-plotting by the military, had ongoing intelligence collection relationships with some plotters, and — because CIA did not discourage the takeover and had sought to instigate a coup in 1970 — probably appeared to condone it. There was no way that anyone, including CIA, could have known that Allende would refuse the putchists' offer of safe passage out of the country and that instead — with *La Moneda* Palace under bombardment from tanks and airplanes and in flames — would take his own life.

Knowledge of Human Rights Violations. CIA officers were aware of and reported to analysts and policymakers in 1973 that General Pinochet and the forces that overthrew the Allende Government were conducting a severe campaign against leftists and perceived political enemies in the early months after the coup. Activities of some security services portended a long-term effort to suppress opponents. In January 1974, CIA officers and assets were tasked to report on human rights violations by the Chilean government....

Note and Questions

The CIA in Chile. The Church Committee reported that at a September 15, 1970, meeting between President Nixon, National Security Adviser Henry Kissinger, DCI Richard Helms, and Attorney General John Mitchell, Nixon and Kissinger directed the CIA to prevent Allende from taking power. According to Helms' notes, they were "not concerned [about the] risks involved," and they wanted Helms to "make the economy scream." *CIA Activities in Chile, supra.* President Nixon instructed Helms and the CIA not to inform the 40 Committee (then the executive decision-making body on covert operations), the State or Defense Departments, or the ambassador in Santiago. Staff of the S. Select Comm. to Study Governmental Operations with Respect to Intelligence Activities, *Covert Action in Chile 1963-1973,* 94th Cong., 41 (Comm. Print 1975). Were the instructions to Helms lawful? Do you think Congress would have approved of the CIA's involvement there if it had been informed? Would the American people have approved?

2. The Hughes-Ryan Amendment of 1974 and the Intelligence Oversight Act of 1980

Any remaining doubt that Congress had by legislation recognized the CIA's covert action function ended in 1974, when the Hughes-Ryan Amendment to the Foreign Assistance Act was enacted. But Hughes-Ryan also signaled Congress's determination to keep an eye on the Agency's secret activities.

Hughes-Ryan Amendment

Foreign Assistance Act of 1974, Pub. L. No. 93-559, §32, 88 Stat. 1795, 1804

Limitation on Intelligence Activities. (a) No funds appropriated under the authority of this or any other Act may be expended by or on behalf of the Central Intelligence Agency for operations in foreign countries, other than activities intended solely for obtaining necessary intelligence, unless and until the President finds that each such operation is important to the national security of the United States and reports, in a timely fashion, a description and scope of such operation to the appropriate committees of the Congress, including the Committee on Foreign Relations of the United States Senate and the Committee on Foreign Affairs of the United States House of Representatives. . . .

Before Hughes-Ryan, the CIA reported to the Armed Services Committees and the Appropriations Committees of both Houses. Hughes-Ryan added the House Foreign Affairs and the Senate Foreign Relations Committees. The seventh and eighth oversight committees were added following the Church Committee investigations in

1975-1976, when each chamber established a special committee for oversight of intelligence.

One clear purpose of Hughes-Ryan was to end the practice of "plausible deniability" for the President, at least in his relations with Congress. *See* Church Comm., bk. I, at 58 ("The concept of plausible denial . . . is dead."). In addition to enhancing accountability for covert operations, requiring the President's approval was supposed to assure the President's careful review of proposals and promote effective internal debate in the executive branch. *CNSS, supra* p. 546, at 37-41. Meanwhile, CIA General Counsel Rogovin maintained that the amendment "clearly implies that the CIA is authorized to plan and conduct covert action." Statement of Mitchell Rogovin, *supra* p. 546, at 1737.

Subsequently, with the seizure of 52 American hostages by Iranian militants on November 4, 1979, and the Soviet invasion of Afghanistan six weeks later, the tide effectively swung away from regulation of the intelligence community and toward an enhanced intelligence capability.

As a result, the Intelligence Oversight Act of 1980, Pub. L. No. 96-450, 94 Stat. 1975 (1981), was an especially modest product, mainly codifying oversight measures already embodied in President Carter's Executive Order No. 12,036, §§3-4, 43 Fed. Reg. 3674, 3688-3692 (Jan. 24, 1978). Still, it beefed up the Hughes-Ryan reporting requirement by instructing heads of entities involved in intelligence activities to "keep [the intelligence committees] fully and currently informed of all intelligence activities" for which the United States is responsible, "including any significant anticipated intelligence activity." Intelligence Oversight Act of 1980, §407(b)(1) (adding new §501 of the National Security Act of 1947, codified today as amended at 50 U.S.C. §3092(a)(1)). The 1980 act provided that the notice provisions did not constitute a prior approval requirement for covert actions, and it permitted the President to limit notice to a "Gang of Eight" — the Speaker of the House and House Minority Leader; the Senate Majority and Minority Leaders; and the Chair and Ranking Members of the two intelligence committees — when necessary "to meet extraordinary circumstances affecting vital interests of the United States." *Id.* The act also required intelligence agencies to report to the intelligence committees "in a timely fashion . . . any illegal intelligence activity or significant intelligence failure and any corrective action" taken or planned in connection with illegal activity or intelligence failure. *Id.*

Notes and Questions

1. *Authorization of Covert Actions?* Did the Hughes-Ryan Amendment provide statutory authority for covert actions? If so, was it wise to do so? Was it preferable to the cryptic fifth function provision of the 1947 Act?

2. *Implementing Hughes-Ryan.* Consider the threshold for invoking Hughes-Ryan — that an operation be "important to the national security." What showing must the President have made to satisfy this standard? Should Congress have substituted "essential" or "grave threats" for "important"?

Should Congress have required the reports to be in writing prior to implementing a covert operation? Should it have required that each project be approved by

Congress in advance? Note that Hughes-Ryan was an exercise of Congress's defense appropriations power. How, if at all, does that fact affect your answers to these questions?

3. Budget Oversight

The importance of the defense appropriations power as a means of ensuring congressional participation in national security decision making is clear. Once funds are appropriated for covert actions, however, the open-ended authority given to the CIA in the National Security Act, along with the secret nature of intelligence operations, may make oversight of the expenditure of those funds especially difficult.

The 1949 Central Intelligence Agency Act grants expansive authority to the CIA concerning the transfer and use of public funds. The act states that sums made available to the CIA "may be expended without regard to the provisions of law and regulations relating to the expenditure of Government funds." 50 U.S.C. §3510(b) (2018). Moreover, instead of direct appropriations to the CIA, the 1949 Act authorizes the Agency to transfer to and receive from other government agencies "such sums as may be approved" by the Office of Management and Budget (OMB) for any of the functions or activities authorized by the National Security Act of 1947. *Id.* §3506(a)(1). Other agencies are also permitted to transfer to or receive from the CIA such sums "without regard to any provisions of law limiting or prohibiting transfers between appropriations." *Id.* Thus, funds for the intelligence community are first concealed in various inflated appropriation bills and then secretly transferred by OMB to the intelligence agencies after the bills are enacted.

> In the formulation of the president's budget, the requests of the intelligence agencies are first coordinated by representatives of sponsoring agencies before being submitted to OMB for careful review of justifications and further coordination within the intelligence community. Once the president's budget is submitted to Congress, the portion for the intelligence agencies is segregated from the rest and discussed by members of the House and Senate Intelligence Committees and the relevant defense appropriations subcommittees meeting in executive session. The committees hold closed hearings at which agency staff answer questions and supply additional detail for the written budget justifications.
>
> Once an NFIP [National Foreign Intelligence Program, now NIP] budget is approved by the intelligence and defense appropriation committees, a classified schedule of the authorizations and an explanation of the budget issues considered by the intelligence committees is made available to the executive branch and to the appropriations and armed services committees. This classified schedule lists the recommended allocation for all intelligence programs. When floor debate on the larger appropriation bills begins, the [NIP] budget is hidden within the recommended appropriations for other agencies, recently DOD. These appropriation accounts are inflated to reflect the pending budget transfers, but the members of Congress who are debating the budget and voting on appropriations do not know which figures are inflated or by how much. Congress is thus only mechanically involved in approving the budget. . . and its action in approving the remainder of the budget is clouded with the shell game of hiding the intelligence figures within other accounts.
>
> After a budget is approved by Congress and the president, OMB receives instructions from the chair of the House Appropriations Committee as to the amounts and sources of budget transfers to be made to the intelligence agencies. OMB then carries out the transfers through its own highly secretive process. [William C. Banks & Peter Raven-Hansen, *National Security Law and the Power of the Purse* 52 (1994) (footnotes omitted).]

In 2007, Congress required that the DNI disclose the aggregate amount of funds appropriated by Congress to the NIP for the fiscal year within 30 days of the end of the fiscal year unless the President filed a written statement with Congress declaring that revealing the number "would damage national security." Implementing Recommendations of the 9/11 Commission Act of 2007, Pub. L. No. 110-53, §601, 121 Stat. 266, 335 (codified as amended at 50 U.S.C. §3306 (2018)). Yet while this measure may give the public a better sense of the overall scope of intelligence spending, it does not help Congress conduct meaningful oversight.

Notes and Questions

1. *Refining Congress's Budget and Oversight Authority?* Article I, Section 8 of the Constitution gives Congress the responsibility for approving government expenditures, while Section 9 bars the spending of unappropriated funds. For practical reasons, of course, appropriations measures are normally drawn in fairly general terms. But can you think of any legal reason that Congress could not restrict funding of covert operations to those specifically approved in advance by Congress? Would it be wise to do so?

In a case seeking public disclosure of the CIA's budget, the Supreme Court declared that "Congress has plenary power to exact any reporting and accounting requirement it considers appropriate." *United States v. Richardson*, 418 U.S. 166, 178 n.11 (1974). Do you think this means that Congress could require intelligence agencies to report to Congress any expenditures for covert operations? Possible constitutional constraints on such oversight efforts are explored in Chapter 4.

2. *Congressional Authority to Limit Public Disclosure?* Article I, Section 9, Clause 7 of the Constitution provides that "a regular Statement and Account of the Receipts and Expenditures of all public Money shall be published from time to time." Does the Constitution thus require that spending for intelligence programs, including covert action, be made public? If the "from time to time" qualifier affords some discretion to delay disclosure, is permanent budget secrecy foreclosed by the Constitution?

In the *Richardson* case, *supra*, a taxpayer-plaintiff asserted that the Statement and Account Clause required publication of the CIA budget, and that Congress's grant of discretion to withhold details of that budget in the Central Intelligence Agency Act of 1949 was unconstitutional. The Third Circuit, sitting en banc, had this to say about the Statement and Account Clause:

> A responsible and intelligent taxpayer and citizen, of course, wants to know how his tax money is being spent. Without this information he cannot intelligently follow the actions of the Congress or of the Executive. Nor can he properly fulfill his obligations as a member of the electorate. The Framers of the Constitution deemed fiscal information essential if the electorate was to exercise any control over its representatives and meet their new responsibilities as citizens of the Republic. [*Richardson v. United States*, 465 F.2d 844, 853 (3d Cir. 1972) (en banc).]

But the Supreme Court dismissed on standing grounds without reaching the disclosure issue. 418 U.S. 166.

3. Congressional Authority to Require Public Disclosure? Would a statutory requirement to publish the CIA budget be constitutional? Or *must* the Congress keep the CIA budget secret in the interest of national security? *See generally* Banks & Raven-Hansen, *supra*, at 105 (arguing that a requirement to disclose would be constitutional). Is there a lawful middle ground, such as required publication of the aggregate spending for intelligence programs without any detail? Do you think a federal court would decide this issue?

D. THE IRAN-CONTRA AFFAIR

In 1984, news reached Congress that the CIA had secretly mined seaports in Nicaragua, as part of the Reagan administration's program to support the Contras — an insurgent group — against the left-wing Sandinista government. Congress then passed the 1984 Boland Amendment, tightening prior restrictions on aid to the Contras:

> No appropriations or funds made available pursuant to this [authorization bill] to the Central Intelligence Agency, the Department of Defense, or any other agency or entity of the United States involved in intelligence activities may be obligated or expended for the purpose or which would have the effect of supporting, directly or indirectly, military or paramilitary operations in Nicaragua by any nation, group, organization, movement, or individual. [Pub. L. No. 98-473, §8066(a), 98 Stat. 1837, 1935 (1984).]

On November 3, 1986, *Al-Shiraa*, a Beirut weekly, reported that the United States had secretly sold arms to Iran, using Israel as an intermediary. Reports soon followed that linked the arms sales to a plan to gain the release of American hostages in Lebanon. After a brief investigation by the Justice Department, it was revealed that some proceeds from the arms sales to Iran had been diverted to the Contras in apparent violation of the 1984 Boland Amendment. A member of the staff of the NSC, Lieutenant Colonel Oliver L. North, was effectively in charge of both operations. He was supported by National Security Advisers Robert McFarlane and Vice Admiral John Poindexter and by CIA Director William Casey. A major scandal suddenly burst onto the scene: the Iran-Contra Affair.

The principal congressional and executive branch investigations of the Iran-Contra Affair shared a basic conclusion — that the scandal was not due to the patchwork legal controls of the national security system. The Tower Commission, appointed by President Reagan and made up of former Senator John Tower, former Senator/Secretary of State Edmund Muskie, and former National Security Adviser Brent Scowcroft, emphasized human failings, criticized the President's lax "management style," and concluded that, while systemic problems were found, "their solution does not lie in revamping the National Security Council system." President's Special Review Bd., *The Tower Commission Report* 1-4 (Feb. 26, 1987).

The congressional committees looking into the affair, formed in January 1987 in the Senate and House, merged to conduct a ten-month investigation that included 40 days of public hearings, review of more than 300,000 documents, and examination or interview of more than 500 witnesses. Their final report concluded "that the Iran-Contra Affair resulted from the failure of individuals to observe the law, not from deficiencies in existing law or in our system of governance." H. Select Comm. to

Investigate Covert Arms Transactions with Iran and S. Select Comm. on Secret Military Assistance to Iran and the Nicaraguan Opposition, *Report of the Congressional Committees Investigating the Iran-Contra Affair (Iran-Contra Report)*, S. Rep. No. 100-216, H.R. Rep. No. 100-433, at 423 (1987).

The affair raised important questions about compliance with various laws, including those restricting covert intelligence operations. It also provoked the enactment of new legislation to improve congressional oversight of such operations.

Notes and Questions

1. Arms for Hostages as a Covert Operation? A central issue in the Iran-Contra Affair was whether the President had authority to transfer arms to Iran. Did the President have the power to transfer arms as part of a covert intelligence operation, subject to the finding and reporting requirements of the Intelligence Oversight Act of 1980?

The Arms Export Control Act (AECA), 22 U.S.C. §§2751 to 2799aa-2 (2018), allows the President to sell arms to foreign countries under certain conditions, including advance notice to Congress, but it gives Congress the opportunity to veto sales over certain dollar amounts. The act also barred transfers of weapons to states that aided or abetted international terrorism, such as Iran, unless the President made a finding that "national security" required it, and notice of the finding was sent to Congress. *See id.* §2780. No notice of the transfers was given to Congress, however. The transfers also violated a U.S. arms embargo on Iran. Did the Reagan administration's characterization of the arms transfers as part of a covert intelligence operation excuse compliance with the AECA?

Another statute, the Economy Act, 31 U.S.C. §1535 (2018), permits the President to transfer functions and property from one executive agency to another. The Reagan administration argued that this statute allowed the Defense Department to transfer weapons to the CIA, which could then ship them to Iran as a covert action, free of the constraints of the AECA. Do you agree?

2. Oral Findings? If findings for the arms sales to Iran were required by Hughes-Ryan, what form should those findings have taken? Attorney General Meese testified that President Reagan's tacit oral approval of the early Israeli shipments established legal authorization for the covert direct sales. *Iran-Contra Report,* at 488. Was the Meese opinion sound in light of §501? In light of the Hughes-Ryan Amendment?

3. Constitutional Limits on Oversight? Section 501 stated that its notice requirements applied "to the extent consistent with all applicable authorities and duties, including those conferred by the Constitution upon the executive and legislative branches of the government."

President Reagan's January 17, 1986, finding that authorized direct arms sales to Iran was never reported to Congress. Like the rest of us, Congress learned of the sales through the November 1986 Beirut, Lebanon newspaper story. At a news conference shortly after the story broke, President Reagan said, "I have the right under the law to defer reporting to Congress . . . and defer it until such time as I believe it can safely be done with no risk to others." *See* Ruth Marcus, *Intelligence Law: What Notice Does It Require?*, Wash. Post, Dec. 21, 1986. Do you agree with the President's interpretation?

4. The Applicability and Constitutionality of Boland II. Supporters of the Reagan administration, and the minority report on the Iran-Contra Affair, argued that the 1984 Boland Amendment did not apply to activities of the NSC. Compare its language, *supra* p. 554, with the National Security Act of 1947 provision creating the NSC, *supra* p. 511. Was the NSC covered? Other supporters argued that if the 1984 Boland Amendment did apply to the NSC, then it impermissibly infringed on the President's Article II powers. *See* Eugene V. Rostow, *President, Prime Minister, or Constitutional Monarch?* 18, 22-23 (Institute for Nat'l Strategic Studies 1989). This argument posed a separation-of-powers clash seemingly falling into Justice Jackson's third category.

How would you resolve that clash? Does the Commander-in-Chief Clause empower the President to conduct covert operations without regard for funding restrictions enacted by Congress? Of what relevance is Justice Jackson's dictum in *The Steel Seizure Case* that, while the President's power of command is plenary, "only Congress can provide him an army or navy to command"? *Youngstown Sheet & Tube Co. v. Sawyer*, 343 U.S. 579, 644 (1952) (Jackson, J., concurring). Does Justice Jackson's proposition apply as much to secret or proxy armies as to public armies? Is the Marque and Reprisal Clause relevant? The Appropriations Clause? If there was a clash, which branch should prevail and why?

5. Congressional Limits on Spending Third-Party Contributions. Instead of attacking the Boland Amendment head-on, the Reagan administration sought another way around. It solicited contributions for the Contras from private donors and foreign governments. Did these solicitations run afoul of Boland or other statutes?

> The Government may, of course, receive gifts. However, consistent with Congress' constitutionally exclusive power of the purse, gifts, like all other "miscellaneous receipts," must by statute (31 U.S.C. Section 484) be placed directly into the Treasury of the United States, and may be spent only pursuant to a Congressional appropriation....
>
> The Constitutional process that lodges control of Government expenditures exclusively in Congress is further enforced by the Anti-Deficiency Act (31 U.S.C. Section 1341), which prohibits an officer of the United States from authorizing an expenditure that has not been the subject of a Congressional appropriation, or that exceeds the amount of any applicable appropriation. Thus it provides: "An officer or employee of the United States government may not make or authorize an expenditure or obligation exceeding an amount available in an appropriation or fund for the expenditure or obligation; or involve [the] government in a contract or obligation for the payment of money before an appropriation is made unless authorized by law." Violations of the Anti-Deficiency Act are made crimes by 31 U.S.C. Section 1350. [*Iran-Contra Report*, at 412.]

At least as early as June 25, 1984, months before the strictest funding restriction was enacted, at a National Security Planning Group meeting attended by President Reagan, Secretary of State George Schultz reported an opinion of White House Chief of Staff James Baker that it would be an "impeachable offense" if the United States served as a conduit for third-country funding to the Contras. *Id.* at 39. Regarding U.S. solicitation of third-country support for the Contras, President Reagan remarked, "If such a story gets out, we'll all be hanging by our thumbs in front of the White House until we find out who did it." Nat'l Security Council, *National Security Planning Group Meeting, June 25, 1984, Minutes*, at 14.

6. *The Neutrality Act.* The United States was formally "at peace" with Nicaragua throughout the 1980s, when the United States attacked that country directly and furnished support in various forms to the Contra rebels. Did members of the Reagan administration violate the Neutrality Act, *supra* p. 544? In *United States v. Terrell,* 731 F. Supp. 473, 477 (S.D. Fla. 1989), involving a criminal prosecution under the Neutrality Act for shipping arms to the Contras, the court dismissed an argument that United States was "at peace" with Nicaragua within the meaning of the Act as "absurd," given the "unceasing efforts of the executive branch to support the Contra cause," notwithstanding the executive's "indisputable" conflict with Congress.

Could any violation of the Neutrality Act have been excused as a covert intelligence operation?

E. CONTINUING OVERSIGHT REFORMS

The congressional committees investigating the Iran-Contra Affair determined that the "Administration's conduct in the Iran-Contra Affair was inconsistent" with §501 of the National Security Act of 1947 (as added by the 1980 Intelligence Oversight Act) because the Intelligence Committees were never informed by the President of the arms sales to Iran. *Iran-Contra Report,* at 415. Both the House and Senate Intelligence Committees introduced several bills seeking generally to strengthen the oversight process.

Congressional advocates of oversight reform differed sharply with Administration officials concerning the timing for notification of congressional leaders of a presidential finding authorizing a covert action. Instead of the "in a timely fashion" language first incorporated into the Hughes-Ryan Amendment, the congressional reformers wanted presidential notification within 48 hours of a finding.

In 1991, the intelligence committees and White House agreed to a new set of oversight rules. After repealing the Hughes-Ryan Amendment, they substituted the following provisions for the Intelligence Oversight Act of 1980:

Intelligence Authorization Act, Fiscal Year 1991

Pub. L. No. 102-88, §§601-603, 105 Stat. 429, 441-445 (codified as amended at 50 U.S.C. §§3091-3094 (2018))

§3091. GENERAL CONGRESSIONAL OVERSIGHT PROVISIONS

(a) (1) The President shall ensure that the congressional intelligence committees are kept fully and currently informed of the intelligence activities of the United States, including any significant anticipated intelligence activity as required by this subchapter.

(2) Nothing in this subchapter shall be construed as requiring the approval of the congressional intelligence committees as a condition precedent to the initiation of any significant anticipated intelligence activity.

(b) The President shall ensure that any illegal intelligence activity is reported promptly to the intelligence committees, as well as any corrective action that has been taken or is planned in connection with such illegal activity.

(c) The President and the congressional intelligence committees shall each establish such written procedures as may be necessary to carry out the provisions of this subchapter.

(d) The House of Representatives and the Senate shall each establish, by rule or resolution of such House, procedures to protect from unauthorized disclosure all classified information, and all information relating to intelligence sources and methods, that is furnished to the congressional intelligence committees or to Members of Congress under this subchapter. Such procedures shall be established in consultation with the Director of National Intelligence. . . .

(e) Nothing in this chapter shall be construed as authority to withhold information from the congressional intelligence committees on the grounds that providing the information to the congressional intelligence committees would constitute the unauthorized disclosure of classified information or information relating to intelligence sources and methods.

(f) As used in this section, the term "intelligence activities" includes covert actions as defined in section 3093(e) of this title, and includes financial intelligence activities.

3092. REPORTING OF INTELLIGENCE ACTIVITIES OTHER THAN COVERT ACTIONS

(a) To the extent consistent with due regard for the protection from unauthorized disclosure of classified information relating to sensitive intelligence sources and methods or other exceptionally sensitive matters, the Director of National Intelligence and the heads of all departments, agencies, and other entities of the United States Government involved in intelligence activities shall—

(1) keep the congressional intelligence committees fully and currently informed of all intelligence activities, other than a covert action (as defined in section 3093(e) of this title), which are the responsibility of, are engaged in by, or are carried out for or on behalf of, any department, agency, or entity of the United States Government, including any significant anticipated intelligence activity and any significant intelligence failure; and

(2) furnish the congressional intelligence committees any information or material concerning intelligence activities (including the legal basis under which the intelligence activity is being or was conducted), other than covert actions, which is within their custody or control, and which is requested by either of the congressional intelligence committees in order to carry out its authorized responsibilities. . . .

§3093. PRESIDENTIAL APPROVAL AND REPORTING OF COVERT ACTIONS

(a) The President may not authorize the conduct of a covert action by departments, agencies, or entities of the United States Government unless the President determines such an action is necessary to support identifiable foreign policy objectives of the United States and is important to the national security of the United States, which determination shall be set forth in a finding that shall meet each of the following conditions:

(1) Each finding shall be in writing, unless immediate action by the United States is required and time does not permit the preparation of a written finding, in which case a written record of the President's decision shall be contemporaneously made and shall be reduced to a written finding as soon as possible but in no event more than 48 hours after the decision is made.

(2) Except as permitted by paragraph (1), a finding may not authorize or sanction a covert action, or any aspect of any such action, which already has occurred.

(3) Each finding shall specify each department, agency, or entity of the United States Government authorized to fund or otherwise participate in any significant way in such action. Any employee, contractor, or contract agent of a department, agency, or entity of the United States Government other than the Central Intelligence Agency directed to participate in any way in a covert action shall be subject either to the policies and regulations of the Central Intelligence Agency, or to written policies or regulations adopted by such department, agency, or entity, to govern such participation.

(4) Each finding shall specify whether it is contemplated that any third party which is not an element of, or a contractor or contract agent of, the United States Government, or is not otherwise subject to United States Government policies and regulations, will be used to fund or otherwise participate in any significant way in the covert action concerned, or be used to undertake the covert action concerned on behalf of the United States.

(5) A finding may not authorize any action that would violate the Constitution or any statute of the United States.

(b) To the extent consistent with due regard for the protection from unauthorized disclosure of classified information relating to sensitive intelligence sources and methods or other exceptionally sensitive matters, the Director of National Intelligence and the heads of all departments, agencies, and entities of the United States Government involved in a covert action —

(1) shall keep the congressional intelligence committees fully and currently informed of all covert actions which are the responsibility of, are engaged in by, or are carried out for or on behalf of, any department, agency, or entity of the United States Government, including significant failures; and

(2) shall furnish to the congressional intelligence committees any information or material concerning covert actions (including the legal basis under which the covert action is being or was conducted) which is in the possession, custody, or control of any department, agency, or entity of the United States Government and which is requested by either of the congressional intelligence committees in order to carry out its authorized responsibilities.

(c)(1) The President shall ensure that any finding approved pursuant to subsection (a) shall be reported in writing to the congressional intelligence committees as soon as possible after such approval and before the initiation of the covert action authorized by the finding, except as otherwise provided in paragraph (2) and paragraph (3).

(2) If the President determines that it is essential to limit access to the finding to meet extraordinary circumstances affecting vital interests of the United States, the finding may be reported to the chairmen and ranking minority members of the congressional intelligence committees, the Speaker and minority leader of the House of Representatives, the majority and minority leaders of the

Senate, and such other member or members of the congressional leadership as may be included by the President.

(3) Whenever a finding is not reported pursuant to paragraph (1) or (2) of this [sub]section, the President shall fully inform the congressional intelligence committees in a timely fashion and shall provide a statement of the reasons for not giving prior notice.

(4) In a case under paragraph (1), (2), or (3), a copy of the finding, signed by the President, shall be provided to the chairman of each congressional intelligence committee.

(5)(A) When access to a finding, or a notification provided under subsection (d)(1), is limited to the Members of Congress specified in paragraph (2), a written statement of the reasons for limiting such access shall also be provided.

(B) Not later than 180 days after a statement of reasons is submitted in accordance with subparagraph (A) or this subparagraph, the President shall ensure that—

(i) all members of the congressional intelligence committees are provided access to the finding or notification; or

(ii) a statement of reasons that it is essential to continue to limit access to such finding or such notification to meet extraordinary circumstances affecting vital interests of the United States is submitted to the Members of Congress specified in paragraph (2).

(d)(1) The President shall ensure that the congressional intelligence committees, or, if applicable, the Members of Congress specified in subsection (c)(2) [of this section,] are notified in writing of any significant change in a previously approved covert action, or any significant undertaking pursuant to a previously approved finding, in the same manner as findings are reported pursuant to subsection (c) of this section.

(2) In determining whether an activity constitutes a significant undertaking for purposes of paragraph (1), the President shall consider whether the activity—

(A) involves significant risk of loss of life;

(B) requires an expansion of existing authorities, including authorities relating to research, development, or operations;

(C) results in the expenditure of significant funds or other resources;

(D) requires notification under section 3094 of this title;

(E) gives rise to a significant risk of disclosing intelligence sources or methods; or

(F) presents a reasonably foreseeable risk of serious damage to the diplomatic relations of the United States if such activity were disclosed without authorization.

(e) As used in this subchapter, the term "covert action" means an activity or activities of the United States Government to influence political, economic, or military conditions abroad, where it is intended that the role of the United States Government will not be apparent or acknowledged publicly, but does not include—

(1) activities the primary purpose of which is to acquire intelligence, traditional counterintelligence activities, traditional activities to improve or maintain the operational security of United States Government programs, or administrative activities;

(2) traditional diplomatic or military activities or routine support to such activities;

(3) traditional law enforcement activities conducted by United States Government law enforcement agencies or routine support to such activities; or

(4) activities to provide routine support to the overt activities (other than activities described in paragraph (1), (2), or (3)) of other United States Government agencies abroad.

(f) No covert action may be conducted which is intended to influence United States political processes, public opinion, policies, or media.

(g) (1) In any case where access to a finding reported under subsection (c) or notification provided under subsection (d) (1) is not made available to all members of a congressional intelligence committee in accordance with subsection (c) (2), the President shall notify all members of such committee that such finding or such notification has been provided only to the members specified in subsection (c) (2).

(2) In any case where access to a finding reported under subsection (c) or notification provided under subsection (d) (1) is not made available to all members of a congressional intelligence committee in accordance with subsection (c) (2), the President shall provide to all members of such committee a general description regarding the finding or notification, as applicable, consistent with the reasons for not yet fully informing all members of such committee.

(3) The President shall maintain —

(A) a record of the members of Congress to whom a finding is reported under subsection (c) or notification is provided under subsection (d) (1) and the date on which each member of Congress receives such finding or notification; and

(B) each written statement provided under subsection (c) (5).

(h) For each type of activity undertaken as part of a covert action, the President shall establish in writing a plan to respond to the unauthorized public disclosure of that type of activity.

§3094. FUNDING OF INTELLIGENCE ACTIVITIES . . .

(c) No funds appropriated for, or otherwise available to, any department, agency, or entity of the United States Government may be expended, or may be directed to be expended, for any covert action, as defined in section 3093(e), unless and until a Presidential finding required by subsection (a) of section 3093 has been signed or otherwise issued in accordance with that subsection.

(d) (1) Except as otherwise specifically provided by law, funds available to an intelligence agency that are not appropriated funds may be obligated or expended for an intelligence or intelligence-related activity only if those funds are used for activities reported to the appropriate congressional committees pursuant to procedures which identify —

(A) the types of activities for which non-appropriated funds may be expended; and

(B) the circumstances under which an activity must be reported as a significant anticipated intelligence activity before such funds can be expended.

(2) Procedures for purposes of paragraph (1) shall be jointly agreed upon by the congressional intelligence committees and, as appropriate, the Director of National Intelligence or the Secretary of Defense. . . .

Notes and Questions

1. Congressional Approval of Covert Operations? The 1991 oversight legislation surely eliminated any lingering doubt that Congress approves covert operations generally, albeit with strict limitations. But consider the 1991 act's definition of "covert action." Is the revised definition clear and unambiguous? Is it an improvement over no definition at all? Does it contain all the relevant categories of activities? Does it, for example, apply to secret U.S. cyber operations? Is this definition an improvement over the one contained in Executive Order No. 12,333?

2. Gang-of-Eight Notice. One contentious provision of the Intelligence Authorization Act for Fiscal Year 2010, Pub. L. No. 111-259, §331(c)(4), 124 Stat. 2654, 2686, limited the President's power in §3093(c)(2) to restrict distribution of a covert action finding in exceptional cases to the Gang of Eight. The President now must alert other members of the intelligence committees and provide them with a "general description" of the finding. 50 U.S.C. §3093(g)(1), (2). Do you think this change significantly improves the oversight process? What about new provisions that require every procedure, statement, report, and notice to be in writing?

A few weeks after enactment of the 2010 Act, the House Intelligence Committee found in a classified report that in 16 cases since the 1990s, agencies of the intelligence community failed to provide Congress with "complete, timely and accurate information" about their activities. Scott Shane, *Intelligence Bodies Faulted on Disclosure,* N.Y. Times, Nov. 18, 2010. The lapses included a CIA targeted killing program, the destruction of interrogation videotapes made in secret CIA prisons, CIA involvement in shooting down a missionary flight in Peru, NSA compliance with surveillance laws, and FBI surveillance of a Russian spy ring. *Id.* Do you think the 2010 reforms closed the loop on oversight lapses? How could Congress encourage better compliance with the information requirement?

3. Legal Rationale for Activities. In the FY 2010 Intelligence Authorization Act, Congress required the furnishing of information about "the legal basis" for a reported intelligence activity or covert action when requested by either of the intelligence committees. Intelligence Authorization Act for Fiscal Year 2010 §333(a)(2). However, a letter from the ODNI General Counsel approving of the compromise legislation stated that the Administration understood that the new provision "would not require disclosure of any privileged information or disclosure of information in any particular form." Letter from Robert Litt, ODNI General Counsel, to Dianne Feinstein, Chair & Christopher Bond, Vice Chair, S. Select Comm. on Intelligence (Sept. 27, 2010), *available at* http://www.fas.org/irp/congress/2010_cr/sen-fy10auth.html. The "legal basis" for a particular intelligence activity typically (although not always) may be found in an Office of Legal Counsel opinion. Could Congress constitutionally amend the statute to make it clearer that such an opinion must be furnished to the committees upon request? *See Constitutionality of Statute Requiring Executive Agency to Report Directly to Congress,* 6 Op. O.L.C. 632, 638-639 (1982).

4. Findings and Deniability. Presidential findings in support of covert action must be in writing, and they must be reported to the congressional intelligence committees. Can you tell from reading the oversight legislation how much detail the findings must provide about a planned covert action? Are the procedural requirements fashioned by Congress more about form than substance? May the President still deny U.S. involvement in a particular covert operation while complying with the statutory requirements? *See* A. John Radsan, *An Overt Turn on Covert Action,* 53 St. Louis U. L.J. 485, 539 (2009) (so arguing).

5. *The Continuing Importance of Executive Order No. 12,333.* Compare the reforms enacted by Congress with the executive branch oversight provided by Executive Order No. 12,333. See *supra* p. 521. See if you can identify provisions of the executive order that have practical and legal significance beyond the requirements imposed by statute. Consider in particular §§1.3, 1.6, 2.3, 2.5, and 3.1.

6. *Which Agencies May Lawfully Conduct Covert Action?* Is it lawful for an agency other than the CIA to conduct covert action? Review the pertinent provisions of Executive Order No. 12,333 and the various relevant statutes. Could the NSA conduct a covert operation? How about the Department of State? The Department of Agriculture?

7. *Covert Action and International Law.* Apart from oversight legislation and Executive Order No. 12,333, under what circumstances must a covert action comply with treaties to which the United States is a party and customary international law? Might the answer turn on whether the treaty in question, say the U.N. Charter or Geneva Conventions, is self-executing? *See* Ashley Deeks, *Covert Action and International Law Compliance,* Lawfare, Dec. 18, 2013 (acknowledging the U.S. government view that its intelligence operations can lawfully violate non-self-executing treaties).

F. SPECIAL MILITARY OPERATIONS

Independently of the CIA, the Department of Defense (DOD) has a variety of intelligence collection responsibilities. But outside of its own regulations, it is nowhere explicitly tasked with covert or clandestine operations. Section 1.7(a)(4) of Executive Order No. 12,333 explains that

> No agency except the Central Intelligence Agency (or the Armed Forces of the United States in time of war declared by the Congress or during any period covered by a report from the President to the Congress consistent with the War Powers Resolution, Public Law 93-148) may conduct any covert action activity unless the President determines that another agency is more likely to achieve a particular objective....

Nevertheless, such operations have always been part of DOD's military repertoire. Thus, like the amended Intelligence Oversight Act, the executive order now defines "covert action" as not including "[t]raditional . . . military activities or routine support to such activities." *Id.* §3.5(b)(2).

In recent years, however, so-called special military operations, or SMOs, have generated continuing controversy and legal problems. Military intelligence operations expanded dramatically following the 9/11 attacks. Beginning with the wars in Afghanistan and Iraq, "[t]he American military [was] dispersed into the dark spaces of American foreign policy, with commando teams running spying missions that

Washington would never dreamed of approving in the years before 9/11." Mark Mazzetti, *The Way of the Knife: The CIA, a Secret Army, and a War at the Ends of the Earth* 4 (2013). And while the CIA increasingly engaged in operations traditionally performed by the military, soldiers did a lot more spying.

Notes and Questions

1. *Secret Military Operations in Principle and Practice.* It is not known publicly how often, if ever, the President directs military personnel to conduct covert operations, in accordance with §1.7(a)(4) of Executive Order No. 12,333, or how often any such operations are reported to Congress. But in the years since the United States began paramilitary operations in Afghanistan, Pakistan, and elsewhere in pursuit of Al Qaeda, Taliban, and ISIS operatives, much attention has focused on the exclusion for "traditional military activities."

Citing "an ongoing process of convergence among military and intelligence activities, institutions, and authorities," Professor Robert Chesney argues that the convergence exposes confusion and disagreement over which laws apply to military and intelligence operations. Robert Chesney, *Military-Intelligence Convergence and Law of the Title 10/Title 50 Debate*, 5 J. Nat'l Security L. & Pol'y 539 (2011). If deniable military operations are exempted from "covert action" reporting, can you say whether secret military operations outside an area of ongoing hostilities must be authorized separately by the President? *See id.* at 543 (maybe as policy, but so far not codified). Should any such operation approved by the President be reported to Congress under the 1991 Intelligence Oversight Act amendments?

The Conference Committee on the 1991 amendments stated that "traditional military activities" include "activities by military personnel under the direction and control of a United States military commander . . . preceding and related to hostilities which are either anticipated . . . to involve U.S. military forces . . . [or are ongoing] and, where the fact of the U.S. role in the overall operation is apparent or to be acknowledged publicly." *Joint Explanatory Statement of the Comm. of Conference*, H.R. Rep. No. 102-166 (1991) (Conf. Rep.).

Consider this assessment:

> [C]ongressional oversight [of special operations] could be hampered by the military's reported practice of labeling its clandestine activities — those that are intended to be secret, but that can be publicly acknowledged if discovered or inadvertently revealed — as "operational preparation of the environment," rather than intelligence activities, even though they may pose the same diplomatic and national security risks. As thus characterized, these activities might not be reported to the intelligence committees.[40] Any oversight that occurred would be conducted instead by the House and Senate Armed Services Committees. Such a division of responsibilities might create dangerous confusion.
>
> Congressional involvement also might be frustrated by the statutory exclusion of "traditional . . . military activities or routine support to such activities" from the definition of "covert action." If secret military preparations . . . are regarded as "traditional military activities," under the rationale outlined above they might escape both the presidential findings

---

40. According to one knowledgeable source, all such activities probably are reported as "intelligence activities" under §3091, although the military regards these reports as voluntary.

requirement for covert actions and any reporting to the intelligence committees. [Stephen Dycus, *Congress's Role in Cyber Warfare,* 4 J. Nat'l Security L. & Pol'y 155, 161-162 (2010).]

How much discretion does DOD have in deciding whether to label a secret military operation a "covert action"? What arguments could you make for avoiding the finding and reporting requirement for an operation conducted by military special forces?

Was the 2011 military operation that resulted in the killing of Osama bin Laden in Pakistan a "covert action" for the purpose of the executive order? For the purpose of the 1991 Act?

2. *Paramilitary or Military?* If Army Special Forces participate in covert actions under the direction of the CIA, are its personnel bound by Army regulations? By the laws of armed conflict? If captured, CIA operatives likely do not enjoy the protections of the Geneva Conventions, including prisoner-of-war status. See *supra* pp. 275-283; Gary D. Solis, *The Law of Armed Conflict: International Humanitarian Law in War* 220-224 (2010) (engaging in hostilities without wearing a uniform likely causes loss of combatant status). Would providing uniforms to CIA operatives, with insignia or some other way to identify them as working for the CIA, solve the Geneva Conventions gap?

3. *Two Paramilitary Organizations or One?* Are there good reasons for the United States to have two paramilitary organizations — one managed by the CIA and one run by DOD? Is there a legal problem with this redundancy?

G. OUTSOURCING SECRET WAR

1. Employment of Foreign Paramilitary Forces

When the United States invaded Afghanistan in pursuit of Al Qaeda and their Taliban supporters after the 9/11 attacks, CIA paramilitary personnel were the first forces on the ground, where they established relationships with members of the Northern Alliance and cooperated with them in planning an offensive against Taliban and Al Qaeda targets. Robert L. Grenier, *88 Days to Kandahar: A CIA Diary* 97-146 (2015). U.S. operations involving foreign paramilitary forces began much earlier, however. Here is just one example.

Case Study: The Armée Clandestine in Laos

After the 1962 Geneva agreements "neutralized" Laos and required all "foreign military personnel" to leave the country (see *supra* p. 321), the CIA took over a U.S. paramilitary operation for control of northern and central Laos in support of the government and against Communist Pathet Lao and North Vietnamese forces. Director of Central Intelligence (DCI) William Colby organized L'Armée Clandestine with a handful of CIA case officers and ran what became the largest paramilitary operation in U.S. history from across the border in Thailand. Tens of thousands of Hmong and other tribesmen were recruited for the CIA's private army. Upwards of 20,000 of them were U.S.-paid "volunteers" who had resigned from the Thai army. Colby and other case officers (substantially made up of Army Special Forces troops who joined the CIA payroll after the 1962 accords) trained, supplied, and transported these volunteers, and sometimes directed and fought alongside them in battles against the Pathet Lao and/or supported them with bombing raids.

Nearly all of the equipment for the Armée Clandestine was supplied by the United States, typically delivered under the cover of the U.S. Agency for International Development (USAID). The CIA also engaged in food drops and various "nation-building" activities in Laos, in pursuit of Laotian support for American policies. As the costs of the program mounted, CIA briefs to subcommittees of the appropriations committees in Congress persuaded members to support ever-increasing spending for the covert program.

By the mid-1960s, about 250 Americans were either in Laos or commuting to assignments there. Air America pilots flew in support of the Laos program during time off from their regular flight routes. The pilots were paid bonuses, given tax breaks, and could earn $40,000 or more on top of their regular salary. Flying out of its Thailand bases, the 1969 Air America fleet had 29 helicopters, 20 light planes, and 19 medium transport planes. The air combat task was carried out by Air Force planes and pilots, not Air America. The U.S. Air Force role eventually grew to 100 fighter-bombers and supporting gunships.

By the late 1960s, CIA veterans grew tired and leery of the Laos operation, not due to the growing dissatisfaction with the larger war, but because the program was cumbersome and increasingly overt rather than smoothly run and covert. Still, until the *New York Times* reported on the U.S. role in Laos in 1969, most Americans and members of Congress were unaware of the paramilitary program there.

More recently, the CIA reportedly created, controlled, and funded a secret 3,000-man paramilitary force in Afghanistan beginning in 2010. The force consisted of local Afghans, known as Counterterrorism Pursuit Teams, trained to conduct covert paramilitary operations in Pakistan against Al Qaeda and Taliban targets. Bob Woodward, *Obama's Wars* 8, 52, 367 (2010).

Notes and Questions

1. The CIA in Laos. By what legal authority did the CIA use L'Armée Clandestine? What purpose was served by keeping this operation secret from members of Congress and from the American people?

The CIA and Air America were passive participants in the lucrative and pervasive drug trade in Laos and Thailand — passive only in the sense that intelligence officials reported on the movement of drugs, sometimes by CIA-paid assets and on proprietary aircraft, but did nothing to stop it. Reporting about these linkages to unsavory elements helped spur congressional hearings and the eventual end of the Laotian secret war. *See* John Prados, *Safe for Democracy: The Secret Wars of the CIA* 344-357 (2006).

2. The CIA in Syria. In 2012, the United States began a covert operation that supplied weapons (from a stockpile seized earlier from the Qaddafi regime in Libya) to rebels fighting the government of Bashar al Assad in Syria. The existence if not the details of the covert operation in Syria was publicly discussed by government officials in the media from the outset, apparently to broadcast that the United States was supporting the Syrian rebels without getting involved in a larger commitment.

Is it legally significant that CIA support for the Syrian rebels was publicly discussed by government officials in the media? A *Washington Post* story claimed that the CIA program was chosen by the Obama administration "to avoid international law restrictions on military efforts to overthrow another government and the need for wider congressional approval." Karen DeYoung, *Congressional Panels Approve Arms Aid to Syrian Opposition,* Wash. Post, July 22, 2013. Does using the CIA to support the rebels legally avoid the use of force restrictions in the U.N. Charter? If so, upon what theory?

Does compliance with congressional oversight requirements suffice as domestic legal authorization for the support of foreign paramilitary forces?

3. Preparing Proxies. The U.S. Army has recently established a security assistance program to train allied local forces — in effect, proxies — to respond to threats to U.S. security interests. The core mission of its Security Force Assistance Brigade (SFAB), https://www.goarmy.com/careers-and-jobs/current-and-prior-service/advance-your-career/security-force-assistance-brigade.html, is to "conduct training, advising, assisting, enabling, and accompanying operations with allied and partner nations." Do you see any downside risks or legal problems with the SFAB?

2. Dirty Assets

The United States sometimes recruits or cooperates with foreign proxies who are directed by their U.S. handlers to carry out missions that violate U.S. law, or who act on their own in ways that are illegal or that offend basic American values. Hence the name "dirty assets." Examples follow, with questions about how to regulate such assets.

- In 2010, Mohammed Zia Salehi was the chief of administration of the Afghan National Security Council. During a U.S.-led corruption investigation, Salehi was overheard on a wiretap soliciting a bribe to intervene in the investigation of a politically connected company suspected of exporting large sums of money from the country. Salehi was arrested and jailed in July 2010, but after intervention by Afghan President Hamid Karzai, he was released and the charges against him were dismissed. At the time of his arrest, Afghan and U.S. officials confirmed that Salehi had been on the CIA's payroll for years.

  It remains unclear what Salehi does or did for the Agency. A U.S. official defended the practice of paying foreign government officials even if they engage in corrupt practices: "If you want intelligence in a war zone, you're not going to get it from Mother Theresa or Mary Poppins." Dexter Filkins & Mark Mazzetti, *Karzai Aide in Corruption Inquiry Is Tied to CIA*, N.Y. Times, Aug. 25, 2010; Rod Norland, *Afghans Drop All Corruption Charges Against Karzai Aide*, N.Y. Times, Nov. 8, 2010.

- Humam Khalil Abu-Mulal al-Balawi, a young Jordanian medical doctor with a foreign wife and two children, was picked up in 2009 by Jordanian intelligence officials for questioning after his pseudonymous postings on extremist websites became especially strident. Sensing an intelligence opportunity, the Jordanians told Balawi that if he traveled to Pakistan and infiltrated extremist groups, he and his family would be left alone. Balawi agreed, and he began working for Jordanian and, later, American intelligence handlers after Balawi promised to lead them to Ayman al-Zawahiri, the deputy leader of Al Qaeda.

  Balawi produced credible information about extremists inside Pakistan, and the CIA relied on his information in conducting operations there. Then, on December 30, 2009, Balawi drove a red station wagon from Pakistan to a CIA installation in Afghanistan, where he was greeted by a CIA expert on Al Qaeda, who hoped to learn how the Americans could kill or capture al-Zawahiri. When an American security guard approached Balawi to conduct a pat-down search, Balawi triggered a switch and the ensuing blast killed everyone in the immediate area, including the CIA expert, an analyst, and three other CIA officers, along with two American security guards on contract to the Agency, a Jordanian intelligence officer, and the car's driver. *See* Joby Warrick, *The Triple Agent* (2012).

- In the early 1970s, the CIA managed to penetrate what was then the most feared terrorist organization that had targeted the United States and U.S. citizens in the Middle East — the Palestine Liberation Organization (PLO). Through a secret arrangement with Ali Hassan Salameh, the PLO's chief of intelligence, the CIA obtained extensive information about terrorist activities and groups, and Salameh himself intervened to stop planned attacks. Part of Salameh's motivation was his belief that working for the CIA could help the PLO achieve its political goals in the Middle East.

  Salameh was, however, a member of Yasir Arafat's "Black September" organization, and he may have helped plan the slaughter of Israeli athletes at the Munich Olympics in 1972. Although the CIA subsequently targeted Salameh for assassination, agents continued to work with him until the Israelis killed him in 1979. *See* David Ignatius, *Penetrating Terrorist Networks*, Wash. Post, Sept. 16, 2001.

Notes and Questions

1. Regulating Dirty Assets. One of the risks of recruiting or collaborating with a foreign asset to assist in intelligence work is the relative inability to control that asset's behavior as an employee or to anticipate problems through vetting prior to employment. How should Congress or the executive branch regulate the CIA in its use of such assets to ensure that they operate within a prescribed range of activities? What should that range be? What remedies should exist when abuses occur?

2. *Cooperating with Foreign Intelligence Agencies.* What, if any, legal rules should govern cooperation with foreign governments' intelligence agencies? Was it the Jordanians' fault that Abu-Mulal al-Balawi successfully duped the CIA?

For several years a Baltimore-based company, Cyber Point, contracted with the United Arab Emirates (UAE) to assist its recently established signals intelligence agency. Cyber Point eventually hired a group of ex-NSA employees to work in the UAE on a signals intelligence matter called Project Raven. Although Project Raven was later transferred to a different UAE-based company, along the way the Americans learned that Project Raven was collecting information on Americans. It is unclear whether the Americans were themselves targeting other Americans. Christopher Bing & Joel Schectman, *Special Report: Inside the UAE's Secret Hacking Team of U.S. Mercenaries,* Reuters, Jan. 30, 2019. Should the U.S. engage in vetting American employees of foreign governments? Should their activities be monitored in some way?

Under the Arms Export Control Act (AECA), *supra,* the executive branch is authorized to prohibit the unlicensed export of "defense articles" and "defense services." Items that fall within a lengthy list of prohibited articles and services are prescribed in the International Traffic in Arms Regulations (ITAR) and the U.S. Munitions List (USML). The regulations are enforced by a licensing scheme managed by the State Department's Director of Defense Trade Controls (DDTC). Although Cyber Point applied for and received a license from DDTC, it is unclear whether the license significantly restricted the intelligence services Cyber Point could provide to the UAE so as to protect U.S. national security interests and the rights of Americans. It is also unclear when Project Raven transitioned to the UAE-based company, thus removing its work from DDTC oversight. Can you sketch the outlines of a licensing program that would protect U.S. national security while permitting services of this kind?

The United States could ban foreign intelligence service by Americans, just as we ban foreign military service. *See* 18 U.S.C. §959 (2018). But a ban would prevent Americans from contributing their counterterrorism expertise to the intelligence services of U.S. allies. Should a ban apply instead to former U.S. intelligence employees? For thoughtful analysis of these and related issues, see Robert Chesney, *Project Raven: What Happens When U.S. Personnel Serve a Foreign Intelligence Agency?,* Lawfare, Feb. 11, 2019.

3. *Mother Teresa or Mary Poppins?* Should recruiting of a foreign asset for U.S. intelligence agencies be predicated upon a finding of good moral character? If not, should Congress impose a requirement that the asset not break local or U.S. laws? Would such a requirement be lawful? Apart from the embarrassment of having the CIA asset "outed" by what was, for practical purposes, a U.S. anti-corruption investigation, was any harm caused by Mohammed Zia Salehi's soliciting bribes?

What lesson should we take from our experience with Ali Hassan Salameh? Are the recruitment and use of intelligence assets like Salameh constrained by Executive Order No. 12,333? Does law have any role to play in using dirty assets in counterterrorism?

4. *The Value of Vetting.* After U.S. and coalition forces failed to find any of the weapons of mass destruction (WMD) used to justify the invasion of Iraq in 2003, President Bush appointed a commission to investigate the failure. Comm'n on the Intelligence Capabilities of the United States Regarding Weapons of Mass Destruction

(Robb-Silberman Commission), *Report to the President of the United States* (Mar. 31, 2005). The commission reported that "the Intelligence Community was dead wrong in almost all of its pre-war judgments about Iraq's weapons of mass destruction. This was a major intelligence failure. Its principal causes [included] the Intelligence Community's inability to collect good information about Iraq's WMD programs." *Id.* at 2.

The commission found that the story of a "pivotal" source code-named "Curveball," who lied to intelligence officials about an Iraqi biological weapons program, was "an all-too-familiar one." *Id.* at 27, 367. It recommended that the CIA "take the lead in systematizing and standardizing the Intelligence Community's asset validation procedures . . . ways in which intelligence collectors ensure that the information provided to them is truthful and accurate." *Id.* at 372.

In fact, the CIA had issued guidelines in June 1995 to make case officers more selective in their recruiting. Apparently, the guidelines required case officers to obtain a waiver from CIA headquarters before employing any asset whose background included assassinations, torture, or other serious criminal activities. In the wake of the September 11, 2001, terrorist attacks, Congress enacted legislation directing the DCI to rescind portions of the 1995 guidelines pertaining to the recruitment of counterterrorism assets. Intelligence Authorization Act for Fiscal Year 2002, Pub. L. No. 107-108, §403, 115 Stat. 1394, 1402 (2001). Former CIA Inspector General Frederick Hitz wrote that new guidelines "retained the requirement of an audit trail in . . . recognition of a need for some explanation to headquarters why a dirty asset ought to be on the payroll." Frederick P. Hitz, *Unleashing the Rogue Elephant: September 11 and Letting the CIA Be the CIA*, 25 Harv. J.L. & Pub. Pol'y 765, 769 (2002). Does this assurance compensate for whatever was lost in the rescission?

3. Privatization

In recent years the CIA and the U.S. military have increasingly relied on private contractors both to collect and analyze intelligence and to conduct other secret missions. With certain exceptions, only federal employees may legally perform "inherently governmental functions" — those that are "so intimately related to the public interest as to require performance by Federal Government employees," including activities that "require . . . the exercise of discretion in applying Federal Government authority." Federal Activities Inventory Reform (FAIR) Act of 1998, Pub. L. No. 105-270, §5(2), 112 Stat. 2382, 2384-2385 (codified at 31 U.S.C. §501 note (2018)); *see also* Off. of Mgmt. & Budget, Circular No. A-76 (Revised), *Performance of Commercial Activities* (2003). Nevertheless, "[c]ontractors kill enemy fighters. They spy on foreign governments and eavesdrop on terrorist networks. They help craft war plans. They gather information on local factions in war zones. They are the historians, the architects, the recruiters in the nation's most secretive agencies." Dana Priest & William M. Arkin, *National Security Inc.*, Wash. Post, July 20, 2010. Since 9/11, contractors have also been used as military prison guards, they have interrogated terrorist suspects in U.S. custody, and they have secretly transported (rendered) prisoners for interrogation by foreign agents. For example, the contractor CACI was hired to provide interrogation and translation services at the Abu Ghraib prison in Iraq, later giving rise to prisoners' claims against it for torture and other mistreatment. See *infra* p. 1022.

The use of contractors is said to provide unique expertise and flexibility to meet unpredictable needs. Or it may spare military or intelligence professionals to do jobs for which they are best suited. It is also based on the assumption that contractors will perform the same work that government personnel do, but more efficiently, thereby saving taxpayer dollars. This assumption is widely disputed, however. Among other concerns, contractors commonly employ former military and intelligence personnel who are lured away from government service by much higher private salaries.

This skepticism was on display when the Trump administration announced reductions in the U.S. military force fighting the Taliban and remnants of ISIS in Afghanistan. At the time, some 27,000 U.S. contractor personnel there outnumbered military personnel by more than two to one. Kyle T. Gaines, *Contractors in Afghanistan Are Fleecing the American Taxpayer*, Small Wars J., Feb. 19, 2019. But when Blackwater (now Academi) head Erik Prince appealed directly to the Afghan government to replace U.S. troops with a large private security force, Afghan President Ashraf Ghani proclaimed that he would not outsource Afghanistan's fight against terrorism, and General Joseph Vogel, head of U.S. Central Command, stated that he did not agree with Prince that his private force could win the war more cheaply and effectively. *See* Karen DeYoung, Shane Harris & Dan LaMothe, *Erik Prince, in Kabul, Pushes Privatization of the Afghan War*, Wash. Post, Oct. 4, 2018.

What is undisputed is that privatization poses significant risks that the outsourced work will be conducted without adequate supervision, oversight, and accountability. This employment of private surrogates has occasionally produced nasty surprises.

Case Study: Nisour Square

On September 16, 2007, Blackwater Security Consulting, a private security company operating in Baghdad on a contract with the State Department, was deployed to provide security in the evacuation of a U.S. diplomat from Baghdad. The Blackwater security convoy of four vehicles approached Nisour Square, a traffic circle in downtown Baghdad with multiple checkpoints and a heavy Iraqi security presence due to a car bomb detonation there earlier that year.

The Blackwater convoy came to a stop at the south end of the Square and, together with Iraqi police, brought all traffic to a halt. Two or three minutes later, witnesses reported hearing shots fired and a woman screaming for her son. A white Kia sedan, a type of car flagged by a Blackwater intelligence analyst as one that might be used as a car bomb, had been hit. The driver's side windshield had a bullet hole in it and was splattered with blood.

Two nearby Iraqi police officers approached the Kia, where they found the driver slumped, with a bloody face and a bullet hole in the middle of his forehead. The officers then turned toward the Blackwater convoy, waving their arms to indicate that the shooting should stop. But when the vehicle in front of the Kia moved away, causing the Kia to roll forward, heavy gunfire erupted from the Blackwater convoy. The Iraqi police officers sought cover, as multiple grenades were fired at the Kia, causing it to catch fire, while the car's passenger was shot and killed.

Indiscriminate shooting from the convoy then continued to the south of the Square. Multiple victims were killed while seeking cover or trying to escape. One Blackwater guard radioed that his convoy was taking incoming fire, but others in his group could not locate or verify such a threat. One member of the Blackwater security team continued to fire at civilians, even after repeated cease-fire calls from colleagues. It is unclear whether the team member mistook the civilians for insurgents. After the shooting died down, one Blackwater employee saw another team member shoot an Iraqi in the stomach while the Iraqi's hands were up. The convoy then moved slowly around the circle and north out of the Square, while isolated shooting continued. By the time the convoy exited Nisour Square, at least 31 Iraqi civilians had been killed or wounded.

The killings outraged Iraqis, strained relations with the United States, and prompted multiple investigations. Although Blackwater claimed that the convoy was ambushed and that its employees fired in self-defense, Iraqi and U.S. investigations found that at least 14 of the 17 deaths in Nisour Square that day were without cause. Nevertheless, the United States allowed Blackwater to continue operating in Iraq until January 2009, when a new U.S.-Iraq Status of Forces Agreement took effect.

In December 2008, the United States filed criminal charges against five of the Blackwater guards. Four were eventually convicted of murder, manslaughter, and weapons violations. A fifth pleaded guilty to manslaughter. A civil action brought by six Nisour Square victims was settled in 2012 for an unannounced sum.

Private contractors have also been employed extensively in the fight against international terrorism. The *New York Times* has described a "shadow war against Al Qaeda and its allies" this way:

> In roughly a dozen countries — from the deserts of North Africa, to the mountains of Pakistan, to former Soviet republics crippled by ethnic and religious strife — the United States has significantly increased military and intelligence operations, pursuing the enemy using robotic drones and commando teams, paying contractors to spy and training local operatives to chase terrorists. [Scott Shane, Mark Mazzetti & Robert F. Worth, *Secret Assault on Terrorism Widens on Two Continents*, N.Y. Times, Aug. 14, 2010.]

In tandem with military raids against suspected Al Qaeda operatives in Yemen, Somalia, Kenya, and various locations in North Africa, private contractors have been hired to gather intelligence about insurgent activities in Pakistan. *Id.* At the same time, U.S. incursions beyond the traditional battlefields in Afghanistan and Iraq have increasingly been outsourced to private armies.

Notes and Questions

1. Growing Reliance on Contractors. Efforts to outsource a variety of military and intelligence functions to private contractors began in earnest during the Reagan administration. By 2019, about 90 percent of some 34,000 persons employed by the State Department's Bureau of Diplomatic Security, which is responsible for the safety of the department's missions and personnel worldwide, were private contractors like Blackwater. Numbers for other agencies are hard to come by, even within the executive branch. *See* Gov't Accountability Off., *Civilian Intelligence Community* (GAO-14-204), Jan. 2014. But according to one estimate, in 2016 about one-third of roughly 183,000 military and other intelligence personnel were contractors. Tim Shorrock, *5 Corporations Now Dominate Our Privatized Intelligence Industry*, The Nation, Sept. 8, 2016. And in some agencies, like the CIA's National Clandestine Service and the Defense Intelligence Agency (DIA), a majority of personnel reportedly are contractors. *See* Simon Chesterman, *We Can't Spy . . . If We Can't Buy!: The Privatization of Intelligence and the Limits of Outsourcing "Inherently Governmental Functions,"* 19 Eur. J. Int'l L. 1055, 1056 (2008).

2. *Inherently Governmental Functions?* Why do you think Congress has forbidden the use of contractors to perform "inherently governmental functions"? Can you say what functions are inherently governmental? The Defense Department offers this guidance in the context of war fighting:

> The U.S. government has exclusive responsibility for discretionary decisions concerning the appropriate, measured use of combat power. . . . Since combat operations authorized by the U.S. government entail the exercise of sovereign Government authority and involve substantial discretion — i.e., can significantly affect the life, liberty, or property of private persons or international relations — they are IG [inherently governmental]. . . . [U.S. Dep't of Defense, DOD Instr. 1100.22, *Policy and Procedures for Determining Workforce Mix* 18 (Apr. 12, 2010).]

Does this instruction help distinguish military personnel who may legally engage in special operations from contractors, who may not? Would it be helpful in identifying contractors who could be involved in CIA covert operations? *See* L. Elaine Halchin, *The Intelligence Community and Its Use of Contractors: Congressional Oversight Issues* (Cong. Res. Serv. R44157), Aug. 18, 2015.

3. *Authority for the Use of Contractors?* Does any provision of the National Security Act, *supra* p. 507, authorize the use of private contractors by the Defense Department or other members of the intelligence community? Has Congress implicitly approved their use by prohibiting their performance of inherently governmental functions?

Recall that Executive Order No. 12,333 includes this provision:

> **2.7 Contracting.** Agencies within the Intelligence Community are authorized to enter into contracts or arrangements for the provision of goods or services with private companies or institutions in the United States and need not reveal the sponsorship of such contracts or arrangements for authorized intelligence purposes. Contracts or arrangements with academic institutions may be undertaken only with the consent of appropriate officials of the institution.

Does the executive order supply any needed authority for the use of contractors? Does it limit their use?

Then-Secretary of Defense Robert Gates testified in Congress after the Nisour Square incident that the Defense Department has adequate legal authority to control contractors, but that commanders lack sufficient "means and . . . resources" to exercise adequate oversight. *Examining the President's Fiscal Year 2008 Supplemental Request for the*

Wars in Iraq and Afghanistan: Hearing Before the S. Comm. on Appropriations, 110th Cong. 13 (2007). Can you think of reforms that would make tragedies like the one in Nisour Square less likely? Does the Neutrality Act of 1794, 18 U.S.C. §960 (2018), *supra* p. 544, limit the use of contractors? Might the answer depend on what they are hired to do or where they are directed to do it? Does that act's reference to "whoever" include lawful government employees or contractors? Consider this OLC opinion:

> [The Neutrality Act] is intended solely to prohibit persons acting in a private capacity from taking actions that might interfere with the foreign policy and relations of the United States. It does not proscribe activities conducted by Government officials acting within the course and scope of their duties as officers of the United States. [*Application of the Neutrality Act to Official Government Activities*, 8 Op. O.L.C. 58 (1984).]

4. *Accountability of Nations for Contractors?* In 2008, 17 countries signed the Int'l Comm. of the Red Cross, *The Montreux Document on Pertinent International Legal Obligations and Good Practices for States Related to Operations of Private Military and Security Companies During Armed Conflict* (Sept. 17, 2008), an informal restatement of existing international law applicable to private military and security companies operating in areas of armed conflict. *See* Faiza Patel, *A Primer on Legal Developments Regarding Private Military Contractors*, Brennan Ctr. for Just. Blog, July 18, 2014. A 2013 report by a group of academics and human rights experts found that the United States had adopted only some of the practices recommended in the Montreux Document. Rebecca Winter-Schmitt, *Montreux Five Years On: An Analysis of State Effort to Implement Montreux Document Legal Obligations and Good Practices* 157-158 (2013), https://novact.org/wp-content/uploads/2013/12/MontreuxFinal.pdf.

If private contractors working for a U.S. agency engage in unlawful conduct during armed conflict, is the United States liable? Common Article 1 of the Geneva Conventions provides that "[t]he High Contracting Parties undertake to respect and to ensure respect for the present Convention in all circumstances." Under the "effective control" test employed by the International Court of Justice in the *Nicaragua* case (*supra* p. 249), would the United States be responsible for violations of the Conventions by its contractors? What about violations by U.S. contractors working for the Afghan government? *See* Laura Dickinson, *A Legal and Policy Risk Analysis of the Erik Prince Plan to Privatize War in Afghanistan*, Just Security, Aug. 10, 2017.

5. *Accountability of Contractors Under International Law?* A 2010 International Code of Conduct for Private Security Service Providers includes a voluntary commitment by contractors to "operate in a manner that recognizes and supports the rule of law; respects human rights, and protects the interests of their clients"; and to "take steps to establish and maintain an effective internal governance framework in order to deter, monitor, report, and effectively address adverse impacts on human rights," although it "creates no legal obligations and no legal liabilities" for signatory companies. ¶¶6, 14. By 2019, 86 companies, including Blackwater's successor, Academi, had signed on to the Code and its operational framework.

Do the laws of war, including the combatant's privilege, apply to contract personnel? *See* Jens David Ohlin, *The Combatant's Privilege in Asymmetric and Covert Conflicts*, 40 Yale J. Int'l L. 337, 339 (2015) (the privilege may apply if the force meets the classical requirements for lawful belligerency, but only when the government acknowledges the use of force).

Civil and criminal liability of contractors in U.S. courts is addressed *infra* pp. 1020-1022.

6. Congressional Oversight of Contractors. Review the oversight requirements for intelligence activities enacted in 1991, *supra* p. 557. Do you think those requirements will keep Congress adequately informed about the work of contractors employed by members of the intelligence community?

COVERT OPERATIONS: SUMMARY OF BASIC PRINCIPLES

- The Neutrality Act forbids private military initiatives against nations with which the United States is "at peace," while the Logan Act bars private diplomatic efforts to resolve disputes with foreign governments.

- Covert operations conducted by or on behalf of the U.S. government are intended to be plausibly deniable to the public. They may not always harmonize with U.S. public policy or even basic American principles. The assassination of a foreign official and bribes of foreign politicians are examples.

- Clandestine operations, by contrast, are typically military operations intended to be secret as they are conducted, but not to remain secret or be plausibly deniable after they are concluded. A Special Forces operation to take out enemy radar and anti-aircraft installations before an overt bombing raid (as occurred in the Persian Gulf War) is an example.

- CIA-sponsored paramilitary operations may qualify as "war" under the Constitution, requiring congressional approval under the Declare War Clause or, arguably, the Marque and Reprisal Clause. Either form of approval typically requires transparency inconsistent with "covertness."

- To increase accountability for covert operations, in 1974 Congress required presidential findings (ending the President's plausible deniability within the executive branch, but cementing his control over covert operatives) and notice to Congress of "operations in foreign countries other than activities intended solely for obtaining necessary intelligence."

- After the Church Committee documented covert action abuses by the CIA, Congress shored up legislative oversight of covert operations in 1980 by creating the intelligence committees and requiring the Administration to keep the committees "currently informed of all intelligence activities, including any significant anticipated intelligence activity," but it permitted the President in some cases to limit notice to the Gang of Eight.

- Spurred by further secret abuses in the Iran-Contra Affair, Congress strengthened intelligence oversight mechanisms in the Intelligence Authorization Act of 1991 by:

- defining "covert action," but excluding "traditional" military activities from the definition;
- requiring presidential findings to be in writing;
- forbidding the use of appropriations for actions that violate its oversight requirements.

- The 1949 CIA Act hides the details of intelligence budgets and spending from the public. The Supreme Court has found that ordinary citizens lack standing to enforce the disclosure of these details under the Statement and Account Clause, although Congress could require their publication.
- Congressional oversight is challenged by several developments:
  - The CIA may employ paramilitary forces or dirty assets that are not fully amenable to agency control;
  - Military special forces personnel, who may not be subject to traditional intelligence oversight, may perform tasks traditionally conducted by intelligence agents;
  - Both CIA and DOD employ private contractors to collect intelligence or participate in covert operations, although contractors are not accountable to Congress or the President in the same ways that members of the intelligence community are.
- The use of contractors is limited to functions that are not "inherently governmental." Such use poses various oversight problems, as well as practical issues of control, accountability, and amenability to regulation under the laws of armed conflict.
- Intra-agency vetting of secret foreign assets or of contractors could limit potential abuses and promote accountability for their use, but could also limit access to critically helpful surrogates.

20

The Fourth Amendment and National Security

Since the birth of our nation, Americans have worried about espionage committed by hostile foreign agents. In recent times, we have also become the targets of violent terrorist acts and persistent cyber attacks at home and abroad. To gather information about these threats to national security, we have employed many of the same techniques that are used in ordinary criminal investigations, including undercover agents and informants, physical searches of persons and places, and, increasingly, sophisticated computer technologies, including a variety of electronic intercepts and data mining.

In almost every instance, these measures have succeeded in protecting the American people from harm. In the process, however, government officials have occasionally lost sight of their mission, or strayed from it, and have violated individual privacy rights, just as in any criminal investigation gone awry. Where the subject of a probe is a possible terrorist act or cyber intrusion, which may be politically motivated, First Amendment freedoms of assembly and expression may be implicated as well. Special care is thus required in sorting out protected activities from those that could lead to violence or serious disruption of society, and in selecting appropriate investigative techniques for each. *See* William C. Banks & M.E. Bowman, *Executive Authority for National Security Surveillance,* 50 Am. U. L. Rev. 1, 92-94 (2001).

This sorting-out process is often complicated by a lack of information about the exact nature of suspected threats. While few would argue that a mere hunch about anticipated violent acts or other serious threats will justify surveillance of potential targets, something less than a completed illegal act must suffice. Thus, the development of standards for approval of investigations into national security threats is a critical legal issue.

In this chapter, we provide a baseline for the study of intelligence collection and surveillance by starting with the Fourth Amendment. First we offer a short primer on the Fourth Amendment and the "special needs" exceptions to its warrant requirement, then we examine the Supreme Court's seminal analysis of the President's claim of inherent authority to conduct warrantless electronic surveillance in domestic security investigations. Next we consider whether there is a "foreign intelligence" exception to the warrant requirement of the Fourth Amendment, assessing evolving challenges for Fourth Amendment analysis posed by new technologies — both those that enable more intrusive government surveillance and those that we rely on increasingly in our daily lives. At the end of the chapter we consider whether and to what extent Fourth Amendment protections apply to investigations abroad.

A. THE FOURTH AMENDMENT FRAMEWORK

An introduction to the Fourth Amendment necessarily starts in colonial America. The British used a "general warrant" to conduct searches without probable cause — essentially fishing expeditions.

> The British general warrant was a search tool employed without limitation on location, and without any necessity to precisely describe the object or person sought. British authorities were simply given license to "break into any shop or place suspected" wherever they chose. With that kind of unfettered discretion, the general warrant could be, and often was, used to intimidate. General warrants executed during the reign of Charles I sought to intimidate dissidents, authors, and printers of seditious material by ransacking homes and seizing personal papers. In 1765, the courts declared general warrants illegal, and Parliament followed a year later.
>
> In the colonies, complaints that royal officials were violating the privacy of colonists through the use of writs of assistance, equivalent to general warrants, grew. Because English law did not, as yet, recognize a right of personal privacy, the crown's abuses in the colonies were not remediable at law. It was thus no surprise that the new American Constitution and the government it created would respect a series of individual freedoms. . . . [*Id.* at 2-3.]

In reaction to the general warrant, the Framers adopted the Fourth Amendment to the U.S. Constitution. It provides:

> The right of the people to be secure in their persons, houses, papers, and effects, against unreasonable searches and seizures shall not be violated, and no Warrants shall issue, but upon probable cause, supported by Oath or affirmation, and particularly describing the place to be searched, and the persons or things to be seized.

The Amendment presents several threshold issues. First, federal agents can "search" a property just by looking at it from the street, as any member of the public can. Does the Fourth Amendment apply to such a search? In *Katz v. United States,* 389 U.S. 347 (1967), FBI agents placed an electronic listening device on the roof of a public telephone booth in Los Angeles. They did not seek a warrant. *Id.* at 348-349. The agents recorded the voice of Charles Katz as he engaged in illegal gambling with contacts in other cities. *Id.* Repudiating earlier Supreme Court precedents that limited Fourth Amendment coverage to situations in which a physical penetration of a constitutionally protected place occurred, the *Katz* Court ruled that "the Fourth Amendment protects people, not places." *Id.* at 351. But if the applicability of Fourth Amendment privacy focuses on people rather than places, what circumstances determine whether personal privacy concerns trigger the protection of the Constitution? Concurring, Justice Harlan suggested that Fourth Amendment protection turns on the subjective existence of "a reasonable expectation of privacy." *Id.* at 360 (Harlan, J., concurring). The Harlan formulation thus supplies an answer to the question about a "search" of property in the public view. The Fourth Amendment does not bar such a search because the property owners have no reasonable expectation of freedom from public scrutiny.

A majority of the Court subsequently adopted Justice Harlan's approach, concluding that "a 'search' occurs when an expectation of privacy that society is prepared to consider reasonable is infringed." *United States v. Jacobsen*, 466 U.S. 109, 113 (1984); *see also Skinner v. Ry. Labor Executives' Ass'n*, 489 U.S. 602 (1989). Applying that reasoning, the Court has held that when the government collects data from third parties — like the phone company — to which a person has voluntarily submitted the data, it has not conducted a search regulated by the Fourth Amendment. *See, e.g., Smith v. Maryland*, 442 U.S. 735 (1979) (upholding collection of dialed telephone numbers); *United States v. Miller*, 425 U.S. 435 (1976) (upholding collection of bank records from bank). More recently, the Court declined to extend the resulting "third-party records" doctrine to historical cell-site location information (CSLI), holding "that an individual maintains a legitimate expectation of privacy in the record of his physical movements as captured through CSLI." *Carpenter v. United States*, 138 S. Ct. 2206, 2217 (2018). Dissents by Justices Kennedy, Alito, and Thomas argued that *Katz* should be repudiated on grounds that it is countertextual (the Fourth Amendment does not mention "privacy"); it ignores the property-based history of the Fourth Amendment (which regulates searches only of "persons, houses, papers, and effects"); and it is necessarily subjective and difficult to apply. *Id.* at 2238-2241, 2243-2246 (Thomas, J., dissenting). This and the following chapters will explore the evolving understanding of key Fourth Amendment terms.

Second, how does the Warrant Clause in the Fourth Amendment relate to the reasonableness requirement? Is a warrantless search unreasonable *per se*? In 1967, the Supreme Court held that warrantless searches "are *per se* unreasonable under the Fourth Amendment — subject only to a few specifically established and well-delineated exceptions." *Katz*, 389 U.S. at 357. The Court has also stated that probable cause is a "practical, nontechnical conception affording the best compromise that has been found for accommodating . . . opposing interests." *Brinegar v. United States*, 338 U.S. 160, 176 (1949). The determination of probable cause by a neutral magistrate makes a search pursuant to a warrant presumptively reasonable; without a warrant, a search is presumptively unreasonable, unless it fits one of the few exceptions.

Warrants, however, are now "more the exception than the rule." Joshua Dressler, Alan C. Michaels & Ric Simmons, *Understanding Criminal Procedure, Volume I: Investigation* 293 (7th ed. 2017). Some exceptions, said to be grounded in necessity, have been recognized even in ordinary criminal investigations:

- searches incident to arrest, *United States v. Robinson*, 414 U.S. 218 (1973);
- automobile searches, *Michigan v. Long*, 463 U.S. 1032 (1983);
- "hot pursuit" or exigent circumstance searches, *Michigan v. Tyler*, 436 U.S. 499 (1978); and
- "stop and frisk" searches, *Terry v. Ohio*, 392 U.S. 1 (1968) (based on "reasonable suspicion," not probable cause, to believe a person is armed and dangerous or is engaged or about to engage in criminal activity).

Other exceptions have been recognized because "special needs, beyond the normal need for [criminal] law enforcement, make the warrant and probable-cause requirement impracticable." *Griffin v. Wisconsin*, 483 U.S. 868, 873 (1987) (quoting *New Jersey v. T.L.O.*, 469 U.S. 325, 351 (1985) (Blackmun, J., concurring in the judgment)). Although "special needs" may be "no more than a label that indicates a lax standard will apply," William J. Stuntz, *Implicit Bargains, Government Power, and the Fourth Amendment*, 44 Stan. L. Rev. 553, 554 (1992), that standard still demands reasonableness of the search or seizure. Dressler & Michaels, *supra*, at 306. "Special needs searches" conducted for purposes other than criminal investigation, such as accident prevention, protection of public health, or administrative compliance, where no individualized suspicion is required, include:

- searches to prevent railroad accidents that cause "great human loss," *Skinner*, 489 U.S. at 628;
- searches to help prevent the spread of disease or contamination during a public health crisis, *Camara v. Municipal Court*, 387 U.S. 523 (1967);
- sobriety checkpoints, *Mich. Dep't of State Police v. Sitz*, 496 U.S. 444 (1990); and
- checkpoint searches designed to adduce evidence of criminal activity by individuals *other* than the vehicle's occupants, *Illinois v. Lidster*, 540 U.S. 419 (2004).

Finally, some warrantless searches are permitted at national borders, on the high seas, or of passengers and planes at an airport, on theories of traditional border control and/or the special need to ensure public safety:

- searches of persons and things entering and leaving the United States, *United States v. Montoya de Hernandez*, 473 U.S. 531 (1985);
- searches of boats on navigable waters, *United States v. Villamonte-Marquez*, 462 U.S. 579 (1983); and
- searches of airplanes, *United States v. Nigro*, 727 F.2d 100 (6th Cir. 1984) (en banc).

In view of the devastation wrought by the airline hijackings on September 11, 2001, the reasonableness required for special needs searches has not been a hard standard to meet:

> When the risk is the jeopardy to hundreds of human lives and millions of dollars of property inherent in the pirating or blowing up of a large airplane, that danger alone meets the test of reasonableness, so long as the search is conducted in good faith for the purpose of preventing hijacking or like damage and with reasonable scope and the passenger has been given advance notice of his liability to such a search so that he can avoid it by choosing not to travel by air. [*United States v. Edwards*, 498 F.2d 496, 500 (2d Cir. 1974).]

What about a search prompted by nothing more than an anonymous tip of a planned bombing? In one case the Supreme Court remarked that it did not need to

> speculate about the circumstances under which the danger alleged in an anonymous tip might be so great as to justify a search even without a showing of reliability. We do not say, for example, that a report of a person carrying a bomb need bear the indicia of

reliability we demand for a report of a person carrying a firearm before the police can constitutionally conduct a frisk. [*Florida v. J.L.*, 529 U.S. 266, 273-274 (2000); *see also Navarette v. California*, 134 S. Ct. 1683, 1692 (2014) (holding that an anonymous tip can provide the "reasonable suspicion" required for a *Terry* stop).]

Should concern for national security justify warrantless electronic surveillance of Americans suspected in some way of being connected to terrorist threats? Should it provide the basis for video surveillance of streets, parks, and other public places? In other words, is national security *itself* a special need that excuses the warrant requirement? If there is a national security exception to the warrant requirement, what is the scope of the exception, and what procedures should substitute for the warrant process?

B. A NATIONAL SECURITY EXCEPTION?

Foreign Intelligence Surveillance Act of 1977

S. Rep. No. 95-604, at 9-12 (1977)

. . . In 1928, the Supreme Court in *Olmstead v. United States* [277 U.S. 468] held that wiretapping was not within the coverage of the Fourth Amendment. Three years later, Attorney General William D. Mitchell authorized telephone wiretapping, upon the personal approval of bureau chiefs, of syndicated bootleggers and in "exceptional cases where the crimes are substantial and serious, and the necessity is great and [the bureau chief and the Assistant Attorney General] are satisfied that the persons whose wires are to be tapped are of the criminal type." These general guidelines governed the Department's practice through the thirties and telephone wiretapping was considered to be an important law enforcement tool.

Congress placed the first restrictions on wiretapping in the Federal Communications Act of 1934, which made it a crime for any person "to intercept and divulge or publish the contents of wire and radio communications." [48 Stat. 1103.] The Supreme Court construed this section to apply to Federal agents and held that evidence obtained from the interception of wire and radio communications and the fruits of the evidence, were inadmissible in court. [*Nardone v. United States*, 302 U.S. 379 (1937); 308 U.S. 338 (1939).] However, the Justice Department did not interpret the Federal Communications Act or the *Nardone* decision as prohibiting the interception of wire communications per se; rather only the interception and divulgence of their contents outside the Federal establishment was considered to be unlawful. Thus, the Justice Department found continued authority for its national security wiretaps.

In 1940, President Roosevelt issued a memorandum to the Attorney General stating his view that electronic surveillance would be proper under the Constitution where "grave matters involving defense of the nation" were involved. The President authorized and directed the Attorney General "to secure information by listening devices [directed at] the conversation or other communications of persons suspected of subversive activities against the Government of the United States, including suspected spies." The Attorney General was requested "to limit these investigations so conducted to a minimum and to limit them insofar as possible to aliens."

This practice was continued in successive administrations. . . .

In the early fifties, however, Attorney General J. Howard McGrath took the position that he would not approve or authorize the installation of microphone surveillances by means of trespass. This policy was quickly reversed by Attorney General Herbert Brownell in 1954 in a sweeping memorandum to FBI Director Hoover instructing him that the Bureau was indeed authorized to conduct such trespassory surveillances regardless of the fact of surreptitious entry, and without the need to first acquire the Attorney General's authorization. Such surveillance was simply authorized whenever the Bureau concluded that the "national interest" so required. . . .

In *Katz v. United States*, 389 U.S. 347 (1967), the Supreme Court finally discarded the *Olmstead* doctrine and held that the Fourth Amendment's warrant provision did apply to electronic surveillance. The Court explicitly declined, however, to extend its holding to cases "involving the national security." 389 U.S. at 358 n.23. The next year, Congress followed suit: responding to the *Katz* case, Congress enacted the Omnibus Crime Control and Safe Streets Act (18 U.S.C. §§2510-2520). Title III of that Act established a procedure for the judicial authorization of electronic surveillance for the investigation and prevention of specified types of serious crimes and the use of the product of such surveillance in court proceedings. It prohibited wiretapping and electronic surveillance by persons other than duly authorized law enforcement officers, personnel of the Federal Communications Commission, or communication common carriers monitoring communications in the normal course of their employment.

Title III, however, disclaimed any intention of legislating in the national security area. . . .

Reading the *Keith* Case

In 1968, opposition to the Vietnam War spawned extremist violence in the United States. One violent group, styling itself the White Panther Party, was charged with bombing a CIA office in Ann Arbor, Michigan. Lawrence Robert Plamondon, a member of the group, fled the country but was arrested on re-entry. At his criminal trial, he moved to suppress evidence against him on the grounds that it was obtained by warrantless wiretaps. His case thus posed the question whether domestic security is a special need that excuses a warrantless search.

- Even though Title III does not explicitly authorize warrantless wiretaps, it appears to recognize constitutional power in the President to conduct national security surveillance. Review §2511(3) carefully. Why did the Court decline to find that this provision at least affirmed the power to wiretap Plamondon without a warrant?
- Title III aside, does the Constitution impliedly vest power in the President to conduct warrantless surveillance for reasons of national security? What three reasons did the government offer to support an affirmative answer? Why did the Court reject them?
- What *precisely* did the Court hold?
- If the Fourth Amendment requires a warrant to wiretap someone like Plamondon, then the government must meet the standards of Title III unless Congress enacts another statute with different standards. How could the standards in the new statute be different without violating the Fourth Amendment?

United States v. United States District Court (*Keith*)[1]

United States Supreme Court, 1972
407 U.S. 297

Mr. Justice POWELL delivered the opinion of the Court. The issue before us is an important one for the people of our country and their Government. It involves the delicate question of the President's power, acting through the Attorney General, to authorize electronic surveillance in internal security matters without prior judicial approval. . . . This case brings the issue here for the first time. Its resolution is a matter of national concern, requiring sensitivity both to the Government's right to protect itself from unlawful subversion and attack and to the citizen's right to be secure in his privacy against unreasonable Government intrusion.

Associate Justice Lewis F. Powell Jr.

This case arises from a criminal proceeding in the United States District Court for the Eastern District of Michigan, in which the United States charged three defendants with conspiracy to destroy Government property in violation of 18 U.S.C. §371. One of the defendants, Plamondon, was charged with the dynamite bombing of an office of the Central Intelligence Agency in Ann Arbor, Michigan.

During pretrial proceedings, the defendants moved to compel the United States to disclose certain electronic surveillance information and to conduct a hearing to determine whether this information "tainted" the evidence on which the indictment was based or which the Government intended to offer at trial. In response, the Government filed an affidavit of the Attorney General, acknowledging that its agents had overheard conversations in which Plamondon had participated. The affidavit also stated that the Attorney General approved the wiretaps "to gather intelligence information deemed necessary to protect the nation from attempts of domestic organizations to attack and subvert the existing structure of the Government." The logs of the surveillance were filed in a sealed exhibit for *in camera* inspection by the District Court.

On the basis of the Attorney General's affidavit and the sealed exhibit, the Government asserted that the surveillance was lawful, though conducted without prior judicial approval, as a reasonable exercise of the President's power (exercised through the Attorney General) to protect the national security. The District Court held that the surveillance violated the Fourth Amendment, and ordered the Government to make full disclosure to Plamondon of his overheard conversations.

[1. This case is commonly referred to by the name of the federal district court judge who first heard it, Damon J. Keith, since the case came to the Supreme Court on the government's appeal of the denial of a petition for a writ of mandamus directed to Judge Keith. — Eds.]

... [T]he Court of Appeals for the Sixth Circuit... held that the surveillance was unlawful and that the District Court had properly required disclosure of the overheard conversations....

I

Title III of the Omnibus Crime Control and Safe Streets Act, 18 U.S.C. §§2510-2520, authorizes the use of electronic surveillance for classes of crimes carefully specified in 18 U.S.C. §2516. Such surveillance is subject to prior court order. Section 2518 sets forth the detailed and particularized application necessary to obtain such an order as well as carefully circumscribed conditions for its use. The Act represents a comprehensive attempt by Congress to promote more effective control of crime while protecting the privacy of individual thought and expression. Much of Title III was drawn to meet the constitutional requirements for electronic surveillance enunciated by this Court in *Berger v. New York*, 388 U.S. 41 (1967), and *Katz v. United States*, 389 U.S. 347 (1967).

Together with the elaborate surveillance requirements in Title III, there is the following proviso, 18 U.S.C. §2511(3):

> Nothing contained in this chapter or in section 605 of the Communications Act of 1934 (48 Stat. 1143; 47 U.S.C. 605) shall limit the constitutional power of the President to take such measures as he deems necessary to protect the Nation against actual or potential attack or other hostile acts of a foreign power, to obtain foreign intelligence information deemed essential to the security of the United States, or to protect national security information against foreign intelligence activities. *Nor shall anything contained in this chapter be deemed to limit the constitutional power of the President to take such measures as he deems necessary to protect the United States against the overthrow of the Government by force or other unlawful means, or against any other clear and present danger to the structure or existence of the Government.* The contents of any wire or oral communication intercepted by authority of the President in the exercise of the foregoing powers may be received in evidence in any trial hearing, or other proceeding only where such interception was reasonable, and shall not be otherwise used or disclosed except as is necessary to implement that power. (Emphasis supplied.)

The Government relies on §2511(3). It argues that "in excepting national security surveillances from the Act's warrant requirement Congress recognized the President's authority to conduct such surveillances without prior judicial approval." The section thus is viewed as a recognition or affirmance of a constitutional authority in the President to conduct warrantless domestic security surveillance such as that involved in this case.

We think the language of §2511(3), as well as the legislative history of the statute, refutes this interpretation. The relevant language is that: "Nothing contained in this chapter... shall limit the constitutional power of the President to take such measures as he deems necessary to protect..." against the dangers specified. At most, this is an implicit recognition that the President does have certain powers in the specified areas. Few would doubt this, as the section refers — among other things — to protection "against actual or potential attack or other hostile acts of a foreign power." But so far as the use of the President's electronic surveillance power is concerned, the language is essentially neutral.

Section 2511(3) certainly confers no power, as the language is wholly inappropriate for such a purpose. It merely provides that the Act shall not be interpreted to limit or disturb such power as the President may have under the Constitution. In short, Congress simply left presidential powers where it found them....

... [I]t would have been incongruous for Congress to have legislated with respect to the important and complex area of national security in a single brief and nebulous paragraph. This would not comport with the sensitivity of the problem involved or with the extraordinary care Congress exercised in drafting other sections of the Act. We therefore think the conclusion inescapable that Congress only intended to make clear that the Act simply did not legislate with respect to national security surveillances....

... [V]iewing §2511(3) as a congressional disclaimer and expression of neutrality, we hold that the statute is not the measure of the executive authority asserted in this case. Rather, we must look to the constitutional powers of the President.

II

It is important at the outset to emphasize the limited nature of the question before the Court. This case raises no constitutional challenge to electronic surveillance as specifically authorized by Title III of the Omnibus Crime Control and Safe Streets Act of 1968. Nor is there any question or doubt as to the necessity of obtaining a warrant in the surveillance of crimes unrelated to the national security interest. Further, the instant case requires no judgment on the scope of the President's surveillance power with respect to the activities of foreign powers, within or without this country. The Attorney General's affidavit in this case states that the surveillances were "deemed necessary to protect the nation from attempts of *domestic organizations* to attack and subvert the existing structure of Government" (emphasis supplied). There is no evidence of any involvement, directly or indirectly, of a foreign power.[8]

Our present inquiry, though important, is therefore a narrow one. It addresses a question left open by *Katz*: "Whether safeguards other than prior authorization by a magistrate would satisfy the Fourth Amendment in a situation involving the national security...." The determination of this question requires the essential Fourth Amendment inquiry into the "reasonableness" of the search and seizure in question, and the way in which that "reasonableness" derives content and meaning through reference to the warrant clause.

... [T]he President of the United States has the fundamental duty, under Art. II, §1, of the Constitution, to "preserve, protect and defend the Constitution of the United States." Implicit in that duty is the power to protect our Government against

---

8. Section 2511(3) refers to "the constitutional power of the President" in two types of situations: (i) where necessary to protect against attack, other hostile acts or intelligence activities of a "foreign power"; or (ii) where necessary to protect against the overthrow of the Government or other clear and present danger to the structure or existence of the Government. Although both of the specified situations are sometimes referred to as "national security" threats, the term "national security" is used only in the first sentence of §2511(3) with respect to the activities of foreign powers. This case involves only the second sentence of §2511(3), with the threat emanating—according to the Attorney General's affidavit—from "domestic organizations." Although we attempt no precise definition, we use the term "domestic organization" in this opinion to mean a group or organization (whether formally or informally constituted) composed of citizens of the United States and which has no significant connection with a foreign power, its agents or agencies. No doubt there are cases where it will be difficult to distinguish between "domestic" and "foreign" unlawful activities directed against the Government of the United States where there is collaboration in varying degrees between domestic groups or organizations and agents or agencies of foreign powers. But this is not such a case.

those who would subvert or overthrow it by unlawful means. In the discharge of this duty, the President — through the Attorney General — may find it necessary to employ electronic surveillance to obtain intelligence information on the plans of those who plot unlawful acts against the Government. The use of such surveillance in internal security cases has been sanctioned more or less continuously by various Presidents and Attorneys General since July 1946....

Though the Government and respondents debate their seriousness and magnitude, threats and acts of sabotage against the Government exist in sufficient number to justify investigative powers with respect to them. The covertness and complexity of potential unlawful conduct against the Government and the necessary dependency of many conspirators upon the telephone make electronic surveillance an effective investigatory instrument in certain circumstances. The marked acceleration in technological developments and sophistication in their use have resulted in new techniques for the planning, commission, and concealment of criminal activities. It would be contrary to the public interest for Government to deny to itself the prudent and lawful employment of those very techniques which are employed against the Government and its law-abiding citizens....

But a recognition of these elementary truths does not make the employment by Government of electronic surveillance a welcome development — even when employed with restraint and under judicial supervision. There is, understandably, a deep-seated uneasiness and apprehension that this capability will be used to intrude upon cherished privacy of law-abiding citizens. We look to the Bill of Rights to safeguard this privacy. Though physical entry of the home is the chief evil against which the wording of the Fourth Amendment is directed, its broader spirit now shields private speech from unreasonable surveillance. Our decision in *Katz* refused to lock the Fourth Amendment into instances of actual physical trespass. Rather, the Amendment governs "not only the seizure of tangible items, but extends as well to the recording of oral statements . . . without any 'technical trespass under . . . local property law.'" . . . *Katz, supra,* at 353. . . .

National security cases, moreover, often reflect a convergence of First and Fourth Amendment values not present in cases of "ordinary" crime. Though the investigative duty of the executive may be stronger in such cases, so also is there greater jeopardy to constitutionally protected speech. "Historically the struggle for freedom of speech and press in England was bound up with the issue of the scope of the search and seizure power," *Marcus v. Search Warrant,* 367 U.S. 717, 724 (1961). History abundantly documents the tendency of Government — however benevolent and benign its motives — to view with suspicion those who most fervently dispute its policies. Fourth Amendment protections become the more necessary when the targets of official surveillance may be those suspected of unorthodoxy in their political beliefs. The danger to political dissent is acute where the Government attempts to act under so vague a concept as the power to protect "domestic security." Given the difficulty of defining the domestic security interest, the danger of abuse in acting to protect that interest becomes apparent....

III

As the Fourth Amendment is not absolute in its terms, our task is to examine and balance the basic values at stake in this case: the duty of Government to protect the domestic security, and the potential danger posed by unreasonable surveillance to individual privacy and free expression. If the legitimate need of Government to safeguard domestic security requires the use of electronic surveillance, the question is whether the needs of citizens for privacy and free expression may not be better protected by requiring a warrant before such surveillance is undertaken. We must also ask whether a warrant requirement would unduly frustrate the efforts of Government to protect itself from acts of subversion and overthrow directed against it.

Though the Fourth Amendment speaks broadly of "unreasonable searches and seizures," the definition of "reasonableness" turns, at least in part, on the more specific commands of the warrant clause. . . .

. . . [W]here practical, a governmental search and seizure should represent both the efforts of the officer to gather evidence of wrongful acts and the judgment of the magistrate that the collected evidence is sufficient to justify invasion of a citizen's private premises or conversation. Inherent in the concept of a warrant is its issuance by a "neutral and detached magistrate." The further requirement of "probable cause" instructs the magistrate that baseless searches shall not proceed.

These Fourth Amendment freedoms cannot properly be guaranteed if domestic security surveillances may be conducted solely within the discretion of the Executive Branch. . . . The historical judgment, which the Fourth Amendment accepts, is that unreviewed executive discretion may yield too readily to pressures to obtain incriminating evidence and overlook potential invasions of privacy and protected speech.

It may well be that, in the instant case, the Government's surveillance of Plamondon's conversations was a reasonable one which readily would have gained prior judicial approval. But this Court "has never sustained a search upon the sole ground that officers reasonably expected to find evidence of a particular crime and voluntarily confined their activities to the least intrusive means consistent with that end." *Katz, supra,* at 356-357. The Fourth Amendment contemplates a prior judicial judgment, not the risk that executive discretion may be reasonably exercised. This judicial role accords with our basic constitutional doctrine that individual freedoms will best be preserved through a separation of powers and division of functions among the different branches and levels of Government. The independent check upon executive discretion is not satisfied, as the Government argues, by "extremely limited" post-surveillance judicial review. Indeed, post-surveillance review would never reach the surveillances which failed to result in prosecutions. . . .

It is true that there have been some exceptions to the warrant requirement. But those exceptions are few in number and carefully delineated; in general, they serve the legitimate needs of law enforcement officers to protect their own well-being and preserve evidence from destruction. Even while carving out those exceptions, the Court has reaffirmed the principle that the "police must, whenever practicable, obtain advance judicial approval of searches and seizures through the warrant procedure," *Terry v. Ohio,* [392 U.S. 1, 20 (1968)].

The Government argues that the special circumstances applicable to domestic security surveillances necessitate a further exception to the warrant requirement. It is urged that the requirement of prior judicial review would obstruct the President in the discharge of his constitutional duty to protect domestic security. We are told further that these surveillances are directed primarily to the collecting and maintaining of intelligence with respect to subversive forces, and are not an attempt to gather evidence for specific criminal prosecutions. It is said that this type of surveillance should not be subject to traditional warrant requirements which were established to govern investigation of criminal activity, not ongoing intelligence gathering.

The Government further insists that courts "as a practical matter would have neither the knowledge nor the techniques necessary to determine whether there was probable cause to believe that surveillance was necessary to protect national security." These security problems, the Government contends, involve "a large number of complex and subtle factors" beyond the competence of courts to evaluate.

As a final reason for exemption from a warrant requirement, the Government believes that disclosure to a magistrate of all or even a significant portion of the information involved in domestic security surveillances "would create serious potential dangers to the national security and to the lives of informants and agents. . . . Secrecy is the essential ingredient in intelligence gathering; requiring prior judicial authorization would create a greater 'danger of leaks . . . because in addition to the judge, you have the clerk, the stenographer and some other officer like a law assistant or bailiff who may be apprised of the nature' of the surveillance." . . .

. . . There is, no doubt, pragmatic force to the Government's position.

But we do not think a case has been made for the requested departure from Fourth Amendment standards. . . . Security surveillances are especially sensitive because of the inherent vagueness of the domestic security concept, the necessarily broad and continuing nature of intelligence gathering, and the temptation to utilize such surveillances to oversee political dissent. We recognize, as we have before, the constitutional basis of the President's domestic security role, but we think it must be exercised in a manner compatible with the Fourth Amendment. In this case we hold that this requires an appropriate prior warrant procedure.

We cannot accept the Government's argument that internal security matters are too subtle and complex for judicial evaluation. Courts regularly deal with the most difficult issues of our society. There is no reason to believe that federal judges will be insensitive to or uncomprehending of the issues involved in domestic security cases. . . . If the threat is too subtle or complex for our senior law enforcement officers to convey its significance to a court, one may question whether there is probable cause for surveillance.

Nor do we believe prior judicial approval will fracture the secrecy essential to official intelligence gathering. The investigation of criminal activity has long involved imparting sensitive information to judicial officers who have respected the confidentialities involved. Judges may be counted upon to be especially conscious of security requirements in national security cases. Title III of the Omnibus Crime Control and Safe Streets Act already has imposed this responsibility on the judiciary in connection with such crimes as espionage, sabotage, and treason, §2516(1)(a) and (c), each of which may involve domestic as well as foreign security threats. Moreover, a warrant application involves no public or adversary proceedings: it is an *ex parte* request before a magistrate or judge. Whatever security dangers clerical and secretarial personnel may pose can be minimized by proper administrative measures, possibly to the point of allowing the Government itself to provide the necessary clerical assistance.

Thus, we conclude that the Government's concerns do not justify departure in this case from the customary Fourth Amendment requirement of judicial approval prior to initiation of a search or surveillance. Although some added burden will be imposed upon the Attorney General, this inconvenience is justified in a free society to protect constitutional values. Nor do we think the Government's domestic surveillance powers will be impaired to any significant degree. A prior warrant establishes presumptive validity of the surveillance and will minimize the burden of justification in post-surveillance judicial review. By no means of least importance will be the reassurance of the public generally that indiscriminate wiretapping and bugging of law-abiding citizens cannot occur.

IV

... [W]e do not hold that the same type of standards and procedures prescribed by Title III are necessarily applicable to this case. We recognize that domestic security surveillance may involve different policy and practical considerations from the surveillance of "ordinary crime." The gathering of security intelligence is often long range and involves the interrelation of various sources and types of information. The exact targets of such surveillance may be more difficult to identify than in surveillance operations against many types of crime specified in Title III. Often, too, the emphasis of domestic intelligence gathering is on the prevention of unlawful activity or the enhancement of the Government's preparedness for some possible future crisis or emergency. Thus, the focus of domestic surveillance may be less precise than that directed against more conventional types of crime.

Given these potential distinctions between Title III criminal surveillances and those involving the domestic security, Congress may wish to consider protective standards for the latter which differ from those already prescribed for specified crimes in Title III. Different standards may be compatible with the Fourth Amendment if they are reasonable both in relation to the legitimate need of Government for intelligence information and the protected rights of our citizens. For the warrant application may vary according to the governmental interest to be enforced and the nature of citizen rights deserving protection....

... We ... hold ... that prior judicial approval is required for the type of domestic security surveillance involved in this case and that such approval may be made in accordance with such reasonable standards as the Congress may prescribe.

V

As the surveillance of Plamondon's conversations was unlawful, because conducted without prior judicial approval, the courts below correctly held that *Alderman v. United States*, 394 U.S. 165 (1969), is controlling and that it requires disclosure to the accused of his own impermissibly intercepted conversations. As stated in *Alderman*, "the trial court can and should, where appropriate, place a defendant and his counsel under enforceable orders against unwarranted disclosure of the materials which they may be entitled to inspect." 394 U.S. at 185.

The judgment of the Court of Appeals is hereby affirmed.

The Chief Justice concurs in the result.

[The concurring opinions of Douglas and White, JJ., are omitted.]

Notes and Questions

1. *The Nature of the Privacy Interest.* Has your phone ever been tapped, or have you suspected that it was? Ever had your mail opened? Your e-mail or the history of

your Internet use read by others without your permission? How did you feel (or how do you think you would feel) upon discovering such an intrusion? Would you feel better knowing that a judge had issued a warrant to authorize it?

While acknowledging that "physical entry of the home is the chief evil" addressed by the Fourth Amendment, the Court found in *Keith,* as it had in *Katz,* that the "broader spirit" of the Amendment protects telephone conversations as well. *Keith,* 407 U.S. at 313. But what is it about electronic surveillance that the Court found objectionable? Is it that a "search" of private conversations is being conducted, or is it the "convergence of First and Fourth Amendment values"? Does the privacy protected by the Court cover only governmental acquisition of personal or intimate information?

2. *The Relevance of Title III.* Title III requires that an application for authorization to conduct electronic surveillance contain detailed information about an alleged criminal offense, the facilities and type of communication to be targeted, the identity of the target (if known), the period of time for surveillance, and whether other investigative methods have failed or why they are unlikely to succeed or are too dangerous. 18 U.S.C. §2518(1)(b)-(d) (2018). A court may issue an order approving electronic surveillance only if it finds probable cause to believe that communications related to the commission of a crime will be obtained through the surveillance. *Id.* §2518(3)(b). Can you see why intelligence agencies would seek to avoid the strictures of Title III in conducting electronic surveillance for intelligence purposes?

But Title III also contained a disclaimer of any intent to limit the "constitutional power of the President." What does the *Keith* Court conclude is the effect of this disclaimer? Should the Court have considered the argument that the last sentence in §2511(3) impliedly permits the admission into evidence of communications intercepted pursuant to such constitutional authority?

Do you agree that §2511(3) "is essentially neutral," as concluded by Justice Powell?

3. *Deciding Whether a Warrant Should Issue.* Is probable cause the sole criterion for authorizing a warrant? Might a magistrate also appropriately consider the extent to which the information sought is of an intimate nature? Or what uses the government intends for the information? *See* Russell D. Covey, *Pervasive Surveillance and the Future of the Fourth Amendment,* 80 Miss. L.J. 1289 (2011) (so arguing). Or the consequences of a future development the government seeks to prevent, such as an organization's acquisition of a WMD? *See* Scott J. Glick, *Consequence, Weapons of Mass Destruction, and the Fourth Amendment's "No-Win" Scenario,* 90 Ind. L.J. 1 (2015) (so arguing).

4. *Inherent Surveillance Authority?* Do the President's implied constitutional powers, if any, apply equally to surveillance against domestic security threats and foreign ones? Justice Powell's willingness to draw a sharp distinction between the two became the predicate for establishing the Fourth Amendment warrant requirement for "domestic" national security investigations. Why is the power to protect domestic security viewed with greater skepticism by the Court than the power to protect against foreign perils?

Or does the *Keith* Court's reasoning make unlawful *any* warrantless wiretap ordered by the President? If not, which ones are lawful?

5. *Balancing Away the Warrant Requirement.* Does the Warrant Clause of the Fourth Amendment adequately protect privacy interests? What is the function of a "neutral and detached magistrate" in a warrant proceeding?

According to one scholar, the Warrant Clause plays only a modest role in national security investigations, because courts are poorly equipped to decide whether a warrant requirement would be reasonable in a national security setting. Orin S. Kerr, *The Modest Role of the Warrant Clause in National Security Investigations,* 88 Tex. L. Rev. 1669 (2010). Professor Kerr explains that, unlike the usual Fourth Amendment case, in which police conduct a search and a court then decides whether the already executed, judicially warranted search met Fourth Amendment requirements, judges in national security investigations must decide in advance about hypothetical facts concerning hypothetical investigations, based on an unclear standard:

> Under . . . *Keith* . . . whether a warrant is required is based on whether requiring a warrant is workable, but that depends on what standard is required for obtaining a warrant. . . . [W]hat standard is required for obtaining a warrant depends on what kind of standard would make a warrant standard workable. [*Id.* at 1678.]

Does Kerr accurately describe the way the Warrant Clause was applied in *Keith*? Would you expect the Warrant Clause to diminish in importance in national security investigations? If so, what would take its place?

6. *Should Place Matter?* Although the Supreme Court in *Katz* famously proclaimed that the Fourth Amendment protects people, not places, even in *Katz* the telephone booth became a "temporarily private place whose momentary occupants' expectations of freedom from intrusion are recognized as reasonable." 389 U.S. at 361 (Harlan, J., concurring). The distinction between people and places, perpetuated by Justice Harlan's reasonable expectation of privacy test, may thus be blurry. Can you think of a better test that takes into account the nature of the intrusion, the type of privacy at risk, and the government's interests in acquiring and perhaps using the information?

Unlike a physical search, most computer searches involve the remote collection of digital electronic data. Is a computer search therefore a "search" under the Fourth Amendment? Under what circumstances are computer data "seized," and when would such a search or seizure be "reasonable"? Computer searches "challenge several of the basic assumptions underlying Fourth Amendment doctrine. Computers are like containers in a physical sense, homes in a virtual sense, and vast warehouses in an informational sense." Orin S. Kerr, *Searches and Seizures in a Digital World,* 119 Harv. L. Rev. 531, 533 (2005). Which perspective do you find most helpful in thinking about application of the Fourth Amendment to Internet and computer searches?

7. *Warrantless Surveillance "to Save American Lives."* In December 2005, the *New York Times* revealed the existence of a four-year, large-scale warrantless electronic surveillance program that intercepted communications of some U.S. citizens. James Risen & Eric Lichtblau, *Bush Lets U.S. Spy on Callers Without Courts,* N.Y. Times, Dec. 16, 2005. At a White House press conference, President Bush offered this explanation for the warrantless surveillance:

> We know that a two-minute phone conversation between somebody linked to al Qaeda here and an operative overseas could lead directly to the loss of thousands of lives. To save

> American lives, we must be able to act fast and to detect these conversations so that we can prevent new attacks.
>
> So, consistent with U.S. law and the Constitution, I authorized the interception of international communications of people with known links to al Qaeda and related terrorist organizations. . . .
>
> . . . I've reauthorized this program more than 30 times since the September 11th attacks, and I intend to do so for so long as our nation . . . faces the continuing threat of an enemy that wants to kill American citizens. [Press Conference of the President (Dec. 19, 2005).]

Assuming, arguendo, that Congress has enacted no applicable statute, would you agree, based on *Keith,* that the program described by the President is constitutional? Other aspects of this program are considered in Chapter 22.

C. A FOREIGN INTELLIGENCE EXCEPTION?

In *Keith,* Justice Powell suggested that national security wiretaps may not have to meet all the Fourth Amendment requirements applicable in criminal investigations, but he did not specify what alternative processes might be appropriate in such cases. Nor did the Court refer to the constitutional requirements for other forms of surveillance, such as searches of the home and person. The Court emphasized, however, that *Keith* did not involve any foreign power, but was strictly a case involving "domestic security."

Meanwhile, the agencies within the intelligence community had, since World War II, been developing their own guidelines for national security surveillance. After *Keith,* several lower courts considered the applicability of the Fourth Amendment to surveillance to obtain foreign intelligence. For example, in *United States v. Brown,* 484 F.2d 418 (5th Cir. 1973), and *United States v. Butenko,* 494 F.2d 593 (3d Cir. 1974), courts of appeals upheld the lawfulness of surveillance of American citizens' conversations incidentally overheard when the surveillance was authorized by the Attorney General for the purpose of gathering foreign intelligence. Yet in *Zweibon v. Mitchell,* 516 F.2d 594 (D.C. Cir. 1975), the D.C. Circuit upheld a warrant requirement in the surveillance of a domestic organization without ties to a foreign power. A similar result was reached in *Berlin Democratic Club v. Rumsfeld,* 410 F. Supp. 144, 157 (D.D.C. 1976), where a warrant was required to wiretap Americans living in West Germany, despite Department of Defense arguments about dangers to U.S. forces and to American foreign policy.

While these decisions reinforcing the domestic vs. foreign intelligence bases for lawful intelligence gathering concerned wiretaps, the FBI also conducted warrantless physical searches. The Church Committee reviewed hundreds of so-called "black bag jobs" and other surreptitious entries against domestic targets and found that their use dropped dramatically after FBI Director J. Edgar Hoover banned such operations in 1966. S. Select Comm. to Study Governmental Operations with Respect to Intelligence Activities (Church Committee), *Intelligence Activities and the Rights of Americans,* S. Rep. No. 94-755, bk. III, at 355 (1976).

A foreign intelligence exception to the warrant requirement has been asserted more recently in connection with electronic collection in the digital age. Consider the following case.

Reading *In re Directives*

In 2005, the *New York Times* exposed a warrantless surveillance program that President Bush had approved shortly after 9/11. In 2007, Congress amended the 1978 Foreign Intelligence Surveillance Act (FISA) to permit the NSA to continue a similar program to collect communications to and from persons reasonably believed to be located outside the United States. Under that statute, instead of issuing a warrant, a special court, the Foreign Intelligence Surveillance Court, had merely to approve certain procedures for a *program* to obtain intelligence based on probable cause to believe that any particular target was a foreign power or agent of a foreign power. But judicial approval of individual targets or searches was not required. (We study the origins and legality of this programmatic collection effort in detail in Chapter 21.) In reviewing the following Fourth Amendment challenge to this form of warrantless surveillance, consider these questions:

- Why doesn't the Warrant Clause apply to this programmatic intelligence collection?
- Does the court's opinion finally resolve the question whether there is a foreign intelligence exception to the Warrant Clause?
- Once the court finds the Warrant Clause inapplicable (or excused), is that the end of the challenge? What is the alternative argument under the Fourth Amendment?
- Is there any surveillance to which *neither* part of the Fourth Amendment applies? If so, what is it?

In re Directives to Yahoo! Inc. Pursuant to Section 105B of the Foreign Intelligence Surveillance Act

Foreign Intelligence Surveillance Court of Review, Aug. 22, 2008
No. 08-01, 2008 WL 10632524

SELYA, Chief Judge. This petition for review stems from directives issued to the petitioner Yahoo! Inc., pursuant to a now-expired set of amendments to the Foreign Intelligence Surveillance Act of 1978 (FISA) [50 U.S.C. §§1801-1885c (2012 & Supp. III 2015)]. Among other things, those amendments, known as the Protect America Act of 2007 (PAA), Pub. L. No. 110-55, 121 Stat. 552, authorized the United States to direct communications service providers to assist it in acquiring foreign intelligence when those acquisitions targeted third persons (such as the service provider's customers) reasonably believed to be located outside the United States. Having received [redacted text] such directives, the petitioner challenged their legality before the Foreign Intelligence Surveillance Court (FISC). When that court found the directives lawful and compelled obedience to them, the petitioner brought this petition for review. . . .

I. THE STATUTORY FRAMEWORK

On August 5, 2007, Congress enacted the PAA, codified in pertinent part at 50 U.S.C. §§1805a to 1805c, as a measured expansion of FISA's scope. Subject to certain conditions, the PAA allowed the government to conduct warrantless foreign intelligence surveillance on targets (including United States persons) "reasonably believed" to be located outside the United States. 50 U.S.C. §1805b(a). This proviso is of critical importance here.

Under the new statute, the Director of National Intelligence (DNI) and the Attorney General (AG) were permitted to authorize, for periods of up to one year, "the acquisition of foreign intelligence information concerning persons reasonably believed to be outside the United States" if they determined that the acquisition met five specified criteria. . . . Pursuant to this authorization, the DNI and the AG were allowed to issue directives to "person[s]" — a term that includes agents of communications service providers — delineating the assistance needed to acquire the information. *Id.* §1805b(e); *see id.* §1805b(a)(3). . . .

II. BACKGROUND

Beginning in November of 2007, the government issued directives to the petitioner commanding it to assist in warrantless surveillance of certain customers' [redacted]. These directives were issued pursuant to certifications that purported to contain all the information required by the PAA. . . .

. . . In essence, as implemented, the certifications permit surveillances conducted to obtain foreign intelligence for national security purposes when those surveillances are directed against foreign powers or agents of foreign powers reasonably believed to be located outside the United States.

The . . . petitioner . . . refused to comply with the directives. On November 21, 2007, the government moved to compel compliance. Following amplitudinous briefing, the FISC handed down a meticulous opinion validating the directives and granting the motion to compel. . . .

III. ANALYSIS . . .

B. The Fourth Amendment Challenge. . . .

The petitioner's remonstrance has two main branches. First, it asserts that the government, in issuing the directives, had to abide by the requirements attendant to the Warrant Clause of the Fourth Amendment. Second, it argues that even if a foreign intelligence exception to the warrant requirements exists and excuses compliance with the Warrant Clause, the surveillances mandated by the directives are unreasonable and, therefore, violate the Fourth Amendment. The petitioner limits each of its claims to the harm that may be inflicted upon United States persons. . . .

2. The Foreign Intelligence Exception

The recurrent theme permeating the petitioner's arguments is the notion that there is no foreign intelligence exception to the Fourth Amendment's Warrant

Clause. The FISC rejected this notion, positing that our decision in *In re Sealed Case* [310 F.3d 717, 721 (FISA Ct. Rev. 2002)] confirmed the existence of a foreign intelligence exception to the warrant requirement.

While the *Sealed Case* court avoided an express holding that a foreign intelligence exception exists by assuming arguendo that whether or not the warrant requirements were met, the statute could survive on reasonableness grounds, *see* 310 F.3d at 741-42, we believe that the FISC's reading of that decision is plausible.

The petitioner argues correctly that the Supreme Court has not explicitly recognized such an exception; indeed, the Court reserved that question in *United States v. United States District Court* (*Keith*), 407 U.S. 297, 308-09 (1972). But the Court has recognized a comparable exception, outside the foreign intelligence context, in so-called "special needs" cases. In those cases, the Court excused compliance with the Warrant Clause when the purpose behind the governmental action went beyond routine law enforcement and insisting upon a warrant would materially interfere with the accomplishment of that purpose. *See, e.g., Vernonia Sch. Dist. 47J v. Acton,* 515 U.S. 646, 653 (1995) (upholding drug testing of high-school athletes and explaining that the exception to the warrant requirement applied "when special needs, beyond the normal need for law enforcement, make the warrant and probable-cause requirement[s] impracticable" (quoting *Griffin v. Wisconsin,* 483 U.S. 868, 873 (1987))); *Skinner v. Ry. Labor Execs. Ass'n,* 489 U.S. 602, 620 (1989) (upholding regulations instituting drug and alcohol testing of railroad workers for safety reasons); *cf. Terry v. Ohio,* 392 U.S. 1, 23-24 (1968) (upholding pat-frisk for weapons to protect officer safety during investigatory stop).

The question, then, is whether the reasoning of the special needs cases applies by analogy to justify a foreign intelligence exception to the warrant requirement for surveillance undertaken for national security purposes and directed at a foreign power or an agent of a foreign power reasonably believed to be located outside the United States. Applying principles derived from the special needs cases, we conclude that this type of foreign intelligence surveillance possesses characteristics that qualify it for such an exception.

For one thing, the purpose behind the surveillances ordered pursuant to the directives goes well beyond any garden-variety law enforcement objective. It involves the acquisition from overseas foreign agents of foreign intelligence to help protect national security. Moreover, this is the sort of situation in which the government's interest is particularly intense.

The petitioner has a fallback position. Even if there is a narrow foreign intelligence exception, it asseverates, a definition of that exception should require the foreign intelligence purpose to be the primary purpose of the surveillance. For that proposition, it cites the Fourth Circuit's decision in *United States v. Truong Dinh Hung,* 629 F.2d 908, 915 (4th Cir. 1980). [*Truong* had upheld warrantless surveillance only for as long as the "primary purpose" of the surveillance was collecting foreign intelligence rather than criminal evidence, and it required traditional probable cause after a foreign intelligence investigation "becomes primarily a criminal investigation. . . ." 629 F.2d at 915. The Patriot Act thereafter substituted "significant purpose" for "primary purpose" in the certification requirement for foreign intelligence surveillance. Pub. L. No. 107-56, §218, 115 Stat. 272, 291 (2001).] That dog will not hunt.

This court previously has upheld as reasonable under the Fourth Amendment the Patriot Act's substitution of "a significant purpose" for the talismanic phrase "primary purpose." . . . In our view the more appropriate consideration is the programmatic purpose of the surveillances and whether — as in the special needs cases — that programmatic purpose involves some legitimate objective beyond ordinary crime control.

Under this analysis, the surveillances authorized by the directives easily pass muster. Their stated purpose centers on garnering foreign intelligence. There is no indication that the collections of information are primarily related to ordinary criminal-law enforcement purposes. Without something more than a purely speculative set of imaginings, we cannot infer that the purpose of the directives (and, thus, of the surveillances) is other than their stated purpose.

We add, moreover, that there is a high degree of probability that requiring a warrant would hinder the government's ability to collect time-sensitive information and, thus, would impede the vital national security interests that are at stake. *See, e.g., Truong Dinh Hung,* 629 F.2d at 915 (explaining that when the object of a surveillance is a foreign power or its collaborators, "the government has the greatest need for speed, stealth, and secrecy").... Compulsory compliance with the warrant requirement would introduce an element of delay, thus frustrating the government's ability to collect information in a timely manner....

For these reasons, we hold that a foreign intelligence exception to the Fourth Amendment's warrant requirement exists when surveillance is conducted to obtain foreign intelligence for national security purposes and is directed against foreign powers or agents of foreign powers reasonably believed to be located outside the United States....

[The court went on to hold that a variety of procedures internal and external to the PAA insured the Fourth Amendment reasonableness of the warrantless surveillance.]

Notes and Questions

1. *Special Needs.* The court holds that the Warrant Clause does not apply because the collection program qualifies for a special needs exception. What special needs? How is the collection like or different from the other recognized special needs examples cited by the court?

2. *Dropping the Other (Fourth Amendment) Shoe.* If there is a foreign intelligence exception, it is only an exception to the Warrant Clause. Even a warrantless search must still be reasonable, because the Fourth Amendment forbids "unreasonable searches." The court in *In re Directives* found that various safeguards (chiefly involving "minimization procedures" for dealing with the retention and dissemination of collected intelligence, which we consider in Chapter 22) made the collection program reasonable.

3. *Comparing Physical Searches and Electronic Surveillance.* Is physical entry of the home more threatening to civil liberties than a wiretap? In *United States v. Ehrlichman,* 376 F. Supp. 29, 33 (D.D.C. 1974), *aff'd,* 546 F.2d 910 (D.C. Cir. 1976), the court ruled that

> the Government must comply with the strict constitutional and statutory limitations on trespassory searches and arrests even when known foreign agents are involved. To hold otherwise, except under the most exigent circumstances, would be to abandon the Fourth Amendment to the whim of the Executive in total disregard of the Amendment's history and purpose.

> Defendants contend that, over the last few years, the courts have begun to carve out an exception to this traditional rule for purely intelligence-gathering searches deemed necessary for the conduct of foreign affairs. However, the cases cited are carefully limited to the issue of wiretapping, a relatively nonintrusive search. [*Id.*]

Microphone surveillance at one time required entry to install the device, which would, like a wiretap, transmit all conversations, including those not subject to the investigation. If a physical search is controlled, it will take less time and may focus only on material relevant to the investigation. Yet for many of us, invasion of our physical space is more threatening than the prospect of electronic surveillance. Why is that so? Can you make an argument that the Fourth Amendment's text or history reflects this sense?

In Chapter 21, we will learn that subsequent legislation enabled physical searches for foreign intelligence subject to special procedures different from the traditional warrant requirement.

4. The Impact of New Technology. Changing technology is undeniably affecting the meaning and application of the Fourth Amendment in national security settings. Consider these developments:

- *Intrusiveness of the Surveillance.* By one common sense measure, you might expect that Fourth Amendment protections surrounding uses of new technology would track the intrusiveness of the surveillance. For example, in 1983, the monitoring of beeper signals from a radio transmitter placed in contraband material in an area that was open to visual surveillance did not trigger Fourth Amendment protections, because the target had no legitimate expectation of privacy in such an open area. *United States v. Knotts*, 460 U.S. 276, 284-285 (1983). That reduced expectation of privacy arguably exists in all public spaces, such as malls, banks, mass transit facilities, and places where crowds gather. But suppose the surveillance is 24/7 using a camera mounted surreptitiously on a utility pole and pointed toward a yard and home open to public view. *See United States v. Vargas*, No. 13-6025 (E.D. Wash. Dec. 15, 2014), https://www.eff.org/files/2014/12/15/vargas_order.pdf (because the camera is covert and always on, it is more intrusive than general physical observation of the same place, and a warrant is required). Does the growing power and ubiquity of such surveillance devices support an emerging right to privacy in public places, or just the opposite?

- *Global Positioning and Other Monitoring Devices.* Location services on our devices — including GPS, Bluetooth, crowd-sourced Wi-Fi hotspots, and cell tower locations — are now ubiquitous. In *United States v. Jones*, 565 U.S. 400 (2012), the Supreme Court agreed that the government's monitoring of a GPS tracking device left attached to a criminal defendant's car after a warrant had expired violated the Fourth Amendment. Justice Scalia's opinion for the Court found that the trespassory intrusion on defendant's property constituted a search. Concurring, Justice Sotomayor worried more generally about the impacts of changing technologies on privacy and free expression:

  > GPS monitoring generates a precise, comprehensive record of a person's public movements that reflects a wealth of detail about her familial, political,

professional, religious, and sexual associations. See, *e.g.*, *People v. Weaver*, 12 N.Y. 3d 433, 441-442 (2009) ("Disclosed in [GPS] data . . . will be trips the indisputably private nature of which takes little imagination to conjure: trips to the psychiatrist, the plastic surgeon, the abortion clinic, the AIDS treatment center, the strip club, the criminal defense attorney, the by-the-hour motel, the union meeting, the mosque, synagogue or church, the gay bar and on and on"). The Government can store such records and efficiently mine them for information years into the future. And because GPS monitoring is cheap in comparison to conventional surveillance techniques and, by design, proceeds surreptitiously, it evades the ordinary checks that constrain abusive law enforcement practices: "limited police resources and community hostility." *Illinois v. Lidster*, 540 U.S. 419, 426 (2004).

Awareness that the Government may be watching chills associational and expressive freedoms. And the Government's unrestrained power to assemble data that reveal private aspects of identity is susceptible to abuse. The net result is that GPS monitoring — by making available at a relatively low cost such a substantial quantum of intimate information about any person whom the Government, in its unfettered discretion, chooses to track — may "alter the relationship between citizen and government in a way that is inimical to democratic society." *United States v. Cuevas-Perez*, 640 F.3d 272, 285 (C.A.7 2011) (Flaum, J., concurring). [565 U.S. at 415-416 (Sotomayor, J., concurring).]

Justice Alito, concurring only in the judgment (and joined by Justices Ginsburg, Breyer, and Kagan), found a Fourth Amendment violation relying on *Katz*. But he questioned the adequacy of the *Katz* expectation-of-privacy test for evaluating emerging technologies under the Fourth Amendment:

The *Katz* expectation-of-privacy test avoids the problems and complications [with Justice Scalia's trespassory approach] . . . , but it is not without its own difficulties. It involves a degree of circularity, and judges are apt to confuse their own expectations of privacy with those of the hypothetical reasonable person to which the *Katz* test looks. In addition, the *Katz* test rests on the assumption that this hypothetical reasonable person has a well-developed and stable set of privacy expectations. But technology can change those expectations. Dramatic technological change may lead to periods in which popular expectations are in flux and may ultimately produce significant changes in popular attitudes. New technology may provide increased convenience or security at the expense of privacy, and many people may find the tradeoff worthwhile. And even if the public does not welcome the diminution of privacy that new technology entails, they may eventually reconcile themselves to this development as inevitable. [*Id.* at 427 (Alito, J., concurring in the judgment).]

Toward the end of his opinion, Justice Alito noted that the Court need not consider whether long-term GPS monitoring during investigations involving "extraordinary offenses" should be guided by different privacy considerations than those in *Jones*. Can you articulate the parameters of an "extraordinary offenses exception" to the warrant requirement? Would you create one?

- *Cell Phone Searches Incident to Arrest.* In *Riley v. California*, 573 U.S. 373 (2014), the Supreme Court unanimously held that the police must normally obtain a warrant before searching the data on a cell phone, even when the phone is obtained incident to an arrest. The Court thus created an exception to the categorical rule articulated in *United States v. Robinson*, 414 U.S. 218 (1973), that a search of all items in a suspect's possession incident to his arrest requires no additional justification. The *Riley* Court noted that a cell phone cannot itself be used as a weapon. 573 U.S. at 387. Any government interest in preventing the destruction of data on a cell phone, the Court found, had not been demonstrated to date and might be met by means other than a warrantless search. *Id.* at 388.

The Court recognized the important privacy concerns implicated by cell phones:

> Modern cell phones, as a category, implicate privacy concerns far beyond those implicated by the search of a cigarette pack, a wallet, or a purse....
>
> Cell phones differ in both a quantitative and a qualitative sense from other objects that might be kept on an arrestee's person. The term "cell phone" is itself misleading shorthand; many of these devices are in fact minicomputers that also happen to have the capacity to be used as a telephone. They could just as easily be called cameras, video players, rolodexes, calendars, tape recorders, libraries, diaries, albums, televisions, maps, or newspapers....
>
> ... [A] cell phone search would typically expose to the government far *more* than the most exhaustive search of a house: A phone not only contains in digital form many sensitive records previously found in the home; it also contains a broad array of private information never found in a home in any form — unless the phone is. [*Id.* at 393, 396-397.]

The Court reasoned that the exigent circumstances exception may still justify a warrantless search of a particular phone and that, in any case, a search may be carried out after obtaining a warrant.

■ *Going Dark?* After the December 2015 terrorist attack in San Bernardino, California that killed 14 people, the FBI rushed to learn whether the husband-wife terrorist team was part of a wider plot or was otherwise affiliated with known terrorist organizations. The FBI tried and at first was unable to unlock gunman Syed Rizwan Farook's iPhone. After Apple refused to assist the Bureau, the FBI sued to compel Apple to unlock the phone by writing a software update undoing its security protections. The litigation ended when the government announced that it had found a way to unlock the phone without help from Apple. Katie Benner & Eric Lichtblau, *U.S. Says It Has Unlocked iPhone Without Apple*, N.Y. Times, Mar. 28, 2016.

What law enforcement and intelligence officials call "going dark" has focused attention on whether the government should have some form of exceptional access to overcome encryption of information of electronic devices, and of e-mail and other Internet communications. Meanwhile, the FBI and law enforcement agencies across the country have hired hackers to break into locked phones, and cell phone makers have enhanced security protections to disable the hackers. What are the arguments for and against granting exceptional access when investigating potential terrorist attacks or other serious national security threats? If Apple or another provider were ordered by a court to build software that would unlock an accused terrorist's phone, would that software make all phones less secure? *See* Susan Landau, *Revelations on the FBI's Unlocking of the San Bernardino iPhone: Maybe the Future Isn't Going Dark After All*, Lawfare, Mar. 30, 2018.

D. SURVEILLANCE ABROAD

In re Terrorist Bombings of U.S. Embassies in East Africa (Fourth Amendment Challenges)

United States Court of Appeals, Second Circuit, 2008
552 F.3d 157

JOSÉ A. CABRANES, Circuit Judge. Defendant-appellant Wadih El-Hage, a citizen of the United States, challenges his conviction in the United States District Court for the Southern District of New York (Leonard B. Sand, *Judge*) on numerous charges arising from his involvement in the August 7, 1998 bombings of the American Embassies in Nairobi, Kenya and Dar es Salaam, Tanzania. . . .

El-Hage contends that the District Court erred by (1) recognizing a foreign intelligence exception to the Fourth Amendment's warrant requirement, (2) concluding that the search of El-Hage's home and surveillance of his telephone lines qualified for inclusion in that exception. . . . Because we hold that the Fourth Amendment's requirement of reasonableness — and not the Warrant Clause — governs extraterritorial searches of U.S. citizens and that the searches challenged on this appeal were reasonable, we find no error in the District Court's denial of El-Hage's [motion to suppress illegally obtained evidence]. . . . El-Hage's challenge to his conviction is therefore without merit.

I. BACKGROUND

A. Factual Overview

American intelligence became aware of al Qaeda's presence in Kenya by mid-1996 and identified five telephone numbers used by suspected al Qaeda associates. From August 1996 through August 1997, American intelligence officials monitored these telephone lines, including two El-Hage used: a phone line in the building where El-Hage lived and his cell phone. The Attorney General of the United States then authorized intelligence operatives to target El-Hage in particular. This authorization, first issued on April 4, 1997, was renewed in July 1997. Working with Kenyan authorities, U.S. officials searched El-Hage's home in Nairobi on August 21, 1997, pursuant to a document shown to El-Hage's wife that was "identified as a Kenyan warrant authorizing a search for 'stolen property.'" At the completion of the search, one of the Kenyan officers gave El-Hage's wife an inventory listing the items seized during the search. El-Hage was not present during the search of his home. It is uncontested that the agents did not apply for or obtain a warrant from a U.S. court. . . .

II. DISCUSSION . . .

B. The District Court's Denial of El-Hage's Motion to Suppress Evidence . . .

2. Extraterritorial Application of the Fourth Amendment

In order to determine whether El-Hage's suppression motion was properly denied by the District Court, we must first determine whether and to what extent the Fourth Amendment's safeguards apply to overseas searches involving U.S. citizens. In *United States v. Toscanino,* a case involving a Fourth Amendment challenge to overseas wiretapping of a non-U.S. citizen, we observed that it was "well settled" that "the Bill of Rights has extraterritorial application to the conduct abroad of federal agents directed against United States citizens." 500 F.2d 267, 280-81 (2d Cir. 1974); *see also United States v. Verdugo-Urquidez,* 494 U.S. 259, 283 n.7 (1990) (Brennan, J., dissenting) (recognizing "the rule, accepted by every Court of Appeals to have considered the question, that the Fourth Amendment applies to searches conducted by the United States Government against United States citizens abroad"). Nevertheless, we have not yet determined the specific question of the applicability of the Fourth Amendment's Warrant Clause to overseas searches. Faced with that question now, we hold that the Fourth Amendment's warrant requirement does not govern searches conducted abroad by U.S. agents; such searches of U.S. citizens need only satisfy the Fourth Amendment's requirement of reasonableness. . . .

. . . While never addressing the question directly, the Supreme Court provided some guidance on the issue in *United States v. Verdugo-Urquidez.* . . .

. . . [That guidance] and the following reasons weigh against imposing a warrant requirement on overseas searches.

First, there is nothing in our history or our precedents suggesting that U.S. officials must first obtain a warrant before conducting an overseas search. El-Hage has pointed to no authority — and we are aware of none — directly supporting the proposition that warrants are necessary for searches conducted abroad by U.S. law enforcement officers or local agents acting in collaboration with them; nor has El-Hage identified any instances in our history where a foreign search was conducted pursuant to an American search warrant. This dearth of authority is not surprising in light of the history of the Fourth Amendment and its Warrant Clause as well as the history of international affairs. . . . [Here the court reviews the *Verdugo-Urquidez* Court's analysis of the history of the drafting of the Fourth Amendment.] Accordingly, we agree with the Ninth Circuit's observation that "foreign searches have neither been historically subject to the warrant procedure, nor could they be as a practical matter." *United States v. Barona,* 56 F.3d 1087, 1092 n.1 (9th Cir. 1995).[7]

Second, nothing in the history of the foreign relations of the United States would require that U.S. officials obtain warrants from foreign magistrates before conducting searches overseas or, indeed, [lead us] to suppose that all other states have search and

---

7. A U.S. citizen who is a target of a search by our government executed in a foreign country is not without constitutional protection — namely, the Fourth Amendment's guarantee of reasonableness which protects a citizen from unwarranted government intrusions. Indeed, in many instances, as appears to have been the case here, searches targeting U.S. citizens on foreign soil will be supported by probable cause.

The interest served by the warrant requirement in having a "neutral and detached magistrate" evaluate the reasonableness of a search is, in part, based on separation of powers concerns — namely, the need to interpose a judicial officer between the zealous police officer ferreting out crime and the subject of the search. These interests are lessened in the circumstances presented here for two reasons. First, a domestic judicial officer's ability to determine the reasonableness of a search is diminished where the search occurs on foreign soil. Second, the acknowledged wide discretion afforded the executive branch in foreign affairs ought to be respected in these circumstances.

A warrant serves a further purpose in limiting the scope of the search to places described with particularity or "the persons or things to be seized" in the warrant. U.S. Const. amend. IV. In the instant case, we are satisfied that the scope of the searches at issue was not unreasonable. *See* Parts II.B.3, *post.*

investigation rules akin to our own. As the Supreme Court explained in *Verdugo-Urquidez*:

> For better or for worse, we live in a world of nation-states in which our Government must be able to function effectively in the company of sovereign nations. Some who violate our laws may live outside our borders under a regime quite different from that which obtains in this country. Situations threatening to important American interests may arise halfway around the globe, situations which in the view of the political branches of our Government require an American response with armed force. If there are to be restrictions on searches and seizures which occur incident to such American action, they must be imposed by the political branches through diplomatic understanding, treaty, or legislation.

494 U.S. at 275 (internal citation, quotation marks, and brackets omitted). The American procedure of issuing search warrants on a showing of probable cause simply does not extend throughout the globe and, pursuant to the Supreme Court's instructions, the Constitution does not condition our government's investigative powers on the practices of foreign legal regimes "quite different from that which obtains in this country." *Id.*

Third, if U.S. judicial officers were to issue search warrants intended to have extraterritorial effect, such warrants would have dubious legal significance, if any, in a foreign nation. *Cf. The Schooner Exchange v. M'Faddon*, 11 U.S. 116, 135 (1812) ("The jurisdiction of the nation within its own territory is necessarily exclusive and absolute. It is susceptible of no limitation not imposed by itself."). As a District Court in this Circuit recently observed, "it takes little to imagine the diplomatic and legal complications that would arise if American government officials traveled to another sovereign country and attempted to carry out a search of any kind, professing the authority to do so based on an American-issued search warrant." *United States v. Vilar*, No. 05-CR-621, 2007 WL 1075041, at *52 (S.D.N.Y. Apr. 4, 2007). We agree with that observation. A warrant issued by a U.S. court would neither empower a U.S. agent to conduct a search nor would it necessarily compel the intended target to comply. It would be a nullity, or in the words of the Supreme Court, "a dead letter." *Verdugo-Urquidez*, 494 U.S. at 274.

Fourth and finally, it is by no means clear that U.S. judicial officers could be authorized to issue warrants for overseas searches, *cf. Weinberg v. United States*, 126 F.2d 1004, 1006 (2d Cir. 1942) (statute authorizing district court to issue search warrants construed to limit authority to the court's territorial jurisdiction), although we need not resolve that issue here.

For these reasons, we hold that the Fourth Amendment's Warrant Clause has no extraterritorial application and that foreign searches of U.S. citizens conducted by U.S. agents are subject only to the Fourth Amendment's requirement of reasonableness.

The District Court's recognition of an exception to the warrant requirement for foreign intelligence searches finds support in the pre-FISA law of other circuits. *See United States v. Truong Dinh Hung*, 629 F.2d 908, 913 (4th Cir. 1980); *United States v. Buck*, 548 F.2d 871, 875 (9th Cir. 1977); *United States v. Butenko*, 494 F.2d 593, 605 (3d Cir. 1974); *United States v. Brown*, 484 F.2d 418, 426 (5th Cir. 1973). We decline to adopt this view, however, because the exception requires an inquiry into whether the "primary purpose" of the search is foreign intelligence collection. *See* [*United States v.*

Bin Laden, 126 F. Supp. 2d 264 (S.D.N.Y. 2000),] at 277. This distinction between a "primary purpose" and other purposes is inapt. As the U.S. Foreign Intelligence Surveillance Court of Review has explained:

> [The primary purpose] analysis, in our view, rested on a false premise and the line the court sought to draw was inherently unstable, unrealistic, and confusing. The false premise was the assertion that once the government moves to criminal prosecution, its "foreign policy concerns" recede. . . . [T]hat is simply not true as it relates to counterintelligence. In that field the government's primary purpose is to halt the espionage or terrorism efforts, and criminal prosecutions can be, and usually are, interrelated with other techniques used to frustrate a foreign power's efforts.

In re Sealed Case No. 02-001, 310 F.3d 717, 743 (Foreign Int. Surv. Ct. Rev. 2002).

In addition, the purpose of the search has no bearing on the factors making a warrant requirement inapplicable to foreign searches — namely, (1) the complete absence of any precedent in our history for doing so, (2) the inadvisability of conditioning our government's surveillance on the practices of foreign states, (3) a U.S. warrant's lack of authority overseas, and (4) the absence of a mechanism for obtaining a U.S. warrant. Accordingly, we cannot endorse the view that the normal course is to obtain a warrant for overseas searches involving U.S. citizens unless the search is "primarily" targeting foreign powers.

3. The Kenyan Searches Were Reasonable and Therefore Did Not Violate the Fourth Amendment

. . . First, El-Hage insists that his Nairobi home deserves special consideration in light of the home's status as "the most fundamental bastion of privacy protected by the Fourth Amendment." Second, he contends that the electronic surveillance was far broader than necessary because it encompassed "[m]any calls, if not the predominant amount, [that] were related solely to legitimate commercial purposes, and/or purely family and social matters."

To determine whether a search is reasonable under the Fourth Amendment, we examine the "totality of the circumstances" to balance "on the one hand, the degree to which it intrudes upon an individual's privacy and, on the other, the degree to which it is needed for the promotion of legitimate governmental interests." *Samson v. California*, 547 U.S. 843, 848 (2006). . . .

a. The Search of El-Hage's Home in Nairobi Was Reasonable . . .

Applying that test to the facts of this case, we first examine the extent to which the search of El-Hage's Nairobi home intruded upon his privacy. The intrusion was minimized by the fact that the search was not covert; indeed, U.S. agents searched El-Hage's home with the assistance of Kenyan authorities, pursuant to what was identified as a "Kenyan warrant authorizing [a search]." The search occurred during the daytime and in the presence of El-Hage's wife. At the conclusion of the search, an inventory listing the items seized during the search was prepared and given to El-Hage's wife. In addition, the District Court found that "[t]he scope of the search was limited to those items which were believed to have foreign intelligence value[,] and retention and dissemination of the evidence acquired during the search were minimized."

As described above, U.S. intelligence officers became aware of al Qaeda's presence in Kenya in the spring of 1996. At about that time, they identified five telephone lines used by suspected al Qaeda associates, one of which was located in the same building as El-Hage's Nairobi home; another was a cellular phone used by El-Hage. After these telephone lines had been monitored for several months, the Attorney General of the United States authorized surveillance specifically targeting El-Hage. That authorization was renewed four months later, and, one month after that, U.S. agents searched El-Hage's home in Nairobi. This sequence of events is indicative of a disciplined approach to gathering indisputably vital intelligence on the activities of a foreign terrorist organization. U.S. agents did not breach the privacy of El-Hage's home on a whim or on the basis of an unsubstantiated tip; rather, they monitored telephonic communications involving him for nearly a year and conducted surveillance of his activities for five months before concluding that it was necessary to search his home. In light of these findings of fact, which El-Hage has not contested as clearly erroneous, we conclude that the search, while undoubtedly intrusive on El-Hage's privacy, was restrained in execution and narrow in focus.

Balanced against this restrained and limited intrusion on El-Hage's privacy, we have the government's manifest need to investigate possible threats to national security. As the District Court noted, al Qaeda "declared a war of terrorism against all members of the United States military worldwide" in 1996 and later against American civilians. The government had evidence establishing that El-Hage was working with al Qaeda in Kenya. On the basis of these findings of fact, we agree with the District Court that, at the time of the search of El-Hage's home, the government had a powerful need to gather additional intelligence on al Qaeda's activities in Kenya, which it had linked to El-Hage.

Balancing the search's limited intrusion on El-Hage's privacy against the manifest need of the government to monitor the activities of al Qaeda, which had been connected to El-Hage through a year of surveillance, we hold that the search of El-Hage's Nairobi residence was reasonable under the Fourth Amendment.

b. The Surveillance of El-Hage's Kenyan Telephone Lines Was Also Reasonable

El-Hage appears to challenge the reasonableness of the electronic surveillance of the Kenyan telephone lines on the grounds that (1) they were overbroad, encompassing calls made for commercial, family or social purposes and (2) the government failed to follow procedures to "minimize" surveillance. Indeed, pursuant to defense counsel's analysis, "as many as 25 percent of the calls were either made by, or to" a Nairobi businessman not alleged to have been associated with al Qaeda. El-Hage also criticizes the government for retaining transcripts of irrelevant calls — such as conversations between El-Hage and his wife about their children — despite the government's assurance to the District Court that the surveillance had been properly "minimized." *See United States v. Ruggiero,* 928 F.2d 1289, 1302 (2d Cir. 1991) ("[A]ny [electronic] interception 'shall be conducted in such a way as to minimize the interception of communications not otherwise subject to interception.'" (quoting 18 U.S.C. §2518(5))).

It cannot be denied that El-Hage suffered, while abroad, a significant invasion of privacy by virtue of the government's year-long surveillance of his telephonic communications. The Supreme Court has recognized that, like a physical search, electronic monitoring intrudes on "the innermost secrets of one's home or office" and that "[f]ew threats to liberty exist which are greater than that posed by the use of eavesdropping devices." *Berger v. New York*, 388 U.S. 41, 63 (1967); *cf. Katz v. United States*, 389 U.S. 347, 352-54 (1967). For its part, the government does not contradict El-Hage's claims that the surveillance was broad and loosely "minimized." Instead, the government sets forth a variety of reasons justifying the breadth of the surveillance. These justifications, regardless of their merit, do not lessen the intrusion El-Hage suffered while abroad, and we accord this intrusion substantial weight in our balancing analysis.

Turning to the government's interest, we encounter again the self-evident need to investigate threats to national security presented by foreign terrorist organizations. When U.S. intelligence learned that five telephone lines were being used by suspected al Qaeda operatives, the need to monitor communications traveling on those lines was paramount, and we are loath to discount — much less disparage — the government's decision to do so.

Our balancing of these compelling, and competing, interests turns on whether the scope of the intrusion here was justified by the government's surveillance needs. We conclude that it was, for at least the following four reasons.

First, complex, wide-ranging, and decentralized organizations, such as al Qaeda, warrant sustained and intense monitoring in order to understand their features and identify their members. *See In re Sealed Case No. 02-001*, 310 F.3d 717, 740-41 (Foreign Int. Surv. Ct. Rev. 2002) ("Less minimization in the acquisition stage may well be justified to the extent . . . 'the investigation is focusing on what is thought to be a widespread conspiracy[,] [where] more extensive surveillance may be justified in an attempt to determine the precise scope of the enterprise.'" (quoting *Scott v. United States*, 436 U.S. 128, 140 (1978) (alteration in original))).

Second, foreign intelligence gathering of the sort considered here must delve into the superficially mundane because it is not always readily apparent what information is relevant. *Cf. United States v. Rahman*, 861 F. Supp. 2d 247, 252-53 (S.D.N.Y. 1994) (recognizing the "argument that when the purpose of surveillance is to gather intelligence about international terrorism, greater flexibility in acquiring and storing information is necessary, because innocent-sounding conversations may later prove to be highly significant, and because individual items of information, not apparently significant when taken in isolation, may become highly significant when considered together over time").

Third, members of covert terrorist organizations, as with other sophisticated criminal enterprises, often communicate in code, or at least through ambiguous language. *See, e.g., United States v. Salameh*, 152 F.3d 88, 108 (2d Cir. 1998) ("Because Ajaj was in jail and his telephone calls were monitored, Ajaj and Yousef spoke in code when discussing the bomb plot."). Hence, more extensive and careful monitoring of these communications may be necessary.

Fourth, because the monitored conversations were conducted in foreign languages, the task of determining relevance and identifying coded language was further complicated.

Because the surveillance of suspected al Qaeda operatives must be sustained and thorough in order to be effective, we cannot conclude that the scope of the government's electronic surveillance was overbroad. While the intrusion on El-Hage's privacy was great, the need for the government to so intrude was even greater. Accordingly, the electronic surveillance, like the search of El-Hage's Nairobi residence, was reasonable under the Fourth Amendment.

In sum, because the searches at issue on this appeal were reasonable, they comport with the applicable requirement of the Fourth Amendment and, therefore, El-Hage's motion to suppress the evidence resulting from those searches was properly denied by the District Court.

III. CONCLUSION . . .

For these reasons, and for those set forth in [related appeals] *In re Terrorist Bombings of U.S. Embassies in East Africa,* [552 F.3d 177] (2d Cir. 2008), the judgment of conviction entered by the District Court against El-Hage is **AFFIRMED** in all respects except that the sentence is **VACATED**, and the case is **REMANDED** to the District Court for the sole purpose of resentencing El-Hage as directed in *In re Terrorist Bombings of U.S. Embassies in East Africa,* [552 F.3d 93] (2d Cir. 2008).

Notes and Questions

1. Foreign Intelligence Exception? The district court in El-Hage's case found a foreign intelligence exception to the Fourth Amendment's warrant requirement. Why did the Court of Appeals not base its decision on such an exception? Suppose several of El-Hage's at-large associates were secretly indicted with him, and surveillance of them continued until they were apprehended. Would the fruits of that surveillance fall within a foreign intelligence exception?

2. Warrants for Searches Abroad? The court in *In re Terrorist Bombings* recalled its own declaration in an earlier case that it was "well settled" that "the Bill of Rights has extraterritorial application to the conduct abroad of federal agents directed against United States citizens." *Toscanino, supra,* 500 F.2d at 280. Yet its application of the Fourth Amendment, omitting the warrant requirement, reflects Justice Harlan's pragmatism more than Justice Black's absolutism in *Reid v. Covert,* 354 U.S. 1 (1957), *supra* p. 180. What practical considerations prompted the court to suspend this requirement?

The USA Patriot Act, enacted shortly after the September 11 terrorist attacks, amends Rule 41 of the Federal Rules of Criminal Procedure to authorize a federal magistrate "in any district in which activities related to terrorism may have occurred" to issue a warrant for a search of property or a person "within or outside the district." Pub. L. No. 107-56, §219, 115 Stat. 272, 291 (2001). Should this provision be interpreted to require judicial authorization for searches abroad?

3. Reasonableness of Searches Abroad. The *In re Terrorist Bombings* court held that even though the warrant requirement is inapplicable, searches of U.S. citizens conducted abroad still must be reasonable. How does the court test for reasonableness? Was its test for the physical search of El-Hage's home different from that for the tap on his telephone? Can you derive a general test from its analysis?

In *United States v. Barona,* 56 F.3d 1087 (9th Cir. 1995), a divided court came up with different tests for reasonableness of warrantless surveillance of U.S. citizens abroad in a drug-smuggling investigation. The majority looked to good faith compliance with the law of the foreign country where the surveillance was conducted, absent conduct that shocks the conscience. *Id.* at 1092-1093. In fact, the United States has entered into a growing number of bilateral mutual legal assistance treaties (MLATs), which independently require U.S. officials operating abroad to comply with the law of the foreign state. *See, e.g.*, Treaty Between the United States and the Government of Mexico on Mutual Legal Assistance in Criminal Matters, Dec. 9, 1987, U.S.-Mex., art. 12, 1987 U.S.T. LEXIS 208 ("A request for search, seizure, and delivery of any object acquired thereby to the requesting State shall be executed if it includes the information justifying such action *under the laws of the requested Party*.") (emphasis added). Such treaties confer no private rights, but their very existence may support the *Barona* court's incorporation of a compliance-with-foreign-law requirement into the Fourth Amendment's reasonableness standard. (They also create formal methods for U.S. law enforcement authorities to obtain help with investigations abroad.)

Judge Reinhardt dissented vigorously. Under the majority's reasoning, he argued, Americans are not only relegated to the "vagaries of foreign law," they are given

> *even less* protection than foreign law since . . . the Constitution does not even require foreign officials to comply with their own law; all that is required is that American officials have a good faith belief that they did so. . . . [W]hen Americans enter Iraq, Iran, Singapore, Kuwait, China, or other similarly inclined foreign lands, they can be treated by the United States government exactly the way those foreign nations treat their own citizens — at least for Fourth Amendment purposes. [56 F.3d at 1101 (Reinhardt, J., dissenting).]

Instead, Judge Reinhardt argued, the government still should have probable cause for a foreign search, even if a warrant is impractical. *Id.* at 1102. On a motion to suppress, a court would make a post hoc determination of probable cause based on the government's explanation of why it initiated the search. *Id.* "Because judicial scrutiny of the search will always take place *after* it has been conducted, there is no conceivable way that imposing such a requirement would hinder law enforcement efforts abroad — except to the extent that those efforts violate our own Constitution." *Id.*

In determining the reasonableness of requiring a judicial warrant in domestic terrorism investigations, the Court in *Keith* expressed concern that "unreviewed executive discretion may yield too readily to pressures to obtain incriminating evidence and overlook potential invasions of privacy and protected speech." 407 U.S. at 317. How did the *In re Terrorist Bombings* court address this concern? The *Barona* court?

4. The Silver Platter Doctrine. Suppose the Kenyan police *alone* had conducted the warrantless surveillance of El-Hage without probable cause and in flagrant violation of their own laws. Should a U.S. court suppress the fruits of such a foreign police surveillance? With two exceptions noted below, the courts have uniformly held no. *See, e.g., United States v. Defreitas*, 701 F. Supp. 2d 297, 304-305 (E.D.N.Y. 2010). Because the Bill of Rights does not protect Americans from the acts of foreign sovereigns and because applying the exclusionary rule to such acts would not deter them, such evidence can be turned over to U.S. law enforcement officials on a "silver platter" and admitted in U.S. criminal prosecutions.

5. *The Joint Venture Exception.* Courts have recognized an exception to the silver platter doctrine for searches that are "joint ventures" between U.S. and foreign officials. Unfortunately, the courts have not reached a consensus on what constitutes a joint venture. Most agree that merely providing a tip to foreign police will not trigger the protections of the Fourth Amendment, and many hold that U.S. agents may request, be present during, or even participate in a search as long as they did not initiate and control it. The *Restatement* declares, unhelpfully, that the exclusionary rule applies only when "the participation of United States law enforcement officers in the investigation, arrest, search, or interrogation through which the evidence was obtained was so substantial as to render the action that of the United States." *Restatement (Third) of Foreign Relations Law of the United States* §433(3) (1987). The Second Circuit has cut its own path by asking whether foreign police are acting as agents of the United States or whether U.S. law enforcement agents are evading our law by using foreign police. *See United States v. Maturo,* 982 F.2d 57, 61 (2d Cir. 1992). Apparently, U.S. participation in the Kenyan search was so substantial that the government did not contest responsibility. In one significant post-9/11 terrorism case, a Fourth Circuit panel divided over whether the "joint venture" exception applied to a Saudi interrogation of a U.S. citizen observed (and which included questions suggested) by FBI agents. *See United States v. Abu Ali,* 528 F.3d 210, 228-230 & nn.5-6 (4th Cir. 2008).

6. *The Shocks-the-Conscience Exception.* A second exception to the silver platter doctrine exists for conduct that shocks the judicial conscience. It was articulated in *Toscanino,* 500 F.2d at 267, a forcible abduction case, and applied in *United States v. Fernandez-Caro,* 677 F. Supp. 893, 894 (S.D. Tex. 1987), in which Mexican authorities "threatened to kill [the defendant], beat him about the face and body, poured water through his nostrils while he was stripped, bound and gagged, and applied electrical shocks to his wet body, among other things." *Id.* at 894. Exclusion of a forced confession is "not based on our Fourth Amendment jurisprudence," said the majority in *Barona,* "but rather on the recognition that we may employ our supervisory powers when absolutely necessary to preserve the integrity of the criminal justice system." 56 F.3d at 1091. Such evidence may be excluded even when obtained by foreign officials not acting as agents of the United States. *Maturo,* 982 F.2d at 60-61.

The joint venture and shocks-the-conscience exceptions to the silver platter doctrine are explored further in Chapter 35, where we consider the U.S. practice of rendering terrorist suspects to a third country for interrogation (and likely harsh treatment) by that country's police or intelligence officials.

7. *Statutory Authorization of Collection Abroad.* Six years after *Verdugo-Urquidez* held that the Fourth Amendment does not apply to noncitizens lacking substantial, voluntary connections to the United States, Congress authorized elements of the intelligence community (excluding the military service branches) to collect information outside the United States against non-U.S. persons at the request of law enforcement agencies, "notwithstanding that the law enforcement agency intends to use the information collected for purposes of a law enforcement investigation or counterintelligence investigation." 50 U.S.C. §3039(a) (2018).

As noted in the introduction to *In re Directives,* the FISA Amendments Act of 2008, Pub. L. No. 110-261, 122 Stat. 2436 (codified as amended at 50 U.S.C. §§1881-1885c (2018)), authorizes the Attorney General and the Director of National Intelligence, acting jointly, to approve the programmatic targeting of "persons reasonably believed to be located outside the United States to acquire foreign intelligence information." 50 U.S.C. §1881a. The measure responds to a dramatic increase in communications using the Internet and fiber-optic cable and to greater concern about the threat of international terrorism after 9/11. Once the Foreign Intelligence Surveillance Court (FISC) approves a program for collection, based on assurances that a "significant purpose" of any acquisition is to obtain foreign intelligence information and that the usual FISA minimization procedures will be followed, intelligence agencies like the NSA may monitor and collect electronic data — e-mail and telephone calls, for example — on a wholesale basis, without an individualized judicial order normally required for the targeting of any particular person. The collected data are then mined, using keyword and pattern-recognition algorithms, for whatever information might be of interest.

The FISA Amendments Act also for the first time authorized collections inside the United States of electronic data about U.S. persons located abroad, 50 U.S.C. §1881b, and collections abroad against U.S. persons. *Id.* §1881c. In these latter two instances, the FISC must approve the collection on an individualized basis, applying generally the same standards that it does for domestic targets. The 2008 legislation is analyzed in greater detail in Chapter 22.

Applying the lessons learned in this chapter, do you think these two measures satisfy the requirements of the Fourth Amendment? Specifically, will information collected following the statutory procedures described here be admissible as evidence in a criminal trial? Will a targeted individual be successful in a *Bivens* claim asserting that the collection violated her privacy rights?

THE FOURTH AMENDMENT AND NATIONAL SECURITY: SUMMARY OF BASIC PRINCIPLES

- The government conducts a search subject to the Fourth Amendment if it physically intrudes on private property for the purpose of collecting information or if its collection invades a person's reasonable expectation of privacy.

- The Fourth Amendment prohibits "unreasonable" searches and seizures. A search pursuant to a search warrant issued by a neutral magistrate based on probable cause to believe that evidence of a crime will be collected is presumptively reasonable. A warrantless search is *per se* unreasonable, unless it fits an exception to the Warrant Clause.

- The Supreme Court has recognized exceptions to the Warrant Clause for searches incident to arrest or in "hot pursuit," searches at the border, and searches to meet special needs such as the protection of public health or safety, rather than solely or primarily to collect evidence of criminal activity, among others.

- There is no exception to the Warrant Clause for searches to protect domestic security that do not involve foreign powers. But "different policy and practical considerations" between surveillance of "ordinary crime" and domestic security surveillance may justify different (more lenient) statutory standards for the latter than for the former.

- The Supreme Court has not yet decided whether there is a *foreign intelligence* exception to the Warrant Clause, although some lower federal courts have found one. Lower courts have disagreed, however, on whether such an exception applies only when the collection of foreign intelligence surveillance is the "primary" purpose of the search, or whether foreign intelligence need only be a "significant" purpose. The USA Patriot Act now requires the government only to certify that a "significant purpose" (rather than "primary purpose") of requested surveillance is the collection of foreign intelligence.
- The application of the Warrant Clause to new technology is being decided case by case, occasionally based on the physical trespass test, but more commonly based on shifting and hard-to-predict applications of the expectation-of-privacy test.
- Even when the Warrant Clause does not apply to a government search, the search must still be reasonable, balancing the degree of intrusion against the government's purposes.
- The Fourth Amendment's application to searches abroad depends on the target and possibly the object of the search. It does not apply to searches abroad of aliens who lack a substantial connection to the United States. The Warrant Clause may not apply to searches abroad even of U.S. persons if the purpose is to collect foreign intelligence or if pragmatic reasons make a warrant impractical, but such searches must still be reasonable.

Congressional Authority for Foreign Intelligence Surveillance

Communications and surveillance technologies have undergone explosive growth since the digital and dot-com revolutions of the 1980s and 1990s. Both ordinary and Internet communications can be intercepted, and cell phone calls can be traced to the phone's location. Hidden recorders may preserve conversations, while parabolic microphones capture voices at long distances. Video surveillance cameras permit government officials to monitor public areas by closed-circuit television. Global positioning system (GPS) devices and electronic toll systems permit remote, 24/7 tracing of an individual's movements. Computer-driven scanners can search through millions of e-mail messages in a heartbeat. Emerging nanotechnology and bioengineering will expand further the horizons of the government's capabilities for surveillance.

By providing the means to watch and listen to people and to trace their movements, electronic surveillance can help to detect and prevent terrorism and other security threats. It also may help to find those responsible for security-related crimes after the fact.

Yet unlike physical searches for particular information or things, electronic surveillance records everything a target says or does. Especially when undertaken over a long period on a continual basis, electronic surveillance casts a wide and open-ended net, capturing data that may be at best irrelevant and at worst deeply personal.

The Constitution contains two provisions that can guard against government abuses of such advanced technology. The Fourth Amendment was included in the Bill of Rights to counter any tendency toward the kind of intimidation practiced by the English Crown against its citizens. The First Amendment was added as a bulwark against government intrusions that could dampen political expression. While these are the constitutional backstops for protecting our privacy and expression, however, Congress by statute supplies both the first lines of defense and the authorizations for national security-based intrusions.

This chapter turns from the evolution of Fourth Amendment and national security surveillance law in the courts, discussed in the preceding chapter, to statutory authorization for foreign intelligence surveillance in the Foreign Intelligence Surveillance Act (FISA), 50 U.S.C. §§1801-1885c (2018). We begin by introducing the core FISA requirements and procedures for electronic surveillance and physical searches. We then consider the tension — and, for a time, the "wall" — between surveillance to collect evidence for criminal law enforcement and surveillance to collect foreign intelligence. Then, looking ahead, we briefly assess trends in FISA electronic and physical surveillance.

A. THE FOREIGN INTELLIGENCE SURVEILLANCE ACT: CORE REQUIREMENTS AND PROCEDURES

Two events prompted congressional enactment of FISA in 1978. First, the Supreme Court decision in *Keith* ended by asserting that "Congress may wish to consider protective standards for [domestic security surveillance] . . . which differ from those already prescribed for specified crimes in Title III." *United States v. U.S. Dist. Ct.* (*Keith*), 407 U.S. 297, 322 (1972). Second, in addition to the Watergate scandal, the early 1970s saw startling revelations of illegal spying and other activities by U.S. intelligence agencies, including the FBI and CIA, and by the IRS and the military. These agencies sought to target and disrupt politically active domestic groups (principally civil rights and antiwar organizations), and they engaged in widespread warrantless surveillance. The Senate Select Committee to Study Government Operations with Respect to Intelligence Activities (known as the Church Committee, after its chairman Senator Frank Church) summarized the effects of these domestic intelligence abuses in a 1976 report:

> . . . FBI headquarters alone has developed over 500,000 domestic intelligence files, and these have been augmented by additional files at FBI Field Offices. The FBI opened 65,000 of these domestic intelligence files in 1972 alone. In fact, substantially more individuals and groups are subject to intelligence scrutiny than the number of files would appear to indicate, since typically, each domestic intelligence file contains information on more than one individual or group, and this information is readily retrievable through the FBI General Name Index.
>
> The number of Americans and domestic groups caught in the domestic intelligence net is further illustrated by the following statistics:
>
> - Nearly a quarter of a million first class letters were opened and photographed in the United States by the CIA between 1953-1973, producing a CIA computerized index of nearly one and one-half million names.
> - At least 130,000 first class letters were opened and photographed by the FBI between 1940-1966 in eight U.S. cities.
> - Some 300,000 individuals were indexed in a CIA computer system and separate files were created on approximately 7,200 Americans and over 100 domestic groups during the course of CIA's Operation CHAOS (1967-1973).
> - Millions of private telegrams sent from, to, or through the United States were obtained by the National Security Agency from 1947 to 1975 under a secret arrangement with three United States telegraph companies.
> - An estimated 100,000 Americans were the subjects of United States Army intelligence files created between the mid-1960's and 1971.
> - Intelligence files on more than 11,000 individuals and groups were created by the Internal Revenue Service between 1969 and 1973 and tax investigations were started on the basis of political rather than tax criteria.

- At least 26,000 individuals were at one point catalogued on an FBI list of persons to be rounded up in the event of a "national emergency."

[S. Select Comm. to Study Government Operations with Respect to Intelligence Activities (Church Committee), *Intelligence Activities and the Rights of Americans,* S. Rep. No. 94-755, bk. II, at 6-7 (1976).]

Most of these surveillance and collection abuses were rationalized as foreign intelligence gathering. When Congress responded to the Supreme Court's invitation in *Keith,* therefore, it enacted standards for *foreign intelligence* surveillance inside the United States, not *domestic security* surveillance. In *United States v. Duggan,* 743 F.2d 59 (2d Cir. 1984), the court opined that

> Congress passed FISA to settle what it believed to be the unresolved question of the applicability of the Fourth Amendment warrant requirement to electronic surveillance for foreign intelligence purposes, and to "remove any doubt as to the lawfulness of such surveillance." H.R. Rep. 1283, pt. I, 95th Cong., 2d Sess. 25 (1978). FISA reflects both Congress's "legislative judgment" that the court orders and other procedural safeguards laid out in the Act "are necessary to insure that electronic surveillance by the U.S. Government within this country conforms to the fundamental principles of the fourth amendment," S. Rep. No. 701, 95th Cong., 2d Sess. 13, *reprinted in* 1978 U.S. Code Cong. & Ad. News 3973, 3982, and its attempt to fashion a "secure framework by which the Executive Branch may conduct legitimate electronic surveillance for foreign intelligence purposes within the context of this Nation's commitment to privacy and individual rights." S. Rep. No. 604, 95th Cong., 1st Sess. 15, *reprinted in* 1978 U.S. Code Cong. & Ad. News 3904, 3916. [743 F.2d at 73.]

Domestic security surveillance, on the other hand, was by default left subject to the existing Title III criminal law enforcement framework.

Consider how FISA applied to the defendants in the following case.

Reading *United States v. Rosen*

The following case provides an overview of the FISA process and terminology. Rosen, Weissman, and co-conspirator Lawrence Franklin were charged with violating the Espionage Act, *infra* p. 1235, by communicating or conspiring to communicate national defense information to persons not entitled to receive it. The government alleged that DOD employee Franklin delivered classified information to Rosen and Weissman, then lobbyists for AIPAC, who in turn gave it to the media, foreign policy analysts, and foreign officials. The government utilized FISA procedures to engage in electronic surveillance and physical searches of the defendants. Consider these questions as you read the decision:

- What is "foreign intelligence"? How, if at all, is it different from criminal evidence?
- What must an application for a FISA order contain?
- What must the Foreign Intelligence Surveillance Court (FISC) find to approve an application? The court refers to "probable cause." Probable cause to believe what? How is FISA probable cause different from ordinary probable cause?

- Who is an "agent of a foreign power"?
- Why did collection pursuant to a FISA order not violate the defendants' First Amendment rights?
- What is "minimization," and what is its purpose?
- How did the defendants learn that they had been subjected to FISA surveillance and searches? If there had been no criminal prosecution, how would they have learned about the government's use of FISA procedures?

United States v. Rosen

United States District Court, Eastern District of Virginia, 2006
447 F. Supp. 2d 538

ELLIS, District Judge. Defendants, Steven J. Rosen and Keith Weissman, are charged . . . with one count of conspiring to communicate national defense information to persons not entitled to receive it, in violation of 18 U.S.C. §793(d), (e) and (g). More specifically, Count One . . . alleges that between April 1999 and continuing until August 2004, Rosen and Weissman along with alleged co-conspirator Lawrence Franklin, then an employee of the Department of Defense ("DOD"), were engaged in a conspiracy to communicate information relating to the national defense to those not entitled to receive it. According to the superseding indictment, Franklin and certain other unnamed government officials with authorized possession of classified national defense information communicated that information to Rosen and Weissman, who were employed at the time as lobbyists for the American-Israel Public Affairs Committee (AIPAC). It is further alleged that Rosen and Weissman then communicated the information received from their government sources to members of the media, other foreign policy analysts, and certain foreign officials, none of whom were authorized to receive this information. . . .

In the course of its investigation of the alleged conspiracy, the government sought and obtained orders issued by the Foreign Intelligence Surveillance Court ("FISC") pursuant to the Foreign Intelligence Surveillance Act ("FISA"), 50 U.S.C. §1801 *et seq.*, authorizing certain physical searches and electronic surveillance. As the investigation pertained to national security, these applications and orders were classified. Because the government intends to offer evidence obtained or derived from physical searches and electronic surveillance authorized by these orders, defendants seek by motion (1) to obtain disclosure of the classified applications submitted to the FISC, the FISC's orders, and related materials, and/or (2) to suppress the evidence obtained or derived from any searches or surveillance conducted pursuant to the issued FISA orders. . . .

I.

FISA, enacted in 1978, was Congress's response to three related concerns: (1) the judicial confusion over the existence, nature and scope of a foreign intelligence exception to the Fourth Amendment's warrant requirement that arose in the wake of the Supreme Court's 1972 decision in *United States v. United States District*

Court, 407 U.S. 297 (1972); (2) the Congressional concern over perceived Executive Branch abuses of such an exception;[1] and (3) the felt need to provide the Executive Branch with an appropriate means to investigate and counter foreign intelligence threats.[2] FISA accommodates these concerns by establishing a detailed process the Executive Branch must follow to obtain orders allowing it to collect foreign intelligence information "without violating the rights of citizens of the United States." *United States v. Hammoud,* 381 F.3d 316, 332 (4th Cir. 2004) (en banc), *vacated on other grounds,* 543 U.S. 1097 (2005), *reinstated in pertinent part,* 405 F.3d 1034 (2005). Although originally limited to electronic surveillance, FISA's coverage has now been expanded to include physical searches, as well. . . .

FISA's detailed procedure for obtaining orders authorizing electronic surveillance or physical searches of a foreign power or an agent of a foreign power begins with the government's filing of an *ex parte,* under seal application with the FISC.[4] Such an application must be approved by the Attorney General and must include certain specified information. *See* 50 U.S.C. §§1804(a) and 1823(a). A FISC judge considering the application may also require the submission of additional information necessary to make the requisite findings under §§1805(a) and 1824(a).

After review of the application, a single judge of the FISC must enter an *ex parte* Order granting the government's application for electronic surveillance or a physical search of a foreign power or an agent of a foreign power provided the judge makes certain specific findings, including most importantly, that on the basis of the facts submitted by the applicant there is probable cause to believe that—

> (1) the target of the electronic surveillance or physical search is a foreign power or an agent of a foreign power, except that no United States person may be considered a foreign power or an agent of a foreign power solely upon the basis of activities protected by the First Amendment to the Constitution of the United States; and
>
> (2) for electronic surveillance, each of the facilities or places at which the electronic surveillance is directed is being used, or is about to be used, by a foreign power or an agent of a foreign power; or
>
> (3) for physical searches, the premises or property to be searched is owned, used, possessed by, or is in transit to or from an agent of a foreign power or a foreign power.

See 50 U.S.C. §§1805(a) and 1823(a).[5] If the FISC judge's findings reflect that the government has satisfied the statute's requirements, the judge must issue an order

---

1. *See* S. Rep. No. 95-604(I), at 7, 1978 U.S.C.C.A.N. 3904, 3908 [hereinafter S. Judiciary Comm. Rep.] ("This legislation is in large measure a response to the revelations that warrantless electronic surveillance in the name of national security has been seriously abused.").

2. *See generally* William C. Banks and M.E. Bowman, *Executive Authority for National Security Surveillance,* 50 Am. U. L. Rev. 1, 75-76 (2000) (describing the impetus for FISA).

4. The FISC consists of eleven district court judges selected by the Chief Justice from at least seven judicial circuits and serving staggered seven year terms. *See* 50 U.S.C. §1803(a). At least three of the FISC's judges must reside within twenty miles of Washington, D.C. *Id.* In the unlikely event that a FISA application is denied by a judge of the FISC, the government may seek review of such denial in the Foreign Intelligence Surveillance Court of Review (FISCR), and if necessary, in the Supreme Court of the United States. *See* 50 U.S.C. §1803(b).

5. In addition to these probable cause findings, the FISC judge must also find that: (1) the President has authorized the Attorney General to approve applications for electronic surveillance or physical searches for foreign intelligence information; (2) that the application has been made by a Federal officer and approved by the Attorney General; (3) that the proposed minimization procedures meet the

approving the surveillance or search. Such an order must describe the target, the information sought, and the means of acquiring such information. *See* 50 U.S.C. §§1805(c)(1) and 1824(c)(1). The order must also set forth the period of time during which the electronic surveillance or physical searches are approved, which is generally ninety days or until the objective of the electronic surveillance or physical search has been achieved. *See* 50 U.S.C. §§1805(e)(1) and 1824(d)(1). Applications for a renewal of the order must generally be made upon the same basis as the original application and require the same findings by the FISC. *See* 50 U.S.C. §§1805(e)(2) and 1824(d)(2).

Although FISA is chiefly directed to obtaining "foreign intelligence information,"[6] the Act specifically contemplates cooperation between federal authorities conducting electronic surveillance and physical searches pursuant to FISA and federal law enforcement officers investigating clandestine intelligence activities. In this respect, FISA explicitly allows the use of evidence derived from FISA surveillance and searches in criminal prosecutions. *See* 50 U.S.C. §§1806(k) and 1825(k).

If the Attorney General approves the use of evidence collected pursuant to FISA in a criminal prosecution, and the government intends to use or disclose FISA evidence at the trial of an "aggrieved person,"[7] the government must first notify the aggrieved person and the district court that the government intends to disclose or use the FISA evidence. *See* 50 U.S.C. §§1806(c) and 1825(d). On receiving such notification, an aggrieved person may seek to suppress any evidence derived from FISA surveillance or searches on the grounds that: (1) the evidence was unlawfully acquired; or (2) the electronic surveillance or physical search was not conducted in conformity with the Order of authorization or approval. *See* 50 U.S.C. §§1806(e) and 1825(f). And, if an aggrieved person moves to suppress FISA evidence or to

---

respective definitions of minimization procedures for electronic surveillance and physical searches; and (4) that the application contains all statements and certifications required by 50 U.S.C. §1804 for electronic surveillance and 50 U.S.C. §1823 for physical searches and, if the target is a United States person, the certification or certifications are not clearly erroneous on the basis of the statement made under sections 1804(a)(7)(E) and 1823(a)(7)(E) of title 18 and any other information furnished under sections 1804(d) and 1823(c) of this title. *See* 50 U.S.C. §§1805(a) and 1823(a).

6. FISA defines "foreign intelligence information" as—

> (1) information that relates to, and if concerning a United States person is necessary to, the ability of the United States to protect against—
>
> > (A) actual or potential attack or other grave hostile acts of a foreign power or an agent of a foreign power;
> >
> > (B) sabotage or international terrorism by a foreign power or an agent of a foreign power; or
> >
> > (C) clandestine intelligence activities by an intelligence service or network of a foreign power or by an agent of a foreign power; or
>
> (2) information with respect to a foreign power or foreign territory that relates to, and if concerning a United States person is necessary to—
>
> > (A) the national defense or the security of the United States; or
> >
> > (B) the conduct of the foreign affairs of the United States.

50 U.S.C. §1801(e).

7. FISA defines an "aggrieved person" with respect to electronic surveillance as "a person who is the target of an electronic surveillance or any other person whose communications or activities were subject to electronic surveillance." 50 U.S.C. §1801(k). With respect to physical searches, FISA similarly defines an "aggrieved person" as a "person whose premises, property, information, or material is the target of physical search or any other person whose premises, property, information, or material was subject to physical search." 50 U.S.C. §1821(2).

obtain FISA material, then upon the filing of an affidavit by the Attorney General stating under oath that disclosure of such material would harm national security, the district court must review the FISA warrant applications and related materials *in camera* and *ex parte* to determine whether the surveillance or search "of the aggrieved person was lawfully authorized and conducted." 50 U.S.C. §§1806(f) and 1825(g).

This review is properly *de novo,* especially given that the review is *ex parte* and thus unaided by the adversarial process. Thus, the government's contention here that a reviewing district court must accord the FISC's probable cause determination "substantial deference" cannot be sustained in light of the Fourth Circuit's clear contrary statement on the issue. But the government is correct that the certifications contained in the applications should be "presumed valid." *See* 50 U.S.C. §1805(a)(5) (applying "clearly erroneous" standard to factual averments contained in certification when the target is a United States person)....

II.

At the threshold, defendants seek disclosure of the FISA applications, orders, and related materials at issue in this case so they may effectively participate in the review process. On this point FISA is clear: It allows a reviewing court to disclose such materials "only where such disclosure is necessary to make an accurate determination of the legality of the surveillance." 50 U.S.C. §1806(f). Defendants claim this condition is met, by arguing (1) that the FISC's determination that they were agents of a foreign power was surely wrong; and (2) that evidence of the government's evident failure to comply with FISA's minimization procedures requires disclosure. Neither argument is persuasive....

Review of the FISA applications, orders and other materials in this case presented none of the concerns that might warrant disclosure to defendants. The FISA dockets contained no facial inconsistencies, nor did they disclose any reason to doubt any of the representations made by the government in its applications. Likewise, the targets of the surveillance are precisely defined. Finally, although defendants claim that the discovery obtained from the government contains a significant amount of non-foreign intelligence information, this contention relies upon an inordinately narrow view of what constitutes foreign intelligence information, and therefore is unavailing. For these reasons, and given the government's legitimate national security interest in maintaining the secrecy of the information contained in the FISA applications, disclosure of the FISA materials to defendants is not warranted in this case.

III.

Defendants' attack on the lawfulness of the FISA surveillance in this case focuses chiefly on two issues: (1) whether the FISC had probable cause to believe that the targets of the sanctioned surveillance were "agents of a foreign power," as required by FISA, and (2) whether there was proper compliance with the minimization procedures subsequent to the surveillance. Review of the FISA material confirms that both of these issues must be resolved in favor of the lawfulness of the surveillance.

Defendants' necessarily speculative contention that the FISC must have erred when it found probable cause to believe that the targets are agents of a foreign power is without merit. An agent of a foreign power is defined by the statute, in pertinent part, as any person who—

> (A) knowingly engages in clandestine intelligence gathering activities for or on behalf of a foreign power, which activities involve or may involve a violation of the criminal statutes of the United States;
>
> (B) pursuant to the direction of an intelligence service or network of a foreign power, knowingly engages in any other clandestine intelligence activities for or on behalf of such power, which activities involve or are about to involve a violation of the criminal statutes of the United States; . . . or
>
> (E) knowingly aids or abets any person in the conduct of activities described in [the subparagraphs above] or knowingly conspires with any person to engage in activities described in [the subparagraphs above].

50 U.S.C. §1801(b)(2). Although the phrase "clandestine intelligence gathering activities" is not defined in FISA, the legislative history demonstrates that the drafters viewed these "activities" in light of the criminal espionage laws, including 18 U.S.C. §§793 and 794, and considered that such "activities" would include, for example, "collection or transmission of information or material that is not generally available to the public." *See* S. Rep. No. 95-701, at 21-22 (1978), 1978 U.S.C.C.A.N. 3973, 3990-91 [hereinafter S. Intelligence Rep.]. . . .

Importantly, FISA is clear that in determining whether there is probable cause to believe that a potential target of FISA surveillance or a FISA search is an agent of a foreign power, the FISC judge may not consider a United States person an agent of a foreign power "*solely* upon the basis of activities protected by the First Amendment." 50 U.S.C. §1805(a) (emphasis added). From this plain language, it follows that the probable cause determination may rely in part on activities protected by the First Amendment, provided the determination also relies on activities not protected by the First Amendment. This issue received extensive treatment in the legislative history, which, consistent with the statute's plain language, makes clear that First Amendment activities cannot form the *sole* basis for concluding a U.S. person is an agent of a foreign power. The following excerpt from the legislative history illustrates this point:

> The Bill is not intended to authorize electronic surveillance when a United States person's activities, even though secret and conducted for a foreign power, consist entirely of lawful acts such as lobbying or the use of confidential contacts to influence public officials, directly or indirectly, through the dissemination of information. Individuals exercising their right to lobby public officials or to engage in political dissent from official policy may well be in contact with representatives of foreign governments and groups when the issues concern foreign affairs or international economic matters.
>
> They must continue to be free to communicate about such issues and to obtain information or exchange views with representatives of foreign governments or with foreign groups, free from any fear that such contact might be the basis for probable cause to believe they are acting at the direction of a foreign power thus triggering the government's power to conduct electronic surveillance.

See S. Intelligence Rep. at 29.

The legislative history makes equally clear, however, that this protection extends only to the "*lawful* exercise of First Amendment rights of speech, petition, assembly and association." *Id.* (emphasis added). Similarly, the House Report (Intelligence

Committee) emphasized that FISA "would not authorize surveillance of ethnic Americans who *lawfully* gather political information and perhaps even *lawfully* share it with the foreign government of their national origin." *See In re Sealed Case,* 310 F.3d 717, 739 (FISCR 2002) (emphasis added) (quoting H. Rep. No. 95-1283, at 40). For example, electronic surveillance might be appropriate if there is probable cause to believe that—

> foreign intelligence services [are] hid[ing] behind the cover of some person or organization in order to influence American political events and deceive Americans into believing that the opinions or influence are of domestic origin and initiative and such deception is willfully maintained in violation of the Foreign Agents Registration Act.

S. Intelligence Rep. at 29. Thus, if the FISC judge has probable cause to believe that the potential target is engaged in *unlawful* activities in addition to those protected by the First Amendment, the FISC may authorize surveillance of a U.S. person.

In this respect, it is important to emphasize the significant difference between FISA's probable cause requirement and the government's ultimate burden to prove the existence of criminal activity beyond a reasonable doubt. Indeed, the Fourth Circuit has described probable cause in this context as "a fluid concept—turning on the assessment of probabilities in particular factual contexts—not readily, or even usefully, reduced to a neat set of rules." *United States v. Hammoud,* 381 F.3d [316 (4th Cir. 2004),] at 332 (upholding probable cause finding that Hammoud was an agent of Hizballah). Furthermore, "[i]n evaluating whether probable cause exists, it is the task of the issuing judge 'to make a practical, common-sense decision, whether, given all the circumstances set forth in the affidavit, there is a fair probability' that the search will be fruitful." *Id.* (quoting *Illinois v. Gates,* 462 U.S. 213, 238 (1983)); *see also Mason v. Godinez,* 47 F.3d 852, 855 (7th Cir. 1995) ("Probable cause means more than bare suspicion but less than absolute certainty that a search will be fruitful."). And, in making the probable cause determination, FISA permits a judge to "consider past activities of the target, as well as facts and circumstances relating to current or future activities of the target." 50 U.S.C. §1805(b). Furthermore, with respect to those U.S. persons suspected of involvement in clandestine intelligence activities, the probable cause determination "does not necessarily require a showing of an imminent violation of criminal law" because "Congress clearly intended a lesser showing of probable cause for these activities than that applicable to ordinary cases." *In re Sealed Case,* 310 F.3d at 738. Illustrative of this intent is FISA's description of clandestine intelligence activities as those that "involve or *may* involve a violation of the criminal statutes of the United States." 50 U.S.C. §1801(b)(2)(A); *see In re Sealed Case,* 310 F.3d at 738. As FISA's drafters made clear: "The term 'may involve' not only requires less information regarding the crime involved, but also permits electronic surveillance at some point prior to the time when a crime sought to be prevented, as for example, the transfer of classified documents, actually occurs." *In re Sealed Case,* 310 F.3d at 738 (quoting H. Rep. No. 95-1283, at 40). Thus, while the statute is intended to avoid permitting electronic surveillance solely on the basis of First Amendment activities, it plainly allows a FISC judge to issue an order allowing the surveillance or physical search if there is probable cause to believe that the target, even if engaged in First Amendment activities, may also be involved in unlawful clandestine intelligence activities, or in knowingly aiding and abetting such activities. In these circumstances, the fact that a target is also involved in protected First Amendment activities is no bar to electronic surveillance pursuant to FISA.

A thorough review of the FISA dockets in issue confirms that the FISC had ample probable cause to believe that the targets were agents of a foreign power quite apart from their First Amendment lobbying activities. While the defendants' lobbying activities are generally protected by the First Amendment, willful violations of §793 are not, and as is demonstrated by the allegations contained in the superseding indictment, the FISC had probable cause to believe that such violations had occurred in this case.

Defendants' second argument in support of their motion is that the government failed to follow the applicable minimization procedures. In this regard, it is true that once the electronic surveillance or the physical search has been approved, the government must apply the specific minimization procedures contained in the application to the FISC. These minimization procedures are "designed to protect, as far as reasonable, against the acquisition, retention, and dissemination of nonpublic information which is not foreign intelligence information." *In re Sealed Case,* 310 F.3d 717, 731 (FISCR 2002). While the specific minimization procedures for each application are classified, they must meet the definition of minimization procedures under §1801(h) for electronic surveillance and §1821(4) for physical searches. FISA minimization procedures include, in pertinent part—

> (1) specific procedures adopted by the Attorney General that are reasonably designed in light of the purpose and technique of the particular surveillance or search, to minimize the acquisition and retention, and prohibit the dissemination, of nonpublicly available information concerning unconsenting United States persons consistent with the need of the United States to obtain, produce, and disseminate foreign intelligence information;
>
> (2) procedures that require that nonpublicly available information, which is not foreign intelligence information, shall not be disseminated in a manner that identifies any United States person, without such person's consent, unless such person's identity is necessary to understand foreign intelligence information or assess its importance;
>
> (3) notwithstanding paragraphs (1) and (2), procedures that allow for the retention and dissemination of information that is evidence of a crime which has been, is being, or is about to be committed and that is to be retained or disseminated for law enforcement purposes.

See 50 U.S.C. §§1801(h) and 1821(4). Congress intended these minimization procedures to act as a safeguard for U.S. persons at the acquisition, retention and dissemination phases of electronic surveillance and searches. *See* S. Intelligence Rep. at 39. Thus, for example, minimization at the acquisition stage is designed to insure that the communications of non-target U.S. persons who happen to be using a FISA target's telephone, or who happen to converse with the target about non-foreign intelligence information, are not improperly disseminated. *See id.* Similarly, minimization at the retention stage is intended to ensure that "information acquired, which is not necessary for obtaining, producing, or disseminating foreign intelligence information, be destroyed where feasible." *See In re Sealed Case,* 310 F.3d at 731 (quoting H. Rep. No. 95-1283, at 56). Finally, the dissemination of foreign intelligence information "needed for an approved purpose . . . should be restricted to those officials with a need for such information." *Id.* As the Foreign Intelligence Surveillance Court of Review has recently made clear, these procedures do not prohibit the sharing of foreign intelligence information between FBI intelligence officials and criminal prosecutors when there is evidence of a crime. *Id.* . . .

. . . As the Fourth Circuit pointed out, "[i]t is not always immediately clear" whether a particular conversation must be minimized because "[a] conversation that seems innocuous on one day may later turn out to be of great significance, particularly if the individuals involved are talking in code." *Hammoud,* 381 F.3d at 334. For this reason, "when the government eavesdrops on clandestine groups . . . investigators often find it necessary to intercept all calls in order to record possible code language or oblique references to the illegal scheme." *United States v. Truong,* 629 F.2d 908, 917 (4th Cir. 1980). This latitude was intended by FISA's drafters who understood that it may be necessary to "acquire, retain and disseminate information concerning . . . the known contacts" of a U.S. person engaged in clandestine intelligence activities even though some of those contacts will invariably be innocent of any wrong-doing. H. Rep. No. 95-1283, at 58.

Given the breadth of the term "foreign intelligence information" in the context of investigating clandestine intelligence activities and the rule of reason that applies to the government's obligation to minimize non-pertinent information, defendants' motion to suppress for failure to properly minimize must be denied. The *ex parte, in camera* review of the FISA dockets discloses that any failures to minimize properly the electronic surveillance of the defendants were (i) inadvertent, (ii) disclosed to the FISC on discovery, and (iii) promptly rectified. . . .

Notes and Questions

a. Title III Warrants for Ordinary Criminal Investigations

The general standard for searches in criminal investigations is set out in Federal Rule of Criminal Procedure 41. Among other things, Rule 41 permits warrants for a search and seizure of property that constitutes evidence of or is related to the commission of a crime. For physical searches (but not electronic surveillance), Rule 41 also requires that the target receive a copy of the warrant and an inventory of seized property, and that the investigator show "reasonable cause" for serving the warrant at night rather than in daylight.

As you read the following Notes and Questions, consider how FISA orders for electronic surveillance or physical searches are different, and why. After reading *Rosen,* would you say that FISA supplies a constitutionally adequate substitute for the traditional law enforcement warrant? If FISA had not been enacted, how and pursuant to what authority would investigators have learned about the alleged criminal activities of the co-conspirators charged in *Rosen?* To what extent does the legality of FISA surveillance turn on whether the objective of the investigation is a criminal prosecution?

b. The Scope of FISA Electronic Surveillance and Physical Searches

1. Foreign Intelligence Information. Review the definition of "foreign intelligence information" quoted in *Rosen, supra* p. 616, n.6. "International terrorism," which forms part of that definition, is itself defined in FISA to include activities that—

> (1) involve violent acts or acts dangerous to human life that . . . would be a criminal violation if committed within the jurisdiction of the United States or any State;
>
> (2) appear to be intended

> (A) to intimidate or coerce a civilian population;
> (B) to influence the policy of a government by intimidation or coercion; or
> (C) to affect the conduct of a government by assassination or kidnapping;
>
> and
>
> (3) occur totally outside the United States, or transcend national boundaries in terms of the means by which they are accomplished, the persons they appear intended to coerce or intimidate, or the locale in which their perpetrators operate or seek asylum. [50 U.S.C. §1801(c).]

Can you think of some kinds of information that investigators of possible terrorism would be interested in having that could not be collected pursuant to FISA?

2. Electronic Surveillance. The form of the electronic surveillance used in *Rosen* was not specified. However, FISA defines four categories of electronic surveillance, some of which go beyond conventional telephone wiretaps and hidden microphones:

> (f) "Electronic surveillance" means—
>
> (1) the acquisition by an electronic, mechanical, or other surveillance device of the contents of any wire or radio communication sent by or intended to be received by a particular, known United States person who is in the United States, if the contents are acquired by intentionally targeting that United States person, under circumstances in which a person has a reasonable expectation of privacy and a warrant would be required for law enforcement purposes;
>
> (2) the acquisition by an electronic, mechanical, or other surveillance device of the contents of any wire communication to or from a person in the United States, without the consent of any party thereto, if such acquisition occurs in the United States . . . ;
>
> (3) the intentional acquisition by an electronic, mechanical, or other surveillance device of the contents of any radio communication, under circumstances in which a person has a reasonable expectation of privacy and a warrant would be required for law enforcement purposes, and if both the sender and all intended recipients are located within the United States; or
>
> (4) the installation or use of an electronic, mechanical, or other surveillance device in the United States for monitoring to acquire information, other than from a wire or radio communication, under circumstances in which a person has a reasonable expectation of privacy and a warrant would be required for law enforcement purposes. [50 U.S.C. §1801(f)(1)-(4).]

Does this definition cover surveillance by hidden microphones installed in a person's home or office? What about a listening device in a person's car? Is video surveillance covered? *See United States v. Koyomejian*, 946 F.2d 1450, 1451 (9th Cir. 1991) (video surveillance is covered), *aff'd in part, rev'd in part*, 970 F.2d 536 (9th Cir. 1992) (en banc).

3. The Geographical Scope of FISA Electronic Surveillance and Executive Order No. 12,333. Does FISA cover the surveillance of communications from Afghanistan to the United States? From the United States to Afghanistan? From one city to another within Afghanistan? If not the last, why do you think Congress did not require FISA authorization for such communications? Upon what authority would such surveillance be conducted?

In general, Executive Order No. 12,333 limits the collection, retention, and dissemination of U.S. person information where FISA does not apply. Review in particular §§2.3 and 2.5, *supra* pp. 526, 528. What limits apply to electronic surveillance that is not governed by FISA or traditional law enforcement procedures?

4. Physical Searches. A "physical search" under FISA involves a "physical intrusion within the United States into premises or property . . . under circumstances in which a person has a reasonable expectation of privacy and a warrant would be required for law enforcement purposes." 50 U.S.C. §1821(5). The substantive provisions for physical searches track those for electronic surveillance. The procedures are somewhat different. A physical search may be approved "for the period necessary to achieve its purpose, or for ninety days, whichever is less." *Id.* §1824(d)(1). But a search may continue for up to one year if it is directed against a "foreign power," or up to 120 days if the target is an agent of a foreign power. *Id.* §1824(d)(1)(A) and (B). Unlike the usual procedure for a search pursuant to a warrant, FISA does not require that agents knock before entry, supply notice of the search, particularize the object of the search, or inventory what is found for the target. The difference is based on practical considerations: "Physical searches to gather foreign intelligence depend upon stealth. If the targets of such searches discovered that the United States Government had obtained significant information about their activities, those activities would likely be altered, rendering the information useless." William F. Brown & Americo R. Cinquegrana, *Warrantless Physical Searches for Foreign Intelligence Purposes: Executive Order 12,333 and the Fourth Amendment*, 35 Cath. L. Rev. 97, 131 (1985). Does this explanation provide constitutional justification for either the FISA procedure or a wholly untethered warrantless search?

5. Who May Be Targeted? In an espionage prosecution, it may be easy to see how the target of FISA surveillance falls within the definition of "agent of a foreign power." How do you suppose these determinations are made in other national security or counterterrorism investigations? In addition to the portions of definitions reproduced in *Rosen*, FISA sets out two kinds of potential targets:

§1801. Definitions.

As used in this subchapter:

(a) "Foreign power" means—

(1) a foreign government or any component thereof, whether or not recognized by the United States;

(2) a faction of a foreign nation or nations, not substantially composed of United States persons;

(3) an entity that is openly acknowledged by a foreign government or governments to be directed and controlled by such foreign government or governments;

(4) a group engaged in international terrorism or activities in preparation therefor;

(5) a foreign-based political organization, not substantially composed of United States persons; or

(6) an entity that is directed and controlled by a foreign government or governments. . . .

(b) "Agent of a foreign power" means—

(1) any person other than a United States person, who—

(A) acts in the United States as an officer or employee of a foreign power, or as a member of a foreign power as defined in subsection (a)(4), irrespective of whether the person is inside the United States;

> (B) acts for or on behalf of a foreign power which engages in clandestine intelligence activities in the United States contrary to the interests of the United States, when the circumstances indicate that such person may engage in such activities, or when such person knowingly aids or abets any person in the conduct of such activities or knowingly conspires with any person to engage in such activities;
>
> (C) engages in international terrorism or activities in preparation therefore [sic];
>
> (D) engages in the international proliferation of weapons of mass destruction, or activities in preparation therefor; or
>
> (E) engages in the international proliferation of weapons of mass destruction, or activities in preparation therefor, for or on behalf of a foreign power, or knowingly aids or abets any person in the conduct of such proliferation or activities in preparation therefor, or knowingly conspires with any person to engage in such proliferation or activities in preparation therefor; or
>
> (2) any person who — . . .
>
> (C) knowingly engages in sabotage or international terrorism, or activities that are in preparation therefor, for or on behalf of a foreign power;
>
> (D) knowingly enters the United States under a false or fraudulent identity for or on behalf of a foreign power or, while in the United States, knowingly assumes a false or fraudulent identity for or on behalf of a foreign power. . . .

Subsections (A), (B), and (E) of §1801(b)(2) are set out in *Rosen* at p. 618.

Can you now describe the categories of targets that may be subjected to electronic surveillance or a physical search pursuant to FISA? Taking into account that to be an "agent of a foreign power" requires that the target work for or act on behalf of a "foreign power" (except for the "lone wolf" category described below), can you think of examples of a "foreign power" or "agent of foreign power"?

A "United States person" is defined as "a citizen of the United States, an alien lawfully admitted for permanent residence . . . , an unincorporated association a substantial number of members of which are citizens of the United States or aliens lawfully admitted for permanent residence, or a corporation which is incorporated in the United States, but does not include a corporation or an association which is a foreign power. . . ." 50 U.S.C. §1801(i). Under what circumstances could a "United States person" be treated as an agent of a foreign power? How did these definitions apply to the subjects of surveillance in *Rosen*?

The so-called "lone wolf" provision, 50 U.S.C. §1801(b)(1)(C), was added by section 6001 of the Intelligence Reform and Terrorism Prevention Act of 2004, Pub. L. No. 108-458, 118 Stat. 3638, 3742. If the lone wolf need not be linked in any way to a foreign power, has the "foreign agent" requirement effectively been eliminated for foreign intelligence surveillance? Can you identify any downside risks to the expanded definition?

On the basis of what information would investigators make a "foreign agency" determination before seeking FISA surveillance? Can the FBI make such a determination without the surveillance permitted by FISA?

c. The FISA Application Process for Electronic Surveillance or a Physical Search

1. The Special Court. Congress relied on its constitutional power to "ordain and establish" the lower federal courts when it created the Foreign Intelligence

Surveillance Court (FISC) and Foreign Intelligence Surveillance Court of Review (FISCR). Even though these courts sit only to hear a hyper-specialized set of cases, there is no question that they are Article III courts, since they are staffed by Article III judges and exercise "the judicial power of the United States." *See In re Motion for Release of Court Records,* 526 F. Supp. 2d 484, 486 (FISA Ct. 2007).

2. *An Overview of the Process for Obtaining a FISA Order for Electronic Surveillance or a Physical Search.* As shown by the flow chart below, after an investigation indicates a need for foreign intelligence, an application is prepared (by lawyers in the Department of Justice, typically supported by one or more affidavits from investigating agencies) and submitted to the FISC. The FISC considers the application in camera and ex parte; the targets of the proposed surveillance are not informed. In response to representations by President Trump and others that a FISA surveillance order directed at Trump campaign adviser Carter Page was flawed because it was politically motivated, and because there was no hearing to adjudicate the application for surveillance, a former Assistant Attorney General for the National Security Division explained that an informal but rigorous back-and-forth between DOJ lawyers and FISA Court staff reviewing the applications often substitutes for a formal hearing. The informal process often includes secure phone conversations in which Court staff ask questions or ask for clarification concerning an application. At other times, Court staff and DOJ lawyers meet to discuss an application or its components, and to request additional information to justify the government's claim that the proposed target of surveillance is a foreign power or agent of a foreign power. In short, the absence of a formal hearing on a FISA application does not mean that a rigorous legal and factual review is not conducted. *See* David Kris, *How the FISA Court Really Works,* Lawfare, Sept. 2, 2018; David Kris, *What to Make of the Carter Page FISA Applications,* Lawfare, July 21, 2018.

In response to a Freedom of Information Act lawsuit, the Justice Department released a redacted copy of the application for a FISA order targeting Carter Page. The redacted 412-page application is available at https://www.lawfareblog.com/document-justice-department-releases-carter-page-fisa-application.

If the FISC approves the order, it is executed by the NSA or the FBI in most cases. If the government subsequently seeks to introduce information obtained from the FISA surveillance as evidence in a criminal prosecution, the government must inform the defendant of that intent, as it did in *Rosen.* The defendant may then seek to suppress the materials on the grounds that the evidence was unlawfully acquired or that the surveillance or search was not conducted in conformity with the FISC order. In *Rosen,* the defendant sought disclosure of the FISA application and supporting materials in connection with its motion to suppress. If the Attorney General avers that such disclosure would harm national security, the criminal court will review the materials in camera and ex parte to decide de novo whether the FISC order and its execution by the government were lawful. The *Rosen* court thus took a "second look" at the FISA order, but its nominally de novo review standard considered only whether, for U.S. persons, the certifications contained in the original FISA application were "clearly erroneous" (*Rosen* construed them to be "presum[ptively] valid") or whether, for all other targets, the certifications were complete.

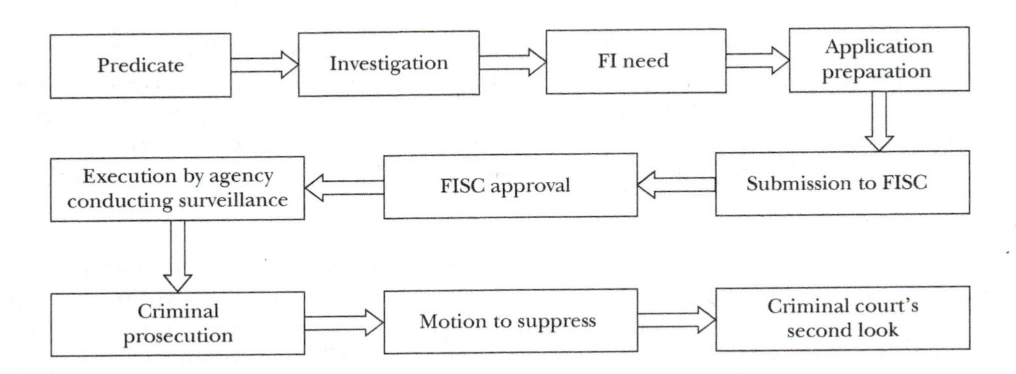

3. What Must an Application Contain? What are the essential components of an application for FISA surveillance? How do they differ from the elements of an application for a traditional warrant for law enforcement purposes?

In addition to the requirements summarized in *Rosen*, the Attorney General must find that the information sought "cannot reasonably be obtained by normal investigative techniques." 50 U.S.C. §1804(a)(6)(C). The application also must describe any past surveillance involving the same target, the surveillance devices to be employed, the means of installation (including whether physical entry will be required), and the period of time for conducting the surveillance. *Id.* §1804(a)(7), (8), (9).

4. The FISA Order for Electronic Surveillance or a Physical Search.

a. *Foreign Power or Agent Target.* FISA "probable cause" is fundamentally different from Title III probable cause. Under FISA, the FISC must find probable cause to believe what? Is the FISA probable cause standard quoted in *Rosen* more or less onerous than the general criminal probable cause standard? Is the FISA standard the same for U.S. persons as for non-U.S. persons? If not, how is it different?

Both FISA and federal criminal laws require something like the probability of a certain fact. But unlike Title III warrants, FISA orders are based "upon the probability of a possibility; the probability to believe that the foreign target of the order *may* engage in spying, or the probability to believe that the American target of the order *may* engage in criminal spying activities." Charles Doyle, *Memorandum to Senate Select Committee on Intelligence: Probable Cause, Reasonable Suspicion, and Reasonableness Standards in the Context of the Fourth Amendment and the Foreign Intelligence Surveillance Act* (Cong. Res. Serv.), Jan. 30, 2006. Under what circumstances and according to what standard may the FISC question the determinations made in the application for surveillance?

What justifies the lesser probable cause requirement in FISA? The purpose of law enforcement is to prosecute those guilty of committing a crime, while intelligence investigations have a broader scope and seek to protect the nation from foreign enemies. Foreign intelligence investigations are often more open-ended. What are the legal implications if law enforcement and intelligence surveillance objectives blur or even merge, when intelligence information produces evidence that is used in a criminal prosecution? What answer does *Rosen* suggest?

b. *Foreign Power or Agent Locus.* The FISC must also find that there is probable cause to believe that the locus of the surveillance is being used or about to be used by, or, for physical searches, owned, used, or possessed by or in transit to or from, a foreign power or agent of a foreign power. This seemingly simple requirement was complicated by the increasing use of cell phones instead of the geographically fixed landlines that existed when FISA was adopted in 1978.

To cope with this change in technology, Federal Rule of Criminal Procedure 41(a) was amended in 2001 to permit a single law enforcement warrant to be used "in any district in which activities related to the terrorism may have occurred" in conducting "an investigation of domestic terrorism or international terrorism." USA PATRIOT Act of 2001, Pub. L. No. 107-56, §219, 115 Stat. 272, 291. FISA was also amended in 2001 to permit the FISC to order these so-called "roving wiretaps." A roving wiretap permits investigators to listen in on any phone a target might use. If the judge "finds that the actions of the target of the application may have the effect of thwarting" the ability of the investigators to identify a specific communications carrier, Internet service provider, or other person needed to assist in the effective and secret execution of the surveillance, the order may authorize such assistance from multiple parties. *Id.* §206, 115 Stat. at 282 (amending 50 U.S.C. §1805(c)(2)(B)).

To complete the authorization for roving wiretaps, the FISA requirement that the FISC "specify . . . the nature and location of each of the facilities or places at which the electronic surveillance will be directed" was also amended in 2001 by adding "if known" at the end. 50 U.S.C. §1805(c)(1)(B).

c. *Minimization.* The FISC must also find that proposed minimization procedures meet statutory requirements. What is minimization, and why is it required? Do you agree with the *Rosen* court that the potential minimization breach in the *Rosen* investigation did not justify suppressing the FISA-derived evidence?

Part of the minimization process involves masking the identities of U.S. persons who are mentioned in intelligence reports. For example, a report derived from surveillance authorized by FISA might say, "non-U.S. person Paul mentioned to [U.S. person # 1] his interest in acquiring schematic drawings of water filtration plants in the New York City area." The U.S. person's identity is masked to protect her privacy. If, however, on the basis of surveillance the unidentified U.S. person is believed to be willing to assist the non-U.S. person in obtaining the schematics, government officials or agencies authorized to receive classified intelligence reports will undoubtedly need to know the identity of that person's identity.

"Unmasking" such a person's identity has historically occurred pursuant to intelligence community rules. Pertinent procedures are found in United States Signals Intelligence Directive 18, *Legal Compliance and U.S. Persons Minimization Procedures,* Jan. 25, 2011, https://www.dni.gov/files/documents/1118/CLEANEDFinal%20USSID%20SP0018.pdf. In general, "for non-public information concerning an unconsenting U.S. person, agencies may only [reveal to an authorized recipient] the identity of the U.S. person if it itself constitutes foreign intelligence, is necessary for the recipient to understand the foreign intelligence being transmitted, or is evidence of a crime." Off. of the Dir. of Nat'l Intelligence, *Protecting U.S. Person Identities in FISA Disseminations,* Nov. 20, 2017, https://icontherecord.tumblr.com/post/167710124123/protecting-us-person-identities-in-fisa-disseminations. Can you see how it might be difficult to apply the unmasking criteria? For examples of U.S. person intelligence that NSA believes may satisfy those criteria, see Robert Chesney, *Unmasking: A Primer on the Issues, Rules, and Possible Reforms,* Lawfare, Apr. 6, 2017.

Requests for unmasking may be made by senior level officials in the NSA, CIA, NCTC, or FBI who need to know the information to perform their lawful functions. Such requests are subject to internal and external oversight and review. If approved, the identity is released only to the requester. *Id.* At least partly in response to political controversy surrounding the unmasking of Donald Trump campaign officials about whom information was collected when they were targeted by a foreign intelligence service (*see id.*), the ODNI has promulgated an intelligence community-wide policy guidance on unmasking, *Intelligence Community Policy Guidance 107.1, Requests for Identities of U.S. Persons in Disseminated Intelligence Reports,* Jan. 11, 2018, https://www.dni.gov/files/documents/ICPG/ICPG-107.1.pdf. The guidance document requires agencies of the intelligence community to develop and maintain procedures to respond to unmasking requests, including a "fact-based justification describing why such U.S. person identity information is required" by the requesting intelligence official. *Id.*

Note that minimization is required only to the extent "consistent with the need of the United States to obtain, produce, and disseminate foreign intelligence information." 50 U.S.C. §§1801(h), 1821(4). Thus, if the name of the U.S. person is required to understand the foreign intelligence value of the information, minimization is not required. When Trump administration National Security Adviser Michael Flynn resigned in the wake of conflicting statements that he made about the contents of wire-tapped telephone calls with an agent of a foreign power, Russian Ambassador Kislyak, prior to President Trump's inauguration, it was thus lawful to disclose Flynn's identity. David Kris, *The Treatment of Flynn's Phone Calls Complies with FISA Minimization Procedures,* Lawfare, Feb. 14, 2017.

5. Provisions for Emergency Surveillance. FISA authorizes electronic surveillance without a court order in certain emergency circumstances. Such surveillance is permitted for up to a year when directed solely at communications between or among foreign powers or focused on their property, when there is "no substantial likelihood" that a communication involving a U.S. person will be acquired. 50 U.S.C. §1802.

More importantly, FISA states that when the Attorney General reasonably determines that "an emergency situation exists" regarding the employment of electronic surveillance to obtain foreign intelligence information "before an order authorizing such surveillance can with due diligence be obtained" and that there is a "factual basis for issuance of an order," the Attorney General may authorize the surveillance if a FISC judge is simultaneously informed and if an application is made to that judge "as soon as practicable, but not later than 7 days" after the Attorney General authorization. *Id.* §1805(e). If the FISC does not issue a judicial order, the surveillance must stop "when the information sought is obtained, when the application for the order is denied, or after the expiration of 7 days from the time of authorization by the Attorney General, whichever is earliest." *Id.* If no order is obtained, the information collected may not be used without consent "except with the approval of the Attorney General if the information indicates a threat of death or serious bodily harm to any person." *Id.*

Provision for physical searches in emergency circumstances is made on a basis parallel to that for electronic surveillance; the authority lasts for up to 7 days, by which time an application for approval must be made to the FISC. *Id.* §§1822(a), 1824(e); *see also id.* §§1843(a), (b) (parallel emergency authorities for pen register and trap and trace devices).

Between FISA's enactment in 1978 and September 11, 2001, Attorneys General issued 47 emergency authorizations under FISA. In the 18 months after September 11, 2001, the Attorney General authorized more than 170 emergency wiretaps and/or physical searches under FISA. Dan Eggen & Robert O'Harrow Jr., *U.S. Steps Up Secret Surveillance,* Wash. Post, Mar. 24, 2003. Under 50 U.S.C. §1808(a)(1), (2), the Attorney General must report semiannually to the intelligence and judiciary committees the total number of emergency employments of physical searches and electronic surveillance. The reports are not publicly available.

How can responsible officials be certain that these decisions satisfy statutory and constitutional norms? Given the availability of these FISA emergency provisions, can you envision any emergency that would justify foreign intelligence surveillance in the United States *without* complying with FISA?

6. Judicial Review of FISA Surveillance. If no criminal prosecution is initiated following FISA surveillance, how would an individual subjected to unlawful surveillance under FISA be able to challenge the illegal conduct in court? The FISC does not ordinarily publish its decisions, and its orders are sealed. Proceedings are ex parte and are thus normally not known to the targets of surveillance. 50 U.S.C. §§1802(a)(3), 1806(f)-(g).

However, 50 U.S.C. §1810 creates a private right of action for an "aggrieved" person subjected to electronic surveillance in violation of FISA procedures. In *Fazaga v. FBI,* 916 F.3d 1202 (9th Cir. 2019), three Muslims living in Southern California alleged that the FBI paid a confidential informant to install listening devices in their mosque based solely on their religious identity. (*See* 50 U.S.C. §1801(f)(4), *supra* p. 622.) Accepting the plaintiffs' allegations as true following the government's motion to dismiss, the Ninth Circuit agreed that the plaintiffs were "aggrieved" persons under §1810, and held that FISA contemplates the §1806 ex parte, in camera hearing and review of any FISA surveillance relevant to plaintiffs' claims. 916 F.3d at 1216. Thus, while the plaintiffs and their lawyers cannot examine any pertinent FISA surveillance materials, the lawyers will be involved in helping the trial court judge decide whether the surveillance violated FISA or the Constitution. In addition, the Ninth Circuit found that the combination of the judicial review procedures in §§1810 and 1806 overcame the government's principal defense — the state secrets privilege. *Id.* at 1229. See Chapter 5. Can you see why the state secrets privilege did not require dismissal of the *Fazaga* case?

As the *Rosen* defendants learned, even if targets of surveillance do find out, they may not be able to examine materials related to the surveillance as part of the criminal court's "second look" if the Attorney General files a claim of privilege under §1806(f). Can you see why FISA permits the government to withhold the applications and accompanying affidavits and certifications from discovery in an adversarial proceeding? If the reviewing judge exercises his statutory discretion not to disclose portions of the documents, how will the targets of surveillance be able to appeal the judge's decision? On what basis could a court of appeals overturn the nondisclosure decision? *See ACLU v. Barr,* 952 F.2d 457 (D.C. Cir. 1991) (reviewing court may overturn a nondisclosure decision if the certifications of compliance with FISA requirements are clearly erroneous).

d. Constitutional Concerns

1. Article III Case or Controversy? The FISC receives applications and issues orders solely on an ex parte basis without any adversarial proceedings. Do such matters meet the Article III "case or controversy" requirement? *United States v. Megahey*, 553 F. Supp. 1180 (E.D.N.Y. 1982), held that FISA proceedings before the FISC "involve concrete questions respecting the application of the Act and are in a form such that a judge is capable of acting on them." *Id.* at 1197. At the time FISA was enacted, the Justice Department's Office of Legal Counsel concluded that FISC proceedings did not violate Article III because, like ordinary warrant applications, they were merely ancillary to subsequent criminal or civil proceedings. *Foreign Intelligence Electronic Surveillance: Hearings on H.R. 5794, H.R. 9745, H.R. 7308, and H.R. 5632 Before the Subcomm. on Legislation of the H. Permanent Select Comm. on Intelligence*, 95th Cong. 21-24 (1978) (statement of John M. Harmon, Ass't Att'y Gen., Off. of Legal Counsel). Note the two premises undergirding this argument: that (1) all the FISC is doing is issuing warrants; and (2) those warrants *will* generally be subject to collateral attack in future civil or criminal proceedings. Were those premises accurate in 1978? Are they accurate today?

2. Political Question Doctrine. The courts that have heard challenges to FISA surveillance orders have ruled that their review is not barred by the political question doctrine. *See, e.g., United States v. Duggan*, 743 F.2d 59, 74-75 (2d Cir. 1984) (limited judicial role in determining whether the target of a warrant is properly subject to the prescribed procedure does not threaten political question values and does not inject courts into the making of foreign policy).

3. Confrontation. Did the *Rosen* court's refusal to disclose the FISA materials to the defendants violate their due process confrontation rights? Although the Supreme Court has never decided a FISA appeal, the Court did deny review in a challenge to the government's refusal to disclose materials that supported an application for FISA surveillance. In *United States v. Squillacote*, 221 F.3d 542 (4th Cir. 2000), a married couple were convicted of conspiring to commit espionage on behalf of East Germany, the Soviet Union, Russia, and South Africa. The FBI obtained 20 separate FISA orders for surveillance that lasted 550 days. Based almost exclusively on the FISA-derived evidence, the parties were sentenced to 22 and 17 years in prison, respectively. Although FISA and the Due Process Clause entitled the accused to question the basis for the government's surveillance, counsel for the accused spies were never permitted to see the underlying documentation that supported the applications for surveillance because the government invoked §1806(f) and filed a claim of privilege. Does §1806(f) comply with the Due Process Clause?

4. FISA and Franks. In *Franks v. Delaware*, 438 U.S. 154 (1978), the Supreme Court held that a criminal defendant had a Fourth Amendment right collaterally to attack a search warrant if he could show that (1) the warrant was based upon false statements that were either deliberately or recklessly made, and (2) the false statements tainted the affidavit such that the remainder of the affidavit was insufficient to establish probable cause for the search. FISA authorizes a *Franks*-like procedure, but, as noted above, leaves it to the district court to resolve the issue in camera and ex parte, and only authorizes disclosure of supporting materials to the defendant and his lawyer "where such disclosure is necessary to make an accurate determination of the legality of the surveillance." 50 U.S.C. §1806(f). Will a district judge be able to determine that disclosure is necessary *without* the benefit of adversarial presentation? As one federal circuit judge has complained,

> A *Franks* motion is premised on material misrepresentations and omissions in the warrant affidavit; but without access to that affidavit, a defendant cannot identify such misrepresentations or omissions, let alone establish that they were intentionally or recklessly made. As a practical matter, the secrecy shrouding the FISA process renders it impossible for a defendant to meaningfully obtain relief under *Franks* absent a patent inconsistency in the FISA application itself or a *sua sponte* disclosure by the government that the FISA application contained a material misstatement or omission. To date, courts have either overlooked the problem or acknowledged it without being able to identify a satisfactory work-around. [*United States v. Daoud,* 755 F.3d 479, 486 (7th Cir. 2014) (Rovner, J., concurring).]

Is this a problem worth a solution? If so, how might §1806(f) be amended better to protect a defendant's rights in such cases?

5. *First Amendment.* What protections does FISA provide against surveillance that would burden expressive freedoms? What is meant by the prohibition against finding a U.S. person to be an agent of a foreign power "solely upon the basis of activities protected by the first amendment"? 50 U.S.C. §1805(a)(2)(A). A 1977 Senate Judiciary Committee report on FISA stated that activities protected by the First Amendment may not "form *any part* of the basis" for identifying a FISA target. S. Rep. No. 95-604, at 8 (1977) (emphasis added). Did the *Rosen* court take this legislative history into account in evaluating the rules for identifying a potential FISA target?

Did the court in *Rosen* fairly separate the defendants' activities that might be protected from those that are not so protected?

B. FISA, LAW ENFORCEMENT, AND THE FOURTH AMENDMENT

In *United States v. Duggan,* 743 F.2d 59 (2d Cir. 1984), alleged members of the Provisional Irish Republican Army faced a number of charges relating to the export, transportation, and delivery of explosives and firearms. Some of the evidence against them was derived from electronic surveillance pursuant to FISA. The defendants contended that FISA is unconstitutional on grounds that it violates the probable cause requirement of the Fourth Amendment. The court rejected their argument:

> We regard the procedures fashioned in FISA as a constitutionally adequate balancing of the individual's Fourth Amendment rights against the nation's need to obtain foreign intelligence information. The governmental concerns . . . make reasonable the adoption of prerequisites to surveillance that are less stringent than those precedent to the issuance of a warrant for a criminal investigation. . . .

> We conclude that these requirements provide an appropriate balance between the individual's interest in privacy and the government's need to obtain foreign intelligence information, and that FISA does not violate the probable cause requirement of the Fourth Amendment. [*Id.* at 73-74.]

Although the Supreme Court has not considered the constitutionality of FISA, the lower courts have uniformly followed *Duggan* in upholding the FISA procedures. How does this "FISA as compromise" view compare with your understanding of the constitutionality of FISA?

Some defendants in criminal cases have moved to suppress FISA-acquired evidence on the ground that the FISA surveillance was unlawful, because the evidence was originally sought as part of a criminal investigation. They maintain that the government has thus misused FISA to do an end run around Title III and the ordinary warrant and probable cause requirements of the Fourth Amendment. The government usually replies that the investigators sought only foreign intelligence information. Is it possible, indeed likely, that both sides are correct? In *Duggan*, the court concluded that an "otherwise valid FISA surveillance is not tainted" simply because the government anticipates that its fruits *may* be used in a criminal prosecution. *Id.* at 78. But how can a judge determine that the government has not used FISA simply to avoid having to comply with Rule 41? *See United States v. Rahman*, 861 F. Supp. 247 (S.D.N.Y. 1994) (refusing to find an end run), *aff'd*, 189 F.2d 88 (2d Cir. 1999).

Before 2002, courts followed *United States v. Truong Dinh Hung*, 629 F.2d 908 (4th Cir. 1980), and allowed evidence gathered during FISA surveillance to support a criminal conviction only after finding that intelligence collection was the "primary" purpose of the surveillance, *United States v. Johnson*, 952 F.2d 565 (1st Cir. 1991), or at least *a* purpose (not necessarily primary), *United States v. Sarkissian*, 841 F.2d 959, 964 (9th Cir. 1988). The assumption seemed to be that if the original purpose of the surveillance was intelligence gathering, there was no reason not to use the collected information in a criminal prosecution.

In the days and weeks after the September 11, 2001, terrorist attacks, it was widely reported that an investigative failure may have permitted a twentieth hijacker to escape pre-attack detection because of a concern based on "primary purpose." Zacarias Moussaoui was arrested on immigration charges a few weeks before the attacks. Officials at a private flight-training school had grown suspicious when Moussaoui said that he wanted to learn to fly large jet aircraft, but that he had no interest in becoming a commercial pilot. At about the same time, a French intelligence agency warned the FBI in a classified cable that Moussaoui had "Islamic extremist beliefs." David Johnston & Philip Shenon, *F.B.I. Curbed Scrutiny of Man Now a Suspect in Attacks*, N.Y. Times, Oct. 6, 2001. When FBI field agents in Minneapolis sought headquarters approval for a FISA search, they were turned down, apparently because there was insufficient indication that Moussaoui was an agent of a foreign power. The field agents then also failed to persuade headquarters to open a criminal investigation that would have employed grand jury subpoenas and law enforcement warrants to examine Moussaoui's computer and telephone records. Apparently, this request was denied because senior FBI officials worried that an open criminal investigation might thwart a later FISA application by defeating the primary purpose requirement. They were concerned in part because FISC Chief Judge Royce Lamberth had recently questioned the candor of Justice Department officials who sought FISA orders for targets who were already the subjects of criminal investigations. A criminal case was eventually opened and a FISA order was obtained, but only after the September 11 attacks. *Id.*

The belief that a full investigation of Moussaoui before September 11 might have led to exposure of the hijackers' plot helped spur enactment of the USA Patriot Act and, three years later, the lone-wolf provision in the Intelligence Reform and Terrorism Prevention Act of 2004, *supra* p. 624. The criminal prosecution of Moussaoui is considered *infra* p. 1108.

Concerns about the primary purpose requirement produced an amendment to FISA in the USA Patriot Act. The meaning and constitutionality of the amendment are addressed in the following case.

Reading *In re Sealed Case*

The following opinion, unlike *In re Directives to Yahoo*, is based on traditional FISA surveillance that resulted in the first-ever appeal from the FISC to the FISCR. Department of Justice procedures first erected a "wall" to keep foreign intelligence and counterintelligence investigations separate from criminal investigations, and the FISC adopted those procedures. The case below concerns Justice Department efforts to dismantle the wall after the USA Patriot Act amended FISA.

- Why had Justice erected the wall? What was its practical effect on foreign intelligence investigations and prosecutions for national security crimes?
- Originally, FISA required that a FISA application certify "that the purpose of the surveillance is to obtain foreign intelligence information." The Patriot Act substituted "a significant purpose." How did this change affect the need for maintenance of the wall?
- If the wall is constitutionally required, even the USA Patriot Act amendment could not lower it. Upon what theory did the FISCR say the revised "purpose" standard meets the requirements of the Fourth Amendment?
- Upon what theory does the court conclude that "FISA could not encroach on the President's constitutional power" to conduct warrantless searches for foreign intelligence information?

In re Sealed Case

Foreign Intelligence Surveillance Court of Review, 2002
310 F.3d 717

GUY, Senior Circuit Judge, presiding; SILBERMAN and LEAVY, Senior Circuit Judges.

PER CURIAM: This is the first appeal from the Foreign Intelligence Surveillance Court to the Court of Review since the passage of the Foreign Intelligence Surveillance Act (FISA), 50 U.S.C. §§1801-1862 (West 1991 and Supp. 2002), in 1978. The appeal is brought by the United States from a FISA court surveillance order which imposed certain restrictions on the government. . . .

I.

... [T]he court ordered that

> law enforcement officials shall not make recommendations to intelligence officials concerning the initiation, operation, continuation or expansion of FISA searches or surveillances. Additionally, the FBI and the Criminal Division [of the Department of Justice] shall ensure that law enforcement officials do not direct or control the use of the FISA procedures to enhance criminal prosecution, and that advice intended to preserve the option of a criminal prosecution does not inadvertently result in the Criminal Division's directing or controlling the investigation using FISA searches and surveillances toward law enforcement objectives.

To ensure the Justice Department followed these strictures the court also fashioned what the government refers to as a "chaperone requirement"; that a unit of the Justice Department, the Office of Intelligence Policy and Review (OIPR) (composed of 31 lawyers and 25 support staff), "be invited" to all meetings between the FBI and the Criminal Division involving consultations for the purpose of coordinating efforts "to investigate or protect against foreign attack or other grave hostile acts, sabotage, international terrorism, or clandestine intelligence activities by foreign powers or their agents." If representatives of OIPR are unable to attend such meetings, "OIPR shall be appri[s]ed of the substance of the meetings forthwith in writing so that the Court may be notified at the earliest opportunity." ...

... [T]he May 17 opinion of the FISA court ... appears to proceed from the assumption that FISA constructed a barrier between counterintelligence/intelligence officials and law enforcement officers in the Executive Branch — indeed, it uses the word "wall" popularized by certain commentators (and journalists) to describe that supposed barrier.

The "wall" emerges from the court's implicit interpretation of FISA. The court apparently believes it can approve applications for electronic surveillance only if the government's objective is *not* primarily directed toward criminal prosecution of the foreign agents for their foreign intelligence activity. But the court neither refers to any FISA language supporting that view, nor does it reference the Patriot Act amendments, which the government contends specifically altered FISA to make clear that an application could be obtained even if criminal prosecution is the primary counter mechanism....

II....

The origin of what the government refers to as the false dichotomy between foreign intelligence information that is evidence of foreign intelligence crimes and that which is not appears to have been a Fourth Circuit case decided in 1980. *United States v. Truong Dinh Hung*, 629 F.2d 908 (4th Cir. 1980). That case, however, involved an electronic surveillance carried out prior to the passage of FISA and predicated on the President's executive power. In approving the district court's exclusion of evidence obtained through a warrantless surveillance subsequent to the point in time when the government's investigation became "primarily" driven by law enforcement objectives, the court held that the Executive Branch should be excused from securing a warrant only when "the object of the search or the surveillance is a foreign power, its agents or collaborators," and "the surveillance is conducted 'primarily' for foreign intelligence reasons." *Id.* at 915. . . .

. . . [S]ome time in the 1980s — the exact moment is shrouded in historical mist — the Department [of Justice] applied the *Truong* analysis to an interpretation of the FISA statute. What is clear is that in 1995 the Attorney General adopted "Procedures for Contacts between the FBI and the Criminal Division Concerning Foreign Intelligence and Foreign Counterintelligence Investigations."

Apparently to avoid running afoul of the primary purpose test used by some courts, the 1995 Procedures limited contacts between the FBI and the Criminal Division in cases where FISA surveillance or searches were being conducted by the FBI for foreign intelligence (FI) or foreign counterintelligence (FCI) purposes. The procedures state that "the FBI and Criminal Division should ensure that advice intended to preserve the option of a criminal prosecution does not inadvertently result in either the fact or the appearance of the Criminal Division's *directing or controlling* the FI or FCI investigation toward law enforcement objectives." 1995 Procedures at 2, ¶6 (emphasis added). Although these procedures provided for significant information sharing and coordination between criminal and FI or FCI investigations, based at least in part on the "directing or controlling" language, they eventually came to be narrowly interpreted within the Department of Justice, and most particularly by OIPR, as requiring OIPR to act as a "wall" to prevent the FBI intelligence officials from communicating with the Criminal Division regarding ongoing FI or FCI investigations. . . .

The Patriot Act and the FISA Court's Decision

The passage of the Patriot Act altered and to some degree muddied the landscape. In October 2001, Congress amended FISA to change "the purpose" language in 1804(a)(7)(B) to "a significant purpose." It also added a provision allowing "Federal officers who conduct electronic surveillance to acquire foreign intelligence information" to "consult with Federal law enforcement officers to coordinate efforts to investigate or protect against" attack or other grave hostile acts, sabotage or international terrorism, or clandestine intelligence activities, by foreign powers or their agents. 50 U.S.C. §1806(k)(1). And such coordination "shall not preclude" the government's certification that a significant purpose of the surveillance is to obtain foreign intelligence information, or the issuance of an order authorizing the surveillance. *Id.* §1806(k)(2). . . .

. . . [T]he Patriot Act amendments clearly disapprove the primary purpose test. And as a matter of straightforward logic, if a FISA application can be granted even if "foreign intelligence" is only a significant — not a primary — purpose, another purpose can be primary. One other legitimate purpose that could exist is to prosecute a target for a foreign intelligence crime. . . .

. . . [I]t is our task to do our best to read the statute to honor congressional intent. The better reading, it seems to us, excludes from the purpose of gaining foreign intelligence information a sole objective of criminal prosecution. We therefore reject the government's argument to the contrary. Yet this may not make much practical difference. Because, as the government points out, when it commences an electronic surveillance of a foreign agent, typically it will not have decided whether to prosecute the agent (whatever may be the subjective intent of the investigators or lawyers who initiate an investigation). So long as the government entertains a realistic option of dealing with the agent other than through criminal prosecution, it satisfies the significant purpose test.

The important point is — and here we agree with the government — the Patriot Act amendment, by using the word "significant," eliminated any justification for the FISA court to balance the relative weight the government places on criminal prosecution as compared to other counterintelligence responses. If the certification of the application's purpose articulates a broader objective than criminal prosecution — such as stopping an ongoing conspiracy — and includes other potential non-prosecutorial responses, the government meets the statutory test. Of course, if the court concluded that the government's sole objective was merely to gain evidence of past criminal conduct — even foreign intelligence crimes — to punish the agent rather than halt ongoing espionage or terrorist activity, the application should be denied.

... It can be argued, however, that by providing that an application is to be granted if the government has only a "significant purpose" of gaining foreign intelligence information, the Patriot Act allows the government to have a primary objective of prosecuting an agent for a non-foreign intelligence crime. Yet we think that would be an anomalous reading of the amendment. For we see not the slightest indication that Congress meant to give that power to the Executive Branch. Accordingly, the manifestation of such a purpose, it seems to us, would continue to disqualify an application. That is not to deny that ordinary crimes might be inextricably intertwined with foreign intelligence crimes. For example, if a group of international terrorists were to engage in bank robberies in order to finance the manufacture of a bomb, evidence of the bank robbery should be treated just as evidence of the terrorist act itself. But the FISA process cannot be used as a device to investigate wholly unrelated ordinary crimes. . . .

III. . . .

The FISA court expressed concern that unless FISA were "construed" in the fashion that it did, the government could use a FISA order as an improper substitute for an ordinary criminal warrant under Title III. That concern seems to suggest that the FISA court thought Title III procedures are constitutionally mandated if the government has a prosecutorial objective regarding an agent of a foreign power. But in *United States v. United States District Court* (*Keith*), 407 U.S. 297, 322 (1972) — in which the Supreme Court explicitly declined to consider foreign intelligence surveillance — the Court indicated that, even with respect to domestic national security intelligence gathering for prosecutorial purposes where a warrant was mandated, Title III procedures were not constitutionally required: "[W]e do not hold that the same type of standards and procedures prescribed by Title III are necessarily applicable to this case. We recognize that domestic security surveillance may involve different policy and practical considerations from the surveillance of 'ordinary crime.'" Nevertheless, in asking whether FISA procedures can be regarded as reasonable under the Fourth Amendment, we think it is instructive to compare those procedures and requirements with their Title III counterparts. Obviously, the closer those FISA procedures are to Title III procedures, the lesser are our constitutional concerns. . . .

... [W]hile Title III contains some protections that are not in FISA, in many significant respects the two statutes are equivalent, and in some, FISA contains additional protections. Still, to the extent the two statutes diverge in constitutionally relevant areas — in particular, in their probable cause and particularity showings — a FISA order may not be a "warrant" contemplated by the Fourth Amendment. . . . We do not decide the issue but note that to the extent a FISA order comes close to meeting Title III, that certainly bears on its reasonableness under the Fourth Amendment. . . .

Ultimately, the question becomes whether FISA, as amended by the Patriot Act, is a reasonable response based on a balance of the legitimate need of the government for foreign intelligence information to protect against national security threats with the protected rights of citizens. . . .

It will be recalled that the case that set forth the primary purpose test *as constitutionally required* was *Truong*. The Fourth Circuit thought that *Keith*'s balancing standard implied the adoption of the primary purpose test. We reiterate that *Truong* dealt with a pre-FISA surveillance based on the President's constitutional responsibility to conduct the foreign affairs of the United States. 629 F.2d at 914. Although *Truong* suggested the line it drew was a constitutional minimum that would apply to a FISA surveillance, *see id.* at 914 n.4, it had no occasion to consider the application of the statute carefully. The *Truong* court, as did all the other courts to have decided the issue, held that the President did have inherent authority to conduct warrantless searches to obtain foreign intelligence information. . . . We take for granted that the President does have that authority and, assuming that is so, FISA could not encroach on the President's constitutional power. The question before us is the reverse, does FISA amplify the President's power by providing a mechanism that at least approaches a classic warrant and which therefore supports the government's contention that FISA searches are constitutionally reasonable. . . .

. . . [The *Truong*] analysis, in our view, rested on a false premise and the line the court sought to draw was inherently unstable, unrealistic, and confusing. The false premise was the assertion that once the government moves to criminal prosecution, its "foreign policy concerns" recede. As we have discussed in the first part of the opinion, that is simply not true as it relates to counterintelligence. In that field the government's primary purpose is to halt the espionage or terrorism efforts, and criminal prosecutions can be, and usually are, interrelated with other techniques used to frustrate a foreign power's efforts. . . .

CONCLUSION

. . . Even without taking into account the President's inherent constitutional authority to conduct warrantless foreign intelligence surveillance, we think the procedures and government showings required under FISA, if they do not meet the minimum Fourth Amendment warrant standards, certainly come close. We, therefore, believe firmly, applying the balancing test drawn from *Keith*, that FISA as amended is constitutional because the surveillances it authorizes are reasonable. . . .

Notes and Questions

1. The Holding. What is the holding of *In re Sealed Case*? Is the holding based on FISA, on the Constitution, or both? Can you reconcile the holding with *Keith*? Does

Truong have any continuing relevance to the law of national security surveillance? Does *In re Sealed Case* say anything about the foreign intelligence exception to the Warrant Clause?

2. *Limits to the Foreign Intelligence Exception?* If some evidence of criminal activity may be collected during what was otherwise a foreign intelligence investigation, may the government rely on the foreign intelligence exception to *continue* a warrantless surveillance even after its purpose shifts to criminal prosecution? The Fourth Circuit in *Truong* decided that the exception is available

> only when the surveillance is conducted "primarily" for foreign intelligence reasons. . . . [O]nce surveillance becomes primarily a criminal investigation, the courts are entirely competent to make the usual probable cause determination, and . . . , importantly, individual privacy interests come to the fore and government foreign policy concerns recede when the government is primarily attempting to form the basis for a criminal prosecution. [629 F.2d at 915.]

How significant is the difference between *Truong*'s conception of a "foreign intelligence" exception to the Warrant Clause — as being limited to cases in which foreign intelligence surveillance is the "primary purpose" of the search — and the version upheld in *In re Directives to Yahoo, supra* p. 593 (a "programmatic purpose" that "involves some legitimate objective beyond ordinary crime control[,]" 2008 WL 10632524, at *6)?

3. *Purpose vs. Use.* In an omitted portion of *In re Sealed Case,* the FISCR found it "virtually impossible to read the 1978 FISA to exclude from its purpose the prosecution of foreign intelligence crimes, most importantly because . . . the definition of an agent of a foreign power — if he or she is a U.S. person — is grounded in criminal conduct." 310 F.3d 723. Is the FBI now permitted to conduct a secret search or wiretap for the primary purpose of investigating possible criminal activity even though there is no probable cause to suspect the commission of a crime? Although terrorism itself is criminal, terrorists may also engage in a variety of common criminal activities — credit card fraud, for example. If the USA Patriot Act amendment makes it easier for the FBI to manage parallel criminal and foreign intelligence investigations, is the gain in effectiveness worth the risk of misuse of the process?

4. *"Special Needs."* In another part of *In re Sealed Case* omitted here, the FISCR analogized its support of the lowered wall to the Supreme Court's approval of warrantless and sometimes suspicionless searches that are designed to serve the government's "special needs, beyond the normal need for law enforcement." *In re Sealed Case,* 310 F.3d at 743 (quoting *Vernonia School Dist. 47J v. Acton,* 515 U.S. 646, 653 (1995)). As noted in the preceding chapter, the Court has upheld searches that do not satisfy conventional Fourth Amendment standards in cases that involve suspicionless drug testing of student athletes, government employees, and railroad workers, along with administrative searches of residences and certain highly regulated businesses. Are you persuaded that the Supreme Court's "special needs" cases are based on considerations analogous to the Justice Department procedures at issue in the principal case?

C. FISA TRENDS

The FISC has been active. More than 30,000 applications for surveillance or searches have been approved by it since 1979. Brief annual FISA reports from the Administrative Office of the U.S. Courts, including the volume of applications approved for the year, are posted at http://www.fas.org/irp/agency/doj/fisa/. *See, e.g.*, Letter from James C. Duff, Director, to Reps. Jerrold Nadler and Adam B. Schiff, and Senators Richard Burr and Lindsey Graham (Apr. 25, 2019). Additional reporting requirements were added by statute in 2015 and expanded in 2017. FISA Amendments Reauthorization Act of 2017, 50 U.S.C. §1873(b)(1)(A) (2018). Based on statutory requirements, the *ODNI Statistical Transparency Report Regarding the Use of National Security Authorities*, ODNI Off. of Civil Liberties, Privacy & Transparency (Apr. 2019), https://icontherecord.tumblr.com/post/184553467393/odni-releases-annual-intelligence-community, states that in calendar year 2018, 1,184 FISA "probable cause" orders were issued involving an estimated 1,833 targets. Of the targets, an estimated 1,601 were non-U.S. persons and 232 were U.S. persons. As then-presiding Judge Reggie Walton explained in a 2013 letter, the final reported statistics on the activities of the FISA courts "do not reflect the fact that many applications are altered prior to final submission or even withheld from final submission entirely, often after an indication that a judge would not approve them." Letter from Reggie B. Walton, Presiding Judge, to Hon. Patrick J. Leahy, Chairman, S. Comm. on the Judiciary (July 29, 2013), at 3, http://www.fisc.uscourts.gov/public-filings/july-29-2013-letter-chairman-leahy-chairman-committee-judiciary-united-states-senate. By comparison, an average of about 600-700 requests for electronic surveillance are submitted to federal courts by law enforcement officials under 18 U.S.C. §2518 annually. What do the numbers suggest?

Far more substantial disclosures of surveillance activity were made by NSA contractor Edward Snowden beginning in June 2013. Subsequent government declassification of pertinent intelligence records has nearly kept pace with the Snowden disclosures. These developments are treated in the next chapter. A website for the Foreign Intelligence Surveillance Court contains significantly more useful information than DOJ's annual reports to Congress. *See* http://www.fisc.uscourts.gov/.

CONGRESSIONAL AUTHORITY FOR FOREIGN INTELLIGENCE SURVEILLANCE: SUMMARY OF BASIC PRINCIPLES

- FISA was a compromise between the President's insistence on inherent constitutional authority to collect foreign intelligence and Congress's insistence on a judicial role. FISA avoided the question whether there is a foreign intelligence exception to the Fourth Amendment warrant requirement by authorizing a secret Article III court to approve foreign intelligence surveillance based upon a unique probable cause requirement.

- Electronic surveillance pursuant to FISA must concern "foreign" intelligence and (with exceptions created by 2008 amendments discussed in the next chapter) must be conducted inside the United States. FISA therefore did not originally regulate surveillance outside the United States.

- While a FISA order cannot be granted solely to collect criminal evidence of a non – national security crime, it need only have "a" significant," and not sole or even primary, purpose of collecting foreign intelligence.

- Instead of probable cause to believe that evidence of a crime will be collected, an application for a FISA order requires only a showing of probable cause to believe, inter alia, that a target is a foreign power or agent of a foreign power.

- A FISA application also must describe "minimization procedures" to limit the collection, retention, and dissemination of nonpublic information — typically information that was "incidentally" collected, like the innocent telephone conversation of a target's teenager.

- FISA gives "United States persons" (citizens and permanent resident aliens) more protection than non-U.S. persons, in recognition of U.S. persons' constitutional rights. Thus, the FISA probable cause standard is higher for U.S. persons, probable cause cannot be based solely on the basis of their First Amendment activities, and the application for surveillance of them must be not only complete, but also not "clearly erroneous."

- Core FISA procedures (as contrasted with certain kinds of bulk collection discussed in Chapter 24) have survived Article III, First Amendment, Fourth Amendment, Fifth Amendment, and Sixth Amendment challenges.

Programmatic Electronic Surveillance for Foreign Intelligence

With the ongoing revolution in digital communications, the geographical border has become an increasingly imperfect line of demarcation for legal authorities and their limits. So has the citizenship or status of a target of electronic surveillance. Packets of data that constitute messages travel in disparate ways on the Internet through global networks, many of which come through or end up in the United States even when the senders or recipients (or both) are abroad. Moreover, it may or may not be possible to identify senders or recipients by the digital signatures or phone numbers they use to communicate.

Because FISA was written to apply to broadly defined categories of "electronic surveillance" inside the United States, recent developments in technology have brought the interception of many previously unregulated communications — e-mail is the most prominent example — inside the FISA scheme.

Evolving technologies have also turned the traditional sequence of FISA processes on its head. Now data analytics — the application of algorithms or other database techniques to reveal hidden characteristics or relationships — may be used to develop a list of targets for traditional FISA surveillance. We discovered after 9/11, for example, that investigators could analyze transactional data about potential terrorists in previously collected databases and come up with a list that included four of the hijackers — the reverse of a typical FISA investigation.

In order to collect foreign intelligence data, whether domestic or foreign in origin, officials need access to telecom switches inside the United States, or to records of Internet traffic residing on servers in the United States. Thus, with FISA's traditional focus on domestic collection, even a foreign-to-foreign text message intercepted from a server inside the United States requires compliance with FISA procedures. Whatever the source or destination of the traffic, the collected data could be expected to often include information about U.S. persons.

After 9/11, in response to the intelligence opportunities afforded by these technological changes, the George W. Bush administration authorized the NSA to collect electronic communications data from Internet service providers and from the fiber-optic cables that serve them without first having to identify individual targets and without seeking approval from the FISC. The so-called Terrorist Surveillance Program (TSP) was hidden from public view for more than four years, at least in part because it was so controversial. In this chapter we begin by exploring that program and the Administration's defense of it. Ultimately, the Administration successfully asked Congress to amend FISA by adding "Section 702" to authorize such "programmatic" surveillance. We consider the resulting statutory framework, operation, and legality of Section 702 surveillance in some detail.

A. CASE STUDY: THE TERRORIST SURVEILLANCE PROGRAM

On December 16, 2005, the *New York Times* reported that, according to government officials, "President Bush secretly authorized the National Security Agency to eavesdrop on Americans and others inside the United States to search for evidence of terrorist activity without the court-approved warrants ordinarily required for domestic spying." James Risen & Eric Lichtblau, *Bush Lets U.S. Spy on Callers Without Courts,* N.Y. Times, Dec. 16, 2005. Pursuant to a still-secret executive order signed by the President in October 2001, the NSA had — without warrants — monitored the contents of telephone and Internet communications of thousands of persons inside the United States, where one end of the communication was outside the United States, in an effort to learn more about possible terrorist plots. Later called the Terrorist Surveillance Program (TSP) by the Administration, the NSA surveillance created a major controversy, drawing out prominent critics and proponents alike, provoking hearings in Congress, prompting lawsuits by civil liberties organizations and by criminal defendants who challenged their previous pleas or convictions, and generating countless op-ed pieces, blog debates, and commentaries. At the same time, President Bush authorized the NSA to collect telephony and Internet non-content information (metadata) in bulk. The details and legal issues involved in bulk collection of metadata will be explored in Chapter 24.

The Bush administration vigorously defended the TSP. President Bush issued authorizations for the program every 30-60 days. According to a 2013 disclosure of Bush administration intelligence collection activities by the Director of National Intelligence, "each presidential authorization required the minimization of information collected concerning American citizens to the extent consistent with the effective accomplishment of the mission of detection and prevention of acts of terrorism within the United States." Off. of the Dir. of Nat'l Intelligence, *DNI Announces the Declassification of the Existence of Collection Activities Authorized by President George W. Bush Shortly After the Attacks of September 11, 2001* (2013). According to the President, the program had to be approved "by our nation's top legal officials, including the Attorney General and the Counsel to the President." *President's Radio Address* (Dec. 17, 2005).

Shortly after the story broke in the *New York Times,* the Justice Department's Office of Legislative Affairs prepared a letter for congressional leaders summarizing the legal rationale for the NSA surveillance. Excerpts from that letter follow:

Letter from William E. Moschella, Assistant Attorney General, to The Honorable Pat Roberts, Chairman, Senate Select Committee on Intelligence, et al.

Dec. 22, 2005

http://www.fas.org/irp/agency/doj/fisa/doj122205.pdf

As you know, in response to unauthorized disclosures in the media, the President has described certain activities of the National Security Agency ("NSA") that he has authorized since shortly after September 11, 2001. As described by the President, the NSA intercepts certain international communications into and out of the United States of people linked to al Qaeda or an affiliated terrorist organization. The purpose of these intercepts is to establish an early warning system to detect and prevent another catastrophic terrorist attack on the United States. The President has made clear that he will use his constitutional and statutory authorities to protect the American people from further terrorist attacks, and the NSA activities the President described are part of that effort. Leaders of the Congress were briefed on these activities more than a dozen times.

The purpose of this letter is to provide an additional brief summary of the legal authority supporting the NSA activities described by the President.

As an initial matter, I emphasize a few points. The President stated that these activities are "crucial to our national security." The President further explained that "the unauthorized disclosure of this effort damages our national security and puts our citizens at risk. Revealing classified information is illegal, alerts our enemies, and endangers our country." These critical national security activities remain classified. All United States laws and policies governing the protection and nondisclosure of national security information, including the information relating to the activities described by the President, remain in full force and effect. The unauthorized disclosure of classified information violates federal criminal law. The Government may provide further classified briefings to the Congress on these activities in an appropriate manner. Any such briefings will be conducted in a manner that will not endanger national security.

Under Article II of the Constitution, including in his capacity as Commander in Chief, the President has the responsibility to protect the Nation from further attacks, and the Constitution gives him all necessary authority to fulfill that duty. *See, e.g., Prize Cases,* 67 U.S. (2 Black) 635, 668 (1863) (stressing that if the Nation is invaded, "the President is not only authorized but bound to resist by force . . . without waiting for any special legislative authority"); *Campbell v. Clinton,* 203 F.3d 19, 27 (D.C. Cir. 2000) (Silberman, J., concurring) ("[T]he *Prize Cases* . . . stand for the proposition that the President has independent authority to repel aggressive acts by third parties even without specific congressional authorization, and courts may not review the level of force selected."); *id.* at 40 (Tatel, J., concurring). The Congress recognized this constitutional authority in the preamble to the Authorization for the Use of Military Force ("AUMF") of September 18, 2001, 115 Stat. 224 (2001) ("[T]he President has authority under the Constitution to take action to deter and prevent acts of international terrorism against the United States."), and in the War Powers Resolution, *see* 50 U.S.C. §1541(c) ("The constitutional powers of the President as Commander in Chief to introduce United States Armed Forces into hostilities [] . . . [extend to] a national emergency created by attack upon the United States, its territories or possessions, or its armed forces.").

This constitutional authority includes the authority to order warrantless foreign intelligence surveillance within the United States, as all federal appellate courts, including at least four circuits, to have addressed the issue have concluded. *See, e.g., In re Sealed Case,* 310 F.3d 717, 742 (FISA Ct. of Rev. 2002) ("[A]ll the other courts to have decided the issue [have] held that the President did have inherent authority to conduct warrantless searches to obtain foreign intelligence information. . . . We take for granted that the President does have that authority. . . ."). The Supreme Court has said that warrants are generally required in the context of purely *domestic* threats, but it expressly distinguished *foreign* threats. *See United States v. United States District Court,* 407 U.S. 297, 308 (1972). As Justice Byron White recognized almost 40 years ago, Presidents have long exercised the authority to conduct warrantless surveillance for national security purposes, and a warrant is unnecessary "if the President of the United States or his chief legal officer, the Attorney General, has considered the requirements of national security and authorized electronic surveillance as reasonable." *Katz v. United States,* 389 U.S. 347, 363-364 (1967) (White, J., concurring).

The President's constitutional authority to direct the NSA to conduct the activities he described is supplemented by statutory authority under the AUMF. The AUMF authorizes the President "to use all necessary and appropriate force against those nations, organizations, or persons he determines planned, authorized, committed, or aided the terrorists attacks of September 11, 2001, . . . in order to prevent any future acts of international terrorism against the United States." §2(a). The AUMF clearly contemplates action within the United States, *see also id.* pmbl. (the attacks of September 11 "render it both necessary and appropriate that the United States exercise its rights to self-defense and to protect United States citizens both at home and abroad"). The AUMF cannot be read as limited to authorizing the use of force against Afghanistan, as some have argued. Indeed, those who directly "committed" the attacks of September 11 resided in the United States for months before those attacks. The reality of the September 11 plot demonstrates that the authorization of force covers activities both on foreign soil and in America.

In *Hamdi v. Rumsfeld,* 542 U.S. 507 (2004), the Supreme Court addressed the scope of the AUMF. At least five Justices concluded that the AUMF authorized the President to detain a U.S. citizen in the United States because "detention to prevent a combatant's return to the battlefield is a fundamental incident of waging war" and is therefore included in the "necessary and appropriate force" authorized by the Congress. *Id.* at 518-519 (plurality opinion of O'Connor, J.); *see id.* 587 (Thomas, J., dissenting). These five Justices concluded that the AUMF "clearly and unmistakably authorize[s]" the "fundamental incident[s] of waging war." *Id.* at 518-19 (plurality opinion); *see id.* at 587 (Thomas, J., dissenting).

Communications intelligence targeted at the enemy is a fundamental incident of the use of military force. Indeed, throughout history, signals intelligence has formed a critical part of waging war. In the Civil War, each side tapped the telegraph lines of the other. In the World Wars, the United States intercepted telegrams into and out of the country. The AUMF cannot be read to exclude this long-recognized and essential authority to conduct communications intelligence targeted at the enemy. We cannot fight a war blind. Because communications intelligence activities constitute, to use the language of *Hamdi*, a fundamental incident of waging war, the AUMF *clearly and unmistakably authorizes* such activities directed against the communications of our enemy. Accordingly, the President's "authority is at its maximum." *Youngstown Sheet & Tube Co. v. Sawyer*, 343 U.S. 579, 635 (1952) (Jackson, J., concurring); *see Dames & Moore v. Regan*, 453 U.S. 654, 668 (1981); *cf. Youngstown*, 343 U.S. at 585 (noting the absence of a statute "from which [the asserted authority] c[ould] be fairly implied").

The President's authorization of targeted electronic surveillance by the NSA is also consistent with the Foreign Intelligence Surveillance Act ("FISA"). Section 2511(2)(f) of title 18 provides, as relevant here, that the procedures of FISA and two chapters of title 18 "shall be the exclusive means by which electronic surveillance . . . may be conducted." Section 109 of FISA, in turn, makes it unlawful to conduct electronic surveillance, "except as authorized by statute." 50 U.S.C. §1809(a)(1). Importantly, section 109's exception for electronic surveillance "authorized by statute" is broad, especially considered in the context of surrounding provisions. *See* 18 U.S.C. §2511(1) ("Except as otherwise specifically provided *in this chapter* any person who — (a) intentionally intercepts . . . any wire, oral or electronic communication [] . . . shall be punished. . . .") (emphasis added); *id.* §2511(2)(e) (providing a defense to liability to individuals "conduct[ing] electronic surveillance, . . . as authorized by *that Act [FISA]*") (emphasis added).

By expressly and broadly excepting from its prohibition electronic surveillance undertaken "as authorized by statute," section 109 of FISA permits an exception to the "procedures" of FISA referred to in U.S.C. §2511(2)(f) where authorized by another statute, even if the other authorizing statute does not specifically amend section 2511(2)(f). The AUMF satisfies section 109's requirement for statutory authorization of electronic surveillance, just as a majority of the Court in *Hamdi* concluded that it satisfies the requirement in 18 U.S.C. §4001(a) that no U.S. citizen be detained by the United States "except pursuant to an Act of Congress." *See Hamdi*, 542 U.S. at 519 (explaining that "it is of no moment that the AUMF does not use specific language of detention"); *see id.* at 587 (Thomas, J., dissenting).

Some might suggest that FISA could be read to require that a subsequent statutory authorization must come in the form of an amendment to FISA itself. But under established principles of statutory construction, the AUMF and FISA must be construed in harmony to avoid any potential conflict between FISA and the President's Article II authority as Commander in Chief. *See, e.g., Zadvydas v. Davis*, 533 U.S. 678, 689 (2001); *INS v. St. Cyr*, 533 U.S. 289, 300 (2001). Accordingly, any ambiguity as to whether the AUMF is a statute that satisfies the requirements of FISA and allows electronic surveillance in the conflict with al Qaeda without complying with FISA procedures must be resolved in favor of an interpretation that is consistent with the President's long-recognized authority.

The NSA activities described by the President are also consistent with the Fourth Amendment and the protection of civil liberties. The Fourth Amendment's "central requirement is one of reasonableness." *Illinois v. McArthur*, 531 U.S. 326, 330 (2001) (internal quotation marks omitted). For searches conducted in the course of ordinary criminal law enforcement, reasonableness generally requires securing a warrant. *See Bd. of Educ. v. Earls*, 536 U.S. 822, 828 (2002). Outside the ordinary criminal law enforcement context, however, the Supreme Court has, at times, dispensed with the warrant, instead adjudging the reasonableness of a search under the totality of the circumstances. *See United States v. Knights*, 534 U.S. 112, 118 (2001). In particular, the Supreme Court has long recognized that "special needs, beyond the normal need for law enforcement," can justify departure from the usual warrant requirement. *Vernonia School Dist. 47J v. Acton*, 515 U.S. 646, 653 (1995); *see also City of Indianapolis v. Edmond*, 531 U.S. 32, 41-42 (2000) (striking down checkpoint where "primary purpose was to detect evidence of ordinary criminal wrongdoing").

Foreign intelligence collection, especially in the midst of an armed conflict in which the adversary has already launched catastrophic attacks within the United States, fits squarely within the "special needs" exception to the warrant requirement. Foreign intelligence collection undertaken to prevent further devastating attacks on our Nation serves the highest government purpose through means other than traditional law enforcement. *See In re Sealed Case*, 310 F.3d at 745; *United States v. Duggan*, 743 F.2d 59, 72 (2d Cir. 1984) (recognizing that the Fourth Amendment implications of foreign intelligence surveillance are far different from ordinary wiretapping, because they are not principally used for criminal prosecution).

Intercepting communications into and out of the United States of persons linked to al Qaeda in order to detect and prevent a catastrophic attack is clearly *reasonable*. Reasonableness is generally determined by "balancing the nature of the intrusion on the individual's privacy against the promotion of legitimate governmental interests." *Earls*, 536 U.S. at 829. There is undeniably an important and legitimate privacy interest at stake with respect to the activities described by the President. That must be balanced, however, against the Government's compelling interest in the security of the Nation, *see, e.g., Haig v. Agee*, 453 U.S. 280, 307 (1981) ("It is obvious and unarguable that no governmental interest is more compelling than the security of the Nation.") (citation and quotation marks omitted). The fact that the NSA activities are reviewed and reauthorized approximately every 45 days to ensure that they continue to be necessary and appropriate further demonstrates the reasonableness of these activities.

As explained above, the President determined that it was necessary following September 11 to create an early warning detection system. FISA could not have provided the speed and agility required for the early warning detection system. In addition, any legislative change, other than the AUMF, that the President might have sought specifically to create such an early warning system would have been public and would have tipped off our enemies concerning our intelligence limitations and capabilities. Nevertheless, I want to stress that the United States makes full use of FISA to address the terrorist threat, and FISA has proven to be a very important tool, especially in longer-term investigations. In addition, the United States is constantly assessing all available legal options, taking full advantage of any developments in the law.

We hope this information is helpful.

Sincerely,
William E. Moschella
Assistant Attorney General

Notes and Questions

1. *The Predicate Legal Standard for Surveillance.* As indicated in the Justice Department letter, the TSP conducted surveillance of persons "linked to al Qaeda or an affiliated terrorist organization." How do you suppose it was determined whether a

person fit that description? What legal standard would govern such a determination? In written answers to questions raised by Senators at a July 26, 2006, Senate Judiciary Committee hearing, NSA Director Keith B. Alexander stated that

> professional intelligence officers at [NSA], with the assistance of other elements of the Intelligence Community and subject to appropriate and vigorous oversight by the NSA Inspector General and General Counsel, among others, would rely on the best available intelligence information to determine whether there are reasonable grounds to believe that a party to an international communication is affiliated with al Qaeda. [Senator Edward M. Kennedy, *FISA for the 21st Century: Questions for Lt. General Keith B. Alexander* (July 26, 2006), *available at* http://www.fas.org/irp/congress/2006_hr/alexander-qfr.pdf.]

Do you see any legal shortcomings in this description of the decision process and the legal standard for implementing TSP surveillance?

2. *Applicability of FISA.* In considering the applicability of FISA to the TSP, you will want to look in particular at the language of 50 U.S.C. §1801(f):

> (f) "Electronic surveillance" means —
>
> (1) the acquisition by an electronic, mechanical, or other surveillance device of the contents of any wire or radio communication sent by or intended to be received by a particular, known United States person who is in the United States, if the contents are acquired by intentionally targeting that United States person, under circumstances in which a person has a reasonable expectation of privacy and a warrant would be required for law enforcement purposes;
>
> (2) the acquisition by an electronic, mechanical, or other surveillance device of the contents of any wire communication to or from a person in the United States, without the consent of any party thereto, if such acquisition occurs in the United States, but does not include the acquisition of those communications of computer trespassers that would be permissible under section 2511(2)(i) of Title 18;
>
> (3) the intentional acquisition by an electronic, mechanical, or other surveillance device of the contents of any radio communication, under circumstances in which a person has a reasonable expectation of privacy and a warrant would be required for law enforcement purposes, and if both the sender and all intended recipients are located within the United States....

Consider also the complete text of 18 U.S.C. §2511(2)(e) and (f), governing ordinary criminal warrants:

> (e) Notwithstanding any other provision of this title or section 705 or 706 of the Communications Act of 1934, it shall not be unlawful for an officer, employee, or agent of the United States in the normal course of his official duty to conduct electronic surveillance, as defined in section 101 of the Foreign Intelligence Surveillance Act of 1978, as authorized by that Act.
>
> (f) Nothing contained in this chapter or chapter 121 or 206 of this title, or section 705 of the Communications Act of 1934, shall be deemed to affect the acquisition by the United States Government of foreign intelligence information from international or foreign communications, or foreign intelligence activities conducted in accordance with otherwise applicable Federal law involving a foreign electronic communications system, utilizing a means other than electronic surveillance as defined in section 101 of the Foreign Intelligence Surveillance Act of 1978 [50 U.S.C. §1801], and procedures in this

chapter or chapter 121 and the Foreign Intelligence Surveillance Act of 1978 shall be the exclusive means by which electronic surveillance, as defined in section 101 of such Act, and the interception of domestic wire, oral, and electronic communications may be conducted.

In addition, consider §1809(a) of FISA (making unauthorized electronic surveillance a criminal offense) as it existed in 2001:

> A person is guilty of an offense if he intentionally—
>
> (1) engages in electronic surveillance under color of law except as authorized by statute; or
>
> (2) discloses or uses information obtained under color of law by electronic surveillance, knowing or having reason to know that the information was obtained through electronic surveillance not authorized by statute.

Are you persuaded by the DOJ analysis that FISA was inapplicable to the TSP?

3. Why Not FISA? The government has an enviable track record in the FISC. Why did it not seek a FISA order or orders for the TSP? In a January 2006 address, Attorney General Alberto R. Gonzales defended the decision not to rely on FISA:

> Some have pointed to the provision in FISA that allows for so-called "emergency authorizations" of surveillance for 72 hours without a court order. There's a serious misconception about these emergency authorizations. People should know that we do not approve emergency authorizations without knowing that we will receive court approval within 72 hours. FISA requires the Attorney General to determine IN ADVANCE that a FISA application for that particular intercept will be fully supported and will be approved by the court before an emergency authorization may be granted. That review process can take precious time. Thus, to initiate surveillance under a FISA emergency authorization, it is not enough to rely on the best judgment of our intelligence officers alone. Those intelligence officers would have to get the sign-off of lawyers at the NSA that all provisions of FISA have been satisfied, then lawyers in the Department of Justice would have to be similarly satisfied, and finally as Attorney General, I would have to be satisfied that the search meets the requirements of FISA. And we would have to be prepared to follow up with a full FISA application within the 72 hours. [Prepared Remarks for Attorney General Alberto R. Gonzales, Georgetown University Law Center (Jan. 24, 2006), *available at* http://www.justice.gov/archive/ag/speeches/2006/ag_speech_0601241.html.]

In evaluating the Attorney General's statement, consider FISA's emergency surveillance provisions, quoted *supra* p. 628. Do you believe he was justified in bypassing the FISA procedures?

4. The AUMF as Authority for the TSP? Recall that the September 18, 2001, Authorization for the Use of Military Force (AUMF), authorizes the President to

> use all necessary and appropriate force against those nations, organizations, or persons he determines planned, authorized, committed, or aided the terrorist attacks that occurred on September 11, 2001, or harbored such organizations, or persons, in order to prevent any future acts of international terrorism against the United States by such nations, organizations or persons. [Pub. L. No. 107-40, §2(a), 115 Stat. 224, 224 (2001).]

Did it thereby authorize the TSP? Is it relevant to your answer that in the USA Patriot Act, enacted in October 2001, *after* the AUMF, Congress amended FISA by, *inter alia,* extending the period of emergency surveillance from 24 hours to 72 hours, or that it left in place the following FISA provision?

> Notwithstanding any other law, the President, through the Attorney General, may authorize electronic surveillance without a court order under this subchapter to acquire foreign intelligence information for a period not to exceed fifteen calendar days following a declaration of war by the Congress. [50 U.S.C. §1811 (2018).]

In light of the comprehensive scheme detailed in FISA, should the more open-ended grant of authority in the AUMF be read to have authorized the TSP? Does that grant satisfy the "clear statement" requirement of decisions like *Greene v. McElroy*, 360 U.S. 474 (1959), *supra* p. 101?

5. *Inherent Constitutional Authority?* In light of all the foregoing, did President Bush have inherent constitutional authority to order the TSP? Consider the President's exchange with a reporter at a December 19, 2005, press conference:

> Q... [W]hy did you skip the basic safeguards of asking courts for permission for the intercepts?
>
> THE PRESIDENT: First of all, I — right after September the 11th, I knew we were fighting a different kind of war. And so I asked people in my administration to analyze how best for me and our government to do the job people expect us to do, which is to detect and prevent a possible attack. That's what the American people want. We looked at the possible scenarios. And the people responsible for helping us protect and defend came forth with the current program, because it enables us to move faster and quicker. And that's important. We've got to be fast on our feet, quick to detect and prevent.
>
> We use FISA still — you're referring to the FISA court in your question — of course, we use FISA. But FISA is for long-term monitoring. What is needed in order to protect the American people is the ability to move quickly to detect.
>
> Now, having suggested this idea, I then, obviously, went to the question, is it legal to do so? I am — I swore to uphold the laws. Do I have the legal authority to do this? And the answer is, absolutely. As I mentioned in my remarks, the legal authority is derived from the Constitution, as well as the authorization of force by the United States Congress. [Press Conference of the President, 2 Pub. Papers 1875 (Dec. 19, 2005), https://georgewbush-whitehouse.archives.gov/news/releases/2005/12/text/20051219-2.html.]

Are you persuaded by the President's statement? Consider the arguments made in the Justice Department letter. If you think there is a clash between the President's claim of authority and the statutes — placing the TSP in Justice Jackson's third category — how should we resolve it?

6. *The Fourth Amendment.* If the President had inherent constitutional authority for the TSP, notwithstanding any statute, did he also escape the strictures of the Fourth Amendment? If not, did the program violate that provision? A few weeks after the September 11 attacks, Office of Legal Counsel (OLC) lawyers John Yoo and Robert Delahunty prepared a memorandum for White House Counsel Gonzales and DOD General Counsel William J. Haynes II, offering advice on the authority for the use of

military force to prevent or deter terrorist activity inside the United States. *Memorandum for Alberto R. Gonzales & William J. Haynes, II, Authority for Use of Military Force to Combat Terrorist Activities Within the United States* (Oct. 23, 2001), *available at* http://www.fas.org/irp/agency/doj/olc/milforce.pdf. The authors argued that the President has expanded wartime powers that overcome Fourth Amendment requirements:

> [H]owever well suited the warrant and probable cause requirements may be as applied to criminal investigations or to other law enforcement activities, they are unsuited to the demands of wartime and the military necessity to successfully prosecute a war against an enemy. In the circumstances created by the September 11 attacks, the Constitution provides the Government with expanded powers to prosecute the war effort. . . .
>
> In light of the well-settled understanding that constitutional constraints must give way in some respects to the exigencies of war, we think that the better view is that the Fourth Amendment does *not* apply to domestic military operations designed to deter and prevent further terrorist attacks. [*Id.* at 24-25.]

Are you persuaded?

7. *Investigating the DOJ Lawyers?* In March 2004, then-Deputy Attorney General (later FBI Director) James B. Comey, acting for a hospitalized Attorney General John Ashcroft, refused to sign off on a reauthorization of the TSP. *See* Harold H. Bruff, *Bad Advice: Bush's Lawyers in the War on Terror* 152-154 (2009). The expiring TSP was reauthorized the next day without DOJ approval. Comey considered resigning, and he learned that Ashcroft, FBI Director Mueller, and OLC head Jack Goldsmith would join him. *Id.* at 154. In a later speech to the staff at the NSA, Comey said that the lawyer is

> the custodian of our Constitution and the rule of law. It is the job of a good lawyer to say "yes." It is as much the job of a good lawyer to say "no." "No" is much, much harder. "No" must be spoken into a storm of crisis, with loud voices all around, with lives hanging in the balance. . . . It takes an understanding that, in the long-run, intelligence under law is the only sustainable intelligence in this country. [James B. Comey, *Intelligence Under the Law,* 10 Green Bag 2d 439, 444 (2007).]

In 2006, more than 40 members of Congress requested that the Department of Justice Office of Professional Responsibility (OPR) investigate whether DOJ lawyers acted properly in approving the TSP. After OPR opened an investigation, the head of OPR requested that he and six OPR employees be given security clearances so that they could start their work. Apparently on the advice of Attorney General Alberto Gonzales, President Bush denied the clearances, blocking the investigation. *See* Kathleen Clark, *The Architecture of Accountability: A Case Study of the Warrantless Surveillance Program,* 2010 BYU L. Rev. 357, 402.

B. THE FISA AMENDMENTS ACT AND THE FUTURE OF PROGRAMMATIC SURVEILLANCE

After the *New York Times* story broke in December 2005, the new NSA Director, Gen. Keith B. Alexander, briefed all FISC judges on the TSP in January 2006. On January 17, 2007, Attorney General Gonzales wrote to Senators Leahy and Specter of the Senate Judiciary Committee and advised them that on January 10, a FISC judge "issued orders authorizing the Government to target for collection international communications into or out of the United States where there is probable cause to believe that one of the communicants is a member or agent of al Qaeda or an associated terrorist organization." Letter from Attorney General Alberto R. Gonzales to Sens. Leahy and Specter (Jan. 17, 2007), *available at* http://www.fas.org/irp/congress/2007_cr/fisa011707.html. According to the Attorney General, these orders would "allow the necessary speed and agility" and, accordingly, all surveillance previously occurring under the TSP would thereafter be conducted with the approval of the FISC. *Id.* The initial FISC order reportedly approved the programmatic collection component of the TSP in part on the government's theory that the U.S. gateway or cable head through which communications passed were facilities used by agents of foreign powers under traditional FISA definitions.

However, a different FISC judge decided in May 2007 not to continue approval of the program. After a backlog in applications for traditional FISA orders developed, the Bush administration quickly urged Congress to pass specific statutory authorization for the program. In August 2007, Congress enacted the temporary Protect America Act (PAA), Pub. L. No. 110-55, 121 Stat. 552, which permitted the DNI and the Attorney General to authorize collection of foreign intelligence concerning persons reasonably believed to be outside the United States, without obtaining an order from the FISC, even if one party to the communication was a U.S. citizen inside the United States. The Protect America Act expired by its own terms in February 2008.

1. The Statutory Framework of the FAA

In July 2008, Congress enacted the FISA Amendments Act (FAA), Pub. L. No. 110-261, 122 Stat. 2436 (codified as amended at 50 U.S.C. §§1881a-1881g (2018)), adding Section 702 of FISA to authorize suspicionless programmatic surveillance targeting individuals outside the United States. As the ODNI General Counsel later explained it, Section 702 "extended the FISA Court's oversight to a kind of surveillance that Congress had originally placed outside of that oversight: the surveillance, for foreign intelligence purposes, of foreigners overseas," because Congress had originally (in 1978) not foreseen that the foreigners would be communicating by Internet communications routed through the United States. Robert S. Litt, *Privacy, Technology and National Security: An Overview of Intelligence Collection* (July 19, 2013). Although the FAA was originally scheduled to sunset at the end of 2012, the statutory authority as amended now extends to December 31, 2023.

In relevant part, Section 702 of FISA authorizes targeting of certain non-U.S. persons outside the United States and forbids "intentionally" targeting U.S. persons, subject to minimization procedures designed to limit the incidental and inadvertent collection, as well as the retention and dissemination, of U.S. person data. The FISC must find that the programmatic targeting and minimization procedures comply with Section 702 and the Fourth Amendment. The FISC does not review the foreign agency of particular targets or otherwise review individual applications under Section 702. Once that court approves the targeting *procedures*, the government may issue directives to electronic communication service providers compelling their assistance in acquiring communications. Pertinent parts of the Section 702 scheme appear below. Although we will generally use the Section 702 descriptor to refer to the programmatic surveillance program and its component parts, you should pay careful attention to the U.S.C. provisions so that you can match the text below to the programmatic elements.

50 U.S.C. §1881a. Procedures for targeting certain persons outside the United States other than United States persons

(a) Authorization — Notwithstanding any other provision of law, upon the issuance of an order in accordance with subsection (j)(3) or a determination under subsection (c)(2), the Attorney General and the Director of National Intelligence may authorize jointly, for a period of up to 1 year from the effective date of the authorization, the targeting of persons reasonably believed to be located outside the United States to acquire foreign intelligence information.

(b) Limitations — An acquisition authorized under subsection (a) —

(1) may not intentionally target any person known at the time of acquisition to be located in the United States;

(2) may not intentionally target a person reasonably believed to be located outside the United States if the purpose of such acquisition is to target a particular, known person reasonably believed to be in the United States;

(3) may not intentionally target a United States person reasonably believed to be located outside the United States;

(4) may not intentionally acquire any communication as to which the sender and all intended recipients are known at the time of the acquisition to be located in the United States;

(5) may not intentionally acquire communications that contain a reference to, but are not to or from, a target of an acquisition authorized under subsection (a), except as provided under section 103(b) of the FISA Amendments Reauthorization Act of 2017 [which allows NSA to restart such collection following a 30-day notice to Congress, which may act to stop the renewal of the practice with new legislation]; and

(6) shall be conducted in a manner consistent with the fourth amendment to the Constitution of the United States.

(c) Conduct of acquisition

(1) In general. An acquisition authorized under subsection (a) shall be conducted only in accordance with —

(A) the targeting and minimization procedures adopted in accordance with subsections (d) and (e); and

(B) upon submission of a certification in accordance with subsection (h), such certification. . . .

(d) Targeting procedures

(1) Requirement to adopt. The Attorney General, in consultation with the Director of National Intelligence, shall adopt targeting procedures that are reasonably designed to —

(A) ensure that any acquisition authorized under subsection (a) is limited to targeting persons reasonably believed to be located outside the United States; and

(B) prevent the intentional acquisition of any communication as to which the sender and all intended recipients are known at the time of the acquisition to be located in the United States. . . .

(e) Minimization procedures

(1) Requirement to adopt. The Attorney General, in consultation with the Director of National Intelligence, shall adopt minimization procedures that meet

the definition of minimization procedures under [§§1801(h), 1821(4)], as appropriate, for acquisitions authorized under subsection (a)....

(3) Publication. The Director of National Intelligence, in consultation with the Attorney General, shall —

(A) conduct a declassification review of any minimization procedures adopted or amended in accordance with paragraph (1); and

(B) consistent with such review, and not later than 180 days after conducting such review, make such minimization procedures publicly available to the greatest extent practicable, which may be in redacted form.

(f) Queries

(1) Procedures required

(A) Requirement to adopt. The Attorney General, in consultation with the Director of National Intelligence, shall adopt querying procedures consistent with the requirements of the fourth amendment to the Constitution . . . for information collected pursuant to an authorization under subsection (a).

(B) Record of United States person query terms. The Attorney General, in consultation with the Director of National Intelligence, shall ensure that the procedures adopted under subparagraph) include a technical procedure whereby a record is kept of each United States person query term used for a query.

(C) Judicial Review. The procedures adopted in accordance with subparagraph (A) shall be subject to judicial review pursuant to subsection (j).

(2) Access to results of certain queries conducted by FBI.

(A) Court order required for FBI review of certain query results in criminal investigations unrelated to national security. Except as provided in subparagraph (E), in connection with a predicated criminal investigation opened by the [FBI] that does not relate to the national security of the United States, the [FBI] may not access the contents of communications acquired under subsection (a) that were retrieved pursuant to a query made using a United States person query term that was not designed to find and extract foreign intelligence information unless —

(i) the [FBI] applies for an order of the Court under subparagraph (C); and

(ii) the Court enters an order under subparagraph (D) approving such application....

(E) Exception. The requirement for an order of the court order under subparagraph (A) to access the contents of communications . . . shall not apply with respect to a query if the [FBI] determines there is a reasonable belief that such contents could assist in mitigating or eliminating a threat to life or serious bodily harm.

(F) Rule of construction. Nothing in this paragraph may be construed as —

(i) limiting the authority of the [FBI] to conduct lawful queries of information acquired under subsection (a);

(ii) limiting the authority of the [FBI] to review, without a court order, the results of any query of any information acquired under subsection (a) that was reasonably designed to find and extract foreign intelligence information, regardless of whether such foreign intelligence information could also be considered evidence of a crime; or

(iii) prohibiting or otherwise limiting the ability of the [FBI] to access the results of queries conducted when evaluating whether to open an assessment or predicated investigation relating to the national security of the United States....

(h) Certification

(1) In general

(A) Requirement. Subject to subparagraph (B) [regarding exigent circumstances], prior to the implementation of an authorization under subsection (a), the Attorney General and the Director of National Intelligence shall provide to the Foreign Intelligence Surveillance Court a written certification [of compliance with targeting and minimization requirements] and any supporting affidavit, under oath and under seal, in accordance with this subsection....

(j) Judicial review of certifications and procedures

(1) In general

(A) Review by the Foreign Intelligence Surveillance Court. The Foreign Intelligence Surveillance Court shall have jurisdiction to review a certification submitted in accordance with subsection [(h)] and the targeting, minimization, and querying procedures adopted in accordance with subsections (d), (e), and (f)(1), and amendments to such certification or such procedures....

(3) Orders

(A) Approval. If the Court finds that a certification submitted in accordance with subsection (h) contains all the required elements and that the targeting, minimization, and querying procedures adopted in accordance with subsections (d), (e), and (f)(1) are consistent with the requirements of those subsections and with the fourth amendment to the Constitution of the United States, the Court shall enter an order approving the certification and the use, or continued use in the case of an acquisition authorized pursuant to a determination under subsection (c)(2), of the procedures for the acquisition....

50 U.S.C. §1881b. Certain acquisitions inside the United States targeting United States persons outside the United States

(a) Jurisdiction of the Foreign Intelligence Surveillance Court

(1) In general. The Foreign Intelligence Surveillance Court shall have jurisdiction to review an application and to enter an order approving the targeting of a United States person reasonably believed to be located outside the United States to acquire foreign intelligence information, if the acquisition constitutes electronic surveillance or the acquisition of stored electronic communications or stored electronic data that requires an order under this chapter, and such acquisition is conducted within the United States....

50 U.S.C. §1881c. Other acquisitions targeting United States persons outside the United States

(a) Jurisdiction and Scope...

(2) Scope. No element of the intelligence community may intentionally target, for the purpose of acquiring foreign intelligence information, a United States person reasonably believed to be located outside the United States under circumstances in which the targeted United States person has a reasonable expectation of privacy and a warrant would be required if the acquisition were conducted inside the United States for law enforcement purposes, unless a judge of the Foreign Intelligence Surveillance Court has entered an order with respect to such targeted United States person or the Attorney General has authorized an emergency acquisition pursuant to subsection (c) or (d), respectively, or any other provision of this chapter....

2. How 702 Collection Has Worked

Privacy and Civil Liberties Oversight Board,[1] Report on the Surveillance Program Operated Pursuant to Section 702 of the Foreign Intelligence Surveillance Act

pp. 5-8, July 2, 2014
available at https://www.pclob.gov/library/702-Report.pdf

A. Description and History of the Section 702 Program . . .

Section 702 permits the Attorney General and the Director of National Intelligence to jointly authorize surveillance targeting persons who are not U.S. persons, and who are reasonably believed to be located outside the United States, with the compelled assistance of electronic communication service providers, in order to acquire foreign intelligence information. Thus, the persons who may be targeted under Section 702 cannot intentionally include U.S. persons or anyone located in the United States, and the targeting must be conducted to acquire foreign intelligence information as defined in FISA. Executive branch authorizations to acquire designated types of foreign intelligence under Section 702 must be approved by the FISA court, along with procedures governing targeting decisions and the handling of information acquired.

Although U.S. persons may not be targeted under Section 702, communications of or concerning U.S. persons may be acquired in a variety of ways. An example is when a U.S. person communicates with a non-U.S. person who has been targeted, resulting in what is termed "incidental" collection. Another example is when two non-U.S. persons discuss a U.S. person. Communications of or concerning U.S. persons that are acquired in these ways may be retained and used by the government, subject to applicable rules and requirements. The communications of U.S. persons may also be collected by mistake, as when a U.S. person is erroneously targeted or in the event of a technological malfunction, resulting in "inadvertent" collection. In such cases, however, the applicable rules generally require the communications to be destroyed.

Under Section 702, the Attorney General and Director of National Intelligence make annual certifications authorizing this targeting to acquire foreign intelligence information, without specifying to the FISA court the particular non-U.S. persons who will be targeted. There is no requirement that the government demonstrate probable cause to believe that an individual targeted is an agent of a foreign power, as is generally required in the "traditional" FISA process under Title I of the statute. Instead, the Section 702 certifications identify categories of information to be collected, which must meet the statutory definition of foreign intelligence information. The certifications that have been authorized include information concerning international terrorism and other topics, such as the acquisition of weapons of mass destruction.

[1. In its 2004 report, the National Commission on Terrorist Attacks Upon the United States, known as the 9/11 Commission, recommended the creation of what is now the Privacy and Civil Liberties Oversight Board (PCLOB). An independent agency inside the executive branch, the PCLOB was established by statute in 2007 to ensure that efforts by the government to protect the nation from terrorism appropriately safeguard privacy and civil liberties. https://www.pclob.gov/. — Eds.]

Section 702 requires the government to develop targeting and "minimization" procedures that must satisfy certain criteria. As part of the FISA court's review and approval of the government's annual certifications, the court must approve these procedures and determine that they meet the necessary standards. The targeting procedures govern how the executive branch determines that a particular person is reasonably believed to be a non-U.S. person located outside the United States, and that targeting this person will lead to the acquisition of foreign intelligence information. The minimization procedures cover the acquisition, retention, use, and dissemination of any non-publicly available U.S. person information acquired through the Section 702 program.

Once foreign intelligence acquisition has been authorized under Section 702, the government sends written directives to electronic communication service providers compelling their assistance in the acquisition of communications. The government identifies or "tasks" certain "selectors," such as telephone numbers or email addresses, that are associated with targeted persons, and it sends these selectors to electronic communications service providers to begin acquisition. There are two types of Section 702 acquisition: what has been referred to as "PRISM" collection and "upstream" collection.

In PRISM collection, the government sends a selector, such as an email address, to a United States-based electronic communications service provider, such as an Internet service provider ("ISP"), and the provider is compelled to give the communications sent to or from that selector to the government. PRISM collection does not include the acquisition of telephone calls. The National Security Agency ("NSA") receives all data collected through PRISM. In addition, the Central Intelligence Agency ("CIA") and the Federal Bureau of Investigation ("FBI") each receive a select portion of PRISM collection.

Upstream collection differs from PRISM collection in several respects. First, the acquisition occurs with the compelled assistance of providers that control the telecommunications "backbone" over which telephone and Internet communications transit, rather than with the compelled assistance of ISPs or similar companies. Upstream collection also includes telephone calls in addition to Internet communications. Data from upstream collection is received only by the NSA: neither the CIA nor the FBI has access to unminimized upstream data. Finally, the upstream collection of Internet communications includes two features that are not present in PRISM collection: the acquisition of so-called "about" communications and the acquisition of so-called "multiple communications transactions" ("MCTs"). An "about" communication is one in which the selector of a targeted person (such as that person's email address) is contained within the communication but the targeted person is not necessarily a participant in the communication. Rather than being "to" or "from" the selector that has been tasked, the communication may contain the selector in the body of the communication, and thus be "about" the selector. An MCT is an Internet "transaction" that contains more than one discrete communication within it. If one of the communications within an MCT is to, from, or "about" a tasked selector, and if one end of the transaction is foreign, the NSA will acquire the entire MCT through upstream collection, including other discrete communications within the MCT that do not contain the selector.

Each agency that receives communications under Section 702 has its own minimization procedures, approved by the FISA court, that govern the agency's use, retention, and dissemination of Section 702 data. Among other things, these procedures include rules on how the agencies may "query" the collected data. The NSA, CIA, and FBI minimization procedures all include provisions permitting these agencies to query data acquired through Section 702, using terms intended to discover or retrieve communications content or metadata that meets the criteria specified in the query. These queries may include terms that identify specific U.S. persons and can be used to retrieve the already acquired communications of specific U.S. persons. Minimization procedures set forth the standards for conducting queries. For example, the NSA's minimization procedures require that queries of Section 702-acquired information be designed so that they are "reasonably likely to return foreign intelligence information."

The minimization procedures also include data retention limits and rules outlining circumstances under which information must be purged. Apart from communications acquired by mistake, U.S. persons' communications are not typically purged or eliminated from agency databases, even when they do not contain foreign intelligence information, until the data is aged off in accordance with retention limits.

Each agency's adherence to its targeting and minimization procedures is subject to extensive oversight within the executive branch, including internal oversight within individual agencies as well as regular reviews conducted by the Department of Justice ("DOJ") and the Office of the Director of National Intelligence ("ODNI"). The Section 702 program is also subject to oversight by the FISA court, including during the annual certification process and when compliance incidents are reported to the court. Information about the operation of the program also is reported to congressional committees. Although there have been various compliance incidents over the years, many of these incidents have involved technical issues resulting from the complexity of the program, and the Board has not seen any evidence of bad faith or misconduct. . . .

NSA Director of Civil Liberties and Privacy Office, NSA's Implementation of Foreign Intelligence Surveillance Act Section 702

pp. 4-8, Apr. 16, 2014
available at fas.org/irp/nsa/clpo-702.pdf

IDENTIFYING AND TASKING A SELECTOR

Next in the Section 702 process is for an NSA analyst to identify a non-U.S. person located outside the U.S. who has and/or is likely to communicate foreign intelligence information as designated in a certification. For example, such a person might be an individual who belongs to a foreign terrorist organization or facilitates the activities of that organization's members. Non-U.S. persons are not targeted unless NSA has reason to believe that they have and/or are likely to communicate foreign intelligence information as designated in a certification; U.S. persons are never targeted.

Once the NSA analyst has identified a person of foreign intelligence interest who is an appropriate target under one of the FISC-approved Section 702 certifications, that person is considered the target. The NSA analyst attempts to determine how, when, with whom, and where the target communicates. Then the analyst identifies specific communications modes used by the target and obtains a unique identifier associated with the target—for example, a telephone number or an email address. This unique identifier is referred to as a selector. The selector is not a "keyword" or particular term (e.g., "nuclear" or "bomb"), but must be a specific communications identifier (e.g., e-mail address).

Next the NSA analyst must verify that there is a connection between the target and the selector and that the target is reasonably believed to be (a) a non-U.S. person and (b) located outside the U.S. This is not a 51% to 49% "foreignness" test. Rather the NSA analyst will check multiple sources and make a decision based on the totality of the information available. If the analyst discovers any information indicating the targeted person may be located in the U.S. or that the target may be a U.S. person, such information must be considered. In other words, if there is conflicting information about the location of the person or the status of the person as a non-U.S. person, that conflict must be resolved before targeting can occur.

For each selector, the NSA analyst must document the following information: (1) the foreign intelligence information expected to be acquired, as authorized by a certification, (2) the information that would lead a reasonable person to conclude the selector is associated with a non-U.S. person, and (3) the information that would similarly lead a reasonable person to conclude that this non-U.S. person is located outside the U.S. This documentation must be reviewed and approved or denied by two senior NSA analysts who have satisfied additional training requirements.... Upon approval, the selector may be used as the basis for compelling a service provider to forward communications associated with the given selector. This is generally referred to as "tasking" the selector....

ACCESSING AND ASSESSING COMMUNICATIONS OBTAINED UNDER SECTION 702 AUTHORITY...

The NSA analyst must review a sample of communications received from the selectors to ensure that they are in fact associated with the foreign intelligence target and that the targeted individual or entity is not a U.S. person and is not currently located in the U.S. If the NSA analyst discovers that NSA is receiving communications that are not in fact associated with the intended target or that the user of a tasked selector is determined to be a U.S. person or is located in the U.S., the selector must be promptly "detasked." As a general rule, in the event that the target is a U.S. person or in the U.S., all other selectors associated with the target also must be detasked....

NSA PROCESSING AND ANALYSIS OF COMMUNICATIONS OBTAINED UNDER SECTION 702 AUTHORITY

Communications provided to NSA under Section 702 are processed and retained in multiple NSA systems and data repositories. One data repository, for example, might hold the contents of communications such as the texts of emails and recordings of conversations, while another, may only include metadata, i.e., basic information about the communication, such as the time and duration of a telephone call, or sending and receiving email addresses.

NSA analysts may access communications obtained under Section 702 authority for the purpose of identifying and reporting foreign intelligence. They access the information via "queries," which may be date-bound, and may include alphanumeric strings such as telephone numbers, email addresses, or terms that can be used individually or in combination with one another. FISC-approved minimization procedures govern any queries done on Section 702-derived information. NSA analysts with access to Section 702-derived information are trained in the proper construction of a query so that the query is reasonably likely to return valid foreign intelligence and minimizes the likelihood of returning non-pertinent U.S. person information. Access by NSA analysts to each repository is controlled, monitored, and audited. There are, for example, automated checks to determine if an analyst has completed all required training prior to returning information responsive to a query. Further, periodic spot checks on queries by NSA analysts are conducted.

Since October 2011 and consistent with other agencies' Section 702 minimization procedures, NSA's Section 702 minimization procedures have permitted NSA personnel to use U.S. person identifiers to query Section 702 collection when such a query is reasonably likely to return foreign intelligence information. NSA distinguishes between queries of communications content and communications metadata. NSA analysts must provide justification and receive additional approval before a content query using a U.S. person identifier can occur. . . . For example, NSA may seek to query a U.S. person identifier when there is an imminent threat to life, such as a hostage situation. NSA is required to maintain records of U.S. person queries and the records are available for review by both DOJ and ODNI as part of the external oversight process for this authority. Additionally, NSA's procedures prohibit NSA from querying Upstream data with U.S. person identifiers. . . .

NSA DISSEMINATION OF INTELLIGENCE DERIVED FROM COMMUNICATIONS OBTAINED UNDER SECTION 702 AUTHORITY

NSA only generates signals intelligence reports when the information meets a specific intelligence requirement, regardless of whether the proposed report contains U.S. person information. Dissemination of information about U.S. persons in any NSA foreign intelligence report is expressly prohibited unless that information is necessary to understand foreign intelligence information or assess its importance, contains evidence of a crime, or indicates a threat of death or serious bodily injury. Even if one or more of these conditions apply, NSA may include no more than the minimum amount of U.S. person information necessary to understand the foreign intelligence or to describe the crime or threat. For example, NSA typically "masks" the true identities of U.S. persons through use of such phrases as "a U.S. person" and the suppression of details that could lead to him or her being successfully identified by the context. Recipients of NSA reporting can request that NSA provide the true identity of a masked U.S. person referenced in an intelligence report if the recipient has a legitimate need to know the identity. Under NSA policy, NSA is allowed to unmask the identity only under certain conditions and where specific additional controls are in place to preclude its further dissemination, and additional approval has been provided by one of seven designated positions at NSA. Additionally, together DOJ and ODNI review the vast majority of disseminations of information about U.S. persons obtained pursuant to Section 702 as part of their oversight process. . . .

RETENTION OF UNEVALUATED COMMUNICATIONS OBTAINED UNDER SECTION 702 AUTHORITY

The maximum time that specific communications' content or metadata may be retained by NSA is established in the FISC-approved minimization procedures. The unevaluated content and metadata for PRISM or telephony data collected under Section 702 is retained for no more than five years. Upstream data collected from Internet activity is retained for no more than two years. NSA complies with these retention limits through an automated process.

NSA's procedures also specify several instances in which NSA must destroy U.S. person collection promptly upon recognition. In general, these include any instance where NSA analysts recognize that such collection is clearly not relevant to the authorized purpose of the acquisition nor includes evidence of a crime. Additionally, absent limited exceptions, NSA must destroy any communications acquired when any user of a tasked account is found to have been located in the U.S. at the time of acquisition. . . .

Notes and Questions

1. *Making Sense of the Statutory Framework.* Once technology evolved to the point where most Internet communications were routed through powerful hubs in the United States, intelligence agencies could keep tabs on non-U.S. persons abroad through surveillance tools available inside the United States. Instead of separate demonstrations of "foreign agency" for individual targets — so-called "retail surveillance" — the core purpose of Section 702 is to enable "wholesale surveillance" — broadly authorized collection inside the United States targeting non-U.S. persons reasonably believed to be abroad. No FISC or other judicial process authorizes or reviews the specific collection activities. Do you see how §1881a authorizes this broad scheme of programmatic intelligence collection?

2. *Role of the Attorney General and Director of National Intelligence.* What are the statutory responsibilities of the Attorney General and DNI in implementing Section 702? Note that the targeting and minimization procedures, as well as the certification to the FISC, are focused on the collection parameters mentioned above and the duty to prevent intentional collection of communications in which the sender and recipients are known to be in the United States. It is also important to recognize that these senior officials do not review proposed targets, only the procedures intelligence agencies will use to develop lists of targets. On the basis of what criteria will the Attorney General and DNI review the targeting and minimization procedures for each agency involved in the Section 702 program?

3. *Role of the Electronic Communication Providers.* Note that Section 702 compels the cooperation of ISPs and other communication providers in applying the selectors identified by the government. The service provider may, however, refuse to comply with a directive, thus requiring the government to petition the FISC to enforce the directive. On what possible bases could the FISC overturn a directive?

A service provider may object on behalf of the privacy interests of its customers. If a customer cannot object because she does not know of the planned surveillance, is the service provider an adequate stand-in for the customer before the FISC?

4. PRISM and Upstream Collection. The paradigmatic PRISM collection is a directive to Google or some other ISP to identify and deliver to NSA e-mail addresses associated with targeted persons. Telephone calls are not acquired through PRISM.

Upstream collection includes telephone and Internet communications, and it is implemented earlier in the communications cycle. In upstream collection, directives are delivered to the companies that control the "backbone" over which communications transit through the United States. An example could be a directive to capture screenshots of communications to, from, or about identified selector e-mail addresses or phone numbers that use an ISP in Pakistan. The upstream collection includes multiple communications transactions (MCTs), which will very often contain communications that do not involve the selector.

Which program is more prone to inadvertent collection of U.S. persons' communications?

5. Reverse Targeting. Can you see how the government could use the Section 702 process as a back-door method for collecting foreign intelligence on a target it knows to be in the United States? Do the safeguards in §1881a(b) convince you that such reverse targeting will not occur? What wiggle room remains for potential government overreach in reverse targeting, and how would you revise the scheme to make abuses less likely? Or is the problem not so much safeguarding against over-collection as it is protecting the collected data from untethered queries? See *infra* p. 675.

6. Extending FISA to U.S. Persons Abroad. In 50 U.S.C. §§1881b and 1881c, the FAA for the first time requires judicial approval of surveillance intentionally targeting a U.S. person reasonably believed to be abroad. Note that, unlike the programmatic collection authorized in 50 U.S.C. §1881a, these new provisions demand adherence to traditional FISC procedures for approval of collection from specific targets. What do you think might have prompted this change? Which Fourth Amendment test would apply to the intentional targeting of U.S. persons abroad? *See In re Terrorist Bombings of U.S. Embassies in East Africa (Fourth Amendment Challenges),* 552 F.3d 157 (2d Cir. 2008), *supra* p. 600.

7. Reforms. Aspects of the Section 702 program have been revised, particularly by the FISA Amendments Reauthorization Act of 2017, signed by President Trump after a short-term extension in January 2018, Pub. L. No. 115-118, 132 Stat. 3, and by executive branch reforms instituted independently of Congress.

3. Legal Analysis of 702 Collection

Reading *Case Title Redacted*

This peculiar title stems from redactions in this declassified 2011 opinion by a FISC judge. The FISC had previously approved collection programs under Section 702, and the Foreign Intelligence Court of Review had upheld a similar program under the 2007 Protect America Act in *In re Directives to Yahoo*, No. 08-01, 2008 WL 10632524 (FISA Ct. Rev. Aug. 22, 2008), *supra* p. 593. The following FISC opinion resulted from a government application for the court's reapproval of Section 702 collection. As the opinion reflects, the court originally understood the 702 collection effort to be narrower than the government later described it, "complicat[ing] its review."

- What was the court's original understanding of the 702 collection program? How did that change?
- How did the change affect the risk of collecting information about U.S. persons?
- Did the expansion of collection to include acquisition of Internet "MCTs" through the NSA's upstream collection violate Section 702's targeting limits?
- Did it violate Section 702's minimization requirements? If so, how?
- Did it violate the Fourth Amendment? If so, how?

[Case Title Redacted]

Foreign Intelligence Surveillance Court, Oct. 3, 2011
2011 WL 10945618

JOHN D. BATES, Judge. These matters are before the Foreign Intelligence Surveillance Court ("FISC" or "Court") on [the Government's Ex Parte Submissions of Reauthorization Certification and Related Procedures]....

I. BACKGROUND . . .

B. The May 2 "Clarification" Letter

On May 2, 2011, the government filed with the Court a letter pursuant to FISC Rule 13(a) titled "Clarification of National Security Agency's Upstream Collection Pursuant to Section 702 of FISA" ("May 2 Letter"). The May 2 Letter disclosed to the Court for the first time that NSA's "upstream collection" of Internet communications includes the acquisition of entire "transaction[s]" [redacted] According to the May 2 Letter, such transactions may contain data that is wholly unrelated to the tasked selector, including the full content of discrete communications that are not to, from, or about the facility tasked for collection. The letter noted that NSA uses [redacted] to ensure that "the person from whom it seeks to obtain foreign intelligence information is located overseas," but suggested that the government might lack confidence in the effectiveness of such measures as applied to Internet transactions....

[The Court first found that the NSA certification "contain[s] all the required elements" set forth in 50 U.S.C. §1881a(j)(2)(A).]

IV. REVIEW OF THE TARGETING AND MINIMIZATION PROCEDURES . . .

[The Court's review of NSA's targeting and minimization procedures revealed significant collection and use by NSA of U.S. person communications in the upstream variant of the Section 702 program. Recall that upstream collection of Internet communications included "about," as opposed to just "to/from" communications, and multiple communications transactions (MCTs) that contain more than one discrete communication inside the collected transaction. In addition to analyzing compliance with statutory requirements, the Court reviewed the upstream procedures for their consistency with the Fourth Amendment.]

D. The Effect of the Government's Disclosures Regarding NSA's Acquisition of Internet Transactions . . .

1. The Scope of NSA's Upstream Collection

NSA acquires more than two hundred fifty million Internet communications each year pursuant to Section 702, but the vast majority of these communications are obtained from Internet service providers and are not at issue here. Indeed, NSA's upstream collection constitutes only approximately 9% of the total Internet communications being acquired by NSA under Section 702.

Although small in relative terms, NSA's upstream collection is significant for three reasons. First, NSA's upstream collection is "uniquely capable of acquiring certain types of targeted communications containing valuable foreign intelligence information." [redacted]. Second, the Court now understands that, in order to collect those targeted Internet communications, NSA's upstream collection devices acquire Internet transactions, and NSA acquires millions of such transactions each year. Third, the government has acknowledged that, due to the technological challenges associated with acquiring Internet transactions, NSA is unable to exclude certain Internet transactions from its upstream collection.

In its June 1 Submission, the government explained that NSA's upstream collection devices have technological limitations that significantly affect the scope of collection. [redacted]. Moreover, at the time of acquisition, NSA's upstream Internet collection devices are generally incapable of distinguishing between transactions containing only a single discrete communication to, from, or about a tasked selector and transactions containing multiple discrete communications, not all of which may be to, from, or about a tasked selector.

As a practical matter, this means that NSA's upstream collection devices acquire any Internet transaction transiting the device if the transaction contains a targeted selector anywhere within it. . . .

. . . The Court now understands . . . that NSA has acquired, is acquiring, and, if the certifications and procedures now before the Court are approved, will continue to acquire, tens of thousands of wholly domestic communications. NSA's manual review of a statistically representative sample drawn from its upstream collection reveals that NSA acquires approximately 2,000-10,000 MCTs each year that contain *at least* one wholly domestic communication. In addition to these MCTs, NSA likely acquires tens of thousands *more* wholly domestic communications every year, given that NSA's upstream collection devices will acquire a wholly domestic "about" SCT if it is routed internationally. Moreover, the actual number of wholly domestic communications acquired may be still higher in view of NSA's inability conclusively to determine whether a significant portion of the MCTs within its sample contained wholly domestic communications. . . .

. . . [T]he Court previously understood that NSA's upstream collection would only acquire the communication of a United States person or a person in the United States if: 1) that person was in direct contact with a targeted selector; 2) the communication referenced the targeted selector, and the communication fell into one of [redacted] specific categories of "about" communications; or 3) despite the operation of the targeting procedures, United States persons or persons inside the United States were mistakenly targeted. [redacted]. But the Court now understands that, in addition to these communications, NSA's upstream collection also acquires: a) the communications of United States persons and persons in the United States that are not to, from, or about a tasked selector and that are acquired solely because the communication is contained within an MCT that somewhere references a tasked selector [redacted] and b) any Internet transaction that references a targeted selector, regardless of whether the transaction falls within one of the [redacted] previously identified categories of "about communications." . . .

In sum, then, NSA's upstream collection is a small, but unique part of the government's overall collection under Section 702 of the FAA. NSA acquires valuable information through its upstream collection, but not without substantial intrusions on Fourth Amendment-protected interests. Indeed, the record before this Court establishes that NSA's acquisition of Internet transactions likely results in NSA acquiring annually tens of thousands of wholly domestic communications, and tens of thousands of non-target communications of persons who have little or no relationship to the target but who are protected under the Fourth Amendment. Both acquisitions raise questions as to whether NSA's targeting and minimization procedures comport with FISA and the Fourth Amendment.

2. NSA's Targeting Procedures . . .

a. Targeting Persons Reasonably Believed to Be Located Outside the United States . . .

. . . With regard to "about" communications, the Court previously found that the user of the tasked facility was the "target" of the acquisition, because the government's purpose in acquiring such communications is to obtain information about that user. Moreover, the communication is not acquired because the government has any interest in the parties to the communication, other than their potential relationship to the user of the tasked facility, and the parties to an "about" communication do not become targets unless and until they are separately vetted under the targeting procedures. In the case of "about" MCTs — *i.e.*, MCTs that are acquired because a targeted selector is referenced somewhere in the transaction — NSA acquires not only the discrete communication that references the tasked selector, but also in many cases the contents of other discrete communications that do not reference the tasked selector and to which no target is a party. [redacted] By acquiring such MCTs, NSA likely acquires tens of thousands of additional communications of non-targets each year, many of whom have no relationship whatsoever with the user of the tasked selector. While the Court has concerns about NSA's acquisition of these non-target communications, the Court accepts the government's representation that the "sole reason [a non-target's MCT] is selected for acquisition is that it contains the presence of a tasked selector used by a person who has been subjected to NSA's targeting procedures." Moreover, at the time of acquisition, NSA's upstream collection devices often lack the capability to determine whether a transaction contains a single communication or multiple communications, or to identify the parties to any particular communication within a transaction. *See id.* Therefore, the Court has no reason to believe that NSA, by acquiring Internet transactions containing multiple communications, is targeting anyone other than the user of the tasked selector. *See United States v. Chemical Found., Inc.*, 272 U.S. 1, 14-15 (1926) ("The presumption of regularity supports the official acts of public officers, and, in the absence of clear evidence to the contrary, courts presume that they have properly discharged their official duties.").

b. Acquisition of Wholly Domestic Communications

... [T]he government knowingly acquires tens of thousands of wholly domestic communications each year. At first blush, it might seem obvious that targeting procedures that permit such acquisitions could not be "reasonably designed... to prevent the intentional acquisition of any communication as to which the sender and all intended recipients are known at the time of the acquisition to be located in the United States." 50 U.S.C. §1881a(d)(1)(B). However, a closer examination of the language of the statute leads the Court to a different conclusion.

The government focuses primarily on the "intentional acquisition" language in Section 1881a(d)(1)(B). Specifically, the government argues that NSA is not "intentionally" acquiring wholly domestic communications because the government does not intend to acquire transactions containing communications that are wholly domestic and has implemented technical means to prevent the acquisition of such transactions. This argument fails for several reasons.

NSA targets a person under Section 702 certifications by acquiring communications to, from, or about a selector used by that person. Therefore, to the extent NSA's upstream collection devices acquire an Internet transaction containing a single, discrete communication that is to, from, or about a tasked selector, it can hardly be said that NSA's acquisition is "unintentional." In fact, the government has argued, and the Court has accepted, that the government intentionally acquires communications to and from a target, even when NSA reasonably—albeit mistakenly—believes that the target is located outside the United States. *See* Docket No. [redacted].

With respect to MCTs, the sole reason NSA acquires such transactions is the presence of a tasked selector within the transaction. Because it is technologically infeasible for NSA's upstream collection devices to acquire only the discrete communication to, from, or about a tasked selector that may be contained within an MCT, however, the government argues that the only way to obtain the foreign intelligence information found within the discrete communication is to acquire the entire transaction in which it is contained. As a result, the government intentionally acquires all discrete communications within an MCT, including those that are not to, from or about a tasked selector....

The government argues that an NSA analyst's post-acquisition discovery that a particular Internet transaction contains a wholly domestic communication should retroactively render NSA's acquisition of that transaction "unintentional." That argument is unavailing. NSA's collection devices are set to acquire transactions that contain a reference to the targeted selector. When the collection device acquires such a transaction, it is functioning precisely as it is intended, even when the transaction includes a wholly domestic communication. The language of the statute makes clear that it is the government's intention at the *time of acquisition* that matters, and the government conceded as much at the hearing in this matter.

Accordingly, the Court finds that NSA intentionally acquires Internet transactions that reference a tasked selector through its upstream collection with the knowledge that there are tens of thousands of wholly domestic communications contained within those transactions. But this is not the end of the analysis. To return to the language of the statute, NSA's targeting procedures must be reasonably designed to prevent the intentional acquisition of "*any communication* as to which the sender and all intended recipients are *known at the time of acquisition* to be located in the United States." 50 U.S.C. §1881a(d)(1)(B) (emphasis added). The underscored language requires an acquisition-by-acquisition inquiry. Thus, the Court must consider whether, at the time NSA intentionally acquires a transaction through its upstream collection, NSA will know that the sender and all intended recipients of any particular communication within that transaction are located in the United States. . . .

Given that NSA's upstream collection devices lack the capacity to detect wholly domestic communications at the time an Internet transaction is acquired, the Court is inexorably led to the conclusion that the targeting procedures are "reasonably designed" to prevent the intentional acquisition of any communication as to which the sender and all intended recipients are known at the time of the acquisition to be located in the United States. This is true despite the fact that NSA knows with certainty that the upstream collection, viewed as a whole, results in the acquisition of wholly domestic communications.

By expanding its Section 702 acquisitions to include the acquisition of Internet transactions through its upstream collection, NSA has, as a practical matter, circumvented the spirit of Section 1881a(b)(4) and (d)(1) with regard to that collection. NSA's knowing acquisition of tens of thousands of wholly domestic communications through its upstream collection is a cause of concern for the Court. But the meaning of the relevant statutory provision is clear and application to the facts before the Court does not lead to an impossible or absurd result. The Court's review does not end with the targeting procedures, however. The Court must also consider whether NSA's minimization procedures are consistent with §1881a(e)(1) and whether NSA's targeting and minimization procedures are consistent with the requirements of the Fourth Amendment.

3. NSA's Minimization Procedures, As Applied to MCTs in the Manner Proposed by the Government Do Not Meet FISA's Definition of "Minimization Procedures". . .

b. Proposed Minimization Measures for MCTs

The government proposes that NSA's minimization procedures be applied to MCTs in the following manner. After acquisition, upstream acquisitions, including MCTs, will reside in NSA repositories until they are accessed (*e.g.*, in response to a query) by an NSA analyst performing his or her day-to-day work. NSA proposes adding a "cautionary banner" to the tools its analysts use to view the content of communications acquired through upstream collection under Section 702. The banner, which will be "broadly displayed on [such] tools," will "direct analysts to consult guidance on how to identify MCTs and how to handle them." Analysts will be trained to identify MCTs and to recognize wholly domestic communications contained within MCTs.

When an analyst identifies an upstream acquisition as an MCT, the analyst will decide whether or not he or she "seek[s] to use a discrete communication within

[the] MCT," presumably by reviewing some or all of the MCT's contents. *Id.* at 8. "NSA analysts seeking to use a discrete communication contained in an MCT (for example, in a FISA application, intelligence report, or Section 702 targeting) will assess whether the discrete communication is to, from, or about a tasked selector." *Id.* [NSA then applies an internal framework in deciding whether to use an MCT.] . . .

c. Statutory Analysis

i. Acquisition

. . . Insofar as NSA likely acquires approximately 2,000-10,000 MCTs each year that contain at least one wholly domestic communication that is neither to, from, nor about a targeted selector, and tens of thousands of communications of or concerning United States persons with no direct connection to any target, the Court has serious concerns. The acquisition of such non-target communications, which are highly unlikely to have foreign intelligence value, obviously does not by itself serve the government's need to "obtain, produce, and disseminate foreign intelligence information." *See* 50 U.S.C. §1801(h)(1).

The government submits, however, that the portions of MCTs that contain references to targeted selectors are likely to contain foreign intelligence information, and that it is not feasible for NSA to limit its collection only to the relevant portion or portions of each MCT — *i.e.*, the particular discrete communications that are to, from, or about a targeted selector. The Court accepts the government's assertion that the collection of MCTs yields valuable foreign intelligence information that by its nature cannot be acquired except through upstream collection. For purposes of this discussion, the Court further accepts the government's assertion that it is not feasible for NSA to avoid the collection of MCTs as part of its upstream collection or to limit its collection only to the specific portion or portions of each transaction that contains the targeted selector. The Court therefore concludes that NSA's minimization procedures are, given the current state of NSA's technical capability, reasonably designed to minimize the acquisition of nonpublicly available information concerning unconsenting United States persons consistent with the need of the United States to obtain, produce, and disseminate foreign intelligence information.

ii. Retention

The principal problem with the government's proposed handling of MCTs relates to what will occur, and what will *not* occur, following acquisition. . . . Rather than attempting to identify and segregate information "not relevant to the authorized purpose of the acquisition" or to destroy such information promptly following acquisition, NSA's proposed handling of MCTs tends to maximize the retention of such information, including information of or concerning United States persons with no direct connection to any target. *See* [NSA Minimization Procedures] §3(b)(1). . . .

It appears that NSA could do substantially more to minimize the retention of information concerning United States persons that is unrelated to the foreign intelligence purpose of its upstream collection. The government has not, for instance, demonstrated why it would not be feasible to limit access to upstream acquisitions to a smaller group of specially-trained analysts who could develop expertise in identifying and scrutinizing MCTs for wholly domestic communications and other discrete communications of or concerning United States persons. Alternatively, it is unclear why an analyst working within the framework proposed by the government should not be required, after identifying an MCT, to apply Section 3(b)(4) of the NSA minimization procedures to each discrete communication within the transaction. . . . Another potentially helpful step might be to adopt a shorter retention period for MCTs and unreviewed upstream communications so that such information "ages off" and is deleted from NSA's repositories in less than five years.

. . . Under the circumstances, the Court is unable to find that, as applied to MCTs in the manner proposed by the government, NSA's minimization procedures are "reasonably designed in light of the purpose and technique of the particular surveillance to minimize the . . . retention . . . of nonpublicly available information concerning unconsenting United States persons consistent with the need of the United States to obtain, produce, and disseminate foreign intelligence information." *See* 50 U.S.C. §§1801(h)(1) & 1821(4)(A).

iii. Dissemination . . .

As the Court understands it, no United States-person-identifying information contained in any MCT will be disseminated except in accordance with the general requirements of NSA's minimization procedures for "foreign communications" "of or concerning United States persons" that are discussed above. Specifically, "[a] report based on communications of or concerning a United States person may be disseminated" only "if the identity of the United States person is deleted and a generic term or symbol is substituted so that the information cannot reasonably be connected with an identifiable United States person." NSA Minimization Procedures §6(b). A report including the identity of the United States person may be provided to a "recipient requiring the identity of such person for the performance of official duties," but only if at least one of eight requirements is also met — for instance, if "the identity of the United States person is necessary to understand foreign intelligence information or assess its importance." . . . *Id.*

Communications as to which a United States person or a person inside the United States is a party are more likely than other communications to contain information concerning United States persons. And when such a communication is neither to, from, nor about a targeted facility, it is highly unlikely that the "need of the United States to disseminate foreign intelligence information" would be served by the dissemination of United States-person information contained therein. Hence, taken together, these measures will tend to prohibit the dissemination of information concerning unconsenting United States persons when there is no foreign-intelligence need to do so. Of course, the risk remains that information concerning United States persons will not be recognized by NSA despite the good-faith application of the measures it proposes. But the Court cannot say that the risk is so great that it undermines the reasonableness of the measures proposed by NSA with respect to the dissemination of information concerning United States persons. Accordingly, the Court concludes that NSA's minimization procedures are reasonably designed to "prohibit the dissemination[ ] of nonpublicly available information concerning unconsenting United States persons consistent with the need of the United States to . . . disseminate foreign intelligence information." *See* 50 U.S.C. §1801(h)(1).

4. *NSA'S Targeting and Minimization Procedures Do Not, as Applied to Upstream Collection that Includes MCTs, Satisfy the Requirements of the Fourth Amendment*...

The Court has assumed in the prior Section 702 Dockets that at least in some circumstances, account holders have a reasonable expectation of privacy in electronic communications, and hence that the acquisition of such communications can result in a "search" or "seizure" within the meaning of the Fourth Amendment. The government accepts the proposition that the acquisition of electronic communications can result in a "search" or "seizure" under the Fourth Amendment. Indeed, the government has acknowledged in prior Section 702 matters that the acquisition of communications from facilities used by United States persons located outside the United States "must be in conformity with the Fourth Amendment." The same is true of the acquisition of communications from facilities used by United States persons and others within the United States. *See United States v. Verdugo-Urquidez,* 494 U.S. 259, 271 (1990) (recognizing that "aliens receive constitutional protections when they have come within the territory of the United States and developed substantial connections with this country").

a. The Warrant Requirement

The Court has previously concluded that the acquisition of foreign intelligence information pursuant to Section 702 falls within the "foreign intelligence exception" to the warrant requirement of the Fourth Amendment. The government's recent revelations regarding NSA's acquisition of MCTs do not alter that conclusion. To be sure, the Court now understands that, as a result of the transactional nature of the upstream collection, NSA acquires a substantially larger number of communications of or concerning United States persons and persons inside the United States than previously understood. Nevertheless, the collection as a whole is still directed at [redacted] conducted for the purpose of national security — a purpose going "'well beyond any garden-variety law enforcement objective.'" *See id.* (quoting *In re Directives,* Docket No. 08-01, Opinion at 16 (FISA Ct. Rev. Aug. 22, 2008) (hereinafter "*In re Directives*")). Further, it remains true that the collection is undertaken in circumstances in which there is a "'high degree of probability that requiring a warrant would hinder the government's ability to collect time-sensitive information and, thus, would impede the vital national security interests that are at stake.'" *Id.* at 36 (quoting *In re Directives* at 18). Accordingly, the government's revelation that NSA acquires MCTs as part of its Section 702 upstream collection does not disturb the Court's prior conclusion that the government is not required to obtain a warrant before conducting acquisitions under NSA's targeting and minimization procedures.

b. Reasonableness

...As the Foreign Intelligence Surveillance Court of Review ("Court of Review") has explained, a court assessing reasonableness in this context must consider "the nature of the government intrusion and how the government intrusion is implemented. The more important the government's interest, the greater the intrusion that may be constitutionally tolerated." *In re Directives* at 19-20 (citations omitted), *quoted in* Docket No. [redacted]. The court must therefore

> balance the interests at stake. If the protections that are in place for individual privacy interests are sufficient in light of the government interest at stake, the constitutional scales will tilt in favor of upholding the government's actions. If, however, those protections are insufficient to alleviate the risks of government error and abuse, the scales will tip toward a finding of unconstitutionality.

Id. at 20 (citations omitted), *quoted in* Docket No. [redacted]. In conducting this balancing, the Court must consider the "totality of the circumstances." *Id.* at 19. Given the all-encompassing nature of Fourth Amendment reasonableness review, the targeting and minimization procedures are most appropriately considered collectively.

The Court has previously recognized that the government's national security interest in conducting acquisitions pursuant to Section 702 "'is of the highest order of magnitude.'" Docket No. [redacted] (quoting *In re Directives* at 20). The Court has further accepted the government's representations that NSA's upstream collection is "'uniquely capable of acquiring certain types of targeted communications containing valuable foreign intelligence information.'" Docket No. [redacted] (quoting government filing). There is no reason to believe that the collection of MCTs results in the acquisition of less foreign intelligence information than the Court previously understood.

Nevertheless, it must be noted that NSA's upstream collection makes up only a very small fraction of the agency's total collection pursuant to Section 702. As explained above, the collection of telephone communications under Section 702 is not implicated at all by the government's recent disclosures regarding NSA's acquisition of MCTs. Nor do those disclosures affect NSA's collection of Internet communications directly from Internet service providers [redacted], which accounts for approximately 91% of the Internet communications acquired by NSA each year under Section 702. And the government recently advised that NSA now has the capability, at the time of acquisition, to identify approximately 40% of its upstream collection as constituting discrete communications (non-MCTs) that are to, from, or about a targeted selector. Accordingly, only approximately 5.4% (40% of 9%) of NSA's aggregate collection of Internet communications (and an even smaller portion of the total collection) under Section 702 is at issue here. The national security interest at stake must be assessed bearing these numbers in mind....

Both in terms of its size and its nature, the intrusion resulting from NSA's acquisition of MCTs is substantial. The Court now understands that each year, NSA's upstream collection likely results in the acquisition of roughly two to ten thousand discrete wholly domestic communications that are neither to, from, nor about a targeted selector, as well as tens of thousands of other communications that are to or from a United States person or a person in the United States but that are neither to, from, nor about a targeted selector. In arguing that NSA's targeting and minimization procedures satisfy the Fourth Amendment notwithstanding the acquisition of MCTs, the government stresses that the number of protected communications acquired is relatively small in comparison to the total number of Internet communications obtained by NSA through its upstream collection. That is true enough, given the enormous volume of Internet transactions acquired by NSA through its upstream collection (approximately 26.5 million annually). But the number is small only in that relative sense. The Court recognizes that the ratio of non-target, Fourth Amendment-protected communications to the total number of communications must be considered in the Fourth Amendment balancing. But in conducting a review under the Constitution that requires consideration of the totality of the circumstances, *see In re Directives* at 19, the Court must also take into account the absolute number of non-target, protected communications that are acquired. In absolute terms, tens of thousands of non-target, protected communications annually is a *very* large number.

The nature of the intrusion at issue is also an important consideration in the Fourth Amendment balancing. *See, e.g., Board of Educ. v. Earls,* 536 U.S. 822, 832 (2002); *Vernonia Sch. Dist. 47J v. Acton,* 515 U.S. 646, 659 (1995). At issue here are the personal [redacted] communications of U.S. persons and persons in the United States. A person's "papers" are among the four items that are specifically listed in the Fourth Amendment as subject to protection against unreasonable search and seizure. Whether they are transmitted by letter, telephone or e-mail, a person's private communications are akin to personal papers. Indeed, the Supreme Court has held that the parties to telephone communications and the senders and recipients of written communications generally have a reasonable expectation of privacy in the contents of those communications. *See Katz* [*v. United States,* 389 U.S. 347 (1967),] at 352; *United States v. United States Dist. Ct. (Keith),* 407 U.S. 297, 313 (1972); *United States v. Jacobsen,* 466 U.S. 109, 114 (1984). The intrusion resulting from the interception of the contents of electronic communications is, generally speaking, no less substantial.

. . . [A]s the government correctly recognizes, the acquisition of non-target information is not necessarily reasonable under the Fourth Amendment simply because its collection is incidental to the purpose of the search or surveillance. There surely are circumstances in which incidental intrusions can be so substantial as to render a search or seizure unreasonable. To use an extreme example, if the only way for the government to obtain communications to or from a particular targeted [redacted] required also acquiring all communications to or from every other [redacted], such collection would certainly raise very serious Fourth Amendment concerns. Here, the quantity and nature of the information that is "incidentally" collected distinguishes this matter from the prior instances in which this Court and the Court of Review have considered incidental acquisitions. As explained above, the quantity of incidentally-acquired, non-target, protected communications being acquired by NSA through its upstream collection is, in absolute terms, very large, and the resulting intrusion is, in each instance, likewise very substantial. And with regard to the nature of the acquisition, the government acknowledged in a prior Section 702 docket that the term "incidental interception" is "most commonly understood to refer to an intercepted communication between a target using a facility subject to surveillance and a third party using a facility not subject to surveillance." Docket Nos. [redacted]. This is the sort of acquisition that the Court of Review was addressing in *In re Directives* when it stated that "incidental collections occurring as a result of constitutionally permissible acquisitions do not render those acquisitions unlawful." *In re Directives* at 30. But here, by contrast, the incidental acquisitions of concern are not direct communications between a non-target third party and the user of the targeted facility. Nor are they the communications of non-targets that refer directly to a targeted selector. Rather, the communications of concern here are acquired simply because they appear somewhere in the same *transaction* as a separate communication that is to, from, or about the targeted facility.

The distinction is significant and impacts the Fourth Amendment balancing. A discrete communication as to which the user of the targeted facility is a party or in which the targeted facility is mentioned is much more likely to contain foreign intelligence information than is a separate communication that is acquired simply because it happens to be within the same transaction as a communication involving a targeted facility. Hence, the national security need for acquiring, retaining, and disseminating the former category of communications is greater than the justification for acquiring, retaining, and disseminating the latter form of communication.

The Court of Review and this Court have recognized that the procedures governing retention, use, and dissemination bear on the reasonableness under the Fourth Amendment of a program for collecting foreign intelligence information. *See In re Directives* at 29-30; Docket No. [redacted] As explained in the discussion of NSA's minimization procedures above, the measures proposed by NSA for handling MCTs tend to maximize, rather than minimize, the retention of non-target information, including information of or concerning United States persons. Instead of requiring the prompt review and proper disposition of non-target information (to the extent it is feasible to do so), NSA's proposed measures focus almost exclusively on those portions of an MCT that an analyst decides, after review, that he or she wishes to use. . . . Accordingly, each analyst who retrieves an MCT and wishes to use a portion thereof is left to apply the proposed minimization measures alone, from beginning to end, and without the benefit of his colleagues' prior review and analysis. Given the limited review of MCTs that is required, and the difficulty of the task of identifying protected information within an MCT, the government's proposed measures seem to enhance, rather than reduce, the risk of error, overretention, and dissemination of non-target information, including information protected by the Fourth Amendment.

In sum, NSA's collection of MCTs results in the acquisition of a very large number of Fourth Amendment-protected communications that have no direct connection to any targeted facility and thus do not serve the national security needs underlying the Section 702 collection as a whole. . . . Under the totality of the circumstances, then, the Court is unable to find that the government's proposed application of NSA's targeting and minimization procedures to MCTs is consistent with the requirements of the Fourth Amendment. The Court does not foreclose the possibility that the government might be able to tailor the scope of NSA's upstream collection, or adopt more stringent post-acquisition safeguards, in a manner that would satisfy the reasonableness requirement of the Fourth Amendment.

V. CONCLUSION

For the foregoing reasons, the government's requests for approval of the certifications and procedures contained in the April 2011 Submissions are granted in part and denied in part. The Court concludes that one aspect of the proposed collection — the "upstream collection" of Internet transactions containing multiple communications, or MCTs — is, in some respects, deficient on statutory and constitutional grounds. . . .

Notes and Questions

1. The Aftermath. On November 30, 2011, less than two months after writing the opinion excerpted above, Judge Bates issued another opinion for the FISC approving amended NSA procedures. Later declassified, the more recent opinion, also heavily redacted, is available at http://www.dni.gov/files/documents/November%202011%20Bates%20Opinion%20and%20Order%20Part%201.pdf.

The amended procedures required NSA to restrict access to the portions of its ongoing upstream collection that are most likely to contain wholly domestic communications and non-target information that is subject to statutory or Fourth Amendment protection. Segregated Internet transactions can be moved to NSA's general repositories only after having been determined by a specially trained analyst not to contain a wholly domestic communication. Any transaction containing a wholly domestic communication (whether segregated or not) must be purged upon recognition. Any transaction moved from segregation to NSA's general repositories is permanently marked as having previously been segregated. On the non-segregated side, any discrete communication within an Internet transaction that an analyst wishes to use is subject to additional checks. NSA is not permitted to use any discrete, non-target communication that is determined to be to or from a U.S. person or a person who appears to be in the United States, other than to protect against an immediate threat to human life. Finally, all upstream acquisitions are retained for a default maximum period of two, rather than five, years.

Do these amendments to NSA procedures satisfy Section 702 requirements? Do they comply with the Fourth Amendment? As noted below, NSA eventually abandoned a portion of its upstream collection program. The targeting and minimization procedures have also been further revised.

2. *Upstream Targeting Redux — Identifying and Tasking a Selector.* NSA apparently relies on Section 702 collection to provide the basis for a form of link analysis, known as contact chaining, in which an analyst begins with some form of Internet identifier, typically an e-mail address — a "selector" — and then mines a database containing the collected information using algorithms to find other communications linked to the original source. Consider the following issues:

a. *Avoiding U.S. Persons — Section 702?* Does the process for identifying and tasking a selector sufficiently protect U.S. persons? A U.S. person is more likely to have her communications collected if she communicates with someone abroad. Given that U.S. person communications are intermingled with foreign communications collected from U.S. companies' fiberoptic cables in the United States, NSA collection has no way of ensuring that only non-U.S. person communications are scooped up. Upstream collection thus may inadvertently and incidentally acquire (many) communications of U.S. persons.

Why did the court reject the NSA's defense that incidental programmatic collection of U.S. person information is acceptable because it is *merely* incidental? What protections against collection from U.S. persons or others inside the United States are embedded in Section 702? *See* §1881a(b)(3), *supra* p. 652.

b. *Avoiding U.S. Persons — Fourth Amendment?* Even if the targeting and minimization procedures all satisfy Section 702, they also have to satisfy the Fourth Amendment, as there is no dispute that the government is conducting a search when it collects the content of Internet communications. But why does the Fourth Amendment apply at all when the NSA is chiefly targeting non-U.S. persons reasonably believed to be located outside the United States?

Assuming that the Fourth Amendment applies, why did the court excuse the warrant requirement?

Even though no warrant was required, the court applied a totality-of-the-circumstances test to determine the Section 702 program's reasonableness for purposes of the Fourth Amendment. Note that these circumstances included both the absolute and relative number of communications collected, the nature of the communications, and the scope and effectiveness of the minimization procedures. Do you agree with the court's balancing?

c. *Foreign Intelligence and Location.* The phrase "foreign intelligence" is pervasive in describing authorized collection activities, including programmatic collection under Section 702. Significantly, the term is still defined by geography: targeting under Section 702 is permitted only against those reasonably believed to be outside the United States. Massive quantities of the contents of e-mails and other electronic communications are collected on the basis of location. But how is location determined for this purpose? Can location abroad reasonably be presumed on the basis of a domain name or the identity of a service provider? If not, then how? Won't the adoption of such a presumption lead inevitably to collection from individuals inside the United States? If it will, does collection on this basis violate Section 702?

Look again at the NSA's own description of its targeting practices. Do they show that compliance with the statute's geographical limitations is either practical or possible?

3. Queries of Section 702 Data. The 2017 amendments to Section 702 require that intelligence agencies obtain FISC approval of rules for queries of incidentally collected data on Americans, 50 U.S.C. §1881a(f) (2018), *supra* p. 653. October 2019 releases of previously classified records and judicial opinions show that the FBI resisted the new requirements, however, and continued to query collected data for information involving large numbers of Americans who fit within general categories of intelligence interest, but against whom there was no individualized basis for suspicion. *See* Charlie Savage, *F.B.I. Practices for Intercepted Emails Violated 4th Amendment, Judge Ruled,* N.Y. Times, Oct. 8, 2019. In October 2018, the FISC approved querying procedures submitted by the CIA and the NSA, but rejected the FBI procedures as "inconsistent with statutory minimization requirements and the requirements of the Fourth Amendment." *Redacted,* 402 F. Supp. 3d 45, 51 (FISA Ct. 2018). The Bureau had been keeping track of all queries without distinguishing which sought information about Americans and which were focused on foreigners. The FBI also initially resisted the insistence of FISC Judge James E. Boasberg that in fashioning its queries the FBI document in writing how a proposed search term — such as an e-mail address or phone number — would be likely to return foreign intelligence or criminal evidence. Savage, *supra.* Rather than complying with the ruling and adjusting the rules, the FBI appealed to the FISCR, which affirmed the FISC decision in July 2019. *In re: DNI/AG 702(h) Certifications 2018* [*Redacted*], 941 F.3d 547 (FISA Ct. Rev. 2019). The Bureau then revised its procedures, and they were approved by the FISC. Document Regarding the Section 702 Certification (FISC Sept. 4, 2019).

The Bureau now presumably conducts large-batch queries trying to identify threats within the information the government has collected without waiting for a tip or criminal referral. Can you see a threat to Americans' Fourth Amendment privacy by such queries of data incidentally collected pursuant to Section 702? The pertinent documents and FISC and FISCR rulings pertaining to these Section 702 certifications may be found at https://icontherecord.tumblr.com/post/188217887058/release-of-documents-related-to-the-2018-fisa.

4. Ending Upstream "About" Collection. Perhaps because NSA was unable to develop technology to end the over-collection of U.S. person communications in its upstream program, it announced on April 28, 2017, that it would no longer collect "about" e-mails and texts exchanged by U.S. persons with persons abroad — those that simply mention identifying terms for foreign targets, but that are neither to nor from those targets. The announcement came after it was revealed that NSA analysts had violated the minimization procedures approved by the FISC in November 2011. Charlie Savage, *N.S.A. Halts Collection of Americans' Emails About Foreign Targets*, N.Y. Times, Apr. 28, 2017. The NSA called its failures to comply with the rules "inadvertent."

Why would NSA have decided to end "about" collection without being ordered to do so by a court? Can you predict the net intelligence losses and privacy gains likely to result from ending "about" collection?

Although reform advocates sought to codify the voluntary decision by NSA to end "about" collection in the upstream program, §1881a(b)(5), *supra* p. 652 (added by the 2017 amendments to the Section 702 program), allows NSA to restart "about" collection following notice to Congress, which may act to stop the renewal with new legislation. The 2017 reforms did not further limit incidental collection from U.S. persons.

Recall that the PRISM program does not collect "about" communications. Nor does the end of upstream "about" collection affect surveillance that occurs abroad, where most intelligence collection is governed by Executive Order No. 12,333.

5. Revising and Tightening Minimization Procedures. In 2016, the NSA informed the FISC that there had been "significant noncompliance" with procedures it submitted for the court's approval. *See* Jordan Brunner et al., *Foreign Intelligence Surveillance Court Approves New Targeting and Minimization Procedures: A Summary*, Lawfare, May 15, 2017. After reprimands from the FISC for the NSA's "lack of candor," the court approved new NSA Minimization Procedures, https://www.dni.gov/files/documents/icotr/51117/2016-NSA-702-Minimization-Procedures_Mar_30_17.pdf, and NSA Targeting Procedures, https://www.dni.gov/files/documents/icotr/51117/2016_NSA_702_Targeting_Procedures_Mar_30_17.pdf. *See [Case Title Redacted]* (FISA Ct. Apr. 26, 2017), https://www.dni.gov/files/documents/icotr/51117/2016_Cert_FISC_Memo_Opin_Order_Apr_2017.pdf.

Should Congress eliminate the geographic limiter altogether in favor of tighter minimization procedures for inevitably collected U.S. person communications under Section 702? If so, how should they be tightened? What did Judge Bates suggest?

Proposals include using automated filters to segregate communications involving U.S. persons from others, allowing the latter to be handled without much restriction; setting limits on the use of data that have been collected (e.g., for foreign intelligence purposes, not for unrelated criminal prosecution); requiring judicial approval before disseminating collected data; and using audit trails to hold officials accountable if they use data for impermissible purposes. *See* Markle Found., *Mobilizing Information to Prevent Terrorism* 65-71 (2006). Would some version of the proposed authorized-use rules would be preferable to minimization?

6. Presumption of Regularity. In finding that upstream collection of MCTs satisfies Section 702, Judge Bates invoked an administrative law "presumption of regularity" by which courts presume that government officials have properly discharged their duties. *Supra* p. 665. But that presumption is typically applied to the transparent actions of government officials acting on records available to the public, and subject, usually, to judicial review in public proceedings. The NSA, by contrast, acts in secret, on classified information, by processes unknown to the public (absent leaks). When those processes are subject to judicial review, they are reviewable ex parte and in camera before a largely secret court. The *Case Title Redacted* decision is a rare publicly released decision, yet still partially redacted.

Should the NSA be denied the benefit of the presumption in these circumstances? Or just the opposite — is it especially entitled to that benefit, given the extraordinary complexity of the technology it employs, the unusual burden a lay federal judge faces in understanding that technology, the national security sensitivity of the data, and the life-and-death stakes of the investigations and watch lists it supports?

In May 2012, an internal NSA audit, based only on Washington-area NSA facilities, found 2,776 incidents in the preceding 12 months of unauthorized collection, retention, access to, or distribution of protected communications. *NSAW SID Intelligence Oversight (IO) Quarterly Report — First Quarter Calendar Year 2012 (1 January-31 March 2012) — EXECUTIVE SUMMARY*, May 3, 2012, http://nsarchive.gwu.edu/NSAEBB/NSAEBB436/docs/EBB-044.pdf (classified "Top Secret"). Most of the incidents involved "roamers," foreign intelligence targets who entered the United States (thus negating the lawfulness of the targeting), unintentional database query errors, or similar mistakes. Scores of media reports decried the "thousands of privacy violations," while NSA compliance officers put the number in context. At 20 million agency queries of data each month, the error rate during the examined period in 2012 was asserted to be .00001156666. *See* Jennifer Rubin, *NSA Scandal or Near-Perfection?*, Wash. Post, Aug. 18, 2013. Does this relatively modest error rate support the presumption of regularity?

7. New Transparency. In response to FOIA lawsuits by the Electronic Frontier Foundation, the ACLU, and the *New York Times*, the ODNI has released a number of newly declassified Section 702 documents. These are collected at Off. of the Dir. of Nat'l Intelligence, *IC on the Record*, http://icontherecord.tumblr.com/tagged/declassified. Semi-annual reports on Section 702 compliance across the IC are available at https://icontherecord.tumblr.com/.

The growing number of such reports, along with other official disclosures by the FISC and the IC, have enabled the creation of a searchable table of violations. Robyn Greene, *A History of FISA Section 702 Compliance Violations*, New America Found., Sept. 28, 2017, https://www.newamerica.org/oti/blog/history-fisa-section-702-compliance-violations/.

8. Exclusivity Redux. The FAA includes this language regarding exclusivity:

> (a) Except as provided in subsection (b), the procedures of chapters 119, 121, and 206 of title 18 and this Act shall be the exclusive means by which electronic surveillance and the interception of domestic wire, oral, or electronic communications may be conducted.

> (b) Only an express statutory authorization for electronic surveillance or the interception of domestic wire, oral, or electronic communications, other than as an amendment to this Act or chapters 119, 121, or 206 of title 18 shall constitute an additional exclusive means for the purpose of subsection (a). [50 U.S.C. §1812.]

Why do you suppose this provision was enacted? Does it adequately express congressional determination to provide the exclusive rules for conducting electronic surveillance for foreign intelligence purposes? After its passage, could the President ever have a legal justification for circumventing the FAA?

9. The Constitutionality of Section 702 Redux. Would a lawsuit challenging the constitutionality of Section 702 on behalf of non-U.S. persons outside the United States have any chance of success after the Supreme Court's decision in *United States v. Verdugo-Urquidez*, 494 U.S. 259 (1990)? See *supra* p. 213. What about a case brought by U.S. persons? How would they be able to show an injury sufficient to confer standing? See *supra* p. 137. If a citizen or public interest organization has standing, would any such lawsuit survive invocation of the state secrets privilege? See *supra* p. 154.

Consider the use of intelligence derived from Section 702 surveillance in criminal prosecutions. Mohamed Osman Mohamud, a lawful permanent resident, was convicted of attempting to detonate a large bomb during the annual Christmas tree lighting ceremony in Pioneer Courthouse Square in Portland, Oregon in violation of 18 U.S.C. §2332a(a)(2)(A). *United States v. Mohamud*, No. 3:10-CR-475, 2014 WL 2866749 (D. Or. June 24, 2014). Mohamud challenged his conviction on multiple grounds, and after the government filed a notice that it had offered evidence derived from collection pursuant to Section 702 at trial, he moved to suppress any FISA-derived evidence on the ground that Section 702 violates the Fourth Amendment. The foreign intelligence the government used in prosecuting Mohamud, a U.S. person, was incidentally collected while targeting a non-U.S. person or persons reasonably believed to be abroad.

In *United States v. Mohamud*, 843 F.3d 420 (9th Cir. 2016), *cert. denied*, 138 S. Ct. 636 (2018), the Ninth Circuit affirmed the denial of a motion to suppress, holding that Section 702 does not violate the Fourth Amendment. The court found "that the most troubling aspect of this 'incidental' collection is . . . its volume, which is vast." *Id.* at 440. However, the court applied traditional Fourth Amendment reasonableness review to uphold the collection and noted that Section 702 collection "does increase the importance of minimization procedures once the communications are collected." *Id.* Because the target of the surveillance was a non-U.S. person located outside the United States at the time of the surveillance, no warrant was required to collect Mohamud's e-mails with that foreign national as an incident to its lawful surveillance. *Id.* How would you assess the Fourth Amendment privacy rights of Mohamud?

PROGRAMMATIC ELECTRONIC SURVEILLANCE FOR FOREIGN INTELLIGENCE: SUMMARY OF BASIC PRINCIPLES

- After 9/11, President George W. Bush secretly authorized the Terrorist Surveillance Program, which included (but was not limited to) warrantless surveillance of the content of international telephone and Internet communications to, from, or through the United States if there was probable cause to believe that any communicant was an agent of Al Qaeda or an associated terrorist organization.

- That surveillance was initially conducted without FISC authorization, based on claims of authority from the AUMF and from the President's inherent Article II authority. A FISC judge subsequently approved that surveillance under FISA, but another FISC judge refused to continue its approval.

- The Administration therefore sought and Congress approved an amendment to FISA adding Section 702, which authorizes programmatic surveillance. In relevant part, it:

  (a) authorizes acquisition of the content of electronic communications based upon the targeting of certain non-U.S. persons reasonably believed to be outside the United States;

  (b) forbids the direct or indirect intentional targeting of U.S. persons without a traditional FISA order (except in emergencies); and

  (c) requires periodic FISC approval that the government's programmatic procedures for targeting and minimization of acquired information comply with Section 702 and the Fourth Amendment, rather than approval of individual surveillance targets.

- "Discrete" Section 702 collection of communications to/from/about certain identifiers or selectors and attendant (not fully known) minimization procedures have been held to comply with both Section 702 and the Fourth Amendment. NSA abandoned "about" collection in 2017 due to technical limitations that prevent filtering out U.S. person communications.

- NSA targeting and minimization procedures for upstream Internet collection —collection of communications content as its transits Internet devices—of multi-communication transactions were initially held unreasonable under the Fourth Amendment, because of the inevitable acquisition of many wholly domestic and U.S. person communications that were neither to, from, nor about otherwise permissible selectors.

- Subsequently, the NSA's revised procedures for upstream collection have been held to satisfy the Fourth Amendment.

- Programmatic Section 702 surveillance poses several unresolved policy questions, among them whether U.S. person-based or geographical limitations are still practical for programmatic surveillance, and what minimization requirements can best protect privacy in light of the national security need for collection.

23

The Third-Party Doctrine: Origins and Applications

The conventional wisdom following the 9/11 terrorist attacks was that U.S. national security agencies failed to "connect the dots" before the attacks. But some experts noted that while there "certainly was a lack of dot-connecting before September 11," the more critical failure was that "[t]here were too few useful dots." Robert Bryant et al., *America Needs More Spies,* The Economist, July 12, 2003, at 30. In this chapter, we consider dots in the form of records about individuals and their transactions held by third parties like phone companies, Internet service providers, and banks.

We begin by exploring the origin and evolution of the "third-party doctrine," which holds that one who "voluntarily" conveys data to a third party has no reasonable expectation of privacy in those data. We then briefly summarize some applications of the doctrine to evolving kinds of records.

A. ORIGINS OF THE THIRD-PARTY DOCTRINE

Reading *Smith v. Maryland*

In this case, without first obtaining a warrant, the police placed a "pen register" on a criminal defendant's home landline telephone to record the numbers he dialed. He challenged the introduction of those numbers into evidence, raising the question whether the warrantless collection constituted a search subject to the Fourth Amendment. Applying the reasoning of its earlier decision in *Katz v. United States*, 389 U.S. 347 (1967), the Court considered whether Smith had a subjective expectation of privacy in the numbers he dialed, and whether that expectation was reasonable.

- What, exactly, is the information recorded by a pen register? How does it compare to information conveyed by a letter? What could it tell the government about a caller?
- Did Smith know he was conveying this information to the phone company? Why did he convey it? Did he have a choice? Should his knowledge or motives, or the voluntariness of his actions, have affected the outcome of his case?
- Does the Court conclude that we have no privacy interest in *any* information we voluntarily convey to a third party? If not, how is its holding limited?

Smith v. Maryland

United States Supreme Court, 1979
442 U.S. 735

Mr. Justice Blackmun delivered the opinion of the Court. This case presents the question whether the installation and use of a pen register[1] constitutes a "search" within the meaning of the Fourth Amendment, made applicable to the States through the Fourteenth Amendment.

I

On March 5, 1976, in Baltimore, Md., Patricia McDonough was robbed. She gave the police a description of the robber and of a 1975 Monte Carlo automobile she had observed near the scene of the crime. After the robbery, McDonough began receiving threatening and obscene phone calls from a man identifying himself as the robber. On one occasion, the caller asked that she step out on her front porch; she did so, and saw the 1975 Monte Carlo she had earlier described to police moving slowly past her home. On March 16, police spotted a man who met McDonough's description driving a 1975 Monte Carlo in her neighborhood. By tracing the license plate number, police learned that the car was registered in the name of petitioner, Michael Lee Smith.

The next day, the telephone company, at police request, installed a pen register at its central offices to record the numbers dialed from the telephone at petitioner's home. The police did not get a warrant or court order before having the pen register installed. The register revealed that on March 17 a call was placed from petitioner's home to McDonough's phone. On the basis of this and other evidence, the police obtained a warrant to search petitioner's residence. The search revealed that a page in petitioner's phone book was turned down to the name and number of Patricia

1. "A pen register is a mechanical device that records the numbers dialed on a telephone by monitoring the electrical impulses caused when the dial on the telephone is released. It does not overhear oral communications and does not indicate whether calls are actually completed." *United States v. New York Tel. Co.*, 434 U.S. 159, 161 n.1 [(1977)]. A pen register is "usually installed at a central telephone facility [and] records on a paper tape all numbers dialed from [the] line" to which it is attached. *United States v. Giordano*, 416 U.S. 505, 549 n.1 (1974).

McDonough; the phone book was seized. Petitioner was arrested, [convicted, and sentenced to six years' imprisonment]....

II

A

...In determining whether a particular form of government-initiated electronic surveillance is a "search" within the meaning of the Fourth Amendment, our lodestar is *Katz v. United States*, 389 U.S. 347 (1967)....

Consistently with *Katz*, this Court uniformly has held that the application of the Fourth Amendment depends on whether the person invoking its protection can claim a "justifiable," a "reasonable," or a "legitimate expectation of privacy" that has been invaded by government action. This inquiry, as Mr. Justice Harlan aptly noted in his *Katz* concurrence, normally embraces two discrete questions. The first is whether the individual, by his conduct, has "exhibited an actual (subjective) expectation of privacy," 389 U.S., at 361 — whether, in the words of the *Katz* majority, the individual has shown that "he seeks to preserve [something] as private." *Id.*, at 351. The second question is whether the individual's subjective expectation of privacy is "one that society is prepared to recognize as 'reasonable,'" *id.*, at 361 — whether, in the words of the *Katz* majority, the individual's expectation, viewed objectively, is "justifiable" under the circumstances. *Id.*, at 353.[5]

B

In applying the *Katz* analysis to this case, it is important to begin by specifying precisely the nature of the state activity that is challenged. The activity here took the form of installing and using a pen register. Since the pen register was installed on telephone company property at the telephone company's central offices, petitioner obviously cannot claim that his "property" was invaded or that police intruded into a "constitutionally protected area." Petitioner's claim, rather, is that, notwithstanding the absence of a trespass, the State, as did the Government in *Katz*, infringed a "legitimate expectation of privacy" that petitioner held. Yet a pen register differs significantly from the listening device employed in *Katz*, for pen registers do not acquire the *contents* of communications. This Court recently noted:

> "Indeed, a law enforcement official could not even determine from the use of a pen register whether a communication existed. These devices do not hear sound. They disclose only the telephone numbers that have been dialed — a means of establishing

---

5. Situations can be imagined, of course, in which *Katz*'s two-pronged inquiry would provide an inadequate index of Fourth Amendment protection. For example, if the Government were suddenly to announce on nationwide television that all homes henceforth would be subject to warrantless entry, individuals thereafter might not in fact entertain any actual expectation [of] of privacy regarding their homes, papers, and effects. Similarly, if a refugee from a totalitarian country, unaware of this Nation's traditions, erroneously assumed that police were continuously monitoring his telephone conversations, a subjective expectation of privacy regarding the contents of his calls might be lacking as well. In such circumstances, where an individual's subjective expectations had been "conditioned" by influences alien to well-recognized Fourth Amendment freedoms, those subjective expectations obviously could play no meaningful role in ascertaining what the scope of Fourth Amendment protection was. In determining whether a "legitimate expectation of privacy" existed in such cases, a normative inquiry would be proper.

> communication. Neither the purport of any communication between the caller and the recipient of the call, their identities, nor whether the call was even completed is disclosed by pen registers." *United States v. New York Tel. Co.*, 434 U.S. 159, 167 (1977).

Given a pen register's limited capabilities, therefore, petitioner's argument that its installation and use constituted a "search" necessarily rests upon a claim that he had a "legitimate expectation of privacy" regarding the numbers he dialed on his phone.

This claim must be rejected. First, we doubt that people in general entertain any actual expectation of privacy in the numbers they dial. All telephone users realize that they must "convey" phone numbers to the telephone company, since it is through telephone company switching equipment that their calls are completed. All subscribers realize, moreover, that the phone company has facilities for making permanent records of the numbers they dial, for they see a list of their long-distance (toll) calls on their monthly bills. In fact, pen registers and similar devices are routinely used by telephone companies "for the purposes of checking billing operations, detecting fraud and preventing violations of law." *United States v. New York Tel. Co.*, 434 U.S., at 174-175. . . .

. . . Most phone books tell subscribers, on a page entitled "Consumer Information," that the company "can frequently help in identifying to the authorities the origin of unwelcome and troublesome calls." Telephone users, in sum, typically know that they must convey numerical information to the phone company; that the phone company has facilities for recording this information; and that the phone company does in fact record this information for a variety of legitimate business purposes. Although subjective expectations cannot be scientifically gauged, it is too much to believe that telephone subscribers, under these circumstances, harbor any general expectation that the numbers they dial will remain secret. . . .

. . . [E]ven if petitioner did harbor some subjective expectation that the phone numbers he dialed would remain private, this expectation is not "one that society is prepared to recognize as 'reasonable.'" This Court consistently has held that a person has no legitimate expectation of privacy in information he voluntarily turns over to third parties. E.g., *United States v. Miller*, 425 U.S. [435] at 442-444 [1976]. In *Miller*, for example, the Court held that a bank depositor has no "legitimate 'expectation of privacy'" in financial information "voluntarily conveyed to . . . banks and exposed to their employees in the ordinary course of business." 425 U.S. at 442. The Court explained:

> "The depositor takes the risk, in revealing his affairs to another, that the information will be conveyed by that person to the Government. . . . This Court has held repeatedly that the Fourth Amendment does not prohibit the obtaining of information revealed to a third party and conveyed by him to Government authorities, even if the information is revealed on the assumption that it will be used only for a limited purpose and the confidence placed in the third party will not be betrayed." *Id.* at 443.

Because the depositor "assumed the risk" of disclosure, the Court held that it would be unreasonable for him to expect his financial records to remain private.

This analysis dictates that petitioner can claim no legitimate expectation of privacy here. When he used his phone, petitioner voluntarily conveyed numerical information to the telephone company and "exposed" that information to its equipment in the ordinary course of business. In so doing, petitioner assumed the risk that the company would reveal to police the numbers he dialed. The switching equipment that processed those numbers is merely the modern counterpart of the operator who, in an earlier day, personally completed calls for the subscriber. Petitioner concedes that if he had placed his calls through an operator, he could claim no legitimate expectation of privacy. We are not inclined to hold that a different constitutional result is required because the telephone company has decided to automate. . . .

. . . We therefore conclude that petitioner in all probability entertained no actual expectation of privacy in the phone numbers he dialed, and that, even if he did, his expectation was not "legitimate." The installation and use of a pen register, consequently, was not a "search," and no warrant was required. . . .

Mr. Justice POWELL took no part in the consideration or decision of this case.

[The dissenting opinion of Justice STEWART, with whom Justice BRENNAN joined, is omitted.]

Mr. Justice MARSHALL, with whom Mr. Justice BRENNAN joins, dissenting. . . . [E]ven assuming . . . that individuals "typically know" that a phone company monitors calls for internal reasons, it does not follow that they expect this information to be made available to the public in general or the government in particular. Privacy is not a discrete commodity, possessed absolutely or not at all. Those who disclose certain facts to a bank or phone company for a limited business purpose need not assume that this information will be released to other persons for other purposes.

The crux of the Court's holding, however, is that whatever expectation of privacy petitioner may in fact have entertained regarding his calls, it is not one "society is prepared to recognize as 'reasonable.'" In so ruling, the Court determines that individuals who convey information to third parties have "assumed the risk" of disclosure to the government. This analysis is misconceived in two critical respects.

Implicit in the concept of assumption of risk is some notion of choice. At least in the third-party consensual surveillance cases, which first incorporated risk analysis into Fourth Amendment doctrine, the defendant presumably had exercised some discretion in deciding who should enjoy his confidential communications. By contrast here, unless a person is prepared to forgo use of what for many has become a personal or professional necessity, he cannot help but accept the risk of surveillance. It is idle to speak of "assuming" risks in contexts where, as a practical matter, individuals have no realistic alternative.

More fundamentally, to make risk analysis dispositive in assessing the reasonableness of privacy expectations would allow the government to define the scope of Fourth Amendment protections. For example, law enforcement officials, simply by announcing their intent to monitor the content of random samples of first-class mail or private phone conversations, could put the public on notice of the risks they would thereafter assume in such communications. Yet, although acknowledging this implication of its analysis, the Court is willing to concede only that, in some circumstances, a further "normative inquiry would be proper." No meaningful effort is made to explain what those circumstances might be, or why this case is not among them.

In my view, whether privacy expectations are legitimate within the meaning of *Katz* depends not on the risks an individual can be presumed to accept when imparting information to third parties, but on the risks he should be forced to assume in a free and open society. . . .

The use of pen registers, I believe, constitutes such an extensive intrusion. To hold otherwise ignores the vital role telephonic communication plays in our personal and professional relationships, as well as the First and Fourth Amendment interests implicated by unfettered official surveillance. Privacy in placing calls is of value not only to those engaged in criminal activity. The prospect of unregulated governmental monitoring will undoubtedly prove disturbing even to those with nothing illicit to hide. Many individuals, including members of unpopular political organizations or journalists with confidential sources, may legitimately wish to avoid disclosure of their personal contacts. Permitting governmental access to telephone records on less than probable cause may thus impede certain forms of political affiliation and journalistic endeavor that are the hallmark of a truly free society. Particularly given the Government's previous reliance on warrantless telephonic surveillance to trace reporters' sources and monitor protected political activity, I am unwilling to insulate use of pen registers from independent judicial review. . . .

Reading *Carpenter v. United States*

Timothy Carpenter was arrested on suspicion of robbing a series of Radio Shack and T-Mobile stores. Based on cell phone numbers provided by an accomplice, police sought court orders to obtain cell phone records for Carpenter under the Stored Communications Act, which authorizes such orders when the government "offers specific and articulable facts showing that there are reasonable grounds to believe" that the records sought "are relevant and material to an ongoing criminal investigation." 18 U.S.C. §2703(d) (2018).

A cell phone constantly searches for a nearby cell tower to connect it to a mobile network, even when the phone is not in use. The cell phone service provider creates and stores a record of the time and duration of each connection. This cell site location information (CSLI) is thus a history of the approximate location of each phone at any given time. (Some phones also collect and store locational data from the Global Positioning System (GPS).) *See* Elec. Frontier Found., *Cell Site Location Information: What Is It?* (n.d.), https://www.eff.org/criminaldefender/cell-site-location.

A court ordered Carpenter's wireless carriers to disclose "cell/site sector [information] for [Carpenter's] telephone[] at call origination and at call termination for incoming and outgoing calls" during the four-month period when the string of robberies occurred. The order produced records spanning 129 days when Carpenter's phone was "roaming" in northeastern Ohio. They included 12,898 location points cataloging Carpenter's movements — an average of 101 data points per day.

At his subsequent trial for robbery, Carpenter unsuccessfully moved to suppress cell-site data that placed him near four of the charged robberies. His conviction was affirmed on appeal, and the Supreme Court granted certiorari.

- How was the privacy interest asserted by Carpenter in his CSLI different from that implicated in the numbers Smith dialed on his landline telephone? Should the law treat the two differently?
- Smith "gave" each number he dialed to the phone company. Carpenter "gave" the service provider periodic CSLI by turning his phone on. Was either act truly "voluntary"?
- The *Carpenter* Court declined to extend *Smith* to CSLI for several reasons. What are they? Based on those reasons, can you articulate a test for deciding whether other applications of the third-party doctrine are still good?
- The dissenters assert that a property-based Fourth Amendment analysis would adhere more closely to the original understanding and yield clearer answers. How would that analysis apply to CSLI? To credit card information? To travel records?

Carpenter v. United States

United States Supreme Court, 2018
138 S. Ct. 2206

Chief Justice ROBERTS delivered the opinion of the Court. This case presents the question whether the Government conducts a search under the Fourth Amendment when it accesses historical cell phone records that provide a comprehensive chronicle of the user's past movements.

I

A

There are 396 million cell phone service accounts in the United States — for a Nation of 326 million people. Cell phones perform their wide and growing variety of functions by connecting to a set of radio antennas called "cell sites." Although cell sites are usually mounted on a tower, they can also be found on light posts, flagpoles, church steeples, or the sides of buildings. Cell sites typically have several directional antennas that divide the covered area into sectors.

Cell phones continuously scan their environment looking for the best signal, which generally comes from the closest cell site. Most modern devices, such as smartphones, tap into the wireless network several times a minute whenever their signal is on, even if the owner is not using one of the phone's features. Each time the phone connects to a cell site, it generates a time-stamped record known as cell-site location information (CSLI). The precision of this information depends on the size of the geographic area covered by the cell site. The greater the concentration of cell sites, the smaller the coverage area. As data usage from cell phones has increased, wireless carriers have installed more cell sites to handle the traffic. That has led to increasingly compact coverage areas, especially in urban areas.

Wireless carriers collect and store CSLI for their own business purposes, including finding weak spots in their network and applying "roaming" charges when another carrier routes data through their cell sites. In addition, wireless carriers often sell aggregated location records to data brokers, without individual identifying information of the sort at issue here. While carriers have long retained CSLI for the start and end of incoming calls, in recent years phone companies have also collected location information from the transmission of text messages and routine data connections. Accordingly, modern cell phones generate increasingly vast amounts of increasingly precise CSLI. . . .

III

The question we confront today is how to apply the Fourth Amendment to a new phenomenon: the ability to chronicle a person's past movements through the record of his cell phone signals. Such tracking partakes of many of the qualities of the GPS monitoring we considered in [*United States v. Jones*, 565 U.S. 400 (2012)]. Much like GPS tracking of a vehicle, cell phone location information is detailed, encyclopedic, and effortlessly compiled.

At the same time, the fact that the individual continuously reveals his location to his wireless carrier implicates the third-party principle of *Smith* [*v. Maryland*, 442 U.S. 735 (1979)] and [*United States v. Miller*, 425 U.S. 435 (1976)]. But while the third-party doctrine applies to telephone numbers and bank records, it is not clear whether its logic extends to the qualitatively different category of cell-site records. After all, when *Smith* was decided in 1979, few could have imagined a society in which a phone goes wherever its owner goes, conveying to the wireless carrier not just dialed digits, but a detailed and comprehensive record of the person's movements.

We decline to extend *Smith* and *Miller* to cover these novel circumstances. Given the unique nature of cell phone location records, the fact that the information is held by a third party does not by itself overcome the user's claim to Fourth Amendment protection. Whether the Government employs its own surveillance technology as in *Jones* or leverages the technology of a wireless carrier, we hold that an individual maintains a legitimate expectation of privacy in the record of his physical movements as captured through CSLI. The location information obtained from Carpenter's wireless carriers was the product of a search.

A

A person does not surrender all Fourth Amendment protection by venturing into the public sphere. To the contrary, "what [one] seeks to preserve as private, even in an area accessible to the public, may be constitutionally protected." [*Katz v. United States*, 389 U.S. 347, 351-352 (1967).] A majority of this Court has already recognized that individuals have a reasonable expectation of privacy in the whole of their physical movements. *Jones,* 565 U.S., at 430 (Alito, J., concurring in judgment); *id.,* at 415 (Sotomayor, J., concurring). Prior to the digital age, law enforcement might have pursued a suspect for a brief stretch, but doing so "for any extended period of time was difficult and costly and therefore rarely undertaken." *Id.,* at 429 (opinion of Alito, J.). For that reason, "society's expectation has been that law enforcement agents and others would not — and indeed, in the main, simply could not — secretly monitor and catalogue every single movement of an individual's car for a very long period." *Id.,* at 430.

Allowing government access to cell-site records contravenes that expectation. Although such records are generated for commercial purposes, that distinction does not negate Carpenter's anticipation of privacy in his physical location. Mapping a cell phone's location over the course of 127 days provides an all-encompassing record of the holder's whereabouts. As with GPS information, the time-stamped data provides an intimate window into a person's life, revealing not only his particular movements, but through them his "familial, political, professional, religious, and sexual associations." *Id.,* at 415 (opinion of Sotomayor, J.). These location records "hold for many Americans the 'privacies of life.'" *Riley v. California,* 573 U.S. ___ (2014) (slip op., at 28) (quoting [*Boyd v. United States,* 116 U.S. 616, 630 (1886)]. And like GPS monitoring, cell phone tracking is remarkably easy, cheap, and efficient compared to traditional investigative tools. With just the click of a button, the Government can access each carrier's deep repository of historical location information at practically no expense.

In fact, historical cell-site records present even greater privacy concerns than the GPS monitoring of a vehicle we considered in *Jones.* Unlike the bugged container in [*United States v. Knotts,* 460 U.S. 276 (1983)] or the car in *Jones,* a cell phone — almost a "feature of human anatomy," *Riley,* 573 U.S., at ___ (slip op., at 9) — tracks nearly exactly the movements of its owner. While individuals regularly leave their vehicles, they compulsively carry cell phones with them all the time. A cell phone faithfully follows its owner beyond public thoroughfares and into private residences, doctor's offices, political headquarters, and other potentially revealing locales. See *id.,* at ___ (slip op., at 19) (noting that "nearly three-quarters of smart phone users report being within five feet of their phones most of the time, with 12% admitting that they even use their phones in the shower"); contrast *Cardwell v. Lewis,* 417 U.S. 583, 590 (1974) (plurality opinion) ("A car has little capacity for escaping public scrutiny."). Accordingly, when the Government tracks the location of a cell phone it achieves near perfect surveillance, as if it had attached an ankle monitor to the phone's user.

Moreover, the retrospective quality of the data here gives police access to a category of information otherwise unknowable. In the past, attempts to reconstruct a person's movements were limited by a dearth of records and the frailties of recollection. With access to CSLI, the Government can now travel back in time to retrace a person's whereabouts, subject only to the retention policies of the wireless carriers, which currently maintain records for up to five years. Critically, because location information is continually logged for all of the 400 million devices in the United States — not just those belonging to persons who might happen to come under investigation — this newfound tracking capacity runs against everyone. Unlike with the GPS device in *Jones,* police need not even know in advance whether they want to follow a particular individual, or when.

Whoever the suspect turns out to be, he has effectively been tailed every moment of every day for five years, and the police may — in the Government's view — call upon the results of that surveillance without regard to the constraints of the Fourth Amendment. Only the few without cell phones could escape this tireless and absolute surveillance.

The Government and Justice Kennedy contend, however, that the collection of CSLI should be permitted because the data is less precise than GPS information. Not to worry, they maintain, because the location records did "not on their own suffice to place [Carpenter] at the crime scene"; they placed him within a wedge-shaped sector ranging from one-eighth to four square miles. Yet the Court has already rejected the proposition that "inference insulates a search." [*Kyllo v. United States,* 533 U.S. 27, 36 (2001).] From the 127 days of location data it received, the Government could, in combination with other information, deduce a detailed log of Carpenter's movements, including when he was at the site of the robberies. And the Government thought the CSLI accurate enough to highlight it during the closing argument of his trial.

At any rate, the rule the Court adopts "must take account of more sophisticated systems that are already in use or in development." *Kyllo,* 533 U.S., at 36. While the records in this case reflect the state of technology at the start of the decade, the accuracy of CSLI is rapidly approaching GPS-level precision. As the number of cell sites has proliferated, the geographic area covered by each cell sector has shrunk, particularly in urban areas. In addition, with new technology measuring the time and angle of signals hitting their towers, wireless carriers already have the capability to pinpoint a phone's location within 50 meters.

Accordingly, when the Government accessed CSLI from the wireless carriers, it invaded Carpenter's reasonable expectation of privacy in the whole of his physical movements.

B

The Government's primary contention to the contrary is that the third-party doctrine governs this case. In its view, cell-site records are fair game because they are "business records" created and maintained by the wireless carriers. The Government (along with Justice Kennedy) recognizes that this case features new technology, but asserts that the legal question nonetheless turns on a garden-variety request for information from a third-party witness.

The Government's position fails to contend with the seismic shifts in digital technology that made possible the tracking of not only Carpenter's location but also everyone else's, not for a short period but for years and years. Sprint Corporation and its competitors are not your typical witnesses. Unlike the nosy neighbor who keeps an eye on comings and goings, they are ever alert, and their memory is nearly infallible. There is a world of difference between the limited types of personal information addressed in *Smith* and *Miller* and the exhaustive chronicle of location information casually collected by wireless carriers today. The Government thus is not asking for a straightforward application of the third-party doctrine, but instead a significant extension of it to a distinct category of information.

The third-party doctrine partly stems from the notion that an individual has a reduced expectation of privacy in information knowingly shared with another. But the fact of "diminished privacy interests does not mean that the Fourth Amendment falls out of the picture entirely." *Riley,* 573 U.S., at ___ (slip op., at 16). *Smith* and *Miller,* after all, did not rely solely on the act of sharing. Instead, they considered "the nature of the particular documents sought" to determine whether "there is a legitimate 'expectation of privacy' concerning their contents." *Miller,* 425 U.S., at 442. *Smith* pointed out the limited capabilities of a pen register; as explained in *Riley,* telephone call logs reveal little in the way of "identifying information." *Smith,* 442 U.S., at 742; *Riley,* 573 U.S., at ___ (slip op., at 24). *Miller* likewise noted that checks were "not confidential communications but negotiable instruments to be used in commercial transactions." 425 U.S., at 442. In mechanically applying the third-party doctrine to this case, the Government fails to appreciate that there are no comparable limitations on the revealing nature of CSLI.

The Court has in fact already shown special solicitude for location information in the third-party context. In *Knotts,* the Court relied on *Smith* to hold that an individual has no reasonable expectation of privacy in public movements that he "voluntarily conveyed to anyone who wanted to look." *Knotts,* 460 U.S., at 281; see *id.,* at 283 (discussing *Smith*). But when confronted with more pervasive tracking, five Justices agreed that longer term GPS monitoring of even a vehicle traveling on public streets constitutes a search. *Jones,* 565 U.S., at 430 (Alito, J., concurring in judgment); *id.,* at 415 (Sotomayor, J., concurring). Justice Gorsuch wonders why "someone's location when using a phone" is sensitive, and Justice Kennedy assumes that a person's discrete movements "are not particularly private." Yet this case is not about "using a phone" or a person's movement at a particular time. It is about a detailed chronicle of a person's physical presence compiled every day, every moment, over several years. Such a chronicle implicates privacy concerns far beyond those considered in *Smith* and *Miller.*

Neither does the second rationale underlying the third-party doctrine — voluntary exposure — hold up when it comes to CSLI. Cell phone location information is not truly "shared" as one normally understands the term. In the first place, cell phones and the services they provide are "such a pervasive and insistent part of daily life" that carrying one is indispensable to participation in modern society. *Riley,* 573 U.S., at ___ (slip op., at 9). Second, a cell phone logs a cell-site record by dint of its operation, without any affirmative act on the part of the user beyond powering up. Virtually any activity on the phone generates CSLI, including incoming calls, texts, or e-mails and countless other data connections that a phone automatically makes when checking for news, weather, or social media updates. Apart from disconnecting the phone from the network, there is no way to avoid leaving behind a trail of location data. As a result, in no meaningful sense does the user voluntarily "assume[] the risk" of turning over a comprehensive dossier of his physical movements. *Smith,* 442 U.S., at 745.

We therefore decline to extend *Smith* and *Miller* to the collection of CSLI. Given the unique nature of cell phone location information, the fact that the Government obtained the information from a third party does not overcome Carpenter's claim to Fourth Amendment protection. The Government's acquisition of the cell-site records was a search within the meaning of the Fourth Amendment.

* * *

Our decision today is a narrow one. We do not express a view on matters not before us: real-time CSLI or "tower dumps" (a download of information on all the devices that connected to a particular cell site during a particular interval). We do not disturb the application of *Smith* and *Miller* or call into question conventional surveillance techniques and tools, such as security cameras. Nor do we address other business records that might incidentally reveal location information. Further, our opinion does not consider other collection techniques involving foreign affairs or national security. As Justice Frankfurter noted when considering new innovations in airplanes and radios, the Court must tread carefully in such cases, to ensure that we do not "embarrass the future." *Northwest Airlines, Inc. v. Minnesota,* 322 U.S. 292, 300 (1944).

IV

Having found that the acquisition of Carpenter's CSLI was a search, we also conclude that the Government must generally obtain a warrant supported by probable cause before acquiring such records. Although the "ultimate measure of the constitutionality of a governmental search is 'reasonableness,'" our cases establish that warrantless searches are typically unreasonable where "a search is undertaken by law enforcement officials to discover evidence of criminal wrongdoing." *Vernonia School Dist. 47J v. Acton,* 515 U.S. 646, 652-653 (1995). Thus, "[i]n the absence of a warrant, a search is reasonable only if it falls within a specific exception to the warrant requirement." *Riley,* 573 U.S., at ____ (slip op., at 5).

The Government acquired the cell-site records pursuant to a court order issued under the Stored Communications Act, which required the Government to show "reasonable grounds" for believing that the records were "relevant and material to an ongoing investigation." 18 U.S.C. §2703(d). That showing falls well short of the probable cause required for a warrant.... Before compelling a wireless carrier to turn over a subscriber's CSLI, the Government's obligation is a familiar one — get a warrant.

* * *

As Justice Brandeis explained in his famous dissent, the Court is obligated — as "[s]ubtler and more far-reaching means of invading privacy have become available to the Government" — to ensure that the "progress of science" does not erode Fourth Amendment protections. *Olmstead v. United States,* 277 U.S. 438, 473-474 (1928). Here the progress of science has afforded law enforcement a powerful new tool to carry out its important responsibilities. At the same time, this tool risks Government encroachment of the sort the Framers, "after consulting the lessons of history," drafted the Fourth Amendment to prevent....

The judgment of the Court of Appeals is reversed, and the case is remanded for further proceedings consistent with this opinion.

It is so ordered.

Justice KENNEDY, with whom Justice THOMAS and Justice ALITO join, dissenting....

II...

Here the only question necessary to decide is whether the Government searched anything of Carpenter's when it used compulsory process to obtain cell-site records from Carpenter's cell phone service providers. This Court's decisions in *Miller* and *Smith* dictate that the answer is no, as every Court of Appeals to have considered the question has recognized.

A...

... *Miller* and *Smith* placed necessary limits on the ability of individuals to assert Fourth Amendment interests in property to which they lack a "requisite connection." *Minnesota v. Carter,* 525 U.S. 83, 99 (1998) (Kennedy, J., concurring). Fourth Amendment rights, after all, are personal. The Amendment protects "[t]he right of the people to be secure in *their*... persons, houses, papers, and effects" — not the persons, houses, papers, and effects of others. (Emphasis added.)

The concept of reasonable expectations of privacy, first announced in *Katz v. United States,* 389 U.S. 347 (1967), sought to look beyond the "arcane distinctions developed in property and tort law" in evaluating whether a person has a sufficient connection to the thing or place searched to assert Fourth Amendment interests in it. *Rakas v. Illinois,* 439 U.S. 128, 143 (1978). Yet "property concepts" are, nonetheless, fundamental "in determining the presence or absence of the privacy interests protected by that Amendment." *Id.,* at 143-144, n.12. This is so for at least two reasons. First, as a matter of settled expectations from the law of property, individuals often have greater expectations of privacy in things and places that belong to them, not to others. And second, the Fourth Amendment's protections must remain tethered to the text of that Amendment, which, again, protects only a person's own "persons, houses, papers, and effects." . . .

Miller and *Smith* set forth an important and necessary limitation on the *Katz* framework. They rest upon the commonsense principle that the absence of property law analogues can be dispositive of privacy expectations. The defendants in those cases could expect that the third-party businesses could use the records the companies collected, stored, and classified as their own for any number of business and commercial purposes. The businesses were not bailees or custodians of the records, with a duty to hold the records for the defendants' use. The defendants could make no argument that the records were their own papers or effects. See *Miller, supra,* at 440 ("the documents subpoenaed here are not respondent's 'private papers'"); *Smith, supra,* at 741 ("petitioner obviously cannot claim that his 'property' was invaded"). The records were the business entities' records, plain and simple. The defendants had no reason to believe the records were owned or controlled by them and so could not assert a reasonable expectation of privacy in the records.

The second principle supporting *Miller* and *Smith* is the longstanding rule that the Government may use compulsory process to compel persons to disclose documents and other evidence within their possession and control. See *United States v. Nixon,* 418 U.S. 683, 709 (1974) (it is an "ancient proposition of law" that "the public has a right to every man's evidence" (internal quotation marks and alterations omitted)). A subpoena is different from a warrant in its force and intrusive power. While a warrant allows the Government to enter and seize and make the examination itself, a subpoena simply requires the person to whom it is directed to make the disclosure. A subpoena, moreover, provides the recipient the "opportunity to present objections" before complying, which further mitigates the intrusion. *Oklahoma Press Publishing Co. v. Walling,* 327 U.S. 186, 195 (1946).

For those reasons this Court has held that a subpoena for records, although a "constructive" search subject to Fourth Amendment constraints, need not comply with the procedures applicable to warrants — even when challenged by the person to whom the records belong. Rather, a subpoena complies with the Fourth Amendment's reasonableness requirement so long as it is "'sufficiently limited in scope, relevant in purpose, and specific in directive so that compliance will not be unreasonably burdensome.'" *Donovan v. Lone Steer, Inc.,* 464 U.S. 408, 415 (1984). Persons with no meaningful interests in the records sought by a subpoena, like the defendants in *Miller* and *Smith,* have no rights to object to the records' disclosure — much less to assert that the Government must obtain a warrant to compel disclosure of the records.

Based on *Miller* and *Smith* and the principles underlying those cases, it is well established that subpoenas may be used to obtain a wide variety of records held by businesses, even when the records contain private information. Credit cards are a prime example. State and federal law enforcement, for instance, often subpoena credit card statements to develop probable cause to prosecute crimes ranging from drug trafficking and distribution to healthcare fraud to tax evasion. Subpoenas also may be used to obtain vehicle registration records, hotel records, employment records, and records of utility usage, to name just a few other examples. . . .

B . . .

All this is not to say that *Miller* and *Smith* are without limits. *Miller* and *Smith* may not apply when the Government obtains the modern-day equivalents of an individual's own "papers" or "effects," even when those papers or effects are held by a third party. See *Ex parte Jackson,* 96 U.S. 727, 733 (1878) (letters held by mail carrier); *United States v. Warshak,* 631 F.3d 266, 283-288 (C.A.6 2010) (e-mails held by Internet service provider). As already discussed, however, this case does not involve property or a bailment of that sort. Here the Government's acquisition of cell-site records falls within the heartland of *Miller* and *Smith*. . . .

III . . .

B . . .

The Court appears, in my respectful view, to read *Miller* and *Smith* to establish a balancing test. For each "qualitatively different category" of information, the Court suggests, the privacy interests at stake must be weighed against the fact that the information has been disclosed to a third party. When the privacy interests are weighty enough to "overcome" the third-party disclosure, the Fourth Amendment's protections apply.

That is an untenable reading of *Miller* and *Smith.* As already discussed, the fact that information was relinquished to a third party was the entire basis for concluding that the defendants in those cases lacked a reasonable expectation of privacy. *Miller* and *Smith* do not establish the kind of category-by-category balancing the Court today prescribes.

But suppose the Court were correct to say that *Miller* and *Smith* rest on so imprecise a foundation. Still the Court errs, in my submission, when it concludes that cell-site records implicate greater privacy interests — and thus deserve greater Fourth Amendment protection — than financial records and telephone records.

Indeed, the opposite is true. A person's movements are not particularly private. As the Court recognized in *Knotts,* when the defendant there "traveled over the public streets he voluntarily conveyed to anyone who wanted to look the fact that he was traveling over particular roads in a particular direction, the fact of whatever stops he made, and the fact of his final destination." 460 U.S., at 281-282. Today expectations of privacy in one's location are, if anything, even less reasonable than when the Court decided *Knotts* over 30 years ago. Millions of Americans choose to share their location on a daily basis, whether by using a variety of location-based services on their phones, or by sharing their location with friends and the public at large via social media. . . .

Still, the Court maintains, cell-site records are "unique" because they are "comprehensive" in their reach; allow for retrospective collection; are "easy, cheap, and efficient compared to traditional investigative tools"; and are not exposed to cell phone service providers in a meaningfully voluntary manner. But many other kinds of business records can be so described. Financial records are of vast scope. Banks and credit card companies keep a comprehensive account of almost every transaction an individual makes on a daily basis. "With just the click of a button, the Government can access each [company's] deep repository of historical [financial] information at practically no expense." And the decision whether to transact with banks and credit card companies is no more or less voluntary than the decision whether to use a cell phone. Today, just as when *Miller* was decided, "'it is impossible to participate in the economic life of contemporary society without maintaining a bank account.'" 425 U.S., at 451 (Brennan, J., dissenting). But this Court, nevertheless, has held that individuals do not have a reasonable expectation of privacy in financial records. . . .

C

The Court says its decision is a "narrow one." But its reinterpretation of *Miller* and *Smith* will have dramatic consequences for law enforcement, courts, and society as a whole.

Most immediately, the Court's holding that the Government must get a warrant to obtain more than six days of cell-site records limits the effectiveness of an important investigative tool for solving serious crimes. As this case demonstrates, cell-site records are uniquely suited to help the Government develop probable cause to apprehend some of the Nation's most dangerous criminals: serial killers, rapists, arsonists, robbers, and so forth. These records often are indispensable at the initial stages of investigations when the Government lacks the evidence necessary to obtain a warrant. And the long-term nature of many serious crimes, including serial crimes and terrorism offenses, can necessitate the use of significantly more than six days of cell-site records. The Court's arbitrary 6-day cutoff has the perverse effect of nullifying Congress' reasonable framework for obtaining cell-site records in some of the most serious criminal investigations.

The Court's decision also will have ramifications that extend beyond cell-site records to other kinds of information held by third parties, yet the Court fails "to provide clear guidance to law enforcement" and courts on key issues raised by its reinterpretation of *Miller* and *Smith*. *Riley v. California*, 573 U.S. ____, ____ (2014) (slip op., at 22).

First, the Court's holding is premised on cell-site records being a "distinct category of information" from other business records. But the Court does not explain what makes something a distinct category of information. Whether credit card records are distinct from bank records; whether payment records from digital wallet applications are distinct from either; whether the electronic bank records available today are distinct from the paper and microfilm records at issue in *Miller*; or whether cell-phone call records are distinct from the home-phone call records at issue in *Smith*, are just a few of the difficult questions that require answers under the Court's novel conception of *Miller* and *Smith*.

Second, the majority opinion gives courts and law enforcement officers no indication how to determine whether any particular category of information falls on the financial-records side or the cell-site-records side of its newly conceived constitutional line. The Court's multifactor analysis — considering intimacy, comprehensiveness, expense, retrospectivity, and voluntariness — puts the law on a new and unstable foundation. . . .

In short, the Court's new and uncharted course will inhibit law enforcement and "keep defendants and judges guessing for years to come." *Riley,* 573 U.S., at ___ (slip op., at 25) (internal quotation marks omitted)....

These reasons all lead to this respectful dissent....

Justice THOMAS, dissenting. [Omitted.]

Justice ALITO, with whom Justice THOMAS joins, dissenting....

II...

B

In the days when this Court followed an exclusively property-based approach to the Fourth Amendment, the distinction between an individual's Fourth Amendment rights and those of a third party was clear cut. We first asked whether the object of the search — say, a house, papers, or effects — belonged to the defendant, and, if it did, whether the Government had committed a "trespass" in acquiring the evidence at issue. *Jones,* 565 U.S., at 411, n.8....

... Carpenter indisputably lacks any meaningful property-based connection to the cell-site records owned by his provider. Because the records are not Carpenter's in any sense, Carpenter may not seek to use the Fourth Amendment to exclude them.

By holding otherwise, the Court effectively allows Carpenter to object to the "search" of a third party's property, not recognizing the revolutionary nature of this change. The Court seems to think that *Miller* and *Smith* invented a new "doctrine" — "the third-party doctrine" — and the Court refuses to "extend" this product of the 1970's to a new age of digital communications. But the Court fundamentally misunderstands the role of *Miller* and *Smith.* Those decisions did not forge a new doctrine; instead, they rejected an argument that would have disregarded the clear text of the Fourth Amendment and a formidable body of precedent.

In the end, the Court never explains how its decision can be squared with the fact that the Fourth Amendment protects only "[t]he right of the people to be secure in *their* persons, houses, papers, and effects." (Emphasis added.) ...

* * *

Although the majority professes a desire not to "'embarrass the future,'" we can guess where today's decision will lead.

One possibility is that the broad principles that the Court seems to embrace will be applied across the board. All subpoenas *duces tecum* and all other orders compelling the production of documents will require a demonstration of probable cause, and individuals will be able to claim a protected Fourth Amendment interest in any sensitive personal information about them that is collected and owned by third parties. Those would be revolutionary developments indeed.

The other possibility is that this Court will face the embarrassment of explaining in case after case that the principles on which today's decision rests are subject to all sorts of qualifications and limitations that have not yet been discovered. If we take this latter course, we will inevitably end up "mak[ing] a crazy quilt of the Fourth Amendment." *Smith, supra,* at 745.

All of this is unnecessary. In the Stored Communications Act, Congress addressed the specific problem at issue in this case. The Act restricts the misuse of cell-site records by cell service providers, something that the Fourth Amendment cannot do. The Act also goes beyond current Fourth Amendment case law in restricting access by law enforcement. It permits law enforcement officers to acquire cell-site records only if they meet a heightened standard and obtain a court order. If the American people now think that the Act is inadequate or needs updating, they can turn to their elected representatives to adopt more protective provisions. Because the collection and storage of cell-site records affects nearly every American, it is unlikely that the question whether the current law requires strengthening will escape Congress's notice. . . .

Justice GORSUCH, dissenting. . . . What's left of the Fourth Amendment? Today we use the Internet to do most everything. Smartphones make it easy to keep a calendar, correspond with friends, make calls, conduct banking, and even watch the game. Countless Internet companies maintain records about us and, increasingly, *for* us. Even our most private documents — those that, in other eras, we would have locked safely in a desk drawer or destroyed — now reside on third party servers. *Smith* and *Miller* teach that the police can review all of this material, on the theory that no one reasonably expects any of it will be kept private. But no one believes that, if they ever did.

What to do? It seems to me we could respond in at least three ways. The first is to ignore the problem, maintain *Smith* and *Miller,* and live with the consequences. If the confluence of these decisions and modern technology means our Fourth Amendment rights are reduced to nearly nothing, so be it. The second choice is to set *Smith* and *Miller* aside and try again using the *Katz* "reasonable expectation of privacy" jurisprudence that produced them. The third is to look for answers elsewhere. [Justice Gorsuch rejects the first two options.] . . .

* * *

There is another way. From the founding until the 1960s, the right to assert a Fourth Amendment claim didn't depend on your ability to appeal to a judge's personal sensibilities about the "reasonableness" of your expectations or privacy. It was tied to the law. [*Florida v. Jardines,* 569 U.S. 1, 11 (2013)]; *United States v. Jones,* 565 U.S. 400, 405 (2012). The Fourth Amendment protects "the right of the people to be secure in their persons, houses, papers and effects, against unreasonable searches and seizures." True to those words and their original understanding, the traditional approach asked if a house, paper or effect was *yours* under law. No more was needed to trigger the Fourth Amendment. Though now often lost in *Katz*'s shadow, this traditional understanding persists. *Katz* only "supplements, rather than displaces the traditional property-based understanding of the Fourth Amendment." *Byrd* [*v. United States,* 584 U.S. ____ (2018)], at ____ (slip op., at 7) (internal quotation marks omitted); *Jardines, supra,* at 11 (same); *Soldal v. Cook County,* 506 U.S. 56, 64 (1992) (*Katz* did not "snuf[f] out the previously recognized protection for property under the Fourth Amendment").

Beyond its provenance in the text and original understanding of the Amendment, this traditional approach comes with other advantages. Judges are supposed to decide cases based on "democratically legitimate sources of law" — like positive law or analogies to items protected by the enacted Constitution — rather than "their own biases or personal policy preferences." Pettys, Judicial Discretion in

Constitutional Cases, 26 J.L. & Pol. 123, 127 (2011). A Fourth Amendment model based on positive legal rights "carves out significant room for legislative participation in the Fourth Amendment context," too, by asking judges to consult what the people's representatives have to say about their rights. [Baude & Stern, The Positive Law Model of the Fourth Amendment, 129 Harv. L. Rev. 1821, 1852 (2016).] Nor is this approach hobbled by *Smith* and *Miller,* for those cases are just *limitations* on *Katz,* addressing only the question whether individuals have a reasonable expectation of privacy in materials they share with third parties. Under this more traditional approach, Fourth Amendment protections for your papers and effects do not automatically disappear just because you share them with third parties.

Given the prominence *Katz* has claimed in our doctrine, American courts are pretty rusty at applying the traditional approach to the Fourth Amendment. We know that if a house, paper, or effect is yours, you have a Fourth Amendment interest in its protection. But what kind of legal interest is sufficient to make something *yours*? And what source of law determines that? Current positive law? The common law at 1791, extended by analogy to modern times? Both? Much work is needed to revitalize this area and answer these questions. I do not begin to claim all the answers today, but (unlike with *Katz*) at least I have a pretty good idea what the questions *are.* And it seems to me a few things can be said.

First, the fact that a third party has access to or possession of your papers and effects does not necessarily eliminate your interest in them. Ever hand a private document to a friend to be returned? Toss your keys to a valet at a restaurant? Ask your neighbor to look after your dog while you travel? You would not expect the friend to share the document with others; the valet to lend your car to his buddy; or the neighbor to put Fido up for adoption. Entrusting your stuff to others is a *bailment.* A bailment is the "delivery of personal property by one person (the *bailor*) to another (the *bailee*) who holds the property for a certain purpose." Black's Law Dictionary 169 (10th ed. 2014). A bailee normally owes a legal duty to keep the item safe, according to the terms of the parties' contract if they have one, and according to the "implication[s] from their conduct" if they don't. 8 C.J.S., Bailments §36, pp. 468-469 (2017). A bailee who uses the item in a different way than he's supposed to, or against the bailor's instructions, is liable for conversion. This approach is quite different from *Smith* and *Miller's* (counter)-intuitive approach to reasonable expectations of privacy; where those cases extinguish Fourth Amendment interests once records are given to a third party, property law may preserve them.

Our Fourth Amendment jurisprudence already reflects this truth. In *Ex parte Jackson,* 96 U.S. 727 (1878), this Court held that sealed letters placed in the mail are "as fully guarded from examination and inspection, except as to their outward form and weight, as if they were retained by the parties forwarding them in their own domiciles." *Id.,* at 733. The reason, drawn from the Fourth Amendment's text, was that "[t]he constitutional guaranty of the right of the people to be secure in their papers against unreasonable searches and seizures extends to *their papers,* thus closed against inspection, *wherever they may be.*" *Ibid.* (emphasis added). It did not matter that letters were bailed to a third party (the government, no less). The sender enjoyed the same Fourth Amendment protection as he does "when papers are subjected to search in one's own household." *Ibid.*

These ancient principles may help us address modern data cases too. Just because you entrust your data — in some cases, your modern-day papers and effects — to a third party may not mean you lose any Fourth Amendment interest in its contents. Whatever may be left of *Smith* and *Miller,* few doubt that e-mail should be treated much like the traditional mail it has largely supplanted — as a bailment in which the owner retains a vital and protected legal interest.

Second, I doubt that complete ownership or exclusive control of property is always a necessary condition to the assertion of a Fourth Amendment right. Where houses are concerned, for example, individuals can enjoy Fourth Amendment protection without fee simple title. Both the text of the Amendment and the common law rule support that conclusion. "People call a house 'their' home when legal title is in the bank, when they rent it, and even when they merely occupy it rent free." *Carter,* 525 U.S., at 95-96 (Scalia, J., concurring). That rule derives from the common law. That is why tenants and resident family members — though they have no legal title — have standing to complain about searches of the houses in which they live.

Another point seems equally true: just because you *have* to entrust a third party with your data doesn't necessarily mean you should lose all Fourth Amendment protections in it. Not infrequently one person comes into possession of someone else's property without the owner's consent. Think of the finder of lost goods or the policeman who impounds a car. The law recognizes that the goods and the car still belong to their true owners, for "where a person comes into lawful possession of the personal property of another, even though there is no formal agreement between the property's owner and its possessor, the possessor will become a constructive bailee when justice so requires." *Christensen v. Hoover,* 643 P.2d 525, 529 (Colo. 1982) (en banc). At least some of this Court's decisions have already suggested that use of technology is functionally compelled by the demands of modern life, and in that way the fact that we store data with third parties may amount to a sort of involuntary bailment too.

Third, positive law may help provide detailed guidance on evolving technologies without resort to judicial intuition. State (or sometimes federal) law often creates rights in both tangible and intangible things. In the context of the Takings Clause we often ask whether those state-created rights are sufficient to make something someone's property for constitutional purposes. A similar inquiry may be appropriate for the Fourth Amendment. Both the States and federal government are actively legislating in the area of third party data storage and the rights users enjoy. . . . If state legislators or state courts say that a digital record has the attributes that normally make something property, that may supply a sounder basis for judicial decisionmaking than judicial guesswork about societal expectations.

Fourth, while positive law may help establish a person's Fourth Amendment interest there may be some circumstances where positive law cannot be used to defeat it. *Ex parte Jackson* reflects that understanding. There this Court said that "[n]o law of Congress" could authorize letter carriers "to invade the secrecy of letters." 96 U.S., at 733. So the post office couldn't impose a regulation dictating that those mailing letters surrender all legal interests in them once they're deposited in a mailbox. If that is right, *Jackson* suggests the existence of a constitutional floor below which Fourth Amendment rights may not descend. Legislatures cannot pass laws declaring your house or papers to be your property except to the extent the police wish to search them without cause. As the Court has previously explained, "we must 'assur[e] preservation of that degree of privacy against government that existed when the Fourth Amendment was adopted.'" *Jones,* 565 U.S., at 406 (quoting *Kyllo v. United States,* 533 U.S. 27, 34 (2001)). Nor does this mean protecting only the specific rights known at the founding; it means protecting their modern analogues too. So, for example, while thermal imaging was unknown in 1791, this Court has recognized that using that technology to look inside a home constitutes a Fourth Amendment "search" of that "home" no less than a physical inspection might. *Id.,* at 40.

Fifth, this constitutional floor may, in some instances, bar efforts to circumvent the Fourth Amendment's protection through the use of subpoenas. No one thinks the government can evade *Jackson*'s prohibition on opening sealed letters without a warrant simply by issuing a subpoena to a postmaster for "all letters sent by John Smith" or, worse, "all letters sent by John Smith concerning a particular transaction." So the question courts will confront will be this: What other kinds of records are sufficiently similar to letters in the mail that the same rule should apply? . . .

* * *

What does all this mean for the case before us? To start, I cannot fault the Sixth Circuit for holding that *Smith* and *Miller* extinguish any *Katz*-based Fourth Amendment interest in third party cell-site data. That is the plain effect of their categorical holdings. Nor can I fault the Court today for its implicit but unmistakable conclusion that the rationale of *Smith* and *Miller* is wrong; indeed, I agree with that. The Sixth Circuit was powerless to say so, but this Court can and should. At the same time, I do not agree with the Court's decision today to keep *Smith* and *Miller* on life support and supplement them with a new and multilayered inquiry that seems to be only *Katz*-squared. Returning there, I worry, promises more trouble than help. Instead, I would look to a more traditional Fourth Amendment approach. Even if *Katz* may still supply one way to prove a Fourth Amendment interest, it has never been the only way. Neglecting more traditional approaches may mean failing to vindicate the full protections of the Fourth Amendment.

Our case offers a cautionary example. It seems to me entirely possible a person's cell-site data could qualify as *his* papers or effects under existing law. Yes, the telephone carrier holds the information. But 47 U.S.C. §222 designates a customer's cell-site location information as "customer proprietary network information" (CPNI), §222(h)(1)(A), and gives customers certain rights to control use of and access to CPNI about themselves. The statute generally forbids a carrier to "use, disclose, or permit access to individually identifiable" CPNI without the customer's consent, except as needed to provide the customer's telecommunications services. §222(c)(1). It also requires the carrier to disclose CPNI "upon affirmative written request by the customer, to any person designated by the customer." §222(c)(2). Congress even afforded customers a private cause of action for damages against carriers who violate the Act's terms. §207. Plainly, customers have substantial legal interests in this information, including at least some right to include, exclude, and control its use. Those interests might even rise to the level of a property right.

The problem is that we do not know anything more. Before the district court and court of appeals, Mr. Carpenter pursued only a *Katz* "reasonable expectations" argument. He did not invoke the law of property or any analogies to the common law, either there or in his petition for certiorari. Even in his merits brief before this Court, Mr. Carpenter's discussion of his positive law rights in cell-site data was cursory. He offered no analysis, for example, of what rights state law might provide him in addition to those supplied by §222. In these circumstances, I cannot help but conclude — reluctantly — that Mr. Carpenter forfeited perhaps his most promising line of argument. . . .

Notes and Questions

1. Pen Registers and Trap and Trace Devices vs. Wiretaps. What is it about a pen register or trap and trace device that makes it so different from a wiretap? Should the differences have such constitutional significance? Consider the analogy to a mailed letter. The letter contains protected content, while the envelope contains only the mailing and return addresses and postage information. Thus, the contents of the letter are afforded protection, but the envelope, which the post office must be able to read in order to route the letter correctly, is not. Does the same contents/envelope distinction fit the pen register/trap and trace scenarios? What "content" is arguably revealed by a pen register?

2. Comparing Katz. Is the privacy interest recognized by the Court in *Katz* different in any appreciable way from the interest asserted in *Smith*? If the telephone company had the technical means to listen in on the phone calls in both cases, why protect one caller but not the other? Are the phone numbers that one dials private? Should they be? When you provide phone numbers to the phone company, do you expect that it will turn them over to Big Brother? Have you knowingly and willingly "assumed the risk" of such disclosure?

Alternatively, is the outcome in *Smith* best understood as reflecting a judgment that it doesn't really matter much, because the phone numbers were not of much value to the individual? If so, why is cell phone locational data of any more value? Of course, such data *are* valuable now to Carpenter. Should we assess value to the reasonable person, to society, or to the individual whose data are at issue?

3. All Third-Party Records? If an unstated premise of *Smith* is that the telephone numbers just aren't that important (private) to most people, does it follow that other kinds of third-party records have no greater value and are no more private? After all, we convey private medical information to our doctors, insurers, and pharmacies, and we e-mail personal stuff to our friends, even though we also knowingly send it through an Internet service provider that stores the e-mails for us. What if information that we have voluntarily provided to a number of different third parties were assembled in a single database? Might we have a reasonable expectation that such aggregated information would not be shared with the government without a warrant? Should we distinguish for Fourth Amendment purposes among different kinds of third-party records or how they are aggregated? If so, how? Can you root such distinctions in some language or reasoning of *Smith* or *Miller* (which involved banking records, which are arguably more sensitive than mere telephone numbers)? Does *Smith* offer other limiting principles to the third-party doctrine?

Carpenter now confirms that not all third-party data are created equal, but does the Court supply a functional metric for differentiating such data? What is it? *See generally* Susan Freiwald & Stephen Wm. Smith, *The Supreme Court, 2017 Term — Comment: The Carpenter Chronicle: A Near-Perfect Surveillance,* 132 Harv. L. Rev. 205, 219 (2018) (asserting that central to *Carpenter*'s holding was whether the technique was (1) hidden, (2) continuous, (3) indiscriminate, and (4) intrusive).

4. *A Statutory Remedy?* After *Smith*, Congress enacted the Pen Register Act, 18 U.S.C. §§3121-3127 (2018). The Act requires a court order for the installation of a pen register. *Id.* §3121(a). However, in contrast to a traditional Fourth Amendment warrant based on probable cause, the government may obtain an order for a pen register simply by showing that its use is "relevant to an ongoing investigation." *Id.* §3123(a).

5. *Some of the Dots: Transactional Data.* "'Transactional' information broadly describes information that documents financial or communications transactions without necessarily revealing the substance of those transactions." Michael J. Woods, *Counterintelligence and Access to Transactional Records: A Practical History of USA PATRIOT Act Section 215*, 1 J. Nat'l Security L. & Pol'y 37, 41 (2005). Such information includes telephone billing records that list numbers dialed, an Internet service provider's records showing a customer's Internet use, records of banking transactions and money transfers, credit card records, and travel records. It has reportedly proven invaluable in counterterrorist investigations. Terrorists can try to encrypt or otherwise disguise the substance of their communications, but "[i]t is far more difficult for them to cover their transactional footsteps." *Id.* at 41-42. Counterterrorism analysts can use transactional information to perform "link analysis" to tie suspects together and thus help identify terror cells. An example is the retrospective link analysis of the 9/11 hijackers. *Id.* at 42. It can also be used for pattern recognition and data matching to identify suspects.

6. *The Expectation of Privacy in Transactional Records.* Do you, subjectively, have any expectation of privacy when you convey data to a bank or commercial vendor, dial a telephone number, or transmit an e-mail message? Of course, you do not expect to keep the information private from the bank, vendor, phone company, or Internet service provider. The entities with which you deal directly need the data to complete the transaction that you initiate. But do you also expect those entities to share the information with others? In fact, don't some vendors promise you just the opposite, and sometimes even provide a box to check or button for you to indicate whether you want such data to be shared? Have the dramatic changes in patterns of commercial activity and communications in the decades since *Smith* and *Miller* made such an expectation of privacy for such transactions reasonable? *See* Christopher Slobogin & Joseph E. Schumacher, *Reasonable Expectations of Privacy and Autonomy in Fourth Amendment Cases: An Empirical Look at "Understandings Recognized and Permitted by Society,"* 42 Duke L.J. 727 (1993) (reporting a survey suggesting that the public finds government perusal of bank records highly invasive).

7. *Privacy vs. Property, Again.* The *Carpenter* dissenters apparently share the view that property-based distinctions are clearer and easier to apply than privacy-based distinctions, deriding the subjectivity of "reasonable expectation." This view is perhaps most plausible when the property is tangible, with physical attributes. Is it equally plausible when the property is intangible? Do you have a protected property interest in an Internet search term or even a text message? If so, is it because you credibly *believe* that you "own" it? Is one's belief in ownership of intangible property any less subjective than one's expectation of privacy? How is the hoary law of "bailment" going to help assess the privacy interest in such property? For the following applications of the third-party doctrine, consider whether a property-based approach yields a

different answer than a privacy-based approach, and which approach is more easily administered.

B. APPLICATIONS OF THE THIRD-PARTY DOCTRINE

1. Telephone Conversations

Easy case, isn't it? The pen register in *Smith* recorded only the numbers Smith dialed — the telephone analogue to the address on the front of the envelope, not the telephone conversations themselves, i.e., content information. Even if a telephone operator could eavesdrop on the conversations, neither the caller nor society expects the operator or telephone company to do so, and the telephone company does not normally record or retain content information.

2. E-mail Content

This may seem easy, given the analogy to telephone content information. But e-mail content, unlike telephone content, is stored on servers. The Stored Communications Act (SCA) authorizes the government to compel an Internet service provider (ISP) to disclose contents of stored electronic communications without a warrant in some circumstances. 18 U.S.C. §§2701-2712 (2018). *See generally* Richard M. Thompson II & Jared P. Cole, *Stored Communications Act: Reform of the Electronic Communications Privacy Act (ECPA)* (Cong. Res. Serv. R44036), May 19, 2015.

In *United States v. Warshak*, 631 F.3d 266 (6th Cir. 2010), the court considered whether such compelled but warrantless disclosure violated the Fourth Amendment, given Steven Warshak's unquestioned subjective expectation of privacy in his electronic correspondence.

> If we accept that an email is analogous to a letter or a phone call, it is manifest that agents of the government cannot compel a commercial ISP to turn over the contents of an email without triggering the Fourth Amendment. An ISP is the intermediary that makes email communication possible. Emails must pass through an ISP's servers to reach their intended recipient. Thus, the ISP is the functional equivalent of a post office or a telephone company. As we have discussed above, the police may not storm the post office and intercept a letter, and they are likewise forbidden from using the phone system to make a clandestine recording of a telephone call — unless they get a warrant, that is. It only stands to reason that, if government agents compel an ISP to surrender the contents of a subscriber's emails, those agents have thereby conducted a Fourth Amendment search, which necessitates compliance with the warrant requirement absent some exception. . . .
>
> . . . [*United States v. Miller*, 425 U.S. 435 (1976)] is distinguishable. First, *Miller* involved simple business records, as opposed to the potentially unlimited variety of "confidential communications" at issue here. Second, the bank depositor in *Miller* conveyed information to the bank so that the bank could put the information to use "in the ordinary course of business." By contrast, Warshak received his emails through NuVox [an Internet service provider]. NuVox was an *intermediary*, not the intended recipient of the emails. *See* [Patricia L. Bellia & Susan Freiwald, *Fourth Amendment Protection for Stored E-Mail*, 2008 U. Chi. Legal F. 121,] 165 ("[W]e view the best analogy for this scenario as the cases in which a

> third party carries, transports, or stores property for another. In these cases, as in the stored e-mail case, the customer grants access to the ISP because it is essential to the customer's interests."). Thus, *Miller* is not controlling.
>
> Accordingly, we hold that a subscriber enjoys a reasonable expectation of privacy in the contents of emails "that are stored with, or sent or received through, a commercial ISP." *Warshak* [*v. United States,* 490 F.3d 455 (6th Cir. 2007),] at 473; *see* [*United States v. Forrester,* 512 F.3d 500 (9th Cir. 2008),] at 511 (suggesting that "[t]he contents [of e-mail messages] may deserve Fourth Amendment protection"). The government may not compel a commercial ISP to turn over the contents of a subscriber's emails without first obtaining a warrant based on probable cause. Therefore, because they did not obtain a warrant, the government agents violated the Fourth Amendment when they obtained the contents of Warshak's emails. Moreover, to the extent that the SCA purports to permit the government to obtain such emails warrantlessly, the SCA is unconstitutional.... [631 F.3d at 286-288.]

Should it make a difference whether the ISP can access e-mails stored on its server? Warshak's ISP had a contractual right of access to his e-mail for certain purposes. Hotel managers, too, reserve a right of access to rooms they rent to guests (to fix the plumbing or replace the towels). A guest nevertheless has a reasonable expectation of privacy in her room. Drawing on this analogy, the court in *Warshak* found that the mere ability or right of Warshak's ISP to access his stored e-mails was not decisive. *Id.* at 287. But suppose Warshak's subscriber agreement gave his ISP the right to "audit, inspect, and monitor" his e-mails. Would his expectation of privacy then be unreasonable?

3. E-mail Headers, Addressing Information, and URLs

The USA Patriot Act extended the pen register and trap and trace authorities to include "dialing, routing, addressing, or signaling information transmitted by an instrument or facility from which a wire or electronic communication is transmitted, provided... that such information shall not include the contents of any communication." Pub. L. No. 107-56, §216(c), 115 Stat. 272, 290 (2001) (codified at 18 U.S.C. §3127(3), (4) (2018)). At first glance, the constitutionality of collecting this kind of third-party records also seems uncontroversial. Such addressing information, after all, sounds like telephone numbers or classic envelope information used to route a communication, as opposed to content. Should the third-party doctrine apply to such addresses?

In *United States v. Forrester,* 512 F.3d 500 (9th Cir. 2008), the Ninth Circuit ruled, based on *Smith,* that the government did not trigger Fourth Amendment requirements when it asked an ISP to install a monitoring device that recorded a target's IP addresses, to/from addresses for e-mails, and the volume of messages sent from the target's account.

> We conclude that the surveillance techniques the government employed here are constitutionally indistinguishable from the use of a pen register that the Court approved in *Smith.* First, e-mail and Internet users, like the telephone users in *Smith,* rely on third-party equipment in order to engage in communication.... [E-]mail and Internet users have no expectation of privacy in the to/from addresses of their messages or the IP addresses of the websites they visit because they should know that this information is

provided to and used by Internet service providers for the specific purpose of directing the routing of information. . . .

Second, e-mail to/from addresses and IP addresses constitute addressing information and do not necessarily reveal any more about the underlying contents of communication than do phone numbers. When the government obtains the to/from addresses of a person's e-mails or the IP addresses of websites visited, it does not find out the contents of the messages or know the particular pages on the websites the person viewed. At best, the government may make educated guesses about what was said in the messages or viewed on the websites based on its knowledge of the e-mail to/from addresses and IP addresses, but this is no different from speculation about the contents of a phone conversation on the basis of the identity of the person or entity that was dialed. . . . [T]he Court in *Smith* and *Katz* drew a clear line between unprotected addressing information and protected content information that the government did not cross here.

The government's surveillance of e-mail addresses also may be technologically sophisticated, but it is conceptually indistinguishable from government surveillance of physical mail. [*Id.* at 510-511.]

An IP address is a numerical code, not unlike a phone number. An e-mail address is different only in the sense that a government agency monitoring an individual's Internet use would not have to associate a code number with the identity of an addressee. While either might suggest the content of a communication, as the *Forrester* court noted, neither, according to the court, would implicate the Fourth Amendment. On the other hand,

> Surveillance techniques that enable the government to determine not only the IP addresses that a person accesses but also the uniform resource locators ("URL") of the pages visited might be more constitutionally problematic. A URL, unlike an IP address, identifies the particular document within a website that a person views and thus reveals much more information about the person's Internet activity. For instance, a surveillance technique that captures IP addresses would show only that a person visited the New York Times' website at http://www.nytimes.com, whereas a technique that captures URLs would also divulge the particular articles the person viewed. *See* [*In re Application of the United States of America for an Order Authorizing the Use of a*] *Pen Register* [*and Trap on [xxx] Internet Service Account/User Name [xxxxxxxx@xxx.com]*, 396 F. Supp. 2d 45, 49 (D. Mass. 2005)] ("[I]f the user then enters a search phrase [in the Google search engine], that search phrase would appear in the URL after the first forward slash. This would reveal content. . . ."). [512 F.3d at 510 n.6.]

4. Text Messages

This one also seems easy. Text messages are quintessentially content. In a suit brought by a city police officer against city and police officials for allegedly violating the Fourth Amendment when they reviewed the contents of stored text messages sent and received on the officer's city-issued alphanumeric pager without a warrant, the Supreme Court was willing to assume for the sake of argument that the police officer had a reasonable expectation of privacy in the messages and that the review was a search. It then held that the assumed warrantless search was nevertheless reasonable, on the strength of the "special needs" exception. *City of Ontario v. Quon*, 560 U.S. 746 (2010).

Why did the Court only assume, *arguendo,* that the review constituted a search, instead of so ruling?

> The Court must proceed with care when considering the whole concept of privacy expectations in communications made on electronic equipment owned by a government employer. The judiciary risks error by elaborating too fully on the Fourth Amendment implications of emerging technology before its role in society has become clear. In *Katz,* the Court relied on its own knowledge and experience to conclude that there is a reasonable expectation of privacy in a telephone booth. It is not so clear that courts at present are on so sure a ground. Prudence counsels caution before the facts in the instant case are used to establish far-reaching premises that define the existence, and extent, of privacy expectations enjoyed by employees when using employer-provided communication devices.
>
> Rapid changes in the dynamics of communication and information transmission are evident not just in the technology itself but in what society accepts as proper behavior. [*Id.* at 759.]

Context, therefore, matters even for content. If you text using a device supplied by your employer, "employer policies concerning communications will . . . shape the reasonable expectations of their employees, especially to the extent that such policies are clearly communicated." *Id.* at 760.

5. Telephony Metadata

So far, the examples we have considered concern *targeted* collection of third-party data — data about Carpenter's location during a certain period of time or Warshak's e-mails. Suppose, however, that the government asks Verizon to supply *all of its "call detail records"*— records of telephony metadata like numbers called, time and length of call, etc., but not contents of conversations — for *all of its customers* on a continuing basis, for the purpose of creating a massive database that the government can later "query" with identifiers like Carpenter's number or the date of the day before the Boston Marathon bombing? Should this kind of quantitatively greater collection change the qualitative Fourth Amendment analysis described above? We consider such "bulk collection" of third-party information in the next chapter.

6. Voiceprints and Voice Data Stored by Smart Speakers

Do you talk to your smart speakers such as Amazon Echo, Google Home, or Apple Homepod? Have you granted them access to your smart phone calendar and contacts or your e-mail account? Do you permit them to share your voiceprints with their manufacturer to "improve" recognition? Have you ever looked at the "history" of your voice commands (or of overheard conversations) that your speaking can create? Have you ever purged that history, if you can?

These questions all present many of the same issues addressed in this chapter, with the added nuances that the device may record some speech that you do not "voluntarily" wish to convey to it and that the device is undeniably your property located inside your home. *See* Note, *If These Walls Could Talk: The Smart Home and the Fourth Amendment Limits of the Third Party Doctrine,* 130 Harv. L. Rev. 1924 (2017); Andrew

Guthrie Ferguson, *Alexa, What Is Probable Cause?*, Slate, Nov. 20, 2018; Judith Shulevitz, *Alexa, Should We Trust You?*, The Atlantic, Nov. 2018. Try to fit the legal principles you now know to this medium, and you begin to get a sense of how difficult it is for courts — and the Fourth Amendment — to keep up with the technology.

THE THIRD-PARTY DOCTRINE: ORIGINS AND APPLICATIONS: SUMMARY OF BASIC PRINCIPLES

- The third-party doctrine established by *Smith v. Maryland* (the pen register case) and *United States v. Miller* (the bank records case) asserts that the government's collection of third-party records — records or information voluntarily conveyed to a third party, usually to effect a transaction — is not a search subject to the Fourth Amendment, because there is no reasonable expectation of privacy in such records.

- The third-party doctrine originally applied to telephone numbers dialed by a criminal defendant, not to the contents of his conversations, suggesting a distinction between "envelope information" (addressing, routing, and related customer or subscriber information), and "content information." Application of the same distinction to Internet routing information, however, has proven difficult.

- In *Carpenter v. United States*, the Supreme Court declined to extend the third-party doctrine to cell-site records. It held that the detailed physical map of a person's location that such records could provide "implicates privacy concerns far beyond those considered in *Smith* and *Miller*," and that cell phone locational information is not "truly 'shared,'" as it requires no affirmative act by the user beyond powering up the phone and because there is no way to avoid leaving a locational trail apart from disconnecting from the network.

- But neither such privacy implications nor such "involuntariness" is unique to cell-site records. The volume of transactional information a person now generates, the ubiquity of the methods by which such information is transmitted, and the retention by third parties of much of such information in computer-manipulable digital form, all raise concerns that are distinct from those considered in *Smith* and *Miller.* Partly for these reasons, social expectations of privacy in third-party records, and with them, the scope of the third-party doctrine, are in flux. Stressing that "the fact that the information is held by a third party does not by itself overcome the user's claim to Fourth Amendment protection," *Carpenter* seems unlikely to be a stopping point in the erosion of the doctrine.

24

The Collection and Use of Third-Party Records

The third-party doctrine often provides the government with a defense to a Fourth Amendment challenge, but an agency still needs affirmative authority for the collection of third-party records. When a collection effort uses identifiers relevant to current targets, it is sometimes called "targeted collection." Nat'l Research Council, *Bulk Collection of Signals Intelligence: Technical Options* 34 (2015) (*supra* p. 495). By contrast, "bulk collection" is the collection of records most of which are not (yet) relevant to current targets, usually because it is not yet possible to know whether the records have or will have intelligence value. *Id.*

A multitude of statutes authorize targeted collection, including provisions authorizing the use of "national security letters" (NSLs) from the Federal Bureau of Investigation (FBI) to a record-holder, as well as the business records provision of FISA, Section 501 (as amended by Section 215 of the USA Patriot Act and therefore usually called the Section 215 authority, codified as amended at 50 U.S.C. §1861 (2018)).

Until 2013, most observers expected that the FBI would use Section 215 orders for the targeted collection of transactional data for particular persons or other discrete identifiers (like a telephone number) on a case-by-case basis. In fact, some thought that the FBI would more likely use NSLs to collect most third-party records, because NSLs do not require prior Foreign Intelligence Surveillance Court (FISC) or other judicial approval.

Many were therefore shocked when documents leaked by Edward Snowden in 2013 revealed the aggressive use of Section 215 authority for the bulk collection of vast amounts of telephony metadata (essentially data about telephone calls without the contents of those calls) from millions of U.S. persons making calls within the

United States[1] "to create giant databases . . . that might *later* be queried on a case-by-case basis." Robert Chesney & Benjamin Wittes, *A Tale of Two NSA Leaks,* New Republic, June 10, 2013 (emphasis added).

In this chapter, we first consider and compare the authorities for targeted collection, and then turn to the authority for bulk collection both before Snowden's disclosure and after Congress enacted new legislation in response. We then conclude by considering the data mining of the databases collected from third-party records.

A. TARGETED COLLECTION OF THIRD-PARTY RECORDS

Below is a heavily redacted example of a national security letter issued in a targeted collection effort, followed by a judicial decision in a case testing the legality of such letters and comparing other government methods for collecting transactional data.

1. Even before the Section 215 bulk orders, certain "Internet metadata" were collected without any court order or any apparent statutory authority, according to a classified 2009 report of the Inspector General of the NSA. *See* Off. of the Inspector Gen., Nat'l Security Agency/Cent. Security Serv., *1109-0002 Working Draft,* Mar. 24, 2009, *available at* http://www.guardian.co.uk/world/interactive/2013/jun/27/nsa-inspector-general-report-document-data-collection. This collection was temporarily halted in 2004 by a "palace revolt" by Department of Justice officials, who resisted White House efforts to have the then-seriously-ill Attorney General John Ashcroft sign an order authorizing the program's continuation. The collection effort was then resumed after an order was obtained from the FISC. This program was reportedly discontinued in 2011 as a result of an interagency review.

ALL INFORMATION CONTAINED HEREIN IS UNCLASSIFIED EXCEPT WHERE SHOWN OTHERWISE

U.S. Department of Justice

Federal Bureau of Investigation

In Reply, Please Refer to File No

[Drafting] Field Division
[Street Address]
[City, State, Zip]

[Month Date, Year]

[Mr /Mrs.] [COMPANY POINT OF CONTACT]
[TITLE]
[COMPANY]
[STREET ADDRESS]
[CITY, STATE No Zip Code]

Dear [Mr /Mrs] [LAST NAME]:

Under the authority of Executive Order 12333, dated December 4, 1981, and pursuant to Title 18, United States Code (U S.C), Section 2709 (as amended, October 26, 2001), you are hereby directed to provide the Federal Bureau of Investigation

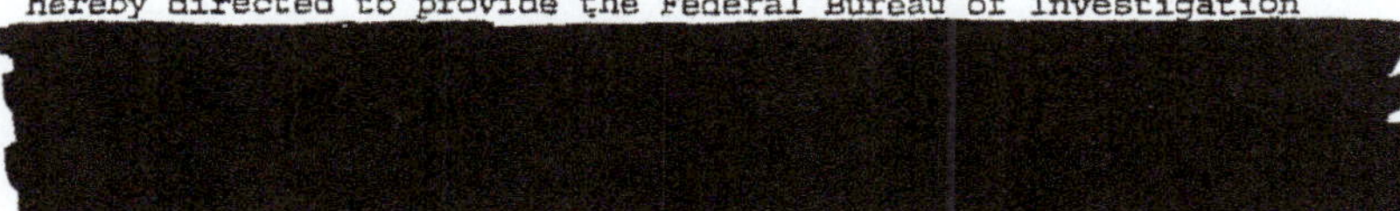

b2-2
b7E-1

In accordance with Title 18, U.S.C., Section 2709(b), I certify that the information sought is relevant to an authorized investigation to protect against international terrorism or clandestine intelligence activities, and that such an investigation of a United States person is not conducted solely on the basis of activities protected by the first amendment of the Constitution of the United States

You are further advised that Title 18, U.S C , Section 2709(c), prohibits any officer, employee or agent of yours from disclosing to any person that the FBI has sought or obtained access to information or records under these provisions.

b2-2
b7E-1

CLASSIFIED DECISIONS FINALIZED BY DEPARTMENT REVIEW COMMITTEE (DRC)
DATE: 07-01-2004

CA# 03-2522

CLASSIFIED BY 65179 dmt/bcs/amw 6/5/2004
REASON: 1.4 (c)
DECLASSIFY ON: x 6/5/2029

Patriot Act II-828

SECRET

DECLASSIFIED BY 65179dmt/bcs/amw
ON 8/3/2004

[Mr /Mrs] [COMPANY POINT OF CONTACT]

Your cooperation in this matter is greatly appreciated

Sincerely,

[ADIC/SAC Name]
Assistant Director/Special
Agent in Charge

CLASSIFIED DECISIONS FINALIZED BY
DEPARTMENT REVIEW COMMITTEE (DRC)
DATE: 07-01-2004

CA# 03-2522

ALL INFORMATION CONTAINED
HEREIN IS UNCLASSIFIED EXCEPT
WHERE SHOWN OTHERWISE

CLASSIFIED BY 65179 dmb/bcs/smw 6/30/2004
REASON: 1.4 (c)
DECLASSIFY ON: X 6/30/2029

2

Patriot Act II-829

SECRET

DECLASSIFIED BY 65179 dmb/bcs/smw
ON 8/3/2004

Reading *Doe v. Ashcroft* (*Doe I*)

In the following case, the recipient of an NSL challenged it on First and Fourth Amendment grounds. Consider these questions:

- Who issues an NSL? What is the statutory standard for its issuance? Who applies that standard?
- Who issues an administrative subpoena? What is the standard for its issuance? How can such a subpoena be subjected to judicial review? What is the judicial standard for review?
- How is an NSL different from an administrative subpoena? Why doesn't the recipient of an NSL simply file a challenge to it in court?
- The NSL in *Doe I* sought "subscriber information and toll billing records," not content. Assuming the third-party record doctrine applies, how can Doe assert any Fourth Amendment right in its challenge to the NSL? *Whose* Fourth Amendment right? What about a First Amendment right? *Whose* First Amendment right?

Doe v. Ashcroft (*Doe I*)

United States District Court, Southern District of New York, 2004
334 F. Supp. 2d 471, *vacated and remanded sub nom.*
Doe v. Gonzales, 449 F.3d 415 (2d Cir. 2006)

MARRERO, J. . . . Plaintiffs in this case challenge the constitutionality of 18 U.S.C. §2709 ("§2709").[2] That statute authorizes the Federal Bureau of Investigation ("FBI") to compel communications firms, such as internet service providers ("ISPs") or telephone companies, to produce certain customer records whenever the FBI certifies that those records are "relevant to an authorized investigation to protect against international terrorism or clandestine intelligence activities." [*Id.*] The FBI's demands under §2709 are issued in the form of national security letters ("NSLs"), which constitute a unique form of administrative subpoena cloaked in secrecy and pertaining to national security issues. The statute bars all NSL recipients from ever disclosing that the FBI has issued an NSL.

The lead plaintiff, called "John Doe" ("Doe") for purposes of this litigation, is described in the complaint as an internet access firm that received an NSL. . . .

II. BACKGROUND. . . .

A. Doe's Receipt of an NSL

After receiving a call from an FBI agent informing him that he would be served with an NSL, Doe received a document, printed on FBI letterhead, which stated that, "pursuant to Title 18, United States Code (U.S.C.), Section 2709" Doe was "directed"

[2. This section was amended by the USA Patriot Improvement and Reauthorization Act in 2006, as explained in the following Notes and Questions. — Eds.]

to provide certain information to the Government. As required by the terms of §2709, in the NSL the FBI "certif[ied] that the information sought [was] relevant to an authorized investigation to protect against international terrorism or clandestine intelligence activities." Doe was "further advised" that §2709(c) prohibited him, or his officers, agents, or employees, "from disclosing to *any person* that the FBI has sought or obtained access to information or records under these provisions." Doe was "requested to provide records responsive to [the] request *personally*" to a designated individual, and to not transmit the records by mail or even mention the NSL in *any* telephone conversation. . . .

. . . Doe has not complied with the NSL request, and has instead engaged counsel to bring the present lawsuit.

B. §2709 in General

As stated above, §2709 authorizes the FBI to issue NSLs to compel communications firms to produce certain customer records whenever the FBI certifies that those records are relevant to an authorized international terrorism or counterintelligence investigation, and the statute also categorically bars NSL recipients from disclosing the inquiry. In relevant part, it states:

> (a) Duty to provide. — A wire or electronic communication service provider shall comply with a request for subscriber information and toll billing records information, or electronic communication transactional records in its custody or possession made by the Director of the Federal Bureau of Investigation under subsection (b) of this section.
>
> (b) Required certification. — The Director of the Federal Bureau of Investigation, or his designee in a position not lower than Deputy Assistant Director at Bureau headquarters or a Special Agent in Charge in a Bureau field office designated by the Director, may — (1) request the name, address, length of service, and local and long distance toll billing records of a person or entity if the Director (or his designee) certifies in writing to the wire or electronic communication service provider to which the request is made that the name, address, length of service, and toll billing records sought are relevant to an authorized investigation to protect against international terrorism or clandestine intelligence activities, provided that such an investigation of a United States person is not conducted solely on the basis of activities protected by the first amendment to the Constitution of the United States. . . .
>
> (c) Prohibition of certain disclosure. — No wire or electronic communication service provider, or officer, employee, or agent thereof, shall disclose to any person that the Federal Bureau of Investigation has sought or obtained access to information or records under this section. . . .

Section 2709 is one of only a handful of statutes authorizing the Government to issue NSLs. The other NSL statutes authorize the Government to compel disclosure of certain financial and credit records which it certifies are relevant to international terrorism or counter-intelligence investigations, and to compel disclosure of certain records of current or former government employees who have (or have had) access to classified information. . . .

D. NSLs and Other Information-Gathering Authority

It is instructive to place the Government's NSL authority in the context of other means by which the Government gathers information of the type covered by §2709 because Congress (in passing and amending the NSL statutes) and the parties here (in contesting §2709's constitutionality) have drawn analogies to those other authorities as grounds for or against its validity. The relationship of §2709 to other related statutes supplies a backdrop for assessing congressional intent and judging the validity of the law on its face and as applied. In addition, an analysis of these analogous information-gathering methods indicates that NSLs such as the ones authorized by §2709 provide fewer procedural protections to the recipient than any other information-gathering technique the Government employs to procure information similar to that which it obtains pursuant to §2709.

1. Administrative Subpoenas

The most important set of statutes relevant to this case are those authorizing federal agencies to issue administrative subpoenas for the purpose of executing the particular agency's function. Ordinary administrative subpoenas, which are far more common than NSLs, may be issued by most federal agencies, as authorized by the hundreds of applicable statutes in federal law. For example, the Internal Revenue Service (IRS) may issue subpoenas to investigate possible violations of the tax code, and the Securities Exchange Commission (SEC) may issue subpoenas to investigate possible violations of the securities laws. . . .

There is a wide body of law which pertains to administrative subpoenas generally. According to the Government's central theory in this case, those standing rules would presumably also apply to NSLs, even if not so explicitly stated in the text of the statute. Where an agency seeks a court order to enforce a subpoena against a resisting subpoena recipient, courts will enforce the subpoena as long as: (1) the agency's investigation is being conducted pursuant to a legitimate purpose, (2) the inquiry is relevant to that purpose, (3) the information is not already within the agency's possession, and (4) the proper procedures have been followed. The Second Circuit has described these standards as "minimal." Even if an administrative subpoena meets these initial criteria to be enforceable, its recipient may nevertheless affirmatively challenge the subpoena on other grounds, such as an allegation that it was issued with an improper purpose or that the information sought is privileged.

Unlike the NSL statutes, most administrative subpoena laws either contain no provision requiring secrecy, or allow for only limited secrecy in special cases. For example, some administrative subpoena statutes permit the investigating agency to apply for a court order to temporarily bar disclosure of the inquiry, generally during specific renewable increments or for an appropriate period of time fixed by the court, where such disclosure could jeopardize the investigation. . . .

2. Subpoena Authority in the Criminal Context

In its role as a party to a federal criminal proceeding (including a grand jury proceeding), the Government has broad authority to issue a subpoena to obtain witness testimony or "*any* books, papers, documents, data, or other objects the subpoena designates."[52] Although such subpoenas "are issued in the name of the district court over

52. Fed. R. Crim. P. 17(a), (c)(1) (emphasis added).

the signature of the clerk, they are issued pro forma and in blank to anyone requesting them," and the "court exercises no prior control whatsoever upon their use."[53]

The court becomes involved in the subpoena process only if the subpoenaed party moves to quash the request as "unreasonable or oppressive,"[54] or if the Government seeks to compel compliance with the subpoena. The reasonableness of a subpoena depends on the context. For example, to survive a motion to quash, a subpoena issued in connection with a criminal trial "must make a reasonably specific request for information that would be both relevant and admissible at trial."[55] By contrast, a grand jury subpoena is generally enforced as long as there is a "reasonable possibility that the category of materials the Government seeks will produce information relevant to the general subject of the grand jury's investigation."[56] Considering the grand jury's broad investigatory power and minimal court supervision, it is accurate to observe, as the Second Circuit did long ago, that "[b]asically the grand jury is a law enforcement agency."[57]

While materials presented in a criminal trial setting are generally public, the federal rules impose stringent secrecy requirements on certain grand jury participants, including the attorneys, court reporters, and grand jurors.[58] . . .

In certain contexts, the Government may issue subpoenas related to criminal investigations even without initiating a formal criminal proceeding. For example, the United States Attorney General is authorized to issue administrative subpoenas, without convening a grand jury, to investigate federal narcotics crimes, racketeering crimes, health care related crimes, and crimes involving the exploitation of children. In each of these instances, the administrative process is governed by the general rules described above, providing safeguards of judicial review.

3. Background Rules Governing Disclosure of Stored Electronic Communications

Title II of the ECPA [also called the Stored Communications Act], in which §2709 was enacted, sets forth an intricate framework by which electronic communications providers, such as ISPs and phone companies, may be compelled to disclose stored electronic information to the Government. The framework described below operates independently of the rules governing NSLs issued pursuant to §2709, but may aid with interpretation of §2709.

The Government may obtain basic subscriber information[69] merely by issuing an authorized administrative subpoena, trial subpoena, or grand jury subpoena, and the Government need not notify the subscriber of the request.

---

53. *In re Grand Jury Proceedings*, 486 F.2d 85, 90 (3d Cir. 1973).

54. Fed. R. Crim. P. 17(c)(2).

55. *United States v. R. Enters., Inc.*, 498 U.S. 292, 299 (1991) (*citing United States v. Nixon*, 418 U.S. 683, 700 (1974)).

56. *Id.* at 301.

57. *United States v. Cleary*, 265 F.2d 459, 461 (2d Cir. 1959).

58. *See* Fed. R. Crim. P. 6(e).

69. Basic subscriber information includes: (1) a subscriber's name and (2) address; (3) the subscriber's local and long distance telephone connection records, or records of session times and durations; (4) the subscriber's length of service and types of service he has utilized; (5) any telephone or instrument

If the Government gives prior notice to the subscriber, or otherwise complies with certain delayed notice procedures, the Government may also subpoena the *contents* of electronic communications which are either (1) retained on a system for storage purposes (*e.g.*, opened email which remains on an ISP's server), or (2) retained, for more than 180 days, in intermediate or temporary storage (*e.g.*, unopened email on an ISP's server). For the Government to obtain the contents of electronic communications kept for 180 days or less in intermediate or temporary storage (e.g., unopened email on an ISP's server), it must obtain a search warrant under Federal Rule of Criminal Procedure 41, or the state equivalent. In other words, the Government would have to appear before a neutral magistrate and make a showing of probable cause. The Government may also obtain a court order requiring an electronic communications service provider to turn over transactional and content information by setting forth "specific and articulable facts showing that there are reasonable grounds to believe that" the information sought is "relevant and material to an ongoing criminal investigation."[75]

The ECPA permits the Government to seek a court order prohibiting the communications provider from revealing the Government's inquiry "for such period as the court deems appropriate" if the court determines that such disclosure, among other things, would result in "destruction of or tampering with evidence" or "seriously jeopardizing an investigation or unduly delaying a trial."[76]

4. Mail

Government law enforcement agencies are authorized to request the Postal Inspector to initiate a so-called "mail cover" to obtain any information appearing on the outside of a particular piece of mail.[77] Among other grounds, the law enforcement agency can obtain a mail cover by "specify[ing] the reasonable grounds to demonstrate the mail cover is necessary" to "[p]rotect the national security" or to "[o]btain information regarding the commission or attempted commission of a crime." There is no requirement that the mail sender or recipient be notified of the mail cover.

The Government must obtain a warrant based upon probable cause to open and inspect sealed mail because the contents of mail are protected by the Fourth Amendment. As the Supreme Court established long ago: "Whilst in the mail, [a person's papers] can only be opened and examined under like warrant, issued upon similar oath or affirmation, particularly describing the thing to be seized, as is required when papers are subjected to search in one's own household."[80]

5. Pen Registers and Trap and Trace Devices

Pen registers and trap and trace devices record certain electronic communications data indicating the origins and destinations of various "dialing, routing,

---

number or other subscriber number or identity, including any temporarily assigned network address; and (6) the subscriber's means and source of payment for the service. *See* 18 U.S.C. §2703(c)(2).

75. 18 U.S.C. §2703(d).

76. *Id.* §2705(b).

77. *See* 39 C.F.R. §233.3.

80. *See Ex parte Jackson*, 96 U.S. 727, 733 (1877).

addressing, or signaling information," *e.g.*, the phone numbers dialed to and from a telephone.[81] In criminal investigations, the Government must apply for a court order, renewable in 60-day increments, to install or collect data from such devices, though the standard for issuing such an order is relatively low. The Government need only show that "the information likely to be obtained by such installation and use is relevant to an ongoing criminal investigation."[83]

The person owning the communications device is prohibited, unless otherwise directed by court order, from disclosing the fact that a pen register or trap and trace device is in effect.

6. Wiretaps and Electronic Eavesdropping

The Fourth Amendment protects against warrantless Government wiretapping. Federal legislation specifies the procedures by which law enforcement officials may obtain a court order to conduct wiretaps and other forms of electronic eavesdropping. The requirements are rigorous. Among other things, the Government must show that: (1) "there is probable cause for belief that an individual is committing, has committed, or is about to commit" one of a list of enumerated crimes; (2) "there is probable cause for belief that particular communications concerning that offense will be obtained through such interception"; and (3) "normal investigative procedures have been tried and have failed or reasonably appear to be unlikely to succeed if tried or to be too dangerous."[87] Such orders are not available "for any period longer than is necessary to achieve the objective of the authorization," subject to a renewable maximum of 30 days.[88] The communications provider is prohibited from disclosing that a wiretap or electronic surveillance is in place, "except as may otherwise be required by legal process and then only after prior notification" to the appropriate law enforcement authorities.[89] . . .

IV. DISCUSSION. . . .

B. As Applied Here, Section 2709 Lacks Procedural Protections Necessary to Vindicate Constitutional Rights

1. Section 2709 and the Fourth Amendment[118] . . .

. . . The Fourth Amendment's protection against unreasonable searches applies to administrative subpoenas, even though issuing a subpoena does not involve a

---

81. *See* 18 U.S.C. §3127(3)-(4).

83. *Id.* §3123(a).

87. *Id.* §2518(3).

88. *Id.* §2518(5).

89. *Id.* §2511(2)(a)(ii).

118. To be clear, the Fourth Amendment rights at issue here belong to the person or entity receiving the NSL, not to the person or entity to whom the subpoenaed records pertain. Individuals possess a limited Fourth Amendment interest in records which they voluntarily convey to a third party. *See* [*Smith v. Maryland,* 442 U.S. 735, 742-746 (1979), *supra* p. 680; *United States v. Miller*, 425 U.S. 435, 440-443 (1976).]

literal physical intrusion or search. In so doing, the Supreme Court explained that the Fourth Amendment is not "confined literally to searches and seizures as such, but extends as well to the orderly taking under compulsion of process."[122]

However, because administrative subpoenas are "at best, constructive searches," there is no requirement that they be issued pursuant to a warrant or that they be supported by probable cause. Instead, an administrative subpoena needs only to be "reasonable," which the Supreme Court has interpreted to mean that (1) the administrative subpoena is "within the authority of the agency;" (2) that the demand is "not too indefinite;" and (3) that the information sought is "reasonably relevant" to a proper inquiry.[124]

While the Fourth Amendment reasonableness standard is permissive in the context of administrative subpoenas, the constitutionality of the administrative subpoena is predicated on the availability of a neutral tribunal to determine, after a subpoena is issued, whether the subpoena actually complies with the Fourth Amendment's demands. In contrast to an actual physical search, which must be justified by the warrant and probable cause requirements occurring *before* the search, an administrative subpoena "is regulated by, and its justification derives from, [judicial] process" available *after* the subpoena is issued.[125]

Accordingly, the Supreme Court has held that an administrative subpoena "may not be made and enforced" by the administrative agency; rather, the subpoenaed party must be able to "obtain judicial review of the reasonableness of the demand prior to suffering penalties for refusing to comply."[126] In sum, longstanding Supreme Court doctrine makes clear that an administrative subpoena statute is consistent with the Fourth Amendment when it is subject to "judicial supervision" and "surrounded by every safeguard of judicial restraint."[127]

Plaintiffs contend that §2709 violates this Fourth Amendment process-based guarantee because it gives the FBI alone the power to issue as well as enforce its own NSLs, instead of contemplating some form of judicial review. Although Plaintiffs appear to concede that the statute does not authorize the FBI to literally enforce the terms of an NSL by, for example, unilaterally seizing documents or imposing fines, Plaintiffs contend that §2709 has the *practical* effect of coercing compliance. . . .

Nevertheless, as discussed below, many potential NSL recipients may have particular interests in resisting an NSL, *e.g.*, because they have contractually obligated themselves to protect the anonymity of their subscribers or because their own rights are uniquely implicated by what they regard as an intrusive and secretive NSL regime. For example, since the definition of "wire or electronic communication service provider," 18 U.S.C. §2709(a), is so vague, the statute could (and may currently) be used to seek subscriber lists or other information from an association that also provides electronic communication services (e.g., email addresses) to its members, or to seek records from libraries that many, including the *amici* appearing in this proceeding, fear will chill speech and use of these invaluable public institutions. . . .

122. [*See United States v. Morton Salt Co.*, 338 U.S. 632, 651-652 (1950).]

124. *Id.* at 652.

125. *United States v. Bailey (In re Subpoena Duces Tecum)*, 228 F.3d 341, 348 (4th Cir. 2000).

126. *See v. City of Seattle*, 387 U.S. 541, 544-45 (1967); *see also Oklahoma Press Publishing Co. v. Walling*, 327 U.S. 186, 217 (1946).

127. *Oklahoma Press*, 327 U.S. at 217.

The crux of the problem is that the form NSL, like the one issued in this case, which is preceded by a personal call from an FBI agent, is framed in imposing language on FBI letterhead and which, citing the authorizing statute, orders a combination of disclosure in person and in complete secrecy, essentially coerces the reasonable recipient into immediate compliance. Objectively viewed, it is improbable that an FBI summons invoking the authority of a certified "investigation to protect against international terrorism or clandestine intelligence activities," and phrased in tones sounding virtually as biblical commandment, would not be perceived with some apprehension by an ordinary person and therefore elicit passive obedience from a reasonable NSL recipient. The full weight of this ominous writ is especially felt when the NSL's plain language, in a measure that enhances its aura as an expression of public will, prohibits disclosing the issuance of the NSL to "any person." Reading such strictures, it is also highly unlikely that an NSL recipient reasonably would know that he may have a right to contest the NSL, and that a process to do so may exist through a judicial proceeding.

Because neither the statute, nor an NSL, nor the FBI agents dealing with the recipient say as much, all but the most mettlesome and undaunted NSL recipients would consider themselves effectively barred from consulting an attorney or anyone else who might advise them otherwise, as well as bound to absolute silence about the very existence of the NSL. . . .

The evidence in this case bears out the hypothesis that NSLs work coercively in this way. The ACLU obtained, via the Freedom of Information Act ("FOIA"), and presented to the Court in this proceeding, a document listing all the NSLs the Government issued from October 2001 through January 2003. Although the entire substance of the document is redacted, it is apparent that hundreds of NSL requests were made during that period. Because §2709 has been available to the FBI since 1986 (and its financial records counterpart in RFPA since 1978), the Court concludes that there must have been hundreds more NSLs issued in that long time span. The evidence suggests that, until now, none of those NSLs was ever challenged in any court. . . .

. . . The Court thus concludes that in practice NSLs are essentially unreviewable because, as explained, given the language and tone of the statute as carried into the NSL by the FBI, the recipient would consider himself, in virtually every case, obliged to comply, with no other option but to immediately obey and stay quiet. . . .

Accordingly, the Court concludes that §2709, as applied here, must be invalidated because in all but the exceptional case it has the effect of authorizing coercive searches effectively immune from any judicial process, in violation of the Fourth Amendment. . . .

2. NSLs May Violate ISP Subscribers' Rights

Plaintiffs have focused on the possibility that §2709 could be used to infringe subscribers' First Amendment rights of anonymous speech and association. Though it is not necessary to precisely define the scope of ISP subscribers' First Amendment rights, the Court concludes that §2709 may, in a given case, violate a subscriber's First Amendment privacy rights, as well as other legal rights, if judicial review is not readily available to an ISP that receives an NSL. . . .

The Supreme Court has recognized the First Amendment right to anonymous speech at least since *Talley v. California*,[161] which invalidated a California law requiring that handbills distributed to the public contain certain identifying information about the source of the handbills. The Court stated that the "identification requirement would tend to restrict freedom to distribute information and thereby freedom of expression."[162] The Supreme Court has also invalidated identification requirements pertaining to persons distributing campaign literature, persons circulating petitions for state ballot initiatives, and persons engaging in door-to-door religious advocacy.

In a related doctrine, the Supreme Court has held that "compelled disclosure of affiliation with groups engaged in advocacy" amounts to a "restraint on freedom of association" where disclosure could expose the members to "public hostility."[166] Laws mandating such disclosures will be upheld only where the Government interest is compelling.

The Court concludes that such First Amendment rights may be infringed by application of §2709 in a given case. For example, the FBI theoretically could issue to a political campaign's computer systems operator a §2709 NSL compelling production of the names of all persons who have email addresses through the campaign's computer systems. The FBI theoretically could also issue an NSL under §2709 to discern the identity of someone whose anonymous online web log, or "blog," is critical of the Government. Such inquiries might be beyond the permissible scope of the FBI's power under §2709 because the targeted information might not be relevant to an authorized investigation to protect against international terrorism or clandestine intelligence activities, or because the inquiry might be conducted solely on the basis of activities protected by the First Amendment. These prospects only highlight the potential danger of the FBI's self-certification process and the absence of judicial oversight.

Other rights may also be violated by the disclosure contemplated by the statute; the statute's reference to "transactional records" creates ambiguity regarding the scope of the information required to be produced by the NSL recipient. If the recipient — who in the NSL is called upon to exercise judgment in determining the extent to which complying materials constitute transactional records rather than content — interprets the NSL broadly as requiring production of all e-mail header information, including subject lines, for example, some disclosures conceivably may reveal information protected by the subscriber's attorney-client privilege, *e.g.*, a communication with an attorney where the subject line conveys privileged or possibly incriminating information. Indeed, the practical absence of judicial review may lead ISPs to disclose information that is protected from disclosure by the NSL statute itself, such as in a case where the NSL was initiated solely in retaliation for the subscriber's exercise of his First Amendment rights, as prohibited by §2709(b)(1)-(b)(2). Only a court would be able to definitively construe the statutory and First Amendment rights at issue in the "First Amendment retaliation" provision of the statute, and to strike a proper balance among those interests.

---

161. 362 U.S. 60 (1960).

162. *Id.* at 64.

166. *NAACP v. State of Alabama ex rel. Patterson*, 357 U.S. 449, 462 (1958).

The Government asserts that disclosure of the information sought under §2709 could not violate a subscriber's rights (and thus demands no judicial process) because the information which a §2709 NSL seeks has been voluntarily conveyed to the ISP who receives the NSL. According to the Government, an internet speaker relinquishes any interest in any anonymity, and any protected claim to that information, as soon as he releases his identity and other information to his ISP. In support of its position, the Government cites the Supreme Court's holding [in *Smith* and *Miller*] that, at least in the Fourth Amendment context involving the Government installing a pen register or obtaining bank records, when a person voluntarily conveys information to third parties, he assumes the risk that the information will be turned over to the Government. . . .

The evidence on the record now before this Court demonstrates that the information available through a §2709 NSL served upon an ISP could easily be used to disclose vast amounts of anonymous speech and associational activity. For instance, §2709 imposes a duty to provide "electronic communication transactional records," a phrase which, though undefined in the statute, certainly encompasses a log of email addresses with whom a subscriber has corresponded and the web pages that a subscriber visits. Those transactional records can reveal, among other things, the anonymous message boards to which a person logs on or posts, the electronic newsletters to which he subscribes, and the advocacy websites he visits. Moreover, §2709 imposes a duty on ISPs to provide the names and addresses of subscribers, thus enabling the Government to specifically identify someone who has written anonymously on the internet.[175] As discussed above, given that an NSL recipient is directed by the FBI to turn over all information "*which you consider to be* an electronic communication transactional record," the §2709 NSL could also reasonably be interpreted by an ISP to require, at minimum, disclosure of all e-mail header information, including subject lines.

In stark contrast to this potential to compile elaborate dossiers on internet users, the information obtainable by a pen register is far more limited. As the Supreme Court in *Smith* was careful to note:

> [Pen registers] disclose only the telephone numbers that have been dialed — a means of establishing communication. Neither the purport of any communication between the caller and the recipient of the call, their identities, nor whether the call was even completed is disclosed by pen registers.

The Court doubts that the result in *Smith* would have been the same if a pen register operated as a key to the most intimate details and passions of a person's private life.

The more apt Supreme Court case for evaluating the assumption of risk argument at issue here is *Katz v. United States*, the seminal decision underlying both

---

175. NSLs can potentially reveal far more than constitutionally-protected associational activity or anonymous speech. By revealing the websites one visits, the Government can learn, among many other potential examples, what books the subscriber enjoys reading or where a subscriber shops. As one commentator has observed, the records compiled by ISPs can "enable the government to assemble a profile of an individual's finances, health, psychology, beliefs, politics, interests, and lifestyle." Daniel J. Solove, *Digital Dossiers and the Dissipation of Fourth Amendment Privacy*, 75 S. Cal. L. Rev. 1083, 1084 (2002).

Smith and *Miller*. *Katz* held that the Fourth Amendment's privacy protections applied where the Government wiretapped a telephone call placed from a public phone booth. Especially noteworthy and pertinent to this case is the Supreme Court's remark that: "The Government's activities in electronically listening to and recording the petitioner's words violated the privacy upon which he justifiably relied while using the telephone booth and thus constituted a 'search and seizure' within the meaning of the Fourth Amendment." The Supreme Court also stated that a person entering a phone booth who "shuts the door behind him" is "surely entitled to assume that the words he utters into the mouthpiece will not be broadcast to the world," and held that, "[t]o read the Constitution more narrowly is to ignore the vital role that the public telephone has come to play in private communication."

Applying that reasoning to anonymous internet speech and associational activity is relatively straightforward. A person who signs onto an anonymous forum under a pseudonym, for example, is essentially "shut[ting] the door behind him," and is surely entitled to a reasonable expectation that his speech, whatever form the expression assumes, will not be accessible to the Government to be broadcast to the world absent appropriate legal process. To hold otherwise would ignore the role of the internet as a remarkably powerful forum for private communication and association. Even the Government concedes here that the internet is an "important vehicle for the free exchange of ideas and facilitates associations."

To be sure, the Court is keenly mindful of the Government's reminder that the internet may also serve as a vehicle for crime. The Court equally recognizes that circumstances exist in which the First Amendment rights of association and anonymity must yield to a more compelling Government interest in obtaining records from internet firms. To this end, the Court re-emphasizes that it does not here purport to set forth the scope of these First Amendment rights in general, or define them in this or any other case. The Court holds only that such fundamental rights are certainly implicated in some cases in which the Government may employ §2709 broadly to gather information, thus requiring that the process incorporate the safeguards of some judicial review to ensure that if an infringement of those rights is asserted, they are adequately protected through fair process in an independent neutral tribunal. Because the necessary procedural protections are wholly absent here, the Court finds on this ground additional cause for invalidating §2709 as applied.

C. Constitutionality of the Non-Disclosure Provision

Finally, the Court turns to the issue of whether the Government may properly enforce §2709(c), the non-disclosure provision, against Doe or any other person who has previously received an NSL. . . .

[The court held that the nondisclosure provision imposed a content-based prior restraint on speech, subject to strict scrutiny.]

. . . [T]he Government cites no authority supporting the open-ended proposition that it may universally . . . impose perpetual secrecy upon an entire category of future cases whose details are unknown and whose particular twists and turns may not justify, for all time and all places, demanding unremitting concealment and imposing a disproportionate burden on free speech. . . .

VI. CONCLUSION

To summarize, the Court concludes that the compulsory, secret, and unreviewable production of information required by the FBI's application of 18 U.S.C. §2709 violates the Fourth Amendment, and that the non-disclosure provision of 18 U.S.C. §2709(c) violates the First Amendment. The Government is therefore enjoined from issuing NSLs under §2709 or from enforcing the non-disclosure provision in this or any other case, but enforcement of the Court's judgment will be stayed pending appeal, or if no appeal is filed, for 90 days. . . .[3]

Carpenter v. United States

United States Supreme Court, 2018
138 S. Ct. 2206

[A portion of the opinion is set out *supra* p. 685.]

Chief Justice Roberts delivered the opinion of the Court. . . .

IV . . .

Justice Alito contends that the warrant requirement simply does not apply when the Government acquires records using compulsory process. Unlike an actual search, he says, subpoenas for documents do not involve the direct taking of evidence; they are at most a "constructive search" conducted by the target of the subpoena. . . .

But this Court has never held that the Government may subpoena third parties for records in which the suspect has a reasonable expectation of privacy. Almost all of the examples Justice Alito cites contemplated requests for evidence implicating diminished privacy interests or for a corporation's own books. The lone exception, of course, is *Miller,* where the Court's analysis of the third-party subpoena merged with the application of the third-party doctrine. 425 U.S., at 444 (concluding that Miller lacked the necessary privacy interest to contest the issuance of a subpoena to his bank).

Justice Alito overlooks the critical issue. At some point, the dissent should recognize that CSLI is an entirely different species of business record — something that implicates basic Fourth Amendment concerns about arbitrary government power much more directly than corporate tax or payroll ledgers. . . .

If the choice to proceed by subpoena provided a categorical limitation on Fourth Amendment protection, no type of record would ever be protected by the warrant requirement. Under Justice Alito's view, private letters, digital contents of

---

[3. After a different district court also found that the nondisclosure provisions of the NSL legislation violated the First Amendment, *Doe v. Gonzales* (*Doe II*), 386 F. Supp. 2d 66 (D. Conn. 2004), the two cases were consolidated on appeal. The appeal was then dismissed as moot after Congress amended the relevant NSL statute in response to these decisions, as described *infra. See Doe v. Gonzales,* 449 F.3d 415 (2d Cir. 2006). — Eds.]

a cell phone — any personal information reduced to document form, in fact — may be collected by subpoena for no reason other than "official curiosity." *United States v. Morton Salt Co.,* 338 U.S. 632, 652 (1950). Justice Kennedy declines to adopt the radical implications of this theory, leaving open the question whether the warrant requirement applies "when the Government obtains the modern-day equivalents of an individual's own 'papers' or 'effects,' even when those papers or effects are held by a third party." *Post,* at 13 (citing *United States v. Warshak,* 631 F.3d 266, 283-288 (C.A.6 2010)). That would be a sensible exception, because it would prevent the subpoena doctrine from overcoming any reasonable expectation of privacy. If the third-party doctrine does not apply to the "modern-day equivalents of an individual's own 'papers' or 'effects,'" then the clear implication is that the documents should receive full Fourth Amendment protection. We simply think that such protection should extend as well to a detailed log of a person's movements over several years.

This is certainly not to say that all orders compelling the production of documents will require a showing of probable cause. The Government will be able to use subpoenas to acquire records in the overwhelming majority of investigations. We hold only that a warrant is required in the rare case where the suspect has a legitimate privacy interest in records held by a third party.

Further, even though the Government will generally need a warrant to access CSLI, case-specific exceptions may support a warrantless search of an individual's cell-site records under certain circumstances. "One well-recognized exception applies when '"the exigencies of the situation" make the needs of law enforcement so compelling that [a] warrantless search is objectively reasonable under the Fourth Amendment.'" *Kentucky v. King,* 563 U.S. 452, 460 (2011) (quoting *Mincey v. Arizona,* 437 U.S. 385, 394 (1978)). Such exigencies include the need to pursue a fleeing suspect, protect individuals who are threatened with imminent harm, or prevent the imminent destruction of evidence. 563 U.S., at 460, and n.3.

As a result, if law enforcement is confronted with an urgent situation, such fact-specific threats will likely justify the warrantless collection of CSLI. Lower courts, for instance, have approved warrantless searches related to bomb threats, active shootings, and child abductions. Our decision today does not call into doubt warrantless access to CSLI in such circumstances. While police must get a warrant when collecting CSLI to assist in the mine-run criminal investigation, the rule we set forth does not limit their ability to respond to an ongoing emergency.

Justice Alito, with whom Justice Thomas joins, dissenting. . . .

I . . .

D . . .

As a matter of modern doctrine, this case is . . . straightforward. As Justice Kennedy explains, no search or seizure of Carpenter or his property occurred in this case. But even if the majority were right that the Government "searched" Carpenter, it would at most be a "figurative or constructive search" governed by the *Oklahoma Press* standard, not an "actual search" controlled by the Fourth Amendment's warrant requirement.

And there is no doubt that the Government met the *Oklahoma Press* standard here. Under *Oklahoma Press,* a court order must "'be sufficiently limited in scope, relevant in purpose, and specific in directive so that compliance will not be unreasonably burdensome.'" *Lone Steer, Inc., supra* at 415. Here, the type of order obtained by the Government almost necessarily satisfies that standard. The Stored Communications Act allows a court to issue the relevant type of order "only if the governmental entity offers specific and articulable facts showing that there are reasonable grounds to believe that... the records... sough[t] are relevant and material to an ongoing criminal investigation." 18 U.S.C. §2703(d). And the court "may quash or modify such order" if the provider objects that the "records requested are unusually voluminous in nature or compliance with such order otherwise would cause an undue burden on such provider." *Ibid.* No such objection was made in this case, and Carpenter does not suggest that the orders contravened the *Oklahoma Press* standard in any other way....

Notes and Questions

1. NSLs, Administrative Subpoenas, and Warrants. An NSL is issued by the FBI or another federal agency without a court order. The agency head or her designate decides that the NSL should be used for an intelligence, counterintelligence, law enforcement, or international terrorism investigation. The purpose, procedure, third-party record holder, and type of record available vary with the particular authorizing statute. If the recipient refuses, the agency may seek judicial enforcement. A former General Counsel to the FBI asserts that "it is not an exaggeration to say that virtually every significant national security investigation... requires the use of NSLs for at least some critical [transactional] information." Michael German et al., *National Security Letters: Building Blocks for Investigations or Intrusive Tools?*, A.B.A. J., Sept. 1, 2012 (comments by Valerie Caproni and Steven Siegel), *available at* http://www.abajournal.com/magazine/article/national_security_letters_building_blocks_for_investigations_or_intrusive_t/.

Administrative subpoenas are issued by a wider variety of agencies for authorized investigations that may or may not relate to national security. As with an NSL, if the recipient of a subpoena refuses to comply, the agency must go to court to enforce the subpoena. Alternatively, the recipient may file a judicial challenge by a motion to quash the subpoena. In either case, the court will enforce the subpoena only if it meets the four-part (judicially crafted) test set out in the *Doe I* decision, *supra* p. 711.

Subpoenas have traditionally not required probable cause for several reasons. First, the search conducted by subpoena is at best a "constructive search," in that it is conducted by the subject of the subpoena, not by government agents, as the dissenters in *Carpenter* stress. Second, the subject can refuse to comply, which may trigger pre-enforcement judicial review. Why do NSLs not require probable cause?

Does *Carpenter* blur the distinction between warrants and subpoenas, as the dissenters suggest? If so, how, and how much?

Profile of the Current NSL Statutes

NSL statute	18 U.S.C. 2709	12 U.S.C. 3414	15 U.S.C. 1681u	15 U.S.C. 1681v	50 U.S.C. 3162
Addressee	communications providers	financial institutions	consumer credit agencies	consumer credit agencies	financial institutions, consumer credit agencies, travel agencies
Certifying officials	senior FBI officials and SACs	senior FBI officials and SACs	senior FBI officials and SACs	supervisory official of an agency investigating, conducting intelligence activities relating to or analyzing int'l terrorism	senior officials no lower than Ass't Secretary or Ass't Director of agency w/ employees w/ access to classified material
Information covered	identified customer's name, address, length of service, and billing info	identified customer financial records	identified consumer's name, address, former address, place and former place of employment	all information relating to an identified consumer	all financial information relating to consenting, identified employee
Standard/ Purpose	relevant to an investigation to protect against int'l terrorism or clandestine intelligence activities	sought for foreign counter-intelligence purposes to protect against int'l terrorism or clandestine intelligence activities	sought for an investigation to protect against int'l terrorism or clandestine intelligence activities	necessary for the agency's investigation, activities, or analysis relating to int'l terrorism	necessary to conduct a law enforcement investigation, counter-intelligence inquiry or security determination
Dissemination	only per Att'y Gen. guidelines	only per Att'y Gen. guidelines	w/i FBI, to secure approval for intell. investigation, to military investigators when inform. relates to military member	no statutory provision	only to agency of employee under investigation, DOJ for law enforcement or intell. purposes, or fed. agency when clearly relevant to mission
Immunity/fees	no provisions	no provisions	fees; immunity for good faith compliance with an NSL	immunity for good faith compliance with an NSL	reimbursement; immunity for good faith compliance with an NSL

Source: Congressional Research Service, based on the statutes cited in the table.

Charles Doyle, *National Security Letters in Foreign Intelligence Investigations: Legal Background* 24 (Cong. Res. Serv. RL33320), July 30, 2015.

2. *Judicial Review of NSLs.* Neither administrative subpoenas nor NSLs require a prior court order. Why are the former lawful under the Fourth Amendment but not the latter (in their then-existing form), according to the court in *Doe I*? Doe obviously

could go to court; he *did* go to court. Why didn't the court find this to be evidence that NSL recipients had available constitutionally adequate pre-compliance judicial review?

How, if at all, can the infirmity of NSLs be cured without compromising national security? In the USA Patriot Improvement and Reauthorization Act, Pub. L. No. 109-177, 120 Stat. 192 (2006), Congress for the first time authorized the recipient of an NSL to petition a federal court to modify or set aside the letter "if compliance would be unreasonable, oppressive, or otherwise unlawful." *Id.* §115. (It also authorized the government to seek enforcement of an NSL from a federal court.) Does the opportunity for judicial review now afforded an NSL recipient satisfy the Fourth Amendment concern identified in *Doe I*?

3. Matching Legal Thresholds and Processes with Government Surveillance and Collection Techniques. Professor Orin Kerr identifies the following legal thresholds (standards for obtaining the information) and attendant processes (administrative or judicial or both) for government surveillance, in ascending order of strictness:

a. *No standard or legal process:* The government just gets the information it seeks.
b. *Internal administrative process:* There is no bifurcation between the issuing and enforcing authority.
c. *Grand jury or administrative subpoena:* The issuing and enforcing authority are bifurcated.
d. *Certification court order:* The government needs a court order, but gets it simply by certifying relevancy. The court does not decide whether the certification is justified.
e. *Articulable facts court order:* The government needs a court order and must offer specific and articulable facts to establish relevancy.
f. *Probable cause search warrant:* The traditional criminal law standard and the predicate preferred by the Fourth Amendment.
g. *"Super" search warrant:* Same, but government must first exhaust all other investigatory techniques or meet some other "plus" requirement beyond showing probable cause.
h. *Prohibition:* The government is forbidden from getting the information.

Adapted from Orin Kerr, *Internet Surveillance Law After the USA Patriot Act: The Big Brother That Isn't*, 97 Nw. U. L. Rev. 607, 620-621 (2003). Match one of these thresholds to each of the surveillance and collection techniques catalogued in *Doe I.*

Recall that FISA electronic surveillance has its own unique threshold. See *supra* p. 626. Where would you place it in the hierarchy of thresholds? What about the threshold for national security surveillance ordered by the President on the basis of his own claimed unilateral authority? See *supra* p. 649. You may need to prepare a table of techniques and standards to do this exercise. Is there any logic or pattern to the matches reflected in your table?

Should one have to make a table to figure all this out? Looking just at electronic surveillance techniques, Professor Daniel Solove remarks, "The intricacy of electronic surveillance law is remarkable because it is supposed to apply not just to the FBI, but to state and local police — and even to private citizens. Given its complexity, however, it is unfair to expect these varying groups to comprehend what they can and cannot do." Daniel J. Solove, *Reconstructing Electronic Surveillance Law,*

72 Geo. Wash. L. Rev. 1264, 1293 (2004). If you agree, and if you believe that inclusion of nonelectronic surveillance techniques only compounds the complexity, should the law be simplified? How?

4. Whose Rights? Are the subscriber information and toll billing information meaningfully different from the telephone numbers Smith dialed? What are the First Amendment implications of government access to this information?

Whether or not subscribers have reasonable expectations concerning their information, doesn't the service provider have its own expectations regarding protection of subscriber information? After all, the third-party records are now its records. Does the reasonableness of any such expectations depend on the ISP's desire to attract subscribers by ensuring their privacy? On some loftier principle of avoiding unnecessary government intrusion into private affairs? Of course, not every service provider will want to stand on any such expectation-based rights (absent subscriber pressure), which is one reason that Doe was apparently the first to go to court over an NSL.

5. Pen Registers and Trap and Trace Devices. The USA Patriot Act of 2001, Pub. L. No. 107-56, 115 Stat. 272, amended FISA to permit the use of pen registers and trap and trace devices:

> to obtain foreign intelligence information not concerning a United States person or to protect against international terrorism or clandestine intelligence activities, provided that such investigation of a United States person is not conducted solely upon the basis of activities protected by the first amendment to the Constitution. [*Id.* §214, 115 Stat. at 286 (codified at 50 U.S.C. §1842(a)(1) (2018)).]

When is such use authorized to investigate a U.S. person? The USA Freedom Act of 2015, Pub. L. No. 114-23, 129 Stat. 268, added a requirement that an application for a pen register or trap and trace device under FISA include "a specific selection term to be used as the basis for the use of the pen register or trap and trace device"—a term that specifically identifies a person, account, address, personal device, or other specific identifier, depending on the type of record. *Id.* §201(a) (codified at 50 U.S.C. §1842(c)(3)).

6. Section 215 Orders. As *Doe I* notes, agencies and grand juries have long enjoyed subpoena power to collect third-party records. The 2001 USA Patriot Act amended FISA to give the FBI equivalent authority. It provided authorization for the Foreign Intelligence Surveillance Court to issue orders for the production of "any tangible things (including books, records, papers, documents, and other items)." Pub. L. No. 107-56, §215, 115 Stat. at 287 (usually called "Section 215" or the "business records" provision) (codified as amended at 50 U.S.C. §§1861-1862 (2018)).

As amended, Section 215 includes a relevancy standard, requiring an application for an order to include:

> a statement of facts showing that there are reasonable grounds to believe that the tangible things sought are relevant to an authorized investigation (other than a threat assessment) conducted in accordance with subsection (a)(2) to obtain foreign intelligence information not concerning a United States person or to protect against international terrorism or clandestine intelligence activities, such things being presumptively relevant to an

> authorized investigation if the applicant shows in the statement of the facts that they pertain to—
>
> (i) a foreign power or an agent of a foreign power;
>
> (ii) the activities of a suspected agent of a foreign power who is the subject of such authorized investigation; or
>
> (iii) an individual in contact with, or known to, a suspected agent of a foreign power who is the subject of such authorized investigation.... [50 U.S.C. §1861(b)(2)(B).]

The "relevant to an authorized investigation" standard also applies to NSLs.

The USA Freedom Act of 2015 narrowed this standard by adding a requirement that applications include a "specific selection term," just as it did for pen register and trap and trace applications, as noted above. Pub. L. No. 114-23, §§101, 103, 107, 201, 501-503, 129 Stat. at 269-274, 277, 282-291. The change is discussed *infra* p. 736.

Mere relevancy to a foreign intelligence or counterterrorism investigation is a lower standard than probable cause or even relevancy to a criminal investigation. The lenient Section 215 standard has been defended on the grounds that Section 215 collection falls under the third-party doctrine. Section 215, however, is not on its face limited to transactional information; it applies to "any tangible things (including books, records, papers, documents, and other items)." 50 U.S.C. §1861(a)(1). Does the Court's reasoning in *Smith* support the full breadth of Section 215? Suppose you entrust your personal diary to your brother. Would a Section 215 order directed to your brother be supported by *Smith*?

7. *Challenging Nondisclosure.* The USA Freedom Act of 2015 authorizes the recipient of an NSL to disclose it to persons to whom disclosure is necessary in order to comply with the request or to an attorney in order to obtain legal advice regarding the request, after giving notice to the requesting agency of the identity of such persons or attorneys. §502(a), 129 Stat. at 283 (codified at 18 U.S.C. §2709(c)(2)). It also directs the Attorney General to adopt procedures that provide for periodic government review of the continued need for nondisclosure, and for disclosure "if the facts no longer support nondisclosure." *Id.* §502(f), 129 Stat. at 288. Finally, it permits the recipient of an NSL to seek judicial review of the nondisclosure requirement, and it authorizes a court to issue or extend a nondisclosure order if it determines that "there is reason to believe that disclosure of the information subject to the nondisclosure requirement during the applicable time period may result in" danger to national security or the life or physical safety of any person, or interference with criminal, counterterrorism, or counterintelligence investigations or with diplomatic relations. *Id.* §502(g), 129 Stat. at 288-289 (codified at 18 U.S.C. §3511(b)). By removing prior statutory provisions that made the government's certification of the need for nondisclosure conclusive, and now vesting discretion in a court under this new standard, the USA Freedom Act sought to put to rest First Amendment and separation-of-powers concerns about the nondisclosure provisions of NSLs. Did it succeed?

8. *Extraterritoriality of SCA §2703(a).* In its survey of government information-gathering authorities, the *Doe I* court mentions the Stored Communications Act (SCA) authority to access the *contents* of recently stored (less than 180 days) e-mail by obtaining a search warrant on a showing of probable cause under the Federal Rules of Criminal Procedure. In *Microsoft v. United States,* 829 F.3d 197 (2d Cir. 2016), *vacated and remanded as moot,* 138 S. Ct. 1186 (2018) (per curiam), the

government had subpoenaed certain *non-content* subscriber information stored by Microsoft in the United States in a criminal investigation of suspected narcotics trafficking. Microsoft complied with the subpoena. Using the SCA, however, the government had also obtained a search warrant issued on probable cause for *content* information for the same customer(s?) stored by Microsoft in Ireland. When Microsoft refused to comply with the warrant, it was held in contempt and then appealed. Applying the presumption against extraterritoriality (see *supra* p. 235), the court of appeals held that the SCA's warrant provision only applied domestically and therefore did not reach storage in Ireland.

The dispute was mooted in 2018 when Congress amended the SCA to expressly authorize extraterritorial SCA warrants. The Clarifying Lawful Overseas Use of Data (CLOUD) Act, Pub. L. No. 115-141, div. V, §103(a)(1), 132 Stat. 348, 1214 (2018) (codified at 18 U.S.C. §2713 (2018)), states:

> A [service provider] shall comply with the obligations of this chapter to preserve, backup, or disclose the contents of a wire or electronic communication and any record or other information pertaining to a customer or subscriber within such provider's possession, custody, or control, regardless of whether such communication, record, or other information is located within or outside of the United States.

B. BULK COLLECTION OF THIRD-PARTY RECORDS

Recall that Section 215 provides that an application for a Section 215 order from the FISC requires "a statement of facts showing that there are reasonable grounds to believe that the tangible things sought are relevant to an authorized investigation (other than a threat assessment) conducted in accordance with subsection (a)(2) of this section to obtain foreign intelligence information not concerning a United States person or to protect against international terrorism or clandestine intelligence activities." 50 U.S.C. §§1861(a)(1), (b)(2)(B). Edward Snowden's disclosures revealed that the NSA had used Section 215 authority for bulk collection of telephony metadata. In *Am. Civil Liberties Union v. Clapper*, 785 F.3d 787, 815 (2d Cir. 2015), the Second Circuit described telephony metadata and how the government uses such data this way:

> Unlike what is gleaned from the more traditional investigative practice of wiretapping, telephone metadata do not include the voice content of telephone conversations. Rather, they include details about telephone calls, including, for example, the length of a call, the phone number from which the call was made, and the phone number called. Metadata can also reveal the user or device making or receiving a call through unique "identity numbers" associated with the equipment (although the government maintains that the information collected does not include information about the identities or names of individuals), and provide information about the routing of a call through the telephone network, which can sometimes (although not always) convey information about a caller's general location. . . .
>
> The government explains that it uses the bulk metadata . . . by making "queries" using metadata "identifiers" (also referred to as "selectors"), or particular phone numbers that it believes, based on "reasonable articulable suspicion," to be associated with a foreign terrorist organization. The identifier is used as a "seed" to search across the government's database; the search results yield phone numbers, and the metadata associated with them, that have been in contact with the seed. That step is referred to as the first "hop." The NSA can then also search for the numbers, and associated metadata, that have been in contact with the numbers resulting from the first search — conducting a second "hop." Until

> recently, the program allowed for another iteration of the process, such that a third "hop" could be conducted, sweeping in results that include the metadata of, essentially, the contacts of contacts of contacts of the original "seed." The government asserts that it does not conduct any general "browsing" of the data. . . . [*Id.* at 793-794, 797.]

See generally Nat'l Research Council, *Bulk Collection of Signals Intelligence: Technical Options* (2015), *supra* p. 730, at 27-34. The court added, "[I]f the orders challenged by appellants do not require the collection of metadata regarding every telephone call made or received in the United States (a point asserted by appellants and at least nominally contested by the government), they appear to come very close to doing so." *Clapper*, 785 F.3d at 815. The process might be likened to collecting a haystack to find a needle (which might or might not be located in the haystack).

The Office of the Director of National Intelligence showed how the "call event hop scenario" that the court described could generate vast numbers of "call detail records" or "CDRs":

Figure 18: **Call Event Hop Scenario and Method of Counting**

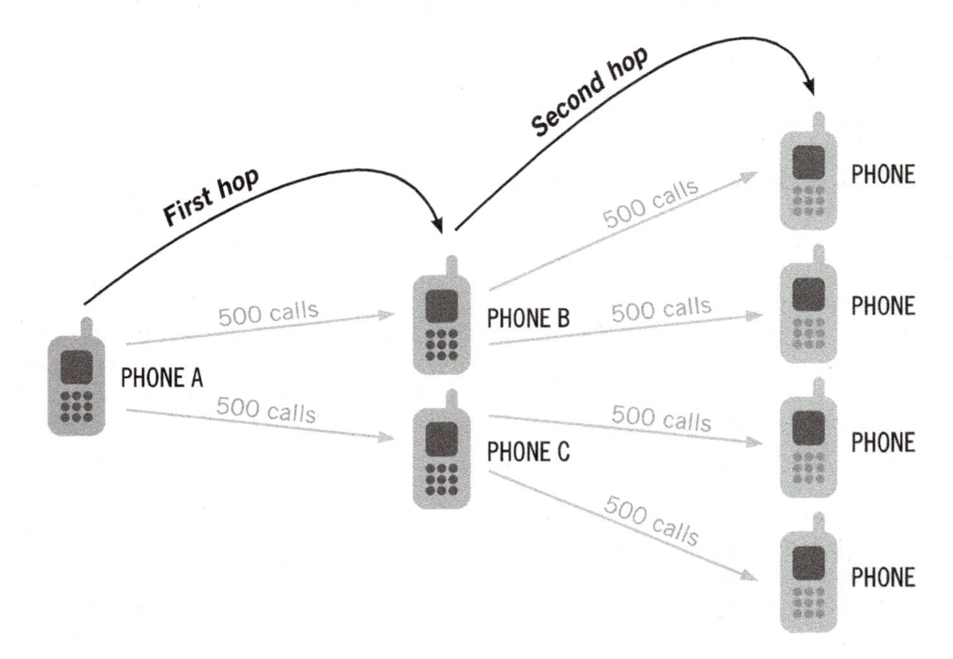

Target uses ***Phone Number A*** *which is the FISC-approved selector in the FISC order. This would be counted as* ***1 order, 1 target, 7 unique identifiers (phone numbers A, B, C, D, E, F, G)*** *and, assuming 500 calls between each party (1,000 records),* ***6000 CDRs.*** *CDRs may include records for both sides of a call (for example, one call from* ***Phone Number A*** *to* ***Phone Number B*** *could result in 2 records).*

ODNI, *Statistical Transparency Report Regarding the Use of National Security Authorities for Calendar Year 2018* (*ODNI Transparency Report*) (Apr. 2019).

Notes and Questions

1. *Bulk vs. Targeted Collection.* The terms "bulk" and "targeted" can be misleading. Collection using a broad identifier like "terrorism" or "Syria" is targeted, but will obviously collect a huge volume of data concerning many persons, the vast majority of whom are not persons of interest. Collecting all the traffic of a single individual is "bulk" collection if there is no other identifier. *See* Nat'l Research Council, *supra*, at 23. The National Research Council therefore suggests this definition: "If a significant portion of the data collected is not associated with current targets, it is bulk collection; otherwise, it is targeted." *Id.* One expert speaks of the "relevance ratio — i.e., the ratio of the number of terrorist-related calls to the total number of calls on which metadata is collected." David S. Kris, *On the Bulk Collection of Tangible Things*, 7 J. Nat'l Security L. & Pol'y 209, 233 (2014). Bulk collection has a much lower relevance ratio than targeted collection. By any standard, then, the telephony metadata collection effort under Section 215 as originally enacted was bulk collection.

2. *Quantity and Quality.* Section 215 also provides that a Section 215 order "may only require the production of a tangible thing if such thing can be obtained with a subpoena duces tecum issued by a court of the United States in aid of a grand jury investigation or with any other order issued by a court of the United States directing the production of records or tangible things." 50 U.S.C. §1861(c)(2)(D). But orders for bulk collection differ from traditional subpoenas in the quantity and quality of information they target. In *Clapper*, the government provided no information to the court to rebut the plaintiffs' claim that the government was using Section 215 to obtain *all* call detail records (and the record showed that it had at least targeted all the records held by Verizon, which handles calls for a vast number of Americans). It therefore had to admit that the quantity of records sought exceeded any quantity ever associated with a grand jury subpoena. That means that the relevance ratio of a Section 215 order is orders of magnitude lower than that of any subpoena.

The quality of information collected was different, too. Can you say why from perusing the *Clapper* court's definition of telephony metadata? How is the database that the government was compiling different from, say, business records of an entity targeted by a traditional grand jury subpoena?

3. *Relevant to What? Statutory Arguments.* To obtain a Section 215 order, the government must provide the FISC with "a statement of facts showing that there are reasonable grounds to believe that the tangible things sought are relevant to an authorized investigation (other than a threat assessment) conducted [under guidelines approved by the Attorney General]." *Id.* §1861(b)(2)(A). *Clapper* rejected as "unprecedented and unwarranted" the government's argument that bulk call detail records are "'relevant' because they may allow the NSA, at some unknown time in the future, utilizing its ability to sift through the trove of irrelevant data it has collected up to that point, to identify information that *is* relevant." 785 F.3d at 812. It noted that Section 215's requirement for relevance to "an authorized investigation" contemplates the "specificity of a particular investigation — not the general

counterterrorism intelligence efforts of the United States government." *Id.* at 816. It gave the example of grand jury investigations that "are investigations of events, enterprises, or persons — the Boston Marathon bombings; Al Capone; or "Fly-by-Night Real Estate Investments," and therefore inherently "constrained by the subject of the investigation." *Id.*

Does this make the wrong comparison?

> [T]he relevant comparison may not be to any grand jury or other subpoena issued in a *single* investigation, but instead to the aggregate of subpoenas that could be or were issued in *all* of what may be thousands of specified terrorism investigations that underlie the bulk metadata collection. In a way, the bulk collection orders represent a kind of aggregation of terrorism-related collection — one-stop shopping across a potentially very large number of ongoing full or enterprise investigations. [Kris, *supra*, at 237.]

But how is this "different, in practical terms, from simply declaring that [call detail records] are relevant to counterterrorism in general"? *Report on the Telephone Records Program Conducted Under Section 215 of the USA PATRIOT ACT and on the Operations of the Foreign Intelligence Surveillance Court* (*PCLOB Report*), Jan. 23, 2014, *at* https://www.pclob.gov/library/215-Report_on_the_Telephone_Records_Program.pdf. Grand jury investigations also have a finite time limit, as do the grand juries themselves. What is the time limit on the government's "counterterrorism investigation"? In fact, is the purpose of "one-stop shopping" to help any pending investigations(s), or it is chiefly to provide a database for some future investigation?

The Foreign Intelligence Surveillance Court (FISC) disagreed with *Clapper*.

> [T]here is nothing "hypothetical" or "future" about the need to conduct searches of the entire volume of records or the investigations giving rise to that need: all the records are searched to uncover contacts with numerous phone numbers or other identifiers approved under a "reasonable articulable suspicion" standard. . . .
>
> Furthermore, the tangible things are being sought in support of individual authorized investigations to protect against international terrorism and concerning various international terrorist organizations. The Court notes that tangible things are "presumptively relevant to an authorized investigation if the applicant shows in the statement of the facts that they pertain to (i) a foreign power or an agent of a foreign power; . . . or (iii) an individual in contact with, or known to, a suspected agent of a foreign power who is the subject of such authorized investigation." FISA §501(b)(2)(A). And . . . it is necessary for the government to collect telephone metadata in bulk in order to find connections between known and unknown international terrorist operatives as part of authorized investigations. [*In re Application of the Federal Bureau of Investigation*, Misc. 15-01, 2015 WL 5637562, at *8 (FISA Ct. June 29, 2015).]

Perhaps all can agree that "relevance" is not an unlimited concept and that Congress must have intended for it to impose *some* constraint on investigations. If so, what is that constraint?

4. Investigations "Other Than a Threat Assessment." Section 215 requires relevance to "an authorized investigation (*other than a threat assessment*)." 50 U.S.C. §1861(b)(2)(B) (emphasis added). Threat assessments are the most preliminary and least intrusive kinds of investigations that the FBI undertakes. More intrusive investigations must be "factually predicated" — that is, they require facts justifying the greater intrusiveness (and the increased commitment of resources). *Clapper* reasoned that

> in limiting the use of §215 to "investigations" rather than "threat assessments," Congress clearly meant to prevent §215 orders from being issued where the FBI, without any particular, defined information that would permit the initiation of even a preliminary investigation, sought to conduct an inquiry in order to identify a potential threat in advance. [785 F.3d at 817.]

If the government's argument is one-stop shopping to prevent terrorism, is that different from "threat assessment"?

5. Acquisition vs. Retention and Analysis. Even if the acquisition and retention of data (what might be called the front end of the process) were in bulk, subsequent analysis of the resulting database (the back end of the process) uses identifiers approved under a "reasonable articulable suspicion" standard. Some defenders of bulk collection have argued that people have no privacy interest in the front end of the process, because no human being initially looks at the acquired and stored data, even if it is initially filtered by computers in some crude way. *See* Richard A. Posner, Opinion, *Our Domestic Intelligence Crisis,* Wash. Post, Dec. 21, 2005 ("[M]achine collection and processing of data cannot, as such, invade privacy. . . . [The] initial sifting [by computer], far from invading privacy (a computer is not a sentient being), keeps most private data from being read by any intelligence officer."). Privacy is first implicated at the back end of the process, they say, when the database is queried and human analysts examine the results.

Do you have any privacy interest in the mere acquisition and retention of your data by the government? If not, would you object to government recording of bedroom or bathroom activities, as long as the resulting data are not analyzed? Interestingly, Congress has criminalized the mere non-consensual *interception* of various electronic communications, as well as their disclosure. 18 U.S.C. §2511(1) (2018).

6. The Fourth Amendment Challenge. The FISC held that bulk collection of telephony metadata was authorized by the third-party records doctrine established by the Supreme Court's ruling in *Smith v. Maryland. In re Application of the FBI,* 2015 WL 5637562, at *9-13. Not only did it view such metadata as analogous to the numbers that Smith had called, but it thought that the quantity of call data made no difference. If each caller abandoned privacy by dialing a number, then a database of a million call details is just one million times zero — still zero. The FISC also saw no constitutionally protected privacy interest implicated in the analysis of the data either, because, under *Smith*'s reasoning, the caller voluntarily abandoned any such interest simply by using the phone to make a call.

Is this reasoning still sound after *Carpenter v. United States, supra* p. 685? The telephone numbers collected in *Smith* connected him to the crime, but they did not track his daily activities to create "an all-encompassing record," *Carpenter,* 138 S. Ct. at 2217, of his phone usage over an extended period. Even if the creation of telephony metadata is "voluntary" when a phone is used to make a single call, can the same be said for the compilation of such data over an extended period of time? *See generally* Sharon Bradford Franklin, *Carpenter and the End of Bulk Surveillance of Americans,* Lawfare, July 25, 2018.

In another judicial challenge to bulk collection, then-Judge Kavanaugh voted to deny rehearing of a procedural ruling by relying on *Smith v. Maryland* to conclude that the collection of telephony metadata was not a search. But even if it were, he went on, it was constitutional under the special needs exception to the Fourth Amendment. "The Government's program for bulk collection of telephony metadata serves a critically important special need — preventing terrorist attacks on the United States. In my view, that critical national security need outweighs the impact on privacy occasioned by this program." *Klayman v. Obama*, 805 F.3d 1148, 1149 (D.C. Cir. 2015) (Kavanaugh, J., concurring in denial of rehearing en banc). Would the same special needs rationale also support continuing government collection of all credit card records? If not, why not?

7. *Does Bulk Collection Work?* The PCLOB could not identify "a single instance involving a threat to the United States in which the [Section 215] Program made a concrete difference in the outcome of a counterterrorism investigation." *PCLOB Report, supra*, at 11. The telephony metadata collected by the NSA did, however, provide additional leads regarding contacts of terrorism suspects already known to investigators or demonstrating that foreign terrorist plots do *not* have a U.S. nexus. *Id.* If these conclusions were accurate (they are disputed by the government), do they condemn or justify the collection program?

The Second Circuit did not initially reach the constitutional question in *Clapper*, because it found that the bulk collection of telephony metadata was not authorized by Section 215. It also avoided the constitutional claim because it believed that Congress's judgment about the reasonableness of a measure could influence a court's judgment about whether that measure is reasonable under the Fourth Amendment. Congress subsequently approved a more limited kind of bulk collection when it enacted the USA Freedom Act of 2015, Pub. L. No. 114-23, 129 Stat. 268, amending Section 215. The limitations may be seen in the excerpt of Section 215, as amended, set out below.

Access to Certain Business Records for Foreign Intelligence and International Terrorism Investigations

50 U.S.C. §1861 (2018)

(b) Recipient and Contents of Application . . .

Each application [from the FBI Director or a designee for an order] under this section . . .

(2) shall include —

(A) a specific selection term to be used as the basis for the production of the tangible things sought; . . .

(C) in the case of an application for the production on an ongoing basis of call detail records created before, on, or after the date of the application relating to an authorized investigation (other than a threat assessment) conducted in accordance with subsection (a)(2) to protect against international terrorism, a statement of facts showing that —

(i) there are reasonable grounds to believe that the call detail records sought to be produced based on the specific selection term required under subparagraph (A) are relevant to such investigation; and

(ii) there is a reasonable, articulable suspicion that such specific selection term is associated with a foreign power engaged in international terrorism or activities in preparation therefor, or an agent of a foreign power engaged in international terrorism or activities in preparation therefor....

(c) Ex Parte Judicial Order of Approval...

(2) An order under this subsection — ...

(F) in the case of an application described in subsection (b)(2)(C), shall —

(i) authorize the production on a daily basis of call detail records for a period not to exceed 180 days;

(ii) provide that an order for such production may be extended upon application under subsection (b) and the judicial finding under paragraph (1) of this subsection;

(iii) provide that the Government may require the prompt production of a first set of call detail records using the specific selection term that satisfies the standard required under subsection (b)(2)(C)(ii);

(iv) provide that the Government may require the prompt production of a second set of call detail records using session-identifying information or a telephone calling card number identified by the specific selection term used to produce call detail records under clause (iii);... and

(vii) direct the Government to —

(I) adopt minimization procedures that require the prompt destruction of all call detail records produced under the order that the Government determines are not foreign intelligence information; and

(II) destroy all call detail records produced under the order as prescribed by such procedures.

(3) No order issued under this subsection may authorize the collection of tangible things without the use of a specific selection term that meets the requirements of subsection (b)(2)....

(k) Definitions

In this section:...

(2) Address. The term "address" means a physical address or electronic address, such as an electronic mail address or temporarily assigned network address (including an Internet protocol address).

(3) Call detail record. The term "call detail record" —

(A) means session-identifying information (including an originating or terminating telephone number, an International Mobile Subscriber Identity number, or an International Mobile Station Equipment Identity number), a telephone calling card number, or the time or duration of a call; and

(B) does not include —

(i) the contents (as defined in section 2510(8) of title 18) of any communication;

(ii) the name, address, or financial information of a subscriber or customer; or

(iii) cell site location or global positioning system information.

(4) Specific selection term

(A) Tangible things

(i) In general. Except as provided in subparagraph (B), a "specific selection term"—

(I) is a term that specifically identifies a person, account, address, or personal device, or any other specific identifier; and

(II) is used to limit, to the greatest extent reasonably practicable, the scope of tangible things sought consistent with the purpose for seeking the tangible things.

(ii) Limitation. A specific selection term under clause (I) does not include an identifier that does not limit, to the greatest extent reasonably practicable, the scope of tangible things sought consistent with the purpose for seeking the tangible things, such as an identifier that—

(I) identifies an electronic communication service provider (as that term is defined in section 1881 of this title) or a provider of remote computing service (as that term is defined in section 2711 of title 18), when not used as part of a specific identifier as described in clause (I), unless the provider is itself a subject of an authorized investigation for which the specific selection term is used as the basis for the production; or

(II) identifies a broad geographic region, including the United States, a city, a county, a State, a zip code, or an area code, when not used as part of a specific identifier as described in clause (I).

(iii) Rule of construction. Nothing in this paragraph shall be construed to preclude the use of multiple terms or identifiers to meet the requirements of clause (I).

(B) Call detail record applications. For purposes of an application submitted under subsection (b)(2)(C), the term "specific selection term" means a term that specifically identifies an individual, account, or personal device. . . .

Notes and Questions

1. *Use of Bulk Collection.* The Office of the Director of National Intelligence (ODNI) reported that in 2018, the FISC issued 56 orders under its 50 U.S.C. §1861(b)(2)(B) authority, with 60 targets and 214,860 unique identifiers, as well as 14 orders for call detail records (telephony metadata) under its §1861(b)(2)(C) authority, with 11 targets, generating 434,255,543 call detail records, containing 19,372,544 telephone numbers, which it queried with 164,682 search terms. ODNI, *Statistical Transparency Report Regarding the Use of National Security Authorities for Calendar Year 2018* (*ODNI Transparency Report*) (Apr. 2019), https://www.dni.gov/index.php/newsroom/reports-publications/item/1987-statistical-transparency-report-regarding-national-security-authorities-calendar-year-2018.

2. *Specific Selection Term.* The USA Freedom Act adopted the relevancy standard of the USA Patriot Act, with a significant restriction: it requires all applications to include a "specific selection term." 50 U.S.C. §1861(b)(2)(A) (2018) (as amended). How does this requirement attempt to solve the statutory problem identified by *Clapper*? Why can't the government do an end run around the new specific selection

requirement by using a term like "202" (the D.C. area code) or "20052" (a D.C. zip code)?

3. Use of NSLs. In the USA Freedom Act, Congress also restricted the use of NSLs for bulk collection. For example, the authority construed in *Doe I, supra* p. 711, was amended to provide that the Director of the FBI or his designee "may, using a term that *specifically identifies* a person, entity, telephone number, or account as the basis for a request," request the billing records and related subscriber information "relevant to an authorized investigation to protect against international terrorism. . . ." 18 U.S.C. §2709(b) (2018) (as amended by USA Freedom Act §501, 129 Stat. at 282) (emphasis added).

4. The End of Bulk Collection of Telephone Metadata (As We Know It?). After Edward Snowden's disclosure of NSA's bulk collection of telephone metadata, and despite the USA Freedom Act amendments, such collection — as we know it — may become a thing of the past. First, the NSA announced that it had destroyed the mass of metadata collected after the Act took effect because some telecom companies had erroneously provided it with metadata to which it was not entitled under the Act. Charlie Savage, *N.S.A. Purges Hundreds of Millions of Call and Text Records,* N.Y. Times, June 29, 2018. Second, a national security adviser for the House Minority Leader revealed that the NSA had stopped using its metadata collection authority for call detail records, *see* Robert Chesney, *Telephony Metadata: Is the Contact-Chaining Program Unsalvageable?,* Lawfare, Mar. 5, 2019, which the Director of National Intelligence subsequently confirmed. Letter from Dan R. Coats (DNI) to Chairman Richard Burr, et al. (Aug. 14, 2019), *available at* https://int.nyt.com/data/documenthelper/1640-odni-letter-to-congress-about/20bfc7d1223dba027e55/optimized/full.pdf. Third, the program is scheduled to sunset in March 2020. But in his letter to Congress, the DNI asked Congress to permanently reauthorize the provisions that were set to expire. *Id.*

Commentators point out that telephony metadata have grown increasingly less useful as apps for alternative means of communication — including some that are encrypted end-to-end — have grown more popular. On the other hand, Section 215 collection is still useful for information other than telephony metadata, and therefore may survive the March 2020 sunset in some form. *Id.*

C. DATA MINING

Data collected in bulk can used in a variety of kinds of data mining.

> Data mining involves the use of sophisticated data analysis tools to discover previously unknown, valid patterns and relationships in large data sets. . . .
>
> . . . Data mining applications can use a variety of parameters to examine the data. They include association (patterns where one event is connected to another event, such as purchasing a pen and purchasing paper), sequence or path analysis (patterns where one event leads to another event, such as the birth of a child and purchasing diapers), classification (identification of new patterns, such as coincidences between duct tape purchases and plastic sheeting purchases), clustering (finding and visually documenting groups of previously unknown facts, such as geographic location and brand preferences),

> and forecasting (discovering patterns from which one can make reasonable predictions regarding future activities, such as the prediction that people who join an athletic club may take exercise classes). [Jeffrey W. Seifert, *Data Mining and Homeland Security: An Overview* 1 (Cong. Res. Serv. RL31798), Aug. 27, 2008.]

In a counterterrorism effort, "data mining can be a potential means to identify terrorist activities, such as money transfers and communications, and to identify and track individual terrorists themselves, such as through travel and immigration records." Seifert, *supra*, Summary. *See generally* K.A. Taipale, *Data Mining and Domestic Security: Connecting the Dots to Make Sense of Data*, 5 Colum. Sci. & Tech. L. Rev. 2 (2003) (describing and assessing the technology).

The telephony metadata program is only the latest example of data mining for counterterrorism purposes. For example, the Computer-Assisted Passenger Prescreening System (CAPPS II) was an airline passenger prescreening program that used computer-generated profiles to select passengers for additional security screening — technically data matching. It would have relied on commercial data to calculate "scores" for passengers. In fact, the Transportation Security Administration obtained such data from at least four airlines and two travel companies. But litigation made airlines wary of voluntarily sharing such data, the European Union objected, and Congress became concerned about false positives and a lack of procedures for correcting errors. In 2005, Congress prohibited the use of appropriated funds for CAPPS II or its successor, Secure Flight, until the Government Accountability Office certified that the system met certain privacy requirements. Seifert, *supra*, at 7-11. TSA put the Secure Flight requirements into effect in 2009, and airlines fully implemented the program in November 2010. *See, e.g.*, Am. Airlines, *TSA Secure Flight* (n.d.), https://www.aa.com/i18n/utility/secureFlight.jsp.

Notes and Questions

1. *Just Finding Clues?* Police investigators have always conducted "link analysis" when they interview witnesses who saw a crime committed or who know the victim, then looked for connections in the information obtained in the interviews. "Data mining is no more than the computational automation of traditional investigative skills — that is, the intelligent analysis of myriad 'clues' in order to develop a theory of the case." Taipale, *supra*, at 21. Does it follow that "using computers to analyze data is similar to a police officer examining the same information and does not violate personal privacy"? McCormick Trib. Found., *Counterterrorism Technology and Privacy* 27 (2005). Do the two processes have different implications for personal privacy or expectations of privacy? Should we distinguish, for example, between searches using specific identifiers (special selection terms) and generalized undirected data mining to derive or to match patterns? If so, how is computerized pattern matching different, from a privacy perspective, from a police officer's observation of a masked individual running on a public street? *See* Taipale, *supra*, at 64.

2. *Privacy of Aggregated Data: A Question Smith and Miller Did Not Ask.* In its 2015 ruling, described above, the FISC rejected a Fourth Amendment challenge to the Section 215 telephony metadata collection partly by invoking *Smith v. Maryland.*

But in *Smith* and *Miller* the Supreme Court focused on the collection techniques (pen registers recording dialed numbers and subpoenas for bank records), not on what became of the information they yielded. The Court's focus was understandable from the perspective of traditionally reactive "retail" criminal law enforcement, which builds one case at a time. In the fight against terrorism, however, reactive law enforcement has given way to proactive and preventive law enforcement. Data are collected and retained in databases for future uses in a continuing preventive effort. Even if they are not immediately archived with other data, they can be "virtually aggregated" at any moment to create a dynamic mega-database. *See* Taipale, *supra,* at 42.

Does the prospect of such prolonged retention and aggregation have any bearing on the expectation of privacy? Do you have a greater expectation of privacy in your aggregated data than in their parts? For example, are you willing to risk that airlines will disclose your travel plans to the government, yet not want those data linked to your other consumer and credit information? Should courts gauge the legitimacy of privacy expectations in each collected item of personal information by the possibility that it will be aggregated for data mining to establish personal behavior patterns and profiles?

> [W]hen combined together, bits and pieces of data begin to form a portrait of a person. The whole becomes greater than the parts. This occurs because combining information creates synergies. When analyzed, aggregated information can reveal new facts about a person that she did not expect would be known about her when the original, isolated data was collected. [Daniel J. Solove, *A Taxonomy of Privacy,* 154 U. Pa. L. Rev. 477, 507 (2006).]

In *U.S. Dep't of Justice v. Reporters Committee for Freedom of the Press,* 489 U.S. 749 (1989), Justice Stevens, writing for the Court, acknowledged that even public personal data enjoy a certain "practical obscurity" that may be altered by its aggregation into an easily searched database. Posing the issue as "whether the compilation of otherwise hard-to-obtain information alters the privacy interest implicated by disclosure of that information," he asserted that "there is a vast difference between the public records" accessible by diligent effort in sundry locations throughout the country and "a computerized summary located in a single clearinghouse of information." *Id.* at 764. But today many public records exist in easily searchable computer databases. Are any computerized records still "practically obscure," in the same sense that hard-copy records at the courthouse or land office once were? Does the ever-increasing use of data mining — in both the public and private sectors — suggest a diminishing expectation of privacy in data? *See Kyllo v. United States,* 533 U.S. 27, 34 (2001) (holding that the use of heat-sensing technology was an unreasonable search, "*at least where (as here) the technology in question is not in general public use*") (emphasis added); *see also City of Ontario v. Quon,* 560 U.S. 746, 759 (2010) ("[r]apid changes in the dynamics of communication and information transmission" are causing privacy expectations to evolve).

Carpenter v. United States, supra p. 685, dealt only with the extended collection of locational data, but the Supreme Court thought that both quantity and duration mattered to the Fourth Amendment analysis. Can you analogize or extrapolate from *Carpenter* to address the constitutionality of an aggregate government database of transactional data? Amazon and Facebook apparently already have such databases. Does that fact influence your constitutional analysis? *Cf.* Franklin, *supra* p. 733

("Although it did not explicitly say so, the *Carpenter* court recognized that metadata at scale implicates protected privacy interests, noting that [cell-site location information] provides 'a detailed chronicle of a person's physical presence compiled every moment, over several years.'").

3. False Positives. Credit card data have several attributes that contribute to the success of data mining: a large number of valid transactions, a large number of fraudulent transactions, repetitive fraudulent use that generates common data patterns, and a relatively low cost to "false positives" — valid purchases that are incorrectly flagged as fraudulent — since they usually simply trigger a confirming phone call to the credit card holder. *See* Peter P. Swire, *Privacy and Information Sharing in the War on Terrorism,* 51 Vill. L. Rev. 951 (2006). In contrast, the number of terrorist attacks is extremely low, terrorist attacks are far less likely to be repetitive, rather than one of a kind, and the cost of false positives is far higher, both to the falsely identified innocent person and to the government, which must use substantial resources to investigate that person. *Id. But see* Paul Rosenzweig, Heritage Found., *Proposals for Implementing the Terrorist Information Awareness System* 4 (Aug. 7, 2003) (suggesting that costs of false positives are "relatively modest"). These differences do not rule out data mining for counterterrorism purposes, but they might suggest the need for special rules for dealing with false positives. *See* Rosenzweig, *supra* (suggesting that "robust" mechanisms to correct false positives from counterterrorist data mining would make the high false positive rate acceptable in light of the consequences of failing to data mine). Can you think of special rules to address these differences?

THE COLLECTION AND USE OF THIRD-PARTY RECORDS: SUMMARY OF BASIC PRINCIPLES

- The government needs affirmative authority for the collection of third-party records. In the national security field, such authority is provided by statutes approving the use of national security letters (NSLs) to collect particular kinds of third-party records, Section 215 authority for the collection of business records and other "tangible things," and FISA authority for pen registers and trap and trace devices, in addition to traditional authorities in criminal law.
- Most of these authorities for the collection of third-party records require that the collection be relevant to an authorized foreign intelligence or counterterrorism investigation — a subpoena-like standard well below traditional probable cause or even FISA probable cause.
- Section 215 authorizes the FISC to issue an order for production of tangible things relevant to an authorized investigation other than a threat assessment, if such things could be obtained with a grand jury subpoena. It was originally intended for use in targeted collection, but after 9/11 it was used for bulk collection of both Internet and telephony metadata.

- Courts disagreed about whether the use of Section 215 for bulk collection of telephony metadata was authorized by Section 215 or consistent with the Fourth Amendment. The FISC invoked the third-party doctrine from *Smith v. Maryland* to reject a Fourth Amendment challenge to Section 215 bulk collection of telephony metadata. But *Carpenter v. United States* has narrowed the scope of the third-party doctrine, and telephony metadata is arguably distinguishable both in quantity and quality from the telephone numbers at issue in *Smith*.

- The USA FREEDOM Act of 2015 narrowed Section 215 authority to require the government to include an identifier called a "special selection term" in its Section 215 applications. The Act also provides that a Section 215 application for production of telephony metadata ("call detail records") must include a statement of reasonable grounds to believe that records based on a specified selection term are relevant to an authorized counterterrorism investigation, as well as a reasonable articulable suspicion that the term is associated with a foreign power (or its agent) engaged in or preparing for international terrorism.

- The collection and retention of bulk data by the government raises the question whether a person has a constitutionally protected privacy interest in the government's aggregation of data that has been lawfully collected under the third-party doctrine. The substantial risks of false positives in the government's use of such data also raises the question whether it should be subjected to tighter statutory regulation.

25

Screening for Security

On September 11, 2001, Mohamed Atta and Abdul Aziz al Omari boarded a 6 A.M. flight from Portland, Maine, to Boston's Logan International Airport. A program called Computer Assisted Passenger Prescreening System (CAPPS) selected Atta for special security measures, which consisted at the time of holding his checked bags until he was on board the airplane. At Logan, Atta and al Omari, and eight colleagues who joined them, went through security checkpoints to board two different planes, both bound for Los Angeles. They were screened by metal detectors calibrated to detect items with the metal content of at least a .22-caliber handgun. Some of these men are now thought to have carried box cutters or pocket utility knives (defined as having blades less than four inches long and permitted on flights at the time).

In the meantime, four out of five more colleagues were flagged by CAPPS at Dulles International Airport en route to board another flight bound for Los Angeles. Two of them — brothers — were selected for extra scrutiny by the airline customer representative at the check-in counter because one of the brothers lacked a photo identification and could not speak English, and they seemed suspicious. Again, the consequence was that their bags were held until they were on board the airplane. Several of the men at Dulles set off the metal detectors at the security checkpoint and were hand-wanded before being passed. One had his carry-on bag swiped by an explosive trace detector. All were videotaped at the checkpoint. Four additional colleagues boarded yet another Los Angeles-bound plane in Newark at about the same time.

Of the 19 men who eventually boarded the fateful flights in this fashion on September 11, seven used Virginia driver's licenses as their identification at check-in. None of them lived in Virginia. They had obtained the licenses there because they learned that one could get a genuine driver's license in Virginia in one day for approximately $100 cash, with no questions asked.

The *9/11 Commission Report* tells the rest of the story.

> The 19 men were aboard four transcontinental flights. They were planning to hijack these planes and turn them into large guided missiles, loaded with up to 11,400 gallons of jet fuel. By 8:00 A.M. on the morning of Tuesday, September 11, 2001, they had defeated all

the security layers that America's civil aviation system then had in place to prevent a hijacking. [*Final Report of the National Commission on Terrorist Attacks Upon the United States* (*9/11 Commission Report*) (2004), at 4.]

This chapter explores some of the legal issues raised by this defeat of what was and still is essentially a system designed to screen terrorists from entry to transportation systems and other high-risk targets. We begin with an analysis of checkpoint searches, then consider the narrower concerns of identification and watch list screening.

A. CHECKPOINT SEARCHES

We are all required to show some identification when we board a flight, and sometimes even just when we enter a government building or other facility. The courts have long upheld an identification requirement in such settings. Thus, "'[A] request for identification by the police does not, by itself, constitute a Fourth Amendment seizure. Rather, '[a]n individual is seized within the meaning of the fourth amendment only if, in view of all of the circumstances surrounding the incident, a reasonable person would have believed that he was not free to leave.'" *Gilmore v. Gonzales,* 435 F.3d 1125, 1137-1138 (9th Cir. 2006) (alterations in original; internal citations omitted). If you don't want to provide an identification to the gate agent, the theory goes, you can go home. If you decide to comply, you have consented. There is no seizure in either case.

We have also all grown accustomed to — if sometimes still annoyed by — security lines and checks at airports and, far less commonly, by the demand that we boot up our laptops as we go through the checkpoint. But have you had TSA or Customs and Border Protection (CBP) agents look through the files on your laptop or the data on your smart phone? Would such a search prevent or deter "the carrying of weapons or explosives aboard aircraft," one ostensible special need for searches at airports? *See United States v. Davis,* 482 F.2d 893, 898 (9th Cir. 1973). If not, would it be lawful?

Reading *United States v. Saboonchi*

Saboonchi was a dual U.S.-Iranian citizen who was trying to re-enter the United States after a day trip in Canada. Because his name was on a watch list, he was taken aside by CBP agents for "secondary screening," and his smart phones and flash drive were seized for closer examination. Although he was then released, he was later prosecuted for violating sanctions-related export controls based in part on evidence retrieved from his seized devices.

- Why doesn't the government need a warrant or even reasonable suspicion for a "routine" border search? What is the object of a routine border search?
- What is a non-routine border search?
- What is the difference between a conventional search of electronic devices at the border and a forensic search? Why does the court treat a conventional search of such devices as a routine border search, not requiring any level of suspicion, but the forensic search as a non-routine search, requiring reasonable suspicion?
- What is "reasonable suspicion"?

United States v. Saboonchi

United States District Court, District of Maryland, 2014
990 F. Supp. 2d 536

PAUL W. GRIMM, District Judge. Defendant Ali Saboonchi is alleged to have violated U.S. export restrictions on trade with the Islamic Republic of Iran. On July 18, 2013, Saboonchi moved to suppress the fruits of warrantless forensic searches of his smart phones and flash drive performed under the authority of the border search doctrine after they were seized at the U.S.-Canadian border. . . . I now hold that, under the facts presented by this case, a forensic computer search cannot be performed under the border search doctrine in the absence of reasonable suspicion. Because the officials here reasonably suspected that Saboonchi was violating export restrictions, Defendant's Motion to Suppress is denied.

I. BACKGROUND . . .

. . . Saboonchi and his wife were allowed to reenter the United States, but an Apple iPhone, a Sony Xperia phone, and a Kingston DT101 G2 USB flash drive (the "Devices") were seized. . . .

. . . [A] Homeland Security Investigations ("HSI") special agent imaged each of the Devices.[2] Thereafter, the image of each device was forensically searched using specialized software. . . .

II. THE BORDER SEARCH DOCTRINE

A. Types of Border Searches

Any analysis of a border search must begin from the proposition that "[t]he Government's interest in preventing the entry of unwanted persons and effects is at its zenith at the international border." *United States v. Flores-Montano,* 541 U.S. 149, 152 (2004). It therefore is well-established "[t]hat searches made at the border, pursuant to the long-standing right of the sovereign to protect itself by stopping and examining persons and property crossing into this country, are reasonable simply by virtue of the fact that they occur at the border." *United States v. Ramsey,* 431 U.S. 606, 616 (1977). "Routine searches of the persons and effects of entrants are not subject to any requirement of reasonable suspicion, probable cause, or warrant. . . ." *United States v. Montoya de Hernandez,* 473 U.S. 531, 538 (1985).

But even at the border, the Fourth Amendment continues to protect against *unreasonable* searches and seizures; the only difference is that, at the border, routine searches become reasonable because the interest of the Government is far stronger and the reasonable expectation of privacy of an individual seeking entry is considerably weaker. *See Carroll v. United States,* 267 U.S. 132, 154 (1925) ("Travelers may be [ ] stopped in crossing an international boundary because of national self-protection reasonably requiring

---

2. Imaging a hard drive is the first step of a forensic search and involves making a copy of a storage device that is known as an "image," "bitstream" copy, or "forensic" copy. *See* Orin S. Kerr, *Searches and Seizures in a Digital World,* 119 Harv. L. Rev. 531, 540-41 (2005). "A Bit Stream Backup is an exact copy of a hard drive, preserving all latent data in addition to the files and directory structures." *The Sedona Conference Glossary: E-Discovery & Digital Information Management* 6 (3d ed. 2010)."

one entering the country to identify himself as entitled to come in, and his belongings as effects which may lawfully be brought in."). When a search stretches beyond the routine, it must rest on reasonable, particularized suspicion, *Montoya de Hernandez,* 473 U.S. at 541, which is significantly less demanding than the showing of probable cause required to secure a warrant for a domestic search, *see* U.S. Const. amend. IV. It is not so easy to divine precisely where a border search falls along the continuum from reasonable to unreasonable, particularly when the search involves imaging the entire contents of two smart phones and a flash drive.

The Supreme Court has not addressed the issue often, but it has laid out the broad strokes of what constitutes a routine, versus a nonroutine, search. On the one hand, in *United States v. Flores-Montano,* the Court held that "the Government's authority to conduct suspicionless inspections at the border includes the authority to remove, disassemble, and reassemble a vehicle's fuel tank." 541 U.S. at 155. In so holding, the Court found that the privacy interest in the contents of a person's gas tank was less than that in the contents of a passenger compartment, that such searches were relatively brief, and that the possibility of permanent damage to a car was so remote that it did not implicate a legitimate property interest, particularly because an owner of a damaged car might be entitled to recover damages. *Id.* at 154-55.

On the other hand, *United States v. Montoya de Hernandez* presents an extreme factual situation that clearly exceeded a mere routine search or seizure, in which a defendant suspected of smuggling drugs in her alimentary canal was told that she would not be released into the United States until she submitted to an x-ray or "produced a monitored bowel movement that would confirm or rebut the inspectors' suspicions." 473 U.S. at 534-35. As a result, she "was detained incommunicado for almost 16 hours before inspectors sought a warrant." *Id.* at 542. In holding that the detention required, and in that particular case was justified by, reasonable suspicion, the Court expressly refrained from defining "what level of suspicion, if any, is required for nonroutine border searches such as strip, body cavity, or involuntary x-ray searches," *id.* at 541 n. 4. . . .

B. Location of Border Searches

A border search need not take place *at* the border — indeed, here it appears that Saboonchi's Devices were seized at a border but actually were searched in Baltimore, well within the territory of the United States. Courts have recognized two different ways that a search may fall within the border search doctrine even though it does not occur at a physical border. First, border searches "may in certain circumstances take place not only at the border itself, but at its functional equivalents as well." *Almeida-Sanchez v. United States,* 413 U.S. 266, 272 (1973). The "functional equivalent" of a border may include "an established station near the border, at a point marking the confluence of two or more roads that extend from the border," or the search of passengers and cargo arriving at an airport within the United States after a nonstop flight from abroad. *Id.* at 273. As these locations are the functional equivalent of a border, the analysis is no different from a search at an actual, physical border and no additional suspicion is required.

Second, courts have permitted "'extended border searches,' under which 'border' is given a geographically flexible reading within limits of reason related to the underlying constitutional concerns to protect against unreasonable searches." *United States v. Bilir,* 592 F.2d 735, 740 (4th Cir. 1979). "[T]he 'extended border search' doctrine has been applied to entry border searches conducted some time after the border was crossed." *United States v. Cardona,* 769 F.2d 625, 628 (9th Cir. 1985) (citing *United States v. Caicedo-Guarnizo,* 723 F.2d 1420, 1422 (9th Cir. 1984)). An extended border search may be necessary because the first contact with a customs official occurs away from the border, or because officers have elected to allow a suspect to pass through the border in order to perform a search at a later time. Unlike searches that actually occur at a border or the functional equivalent thereof, an extended border search requires reasonable suspicion with respect to the criminal nature of the person or thing searched as well as reasonable suspicion that the subject of the search has crossed a border "within a reasonably recent time."

III. DISCUSSION . . .

A. Analytical Framework . . .

The searches of the Devices in this case cannot be an extended border search because Saboonchi was not allowed to bring them across the border. *See United States v. Stewart,* 729 F.3d 517, 525 (6th Cir. 2013) (finding no extended border search under similar circumstances "because [defendant's] laptop computers never cleared the border"). The seizure of the Devices occurred at the border itself. They then were shipped to Baltimore and were transferred from CBP to HSI, both of which play a role in securing the border. And once the devices were cleared for entry, they were returned, in Baltimore, to Saboonchi. "A border search of a computer is not transformed into an extended border search simply because the device is transported and examined beyond the border." *United States v. Cotterman,* 709 F.3d 952, 961 (9th Cir. 2013). Thus, I find that this was not an extended border search; to the contrary, Saboonchi's Devices were not permitted to enter into the United States until they were returned to him in Baltimore, and any searches of those devices were pursuant to the general border search doctrine.

Therefore, the level of suspicion required depends on whether the forensic search of the Devices was a routine search or a nonroutine search. . . .

B. Routine Versus Nonroutine Searches Generally

Unsurprisingly, the overwhelming majority of searches that one would expect to encounter at the border fall into the category of conventional, routine border searches. This includes pat-downs, pocket-dumps, and even searches that require moving or adjusting clothing without disrobing, and also may include scanning, opening, and rifling through the contents of bags or other closed containers. But a routine search also may go beyond what a traveler otherwise may consider routine. For example, a routine search may extend to the inside of an automobile gas tank, *United States v. Flores-Montano,* 541 U.S. 149, 155 (2004), to the contents of photograph albums or information encoded on video tapes, *United States v. Ickes,* 393 F.3d 501, 502-03 (4th Cir. 2005), or to password protected or locked items, *United States v. McAuley,* 563 F. Supp. 2d 672, 678 (W.D. Tex. 2008). Insofar as the "touchstone of the Fourth Amendment is reasonableness," *Florida v. Jimeno,* 500 U.S. 248, 250 (1991) (citing *Katz v. United States,* 389 U.S. 347, 360 (1967)), it does not require Napoleonic insight to see how the power to conduct searches of this kind on a routine basis, without suspicion, is the *sine qua non* of customs and border enforcement; otherwise there would be nothing to stop travelers or commercial shippers from dodging our customs laws with impunity so long as they avoid drawing attention. *See, e.g., United States v. Johnson,* 991 F.2d 1287, 1292 (7th Cir. 1993) ("A customs official might have to rummage through any border entrant's luggage to ascertain whether all items have been declared properly.").

A wide range of searches of persons also have been upheld as routine even if they involve some level of indignity or intrusiveness, so long as they fall short of a strip search and do not expose the cavities of the body.

On the other hand, *United States v. Ramsey* left open the possibility that "a border search might be deemed 'unreasonable' because of the particularly offensive manner in which it is carried out." 431 U.S. 606, 618 n. 13 (1977). For example, there is a general consensus that even the border search power cannot justify a strip search without any particularized suspicion. . . .

Courts have struggled to define a clear dividing line between routine and non-routine searches. In *United States v. Braks,* 842 F.2d 509 (1st Cir. 1988), the First Circuit listed the following relevant factors:

> (i) whether the search results in the exposure of intimate body parts or requires the suspect to disrobe;
> (ii) whether physical contact between Customs officials and the suspect occurs during the search;
> (iii) whether force is used to effect the search;
> (iv) whether the type of search exposes the suspect to pain or danger;
> (v) the overall manner in which the search is conducted; and
> (vi) whether the suspect's reasonable expectations of privacy, if any, are abrogated by the search.

842 F.2d at 512 (footnotes omitted). These factors did not represent "an exhaustive list of equally-weighted concerns," and each search was a fact-specific inquiry in which those factors were among the relevant considerations. *Id.* at 513.

Other courts have focused specifically on familiar touchstones such as the exposure of intimate body parts and details, as well as a suspect's reasonable expectations of privacy. . . .

. . . Accordingly, even if a search is not destructive or damaging, if it is sufficiently invasive or intrusive, or butts up against other Fourth Amendment values, it may be nonroutine in any event.

C. Prior Case Law on Searches of Electronic Media

Ickes makes it clear that a routine border search may include a conventional inspection of electronic media and a review of the files on them just as it may include physical papers. . . .

But courts have disagreed on whether the same principles apply to forensic searches of electronic devices. . . .

United States v. Cotterman [709 F.3d 952 (9th Cir. 2013) (en banc)] is the first (and as far as I have found, the only) circuit court case to address the issue, and it held that a forensic search of electronic media could not be a routine search. . . .

The Ninth Circuit found no problem with the initial search of Cotterman's devices at the border itself, but held that "the comprehensive and intrusive nature of a forensic examination . . . trigger[s] the requirement of reasonable suspicion here," *id.* at 962, because the material that can be gleaned from a forensic search of an electronic device differed not only in quantity, but in kind, from that which previously had been upheld. . . .

[*Abidor v. Napolitano*, 990 F. Supp. 2d 260 (E.D.N.Y. 2013)] seems to proceed from the view that, "it would be foolish, if not irresponsible, for plaintiffs to store truly private or confidential information on electronic devices that are carried and used overseas." *Abidor*, 990 F. Supp. 2d at 277. The court reasons that, because "'the individual crossing a border is on notice that certain types of searches are likely to be made, . . . he thus has ample opportunity to diminish the impact of that search by limiting the nature and character of the effects which he brings with him.'" *Id.* at 280, at *16.

While this reasoning may make sense with respect to non-digital "effects" carried by international travelers, it misperceives the reality of the capacity and use of digital devices in today's world: Portable electronic devices are ubiquitous. It neither is realistic nor reasonable to expect the average traveler to leave his digital devices at home when traveling. Over ninety percent of American adults own some kind of cellular phone and more than half of those own a smartphone — a category that includes, but is not limited to, iPhones, Android-based phones, and Blackberry devices. The public increasingly is attached to its phones: In 2010 the Pew Research Center found that sixty-five percent of adults — and seventy-two percent of parents — have slept with or near their phones. Although many undoubtedly carry their phones as a convenience or a luxury, for others it is a necessity. . . . And for travelers — whether for business or pleasure — who may leave behind children, sick or pregnant family members, or businesses and professions that depend upon them keeping current, the choice to travel without a reliable means of contact, in reality, is no choice at all. . . .

D. An Analytical Framework for Searches of Electronic Media . . .

A conventional search at the border of a computer or device may include a Customs officer booting it up and operating it to review its contents, and seemingly, also would allow (but is not necessarily limited to) reviewing a computer's directory tree or using its search functions to seek out and view the contents of specific files or file types. Because electronic storage is logical, not spatial or physical, even a cursory search can be tremendously powerful because it can target very specific files or file types. *See* Orin S. Kerr, *Searches and Seizures in a Digital World*, 119 Harv. L. Rev. 531, 540, 544-47 (2005). And, just as a luggage lock does not render the contents of a suitcase immune from search, a password protected file is not unsearchable on that basis alone.

But seizing a digital device, imaging the entirety of its contents, and keeping the imaged file in the possession of the government after the device has been returned for the purpose of subjecting the imaged file to a forensic search, is another matter entirely. In a forensic search of electronic storage, a bitstream copy is created and then is searched by an expert using highly specialized analytical software — often over the course of several days, weeks, or months — to locate specific files or file types, recover hidden, deleted, or encrypted data, and analyze the structure of files and of a drive. It is the potentially limitless duration and scope of a forensic search of the imaged contents of a digital device that distinguishes it from a conventional computer search. The latter may take hours and delve deeply into the contents of the device, but it is difficult to conceive of a conventional search of a computer or similar device at a border lasting days or weeks. A forensic examination of the imaged content, possibly at a location far from the border and using sophisticated electronic search methods designed to recover even deleted information, is of an altogether different scope and magnitude. And while courts may reach different conclusions about whether forensic searches of digital devices seized at the border require reasonable suspicion, they nevertheless should acknowledge the true character of the devices at issue, the amount of data they contain, the mix of personal and business information they store, and the magnitude of what their contents may reveal about the lives of their users. Facile analogies of forensic examination of a computer or smartphone to the search of a briefcase, suitcase, or trunk are no more helpful than analogizing a glass of water to an Olympic swimming pool because both involve water located in a physical container. "Judges and lawyers live on the slippery slope of analogies; they are not supposed to ski it to the bottom." Robert H. Bork, *The Tempting of America: The Political Seduction of the Law* 169 (1990).

The courts that have confronted forensic searches have struggled to differentiate between general characteristics of searches of electronic devices and characteristics unique to forensic searches as such. *See supra* (explaining that neither *Cotterman* nor *Abidor* drew a clear distinction between a forensic search and a conventional one). This distinction seems absolutely necessary for analyzing the constitutional requirements for forensic searches.

1. Issues Raised by Electronic Devices Generally

The proliferation of electronic devices has allowed travelers to carry a tremendous amount of information with them, much of which is likely to be highly personal. The sheer quantity of data strains analogies between computers and other closed containers....

There also is no question that a conventional search allows Customs officers to examine a wealth of information that

> is, by and large, of a highly personal nature: photographs, videos, written and audio messages (text, email, and voicemail), contacts, calendar appointments, web search and browsing history, purchases, and financial and medical records. It is the kind of information one previously would have stored in one's home that would have been off limits to officers performing [a border search].

United States v. Wurie, 728 F.3d 1, 8 (1st Cir. 2013), *cert. granted,* ____ U.S. ____, 134 S. Ct. 999 (2014) (internal citations omitted)....

But even though travelers routinely walk around carrying digital truckloads worth of data, a conventional search of an electronic device does not differ significantly in scope from the search of a suitcase. There is a limited amount of time that can be devoted to this while the owner waits at the border for the search to conclude and, even if "[t]he private information individuals store on digital devices — their personal 'papers' in the words of the Constitution — stands in stark contrast to the generic and impersonal contents of a gas tank," *Cotterman,* 709 F.3d at 964 (citing *United States v. Jones,* 132 S. Ct. 945, 957 (2012) (Sotomayor, J., concurring)), a conventional search of a digital device . . . must focus on turning up evidence of contraband or illegal activity within a reasonably limited amount of time. The mere fact that this information may be located more readily on a computer does not change the nature of the search. *See United States v. Knotts,* 460 U.S. 276, 285 (1983) (using a beeper to augment visual surveillance of a suspect on public roadways was permissible because "scientific enhancement of this sort raises no constitutional issues which visual surveillance would not also raise").

Nor do the privacy concerns raised by such a search differ from where a traveler brings a suitcase full of personal items, files, or a diary. Although it surely is a discomforting concept, there is no principle beyond the shortness of life and the acknowledgement that there is only so much time available to conduct any particular border search that prevents a CBP officer from "reading a diary line by line looking for mention of criminal activity." *Cf. Cotterman,* 709 F.3d at 962-63. But in practice, CBP officers are expected to use their discretion to focus on more likely evidence of contraband or criminality — to ensure that what appears to be a diary is not actually *The Anarchist Cookbook,* and to move on. . . .

In sum, the reason why a conventional search of a computer can be analogized to a conventional search of a suitcase is less because a computer is analogous to a suitcase than it is because a conventional search has the same inherent limitations — and the same inherent risk of invasiveness — irrespective of what is being searched. There is only a finite amount of time available for a CBP agent to detain a traveler at the border to search the contents of his suitcase or laptop. If the collected works of Shakespeare comprise a mere five megabytes of text, a conventional search of a hard drive containing several gigabytes of data cannot possibly encompass every bit of data on the device to be searched any more than a search of an English major's bags would include a full reading of *Hamlet.* There simply is not enough time to do so while both traveler and Customs agent wait at the border.

2. Issues Unique to Forensic Searches

In contrast, a forensic search is a different *search*— not merely a search of a different object — and it fundamentally alters the playing field for all involved. A forensic search requires the creation of a bitstream copy and its thorough analysis with specialized software over an extended period of time. This type of search raises issues that do not arise in conventional searches. First, because the item searched is a bitstream copy of a device, it may take place long after the device itself has been returned to its owner and therefore a forensic search is unbounded in time. Second, a forensic search allows officers to recover a wealth of information even after it has been deleted. And third, a forensic search provides information about a person's domestic activities away from the border that is not otherwise available even in a conventional search taking place at the border. . . .

iv. A Forensic Search Is Sui Generis . . .

. . . Accordingly, under the facts presented to me in this case, I find that a search of imaged hard drives of digital devices taken from the Defendant at the border and subjected to forensic examination days or weeks later cannot be performed in the absence of reasonable suspicion.

v. The Scope of This Ruling

I also must clarify what I do not hold today. First, nothing in this opinion departs from the Fourth Circuit's holding in *Ickes.* It would be unworkable to develop a different set of rules for conventional border searches of computers, not to mention for anything capable of containing expressive material.

I also do not define a forensic search in terms of the amount of data that is recovered, thereby leaving the status of a given search to be resolved later by Customs officers. A forensic search is a different procedure, fundamentally, from a conventional search. It occurs when a computer expert creates a bitstream copy and it analyzes it by means of specialized software. Because the distinction between a conventional computer search at the border that requires no showing of suspicion and a forensic examination of the imaged hard drive of a computer or digital device is easy to distinguish, the narrow holding of this decision does not hamper the ability of Customs officers to perform their duties when conventionally searching digital devices at the border.

Moreover, as explained, forensic searches are not prohibited — or even subject to a difficult or exacting level of constitutional scrutiny. All that is required is that a Customs officer has reasonable suspicion — that is, a "'particularized and objective basis for suspecting the particular'" device to be searched contains contraband or evidence of criminal activity. This standard is far from onerous and still leaves officers with considerable freedom to search suspicious persons and respond to unexpected factual developments.

Nor is my ruling likely meaningfully to change anything that actually happens at the border. The Department of Homeland Security has advised CBP officers that "[i]n the course of a border search, with or without individualized suspicion, an Officer may examine electronic devices and may review and analyze the information encountered at the border." CBP Directive §5.1.2, Privacy Impact Assessment Attachment 1. This has not changed. CBP Officers also might detain an electronic device "to perform a thorough border search." CBP Directive §5.3.1. So long as that search is conventional, and not forensic — and so long as the time for which the device is detained is reasonably related in scope to the circumstances requiring the search — this also remains permissible. . . .

E. The Search of Saboonchi's Devices Was Supported by Reasonable Suspicion

When Saboonchi arrived at the Rainbow Bridge on March 31, 2012, he already was the subject of an investigation. His name had come up in connection with two different investigations of export violations. Several subpoenas seeking evidence about Saboonchi's dealings already had been issued and were returned in early March 2012. The information that was received in response to those subpoenas showed that Saboonchi had purchased two cyclone separators after representing that they would be used domestically, and then shipped them overseas, understating the value of the cyclone separators in a manner consistent with an attempt to avoid scrutiny. Special Agent Baird also had determined that the recipient of the cyclone separators, General DSAZ, was linked to an industrial parts company in Iran.

All of this is more than sufficient to give rise to reasonable, particularized suspicion — if not probable cause — that Saboonchi was involved in violations of export restrictions on Iran. Accordingly, CBP and HSI officers did not violate the Fourth Amendment when they seized Saboonchi's Devices and subjected them to a forensic search.

IV. CONCLUSION

In sum, for the reasons stated above, Defendant's Motion to Suppress is DENIED. . . .

Notes and Questions

1. Consent. If identification requirements are not searches under a consent theory, why treat checkpoint searches any differently? Since air travelers know or should know of the security screening done at the gate, don't they impliedly consent by trying to use air travel? Is this logic compelling for air travelers? *See Davis*, 482 F.2d at 905 (asserting that it would violate the principle that government cannot "avoid the restrictions of the Fourth Amendment by notifying the public that all telephone lines would be tapped or that all homes would be searched"); 5 Wayne R. LaFave, *Search and Seizure* §10.6(g) (4th ed. 2004) (theory of implied consent "diverts attention from the more fundamental question of whether the nature of the regulation undertaken by the government is in fact reasonable under the Fourth Amendment").

Closely related to the consent theory is one that travelers have notice of the inspection and therefore can always refuse inspection and take alternative transportation. A few courts condition their finding that a screening program is reasonable upon the program's inclusion of this option. *See Davis*, 482 F.2d at 910. Does this logic take into account the impact of the walk-away option on the government's security interest? One court said no, reasoning that "such an option would constitute a one-way street for the benefit of a party planning airplane mischief, since there is no guarantee that if he were allowed to leave he might not return and be more successful," and that "the very fact that a safe exit is available if apprehension is threatened would, by diminishing risk, encourage attempts." *United States v. Skipwith*, 482 F.2d 1272, 1282 (5th Cir. 1973) (Aldrich, J., dissenting, but this discussion adopted by majority). Does the apparently heightened risk of terrorism to transportation systems after 9/11 justify finding that a screening system without this option can still be reasonable? Then-Judge Alito, writing for the Third Circuit, thought so in *United States v. Hartwell*, 436 F.3d 174, 179 (3d Cir. 2006) (upholding a non-consensual hand-wanding of Hartwell after he set off the metal detector at an airport).

2. Routine Airport Screening. The legality of warrantless and suspicionless searches at airports rests on two rationales. First, the border searches are tools of "national self-protection" by which the sovereign controls who and what crosses its borders. Second, screening would-be passengers for weapons or explosives helps prevent aircraft hijacking and sabotage. Although any weapons or explosives found could be used as evidence in a criminal prosecution, the primary purpose of the search is not obtaining criminal evidence; it is the "special need" to assure flight safety. Searches like these are "routine" border searches.

3. Laptop and Smart Phone Searches. Requiring the air traveler to boot up her laptop may also serve that special need because it presumably helps show that the laptop is a laptop, and not a box for carrying explosives. Some courts therefore treat the laptop or smart phone as nothing more than another container.

Are searches of files on your laptop or data on your smart phone different from searches of other containers? Does either of the traditional rationales for airport screening justify border searches of data on laptops or smart phones? How?

4. *Forensic Searches.* As *Saboonchi* and *Cotterman* both suggest, perhaps not all border searches of laptop or smart phone data are the same. The court in *Saboonchi* sharply differentiates between conventional searches of electronic media at the border and forensic searches. Why? Is it the quantity of data involved? Why are forensic searches "non-routine"? How do such searches compare with the kinds of searches the Supreme Court has declared non-routine?

The Eleventh Circuit has held that forensic searches of electronic devices at the border do not require reasonable suspicion:

> We see no reason why the Fourth Amendment would require suspicion for a forensic search of an electronic device when it imposes no such requirement for a search of other personal property. Just as the United States is entitled to search a fuel tank for drugs, it is entitled to search a flash drive for child pornography. And it does not make sense to say that electronic devices should receive special treatment because so many people now own them or because they can store vast quantities of records or effects. The same could be said for a recreational vehicle filled with personal effects or a tractor-trailer loaded with boxes of documents. Border agents bear the same responsibility for preventing the importation of contraband in a traveler's possession regardless of advances in technology. Indeed, inspection of a traveler's property at the border "is an old practice and is intimately associated with excluding illegal articles from the country." [*United States v. Touset,* 890 F.3d 1227, 1233 (11th Cir. 2018) (internal citations omitted).]

In *Riley v. California,* 573 U.S. 373 (2014), the Supreme Court considered the warrantless search of data on a cell phone seized incident to an arrest. Distinguishing past precedent for searches incident to an arrest, the Court said:

> [*United States v. Robinson,* 414 U.S. 218 (1973)] concluded that the two risks identified [incident to arrest] . . . — harm to officers and destruction of evidence — are present in all custodial arrests. There are no comparable risks when the search is of digital data. In addition, *Robinson* regarded any privacy interests retained by an individual after arrest as significantly diminished by the fact of the arrest itself. Cell phones, however, place vast quantities of personal information literally in the hands of individuals. A search of the information on a cell phone bears little resemblance to the type of brief physical search considered in *Robinson.*
>
> We therefore decline to extend *Robinson* to searches of data on cell phones, and hold instead that officers must generally secure a warrant before conducting such a search. [573 U.S. at 386.]

Does *Riley* support a distinction between border searches of laptops or cell phones and border searches of other containers, or between conventional and forensic border searches of laptops or cell phones?

5. *Reasonable Suspicion. Saboonchi* sheds little light on the reasonable suspicion standard it applies, except to note that it is less than probable cause. *Cotterman* explained that reasonable suspicion is "'a particularized and objective basis for suspecting the particular person stopped of criminal activity,'" an assessment that is made in light of "'the totality of the circumstances,'" 709 F.3d at 968 (quoting *United States v. Cortez,* 449 U.S. 411, 417-418 (1981)). "[E]ven when factors considered in isolation from each other are susceptible to an innocent explanation, they may collectively amount to a reasonable suspicion." *United States v. Berber-Tinoco,* 510 F.3d 1083, 1087 (9th Cir. 2007).

In *Saboonchi,* the court held that the standard was satisfied by the totality of the circumstances summarized in the penultimate paragraph of the opinion. In *Cotterman,* the court held that reasonable suspicion was established by Cotterman's prior criminal record for sex tourism (though this was not enough, standing alone), his travel to a country with a reputation for such tourism, his other travel patterns, and his use of passwords on his laptop to protect his files (though, again, this would not have been enough, standing alone). In *United States v. Kim,* 103 F. Supp. 3d 32 (D.D.C. 2015), *appeal dismissed,* No. 15-3035, 2015 WL 5237696 (D.C. Cir. Aug. 14, 2015), a series of suspicious e-mails with another person of interest who had been arrested for involvement in illegal exports to Iran, and that person's assertion that Kim knew that certain embargoed goods were destined for customers in Iran, caused Homeland Security agents to conduct a border search of Kim the next time he left the country "to determine if he was engaged in any potential criminal activity while in the United States." *Id.* at 38. The court held that these facts did not satisfy the reasonable suspicion standard, as they suggested no ongoing criminal activity by Kim. "Looking at all of the circumstances presented, . . . while it is a close case, it seems clear to the Court that the search of the laptop was predicated upon the agent's expectation that the computer would contain evidence of past criminal activity, but there was no objective manifestation that Kim was or was 'about to be, engaged in criminal activity' at that time." *Id.* at 46 (quoting *Cortez,* 449 U.S. at 417).

Is this the right standard for a border search of a laptop? Or is the relevant question "whether there is reasonable suspicion that evidence or contraband is presently on the laptop, not whether there is reasonable suspicion to believe that the laptop owner is currently engaged in criminal activity"? Orin Kerr, *Every Computer Border Search Requires Case-by-Case Reasonableness, DC Court Holds,* Volokh Conspiracy, May 12, 2015.

6. CBP Policy for Border Searches of Electronic Devices. On January 4, 2018, U.S. Customs and Border Protection (CBP) announced a new directive for border searches of electronic devices. CBP Directive No. 3340-049A. It cites a "well-established" "plenary authority of the Federal Government to conduct searches and inspections of persons and merchandise crossing our nation's borders . . . premised in part on a reduced expectation of privacy associated with international travel." *Id.* §4. The directive authorizes CBP officers to conduct a "basic search," without suspicion, of information stored on a traveler's electronic device and accessible through a device's operating system and applications. Officers are not authorized to access information that is stored remotely, *id.* §5.1.2, presumably including data residing on the cloud. If they form a reasonable suspicion of activity that violates laws administered by the CBP or raises a "national security concern," however, they may conduct an "advanced search" using external equipment to access, copy, and analyze the contents of a device. Examples of factors in deciding reasonable suspicion include "the existence of a national security-related lookout in combination with other articulable factors as appropriate, or the presence of an individual on a government operated and government-vetted terrorist watch list." *Id.* §5.1.4.

For the first time, CBP officers are also expressly authorized to request passwords from travelers, and travelers are "obligated" to present their devices "in a condition that allows inspection of the device and its contents." *Id.* §5.3.1. If a traveler refuses to provide a password or if contents are encrypted, officers may detain her device. The default period for any detention of a device is five days, but it may be extended with appropriate approvals. *Id.* §5.3.3. Although the directive asserts that officers who encounter information that may be protected as attorney-client or work product material must seek clarification from the individual carrying the device, and coordinate with a U.S. Attorney's Office, as needed, to segregate such materials, it more vaguely provides that sensitive medical records and journalists' notes shall be handled in accordance with applicable laws and policy, and that officers shall treat sensitive commercial information as "business confidential information." *Id.* §5.2.

Does this directive pass muster under the reasoning of *Saboonchi*? *See Alasaad v. Nielsen*, No. 17-CV-11730-DJC, 2019 WL 5899371 (D. Mass. Nov. 12, 2019) (declaring that CBP policy for "non-cursory searches" of electronic devices without reasonable suspicion violates the Fourth Amendment). *See generally Privacy Impact Assessment Update for CBP Border Searches of Electronic Devices*, DHS/CBP/PIA-008(a) (Jan. 4, 2018), https://www.dhs.gov/sites/default/files/publications/PIA-CBP%20-%20Border-Searches-of-Electronic-Devices%20-January-2018%20-%20Compliant.pdf.

7. *Compelled Passwords?* The CBP Directive permits CBP agents to ask travelers for their passwords, on penalty of loss of their devices for days. More generally, your e-mail, text messages, and some files resident on your laptop or smart phone are all often protected by passwords or passcodes. Even some smart speakers are coded to your voice alone.

Such security protections pose a distinct constitutional question: can you be compelled to give the government your password, passcode, or voiceprint? Some courts say no, citing a Fifth Amendment privilege against testimonial self-incrimination. But suppose the materials can be accessed by a biometric decrypter, like a fingerprint ("Touch ID"), face recognition, or retinal scan? *See* Christopher Elliot, *What Does the Future of Airport Screening Hold?*, Wash. Post, Feb. 14, 2019 (reporting introduction of first "biometric" terminal at Hartsfield-Jackson Atlanta International Airport). Some courts reason that compelling a person to do something that displays a physical characteristic is not "testimonial" and therefore falls outside the privilege. *See generally* Thomas Brewster, *The U.S. Government Can't Force You to Unlock Your Phone with Your Fingerprint, Another Judge Rules*, Forbes, May 10, 2019.

8. *Whole Body Imaging.* In 2010, TSA introduced whole body imaging (WBI) systems at airport checkpoints, and these systems are now the primary screening method at the busiest airports. Bart Elias, *Changes in Airport Passenger Screening Technologies and Procedures: Frequently Asked Questions* 1 (Cong. Res. Serv. R41502), Jan. 26, 2011. WBI systems notoriously capture a crude image of a passenger's body, causing some critics to call a WBI scan a "virtual strip search." *Id.* But TSA gives passengers the option of submitting to a pat-down search instead.

Is a WBI scan a routine search, permissible without suspicion, or a "non-routine" search requiring reasonable and particularized suspicion? Does the pat-down option affect your answer?

9. *Subway and Train Searches.* After terrorist bombings of trains killed more than 200 in Madrid in 2004, and subway bombings killed 52 in London in 2005, the New York City subway system instituted a random container inspection program, whereby subway passengers were randomly selected for inspection of knapsacks, parcels, and purses (confined to "what is minimally necessary to ensure that the . . . item does not

contain an explosive device"). Selected passengers were afforded the option of leaving rather than submitting to inspection.

Clearly, the border search rationale does completely not fit these subway inspections, and they are conducted without reasonable suspicion or a warrant. How, then, are they reasonable? In a challenge to the program, a court described the rationale as follows:

> First, as a threshold matter, the search must "serve as [its] immediate purpose an objective distinct from the ordinary evidence gathering associated with crime investigation." *Nicholas v. Goord*, 430 F.3d 652, 663 (2d Cir. 2005). Second, once the government satisfies that threshold requirement, the court determines whether the search is reasonable by balancing several competing considerations. These balancing factors include (1) the weight and immediacy of the government interest, [*Bd. of Educ. v. Earls*, 536 U.S. 822 (2002),] at 834; (2) "the nature of the privacy interest allegedly compromised by" the search, *id.* at 830; (3) "the character of the intrusion imposed" by the search, *id.* at 832; and (4) the efficacy of the search in advancing the government interest. [*MacWade v. Kelly*, 460 F.3d 260, 268-269 (2d Cir. 2006).]

The court then found that the New York City subway container inspection program served the immediate and substantial "special need of preventing a terrorist attack on the subway." While it acknowledged the subway rider's full expectation of privacy in his containers, it also found the search "minimally intrusive" and "reasonably effective" (perhaps doubtful, given the walk-away option), and therefore that the program was, on balance, constitutional. *Id.* at 270, 273-275. Will any inspection program intended to prevent a terrorist attack *ever* be, on balance, unconstitutional? What kind of subway security check would fail the special needs test?

10. Identification for Screening Purposes and the Fourth Amendment. "Effective checking of names against watch lists . . . requires that every person carry an accurate and secure form of identification." Daniel J. Steinbock, *Designating the Dangerous: From Blacklists to Watch Lists*, 30 Seattle U. L. Rev. 65, 113 (2006). Watch listing is thus linked closely to the asserted need for more secure identification and to more frequent identification stops or checkpoints. *Id.*

Identification is mandatory for boarding flights. As we note, the Fourth Amendment poses no barrier to suspicionless government requests for identification at check-in or the security checkpoint, provided that a reasonable requested person would feel free to terminate the encounter. David J. Steinbock, *National Identity Cards: Fourth and Fifth Amendment Issues*, 56 Fla. L. Rev. 697, 711-714 (2004). Furthermore, the *MacWade* (subway search) analysis suggests that "regulatory" (administrative) demands for identification at airport, transit system, and many building checkpoints would pass Fourth Amendment muster as well. *Id.* at 725-743. How would you apply that analysis to mandatory identification at the entrance to a federal building? What about a random demand for "your papers, please" made by police in a public street? *Cf. Hiibel v. Sixth Jud. Dist. Ct. of Nev.*, 542 U.S. 177 (2004) (upholding a Nevada "stop-and-identify" statute that requires individuals lawfully subjected to a *Terry* stop to identify themselves).

11. A National Identity Card or Other Identifier? Some have argued that after 9/11 we need a national identity card system. *See* Alan Dershowitz, Opinion, *Why Fear*

National ID Cards?, N.Y. Times, Oct. 13, 2001. *See generally* Steinbock, *Designating the Dangerous, supra* (citing proponents). An effective system "necessitates mandatory participation, both in the sense of having an identity within the system and in presenting identification when required." Steinbock, *National Identity Cards, supra*, at 708.

A mandatory national identifier requirement would pose at least three kinds of legal issues. First, there may be a Fourth Amendment question if identification is demanded randomly in some places, such as public streets, as suggested above. "[O]ne of the primary reasons that governments created passports and identity cards was to restrict movement, alter patterns of migration, and control the movements of poor people and others viewed as undesirable." Daniel J. Solove, *A Taxonomy of Privacy*, 154 U. Pa. L. Rev. 477, 514 n.183 (2006).

Second, the "main point of identity checking is to make a connection between the identified individual and collection of data." Steinbock, *National Identity Cards, supra*, at 700. A national identifier "would likely be but one component of a large and complex nationwide identity system, the core of which could be a database of personal information on the U.S. population." Computer Sci. & Telecomms. Bd., National Research Council, *IDs — Not That Easy: Questions About Nationwide Identity Systems* 7 (2002). The legality of a national identifier system thus turns in part on the legality of the associated database or watch list.

Third, identity checking may also generate data that can be used to track movements and purchases (e.g., subject was identified at 11:06 A.M. on June 20, 2006, at Constitution Ave. entrance to Department of Justice). The use of such data in a computer database raises some of the same privacy concerns created by government access to and use of third-party records. *See Carpenter v. United States*, 138 S. Ct. 2206 (2018) (cell-site location information), *supra* p. 685. By providing identification on demand, does a person waive her privacy interest in the data? *See* Steinbock, *National Identity Cards, supra*, at 748-752 (no, because identification is different from providing telephone numbers or banking information). Even if a single identification encounter does not offend privacy, does its retention (and possibly aggregation) into a database do so?

12. The REAL ID Act — A Step in the Direction of a National ID Card? In 2005, Congress enacted the REAL ID Act, Pub. L. No. 109-13, div. B, 119 Stat. 231, 302 (2005) (codified in scattered sections of 8 and 49 U.S.C.). The REAL ID Act forbids any federal agency, beginning three years after the Act's enactment, from accepting for any official purpose a state-issued driver's license or identification card unless it meets certain requirements. The identification must include the licensee's name, address, date of birth, gender, a digital photo, signature, anti-tampering security features, and "[a] common machine-readable technology, with defined minimum data elements." *Id.* §202(b)(9), 119 Stat. at 312. In addition, the state must insist on and verify certain identifying information and evidence of lawful status to issue such an identification. Finally, each state must "provide electronic access to all other States to information contained in the motor vehicle database of the States," which must include, at a minimum, "all data fields printed on drivers' licenses and identification cards issued by the State." *Id.* §202(d)(13)(A), 119 Stat. at 316. How is the REAL ID different from a national identity card? Which poses the larger privacy concern, the REAL ID or the database the Act requires? In *Whalen v. Roe*, 429 U.S. 589 (1977), the Supreme Court found reasonable a mandatory prescription-reporting system tied to a centralized database, but only because the system limited access to the database and criminalized unauthorized disclosures. What protections, if any, are necessary to make the motor vehicle database contemplated by the REAL ID Act reasonable?

For an argument that "state governments are quietly developing national ID systems in a variety of forms," including the identity card system envisioned by the REAL ID Act, state promotion of the E-Verify background check for employment, and other identity-tracking systems, see Jim Harper, *The New National ID Systems*, Cato Inst. Policy Analysis No. 831 (Jan. 30, 2018).

B. WATCH LISTING

Watch lists are automated databases used to identify individuals or entities for consequences (such as denial of entry or boarding) based solely on their inclusion ("listing") in the database. Two of the 9/11 hijackers had been identified by the CIA as possible terrorist suspects and added to a State Department watch list of such suspects called "TIPOFF" on August 24, 2001. *9/11 Commission Report, supra* p. 744, at 270. But TIPOFF was intended primarily to keep terrorists from getting visas to the United States. It was not shared with the FAA, which maintained a separate "no-fly list" of persons banned for air travel because of the threat they were thought to pose to civil aviation, as well as a "selectee list" of persons selected for further screening, such as hand-wanding and questioning. None of the hijackers was on either FAA list. *The 9/11 Investigations* 27 (Steve Strasser ed., 2004).

In 2003, President George W. Bush issued Homeland Security Presidential Directive 6 (HSPD-6) (Sept. 16, 2003), establishing a Terrorist Screening Center to consolidate the government's watch listing and screening. *See generally* William J. Krouse & Bart Elias, *Terrorist Watchlist Checks and Air Passenger Prescreening* 2 (Cong. Res. Serv. RL33645), Dec. 30, 2009. Subsequently, based partly on TIPOFF data, the National Counterterrorism Center (NCTC), under the Office of the Director of National Intelligence, created the Terrorist Identities Datamart Environment (TIDE) as the master repository for international terrorism data. TIDE "includes information the US Government possesses related to the identities of individuals known or appropriately suspected to be or to have been involved in activities constituting, in preparation for, in aid of, or related to terrorism (with the exception of purely domestic terrorism information)." Nat'l Counterterrorism Ctr., *Terrorist Identities Datamart Environment (TIDE)* (2017), *available at* https://www.dni.gov/files/NCTC/documents/features_documents/TIDEfactsheet10FEB2017.pdf.

As of February 2017, TIDE contained about 1.6 million people, of which "US Persons" (both citizens and lawful permanent residents) accounted for approximately 16,000. *Id.*

In theory, the watch list process begins when a member of the intelligence community shares newly acquired information about suspected terrorists or their supporters with NCTC's TIDE. See the chart below. The standards applied are not public, although some anecdotal evidence suggests that they are at least partly subjective, that they may rest on indirect and possibly innocent connections to suspected terrorists as well as informant information of doubtful reliability, and that they err on the side of inclusion. NCTC nominates some of these persons, and the FBI-administered inter-agency Terrorist Screening Center (TSC) decides whether to accept the nomination for inclusion in the Consolidated Terrorist Screening

Database (TSDB). Krouse & Elias, *supra,* at 203. The FBI also provides data about domestic terrorist suspects to the TSDB. To be included in the TSDB,

> the "biographic information associated with a nomination must contain sufficient identifying data so that a person being screened can be matched or disassociated from a watch-listed terrorist." Second, the "facts and circumstances" must "meet the reasonable suspicion standard of review." This means "articulable facts which, taken together with rational inferences, reasonably warrant the determination that an individual is known or suspected to be or has been engaged in conduct constituting, in preparation for, in aid of, or related to terrorism and terrorist activities." This standard was not mandated by statute, but was "adopted by internal Executive Branch policy and practice." In addition, a recent district court case indicates that there is a "secret exception to the reasonable suspicion standard," but the "nature of the exception and the reasons . . . for nomination are claimed to be state secrets." [Jared P. Cole, *Terrorist Databases and the No Fly List: Procedural Due Process and Hurdles to Litigation* 3 (Cong. Res. Serv. R43730), Apr. 2, 2015 (citations omitted).]

As of 2017, it was reported that the TSDB contained records for more than 1.2 million people, including 4,600 Americans. Charlie Savage, *Judge Rules Terrorism Watchlist Violates Constitutional Rights,* N.Y. Times, Sept. 4, 2019.

The TSC then distributes TSDB-generated watch lists to end users — including all frontline screening agencies — such as the Transportation Security Administration (administering the no-fly and selectee lists), U.S. Customs and Border Protection, the State Department's Bureau of Consular Affairs, the FBI, and state and local governments through the National Crime Information Center. A 2007 study identified nine different end users, although the number and names of users has changed since then. *See* Peter M. Shane, *The Bureaucratic Due Process of Government Watch Lists,* 75 Geo. Wash. L. Rev. 804 (2007). In a 2014 case, the court asserted that there were 17 end users. *Ibrahim v. Dep't of Homeland Security,* 62 F. Supp. 3d 909, 918 (N.D. Cal. 2014) (*infra* p. 762).

The 9/11 Commission expressly recommended expanding traveler intelligence and traveler screening, with priority given to screening airline passengers for explosives. *9/11 Commission Report, supra,* at 385, 393. After a number of false starts, TSA adopted a program called Secure Flight that screens air travelers based in part on the collection of pre-flight information from them. No-fly and selectee watch lists were consolidated into the TSDB sometime in 2004, although they form only a small subset of the TSDB. In 2007, the head of TSA testified to efforts by TSA and TSC to reduce the number of persons on the no-fly list by as much as 50 percent, partly in response to the DHS Privacy Office's criticism of the quality of the list. Krouse & Elias, *supra,* at 12-13. It was reported in 2014 that there were still 47,000 people on the list, including 800 Americans. Cole, *supra,* at 1 n.3.

But the listing process has been beset with errors. In 2012, a court of appeals asserted that

> [t]ens of thousands of travelers have been misidentified because of misspellings and transcription errors in the nomination process, and because of computer algorithms that imperfectly match travelers against the names on the list. TSA maintains a list of approximately 30,000 individuals who are commonly confused with those on the No-Fly and Selectee Lists. One major air carrier reported that it encountered 9,000 erroneous terrorist watchlist matches every day during April 2008. [*Ibrahim v. Dep't of Homeland Security,* 669 F.3d 983, 990 (9th Cir. 2012).]

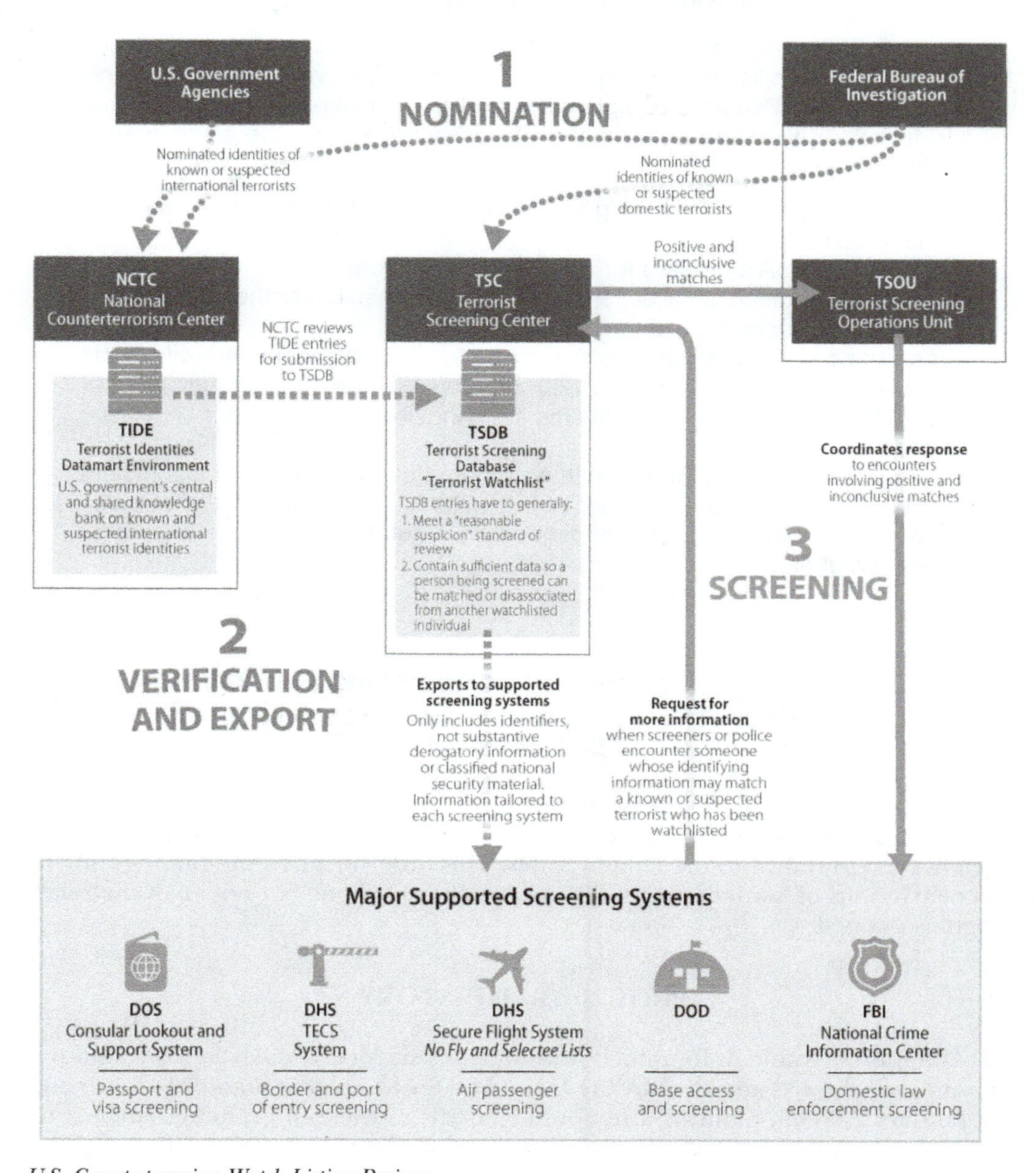

U.S. Counterterrorism Watch Listing Regime

From Jerome P. Bjelopera, Bart Elias & Alison Siskin, *The Terrorist Screening Database and Preventing Terrorist Travel* 3 (Cong. Res. Serv. RL44678), Nov. 7, 2016.

Reading *Ibrahim v. Department of Homeland Security*

In the following case, a lawfully admitted student was erroneously placed on a no-fly watch list and then had her visa revoked, leaving her unable to re-enter the United States to complete her studies, visit with her ill thesis adviser and friend, or even attend the trial in this case challenging the government's actions.

- What is the process for adding a name to the no-fly list? What went wrong in that process here?
- What is the TSA's process for correcting such errors?
- Why is Dr. Ibrahim, an alien, entitled to due process under the Fifth Amendment? (See *supra* pp. 219-220.)
- Assuming she was entitled to due process, what balancing determined the process due? Why wasn't the TRIP process sufficient? What judicial remedy did the court provide? Why did it not include restoration of her student visa?
- To err is human. Was the human error here truly a reflection of insufficient "front-end" process — process in the making of the watch list? Does due process require governmental perfection? If not, how was there a denial of process at all?

Ibrahim v. Department of Homeland Security

United States District Court, Northern District of California, 2014
62 F. Supp. 3d 909

William Alsup, J.: In this terrorist-watchlist challenge, a nonimmigrant alien seeks relief after having been barred airplane-boarding privileges and after having been denied a visa to return to the United States. This order includes the findings of fact and conclusions of law following a five-day bench trial. Some but not all of the relief sought is granted.

PROCEDURAL HISTORY

Plaintiff Dr. Rahinah Ibrahim is Muslim and a subject of Malaysia. Pursuant to a student visa, she was admitted to the United States to study at Stanford University. On January 2, 2005, plaintiff attempted to fly from the San Francisco airport to Hawaii but was handcuffed and led away because she was on a federal no-fly list. After being held, she was eventually (the next day) allowed to fly to Hawaii and then back to Los Angeles and then to Malaysia. While she was in Malaysia, her student visa was revoked.

In January 2006, plaintiff commenced this civil action against multiple state and federal agencies alleging Section 1983 claims, state law tort claims, and several constitutional claims based on the inclusion of her name on government terrorist watchlists. . . .

FINDINGS OF FACT

Plaintiff . . .

5. Government counsel has conceded at trial that Dr. Ibrahim is not a threat to our national security. She does not pose (and has not posed) a threat of committing an act of international or domestic terrorism with respect to an aircraft, a threat to airline passenger or civil aviation security, or a threat of domestic terrorism. This the government admits and this order finds. . . .

7. In November 2004, FBI Special Agent Kevin Michael Kelley, located in San Jose, nominated Dr. Ibrahim, who was then at Stanford, to various federal watchlists using the NCIC Violent Gang and Terrorist Organizations File Gang Member Entity Form ("VGTOF"). VGTO, also known as Violent Gang and Terrorist Organization, was an office within the FBI's National Crime Information Center ("NCIC"). VGTOF was a file within the FBI's NCIC.

Agent Kelley misunderstood the directions on the form and erroneously nominated Dr. Ibrahim to the TSA's no-fly list and the Interagency Border Information System ("IBIS"). He did not intend to do so. This was a mistake, he admitted at trial. He intended to nominate her to the Consular Lookout and Support System ("CLASS"), the TSA selectee list, TUSCAN (information exported to Canada), and TACTICS (information exported to Australia). He checked the wrong boxes, filling out the form exactly the opposite way from the instructions on the form. He made this mistake even though the form stated, "It is recommended the subject NOT be entered into the following selected terrorist screening databases." An excerpt of Agent Kelley's nomination is provided below:

> It is recommended the subject NOT be entered into the following selected terrorist screening databases
>
> ☒ Consular Lookout and Support System (CLASS)
> ☐ Interagency Border Information System (IBIS)
> ☐ TSA No Fly List
> ☒ TSA Selectee List
> ☒ TUSCAN
> ☒ TACTICS

Based on the way Agent Kelley checked the boxes on the form, plaintiff was placed on the no-fly list and IBIS (but not on CLASS, the selectee list, TUSCAN, or TACTICS). So, the way in which plaintiff got on the no-fly list in the first place was human error by the FBI. Agent Kelley did not learn of this error until his deposition in September 2013. . . .

Terrorist Screening Database and Related Watchlists . . .

20. FBI agents and other government employees normally nominate individuals to the TSDB using a "reasonable suspicion standard," meaning articulable facts which, taken together with rational inferences, reasonably warrant the determination that an individual is known or suspected to be or has been engaged in conduct constituting, in preparation for, in aid of, or related to terrorism and terrorist activities. Unlike a standard codified by Congress or rendered by judicial decision, this "reasonable suspicion" standard was adopted by internal Executive Branch policy and

practice. From 2004 to 2007, there was no uniform standard for TSDB nominations. Each agency promulgated its own nominating procedures for inclusion in the TSDB based on its interpretation of homeland security presidential directives and the memorandum of opinion that established the TSC. One such directive was Homeland Security Presidential Directive 6 ("HSPD-6") which stated, "[t]his directive shall be implemented in a manner consistent with the provisions of the Constitution and applicable laws, including those protecting the rights of all Americans." Agents now interpret this guideline, and others, as meaning that it would not be appropriate to watchlist someone based upon their religion, religious practices, and any other First Amendment activity.

21. For each nominee, the TSDB calls out which particular watchlists the nominee should be on and which he or she should not be on.... If nominated, designations in the TSDB are then exported to the nominated downstream customer watchlists operated by various government entities. For example, information in the TSDB (if selected) is sent to the Department of State for inclusion in CLASS-Visa or CLASS-Passport.

22. Due to Agent Kelley's mistake, Dr. Ibrahim was nominated to the no-fly and IBIS watchlists. She was placed in the TSDB and her information was exported to the no-fly list and IBIS. Thus, when she arrived at the ticket counter, the airline (which has and had access to the no-fly list), was obligated to deny her boarding (and then called the police).

23. When persons are placed on the no-fly list or any other watchlist, they receive no formal notice of such placement and may never learn of such placement until, if ever, they attempt to board a plane or do any other act covered by the watchlist.

24. When an agency "encounters" an individual via a visa application, airport boarding, border entry, to take three examples, the agency official searches for the individual's identity on applicable watchlists. If there is a potential name match, the individual's name is forwarded to the TSC. The TSC, in turn, reviews the TSDB record and an appropriate counterterrorism response may be made.

Travel Redress Inquiry Program (TRIP)

25. Under Section 44926(a) of Title 49 of the United States Code:

> The Secretary of Homeland Security shall establish a timely and fair process for individuals who believe they have been delayed or prohibited from boarding a commercial aircraft because they were wrongly identified as a threat under the regimes utilized by the Transportation Security Administration, United States Customs and Border Protection, or any other office or component of the Department of Homeland Security.

Prior to 2007, individuals who claimed they were denied or delayed boarding or entry to the United States or repeatedly subjected to additional screening or inspection could submit a Passenger Identity Verification Form (PIVF) to the TSA. This program was succeeded by the DHS's TRIP process in 2007.

26. If DHS determines that the complainant is an exact or near match to an identity in the TSDB, the match is referred to the TSC's redress unit.

27. The TSC's redress unit reviews the information available to determine (1) whether the individual's status is an exact match to an identity in the TSDB; (2) if an exact match, whether the traveler should continue to be in the TSDB; and

(3) if the traveler should continue to be in the TSDB, whether the traveler meets additional criteria for placement on the no-fly or selectee lists.

28. The TSC's redress unit does not undertake additional fieldwork in determining whether an individual was properly placed in the TSDB or customer databases. The review is based on existing records and may (or may not) include contacting the nominating agency to obtain any new derogatory information that supports a nomination. The TSC's redress unit then notifies DHS TRIP of any modification or removal of the individual's record.

29. A letter responding to the request for redress is eventually sent to the complainant. Dr. Ibrahim attempted to use this redress method and received a vague and inconclusive response, described below....

Plaintiff and the Watchlists

36. Dr. Ibrahim obtained a F-1 student visa to attend Stanford University for her Ph.D. for at least the duration of 2000 to 2005....

39. In an e-mail dated January 3, 2005, between two officials in the coordination division of the visa office, one wrote (emphasis in original):

> As I mentioned to you, I have a stack of pending revocations that are based on VGTO entries. These revocations contain virtually no derogatory information. After a *long* and frustrating game of phone tag with INR, TSC, and Steve Naugle of the FBI's VGTO office, finally we're going to revoke them.
>
> Per my conversation with Steve, there is no practical way to determine what the basis of the investigation is for these applicants. The only way to do it would be to contact the case agent for each case individually to determine what the basis of the investigation is. Since we don't have the time to do that (and, in my experience, case agents don't call you back promptly, if at all), we will accept that the opening of an investigation itself is a prima facie indicator of potential ineligibility under 3(B)....

40. A pending revocation for Dr. Ibrahim was in the above-referenced stack. (Again, VGTO referred to the FBI's Violent Gang and Terrorist Organization office; INR refers to the Department of State's Bureau of Intelligence and Research; and the term 3(B) referred to Section 212(a)(3)(B) of the Immigration and Nationality Act, 8 U.S.C. 1182(a)(3)(B).)

41. Dr. Ibrahim's F-1 student visa was revoked on January 31, 2005. The certificate of revocation stated: "subsequent to visa issuance, information has come to light indicating that the alien may be inadmissible to the United States and ineligible to receive a visa under section 212(a)(3)(B) of the Immigration and Nationality Act, such that the alien should reappear before a U.S. Consular Officer to establish his eligibility for a visa before being permitted to apply for entry to the United States." The trial record does not explain what "information" had come to light. After Dr. Ibrahim's visa was revoked, the Department of State entered a record into CLASS that would notify any consular officer adjudicating a future visa application submitted by Dr. Ibrahim that Dr. Ibrahim may be inadmissible under 8 U.S.C. 1182(a)(3)(B).

42. The revocation was pursuant to Section 212(a)(3)(B) of the Immigration and Nationality Act, 8 U.S.C. 1182(a)(3)(B). The revocation itself was on January 31, 2005, and Dr. Ibrahim learned of the revocation in March 2005.

43. In an e-mail dated February 8, 2005, between the chief of the consular section at the United States Embassy in Kuala Lumpur and an official in the coordination division of the visa office of the Department of State, the chief asked about a prudential visa revocation cable he had received concerning the events Dr. Ibrahim experienced in January 2005. The Department of State employee replied in e-mail stating:

> Paul asked me to respond to you on this case, as I handle revocations in VO/L/C. The short version is that this person's visa was revoked because there is law enforcement interest in her as a potential terrorist. This is sufficient to prudentially revoke a visa but doesn't constitute a finding of ineligibility. The idea is to revoke first and resolve the issues later in the context of a new visa application.... My guess based on past experience is that she's probably issuable. However, there's no way to be sure without putting her through the interagency process. I'll gin up the revocation. VO/L/C is the designation of the coordination division within the visa office.

44. After she tried unsuccessfully to return to the United States in March 2005, using what she thought was a valid student visa, a letter arrived for Dr. Ibrahim, dated April 2005, stating: "[t]he revocation of your visa does not necessarily indicate that you are ineligible to receive a U.S. visa in future [sic]. That determination can only be made at such time as you apply for a new visa. Should you choose to do so, instructions can be found on the Embassy web site at http://malaysia.usembassy.gov."...

[Subsequently, Dr. Ibrahim re-applied for a visa.]

60. On December 14, 2009, Dr. Ibrahim's visa application was denied. Dr. Ibrahim was given a letter by the consular officer informing her that the Department of State was unable to issue her a visa pursuant to Section 212(a)(3)(B). The consular officer wrote the word "(Terrorist)" on the form beside Section 212(a)(3)(B) to explain why she was deemed inadmissible. [She was not informed of her right to apply for a waiver.]...

65. In September 2013, Dr. Ibrahim submitted a visa application so that she could attend the trial on this matter. She attended a consular officer interview in October 2013. At the interview, she was asked to provide supplemental information via e-mail. Trial in this action began on December 2 and ended on December 6. As of December 6, Dr. Ibrahim had not received a response to her visa application. At trial, however, government counsel stated verbally that the visa had been denied. Plaintiff's counsel said that they had not been so aware and that Dr. Ibrahim had not been so notified.

Dr. Ibrahim Today...

70. Since 2005, Dr. Ibrahim has never been permitted to enter the United States....

CONCLUSIONS OF LAW

Due Process

At long last, the government has conceded that plaintiff poses no threat to air safety or national security and should never have been placed on the no-fly list. She got there by human error within the FBI. This too is conceded. This was no minor human error but an error with palpable impact, leading to the humiliation, cuffing, and incarceration of an innocent and incapacitated air traveler. That it was human error may seem hard to accept — the FBI agent filled out the nomination form in a way *exactly* opposite from the instructions on the form, a bureaucratic analogy to a surgeon amputating the wrong digit — human error, yes, but of considerable consequence. Nonetheless, this order accepts the agent's testimony.

Since her erroneous placement on the no-fly list, plaintiff has endured a litany of troubles in getting back into the United States. Whether true or not, she reasonably suspects that those troubles are traceable to the original wrong that placed her on the no-fly list. Once derogatory information is posted to the TSDB, it can propagate extensively through the government's interlocking complex of databases, like a bad credit report that will never go away. As a post-deprivation remedy, therefore, due process requires, and this order requires, that the government remediate its wrong by cleansing and/or correcting all of its lists and records of the mistaken 2004 derogatory designation and by certifying that such cleansing and/or correction has been accurately done as to every single government watchlist and database. This will not implicate classified information in any way but will give plaintiff assurance that, going forward, her troubles in returning to the United States, if they continue, are unaffected by the original wrong.

The basic issue is what due process of law requires in these circumstances. . . .

Due process provides heightened protection against government interference when certain fundamental rights and liberty interests are involved. *Washington v. Glucksberg*, 521 U.S. 702, 720 (1997).

With respect to Dr. Ibrahim, the private interests at stake in her 2005 deprivations were the right to travel, *Kent v. Dulles*, 357 U.S. 116, 125 (1958), and the right to be free from incarceration, *Hamdi v. Rumsfeld*, 542 U.S. 507, 529 (2004), and from the stigma and humiliation of a public denial of boarding and incarceration, *Paul v. Davis*, 424 U.S. 693, 701, 711 (1976), any one of which would be sufficient and all three of which apply on this record.

With respect to the government's interest, all would surely agree that our government must and should track terrorists who pose a threat to America — not just to its air travel — but to any aspect of our national security. In this connection, however, the government concedes that Dr. Ibrahim herself poses no such threat (nor did she in 2005). . . .

Significantly, therefore, our case involves a conceded, proven, undeniable, and serious error by the government — not merely a risk of error. Consequently, this order holds that due process entitles Dr. Ibrahim to a correction in the government's records to prevent the 2004 error from further propagating through the various agency databases and from causing further injury to Dr. Ibrahim. By this order, all defendants shall specifically and thoroughly query the databases maintained by them, such as the TSDB, TIDE, CLASS, KSTF, TECS, IBIS, TUSCAN, TACTICS, and the no-fly and selectee lists, and to remove all references to the designations made by the defective 2004 nomination form or, if left in place, to add a correction in the same paragraph that the designations were erroneous and should not be relied upon for any purpose. To be clear, no agency should even rely on Agent Kelley's actual unexpressed intention to nominate to certain lists in 2004, for the form instructions were not properly followed. The designations in the November 2004 form should be disregarded for all purposes. The government is always free to make a new nomination doing it the right way. A deadline will be set for defendants to file declarations under oath attesting to compliance.

It is perhaps true that the error has already been corrected, at least in part, but there is reason to doubt that the error and all of its echoes have been traced and cleansed from all interlocking databases. A correction in the TSDB REDACTED would *not* have automatically expunged incorrect data previously exported from the TSDB REDACTED to the customer agency databases. For example, the Department of State separately maintains its CLASS database. If the bad information was transferred from the TSDB REDACTED to CLASS in the 2004 period, then that bad information may remain there and may linger on there notwithstanding a correction in the TSDB REDACTED. This order will require defendants to trace through each agency database employing the TSDB REDACTED and make sure the correction or deletion has actually been made.

This order finds that suspicious adverse effects continued to haunt Dr. Ibrahim in 2005 and 2006, even though the government claims to have learned of and corrected the mistake. For example, after her name was removed from the no-fly list, the next day, Dr. Ibrahim was issued a bright red "SSSS" pass. Less than a month after she was removed from the no-fly list, her visa was "prudentially" revoked. In March 2005, she was not permitted to fly to the United States. Her daughter was not allowed to fly to the United States even to attend this trial despite the fact that her daughter is a United States citizen. After so much gnashing of teeth and so much on-the-list-off-the-list machinations, the government is ordered to provide the foregoing relief to remediate its wrong. If the government has already cleansed its records, then no harm will be done in making sure again and so certifying to the Court.

With respect to the government's TRIP program, which does provide a measure of post-deprivation relief, this order holds that it is inadequate, at least on this record. After Dr. Ibrahim was denied boarding on January 2, 2005, and denied boarding to return in March 2005, she submitted a Passenger Identity Verification Form (PIVF), a program that eventually morphed into the TRIP program by 2007. Approximately one year later, the TSA responded to her PIVF form with the following vague response:

> Where it has been determined that a correction to records is warranted, these records have been modified to address any delay or denial of boarding that you may have experienced as a result of the watchlist screening process.

Noticeably missing from the response to Dr. Ibrahim was whether there had been errors in her files and whether all errors in customer databases had been corrected. This vague response fell short of providing any assurance to Dr. Ibrahim — who the government concedes is not a national security threat and was the victim of concrete, reviewable adverse government action caused by government error — that the mistake had been traced down in all its forms and venues and corrected.

This order provides only a post-deprivation remedy, to be sure, but post-deprivation remedies are efficacious, especially where, as here, it would be impractical and harmful to national security to routinely provide a pre-deprivation opportunity to be heard of the broad and universal type urged by plaintiff's counsel. *Haig v. Agee,* 453 U.S. 280, 309-10 (1981). Such advance notice to all nominees would aid terrorists in their plans to bomb and kill Americans. Moreover, at the time of listing, the government would have no way of knowing which nonimmigrant aliens living abroad would enjoy standing under *Ibrahim II.* Instead, any remedy must await the time when, if ever, concrete, reviewable adverse action is taken against the nominee.

Put differently, until concrete, reviewable adverse action occurs against a nominee, the Executive Branch must be free to maintain its watchlists in secret, just as federal agents must be able to maintain in secret its investigations into organized crime, drug trafficking organizations, prostitution, child-pornography rings, and so forth. To publicize such investigative details would ruin them. Once concrete, reviewable adverse action is taken against a target, then there is and will be time enough to determine what post-deprivation process is due the individual affected. In this connection, since the reasonable suspicion standard is an internal guideline used within the Executive Branch for watchlisting and not imposed by statute (or by specific judicial holding), the Executive Branch is free to modify its own standard as needed by exception, even if the exception is cloaked in state secrets. Any other rule requiring reviewability before concrete adverse action would be manifestly unworkable.*

Given the Kafkaesque on-off-on-list treatment imposed on Dr. Ibrahim, the government is further ordered expressly to tell Dr. Ibrahim that she is no longer on the no-fly list and has not been on it since 2005 (always subject, of course, to future developments and evidence that might warrant reinstating her to the list). This relief is appropriate and warranted because of the confusion generated by the government's own mistake and the very real misapprehension on her part that the later visa denials are traceable to her erroneous 2004 placement on the no-fly list, suggesting (reasonably from her viewpoint) that she somehow remains on the no-fly list.

It is true, as the government asserts as part of its ripeness position, that she cannot fly to the United States without a visa, but she is entitled to try to solve one hurdle at a time and perhaps the day will come when all hurdles are cleared and she can fly back to our country. The government's legitimate interest in keeping secret the composition of the no-fly list should yield, on the facts of this case, to a particularized remedy isolated by this order only to someone even the government concludes poses no threat to the United States. Everyone else in this case knows it. As a matter of remedy, she should be told that the no-fly hurdle has been cleared. . . .

In sum, after what our government has done by error to Dr. Ibrahim, this order holds that she is entitled to the post-deprivation remedy described above, that the government's post-deprivation administrative remedies fall far short of such relief, and to deny her such relief would deprive her of due process of law. This order will supply the due process that otherwise has been denied to plaintiff. . . .

---

* In the instant case, the nomination in 2004 to the no-fly list was conceded at trial to have been a mistake. In this sense, this is an easier case to resolve. Harder no-fly cases surely exist. For example, the government uses "derogatory" information to place individuals on the no-fly list. When an individual is refused boarding, does he or she have a right to know the specific information that led to the listing? Certainly in some (but not all) cases, providing the specifics would reveal sources and methods used in our counterterrorism defense program and disclosure would unreasonably jeopardize our national security. Possibly, instead, a general summary might provide a degree of due process, allowing the nominee an opportunity to refute the charge. Or, agents might interview the nominee in such a way as to address the points of concern without revealing the specifics. Possibly (or possibly not), even that much process would betray our defense systems to our enemies. This order need not and does not reach this tougher, broader issue, for, again, the listing of Dr. Ibrahim was concededly based on human error. Revealing this error could not and has not betrayed any worthwhile methods or sources.

Notes and Questions

1. The Nomination Process. Although the *Ibrahim* court speaks of an FBI "reasonable suspicion" standard for nominations to the TSDB, it also states that over the period relevant to Dr. Ibrahim's case, there was no uniform standard. Neither we nor Dr. Ibrahim know what information Agent Kelly had concerning Dr. Ibrahim, but we do know that he misread the rather confusingly written direction on the VGTOF form (which requires a checkmark for a non-listing, thus making the default result a recommendation for listing).

When an innocent person is erroneously included on a watch list or has the same name as someone on the list, the listing generates a "false positive." With approximately 8 percent of all air travelers being stopped each day and an estimated 70 million secondary screening searches being conducted annually, even a small rate of false positives will snare many innocent travelers. *See* Paul Rosenzweig & Jeff Jonas, *Correcting False Positives: Redress and the Watch List Conundrum*, 17 Legal Mem. (Heritage Found.) 2 n.3 (June 17, 2005), *available at* http://www.heritage.org/Research/HomelandDefense/lm17.cfm.

2. Blacklists and Watch Lists. The use of lists did not start with the counterterrorist efforts of the 1990s and later. The infamous "blacklists" of the McCarthy era — listing "known" Communists and their "fellow travelers" — are a disturbing antecedent. Professor Steinbock summarizes the blacklists, and the loyalty screening programs with which they were associated, as follows:

> Little or no effort was made to identify specific workers whose presence would actually pose some realistic threat to national security. Because Communist Party membership or "sympathetic association" with "subversive organizations," even long in the past, were [*sic*] deemed to be adequate proxies for dangerousness, large numbers of people were labeled disloyal or security threats who factually were not. In practice these programs often amounted, instead, to widespread punishment for the exercise of rights of belief, speech, and association. More broadly, they were also about public shaming and enforcing ideological conformity. [Steinbock, *Designating the Dangerous, supra* p. 757, at 77.]

Some procedural protections were eventually required by the courts or by Congress to protect victims of blacklisting and loyalty screening programs. Remarkably, "even [these] are wholly absent from twenty-first century listing. The result [today], in all likelihood, is a glut of both false positives and false negatives." *Id.* at 99.

3. Protected Interests. When the federal government watch lists or takes action on the basis of a watch list, the chief procedural protection may be the Fifth Amendment's guarantee of due process. Did Dr. Ibrahim have a right to process under the Fifth Amendment? The answer involves two inquiries.

First, as an alien, did she have a sufficient connection to the United States to invoke the Constitution at all? See *supra* p. 220.

Second, did the government deprive her of life or a constitutionally protected liberty or property interest? In *Gilmore v. Gonzales*, 435 F.3d 1125 (9th Cir. 2006), the Ninth Circuit held that there was no fundamental right to travel by airplane (or by the most convenient mode of transportation). But Gilmore was a domestic air traveler; Dr. Ibrahim was an international traveler without any convenient alternative to air travel. *See Tarhuni v. Holder*, 8 F. Supp. 3d 1253 (D. Or. 2014) (right to international air travel is protected when air travel is only practical means of passenger travel); *Latif v. Holder*, 969 F. Supp. 2d 1293 (D. Or. 2013) (burden on international travel is greater than on interstate travel).

The Supreme Court has held that something more than a mere reputational injury or "stigma" from the government action is required to make out a liberty interest. It requires "stigma-plus," the plus being some tangible burden such as loss of employment or of the opportunity to purchase alcohol. *See, e.g.*, *Paul v. Davis*, 424 U.S. 693 (1976); *Wisconsin v. Constantineau*, 400 U.S. 433 (1971). Does a person who is singled out for further screening or is barred from boarding by his identification on a no-fly or TSDB list meet this requirement?

As applied to U.S. citizens, a federal court ruled in 2019 that the standard for inclusion in the database was too vague: "[T]he risk of erroneous deprivation of plaintiffs' travel-related and reputational liberty interests is high, and the currently existing procedural safeguards are not sufficient to address that risk." *Elhady v. Kable*, 391 F. Supp. 3d 562, 582 (E.D. Va. 2019). Although the group of 23 American plaintiffs obtained summary judgment following their reports of being detained and harassed when trying to enter the country, the court stopped short of providing a remedy. Can you outline relief that will protect due process and not unduly compromise national security?

Dr. Ibrahim's argument for a protected interest was easier, once she established a sufficient connection to the United States. Can you say why?

4. Process Due in Watch List Making or Correction. Once Dr. Ibrahim showed that the government had deprived her of a protected interest, the process due her was determined by balancing the three factors described by *Mathews v. Eldridge*, 424 U.S. 319 (1976). Be sure you can identify those factors in *Ibrahim*. The most important is arguably the contribution that existing and additional procedures would make to reducing the risk of error.

Critics of watch lists have suggested several procedural fixes for false positives and misidentification. A "front-end" fix is to institute more careful vetting procedures for placing a name on the list and tighter, more transparent standards. *See* Shane, *supra*, at 819-836. What "front-end" procedure would have eliminated the risk of the human error that started Dr. Ibrahim's parade of horribles? Professor Steinbock raises the question whether the cost of such additional procedure and/or higher evidentiary standards for watch listing may be too high for effective prevention of terrorist entry. Given the magnitude of the risk, should doubts be resolved in favor of including doubtful names of the lists? *See* Steinbock, *Designating the Dangerous, supra* p. 757; *Kashem v. Barr*, 941 F.3d 358, 374 (9th Cir. 2019) (finding TSA criteria constitutionally sufficient).

Another fix is "back-end": providing some procedure for the victim of misidentification or other false positive to clear his name from the list. *See* Rosenzweig & Jonas, *supra*, at 4-12 (suggesting administrative procedures for deciding passenger complaints, with a right of appeal to federal court, as well as "wrong matching" procedures for full attribution of list entries and for a wrongly matched person to supply additional information to correct an error); Florence, *supra*, at 2166-2178 (suggesting that passengers be given "advance notice" of watch listing on inquiry and the right to an administrative hearing about the alleged listing error through a government-appointed and security-cleared "compensatory counsel"). *But see Kashem*, 941 F.3d at

382-385 (finding that a no fly notification letter was constitutionally sufficient even without providing a complete list of reasons for listing). Professor Steinbock suggests a different and simpler kind of back-end protection: restricting the consequences of being listed just to selection for further investigation, thus "putting the *watch* back in watch lists." Steinbock, *Designating the Dangerous, supra,* at 110.

The Intelligence Reform and Terrorism Prevention Act of 2004 (IRTPA), Pub. L. No. 108-458, §4012(a)(1), 118 Stat. 3638, 3714-3715 (codified at 49 U.S.C. §44903(j)(2)(C)(iii)(I) (2018)), required TSA and DHS to create appeals procedures for listed persons to challenge their listings. DHS therefore established a Traveler Redress Inquiry Program (TRIP) for taking complaints. Congress also conditioned implementation of "Secure Flight" — the program for collecting preflight information on passengers for watch list screening — on development of procedures for protecting privacy and providing redress for victims of false positives. Department of Homeland Security Appropriations Act of 2006, Pub. L. No. 109-90, §518, 119 Stat. 2064, 2085 (2005). Why did the *Ibrahim* court find this back-end procedure inadequate?

In *Beydoun v. Sessions,* 871 F.3d 459 (6th Cir. 2017), the plaintiffs-appellants challenged their inclusion on the Selectee List, a subset of the Terrorist Screening Database identifying travelers for enhanced screening at the airport, on *substantive* due process grounds. Noting that the interests protected by substantive due process are much narrower than those protected by procedural due process, *id.* at 466, the court of appeals held that the delays occasioned by enhanced screening were "negligible" and did not rise to the level of being denied boarding or, therefore, the right to travel, and that there was also therefore no "plus" for the plaintiffs' stigma-plus claims. *Id.* at 468-469. But one of the plaintiffs alleged that he had missed "countless flights" as a result of the delay, and the other alleged that he had canceled a planned trip to avoid the stress and embarrassment of enhanced screening. Should the court have taken into account the frequency and not just the duration of the delays the plaintiffs suffered? Is the right to travel all or nothing, or is it also implicated by frequent, if not routine, delays from enhanced screening?

5. A Lawsuit: The Process Due? Clearly, the only effective back-end process for Dr. Ibrahim was judicial review of her due process claim. If the availability of judicial review is part of the process, is it, together with the admittedly imperfect TRIP process, enough process to satisfy the Fifth Amendment? *See Tarhuni,* 8 F. Supp. 3d at 1276 (finding, on motion to dismiss, that plaintiff had "plausibly alleged the procedures in the DHS TRIP process *and subsequent judicial review* do not strike the proper balance under *Mathews* and, therefore, violate due process") (emphasis added).

The 2014 decision in *Latif* also noted the apparent inefficacy of the TRIP regime for correcting no-fly listings, citing *Ibrahim.* But it added this:

> [T]he DHS TRIP process suffers from an even more fundamental deficiency. As noted, the reasonable suspicion standard used to accept nominations to the TSDB is a low evidentiary threshold. This low standard is particularly significant in light of Defendants' refusal to reveal whether travelers who have been denied boarding and who submit DHS TRIP inquiries are on the No-Fly List and, if they are on the List, to provide the travelers with reasons for their inclusion on the List. "Without knowledge of a charge, even simple factual errors may go uncorrected despite potentially easy, ready, and persuasive explanations." *Al Haramain Islamic Found., Inc. v. United States Dep't of Treasury,* 686 F.3d 965, 982 (9th Cir. 2012).

> The availability of judicial review does little to cure this risk of error. While judicial review provides an independent examination of the existing administrative record, that review is of [sic] the same one-sided and potentially insufficient administrative record that TSC relied on in its listing decision without any additional meaningful opportunity for the aggrieved traveler to submit evidence intelligently in order to correct anticipated errors in the record. Moreover, judicial review only extends to whether the government reasonably determined the traveler meets the minimum substantive derogatory criteria; i.e., the reasonable suspicion standard. Thus, the fundamental flaw at the administrative-review stage (the combination of a one-sided record and a low evidentiary standard) carries over to the judicial-review stage. [28 F. Supp. 3d at 1152-1153.]

6. The Remedy Due? In *Ibrahim,* the remedy was straightforward and dictated by the very specific human error that cascaded through the watch listing system: purging the error. In *Latif,* the court was more ambitious:

> Because due process requires Defendants to provide Plaintiffs (who have all been denied boarding flights and who have submitted DHS TRIP inquiries without success) with notice regarding their status on the No-Fly List and the reasons for placement on that List, it follows that such notice must be reasonably calculated to permit each Plaintiff to submit evidence relevant to the reasons for their respective inclusions on the No-Fly List. In addition, Defendants must include any responsive evidence that Plaintiffs submit in the record to be considered at both the administrative and judicial stages of review. As noted, such procedures could include, but are not limited to, the procedures identified by the Ninth Circuit in *Al Haramain*; that is, Defendants may choose to provide Plaintiffs with unclassified summaries of the reasons for their respective placement on the No-Fly List or disclose the classified reasons to properly-cleared counsel.
>
> Although this Court cannot foreclose the possibility that in some cases such disclosures may be limited or withheld altogether because any such disclosure would create an undue risk to national security, Defendants must make such a determination on a case-by-case basis including consideration of, at a minimum, the factors outlined in *Al Haramain*; i.e., (1) the nature and extent of the classified information, (2) the nature and extent of the threat to national security, and (3) the possible avenues available to allow the Plaintiff to respond more effectively to the charges. *See Al Haramain,* 686 F.3d at 984. Such a determination must be reviewable by the relevant court. [28 F. Supp. 3d at 1162.]

Subsequently, in *Latif,* the government informed plaintiffs of their status on or off the no-fly list, the substantive criteria used to determine that status, and unclassified summaries of how the plaintiffs met that criteria. The plaintiffs were allowed to respond, and the government committed to reviewing those responses. Cole, *supra* p. 760, at 18-19.

After Dr. Ibrahim prevailed, the district court allowed less than $35,000 in fees out of $294,000 her lawyers sought, applying the statutory standard whether the government's losing position was "substantially justified." The court of appeals reversed en banc, declaring that "the agency position upon which these going-on-thirteen years of litigation was based was not justified at all, much less substantially." *Ibrahim v. U.S. Dep't of Homeland Sec.,* 912 F.3d 1147, 1170 (9th Cir. 2019) (en banc), *cert. denied,* 140 S. Ct. 424 (2019).

> Dr. Ibrahim refined federal watchlisting policy by creating a roadmap for other similarly situated plaintiffs to seek judicial redress for alleged wrongful placement on government watchlists.

> The significance of Dr. Ibrahim's roadmap cannot be overstated. Any person could have the misfortune of being mistakenly placed on a government watchlist, and the consequences are severe. Placement on the No Fly list, if left unchanged, prevents an individual from ever boarding an airplane that touches the vast expanse of U.S. airspace. Travel by air has become a normal part of our lives, whether for work, vacations, funerals, weddings, or to visit friends and family. In 2017 alone, there were 728 million airline passengers in the United States. It is debilitating to lose the option to fly to one's intended destination. Today, those misplaced on the No Fly list can contest that placement, and, if misplaced, regain their right to flight. [*Id.* at 1178-1179.]

7. *Mission Creep?* Watch lists are already used to control visa eligibility, entry, and departure; to screen airline passengers; to screen employees for sensitive jobs; and to trigger surveillance. "Mission creep" — using lists for more and more purposes, including ordinary criminal and regulatory purposes, such as denial of firearms purchases — is a continuing risk.

Immediately after Pearl Harbor, for example, some 2,500 Japanese Americans were immediately arrested by the FBI because their names appeared on a "custodial detention list" prepared before the attack. Later, the FBI prepared lists of "dangerous persons" who might be taken into custody under the Emergency Detention Act of 1950, Pub. L. No. 81-831, 64 Stat. 1019, *repealed by* Act of Sept. 25, 1971, Pub. L. No. 92-128, §2(a), 85 Stat. 347, 348. By 1966, the FBI's "Security Index," which included a number of civil rights and anti-war protestors, had grown to 26,000 names. Steinbock, *Designating the Dangerous, supra,* at 89.

The "mission creep" concern has taken on added urgency with the disclosure in watch list litigation that more than 1,441 *private* entities have access to a government terrorism watch list. *See* Rachel Weiner, *More Than 1,000 Private Entities Have Access to Terrorism Watch List, Government Says,* Wash. Post, Feb. 20, 2019. They reportedly include private prisons, university police, and private security companies that work in government facilities or hospitals, as well as animal shelters. *See* Ibrahim Hooper, *CAIR Calls on FBI to Cease Dissemination of Government Watchlist to Animal Shelters, Private Investigators, Megachurch, Others,* CAIR, Mar. 11, 2019. One court in a challenge to no-fly listing found that "[t]he dissemination of an individual's TSDB status to these entities would reasonably be expected to affect any interaction an individual on the Watchlist has with law enforcement agencies and private entities that use TSDB information to screen individuals they encounter in traffic stops, field interviews, house visits, municipal permit processes, firearm purchases, certain licensing applications, and other scenarios." *Elhady,* 391 F. Supp. 3d at 580.

Should the reasonableness of a watch list turn in part on some statutory control of the purposes for which it may be used?

SCREENING FOR SECURITY: SUMMARY OF BASIC PRINCIPLES

- The Fourth Amendment permits "routine" warrantless and suspicionless searches at the border. They are presumptively reasonable because national self-protection requires control of cross-border movements of people and things, and because there is a "special need" to assure aircraft and airport security. Such routine searches include "conventional" (e.g., limited by time and location) searches of electronic media.

- But reasonable suspicion is required for "non-routine" border searches — highly intrusive searches of persons, destructive searches, and searches conducted in a particularly offensive manner. Reasonable suspicion requires a particularized and objective basis (less than probable cause) for suspecting criminal activity in the totality of the circumstances.

- Some lower courts have held that more extensive, "forensic" border searches of electronic media are non-routine and therefore require reasonable suspicion, but they are agreed neither on a definition of such searches nor on a rationale for applying the reasonable suspicion standard.

- Watch lists are government-maintained databases for identifying suspects for screening or other legal consequences. The reported administrative standard for nominating persons to the Consolidated Terrorist Screening Database is reasonable suspicion, but there is little public oversight of the nominating process.

- Citizens and aliens with a substantial connection to the United States are constitutionally entitled to due process before the federal government deprives them of liberty or property, but the lower courts are divided about whether the right to board a flight is a liberty interest, either alone or in combination with the stigma associated with being denied boarding or selected for secondary screening.

- Courts that have recognized that denial of boarding to a person on a no-fly list implicates a constitutionally protected interest have held that the administrative process for watch list–related complaints — TRIP — is inadequate, but they have not agreed on what further process is due.

26

Profiling and Travel Bans

It is not just watch listing that causes the government to single out individuals for further investigation or other consequences, but also observations or reports of particular behaviors, mediated by institutional assumptions, individual biases, and experience. When the singling out is based on race, national origin, or religion, the government is often said to be profiling. Whether such profiling is lawful depends partly on the justification for the profiling, as well as its operation.

In this chapter, we start with a case in which airport police singled out air passengers based on their apparent "Arab ethnicity," and use that incident to consider the legality, practicality, and utility of profiling. We then consider the travel bans first imposed on Muslim travelers to the United States, and later on travelers from some, but not all, predominantly Muslim countries, as well as other profiling practices at the nation's borders.

A. PROFILING

Reading *Farag v. United States*

In *Farag*, the plaintiffs' behavior during a flight was alleged to give probable cause for their arrest and detention as they deplaned, but their apparent "Arab ethnicity" was also a factor. Was their arrest therefore the product of unlawful ethnic profiling?

- What is the probable cause standard for arrest? Does it matter *for Fourth Amendment purposes* whether the arresting officers had ulterior motives (perhaps ethnic biases) for the arrests? If not, why not? Would it matter *for Fifth Amendment equal protection purposes*?

- Do you think there was probable cause for the plaintiffs' arrests based on non-ethnic factors? If not, why didn't the addition of the ethnic factor tip the scale to establish probable cause?
- Could an ethnic or racial factor ever lawfully tip the scales? When? To put it more colloquially, is ethnic or racial profiling *ever* unlawful?
- Are there benefits as well as costs of racial or ethnic profiling in counterterrorism investigations? What are they, and how should they be balanced?

Farag v. United States

United States District Court, Eastern District of New York, 2008
587 F. Supp. 2d 436

BLOCK, Senior District Judge: . . . On August 22, 2004, weeks away from the third anniversary of 9/11, plaintiffs Tarik Farag ("Farag") and Amro Elmasry ("Elmasry"), both Arabs, flew from San Diego to New York's John F. Kennedy Airport ("JFK") on American Airlines Flight 236. [Farag and Elmasry, longtime friends, were flying to JFK after vacationing in California. Both were born in Egypt, but Farag, 36, had moved to the United States in 1971 at age five and later became an American citizen. He was a retired New York City police officer, and was then employed by the United States Bureau of Prisons as a corrections officer. Elmasry, 37, was an Egyptian citizen; he was employed in Egypt by General Electric as an area sales manager for its Africa-East Mediterranean region and had a valid U.S. visa.] They claim that when they deplaned they were met by at least ten armed police officers in SWAT gear with shotguns and police dogs, ordered to raise their hands, frisked, handcuffed and taken to a police station, where they were placed in jail cells; they were not released until about four hours later, after having been interrogated at length during their imprisonment regarding suspected terrorist surveillance activity aboard the plane. The investigation yielded absolutely no evidence of wrongdoing.

Alleging that they were unlawfully seized and imprisoned, Farag and Elmasry have each brought an action under *Bivens v. Six Unknown Named Agents of Federal Bureau of Narcotics*, 403 U.S. 388 (1971), against defendants FBI Special Agent William Ryan Plunkett ("Plunkett") and New York City Police Department Detective Thomas P. Smith ("Smith"), two counterterrorism agents responsible for plaintiffs' seizures, detentions and interrogations. . . . Plunkett and Smith seek summary judgment as to plaintiffs' *Bivens* claims on the ground of qualified immunity. . . .

THE GOVERNMENT'S JUSTIFICATION FOR ITS CONDUCT

The Government lists the following actions of Farag and Elmasry on the aircraft, which, they argue, supported the agents' "concern that [plaintiffs] may [have been] conducting [terrorist] surveillance or probing operations,"[20] and justified the agents' seizures, detentions, and interrogations of plaintiffs:

---

20. In particular, the Government argues that "there was probable cause to believe that Plaintiffs were violating the Destruction of Aircraft Act, 18 U.S.C. §32, and the federal conspiracy statute, 18 U.S.C.

- At the beginning of the flight, despite sitting on opposite sides of the aisle, plaintiffs spoke to each other over the heads of other passengers in a mixture of Arabic and English;
- Elmasry made an allegedly "unusual" initial seat change "from a window seat . . . to a middle seat . . . between two other male passengers";
- After Elmasry changed seats, he and Farag talked to each other "loudly" over the heads of other passengers in a mixture of Arabic and English;
- Elmasry looked at his watch when the plane took off, when the plane landed, and at other points during the flight;
- After the meal service, Elmasry "got out of his seat . . . , went into the aisle, leaned over to Farag, and spoke a 'very short sentence' to Farag in a mixture of Arabic and English";
- Immediately thereafter, plaintiffs moved together to the back of the plane, and did not take their carry-on luggage with them;
- Plaintiffs got up to return to the front of the cabin at the very end of the flight, after the "fasten seatbelt" indicator was lit;
- Upon returning to the front of the plane, Farag did not sit in his original seat (17E), but rather, in Elmasry's original seat (18A), which was located directly behind Smith;
- After the plane landed, Elmasry took out his cellular phone and deleted five or six numbers;
- While the plane was taxiing to the gate, Elmasry told Smith that "he is from Egypt, that he works for GE, and that '[his] work is always traveling.'"

The Government lists the following events that took place in the terminal at JFK, after plaintiffs were first detained, as further support for the agents' actions:

- Farag told Smith that "after 9/11, when the CIA had c[o]me into the Federal Bureau of Prisons, my supervisors had asked me to translate documents, to translate tapes, [and] in fact I did translate tapes";
- Farag told Smith that "I had guns pointed at me as a police officer";
- While Farag was telling these things to Smith, Farag was "jittery" and "shaking" and "[his] speech was not calm." He appeared "nervous" and seemed "jumpy and agitated," and he raised his voice. . . .

II. ANALYSIS . . .

B. Was There Probable Cause for the Arrests?

Probable cause to arrest exists "where the arresting officer has 'knowledge or reasonably trustworthy information of facts and circumstances that are sufficient to warrant a person of reasonable caution in the belief that the person to be arrested has committed or is committing a crime.'" [*United States v. Delossantos*, 536 F.3d 155, 158 (2d Cir. 2008) (quoting *Walczyk v. Rio*, 496 F.3d 139, 156 (2d Cir. 2007))]. Only "those facts available to the officer at the time of the arrest and immediately before it" may be considered. *Lowth v. Town of Cheektowaga*, 82 F.3d 563, 569 (2d Cir. 1996) (citation omitted). Moreover, "[p]robable cause is to be assessed on an objective basis[,]" *Zellner v. Summerlin*, 494 F.3d 344, 369 (2d Cir. 2007); thus, "[a]n arresting officer's state of mind (*except for the facts that he knows*) is irrelevant. . . ." *Id.* The standard is a

---

§371, both of which have been upheld by the Second Circuit as providing legitimate grounds for prosecuting potential terrorist plots against United States-flag aircraft." Gov't Br. at 25 (citing *United States v. Yousef*, 327 F.3d 56, 86-88 (2d Cir. 2003)).

"fluid and contextual" one, requiring "examin[ation of] the totality of the circumstances of a given arrest." *Delossantos*, 536 F.3d at 159 (citations omitted)....

1. Was There Probable Cause Based on Non-Ethnic Factors Alone?

The Government contends that even if the Court does not consider that plaintiffs were Arabs and that they were at times conversing in Arabic, the other factors relied upon by the Government constitute probable cause. The Court disagrees. The Government tacks together a number of benign circumstances in the apparent belief that their numerosity will carry the day. The Court acknowledges that the Second Circuit has cautioned district courts not to "engage[ ] in erroneous 'divide-and-conquer analysis'" by "declining to give weight to [individual] observation[s] 'that [were] by [themselves] readily susceptible to . . . innocent explanation[s].'" *Id.* at 161 (quoting *United States v. Arvizu*, 534 U.S. 266, 274 (2002)); *accord* [*United States v. Sokolow*, 490 U.S. 1, 9 (1989)] ("Any one of these factors is . . . quite consistent with innocent travel. But we think taken together they amount to reasonable suspicion."). Yet, even viewing all of these circumstances as a whole, it cannot rationally be held that if, hypothetically, the plaintiffs were two Caucasian traveling companions speaking French, or another non-Arabic language which the agents did not understand, "a person of reasonable caution" would have believed that they were engaged in terrorist surveillance. *Delossantos*, 536 F.3d at 158.

Principally, the Government relies on the agents' observations of plaintiffs' seat-changing and Elmasry's "timing" events with his watch. But the agents acknowledged in their incident report that they knew the plaintiffs were friends; quite logically, friends would want to sit as close to each other as possible, and they would also logically return to the vicinity of their original seats when the plane was landing to retrieve their carry-on luggage. As for Elmasry looking at his watch upon takeoff, landing, and at various other times during the flight, the proportion of airline passengers who do this is probably higher than the proportion who do not. *See United States v. Jones*, 149 F.3d 364, 369 (5th Cir. 1998) ("A factual condition which is consistent with [criminal activity] will not predicate reasonable suspicion, if that factual condition occurs even more frequently among the law abiding public. . . .").

The Government also argues that Elmasry's deletion of five or six telephone numbers from his cellular phone while he waited for the plane to reach the gate "could have been interpreted as destroying evidence[,]" Gov't Br. at 16. This conclusion, however, is utter speculation; the Government's Rule 56.1 Statement does not assert that Elmasry made any telephone calls during or after the flight, and the record gives no indication that Elmasry suspected he was about to be caught sufficient to imbue his acts with a suggestion of guilt.

Most troubling, the heavy reliance which the Government places on the plaintiffs' speaking "loudly" to each other over the heads of other passengers and otherwise drawing attention to themselves is counterintuitive: it simply makes no sense that if Elmasry were a terrorist on a surveillance mission, he would speak "loudly" across the aisle to his companion before takeoff, seek out and converse with the flight attendant, relocate to a seat "between two large men," or volunteer to one of those "large men" that he was from Egypt. What terrorist engaged in surveillance activity would behave so conspicuously? One would expect that such activity would be characterized by secrecy.

Nor could plaintiffs' conduct in the terminal be reasonably viewed as an escalation of events that would then have given rise to probable cause. The Court fails to grasp the significance of Farag telling Smith that because he spoke Arabic he had been asked by the Bureau of Prisons to translate tapes, and that guns had been pointed at him as a police officer — both logical consequences of his past and present employments.

Reliance on Farag's nervousness and raised voice is also problematic. *See, e.g., United States v. Ten Thousand Seven Hundred Dollars and No Cents in U.S. Currency*, 258 F.3d 215, 226-27 (3d Cir. 2001) ("[C]laimants' apparent nervousness is of minimal probative value, given that many, if not most, individuals can become nervous or agitated when detained by police officers." (citation omitted)). Moreover, Farag's "nervous" response to an unlawful show of force could not retroactively justify plaintiffs' arrests.

In sum, viewed in the light most favorable to plaintiffs, the non-ethnic factors cited by the Government do not constitute probable cause.

2. *Would Consideration of Plaintiffs' Ethnicity Warrant a Finding of Probable Cause?*

Allowing consideration of the plaintiffs' ethnicity and their use of Arabic would still not warrant a finding, in the context of the defendants' summary-judgment motion, that there was probable cause to arrest them. In other words, if the plaintiffs' view of events holds up at trial, their conduct was so benign that the ethnicity factor — even if it could be considered — would not change the outcome.

Nonetheless, the Court will address the ethnicity issue since the Government, given the importance it ascribes to the issue, would otherwise undoubtedly raise it at trial; moreover, the issue would probably surface if Smith and Plunkett were to take an interlocutory appeal from the Court's denial of that aspect of their motion seeking qualified immunity.

3. *Can Plaintiffs' Arab Ethnicity Serve as a Probable Cause Factor?*

The Government argues that plaintiffs' Arab ethnicity and use of the Arabic language are relevant factors in the probable-cause, as well as the reasonable-suspicion, calculus because "all of the persons who participated in the 9/11 terrorist attacks were Middle Eastern males[,]" Tr. of Oral Argument, July 18, 2008, at 18, and "the United States continues to face a very real threat of domestic terrorism from Islamic terrorists." Gov't Br. at 17.

The Government's position has some superficial appeal. After all, probable cause, and undoubtedly reasonable suspicion as well, is, once again, "a practical, nontechnical conception that deals with the factual and practical considerations of everyday life," *Delossantos*, 536 F.3d at 159 (internal quotation marks and citation omitted), and what American would not acknowledge that everyday life has changed in myriad ways, both great and small, since 9/11? Indeed, earlier this fall, the Second Circuit upheld a government program "that singled out male immigrants from two dozen predominantly Arab and Muslim countries for accelerated deportation after the Sept. 11, 2001, terrorist attacks[,]" Mark Hamblett, *Circuit*

Upholds Post-9/11 Effort That Singled Out Muslim Men, N.Y.L.J., Sept. 25, 2008 at 1, finding it a "plainly rational attempt to enhance national security." *Rajah v. Mukasey,* 544 F.3d 427, [439 (2d Cir. 2008)].

Rajah, however, did not deal with ethnicity in the context of probable cause or reasonable suspicion. Indeed, the Government recognizes that "[t]here is no single precedent that resolves this case," Tr. of Oral Argument, July 18, 2008, at 17, which presumably accounts for its view of the case as one of first impression. Nevertheless, the interplay between race[33] and the Fourth Amendment is not a recent phenomenon; courts and commentators have long struggled with the issue of whether and to what extent race can be a relevant consideration in the decision to detain an individual. That legal backdrop obviously bears on the Court's analysis here.

At the outset, it should be understood that the Fourth Amendment — unlike the Equal Protection Clause — imposes no *a priori* restriction on race-based governmental action. As the Supreme Court noted in *Whren v. United States,* 517 U.S. 806 (1996):

> [T]he Constitution prohibits selective enforcement of the law based on considerations such as race. But the constitutional basis for objecting to intentionally discriminatory application of laws is the Equal Protection Clause, not the Fourth Amendment. Subjective intentions play no role in ordinary, probable-cause Fourth Amendment analysis.

Id. at 813; *see also United States v. Scopo,* 19 F.3d 777, 786 (2d Cir. 1994) (Newman, J., concurring) ("Though the Fourth Amendment permits a pretext arrest, if otherwise supported by probable cause, the Equal Protection Clause still imposes restraint on impermissibly class-based discriminations.").

In *Whren,* the existence of probable cause based on non-racial factors was conceded. *See* 517 U.S. at 810 ("Petitioners accept that Officer Soto had probable cause to believe that various provisions of the District of Columbia traffic code had been violated."). Thus, the Court opined only that an officer's subjective, potentially race-based motivations were irrelevant to the Fourth Amendment *once probable cause is established;* it was not called upon to address whether race might be relevant to the probable-cause analysis itself.

Although the Fourth Amendment does not single out race as a matter of special concern, it does impose a general requirement that *any* factor considered in a decision to detain must contribute to "a particularized and objective basis for suspecting the particular person stopped of criminal activity." *United States v. Cortez,* 449 U.S. 411, 417-18 (1981). Thus, as one commentator has observed, "race cannot affect probable cause or reasonable suspicion calculations unless it is statistically related to suspected criminal activity." [Sheri Lynn Johnson, *Race and the Decision to Detain a Suspect,* 93 Yale L.J. 214, 237 (1983).] Whether such a relationship exists in a given case is necessarily a fact-specific inquiry; nevertheless, the case law reveals some recurring themes.

Perhaps the least controversial use of race in the context of the Fourth Amendment is its use as an *identifying* factor. If the victim of, or witness to, a crime describes

---

33. For present purposes, the Court treats the "technically" distinct concepts of race and ethnicity as legal equivalents. *Iqbal v. Hasty,* 490 F.3d 143, 148 n.2 (2d Cir. 2007), *cert. granted sub nom. Ashcroft v. Iqbal,* ___ U.S. ___, 128 S. Ct. 2931 (2008). Moreover, the Court considers the fact that the plaintiffs spoke their native tongue, Arabic — as opposed to some other language equally unfamiliar to the agents — as inextricably related to, and legally indistinguishable from, plaintiffs' ethnicity per se.

the perpetrator as a young white male wearing a white shirt and black pants, there can be little doubt that law enforcement officials may consider that description in deciding whom to detain, even though the description is based, in part, on race.

Courts have also confronted the so-called "racial incongruity" argument — i.e., that race is indicative of criminality when members of a particular race seem "out of place" in a particular location. Some courts — including the Second Circuit — have sidestepped the issue by finding probable cause or reasonable suspicion based on other, non-racial factors. For example, in *United States v. Magda*, 409 F. Supp. 734 (S.D.N.Y. 1976), the district court found reasonable suspicion lacking where "[t]he reason for the stop was primarily because of an observed exchange . . . between a young black man and a young white man in an area of the city defined as 'narcotics prone.'" *Id.* at 740. The Second Circuit reversed, concluding that the circumstances and location of the transaction were sufficient to create reasonable suspicion; the circuit court made no mention of the race of the participants. *See United States v. Magda*, 547 F.2d 756, 758-59 (2d Cir. 1976); *see also United States v. Richard*, 535 F.2d 246, 248-249 (3d Cir. 1976) (noting that "the presence of two black males cruising in a car in a predominately white neighborhood is, by itself, insufficient cause for a belief that those persons have participated in a recent crime in the neighborhood," but reversing suppression order based on other factors); *State v. Wilson*, 775 So. 2d 1051, 1052 (La. 2000) ("[T]he officer made clear . . . that while racial incongruity 'did factor in,' he considered other circumstances more important in his decision to make an investigatory stop.").

Those courts that have squarely addressed the incongruity argument have uniformly rejected it. *See People v. Bower*, 24 Cal. 3d 638 (1979) ("[T]he presence of an individual of one race in an area inhabited primarily by members of another race is not a sufficient basis to suggest that crime is afoot."); *State v. Barber*, 118 Wash. 2d 335 (1992) ("It is the law that racial incongruity, i.e., a person of any race being allegedly 'out of place' in a particular geographic area, should never constitute a finding of reasonable suspicion of criminal activity); *Phillips v. State*, 781 So. 2d 477, 479 (Fla. Dist. Ct. App. 2001) ("Clearly, the fact that a black person is merely walking in a predominantly white neighborhood does not indicate that he has committed, is committing, or is about to commit a crime."). . . .

But this case involves neither identification nor racial incongruity. Rather, defendants' argument that plaintiffs' Arab ethnicity is a relevant consideration is premised on the notion that Arabs have a greater *propensity* than non-Arabs toward criminal activity — namely, terrorism.

In support of this argument, defendants rely principally on language from the Supreme Court's opinion in *United States v. Brignoni-Ponce*, 422 U.S. 873 (1975). There, a roving border patrol agent had made a traffic stop based on nothing more than "the apparent Mexican ancestry" of the car's occupants. *Id.* at 885. The Supreme Court held that "this factor alone would [not] justify . . . a reasonable [suspicion]" of an immigration violation. *Id.* at 886. But it stated — in dictum — that "[t]he likelihood that any given person of Mexican ancestry is an alien is high enough to make Mexican appearance *a relevant factor*" in the Fourth Amendment calculus, if it were not *the only* basis for suspicion. *Id.* at 886-87 (emphasis added).[34]

---

34. A year after *Brignoni-Ponce*, the Supreme Court held that officials at a border-control checkpoint could constitutionally single out motorists for inspection "even if it be assumed that such referrals are made largely on the basis of apparent Mexican ancestry." *United States v. Martinez-Fuerte*, 428 U.S. 543, 563

Brignoni-Ponce's dictum was predicated on 1970 census figures establishing that in the border states between 8.5% and 20.4% of the ethnic-Mexican population self-registered as aliens. *Id.* at 886-87 & n.12. To the Court's knowledge, no court has ever marshaled statistics to conclude that racial or ethnic appearance is correlated with, and thus probative of, any type of criminal conduct *other than* immigration violations. *See, e.g., United States v. Avery*, 137 F.3d 343, 354 (6th Cir. 1997) ("[A]lthough the Court in *Brignoni-Ponce* stated 'the likelihood that any given person of Mexican ancestry is an alien is high enough to make Mexican appearance a relevant factor,' we refuse to adopt, by analogy, the concept that 'the likelihood that any given person of African ancestry is involved in drug trafficking is high enough to make African ancestry a relevant fact' in investigating drug trafficking. . . ." (citation omitted)).

Moreover, the statistical rationale behind the *Brignoni-Ponce* dictum does not translate to the present case: Even granting that all of the participants in the 9/11 attacks were Arabs, and even assuming *arguendo* that a large proportion of would-be anti-American terrorists are Arabs, the likelihood that *any given airline passenger* of Arab ethnicity is a terrorist is so negligible that Arab ethnicity has no probative value in a particularized reasonable-suspicion or probable-cause determination. *Accord United States v. Ramos*, [591 F. Supp. 2d 93, 104 (D. Mass. 2008)] (considering, in dicta, the applicability of *Brignoni-Ponce* to Arabs suspected of terrorist activity post-9/11, and noting that "[a]mong other things, the type of statistics relied upon in *Brignoni-Ponce*... have not been presented here.") [, *aff'd*, 629 F.3d 60 (1st Cir. 2010)]. . . .

Indeed, the Ninth Circuit, whose judgment the Supreme Court upheld in *Brignoni-Ponce*, revisited *Brignoni-Ponce*'s dictum 25 years later and held, albeit also in dicta, that the statistical inference on which it was based was no longer valid, even in its original illegal-immigration context:

> The Hispanic population of this nation, and of the Southwest and Far West in particular, has grown enormously. . . . Accordingly, Hispanic appearance is of little or no use in determining which particular individuals among the vast Hispanic populace should be stopped by law enforcement officials on the lookout for illegal aliens. Reasonable suspicion requires *particularized* suspicion, and in an area in which a large number of people share a specific characteristic, that characteristic casts too wide a net to play any part in a particularized reasonable suspicion determination.

[*United States v. Montero-Camargo*, 208 F.3d 1122, 1133-34 (9th Cir. 2000) (emphasis in original).] . . .

There is no doubt that the specter of 9/11 looms large over this case. Although this is the first post-9/11 case to address whether race may be used to establish criminal propensity under the Fourth Amendment, the Court cannot subscribe to the notion that in the wake of 9/11 this may now be permissible. As the Second Circuit recently admonished, "the strength of our system of constitutional rights derives from

---

(1976). The Court recognized that such a criterion "would not sustain a roving-patrol stop," *id.*, but concluded that border-control checkpoints were exempt from the usual Fourth Amendment requirement of individualized suspicion. *See id.* at 562 ("[W]e hold that the stops and questioning at issue may be made in the absence of any individualized suspicion at reasonably located checkpoints."). Since there is obviously no contention that a traditional arrest or *Terry* stop is similarly exempt from that requirement, *Martinez-Fuerte* cannot support plaintiffs' detention.

the steadfast protection of those rights in both normal and unusual times." *Iqbal v. Hasty*, 490 F.3d 143, 159 (2d Cir. 2007) [*rev'd on other grounds and remanded sub nom. Ashcroft v. Iqbal*, 129 S. Ct. 1937, 1954 (2009), *cert. granted and remanded*, 129 S. Ct. 2430 (2009), *cert. granted and remanded sub nom. Sawyer v. Iqbal*, 129 S. Ct. 2431 (2009)].

History teaches much the same lesson: The Supreme Court's approval of the internment of large numbers of Japanese-Americans during World War II, *see Korematsu v. United States*, 323 U.S. 214 (1945), is now widely regarded as a black mark on our constitutional jurisprudence. The daughter of two such internees — Kiyo Matsumoto — recently became the third Asian-American woman to be elevated to the federal bench. At her induction ceremony, Judge Matsumoto recalled the closing words of Justice Murphy's dissent in *Korematsu*; they are equally apt here:

> All residents of this nation are kin in some way by blood or culture to a foreign land. Yet they are primarily and necessarily a part of the new and distinct civilization of the United States. They must accordingly be treated at all times as the heirs of the American experiment and as entitled to all the rights and freedoms guaranteed by the Constitution.

323 U.S. at 206.

The Court "fully recognize[s] the gravity of the situation that confront[s] investigative officials of the United States as a consequence of the 9/11 attack[,]" *Iqbal*, 490 F.3d at 159 (2d Cir. 2007), and that the mindset of airline travelers has understandably been altered by 9/11. This justifiable apprehension must be assuaged by ensuring that security is strictly enforced, and by the passage of time without, hopefully, other episodic affronts to our country; but fear cannot be a factor to allow for the evisceration of the bedrock principle of our Constitution that no one can be arrested without probable cause that a crime has been committed. . . .

CONCLUSION

For the reasons described above, the Court grants summary judgment in the Government's favor with respect to plaintiffs' conspiracy claims, plaintiffs' common-law claims against Smith, and plaintiffs' §1981 claims. The Court denies summary judgment with respect to plaintiffs' *Bivens* claims against Smith and Plunkett, plaintiffs' FTCA claims against the United States, and Smith and Plunkett's qualified-immunity defense.

So ordered.

Notes and Questions

a. Legal Analysis of Profiling

1. Probable Cause and Subjective Intention. The traditional Fourth Amendment standard of probable cause for arrest is "'knowledge or reasonably trustworthy information of facts and circumstances that are sufficient to warrant a person of reasonable caution in the belief that the person to be arrested has committed or is committing a crime.'" *United States v. Delossantos*, 536 F.3d 155, 158 (2d Cir. 2008) (quoting *Walczyk v. Rio*, 496 F.3d 139, 156 (2d Cir. 2007)). The standard, however, is objective. It does not matter for Fourth Amendment purposes that the arresting officer subjectively has some ulterior motive for the arrest, even a discriminatory one — pretextual arrests do not offend the Fourth Amendment, as long as there is objective probable cause. *Whren v. United States*, 517 U.S. 806 (1996). The reason is practical: not only would inquiries into motives invite time-consuming challenges to every arrest, but an arresting officer's ulterior motives could well result in guilty parties going free. *But see* Gabriel J. Chin & Charles J. Vernon, *Reasonable but Unconstitutional: Racial Profiling and the Radical Objectivity of Whren v. United States*, 83 Geo. Wash. L. Rev. 882 (2015) (arguing that *Whren* was wrongly decided because even when there is probable cause, arrest can be unreasonable if based on constitutionally impermissible factors); L. Song Richardson, *Implicit Racial Bias and the Perpetrator Perspective: A Response to Reasonable but Unconstitutional*, 83 Geo. Wash. L. Rev. 1008 (2015) (agreeing that *Whren* should be discarded, but going further than Chin & Vernon).

But motive aside, race or ethnicity must still sufficiently contribute to a particularized and objective basis to suspect possible criminal activity for such a factor to influence a Fourth Amendment probable cause inquiry. Given the court's conclusion that the non-ethnic factors in *Farag* were insufficient to establish probable cause, the Fourth Amendment issue was therefore whether consideration of the plaintiffs' "Arab ethnicity" was related to possible criminal activity and tipped the probable-cause scale.

2. *The Easy Case: Individualized Description?* It may seem obvious that a suspect's race or ethnicity might qualify as a factor when the arresting officers use it as an identifying factor — for example, when an arresting officer identifies an arrestee based on a crime report that a person of that race or ethnicity committed an assault proximate in time and place to the arrest. Thus, the Department of Justice provides the following guidance to federal law enforcement agencies:

> *In making routine or spontaneous law enforcement decisions*, such as ordinary traffic stops, Federal law enforcement officers may not use race, ethnicity, gender, national origin, religion, sexual orientation, or gender identity to any degree, *except that officers may rely on the listed characteristics in a specific suspect description*. This prohibition applies even where the use of a listed characteristic might otherwise be lawful. [Civil Rights Div., U.S. Dep't of Justice, *Guidance for Federal Law Enforcement Agencies Regarding the Use of Race, Ethnicity, Gender, National Origin, Religion, Sexual Orientation, or Gender Identity* 2 (Dec. 2014) ("*DOJ Guidance*") (emphasis added).]

It explains that an officer who is "'on the lookout' for specific individuals identified at least in part by a specific listed characteristic . . . is not acting on a generalized assumption about individuals possessing certain characteristics; rather, the officer is helping locate specific individuals previously identified as involved in a crime." *Id.* at 3. "To act on the basis of a particular suspect's description as belonging to a given race is certainly to take race into account," Professor Ellmann explains, "but it is not to take *generalizations* about race into account." Stephen J. Ellmann, *Racial Profiling and Terrorism*, 46 N.Y.L. Sch. L. Rev. 675, 676 n.4 (2003).

3. *Profiling for National Security*. The *DOJ Guidance* provides a different rule for "activities other than routine or spontaneous law enforcement activities."

> In conducting all activities other than routine or spontaneous law enforcement activities, Federal law enforcement officers may consider race, ethnicity, gender, national origin, religion, sexual orientation, or gender identity only *to the extent that there is trustworthy information, relevant to the locality or time frame, that links persons possessing a particular listed characteristic to an identified criminal incident, scheme, or organization, a threat to national or homeland security, a violation of Federal immigration law, or an authorized intelligence activity*. In order to rely on a listed characteristic, law enforcement officers must also reasonably believe that the law enforcement, security, or intelligence activity to be undertaken is merited under the totality of the circumstances, such as any temporal exigency and the nature of any potential harm to be averted. This standard applies even where the use of a listed characteristic might otherwise be lawful. [*DOJ Guidance*, *supra*, at 4 (emphasis added).]

In other words, officers may consider ethnic or racial factors that "link" a suspect to an identified organization, or just to "a threat to national or homeland security." It gives these examples:

> **Example**: A terrorist organization that is made up of members of a particular ethnicity sets off a bomb in a foreign country. There is no specific information that the organization is currently a threat to the United States. To gain intelligence on the evolving threat posed by the organization, and to gain insight into its intentions regarding the U.S. homeland and U.S. interests, the FBI may properly consider ethnicity when developing sources with information that could assist the FBI in mitigating any potential threat from the organization. . . .
>
> **Example**. The FBI receives reliable information that persons affiliated with a foreign ethnic insurgent group intend to use suicide bombers to assassinate that country's president and his entire entourage during an official visit to the United States. Agents may appropriately focus investigative attention on identifying members of that ethnic insurgent group who may be present and active in the United States and who, based on other available information, might be involved in planning some such attack during the state visit. [*Id.* at 8, 10.]

Neither of these examples would justify the arrests in *Farag*. Suppose that the Department of Homeland Security had information that an Egyptian terrorist group that had set off bombs at police stations in Egypt planned to use suicide bombers to set off an explosion in an American airport. Would that have been sufficient to permit the arrests of the plaintiffs in *Farag*? The *DOJ Guidance* still forbids "[r]eliance upon generalized stereotypes," and requires that the information or characteristics used in such examples be relevant to the locality or time frame of the threat, trustworthy, and "tied to a particular" organization or threat. *Id.* at 4.

4. Equal Protection Analysis: Stricter Scrutiny and Necessity? Even if the arrest of Farag and Elmasry had survived a Fourth Amendment challenge, it would have raised questions under the Equal Protection Clause. At least as early as 1944, the Supreme Court declared that "all legal restrictions which curtail the rights of a single racial group are immediately suspect" and therefore subject to the "most rigid scrutiny." *Korematsu v. United States*, 323 U.S. 214, 216 (1944), *infra* p. 876. Since *Korematsu*, the Court has refined its equal protection analysis. When government action is challenged on equal protection grounds, "the issue is whether the government can identify a sufficiently important objective for its discrimination. What is a sufficient justification depends entirely on the type of discrimination." Erwin Chemerinsky, *Constitutional Law* 684

(6th ed. 2019). When the government discriminates on the basis of race, national origin, or, for some actions, alienage, its justification will be subject to "strict scrutiny" and upheld only "if it proves that they are necessary to achieve a compelling government purpose." *Id.* (footnote omitted). Other classifications may require only "rational basis" review, under which the law need only be rationally related to a legitimate government purpose, or "intermediate scrutiny." *Id.*

Can you formulate an argument for the legality of ethnic profiling of Farag and Elmasry under modern equal protection analysis? Do you think that an ostensibly national security-based reason for discrimination should justify lowering the review standard to rational basis? Would a national security-based discriminatory action ever fail that standard? *See Trump v. Hawaii,* 138 S. Ct. 2392 (2018) (*infra* p. 798).

5. *Profiling at the Border?* Farag and Elmasry were apparently not pulled aside for secondary screening when they boarded. But routine border searches do not require probable cause or even reasonable suspicion. What then was to prevent government agents from using their supposed "Arab appearance" or Egyptian birth to subject them to secondary screening? One study concludes that "the absence of any requisite level of suspicion to conduct border searches opens the door to racial or religious profiling." Const. Proj., *Suspicionless Border Searches of Electronic Devices: Legal and Privacy Concerns with the Department of Homeland Security's Policy* 6 (2011); *see also* Sharon L. Davies, *Profiling Terror,* 1 Ohio St. J. Crim. L. 45, 60-61 (2003) (noting that courts have required profiles to be based on more than racial or ethnic elements alone to withstand an equal protection challenge).

The *DOJ Guidance* reportedly reflects a compromise between concerns about ethnic and racial profiling and the asserted needs of border security.

> [T]he Department of Homeland Security resisted efforts to limit the factors it can consider when looking for illegal immigrants. Department officials argued that it was impractical to ignore ethnicity when it came to border enforcement.
>
> "The immigration investigators have said, 'We can't do our job without taking ethnicity into account. We are very dependent on that,'" said one official briefed on the new rules. "They want to have the least amount of restrictions holding them back." [Matt Apuzzo & Michael S. Schmidt, *U.S. to Continue Racial, Ethnic Profiling in Border Policy,* N.Y. Times, Dec. 5, 2014.]

b. Practical Problems and Assessment of Profiling

1. *Problems of Applying Racial and Ethnic Classifications in Screening.* The *DOJ Guidance* approves the use of "specific suspect description[s]" as identifiers. But what if the description is "Middle Eastern male," "Arab ethnicity," or "Muslim male"? Are these useful identifiers, or stereotypes that invite error? Is being on the lookout for "Middle Eastern men" in their early 20s merely taking into account the fact that the original Al Qaeda membership seemed overwhelmingly to have included such men, or does it assume that they are more likely to commit future terrorist acts than, say, Swedish grandmothers? Does the "look-out" profile stigmatize all young Middle Eastern men?

One journalist characterized the New York subway system's random container inspection as an "obvious absurdity" and an "appalling waste of effort." Charles Krauthammer, *Give Grandma a Pass: Politically Correct Screening Won't Catch Jihadists,*

Wash. Post, July 29, 2005. Since "jihadist terrorism has been carried out . . . by young Muslim men," he reasoned, we should give "special scrutiny to *young Islamic men.*" *Id.* (emphasis added). Could you explain to subway security officers how to identify "Islamic men"? What about persons "of Middle Eastern appearance"? *See* John Derbyshire, *At First Glance: Racial Profiling, Burning Hotter,* Nat'l Rev. Online (Oct. 5, 2001). What about "Arab-looking" men? *See* Stuart Taylor Jr., *D.C. Dispatch: Politically Incorrect Profiling: A Matter of Life or Death,* Nat'l J., Nov. 6, 2001; Davies, *supra,* at 51 n.29 ("It is a common misconception that all Arabs are racially identifiable by their darker skin. In fact, Arabs may have white skin and blue eyes, olive or dark skin and brown eyes, and hair in a variety of textures.").

"Defenses of racial and ethnic profiling depend upon the ability of law enforcement officers to do it — to distinguish racial and ethnic groups from one another." Albert W. Alschuler, *Racial Profiling and the Constitution,* 2002 U. Chi. Legal F. 163, 224. One danger of vague classifications is therefore that they leave the screeners too much discretion, creating space for conscious or unconscious application of the screeners' own prejudices. The same may be true even of profiling that includes behavioral factors, such as unusual passenger nervousness or sweating or failure to make eye contact, in a profile together with racial or ethnic factors. After 9/11, for example, the American Civil Liberties Union reported that 67 percent of airline passengers subjected to personal searches upon entering the United States were people of color; blacks and Hispanics were four to nine times as likely as white Americans to be x-rayed after being frisked or patted down; and black women were more likely than any other U.S. citizens to be strip-searched. *See* R. Spencer McDonald, Note, *Rational Profiling in America's Airports,* 17 BYU J. Pub. L. 113, 136 (2002) (citing Am. Civil Liberties Union press release (Mar. 26, 2002)).

In light of these considerations, were the "non-ethnic" factors that caused agents to "arrest" Farag and Elmasry objective or subjective — reasonable intuitions or masked discrimination? Consider this view:

> To insist that an experienced bomb-dog handler or baggage screener ignore any hunches while mindlessly sticking to random passenger screening is, at best, a waste of limited resources. Sky marshals, Transportation Security Administration screeners, and others on the front lines of counterterrorism should be afforded sufficient discretion to draw upon their common sense and experience regarding people who exhibit nonbehavioral risk factors. [John Winn, *The Legitimacy of Profiling,* Wash. Times, Dec. 30, 2009.]

Should the court in *Farag* have paid more deference to the "common sense and experience" of security professionals? A Government Accountability Office study of TSA behavior detection activities concluded that "the ability of human observers to accurately identify deceptive behavior based on behavioral cues or indicators is the same as or slightly better than chance." Gov't Accountability Off., *Aviation Security: TSA Should Limit Future Funding for Behavior Detection Activities,* GAO-14-159, at 16 (Nov. 2013), *available at* http://www.gao.gov/assets/660/658923.pdf.

2. Empirical Nexus? In *United States v. Lopez,* 328 F. Supp. 1077 (E.D.N.Y. 1971), the court initially upheld the use of a passenger profile in the pre-1973 selective anti-skyjacking screening program and follow-up frisk. But when discovery revealed that the airline had unilaterally eliminated one element of the FAA-established profile and added "an ethnic element for which there was no experimental basis, thus raising serious equal protection problems," the court suppressed the evidence from the frisk. *Id.* at 1101. "The approved [FAA] system survives constitutional scrutiny only by its careful adherence to absolute objectivity and neutrality," the court explained. "When elements of discretion and prejudice are interjected it becomes constitutionally impermissible." *Id.*

Does this mean that any ethnic, religious, or national origin element of a screening profile must have at least "an experimental basis" to find a nexus between the element and the probability of a terrorist act? If so, does "Islamic men" or "Middle Eastern appearance" have such a nexus to terrorism, in light of the fact that all 19 of the 9/11 hijackers were apparently Muslims from the Middle East? *Compare* Thomas W. Joo, *Presumed Disloyal: Executive Power, Judicial Deference, and the Construction of Race Before and After September 11*, 34 Colum. Hum. Rts. L. Rev. 1, 41-42 (2002) (the "categories of 'Arab' and 'Muslim' are simply too broad"; "even if a man of Arab descent is relatively more likely to be a terrorist than a non-Arab, the likelihood that any given Arab man is a terrorist remains negligible"), *with* Ellmann, *supra* p. 786, at 698 ("People sharing all of Al Qaeda's background characteristics still seem more likely to be our adversaries than most of the people who share none of them — even though the great majority of people sharing all of these characteristics have no connection to terrorism whatsoever.").

Professor Alschuler suggests that "when a police practice systematically subjects the members of a race to searches and seizures at a higher rate than their rate of offending, a court should hold the practice unconstitutional unless it is appropriately tailored to advance a significant state interest." Alschuler, *supra*, at 223. Would profiling of "Middle Eastern men" satisfy this test? *See id.* at 265 ("special screening of people of Arab ethnicity at airports . . . should be impermissible"). How would we measure their "rate of offending"?

Professor Harcourt suggests that the success and justification of profiling depend on more than "identifying a stable group trait that correlates with higher offending." It also depends on "how responsive different groups are to the targeted policing and whether they engage in forms of substitution" by recruiting from nonprofiled groups or substituting different types of attacks that are more immune to profiling. *See* Bernard E. Harcourt, *Muslim Profiles Post 9/11: Is Racial Profiling an Effective Counterterrorist Measure and Does It Violate the Right to Be Free from Discrimination?*, at 9-10 (Univ. of Chi. Law Sch., John M. Olin Law & Econ. Working Paper No. 288 (2d Series), Mar. 2006, *available at* http://ssrn.com/abstract=893905.

> The central question [is] whether racial profiling of young Muslim men in the New York subways will likely detect a terrorist attack or instead lead to the recruitment of nonprofiled persons and the substitution of other acts for subway attacks — in other words, whether profiling will detect or increase terrorist attacks. The answer to this question is pure speculation. In the end, then, there is no need or reason to engage in a rights trade-off by racial profiling as part of any subway screening. [*Id.* at 27-28.]

That is, without empirical evidence that racial profiling works, there is no need for it. Do you agree?

3. Costs and Benefits of Profiling. Proponents of counterterrorism profiling have argued that the cost to a victim of frequent false positives "is minuscule," while the cost to society of a false negative (letting a terrorist through) could be enormous. They conclude that racial profiling is justified by a cost-benefit analysis. *See* LaFave, *supra* p. 753 (summarizing arguments of some proponents); Ellman, *supra,* at 698-707. Does this analysis consider all the costs? What about the risk that Al Qaeda will respond to the profile by selecting terrorists who do not look "Islamic" or "Middle Eastern," including Americans like José Padilla (see *infra* p. 902), thus increasing the rate of false negatives? What about the cost of creating hostility and anxiety in the U.S. community of persons from the Middle East, and discouraging its members from voluntary cooperation? *See generally* Ellman, *supra,* at 705-707; Davies, *supra,* at 73-74. How would you inventory and balance all the benefits and costs of racial profiling in security screening and counterterrorism investigations?

c. National Origin and Religious Profiling

Case Study: *Hassan v. City of New York*

Following the 9/11 attacks, the New York Police Department launched a surveillance program allegedly directed at Muslims and Muslim communities in and around New York City. It involved taking pictures and making video recordings of Muslims and mosques, collecting license plate numbers of congregants at area mosques, using undercover officers (sometimes called "mosque crawlers or rakers") in mosques, organizations, businesses, and neighborhoods believed to be heavily Muslim, and other surveillance techniques. The program generated a series of intelligence reports focusing on the Muslim community in Newark, mapping the location of mosques and Muslim businesses, identifying them as "locations of concern," compiling pictures and license plate numbers of mosque congregants, and listing names of persons affiliated with Muslim student organizations. Authorities eventually publicized and defended parts of the program.

A group of Muslim plaintiffs sued New York City for injunctive relief and damages, alleging that its program of "selective investigation" not only stigmatized them and caused them financial harm, but also violated their First Amendment rights of free expression, association, and religion, as well as their right of equal protection under the Fourteenth Amendment. *Hassan v. City of New York,* Civ. No. 2:12-3401 (WJM), 2014 WL 654604 (D.N.J. Feb. 20, 2014). After the district court dismissed the action for lack of standing and failure to state a claim, the Third Circuit reversed. 804 F.3d 277 (3d Cir. 2016) (as amended).

Regarding the equal protection claim, the court held:

> Here, Plaintiffs . . . [argue that their] "allegations leave no doubt that the . . . [Program] relies on an express classification of Muslims for disfavored treatment." This is a viable legal theory. Where a plaintiff can point to a facially discriminatory policy, "the protected trait by definition plays a role in the decision-making process, inasmuch as the policy explicitly classifies people on that basis." *Cmty. Servs. v. Wind Gap Mun. Auth.,* 421 F.3d 170, 177 (3d Cir. 2005) (quoting

> *DiBiase v. SmithKline Beecham Corp.*, 48 F.3d 719, 726 (3d Cir. 1995)). Put another way, direct evidence of intent is "supplied by the policy itself." *Massarsky v. Gen. Motors Corp.*, 706 F.2d 111, 128 (3d Cir. 1983) (Sloviter, J., dissenting). . . .
>
> Finally, because Plaintiffs allege that all of these persons and entities were surveilled without any reasonable suspicion of wrongdoing (as noted above, they assert that, "[i]n all its years of operation, the Program has never generated a single [criminal] lead," id. ¶2), this case can be easily contrasted with others where the law-enforcement investigation at issue was almost certainly explained by a reasonable suspicion of wrongdoing. *Cf. George v. Rehiel*, 738 F.3d 562, 586 (3d Cir. 2013) ("The TSA Officials' suspicion was an obvious alternative explanation for their conduct, which negates any inference of retaliation."). That we might be able to conjure up some non-discriminatory motive to explain the City's alleged conduct is not a valid basis for dismissal. It is "only when [a] defendant's plausible alternative explanation is so convincing" to render the "plaintiff's explanation . . . implausible" that a court may dismiss a complaint. *Starr v. Baca*, 652 F.3d 1202, 1216 (9th Cir. 2011) (emphasis in original). [804 F.3d at 295-297.]

The Court added that the City's alleged good motive for the program (protecting public safety rather than discriminating against Muslims) was no defense to *intentionally* discriminatory conduct. *Id.* at 297. The Court reached the same conclusion concerning the City's "threadbare" defense of the First Amendment religion claim. *Id.* at 309.

Concluding that religious discrimination is subject to heightened scrutiny, the Court also held, "No matter how tempting it might be to do otherwise, we must apply the same rigorous standards even where national security is at stake. We have learned from experience that it is often where the asserted interest appears most compelling that we must be most vigilant in protecting constitutional rights." *Id.* at 307 (citing, *inter alia, Korematsu v. United States*, 323 U.S. 214 (1944), *infra* p. 876). It found that the City had not met its burden of justification by simply invoking generalized national security and public safety concerns. *Id.*

The Court then summarized its conclusion:

> The allegations in Plaintiffs' Complaint tell a story in which there is standing to complain and which present constitutional concerns that must be addressed and, if true, redressed. Our job is judicial. We "can apply only law, and must abide by the Constitution, or [we] cease to be civil courts and become instruments of [police] policy." *Korematsu*, 323 U.S. at 247 (Jackson, J., dissenting).
>
> We believe that statement of Justice Jackson to be on the right side of history, and for a majority of us in quiet times it remains so . . . until the next time there is the fear of a few who cannot be sorted out easily from the many. Even when we narrow the many to a class or group, that narrowing — here to those affiliated with a major worldwide religion — is not near enough under our Constitution. "[T]o infer that examples of individual disloyalty prove group disloyalty and justify discriminatory action against the entire group is to deny that under our system of law individual guilt is the sole basis for deprivation of rights." *Id.* at 240 (Murphy, J., dissenting).
>
> What occurs here in one guise is not new. We have been down similar roads before. Jewish-Americans during the Red Scare, African-Americans during the

> Civil Rights Movement, and Japanese-Americans during World War II are examples that readily spring to mind. We are left to wonder why we cannot see with foresight what we see so clearly with hindsight — that "[l]oyalty is a matter of the heart and mind[,] not race, creed, or color." *Ex parte Mitsuye Endo,* 323 U.S. 283, 302 (1944). [804 F.3d at 309.]

Notes and Questions

1. *National Origin Profiling of Post-9/11 Detainees and Interviewees.* Following the September 11 attacks, law enforcement and immigration authorities detained more than 1,100 persons as part of their investigation. On November 27, 2001, the Bush administration provided a breakdown of some 600 persons still being held. According to the report, 548 detained on immigration charges hailed from 47 countries, including more than 200 from Pakistan, and smaller numbers from Egypt, Turkey, Yemen, and India. Dan Eggen, *About 600 Still Held in Connection with Attacks, Ashcroft Says,* Wash. Post, Nov. 28, 2001. An earlier newspaper investigation of 235 detainees found that the largest numbers were from Saudi Arabia, Egypt, and Pakistan, and that almost all of them were men in their 20s and 30s. Amy Goldstein, *A Deliberate Strategy of Disruption,* Wash. Post, Nov. 4, 2001. When these figures were reported, none of the detainees had been charged with any terrorist activity. Subsequently, the Administration conducted "voluntary" interviews targeting 5,000 mostly Middle Eastern aliens holding tourist, student, or business visas. *See* Allan Lengel, *Arab Men in Detroit to Be Asked to See U.S. Attorney,* Wash. Post, Nov. 27, 2001.

Did these actions constitute constitutionally suspect profiling? Did they violate the *DOJ Guidance*? *Compare* Davies, *supra,* at 80-81, *and* Ellmann, *supra,* at 726-727 (because mass interviews were based on stigmatizing racial generalization that promoted public stereotypes, created great resentment in the targeted community, and probably generated few, if any leads, they were "unjustifiable discrimination"), *with* Samuel R. Gross & Debra Livingston, *Racial Profiling Under Attack,* 102 Colum. L. Rev. 1413, 1436 (2002) (concluding that the interview campaign was profiling to the extent that the FBI assumed that Middle Eastern men were more likely than others to commit acts of terror but was not profiling to the extent that FBI agents were "pursuing case-specific information about the September 11 attacks, albeit in dragnet fashion"). Does it matter? Professor Gross and (now-Judge) Livingston suggest that how the FBI selects its interviewees matters less than how they carry out the interviews. Gross & Livingston, *supra,* at 1436-1437 ("Are the interviews conducted respectfully . . . ?"). Do you agree?

2. *Singling Out Muslim Immigrants?* Muslim men who were detained for immigration violations after they had been identified as persons of "high interest" in the investigation following 9/11 claimed that they had been impermissibly selected on the basis of their national origin. The Second Circuit rejected their claim.

> [P]laintiffs point to no authority clearly establishing an equal protection right to be free of selective enforcement of the immigration laws based on national origin, race, or religion at the time of plaintiffs' detentions. *See Reno v. American-Arab Anti-Discrimination Comm.,*

> 525 U.S. 471, 490-91 (1999) ("What will be involved in deportation cases is not merely the disclosure of normal domestic law enforcement priorities and techniques, but often the disclosure of foreign-policy objectives and (as in this case) foreign-intelligence products and techniques. The Executive should not have to disclose its 'real' reasons for deeming nationals of a particular country a special threat — or indeed for simply wishing to antagonize a particular foreign country by focusing on that country's nationals — and even if it did disclose them a court would be ill equipped to determine their authenticity and utterly unable to assess their adequacy"); *see also Zadvydas* [*v. Davis,* 533 U.S. 678, 696 (2001)] ("terrorism" might warrant "special arguments" for "heightened deference to the judgments of the political branches with respect to matters of national security"); *Mathews v. Diaz,* 426 U.S. 67, 81-82 (1976) ("The reasons that preclude judicial review of political questions also dictate a narrow standard of review of decisions made by the Congress or the President in the area of immigration and naturalization."); *but see Iqbal v. Hasty,* 490 F.3d 143, 175 (2d Cir. 2007) (determining that *Reno* "does not stand for the proposition that the Government may subject members of a particular race, ethnicity, or religion to more restrictive conditions of confinement than members of other races, ethnic backgrounds, or religions"), *rev'd on other grounds and remanded, Ashcroft v. Iqbal,* 129 S. Ct. 1937, 1954 (2009). [*Turkmen v. Ashcroft,* 589 F.3d 542, 550 (2d Cir. 2009).]

How was the program of targeting Muslims in *Hassan* different?

B. THE TRUMP ADMINISTRATION TRAVEL BANS[1]

In December 2015, then-presidential candidate Donald Trump published a statement on his campaign website proposing "a total and complete shutdown of Muslims entering the United States until our country's representatives can figure out what is going on." In tweets and media interviews he explained, "We're having problems with Muslims, and we're having problems with Muslims coming into the country," and "you have to deal with the mosques whether you like it or not." In an interview with CNN he added, "I think Islam hates us," and "[W]e can't allow people coming into the country who have this hatred."

When these and other statements drew criticism, he responded, "Calls to ban Muslims from entering the U.S. are offensive and unconstitutional. So you call it territories. OK? We're gonna do territories." He later added, "I'm looking now at territories. People were so upset when I used the word Muslim. Oh, you can't use the word Muslim. Remember this. I'm okay with that, because I'm talking territory instead of Muslim."

Just a week after taking office, President Trump signed Executive Order No. 13,769 [EO-1], *Protecting the Nation from Foreign Terrorist Entry into the United States,* which suspended travel for 90 days from Iran, Libya, Somalia, Sudan, Syria, Yemen,

---

1. This history is drawn from reported cases, as well as from Joanna Walters, Edward Helmore & Saeed Kamali, *US Airports on Frontline as Donald Trump's Travel Ban Causes Chaos and Protests,* The Guardian, Jan. 28, 2017; Dan Merica, *How Trump's Travel Ban Affects Green Card Holders and Dual Citizens,* CNN, Jan. 29, 2017, http://www.cnn.com/2017/01/29/politics/donald-trump-travel-ban-green-card-dual-citizens/index.html; Glenn Kessler, *The Number of People Affected by Trump's Travel Ban: About 90,000,* Wash. Post, Jan. 30, 2017; and Louis Jacobson, *Trump's Travel Ban Executive Order, Take 2,* Politifact, Mar. 6, 2017, http://www.politifact.com/truth-o-meter/article/2017/mar/06/trumps-travel-ban-executive-order-take-2/.

We use the term "travel ban" because the President did. *See* Eugene Scott, *Trump Criticizes Latest Court Ruling Against Travel Ban,* CNN, June 13, 2017, http://www.cnn.com/2017/06/13/politics/trump-tweet-ban-ninth-court/index.html.

and Iraq (all Muslim-majority countries),[2] blocked the admittance of all Syrian refugees indefinitely, and halted other refugee admissions for 120 days.[3] He said, "This is the 'Protection of the Nation from Foreign Terrorist Entry into the United States.' We all know what that means." The next day, presidential adviser Rudolph Giuliani explained, "So when [the President] first announced it, he said 'Muslim ban.' He called me up. He said, 'Put a commission together. Show me the right way to do it legally.'" Giuliani then said that he had assembled a group of lawyers who "focused on, instead of religion, danger — the areas of the world that create danger for us."

EO-1 went into effect immediately and applied to permanent U.S. residents (green-card holders) as well as foreign visitors. Confusion and uncertainty surrounding the implementation of the order resulted in hundreds being detained at airports or in transit, including lawful permanent residents, students, work and tourist visa holders, and pre-approved refugees. The application of the order to lawful permanent residents was reversed two days later under political pressure.

Following partly successful challenges to EO-1, the Administration rescinded it and published a superseding executive order with the same name, Executive Order No. 13,780 [EO-2], on March 6, 2017.[4] EO-2 denied that EO-1 had any religious animus, and then ordered "a temporary pause on the entry of nationals from Iran, Libya, Somalia, Sudan, Syria, and Yemen" until the Administration completed a "worldwide review to identify whether, and if so what, additional information will be needed from each foreign country to adjudicate an application by a national of that country for a visa, admission, or other benefit" under the Immigration and Nationality Act (INA).

Lawsuits were immediately filed challenging EO-2, asserting both statutory and constitutional (chiefly Establishment Clause) claims. In *International Refugee Assistance Project v. Trump* (*IRAP*), 241 F. Supp. 3d 539 (D. Md. 2017), *aff'd in part, vacated in part,* 857 F.3d 554 (4th Cir. 2017) (en banc), the parties relied partly on the INA. The government invoked the President's authority under INA §1182(f), while the plaintiffs argued that this authority was subject to INA §1152(a)(1)(A), the INA's anti-discrimination provision.

Immigration and Nationality Act

8 U.S.C. §1101-1537 (2018)

§1152. Numerical Limitations on Individual Foreign States

(a) Per Country Level

(1) Nondiscrimination

(A) Except as specifically provided in paragraph (2) and in sections 1101(a)(27), 1151(b)(2)(A)(i), and 1153 of this title, no person shall receive any preference or priority or be discriminated against

---

2. At the time EO-1 was promulgated, Iraq's population was 99 percent Muslim, Iran's was 99.5 percent, Libya's was 96.6 percent, Sudan's was 90.7 percent, Somalia's was 99.8 percent, Syria's was 92.8 percent, and Yemen's was 99.1 percent. *See Int'l Refugee Assistance Proj. v. Trump* (*IRAP*), 857 F.3d 554 (4th Cir. 2017) (en banc), at 572 n.2 (citing Pew Research Ctr., *The Global Religious Landscape* 45-50 (2012)).

3. Exec. Order No. 13,769, 82 Fed. Reg. 8977 (Jan. 27, 2017).

4. 82 Fed. Reg. 13,209 (Mar. 6, 2017).

> in the issuance of an immigrant visa because of the person's race, sex, nationality, place of birth, or place of residence....
>
> **§1182. Inadmissible Aliens** . . .
>
> (f) Suspension of Entry or Imposition of Restrictions by President. Whenever the President finds that the entry of any aliens or of any class of aliens into the United States would be detrimental to the interests of the United States, he may by proclamation, and for such period as he shall deem necessary, suspend the entry of all aliens or any class of aliens as immigrants or nonimmigrants, or impose on the entry of aliens any restrictions he may deem to be appropriate....

In the Maryland case, the district court agreed with plaintiffs, holding:

> Because there is no clear basis to conclude that [the President's authority under] §1182(f) is exempt from the non-discrimination provision of §1152(a) or that the President is authorized to impose nationality-based distinctions on the immigrant visa issuance process through another statutory provision, the Court concludes that Plaintiffs have shown a likelihood of success on the merits of their claim that the Second Executive Order violates §1152(a), but only as to the issuance of immigrant visas, which the statutory language makes clear is the extent of the scope of that anti-discrimination requirement. [*IRAP*, 241 F. Supp. 3d at 556.]

It also concluded that the plaintiffs had established a likelihood of success on their Establishment Clause claim, holding that

> while the travel ban bears no resemblance to any response to a national security risk in recent history, it bears a clear resemblance to the precise action that President Trump described as effectuating his Muslim ban. Thus, it is more likely that the primary purpose of the travel ban was grounded in religion, and even if the Second Executive Order has a national security purpose, it is likely that its primary purpose remains the effectuation of the proposed Muslim ban. [*Id.* at 563.]

The court then enjoined enforcement of Section 2(c) of EO-2 (the ban on the entry of citizens from the six Muslim-majority countries) nationwide. On the government's appeal, the Court of Appeals for the Fourth Circuit, sitting en banc, affirmed the district court ruling in substantial part by a 10-3 vote. 857 F.3d 554.

In *Hawai'i v. Trump*, 241 F. Supp. 3d 1119 (D. Haw. 2017), *affirmed in part, vacated in part*, 859 F.3d 741 (9th Cir. 2017) (per curiam), the district court relied on statements by both candidate and President Trump and his advisers, in ruling for the plaintiffs on their Establishment Clause claim.

> These plainly-worded statements, made in the months leading up to and contemporaneous with the signing of the Executive Order, and, in many cases, made by the Executive himself, betray the Executive Order's stated secular purpose. Any reasonable, objective observer would conclude, as does the Court for purposes of the instant Motion for TRO,

> that the stated secular purpose of the Executive Order is, at the very least, "secondary to a religious objective" of temporarily suspending the entry of Muslims. [241 F. Supp. 3d at 1137 (citation omitted).]

The court issued a nationwide temporary restraining order of EO-2's 120-day ban on the admission of refugees and its 90-day ban on immigrants from listed countries, which it subsequently converted to a preliminary injunction. On the government's appeal, the Court of Appeals for the Ninth Circuit affirmed on statutory grounds without reaching the constitutional claims, though it slightly narrowed the scope of the preliminary injunction to exclude purely internal review processes within the executive branch. 859 F.3d 741.

The Supreme Court granted the government's petitions for certiorari from both the Fourth and Ninth Circuit rulings and entered a partial (but not complete) stay of the lower courts' injunctions. *Trump v. Int'l Refugee Assistance Proj.*, 137 S. Ct. 2080 (2017) (per curiam).

After the completion of the worldwide review ordered by EO-2, on September 24, 2017 the President issued Proclamation No. 9645, *Enhancing Vetting Capabilities and Processes for Detecting Attempted Entry into the United States by Terrorists or Other Public-Safety Threats.* 82 Fed. Reg. 45,161, *modified by* Pres. Proclamation 9723, *Maintaining Enhanced Vetting Capabilities and Processes for Detecting Attempted Entry into the United States by Terrorists or Other Public-Safety Threats,* 83 Fed. Reg. 15,937 (Apr. 10, 2018) (removing certain visa restrictions on nationals of Chad). Its provisions are summarized in the Supreme Court opinion excerpted below.

Reading *Trump v. Hawaii*

The State of Hawai'i and other plaintiffs challenged Proclamation No. 9645 on statutory as well as Establishment Clause grounds. After the court granted a nationwide preliminary injunction barring enforcement of the entry restrictions, *State v. Trump*, 265 F. Supp. 3d 1140 (D. Haw. 2017), the Court of Appeals for the Ninth Circuit affirmed on statutory grounds without reaching the Establishment Clause claim. *Hawaii v. Trump*, 878 F.3d 662 (9th Cir. 2017). The Supreme Court granted certiorari and handed down the decision set out below. After the Court granted certiorari but before the Court's decision, the President issued Proclamation No. 9723, 83 Fed. Reg. 15937 (2018), lifting restrictions on nationals of Chad.

- Should the Court have heard this case at all? Since it touches on foreign relations, why wasn't it non-justiciable under the political question doctrine?
- The majority finds that INA §1182(f) "exudes deference to the President." Why doesn't it find such deference sharply bounded by §1152(a)(1)'s nondiscrimination clause?
- The Court has usually applied heightened scrutiny to claims of religious discrimination, as the dissent notes. Why did the majority instead opt for rational basis review, especially given its candid admission that "the Court hardly ever strikes down a policy as illegitimate under rational basis scrutiny"?
- Under a more relaxed standard of review, the authority that the majority cites (*Kleindienst v. Mandel*) still looks to whether the government has provided "a

facially legitimate and bona fide reason." Whether or not the Proclamation is facially neutral, is it "bona fide," given the "Muslim ban" rhetoric by President Trump and his advisers? The majority "assume[s] that we may look behind the face of the Proclamation" to decide this question, but does it do that? If you think that it should, what kinds of evidence should it consider?

- What do you suppose is the meaning or intent of Justice Kennedy's "further observation"?

Trump v. Hawaii

United States Supreme Court, 2018
138 S. Ct. 2392

Chief Justice Roberts delivered the opinion of the Court. . . .

I

A. . .

On September 24, 2017, after completion of the worldwide review, the President issued the Proclamation before us — Proclamation No. 9645, Enhancing Vetting Capabilities and Processes for Detecting Attempted Entry Into the United States by Terrorists or Other Public-Safety Threats. 82 Fed. Reg. 45161. The Proclamation (as its title indicates) sought to improve vetting procedures by identifying ongoing deficiencies in the information needed to assess whether nationals of particular countries present "public safety threats." §1(a). To further that purpose, the Proclamation placed entry restrictions on the nationals of eight foreign states whose systems for managing and sharing information about their nationals the President deemed inadequate.

The Proclamation described how foreign states were selected for inclusion based on the review undertaken pursuant to EO-2. As part of that review, the Department of Homeland Security (DHS), in consultation with the State Department and several intelligence agencies, developed a "baseline" for the information required from foreign governments to confirm the identity of individuals seeking entry into the United States, and to determine whether those individuals pose a security threat. §1(c). . . .

DHS collected and evaluated data regarding all foreign governments. §1(d). It identified 16 countries as having deficient information-sharing practices and presenting national security concerns, and another 31 countries as "at risk" of similarly failing to meet the baseline. §1(e). The State Department then undertook diplomatic efforts over a 50-day period to encourage all foreign governments to improve their practices. §1(f). As a result of that effort, numerous countries provided DHS with travel document exemplars and agreed to share information on known or suspected terrorists. *Ibid.*

Following the 50-day period, the Acting Secretary of Homeland Security concluded that eight countries — Chad, Iran, Iraq, Libya, North Korea, Syria, Venezuela, and Yemen — remained deficient in terms of their risk profile and willingness to provide requested information. The Acting Secretary recommended that the President impose entry restrictions on certain nationals from all of those countries except Iraq.

§§1(g), (h). She also concluded that although Somalia generally satisfied the information-sharing component of the baseline standards, its "identity-management deficiencies" and "significant terrorist presence" presented special circumstances justifying additional limitations. She therefore recommended entry limitations for certain nationals of that country. §1(i). As for Iraq, the Acting Secretary found that entry limitations on its nationals were not warranted given the close cooperative relationship between the U.S. and Iraqi Governments and Iraq's commitment to combating ISIS. §1(g).

After consulting with multiple Cabinet members and other officials, the President adopted the Acting Secretary's recommendations and issued the Proclamation. Invoking his authority under 8 U.S.C. §§1182(f) and 1185(a), the President determined that certain entry restrictions were necessary to "prevent the entry of those foreign nationals about whom the United States Government lacks sufficient information"; "elicit improved identity-management and information-sharing protocols and practices from foreign governments"; and otherwise "advance [the] foreign policy, national security, and counterterrorism objectives" of the United States. Proclamation §1(h). The President explained that these restrictions would be the "most likely to encourage cooperation" while "protect[ing] the United States until such time as improvements occur." *Ibid.*

The Proclamation imposed a range of restrictions that vary based on the "distinct circumstances" in each of the eight countries. *Ibid.* . . .

The Proclamation exempts lawful permanent residents and foreign nationals who have been granted asylum. §3(b). It also provides for case-by-case waivers when a foreign national demonstrates undue hardship, and that his entry is in the national interest and would not pose a threat to public safety. §3(c)(i); see also §3(c)(iv) (listing examples of when a waiver might be appropriate, such as if the foreign national seeks to reside with a close family member, obtain urgent medical care, or pursue significant business obligations). The Proclamation further directs DHS to assess on a continuing basis whether entry restrictions should be modified or continued, and to report to the President every 180 days. §4. Upon completion of the first such review period, the President, on the recommendation of the Secretary of Homeland Security, determined that Chad had sufficiently improved its practices, and he accordingly lifted restrictions on its nationals. Presidential Proclamation No. 9723, 83 Fed. Reg. 15937 (2018).

B

Plaintiffs in this case are the State of Hawaii, three individuals (Dr. Ismail Elshikh, John Doe #1, and John Doe #2), and the Muslim Association of Hawaii. The State operates the University of Hawaii system, which recruits students and faculty from the designated countries. The three individual plaintiffs are U.S. citizens or lawful permanent residents who have relatives from Iran, Syria, and Yemen applying for immigrant or nonimmigrant visas. The Association is a nonprofit organization that operates a mosque in Hawaii.

Plaintiffs challenged the Proclamation — except as applied to North Korea and Venezuela — on several grounds. As relevant here, they argued that the Proclamation contravenes provisions in the Immigration and Nationality Act (INA), 66 Stat. 187, as amended. Plaintiffs further claimed that the Proclamation violates the Establishment Clause of the First Amendment, because it was motivated not by concerns pertaining to national security but by animus toward Islam. . . .

II . . .

The justiciability of plaintiffs' challenge under the INA presents a difficult question. . . . The Government does not argue that the doctrine of consular nonreviewability goes to the Court's jurisdiction, nor does it point to any provision of the INA that expressly strips the Court of jurisdiction over plaintiffs' claims, see *Sebelius v. Auburn Regional Medical Center*, 568 U.S. 145, 153 (2013) (requiring Congress to "clearly state[ ]" that a statutory provision is jurisdictional). As a result, we may assume without deciding that plaintiffs' statutory claims are reviewable, notwithstanding consular nonreviewability or any other statutory nonreviewability issue, and we proceed on that basis.

III . . .

Plaintiffs argue that the Proclamation is not a valid exercise of the President's authority under the INA. In their view, §1182(f) confers only a residual power to temporarily halt the entry of a discrete group of aliens engaged in harmful conduct. They also assert that the Proclamation violates another provision of the INA — 8 U.S.C. §1152(a)(1)(A) — because it discriminates on the basis of nationality in the issuance of immigrant visas. [Both statutory provisions are set forth above.]

By its plain language, §1182(f) grants the President broad discretion to suspend the entry of aliens into the United States. The President lawfully exercised that discretion based on his findings — following a worldwide, multi-agency review — that entry of the covered aliens would be detrimental to the national interest. And plaintiffs' attempts to identify a conflict with other provisions in the INA, and their appeal to the statute's purposes and legislative history, fail to overcome the clear statutory language.

A . . .

By its terms, §1182(f) exudes deference to the President in every clause. It entrusts to the President the decisions whether and when to suspend entry ("[w]henever [he] finds that the entry" of aliens "would be detrimental" to the national interest); whose entry to suspend ("all aliens or any class of aliens"); for how long ("for such period as he shall deem necessary"); and on what conditions ("any restrictions he may deem to be appropriate"). It is therefore unsurprising that we have previously observed that §1182(f) vests the President with "ample power" to impose entry restrictions in addition to those elsewhere enumerated in the INA. *Sale*, 509 U.S., at 187 (finding it "perfectly clear" that the President could "establish a naval blockade" to prevent illegal migrants from entering the United States); see also *Abourezk v. Reagan*, 785 F. 2d 1043, 1049, n.2 (CADC 1986) (describing the "sweeping proclamation power" in §1182(f) as enabling the President to supplement the other grounds of inadmissibility in the INA).

The Proclamation falls well within this comprehensive delegation. The sole prerequisite set forth in §1182(f) is that the President "find[ ]" that the entry of the covered aliens "would be detrimental to the interests of the United States." The President has undoubtedly fulfilled that requirement here. He first ordered DHS and other agencies to conduct a comprehensive evaluation of every single country's compliance with the information and risk assessment baseline. The President then issued a Proclamation setting forth extensive findings describing how deficiencies in the practices of select foreign governments — several of which are state sponsors of terrorism — deprive the Government of "sufficient information to assess the risks [those countries' nationals] pose to the United States." Proclamation §1(h)(i). Based on that review, the President found that it was in the national interest to restrict entry of aliens who could not be vetted with adequate information — both to protect national security and public safety, and to induce improvement by their home countries. The Proclamation therefore "craft[ed] . . . country-specific restrictions that would be most likely to encourage cooperation given each country's distinct circumstances," while securing the Nation "until such time as improvements occur." *Ibid.*

Plaintiffs believe that these findings are insufficient. They argue, as an initial matter, that the Proclamation fails to provide a persuasive rationale for why nationality alone renders the covered foreign nationals a security risk. And they further discount the President's stated concern about deficient vetting because the Proclamation allows many aliens from the designated countries to enter on nonimmigrant visas.

Such arguments are grounded on the premise that §1182(f) not only requires the President to *make* a finding that entry "would be detrimental to the interests of the United States," but also to explain that finding with sufficient detail to enable judicial review. That premise is questionable. See *Webster v. Doe*, 486 U.S. 592, 600 (1988) (concluding that a statute authorizing the CIA Director to terminate an employee when the Director "shall deem such termination necessary or advisable in the interests of the United States" forecloses "any meaningful judicial standard of review"). But even assuming that some form of review is appropriate, plaintiffs' attacks on the sufficiency of the President's findings cannot be sustained. The 12-page Proclamation — which thoroughly describes the process, agency evaluations, and recommendations underlying the President's chosen restrictions — is more detailed than any prior order a President has issued under §1182(f). . . .

Moreover, plaintiffs' request for a searching inquiry into the persuasiveness of the President's justifications is inconsistent with the broad statutory text and the deference traditionally accorded the President in this sphere. "Whether the President's chosen method" of addressing perceived risks is justified from a policy perspective is "irrelevant to the scope of his [§1182(f)] authority." *Sale*, 509 U.S., at 187-188. And when the President adopts "a preventive measure . . . in the context of international affairs and national security," he is "not required to conclusively link all of the pieces in the puzzle before [courts] grant weight to [his] empirical conclusions." *Holder v. Humanitarian Law Project*, 561 U.S. 1, 35 (2010). . . .

In short, the language of §1182(f) is clear, and the Proclamation does not exceed any textual limit on the President's authority.

B . . .

1

Plaintiffs' structural argument starts with the premise that §1182(f) does not give the President authority to countermand Congress's considered policy judgments. The President, they say, may supplement the INA, but he cannot supplant it. And in their view, the Proclamation falls in the latter category because Congress has already specified a two-part solution to the problem of aliens seeking entry from countries that do not share sufficient information with the United States. First, Congress designed an individualized vetting system that places the burden on the alien to prove his admissibility. See §1361. Second, instead of banning the entry of nationals from particular countries, Congress sought to encourage information sharing through a Visa Waiver Program offering fast-track admission for countries that cooperate with the United States. See §1187.

We may assume that §1182(f) does not allow the President to expressly override particular provisions of the INA. But plaintiffs have not identified any conflict between the statute and the Proclamation that would implicitly bar the President from addressing deficiencies in the Nation's vetting system.

To the contrary, the Proclamation supports Congress's individualized approach for determining admissibility. The INA sets forth various inadmissibility grounds based on connections to terrorism and criminal history, but those provisions can only work when the consular officer has sufficient (and sufficiently reliable) information to make that determination. The Proclamation promotes the effectiveness of the vetting process by helping to ensure the availability of such information.

Plaintiffs suggest that the entry restrictions are unnecessary because consular officers can simply deny visas in individual cases when an alien fails to carry his burden of proving admissibility — for example, by failing to produce certified records regarding his criminal history. But that misses the point: A critical finding of the Proclamation is that the failure of certain countries to provide reliable information prevents the Government from accurately determining whether an alien is inadmissible or poses a threat. Proclamation §1(h). Unless consular officers are expected to apply categorical rules and deny entry from those countries across the board, fraudulent or unreliable documentation may thwart their review in individual cases. And at any rate, the INA certainly does not *require* that systemic problems such as the lack of reliable information be addressed only in a progression of case-by-case admissibility determinations. One of the key objectives of the Proclamation is to encourage foreign governments to improve their practices, thus facilitating the Government's vetting process overall. *Ibid.*...

Because plaintiffs do not point to any contradiction with another provision of the INA, the President has not exceeded his authority under §1182(f).

2

Plaintiffs seek to locate additional limitations on the scope of §1182(f) in the statutory background and legislative history. Given the clarity of the text, we need not consider such extra-textual evidence. At any rate, plaintiffs' evidence supports the plain meaning of the provision....

Plaintiffs also strive to infer limitations from executive practice. By their count, every previous suspension order under §1182(f) can be slotted into one of two categories. The vast majority targeted discrete groups of foreign nationals engaging in conduct "deemed harmful by the immigration laws." And the remaining entry restrictions that focused on entire nationalities — namely, President Carter's response to the Iran hostage crisis and President Reagan's suspension of immigration from Cuba — were, in their view, designed as a response to diplomatic emergencies "that the immigration laws do not address."

Even if we were willing to confine expansive language in light of its past applications, the historical evidence is more equivocal than plaintiffs acknowledge. Presidents have repeatedly suspended entry not because the covered nationals themselves engaged in harmful acts but instead to retaliate for conduct by their governments that conflicted with U.S. foreign policy interests. . . . And while some of these reprisals were directed at subsets of aliens from the countries at issue, others broadly suspended entry on the basis of nationality due to ongoing diplomatic disputes. . . .

More significantly, plaintiffs' argument about historical practice is a double-edged sword. The more ad hoc their account of executive action — to fit the history into their theory — the harder it becomes to see such a refined delegation in a statute that grants the President sweeping authority to decide whether to suspend entry, whose entry to suspend, and for how long.

C

Plaintiffs' final statutory argument is that the President's entry suspension violates §1152(a)(1)(A) [*supra* p. 795], which provides that "no person shall . . . be discriminated against in the issuance of an immigrant visa because of the person's race, sex, nationality, place of birth, or place of residence." They contend that we should interpret the provision as prohibiting nationality-based discrimination throughout the *entire* immigration process, despite the reference in §1152(a)(1)(A) to the act of visa issuance alone. Specifically, plaintiffs argue that §1152(a)(1)(A) applies to the predicate question of a visa applicant's eligibility for admission and the subsequent question whether the holder of a visa may in fact enter the country. Any other conclusion, they say, would allow the President to circumvent the protections against discrimination enshrined in §1152(a)(1)(A). . . .

. . . [W]e reject plaintiffs' interpretation because it ignores the basic distinction between admissibility determinations and visa issuance that runs throughout the INA. Section 1182 defines the pool of individuals who are admissible to the United States. Its restrictions come into play at two points in the process of gaining entry (or admission) into the United States. First, any alien who is inadmissible under §1182 (based on, for example, health risks, criminal history, or foreign policy consequences) is screened out as "ineligible to receive a visa." 8 U.S.C. §1201(g). Second, even if a consular officer issues a visa, entry into the United States is not guaranteed. As every visa application explains, a visa does not entitle an alien to enter the United States "if, upon arrival," an immigration officer determines that the applicant is "inadmissible under this chapter, or any other provision of law" — including §1182(f). §1201(h).

Sections 1182(f) and 1152(a)(1)(A) thus operate in different spheres: Section 1182 defines the universe of aliens who are admissible into the United States (and therefore eligible to receive a visa). Once §1182 sets the boundaries of admissibility into the United States, §1152(a)(1)(A) prohibits discrimination in the allocation of immigrant visas based on nationality and other traits. The distinction between admissibility — to which §1152(a)(1)(A) does not apply — and visa issuance — to which it does — is apparent from the text of the provision, which specifies only that its protections apply to the "issuance" of "immigrant visa[s]," without mentioning admissibility or entry. Had Congress instead intended in §1152(a)(1)(A) to constrain the President's power to determine who may enter the country, it could easily have chosen language directed to that end. See, *e.g.*, §§1182(a)(3)(C)(ii), (iii) (providing that certain aliens "*shall not be excludable or subject to restrictions or conditions on entry* . . . because of the alien's past, current, or expected beliefs, statements, or associations" (emphasis added)). "The fact that [Congress] did not adopt [a] readily available and apparent alternative strongly supports" the conclusion that §1152(a)(1)(A) does not limit the President's delegated authority under §1182(f). *Knight v. Commissioner*, 552 U.S. 181, 188 (2008).

Common sense and historical practice confirm as much. Section 1152(a)(1)(A) has never been treated as a constraint on the criteria for admissibility in §1182. Presidents have repeatedly exercised their authority to suspend entry on the basis of nationality. As noted, President Reagan relied on §1182(f) to suspend entry "as immigrants by all Cuban nationals," subject to exceptions. Proclamation No. 5517, 51 Fed. Reg. 30470 (1986). Likewise, President Carter invoked §1185(a)(1) to deny and revoke visas to all Iranian nationals. See Exec. Order No. 12172, 3 CFR 461 (1979), as amended by Exec. Order No. 12206, 3 CFR 249 (1980); Public Papers of the Presidents, Jimmy Carter, Sanctions Against Iran, Vol. 1, Apr. 7, 1980, pp. 611-612 (1980).

On plaintiffs' reading, those orders were beyond the President's authority. The entry restrictions in the Proclamation on North Korea (which plaintiffs do not challenge in this litigation) would also be unlawful. Nor would the President be permitted to suspend entry from particular foreign states in response to an epidemic confined to a single region, or a verified terrorist threat involving nationals of a specific foreign nation, or even if the United States were on the brink of war....

* * *

The Proclamation is squarely within the scope of Presidential authority under the INA. Indeed, neither dissent even attempts any serious argument to the contrary, despite the fact that plaintiffs' primary contention below and in their briefing before this Court was that the Proclamation violated the statute.

IV

A

We now turn to plaintiffs' claim that the Proclamation was issued for the unconstitutional purpose of excluding Muslims....

...We agree that a person's interest in being united with his relatives is sufficiently concrete and particularized to form the basis of an Article III injury in fact....

...We therefore conclude that the individual plaintiffs have Article III standing to challenge the exclusion of their relatives under the Establishment Clause.

B

The First Amendment provides, in part, that "Congress shall make no law respecting an establishment of religion, or prohibiting the free exercise thereof." Our cases recognize that "[t]he clearest command of the Establishment Clause is that one religious denomination cannot be officially preferred over another." *Larson v. Valente*, 456 U.S. 228, 244 (1982). Plaintiffs believe that the Proclamation violates this prohibition by singling out Muslims for disfavored treatment. The entry suspension, they contend, operates as a "religious gerrymander," in part because most of the countries covered by the Proclamation have Muslim-majority populations. And in their view, deviations from the information-sharing baseline criteria suggest that the results of the multi-agency review were "foreordained." Relying on Establishment Clause precedents concerning laws and policies applied domestically, plaintiffs allege that the primary purpose of the Proclamation was religious animus and that the President's stated concerns about vetting protocols and national security were but pretexts for discriminating against Muslims.

At the heart of plaintiffs' case is a series of statements by the President and his advisers casting doubt on the official objective of the Proclamation. For example, while a candidate on the campaign trail, the President published a "Statement on Preventing Muslim Immigration" that called for a "total and complete shutdown of Muslims entering the United States until our country's representatives can figure out what is going on." That statement remained on his campaign website until May 2017. Then-candidate Trump also stated that "Islam hates us" and asserted that the United States was "having problems with Muslims coming into the country." Shortly after being elected, when asked whether violence in Europe had affected his plans to "ban Muslim immigration," the President replied, "You know my plans. All along, I've been proven to be right."

One week after his inauguration, the President issued EO-1. In a television interview, one of the President's campaign advisers explained that when the President "first announced it, he said, 'Muslim ban.' He called me up. He said, 'Put a commission together. Show me the right way to do it legally.'" The adviser said he assembled a group of Members of Congress and lawyers that "focused on, instead of religion, danger. . . . [The order] is based on places where there [is] substantial evidence that people are sending terrorists into our country."

Plaintiffs also note that after issuing EO-2 to replace EO-1, the President expressed regret that his prior order had been "watered down" and called for a "much tougher version" of his "Travel Ban." Shortly before the release of the Proclamation, he stated that the "travel ban . . . should be far larger, tougher, and more specific," but "stupidly that would not be politically correct." More recently, on November 29, 2017, the President retweeted links to three anti-Muslim propaganda videos. In response to questions about those videos, the President's deputy press secretary denied that the President thinks Muslims are a threat to the United States, explaining that "the President has been talking about these security issues for years now, from the campaign trail to the White House" and "has addressed these issues with the travel order that he issued earlier this year and the companion proclamation." *IRAP v. Trump*, 883 F.3d 233, 267 (CA4 2018). . . .

Plaintiffs argue that this President's words strike at fundamental standards of respect and tolerance, in violation of our constitutional tradition. But the issue before us is not whether to denounce the statements. It is instead the significance of those statements in reviewing a Presidential directive, neutral on its face, addressing a matter within the core of executive responsibility. In doing so, we must consider not only the statements of a particular President, but also the authority of the Presidency itself.

The case before us differs in numerous respects from the conventional Establishment Clause claim. Unlike the typical suit involving religious displays or school prayer, plaintiffs seek to invalidate a national security directive regulating the entry of aliens abroad. Their claim accordingly raises a number of delicate issues regarding the scope of the constitutional right and the manner of proof. The Proclamation, moreover, is facially neutral toward religion. Plaintiffs therefore ask the Court to probe the sincerity of the stated justifications for the policy by reference to extrinsic statements — many of which were made before the President took the oath of office. These various aspects of plaintiffs' challenge inform our standard of review.

C

For more than a century, this Court has recognized that the admission and exclusion of foreign nationals is a "fundamental sovereign attribute exercised by the Government's political departments largely immune from judicial control." *Fiallo v. Bell*, 430 U.S. 787, 792 (1977); see *Harisiades v. Shaughnessy*, 342 U.S. 580, 588-589 (1952) ("[A]ny policy toward aliens is vitally and intricately interwoven with contemporaneous policies in regard to the conduct of foreign relations [and] the war power."). Because decisions in these matters may implicate "relations with foreign powers," or involve "classifications defined in the light of changing political and economic circumstances," such judgments "are frequently of a character more appropriate to either the Legislature or the Executive." *Mathews v. Diaz*, 426 U.S. 67, 81 (1976).

Nonetheless, although foreign nationals seeking admission have no constitutional right to entry, this Court has engaged in a circumscribed judicial inquiry when the denial of a visa allegedly burdens the constitutional rights of a U.S. citizen. In *Kleindienst v. Mandel* [408 U.S. 753 (1972)], . . . we held that "when the Executive exercises this [delegated] power negatively on the basis of a facially legitimate and bona fide reason, the courts will neither look behind the exercise of that discretion, nor test it by balancing its justification" against the asserted constitutional interests of U.S. citizens. *Id.*, at 770. . . .

Mandel's narrow standard of review "has particular force" in admission and immigration cases that overlap with "the area of national security." [*Kerry v. Din*, 576 U.S., at ___ (2015)] (Kennedy, J., concurring in judgment) (slip op., at 3). For one, "[j]udicial inquiry into the national-security realm raises concerns for the separation of powers" by intruding on the President's constitutional responsibilities in the area of foreign affairs. *Ziglar v. Abbasi*, 582 U.S. ___, ___ (2017) (slip op., at 19) (internal quotation marks omitted). For another, "when it comes to collecting evidence and drawing inferences" on questions of national security, "the lack of competence on the part of the courts is marked." *Humanitarian Law Project*, 561 U.S., at 34.

The upshot of our cases in this context is clear: "Any rule of constitutional law that would inhibit the flexibility" of the President "to respond to changing world conditions should be adopted only with the greatest caution," and our inquiry into matters of entry and national security is highly constrained. *Mathews*, 426 U.S., at 81-82. We need not define the precise contours of that inquiry in this case. A conventional application of *Mandel*, asking only whether the policy is facially legitimate and bona fide, would put an end to our review. But the Government has suggested that it may be appropriate here for the inquiry to extend beyond the facial neutrality of the order. For our purposes today, we assume that we may look behind the face of the Proclamation to the extent of applying rational basis review. That standard of review considers whether the entry policy is plausibly related to the Government's stated objective to protect the country and improve vetting processes. See *Railroad Retirement Bd. v. Fritz*, 449 U.S. 166, 179 (1980). As a result, we may consider plaintiffs' extrinsic evidence, but will uphold the policy so long as it can reasonably be understood to result from a justification independent of unconstitutional grounds.

D

Given the standard of review, it should come as no surprise that the Court hardly ever strikes down a policy as illegitimate under rational basis scrutiny. On the few occasions where we have done so, a common thread has been that the laws at issue lack any purpose other than a "bare . . . desire to harm a politically unpopular group." *Department of Agriculture v. Moreno*, 413 U.S. 528, 534 (1973). . . .

The Proclamation does not fit this pattern. It cannot be said that it is impossible to "discern a relationship to legitimate state interests" or that the policy is "inexplicable by anything but animus." Indeed, the dissent can only attempt to argue otherwise by refusing to apply anything resembling rational basis review. But because there is persuasive evidence that the entry suspension has a legitimate grounding in national security concerns, quite apart from any religious hostility, we must accept that independent justification.

The Proclamation is expressly premised on legitimate purposes: preventing entry of nationals who cannot be adequately vetted and inducing other nations to improve their practices. The text says nothing about religion. Plaintiffs and the dissent nonetheless emphasize that five of the seven nations currently included in the Proclamation have Muslim-majority populations. Yet that fact alone does not support an inference of religious hostility, given that the policy covers just 8% of the world's Muslim population and is limited to countries that were previously designated by Congress or prior administrations as posing national security risks. . . .

The Proclamation, moreover, reflects the results of a worldwide review process undertaken by multiple Cabinet officials and their agencies. Plaintiffs seek to discredit the findings of the review, pointing to deviations from the review's baseline criteria resulting in the inclusion of Somalia and omission of Iraq. But as the Proclamation explains, in each case the determinations were justified by the distinct conditions in each country. . . . It is, in any event, difficult to see how exempting one of the largest predominantly Muslim countries in the region from coverage under the Proclamation can be cited as evidence of animus toward Muslims. . . .

More fundamentally, plaintiffs and the dissent challenge the entry suspension based on their perception of its effectiveness and wisdom. They suggest that the policy is overbroad and does little to serve national security interests. But we cannot substitute our own assessment for the Executive's predictive judgments on such matters, all of which "are delicate, complex, and involve large elements of prophecy." *Chicago & Southern Air Lines, Inc. v. Waterman S. S. Corp.*, 333 U.S. 103, 111 (1948); see also *Regan v. Wald*, 468 U.S. 222, 242-243 (1984) (declining invitation to conduct an "independent foreign policy analysis"). While we of course "do not defer to the Government's reading of the First Amendment," the Executive's evaluation of the underlying facts is entitled to appropriate weight, particularly in the context of litigation involving "sensitive and weighty interests of national security and foreign affairs." *Humanitarian Law Project*, 561 U.S., at 33-34.

Three additional features of the entry policy support the Government's claim of a legitimate national security interest. First, since the President introduced entry restrictions in January 2017, three Muslim-majority countries — Iraq, Sudan, and Chad — have been removed from the list of covered countries. . . .

Second, for those countries that remain subject to entry restrictions, the Proclamation includes significant exceptions for various categories of foreign nationals. . . .

Third, the Proclamation creates a waiver program open to all covered foreign nationals seeking entry as immigrants or nonimmigrants. . . .

Finally, the dissent invokes *Korematsu v. United States*, 323 U.S. 214 (1944). Whatever rhetorical advantage the dissent may see in doing so, *Korematsu* has nothing to do with this case. The forcible relocation of U.S. citizens to concentration camps, solely and explicitly on the basis of race, is objectively unlawful and outside the scope of Presidential authority. But it is wholly inapt to liken that morally repugnant order to a facially neutral policy denying certain foreign nationals the privilege of admission. The entry suspension is an act that is well within executive authority and could have been taken by any other President — the only question is evaluating the actions of this particular President in promulgating an otherwise valid Proclamation.

The dissent's reference to *Korematsu,* however, affords this Court the opportunity to make express what is already obvious: *Korematsu* was gravely wrong the day it was decided, has been overruled in the court of history, and — to be clear — "has no place in law under the Constitution." 323 U.S., at 248 (Jackson, J., dissenting).

* * *

Under these circumstances, the Government has set forth a sufficient national security justification to survive rational basis review. We express no view on the soundness of the policy. We simply hold today that plaintiffs have not demonstrated a likelihood of success on the merits of their constitutional claim....

The judgment of the Court of Appeals is reversed, and the case is remanded for further proceedings consistent with this opinion.

It is so ordered.

Justice KENNEDY, concurring. I join the Court's opinion in full.

There may be some common ground between the opinions in this case, in that the Court does acknowledge that in some instances, governmental action may be subject to judicial review to determine whether or not it is "inexplicable by anything but animus," *Romer v. Evans,* 517 U.S. 620, 632 (1996), which in this case would be animosity to a religion. Whether judicial proceedings may properly continue in this case, in light of the substantial deference that is and must be accorded to the Executive in the conduct of foreign affairs, and in light of today's decision, is a matter to be addressed in the first instance on remand. And even if further proceedings are permitted, it would be necessary to determine that any discovery and other preliminary matters would not themselves intrude on the foreign affairs power of the Executive.

In all events, it is appropriate to make this further observation. There are numerous instances in which the statements and actions of Government officials are not subject to judicial scrutiny or intervention. That does not mean those officials are free to disregard the Constitution and the rights it proclaims and protects. The oath that all officials take to adhere to the Constitution is not confined to those spheres in which the Judiciary can correct or even comment upon what those officials say or do. Indeed, the very fact that an official may have broad discretion, discretion free from judicial scrutiny, makes it all the more imperative for him or her to adhere to the Constitution and to its meaning and its promise.

The First Amendment prohibits the establishment of religion and promises the free exercise of religion. From these safeguards, and from the guarantee of freedom of speech, it follows there is freedom of belief and expression. It is an urgent necessity that officials adhere to these constitutional guarantees and mandates in all their actions, even in the sphere of foreign affairs. An anxious world must know that our Government remains committed always to the liberties the Constitution seeks to preserve and protect, so that freedom extends outward, and lasts.

[Concurring opinion of Justice THOMAS omitted.]

Justice BREYER, with whom Justice KAGAN joins, dissenting. . . . [G]iven the importance of the decision in this case, the need for assurance that the Proclamation does not rest upon a "Muslim ban," and the assistance in deciding the issue that answers to the "exemption and waiver" questions may provide, I would send this case back to the District Court for further proceedings. And, I would leave the injunction in effect while the matter is litigated. Regardless, the Court's decision today leaves the District Court free to explore these issues on remand.

If this Court must decide the question without this further litigation, I would, on balance, find the evidence of antireligious bias, including statements on a website taken down only after the President issued the two executive orders preceding the Proclamation, along with the other statements also set forth in Justice Sotomayor's opinion, a sufficient basis to set the Proclamation aside. And for these reasons, I respectfully dissent.

Justice SOTOMAYOR, with whom Justice GINSBURG joins, dissenting. The United States of America is a Nation built upon the promise of religious liberty. Our Founders honored that core promise by embedding the principle of religious neutrality in the First Amendment. The Court's decision today fails to safeguard that fundamental principle. It leaves undisturbed a policy first advertised openly and unequivocally as a "total and complete shutdown of Muslims entering the United States" because the policy now masquerades behind a facade of national-security concerns. But this repackaging does little to cleanse Presidential Proclamation No. 9645 of the appearance of discrimination that the President's words have created. Based on the evidence in the record, a reasonable observer would conclude that the Proclamation was motivated by anti-Muslim animus. That alone suffices to show that plaintiffs are likely to succeed on the merits of their Establishment Clause claim. The majority holds otherwise by ignoring the facts, misconstruing our legal precedent, and turning a blind eye to the pain and suffering the Proclamation inflicts upon countless families and individuals, many of whom are United States citizens. Because that troubling result runs contrary to the Constitution and our precedent, I dissent.

I . . .

A

The Establishment Clause forbids government policies "respecting an establishment of religion." U.S. Const., Amdt. 1. The "clearest command" of the Establishment Clause is that the Government cannot favor or disfavor one religion over another. *Larson v. Valente*, 456 U.S. 228, 244 (1982). Consistent with that clear command, this Court has long acknowledged that governmental actions that favor one religion "inevitabl[y]" foster "the hatred, disrespect and even contempt of those who [hold] contrary beliefs." *Engel v. Vitale*, 370 U.S. 421, 431 (1962). That is so, this Court has held, because such acts send messages to members of minority faiths "'that they are outsiders, not full members of the political community.'" *Santa Fe Independent School Dist. v. Doe*, 530 U.S. 290, 309 (2000). To guard against this serious harm, the Framers mandated a strict "principle of denominational neutrality." *Larson*, 456 U.S., at 246; *Board of Ed. of Kiryas Joel Village School Dist. v. Grumet*, 512 U.S. 687, 703 (1994) (recognizing the role of courts in "safeguarding a principle at the heart of the Establishment Clause, that government should not prefer one religion to another, or religion to irreligion").

"When the government acts with the ostensible and predominant purpose" of disfavoring a particular religion, "it violates that central Establishment Clause value of official religious neutrality, there being no neutrality when the government's ostensible object is to take sides." *McCreary County v. American Civil Liberties Union of Ky.*, 545 U.S. 844, 860 (2005). To determine whether plaintiffs have proved an Establishment Clause violation, the Court asks whether a reasonable observer would view the government action as enacted for the purpose of disfavoring a religion. See *id.*, at 862, 866; accord, *Town of Greece v. Galloway*, 572 U.S. ____, ____ (2014) (plurality opinion) (slip op., at 19).

In answering that question, this Court has generally considered the text of the government policy, its operation, and any available evidence regarding "the historical background of the decision under challenge, the specific series of events leading to the enactment or official policy in question, and the legislative or administrative history, including contemporaneous statements made by" the decisionmaker. [*Church of Lukumi Babalu Aye, Inc. v. Hialeah*, 508 U.S. 520 (1993)], at 540 (opinion of Kennedy, J.); *McCreary*, 545 U.S., at 862 (courts must evaluate "text, legislative history, and implementation . . . , or comparable official act" (internal quotation marks omitted)). At the same time, however, courts must take care not to engage in "any judicial psychoanalysis of a drafter's heart of hearts." *Id.*, at 862.

B . . .

2 . . .

Taking all the relevant evidence together, a reasonable observer would conclude that the Proclamation was driven primarily by anti-Muslim animus, rather than by the Government's asserted national-security justifications. Even before being sworn into office, then-candidate Trump stated that "Islam hates us," warned that "[w]e're having problems with the Muslims, and we're having problems with Muslims coming into the country," promised to enact a "total and complete shutdown of Muslims entering the United States," and instructed one of his advisers to find a "lega[l]" way to enact a Muslim ban.[3] The President continued to make similar statements well after his inauguration. . . .

---

3. The Government urges us to disregard the President's campaign statements. But nothing in our precedent supports that blinkered approach. To the contrary, courts must consider "the historical background of the decision under challenge, the specific series of events leading to the enactment or official policy in question, and the legislative or administrative history." *Church of Lukumi Babalu Aye, Inc. v. Hialeah*, 508 U.S. 520, 540 (1993) (opinion of Kennedy, J.). Moreover, President Trump and his advisers have repeatedly acknowledged that the Proclamation and its predecessors are an outgrowth of the President's campaign statements. For example, just last November, the Deputy White House Press Secretary reminded the media that the Proclamation addresses "issues" the President has been talking about "for years," including on "the campaign trail." *IRAP II*, 883 F.3d 233, 267 (CA4 2018). In any case, as the Fourth Circuit correctly recognized, even without relying on any of the President's campaign statements, a reasonable observer would conclude that the Proclamation was enacted for the impermissible purpose of disfavoring Muslims. *Id.*, at 266, 268.

Moreover, despite several opportunities to do so, President Trump has never disavowed any of his prior statements about Islam. Instead, he has continued to make remarks that a reasonable observer would view as an unrelenting attack on the Muslim religion and its followers. Given President Trump's failure to correct the reasonable perception of his apparent hostility toward the Islamic faith, it is unsurprising that the President's lawyers have, at every step in the lower courts, failed in their attempts to launder the Proclamation of its discriminatory taint. See *United States v. Fordice*, 505 U.S. 717, 746-747 (1992) ("[G]iven an initially tainted policy, it is eminently reasonable to make the [Government] bear the risk of nonpersuasion with respect to intent at some future time, both because the [Government] has created the dispute through its own prior unlawful conduct, and because discriminatory intent does tend to persist through time" (citation omitted)). Notably, the Court recently found less pervasive official expressions of hostility and the failure to disavow them to be constitutionally significant. Cf. *Masterpiece Cakeshop, Ltd. v. Colorado Civil Rights Comm'n*, 584 U.S. ____, ____ (2018) (slip op., at 18) ("The official expressions of hostility to religion in some of the commissioners' comments — comments that were not disavowed at the Commission or by the State at any point in the proceedings that led to the affirmance of the order — were inconsistent with what the Free Exercise Clause requires"). It should find the same here.

Ultimately, what began as a policy explicitly "calling for a total and complete shutdown of Muslims entering the United States" has since morphed into a "Proclamation" putatively based on national-security concerns. But this new window dressing cannot conceal an unassailable fact: the words of the President and his advisers create the strong perception that the Proclamation is contaminated by impermissible discriminatory animus against Islam and its followers.

II

Rather than defend the President's problematic statements, the Government urges this Court to set them aside and defer to the President on issues related to immigration and national security. The majority accepts that invitation and incorrectly applies a watered-down legal standard in an effort to short circuit plaintiffs' Establishment Clause claim. . . .

In light of the Government's suggestion "that it may be appropriate here for the inquiry to extend beyond the facial neutrality of the order," the majority rightly declines to apply *Mandel*'s "narrow standard of review" and "assume[s] that we may look behind the face of the Proclamation." In doing so, however, the Court, without explanation or precedential support, limits its review of the Proclamation to rational-basis scrutiny. That approach is perplexing, given that in other Establishment Clause cases, including those involving claims of religious animus or discrimination, this Court has applied a more stringent standard of review. See, *e.g.*, *McCreary*, 545 U.S., at 860-863; *Larson*, 456 U.S., at 246; *Presbyterian Church in U.S. v. Mary Elizabeth Blue Hull Memorial Presbyterian Church*, 393 U.S. 440, 449-452 (1969); see also *Colorado Christian Univ. v. Weaver*, 534 F.3d 1245, 1266 (CA10 2008) (McConnell, J.) (noting that, under Supreme Court precedent, laws "involving discrimination on the basis of religion, including interdenominational discrimination, are subject to heightened scrutiny whether they arise under the Free Exercise Clause, the Establishment Clause, or the Equal Protection Clause" (citations omitted)).[6] As explained above, the Proclamation is plainly unconstitutional under that heightened standard.

But even under rational-basis review, the Proclamation must fall. That is so because the Proclamation is "'divorced from any factual context from which we could discern a relationship to legitimate state interests,' and 'its sheer breadth [is] so discontinuous with the reasons offered for it'" that the policy is "'inexplicable by anything but animus.'" *Ante,* at 33 (quoting *Romer v. Evans,* 517 U.S. 620, 632, 635 (1996)); see also *Cleburne v. Cleburne Living Center, Inc.,* 473 U.S. 432, 448 (1985) (recognizing that classifications predicated on discriminatory animus can never be legitimate because the Government has no legitimate interest in exploiting "mere negative attitudes, or fear" toward a disfavored group). The President's statements, which the majority utterly fails to address in its legal analysis, strongly support the conclusion that the Proclamation was issued to express hostility toward Muslims and exclude them from the country. Given the overwhelming record evidence of anti-Muslim animus, it simply cannot be said that the Proclamation has a legitimate basis. *IRAP II,* 883 F.3d, at 352 (Harris, J., concurring) (explaining that the Proclamation contravenes the bedrock principle "that the government may not act on the basis of *animus* toward a disfavored religious minority" (emphasis in original)). . . .

. . . [E]ven a cursory review of the Government's asserted national-security rationale reveals that the Proclamation is nothing more than a "'religious gerrymander.'" *Lukumi,* 508 U.S., at 535.

The majority first emphasizes that the Proclamation "says nothing about religion." Even so, the Proclamation, just like its predecessors, overwhelmingly targets Muslim-majority nations. Given the record here, including all the President's statements linking the Proclamation to his apparent hostility toward Muslims, it is of no moment that the Proclamation also includes minor restrictions on two non-Muslim majority countries, North Korea and Venezuela, or that the Government has removed a few Muslim-majority countries from the list of covered countries since EO-1 was issued. Consideration of the entire record supports the conclusion that the inclusion of North Korea and Venezuela, and the removal of other countries, simply reflect subtle efforts to start "talking territory instead of Muslim," precisely so the Executive

6. The majority chides as "problematic" the importation of Establishment Clause jurisprudence "in the national security and foreign affairs context." As the majority sees it, this Court's Establishment Clause precedents do not apply to cases involving "immigration policies, diplomatic sanctions, and military actions." But just because the Court has not confronted the precise situation at hand does not render these cases (or the principles they announced) inapplicable. Moreover, the majority's complaint regarding the lack of direct authority is a puzzling charge, given that the majority itself fails to cite any "authority for its proposition" that a more probing review is inappropriate in a case like this one, where United States citizens allege that the Executive has violated the Establishment Clause by issuing a sweeping executive order motivated by animus. In any event, even if there is no prior case directly on point, it is clear from our precedent that "[w]hatever power the United States Constitution envisions for the Executive" in the context of national security and foreign affairs, "it most assuredly envisions a role for all three branches when individual liberties are at stake." *Hamdi v. Rumsfeld,* 542 U.S. 507, 536 (2004) (plurality opinion). This Court's Establishment Clause precedents require that, if a reasonable observer would understand an executive action to be driven by discriminatory animus, the action be invalidated. See *McCreary,* 545 U.S., at 860. That reasonable-observer inquiry includes consideration of the Government's asserted justifications for its actions. The Government's invocation of a national-security justification, however, does not mean that the Court should close its eyes to other relevant information. Deference is different from unquestioning acceptance. Thus, what is "far more problematic" in this case is the majority's apparent willingness to throw the Establishment Clause out the window and forgo any meaningful constitutional review at the mere mention of a national-security concern.

Branch could evade criticism or legal consequences for the Proclamation's otherwise clear targeting of Muslims. . . .

The majority next contends that the Proclamation "reflects the results of a worldwide review process undertaken by multiple Cabinet officials." . . .

. . . [T]he worldwide review does little to break the clear connection between the Proclamation and the President's anti-Muslim statements. . . .

. . . [T]he majority empowers the President to hide behind an administrative review process that the Government refuses to disclose to the public. See *IRAP II*, 883 F.3d, at 268 ("[T]he Government chose not to make the review publicly available" even in redacted form); *IRAP v. Trump*, No. 17-2231 (CA4), Doc. 126 (Letter from S. Swingle, Counsel for Defendants-Appellants, to P. Connor, Clerk of the United States Court of Appeals for the Fourth Circuit (Nov. 24, 2017)) (resisting Fourth Circuit's request that the Government supplement the record with the reports referenced in the Proclamation). Furthermore, evidence of which we can take judicial notice indicates that the multiagency review process could not have been very thorough. . . .

Beyond that, Congress has already addressed the national-security concerns supposedly undergirding the Proclamation through an "extensive and complex" framework governing "immigration and alien status." *Arizona v. United States*, 567 U.S. 387, 395 (2012). The Immigration and Nationality Act sets forth, in painstaking detail, a reticulated scheme regulating the admission of individuals to the United States. . . .

. . . Tellingly, the Government remains wholly unable to articulate any credible national-security interest that would go unaddressed by the current statutory scheme absent the Proclamation. . . .

Moreover, the Proclamation purports to mitigate national-security risks by excluding nationals of countries that provide insufficient information to vet their nationals. Yet, as plaintiffs explain, the Proclamation broadly denies immigrant visas to all nationals of those countries, including those whose admission would likely not implicate these information deficiencies (*e.g.*, infants, or nationals of countries included in the Proclamation who are long-term residents of and traveling from a country not covered by the Proclamation). In addition, the Proclamation permits certain nationals from the countries named in the Proclamation to obtain nonimmigrant visas, which undermines the Government's assertion that it does not already have the capacity and sufficient information to vet these individuals adequately. . . .

In sum, none of the features of the Proclamation highlighted by the majority supports the Government's claim that the Proclamation is genuinely and primarily rooted in a legitimate national-security interest. What the unrebutted evidence actually shows is that a reasonable observer would conclude, quite easily, that the primary purpose and function of the Proclamation is to disfavor Islam by banning Muslims from entering our country. . . .

IV . . .

Today's holding is all the more troubling given the stark parallels between the reasoning of this case and that of *Korematsu v. United States*, 323 U.S. 214 (1944). In *Korematsu*, the Court gave "a pass [to] an odious, gravely injurious racial classification" authorized by an executive order. *Adarand Constructors, Inc. v. Peña*, 515 U.S. 200, 275 (1995) (Ginsburg, J., dissenting). As here, the Government invoked an ill-defined national-security threat to justify an exclusionary policy of sweeping proportion. As here, the exclusion order was rooted in dangerous stereotypes about, *inter alia*, a particular group's supposed inability to assimilate and desire to harm the United States. See *Korematsu*, 323 U.S., at 236-240 (Murphy, J., dissenting). As here, the Government was unwilling to reveal its own intelligence agencies' views of the alleged security concerns to the very citizens it purported to protect. Compare *Korematsu v. United States*, 584 F. Supp. 1406, 1418-1419 (ND Cal. 1984) (discussing information the Government knowingly omitted from report presented to the courts justifying the executive order); Brief for Karen Korematsu et al. as *Amici Curiae* 35-36, and n. 5 (noting that the Government "has gone to great lengths to shield [the Secretary of Homeland Security's] report from view"). And as here, there was strong evidence that impermissible hostility and animus motivated the Government's policy.

Although a majority of the Court in *Korematsu* was willing to uphold the Government's actions based on a barren invocation of national security, dissenting Justices warned of that decision's harm to our constitutional fabric. Justice Murphy recognized that there is a need for great deference to the Executive Branch in the context of national security, but cautioned that "it is essential that there be definite limits to [the government's] discretion," as "[i]ndividuals must not be left impoverished of their constitutional rights on a plea of military necessity that has neither substance nor support." 323 U.S., at 234 (Murphy, J., dissenting). Justice Jackson lamented that the Court's decision upholding the Government's policy would prove to be "a far more subtle blow to liberty than the promulgation of the order itself," for although the executive order was not likely to be long lasting, the Court's willingness to tolerate it would endure. *Id.*, at 245-246.

In the intervening years since *Korematsu*, our Nation has done much to leave its sordid legacy behind. See, *e.g.*, Civil Liberties Act of 1988, 50 U.S.C. App. §4211 *et seq.* (setting forth remedies to individuals affected by the executive order at issue in *Korematsu*); Non-Detention Act of 1971, 18 U.S.C. §4001(a) (forbidding the imprisonment or detention by the United States of any citizen absent an Act of Congress). Today, the Court takes the important step of finally overruling *Korematsu*, denouncing it as "gravely wrong the day it was decided." (citing *Korematsu*, 323 U.S., at 248 (Jackson, J., dissenting)). This formal repudiation of a shameful precedent is laudable and long overdue. But it does not make the majority's decision here acceptable or right. By blindly accepting the Government's misguided invitation to sanction a discriminatory policy motivated by animosity toward a disfavored group, all in the name of a superficial claim of national security, the Court redeploys the same dangerous logic underlying *Korematsu* and merely replaces one "gravely wrong" decision with another.

Our Constitution demands, and our country deserves, a Judiciary willing to hold the coordinate branches to account when they defy our most sacred legal commitments. Because the Court's decision today has failed in that respect, with profound regret, I dissent.

Notes and Questions

1. Justiciability. The government made a double-barreled attack on justiciability in the travel ban cases. First, it argued for "consular nonreviewability," the doctrine that a decision to issue or withhold a visa is not subject to judicial review.

See Li Hing of Hong Kong, Inc. v. Levin, 800 F.2d 970, 971 (9th Cir. 1986) ("[I]t has been consistently held that the consular official's decision to issue or withhold a visa is not subject either to administrative or judicial review."). Given the sweep of the travel ban orders and the Proclamation, and the constitutional bases of some of the plaintiffs' claims, can you rebut this argument? *See Hawaii,* 859 F.3d at 768 ("Plaintiffs do not seek review of an individual consular officer's decision to grant or to deny a visa pursuant to valid regulations, which could implicate the consular nonreviewability doctrine. Plaintiffs instead challenge 'the President's *promulgation* of sweeping immigration policy.' Courts can and do review both constitutional and statutory 'challenges to the substance and implementation of immigration policy.'") (citations omitted); *see also Kerry v. Din,* 135 S. Ct. 2128 (2015) (reaching a due process claim in the face of an assertion of consular non-reviewability). Second, the government sometimes argued that the President's immigration decisions, *particularly when motivated by national security concerns,* were unreviewable. Do the national security cases you have read elsewhere in the casebook support such a claim? Is it consistent with what you understand to be the constitutional structure?

In *Trump v. Hawaii,* the Supreme Court dodged the issue, "assuming without deciding that plaintiffs' statutory claims are reviewable." Why do you think it did so?

2. The Statutory Claims. The plaintiffs argued that what Justice Sotomayor with considerable understatement calls the INA's "reticulated scheme" for admission of aliens already addressed the risk that the Proclamation purportedly addressed, and that the President lacked the authority to override the congressional judgments reflected in that scheme. Even if the INA scheme and the Proclamation targeted the same risk, did the Proclamation countermand or just supplement the former? *See* Marty Lederman, *Travel Ban III: Why the Court Does Not Have to Second-Guess Any (Nonexistent) Presidential National Security Decisions,* Just Security, Apr. 26, 2018. What answer did the majority give?

At first glance, 8 U.S.C. §1152(a) (2018) (see *supra* p. 795) (banning "discrimination . . . because of the person's . . . nationality"), appears to apply unambiguously to the travel bans. Why did the majority reject the statutory challenge based on this provision? Identify the specific executive action to which the provision applies. How, if at all, is the executive action described in 8 U.S.C. §1182(f) different?

3. The Rational Basis Standard of Review. As Justice Sotomayor points out, the courts have usually applied strict scrutiny to Establishment Clause challenges to government action. The majority, however, reads *Kleindienst v. Mandel,* 408 U.S. 753 (1972), to dilute that rigorous standard into mere rational basis review. Once a court applies mere rational basis review to a challenged government action, the answer is usually foreordained: the government wins. See *supra* pp. 806-807 ("[I]t should come as no surprise that the Court hardly ever strikes down a policy as illegitimate under rational basis scrutiny").

But was rational basis the right standard? The majority cited no authority other than *Mandel* for this standard, and then described it by reference to an equal protection challenge to a retirement scheme that distinguished among classes of annuitants. *See U.S. Railroad Retirement Board v. Fritz,* 449 U.S. 166, 179 (1980). The alleged discrimination against one class there was not based on any invidious classification or religious identification. Granted that the courts have generally been deferential to the executive branch in matters of national security or foreign policy, should they also defer to the same extent in assessing substantial claims of religious discrimination or other civil rights deprivations? That is, should national security deference trump strict scrutiny? Or is it precisely when the government invokes national security to affect core constitutional rights that a more rigorous standard of review is needed for their protection?

Does *Hassan v. City of New York* (*supra* p. 791) survive *Trump v. Hawaii*?

4. The "Facial" Standard of Review. The majority in *Trump v. Hawaii* looked chiefly to *Mandel* for its standard of review for the Establishment Clause claim. In that 1972 case the Court declared that when the executive supplies "a facially legitimate and bona fide reason for its action, the courts will neither look behind the exercise of that discretion, nor test it by balancing its justification against the asserted constitutional interests of U.S. citizens." 408 U.S. at 770. In other words, the majority reasoned, such a reason "would put an end to our review."

But did the *Hawaii* majority read *Mandel* correctly? It requires "a facially legitimate *and* bona fide reason" (emphasis added). Didn't the Court have to look behind a facially legitimate Proclamation to satisfy itself that the Proclamation was also "bona fide"? The Court says "we may consider plaintiffs' extrinsic evidence." But where in the majority opinion is there evidence that it did so?

5. Looking Behind the Curtain. If the Court could look "behind the face of the Proclamation to the extent of applying rational basis review," what "extrinsic evidence" do you think it should have considered?

The evolution of the executive policies? Recall that EO-1, banning entry, morphed into EO-2, temporarily suspending entry pending a worldwide review, and then into the Proclamation, narrowing slightly, but continuing the suspension based upon that review. What about public comments by the President? Or his tweets? (Justice Sotomayor noted that "[a]ccording to the White House, President Trump's statements on Twitter are 'official statements.'" *See also Knight First Amendment Inst. at Columbia Univ. v. Trump,* 928 F.3d 226 (2d Cir. 2019) (holding that control of the @realDonaldTrump account is governmental)). What about comments by other members of the executive branch? If so, which ones? "Informal consultants" like former Mayor Giuliani? How formal and how nearly contemporaneous must such comments be? What about statements by *candidate* Trump during the presidential campaign? How are they different from his tweets as President?

If you think the Court should have considered *all* of this evidence, would you trust the Court not to cherry-pick the elements that support a desired outcome? Would considering all such evidence risk confusing "the statements of a particular President" with "the authority of the Presidency itself," as the majority seems to worry? Would it over-empower the courts?

Suppose you look just at the text of the Proclamation. Might the Court uphold an order on the basis of its "facial neutrality," even though the President tweets, "I just told my lawyers to call it something else, but this is the ban on Muslims that I promised"? In the alternative, if in a constitutional challenge to the order extrinsic evidence of pretext is considered, under the majority's conflation of *Mandel* and rational basis review, how should it view this particular piece of evidence?

The majority clearly was uncomfortable with some of the extrinsic evidence. Indeed, after asserting that it would look behind the face of the Proclamation, it did not cite a single statement or tweet by the President. *See* Elizabeth Goitein, *Trump v. Hawaii: Giving Pretext a Pass,* Just Security (June 27, 2018) ("The section of the opinion that performs the 'rational basis' review contains not a single word about the president's anti-Muslim statements.... The court did not expressly hold that a president may intentionally discriminate on the basis of race or religion in national security policies, as long as he comes up with a pretext that has some minimal quantum of evidentiary support. But that is the functional outcome of the court's approach."). It defended its approach by explaining that "we must consider not only the statements of a particular President, but also the authority of the Presidency itself." But how clear is the line between the "particular President" and the "authority of the Presidency," when the challenged executive orders or proclamations are not mandated by statute and deliberately reverse past executive actions? Would the *Hawaii* Court have been better off saying nothing at all about the President's statements?

6. Lost in Litigation: The Policy Question. Is banning Muslims, or even just travelers from the Muslim-majority countries named in the Proclamation (as amended), good antiterrorist policy? Consider the practical problems and costs and benefits of profiling discussed in the casebook (*supra* pp. 790-791, as well as the likely impact on Muslim immigrant communities *already* legally resident in the United States, not to mention Muslim citizens. Is there any way other than a ban to reduce the likelihood that dangerous persons will enter the United States from areas abroad that are experiencing serious terrorist violence? If you have read *Korematsu v. United States,* 323 U.S. 214 (1944) (*infra* p. 876), you will recognize this as a variant on a question posed by *Korematsu*: Was there any way other than wholesale internment to reduce any threat to national security posed by Japanese-Americans in the United States during World War II? One of the many reasons for *Korematsu*'s infamy is that the answer in that case was "yes," but the Justices were kept in the dark thanks to a misleading (if not affirmatively untruthful) brief filed by the Justice Department (one for which the Acting Solicitor General formally apologized in 2011). Is there reason to worry that the Court relied upon a similarly pretextual assertion of national security here?

7. Still Looking Behind the Curtain. The Supreme Court's decision did not necessarily prevent other courts from looking behind the curtain, because it stressed that, "*[u]nder these circumstances,* the Government has set forth a sufficient national security justification to survive rational basis review." 138 S. Ct. at 2423 (emphasis added). In *Arab American Civil Rights League v. Trump,* 399 F. Supp. 3d 717 (E.D. Mich. 2019), *appeal docketed sub. nom In re Trump,* No. 19-114 (6th Cir. Nov. 8, 2019), the court looked to what it characterized as different circumstances to deny the government's motion to dismiss another challenge to the latest travel ban:

> The same day the Proclamation was issued, President Trump's deputy press secretary said that "the companion [P]roclamation" — i.e., a companion to EO-1 and EO2 — addresses the issues President Trump had been talking about for years, "from the campaign trail to the White House." Notably, what President Trump made explicit while on the campaign trail was his desire and intention to ban Muslims from entering the United States — even if it meant framing the ban in terms of "territories." President Trump has

> never disguised his true goal or the purpose of the ban; at all steps up to and after issuing the Proclamation, he has admitted that "[t]he Muslim Ban is something that in some form has morphed into extreme vetting from certain areas of the world" because "[p]eople were so upset when I used the word 'Muslim.'"
>
> Accepting Plaintiffs' allegations as true and drawing all inferences in their favor — as is required at this stage — it is reasonable to infer that the "morphed" executive orders and "companion" Proclamation "rest on an irrational prejudice against [Muslims]," [*City of Cleburne v. Cleburne Living Center,* 473 U.S. 432, 450 (1985)] at 450, and are "inexplicable by anything but animus toward [Muslims]," [*Romer v. Evans,* 517 U.S. 620, 632, 632 (1996)], especially considering that President Trump admitted that the "Muslim ban" only morphed into "extreme vetting" because "people were so upset" when he vociferously discriminated against Muslims.
>
> Plaintiffs plausibly allege sufficient facts to demonstrate that the Proclamation is not rationally related to national security goals of preventing inadequately vetted individuals and inducing other nations to improve information sharing. *See IRAP,* 373 F. Supp. 3d at 676. Indeed, Plaintiffs present sufficient evidence that the Proclamation is unable to be explained by anything but animus towards Muslims. [399 F. Supp. 3d at 729.]

Is the district court's consideration of this evidence consistent with *Trump v. Hawaii*?

8. Nationality/Religion-Based Profiling at the Border. In *Tabbaa v. Chertoff,* 509 F.3d 89 (2d Cir. 2007), Customs and Border Protection agents received classified information giving them reason to believe that terrorists or persons with terrorist ties would be attending a Muslim religious conference in Canada, which drew 13,000 individuals from across North America. Without any particularized suspicion, the agents then stopped a group of Muslim U.S. citizens at the border on their return from the conference and frisked, fingerprinted, photographed, questioned, and detained them for four to six hours, without telling them why they had been pulled aside. When these citizens challenged these actions in court, the court of appeals ultimately ruled that, as "routine" border searches, the actions did not violate the Fourth Amendment. It also held that the actions did not violate the plaintiffs' First Amendment rights of association or religious freedom under a strict scrutiny test, because they served a compelling counterterrorism need, and, *at the border,* this need could not have been satisfied by any significantly less restrictive means. *Id.* at 102-105.

Compare *Tabbaa* with *Tanvir v. Tanzin,* 894 F.3d 449 (2d Cir. 2018), *cert. granted,* No. 19-71, 2019 WL 6222538 (U.S. Nov. 22, 2019). Tanvir and his fellow Muslim plaintiffs had become either citizens or permanent resident aliens after immigrating to the United States. They had family in Pakistan (and possibly Afghanistan) whom they desired to visit from time to time. Alleging that the FBI threatened to and did place them on the no-fly list unless they agreed to spy and inform on their Muslim communities abroad, they brought claims for damages under the First Amendment and the Religious Freedom Restoration Act (RFRA). The court of appeals concluded, "[W]e hold that RFRA, like Section 1983, authorizes a plaintiff to bring individual capacity claims against federal officials or other 'person[s] acting under color of [federal] law.'" *Id.* at 462. Can you see how the border search doctrine does not insulate the alleged FBI conduct in *Tanvir*? After *Trump v. Hawaii,* should the court apply heightened scrutiny or rational basis review to the Establishment Clause claim in *Tanvir*? Do you think it would make any difference to the outcome? If so, why?

SUMMARY OF BASIC PRINCIPLES: PROFILING AND TRAVEL BANS

- Probable-cause arrests may not be based on ethnic or racial factors alone, but such factors may be considered when they contribute to a particularized and objective basis for suspecting criminal activity, such as when they are used in a specific suspect description.

- However, ambiguities in suspect descriptions may leave too much discretion to the screeners or arresting officers, enabling stereotyping, with both individual and systemic costs.

- The Department of Justice has barred the use of racial and other suspect characteristics in routine or spontaneous law enforcement decisions, except in a specific suspect description.

- The Department of Justice permits broader use of racial and other suspect characteristics (and resulting profiling) for some non-routine law enforcement activities, notably to link persons to an identified criminal organization or to a national security threat, provided the characteristics meet certain requirements designed to prevent reliance on generalized stereotypes.

- The President has broad statutory discretion to restrict entry to the United States on the basis of nationality, and the Supreme Court ruled in *Trump v. Hawaii* that President Trump acted within his statutory authority in issuing the facially neutral Proclamation No. 9645, banning travel from some Muslim-majority countries (subject to waivers).

- Rational basis review, rather than heightened scrutiny, may apply to Establishment Clause (and possibly Equal Protection Clause) challenges to executive action involving immigration, diplomatic sanctions, or military actions.

- Even when the President and his advisers have made statements at odds with the facial justification of some government action, courts must consider not just "the statements of a particular President, but also the authority of the Presidency itself," in deciding the legality of the action. In practice, this may mean discounting such statements.

PART V DETAINING TERRORIST SUSPECTS

27

Habeas Corpus: The Structure of the Suspension Clause

In what circumstances, if any, may the U.S. government imprison individuals who have not been charged with a crime? Although this question may arise in contexts far removed from national security law, it is of especial significance here, where the government often claims the need to incapacitate individuals for reasons other than criminal punishment. In this part of the casebook, we turn to the important and intricate legal questions raised by such detention, both in the abstract and in the more specific context of contemporary counterterrorism operations.

We begin with the writ of habeas corpus *ad subjiciendum*— the "Great Writ," as Blackstone put it. At common law, such a writ was a judicial order directing a jailor to return to court with the body of a named detainee (hence the title of a popular historical novel set during Henry VIII's reign: *Bring Up the Bodies*, by Hilary Mantel), so that the issuing judge could inquire into the legality of the detainee's confinement. Colloquially, the writ of habeas corpus could be styled a protection against being "disappeared." Blackstone thought of it as the very core of liberty:

> Of great importance to the public is the preservation of this personal liberty: for if once it were left in the power of any, the highest, magistrate to imprison arbitrarily whomever he or his officers thought proper . . . there would soon be an end of all other rights and immunities. . . . To bereave a man of life, or by violence to confiscate his estate, without accusation or trial, would be so gross and notorious an act of despotism, as must at once convey the alarm of tyranny throughout the whole kingdom. But confinement of the person, by secretly hurrying him to gaol, where his sufferings are unknown or forgotten; is a less public, a less striking, and therefore a more dangerous engine of arbitrary government. . . .
>
> To make imprisonment lawful, it must either be, by process from the courts of judicature, or by warrant from some legal officer, having authority to commit to prison; which warrant must be in writing, under the hand and seal of the magistrate, and express the causes of the commitment, in order to be examined into (if necessary) upon a *habeas corpus*. If there be no cause expressed, the gaoler is not bound [permitted] to detain the prisoner. For the law judges in this respect, . . . that it is unreasonable to send a prisoner, and

> not to signify withal the crimes alleged against him. [1 William Blackstone, *Commentaries* *132-133 (1765), *quoted in Hamdi v. Rumsfeld*, 542 U.S. 507, 555 (2004) (Scalia, J., dissenting).]

In other words, Blackstone argued that the right to petition for the writ and have a neutral magistrate judge the legality of one's imprisonment is the most basic right, essential to the exercise of all others, because a person who is disappeared — seized by the government and secretly locked away in a dungeon — cannot exercise any other right from that black hole.

The right to petition for the writ of habeas corpus was not created by the U.S. Constitution. Instead, the so-called Suspension Clause provides that "the Privilege of the Writ of Habeas Corpus shall not be suspended unless when in cases of Rebellion or Invasion the public Safety may require it." U.S. Const. art. I, §9, cl. 2. All agree that the Suspension Clause has some bearing on when and how the U.S. government can hold at least *some* individuals without charges or trial. Beyond that, however, questions about the Suspension Clause abound. For example:

- What is the "Privilege of the Writ of Habeas Corpus" that, absent suspension, the Constitution protects?
- Who may claim that privilege?
- Which branch may suspend the privilege?
- What does it mean to suspend the privilege?
- When, in "cases of Rebellion or Invasion," would "the public Safety" require suspension of the privilege?

Complicating matters, the Supreme Court has seldom even *construed* the Suspension Clause. Instead, the Justices have routinely invoked the difficulty of asking (let alone answering) these questions as a reason to interpret various statutes to *not* implicate the Suspension Clause. *See, e.g., INS v. St. Cyr*, 533 U.S. 289, 301 n.13 (2001) ("The fact that this Court would be required to answer the difficult question of what the Suspension Clause protects is in and of itself a reason to avoid answering the constitutional questions that would be raised by concluding that review was barred entirely."). Thus, before turning to more specific questions concerning the contemporary scope of the Suspension Clause in Chapter 28 (and to the substantive detention authorities available to the government in Chapters 29, 30, and 31), this chapter aims to introduce the Suspension Clause through its history and structure. We begin with the origins of the Suspension Clause in pre-1787 British practice and precedent, then carry the story forward by introducing the current statutory provisions regarding habeas corpus — and their relatively staid history. Next we turn to the Civil War-era debate over *which* branch of the government may suspend the writ. Finally, we describe the technical but significant debate over what actually *happens* in the exceptionally rare cases in which habeas is properly suspended.

A. THE ORIGINS OF THE SUSPENSION CLAUSE

The Supreme Court has assumed that, at a minimum, the Constitution protects the scope of the writ of habeas corpus "as it existed in 1789." *St. Cyr*, 533 U.S. at 301.

For that reason, and to inform what the Constitution's drafters understood the "Privilege of the Writ of Habeas Corpus" to entail, any study of the Suspension Clause must begin with pre-revolutionary English practice.

As one comprehensive archival study of that practice has demonstrated, habeas corpus emerged in the seventeenth century not out of a desire to guard against arbitrary, indefinite executive imprisonment, but rather as an instrument of increasing judicial power — as the means by which the King's Bench increasingly came to assert its authority, first at the expense of other judicial tribunals, and eventually at the expense of Parliament and the King himself. *See* Paul Halliday, *Habeas Corpus: From England to Empire* 160 (2010). "At the center of this jurisprudence stood the idea that the court might inspect imprisonment orders made at any time, anywhere, by any authority. This simple idea, grounded in the prerogative, marked the point from which the justices' use of the writ expanded." *Id.* at 160. To be sure, the increased judicial power that resulted from this practice enabled English judges better to vindicate the (ever-expanding) rights of those held unlawfully, but the protection of individual rights was only a side effect of the more fundamental goal of providing an institutional check on parliamentary (and, increasingly, royal) authority.

Importantly, most of this practice was grounded in the common law — and not statutes. Although Parliament sought to codify at least some of the writ's expanding scope in the Habeas Corpus Act of 1679, pre-revolutionary English judicial practice was replete with examples of judges blending principles of common law and equity to allow them to decide challenges to all forms of detention through habeas corpus, within and without the realm, and without regard for what Parliament had and had not authorized.

The rise of such judicial power eventually provoked a backlash from Parliament, which began passing acts in the 1680s that were somewhat misleadingly called "suspension acts" — measures that, for example, empowered the Privy Council to imprison individuals alleged to have committed treason, or held on suspicion of treason, without "Baile or Mainprize." As importantly, suspension acts typically provided for a period of imprisonment, "any Law or Statute to the contrary notwithstanding." *See, e.g.*, 1 W. & M., c. 2 (Eng.). Thus, a suspension act "operated not by [literally] suspending habeas corpus, but by expanding detention powers," Halliday, *supra*, at 249, mooting the immediate effect of the writ by suspending the relief it could provide, albeit for a finite (and very short) period of time. In pre-revolutionary England, then, "suspension" of habeas had the effect of authorizing detention without trial by displacing judicial review, at least temporarily.

The U.S. Constitution's Suspension Clause was a direct response to the broadest of these suspension acts — which Parliament enacted in 1777. As one of us has written,

> What changed in 1777 was, candidly, our fault. With rebellion afoot in the North American colonies, Parliament faced growing numbers of American sailors in English captivity. Holding the captives as prisoners of war would lend legitimacy to American claims of independence. Instead, Parliament suspended habeas corpus in an unprecedented manner. First, there was no claim of domestic emergency — no rebellion on the home island or threat of invasion that might provide the "necessity" that Parliament had previously relied upon as the basis for suspending the writ. Second, the period of suspension would eventually last for six years — all the way through the beginning of

> 1783 — by far the longest of any suspension Parliament had enacted to date. Third, the 1777 suspension distinguished among subjects for the first time, applying only to those arrested for treason in any colony, on the high seas, or for piracy, and exempting from its scope "any other Prisoner or Prisoners than such as shall have been out of the Realm at the Time or Times of the Offence or Offences wherewith he or they shall be charged." [Stephen I. Vladeck, *The New Habeas Revisionism*, 124 Harv. L. Rev. 941, 957 (2011) (reviewing Halliday, *supra*).]

Negative reaction to the 1777 Suspension Act meant that, at the 1787 Constitutional Convention in Philadelphia, the question was not whether the new Constitution would try to protect habeas corpus, but how it would do so.

Neither the debates at Philadelphia nor those that took place in the ratification conventions that followed shed specific light onto what the Constitution's drafters understood "the privilege of the writ of habeas corpus" to encompass. Nevertheless, "the framers of the Suspension Clause implicitly restored the traditional order of writs and suspensions that had existed before the Parliamentary suspension acts that began in 1777." Paul D. Halliday & G. Edward White, *The Suspension Clause: English Text, Imperial Contexts, and American Implications*, 94 Va. L. Rev. 575, 671 (2008).

Congress almost immediately codified the habeas privilege by statute — and, at least until 1996, gradually expanded its scope to encompass claims brought by individuals detained pursuant to virtually all state or federal criminal convictions. Thus, as the Supreme Court has observed,

> the habeas statute clearly has expanded habeas corpus "beyond the limits that obtained during the 17th and 18th centuries." But "[a]t its historical core, the writ of habeas corpus has served as a means of reviewing the legality of Executive detention, and it is in that context that its protections have been strongest." [*Rasul v. Bush*, 542 U.S. 466, 474 (2004) (internal citations omitted).]

B. THE HABEAS CORPUS STATUTE(S)

Whereas pre-revolutionary English practice primarily derived from the common law, habeas corpus practice in the U.S. federal courts has principally been a creature of statute since almost immediately after the Constitution was ratified — when Congress enacted Section 14 of the Judiciary Act of 1789.

Reading the Habeas Statute

The current habeas corpus statute describes the qualifications of persons entitled to seek the writ, as well as basic procedures for a court to follow in considering a petition for a writ.

- Who may seek the writ?
- Who bears the burden of demonstrating or disproving a legal justification for detention?
- What kind of hearing does the statute prescribe?
- What kind of relief may a court provide?

Habeas Corpus

28 U.S.C. §§2241-2255 (2018)

§2241. POWER TO GRANT WRIT

(a) Writs of habeas corpus may be granted by the Supreme Court, any justice thereof, the district courts and any circuit judge within their respective jurisdictions. . . .

(c) The writ of habeas corpus shall not extend to a prisoner unless —

(1) He is in custody under or by color of the authority of the United States or is committed for trial before some court thereof; or

(2) He is in custody for an act done or omitted in pursuance of an Act of Congress, or an order, process, judgment or decree of a court or judge of the United States; or

(3) He is in custody in violation of the Constitution or laws or treaties of the United States. . . .

§2243. ISSUANCE OF WRIT; RETURN; HEARING; DECISION

A court, justice or judge entertaining an application for a writ of habeas corpus shall forthwith award the writ or issue an order directing the respondent to show cause why the writ should not be granted, unless it appears from the application that the applicant or person detained is not entitled thereto.

The writ, or order to show cause shall be directed to the person having custody of the person detained. It shall be returned within three days unless for good cause additional time, not exceeding twenty days, is allowed.

The person to whom the writ or order is directed shall make a return certifying the true cause of the detention.

When the writ or order is returned a day shall be set for hearing, not more than five days after the return unless for good cause additional time is allowed.

Unless the application for the writ and the return present only issues of law the person to whom the writ is directed shall be required to produce at the hearing the body of the person detained.

The applicant or the person detained may, under oath, deny any of the facts set forth in the return or allege any other material facts. . . .

The court shall summarily hear and determine the facts, and dispose of the matter as law and justice require.

Notes and Questions

1. Common Law Habeas vs. Statutory Habeas. Did enactment of a habeas statute replace the common law writ? In *Ex parte Bollman*, 8 U.S. (4 Cranch) 75 (1807), Chief Justice Marshall disclaimed the power of the federal courts to issue "common law" writs of habeas corpus, holding that federal jurisdiction over habeas petitions came exclusively from Section 14 of the Judiciary Act of 1789. Because common law habeas relief was unquestionably available at that time in state courts, such a conclusion raised no Suspension Clause questions. But the Supreme Court later rejected the power of state courts to provide habeas relief to those in *federal* custody in *Tarble's Case*, 80 U.S. (13 Wall.) 371 (1872). After *Tarble's Case*, should *Bollman* still be good law? If so, don't *Bollman* and *Tarble* suggest that relief for federal prisoners is entirely a creature of statute, since federal courts cannot issue common law writs and state courts cannot issue writs to individuals in federal custody? On that reading, won't courts be powerless to vindicate the Suspension Clause unless and until Congress specifically empowers them to do so? *See St. Cyr*, 533 U.S. at 341-342 (Scalia, J., dissenting). Wouldn't such a result radically undermine the purpose of the Suspension Clause?

2. Producing the Body — or Not. Both Section 14 of the Judiciary Act of 1789 and present-day 28 U.S.C. §2243 contemplate the physical production of the prisoner before the judge in the typical case. But, in keeping with the actual common law practice, virtually all statutory habeas petitions are resolved *before* the writ formally "issues," through "show cause" proceedings that allow for adjudication of the petitioner's claims without his actual appearance in court. The Supreme Court blessed this practice in *Walker v. Johnston*, 312 U.S. 275 (1941). Thus, today the "writ" typically issues only at the conclusion of the proceeding — to order the petitioner's release once the court has determined that his detention is unlawful.

3. The Broad Meaning of "Custody." Consider the breadth of 28 U.S.C. §2241(c)(3), which empowers the federal courts to review claims by anyone that they are "in custody in violation of the Constitution or laws or treaties of the United States." "Custody," in this context, could mean any number of things — and does not require current, physical confinement by the state or federal government. Thus, the Supreme Court has held that a petitioner can be in "custody" for purposes of the habeas statute sufficient to challenge a criminal conviction even if he is at liberty, so long as he is still serving some aspect of his sentence — including parole. *See Jones v. Cunningham*, 371 U.S. 236 (1963). The statute also encompasses potentially unlawful detention by non-governmental actors (for example, detention in violation of the Thirteenth Amendment). And the statute allows individuals to challenge their detention by *foreign* governments insofar as they allege that they are held at the behest of the United States — and that they are therefore in the "constructive custody" of the United States. *See, e.g., Abu Ali v. Ashcroft*, 350 F. Supp. 2d 28 (D.D.C. 2004).

4. The Territorial Scope of Section 2241(a). Section 2241(a) allows federal judges to provide habeas relief "within their respective jurisdictions." Before 1948 (and since 1973), this language was interpreted to confer subject-matter jurisdiction so long as a district court could lawfully assert personal jurisdiction over a proper respondent (typically, the jailor or his superior) — and so the *petitioner's* location was irrelevant. In *Ahrens v. Clark*, 335 U.S. 188 (1948), however, the Supreme Court read this same language to require habeas petitioners to file in the district in which they were confined. Although the Justices reserved "the question of what process, if any, a person confined in an area not subject to the jurisdiction of any district court may employ to assert federal rights," *id.* at 192 n.4, the decision was soon understood to foreclose statutory jurisdiction in such cases — raising the question whether detainees held overseas had a *constitutional* right of access to habeas (and provoking *Johnson v. Eisentrager*, 339 U.S. 763 (1950), discussed *infra* pp. 847-848).

In *Braden v. 30th Judicial Circuit Court of Kentucky*, 410 U.S. 484 (1973), the Court reverted to the pre-*Ahrens* understanding. Thus, when the first round of habeas petitions from Guantánamo detainees reached the Supreme Court in *Rasul v. Bush*, 542 U.S. 466 (2004), the Court held that the federal courts' statutory jurisdiction followed from *Braden*—because the district courts had personal jurisdiction over the government respondents (including President Bush, who was located in the District of Columbia).

C. SUSPENDING THE WRIT

Although the Suspension Clause appears in that part of the Constitution devoted to legislative powers, there is no express language clarifying which branch or branches possess the power to suspend the writ. The question arose in an early Civil War-era case, *Ex parte Merryman*, 17 F. Cas. 144 (C.C.D. Md. 1861) (No. 9487), when Chief Justice Taney ordered the release of a Southern sympathizer imprisoned without charge at Fort McHenry. John Merryman had been seized after President Lincoln signed an order authorizing suspension of the writ of habeas corpus. Said the Chief Justice, "I had supposed it to be one of those points in constitutional law upon which there was no difference of Opinion . . . that the privilege of the writ could not be suspended, except by act of congress." *Id.* at 148. However, Taney's decree was ignored by the President, and Merryman remained in military detention for a time. A month later, in a message to a special session of Congress, Lincoln remarked that Taney's interpretation of the constitutional requirement

> would allow all the laws, but one, to go unexecuted, and the government itself go to pieces, lest that one be violated. . . . [T]he Constitution itself, is silent as to which, or who, is to exercise the power; and as the provision was plainly made for a dangerous emergency, it cannot be believed the framers of the instrument intended, that in every case, the danger should run its course, until Congress could be called together; the very assembling of which might be prevented, as was intended in this case, by the rebellion. [4 *The Collected Works of Abraham Lincoln* 430-431 (Roy P. Basler ed., 1953).]

Five years later, the full Supreme Court made it clear that under some circumstances Congress may authorize the suspension of the writ by the President.

Reading *Ex parte Milligan*

The Supreme Court's 1866 decision in *Ex parte Milligan* is most famous for its unanimous (and heavy-handed) invalidation of military commissions unilaterally established by President Lincoln to try Confederate sympathizers during the Civil War — to which we will return in Chapter 36. But *Milligan* also includes the Supreme Court's most extended discussion of congressional authority for suspension of habeas corpus — to wit, the Habeas Corpus Act of 1863. As you read the following excerpt, consider these questions:

- Given Congress's authorization to suspend habeas corpus in the 1863 Act, how did the Supreme Court even have the power to hear Milligan's (habeas!) challenge to his trial by military commission?
- Which branch did the Court say had the power to suspend the privilege of the writ?

Ex parte Milligan

United States Supreme Court, 1866
71 U.S. (4 Wall.) 2

[The Habeas Corpus Act of 1863 authorized President Abraham Lincoln to suspend the writ of habeas corpus, subject to certain limitations. The statute was summarized in the headnotes to this case as follows:

> The first section authorizes the suspension, during the Rebellion, of the writ of habeas corpus, throughout the United States, by the President.
>
> Two following sections limited the authority in certain respects.
>
> The second section required that lists of all persons, being citizens of States in which the administration of the laws had continued unimpaired in the Federal courts, who were then held, or might thereafter be held, as prisoners of the United States, under the authority of the President, otherwise than as prisoners of war, should be furnished by the Secretary of State and Secretary of War to the judges of the Circuit and District Courts. These lists were to contain the names of all persons, residing within their respective jurisdictions, charged with violation of national law. And it was required, in cases where the grand jury in attendance upon any of these courts should terminate its session without proceeding by indictment or otherwise against any prisoner named in the list, that the judge of the court should forthwith make an order that such prisoner, desiring a discharge, should be brought before him or the court to be discharged, on entering into recognizance, if required, to keep the peace and for good behavior, or to appear, as the court might direct, to be further dealt with according to law. Every officer of the United States having custody of such prisoners was required to obey and execute the judge's order, under penalty, for refusal or delay, of fine and imprisonment.
>
> The third section enacts, in case lists of persons other than prisoners of war then held in confinement, or thereafter arrested, should not be furnished within twenty days after the passage of the act, or, in cases of subsequent arrest, within twenty days after the time of arrest, that any citizen, after the termination of a session of the grand jury without indictment or presentment, might, by petition alleging the facts and verified by oath, obtain the judge's order of discharge in favor of any person so imprisoned, on the terms and conditions prescribed in the second section. [*Ex parte Milligan*, 71 U.S. (4 Wall.) 2, 4-5 (1866).]

Lambdin P. Milligan, a resident of Indiana, was arrested at his home in October 1864 by order of General Alvin P. Hovey, commander of the military district of Indiana, and held in close confinement "otherwise than as [a] prisoner[] of war." He was then brought before a military tribunal in Indianapolis, tried on charges ranging from conspiracy against the government to inciting insurrection, found guilty, and sentenced to be hanged.

In the meantime, on January 2, 1865, the United States Circuit Court for Indiana had met at Indianapolis and empaneled a grand jury to inquire whether any laws of the United States had been broken by anyone and to make presentments. The grand jury did not find any bill of indictment or make any presentment against Milligan, and on January 27 the court adjourned after discharging the grand jury from further service.

Milligan then petitioned the Circuit Court for his release, citing the foregoing statute and arguing that the military tribunal had no jurisdiction to try him. We provide here only the first part of the resulting opinion, respecting the suspension of the writ of habeas corpus. We take up later parts of the majority opinion *infra* pp. 1124 and 1209.]

Mr. Justice DAVIS delivered the opinion of the court. . . . The importance of the main question presented by this record cannot be overstated; for it involves the very framework of the government and the fundamental principles of American liberty.

During the late wicked Rebellion, the temper of the times did not allow that calmness in deliberation and discussion so necessary to a correct conclusion of a purely judicial question. *Then,* considerations of safety were mingled with the exercise of power; and feelings and interests prevailed which are happily terminated. *Now* that the public safety is assured, this question, as well as all others, can be discussed and decided without passion or the admixture of any element not required to form a legal judgment. . . .

Milligan claimed his discharge from custody by virtue of the act of Congress "relating to *habeas corpus* and regulating judicial proceedings in certain cases," approved March 3d, 1863. Did that act confer jurisdiction on the Circuit Court of Indiana to hear this case?

In interpreting a law, the motives which must have operated with the legislature in passing it are proper to be considered. This law was passed in a time of great national peril, when our heritage of free government was in danger. An armed rebellion against the national authority, of greater proportions than history affords an example of, was raging; and the public safety required that the privilege of the writ of *habeas corpus* should be suspended. The President had practically suspended it, and detained suspected persons in custody without trial; but his authority to do this was questioned. It was claimed that Congress alone could exercise this power; and that the legislature, and not the President, should judge of the political considerations on which the right to suspend it rested. The privilege of this great writ had never before been withheld from the citizen; and as the exigence of the times demanded immediate action, it was of the highest importance that the lawfulness of the suspension should be fully established. It was under these circumstances, which were such as to arrest the attention of the country, that this law was passed. The President was authorized by it to suspend the privilege of the writ of *habeas corpus,* whenever, in his judgment, the public safety required; and he did, by proclamation, bearing date the 15th of September, 1863, reciting, among other things, the authority of this statute, suspend it. The suspension of the writ does not authorize the arrest of any one, but simply denies to one arrested the privilege of this writ in order to obtain his liberty.

It is proper, therefore, to inquire under what circumstances the courts could rightfully refuse to grant this writ, and when the citizen was at liberty to invoke its aid.

The second and third sections of the law are explicit on these points. The language used is plain and direct, and the meaning of the Congress cannot be mistaken. The public safety demanded, if the President thought proper to arrest a suspected person, that he should not be required to give the cause of his detention on return to a writ of *habeas corpus.* But it was not contemplated that such person should be detained in custody beyond a certain fixed period, unless certain judicial proceedings, known to the common law, were commenced against him....

Milligan, in his application to be released from imprisonment, averred the existence of every fact necessary under the terms of this law to give the Circuit Court of Indiana jurisdiction. If he was detained in custody by the order of the President, otherwise than as a prisoner of war; if he was a citizen of Indiana and had never been in the military or naval service, and the grand jury of the district had met, after he had been arrested, for a period of twenty days, and adjourned without taking any proceedings against him, *then* the court had the right to entertain his petition and determine the lawfulness of his imprisonment....

The controlling question in the case is this: Upon the *facts* stated in Milligan's petition, and the exhibits filed, had the military commission mentioned in it *jurisdiction,* legally, to try and sentence him?...

No graver question was ever considered by this court, nor one which more nearly concerns the rights of the whole people; for it is the birthright of every American citizen when charged with crime, to be tried and punished according to law. The power of punishment is, alone through the means which the laws have provided for that purpose, and if they are ineffectual, there is an immunity from punishment, no matter how great an offender the individual may be, or how much his crimes may have shocked the sense of justice of the country, or endangered its safety. By the protection of the law human rights are secured; withdraw that protection, and they are at the mercy of wicked rulers, or the clamor of an excited people. If there was law to justify this military trial, it is not our province to interfere; if there was not, it is our duty to declare the nullity of the whole proceedings. The decision of this question does not depend on argument or judicial precedents, numerous and highly illustrative as they are. These precedents inform us of the extent of the struggle to preserve liberty and to relieve those in civil life from military trials. The founders of our government were familiar with the history of that struggle; and secured in a written constitution every right which the people had wrested from power during a contest of ages. By that Constitution and the laws authorized by it this question must be determined. The provisions of that instrument on the administration of criminal justice are too plain and direct, to leave room for misconstruction or doubt of their true meaning. Those applicable to this case are found in that clause of the original Constitution which says, "That the trial of all crimes, except in case of impeachment, shall be by jury;" and in the fourth, fifth, and sixth articles of the amendments. The fourth proclaims the right to be secure in person and effects against unreasonable search and seizure; and directs that a judicial warrant shall not issue "without proof of probable cause supported by oath or affirmation." The fifth declares "that no person shall be held to answer for a capital or otherwise infamous crime unless on presentment by a grand jury, except in cases arising in the land or naval forces, or in the militia, when in actual service in time of war or public danger, nor be deprived of life, liberty, or property, without due process of law." And the sixth guarantees the right of trial by jury, in such manner and with such regulations that with upright judges, impartial juries, and an able bar, the innocent will be saved and the guilty punished....

Time has proven the discernment of our ancestors; for even these provisions, expressed in such plain English words, that it would seem the ingenuity of man could not evade them, are *now*, after the lapse of more than seventy years, sought to be avoided. Those great and good men foresaw that troublous times would arise, when rulers and people would become restive under restraint, and seek by sharp and decisive measures to accomplish ends deemed just and proper; and that the principles of constitutional liberty would be in peril, unless established by irrepealable law. The history of the world had taught them that what was done in the past might be attempted in the future. The Constitution of the United States is a law for rulers and people, equally in war and in peace, and covers with the shield of its protection all classes of men, at all times, and under all circumstances. No doctrine, involving more pernicious consequences, was ever invented by the wit of man than that any of its provisions can be suspended during any of the great exigencies of government. Such a doctrine leads directly to anarchy and despotism, but the theory of necessity on which it is based is false; for the government, within the Constitution, has all the powers granted to it, which are necessary to preserve its existence; as has been happily proved by the result of the great effort to throw off its just authority.

Have any of the rights guaranteed by the Constitution been violated in the case of Milligan? and if so, what are they?

Every trial involves the exercise of judicial power; and from what source did the military commission that tried him derive their authority? Certainly no part of the judicial power of the country was conferred on them; because the Constitution expressly vests it "in one supreme court and such inferior courts as the Congress may from time to time ordain and establish," and it is not pretended that the commission was a court ordained and established by Congress. They cannot justify on the mandate of the President; because he is controlled by law, and has his appropriate sphere of duty, which is to execute, not to make, the laws; and there is "no unwritten criminal code to which resort can be had as a source of jurisdiction."

But it is said that the jurisdiction is complete under the "laws and usages of war."

It can serve no useful purpose to inquire what those laws and usages are, whence they originated, where found, and on whom they operate; they can never be applied to citizens in states which have upheld the authority of the government, and where the courts are open and their process unobstructed. This court has judicial knowledge that in Indiana the Federal authority was always unopposed, and its courts always open to hear criminal accusations and redress grievances; and no usage of war could sanction a military trial there for any offence whatever of a citizen in civil life, in nowise connected with the military service. Congress could grant no such power; and to the honor of our national legislature be it said, it has never been provoked by the state of the country even to attempt its exercise. One of the plainest constitutional provisions was, therefore, infringed when Milligan was tried by a court not ordained and established by Congress, and not composed of judges appointed during good behavior.

Why was he not delivered to the Circuit Court of Indiana to be proceeded against according to law? No reason of necessity could be urged against it; because Congress had declared penalties against the offences charged, provided for their punishment, and directed that court to hear and determine them. And soon after this military tribunal was ended, the Circuit Court met, peacefully transacted its business, and adjourned. It needed no bayonets to protect it, and required no military aid to execute its judgments. It was held in a state, eminently distinguished for patriotism, by judges commissioned during the Rebellion, who were provided with juries, upright, intelligent, and selected by a marshal appointed by the President. The government had no right to conclude that Milligan, if guilty, would not receive in that court merited punishment; for its records disclose that it was constantly engaged in the trial of similar offences, and was never interrupted in its administration of criminal justice. If it was dangerous, in the distracted condition of affairs, to leave Milligan unrestrained of his liberty because he "conspired against the government, afforded aid and comfort to rebels, and incited the people to insurrection," the *law* said arrest him, confine him closely, render him powerless to do further mischief; and then present his case to the grand jury of the district, with proofs of his guilt, and, if indicted, try him according to the course of the common law. If this had been done, the Constitution would have been vindicated, the law of 1863 enforced, and the securities for personal liberty preserved and defended. . . .

This nation, as experience has proved, cannot always remain at peace, and has no right to expect that it will always have wise and humane rulers, sincerely attached to the principles of the Constitution. Wicked men, ambitious of power, with hatred of liberty and contempt of law, may fill the place once occupied by Washington and Lincoln; and if this right is conceded, and the calamities of war again befall us, the dangers to human liberty are frightful to contemplate. If our fathers had failed to provide for just such a contingency, they would have been false to the trust reposed in them. They knew — the history of the world told them — the nation they were founding, be its existence short or long, would be involved in war; how often or how long continued, human foresight could not tell; and that unlimited power, wherever lodged at such a time, was especially hazardous to freemen. For this, and other equally weighty reasons, they secured the inheritance they had fought to maintain, by incorporating in a written constitution the safeguards which *time* had proved were essential to its preservation. Not one of these safeguards can the President, or Congress, or the Judiciary disturb, except the one concerning the writ of *habeas corpus.*

It is essential to the safety of every government that, in a great crisis, like the one we have just passed through, there should be a power somewhere of suspending the writ of *habeas corpus.* In every war, there are men of previously good character, wicked enough to counsel their fellow-citizens to resist the measures deemed necessary by a good government to sustain its just authority and overthrow its enemies; and their influence may lead to dangerous combinations. In the emergency of the times, an immediate public investigation according to law may not be possible; and yet, the peril to the country may be too imminent to suffer such persons to go at large. Unquestionably, there is then an exigency which demands that the government, if it should see fit in the exercise of a proper discretion to make arrests, should not be required to produce the persons arrested in answer to a writ of *habeas corpus.* The Constitution goes no further. It does not say after a writ of *habeas corpus* is denied a citizen, that he shall be tried otherwise than by the course of the common law. . . .

If the military trial of Milligan was contrary to law, then he was entitled, on the facts stated in his petition, to be discharged from custody by the terms of the act of Congress of March 3d, 1863. . . .

The Chief Justice delivered the following opinion [in which Wayne, Swayne, and Miller, JJ., concurred]. . . . [The Chief Justice agreed that the military commission was without lawful jurisdiction to try Milligan.] But the opinion which has just been read goes further; and as we understand it, asserts not only that the military commission held in Indiana was not authorized by Congress, but that it was not in the power of Congress to authorize it. . . .

We think that Congress had power, though not exercised, to authorize the Military Commission which was held in Indiana. . . .

Congress cannot direct the conduct of campaigns, nor can the President, or any commander under him, without the sanction of Congress, institute tribunals for the trial and punishment of offences, either of soldiers or civilians, unless in cases of a controlling necessity, which justifies what it compels, or at least insures acts of indemnity from the justice of the legislature.

We by no means assert that Congress can establish and apply the laws of war where no war has been declared or exists.

Where peace exists the laws of peace must prevail. What we do maintain is, that when the nation is involved in war, and some portions of the country are invaded, and all are exposed to invasion, it is within the power of Congress to determine in what states or district such great and imminent public danger exists as justifies the authorization of military tribunals for the trial of crimes and offences against the discipline or security of the army or against the public safety. . . .

Notes and Questions

1. *Presidential Authority to Suspend the Writ?* Although the privilege of the writ has been suspended on several other occasions, the question raised by *Merryman* has not yet been squarely decided by the full Supreme Court. *But see Hamdi v. Rumsfeld*, 542 U.S. 507, 536 (2004) (plurality opinion) ("[U]nless Congress acts to suspend it, the Great Writ of habeas corpus allows the Judicial Branch to . . . [serve] as an important judicial check on the Executive's discretion in the realm of detentions."); *Bollman*, 8 U.S. (4 Cranch) at 101 (dictum) ("If at any time the public safety should require the suspension of the powers vested by this act in the courts of the United States, it is for the legislature to say so. That question depends on political considerations, on which the legislature is to decide."). Do you see any danger in allowing the President, acting alone, to suspend the writ, as Lincoln did?

What about a danger in *not* allowing the President, acting alone, to suspend? During the War of 1812, the British burned the Capitol building (after several tries). If Congress was unable to assemble, but British sympathizers had to be imprisoned for reasons of national security, which branch would best be able to suspend the writ to prevent challenges to such detentions? How, if at all, could the Suspension Clause be interpreted to balance the dangers?

2. *Non-Suspension Statutes and Constitutional Avoidance.* By the usual rules of statutory construction, courts should construe legislation or executive orders, when "fairly possible," to avoid significant constitutional questions. *See St. Cyr*, 533 U.S. at 299-300. It may be especially desirable to avoid having to decide whether the Executive alone may cut off access to the courts, because, "[a]t its historical core, the writ of habeas corpus has served as a means of reviewing the legality of executive detention, and it is in that context that its protections have been the strongest."

Id. at 301. Thus, in *St. Cyr*, the Court construed a statute to allow habeas access to the courts, even though the provision at issue was titled "Elimination of Custody Review by Habeas Corpus." The Court insisted that any effort to restrict the privilege of seeking the writ must be more clearly stated! *Id.* at 308-309 (finding that the provision's title was not controlling, where the actual statutory text never expressly mentioned habeas corpus). Justice Scalia criticized the majority for "fabricat[ing] a superclear statement, 'magic words' requirement for the congressional expression of such an intent, unjustified in law and unparalleled in any other area of our jurisprudence." *Id.* at 327. Given the implications of reading a statute otherwise, *was* it unjustified?

3. *"Magic Words."* Consider Section 7(a) of the Military Commissions Act of 2006, Pub. L. No. 109-366, 120 Stat. 2600, 2635-2636 (codified at 28 U.S.C. §2241(e)(1) (2018)):

> No court, justice, or judge shall have jurisdiction to hear or consider an application for a writ of habeas corpus filed by or on behalf of an alien detained by the United States who has been determined by the United States to have been properly detained as an enemy combatant or is awaiting such determination.

Does this statute satisfy *St. Cyr*'s "magic words" requirement? If so, is it a valid suspension of habeas corpus? What additional information would you need in order to answer this question? Most importantly, *who* should answer the question?

D. THE EFFECTS OF A VALID SUSPENSION

What actually happens when the privilege of the writ of habeas corpus is suspended? Obviously, the immediate, practical effect of a suspension is that prisoners covered by it remain in custody for as long as the Executive chooses to hold them. But is that because the act of suspension does nothing other than prevent the judicial review that might otherwise have produced their release, or because it provides affirmative authorization for their detention, such that any judicial review would necessarily be unsuccessful? In *Ex parte Milligan*, Justice Davis suggested in a dictum that "[t]he suspension of the writ does not authorize the arrest of any one, but simply denies to one arrested the privilege of this writ in order to obtain his liberty." 71 U.S. (4 Wall.) at 115. As recent scholarship has suggested, though, the historical evidence on this point is rather equivocal.

This might seem like a purely semantic distinction, but it matters in two different respects: *First*, if suspension of habeas merely forecloses judicial review, then detainees might seek legal relief once the suspension has ended — including, perhaps, through suits for damages. *Second*, and more importantly, if suspension actually *authorizes* detention, then suspending habeas arguably is the only lawful way to authorize non-criminal detention. In other words, *all* statutes that authorize non-criminal detention would have to comply with the substantive limits of the Suspension Clause, to wit, "cases of rebellion or invasion when the public safety requires" detention. Because Congress has not authorized the suspension of habeas since 1871 (see the Ku Klux Act, 17 Stat. 13), this question has largely been left to academic debate. But consider the position taken by Justice Scalia (joined by Justice Stevens) in the following case — and what it would mean if it were correct.

Reading Justice Scalia's Dissent in *Hamdi v. Rumsfeld*

In *Hamdi v. Rumsfeld*, 542 U.S. 507 (2004), to which we return in more detail in Chapter 29, the Supreme Court held that the Authorization for the Use of Military Force (AUMF), Pub. L. No. 107-40, 115 Stat. 224 (2001), authorized the military detention of a U.S. citizen who was captured in Afghanistan, allegedly while engaged in hostilities against U.S. forces there.

In a four-Justice plurality opinion, Justice O'Connor wrote that, while the AUMF *could* authorize the detention of U.S. citizens like Hamdi, the Constitution required that Hamdi have a fair opportunity to contest the government's factual basis for his detention. Justice Thomas agreed that Hamdi's detention was authorized, and disagreed that Hamdi was entitled to any additional process. Justices Souter and Ginsburg would have held that Hamdi's detention was not authorized by the AUMF, even if the government's allegations were true.

In the dissent that follows, Justice Scalia, joined by Justice Stevens, agreed with Justices Souter and Ginsburg that Congress *had not* authorized Hamdi's detention in the AUMF. In his view, Congress *could not* so provide. As you read Scalia's dissent, consider the following questions:

- What textual and historical evidence does Justice Scalia rely upon in concluding that U.S. citizens may be detained without trial only if habeas is properly suspended? What role does the Treason Clause (and statute) play in his analysis?
- How does Justice Scalia distinguish *Ex parte Quirin*, 317 U.S. 1 (1942), in which the Supreme Court (unanimously) upheld the detention and military commission trial of eight Nazi saboteurs, at least one of whom was a U.S. citizen? Given that *Quirin* (which we cover in more detail in Chapter 36) is not about the Suspension Clause, why does it appear to pose so much trouble for Justice Scalia's argument?
- According to Justice Scalia, what is the *purpose* of a proper suspension of habeas corpus? Is it to displace judicial review, or affirmatively to authorize non-criminal detention?

Hamdi v. Rumsfeld

United States Supreme Court, 2004
542 U.S. 507

Justice Scalia, with whom Justice Stevens joins, dissenting. . . . Where the Government accuses a citizen of waging war against it, our constitutional tradition has been to prosecute him in federal court for treason or some other crime. Where the exigencies of war prevent that, the Constitution's Suspension Clause, Art. I, §9, cl. 2, allows Congress to relax the usual protections temporarily. Absent suspension, however, the Executive's assertion of military exigency has not been thought sufficient to permit detention without charge. No one contends that the congressional Authorization for Use of Military Force, on which the Government relies to justify its actions here, is an implementation of the Suspension Clause. Accordingly, I would reverse the decision below.

I

The very core of liberty secured by our Anglo-Saxon system of separated powers has been freedom from indefinite imprisonment at the will of the Executive. Blackstone stated this principle clearly: [The passage quoted here by Justice Scalia is set forth *supra* pp. 823-824.] . . .

These words were well known to the Founders. Hamilton quoted from this very passage in The Federalist No. 84, p. 444 (G. Carey & J. McClellan eds., 2001). The two ideas central to Blackstone's understanding — due process as the right secured, and habeas corpus as the instrument by which due process could be insisted upon by a citizen illegally imprisoned — found expression in the Constitution's Due Process and Suspension Clauses. See Amdt. 5; Art. I, §9, cl. 2.

The gist of the Due Process Clause, as understood at the founding and since, was to force the Government to follow those common-law procedures traditionally deemed necessary before depriving a person of life, liberty, or property. When a citizen was deprived of liberty because of alleged criminal conduct, those procedures typically required committal by a magistrate followed by indictment and trial. . . .

II

The allegations here, of course, are no ordinary accusations of criminal activity. Yaser Esam Hamdi has been imprisoned because the Government believes he participated in the waging of war against the United States. The relevant question, then, is whether there is a different, special procedure for imprisonment of a citizen accused of wrongdoing *by aiding the enemy in wartime.*

A

Justice O'Connor, writing for a plurality of this Court, asserts that captured enemy combatants (other than those suspected of war crimes) have traditionally been detained until the cessation of hostilities and then released. That is probably an accurate description of wartime practice with respect to enemy *aliens.* The tradition with respect to American citizens, however, has been quite different. Citizens aiding the enemy have been treated as traitors subject to the criminal process. . . .

The modern treason statute is 18 U.S.C. §2381; it basically tracks the language of the constitutional provision. Other provisions of Title 18 criminalize various acts of warmaking and adherence to the enemy. The only citizen other than Hamdi known to be imprisoned in connection with military hostilities in Afghanistan against the United States *was* subjected to criminal process and convicted upon a guilty plea. See *United States v. Lindh,* 212 F. Supp. 2d 541 (E.D. Va. 2002) (denying motions for dismissal).

B

There are times when military exigency renders resort to the traditional criminal process impracticable. English law accommodated such exigencies by allowing legislative suspension of the writ of habeas corpus for brief periods. Blackstone explained:

> "And yet sometimes, when the state is in real danger, even this [*i.e.*, executive detention] may be a necessary measure. But the happiness of our constitution is, that it is not left to the executive power to determine when the danger of the state is so great, as to render this measure expedient. For the parliament only, or legislative power, whenever it seems proper, can authorize the crown, by suspending the *habeas corpus* act for a short and limited time, to imprison suspected persons without giving any reason for so doing. . . . In like manner this experiment ought only to be tried in case of extreme emergency; and in these the nation parts with it[s] liberty for a while, in order to preserve it for ever." 1 Blackstone 132. . . .

Our Federal Constitution contains a provision explicitly permitting suspension, but limiting the situations in which it may be invoked: "The privilege of the Writ of Habeas Corpus shall not be suspended, unless when in Cases of Rebellion or Invasion the public Safety may require it." Art. I, §9, cl. 2. Although this provision does not state that suspension must be effected by, or authorized by, a legislative act, it has been so understood, consistent with English practice and the Clause's placement in Article I.

The Suspension Clause was by design a safety valve, the Constitution's only "express provision for exercise of extraordinary authority because of a crisis," *Youngstown Sheet & Tube Co. v. Sawyer*, 343 U.S. 579, 650 (1952) (Jackson, J., concurring). . . .

III . . .

Writings from the founding generation also suggest that, without exception, the only constitutional alternatives are to charge the crime or suspend the writ. In 1788, Thomas Jefferson wrote to James Madison questioning the need for a Suspension Clause in cases of rebellion in the proposed Constitution. His letter illustrates the constraints under which the Founders understood themselves to operate:

> "Why suspend the Hab. corp. in insurrections and rebellions? The parties who may be arrested may be charged instantly with a well defined crime. Of course the judge will remand them. If the publick safety requires that the government should have a man imprisoned on less probable testimony in those than in other emergencies; let him be taken and tried, retaken and retried, while the necessity continues, only giving him redress against the government for damages." 13 Papers of Thomas Jefferson 442 (July 31, 1788) (J. Boyd ed. 1956). . . .

Further evidence comes from this Court's decision in *Ex parte Milligan*, [71 U.S. (4 Wall.) 2] (1866). There, the Court issued the writ to an American citizen who had been tried by military commission for offenses that included conspiring to overthrow the Government, seize munitions, and liberate prisoners of war. The Court rejected in no uncertain terms the Government's assertion that military jurisdiction was proper "under the 'laws and usages of war,'" *id.*, at 121:

> "It can serve no useful purpose to inquire what those laws and usages are, whence they originated, where found, and on whom they operate; they can never be applied to citizens

in states which have upheld the authority of the government, and where the courts are open and their process unobstructed." *Ibid.*

Milligan is not exactly this case, of course, since the petitioner was threatened with death, not merely imprisonment. But the reasoning and conclusion of *Milligan* logically cover the present case. The Government justifies imprisonment of Hamdi on principles of the law of war and admits that, absent the war, it would have no such authority. But if the law of war cannot be applied to citizens where courts are open, then Hamdi's imprisonment without criminal trial is no less unlawful than Milligan's trial by military tribunal.

Milligan responded to the argument, repeated by the Government in this case, that it is dangerous to leave suspected traitors at large in time of war:

> "If it was dangerous, in the distracted condition of affairs, to leave Milligan unrestrained of his liberty, because he 'conspired against the government, afforded aid and comfort to rebels, and incited the people to insurrection,' the *law* said arrest him, confine him closely, render him powerless to do further mischief; and then present his case to the grand jury of the district, with proofs of his guilt, and, if indicted, try him according to the course of the common law. If this had been done, the Constitution would have been vindicated, the law of 1863 enforced, and the securities for personal liberty preserved and defended." *Id.*, at 122.

Thus, criminal process was viewed as the primary means — and the only means absent congressional action suspending the writ — not only to punish traitors, but to incapacitate them.

The proposition that the Executive lacks indefinite wartime detention authority over citizens is consistent with the Founders' general mistrust of military power permanently at the Executive's disposal. In the Founders' view, the "blessings of liberty" were threatened by "those military establishments which must gradually poison its very fountain." The Federalist No. 45, p. 238 (J. Madison). No fewer than 10 issues of the Federalist were devoted in whole or part to allaying fears of oppression from the proposed Constitution's authorization of standing armies in peacetime. Many safeguards in the Constitution reflect these concerns. Congress's authority "[t]o raise and support Armies" was hedged with the proviso that "no Appropriation of Money to that Use shall be for a longer Term than two Years." U.S. Const., Art. 1, §8, cl. 12. Except for the actual command of military forces, all authorization for their maintenance and all explicit authorization for their use is placed in the control of Congress under Article I, rather than the President under Article II. . . . A view of the Constitution that gives the Executive authority to use military force rather than the force of law against citizens on American soil flies in the face of the mistrust that engendered these provisions.

IV

The Government argues that our more recent jurisprudence ratifies its indefinite imprisonment of a citizen within the territorial jurisdiction of federal courts. It places primary reliance upon *Ex parte Quirin*, 317 U.S. 1 (1942), a World War II case upholding the trial by military commission of eight German saboteurs, one of whom, Hans Haupt, was a U.S. citizen. The case was not this Court's finest hour. The Court upheld the commission and denied relief in a brief *per curiam* issued the day after oral argument concluded; a week later the Government carried out the commission's death sentence upon six saboteurs, including Haupt. The Court eventually explained its reasoning in a written opinion issued several months later.

Only three paragraphs of the Court's lengthy opinion dealt with the particular circumstances of Haupt's case. The Government argued that Haupt, like the other petitioners, could be tried by military commission under the laws of war. In agreeing with that contention, *Quirin* purported to interpret the language of *Milligan* quoted above (the law of war "can never be applied to citizens in states which have upheld the authority of the government, and where the courts are open and their process unobstructed") in the following manner:

> "Elsewhere in its opinion . . . the Court was at pains to point out that Milligan, a citizen twenty years resident in Indiana, who had never been a resident of any of the states in rebellion, was not an enemy belligerent either entitled to the status of a prisoner of war or subject to the penalties imposed upon unlawful belligerents. We construe the Court's statement as to the inapplicability of the law of war to Milligan's case as having particular reference to the facts before it. From them the Court concluded that Milligan, not being a part of or associated with the armed forces of the enemy, was a nonbelligerent, not subject to the law of war. . . ." 317 U.S., at 45.

In my view this seeks to revise *Milligan* rather than describe it. *Milligan* had involved (among other issues) two separate questions: (1) whether the military trial of Milligan was justified by the laws of war, and if not (2) whether the President's suspension of the writ, pursuant to congressional authorization, prevented the issuance of habeas corpus. The Court's categorical language about the law of war's inapplicability to citizens where the courts are open (with no exception mentioned for citizens who were prisoners of war) was contained in its discussion of the first point. See 4 Wall., at 121. The factors pertaining to whether Milligan could reasonably be considered a belligerent and prisoner of war, while mentioned earlier in the opinion, were made relevant and brought to bear in the Court's later discussion of whether Milligan came within the statutory provision that effectively made an exception to Congress's authorized suspension of the writ for (as the Court described it) "all parties, not prisoners of war, resident in their respective jurisdictions, . . . who were citizens of states in which the administration of the laws in the Federal tribunals was unimpaired," *id.* at 116. *Milligan* thus understood was in accord with the traditional law of habeas corpus I have described: Though treason often occurred in wartime, there was, absent provision for special treatment in a congressional suspension of the writ, no exception to the right to trial by jury for citizens who could be called "belligerents" or "prisoners of war."

But even if *Quirin* gave a correct description of *Milligan,* or made an irrevocable revision of it, *Quirin* would still not justify denial of the writ here. In *Quirin* it was uncontested that the petitioners were members of enemy forces. They were "*admitted* enemy invaders," 317 U.S., at 47 (emphasis added), and it was "undisputed" that they had landed in the United States in service of German forces, *id.*, at 20. The specific holding of the Court was only that, "upon the *conceded* facts," the petitioners were "plainly within [the] boundaries" of military jurisdiction, *id.*, at 46 (emphasis added). But where those jurisdictional facts are *not* conceded — where the petitioner insists that he is *not* a belligerent — *Quirin* left the pre-existing law in place: Absent suspension of the writ, a citizen held where the courts are open is entitled either to criminal trial or to a judicial decree requiring his release.

V

It follows from what I have said that Hamdi is entitled to a habeas decree requiring his release unless (1) criminal proceedings are promptly brought, or (2) Congress has suspended the writ of habeas corpus. A suspension of the writ could, of course, lay down conditions for continued detention, similar to those that today's opinion prescribes under the Due Process Clause. But there is a world of difference between the people's representatives' determining the need for that suspension (and prescribing the conditions for it), and this Court's doing so.

The plurality finds justification for Hamdi's imprisonment in the Authorization for Use of Military Force, 115 Stat. 224. . . . This is not remotely a congressional suspension of the writ, and no one claims that it is. Contrary to the plurality's view, I do not think this statute even authorizes detention of a citizen with the clarity necessary to satisfy the interpretive canon that statutes should be construed so as to avoid grave constitutional concerns; with the clarity necessary to comport with cases such as *Ex parte Endo*, 323 U.S. 283, 300 (1944), and *Duncan v. Kahanamoku*, 327 U.S. 304, 314-316, 324 (1946); or with the clarity necessary to overcome the statutory prescription that "[n]o citizen shall be imprisoned or otherwise detained by the United States except pursuant to an Act of Congress." 18 U.S.C. §4001(a). But even if it did, I would not permit it to overcome Hamdi's entitlement to habeas corpus relief. The Suspension Clause of the Constitution, which carefully circumscribes the conditions under which the writ can be withheld, would be a sham if it could be evaded by congressional prescription of requirements *other than the common-law requirement of committal for criminal prosecution* that render the writ, though available, unavailing. If the Suspension Clause does not guarantee the citizen that he will either be tried or released, unless the conditions for suspending the writ exist and the grave action of suspending the writ has been taken; if it merely guarantees the citizen that he will not be detained unless Congress by ordinary legislation says he can be detained; it guarantees him very little indeed.

It should not be thought, however, that the plurality's evisceration of the Suspension Clause augments, principally, the power of Congress. As usual, the major effect of its constitutional improvisation is to increase the power of the Court. Having found a congressional authorization for detention of citizens where none clearly exists; and having discarded the categorical procedural protection of the Suspension Clause; the plurality then proceeds, under the guise of the Due Process Clause, to prescribe what procedural protections *it* thinks appropriate. . . .

. . . This judicial remediation of executive default is unheard of. The role of habeas corpus is to determine the legality of executive detention, not to supply the omitted process necessary to make it legal. . . .

There is a certain harmony of approach in the plurality's making up for Congress's failure to invoke the Suspension Clause and its making up for the Executive's failure to apply what it says are needed procedures — an approach that reflects what might be called a Mr. Fix-it Mentality. The plurality seems to view it as its mission to Make Everything Come Out Right, rather than merely to decree the consequences, as far as individual rights are concerned, of the other two branches' actions and omissions. Has the Legislature failed to suspend the writ in the current dire emergency? Well, we will remedy that failure by prescribing the reasonable conditions that a suspension should have included. And has the Executive failed to live up to those reasonable conditions? Well, we will ourselves make that failure good, so that this dangerous fellow (if he is dangerous) need not be set free. The problem with this approach is not only that it steps out of the courts' modest and limited role in a democratic society; but that by repeatedly doing what it thinks the political branches ought to do it encourages their lassitude and saps the vitality of government by the people.

VI

Several limitations give my views in this matter a relatively narrow compass. They apply only to citizens, accused of being enemy combatants, who are detained within the territorial jurisdiction of a federal court. This is not likely to be a numerous group; currently we know of only two, Hamdi and Jose Padilla. Where the citizen is captured outside and held outside the United States, the constitutional requirements may be different. Cf. *Johnson v. Eisentrager*, 339 U.S. 763, 769-771 (1950); *Reid v. Covert*, 354 U.S. 1, 74-75 (1957) (Harlan, J., concurring in result); *Rasul v. Bush*, [542 U.S. 466 (2004)] (Scalia, J., dissenting). Moreover, even within the United States, the accused citizen-enemy combatant may lawfully be detained once prosecution is in progress or in contemplation . . .

. . . If the situation demands it, the Executive can ask Congress to authorize suspension of the writ — which can be made subject to whatever conditions Congress deems appropriate, including even the procedural novelties invented by the plurality today. To be sure, suspension is limited by the Constitution to cases of rebellion or invasion. But whether the attacks of September 11, 2001, constitute an "invasion," and whether those attacks still justify suspension several years later, are questions for Congress rather than this Court. . . .

Notes and Questions

1. Justice Scalia's "Limited Compass." Note the practical limitations of Justice Scalia's argument: although he reads the Constitution as categorically forbidding non-criminal detention absent suspension of habeas corpus, that only applies, in his view, to U.S. citizens detained within the United States. What about (1) U.S. citizens detained overseas; (2) non-citizens detained within the United States; or (3) non-citizens detained overseas? We'll encounter Justice Scalia's views about the third category in the next chapter. But what about the first two? How useful would the Suspension Clause be if the government could avoid it merely by shipping U.S. citizen detainees elsewhere (or not bringing them home)? Note that Hamdi was captured in Afghanistan, and was only brought back to the United States *by* the U.S. government — and then only after a short stint at Guantánamo.

2. The Suspension Clause and Other Non-Criminal Detention. As we'll see in Chapter 31, the Supreme Court has blessed various forms of *civil* detention without trial — including the civil commitment of dangerous sex offenders after they have served their criminal sentences — in opinions that Justice Scalia has joined without reservation. Could statutes authorizing *those* detentions be justified as "suspensions" of habeas corpus? If not, why doesn't the Suspension Clause, on Justice Scalia's reading, prohibit those detentions as well? Is there a principled basis for distinguishing between different kinds of non-criminal detention based upon whether the detention is at the hands of the military or of civilian authorities, or whether the detainee is accused of hostilities against the United States as opposed to posing a danger to those around him?

3. *Could the AUMF Have Been a Suspension?* Justice Scalia implies that Congress *could* have suspended habeas corpus for U.S. citizens in the AUMF, even though it was quite clear that the AUMF was *not* meant as a suspension. Do you agree? Certainly, it shouldn't be difficult to accept that the 9/11 attacks constituted an "Invasion." But the Suspension Clause allows suspension only "when in Cases of Rebellion or Invasion the public Safety may require it." What factors are relevant in deciding whether the public safety requires suspension? Did those factors apply in the aftermath of 9/11? Do they still apply? Who decides?

4. *The Significance of Hamdi.* Although *Hamdi* is not about the Suspension Clause, it is important to our understanding of that constitutional provision: Five Justices expressly held that the non-criminal detention of a U.S. citizen was authorized by an Act of Congress that (all agree) was *not* a suspension of habeas corpus. *Hamdi* therefore held that Congress *may* authorize the detention of U.S. citizens within the United States *without* suspending habeas corpus. In rejecting Justice Scalia's alternative reading of the Suspension Clause, both the *Hamdi* plurality and Justice Thomas thereby endorsed, however implicitly, the view that a valid suspension serves only to displace judicial review for the duration of the suspension. On that view, (1) suspension does not authorize detention; and (2) authorizations of detention (in *Hamdi*, the AUMF) do not displace judicial review.

HABEAS CORPUS: THE STRUCTURE OF THE SUSPENSION CLAUSE: SUMMARY OF BASIC PRINCIPLES

- The writ of habeas corpus *ad subjiciendum* is a judicial order directed to a jailor that compels him to return to court with a named prisoner, so that the issuing judge may inquire into the legality of the prisoner's confinement.

- In practice, virtually all habeas petitions are resolved *before* the writ formally "issues," through "show cause" proceedings that allow for adjudication of the petitioner's claims *without* his physical presence in court.

- At an absolute minimum, the Suspension Clause of the Constitution protects the writ of habeas corpus "as it existed in 1789." It thereby incorporates the scope of habeas corpus as it existed in pre-revolutionary England.

- When habeas corpus is not validly suspended, the Suspension Clause requires access to judicial review in *some* U.S. forum for at least *some* executive branch detainees — including, at a minimum, U.S. citizens held without charges within the territorial United States.

- Congress has historically provided for more review than that, in statutes dating back to the Judiciary Act of 1789, which gave the lower federal courts jurisdiction to issue statutory writs of habeas corpus.

- Because the Supreme Court has separately disavowed the power of state courts to issue writs of habeas corpus to *federal* jailors, and denied the power of federal courts to issue *common law* writs, the federal habeas statutes historically provided all of the habeas review that is available to federal prisoners. Until 2008, the Supreme Court never had to decide what happened in cases in which the Suspension Clause applies but no statute provides jurisdiction.

- Although the Supreme Court has never squarely so held, it has suggested, and scholars generally agree, that *only Congress* may suspend or authorize suspension of habeas corpus absent truly exigent circumstances, such as those that might justify a declaration of martial law. Such suspensions must be explicit; courts will bend over backward to avoid interpreting statutes as limiting access to habeas corpus.

- The Supreme Court has also suggested that a valid suspension of habeas corpus is not a freestanding authorization of indefinite non-criminal detention, but rather only a temporary displacement of judicial review for the duration of the suspension. Thus, non-criminal detention must rest on some *other*, affirmative authority in order to be lawful.

Habeas Corpus: The Scope of the Suspension Clause

The last chapter introduced the historical origins and constitutional structure of the "great writ" of habeas corpus. No less important to contemporary national security law is the *scope* of the Suspension Clause — the cases to which it applies, and the kind of judicial review it requires in those cases. And even when it is clear *where* the Suspension Clause applies, what is its *practical effect*? What kinds of claims must detainees be allowed to bring via habeas petitions, and how vigorous must judicial review of those claims be? In addition to substantive law questions provoked by the detention of noncitizens at Guantánamo (to which we turn in Chapter 30), federal courts have also had to address fundamental procedural issues involving the "great writ," and, in the process, to answer basic questions about the purpose and role of judicial review in supervising executive detention.

A. GEOGRAPHIC SCOPE OF THE SUSPENSION CLAUSE

Before the September 11 attacks, the Supreme Court rarely had occasion to address the *geographical* scope of the Suspension Clause and, in particular, whether it protected noncitizens captured and detained outside the territorial United States.[1] The only significant decision in which that question was even implicated was *Johnson v. Eisentrager*, 339 U.S. 763 (1950), a post-World War II case brought by 21 German nationals held in a German prison operated by the U.S. Army. They sought to challenge the jurisdiction of an American military commission in China that had convicted them for war crimes committed after Germany's unconditional surrender. As noted above, *supra* pp. 828-829, the Supreme Court at that time understood the habeas statute to allow habeas petitions to be brought only in a detainee's "district of confinement."

1. The Supreme Court has long assumed (although it has never expressly held) that U.S. persons are fully protected by the Suspension Clause overseas. *See, e.g.*, *Rasul v. Bush*, 542 U.S. 466, 497 (2004) (Scalia, J., dissenting); *Ex parte Hayes*, 414 U.S. 1327, 1328-1329 (Douglas, Circuit Justice 1973).

The district court in *Eisentrager* held that it therefore lacked statutory jurisdiction over the petitioners' habeas claims. The D.C. Circuit reversed, holding that the detainees had an absolute *constitutional* right to habeas corpus even though they were noncitizens held outside the United States, so it did not matter that the statute failed to confer jurisdiction. *Eisentrager v. Forrestal*, 174 F.2d 961 (D.C. Cir. 1949).

In a 6-3 decision, the Supreme Court reversed the D.C. Circuit. As Justice Jackson explained for the Court, no historical precedent supported the conclusion reached by the appellate court below, and recognition of such unlimited constitutional protections for enemy soldiers would create a wide range of practical and logistical problems, especially given the large number of enemy soldiers still in U.S. custody overseas at that time. Thus, Jackson explained, because each of the petitioners "(a) is an enemy alien; (b) has never been or resided in the United States; (c) was captured outside of our territory and there held in military custody as a prisoner of war; (d) was tried and convicted by a Military Commission sitting outside the United States; (e) for offences against laws of war committed outside the United States; (f) and is at all times imprisoned outside the United States, . . . no right to the writ of habeas corpus appears." 339 U.S. at 777, 781.

But Justice Jackson's opinion was unclear about whether "no right to the writ of habeas corpus appear[ed]" because (1) noncitizens outside the United States are not protected by the Suspension Clause; or (2) the petitioners' challenge to the jurisdiction of the military commission that convicted them (the only claim then cognizable via such a habeas petition) was without merit. The former holding would mean that the federal courts lacked the authority to hear even meritorious habeas claims; the latter would mean simply that the *Eisentrager* petitioners had no legal rights to vindicate by granting their petition — in other words, that there was nothing for habeas to *do* in their case.

Uncertainty over *Eisentrager*'s holding caused significant debate after September 11, especially once the U.S. government began holding noncitizens captured overseas at the U.S. Naval Station at Guantánamo Bay, Cuba. The government argued that *Eisentrager* foreclosed federal jurisdiction over habeas petitions from such prisoners. The prisoners argued, to the contrary, that *Eisentrager* merely rejected the earlier petitioners' challenge to the jurisdiction of their military commission on the merits — and so had no bearing on federal jurisdiction over Guantánamo. The lower courts initially divided on the question.

In *Rasul v. Bush*, 542 U.S. 466 (2004), the Supreme Court sided with the prisoners, and ruled that, *Eisentrager* notwithstanding, federal courts had *statutory* habeas jurisdiction over claims brought by noncitizens held at Guantánamo. As Justice Stevens explained for a 6-3 majority, a post-*Eisentrager* case — *Braden v. 30th Judicial Cir. Ct. of Kentucky*, 410 U.S. 484 (1973) — had held that the habeas statute only requires jurisdiction over the detainee's *custodian*, which the *Rasul* petitioners satisfied because they had sued President Bush, Secretary Rumsfeld, and a host of other officials responsible for Guantánamo. Thus, *Rasul* concluded, whatever *Eisentrager* might have held concerning the scope of the constitutional writ was irrelevant, all the more so given the myriad factual distinctions between the cases.

Congress sought to overrule *Rasul* in the Detainee Treatment Act of 2005 (DTA), Pub. L. No. 109-148, §1005(e), 119 Stat. 2680, 2739-2740. The DTA authorized direct appeals to the D.C. Circuit of some (but not all) military commission convictions and of final decisions by "Combatant Status Review Tribunals" (CSRTs) — executive branch tribunals created after *Rasul* to provide some modicum of process to detainees who sought to challenge the government's determination that they were "enemy combatants." Otherwise, however, the DTA purported to bar *all* federal jurisdiction over any claim, including habeas petitions, brought by or on behalf of the Guantánamo detainees.

The following year, in *Hamdan v. Rumsfeld*, 548 U.S. 557 (2006), the Supreme Court held, among other things, that the DTA's jurisdiction-stripping provisions did not apply to "pending" cases — including all of the Guantánamo habeas petitions. *See id.* at 572-584. Congress then responded to *Hamdan* by enacting the Military Commissions Act of 2006 (MCA), Pub. L. No. 109-366, 120 Stat. 2600, which, among many other things, provided:

> No court, justice, or judge shall have jurisdiction to hear or consider an application for a writ of habeas corpus filed by or on behalf of an alien detained by the United States who has been determined by the United States to have been properly detained as an enemy combatant or is awaiting such determination. [*Id.* §7(a), 120 Stat. at 2635-2636 (codified at 28 U.S.C. §2241(e)(1)(2018)).]

Reading the First Holding in *Boumediene v. Bush*

In *Boumediene v. Bush*, 476 F.3d 981 (D.C. Cir. 2007), a divided appeals panel upheld §7(a) of the MCA, holding that, especially in light of *Eisentrager*, the Guantánamo detainees were not protected by the Suspension Clause. The Supreme Court subsequently reversed the D.C. Circuit panel. In the excerpt that follows, the Court held (over a bitter dissent from Justice Scalia) that the Suspension Clause "has full effect" at Guantánamo. Later in the chapter, we'll return to *Boumediene* and its second holding — that the MCA *violates* the Suspension Clause by failing to provide the detainees with an adequate alternative to habeas corpus. For now, though, start with these questions:

- How does Justice Kennedy use the history of habeas corpus — some of which we studied in the last chapter — to amplify his analysis? Given that ultimately he declines "to infer too much, one way or the other, from the lack of historical evidence on point," what is the purpose of Part III of his opinion?
- In Part IV, Justice Kennedy turns far more specifically to the unique status of Guantánamo. Why does he reject the government's "formal," "sovereignty-based" test for the applicability of the Suspension Clause? What test does he fashion (and then apply) in its stead?
- What is the significance, if any, of Justice Kennedy's basing so much of his analysis on the status of Guantánamo? Given the separation-of-powers principles to which he repeatedly alludes, should the scope of the writ turn on the kinds of practical, functional considerations upon which he ultimately relies?
- Justice Scalia's dissent makes much out of *Eisentrager*. Is Justice Kennedy's response convincing? *Eisentrager* aside, why does Justice Scalia believe that it is so dangerous to confer at least some constitutional protections upon noncitizens outside the United States? Is there a difference, in this regard, between applying the Suspension Clause and, for example, the Due Process Clause abroad?

Boumediene v. Bush

United States Supreme Court, 2008
553 U.S. 723

Justice KENNEDY delivered the opinion of the Court. . . . Petitioners present a question not resolved by our earlier cases relating to the detention of aliens at Guantanamo: whether they have the constitutional privilege of habeas corpus, a privilege not to be withdrawn except in conformance with the Suspension Clause, Art. I, §9, cl. 2. We hold these petitioners do have the habeas corpus privilege. . . . We do not address whether the President has authority to detain these petitioners nor do we hold that the writ must issue. These and other questions regarding the legality of the detention are to be resolved in the first instance by the District Court.

I . . .

Interpreting the AUMF [Authorization for Use of Military Force, Pub. L. No. 107-40 (2001), *supra* p. 88], the Department of Defense ordered the detention of these petitioners, and they were transferred to Guantanamo. Some of these individuals were apprehended on the battlefield in Afghanistan, others in places as far away from there as Bosnia and Gambia. All are foreign nationals, but none is a citizen of a nation now at war with the United States. Each denies he is a member of the al Qaeda terrorist network that carried out the September 11 attacks or of the Taliban regime that provided sanctuary for al Qaeda. Each petitioner appeared before a separate CSRT; was determined to be an enemy combatant; and has sought a writ of habeas corpus in the United States District Court for the District of Columbia. . . .

III . . .

We begin with a brief account of the history and origins of the writ. Our account proceeds from two propositions. First, protection for the privilege of habeas corpus was one of the few safeguards of liberty specified in a Constitution that, at the outset, had no Bill of Rights. In the system conceived by the Framers the writ had a centrality that must inform proper interpretation of the Suspension Clause. Second, to the extent there were settled precedents or legal commentaries in 1789 regarding the extraterritorial scope of the writ or its application to enemy aliens, those authorities can be instructive for the present cases.

A

The Framers viewed freedom from unlawful restraint as a fundamental precept of liberty, and they understood the writ of habeas corpus as a vital instrument to secure that freedom. Experience taught, however, that the common-law writ all too often had been insufficient to guard against the abuse of monarchial power. That history counseled the necessity for specific language in the Constitution to secure the writ and ensure its place in our legal system. . . .

This history was known to the Framers. It no doubt confirmed their view that pendular swings to and away from individual liberty were endemic to undivided, uncontrolled power. The Framers' inherent distrust of governmental power was the driving force behind the constitutional plan that allocated powers among three independent branches. This design serves not only to make Government accountable but also to secure individual liberty. Because the Constitution's separation-of-powers structure, like the substantive guarantees of the Fifth and Fourteenth Amendments, *see Yick Wo v. Hopkins,* 118 U.S. 356, 374 (1886), protects persons as well as citizens, foreign nationals who have the privilege of litigating in our courts can seek to enforce separation-of-powers principles, see, *e.g., INS v. Chadha,* 462 U.S. 919, 958-959 (1983).

That the Framers considered the writ a vital instrument for the protection of individual liberty is evident from the care taken to specify the limited grounds for its suspension: "The Privilege of the Writ of Habeas Corpus shall not be suspended, unless when in Cases of Rebellion or Invasion the public Safety may require it." Art. I, §9, cl. 2; *see* Amar, *Of Sovereignty and Federalism,* 96 Yale L.J. 1425, 1509 n.329 (1987) ("[T]he non-suspension clause is the original Constitution's most explicit reference to remedies")....

In our own system the Suspension Clause is designed to protect against these cyclical abuses. The Clause protects the rights of the detained by a means consistent with the essential design of the Constitution. It ensures that, except during periods of formal suspension, the Judiciary will have a time-tested device, the writ, to maintain the "delicate balance of governance" that is itself the surest safeguard of liberty. *See Hamdi* [*v. Rumsfeld,* 542 U.S. 507 (2004)], at 536 (plurality opinion). The Clause protects the rights of the detained by affirming the duty and authority of the Judiciary to call the jailer to account. The separation-of-powers doctrine, and the history that influenced its design, therefore must inform the reach and purpose of the Suspension Clause.

B...

To support their arguments, the parties in these cases have examined historical sources to construct a view of the common-law writ as it existed in 1789 — as have *amici* whose expertise in legal history the Court has relied upon in the past. The Government argues the common-law writ ran only to those territories over which the Crown was sovereign. Petitioners argue that jurisdiction followed the King's officers. Diligent search by all parties reveals no certain conclusions....

...We decline, therefore, to infer too much, one way or the other, from the lack of historical evidence on point.

IV

Drawing from its position that at common law the writ ran only to territories over which the Crown was sovereign, the Government says the Suspension Clause affords petitioners no rights because the United States does not claim sovereignty over the place of detention.

Guantanamo Bay is not formally part of the United States. *See* DTA §1005(g), 119 Stat. 2743. And under the terms of the lease between the United States and Cuba, Cuba retains "ultimate sovereignty" over the territory while the United States exercises "complete jurisdiction and control." *See* Lease of Lands for Coaling and Naval Stations, Feb. 23, 1903, U.S.-Cuba, Art. III, T.S. No. 418 (hereinafter 1903 Lease

Agreement); *Rasul,* 542 U.S., at 471. Under the terms of the 1934 Treaty, however, Cuba effectively has no rights as a sovereign until the parties agree to modification of the 1903 Lease Agreement or the United States abandons the base. *See* Treaty Defining Relations with Cuba, May 29, 1934, U.S.-Cuba, Art. III, 48 Stat. 1683, T.S. No. 866.

The United States contends, nevertheless, that Guantanamo is not within its sovereign control. This was the Government's position well before the events of September 11, 2001. And in other contexts the Court has held that questions of sovereignty are for the political branches to decide. Even if this were a treaty interpretation case that did not involve a political question, the President's construction of the lease agreement would be entitled to great respect.

We therefore do not question the Government's position that Cuba, not the United States, maintains sovereignty, in the legal and technical sense of the term, over Guantanamo Bay. But this does not end the analysis. Our cases do not hold it is improper for us to inquire into the objective degree of control the Nation asserts over foreign territory. . . .

A

The Court has discussed the issue of the Constitution's extraterritorial application on many occasions. These decisions undermine the Government's argument that, at least as applied to noncitizens, the Constitution necessarily stops where *de jure* sovereignty ends.

[The Court reviewed cases, including the *Insular Cases* and *Reid v. Covert,* 354 U.S. 1 (1957), as standing for the proposition that "whether a constitutional provision has extraterritorial effect depends upon the 'particular circumstances, the practical necessities, and the possible alternatives which Congress had before it' and, in particular, whether judicial enforcement of the provision would be 'impracticable and anomalous.'" (quoting Justice Harlan's opinion concurring in the judgment in *Reid*).] . . .

Practical considerations weighed heavily as well in *Johnson v. Eisentrager,* 339 U.S. 763 (1950), where the Court addressed whether habeas corpus jurisdiction extended to enemy aliens who had been convicted of violating the laws of war. The prisoners were detained at Landsberg Prison in Germany during the Allied Powers' postwar occupation. The Court stressed the difficulties of ordering the Government to produce the prisoners in a habeas corpus proceeding. It "would require allocation of shipping space, guarding personnel, billeting and rations" and would damage the prestige of military commanders at a sensitive time. *Id.,* at 779. In considering these factors the Court sought to balance the constraints of military occupation with constitutional necessities. *Id.,* at 769-779; *see Rasul,* 542 U.S., at 475-476 (discussing the factors relevant to *Eisentrager*'s constitutional holding); 542 U.S., at 486 (Kennedy, J., concurring in judgment) (same).

True, the Court in *Eisentrager* denied access to the writ, and it noted the prisoners "at no relevant time were within any territory over which the United States is sovereign, and [that] the scenes of their offense, their capture, their trial and their punishment were all beyond the territorial jurisdiction of any court of the United States." 339 U.S., at 778. The Government seizes upon this language as proof positive that the *Eisentrager* Court adopted a formalistic, sovereignty-based test for determining the reach of the Suspension Clause. We reject this reading for three reasons.

First, we do not accept the idea that the above-quoted passage from *Eisentrager* is the only authoritative language in the opinion and that all the rest is dicta. The Court's further determinations, based on practical considerations, were integral to Part II of its opinion and came before the decision announced its holding. *See* 339 U.S., at 781.

. . . Even if we assume the *Eisentrager* Court considered the United States' lack of formal legal sovereignty over Landsberg Prison as the decisive factor in that case, its holding is not inconsistent with a functional approach to questions of extraterritoriality. The formal legal status of a given territory affects, at least to some extent, the political branches' control over that territory. *De jure* sovereignty is a factor that bears upon which constitutional guarantees apply there.

Third, if the Government's reading of *Eisentrager* were correct, the opinion would have marked not only a change in, but a complete repudiation of, the *Insular Cases*' (and later *Reid*'s) functional approach to questions of extraterritoriality. We cannot accept the Government's view. Nothing in *Eisentrager* says that *de jure* sovereignty is or has ever been the only relevant consideration in determining the geographic reach of the Constitution or of habeas corpus. Were that the case, there would be considerable tension between *Eisentrager,* on the one hand, and the *Insular Cases* and *Reid,* on the other. Our cases need not be read to conflict in this manner. A constricted reading of *Eisentrager* overlooks what we see as a common thread uniting the *Insular Cases, Eisentrager,* and *Reid:* the idea that questions of extraterritoriality turn on objective factors and practical concerns, not formalism.

B

The Government's formal sovereignty-based test raises troubling separation-of-powers concerns as well. The political history of Guantanamo illustrates the deficiencies of this approach. The United States has maintained complete and uninterrupted control of the bay for over 100 years. . . . The necessary implication of the argument is that by surrendering formal sovereignty over any unincorporated territory to a third party, while at the same time entering into a lease that grants total control over the territory back to the United States, it would be possible for the political branches to govern without legal constraint.

Our basic charter cannot be contracted away like this. The Constitution grants Congress and the President the power to acquire, dispose of, and govern territory, not the power to decide when and where its terms apply. Even when the United States acts outside its borders, its powers are not "absolute and unlimited" but are subject "to such restrictions as are expressed in the Constitution." *Murphy v. Ramsey,* 114 U.S. 15, 44 (1885). Abstaining from questions involving formal sovereignty and territorial governance is one thing. To hold the political branches have the power to switch the Constitution on or off at will is quite another. The former position reflects this Court's recognition that certain matters requiring political judgments are best left to the political branches. The latter would permit a striking anomaly in our tripartite system of government, leading to a regime in which Congress and the President, not this Court, say "what the law is." *Marbury v. Madison,* 1 Cranch 137, 177 (1803).

These concerns have particular bearing upon the Suspension Clause question in the cases now before us, for the writ of habeas corpus is itself an indispensable mechanism for monitoring the separation of powers. The test for determining the scope of this provision must not be subject to manipulation by those whose power it is designed to restrain.

C

As we recognized in *Rasul,* 542 U.S., at 476; *id.,* at 487 (Kennedy, J., concurring in judgment), the outlines of a framework for determining the reach of the Suspension Clause are suggested by the factors the Court relied upon in *Eisentrager.* In addition to the practical concerns discussed above, the *Eisentrager* Court found relevant that each petitioner:

> "(a) is an enemy alien; (b) has never been or resided in the United States; (c) was captured outside of our territory and there held in military custody as a prisoner of war; (d) was tried and convicted by a Military Commission sitting outside the United States; (e) for offenses against laws of war committed outside the United States; (f) and is at all times imprisoned outside the United States." 339 U.S., at 777.

Based on this language from *Eisentrager,* and the reasoning in our other extraterritoriality opinions, we conclude that at least three factors are relevant in determining the reach of the Suspension Clause: (1) the citizenship and status of the detainee and the adequacy of the process through which that status determination was made; (2) the nature of the sites where apprehension and then detention took place; and (3) the practical obstacles inherent in resolving the prisoner's entitlement to the writ.

Applying this framework, we note at the onset that the status of these detainees is a matter of dispute. The petitioners, like those in *Eisentrager,* are not American citizens. But the petitioners in *Eisentrager* did not contest, it seems, the Court's assertion that they were "enemy alien[s]." In the instant cases, by contrast, the detainees deny they are enemy combatants. They have been afforded some process in CSRT proceedings to determine their status; but, unlike in *Eisentrager,* there has been no trial by military commission for violations of the laws of war. The difference is not trivial. The records from the *Eisentrager* trials suggest that, well before the petitioners brought their case to this Court, there had been a rigorous adversarial process to test the legality of their detention. The *Eisentrager* petitioners were charged by a bill of particulars that made detailed factual allegations against them. To rebut the accusations, they were entitled to representation by counsel, allowed to introduce evidence on their own behalf, and permitted to cross-examine the prosecution's witnesses.

In comparison, the procedural protections afforded to the detainees in the CSRT hearings are far more limited, and, we conclude, fall well short of the procedures and adversarial mechanisms that would eliminate the need for habeas corpus review. Although the detainee is assigned a "Personal Representative" to assist him during CSRT proceedings, the Secretary of the Navy's memorandum makes clear that person is not the detainee's lawyer or even his "advocate." The Government's evidence is accorded a presumption of validity. The detainee is allowed to present "reasonably available" evidence, but his ability to rebut the Government's evidence against him is limited by the circumstances of his confinement and his lack of counsel at this stage. And although the detainee can seek review of his status determination in the Court of Appeals, that review process cannot cure all defects in the earlier proceedings. *See* Part V, *infra.*

As to the second factor relevant to this analysis, the detainees here are similarly situated to the *Eisentrager* petitioners in that the sites of their apprehension and detention are technically outside the sovereign territory of the United States. As noted earlier, this is a factor that weighs against finding they have rights under the Suspension

Clause. But there are critical differences between Landsberg Prison, circa 1950, and the United States Naval Station at Guantanamo Bay in 2008. Unlike its present control over the naval station, the United States' control over the prison in Germany was neither absolute nor indefinite. Like all parts of occupied Germany, the prison was under the jurisdiction of the combined Allied Forces. The United States was therefore answerable to its Allies for all activities occurring there. The Court's holding in *Eisentrager* was thus consistent with the *Insular Cases*, where it had held there was no need to extend full constitutional protections to territories the United States did not intend to govern indefinitely. Guantanamo Bay, on the other hand, is no transient possession. In every practical sense Guantanamo is not abroad; it is within the constant jurisdiction of the United States.

As to the third factor, we recognize, as the Court did in *Eisentrager,* that there are costs to holding the Suspension Clause applicable in a case of military detention abroad. Habeas corpus proceedings may require expenditure of funds by the Government and may divert the attention of military personnel from other pressing tasks. While we are sensitive to these concerns, we do not find them dispositive. Compliance with any judicial process requires some incremental expenditure of resources. Yet civilian courts and the Armed Forces have functioned along side each other at various points in our history. *See, e.g., Duncan v. Kahanamoku,* 327 U.S. 304 (1946); *Ex parte Milligan,* 4 Wall. 2 (1866). The Government presents no credible arguments that the military mission at Guantanamo would be compromised if habeas corpus courts had jurisdiction to hear the detainees' claims. And in light of the plenary control the United States asserts over the base, none are apparent to us.

The situation in *Eisentrager* was far different, given the historical context and nature of the military's mission in post-War Germany. When hostilities in the European Theater came to an end, the United States became responsible for an occupation zone encompassing over 57,000 square miles with a population of 18 million. In addition to supervising massive reconstruction and aid efforts the American forces stationed in Germany faced potential security threats from a defeated enemy. In retrospect the post-War occupation may seem uneventful. But at the time *Eisentrager* was decided, the Court was right to be concerned about judicial interference with the military's efforts to contain "enemy elements, guerilla fighters, and 'were-wolves.'" 339 U.S., at 784.

Similar threats are not apparent here; nor does the Government argue that they are. The United States Naval Station at Guantanamo Bay consists of 45 square miles of land and water. The base has been used, at various points, to house migrants and refugees temporarily. At present, however, other than the detainees themselves, the only long-term residents are American military personnel, their families, and a small number of workers. The detainees have been deemed enemies of the United States. At present, dangerous as they may be if released, they are contained in a secure prison facility located on an isolated and heavily fortified military base.

There is no indication, furthermore, that adjudicating a habeas corpus petition would cause friction with the host government. . . . [I]f the detention facility were located in an active theater of war, arguments that issuing the writ would be "impracticable or anomalous" would have more weight. *See Reid,* 354 U.S., at 74 (Harlan, J., concurring in result). Under the facts presented here, however, there are few practical barriers to the running of the writ. To the extent barriers arise, habeas corpus procedures likely can be modified to address them.

It is true that before today the Court has never held that noncitizens detained by our Government in territory over which another country maintains *de jure* sovereignty have any rights under our Constitution. But the cases before us lack any precise historical parallel. They involve individuals detained by executive order for the duration of a conflict that, if measured from September 11, 2001, to the present, is already among the longest wars in American history. The detainees, moreover, are held in a territory that, while technically not part of the United States, is under the complete and total control of our Government. Under these circumstances the lack of a precedent on point is no barrier to our holding.

We hold that Art. I, §9, cl. 2, of the Constitution has full effect at Guantanamo Bay. If the privilege of habeas corpus is to be denied to the detainees now before us, Congress must act in accordance with the requirements of the Suspension Clause. *Cf. Hamdi,* 542 U.S., at 564 (Scalia, J., dissenting) ("[I]ndefinite imprisonment on reasonable suspicion is not an available option of treatment for those accused of aiding the enemy, absent a suspension of the writ"). This Court may not impose a *de facto* suspension by abstaining from these controversies. The MCA does not purport to be a formal suspension of the writ; and the Government, in its submissions to us, has not argued that it is. Petitioners, therefore, are entitled to the privilege of habeas corpus to challenge the legality of their detention.

V

In light of this holding the question becomes whether the statute stripping jurisdiction to issue the writ avoids the Suspension Clause mandate because Congress has provided adequate substitute procedures for habeas corpus. . . . [We return to this part of the Court's analysis later in the chapter, *infra* p. 864.]

* * *

In considering both the procedural and substantive standards used to impose detention to prevent acts of terrorism, proper deference must be accorded to the political branches. *See United States v. Curtiss-Wright Export Corp.,* 299 U.S. 304, 320 (1936). Unlike the President and some designated Members of Congress, neither the Members of this Court nor most federal judges begin the day with briefings that may describe new and serious threats to our Nation and its people. The law must accord the Executive substantial authority to apprehend and detain those who pose a real danger to our security.

Officials charged with daily operational responsibility for our security may consider a judicial discourse on the history of the Habeas Corpus Act of 1679 and like matters to be far removed from the Nation's present, urgent concerns. Established legal doctrine, however, must be consulted for its teaching. Remote in time it may be; irrelevant to the present it is not. Security depends upon a sophisticated intelligence apparatus and the ability of our Armed Forces to act and to interdict. There are further considerations, however. Security subsists, too, in fidelity to freedom's first principles. Chief among these are freedom from arbitrary and unlawful restraint and the personal liberty that is secured by adherence to the separation of powers. It is from these principles that the judicial authority to consider petitions for habeas corpus relief derives.

Our opinion does not undermine the Executive's powers as Commander in Chief. On the contrary, the exercise of those powers is vindicated, not eroded, when confirmed by the Judicial Branch. Within the Constitution's separation-of-powers structure, few exercises of judicial power are as legitimate or as necessary as the responsibility to hear challenges to the authority of the Executive to imprison a person. Some of these petitioners have been in custody for six years with no definitive judicial determination as to the legality of their detention. Their access to the writ is a necessity to determine the lawfulness of their status, even if, in the end, they do not obtain the relief they seek.

Because our Nation's past military conflicts have been of limited duration, it has been possible to leave the outer boundaries of war powers undefined. If, as some fear, terrorism continues to pose dangerous threats to us for years to come, the Court might not have this luxury. This result is not inevitable, however. The political branches, consistent with their independent obligations to interpret and uphold the Constitution, can engage in a genuine debate about how best to preserve constitutional values while protecting the Nation from terrorism. *Cf. Hamdan* [*v. Rumsfeld,* 548 U.S. 557 (2006)], at 636 (Breyer, J., concurring) ("[J]udicial insistence upon that consultation does not weaken our Nation's ability to deal with danger. To the contrary, that insistence strengthens the Nation's ability to determine — through democratic means — how best to do so").

It bears repeating that our opinion does not address the content of the law that governs petitioners' detention. That is a matter yet to be determined. We hold that petitioners may invoke the fundamental procedural protections of habeas corpus. The laws and Constitution are designed to survive, and remain in force, in extraordinary times. Liberty and security can be reconciled; and in our system they are reconciled within the framework of the law. The Framers decided that habeas corpus, a right of first importance, must be a part of that framework, a part of that law.

The determination by the Court of Appeals that the Suspension Clause and its protections are inapplicable to petitioners was in error. The judgment of the Court of Appeals is reversed. The cases are remanded to the Court of Appeals with instructions that it remand the cases to the District Court for proceedings consistent with this opinion.

It is so ordered.

[The concurring opinion of Justice SOUTER, with whom Justice GINSBURG and Justice BREYER joined, is omitted.]

[The dissenting opinion of Chief Justice ROBERTS, with whom Justice SCALIA, Justice THOMAS, and Justice ALITO joined, is excerpted below, *infra* p. 870.]

Justice SCALIA, with whom THE CHIEF JUSTICE, Justice THOMAS, and Justice ALITO join, dissenting. . . . Contrary to my usual practice, . . . I think it appropriate to begin with a description of the disastrous consequences of what the Court has done today.

I

America is at war with radical Islamists. . . .

The game of bait-and-switch that today's opinion plays upon the Nation's Commander in Chief will make the war harder on us. It will almost certainly cause more

Americans to be killed. That consequence would be tolerable if necessary to preserve a time-honored legal principle vital to our constitutional Republic. But it is this Court's blatant *abandonment* of such a principle that produces the decision today. The President relied on our settled precedent in *Johnson v. Eisentrager*, 339 U.S. 763 (1950), when he established the prison at Guantanamo Bay for enemy aliens. Citing that case, the President's Office of Legal Counsel advised him "that the great weight of legal authority indicates that a federal district court could not properly exercise habeas jurisdiction over an alien detained at [Guantanamo Bay]." Memorandum from Patrick F. Philbin and John C. Yoo, Deputy Assistant Attorneys General, Office of Legal Counsel, to William J. Haynes II, General Counsel, Dept. of Defense (Dec. 28, 2001). Had the law been otherwise, the military surely would not have transported prisoners there, but would have kept them in Afghanistan, transferred them to another of our foreign military bases, or turned them over to allies for detention. Those other facilities might well have been worse for the detainees themselves.

In the long term, then, the Court's decision today accomplishes little, except perhaps to reduce the well-being of enemy combatants that the Court ostensibly seeks to protect. In the short term, however, the decision is devastating. At least 30 of those prisoners hitherto released from Guantanamo Bay have returned to the battlefield. Some have been captured or killed. But others have succeeded in carrying on their atrocities against innocent civilians. . . .

These, mind you, were detainees whom *the military* had concluded were not enemy combatants. Their return to the kill illustrates the incredible difficulty of assessing who is and who is not an enemy combatant in a foreign theater of operations where the environment does not lend itself to rigorous evidence collection. Astoundingly, the Court today raises the bar, requiring military officials to appear before civilian courts and defend their decisions under procedural and evidentiary rules that go beyond what Congress has specified. As the Chief Justice's dissent makes clear, we have no idea what those procedural and evidentiary rules are, but they will be determined by civil courts and (in the Court's contemplation at least) will be more detainee-friendly than those now applied, since otherwise there would no reason to hold the congressionally prescribed procedures unconstitutional. If they impose a higher standard of proof (from foreign battlefields) than the current procedures require, the number of the enemy returned to combat will obviously increase.

But even when the military has evidence that it can bring forward, it is often foolhardy to release that evidence to the attorneys representing our enemies. And one escalation of procedures that the Court *is* clear about is affording the detainees increased access to witnesses (perhaps troops serving in Afghanistan?) and to classified information. During the 1995 prosecution of Omar Abdel Rahman, federal prosecutors gave the names of 200 unindicted co-conspirators to the "Blind Sheik's" defense lawyers; that information was in the hands of Osama Bin Laden within two weeks. In another case, trial testimony revealed to the enemy that the United States had been monitoring their cellular network, whereupon they promptly stopped using it, enabling more of them to evade capture and continue their atrocities. . . .

. . . The Court today decrees that no good reason to accept the judgment of the other two branches is "apparent." "The Government," it declares, "presents no credible arguments that the military mission at Guantanamo would be compromised if habeas corpus courts had jurisdiction to hear the detainees' claims." What competence does the Court have to second-guess the judgment of Congress and the President on such a point? None whatever. But the Court blunders in nonetheless. Henceforth, as today's opinion makes unnervingly clear, how to handle enemy prisoners in this war will ultimately lie with the branch that knows least about the national security concerns that the subject entails.

II

A...

...The Court admits that it cannot determine whether the writ historically extended to aliens held abroad, and it concedes (necessarily) that Guantanamo Bay lies outside the sovereign territory of the United States. Together, these two concessions establish that it is (in the Court's view) perfectly ambiguous whether the common-law writ would have provided a remedy for these petitioners. If that is so, the Court has no basis to strike down the Military Commissions Act, and must leave undisturbed the considered judgment of the coequal branches.

How, then, does the Court weave a clear constitutional prohibition out of pure interpretive equipoise? The Court resorts to "fundamental separation-of-powers principles" to interpret the Suspension Clause. According to the Court, because "the writ of habeas corpus is itself an indispensable mechanism for monitoring the separation of powers," the test of its extraterritorial reach "must not be subject to manipulation by those whose power it is designed to restrain."

That approach distorts the nature of the separation of powers and its role in the constitutional structure. The "fundamental separation-of-powers principles" that the Constitution embodies are to be derived not from some judicially imagined matrix, but from the sum total of the individual separation-of-powers provisions that the Constitution sets forth. Only by considering them one-by-one does the full shape of the *Constitution's* separation-of-powers principles emerge. It is nonsensical to interpret those provisions themselves in light of some general "separation-of-powers principles" dreamed up by the Court. Rather, they must be interpreted to mean what they were understood to mean when the people ratified them. And if the understood scope of the writ of habeas corpus was "designed to restrain" (as the Court says) the actions of the Executive, the understood *limits* upon that scope were (as the Court seems not to grasp) just as much "designed to restrain" the incursions of the Third Branch. "Manipulation" of the territorial reach of the writ by the Judiciary poses just as much a threat to the proper separation of powers as "manipulation" by the Executive. As I will show below, manipulation is what is afoot here. The understood limits upon the writ deny our jurisdiction over the habeas petitions brought by these enemy aliens, and entrust the President with the crucial wartime determinations about their status and continued confinement.

B

The Court purports to derive from our precedents a "functional" test for the extraterritorial reach of the writ, which shows that the Military Commissions Act unconstitutionally restricts the scope of habeas. That is remarkable because the most pertinent of those precedents, *Johnson v. Eisentrager*, 339 U.S. 763, conclusively establishes the opposite....

. . . *Eisentrager* nowhere mentions a "functional" test, and the notion that it is based upon such a principle is patently false. . . .

The category of prisoner comparable to these detainees are not the *Eisentrager* criminal defendants, but the more than 400,000 prisoners of war detained in the United States alone during World War II. Not a single one was accorded the right to have his detention validated by a habeas corpus action in federal court — and that despite the fact that they were present on U.S. soil. The Court's analysis produces a crazy result: Whereas those convicted and sentenced to death for war crimes are without judicial remedy, all enemy combatants detained during a war, at least insofar as they are confined in an area away from the battlefield over which the United States exercises "absolute and indefinite" control, may seek a writ of habeas corpus in federal court. And, as an even more bizarre implication from the Court's reasoning, those prisoners whom the military plans to try by full-dress Commission at a future date may file habeas petitions and secure release before their trials take place. . . .

III

Putting aside the conclusive precedent of *Eisentrager,* it is clear that the original understanding of the Suspension Clause was that habeas corpus was not available to aliens abroad. . . .

. . . *[A] ll* available historical evidence points to the conclusion that the writ would not have been available at common law for aliens captured and held outside the sovereign territory of the Crown. Despite three opening briefs, three reply briefs, and support from a legion of *amici,* petitioners have failed to identify a single case in the history of Anglo-American law that supports their claim to jurisdiction. The Court finds it significant that there is no recorded case *denying* jurisdiction to such prisoners either. But a case standing for the remarkable proposition that the writ could issue to a foreign land would surely have been reported, whereas a case denying such a writ for lack of jurisdiction would likely not. At a minimum, the absence of a reported case either way leaves unrefuted the voluminous commentary stating that habeas was confined to the dominions of the Crown.

What history teaches is confirmed by the nature of the limitations that the Constitution places upon suspension of the common-law writ. It can be suspended only "in Cases of Rebellion or Invasion." Art. I, §9, cl. 2. The latter case (invasion) is plainly limited to the territory of the United States; and while it is conceivable that a rebellion could be mounted by American citizens abroad, surely the overwhelming majority of its occurrences would be domestic. If the extraterritorial scope of habeas turned on flexible, "functional" considerations, as the Court holds, why would the Constitution limit its suspension almost entirely to instances of domestic crisis? Surely there is an even greater justification for suspension in foreign lands where the United States might hold prisoners of war during an ongoing conflict. And correspondingly, there is less threat to liberty when the Government suspends the writ's (supposed) application in foreign lands, where even on the most extreme view prisoners are entitled to fewer constitutional rights. It makes no sense, therefore, for the Constitution generally to forbid suspension of the writ abroad if indeed the writ has application there. . . .

The Nation will live to regret what the Court has done today. I dissent.

Notes and Questions

1. Form or Function? Justice Kennedy's majority opinion refers to the role of the Suspension Clause in the separation of powers at least 11 different times, but ultimately settles upon a functional test for assessing its extraterritorial applicability to noncitizens, balancing "(1) the citizenship and status of the detainee and the adequacy of the process through which that status determination was made; (2) the nature of the sites where apprehension and then detention took place; and (3) the practical obstacles inherent in resolving the prisoner's entitlement to the writ." Is there a fundamental tension between these two approaches (and, thus, between Parts III and IV of Justice Kennedy's opinion)? At the end of the day, if the Suspension Clause is such a vital element of constitutional checks and balances, should its applicability turn on this litany of other considerations? In the opposite direction, if the Suspension Clause depends upon these kinds of practical concerns, just how critical is it to the separation of powers?

2. Does the Constitutional Writ Extend Beyond Guantánamo Bay? While *Boumediene* dealt only with detainees held at Guantánamo, its functional test for extraterritorial application of the Suspension Clause has been applied elsewhere. In *Al Maqaleh v. Gates*, 605 F.3d 84 (D.C. Cir. 2010), petitioners were three prisoners at Bagram Air Force Base in Afghanistan, none of whom was either (1) a citizen of Afghanistan or (2) captured in Afghanistan. Regarding citizenship, the court found these petitioners (two Yemenis and a Tunisian) no different from those in *Boumediene.* The relatively scant process they received from an "Unlawful Enemy Combatant Review Board" (UECRB) weighed in their favor. But the location of their detention weighed the other way: "While it is certainly realistic to assert that the United States has *de facto* sovereignty over Guantánamo, the same simply is not true with respect to Bagram." *Id.* at 97. The tie-breaker was the third factor, "the practical obstacles inherent in resolving the prisoner's entitlement to the writ." Bagram was, the court noted, located in an active theater of war. "The United States asserts, and petitioners cannot credibly dispute, that all of the attributes of a facility exposed to the vagaries of war are present in Bagram." Accordingly, the court held, "[w]e cannot, consistent with *Eisentrager* as elucidated by *Boumediene*, hold that the right to the writ of habeas corpus and the constitutional protections of the Suspension Clause extend to Bagram detention facility in Afghanistan." *Id.* at 97-98.

Even as the nature of the U.S. military presence in Afghanistan has evolved, the D.C. Circuit has reaffirmed this reasoning, despite renewed claims from the petitioners that they were detained in a combat theater largely to *avoid* federal habeas jurisdiction. *See Al-Maqaleh v. Hagel*, 738 F.3d 312, 335-336 (D.C. Cir. 2013) (holding that alleged government manipulation of the location of detention is not part of the *Boumediene* analysis). Did *Al Maqaleh* thereby allow the Administration to create a new "black hole" for detainees? Based on the analysis in *Al Maqaleh*, how would you decide the extraterritorial application of the Suspension Clause to noncitizen detainees at a CIA detention facility in Poland? On a U.S. naval vessel in the Indian Ocean?

3. Does the Constitutional Writ Apply Throughout the Territorial United States? Although the Supreme Court in *Boumediene* appeared to assume that the Suspension

Clause protects all noncitizens within the United States, the Third Circuit held otherwise in *Castro v. U.S. Dep't of Homeland Security*, 835 F.3d 422 (3d Cir. 2016), concluding that undocumented immigrants "apprehended within hours of surreptitiously entering the United States" are functionally equivalent to "arriving aliens . . . stopped at the border," and that they are not constitutionally entitled to habeas review even after — and notwithstanding — *Boumediene. See id.* at 445-449 & n.22. (In so holding, the Court of Appeals upheld a statute, 8 U.S.C. §1252(a)(2)(A)(2018), that took away federal habeas jurisdiction in such cases.) Indeed, the court held that *Boumediene*'s multi-factor test "provide[s] little guidance" for the constitutional entitlement to habeas within the United States because "the [*Boumediene*] Court derived the factors from its extraterritoriality jurisprudence in order to assess the reach of the Suspension Clause to a territory where the United States is not sovereign." *Id.* at 445 n.25. "In our case, of course, there is no question that Petitioners were apprehended within the sovereign territory of the United States; thus, the *Boumediene* factors are of limited utility in determining Petitioners' entitlement to the protections of the Suspension Clause." *Id.*

But aren't *Boumediene*'s factors of limited utility because there's a *stronger* case for habeas for persons already within the United States at the time of their detention? After all, *Boumediene* derived its "factors" to decide whether habeas protections should be extended extraterritorially. Do we need them to decide whether habeas protection applies *intra*territorially? What is the argument for why noncitizen terrorism suspects captured overseas (and who have never set foot on U.S. soil) are protected by the Suspension Clause, but undocumented immigrants arrested within the territorial United States — or even those stopped at the border — are not?

The Ninth Circuit has since disagreed with *Castro*, and held that the Suspension Clause does apply to undocumented immigrants arrested shortly after entering the country. *See Thuraissigiam v. U.S. Dep't of Homeland Security*, 917 F.3d 1097, 1108 (9th Cir. 2019) (noting that *Boumediene* factors "do not map precisely onto this case because Thuraissigiam was apprehended and is detained on U.S. soil," but finding that *Boumediene*'s emphasis also on the "1789-era historical application of the writ" supports the intraterritorial application of the Suspension Clause). The Supreme Court granted certiorari in *Thuraissigiam* in October 2019, with the federal government urging the Court to side with the Third Circuit. *Dep't of Homeland Security v. Thuraissigiam*, 140 S. Ct. 427 (2019). On which side should the Court come down — and why?

4. What Kinds of Claims Are Cognizable Via Habeas? In all of the cases we have considered so far, prisoners have sought to use the vehicle of a habeas petition to challenge either the "fact" or the "duration" of their confinement — what the Supreme Court has described as the "core" of habeas corpus. *See Preiser v. Rodriguez*, 411 U.S. 475, 477 (1973). But there are other ways in which a prisoner's detention could be unlawful — including if the *conditions* of his confinement violate applicable constitutional, statutory, or international law protections, or if he is subjected to some other legally objectionable process (e.g., a military commission) while lawfully detained. Can those claims also be brought through habeas petitions?

The distinction between "core" habeas claims and what we might call "noncore" claims is especially important under the MCA, which, in addition to the jurisdiction-stripping provision invalidated in *Boumediene*, also forecloses jurisdiction over "any other action against the United States or its agents relating to any aspect of the detention, transfer, treatment, trial, or conditions of confinement" of noncitizen detainees. 28 U.S.C. §2241(e)(2); *see Al Zahrani v. Rodriguez*, 669 F.3d 315 (D.C. Cir. 2012) (upholding this provision as applied to *Bivens* suits for damages by former detainees); *see also Janko v. Gates*, 741 F.3d 136 (D.C. Cir. 2014) (applying *Al Zahrani* to a case in which the detainee had prevailed in his habeas petition prior to his release). If noncitizen detainees may obtain judicial review only through habeas petitions (the practical result of reading *Boumediene* together with *Al Zahrani* and *Janko*), and if habeas petitions become moot upon a detainee's release from custody, *see Gul v. Obama*, 652 F.3d 12 (D.C. Cir. 2011), then quite a lot turns on the kinds of claims that may properly be brought in a habeas petition.

The D.C. Circuit's decision in *Aamer v. Obama*, 742 F.3d 1023 (D.C. Cir. 2014), simplified matters dramatically — holding that the Supreme Court not only invalidated the MCA's habeas-stripping provision as applied to "core" claims from the Guantánamo detainees, but that it also thereby returned the habeas statute to the pre-2005 status quo for *all* claims. Thus, instead of having to resolve whether the *Suspension Clause* protects a particular kind of "non-core" habeas claim, courts applying *Aamer* need only resolve whether the federal habeas *statute* encompassed such a claim at the time *Rasul* was decided. And in *Aamer*, the D.C. Circuit held that the habeas statute *did* then encompass challenges to the conditions of confinement, *see id.* at 1028-1038, even though the court went on to reject the petitioners' challenge on the merits, *see id.* at 1038-1044.

B. REVIEW REQUIRED BY THE SUSPENSION CLAUSE

It is one thing to conclude that the Suspension Clause applies in a particular context, and that it therefore requires courts to entertain claims from federal prisoners that are properly cognizable via habeas petitions. But what must such judicial review look like? Does the Suspension Clause simply require federal courts to formally provide a remedy called "habeas," no matter how cursory or superficial the underlying review might be? Or does it instead require something more functional — judicial review that meets certain substantive benchmarks, regardless of what it is actually called?

In a pair of older cases, the Supreme Court suggested that the answer was the latter, twice upholding statutes that created "substitutes" to the habeas petitions authorized by 28 U.S.C. §2241 for no other reason than administrative convenience. *See Swain v. Pressley*, 430 U.S. 372 (1977); *United States v. Hayman*, 342 U.S. 205 (1952). Although the statutes at issue both displaced habeas corpus, they not only authorized comparable judicial review, but they also included "safety valves" — provisions expressly allowing resort to habeas itself if the substitute remedy proved "inadequate or ineffective to test the legality of [the prisoner's] detention." It therefore followed that these statutes satisfied the Suspension Clause, the Supreme Court concluded, because the protection afforded by the Suspension Clause was left intact. On that logic, the Suspension Clause does not formally require something *called* "habeas"; it requires *a* remedy, however named, that is functionally adequate and effective to test the legality of a prisoner's detention.

Reading the Second Holding in *Boumediene v. Bush*

What if Congress replaces habeas with an alternative that lacks a safety valve? In effect, that's what the Military Commissions Act of 2006 (MCA) did when it stripped Article III courts of habeas jurisdiction in cases brought by noncitizens detained by the military. Would-be habeas petitioners were left instead with only a heavily circumscribed appeal to the D.C. Circuit of a status determination by a Combatant Status Review Tribunal (CSRT) — an appeal right created in the Detainee Treatment Act of 2005 (DTA). After holding that the Suspension Clause "has full effect" at Guantánamo Bay, see *supra* p. 856, the Supreme Court in *Boumediene v. Bush* turned to whether this review scheme satisfied the Suspension Clause — and concluded that it did not. In the process, both Justice Kennedy's majority opinion and Chief Justice Roberts' dissent had a lot to say about what makes a remedy "adequate and effective" under the Suspension Clause. Consider these questions as you read their analyses:

- Read very carefully through Justice Kennedy's comparison of habeas cases challenging executive detention and the more common use of habeas to collaterally attack criminal convictions. Why, in Justice Kennedy's view, is more robust judicial review required in the former context? Do you agree? Does Chief Justice Roberts disagree?
- What are some of the basic requirements, according to Justice Kennedy, of an "adequate" and "effective" remedy to challenge unlawful detention? How, in his view, does the CSRT (and D.C. Circuit appeal thereof) fail to satisfy those requirements? What kinds of arguments are detainees not allowed to make to the CSRT and D.C. Circuit on appeal that they *would* be allowed to press in a habeas petition?
- Chief Justice Roberts makes much in his dissent about how the Court should at least allow the CSRTs to operate for a time before passing on their adequacy and effectiveness. After all, how can the Court decide in advance whether the CSRTs satisfy due process? How does Justice Kennedy (indirectly) respond to this argument? Is he worried about due process? Or is he worried about something else? If the latter, *what* is he worried about?

Boumediene v. Bush

United States Supreme Court, 2008
553 U.S. 723

[Other parts of the decision are set forth *supra* p. 850.]

Justice KENNEDY delivered the opinion of the Court. . . . If the privilege of habeas corpus is to be denied to the detainees now before us, Congress must act in accordance with the requirements of the Suspension Clause. *Cf. Hamdi* [*v. Rumsfeld,* 542 U.S. 507 (2004)], at 564 (Scalia, J., dissenting) ("[I]ndefinite imprisonment on reasonable suspicion is not an available option of treatment for those accused of aiding the enemy, absent a suspension of the writ"). . . .

V

. . . The Government submits there has been compliance with the Suspension Clause because the DTA review process in the Court of Appeals, *see* DTA §1005(e), provides an adequate substitute. Congress has granted that court jurisdiction to consider

> "(i) whether the status determination of the [CSRT] . . . was consistent with the standards and procedures specified by the Secretary of Defense . . . and (ii) to the extent the Constitution and laws of the United States are applicable, whether the use of such standards and procedures to make the determination is consistent with the Constitution and laws of the United States." §1005(e)(2)(C), 119 Stat. 2742. . . .

A

Our case law does not contain extensive discussion of standards defining suspension of the writ or of circumstances under which suspension has occurred. This simply confirms the care Congress has taken throughout our Nation's history to preserve the writ and its function. Indeed, most of the major legislative enactments pertaining to habeas corpus have acted not to contract the writ's protection but to expand it or to hasten resolution of prisoners' claims. . . .

. . . [Unlike those statutes], here we confront statutes, the DTA and the MCA, that were intended to circumscribe habeas review. Congress' purpose is evident not only from the unequivocal nature of MCA §7's jurisdiction-stripping language, 28 U.S.C.A. §2241(e)(1) (Supp. 2007) ("No court, justice, or judge shall have jurisdiction to hear or consider an application for a writ of habeas corpus . . . "), but also from a comparison of the DTA to the statutes at issue in [*United States v. Hayman,* 342 U.S. 205 (1952), and *Swain v. Pressley,* 430 U.S. 372 (1977), both of which included safety-valve provisions preserving habeas in circumstances in which the alternative proved inadequate or ineffective]. . . . When Congress has intended to replace traditional habeas corpus with habeas-like substitutes, . . . it has granted to the courts broad remedial powers to secure the historic office of the writ. . . .

In contrast, the DTA's jurisdictional grant is quite limited. The Court of Appeals has jurisdiction not to inquire into the legality of the detention generally but only to assess whether the CSRT complied with the "standards and procedures specified by the Secretary of Defense" and whether those standards and procedures are lawful. DTA §1005(e)(2)(C), 119 Stat. 2742. If Congress had envisioned DTA review as coextensive with traditional habeas corpus, it would not have drafted the statute in this manner. . . . [M]oreover, there has been no effort to preserve habeas corpus review as an avenue of last resort. No saving clause exists in either the MCA or the DTA. And MCA §7 eliminates habeas review for these petitioners. . . .

B

We do not endeavor to offer a comprehensive summary of the requisites for an adequate substitute for habeas corpus. We do consider it uncontroversial, however, that the privilege of habeas corpus entitles the prisoner to a meaningful opportunity to demonstrate that he is being held pursuant to "the erroneous application or interpretation" of relevant law. [*INS v. St. Cyr,* 533 U.S. 289 (2001),] at 302. And the habeas court must have the power to order the conditional release of an individual unlawfully detained — though release need not be the exclusive remedy and is not the appropriate one in every case in which the writ is granted. These are the easily identified attributes of any constitutionally adequate habeas corpus proceeding. But, depending on the circumstances, more may be required.

Indeed, common-law habeas corpus was, above all, an adaptable remedy. Its precise application and scope changed depending upon the circumstances. It appears the common-law habeas court's role was most extensive in cases of pretrial and noncriminal detention, where there had been little or no previous judicial review of the cause for detention. . . .

The idea that the necessary scope of habeas review in part depends upon the rigor of any earlier proceedings accords with our test for procedural adequacy in the due process context. *See Mathews v. Eldridge*, 424 U.S. 319, 335 (1976) (noting that the Due Process Clause requires an assessment of, *inter alia*, "the risk of an erroneous deprivation of [a liberty interest;] and the probable value, if any, of additional or substitute procedural safeguards"). . . .

Accordingly, where relief is sought from a sentence that resulted from the judgment of a court of record, . . . considerable deference is owed to the court that ordered confinement. Likewise in those cases the prisoner should exhaust adequate alternative remedies before filing for the writ in federal court. Both aspects of federal habeas corpus review are justified because it can be assumed that, in the usual course, a court of record provides defendants with a fair, adversary proceeding. . . . The present cases fall outside these categories, however; for here the detention is by executive order.

Where a person is detained by executive order, rather than, say, after being tried and convicted in a court, the need for collateral review is most pressing. A criminal conviction in the usual course occurs after a judicial hearing before a tribunal disinterested in the outcome and committed to procedures designed to ensure its own independence. These dynamics are not inherent in executive detention orders or executive review procedures. In this context the need for habeas corpus is more urgent. The intended duration of the detention and the reasons for it bear upon the precise scope of the inquiry. Habeas corpus proceedings need not resemble a criminal trial, even when the detention is by executive order. But the writ must be effective. The habeas court must have sufficient authority to conduct a meaningful review of both the cause for detention and the Executive's power to detain.

To determine the necessary scope of habeas corpus review, therefore, we must assess the CSRT process, the mechanism through which petitioners' designation as enemy combatants became final. . . .

Petitioners identify what they see as myriad deficiencies in the CSRTs. The most relevant for our purposes are the constraints upon the detainee's ability to rebut the factual basis for the Government's assertion that he is an enemy combatant. As already noted, at the CSRT stage the detainee has limited means to find or present evidence to challenge the Government's case against him. He does not have the assistance of counsel and may not be aware of the most critical allegations that the Government relied upon to order his detention. *See* App. to Pet. for Cert. in No. 06-1196, at 156, ¶F(8) (noting that the detainee can access only the "unclassified portion of the Government Information"). The detainee can confront witnesses that testify during the CSRT proceedings. *Id.*, at 144, ¶*g*(8). But given that there are in effect no limits on the admission of hearsay evidence — the only requirement is that the tribunal deem the evidence "relevant and helpful," *ibid.*, ¶*g*(9) — the detainee's opportunity to question witnesses is likely to be more theoretical than real. . . .

Even if we were to assume that the CSRTs satisfy due process standards, it would not end our inquiry. Habeas corpus is a collateral process that exists, in Justice Holmes' words, to "cu[t] through all forms and g[o] to the very tissue of the structure. It comes in from the outside, not in subordination to the proceedings, and although every form may have been preserved opens the inquiry whether they have been more than an empty shell." *Frank v. Mangum*, 237 U.S. 309, 346 (1915) (dissenting opinion). Even when the procedures authorizing detention are structurally sound, the Suspension Clause remains applicable and the writ relevant. *See* 2 Chambers, Course of Lectures on English Law 1767-1773, at 6 ("Liberty may be violated either by arbitrary *imprisonment* without law or the appearance of law, or by a lawful magistrate for an unlawful reason"). . . .

Although we make no judgment as to whether the CSRTs, as currently constituted, satisfy due process standards, we agree with petitioners that, even when all the parties involved in this process act with diligence and in good faith, there is considerable risk of error in the tribunal's findings of fact. This is a risk inherent in any process that, in the words of the former Chief Judge of the Court of Appeals, is "closed and accusatorial." *See* [*Bismullah v. Gates*, 514 F.3d 1291, 1296 (D.C. Cir. 2008)] (Ginsburg, C.J., concurring in denial of rehearing en banc). And given that the consequence of error may be detention of persons for the duration of hostilities that may last a generation or more, this is a risk too significant to ignore.

For the writ of habeas corpus, or its substitute, to function as an effective and proper remedy in this context, the court that conducts the habeas proceeding must have the means to correct errors that occurred during the CSRT proceedings. This includes some authority to assess the sufficiency of the Government's evidence against the detainee. It also must have the authority to admit and consider relevant exculpatory evidence that was not introduced during the earlier proceeding. . . .

The extent of the showing required of the Government in these cases is a matter to be determined. We need not explore it further at this stage. We do hold that when the judicial power to issue habeas corpus properly is invoked the judicial officer must have adequate authority to make a determination in light of the relevant law and facts and to formulate and issue appropriate orders for relief, including, if necessary, an order directing the prisoner's release.

C

We now consider whether the DTA allows the Court of Appeals to conduct a proceeding meeting these standards. "[W]e are obligated to construe the statute to avoid [constitutional] problems" if it is "'fairly possible'" to do so. *St. Cyr*, 533 U.S., at 299-300 (quoting *Crowell v. Benson*, 285 U.S. 22, 62 (1932)). . . .

The DTA does not explicitly empower the Court of Appeals to order the applicant in a DTA review proceeding released should the court find that the standards and procedures used at his CSRT hearing were insufficient to justify detention. This is troubling. Yet, for present purposes, we can assume congressional silence permits a constitutionally required remedy. . . .

The absence of a release remedy and specific language allowing AUMF challenges are not the only constitutional infirmities from which the statute potentially suffers, however. The more difficult question is whether the DTA permits the Court of Appeals to make requisite findings of fact. The DTA enables petitioners to request "review" of their CSRT determination in the Court of Appeals, DTA §1005(e)(2)(B)(i), 119 Stat. 2742; but the "Scope of Review" provision confines the Court of Appeals' role to reviewing whether the CSRT followed the "standards and procedures" issued by the Department of Defense and assessing whether those "standards and procedures" are lawful. §1005(e)(C), *ibid.* Among these standards is "the requirement that the conclusion of the Tribunal be supported by a preponderance of the evidence... allowing a rebuttable presumption in favor of the Government's evidence." §1005(e)(C)(i), *ibid.*

Assuming the DTA can be construed to allow the Court of Appeals to review or correct the CSRT's factual determinations, as opposed to merely certifying that the tribunal applied the correct standard of proof, we see no way to construe the statute to allow what is also constitutionally required in this context: an opportunity for the detainee to present relevant exculpatory evidence that was not made part of the record in the earlier proceedings.

On its face the statute allows the Court of Appeals to consider no evidence outside the CSRT record....

By foreclosing consideration of evidence not presented or reasonably available to the detainee at the CSRT proceedings, the DTA disadvantages the detainee by limiting the scope of collateral review to a record that may not be accurate or complete. In other contexts, *e.g.*, in post-trial habeas cases where the prisoner already has had a full and fair opportunity to develop the factual predicate of his claims, similar limitations on the scope of habeas review may be appropriate. In this context, however, where the underlying detention proceedings lack the necessary adversarial character, the detainee cannot be held responsible for all deficiencies in the record....

Although we do not hold that an adequate substitute must duplicate §2241 in all respects, it suffices that the Government has not established that the detainees' access to the statutory review provisions at issue is an adequate substitute for the writ of habeas corpus. MCA §7 thus effects an unconstitutional suspension of the writ. In view of our holding we need not discuss the reach of the writ with respect to claims of unlawful conditions of treatment or confinement....

VI

A

In light of our conclusion that there is no jurisdictional bar to the District Court's entertaining petitioners' claims the question remains whether there are prudential barriers to habeas corpus review under these circumstances....

In cases involving foreign citizens detained abroad by the Executive, it likely would be both an impractical and unprecedented extension of judicial power to assume that habeas corpus would be available at the moment the prisoner is taken into custody. If and when habeas corpus jurisdiction applies, as it does in these cases, then proper deference can be accorded to reasonable procedures for screening and initial detention under lawful and proper conditions of confinement and treatment for a reasonable period of time. Domestic exigencies, furthermore, might also impose such onerous burdens on the Government that here, too, the Judicial Branch would be required to devise sensible rules for staying habeas corpus proceedings until the

Government can comply with its requirements in a responsible way. Here, as is true with detainees apprehended abroad, a relevant consideration in determining the courts' role is whether there are suitable alternative processes in place to protect against the arbitrary exercise of governmental power.

The cases before us, however, do not involve detainees who have been held for a short period of time while awaiting their CSRT determinations. Were that the case, or were it probable that the Court of Appeals could complete a prompt review of their applications, the case for requiring temporary abstention or exhaustion of alternative remedies would be much stronger. These qualifications no longer pertain here. In some of these cases six years have elapsed without the judicial oversight that habeas corpus or an adequate substitute demands. And there has been no showing that the Executive faces such onerous burdens that it cannot respond to habeas corpus actions. To require these detainees to complete DTA review before proceeding with their habeas corpus actions would be to require additional months, if not years, of delay. The first DTA review applications were filed over a year ago, but no decisions on the merits have been issued. While some delay in fashioning new procedures is unavoidable, the costs of delay can no longer be borne by those who are held in custody. The detainees in these cases are entitled to a prompt habeas corpus hearing.

Our decision today holds only that the petitioners before us are entitled to seek the writ; that the DTA review procedures are an inadequate substitute for habeas corpus; and that the petitioners in these cases need not exhaust the review procedures in the Court of Appeals before proceeding with their habeas actions in the District Court. The only law we identify as unconstitutional is MCA §7, 28 U.S.C.A. §2241(e) (Supp. 2007). Accordingly, both the DTA and the CSRT process remain intact. Our holding with regard to exhaustion should not be read to imply that a habeas court should intervene the moment an enemy combatant steps foot in a territory where the writ runs. The Executive is entitled to a reasonable period of time to determine a detainee's status before a court entertains that detainee's habeas corpus petition. The CSRT process is the mechanism Congress and the President set up to deal with these issues. Except in cases of undue delay, federal courts should refrain from entertaining an enemy combatant's habeas corpus petition at least until after the Department, acting via the CSRT, has had a chance to review his status.

B

Although we hold that the DTA is not an adequate and effective substitute for habeas corpus, it does not follow that a habeas corpus court may disregard the dangers the detention in these cases was intended to prevent. . . . [T]he Suspension Clause does not resist innovation in the field of habeas corpus. Certain accommodations can be made to reduce the burden habeas corpus proceedings will place on the military without impermissibly diluting the protections of the writ.

In the DTA Congress sought to consolidate review of petitioners' claims in the Court of Appeals. Channeling future cases to one district court would no doubt reduce administrative burdens on the Government. This is a legitimate objective that might be advanced even without an amendment to §2241. . . .

Another of Congress' reasons for vesting exclusive jurisdiction in the Court of Appeals, perhaps, was to avoid the widespread dissemination of classified information. The Government has raised similar concerns here and elsewhere. We make no attempt to anticipate all of the evidentiary and access-to-counsel issues that will arise during the course of the detainees' habeas corpus proceedings. We recognize, however, that the Government has a legitimate interest in protecting sources and methods of intelligence gathering; and we expect that the District Court will use its discretion to accommodate this interest to the greatest extent possible. *Cf. United States v. Reynolds,* 345 U.S. 1, 10 (1953) (recognizing an evidentiary privilege in a civil damages case where "there is a reasonable danger that compulsion of the evidence will expose military matters which, in the interest of national security, should not be divulged").

These and the other remaining questions are within the expertise and competence of the District Court to address in the first instance....

[The concurring opinion of Justice SOUTER, with whom Justice GINSBURG and Justice BREYER join, is omitted.]

Chief Justice ROBERTS, with whom Justice SCALIA, Justice THOMAS, and Justice ALITO join, dissenting. Today the Court strikes down as inadequate the most generous set of procedural protections ever afforded aliens detained by this country as enemy combatants. The political branches crafted these procedures amidst an ongoing military conflict, after much careful investigation and thorough debate. The Court rejects them today out of hand, without bothering to say what due process rights the detainees possess, without explaining how the statute fails to vindicate those rights, and before a single petitioner has even attempted to avail himself of the law's operation. And to what effect? The majority merely replaces a review system designed by the people's representatives with a set of shapeless procedures to be defined by federal courts at some future date. One cannot help but think, after surveying the modest practical results of the majority's ambitious opinion, that this decision is not really about the detainees at all, but about control of federal policy regarding enemy combatants....

...The important point for me, however, is that the Court should have resolved these cases on other grounds. Habeas is most fundamentally a procedural right, a mechanism for contesting the legality of executive detention. The critical threshold question in these cases, prior to any inquiry about the writ's scope, is whether the system the political branches designed protects whatever rights the detainees may possess. If so, there is no need for any additional process, whether called "habeas" or something else....

II...

...After much hemming and hawing, the majority appears to concede that the DTA provides an Article III court competent to order release. The only issue in dispute is the process the Guantanamo prisoners are entitled to use to test the legality of their detention....

A...

Hamdi merits scant attention from the Court — a remarkable omission, as *Hamdi* bears directly on the issues before us. The majority attempts to dismiss *Hamdi*'s relevance by arguing that because the availability of §2241 federal habeas was never in doubt in that case, "the Court had no occasion to define the necessary scope of habeas review . . . in the context of enemy combatant detentions." Hardly. *Hamdi* was all about the scope of habeas review in the context of enemy combatant detentions. The petitioner, an American citizen held within the United States as an enemy combatant, invoked the writ to challenge his detention. After "a careful examination both of the writ . . . and of the Due Process Clause," this Court enunciated the "basic process" the Constitution entitled Hamdi to expect from a habeas court under §2241. That process consisted of the right to "receive notice of the factual basis for his classification, and a fair opportunity to rebut the Government's factual assertions before a neutral decisionmaker." In light of the Government's national security responsibilities, the plurality found the process could be "tailored to alleviate [the] uncommon potential to burden the Executive at a time of ongoing military conflict." For example, the Government could rely on hearsay and could claim a presumption in favor of its own evidence.

Hamdi further suggested that this "basic process" on collateral review could be provided by a military tribunal. It pointed to prisoner-of-war tribunals as a model that would satisfy the Constitution's requirements. Only "[i]n the *absence* of such process" before a military tribunal, the Court held, would Article III courts need to conduct full-dress habeas proceedings to "ensure that the minimum requirements of due process are achieved." *Ibid.* (emphasis added). And even then, the petitioner would be entitled to no more process than he would have received from a properly constituted military review panel, given his limited due process rights and the Government's weighty interests.

Contrary to the majority, *Hamdi* is of pressing relevance because it establishes the procedures American *citizens* detained as enemy combatants can expect from a habeas court proceeding under §2241. The DTA system of military tribunal hearings followed by Article III review looks a lot like the procedure *Hamdi* blessed. If nothing else, it is plain from the design of the DTA that Congress, the President, and this Nation's military leaders have made a good-faith effort to follow our precedent.

The Court, however, will not take "yes" for an answer. . . .

I respectfully dissent.

[The dissenting opinion of Justice SCALIA, with whom THE CHIEF JUSTICE, Justice THOMAS, and Justice ALITO join, is set forth *supra* p. 857.]

Notes and Questions

1. *The Ripeness of "Adequacy."* Chief Justice Roberts' dissent offered any number of ways in which the CSRTs (and the D.C. Circuit's appellate review thereof) *might* have satisfied whatever due process rights the detainees may have had. Thus, he argued, the majority could (and should) have waited for the CSRT process to unfold before holding that it was an inadequate alternative to habeas. His argument may help explain why the Justices originally denied certiorari in *Boumediene*, with Justices Stevens and Kennedy invoking "our practice of requiring the exhaustion of available remedies as a precondition to accepting jurisdiction over applications for the writ of habeas corpus." *Boumediene v. Bush*, 549 U.S. 1328, 1329 (2007) (statement of Stevens & Kennedy, JJ., respecting the denial of certiorari). Three months later, the Court changed its mind and granted review on rehearing. Why might Justices Stevens and

Kennedy have changed their minds? Justice Kennedy, who seldom responded to dissents, did so in his majority opinion only indirectly — especially in his discussion of why, even assuming that the CSRTs satisfied due process, the writ remains "relevant." What were his arguments? Should the Court have waited?

2. *The Significance of Congress's Intent.* One of the other central differences between the majority and the dissent is how far the Court should go to rewrite the DTA to save it — and to read into the statute procedures and authorities that Congress did not provide, in order to render it an adequate alternative to habeas. Who had the better side of this argument? Given what you know about the background of the enactment of the DTA and MCA, do you think Congress intended the statutes to provide a constitutionally adequate alternative to habeas?

3. *The New "Common Law" of Habeas.* Quite consciously, the *Boumediene* Court made no effort "to anticipate all of the evidentiary and access-to-counsel issues that will arise during the course of the detainees' habeas corpus proceedings." Given the absence of detailed statutory procedures and evidentiary rules, the effect of this avoidance, coupled with the abrogation of the CSRT process, was to leave a bevy of complex questions to be resolved by the D.C. district courts and the D.C. Circuit Court of Appeals in the first instance through habeas litigation. The result has been described as a new "common law" of habeas. *See, e.g.*, Baher Azmy, *Executive Detention, Boumediene, and the New Common Law of Habeas*, 95 Iowa L. Rev. 445 (2010). Some judges, though, have vehemently criticized this role, wondering rhetorically if "a court-driven process is best suited to protecting both the rights of petitioners and the safety of our nation," and suggesting that "in the midst of an ongoing war, time to entertain a process of literal trial and error is not a luxury we have." *Al-Bihani v. Obama*, 590 F.3d 866, 881-882 (D.C. Cir. 2010) (Brown, J., concurring). Would it have been better for the Supreme Court itself to articulate the relevant procedural and evidentiary rules? Failing that, and failing a statutory framework, what else could the lower courts have done after *Boumediene*?

4. *The D.C. Circuit and Boumediene.* In the first post-*Boumediene* habeas case in which the merits of the prisoner's detention reached the D.C. Circuit, the Court of Appeals framed its assessment of the applicable procedural and evidentiary baseline as follows:

> Habeas review for Guantanamo detainees need not match the procedures developed by Congress and the courts specifically for habeas challenges to criminal convictions. *Boumediene*'s holding explicitly stated that habeas procedures for detainees "need not resemble a criminal trial," 128 S. Ct. at 2269. . . . The Suspension Clause protects only the fundamental character of habeas proceedings, and any argument equating that fundamental character with all the accoutrements of habeas for domestic criminal defendants is highly suspect. [*Al-Bihani*, 590 F.3d at 876.]

Reread the second and third sentences quoted above. Isn't there a (material) difference between the procedures of a "criminal trial" and the "accoutrements of habeas for domestic criminal defendants"? Didn't Justice Kennedy expressly state that habeas must be *more* rigorous in the context of challenges to executive detention than in collateral attacks on criminal convictions? Did the Court of Appeals simply misread *Boumediene*?

HABEAS CORPUS: THE SCOPE OF THE SUSPENSION CLAUSE: SUMMARY OF BASIC PRINCIPLES

- For noncitizens captured and detained outside the territorial United States, whether the Suspension Clause applies to their detention depends upon a balance of: (1) the citizenship and status of the detainee and the adequacy of the process through which that status determination was made; (2) the nature of the sites where apprehension and then detention took place; and (3) the practical obstacles inherent in resolving the prisoner's entitlement to the writ.

- Applying these tests, the Supreme Court has held that the Suspension Clause "has full effect" at Guantánamo, and the D.C. Circuit has held that the Suspension Clause does not apply at the Bagram Air Base in Afghanistan — although a subsequent D.C. Circuit decision has suggested that the habeas *statute* now applies globally.

- The Suspension Clause protects claims going to the "core" of habeas, i.e., challenges to the legal basis for and/or duration of an individual's confinement. Whether the Suspension Clause goes further — and protects, among other claims, challenges to the conditions of confinement — has not yet been resolved by the courts. Most lower courts, including the D.C. Circuit, have held that the habeas *statute* allows challenges to conditions of confinement, mooting the constitutional question. Lower courts have also, however, upheld a jurisdiction-stripping statute as applied to non-habeas claims by noncitizen military detainees, meaning that claims that are not cognizable via habeas are not available *at all*.

- In cases in which the Suspension Clause applies, Congress can provide alternatives to habeas corpus, but those alternatives must provide the detainee with an "adequate" and "effective" means of obtaining judicial review of the legality of his detention. Although the Supreme Court has not provided "a comprehensive summary of the requisites for an adequate substitute for habeas corpus," it has held that a detainee must be able to demonstrate that he is being held pursuant to "the erroneous application or interpretation" of relevant law, and that the habeas court must have the power to order the conditional release of an individual unlawfully detained. The Court has also suggested that, depending on the circumstances, more may be required, including an opportunity to prevent extra-record exculpatory evidence and to enlist the assistance of counsel.

29

Military Detention of U.S. Persons

For obvious reasons, few subjects are as controversial in U.S. national security law as the detention without trial of U.S. persons — a term we use to encompass citizens everywhere and noncitizens lawfully present within the territorial United States. This chapter introduces the legal bases for, and statutory and constitutional limits upon, their detention on national security grounds, but without the legal process normally available to criminal defendants.

A. THE INTERNMENT CAMPS AND THE NON-DETENTION ACT

Alien Enemy Act of 1798

50 U.S.C. §21 (2018)

Whenever there is a declared war between the United States and any foreign nation or government, or any invasion or predatory incursion is perpetrated, attempted, or threatened against the territory of the United States by any foreign nation or government, and the President makes public proclamation of the event, all natives, citizens, denizens, or subjects of the hostile nation or government, being of the age of fourteen years and upward, who shall be within the United States and not actually naturalized, shall be liable to be apprehended, restrained, secured, and removed as alien enemies. . . .

Reading *Korematsu v. United States*

After Pearl Harbor, President Roosevelt, ostensibly fearing a potential Japanese invasion of the West Coast, signed an executive order authorizing the designation of certain "military zones" within the United States, and restriction of access to those zones. This order led to a series of military orders (1) identifying the entire West Coast as a "military zone"; (2) setting up a curfew for individuals of Japanese descent living within the zone; and (3) then categorically excluding those individuals from the zone — requiring them to abandon their homes, farms, and businesses and relocate to internment camps in the interior of the country, where they would remain under military guard for several years. Congress enacted a statute that made violation of the military orders a criminal offense. More than 110,000 individuals (some 70,000 of them U.S. citizens) were confined in the camps.

In *Hirabayashi v. United States*, 320 U.S. 81 (1943), the Supreme Court unanimously (but narrowly) sustained the conviction of a Japanese American for violating the curfew order. In the decision excerpted below, the Court was faced with the far broader question of whether Fred Korematsu, a U.S. citizen of Japanese descent living in San Leandro, California, could constitutionally be tried and convicted under the statute for violating an exclusion order. In a deeply controversial 6-3 decision, the Supreme Court answered that question in the affirmative. As you read excerpts from the various opinions, consider these questions:

- How did Justice Black's majority opinion respond to the dissenters' charge that the exclusion was motivated solely by racism, and not by legitimate military necessity? How did the majority know that the categorical exclusion of all individuals of Japanese descent from the West Coast (as opposed to, say, only those whom the government suspected of disloyalty) was militarily necessary? What kind of scrutiny did Justice Black actually apply?
- Why, according to Justice Murphy, were the exclusion orders unconstitutional? In strict scrutiny terms, was the problem the government's lack of a sufficiently compelling interest? Absence of narrow tailoring? Something else?
- Review Justice Jackson's dissent carefully. His famous "loaded weapon" rhetoric aside, what was his actual point? If it had been up to him, what would the Supreme Court have done in Korematsu's case? Would that course have been better than the ones pursued by either the majority or the other dissenters?

Korematsu v. United States

United States Supreme Court, 1944
323 U.S. 214

Mr. Justice Black delivered the opinion of the Court. The petitioner, an American citizen of Japanese descent, was convicted in a federal district court for remaining in San Leandro, California, a "Military Area," contrary to Civilian Exclusion Order No. 34 of the Commanding General of the Western Command, U.S. Army, which directed that after May 9, 1942, all persons of Japanese ancestry should be excluded from that area. No question was raised as to petitioner's loyalty to the United States. The Circuit Court of Appeals affirmed, and the importance of the constitutional question involved caused us to grant certiorari.

It should be noted, to begin with, that all legal restrictions which curtail the civil rights of a single racial group are immediately suspect. That is not to say that all such restrictions are unconstitutional. It is to say that courts must subject them to the most rigid scrutiny. Pressing public necessity may sometimes justify the existence of such restrictions; racial antagonism never can.

In the instant case prosecution of the petitioner was begun by information charging violation of an Act of Congress, of March 21, 1942, 56 Stat. 173, which provides that

> . . . whoever shall enter, remain in, leave, or commit any act in any military area or military zone prescribed, under the authority of an Executive order of the President, by the Secretary of War, or by any military commander designated by the Secretary of War, contrary to the restrictions applicable to any such area or zone or contrary to the order of the Secretary of War or any such military commander, shall, if it appears that he knew or should have known of the existence and extent of the restrictions or order and that his act was in violation thereof, be guilty of a misdemeanor and upon conviction shall be liable to a fine of not to exceed $5,000 or to imprisonment for not more than one year, or both, for each offense.

Exclusion Order No. 34, which the petitioner knowingly and admittedly violated, was one of a number of military orders and proclamations, all of which were substantially based upon Executive Order No. 9066, 7 Fed. Reg. 1407. That order, issued after we were at war with Japan, declared that "the successful prosecution of the war requires every possible protection against espionage and against sabotage to national-defense material, national-defense premises, and national-defense utilities. . . ." [The order also authorized the designation of "military areas . . . from which any and all persons may be excluded."]

One of the series of orders and proclamations, a curfew order, which like the exclusion order here was promulgated pursuant to Executive Order 9066, subjected all persons of Japanese ancestry in prescribed West Coast military areas to remain in their residences from 8 P.M. to 6 A.M. As is the case with the exclusion order here, that prior curfew order was designed as a "protection against espionage and against sabotage." In *Hirabayashi v. United States*, 320 U.S. 81, we sustained a conviction obtained for violation of the curfew order. The Hirabayashi conviction and this one thus rest on the same 1942 Congressional Act and the same basic executive and military orders, all of which orders were aimed at the twin dangers of espionage and sabotage.

The 1942 Act was attacked in the *Hirabayashi* case as an unconstitutional delegation of power; it was contended that the curfew order and other orders on which it rested were beyond the war powers of the Congress, the military authorities and of the President, as Commander in Chief of the Army; and finally that to apply the curfew order against none but citizens of Japanese ancestry amounted to a constitutionally prohibited discrimination solely on account of race. To these questions, we gave the consideration which their importance justified. We upheld the curfew order as an exercise of the power of the government to take steps necessary to prevent espionage and sabotage in an area threatened by Japanese attack.

In the light of the principles we announced in the *Hirabayashi* case, we are unable to conclude that it was beyond the war power of Congress and the Executive to exclude those of Japanese ancestry from the West Coast war area at the time they did. True, exclusion from the area in which one's home is located is a far greater deprivation than constant confinement to the home from 8 P.M. to 6 A.M. Nothing short of apprehension by the proper military authorities of the gravest imminent danger to the public safety can constitutionally justify either. But exclusion from a threatened area, no less than curfew, has a definite and close relationship to the prevention of espionage and sabotage....

Here, as in the *Hirabayashi* case, *supra*, at p. 99, "...we cannot reject as unfounded the judgment of the military authorities and of Congress that there were disloyal members of that population, whose number and strength could not be precisely and quickly ascertained. We cannot say that the war-making branches of the Government did not have ground for believing that in a critical hour such persons could not readily be isolated and separately dealt with, and constituted a menace to the national defense and safety, which demanded that prompt and adequate measures be taken to guard against it."...

We uphold the exclusion order as of the time it was made and when the petitioner violated it. In doing so, we are not unmindful of the hardships imposed by it upon a large group of American citizens. But hardships are part of war, and war is an aggregation of hardships. All citizens alike, both in and out of uniform, feel the impact of war in greater or lesser measure. Citizenship has its responsibilities as well as its privileges, and in time of war the burden is always heavier. Compulsory exclusion of large groups of citizens from their homes, except under circumstances of direst emergency and peril, is inconsistent with our basic governmental institutions. But when under conditions of modern warfare our shores are threatened by hostile forces, the power to protect must be commensurate with the threatened danger....

It is said that we are dealing here with the case of imprisonment of a citizen in a concentration camp solely because of his ancestry, without evidence or inquiry concerning his loyalty and good disposition towards the United States. Our task would be simple, our duty clear, were this a case involving the imprisonment of a loyal citizen in a concentration camp because of racial prejudice. Regardless of the true nature of the assembly and relocation centers — and we deem it unjustifiable to call them concentration camps with all the ugly connotations that term implies — we are dealing specifically with nothing but an exclusion order. To cast this case into outlines of racial prejudice, without reference to the real military dangers which were presented, merely confuses the issue. Korematsu was not excluded from the Military Area because of hostility to him or his race. He *was* excluded because we are at war with the Japanese Empire, because the properly constituted military authorities feared an invasion of our West Coast and felt constrained to take proper security measures, because they decided that the military urgency of the situation demanded that all citizens of Japanese ancestry be segregated from the West Coast temporarily, and finally, because Congress, reposing its confidence in this time of war in our military leaders — as inevitably it must — determined that they should have the power to do just this. There was evidence of disloyalty on the part of some, the military authorities considered that the need for action was great, and time was short. We cannot — by availing ourselves of the calm perspective of hindsight — now say that at that time these actions were unjustified.

Affirmed.

Japanese American heads of families line up for relocation, San Francisco, 1942.

Photo courtesy The National Archives.

[The concurring opinion of FRANKFURTER, J., and the dissenting opinion of ROBERTS, J., are omitted.]

Mr. Justice MURPHY, dissenting. This exclusion of "all persons of Japanese ancestry, both alien and non-alien," from the Pacific Coast area on a plea of military necessity in the absence of martial law ought not to be approved. Such exclusion goes over "the very brink of constitutional power" and falls into the ugly abyss of racism.

In dealing with matters relating to the prosecution and progress of a war, we must accord great respect and consideration to the judgments of the military authorities who are on the scene and who have full knowledge of the military facts. The scope of their discretion must, as a matter of necessity and common sense, be wide. And their judgments ought not to be overruled lightly by those whose training and duties ill-equip them to deal intelligently with matters so vital to the physical security of the nation.

At the same time, however, it is essential that there be definite limits to military discretion, especially where martial law has not been declared. Individuals must not be left impoverished of their constitutional rights on a plea of military necessity that has neither substance nor support. Thus, like other claims conflicting with the asserted constitutional rights of the individual, the military claim must subject itself to the judicial process of having its reasonableness determined and its conflicts with other interests reconciled. "What are the allowable limits of military discretion, and whether or not they have been overstepped in a particular case, are judicial questions." *Sterling v. Constantin*, 287 U.S. 378, 401.

The judicial test of whether the Government, on a plea of military necessity, can validly deprive an individual of any of his constitutional rights is whether the deprivation is reasonably related to a public danger that is so "immediate, imminent, and impending" as not to admit of delay and not to permit the intervention of ordinary constitutional processes to alleviate the danger. *United States v. Russell*, 13 Wall. 623, 627-628; *Mitchell v. Harmony*, 13 How. 115, 134-135; *Raymond v. Thomas*, 91 U.S. 712, 716. Civilian Exclusion Order No. 34, banishing from a prescribed area of the Pacific Coast "all persons of Japanese ancestry, both alien and non-alien," clearly does not meet that test. Being an obvious racial discrimination, the order deprives all those within its scope of the equal protection of the laws as guaranteed by the Fifth Amendment. It further deprives these individuals of their constitutional rights to live and work where they will, to establish a home where they choose and to move about freely. In excommunicating them without benefit of hearings, this order also deprives them of all their constitutional rights to procedural due process. Yet no reasonable relation to an "immediate, imminent, and impending" public danger is evident to support this racial restriction which is one of the most sweeping and complete deprivations of constitutional rights in the history of this nation in the absence of martial law. . . .

Mr. Justice Jackson, dissenting. . . . [I]t is said that if the military commander had reasonable military grounds for promulgating the orders, they are constitutional and become law, and the Court is required to enforce them. There are several reasons why I cannot subscribe to this doctrine.

It would be impracticable and dangerous idealism to expect or insist that each specific military command in an area of probable operations will conform to conventional tests of constitutionality. When an area is so beset that it must be put under military control at all, the paramount consideration is that its measures be successful, rather than legal. The armed services must protect a society, not merely its Constitution. The very essence of the military job is to marshal physical force, to remove every obstacle to its effectiveness, to give it every strategic advantage. Defense measures will not, and often should not, be held within the limits that bind civil authority in peace. No court can require such a commander in such circumstances to act as a reasonable man; he may be unreasonably cautious and exacting. Perhaps he should be. But a commander in temporarily focusing the life of a community on defense is carrying out a military program; he is not making law in the sense that the courts know the term. He issues orders, and they may have a certain authority as military commands, although they may be very bad as constitutional law.

But if we cannot confine military expedients by the Constitution, neither would I distort the Constitution to approve all that the military may deem expedient. That is what the Court appears to be doing, whether consciously or not. I cannot say, from any evidence before me, that the orders of General DeWitt were not reasonably expedient military precautions, nor could I say that they were. But even if they were permissible military procedures, I deny that it follows that they are constitutional. If, as the Court holds, it does follow, then we may as well say that any military order will be constitutional and have done with it.

The limitation under which courts always will labor in examining the necessity for a military order [is] illustrated by this case. How does the Court know that these orders have a reasonable basis in necessity? No evidence whatever on that subject has been taken by this or any other court. . . .

In the very nature of things, military decisions are not susceptible of intelligent judicial appraisal. They do not pretend to rest on evidence, but are made on information that often would not be admissible and on assumptions that could not be proved.

Information in support of an order could not be disclosed to courts without danger that it would reach the enemy. Neither can courts act on communications made in confidence. Hence courts can never have any real alternative to accepting the mere declaration of the authority that issued the order that it was reasonably necessary from a military viewpoint.

Much is said of the danger to liberty from the Army program for deporting and detaining these citizens of Japanese extraction. But a judicial construction of the due process clause that will sustain this order is a far more subtle blow to liberty than the promulgation of the order itself. A military order, however unconstitutional, is not apt to last longer than the military emergency. Even during that period a succeeding commander may revoke it all. But once a judicial opinion rationalizes such an order to show that it conforms to the Constitution, or rather rationalizes the Constitution to show that the Constitution sanctions such an order, the Court for all time has validated the principle of racial discrimination in criminal procedure and of transplanting American citizens. The principle then lies about like a loaded weapon ready for the hand of any authority that can bring forward a plausible claim of an urgent need. Every repetition imbeds that principle more deeply in our law and thinking and expands it to new purposes. . . .

I should hold that a civil court cannot be made to enforce an order which violates constitutional limitations even if it is a reasonable exercise of military authority. The courts can exercise only the judicial power, can apply only law, and must abide by the Constitution, or they cease to be civil courts and become instruments of military policy.

Of course the existence of a military power resting on force, so vagrant, so centralized, so necessarily heedless of the individual, is an inherent threat to liberty. But I would not lead people to rely on this Court for a review that seems to me wholly delusive. The military reasonableness of these orders can only be determined by military superiors. If the people ever let command of the war power fall into irresponsible and unscrupulous hands, the courts wield no power equal to its restraint. The chief restraint upon those who command the physical forces of the country, in the future as in the past, must be their responsibility to the political judgments of their contemporaries and to the moral judgments of history.

My duties as a justice as I see them do not require me to make a military judgment as to whether General DeWitt's evacuation and detention program was a reasonable military necessity. I do not suggest that the courts should have attempted to interfere with the Army in carrying out its task. But I do not think they may be asked to execute a military expedient that has no place in law under the Constitution. I would reverse the judgment and discharge the prisoner.

Notes and Questions

1. Alien Enemies? The U.S. government imprisoned thousands of German and Italian nationals, and some Japanese citizens, within the United States during World War II under the Alien Enemy Act. *See, e.g., Ludecke v. Watkins*, 335 U.S. 160 (1948). Why did the government not invoke the same statute to confine Fred Korematsu and more than 110,000 other ethnic Japanese internees?

2. *Strict Scrutiny?* What, exactly, was the constitutional ground upon which Korematsu challenged his conviction (and upon which Justice Murphy relied in his dissent)? The Supreme Court would not formally establish that the federal government was bound by equal protection principles (through the Fifth Amendment's Due Process Clause) until *Bolling v. Sharpe*, 347 U.S. 497 (1954). But recall that the Court had already hinted, in *United States v. Carolene Products Co.*, 304 U.S. 144 (1938), that "prejudice against discrete and insular minorities may be a special condition" justifying heightened judicial scrutiny of government regulation. *Id.* at 152 n.4. From Justice Murphy's perspective, did the majority err by failing to *apply* strict scrutiny, or by applying it incorrectly?

3. *Jackson's Dissent.* Justices Murphy and Roberts used their dissents to object to the Court's resolution of Korematsu's case on the merits. Justice Jackson's dissent takes a different tack, arguing that the real constitutional evil was not the exclusion orders, but rather the *Korematsu* majority's legal rationalization of them. From Jackson's perspective, courts are in no position to assess "military necessity," and should therefore not even bother trying to do so — a suggestion that courts would be better off staying away from such disputes whenever possible. Shortly after it was written, Jackson's opinion was described as a "fascinating and fantastic essay in nihilism." Eugene V. Rostow, *The Japanese-American Cases — A Disaster*, 54 Yale L.J. 489, 511 (1945). Do you agree?

4. *Korematsu's Infamy.* The Supreme Court's decision in *Korematsu* has been so thoroughly criticized and debunked that it has become part of what one scholar calls "the anticanon" — "the set of cases whose central propositions all legitimate decisions must refute." Jamal Greene, *The Anticanon*, 125 Harv. L. Rev. 379 (2011). Why? The answer, it would seem, has two parts: First, unlike German and Italian alien enemies, none of the Japanese American internees received individualized hearings. Instead, all were subjected to categorical curfew and exclusion orders based solely upon their Japanese heritage. Second, some two-thirds of the internees were *nisei*— second-generation children born to first-generation Japanese immigrants (*issei*) who, by dint of the Citizenship Clause of the Fourteenth Amendment, were U.S. citizens. Thus, *Korematsu* appeared to sustain the mass, suspicionless exclusion and subsequent detention not only of Japanese nationals, but also of their U.S. citizen children and grandchildren.

But the evils embodied in *Korematsu* ran much deeper. A 1982 congressional commission concluded that Executive Order No. 9066, the military orders that followed, and the act of Congress that criminalized violations, all adopted in the atmosphere of fear and anger that followed the attack on Pearl Harbor, were chiefly motivated not by military necessity, as the Court concluded, but by racism and avarice on the part on California farmers and commercial interests, who seized the opportunity to get rid of critical competition. *See* Comm'n on Wartime Relocation & Internment of Civilians, *Personal Justice Denied* 67-72 (1982). Moreover, "not a single documented act of espionage, sabotage, or fifth column activity was committed by an American citizen of Japanese ancestry or by a resident Japanese alien on the West Coast.... [T]here was no justification in military necessity for the exclusion,... there was no basis for the detention." *Id.* at 3, 10. Finally, the release of the internees was delayed, even after it was evident that they posed no danger to anybody, by President Roosevelt, who worried about a possible reaction by California voters in the November 1944 national election. "The inescapable conclusion . . . is that the delay was motivated by political considerations." *Id.* at 15.

5. Fraud on the Court. Although the decision in *Korematsu* is troubling enough in its own right, the *Korematsu* Court's extremely deferential review of the government's claim of military necessity enabled a stunning act of official fraud that was not revealed until nearly four decades later. In 1982, Professor Peter Irons of the University of California at San Diego initiated a Freedom of Information Act request to obtain access to Justice Department records from its prosecution of the *Korematsu* case in 1944. His discoveries encouraged Fred Korematsu to file a petition for a writ of *coram nobis* in the court where he was tried 40 years earlier to vacate his conviction on grounds of government misconduct. Setting aside Korematsu's conviction, the court found that

> the government knowingly withheld information from the courts when they were considering the critical question of military necessity in this case. A series of correspondence regarding what information should be included in the government's brief before the Supreme Court culminated in two different versions of a footnote that was to be used to specify the factual data upon which the government relied for its military necessity justification. The first version read as follows:
>
>> The Final Report of General DeWitt (which is dated June 5, 1943, but which was not made public until January 1944) is relied on in this brief for statistics and other details concerning the actual evacuation and the events that took place subsequent thereto. *The recital of the circumstances justifying the evacuation as a matter of military necessity, however, is in several respects,* particularly with reference to the use of illegal radio transmitters and to shore-to-ship signalling by persons of Japanese ancestry, *in conflict with information in the possession of the Department of Justice. In view of the contrariety of the reports on this matter we do not ask the Court to take judicial notice of the recital of those facts contained in the Report.* Petitioner's Exhibit AA, Memorandum of John L. Burling to Assistant Attorney General Herbert Wechsler, September 11, 1944 [emphasis added]. . . .
>
> The footnote that appeared in the final version of the brief merely read as follows:
>
>> The Final Report of General DeWitt (which is dated June 5, 1943, but which was not made public until January 1944), hereinafter cited as Final Report, is relied on in this brief for statistics and other details concerning the actual evacuation and the events that took place subsequent thereto. *We have specifically recited in this brief the facts relating to the justification for the evacuation, of which we ask the Court to take judicial notice, and we rely upon the Final Report only to the extent that it relates to such facts.*
>
> Brief for the United States, *Korematsu v. United States,* October Term, 1944, No. 22, at 11. The final version made no mention of the contradictory reports. The record is replete with protestations of various Justice Department officials that the government had the obligation to advise the courts of the contrary facts and opinions. In fact, several Department of Justice officials pointed out to their superiors and others the "wilful historical inaccuracies and intentional falsehoods" contained in the DeWitt Report. . . .
>
> . . . Omitted from the reports presented to the courts was information possessed by the Federal Communications Commission, the Department of the Navy, and the Justice Department which directly contradicted General DeWitt's statements. Thus, the court had before it a selective record. [*Korematsu v. United States,* 584 F. Supp. 1406, 1417-1419 (N.D. Cal. 1984).]

The circumstances leading up to the 1984 decision are described in Peter Irons, *Justice at War: The Story of the Japanese American Internment Cases* (1983); *see also Hirabayashi v. United States,* 828 F.2d 591 (9th Cir. 1987).

Separate from the affirmative misstatements in the government's briefs, the Acting Solicitor General in 2011 suggested that those cases might have been decided differently if the Solicitor General at the time, Charles Fahy, had been candid in his oral arguments before the Court about the lack of any evidence of military necessity. Neal Katyal, *Confession of Error: The Solicitor General's Mistakes During the Japanese-American Internment Cases,* The Justice Blog (May 20, 2011), http://blogs.usdoj.gov/blog/archives/1346.

Do these revelations vindicate Justice Jackson's concern about the Court's comparative inability adequately to assess military necessity? Judge Marilyn Patel, who granted Fred Korematsu's 1984 *coram nobis* petition, came to a different conclusion:

> *Korematsu* . . . stands as a constant caution that in times of war or declared military necessity our institutions must be vigilant in protecting constitutional guarantees. It stands as a caution that in times of distress the shield of military necessity and national security must not be used to protect governmental actions from close scrutiny and accountability. It stands as a caution that in times of international hostility and antagonisms our institutions, legislative, executive and judicial, must be prepared to exercise their authority to protect all citizens from the petty fears and prejudices that are so easily aroused. [584 F. Supp. at 1420.]

6. Korematsu's Forgotten Companion. In *Ex parte Endo,* 323 U.S. 283 (1944), decided the same day as *Korematsu,* the Court held that a Japanese American citizen whose loyalty to the United States was conceded by the government could not be detained in a relocation center. Unlike Korematsu, who was convicted of violating a criminal statute, Mitsuye Endo — like almost all of the other internees — was held without a criminal conviction. The Court ordered her freed not because the Constitution forbade her imprisonment, but because no statute or executive order authorized it. Should we infer from *Endo* that internment based on race or ethnic background *might* be permissible if it were approved either by an act of Congress or a clear presidential directive?

Despite the narrowness of its holding, *Endo* clearly indicated that the majority of the internees, who were also U.S. citizens, were unlawfully held. Reportedly tipped off that the *Endo* decision was forthcoming, the Roosevelt administration formally announced the closure of the internment camps on Sunday, December 17, 1944 — the day before *Korematsu* and *Endo* were handed down. If *Endo* had in fact closed the internment camps, might *Korematsu* (and the Supreme Court's role in defending exclusion) not be so reviled? *See* Patrick O. Gudridge, *Remember Endo?,* 116 Harv. L. Rev. 1933 (2003).

7. Apology and Payment. In 1948, Congress passed the American-Japanese Evacuation Claims Act, Pub. L. 80-866, 62 Stat. 1231, authorizing payment of up to $100,000 to each internee for loss of real or personal property occasioned by the evacuation. On February 19, 1976, President Gerald Ford rescinded Executive Order No. 9066, 34 years to the day after its issuance. Proclamation No. 4417, 41 Fed. Reg. 7741 (Feb. 20, 1976).

After the publication of *Personal Justice Denied,* Congress in the Civil Liberties Act of 1988 voted to give $20,000 and an apology to each of the 60,000 surviving internees. The measure was signed into law by President Reagan, and is codified today at 50 U.S.C. §§4201-4251 (2018). Acceptance of the $20,000 payment "shall be in full satisfaction of all claims" against the government for damages. *Id.* §4215(a)(4)(A). When those payments were finally made in 1991, they were accompanied by a letter from President George H.W. Bush, formally apologizing for the "serious injustices" that "were done to Japanese Americans during World War II." Do you believe these measures provided sufficient accountability for the underlying abuses? Why or why not?

8. The Non-Detention Act. In 1971, Congress passed the so-called Non-Detention Act, Pub. L. No. 92-128, §1(a), 85 Stat. 347 (codified at 18 U.S.C. §4001(a) (2018)). It provides that "No citizen shall be imprisoned or otherwise detained by the United States except pursuant to an Act of Congress." Enacted during the Vietnam War, the Non-Detention Act was a response to two separate developments: (1) growing concerns over a Cold War statute — the Emergency Detention Act of 1950 — which would have authorized mass detentions without trial during an "internal security emergency," and (2) increasing backlash against the World War II internment camps. The Non-Detention Act thus also repealed the 1950 measure. But did it prohibit detention without trial? Or did it simply require specific congressional authorization for such detention? If the latter, would Korematsu's detention have violated §4001(a)? Would Endo's? How specific must an act of Congress be in order to satisfy §4001(a)?

9. Korematsu Overruled. In *Trump v. Hawaii*, 138 S. Ct. 2392 (2018), *supra* p. 797, the Supreme Court finally repudiated *Korematsu.* Stung by the dissent's comparison of the Trump administration travel ban to the forced relocation of U.S. citizens to concentration camps based solely on race approved by the Court in 1944, Chief Justice Roberts not only denied the comparison, but took the opportunity "to make express what is already obvious: *Korematsu* was gravely wrong the day it was decided, has been overruled in the court of history, and — to be clear — 'has no place in law under the Constitution.'" *Id.* at 2423 (quoting *Korematsu v. United States*, 323 U.S. 214, 248 (1944) (Jackson, J., dissenting)). Justice Sotomayor, however, saw "stark parallels between the reasoning of this case and that of *Korematsu*," when "the Court gave 'a pass [to] an odious, gravely injurious racial classification' authorized by an executive order." 138 S. Ct. at 2447 (Sotomayor, J., dissenting) (quoting *Adarand Constructors, Inc. v. Peña*, 515 U.S. 200, 275 (1995) (Ginsburg, J., dissenting)).

> By blindly accepting the Government's misguided invitation to sanction a discriminatory policy motivated by animosity toward a disfavored group, all in the name of a superficial claim of national security, the Court redeploys the same dangerous logic underlying *Korematsu* and merely replaces one "gravely wrong" decision with another.
>
> Our Constitution demands, and our country deserves, a Judiciary willing to hold the coordinate branches to account when they defy our most sacred legal commitments. . . . [T]he Court's decision today has failed in that respect. [*Id.* at 2448.]

Others put it even more bluntly: "In national security cases after June 2018, judges possess a citation to bolster an exceedingly deferential judicial posture without having to draw, at least implicitly, on *Korematsu.* What could not be comfortably cited earlier can be openly cited now — as *Trump v. Hawai'i*." Eric K. Yamamoto & Rachel Oyama, *Masquerading Behind a Facade of National Security*, 128 Yale L.J. F. 688, 716 (2019).

On the fiftieth anniversary of the internments, Fred Korematsu remarked, "The constitutional violations that were committed have been cleared. This will never happen again." Katherine Bishop, *Japanese-Americans Treat Pain of Internment in World War II*, N.Y. Times, Feb. 19, 1992. Do you share Korematsu's optimism?

B. MILITARY DETENTION OF U.S. PERSONS CAPTURED OVERSEAS

Reading *Hamdi v. Rumsfeld*

Three days after the September 11 attacks, Congress enacted the Authorization for the Use of Military Force (AUMF), and the United States began offensive military operations in and around Afghanistan under its auspices a few weeks later. As part of those operations, U.S. forces began taking military prisoners almost immediately. One such prisoner was Yasser Hamdi, who was initially captured by Northern Alliance forces under circumstances that remain unclear. Hamdi was subsequently transferred to U.S. military custody, then sent to the Guantánamo Bay Naval Base in Cuba. When it was discovered that he was born in Louisiana (and was therefore a U.S. citizen), he was transferred to a Navy brig in Virginia and, later, to one in South Carolina. He was described by the government as an "enemy combatant." But he was not charged with any crime, and he was denied access to a lawyer.

Hamdi's father filed a habeas petition on behalf of his son under 28 U.S.C. §2241, alleging that the government held him in violation of the Fifth Amendment and the Non-Detention Act. In the ensuing proceeding, the government filed an affidavit by a DOD official named Michael Mobbs, purporting to set forth the factual basis for Hamdi's detention, but based entirely upon hearsay. When the case reached the Supreme Court, the Justices reached two conclusions: (1) the AUMF authorized Hamdi's detention (and thereby satisfied the Non-Detention Act); but (2) Mobbs' affidavit, by itself, was insufficient process to justify Hamdi's detention. As you read the Court's opinions in *Hamdi*, consider the following questions:

- What, precisely, is the holding regarding the effect of the AUMF, and how many Justices voted for it? How does Justice O'Connor find in the AUMF — a statute that says nothing about detention — sufficient authority to satisfy the Non-Detention Act?
- Why does the plurality conclude that Hamdi's citizenship is no barrier to his detention? Why do Justices Souter and Ginsburg disagree?
- With regard to the process that is due to Hamdi, what is the vote on this holding? What evidence, according to Justice O'Connor, would have justified Hamdi's continued detention? Why is "some evidence" not enough? Is it clear to you how much more is required by the Due Process Clause? Would — or should — more be required for individuals, unlike Hamdi, who are captured inside the United States?
- For Justice Thomas, is there any meaningful role for courts to play in these cases? If so, what is it?

Hamdi v. Rumsfeld

United States Supreme Court, 2004
542 U.S. 507

Justice O'CONNOR announced the judgment of the Court and delivered an opinion, in which THE CHIEF JUSTICE, Justice KENNEDY, and Justice BREYER join....

II

The threshold question before us is whether the Executive has the authority to detain citizens who qualify as "enemy combatants." There is some debate as to the proper scope of this term, and the Government has never provided any court with the full criteria that it uses in classifying individuals as such. It has made clear, however, that, for purposes of this case, the "enemy combatant" that it is seeking to detain is an individual who, it alleges, was "part of or supporting forces hostile to the United States or coalition partners" in Afghanistan and who "engaged in an armed conflict against the United States" there. We therefore answer only the narrow question before us: whether the detention of citizens falling within that definition is authorized.

The Government maintains that no explicit congressional authorization is required, because the Executive possesses plenary authority to detain pursuant to Article II of the Constitution. We do not reach the question whether Article II provides such authority, however, because we agree with the Government's alternative position, that Congress has in fact authorized Hamdi's detention, through the AUMF [*supra* p. 88].

Our analysis on that point, set forth below, substantially overlaps with our analysis of Hamdi's principal argument for the illegality of his detention. He posits that his detention is forbidden by 18 U.S.C. §4001(a). Section 4001(a) states that "[n]o citizen shall be imprisoned or otherwise detained by the United States except pursuant to an Act of Congress." Congress passed §4001(a) in 1971 as part of a bill to repeal the Emergency Detention Act of 1950, 50 U.S.C. §811 *et seq.*, which provided procedures for executive detention, during times of emergency, of individuals deemed likely to engage in espionage or sabotage. Congress was particularly concerned about the possibility that the Act could be used to reprise the Japanese internment camps of World War II. The Government again presses two alternative positions. First, it argues that §4001(a), in light of its legislative history and its location in Title 18, applies only to "the control of civilian prisons and related detentions," not to military detentions. Second, it maintains that §4001(a) is satisfied, because Hamdi is being detained "pursuant to an Act of Congress" — the AUMF. Again, because we conclude that the Government's second assertion is correct, we do not address the first. In other words, for the reasons that follow, we conclude that the AUMF is explicit congressional authorization for the detention of individuals in the narrow category we describe (assuming, without deciding, that such authorization is required), and that the AUMF satisfied §4001(a)'s requirement that a detention be "pursuant to an Act of Congress" (assuming, without deciding, that §4001(a) applies to military detentions).

The AUMF authorizes the President to use "all necessary and appropriate force" against "nations, organizations, or persons" associated with the September 11, 2001, terrorist attacks. 115 Stat. 224. There can be no doubt that individuals who fought against the United States in Afghanistan as part of the Taliban, an organization known to have supported the al Qaeda terrorist network responsible for those attacks, are individuals Congress sought to target in passing the AUMF. We conclude that detention of individuals falling into the limited category we are considering, for the duration of the particular conflict in which they were captured, is so fundamental and accepted an incident to war as to be an exercise of the "necessary and appropriate force" Congress has authorized the President to use.

The capture and detention of lawful combatants and the capture, detention, and trial of unlawful combatants, by "universal agreement and practice," are "important incident[s] of war." *Ex parte Quirin,* 317 U.S. [1 (1942)], at 28. The purpose of detention is to prevent captured individuals from returning to the field of battle and taking up arms once again.

There is no bar to this Nation's holding one of its own citizens as an enemy combatant. In *Quirin,* one of the detainees, Haupt, alleged that he was a naturalized United States citizen. 317 U.S., at 20. We held that "[c]itizens who associate themselves with the military arm of the enemy government, and with its aid, guidance and direction enter this country bent on hostile acts, are enemy belligerents within the meaning of . . . the law of war." *Id.,* at 37-38. While Haupt was tried for violations of the law of war, nothing in *Quirin* suggests that his citizenship would have precluded his mere detention for the duration of the relevant hostilities. See *id.,* at 30-31. Nor can we see any reason for drawing such a line here. A citizen, no less than an alien, can be "part of or supporting forces hostile to the United States or coalition partners" and "engaged in an armed conflict against the United States"; such a citizen, if released, would pose the same threat of returning to the front during the ongoing conflict.

In light of these principles, it is of no moment that the AUMF does not use specific language of detention. Because detention to prevent a combatant's return to the battlefield is a fundamental incident of waging war, in permitting the use of "necessary and appropriate force," Congress has clearly and unmistakably authorized detention in the narrow circumstances considered here. . . .

Hamdi contends that the AUMF does not authorize indefinite or perpetual detention. Certainly, we agree that indefinite detention for the purpose of interrogation is not authorized. Further, we understand Congress' grant of authority for the use of "necessary and appropriate force" to include the authority to detain for the duration of the relevant conflict, and our understanding is based on longstanding law-of-war principles. If the practical circumstances of a given conflict are entirely unlike those of the conflicts that informed the development of the law of war, that understanding may unravel. But that is not the situation we face as of this date. Active combat operations against Taliban fighters apparently are ongoing in Afghanistan. The United States may detain, for the duration of these hostilities, individuals legitimately determined to be Taliban combatants who "engaged in an armed conflict against the United States." If the record establishes that United States troops are still involved in active combat in Afghanistan, those detentions are part of the exercise of "necessary and appropriate force," and therefore are authorized by the AUMF.

Ex parte Milligan, [71 U.S. (4 Wall.) 2 (1866)], does not undermine our holding about the Government's authority to seize enemy combatants, as we define that term today. In that case, the Court made repeated reference to the fact that its inquiry into whether the military tribunal had jurisdiction to try and punish Milligan turned in large part on the fact that Milligan was not a prisoner of war, but a resident of Indiana arrested while at home there. *Id.*, at 118, 131. That fact was central to its conclusion. Had Milligan been captured while he was assisting Confederate soldiers by carrying a rifle against Union troops on a Confederate battlefield, the holding of the Court might well have been different. The Court's repeated explanations that Milligan was not a prisoner of war suggest that had these different circumstances been present he could have been detained under military authority for the duration of the conflict, whether or not he was a citizen. . . .

III

Even in cases in which the detention of enemy combatants is legally authorized, there remains the question of what process is constitutionally due to a citizen who disputes his enemy-combatant status. . . .

A

Though they reach radically different conclusions on the process that ought to attend the present proceeding, the parties begin on common ground. All agree that, absent suspension, the writ of habeas corpus remains available to every individual detained within the United States. U.S. Const., Art. I, §9, cl. 2 ("The Privilege of the Writ of Habeas Corpus shall not be suspended, unless when in Cases of Rebellion or Invasion the public Safety may require it"). Only in the rarest of circumstances has Congress seen fit to suspend the writ. . . . All agree suspension of the writ has not occurred here. Thus, it is undisputed that Hamdi was properly before an Article III court to challenge his detention under 28 U.S.C. §2241. Further, all agree that §2241 and its companion provisions provide at least a skeletal outline of the procedures to be afforded a petitioner in federal habeas review. Most notably, §2243 provides that "the person detained may, under oath, deny any of the facts set forth in the return or allege any other material facts," and §2246 allows the taking of evidence in habeas proceedings by deposition, affidavit, or interrogatories.

The simple outline of §2241 makes clear both that Congress envisioned that habeas petitioners would have some opportunity to present and rebut facts and that courts in cases like this retain some ability to vary the ways in which they do so as mandated by due process. The Government recognizes the basic procedural protections required by the habeas statute, but asks us to hold that, given both the flexibility of the habeas mechanism and the circumstances presented in this case, the presentation of the Mobbs Declaration to the habeas court completed the required factual development. It suggests two separate reasons for its position that no further process is due.

B

First, the Government urges the adoption of the Fourth Circuit's holding below — that because it is "undisputed" that Hamdi's seizure took place in a combat zone, the habeas determination can be made purely as a matter of law, with no further hearing or factfinding necessary. This argument is easily rejected. As the dissenters from the denial of rehearing en banc noted, the circumstances surrounding Hamdi's seizure cannot in any way be characterized as "undisputed," as "those circumstances are neither conceded in fact, nor susceptible to concession in law, because Hamdi has not been permitted to speak for himself or even through counsel as to those circumstances." 337 F.3d 335, 357 (Luttig, J., dissenting from denial of rehearing en banc). Further, the "facts" that constitute the alleged concession are insufficient to support Hamdi's detention. Under the definition of enemy combatant that we accept today as falling within the scope of Congress' authorization, Hamdi would need to be "part of or supporting forces hostile to the United States or coalition partners" and "engaged in an armed conflict against the United States" to justify his detention in the United States for the duration of the relevant conflict. The habeas petition states only that "[w]hen seized by the United States Government, Mr. Hamdi resided in Afghanistan." An assertion that one *resided* in a country in which combat operations are taking place is not a concession that one was "*captured* in a zone of active combat operations in a foreign theater of war," 316 F.3d, at 459 (emphasis added), and certainly is not a concession that one was "part of or supporting forces hostile to the United States or coalition partners" and "engaged in an armed conflict against the United States." Accordingly, we reject any argument that Hamdi has made concessions that eliminate any right to further process.

C

The Government's second argument requires closer consideration. This is the argument that further factual exploration is unwarranted and inappropriate in light of the extraordinary constitutional interests at stake. Under the Government's most extreme rendition of this argument, "[r]espect for separation of powers and the limited institutional capabilities of courts in matters of military decision-making in connection with an ongoing conflict" ought to eliminate entirely any individual process, restricting the courts to investigating only whether legal authorization exists for the broader detention scheme. At most, the Government argues, courts should review its determination that a citizen is an enemy combatant under a very deferential "some evidence" standard. [Brief for Respondents] 34 ("Under the some evidence standard, the focus is exclusively on the factual basis supplied by the Executive to support its own determination" (citing *Superintendent, Mass. Correctional Institution at Walpole v. Hill*, 472 U.S. 445, 455-457 (1985) (explaining that the some evidence standard "does not require" a "weighing of the evidence," but rather calls for assessing "whether there is any evidence in the record that could support the conclusion")). Under this review, a court would assume the accuracy of the Government's articulated basis for Hamdi's detention, as set forth in the Mobbs Declaration, and assess only whether that articulated basis was a legitimate one. In response, Hamdi emphasizes that this Court consistently has recognized that an individual challenging his detention may not be held at the will of the Executive without recourse to some proceeding before a neutral tribunal to determine whether the Executive's asserted justifications for that detention have basis in fact and warrant in law. *See, e.g., Zadvydas v. Davis*, 533 U.S. 678, 690 (2001)....

...The ordinary mechanism that we use for balancing such serious competing interests, and for determining the procedures that are necessary to ensure that a citizen is not "deprived of life, liberty, or property, without due process of law," U.S. Const., Amdt. 5, is the test that we articulated in *Mathews v. Eldridge*, 424 U.S. 319 (1976). *Mathews* dictates that the process due in any given instance is determined by weighing "the private interest that will be affected by the official action" against the Government's asserted interest, "including the function involved" and the burdens the Government would face in providing greater process. 424 U.S., at 335. The *Mathews* calculus then contemplates a judicious balancing of these concerns, through an analysis of "the risk of an erroneous deprivation" of the private interest if the process were reduced and the "probable value, if any, of additional or substitute safeguards." *Ibid.* We take each of these steps in turn.

1

It is beyond question that substantial interests lie on both sides of the scale in this case. Hamdi's "private interest . . . affected by the official action," *ibid.*, is the most elemental of liberty interests — the interest in being free from physical detention by one's own government. "In our society liberty is the norm," and detention without trial "is the carefully limited exception." [*United States v. Salerno*, 481 U.S. 739 (1987),] at 755. . . .

Nor is the weight on this side of the *Mathews* scale offset by the circumstances of war or the accusation of treasonous behavior, for "[i]t is clear that commitment for *any* purpose constitutes a significant deprivation of liberty that requires due process protection," *Jones v. United States*, 463 U.S. 354, 361 (1983) (emphasis added; internal quotation marks omitted), and at this stage in the *Mathews* calculus, we consider the interest of the *erroneously* detained individual. Indeed, as *amicus* briefs from media and relief organizations emphasize, the risk of erroneous deprivation of a citizen's liberty in the absence of sufficient process here is very real. See Brief for AmeriCares et al. as *Amici Curiae* 13-22 (noting ways in which "[t]he nature of humanitarian relief work and journalism present a significant risk of mistaken military detentions"). Moreover, as critical as the Government's interest may be in detaining those who actually pose an immediate threat to the national security of the United States during ongoing international conflict, history and common sense teach us that an unchecked system of detention carries the potential to become a means for oppression and abuse of others who do not present that sort of threat. . . .

2

On the other side of the scale are the weighty and sensitive governmental interests in ensuring that those who have in fact fought with the enemy during a war do not return to battle against the United States. As discussed above, the law of war and the realities of combat may render such detentions both necessary and appropriate, and our due process analysis need not blink at those realities. Without doubt, our Constitution recognizes that core strategic matters of warmaking belong in the hands of those who are best positioned and most politically accountable for making them. *Department of Navy v. Egan*, 484 U.S. 518, 530 (1988) (noting the reluctance of the courts "to intrude upon the authority of the Executive in military and national security affairs"); *Youngstown Sheet & Tube Co. v. Sawyer*, 343 U.S. 579, 587 (1952) (acknowledging "broad powers in military commanders engaged in day-to-day fighting in a theater of war").

The Government also argues at some length that its interests in reducing the process available to alleged enemy combatants are heightened by the practical difficulties that would accompany a system of trial-like process. In its view, military officers who are engaged in the serious work of waging battle would be unnecessarily and dangerously distracted by litigation half a world away, and discovery into military operations would both intrude on the sensitive secrets of national defense and result in a futile search for evidence buried under the rubble of war. To the extent that these burdens are triggered by heightened procedures, they are properly taken into account in our due process analysis.

3

Striking the proper constitutional balance here is of great importance to the Nation during this period of ongoing combat. But it is equally vital that our calculus not give short shrift to the values that this country holds dear or to the privilege that is American citizenship. It is during our most challenging and uncertain moments that our Nation's commitment to due process is most severely tested; and it is in those times that we must preserve our commitment at home to the principles for which we fight abroad.

With due recognition of these competing concerns, we believe that neither the process proposed by the Government nor the process apparently envisioned by the District Court below strikes the proper constitutional balance when a United States citizen is detained in the United States as an enemy combatant. That is, "the risk of erroneous deprivation" of a detainee's liberty interest is unacceptably high under the Government's proposed rule, while some of the "additional or substitute procedural safeguards" suggested by the District Court are unwarranted in light of their limited "probable value" and the burdens they may impose on the military in such cases. *Mathews,* 424 U.S., at 335.

We therefore hold that a citizen-detainee seeking to challenge his classification as an enemy combatant must receive notice of the factual basis for his classification, and a fair opportunity to rebut the Government's factual assertions before a neutral decisionmaker. "For more than a century the central meaning of procedural due process has been clear: 'Parties whose rights are to be affected are entitled to be heard; and in order that they may enjoy that right they must first be notified.' It is equally fundamental that the right to notice and an opportunity to be heard 'must be granted at a meaningful time and in a meaningful manner.'" *Fuentes v. Shevin,* 407 U.S. 67, 80 (1972). These essential constitutional promises may not be eroded.

At the same time, the exigencies of the circumstances may demand that, aside from these core elements, enemy combatant proceedings may be tailored to alleviate their uncommon potential to burden the Executive at a time of ongoing military conflict. Hearsay, for example, may need to be accepted as the most reliable available evidence from the Government in such a proceeding. Likewise, the Constitution would not be offended by a presumption in favor of the Government's evidence, so long as that presumption remained a rebuttable one and fair opportunity for rebuttal were provided. Thus, once the Government puts forth credible evidence that the habeas petitioner meets the enemy-combatant criteria, the onus could shift to the petitioner to rebut that evidence with more persuasive evidence that he falls outside the criteria. A burden-shifting scheme of this sort would meet the goal of ensuring that the errant tourist, embedded journalist, or local aid worker has a chance to prove military error while giving due regard to the Executive once it has put forth meaningful support for its conclusion that the detainee is in fact an enemy combatant. In the words of *Mathews,* process of this sort would sufficiently address the "risk of erroneous deprivation" of a detainee's liberty interest while eliminating certain procedures that have questionable additional value in light of the burden on the Government. 424 U.S., at 335.

We think it unlikely that this basic process will have the dire impact on the central functions of warmaking that the Government forecasts. The parties agree that initial captures on the battlefield need not receive the process we have discussed here; that process is due only when the determination is made to *continue* to hold those who have been seized. The Government has made clear in its briefing that documentation regarding battlefield detainees already is kept in the ordinary course of military affairs. Any factfinding imposition created by requiring a knowledgeable affiant to summarize these records to an independent tribunal is a minimal one. Likewise, arguments that military officers ought not have to wage war under the threat of litigation lose much of their steam when factual disputes at enemy-combatant hearings are limited to the alleged combatant's acts. This focus meddles little, if at all, in the strategy or conduct of war, inquiring only into the appropriateness of continuing to detain an individual claimed to have taken up arms against the United States. While we accord the greatest respect and consideration to the judgments of military authorities in matters relating to the actual prosecution of a war, and recognize that the scope of that discretion necessarily is wide, it does not infringe on the core role of the military for the courts to exercise their own time-honored and constitutionally mandated roles of reviewing and resolving claims like those presented here. Cf. *Korematsu v. United States,* 323 U.S. 214, 233-234 (1944) (Murphy, J., dissenting) ("[L]ike other claims conflicting with the asserted constitutional rights of the individual, the military claim must subject itself to the judicial process of having its reasonableness determined and its conflicts with other interests reconciled"); *Sterling v. Constantin,* 287 U.S. 378, 401 (1932) ("What are the allowable limits of military discretion, and whether or not they have been overstepped in a particular case, are judicial questions").

In sum, while the full protections that accompany challenges to detentions in other settings may prove unworkable and inappropriate in the enemy-combatant setting, the threats to military operations posed by a basic system of independent review are not so weighty as to trump a citizen's core rights to challenge meaningfully the Government's case and to be heard by an impartial adjudicator.

D

In so holding, we necessarily reject the Government's assertion that separation of powers principles mandate a heavily circumscribed role for the courts in such circumstances. Indeed, the position that the courts must forgo any examination of the individual case and focus exclusively on the legality of the broader detention scheme cannot be mandated by any reasonable view of separation of powers, as this approach serves only to *condense* power into a single branch of government. We have long since made clear that a state of war is not a blank check for the President when it comes to the rights of the Nation's citizens. *Youngstown Sheet & Tube,* 343 U.S., at 587. Whatever power the United States Constitution envisions for the Executive in its exchanges with other nations or with enemy organizations in times of conflict, it most assuredly envisions a role for all three branches when individual liberties are at stake. *Mistretta v. United States,* 488 U.S. 361, 380 (1989) (it was "the central judgment of the Framers of the Constitution that, within our political scheme, the separation of governmental powers into three coordinate Branches is essential to the preservation of liberty"); *Home Building & Loan Assn. v. Blaisdell,* 290 U.S. 398, 426 (1934) (The war power "is a power to wage war successfully, and thus it permits the harnessing of the entire energies of the people in a supreme cooperative effort to preserve the nation. But even the war power does not remove constitutional limitations safeguarding essential liberties"). Likewise, we have made clear that, unless Congress acts to suspend it, the Great Writ of habeas corpus allows the Judicial Branch to play a necessary role in maintaining this delicate balance of governance, serving as an important judicial check on the Executive's discretion in the realm of detentions. See *INS v. St. Cyr*, 533 U.S. 289, 301 (2001) ("At its historical core, the writ of habeas corpus has served as a means of reviewing the legality of Executive detention, and it is in that context that its protections have been strongest"). Thus, while we do not question that our due process assessment must pay keen attention to the particular burdens faced by the Executive in the context of military action, it would turn our system of checks and balances on its head to suggest that a citizen could not make his way to court with a challenge to the factual basis for his detention by his government, simply because the Executive opposes making available such a challenge. Absent suspension of the writ by Congress, a citizen detained as an enemy combatant is entitled to this process.

Because we conclude that due process demands some system for a citizen detainee to refute his classification, the proposed "some evidence" standard is inadequate. Any process in which the Executive's factual assertions go wholly unchallenged or are simply presumed correct without any opportunity for the alleged combatant to demonstrate otherwise falls constitutionally short. As the Government itself has recognized, we have utilized the "some evidence" standard in the past as a standard of review, not as a standard of proof. That is, it primarily has been employed by courts in examining an administrative record developed after an adversarial proceeding — one with process at least of the sort that we today hold is constitutionally mandated in the citizen enemy-combatant setting. This standard therefore is ill suited to the situation in which a habeas petitioner has received no prior proceedings before any tribunal and had no prior opportunity to rebut the Executive's factual assertions before a neutral decisionmaker.

Today we are faced only with such a case. Aside from unspecified "screening" processes, and military interrogations in which the Government suggests Hamdi could have contested his classification, Hamdi has received no process. An interrogation by one's captor, however effective an intelligence-gathering tool, hardly constitutes a constitutionally adequate factfinding before a neutral decisionmaker. That even purportedly fair adjudicators "are disqualified by their interest in the controversy to be decided is, of course, the general rule." *Tumey v. Ohio*, 273 U.S. 510, 522 (1927). Plainly, the "process" Hamdi has received is not that to which he is entitled under the Due Process Clause.

There remains the possibility that the standards we have articulated could be met by an appropriately authorized and properly constituted military tribunal. Indeed, it is notable that military regulations already provide for such process in related instances, dictating that tribunals be made available to determine the status of enemy detainees who assert prisoner-of-war status under the Geneva Convention. See Enemy Prisoners of War, Retained Personnel, Civilian Internees and Other Detainees, Army Regulation 190-8, §1-6 (1997). In the absence of such process, however, a court that receives a petition for a writ of habeas corpus from an alleged enemy combatant must itself ensure that the minimum requirements of due process are achieved. . . . As we have discussed, a habeas court in a case such as this may accept affidavit evidence like that contained in the Mobbs Declaration, so long as it also permits the alleged combatant to present his own factual case to rebut the Government's return. We anticipate that a District Court would proceed with the caution that we have indicated is necessary in this setting, engaging in a factfinding process that is both prudent and incremental. We have no reason to doubt that courts faced with these sensitive matters will pay proper heed both to the matters of national security that might arise in an individual case and to the constitutional limitations safeguarding essential liberties that remain vibrant even in times of security concerns. . . .

The judgment of the United States Court of Appeals for the Fourth Circuit is vacated, and the case is remanded for further proceedings.

It is so ordered.

Justice SOUTER, with whom Justice GINSBURG joins, concurring in part, dissenting in part, and concurring in the judgment. . . . The plurality rejects [the government's "some evidence"] limit on the exercise of habeas jurisdiction and so far I agree with its opinion. The plurality does, however, accept the Government's position that if Hamdi's designation as an enemy combatant is correct, his detention (at least as to some period) is authorized by an Act of Congress as required by §4001(a), that is, by the Authorization for Use of Military Force, 115 Stat. 224 (hereinafter Force Resolution). Here, I disagree and respectfully dissent. . . .

II

The threshold issue is how broadly or narrowly to read the Non-Detention Act, the tone of which is severe: "No citizen shall be imprisoned or otherwise detained by the United States except pursuant to an Act of Congress." . . . For a number of reasons, the prohibition within §4001(a) has to be read broadly to accord the statute a long reach and to impose a burden of justification on the Government.

First, the circumstances in which the Act was adopted point the way to this interpretation. The provision superseded a cold-war statute, the Emergency Detention Act of 1950, which had authorized the Attorney General, in time of emergency, to detain anyone reasonably thought likely to engage in espionage or sabotage. That statute was repealed in 1971 out of fear that it could authorize a repetition of the World War II internment of citizens of Japanese ancestry; Congress meant to preclude another episode like the one described in *Korematsu v. United States*, 323 U.S. 214 (1944). . . .

. . . To appreciate what is most significant, one must only recall that the internments of the 1940's were accomplished by Executive action. Although an Act of Congress ratified and confirmed an Executive order authorizing the military to exclude individuals from defined areas and to accommodate those it might remove, see *Ex parte Endo*, 323 U.S. 283, 285-288 (1944), the statute said nothing whatever about the detention of those who might be removed; internment camps were creatures of the Executive, and confinement in them rested on assertion of Executive authority. When, therefore, Congress repealed the 1950 Act and adopted §4001(a) for the purpose of avoiding another *Korematsu*, it intended to preclude reliance on vague congressional authority (for example, providing "accommodations" for those subject to removal) as authority for detention or imprisonment at the discretion of the Executive (maintaining detention camps of American citizens, for example). In requiring that any Executive detention be "pursuant to an Act of Congress," then, Congress necessarily meant to require a congressional enactment that clearly authorized detention or imprisonment.

Second, when Congress passed §4001(a) it was acting in light of an interpretive regime that subjected enactments limiting liberty in wartime to the requirement of a clear statement and it presumably intended §4001(a) to be read accordingly. This need for clarity was unmistakably expressed in *Ex parte Endo, supra,* decided the same day as *Korematsu*. . . . The petitioner was held entitled to habeas relief in an opinion that set out this principle for scrutinizing wartime statutes in derogation of customary liberty:

> "In interpreting a wartime measure we must assume that [its] purpose was to allow for the greatest possible accommodation between . . . liberties and the exigencies of war. We must assume, when asked to find implied powers in a grant of legislative or executive authority, that the law makers intended to place no greater restraint on the citizen than was clearly and unmistakably indicated by the language they used." *Id.*, at 300.

Congress's understanding of the need for clear authority before citizens are kept detained is itself therefore clear, and §4001(a) must be read to have teeth in its demand for congressional authorization.

Finally, even if history had spared us the cautionary example of the internments in World War II, even if there had been no *Korematsu,* and *Endo* had set out no principle of statutory interpretation, there would be a compelling reason to read §4001(a) to demand manifest authority to detain before detention is authorized. The defining character of American constitutional government is its constant tension between security and liberty, serving both by partial helpings of each. In a government of separated powers, deciding finally on what is a reasonable degree of guaranteed liberty whether in peace or war (or some condition in between) is not well entrusted to the Executive Branch of Government, whose particular responsibility is to maintain security. For reasons of inescapable human nature, the branch of the Government asked to counter a serious threat is not the branch on which to rest the Nation's entire reliance in striking the balance between the will to win and the cost in liberty on the way to victory; the responsibility for security will naturally amplify the claim that security legitimately raises. A reasonable balance is more likely to be reached on the judgment of a different branch, just as Madison said in remarking that "the constant aim is to divide and arrange the several offices in such a manner as that each may be a check on the other — that the private interest of every individual may be a sentinel over the public rights." The Federalist No. 51, p. 349 (J. Cooke ed. 1961). Hence the need for an assessment by Congress before citizens are subject to lockup, and likewise the need for a clearly expressed congressional resolution of the competing claims.

III . . .

C

. . . [T]here is one argument for treating the Force Resolution as sufficiently clear to authorize detention of a citizen consistently with §4001(a). Assuming the argument to be sound, however, the Government is in no position to claim its advantage.

Because the Force Resolution authorizes the use of military force in acts of war by the United States, the argument goes, it is reasonably clear that the military and its Commander in Chief are authorized to deal with enemy belligerents according to the treaties and customs known collectively as the laws of war. Accordingly, the United States may detain captured enemies, and *Ex parte Quirin,* 317 U.S. 1 (1942), may perhaps be claimed for the proposition that the American citizenship of such a captive does not as such limit the Government's power to deal with him under the usages of war. Thus, the Government here repeatedly argues that Hamdi's detention amounts to nothing more than customary detention of a captive taken on the field of battle: if the usages of war are fairly authorized by the Force Resolution, Hamdi's detention is authorized for purposes of §4001(a). . . .

By holding him incommunicado, however, the Government obviously has not been treating him as a prisoner of war, and in fact the Government claims that no Taliban detainee is entitled to prisoner of war status. This treatment appears to be a violation of the Geneva Convention provision that even in cases of doubt, captives are entitled to be treated as prisoners of war "until such time as their status has been determined by a competent tribunal." Art. 5, 6 U.S.T., at 3324. . . .

Whether, or to what degree, the Government is in fact violating the Geneva Convention and is thus acting outside the customary usages of war are not matters I can resolve at this point. What I can say, though, is that the Government has not made out its claim that in detaining Hamdi in the manner described, it is acting in accord with the laws of war authorized to be applied against citizens by the Force Resolution. I conclude accordingly that the Government has failed to support the position that the Force Resolution authorizes the described detention of Hamdi for purposes of §4001(a).

It is worth adding a further reason for requiring the Government to bear the burden of clearly justifying its claim to be exercising recognized war powers before declaring §4001(a) satisfied. Thirty-eight days after adopting the Force Resolution, Congress passed the statute entitled Uniting and Strengthening America by Providing Appropriate Tools Required to Intercept and Obstruct Terrorism Act of 2001 (USA PATRIOT ACT), 115 Stat. 272; that Act authorized the detention of alien terrorists for no more than seven days in the absence of criminal charges or deportation proceedings, 8 U.S.C. §1226a(a)(5) (2000 ed., Supp. I). It is very difficult to believe that the same Congress that carefully circumscribed Executive power over alien terrorists on home soil would not have meant to require the Government to justify clearly its detention of an American citizen held on home soil incommunicado.

D

Since the Government has given no reason either to deflect the application of §4001(a) or to hold it to be satisfied, I need to go no further; the Government hints of a constitutional challenge to the statute, but it presents none here. I will, however, stray across the line between statutory and constitutional territory just far enough to note the weakness of the Government's mixed claim of inherent, extrastatutory authority under a combination of Article II of the Constitution and the usages of war. It is in fact in this connection that the Government developed its argument that the exercise of war powers justifies the detention, and what I have just said about its inadequacy applies here as well. Beyond that, it is instructive to recall Justice Jackson's observation that the President is not Commander in Chief of the country, only of the military. *Youngstown Sheet & Tube Co. v. Sawyer*, 343 U.S. 579, 643-644 (1952) (concurring opinion); see also *id.*, at 637-638 (Presidential authority is "at its lowest ebb" where the President acts contrary to congressional will).

There may be room for one qualification to Justice Jackson's statement, however: in a moment of genuine emergency, when the Government must act with no time for deliberation, the Executive may be able to detain a citizen if there is reason to fear he is an imminent threat to the safety of the Nation and its people (though I doubt there is any want of statutory authority). This case, however, does not present that question, because an emergency power of necessity must at least be limited by the emergency; Hamdi has been locked up for over two years. Cf. *Ex parte Milligan,* 4 Wall. 2, 127 (1866) (martial law justified only by "actual and present" necessity as in a genuine invasion that closes civilian courts). . . .

IV . . .

It should go without saying that in joining with the plurality to produce a judgment, I do not adopt the plurality's resolution of constitutional issues that I would not reach. It is not that I could disagree with the plurality's determinations (given the plurality's view of the Force Resolution) that someone in Hamdi's position is entitled at a minimum to notice of the Government's claimed factual basis for holding him, and to a fair chance to rebut it before a neutral decision maker; nor, of course, could I disagree with the plurality's affirmation of Hamdi's right to counsel. On the other hand, I do not mean to imply agreement that the Government could claim an evidentiary presumption casting the burden of rebuttal on Hamdi, or that an opportunity to litigate before a military tribunal might obviate or truncate enquiry by a court on habeas.

Subject to these qualifications, I join with the plurality in a judgment of the Court vacating the Fourth Circuit's judgment and remanding the case.

[The dissenting opinion of Justice SCALIA, joined by Justice STEVENS, who would have held that the Suspension Clause bars the detention of U.S. citizens without charges — and that Hamdi's detention without a valid suspension of habeas corpus was therefore unconstitutional — is excerpted *supra* p. 837.]

Justice THOMAS, dissenting. The Executive Branch, acting pursuant to the powers vested in the President by the Constitution and with explicit congressional approval, has determined that Yaser Hamdi is an enemy combatant and should be detained. This detention falls squarely within the Federal Government's war powers, and we lack the expertise and capacity to second-guess that decision. As such, petitioners' habeas challenge should fail, and there is no reason to remand the case. . . . I do not think that the Federal Government's war powers can be balanced away by this Court. Arguably, Congress could provide for additional procedural protections, but until it does, we have no right to insist upon them. But even if I were to agree with the general approach the plurality takes, I could not accept the particulars. The plurality utterly fails to account for the Government's compelling interests and for our own institutional inability to weigh competing concerns correctly. I respectfully dissent. . . .

Notes and Questions

1. The AUMF and the Non-Detention Act. The AUMF (see *supra* p. 88 for the full version) authorizes the President to use "all necessary and appropriate force," but it is completely silent about detention authority. Why does the plurality hold that it nevertheless authorizes detention? By what standards or principles does the Court measure necessity and appropriateness? Why does Justice Souter (joined by Justice

Ginsburg) insist that the AUMF fails to satisfy the Non-Detention Act? Who, in your view, has the better of the argument, and why?

2. *The Holding in Hamdi?* What is the actual holding of *Hamdi*? Five Justices (the plurality joined by Justice Thomas) believed that Hamdi's detention was authorized, but the plurality repeatedly stressed the "limited category" of individuals to whom its reasoning applies, i.e., "individuals who fought against the United States in Afghanistan as part of the Taliban." As Justice Breyer explained nearly a decade later in a different case, *Hamdi* said nothing about two vital questions: "whether the AUMF authorizes, and the Constitution permits, detention on the basis that an individual was part of al Qaeda, or part of the Taliban, but was *not* 'engaged in an armed conflict against the United States' in Afghanistan prior to his capture," and "whether, assuming detention . . . is [otherwise] permissible, either the AUMF or the Constitution limits the *duration* of detention." *Hussain v. Obama*, 134 S. Ct. 1621, 1622 (2014) (Breyer, J., respecting the denial of certiorari) (emphases added); *see also al-Alwi v. Trump*, 139 S. Ct. 1893, 1894 (2019) (Breyer, J., respecting the denial of certiorari) ("In my judgment, it is past time to confront the difficult question left open by *Hamdi*."). Does anything in Justice O'Connor's opinion hint at how she might have answered these two questions, especially when the detainee is a U.S. citizen?

3. *"Longstanding Law-of-War Principles."* The *Hamdi* plurality appeals to "longstanding law-of-war principles." What, exactly, are those principles, and where can they be found? See Chapter 9. How are they relevant here?

The assertion of law-of-war principles presents several thorny questions. First, if their application presupposes a war or armed conflict, must U.S. involvement in that conflict be expressly authorized by Congress? If law-of-war principles apply, do all of the President's war powers apply, as well, or just some of them? *See Hamdan v. Rumsfeld*, 548 U.S. 557, 594 (2006) (declaring that "there is nothing in the text or legislative history of the AUMF even hinting that Congress intended to expand or alter" the President's existing authority to convene a military commission).

Second, how does the *Hamdi* Court define "enemy combatants" — persons subject to military detention under the law of war? If war is authorized by declaration or by a use-of-force statute like the AUMF, should we not look to the congressional authorization for a definition of the enemy, rather than the law of war? Suppose Congress had not authorized the use of force against terrorist organizations like Al Qaeda, but the President had launched military strikes on Al Qaeda targets anyway, relying on his inherent power to repel attacks. Would military detention of combatants in that war be authorized? How would they be defined? What about persons detained as terrorists generally in an undeclared "war on terrorism"?

Third, even if the AUMF suffices to authorize military detention "in the field," does it apply in the United States? Unlike Afghanistan, where Hamdi was captured, in the United States civilian courts are open and the criminal process is available. Should this make a difference?

Fourth, the principles of the law of war may be "longstanding," but will they be long-lasting? Under what changed circumstances could the majority's understanding of these principles "unravel," as the plurality opinion warns? Note, again, Justice Breyer's suggestion in *Hussain, supra*, that *Hamdi* said nothing about U.S. law limits on the duration of detention. Should law-of-war detention continue until the end of hostilities? What if the hostilities never end?

4. *The Greater Includes the Lesser?* In *Hamdi,* the Court assumed that Supreme Court precedents concerning trial by military commission, especially *Ex parte Quirin,* 317 U.S. 1 (1942), were apposite to the legality of military detention. *Quirin* did say that both lawful and unlawful combatants "are subject to capture and detention," and that unlawful combatants are additionally subject to military trial and punishment. See *infra* p. 1125. A lower court in a separate detention case understood *Quirin* to reflect the Supreme Court's belief that "detention alone . . . [is] certainly the lesser of the consequences an unlawful combatant could face." *Padilla ex rel. Newman v. Bush,* 233 F. Supp. 2d 564, 595 (S.D.N.Y. 2002), *rev'd sub nom. Rumsfeld v. Padilla,* 352 F.3d 685 (2d Cir. 2003), *rev'd,* 542 U.S. 426 (2004).

But is that always true? The unlawful combatant who is tried at least will see a resolution of his status. *See Rasul v. Bush,* 542 U.S. 466, 488 (2004) (Kennedy, J., concurring in the judgment) (distinguishing *Johnson v. Eisentrager,* which involved aliens detained after conviction by military commission, from *Rasul,* which involved aliens "being held indefinitely, and without benefit of any legal proceeding to determine their status"). If detention is not the "lesser" consequence for such a combatant, is case law establishing the legality of a military *trial* really apposite to the legality of *detention?*

5. *"Plenary" Military Authority.* In *Hamdi,* the government also argued that the Executive has plenary authority under Article II to detain enemy combatants, presumably a "war power" of the Commander in Chief. Although the plurality did not reach this claim, it agreed that the capture and military detention of combatants are "important incident[s] of war," quoting *Quirin,* and Justice Thomas dissented on the ground that Hamdi's "detention falls squarely within the Federal Government's war powers" vested in the executive branch. Could this mean that the President did not need the delegated authority of the AUMF to capture the detainees? Might there be a constitutionally significant distinction between capture and *short-term* military detention (which may be necessary steps taken in self-defense) versus *long-term* military detention? Isn't *Hamdi* clearly an example of the latter?

6. *The Process Point: Determining the Combatant Status of U.S. Citizens.* The plurality in *Hamdi* employed conventional due process balancing analysis to identify the procedures required for determining a U.S. citizen detainee's status. Why did the Court reject the government's argument that Hamdi's status was undisputed? If the detainee's combatant status is disputed and he is entitled to petition for a writ of habeas corpus, then the habeas corpus statute, 28 U.S.C. §2243, *supra* p. 827, itself (and, barring that, the Suspension Clause) mandates some evidentiary proceeding. Can you see why from examining the statute?

But what evidence and what kind of proceeding? The government suggested that "some evidence" would suffice, and that a court's role in a habeas corpus proceeding was only to decide whether the evidence stated in the Mobbs Declaration was sufficient standing alone. Is that argument consistent with the habeas corpus statute? Or with due process?

The plurality, joined on this point by Justices Souter and Ginsburg, rejected the "some evidence" standard partly on the ground that "it primarily has been employed by courts in examining an administrative record developed after an adversarial proceeding. . . ." *Hamdi,* 542 U.S. at 537 (plurality opinion). But the government asserted that it had developed an administrative record after an elaborate internal process for determining the combatant status of U.S. citizens, incorporating information developed by the Department of Defense, the Central Intelligence Agency, and the Department of Justice; written assessments by the same agencies; a formal legal opinion by the Office of Legal Counsel; recommendations by the Attorney General and the Secretary of Defense; and a final recommendation to and briefing for the President by the White House Counsel.[1] If such procedures were actually used to designate Hamdi as an enemy combatant and to generate the factual predicates for his military detention, why was the "some evidence" standard still not sufficient?

Finally, consider the procedures that the plurality in *Hamdi* found were required by a due process balancing. Are these procedures sufficient to reduce the risk of inaccuracy in light of the interests at stake? What more would Justices Souter and Ginsburg require if they found that Congress had authorized military detention? What would you find necessary if you performed the balancing? How critical is it, to your due process analysis, that Hamdi is a U.S. citizen?

7. Hamdi After Remand. After the Supreme Court remanded Hamdi's case with the command that Hamdi receive additional process, Hamdi and the government negotiated an agreement for his release to his family in Saudi Arabia. The government asserted that he no longer had any intelligence value and posed no threat. Under the agreement, Hamdi gave up his U.S. citizenship, renounced terrorism, waived any civil claim he had for his detention, and accepted certain travel restrictions, including a ten-year ban on returning to the United States. *See* Motion to Stay Proceedings, *Hamdi v. Rumsfeld,* No. 2:02CV439 (E.D. Va. Sept. 24, 2004), *available at* http://notablecases.vaed.uscourts.gov/2:02-cv-00439/docs/70223/0.pdf.

Why do you suppose the government agreed to Hamdi's release after fighting his case all the way to the Supreme Court? Might the Court's due process holding have had anything to do with it? Why do you think Hamdi agreed to the terms of his release?

8. The Alsheikh Case. To date, the only other U.S. person captured outside the United States and detained under the 2001 AUMF is Abdulrahman Ahmad Alsheikh — a dual U.S.-Saudi citizen who surrendered to Syrian militia forces in Syria in September 2017 while allegedly fighting on behalf of the Islamic State, and who was then transferred to U.S. custody in Iraq. The government initially objected to a habeas petition filed by the ACLU on Alsheikh's behalf, arguing that the ACLU had no prior relationship with the detainee, and so could not be his "next friend." The district court sided with the ACLU, however, and ordered the government to provide the ACLU with unmonitored access to Alsheikh. *See ACLU Found. ex rel. Unnamed U.S. Citizen v. Mattis,* 286 F. Supp. 3d 53 (D.D.C. 2017). By the time the district court ruled that Alsheikh was entitled to meet with counsel to challenge his detention, 100 days had elapsed since his initial capture.

9. Transferring U.S.-Person Detainees. Alsheikh's case never produced a substantive ruling as to the legality of his detention. Instead, it devolved into a dispute over whether the government could "transfer" Alsheikh to one of two (initially)

---

1. Alberto R. Gonzales, Counsel to the President, Remarks at an American Bar Ass'n Standing Comm. on Law and Nat'l Security program (Feb. 24, 2004), *available at* http://www.fas.org/irp/news/2004/02/gonzales.pdf. Gonzales also asserted, however, that neither these procedures nor any other specific procedures were required by law, but were adopted only as a matter of administrative grace.

unidentified countries. For U.S. persons within the United States, the Supreme Court had long held that the government must identify a source of "positive legal authority" to justify a transfer, such as an extradition treaty. *See Valentine v. United States ex rel. Neidecker*, 299 U.S. 5 (1936). But in *Munaf v. Geren*, 553 U.S. 674 (2008), the Supreme Court allowed the government to transfer two U.S. citizens from U.S. military custody to the custody of the Iraqi government *without* such authority, when those two individuals had voluntarily traveled to Iraq prior to their capture. In *Doe v. Mattis*, 889 F.3d 745 (D.C. Cir. 2018), a divided panel of the Court of Appeals held that Alsheikh's case was governed by *Valentine*, not *Munaf*—and that the government therefore could only transfer Alsheikh to a third country if it had positive legal authority for the transfer. Although the D.C. Circuit held that, even in the absence of an extradition treaty with the relevant country, the AUMF *could* provide such authority, it would only do so if Alsheikh was *lawfully* detained under the AUMF—which had not yet been resolved. Rather than pursue that claim on remand, the government ultimately agreed to release Alsheikh in October 2018—13 months after his capture. *See* Charlie Savage, Rukmini Callimachi & Eric Schmitt, *American ISIS Suspect Is Freed After Being Held More Than a Year*, N.Y. Times, Oct. 29, 2018. The *Doe* decision is significant in how it constrains the government's ability to transfer U.S. persons in military custody to foreign countries, but it is also likely *limited* to U.S. persons. *See, e.g., Kiyemba v. Obama*, 561 F.3d 509 (D.C. Cir. 2009) (holding that noncitizens detained at Guantánamo have no right to notice or a hearing before being transferred to a foreign country).

C. MILITARY DETENTION OF U.S. PERSONS CAPTURED IN THE UNITED STATES

1. José Padilla

> Al Qaeda operatives recruited Jose Padilla, a United States citizen, to train for jihad in Afghanistan in February 2000, while Padilla was on a religious pilgrimage to Saudi Arabia. Subsequently, Padilla met with al Qaeda operatives in Afghanistan, received explosives training in an al Qaeda-affiliated camp, and served as an armed guard at what he understood to be a Taliban outpost. When United States military operations began in Afghanistan, Padilla and other al Qaeda operatives moved from safehouse to safehouse to evade bombing or capture. Padilla was, on the facts with which we are presented, "armed and present in a combat zone during armed conflict between al Qaeda/Taliban forces and the armed forces of the United States." Padilla eventually escaped to Pakistan, armed with an assault rifle. Once in Pakistan, Padilla met with Khalid Sheikh Mohammad, a senior al Qaeda operations planner, who directed Padilla to travel to the United States for the purpose of blowing up apartment buildings, in continued prosecution of al Qaeda's war of terror against the United States. After receiving further training, as well as cash, travel documents, and communication devices, Padilla flew to the United States in order to carry out his accepted assignment. [*Padilla v. Hanft*, 423 F.3d 386, 389-390 (4th Cir. 2005) (describing facts that were stipulated solely for purposes of summary judgment motion—and which remain in dispute).]

Padilla was arrested as a material witness when he stepped off the plane at O'Hare International Airport in Chicago on May 8, 2002. He was then moved to a civilian correctional facility in New York City, where a grand jury had been convened.

Shortly before he was scheduled to go before a federal judge for a hearing on his detention as material witness, President George W. Bush declared Padilla "an enemy combatant" and ordered the Secretary of Defense to detain him "consistent with U.S. law and the laws of war. . . ." Order by President George W. Bush to the Secretary of Defense (June 9, 2002), *reproduced in Padilla v. Rumsfeld,* 352 F.3d 695, 724-725 app. A (2d Cir. 2003). He was then transferred to military custody in South Carolina.

Initially, Padilla challenged his detention by filing a habeas petition in the Southern District of New York. After the district court held that the government was authorized to detain him if it could adduce "some evidence" that he was an enemy combatant, *Padilla ex rel. Newman v. Bush,* 233 F. Supp. 2d 564 (S.D.N.Y. 2002), the Second Circuit reversed on the merits, 352 F.3d 695, holding that Padilla's detention violated the Non-Detention Act. The Supreme Court, however, then reversed the Second Circuit on jurisdictional grounds, holding that Padilla (who, unbeknownst to his lawyers, was moved from New York to South Carolina just before his habeas petition was filed) had brought his suit in the wrong court. *Rumsfeld v. Padilla,* 542 U.S. 426 (2004).

Importantly, though, Justice Breyer — who joined the plurality in *Hamdi* — joined Justice Stevens' *Padilla* dissent in full, including its conclusion that "the Non-Detention Act prohibits — and the Authorization for Use of Military Force does not authorize — the protracted, incommunicado detention of American citizens arrested in the United States." *Id.* at 464 n.8 (Stevens, J., dissenting). Assuming that Justice Scalia's and Justice Souter's *Hamdi* dissents would apply with equal (if not greater) force to a U.S. citizen arrested within the United States, the *Padilla* footnote strongly suggested that at least five Justices — Stevens, Scalia, Souter, Ginsburg, and Breyer — believed that, on the merits, Padilla's detention was unlawful.

Padilla then refiled his habeas petition in a federal district court in South Carolina, where he was being held in military custody. That court granted the petition. *Padilla v. Hanft,* 389 F. Supp. 2d 678 (D.S.C. 2005). Relying on *Hamdi,* the Fourth Circuit reversed. 423 F.3d 386 (4th Cir. 2005). Before the Supreme Court could decide Padilla's petition for certiorari, however, the government announced that it was transferring Padilla back to law enforcement custody for criminal prosecution. He was then ultimately convicted of criminal conspiracy to commit murder and providing material support to terrorists, and ultimately sentenced to 21 years in prison — a total that was increased on appeal in order to *not* include his time in military detention as "time served." *See United States v. Jayyousi,* 657 F.3d 1085, 1115-1119 (11th Cir. 2011).

2. Ali Saleh Kahlah al-Marri

Al-Marri was a lawful resident alien arrested in Peoria, Illinois, as a material witness who was then was indicted for credit card fraud and lying to the FBI. When he moved to suppress certain evidence in civil court, the government moved ex parte to dismiss the indictment based upon an order signed by the President that declared al-Marri to be an enemy combatant and ordered his transfer to military custody. Al-Marri petitioned for a writ of habeas corpus, to which the government filed a declaration asserting that

> al-Marri: (1) is "closely associated with al Qaeda, an international terrorist organization with which the United States is at war"; (2) trained at an al Qaeda terrorist training camp in

> Afghanistan sometime between 1996 and 1998; (3) in the summer of 2001, was introduced to Osama Bin Laden by Khalid Shaykh Muhammed; (4) at that time, volunteered for a "martyr mission" on behalf of al Qaeda; (5) was ordered to enter the United States sometime before September 11, 2001, to serve as a "sleeper agent" to facilitate terrorist activities and explore disrupting this country's financial system through computer hacking; (6) in the summer of 2001, met with terrorist financier Mustafa Ahmed al-Hawsawi, who gave al-Marri money, including funds to buy a laptop; (7) gathered technical information about poisonous chemicals on his laptop; (8) undertook efforts to obtain false identification, credit cards, and banking information, including stolen credit card numbers; (9) communicated with known terrorists, including Khalid Shaykh Muhammed and al-Hawsawi, by phone and e-mail; and (10) saved information about jihad, the September 11th attacks, and Bin Laden on his laptop computer. [*Al-Marri v. Pucciarelli*, 534 F.3d 213, 220 (4th Cir. 2008) (en banc), *vacated and remanded sub nom. Al-Marri v. Spagone*, 555 U.S. 1220 (2009).]

The district court denied relief, and al-Marri appealed. A divided panel of the Fourth Circuit reversed, and the government petitioned for rehearing en banc. A sharply divided en banc court produced multiple concurring and dissenting opinions. Judge Motz first opined that the Executive lacked authority for the military detention of al-Marri, but only three of the other eight judges joined her on this question. Thus, a bare 5-4 majority of the court upheld the government's authority to detain al-Marri. Judge Traxler then abandoned that majority to form a different majority for the proposition that the process afforded al-Marri to challenge his designation did not meet *Hamdi*'s due process standards. These five votes sufficed to send the case back to the district court. Al-Marri then successfully petitioned the Supreme Court for certiorari on the authority question. But while his appeal was being briefed on the merits, the government obtained a new criminal indictment against al-Marri, and returned him to civilian custody, just as it had with José Padilla. The Supreme Court then issued an order vacating the en banc Fourth Circuit's judgment and dismissing al-Marri's appeal as moot. Thus, whereas the dueling Second and Fourth Circuit opinions in *Padilla* created conflicting law concerning the military detention under the AUMF of U.S. citizens captured within the United States, the Supreme Court's order in *al-Marri* left *no* law under the AUMF for noncitizens captured stateside.

Notes and Questions

1. The Non-Detention Act Redux. In the Second Circuit's ruling in *Padilla*, it read the Non-Detention Act, 18 U.S.C. §4001(a), to require not just congressional authorization for the detention of U.S. citizens, but a "clear statement" from Congress to that effect. Clearly, such a rule as a general proposition is incompatible with the Supreme Court's subsequent decision in *Hamdi*. But is there any argument that, where the citizen in question is apprehended within the United States, §4001(a) *should* be read as a "clear statement" rule? Even without insisting upon a clear statement, does a natural reading of the AUMF embrace uses of force (and, by implication, military detention) *within* the United States, or just in Afghanistan or wherever else the armed forces are actively deployed in combat abroad? *See* Stephen I. Vladeck, Comment, *A Small Problem of Precedent: 18 U.S.C. §4001(a) and the Detention of U.S. Citizen "Enemy Combatants,"* 112 Yale L.J. 961, 967 (2003) (offering a pre-*Hamdi* argument for why the AUMF fails to satisfy §4001(a)).

2. Mooting the Issue. As should by now be clear, the government managed to convince the Supreme Court to avoid reaching the merits in both *Padilla* and *al-Marri* by transferring the detainees to civilian criminal custody on the eve of the Justices' review. As the Fourth Circuit complained in *Padilla,* the timing of the government's actions "have given rise to at least an appearance that the purpose of these actions may be to avoid consideration of our decision by the Supreme Court." *Padilla v. Hanft,* 432 F.3d 582, 585 (4th Cir. 2005). Indeed,

> [the government's] actions have left not only the impression that Padilla may have been held for these years, even if justifiably, by mistake — an impression we would have thought the government could ill afford to leave extant. They have left the impression that the government may even have come to the belief that the principle in reliance upon which it has detained Padilla for this time, that the President possesses the authority to detain enemy combatants who enter into this country for the purpose of attacking America and its citizens from within, can, in the end, yield to expediency with little or no cost to its conduct of the war against terror — an impression we would have thought the government likewise could ill afford to leave extant. [*Id.* at 587.]

Although the Supreme Court unanimously acquiesced in *al-Marri* (and vacated the decision below), three Justices dissented from the Court's denial of certiorari in *Padilla II* (which left the Fourth Circuit's ruling in that case intact). *See Padilla v. Hanft,* 547 U.S. 1062, 1062, 1064 (2006) (Ginsburg, J., dissenting). Specifically, Justice Ginsburg argued that the case was not formally moot, and that the gravity of the questions presented justified the Court's intervention — even if Padilla's transfer mitigated the effects of such a ruling. Assuming that it *could* have reviewed the Fourth Circuit's decisions in *Padilla II* and/or *al-Marri, should* the Supreme Court have done so? Why or why not?

D. CODIFICATION OF MILITARY DETENTION

In 2011, Congress purported to "clarify" the military detention authority provided by the AUMF in the National Defense Authorization Act (NDAA) for Fiscal Year 2012. Whether and to what extent it did so is a matter of ongoing debate, as applied to both U.S. persons and non-U.S. persons.

National Defense Authorization Act for Fiscal Year 2012

Pub. L. No. 112-81, 125 Stat. 1298, 1562-1564 (2011)

§1021. Affirmation of Authority of the Armed Forces of the United States to Detain Covered Persons Pursuant to the Authorization for Use of Military Force

(a) In General. — Congress affirms that the authority of the President to use all necessary and appropriate force pursuant to the Authorization for Use of Military Force (Public Law 107-40; 50 U.S.C. 1541 note) includes the authority for the Armed Forces of the United States to detain covered persons (as defined in subsection (b)) pending disposition under the law of war.

(b) Covered Persons. — A covered person under this section is any person as follows:

(1) A person who planned, authorized, committed, or aided the terrorist attacks that occurred on September 11, 2001, or harbored those responsible for those attacks.

(2) A person who was a part of or substantially supported al-Qaeda, the Taliban, or associated forces that are engaged in hostilities against the United States or its coalition partners, including any person who has committed a belligerent act or has directly supported such hostilities in aid of such enemy forces.

(c) Disposition under Law of War. — The disposition of a person under the law of war as described in subsection (a) may include the following:

(1) Detention under the law of war without trial until the end of the hostilities authorized by the Authorization for Use of Military Force.

(2) Trial under chapter 47A of title 10, United States Code (as amended by the Military Commissions Act of 2009).

(3) Transfer for trial by an alternative court or competent tribunal having lawful jurisdiction.

(4) Transfer to the custody or control of the person's country of origin, any other foreign country, or any other foreign entity.

(d) Construction. — Nothing in this section is intended to limit or expand the authority of the President or the scope of the Authorization for Use of Military Force.

(e) Authorities. — Nothing in this section shall be construed to affect existing law or authorities relating to the detention of United States citizens, lawful resident aliens of the United States, or any other persons who are captured or arrested in the United States. . . .

§1022. Military Custody for Foreign al-Qaeda Terrorists

[This section *requires* the military detention pending disposition under the law of war (as under §1021(c)) of any person captured in the course of hostilities authorized by the 2001 AUMF who is determined to "be a member of, or part of, al-Qaeda or an associated force that acts in coordination with or pursuant to the direction of al-Qaeda," and who "participated in the course of planning or carrying out an attack or attempted attack against the United States or its coalition partners," §1022(a)(2), unless waived by the President on national security grounds. §1022(a)(4). This section does not apply to U.S. citizens, or to lawful resident aliens based on "conduct taking place within the United States, except to the extent permitted by the Constitution." §1022(b).]

Notes and Questions

1. Who Is Covered? Recall that in *Hamdi* the four-Justice plurality was careful to limit its holding as to the rights of purported "enemy combatants" to individuals who allegedly were "'part of or supporting forces hostile to the United States or coalition partners' in Afghanistan and who 'engaged in an armed conflict against the

United States' there." 542 U.S. at 516 (plurality opinion). In §1021(b), "covered persons" are described quite differently. Does §1021(b) describe Yasir Hamdi? How about José Padilla? Ali Saleh Kahlah al-Marri? Why or why not?

Who else is described by §1021(b) as a covered person? Shortly after the law was enacted, a group of writers, journalists, and political activists mounted a facial challenge to the NDAA on First and Fifth Amendment grounds. They alleged, *inter alia,* that the terms "associated forces," "substantially supported," and "directly supported" in §1021(b) were overbroad and impermissibly vague, exposing them to indefinite military imprisonment without due process. They worried, for example, that a news article based on an interview with an Al Qaeda leader could be interpreted as "substantial support," leading to their arrest. A federal district court agreed with them. *Hedges v. Obama,* 890 F. Supp. 2d 424 (S.D.N.Y. 2012); *see also* Steve Vladeck, *What Hedges Could Have Said...*, Lawfare, Sept. 18, 2012 (meaning of "substantial support" is "unclear"). Is the meaning of these terms clear to you?

2. *The Feinstein Amendment.* Following a heated and contentious debate over the potential effect of the NDAA's detention provision on U.S. persons, Senator Dianne Feinstein proposed — and Congress adopted — §1021(e) of the act. After the district court in the *Hedges* case, *supra,* found §1021(b) unconstitutional, the Second Circuit reversed, partly on grounds that U.S. persons among the plaintiffs had no standing to challenge the law: "Section 1021 cannot itself be challenged as unconstitutional by citizens on the grounds advanced by plaintiffs because as to them it neither adds to nor subtracts from whatever authority would have existed in its absence." *Hedges v. Obama,* 724 F.3d 170, 193 (2d Cir. 2013).

If, as the Second Circuit indicated, the Feinstein Amendment merely codified the status quo (as of the end of 2011) with regard to the detention of U.S. persons, can you say what the status quo was? Might one of the U.S.-person plaintiffs in *Hedges* be confined in a military brig for "substantially supporting" Al Qaeda under pre-NDAA law? *See* Vladeck, *What Hedges Could Have Said, supra* (suggesting that, if so, the "new" statutory criterion for detention should have provided standing).

MILITARY DETENTION OF U.S. PERSONS: SUMMARY OF BASIC PRINCIPLES

- Long-term military detention of U.S. persons today will typically require (1) statutory authority, and (2) individualized administrative (and, subsequently, judicial) assessments of the factual basis for the detention.

- The Non-Detention Act requires specific statutory authorization to hold a U.S. citizen as a military prisoner, and it may require a clear statement of that authority to detain individuals captured outside zones of active combat operations.

- The 2001 Authorization for the Use of Military Force satisfies the Non-Detention Act for U.S. citizens captured in Afghanistan while fighting for or on behalf of Al Qaeda or the Taliban against the United States. Whether it does so for U.S. citizens captured elsewhere, including within the territorial United States, has produced conflicting circuit-level precedents, but no decisive Supreme Court ruling. Even under the circuit court rulings, however, the AUMF would satisfy the Non-Detention Act only if the detainee had been actively involved in combat activities overseas.

- For noncitizens lawfully present within the United States at the time of their capture, the Non-Detention Act does not apply. But the Due Process Clause of the Fifth Amendment (which unquestionably protects such individuals) likely requires a specific statutory basis for their detention and, as with U.S. citizens captured in Afghanistan, a meaningful opportunity to contest the government's factual basis for their detention before a neutral decision maker. In such a hearing, "some evidence" will not be a sufficient evidentiary standard, and the detainee must be allowed, among other things, access to counsel and an opportunity to present potentially exculpatory extra-record evidence.
- In 2011, Congress sought to "affirm" the government's right under the AUMF to detain terrorist suspects in military custody indefinitely without trial. But it raised new questions about who could be detained, including U.S. persons, and about what rights such detainees might have.

Military Detention of Non-U.S. Persons

Only three U.S. persons have been subjected to long-term military detention inside the United States since 9/11. In contrast, thousands of non-U.S. persons have been imprisoned without trial by the military under the AUMF in Afghanistan, at Guantánamo, and elsewhere.

Because the Supreme Court ruled in *Boumediene v. Bush*, 553 U.S. 723 (2008), that at least under certain circumstances non-U.S. persons held as prisoners by the military abroad are entitled to judicial review of their detentions via the Suspension Clause, see *supra* p. 849, much substantive law has emerged from the resulting habeas cases concerning the scope of the government's authority to detain such persons. We also know more now than previously about the procedural and evidentiary burdens that the government must bear in such cases. Yet even as the number of non-U.S. persons in U.S. custody has shrunk to a matter of dozens, the relevant legal rules remain a work in progress.

A. SUBSTANTIVE AUTHORITY TO DETAIN NON-U.S. PERSONS

Although the Supreme Court's decision in *Hamdi v. Rumsfeld*, 542 U.S. 507 (2004), *supra* p. 886, involved a U.S. citizen, its endorsement of at least some law-of-war detentions under the 2001 AUMF applies *a fortiori* to non-U.S. persons. Once the Supreme Court conclusively opened the door to habeas petitions from Guantánamo detainees in *Boumediene*, *supra* p. 849, the D.C. federal courts began to consider the applicability of law-of-war principles in dozens of habeas cases. At first, the district courts reached varying conclusions about whether law-of-war detention authority under the AUMF extended only to the Al Qaeda "command structure," to all "members" of Al Qaeda or the Taliban, to those who "substantially supported" Al Qaeda or the Taliban, or to anyone who provided any "material" support to them. These courts also struggled with whether the scope of such authority is informed or limited by the laws of war in light of the Obama administration's reliance strictly on the AUMF. Procedurally, the courts also disagreed about whether (and how far) the government's evidentiary bar moves up or down over time with a prisoner's continued detention, an issue related to the substantive question raised but not answered in *Hamdi* about whether detention status is permanent or might change over time. These courts diverged less sharply on the quality of admissible hearsay and other evidentiary issues raised but not resolved in *Hamdi.*

The following decision by a D.C. Circuit panel resolved some, but by no means all, of the conflicts among the district court opinions.

Reading *Al-Bihani v. Obama*

Ghaleb Nassar Al-Bihani is a Yemeni citizen who traveled to Afghanistan to defend the Taliban's Islamic state against the Northern Alliance. The government alleged that he stayed at Al Qaeda-affiliated guesthouses and may also have received instruction at Al Qaeda terrorist training camps. Al-Bihani did not dispute that he eventually accompanied and served as a cook for a paramilitary group allied with the Taliban, known as the 55th Arab Brigade, which included Al Qaeda members within its command structure and which fought on the front lines against the Northern Alliance. He carried a brigade-issued weapon, but never fired it in combat. Al-Bihani and the rest of the brigade eventually surrendered, under orders, to Northern Alliance forces, which kept him in custody until his handover to U.S. coalition forces in early 2002. The U.S. military sent al-Bihani to Guantánamo for detention and interrogation. Al-Bihani unsuccessfully petitioned for a writ of habeas corpus, then brought this appeal — the first post-*Boumediene* Guantánamo habeas petition to reach the D.C. Circuit on the "merits," and thus a case that required the D.C. Circuit to resolve a number of questions of first impression, including:

- What is the exact scope of the government's substantive detention authority under the AUMF? Is it informed by international law? If not, how should courts evaluate the scope of "necessary and appropriate" force under the 2001 statute? How did Judge Williams depart from the majority in answering these questions?
- How long does such detention authority continue?
- What is the burden of proof on the government in these cases? Why is that standard appropriate? What role, if any, can hearsay evidence play?

Al-Bihani v. Obama

United States Court of Appeals, District of Columbia Circuit, 2010
590 F.3d 866, *rehearing en banc denied*, 619 F.3d 1 (D.C. Cir. 2010)

Brown, Circuit Judge: . . .

II

Al-Bihani's many arguments present this court with two overarching questions regarding the detainees at the Guantánamo Bay naval base. The first concerns whom the President can lawfully detain pursuant to statutes passed by Congress. The second asks what procedure is due to detainees challenging their detention in habeas corpus proceedings. The Supreme Court has provided scant guidance on these questions, consciously leaving the contours of the substantive and procedural law of detention open for lower courts to shape in a common law fashion. In this decision, we aim to narrow the legal uncertainty that clouds military detention.

A

Al-Bihani challenges the statutory legitimacy of his detention by advancing a number of arguments based upon the international laws of war. He first argues that relying on "support," or even "substantial support" of Al Qaeda or the Taliban as an independent basis for detention violates international law. As a result, such a standard should not be read into the ambiguous provisions of the Authorization for Use of Military Force (AUMF), Pub. L. No. 107-40, §2(a), 115 Stat. 224, 224 (2001), the Act empowering the President to respond to the attacks of September 11, 2001. Al-Bihani interprets international law to mean anyone not belonging to an official state military is a civilian, and civilians, he says, must commit a direct hostile act, such as firing a weapon in combat, before they can be lawfully detained. Because Al-Bihani did not commit such an act, he reasons his detention is unlawful. Next, he argues the members of the 55th Arab Brigade were not subject to attack or detention by U.S. Coalition forces under the laws of co-belligerency because the 55th, although allied with the Taliban against the Northern Alliance, did not have the required opportunity to declare its neutrality in the fight against the United States. His third argument is that the conflict in which he was detained, an international war between the United States and Taliban-controlled Afghanistan, officially ended when the Taliban lost control of the Afghan government. Thus, absent a determination of future dangerousness, he must be released. *See* Geneva Convention Relative to the Treatment of Prisoners of War (Third Geneva Convention) art. 118, Aug. 12, 1949, 6 U.S.T. 3316, 75 U.N.T.S. 135. Lastly, Al-Bihani posits a type of "clean hands" theory by which any authority the government has to detain him is undermined by its failure to accord him the prisoner-of-war status to which he believes he is entitled by international law.

Before considering these arguments in detail, we note that all of them rely heavily on the premise that the war powers granted by the AUMF and other statutes are limited by the international laws of war. This premise is mistaken. There is no indication in the AUMF, the Detainee Treatment Act of 2005 [DTA], Pub. L. No. 109-148, div. A, tit. X, 119 Stat. 2739, 2741-43, or the MCA of 2006 or 2009 [Military Commissions Act of 2006, Pub. L. No. 109-366, 120 Stat. 2600; Military Commissions Act of 2009, Pub. L. No. 111-84, 123 Stat. 2190], that Congress intended the international laws of war to act as extra-textual limiting principles for the President's war powers under the AUMF. The international laws of war as a whole have not been implemented domestically by Congress and are therefore not a source of authority for U.S. courts. *See* Restatement (Third) of Foreign Relations Law of the United States §111(3)-(4) (1987). Even assuming Congress had at some earlier point implemented the laws of war as domestic law through appropriate legislation, Congress had the power to authorize the President in the AUMF and other later statutes to exceed those bounds. *See id.* §115(1)(a). Further weakening their relevance to this case, the international laws of war are not a fixed code. Their dictates and application to actual events are by nature contestable and fluid. *See id.* §102 cmts. b & c (stating there is "no precise formula" to identify a practice as custom and that "[i]t is often difficult to determine when [a custom's] transformation into law has taken place"). Therefore, while the international laws of war are helpful to courts when identifying the general set of war powers to which the AUMF speaks, *see Hamdi*, 542 U.S. at 520, their lack of controlling legal force and firm definition render their use both inapposite and inadvisable when courts seek to determine the limits of the President's war powers.

Therefore, putting aside that we find Al-Bihani's reading of international law to be unpersuasive, we have no occasion here to quibble over the intricate application of vague treaty provisions and amorphous customary principles. The sources we look to for resolution of Al-Bihani's case are the sources courts always look to: the text of relevant statutes and controlling domestic case law.

Under those sources, Al-Bihani is lawfully detained. . . . The statutes authorizing the use of force and detention not only grant the government the power to craft a workable legal standard to identify individuals it can detain, but also cabin the application of these definitions. The AUMF authorizes the President to "use all necessary and appropriate force against those nations, organizations, or persons he determines planned, authorized, committed, or aided the terrorist attacks that occurred on September 11, 2001, or harbored such organizations or persons." AUMF §2(a). The Supreme Court in *Hamdi* ruled that "necessary and appropriate force" includes the power to detain combatants subject to such force. 542 U.S. at 519. Congress, in the 2006 MCA, provided guidance on the class of persons subject to detention under the AUMF by defining "unlawful enemy combatants" who can be tried by military commission. 2006 MCA sec. 3, §948a(1). The 2006 MCA authorized the trial of an individual who "engaged in hostilities or who has purposefully and materially supported hostilities against the United States or its co-belligerents who is not a lawful enemy combatant (including a person who is part of the Taliban, al Qaeda, or associated forces)." *Id.* §948a(1)(A)(i). In 2009, Congress enacted a new version of the MCA with a new definition that authorized the trial of "unprivileged enemy belligerents," a class of persons that includes those who "purposefully and materially supported hostilities against the United States or its coalition partners." Military Commissions Act of 2009 sec. 1802, §§948a(7), 948b(a), 948c, 123 Stat. 2575-76. The provisions of the 2006 and 2009 MCAs are illuminating in this case because the government's detention authority logically covers a category of persons no narrower than is covered by its military commission authority. Detention authority in fact sweeps wider, also extending at least to traditional P.O.W.s, *see id.* §948a(6), and arguably to other categories of persons. But for this case, it is enough to recognize that any person subject to a military commission trial is also subject to detention, and that category of persons includes those who are part of forces associated with Al Qaeda or the Taliban or those who purposefully and materially support such forces in hostilities against U.S. Coalition partners.

In light of these provisions of the 2006 and 2009 MCAs, the facts that were both found by the district court and offered by Al-Bihani . . . place Al-Bihani within the "part of" and "support" prongs of the relevant statutory definition. . . . His acknowledged actions — accompanying the brigade on the battlefield, carrying a brigade-issued weapon, cooking for the unit, and retreating and surrendering under brigade orders — strongly suggest, in the absence of an official membership card, that he was part of the 55th. Even assuming, as he argues, that he was a civilian "contractor" rendering services, those services render Al-Bihani detainable under the "purposefully and materially supported" language of both versions of the MCA. That language constitutes a standard whose outer bounds are not readily identifiable. But wherever the outer bounds may lie, they clearly include traditional food operations essential to a fighting force and the carrying of arms. Viewed in full, the facts show Al-Bihani was part of and supported a group — prior to and after September 11 — that was affiliated with Al Qaeda and Taliban forces and engaged in hostilities against a U.S. Coalition partner. Al-Bihani, therefore, falls squarely within the scope of the President's statutory detention powers.

The government can also draw statutory authority to detain Al-Bihani directly from the language of the AUMF. The AUMF authorizes force against those who "harbored . . . organizations or persons" the President determines "planned, authorized, committed, or aided the terrorist attacks of September 11, 2001." AUMF §2(a). It is not in dispute that Al Qaeda is the organization responsible for September 11 or that it was harbored by the Taliban in Afghanistan. It is also not in dispute that the 55th Arab Brigade defended the Taliban against the Northern Alliance's efforts to oust the regime from power. Drawing from these facts, it cannot be disputed that the actual and foreseeable result of the 55th's defense of the Taliban was the maintenance of Al Qaeda's safe haven in Afghanistan. This result places the 55th within the AUMF's wide ambit as an organization that harbored Al Qaeda, making it subject to U.S. military force and its members and supporters — including Al-Bihani — eligible for detention. . . .

With the government's detention authority established as an initial matter, we turn to the argument that Al-Bihani must now be released according to longstanding law of war principles because the conflict with the Taliban has allegedly ended. Al-Bihani offers the court a choice of numerous event dates — the day Afghans established a post-Taliban interim authority, the day the United States recognized that authority, the day Hamid Karzai was elected President — to mark the official end of the conflict. No matter which is chosen, each would dictate the release of Al-Bihani if we follow his reasoning. His argument fails on factual and practical grounds. First, it is not clear if Al-Bihani was captured in the conflict with the Taliban or with Al Qaeda; he does not argue that the conflict with Al Qaeda is over. Second, there are currently 34,800 U.S. troops and a total of 71,030 Coalition troops in Afghanistan, with tens of thousands more to be added soon. The principle Al-Bihani espouses — were it accurate — would make each successful campaign of a long war but a Pyrrhic prelude to defeat. The initial success of the United States and its Coalition partners in ousting the Taliban from the seat of government and establishing a young democracy would trigger an obligation to release Taliban fighters captured in earlier clashes. Thus, the victors would be commanded to constantly refresh the ranks of the fledgling democracy's most likely saboteurs. . . .

Even so, we do not rest our resolution of this issue on international law or mere common sense. The determination of when hostilities have ceased is a political decision, and we defer to the Executive's opinion on the matter, at least in the absence of an authoritative congressional declaration purporting to terminate the war. *See Ludecke v. Watkins*, 335 U.S. 160, 168-70 & n.13 (1948) ("[T]ermination [of a state of war] is a political act.") . . . . In the absence of a determination by the political branches that hostilities in Afghanistan have ceased, Al-Bihani's continued detention is justified.

Al-Bihani also argues he should be released because the government's failure to accord him P.O.W. status violated international law and undermined its otherwise lawful authority to detain him. Even assuming Al-Bihani is entitled to P.O.W. status, we find no controlling authority for this "clean hands" theory in statute or in caselaw. The AUMF, DTA, and MCA of 2006 and 2009 do not hinge the government's detention authority on proper identification of P.O.W.s or compliance with international law in general. In fact, the MCA of 2006, in a provision not altered by the MCA of 2009, explicitly precludes detainees from claiming the Geneva conventions — which include criteria to determine who is entitled to P.O.W. status — as a source of rights. *See* 2006 MCA sec. 5(a). . . .

B . . .

[The *Al-Bihani* court's discussion of the appropriate procedures appears *infra* p. 921.]

III

Al-Bihani's detention is authorized by statute and there was no constitutional defect in the district court's habeas procedure that would have affected the outcome of the proceeding. For these reasons, the order of the district court denying Al-Bihani's petition for a writ of habeas corpus is

Affirmed.

[Concurring opinion of BROWN, Circuit Judge, is omitted.]

WILLIAMS, Senior Circuit Judge, concurring in part and concurring in the judgment: . . . The petitioner's detention is legally permissible by virtue of facts that he himself has conceded. . . .

Within the portion of the opinion addressing the petitioner's substantive argument that his activities in Afghanistan do not put him in the class of people whom the President may detain pursuant to the AUMF, the majority unnecessarily addresses a number of other points. Most notable is the paragraph that begins, "Before considering these arguments in detail," and that reaches the conclusion that "the premise that the war powers granted by the AUMF and other statutes are limited by the international laws of war . . . is mistaken." The paragraph appears hard to square with the approach that the Supreme Court took in *Hamdi*. See 542 U.S. at 521 (O'Connor, J.) (plurality opinion) ("[W]e understand Congress' grant of authority for the use of 'necessary and appropriate force' to include the authority to detain for the duration of the relevant conflict, and our understanding is based on longstanding law-of-war principles."); *id.* at 548-49 (Souter, J., opinion concurring in part and dissenting in part) (advocating a more substantial role for the laws of war in interpretations of the President's authority under the AUMF). In any event, there is no need for the court's pronouncements, divorced from application to any particular argument. Curiously, the majority's dictum goes well beyond what even the *government* has argued in this case.

Because the petitioner's detention is lawful by virtue of facts that he has conceded — a conclusion that the majority seems not to dispute — the majority's analysis of the constitutionality of the *procedures* the district court used is unnecessary. . . .

[Portions of the decision denying rehearing en banc in this case, and the opinions concurring therein, *see* 619 F.3d 1 (D.C. Cir. 2010), are reproduced *supra* p. 188.]

Notes and Questions

1. *Substantive Detention Authority and the Military Commissions Act.* The *Al-Bihani* panel looked first to the AUMF's identification of those against whom the President could use "necessary and appropriate force" to determine the government's detention authority. It then looked to the Military Commissions Act (MCA), and its definition of who may be tried by military commission (a subject we return to in Chapter 36) to support its interpretation of the AUMF as encompassing non-members of Al Qaeda or the Taliban who provide only "material support" to those organizations.

But as a general proposition, does it make sense to understand the scope of the government's power to *detain without charges* as derivative of its power to *try* enemy belligerents by military commission, given the significant differences between the authorities for and purposes of the different regimes? See *supra* p. 900. When Congress revised the MCA in 2009, it specifically *disclaimed* the precise reading Judge Brown adopted. *See* H.R. Conf. Rep. No. 111-288, at 862-863 (2009) (explaining that the definition of who can be tried "is not intended to address the scope of the authority of the United States to detain individuals in accordance with the laws of war or for any other purpose"). Why, then, do you suppose Judge Brown looked to the MCA?

2. *Law-of-War Limits?* Writing for herself and then-Judge Kavanaugh, Judge Brown went out of her way to reject al-Bihani's argument that any detention authority conferred by the AUMF was subject to or incorporated limits set by the law of war. In other words, they considered detention authority to be exclusively a question of domestic law. Judge Williams, the third member of the panel, disassociated himself from what he described as *dicta* that went well beyond any argument that even the government had made. In denying en banc review, the full court (besides the two judges in the majority on the *Al-Bihani* panel) agreed, asserting that a determination of "the role of international law-of-war principles in interpreting the AUMF . . . is not necessary to the disposition of the merits." *Al-Bihani v. Obama*, 619 F.3d 1, 1 (D.C. Cir. 2010) (Sentelle, C.J., and Ginsburg, Henderson, Rogers, Tatel, Garland & Griffith, JJ., concurring in the denial of rehearing en banc).

So what is the role of international law-of-war principles? One view is that Congress was oblivious to the law of war when it enacted the AUMF, and that the scope of the AUMF is to be found entirely in its plain words (and perhaps, legislative intent). While "necessary and appropriate" is hardly helpful in describing the kinds of force the AUMF authorizes, its identification of the targets of force at least permits some group identification. It is left then to courts to determine individual identification — what degree of association to a targeted group is necessary to justify "AUMF detention."

But Congress does not legislate in a vacuum. If the plain words and legislative history are not dispositive, courts interpret statutes against shared background understandings, often those reflected in like cases. There is a broad background understanding of law enforcement detention in U.S. law, driven by or under the shadow of the Fourth Amendment, but the understanding concerning wartime detention is reflected chiefly in *Ex parte Milligan*, 71 U.S. (4 Wall.) 2 (1866), *supra* p. 829, and *Ex parte Quirin*, 317 U.S. 1 (1942), *infra* p. 1125. Ironically, each discusses the law of war. In *Quirin*, the Court said that "[f]rom the very beginning of its history this Court has recognized and applied the law of war as including that part of the law of nations which prescribes, for the conduct of war, the status, rights and duties of enemy nations as well as of enemy individuals." 317 U.S. at 27. Our armed services have also long followed the law of war, dating back at least to the Lieber Code of 1863. Is that law not therefore part of the background understanding for interpreting the AUMF? Indeed, wasn't Congress's affirmative incorporation of that background understanding crucial to the Supreme Court's conclusion in *Hamdi* that the AUMF satisfied the Non-Detention Act despite its silence as to detention? *See* Marty Lederman & Steve Vladeck, *The NDAA: The Good, the Bad, and the Laws of War — Part II*, Lawfare, Dec. 31, 2011 (so arguing).

3. The Government's Standard. The AUMF targets organizations and persons who "planned, authorized, committed, or aided" the 9/11 attacks, or harbored such organizations or persons. In the post-*Boumediene* habeas litigation, the government proposed the following standard for detention under the AUMF:

> The President has the authority to detain persons that the President determines planned, authorized, committed, or aided the terrorist attacks that occurred on September 11, 2001, and persons who harbored those responsible for those attacks. The President also has the authority to detain persons who were part of, or substantially supported, Taliban or al Qaida forces or associated forces that are engaged in hostilities against the United States or its coalition partners, including any person who has committed a belligerent act, or has directly supported hostilities, in aid of such enemy armed forces. [*Hamlily v. Obama*, 616 F. Supp. 2d 63, 67 (D.D.C. 2009) (quoting government brief).]

Al-Bihani was a brigade cook; the government made no claim that he was involved in the 9/11 attacks. Does he meet the proposed standard to justify detention? If that standard is different from the AUMF standard, does he meet the latter? The court deemed cooking for a Taliban combat unit sufficient. But is that because he was present in the field with the brigade, because it had Al Qaeda members in its command structure, or because he carried a weapon (although he says he never fired it)?

Suppose al-Bihani was not in the field, but merely purchased food for the brigade in a Pakistani marketplace? Suppose he only donated money for that purpose? *See* Charlie Savage, *Obama Team Is Divided on Anti-Terror Tactics*, N.Y. Times, Mar. 28, 2010 (reporting that the Justice Department's Office of Legal Counsel "found no precedents justifying detention of mere supporters of Al Qaeda who were picked up far away from enemy forces, [but] it was not prepared to state any definitive conclusion"). Suppose he quit as cook and left the brigade because he was unhappy with the pay? Suppose he was trained in an Al Qaeda camp, but as a cook, not a terrorist? Suppose he received weapons training in a camp in Pakistan, but the camp was neither Al Qaeda nor Taliban, but instead something like the local boy scouts? Can you see why the habeas courts might diverge in deciding who can be detained? More fundamentally, can you see why the relevant procedural rules are so crucial in both the presumptions they create and in how they apportion the relevant evidentiary burdens?

4. *"Leaving" Al Qaeda.* By rejecting the "command structure" test, and tying at least one basis for detention authority to mere "membership," *Al-Bihani* opens the door to detention of individuals who may have done very little, indeed, to support Al Qaeda's hostilities against the United States — including one noteworthy case in which most of the government's evidence of a detainee's membership pre-dated September 11 by almost a decade. *See Salahi v. Obama,* 625 F.3d 745 (D.C. Cir. 2010). If detention can be based upon membership, then does the government have the authority to detain someone who has withdrawn from or otherwise abandoned his membership in Al Qaeda? The D.C. Circuit has not squarely answered this question, but one district court has held that "a prior relationship between a detainee and Al Qaeda (or the Taliban) can be sufficiently vitiated by the passage of time, intervening events, or both." *Al Ginco v. Obama,* 626 F. Supp. 2d 123, 128 (D.D.C. 2009). In *Al Ginco,* the relevant evidence of vitiation was the detainee's 18-month imprisonment and torture *by* Al Qaeda — which, in the district judge's view, made his an easy case. What *other* evidence would you accept as sufficient to demonstrate vitiation? Would you require more from a detainee for vitiation after the September 11 attacks as compared to before them?

5. *Mooting Al-Bihani?* Some of the questions about the scope of the AUMF raised but not answered by *Al-Bihani* (and the subsequent en banc maneuverings) seemed to be settled by Congress when it enacted the National Defense Authorization Act (NDAA) for Fiscal Year 2012, Pub. L. No. 112-81, §§1021-1022, 125 Stat. 1298, 1562-1564 (2011), *supra* p. 905. Whatever uncertainty may exist about its applicability to U.S. persons, it clearly applies to non-U.S. persons. But it makes such persons subject to possible military detention not only for membership in Al Qaeda, the Taliban, or "associated forces," but also for "substantial support" of these groups. *Id.* §1021(b).

The NDAA thus clearly endorses *Al-Bihani*'s focus on membership or support, but how *much* support? The government has never publicly relied upon "substantial support" (as opposed to membership) as the basis for detention in a Guantánamo habeas case. Instead, the question of what that term means has only arisen in a rather different context — when a group of writers, journalists, and activists brought an anticipatory action seeking to enjoin the enforcement of §1021(b) because they feared it authorized *their* military detention.

Reading *Hedges v. Obama*

Hedges is a strange case. The plaintiffs weren't detained by the federal government, but they brought suit because they feared that, under the terms of NDAA §1021(b), they could be detained in military custody indefinitely and without trial based upon constitutionally protected activities (including investigative reporting, human rights advocacy, and legal representation). The district court granted the injunction. The court first held that "[m]ilitary detention based on allegations of 'substantially supporting' or 'directly supporting' the

Taliban, al-Qaeda or associated forces, is not encompassed within the AUMF." 890 F. Supp. 2d 424, 472 (S.D.N.Y. 2012). It then went on to rule that, because the amorphous language in the NDAA might allow the detention of individuals based upon their constitutionally protected speech, and because of the vagueness of the terminology in the statute, it violated both the First and Fifth Amendments. In the opinion that follows, the Second Circuit reversed — albeit not on the merits. As you read its decision, consider these questions:

- In the Second Circuit's view, what is the relationship between the NDAA and the AUMF?
- What does it mean to "substantially support" Al Qaeda or associated forces?
- Why does the Second Circuit hold that the plaintiffs are not entitled to injunctive relief? Why couldn't they establish to the Second Circuit's satisfaction that §1021(b) might be applied to them?
- What, if any, precedent does *Hedges* set for the scope of (and limits upon) the government's power to detain non-U.S. persons under the NDAA?

Hedges v. Obama

United States Court of Appeals, Second Circuit, 2013
724 F.3d 170, *cert. denied*, 572 U.S. 1087 (2014)

Lewis A. Kaplan, District Judge [sitting by designation]: . . .

II. DISCUSSION . . .

B. The Proper Construction of Section 1021 . . .

At first blush, Section 1021 may seem curious, if not contradictory. While Section 1021(b)(1) mimics language in the AUMF, Section 1021(b)(2) adds language absent from the AUMF. Yet Section 1021(a) states that it only "affirms" authority included under the AUMF, and Section 1021(d) indicates that Section 1021 is not "intended to limit or expand the authority of the President or the scope of the [AUMF]."

Fortunately, this apparent contradiction — that Section 1021 merely affirms AUMF authority even while it adds language not used in the AUMF — is readily resolved. It is true that the language regarding persons who "planned, authorized, committed, or aided" the 9/11 attacks (or harbored those who did) is identical in the AUMF and Section 1021(b)(1). The AUMF, however, does not merely define persons who may be detained, as does Section 1021(b). Instead, it provides the President authority to use "force" against the "nations, organizations, or persons" responsible for 9/11. Section 1021(b)(1) (read with Section 1021(a)) affirms that the AUMF authority to use force against the persons responsible for 9/11 includes a power to detain such persons. But it does not speak to what additional detention authority, if any, is included in the President's separate AUMF authority to use force against the organizations responsible for 9/11.

This is where Section 1021(b)(2), a provision concerned with the organizations responsible for 9/11—al-Qaeda and the Taliban—plays a role. Section 1021(b)(2) naturally is understood to affirm that the general AUMF authority to use force against these organizations includes the more specific authority to detain those who were part of, or those who substantially supported, these organizations or associated forces. Because one obviously cannot "detain" an organization, one must explain how the authority to use force against an organization translates into detention authority. Hence, it is not surprising that Section 1021(b)(2) contains language that does not appear in the AUMF, notwithstanding Section 1021(d). Plaintiffs create a false dilemma when they suggest that either Section 1021 expands the AUMF detention authority or it serves no purpose.

Indeed, there are perfectly sensible and legitimate reasons for Congress to have affirmed the nature of AUMF authority in this way. To the extent that reasonable minds might have differed—and in fact very much did differ—over whether the administration could detain those who were part of or substantially supported al-Qaeda, the Taliban, and associated forces under the AUMF authority to use force against the "organizations" responsible for 9/11, Section 1021(b)(2) eliminates any confusion on that particular point. At the same time, Section 1021(d) ensures that Congress' clarification may not properly be read to suggest that the President did not have this authority previously—a suggestion that might have called into question prior detentions. This does not necessarily make the section a "'legislative attempt at an ex post facto "fix" . . . to try to ratify past detentions which may have occurred under an overly-broad interpretation of the AUMF,'" as plaintiffs contend. Rather, it is simply the 112th Congress' express resolution of a previously debated question about the scope of AUMF authority. . . .

We thus conclude, consistent with the text and buttressed in part by the legislative history, that Section 1021 means this: With respect to individuals who are not citizens, are not lawful resident aliens, and are not captured or arrested within the United States, the President's AUMF authority includes the authority to detain those responsible for 9/11 as well as those who were a part of, or substantially supported, al-Qaeda, the Taliban, or associated forces that are engaged in hostilities against the United States or its coalition partners—a detention authority that Section 1021 concludes was granted by the original AUMF. . . .

[The court of appeals went on to hold that, in light of its interpretation of Section 1021, the plaintiffs had not alleged facts sufficient to establish their standing because they could not show that they reasonably feared being detained under the NDAA.]

III. CONCLUSION

In sum, . . . [w]hile Section 1021 does have meaningful effect regarding the authority to detain individuals who are not citizens or lawful resident aliens and are apprehended abroad, [the noncitizen plaintiffs] have not established standing on this record. We VACATE the permanent injunction and remand for further proceedings consistent with this opinion.

Notes and Questions

1. *What Is the Purpose?* The *Hedges* appellate court observed that "Section 1021 may seem curious, if not contradictory," referring to the fact that while §1021(a) "affirms" the authority of the President, acting under the 2001 AUMF, to order military forces to imprison certain individuals without criminal charges or trial, §1021(d) states that the section neither limits nor expands the authority of the President or the scope of the AUMF. What, then, do you suppose was the purpose of this legislation? *See* Benjamin Wittes & Robert Chesney, *NDAA FAQ: A Guide for the Perplexed,* Lawfare, Dec. 19, 2011 ("[I]t puts the legislature squarely behind a set of policies on which it had always retained a kind of strategic ambiguity—a tolerance for detention without a clear endorsement of it of the sort that would make members accountable."). But does the relationship between the AUMF and NDAA actually matter? Put another way, can you describe an individual who was not subject to military detention on the day before the NDAA was enacted, but who is subject to military detention now? If not, what's all the fuss about?

2. *The Government's Rejected Invitation: Substantial Support and the Laws of War.* The heart of the issue in *Hedges* is the language of §1021(b)(2) that authorizes detention of individuals who "substantially support" Al Qaeda or its affiliates in hostilities against the United States. What does "substantial[]" support mean? In enjoining the enforcement of §1021(b)(2), the district court held, in part, that the phrase was unconstitutionally vague because a reasonable person would not know what activity might actually subject him to detention. *See Hedges v. Obama,* 890 F. Supp. 2d 424, 466-471 (S.D.N.Y. 2012).

On appeal, the government argued that one way to understand the term is by reference to the laws of war: the NDAA clearly did not authorize detention of *civilians* (such as the *Hedges* plaintiffs). So understood, *Hedges* would have been an easy case, as the court could then have held that, since the NDAA expressly incorporated the laws of war, individuals who were not belligerents under the laws of war clearly lacked standing to challenge it. Instead, the court of appeals declined to take up the government's invitation, and instead held that the plaintiffs lacked standing—simply because the government had disavowed even the possibility that the plaintiffs could be subject to military detention under the NDAA.

By that logic, though, the government arguably could control who has standing to challenge its detention authority merely by disclaiming (in legal briefs) a general desire to detain certain groups of individuals. Is that a satisfying result?

B. THE PROCESS FOR PROVING DETAINABILITY

Because of the D.C. Circuit's endorsement of membership in Al Qaeda or the Taliban as sufficient to justify the detention of non-U.S. persons under the AUMF, much has turned on how the government proves that a particular detainee was "part of" Al Qaeda or the Taliban. In three separate decisions, the D.C. Circuit addressed: (1) the burden of proof and role of hearsay evidence; (2) the relevance of "conditional probability analysis" in ascertaining whether the government has carried its burden; and (3) the "presumption of regularity" owed to government intelligence reports.

1. The Burden of Proof and Role of Hearsay Evidence

In *Al-Bihani v. Obama*, 590 F.3d 866 (D.C. Cir. 2010), *supra* p. 910, after discussing the scope of the government's detention authority, the D.C. Circuit turned to the burden of proof and the role of hearsay evidence:

> The question of what standard of proof is due in a habeas proceeding like Al-Bihani's has not been answered by the Supreme Court. *See Boumediene*, 128 S. Ct. at 2271 ("The extent of the showing required of the Government in these cases is a matter to be determined."). Attempting to fill this void, Al-Bihani argues the prospect of indefinite detention in this unconventional war augurs for a reasonable doubt standard or, in the alternative, at least a clear and convincing standard. . . .
>
> . . . [But] [i]n addition to the *Hamdi* plurality's approving treatment of military tribunal procedure, it also described as constitutionally adequate — even for the detention of U.S. citizens — a "burden-shifting scheme" in which the government need only present "credible evidence that the habeas petitioner meets the enemy-combatant criteria" before "the onus could shift to the petitioner to rebut that evidence with more persuasive evidence that he falls outside the criteria." *Hamdi,* 542 U.S. at 533-34. That description mirrors a preponderance standard. . . .
>
> . . . [T]raditional habeas review did not entail review of factual findings, particularly in the military context. *See In re Yamashita,* 327 U.S. 1, 8 (1946) ("If the military tribunals have lawful authority to hear, decide and condemn, their action is not subject to judicial review merely because they have made a wrong decision on disputed facts."). Where factual review has been authorized, the burden in some domestic circumstances has been placed *on the petitioner* to prove his case under a clear and convincing standard. *See* 28 U.S.C. §2254(e)(1) (regulating federal review of state court factual findings). If it is constitutionally permissible to place that higher burden on a citizen petitioner in a routine case, it follows a priori that placing a lower burden on the government defending a wartime detention — where national security interests are at their zenith and the rights of the alien petitioner at their nadir — is also permissible.
>
> We find Al-Bihani's hearsay challenges to be similarly unavailing. Al-Bihani claims that government reports of his interrogation answers — which made up the majority, if not all, of the evidence on which the district court relied — and other informational documents were hearsay improperly admitted absent an examination of reliability and necessity. He contends, in fact, that government reports of his interrogation answers were "*double* hearsay" because his answers were first translated by an interpreter and then written down by an interrogator. We first note that Al-Bihani's interrogation answers themselves were not hearsay; they were instead party-opponent admissions that would have been admitted in any U.S. court. *See* Fed. R. Evid. 801(d)(2)(A). That they were translated does not affect their status. *See United States v. Da Silva,* 725 F.2d 828, 831-32 (2d Cir. 1983). However, that the otherwise admissible answers were relayed through an interrogator's account does introduce a level of technical hearsay because the interrogator is a third party unavailable for cross examination. Other information, such as a diagram of Al Qaeda's leadership structure, was also hearsay.
>
> But that such evidence was hearsay does not automatically invalidate its admission — it only begins our inquiry. . . .
>
> . . . [T]he question a habeas court must ask when presented with hearsay is not whether it is admissible — it is always admissible — but what probative weight to ascribe to whatever indicia of reliability it exhibits. . . .
>
> In Al-Bihani's case, the district court clearly reserved that authority in its process and assessed the hearsay evidence's reliability as required by the Supreme Court. First, the district court retained the authority to assess the weight of the evidence. Second, the district

> court had ample contextual information about evidence in the government's factual return to determine what weight to give various pieces of evidence. Third, the district court afforded Al-Bihani the opportunity... to rebut the evidence and to attack its credibility. Further, Al-Bihani did not contest the truth of the majority of his admissions upon which the district court relied, enhancing the reliability of those reports. We therefore find that the district court did not improperly admit hearsay evidence.... [590 F.3d at 878-881.]

2. The Relevance of "Conditional Probability Analysis"

How does the government show that a "preponderance" of the evidence supports the conclusion that an individual detainee is "part of" Al Qaeda or the Taliban? The cases that have been litigated have generally involved circumstantial evidence in which courts are asked to draw inferences from the detainee's movements, associations, and otherwise. In *Al-Adahi v. Obama*, 613 F.3d 1102 (D.C. Cir. 2010), the D.C. Circuit chastised the district court for failing to follow "conditional probability analysis" in weighing the government's evidence, even though factual findings are usually only overturned when they are clearly erroneous. As Judge Randolph explained,

> The key consideration is that although some events are independent (coin flips, for example), other events are dependent: "the occurrence of one of them makes the occurrence of the other more or less likely...." John Allen Paulos, *Beyond Numeracy: Ruminations of a Numbers Man* 189 (1991). Dr. Paulos gives this example: "the probability that a person chosen at random from the phone book is over 250 pounds is quite small. However, if it's known that the person chosen is over six feet four inches tall, then the conditional probability that he or she also weighs more than 250 pounds is considerably higher." [613 F.3d at 1105.]

Thus, as the D.C. Circuit would explain in a subsequent case,

> Merely because a particular piece of evidence is insufficient, standing alone, to prove a particular point does not mean that the evidence "may be tossed aside and the next [piece of evidence] may be evaluated as if the first did not exist." The evidence must be considered in its entirety in determining whether the government has satisfied its burden of proof. [*Salahi v. Obama*, 625 F.3d 745, 753 (D.C. Cir. 2010) (quoting *Al-Adahi*, 613 F.3d at 1105).]

As a result of *Al-Adahi*, the government can make its case oftentimes through use of a "mosaic theory," where different pieces of circumstantial evidence, aggregated together, make it "more likely than not" that the detainee in question was "part of" Al Qaeda or the Taliban. To that end, *Al-Adahi* was the first of six different cases in which the D.C. Circuit vacated or reversed a grant of habeas relief by the district court—all of which were based on disagreements between the trial and appellate courts over the weight that ought to have been given to the government's circumstantial evidence. Can you see why *Al-Adahi* had such a significant impact on these cases? Indeed, some detainees have lost their habeas petitions even in cases in which, in the district court's own words, the evidence against them was "gossamer thin." *Awad v. Obama*, 646 F. Supp. 2d 20, 27 (D.D.C. 2009).

3. The "Presumption of Regularity"

Understanding the significance of *Al-Adahi* also helps to crystallize the dispute between the majority and dissenting judges in *Latif v. Obama,* 677 F.3d 1175 (D.C. Cir. 2011). There, the question was what weight should be accorded to a heavily redacted government intelligence report that apparently included statements made by the detainee while he was in custody. The district court had granted Latif's petition, holding that there was serious question as to whether "the Report accurately reflected Latif's words," "the incriminating facts in the [Report] are not corroborated," and "Latif has presented a plausible alternative story to explain his travel." *Id.* at 1178. In reversing the district court, Judge Brown held that the government's report was entitled to a "presumption of regularity" — that is, that the report should be presumed to be accurate, and treated as such unless the detainee could introduce facts tending to disprove its accuracy:

> "The presumption of regularity supports the official acts of public officers and, in the absence of clear evidence to the contrary, courts presume that they have properly discharged their official duties." *Sussman v. U.S. Marshals Serv.*, 494 F.3d 1106, 1117 (D.C. Cir. 2007). The presumption applies to government-produced documents no less than to other official acts. But Latif (and our dissenting colleague) argue no such presumption can be applied in Guantanamo cases — at least not to interrogation reports prepared in stressful and chaotic conditions, filtered through interpreters, subject to transcription errors, and heavily redacted for national security purposes.
>
> Since the problems Latif cites are typical of Guantanamo detainees' interrogation reports, the rule he proposes would subject all such documents to the he-said/she-said balancing of ordinary evidence. It is impossible to cure the conditions under which these documents were created, so Latif's proposed rule would render the traditional presumption of regularity wholly illusory in this context. We conclude first that intelligence documents of the sort at issue here are entitled to a presumption of regularity, and second that neither internal flaws nor external record evidence rebuts that presumption in this case. [*Latif,* 677 F.3d at 1178-1179.]

In a sharply worded dissent, Judge Tatel objected that intelligence reports aren't typical government documents and should therefore receive no such presumption:

> [E]very case applying the presumption of regularity . . . [has] something in common: actions taken or documents produced within a process that is generally reliable because it is, for example, transparent, accessible, and often familiar. As a result, courts have no reason to question the output of such processes in any given case absent specific evidence of error. Such a presumption rests on common sense. . . . Courts presume accuracy because they can trust the reliability of documents produced by such processes. Courts and agencies are hardly infallible, but for the most part we have sufficient familiarity and experience with such institutions to allow us to comfortably rely on documents they produce in the ordinary course of business. . . .
>
> By contrast, the Report at issue here was produced in the fog of war by a clandestine method that we know almost nothing about. It is not familiar, transparent, generally understood as reliable, or accessible; nor is it mundane, quotidian data entry akin to state court dockets or tax receipts. Its output, a [REDACTED] intelligence report, was, in this court's own words, "prepared in stressful and chaotic conditions, filtered through interpreters, subject to transcription errors, and heavily redacted for national security

purposes." Maj. Op. at 1179. Needless to say, this is quite different from assuming the mail is delivered or that a court employee has accurately jotted down minutes from a meeting.

To support its approach here, this court invokes presumptions of regularity for state court fact-finding and for final judgments in criminal habeas proceedings. *See id.* at 1181-82. Aside from the abstract and uncontroversial proposition that courts should be sensitive to the separation of powers as well as to federalism, *id.* at 1181-82, the analogy makes little sense. State court judgments and fact findings arise out of a formal and public adversarial process where parties generally have attorneys to zealously guard their interests, and where neutral state court judges, no less than federal judges, pledge to apply the law faithfully. That federal courts give a presumption of regularity to judgments and fact findings that emerge from such a process, where criminal defendants have ample opportunity to challenge adverse evidence, provides no reason for habeas courts also to presume the accuracy of [REDACTED] intelligence reports prepared in the fog of war. Indeed, unlike statutory habeas, where federal review follows state court proceedings, constitutional habeas is the only process afforded Guantanamo detainees . . .

To be sure, the government in this case has produced a declaration stating [REDACTED] *see* Maj. Op. at 1186 (quoting this affidavit). But we have no idea what the [REDACTED] is, nor anywhere near the level of familiarity or experience with that course of business that would allow us to comfortably make presumptions about whether the output of that process is reliable. Of course, we may take some assurance from the fact that the Executive Branch acts in good faith when carrying out its duties. But the very point of *Boumediene* is to ensure that detainees have a "meaningful opportunity" to subject the Executive's detention decisions to scrutiny by an independent Article III court.

This is not to say that reports similar to the one at issue here are necessarily unreliable. Perhaps after careful scrutiny district courts will conclude that many are reliable. *See, e.g., Khan v. Obama,* 655 F.3d 20, 24-26 (D.C. Cir. 2011). My point is far more modest: because we are unfamiliar with this highly secretive process, and because we have no basis on which to draw conclusions about the general reliability of its output, we should refrain from categorically affording it presumptions one way or the other. This approach does not reflect "skeptic[ism]" or "cynic[ism]" about the Executive Branch, Maj. Op. at 1179-80 — it is nothing more than what *Boumediene* directs us to do. And indeed, from time immemorial courts have been skeptical of hearsay evidence without implying bad faith or cynicism about the Executive (or whoever is attempting to present that evidence). . . .

. . . [T]his court goes well beyond these modest conclusions — and well beyond what the government actually argues in its briefs — when it relies on the bare fact that government officials have incentives to maintain careful intelligence reports as a reason to require district courts to presume that such reports are not only authentic, but also accurate, despite circumstances casting their reliability into serious doubt. One need imply neither bad faith nor lack of incentive nor ineptitude on the part of government officers to conclude that [REDACTED] compiled in the field by [REDACTED] in a [REDACTED] [REDACTED] near an [REDACTED] that contain multiple layers of hearsay, depend on translators of unknown quality, and include cautionary disclaimers that [REDACTED] are prone to significant errors; or, at a minimum, that such reports are insufficiently regular, reliable, transparent, or accessible to warrant an automatic presumption of regularity. [*Latif,* 677 F.3d at 1207-1210 (Tatel, J., dissenting).]

Notes and Questions

1. The Burden of Proof. In *Al-Bihani,* Judge Brown defends the "preponderance" burden by reference to the burden placed on convicted criminals who file habeas petitions to collaterally attack their convictions. But isn't there a world of difference (as *Boumediene* recognized) between habeas to challenge a criminal conviction and habeas to challenge executive detention, where there is no other judicial review standing between a detainee and potentially decades of non-criminal confinement? See *supra* p. 872. Shouldn't the government's burden be far *higher* in the latter cases — closer to the "clear and convincing evidence" standard for which the detainees argued?

In an unusual turn of events, some D.C. Circuit judges subsequently criticized the federal government for not seeking an even *lower* burden of proof. As Judge Randolph wrote in *Al-Adahi,* "we doubt . . . that the Suspension Clause requires the use of the preponderance standard," but because the government had failed to argue as much, "we will not decide the question in this case." 613 F.3d at 1105. In essence, the D.C. Circuit is arguing for the very "some evidence" standard that the Supreme Court rejected in *Hamdi,* presumably because of the differences in how the Due Process Clause applies to citizens versus the noncitizen Guantánamo detainees. Is "some evidence" somehow more reliable when a non-U.S. person is the detainee than it was in *Hamdi*? If not, why do you suppose the D.C. Circuit was so critical of the government for not arguing for such a low burden? *See Esmail v. Obama,* 639 F.3d 1075, 1078 (D.C. Cir. 2011) (Silberman, J., concurring) ("[T]he preponderance of evidence standard is unnecessary — and, moreover, unrealistic. I doubt any of my colleagues will vote to grant a petition if he or she believes that it is somewhat likely that the petitioner is an Al Qaeda adherent or an active supporter.").

2. Conditional Probability Analysis and the "Mosaic Theory." In many ways, *Al-Adahi* is a more important decision than *Al-Bihani,* since it expressly rejected the manner in which the district courts had been looking at the government's evidence. But is the mosaic theory it thereby defends so obviously valid? As one of us has written,

> If there are reasons why individual pieces of evidence are insufficient to satisfy a "preponderance" standard, including a lack of reliability, those reasons do not dissipate merely because there is additional evidence that suffers from comparable reliability concerns. Thus, whereas the whole may often be greater than the sum of its parts, it may just as easily represent the aggregation of unreliable evidence, which is no more reliable taken as a whole than the individual items were taken individually. [Stephen I. Vladeck, *The D.C. Circuit After Boumediene,* 41 Seton Hall L. Rev. 1451, 1472 n.112 (2011).]

Put another way, if four pieces of evidence come from the same potentially unreliable source (as opposed to different, independent sources), does the fact that there are four pieces, rather than one, somehow change how courts should assess the source's reliability? More generally, how can courts tell whether, in an individual case, resort to the mosaic theory is more or less justified? How do *Latif* and the "presumption of authenticity" factor into this analysis?

3. The Presumption of Regularity. Although it is the farthest into the weeds, *Latif* is in many ways the most interesting of these decisions, at least in part because of Judge Tatel's unusual and sharp dissent. If the burden is on the government to demonstrate detainability by a preponderance of the evidence, is it fair to require a detainee to rebut the presumption of regularity? How might a detainee do that, especially if he doesn't have access to classified information, like the report in *Latif*? At a more basic level, do you see how the presumption of regularity, together with conditional probability analysis, makes it so much easier for the government to meet its burden than might otherwise have been true?

4. *The Scorecard.* Given these decisions, one might expect that the government prevailed in most — if not all — of the post-*Boumediene* Guantánamo habeas cases. In fact, of the 64 detainees who have had their habeas claims adjudicated on the merits as of December 1, 2019, 39 (60.9%) prevailed in the district court. Three of those rulings were subsequently dismissed or held in abeyance pending the detainees' transfer, and another six were reversed by the D.C. Circuit. But that still left 30 out of 61 detainees (not counting the dismissed or stayed cases) who prevailed even under the D.C. Circuit's decisional law. Does this figure surprise you, given that these were detainees who remained at Guantánamo after *Boumediene* was decided (in contrast to the more than 500 who had been transferred or released)?

5. *What Happens When a Detainee "Wins"?* If a detainee prevails, what happens next? In a habeas hearing, a finding that detention is unjustified is ordinarily followed by an order for a prisoner's release (or, where the writ challenges a criminal conviction, retrial). But how can a detainee be judicially "released" from Guantánamo?

Consider the case of the Uighurs — 17 ethnically Turkic Chinese Muslim detainees who, after prevailing in CSRT and habeas litigation, could not be sent home because they credibly feared persecution at the hands of the Chinese government. In October 2009, one district judge ordered the government to produce the detainees in his Washington courtroom, presumably so they could be released into the United States. The D.C. Circuit quickly reversed, holding that just because a detainee held overseas had won his habeas petition did not mean that a judge could thereby override the political branches' plenary power over immigration into the United States. *See Kiyemba v. Obama*, 555 F.3d 1022 (D.C. Cir. 2009), *vacated*, 559 U.S. 131 (2010) (per curiam), *reinstated on remand*, 605 F.3d 1046 (D.C. Cir. 2010) (per curiam), *cert. denied*, 563 U.S. 954 (2011). After back-and-forth procedural maneuvers, the Supreme Court ultimately declined review because the detainees had received genuine offers to resettle to third-party countries, and so the case no longer presented the question "whether a district court may order the release of an unlawfully held prisoner into the United States *where no other remedy is available*." 563 U.S. at 955 (Breyer, J., respecting the denial of certiorari) (emphasis added). But what if no such offers had been made? As between the plenary power of the political branches over immigration and the right to release from unlawful custody at the heart of the Suspension Clause, which constitutional imperative should yield? Would *Kiyemba* allow the government to simply ignore a writ of habeas corpus, much as President Lincoln did at the outset of the Civil War (see *supra* p. 829)?

6. *Transfers.* Another question raised by the Uighurs' cases was whether detainees had any right to *object* to their transfer, especially if it was to a country where they might credibly fear torture or other forms of cruel, inhuman, or degrading treatment. In "*Kiyemba II*," a divided panel of the D.C. Circuit held that the answer was no — and that, so long as the government averred that it does not transfer to torture, the federal courts lack the power to consider a detainee's claim that he nevertheless credibly

fears mistreatment once transferred, and so a detainee had no right to notice and a hearing prior to such a transfer. *See Kiyemba v. Obama*, 561 F.3d 509 (D.C. Cir. 2009), *cert. denied*, 559 U.S. 1005 (2010). Although the majority purported to rest such a holding on the Supreme Court's decision in *Munaf v. Geren*, 553 U.S. 674 (2008) (which had rejected efforts by two U.S. citizens detained by the United States in Iraq to block their transfer to Iraqi custody), Judge Griffith argued in his dissent that *Munaf* was easily distinguishable, and that, in any event, the Suspension Clause required courts to reach the underlying legal question (whether it was actually more likely than not that the petitioners would be mistreated), even if the U.S. government took the contrary position. *See Kiyemba II*, 561 F.3d at 522-526 (Griffith, J., concurring in the judgment in part and dissenting in part); *see also Abdah v. Obama*, 630 F.3d 1047, 1048-1054 (D.C. Cir. 2011) (Griffith, J., dissenting from the denial of rehearing en banc); *Mohammed v. Obama*, 561 U.S. 1042 (2010) (Ginsburg, J., dissenting from the denial of a stay). Whoever has the better of this legal argument, note the practical effect of *Kiyemba II* — making it much easier, at least legally, for the government to transfer non-U.S. person detainees to third-party countries.

7. *"Hostility" to Boumediene?* In response to the decisions discussed above, along with a thinly veiled contempt expressed by at least some judges for the outcome in *Boumediene, see, e.g., Esmail*, 639 F.3d at 1078 (Silberman, J., concurring) (describing the habeas litigation as "a charade prompted by the Supreme Court's defiant — if only theoretical — assertion of judicial supremacy"), the D.C. Circuit has received significant criticism from civil liberties groups, human rights organizations, detainee lawyers, and the editorial pages of major media outlets. Indeed, senior D.C. Circuit Judge Harry Edwards has written that he is "disquieted by our jurisprudence," *Hussain v. Obama*, 718 F.3d 964, 973 (D.C. Cir. 2013) (Edwards, J., concurring in the judgment). As he explained in one case, "[t]he troubling question in these detainee cases is whether the law of the circuit has stretched the meaning of the AUMF and the NDAA so far beyond the terms of these statutory authorizations that habeas corpus proceedings . . . are functionally useless." *Ali v. Obama*, 736 F.3d 542, 553-554 (D.C. Cir. 2013) (Edwards, J., concurring in the judgment). How would you answer that charge? How would Justice Kennedy, who wrote the opinion for the Court in *Boumediene*, answer?

C. THE NEXT GENERATION OF GUANTÁNAMO LITIGATION

No new detainees were sent to Guantánamo after 2008. By the end of 2019, it appeared that the U.S. government had, at least for the time being, generally eschewed long-term military detention as a means of incapacitating terrorism suspects. As a result, the focus of contemporary litigation has shifted away from the substantive and procedural questions raised in the first round of Guantánamo habeas litigation, and toward "legacy" questions concerning the conditions and legality of the continuing confinement of the 40 detainees who were still in custody on December 1, 2019. In Chapter 28, we considered which of these claims are properly cognizable in habeas petitions. Here, we return to those cases to examine how courts considered their merits.

Reading *Aamer v. Obama*

We first confronted *Aamer* in Chapter 28, and its holding that the federal courts can entertain challenges to the conditions of the Guantánamo detainees via habeas petitions. Here, we turn to the merits of the *Aamer* petitioners' challenge — that the government's use of force-feeding in response to their hunger strikes violated their rights. As you read the D.C. Circuit's analysis, consider the following questions:

- What "rights" do the detainees maintain that their force-feeding violates?
- What test does the court apply to determine whether the challenged conditions are justified? Does it make sense to apply that test to military detention at Guantánamo?
- Why does the D.C. Circuit conclude that the government has a sufficient justification for its conduct? What analogies does it draw?
- The petitioners in *Aamer* were seeking only a preliminary injunction. What additional evidence might they have provided on remand to show that the force-feeding was, in fact, unlawful?

Aamer v. Obama

United States Court of Appeals, District of Columbia Circuit, 2014
742 F.3d 1023

TATEL, Circuit Judge: Petitioners Ahmed Belbacha, Abu Dhiab, and Shaker Aamer are detainees who, although cleared for release, remain held at the United States Naval Station at Guantanamo Bay, Cuba. Protesting their continued confinement, they and other similarly situated detainees have engaged in a hunger strike, refusing to eat unless and until released. In response, the government instituted a force-feeding protocol. Petitioners, each of whom had already sought release via a writ of habeas corpus, moved in those habeas actions for a preliminary injunction preventing the government from subjecting them to force-feeding. . . . We . . . conclude . . . that although their claims are not insubstantial, petitioners have failed to establish their entitlement to preliminary injunctive relief. . . .

III.

"'A plaintiff seeking a preliminary injunction must establish [1] that he is likely to succeed on the merits, [2] that he is likely to suffer irreparable harm in the absence of preliminary relief, [3] that the balance of equities tips in his favor, and [4] that an injunction is in the public interest.'" *Sherley v. Sebelius*, 644 F.3d 388, 392 (D.C. Cir. 2011) (alteration in original) (quoting *Winter v. Natural Resources Defense Council, Inc.*, 555 U.S. 7, 20 (2008)). We review the district court's balancing of these four factors for abuse of discretion, while reviewing de novo the questions of law involved in that inquiry. *Id.* at 393.

A.

We begin with the first and most important factor: whether petitioners have established a likelihood of success on the merits. Petitioners advance two separate substantive claims regarding the legality of force-feeding.

Their first and central claim is that the government's force-feeding of hunger-striking detainees violates their constitutionally protected liberty interest — specifically, the right to be free from unwanted medical treatment, *see Cruzan v. Director, Missouri Department of Health*, 497 U.S. 261, 278-79 (1990) — and that the government is unable to justify the practice of force-feeding under the standard established in *Turner v. Safley*, 482 U.S. 78 (1987). In *Turner*, the Supreme Court set forth the general test for assessing the legality of a prison regulation that "impinges on" an inmate's constitutional rights, holding that such a regulation is "valid if it is reasonably related to legitimate penological interests." *Id.* at 89. As the government does not press the issue, we shall, for purposes of this case, assume without deciding that the constitutional right to be free from unwanted medical treatment extends to nonresident aliens detained at Guantanamo and that we should use the *Turner* framework to evaluate petitioners' claim. . . .

For petitioners to be entitled to injunctive relief, . . . it is not enough for us to say that force-feeding may cause physical pain, invade bodily integrity, or even implicate petitioners' fundamental individual rights. This is a court of law, not an arbiter of medical ethics, and as such we must view this case through *Turner*'s restrictive lens. The very premise of *Turner* is that a "prison regulation [that] impinges on inmates' constitutional rights" may nonetheless be "valid." *Turner*, 482 U.S. at 89. That is, although "[p]rison walls do not form a barrier separating prison inmates from the protections of the Constitution," they do substantially change the nature and scope of those constitutional protections, as well as the degree of scrutiny that courts will employ in assessing alleged violations. *Id.* at 84. Thus, even if force-feeding "burdens fundamental rights," *Turner*, 482 U.S. at 87. *Turner* makes clear that a federal court may step in only if the practice is not "reasonably related to legitimate penological interests," *id.* at 89.

The government has identified two penological interests at stake here: preserving the lives of those in its custody and maintaining security and discipline in the detention facility. As the government emphasizes, many courts have concluded that such interests are legitimate and justify prison officials' force-feeding of hunger-striking inmates. The New York Court of Appeals recently explained that prison officials faced with a hunger-striking inmate whose behavior is life-threatening would, absent force-feeding, face two choices: (1) give in to the inmate's demands, which would lead other inmates to "copy the same tactic, manipulating the system to get a change in conditions"; or (2) let the inmate die, which is a harm in its own right, and would often "evoke[ ] a strong reaction from the other inmates and create[ ] serious safety and security concern[s]." *Matter of Bezio* [*v. Dorsey*], 989 N.E.2d [942,] 951 [(N.Y. 2013)] (internal quotation marks omitted). Although a handful of state appellate courts have rejected prison officials' attempts to force-feed particular inmates, those courts have largely done so while applying state law and under unique factual circumstances. But such an approach is not constitutionally compelled because it fails to similarly achieve the government's legitimate penological interests — including, most obviously, the interest in preserving the inmate's life.

Thus, the overwhelming majority of courts have concluded, as did Judge Collyer and as we do now, that absent exceptional circumstances prison officials may force-feed a starving inmate actually facing the risk of death. Petitioners point to nothing specific to their situation that would give us a basis for concluding that the government's legitimate penological interests cannot justify the force-feeding of hunger-striking detainees in Guantanamo.

Instead, petitioners attempt to distinguish the many decisions upholding the lawfulness of force-feeding by tying their challenge to an attack on the legality of the fact of their detention itself, arguing that "[t]here cannot be a legitimate penological interest in force-feeding the Guantanamo Bay detainees to prolong their indefinite detention" because force-feeding then simply "facilitates the violation of a fundamental human right." Appellants' Br. 40. But this court has repeatedly held that under the Authorization for the Use of Military Force, Pub. L. No. 107-40, 115 Stat. 224 (2001), individuals may be detained at Guantanamo so long as they are determined to have been part of Al Qaeda, the Taliban, or associated forces, and so long as hostilities are ongoing. *See, e.g., Al-Bihani v. Obama,* 590 F.3d 866, 873-74 (D.C. Cir. 2010). Given that such continued detention is lawful, force-feeding that furthers this detention serves the same legitimate penological interests as it would if petitioners were serving determinate sentences in state or federal prison.

In reaching this conclusion, we emphasize that we are addressing only petitioners' *likelihood* of success on the merits, not the actual merits of their claim. It is conceivable that petitioners could establish that the government's interest in preserving the lives of those detained at Guantanamo is somehow reduced, or demonstrate that the government has such complete control over Guantanamo detainees that hunger-striking inmates present no threat to order and security, or even show that there are "ready alternatives" to force-feeding that the government might employ to achieve these same legitimate interests. *Turner,* 482 U.S. at 90. We leave it to the district court to decide in the first instance what procedures may be necessary to provide petitioners a "meaningful opportunity" to make this showing. *Boumediene,* 553 U.S. at 779. . . .

B.

. . . [T]he remaining factors do not . . . weigh in petitioners' favor. The primary "purpose of a preliminary injunction is to preserve the object of the controversy in its then existing condition — to preserve the status quo." *Doeskin Products, Inc. v. United Paper Co.,* 195 F.2d 356, 358 (7th Cir. 1952). In this case, even if petitioners might eventually prevail in their challenge to the government's force-feeding protocol, we see especially good reasons for preserving the status quo by denying petitioners' request. Were we to now conclude that a preliminary injunction should issue, and then the district court, this court, or the Supreme Court later determined that the petitioners' claims lacked merit, the petitioners could very well die before the government would ever receive the benefit of that decision. But were we to uphold the district court's denial of a preliminary injunction, and it was later determined that force-feeding as practiced at Guantanamo violates petitioners' rights, petitioners would suffer by being compelled to endure force-feeding or the threat of force-feeding in the interim, but they would ultimately be able to engage in an uninterrupted hunger strike as they wish. Given that the risk of error is greater if a preliminary injunction is granted than if it is denied, we conclude, as did Judge Collyer, that the balance of equities and public interest support denying petitioners' request for interim relief.

IV.

For the forgoing reasons, we affirm the district courts' denials of petitioners' applications for a preliminary injunction.

So ordered.

[The opinion of WILLIAMS, Senior Circuit Judge, dissenting, is omitted.]

Notes and Questions

1. *Turner v. Safley at Guantánamo.* The detainees claimed that the force-feeding violated their constitutional rights and the Religious Freedom Restoration Act (RFRA), 42 U.S.C. §2000bb-1 (2018). The D.C. Circuit ruled against them on the merits in principal part because it concluded that "force-feeding that furthers this detention serves the same legitimate penological interests as it would if petitioners were serving determinate sentences in state or federal prison." 742 F.3d at 1041. Do you agree with Judge Tatel that the government's "penological interests" vis-à-vis the Guantánamo detainees are the same as its interests with respect to ordinary criminal prisoners? Are there significant differences between the goals (and the government's interests) in military versus criminal detention? If there are, which way would that cut under *Turner*?

2. *Duration of Detention Redux.* In *Al-Alwi v. Trump*, 901 F.3d 294 (D.C. Cir. 2018), the D.C. Circuit held that the detention authority provided by the AUMF had neither "unraveled" nor "expired" because "[a]lthough United States troops are involved in combat with a different operation name, they nonetheless remain in active combat with the Taliban and al Qaeda. Accordingly, the 'relevant conflict' has not ended." *Id.* at 300. When the Supreme Court denied al-Alwi's petition for certiorari in June 2019, Justice Breyer wrote separately to argue that "it is past time to confront the difficult question left open by *Hamdi*" concerning the temporal scope of detention authority under the 2001 AUMF. *Al-Alwi v. Trump*, 139 S. Ct. 1893, 1894 (2019) (Breyer, J., respecting the denial of certiorari). As Breyer noted,

> al-Alwi faces the real prospect that he will spend the rest of his life in detention based on his status as an enemy combatant a generation ago, even though today's conflict may differ substantially from the one Congress anticipated when it passed the AUMF, as well as those "conflicts that informed the development of the law of war." [*Id.* (quoting *Hamdi*, 542 U.S. at 521 (plurality opinion)).]

Thus, Breyer explained, "I would, in an appropriate case, grant certiorari to address whether, in light of the duration and other aspects of the relevant conflict, Congress has authorized and the Constitution permits continued detention." *Id.* Even if you believe that "Congress has authorized and the Constitution permits [such] continued detention," do you agree with Justice Breyer that, more than 15 years after *Hamdi*, the Supreme Court ought to weigh in again?

Part of why Justice Breyer may nevertheless have thought *Al-Alwi* was not necessarily an appropriate case for review is because the D.C. Circuit did not reach the petitioner's claim that, even if his potentially indefinite detention was authorized by the AUMF, it violates the Due Process Clause of the Fifth Amendment. *See Al-Alwi*, 901 F.3d at 301. Shortly after *Al-Alwi*, however, the Court of Appeals clarified that it was still an open question whether the Due Process Clause *applies* to Guantánamo detainees — leaving open the possibility that a duration-of-detention challenge could be mounted on due process grounds. *See Qassim v. Trump*, 927 F.3d 522 (D.C. Cir. 2019). *But see Qassim v. Trump*, 938 F.3d 375, 376 (D.C. Cir. 2019) (Henderson, J., dissenting from the denial of rehearing en banc) (disputing the panel's conclusion that the due process question was open). It is a telling reflection that, more than 17 years after the first court cases arising out of Guantánamo, such basic questions still have not been conclusively answered by the courts.

D. "CLOSING" GUANTÁNAMO

Despite his repeated pledges to close Guantánamo, President Obama was unable to do so, and 41 detainees remained at the end of his tenure — including at least two dozen who had been "cleared for transfer" under the government's own criteria (one detainee was released pursuant to a military commission plea agreement in May 2018). Part of the reason for the difficulty President Obama encountered was a series of spending restrictions that Congress began imposing in 2011 on the transfer of detainees either into the United States or to foreign countries. The following provision, for example, appeared in the National Defense Authorization Act for FY2013:

> None of the funds authorized to be appropriated by this Act for fiscal year 2013 may be used to transfer, release, or assist in the transfer or release to or within the United States, its territories, or possessions of Khalid Sheikh Mohammed or any other detainee who —
>
> (1) is not a United States citizen or a member of the Armed Forces of the United States; and
>
> (2) is or was held on or after January 20, 2009, at United States Naval Station, Guantanamo Bay, Cuba, by the Department of Defense.

Pub. L. No. 112-239, §1027, 126 Stat. 1632, 1914 (2012).

Section 1028 of the same act prohibited the transfer of detainees elsewhere unless ordered by a court, or unless the Secretary of Defense certified, at least 30 days in advance of the transfer, that the country to which the detainee was to be transferred:

> (A) is not a designated state sponsor of terrorism or designated foreign terrorist organization;
>
> (B) maintains control over each detention facility in which the individual is to be detained if the individual is to be housed in a detention facility;
>
> (C) is not, as of the date of the certification, facing a threat that is likely to substantially affect its ability to exercise control over the individual;
>
> (D) has taken or agreed to take effective actions to ensure that the individual cannot take action to threaten the United States, its citizens, or its allies in the future;

> (E) has taken or agreed to take such actions as the Secretary of Defense determines are necessary to ensure that the individual cannot engage or reengage in any terrorist activity; and
>
> (F) has agreed to share with the United States any information that—
>
> (i) is related to the individual or any associates of the individual; and
>
> (ii) could affect the security of the United States, its citizens, or its allies. . . .

Id. §1028(b)(1), 126 Stat. at 1915. Although the measure included authority for the Secretary to waive some of these certifications, *see id.* §1028(d), 126 Stat. at 1915-1916, the difficulties inherent in making these showings may have helped to account for the total absence of such certifications—and, as such, of non-court-ordered foreign transfers—between 2011 and 2013. These restrictions also provoked annual signing statements from President Obama, who objected that the provisions

> hinder[] the executive's ability to carry out its military, national security, and foreign relations activities and . . . would, under certain circumstances, violate constitutional separation of powers principles. The executive branch must have the flexibility to act swiftly in conducting negotiations with foreign countries regarding the circumstances of detainee transfers. In the event that the statutory restrictions . . . operate in a manner that violates constitutional separation of powers principles, my Administration will interpret them to avoid the constitutional conflict.

Statement by the President on H.R. 1540 (Dec. 31, 2011), http://www.whitehouse.gov/the-press-office/2011/12/31/statement-president-hr-1540.

In the NDAA for Fiscal Year 2014, Congress left the ban on transfers into the United States intact, but relaxed the foreign transfer restrictions. Instead of requiring onerous certifications from the Secretary of Defense before detainees could be transferred, it authorized transfers if (a) "the Secretary determines, following a review conducted in accordance with [prior statutes and executive orders] that the individual is no longer a threat to the national security of the United States," or (b) he determines that:

> (1) actions that have been or are planned to be taken will substantially mitigate the risk of such individual engaging or reengaging in any terrorist or other hostile activity that threatens the United States or United States persons or interests; and
>
> (2) the transfer is in the national security interest of the United States.

Pub. L. No. 113-66, §1035(b), 127 Stat. 622, 851 (2013). In all such cases, §1035(d) mandated that "[t]he Secretary of Defense shall notify the appropriate committees of Congress of a determination of the Secretary under subsection (a) or (b) not later than 30 days before the transfer or release of the individual under such subsection." *Id.* §1035(d), 127 Stat. at 853. Thanks in part to these more relaxed provisions, ten detainees were transferred out of Guantánamo between December 2013 and April 2014.

On May 31, 2014, the Obama administration announced the transfer of five additional Taliban detainees at Guantánamo to Qatar as part of an exchange for Sergeant Bowe Bergdahl, the one U.S. soldier held by Taliban forces in Afghanistan as a prisoner of war. Whatever the policy merits of the exchange, many objected that the transfer was unlawful, insofar as the government had failed to satisfy the notice requirements of §1035(d). In response, the National Security Council issued a statement explaining that

> the Administration determined that the notification requirement should be construed not to apply to this unique set of circumstances, in which the transfer would secure the release of a captive U.S. soldier and the Secretary of Defense, acting on behalf of the President, has determined that providing notice as specified in the statute could endanger the soldier's life.
>
> In these circumstances, delaying the transfer in order to provide the 30-day notice would interfere with the Executive's performance of two related functions that the Constitution assigns to the President: protecting the lives of Americans abroad and protecting U.S. soldiers. Because such interference would significantly alter the balance between Congress and the President, and could even raise constitutional concerns, we believe it is fair to conclude that Congress did not intend that the Administration would be barred from taking the action it did in these circumstances.

E-mail from NSC Press Office (June 3, 2014, 1:27 P.M.), *available at* http://www.scribd.com/doc/228207506/NSC-Statement-On-30-Day-Transfer-Notice-Requirement-In-2014-NDAA.

Notes and Questions

1. A Statutory Argument, or a Constitutional One? Reread the NSC statement about the Bergdahl swap carefully. Is this an example of a President's assertion that a statute unconstitutionally interferes with executive power? Or is the argument, instead, that the statutory notice requirement shouldn't be read to apply to unique cases like Bergdahl's — that Congress wasn't contemplating either (1) prisoner exchanges generally, or (2) cases where the notice requirement might negatively affect the health of a servicemember, specifically. Are you convinced by either or both of these arguments? Does it make a difference that the provision President Obama arguably violated was a procedural, rather than substantive, constraint on detainee transfers? Could anyone bring a lawsuit challenging President Obama's allegedly unlawful conduct?

2. Moving the Detainees into the United States. Suppose the federal government ultimately closes Guantánamo by moving those detainees whom the government refused to transfer or release into the United States for continuing long-term military detention. So long as the AUMF remains on the books and "active hostilities" remain ongoing, would the move change either the government's substantive detention authority or limits on the duration or conditions of the detainees' confinement? If not, then why do you suppose closing Guantánamo has been so politically fraught?

3. The Periodic Review Board (PRB) Process. In 2011, President Obama issued an executive order creating an internal, administrative review process for prisoners subject to continuing detention under the AUMF. *See* Exec. Order No. 13,567, 76 Fed. Reg. 13,277 (Mar. 7, 2011). Among other things, the order provides that a prisoner's "[c]ontinued law of war detention is warranted" only "if it is necessary to protect against a significant threat to the security of the United States," and it mandates both an initial review of all detainees who have not already been cleared for transfer, and periodic file reviews every six months for all detainees who remain uncleared. *Id.*

§§2-3. Although the PRB process has moved at a snail's pace (with one detainee going so far as to sue the government to *force* it to provide him with a PRB), the PRBs cleared 13 of the first 15 prisoners whose cases it heard. On paper, the result is to increase the number of detainees who have been cleared for transfer, and decrease the number of detainees whom the government refuses to release. But given the difficulties the Obama administration encountered in transferring detainees who had been cleared, and the seeming refusal of the Trump administration to transfer such detainees, what purpose, if any, do the PRBs actually serve? Why do you suppose President Obama went out of his way to both (1) create the PRBs, and (2) charge them with a higher standard for continuing detention than either international or domestic law requires? Why do you suppose President Trump, who rescinded President Obama's "close Guantánamo" executive order, has not also rescinded the PRB order?

MILITARY DETENTION OF NON-U.S. PERSONS: SUMMARY OF BASIC PRINCIPLES

- Because non-U.S. citizens are not covered by the Non-Detention Act, and non-U.S. persons who lack substantial connections to the United States may lack the protection of the Due Process Clause (a question not yet definitively decided), the government's domestic legal authority to detain such individuals without criminal charges or trial is usually circumscribed only by the scope of some relevant statutory authorization.

- The FY2012 NDAA provides that noncitizens may be subjected to long-term military detention if they are "part of or substantially supported al-Qaeda, the Taliban, or associated forces that are engaged in hostilities against the United States or its coalition partners."

- Lower federal courts have assumed (without deciding) that the government must show by a preponderance of the evidence that a non-U.S. person meets that definition. In doing so, hearsay evidence is admissible, courts may rely upon "conditional probability analysis," and government intelligence reports are entitled to a "presumption of regularity."

- Although non-U.S. persons held at Guantánamo have been allowed to pursue challenges to the conditions of their confinement, courts have applied the Supreme Court's deferential *Turner v. Safley* reasonably-related-to-a-legitimate-penological-purpose test to such claims — and have sustained an array of government policies including, among other things, restrictive genital searches.

- Whereas the government has not subjected any new individuals to long-term military detention since 2008, statutory restrictions on the government's power to transfer or release detainees from Guantánamo have dramatically complicated efforts to close the facility and/or end the detention program, even as a growing number of the existing detainees have been cleared for transfer.

31

Preventive Detention

In some cases, national security-related and otherwise, the government would like to be able to take individuals into custody when there is insufficient (or insufficiently reliable) evidence to pursue criminal charges against them, but without relying (or being legally able to rely) upon the military to hold them.

Consider, in this regard, the FBI's investigation of the September 11 terrorist attacks (dubbed the PENTTBOM investigation), which began even before the last hijacked plane crashed in Pennsylvania. From the start, the government needed to do more than simply identify, apprehend, and convict the perpetrators in the time-honored fashion of criminal investigations. As then-Assistant Attorney General Michael Chertoff would later explain,

> In past terrorist investigations, you usually had a defined event and you're investigating it after the fact. That's not what we had here.... From the start, there was every reason to believe that there is more to come.... So we thought that we were getting information to prevent more attacks, which was even more important than trying any case that came out of the attacks. [*Quoted in* Jeffrey Toobin, *Crackdown*, New Yorker, Nov. 5, 2001, at 56.]

To that end, the FBI immediately checked passenger manifests, airport terminal and parking garage videotapes, car rental agreements, credit card receipts, telephone records, and numerous other data sources to help identify the hijackers. It then extended its investigation to persons who lived or worked with the hijackers or otherwise crossed paths with them. Most of those interviewed were foreign nationals.

The FBI itself detained some (or had state and local authorities detain them) on suspicion of committing a variety of minor crimes. The Bureau also asked the INS to detain many others who were in technical violation of their immigration status (out-of-status immigrants), even if they had broken no criminal laws.

In January 2002, the government initiated the "Absconder Apprehension Initiative" to locate and deport 6,000 Arabs and Muslims with outstanding deportation orders (among more than 300,000 foreign nationals subject to similar orders whose deportation was not actively sought). By May 2003, another 2,747 noncitizens had been detained as part of a special registration program directed at Arabs and

Muslims. In addition, the FBI detained several individuals as "material witnesses" to the ongoing investigation.

"We're clearly not standing on ceremony, and if there is a basis to hold them we're going to hold them," Chertoff said in reference to the detentions. Attorney General John Ashcroft was even more blunt: "We have waged a deliberate campaign of arrest and detention to remove suspected terrorists who violate the law from our streets." *Preserving Our Freedom While Defending Against Terrorism: Hearing on DOJ Oversight Before the S. Comm. on the Judiciary*, 107th Cong. (2001) (statements of John Ashcroft, Attorney General, and Michael Chertoff, Assistant Attorney General).

Within weeks of the 9/11 attacks, the media reported that more than 1,100 persons had been or were being detained by law enforcement authorities. Although the government declined to release a breakdown of this number, a newspaper investigation of 235 detainees whom it could identify indicated that the largest number were from Egypt, Saudi Arabia, and Pakistan. By the end of November, federal criminal charges had been brought against 104 individuals (most relating to possession of false identification or other fraud), of whom 55 were then in custody, while the INS had detained 548 persons for immigration violations.

Were these arrests and detentions lawful? What other options were available to the government? What are the limits on the government's power to detain individuals without charges? This chapter is devoted to answering these questions.

A. CONSTITUTIONAL LIMITS ON PREVENTIVE DETENTION

One scholar has described circumstances in which the government might want to detain a suspected terrorist but is not ready "to file charges in open court as required for a criminal prosecution."

> The government may have learned of the individual from a confidential or foreign-government source that it cannot publicly disclose, or from an ongoing investigation. It may lack sufficient evidence to convict beyond a reasonable doubt, but have substantial grounds to believe that the individual was actively engaged in armed conflict for al Qaeda. The disclosures necessary for a public trial might seriously compromise the military struggle against the Taliban and al Qaeda. U.S. law has no formal statutory mechanism by which the government could detain such a person. [David Cole, *Out of the Shadows: Preventive Detention, Suspected Terrorists, and War*, 97 Cal. L. Rev. 693, 693 (2009).]

Notwithstanding the view that the Suspension Clause bars the non-criminal detention of U.S. citizens, articulated by Justice Scalia in his dissent in *Hamdi v. Rumsfeld*, 542 U.S. 507 (2004), *supra* p. 837, the Supreme Court has upheld civil detention of certain persons who have not been convicted of a crime: (1) criminal arrestees pending their trial who are flight risks or dangers to the community (or who can't make bail); (2) some noncitizens facing deportation; (3) the mentally ill when they pose a danger to themselves or those around them; (4) violent sexual offenders who continue to pose a threat to the community even after they have served their criminal sentences; (5) people with communicable diseases (see Chapter 37); and (6) various persons (drunks, addicts, and the homeless) for their own protection. *See* Adam Klein & Benjamin Wittes, *Preventive Detention in American Theory and Practice*, 2 Harv. Nat'l Security J. 85 (2011) (exploring each kind of existing detention authority). Some scholars have therefore argued that any purported presumption against preventive detention is a "civic myth," *id.* at 87, and others agree that "[p]reventive detention is in fact an established part of U.S. law." Cole, *supra*, at 695.

Yet there are strong reasons to be skeptical of preventive detention.

> First, preventive detention rests on a prediction about future behavior, and no one can predict the future. Decision makers all too often fall back on stereotypes and prejudices as proxies for dangerousness. . . .
>
> Second, the risk of unnecessarily detaining innocent people is high, because decision makers are likely to err on the side of detention. . . .
>
> Third, preventive detention is inconsistent with basic notions of human autonomy and free will. We generally presume that individuals have a choice to conform their conduct to the law. Thus, we do not criminalize thought or intentions, but only actions. . . .
>
> While it is not always explicitly rationalized in such terms, constitutional doctrine governing preventive detention is best understood as reflecting a strong presumption that the criminal process is the preferred means for addressing socially dangerous behavior. [Cole, *supra*, at 696-697.]

Any detention is subject not only to the procedural and substantive requirements of the Fifth Amendment's Due Process Clause; it is also circumscribed by the Fourth Amendment, which insists on "[t]he right of the people to be secure in their persons . . . against unreasonable . . . seizures," and which provides that no arrest warrants shall issue except upon probable cause. Since there is usually no probable cause (as that term is used in the Fourth Amendment) to believe that a preventive detainee has yet committed or is committing a crime, a warrant for her detention is unavailable. And even if compliance with the warrant requirement is excused for some reason, the detention must still be reasonable under the circumstances.

Finally, recall that the Non-Detention Act, 18 U.S.C. §4001(a), provides that "No citizen shall be imprisoned or otherwise detained by the United States except pursuant to an Act of Congress." Thus, civil detention of U.S. citizens would appear to require explicit statutory authority.

Notes and Questions

1. Constitutional Standards for Detention. Generally, the Fourth Amendment requires that before police make an arrest, they must have probable cause to believe that a suspect has committed a crime. However, they are allowed to stop a person when there is an "articulable suspicion that the person has been, is, or is about to be engaged in criminal activity." *United States v. Place*, 462 U.S. 696, 702 (1983); *see Terry v. Ohio*, 392 U.S. 1, 9 (1968). Nevertheless, "reasonable suspicion of criminal activity," short of probable cause, only "warrants a temporary seizure for the purpose of questioning limited to the purpose of the stop," and not longer confinement. *Florida v. Royer*, 460 U.S. 491, 498 (1983). Even where suspects are lawfully arrested without a warrant, they are entitled to a probable cause hearing no more than 48 hours after their arrest. *See County of Riverside v. McLaughlin*, 500 U.S. 44 (1991).

Immigration officials may stop and detain persons for questioning about their citizenship upon a *reasonable suspicion* that they are present in the United States unlawfully. *See United States v. Brignoni-Ponce*, 422 U.S. 873, 882-883 (1975). Congress has authorized the arrest and detention of such persons pending a decision about their removal. 8 U.S.C. §1226 (2018). But the Supreme Court has ruled that after a decision is made to remove, continued indefinite detention presents a serious due process issue, at least as to aliens already in the country, who enjoy settled Fifth Amendment protections. *See Zadvydas v. Davis,* 533 U.S. 678 (2001).

Zadvydas did not, however, involve an individual suspected of terrorism. The Court emphasized that the detention there at issue did not concern " 'a small segment of particularly dangerous individuals,' say suspected terrorists." *Id.* at 691 (quoting *Kansas v. Hendricks,* 521 U.S. 346, 368 (1997) (upholding the preventive detention of a convicted sexual predator longer than his criminal sentence, until he is no longer dangerous)). "Neither do we consider terrorism or other special circumstances," it added, "where special arguments might be made for forms of preventive detention and for heightened deference to the judgments of the political branches with respect to matters of national security." *Id.* at 696.

Was the Court suggesting a "national security exception" to the Fifth Amendment guarantee of due process? Could there be such an exception to the Fourth Amendment's protection against unreasonable seizure? (Recall that, before enactment of the Foreign Intelligence Surveillance Act (FISA) in 1978, some lower courts found a national security exception to the warrant requirement for some kinds of searches and electronic surveillance. See *supra* p. 592.) How would you define such an exception? What limitations, if any, would the Fourth or Fifth Amendment place on how long a terrorism suspect could be detained before criminal proceedings were commenced against him?

2. *Due Process Requirements for Statutory Detention.* In *Demore v. Hyung Joon Kim,* 538 U.S. 510 (2003), Justice Souter summarized the due process requirements for preventive detention as follows:

> [D]ue process requires a "special justification" for physical detention that "outweighs the individual's constitutionally protected interest in avoiding physical restraint" as well as "adequate procedural protections." "There must be a 'sufficiently compelling' governmental interest to justify such an action, usually a punitive interest in imprisoning the convicted criminal or a regulatory interest in forestalling danger to the community." The class of persons subject to confinement must be commensurately narrow and the duration of confinement limited accordingly. . . . Finally, procedural due process requires, at a minimum, that a detainee have the benefit of an impartial decisionmaker able to consider particular circumstances on the issue of necessity. [*Id.* at 557 (Souter, J., concurring in part and dissenting in part) (internal citations omitted).]

Compare Klein & Wittes, *supra,* at 89 (arguing for "a relatively simply test" for counterterrorism detention: "Does America really need to do it, and if so, how can it do it in a fashion that minimizes erroneous incarcerations?").

Applying similar standards in *United States v. Salerno,* 481 U.S. 739 (1987), a divided Supreme Court upheld a provision of the Bail Reform Act of 1984, 18 U.S.C. §3142(e) (2018), which authorizes preventive detention (denial of bail) of arrestees on the grounds of flight risk or future dangerousness — if a neutral magistrate determines that "no condition or combination of conditions will reasonably assure the appearance of the person as required and the safety of any other person and the community." The majority found that the Act authorized a "regulatory," rather than punitive, detention that was reasonably related to compelling government interests. The Court noted that regulatory interests in community safety can outweigh an individual's liberty interest, "[f]or example, in times of war and insurrection." *Salerno,* 481 U.S. at 748. But the Court emphasized that the Bail Reform Act authorized detention of an arrestee only when: (a) he has been arrested and indicted on probable cause of having committed one or more specified extremely dangerous offenses, (b) a court conducts a full-blown adversary hearing on the denial of bail, at which the arrestee is entitled to be represented by his own counsel, (c) the government persuades the court by clear and convincing evidence that no conditions of release can assure the presence of the arrestee or the safety of the community, and (d) the arrestee is given a right of appeal from the court's decision.

Did the post-September 11 detentions described above satisfy *Salerno*'s due process standards? How important might it have been to the *Salerno* Court that pretrial detention invariably culminates in a *trial* — as opposed to potentially indefinite detention *without* trial?

B. "SPITTING ON THE SIDEWALK": PRETEXTUAL(?) CRIMINAL DETENTION

Explaining the PENTTBOM detentions, Attorney General John Ashcroft likened some of the arrests of terrorist suspects for minor crimes to Attorney General Robert Kennedy's policy of "arrest[ing] mobsters [for] spitting on the sidewalk if it would help in the battle against organized crime." Amy Goldstein, *A Deliberate Strategy of Disruption; Massive, Secretive Detention Effort Aimed Mainly at Preventing More Terror,* Wash. Post, Nov. 4, 2001. Identity fraud, credit card fraud, forgery, and larceny were among the criminal charges brought against some of the detainees. (Prosecution of suspected terrorists for crimes directly related to acts of terrorism is addressed in Chapters 35-36.)

Notes and Questions

1. Pretextual Arrest — The Whren Principle. A terrorism suspect taken into custody for "spitting on the sidewalk" has been arrested on a pretext: the government's real reason for the arrest is that it suspects he has committed or will commit a terrorist act, or knows information about a planned future act. Does a pretextual arrest violate the Fourth Amendment? The Supreme Court said no in *Whren v. United States,* 517 U.S. 806, 813 (1996), as long as there is objective probable cause for the actual arrest: "[s]ubjective intent [to detain the arrestee for terrorism-related conduct or information] . . . does not make otherwise lawful conduct [the arrest] illegal or unconstitutional." Note, however, that *Whren* involved only a Fourth Amendment challenge; pretextual arrests may be unlawful on *other* grounds — e.g., if the arrest was made with the intent to discriminate on the basis of race. *See, e.g., United States v. Armstrong,* 517 U.S. 456 (1996).

2. The Practical Problem. One difficulty with the spitting-on-the-sidewalk policy is that persons charged with such minor offenses are usually released on bail. Indeed, even *conviction* on such a charge often yields no (or a rather modest) term of imprisonment. Rising to the occasion, however, one federal magistrate denied bail for an immigrant from El Salvador who had allegedly helped some of the September 11 hijackers obtain false identity papers (apparently without knowing that they were terrorists), explaining that "[o]ne of the unspoken issues today is, after the events of September 11, is it going to be business as usual? I suspect not. The defendant, either wittingly or unwittingly, certainly contributed [to the attacks]." T.R. Reid & Allen Lengel, *Scotland Yard Says Hijackers May Have Trained in Britain; Terror Suspects Arrested in Spain, Holland,* Wash. Post, Sept. 27, 2001. Should judges be allowed to take these considerations into play in cases in which the (minor) charges have nothing to do with terrorism?

3. PENTTBOM Convictions. In mid-2005, the Bush administration asserted that terrorism investigations had resulted in charges against more than 400 suspects, half of whom were convicted. A *Washington Post* study of the Department of Justice's own list of prosecutions, however, indicated that only 39 of these convictions were for crimes remotely related to terrorism or national security. Dan Eggen & Julie Tate, *U.S. Campaign Produces Few Convictions on Terrorism Charges,* Wash. Post, June 12, 2005. The majority were for minor crimes such as fraud, making false statements, and passport violations, for which the median sentence was just 11 months.

The Justice Department defended the numbers by arguing that many defendants were prosecuted for such crimes in exchange for nonpublic information that was valuable in other terrorism probes. *Id.* The former Associate Attorney General who headed the Office of Legal Policy had an additional explanation: "You're talking about a violation of law that may or may not rise to the level of what might usually be called a federal case. But the calculation does not happen in isolation; you are not just talking about the [minor] crime itself, but the suspicion of terrorism. . . . That skews the calculation in favor of prosecution." *Id.* (quoting Viet D. Dinh). In other words, the *Post* paraphrased, "the primary strategy is to use 'prosecutorial discretion' to detain suspicious individuals by charging them with minor crimes." *Id.* Replied a defense attorney, "That's fine if you take it as a given that you have the devil here," citing Al Capone (who was eventually prosecuted for income tax evasion) as an example, but "[t]he problem is . . . that you're going to make mistakes and you're going to hurt innocent people." *Id.*

C. THE POST-9/11 ROUNDUP OF "HIGH INTEREST" DETAINEES

Reading *Turkmen v. Hasty*

One major component of the PENTTBOM investigation was the use of immigration authorities to arrest and detain noncitizens who were "out of status," even if the detainees could not be connected to terrorism — or any other criminal activity. These arrests resulted from a policy to detain any man believed to be Muslim or of Arab descent who was encountered during the investigation of a tip in the 9/11 terrorism investigation and who was discovered to be a noncitizen out of status. The government also created a "hold-until-cleared" policy, pursuant to which such individuals, once arrested, could not be released from custody until the FBI affirmatively cleared them of terrorist ties. As a result, nearly 800 noncitizens (most of whom lived in and around New York City) were held for up to several months, with almost 200 subjected to especially harsh conditions of confinement, even though many were ultimately released without being prosecuted or deported.

In *Ashcroft v. Iqbal*, 556 U.S. 662 (2009), the Supreme Court threw out one suit challenging these arrests and detentions, holding that the plaintiff — a Muslim Pakistani — had failed to plead sufficient facts to state his claim for purposeful and unlawful discrimination against Attorney General Ashcroft and FBI Director Robert Mueller (and holding that claims under *Bivens v. Six Unknown Named Agents of the Federal Bureau of Narcotics*, 403 U.S. 388 (1971), cannot be predicated on supervisory liability). The case that follows arose out of the same facts, but involved different plaintiffs asserting claims tied much more specifically to conditions of detention, as opposed to the initial arrests and length of detention. And although the Supreme Court would reverse in part and vacate in part the majority's decision in *Ziglar v. Abbasi*, 137 S. Ct. 1843 (2017) (treating availability of a *Bivens* claim and of qualified immunity defenses), see *supra* p. 150, the contrast between the majority and dissenting opinions in the Second Circuit is still deeply relevant to the material in this chapter. As you read through the excerpts from those opinions, consider the following questions:

- What are the plaintiffs' central claims against the various government defendants? Which claims did the majority allow to go forward, and against which defendants? Which claims did the court throw out? Why? Do you find the distinctions upon which the majority relies persuasive?
- Judge Raggi's dissent argues, forcefully, that in the days and weeks after the September 11 attacks the law did not clearly provide that the government could not, in fact, choose especially restrictive conditions of confinement for out-of-status noncitizens of Muslim and/or Arab descent without some showing that those conditions were appropriate in individual cases. What is the majority's support for its conclusion that the relevant law *was* "clearly established" at the relevant time? Whose analysis do you find more convincing?

Turkmen v. Hasty

United States Court of Appeals, Second Circuit, 2015

789 F.3d 218, *rev'd in part and vacated in part sub nom. Ziglar v. Abbasi*, 137 S. Ct. 1843 (2017)

Pooler and Wesley, Circuit Judges: . . . This case raises a difficult and delicate set of legal issues concerning individuals who were caught up in the post-9/11 investigation even though they were unquestionably never involved in terrorist activity. Plaintiffs are eight male, "out-of-status" aliens who were arrested on immigration charges and detained following the 9/11 attacks. Plaintiffs were held at the Metropolitan Detention Center (the "MDC") in Brooklyn, New York, or the Passaic County Jail ("Passaic") in Paterson, New Jersey; their individual detentions generally ranged from approximately three to eight months. [They sued on behalf of a class of similarly situated noncitizens who were Arab or Muslim, or were perceived by Defendants as Arab or Muslim, and were arrested and detained in response to the 9/11 attacks.]

The operative complaint, a putative class action, asserts various claims against former Attorney General John Ashcroft; former Director of the Federal Bureau of Investigation (the "FBI") Robert Mueller; former Commissioner of the Immigration and Naturalization Service (the "INS") James Ziglar [herein collectively called the "DOJ Defendants"]; former MDC Warden Dennis Hasty; former MDC Warden Michael Zenk; and former MDC Associate Warden James Sherman [herein collectively called "the MDC Defendants"]. All claims arise out of allegedly discriminatory and punitive treatment Plaintiffs suffered while confined at the MDC or Passaic.

BACKGROUND

I. PROCEDURAL HISTORY . . .

The Complaint . . . alleges seven claims against eight defendants. The first six claims, all brought pursuant to *Bivens v. Six Unknown Named Agents of Federal Bureau of Narcotics*, 403 U.S. 388 (1971), are: (1) a conditions of confinement claim under the Due Process Clause; (2) an equal protection claim alleging that Defendants subjected Plaintiffs to the challenged conditions because of their, or their perceived, race, religion, ethnicity, and/or national origin; (3) a claim arising under the Free Exercise Clause; (4) and (5) two claims generally alleging interference with counsel; and (6) a claim under the Fourth and Fifth Amendments alleging unreasonable and punitive strip searches. The seventh and final claim alleges a conspiracy under 42 U.S.C. §1985(3). The DOJ and MDC Defendants moved to dismiss the Complaint for failure to state a claim, on qualified immunity grounds, and, in some instances, based on a theory that *Bivens* relief did not extend to the claim at issue.

II. THE OIG REPORTS

Plaintiffs supplemented the factual allegations in their amended complaints with information gleaned from two reports by the Office of the Inspector General of the United States Department of Justice (the "OIG reports")[5] that documented the federal law enforcement response to 9/11 and conditions at the MDC and Passaic. . . .

III. PLAINTIFFS' ALLEGATIONS

In the aftermath of the 9/11 attacks, the FBI and other agencies within the DOJ immediately initiated an immense investigation aimed at identifying the 9/11 perpetrators and preventing any further attacks. PENTTBOM, the Pentagon/Twin Towers Bombings investigation, was initially run out of the FBI's field offices, but shortly

---

5. There are two OIG reports. The first OIG report, published in June 2003, covers multiple aspects of law enforcement's response to 9/11. *See* U.S. Dep't of Justice, Office of the Inspector General, The September 11 Detainees: A Review of the Treatment of Aliens Held on Immigration Charges in Connection with the Investigation of the September 11 Attacks (April 2003) (the "OIG Report"), *available at* http://www.justice.gov/oig/special/0306/full.pdf. The second OIG report, published in December 2003, focuses on abuses at the MDC. *See* U.S. Dep't of Justice, Office of the Inspector General, Supplemental Report on September 11 Detainees' Allegations of Abuse at the Metropolitan Detention Center in Brooklyn, New York (Dec. 2003) (the "Supplemental OIG Report"), *available at* http://www.justice.gov/oig/special/0312/final.pdf.

thereafter, Mueller ordered that management of the investigation be switched to the FBI's Strategic Information and Operations Center (the "SIOC") at FBI Headquarters in Washington, D.C. Mueller personally directed PENTTBOM from the SIOC and remained in daily contact with FBI field offices. . . .

Given that the 9/11 hijackers were all foreign nationals, the DOJ response carried a major immigration law component. Ashcroft and Mueller developed "a policy whereby any Muslim or Arab man encountered during the investigation of a tip received in the 9/11 terrorism investigation . . . and discovered to be a non-citizen who had violated the terms of his visa, was arrested." Ashcroft also created the related "hold-until-cleared" policy, which mandated that individuals arrested in the wake of 9/11 not be released from "custody until [FBI Headquarters] affirmatively cleared them of terrorist ties."

. . . Ultimately, 762 detainees were placed on the INS Custody List (the "INS List") that then made them subject to Ashcroft's hold-until-cleared policy.

In the months following 9/11, the DOJ Defendants "received detailed daily reports of the arrests and detentions." Ashcroft and Mueller also "met regularly with a small group of government officials in Washington, D.C., and mapped out ways to exert maximum pressure on the individuals arrested in connection with the terrorism investigation." This small group "discussed and decided upon a strategy to restrict the 9/11 detainees' ability to contact the outside world and delay their immigration hearings. The group also decided to spread the word among law enforcement personnel that the 9/11 detainees were suspected terrorists[ ] . . . and that they needed to be encouraged in any way possible to cooperate."

Plaintiffs, with the exception of Turkmen and Sachdeva, were held at the MDC. Under MDC confinement policy, the 9/11 detainees placed in the MDC were held in the MDC's Administrative Maximum Special Housing Unit (the "ADMAX SHU") — "a particularly restrictive type of SHU not found in most [Bureau of Prisons ('BOP')] facilities because the normal SHU is usually sufficient for correcting inmate misbehavior and addressing security concerns." The confinement policy was created by the MDC Defendants "in consultation with the FBI."

Conditions in the ADMAX SHU were severe and began to receive media attention soon after detentions began. Detainees were: "placed in tiny cells for over 23 hours a day"; "strip-searched every time they were removed from or returned to their cell[s], . . . even when they had no conceivable opportunity to obtain contraband"; provided with "meager and barely edible" food; denied sleep by "bright lights" that were left on in their cells for 24 hours a day; and, "[o]n some occasions, correctional officers walked by every 20 minutes throughout the night, kicked the doors to wake up the detainees, and yelled" highly degrading and offensive comments; constructively denied recreation and exposed to the elements; "denied access to basic hygiene items like toilet paper, soap, towels, toothpaste, [and] eating utensils"; and prohibited from moving around the unit, using the telephone freely, using the commissary, or accessing MDC handbooks, which explained how to file complaints about mistreatment.

MDC staff also subjected the 9/11 detainees to frequent physical and verbal abuse. The abuse included slamming the 9/11 detainees into walls; bending or twisting their arms, hands, wrists, and fingers; lifting them off the ground by their arms; pulling on their arms and handcuffs; stepping on their leg restraints; restraining them with handcuffs and/or shackles even while in their cells; and handling them in other rough and inappropriate ways. MDC staff also referred to the 9/11 detainees as " 'terrorists,' and other offensive names; threaten[ed] them with violence; curs[ed] at them; insult[ed] their religion; and ma[de] humiliating sexual comments during strip-searches." Specifically, Plaintiffs and putative class members at the MDC were referred to by staff as "camel[s]," "fucking Muslims," and "Arabic asshole[s]."

The MDC Plaintiffs did not receive copies of the Koran for weeks or months after requesting them, and one Plaintiff never received a copy, "pursuant to a written MDC policy . . . that prohibited the 9/11 detainees from keeping anything, including a Koran, in their cell[s]." The MDC Plaintiffs were also "denied the Halal food required by their Muslim faith." And "MDC staff frequently interrupted Plaintiffs' and class members' prayers," including "by banging on cell doors," yelling derogatory comments, and mocking the detainees while they prayed. . . .

IV. THE NEW YORK LIST AND THE "OF INTEREST" DESIGNATION

As originally articulated by Ashcroft, following 9/11, the DOJ sought to prevent future terrorism by arresting and detaining those people who "have been identified as persons who participate in, or lend support to, terrorist activities." OIG Report at 12 (internal quotation marks omitted). To that end, . . . [a] September 22, 2001 order instructed agents to "exercise sound judgment" and to limit arrests to those aliens in whom the FBI had an "interest" and discouraged arrest in cases that were "clearly of no interest in furthering the investigation of the terrorist attacks of September 11th." *Id.* at 45 (internal quotation marks omitted). The "of interest" designation by an FBI agent had significant implications for a detainee. "Of interest" detainees were placed on the INS List, subject to the hold-until-cleared policy, and required FBI clearance of any connection to terrorism before they could be released or removed from the United States. Detainees who were not designated "of interest" to the FBI's PENTTBOM investigation were not placed on the INS List, did not require clearance by the FBI, and could be processed according to normal INS procedures. *Id.* at 40.

The arrest and detention mandate was not uniformly implemented throughout the country. Specifically, the New York FBI investigated all PENTTBOM leads without vetting the initial tip and designated as "of interest" "anyone picked up on a PENTTBOM lead . . . regardless of the strength of the evidence or the origin of the lead." *Id.* at 41. For instance, days after 9/11, New York City police stopped three Middle Eastern men in Manhattan on a traffic violation and found plans to a public school in the car. The next day, their employer confirmed that the men had the plans because they were performing construction work on the school. Nonetheless, the men were arrested and detained. In another instance, a Middle Eastern man was arrested for illegally crossing into the United States from Canada over a week before 9/11. After the attacks, the man was placed on New York's "'special interest' list even though a document in his file, dated September 26, 2001, stated that FBI New York had no knowledge of the basis for his detention." *Id.* at 64 (internal quotation marks omitted).

In many cases, the New York FBI did not even attempt to determine whether the alien was linked to terrorism, and it "never labeled a detainee 'no interest' until *after* the clearance process was complete," *id.* at 18 (emphasis added). Thus, aliens encountered and arrested pursuant to a PENTTBOM lead in New York were designated "of interest" (or special interest) and held until the local field office confirmed they had no ties to terrorism. The result was that the MDC Plaintiffs and others similarly situated in New York were held at the MDC ADMAX SHU as if they met the national "of interest" designation. These practices — specifically the absolute lack of triage — appear to have been unique to New York. . . .

After INS Headquarters learned of the separate New York List, small groups of senior officials from the DAG's Office, the FBI, and the INS convened on at least two occasions in October and November 2001 to suggest how to deal with the two separate lists of detainees. In discussing how to address the New York List, "officials at the INS, FBI, and [DOJ] raised concerns about, among other things, whether the aliens [on the New York List] had any nexus to terrorism." *Id.* at 53. Nonetheless, this list was merged with the INS List due to the concern that absent further investigation, "the FBI could unwittingly permit a dangerous individual to leave the United States." *Id.* The decision to merge the lists ensured that some of the individuals on the New York List would remain detained in the challenged conditions of confinement as if there were some suspicion that those individuals were tied to terrorism, even though no such suspicion existed. . . .

DISCUSSION . . .

II. AVAILABILITY OF A *BIVENS* REMEDY FOR PLAINTIFFS' CLAIMS . . .

. . . [W]e conclude that a *Bivens* remedy is available for Plaintiffs' conditions of confinement claims, under both the Due Process and Equal Protection Clauses of the Fifth Amendment, and Fourth Amendment unreasonable and punitive strip searches claim. However, Plaintiffs' free exercise claim would require extending *Bivens* to a new context, a move we decline to make absent guidance from the Supreme Court.

III. CLAIM 1: SUBSTANTIVE DUE PROCESS CONDITIONS OF CONFINEMENT

The MDC Plaintiffs allege that the harsh conditions of confinement in the MDC violated their Fifth Amendment substantive due process rights and that all Defendants are liable for this harm. Plaintiffs present distinct theories of liability as to the DOJ and MDC Defendants. . . .

B. The DOJ Defendants . . .

The MDC Plaintiffs concede that the DOJ Defendants did not create the particular conditions in question. The MDC Plaintiffs similarly fail to plead that Ashcroft's initial arrest and detention mandate required subordinates to apply excessively restrictive conditions to civil detainees against whom the government lacked individualized suspicion of terrorism. Given the mandate's facial validity, the DOJ Defendants had a right to presume that subordinates would carry it out in a constitutional manner. But that is not the end of the matter.

The MDC Plaintiffs plausibly plead that the DOJ Defendants were aware that illegal aliens were being detained in punitive conditions of confinement in New York and further knew that there was no suggestion that those detainees were tied to terrorism except for the fact that they were, or were perceived to be, Arab or Muslim. The MDC Plaintiffs further allege that while knowing these facts, the DOJ Defendants were responsible for a decision to merge the New York List with the national INS List, which contained the names of detainees whose detention was dependent not only on their illegal immigrant status and their perceived Arab or Muslim affiliation, but also a suspicion that they were connected to terrorist activities. The merger ensured that the MDC Plaintiffs would continue to be confined in punitive conditions. This is sufficient to plead a Fifth Amendment substantive due process violation. Given the lack of individualized suspicion, the decision to merge the lists was not "reasonably related to a legitimate goal." The only reason why the MDC Plaintiffs were held as if they were suspected of terrorism was because they were, or appeared to be, Arab or Muslim. We conclude that this plausibly pleads punitive intent. . . .

4. Punitive Intent . . .

To be clear, it is "no surprise" — nor is it constitutionally problematic — that the enforcement of our immigration laws in the wake of 9/11 had a "disparate, incidental impact on Arab Muslims." *Iqbal*, 556 U.S. at 682. And we do not contend that Supreme Court, or our own, precedent requires individualized suspicion to subject detainees to generally restrictive conditions of confinement; restriction is an incident of detention. Rather, we simply acknowledge that "if a restriction or condition is not reasonably related to a legitimate goal — if it is arbitrary or purposeless — a court permissibly may infer that the purpose of the governmental action is punishment that may not constitutionally be inflicted upon detainees qua detainees." [*Bell v. Wolfish*, 441 U.S. 520 (1979)], at 539. We believe, then, that the challenged conditions — keeping detainees in their cells for twenty-three hours a day, constructively denying them recreation and exposing them to the elements, strip searching them whenever they were removed from or returned to their cells, denying them sleep by bright lights — were not reasonably related to a legitimate goal, but rather were punitive and unconstitutional.

While national security concerns could justify detaining those individuals with suspected ties to terrorism in these challenged conditions for the litany of reasons articulated by the dissent, those concerns do not justify detaining individuals solely on the basis of an immigration violation and their perceived race or religion in those same conditions. . . .[31]

. . . Placing the MDC Plaintiffs in chains and shackles and throwing them in the ADMAX SHU ensured that they posed no threat in the aftermath of 9/11; but we can reach no conclusion other than that the DOJ Defendants' decision to do so was made with punitive intent.

In view of the foregoing, we hold that the MDC Plaintiffs fail to plausibly plead a substantive due process claim against the DOJ Defendants coextensive with the entire post-9/11 investigation and reaching back to the time of Plaintiffs' initial detention. Nonetheless, Plaintiffs' well-pleaded allegations, in conjunction with the OIG Report's documentation of events such as the New York List controversy, render

---

31. The dissent cites several cases that it claims demonstrate that individualized suspicion is not required for imposing restrictive conditions of confinement. We do not disagree: individualized suspicion is not required to impose conditions that are reasonably related to a legitimate governmental objective. Thus, in each of the cases cited by the dissent, rather than announce that individualized suspicion was not required, the Supreme Court determined that the restrictions at issue in each of those cases were related to the legitimate goal of prison security and, therefore, were not punitive. Thus, the cases cited by the dissent do not change our conclusion here, where the challenged conditions — the most restrictive available and imposed on detainees *qua* detainees — are not reasonably related to either the goal of prison security, or national security.

plausible the claim that by the beginning of November 2001, Ashcroft knew of, and approved, the MDC Plaintiffs' confinement under severe conditions, and that Mueller and Ziglar complied with Ashcroft's order notwithstanding their knowledge that the government had no evidence linking the MDC Plaintiffs to terrorist activity. Discovery may ultimately prove otherwise, but for present purposes, the MDC Plaintiffs' substantive due process claim — with the exception of the temporal limitation noted above — may proceed against the DOJ Defendants.

5. Qualified Immunity . . .

. . . [T]he law regarding the punishment of pretrial detainees was clearly established in the fall of 2001. As discussed, *Wolfish* made clear that a particular condition or restriction of pretrial detention not reasonably related to a legitimate governmental objective is punishment in violation of the constitutional rights of detainees. And in [*Iqbal v. Hasty* (*Hasty*), 490 F.3d 143 (2d Cir. 2007)], this Court denied qualified immunity with respect to a materially identical conditions claim against Hasty. 490 F.3d at 168-69. We explained that "[t]he right of pretrial detainees to be free from punitive restraints was clearly established at the time of the events in question, and no reasonable officer could have thought that he could punish a pretrial detainee by subjecting him to the practices and conditions alleged by the Plaintiff." *Id.* at 169.

Hasty further rejected the argument that the post-9/11 context warranted qualified immunity even if it was otherwise unavailable. Recognizing the "gravity of the situation" that 9/11 presented, we explained that qualified immunity remained inappropriate because a pretrial detainee's right to be free from punishment does not vary with the surrounding circumstances. Nothing has undermined the logic or precedential authority of our qualified immunity holding in *Hasty*. We therefore conclude that the DOJ Defendants are not entitled to qualified immunity on the MDC Plaintiffs' conditions of confinement claim.

C. The MDC Defendants . . .

Plaintiffs' allegations, the OIG Report, and the MDC Defendants' arguments confirm that Hasty and Sherman housed 9/11 detainees for extended periods of time in highly restrictive conditions without ever obtaining individualized information that would warrant this treatment. Because Plaintiffs' allegations support an inference of punitive intent, and it would be inappropriate to wrestle with competing factual accounts at this stage of the litigation, we hold that a reasonable officer in the MDC Defendants' position would have concluded that this treatment was not reasonably related to a legitimate goal.

IV. CLAIM 2: EQUAL PROTECTION — CONDITIONS OF CONFINEMENT

Plaintiffs next assert a claim that Defendants subjected them to the harsh conditions of confinement detailed above based on their race, ethnicity, religion, and/or national origin, in violation of the equal protection guarantee of the Fifth Amendment. . . .

B. The DOJ Defendants

. . . In view of our analysis of Plaintiffs' substantive due process claim against the DOJ Defendants, and particularly these Defendants' roles with respect to the merger of the New York List, we hold that the MDC Plaintiffs have adequately alleged an equal protection claim against Ashcroft, Mueller, and Ziglar.

Plaintiffs' well-pleaded allegations and the OIG Report give rise to the following reasonable inferences, which render plausible the MDC Plaintiffs' equal protection claim against the DOJ Defendants: (1) the New York FBI field office discriminatorily targeted individuals in the 9/11 investigation not based on individualized suspicion, but rather based on race, ethnicity, religion, and/or national origin, and those individuals were then placed on the New York List; (2) the DOJ Defendants knew about the discriminatory manner in which the New York FBI field office placed individuals on the New York List; and (3) the DOJ Defendants condoned the New York FBI's discrimination by merging the New York List with the INS List, thereby ensuring that some of the individuals on the New York List would be subjected to the challenged conditions of confinement. . . .

The DOJ Defendants' condonation of the New York FBI field office's purposeful discrimination allows us to reasonably infer at the motion to dismiss stage that the DOJ Defendants themselves acted with discriminatory purpose. . . .

In this case, unlike in *Iqbal*, it is not "more likely" that the MDC Plaintiffs were detained in the challenged conditions because of their suspected ties to the 9/11 attacks. Indeed, as discussed at length earlier, Plaintiffs have plausibly alleged that they were detained without *any* suspicion of a link to terrorist activity and that the DOJ Defendants knew that the government lacked information tying Plaintiffs to terrorist activity, but decided to merge the lists anyway.[37] Thus, unlike in *Iqbal*, there was no legitimate reason to detain the MDC Plaintiffs in the challenged conditions and, thus, no obvious, more likely explanation for the DOJ Defendants' actions with respect to the New York List merger. . . .

C. The MDC Defendants . . .

. . . [T]he MDC Plaintiffs have stated a plausible claim that Hasty and Sherman detained them in the challenged conditions because of their race, ethnicity, religion, and/or national origin. These Defendants' approval of the false document, and Hasty's use of charged language in the particular context of the MDC Plaintiffs' detention, support the reasonable inference that Hasty and Sherman subjected the MDC Plaintiffs to harsh conditions of confinement based on suspect classifications.

With respect to Zenk, the MDC Plaintiffs' allegations are more limited and fail to support the reasonable inference that he established or implemented the alleged

---

37. Given the clear language used by the Supreme Court in *Iqbal* regarding the detainees' connections to terrorism, we understand the *Iqbal* Court to have rejected as conclusory the allegation in the *Iqbal* complaint identified by the dissent, which only pleads in the broadest terms that the *Iqbal* plaintiffs were confined without "any individual determination" that such restrictions were "appropriate or should continue." Here, in contrast, the well-pleaded allegations, as supported by the OIG reports, allege that the DOJ Defendants made, and complied with, the decision to merge the New York List with the national INS List, thereby ensuring that the MDC Plaintiffs, and others, remained in the challenged conditions of confinement despite the absence of any suspicion that they were tied to terrorism.

conditions of confinement based on animus that offends notions of equal protection.

D. Qualified Immunity . . .

. . . [I]t was clearly established at the time of Plaintiffs' detention that it was illegal to hold individuals in harsh conditions of confinement and otherwise target them for mistreatment because of their race, ethnicity, religion, and/or national origin. . . .

V. CLAIM 6: UNREASONABLE AND PUNITIVE STRIP SEARCHES . . .

Plaintiffs allege that the 9/11 detainees at the MDC were strip searched upon arrival, and again after they had been escorted in shackles and under continuous guard to the ADMAX SHU. They were also strip searched every time they were taken from or returned to their cells, including after non-contact attorney visits, when "physical contact between parties was prevented by a clear partition," OIG Report at 123, and when being transferred from one cell to another. [Plaintiff Benamar] Benatta was strip searched on September 23, 24, and 26 of 2001, even though he was not let out of his cell on any of those days. Numerous strip searches were documented in a "visual search log" that was created for review by MDC management, including Hasty.

Plaintiffs' allegations regarding the strip searches are supported by the Supplemental OIG Report, which concluded that MDC staff "inappropriately used strip searches to intimidate and punish detainees." Supplemental OIG Report at 35. That report also "questioned the need for the number of strip searches, such as after attorney and social visits in non-contact rooms." *Id.*

The foregoing allegations, supported as they are by the Supplemental OIG Report, are sufficient to establish at this stage of the litigation that Hasty and Sherman were personally involved in creating and executing a strip-search policy that was not reasonably related to legitimate penological interests. Hasty ordered the policy, and both he and Sherman approved and implemented it. Under that policy, the MDC Plaintiffs were strip searched when there was no possibility that they could have obtained contraband. Plaintiffs have alleged that Hasty and Sherman were aware of these searches either based on the search log that was created for review by MDC management, or because they were involved in the implementation of the strip-search policy. These allegations give rise to a plausible Fourth Amendment claim against Hasty and Sherman. . . .

VII. FINAL THOUGHTS

If there is one guiding principle to our nation it is the rule of law. It protects the unpopular view, it restrains fear-based responses in times of trouble, and it sanctifies individual liberty regardless of wealth, faith, or color. The Constitution defines the limits of the Defendants' authority; detaining individuals as if they were terrorists, in the most restrictive conditions of confinement available, simply because these individuals were, or appeared to be, Arab or Muslim exceeds those limits. It might well be that national security concerns motivated the Defendants to take action, but that is of little solace to those who felt the brunt of that decision. The suffering endured by those who were imprisoned merely because they were caught up in the hysteria of the days immediately following 9/11 is not without a remedy.

Holding individuals in solitary confinement twenty-three hours a day with regular strip searches because their perceived faith or race placed them in the group targeted for recruitment by al Qaeda violated the detainees' constitutional rights. To use such a broad and general basis for such severe confinement without any further particularization of a reason to suspect an individual's connection to terrorist activities requires certain assumptions about the "targeted group" not offered by Defendants nor supported in the record. It assumes that members of the group were already allied with or would be easily converted to the terrorist cause, until proven otherwise. Why else would no further particularization of a connection to terrorism be required? Perceived membership in the "targeted group" was seemingly enough to justify extended confinement in the most restrictive conditions available.

Discovery may show that the Defendants — the DOJ Defendants, in particular — are not personally responsible for detaining Plaintiffs in these conditions. But we simply cannot conclude at this stage that concern for the safety of our nation justified the violation of the constitutional rights on which this nation was built. The question at this stage of the litigation is whether the MDC Plaintiffs have plausibly pleaded that the Defendants exceeded the bounds of the Constitution in the wake of 9/11. We believe that they have....

REENA RAGGI, Circuit Judge, concurring in part in judgment and dissenting in part: Today, our court becomes the first to hold that a *Bivens* action can be maintained against the nation's two highest ranking law enforcement officials — the Attorney General of the United States and the Director of the Federal Bureau of Investigation ("FBI") — for policies propounded to safeguard the nation in the immediate aftermath of the infamous al Qaeda terrorist attacks of September 11, 2001 ("9/11")....

... [B]ecause I conclude both that a *Bivens* remedy should not be extended to plaintiffs' policy-challenging claims and that the DOJ and MDC defendants are entitled, in any event, to qualified immunity, I dissent from the majority's refusal to dismiss these claims.[2]

I. *BIVENS* SHOULD NOT BE EXTENDED TO PLAINTIFFS' POLICY-CHALLENGING CLAIMS...

[In Part I, Judge Raggi argued against recognition of a *Bivens* remedy for many of the reasons subsequently adopted by the Supreme Court in *Abbasi, supra* p. 150.]

---

2. In concluding its opinion, the majority asserts that plaintiffs' claims cannot be dismissed because "[i]f there is one guiding principle to our nation it is the rule of law." The rule of law, however, is embodied not only in amendments to the Constitution, but also, and first, in that document's foundational structure of separated powers. Thus, it is the rule of law that demands that a court do more than identify a possible wrong; it must consider what authority the judiciary has to imply a remedy — specifically, a damages remedy — in the absence of legislative action.

It is also the rule of law — to which both sides in a lawsuit have a right — that requires a court to consider whether certain defenses, such as qualified immunity, shield a particular defendant in any event from a suit for damages.

Thus, the rule of law animates this dissent no less than the majority opinion.

II. DEFENDANTS ARE ENTITLED TO QUALIFIED IMMUNITY

A. The Concept of Qualified Immunity

Whether or not a *Bivens* action is available to challenge the executive policy at issue, defendants are entitled to dismissal on grounds of qualified immunity. . . .

It is difficult to imagine a public good more demanding of decisiveness or more tolerant of reasonable, even if mistaken, judgments than the protection of this nation and its people from further terrorist attacks in the immediate aftermath of the horrific events of 9/11. Whatever lessons hindsight might teach about how best to achieve this legitimate government objective within our system of laws, I cannot conclude that defendants here were plainly incompetent or defiant of established law in instituting or maintaining the challenged restrictive confinement policy. Insofar as the majority decides otherwise based on its determinations that plaintiffs have (1) plausibly pleaded violations of Fourth and Fifth Amendment rights, (2) which rights were clearly established at the time of defendants' actions, I respectfully dissent. As to the second point in particular, I think the majority defines established law at an impermissibly "high level of generality."

B. Punitive Confinement . . .

With the benefit — or handicap — of hindsight, persons might now debate how well the challenged restrictive confinement policy at the MDC served national security interests. But it is no more a judicial function to decide how best to ensure national security than it is to decide how best to operate a detention facility. Rather, on qualified immunity review, our task is to determine whether the MDC Plaintiffs plausibly allege a substantive due process violation that, in late 2001, was so clearly established by precedent as to put the illegality of the DOJ Defendants' actions beyond debate. . . . I conclude that is not this case and that the DOJ Defendants are, therefore, entitled to dismissal of plaintiffs' punitive confinement claim on the ground of qualified immunity.

By contrast to the DOJ Defendants, MDC Defendants Hasty and Sherman were personally involved in the MDC Plaintiffs' restrictive confinement in the ADMAX SHU both before and after the November 2001 merger decision. As warden and deputy warden of the MDC, however, these defendants have a particular claim to judicial deference in determining the confinement conditions reasonably related to legitimate security interests. . . .

. . . [P]laintiffs' pleadings do not admit a plausible inference that Hasty and Sherman imposed restrictive conditions of confinement without any supporting information or assessment of propriety. As to the latter, the OIG Report recounts that, immediately after the 9/11 attacks, BOP Headquarters ordered that "all detainees who were 'convicted of, charged with, associated with, or in any way linked to terrorist activities' . . . be placed in the highest level of restrictive detention." OIG Report 112. A plausible inference of punitive intent cannot reasonably be drawn from the MDC Defendants' carrying out this order without making an independent assessment of its categorical need. The obvious and more likely motivation for their doing so is national and prison security. Defendants reasonably deferred to their superiors' assessment that, in the aftermath of a devastating terrorist attack, lawfully arrested illegal aliens, whom the FBI and CIA were investigating for possible terrorist connections, should be kept "in the most secure conditions available until the suspects could be cleared of terrorist activity." *Ashcroft v. Iqbal,* 556 U.S. at 683. The Supreme Court has already held that such motivation does not admit a plausible inference of discriminatory intent. No more will it admit a plausible inference of punitive intent.

[C]. Discriminatory Confinement

To state a Fifth Amendment claim for discriminatory confinement, a plaintiff must plead sufficient factual matter to show that defendants adopted the challenged restrictive confinement policy not for a neutral reason "but for the purpose of discriminating on account of race, religion, or national origin." *Ashcroft v. Iqbal,* 556 U.S. at 676-77. The Supreme Court articulated this standard in reversing this court's determination that these plaintiffs' original complaint stated a plausible claim for discriminatory confinement based on race, religion, or national origin. While acknowledging that plaintiffs had pleaded facts "consistent with" purposeful discrimination, the Court concluded that such a claim was not plausible in light of the "obvious," and "more likely" non-discriminatory reason for the challenged confinement policy, specifically, national security concerns about "potential connections" between illegal aliens identified in the course of the FBI's investigation of the 9/11 attacks and Islamic terrorism. . . .

. . . I am not persuaded.

First, the amended complaint's pleadings of purposeful FBI discrimination are not materially different from those considered in *Ashcroft v. Iqbal.* Thus, we are bound by the Supreme Court's holding that such allegations are inadequate to plead plausible discriminatory intent in light of the obvious and more likely national security explanation for the challenged confinement.

Not insignificantly, in reaching this conclusion, the Supreme Court acknowledged that it was the perpetrators of the 9/11 attacks who injected religion and ethnicity into the government's investigative and preventative efforts. The Court stated that the attacks "were perpetrated by 19 Arab Muslim hijackers who counted themselves members in good standing of al Qaeda, an Islamic fundamentalist group. Al Qaeda was headed by another Arab Muslim — Osama bin Laden — and composed in large part of his Arab Muslim disciples." *Id.* at 682. Where a terrorist group thus effectively defines itself by reference to religion and ethnicity, the Constitution does not require investigating authorities to ignore that reality nor to dilute limited resources casting a wider net for no good reason. It is "no surprise" then that a law enforcement policy — including a restrictive confinement policy — legitimately aimed at identifying persons with connections to the 9/11 attacks and preventing further attacks "would produce a disparate, incidental impact on Arab Muslims, even though the purpose of the policy was to target neither Arabs nor Muslims." *Ashcroft v. Iqbal,* 556 U.S. at 682.[42]

---

42. In recently forbidding investigative stereotyping, the Department of Justice nevertheless stated that, "in conducting activities directed at a specific criminal organization or terrorist group whose membership has been identified as overwhelmingly possessing a listed characteristic, law enforcement should not be expected to disregard such facts in taking investigative or preventive steps aimed at the organizations' activities." U.S. Dep't of Justice, *Guidance for Federal Law Enforcement Agencies Regarding the Use of Race, Ethnicity, Gender, National Origin, Religion, Sexual Orientation, or Gender Identity* 4 (Dec. 2014), *available at* http://1.usa.gov/1ytxRoa.

Thus, as in *Ashcroft v. Iqbal*, plaintiffs cannot plausibly imply proscribed discriminatory intent from pleadings merely "consistent with" the New York FBI's alleged purposeful targeting and detention of aliens based on ethnicity and religion. Here, those characteristics originated with the terrorists not the state, the FBI actions were limited to aliens not lawfully in this country and encountered in the course of the 9/11 investigation, and the obvious and more likely reason for the challenged confinement was ensuring national security in the face of an Islamic terrorist threat.[43]

Second, the DOJ Defendants' purported involvement with the lists-merger decision also cannot imply these defendants' discriminatory intent....

...The reality that most Arab Muslim detainees on the New York list were *not* held in restrictive confinement precludes a plausible inference that arresting FBI agents were intent on discriminating against Arab Muslims in assigning a minority of New York detainees to the MDC. Thus, even if the lists-merger decision can be understood to manifest the DOJ Defendants' "deference to others' designation of detainees for particular facilities," that is not a factual basis for plausibly inferring their discriminatory intent against MDC detainees....

...[*Third*,] as already explained, courts have upheld the imposition of restrictive conditions of confinement on lawfully arrested persons without requiring individualized suspicion of a security threat, recognizing both the difficulty in identifying which detainees pose the particular risk needing to be addressed, and the serious harm that can ensue from a failure to do so. Thus, no clearly established law would have alerted reasonable officials that restrictive confinement without individualized suspicion was unconstitutionally punitive or discriminatory in the circumstances presented here....

[D]. Fourth Amendment Claim...

First, insofar as plaintiffs challenge the frequency of the strip searches, it is their burden to plead facts sufficient to demonstrate that the challenged policy lacked a rational relationship to a legitimate government objective, specifically, prison security. *See Turner v. Safley*, 482 U.S. [78 (1987),] at 89. That burden is, moreover, a heavy one because it requires a showing that the "logical connection between the regulation and the asserted goal is so remote as to render the policy arbitrary or irrational." *Turner v. Safley*, 482 U.S. at 89-90. I do not think plaintiffs' pleadings plausibly allege that the frequency with which they were strip searched was so unrelated to prison security as to be arbitrary or irrational.

Plaintiffs assert that they were strip searched "even when they had no conceivable opportunity to obtain contraband."...In the aftermath, however, of an all-too-successful attack on a BOP guard by a restrictively confined terrorist suspect, it was hardly irrational for prison authorities to conclude that persons under investigation for terrorist connections should be strip searched both randomly in their cells and whenever they were moved from one location to another to ensure prison security....

---

43. In discussing the actions of the New York FBI office — and particularly its maintenance of its own list of 9/11 detainees — the OIG and the majority reference that office's tradition of independence from headquarters. Such independence does not plausibly imply rogue conduct. To the contrary, in the years before 9/11, the New York FBI office led the nation's pursuit of Islamic terrorism, as is evident in a number of exemplary investigations. In short, at the time of the 9/11 investigation, there was no FBI field office with greater knowledge of, or experience investigating, Islamic terrorism than that in New York. This, and not invidious discriminatory intent, is the obvious and more likely explanation for its independence.

Second, with respect to the manner in which the searches were conducted, plaintiffs' claims against Hasty and Sherman depend on these defendants' review of a visual search log allegedly created by MDC staff for management. The "possibility" that defendants reviewed such logs is not enough, however, to state a plausible claim against them for the manner of the searches. *Ashcroft v. Iqbal*, 556 U.S. at 678. Indeed, even if their review of the logs were plausible, it would, at best, support an inference of Hasty's and Sherman's knowledge of the manner in which the searches were being conducted. Further facts indicating more than negligence in these defendants' failure to take corrective action would be necessary plausibly to plead that through their "own individual actions," each had "violated the Constitution." *Id.* at 676.

I would thus grant Hasty and Sherman dismissal of the MDC Plaintiffs' Fourth Amendment claim on the ground of qualified immunity. . . .

Notes and Questions

1. Immigration Detention. At the heart of *Turkmen* is the government's power to detain immigrants pending their deportation — and whether that authority was abused in the context of the post-9/11 roundup. Aliens who have been found either inadmissible or removable for terrorist activity are subject to mandatory detention under the immigration laws until their removal can be effected. *See, e.g.*, 8 U.S.C. §§1182(a)(3)(B), 1227(a)(4)(B) (2018). As the Second Circuit explained, though, most of the post-9/11 detainees were not charged with (or even suspected of) terrorist activity.

Prolonged detention for minor "overstays" has historically been highly unusual, according to immigration lawyers. *See* Pat Leisner, *Detention After Attacks Challenged*, AP Online, Dec. 1, 2001. INS regulations before the September 11 attacks provided that persons suspected of immigration violations could be held for 24 hours before being charged. After the attacks, the Department of Justice lengthened the period to 48 hours, then authorized the Attorney General to stay for ten days the release of immigrants granted bond in order to allow the government to appeal. *Review of Custody Determinations*, 66 Fed. Reg. 54,909 (Oct. 31, 2001). Asked to explain what standard he used for staying releases ordered by immigration judges, Attorney General Ashcroft testified that "if the attorney general develops an understanding that it's against the national interest and would in some way potentially violate or jeopardize the national security, then those orders are overruled." *Preserving Our Freedom While Defending Against Terrorism: Hearing on DOJ Oversight Before the S. Comm. on the Judiciary*, 107th Cong. (2001) (statement of John Ashcroft, Attorney General); *see also Continued Detention of Aliens Subject to Final Orders of Removal*, 66 Fed. Reg. 56,967 (Nov. 14, 2001) (providing for indefinite detention of suspected terrorist aliens after expiration of removal period). Authorities explained that immigration charges are a good way to detain persons suspected of terrorist connections when the government lacks sufficient evidence to prove the connections.

The *Washington Post* reported in 2005 that most of the nearly 800 individuals who were "secretly processed on immigration charges" in the post-9/11 investigation were deported after being cleared of terrorism connections. Mary Beth Sheridan, *Immigration Law as an Anti-Terrorism Tool*, Wash. Post, June 13, 2005. Would your assessment of the *Turkmen* plaintiffs' claims change if more of the individuals arrested and detained on comparatively minor immigration charges had actually been connected to terrorist plots?

2. *Pretext and Immigration Detention.* Is *Turkmen* a case in which the government used immigration detention authorities as a pretext for detaining terrorism suspects? Note the majority's focus on the government's concession that many of the plaintiffs were both arrested and placed in the ADMAX SHU, even though the government knew that they had no connection to terrorists — that the government had no basis for individualized suspicion of most of the detainees. If these immigration detention authorities weren't being used as a pretext to round up terrorism suspects, what were they being used for? Does Judge Raggi's dissent offer a compelling (and legitimate) explanation?

3. *Back to Profiling?* In a telling passage in her dissent, Judge Raggi argues that "[w]here a terrorist group . . . effectively defines itself by reference to religion and ethnicity, the Constitution does not require investigating authorities to ignore that reality nor to dilute limited resources casting a wider net for no good reason." If that's true, then where would you draw the line between permissible counterterrorism investigations and impermissible racial profiling? If the *Turkmen* plaintiffs' allegations are true, on which side of the line does the post-9/11 roundup fall? Why?

4. *The USA Patriot Act Preventive Detention Provision.* Immediately after the 9/11 attacks, Attorney General Ashcroft asked Congress for authority to hold suspected alien terrorists indefinitely. Would such legislation be constitutional? Congress rebuffed this request, providing instead in the USA Patriot Act that the INS could hold immigrants for up to seven days before charging them with either immigration or criminal offenses, and could then hold them while immigration proceedings were pending if the Attorney General certified, at least every six months, that their release would threaten national security. Pub. L. No. 107-56, §412, 115 Stat. 272, 350-351 (2001) (codified at 8 U.S.C. §1226a (2012)). How, if at all, might you argue that this legislation affected the legality of subsequent immigration detentions in the PENTTBOM investigation? Is the detention without *any* charge during the seven days authorized by the statute constitutional? Could the statute be used as an alternative basis for holding the Guantánamo detainees if and when they are moved into the United States? *See, e.g.*, Stephen I. Vladeck, *Detention After the AUMF*, 82 Fordham L. Rev. 2189 (2014) (explaining how the statute could be interpreted — or easily amended — to provide such authority, and arguing that, in the specific case of those Guantánamo detainees who have not been cleared for release, it would arguably satisfy due process).

5. *A Section 412 Test Case.* Although the USA Patriot Act provision discussed in the previous note went unused over its first 18 years, a test case finally emerged in mid-2019. Adham Hassoun, a Palestinian computer programmer who was convicted of serious terrorism-related criminal charges in 2007, served almost 14 years of a 15-year sentence (including time served in pretrial detention and "good time" credit), and was placed in immigration detention pending his removal from the country after he finished serving his criminal sentence in October 2017. Because there is no country to which Hassoun can be removed (Israel refuses to accept Palestinian deportees), his immigration detention is potentially indefinite. When Hassoun invoked *Zadvydas* to argue that the Constitution limits how long he can remain in immigration detention, the government responded that it was holding him under Section 412 of the

USA Patriot Act—which expressly contemplates long-term immigration detention subject to periodic review. *See* Spencer Ackerman, *Trump Is First to Use PATRIOT Act to Detain a Man Forever,* Daily Beast, Nov. 29, 2019. Hassoun's case therefore raises difficult and important questions about Section 412. For instance, given that it authorizes initially holding a noncitizen for seven days with no charges, should it *ever* provide a mechanism for detaining noncitizen terrorism suspects on the far side of their criminal sentence for terrorism-related convictions? Even if the answer is yes, what burden should the government face in demonstrating that a detainee's release truly would "threaten the national security of the United States or the safety of the community or any person," and does that burden change over time? *See* 8 U.S.C. §1226a(a)(6). Is *Hamdi v. Rumsfeld, supra* p. 886, instructive? Why or why not? *See Hassoun v. Searls,* No. 19-cv-370, 2019 WL 6798903 (W.D.N.Y. Dec. 13, 2019) (ordering an evidentiary hearing into the factual and legal basis for the government's authority to detain Hassoun under Section 412).

6. The Ethics of Immigration Bond Hearings. As the Second Circuit's discussion suggests, immigration laws, like the Bail Reform Act, authorize immigration judges to deny bond for a detained immigrant if the government provides evidence of flight risk or dangerousness. The FBI, however, provided no information to sustain such determinations in many cases. Nevertheless, INS lawyers were apparently ordered to argue the "no bond" position in court without any evidence, using "boilerplate" language. *See* OIG Report, *supra* p. 944 n.5, at 78-80. Was this ethical? In some cases, the alien succeeded in obtaining a bond order and in posting bond, but the INS, without appealing the order, continued to hold him anyway. Was this lawful? *See id.* at 87 (reporting that one INS official admitted not knowing what to tell the immigrant's lawyer, "because I cannot bring myself to say that the INS no longer feels compelled to obey the law"). How far may a government lawyer go in defending preventive detention if she is instructed that it is essential to a terrorism investigation?

7. The Length of Immigration Detentions. In *Demore v. Hyung Joon Kim,* 538 U.S. 510 (2003), the Supreme Court revisited the permissible length of immigration detention, this time considering a statutory provision for mandatory detention of criminal aliens pending their removal hearings. Conceding that individualized bond hearings might be feasible, the majority nevertheless concluded that "when the Government deals with deportable aliens, the Due Process Clause does not require it to employ the least burdensome means to accomplish its goal." *Id.* at 528. It therefore upheld the mandatory detention law but emphasized that such detentions pending removal were for less than 90 days in the majority of cases. Joining in the opinion, Justice Kennedy noted that if the removal proceedings were unreasonably delayed, "it could become necessary then to inquire whether the detention is not to facilitate deportation, or to protect against risk of flight or dangerousness, but to incarcerate for other reasons." *Id.* at 532-533 (Kennedy, J., concurring). How would the post-September 11 immigration detentions described in *Turkmen* fare by these standards?

8. Jennings v. Rodriguez. The Supreme Court has not addressed the constitutional limits on the length of immigration detention since *Demore.* But in *Jennings v. Rodriguez,* 138 S. Ct. 830 (2018), the Court reversed a lower-court ruling that had read into federal immigration law a host of limits on the length of immigration detention in cases not expressly covered by *Zadvydas,* including those in which the noncitizens were detained either while attempting to enter the United States or shortly thereafter. Writing for the majority, Justice Alito held that in those cases the relevant statutes were sufficiently clear to preclude invocation of the constitutional avoidance canon, and therefore that the Court need not address whether the absence of such limits raised due process concerns. *See id.* at 842. Dissenting, Justice Breyer (who wrote the majority opinion in *Zadvydas*) argued at length that, as construed by the majority, the relevant statutory provisions probably *would* violate the Due Process Clause. *See id.* at 861-869 (Breyer, J., dissenting). If nothing else, *Jennings* underscores that, even after *Zadvydas*, the constitutional limits on the length of immigration detention remain to a significant degree unsettled.

D. MATERIAL WITNESS DETENTIONS

As we saw in Chapter 29, the two U.S. persons arrested in the United States and subjected to military detention after September 11—José Padilla and Ali Saleh Kahlah al-Marri—were previously held for some time under "material witness" warrants, i.e., court orders authorizing the detention of individuals believed to have testimony "material in a criminal proceeding" where the government can demonstrate probable cause to believe that "it may become impracticable to secure the presence of the person by subpoena." As you read the full statute below, consider two questions: (1) should "criminal proceeding" include grand jury proceedings (which would give the statute a very broad ambit), or should it be limited to testimony at criminal trials?; and (2) either way, does it make sense to treat material witnesses the same way as individuals who have been arrested and charged with a crime, and are pending trial under the Bail Reform Act?

Release or Detention of a Material Witness

18 U.S.C. §3144 (2018)

If it appears from an affidavit filed by a party that the testimony of a person is material in a criminal proceeding, and if it is shown that it may become impracticable to secure the presence of the person by subpoena, a judicial officer may order the arrest of the person and treat the person in accordance with the provisions of section 3142 of this title [governing release on bond and requiring a judicial hearing]. No material witness may be detained because of inability to comply with any condition of release if the testimony of such witness can adequately be secured by deposition, and if further detention is not necessary to prevent a failure of justice. Release of a material witness may be delayed for a reasonable period of time until the deposition of the witness can be taken pursuant to the Federal Rules of Criminal Procedure.

The material witness statute apparently was first used in a terrorism investigation to detain Terry Nichols, who was eventually convicted in connection with the 1995 Oklahoma City bombing. *See United States v. McVeigh*, 940 F. Supp. 1541, 1562 (D. Colo. 1996) (finding that Nichols' renunciation of U.S. citizenship and his association with

Timothy McVeigh sufficiently showed probable cause to believe that it "may become impracticable" to rely on a subpoena to secure his testimony). After 9/11, it was used for the first time on a broader scale to detain persons suspected of having a connection with or information about terrorism — with the government asserting that these individuals were material witnesses to an ongoing grand jury investigation (the investigation into the 9/11 attacks), as opposed to a specific, pending criminal trial. Although the government has not disclosed exactly how many persons it held as material witnesses in the PENTTBOM and subsequent counterterrorism investigations, Human Rights Watch reported that its research identified at least 70 such individuals as of June 2005. Human Rights Watch, *Witness to Abuse: Human Rights Abuses Under the Material Witness Law Since September 11,* 17 Hum. Rts. Watch 1 (June 2005). The plaintiff in the following case may have been typical.

Reading *Ashcroft v. al-Kidd*

Abdullah al-Kidd was born in Kansas and converted to Islam while attending (and playing football for) the University of Idaho. In the spring of 2003, al-Kidd was arrested at the airport on "a material witness warrant" as he prepared to fly to Saudi Arabia to study Arabic and Islamic law on a scholarship. The warrant had been issued on the strength of an FBI affidavit asserting that al-Kidd was believed to have information crucial to the criminal prosecution of Sami Omar Al-Hussayen for visa fraud and false statements — and that he had paid cash for a one-way, first-class plane ticket to Saudi Arabia (in fact, it was a roundtrip, coach ticket). Al-Kidd was handcuffed, interrogated, and then detained for 16 days, during which he was strip-searched on multiple occasions, handcuffed and shackled, confined in a high-security unit, and allowed to leave his continuously lit cell for only one to two hours each day.

He was released under supervision after he surrendered his passport. These conditions were only lifted 15 months later, after Al-Hussayen's trial was completed. (Al-Hussayen, a suspected webmaster of an allegedly jihadist website, was not convicted of any charges against him but was deported to Saudi Arabia for visa violations.) Al-Kidd was never called as a witness, and no evidence of any criminal activity by him was ever discovered. Nevertheless, he was fired from his job, separated from his wife, deprived of his scholarship for study in Saudi Arabia, and unable afterward to find steady employment.

Al-Kidd then sued Attorney General Ashcroft and others for injuries resulting from the alleged misuse of the material witness statute and for the conditions of his confinement. The Ninth Circuit held that Ashcroft was not entitled to absolute or qualified immunity because pretextual arrests absent probable cause of criminal wrongdoing violate the material witness statute and are thus unreasonable under the Fourth Amendment. In the decision that follows, the Supreme Court reversed — kind of. As you read it, consider these questions:

- Recall from above that, in *Whren*, the Supreme Court held that arrests supported by probable cause do not violate the Fourth Amendment even where they are pretextual. Does Justice Scalia's analysis simply follow from *Whren*? Is there anything different where the "arrest" is not based upon suspicion of criminal activity? Should there be?

- How does Justice Scalia conclude that the underlying material witness warrant was "valid," a determination that drives the rest of his analysis of qualified immunity? Justice Kennedy's concurrence maintains that the opinion leaves unresolved whether the government's use of the statute was "lawful." And Justice Ginsburg suggests that it may well have been unlawful. If that is so, then how/why did al-Kidd lose?
- Count the votes carefully. All eight participating Justices agreed that Ashcroft was entitled to qualified immunity. But how many concluded on the merits that he did not actually violate the Fourth Amendment? How many concluded on the merits that he did not actually violate the material witness statute? What precedent does al-Kidd actually set, going forward?

Ashcroft v. al-Kidd

United States Supreme Court, 2011
563 U.S. 731

Justice SCALIA delivered the opinion of the Court. . . .

II

Qualified immunity shields federal and state officials from money damages unless a plaintiff pleads facts showing (1) that the official violated a statutory or constitutional right, and (2) that the right was "clearly established" at the time of the challenged conduct. *Harlow v. Fitzgerald*, 457 U.S. 800, 818 (1982). . . . In this case, the Court of Appeals' analysis at both steps of the qualified-immunity inquiry needs correction.

A

The Fourth Amendment protects "[t]he right of the people to be secure in their persons, houses, papers, and effects, against unreasonable searches and seizures." An arrest, of course, qualifies as a "seizure" of a "person" under this provision, *Dunaway v. New York*, 442 U.S. 200, 207-208 (1979), and so must be reasonable under the circumstances. Al-Kidd does not assert that Government officials would have acted unreasonably if they had used a material-witness warrant to arrest him for the purpose of securing his testimony for trial. He contests, however (and the Court of Appeals here rejected), the reasonableness of using the warrant to detain him as a suspected criminal.

Fourth Amendment reasonableness "is predominantly an objective inquiry." [*Indianapolis v. Edmond*, 531 U.S. 32, 47 (2000).] We ask whether "the circumstances, viewed objectively, justify [the challenged] action." *Scott v. United States*, 436 U.S. 128, 138 (1978). If so, that action was reasonable "*whatever* the subjective intent" motivating the relevant officials. *Whren v. United States*, 517 U.S. 806, 814 (1996). This approach recognizes that the Fourth Amendment regulates conduct rather than thoughts, *Bond v. United States*, 529 U.S. 334, 338, n.2 (2000); and it promotes evenhanded, uniform enforcement of the law, *Devenpeck v. Alford*, 543 U.S. 146, 153-154 (2004).

Two "limited exception[s]" to this rule are our special-needs and administrative-search cases, where "actual motivations" do matter. *United States v. Knights*, 534 U.S.

112, 122 (2001) (internal quotation marks omitted). A judicial warrant and probable cause are not needed where the search or seizure is justified by "special needs, beyond the normal need for law enforcement," such as the need to deter drug use in public schools, *Vernonia School Dist. 47J v. Acton*, 515 U.S. 646, 653 (1995) (internal quotation marks omitted), or the need to assure that railroad employees engaged in train operations are not under the influence of drugs or alcohol, *Skinner v. Railway Labor Executives' Assn.*, 489 U.S. 602 (1989); and where the search or seizure is in execution of an administrative warrant authorizing, for example, an inspection of fire-damaged premises to determine the cause, *Michigan v. Clifford*, 464 U.S. 287, 294 (1984) (plurality opinion), or an inspection of residential premises to assure compliance with a housing code, *Camara v. Municipal Court of City and County of San Francisco*, 387 U.S. 523, 535-538 (1967). But those exceptions do not apply where the officer's purpose is not to attend to the special needs or to the investigation for which the administrative inspection is justified. The Government seeks to justify the present arrest on the basis of a properly issued judicial warrant — so that the special-needs and administrative-inspection cases cannot be the basis for a purpose inquiry here.

Apart from those cases, we have almost uniformly rejected invitations to probe subjective intent. See *Brigham City v. Stuart*, 547 U.S. 398, 404 (2006). There is one category of exception, upon which the Court of Appeals principally relied. In *Edmond*, 531 U.S. 32, we held that the Fourth Amendment could not condone suspicionless vehicle checkpoints set up for the purpose of detecting illegal narcotics. Although we had previously approved vehicle checkpoints set up for the purpose of keeping off the road unlicensed drivers, *Delaware v. Prouse*, 440 U.S. 648, 663 (1979), or alcohol-impaired drivers, *Michigan Dept. of State Police v. Sitz*, 496 U.S. 444 (1990); and for the purpose of interdicting those who illegally cross the border, *United States v. Martinez-Fuerte*, 428 U.S. 543 (1976); we found the drug-detection purpose in *Edmond* invalidating because it was "ultimately indistinguishable from the general interest in crime control," 531 U.S., at 44. In the Court of Appeals' view, *Edmond* established that " 'programmatic purpose' is relevant to Fourth Amendment analysis of programs of seizures without probable cause." 580 F.3d, at 968.

That was mistaken. It was not the absence of probable cause that triggered the invalidating-purpose inquiry in *Edmond*. To the contrary, *Edmond* explicitly said that it would approve checkpoint stops for "general crime control purposes" that were based upon merely "some quantum of individualized suspicion." 531 U.S., at 47. Purpose was relevant in *Edmond* because "programmatic purposes may be relevant to the validity of Fourth Amendment intrusions undertaken *pursuant to a general scheme without individualized suspicion*," *id.*, at 45-46 (emphasis added).

Needless to say, warrantless, "suspicionless intrusions pursuant to a general scheme," *id.*, at 47, are far removed from the facts of this case. A warrant issued by a neutral Magistrate Judge authorized al-Kidd's arrest. The affidavit accompanying the warrant application (as al-Kidd concedes) gave individualized reasons to believe that he was a material witness and that he would soon disappear. The existence of a judicial warrant based on individualized suspicion takes this case outside the domain of not only our special-needs and administrative-search cases, but of *Edmond* as well.

A warrant based on individualized suspicion in fact grants more protection against the malevolent and the incompetent than existed in most of our cases eschewing inquiries into intent. In *Whren* and *Devenpeck*, we declined to probe the motives behind seizures supported by probable cause but lacking a warrant approved by a detached magistrate. *Terry v. Ohio*, 392 U.S. 1, 21-22 (1968), and *Knights*, 534 U.S., at

121-122, applied an objective standard to warrantless searches justified by a lesser showing of reasonable suspicion. We review even some suspicionless searches for objective reasonableness. See *Bond*, 529 U.S., at 335-336, 338, n.2. If concerns about improper motives and pretext do not justify subjective inquiries in those less protective contexts, we see no reason to adopt that inquiry here.

Al-Kidd would read our cases more narrowly. He asserts that *Whren* establishes that we ignore subjective intent only when there exists "probable cause to believe that a violation of law has occurred," 517 U.S., at 811 — which was not the case here. That is a distortion of *Whren*. Our unanimous opinion held that we would not look behind an objectively reasonable traffic stop to determine whether racial profiling or a desire to investigate other potential crimes was the real motive. In the course of our analysis, we dismissed Whren's reliance on our inventory-search and administrative-inspection cases by explaining that those cases do not "endors[e] the principle that ulterior motives can invalidate police conduct that is justifiable on the basis of probable cause to believe that a violation of law has occurred," *id.*, at 811. But to say that ulterior motives do *not* invalidate a search that is legitimate because of probable cause to believe a crime has occurred is not to say that it *does* invalidate all searches that are legitimate for other reasons.

"[O]nly an undiscerning reader," *ibid.*, would think otherwise. We referred to probable cause to believe that a violation of law had occurred because that was the legitimating factor in the case at hand. But the analysis of our opinion swept broadly to reject inquiries into motive generally. See *id.*, at 812-815. We remarked that our special-needs and administrative-inspection cases are unusual in their concern for pretext, and do nothing more than "explain that the exemption from the need for probable cause (and warrant), which is accorded to searches made for the purpose of inventory or administrative regulation, is not accorded to searches that are *not* made for those purposes," *id.*, at 811-812. And our opinion emphasized that we had at that time (prior to *Edmond*) rejected every request to examine subjective intent outside the narrow context of special needs and administrative inspections. Thus, al-Kidd's approach adds an "only" to a sentence plucked from the *Whren* opinion, and then elevates that sentence (as so revised) over the remainder of the opinion, and over the consistent holdings of our other cases.

Because al-Kidd concedes that individualized suspicion supported the issuance of the material-witness arrest warrant; and does not assert that his arrest would have been unconstitutional absent the alleged pretextual use of the warrant; we find no Fourth Amendment violation.[3] Efficient and evenhanded application of the law demands that we look to whether the arrest is objectively justified, rather than to the motive of the arresting officer.

B

A Government official's conduct violates clearly established law when, at the time of the challenged conduct, "[t]he contours of [a] right [are] sufficiently clear" that

---

3. The concerns of Justices Ginsburg and Sotomayor about the validity of the warrant in this case are beside the point. The validity of the warrant is not *our* "opening assumption," it is the premise of al-Kidd's argument. Al-Kidd does not claim that Ashcroft is liable because the FBI agents failed to obtain a valid warrant. He takes the validity of the warrant as a given, and argues that his arrest nevertheless violated the Constitution because it was motivated by an illegitimate purpose. His separate Fourth Amendment and statutory claims against the FBI agents who sought the material-witness warrant, which are the focus of both concurrences, are not before us.

every "reasonable official would have understood that what he is doing violates that right." *Anderson v. Creighton*, 483 U.S. 635, 640 (1987). We do not require a case directly on point, but existing precedent must have placed the statutory or constitutional question beyond debate. See *ibid.*; *Malley v. Briggs*, 475 U.S. 335, 341 (1986). The constitutional question in this case falls far short of that threshold.

At the time of al-Kidd's arrest, not a single judicial opinion had held that pretext could render an objectively reasonable arrest pursuant to a material-witness warrant unconstitutional. . . .

The Court of Appeals also found clearly established law lurking in the broad "history and purposes of the Fourth Amendment." 580 F.3d, at 971. We have repeatedly told courts — and the Ninth Circuit in particular, see *Brosseau v. Haugen*, 543 U.S. 194, 198-199 (2004) (*per curiam*) — not to define clearly established law at a high level of generality. The general proposition, for example, that an unreasonable search or seizure violates the Fourth Amendment is of little help in determining whether the violative nature of particular conduct is clearly established.

The same is true of the Court of Appeals' broad historical assertions. The Fourth Amendment was a response to the English Crown's use of general warrants, which often allowed royal officials to search and seize whatever and whomever they pleased while investigating crimes or affronts to the Crown. According to the Court of Appeals, Ashcroft should have seen that a pretextual warrant similarly "gut[s] the substantive protections of the Fourth Amendmen[t]" and allows the State "to arrest upon the executive's mere suspicion." 580 F.3d, at 972.

Ashcroft must be forgiven for missing the parallel, which escapes us as well. The principal evil of the general warrant was addressed by the Fourth Amendment's particularity requirement which Ashcroft's alleged policy made no effort to evade. The warrant authorizing al-Kidd's arrest named al-Kidd and only al-Kidd. It might be argued, perhaps, that when, in response to the English abuses, the Fourth Amendment said that warrants could only issue "on probable cause" it meant only probable cause to suspect a violation of law, and not probable cause to believe that the individual named in the warrant was a material witness. But that would make *all* arrests pursuant to material-witness warrants unconstitutional, whether pretextual or not — and that is not the position taken by al-Kidd in this case. . . .

Qualified immunity gives government officials breathing room to make reasonable but mistaken judgments about open legal questions. When properly applied, it protects "all but the plainly incompetent or those who knowingly violate the law." *Malley*, 475 U.S., at 341. Ashcroft deserves neither label, not least because eight Court of Appeals judges agreed with his judgment in a case of first impression. He deserves qualified immunity even assuming — contrafactually — that his alleged detention policy violated the Fourth Amendment.

* * *

We hold that an objectively reasonable arrest and detention of a material witness pursuant to a validly obtained warrant cannot be challenged as unconstitutional on the basis of allegations that the arresting authority had an improper motive. Because Ashcroft did not violate clearly established law, we need not address the more difficult question whether he enjoys absolute immunity. The judgment of the Court of Appeals is reversed, and the case is remanded for further proceedings consistent with this opinion.

It is so ordered.

Justice KAGAN took no part in the consideration or decision of this case.

Justice KENNEDY, with whom Justice GINSBURG, Justice BREYER, and Justice SOTOMAYOR join as to Part I, concurring. I join the opinion of the Court in full. In holding that the Attorney General could be liable for damages based on an unprecedented constitutional rule, the Court of Appeals for the Ninth Circuit disregarded the purposes of the doctrine of qualified immunity. This concurring opinion makes two additional observations.

I

The Court's holding is limited to the arguments presented by the parties and leaves unresolved whether the Government's use of the Material Witness Statute in this case was lawful. See *ante* (noting that al-Kidd "does not assert that his arrest would have been unconstitutional absent the alleged pretextual use of the warrant"). Under the statute, a Magistrate Judge may issue a warrant to arrest someone as a material witness upon a showing by affidavit that "the testimony of a person is material in a criminal proceeding" and "that it may become impracticable to secure the presence of the person by subpoena." 18 U.S.C. §3144. The scope of the statute's lawful authorization is uncertain. For example, a law-abiding citizen might observe a crime during the days or weeks before a scheduled flight abroad. It is unclear whether those facts alone might allow police to obtain a material witness warrant on the ground that it "may become impracticable" to secure the person's presence by subpoena. *Ibid.* The question becomes more difficult if one further assumes the traveler would be willing to testify if asked; and more difficult still if one supposes that authorities delay obtaining or executing the warrant until the traveler has arrived at the airport. These possibilities resemble the facts in this case.

In considering these issues, it is important to bear in mind that the Material Witness Statute might not provide for the issuance of warrants within the meaning of the Fourth Amendment's Warrant Clause. The typical arrest warrant is based on probable cause that the arrestee has committed a crime; but that is not the standard for the issuance of warrants under the Material Witness Statute. See *ante,* at 11 (reserving the possibility that probable cause for purposes of the Fourth Amendment's Warrant Clause means "only probable cause to suspect a violation of law"). If material witness warrants do not qualify as "Warrants" under the Fourth Amendment, then material witness arrests might still be governed by the Fourth Amendment's separate reasonableness requirement for seizures of the person. Given the difficulty of these issues, the Court is correct to address only the legal theory put before it, without further exploring when material witness arrests might be consistent with statutory and constitutional requirements. . . .

Justice GINSBURG, with whom Justice BREYER and Justice SOTOMAYOR join, concurring in the judgment. Is a former U.S. Attorney General subject to a suit for damages on a claim that he instructed subordinates to use the Material Witness Statute as a pretext to detain terrorist suspects preventively? Given *Whren v. United States,* 517 U.S. 806 (1996), I agree with the Court that no "clearly established law" renders Ashcroft answerable in damages for the abuse of authority al-Kidd charged. But I join Justice Sotomayor in objecting to the Court's disposition of al-Kidd's Fourth Amendment claim on the merits; as she observes, *post*, at 1 (opinion concurring in judgment), that claim involves novel and trying questions that will "have no effect on the outcome of th[is] case." *Pearson v. Callahan*, 555 U.S. 223, 236-237 (2009).

In addressing al-Kidd's Fourth Amendment claim against Ashcroft, the Court assumes at the outset the existence of a *validly obtained* material witness warrant. That characterization is puzzling. See *post*, at 2 (opinion of Sotomayor, J.).[1] Is a warrant "validly obtained" when the affidavit on which it is based fails to inform the issuing Magistrate Judge that "the Government has no intention of using [al-Kidd as a witness] at [another's] trial," *post*, at 1, and does not disclose that al-Kidd had cooperated with FBI agents each of the several times they had asked to interview him . . . ?

Casting further doubt on the assumption that the warrant was validly obtained, the Magistrate Judge was not told that al-Kidd's parents, wife, and children were all citizens and residents of the United States. In addition, the affidavit misrepresented that al-Kidd was about to take a one-way flight to Saudi Arabia, with a first-class ticket costing approximately $5,000; in fact, al-Kidd had a round-trip, coach-class ticket that cost $1,700. Given these omissions and misrepresentations, there is strong cause to question the Court's opening assumption — a valid material-witness warrant — and equally strong reason to conclude that a merits determination was neither necessary nor proper.

I also agree with Justice Kennedy that al-Kidd's treatment presents serious questions, unaddressed by the Court, concerning "the [legality of] the Government's use of the Material Witness Statute in this case." In addition to the questions Justice Kennedy poses, and even if the initial material witness classification had been proper, what even arguably legitimate basis could there be for the harsh custodial conditions to which al-Kidd was subjected: Ostensibly held only to secure his testimony, al-Kidd was confined in three different detention centers during his 16 days' incarceration, kept in high-security cells lit 24 hours a day, strip-searched and subjected to body-cavity inspections on more than one occasion, and handcuffed and shackled about his wrists, legs, and waist. App. 29-36; cf. *Bell v. Wolfish*, 441 U.S. 520, 539, n.20 (1979) ("[L]oading a detainee with chains and shackles and throwing him in a dungeon may ensure his presence at trial and preserve the security of the institution. But it would be difficult to conceive of a situation where conditions so harsh, employed to achieve objectives that could be accomplished in so many alternative and less harsh methods, would not support a conclusion that the purpose for which they were imposed was to punish.").

However circumscribed al-Kidd's *Bivens* claim against Ashcroft may have been, see *Bivens v. Six Unknown Fed. Narcotics Agents*, 403 U.S. 388 (1971), his remaining claims against the FBI agents who apprehended him invite consideration of the issues Justice Kennedy identified. His challenges to the brutal conditions of his confinement have been settled. But his ordeal is a grim reminder of the need to install safeguards against disrespect for human dignity, constraints that will control officialdom even in perilous times.

Justice SOTOMAYOR, with whom Justice GINSBURG and Justice BREYER join, concurring in the judgment. I concur in the Court's judgment reversing the Court of

---

1. Nowhere in al-Kidd's complaint is there any concession that the warrant gained by the FBI agents was validly obtained.

Appeals because I agree with the majority's conclusion that Ashcroft did not violate clearly established law. I cannot join the majority's opinion, however, because it unnecessarily "resolve[s] [a] difficult and novel questio[n] of constitutional . . . interpretation that will 'have no effect on the outcome of the case.'" *Ante*, at 3 (quoting *Pearson v. Callahan*, 555 U.S. 223, 237 (2009)).

Whether the Fourth Amendment permits the pretextual use of a material witness warrant for preventive detention of an individual whom the Government has no intention of using at trial is, in my view, a closer question than the majority's opinion suggests. Although the majority is correct that a government official's subjective intent is generally "irrelevant in determining whether that officer's actions violate the Fourth Amendment," *Bond v. United States*, 529 U.S. 334, 338, n.2 (2000), none of our prior cases recognizing that principle involved prolonged detention of an individual without probable cause to believe he had committed any criminal offense. We have never considered whether an official's subjective intent matters for purposes of the Fourth Amendment in that novel context, and we need not and should not resolve that question in this case. All Members of the Court agree that, whatever the merits of the underlying Fourth Amendment question, Ashcroft did not violate clearly established law. . . .

Notes and Questions

1. *Probable Cause.* The Ninth Circuit had distinguished *Whren* on the grounds that it presupposes "ordinary" probable cause to believe that the arrestee has committed a crime, and that material witness arrests are based neither on ordinary probable cause nor even reasonable suspicion to believe that the arrestee has committed or is committing a crime. What was the Supreme Court's answer? It asserted that al-Kidd conceded that "individualized suspicion" justified his search, but individualized suspicion of what?

Has the Court definitively decided the legality of material witness detentions? If not, what is left open? Under what circumstances would a material witness arrest be unlawful, either under the statute or under the Constitution? Consider this assessment:

> [I]t is quite possible that section 3144 going forward will turn out to be problematic under the Fourth Amendment quite apart from the question of pretext, at least when applied in some settings that appear particularly harsh. Second, the lingering prospect of *Bivens* liability for FBI agents who misstate or misrepresent facts in the underlying 3144 warrant application to some degree will check the prextual use of 3144. . . . Where the case can actually be made that the person's testimony is needed and at risk, however, this decision should pave the way for reliance on 3144 even if the underlying motivation is primarily to incapacitate a potentially dangerous person. . . . [Robert Chesney, *Supreme Court Rejects Fourth Amendment Challenge to Material Witness Detention in Al-Kidd v. Ashcroft*, Lawfare, May 31, 2011.]

2. *Obtaining Testimony?* Human Rights Watch found that fewer than half of the 9/11 material witnesses were ever brought before a grand jury or court to testify; many were apparently held as suspects rather than as witnesses. *Witness to Abuse, supra* p. 960, at 2. The government has not been shy about explaining this use of the statute.

For example, after acknowledging that the United States has no general preventive detention law, one architect of the post-9/11 detention policy said that "the material witness statute *gives the government effectively the same power.* . . . To the extent that it is a suspect involved in terror, you hold them on a material witness warrant, and you get the information until you find out what's going on." *Id.* at 19 (quoting Mary Jo White, former U.S. Attorney for the Southern District of New York) (emphasis added). In another case in which the material witness's lawyer argued that the government was holding his client as a criminal suspect, not as a witness, the government responded, "Based on evidence collected to date, the government cannot exclude the possibility that [the detainee] was criminally, rather than innocently, involved in how his fingerprint got to Spain." *See* Ricardo J. Bascuas, *The Unconstitutionality of "Hold Until Cleared": Reexamining Material Witness Detentions in the Wake of the September 11th Dragnet,* 58 Vand. L. Rev. 677, 679 (2005) (citation omitted).

Here is what the Court of Appeals said about the government's motives in detaining al-Kidd:

- Al-Kidd's arrest was sought a month *after* Al-Hussayen was indicted, and more than a year *before* trial began, temporally distant from the time any testimony would have been needed.
- The FBI had previously investigated and interviewed al-Kidd, but had never suggested, let alone demanded, that he appear as a witness.
- The FBI conducted lengthy interrogations with al-Kidd while in custody, including about matters apparently unrelated to Al-Hussayen's alleged visa violations.
- Al-Kidd *never actually testified* for the prosecution in Al-Hussayen's or any other case, despite his assurances that he would be willing to do so.
- Ashcroft's immediate subordinate, FBI Director Mueller, testified before Congress that al-Kidd's *arrest* (rather than, say, the obtaining of the evidence he was supposedly going to provide against Al-Hussayen) constituted a "major success[ ]" in "identifying and dismantling terrorist networks." [*Al-Kidd v. Ashcroft,* 580 F.3d 949, 963-964 (9th Cir. 2009).]

Is there any doubt that al-Kidd was detained primarily for reasons other than to obtain his testimony for the Al-Hussayen case?

3. Clearly Established? The Court held unanimously (with Justice Kagan recused) that Ashcroft did not violate clearly established law. Was the rest of the majority opinion necessary to the result? If not, why do you suppose the Justices reached these other questions? How (and why) did their conclusions differ?

4. Testimony: A Key to the Material Witness's Jail Cell? The material witness statute makes a deposition an alternative to detention for obtaining grand jury testimony, effectively giving the detainee a key to his jail cell. Human Rights Watch reports, however, that the government has consistently opposed depositions or stalled taking them, citing national security reasons. *Witness to Abuse, supra,* at 79. Moreover, the government reportedly failed to advise many detainees of the reasons for their arrests, of their right to an attorney and to have an attorney present at their interrogations, and of their right to remain silent. *Id.* at 4.

5. *Al-Kidd's Tort Claims.* Although the Supreme Court threw out al-Kidd's claims under the Fourth Amendment and the material witness statute, al-Kidd also sued the United States under the Federal Tort Claims Act, on the ground that the government agents who arrested him were liable for both false imprisonment and abuse of process. In September 2012, the U.S. District Court for the District of Idaho granted summary judgment to al-Kidd on his false imprisonment claim, and ordered that his abuse-of-process claim proceed to trial. *See Al-Kidd v. Gonzales,* No. 05-093, 2012 WL 4470782 (D. Idaho Sept. 27, 2012). In 2015, the government settled out of court with al-Kidd for $385,000 — one of the few examples (along with *Iqbal*) of a civil suit arising out of alleged post-September 11 counterterrorism abuses that resulted in compensation to the plaintiff. *See Idaho Student Receives Official Regrets and Compensation for Post-9/11 Arrest,* Associated Press, Jan. 16, 2015, http://www.theguardian.com/us-news/2015/jan/16/idaho-student-regrets-compensation-post-911-arrest.

6. *Material Witness Detentions Going Forward.* Review the material witness statute, *supra* p. 959. What aspect of the procedure for detaining material witnesses might deter the government from making wider use of this legal basis for detention? Under what circumstances might material witness detention appeal to the government? (Recall, in this context, that both José Padilla and Ali al-Marri — who were subsequently detained as enemy combatants and then prosecuted in civilian courts — were initially detained pursuant to material witness warrants.)

PREVENTIVE DETENTION: SUMMARY OF BASIC PRINCIPLES

- Preventive detention is usually authorized by an express statute.
- The Constitution does not categorically forbid preventive detention by civil authorities. But such detention (like all others) is circumscribed by the Fourth Amendment's requirement of reasonable seizures, as well as by the Fifth Amendment's requirement of procedural (and substantive) due process.
- Warrantless detentions not based on express statutory authority are usually permissible only in narrow circumstances, when, among other things, the government can show both (1) a compelling interest in the individual's detention, and (2) that the detainee would otherwise pose a danger to himself or others. Even then, such detentions might be challenged on other constitutional grounds, including the equal protection component of the Fifth Amendment's Due Process Clause.
- The Constitution does not categorically forbid pretextual arrests, so long as they are otherwise lawful — the *Whren* principle. Thus, after the 9/11 attacks, the government often relied upon non-terrorism-related authorities to arrest and detain individuals who were either suspects or persons with information relevant to the government's broader investigation into 9/11. Such detentions may raise relatively modest Fourth and Fifth Amendment concerns.

- In addition to arrests for minor ("spitting on the sidewalk") offenses, in the weeks and months after 9/11 the government routinely used immigration authorities to arrest and detain noncitizens, including (but not limited to) individuals of perceived Arab or Muslim descent, for conduct that was overlooked in other immigrant populations.

- The government has also relied upon its authority to detain "material witnesses" to hold terrorism suspects without trial, albeit for relatively brief periods. This authority is available if the government can show that the individual in question has information that is relevant to an ongoing (petit or grand) jury proceeding, and that there is reason to believe that the witness will not appear if called to testify.

- The Supreme Court threw out the two major challenges to these authorities in the *Iqbal* and *al-Kidd* cases, respectively. But it left unanswered some key questions about limits on the government's authority in this field, including whether and to what extent the government may use the material witness statute to hold suspects, as opposed to witnesses, and how long immigrants who are arrested in anticipation of their deportation (rather than on criminal charges) can be held before they must be released.

PART VI INTERROGATING TERRORIST SUBJECTS

32

Interrogating Terrorist Suspects

Torture is as old as human violence. Sometimes it has been used simply to inflict pain on an enemy. Sometimes it is used to extract confessions. Before and during the Inquisition, trial by ordeal employed torture to supplement circumstantial evidence in a criminal case. If an accused confessed during torture, he could be convicted. John H. Langbein, *The Legal History of Torture*, in *Torture: A Collection* 93, 93-95 (Sanford Levinson ed., 2004).

More recently, torture has been used primarily to extract information. When information is needed to anticipate an enemy or terrorist attack, its time urgency and life-or-death significance may combine with an interrogator's hatred of the enemy (or perhaps sadism) to encourage ever-escalating efforts to make a subject talk. Experts hotly dispute whether torture is effective in obtaining information, either at all or by comparison with less harsh methods of interrogation. There is no disputing, of course, that it fails when the suspect knows nothing.

Some say, however, its effectiveness is immaterial given its moral cost. When grotesque photographs of detainees being abused by U.S. personnel at the Abu Ghraib detention facility in Iraq became primetime news in 2004, this nation's leaders engaged in an often vituperative debate about whether gathering intelligence through torture is effective — whether the gain is worth the pain. Two former U.S. military commanders responded in 2007:

> These assertions that "torture works" may reassure a fearful public, but it is a false security . . . and any "flexibility" about torture at the top drops down the chain of command like a stone. . . . If we forfeit our values by signaling that they are negotiable in situations of grave or imminent danger, we drive those undecideds into the arms of the enemy. [Charles C. Krulak & Joseph P. Hoar, Opinion, *It's Our Cage, Too*, Wash. Post, May 17, 2007.]

Similarly polarized opinions followed the 2014 partial release of a Senate Select Committee on Intelligence (SSCI) study of the CIA's detention and interrogation activities after 9/11.

How should legal rules guide this controversial and uncertain quest for information? If the human instinct in war or emergency is to extract information by any means necessary, is abusive interrogation inevitable unless we forbid it absolutely? *See* Joseph Margulies, *Guantanamo and the Abuse of Presidential Power* 29 (2006) (so arguing). This chapter explores these and related questions of interrogation. We begin by reviewing our government's own account of so-called Enhanced Interrogation Techniques (EITs) after 9/11, then consider where to draw the line between permissible interrogation and torture. We then use a judicial decision interpreting anti-torture laws to explore the legal landscape that governs interrogation for intelligence purposes.

In the next chapter, we apply this legal framework to a case study of coercive interrogation during the war on terror.

A. WHEN IS INTERROGATION TORTURE?

On September 17, 2001, President George W. Bush reportedly signed a memorandum that gave the CIA "unprecedented, broad authority to render [to 'surrender' or 'hand over' persons from one jurisdiction to another for purposes of detention, interrogation, and/or trial] individuals who 'pose continuing or serious threats of violence or death to U.S. persons or interests or who are planning terrorist attacks.'" *See CIA Comments on the Senate Select Committee on Intelligence Report on the Rendition, Detention, and Interrogation Program*, Conclusion 1, at 1, June 27, 2013, *at* https://www.cia.gov/library/reports/CIAs_June2013_Response_to_the_SSCI_Study_on_the_Former_Detention_and_Interrogation_Program.pdf. The President's memorandum, which is still classified, apparently said nothing explicitly about interrogation. Nevertheless, the CIA began a detention and interrogation program soon thereafter, and the program continued until it was stopped by President Obama in 2009.

The CIA concluded that some persons in its custody who were labeled "High Value Detainees" (HVDs) — believed to possess actionable knowledge about imminent terrorist threats against the United States — were resisting ordinary interrogation techniques. These "ordinary" techniques, employed by U.S. law enforcement and military interrogators, did not incorporate significant physical or psychological pressure. The CIA then began subjecting HVDs to "Enhanced Interrogation Techniques" (EITs). A 2007 Justice Department memorandum explained that the CIA program

> is limited to persons whom the Director of the CIA determines to be a member or part of al Qaeda, the Taliban, or associated terrorist organizations and likely to possess information that could prevent terrorist attacks against the United States or its interests or that could help locate senior leadership of al Qaeda who are conducting its campaign of terror against the United States. . . . The program is designed to dislodge the detainee's expectations about how he will be treated in U.S. custody, to create a situation in which he feels that he is not in control, and to establish a relationship of dependence on the part of the detainee. Accordingly, the program's intended effect is psychological; it is not intended to extract information through the imposition of physical pain. [Memorandum from

Stephen Bradbury, Principal Deputy Ass't Attorney General, to John Rizzo, Acting CIA General Counsel, *Application of the War Crimes Act, the Detainee Treatment Act, and Common Article 3 of the Geneva Conventions to Certain Techniques that May Be Used by the CIA in the Interrogation of High Value al Qaeda Detainees*, at 5-6 (July 20, 2007).]

A 2004 report by the CIA Inspector General compiled the following list of EITs.

Enhanced Interrogation Techniques

- The *attention grasp* consists of grasping the detainee with both hands, with one hand on each side of the collar opening, in a controlled and quick motion. In the same motion as the grasp, the detainee is drawn toward the interrogator.
- During the *walling technique*, the detainee is pulled forward and then quickly and firmly pushed into a flexible false wall so that his shoulder blades hit the wall. His head and neck are supported with a rolled towel to prevent whiplash.
- The *facial hold* is used to hold the detainee's head immobile. The interrogator places an open palm on either side of the detainee's face and the interrogator's fingertips are kept well away from the detainee's eyes.
- With the *facial or insult slap*, the fingers are slightly spread apart. The interrogator's hand makes contact with the area between the tip of the detainee's chin and the bottom of the corresponding earlobe.
- In *cramped confinement*, the detainee is placed in a confined space, typically a small or large box, which is usually dark. Confinement in the smaller space lasts no more than two hours and in the larger space it can last up to 18 hours.
- *Insects* placed in a confinement box involve placing a harmless insect in the box with the detainee.
- During *wall standing*, the detainee may stand about 4 to 5 feet from a wall with his feet spread approximately to his shoulder width. His arms are stretched out in front of him and his fingers rest on the wall to support all of his body weight. The detainee is not allowed to reposition his hands or feet.
- The application of *stress positions* may include having the detainee sit on the floor with his legs extended straight out in front of him with his arms raised above his head or kneeling on the floor while leaning back at a 45 degree angle.
- *Sleep deprivation* will not exceed 11 days at a time.
- The application of the *waterboard technique* involves binding the detainee to a bench with his feet elevated above his head. The detainee's head is immobilized and an interrogator places a cloth over the detainee's mouth and nose while pouring water onto the cloth in a controlled manner. Airflow is restricted for 20 to 40 seconds and the technique produces the sensation of drowning and suffocation. [Off. of the Inspector Gen., *Special Review: Counterterrorism Detention and Interrogation Activities (September 2001-October 2003)*, at 15 (Report No. 2003-7123-IG) (2004).]

More than a decade later, the Senate Select Committee on Intelligence (SSCI) released a 500-page Executive Summary of its much anticipated 6,700-page study of the CIA's detention and interrogation activities after 9/11. The balance of the study remains classified. The SSCI study comprehensively reviewed the CIA's detention of 119 foreign nationals and its use of EITs on them between 2002 and 2007. The following brief excerpts describe the application of EITs by the CIA to two detainees.

Senate Select Committee on Intelligence, Committee Study of the Central Intelligence Agency's Detention and Interrogation Program (SSCI Study)

Dec. 13, 2012 (released in part on Dec. 3, 2014)
available at http://www.intelligence.senate.gov/sites/default/files/press/executive-summary_0.pdf

THE CIA USES THE WATERBOARD AND OTHER ENHANCED INTERROGATION TECHNIQUES AGAINST ABU ZUBAYDAH

On August 3, 2002, CIA Headquarters informed the interrogation team at DETENTION SITE GREEN that it had formal approval to apply the CIA's enhanced interrogation techniques, including the waterboard, against Abu Zubaydah. According to CIA records, only the two CIA contractors, SWIGERT and DUNBAR [James Mitchell and Bruce Jessen], were to have contact with Abu Zubaydah. Other CIA personnel at DETENTION SITE GREEN — including CIA medical personnel and other CIA "interrogators with whom he is familiar" — were only to observe.

From August 4, 2002, through August 23, 2002, the CIA subjected Abu Zubaydah to its enhanced interrogation techniques on a near 24-hour-per-day basis. After Abu Zubaydah had been in complete isolation for 47 days, the most aggressive interrogation phase began at approximately 11:50 AM on August 4, 2002. Security personnel entered the cell, shackled and hooded Abu Zubaydah, and removed his towel (Abu Zubaydah was then naked). Without asking any questions, the interrogators placed a rolled towel around his neck as a collar, and backed him up into the cell wall (an interrogator later acknowledged the collar was used to slam Abu Zubaydah against a concrete wall). The interrogators then removed the hood, performed an attention grab, and had Abu Zubaydah watch while a large confinement box was brought into the cell and laid on the floor. A cable states Abu Zubaydah "was unhooded and the large confinement box was carried into the interrogation room and paced [sic] on the floor so as to appear as a coffin." The interrogators then demanded detailed and reliable information on terrorist operations planned against the United States, including the names, phone numbers, email addresses, weapon caches, and safe houses of anyone involved. CIA records describe Abu Zubaydah as appearing apprehensive. Each time Abu Zubaydah denied having additional information, the interrogators would perform a facial slap or face grab. At approximately 6:20 PM, Abu Zubaydah was waterboarded for the first time. Over a two-and-a-half-hour period, Abu Zubaydah coughed, vomited, and had "involuntary spasms of the torso and extremities" during waterboarding. Detention site personnel noted that "throughout the process [Abu Zubaydah] was asked and given the opportunity to respond to questions about threats" to the United States, but Abu Zubaydah continued to maintain that he did not have any additional information to provide. In an email to OMS leadership entitled, "So it begins," a medical officer wrote:

> "The sessions accelerated rapidly progressing quickly to the water board after large box, walling, and small box periods. [Abu Zubaydah] seems very resistant to the water board. Longest time with the cloth over his face so far has been 17 seconds. This is sure to increase shortly. NO useful information so far.... He did vomit a couple of times during the water board with some beans and rice. It's been 10 hours since he ate so this is

> surprising and disturbing. We plan to only feed Ensure for a while now. I'm head[ing] back for another water board session."

The use of the CIA's enhanced interrogation techniques — including "walling, attention grasps, slapping, facial hold, stress positions, cramped confinement, white noise and sleep deprivation" — continued in "varying combinations, 24 hours a day" for 17 straight days, through August 20, 2002. When Abu Zubaydah was left alone during this period, he was placed in a stress position, left on the waterboard with a cloth over his face, or locked in one of two confinement boxes. According to the cables, Abu Zubaydah was also subjected to the waterboard "2-4 times a day . . . with multiple iterations of the watering cycle during each application."

The "aggressive phase of interrogation" continued until August 23, 2002. Over the course of the entire 20 day "aggressive phase of interrogation," Abu Zubaydah spent a total of 266 hours (11 days, 2 hours) in the large (coffin size) confinement box and 29 hours in a small confinement box, which had a width of 21 inches, a depth of 2.5 feet, and a height of 2.5 feet. The CIA interrogators told Abu Zubaydah that the only way he would leave the facility was in the coffin-shaped confinement box.

According to the daily cables from DETENTION SITE GREEN, Abu Zubaydah frequently "cried," "begged," "pleaded," and "whimpered," but continued to deny that he had any additional information on current threats to, or operatives in, the United States. . . .

From Abu Zubaydah's capture on March 28, 2002, to his transfer to Department of Defense custody on September 5, 2006, information provided by Abu Zubaydah resulted in 766 disseminated intelligence reports. According to CIA documents, Abu Zubaydah provided information on "al-Qa'ida activities, plans, capabilities, and relationships," in addition to information on "its leadership structure, including personalities, decision-making processes, training, and tactics." As noted, this type of information was provided by Abu Zubaydah before, during, and after the use of the CIA's enhanced interrogation techniques. At no time during or after the use of the CIA's enhanced interrogation techniques did Abu Zubaydah provide information about operatives in, or future attacks against, the United States. . . .

THE DETENTION AND INTERROGATION OF ABD AL-RAHIM AL-NASHIRI . . .

Abd al-Rahim al-Nashiri, assessed by the CIA to be an al-Qa'ida "terrorist operations planner" who was "intimately involved" in planning both the *USS Cole* bombing and the 1998 East Africa U.S. Embassy bombings, was captured in the United Arab Emirates in mid-October 2002. He provided information while in the custody of a foreign government, including on plotting in the Persian Gulf, and was then rendered by the CIA to DETENTION SITE COBALT in Country I on November 11, 2002, where he was held for [ ] days before being transferred to DETENTION SITE GREEN on November [ ], 2002. At DETENTION SITE GREEN, al-Nashiri was interrogated using the CIA's enhanced interrogation techniques, including being subjected to the waterboard at least three times. In December 2002, when DETENTION SITE GREEN was closed, al-Nashiri and Abu Zubaydah were rendered to DETENTION SITE BLUE.

In total, al-Nashiri was subjected to the CIA's enhanced interrogation techniques during at least four separate periods. . . .

It was later learned that during these interrogation sessions, [CIA OFFICER 2], with the permission and participation of the DETENTION SITE BLUE chief of Base, who also had not been trained and qualified as an interrogator, used a series of unauthorized interrogation techniques against al-Nashiri. For example, [CIA OFFICER 2] placed al-Nashiri in a "standing stress position" with "his hands affixed over his head" for approximately two and a half days. Later, during the course of al-Nashiri's debriefings, while he was blindfolded, [CIA OFFICER 2] placed a pistol near al-Nashiri's head and operated a cordless drill near al-Nashiri's body. Al-Nashiri did not provide any additional threat information during, or after, these interrogations. . . .

In October 2004, 21 months after the final documented use of the CIA's enhanced interrogation techniques against al-Nashiri, an assessment by CIA contract interrogator DUNBAR and another CIA interrogator concluded that al-Nashiri provided "essentially no actionable information," and that "the probability that he has much more to contribute is low." Over the course of al-Nashiri's detention and interrogation by the CIA, the CIA disseminated 145 intelligence reports based on his debriefings. Al-Nashiri provided information on past operational plotting, associates whom he expected to participate in plots, details on completed operations, and background on al-Qa'ida's structure and methods of operation. Al-Nashiri did not provide the information that the CIA's ALEC Station sought and believed al-Nashiri possessed, specifically "perishable threat information to help [CIA] thwart future attacks and capture additional operatives." . . .

Notes and Questions

1. *Definitions: Do You Know It When You See It?* The ban on torture is widely said to be *jus cogens* — a universal norm. *See, e.g., Filartiga v. Peña-Irala*, 630 F.2d 876, 884 (2d Cir. 1980) (finding that "official torture is now prohibited by the law of nations"); *Tel-Oren v. Libyan Arab Republic*, 726 F.2d 774, 781, 791 n.20 (D.C. Cir. 1984) (Edwards, J., concurring) (asserting that "commentators have begun to identify a handful of heinous actions — each of which violates definable, universal and obligatory norms," including, at a minimum, bans on governmental "torture").

We consider the attempted legal definitions of torture later in this chapter, but if the ban on torture is *jus cogens*, do we need a legal definition? Which, if any, of the techniques described above do you consider torture? Why?

Even if you are unclear whether a technique — or battery of techniques — is torture, you might well conclude that it is inhumane and offensive to human dignity. For example, after objections to Israeli mistreatment of detainees during the Palestinian Intifada, the Israeli Supreme Court ruled that certain interrogation methods approved for use by Israel's security services — hooding, shaking, forced crouch on toes, painful handcuffing, seating detainees on low and inclined stools, sleep deprivation, and prolonged extremely loud music — violated the detainees' constitutional protections to a right of dignity, based on Israeli domestic law. *Public Committee Against Torture in Israel v. State of Israel*, HC 5100/94 (1999). Are any of the EITs inhumane and offensive to human dignity?

2. *Waterboarding.* Waterboarding pre-dates the Inquisition and owes its longevity and apparent appeal to the fact that it causes extreme physical and mental suffering, but leaves no marks on the body. Eric Weiner, *Waterboarding: A Tortured History*, Nat'l Pub. Radio, Nov. 3, 2007, *available at* http://www.npr.org/2007/11/03/15886834/waterboarding-a-tortured-history.

Does waterboarding constitute torture? As early as 1902, the U.S. Army court-martialed an officer for administering the "water cure" to a suspect during U.S. military activities against Filipino guerrillas. Court-Martial of Major Edwin F. Glenn, S. Doc. No. 213, 57th Cong. 20-28 (1902). Federal courts in the United States have also punished law enforcement personnel for waterboarding, including local sheriffs and Philippine government agents. *See United States v. Lee*, 744 F.2d 1124 (5th Cir. 1984); *In re Estate of Ferdinand E. Marcos, Human Rights Litig.*, 910 F. Supp. 1460, 1463 (D. Haw. 1995).

Can you draft language for a law that would forbid use of waterboarding? Would a ban on "torture" accomplish the objective?

3. *Who Decides What Interrogation Conduct Is Unlawful?* The official policy of the United States is to condemn and prohibit torture. *See generally* U.S. Dep't of State, *Initial Report of the United States of America to the UN Committee Against Torture* (Oct. 15, 1999), *available at* https://1997-2001.state.gov/policy_remarks/1999/991015_koh_rpt_torture.html ("Torture is prohibited by law throughout the United States. It is categorically denounced as a matter of policy and as a tool of state authority."); *Second Periodic Report of the United States of America to the Committee Against Torture* (May 6, 2005), *available at* https://2009-2017.state.gov/j/drl/rls/45738.htm ("[The] United States is unequivocally opposed to the use and practice of torture.... No circumstance whatsoever... may be invoked as a justification for or defense to committing torture."). Who decides how to translate the policy into enforceable rules?

4. *The Ticking Bomb: Utilitarianism vs. Morality?* A common utilitarian objection to using torture to obtain information is that it is ineffective because the person being interrogated will say anything to stop the pain. Thus, information procured by torture is said to be inherently unreliable. *See* Jeannine Bell, *"Behind This Mortal Bone": The (In)effectiveness of Torture*, 83 Ind. L.J. 339 (2008). But defenders of harsh interrogation techniques respond that if a person will say anything, then he will also tell what he knows (if he knows anything). Of course, his information will need to be corroborated, if possible, but that is true of all intelligence. If, however, this rebuttal suggests that torture can sometimes obtain useful information, it still leaves the question whether other less "enhanced" methods of interrogation are *equally* or *more* effective.

In any case, many reject the utilitarian analysis altogether. Is it *ever* morally justifiable to torture a detainee? The mere possibility that coercive interrogation could save many lives creates an undoubted and morally complex tension between the need to obtain information and the condemnation of torture. Assume, for example, that authorities have in custody someone whom they feel certain has placed an especially destructive explosive device somewhere in a large shopping mall. The explosive may go off at any time, and there may not be enough time to evacuate the mall. If the bomb detonates, thousands will die. The detainee is believed to be the only person with knowledge of the bomb, and he will not talk. Should the interrogators torture the detainee in hopes of learning the location of the bomb before it is too late?

Should either analysis — utilitarian or moral — also take into account the effect on the torturers of using torture?

B. THE LEGAL STANDARDS AND THEIR APPLICATION

Reading *United States v. Charles Emmanuel*

On March 30, 2006, Charles Emmanuel, a/k/a Chuckie Taylor, the son of the infamous president of Liberia, Charles Taylor, was arrested when he attempted to enter the United States with a passport obtained through false statements on his passport application. After he pleaded guilty to the passport fraud charge and was sentenced to 11 months in prison in December 2007, a 2008 Justice Department indictment charged Emmanuel with participating in torture in Liberia between 1999 and 2003. The opinion below, issued in response to a pretrial motion to dismiss the indictment, is the first judicial interpretation of the Torture Act, 18 U.S.C. §§2340-2340A (2018), which criminalizes acts of torture committed outside the United States if the offender is a U.S. national or, regardless of nationality, is present in the United States.

- What does the Convention Against Torture (CAT) forbid?
- How, if at all, was the CAT prohibition on torture changed by the conditions attached to the U.S. ratification of the CAT? Did they broaden or narrow the prohibition?
- What does the Torture Act prohibit? How, if at all, is it different from the CAT prohibition? Why is it different? Does the Torture Act leave room for the use of torture for the purpose of obtaining information?
- By what authorities can Congress implement the CAT? Do they permit it to depart from the CAT's definition of torture?
- Was the indictment vague as applied to Emmanuel's acts? Would he have known that they constituted torture within the meaning of the Torture Act?

United States v. Charles Emmanuel

United States District Court, Southern District of Florida, July 5, 2007
No. 06-20758-CR, 2007 WL 2002452

Cecilia M. Altonaga, United States District Judge. This cause is before the Court on Defendant, Charles Emmanuel's Motion to Dismiss the Indictment Based on the Unconstitutionality of 18 U.S.C. §2340A. . . .

I. BACKGROUND

A. International and National Prohibitions of Torture

International prohibition against torture is a *jus cogens* norm of international law. *See Nuru v. Gonzales*, 404 F.3d 1207, 1222-23 (9th Cir. 2005) ("torture is illegal under the law of virtually every country in the world and under the international law of human rights") (internal footnotes omitted). The Universal Declaration of Human Rights, adopted by the United Nations in 1948, states that "no one shall be subjected to torture or to cruel, inhuman or degrading treatment or punishment." Universal Decl. of Human Rights, Dec. 10, 1948, U.N. Doc. A/810, art. 5. The International Covenant on Civil and Political Rights, Dec. 16, 1966, art. 7, 999 U.N.T.S. 171, 6 I.L.M. 368, states that "[n]o one shall be subjected to torture or to cruel, inhuman or degrading treatment or punishment."

On December 10, 1984, the United Nations General Assembly unanimously adopted the Convention Against Torture and Other Cruel, Inhuman or Degrading Treatment or Punishment ("Convention Against Torture" or "Convention"). G.A. Res. 39/46, U.N. GAOR, 39th Sess., Supp. No. 51 at 197, U.N. Doc. A/RES/39/46, S. Treaty Doc. No. 100-20, 1465 U.N.T.S. 85 (Dec. 10, 1984). It was adopted "with the stated purpose to 'make more effective the struggle against torture and other cruel, inhuman or degrading treatment or punishment throughout the world.'" *Auguste v. Ridge*, 395 F.3d 123, 130 (3d Cir. 2005) (quoting the Preamble to the Convention, S. Treaty Doc. No. 100-20, 1465 U.N.T.S. 85)). The Convention entered into force on June 26, 1987. *See id.* It has been described as the "most important U.N. treaty for controlling, regulating, and prohibiting torture and related practices." Winston Nagan & Lucie Atkins, *The International Law of Torture: From Universal Proscription to Effective Application and Enforcement*, 14 Harv. Hum. Rts. J. 87, 97 (2001).

On April 18, 1988, President Ronald Reagan signed the Convention, with the caveat that the United States reserved the right to communicate such reservations, interpretive understandings, or declarations as were deemed necessary. President Reagan submitted the Convention Against Torture to the Senate for advice and consent to ratification on May 20, 1988, with seventeen proposed conditions (four reservations, nine understandings, and four declarations).

In January 1990, President George H.W. Bush submitted a revised and reduced list of proposed conditions. One of the proposed conditions was that in order to constitute torture, the "act must be specifically intended to inflict severe physical or mental pain or suffering." [*Auguste*, 395 F.3d at 131 (quoting S. Exec. Rep. 101-30 at 9, 36).] On January 30, 1990, the Senate Foreign Relations Committee held a hearing and thereafter, on August 30, 1990, issued a report recommending that the Senate give its advice and consent to ratification of the Convention Against Torture, subject to reservations, understandings and declarations.[2] S. Exec. Rep. 101-30 (1990). The full Senate gave its advice and consent to ratification, again, subject to several reservations, understandings and declarations.

On October 21, 1994 and pursuant to Article 26 of the Convention, when President William Clinton deposited the instrument for ratification with the United Nations, the United States became a party to the Convention. "Notably, the President included the Senate understandings in the instrument of ratification." *Auguste*, 395 F.3d at 132 (citing 1830 U.N.T.S. 320, 321, 322 (1994)); Declarations and Reservations made upon Ratification, Accession, or Succession (visited Nov. 24, 2004)

---

2. The Senate gave advice and consent subject to the reservation that the term "cruel, inhuman or degrading treatment or punishment" is to have a meaning as prohibited by the Fifth, Eighth, and/or Fourteenth Amendments to the U.S. Constitution, and subject to additional understandings, including that the provisions of the Convention are not self-executing. For a complete listing of the reservations, understandings and declarations of the United States Senate, see [https://treaties.un.org/Pages/ViewDetails.aspx?src=treaty&mtdsg_no=iv-9&chapter=4&lang=en#EndDec].

(http://untreaty.un.org/ENGLISH/bible/englishinternetbible/partI/chapterIV/treaty14.asp).

In consenting to ratification of the Convention Against Torture, the Senate acknowledged that existing U.S. federal and state criminal statutes prohibited acts of torture occurring within the United States. *See Summary and Analysis of the Convention Against Torture and Other Cruel, Inhuman or Degrading Treatment*, S. Treaty Doc. 100-20, 9-10 (1988). The Senate recognized that in order for the United States to comply with its obligations under the treaty, it would need to enact a criminal statute prohibiting acts of torture by the defendants specified in Article 5 of the Convention, committed outside the United States. *Id.*

There are 144 parties to the Convention Against Torture, representing approximately 75% of the member states of the United Nations, including the United States and Liberia. The Convention defines "torture" as

> any act by which severe pain or suffering, whether physical or mental, is intentionally inflicted on a person for such purposes as obtaining from him or a third person information or a confession, punishing him for an act he or a third person has committed or is suspected of having committed, or intimidating or coercing him or a third person, or for any reason based on discrimination of any kind, when such pain or suffering is inflicted by or at the instigation of or with the consent or acquiescence of a public official or other person acting in an official capacity.

Convention, Article 1(1).

Article 2(1) of the Convention requires each State Party to "take effective legislative, administrative, judicial or other measures to prevent acts of torture in any territory under its jurisdiction." Article 4 requires each State Party to "ensure that all acts of torture are offences under its criminal law. The same shall apply to any attempt to commit torture and to any act by any person which constitutes complicity or participation in torture." Article 5(1) requires each State Party to "take such measures as may be necessary to establish its jurisdiction over the offences ... (b) When the alleged offender is a national of that State," and "2. ... where the alleged offender is present in any territory under its jurisdiction and it does not extradite him. ..."

The Convention ... was not intended to be self-executing. ... The United States therefore enacted 18 U.S.C. §§2340-2340A of the United States Criminal Code pursuant to Articles 4 and 5 of the Convention. The Torture Convention Implementation Act ("Torture Act"), 18 U.S.C. §§2340 and 2340A, contains a definitional section, section 2340, and a section listing proscriptive elements and jurisdictional requirements, section 2340A.

The Torture Act states that "[w]hoever outside the United States commits or attempts to commit torture shall be fined ... or imprisoned not more than 20 years, or both, and if death results ... shall be punished by death or imprisoned for any term of years or for life." Federal courts have jurisdiction if "the alleged offender is a national of the United States; or the alleged offender is present in the United States, irrespective of the nationality of the victim or alleged offender." 18 U.S.C. §2340A(b). A person who conspires to commit an offense under the Act is subject to the same penalties prescribed for the offense under section 2340A(c).

Under the Torture Act, torture is defined in a slightly different manner from its definition in the Convention. Torture is defined in the Torture Act as "an act committed by a person acting under the color of law specifically intended to inflict severe physical or mental pain or suffering (other than pain or suffering incidental to lawful sanctions) upon another person within his custody or physical control." 18 U.S.C. §2340(1). "Severe mental pain or suffering" is

> the prolonged mental harm caused by or resulting from —
>
> (A) the intentional infliction or threatened infliction of severe physical pain or suffering;
>
> (B) the administration or application, or threatened administration or application, of mind-altering substances or other procedures calculated to disrupt profoundly the senses or the personality;
>
> (C) the threat of imminent death; or
>
> (D) the threat that another person will imminently be subjected to death, severe physical pain or suffering, or the administration or application of mind-altering substances or other procedures calculated to disrupt profoundly the senses or personality.

18 U.S.C. §2340(2).

. . . Pursuant to Article 27 of the Convention, the Torture Act entered into force for the United States on November 20, 1994, thirty days after it was deposited for ratification with the United Nations. The conspiracy offense was added in the 2001 amendments. . . .

B. This Prosecution

On December 6, 2006, the Grand Jury returned an Indictment against Defendant, Charles Emmanuel, charging Defendant with conspiracy to commit, and the commission of acts of torture upon an unidentified person ("victim") in the country of Liberia. The Indictment alleges that Defendant was born in Boston, Massachusetts, was present in the United States as a result of his arrival at Miami International Airport, and at relevant times, was present in the country of Liberia, located in West Africa. Because his father, Charles McArthur Taylor, was president of Liberia, Defendant allegedly had authority to command members of the Liberian Antiterrorist Unit and participated in activities of the Liberian security forces, including the Antiterrorist Unit, a Special Security Service, and the Liberian National Police. During 2002, Liberia had non-violent groups and armed rebel groups opposed to the presidency of Defendant's father.

Count One of the Indictment charges Defendant with knowingly conspiring with others to commit torture by conspiring with others to commit acts, under the color of law, with the specific intent to inflict severe physical pain and suffering upon a person within their custody and control. The object of the conspiracy was to obtain information from the alleged victim about actual, perceived, or potential opponents of the Taylor presidency by, *inter alia*, committing torture, in violation of Title 18, United States Code, §§2340A and 2340(1). The interrogation and torture are alleged to have taken place in various locations in Liberia, on or about July 24, 2002. Among other things, Defendant allegedly made the victim hold scalding water in his hands and repeatedly shocked the victim's genitalia and other body parts, and a co-conspirator poured scalding water on other locations of the victim's body, applied a hot iron to the victim's flesh, and rubbed salt into the victim's open wounds. All acts are alleged to violate 18 U.S.C. §2340A(c).

Count Two alleges that Defendant and others, while intending to inflict severe physical pain and suffering, committed and attempted to commit torture, while acting under color of law, by committing [the acts described above], in violation of 18 U.S.C. §§2340A and 2340(1), and 18 U.S.C. §2....

Defendant's Motion to Dismiss challenges the Indictment on several constitutional grounds. The "core problem with this case," according to Defendant, is that "the government seeks to oversee, through the open-ended terms of federal criminal law — the internal and wholly domestic actions of a foreign government." The essence of the challenge to the prosecution is the constitutional infirmity of 18 U.S.C. §2340A, a law that has been in place for over a decade, and under which Defendant is the first person to be prosecuted....

II. ANALYSIS

A. Congress' Power to Enact the Torture Act

To paraphrase Defendant, he argues that the Torture Act does not implement the Convention Against Torture, but rather, creates a different crime from the act of torture defined in the Convention. According to Defendant, the Torture Act has an expansive statutory prohibition of torture, where pain and suffering need not be inflicted for purposes of intimidation, coercion, or for obtaining a confession. That definition is at odds with the limited treaty terms, which define torture as an act by which severe pain or suffering is intentionally inflicted for such purposes as obtaining information or a confession when inflicted by a public official in an official capacity. Because the definition of torture in the Torture Act, in essence, a definition amounting to aggravated battery, does not track the treaty language, the definition varies sharply from the international understanding of torture as set forth in the Convention, and the statute thus cannot be said to effectuate, or be necessary to or proper for, compliance with the treaty.

Defendant's argument fails to persuade that Congress lacked authorization, under the Necessary and Proper Clause or the Offences Clause of Article I of the Constitution, to enact the Torture Act.

1. Necessary and Proper Clause and the Treaty Power

... Congress certainly had the authority to pass the Torture Act under the Necessary and Proper Clause of Article I, as an adjunct to the Executive's authority under Article II to enter into treaties, with the advice and consent of the Senate....

In determining the intended meaning of the parties, a court should look to a treaty's negotiating and drafting history, as well as the subsequent practice of the parties in their application of the treaty. Also, because a treaty implicates questions of foreign policy, the construction given by the Executive Branch, although not binding on the court, is entitled to great weight. *See Factor v. Laubenheimer*, 290 U.S. 276, 295 (1933). Furthermore, "if a treaty fairly admits of two constructions, one restricting the rights that may be claimed under it, and the other enlarging it, the more liberal construction is to be preferred." *Id.* at 293-94. Lastly, a court is under a duty to interpret a statute in a manner consonant with treaty obligations, because "an act of Congress ought never to be construed to violate the law of nations, if any other possible construction remains...." *United States v. PLO*, 695 F. Supp. 1456, 1465 (S.D.N.Y. 1988) (quoting *Murray v. The Charming Betsy*, 6 U.S. (2 Cranch) 64, 118 (1804)).

When the Convention was ratified by the United States, it was explicitly ratified subject to certain understandings and restrictions. Those understandings and limitations were subsequently incorporated into the legislative scheme that effectuated it, including the statutory definition of torture. Defendant cites to no case that compels a finding that where legislation that implements a treaty varies from the language or scope of the treaty, it is constitutionally infirm, or is less necessary and proper to carry out the powers exercised by the Executive under Article II than legislation that mirrors verbatim the language used in the treaty....

Here, the definition of torture in the Torture Act admittedly does not "track the language of the Convention in all material respects." The statutory definition of torture does, however, parallel the definition found in the Convention, in that both texts define torture to include the intentional infliction of severe pain or suffering by a public official or person acting under color of law. The element missing from the statutory definition, that is, that the torture be inflicted for the purposes of obtaining a confession, for punishment, or for intimidation or coercion, does not take the Torture Act outside the authorization given Congress in the Necessary and Proper Clause. Indeed, the more expansive statutory definition, which captures more acts of torture than does the definition contained in the Convention, is consistent with the international community's near universal condemnation of torture and cruel, inhuman or degrading treatment, and is consistent with repeated calls for the international community to be more "effective [in] the struggle against torture." *Convention Preamble*....

... [T]he Torture Act plainly bears a rational relationship to the stated objectives of the Convention, and thus passes constitutional muster under the Necessary and Proper Clause.

2. Offenses Clause

Alternatively, assuming Defendant was correct, and Congress' more expansive definition of torture took the Torture Act outside the realm of the Necessary and Proper Clause, one additional source of constitutional authority for the Torture Act may be found in Article I, §8, cl.10 of the Constitution, that is the "offences against the Law of Nations" Clause. That clause gives Congress the power "[t]o define and punish Piracies and Felonies on the high Seas, and Offences against the Law of Nations." *Id.* Because of the way the clause is written, and contrary to Defendant's proposed interpretation of it, Congress has the power to define and punish offenses against the law of nations, independent of any piracies or felonies that occur on the high seas....

The prohibition against official torture has attained the status of a *jus cogens* norm, not merely the status of customary international law. *See* [*Siderman de Blake v. Republic of Argentina*, 965 F.2d 699, 714, 717 (9th Cir. 1992)] (collecting authorities). In reaching the not surprising conclusion that prohibition of official torture was a *jus cogens* norm, the Ninth Circuit explained:

> [W]e conclude that the right to be free from official torture is fundamental and universal, a right deserving of the highest status under international law, a norm of *jus cogens.* The crack of the whip, the clamp of the thumb screw, the crush of the iron maiden, and, in these more efficient modern times, the shock of the electric cattle prod are forms of torture that the international order will not tolerate. To subject a person to such horrors is to commit one of the most egregious violations of the personal security and dignity of a human being. That states engage in official torture cannot be doubted, but all states

> believe it is wrong, all that engage in torture deny it, and no state claims a sovereign right to torture its own citizens.

Id. at 717 (citations omitted).

It is beyond peradventure that torture and acts that constitute cruel, inhuman or degrading punishment, acts prohibited by *jus cogens*, are similarly abhorred by the law of nations. *See, e.g., Sosa v. Alvarez-Machain*, 542 U.S. 692, 732 (2004) ("'[F]or purposes of civil liability, the torturer has become — like the pirate and slave trader before him — *hostis humani generis*, an enemy of all mankind.'") (quoting *Filartiga v. Peña-Irala*, 630 F.2d 876, 890 (2d Cir. 1980)). Certainly the numerous international treaties and agreements, and several domestic statutes that contain varying proscriptions against torture, addressing both civil and criminal reparation, demonstrate the law of nations' repudiation of torture.

Over a century ago, the Supreme Court stated that "if the thing made punishable is one which the United States are required by their international obligations to use due diligence to prevent, it is an offense against the law of nations." *United States v. Arjona*, 120 U.S. 479, 488 (1887). In the present international community, it cannot be said that the Torture Act, legislation that criminalizes acts of torture by U.S. nationals or persons present in the United States, committed outside the United States, does not address an act made punishable by the Government's international obligations under the Convention, and which the Government is required to use due diligence to prevent. Thus, the Torture Act also finds constitutional protection as a law enacted by Congress to punish offences against the law of nations. . . .

D. Whether Sections 2340-2340A Are Unconstitutionally Vague

Defendant argues that the Torture Act, 18 U.S.C. §§2340-2340A, does not give fair warning of what is outlawed, is void for vagueness, and therefore violates the Due Process Clause of the Fifth Amendment. Specifically, Defendant maintains that the definitions of "torture" and "severe mental pain or suffering," and the various terms used in those definitions, such as "acting under the color of law," and "incidental to lawful sanction," included in the Torture Act, 18 U.S.C. §2340, do "not provide the kind of notice that will allow ordinary people to understand what conduct is prohibited." Defendant also argues that because the statute is vague, a prosecutor may use it as a tool of foreign affairs, and it may consequently authorize or encourage arbitrary and discriminatory enforcement. Defendant challenges the Torture Act as vague on its face and as applied, and as additional support for his position regarding vagueness, Defendant submits with his Reply memorandum two Justice Department memoranda which offer varying interpretations of torture as defined in the Torture Act.[8]

. . . "Vagueness may invalidate a criminal statute if it either (1) fails 'to provide the kind of notice that will enable ordinary people to understand what conduct it

---

8. An August 1, 2002 memorandum from Assistant Attorney General Jay S. Bybee to Alberto R. Gonzales, then Counsel to the President, states, for example, that "certain acts may be cruel, inhuman, or degrading, but still not produce pain and suffering of the requisite intensity to fall within Section 2340A's proscription against torture." The memorandum goes on to examine possible defenses that would negate a claim that interrogation methods violate the statute. A December 30, 2004 Justice Department memorandum "supercedes" the August 2002 memorandum "in its entirety," because the discussion contained within the latter was "unnecessary."

prohibits' or (2) authorizes or encourages 'arbitrary and discriminatory enforcement.'" *United States v. Eckhardt,* 466 F.3d 938, 944 (11th Cir. 2006) (quoting *City of Chicago v. Morales,* 527 U.S. 41, 56 (1999) (citation omitted)). . . .

The Torture Statute contains specific intent as one of its elements, as it defines "torture" to be "an act committed by a person acting under the color of law specifically intended to inflict severe physical or mental pain or suffering. . . ." The Indictment informs Defendant that he and his co-conspirators, acting under color of law and with the specific intent to inflict severe physical pain and suffering, burned the alleged victim's flesh with a hot iron, forced the alleged victim at gunpoint to hold scalding water in his hands, burned parts of the victim's body with scalding water, repeatedly shocked the genitalia and other parts of the body with an electrical device, and rubbed salt into the alleged victim's wounds. Such allegations, coupled with the statutory language contained in the Torture Statute, certainly advise the ordinary person of prohibited conduct with sufficient definiteness. The Torture Statute, enacted to fulfill the United States' treaty obligations with most of the countries of the world, certainly put the Defendant, a person born in the United States, on notice of conduct prohibited not only in this country, but in much of the civilized world. . . .

[The court also held that, because the defendant is a U.S. citizen by birth, extraterritorial application of the Torture Statute does not violate Fifth Amendment Due Process Clause rights. Nor were his Sixth Amendment speedy trial or venue rights violated because, although his alleged crimes occurred years earlier in Liberia, the indictment was only months old and he had not shown that he would be unable to mount a constitutionally adequate defense in Miami. As a result, the court denied the motion to dismiss.]

Notes and Questions

a. The Convention Against Torture

1. Interpreting the Convention Against Torture (CAT). Is the meaning of the CAT prohibition in Article 1(1) clear? Note that the ban is unconditional: "No exceptional circumstances whatsoever, whether a state of war or a threat of war, internal political instability or any other public emergency, may be invoked as a justification of torture." CAT art. 2(2). Surely the CAT drafters were aware of the so-called "ticking bomb" scenario, in which torture is justified on grounds of saving lives in a crisis. Why do you suppose the CAT did not preserve an exception for the ticking bomb?

2. Comparing the Definitions of Torture. As noted in the *Emmanuel* case, when the U.S. Senate gave its consent to the CAT in 1990, it attached a variety of reservations, declarations, and understandings. Included was an understanding about the meaning of the term "torture":

> that, in order to constitute torture, an act must be specifically intended to inflict severe physical or mental pain or suffering and that mental pain or suffering refers to prolonged mental harm caused by or resulting from (1) the intentional infliction or threatened infliction of severe physical pain or suffering; (2) the administration or application, or

threatened administration or application, of mind altering substances or other procedures calculated to disrupt profoundly the senses or the personality; (3) the threat of imminent death; or (4) the threat that another person will imminently be subjected to death, severe physical pain or suffering, or the administration or application of mind altering substances or other procedures calculated to disrupt profoundly the senses or personality. [Resolution of Advice and Consent to the Ratification of the Convention Against Torture and Other Forms of Cruel, Inhuman or Degrading Treatment or Punishment ¶II(1)(a), 136 Cong. Rec. S17491 (Oct. 27, 1990).]

Congress then implemented the CAT in part by passing the Torture Act, containing this definition of torture:

Torture Act

18 U.S.C. §2340 (2018)

As used in this chapter —

(1) "torture" means an act committed by a person acting under the color of law specifically intended to inflict severe physical or mental pain or suffering (other than pain or suffering incidental to lawful sanctions) upon another person within his custody or physical control;

(2) "severe mental pain or suffering" means the prolonged mental harm caused by or resulting from —

(A) the intentional infliction or threatened infliction of severe physical pain or suffering;

(B) the administration or application, or threatened administration or application, of mind-altering substances or other procedures calculated to disrupt profoundly the senses or the personality;

(C) the threat of imminent death; or

(D) the threat that another person will imminently be subjected to death, severe physical pain or suffering, or the administration or application of mind-altering substances or other procedures calculated to disrupt profoundly the senses or personality. . . .

As the court in *Emmanuel* noted, the statutory definition differs in some respects from the CAT. Yet in its Initial Report to the U.N. Committee against Torture in 1999 (CAT/C/28/Add.5), the United States declared: "In 1994, Congress enacted a new federal law to implement the requirements of the Convention against Torture relating to acts of torture committed outside United States territory. . . . The statute adopts the Convention's definition of torture, consistent with the terms of United States ratification." *Id.* ¶47.

How do the two authorities differ in their definitions of torture? How does the meaning of mental suffering differ? Why would the Senate, in approving the CAT, and later Congress, in passing the Torture Act, have added a specific intent requirement to the definition? If causing pain is a purposeful means to the end of obtaining desired intelligence, is there a meaningful distinction between specific intent and knowledge of the consequences?

3. The Legislative Authorities. What test does the *Emmanuel* court apply to decide whether the Torture Act passes constitutional muster under the Necessary and Proper Clause? What is the test under the Offenses Clause? Which is broader?

4. The CAT and "Cruel, Inhuman, or Degrading Treatment." Article 16 of the CAT requires that states "undertake to prevent . . . other acts of cruel, inhuman or degrading treatment or punishment which do not amount to torture." How does this requirement differ from the Convention's ban on torture?

One of the reservations attached to the CAT by the U.S. Senate provides that "the United States considers itself bound by the obligation under article 16 to prevent 'cruel, inhuman or degrading treatment or punishment,' only insofar as [that term] means the cruel, unusual and inhumane treatment or punishment prohibited by the Fifth, Eighth, and/or Fourteenth Amendments to the Constitution of the United States." Resolution of Advice and Consent *supra,* ¶I(1), 136 Cong. Rec. S17491 (Oct. 27, 1990). Why might the Senate have insisted on (and the President have supported) this reservation?

Why do you suppose that Congress failed to include criminal sanctions for cruel, inhuman, or degrading treatment (CIDT) in the Torture Act? How did this failure affect the U.S. obligation under the Torture Convention not to engage in such treatment?

b. Incorporating the Geneva Conventions

1. Geneva Conventions, Common Article 3. Common Article 3 applies to armed conflicts not of an international character and prohibits, "at any time and in any place whatsoever," with respect to non-combatants or combatants placed *hors de combat,* "[v]iolence to life and person, in particular . . . cruel treatment and torture," as well as "[o]utrages upon personal dignity, in particular, humiliating and degrading treatment." Geneva Convention Relative to the Treatment of Prisoners of War, art. 3, Aug. 12, 1949, 75 U.N.T.S. 135, 136-138. See *supra* p. 270.

2. The War Crimes Act and Grave Breaches of the Geneva Conventions. The War Crimes Act (WCA), 18 U.S.C. §2441 (2018), provides criminal sanctions for, *inter alia,* "grave breaches" of the Geneva Conventions:

War Crimes Act

18 U.S.C. §2441 (2018)

(a) Offense. — Whoever, whether inside or outside the United States, commits a war crime, in any of the circumstances described in subsection (b), shall be fined under this title or imprisoned for life or any term of years, or both, and if death results to the victim, shall also be subject to the penalty of death.

(b) Circumstances. — The circumstances referred to in subsection (a) are that the person committing such war crime or the victim of such war crime is a member of the Armed Forces of the United States or a national of the United States. . . .

> (c) Definition. — As used in this section the term "war crime" means any conduct —
>
> (1) defined as a grave breach in any of the international conventions signed at Geneva 12 August 1949, or any protocol to such convention to which the United States is a party . . . [or]
>
> (3) which constitutes a grave breach of common Article 3 . . . when committed in the context of and in association with an armed conflict not of an international character. . . .
>
> (d) Common Article 3 violations.
>
> (1) . . . [T]he term "grave breach of common Article 3" [includes torture, cruel or inhuman treatment, performing biological experiments, murder, mutilation or maiming, intentionally causing serious bodily injury, rape, sexual assault or abuse, and taking hostages]. . . .

Common Article 3 does not expressly condemn grave breaches. Article 130 of Geneva Convention III on POWs defines a grave breach as

> willful killing, torture or inhuman treatment, including biological experiments, willfully causing great suffering or serious injury to body or health, compelling a prisoner of war to serve in the forces of the hostile Power, or willfully depriving a prisoner of war of the rights of fair and regular trial prescribed in this Convention.

Applying the language of the Geneva Conventions, as incorporated through the WCA, what threshold determinations must be made to establish criminal liability, and by whom?

a. *What Conduct Is Covered?* If not just "torture," however defined, but also "cruel treatment, . . . [and] outrages upon personal dignity, in particular humiliating and degrading treatment" are grave breaches under the Geneva Conventions, does it make sense to engage in hairsplitting definitional debates about permissible interrogation? What interrogation techniques would be proscribed by these rules? *See* Jennifer K. Elsea, *Lawfulness of Interrogation Techniques Under the Geneva Conventions* 23-35 (Cong. Res. Serv. RL32567), Sept. 8, 2004.

b. *Are the Conventions Judicially Enforceable?* In *Hamdan v. Rumsfeld*, 548 U.S. 557 (2006), the Supreme Court held that Common Article 3 is applicable to the non-international armed conflict between the United States and Al Qaeda. Even though its protections in such a conflict fall "short of full protection under the Conventions," the Court ruled that Hamdan had to be tried by a " 'regularly constituted court affording all the judicial guarantees which are recognized as indispensable by civilized peoples.' " *Id.* at 630 (quoting Common Article 3(1)(d)). Does it follow that the rest of Common Article 3 applies as well?

3. The International Covenant on Civil and Political Rights (ICCPR). The ICCPR, like the CAT, forbids torture and cruel, inhuman, and degrading conduct, and was approved as a treaty by the Senate. The ICCPR is non-self-executing, and lower federal courts have found that the ICCPR creates no privately enforceable rights in U.S. courts. *See, e.g., Buell v. Mitchell*, 274 F.3d 337 (6th Cir. 2001). However, some courts cite the ICCPR as evidence that customary international law prohibits arbitrary arrest, prolonged detention, and torture. *See* Elsea, *supra*, at 12-13 (noting that the United States "has not officially proclaimed an emergency or named measures that would derogate from the ICCPR").

4. The Role of Customary International Law and Jus Cogens. The substantive content of customary international law on the subject of torture is embodied in the CAT and ICCPR, among other instruments. As noted above, the United States has recognized Article 75 of Additional Protocol I to the Geneva Conventions as customary international law. It forbids "torture of all kinds, whether physical or mental," as well as "outrages upon personal dignity, in particular humiliating and degrading treatment, . . . any form of indecent assault, . . . and threats to commit any of the foregoing acts." Additional Protocol I, art. 75(2). Technically, Protocol I applies only to conflicts of an international character. But as customary law, does Article 75 set a baseline for *all* "persons who are in the power of a Party"?

The torture prohibition is also part of *jus cogens* and is so recognized by U.S. courts. *See Restatement (Third) of Foreign Relations Law of the United States* §702 (1986). It remains unclear, however, whether the prohibition against cruel, inhuman, or degrading treatment is also part of *jus cogens*.

c. Domestic Law on Torture

1. A Domestic Baseline: How We Treat Our Own? The U.S. reservation to Article 16 of the CAT limits "cruel, inhuman or degrading conduct" to that which violates that Fifth, Eighth, and/or Fourteenth Amendments. What is the content of those constitutional protections? It was not until 1936 that the Supreme Court barred the use in a state criminal trial of a confession obtained by brutally beating a suspect. In *Brown v. Mississippi*, 297 U.S. 278 (1936), the confessions were thrown out on the grounds that interrogation is part of the state machinery for obtaining convictions and is thus subject to the requirements of the Due Process Clause. In *Rogers v. Richmond*, 365 U.S. 534 (1961), the Court extended the Due Process Clause ban to abusive police conduct even where the reliability of a confession was not at issue.

In *Chavez v. Martinez*, 538 U.S. 760 (2003), a badly fractured Supreme Court ruled on claims of liability asserted by a plaintiff who had been subjected to persistent police questioning while he was in the hospital incapacitated by extreme pain. Five Justices voted to remand the question of whether the plaintiff could pursue a claim for violation of his substantive due process rights, but the Court could not agree about the scope and applicability of those rights or the related right against self-incrimination.

Chief Justice Rehnquist and Justice Scalia joined part of an opinion by Justice Thomas asserting that the interrogation was not egregious or conscience-shocking enough to violate the plaintiff's substantive due process rights. They reasoned that "freedom from unwanted police questioning is [not] a right so fundamental that it cannot be abridged absent a 'compelling state interest.'" *Id.* at 776 (plurality opinion). For them, it was enough that the questioning was justified by *some* government interest — here, the need to preserve critical evidence concerning a shooting by a police officer — and that it was not "conduct intended to injure in some way unjustifiable by any government interest." *Id.* at 775. Justice Stevens concluded that "the interrogation of respondent was the functional equivalent of an attempt to obtain an involuntary confession from a prisoner by torturous methods," which is "a classic example of a violation of a constitutional right 'implicit in the concept of ordered liberty.'" *Id.* at 788 (Stevens, J., concurring in part and dissenting in part).

Justice Kennedy (joined on this point by Justices Stevens and Ginsburg) agreed that the use of investigatory torture violates a person's fundamental right to liberty but noted that interrogating suspects who are in pain or anguish is not necessarily torture when the police have "legitimate reasons, borne of exigency... [such as] [l]ocating the victim of a kidnapping, ascertaining the whereabouts of a dangerous assailant or accomplice, or determining whether there is a rogue police officer at large." *Id.* at 796 (Kennedy, J., concurring in part and dissenting in part). On the other hand, he added, the police may not prolong or increase the suspect's suffering or threaten to do so to elicit a statement. *Id.* at 797. The test for a constitutional violation, in Justice Kennedy's view, was whether the police "exploited" the suspect's pain to secure his statement. *Id.* He found that they had done so in *Chavez*.

Under any of the tests in *Chavez*, would torture in the United States of a suspected terrorist to obtain information about a possibly imminent terrorist attack violate substantive due process? How about practices such as hooding and sleep deprivation? Do military or civilian investigators in the war on terrorism have broader authority than the police do to use coercive interrogation techniques because of their different goals in an interrogation?

The Eighth Amendment ban on "cruel and unusual punishment" applies to persons detained after a finding of guilt. *See Ingraham v. Wright*, 430 U.S. 651, 671 n.40 (1977) ("[T]he State does not acquire the power to punish with which the Eighth Amendment is concerned until after it has secured a formal adjudication of guilt in accordance with due process of law."). Is it therefore irrelevant to detainees in the war on terror who have not yet been tried? More fundamentally, if the U.S. position is that torture is to be defined by reference to the Bill of Rights, what about cases, such as the detention of noncitizens overseas, where the Bill of Rights might not apply?

2. A Congressional Prohibition. In 2005, over the strenuous objection of the Bush administration, Congress enacted the Detainee Treatment Act, which provides in part:

Detainee Treatment Act

Pub. L. No. 109-148, §§1001-1006, 119 Stat. 2680, 2739-2744 (2005)
(codified in part at 42 U.S.C. §2000dd (2018))

§2000dd. Prohibition on cruel, inhuman, or degrading treatment or punishment of persons under custody or control of the United States Government

(a) In General. — No individual in the custody or under the physical control of the United States Government, regardless of nationality or physical location, shall be subject to cruel, inhuman, or degrading treatment or punishment.

(b) Construction. — Nothing in this section shall be construed to impose any geographical limitation on the applicability of the prohibition against cruel, inhuman, or degrading treatment or punishment under this section.

(c) Limitation on Supersedure. — The provisions of this section shall not be superseded, except by a provision of law enacted after the date of the enactment of this Act which specifically repeals, modifies, or supersedes the provisions of this section.

(d) Cruel, Inhuman, or Degrading Treatment or Punishment Defined. — In this section, the term "cruel, inhuman, or degrading treatment or punishment" means the cruel, unusual, and inhumane treatment or punishment prohibited by the Fifth, Eighth, and Fourteenth Amendments to the Constitution of the United States, as defined in the United States Reservations, Declarations and Understandings to the United Nations Convention Against Torture and Other Forms of Cruel, Inhuman or Degrading Treatment or Punishment done at New York, December 10, 1984.

The language of the Detainee Treatment Act also appears in Pub. L. No. 109-163, §§1401-1406, 119 Stat. 3136, 3474-3480 (2006).

Does the phrase "regardless of nationality or physical location" really make the location of the interrogation immaterial, when "cruel, inhuman, or degrading treatment" is defined just as conduct prohibited by the Fifth, Eighth, and Fourteenth Amendments? Does it apply to extraterritorial interrogations of persons who are not U.S. citizens or permanent resident aliens? Or does the Act prohibit subjecting anyone to any conduct abroad that would be unconstitutional if it occurred in the United States?

If the meaning of the constitutional protections changes over time, the treatment forbidden by the Act presumably will change as well.

3. The Army Field Manual. The Detainee Treatment Act also forbids exposure of persons in the custody or under the effective control of the Department of Defense (DOD) to any interrogation techniques not listed in the U.S. Army's field manual, *Human Intelligence Collector Operations* (FM 2-22.3) (Sept. 6, 2006). *See* DTA §1002(a), 119 Stat. at 2739; Pub. L. No. 109-163, §1402(a), 119 Stat. at 3475. The manual states that "[a]cts of violence or intimidation, including physical or mental torture, or exposure to inhumane treatment as a means of or aid to interrogation are expressly prohibited." FM 2-22.3, at 5-26. It also asserts that the use of torture "is a poor technique that yields unreliable results, may damage subsequent collection efforts, and can induce the source to say what he thinks the HUMINT collector wants to hear." *Id.* at 5-21. What is the legal significance of limiting DOD interrogators to techniques in an Army field manual?

In 2015 Congress enacted the McCain-Feinstein Amendment as part of the National Defense Authorization Act for Fiscal Year 2016, Pub. L. No. 114-92, 129 Stat. 726 (2015), which likewise limits U.S. interrogations to methods that are listed in Army Field Manual 2-22.3. However, the McCain-Feinstein Amendment applies to any "officer, employee, or agent of the United States government" (outside of the law enforcement context), and limits the interrogation methods that can be deployed against any individual "detained within a facility owned, operated, or controlled by a department or agency of the United States in any armed conflict." §1045(a)(2)(B), 129 Stat. at 977. The McCain-Feinstein Amendment further provides that the Manual may be revised "[n]ot sooner than three years after the date of enactment of this Act, and once every three years thereafter." §1045(a)(6)(A), 129 Stat. at 978. Can you see why Congress favored this broader set of limits on interrogation — enumerating the *permissible* interrogation methods rather than imposing rights-based limits on unenumerated methods?

4. The Military Commissions Act (MCA). The Military Commissions Act of 2006 (MCA), Pub. L. No. 109-366, §6, 120 Stat. 2600, which was otherwise focused on the Guantánamo military commissions, also amended the War Crimes Act, *supra*, which punishes in civilian court, *inter alia*, some violations of the Geneva Conventions. As to Common Article 3, it narrowed the offense from "a violation" to "a grave breach." It also added an exclusive list of grave breaches that defines "torture" as "an act specifically intended to inflict severe physical or mental pain or suffering," and "cruel or inhuman treatment" as "an act intended to inflict severe or serious physical or mental pain or suffering." It then defined "severe physical pain or suffering" to mean "bodily injury that involves — (i) a substantial risk of death; (ii) extreme physical pain; (iii) a burn or physical disfigurement of a serious nature (other than cuts, abrasions, or bruises); or (iv) significant loss or impairment of the function of a bodily member, organ, or mental faculty." The 2006 measure went on to authorize the President to interpret the meaning and application of the Geneva Conventions, while at the same time declaring that the War Crimes Act, as amended, satisfies the U.S. obligations under the Geneva Convention to punish grave breaches encompassed in Common Article 3 in an armed conflict not of an international character.

The MCA did not criminalize degrading treatment. Nor did it specifically prohibit techniques such as waterboarding. The added flexibility afforded by the MCA permitted President Bush to issue an executive order restoring discretion for CIA personnel to undertake "enhanced" interrogation techniques, without fear of prosecution under the War Crimes Act.

Do you think the definition of torture in the amended War Crimes Act satisfies U.S. obligations under either the Geneva Conventions or the Convention Against Torture? Does it hold U.S. government personnel to the same standard as the one applied to the defendant in the *Emmanuel* case?

5. Other Criminal Sanctions. The Uniform Code of Military Justice (UCMJ) provides for courts-martial to prosecute torture or inhumane acts committed within or outside the United States by members of the military and certain accompanying civilians. 10 U.S.C. §805 (UCMJ applies worldwide); *id.* §802 (to any servicemember); *id.* §802(a)(10) (to certain accompanying civilians); *id.* §818 (for an offense against the laws of war); *id.* §855 (torture or cruel or unusual punishment); *id.* §934 ("disorders and neglects to the prejudice of good order and discipline in the armed forces"). The Torture Act criminalizes torture outside the United States. Why do you suppose Congress has not enacted a general criminal statute specifically outlawing torture *within* the United States?

6. Criminal and Civil Defenses to Torture Actions. One part of the Detainee Treatment Act provides a legal defense for U.S. personnel in any criminal or civil action brought against them based on their involvement in an authorized interrogation of suspected foreign terrorists. The defense exists when the U.S. interrogator "did not know that the [interrogation] practices were unlawful and a person of ordinary sense and understanding would not know the practices were unlawful." DTA §1004(a), 119 Stat. at 2740; Pub. L. No. 109-163, §1404, 119 Stat. at 3475-3476. A good faith reliance on the advice of counsel may be "an important factor" in measuring the accused's culpability. *Id.* Does the codification of this defense *support* the availability of damages for detainees subjected to unlawful treatment while in U.S. custody?

7. *Civil Sanctions.* The Foreign Claims Act (FCA), 10 U.S.C. §2734(a) (2018), permits recovery of up to $100,000 from the United States for a claim brought by a resident of a foreign country where the injury occurred outside the United States "and is caused by, or is otherwise incident to [the] noncombat activities of" the U.S. military. "Noncombat activity" is defined to include any "activity, other than combat, war or armed conflict, that is particularly military in character and has little parallel in the civilian community." 32 C.F.R. §842.41(c) (2014). Under the FCA, claims commissions, consisting of commissioned military officers, are established for each service branch and are in place wherever the military has a significant presence. However, experience with the FCA in Iraq and Afghanistan suggests that complex procedures and stringent policies have prevented most injured Afghans and Iraqis from obtaining compensation for their injuries. Scott Borrowman, *Sosa v. Alvarez-Machain and Abu Ghraib — Civil Remedies for Victims of Extraterritorial Torts by U.S. Military Personnel and Civilian Contractors*, 2005 BYU L. Rev. 371, 376.

The Alien Tort Claims Act (ATCA), 28 U.S.C. §1350 (2018), confers jurisdiction on federal district courts over tort suits by aliens where a violation of the law of nations or a treaty of the United States is alleged. In *Sosa v. Alvarez-Machain*, 542 U.S. 692 (2004), *supra* p. 149, the Supreme Court rejected the ATCA as a basis for jurisdiction in the federal courts over a tort claim related to the abduction of one Mexican national by another who acted with the approval of the Drug Enforcement Administration (DEA). The Court agreed with the plaintiff that the ATCA was intended to create jurisdiction to hear suits based on current international norms, but only those whose "content and acceptance among civilized nations" is no less definite than the small number of "historical paradigms" familiar when the statute was passed in 1789. *Id.* at 718. In the course of its opinion, however, the Court cited with evident approval the decision in *Filartiga v. Peña-Irala*, 630 F.2d 876 (2d Cir. 1980), which applied the ATCA in a torture case.

The Torture Victim Protection Act (TVPA), Pub. L. No. 102-256, 106 Stat. 73 (1992) (codified at 28 U.S.C. §1350 note (2018)), provides a civil remedy in the federal courts for individuals, including U.S. persons, who have been victims of torture or extrajudicial killing. The TVPA thus may offer relief for U.S. persons that would be unavailable under the ATCA. However, the TVPA only provides a cause of action for torture or extrajudicial killing "under color of law, of any *foreign* nation." *Id.* §2a (emphasis added). Do you think that the TVPA would support an action for improper removal by U.S. officials of an individual who might be subjected to torture abroad? Would it apply where U.S. officials allegedly direct foreign officials to carry out acts of torture against a non-U.S. citizen? *See Arar v. Ashcroft*, 585 F.3d 559 (2d Cir. 2009) (en banc) (no).

INTERROGATING TERRORIST SUSPECTS: SUMMARY OF BASIC PRINCIPLES

- The prohibition against torture is *jus cogens*, a universal norm based upon values held fundamental by the international community. Notwithstanding the universality of the prohibition, there is continuing debate about what conduct qualifies as torture and about its effectiveness, and as well as its morality in a ticking bomb scenario.

- The Convention Against Torture (CAT) can be viewed simply as the codification of *jus cogens* — what the law would be without the Convention. The United States has ratified the CAT with the understanding that it is not self-executing, and with the reservation that its prohibition of "cruel, inhuman or degrading treatment or punishment" means conduct prohibited by the Fifth, Eighth, and/or Fourteenth Amendments.

- The Torture Act, 18 U.S.C. §2340A, implements the CAT by adding a specific intent requirement and a definition of "severe mental pain and suffering," but it omits criminal penalties for cruel, inhuman, and degrading treatment.

- Common Article 3 of the Geneva Conventions forbids torture and humiliating and degrading treatment in armed conflicts not of an international character, and it defines torture and inhuman treatment as a grave breach of the Conventions. The U.S. Supreme Court has held that it applies to the post-9/11 conflict in Afghanistan. The War Crimes Act, 18 U.S.C. §2441, criminalizes grave breaches of the Geneva Conventions committed by or against members of the U.S. armed forces or U.S. nationals.

- The Detainee Treatment Act prohibits subjecting persons under the custody or control of the United States to cruel, inhuman, or degrading treatment or punishment, but (like the U.S. reservation to the CAT) defines such treatment as treatment or punishment prohibited by the Fifth, Eighth, and/or Fourteenth Amendments. It also forbids subjecting a person in custody or control of the Department of Defense to any interrogation techniques not listed in the *Army Field Manual*, which in turn prohibits any inhumane treatment.

- The 2015 McCain-Feinstein Amendment broadly limits interrogation during an armed conflict by any employee or agent of the United States of persons detained in any U.S. facility to the techniques listed in the Army Field Manual.

- Neither the U.S. reservation to the CAT nor the Detainee Treatment Act indicates whether the reference to the Fifth, Eighth, and/or Fourteenth Amendments is based on the application of those amendments domestically or abroad, or to U.S. or non-U.S. persons.

- The Torture Victim Protection Act provides a civil remedy for individuals who are tortured by persons acting "under actual or apparent authority, or color of law, of any foreign nation."

33

Case Study of Coercive Interrogation of Detainees in U.S. Custody After 9/11

As early as December 2002, U.S. military and civilian interrogators are reported to have abused individuals captured and detained in the war on terrorism by beating them and subjecting them to prolonged sleep and sensory deprivation, as well as to sexual humiliation. The abuse began in Afghanistan, then spread to Guantánamo Bay, Cuba, and other offshore U.S. interrogation centers, and later to Iraq.

In this chapter, we briefly review U.S. interrogation practices after 9/11, then apply laws reviewed in the preceding chapter to those practices.

A. THE EVOLVING HISTORY OF U.S. INTERROGATION OF SUSPECTED TERRORISTS[1]

Beginning with the capture in Afghanistan of senior Al Qaeda operatives, the Bush administration had to determine how best to extract intelligence information from individuals detained by U.S. forces. "Setting" the methods and parameters of interrogation thus became an integral part of counterterrorism planning. Should Al

1. Several collections of documents relating to U.S. interrogation of its detainees may be found online. Among the most extensive are N.Y. Times, *A Guide to the Memos on Torture* (n.d.), *at* http://www.nytimes.com/ref/international/24MEMO-GUIDE.html; Nat'l Security Archive, *Torturing Democracy* (2008), *available at* http://www.gwu.edu/~nsarchiv/torturingdemocracy/timelines/index2.html. Regarding CIA interrogation specifically, see S. Select Comm. on Intelligence, *Committee Study of the Central Intelligence Agency's Detention and Interrogation Program* (SSCI Study) (Dec. 13, 2012) (released in part on Dec. 3, 2014), *available at* http://www.intelligence.senate.gov/press/committee-releases-study-cias-detention-and-interrogation-program. The Department of Defense website also provides links to DOD reports, independent panel and inspector general reports, briefing transcripts, and news releases and articles. http://www.defense.gov/news. Many of the key documents are collected in Mark Danner, *Torture and Truth: America, Abu Ghraib, and the War on Terror* (2004); and *The Torture Papers, The Road to Abu Ghraib* (Karen J. Greenberg & Joshua L. Dratel eds., 2005).

Qaeda figures be questioned by the FBI, using traditional methods? By military interrogators, following service branch rules? By the CIA, perhaps using harsher techniques in secret locations?

Answering these questions became intensely political and legally contentious inside the Bush administration. Although FBI interrogators were involved on occasion, most interrogations were conducted by military and CIA personnel and their contractors. At times, the two sets of interrogators operated separately, at other times they were co-located, and military personnel often had responsibility for capturing and holding the suspects who were later subjected to CIA interrogation. As a result, the two intelligence-gathering efforts tended to overlap if not merge.

While the Administration's early legal guidance on interrogation was prepared for the CIA, the Department of Defense later relied on some of the analysis in those memoranda to develop guidance for its own military interrogators. When abusive interrogations by U.S. officials began to be revealed, Congress adopted reforms that covered the military, but apparently not the CIA until much later.

The Bush administration decided early on to create a new detention facility at the U.S. Navy base at Guantánamo Bay to hold at least some of the individuals captured on the battlefields in Afghanistan (and elsewhere). The first detainees taken there in January 2002 were designated "unlawful combatants" by President Bush.

Earlier still, on September 17, 2001, President Bush reportedly signed a still-secret memorandum that apparently was interpreted as directing the CIA to detain and interrogate certain "high value" terrorism suspects. Because of statutory authorities that enable the CIA to operate in secret, the Administration may have believed it could hold detainees in secret prisons where no one would know who was being held or what the CIA was doing to them in detention. Yet so far as is publicly known, the memorandum did not provide additional guidance on detention or interrogation. And because the CIA had little interrogation experience, the Agency sought guidance from decades-old manuals to reverse-engineer a "survive, evade, resist, escape" (SERE) program used in training U.S. service personnel to withstand the effects of enemy torture.[2]

In early 2002, senior Al Qaeda operative Abu Zubaydah was captured in a firefight in Pakistan and flown to a secret CIA facility in Thailand. After the Federal Bureau of Investigation (FBI) interrogated Zubaydah in a non-coercive manner and learned that Khalid Sheikh Mohammed (KSM) was the apparent mastermind of the September 11 attacks, Zubaydah began to resist interrogation. The CIA then took over the interrogation and subjected Zubaydah to waterboarding, reportedly ending his resistance. Eventually, Zubaydah was moved to another CIA site in Poland, and then to Guantánamo.[3] KSM was captured in March 2003 in Pakistan, then transported to Afghanistan and subsequently to the CIA site in Poland, where he was waterboarded and otherwise subjected to harsh interrogation techniques (he, too, was subsequently transferred to Guantánamo).[4] The CIA Inspector General later

---

2. Scott Shane, David Johnston & James Risen, *Secret U.S. Endorsement of Severe Interrogations,* N.Y. Times, Oct. 4, 2007.

3. David Johnston, *At a Secret Interrogation, Dispute Flared over Tactics,* N.Y. Times, Sept. 10, 2006; Scott Shane, *Inside a 9/11 Mastermind's Interrogation,* N.Y. Times, June 22, 2008.

4. Jane Mayer, *The Dark Side: The Inside Story of How the War on Terror Turned into a War on American Ideals* 270-274 (2008).

found that the CIA waterboarded Zubaydah 83 times in August 2002, and employed the same technique with KSM 183 times in March 2003.[5]

President Bush announced in a February 7, 2002 order, *Humane Treatment of Al Qaeda and Taliban Detainees*,[6] that the United States would voluntarily extend the protections of the Third Geneva Convention to captured Taliban fighters, although such fighters were not regarded as lawful combatants entitled to prisoner-of-war (POW) status. Captured members of Al Qaeda would be treated "humanely," even though the Geneva Conventions were said not to apply to Al Qaeda members at all. This followed advice in a January 9, 2002, memorandum from the Justice Department's Office of Legal Counsel (OLC) to the Defense Department, *Application of Treaties and Laws to Al Qaeda and Taliban Detainees*,[7] written by John Yoo and Robert Delahunty, concluding that the President had constitutional authority to suspend application of the Geneva Conventions in Afghanistan, or to decide that the Conventions did not apply to captured Al Qaeda and Taliban detainees. The "humane treatment" order applied only to the armed forces, moreover, not the CIA, which presumably was free to continue utilizing more aggressive interrogation techniques.

In the summer of 2002, the Justice Department was asked to advise what interrogation techniques would violate U.S. or international law. In August, the OLC opined that

> for an act to constitute torture as defined in [the Torture Act], it must inflict pain that is difficult to endure. Physical pain amounting to torture must be equivalent in intensity to the pain accompanying serious physical injury, such as organ failure, impairment of bodily function, or even death. For purely mental pain or suffering to amount to torture . . . it must result in significant psychological harm of significant duration, e.g., lasting for months or even years. We conclude that the mental harm also must result from one of the predicate acts listed in the statute, namely: threats of imminent death; threats of the infliction of the kind of pain that would amount to physical torture; infliction of such physical pain as a means of psychological torture; use of drugs or other procedures designed to deeply disrupt the senses, or fundamentally alter an individual's personality; or threatening to do any of these things to a third party.[8]

The memorandum suggested that a one-time kick to a prisoner's stomach with military boots while forcing him into a kneeling position would not amount to "torture" that would be subject to prosecution. The OLC memorandum even concluded that torture might be justified in some circumstances, and that the statutory prohibition on torture would not apply to actions taken by the President as Commander in Chief. *Id.* at 33-39.

---

5. *See* Office of Inspector Gen., Cent. Intelligence Agency, *Special Review: Counterterrorism Detention and Interrogation Activities (September 2001-October 2003)*, at 12-23, 44-45 (May 7, 2004), *available at* https://fas.org/irp/cia/product/ig-interrog.pdf.

6. *Reprinted in The Torture Papers: The Road to Abu Ghraib* 134 (Karen J. Greenberg & Joshua L. Dratel eds., 2005).

7. *Reprinted in id.* at 38.

8. Office of Legal Counsel, U.S. Dep't of Justice, *Memorandum for Alberto R. Gonzales, Counsel to the President, Re: Standards of Conduct for Interrogation Under 18 U.S.C. §§2340-2340A*, at 1 (Aug. 1, 2002) (commonly referred to as the Bybee Memo, for Ass't Att'y Gen. Jay S. Bybee, who signed it, although it is generally believed to have been written by John Yoo), *available at* http://nsarchive.gwu.edu/NSAEBB/NSAEBB127/02.08.01.pdf.

By the summer of 2002, there were about 600 detainees at Guantánamo. Military interrogators there knew from the President's order that the Geneva Convention POW protections did not apply, and that detainees should be treated "humanely," but they had no clear guidance on the limits of their interrogations other than the statutes reviewed in Chapter 32.

After the United States and its allies invaded Iraq in March 2003, there reportedly was widespread confusion about permissible techniques for interrogating prisoners there. The Geneva Conventions clearly applied in Iraq to captured Iraqis (since, at least at first, the war was an international armed conflict), but the detention facilities also included members of Al Qaeda and other foreign fighters whose status was unclear based on Administration determinations concerning those held at Guantánamo. A March 14, 2003, OLC opinion written by John Yoo, *Military Interrogation of Alien Unlawful Combatants Held Outside the United States,*[9] contained extensive analysis of supposed broad authorities of the President to make rules for interrogation that fail to comply with either the CAT or the Geneva Conventions. The opinion also suggested defenses that the President would have available if any executive official were charged with abusive interrogation. The opinion failed, however, to take into account application of the Uniform Code of Military Justice (UCMJ) or the Army field manual on interrogation.

The U.S. military command authority initially ordered that rules set out in another Army field manual, *Intelligence Interrogation* (FM 34-52) (Sept. 28, 1992), be followed in Iraq. In August 2003, however, Defense Secretary Rumsfeld sent the military overseer of interrogation at Guantánamo — Major General Geoffrey Miller — to Iraq to "rapidly exploit internees for actionable intelligence."[10] General Miller brought with him the techniques approved by Secretary Rumsfeld for Guantánamo, some of which exceeded the limits of the Army field manuals, although he noted that the Geneva Conventions were supposed to apply in Iraq. In September, the military commander in Iraq approved a policy on interrogation that included portions of the Guantánamo policy and elements of policies then used by special forces.[11] Central Command disapproved the September policy, however, and in October approved rules that mirrored an outdated version of FM 34-52, which permitted interrogators to control "lighting and heating, as well as food, clothing, and shelter given to detainees."[12] The policy on interrogation in Iraq changed again later in October, the third amendment in less than 30 days.[13]

---

9. *Available at* http://www.justice.gov/olc/docs/memo-combatantsoutsideunitedstates.pdf.

10. General Antonio M. Taguba, *Article 15-6 Investigation of the 800th Military Police Brigade* 7 (hereinafter *Taguba Report*) (Jan. 31, 2004), *available at* http://hrlibrary.umn.edu/OathBetrayed/Taguba-Report.pdf.

11. Subsequent investigators described a migration to Iraq of Guantánamo techniques — such as the use of dogs and forced nudity — to intimidate and dehumanize detainees. *See Final Report of the Independent Panel to Review DoD Detention Operations* 36 (Aug. 24, 2004) (hereinafter *Schlesinger Report*), *available at* http://pdf.prisonexp.org/SchlesingerReport.pdf; Maj. Gen. George R. Fay, *AR 15-6 Investigation of the Abu Ghraib Prison and 205th Military Intelligence Brigade* 10 (Aug. 25, 2004) (hereinafter *Fay Report*), *available at* http://www.washingtonpost.com/wp-srv/nationi/documents/fay_report_8-25-04.pdf.

12. *Schlesinger Report, supra* note 11, at 37-38, ch. 3.

13. *Fay Report, supra* note 11, at 28.

In January 2004, following public reports of detainee abuse, Lieutenant General Ricardo S. Sanchez, Commander of Combined Joint Task Force Seven in Iraq, requested an investigation of the operations of the 800th Military Police Brigade, the unit in charge of Abu Ghraib prison near Baghdad. Major General Antonio M. Taguba, who was appointed to conduct the investigation, found "numerous incidents of sadistic, blatant, wanton criminal abuses" at the prison, "intentionally perpetrated by several members of the military police guard force." The abuses included "punching, slapping, and kicking detainees," a litany of sexual and vulgar insults and attacks, and threats with loaded weapons.[14] In February 2004, the International Committee of the Red Cross (ICRC) issued a report detailing a number of serious human rights abuses by coalition forces in Iraq between March and November 2003.[15] A March 2004 classified report by the CIA inspector general concluded that some of the interrogation techniques approved for CIA use by the Department of Justice in 2002 might violate the prohibition on "cruel, inhuman, or degrading" treatment in the Convention Against Torture.[16] Finally, in May 2004, public attention focused on Abu Ghraib after graphic photos of prisoner abuse were exposed by the media.[17]

In June 2004, the OLC memos were leaked. Two months after the public disclosure of abuses at Abu Ghraib, the August 2002 Bybee Memo was withdrawn by new OLC head Jack Goldsmith because he thought it was "sloppily reasoned, overbroad, and incautious in asserting extraordinary constitutional authorities on behalf of the President."[18] A new opinion superseding the Bybee Memo was delivered on December 30, 2004.[19] The new memorandum questioned "the appropriateness and relevance of the non-statutory discussion . . . and various aspects of the statutory analysis" in the earlier memo — namely, the assertion that torture required organ failure, impaired bodily function, or death.[20] However, the new memorandum did not disagree with any substantive conclusions offered by the 2002 memorandum. Moreover, it continued to maintain that it was unlikely that a person who "acted in good faith, and only after reasonable investigation establishing that his conduct would not inflict

---

14. *Taguba Report, supra* note 10.

15. *Report of the International Committee of the Red Cross (ICRC) on the Treatment by the Coalition Forces of Prisoners of War and Other Protected Persons by the Geneva Conventions in Iraq during Arrest, Internment and Interrogation* (Feb. 2004), *available at* http://www.derechos.org/nizkor/us/doc/icrc-prisoner-report-feb-2004.pdf.

16. Douglas Jehl, *Report Warned on CIA's Tactics in Interrogation*, N.Y. Times, Nov. 9, 2005.

17. The Abu Ghraib photos are collected at http://www.salon.com/2006/03/14/introduction_2/. In November 2009, Secretary of Defense Robert Gates blocked the release of 2,000 additional photos depicting detainee abuse in Iraq and Afghanistan. Gates acted on the basis of authority granted in the Protected National Security Documents Act of 2009, Pub. L. No. 111-83, §565, 123 Stat. 2142, 2184 (codified at 5 U.S.C. §552 note (2018)), which Congress enacted in response to the Second Circuit's decision in *ACLU v. Dep't of Defense*, 543 F.3d 59 (2d Cir. 2008), *vacated*, 558 U.S. 1042 (2009) (mem.). *Gates Blocks Detainee Abuse Photos*, CBS News, Nov. 14, 2009, *at* http://www.cbc.ca/news/world/story/2009/11/14/prisoner-abuse-photos014.html.

18. Jack Goldsmith, *The Terror Presidency* 10 (2007).

19. Memorandum for James B. Comey, Deputy Att'y Gen., from Daniel Levin, Acting Ass't Att'y Gen., *Legal Standards Applicable Under 18 U.S.C. 2340-2340A*, (Dec. 30, 2004), *at* http://www.thetorturedatabase.org/document/olc-memo-legal-standards-applicable-under-18-usc-§§-2340-2340a.

20. *Id.* at 1-2.

severe physical or mental pain or suffering," would possess the specific intent required to violate the torture statute.[21]

A February 2006 United Nations report on the Guantánamo Bay detentions, compiled by U.N. envoys who interviewed former detainees, their families, and their lawyers, along with U.S. officials, concluded that U.S. treatment of detainees there violated the detainees' rights to physical and mental health and, in some cases, constituted torture. U.N. Comm'n on Human Rights, *Situation of Detainees at Guantanamo Bay* (Feb. 17, 2006), *available at* http://www.refworld.org/docid/45377b0b0.html. The United States replied to the U.N. report with a factual and legal defense, *Reply of the Government of the United States of America to the Report of the Five UNCHR Special Rapporteurs on Detainees in Guantanamo Bay, Cuba* (Mar. 10, 2006), *available at* http://www.state.gov/documents/organization/98969.pdf.

B. APPLYING THE INTERROGATION LAWS

On April 16, 2009, President Obama authorized the release of four previously undisclosed OLC memos describing interrogation techniques used by the CIA between 2002 and 2005. One, signed by Jay S. Bybee in 2002, purported to give the CIA legal approval for waterboarding and other harsh treatment, including forced nudity, slamming detainees into walls, and prolonged sleep deprivation. Three others, signed by Stephen G. Bradbury in May 2005, also concluded that the harsh techniques were lawful, even when multiple methods were used in combination. The memos are available at http://www.fas.org/irp/agency/doj/olc/index.html.

More than five years later, the Senate Select Committee on Intelligence (SSCI) released a 500-page Executive Summary of its much anticipated 6,700-page study of the CIA's detention and interrogation activities after 9/11. The following excerpts provide the Findings and Conclusions of the SSCI.

Senate Select Committee on Intelligence, Committee Study of the Central Intelligence Agency's Detention and Interrogation Program (SSCI Study)

S. Rep. No. 113-288 (2012) (released in part on Dec. 3, 2014)
https://www.intelligence.senate.gov/sites/default/files/publications/CRPT-113srpt288.pdf

(U) The Committee's Study is the most comprehensive review ever conducted of the CIA's Detention and Interrogation Program. The CIA has informed the Committee that it has provided the Committee with all CIA records related to the CIA's Detention and Interrogation Program. The document production phase lasted more than three years, produced more than six million pages of material, and was completed in July 2012. The Committee Study is based primarily on a review of these documents, which include CIA operational cables, reports, memoranda, intelligence products, and numerous interviews conducted of CIA personnel by various entities

---

21. *Id.* at 17.

within the CIA, in particular the CIA's Office of Inspector General and the CIA's Oral History Program, as well as internal email and other communications....

FINDINGS AND CONCLUSIONS

#1: The CIA's use of its enhanced interrogation techniques was not an effective means of acquiring intelligence or gaining cooperation from detainees.

The Committee finds, based on a review of CIA interrogation records, that the use of the CIA's enhanced interrogation techniques was not an effective means of obtaining accurate information or gaining detainee cooperation.

For example, according to CIA records, seven of the 39 CIA detainees known to have been subjected to the CIA's enhanced interrogation techniques produced no intelligence while in CIA custody.... Other detainees provided significant accurate intelligence prior to, or without having been subjected to these techniques.

While being subjected to the CIA's enhanced interrogation techniques and afterwards, multiple CIA detainees fabricated information, resulting in faulty intelligence. Detainees provided fabricated information on critical intelligence issues, including the terrorist threats which the CIA identified as its highest priorities....

#2: The CIA's justification for the use of its enhanced interrogation techniques rested on inaccurate claims of their effectiveness....

The Committee reviewed 20 of the most frequent and prominent examples of purported counterterrorism successes that the CIA has attributed to the use of its enhanced interrogation techniques, and found them to be wrong in fundamental respects. In some cases, there was no relationship between the cited counterterrorism success and any information provided by detainees during or after the use of the CIA's enhanced interrogation techniques. In the remaining cases, the CIA inaccurately claimed that specific, otherwise unavailable information was acquired from a CIA detainee "as a result" of the CIA's enhanced interrogation techniques, when in fact the information was either: (1) corroborative of information already available to the CIA or other elements of the U.S. Intelligence Community from sources other than the CIA detainee, and was therefore not "otherwise unavailable"; or (2) acquired from the CIA detainee prior to the use of the CIA's enhanced interrogation techniques. The examples provided by the CIA included numerous factual inaccuracies....

#3: The interrogations of CIA detainees were brutal and far worse than the CIA represented to policymakers and others.

Beginning with the CIA's first detainee, Abu Zubaydah, and continuing with numerous others, the CIA applied its enhanced interrogation techniques with significant repetition for days or weeks at a time. Interrogation techniques such as slaps and "wallings" (slamming detainees against a wall) were used in combination, frequently concurrent with sleep deprivation and nudity. Records do not support CIA representations that the CIA initially used "an open, non-threatening approach," or that interrogations began with the "least coercive technique possible" and escalated to more coercive techniques only as necessary.

The waterboarding technique was physically harmful, inducing convulsions and vomiting. Abu Zubaydah, for example, became "completely unresponsive, with bubbles rising through his open, full mouth." Internal CIA records describe the waterboarding of Khalid Shaykh Mohammad as evolving into a "series of near drownings."

Sleep deprivation involved keeping detainees awake for up to 180 hours, usually standing or in stress positions, at times with their hands shackled above their heads. At least five detainees experienced disturbing hallucinations during prolonged sleep deprivation and, in at least two of those cases, the CIA nonetheless continued the sleep deprivation.

Contrary to CIA representations to the Department of Justice, the CIA instructed personnel that the interrogation of Abu Zubaydah would take "precedence" over his medical care, resulting in the deterioration of a bullet wound Abu Zubaydah incurred during his capture. In at least two other cases, the CIA used its enhanced interrogation techniques despite warnings from CIA medical personnel that the techniques could exacerbate physical injuries. CIA medical personnel treated at least one detainee for swelling in order to allow the continued use of standing sleep deprivation.

At least five CIA detainees were subjected to "rectal rehydration" or rectal feeding without documented medical necessity. The CIA placed detainees in ice water "baths." The CIA led several detainees to believe they would never be allowed to leave CIA custody alive, suggesting to one detainee that he would only leave in a coffin-shaped box. One interrogator told another detainee that he would never go to court, because "we can never let the world know what I have done to you." CIA officers also threatened at least three detainees with harm to their families — to include threats to harm the children of a detainee, threats to sexually abuse the mother of a detainee, and a threat to "cut [a detainee's] mother's throat."

#4: The conditions of confinement for CIA detainees were harsher than the CIA had represented to policymakers and others.

Conditions at CIA detention sites were poor, and were especially bleak early in the program. CIA detainees at the COBALT detention facility were kept in complete darkness and constantly shackled in isolated cells with loud noise or music and only a bucket to use for human waste. Lack of heat at the facility likely contributed to the death of a detainee. The chief of interrogations described COBALT as a "dungeon." Another senior CIA officer stated that COBALT was itself an enhanced interrogation technique.

At times, the detainees at COBALT were walked around naked or were shackled with their hands above their heads for extended periods of time. Other times, the detainees at COBALT were subjected to what was described as a "rough takedown," in which approximately five CIA officers would scream at a detainee, drag him outside of his cell, cut his clothes off, and secure him with Mylar tape. The detainee would then be hooded and dragged up and down a long corridor while being slapped and punched. . . .

#5: The CIA repeatedly provided inaccurate information to the Department of Justice, impeding a proper legal analysis of the CIA's Detention and Interrogation Program.

From 2002 to 2007, the Office of Legal Counsel (OLC) within the Department of Justice relied on CIA representations regarding: (1) the conditions of confinement for detainees, (2) the application of the CIA's enhanced interrogation techniques, (3) the physical effects of the techniques on detainees, and (4) the effectiveness of the techniques. Those representations were inaccurate in material respects. . . .

Prior to the initiation of the CIA's Detention and Interrogation Program and throughout the life of the program, the legal justifications for the CIA's enhanced interrogation techniques relied on the CIA's claim that the techniques were necessary to save lives. In late 2001 and early 2002, senior attorneys at the CIA Office of General Counsel first examined the legal implications of using coercive interrogation techniques. CIA attorneys stated that "a novel application of the necessity defense" could be used "to avoid prosecution of U.S. officials who tortured to obtain information that saved many lives."

Having reviewed information provided by the CIA, the OLC included the "necessity defense" in its August 1, 2002, memorandum to the White House counsel on *Standards of Conduct for Interrogation.* The OLC determined that "under the current circumstances, necessity or self-defense may justify interrogation methods that might violate" the criminal prohibition against torture.

On the same day, a second OLC opinion approved, for the first time, the use of 10 specific coercive interrogation techniques against Abu Zubaydah — subsequently referred to as the CIA's "enhanced interrogation techniques." The OLC relied on inaccurate CIA representations about Abu Zubaydah's status in al-Qa'ida and the interrogation team's "certain[ty]" that Abu Zubaydah was withholding information about planned terrorist attacks. The CIA's representations to the OLC about the techniques were also inconsistent with how the techniques would later be applied.

In March 2005, the CIA submitted to the Department of Justice various examples of the "effectiveness" of the CIA's enhanced interrogation techniques that were inaccurate. OLC memoranda signed on May 30, 2005, and July 20, 2007, relied on these representations, determining that the techniques were legal in part because they produced "specific, actionable intelligence" and "substantial quantities of otherwise unavailable intelligence" that saved lives.

#6: The CIA has actively avoided or impeded congressional oversight of the program.

The CIA did not brief the leadership of the Senate Select Committee on Intelligence on the CIA's enhanced interrogation techniques until September 2002, after the techniques had been approved and used. . . .

The CIA restricted access to information about the program from members of the Committee beyond the chairman and vice chairman until September 6, 2006, the day the president publicly acknowledged the program. . . .

Prior to September 6, 2006, the CIA provided inaccurate information to the leadership of the Committee. Briefings to the full Committee beginning on September 6, 2006, also contained numerous inaccuracies, including inaccurate descriptions of how interrogation techniques were applied and what information was obtained from CIA detainees. The CIA misrepresented the views of members of Congress on a number of occasions. After multiple senators had been critical of the program and written letters expressing concerns to CIA Director Michael Hayden, Director Hayden nonetheless told a meeting of foreign ambassadors to the United States that every Committee member was "fully briefed," and that "[t]his is not CIA's program. This is not the

President's program. This is America's program." The CIA also provided inaccurate information describing the views of U.S. senators about the program to the Department of Justice.

A year after being briefed on the program, the House and Senate Conference Committee considering the Fiscal Year 2008 Intelligence Authorization bill voted to limit the CIA to using only interrogation techniques authorized by the Army Field Manual. That legislation was approved by the Senate and the House of Representatives in February 2008, and was vetoed by President Bush on March 8, 2008.

#7: The CIA impeded effective White House oversight and decision-making.

The CIA provided extensive amounts of inaccurate and incomplete information related to the operation and effectiveness of the CIA's Detention and Interrogation Program to the White House, the National Security Council principals, and their staffs. This prevented an accurate and complete understanding of the program by Executive Branch officials, thereby impeding oversight and decision-making.

According to CIA records, no CIA officer, up to and including CIA Directors George Tenet and Porter Goss, briefed the president on the specific CIA enhanced interrogation techniques before April 2006. . . .

At the direction of the White House, the secretaries of state and defense . . . were not briefed on program specifics until September 2003. An internal CIA email from July 2003 noted that ". . . the WH [White House] is extremely concerned [Secretary] Powell would blow his stack if he were to be briefed on what's been going on." Deputy Secretary of State Armitage complained that he and Secretary Powell were "cut out" of the National Security Council coordination process. . . .

#8: The CIA's operation and management of the program complicated, and in some cases impeded, the national security missions of other Executive Branch agencies.

The CIA, in the conduct of its Detention and Interrogation Program, complicated, and in some cases impeded, the national security missions of other Executive Branch agencies . . . . The CIA withheld or restricted information relevant to these agencies' missions and responsibilities, denied access to detainees, and provided inaccurate information on the CIA's Detention and Interrogation Program to these agencies.

The use of coercive interrogation techniques and covert detention facilities that did not meet traditional U.S. standards resulted in the FBI and the Department of Defense limiting their involvement in CIA interrogation and detention activities. This reduced the ability of the U.S. Government to deploy available resources and expert personnel to interrogate detainees and operate detention facilities. The CIA denied specific requests from FBI Director Robert Mueller III for FBI access to CIA detainees that the FBI believed was necessary to understand CIA detainee reporting on threats to the U.S. Homeland. Information obtained from CIA detainees was restricted within the Intelligence Community, leading to concerns among senior CIA officers that limitations on sharing information undermined government-wide counterterrorism analysis. . . .

#9: The CIA impeded oversight by the CIA's Office of Inspector General.

The CIA avoided, resisted, and otherwise impeded oversight of the CIA's Detention and Interrogation Program by the CIA's Office of Inspector General (OIG). The CIA did not brief the OIG on the program until after the death of a detainee, by which time the CIA had held at least 22 detainees at two different CIA detention sites. Once notified, the OIG reviewed the CIA's Detention and Interrogation Program and issued several reports, including an important May 2004 "Special Review" of the program that identified significant concerns and deficiencies. . . .

In 2005, CIA Director Goss requested in writing that the inspector general not initiate further reviews of the CIA's Detention and Interrogation Program until reviews already underway were completed. In 2007, Director Hayden ordered an unprecedented review of the OIG itself in response to the OIG's inquiries into the CIA's Detention and Interrogation Program.

#10: The CIA coordinated the release of classified information to the media, including inaccurate information concerning the effectiveness of the CIA's enhanced interrogation techniques.

The CIA's Office of Public Affairs and senior CIA officials coordinated to share classified information on the CIA's Detention and Interrogation Program to select members of the media to counter public criticism, shape public opinion, and avoid potential congressional action to restrict the CIA's detention and interrogation authorities and budget. These disclosures occurred when the program was a classified covert action program, and before the CIA had briefed the full Committee membership on the program. . . .

#11: The CIA was unprepared as it began operating its Detention and Interrogation Program more than six months after being granted detention authorities. . . .

The CIA was not prepared to take custody of its first detainee. In the fall of 2001, the CIA explored the possibility of establishing clandestine detention facilities in several countries. The CIA's review identified risks associated with clandestine detention that led it to conclude that U.S. military bases were the best option for the CIA to detain individuals under the [September 17 memorandum from President Bush] authorities. In late March 2002, the imminent capture of Abu Zubaydah prompted the CIA to again consider various detention options. In part to avoid declaring Abu Zubaydah to the International Committee of the Red Cross, which would be required if he were detained at a U.S. military base, the CIA decided to seek authorization to clandestinely detain Abu Zubaydah at a facility in Country [] — a country that had not previously been considered as a potential host for a CIA detention site. A senior CIA officer indicated that the CIA "will have to acknowledge certain gaps in our planning/preparations," but stated that this plan would be presented to the president. At a Presidential Daily Briefing session that day, the president approved CIA's proposal to detain Abu Zubaydah in Country []. . . .

In July 2002, on the basis of consultations with contract psychologists, and with very limited internal deliberation, the CIA requested approval from the Department of Justice to use a set of coercive interrogation techniques. The techniques were adapted from the training of U.S. military personnel at the U.S. Air Force Survival, Evasion, Resistance and Escape (SERE) school, which was designed to prepare U.S. military personnel for the conditions and treatment to which they might be subjected if taken prisoner by countries that do not adhere to the Geneva Conventions.

As it began detention and interrogation operations, the CIA deployed personnel who lacked relevant training and experience. The CIA began interrogation training more than seven months after taking custody of Abu Zubaydah, and more than three months after the CIA began using its "enhanced interrogation techniques." CIA Director George Tenet issued formal guidelines for interrogations and conditions of confinement at detention sites in January 2003, by which time 40 of the 119 known detainees had been detained by the CIA.

#12: The CIA's management and operation of its Detention and Interrogation Program was deeply flawed throughout the program's duration, particularly so in 2002 and early 2003.

The CIA's COBALT detention facility in Country [] began operations in September 2002 and ultimately housed more than half of the 119 CIA detainees identified in this Study. The CIA kept few formal records of the detainees in its custody at COBALT. Untrained CIA officers at the facility conducted frequent, unauthorized, and unsupervised interrogations of detainees using harsh physical interrogation techniques that were not — and never became — part of the CIA's formal "enhanced" interrogation program. The CIA placed a junior officer with no relevant experience in charge of COBALT. On November [], 2002, a detainee who had been held partially nude and chained to a concrete floor died from suspected hypothermia at the facility. At the time, no single unit at CIA Headquarters had clear responsibility for CIA detention and interrogation operations. In interviews conducted in 2003 with the Office of Inspector General, CIA's leadership and senior attorneys acknowledged that they had little or no awareness of operations at COBALT, and some believed that enhanced interrogation techniques were not used there.

Although CIA Director Tenet in January 2003 issued guidance for detention and interrogation activities, serious management problems persisted. For example, in December 2003, CIA personnel reported that they had made the "unsettling discovery" that the CIA had been "holding a number of detainees about whom" the CIA knew "very little" at multiple detention sites in Country [].

Divergent lines of authority for interrogation activities persisted through at least 2003. Tensions among interrogators extended to complaints about the safety and effectiveness of each other's interrogation practices. . . .

#13: Two contract psychologists devised the CIA's enhanced interrogation techniques and played a central role in the operation, assessments, and management of the CIA's Detention and Interrogation Program. By 2005, the CIA had overwhelmingly outsourced operations related to the program.

The CIA contracted with two psychologists to develop, operate, and assess its interrogation operations. The psychologists' prior experience was at the U.S. Air Force Survival, Evasion, Resistance and Escape (SERE) school. Neither psychologist had any experience as an interrogator, nor did either have specialized knowledge of al-Qa'ida, a background in counterterrorism, or any relevant cultural or linguistic expertise.

On the CIA's behalf, the contract psychologists developed theories of interrogation based on "learned helplessness," and developed the list of enhanced interrogation techniques that was approved for use against Abu Zubaydah and subsequent CIA detainees. The psychologists personally conducted interrogations of some of the CIA's most significant detainees using these techniques. They also evaluated whether detainees' psychological state allowed for the continued use of the CIA's enhanced interrogation techniques, including some detainees whom they were themselves interrogating or had interrogated. The psychologists carried out inherently governmental functions, such as acting as liaison between the CIA and foreign intelligence services, assessing the effectiveness of the interrogation program, and participating in the interrogation of detainees held in foreign government custody.

In 2005, the psychologists formed a company specifically for the purpose of conducting their work with the CIA. Shortly thereafter, the CIA outsourced virtually all aspects of the program. . . .

#14: CIA detainees were subjected to coercive interrogation techniques that had not been approved by the Department of Justice or had not been authorized by CIA Headquarters.

Prior to mid-2004, the CIA routinely subjected detainees to nudity and dietary manipulation. The CIA also used abdominal slaps and cold water dousing on several detainees during that period. None of these techniques had been approved by the Department of Justice.

At least 17 detainees were subjected to CIA enhanced interrogation techniques without authorization from CIA Headquarters. Additionally, multiple detainees were subjected to techniques that were applied in ways that diverged from the specific authorization, or were subjected to enhanced interrogation techniques by interrogators who had not been authorized to use them. Although these incidents were recorded in CIA cables and, in at least some cases were identified at the time by supervisors at CIA Headquarters as being inappropriate, corrective action was rarely taken against the interrogators involved.

#15: The CIA did not conduct a comprehensive or accurate accounting of the number of individuals it detained, and held individuals who did not meet the legal standard for detention. The CIA's claims about the number of detainees held and subjected to its enhanced interrogation techniques were inaccurate.

The CIA never conducted a comprehensive audit or developed a complete and accurate list of the individuals it had detained or subjected to its enhanced interrogation techniques. CIA statements to the Committee and later to the public that the CIA detained fewer than 100 individuals, and that less than a third of those 100 detainees were subjected to the CIA's enhanced interrogation techniques, were inaccurate. The Committee's review of CIA records determined that the CIA detained at least 119 individuals, of whom at least 39 were subjected to the CIA's enhanced interrogation techniques.

Of the 119 known detainees, at least 26 were wrongfully held and did not meet the detention standard in the September 2001 Memorandum. . . . These included an "intellectually challenged" man whose CIA detention was used solely as leverage to get a family member to provide information, two individuals who were intelligence sources for foreign liaison services and were former CIA sources, and two individuals whom the CIA assessed to be connected to al-Qa'ida based solely on information fabricated by a CIA detainee subjected to the CIA's enhanced interrogation techniques. Detainees often remained in custody for months after the CIA determined that they did not meet the [] standard. CIA records provide insufficient information to justify the detention of many other detainees. . . .

#16: The CIA failed to adequately evaluate the effectiveness of its enhanced interrogation techniques.

The CIA never conducted a credible, comprehensive analysis of the effectiveness of its enhanced interrogation techniques, despite a recommendation by the CIA inspector general and similar requests by the national security advisor and the leadership of the Senate Select Committee on Intelligence.

Internal assessments of the CIA's Detention and Interrogation Program were conducted by CIA personnel who participated in the development and management of the program, as well as by CIA contractors who had a financial interest in its continuation and expansion. . . .

In 2005, in response to the recommendation by the inspector general for a review of the effectiveness of each of the CIA's enhanced interrogation techniques, the CIA asked two individuals not employed by the CIA to conduct a broader review of "the entirety of" the "rendition, detention and interrogation program." According to one individual, the review was "heavily reliant on the willingness of [CIA Counterterrorism Center] staff to provide us with the factual material that forms the basis of our conclusions." That individual acknowledged lacking the requisite expertise to review the effectiveness of the CIA's enhanced interrogation techniques, and concluded only that "the program," meaning all CIA detainee reporting regardless of whether it was connected to the use of the CIA's enhanced interrogation techniques, was a "great success." The second reviewer concluded that "there is no objective way to answer the question of efficacy" of the techniques.

There are no CIA records to indicate that any of the reviews independently validated the "effectiveness" claims presented by the CIA, to include basic confirmation that the intelligence cited by the CIA was acquired from CIA detainees during or after the use of the CIA's enhanced interrogation techniques. Nor did the reviews seek to confirm whether the intelligence cited by the CIA as being obtained "as a result" of the CIA's enhanced interrogation techniques was unique and "otherwise unavailable," as claimed by the CIA, and not previously obtained from other sources.

#17: The CIA rarely reprimanded or held personnel accountable for serious and significant violations, inappropriate activities, and systemic and individual management failures. CIA officers and CIA contractors who were found to have violated CIA policies or performed poorly were rarely held accountable or removed from positions of responsibility.

Significant events, to include the death and injury of CIA detainees, the detention of individuals who did not meet the legal standard to be held, the use of unauthorized interrogation techniques against CIA detainees, and the provision of inaccurate information on the CIA program did not result in appropriate, effective, or in many cases, any corrective actions. CIA managers who were aware of failings and shortcomings in the program but did not intervene, or who failed to provide proper leadership and management, were also not held to account.

On two occasions in which the CIA inspector general identified wrongdoing, accountability recommendations were overruled by senior CIA leadership. . . .

#18: The CIA marginalized and ignored numerous internal critiques, criticisms, and objections concerning the operation and management of the CIA's Detention and Interrogation Program.

Critiques, criticisms, and objections were expressed by numerous CIA officers, including senior personnel overseeing and managing the program, as well as analysts, interrogators, and medical officers involved in or supporting CIA detention and interrogation operations. . . .

The CIA was also resistant to, and highly critical of more formal critiques. The deputy director for operations stated that the CIA inspector general's draft Special Review should have come to the "conclusion that our efforts have thwarted attacks and saved lives," while the CIA general counsel accused the inspector general of presenting "an imbalanced and inaccurate picture" of the program. A February 2007 report from the International Committee of the Red Cross (ICRC), which the CIA acting general counsel initially stated "actually does not sound that far removed from the reality," was also criticized. . . .

#19: The CIA's Detention and Interrogation Program was inherently unsustainable and had effectively ended by 2006 due to unauthorized press disclosures, reduced cooperation from other nations, and legal and oversight concerns.

The CIA required secrecy and cooperation from other nations in order to operate clandestine detention facilities, and both had eroded significantly before President Bush publicly disclosed the program on September 6, 2006. From the beginning of the program, the CIA faced significant challenges in finding nations willing to host CIA clandestine detention sites. These challenges became increasingly difficult over time. With the exception of Country [], the CIA was forced to relocate detainees out of every country in which it established a detention facility because of pressure from the host government or public revelations about the program. Beginning in early 2005, the CIA sought unsuccessfully to convince the U.S. Department of Defense to allow the transfer of numerous CIA detainees to U.S. military custody. By 2006, the CIA admitted in its own talking points for CIA Director Porter Goss that, absent an Administration decision on an "endgame" for detainees, the CIA was "stymied" and "the program could collapse of its own weight." . . .

After detaining at least 113 individuals through 2004, the CIA brought only six additional detainees into its custody: four in 2005, one in 2006, and one in 2007. By March 2006, the program was operating in only one country. The CIA last used its enhanced interrogation techniques on November 8, 2007. The CIA did not hold any detainees after April 2008.

#20: The CIA's Detention and Interrogation Program damaged the United States' standing in the world, and resulted in other significant monetary and non-monetary costs.

The CIA's Detention and Interrogation Program created tensions with U.S. partners and allies, leading to formal *demarches* to the United States, and damaging and complicating bilateral intelligence relationships. . . .

More broadly, the program caused immeasurable damage to the United States' public standing, as well as to the United States' longstanding global leadership on human rights in general and the prevention of torture in particular. . . .

Notes and Questions

a. The SSCI Study

1. Perspectives on the SSCI Study. Senator Dianne Feinstein, chair of the SSCI at the time the report was released, summed up the Committee's work in her Foreword to the Executive Summary:

> I have attempted throughout to remember the impact on the nation and to the CIA workforce from the attacks of September 11, 2001. I can understand the CIA's impulse to consider the use of every possible tool to gather intelligence and remove terrorists from the battlefield, and CIA was encouraged by political leaders and the public to do whatever it could to prevent another attack. . . .
>
> Nevertheless, such pressure, fear, and expectation of further terrorist plots do not justify, temper, or excuse improper actions taken by individuals or organizations in the name of national security. The major lesson of this report is that regardless of the pressures and the need to act, the Intelligence Community's actions must always reflect who we are as a nation, and adhere to our laws and standards. It is precisely at these times of national crisis that our government must be guided by the lessons of our history and subject decisions to internal and external review.
>
> Instead, CIA personnel, aided by two outside contractors, decided to initiate a program of indefinite secret detention and the use of brutal interrogation techniques in violation of U.S. law, treaty obligations, and our values. . . .
>
> . . . [P]rior to the attacks of September 2001, the CIA itself determined from its own experience with coercive interrogations, that such techniques "do not prōduce intelligence," "will probably result in false answers," and had historically proven to be ineffective. Yet these conclusions were ignored. . . .
>
> . . . [E]xisting U.S. law and treaty obligations should have prevented many of the abuses and mistakes made during this program. While the Office of Legal Counsel found otherwise between 2002 and 2007, it is my personal conclusion that, under any common meaning of the term, CIA detainees were tortured. I also believe that the conditions of confinement and the use of authorized and unauthorized interrogation and conditioning techniques were cruel, inhuman, and degrading. I believe the evidence of this is

> overwhelming and incontrovertible. . . . [S. Select Comm. on Intelligence, *Committee Study of the Central Intelligence Agency's Detention and Interrogation Program: Foreword by S. Select Comm. on Intelligence Chairman Dianne Feinstein* (Dec. 3, 2014), *available at* http://www.feinstein.senate.gov/public/index.cfm/files/serve?File_id=7c85429a-ec38-4bb5-968f-289799bf6d0e&SK=D500C4EBC500E1D256BA519211895909.]

Republican members of the committee, led by SSCI Vice Chairman Saxby Chambliss, emphatically disagreed in a statement of minority views:

> (U) . . . In reviewing the information the CIA provided for the Study . . . we were in awe of what the men and women of the CIA accomplished in their efforts to prevent another attack. The rendition, detention, and interrogation program they created, of which enhanced interrogation was only a small part, enabled a stream of collection and intelligence validation that was unprecedented. The most important capability this program provided had nothing to do with enhanced interrogation — it was the ability to hold and question terrorists, who, if released, would certainly return to the fight, but whose guilt would be difficult to establish in a criminal proceeding without compromising sensitive sources and methods. The CIA called the detention program a "crucial pillar of US counterterrorism efforts, aiding intelligence and law enforcement operations to capture additional terrorists, helping to thwart terrorist plots, and advancing our analysis of the al-Qa'ida target." We agree. We have no doubt that the CIA's detention program saved lives and played a vital role in weakening al-Qa'ida while the Program was in operation. When asked about the value of detainee information and whether he missed the intelligence from it, one senior CIA operator [] told members, "I miss it every day." We understand why. [S. Select Comm. on Intelligence, *Committee Study of the Central Intelligence Agency's Detention and Interrogation Program: Minority Views* 106 (June 20, 2014), *available at* http://www.intelligence.senate.gov/sites/default/files/press/minority-views.pdf.]

The CIA released its own extensive rebuttal of the *SSCI Study. CIA Comments on the Senate Select Committee on Intelligence Report on the Rendition, Detention, and Interrogation Program* (June 27, 2013, released Dec. 8, 2014), *available at* https://www.cia.gov/library/reports/CIAs_June2013_Response_to_the_SSCI_Study_on_the_Former_Detention_and_Interrogation_Program.pdf. The CIA and SSCI minority rebuttals were also published in book form, alongside essays from former CIA officials knowledgeable about the interrogation program. *Rebuttal: The CIA Responds to the Senate Intelligence Committee's Study of Its Detention and Interrogation Program* (Bill Harlow ed., 2015).

The full 6,700-page Senate report has not been made publicly available. Although the SSCI sent copies of the full report to at least eight federal agencies and asked that they incorporate the report into their records, the agencies refused. The ACLU sued the CIA and argued that the report was an "agency record" subject to FOIA, but the D.C. Circuit ruled that the Senate report remains a congressional document and is not subject to disclosure under FOIA. *ACLU v. CIA*, 823 F.3d 655 (D.C. Cir. 2016), *cert. denied*, 137 S. Ct. 1837 (2017).

Putting partisan differences aside, after reviewing the SSCI Findings and Conclusions, can you determine whether the CIA interrogation program was lawful? What additional information, if any, would you need to make such an assessment? Was the failure of the CIA to brief the entire Intelligence Committee at the outset of the program not just a mistake, but unlawful? See Chapter 18.

2. Efficacy of the EITs. The Bush administration consistently maintained that its harsh interrogation techniques produced intelligence that helped prevent terrorist attacks. For example, officials claimed that Khalid Sheikh Mohammed (KSM), the mastermind of the 9/11 attacks, provided detailed intelligence about the Al Qaeda network after being subjected to waterboarding, and that Abu Zubaydah, an alleged top Al Qaeda strategist, implicated José Padilla in a dirty-bomb plot after EITs. Stephen Grey, *Ghost Plane: The True Story of the CIA Torture Program* 242-243 (2006). However, the SSCI study concluded that much of the disseminated intelligence from KSM that the CIA identified as important was fabricated, and that Zubaydah provided all his key statements to FBI special agents shortly after his capture. *SSCI Study, supra,* at 47, 96. CIA Director John Brennan had this to say: "We have not concluded that it was the use of EITs . . . that allowed us to obtain useful information from detainees subjected to them. The cause and effect relationship between the use of EITs and useful information subsequently provided by the detainees is, in my view, unknowable." John Brennan, *Response to SSCI Study on the Former Detention and Interrogation Program,* Dec. 11, 2014.

3. Who Decides? Who was responsible for deciding whether the use of EITs was effective? If there is no unequivocal yes or no answer on effectiveness, which agency or officials should make judgments on whether to permit the harsher techniques?

4. The EITs and Torture. Review the list of EITs and the excerpts from the SSCI Study. Were the interrogations of Zubaydah and al-Nashiri unlawful? If so, which authorities were violated, and which techniques caused the violations?

5. The Impact of Inaccurate, Misleading, and False Information. The SSCI Study recounts repeated instances in which the CIA provided false or misleading statements that impeded congressional, executive branch, and inspector general oversight of the interrogation program. What steps could DOD or lawyers inside CIA take to make inaccurate or misleading reporting less likely? In light of intelligence oversight laws and the committee structure inside Congress, what legal or structural reforms might improve accountability, control, and oversight of CIA interrogation activities?

6. The Role of Contractors and Psychologists. Inexperience clearly affected at least the early stages of the CIA interrogation program. In relying on contract psychologists to develop and implement the interrogation program and techniques adapted from the SERE school, the CIA was operating ad hoc, with little internal deliberation. What is the legal significance of the SSCI's conclusion that the psychologists carried out inherently governmental functions? How would you advise the CIA or any other intelligence agency to avoid these pitfalls in the future?

On the heels of the release of the SSCI Study Executive Summary, the American Psychological Association's Council of Representatives voted overwhelmingly in August 2015 in favor of a resolution that "prohibits psychologists from participating in national security investigations." Am. Psychological Ass'n, *Resolution to Amend the 2006 and 2013 Council Resolutions to Clarify the Roles of Psychologists Related to Interrogation and Detainee Welfare in National Security Settings, to Further Implement the 2008 Petition Resolution, and to Safeguard Against Acts of Torture and Cruel, Inhuman, or Degrading Treatment or Punishment in All Settings* (2015), *available at* https://www.justsecurity.org/wp-content/uploads/2015/08/apa.Approved_Resolution_23B.pdf. The participation ban adds to an existing APA ethical prohibition declaring that psychologists "may not engage directly or indirectly in any act of torture or cruel, inhuman, or degrading treatment or punishment" applied to any person held in any place. *Id.* The resolution also states that

> psychologists shall not conduct, supervise, be in the presence of, or otherwise assist any national security interrogations for any military or intelligence entities, including private contractors working on their behalf. . . . [Psychologists] may provide consultation with regard to policy pertain to information gathering methods which are humane so long as they do not violate the prohibitions of this Resolution. *Id.*

What do you think will be the impact of the APA Resolution on U.S. intelligence interrogations? Does the resolution apply to psychologists who are also military officers? *See* James Risen, *Psychologists Approve Ban on Role in National Security Investigations,* N.Y. Times, Aug. 7, 2015.

b. Legality Under International Law

1. The CAT and the Torture Act. Do any of the techniques on the CIA IG list exceed the limits set out in the Torture Convention or the U.S. understandings? Did the use of EITs by CIA interrogators on detainees Zubaydah and al-Nashiri violate the CAT?

For the purposes of compliance with the CAT, would it matter *where* the mistreatment of a prisoner by U.S. officials took place? If the measures of compliance with the CAT prohibition against "cruel, inhuman, or degrading treatment" are the Fifth, Eighth, and Fourteenth Amendments, as stated in the U.S. reservation upon ratification, do aliens held by the United States overseas have any protection from such treatment by U.S. officials under the CAT? *See United States v. Verdugo-Urquidez,* 494 U.S. 259 (1990) (holding the Fourth Amendment inapplicable to the search abroad of an alien who lacks substantial connections to the United States); *Johnson v. Eisentrager,* 339 U.S. 763 (1950) (suggesting that the Fifth Amendment has no extraterritorial application to "enemy aliens"). For more on extraterritoriality, see *supra* Chapter 7.

Do any of the techniques exceed the limits of the Torture Act? Recall that in August 2002 the Justice Department's OLC offered a very narrow definition of "torture," and argued that in any case the President could authorize torture. It also indicated that interrogation activities "may be cruel, inhuman, or degrading, but still not produce pain and suffering of the requisite intensity" to violate §2340. Bybee Memo, *supra,* at 1. The memorandum also asserted that a specific intent to torture is required to violate the torture statute. *Id.* at 4. How would you rate this definition of the key terms against those set out in the Torture Convention, the Torture Act, and the U.S. understanding? Could the Bybee Memo effectively exempt the CIA from complying with either the CAT or the Torture Act?

2. Applying the Geneva Conventions. Recall from our consideration of the Geneva Conventions in Chapters 9 and 32 that each one requires nations to criminalize "grave breaches," including acts of "torture or inhuman treatment." Common Article 3 requires detainees of every description to be treated humanely, and it forbids "cruel treatment and torture," as well as "outrages on personal dignity, in particular, humiliating and degrading treatment." Each Convention calls on nations to "take measures necessary for the suppression of all acts contrary to the provisions of the present Convention other than the grave breaches." The War Crimes Act, *supra* p. 989, was supposed to satisfy U.S. obligations under the Geneva Conventions in this regard by criminalizing grave breaches as well as violations of Common Article 3.

The Bush administration took the position in early 2002 that Al Qaeda and Taliban prisoners were "unlawful combatants" not protected by the Geneva Convention Relative to the Treatment of Prisoners of War (Geneva III), the one most clearly relevant here. Because Geneva III was inapplicable, it argued, the War Crimes Act incorporating it by reference necessarily did not apply to U.S. officials interrogating such prisoners. President George W. Bush, *Memorandum for the Vice President et al.: Humane Treatment of al Qaeda and Taliban Detainees* (Feb. 7, 2002), *available at* http://www.aclu.org/files/assets/CIA.pdf. The Administration's arguments are reviewed in the following paragraphs.

a. *Terrorists as Protected Belligerents?* The Bush administration first argued that the Geneva Conventions did not apply to members of Al Qaeda, because Al Qaeda is not a High Contracting Party to the Conventions. On the other hand, members of the Taliban, as a group representing the de facto government of Afghanistan, a High Contracting Party, were said to be covered by the Conventions.

As a practical matter, of course, Al Qaeda depended heavily on Taliban support — bordering on sponsorship — in order to carry out its terrorist attacks against the United States. At the same time, the Taliban appear to have been heavily influenced by Al Qaeda. Under the circumstances, does it make sense to apply the Conventions differently to members of the two enemy groups?

b. *Character of the Conflict.* The Administration maintained that neither Al Qaeda nor Taliban members were entitled to the protection of Common Article 3, however, because the conflict was, at least initially, international, not one described as "not of an international character." Is this argument consistent with the contention that the Taliban were covered by the Conventions generally because the Taliban were the de facto government of Afghanistan? In *Hamdan v. Rumsfeld*, 548 U.S. 557, 562 (2006), the Supreme Court found that Common Article 3 affords some protection to persons who are not associated with a signatory or nonsignatory "Power" but who are involved in a conflict "in the territory of" a signatory. The Court construed the phrase "not of an international character" literally to distinguish conflicts between nations. *Id.*

c. *Status as POWs?* The Administration also insisted that the Taliban were not entitled to protections afforded prisoners of war under Geneva III. Article 4 of that Convention defines POWs as combatants who have a "fixed distinctive sign recognizable at a distance," carry arms openly, and conduct operations in accordance with the laws and customs of war. The government was supported in this argument in *United States v. Lindh*, 212 F. Supp. 2d 541 (E.D. Va. 2002), which emphasized that the requirements in question are designed to enable belligerents on one side to distinguish those on the other from noncombatants, who must not be attacked.

A POW must be "humanely treated," and he may not be required to divulge more than his name, rank, serial number, and age. Once a prisoner of any sort is in custody, should his failure to fit the definition of a POW expose him to torture or inhumane treatment? Note that Common Article 3 applies to all prisoners, regardless of their status.

3. The New Paradigm? In 2002, White House Counsel Alberto R. Gonzales argued in a memorandum to President Bush that the "nature of the new war" and the "new paradigm render[] obsolete Geneva's strict limitations" on questioning and make other Geneva provisions "quaint." *Decision Re Application of the Geneva Convention on Prisoners of War to the Conflict with Al Qaeda and the Taliban* (Jan. 25, 2002), *available at* http://www.slate.com/features/whatistorture/pdfs/020125.pdf. How would you rebut Gonzales' interpretation? Do Gonzales' arguments apply with equal force in Afghanistan and in Iraq? To detainees captured elsewhere?

Review the provisions of the Detainee Treatment Act, *supra* p. 992, and the McCain-Feinstein Amendment, *supra* p. 993. If these measures had been in place beginning in October 2001, in what respects, if at all, would the lawfulness of U.S. interrogation practices have been different?

c. Domestic Law

The CIA and Contractors. Not long after CIA black sites (and the Agency's detention and interrogation program at those sites) were exposed in media reports and publicly acknowledged by the Bush administration, the sites were closed and remaining detainees were transferred to Guantánamo Bay. On July 20, 2007, President Bush signed Executive Order No. 13,340, *Interpretation of the Geneva Conventions Common Article 3 as Applied to a Program of Detention and Interrogation Operated by the Central Intelligence Agency,* 72 Fed. Reg. 40,707. The executive order did not authorize the use of any particular interrogation techniques. Instead, it barred the CIA and presumably its contractors from certain practices, including those forbidden by the Torture Act, the DTA, and the MCA. However, the order did not expressly forbid techniques denied to the military by the 2006 *Army Field Manual*—such as waterboarding, hooding, sleep deprivation, or forced standing for long periods.

President Obama revoked the Bush order in 2009, in Executive Order No. 13,491, *Ensuring Lawful Interrogations,* 74 Fed. Reg. 4893 (Jan. 22, 2009). The core of the Obama order provides:

Sec. 3. Standards and Practices for Interrogation of Individuals in the Custody or Control of the United States in Armed Conflicts.

(a) Common Article 3 Standards as a Minimum Baseline. Consistent with the requirements of the Federal torture statute, 18 U.S.C. 2340-2340A, section 1003 of the Detainee Treatment Act of 2005, 42 U.S.C. 2000dd, the Convention Against Torture, Common Article 3, and other laws regulating the treatment and interrogation of individuals detained in any armed conflict, such persons shall in all circumstances be treated humanely and shall not be subjected to violence to life and person (including murder of all kinds, mutilation, cruel treatment, and torture), nor to outrages upon personal dignity (including humiliating and degrading treatment), whenever such individuals are in the custody or under the effective control of an officer, employee, or other agent of the United States Government or detained within a facility owned, operated, or controlled by a department or agency of the United States.

(b) Interrogation Techniques and Interrogation-Related Treatment. Effective immediately, an individual in the custody or under the effective control of an officer, employee, or other agent of the United States Government, or detained within a facility owned, operated, or controlled by a department or agency of the United States, in any armed conflict, shall not be subjected to any interrogation technique or approach, or any treatment related to interrogation, that is not authorized by and listed in Army Field Manual 2-22.3. . . .

Sec. 4. Prohibition of Certain Detention Facilities, and Red Cross Access to Detained Individuals.

(a) CIA Detention. The CIA shall close as expeditiously as possible any detention facilities that it currently operates and shall not operate any such detention facility in the future.

(b) International Committee of the Red Cross Access to Detained Individuals. All departments and agencies of the Federal Government shall provide the International Committee of the Red Cross with notification of, and timely access to, any individual detained in any armed conflict in the custody or under the effective control of an officer, employee, or other agent of the United States Government or detained within a facility owned, operated, or controlled by a department or agency of the United States Government, consistent with Department of Defense regulations and policies. . . .

In what respects did the Obama executive order change the law concerning interrogations for intelligence purposes? Are torture and cruel, inhuman, and degrading treatment now unlawful if carried out by any person working on behalf of the United States? How durable are the rules contained in the executive order?

d. Responsibility for Abuse

1. Assigning Responsibility. Guidance for interrogations at Abu Ghraib prison came from three different sources at different times — from Army field manuals, from personnel who had worked earlier in Afghanistan, and from Guantánamo. Craig Gordon, *High-Pressure Tactics: Critics Say Bush Policies — Post 9/11 — Gave Interrogators Leeway to Push Beyond Normal Limits,* Newsday, May 23, 2004.

The overall detention and interrogation picture that has emerged from official statements and documents reveals "a trail of fitful ad hoc policymaking" where interrogation techniques were authorized, then rescinded or modified, at times leading to decisions made in the field or at the Pentagon on a case-by-case basis. Dana Priest & Bradley Graham, *U.S. Struggled Over How Far to Push Tactics,* Wash. Post, June 24, 2004. Unlike CIA requests for expanded interrogation authority that were reviewed by the Department of Justice and the National Security Council, Defense Department interrogation policy decisions were not subjected to outside review. *Id.*

2. Investigating Interrogation Abuses. Before the SSCI decided to investigate the CIA interrogations, an investigation led by former Secretary of Defense James Schlesinger found 300 allegations of abuse and 66 substantiated cases of confirmed or possible abuse in Iraq.[22] The Army decided not to charge any soldiers or officers with wrongdoing, however, finding some senior officers "responsible" but not "culpable."[23]

---

22. *Schlesinger Report, supra* note 11, at 5.

23. Josh White & Thomas E. Ricks, *Officers Won't Be Charged in Prison Scandal,* Wash. Post, Aug. 27, 2004.

By contrast, the Schlesinger investigation found that the abuses were "more than the failure of a few leaders to enforce proper discipline. There is both institutional and personal responsibility at higher levels."[24] On March 22, 2006, an Army spokesman reported more than 600 accusations of detainee abuse in Iraq and Afghanistan since October 2001.[25]

e. Criminal Liability

1. Prosecuting Abuses. Seven Military Police and two military intelligence soldiers were convicted under the UCMJ of abusing detainees at Abu Ghraib, while 251 other soldiers and officers were punished in some way for detainee abuse in Iraq and Afghanistan.[26] Three of the five officers investigated by the Army for their role in the Abu Ghraib abuses were cleared; Colonel Thomas Pappas, commander of Abu Ghraib prison, was reprimanded and fined, while Brigadier General Janis Karpinski, another commander of Abu Ghraib, was demoted to the rank of colonel.[27] Only one person connected to the post-9/11 interrogations has been criminally prosecuted in U.S. civilian courts for detainee abuse.

At a news conference called in response to the Abu Ghraib publicity in June 2004, White House Counsel Alberto Gonzales denied that "the president . . . authorized, ordered or directed" violations of "the standards of the torture conventions or the torture statute." *Transcript of Press Briefing by Alberto Gonzales* (June 22, 2004). What legal wiggle room did the Gonzales statement leave for the President? Did it mean that President Bush was not responsible for the reported abuses?

2. Possible Defenses to Torture Charges: Article II as a Trump Card? The August 2002 OLC memo, *supra* p. 999, at 36, 39, asserted that "Congress can no more interfere with the President's conduct of the interrogation of enemy combatants than it can dictate strategic or tactical decisions on the battlefield." In what particular settings is the Article II argument most persuasive? Unlike the Bybee Memo, *supra* p. 999, the December 30, 2004, OLC memo, *supra* p. 1001, made no mention of the constitutional authority of the President to disregard statutory or treaty obligations regarding torture. Of what significance is the revision?

Compare detention and on-the-spot interrogations of those seized on the battlefield during combat with long-term detentions in remote locations away from the battle. Al Qaeda and ISIS reportedly continue to plan and carry out terrorist acts that threaten national security. Does that ongoing threat give the Commander in Chief a tactical choice to capture and interrogate Al Qaeda and ISIS operatives using torture?

If you agree that there is a constitutional limit to the authority of Congress to regulate interrogation, can you construe the laws reviewed in this section to avoid the potential constitutional problem? Is the constitutional authority of the President

---

24. *Schlesinger Report, supra* note 11, at 5.

25. Eric Schmitt, *Iraq Abuse Trial Is Again Limited to Lower Ranks*, N.Y. Times, Mar. 23, 2006.

26. *Id.*; Eric Schmitt, *Army Dog Handler Is Convicted in Detainee Abuse at Abu Ghraib*, N.Y. Times, Mar. 22, 2006.

27. *Army Releases Findings, supra*; Frontline, *The Torture Question: Frequently Asked Questions*, PBS, Oct. 18, 2005, *at* http://www.pbs.org/wgbh/pages/frontline/torture/etc/faqs.html#8.

relevant to the international legality of the abusive conduct? *See* W. Michael Reisman, Editorial Comment, *Holding the Center of the Law of Armed Conflict,* 100 Am. J. Int'l L. 852, 854 (2006) (no).

3. Prosecuting Civilian Contractors? In June 2004 a federal grand jury in North Carolina indicted a contractor employed by the CIA on assault charges for allegedly beating a detainee in Afghanistan over two days in 2003. The detainee died the next day. The former contractor was found guilty of assault and sentenced to eight years and four months in prison. Elizabeth Dunbar, *Ex-CIA Contractor Sentenced to Prison,* Wash. Post, Feb. 13, 2007. How might the War Crimes Act, 18 U.S.C. §2441, *supra* p. 989, apply to the accused in this case?

Generally, the UCMJ has not been used to criminally prosecute civilians accompanying military units in peacetime. *See, e.g., Willenbring v. Neurauter,* 48 M.J. 152, 157 (C.A.A.F. 1998). The Military Extraterritorial Jurisdiction Act of 2000 (MEJA), however, provides for federal civilian jurisdiction over crimes committed abroad by civilians who are "accompanying or employed by" the U.S. military. 18 U.S.C. §§3261-3267 (2018). MEJA creates no new substantive crimes but incorporates a range of existing offenses, such as murder, assault, sexual abuse, and deprivation of rights under color of law.

The Fiscal Year 2005 National Defense Authorization Act broadened the range of potential defendants under MEJA to include civilian employees, contractors or subcontractors, and their employees, of DOD or "any other Federal agency, or any provisional authority, to the extent such employment relates to supporting the mission of the Department of Defense overseas." Pub. L. No. 108-375, §1088, 118 Stat. 1811, 2066-2067 (2004) (amending 18 U.S.C. §3267(1)(A)). Do these amendments to MEJA plug all the holes? Would they reach State Department or FBI contractors? CIA contractors?

The National Defense Authorization Act for Fiscal Year 2010, Pub. L. No. 111-84, §1038, 123 Stat. 2190, 2451-2452 (2009) (codified at 10 U.S.C. §801 note), prohibits contractor personnel from interrogating detainees under the control of the Department of Defense, unless the Secretary waives the ban for up to 60 days after he determines that the waiver is "vital to the national security interests of the United States." *Id.* §1038(d). The Defense Department has issued rules implementing the contractor restrictions. 48 C.F.R. §237.173 (2018). Do these provisions provide adequate controls on contract personnel?

Finally, note that Congress in 2006 also expanded the jurisdiction of courts-martial, which already encompassed "persons serving with or accompanying an armed force in the field" during a time of (formally declared) war, to also apply during a "contingency operation," as defined by 10 U.S.C. §101(a)(13). *See* 10 U.S.C. §802(a)(10)(2018). As a practical matter, this amendment allows the trial by court-martial of civilian contractors serving alongside the military virtually anywhere in the world. Is it constitutional? To date, the highest court in the military justice system — the Court of Appeals for the Armed Forces — has said yes, but only in the very narrow context of a noncitizen lacking substantial voluntary connections to the United States, i.e., a defendant lacking the constitutional rights to due process and jury trial that might otherwise bar such military jurisdiction. *See United States v. Ali,* 71 M.J. 256 (C.A.A.F. 2012).

4. Lawyers and Their Role. The *Schlesinger Report, supra* p. 1000, n.11, found that in the development of Defense Department detention and interrogation policies in

2002 and 2003, "the legal resources of the Services' Judge Advocate General and General Counsels were not utilized to their full potential. Had the Secretary of Defense had a wider range of legal opinions and more robust debate regarding detainee policies and operations," the frequent policy changes between December 2002 and April 2003 might have been avoided. *Id.* at 8. Why would the Secretary not have sought more advice from JAG lawyers and General Counsels? What might have been gained by their perspectives?

The Office of Professional Responsibility of the Department of Justice completed an investigation of OLC lawyers John Yoo and Jay S. Bybee in 2009, concluding that they engaged in "professional misconduct" by authorizing enhanced interrogation techniques. Office of Prof'l Responsibility, Dep't of Justice, *Report* 260 (2009), *available at* nsarchive.gwu.edu/news/20100312/OPRFinalReport090729.pdf. A second report from the Associate Deputy Attorney General, David Margolis, said only that the two lawyers exercised "poor judgment," but that he would not recommend referring them for discipline because they did not, in his view, knowingly provide false advice. Memorandum from David Margolis, Assoc. Att'y Gen., to the Att'y Gen. (Jan. 5, 2010), *available at* http://graphics8.nytimes.com/packages/pdf/politics/20100220JUSTICE/20100220JUSTICE-DAGMargolisMemo.pdf.

The latter conclusion thus excused what might otherwise have been an obligation by the Department of Justice to refer Yoo and Bybee to state bar associations for disciplinary proceedings. President Obama also stated that he would not advocate prosecuting the OLC lawyers. *See* Press Release, White House Off. of the Press Sec'y, *Statement of President Barack Obama on Release of the OLC Memos* (Apr. 16, 2009) ("[N]othing will be gained by spending our time and energy laying blame for the past."). Do you believe that these lawyers and/or their highest-ranking superiors broke the law? Which laws? Do you agree that nothing would be gained by a prosecution? What about an ethics referral to state bar associations?

f. Civil Liability

1. *Civil Liability for U.S. Government Interrogators?* Should individual interrogators or their superiors be held liable for abusive interrogation? In February 2006, a federal district court dismissed most of a civil suit for damages brought by Guantánamo detainees who alleged that they were tortured in violation of the Geneva Conventions, the law of nations, and the Constitution. *Rasul v. Rumsfeld*, 414 F. Supp. 2d 26 (D.D.C. 2006). The court held that sovereign immunity barred the law of nations and Geneva Conventions claims, and that qualified immunity of individual government officials required dismissal of the constitutional claims because the rights at stake were not "clearly established." *Id.* at 31, 44. For sovereign immunity to apply to the international law claims, however, the court had to find that the defendants were acting within their scope of employment. How could U.S. officials act within their scope of employment when they torture detainees? The Court of Appeals voted to dismiss all the claims, *Rasul v. Myers*, 512 F.3d 644 (D.C. Cir. 2008), but the Supreme Court reversed and remanded so the D.C. Circuit could reconsider the constitutional claims in light of the Court's 2008 decision in *Boumediene v. Bush*, 553 U.S. 723 (2008), *supra* p. 850. *See Rasul v. Myers*, 555 U.S. 1083 (2008) (mem.). On remand, the Court of Appeals again dismissed all of the detainees' claims after concluding that the alien detainees lacked clearly established constitutional rights under the Fifth or Eighth

Amendments, inasmuch as the Supreme Court has yet to squarely overrule the part of *Johnson v. Eisentrager*, 339 U.S. 763 (1950), suggesting that aliens abroad do not have Fifth Amendment rights. *Rasul v. Myers*, 563 F.3d 527 (D.C. Cir. 2009) (per curiam). Moreover, the court concluded, even if the detainees *were* protected by the Constitution, "special factors" militated against recognizing the kind of damages remedy provided by *Bivens* (see *supra* p. 150). *Id.* at 532 n.5. *Rasul* is not alone in this regard; as we discovered in Chapter 5, the absence of a cause of action, qualified immunity, and other procedural and evidentiary doctrines have made it very difficult for victims of post-September 11 abuses — including abusive interrogations — to obtain damages from the responsible government officers. In addition, a provision of the Detainee Treatment Act, *supra* p. 992, protects U.S. government personnel against liability for torture "in any civil action or criminal prosecution" where the interrogation activities "were officially authorized and determined to be lawful at the time they were conducted" and the employee "did not know that the practices were unlawful." 42 U.S.C. §2000dd-1 (2018). What difference do you think this provision will make in providing accountability for abusive interrogation practices?

2. *Civil Liability for Lawyers?* In 2009, a federal district court refused to dismiss most parts of a civil suit by convicted terrorist José Padilla against former OLC lawyer John Yoo. *Padilla v. Yoo*, 633 F. Supp. 2d 1005 (N.D. Cal. 2009). Padilla alleged that he was abused during his confinement in a military brig in South Carolina during his three-year, eight-month detention based on the orders of high-ranking government officials and the legal and policy justifications for abusive interrogation provided by Yoo. *Id.* at 1013-1015. The court noted that Yoo is unlikely to be held accountable for his actions in any other forum, and that a reasonable lawyer in Yoo's position should have known that he was authorizing a violation of Padilla's constitutional rights. *Id.* at 1034. On appeal, after an extensive discussion of the merits, the Ninth Circuit reversed, finding that Yoo was entitled to qualified immunity. *Padilla v. Yoo*, 678 F.3d 748 (9th Cir. 2012). See *supra* p. 153. Despite concluding that Padilla's alleged treatment "appears to have been a violation of his constitutional rights," and assuming (without deciding) that Padilla was tortured, the Ninth Circuit reversed for two reasons. *Id.* at 761. The court found that, at the relevant times, it was not "beyond debate" that Padilla was entitled to the same constitutional protections as an accused or convicted criminal. *Id.* at 764. Second, it was not clearly established in 2001-2003 that the alleged treatment Padilla suffered *was* torture. *Id.* at 768. And as we noted in Chapter 5, the Ninth Circuit also refused to hold that, going forward, Padilla's allegations *did* establish that his treatment was unconstitutional.

3. *Civil Liability for Contractors?* The potential for recovery of damages for abusive interrogation is illustrated by two recent cases. In *Al Shimari v. CACI Premier Tech., Inc.*, 320 F. Supp. 3d 781 (E.D. Va. 2018), Iraqi citizens held at the Abu Ghraib prison alleged torture, CIDT, and war crimes by contractor CACI employees and U.S. military personnel, all in violation of international law and actionable under the Alien Tort Statute (ATS), 28 U.S.C. §1350 (2018). The court held that plaintiffs' allegations described serious misconduct by CACI that violates international law, that their claims were actionable under the ATS, and that the political question doctrine was inapplicable. *Id.* at 785-786. Judge Leonie Brinkema noted that the lawsuit against CACI "fully aligns with the original goals of the ATS: to provide a federal forum for tort suits by aliens against Americans for international law violations." *Id.* at 787.

In 2019, Judge Brinkema ruled that sovereign immunity does not bar ATS claims based on alleged *jus cogens* violations where the state defendant has a sufficient nexus to the alleged violations. *Al Shimari v. CACI Premier Tech., Inc.*, 368 F. Supp. 3d 935 (E.D. Va. 2019). See *supra* p. 196. Because

> the People as sovereign are bound by the nonderogability of *jus cogens* norms . . . the People may not legitimately delegate to the government the power to engage in *jus cogens* violations. Accordingly, the federal government, bounded by its status as a limited government of delegated powers, has no sovereign power to immunize itself from liability for such violations." [*Id.* at 968.]

Thus, the ATS claims that alleged violation of *jus cogens* norms could proceed against both defendants. The Fourth Circuit rejected CACI's effort to take an interlocutory appeal from Judge Brinkema's ruling, *see Al Shimari v. CACI Premier Tech., Inc.*, 775 F. App'x 758 (4th Cir. 2019), and CACI's petition for a writ of certiorari challenging that decision was pending as of December 2019.

A second case involved the CIA's reliance on contract psychologists to develop and implement the early stages of the interrogation program, based on techniques adapted from the U.S. military's SERE schools. Litigation by three former detainees (one of whom died in CIA custody) against CIA contract psychologists James E. Mitchell and Bruce Jessen under the ATS was settled days before a trial was scheduled to begin in September 2017. Sheri Fink, *Settlement Reached in C.I.A. Torture Case,* N.Y. Times, Aug. 17, 2017. Before settlement, however, the court found no bar to justiciability based on either the political question doctrine or sovereign immunity. It found jurisdiction for the lawsuit under the ATS and ruled that the defendants had not met their burden of showing that they were "agents" of the United States within the meaning of a Military Commissions Act (MCA) provision that bars such lawsuits in certain instances. *Salim v. Mitchell,* 183 F. Supp. 3d 1121 (E.D. Wash. 2016); *see also Salim v. Mitchell,* 268 F. Supp. 3d 1132 (E.D. Wash. 2017). The court also ruled that the plaintiffs' evidence generally supported the basic allegations of their complaint, and it affirmed ATS jurisdiction based on the touch and concern test from *Kiobel. Salim,* 268 F. Supp. 3d 1132. Declassified CIA documents and transcripts of the depositions of CIA officials and the psychologists in *Salim v. Mitchell* are available in links in the online version of the *New York Times* story by Sheri Fink, *supra. See also* Sheri Fink & James Risen, *Psychologists Open a Window on Brutal C.I.A. Interrogations,* N.Y. Times, June 21, 2017. A companion video is available at https://www.nytimes.com/interactive/2017/06/20/us/cia-torture.html?_r=0.

If civil suits against the government and government officials are barred, will the prospect of criminal prosecution provide an adequate deterrence to official torture? All things being equal, would an optimal deterrence scheme focus on civil remedies or criminal remedies? And against whom?

4. Extraordinary Rendition. Rendition is generally understood to be the surrender of a person from one state to another state that has requested his transfer, typically pursuant to an agreement or extradition treaty, for the purpose of criminal prosecution. In the mid-1990s, the United States began capturing suspected terrorist operatives and transferring them to foreign countries as part of a CIA program designed to disrupt and dismantle Al Qaeda terrorist operations. Michael Scheuer, *A Fine Rendition,* N.Y. Times, Mar. 11, 2005. The practice is commonly called "extraordinary rendition," because it involves no treaty or formal agreement and is attended by no judicial process.

After September 11, extraordinary renditions expanded, apparently as an adjunct to the CIA interrogations reviewed by the SSCI. Receiving nations included Syria, Jordan, Morocco, and Uzbekistan, as well as Egypt. The renditions were not limited to individuals wanted by third countries, but included transfers, typically on CIA charter flights, to third countries solely for the purpose of interrogation — to extract intelligence, as quickly as possible. Stephen Grey, *Ghost Plane: The True Story of the CIA Torture Program* 148-152 (2006). By 2004, investigative journalists and human rights groups alleged that torture was used against the subjects of extraordinary rendition with the knowledge or acquiescence of the United States.

No one knows for sure how many extraordinary renditions occurred. Some estimate that more than 100 persons were thus rendered by the United States after the September 11 attacks. Dana Priest, *CIA's Assurances on Transferred Suspects Doubted,* Wash. Post, Mar. 17, 2005. The news reports prompted numerous investigations by international organizations and national governments.

a. *The Legal Basis for Extraordinary Rendition.* Is the practice of extraordinary rendition lawful? Review the language of the September 2001 memorandum from President Bush, *supra* p. 998, authorizing the CIA to capture and detain suspected terrorists. Assuming the President's finding complied with the National Security Act, does it confer authority for extraordinary renditions? If it does, what are the limits of that authority? If it does not, what alternative sources of authority can you think of?

Officials denied that renditions occurred for the purpose of torture. R. Jeffrey Smith, *Gonzales Defends Transfer of Detainees,* Wash. Post, Mar. 8, 2005 (quoting Attorney General Gonzales as stating that it is not U.S. policy to send persons "to countries where we believe or we know that they're going to be tortured"); Joel Brinkley, *U.S. Interrogations Are Saving European Lives, Rice Says,* N.Y. Times, Dec. 6, 2005 (quoting Secretary of State Condoleezza Rice as stating that "[t]he United States does not transport and has not transported detainees from one country to another for the purpose of interrogation using torture"). How much legal wiggle room do these statements preserve for the government?

b. *Judicial Remedies for Extraordinary Rendition.* Binyam Mohamed, an Ethiopian national and British resident, was taken into U.S. custody in Pakistan in 2002 and, for two years, was moved between "black sites" in Pakistan, Morocco, and Afghanistan, and then to Guantánamo, where he remained until he was released to Britain in 2009. Before his release, lawyers for Mohamed sued in Britain to obtain disclosure of any information in the possession of the U.K. government that would support Mohamed's claims that he had been tortured by the United States. Eventually, the U.K. courts ordered the release of limited summaries that confirm that Mohamed was subjected to cruel, inhuman, and degrading treatment by U.S. authorities. Richard Norton-Taylor, *Binyam Mohamed Torture Evidence Must Be Revealed,* Guardian, Feb. 10, 2010. Mohamed and other victims of CIA extraordinary rendition then brought suit under the Alien Tort Statute (ATS) against Jeppesen Dataplan, a company allegedly involved in providing flight services that enabled the CIA to carry out the renditions of Mohamed and his co-plaintiffs. *Mohamed v. Jeppesen Dataplan, Inc.,* 579 F.3d 943 (9th Cir. 2009) (en banc). During a corporate meeting, Jeppesen executive Bob Overby stated to his colleagues, "We do all of the extraordinary rendition flights—you know, the torture flights." Jane Mayer, *Outsourcing Torture: The Secret History of America's "Extraordinary Rendition" Program,* New Yorker, Feb. 14, 2005. If the state secrets privilege had not effectively ended the lawsuit against Jeppesen Dataplan, how should the court have ruled on the merits of Mohamed's claims?

The Torture Victim Protection Act (TVPA) provides a remedy in the federal courts for persons who have been victims of torture, but only for torture or extrajudicial killing "under color of law, of any foreign nation." In *Arar v. Ashcroft,* 585 F.3d 559 (2d Cir. 2009) (en banc), the Second Circuit ruled that the TVPA does not support a claim where U.S. officials allegedly *directed* foreign officials to torture a non-U.S. citizen. (The U.S. officials were alleged to be acting under color of federal, not Syrian, law.) Of what value, then, is the TVPA to victims of torture directed by U.S. agents? Would Arar have gotten further if he instead alleged that his arrest, detention, and subsequent rendition by U.S. officials was at the behest of the *Syrian* government?

Finally, as with suits against alleged U.S. government torturers, claims for damages arising out of alleged due process violations have also failed to produce judgments for extraordinary rendition victims in U.S. courts because of "special factors counseling hesitation" against recognizing *Bivens* claims.

c. *International Law Limits on Extraordinary Rendition.* CAT Article 3 provides that "[n]o State Party shall expel, return ('refouler') or extradite a person to another State where there are substantial grounds for believing that he would be in danger of being subjected to torture." An understanding attached to the Convention by the U.S. Senate upon its advice and consent states that the prohibition in Article 3 would apply when it is "more likely than not" that torture would follow such a rendition. S. Exec. Rep. No. 101-30, Resolution of Advice and Consent to Ratification ¶II(2) (1990). What information should lawyers take into account when asked to advise on a "more likely than not" determination? The CAT lacks a parallel provision regarding cruel, inhuman, or degrading treatment following rendition. What is the legal significance of this omission? *See* Michael John Garcia, *Renditions: Constraints Imposed by Laws on Torture* 7 (Cong. Res. Serv. RL32890), Sept. 8, 2009.

In the Foreign Affairs Reform and Restructuring Act of 1998 (FARRA), Congress purported to implement Article 3 of the CAT. Pub. L. No. 105-277, §2242, 112 Stat. 2681, 2681-822 to 2681-823 (codified at 8 U.S.C. §1231 note). The measure states that it is

> the policy of the United States not to . . . effect the involuntary return of any person to a country in which there are substantial grounds for believing the person would be in danger of being subjected to torture, regardless of whether the person is physically present in the United States. [*Id.* §2242(a).]

The Act requires relevant federal agencies to adopt regulations to implement the policy. But it provides no penalties for violation. Article 4(1) of the CAT requires each state party to "ensure that all acts of torture are offenses under its criminal law. The same shall apply to an attempt to commit torture and to an act by any person which constitutes complicity or participation in torture." Does the 1998 legislation satisfy the U.S. obligation under Article 4(1)? How about current Department of Homeland Security regulations that prohibit the removal of all persons to states where they "more likely than not" would be tortured? 8 C.F.R. §§208.16-18, 1208.16-18 (2019). (CIA regulations concerning renditions, if any, are not publicly available.) *See* Garcia, *supra,* at 9. Even if FARRA does not provide its own remedy, can it provide the basis for relief through, e.g., a habeas petition? *See Trinidad y Garcia v. Thomas,* 683 F.3d 952 (9th Cir. 2012) (en banc) (per curiam) (holding that courts have the power to entertain FARRA claims through habeas petitions, but only to ensure that the government has made the requisite determination).

Recall that the Torture Act, 18 U.S.C. §§2340, 2340A (2018), expressly criminalizes acts of torture and attempts to commit torture outside the United States. *Id.* §2340A(a). It also provides punishment for conspiracy to do either of those things. *Id.* §2340A(c). What facts would have to be proven in order to hold a CIA official criminally liable under the statute who arranged for an extraordinary rendition that resulted in torture? Does this statute satisfy the U.S. obligation under CAT Article 4(1)?

A March 2002 memorandum to the General Counsel of the Defense Department, signed by Jay S. Bybee of the Office of Legal Counsel, asserted that "the United States is free from any constraints imposed by the Torture Convention in deciding whether to transfer detainees that it is holding abroad to third countries." *Memorandum from Jay Bybee to William J. Haynes, Re: The President's Power as Commander in Chief to Transfer Captured Terrorists to the Control and Custody of Foreign Nations* (Mar. 13, 2002), *available at* https://fas.org/irp/agency/doj/olc/transfer.pdf (maintaining that the treaty does not apply extraterritorially). Recall that the Bush administration also decided early in 2002 that the Geneva Conventions did not apply to captured Al Qaeda or Taliban detainees. Were these positions legally defensible in 2002? Are they defensible now?

Do the protections of Common Article 3 of the Geneva Conventions apply to renditions of persons to countries where they may be tortured? *See* Garcia, *supra,* at 20 (probably not). Would the War Crimes Act prohibit renditions where torture is likely? *See id.* at 21 (yes, if U.S. personnel conspire with foreign officials and intend to so harm the victim). President Obama prohibited U.S. participation in coercive interrogation when he issued Executive Order No. 13,491, 74 Fed. Reg. 4893 (Jan. 22, 2009), *supra* p. 1017. Does the Obama order categorically forswear U.S. participation in extraordinary rendition operations going forward?

d. *Remedies from International Courts.* Khaled el-Masri, a German citizen of Lebanese descent, was pulled off a bus in Macedonia on New Year's Eve 2003 after border guards apparently confused him with an Al Qaeda operative who had a similar name. He was locked in a hotel room in Skopje for 23 days and told that he would be shot if he attempted to leave. He was then taken to the Skopje airport, where he was transferred to a CIA team. CIA operatives stripped el-Masri, then beat, shackled, hooded, and allegedly sodomized him, before flying him to Afghanistan, where he was detained in solitary confinement for more than four months. Once the mistaken identity was confirmed, he was flown to Albania and left on the side of a road.

When el-Masri sought relief in U.S. courts against the CIA for his rendition and mistreatment, his claims were dismissed on the basis of the state secrets privilege. *El-Masri v. United States,* 479 F.3d 296 (4th Cir. 2007). However, his claim against the government of Macedonia was vindicated when, in December 2012, the 17 judges of the European Court of Human Rights ruled unanimously that Macedonia violated Article 5 the European Convention on Human Rights, which prohibits torture and inhuman or degrading treatment. *El-Masri v. The Former Yugoslav Republic of Macedonia,* 2012-VII Eur. Ct. H.R. 263, *available at* https://www.echr.coe.int/Documents/Reports_Recueil_2012_VI.pdf. The Court awarded el-Masri about $78,000 in damages, finding that his extraordinary rendition was "by [Macedonia's] deliberate circumvention of due process . . . anathema to the rule of law and the values protected by the Convention." *Id.* at 268. Macedonian officials should have known, said the Court, that when el-Masri was handed over to U.S. authorities he faced a considerable risk that his Article 5 rights would be violated. The Macedonian government thus failed in its duty to protect el-Masri from such violations, and it actively facilitated his detention in Afghanistan by handing him over to the CIA. Macedonia also violated Article 5 by holding el-Masri for 23 days in the Skopje hotel.

The same court found multiple violations of the European Convention on Human Rights by the government of Poland when it failed to investigate serious violations of the Convention, including torture, ill-treatment, and undisclosed detention of Khalid Sheikh Mohammed, Abd al-Rahim al-Nashiri, and Abu Zubaydah while they were in CIA custody in a Polish CIA black site in 2002 and 2003. *Al-Nashiri v. Poland,* Former Fourth Section (July 24, 2014), HUDOC, http://hudoc.echr.coe.int/sites/eng/pages/search.aspx?i=001-146044. The Court ordered Poland to pay $262,000 in compensation to KSM and al-Nashiri. The ECHR issued a similar ruling on May 31, 2018, against Lithuania and Romania for their roles in hosting secret CIA prisons where the CIA tortured Abu Zubaydah and Abd al-Rahim al-Nashiri between 2003 and 2006. *Abu Zubahdah v. Lithuania,* First Section (May 31, 2018), HUDOC, https://hudoc.echr.coe.int/eng?i=001-183687; *Al-Nashiri v. Romania,* First Section (May 31, 2018), https://hudoc.echr.coe.int/eng?i=001-183685. The ECHR judges also ruled that Lithuania and Romania enabled the CIA to transfer the suspects to other prisons in Afghanistan and Guantánamo Bay. Alan Cowell & Charlie Savage, *Lithuania and Romania Complicit in C.I.A. Prisons, European Court Says,* N.Y. Times, May 31, 2018.

On May 9, 2018, the British government issued an apology to a Libyan dissident, Abdel Hakim Belhaj, and his wife, Fatima Boudchar, for its role in a CIA abduction in 2004. Declan Walsh, *Britain Apologizes for Role in Libyan Dissident's C.I.A. Nightmare,* N.Y. Times, May 10, 2018. Belhaj and his wife were detained in Malaysia on a tip by British operatives who told U.S. counterparts that the couple were suspected of having ties to Al Qaeda. *Id.* After transfer to a secret CIA site in Thailand, where Belhaj said he was tortured, the couple were transferred to Libya, where Belhaj was tortured and sentenced to death by the Libyan government before being released in 2010. *Id.* Prime Minister Theresa May stated in her letter to the couple that "the U.K. government's actions contributed to your detention, rendition and suffering." *Id.* Ms. Boudchar described her time in the CIA prison in Thailand to include black-clad figures wearing ski masks trussing her, chaining her to a wall, and assaulting her.

If rights violations occurred at U.S. black sites in Afghanistan after 9/11, how will victims hold the perpetrators accountable?

CASE STUDY OF COERCIVE INTERROGATION OF DETAINEES IN U.S. CUSTODY AFTER 9/11: SUMMARY OF BASIC PRINCIPLES

- After 9/11, the Bush administration authorized the CIA to use Enhanced Interrogation Techniques (EITs) to interrogate High Value Detainees (HVDs). The CIA adopted very aggressive interrogation methods reverse-engineered from earlier exercises used to train U.S. service personnel to withstand the effects of torture.

- The CIA sought and obtained opinions from the Office of Legal Counsel approving some of these techniques. These techniques then "migrated" to military interrogation and to the treatment of prisoners detained in Iraq.

- Both the effectiveness of EITs and their legality are hotly contested, as is the CIA's cooperation with its Inspector General and with the intelligence committees.

- The legality of EITs under international law depends on the definitions of torture and of cruel, inhumane, and degrading acts; the applicability of the Geneva Conventions to the conflicts in Afghanistan, Iraq, and elsewhere; and the War Crimes Act's definition of grave breaches of the Conventions.

- The legality of EITs under domestic law depends on compliance with the Torture Act, the Detainee Treatment Act, the War Crimes Act, and the U.S. Constitution. Some assert that the President may ignore any such constraints in his command of military operations, and attendant military intelligence operations, when he acts as Commander in Chief under Article II.

- Assuming that the use of EITs was unlawful in some instances, an interrogator may be able to escape criminal or civil liability by asserting official (and in some cases, sovereign) immunity, reliance on advice of counsel, necessity, or (for civil liability only) either the presumption against extraterritorial jurisdiction or failure to state a claim upon which relief could be granted.

- Extraordinary rendition is the transfer of a person from one jurisdiction to another, without the use of formal treaty or judicial process, for detention and interrogation. After 9/11, the CIA engaged in a program of extraordinary rendition of uncertain scope.

- The CAT prohibits rendition for torture, and the Senate approved this part of the CAT on the understanding that the prohibition applies when it is "more likely than not" that torture will follow a rendition. But the Bush administration initially took the position after 9/11 that the United States was free of the CAT's constraints in making rendering prisoners.

- President Obama issued an executive order in 2009 barring torture and outrages upon human dignity (including humiliating and degrading treatment) of persons in the custody or control of any U.S. employee or agent or detained in any U.S. facility, and directing that interrogation in armed conflict use only the techniques listed in the Army's field manual on interrogation.

PART VII PROSECUTING THREATS TO NATIONAL SECURITY

Criminalizing Terrorism and Its Precursors

A federal statute in the "Terrorism" chapter of the federal criminal code, 18 U.S.C. ch. 113B, defines both international and domestic terrorism:

> (1) The term "international terrorism" means activities that—
>
> (A) involve violent acts or acts dangerous to human life that are a violation of the criminal laws of the United States or of any State, or that would be a criminal violation if committed within the jurisdiction of the United States or of any State;
>
> (B) appear to be intended—
>
> (i) to intimidate or coerce a civilian population;
>
> (ii) to influence the policy of a government by intimidation or coercion; or
>
> (iii) to affect the conduct of a government by mass destruction, assassination or kidnaping; and
>
> (C) occur primarily outside the territorial jurisdiction of the United States, or transcend national boundaries in terms of the means by which they are accomplished, the persons they appear intended to intimidate or coerce, or the locale in which their perpetrators operate or seek asylum....
>
> (5) the term "domestic terrorism" means activities that—
>
> (A) [same as above];
>
> (B) [same as above]; and
>
> (C) occur primarily within the territorial jurisdiction of the United States. [18 U.S.C. §2331 (2018).]

These two definitions do not, however, themselves criminalize the conduct they define. In this chapter we explore some laws that do, and analyze the legal issues that those laws raise.

We begin by briefly considering a swath of federal laws that criminalize some of the means used to conduct terrorism. Although most of these laws have no express "international" or "foreign" element, "the US national security apparatus is fundamentally designed to look outside our borders and to turn inward only when a foreign threat has washed ashore." Susan Hennessey, *The Good Reasons to Not Charge All Terrorists with Terrorism*, Lawfare, Dec. 5, 2015.

In the wake of violence involving white supremacist extremists that appeared to escalate beginning in 2017, however, some have argued for the federal criminalization of domestic terrorism. *See, e.g.*, Mary McCord, *It's Time for Congress to Make Domestic Terrorism a Federal Crime*, Lawfare, Dec. 5, 2018. We therefore also consider the arguments for such legislation.

The crimes we consider initially here concern completed or ongoing acts of terrorism — in the blunt vernacular of FBI agents, "boom" crimes. Barbara McQuade, *Proposed Bills Would Help Combat Domestic Terrorism*, Lawfare, Aug. 20, 2019. But prosecution after the "boom" comes too late to save lives and property. After-boom prosecution is also unlikely to deter others who are religiously or politically motivated to commit terrorist attacks — especially when the perpetrators are themselves killed in, or shortly after, the attack. We therefore also consider "Left of Boom" (what might be termed "precursor") crimes, as well — those that occur at the front end of the terrorist timeline. Because these crimes precede any acts of violence, they present difficult evidentiary and constitutional challenges by criminalizing planning, association, and speech.

Finally, most criminal law enforcement targets conduct within the territorial jurisdiction of the United States. But international terrorism is often directed at U.S. nationals and property outside the United States, like American tourists, U.S. embassies, and U.S. military facilities or personnel. At the end of the chapter we consider the extraterritorial application of federal criminal laws to prosecute international terrorism.

A. "BOOM" TERRORIST CRIMES

Case Study: The 2017 Unite the Right "Rally"[1]

In August 2017, self-identified members of alt-right, white nationalist, neo-Nazi, and right-wing militia groups rallied in Charlottesville, Virginia, to "Unite the Right" and to protest the planned removal of a statue of Confederate General Robert E. Lee from a city park. Some carried Nazi and neo-Nazi flags and symbols as well as semi-automatic weapons, and some shouted racist and anti-Semitic slogans at counter-protesters. Violence between the marchers and counter-protesters resulted in multiple injuries. Counter-protesters were beaten with pipes and boards, and kicked by marchers in violence captured on video.

The governor of Virginia declared a state of emergency, and state police declared the rally to be an unlawful assembly. Not long afterwards, self-

1. Information for this case study was drawn from Michael German & Sara Robinson, *Wrong Priorities on Fighting Terrorism* 16 (Brennan Ctr. for Justice 2018) ("*Brennan Priorities Report*"); Harry Jaffe, *The Trump Appointee Who's Putting White Supremacists in Jail*, Wash. Post Mag., Aug. 7, 2019; C. Thompson, *Once Defiant, All Four White Supremacists Charged in Charlottesville Violence Plead Guilty*, ProPublica, May 6, 2019; Rosie Gray, *Trump Defends White-Nationalist Protesters: "Some Very Fine People on Both Sides,"* The Atlantic, Aug. 25, 2017.

identified white supremacist James Alex Fields Jr. drove his car at high speed into a crowd of counter-protesters, killing one and severely injuring more than a dozen others.

President Trump's first public comments on the violence included his observation that there were "very fine people on both sides," although he later condemned neo-Nazis and white nationalists. Attorney General Sessions called Fields' attack an act of "domestic terrorism."

Fields was subsequently arrested by state law enforcement officers. He was tried in a Virginia state court for the state crimes of first-degree murder and malicious wounding (among others), convicted, and sentenced to life imprisonment plus 419 years. He was also later charged by federal authorities with hate crimes under federal law, for which prosecutors sought the death penalty. Fields pleaded guilty to these federal crimes in exchange for the federal prosecutors' agreement to drop the death penalty.

The FBI announced that it would open a civil rights investigation of the violence. Four of the Unite the Right marchers whose violence was caught on video were subsequently identified by online sleuths as California residents associated with the "Rise Above Movement," allegedly a white supremacist organization. Federal prosecutors had the four arrested and brought back to Virginia to stand trial for traveling in interstate commerce with the intent to riot under 18 U.S.C. §2101 (2018) ("Anti-Riot Act") and for conspiracy under 18 U.S.C. §371 (2018) (conspiracy to commit offenses against the United States). The federal court rejected a broad-gauged constitutional challenge to the indictment, finding, inter alia, that

> §2101 does not proscribe mere advocacy of violence and explicitly excludes from its ambit the "mere oral or written . . . advocacy of ideas or . . . expression of belief." 18 U.S.C. §2102(b). The Act's proscription of use of interstate or foreign facilities with the intent to commit acts of violence in furtherance of a riot or to incite or instigate a riot, coupled with overt acts committed for those purposes, does not render the statute overbroad, as the First Amendment protects neither violence nor the incitement of violence. [United States v. Daley, 378 F. Supp. 3d 539, 554 (W.D. Va. 2019).]

All four defendants ultimately pleaded guilty and were sentenced to 27-37 months in a federal prison.

Notes and Questions

1. State Criminal Laws. Activities that kill or injure people or damage property are typically investigated and prosecuted by state authorities. In our federal system, state investigation and prosecution are the default law enforcement answer to violent acts. Thus, James Fields had already been charged by Virginia with first-degree murder before federal authorities charged him with federal hate crimes in federal court.

Federal criminal laws exist only to protect federal interests, usually with a jurisdictional "hook" in interstate or foreign commerce or involving crimes committed on federal property. *See* Charles Doyle, *Domestic Terrorism: Some Considerations* 2 (Cong. Res. Serv. LSB10340), Apr. 12, 2019. The terrorism chapter of the federal criminal code does include a crime of homicide, but it only applies when a U.S. national is killed *outside* the United States, 18 U.S.C. §2332(a) (2018), and even then no prosecution can proceed unless the Attorney General certifies that the offense "was intended to coerce, intimidate, or retaliate against a government or a civilian population." *Id.* §2332(d). Whether or not the Constitution would allow it to do so, Congress did not want to make every murder a federal terrorism crime, or to make even the murder of a U.S. national abroad a federal offense if it is an ordinary street crime.

2. *Federal Terrorism Crimes?* Notwithstanding various federal statutory definitions of terrorism, Congress has not yet criminalized terrorism, even international terrorism, as such. Instead, it has criminalized various *means* by which terrorist activities are carried out. Thus, 18 U.S.C. §2332b, which sets forth penalties for terrorist acts, somewhat confusingly defines "the federal crime of terrorism" (strictly for the purpose of describing the Attorney General's — i.e., the FBI's — investigatory, not prosecutorial, authority, *id.* §2332b(f)), by combining terrorist intent with violation of any one of more than 50 other federal criminal provisions:

Acts of Terrorism Transcending National Boundaries

18 U.S.C. §2332b (2018)

(g) Definitions. . . .

(5) The term "Federal crime of terrorism" means an offense that —

(A) is calculated to influence or affect the conduct of government by intimidation or coercion, or to retaliate against government conduct; and

(B) is a violation of —

(i) section 32 (relating to destruction of aircraft or aircraft facilities), 37 (relating to violence at international airports), 81 (relating to arson within special maritime and territorial jurisdiction), 175 or 175b (relating to biological weapons), 175c (relating to variola virus), 229 (relating to chemical weapons), subsection (a), (b), (c), or (d) of section 351 (relating to congressional, cabinet, and Supreme Court assassination and kidnaping), 831 (relating to nuclear materials), 832 (relating to participation in nuclear and weapons of mass destruction threats to the United States), 842(m) or (n) (relating to plastic explosives), 844(f)(2) or (3) (relating to arson and bombing of Government property risking or causing death), 844(i) (relating to arson and bombing of property used in interstate commerce), 930(c) (relating to killing or attempted killing during an attack on a Federal facility with a dangerous weapon), 956(a)(1) (relating to conspiracy to murder, kidnap, or maim persons abroad), 1030(a)(1) (relating to protection of computers), 1030(a)(5)(A) resulting in damage as defined in

1030(c)(4)(A)(i)(II) through (VI) (relating to protection of computers), 1114 (relating to killing or attempted killing of officers and employees of the United States), 1116 (relating to murder or manslaughter of foreign officials, official guests, or internationally protected persons), 1203 (relating to hostage taking), 1361 (relating to government property or contracts), 1362 (relating to destruction of communication lines, stations, or systems), 1363 (relating to injury to buildings or property within special maritime and territorial jurisdiction of the United States), 1366(a) (relating to destruction of an energy facility), 1751(a), (b), (c), or (d) (relating to Presidential and Presidential staff assassination and kidnaping), 1992 (relating to terrorist attacks and other acts of violence against railroad carriers and against mass transportation systems on land, on water, or through the air), 2155 (relating to destruction of national defense materials, premises, or utilities), 2156 (relating to national defense material, premises, or utilities), 2280 (relating to violence against maritime navigation), 2280a (relating to maritime safety), 2281 through 2281a (relating to violence against maritime fixed platforms), 2332 (relating to certain homicides and other violence against United States nationals occurring outside of the United States), 2332a (relating to use of weapons of mass destruction), 2332b (relating to acts of terrorism transcending national boundaries), 2332f (relating to bombing of public places and facilities), 2332g (relating to missile systems designed to destroy aircraft), 2332h (relating to radiological dispersal devices), 2332i (relating to acts of nuclear terrorism), 2339 (relating to harboring terrorists), 2339A (relating to providing material support to terrorists), 2339B (relating to providing material support to terrorist organizations), 2339C (relating to financing of terrorism), 2339D (relating to military-type training from a foreign terrorist organization), or 2340A (relating to torture) of this title;

(ii) sections 92 (relating to prohibitions governing atomic weapons) or 236 (relating to sabotage of nuclear facilities or fuel) of the Atomic Energy Act of 1954 (42 U.S.C. 2122 or 2284);

(iii) section 46502 (relating to aircraft piracy), the second sentence of section 46504 (relating to assault on a flight crew with a dangerous weapon), section 46505(b)(3) or (c) (relating to explosive or incendiary devices, or endangerment of human life by means of weapons, on aircraft), section 46506 if homicide or attempted homicide is involved (relating to application of certain criminal laws to acts on aircraft), or section 60123(b) (relating to destruction of interstate gas or hazardous liquid pipeline facility) of title 49; or

(iv) section 1010A of the Controlled Substances Import and Export Act (relating to narco-terrorism).

See generally Brennan Priorities Report, *supra*, at 6; Robert Chesney, *Should We Create a Federal Crime of Domestic Terrorism?*, Lawfare, Aug. 8, 2019.

For example, Abu Khattalah, accused of leading a lethal attack on the U.S. Special Mission compound in Benghazi that killed the U.S. Ambassador, was charged with, *inter alia,* murder of an internationally protected person, 18 U.S.C. §§1116 & 1111 (2018), attempted murder of a U.S. employee, *id.* §§1114 & 1111, and malicious destruction of U.S. property by means of fire and explosives, *id.* §844(f)(1) & (3). When such criminal statutes can be applied extraterritorially (see *infra* Part C), there is ample federal statutory authority for prosecuting international terrorists for foreign attacks, as well as for attacks they might orchestrate in the United States.

Fifty-one of the 57 crimes listed in 18 U.S.C. §2332b(g)(5)(B) are applicable to both international and domestic terrorism. *Brennan Priorities Report, supra,* at 5-6. For example, Timothy McVeigh, the Oklahoma City bomber, was convicted and ultimately executed for conspiring to use a weapon of mass destruction (WMD) to kill and injure persons and damage property of the United States, 18 U.S.C. §2332a(a)(2) & (3) (2018), as well as for the murder of federal officers, *id.* §1114, among other federal crimes. *See United States v. McVeigh,* 940 F. Supp. 1571 (D. Colo. 1996). WMDs are defined to include explosive devices and even large caliber firearms. 18 U.S.C. §921(a)(4). Eric Rudolph, who set off bombs in Olympic Park, Atlanta, and at multiple abortion clinics, pleaded guilty to bombing property used in interstate commerce. *Id.* §844(i). The eventual federal charges against James Fields show that federal hate crime statutes may also be used to prosecute domestic terrorists who cause bodily injury, or attempt to do so, using a dangerous weapon, because of the victim's perceived race, color, religion, national origin, gender, sexual orientation, or disability, where the crime affected interstate or foreign commerce. *Id.* §249; *see also id.* §§241, 245, 247, 3631.

3. Authorizing Federal Investigation? A new federal domestic terrorism statute might be needed not so much to fill an *enforcement* gap as to provide broader *investigative* authority for the FBI. While state law enforcement officials have the authority to investigate in-state boom crimes, if a crime transcends state lines, they may lack both sufficient authority and adequate resources. Thus, the four Unite the Right marchers who were traced to California were ultimately arrested on federal warrants and brought back to Virginia by federal, not state, authorities. "[W]hat's really at stake in the label [given a terrorist incident] . . . is the authority of the federal government to investigate the crime." Hennessey, *supra.*

Yet federal law already authorizes federal investigation of "federal terrorism crimes," as noted above. 18 U.S.C. §2332b(f) (2018) (assigning "primary investigative responsibility for all Federal crimes of terrorism" to the Attorney General). Moreover, the *Attorney General Guidelines for Domestic FBI Operations* (2008) expressly authorize "enterprise investigations" for establishing the factual basis for a belief that a group has committed or intends to commit an act of domestic terrorism within the 18 U.S.C. §2331(5) definition (see *supra* p. 1031). Such investigations may use "all lawful methods" to investigate

> the structure, scope, and nature of the group or organization including: its relationship, if any, to a foreign power; the identity and relationship of its members, employees, or other persons who may be acting in furtherance of its objectives; its finances and resources; its geographical dimensions; and its past and future activities and goals. [*Attorney General Guidelines, supra,* at 23.]

See Hennessey, *supra.* Even the FBI's 2010 *Civil Rights Program Policy Implementation Guide* provides that if the subject of a hate crime investigation has "a nexus to any kind of white supremacy extremist group," the case should be opened as both a domestic terrorism and a civil rights case. Fed. Bureau of Investigation, *Civil Rights Program Policy Implementation Guide* 14-15 (Oct. 18, 2010), https://www.justice.gov/archive/opa/docs/guidelines.pdf. This suggests that the FBI's civil rights investigation into the Unite the Right rally violence could have been conducted as both. *See Brennan Priorities Report, supra,* at 16.

In any case, the most important constraint on any federal investigation of domestic terrorism is constitutional. Any national security exception to the Fourth Amendment warrant requirement that exists may apply only to the collection of foreign intelligence. *See supra* Chapter 20. By contrast, domestic security surveillance normally requires a warrant, *United States v. U.S. Dist. Court (Keith),* 407 U.S. 297 (1972) (*supra* p. 583).

4. The Moral Equivalent of International Terrorism? Even if there is no significant gap in the federal criminal code for terrorism crimes, and sufficient federal investigative authority already exists, formal statutory criminalization of domestic terrorism could serve a signaling function: that domestic terrorism is the "moral equivalent of international terrorism," just as illegitimate, and at least as deserving of prioritization in counterterrorism. *See, e.g.,* McQuade, *supra;* Jason Blazakis, *American Terrorists: Why Current Laws Are Inadequate for Violent Extremists at Home,* Lawfare, Dec. 2, 2018 (criminalization of domestic terrorism "will send an important political message"). Making a federal crime of domestic terrorism "would indicate seriousness of purpose, help steer discretionary allocations of investigative resources, and hopefully help to further delegitimize domestic political violence." Chesney, *supra.* Perhaps the debate about criminalizing domestic terrorism is less about enforcement gaps or investigatory authority than it is a proxy for political leadership in delegitimizing such terrorism and prioritizing it in forming counterterrorist policy.

At this writing, pending bills in Congress that would criminalize domestic terrorism don't actually call the new crime "domestic terrorism" anywhere but in their titles. Instead, they continue to criminalize the *means* of terrorism and add a terrorist intent requirement, essentially criminalizing acts that 18 U.S.C. §2332b(g)(5) (2018) already calls the "[f]ederal crime of terrorism." *See, e.g.,* Confronting the Threat of Domestic Terrorism Act, H.R. 4192, 116th Cong. (2019).

B. "LEFT OF BOOM" (PRECURSOR) CRIMES

Following the 2019 mass shooting of Hispanic victims at a Walmart in El Paso, former Deputy Attorney General Rod Rosenstein told the press, "We need to catch them before they act on their plans." Sabrina Tavernise, *Shootings Renew Debate over How to Combat Domestic Terrorism,* N.Y. Times, Aug. 5, 2019. Both state and federal laws have traditionally used conspiracy principles for such front-end law enforcement, and federal law has added a trio of statutes criminalizing "material support" for terrorists and foreign terrorist organizations. But such front-end enforcement — prosecuting "left of boom" crimes — has presented serious constitutional challenges, insofar as it depends on evidence of speech, association, and advocacy.

1. Conspiracy Crimes

Reading *United States v. Rahman*

In this case, the Second Circuit considered appeals by ten defendants convicted of seditious conspiracy and other offenses arising out of a wide-ranging plot to conduct a campaign of urban terrorism. Among the activities of some or all of the defendants were rendering assistance to those who bombed the World Trade Center in 1993, planning to bomb bridges and tunnels in New York City, murdering Rabbi Meir Kahane, and planning to murder the President of Egypt.

One of the defendants, Abdul Rahman, was an Egyptian-born Islamic scholar and cleric who legally resided in the United States. The government tried Rahman for seditious conspiracy. The seditious conspiracy statute provides:

> If two or more persons in any State or Territory, or in any place subject to the jurisdiction of the United States, conspire to overthrow, put down or to destroy by force the Government of the United States, or to levy war against them, or to oppose by force the authority thereof, or by force to prevent, hinder or delay the execution of any law of the United States, or by force to seize, take, or possess any property of the United States contrary to the authority thereof, they shall each be fined under this title or imprisoned not more than twenty years, or both. [18 U.S.C. §2384 (2018).]

Among other defenses, the court in *Rahman* considered the defendant's argument that the offense of "seditious conspiracy" violated the First Amendment as applied to speech.

- What acts did Rahman perform? Did he do anything more than talk and preach?
- With the exception of the planned murder of Egyptian President Mubarak, all of the terrorist acts Rahman discussed with his co-conspirators were to take place in the United States. Would you call him an international terrorist, a domestic terrorist, or something else? How helpful are these categories?
- Where does the Court of Appeals draw the line between constitutionally protected speech and speech that can appropriately be subject to criminal sanction?
- Why did the Rahman defendants' speech fall on the wrong side of that line? Is it clear to you when speech inciting acts of terrorism will and will not be protected?

United States v. Rahman

United States Court of Appeals, Second Circuit, 1999
189 F.3d 88

Per Curiam: . . . The Government adduced evidence at trial showing the following: Abdel Rahman, a blind Islamic scholar and cleric, was the leader of the seditious conspiracy, the purpose of which was "*jihad*," in the sense of a struggle against the enemies of Islam. Indicative of this purpose, in a speech to his followers Abdel Rahman instructed that they were to "do *jihad* with the sword, with the cannon, with the grenades, with the missile . . . against God's enemies." Abdel Rahman's role in the conspiracy was generally limited to overall supervision and direction of the membership, as he made efforts to remain a level above the details of individual operations. However, as a cleric and the group's leader, Abdel Rahman was entitled to dispense "*fatwas,*" religious opinions on the holiness of an act, to members of the group sanctioning proposed courses of conduct and advising them whether the acts would be in furtherance of *jihad.*

According to his speeches and writings, Abdel Rahman perceives the United States as the primary oppressor of Muslims worldwide, active in assisting Israel to gain power in the Middle East, and largely under the control of the Jewish lobby. Abdel Rahman also considers the secular Egyptian government of Mubarak to be an oppressor because it has abided Jewish migration to Israel while seeking to decrease Muslim births. Holding these views, Abdel Rahman believes that *jihad* against Egypt and the United States is mandated by the Qur'an. Formation of a *jihad* army made up of small "divisions" and "battalions" to carry out this *jihad* was therefore necessary, according to Abdel Rahman, in order to beat back these oppressors of Islam including the United States. . . .

I. CONSTITUTIONAL CHALLENGES . . .

B. Seditious Conspiracy Statute and the First Amendment

Abdel Rahman, joined by the other appellants, contends that the seditious conspiracy statute, 18 U.S.C. §2384, is an unconstitutional burden on free speech and the free exercise of religion in violation of the First Amendment. First, Abdel Rahman argues that the statute is facially invalid because it criminalizes protected expression and that it is overbroad and unconstitutionally vague. Second, Abdel Rahman contends that his conviction violated the First Amendment because it rested solely on his political views and religious practices.

1. Facial Challenge

a. Restraint on Speech. . . . As Section 2384 proscribes "speech" only when it constitutes an agreement to use force against the United States, Abdel Rahman's generalized First Amendment challenge to the statute is without merit. Our court has previously considered and rejected a First Amendment challenge to Section 2384. *See United States v. Lebron,* 222 F.2d 531, 536 (2d Cir. 1955). Although *Lebron*'s analysis of the First Amendment issues posed by Section 2384 was brief, the panel found the question was squarely controlled by the Supreme Court's then-recent decision in *Dennis v. United States,* 341 U.S. 494 (1951). In *Dennis,* the Court upheld the constitutionality of the Smith Act, which made it a crime to advocate, or to conspire to advocate, the overthrow of the United States government by force or violence. *See* 18 U.S.C. §2385; *Dennis,* 341 U.S. at 494. The *Dennis* Court concluded that, while the "element of speech" inherent in Smith Act convictions required that the Act be given close First Amendment scrutiny, the Act did not impermissibly burden the expression of protected speech, as it was properly "directed at advocacy [of overthrow of the government by force], not discussion." *See id.* at 502.

After *Dennis,* the Court broadened the scope of First Amendment restrictions on laws that criminalize subversive advocacy. It remains fundamental that while the state may not criminalize the expression of views — even including the view that violent overthrow of the government is desirable — it may nonetheless outlaw encouragement, inducement, or conspiracy to take violent action. Thus, in *Yates v. United States,* 354 U.S. 298, 318 (1957), overruled in part on other grounds, *Burks v. United States,* 437 U.S. 1, 7 (1978), the Court interpreted the Smith Act to prohibit only the advocacy of concrete violent action, but not "advocacy and teaching of forcible overthrow as an abstract principle, divorced from any effort to instigate action to that end." And in *Brandenburg v. Ohio,* 395 U.S. 444, 447 (1969) (per curiam), the Court held that a state may proscribe subversive advocacy only when such advocacy is directed towards, and is likely to result in, "imminent lawless action."

The prohibitions of the seditious conspiracy statute are much further removed from the realm of constitutionally protected speech than those at issue in *Dennis* and its progeny. To be convicted under Section 2384, one must conspire to *use* force, not just to *advocate* the use of force. We have no doubt that this passes the test of constitutionality. . . .

b. Vagueness and Overbreadth. Abdel Rahman also contends that Section 2384 is overbroad and void for vagueness.

(i) *Overbreadth.* . . . Abdel Rahman argues that Section 2384 is overbroad because Congress could have achieved its public safety aims "without chilling First Amendment rights" by punishing only "substantive acts involving bombs, weapons, or other violent acts." One of the beneficial purposes of the conspiracy law is to permit arrest and prosecution before the substantive crime has been accomplished. The Government, possessed of evidence of conspiratorial planning, need not wait until buildings and tunnels have been bombed and people killed before arresting the conspirators. Accordingly, it is well established that the Government may criminalize certain preparatory steps towards criminal action, even when the crime consists of the use of conspiratorial or exhortatory words. Because Section 2384 prohibits only conspiratorial agreement, we are satisfied that the statute is not constitutionally overbroad.

(ii) *Vagueness.* . . . There is indeed authority suggesting that the word "seditious" does not sufficiently convey what conduct it forbids to serve as an essential element of a crime. *See Keyishian v. Board of Regents,* 385 U.S. 589, 598 (1967) (noting that "dangers fatal to First Amendment freedoms inhere in the word 'seditious,'" and invalidating law that provided, *inter alia,* that state employees who utter "seditious words" may be discharged). But the word "seditious" does not appear in the prohibitory text of the statute; it appears only in the caption. The terms of the statute are far more precise. The portions charged against Abdel Rahman and his co-defendants — conspiracy to levy war against the United States and to oppose by force the authority thereof — do not involve terms of such vague meaning. Furthermore, they unquestionably specify that agreement *to use force* is an essential element of the crime. Abdel Rahman therefore cannot prevail on the claim that the portions of Section 2384 charged against him criminalize mere expressions of opinion, or are unduly vague.

2. *Application of Section 2384 to Abdel Rahman's Case*

Abdel Rahman also argues that he was convicted not for entering into any conspiratorial agreement that Congress may properly forbid, but "solely for his religious words and deeds" which, he contends, are protected by the First Amendment. In support of this claim, Abdel Rahman cites the Government's use in evidence of his speeches and writings.

There are two answers to Abdel Rahman's contention. The first is that freedom of speech and of religion do not extend so far as to bar prosecution of one who uses a public speech or a religious ministry to commit crimes. Numerous crimes under the federal criminal code are, or can be, committed by speech alone. As examples: Section 2 makes it an offense to "counsel[ ]," "command[ ]," "induce[ ]" or "procure[ ]" the commission of an offense against the United States. 18 U.S.C. §2(a). Section 371 makes it a crime to "conspire . . . to commit any offense against the United States." 18 U.S.C. §371. Section 373, with which Abdel Rahman was charged, makes it a crime to "solicit[ ], command[ ], induce[ ], or otherwise endeavor[ ] to persuade" another person to commit a crime of violence. 18 U.S.C. §373(a). Various other statutes, like Section 2384, criminalize conspiracies of specified objectives, *see, e.g.*, 18 U.S.C. §1751(d) (conspiracy to kidnap); 18 U.S.C. §1951 (conspiracy to interfere with commerce through robbery, extortion, or violence); 21 U.S.C. §846 (conspiracy to violate drug laws). All of these offenses are characteristically committed through speech. Notwithstanding that political speech and religious exercise are among the activities most jealously guarded by the First Amendment, one is not immunized from prosecution for such speech-based offenses merely because one commits them through the medium of political speech or religious preaching. Of course, courts must be vigilant to insure that prosecutions are not improperly based on the mere expression of unpopular ideas. But if the evidence shows that the speeches crossed the line into criminal solicitation, procurement of criminal activity, or conspiracy to violate the laws, the prosecution is permissible.

The evidence justifying Abdel Rahman's conviction for conspiracy and solicitation showed beyond a reasonable doubt that he crossed this line. His speeches were not simply the expression of ideas; in some instances they constituted the crime of conspiracy to wage war on the United States under Section 2384 and solicitation of attack on the United States military installations, as well as of the murder of Egyptian President Hosni Mubarak under Section 373.

For example: Abdel Rahman told Salem he "should make up with God . . . by turning his rifle's barrel to President Mubarak's chest, and kill[ing] him." Tr. 4633.

On another occasion, speaking to Abdo Mohammed Haggag about murdering President Mubarak during his visit to the United States, Abdel Rahman told Haggag, "Depend on God. Carry out this operation. It does not require a fatwa. . . . You are ready in training, but do it. Go ahead." Tr. 10108.

The evidence further showed that Siddig Ali consulted with Abdel Rahman about the bombing of the United Nations Headquarters, and Abdel Rahman told him, "Yes, it's a must, it's a duty." Tr. 5527-5529.

On another occasion, when Abdel Rahman was asked by Salem about bombing the United Nations, he counseled against it on the ground that it would be "bad for Muslims," Tr. 6029, but added that Salem should "find a plan to destroy or to bomb or to . . . inflict damage to the American Army." Tr. 6029-6030.

Words of this nature — ones that instruct, solicit, or persuade others to commit crimes of violence — violate the law and may be properly prosecuted regardless of whether they are uttered in private, or in a public speech, or in administering the duties of a religious ministry. The fact that his speech or conduct was "religious" does not immunize him from prosecution under generally-applicable criminal statutes.

Abdel Rahman also protests the Government's use in evidence of his speeches, writings, and preachings that did not in themselves constitute the crimes of solicitation or conspiracy. He is correct that the Government placed in evidence many instances of Abdel Rahman's writings and speeches in which Abdel Rahman expressed his opinions within the protection of the First Amendment. However, while the First Amendment fully protects Abdel Rahman's right to express hostility against the United States, and he may not be prosecuted for so speaking, it does not prevent the use of such speeches or writings in evidence when relevant to prove a pertinent fact in a criminal prosecution. The Government was free to demonstrate Abdel Rahman's resentment and hostility toward the United States in order to show his motive for soliciting and procuring illegal attacks against the United States and against President Mubarak of Egypt.

Furthermore, Judge Mukasey properly protected against the danger that Abdel Rahman might be convicted because of his unpopular religious beliefs that were hostile to the United States. He explained to the jury the limited use it was entitled to make of the material received as evidence of motive. He instructed that a defendant could not be convicted on the basis of his beliefs or the expression of them — even if those beliefs favored violence. He properly instructed the jury that it could find a defendant guilty only if the evidence proved he committed a crime charged in the indictment.

We reject Abdel Rahman's claim that his conviction violated his rights under the First Amendment. . . .

Reading *United States v. Stone*

Defendants in this case were alleged to have been part of an apocalyptic Christian militant group who were plotting to kill local law enforcement officers in order to catalyze a broader antigovernment uprising. *See generally* Nick Bunkley & Charlie Savage, *Militia Charged with Plotting to Murder Officers*, N.Y. Times, Mar. 29, 2010. ("Alleged" is used deliberately here, as the defendants were acquitted of some counts.)

The group called itself Hutaree (a word its leader, David Stone, Sr., apparently invented to mean Christian warriors) and viewed local law enforcement as "foot soldiers" for the federal government. The group was alleged to have acquired firearms, ammunition, explosives, and uniforms, and to have engaged in combat training.

The indictment alleged a multi-phase plot, by which the group would attract the attention of law enforcement by killing an officer after a traffic stop, killing an officer and his or her family at home, ambushing an officer in a rural community, or luring an officer with a false 911 emergency call and then killing him or her. The group then planned to use explosives to attack the ensuing funeral procession, including any federal law enforcement officers in attendance. After that attack, the group would retreat to "rally points" to defend their positions with firearms, hoping that this engagement would be a catalyst for a more widespread uprising against the U.S. government.

The defendants were charged with seditious conspiracy, 18 U.S.C. §2384, conspiracy to use weapons of mass destruction, 18 U.S.C. §2332a(a)(2), and sundry firearms violations. After trial, they moved for judgments of acquittal on all counts.

- Both Abdul Rahman and David Stone, Sr., were tried for seditious conspiracy partly on the basis of their speech. What accounts for the different outcomes?
- The very word "seditious" sounds obsolete, and indeed the seditious conspiracy statute was enacted more than 70 years ago at the start of the McCarthy era in large part to target suspected Communists and their supporters. Can you see why it may not have broad application to domestic terrorism, even apart from any First Amendment issues it raises?
- The charge of conspiracy to use weapons of mass destruction (which are broadly and counterintuitively defined to include ordinary bombs, grenades, and even large-caliber firearms, *see* 18 U.S.C. §§2332a(c)(2)(A) and 921(a)(4) (2018)) does not pose the same definitional challenge as the seditious conspiracy statute, but the court acquits the defendants of this charge as well. Why? What is the evidentiary challenge in proving *any* conspiracy?

United States v. Stone

United States District Court, Eastern District of Michigan, Mar. 27, 2012
No. 10-20123, 2012 WL 1034937

VICTORIA A. ROBERTS, District Judge.

I. INTRODUCTION

This matter is before the Court on Defendants' motions for judgment of acquittal pursuant to Rule 29 of the Federal Rules of Criminal Procedure. . . .

III. ANALYSIS

A. Standard of Review

. . . In reviewing a Rule 29 motion, "the relevant question is whether, after viewing the evidence in the light most favorable to the prosecution, any rational trier of fact could have found the essential elements of the crime beyond a reasonable doubt." *Jackson v. Virginia,* 443 U.S. 307, 319 (1979). . . .

B. Conspiracy Law and the First Amendment

In order to sustain a conviction for conspiracy, the Government must prove that each Defendant: (1) agreed to violate the law; (2) possessed the knowledge and intent to join the conspiracy; and (3) participated in the conspiracy. In addition, a conspiracy requires a specific plan.

"The elements of a conspiracy may be proven entirely by circumstantial evidence, but each element of the offense must be proved beyond a reasonable doubt." *United States v. Wexler,* 838 F.2d 88, 90 (3d Cir. 1988) (citations omitted). Indeed, it is common for a conspiracy to be proved by circumstantial evidence; a criminal agreement is rarely explicit. Thus, in the absence of "proof of a formal agreement among the conspirators . . . a tacit or mutual understanding . . . is sufficient to show a conspiracy." *United States v. Lee,* 991 F.2d 343, 348 (6th Cir. 1993). . . .

The issue of guilt or innocence in a conspiracy is always an individualized inquiry. *Kotteakos v. United States,* 328 U.S. 750, 772 (1946) ("Guilt with us remains individual and personal, even as respects conspiracies. It is not a matter of mass application."). The government must prove the intent of each individual conspirator to enter into the conspiracy, knowing of its objectives, and agreeing to further its goals. . . .

Where a conspiracy implicates First Amendment protections such as freedom of association and freedom of speech, the court must make a "specially meticulous inquiry" into the government's evidence so there is not "an unfair imputation of the intent or acts of some participants to all others." *United States v. Dellinger,* 472 F.2d 340, 392 (7th Cir. 1972). It is black-letter law that "[a] defendant cannot be convicted of conspiracy merely on the grounds of guilt by association, and mere association with the members of the conspiracy without the intention and agreement to accomplish an illegal objective is not sufficient to make an individual a conspirator." *Lee,* 991 F.2d at 348. Likewise, mere presence at the scene does not establish participation in a conspiracy. *United States v. Paige,* 470 F.3d 603, 609 (6th Cir. 2006).

The Government has consistently maintained that this case is not about freedom of speech or association, but about the specific acts of violence alleged in the Indictment. . . . However, much of the Government's evidence against Defendants at trial was in the form of speeches, primarily by Stone, Sr., who frequently made statements describing law enforcement as the enemy, discussing the killing of police officers, and the need to go to war. Indeed, at oral argument on March 26, 2012, the Government asked the Court to find the existence of a seditious conspiracy based primarily on two conversations involving Stone, Sr., and others — the first on August 13, 2009, and the second on February 20, 2010.

Additional evidence the Government relies on includes Defendants' participation in various military-style training exercises, anti-Government literature found in some of the Defendants' homes, and guns and ammunition collected by various Defendants. But, none of these things is inherently unlawful. While this evidence may provide circumstantial proof that some of the Defendants planned to do something unlawful, the Indictment sets forth a specific plot to draw law enforcement to Michigan from around the country by killing a member of local law enforcement. The Indictment alleges the Defendants would then attack the funeral procession and retreat to "rally points" to conduct operations against the government with the intent that these operations would be a catalyst for a more widespread uprising between the Hutaree and the Federal Government.

Because the Government's proofs consist overwhelmingly of speech and association, the Court takes particular care to analyze the evidence against each defendant to determine whether it is capable of convincing beyond a reasonable doubt.

C. Count — I Seditious Conspiracy

1. Seditious Conspiracy Requires that Acts of Force Be Directed Specifically at the Government of the United States

Count One of the Indictment charges Seditious Conspiracy, 18 U.S.C. §2384. . . .

Specifically, the Government charges Defendants with conspiring to "oppose by force the authority" of the United States Government. Essential to that charge, Defendants must have agreed to oppose some positive assertion of authority by the United States Government; mere violations of the law do not suffice. *Baldwin v. Franks,* 120 U.S. 678, 693 (1887). . . .

The law is clear that seditious conspiracy requires an agreement to oppose by force the authority of the United States itself. It must be an offense against the Nation, not local units of government. *See Commonwealth of Pennsylvania v. Nelson,* 350 U.S. 497, 505 (1956) ("Sedition against the United States is not a local offense. It is a crime against the Nation." (citation and quotation marks omitted)). Any overt act in furtherance of seditious conspiracy must further a common plan to oppose the United States by force; otherwise, "the seditious conspiracy statute would expand infinitely to embrace the entire agenda of anyone who violated it. . . ." *United States v. Rahman,* 854 F. Supp. 254, 260 (S.D.N.Y. 1994).

. . . [W]hile the Government presented evidence of vile and often hateful speech, and may have even shown that certain Defendants conspired to commit some crime — perhaps to murder local law enforcement — offensive speech and a conspiracy to do something other than forcibly resist a positive show of authority by the Federal Government is not enough to sustain a charge of seditious conspiracy. A conspiracy to murder law enforcement is a far cry from a conspiracy to forcibly oppose the authority of the Government of the United States. . . .

3. The Evidence Against Defendants Is Insufficient to Sustain the Charge

i. David Stone, Sr. The Government's strongest case is against David Stone, Sr.; however, even the evidence against Stone is not enough to sustain the seditious conspiracy charge. . . .

Essential to the seditious conspiracy charge is evidence of an agreement between David Stone and the coconspirators to spark an uprising with federal law enforcement after attacking a funeral procession. While the record contains evidence that Stone may have wanted to engage in a war with the federal government and/or "the Brotherhood," it is totally devoid of an agreement to do so between Stone and the other Defendants.

. . . The bulk of this evidence includes training sessions where various explosive devices and firearms were used and where Stone makes anti-Government statements. For example, on October 18, 2008, Stone mentions "rally points" and a desire to "kill." On December 8, 2008 Stone tells Murray in an email to "stand ready" to go to war against the ATF if the ATF "pushes further." Likewise, on December 20, 2008, Stone refers to one of his guns as a "cop killer." On August 27, 2009, Stone says a shape charge would definitely take out a convoy. While vile, all of this speech is protected by the First Amendment.

The Court is aware that protected speech and mere words can be sufficient to show a conspiracy. In this case, however, they do not rise to that level. Stones' statements and exercises do not evince a concrete agreement to forcibly resist the authority of the United States Government. His diatribes evince nothing more than his own hatred for — perhaps even desire to fight or kill — law enforcement; this is not the same as seditious conspiracy.

At the hearing, the Government contended that the conspiracy evolved on August 13, 2009 when Stone, Joshua Stone, and others plotted an attack on "the Brotherhood," consisting of all law enforcement, local and federal; they discussed killing a local police officer and attacking the funeral procession. Stone states that in three days 1,000 members of law enforcement would converge for the funeral, and that he would need mortars. This "plan" is utterly short on specifics. Further, it is a stretch to infer that other members of the Hutaree knew of this plan, and agreed to further it. More importantly, though, is that the alleged plan makes no reference to a widespread uprising against the United States Government. That Stone may have had some vague belief that local police officers were members of the "Brotherhood," and were, therefore, somehow connected with federal agents is of no consequence. *See Rahman,* 854 F. Supp. at 259-60 (holding that whether Defendant subjectively believed murder of Israeli citizen would further seditious conspiracy was irrelevant, because the law of seditious conspiracy has objective limits).

The next time Stone mentions "rally points" is on August 22, 2009; then he tells the other Defendants if the Government starts backing them in with swine flu vaccinations, they have a "rally point." This is obviously insufficient to establish an agreement between Stone and others to forcibly oppose the authority of the United States Government.

On September 13, 2009 Stone tells Murray that the Hutaree's goal "is to go to war." He mentions killing police officers and their families and says that fifteen or twenty members of the Hutaree would be ready to pull the trigger. While these statements are offensive and disturbing, the Indictment alleges a specific agreement to forcibly oppose the United States Government — not to go on a shooting rampage, not to go to war with police officers in general. Moreover, a desire or goal to go to war on the part of Stone alone is not enough to sustain the conspiracy charge against him; the Government needs to show Stone agreed with at least one other person to carry out the goal. It did not.

Stone again mentions going to war on February 6, 2010 while attempting to attend a militia summit. He also makes a vague reference to getting to "the feds" and the Hutaree's intention to oppose the Brotherhood. Again, absent more concrete evidence of an agreement to spark the uprising central to the seditious conspiracy charge, Stone's remarks during the road trip evince little more than Stone's distrust of the federal government and desire to fight against it.

That others in the car did not explicitly oppose Stone's remarks does not convince the Court that there was a specific agreement to oppose the United States Government while that Government exercised its authority, and in the manner specified in the Indictment. This would require too many inferences. While it is often necessary to make certain inferences from circumstantial evidence in conspiracy cases, the plethora of inferences the Government asks this Court to make are in excess of what the law allows. But, the Government crosses the line from inference to pure speculation a number of times in this case. Charges built on speculation cannot be sustained.

Finally, on February 20, Stone engages in a conversation with Meeks, Sickles, Piatek, Joshua Stone, and Clough about killing police officers. Stone again brings up the idea of murdering an officer and attacking the funeral procession. Nothing resembling an agreement to spark an uprising with the Federal Government is reached during this conversation. Defendants toss out ideas of ways in which to kill police that are often incredible; more importantly, they never come to a consensus or agreement on ways in which to oppose federal agents by force. Stone even states, "there's a hundred and one scenarios you can use." This back and forth banter, like the other anti-government speech and statements evincing a desire — even a goal — to kill police, is simply insufficient to sustain the seditious conspiracy charge; it requires *an agreement and plan of action, not mere advocacy* or hateful speech. . . .

D. Count II — Conspiracy to Use Weapons of Mass Destruction

Defendants are charged with conspiracy to use weapons of mass destruction in violation of 18 U.S.C. §2332a(a)(2). The allegations of Count II of the Indictment specifically incorporate the factual allegations of Count I. In addition, the Indictment states that Defendants "conspired to use, without lawful authority, one or more weapons of mass destruction, specifically explosive bombs, explosive mines, and other similar explosive devices, against persons and property within the United States, that is, local, state, and federal law enforcement officers and vehicles owned and used by local, state, and federal law enforcement agencies." Second Superseding Indictment p. 11.

The essence of a charge of conspiracy is an agreement, as explained above. For the same reasons the Court does not find the existence of an agreement with respect to Count I, the Court cannot find that the Government proved an agreement among the Defendants to use weapons of mass destruction in the manner described in the Indictment, beyond a reasonable doubt. . . .

IV. CONCLUSION

The Court **GRANTS** Defendants' motions for judgment of acquittal on [the conspiracy counts, but denied them as to certain firearms counts.]

It Is Ordered.

Notes and Questions

1. *Inciting Imminent Harm.* The *Rahman* court's synopsis of the constitutional law governing advocacy of lawless action makes it sound more consistent than it is. In a World War I case under the 1918 Sedition Act, the Supreme Court declared that the government could constitutionally criminalize the utterance of "words . . . used in such circumstances . . . as to create a clear and present danger that they will bring about the substantive evils that Congress has a right to prevent." *Schenck v. United*

States, 249 U.S. 47, 52 (1919). The Court subsequently seemed to relax the clear-and-present-danger test in *Dennis v. United States*, 341 U.S. 494 (1951), by finding that the harm from an overthrow of the government would be so grave that the government need not show its imminence or probability in order to punish advocacy of the overthrow. Dennis and his co-defendants were convicted and sentenced to long prison terms for violating the Smith Act, which made it unlawful "to knowingly or willfully advocate, abet, advise, or teach the duty, necessity, desirability, or propriety of overthrowing or destroying any government in the United States by force or violence." Act of June 28, 1940, 54 Stat. 670, 671. What were their criminal acts? Apparently, according to the evidence adduced by the government, assembling to discuss and plan future teaching of books by Stalin, Marx and Engels, and Lenin.

Finally, without disavowing these chilling precedents, the Court reversed a conviction for "criminal syndicalism" in *Brandenberg v. Ohio*, 395 U.S. 444 (1969). There, the defendant had given a racist and anti-Semitic speech at a Ku Klux Klan rally. The Court held that a State could not criminalize "advocacy of the use of force or of law violation except where such advocacy is directed to inciting or producing imminent lawless action *and* is *likely* to incite or produce such action." *Id.* at 447 (emphases added).

How does the seditious conspiracy statute fare under these tests? As applied in *Rahman* and *Stone*?

2. Distinguishing the Cases. Judging from the quoted evidence, Stone seems to have engaged in much the same kind of speech as Rahman, but without the added cover of religious expression. Why do you suppose that Stone and the Hutaree were acquitted of the conspiracy charges, while Rahman's conviction was affirmed?

3. Conspiracy. Stone was charged with two different counts of conspiracy. What element of the seditious conspiracy count did the government fail to prove? Could the government have charged James Fields or the four marchers from the Charlottesville Unite the Right violence with seditious conspiracy?

The same limiting substantive element did not apply in *Stone* to the count of conspiracy to use WMD. Why did the court acquit on that count? Conspiracy is sometimes called the prosecutor's favorite charge in ordinary criminal cases. Can you say why? What is the downside to a conspiracy count in a case like *Stone*?

4. Criminalizing Domestic Terrorism. How could Congress criminalize domestic terrorism to make prosecution of a case like *Stone* easier? Should it do so?

2. Material Support Crimes

Terrorists often evade capture or die in an attack. For such individuals, criminal sanctions provide neither punishment nor deterrence. But terrorists typically cannot carry out their attacks in the first place without support and encouragement from others. Thus, policymakers and prosecutors have gravitated toward laws criminalizing "material support" for terrorism, often well left of boom. The first material support statute, 18 U.S.C. §2339A (2018), reproduced below, makes it a crime to provide support in preparation for or carrying out specific criminal acts.

The second such statute, 18 U.S.C. §2339B, criminalizes support for any organization that the Secretary of State has designated as a "foreign terrorist organization" (FTO) under 8 U.S.C. §1189(a)(1), if the defendant knows that the organization has been so designated or if he knows that it engages in or has engaged in terrorist activities. The Secretary may designate a foreign organization as an FTO if she finds that it engages in "terrorism," defined as "premeditated, politically motivated violence perpetrated against noncombatant targets by subnational groups or clandestine agents," 22 U.S.C. §2656f(d)(2), or in "terrorist activity," defined as

> any activity which is unlawful under the laws of the place where it is committed (or which, if it had been committed in the United States, would be unlawful under the laws of the United States or any State) and which involves any of the following:
>
> (I) The highjacking or sabotage of any conveyance (including an aircraft, vessel, or vehicle).
>
> (II) The seizing or detaining, and threatening to kill, injure, or continue to detain, another individual in order to compel a third person (including a governmental organization) to do or abstain from doing any act as an explicit or implicit condition for the release of the individual seized or detained.
>
> (III) A violent attack upon an internationally protected person (as defined in section 1116(b)(4) of Title 18) or upon the liberty of such a person.
>
> (IV) An assassination.
>
> (V) The use of any—
>
> (a) biological agent, chemical agent, or nuclear weapon or device, or
>
> (b) explosive, firearm, or other weapon or dangerous device (other than for mere personal monetary gain),
>
> with intent to endanger, directly or indirectly, the safety of one or more individuals or to cause substantial damage to property.
>
> (VI) A threat, attempt, or conspiracy to do any of the foregoing.
>
> [8 U.S.C. §1182(a)(3)(B)(iii).]

The courts have held that an organization with a U.S. presence is entitled to notice and an opportunity to be heard before it is designated as an FTO, but they have also been deferential to the Secretary's underlying determinations, and they have rejected claims that she must reveal classified information that forms part of the basis for the designation. *See, e.g., People's Mojahedin Org. of Iran v. Dep't of State,* 327 F.3d 1238 (D.C. Cir. 2003). Courts have also declined to allow criminal defendants to collaterally attack the Secretary's designation of an FTO in a prosecution under §2339B—albeit not without controversy. *See, e.g., United States v. Afshari,* 446 F.3d 915, 915-922 (9th Cir. 2006) (Kozinski, J., dissenting from denial of rehearing en banc).

As of December 2019, more than 65 entities have been determined by the Secretary to be FTOs (12 other groups have been "delisted"). The list includes Al Qaeda and most of its affiliates, Hamas (Islamic Resistance Movement), Hizballah (Party of God), Kongra-Gel (KGK, formerly Kurdistan Workers' Party, PKK, KADEK), Liberation Tigers of Tamil Eelam (LTTE), Real IRA (RIRA), the Revolutionary Armed Forces of Colombia (FARC), and a number of Islamic State affiliates. Bur. of Counterterrorism and Countering Violent Extremism, U.S. Dep't of State, *Foreign Terrorist Organizations* (updated regularly), *available at* https://www.state.gov/foreign-terrorist-organizations/.

The material support statutes are excerpted below, followed by a Supreme Court decision rejecting a constitutional challenge to one of those statutes. As you read them, consider how broadly some of the key terms — such as "training," "expert advice or assistance," and even "personnel" — might sweep, and whether any of the material support statutes applies to domestic terrorism.

18 U.S.C. §2339A. Providing material support to terrorists

(a) Offense. — Whoever provides material support or resources or conceals or disguises the nature, location, source, or ownership of material support or resources, knowing or intending that they are to be used in preparation for, or in carrying out, a violation of [various specific terrorist crimes] or in preparation for, or in carrying out, the concealment of an escape from the commission of any such violation, or attempts or conspires to do such an act, shall be fined under this title, imprisoned not more than 15 years, or both, and, if the death of any person results, shall be imprisoned for any term of years or for life. A violation of this section may be prosecuted in any Federal judicial district in which the underlying offense was committed, or in any other Federal judicial district as provided by law.

(b) Definitions. — As used in this section —

(1) the term "material support or resources" means any property, tangible or intangible, or service, including currency or monetary instruments or financial securities, financial services, lodging, training, expert advice or assistance, safehouses, false documentation or identification, communications equipment, facilities, weapons, lethal substances, explosives, personnel (1 or more individuals who may be or include oneself), and transportation, except medicine or religious materials.

(2) the term "training" means instruction or teaching designed to impart a specific skill, as opposed to general knowledge; and

(3) the term "expert advice or assistance" means advice or assistance derived from scientific, technical or other specialized knowledge.

18 U.S.C. §2339B. Providing material support or resources to designated foreign terrorist organizations

(a) (1) Unlawful conduct. — Whoever knowingly provides material support or resources to a foreign terrorist organization, or attempts or conspires to do so, shall be fined under this title or imprisoned not more than 15 years, or both, and, if the death of any person results, shall be imprisoned for any term of years or for life. To violate this paragraph, a person must have knowledge that the organization is a designated terrorist organization . . . , that the organization has engaged or engages in terrorist activity . . . , or that the organization has engaged or engages in terrorism. . . .

(g) Definitions. — As used in this section — . . .

(4) the term "material support or resources" has the same meaning given that term in section 2339A. . . .

(h) Provision of personnel. — No person may be prosecuted under this section in connection with the term "personnel" unless that person has knowingly provided, attempted to provide, or conspired to provide a foreign terrorist organization with 1 or more individuals (who may be or include himself) to work under that terrorist organization's direction or control or to organize, manage, supervise, or otherwise direct the operation of that organization. Individuals who act entirely independently of the foreign terrorist organization to advance its goals or objectives shall not be considered to be working under the foreign terrorist organization's direction and control.

(i) Rule of construction. — Nothing in this section shall be construed or applied so as to abridge the exercise of rights guaranteed under the First Amendment to the Constitution of the United States. . . .

18 U.S.C. §2339C. Prohibitions against the financing of terrorism

(a) Offenses.—

(1) In general.—Whoever, in a circumstance described in subsection (b) [prescribing jurisdictional attributes of crime], by any means, directly or indirectly, unlawfully and willfully provides or collects funds with the intention that such funds be used, or with the knowledge that such funds are to be used, in full or in part, in order to carry out— . . .

(B) any . . . act intended to cause death or serious bodily injury to a civilian, or to any other person not taking an active part in the hostilities in a situation of armed conflict, when the purpose of such act, by its nature or context, is to intimidate a population, or to compel a government or an international organization to do or to abstain from doing any act,

shall be punished as prescribed in subsection (d)(1). . . .

Reading *Holder v. Humanitarian Law Project*

The Humanitarian Law Project (HLP) (a human rights organization with consultative status to the United Nations), Ralph Fertig (the HLP's president), and others who wanted to provide support to the Kurdistan Workers' Party (PKK) (founded to establish an independent Kurdish state in southeastern Turkey), and the Liberation Tigers of Tamil Eelam (LTTE) (founded to create an independent Tamil state in Sri Lanka), brought suit in 1998 to challenge the constitutionality of 18 U.S.C. §2339B. Although the PKK and LTTE were each designated as an FTO by the United States, based upon evidence that they committed numerous terrorist attacks, some of which harmed U.S. citizens, the plaintiffs claimed that they wanted to support only the lawful humanitarian and political activities of the PKK and LTTE with monetary contributions, other tangible aid, legal training, and political advocacy.

More than a decade of litigation provoked a series of statutory reforms in which Congress repeatedly either narrowed the scope of §2339B or defined its terms with more precision. Thus, by the time the case reached the Supreme Court in 2010, the plaintiffs were challenging only §2339B's bans on material support in the form of "training," "expert advice or assistance," "service," or "personnel," arguing that each term was both unconstitutionally vague under the Fifth Amendment's Due Process Clause and an unconstitutional restriction on speech under the First Amendment. In the decision that follows, the Supreme Court rejected both arguments. Consider these questions as you read the excerpt:

- In a prior case, the Supreme Court had held that prosecution for *mere membership* in a criminal organization was constitutional only upon proof of knowing membership *and* specific intent to further the organization's criminal goals. Why didn't the majority here require proof of specific intent under the material support statute?
- Why did Chief Justice Roberts conclude that the four contested statutory terms aren't unconstitutionally vague? How significant to his analysis

was the fact that, thanks to this very litigation, Congress had repeatedly narrowed or clarified these terms? Should Congress's efforts at clarification be sufficient to satisfy vagueness concerns? Did the dissenters disagree?

- Even if the terms aren't vague, how does criminalizing support for non-violent activities of an FTO (such as advocacy before the United Nations or charity for widows and orphans) further a legitimate government interest?
- With regard to the plaintiffs' First Amendment claim, note the significance of the distinction Chief Justice Roberts drew between "independent" advocacy and coordinated support. Does §2339B draw such a distinction? If not, where did it come from? Why did Justice Breyer disagree with this analysis? Who, in your view, had the better of the argument? At the end of the day, *could* §2339B be used to impose "guilt by association"?
- Suppose you write a check to the PKK for medical supplies for victims of flooding. Could you constitutionally be prosecuted for providing this support?

Holder v. Humanitarian Law Project

United States Supreme Court, 2010
561 U.S. 1

Chief Justice Roberts delivered the opinion of the Court. . . .

II

. . . Plaintiffs challenge §2339B's prohibition on four types of material support—"training," "expert advice or assistance," "service," and "personnel." They raise three constitutional claims. First, plaintiffs claim that §2339B violates the Due Process Clause of the Fifth Amendment because these four statutory terms are impermissibly vague. Second, plaintiffs claim that §2339B violates their freedom of speech under the First Amendment. Third, plaintiffs claim that §2339B violates their First Amendment freedom of association.

Plaintiffs do not challenge the above statutory terms in all their applications. Rather, plaintiffs claim that §2339B is invalid to the extent it prohibits them from engaging in certain specified activities. With respect to the HLP and Judge Fertig, those activities are: (1) "train[ing] members of [the] PKK on how to use humanitarian and international law to peacefully resolve disputes"; (2) "engag[ing] in political advocacy on behalf of Kurds who live in Turkey"; and (3) "teach[ing] PKK members how to petition various representative bodies such as the United Nations for relief." With respect to the other plaintiffs, those activities are: (1) "train[ing] members of [the] LTTE to present claims for tsunami-related aid to mediators and international bodies"; (2) "offer[ing] their legal expertise in negotiating peace agreements between the LTTE and the Sri Lankan government"; and (3) "engag[ing] in political advocacy on behalf of Tamils who live in Sri Lanka." . . .

III

Plaintiffs claim, as a threshold matter, that we should affirm the Court of Appeals without reaching any issues of constitutional law. They contend that we should interpret the material-support statute, when applied to speech, to require proof that a defendant intended to further a foreign terrorist organization's illegal activities. That interpretation, they say, would end the litigation because plaintiffs' proposed activities consist of speech, but plaintiffs do not intend to further unlawful conduct by the PKK or the LTTE.

We reject plaintiffs' interpretation of §2339B because it is inconsistent with the text of the statute. Section 2339B(a)(1) prohibits "knowingly" providing material support. It then specifically describes the type of knowledge that is required: "To violate this paragraph, a person must have knowledge that the organization is a designated terrorist organization . . . , that the organization has engaged or engages in terrorist activity . . . , or that the organization has engaged or engages in terrorism. . . ." *Ibid.* Congress plainly spoke to the necessary mental state for a violation of §2339B, and it chose knowledge about the organization's connection to terrorism, not specific intent to further the organization's terrorist activities.

Plaintiffs' interpretation is also untenable in light of the sections immediately surrounding §2339B, both of which do refer to intent to further terrorist activity. See §2339A(a) (establishing criminal penalties for one who "provides material support or resources . . . knowing or intending that they are to be used in preparation for, or in carrying out, a violation of" statutes prohibiting violent terrorist acts); §2339C(a)(1) (setting criminal penalties for one who "unlawfully and willfully provides or collects funds with the intention that such funds be used, or with the knowledge that such funds are to be used, in full or in part, in order to carry out" other unlawful acts). Congress enacted §2339A in 1994 and §2339C in 2002. See §120005(a), 108 Stat. 2022 (§2339A); §202(a), 116 Stat. 724 (§2339C). Yet Congress did not import the intent language of those provisions into §2339B, either when it enacted §2339B in 1996, or when it clarified §2339B's knowledge requirement in 2004.

Finally, plaintiffs give the game away when they argue that a specific intent requirement should apply only when the material-support statute applies to speech. There is no basis whatever in the text of §2339B to read the same provisions in that statute as requiring intent in some circumstances but not others. It is therefore clear that plaintiffs are asking us not to interpret §2339B, but to revise it. "Although this Court will often strain to construe legislation so as to save it against constitutional attack, it must not and will not carry this to the point of perverting the purpose of a statute." *Scales v. United States*, 367 U.S. 203, 211 (1961).

Scales is the case on which plaintiffs most heavily rely, but it is readily distinguishable. That case involved the Smith Act, which prohibited membership in a group advocating the violent overthrow of the government. The Court held that a person could not be convicted under the statute unless he had knowledge of the group's illegal advocacy and a specific intent to bring about violent overthrow. *Id.*, at 220-222, 229. This action is different: Section 2339B does not criminalize mere membership in a designated foreign terrorist organization. It instead prohibits providing "material support" to such a group. Nothing about *Scales* suggests the need for a specific intent requirement in such a case. The Court in *Scales*, moreover, relied on both statutory text and precedent that had interpreted closely related provisions of the Smith Act to require specific intent. Plaintiffs point to nothing similar here.

We cannot avoid the constitutional issues in this litigation through plaintiffs' proposed interpretation of §2339B.

IV

We turn to the question whether the material-support statute, as applied to plaintiffs, is impermissibly vague under the Due Process Clause of the Fifth Amendment. "A conviction fails to comport with due process if the statute under which it is obtained fails to provide a person of ordinary intelligence fair notice of what is prohibited, or is so standardless that it authorizes or encourages seriously discriminatory enforcement." *United States v. Williams,* 553 U.S. 285, 304 (2008). We consider whether a statute is vague as applied to the particular facts at issue, for "[a] plaintiff who engages in some conduct that is clearly proscribed cannot complain of the vagueness of the law as applied to the conduct of others." *Hoffman Estates v. Flipside, Hoffman Estates, Inc.,* 455 U.S. 489, 495 (1982). We have said that when a statute "interferes with the right of free speech or of association, a more stringent vagueness test should apply." *Id.,* at 499. "But 'perfect clarity and precise guidance have never been required even of regulations that restrict expressive activity.'" *Williams, supra,* at 304 (quoting *Ward v. Rock Against Racism,* 491 U.S. 781, 794 (1989)). . . .

. . . [Cases establish the] rule that "[a] plaintiff who engages in some conduct that is clearly proscribed cannot complain of the vagueness of the law as applied to the conduct of others." *Hoffman Estates, supra,* at 495. That rule makes no exception for conduct in the form of speech. Thus, even to the extent a heightened vagueness standard applies, a plaintiff whose speech is clearly proscribed cannot raise a successful vagueness claim under the Due Process Clause of the Fifth Amendment for lack of notice. And he certainly cannot do so based on the speech of others. Such a plaintiff may have a valid overbreadth claim under the First Amendment, but our precedents make clear that a Fifth Amendment vagueness challenge does not turn on whether a law applies to a substantial amount of protected expression. Otherwise the doctrines would be substantially redundant.

Under a proper analysis, plaintiffs' claims of vagueness lack merit. Plaintiffs do not argue that the material-support statute grants too much enforcement discretion to the Government. We therefore address only whether the statute "provide[s] a person of ordinary intelligence fair notice of what is prohibited." *Williams,* 553 U.S., at 304.

As a general matter, the statutory terms at issue here are quite different from the sorts of terms that we have previously declared to be vague. We have in the past "struck down statutes that tied criminal culpability to whether the defendant's conduct was 'annoying' or 'indecent'—wholly subjective judgments without statutory definitions, narrowing context, or settled legal meanings." *Id.,* at 306; see also *Papachristou v. Jacksonville,* 405 U.S. 156, n.1 (1972) (holding vague an ordinance that punished "vagrants," defined to include "rogues and vagabonds," "persons who use juggling," and "common night walkers" (internal quotation marks omitted)). Applying the statutory terms in this action—"training," "expert advice or assistance," "service," and "personnel"—does not require similarly untethered, subjective judgments.

Congress also took care to add narrowing definitions to the material-support statute over time. These definitions increased the clarity of the statute's terms. See

§2339A(b)(2) ("'training' means instruction or teaching designed to impart a specific skill, as opposed to general knowledge"); §2339A(b)(3) ("'expert advice or assistance' means advice or assistance derived from scientific, technical or other specialized knowledge"); §2339B(h) (clarifying the scope of "personnel"). And the knowledge requirement of the statute further reduces any potential for vagueness, as we have held with respect to other statutes containing a similar requirement.

Of course, the scope of the material-support statute may not be clear in every application. But the dispositive point here is that the statutory terms are clear in their application to plaintiffs' proposed conduct, which means that plaintiffs' vagueness challenge must fail. Even assuming that a heightened standard applies because the material-support statute potentially implicates speech, the statutory terms are not vague as applied to plaintiffs.

Most of the activities in which plaintiffs seek to engage readily fall within the scope of the terms "training" and "expert advice or assistance." Plaintiffs want to "train members of [the] PKK on how to use humanitarian and international law to peacefully resolve disputes," and "teach PKK members how to petition various representative bodies such as the United Nations for relief." 552 F.3d at 921 n.1. A person of ordinary intelligence would understand that instruction on resolving disputes through international law falls within the statute's definition of "training" because it imparts a "specific skill," not "general knowledge." §2339A(b)(2). Plaintiffs' activities also fall comfortably within the scope of "expert advice or assistance": A reasonable person would recognize that teaching the PKK how to petition for humanitarian relief before the United Nations involves advice derived from, as the statute puts it, "specialized knowledge." §2339A(b)(3). In fact, plaintiffs themselves have repeatedly used the terms "training" and "expert advice" throughout this litigation to describe their own proposed activities, demonstrating that these common terms readily and naturally cover plaintiffs' conduct.

Plaintiffs respond by pointing to hypothetical situations designed to test the limits of "training" and "expert advice or assistance." They argue that the statutory definitions of these terms use words of degree — like "specific," "general," and "specialized" — and that it is difficult to apply those definitions in particular cases. . . .

Whatever force these arguments might have in the abstract, they are beside the point here. Plaintiffs do not propose to teach a course on geography, and cannot seek refuge in imaginary cases that straddle the boundary between "specific skills" and "general knowledge." We emphasized this point in *Scales*, holding that even if there might be theoretical doubts regarding the distinction between "active" and "nominal" membership in an organization — also terms of degree — the defendant's vagueness challenge failed because his "case present[ed] no such problem." 367 U.S. at 223. . . .

Plaintiffs also contend that they want to engage in "political advocacy" on behalf of Kurds living in Turkey and Tamils living in Sri Lanka. They are concerned that such advocacy might be regarded as "material support" in the form of providing "personnel" or "service[s]," and assert that the statute is unconstitutionally vague because they cannot tell.

As for "personnel," Congress enacted a limiting definition in IRTPA that answers plaintiffs' vagueness concerns. Providing material support that constitutes "personnel" is defined as knowingly providing a person "to work under that terrorist organization's direction or control or to organize, manage, supervise, or otherwise direct the operation of that organization." §2339B(h). The statute makes clear that "personnel" does not cover *independent* advocacy: "Individuals who act entirely independently of the foreign terrorist organization to advance its goals or objectives shall not be considered to be working under the foreign terrorist organization's direction and control." *Ibid.*

"[S]ervice" similarly refers to concerted activity, not independent advocacy. See Webster's Third New International Dictionary 2075 (1993) (defining "service" to mean "the performance of work commanded or paid for by another: a servant's duty: attendance on a superior"; or "an act done for the benefit or at the command of another"). Context confirms that ordinary meaning here. The statute prohibits providing a service "*to* a foreign terrorist organization." §2339B(a)(1) (emphasis added). The use of the word "to" indicates a connection between the service and the foreign group. We think a person of ordinary intelligence would understand that independently advocating for a cause is different from providing a service to a group that is advocating for that cause....

V

A

We next consider whether the material-support statute, as applied to plaintiffs, violates the freedom of speech guaranteed by the First Amendment. Both plaintiffs and the Government take extreme positions on this question. Plaintiffs claim that Congress has banned their "pure political speech." It has not. Under the material-support statute, plaintiffs may say anything they wish on any topic. They may speak and write freely about the PKK and LTTE, the governments of Turkey and Sri Lanka, human rights, and international law. They may advocate before the United Nations. As the Government states: "The statute does not prohibit independent advocacy or expression of any kind." Brief for Government 13. Section 2339B also "does not prevent [plaintiffs] from becoming members of the PKK and LTTE or impose any sanction on them for doing so." *Id.*, at 60. Congress has not, therefore, sought to suppress ideas or opinions in the form of "pure political speech." Rather, Congress has prohibited "material support," which most often does not take the form of speech at all. And when it does, the statute is carefully drawn to cover only a narrow category of speech to, under the direction of, or in coordination with foreign groups that the speaker knows to be terrorist organizations....

[But] [t]he Government is wrong that the only thing actually at issue in this litigation is conduct....[Section] 2339B regulates speech on the basis of its content. Plaintiffs want to speak to the PKK and the LTTE, and whether they may do so under §2339B depends on what they say. If plaintiffs' speech to those groups imparts a "specific skill" or communicates advice derived from "specialized knowledge" — for example, training on the use of international law or advice on petitioning the United Nations — then it is barred. On the other hand, plaintiffs' speech is not barred if it imparts only general or unspecialized knowledge....

B

The First Amendment issue before us is more refined than either plaintiffs or the Government would have it. It is not whether the Government may prohibit pure political speech, or may prohibit material support in the form of conduct. It is instead whether the Government may prohibit what plaintiffs want to do — provide material support to the PKK and LTTE in the form of speech.

Everyone agrees that the Government's interest in combating terrorism is an urgent objective of the highest order. Plaintiffs' complaint is that the ban on material support, applied to what they wish to do, is not "necessary to further that interest." The objective of combating terrorism does not justify prohibiting their speech, plaintiffs argue, because their support will advance only the legitimate activities of the designated terrorist organizations, not their terrorism.

Whether foreign terrorist organizations meaningfully segregate support of their legitimate activities from support of terrorism is an empirical question. When it enacted §2339B in 1996, Congress made specific findings regarding the serious threat posed by international terrorism. See AEDPA §§301(a)(1)-(7), 110 Stat. 1247, note following 18 U.S.C. §2339B (Findings and Purpose). One of those findings explicitly rejects plaintiffs' contention that their support would not further the terrorist activities of the PKK and LTTE: "[F]oreign organizations that engage in terrorist activity are so tainted by their criminal conduct that *any contribution to such an organization* facilitates that conduct." §301(a)(7) (emphasis added).

Plaintiffs argue that the reference to "any contribution" in this finding meant only monetary support. There is no reason to read the finding to be so limited, particularly because Congress expressly prohibited so much more than monetary support in §2339B. Congress's use of the term "contribution" is best read to reflect a determination that any form of material support furnished "to" a foreign terrorist organization should be barred, which is precisely what the material-support statute does. Indeed, when Congress enacted §2339B, Congress simultaneously removed an exception that had existed in §2339A(a) (1994 ed.) for the provision of material support in the form of "humanitarian assistance to persons not directly involved in" terrorist activity. AEDPA §323, 110 Stat. 1255. That repeal demonstrates that Congress considered and rejected the view that ostensibly peaceful aid would have no harmful effects.

We are convinced that Congress was justified in rejecting that view. The PKK and the LTTE are deadly groups. "The PKK's insurgency has claimed more than 22,000 lives." Declaration of Kenneth R. McKune, App. 128, ¶5. The LTTE has engaged in extensive suicide bombings and political assassinations, including killings of the Sri Lankan President, Security Minister, and Deputy Defense Minister. *Id.*, at 130-132; Brief for Government 6-7. "On January 31, 1996, the LTTE exploded a truck bomb filled with an estimated 1,000 pounds of explosives at the Central Bank in Colombo, killing 100 people and injuring more than 1,400. This bombing was the most deadly terrorist incident in the world in 1996." McKune Affidavit, App. 131, ¶6.h. It is not difficult to conclude as Congress did that the "tain[t]" of such violent activities is so great that working in coordination with or at the command of the PKK and LTTE serves to legitimize and further their terrorist means. AEDPA §301(a)(7), 110 Stat. 1247.

Material support meant to "promot[e] peaceable, lawful conduct," Brief for Plaintiffs 51, can further terrorism by foreign groups in multiple ways. "Material support" is a valuable resource by definition. Such support frees up other resources within the organization that may be put to violent ends. It also importantly helps lend legitimacy to foreign terrorist groups — legitimacy that makes it easier for those groups to persist, to recruit members, and to raise funds — all of which facilitate more terrorist attacks. "Terrorist organizations do not maintain *organizational* 'firewalls' that would prevent or deter . . . sharing and commingling of support and benefits." McKune Affidavit, App. 135, ¶11. "[I]nvestigators have revealed how terrorist groups systematically conceal their activities behind charitable, social, and political fronts." M. Levitt, Hamas: Politics, Charity, and Terrorism in the Service of Jihad 2-3 (2006). "Indeed, some designated foreign terrorist organizations use social and political components to recruit personnel to carry out terrorist operations, and to provide support to criminal terrorists and their families in aid of such operations." McKune Affidavit, App. 135, ¶11; Levitt, *supra,* at 2 ("Muddying the waters between its political activism, good works, and terrorist attacks, Hamas is able to use its overt political and charitable organizations as a financial and logistical support network for its terrorist operations").

Money is fungible, and "[w]hen foreign terrorist organizations that have a dual structure raise funds, they highlight the civilian and humanitarian ends to which such moneys could be put." McKune Affidavit, App. 134, ¶9. But "there is reason to believe that foreign terrorist organizations do not maintain legitimate *financial* firewalls between those funds raised for civil, nonviolent activities, and those ultimately used to support violent, terrorist operations." *Id.,* at 135, ¶12. Thus, "[f]unds raised ostensibly for charitable purposes have in the past been redirected by some terrorist groups to fund the purchase of arms and explosives." *Id.,* at 134, ¶10. See also Brief for Anti-Defamation League as *Amicus Curiae* 19-29 (describing fundraising activities by the PKK, LTTE, and Hamas); *Regan v. Wald,* 468 U.S. 222, 243 (1984) (upholding President's decision to impose travel ban to Cuba "to curtail the flow of hard currency to Cuba — currency that could then be used in support of Cuban adventurism"). There is evidence that the PKK and the LTTE, in particular, have not "respected the line between humanitarian and violent activities." McKune Affidavit, App. 135, ¶13 (discussing PKK); see *id.,* at 134 (LTTE).

The dissent argues that there is "no natural stopping place" for the proposition that aiding a foreign terrorist organization's lawful activity promotes the terrorist organization as a whole. But Congress has settled on just such a natural stopping place: The statute reaches only material support coordinated with or under the direction of a designated foreign terrorist organization. . . .

C

In analyzing whether it is possible in practice to distinguish material support for a foreign terrorist group's violent activities and its nonviolent activities, we do not rely exclusively on our own inferences drawn from the record evidence. We have before us an affidavit stating the Executive Branch's conclusion on that question. The State Department informs us that "[t]he experience and analysis of the U.S. government agencies charged with combating terrorism strongly suppor[t]" Congress's finding that all contributions to foreign terrorist organizations further their terrorism. McKune Affidavit, App. 133, ¶8. See *Winter v. Natural Resources Defense Council, Inc.,* 129 S. Ct. 365, 376-377 (2008) (looking to similar affidavits to support according weight to national security claims). In the Executive's view: "Given the purposes, organizational structure, and clandestine nature of foreign terrorist organizations, it is highly likely that any material support to these organizations will ultimately inure to the benefit of their criminal, terrorist functions — regardless of whether such support was ostensibly intended to support non-violent, non-terrorist activities." McKune Affidavit, App. 133, ¶8.

That evaluation of the facts by the Executive, like Congress's assessment, is entitled to deference. This litigation implicates sensitive and weighty interests of national security and foreign affairs. The PKK and the LTTE have committed terrorist acts against American citizens abroad, and the material-support statute addresses acute foreign policy concerns involving relationships with our Nation's allies. See *id.*, at 128-133, 137. We have noted that "neither the Members of this Court nor most federal judges begin the day with briefings that may describe new and serious threats to our Nation and its people." *Boumediene v. Bush*, 553 U.S. 723, 797 (2008). It is vital in this context "not to substitute . . . our own evaluation of evidence for a reasonable evaluation by the Legislative Branch." *Rostker v. Goldberg*, 453 U.S. 57, 68 (1981).

Our precedents, old and new, make clear that concerns of national security and foreign relations do not warrant abdication of the judicial role. We do not defer to the Government's reading of the First Amendment, even when such interests are at stake. We are one with the dissent that the Government's "authority and expertise in these matters do not automatically trump the Court's own obligation to secure the protection that the Constitution grants to individuals." But when it comes to collecting evidence and drawing factual inferences in this area, "the lack of competence on the part of the courts is marked," *Rostker, supra*, at 65, and respect for the Government's conclusions is appropriate.

One reason for that respect is that national security and foreign policy concerns arise in connection with efforts to confront evolving threats in an area where information can be difficult to obtain and the impact of certain conduct difficult to assess. The dissent slights these real constraints in demanding hard proof — with "detail," "specific facts," and "specific evidence" — that plaintiffs' proposed activities will support terrorist attacks. That would be a dangerous requirement. In this context, conclusions must often be based on informed judgment rather than concrete evidence, and that reality affects what we may reasonably insist on from the Government. The material-support statute is, on its face, a preventive measure — it criminalizes not terrorist attacks themselves, but aid that makes the attacks more likely to occur. The Government, when seeking to prevent imminent harms in the context of international affairs and national security, is not required to conclusively link all the pieces in the puzzle before we grant weight to its empirical conclusions. See *Zemel v. Rusk*, 381 U.S., at 17 ("[B]ecause of the changeable and explosive nature of contemporary international relations, . . . Congress . . . must of necessity paint with a brush broader than that it customarily wields in domestic areas"). . . .

We also find it significant that Congress has been conscious of its own responsibility to consider how its actions may implicate constitutional concerns. First, §2339B only applies to designated foreign terrorist organizations. There is, and always has been, a limited number of those organizations designated by the Executive Branch, see, *e.g.*, 74 Fed. Reg. 29742 (2009); 62 Fed. Reg. 52650 (1997), and any groups so designated may seek judicial review of the designation. Second, in response to the lower courts' holdings in this litigation, Congress added clarity to the statute by providing narrowing definitions of the terms "training," "personnel," and "expert advice or assistance," as well as an explanation of the knowledge required to violate §2339B. Third, in effectuating its stated intent not to abridge First Amendment rights, see §2339B(i), Congress has also displayed a careful balancing of interests in creating limited exceptions to the ban on material support. The definition of material support, for example, excludes medicine and religious materials. See §2339A(b)(1). In this area perhaps more than any other, the Legislature's superior capacity for weighing competing interests means that "we must be particularly careful not to substitute our judgment of what is desirable for that of Congress." *Rostker, supra*, at 68. Finally, and most importantly, Congress has avoided any restriction on independent advocacy, or indeed any activities not directed to, coordinated with, or controlled by foreign terrorist groups.

At bottom, plaintiffs simply disagree with the considered judgment of Congress and the Executive that providing material support to a designated foreign terrorist organization — even seemingly benign support — bolsters the terrorist activities of that organization. That judgment, however, is entitled to significant weight, and we have persuasive evidence before us to sustain it. Given the sensitive interests in national security and foreign affairs at stake, the political branches have adequately substantiated their determination that, to serve the Government's interest in preventing terrorism, it was necessary to prohibit providing material support in the form of training, expert advice, personnel, and services to foreign terrorist groups, even if the supporters meant to promote only the groups' nonviolent ends.

We turn to the particular speech plaintiffs propose to undertake. First, plaintiffs propose to "train members of [the] PKK on how to use humanitarian and international law to peacefully resolve disputes." 552 F.3d at 92 n.1. Congress can, consistent with the First Amendment, prohibit this direct training. It is wholly foreseeable that the PKK could use the "specific skill[s]" that plaintiffs propose to impart, §2339A(b)(2), as part of a broader strategy to promote terrorism. The PKK could, for example, pursue peaceful negotiation as a means of buying time to recover from short-term setbacks, lulling opponents into complacency, and ultimately preparing for renewed attacks. See generally A. Marcus, Blood and Belief: The PKK and the Kurdish Fight for Independence 286-295 (2007) (describing the PKK's suspension of armed struggle and subsequent return to violence). A foreign terrorist organization introduced to the structures of the international legal system might use the information to threaten, manipulate, and disrupt. This possibility is real, not remote.

Second, plaintiffs propose to "teach PKK members how to petition various representative bodies such as the United Nations for relief." 552 F.3d at 921 n.1. The Government acts within First Amendment strictures in banning this proposed speech because it teaches the organization how to acquire "relief," which plaintiffs never define with any specificity, and which could readily include monetary aid. Indeed, earlier in this litigation, plaintiffs sought to teach the LTTE "to present claims for tsunami-related aid to mediators and international bodies," 552 F.3d at 921 n.1, which naturally included monetary relief. Money is fungible, and Congress logically concluded that money a terrorist group such as the PKK obtains using the techniques plaintiffs propose to teach could be redirected to funding the group's violent activities.

Finally, plaintiffs propose to "engage in political advocacy on behalf of Kurds who live in Turkey," and "engage in political advocacy on behalf of Tamils who live in Sri Lanka." 552 F.3d at 921 n.1. As explained above, plaintiffs do not specify their expected level of coordination with the PKK or LTTE or suggest what exactly their "advocacy" would consist of. Plaintiffs' proposals are phrased at such a high level of generality that they cannot prevail in this preenforcement challenge. See [*Washington State Grange v. Washington State Republican Party*, 552 U.S. 442, 454 (2008)]; *Zemel*, 381 U.S., at 20. . . .

All this is not to say that any future applications of the material-support statute to speech or advocacy will survive First Amendment scrutiny. It is also not to say that any other statute relating to speech and terrorism would satisfy the First Amendment. In particular, we in no way suggest that a regulation of independent speech would pass constitutional muster, even if the Government were to show that such speech benefits foreign terrorist organizations. We also do not suggest that Congress could extend the same prohibition on material support at issue here to domestic organizations. We simply hold that, in prohibiting the particular forms of support that plaintiffs seek to provide to foreign terrorist groups, §2339B does not violate the freedom of speech.

VI

Plaintiffs' final claim is that the material-support statute violates their freedom of association under the First Amendment. Plaintiffs argue that the statute criminalizes the mere fact of their associating with the PKK and the LTTE, thereby running afoul of [prior] decisions . . . and cases in which we have overturned sanctions for joining the Communist Party.

The Court of Appeals correctly rejected this claim because the statute does not penalize mere association with a foreign terrorist organization. As the Ninth Circuit put it: "The statute does not prohibit being a member of one of the designated groups or vigorously promoting and supporting the political goals of the group. . . . What [§2339B] prohibits is the act of giving material support. . . ." 205 F.3d at 1133. Plaintiffs want to do the latter. Our decisions scrutinizing penalties on simple association or assembly are therefore inapposite. *See, e.g., Robel, supra,* at 262 ("It is precisely because th[e] statute sweeps indiscriminately across all types of association with Communist-action groups, without regard to the quality and degree of membership, that it runs afoul of the First Amendment"). . . .

* * *

The Preamble to the Constitution proclaims that the people of the United States ordained and established that charter of government in part to "provide for the common defence." As Madison explained, "[s]ecurity against foreign danger is . . . an avowed and essential object of the American Union." The Federalist No. 41, p. 269 (J. Cooke ed. 1961). We hold that, in regulating the particular forms of support that plaintiffs seek to provide to foreign terrorist organizations, Congress has pursued that objective consistent with the limitations of the First and Fifth Amendments.

The judgment of the United States Court of Appeals for the Ninth Circuit is affirmed in part and reversed in part, and the cases are remanded for further proceedings consistent with this opinion.

It is so ordered.

Justice Breyer, with whom Justices Ginsburg and Sotomayor join, dissenting. Like the Court, and substantially for the reasons it gives, I do not think this statute is unconstitutionally vague. But I cannot agree with the Court's conclusion that the Constitution permits the Government to prosecute the plaintiffs criminally for engaging in coordinated teaching and advocacy furthering the designated organizations' lawful political objectives. In my view, the Government has not met its burden of showing that an interpretation of the statute that would prohibit this speech- and association-related activity serves the Government's compelling interest in combating terrorism. And I would interpret the statute as normally placing activity of this kind outside its scope.

I. . . .

"Coordination" with a group that engages in unlawful activity also does not deprive the plaintiffs of the First Amendment's protection under any traditional "categorical" exception to its protection. The plaintiffs do not propose to solicit a crime. They will not engage in fraud or defamation or circulate obscenity. Cf. *United States v. Stevens*, 130 S. Ct. 1577, 1585 (2010) (describing "categories" of unprotected speech). And the First Amendment protects advocacy even of *unlawful* action so long as that advocacy is not "directed to inciting or producing *imminent lawless action* and . . . *likely to incite or produce* such action." *Brandenburg v. Ohio*, 395 U.S. 444, 447 (1969) (*per curiam*) (emphasis added). Here the plaintiffs seek to advocate peaceful, *lawful* action to secure *political* ends; and they seek to teach others how to do the same. No one contends that the plaintiffs' speech to these organizations can be prohibited as incitement under *Brandenburg*.

Moreover, the Court has previously held that a person who associates with a group that uses unlawful means to achieve its ends does not thereby necessarily forfeit the First Amendment's protection for freedom of association. See *Scales v. United States*, 367 U.S. 203, 229 (1961) ("[Q]uasi-political parties or other groups that may embrace both legal and illegal aims differ from a technical conspiracy, which is defined by its criminal purpose"); see also [*NAACP v. Claiborne Hardware Co.*, 458 U.S. 886, 908 (1982)] ("The right to associate does not lose all constitutional protection merely because some members of the group may have participated in conduct or advocated doctrine that itself is not protected"). Rather, the Court has pointed out in respect to associating with a group advocating overthrow of the Government through force and violence: "If the persons assembling have committed crimes elsewhere . . . , they may be prosecuted for their . . . violation of valid laws. But it is a different matter when the State, instead of prosecuting them for such offenses, seizes upon mere participation in a peaceable assembly and a lawful public discussion as the basis for a criminal charge." [*De Jonge v. Oregon*, 299 U.S. 353, 365 (1937)] (striking down conviction for attending and assisting at Communist Party meeting because "[n]otwithstanding [the party's] objectives, the defendant still enjoyed his personal right of free speech and to take part in peaceable assembly having a lawful purpose"). . . .

Not even the "serious and deadly problem" of international terrorism can require *automatic* forfeiture of First Amendment rights. §301(a)(1), 110 Stat. 1247, note following 18 U.S.C. §2339B. Cf. §2339B(i) (instructing courts not to "constru[e] or appl[y the statute] so as to abridge the exercise of right[s] guaranteed under the First Amendment"). After all, this Court has recognized that not "'[e]ven the war power . . . remove[s] constitutional limitations safeguarding essential liberties.'" *United States v. Robel*, 389 U.S. 258, 264 (1967) (quoting *Home Building & Loan Assn. v. Blaisdell*, 290 U.S. 398, 426 (1934)). See also *Abrams v. United States*, 250 U.S. 616, 628 (1919) (Holmes, J., dissenting) ("[A]s against dangers peculiar to war, as against others, the principle of the right to free speech is always the same"). Thus, there is no general First Amendment exception that applies here. If the statute is constitutional in this context, it would have to come with a strong justification attached. . . .

The Government does identify a compelling countervailing interest, namely, the interest in protecting the security of the United States and its nationals from the threats that foreign terrorist organizations pose by denying those organizations financial and other fungible resources. I do not dispute the importance of this interest. But

I do dispute whether the interest can justify the statute's criminal prohibition. To put the matter more specifically, precisely how does application of the statute to the protected activities before us *help achieve* that important security-related end?

The Government makes two efforts to answer this question. *First,* the Government says that the plaintiffs' support for these organizations is "fungible" in the same sense as other forms of banned support. Being fungible, the plaintiffs' support could, for example, free up other resources, which the organization might put to terrorist ends.

The proposition that the two very different kinds of "support" are "fungible," however, is not *obviously* true. There is no *obvious* way in which undertaking advocacy for political change through peaceful means or teaching the PKK and LTTE, say, how to petition the United Nations for political change is fungible with other resources that might be put to more sinister ends in the way that donations of money, food, or computer training are fungible. It is far from obvious that these advocacy activities can themselves be redirected, or will free other resources that can be directed, towards terrorist ends. Thus, we must determine whether the Government has come forward with evidence to support its claim.

The Government has provided us with no empirical information that might convincingly support this claim. . . .

Second, the Government says that the plaintiffs' proposed activities will "bolste[r] a terrorist organization's efficacy and strength in a community" and "undermin[e] this nation's efforts to *delegitimize and weaken* those groups." Government Brief 56 (emphasis added). In the Court's view, too, the Constitution permits application of the statute to activities of the kind at issue in part because those activities could provide a group that engages in terrorism with "legitimacy." The Court suggests that, armed with this greater "legitimacy," these organizations will more readily be able to obtain material support of the kinds Congress plainly intended to ban — money, arms, lodging, and the like. . . .

But this "legitimacy" justification cannot by itself warrant suppression of political speech, advocacy, and association. Speech, association, and related activities on behalf of a group will often, perhaps always, help to legitimate that group. Thus, were the law to accept a "legitimating" effect, in and of itself and without qualification, as providing sufficient grounds for imposing such a ban, the First Amendment battle would be lost in untold instances where it should be won. Once one accepts this argument, there is no natural stopping place. The argument applies as strongly to "independent" as to "coordinated" advocacy. That fact is reflected in part in the Government's claim that the ban here, so supported, prohibits a lawyer hired by a designated group from filing on behalf of that group an *amicus* brief before the United Nations or even before this Court. . . .

Regardless, the "legitimacy" justification itself is inconsistent with critically important First Amendment case law. Consider the cases involving the protection the First Amendment offered those who joined the Communist Party intending only to further its peaceful activities. In those cases, this Court took account of congressional findings that the Communist Party not only advocated theoretically but also sought to put into practice the overthrow of our Government through force and violence. The Court had previously accepted Congress' determinations that the American Communist Party was a "Communist action organization" which (1) acted under the "control, direction, and discipline" of the world Communist movement, a movement that sought to employ "espionage, sabotage, terrorism, and any other means deemed necessary, to establish a Communist totalitarian dictatorship," and (2) "endeavor[ed]" to bring about "the overthrow of existing governments by . . . force if necessary." *Communist Party of United States v. Subversive Activities Control Bd.*, 367 U.S. 1, 5-6 (1961) (internal quotation marks omitted).

Nonetheless, the Court held that the First Amendment protected an American's right to belong to that party — despite whatever "legitimating" effect membership might have had — as long as the person did not share the party's unlawful purposes. . . . The Government's "legitimating" theory would seem to apply to these cases with equal justifying force; and, if recognized, it would have led this Court to conclusions other than those it reached. . . .

II

For the reasons I have set forth, I believe application of the statute as the Government interprets it would gravely and without adequate justification injure interests of the kind the First Amendment protects. Thus, there is "a serious doubt" as to the statute's constitutionality. [*Crowell v. Benson*, 285 U.S. 22, 62 (1932).] And where that is so, we must "ascertain whether a construction of the statute is fairly possible by which the question may be avoided." *Ibid.*

I believe that a construction that would avoid the constitutional problem is "fairly possible." In particular, I would read the statute as criminalizing First-Amendment-protected pure speech and association only when the defendant knows or intends that those activities will assist the organization's unlawful terrorist actions. Under this reading, the Government would have to show, at a minimum, that such defendants provided support that they knew was significantly likely to help the organization pursue its unlawful terrorist aims.

A person acts with the requisite knowledge if he is aware of (or willfully blinds himself to) a significant likelihood that his or her conduct will materially support the organization's terrorist ends. On the other hand, for the reasons I have set out, knowledge or intent that this assistance (aimed at lawful activities) could or would help further terrorism simply by helping to legitimate the organization is not sufficient. . . .

Thus, textually speaking, a statutory requirement that the defendant *knew* the support was material can be read to require the Government to show that the defendant knew that the consequences of his acts had a significant likelihood of furthering the organization's terrorist, not just its lawful, aims.

I need not decide whether this is the only possible reading of the statute in cases where "material support" takes the form of "currency," "property," "monetary instruments," "financial securities," "financial services," "lodging," "safehouses," "false documentation or identification," "weapons," "lethal substances," or "explosives," and the like. §2339A(b)(1). Those kinds of aid are inherently more likely to help an organization's terrorist activities, either directly or because they are fungible in nature. Thus, to show that an individual has provided support of those kinds will normally prove sufficient for conviction (assuming the statute's other requirements are met). But where support consists of pure speech or association, I would indulge in no such presumption. Rather, the Government would have to prove that the defendant knew he was providing support significantly likely to help the organization pursue its unlawful terrorist aims (or, alternatively, that the defendant intended the support to be so used). . . .

III

Having interpreted the statute to impose the *mens rea* requirement just described, I would remand the cases so that the lower courts could consider more specifically the precise activities in which the plaintiffs still wish to engage and determine whether and to what extent a grant of declaratory and injunctive relief were [*sic*] warranted. . . .

Notes and Questions

1. The Anti-Terrorist Prosecutor's Weapon of Choice? As we noted above, the apparent expansion of the international suicide terrorist threat in the 1990s, and the difficulty of identifying and arresting would-be suicide terrorists in time, have caused the government to begin searching left of boom not only for those who plan, but also for those who support, acts of terrorism — whether directly or indirectly. Abdel Rahman's prosecution was a way station in this shift in prosecutorial focus to "precursor crimes," because he was prosecuted for "overall supervision and direction of the membership," as the *Rahman* court put it, not for involvement in "individual operations." Yet the "seditious conspiracy" crime that the government charged there was anachronistic, notwithstanding the eventual success of the prosecution. Prosecutors needed a tool better suited for going after those who facilitated the work of terrorist organizations through any number of channels.

When Congress responded by expanding material support liability in subsequent legislation, prosecutors used their new weapon enthusiastically. The material support charge has become the government's weapon of choice against suspected terrorists — and shows up in an overwhelming majority of terrorism-related criminal prosecutions, in many of which it is the *only* charge. Given the language of the statute and the Supreme Court's analysis in *Humanitarian Law Project*, can you see why, from a prosecutor's perspective, it is much easier to bring a material support case against a terrorism suspect than a case based upon the suspect's alleged role in a potential future terrorist attack?

2. Knowledge or Specific Intent? The plaintiffs in *Humanitarian Law Project* argued that §2339B required proof that a defendant intended to further an FTO's terrorist activities. What does the statute say? How do its *scienter* (state of mind) requirements compare to its companion material support statutes, §§2339A and 2339C?

If the statute does not require specific intent, why is it not unconstitutional? In the Smith Act, Congress criminalized knowing membership in any organization that advocates the overthrow of the government by force or violence. 18 U.S.C. §2385 (2018). The Act came before the Supreme Court in *Scales v. United States*, 367 U.S. 203 (1961), in which the Court upheld a conviction for membership only on proof of *knowing* membership or affiliation *and specific intent* to further the group's unlawful goals. The Court explained its insistence on these elements of proof by rejecting the concept of guilt by association:

> In our jurisprudence guilt is personal, and when the imposition of punishment on a status or on conduct can only be justified by reference to the relationship of that status or conduct to other concededly criminal activity (here advocacy of violent overthrow), that

> relationship must be sufficiently substantial to satisfy the concept of personal guilt in order to withstand attack under the Due Process Clause of the Fifth Amendment. [*Id.* at 224-225.]

Specific intent implements the requirement of personal guilt by "tying the imposition of guilt to an individually culpable act." David Cole, *Hanging with the Wrong Crowd: Of Gangs, Terrorists, and the Right of Association*, 1999 Sup. Ct. Rev. 203, 217. In First Amendment terms, the specific intent requirement "identifies the only narrowly tailored way to punish individuals for group wrongdoing (essentially by requiring evidence of individual wrongdoing), just as the *Brandenburg* test [*supra* p. 1040] sets forth the narrowly tailored way to respond to advocacy of illegal conduct." Cole, *supra*, at 218. How does the Court distinguish *Scales*? Does §2339B make it a crime to be a member of an FTO? (Hint: What does it mean to provide "personnel" to an FTO?)

3. Vagueness. A law is unconstitutionally vague if a reasonable person cannot tell what expression is prohibited and what is permitted. "Material support," as used in §2339B, is defined in §2339A(b). Is the statute vague as applied to the provision of explosives or safehouses to a terrorist or FTO? What about the donation of money to an FTO? If these applications don't seem unconstitutionally vague, what about providing personnel, training, or expert advice? Why did the majority reject the vagueness challenge to the latter terms?

Did the Court rule that there are no applications of these terms that would be unconstitutionally vague? Consider the case of a lawyer for a convicted terrorist who meets periodically with her client in prison and secretly conveys messages between him and his associates (including members of an FTO) outside prison. Is the term "personnel" unconstitutionally vague as applied to prosecute that lawyer for providing *herself* as "personnel" to a terrorist or FTO? *See United States v. Sattar* (*Sattar I*), 272 F. Supp. 2d 348 (S.D.N.Y. 2003) (too vague; government's assertion in oral argument that "you know it when you see it" is an "insufficient guide by which a person can predict the legality of that person's conduct," whatever merit it may have as a way to identify obscenity). Is it too vague for prosecuting the lawyer for supplying *her client* as "personnel" to the FTO, by making him "available" through communications that she conveys? *See United States v. Sattar* (*Sattar II*), 314 F. Supp. 2d 279, 300 (S.D.N.Y. 2004) (not vague; "the 'provision' of 'personnel' — in this case, by making the imprisoned Sheik Abdel Rahman available as a co-conspirator in a conspiracy to kill and kidnap persons in a foreign country — is conduct that plainly is prohibited by the statute" with sufficient definiteness). How about a U.S. citizen who joins the Taliban to fight alongside Al Qaeda fighters against U.S. armed forces in Afghanistan? *See United States v. Lindh*, 212 F. Supp. 2d 541, 574 (E.D. Va. 2002) (not vague; "personnel" is not unconstitutionally vague as applied to "employees" or "employee-like operatives" who were under the "direction and control" of an FTO).

Suppose a cab driver drives a person he knows to be a member of an FTO to the airport. Can he constitutionally be prosecuted for providing "transportation" to an FTO?

4. The Logic of Criminalizing Humanitarian Support. Some FTOs, such as Hamas, are dual-purpose organizations; they engage in terrorism, but they also provide social services. Some supporters want only to further the non-terrorist purposes of the FTO. Did Congress in §2339B make it a crime to write a check to Hamas to support its social services? If so, why? Why does the majority in *Humanitarian Law Project* not reject Congress's reasoning? Why does the dissent do so?

Did the majority defer too much to congressional "fact" finding? Consider one scholar's discussion of "fact" deference in national security litigation:

> "[N]ational security fact deference" is freighted with constitutional significance. On one hand, it may undermine the capacity of courts to guard against unlawful executive branch actions (in terms of both unjustified assertions of power and violations of individual rights). On the other hand, it may prevent the judicial power from encroaching inappropriately upon executive responsibilities relating to national security, while simultaneously helping to preserve the judiciary's institutional legitimacy. National security fact deference claims, in short, implicate competing values of great magnitude. [Robert M. Chesney, *National Security Fact Deference*, 95 Va. L. Rev. 1361, 1362 (2009).]

5. Protected Expression. Donating money is not membership, but it is also unlike donating weapons, safe houses, or transportation. "The right to join together 'for the advancement of beliefs and ideas' is diluted," the Supreme Court explained, "if it does not include the right to pool money through contributions, for funds are often essential if 'advocacy' is to be truly or optimally 'effective.'" *Buckley v. Valeo*, 424 U.S. 1, 65-66 (1976) (per curiam) (quoting *NAACP v. Alabama ex rel. Patterson*, 357 U.S. 449, 460 (1958)). Why is donating money to an FTO not protected political expression?

One answer is that it *is* protected expression, but that the protection is not absolute. What degree of scrutiny should a court then give to its regulation? *See* Cole, *supra*, at 237-238 (urging strict scrutiny—requiring a close relationship to a compelling government interest—when government's purpose is to regulate association as such).

In *Humanitarian Law Project*, however, the plaintiffs were not making financial contributions to the FTOs; nor were they engaged simply in "pure political speech." Instead, they wanted to provide material support to FTOs "in the form of speech"—by providing training lectures and advice. How did prohibiting such support in the form of speech have a close relationship to the concededly compelling interest of preventing or making more difficult terrorist acts by FTOs? Does *Humanitarian Law Project* "open[] the door for prohibiting any speech related to a terrorist organization, no matter how peaceful it is, as long as it is expressed in coordination with or under the direction of a terrorist organization"? Daphne Barak-Erez & David Scharia, *Freedom of Speech, Support for Terrorism, and the Challenge of Global Constitutional Law*, 2 Harv. Nat'l Security J. 1, 19 (2011).

The dissent in *Humanitarian Law Project* had serious doubts that the prohibition bore the necessary relationship to the counterterrorism interest. How did it avoid the resulting constitutional issue? Does its solution interpret §2339B or rewrite it? Should Congress amend §2339B to require specific intent for support in the form of speech? *See* Const. Proj., *Reforming the Material Support Laws: Constitutional Concerns Presented by Prohibitions on Material Support to "Terrorist Organizations"* (Nov. 17, 2009) (so arguing).

6. Material Support for Domestic Terrorism. A prosecutor in the *Stone* case later explained why the government brought a seditious conspiracy charge: "We found a dearth of federal statutes to use against domestic terrorists, and ended up charging seditious conspiracy, a clumsy statute with an Orwellian name." McQuade, *supra*.

Why didn't the government instead charge Stone with providing the Hutaree with material support in violation of §2339A? It criminalizes providing, or attempting or conspiring to provide, material support — "training, expert advice or assistance, . . . weapons, . . . explosives," and last, but not least, "personnel (one or more individuals who may be or include oneself)" — "knowing or intending that they are to be used in preparation for, or in carrying out," one of the 57 listed crimes. As noted above, 51 of these crimes do not require an international or foreign nexus, including §2332a(a)(2) (using WMD (including explosives) against persons or property in the United States), and 18 U.S.C. §1114 (attempting to kill an officer of the United States in performance of the officer's duties). *See Brennan Priorities Report, supra*, at 18-19 (identifying a small number of domestic terrorism cases in which §2339A has been used). Compare the scienter requirement of §2339A with that of §2339B. Which is easier for the government to satisfy? Is it more difficult to prove material support than to prove seditious conspiracy or conspiracy to use WMD?

7. *Material Support for DTOs?* It is easier to see why the government in *Stone* did not charge Stone with violating §2339B for providing material support to the Hutarees. The Hutarees were not an FTO. This example thus highlights a gap in the government's arsenal against domestic terrorism: there is no equivalent to the "go-to" §2339B charge because there is no domestic equivalent to FTOs. The government does not designate Domestic Terrorist Organizations (DTOs), although the FBI uses the term in its *Civil Rights Program Policy Implementation Guide, supra* p. 1037, at 15.

One scholar has recommended enacting a process for designating as DTOs organizations and groups primarily based in the United States that engage in terrorism, or "have the capability and intent to do so, . . . with a political objective," such as "movements that espouse extremist ideologies of political, religious, social, racial or environmental nature." Blazakis, *supra*. Under his proposal, not only would material support for a DTO be a crime, but a DTO "would be blocked from the formal financial system," and its Internet presence could be curtailed by private service providers under cover of the material support law. *Id.*

Would this proposal permit DTO designation of an extreme environmental group that advocates illegal entry and occupation of logging sites, an animal rights group that advocates trespass to free caged animals, or a Quaker antiwar group that blocks traffic to protest starting a war with Iran? (Even without a formal DTO designation process, FBI agents called "eco-terrorism" the number one terrorism threat in America between 2004 and 2008, despite the fact that no one had been killed by it. *FBI: Eco-Terrorism Remains No. 1 Domestic Terror Threat*, Fox News, Mar. 31, 2008.)

In *Humanitarian Law Project*, 561 U.S. at 39, the Court warned, "We . . . do not suggest that Congress could extend the same prohibition on material support at issue here to domestic organizations." Why not?

C. TREASON

One of the oldest crimes associated with national security is treason. It is also the only crime defined in the Constitution: "Treason against the United States, shall consist only in levying War against them, or in adhering to their Enemies, giving them Aid and Comfort." U.S. Const. art. III, §3. The crime of treason has been codified, as well:

> Whoever, owing allegiance to the United States, levies war against them or adheres to their enemies, giving them aid and comfort within the United States or elsewhere, is guilty of treason and shall suffer death, or shall be imprisoned not less than five years and fined under this title but not less than $10,000; and shall be incapable of holding any office under the United States. [18 U.S.C. §2381 (2018).]

The constitutional text also supplies a special evidentiary rule for treason prosecutions: "No Person shall be convicted of Treason unless on the Testimony of two Witnesses to the same overt Act, or on Confession in open Court." U.S. Const. art. III, §3. This stringent requirement of proof reflects the Framers' fears that the state might use treason prosecutions to suppress dissent.

> The treason clause is a product of the awareness of the Framers of the "numerous and dangerous excrescences" which had disfigured the English law of treason and was therefore intended to put it beyond the power of Congress to "extend the crime and punishment of treason." The debate in the Convention, remarks in the ratifying conventions, and contemporaneous public comment make clear that a restrictive concept of the crime was imposed and that ordinary partisan divisions within political society were not to be escalated by the stronger into capital charges of treason, as so often had happened in England. [S. Doc. No. 92-82, Congressional Research Service, *The Constitution of the United States of America: Analysis and Interpretation* (1973) (citations omitted), *updated version available at* http://www.law.cornell.edu/anncon/authorship.html.]

One statutory limitation on treason not expressed in the constitutional text is its applicability only to U.S. citizens. Nonetheless, in the view of one court, "[t]he reference to treason in the constitutional clause necessarily incorporates the elements of allegiance and betrayal that are essential to the concept of treason." *Rahman*, 189 F.3d at 114.

Neither the constitutional text nor the statute answers important questions that might be raised about their application, however. For example, following President Trump's inauguration in 2017, congressional intelligence committees and a Special Counsel investigated allegations that officials in the Trump presidential campaign colluded with Russia to influence the November 2016 election in Trump's favor. Some argued that any such collusion would amount to treason. *See, e.g.*, Nicholas Kristof, Opinion, *"There's a Smell of Treason in the Air,"* N.Y. Times, Mar. 23, 2017.

One of us responded that such arguments were groundless, because "[w]hatever one thinks of Russia, Vladimir Putin, or the current state of relations between it/them and the United States, we are not at war with Russia. Full stop. Russia is therefore not an 'enemy' of the United States. Full stop." Steve Vladeck, *[Calling It] Treason Doth Never Prosper...* , Just Security, Mar. 24, 2017. But the terms "war" and "enemy" are not defined in either the Constitution or the treason statute. The risk of unwarranted prosecutions of U.S. citizens for treason is an argument for using a declaration or war or authorization for use of military force to demark qualifying hostilities. See *supra* pp. 82-87.

At least during World War II, courts held that individuals could commit "treason" only during the existence of formally declared hostilities against an identified enemy. *See, e.g.*, *United States v. McWilliams*, 54 F. Supp. 791, 793 (D.D.C. 1944) ("The averments as to what happened between 1933 and 1940 cannot be deemed a charge of conspiracy to commit treason since an essential element therein is aid and comfort to 'enemies' and Germany did not become a statutory enemy until December

1941."); *see also* Steve Vladeck, *We Have Met the Enemy, and He Is . . . ?*, Just Security, Mar. 25, 2017 (arguing that liability under the treason statute requires "the existence of an armed conflict under both domestic and international law — something noticeably lacking with regard to the United States and Russia").

While it is true that the United States is not "at war" with Russia in the same sense that we were, say, with France in 1800 (see *Bas v. Tingy*, 4 U.S. (4 Dall.) 37 (1800), *supra* p. 85), relations between our two countries appear to be extremely adversarial. Some might even paraphrase Justice Bushrod Washington in *Bas* to the effect that, if Russia is not our enemy, we know not what constitutes an enemy.

Treason has been only infrequently charged in criminal prosecutions, and no one has been found guilty of treason since World War II. Yet treason may be especially important today. It may provide an additional useful tool for the government in the fight against terrorism. *See* B. Mitchell Simpson, III, *Treason and Terror: A Toxic Brew*, 23 Roger Williams U. L. Rev. 1 (2018) (so arguing).

But treason also may, despite the Framers' efforts to prevent its misuse, be weaponized to threaten political adversaries. At this writing in late 2019, President Trump has been impeached by the House of Representatives and faces a trial in the Senate. The President has responded in part by suggesting that some of his critics might be guilty of treason. In one tweet he wrote that the Chair of the House Intelligence Committee should be "questioned at the highest level for Fraud and Treason." *See* Katie Rogers, *As Impeachment Moves Forward, Trump's Language Turns Darker*, N.Y. Times, Oct. 1, 2019. The President has also accused an intelligence community whistleblower, a Director and Acting Director of the FBI, and the *New York Times* of treasonous behavior. *Id.* Do you think such public statements might stifle dissent or reporting of the news? If so, is there any remedy?

D. THE LONG ARM OF THE LAW: EXTRATERRITORIAL CRIMINAL JURISDICTION

Congress has enacted a variety of statutes aimed at least in part at international terrorism. *See, e.g.*, 18 U.S.C. §§31-32 (2018) (hijacking or sabotaging aircraft); *id.* §§175-178 (developing or possessing biological or toxin weapons); *id.* §§2331-2332 (killing or injuring U.S. citizens abroad); *id.* §2332a (directing weapons of mass destruction against Americans abroad or against anyone within the United States); *id.* §§2339A-2339C (providing material support to terrorists); and 49 U.S.C. §§46,501-46,507 (air piracy). Most of these are now expressly extraterritorial in their application. But some older criminal statutes are not. The following case discusses the interpretative principles governing extraterritorial application of U.S. criminal laws.

Reading *United States v. Bin Laden*

After the 1998 U.S. embassy bombings in East Africa, the U.S. government indicted 15 defendants on a host of charged related to those attacks, even though the defendants — and virtually all of the relevant conduct — took place outside the territorial United States. In the opinion that follows, the district court denied the defendants' motion to dismiss in principal part, holding that most of the relevant offenses *did* apply overseas. As you read its analysis, consider the following questions:

- As we saw in Chapter 7, above, the Supreme Court has become far more skeptical about assuming that most statutes apply extraterritorially. Are there nevertheless reasons to assume that *these* statutes were meant to cover conduct of foreign nationals overseas? What cases and principles does Judge Sand rely upon to so conclude?
- Judge Sand also rejects the defendants' challenge to Congress's constitutional authority to proscribe such conduct. Why? On this logic, what, if anything, would stop Congress from codifying almost *all* terrorism-related offenses committed overseas?

United States v. Bin Laden

United States District Court, Southern District of New York, 2000
92 F. Supp. 2d 189

SAND, District Judge. The sixth superseding indictment in this case ("the Indictment") charges fifteen defendants with conspiracy to murder United States nationals, to use weapons of mass destruction against United States nationals, to destroy United States buildings and property, and to destroy United States defense utilities. The Indictment also charges defendants Mohamed Sadeek Odeh, Mohamed Rashed Daoud al-'Owhali, and Khalfan Khamis Mohamed, among others, with numerous crimes in connection with the August 1998 bombings of the United States Embassies in Nairobi, Kenya, and Dar es Salaam, Tanzania, including 223 counts of murder. . . .

I. EXTRATERRITORIAL APPLICATION

Odeh argues that Counts 5-8, 11-237, and 240-244 must be dismissed because (a) they concern acts allegedly performed by Odeh and his co-defendants outside United States territory, yet (b) are based on statutes that were not intended by Congress to regulate conduct outside United States territory. More specifically, Odeh argues that "the statutes that form the basis for the indictment fail clearly and unequivocally to regulate the conduct of foreign nationals for conduct outside the territorial boundaries of the United States." . . .

A. General Principles of Extraterritorial Application

It is well-established that Congress has the power to regulate conduct performed outside United States territory. It is equally well-established, however, that courts are to presume that Congress has not exercised this power — i.e., that statutes apply only to acts performed within United States territory — unless Congress manifests an intent to reach acts performed outside United States territory. This "clear manifestation" requirement does not require that extraterritorial coverage should be found only if the statute itself explicitly provides for extraterritorial application. Rather, courts should consider "all available evidence about the meaning" of the statute, e.g., its text, structure, and legislative history.

Furthermore, the Supreme Court has established a limited exception to this standard approach for "criminal statutes which are, as a class, not logically dependent on their locality for the Government's jurisdiction, but are enacted because of the right of the Government to defend itself against obstruction, or fraud wherever perpetrated, especially if committed by its own citizens, officers, or agents." *United States v. Bowman,* 260 U.S. 94, 98 (1922). As regards statutes of this type, courts may infer the requisite intent "from the nature of the offense" described in the statute, and thus need not examine its legislative history.[3] *Id.* The Court further observed that "to limit the [] locus [of such a statute] to the strictly territorial jurisdiction [of the United States] would be greatly to curtail the scope and usefulness of the statute and leave open a large immunity for frauds as easily committed by citizens on the high seas and in foreign countries as at home. . . ."

Odeh argues that *Bowman* is "not controlling precedent" because it "involved the application of [a] penal statute[] to United States citizens," i.e., not to foreign nationals such as himself. This argument is unavailing. . . .

. . . Under international law, the primary basis of jurisdiction is the "subjective territorial principle," under which "a state has jurisdiction to prescribe law with respect to . . . conduct that, wholly or in substantial part, takes place within its territory." *Restatement (Third) of the Foreign Relations Law of the United States* §402(1)(a) (1987). International law recognizes five other principles of jurisdiction by which a state may reach conduct *outside* its territory: (1) the objective territorial principle; (2) the protective principle; (3) the nationality principle; (4) the passive personality principle; and (5) the universality principle. The objective territoriality principle provides that a state has jurisdiction to prescribe law with respect to "conduct outside its territory that has or is intended to have substantial effect within its territory." *Restatement* §402(1)(c). The protective principle provides that a state has jurisdiction to prescribe law with respect to "certain conduct outside its territory by *persons not its nationals* that is directed against *the security of the state* or against a limited class of other state interests." *Id.* §402(3) (emphasis added). The nationality principle provides that a state has jurisdiction to prescribe law with respect to "the activities, interests, status, or relations of its nationals outside as well as within its territory." *Id.* §402(2). The passive personality principle provides that "a state may apply law — particularly criminal law — to an act committed outside its territory by a person not its national where the victim of the act was its national." *Id.* §402, cmt. g. The universality principle provides that, "[a] state has jurisdiction to define and prescribe punishment for certain offenses recognized by the community of nations as of universal concern, such as piracy, slave trade, attacks on or hijacking of aircraft, genocide, war crimes, and perhaps *certain acts of terrorism,*" regardless of the locus of their occurrence. *Id.* §404 (emphasis added). Because Congress has the power to override international law if it so chooses, *Restatement* §402, cmt. I., none of these five principles places ultimate limits on Congress's power to reach extraterritorial conduct. At the same time, however, "[i]n determining whether a statute applies extraterritorially, [courts] presume

3. This is not necessarily to say, however, that legislative history is entirely irrelevant under the *Bowman* exception to the standard approach. Given that the *Bowman* rule is ultimately concerned with congressional intent, if the legislative history clearly indicates that Congress intended the statute in question to apply only within the United States, it would be inconsistent with *Bowman* to ignore this evidence, and conclude — in reliance on *Bowman*— that Congress intended the statute to apply extraterritorially. . . .

that Congress does not intend to violate principles of international law . . . [and] in the absence of an explicit Congressional directive, courts do not give extraterritorial effect to any statute that violates principles of international law." *United States v. Vasquez-Velasco*, 15 F.3d 833, 839 (9th Cir. 1994) (citing *McCulloch v. Sociedad Nacional de Marineros de Honduras*, 372 U.S. 10, 21-22 (1963)). Hence, courts that find that a given statute applies extraterritorially typically pause to note that this finding is consistent with one or more of the five principles of extraterritorial jurisdiction under international law.

The *Bowman* rule would appear to be most directly related to the protective principle, which, as noted, explicitly authorizes a state's exercise of jurisdiction over "conduct outside its territory *by persons not its nationals.*" *Restatement* §402(3). Hence, an application of the *Bowman* rule that results in the extraterritorial application of a statute to the conduct of foreign nationals is consistent with international law. . . .

B. 18 U.S.C. §§844, 924, 930, 1114, and 2155

In light of the preceding general principles, we find that Congress intended each of the following statutory provisions to reach conduct by foreign nationals on foreign soil. . . .

1. 18 U.S.C. §844(f), (h), and (n)

The Indictment predicates Count 5 on 18 U.S.C. §§844(f). . . . Subsection 844(f)(1) provides:

> Whoever maliciously damages or destroys, or attempts to damage or destroy, by means of fire or an explosive, any building, vehicle, or other personal or real property in whole or in part owned or possessed by, or leased to, the United States, or any department or agency thereof, shall be imprisoned for not less than 5 years and not more than 20 years, fined under this title, or both.

18 U.S.C. §844(f)(1). Given (i) that this provision is explicitly intended to protect United States property, (ii) that a significant amount of United States property is located outside the United States, and (iii) that, accordingly, foreign nationals are in at least as good a position as are United States nationals to damage such property, we find, under *Bowman*, that Congress intended Section 844(f)(1) to apply extraterritorially — irrespective of the nationality of the perpetrator. . . .

III. CONSTITUTIONAL AUTHORITY

Odeh argues that the Counts based on 18 U.S.C. §§2332 and 2332a must be dismissed because these statutes are unconstitutional in that they exceed Congress's authority to legislate under the Constitution. As noted above, Subsection 2332(b) provides in relevant part that "[w]hoever outside the United States . . . engages in a conspiracy to kill[] a national of the United States shall [be punished as further provided]," 18 U.S.C. §2332(b); and Section 2332a(a) provides in relevant part that, "[a] person who . . . uses, threatens, or attempts or conspires to use, a weapon of mass destruction . . . (1) against a national of the United States while such national is outside of the United States; . . . or (3) against any property that is owned, leased or used by the United States . . . , whether the property is within or outside of the United States, shall [be punished as further provided]." 18 U.S.C. §2332a(a).

Odeh suggests that there is but one constitutional grant of authority to legislate that could support these two statutory provisions: Article I, Section 8, Clause 10. Clause 10 grants Congress the authority "[t]o define and punish Piracies and Felonies committed on the high Seas, and Offenses against the Law of Nations." U.S. Const. art. I, §8, cl. 10. Odeh argues that, as "[t]he acts described in these two statutes . . . are not widely regarded as offenses 'against the law of nations,'" these statutes exceed Congress's authority under Clause 10.

There are two problems with this argument. First, even assuming that the acts described in Sections 2332 and 2332a are not *widely* regarded as violations of international law, it does not necessarily follow that these provisions exceed Congress's authority under Clause 10. Clause 10 does not merely give Congress the authority to punish offenses against the law of nations; it also gives Congress the power to "define" such offenses. Hence, provided that the acts in question are recognized by at least some members of the international community as being offenses against the law of nations, Congress arguably has the power to criminalize these acts pursuant to its power *to define* offenses against the law of nations. *See United States v. Smith*, 18 U.S. (5 Wheat.) 153, 159 (1820) (Story, J.) ("Offenses . . . against the law of nations, cannot, with any accuracy, be said to be completely ascertained and defined in any public code recognized by the common consent of nations. . . . [T]herefore . . . , there is a peculiar fitness in giving the power to define as well as to punish.").

Second, and more important, it is not the case that Clause 10 provides the only basis for Sections 2332 and 2332a. The Supreme Court has recognized that, with regard to foreign affairs legislation, "investment of the federal Government with the powers of external sovereignty did not depend upon the affirmative grants of the Constitution." *United States v. Curtiss-Wright Export Corp.*, 299 U.S. 304, 318 (1936). Rather, Congress's authority to regulate foreign affairs "exist[s] as inherently inseparable from the conception of nationality." *Id.* (citations omitted). More specifically, this "concept of essential sovereignty of a free nation clearly requires the existence and recognition of an inherent power in the state to protect itself from destruction." *United States v. Rodriguez*, 182 F. Supp. 479, 491 (S.D. Cal. 1960), *aff'd in part sub nom. Rocha v. United States*, 288 F.2d 545 (9th Cir.), *cert. denied*, 366 U.S. 948 (1961).

In penalizing extraterritorial conspiracies to kill nationals of the United States, Section 2332(b) is clearly designed to protect a vital United States interest. And, indeed, Congress expressly identified this protective function as the chief purpose of Section 2332. Therefore, we conclude, under *Curtiss-Wright*, that Congress acted within its authority in enacting these provisions. . . .

V. APPLICATION OF 18 U.S.C. §930(c) TO FOREIGN VICTIMS

Odeh argues that interpreting Section 930(c)[2] to reach "the deaths of Kenyan and Tanzanian citizens [as opposed to United States citizens] would be contrary to

[2. 18 U.S.C. §930(c) (2018) provides that "[a] person who kills or attempts to kill any person in the course of a violation of subsection (a) or (b) [involving knowing possession of firearms or other dangerous weapons in a federal facility], or in the course of an attack on a Federal facility involving the use of a firearm or other dangerous weapon, shall be punished [as further provided]." — Eds.]

established principles of international law." More specifically, Odeh advances the following two arguments. First, given (i) that "[u]nder 18 U.S.C. §930(c), the only arguable basis for jurisdiction over the deaths of foreign citizens is the principle of universality," (ii) that "[u]niversal jurisdiction results where there is *universal* condemnation of an offense, and a general interest in cooperating to suppress them, as reflected in *widely accepted* international agreements," and (iii) that "the universality principle does not encompass terrorist actions resulting in the deaths of individuals who are not diplomatic personnel," it follows that applying Section 930(c) to the deaths of "ordinary" foreign nationals on foreign soil would constitute a violation of international law.

There are two problems with this argument. First, because "universal jurisdiction is increasingly accepted for certain acts of terrorism, such as . . . indiscriminate violent assaults on people at large," Restatement §404, cmt. a, a plausible case could be made that extraterritorial application of Section 930(c) in this case *is* supported by the universality principle.

Second, it is not the case that the universality principle is the "only arguable basis for jurisdiction over the deaths of foreign citizens." As indicated by our conclusion . . . that Section 930(c) is designed to *protect* vital United States interests, the protective principle is also an "arguable basis" for the extraterritorial application of Section 930(c). . . . In providing for the death penalty where death results in the course of an attack on a Federal facility, Section 930(c) is clearly designed to deter attacks on Federal facilities. Given the likelihood that foreign nationals will be in or near Federal facilities located in foreign nations, this deterrent effect would be significantly diminished if Section 930(c) were limited to the deaths of United States nationals. . . .

Odeh argues, second, that, even if the universality principle (or one of the four other principles) did authorize the application of Section 930(c) to the deaths of ordinary foreign nationals on foreign soil, such application would violate international law nevertheless, because (i) "[e]ven where one of the principles authorizes jurisdiction, a nation is nevertheless precluded from exercising jurisdiction where jurisdiction would be 'unreasonable,'" and (ii) application of Section 930(c) to the deaths of ordinary foreign nationals on foreign soil would be unreasonable. *Id.* (citations omitted).

According to the Restatement, the following factors are to be taken into account for the purpose of determining whether exercise of extraterritorial jurisdiction is reasonable:

> (a) the link of the activity to the territory of the regulating state, i.e., the extent to which the activity takes place within the territory, or has substantial, direct, and foreseeable effect upon or in the territory;
>
> (b) the connections, such as nationality, residence, or economic activity, between the regulating state and the person principally responsible for the activity to be regulated, or between that state and those whom the regulation is designed to protect;
>
> (c) the character of the activity to be regulated, the importance of regulation to the regulating state, the extent to which other states regulate such activities, and the degree to which the desirability of such regulation is generally accepted;
>
> (d) the existence of justified expectations that might be protected or hurt by the regulation;
>
> (e) the importance of the regulation to the international political, legal, or economic system;

(f) the extent to which the regulation is consistent with the traditions of the international system;

(g) the extent to which another state may have an interest in regulating the activity; and

(h) the likelihood of conflict with regulation by another state.

Restatement §403(2). Given that factor (a) alludes to the subjective territorial principle and the objective territorial principle, it is not especially relevant to a statute, such as Section 930(c), based primarily on the protective principle. Much the same can be said of factor (b), as it alludes to the nationality principle, the subjective territorial principle, and the objective territorial principle. Factor (c), in contrast, is highly relevant to Section 930(c). It is important both to the United States and other nations to prevent the destruction of their facilities — regardless of their location; and such regulation is accordingly widely accepted among the nations of the world. As for factor (d), Section 930(c) protects the expectation of foreign nationals that they will be free of harm while on the premises of United States facilities. We can think of no "justified" expectation, however, that would be hurt by the extraterritorial application of Section 930(c). As for factor (e), in light of the prominent role played by the United States in "the international political, legal, and economic systems," the protection of United States facilities — regardless of their location — is highly important to the stability of these systems. Turning to factor (f), as indicated by the preceding discussion of factor (c), most, if not all, nations are concerned about protecting their facilities, both at home and abroad. Hence, Section 930(c) is highly consistent "with the traditions of the international system." As for (g), it must be acknowledged that when the United States facility is on foreign soil, and when the victims of the attack are nationals of the host nation, the host nation "has a keen interest in regulating and punishing [the] offenders." This is not to say, however, that the host nation has a greater interest than does the United States. Furthermore, even if it were the case that the host nation had a greater interest than the United States, this single factor would be insufficient to support the conclusion that application of Section 930(c) to the bombings of the two Embassies is unreasonable. Coming, finally, to factor (h), Odeh does not argue that application of Section 930(c) to the bombings would conflict with Kenyan and/or Tanzanian law, nor are we otherwise aware of such conflict. On the contrary, the Government informs the Court that "[t]he Kenyan Government voluntarily rendered Odeh (and [co-defendant] al-'Owhali) to the United States, and neither the Kenyan nor the Tanzanian Government has asserted any objection to the United States' exercise of jurisdiction in this case." Factor (h) thus counts in favor of the reasonableness of applying Section 930(c) to the bombings. . . .

Notes and Questions

1. *Extraterritoriality and the Constitution.* No one questions a sovereign state's authority to prescribe laws for its own territory, and the Constitution quite clearly vests limited authority to do so in Congress. But can Congress constitutionally make laws that apply abroad? The Constitution is silent on this question, but Article III states that when a crime is "not committed within any State," trial for the crime shall be conducted where Congress directs. U.S. Const. art. III, §2, cl. 3. Thus, the Framers

clearly contemplated criminal sanctions against acts committed outside any state of the union. Moreover, they vested Congress with the authority to define and punish "Offenses against the Law of Nations." *Id.* art. I, §8, cl. 10. See *supra* pp. 187-188. Because such offenses may be committed abroad, this provision gives Congress extraterritorial lawmaking authority. On what basis does Odeh argue that 18 U.S.C. §§2332 and 2332a exceed Congress's lawmaking authority? Is the court's response consistent with a federal government of limited lawmaking authority?

Assuming that Congress can enact laws with extraterritorial effect, does the Constitution place any limit on extraterritoriality? Civil procedure students may suspect that some "minimum contact" by the defendant or her acts with the United States might be required as a matter of due process. Beyond that, however, customary international law principles of prescriptive jurisdiction might also establish limits as a part of our federal common law. See *supra* pp. 202-203. Indeed, one commentator asserts that "[i]t is arguable that the Constitution permits Congress to make acts committed abroad crimes under United States law only to the extent permitted by international law." Andreas Lowenfeld, *U.S. Law Enforcement Abroad: The Constitution and International Law,* 83 Am. J. Int'l L. 880, 881 (1989). How did the *Bin Laden* court regard this assertion?

If international law does not limit extraterritorial lawmaking by Congress, what role, if any, does it play, according to the court? What rule of statutory construction is implicated by applicable international laws?

2. Presumption Against Extraterritoriality. Why should the courts presume that a statute applies locally only, unless Congress clearly manifests an intent to reach acts performed abroad? Sometimes such an intent is manifested by the plain language of the statute. The statute that makes it a crime to develop, produce, stockpile, transfer, acquire, retain, or possess any biological agent, toxin, or delivery system for use as a weapon, for example, expressly provides that "[t]here is extraterritorial Federal jurisdiction over an offense under this section committed by or against a national of the United States." 18 U.S.C. §175 (2018). Similarly, 18 U.S.C. §2332(b) expressly makes it a crime to engage in a conspiracy "outside the United States" to kill U.S. nationals. *Bowman* created an exception to the presumption against extraterritoriality. Why?

3. The Territoriality and Nationality Principles of Extraterritorial Jurisdiction. The court in *Bin Laden* catalogued principles of jurisdiction under customary international law, but such principles are not equally accepted by all nations, and they may not be helpful for other reasons. The territorial principle, for example, applies both to actors within a sovereign's territory ("subjective territoriality") and to effects in such territory resulting from acts abroad ("objective territoriality"), and it is reflected in *Restatement (Fourth) of Foreign Relations Law* §402(1) (2018). But while it is the most common and widely accepted principle of jurisdiction, it often will be unavailable for prosecution of terrorist or other criminal acts performed abroad, including inchoate acts intended ultimately to cause injury in the United States. The nationality principle—allowing a sovereign to exercise jurisdiction over its nationals for their acts performed abroad—is also accepted by the practice of nations. Roman Boed, *United States Legislative Approach to Extraterritorial Jurisdiction in Connection with Terrorism,* in 2 *International Criminal Law* 147 (M. Cherif Bassiouni ed., 2d ed. 1999). But international terrorists may not be U.S. nationals, just as most of the *Bin Laden* defendants were not.

4. *The Protective Principle of Extraterritorial Jurisdiction.* The protective principle is more likely to apply to acts of international terrorism, but it is limited to offenses against the security of the state or "a limited class of other fundamental U.S. interests." *Restatement (Fourth)* §402(1)(e). It thus is easily applied to the embassy bombings. Would it apply to terrorist acts committed against private U.S. nationals abroad? "The lack of definition of the range of conduct encompassed by the protective principle and the principle's malleability," Professor Boed worries, "could lead to the principle's justification of a wide-ranging exercise of extraterritorial jurisdiction." Boed, *supra,* at 148.

5. *The Passive Personality Principle of Extraterritorial Jurisdiction.* Even if the protective principle does not apply to terrorist acts against private U.S. nationals, such acts would clearly fall under the passive personality principle. But this principle has not traditionally found wide support in the practice of states, and it was squarely rejected by the United States until recently.

In the Omnibus Diplomatic Security and Antiterrorism Act of 1986, however, Congress made it a crime to kill or conspire to kill or cause physical violence to a U.S. national while such national is outside the United States. Pub. L. No. 99-399, §1202, 100 Stat. 853, 896 (codified at 18 U.S.C. §2332 (2018)). The *Bin Laden* defendants were charged with this crime, and it would apply as well to acts of homicide or physical violence against private U.S. nationals traveling abroad. Does that mean that the United States could prosecute an Italian pickpocket for pushing a U.S. tourist in Rome as he extracted the tourist's wallet? Even Congress had doubts about reaching so far, so it added a limitation forbidding any prosecution except upon written certification by the Attorney General or his Deputy that "such offense was intended to coerce, intimidate, or retaliate against a government or a civilian population." 18 U.S.C. §2332(d). Here Congress attempted to narrow the offenses to terrorist offenses without defining them and thus to avoid extending the statute to barroom brawls or ordinary street crimes. But what new problem does this provision arguably create? Who creates jurisdiction under this law, and when is it created? *See* Lowenfeld, *supra,* at 891 (opining that the statute is unconstitutional).

Congress came back to passive personality jurisdiction in the Antiterrorism and Effective Death Penalty Act of 1996, Pub. L. No. 104-132, 110 Stat. 1214. In a section of that Act entitled "Clarification and Extension of Criminal Jurisdiction Over Certain Terrorism Offenses Overseas," Congress systematically amended multiple sections of the criminal code to supply the "clear manifestation" of extraterritoriality that is needed to overcome the presumption against extraterritoriality. *See, e.g., id.* §721. These sections address aircraft piracy, destruction of aircraft, violence at international airports, murder of foreign officials and other persons, protection of the same, threats and extortion against the same, kidnaping of internationally protected persons, and developing or possessing biological weapons. *See* Boed, *supra,* at 159-173. Note, however, that Congress did not apply the material support statutes extraterritorially until *after* September 11 — extending §2339A in the USA Patriot Act of 2001, Pub. L. No. 107-56, §805(a)(1)(F), 115 Stat. 272, 377; and §2339B in the Intelligence Reform and Terrorism Prevention Act of 2004, Pub. L. No. 108-458, §6603(d), 118 Stat. 3638, 3763. Given the breadth of those prohibitions (especially after the Supreme Court's *Humanitarian Law Project* ruling), do you see the significance of having *these* offenses apply to anyone, anywhere in the world?

6. The Universality Principle of Extraterritorial Jurisdiction. Universality is perhaps the most controversial of the principles of extraterritorial jurisdiction, because it could theoretically result in a state's prosecuting a non-national for acts performed abroad against other non-nationals. *See* Kenneth C. Randall, *Universal Jurisdiction Under International Law,* 66 Tex. L. Rev. 785 (1988). It rests on the assumption that there are some crimes so widely regarded as heinous that their perpetrators are enemies of mankind, subject to prosecution the world over. The prosecuting nation acts for all nations to protect their collective interest. See *supra* p. 188 (discussing *jus cogens*).

To which crimes does this principle apply, according to the *Bin Laden* court? Do they include terrorism? In 1984, Judge Edwards of the D.C. Circuit asserted that he was unable to conclude "that the law of nations . . . outlaws politically motivated terrorism, no matter how repugnant it might be to our legal system." *Tel-Oren v. Libyan Arab Republic,* 726 F.2d 774, 796 (D.C. Cir. 1984) (Edwards, J., concurring). Why do you suppose that the law of nations might not subject terrorism to universal jurisdiction? On the other hand, the law of nations is not static. The *Restatement (Fourth)* §404 took a half step after *Bin Laden* by including "certain acts of terrorism," which were undefined, but identified in the reporter's comment by reference to treaties prohibiting particular acts, such as hijackings and bombings.

7. The Rule of Comity. The *Restatement* suggests that traditional principles of extraterritoriality are not to be mechanically applied: "In exercising jurisdiction to prescribe, the United States takes account of the legitimate interests of other nations as a matter of prescriptive comity," and "[a]s a matter of prescriptive comity, courts in the United States may interpret federal statutory provisions to include other limitations on their applicability." *Restatement (Fourth)* §§401(2), 405 (entitled "Reasonableness in Interpretation"). Indeed, the malleability and overlap of the traditional principles of extraterritorial jurisdiction under international law have led to suggestions that reasonableness is today the overriding principle, under which the availability or nonavailability of the traditional principles is just a factor in the equation. *See generally* Christopher L. Blakesley, *Extraterritorial Jurisdiction,* in 2 *International Criminal Law, supra,* at 41. Is extraterritorial jurisdiction in *Bin Laden* "reasonable"? Why or why not?

8. "Substantial Nexus." We suggested that the civil procedure student might speculate whether the Due Process Clause imposes a "minimum contacts" requirement for extraterritorial jurisdiction. In fact, a few cases have spoken of the need for a substantial nexus between the defendant or his acts and the state exercising extraterritorial jurisdiction. *See, e.g., United States v. Davis,* 905 F.2d 245 (9th Cir. 1990). Most courts, however (including the *Bin Laden* court in a portion of the opinion not reproduced here), have concluded that if extraterritorial jurisdiction is justified by the international principles of extraterritorial jurisdiction, due process is satisfied. *Id.* at 249. This seems persuasive when jurisdiction is supported by the territoriality, nationality, or protective principle, because each presumes "contact." Can you explain how? But does it work for jurisdiction supported only by the passive personality or universality principle?

In *United States v. Brehm,* 691 F.3d 547 (4th Cir. 2012), the Court of Appeals upheld a conviction of a South African military contractor under the Military Extraterritorial Jurisdiction Act for an assault committed against a British subject on a

NATO airbase in Afghanistan. Critical to the court's analysis were the facts that (1) the Afghan government had "authorized the American government 'to exercise its criminal jurisdiction over the personnel of the United States'"; and (2) Brehm, as an employee of a U.S. military contractor, had signed an agreement with his employer that stated that he "may be subject to U.S. . . . federal criminal jurisdiction under the [MEJA] by accompanying armed forces outside the United States." *Id.* at 550-551. Thus, the court concluded, Brehm should have known that it would be reasonable "to interpret 'personnel of the United States' to include employees of DynCorp and other American contractors and subcontractors." *Id.* at 553. Do you agree?

CRIMINALIZING TERRORISM AND ITS PRECURSORS: SUMMARY OF BASIC PRINCIPLES

- Federal law defines both international and domestic terrorism, but does not make either a crime as such. However, state criminal laws apply to almost all violent acts that might be performed by terrorists, and more than 50 federal statutes criminalize many such acts (e.g., using explosives or killing or injuring federal officers). The substantial majority of these federal statutes apply to both international and domestic terrorism.

- While the foregoing laws cover a multitude of completed acts of terrorism, counterterrorism efforts also aim "left of boom" to prevent terrorist acts. Traditionally, criminal conspiracy laws have been used for this purpose, but some, like laws punishing seditious conspiracy, are both anachronistic and too narrow to cover some forms of terrorism, and all pose significant evidentiary challenges.

- Federal law has therefore criminalized the "precursor" acts of providing material support to terrorists and foreign terrorist organizations (FTOs). The Supreme Court has upheld the statute punishing material support for FTOs even though the statute (1) does not require specific intent on the part of the defendant, and (2) in some applications may come close to imposing "guilt by association" on persons who knowingly supply even humanitarian or other non-violent support to an FTO. The First Amendment, the Supreme Court has held, protects only independent advocacy on behalf of designated FTOs.

- There is no process yet for formally designating primarily domestic groups as domestic terrorist organizations (DTOs), and no federal statute expressly criminalizes material support of such organizations. In its decision upholding the material support statute for FTOs, the Supreme Court went out of its way to emphasize that it was not suggesting that Congress could extend the same prohibition to DTOs, leaving proposals for doing so under a heavy constitutional cloud.

- The constitutional and statutory crime of treason may be invoked to abate threats or punish acts that jeopardize national security, but only in prosecutions of U.S. citizens based on the testimony of at least two witnesses. The definition of the crime is ambiguous in certain critical respects, however. And the threat of prosecution for treason may be used as a political weapon to stifle dissent.

- Even as the Supreme Court has shown increasing skepticism toward the application of most U.S. laws overseas, courts have broadly construed the territorial reach of criminal counterterrorism laws — and Congress has followed suit, expanding the explicit coverage of the material support statutes to encompass conduct by anyone anywhere in the world. As a result, the U.S. government today has the power to prosecute terrorism suspects across the globe, so long as it can establish that those individuals provided material support to a designated FTO.

Terrorism Trials: Procedure and Evidence

It is not just the crimes that pose legal problems in prosecuting accused terrorists and their supporters, but also the process and evidence. In 1996, Congress for the first time authorized the intelligence community, "upon the request of a United States law enforcement agency, [to] collect information outside the United States about individuals who are not United States persons . . . notwithstanding that the law enforcement agency intends to use the information collected for purposes of a law enforcement investigation or counterintelligence investigation." 50 U.S.C. §3039(a) (2018). Then, after 9/11, Congress expressly authorized and encouraged more sharing of information among intelligence and law enforcement agencies. See *supra* pp. 538-539. Intelligence agencies may even be tasked with information collection for law enforcement, with the understanding that the information collected may be used in criminal prosecutions against alleged terrorists or their supporters.

However, concerns for the security of the information itself, as well as for the intelligence sources or methods used to collect it, may pose serious issues in the criminal prosecution of terrorists. Must a terrorism suspect receive a *Miranda* warning before he is interrogated, and, if so, would such a warning compromise the acquisition of intelligence? How can the intelligence-driven need for lengthy interrogation be reconciled with criminal suspects' rights to a speedy trial? Is a criminal proceeding fatally tainted by claims that the defendant was held in coercive detention, or is coerced evidence inadmissible in a terrorism prosecution? What about evidence that is classified or that the government wishes to keep secret for some other reason? These are only some of the serious questions presented by the clash of intelligence collection, criminal procedure, and the rules of evidence.

Moreover, as Judge Wilkinson explained in his opinion in *Al-Marri v. Pucciarelli*, 534 F.3d 213 (4th Cir. 2008) (en banc), *vacated and remanded sub nom. Al-Marri v. Spagone*, 555 U.S. 1220 (2009):

> The problems presented by the criminal prosecution of terrorists are even more pronounced at trial. . . .

> First, while a showcase of American values, an open and public criminal trial may also serve as a platform for suspected terrorists. Terror suspects may use the bully pulpit of a criminal trial in an attempt to recruit others to their cause. Likewise, terror suspects may take advantage of the opportunity to interact with others during trial to pass critical intelligence to their allies. . . .
>
> Second, and relatedly, the prosecution of some terrorists could present security concerns of a different sort: witnesses and jurors may be subjected to threats of violence or become the targets of attack. . . .
>
> Third, and finally, . . . traditional criminal proceedings, especially public trials, may not be responsive to the executive's legitimate need to protect sensitive information. . . .
>
> However, the government's desire to protect such sensitive intelligence may conflict with a defendant's confrontation and compulsory process rights. By employing those rights, a terror suspect like al-Marri may, in a tactic commonly referred to as "graymail," request highly sensitive materials. Such a request leaves the government facing a Hobson's Choice. The government can withdraw all or part of its case to protect its information, or proceed and surrender its sensitive intelligence and possibly its source. And even if the government is able to suppress the defendant's request, defense counsel will be able to insinuate that the government is hiding information that is favorable to the defendant. . . .
>
> . . . Congress may certainly take [such concerns] into account in deciding that the criminal justice system is not the sole permissible means of dealing with suspected terrorists. . . . [*Id.* at 307-308 (Wilkinson, J., concurring in part and dissenting in part).]

In this chapter, we consider how Congress, the courts, and the Executive have taken such problems into account in criminal prosecutions against accused terrorists and their supporters.

A. NATIONAL SECURITY CRIMINAL PROCEDURE: *MIRANDA*, PRESENTMENT, AND SPEEDY TRIAL

Terrorism prosecutions tend to raise unique evidentiary concerns because they often involve the use, by either the government or the defendant (or both), of classified information. But as we have seen throughout the preceding chapters, the government usually has a *dual* interest in incapacitating terrorism suspects — to neutralize the threat they pose by subjecting them to criminal punishment, as well as to derive actionable intelligence from them. This latter interest, in turn, has generated significant pressure on the government to interrogate terrorism suspects to the fullest extent permitted by law, and it has subjected the government to substantial criticism from some circles for not doing even more.

To that end, some have argued that the government should be able to interrogate terrorism suspects without advising them of their rights to counsel and to remain silent under *Miranda*, at least for some time before criminal proceedings formally begin. Senator Lindsey Graham, among others, urged the Obama administration not to Mirandize Dzokhar Tsarnaev, one of the Boston Marathon bombers, and instead to hold him as an enemy combatant in order to interrogate him for intelligence-gathering purposes. *See, e.g.*, Wells Bennett, *Senator Graham on Tsarnaev and Miranda*, Lawfare, Apr. 23, 2013. Similar calls followed the capture of Abu Khattalah — the alleged ringleader of the September 11, 2012 Benghazi attacks.

The Supreme Court has already recognized an exception to *Miranda* for interrogations motivated by concern for "public safety," as opposed to ordinary law enforcement. *See New York v. Quarles*, 467 U.S. 649 (1984). As you review the materials that follow, consider how, if at all, the *Quarles* exception — and the range of issues that have arisen alongside *Miranda*'s applicability to terrorism cases — illuminate this debate.

U.S. Department of Justice, Federal Bureau of Investigation, Custodial Interrogation for Public Safety and Intelligence-Gathering Purposes of Operational Terrorists Inside the United States[1]

Oct. 21, 2010

Identifying and apprehending suspected terrorists, interrogating them to obtain intelligence about terrorist activities and impending terrorist attacks, and lawfully detaining them so that they do not pose a continuing threat to our communities are critical to protecting the American people. The Department of Justice and the FBI believe that we can maximize our ability to accomplish these objectives by continuing to adhere to FBI policy regarding the use of *Miranda* warnings for custodial interrogation of operational terrorists[2] who are arrested inside the United States:

1. If applicable, agents should ask any and all questions that are reasonably prompted by an immediate concern for the safety of the public or the arresting agents without advising the arrestee of his *Miranda* rights.[3]
2. After all applicable public safety questions have been exhausted, agents should advise the arrestee of his *Miranda* rights and seek a waiver of those rights before any further interrogation occurs, absent exceptional circumstances described below.
3. There may be exceptional cases in which, although all relevant public safety questions have been asked, agents nonetheless conclude that continued unwarned interrogation is necessary to collect valuable and timely intelligence not related to any immediate threat, and that the government's interest in obtaining this intelligence outweighs the disadvantages of proceeding with unwarned interrogation.[4] . . . Presentment of an arrestee may not be

---

1. This guidance applies only to arrestees who have not been indicted and who are not known to be represented by an attorney. . . .

2. For these purposes, an operational terrorist is an arrestee who is reasonably believed to be either a high-level member of an international terrorist group; or an operative who has personally conducted or attempted to conduct a terrorist operation that involved risk to life; or an individual knowledgeable about operational details of a pending terrorist operation.

3. The Supreme Court held in *New York v. Quarles*, 467 U.S. 649 (1984), that if law enforcement officials engage in custodial interrogation of an individual that is "reasonable prompted by a concern for the public safety," any statements the individual provides in the course of such interrogation shall not be inadmissible in any criminal proceeding on the basis that the warnings described in *Miranda v. Arizona*, 384 U.S. 436 (1966), were not provided. The court noted that this exception to the *Miranda* rule is a narrow one and that "in each case it will be circumscribed by the [public safety] exigency which justifies it." 467 U.S. at 657.

4. The Supreme Court has strongly suggested that an arrestee's Fifth Amendment right against self-incrimination is not violated at the time a statement is taken without *Miranda* warnings, but instead may be violated only if and when the government introduces an unwarned statement in a criminal proceeding against the defendant. *See* Chavez v. Martinez, 538 U.S. 760, 769 (2003) (plurality opinion). . . .

> delayed simply to continue the interrogation, unless the defendant has timely waived prompt presentment.

The determination whether particular unwarned questions are justified on public safety grounds must always be made on a case-by-case basis based on all the facts and circumstances. In light of the magnitude and complexity of the threat often posed by terrorist organizations, particularly international terrorist organizations, and the nature of their attacks, the circumstances surrounding an arrest of an operational terrorist may warrant significantly more extensive public safety interrogation without *Miranda* warnings than would be permissible in an ordinary criminal case. Depending on the facts, such interrogation might include, for example, questions about possible impending or coordinated terrorist attacks; the location, nature, and threat posed by weapons that might post an imminent danger to the public; and the identities, locations, and activities or intentions of accomplices who may be plotting additional imminent attacks. . . .

Notes and Questions

1. *Quarles and the Origin of the "Public Safety" Exception.* Although *Quarles* has come to serve as the fountainhead for the "public safety" exception, it was a fairly unexceptional case. There, a rape victim told the police that the perpetrator (who was armed) had just entered a nearby supermarket. When officers arrested the suspect inside the supermarket, they found an empty holster, leading one of the officers to ask the suspect what had happened to the gun. The suspect's answer, which led the officers to where he had hidden the gun, was subsequently suppressed by the trial court on the ground that it was obtained in violation of *Miranda*; it was, after all, a statement made in response to an unwarned custodial interrogation. *See Quarles*, 467 U.S. at 651-653. But the Supreme Court reversed. As then-Justice Rehnquist explained for a 5-4 majority, "Whatever the motivation of individual officers in such a situation, we do not believe that the doctrinal underpinnings of *Miranda* require that it be applied in all its rigor to a situation in which police officers ask questions reasonably prompted by a concern for the public safety." *Id.* at 656.

In other words, where questioning in a custodial interrogation focuses on ongoing concern for public safety, rather than the suspect's specific culpability, statements made by the suspect in response are admissible against him even if they were obtained prior to the administration of the *Miranda* warnings. Otherwise, Rehnquist explained, law enforcement officers would be forced to make a difficult choice — to decide on the spur of the moment and under exigent circumstances

> whether it best serves society for them to ask the necessary questions without the *Miranda* warnings and render whatever probative evidence they uncover inadmissible, or for them to give the warnings in order to preserve the admissibility of evidence they might uncover but possibly damage or destroy their ability to obtain that evidence and neutralize the volatile situation confronting them. [*Id.* at 657-658.]

2. *Justice O'Connor's Objection.* In an unusually strident dissent, Justice O'Connor criticized this reasoning as presenting a false dichotomy grounded in a misunderstanding of *Miranda* — as a bar on interrogations, rather than as an exclusionary rule. (As the FBI guidelines point out in footnote 3, the Supreme Court has all but held

that *Miranda* is only the latter, and does not bar unwarned interrogations in the abstract.) As she elaborated,

> *Miranda* has never been read to prohibit the police from asking questions to secure the public safety. Rather, the critical question *Miranda* addresses is who shall bear the cost of securing the public safety when such questions are asked and answered: the defendant or the State. *Miranda,* for better or worse, found the resolution of that question implicit in the prohibition against compulsory self-incrimination and placed the burden on the State. When police ask custodial questions without administering the required warnings, *Miranda* quite clearly requires that the answers received be presumed compelled and that they be excluded from evidence at trial. [*Id.* at 665 (O'Connor, J., concurring in the judgment in part and dissenting in part).]

Isn't Justice O'Connor correct that *Quarles* would allow law enforcement officers to have their cake and eat it, too? Is that simply a necessary compromise in situations in which there is a serious threat to "public safety"? If so, was such a compromise necessary to deal with the threat to public safety in *Quarles*: a handgun hidden in a grocery store?

3. The FBI's "Exceptional Cases" Category. The FBI guidelines reproduced above are mostly devoted to implementing *Quarles* in practice. But consider the suggestion under point "3" that

> [t]here may be exceptional cases in which, although all relevant public safety questions have been asked, agents nonetheless conclude that continued unwarned interrogation is necessary to collect valuable and timely intelligence not related to any immediate threat, and that the government's interest in obtaining this intelligence outweighs the disadvantages of proceeding with unwarned interrogation.

Are the guidelines suggesting that such statements may nevertheless be admissible under *Quarles*? Or are they suggesting that there will be cases in which the potential fruits of such statements outweigh the government's need to be able to introduce them against the suspect at trial? If these considerations are already applied by the government, doesn't that undermine Justice Rehnquist's reasoning in *Quarles*, which sought to free the government from such calculus? Or might it suggest, in the alternative, that the FBI has a narrower view of the "public safety" exception than the courts?

4. The Scope of the "Public Safety" Exception in Terrorism Cases. How should courts measure the threat to public safety in terrorism cases, where the potential risk to public safety may be far greater than that posed by a single gun hidden in a grocery store, but where it also may be far less imminent and specific? Is there a principled way to define "public safety" in this context? Or was Justice O'Connor correct in *Quarles* when she warned that "[t]he end result will be a finespun new doctrine on public safety exigencies incident to custodial interrogation, complete with the hair-splitting distinctions that currently plague our Fourth Amendment jurisprudence"? 467 U.S. at 663-664 (O'Connor, J., concurring in the judgment in part and dissenting in part).

5. The Abdulmutallab Case. Omar Farouk Abdulmutallab, the "underwear bomber," sustained significant burns while attempting to ignite explosives concealed in his underwear in order to blow up Northwest Flight 253 as it was approaching Detroit, Michigan, on December 25, 2009. He was interrogated for 50 minutes by the FBI after his arrest while undergoing treatment at the University of Michigan Hospital, but before he was advised of his rights under *Miranda v. Arizona*. Among other things, the agents asked him where and when he had traveled, how, and with whom; for details of the explosive device; for details regarding the bomb-maker, including where Abdulmutallab had received the bomb; his intentions in attacking Flight 253; and who else might be planning an attack. In the criminal prosecution that followed, Abdulmutallab moved to suppress statements made by him in response to those questions. The district court denied Abdulmutallab's motion, holding that "[t]he agents' questions were intended to shed light on the obvious public safety concerns in this case and were 'necessary to secure . . . the safety of the public[.]'" *United States v. Abdulmutallab*, No. 10-20005, 2011 WL 4345243, at *5 (E.D. Mich. Sept. 16, 2011) (quoting *Quarles*, 467 U.S. at 659). Why was the "public safety" exception even necessary in Abdulmutallab's case? For a suspect literally caught red-handed, what additional information could the government have needed to prosecute him for attempting to destroy an aircraft? The court's ruling rested heavily on the gravity of the threat that would have been posed to public safety if there had been similar plots against other aircraft. Should the gravity of the apparent threat bear on the timing and scope of admissible, unwarned questioning? Won't that always tip the scales in the government's favor in terrorism cases?

6. *The Other Shoe: Presentment.* Even *Abdulmutallab* upholds only 50 minutes of "public safety" questioning, suggesting, at least implicitly, that the temporal scope of the *Quarles* exception is quite limited. If it is not, then the other relevant consideration is "presentment" — the requirement that individuals arrested without a warrant be brought before a neutral magistrate "without unnecessary delay," Fed. R. Crim. P. 5(a)(1)(A), at which point a suspect will be advised of his rights to counsel and to remain silent, if he has not been already. As a result, under *McNabb v. United States*, 318 U.S. 332 (1943), and *Mallory v. United States*, 354 U.S. 449 (1957), an arrestee's confession is inadmissible if it is given after an unreasonable delay in presentment. And under *County of Riverside v. McLaughlin*, 500 U.S. 44 (1991), the Fourth Amendment itself requires a probable cause finding by a grand jury or neutral magistrate within 48 hours of a warrantless arrest (where no such finding has previously been made). Taken together, these cases might be read to suggest that the government is entitled to no more than 48 hours of "public safety" questioning of a suspect before apprising him of his *Miranda* rights. Is there any argument that the presentment requirement might itself have a "public safety" exception? Would such an exception ever be necessary?

7. *Does Quarles Apply Once a Suspect Invokes His Rights? Quarles* clearly allows law enforcement officers to begin to question a suspect without advising him of his *Miranda* rights. But what if, without being so warned, a suspect nevertheless invokes his right to remain silent and/or consult with an attorney? Of course, the government could continue to question a suspect even after he has invoked his rights; *Miranda*, after all, is only an exclusionary rule. But would *Quarles* apply in such a case to allow for the admission of statements made in response to such post-invocation questioning? What little case law there is on this question suggests that the answer is no. *See Williams v. Jacquez*, No. S-05-0058, 2011 WL 703616, at *14 (E.D. Cal. Feb. 18, 2011) ("The rationale for the *Quarles* exception does not justify continuing a broad ranging interview after the suspect invokes her right to silence."). If *Quarles* means what it says, why should it matter whether or not the suspect has invoked his rights?

8. How Quarles Fits into the Terrorism Disposition Debate. Doesn't *Quarles* strongly support those who favor trying most (if not all) terrorism suspects in civilian courts (who might otherwise object to *Quarles*), insofar as it allows the government both to interrogate terrorism suspects about ongoing threats to public safety without advising them of their *Miranda* rights *and* to use anything the suspects say in response against them at trial? On the flip side, for those who support military detention and/or trial by military commission for new terrorism suspects, and who might otherwise be more sympathetic to *Quarles*, doesn't it militate *against* such arguments insofar as it demonstrates the ability of the civilian courts adequately to accommodate the government's interests in terrorism cases?

9. When Do the Relevant Clocks "Start"? One of the questions not raised in *Quarles* or *Abdulmutallab* is when the relevant *Miranda* and presentment clocks "start." In cases in which suspects are arrested within the United States, the assumption has always been that the clocks begin to run at the moment of arrest. Is that necessarily true in cases in which the suspect is arrested *outside* the United States? What if the suspect is initially held in *military*, rather than *civilian*, detention? In *United States v. Ghailani*, 733 F.3d 29 (2d Cir. 2013), the Second Circuit rejected a Sixth Amendment Speedy Trial Clause challenge brought by a defendant who had spent nearly five years in CIA and then military detention as an "enemy combatant" before being transferred to civilian criminal custody in New York for the purpose of criminal prosecution. At the heart of the court's analysis was the conclusion that "national security" can justify a trial delay that is "not related to the trial itself." *Id.* at 47. To justify this conclusion, the court explained that there is "nothing in the text or history of the Speedy Trial Clause that requires the government to choose between national security and an orderly and fair justice system." *Id.* at 47-48. Is *that* the relevant choice here? Shouldn't there have come a point where Ghailani's continuing detention by the military precluded the government from eventually subjecting him to civilian criminal trial? More generally, shouldn't the delay have to have *something* to do with the trial? If not, will anything prevent the government from holding *other* terrorism suspects in potentially long-term military detention before transferring them to civilian custody for criminal trial? *See* Stephen I. Vladeck, *Terrorism Prosecutions and the Problem of Constitutional Cross-Ruffing*, 36 Cardozo L. Rev. 709 (2014) (arguing that, under current law, the answer is no — and suggesting potential reforms). Note that no court ever ruled on whether Ghailani's CIA or military detention was actually lawful. Should resolution of that question matter here?

10. Abu Khattalah and the "Slow Ship." Perhaps the most relevant precedent thus far on the presentment issue is the case of Ahmed Abu Khattalah, one of the ringleaders of the 2012 Benghazi attack that resulted in the deaths of four Americans, including Ambassador J. Christopher Stevens. In 2014, U.S. Special Forces troops captured Abu Khattalah in Libya, after which he was taken to a U.S. warship positioned off the Libyan coast, which then transported him to the United States — approximately 5,000 miles away. Abu Khatallah was repeatedly interrogated over the course of the 13-day journey, and was advised of his *Miranda* rights only after prolonged and sustained questioning by intelligence agents. When the government sought to introduce at trial some of the statements Abu Khattalah made after he was advised of his *Miranda* rights, he moved to suppress, arguing, among (many) other things, "that his nearly two-week journey across the Atlantic Ocean by boat violated his right to prompt presentment before a magistrate under Federal Rule of Criminal Procedure 5(a)." *United States v. Abu*

Khattalah, 275 F. Supp. 3d 32, 38 (D.D.C. 2017). In support of his claim, Abu Khattalah cited an e-mail from one FBI agent to an agent on the ship with him suggesting that he "is onboard a slow ship somewhere bringing our newest detainee to justice," *id.* at 57, and that the ship "was not traveling at its maximum speed across the Atlantic." *Id.* at 59.

The district court rejected the Rule 5(a) challenge. As Judge Cooper explained, the government's proffered justifications for not pursuing faster means of presentment were reasonable under the circumstances "given the distance between the site of the arrest and the nearest available magistrate, as well as the means of transportation chosen." *Id.* at 60. Among other things, the court found that the government had good reasons for not flying Abu Khatallah to the United States, and that the serious engine troubles encountered by the ship transporting him were genuine. But Judge Cooper also stressed that "[t]he *McNabb-Mallory* framework is not a 'stiff formula' that mechanically permits a prolonged presentment delay in all cases where a defendant is apprehended overseas, or where the government's justifications for delay are buoyed by national security or diplomatic concerns." *Id.* Does that conclusion suggest that a future court might be more skeptical if the government once again uses a "slow ship" to transport a suspect arrested overseas back to the United States?

B. COERCED EVIDENCE

As the above materials underscore, when the government captures a terrorism suspect there is often a felt need to derive as much actionable intelligence from the suspect as the law allows. But when government officials overstep legal limits in their interrogations, how does that affect the admissibility of the suspect's statements, or evidence derived from those statements, at criminal trials? Note that the answer to this question matters for two very different sets of reasons: *First*, limits on the admissibility of such evidence may well create a deterrent to the use of such methods in at least some cases. *Second*, whether those limits can be ameliorated by statute, either within the civilian courts or elsewhere, may have a lot to do with the viability and desirability of an alternative forum for terrorism prosecutions — including military commissions. To illuminate this question, we return to the *Ghailani* case, which, in addition to the speedy trial issues discussed above, also included a series of pretrial challenges to both the prosecution itself and to the admissibility of certain evidence based upon the government's alleged mistreatment of Ghailani himself.

Reading *United States v. Ghailani*

Ghailani is not only the most important speedy trial case involving an alleged terrorist defendant, it is also the most significant post–September 11 prosecution regarding the proper evidentiary sanction for government coercion — whether of the defendant himself, or of witnesses whose testimony the government seeks to introduce. As you read the opinion that follows, consider these questions:

- What is the *Ker-Frisbie* rule, and why is it so central to the district court's analysis of Ghailani's treatment?

■ Although the Supreme Court has recognized dismissal as an appropriate sanction for government conduct that "shocks the conscience," the district court notes that there are significant limits on the circumstances in which such a drastic remedy is appropriate. When should courts dismiss prosecutions under this test? Why weren't Ghailani's allegations enough to satisfy it?

United States v. Ghailani

United States District Court, Southern District of New York, 2010
751 F. Supp. 2d 502

LEWIS A. KAPLAN, District Judge. Ahmed Khalfan Ghailani, an alleged member of Al Qaeda, was indicted in this Court in 1998 and charged with conspiring with Usama Bin Laden and others to kill Americans abroad by, among other means, bombing the United States Embassies in Nairobi, Kenya, and Dar es Salaam, Tanzania, bombings in which 224 people reportedly were killed. Years later, he was captured abroad by a foreign state and subsequently turned over to the Central Intelligence Agency ("CIA"). He was held and interrogated by the CIA at one or more secret locations outside the United States for a substantial period. He then was shifted to a secure facility at the United States naval base at Guantanamo where he remained until June 2009, at which time he was produced in this Court for prosecution on the indictment. Ghailani now moves to dismiss the indictment on the ground that he was tortured by the CIA in violation of his rights under the Due Process Clause of the Constitution.

I . . .

In this case, Ghailani has not identified explicitly the component of his due process rights that allegedly was violated. But he argues that both the CIA's use of "enhanced interrogation techniques" — in his word, torture — to question him and the fact that use of those techniques was authorized by "the highest levels of our government" are "'so fundamentally unfair,' 'shocking to our traditional sense of justice,' and 'outrageous'" that due process requires the indictment to be dismissed. He thereby invokes substantive rather than procedural due process.

The government does not here respond to Ghailani's assertions as to what was done to him while in CIA custody. Nor does it join issue on the question whether those assertions, if true, violated Ghailani's right to due process of law. Rather, it argues that Ghailani's allegations of pretrial custodial abuse are immaterial to this motion because dismissal of the indictment would not be a proper remedy for the government's alleged misconduct. In other words, the government argues that there is no legally significant connection between the alleged torture and any deprivation of the defendant's liberty that might result from this criminal prosecution.

If the government is correct in contending that Ghailani would not be entitled to dismissal of this criminal prosecution on due process grounds even if he was tortured in violation of his constitutional rights, it would be unnecessary for this Court to address the details of Ghailani's alleged treatment while in CIA custody. Nor in that event would it be appropriate to express any opinion as to whether that treatment violated his right to due process of law. The Court therefore passes directly to consideration of the government's argument.

II

The Due Process Clause, so far as is relevant here, protects against deprivations of liberty absent due process of law. The deprivation of liberty that Ghailani claims may occur if this case goes forward is his imprisonment in the event of conviction. In seeking dismissal of the indictment, however, he does not deny that he is being afforded every protection guaranteed to all in the defense of criminal prosecutions. Rather, Ghailani in effect argues that the case should be dismissed to punish the government for its mistreatment of him before he was presented in this Court to face the pending indictment.

For a due process violation to result in consequences adverse to the government in a criminal case — for example, the suppression of evidence or the dismissal of an indictment — there must be a causal connection between the violation and the deprivation of the defendant's life or liberty threatened by the prosecution. That is to say, relief against the government in a criminal case is appropriate if, and only if, a conviction otherwise would be a product of the government misconduct that violated the Due Process Clause. For only in such circumstances may it be said that the deprivation of life or liberty that follows from a criminal conviction flows from the denial of due process. This conclusion thus rests directly on the text of the Due Process Clause itself.

This point finds support also in the Supreme Court's consistent holdings that illegality in arresting or obtaining custody of a defendant does not strip a court of jurisdiction to try that defendant. "An illegal arrest, without more, has never been viewed as a bar to subsequent prosecution, nor as a defense to a valid conviction."

This doctrine, better known as the *Ker-Frisbie* rule,[14] dates back well over a century and "rests on the sound basis that due process of law is satisfied when one present in court is convicted of a crime after being fairly apprized of the charges against him and after a fair trial in accordance with constitutional procedural safeguards."[15] The Court repeatedly has reaffirmed this doctrine even as the concept of substantive due process has expanded. Moreover, the Court explicitly has refused to adopt an exclusionary rule that would operate on the defendant's person:

> "Our numerous precedents ordering the exclusion of such illegally obtained evidence assume implicitly that the remedy does not extend to barring the prosecution altogether. So drastic a step might advance marginally some of the ends served by exclusionary rules, but it would also increase to an intolerable degree interference with the public interest in having the guilty brought to book."[17]

"[A defendant] is not himself a suppressible 'fruit,' and the illegality of his detention cannot deprive the Government of the opportunity to prove his guilt through the

---

14. *See Ker v. Illinois,* 119 U.S. 436 (1886); *Frisbie v. Collins,* 342 U.S. 519 (1952).

15. *Frisbie,* 342 U.S. at 522.

17. *United States v. Blue,* 384 U.S. 251, 255 (1966).

introduction of evidence wholly untainted by the police misconduct."[18] Rather, the proper remedy is money damages or criminal prosecution of the offending officers.

This case follows *a fortiori* from the rationale of the *Ker-Frisbie* rule. Ghailani is charged here with complicity in the murder of 224 people. The government here has stated that it will not use anything that Ghailani said while in CIA custody, or the fruits of any such statement, in this prosecution. In consequence, any deprivation of liberty that Ghailani might suffer as a result of a conviction in this case would be entirely unconnected to the alleged due process violation. Even if Ghailani was mistreated while in CIA custody and even if that mistreatment violated the Due Process Clause, there would be no connection between such mistreatment and this prosecution. If, as *Ker-Frisbie* holds, the illegal arrest of a defendant is not sufficiently related to a prosecution to warrant its dismissal, it necessarily follows that mistreatment of a defendant is not sufficient to justify dismissal where, as here, the connection between the alleged misconduct and the prosecution is non-existent or, at least, even more remote. Certainly the government should not be deprived here "of the opportunity to prove his guilt through the introduction of evidence wholly untainted by [any government] misconduct."[21] Any remedy for any such violation must be found outside the confines of this criminal case.

United States v. Toscanino[22] is not to the contrary. The defendant in that case allegedly was brought before the trial court as a result of being abducted and tortured by government agents, conduct that he claimed violated his right to due process of law. Upon conviction, he appealed on the ground that the agents' actions violated his right to due process and that the district court's jurisdiction over him was a product of that violation. The Second Circuit reversed the conviction and remanded to enable the defendant to attempt to prove that the agents' conduct was sufficiently outrageous to have violated the Due Process Clause. But *Toscanino* does not support Ghailani here.

As an initial matter, *Toscanino* was concerned with "denying the government the fruits of its exploitation of any deliberate and unnecessary lawlessness on its part." To whatever extent it is authoritative, a subject discussed below, the case is limited to situations in which the alleged outrageous government conduct brought the defendant within the court's jurisdiction, and thus was a but-for cause of any resulting conviction, and compromised the fairness and integrity of the criminal proceedings. There is no similar connection between Ghailani's alleged mistreatment while in CIA custody and this prosecution. Hence, to whatever extent that *Toscanino* remains viable, it does not apply here.

Second, as suggested already, it is doubtful that *Toscanino* remains authoritative. Several circuits have expressed doubt as to its continued viability in light of subsequent Supreme Court decisions. Moreover, the Second Circuit itself subsequently has relied heavily on the *Ker-Frisbie* rule in deciding a case very similar to the one currently before this Court.

In *Brown v. Doe*,[27] a defendant convicted of felony murder and robbery in state court sought federal habeas corpus relief on the ground, *inter alia*, that his substantive

---

18. *United States v. Crews*, 445 U.S. 463, 474 (1980).

21. *Crews*, 445 U.S. at 474.

22. 500 F.2d 267 (2d Cir. 1974).

27. 2 F.3d 1236 (2d Cir. 1993).

due process rights had been violated by repeated brutal beatings by police following his arrest. He alleged that this pretrial custodial abuse "was so outrageous and so offensive to due process of law that it bar[red] his prosecution and require[d] dismissal of the indictment."[29]

In affirming the district court's denial of relief, the Second Circuit held that the Due Process Clause was the appropriate source of constitutional protection against the alleged pretrial abuse, but it concluded that the requested remedy was inappropriate. In light of the *Ker-Frisbie* line of cases, the court reasoned that "if there is no authority for barring the prosecution of a defendant who was illegally taken into custody, we are in no position to strip New York State of its power to try a defendant . . . who was lawfully arrested and convicted on untainted evidence."[30] Moreover, "the wrong committed by the police has its own remedies. It is unnecessary to remedy that wrong by absolving [petitioner] of his own crime, and there is no interest of justice served by a result in which the community suffers two unpunished wrongs."[31] The court concluded that "[t]he remedy of dismissal is not required to vindicate [petitioner's] due process rights. Other and more appropriate remedies are available," potentially including civil remedies under 42 U.S.C. §1983 and criminal prosecution of the police who assaulted him.[32]

Brown confirms this Court's view that *Toscanino,* if it retains any force, does so only where the defendant's presence before the trial court is procured by methods that offend the Due Process Clause. Dismissal of the indictment in the absence of a constitutional violation affecting the fairness of the criminal adjudication itself is unwarranted.

CONCLUSION

If, as Ghailani claims, he was tortured in violation of the Due Process Clause, he may have remedies. For the reasons set forth above, however, those remedies do not include dismissal of the indictment. The defendant's motion to dismiss the indictment on the grounds of allegedly outrageous government conduct in violation of his Fifth Amendment due process right is denied.

So ordered.

Notes and Questions

1. *The Ker-Frisbie Doctrine and Unlawful Arrests.* As the court notes, the Supreme Court has declared that *how* a criminal defendant is brought to the court does not affect the court's jurisdiction over him, even if the underlying arrest was itself unlawful. The *Ker-Frisbie* doctrine opened the door to abductions of suspects abroad (by a

---

29. *Id.* at 1242.

30. *Id.* at 1243.

31. *Id.*

32. *Id.*

process sometimes called "informal rendition" — the converse of "extraordinary rendition" discussed in Chapter 33). And a controversial 1989 memorandum by the Justice Department's Office of Legal Counsel even concluded that "the FBI may use its statutory authority to investigate and arrest individuals for violating United States law, even if the FBI's actions contravene customary international law." *Authority of the Federal Bureau of Investigation to Override International Law in Extraterritorial Law Enforcement Activities,* 13 Op. O.L.C. 163, 163 (1989).

But *Toscanino* seemed to limit the *Ker-Frisbie* doctrine by requiring dismissal of an indictment against a defendant who had been abducted by force that "shocked the conscience." See *supra* p. 1093. How does the court in *Ghailani* distinguish *Toscanino*? If this distinction is tenable, when will an unlawful *arrest* (and not just unlawful treatment after arrest) provide a basis for dismissing an indictment in its entirety? On which side of the line would arrests in violation of national sovereignty, but not the individual rights of the suspect, fall? What about arrests in violation of international human rights treaties that the United States either has not ratified, or views as non-self-executing?

2. Using Ghailani's Coerced Testimony Directly. Suppose Ghailani confessed during his alleged torture. Would his coerced confession be admissible against him? The courts have traditionally excluded involuntary confessions for two reasons. First,

> because the methods used to extract them offend an underlying principle in the enforcement of our criminal law: that ours is an accusatorial and not an inquisitorial system — a system in which the State must establish guilt by evidence independently and freely secured and may not by coercion prove its charge against an accused out of his own mouth. "A coerced confession is offensive to basic standards of justice, not because the victim has a legal grievance against the police, but because declarations procured by torture are not premises from which a civilized forum will infer guilt." [*United States v. Karake,* 443 F. Supp. 2d 8, 50 (D.D.C. 2006) (quoting *Lyons v. Oklahoma,* 322 U.S. 596, 605 (1944)).]

Second, involuntary confessions are unreliable.

> [W]hile a confession obtained by means of torture may be excluded on due process grounds as "[in]consistent with the fundamental principles of liberty and justice which lie at the base of all our civil and political institutions," *Brown v. Mississippi,* 297 U.S. 278, 286 (1936), another legitimate reason to suppress it is the "likelihood that the confession is untrue." *Linkletter v. Walker,* 381 U.S. 618, 638 (1965) (quoting *Blackburn v. Alabama,* 361 U.S. 199, 207 (1960)). [*Karake,* 443 F. Supp. 2d at 50-51.]

3. Using Ghailani's Coerced Testimony Indirectly: Fruit of the Poisonous Tree. The government did not try to use Ghailani's confession, however. Instead it wanted to offer the testimony of a witness — Huseein Abebe — the identity of whom "the government obtained only through information it allegedly extracted by physical and psychological abuse of the defendant." *United States v. Ghailani,* 743 F. Supp. 2d 261, 264 (S.D.N.Y. 2010). Although Abebe's testimony was allegedly voluntary, the government conceded for the purpose of Ghailani's motion to preclude Abebe's testimony that Ghailani had been coerced. The district court granted Ghailani's motion to exclude Abebe's testimony, holding that "the link between the CIA's coercion of Ghailani and Abebe's testimony is direct and close," and that the government failed to show "that Abebe's testimony would be so attenuated from Ghailani's coerced statements to permit its use." *Id.* at 265. Why do you suppose the government conceded that Ghailani had been coerced? What might have been the costs to the government of contesting the coercion question in the district court?

Some of the evidence against detainees at Guantánamo Bay is derived from their own statements to interrogators, and some is from fellow detainees. Can you see problems that these latter evidentiary sources could create for criminal prosecutions like Ghailani's? What is the solution? *Should* the *Ghailani* court have taken into account "the perilous world in which we live," *id.* at 288, in applying the relevant legal principles? These principles were, after all, chiefly developed in domestic cases involving police abuse of suspects (often with racist overtones). Are criminal prosecutions of accused terrorists who have been interrogated by military and CIA interrogators different?

4. Ghailani's Conviction: Victory or Defeat? After a jury trial from which Abebe's testimony was excluded, the jury convicted Ghailani on one count of conspiring to commit murder and acquitted him on 280 others. Charlie Savage, *Terror Verdict Tests Obama's Strategy on Trials,* N.Y. Times, Nov. 18, 2010. The court sentenced Ghailani to life in prison.

Representative Peter King called the outcome a "total miscarriage of justice," Editorial, *The Ghailani Verdict,* N.Y. Times, Nov. 19, 2010, and a "tragic wake-up call to the Obama administration to immediately abandon its ill-advised plan to try Guantánamo terrorists" in civilian courts, and he urged the Administration to try them in military commissions instead. Charlie Savage, *Ghailani Verdict Reignites Debate over the Proper Court for Terrorism Trials,* N.Y. Times, Nov. 19, 2010. Justice Department spokespersons, on the other hand, declared it a victory, noting that the judge excluded key evidence (in the excerpted opinion) because of Ghailani's treatment during the prior Administration. *Id.* Others pointed out that neither costly security, public grandstanding by Ghailani, nor disclosures or leaks of classified information had resulted from the prosecution, contrary to critics' predictions. *Id.*

Was the mixed verdict a victory or a defeat for the criminal justice option for dealing with accused terrorists? Regarding Representative King's advice to the Administration, the district court noted that "[i]t is very far from clear that Abebe's testimony would be admissible if Ghailani were being tried by military commission, even without regard to the question whether the Fifth Amendment would invalidate any more forgiving provisions of the rules of evidence otherwise applicable in such a proceeding." 743 F. Supp. 2d at 287 n.182. Had the jury found Ghailani not guilty on all counts, what would the Administration have done in light of Abebe's excluded testimony? Even if the Administration had resorted to a military commission initially, doesn't footnote 182 suggest that it might have stumbled there, as well?

C. SECRET EVIDENCE

Once the government has a terrorism suspect in custody and decides to pursue criminal charges, questions of how classified information can and will be used at trial will often arise. In 1980, Congress enacted the following statute to deal with at least one set of problems raised in such cases.

Classified Information Procedures Act

18 U.S.C. app. III §§1-16 (2018)

§4. DISCOVERY OF CLASSIFIED INFORMATION BY DEFENDANTS

The court, upon a sufficient showing, may authorize the United States to delete specified items of classified information from documents to be made available to the defendant through discovery under the Federal Rules of Criminal Procedure, to substitute a summary of the information for such classified documents, or to substitute a statement admitting relevant facts that the classified information would tend to prove. The court may permit the United States to make a request for such authorization in the form of a written statement to be inspected by the court alone. . . .

§5. NOTICE OF DEFENDANT'S INTENTION TO DISCLOSE CLASSIFIED INFORMATION

(a) Notice by defendant. If a defendant reasonably expects to disclose or to cause the disclosure of classified information in any manner in connection with any trial or pretrial proceeding involving the criminal prosecution of such defendant, the defendant shall, within the time specified by the court or, where no time is specified, within thirty days prior to trial, notify the attorney for the United States and the court in writing. Such notice shall include a brief description of the classified information. Whenever a defendant learns of additional classified information he reasonably expects to disclose at any such proceeding, he shall notify the attorney for the United States and the court in writing as soon as possible thereafter and shall include a brief description of the classified information. . . .

§6. PROCEDURE FOR CASES INVOLVING CLASSIFIED INFORMATION

(a) Motion for hearing. Within the time specified by the court for the filing of a motion under this section, the United States may request the court to conduct a hearing to make all determinations concerning the use, relevance, or admissibility of classified information that would otherwise be made during the trial or pretrial proceeding. Upon such a request, the court shall conduct such a hearing. Any hearing held pursuant to this subsection (or any portion of such hearing specified in the request of the Attorney General) shall be held in camera if the Attorney General certifies to the court in such petition that a public proceeding may result in the disclosure of classified information. As to each item of classified information, the court shall set forth in writing the basis for its determination. Where the United States' motion under this subsection is filed prior to the trial or pretrial proceeding, the court shall rule prior to the commencement of the relevant proceeding.

(b) Notice.

(1) Before any hearing is conducted pursuant to a request by the United States under subsection (a), the United States shall provide the defendant with notice of the classified information that is at issue. Such notice shall identify the specific classified information at issue whenever that information previously has been made

available to the defendant by the United States. When the United States has not previously made the information available to the defendant in connection with the case, the information may be described by generic category, in such form as the court may approve, rather than by identification of the specific information of concern to the United States.

(2) Whenever the United States requests a hearing under subsection (a), the court, upon request of the defendant, may order the United States to provide the defendant, prior to trial, such details as to the portion of the indictment or information at issue in the hearing as are needed to give the defendant fair notice to prepare for the hearing.

(c) Alternative procedure for disclosure of classified information

(1) Upon any determination by the court authorizing the disclosure of specific classified information under the procedures established by this section, the United States may move that, in lieu of the disclosure of such specific classified information, the court order —

(A) the substitution for such classified information of a statement admitting relevant facts that the specific classified information would tend to prove; or

(B) the substitution for such classified information of a summary of the specific classified information.

The court shall grant such a motion of the United States if it finds that the statement or summary will provide the defendant with substantially the same ability to make his defense as would disclosure of the specific classified information. The court shall hold a hearing on any motion under this section. Any such hearing shall be held in camera at the request of the Attorney General.

(2) The United States may, in connection with a motion under paragraph (1), submit to the court an affidavit of the Attorney General certifying that disclosure of classified information would cause identifiable damage to the national security of the United States and explaining the basis for the classification of such information. If so requested by the United States, the court shall examine such affidavit in camera and ex parte. . . .

(e) Prohibition on disclosure of classified information by defendant, relief for defendant when United States opposes disclosure

(1) Whenever the court denies a motion by the United States that it issue an order under subsection (c) and the United States files with the court an affidavit of the Attorney General objecting to disclosure of the classified information at issue, the court shall order that the defendant not disclose or cause the disclosure of such information.

(2) Whenever a defendant is prevented by an order under paragraph (1) from disclosing or causing the disclosure of classified information, the court shall dismiss the indictment or information; except that, when the court determines that the interests of justice would not be served by dismissal of the indictment or information, the court shall order such other action, in lieu of dismissing the indictment or information, as the court determines is appropriate. Such action may include, but need not be limited to —

(A) dismissing specified counts of the indictment or information;

(B) finding against the United States on any issue as to which the excluded classified information relates; or

(C) striking or precluding all or part of the testimony of a witness. . . .

Reading *United States v. Lee*

Dr. Wen Ho Lee was prosecuted on charges of espionage and mishandling of classified information at the Los Alamos National Laboratory. Before utilizing the framework provided by CIPA, Lee challenged that framework on the ground that it violated various of his rights under the Fifth and Sixth Amendments insofar as it required him to disclose to the government significant details concerning his defense strategy and tactics — information that, he claimed, would give the government an unfair advantage. The district court rejected his challenges in their entirety, but not before carefully walking through how the CIPA framework works — and why it doesn't raise any of these constitutional questions. As you read its opinion, consider the following questions:

- Why did the district court conclude that CIPA doesn't violate either the Fifth or Sixth Amendments by tipping off the government to the defendant's tactics and strategy? Was it because similar accommodations have been allowed in other contexts? Because the government's interest in avoiding graymail is sufficiently compelling? Some combination of each?
- The district court agreed that "due process is . . . denied where the balance of discovery is tipped against the defendant and in favor of the government," but then concluded that CIPA doesn't tip the balance, because it also places burdens on the government. Is imposing burdens on both parties equivalent to preserving the "balance of discovery"? Why or why not?
- Does CIPA actually change the substantive *scope* of the discovery to which a defendant is entitled, or merely the way in which challenges to discovery requests are litigated?
- If the court finds that classified information is relevant and admissible, what are the government's options? If the government refuses to disclose the classified information, or provide any satisfactory substitute, what are the court's options?
- Based your understanding of the Fifth Amendment and your reading of CIPA, does CIPA — or *could* CIPA — ever permit the government to use classified information to prosecute a defendant without letting him see it?

United States v. Lee

United States District Court, District of New Mexico, 2000
90 F. Supp. 2d 1324

CONWAY, Chief Judge. . . .

I. CIPA FRAMEWORK

The Classified Information Procedures Act (CIPA), 18 U.S.C. app. III §§1-16 (1988), provides for pretrial procedures to resolve questions of admissibility of classified information in advance of its use in open court.[1] Under CIPA procedures, the defense must file a notice briefly describing any classified information that it "reasonably expects to disclose or to cause the disclosure of" at trial. 18 U.S.C. app. III §5(a). Thereafter, the prosecution may request an *in camera* hearing for a determination of the "use, relevance and admissibility" of the proposed defense evidence. *Id.* at §6(a). If the Court finds the evidence admissible, the government may move for, and the Court may authorize, the substitution of unclassified facts or a summary of the information in the form of an admission by the government.[2] *See id.* at §6(c)(1). Such a motion may be granted if the Court finds that the statement or summary will provide the defendant with "substantially the same ability to make his defense as would disclosure of the specific classified information." *Id.* If the Court does not authorize the substitution, the government can require that the defendant not disclose classified information. *See id.* at §6(e). However, under §6(e)(2), if the government prevents a defendant from disclosing classified information at trial, the court may: (A) dismiss the entire indictment or specific counts, (B) find against the prosecution on any issue to which the excluded information relates, or (C) strike or preclude the testimony of particular government witnesses. *See* 18 U.S.C. app. III §6(e)(2). Finally, CIPA requires that the government provide the defendant with any evidence it will use to rebut the defendant's revealed classified information evidence. *See id.* at §6(f).

II. CONSTITUTIONALITY OF CIPA

Defendant Lee contends that, as applied to him, the notice and hearing requirements of §5 and §6 of CIPA are unconstitutional. . . . Although I find Defendant's claims unjustified, I will nevertheless address them in turn.[3] . . .

A. Defendant's Privilege Against Self-incrimination

Defendant Lee's first contention is that the notice and hearing requirements of §5 and §6 violate his Fifth Amendment privilege against self-incrimination because they force him to reveal classified aspects of his own trial testimony. Defendant argues that by forcing him to reveal portions of his potential testimony, CIPA unconstitutionally infringes upon his right to remain silent until and unless he decides to testify. Similarly, Defendant argues that if he chooses not to comply with the notice requirements, under the penalty of not being able to offer such testimony at trial, CIPA unconstitutionally denies him the right to testify on his own behalf. In either case, Defendant contends that CIPA forces him to pay a price in the form of a costly pretrial decision in order to preserve his constitutional rights at trial.

---

1. Classified information is defined as including "information and material" subject to classification or otherwise requiring protection from public disclosure. *See* 18 U.S.C. app. III §1. Thus, CIPA applies to classified testimony as well as to classified documents.

2. If the court finds that the evidence is not admissible at trial, CIPA is no longer implicated. When determining the use, relevance and admissibility of the proposed evidence, the court may not take into account that the evidence is classified; relevance of classified information in a given case is governed solely by the standards set forth in the Federal Rules of Evidence.

3. Other courts that have considered the constitutionality of CIPA are in accord.

CIPA does not require that a defendant specify whether or not he will testify or what he will testify about. Instead, CIPA requires "merely a general disclosure as to what classified information the defense expects to use at trial, regardless of the witness or the document through which that information is to be revealed." *United States v. Poindexter*, 725 F. Supp. 13, 33 (D.D.C. 1989). Defendant's argument that if he discloses the classified information his right to remain silent has been compromised (or in the alternative that if he refuses to disclose the classified information his right to testify has been compromised) is misplaced. Despite CIPA's requirements, Defendant still has the option of not testifying. Similarly, if the defense does not disclose classified information as required by CIPA, the defendant retains the option of testifying, albeit with the preclusion of any classified information.

In addition, the pretrial disclosure of certain aspects of a criminal defense is hardly a novel concept. Examples of such requirements include Fed. R. Crim. P. 12.1 (alibi defense); Fed. R. Crim. P. 12.2 (insanity defense); Fed. R. Crim. P. 12.3 (public authority defense); and Fed. R. Crim. P. 16 (medical and scientific tests, and tangible objects and certain documents). Such provisions have consistently been held constitutional. . . . CIPA merely provides a mechanism for determining the admissibility of classified information so that classified information is not inadvertently disclosed during open proceedings. Defendant still has the choice of presenting the evidence during trial or not, after it has been deemed admissible. "That the defendant faces . . . a dilemma demanding a choice between complete silence and presenting a defense has never been thought an invasion of the privilege against compelled self-incrimination." *Williams v. Florida*, 399 U.S. 78, 84 (1970).

Defendant also argues that the burdens placed upon him by CIPA unconstitutionally violate his Fifth Amendment rights in that they do not advance any interests related to the fairness and accuracy of the criminal trial. However, Defendant's argument is unconvincing. CIPA is designed to "assure the fairness and reliability of the criminal trial" while permitting the government to "ascertain the potential damage to national security of proceeding with a given prosecution before trial." *See United States v. Ivy*, 1993 WL 316215 at *4 (citations omitted). As the Supreme Court has noted, "it is obvious and unarguable that no governmental interest is more compelling than the security of the Nation." *Poindexter*, 725 F. Supp. at 34 (quoting *Haig v. Agee*, 453 U.S. 280, 307 (1981)). CIPA serves that interest "by providing a mechanism for protecting both the unnecessary disclosure of sensitive national security information and by helping to ensure that those with significant access to such information will not escape the sanctions of the law applicable to others by use of the greymail route."[5] *Id.* at 34. Accordingly, I find that CIPA does not violate Defendant's privilege against self-incrimination by infringing upon either his right to remain silent or his right to testify on his own behalf.

B. Defendant's Right to Confront and Cross-examine Witnesses

Defendant Lee next argues that §5 and §6 of CIPA violate his Sixth Amendment right to confront and cross-examine government witnesses by forcing him to notify the government pretrial (and explain the significance) of all the classified

5. Greymail refers to a tactic employed by a defendant who threatens to disclose classified information with the hopes that the prosecution will choose not to prosecute in order to keep the information protected.

information he reasonably expects to elicit from prosecution witnesses on cross-examination and all such information that will be contained in defense counsel's questions to those witnesses.[6]

Defendant contends that under CIPA, the "prosecution can shape its case-in-chief to blunt the force of the defense cross examination" and that the advance notice under CIPA "will impede effective defense cross-examination." However, the Confrontation Clause does not guarantee the right to undiminished surprise with respect to cross-examination of prosecutorial witnesses. . . .

CIPA does not require that the defense reveal its plan of cross-examination to the government. CIPA also does not require that the defendant reveal what questions his counsel will ask, in which order, and to which witnesses. Likewise, the defendant need not attribute the information to any particular witness. CIPA merely requires that the defendant identify the classified information he reasonably intends to use. Because the only cited tactical disadvantage that may accrue, minimization of surprise, is slight, defendant has failed to demonstrate that the requirements under CIPA render his opportunity for cross-examination ineffective.

C. Defendant's Right to Due Process

Defendant's due process argument is based on the contention that CIPA's disclosure requirements violate the Due Process Clause by imposing a one-sided burden on the defense, without imposing a mandatory reciprocal duty on the prosecution. However, due process is only denied where the balance of discovery is tipped against the defendant and in favor of the government. . . .

Here, the CIPA burdens are not one-sided. First, the government has already agreed to allow Defendant and his counsel access to all classified files at issue in the indictment. Second, the government must produce all discoverable materials before the defense is required to file a §5(a) notice. Third, before a §6 hearing is conducted, the government must reveal details of its case so as to give the defense fair notice to prepare for the hearing. *See* 18 U.S.C. app. III §6(b)(2). Specifically, the government must provide the defense with any portions of any material it may use to establish the "national defense" element of any charges against Lee. Fourth, under §6(f), the government is required to provide notice of any evidence it will use to rebut classified information that the court permits the defense to use at trial. Finally, in addition to the discovery obligations under §6 of CIPA, the government must also comply with the Federal Rules of Criminal Procedure and *Brady v. Maryland*, 373 U.S. 83 (1963).

Despite the fact that the government's reciprocal duties under CIPA are not triggered until it decides to request a §6 hearing, the overall balance of discovery is not tipped against Lee. . . .

III. CONCLUSION

In summary, Defendant Lee has failed to show that the carefully balanced framework for determining the use of classified information by the defense set forth in CIPA violates his Fifth Amendment privilege against self-incrimination, his Fifth

---

6. Under the Sixth Amendment, a criminal defendant "shall enjoy the right . . . to be confronted with the witnesses against him." U.S. Const. amend. VI. Pursuant to the right to confront the witnesses against him, a criminal defendant has the "fundamental right" to cross examine witnesses for the prosecution.

Amendment right to remain silent or his Fifth and Sixth Amendment rights to testify on his own behalf. Defendant has also failed to demonstrate that CIPA violates his Fifth Amendment right to due process of law or his Sixth Amendment right to confront and cross-examine witnesses.

Notes and Questions

1. The Decision to Prosecute. When the government decides whether to mount a criminal prosecution or initiate an immigration proceeding against an alleged terrorist, it must assess the risk that, in going forward, state secrets or classified information will be exposed. Consequently, the Attorney General has instructed federal prosecutors, in deciding whether to prosecute, to weigh (a) the likelihood of such exposure, (b) the resulting damage to national security, (c) the likelihood of success if the case is brought, and (d) the nature and importance of other federal interests that prosecution would promote. U.S. Dep't of Justice, *Attorney General's Guidelines for Prosecutions Involving Classified Information* 4-6 (1981). Sometimes this weighing will dictate not prosecuting. How, if at all, would the enactment of CIPA have affected this process?

2. Is It Classified? How did the *Lee* court decide whether CIPA was applicable — that is, whether the information Wen Ho Lee was planning to use was "classified"? Must the court simply defer to the government's classification stamp? If so, "the government could make CIPA applicable whenever it suited its purpose simply by rubber-stamping documents that have no relevance to the national security." 26 Charles Alan Wright & Kenneth W. Graham, *Federal Practice and Procedure* §5672 (2019). Rules for classifying information are examined in Chapter 39.

3. Graymail. In *United States v. Reynolds*, 345 U.S. 1, 12 (1953), the Supreme Court said that "it is unconscionable to allow [the government] to undertake prosecution and then invoke its governmental privileges to deprive the accused of anything which might be material to his defense." Rejected Federal Rule of Evidence 509 therefore provided that when the state secrets privilege is sustained and a party is thereby deprived of material evidence, the court should make whatever orders "the interests of justice require, including striking the testimony of a witness, declaring a mistrial, finding against the government upon an issue as to which the evidence is relevant, or dismissing the action." 26 Wright & Graham, *supra*, §5661.

Can you see how these principles from civil litigation help set the stage for graymail in criminal trials? How does it work? Is it an unfair tactic by unscrupulous defendants or lawyers? Former Assistant Attorney General Philip Heymann has noted that "[i]t would be a mistake . . . to view the 'greymail' problem as limited to instances of unscrupulous or questionable conduct by defendants since wholly proper defense attempts to obtain or disclose classified information may present the government with the same 'disclose or dismiss' dilemma." S. Rep. No. 96-823, at 3 (1980), *reprinted in* 1980 U.S.C.C.A.N. 4294, 4296-4297. Into which category would the disclose-or-dismiss dilemma in the Wen Ho Lee case fall? *See* Bob Drogin, *Nuke Secrets Deemed Vital to Scientist's Case*, L.A. Times, June 16, 2000 (reporting that a member of Lee's legal team characterized as "graymailing the government" his request for complete computer records and 400,000 pages of classified data for nearly every U.S. nuclear weapon). Has the enactment of CIPA eliminated the possibility of graymail?

4. Defendant's Discovery in Criminal Cases. In criminal cases, defendants have certain limited rights to discovery. The Supreme Court has held that the prosecution must disclose evidence that is favorable to the defendant and "is material either to guilt or to punishment." *Brady v. Maryland,* 373 U.S. 83, 83-87 (1963). Specific defense requests thus require the prosecution to turn over all exculpatory evidence, which may include classified information in national security prosecutions.

In addition, the Jencks Act, 18 U.S.C. §3500 (2018), requires the prosecution to produce statements in its possession by witnesses who have testified on direct examination at trial in order to facilitate cross-examination by the defense. Such statements could include ones made by secret intelligence assets. For example, in the case that gave the Act its name, the statements were confidential reports by paid government informants who were members of the Communist Party. *Jencks v. United States,* 353 U.S. 657 (1957).

Finally, Federal Rule of Criminal Procedure 16(a)(1)(A)-(B) permits criminal defendants to discover their own statements, as well as documents and tangible objects in the possession, custody, or control of the government that are material to the defendant's defense; are intended for use by government as evidence; or were obtained from or belong to the defendant. Here again, the documents or tangible objects might include classified information, or their disclosure might reveal intelligence sources and methods. *See generally* Jonathan M. Fredman, *Intelligence Agencies, Law Enforcement, and the Prosecution Team,* 16 Yale L. & Pol'y Rev. 331 (1998).

Of course, intelligence agencies may hold back classified information or sources and methods and provide only unclassified information to the prosecution. Could the prosecution then argue that it had only the latter in its possession, custody, or control, thus avoiding discovery of classified information by the defense? The cases are neither clear nor consistent, but in general they hold that "federal discovery obligations extend to those government agencies that are so closely 'aligned' with the prosecution of a specific matter that justice requires their records be subject to the respective discovery obligations." *Id.* at 347. The Department of Justice's *Justice Manual* states that "an investigative or prosecutive agency becomes aligned with the government prosecutor when it becomes actively involved in the investigation or the prosecution of a particular case." *Justice Manual* tit. 9, *Criminal Resource Manual* §2052(B)(1) (2018).

Does the tasking of an intelligence agency by the FBI under the 1996 Intelligence Authorization Act (quoted *supra* p. 539) constitute sufficient "active involvement" to align it with the prosecution? *See* Fredman, *supra* at 364 (opining that "a court could well [so] conclude"). Suppose the intelligence community on its own initiative forwards to the FBI foreign surveillance information suggesting criminal wrongdoing. Has it thereby aligned itself with the prosecutors if a criminal prosecution results? *Id.* (probably not). Here the *United States Attorneys' Manual* suggests that its role must first "exceed[] the role of providing mere tips or leads based on information generated independently of the criminal case." *Criminal Resource Manual, supra,* §2052(B)(1).

5. CIPA and Discovery. CIPA permits the government to argue ex parte against the discovery of classified information, 18 U.S.C. app. III §4, but it does not purport to change discovery standards. Nevertheless, some courts and commentators have read CIPA to narrow a defendant's rights or balance them against governmental interests. *See* 26 Wright & Graham, *supra,* §5672. In *United States v. Yunis,* 867 F.2d 617 (D.C. Cir. 1989), for example, the court arguably crafted a new relevancy standard for discovery of classified information by holding that "mere . . . theoretical relevance" was not enough; the defendant was obliged to show that the information is "at least 'helpful to the defense of [the] accused.'" *Id.* at 623 (quoting *Roviaro v. United States,* 353 U.S. 53, 60-61 (1957) (involving informer's privilege)).

When a court in a §4 proceeding *does* find that classified information is discoverable, the government is afforded the option of substituting a summary or a statement admitting relevant facts that the classified information would tend to prove. The courts have also inferred authority from CIPA to order defense counsel to obtain security clearances as a condition of seeing classified information or participating in hearings at which it may be disclosed. *See United States v. Bin Laden,* 58 F. Supp. 2d 113 (S.D.N.Y. 1999) (rejecting the claim that this requirement unconstitutionally interferes with defendant's choice of counsel).

6. CIPA Notice and the Admissibility Hearing. A defendant who wishes to disclose classified information in the case must give specific prior notice to the government pursuant to §5, on penalty of having the court exclude any classified information omitted from the notice. 18 U.S.C. app. III §5. Why is it not unconstitutional to thus require a defendant to tip his hand, according to *Lee*?

Following a §5 notice, the government may request a hearing concerning the use, relevancy, or admissibility of the identified information. 18 U.S.C. app. III §6. This hearing is usually held in camera. CIPA's legislative history is quite clear that it was not intended to change existing rules of evidence applicable in this hearing. *See* 26 Wright & Graham, *supra,* §5672 (discussing history). Some courts have taken this history to heart and even stated that they must disregard the classified nature of the information in ruling on its relevancy and admissibility. Others — notably the Fourth Circuit — have found that CIPA established "a more strict rule of admissibility" for classified information. *United States v. Smith,* 780 F.2d 1102, 1105 (4th Cir. 1985). Moreover, other courts have obtained the same results as *Smith* by narrowly construing defenses, such as reliance on CIA authority, *see United States v. Lopez-Lima,* 738 F. Supp. 1404 (S.D. Fla. 1990), in order to rule the classified information irrelevant. *See* 26 Wright & Graham, *supra,* §5672. In an appropriate case, should the Supreme Court resolve this confusion?

7. CIPA Substitution. Courts may find classified information to be relevant and material. CIPA §6 then affords the government the option of moving to substitute an unclassified statement of admissions or an unclassified summary for the classified information. The court must grant that motion "if it finds that the statement or summary will provide the defendant with substantially the same ability to make his defense as would disclosure." 18 U.S.C. app. III §6(c)(1). Is it clear that courts will always be able to make that determination fairly (as it must) without input from the defendant?

8. CIPA: Disclose or Dismiss. If, on the other hand, the court denies the government's motion, then the Attorney General must decide whether to disclose the information. *Id.* §6(e)(1). If she decides against disclosure, the court may dismiss all or part of the indictment, find against the government on an issue to which the withheld information relates, or strike testimony. *Id.* §6(e)(2). In deciding among these alternatives, the court is not supposed to balance interests, but instead to take whatever action is necessary "to make the defendant whole again." S. Rep. No. 96-823, at 9 (1980). For example, in *United States v. Fernandez*, 913 F.2d 148 (4th Cir. 1990), a prosecution of the CIA station chief in Costa Rica growing out of the Iran-Contra Affair, the defendant sought to introduce classified documents purporting to show the truth of statements he had made concerning the CIA's role in the resupply of the Contras. Using CIPA procedures, the Independent Counsel proposed that an unclassified summary of evidence be used in substitution for the documents, but the court found that the summary would not provide Fernandez with substantially the same ability to make his defense as would disclosure of the classified information. When the Attorney General refused to declassify the information, the court dismissed the indictment over the strenuous objections of the Independent Counsel. Can you think of any way to avoid the potential politicization of such decisions?

The government ended the Wen Ho Lee prosecution by accepting his plea to a single count of mishandling confidential computer files — partly, it is reported, because senior Energy Department officials feared that the judge would otherwise order disclosure of classified information to Lee for use in his defense. *See* Bob Drogin, *How FBI's Flawed Case Against Lee Unraveled*, L.A. Times, Sept. 13, 2000. But the government may also have wished to avoid exposure of information showing that the prosecution was racially biased. The government's insistence that Lee be held for months in solitary confinement without bail apparently was based in part on a racial stereotype. Judge James A. Parker issued a public apology to Dr. Lee: "I am truly sorry that I was led by our Executive Branch of government to order your detention.... I feel I was led astray" by the Justice Department, the FBI, and the U.S. Attorney for New Mexico. *Statement by Judge in Los Alamos Case, with Apology for Abuse of Power*, N.Y. Times, Sept. 14, 2000.

9. Another Option: Lying? In 1983, a former CIA officer named Edwin P. Wilson was tried and convicted for illegally exporting explosives to Libya. He claimed that he was still working for the Agency and acting on its authority. During Wilson's trial, the government introduced an affidavit from a high-ranking CIA official denying Wilson's continued employment. The affidavit was false. Before Wilson was sentenced, attorneys at the CIA and the Justice Department learned of the fabrication, yet they failed to inform either the trial court or the appellate court. When the truth came to light 20 years later, Wilson's conviction was vacated. *United States v. Wilson*, 289 F. Supp. 2d 801 (S.D. Tex. 2003). A clearly incensed judge wrote, "Honesty comes hard to the government." *Id.* at 809. Ultimately, does CIPA make it easier or harder for courts to avoid another travesty of justice like *Wilson*, going forward?

10. The Silent Witness Rule. CIPA deals with one set of "secret evidence" problems, but what if the *government* wishes to introduce classified information at trial without declassifying it? Is there any way to simultaneously satisfy the defendant's Sixth Amendment right to confront the witnesses against him, his Sixth Amendment right to a public trial, and the government's interest in preserving the confidentiality of classified information? Courts have said yes, and have articulated the "silent witness rule" in an effort to accommodate the competing concerns.

Under the rule, a party seeking to introduce a classified document would call a witness who could authenticate the document. While on the stand,

> the witness would not disclose the information from the classified document in open court. Instead, the witness would have a copy of the classified document before him. The court, counsel and the jury would also have copies of the classified document. The witness would refer to specific places in the document in response to questioning. The jury would then refer to the particular part of the document as the witness answered. By this method, the classified information would not be made public at trial but the [party] would be able to present that classified information to the jury. [*United States v. Zettl*, 835 F.2d 1059, 1063 (4th Cir. 1987).]

As long as the *defendant* had access to the classified document, his Sixth Amendment Confrontation Clause rights would not be violated. *See United States v. Abu Ali*, 528 F.3d 210, 253-255 (4th Cir. 2008) (holding that the district court violated the defendant's rights by not providing him with access to a classified document introduced by the government, but that the error was harmless).

As for how to ensure that the silent witness rule does not violate a defendant's right to a public trial, one court has concluded that it should be available

> only when the government establishes (i) an overriding reason for closing the trial, (ii) that the closure is no broader than necessary to protect that interest, (iii) that no reasonable alternatives exist to closure, and (iv) that the use of the [rule] provides defendants with substantially the same ability to make their defense as full public disclosure of the evidence, presented without the use of code. [*United States v. Rosen*, 520 F. Supp. 2d 786, 799 (E.D. Va. 2007).]

In a case in which these criteria are satisfied, are you convinced that the defendant's constitutional rights are adequately protected? Should a court also consider the right of the public to observe the trial, which some have characterized as an important check on criminal prosecutions? See *infra* pp. 1275-1287.

D. ACCESS TO SECRET EXCULPATORY TESTIMONY

Reading *United States v. Moussaoui*

While the "silent witness" rule is a specific accommodation meant to balance governmental secrecy with a defendant's Confrontation Clause (and other) rights, a far larger issue implicating that balance involves a defendant's right of access to potentially exculpatory evidence (including witness testimony) that may itself be classified. As you read the excerpt that follows, consider these questions:

- Did the Fourth Circuit panel disagree with the district court's conclusion that the witnesses at issue had potentially exculpatory testimony to offer, and that the defendant therefore had a constitutional right of access to the witnesses?
- How did the appeals court conclude that the district court erred by striking the death penalty as a sanction for the government's non-compliance?
- What remedy for the district court's error did the Fourth Circuit impose? Was that remedy sufficient, in your view, to make up for the government's intentional withholding of potentially exculpatory testimony?

- The Fourth Circuit referred to CIPA by analogy in fashioning relief in Moussaoui's case. Did that analogy make sense, given the very different concerns CIPA was enacted to address?
- Does *Moussaoui* suggest, as many have argued, that civilian courts simply aren't cut out for these kinds of terrorism prosecutions? Would a trial by military commission be more appropriate?

United States v. Moussaoui

United States Court of Appeals, Fourth Circuit, 2004
365 F.3d 292, *amended on reh'g*, 382 F.3d 453

[Zacarias Moussaoui was arrested before the 9/11 attacks, then later indicted for acts in connection with those attacks. The government sought the death penalty on several of these charges. Subsequently, Witness **** (asterisks are used by the court to indicate redacted material), a suspected member of al Qaeda, was captured by the United States. Moussaoui moved for access to Witness ****, asserting that the witness would be an important part of his defense. Ultimately, he sought access from two additional witnesses in U.S. custody. The government opposed these requests.

The district court found that the requested witnesses were material witnesses who might support Moussaoui's claim that he was not involved in the 9/11 attacks and that he should not receive the death penalty if convicted. It ordered their deposition by remote video, but the government appealed. The Court of Appeals remanded for the District Court to determine whether any substitution existed that would place Moussaoui in substantially the same position as would a deposition. The District Court rejected the government's proposed substitutions and again ordered deposition of the witnesses. When the government refused to comply with this order, the District Court dismissed the death notice and prohibited the government "from making any argument, or offering any evidence, suggesting that the defendant had any involvement in, or knowledge of, the September 11 attacks." This appeal followed.]

WILLIAM W. WILKINS, Chief Judge:...

III....

A. Process Power

The Sixth Amendment guarantees that "[i]n all criminal prosecutions, the accused shall enjoy the right... to have compulsory process for obtaining witnesses in his favor." U.S. Const. amend. VI. The compulsory process right is circumscribed, however, by the ability of the district court to obtain the presence of a witness through service of process. The Government maintains that because the enemy combatant witnesses are foreign nationals outside the boundaries of the United States, they are beyond the process power of the district court and, hence, unavailable to Moussaoui....

The Government's argument overlooks the critical fact that the enemy combatant witnesses are in the custody of an official of the United States Government. Therefore, we are concerned not with the ability of the district court to issue a subpoena to the witnesses, but rather with its power to issue a writ of habeas corpus *ad testificandum* ("testimonial writ") to the witnesses' custodian. . . .

[The court found that Secretary Rumsfeld was the proper custodian and that he was within the process power of the district court.]

IV.

The Government next argues that even if the district court would otherwise have the power to order the production of the witnesses, the January 30 and August 29 orders are improper because they infringe on the Executive's warmaking authority, in violation of separation of powers principles. . . .

B. Governing Principles . . .

This is not a case involving arrogation of the powers or duties of another branch. The district court orders requiring production of the enemy combatant witnesses involved the resolution of questions properly — indeed, exclusively — reserved to the judiciary. Therefore, if there is a separation of powers problem at all, it arises only from the burden the actions of the district court place on the Executive's performance of its duties.

The Supreme Court has explained on several occasions that determining whether a judicial act places impermissible burdens on another branch of government requires balancing the competing interests. *See, e.g., Nixon v. Admin'r of Gen. Servs.*, 433 U.S. 425, 443 (1977). . . .

C. Balancing

1. The Burden on the Government

The Constitution charges the Congress and the Executive with the making and conduct of war. It is not an exaggeration to state that the effective performance of these duties is essential to our continued existence as a sovereign nation. Indeed, "no governmental interest is more compelling than the security of the Nation." *Haig v. Agee*, 453 U.S. 280, 307 (1981). . . .

The Government alleges — and we accept as true — that **** the enemy combatant witnesses is critical to the ongoing effort to combat terrorism by al Qaeda. The witnesses are al Qaeda operatives **** Their value as intelligence sources can hardly be overstated. And, we must defer to the Government's assertion that interruption **** will have devastating effects on the ability to gather information from them. ****, it is not unreasonable to suppose that interruption **** could result in the loss of information that might prevent future terrorist attacks.

The Government also asserts that production of the witnesses would burden the Executive's ability to conduct foreign relations. The Government claims that if the Executive's assurances of confidentiality can be abrogated by the judiciary, the vital ability to obtain the cooperation of other governments will be devastated.

The Government also reminds us of the bolstering effect production of the witnesses might have on our enemies. . . . For example, al Qaeda operatives are trained to disrupt the legal process in whatever manner possible; indications that such techniques may be successful will only cause a redoubling of their efforts.

In summary, the burdens that would arise from production of the enemy combatant witnesses are substantial.

2. Moussaoui's Interest

The importance of the Sixth Amendment right to compulsory process is not subject to question — it is integral to our adversarial criminal justice system:

> The need to develop all relevant facts in the adversary system is both fundamental and comprehensive. The ends of criminal justice would be defeated if judgments were to be founded on a partial or speculative presentation of the facts. The very integrity of the judicial system and public confidence in the system depend on full disclosure of all the facts, within the framework of the rules of evidence. To ensure that justice is done, it is imperative to the function of the courts that compulsory process be available for the production of evidence needed either by the prosecution or by the defense.

United States v. Nixon, 418 U.S. 683, 709 (1974).

The compulsory process right does not attach to any witness the defendant wishes to call, however. Rather, a defendant must demonstrate that the witness he desires to have produced would testify "in his favor." Thus, in order to assess Moussaoui's interest, we must determine whether the enemy combatant witnesses could provide testimony material to Moussaoui's defense.

In the CIPA context,[12] we have adopted the standard articulated by the Supreme Court in *Roviaro v. United States,* 353 U.S. 53 (1957), for determining whether the government's privilege in classified information must give way. Under that standard, a defendant becomes entitled to disclosure of classified information upon a showing that the information "'is relevant and helpful to the defense . . . or is essential to a fair determination of a cause.'" [*United States v. Smith,* 780 F.2d 1102 (4th Cir. 1985)], at 1107 (quoting *Roviaro,* 353 U.S. at 60-61).

Because Moussaoui has not had — and will not receive — direct access to any of the witnesses, he cannot be required to show materiality with the degree of specificity that applies in the ordinary case. Rather, it is sufficient if Moussaoui can make a "plausible showing" of materiality. However, in determining whether Moussaoui has made a plausible showing, we must bear in mind that Moussaoui *does* have access to the **** summaries. . . .

. . . [T]he Government argues that even if the witnesses' testimony would tend to exonerate Moussaoui of involvement in the September 11 attacks, such testimony would not be material because the conspiracies with which Moussaoui is charged

---

12. We adhere to our prior ruling that CIPA does not apply because the January 30 and August 29 orders of the district court are not covered by either of the potentially relevant provisions of CIPA: §4 (concerning deletion of classified information from *documents* to be turned over to the defendant during discovery) or §6 (concerning the disclosure of classified information by the defense during pretrial or trial proceedings). *See Moussaoui I,* 333 F.3d [509, 514-515 (4th Cir. 2003).] Like the district court, however, we believe that CIPA provides a useful framework for considering the questions raised by Moussaoui's request for access to the enemy combatant witnesses.

are broader than September 11. Thus, the Government argues, Moussaoui can be convicted even if he lacked any prior knowledge of September 11. This argument ignores the principle that the scope of an alleged conspiracy is a jury question, and the possibility that Moussaoui may assert that the conspiracy culminating in the September 11 attacks was distinct from any conspiracy in which he was involved. Moreover, even if the jury accepts the Government's claims regarding the scope of the charged conspiracy, testimony regarding Moussaoui's non-involvement in September 11 is critical to the penalty phase. If Moussaoui had no involvement in or knowledge of September 11, it is entirely possible that he would not be found eligible for the death penalty.

We now consider the rulings of the district court regarding the ability of each witness to provide material testimony in Moussaoui's favor.

The district court did not err in concluding that Witness **** could offer material evidence on Moussaoui's behalf. **** Several statements by Witness **** tend to exculpate Moussaoui. For example, the **** summaries state that **** This statement tends to undermine the theory (which the Government may or may not intend to advance at trial) that Moussaoui was to pilot a fifth plane into the White House. Witness **** has also **** This statement is significant in light of other evidence **** indicating that Moussaoui had no contact with any of the hijackers. **** This is consistent with Moussaoui's claim that he was to be part of a post–September 11 operation. . . .

. . . Moussaoui has made a sufficient showing that evidence from Witness **** would be more helpful than hurtful, or at least that we cannot have confidence in the outcome of the trial without Witness **** evidence. . . .

3. Balancing

Having considered the burden alleged by the Government and the right claimed by Moussaoui, we now turn to the question of whether the district court should have refrained from acting in light of the national security interests asserted by the Government. The question is not unique; the Supreme Court has addressed similar matters on numerous occasions. In all cases of this type — cases falling into "what might loosely be called the area of constitutionally guaranteed access to evidence," *Arizona v. Youngblood,* 488 U.S. 51, 55 (1988) (internal quotation marks omitted) — the Supreme Court has held that the defendant's right to a trial that comports with the Fifth and Sixth Amendments prevails over the governmental privilege. Ultimately, as these cases make clear, the appropriate procedure is for the district court to order production of the evidence or witness and leave to the Government the choice of whether to comply with that order. If the government refuses to produce the information at issue — as it may properly do — the result is ordinarily dismissal. . . .

In addition to the pronouncements of the Supreme Court in this area, we are also mindful of Congress' judgment, expressed in CIPA, that the Executive's interest in protecting classified information does not overcome a defendant's right to present his case. Under CIPA, once the district court determines that an item of classified information is relevant and material, that item must be admitted unless the government provides an adequate substitution. If no adequate substitution can be found, the government must decide whether it will prohibit the disclosure of the classified information; if it does so, the district court must impose a sanction, which is presumptively dismissal of the indictment.

In view of these authorities, it is clear that when an evidentiary privilege — even one that involves national security — is asserted by the Government in the context of its prosecution of a criminal offense, the "balancing" we must conduct is primarily, if not solely, an examination of whether the district court correctly determined that the information the Government seeks to withhold is material to the defense. We have determined that the enemy combatant witnesses can offer material testimony that is essential to Moussaoui's defense, and we therefore affirm the January 30 and August 29 orders. Thus, the choice is the Government's whether to comply with those orders or suffer a sanction.

V.

As noted previously, the Government has stated that it will not produce the enemy combatant witnesses for depositions (or, we presume, for any other purpose related to this litigation). We are thus left in the following situation: the district court has the power to order production of the enemy combatant witnesses and has properly determined that they could offer material testimony on Moussaoui's behalf, but the Government has refused to produce the witnesses. Under such circumstances, dismissal of the indictment is the usual course. Like the district court, however, we believe that a more measured approach is required. Additionally, we emphasize that no punitive sanction is warranted here because the Government has rightfully exercised its prerogative to protect national security interests by refusing to produce the witnesses.

Although, as explained above, this is not a CIPA case, that act nevertheless provides useful guidance in determining the nature of the remedies that may be available. Under CIPA, dismissal of an indictment is authorized only if the government has failed to produce an adequate substitute for the classified information, and the interests of justice would not be served by imposition of a lesser sanction. CIPA thus enjoins district courts to seek a solution that neither disadvantages the defendant nor penalizes the government (and the public) for protecting classified information that may be vital to national security.

A similar approach is appropriate here. Under such an approach, the first question is whether there is any appropriate substitution for the witnesses' testimony. Because we conclude, for the reasons set forth below, that appropriate substitutions are available, we need not consider any other remedy. . . .

C. Instructions

. . . [W]e conclude that the district court erred in ruling that any substitution for the witnesses' testimony is inherently inadequate to the extent it is derived from the **** reports. To the contrary, we hold that the **** summaries (which, as the district court determined, accurately recapitulate the **** reports) provide an adequate basis for the creation of written statements that may be submitted to the jury in lieu of the witnesses' deposition testimony.

The crafting of substitutions is a task best suited to the district court, given its greater familiarity with the facts of the case and its authority to manage the presentation of evidence. Nevertheless, we think it is appropriate to provide some guidance to the court and the parties.

First, the circumstances of this case — most notably, the fact that the substitutions may very well support Moussaoui's defense — dictate that the crafting of substitutions be an interactive process among the parties and the district court. Second, we think that accuracy and fairness are best achieved by crafting substitutions that use the exact language of the **** summaries to the greatest extent possible. We believe that the best means of achieving both of these objectives is for defense counsel to identify particular portions of the **** summaries that Moussaoui may want to admit into evidence at trial. The Government may then argue that additional portions must be included in the interest of completeness.... If the substitutions are to be admitted at all (we leave open the possibility that Moussaoui may decide not to use the substitutions in his defense), they may be admitted only by Moussaoui. Based on defense counsel's submissions and the Government's objections, the district court could then create an appropriate set of substitutions....

As previously indicated, the jury must be provided with certain information regarding the substitutions. While we leave the particulars of the instructions to the district court, the jury must be informed, at a minimum, that the substitutions are what the witnesses would say if called to testify; that the substitutions are derived from statements obtained under conditions that provide circumstantial guarantees of reliability; that the substitutions contain statements obtained ****; and that neither the parties nor the district court has ever had access to the witnesses....

Affirmed in part, vacated in part, and remanded.

[The opinions of WILLIAMS, Circuit Judge, and GREGORY, Circuit Judge, each concurring in part and dissenting in part, are omitted.]

Notes and Questions

1. *No "Punitive Sanction."* The Fourth Circuit agreed with the district court that the government's unwillingness to grant access to witnesses in its custody warranted a judicial sanction, and explained that, "[u]nder such circumstances, dismissal of the indictment is the usual course. Like the district court, however, we believe that a more measured approach is required." But whereas the district court's "more measured approach" was to strike the death penalty, the Court of Appeals concluded that such a sanction was "punitive," and that "no punitive sanction is warranted here because the Government has rightfully exercised its prerogative to protect national security interests by refusing to produce the witnesses." What was the source of that prerogative? Is the appeals court's alternative sanction consistent with the Supreme Court cases on which the Fourth Circuit otherwise relies to hold that a sanction is necessary in the first place? Without a "punitive" sanction, what incentive will the government have for producing witnesses such as those at issue here in a future case?

2. *The Analogy to CIPA.* After concluding that no "punitive" sanction was warranted, the court turns to CIPA — and its procedure for providing "substitutes" — to fashion what it deems to be an appropriate remedy. *See also United States v. Paracha*, No. 03 CR. 1197(SHS), 2006 WL 12768 (S.D.N.Y. Jan. 3, 2006) (using CIPA by analogy

to impose a *Moussaoui*-type solution for access to witnesses in U.S. custody in Afghanistan), *aff'd*, 313 F. App'x 347 (2d Cir. 2008). Is the analogy convincing in *Moussaoui*? Recall that the purpose of CIPA is not to protect a defendant's rights under the Due Process and Confrontation Clauses, but rather to protect the government's interests in preserving secrecy. Is it therefore circular to invoke CIPA as a remedy for a violation of a defendant's rights in a case like *Moussaoui*? Or is it, as the Fourth Circuit concluded, justified by the uniquely compelling interests on both sides of the case? If the applicability of CIPA to the *Moussaoui* problem needs to be made clearer, shouldn't it be Congress's job to amend the statute?

3. Deciding a Clash Between Branches: Formalism or Balancing? The *Moussaoui* court concluded that the appropriate separation of powers analysis required by Moussaoui's insistence on access to **** was balancing, as prescribed by *Nixon v. Administrator of General Services*, 433 U.S. 425 (1977), a civil case holding that "the proper inquiry focuses on the extent to which [the judicial act of ordering access, in this instance] prevents the Executive Branch from accomplishing its constitutionally assigned functions, . . . [and whether] that impact is justified by an overriding need to promote objectives within the constitutional authority of [the court]"). *Id.* at 443. But in *Public Citizen v. United States Department of Justice*, 491 U.S. 440 (1989), noted *supra* p. 45, Justice Kennedy indicated that there is "a line of cases of equal weight and authority, . . . where the Constitution by explicit text commits the power at issue to the exclusive control of the President, . . . [and the Court has] refused to tolerate *any* intrusion by [the courts]." *Id.* at 485 (Kennedy, J., concurring). Why isn't *Moussaoui* controlled by *Public Citizen*? Doesn't the Commander in Chief Clause of Article II commit command of the armed forces in war to the President, and isn't the interrogation of enemy combatants in war part of that command? On the other hand, as CIPA itself recognizes, might the government necessarily forfeit some of the constitutional prerogatives against disclosure that it might otherwise possess when it chooses to bring a criminal prosecution?

What other cases would you rely on in making the formalist argument for the government, or, by a balancing analysis, in arguing that court-ordered access to **** would prevent the President from conducting the war?

4. Switching Forums? The district court invited the government to "reconsider whether the civilian criminal courts are the appropriate fora" for trying someone like Moussaoui. *United States v. Moussaoui*, No. Cr-01-455-A, 2003 WL 21263699, at *6 (E.D. Va. Mar. 10, 2003). The alternative is trial by military commission, which we explore in the next chapter. Indeed, even Moussaoui's standby counsel appears to have invited this alternative, gratuitously conceding that the government's authority to try enemy combatants by military commission is "settled," and implying that the government can simply dismiss the criminal prosecution and proceed instead by a military commission to resolve the tension between Moussaoui's Sixth Amendment rights and the war powers. Brief of the Appellee at 3-4, *United States v. Moussaoui*, No. 03-4162 (4th Cir. May 13, 2003).

After you read the materials on military commissions, you can decide for yourself whether this was a wise concession. Do you agree with the apparent assumption upon which that concession and the district court's invitation rested — that the government can switch forums in midstream? Even assuming that the government could lawfully have tried Moussaoui by military commission *ab initio*, does it necessarily follow that the government may start in a civilian court and then dismiss in favor of a military commission when it is unhappy with the civilian court's rulings? Would it matter how far the criminal prosecution had progressed beyond the indictment? If such a switch survived constitutional challenges, would it nevertheless violate the spirit of the law? And in any event, doesn't this all assume that the Sixth Amendment considerations at issue in *Moussaoui* would be inapplicable in a military commission? Is it clear that this would be so?

The government did, in fact, make a switch — actually a triple-switch — in *Al-Marri v. Hanft*, 378 F. Supp. 2d 673 (D.S.C. 2005), noted *supra* p. 903. After al-Marri lawfully entered the United States with his family to obtain a master's degree, he was initially arrested as a material witness in the 9/11 investigation. In the first switch, he was then rearrested and indicted for making false statements and for credit card fraud. More than two years later, President Bush interrupted the course of normal criminal proceedings (trial had not yet begun) by designating al-Marri an enemy combatant, after which he was transferred to military detention in South Carolina in the government's second switch. The government then successfully moved to drop the criminal indictment with prejudice.

Al-Marri argued that his criminal detention was sufficient to thwart any terrorist acts and that there was no necessity for military detention. The district court rejected his argument in part on the reasoning from case law asserting that when a federal investigation of criminal charges pending in state court reveals a federal crime, the state charges can be dismissed and the matter can be transferred to federal jurisdiction. *Id.* at 681. Is the analogy sound?

Al-Marri also protested that while he might have been acquitted of the criminal charges, he had no opportunity to prove his innocence in military detention. The court rejected this claim as well, reasoning that the purpose of military detention is preventive:

> This Court recognizes the natural response to this reasoning that, when a defendant is acquitted of criminal charges, society should not assume that he ever did nor that he will, in the future, engage in the activities for which he was charged. In this case, however, Petitioner was not charged with crimes of terrorism, and thus, an acquittal of various fraud charges does not lead to the conclusion that he will not, in the future, engage in acts of terrorism as alleged by the government. [*Id.* at 681 n.8.]

After the Court of Appeals later divided sharply on the legality of al-Marri's detention as an enemy combatant and the adequacy of the procedure afforded him in deciding his status, the government switched forums for a third time, indicting al-Marri again when his case was already before the Supreme Court. This time, al-Marri entered a guilty plea to one count of conspiracy to provide material support to a foreign terrorist organization. Note how this phenomenon drives home the "cross-ruffing" concerns introduced earlier in this chapter, *supra* p. 1089.

5. Guilty Plea and Sentence. On April 22, 2005, Moussaoui surprised everyone by pleading guilty to the key charges against him, while at the same time denying having any intention to commit mass murder. *See Moussaoui Pleads Guilty to Terror Charges*, CNN.com, Apr. 23, 2005, *at* http://www.cnn.com/2005/LAW/04/22/moussaoui/index.html. He was subsequently sentenced to life in prison. *United States v. Moussaoui*, No. 1:01CR00455-001, Judgment in a Criminal Case at 2 (E.D. Va. May 14, 2006).

6. A Better Forum for Moussaoui? The following assessment was written before the conclusion of the *Moussaoui* trial.

> The United States should drop all criminal charges against Zacarias Moussaoui, not because he is innocent, but because he is a foreign citizen who is (or was) a terrorist bent on killing innocent Americans, destroying American property, and disrupting American society. For less than a nanosecond, Moussaoui should be a free man again. . . .
>
> Before the nanosecond of Moussaoui's freedom ends, he should be transferred to the custody of the United States Department of Defense. After that, based on recommendations coordinated by the National Security Council (NSC) for the President, the Executive Branch should implement a well-conceived decision about Moussaoui's next address. The NSC, rather than a particular United States agency, such as the Justice Department or the Defense Department, is the appropriate forum to vet such policies because they transcend the boundaries between domestic and international spheres, going beyond law enforcement and military issues. . . . The President, in making this decision on Moussaoui's next address, should consider our relations with foreign countries and the safety of our homeland. But whatever happens to Moussaoui, he did not — and does not — belong in criminal custody. [John Radsan, *The Moussaoui Case: The Mess from Minnesota,* 31 Wm. Mitchell L. Rev. 1417, 1417-1419 (2005).]

Do you agree? Did the system work? Or was the system distorted to accommodate national security?

7. The Paracha Case. The *Moussaoui* prosecution was not the only post-September 11 terrorism prosecution in which the government denied a defendant access to potentially exculpatory witnesses. The same thing happened in the case of Uzair Paracha, a Pakistani citizen arrested on a material witness warrant in 2003, and ultimately prosecuted and convicted on multiple terrorism-related charges — and sentenced to 30 years in prison. Paracha had sought to depose Khalid Sheikh Mohammad, Ammar al Baluchi, and Majid Khan, three high value detainees then in CIA custody (and later transferred to Guantánamo), on the ground that they might be able to exculpate him. Relying on *Moussaoui,* the district court limited Paracha to introducing the unclassified summaries of statements made by the detainees while in custody.

After his conviction, Paracha discovered, through a combination of government disclosures and public reporting, that al Baluchi, Khan, and Khalid Sheikh Mohammad had each made numerous statements that tended to contradict at least some of the evidence the government had used against him at trial. In light of this new evidence, a district court — 13 years after Paracha's trial — threw out his conviction and ordered a new trial. *United States v. Paracha,* No. 03-cr-1197, 2018 WL 3238824 (S.D.N.Y. July 3, 2018). The government initially appealed the district court's ruling, but then voluntarily dismissed the appeal in December 2018. Is *Paracha* an example of the system "working," because he received a new trial? Or is it further reason to worry about denying criminal defendants access to potentially exculpatory witnesses, given that what came out later could very well have been elicited in the original proceeding, potentially leading to Paracha's prompt acquittal?

E. DO WE NEED A NATIONAL SECURITY COURT?

The uncomfortable denouement in *Moussaoui*, and, later, the mixed verdict in *United States v. Ghailani*, reviewed earlier in this chapter, both rekindled an acrimonious debate about the ability of the criminal process to handle terrorist cases. In addition to the problems of secret and coerced evidence discussed above, terror prosecutions potentially pose the following problems:

- whether the right to speedy trial has been violated by lengthy detention as an enemy combatant;
- whether the accused terrorist was entitled to *Miranda* warnings ("you have a right to remain silent. . . .") when he was arrested and detained abroad;
- whether the security of the jury and the judge requires special measures, including shackling the defendant or concealing the identity of jurors;
- whether tensions between the accused terrorist and his court-appointed lawyers render the assistance of counsel ineffective or threaten the conduct of the trial;
- whether the criminal justice system can afford the often lengthy, appeal-interrupted, pretrial motion practice and trial of accused terrorists.

Former federal judge and Attorney General Michael B. Mukasey cited the José Padilla saga as evidence that "current institutions and statutes are not well suited to even the limited task of supplementing . . . a military effort to combat Islamic terrorism," even *after* Padilla was convicted on federal criminal charges and sentenced to decades in prison. Michael B. Mukasey, Op-Ed, *Jose Padilla Makes Bad Law*, Wall St. J., Aug. 22, 2007. He noted that Padilla's criminal case took three months to try, and that criminal cases involving the 1993 World Trade Center bombing, 1996 attacks on Khobar Towers, 1998 attacks on U.S. embassies in Africa, and the 2000 bombing of the USS *Cole* "have strained the financial resources and security resources of the federal courts near to the limit." *Id.* He also asserted that such prosecutions risk disclosing methods and sources of intelligence, and, when the courts relax evidentiary rules or criminal procedures, also can distort the rules applicable to ordinary criminal cases. *Id.*

Judge Mukasey therefore urged Congress to consider creating a new Article III "national security court" to deal with national security prosecutions, including terrorism cases. One proposal would model such a court on the Foreign Intelligence Surveillance Court (or even "subsume the FISA court and its obligations within a new National Security Court") and staff it with Article III judges. Andrew C. McCarthy & Alykhan Velshi, *Outsourcing American Law: We Need a National Security Court* 24 & n.61 (American Enter. Inst. Working Paper No. 156, 2009), *available at* http://www.aei.org/docLib/20090820-Chapter6.pdf. Such a court would have concurrent jurisdiction with military commissions to try "alleged offenders . . . if those offenders qualify as alien enemy combatants. . . ." *Id.* at 26. Its priority would be "not justice for the individual but security of the American people," and it would therefore need "clear procedural rules which underscore that the overriding mission — into which the judicial function is being imported for very limited purposes — remains executive and military." *Id.* at 30. The proposal is not specific about those rules, but they would apparently include a "credible and convincing evidence" standard of proof, a systemic "preference . . . that defendants be convicted and harshly sentenced," and strict limits on "judicial excess," to be enforced by a right of interlocutory appeal by the government to challenge any order "by which the court deviates from the procedural rules." *Id.* at 31-32. Finally, the court would be instructed by Congress to apply a much-narrowed *Brady* exculpatory evidence doctrine. *Id.* at 35. In short, they sum up, "[National Security Court] trials would add the Article III judges to the existing military commission format." *Id.* at 32.

Other proposals for a National Security Court would lengthen the speedy trial limitation, ease the government's burden to show a need for closing a trial to the public, require only a two-thirds vote to find proof of guilt beyond a reasonable doubt, relax the hearsay and authentication rules of evidence, and, possibly, permit coerced statements into evidence in some circumstances (although this is unclear). *See* Kevin E. Lunday & Harvey Rishikof, *Due Process Is a Strategic Choice: Legitimacy and the Establishment of an Article III National Security Court*, 39 Cal. W. Int'l L.J. 87 (2008).

Notes and Questions

1. A National Security Court for Detention Decisions. A National Security Court has been proposed both to review detention cases via habeas and to provide a forum for criminal trials of terrorism cases. *See, e.g.*, McCarthy & Velshi, *supra*, at 23-27; Lunday & Rishikof, *supra*, at 113-118. Such a court would relieve the habeas courts of their burden of reviewing wartime detention, and they could also be given jurisdiction to authorize or review preventive detention under a new statute. Several scholars assert that the courts in the D.C. Circuit already *are* National Security Courts by default, because of their handling of habeas petitions and military commission appeals from Guantánamo detainees. *See, e.g.*, Jack Goldsmith, *Long-Term Terrorist Detention and Our National Security Court* 6-8 (Series on Counterterrorism and American Statutory Law, Working Paper No. 5, 2009), *available at* https://www.brookings.edu/research/long-term-terrorist-detention-and-our-national-security-court/. In light of the procedural and evidentiary issues covered in this and the preceding chapter, could one argue that the federal courts *in general* have become de facto national security courts?

2. Need? Proponents of a special National Security Court have cited the aforementioned problems, the length of terrorism trials, and the mixed verdict in *Ghailani* as evidence of the need for a new kind of trial court, but is the anecdotal evidence compelling? Opponents note, first, that convictions were obtained in all of the cited cases. Although some scholars have criticized Department of Justice statistics for being over-inclusive and have pointed to the surprisingly short *average* sentences handed out in cases that DOJ has classified as terrorism-related, more nuanced evaluation of the statistics suggests that the government has obtained lengthy sentences for cases actually based on terrorism and material support charges. *See* Robert M. Chesney, *Federal Prosecution of Terrorism-Related Offenses: Conviction and Sentencing Data in Light of the "Soft-Sentence" and "Data-Reliability" Critiques*, 11 Lewis & Clark L. Rev. 851 (2007). The court of appeals in *Abu Ali* emphasized that "the criminal justice system is not without those attributes of adaptation that will permit it to function in the post-9/11 world." *Abu Ali*, 528 F.3d at 221. A 625-page Federal Judicial Center study has documented hundreds of such adaptations — including many of those found herein. *See* Robert Timothy Reagan, Fed. Jud. Ctr., *National Security Case Studies: Special Case-Management Challenges* (6th ed. 2015).

How much stress on the criminal justice system would be needed to justify creation of a National Security Court? On whom should the burden of proof fall, the proponents of such a court or their opponents? The current criminal justice system assumes that protection of the innocent is worth the cost of letting some guilty defendants go free. Does the same assumption apply to accused terrorists?

3. *Changing the Rules or Changing the Court?* In contrast to footnote 182 in *Ghailani, supra* p. 1096, proponents of a National Security Court assume that evidentiary rules and standards of proof can be relaxed. But if this is true, could those rules and standards not be relaxed for ordinary criminal courts without the need to create a controversial new court? If the answer is no because of constitutional limitations, would the same limitations not apply to the new Article III court? Consider the assessment one of us offered in response to these proposals:

> [E]ither Congress can amend the Federal Rules of Evidence [or CIPA] to allow for the introduction [or the exclusion] of particular forms of evidence in particular cases, or the Constitution prohibits Congress from so acting. The former would suggest that a move to a national security court would be akin to using a bazooka to kill an ant; the latter would suggest that national security courts *couldn't* have a lesser evidentiary burden. [Stephen I. Vladeck, *The Case Against National Security Courts*, 45 Willamette L. Rev. 505, 519-520 (2009).]

But suppose that Congress *could* dilute the evidentiary protections in terrorism cases. Might there be a good reason for it to do so *only* in those cases — perhaps by funneling those trials into an alternative forum?

4. *"Seepage."* Even if some of the challenges facing terrorist prosecutions could constitutionally be alleviated by simple rule changes, are they changes we would want to make to the ordinary criminal justice system? Judge Mukasey expressed concern that "if conventional legal rules are adapted to deal with a terrorist threat, whether by relaxed standards for conviction, searches, the admissibility of evidence or otherwise, those adaptions will infect and change the standards in ordinary cases with ordinary defendants in ordinary courts of law." Mukasey, *supra*. If such rule changes are confined to terrorism cases, then they could effectively convert the criminal courts into a "National Security Court" for purposes of terrorism cases, anyway. Historically, one protection against unfair rules has always been the fact that rules apply the same way to everyone, sometimes expressed in the aphorism that we are measured by how we treat our enemies. On the other hand, some of the innovations that judges have employed in terrorism cases were borrowed from drug or gang cases. Is concern about the "relaxation" or adaptation of rules in terrorism cases overblown?

5. *Legitimacy.* An important attribute of American criminal justice is its transparency. Secret "Star Chamber" courts are contrary to our tradition, and some feel (perhaps unfairly) that the legitimacy of the Foreign Intelligence Surveillance Court is undercut by its closed hearings. Moreover, the United States has traditionally been critical of "special" security courts and military courts used in non-democratic states to stifle opponents and dissidents, as well as to try security risks. "Legitimacy remains

a vital strategic weapon against terrorism." Lunday & Rishikof, *supra*, at 131. Does not the legitimacy of the state's courts therefore also matter? Would a National Security Court have the same legitimacy as ordinary Article III courts have acquired over time? Should we be concerned not only about its legitimacy to Americans, but also about its legitimacy to our foreign allies and enemies? As we turn to military commissions in the next chapter, keep these legitimacy concerns in mind.

TERRORISM TRIALS: PROCEDURE AND EVIDENCE: SUMMARY OF BASIC PRINCIPLES

- Courts have recognized a "public safety" exception to *Miranda* that allows the introduction at trial of unwarned statements made during a custodial interrogation so long as the interrogation was focused on identifying an ongoing threat to public safety, rather than inculpating the defendant. In terrorism cases, courts have allowed up to 50 minutes of "public safety" questioning — even where there was no direct evidence of any ongoing threat.

- To date, courts have held that the Speedy Trial Clause is not violated when terrorism suspects are subjected to CIA and/or military detention for an extended period of time prior to their civilian criminal trial.

- At most, the mistreatment of a defendant prior to his trial will warrant a dismissal of the indictment only if the government abuse truly "shocks the conscience." But the Due Process and Self-Incrimination Clauses of the Fifth Amendment preclude the introduction at trial of evidence obtained from the defendant's mistreatment — and fruits of the poisonous tree.

- National security considerations led Congress to enact the Classified Information Procedures Act (CIPA), which provides a complex series of procedural and evidentiary rules to balance the defendant's Fifth and Sixth Amendment rights against the government's interest in avoiding "graymail."

- Although CIPA requires defendants to make a number of pretrial disclosures that could reveal aspects of their trial strategy and tactics (and thereby arguably give the government a litigation advantage), courts have upheld these regimes against constitutional challenges, concluding that, because CIPA also burdens the government in key respects, these additional burdens on the defendant do not alter the adversarial balance as between the prosecution and the defense.

- To allow for the introduction of classified information at trial without its public disclosure, courts have devised the "silent witness" rule, pursuant to which a witness will identify the relevant portion of a classified document in a manner that is clear to the judge, the jury, the defendant, and counsel, but not to the public.

- Defendants in civilian criminal prosecutions have a clearly established right of access to potentially exculpatory evidence and witness testimony, even if it is classified. When the government has refused to turn over such evidence, courts have required the government to fashion constitutionally suitable alternatives — and have sanctioned the government when it has refused to do so.

- Because of the burdens and obstacles these rules place in the way of secrecy-laden terrorism prosecutions in civilian courts, some have proposed an alternative "National Security Court" with special, looser evidentiary and procedural rules to be applied only in terrorism cases. These proposals raise a number of questions, however, including why, if the rules *can* constitutionally be relaxed in such a new forum, they can't also be similarly loosened within the existing criminal justice system.

36

Trial by Military Commission

Before deploying "necessary and appropriate force" against Al Qaeda and the Taliban in Afghanistan in November 2001, the Bush administration had to decide what it would do with those captured in the fight. Apart from simply detaining them, the authorities for which we explored in Chapters 29 and 30, one possibility was trying them in U.S. criminal courts. But the problems of secret evidence and territorial limits on U.S. criminal laws, analyzed in the preceding chapter, not to mention concerns about security and efficiency, given the sheer numbers of anticipated captives, made this option impractical.

A second option was trying the detainees before some ad hoc international tribunal. The surrender of control that this would entail, coupled with the Administration's repudiation of the International Criminal Court, made this option unappealing.

A third option was trying the detainees by court-martial, using the same rules applicable to U.S. servicemen. This option would have used fair and time-tested procedures at the same time that it conformed with the laws of war. But the very fairness of these procedures may have been a strike against them; they may have seemed too fair and, partly as a result, too cumbersome for terrorists charged with horrific war crimes against civilians. *See* Jane Mayer, *The Hidden Power*, New Yorker, May 3, 2006, at 44 (quoting Vice President Dick Cheney on military commissions: "We think it guarantees that we'll have the kind of treatment of these individuals that we believe they deserve."). Conformity of court-martial trials with the laws of war could have been another strike against them, as long as the Administration insisted that such laws did not apply to terrorists. See Chapter 9.

Whatever the precise reasons, the Bush administration chose a fourth option: to try selected captives by "military commission" under procedures devised for the occasion. Military commissions are tribunals in which military officers sit as judge and jury. Historically, they have been irregular bodies used in the field to try spies, saboteurs, and others who violate the laws of war, and in occupied territories or areas under martial law to try common crimes as well. This chapter introduces the precedents for these tribunals and the specific questions they have confronted after 9/11.

A. TRIAL BY MILITARY COMMISSION BEFORE 9/11

Reading *Ex parte Milligan*

Recall from Chapter ♦♦ that Lambdin Milligan was arrested, detained, and tried by the military during the Civil War. A military commission — composed exclusively of active-duty members of the military — conducted the trial, found him guilty, and sentenced him to death. He first wrote the Secretary of War to ask the President to intervene:

> Indianapolis 28 Dec. 1864
>
> Hon. E. M. Stanton Sect. War.
> Dear Sir I have been condemned to die without evidence. Please examine the facts and advise the President. Do this much for an old acquaintance and friend—
>
> Yours very truly
>
> L. P. Milligan

Courtesy of the National Archives and Records Administration

When that did not work, his lawyers asked the Supreme Court to overturn his conviction.

- What precisely were the charges against Milligan?
- Why did the Court majority conclude that the commission lacked "jurisdiction" to try Milligan?
- What constitutional rights of Milligan did the Court find that the commission had violated?
- By the majority's view, would it ever be constitutional for a military commission to try someone like Milligan? If so, under what conditions? Why?
- In Chief Justice Chase's view, when would it be constitutional to try someone like Milligan before a military commission?
- Suppose Milligan had been a member of the Confederate Army captured on the battlefield at Gettysburg, and had been charged with murdering civilians. Would it have been constitutional then to try him by military commission? Why? Consider both Article I, §8, cl. 14 and the Fifth Amendment when you answer.

Ex parte Milligan

United States Supreme Court, 1866
71 U.S. (4 Wall.) 2

[The opinions are set forth *supra* p. 829 and *infra* p. 1209.]

Reading *Ex parte Quirin*

After war was declared between the United States and Germany in 1941, seven German nationals and Herbert Hans Haupt (a dual U.S.-German national) were trained at a German sabotage school near Berlin. German submarines then carried the saboteurs with a supply of explosives to the United States. They landed on U.S. beaches in the summer of 1942 wearing German marine infantry uniforms, which they immediately buried. Before they could engage in any acts of sabotage, however, they were betrayed to the FBI by one of their number.

After their arrest, President Roosevelt issued an order declaring that nationals of enemy states or those who acted under their direction, who were charged with sabotage, espionage, or "violations of the law of war," were subject to the jurisdiction of military tribunals. Proclamation No. 2561, 7 Fed. Reg. 5101 (July 7, 1942). A military commission then conducted a secret 18-day trial of the saboteurs.

Toward the end of the trial, the Supreme Court decided in an extraordinary summer session to hear argument on the saboteurs' appeal from the refusal of the lower courts to entertain their habeas petitions challenging the commissions. Less than 24 hours after argument, it issued a per curiam ruling that the military commission was lawfully constituted and authorized to try the saboteurs, promising a full opinion later. Six of the saboteurs were executed eight days after the Supreme Court's per curiam ruling (Roosevelt commuted the sentences of the other two to imprisonment). The Court then issued its full opinion three months later.

- Chief Justice Stone's opinion for the Court offers two principal grounds on which to distinguish *Milligan*: (1) the existence of congressional authorization for the commissions; and (2) the inapplicability of the Constitution's jury-trial protections. How does he justify both of these holdings?
- Do you agree that the statute he identifies actually *does* authorize the commissions?
- Do you agree with the exception to the Sixth Amendment he identifies?
- As we will see later in this chapter, one of the lingering constitutional questions after September 11 is whether, in addition to *upholding* military commissions, *Quirin* also articulated constitutional *limits* on their jurisdiction. What, if anything, in Chief Justice Stone's opinion speaks to this question?

Ex parte Quirin

United States Supreme Court, 1942
317 U.S. 1

Mr. Chief Justice STONE delivered the opinion of the Court. . . . We are not here concerned with any question of the guilt or innocence of petitioners. Constitutional safeguards for the protection of all who are charged with offenses are not to be disregarded in order to inflict merited punishment on some who are guilty. *Ex parte*

Milligan, [71 U.S. (4 Wall.) 2 (1866)]. But the detention and trial of petitioners — ordered by the President in the declared exercise of his powers as Commander in Chief of the Army in time of war and of grave public danger — are not to be set aside by the courts without the clear conviction that they are in conflict with the Constitution or laws of Congress constitutionally enacted. . . .

By the Articles of War, 10 U.S.C. §§1471-1593, Congress has provided rules for the government of the Army. . . . But the Articles also recognize the "military commission" appointed by military command as an appropriate tribunal for the trial and punishment of offenses against the law of war not ordinarily tried by court martial. . . . Article 15 declares that "the provisions of these articles conferring jurisdiction upon courts-martial shall not be construed as depriving military commissions . . . or other military tribunals of concurrent jurisdiction in respect of offenders or offenses that by statute or by the law of war may be triable by such military commissions . . . or other military tribunals." . . .

From the very beginning of its history this Court has recognized and applied the law of war as including that part of the law of nations which prescribes, for the conduct of war, the status, rights and duties of enemy nations as well as of enemy individuals. By the Articles of War, and especially Article 15, Congress has explicitly provided, so far as it may constitutionally do so, that military tribunals shall have jurisdiction to try offenders or offenses against the law of war in appropriate cases. . . .

An important incident to the conduct of war is the adoption of measures by the military command not only to repel and defeat the enemy, but to seize and subject to disciplinary measures those enemies who in their attempt to thwart or impede our military effort have violated the law of war. It is unnecessary for present purposes to determine to what extent the President as Commander in Chief has constitutional power to create military commissions without the support of Congressional legislation. For here Congress has authorized trial of offenses against the law of war before such commissions. . . . We may assume that there are acts regarded in other countries, or by some writers on international law, as offenses against the law of war which would not be triable by military tribunal here, either because they are not recognized by our courts as violations of the law of war or because they are of that class of offenses constitutionally triable only by a jury. It was upon such grounds that the Court denied the right to proceed by military tribunal in *Ex parte Milligan, supra.* But as we shall show, these petitioners were charged with an offense against the law of war which the Constitution does not require to be tried by jury. . . .

. . . [B]y the reference in the 15th Article of War to "offenders or offenses that . . . by the law of war may be triable by such military commissions," Congress has incorporated by reference, as within the jurisdiction of military commissions, all offenses which are defined as such by the law of war, and which may constitutionally be included within that jurisdiction. Congress had the choice of crystallizing in permanent form and in minute detail every offense against the law of war, or of adopting the system of common law applied by military tribunals so far as it should be recognized and deemed applicable by the courts. It chose the latter course.

By universal agreement and practice the law of war draws a distinction between the armed forces and the peaceful populations of belligerent nations and also between those who are lawful and unlawful combatants. Lawful combatants are subject to capture and detention as prisoners of war by opposing military forces. Unlawful combatants are likewise subject to capture and detention, but in addition they are subject to trial and punishment by military tribunals for acts which render their belligerency unlawful. The spy who secretly and without uniform passes the military lines of a belligerent in time of war, seeking to gather military information and communicate it to the enemy, or an enemy combatant who without uniform comes secretly through the lines for the purpose of waging war by destruction of life or property, are familiar examples of belligerents who are generally deemed not to be entitled to the status of prisoners of war, but to be offenders against the law of war subject to trial and punishment by military tribunals. . . .

Specification 1 states that petitioners "being enemies of the United States and acting for . . . the German Reich, a belligerent enemy nation, secretly and covertly passed, in civilian dress, contrary to the law of war, through the military and naval lines and defenses of the United States . . . and went behind such lines, contrary to the law of war, in civilian dress . . . for the purpose of committing . . . hostile acts, and, in particular, to destroy certain war industries, war utilities and war materials within the United States."

This specification . . . plainly alleges violation of the law of war. . . .

Citizenship in the United States of an enemy belligerent does not relieve him from the consequences of a belligerency which is unlawful because in violation of the law of war. Citizens who associate themselves with the military arm of the enemy government, and with its aid, guidance and direction enter this country bent on hostile acts are enemy belligerents within the meaning of the Hague Convention and the law of war. It is as an enemy belligerent that petitioner Haupt is charged with entering the United States, and unlawful belligerency is the gravamen of the offense of which he is accused. . . .

But petitioners insist that even if the offenses with which they are charged are offenses against the law of war, their trial is subject to the requirement of the Fifth Amendment that no person shall be held to answer for a capital or otherwise infamous crime unless on a presentment or indictment of a grand jury, and that such trials by Article III, §2, and the Sixth Amendment must be by jury in a civil court. . . .

Presentment by a grand jury and trial by a jury of the vicinage where the crime was committed were at the time of the adoption of the Constitution familiar parts of the machinery for criminal trials in the civil courts. But they were procedures unknown to military tribunals, which are not courts in the sense of the Judiciary Article, and which in the natural course of events are usually called upon to function under conditions precluding resort to such procedures. . . .

. . . [W]e must conclude that §2 of Article III and the Fifth and Sixth Amendments cannot be taken to have extended the right to demand a jury to trials by military commission, or to have required that offenses against the law of war not triable by jury at common law be tried only in the civil courts. . . .

We may assume, without deciding, that a trial prosecuted before a military commission created by military authority is not one "arising in the land . . . forces," when the accused is not a member of or associated with those forces. But even so, the exception cannot be taken to affect those trials before military commissions which are neither within the exception nor within the provisions of Article III, §2, whose guaranty the Amendments did not enlarge. No exception is necessary to exclude from the operation of these provisions cases never deemed to be within their terms. An express exception from Article III, §2, and from the Fifth and Sixth Amendments, of trials of petty offenses and of criminal contempts has not been found necessary in order to preserve the traditional practice of trying those offenses without a jury. It is no more so in order to continue the practice of trying, before military tribunals without a jury, offenses committed by enemy belligerents against the law of war. . . .

Since the [Fifth and Sixth] Amendments, like §2 of Article III, do not preclude all trials of offenses against the law of war by military commission without a jury when the offenders are aliens not members of our Armed Forces, it is plain that they present no greater obstacle to the trial in like manner of citizen enemies who have violated the law of war applicable to enemies. . . .

Petitioners, and especially petitioner Haupt, stress the pronouncement of this Court in the *Milligan* case that the law of war "can never be applied to citizens in states which have upheld the authority of the government, and where the courts are open and their process unobstructed." Elsewhere in its opinion, the Court was at pains to point out that Milligan, a citizen twenty years resident in Indiana, who had never been a resident of any of the states in rebellion, was not an enemy belligerent either entitled to the status of a prisoner of war or subject to the penalties imposed upon unlawful belligerents. We construe the Court's statement as to the inapplicability of the law of war to Milligan's case as having particular reference to the facts before it. From them the Court concluded that Milligan, not being a part of or associated with the armed forces of the enemy, was a non-belligerent, not subject to the law of war save as — in circumstances found not there to be present and not involved here — martial law might be constitutionally established.

The Court's opinion is inapplicable to the case presented by the present record. We have no occasion now to define with meticulous care the ultimate boundaries of the jurisdiction of military tribunals to try persons according to the law of war. It is enough that petitioners here, upon the conceded facts, were plainly within those boundaries, and were held in good faith for trial by military commission, charged with being enemies who, with the purpose of destroying war materials and utilities, entered or after entry remained in our territory without uniform — an offense against the law of war. We hold only that those particular acts constitute an offense against the law of war which the Constitution authorizes to be tried by military commission. . . .

. . . It follows that the orders of the District Court should be affirmed, and that leave to file petitions for habeas corpus in this Court should be denied.

Justice Murphy took no part in the consideration or decision of these cases.

Notes and Questions

1. Statutory Authority? Quirin holds that there was statutory authority for the commission that tried the German saboteurs by reference to Article 15 of the Articles of War, which it quotes *supra* p. 1126. At the time *Quirin* was decided, did Article 15, which is now 10 U.S.C. §821 (2018), authorize military commissions, or is it merely a savings clause? If the latter, what preexisting authority did it save? In another World War II case involving military commissions, *In re Yamashita*, 327 U.S. 1 (1946), the Supreme Court explained that "[b]y thus recognizing military commissions in order to preserve their traditional jurisdiction over enemy combatants unimpaired by the Articles, Congress gave sanction, as we held in *Ex parte Quirin*, to any use of the military commission contemplated by the *common law of war*." *Id.* at 20 (emphasis added).

Whatever the merits of *Quirin*'s reading of Article 15 (which the Supreme Court has since described as "controversial," *see Hamdan v. Rumsfeld,* 548 U.S. 557, 593 (2006)), the United States conducted military commission trials of hundreds of enemy soldiers during and after World War II based upon that reading, and Congress presumably codified that interpretation in 1950, when it reenacted Article 15 as Article 21 of the Uniform Code of Military Justice (UCMJ). But what does Article 21 actually *authorize*? What are the constitutional limits of Congress's power over the jurisdiction of military commissions after *Quirin*?

2. *The Jury-Trial Exception.* Chief Justice Stone places a lot of weight on an exception to the Constitution's jury-trial protections for "offenses committed by enemy belligerents against the laws of war." But other than the historical practice of trials for espionage and aiding the enemy before military commissions, he provided no historical or analytical support for the existence of such an exception; he merely asserted its existence. Should there be such an exception? If so, what should be its limits?

Note how *Quirin*'s reading of Article 15 (as reflecting Congress's acquiescence in military commissions for offenses against the laws of war) dovetails with its reading of the jury-trial clauses. Would the jury-trial clauses limit Congress's power to authorize military commissions to try offenses *not* recognized by the laws of war?

3. *Reconciling Milligan and Quirin.* Although Attorney General Francis Biddle at first asked the Court in *Quirin* to overrule *Milligan,* he later backed off from this demand in his oral argument and asserted that the Court could uphold the use of the military commission to try the saboteurs "without touching a hair of the *Milligan* case." George Lardner Jr., *Nazi Saboteurs Captured!,* Wash. Post Mag., Jan. 13, 2002, at 23. How *did* the Court distinguish *Milligan*? Did the *Quirin* Court distinguish the defendants by their citizenship? *See Mudd v. Caldera,* 134 F. Supp. 2d 138 (D.D.C. 2001) (citizens and noncitizens alike may be subject to the jurisdiction of a military commission for violating the laws of war). By their acts? (Recall that Milligan was charged with "Violation of the laws of war.") If *Milligan* survived *Quirin,* as the later opinion suggests, did *Milligan* nevertheless get a pretty short haircut? How much of it is left?

The *Quirin* Court suggested that *Milligan* should be limited to its facts. On the other hand, Justice Black wrote to the other Justices in *Quirin* that "[i]n this case I want to go no further than to declare that these particular defendants are subject to the jurisdiction of a military tribunal because of the circumstances." *See* Evan P. Schultz, *Now and Later,* Legal Times, Dec. 24, 2001, at 54. Accordingly, the opinion for the Court stated, "We hold only that these particular facts constitute an offense against the law of nations which the Constitution authorizes to be tried by military commission." *Quirin,* 317 U.S. at 20. Do "these particular facts" include the fact of declared war with its attendant limits (including the concession that the defendants were enemy combatants)?

In ascertaining the relationship between *Milligan* and *Quirin,* should it matter that Justice Frankfurter would later describe the case as "not a happy precedent," *see* David J. Danelski, *The Saboteurs' Case,* J. Sup. Ct. Hist., July 1996, at 61, 80, or that Justice Scalia has derided it as "not this Court's finest hour," *Hamdi v. Rumsfeld,* 542 U.S. 507, 569 (2004) (Scalia, J., dissenting)? As between *Milligan* and *Quirin,* which case narrows which?

4. Violations of the Law of War. Were the September 11 attacks acts of war, and did they violate the law of war? Traditionally, states carry out acts of war, and a state's deliberate attack on noncombatant civilians would clearly violate the law of war. *See, e.g.*, Convention Relative to the Protection of Civilian Persons in Time of War (1949 Geneva Convention IV), Aug. 12, 1949, 6 U.S.T. 3516, 75 U.N.T.S. 287, *supra* p. 272. Some have argued that "war crimes" must by definition either be committed during an international armed conflict between *states* or in an internal armed conflict, and that the war conducted by terrorists is neither. *See, e.g.*, Joan Fitzpatrick, *Jurisdiction of Military Commissions and the Ambiguous War on Terrorism*, 96 Am. J. Int'l'l L. 345 (2002).

But the law of war applies also to some nonstate actors, such as insurgents. A.B.A. Task Force on Terrorism and the Law, *Report and Recommendations on Military Commissions* 7 (Jan. 4, 2002). It also presumably applies to terrorists with state sponsors. Does one also violate the law of war solely by conspiring with or aiding and abetting Al Qaeda, as opposed to directly participating in the commission of terrorist attacks? *See* Ass'n of the Bar of the City of New York, Comm. on Military Aff. & Justice, *Inter Arma Silent Leges: In Times of Armed Conflict, Should the Laws Be Silent?* 16 (Dec. 2001) (*N.Y. City Bar Report*) (no).

B. TRIAL BY MILITARY COMMISSION AFTER 9/11: THE FIRST PHASE

Reading the November 2001 OLC Memo

Before the Bush administration turned to the fourth option identified above — trying enemy combatants by military commission — it tasked the Office of Legal Counsel with advising the President on the legality of using military commissions to try enemy combatants in the armed conflict against the Taliban and al Qaeda. That advice resulted in an opinion dated November 6, 2001, which is excerpted below. A week later, President Bush issued a Military Order authorizing trial by military commissions of noncitizens designated as "enemy combatants" for offenses (and pursuant to rules) subsequently identified by the Secretary of Defense. *See, e.g.*, Dep't of Def., *Military Commission Order No. 1* (Mar. 21, 2002); Dep't of Def., *Military Commissions Instructions Nos. 1-10* (various dates). As you read the OLC opinion, consider the following:

- How much does the memorandum rely upon *Quirin*?
- Is it clear from the memo what the key factual (and legal) differences are between the commissions contemplated by the Bush administration and those upheld by the Supreme Court in *Quirin*?

Legality of the Use of Military Commissions to Try Terrorists

U.S. Department of Justice, Office of Legal Counsel
25 Op. O.L.C. 238 (2001)

The President possesses inherent authority under the Constitution, as Chief Executive and Commander in Chief of the Armed Forces of the United States, to establish military commissions to try and punish terrorists captured in connection with the attacks of September 11 or in connection with U.S. military operations in response to those attacks.

Memorandum Opinion for the Counsel to the President

You have asked us to consider whether terrorists captured in connection with the attacks of September 11 or in connection with ongoing U.S. operations in response to those attacks could be subject to trial before a military court. The Uniform Code of Military Justice ("UCMJ"), 10 U.S.C. §§801-946, authorizes military commissions to try "offenders or offenses that by statute or by the law of war may be tried by military commissions." 10 U.S.C. §821 (2000). The Supreme Court has interpreted identical language (then included in Article 15 of the Articles of War in effect during World War II) to incorporate customary practice and to authorize trial by military commission of any person subject to the laws of war for any offense under the laws of war. *See Ex parte Quirin,* 317 U.S. 1, 30 (1942).

We conclude that under 10 U.S.C. §821 and his inherent powers as Commander in Chief, the President may establish military commissions to try and punish terrorists apprehended as part of the investigation into, or the military and intelligence operations in response to, the September 11 attacks....

BACKGROUND

A military commission is a form of military tribunal typically used in three scenarios: (I) to try individuals (usually members of enemy forces) for violations of the laws of war; (ii) as a general court administering justice in occupied territory; and (iii) as a general court in an area where martial law has been declared and the civil courts are closed. *See generally* William Winthrop, *Military Law and Precedents* 836-40 (2d ed. 1920)....

Military commissions have been used throughout U.S. history to prosecute violators of the laws of war. "Since our nation's earliest days, such commissions have been constitutionally recognized agencies for meeting many urgent governmental responsibilities related to war. They have been called our common law war courts." *Madsen v. Kinsella,* 343 U.S. 341, 346-47 (1952). Military commissions have tried offenders drawn from the ranks of aliens and citizens alike charged with war crimes arising as early as the Revolutionary War, the Mexican-American War, and the Civil War, and as recently as World War II. *See Quirin,* 317 U.S. at 32 n.10, 42 n.14. President Lincoln's assassins and their accomplices were imprisoned and even executed pursuant to convictions rendered by military commissions. Their offenses were characterized not as criminal matters but rather as acts of rebellion against the government itself. *See Military Commissions,* 11 Op. Att'y Gen. 297 (1865); *Ex parte Mudd,* 17 F. Cas. 954 (S.D. Fla. 1868) (No. 9899). Such use of military commissions has been repeatedly endorsed by federal courts, including as recently as this year. *See Mudd v. Caldera,* 134 F. Supp. 2d 138 (D.D.C. 2001).

Military commissions are not courts within Article III of the Constitution, nor are they subject to the jury trial requirements of the Fifth and Sixth Amendments of the Constitution. *See Quirin,* 317 U.S. at 40. Unlike Article III courts, the powers of military commissions are derived not from statute, but from the laws of war. *See Ex parte Vallandigham,* 68 U.S. (1 Wall.) 243, 249-53 (1863). That is, their authority derives from the

Constitution's vesting of the power of Commander in Chief in the President. "Neither their procedure nor their jurisdiction has been prescribed by statute. [Instead,] [i]t has been adapted in each instance to the need that called it forth." *Madsen*, 343 U.S. at 347-48. "In general — [Congress] has left it to the President, and the military commanders representing him, to employ the commission, as occasion may require, for the investigation and punishment of violations of the laws of war." *Id.* at 346 n.9 (quoting Winthrop, *supra* at 831).

I. MILITARY COMMISSIONS MAY BE USED TO TRY ALL OFFENSES AGAINST THE LAWS OF WAR. . . .

A. Congress Has Sanctioned the Broad Jurisdiction of Military Commissions to Try All Offenses Against the Laws of War

The UCMJ addresses the jurisdiction of military commissions in article 21, which is section 821 of title 10 of the United States Code. Section 821 is phrased somewhat unusually, because it does not *create* military commissions and define their functions and jurisdiction. Instead, it refers to military commissions primarily to acknowledge their existence and to *preserve* their existing jurisdiction. As explained more fully below, military commissions had been created under the authority of the President as Commander in Chief and used to try offenses against the laws of war before there was any explicit statutory sanction for their use. Section 821, which is entitled "Jurisdiction of courts-martial not exclusive," thus states that "[t]he provisions of this chapter conferring jurisdiction upon courts-martial do not *deprive* military commissions . . . of concurrent jurisdiction with respect to offenders or offenses that by statute or by the law of war may be tried by military commissions." 10 U.S.C. §821 (emphasis added). The jurisdictional provision for courts-martial that is cross-referenced is 10 U.S.C. §818 (2000), which defines the jurisdiction of general courts-martial to include "jurisdiction to try any person who by the law of war is subject to trial by a military tribunal." By its terms, section 821 takes the existence of military commissions as a given and clarifies that the establishment of broad jurisdiction in courts-martial will not curtail the powers of military commissions.

By expressly preserving the jurisdiction of military commissions, section 821 necessarily provides a congressional authorization and sanction for their use. Indeed, the Supreme Court has concluded that identical language in the predecessor provision to section 821 — article 15 of the Articles of War — "*authorized* trial of offenses against the laws of war before such commissions." *Quirin*, 317 U.S. at 29 (emphasis added). . . .

Indeed, if section 821 were read as restricting the use of military commissions and prohibiting practices traditionally followed, it would infringe on the President's express constitutional powers as Commander in Chief. *Cf. Quirin*, 317 U.S. at 47 (declining to "inquire whether Congress may restrict the power of the Commander in Chief to deal with enemy belligerents" by restricting use of military commissions); *id.* (declining also to "consider the question whether the President is compelled by the Articles of War to afford unlawful enemy belligerents a trial before subjecting them to disciplinary measures"). A clear statement of congressional intent would be required before a statute could be read to effect such an infringement on core executive powers. *See, e.g., Public Citizen v. Department of Justice*, 491 U.S. 440, 466 (1989).

The congressional sanction for the use of military commissions is a permissible exercise of Congress's powers under the Constitution. Congress has authority not only to "declare War," but also to "raise and support Armies," and "make Rules for the Government and Regulation of the land and naval Forces." U.S. Const. art. I, §8, cl. 11, 12, 14. . . . Congress has authority to "define and punish . . . Offences against the Law of Nations." *Id.* art. I, §8, cl. 10. Authorizing the use of military commissions to enforce the laws of war — which are considered a part of the "Law of Nations" — is certainly a permissible exercise of these authorities. Or, to be more precise, it is permissible at least so long as any congressional regulations do not interfere with the President's authority as Commander in Chief. *Cf. Quirin,* 317 U.S. at 47 (declining to address "whether Congress may restrict the power of the Commander in Chief to deal with enemy belligerents" through regulations on military commissions); *cf. also Hamilton v. Dillin,* 88 U.S. (21 Wall.) 73, 87 (1874) (stating that the "President alone" is "constitutionally invested with the entire charge of hostile operations"). . . .

B. Even if Congress Had Not Authorized Creation of Military Commissions, the President Would Have Authority as Commander in Chief to Convene Them. . . .

The Commander in Chief Clause, U.S. Const. art. II, §2, cl. 1, vests in the President the full powers necessary to prosecute successfully a military campaign. It has long been understood that the Constitution provides the federal government all powers necessary for the execution of the duties the Constitution describes. As the Supreme Court explained in *Johnson v. Eisentrager,* "[t]he first of the enumerated powers of the President is that he shall be Commander-in-Chief of the Army and Navy of the United States. And, of course, grant of war power includes all that is necessary and proper for carrying these powers into execution." 339 U.S. 763, 788 (1950) (citation omitted). One of the necessary incidents of authority over the conduct of military operations in war is the power to punish enemy belligerents for violations of the laws of war. The laws of war exist in part to ensure that the brutality inherent in war is confined within some limits. It is essential for the conduct of a war, therefore, that an army have the ability to enforce the laws of war by punishing transgressions by the enemy. . . .

C. The Use of Military Commissions to Inflict Punishments Without the Procedures Provided for Criminal Trials Under Article III, Section 2 and the Fifth and Sixth Amendments Is Constitutionally Permissible. . . .

At the time of the Founding, it was well settled that offenses under the laws of war were a distinct category of offense, unlike criminal offenses against the civil law, and were subject to trial in military tribunals without the benefits of the procedures of the common law enshrined in the Constitution. . . . Thus, under the settled understanding that the rights to jury trial and grand jury indictment do not extend beyond the cases where they were available at common law, those rights simply do not extend to trials before military tribunals for offenses against the laws of war. Such trials never included indictment or jury trial at the time of the Founding. . . .

The primary support for constitutional arguments to *restrict* the use of military commissions would be based on the Supreme Court's decision in *Ex parte Milligan,* 71 U.S. (4 Wall.) 2 (1866). . . .

We believe that the broad pronouncements in *Milligan* do not accurately reflect the requirements of the Constitution and that the case has properly been severely limited by the later decision in *Quirin*. . . .

Thus, the line that the Court ultimately drew in *Quirin* to distinguish *Milligan* may be read to suggest that a citizen (not in the U.S. military) can be tried by military commission *when he acts as a belligerent. See* 317 U.S. at 37. That condition was most clearly met where citizens "associate themselves with the military arm of the enemy government." *Id.* The distinction suggests that *Milligan* can be explained on the basis that the actions charged in *Milligan* did not amount to acts of belligerency. Even under this approach to *Quirin*, we conclude that in the context of the current conflict, any actions by U.S. citizens that amount to hostile acts against the United States or its citizens (and certainly participation in biological attacks, the attacks of September 11, or similar attacks) would make a person a "belligerent" subject to trial by military commission under *Quirin*.

We caution, however, that applying this standard may raise some ambiguities. The *Milligan* decision holds out at least the possibility that some charges that may be articulated under the law of war (such as the charge of giving aid and comfort to the enemy used in *Milligan*) may not, in some circumstances, amount to acts of belligerency triable by military commission. Exactly which acts place a person in the category of an "enemy belligerent" under *Quirin* thus may be a subject of litigation. In addition, it might be argued that *Quirin* should be read as imposing a brighter-line test under which citizens are triable by military commission when they "associate themselves with the military arm of the enemy government." 317 U.S. at 37. That standard, it could be claimed, is difficult to apply here because there are no organized armed forces of another belligerent nation facing the United States. For the reasons outlined above, we conclude that such an approach does not reflect the proper constitutional analysis and is not the proper reading of *Quirin*. Nonetheless, it raises a potential source of litigation risk. . . .

2. Enemy Aliens Seized in the United States

Even if *Milligan* might raise litigation risks for the use of military commissions to try citizens, it should not raise the same difficulties for trying *aliens* charged with violations of the law of war. . . .

III. UNDER THE LAWS OF WAR, THE TERRORISTS ARE UNLAWFUL COMBATANTS SUBJECT TO TRIAL AND PUNISHMENT FOR VIOLATIONS OF THE LAWS OF WAR. . . .

As noted above, the terrorists involved in the attacks did not meet even the minimal conditions required to be recognized as lawful combatants. It is open to some doubt whether persons acting without authorization of a state could *ever* undertake hostile acts without violating the laws of war. But we need not reach that theory to conclude that the terrorists did not meet even the most basic requirements for complying with the laws of war as lawful combatants. They were not bearing arms openly and wearing fixed insignia. Thus, all of their hostile acts can be treated as violations of the laws of war. It is settled that any violation of the laws of war may be prosecuted as a "war crime." The U.S. Army Field Manual, *The Law of Land Warfare*, provides that "[a]ny person, whether a member of the armed forces or a civilian, who commits an act which constitutes a crime under international law is responsible therefor and liable to punishment." FM 27-10 ch. 8, par. 498. "The term 'war crime' is the technical expression for a violation of the law of war by any person or persons, military or civilian. Every violation of the laws of war is a war crime." *Id.* ch. 8, par. 499. Specific offenses here could include violations of the rule prohibiting "[u]se of civilian clothing by troops to conceal their military character," *id.* ch. 8, par. 504(g), the rule prohibiting "[f]iring on localities which are undefended and without military significance," *id.* ch. 8, par. 504(d), and the rule prohibiting deliberate targeting of civilian populations.

In addition, individuals can be prosecuted under the laws of armed conflict using standard theories of aiding and abetting and conspiracy. The U.S. Army Field Manual provides that "[c]onspiracy, direct incitement, and attempts to commit, as well as complicity in the commission of, crimes against peace, crimes against humanity, and war crimes are punishable." *Id.* ch. 8, par. 500. Commanders can also be held responsible for war crimes committed either under their orders or by those under their command.

Patrick F. Philbin
Deputy Ass't Attorney General

Notes and Questions

1. *Establishing the Post-9/11 Military Commissions.* President George W. Bush relied upon the OLC memo set out above in promulgating a military order that authorized military commissions to try noncitizen terrorism suspects at Guantánamo, without going to Congress for more specific statutory authority. *See* Military Order of November 13, 2001, *Detention, Treatment, and Trial of Certain Non-Citizens in the War Against Terrorism,* 66 Fed. Reg. 57,833 (Nov. 16, 2001). Critically, the commissions were ordered to follow procedures that were to be established by the Secretary of Defense and that differed from those used in courts-martial.

The military order also gave the commissions jurisdiction to try "any and all offenses triable by military commission." *Id.* §4(a). This language was subsequently interpreted by the Bush administration to include some offenses that were not clearly established as violations of the international laws of war, such as providing "material support" to terrorist organizations, conspiracy, and solicitation. The inclusion of these "associational" offenses was both controversial and critical to the utility of the commissions, since only a handful of the Guantánamo detainees could be tied directly to specific war crimes (such as the 9/11 attacks themselves).

2. *The Hamdan Decision.* Pursuant to the military order, military commissions were instituted in 2003 against four persons, including Salim Ahmed Hamdan, a Yemeni national captured during fighting in Afghanistan, who was initially charged with inchoate "conspiracy." Before his trial began, Hamdan sought to challenge the legality of the commissions pursuant to a habeas petition, which, after the Supreme Court's 2004 decision in *Rasul v. Bush,* 542 U.S. 466 (2004), the federal courts then had the power to hear. The lower courts initially divided on the merits of his challenge, with the district court holding that the commissions were unlawful, *see Hamdan*

v. Rumsfeld, 344 F. Supp. 2d 152 (D.D.C. 2004), before a panel of the D.C. Circuit (including future Chief Justice John Roberts) reversed. *See Hamdan v. Rumsfeld,* 415 F.3d 33 (D.C. Cir. 2005).

In *Hamdan v. Rumsfeld,* 548 U.S. 557 (2006), the Supreme Court sided with the district court and invalidated the military commissions created pursuant to President Bush's November 2001 military order. At the heart of the *Hamdan* Court's analysis was *Quirin,* and the 1942 Court's reliance upon Article 15 of the Articles of War (now Article 21 of the UCMJ). As Justice Stevens wrote for a 5-3 majority (with Chief Justice Roberts recused), "Whether or not the President has independent power, absent congressional authorization, to convene military commissions, he may not disregard limitations that Congress has, in proper exercise of its own war powers, placed on his powers." *Id.* at 593 n.23 (citing *Youngstown Sheet & Tube Co. v. Sawyer,* 343 U.S. 579, 637 (1952) (Jackson, J., concurring)). And, as Justice Stevens explained, the Guantánamo commissions transcended two of those statutory limits, as well as the Geneva Conventions:

- Article 21 of the UCMJ, which, per *Quirin,* authorized military commission trials for offenses against the "laws of war," a body of law that, according to a four-Justice plurality in *Hamdan,* did *not* recognize standalone conspiracy as a triable offense;
- Article 36 of the UCMJ, which, at the time *Hamdan* was decided, required (a) that the rules and regulations governing commissions and other military tribunals be "uniform insofar as practicable," and (b) that the President formally certify when circumstances do not permit such uniformity; and
- Common Article 3 of the Geneva Conventions (which applied because the conflict in Afghanistan was a non-international armed conflict between the United States and Al Qaeda), which requires, among other things, that tribunals adjudicating the status of detainees be "regularly constituted courts" (which, the Court further held, the Guantánamo military commissions were not).

3. Overruling Hamdan? Could Congress simply change the UCMJ, or enact other superseding legislation, to overrule *Hamdan*? The *Hamdan* Court's 177 pages of opinions consisted almost entirely of statutory analysis, so the decision of the Court could effectively be overturned by Congress. But what about the effect of the Court's holding with regard to Common Article 3 of the Geneva Conventions?

4. Hamdan's Collateral Damage to the President's Post-9/11 Initiatives. *Hamdan*'s holding that Common Article 3 applies to the non-international armed conflict between the United States and Al Qaeda had significant implications for the treatment of detainees. See *supra* p. 1016. And its holding in footnote 23 (quoted above) that President Bush could not transcend statutory limits on his authority appeared to repudiate a theory of plenary and exclusive presidential power that had been invoked in numerous other contexts, including, again, detainee treatment and foreign surveillance. See *supra* pp. 643-646; 999; *see also* Stephen I. Vladeck, *Congress, the Commander-in-Chief, and the Separation of Powers After* Hamdan, 16 Transnat'l L. & Contemp. Probs. 933 (2007). Thus, even though *Hamdan* was largely a statutory decision, it remains perhaps the most *politically* significant Supreme Court decision in a post-9/11 counterterrorism case.

C. MILITARY COMMISSIONS AFTER *HAMDAN*

Less than four months after the Supreme Court's *Hamdan* decision, Congress responded by passing the Military Commissions Act of 2006 (MCA), Pub. L. No. 109-366, 120 Stat. 2600 (codified as amended at 10 U.S.C. §§948a-950t (2018)). Among other things, the MCA, which was significantly updated by the Military Commissions Act of 2009,[1] provided the express statutory authorization for military commissions that the *Hamdan* Court had found lacking. It also provided for appellate supervision of the commissions through a newly created Article I Court of Military Commission Review (CMCR) and the U.S. Court of Appeals for the D.C. Circuit, and it created a series of new procedural and evidentiary rules to govern the commissions (that were exempted from the Article 36 uniformity requirement that *Hamdan* had relied upon). In addition, the MCA identified more than two dozen specific substantive offenses that could be tried by the commissions, and it authorized trial for those offenses of any noncitizen who "(A) has engaged in hostilities against the United States or its coalition partners; (B) has purposefully and materially supported hostilities against the United States or its coalition partners; or (C) was a part of Al Qaeda at the time of the alleged offense under this chapter." 10 U.S.C. §948a(7).

Some of the offenses defined by the MCA, such as perfidy and attacking protected targets, are clearly recognized as international war crimes. They thus fall well within the Supreme Court's pre-September 11 precedents for military commissions, especially *Quirin*. Others, such as inchoate conspiracy and "providing material support to terrorism," are not nearly as well established as international offenses, as four Justices emphasized in *Hamdan*.

Critically for present purposes, these latter offenses have formed the basis for *most* of the post-MCA military commission prosecutions, including the convictions of Salim Hamdan (the petitioner in *Hamdan*) on material support charges, and of Al Qaeda propagandist Ali al Bahlul (whose case appears below) on conspiracy, material support, and solicitation charges. These convictions, in turn, provoked a series of challenges to the statutory and constitutional authority of the commissions to try offenses not clearly recognized as international war crimes — by far the most significant constitutional challenges to military commission jurisdiction since *Quirin*.

At first, the litigation focused on the Ex Post Facto Clause, since some detainees were tried for offenses that, whether or not they were violations of the laws of war, were committed prior to the MCA's October 2006 enactment. In July 2014, an en banc majority of the D.C. Circuit held (unanimously) that trial by military commission for material support and solicitation based upon conduct that predated the MCA's enactment in 2006 violated the Ex Post Facto Clause because there was no support, prior to the MCA, for trying such offenses in a military commission. Six of the seven sitting judges then held, however, that it was not plain error[2] under

---

1. For ease of reference, we use "MCA" to refer to the 2006 statute as amended in 2009, and cite to current U.S. Code provisions except where the difference between the two statutes matters.

2. Four of the seven judges concluded that al Bahlul had "forfeited" his ex post facto challenge by failing properly to raise it during his trial, which is why they reviewed the claim pursuant to the highly deferential "plain error" standard, rather than reviewing it de novo. *See Al Bahlul I*, 767 F.3d at 9-10. And although Judges Brown and Kavanaugh applied de novo review, they concluded that, even under that more rigorous standard, Bahlul's conspiracy conviction did not violate the Ex Post Facto Clause. *See id.* at 52 (Brown, J., concurring in the judgment in part and dissenting in part); *id.* at 63 (Kavanaugh, J., concurring in the judgment in part and dissenting in part).

the Ex Post Facto Clause for the commissions to try inchoate conspiracy, given the somewhat stronger historical precedents for military commission trials of that offense. *See Al Bahlul v. United States* (*Al Bahlul I*), 767 F.3d 1 (D.C. Cir. 2014) (en banc).

Reading *Al Bahlul v. United States*

The 2014 en banc Court of Appeals ruling left Al Bahlul's conspiracy conviction intact, but expressly declined to consider Al Bahlul's other constitutional objections to his conviction, including his arguments that military commission trials of domestic offenses like inchoate conspiracy violate Articles I and III of the Constitution. Instead, this and other claims were returned to the original three-judge panel, which handed down the following ruling in June 2015. Even though the decision that follows was vacated by the D.C. Circuit on rehearing en banc (as explained in more detail in the Notes after the decision), it provides the most detailed judicial discussion to date of constitutional limits on the jurisdiction of military commissions.

- Bahlul argued that his trial by military commission for conspiracy violated the separation of powers under both Article III and Article I. How are these arguments distinct from each other?
- Judge Rogers' majority opinion focuses heavily on *Quirin* to reject the Article III argument, concluding from it that law-of-war military commissions may not try "domestic" offenses like conspiracy. How do she and Judge Tatel explain their reading of *Quirin* (which *authorized* military commissions) as imposing constitutional limits upon the commissions? What modes of analysis does Judge Rogers use to support her claim?
- What does the majority say about Al Bahlul's Article I argument? What is Judge Henderson's answer? Do you think that Congress intended to identify conspiracy as a crime under the law of nations? Had it done so, could the court second-guess it?
- The Supreme Court has upheld non-Article III adjudication of some disputes by looking to a balancing test articulated in *Commodity Futures Trading Comm'n v. Schor*, 478 U.S. 833 (1986), that considers the following factors:

  > (1) the extent to which the "essential attributes of judicial power" are reserved to Article III courts, and, conversely, the extent to which the non-Article III forum exercises the range of jurisdiction and powers normally vested only in Article III courts, (2) the origins and importance of the right to be adjudicated, and (3) the concerns that drove Congress to depart from the requirements of Article III. [*Id.* at 851.]

  Why did Judge Henderson find that Bahlul's military commission passed the *Schor* balancing test? How did Judge Rogers respond? Is it clear why this balancing test should apply to military commissions at all?

Al Bahlul v. United States (*Al Bahlul II*)

United States Court of Appeals, District of Columbia Circuit, 2015
792 F.3d 1, *vacated*, 840 F.3d 757 (D.C. Cir. 2016) (en banc)

Rogers, Circuit Judge:... Bahlul contends that his inchoate conspiracy conviction must be vacated because: (1) Congress exceeded its authority under Article I, §8 of the Constitution by defining crimes triable by military commission that are not offenses under the international law of war; (2) Congress violated Article III of the Constitution by vesting military commissions with jurisdiction to try crimes that are not offenses under the international law of war; (3) the government put his thoughts, beliefs, and ideas on trial in violation of the First Amendment of the Constitution; and (4) the 2006 MCA discriminates against aliens in violation of the Equal Protection component of the Due Process Clause of the Fifth Amendment.

Because Bahlul's challenges include a structural objection under Article III that cannot be forfeited, *see Commodity Futures Trading Comm'n v. Schor*, 478 U.S. 833, 850-51 (1986), we review that challenge *de novo*, and we conclude, for the following reasons, that his conviction for inchoate conspiracy must be vacated....

II.

... The Supreme Court, based on the text of Article III and its own precedent, has continued to reaffirm that

> Article III is an inseparable element of the constitutional system of checks and balances that both defines the power and protects the independence of the Judicial Branch. Under the basic concept of separation of powers that flows from the scheme of a tripartite government adopted in the Constitution, the "judicial Power of the United States" can no more be shared with another branch than the Chief Executive, for example, can share with the Judiciary the veto power, or the Congress share with the Judiciary the power to override a Presidential veto.

Stern [*v. Marshall*], 131 S. Ct. [2594 (2011),] at 2608 (alterations and some internal quotation marks omitted) (quoting U.S. Const. art. III, §1).

If a suit falls within the judicial power, then "the responsibility for deciding that suit rests with Article III judges in Article III courts." *Id.* at 2609. There are limited exceptions: Congress may create non-Article III courts to try cases in the District of Columbia and U.S. territories not within a state. It may assign certain criminal prosecutions to courts martial and military commissions, *see Ex parte Quirin*, 317 U.S. 1, 46 (1942). And it may assign to administrative agencies the adjudication of disputes involving "public rights" stemming from federal regulatory programs. Bahlul was tried by a law of war military commission, so the question is whether conspiracy falls within the Article III exception for that type of commission.

A.

...[I]n the seminal case of *Ex parte Quirin*, 317 U.S. 1 (1942)...[t]he Supreme Court held that the law of war military commission had jurisdiction to try "offense[s] against the law of war," of which sabotage was one. *Id.* at 46.... "[S]ince the founding of our government" and continued in the Articles of War, Article III has been construed "as not foreclosing trial by military tribunals, without a jury, of offenses against the law of war committed by enemies not in or associated with our Armed Forces." *Id.* at 41.

In *Quirin,* the Supreme Court described the law of war as a "branch of international law," 317 U.S. at 29, and defined "the law of war as including that part of the law of nations which prescribes, for the conduct of war, the status, rights and duties of enemy nations as well as of enemy individuals." *Id.* at 27-28. The Court stated that Congress had

> exercised its authority to define and punish offenses against the law of nations by sanctioning . . . the jurisdiction of military commissions to try persons for offenses which, according to the rules and precepts of the law of nations, and more particularly the law of war, are cognizable by such tribunals.

Id. at 28. In addition to international precedents, the Court also considered domestic precedents (during the American Revolution, the War of 1812, and the Mexican and Civil Wars), but only as potential limits on the law of war. The Court explained:

> We may assume that there are acts regarded in other countries, or by some writers on international law, as offenses against the law of war which would not be triable by military tribunal here, either because they are not recognized by our courts as violations of the law of war or because they are of that class of offenses constitutionally triable only by a jury.

Id. at 29 (citing, as an example of the latter, *Ex parte Milligan,* 71 U.S. (4 Wall.) 2 (1866)). Thus, "our courts" may recognize fewer law of war offenses than other countries' courts, whether because they disagree about the content of international law or because of independent constitutional limitations. In the same vein, the Supreme Court recognized that Congress had "adopt[ed] the system of common law applied by military tribunals so far as it should be recognized and deemed applicable by the courts." *Id.* at 30. The Court in *Hamdan* [*v. Rumsfeld,* 548 U.S. 557 (2006),] likewise treated "the American common law of war" as a source of constraint, not expansion. 548 U.S. at 613.

The Supreme Court has adhered to *Quirin*'s understanding of the meaning of the "law of war" for over seventy years. . . . More recently, in *Hamdan,* the Supreme Court reaffirmed *Quirin*'s principle that the "law of war" means "the body of international law governing armed conflict." 548 U.S. at 641 (Kennedy, J., concurring in part); *id.* at 603 (plurality op.) (quoting *Quirin,* 317 U.S. at 30, 35-36).

The Supreme Court's reason in *Quirin* for recognizing an exception to Article III — that international law of war offenses did not entail a right to trial by jury at common law — does not apply to conspiracy as a standalone offense. The Court in *Quirin* held that the international law of war offense of unlawful belligerency was triable by law of war military commissions. Although the Court had no occasion to speak more broadly about whether other offenses came within the Article III exception, its reasoning precludes an Article III exception for conspiracy, which did entail a right to trial by jury at common law. . . . The reasoning in *Quirin* also counsels against expanding the exception beyond international law of war offenses. Stating that "[f]rom the very beginning of its history th[e] Court has recognized and applied the law of war as [being] part of the law of nations," *Quirin,* 317 U.S. at 27, the Court explained that some offenses may not be triable by military commission because "they are not recognized by our courts as violations of the law of war," *id.* at 29. No subsequent Supreme Court holding suggests that law of war military commissions may exercise jurisdiction over offenses not recognized by the "law of war" as defined in *Quirin.*

B.

The parties agree that Bahlul was tried by a law of war military commission that had jurisdiction to try charges for offenses against the law of war as defined in *Quirin.* The government concedes that conspiracy is not a violation of the international law of war. The question, therefore, is whether a law of war military commission may try *domestic* offenses — specifically conspiracy — without intruding on the judicial power in Article III.

The government insists that the Article III exception identified in *Quirin* is not limited to international law of war offenses because "the sabotage offense at issue in *Quirin* — which the Court viewed as akin to spying — is not and has never been an offense under the international law of war." Yet the Supreme Court in *Quirin* concluded otherwise. . . . The government points to scholarly criticism of the Court's conclusion, but this court is bound by the Supreme Court's analysis in *Quirin,* which was premised on sabotage being an international offense.

Alternatively, the government maintains that even if *Quirin* did not extend the Article III exception to domestic offenses, historical practice demonstrates that it has been so extended. The Supreme Court, however, when relying on historical practice to analyze the separation of powers, has required much more evidence of a settled tradition than the government has identified. . . .

The history on which the government relies fails to establish a settled practice of trying non-international offenses in law of war military commissions. . . .

. . . [E]ven if spying and aiding the enemy were not international offenses, their historical pedigrees stand in marked contrast to that of conspiracy. Both of those offenses have been subject to military jurisdiction since the ratification of the Constitution. Congress has reenacted the spying and aiding the enemy statutes on multiple occasions, and scores of law of war military tribunals have tried the offenses. . . .

The history of inchoate conspiracy being tried by law of war military tribunals is thin by comparison and equivocal at best. The government has identified only a handful of ambiguous examples, and none in which an inchoate conspiracy conviction was affirmed by the Judicial Branch. The examples are unpersuasive in themselves and insufficient to establish a longstanding historical practice.

First, although the charges against the Lincoln assassins referred to conspiracy, the specifications listed the elements of the completed offense. The Attorney General's formal opinion in 1865 described the charge as "the offence of having assassinated the President." 11 Op. Att'y Gen. at 297; *see id.* at 316-17. At the time, it was unclear that conspiracy could even be charged separately from the object offense, once completed. . . .

Second, although the charges against the Nazi saboteurs in *Quirin* included conspiracy to commit the charged offenses, the Court upheld the jurisdiction of the law of war military commission only as to the charge of sabotage and did not mention the conspiracy charge in its analysis. *See Quirin,* 317 U.S. at 46. . . . Moreover, in both *Quirin* and *Colepaugh* [*v. Looney,* 235 F.2d 429 (10th Cir. 1956),] the charged conspiracies involved completed offenses. By contrast, none of the underlying overt acts for

Bahlul's conspiracy conviction was a law of war offense itself, and the government declined to charge him with vicarious liability under *Pinkerton v. United States*, 328 U.S. 640 (1946), or with joint criminal enterprise....

Finally, the government asserts that any "enemy belligerent" can be tried by a military commission regardless of the offense. But the Supreme Court has focused on "the question whether it is within the constitutional power of the national government to place petitioners upon trial before a military commission for the *offenses* with which they are charged." *Quirin*, 317 U.S. at 29 (emphasis added). Thus, in *Quirin*, the Court "assume[d] that there are *acts*" that could not be tried by military commission "because they are of that class of *offenses* constitutionally triable only by a jury." *Id.* (emphasis added). Likewise, in [*In re*] *Yamashita*, [327 U.S. 1 (1946)], the Court "consider[ed] . . . only the lawful power of the commission to try the petitioner for the *offense* charged." 327 U.S. at 8 (emphasis added). In *Hamdan*, the Court explained that the status of the offender (being a member of a foreign armed force) and the nature of the offense were *both* necessary conditions for the exercise of jurisdiction by a law of war military commission.

C.

This court need not decide the precise relationship between Bahlul's Article I and Article III challenges. In *Quirin*, the Supreme Court's Article III analysis did not look to Article I at all. *See Quirin*, 317 U.S. at 38-46.... Upon examining the government's Article I contentions, we conclude that they do not call into question the conclusion that the Article III exception for law of war military commissions does not extend to the trial of domestic crimes in general, or inchoate conspiracy in particular....

Our dissenting colleague . . . maintains that this court must accord Congress "'extraordinary deference when it acts under its Define and Punish Clause powers.'" Dis. Op. 34 (quoting *Bahlul*, 767 F.3d at 59 (Brown, J., concurring in the judgment in part and dissenting in part)). This court has no occasion to decide the extent of that deference because the government has never maintained that Congress defined conspiracy in the 2006 MCA as a violation of the law of nations.... In maintaining otherwise, the dissent confuses acting pursuant to the Define and Punish Clause with identifying the content of the law of nations; Congress purported to do the former, not the latter. In Bahlul's case, the "law of nations" is not "too vague and deficient to be a rule"; to the contrary, it quite clearly does not view conspiracy to be an independent war crime, as the government has conceded....

Even if Congress has authority to criminalize non-international offenses pursuant to the Define and Punish Clause, as supplemented by the Necessary and Proper Clause, the government fails to explain why such congressional power to prohibit conduct implies the power to establish military jurisdiction over that conduct. Military jurisdiction over the offenses that the Supreme Court has previously upheld under the Define and Punish Clause — such as spying and sabotage — have a textual basis in the Constitution: The "Law of Nations," U.S. Const. art. I, §8, cl. 10, *itself* makes those offenses "cognizable by [military] tribunals." *Quirin*, 317 U.S. at 28. Court-martial jurisdiction similarly has a textual basis in the Constitution, which authorizes Congress to "make Rules for the Government and Regulation of the land and naval Forces," U.S. Const. art. I, §8, cl. 14, and exempts those offenses from trial by jury, *see id.* amend. V. . . . Military jurisdiction over conspiracy, by contrast, has neither an express textual basis nor an established historical tradition.

The government maintains that under the Necessary and Proper Clause, "[i]f commission of the substantive crime that is the conspiracy's object would be within the scope of permissible congressional regulation, then so is the conspiracy." But again, Bahlul's Article III challenge is not that Congress lacks authority to prohibit his conduct; rather, he challenges Congress's authority to confer jurisdiction in a military tribunal. Absent a textual or historical basis for prosecuting conspiracy as a standalone offense in a law of war military commission, the government's position is confounded by the Supreme Court's repeated reluctance to extend military jurisdiction based on the Necessary and Proper Clause. . . .

D.

. . . [T]he dissent maintains that if conspiracy does not fall within the Article III exception for law of war military commissions, then Bahlul's conviction must be affirmed under *Schor*'s multi-factor balancing approach. The Supreme Court has never suggested that an entire criminal adjudication outside an established Article III exception could ever satisfy the *Schor* analysis. . . . But even accepting the dissent's premise, its analysis fails on its own terms. Bahlul's military commission is on the wrong side of nearly every balancing factor that the Supreme Court has applied.

With respect to what the dissent characterizes as the "most important[]" factor, the 2006 MCA provides for appellate review "only with respect to matters of law, including the sufficiency of the evidence to support the verdict," 10 U.S.C. §950g(d). Sufficiency review is "sharply limited," *Wright v. West*, 505 U.S. 277, 296 (1992), and "very deferential[]," *United States v. Harrison*, 931 F.2d 65, 71 (D.C. Cir. 1991). This is exactly the type of limited judicial review the Supreme Court has repeatedly held offends Article III. *See Stern*, 131 S. Ct. at 2611; *Schor*, 478 U.S. at 853; *Northern Pipeline* [*v. Marathon Oil Co.*], 458 U.S. [50,] 85, 86 n.39 [(1982)] (plurality op.); *id.* at 91 (Rehnquist, J., concurring in the judgment); *Crowell v. Benson*, 285 U.S. 22, 57 (1932). . . .

Another factor the Supreme Court has considered is the "concern[] that drove Congress to depart from the requirements of Article III." *Schor*, 478 U.S. at 851. In non-Article III adjudications upheld by the Supreme Court, Congress's "concern" was the fact that an ostensibly "private" claim was so "closely intertwined with a federal regulatory program," *Granfinanciera, S.A. v. Nordberg*, 492 U.S. 33, 54 (1989), that the program would be "confounded" without the ability to adjudicate that claim. *Schor*, 478 U.S. at 856. Neither the government nor the dissent offer[s] any reason to conclude that otherwise-valid military commission prosecutions will be "confounded" by the inability to prosecute non-law of war offenses.

Bahlul's military commission fails a number of other *Schor* factors the dissent neglects to mention. The military commission resolves "all matters of fact and law in whatever domains of the law to which" a charge may lead. *Stern*, 131 S. Ct. at 2610 (internal quotation marks and alterations omitted). It "'issue[s] final judgments, which are binding and enforceable,'" *id.* at 2610-11 (quoting *Northern Pipeline*, 458 U.S. at 85-86 (plurality op.)), and "subject to review only if a party chooses to appeal," *Stern*, 131 S. Ct. at 2619. As for the "origins and importance of the right to be adjudicated," *Schor*, 478 U.S. at 851, the right to "[f]reedom from imprisonment" is one of the oldest and most basic in our legal system. *Zadvydas v. Davis*, 533 U.S. 678, 690

(2001). The circumstances of Bahlul's prosecution thus could not be further from *Schor.* There, Congress added to an Article I tribunal otherwise within an established Article III exception the authority to adjudicate a closely intertwined common-law cause of action, only with the consent of the parties, without authority to issue final enforceable judgments, and with meaningful factual review on appeal. Here, in Bahlul's case, Congress has created a *standalone* Article I tribunal to adjudicate his entire criminal case *without* his consent, *with* the ability to issue final enforceable judgments, and with *almost no* factual review on appeal.

If Bahlul's military commission falls outside the historical Article III exception for law of war military commissions, then there is no question that it usurps "the essential attributes of judicial power." *Schor,* 478 U.S. at 851 (internal quotation marks omitted).... The dissent struggles, unpersuasively, to avoid this conclusion. It suggests that military commissions somehow do not raise the same separation-of-powers concerns as bankruptcy courts, even though bankruptcy judges are appointed, supervised, and removable by Article III courts. It points to the established Article III exception for military commissions, even though the analysis in *Schor* is premised on the adjudication being outside of such an exception, as the dissent elsewhere acknowledges. The government, unsurprisingly, has barely presented any balancing analysis.

III.

For more than seventy years the Supreme Court has adhered to the definition of the law of war articulated in *Quirin,* which the government concedes does not prohibit conspiracy. The government has failed to identify a sufficiently settled historical practice for this court to conclude that the inchoate conspiracy offense of which Bahlul was convicted falls within the Article III exception for law of war military commissions. Absent further guidance from the Supreme Court, this court must apply the settled limitations that Article III places on the other branches with respect to the "judicial Power of the United States." U.S. Const. art. III, §1.

Contrary to the government's suggestion, vacating Bahlul's inchoate conspiracy conviction does not "cast doubt on the constitutional validity of the most prominent military commission precedents in our nation's history." The Lincoln assassins and Colonel Grenfel were tried by mixed commissions, whose jurisdiction was based on martial law. The lawfulness of military commission jurisdiction over the charges against the Nazi saboteurs and Colepaugh was judicially upheld without having to reach the conspiracy charges. Neither does our holding "inappropriately restrict Congress's ability, in the absence of broad concurrence by the international community, to adapt the range of offenses triable by military commission in light of future changes in the practice of modern warfare and the norms that govern it." Military commissions retain the ability to prosecute joint criminal enterprise, aiding and abetting, or any other offenses against the law of war, however it may evolve. Congress retains the authority it has always had to proscribe domestic offenses through the criminal law in the civil courts. The international law of war limits Congress's authority because the Constitution expressly ties that authority to "the Law of Nations," U.S. Const. art. I, §8, cl. 10.

Accordingly, we hold that Bahlul's conviction for inchoate conspiracy by a law of war military commission violated the separation of powers enshrined in Article III §1 and must be vacated. We need not and do not address Bahlul's other contentions.

Tatel, Circuit Judge, concurring: . . . In my view, the weight of the Court's language in *Quirin* strongly indicates that the law-of-war exception is exclusively international. Making this point repeatedly, the Court observed that in sending Quirin and his fellow saboteurs to a military commission, Congress had permissibly "exercised its authority . . . by sanctioning . . . the jurisdiction of military commissions to try persons for offenses which, according to the rules and precepts of *the law of nations,* and more particularly the law of war, are cognizable by such tribunals." [317 U.S.] at 28 (emphasis added); *see also id.* at 29 (calling the law of war a "branch of international law"). The Court made the point even clearer in *Yamashita:* military-commission authority derives from "the Law of Nations . . . *of which the law of war is a part.*" 327 U.S. 1, 7 (1946) (alteration in original) (emphasis added). . . .

. . . [A]lthough the Court held in *Hamdan* that domestic law — namely, the UCMJ — can *limit* the scope of military-commission jurisdiction, only three Justices would have extended that jurisdiction beyond the international law of war to the "American common law of war." Given this, and given that Article III courts are the default, that exceptions must be "delineated in [the Court's] precedents," and that the *Schor* balancing factors favor al Bahlul, this "inferior" court is without authority to go beyond the Supreme Court's clear signal, sent first in *Quirin* and repeated in *Yamashita,* that military-commission jurisdiction is limited to crimes that violate the *international law of war.* Instead, we must leave it to the Supreme Court to take that step.

Moreover, . . . were the government correct about Article I, Congress would have virtually unlimited authority to bring any crime within the jurisdiction of military commissions — even theft or murder — so long as it related in some way to an ongoing war or the armed forces. Congress could simply declare any crime to be a violation of the law of war and then vest military commissions with jurisdiction to try it, thereby gutting Article III's critical protections. The Supreme Court rejected that view of Article I in *Northern Pipeline.* There, the Court concluded that Congress had no authority to establish bankruptcy courts entirely outside of Article III's reach because any limit on such "broad legislative discretion" would prove "wholly illusory." *Northern Pipeline,* 458 U.S. at 73-74. Like the bankruptcy scheme the Court rejected in *Northern Pipeline,* the government's view of Article I would "effectively eviscerate [Article III's] guarantee of an independent Judicial Branch of the Federal Government." *Id.* at 74. . . .

Despite the government's protestations, moreover, this court's holding will not "inappropriately restrict" the nation's ability to ensure that those who conspire to commit terrorism are appropriately punished. After all, the government can always fall back on the apparatus it has used to try federal crimes for more than two centuries: the federal courts. *See* 18 U.S.C. §371 (criminalizing conspiracy). Federal courts hand down thousands of conspiracy convictions each year, on everything from gunrunning to financial fraud to, most important here, terrorism. *See* Center on Law and Security, New York University School of Law, Terrorist Trial Report Card: September 11, 2001-September 11, 2011 at 2, 7, table 1, *available at* http://goo.gl/Ks3Okc (since September 11, 2001, prosecutors have prevailed in almost 200 "jihadist-related" terrorism and national-security cases in federal courts); *id.* at 13 ("the most commonly charged crimes" have included violations of 18 U.S.C. §371, for "general criminal conspiracy"). For instance, Zacarias Moussaoui — the potential 20th 9/11 hijacker — pled guilty in federal court to six counts of conspiracy for his role in planning the 2001 attacks; a federal jury convicted Wadih el Hage, Mohamed

Odeh, and Mohamed al Owhali for conspiring to bomb the American embassies in Kenya and Tanzania; and Ahmed Abu Khattalah, who stands accused of conspiring to attack the American diplomatic mission in Benghazi, Libya, awaits trial in this very courthouse.

By contrast, although the detention camp at the U.S. naval station at Guantánamo Bay has held at least 780 individuals since opening shortly after September 11th, and although military prosecutors have brought charges against some two hundred, the commissions have convicted only eight: al Bahlul, Hamdan, Noor Uthman Muhammed, David Hicks, Omar Khadr, Majid Khan, Ibrahim al Qosi, and Ahmed al Darbi. Furthermore, due to various questions about the military-commission process itself, as of this writing only three of those convictions — Khan's, al Darbi's, and al Qosi's — remain on the books and unchallenged.

KAREN LECRAFT HENDERSON, Circuit Judge, dissenting: . . . My colleagues contend — as a matter of *constitutional law,* not simple comity — that the Congress cannot authorize military-commission trials unless the international community agrees, jot and tittle, that the offense in question violates the law of war. And the content of international law is to be determined by — who else? — the Judiciary, with little or no deference to the political branches. *Contra Rostker v. Goldberg,* 453 U.S. 57, 65-66 (1981) ("perhaps in no other area has the Court accorded Congress greater deference" than "in the context of Congress' authority over national defense and military affairs"). But the definition and applicability of international law is, in large part, a political determination, and the decision to try an alien enemy combatant by military commission is part and parcel of waging war. The majority opinion thereby draws us into a thicket, one in which our "lack of competence . . . is marked," *Rostker,* 453 U.S. at 65, our democratic unaccountability glaring, *Gilligan v. Morgan,* 413 U.S. 1, 10 (1973), and the ramifications of our actions unpredictable, *Holder v. Humanitarian Law Project,* 561 U.S. 1, 34 (2010) ("most federal judges" do not "begin the day with briefings that may describe new and serious threats to our Nation and its people").

The immediate consequences of today's decision are serious enough: my colleagues bar the Government from employing military commissions to try individuals who conspire to commit war crimes against the United States. But the consequences moving forward may prove more alarming still. My colleagues' opinion means that, in future conflicts, the Government cannot use military commissions to try enemy combatants for *any* law-of-war offense the international community has not element-by-element condoned. Their timing could not be worse. *See* Letter from the President to the Congress of the United States — Authorization for the Use of United States Armed Forces in Connection with the Islamic State of Iraq and the Levant (Feb. 11, 2015). And the beneficiary of today's decision could not be less deserving. Ali Hamza Ahmad Suliman al Bahlul (Bahlul) "is an alien unlawful enemy combatant who — like Hitler's Goebbels — led Osama bin Laden's propaganda operation." *Bahlul v. United States,* 767 F.3d 1, 33-34 (D.C. Cir. 2014) (*en banc*) (Henderson, J., concurring). He "freely admitted" — indeed, bragged about — his role in the attacks of September 11, 2001. *Id.* at 34. During his military-commission trial, he never raised any of the arguments we today consider. The *en banc* court deemed his Ex Post Facto challenge forfeited and reviewed it for plain error only. *Id.* at 9-11. We should have taken the same approach here, rather than declaring unconstitutional a provision of the Military Commissions Act of 2006.

Accordingly, I must dissent. . . .

II. THE CONSTITUTIONAL CHALLENGES . . .

A. Article I

Bahlul begins with an uncontroversial premise: "law-of-war military commissions" can try only those "offenses against the law of war." But he then embroiders that premise with needlework that produces naught but knots. First, he insists that the Congress's power to codify a law-of-war offense derives exclusively from the Define and Punish Clause, U.S. Const. art I, §8, cl. 10. Second, he argues that the Define and Punish Clause allows the Congress to codify a law-of-war offense only if the international community has expressly agreed, element-by-element, that the offense is cognizable. And based on the Government's concession that "conspiracy has not attained recognition at this time as an offense under customary international law," Bahlul insists that "[t]he answer . . . is both plain and uncontested": conspiracy falls outside the Congress's Article I power.

Both of Bahlul's embroidered premises are wrong. Even under the Define and Punish Clause alone, the Congress has the constitutional authority to codify conspiracy to commit war crimes by military commission. The international community *does* recognize that Bahlul violated "the principles of the law of nations, as they result from the usages established among civilized peoples, from the laws of humanity and the dictates of the public conscience," *Quirin,* 317 U.S. at 35, and the Congress has done nothing more than provide for "the limits or precise meaning" of those principles in authorizing the trial and sentencing by military commission for the violation thereof. 11 U.S. Op. Atty. Gen. 297, 299 (1865) (then-Attorney General James Speed's review of Lincoln conspirators' trial).

Bahlul's other embroidered premise fares no better. The Congress does not derive its power to enumerate war crimes triable by military commission solely from the Define and Punish Clause. As the Supreme Court has recognized, the "capture, detention, and *trial* of unlawful combatants" are "'important incidents of *war*,'" *Hamdi v. Rumsfeld,* 542 U.S. 507, 518 (2004) (plurality) (quoting *Quirin,* 317 U.S. at 28 (emphases added) (alteration omitted)), and the Congress's power to conduct war, in all of its "incidents," necessarily derives from its several Article I war powers *mutatis mutandis*. . . .

1. Define and Punish Clause

The Define and Punish Clause declares that "[t]he Congress shall have Power . . . [t]o define and punish Piracies and Felonies committed on the high Seas, and Offences against the Law of Nations." U.S. Const. art. I, §8, cl. 10. The power to "define" means that the Congress can "determine," "decide" or "lay down definitely" offenses against the law of nations. *Define,* Oxford English Dictionary (2d ed. 1989). The word "define" — especially joined by the conjunction "and" — has teeth. . . .

The Clause's history and text suggest two principles helpful to our interpretive task. The first is that international law derives from "a myriad of sources" and is "vast and always changing." [Peter Margulies, *Defining, Punishing, and Membership in the Community of Nations: Material Support and Conspiracy Charges in Military Commissions,* 36 Fordham Int'l L.J. 1 (2013)], at 24. . . .

The second principle is that "[t]he judiciary must give Congress extraordinary deference when it acts under its Define and Punish Clause powers." *Bahlul,* 767 F.3d at 59 (Brown, J., concurring/dissenting). The Framers recognized that "[d]efining and enforcing the United States' obligations under international law require the making of extremely sensitive *policy* decisions, decisions which will inevitably color our relationships with other nations." *Finzer* [*v. Barry*, 798 F.2d 1450 (D.C. Cir. 1986),] at 1458 (emphasis added). "[S]uch decisions 'are delicate, complex, and involve large elements of prophecy. . . . They are decisions of a kind for which the Judiciary has neither aptitude, facilities nor responsibility.'" *Id.* at 1458-59 (quoting *Chi. & S. Air Lines, Inc. v. Waterman Steamship Corp.*, 333 U.S. 103, 111 (1948)). Indeed, "[j]udicial deference to such congressional definition is but a corollary to the grant to Congress of *any* Article I power." *Eldred v. Ashcroft*, 537 U.S. 186, 218 (2003) (emphasis added) (quotation marks omitted). . . .

Mindful of the two principles discussed above — the inherently fluid nature of international law and the deference owed to the Congress's power to define offenses against the law of nations — we should examine whether the international community *permits* Bahlul to be tried by military commission rather than requiring that the charge against him, as defined by the Congress, *match*[] an offense expressly recognized by the law of nations as a war crime.

Bahlul was convicted of "conspiracy to commit war crimes." *Bahlul*, 767 F.3d at 5. The 2006 MCA defines conspiracy as including any enemy combatant "who conspires to commit one or more" law-of-war offenses and "who knowingly does any overt act" in furtherance thereof. 10 U.S.C. §950v(28) (2006). As is common in the United States, the conspiracy offense set out in the 2006 MCA has two elements: an agreement to commit a war crime and an overt act in furtherance of that agreement. *Cf.*, *e.g.*, 18 U.S.C. §371. . . .

[Judge Henderson then proceeds to explain how, although civil-law countries view conspiracy as a theory of vicarious liability requiring proof of a completed offense, international criminal courts have recognized at least *some* circumstances in which inchoate conspiracy may be prosecuted — including when the conspiracy is one to commit genocide or wage aggressive war.]

Discernible in this brief discussion is a common animating principle that, notwithstanding the differences in descriptive labels or elements, individuals who join together to further the commission of a war crime violate the law of war. Granted, the Congress did not include proof of a completed war crime as an element of the conspiracy offense included in the 2006 MCA. My colleagues characterize this omission as the *creation* of a new, purely "*domestic*" offense, as if it were made out of whole cloth. In my view, the Congress has taken a preexisting international law-of-war offense — conspiracy to commit war crimes — and eliminated one element. This it is constitutionally authorized to do within its "power to define" that Justice Story wrote about almost 200 years ago. [*United States v. Smith*, 18 U.S. 153 (1820),] at 159.

Nor does the Define and Punish Clause require the Congress to wait for the international community to catch up. The *Yamashita* Court did not play "Mother, may I" with established international law. Instead, it used what it viewed as the international law of war's "presuppos[ition]" and "purpose" in order to uphold Yamashita's conviction of "failure to prevent" war crimes, which failure "result[ed] in" war crimes it was "the purpose of the law of war to prevent." 327 U.S. at 15-16 & n.3. Moreover, it upheld Yamashita's war crimes convictions for *omissions to act;* even more cognizable as war crimes, then, are Bahlul's *commissions*. . . . In my view, the Congress can, consonant with the Define and Punish Clause, track somewhat ahead of the international community. The United States can be the standard bearer and take the reins in resolving difficult questions of international law related to the ongoing threat of international terrorism. . . .

. . . [T]he 2006 MCA . . . expressly enumerates conspiracy as a law-of-war offense triable by military commission. *See* 10 U.S.C. §950v(28) (2006). Inexplicably, my colleagues suggest that the Congress was *not* exercising its power to "define" the law of nations in enacting the challenged provision. The *en banc* court, however, necessarily recognized that the Congress *was* exercising its power to "define" in the 2006 enactment. Moreover, the legislative history accompanying the 2006 MCA makes plain that the Congress viewed itself as acting pursuant to its authority under the Define and Punish Clause. . . . Contrary to my colleagues' suggestion, the Congress does not need to incant any magic words to invoke its "define" power.

Bahlul's conspiracy conviction thus stands on firmer constitutional footing than Hamdan's, Quirin's or even Yamashita's convictions. The Congress has in fact *exercised* its Article I power to "define" conspiracy as an offense against the law of nations. The difference between this case and *Hamdan* is the difference between Justice Jackson's first and third categories, respectively. *See Youngstown*, 343 U.S. at 635-38 (Jackson, J., concurring). . . .

Accordingly, the Congress's decision to define conspiracy to commit war crimes as an offense against the law of war triable by military commission is consistent with international law — even if not a perfect match. Add to that the elevated level of deference we give the Congress in exercising its Article I powers and, to me, the inclusion of conspiracy to commit war crimes in the 2006 MCA is plainly within its authority under the Define and Punish Clause.

2. Necessary and Proper Clause

Next, the Necessary and Proper Clause augments the Congress's already ample Define and Punish Clause authority to codify conspiracy as a law-of-war offense triable by military commission. The Supreme Court has made plain that, "in determining whether the Necessary and Proper Clause grants Congress the legislative authority to enact a particular federal statute," courts "look to see whether the statute constitutes a means that is rationally related to the implementation of a constitutionally enumerated power." *United States v. Comstock*, 560 U.S. 126, 134 (2010). The constitutionally enumerated power here — the Define and Punish Clause — allows the Congress, at a minimum, to codify Bahlul's object offenses (*e.g.*, murder in violation of the law of war) as war crimes triable by military commission. Trying by military commission those who *conspire* to commit war crimes is "convenient," "useful," and "'conducive' to the . . . 'beneficial exercise'" of the Congress's power to authorize the trial of substantive war crimes and doing so is abundantly rational. . . .

3. Broader War Powers . . .

Before moving to Article III, one final point is in order. Both of my colleagues contend that, unless we stringently police the Congress's Article I powers, the Government will possess "virtually unlimited authority" to try enemy combatants by military commission. Yet, when it comes to issues of national security and foreign affairs, abstention — not aggressive policing — has always been our watchword. In addition, several limitations on military commissions remain, including the other jurisdictional requirements identified by Winthrop; the Bill of Rights (for U.S. citizens); and — at the very least — the existence of an ongoing *war.* This last requirement should not be minimized. We would be wise to remember that, in a democracy like ours, not every question calls for a *judicial* answer.

B. Article III

The heart of Bahlul's appeal is his claim that the Congress violated Article III when it made conspiracy triable by military commission. In my view, Bahlul invokes two separate provisions of Article III: the Judicial Power Clause, U.S. Const. art. III, §1, and the Criminal Jury Clause, *id.* §2, cl. 3. I analyze both arguments below.

1. Judicial Power Clause . . .

Section 1 of Article III vests the "judicial Power" in the federal courts, whose judges enjoy life tenure and fixed salaries. *See* U.S. Const. art. III, §1. The "judicial Power," as relevant here, extends to "Cases . . . arising under . . . the Laws of the United States." *Id.* §2, cl. 1. Axiomatically, these provisions require Article III cases to be adjudicated by Article III judges in Article III courts. And they restrain the Congress's authority to assign the judicial power to federal tribunals lacking the insulating protections of Article III.

Despite this analytic simplicity, however, "the literal command of Art. III . . . must be interpreted in light of the historical context in which the Constitution was written, and of the structural imperatives of the Constitution as a whole." *N. Pipeline,* 458 U.S. at 64 (plurality). The Supreme Court has recognized several historical — albeit atextual — "exception[s]" to the Judicial Power Clause. *See id.* at 63-76 (plurality). The deviations are justified by longstanding historical practice and "exceptional constitutional grants of power to Congress" over particular subject matters. *Id.* at 70 & n.25.

The military commission is one such exception. Like courts martial and occupational courts, the constitutionality of the law-of-war military commission is "well-established." [*Johnson v. Eisentrager,* 339 U.S. 339 U.S. 763 (1950),] at 786. Military tribunals predate the ratification of our Constitution and were used — without constitutional incident — during the Revolutionary, Mexican — American and Civil Wars. Moreover, the Constitution vests broad war powers in the Congress, and military-commission trials are part of waging war. Accordingly, placing the military commission outside the confines of Article III is "consistent with, rather than threatening to, the constitutional mandate of separation of powers." *N. Pipeline,* 458 U.S. at 64 (plurality).

As discussed earlier, the Congress acted well within its Article I powers when it made conspiracy triable by military commission. The challenged provision therefore falls within a historical exception to the Judicial Power Clause. The Supreme Court said it well more than 150 years ago:

> Congress has the power to provide for the trial and punishment of military and naval offences in the manner then and now practiced by civilized nations; and . . . the power to do so is given *without any connection* between it and the 3d article of the Constitution defining the judicial power of the United States; indeed, . . . the two powers are *entirely independent* of each other.

Dynes v. Hoover, 61 U.S. 65, 79 (1857) (emphases added). For this reason alone, Bahlul's Article III challenge should fail. . . .

My colleagues suggest, however, that the proper allocation of power between the Congress and the Judiciary turns on the latter's interpretation of *international law.* This approach is troubling enough under Article I; but the notion that international law dictates the operation of the separation of powers under *our* Constitution is outlandish. Indeed, the notion "runs counter to the democratic accountability and federal structure envisioned by our Constitution." Hon. J. Harvie Wilkinson III, *The Use of International Law in Judicial Decisions,* 27 Harv. J.L. & Pub. Pol'y 423, 429 (2004). Instead, if the challenged provision falls outside a historical exception to Article III, we must still assess it under *Schor. Schor*'s balancing test is the only one that considers factors that are *relevant* to the separation-of-powers concerns underlying the Judicial Power Clause. We should look to separation-of-powers interests to decide separation-of-powers questions.

Applying the *Schor* balancing test here, I believe the challenged provision does not violate the Judicial Power Clause. Granted, on one side of the *Schor* balance, a military trial for conspiracy implicates "private," as opposed to public, rights. This observation "does not end our inquiry," *Schor,* 478 U.S. at 853, but it means our review must be "searching." *Id.* at 854. Further, military commissions exercise many, but not all, of the "ordinary powers of district courts." *N. Pipeline,* 458 U.S. at 85 (plurality). . . .

On the other side of the balance, several factors indicate that conspiracy to commit war crimes can be constitutionally tried by military commission. First, and most importantly, the Congress has subjected the military commission to judicial review. The 2009 MCA, like its 2006 predecessor, allows the enemy combatants held at Guantanamo Bay, Cuba, to appeal their convictions to this Court, 10 U.S.C. §950g, after intermediate review by the CMCR, *id.* §950f. We then review *de novo* all "matters of law" that an enemy combatant preserves for appeal, *id.* §950g(d), with the opportunity of certiorari review by the Supreme Court, *id.* §950g(e). This safeguard "provides for the appropriate exercise of the judicial function in this class of cases" and keeps the military commission within the bounds of law. *Crowell v. Benson,* 285 U.S. 22, 54 (1932). . . .

Second, the military commission has very limited jurisdiction under the 2006 MCA. It "deals only with a particularized area of law" — namely, the law of war. *Schor,* 478 U.S. at 852 (quotation marks omitted). The 2006 MCA enumerates, in total, 30 war crimes, 10 U.S.C. §§950r, 950u-950v (2006), and only an "alien unlawful enemy combatant" is subject to military-commission trial, *id.* §948c. No one disputes that military commissions can — consistent with Article III — adjudicate expressly recognized international law-of-war offenses. An inchoate offense like conspiracy adds only a "narrow class of . . . claims . . . incident to the [military commission's] primary, and unchallenged, adjudicative function." [*Wellness International Network, Ltd. v. Sharif,* No. 13-935 (U.S. May 26, 2015)], slip op. at 13. This is not a case in which the Congress "created a phalanx of non-Article III tribunals equipped to handle the entire business of the Article III courts." *Schor,* 478 U.S. at 855. . . .

Third, "the concerns that drove Congress to depart from the requirements of Article III" tilt in favor of the challenged provision's constitutionality. The Congress chose the military commission over [the] Article III court for one overriding reason: national security. Among the discussed concerns were the potential disclosure of highly classified information; the efficiency of military-commission proceedings; the military's expertise in matters of national security; the inability to prosecute enemy combatants due to speedy-trial violations; the inadmissibility of certain forms of evidence; and, later, the risk of terrorist attacks on domestic courts. Unlike my concurring colleague, who believes that Article III courts are well-suited to try conspirators like Bahlul, I would defer to the choice made by the Congress — an institution with real-world expertise in this area that has rejected a one-size-fits-all choice of forum. In any event, the Congress's concerns are plainly legitimate; indeed, "no governmental interest is more compelling than the security of the Nation." *Haig v. Agee*, 453 U.S. 280, 307 (1981). And these legitimate interests demonstrate without question that the Congress did not "transfer jurisdiction to [a] non-Article III tribunal [] for the *purpose* of emasculating constitutional courts." *Schor*, 478 U.S. at 850 (emphasis added) (alterations and quotation marks omitted).

Finally, the system that the Congress has established — military-commission proceedings in the Executive Branch, appellate review in the Judicial Branch — "raises no question of the aggrandizement of congressional power at the expense of a coordinate branch." *Schor*, 478 U.S. at 856. . . . This is not the sort of legislation that raises separation-of-powers hackles. . . .

2. Criminal Jury Clause . . .

. . . As discussed earlier, the Congress has the Article I authority to require Bahlul to be tried by military commission. He therefore has no right to a jury. *See Quirin*, 317 U.S. at 40 ("[section] 2 of Article III and the Fifth and Sixth Amendments cannot be taken to have extended the right to demand a jury to trials by military commission"). . . .

Even if the Criminal Jury Clause did limit military-commission jurisdiction, it has no application here because Bahlul is neither a U.S. citizen nor present on U.S. soil. The Supreme Court has repeatedly held that the Constitution offers no protection to noncitizens outside the United States. . . .

Bahlul has no constitutional right to a jury and neither the Criminal Jury Clause nor the Judicial Power Clause of Article III can invalidate his conspiracy conviction. . . .

For the foregoing reasons, I respectfully dissent.

Notes and Questions

1. The En Banc Court Vacates Al Bahlul II. In *Al Bahlul v. United States* (*Al Bahlul III*), 840 F.3d 757 (D.C. Cir. 2016) (en banc) (per curiam), a fractured Court of Appeals largely sided with Judge Henderson's panel dissent in *Al Bahlul II* and affirmed Al Bahlul's conspiracy conviction — although no single rationale commanded a majority. Nine judges (all of the court's then-active judges, except Chief Judge Garland and Judge Srinivasan) participated in the decision.

Of those nine, six voted to affirm — four (Judges Brown, Griffith, Henderson, and Kavanaugh) on the ground that, "consistent with Articles I and III of the Constitution, Congress may make conspiracy to commit war crimes an offense triable by military commission." *Id.* at 758. Judges Millett and Wilkins, whose votes were necessary to form the majority, voted to affirm on narrower grounds — the former because of her conclusion that Al Bahlul forfeited his jurisdictional challenge, and that his conspiracy conviction was not plainly erroneous; the latter because "the particular features of Bahlul's conviction demonstrate that Bahlul was not convicted of an inchoate conspiracy offense," but rather of conspiracy to commit a completed war crime — on a theory of "joint criminal enterprise" recognized by international criminal law. *See id.* Three judges (Rogers, Tatel, and Pillard) jointly dissented, largely for the reasons set forth in the *Al Bahlul II* panel majority opinion excerpted above.

Note several curious features of this split result:

First, the absence of a majority rationale leaves the major constitutional question — whether the Guantánamo military commissions may try offenses that are not international war crimes — at least formally unsettled. And because the D.C. Circuit's ruling in *Al Bahlul III* leaves intact the Court of Military Commission Review's conclusion that the commissions may try such offenses, it is likely that the commissions will proceed on the assumption that they may continue to try such crimes, until and unless the matter is decisively settled to the contrary.

Second, the absence of a majority rationale may have also weakened the imperative for the Supreme Court to intervene, at least at this point, since either of the narrower grounds offered by Judges Millett and Wilkins might have provided enough of a reason for the Justices to believe that Al Bahlul's case did not require them to reach the major constitutional question. Indeed, one does not have to agree with either of the narrow concurrences (both of which are open to some fairly substantial critiques, *see* Steve Vladeck, *Al Bahlul and the Long Shadow of Illegitimacy*, Lawfare, Oct. 22, 2016), to believe that they complicated the case for further review — perhaps leading to the Supreme Court's denial of certiorari in October 2017. *Al Bahlul v. United States*, 138 S. Ct. 313 (2017) (mem.).

Third, a divided panel of the D.C. Circuit has also held, in *In re Al-Nashiri* (*Al-Nashiri II*), 835 F.3d 110 (D.C. Cir. 2016), that civilian courts should "abstain" from resolving pretrial jurisdictional challenges to military commission proceedings — and should take up such jurisdictional questions only where necessary as part of a defendant's post-conviction appeal. In *Al-Nashiri*, such abstention prevented the civilian courts from resolving in advance the defendant's claim that he could not be tried for his role in orchestrating the October 2000 bombing of the USS *Cole* — an attack that predated the September 11 attacks. *See* 10 U.S.C. §950p(c) ("An offense specified in this subchapter is triable by military commission under this chapter only if the offense is committed in the context of and associated with hostilities."); *see also id.* §948a(9) ("The term 'hostilities' means any conflict subject to the laws of war."). And more generally, *Al-Nashiri II* prevents the civilian courts from resolving the jurisdictional question in *Al Bahlul III* — perhaps the central legal question surrounding the Guantánamo commissions — until a post-conviction appeal of the *next* conviction for a non-international war crime, which, at this writing, does not appear to be on the immediate horizon.

In his concurring opinion in *Al Bahlul III*, then-Judge Kavanaugh decried the D.C. Circuit's refusal to settle the matter, one way or the other:

> The question of whether conspiracy may constitutionally be tried by military commission is extraordinarily important and deserves a "definitive answer." The question implicates an important part of the U.S. Government's war strategy. And other cases in the pipeline require a clear answer to the question. This case unfortunately has been pending in this Court for more than five years. It is long past time for us to resolve the issue squarely and definitively. [840 F.3d at 760 n.1 (Kavanaugh, J., concurring).]

Whatever you think the answer to the jurisdictional question actually is, isn't he absolutely right? Does anyone benefit from leaving this issue unsettled?

2. Defining Offenses. In her panel dissent in *Al Bahlul II*, Judge Henderson explained at some length why Congress should have some leeway, in identifying offenses under the Define and Punish Clause, to decide what the "law of nations" is. Note that the majority did not disagree. Instead, as Judge Rogers explained, "Even if Congress has authority to criminalize non-international offenses pursuant to the Define and Punish Clause, as supplemented by the Necessary and Proper Clause, the government fails to explain why such congressional power to prohibit conduct implies the power to establish military jurisdiction over that conduct." 792 F.3d at 18. Thus, the majority suggested that the "Article I" question (whether Congress can recognize the offense in the abstract) is entirely independent of the "Article III" question (whether Congress can subject that offense to trial by military commission), and so "[t]his court need not decide the precise relationship between Bahlul's Article I and Article III challenges." *Id.* at 14. Do you agree? If so, why did Judge Henderson devote so much attention to the scope of Congress's Article I power? On the majority's logic, could Congress make the "war crime" of inchoate conspiracy an offense triable in civilian, Article III courts?

3. International Law as a Constitutional Constraint? Perhaps the most significant holding of *Al Bahlul II* is the D.C. Circuit's conclusion that the exception to Article III for military commissions is limited, as in *Quirin*, to trials for "offenses committed by enemy belligerents against the law of war." Judge Henderson objected that "the notion that international law dictates the operation of the separation of powers under *our* Constitution is outlandish." *Id.* at 65 (Henderson, J., dissenting).

Note, however, that the *Quirin* Court justified the exception to Article III in the 1942 case by referring to the absence of jury-trial protections for international war crimes. Isn't *Quirin* itself, then, an example of "international law dictat[ing] the operation of the separation of powers" — albeit in *favor* of military commission jurisdiction, as opposed to *against* it? If so, isn't Judge Rogers correct that "the dissent's disagreement is not about *whether* international law constrains congressional authority, only *to what extent*," *id.* at 16 (majority opinion)?

If you agree with the majority on this point, and if Bahlul is otherwise protected by the Constitution's jury-trial provisions (which Judge Henderson disputes), then *Al Bahlul II* becomes an easy case, because the government conceded that conspiracy is not recognized as a war crime under international law. In a harder case, how will courts determine that it is sufficiently clear that a specific offense is recognized by the international laws of war so as to be triable before a U.S. military commission? *See generally* Stephen I. Vladeck, *Military Courts and Article III*, 103 Geo. L.J. 933 (2015) (offering a more detailed analysis of how courts should understand the relationship between international law and the military exception to Article III).

4. Formalism vs. Functionalism. On the "Article III" question, specifically, note the different methodological approaches taken by the majority and dissenting opinions. The majority suggested that the departure from Article III for military commissions should be construed narrowly, and only permitted when consistent with existing precedent. Thus, for the majority, the fatal problem with trying inchoate conspiracy before a military commission was the extent to which *Quirin* sanctioned military commission trials only for violations of the international law of war. As Judge Tatel explained in his concurrence, "The question in this case is whether conspiracy to commit war crimes falls within the military-commission exception to Article III as articulated by the Supreme Court." Contrast this formalistic approach with the more pragmatic "functionalist" analysis of Judge Henderson's dissent, which looked to the multi-factor balancing test the Supreme Court has used to define the permissible scope of other forms of non–Article III adjudication (especially the adjudication of "public rights," like tax claims, suits against the federal government, and other areas of government-driven civil adjudication).

Leaving aside the bottom line, which methodological approach do you find more appropriate in this context? Should courts take practical considerations into account in determining the permissible constitutional scope of military adjudication? If not, why not? If so, which considerations should and should not be relevant?

5. *Taking the Functional Argument Seriously.* According to the *Al Bahlul II* majority, at least, the formalism/functionalism distinction ended up being irrelevant because, "even accepting the dissent's [methodological] premise, its analysis fails on its own terms. Bahlul's military commission is on the wrong side of nearly every balancing factor that the Supreme Court has applied." Do you agree?

If you are inclined, like Judge Henderson, to uphold the jurisdiction of military commissions under *Schor*, how do you respond to Judge Tatel's concern that, under this approach, "Congress would have virtually unlimited authority to bring any crime within the jurisdiction of military commissions — even theft or murder — so long as it related in some way to an ongoing war or the armed forces"? What was Judge Henderson's limiting principle?

6. *Evidentiary Issues.* Although the focus of this chapter has been on jurisdictional questions, the commissions have also raised a bevy of complicated procedural and evidentiary issues — especially relating to the admissibility of evidence obtained through coercion. The November 2001 Military Order and the 2006 MCA were both far more tolerant of admitting evidence obtained through coercion than civilian courts typically are, as we saw in Chapter 35. But one of the major contributions of the 2009 MCA was to bring the military commission's evidentiary rules into closer alignment with the Federal Rules of Evidence:

10 U.S.C. §948r. Exclusion of statements obtained by torture or cruel, inhuman, or degrading treatment; prohibition of self-incrimination; admission of other statements of the accused

(a) EXCLUSION OF STATEMENTS OBTAIN BY TORTURE OR CRUEL, INHUMAN, OR DEGRADING TREATMENT. — No statement obtained by the use of torture or by cruel, inhuman, or degrading treatment (as defined by section 1003 of the Detainee Treatment Act of 2005 (42 U.S.C. 2000dd)), whether or not under color of law, shall be admissible in a military commission under this chapter, except against a person accused of torture or such treatment as evidence that the statement was made.

(b) SELF-INCRIMINATION PROHIBITED. — No person shall be required to testify against himself or herself at a proceeding of a military commission under this chapter.

(c) OTHER STATEMENTS OF THE ACCUSED. — A statement of the accused may be admitted in evidence in a military commission under this chapter only if the military judge finds —

(1) that the totality of the circumstances renders the statement reliable and possessing sufficient probative value; and

(2) that —

(A) the statement was made incident to lawful conduct during military operations at the point of capture or during closely related active combat engagement, and the interests of justice would best be served by admission of the statement into evidence; or

(B) the statement was voluntarily given.

(d) DETERMINATION OF VOLUNTARINESS. — In determining for purposes of subsection (c)(2)(B) whether a statement was voluntarily given, the military judge shall consider the totality of the circumstances, including, as appropriate, the following:

(1) The details of the taking of the statement, accounting for the circumstances of the conduct of military and intelligence operations during hostilities.

(2) The characteristics of the accused, such as military training, age, and education level.

(3) The lapse of time, change of place, or change in identity of the questioners between the statement sought to be admitted and any prior questioning of the accused. . . .

How different are these rules from those followed in civilian courts? Prior to the *Hamdan* decision, Justice Scalia, in an unguarded moment, reportedly said of proposals to try enemy combatants in civil courts:

> Give me a break. If he was captured by my army on the battlefield, that is where he belongs. I had a son on that battlefield and they were shooting at my son and I'm not about to give this man who was captured in a war a full jury trial. I mean it's crazy. [*Supreme Court: Detainees' Rights — Justice Scalia Speaks His Mind,* Newsweek, Apr. 3, 2006.]

Do you think it is crazy? If the military commissions' evidentiary and procedural rules really do increasingly come to resemble those that apply in civilian trials, what purpose would the military commissions serve? And if they really do diverge from those that apply in civilian trials, what does that say about the commissions themselves?

7. *Have the Military Commissions "Failed"?* As Judge Tatel pointed out in his concurrence in *Al Bahlul II*, the Guantánamo military commissions have a rather sobering track record. As of this writing, they have produced a total of eight convictions, only four of which (including only one of the three guilty verdicts in *Al Bahlul*) remain on the books. Six of those eight convictions were obtained via plea bargains; and only one of the other two (*Al Bahlul*) survived a post-conviction appeal to the D.C. Circuit — and barely, at that.

It would be one thing if these were growing pains, but serious problems continue to plague each of the three prosecutions underway at the time of this writing — of the five so-called "9/11 defendants," plus al-Nashiri and Abdul Hadi al Iraqi. In al-Nashiri's case, for example, the D.C. Circuit in April 2019 vacated three-and-a-half years' worth of pretrial rulings after determining that there was at least the appearance of bias from the former presiding judge, Air Force Colonel Vance Spath, who had been (successfully) seeking a job in the Justice Department as an immigration judge while handling pretrial matters in al-Nashiri's case. *See In re Al-Nashiri* (*Al-Nashiri III*), 921 F.3d 224 (D.C. Cir. 2019). That ruling, in turn, mooted (without resolving) a contentious, years-long dispute that had arisen over efforts by al-

Nashiri's civilian counsel to withdraw from the case after discovering evidence that their communications with their client might have been recorded by the government — and being ordered to not discuss that evidence with their client. *See id.* at 228-231 (summarizing the background).

The other two pending prosecutions have been beset with an array of similar (and also distinct) procedural and evidentiary questions — and show no signs of going to trial anytime soon. In the trial of the 9/11 defendants, especially, there continues to be detailed litigation over the extent to which the government can use statements obtained from interrogations of the defendants by an FBI "clean team," and the extent to which the defendants themselves can introduce evidence of their CIA torture.

All of this has led one of us to suggest that, however these legal questions are resolved, at least as a policy matter, "it's time for everyone to admit that the Guantanamo military commissions have failed." Steve Vladeck, *It's Time to Admit That the Military Commissions Have Failed*, Lawfare, Apr. 16, 2019.

> The commissions failed for a host of interrelated reasons. They failed because Congress made some fatally flawed structural choices in creating them in the first place. They failed because they couldn't escape the shadow of CIA torture of many of the defendants, which continues to play a role in so many of the evidentiary disputes in these cases. They failed because the judges refused to show the kind of independence vis-a-vis the government that might have helped to establish the commissions' legitimacy. They failed because the logistical difficulties of holding these trials at Guantanamo created inevitable delays that dragged out even the most mundane and routine aspects of the pretrial proceedings. They failed because no one in a position to make a difference ever stood up and said "enough is enough." The Bush administration didn't. The Obama administration didn't. And the Trump administration hasn't. [*Id.*]

Whatever the merits of this assessment, wouldn't we be better off if, as Attorney General Eric Holder proposed in 2009, these cases were moved into the civilian criminal justice system? Why or why not?

TRIAL BY MILITARY COMMISSION: SUMMARY OF BASIC PRINCIPLES

- Although *Ex parte Milligan* appeared to reject military commissions whenever (and wherever) civilian courts were functioning, *Ex parte Quirin* authorizes trial by military commissions even in those circumstances so long as (1) Congress has authorized the trial, and (2) the commissions are trying "offenses committed by enemy belligerents against the laws of war." *Quirin*, however, did not say whether military commissions might be constitutional under other circumstances.

- After September 11, the Bush administration relied heavily upon *Quirin* in authorizing military commission trials of noncitizen terrorism suspects for a range of offenses, including some (like inchoate conspiracy and providing material support to terrorism) that are not clearly established violations of the laws of war.

- In *Hamdan v. Rumsfeld*, the Supreme Court held that those commissions exceeded the statutory authorization Congress had provided (and also violated Common Article 3 of the Geneva Conventions), and were therefore unlawful.

- Congress responded to *Hamdan* by enacting the Military Commissions Act (MCA), which, in addition to expressly authorizing military commission trials of noncitizen terrorism suspects (and solving most of the other statutory problems identified in *Hamdan*), conferred jurisdiction upon the military commissions to try more than 30 offenses. These included inchoate conspiracy and providing material support to terrorism, even though neither is a clearly established violation of the laws of war.

- Although the D.C. Circuit subsequently held in *Al Bahlul II* that Article III prevents law-of-war military commissions from trying such "domestic" offenses, the en banc Court of Appeals vacated that ruling without settling the matter one way or the other. Thus, it remains an open question whether — and to what extent — the Guantánamo military commissions may try offenses that are not international war crimes.

- Since 2001, the military commissions at Guantánamo have also been beset with a series of challenging procedural and evidentiary questions, even as the rules have evolved to more closely resemble those of civilian criminal trials.

PART VIII HOMELAND SECURITY

37

Homeland Security

Long before the 2001 attacks on the World Trade Center and the Pentagon, the U.S. government had begun to develop extensive plans for a response to asymmetric attacks on the homeland. In Chapters 17-36 we examined the elaborate federal apparatus for detecting and interdicting terrorist threats. Here we consider what to do if and when those prophylactic efforts fail.

Federal government plans for homeland security have evolved considerably, particularly since September 11. As a result, the planning documents, organizational charts of the important players, and directives telling them what to do and when to do it have proven extremely ephemeral. Instead of tracing any particular plan for responding to a terrorist attack, we therefore approach the problem functionally. To set the stage, we begin by describing a credible worst-case scenario — an attack on the U.S. homeland using a weapon of mass destruction, and the responses of various government authorities. We next briefly review current federal government plans and authorities for responding to such an attack, particularly those involving interaction with first responders — local, state, and regional emergency personnel. We then consider the legal authorities for these first responders, focusing especially on the coordination of their roles. At the end of the chapter we examine federal authorities that may be invoked if a bioterrorist attack requires the compulsion of persons — isolation, quarantine, or vaccination — or commandeering of resources.

A. WORST-CASE SCENARIO: A PLAGUE ON YOUR CITY

Thomas V. Inglesby, Rita Grossman & Tara O'Toole, A Plague on Your City: Observations from TOPOFF

32 Clinical Infectious Diseases 436 (2001)

May 17: An aerosol of pneumonic plague (*Yersinia pestis*) bacilli is released covertly from a fire extinguisher at a benefit concert in the Denver Performing Arts Center.

May 20: The Colorado Department of Public Health and Environment receives information that increasing numbers of persons began seeking medical attention at Denver area hospitals for cough and fever during the evening of May 19th. By early afternoon on May 20, 500 persons with these symptoms have received medical care, and 25 of those have died.

The Health Department notifies the CDC of the increased volume of sick. Plague is identified first by the state laboratory and subsequently confirmed in a patient specimen by the CDC lab at Ft. Collins. A public health emergency is declared by the State Health Officer, who immediately requests support from DHHS's Office of Emergency Preparedness. The Governor's Emergency Epidemic Response Committee assembles to respond to the unfolding crisis.

Thirty-one CDC staff are sent to Denver. Hospitals and clinics around the Denver area that just a day earlier were dealing with what appeared to be an unusual increase in influenza cases are now recalling staffs, implementing emergency plans, and seeking assistance in determining treatment protocols and protective measures. By late afternoon, hospital staff are beginning to call in sick, and antibiotics and ventilators are becoming more scarce. Some hospital staff have donned respiratory protective equipment.

The CDC and the FBI are notified by Denver police that a dead man has been found with terrorist literature and paraphernalia in his possession; his cause of death is unknown.

The Governor issues an executive order that restricts travel — including bus, rail and air travel — into or out of 14 Denver Metro counties, and commandeers all antibiotics that can be used to prevent or treat plague. At a press conference, the Governor informs the public that there is a plague outbreak in Denver as a result of a terrorist attack, and he announces his executive order. Citizens are instructed to seek treatment at a medical facility if feeling ill or if they have been in contact with a known or suspected case of plague. Those who are well are directed to stay in their homes and avoid public gatherings. The public is told that the disease is spread from person to person only "if you are within 6 feet of someone who is infected and coughing," and told that dust masks are effective at preventing the spread of disease.

Confirmed cases of plague are identified in Colorado locations other than Denver. Patient interviews suggest that most victims were at the Performing Arts Center days earlier. It is announced that the Governor is working with the President of the United States to resolve the crisis and that federal resources are being brought in to support the state agencies. By the end of the day, 783 cases of pneumonic plague have occurred, and 123 persons have died.

May 21: Broadcast media report that a "national crash effort" is underway to move large quantities of antibiotics to the region, as the CDC brings in its "national stockpile," but the quantity of available antibiotics is uncertain. The report explains that early administration of antibiotics is effective in treating plague but that antibiotics must be started within 24 hours of developing symptoms. A news story a few hours later reports that hospitals are running out of antibiotics.

A shipment from the National Pharmaceutical Stockpile (NPS) arrives in Denver, but there are great difficulties moving antibiotics from the airport to the persons who need it for treatment and prophylaxis. Out-of-state cases begin to be reported. The CDC officially notifies bordering states of the epidemic. Cases are reported in

England and Japan. Both Japan and the World Health Organization request technical assistance from the CDC.

A number of hospitals in Denver are full to capacity and by the end of the day are unable to see or admit new patients. Thirteen hundred ventilators from the NPS are flown to Colorado. Bodies in hospital morgues are reported to have reached critical levels. The U.S. Surgeon General flies to Colorado to facilitate communications. Many states now are requesting supplies from the NPS. By the end of the day, 1,871 plague cases have been diagnosed throughout the U.S. and abroad. Of these, 389 persons have died.

May 22: Hospitals are under-staffed and have insufficient antibiotics, ventilators, and beds to meet demand. They cannot manage the influx of sick patients into the hospitals. Medical care is "beginning to shut down" in Denver.

Officials from the Health Department and the CDC have determined that a secondary spread of disease is occurring. The population in Denver is encouraged to wear face masks. The CDC advises that Colorado state borders be cordoned off in order to limit further spread of plague throughout the U.S. and other countries. Colorado officials express concern about their ability to get food and supplies into the state. The Governor's executive order is extended to prohibit travel into or out of the state of Colorado. By noon, there are 3,060 U.S. and international cases of pneumonic plague, 795 of whom have died.

The following day, May 23, 2000, this frightening exercise, called TOPOFF, was terminated. It had been organized by the Justice Department to test the ability of top officials at all levels of government to respond to a bioterrorist attack. Among the sobering results was the revelation that local health services — medical personnel, hospitals, and pharmaceutical supplies — were not nearly prepared to treat an outbreak of an infectious disease on such a large scale. Communications among local, state, and federal officials were unreliable. And responses were slowed by cumbersome decision-making processes or by a perception that no one was in charge. Other conclusions are described below.

> The unfolding situation precipitated a series of increasingly stringent containment measures. By the end of the first day, [a travel advisory was issued] . . . that restricted travel in 16 Denver Metro counties. . . . Some people, in fact, were reported to be racing out of the state. As part of the travel advisory, persons were advised to stay home unless they were close contacts of diagnosed cases or were feeling sick; in the case of the latter they were directed to seek medical care. . . . [T]he police and National Guard admitted . . . that they would be unable to keep people at home. . . . [B]y the end of the exercise, "people had been asked to stay in their homes for 72 hours. . . . How were they supposed to get food or medicine?"
>
> Throughout the unfolding epidemic, determining what information the public should be given and how quickly was an important and difficult issue. . . . It was clear that the public message itself would affect the capacity to control the epidemic, in that worried or panicked people might not seek the care they needed or, alternatively, might dangerously crowd health care facilities.
>
> Balancing the rights of the uninfected with the rights of the infected was considered a critical issue. One observer commented that a citizen might be expected to respond to the

series of advisories by saying, "You've told me I should just stay in my home, now you have an obligation to give me antibiotics." But there were not enough antibiotics to do this....

Sometime into the exercise, (notional) civil unrest broke out. People had not been allowed to shop. Stores were closed. Food ran out because no trucks were being let into the state. Rioting began to occur. Gridlock occurred around the city, including around health care facilities. The use of snow-plows was proposed as a way of clearing the road of cars. Given the constraints of the exercise, it was not possible to gauge the true extent of social disorder that a bioterrorist attack might evoke, but most observers and participants agreed that serious civil disruption would be a genuine risk in such a crisis.

The wide spectrum of disease containment measures which were considered or implemented illustrated the uncertainty surrounding what measures would, in fact, be feasible and effective. One senior health participant said that sufficient legal powers seemed to exist to carry out the decisions that were being made, and noted that legal authorities were not the problem. The critical issue was having access to the necessary scientific, technical, practical and political expertise, and having sufficient reliable and timely information available (e.g., the number and location of sick persons, etc.) to make sound decisions about how to contain the epidemic....

...Perhaps the most striking observation overall is the recognition that the systems and resources now in place would be hard-pressed to successfully manage a bioweapons attack like that simulated in TOPOFF.... [Inglesby et al., *supra.*]

Notes and Questions

1. Assessing the Emergency. The escalating crisis in the TOPOFF exercise shows the importance of rapid recognition of the nature of an emergency. According to a Department of Homeland Security (DHS) study,

> ER physicians, local hospital staff, infectious disease physicians, medical examiners, epidemiologists, and other public health officials should rapidly recognize the seriousness of the incident. Although laboratory methods to suspect preliminary diagnosis of the plague are available at many local public and private laboratories, there may be delayed recognition of the plague since most hospital ER and laboratory personnel in the United States and Canada have limited or no experience in identifying and/or treating plague.
>
> ...A rapid onset with large numbers of persons presenting at ERs with pneumonia should create high suspicion of a terrorist incident using the plague. Detection of the plague should also initiate laboratory identification of the plague strain and a determination of the potentiality of known antimicrobial drug resistance.... [Dep't of Homeland Security/Homeland Security Council, *National Planning Scenarios* 4-5 (Version 21.3 Final Draft, Mar. 2006), *available at* http://info.publicintelligence.net/DHS%20-%20National%20Planning%20Scenarios%20March%202006.pdf.]

The Centers for Disease Control and Prevention (CDC) encourages the reporting of possible outbreaks of various communicable diseases, including some that might be weaponized by terrorists. *See* Ctrs. for Disease Control & Prevention, National Notifiable Diseases Surveillance System (NNDSS), *Data Collection and Reporting* (updated Sept. 28, 2018), https://wwwn.cdc.gov/nndss/data-collection.html. If a local health official suspects such an outbreak, she should inform the state's health department, which will then notify the CDC. If a terrorist source is confirmed or is thought by the state health department to be probable, the FBI and other predetermined response partners are to be notified. Reports are voluntary, however, and state and local governments have adopted reporting protocols that vary considerably. Should reporting to the CDC be mandatory?

2. First Response. As soon as a bioterrorist attack is detected, a concerted, immediate response will be required to limit the loss of life. What measures would the first responders to such an attack take? The DHS planning document cited above includes this partial catalog:

> Persons with primary aerosol exposure to plague need to receive antibiotic therapy within 24 hours in order to prevent near certain fatality. The prevention of potential secondary person-to-person spread by fleeing victims will be a challenge. Epidemiological assessments, including contact investigation and notification, will be needed. Actions of incident-site personnel . . . include hazard identification and site control, establishment and operation of the ICS [federal Incident Command System], isolation and treatment of exposed victims, mitigation efforts, obtainment of PPE [personal protective equipment] and prophylaxis for responders, site remediation and monitoring, notification of airlines and other transportation providers, provision of public information, and effective coordination with national and international public health and governmental agencies.
>
> Evacuation and treatment of some victims will be required. Self-quarantine through shelter-in-place may be instituted.
>
> Tens of thousands of people will require treatment or prophylaxis with ventilators and antibiotics. Plague prompts antimicrobial prophylaxis of exposed persons, responders, and pertinent health care workers. Thousands will seek care at hospitals with many needing advanced critical care due to pneumonia caused by plague. Exposed persons will also need to be informed of signs and symptoms suggestive of plague as well as measures to prevent person-to-person spread. PPE (e.g., masks) for responders and health care providers should be available. Mobilization of the SNS [Strategic National Stockpile] for additional critical supplies and antibiotics will be necessary. Public information activities will be needed to promote awareness of potential signs and symptoms of plague. Proper control measures will include the need for rapid treatment; contact tracing; and, potentially, self-quarantine through shelter-in-place or other least restrictive means.
>
> Actions of incident-site personnel tested after the attack include protective action decisions, recognition of the hazard and scope, providing emergency response, communication, protection of special populations, treating victims with additional ventilators at hospitals, providing patient screening clinics, and providing treatment or drug distribution centers for prophylactic antibiotics. Mortuary requirements, animal-based surveillance to monitor potential spread of plague via natural methods, and veterinary services also will need to be considered. Since this is an international incident, the U.S. Department of State will provide appropriate assistance to U.S. citizens traveling or residing abroad, including the timely dissemination of information to allow citizens to make informed plans and decisions. [*National Planning Scenarios, supra,* at 4-6 to 4-7.]

Who should be expected to perform all these tasks — state and local personnel, federal officials, or both? What practical and legal problems can you foresee in implementing these measures?

3. Controlling Public Information. When word began to spread about the September 11, 2001, attacks on the World Trade Center and the Pentagon, Americans turned immediately to their televisions for news. They were rewarded with days of nonstop pictures, government press releases, and expert speculation about what had happened.

If an attack affects a wider area, as a chemical or radiological weapon might, or involves an infectious biological agent like plague, the public's involvement and cooperation in the response will be critically important. Members of the public cannot be expected to cooperate, of course, unless they receive some information about the nature of the emergency, as well as credible, authoritative instructions about how to respond. What form should that communication take?

In January 2018, in the midst of a highly public exchange of nuclear threats between the United States and North Korea, the Hawaii Emergency Management Agency broadcast this message to cell phones across the island state: "Ballistic Missile Threat Inbound to Hawaii. Seek Immediate Shelter. This is not a Drill." Emergency sirens were triggered, and widespread panic immediately ensued, with people flocking to shelters and crowding highways. Thirty-eight minutes later, the warning was rescinded — after it was discovered that it was a false alarm caused by a computer operator who mistakenly thought a drill was a true emergency. *See* Adam Nagourney, David E. Sanger & Johanna Barr, *Panic in Hawaii as Missile Alert Is Sent in Error*, N.Y. Times, Jan. 14, 2018.

How would you react upon hearing a message like this on the radio or reading it on your smart phone? If your answer is, "I don't know," or "I would panic," how do you think the message could be crafted to evoke a more helpful response? What other steps could be taken that might secure the desired reaction from the public? *See* Dep't of Homeland Security, *Public Safety Communications: Ten Keys to Improving Emergency Alerts, Warnings & Notifications* (Apr. 2019).

Can you think of reasons that the government might want to regulate media coverage of a catastrophic event? Do you think it should be able to impose limits on the dissemination of news? If so, can you say under what circumstances? See *infra* Chapter 41.

4. Civil Unrest. In the TOPOFF exercise, civil unrest (notionally, but predictably) broke out after a day or two. Can you suggest ways to avoid domestic violence in the wake of a terrorist attack? If such unrest is unavoidable, what government entity should be charged with responsibility for restoring order?

5. Exercising for Disaster. While the TOPOFF exercise was under way in Denver in May 2000, simulated terrorist attacks involving chemical and radiological weapons were occurring in other cities. Similar exercises today, now mandated by 6 U.S.C. §748 (2018 & Supp. I 2019), are conducted biennially. Now called National Level Exercises, they also feature notional attacks using cyber and other weapons, as well as natural disasters. *See* FEMA, *National Exercise Program: Base Plan* (Oct. 22, 2018). In 2014, for example, FEMA practiced responses to a major earthquake in Alaska and a nuclear weapon accident in Colorado. *See* FEMA, *National Exercise Program (NEP), National Level Exercise — Capstone Exercise 2014* (updated Feb. 6, 2014), https://www.fema.gov/media-library/assets/documents/90725.

B. THE FEDERAL RESPONSE ROLE

From 1950, when the Soviet Union tested its first atomic weapon, until the end of the Cold War, the American people lived in constant fear of a nuclear attack. For more than 40 years, the Civil Defense Act of 1950, ch. 1228, 64 Stat. 1245 (1951), as amended, directed the creation of a program to minimize the effects of such an attack on the civilian population and to deal with the resulting emergency conditions. Included in the program were planning for continuity of government, recruitment of emergency personnel, stockpiling of critical materials, and provision of warning systems and shelters. The Act purported to give the President broad powers in a civil defense emergency, for example, to take property "without regard to the limitation of any existing law," *id.* §303(a), 64 Stat. at 1252, and to provide the government with immunity from suits for damages to property, personal injury, or death based on its actions during such an emergency. *Id.* §304, 64 Stat. at 1253. The civil defense program, administered since 1979 by FEMA, was supposed to convince the American people and the Soviet leadership that the United States could not only survive a nuclear war, but also win one.

1. Stafford Act Authorities

The Civil Defense Act also provided for federal responses to natural disasters, such as floods and hurricanes. It was augmented in 1988 by the Robert T. Stafford Disaster Relief and Emergency Assistance Act (Stafford Act), Pub. L. No. 100-707, 102 Stat. 4689 (1988), providing broadly for federal financial and other assistance to states. In 1994, the Civil Defense Act was repealed, then partially reenacted as an amendment to the Stafford Act. National Defense Authorization Act for Fiscal Year 1995, Pub. L. No. 103-337, §§3411, 3412, 108 Stat. 2663, 3100-3111 (1994). The House Armed Services Committee reported at the time, ironically, that "the program has lost its defense emphasis. . . . Rather, the chief threats today come from tornadoes, earthquakes, floods, chemical spills, and the like." H.R. Rep. No. 103-499, at 5 (1994).

The Stafford Act, as amended, 42 U.S.C. §§5121-5207 (2018 & Supp. I 2019), may be invoked in the event of a presidentially declared "major disaster" or "emergency," including "any natural catastrophe . . . or, regardless of cause, any fire, flood, or explosion," when the President finds that "the situation is of such severity and magnitude that effective response is beyond the capabilities of the State and the affected local governments and that Federal assistance is necessary." *Id.* §§5122, 5170(a), 5191(a). While the President's declaration will usually be based on a state governor's request for help, the President may act without such a request in an "emergency" when "the primary responsibility for response rests with the United States." *Id.* §5191(b).

Alfred P. Murrah Federal Building, Oklahoma City, following a terrorist attack on April 19, 1995. FBI photo.

President Clinton declared an emergency under the Stafford Act on April 19, 1995, in response to the terrorist bombing that day of the Alfred P. Murrah Federal

Building in Oklahoma City, and he ordered FEMA to direct and coordinate responses by other federal agencies and provide needed federal assistance. 60 Fed. Reg. 22,579 (May 8, 1995); *see also* 60 Fed. Reg. 21,819 (May 3, 1995) (declaring a "major disaster" and providing public and individual assistance). The Stafford Act was also invoked on September 11, 2001, when President Bush declared a "major disaster" in the State of New York in order to make available various forms of public and individual assistance, 66 Fed. Reg. 48,682-01, and on August 31, 2005, for Louisiana, Mississippi, and Alabama, following the landfall of Hurricane Katrina. The White House, *The Federal Response to Hurricane Katrina: Lessons Learned* 33 (Feb. 2006).

Recent terrorist attacks like shootings in San Bernardino in 2015 and Las Vegas in 2017 caused extensive loss of life but did not prompt Stafford Act declarations, because they did not involve "fire, flood, or explosion." For the same reason, the Stafford Act would not have provided relief in response to the plague attack described in the TOPOFF exercise, *supra.* Proposals to extend coverage of the Act to include such events are outlined in Bruce R. Lindsay, *Stafford Act Assistance and Acts of Terrorism* (Cong. Res. Serv. R44801), Jan. 16, 2019.

2. The Homeland Security Act and Related Directives

The Homeland Security Act of 2002, Pub. L. No. 107-296, 116 Stat. 2135 (codified as amended in scattered sections of 6 U.S.C. and other titles), directed the Secretary of the new Department of Homeland Security (DHS) to "build a comprehensive national incident management system with Federal, State, and local government personnel, agencies, and authorities, to respond to . . . [terrorist] attacks and disasters." 6 U.S.C. §312(5). The Act required the Secretary to "consolidate existing Federal Government emergency response plans into a single, coordinated national response plan." *Id.* §312(6). It merged all or portions of 22 federal agencies and 180,000 employees into the DHS. Included were the Coast Guard, Customs Service, Transportation Security Administration, FEMA, Secret Service, parts of the Immigration and Naturalization Service, and a long list of less well-known federal entities. The Act designated DHS as the lead agency for coordinating disaster and emergency response and recovery assistance with state and local authorities.

In 2003 the White House published Homeland Security Presidential Directive/ HSPD-5, *Management of Domestic Incidents* (Feb. 28, 2003), which is meant to "ensure that all levels of the government across the Nation have the capability to work efficiently and effectively together, using a national approach to domestic incident management." *Id.* ¶(3). It declares that the Secretary of Homeland Security is the "principal Federal official for domestic incident management." *Id.* ¶(4). The Secretary of Health and Human Services (HHS) shares responsibility with DHS for biological incidents, while the Attorney General is given lead responsibility for criminal investigations of terrorist threats or acts within the United States, and is directed to "coordinate the activities of other members of the law enforcement community to detect, prevent, preempt, and disrupt terrorist attacks against the United States." *Id.* ¶(8). In addition, the Defense Department may provide military support to civil authorities in a domestic incident, but always under the command of the Secretary of Defense. *Id.* ¶(9). While states have the primary role in responding to emergencies, DHS responsibilities are triggered when a federal agency acting under its own authority has requested DHS assistance, when state and local resources are overwhelmed and request federal assistance, when more than one federal agency has become involved in responding to an incident, or when the President directs the Secretary of Homeland Security to assume management of an incident. *Id.* ¶¶(4), (6).

HSPD-5 also ordered the creation of a National Incident Management System (NIMS), to provide a flexible national framework within which governments at all levels and private entities can work together to manage domestic "incidents." The NIMS was rolled out a year later. FEMA, *National Incident Management System* (updated Oct. 9, 2019), http://www.fema.gov/national-incident-management-system.

HSPD-5 was augmented in 2011 by Presidential Policy Directive/PPD-8, *National Preparedness* (Mar. 30, 2011), http://www.dhs.gov/xlibrary/assets/presidential-policy-directive-8-national-preparedness.pdf.

3. DHS Response Plans

HSPD-5 called for development of a National Response Plan (NRP) to provide for a coordinated, all-hazards approach to "incident management." Published in January 2005, the NRP spelled out in broad terms the roles of various elements of the national government, and created a framework for federal interaction with state, local, and tribal authorities and with the private sector in an emergency. Weaknesses in the NRP were exposed in the deeply flawed federal response to Hurricane Katrina later in 2005, however, prompting Congress to amend the Stafford Act to allow accelerated federal assistance, without a state request, when necessary to save lives, prevent suffering, and mitigate severe damage. 42 U.S.C. §5170a(6) (2018).

In January 2008 DHS released a reinvented NRP — the National Response Framework (NRF) — now in a fourth version. Dep't of Homeland Security, *National Response Framework* (4th ed. Oct. 28, 2019). The NRF describes in very broad terms federal responses to "incidents that range from the serious but purely local to those that are catastrophic and national in scope." *Id.* at 2. Echoing the language of the Homeland Security Act, it declares that "the Secretary of Homeland Security . . . [p]rovides the Executive Branch with an overall architecture for domestic incident management, and coordinates the Federal response, as required." *Id.* at 34.

FEMA has undertaken more detailed planning in FEMA, *Federal Interagency Operational Plans* (May 2, 2018), http://www.fema.gov/federal-interagency-operational-plans. Five FIOPs, as they are referred to, deal, respectively, with prevention, protection, mitigation, response, and recovery efforts following an incident that warrants federal intervention. They are lengthy, ambitious plans focused on the practical *functions* of relevant federal agencies, rather than on the agencies themselves, and they acknowledge obvious overlaps in responsibilities, thus avoiding to some degree the balkanization that characterized earlier planning efforts.

The *Prevention FIOP* aims to

> unif[y] the collective capabilities of the Federal Government to respond to an imminent threat, terrorist attack, and/or follow-on attack. In the instances of imminent terrorist threats and suspected acts of terrorism, prevention activities include the law enforcement response; public safety; crime scene security and preservation of evidence; render safe of chemical, biological, radiological, nuclear, or high-yield explosive (CBRNE) devices; tactical missions; and counterterrorism, counterintelligence, and criminal investigative activities. [Dep't of Homeland Security, *Response Federal Interagency Operational Plan* 4-5 (2d ed. Aug. 2016).]

It is mainly concerned with what DHS insiders refer to as "left of boom" threats—precursors to actual attacks. Details, however, have not been made public.

The *Mitigation FIOP* seeks to reduce the loss of life and property by lessening the impact of an incident after it occurs. The goal of the *Protection FIOP* is to protect people, communities, and vital facilities in the aftermath of a catastrophic incident. The *Recovery FIOP* is designed to help communities affected by a catastrophe get back on their feet.

The *Response FIOP*, anticipating a worst-case scenario, outlines the federal response to "[m]ultiple catastrophic incidents or attacks [that] occur with little or no warning," with cascading effects, possibly caused by terrorists, when local, state, and tribal resources are exhausted. *Id.* at 9-11. Like the other FIOPs, this one addresses agency interdependencies and integration of agency efforts. It also describes the critical tasks and responsibilities of each agency. For example, it gives the FBI lead agency responsibility for domestic intelligence and counterterrorism investigations, while the Defense Secretary "provides defense support to civil authorities for domestic incidents, as directed by the President, or when consistent with military readiness and appropriate under the circumstances and the law." *Id.* at C-6 to C-7. Individual agencies are left to develop their own detailed response plans, however, and some of these are, predictably, classified.

Notes and Questions

1. *Adequacy of Emergency Response Authority.* The *National Response Framework* is written in very general terms. The more recent FIOPs are more detailed, but only in comparison to the NRF. Without knowing the details of individual agency emergency plans, and based on the brief descriptions of the planning documents outlined here, do you believe that DHS has set the right priorities in planning? Can you guess how to measure progress toward a goal of national preparedness? If you think a different approach is needed, what would it be?

2. *The Importance of Coordination.* The concept of "unified command" is central to the NRF and NIMS. In contrast to a military-type chain of command, unified command takes into account that there may be multiple agencies and jurisdictions responding to an emergency. Designated leaders of those entities work together to establish a common set of objectives, and they agree upon a single operations plan (SOP) for responding to the event. In operational terms unified command under the NRF and NIMS is facilitated through a Joint Field Office (JFO). What will be required in practical terms to create a viable SOP and to implement it in a crisis?

FEMA also coordinates support through 15 Emergency Support Functions (ESFs), each headed by a lead federal agency, as described in the NRF. They are intended to integrate federal capabilities in support of state and local response agencies. How will an official of a federal, state, or local government agency know what is expected of them—and what the limits of their authority are—in the midst of a catastrophic incident?

3. *The Legal Status of Federal Planning Documents.* The Homeland Security Act expressly grants rulemaking authority to DHS and states that the issuance of DHS

regulations is generally governed by the Administrative Procedure Act (APA). 6 U.S.C. §112(e). However, DHS took the position that because the National Response Framework and its associated planning documents are simply guidance documents, intended to create no binding or enforceable norms, it was not required to publish a Notice of Proposed Rulemaking or to invite public comments, as the APA normally requires for binding agency regulations. Might a more transparent and participatory rulemaking process produce better plans? Are there good reasons here to bypass the APA?

4. A Military Role? Each state's National Guard has elements trained and equipped to assist, under the direction of the state governor, in the response to a terrorist attack or a large natural disaster. At the federal level, the Stafford Act, the NRF, and other planning documents assign the Defense Department a supporting role in responding to a terrorist attack, including one involving a weapon of mass destruction. Should the military be given a larger role, or even lead agency responsibility? Consideration was given to such proposals in the wake of the flawed response to Hurricane Katrina. *See* David E. Sanger, *Bush Wants to Consider Broadening of Military's Powers During Natural Disasters,* N.Y. Times, Sept. 27, 2005. Do you think either the states or the federal government could mount a fully effective response to such a calamity without the assistance of military forces? The domestic deployment of troops for various purposes is explored in the next chapter.

5. The Greatest Homeland Security Threat? The Department of Homeland Security believes that "[o]ur daily life, economic vitality, and national security depend on a stable, safe, and resilient cyberspace." Dep't of Homeland Security, *Cybersecurity* (June 5, 2019), https://www.dhs.gov/topic/cybersecurity. It reported in 2018 that Russia had hacked into control systems for U.S. power plants, water supplies, and electrical distribution systems, and planted malware there. Reacting to this and other cyber threats, DHS has announced a new *Cybersecurity Strategy* (May 15, 2018), the goals of which are, *inter alia,* to "partner with key stakeholders to ensure that national cybersecurity risks are adequately managed" and to "minimize consequences from potentially significant cyber incidents through coordinated community-wide response efforts," as well as to fight Internet-based crime. *Id.* at 3.

Couched in very general terms, the *Strategy* calls for promotion of best cyber practices, development of international standards, and improved communications among stakeholders, with DHS playing a coordinating role. It does not call for new regulations that would require private owners of critical infrastructure to do anything, however; compliance apparently would be strictly voluntary. In the event of a "significant cyber incident," the *Strategy* declares, DHS will coordinate a government-wide response. But it offers no details to indicate how, for example, it might respond to an extended, widespread attack on the electric grid, although it expects to plan and exercise for such a response.

The Cybersecurity and Infrastructure Security Agency Act (CISA) of 2018, Pub. L. No. 115-278, 132 Stat. 4168, rebranded the National Protection and Programs Directorate of DHS to create a new Cybersecurity and Infrastructure Security Agency, whose job it is to "coordinate a national effort to secure and protect against critical infrastructure risks." *Id.* §2(c)(4). Included within its responsibilities are assessing the vulnerabilities of key resources and critical infrastructure, developing a plan for securing them, and furnishing technical assistance to entities affected by cyber risks.

It is also directed to facilitate information sharing and coordinate responses to actual threats. *Id.* §2(a)(4). But like the DHS *Cybersecurity Strategy*, the Act did not create new authority to require any non-government entity to do anything under any circumstances.

Do you believe we can, or should, rely on private owner/operators of critical infrastructure to adhere voluntarily to DHS's recommended best cyber practices, or to cooperate in responding to a cyber attack? Can you describe practical and legally enforceable regulations that would require their cooperation?

6. Viability of Plans? Any response plans need to promise some predictability about the future. They should provide reasonable assurance that if all our defenses fail and we suffer another catastrophic terrorist attack, basic government structures will nevertheless survive, citizens will be protected from further harm, and normal life will eventually be substantially restored. Furthermore, both the existence of the plans and their viability must be made widely known. If the worst happens, members of the public must be convinced that it is in their best interests to cooperate in the implementation of the plan. The President should be convinced that even in a great crisis the rule of law can provide needed security — that she need not, for example, declare martial law. And potential terrorists should be deterred by the knowledge that if they attack, the American people will not lose faith in their government.

Do the DHS plans reviewed here provide these assurances? Any thoughtful answer must recognize the staggering complexity of the task, as well as the remarkable progress made since 9/11. Yet much remains to be done.

C. FIRST RESPONDERS: STATE AND LOCAL RESPONSES

State and local authorities are always the first responders. State constitutions and statutes typically give governors and public health officials broad discretion to act to protect public health and safety, and in an emergency to suspend laws and administrative rules, order evacuations and quarantines, commandeer resources, and control property. If terrorists launch an attack in the United States using chemical, biological, radiological, or nuclear weapons or high explosives, the first response will come from local police, EMTs, hospital and other public health personnel, firefighters, HAZMAT teams, National Guard forces, NGOs (like the Red Cross), private sector entities (such as public utilities), and individual citizens — seeking to contain the damage, minister to the injured, restore order, and collect evidence for a criminal prosecution.

Even if the overall scale and complexity of an incident quickly overwhelm local authorities, their initial response will be critically important until federal help arrives, and their cooperation will be essential afterward. Thus, the *National Response Framework* and its supporting guidance documents contemplate a "tiered" response to all types of incidents: (1) relying on state, local, and tribal first responders to the greatest extent possible; (2) providing well-rehearsed and carefully coordinated federal support when necessary, often under the Stafford Act; (3) taking federal control of a response only when there is no reasonable alternative; and (4) returning control to local authorities at the earliest possible moment. "Incident management begins and ends locally, and most incidents are managed or executed at the closest possible geographical, organizational, and jurisdictional levels." *National Response Framework, supra,* at 15.

The critical role of local first responders was apparent in the immediate aftermath of the 9/11 terrorist attacks. When the World Trade Center towers fell, New York City police, fire fighters, and New York National Guard troops displayed enormous bravery and dedication in assisting survivors and restoring order in lower Manhattan. Meanwhile, after American Airlines Flight 77 struck the Pentagon, the reaction of state and local officials in Virginia and surrounding areas demonstrated the importance of planning and cooperation at all levels of government.

The 9/11 Commission Report: Final Report of the National Commission on Terrorist Attacks upon the United States

pp. 311-315 (2004)

The emergency response at the Pentagon represented a mix of local, state, and federal jurisdictions and was generally effective. It overcame the inherent complications of a response across jurisdictions because the Incident Command System, a formalized management structure for emergency response, was in place in the National Capital Region on 9/11.

Because of the nature of the event — a plane crash, fire, and partial building collapse — the Arlington County Fire Department served as incident commander. Different agencies had different roles. The incident required a major rescue, fire, and medical response from Arlington County at the U.S. military's headquarters — a facility under the control of the secretary of defense. Since it was a terrorist attack, the Department of Justice was the lead federal agency in charge (with authority delegated to the FBI for operational response). Additionally, the terrorist attack affected the daily operations and emergency management requirements of Arlington County and all bordering and surrounding jurisdictions.

At 9:37, the west wall of the Pentagon was hit by hijacked American Airlines Flight 77, a Boeing 757. The crash caused immediate and catastrophic damage. All 64 people aboard the airliner were killed, as were 125 people inside the Pentagon (70 civilians and 55 military service members). One hundred six people were seriously injured and transported to area hospitals. . . .

Local, regional, state, and federal agencies immediately responded to the Pentagon attack. In addition to county fire, police, and sheriff's departments, the response was assisted by the Metropolitan Washington Airports Authority, Ronald Reagan Washington National Airport Fire Department, Fort Myer Fire Department, the Virginia State Police, the Virginia Department of Emergency Management, the FBI, FEMA, a National Medical Response Team, the Bureau of Alcohol, Tobacco, and Firearms, and numerous military personnel within the Military District of Washington.

Command was established at 9:41. At the same time, the Arlington County Emergency Communications Center contacted the fire departments of Fairfax County, Alexandria, and the District of Columbia to request mutual aid. The incident command post provided a clear view of and access to the crash site, allowing the incident commander to assess the situation at all times. . . .

Several factors facilitated the response to this incident, and distinguish it from the far more difficult task in New York. There was a single incident, and it was not 1,000 feet above ground. The incident site was relatively easy to secure and contain, and there were no other buildings in the immediate area. There was no collateral damage beyond the Pentagon.

Yet the Pentagon response encountered difficulties that echo those experienced in New York. As the "Arlington County: After-Action Report" notes, there were significant problems with both self-dispatching and communications: "Organizations, response units, and individuals proceeding on their own initiative directly to an incident site, without the knowledge and permission of the host jurisdiction and the Incident Commander, complicate the exercise of command, increase the risks faced by bonafide responders, and exacerbate the challenge of accountability." With respect to communications, the report concludes: "Almost all aspects of communications continue to be problematic, from initial notification to tactical operations. Cellular telephones were of little value.... Radio channels were initially oversaturated....

It is a fair inference, given the differing situations in New York City and Northern Virginia, that the problems in command, control, and communications that occurred at both sites will likely recur in any emergency of similar scale. The task looking forward is to enable first responders to respond in a coordinated manner with the greatest possible awareness of the situation....

Notes and Questions

1. State and Local Response Plans. What plans have your home town, county, and state made in preparation for a great natural disaster or a terrorist attack? Do you know, for example, who would be in charge of the government's response? How would you find out about such plans? How important do you think it is for you and your neighbors to know what any such plans provide?

2. Who's in Charge? If an emergency response plan is to have any hope of success, everyone involved must know that someone is in charge—and they must know who that someone is. They must be able to identify a single individual upon whom they can rely for accurate information and authoritative instructions. How will that individual be recognized in the midst of a great crisis?

In a major incident that exceeds the capabilities of state and local officials, responsibility for managing and coordinating the response will pass from them to designated federal officials, who will implement protocols set out in the *National Response Framework* and its supporting documents. This handoff of responsibility must immediately be clear and widely understood. Yet given the unpredictability of the timing and character of such a development, it might be unwise to adopt fixed criteria for the handoff. Reflecting this need for flexibility, the NRF states merely that "most incidents start at the local or tribal level, and as needs exceed resources and capabilities, additional... federal assets may be required." *National Response Framework, supra,* at 48. It may be possible instead to develop a *procedure* for making the transition, so that all concerned, including members of the public, will be aware of the shift in authority. Can you describe such a procedure?

3. Regional Cooperation. All 50 states and six U.S. territories (including the District of Columbia) have entered into a congressionally approved compact of mutual assistance, including help with evacuations. Emergency Management Assistance Compact,

Pub. L. No. 104-321, 110 Stat. 3877 (1996). *See EMAC: Emergency Management Assistance Compact* (n.d.), *at* http://www.emacweb.org/?9. The compact is designed to aid in planning for emergencies, as well as to sweep aside legal barriers to interstate cooperation. A state requested to provide assistance to another generally must do so. State forces, such as National Guard troops, operating out of their jurisdiction have "the same powers (except that of arrest unless specifically authorized by the receiving state), duties, rights, and privileges as are afforded forces of the state in which they are performing emergency services." EMAC art. IV. Compensation and benefits for such forces are paid by their home states, *id.* art. VIII, although other expenses and damages are reimbursed by the receiving state. *Id.* art. IX. Presumably, sharing of sub-state units must be provided for by enabling legislation within each state. *See generally* Nat'l Emergency Mgmt. Ass'n, *The Emergency Management Assistance Compact: A History and Analysis of the Evolution of National Mutual Aid Policy and Operations* (Sept. 2014).

D. RESPONDING TO BIOLOGICAL THREATS

Threats to public health come in various forms and from various sources. With the growing ease of international travel, communicable diseases that once might have afflicted only local populations in Southeast Asia, the Middle East, or Africa have recently made their way into the United States, presenting special challenges for medical care providers who lack experience in treating them — or effective antidotes. Examples include the H1N1 virus (swine flu), SARS (severe acute respiratory syndrome), MERS (Middle East respiratory syndrome), and, in 2014, the Ebola virus. Some tropical diseases have also begun to extend their historical ranges northward and southward under the influence of climate change.

Additional public health threats come from terrorists, who might be able to weaponize a pathogen like *yersinia pestis*, or pneumonic plague, and release it in the civilian population, with effects described in the TOPOFF exercise at the beginning of this chapter. Perhaps most frightening of all is the prospect of a genetically engineered disease with no known remedy delivered by a terrorist on a suicide mission.

All of these diseases pose threats to national security. Extensive preparations to deal with them are underway at all levels of government. Unfortunately, legal authorities to guide these preparations or their implementation are incomplete or, in some instances, conflicting, as the following case study makes clear.

Case Study: The 2014 Ebola Virus Epidemic

In late 2013, an outbreak of the dreaded, highly contagious Ebola virus was reported in Guinea and several other West African nations. Several months later, President Obama called it "a national security priority." The CDC worked with the World Health Organization to develop a strategy for containment, while hundreds of CDC personnel and U.S. troops traveled to Africa to assist in the treatment of those afflicted and deliver aid from USAID. They also provided diagnostic testing and training for local health care workers.

Several U.S. health care workers were infected with the disease and were placed in isolation when they returned to this country. One of them died. Meanwhile, HHS quickly published special guidance on identification of persons infected with Ebola, along with protocols for their treatment in U.S. hospitals. The CDC also began work on development of a vaccine for the disease, and the Food and Drug Administration granted emergency permits for the use of experimental drugs on infected patients.

By the end of October 2015, the total number of cases reported in West Africa since the outbreak was more than 28,000, of whom some 11,000 had died. No one was then infected in the United States.

Only four persons were diagnosed with the Ebola virus in the United States — two who had contact with Ebola patients in West Africa, and two nurses, who contracted the disease from one of the first two patients. All were hospitalized. Nevertheless, several states, believing that HHS voluntary protocols were inadequate, adopted their own varying policies requiring the monitoring and possible isolation of individuals who had traveled to West Africa or had contact with Ebola patients. The results, predictably, were inconsistent and possibly dangerous. For example, Kaci Hickox, a nurse arriving at Newark Airport from Sierra Leone, where she worked with Doctors Without Borders, was held in involuntary isolation on orders from New Jersey governor Chris Christie for three days, even though she was asymptomatic. Released to travel by car to her home in Maine, she was then placed under a 21-day quarantine there by order of Governor Paul LePage. (Three other states also adopted policies requiring the monitoring for three weeks of individuals who traveled to West Africa.) After Hickox refused to stay home, a Maine court rejected the governor's request for a court order to confine her, saying it was not "necessary to protect other individuals from the dangers of infection." *See* Abby Ohlheiser & Cecelia Kang, *Nurse Quarantined in New Jersey After Returning from Ebola Mission Is Released,* Wash. Post, Oct. 27, 2014; Julia Bayley & Jackie Farwell, *After Kaci Hickox Wins Court Reprieve, LePage Says He Doesn't Trust Her,* BDN Maine, Oct. 31, 2014.

1. Balancing Freedom and Public Health

In general, a person infected with a contagious disease may be isolated to prevent her from infecting others. Healthy but exposed persons may be vaccinated or given medicine or have their movements restricted.

The Supreme Court has long recognized the authority of the government to erect quarantines, both to confine persons and to exclude them, in order to prevent the spread of contagious or infectious diseases. In *Gibbons v. Ogden*, 22 U.S. (9 Wheat.) 1, 25 (1824), the Supreme Court referred to a state's authority to quarantine, noting that even though quarantine laws affect commerce, their objective is to protect public health and they are thus within the authority of state and local governments. In recent times the Court approved the confinement of a sexually violent predator, declaring that

> we have never held that the Constitution prevents a State from civilly detaining those for whom no treatment is available, but who nevertheless pose a danger to others. A State could hardly be seen as furthering a "punitive" purpose by involuntarily confining persons afflicted with an untreatable, highly contagious disease. [*Kansas v. Hendricks,* 521 U.S. 346, 366 (1997).]

See also Jacobson v. Massachusetts, 197 U.S. 11 (1905) (upholding mandatory vaccinations following a smallpox outbreak); *Compagnie Francaise de Navigation a Vapeur v. La. Bd. of Health,* 186 U.S. 380 (1902) (upholding a quarantine in New Orleans following a yellow fever outbreak). And while the Supreme Court has called the constitutional right to travel from one state to another "firmly imbedded in our jurisprudence," *Saenz v. Roe,* 526 U.S. 489, 498 (1999), other courts have held that the right may be curtailed in an emergency. *See, e.g., Smith v. Avino,* 91 F.3d 105 (11th Cir. 1996) (upholding a curfew in South Florida in the wake of Hurricane Andrew). Other constitutional challenges are described in Jared P. Cole, *Federal and State Quarantine Authority* (Cong. Res. Serv. RL33201), Oct. 9, 2014.

Government officials may establish a cordon around an area suspected of containing infected persons. No clear rules exist, however, to say precisely when to establish a quarantine, how long to maintain it, or the size of the area it may cover. *See Empire Kosher Poultry, Inc. v. Hallowell,* 816 F.2d 907 (3d Cir. 1987) (upholding a quarantine of poultry with broad boundaries to combat avian influenza).

In addition to quarantines, involuntary evacuations, and forced inoculations, government responses to a pandemic or a bioterrorist attack may include compulsory physical examinations to determine whether individuals are infected with a contagious disease, inspections of private property, and reviews of personal medical records. *See Camara v. Municipal Court of San Francisco,* 387 U.S. 523, 539 (1967) (observing that warrantless inspections are "traditionally upheld in emergency situations"); *see also* Barry Kellman, *Biological Terrorism: Legal Measures for Preventing Catastrophe,* 24 Harv. J.L. & Pub. Pol'y 417, 478-485 (2001).

As first responders, state and local officials have typically taken the lead in seeking to prevent the spread of contagious diseases. Spurred by the 9/11 and anthrax attacks in 2001, many cities and states have enacted new laws based on the Model State Emergency Health Powers Act (MSEHPA) (draft Dec. 21, 2001), http://www.publichealthlaw.net/MSEHPA/MSEHPA.pdf, drawn up by public health experts at Georgetown and Johns Hopkins Universities.

MSEHPA authorizes governors to declare a "public health emergency," defined as "an occurrence or imminent threat" of illness that is "believed to be caused" by bioterrorism or other disasters and that poses "a high probability" of a large number of deaths, serious or long-term disabilities, or widespread exposure "that poses a significant risk of substantial harm to a large number of people in the affected population." *Id.* §104(m). During such an emergency, a governor may suspend any statute concerning state government procedures or any agency rule, and state officials may close, evacuate, or decontaminate "any facility" or destroy "any material" where "there is a reasonable cause to believe that it may endanger the public health." *Id.* §501. Public health authorities are also given power to condemn or assume control over private property, control and manage health care facilities, and control routes and modes of transportation. *Id.* §502. And they may require the vaccination or treatment of persons, or may order their quarantine or isolation. *Id.* §§603-604.

Notes and Questions

1. *Legal Basis for Compulsory Measures?* The government's interest in protecting members of the public from the spread of disease is, needless to say, very strong. Depending on the virulence of a particular pathogen, its location and the extent of its spread, its susceptibility to treatment, and, perhaps, the method of its introduction into the population, it may pose a threat to national security, another very high government interest. Balanced against these government interests are individual interests protected by the Fourth Amendment (against unreasonable searches or seizures) and the Fifth Amendment (against deprivation of liberty or property without due process). Given the history of Supreme Court cases upholding quarantines and mandatory inoculations, can you think of any way to challenge a quarantine like the one imposed in the TOPOFF exercise? Could you attack the establishment of a cordon on grounds that it was too large or that it remained in place for too long? Do you think a court would rule on your challenge during the continuation of the quarantine?

2. *Viability of Compulsory Measures?* One critique of the 2000 federal TOPOFF exercise described above calls the quarantine of large groups of people "impractical," citing concern about the level of force needed for enforcement:

> Not only were local officials uncertain about their statutory authority to proceed with a quarantine, they believed that the public would probably not cooperate with compulsory orders to commandeer property, restrict movement of people, or forcibly remove them to designated locations. Traditionally, governments have counted upon the public to comply with public health orders on the basis that the good of the community overrides the rights of the individual. These days, however, citizens get angry at forced evacuations for such visible calamities as hurricanes, floods, and wildfires, not to mention a stay-at-home order for a microscopic killer that they may doubt is in their midst. Police also questioned whether their colleagues would recognize the authority of the public health officer to declare a quarantine or would even stick around to enforce the order. Finally, some wondered whether there were enough local and state police to quarantine a large metropolitan area in the first place. [Amy E. Smithson & Leslie-Anne Levy, *Ataxia: The Chemical and Biological Terrorism Threat and the U.S. Response* 269 (Henry L. Stimson Ctr. 2000).]

According to one police captain, "If police officers knew that a biological agent had been released, 99 percent of the cops would not be here. They would grab their families and leave." *Id.* at 270 n.225. Can you think of a practical way to help ensure the effectiveness of a quarantine?

3. *A Military Role in Compulsory Measures?* Could a cordon around a large city, like Denver, be maintained without the use of military forces? Could soldiers shoot individuals trying to escape the quarantine? *See* Jesse T. Greene, *Federal Enforcement of Mass Involuntary Quarantines: Toward a Specialized Standing Rules for the Use of Force*, 6 Harv. Nat'l Security J. 58, 88 (2015) (predicting that troops would take part, but doubting their authority to shoot to kill). Sources and limits of military authority for such domestic deployments are analyzed in the next chapter.

2. Federal Public Health Authorities

The federal responsibility for biological incidents is shared by several agencies, civilian and military. Overall coordination is supposed to be provided by the Department of Homeland Security. The Department of Health and Human Services, acting through the CDC, will play a leading role based on its specialized experience and expertise.

Public Health Service Act

42 U.S.C. §§201 to 300mm-61 (2018)

§243. GENERAL GRANT OF AUTHORITY FOR COOPERATION . . .

(c) Development of plan to control epidemics and meet emergencies or problems resulting from disasters; . . .

(1) The Secretary [of Health and Human Services (the "Service")] is authorized to develop (and may take such action as may be necessary to implement) a plan under which personnel, equipment, medical supplies, and other resources of the Service and other agencies under the jurisdiction of the Secretary may be effectively used to control epidemics of any disease or condition and to meet other health emergencies or problems. . . .

§264. REGULATIONS TO CONTROL COMMUNICABLE DISEASES

(a) Promulgation and Enforcement by Surgeon General. The Surgeon General, with the approval of the Secretary, is authorized to make and enforce such regulations as in his judgment are necessary to prevent the introduction, transmission, or spread of communicable diseases from foreign countries into the States or possessions, or from one State or possession into any other State or possession. For purposes of carrying out and enforcing such regulations, the Surgeon General may provide for such inspection, fumigation, disinfection . . . and other measures, as in his judgment may be necessary.

(b) Apprehension, detention, or conditional release of individuals. Regulations prescribed under this section shall not provide for the apprehension, detention, or conditional release of individuals except for the purpose of preventing the introduction, transmission, or spread of such communicable diseases as may be specified from time to time in Executive orders of the President upon the recommendation of the Secretary, in consultation with the Surgeon General. . . .

(d) Apprehension and examination of persons reasonably believed to be infected.

(1) Regulations prescribed under this section may provide for the apprehension and examination of any individual reasonably believed to be infected with a communicable disease in a qualifying stage and (A) to be moving or about to move from a State to another State; or (B) to be a probable source of infection to individuals who, while infected with such disease in a qualifying stage, will be moving from a State to another State. Such regulations may provide that if upon

examination any such individual is found to be infected, he may be detained for such time and in such manner as may be reasonably necessary....

(e) Preemption. Nothing in this section ... or the regulations promulgated [hereunder] may be construed as superseding any provision under State law ... except to the extent that such a provision conflicts with an exercise of Federal authority under this section....

HHS has adopted the following regulations to implement this statutory authority:

Interstate Quarantine Regulations

42 C.F.R. pt. 70 (2019)

§70.2 MEASURES IN THE EVENT OF INADEQUATE LOCAL CONTROL

Whenever the Director of the Centers for Disease Control and Prevention determines that the measures taken by health authorities of any State or possession (including political subdivisions thereof) are insufficient to prevent the spread of any of the communicable diseases from such State or possession to any other State or possession, he/she may take such measures to prevent such spread of the diseases as he/she deems reasonably necessary, including inspection....

§70.6 APPREHENSION AND DETENTION OF PERSONS WITH QUARANTINABLE COMMUNICABLE DISEASES

(a) The Director may authorize the apprehension, medical examination, quarantine, isolation, or conditional release of any individual for the purpose of preventing the introduction, transmission, and spread of quarantinable communicable diseases, as specified by Executive Order, based upon a finding that:

(1) The individual is reasonably believed to be infected with a quarantinable communicable disease in a qualifying stage and is moving or about to move from a State into another State; or

(2) The individual is reasonably believed to be infected with a quarantinable communicable disease in a qualifying stage and constitutes a probable source of infection to other individuals who may be moving from a State into another State....

§70.12 MEDICAL EXAMINATIONS

(a) The Director may require an individual to undergo a medical examination as part of a Federal order for quarantine, isolation, or conditional release for a quarantinable communicable disease....

(d) Individuals reasonably believed to be infected based on the results of a medical examination may be isolated, or if such results are inconclusive or unavailable, individuals may be quarantined or conditionally released in accordance with this part....

Notes and Questions

1. Responding to Listed Pathogens. The HHS regulations set out above apply only to infectious agents listed by executive order and incorporated by reference in §70.6. In 2019 that list included cholera, diphtheria, infectious tuberculosis, plague, smallpox, yellow fever, viral hemorrhagic fevers (including Lassa, Marburg, and Ebola), severe acute respiratory syndrome (SARS), and influenza that can cause a pandemic. *See* Exec. Order No. 13,295, *Revised List of Quarantinable Communicable Diseases,* 68 Fed. Reg. 17,255 (Apr. 9, 2003), as amended by Exec. Order No. 13,375, 70 Fed. Reg. 17,299 (Apr. 4, 2005); and Exec. Order No. 13,674, 79 Fed. Reg. 45,671 (Aug. 6, 2014).

In the Ebola case study, above, nurse Kaci Hickox was ordered held in isolation by two different state governors. Could she have been legally confined under the federal authorities described here? Would your answer be the same if she had remained in New Jersey? *See* Kayte M. Jobe, Comment, *The Constitutionality of Quarantine and Isolation Orders in the Ebola Epidemic and Beyond,* 51 Wake Forest L. Rev. 165, 188 (2016) (asserting that "the existing overlap in federal and state quarantine and isolation authority needs clarifying").

Not listed in any executive order are tularemia, botulism, and other contagions that could be weaponized and used by terrorists. How should government authorities respond to the terrorist release of an infectious agent not listed or not immediately identifiable?

2. Responding to Anthrax. Anthrax is extremely dangerous but not communicable. In October 2001, letters containing anthrax spores were sent to two U.S. Senators and several news media offices, killing five people and sickening 17 others. Can you explain how various federal agencies might cooperate to prevent such attacks in the future? Do HHS and the CDC have the authority they need to be helpful? *See* David Heyman, *Lessons from the Anthrax Attacks: Implications for U.S. Bioterrorism Preparedness* (Apr. 2002) (concluding that the anthrax letter attacks "revealed weaknesses in almost every aspect of U.S. biopreparedness and response"), http://www.fas.org/irp/threat/cbw/dtra02.pdf; Keith Rhodes, *Diffuse Security Threats: Information on U.S. Domestic Anthrax Attacks* (GAO-03-0323T), Dec. 10, 2002.

3. Responding to Smallpox. Reflecting fears that remaining supplies of smallpox virus in the United States and Russia might fall into the hands of terrorists, the CDC has published a plan for responding to an outbreak of a disease thought to have been eradicated in the 1970s. *See* Ctrs. for Disease Control and Prevention, *Smallpox: Bioterrorism Response Planning* (Jan. 6, 2017), https://www.cdc.gov/smallpox/bioterrorism-response-planning/index.html. The plan calls for employment of a "ring" strategy to isolate confirmed and suspected smallpox cases, vaccinate persons who may have come into contact with them, and keep all possible contacts under close surveillance. The size of a ring is to be determined by state and federal health officials.

4. Federal vs. State Authority. Officially, the success of the federal mission in responding to a biological incident is "contingent upon the coordination with and the success of the community response." *National Biodefense Strategy* 1 (2018).

According to one analysis, however, in the event of a bioterrorist attack, "[a]lmost certainly, a clash would occur between public health and legal officials at the local, state, and national levels about the measures necessary and the entity with jurisdiction to act." Smithson & Levy, *supra* p. 1178, at 269.

What is the relationship between the HHS/CDC authorities and state law? The Public Health Service Act directs the HHS Secretary to "cooperate with and aid State and local authorities in the enforcement of their quarantine and other health regulations." 42 U.S.C. §243(a). But §264(e) of the same title indicates that federal measures trump those of states. If state and federal response efforts do come directly into conflict, the former presumably must give way under the Supremacy Clause.

Still, doubt remains about the primacy of authorities, particularly the power to quarantine or isolate within a single state. The Supreme Court has declared that Congress may "regulate those activities having a substantial relation to interstate commerce," *United States v. Lopez*, 514 U.S. 549, 555 (1995), but also that Congress may not regulate *noneconomic* activities within a state solely on the basis of the effect of those activities on interstate commerce. *United States v. Morrison*, 529 U.S. 598 (2000). But in *Gonzales v. Raich*, 545 U.S. 1 (2005), the Court upheld a federal statute barring the intrastate growing and use of medical marijuana, permitted by state law, on grounds that the forbidden substance might enter interstate commerce.

A 2009 memorandum from the Attorney General concluded that the authority to implement an intrastate federal quarantine is unclear. Memorandum for the President from the Att'y General, *Summary of Legal Authorities for Use in Response to an Outbreak of Pandemic Influenza* (Apr. 25, 2009), *available at* https://www.hsdl.org/?abstract&did=37094. Many scholars disagree. *See, e.g.*, Polly J. Price, *Do State Lines Make Public Health Emergencies Worse? Federal Versus State Control of Quarantine*, 67 Emory L.J. 491, 495 (2018) (arguing that "[s]tatutory authority already exists for preemption of state quarantine laws, even if the political will to assert it has been lacking"). The CDC states flatly that "[i]n the event of a conflict, federal law is supreme." Ctrs. for Disease Control and Prevention, *Legal Authorities for Isolation and Quarantine* (Oct. 8, 2014), https://www.cdc.gov/quarantine/aboutlawsregulationsquarantineisolation.html.

How could potential conflicts between federal and state or local response efforts be minimized?

5. Triage and Surge Control. The CDC maintains the Strategic National Stockpile program. Within 12 hours of a terrorist attack, the Stockpile can deliver "push packages" containing needed pharmaceuticals and other medical supplies anywhere in the country. *See* CDC, *Strategic National Stockpile (SNS)* (updated Nov. 6, 2019), http://www.cdc.gov/phpr/stockpile/stockpile.htm. Inventories are nevertheless limited, and they might not be adequate to treat every person affected by an outbreak of some diseases. Who do you think should receive such limited supplies first? Who should be empowered to choose among potential recipients? Would it be a good idea to decide such questions in advance of a terrorist attack or pandemic? If so, how?

Federal law also authorizes the waiver of various regulatory requirements in the event of a public health emergency. For example, the Food and Drug Administration (FDA) may permit the use of an unapproved drug or device in an emergency involving a biological, chemical, radiological, or nuclear agent. 21 U.S.C. §§360bbb-3 (2018).

HOMELAND SECURITY: SUMMARY OF BASIC PRINCIPLES

- The President's inherent "repel attack" powers authorize measures to protect the United States and its people from serious threats, although the precise circumstances that trigger such powers, as well as their scope and duration, are uncertain. Also uncertain are the limits of Congress's correlative authority to regulate the President's homeland security actions.
- The Homeland Security Act of 2002 created an enormous government structure to protect against natural disasters and terrorist attacks in the United States, and ordered extensive planning to respond to such incidents.
- The Department of Homeland Security (DHS) has developed elaborate plans for responding to emergencies ranging from strictly local to widespread, and from relatively minor to catastrophic. The plans generally call for action at the lowest possible level of government, they vary greatly in detail, and they stress the importance of coordination among government agencies.
- States and first responders at the local level have developed their own protocols, including agreements with neighboring states to share assistance in responding to emergencies.
- Federal assistance to states is prescribed by the Stafford Act and other legislation, which sometimes allow federal intervention without a request from a state.
- Both state and federal laws provide for the detention, isolation, or quarantine of individuals to prevent the spread of contagious diseases. If federal and state authorities conflict, state actions are in principle preempted by the Supremacy Clause, although federal power to regulate entirely intrastate is disputed.
- The government's interest in protecting public health, especially if national security is implicated, has so far generally been found to trump claims that isolation, quarantine, or forced inoculation for contagious diseases violates Fourth or Fifth Amendment rights of affected individuals.

The Military's Domestic Role

Until recently, we tended to think of the Defense Department as organized almost exclusively to fight a conventional war far from America's shores. In part this belief reflected the American public's antipathy toward any sort of military involvement in domestic life. During the Vietnam War, the Supreme Court noted "a traditional and strong resistance of Americans to any military intrusion into civilian affairs." *Laird v. Tatum*, 408 U.S. 1, 15 (1972). Thus, for most of our history the military's domestic role has consisted primarily of preparations for foreign wars and of occasional support for civilian authorities in curbing civil unrest and fighting the "war on drugs."

On September 11, 2001, however, the military's role, like so much else in this country, began to change. The following day the President described the terrorist attacks as "acts of war" — a war in which the battlefield included the U.S. homeland. Armed troops were quickly deployed to protect airports and bridges around the country. In this unfamiliar role, soldiers faced important questions: Could they detain and try suspected terrorists, should they be given other domestic responsibilities, should their Rules of Engagement (ROE) be different from those that applied to military operations abroad, and what legal authorities existed to guide their actions?

In this chapter we address both legal and practical issues that arise in the domestic use of military forces. We also consider the possibility that troops might take over critical government functions by invoking martial law.

A. THE TRADITIONAL ROLE OF THE MILITARY IN AMERICAN SOCIETY

The domestic use of troops has been a fact of life and a matter of controversy at least since President Washington called out the militia to put down the Whiskey Rebellion in 1794. Many other Presidents have deployed federal military forces to help keep the peace, to aid local governments in natural disasters, and to enforce federal and state laws. State governors have called out their militias even more often, especially in the first three decades of the twentieth century. From the earliest days of the Republic, however, Americans have resisted any involvement by military forces in domestic matters. This tradition is spelled out in William C. Banks & Stephen Dycus, *Soldiers on the Home Front: The Domestic Role of the American Military* (2016).

1. The Posse Comitatus Act as a Background Principle

Reading *Bissonnette v. Haig*

In 1973, some 200 Oglala Sioux and American Indian Movement members occupied the village of Wounded Knee on the Pine Ridge Reservation in South Dakota. Their protests grew out of an internal tribal dispute, as well as alleged U.S. government violations of treaty obligations with Indian people. The village was sealed off by agents of the FBI, Bureau of Indian Affairs, and U.S. Marshals Service. The Army provided armored personnel carriers, weapons, and ammunition, as well as two officers who advised civilian officials on tactics. National Guard personnel from two states conducted aerial reconnaissance and maintained military equipment. The standoff continued for ten weeks, during the course of which two protestors were killed.

Native Americans involved in the protest sued for damages on grounds that the government's actions violated their Fourth and Fifth Amendment rights. As you read the following decision, consider these questions, among others:

- What role do U.S. military forces traditionally play in law enforcement, and why?
- How, precisely, does the Posse Comitatus Act limit that role?
- How does compliance with the Posse Comitatus Act affect the court's assessment of the plaintiffs' Fourth Amendment claims?

Bissonette v. Haig

United States Court of Appeals, Eighth Circuit, 1985
776 F.2d 1384, *aff'd*, 800 F.2d 812 (8th Cir. 1986) (en banc), *aff'd*, 485 U.S. 264 (1988)

Arnold, J. . . . In their amended complaint, plaintiffs allege . . . that they were unreasonably seized and confined in the village of Wounded Knee contrary to the Fourth Amendment and their rights to free movement and travel. Second, they claim that they were unreasonably searched by ground and aerial surveillance. In both cases, plaintiffs assert that the seizures and searches were unreasonable because "Defendants accomplished or caused to be accomplished those actions by means of the unconstitutional and felonious use of parts of the United States Army or Air Force. . . ." . . . This case comes to us on appeal from a dismissal for failure to state a claim, and we therefore accept for present purposes the factual allegations of the complaint.

These allegations must be viewed against the background of the Posse Comitatus Act of 1878, 18 U.S.C. §1385 (2012), which plaintiffs claim was violated here. The statute provides:

§1385. Use of Army and Air Force as Posse Comitatus[1]

Whoever, except in cases and under circumstances expressly authorized by the Constitution or Act of Congress, willfully uses any part of the Army or the Air Force as a posse comitatus or otherwise to execute the laws shall be fined not more than $10,000 or imprisoned not more than two years, or both.

A

The first two sets of claims raise the question whether a search or seizure, otherwise permissible, can be rendered unreasonable under the Fourth Amendment because military personnel or equipment were used to accomplish those actions. We believe that the Constitution, certain Acts of Congress, and the decisions of the Supreme Court embody certain limitations on the use of military personnel in enforcing the civil law, and that searches and seizures in circumstances which exceed those limits are unreasonable under the Fourth Amendment.

. . . Reasonableness is determined by balancing the interests for and against the seizure. Usually, the interests arrayed against a seizure are those of the individual in privacy, freedom of movement, or, in the case of a seizure by deadly force, life. Here, however, the opposing interests are more societal and governmental than strictly individual in character. They concern the special threats to constitutional government inherent in military enforcement of civilian law. That these governmental interests should weigh in the Fourth Amendment balance is neither novel nor surprising. In the typical Fourth Amendment case, the interests of the individual are balanced against those of the government. That some of those governmental interests are on the other side of the Fourth Amendment balance does not make them any less relevant or important.

Civilian rule is basic to our system of government. The use of military forces to seize civilians can expose civilian government to the threat of military rule and the suspension of constitutional liberties. On a lesser scale, military enforcement of the civil law leaves the protection of vital Fourth and Fifth Amendment rights in the hands of persons who are not trained to uphold these rights. It may also chill the exercise of fundamental rights, such as the rights to speak freely and to vote, and create the atmosphere of fear and hostility which exists in territories occupied by enemy forces.

The interest in limiting military involvement in civilian affairs has a long tradition beginning with the Declaration of Independence and continued in the Constitution, certain Acts of Congress, and decisions of the Supreme Court. The Declaration of Independence states among the grounds for severing ties with Great Britain that the King "has kept among us, in times of peace, Standing Armies without Consent of our Legislature . . . [and] has affected to render the Military independent of and superior to the Civil power." These concerns were later raised at the Constitutional Convention. Luther Martin of Maryland said, "when a government wishes to deprive its citizens of freedom, and reduce them to slavery, it generally makes use of a standing army."

The Constitution itself limits the role of the military in civilian affairs: it makes the President, the highest civilian official in the Executive Branch, Commander in

[1. The Latin term posse comitatus means, literally, "power or authority of the county," but it connotes a body of persons summoned by a sheriff to assist in preserving the peace or enforcing the law. The persons summoned to assist the sheriff might, of course, be either civilian or military. — Eds.]

Chief of the armed services (Art. II, §2); it limits the appropriations for armed forces to two years and grants to the Congress the power to make rules to govern the armed forces (Art. I, §8, cl. 14); and it forbids the involuntary quartering of soldiers in any house in time of peace (Third Amendment).

Congress has passed several statutes limiting the use of the military in enforcing the civil law [including the Posse Comitatus Act and the Insurrection Act, addressed *infra*]. . . .

The Supreme Court has also recognized the constitutional limitations placed on military involvement in civilian affairs. A leading case is *Ex parte Milligan*, 71 U.S. 2, 124 (1866). . . . More recently, in *Laird v. Tatum*, 408 U.S. 1, 15-16 (1972), statements the Court made in dicta reaffirm these limitations. . . .

The governmental interests favoring military assistance to civilian law enforcement are primarily twofold: first, to maintain order in times of domestic violence or rebellion; and second, to improve the efficiency of civilian law enforcement by giving it the benefit of military technologies, equipment, information, and training personnel. These interests can and have been accommodated by Acts of Congress to the overriding interest of preserving civilian government and law enforcement. At the time of the Wounded Knee occupation, Congress had prohibited the use of the military to execute the civilian laws, except when expressly authorized. 18 U.S.C. §1385. And it had placed specific limits on the President's power to use the national guard and military in emergency situations. 10 U.S.C. [§§251-255]. For example, under 10 U.S.C. [§252], the President may call upon the military only after having determined that domestic unrest makes it "impracticable to enforce the laws of the United States by the ordinary course of judicial proceedings," and under 10 U.S.C. [§254], he may do so only after having issued a proclamation ordering the insurgents to disperse. Those steps were not taken here.

We believe that the limits established by Congress on the use of the military for civilian law enforcement provide a reliable guidepost by which to evaluate the reasonableness for Fourth Amendment purposes of the seizures and searches in question here. Congress has acted to establish reasonable limits on the President's use of military forces in emergency situations, and in doing so has circumscribed whatever, if any, inherent power the President may have had absent such legislation. This is the teaching of *Youngstown Sheet & Tube Co. v. Sawyer*, 343 U.S. 579 (1952). . . .

B

. . . [T]he use of military force for domestic law-enforcement purposes is in a special category, and . . . both the courts and Congress have been alert to keep it there. In short, if the use of military personnel is both unauthorized by any statute, and contrary to a specific criminal prohibition, and if citizens are seized or searched by military means in such a case, we have no hesitation in declaring that such searches and seizures are constitutionally "unreasonable." We do not mean to say that every search or seizure that violates a statute of any kind is necessarily a violation of the Fourth Amendment. But the statute prohibiting (if the allegations in the complaint can be proved) the conduct engaged in by defendants here is, as we have attempted to explain, not just any Act of Congress. It is the embodiment of a long tradition of suspicion and hostility towards the use of military force for domestic purposes.

Plaintiffs' Fourth Amendment case, therefore, must stand or fall on the proposition that military activity in connection with the occupation of Wounded Knee violated the Posse Comitatus Act.

In *United States v. Casper*, 541 F.2d 1275 (8th Cir. 1976) (per curiam), *cert. denied*, 430 U.S. 970 (1977), . . . the District Court had found on a stipulated record that the following activities did not violate the Act: the use of Air Force personnel, planes, and cameras to fly surveillance; the advice of military officers in dealing with the disorder; and the furnishing of equipment and supplies. We affirmed "on the basis of the trial court's thorough and well-reasoned opinion." 541 F.2d at 1276.

. . . Therefore, unless plaintiffs now allege that the defendants took actions that went beyond those alleged in the *Casper* case, the actions alleged in the complaint now before us cannot violate the Act.

In *Casper*, . . . we approved the following standard for determining whether a violation of the Posse Comitatus Act had occurred:

> Were Army or Air Force personnel used by the civilian law enforcement officers at Wounded Knee in such a manner that the military personnel subjected the citizens to the exercise of military power which was regulatory, proscriptive, or compulsory in nature, either presently or prospectively?

541 F.2d at 1278. . . .

When this concept is transplanted into the present legal context, we take it to mean that military involvement, even when not expressly authorized by the Constitution or a statute, does not violate the Posse Comitatus Act unless it actually regulates, forbids, or compels some conduct on the part of those claiming relief. A mere threat of some future injury would be insufficient. . . .

. . . We of course have no way of knowing what plaintiffs would be able to prove if this case goes to trial, but the complaint, considered simply as a pleading, goes well beyond an allegation that defendants simply furnished supplies, aerial surveillance, and advice. It specifically charges that "the several Defendants maintained or caused to be maintained roadblocks and armed patrols constituting an armed perimeter around the village of Wounded Knee. . . ." Defendants' actions, it is charged, "seized, confined, and made prisoners (of plaintiffs) against their will. . . ." These allegations amount to a claim that defendants' activities, allegedly in violation of the Posse Comitatus Act, were "regulatory, proscriptive, or compulsory," in the sense that these activities directly restrained plaintiffs' freedom of movement. No more is required to survive a motion to dismiss. . . .

As to the second set of claims, . . . plaintiffs charge that they were searched and subjected to surveillance against their will by aerial photographic and visual search and surveillance. As we have already noted, *Casper* holds that this sort of activity does not violate the Posse Comitatus Act. It is therefore not "unreasonable" for Fourth Amendment purposes. . . .

Notes and Questions

1. *Origins of the Posse Comitatus Act.* Early acts of Congress authorized the use of the militia to aid in law enforcement, although such use was never so extensive as it was after the Civil War. Reconstruction-era abuses, culminating in the use of federal

troops to police polling stations in Southern states (some say to influence the outcome of the presidential election in 1876; others say to prevent harassment and intimidation of black voters by the Ku Klux Klan), led to passage of the Posse Comitatus Act in 1878.

2. *Elements of a Posse Comitatus Act Violation.* What exactly constitutes use of the armed forces "as a posse comitatus or otherwise to execute the laws"? To the "regulatory, proscriptive, or compulsory" standard set forth in *Bissonette,* we may add criteria from other cases growing out of the Wounded Knee incident: whether there was "direct, active" use of the military in civil law enforcement, *United States v. Red Feather,* 392 F. Supp. 916, 923 (D.S.D. 1975), or whether the use of the Army or the Air Force "pervaded the activities" of the civil law enforcement officers, *United States v. Jaramillo,* 380 F. Supp. 1375, 1379 (D. Neb. 1974), *appeal dismissed,* 510 F.2d 808 (8th Cir. 1975).

The Posse Comitatus Act may be inapplicable when the primary purpose of armed forces involvement is to enforce the Uniform Code of Military Justice or to achieve some distinctly military goal, such as force protection, and any benefits to civilian authorities are merely incidental—the so-called "military purpose" doctrine. *See Applewhite v. U.S. Air Force,* 995 F.2d 997, 1001 (10th Cir. 1993); *United States v. Thompson,* 33 M.J. 218 (C.M.A. 1991).

Are you now prepared to say what particular military activities in aid of law enforcement are forbidden? Do you think the Posse Comitatus Act should be amended to make it easier to predict when the Act would apply? If so, how?

3. *Judicial Remedies for Violations.* There has been no reported criminal prosecution of anyone for violation of the Posse Comitatus Act. Violations of the Act have, however, often been asserted as a defense to charges under other criminal statutes. For example, in *Red Feather* and *Jaramillo, supra,* Native Americans at Wounded Knee were charged with interfering with a "law enforcement officer lawfully engaged in the lawful performance of his official duties." *See* 18 U.S.C. §231(a)(3) (2018). The defendants argued that the federal marshals and FBI agents were not performing their duties lawfully, within the meaning of the statute, because they enlisted military forces as a posse comitatus.

Others apprehended by the military while attempting to smuggle drugs into the United States have asserted that the evidence obtained in their arrests was inadmissible at trial. However, the federal courts have consistently refused to exclude such evidence in the absence of widespread and repeated Posse Comitatus Act violations. In *United States v. Dreyer,* 804 F.3d 1266 (9th Cir. 2015) (en banc), for example, the court declared that suppression *could* be an appropriate remedy in an especially egregious case, but that it was not required in a one-off violation, regardless of the violation's scale.

In *Bissonette v. Haig,* the appellants sought damages for infringement of their constitutional rights resulting from Posse Comitatus Act violations. The Act does not expressly provide a right of action for damages. How was the Act relevant in *Bissonette*? Should such statutory violations give rise to a private cause of action separate and apart from any possible constitutional injury? *See Lamont v. Haig,* 539 F. Supp. 552 (D.S.D. 1982) (no legislative intent to create a private right of action).

4. *Which Military Services Are Covered?* The Posse Comitatus Act expressly refers only to the Army and Air Force, and several cases have found that the Act does not

restrict Navy law enforcement efforts. *See, e.g., United States v. Mendoza-Cecelia,* 963 F.2d 1467, 1477-1478 (11th Cir. 1992). *But cf. United States v. Chon,* 210 F.3d 990 (9th Cir. 2000). Notwithstanding the absence of the Navy from the statute, Defense Department regulations have long prohibited the use of the Navy and Marine Corps as a posse comitatus, with certain exceptions. *See* DOD Instr. 3025.21, *Defense Support of Civilian Law Enforcement Agencies* 24 (Feb. 27, 2013, with change Feb. 8, 2019).

Note that the Coast Guard is "a military service and a branch of the armed forces of the United States at all times," specifically, "a service in the Navy." 14 U.S.C. §§101, 103 (2018). But unless "the President directs" or in a declaration of war Congress so directs, the Coast Guard is "a service in the Department of Homeland Security," where it is given a broad range of statutory law enforcement responsibilities. *Id.* §§102, 103. In this latter role it is therefore exempted from the Posse Comitatus Act.

In the event of a major terrorist attack or natural disaster, it is likely that unfederalized National Guard troops will be dispatched to the scene before federal troops can be deployed. Several courts have held that, until Guard forces are federalized, they are not subject to the strictures of the Posse Comitatus Act. *See, e.g., United States v. Gilbert,* 165 F.3d 470 (6th Cir. 1999). Moreover, Congress has explicitly approved the states' use of the militia for "drug interdiction and counter-drug activities," so long as they remain under state control. 32 U.S.C. §112 (2018).

2. Exceptions to the Posse Comitatus Act

Recall that the Posse Comitatus Act prohibition applies "except in cases and under circumstances expressly authorized by the Constitution or Act of Congress." 18 U.S.C. §1385. The most important exception to the Act is a set of five statutes, referred to collectively as the Insurrection Act. It provides, in part:

Insurrection Act

10 U.S.C. §§251-255 (2018)

§252. USE OF MILITIA AND ARMED FORCES TO ENFORCE FEDERAL AUTHORITY

Whenever the President considers that unlawful obstructions, combinations, or assemblages, or rebellion against the authority of the United States, make it impracticable to enforce the laws of the United States in any State by the ordinary course of judicial proceedings, he may call into Federal service such of the militia of any State, and use such of the armed forces, as he considers necessary to enforce those laws or to suppress the rebellion.

§253. MAJOR PUBLIC EMERGENCIES; INTERFERENCE WITH STATE AND FEDERAL LAW

The President, by using the militia or the armed forces, or both, or by any other means, shall take such measures as he considers necessary to suppress, in a State, any insurrection, domestic violence, unlawful combination, or conspiracy, if it . . .

(2) opposes or obstructs the execution of the laws of the United States or impedes the course of justice under those laws. . . .

§254. PROCLAMATION TO DISPERSE

Whenever the President considers it necessary to use the militia or the armed forces under this chapter, he shall, by proclamation, immediately order the insurgents to disperse and retire peaceably to their abodes within a limited time.[2]

Military Cooperation with Civilian Law Enforcement Officials

10 U.S.C. §§271-284 (2018)

§271. USE OF INFORMATION COLLECTED DURING MILITARY OPERATIONS

(a) The Secretary of Defense may, in accordance with other applicable law, provide to Federal, State, or local civilian law enforcement officials any information collected during the normal course of military training or operations that may be relevant to a violation of any Federal or State law within the jurisdiction of such officials.

(b) The needs of civilian law enforcement officials for information shall, to the maximum extent practicable, be taken into account in the planning and execution of military training or operations.

(c) The Secretary of Defense shall ensure, to the extent consistent with national security, that intelligence information held by the Department of Defense and relevant to drug interdiction or other civilian law enforcement matters is provided promptly to appropriate civilian law enforcement officials. . . .

§275. RESTRICTION ON DIRECT PARTICIPATION BY MILITARY PERSONNEL

The Secretary of Defense shall prescribe such regulations as may be necessary to ensure that any activity (including the provision of any equipment or facility or the assignment or detail of any personnel) under this chapter does not include or permit direct participation by a member of the Army, Navy, Air Force, or Marine Corps in a search, seizure, arrest, or other similar activity unless participation in such activity by such member is otherwise authorized by law. . . .

[2. Section 251 provides for federal military assistance in putting down an insurrection against a state government. Section 255 makes the statutes applicable to Guam and the Virgin Islands. — Eds.]

§282. EMERGENCY SITUATIONS INVOLVING WEAPONS OF MASS DESTRUCTION

(a) In general. — The Secretary of Defense, upon the request of the Attorney General, may provide assistance in support of Department of Justice activities relating to the enforcement of section 175, 229, or 2332a of title 18 during an emergency situation involving a weapon of mass destruction. . . .

(d) Regulations. —

(1) The Secretary of Defense and the Attorney General shall jointly prescribe regulations concerning the types of assistance that may be provided under this section. . . .

(2) (A) Except as provided in subparagraph (B), the regulations may not authorize the following actions:

(i) Arrest.

(ii) Any direct participation in conducting a search for or seizure of evidence related to a violation of section 175, 229, or 2332a of title 18.

(iii) Any direct participation in the collection of intelligence for law enforcement purposes.

(B) The regulations may authorize an action described in subparagraph (A) to be taken under the following conditions:

(i) The action is considered necessary for the immediate protection of human life, and civilian law enforcement officials are not capable of taking the action.

(ii) The action is otherwise authorized under subsection (c) or under otherwise applicable law. . . .[3]

Notes and Questions

1. History of the Insurrection Act. The Insurrection Act had its origin in a 1792 law invoked by President Washington in suppressing the Whiskey Rebellion. The history of its component parts is traced in Stephen I. Vladeck, Note, *Emergency Power and the Militia Acts,* 114 Yale L.J. 149, 159-167 (2004); and William C. Banks, *Providing "Supplemental Security" — The Insurrection Act and the Military Role in Responding to Domestic Crises,* 3 J. Nat'l Security L. & Pol'y 39, 56-72 (2009). In 1827, the Supreme Court indicated that the President had broad discretion in determining when to use these statutes in calling forth the militia, and that his determination was not subject to judicial review. *Martin v. Mott,* 25 U.S. (12 Wheat.) 19, 29-32 (1827); *see also Luther v. Borden,* 48 U.S. (7 How.) 1, 43-45 (1849); *The Prize Cases,* 67 U.S. (2 Black) 635, 668 (1863).

Since that time, the Insurrection Act has been invoked for a variety of purposes, including the breaking of the Pullman Strike in 1894. More recently, it has been used

[3. Other sections of the 1981 Act, as amended, deal variously with the use of military equipment and facilities, training and advising civilian law enforcement officials, maintenance and operation of equipment, reimbursement, the use of Coast Guard personnel for law enforcement, and impacts on military preparedness. References to 18 U.S.C. §§175, 229, and 2332a concern prohibitions on the possession or use of biological or chemical weapons, or weapons of mass destruction, respectively. — Eds.]

to help integrate public schools and universities, to control racial unrest, and to enforce a variety of state and federal laws. It was last invoked by President George H.W. Bush in 1992 to send federalized California National Guard troops, as well as active-duty soldiers from Fort Ord and Marines from Camp Pendleton, to Los Angeles to help control rioting in the wake of the Rodney King trial verdict. Exec. Order No. 12,804, 57 Fed. Reg. 19,361 (May 1, 1992); Proclamation No. 6427, 57 Fed. Reg. 19,359 (May 1, 1992).

2. Insurrection Act as a Challenge to State Authority? When Hurricane Katrina hit New Orleans in 2005, local police and other first responders were overwhelmed. The Governor of Louisiana immediately asked the White House for 40,000 soldiers to help in the recovery effort. The White House delayed sending any active-duty military forces for five days, however, then approved deployment of only 7,200 troops. Some 29,000 National Guard personnel arrived from 49 other states, two territories, and the District of Columbia pursuant to agreements under the Emergency Management Assistance Compact (EMAC). See *supra* p. 1174. These unfederalized state troops, along with those from the Louisiana National Guard, were able to assist with law enforcement, as they were not subject to the Posse Comitatus Act. *See A Failure of Initiative: Final Report of the Select Bipartisan [House] Comm. to Investigate the Preparation for and Response to Hurricane Katrina,* 109th Cong., at 201-238 (Feb. 15, 2006).

The "issue of federalism . . . may have slowed the active duty military response." *Id.* at 222. The President reportedly believed that he would have to federalize Louisiana National Guard forces and invoke the Insurrection Act, then maintain federal control of Guard troops to assist in law enforcement — to stop looting and other lawlessness in the stricken area. But he wanted to avoid the perception that he was seizing command from a female Southern governor of another party. *See* Eric Lipton, Eric Schmitt & Thom Shanker, *Political Issues Snarled Plans for Troop Aid,* N.Y. Times, Sept. 5, 2005.

President George W. Bush did not invoke the Insurrection Act, which he claimed failed to provide the flexible authority he needed to deal with such a crisis. 10 U.S.C. §253 was then amended to give the President even broader powers to deploy troops when, *inter alia,* domestic violence made it impossible for state officials to restore public order. Pub. L. No. 109-364, §1076, 120 Stat. 2083, 2404-2405 (2006). But vigorous opposition from the National Governors Association and others persuaded Congress to repeal the amendment a short time later, restoring the earlier language.

Is the language of §253 broad enough to give the President the flexibility she needs in responding to unforeseeable future emergencies? Does it impose any limit on the President's authority in a crisis to send troops into a state over the governor's objection? If a President were inclined for political reasons either to order federal military intervention or to withhold it in an emergency, would the statute restrict her choice?

3. Military Cooperation with Civilian Law Enforcement Officials. A dramatic surge in illicit drug traffic and related criminal activity during the 1970s and 1980s led President Reagan to declare a "war on drugs." Congress responded by enacting the 1981 legislation excerpted above, allowing the military to furnish equipment, facilities, and training to civilian law enforcement agencies, and to share relevant intelligence. 10 U.S.C. §§271-273. The statute also authorizes military personnel to operate equipment to intercept vessels or aircraft for law enforcement purposes. *Id.* §274. But it expressly forbids "direct participation by a member of the Army, Navy, Air Force, or Marine Corps in a search, seizure, arrest, or other similar activity unless . . . otherwise authorized by law." *Id.* §275. In separate legislation, the Defense Department was designated lead agency for the detection and monitoring of aerial and maritime shipments of illicit drugs into the United States. 10 U.S.C. §124 (2018).

Do you think these measures added to powers already enjoyed by the President under the Insurrection Act? If not, why did Congress bother to pass them?

4. Other Statutory Exceptions. Another exception to the Posse Comitatus Act is found in H.R.J. Res. 1292, Pub. L. No. 90-331, 82 Stat. 170 (1968), which directs federal agencies (including the Department of Defense) to assist the Secret Service in the performance of its protective duties. This authority was used by President Johnson to deploy federal troops in Chicago during the Democratic National Convention in 1968 and by President Nixon to control anti-war demonstrations on several occasions. Congress has also approved emergency military assistance in enforcing a prohibition on the unauthorized possession or use of nuclear material. 18 U.S.C. §831(e), (f) (2018).

5. Constitutional Exceptions. The Posse Comitatus Act includes an exception for "circumstances expressly authorized by the Constitution." One possible express constitutional exception may be found in Article IV, section 4, which provides, "The United States shall guarantee to every State in this Union a Republican Form of Government, and shall protect each of them against invasion; and on Application of the Legislature, or of the Executive (when the Legislature cannot be convened) against domestic Violence." Can you describe the limits of the President's power to use troops for law enforcement under this provision?

A Defense Department regulation once referred to two "constitutional exceptions" to the Posse Comitatus Act "based upon the inherent legal right of the U.S. Government — a sovereign national entity under the Federal Constitution — to insure the preservation of public order and the carrying out of governmental operations within its territorial limits, by force if necessary." 32 C.F.R. §215.4(c)(1) (2017). One exception was described as emergency authority to take

> prompt and vigorous Federal action, including use of military forces, to prevent loss of life or wanton destruction of property and to restore governmental functioning and public order when sudden and unexpected civil disturbances, disasters, or calamities seriously endanger life and property and disrupt normal governmental functions to such an extent that duly constituted local authorities are unable to control the situations. [*Id.* §215.4(c)(1)(i).]

The other was for "protection of Federal property and functions." *Id.* §215.4(c)(1)(ii). President Johnson apparently believed that he was exercising such inherent powers when he ordered the military to suppress rioting in Washington, D.C., following the assassination of Dr. Martin Luther King Jr. in 1968. *See* Proclamation No. 3840, 33 Fed. Reg. 5495 (Apr. 9, 1968). The powers claimed by DOD are not "expressly" set out in the constitutional text, of course. In 2018, the DOD regulation was removed as "outdated and unnecessary," *Employment of Military Resources in the Event of Civil Disturbances,* 83 Fed. Reg. 16774-01 (Apr. 17, 2018), and it has not been replaced.

Has Congress "occupied the field" by its enactment of the Posse Comitatus Act and its exceptions, precluding inconsistent exercise by the President of any inherent constitutional powers? Could Congress do so?

6. Law Enforcement or War Fighting? After being arrested by the FBI at O'Hare Airport, José Padilla was confined in a military brig for more than three years as an "enemy combatant" before finally being charged with criminal offenses related to terrorism. See *supra* p. 902. In responding to his petition for a writ of habeas corpus, one court remarked:

> Padilla argues also that his detention by the military violates the Posse Comitatus Act.... [T]he statute bars use of the military in civilian law enforcement. Padilla is not being detained by the military in order to execute a civilian law or for violating a civilian law, notwithstanding that his alleged conduct may in fact violate one or more such laws. He is being detained in order to interrogate him about the unlawful organization with which he is said to be affiliated and with which the military is in active combat, and to prevent him from becoming reaffiliated with that organization. Therefore, his detention by the military does not violate the Posse Comitatus Act. [*Padilla ex rel. Newman v. Bush,* 233 F. Supp. 2d 564, 588 n.9 (S.D.N.Y. 2002), *rev'd in part on other grounds sub nom. Padilla v. Rumsfeld,* 352 F.3d 695 (2d Cir. 2003), *rev'd,* 542 U.S. 426 (2004).]

Do you think the military can avoid application of the Posse Comitatus Act simply by characterizing a person it suspects of criminal activity as an "enemy combatant"? Or did the same statute that authorized Yaser Hamdi's military detention (*see Hamdi v. Rumsfeld,* 542 U.S. 507 (2004), *supra* p. 887) — the Authorization for the Use of Military Force, Pub. L. No. 107-40, 115 Stat. 224 (*supra* p. 88) — also provide a statutory exception to the Posse Comitatus Act that enabled Padilla's military detention?

If you think the designation of enemy combatants might be subject to abuse, can you suggest some realistic process for distinguishing between law enforcement and war fighting, at least for this purpose? Or can you articulate some other principled basis for limiting the military's role in activities that involve both law enforcement and war fighting?

B. DOMESTIC MILITARY INTELLIGENCE COLLECTION

Since the earliest days of the Republic, military intelligence units have supported domestic uses of military force. General George Washington was America's first spymaster. In principle, domestic intelligence collection by soldiers for force protection or as part of DOD's homeland defense mission has never been controversial. But military intelligence personnel have also been used at times to collect personal information about Americans who pose no real threat to national security. *See* Banks & Dycus, *supra,* at 166-196.

Domestic military intelligence activity reached a peak in the late 1960s, when the Pentagon compiled data on politically active Americans in an effort to quell civil rights and anti–Vietnam War demonstrations and to discredit protestors. The Army deployed 1,500 plainclothes agents to watch demonstrators, infiltrate organizations, and circulate blacklists. Military officials claimed that they were preparing for the use of troops to put down insurrections. *See* Christopher H. Pyle, *Military Surveillance of Civilian Politics, 1961-1971* (1986). In 1976, the Church Committee, looking into a variety of intelligence community abuses, called the Army program "the worst intrusion that military intelligence has ever made into the civilian community." S. Select Comm. to Study Governmental Operations with Respect to Intelligence Activities, *Improper Surveillance of Private Citizens by the Military (Church Committee Report)*, S. Rep. No. 94-755, bk. III, at 792 (1976). The Army surveillance program is also detailed in reports of an earlier committee headed by Senator Sam Ervin. Subcomm. on Constitutional Rights, S. Comm. on the Judiciary, *Military Surveillance of Civilian Politics: A Report*, 93d Cong. (1973). Public disclosure of this activity precipitated the following case.

Reading *Laird v. Tatum*

During the Vietnam War, soldiers watched anti-war demonstrators and infiltrated organizations. They monitored marches, teach-ins, and prayer vigils, and they collected biographical information on 100,000 Americans, including their age, ethnicity, economic status, political views, and education, with particular emphasis on women. Their targets included clergy, lawyers, professors, reporters, factory workers, state governors, members of Congress, and even one Supreme Court Justice.

When this Army intelligence program came to light in 1970, Frank Askin, a Rutgers law professor, and the ACLU filed a class-action lawsuit on behalf of opponents of the Vietnam War, asking for an injunction to stop the military surveillance of their lawful protests, and for an order to destroy the related dossiers, blacklists, and other records. They claimed that the program was intended to harass, intimidate, and deter them from exercising their rights of free expression and association by playing on justifiable fears that the data collected would be used to damage their reputations or opportunities for employment.

In reviewing the opinions that follow, consider these questions:

- Do you believe the Army's surveillance program was needed to prepare for a military response to civil unrest beyond the control of civil authorities?
- Do you think the plaintiffs were justifiably deterred by the program in exercising their First Amendment rights of free expression and association? Were their Fourth Amendment privacy rights implicated?
- How could the plaintiffs have established standing to sue by showing that they were individually targeted by the program?
- Might the Army program have violated the Posse Comitatus Act? If so, could a violation have been avoided by invoking the Insurrection Act?

Laird v. Tatum

United States Supreme Court, 1972
408 U.S. 1

Mr. Chief Justice Burger delivered the opinion of the Court. Respondents brought this class action in the District Court seeking declaratory and injunctive relief on their claim that their rights were being invaded by the Department of the Army's alleged "surveillance of lawful and peaceful civilian political activity." The petitioners in response describe the activity as "gathering by lawful means . . . (and) maintaining and using in their intelligence activities . . . information relating to potential or actual civil disturbances (or) street demonstrations." . . .

The President is authorized by 10 U.S.C. [§251][2] to make use of the armed forces to quell insurrection and other domestic violence if and when the conditions described in that section obtain within one of the States. Pursuant to those provisions, President Johnson ordered federal troops to assist local authorities at the time of the civil disorders in Detroit, Michigan, in the summer of 1967 and during the disturbances that followed the assassination of Dr. Martin Luther King. Prior to the Detroit disorders, the Army had a general contingency plan for providing such assistance to local authorities, but the 1967 experience led Army authorities to believe that more attention should be given to such preparatory planning. The data-gathering system here involved is said to have been established in connection with the development of more detailed and specific contingency planning designed to permit the Army, when called upon to assist local authorities, to be able to respond effectively with a minimum of force. As the Court of Appeals observed,

> In performing this type function the Army is essentially a police force or the back-up of a local police force. To quell disturbances or to prevent further disturbances the Army needs the same tools and, most importantly, the same information to which local police forces have access. Since the Army is sent into territory almost invariably unfamiliar to most soldiers and their commanders, their need for information is likely to be greater than that of the hometown policeman.
>
> No logical argument can be made for compelling the military to use blind force. When force is employed it should be intelligently directed, and this depends upon having reliable information — in time. As Chief Justice John Marshall said of Washington, "A general must be governed by his intelligence and must regulate his measures by his information. It is his duty to obtain correct information; . . . ." So we take it as undeniable that the military, *i.e.*, the Army, need a certain amount of information in order to perform their constitutional and statutory missions. 444 F.2d at 952-953 (footnotes omitted).

The system put into operation as a result of the Army's 1967 experience consisted essentially of the collection of information about public activities that were thought to have at least some potential for civil disorder, the reporting of that information to Army Intelligence headquarters at Fort Holabird, Maryland, the dissemination of these reports from headquarters to major Army posts around the country, and the storage of the reported information in a computer data bank located at Fort Holabird. The information itself was collected by a variety of means, but it is significant that the principal sources of information were the news media and publications in general circulation. Some of the information came from Army Intelligence agents who attended meetings that were open to the public and who wrote field reports describing the meetings, giving such data as the name of the sponsoring organization, the identity of speakers, the approximate number of persons in attendance, and an

---

2. "Whenever there is an insurrection in any State against its government, the President may, upon the request of its legislature or of its governor if the legislature cannot be convened, call into Federal service such of the militia of the other States, in the number requested by that State, and use such of the armed forces, as he considers necessary to suppress the insurrection." . . .

indication of whether any disorder occurred. And still other information was provided to the Army by civilian law enforcement agencies....

In recent years this Court has found in a number of cases that constitutional violations may arise from the deterrent, or "chilling," effect of governmental regulations that fall short of a direct prohibition against the exercise of First Amendment rights. In none of these cases, however, did the chilling effect arise merely from the individual's knowledge that a governmental agency was engaged in certain activities or from the individual's concomitant fear that, armed with the fruits of those activities, the agency might in the future take some other and additional action detrimental to that individual. Rather, in each of these cases, the challenged exercise of governmental power was regulatory, proscriptive, or compulsory in nature, and the complainant was either presently or prospectively subject to the regulations, proscriptions, or compulsions that he was challenging....

The decisions in these cases fully recognize that governmental action may be subject to constitutional challenge even though it has only an indirect effect on the exercise of First Amendment rights. At the same time, however, these decisions have in no way eroded the "established principle that to entitle a private individual to invoke the judicial power to determine the validity of executive or legislative action he must show that he has sustained, or is immediately in danger of sustaining, a direct injury as the result of that action...." *Ex parte Levitt,* 302 U.S. 633 (1937).

The respondents do not meet this test; their claim, simply stated, is that they disagree with the judgments made by the Executive Branch with respect to the type and amount of information the Army needs and that the very existence of the Army's data-gathering system produces a constitutionally impermissible chilling effect upon the exercise of their First Amendment rights. That alleged "chilling" effect may perhaps be seen as arising from respondents' very perception of the system as inappropriate to the Army's role under our form of government, or as arising from respondents' beliefs that it is inherently dangerous for the military to be concerned with activities in the civilian sector, or as arising from respondents' less generalized yet speculative apprehensiveness that the Army may at some future date misuse the information in some way that would cause direct harm to respondents. Allegations of a subjective "chill" are not an adequate substitute for a claim of specific present objective harm or a threat of specific future harm....

The concerns of the Executive and Legislative Branches in response to disclosure of the Army surveillance activities — and indeed the claims alleged in the complaint — reflect a traditional and strong resistance of Americans to any military intrusion into civilian affairs. That tradition has deep roots in our history and found early expression, for example, in the Third Amendment's explicit prohibition against quartering soldiers in private homes without consent and in the constitutional provisions for civilian control of the military. Those prohibitions are not directly presented by this case, but their philosophical underpinnings explain our traditional insistence on limitations on military operations in peacetime. Indeed, when presented with claims of judicially cognizable injury resulting from military intrusion into the civilian sector, federal courts are fully empowered to consider claims of those asserting such injury; there is nothing in our Nation's history or in this Court's decided cases, including our holding today, that can properly be seen as giving any indication that actual or threatened injury by reason of unlawful activities of the military would go unnoticed or unremedied.

Reversed.

Mr. Justice DOUGLAS, with whom Mr. Justice MARSHALL concurs, dissenting.

I...

... [W]e have until today consistently adhered to the belief that "[i]t is an unbending rule of law, that the exercise of military power, where the rights of the citizen are concerned, shall never be pushed beyond what the exigency requires." *Raymond v. Thomas*, 91 U.S. 712, 716....

The act of turning the military loose on civilians even if sanctioned by an Act of Congress, which it has not been, would raise serious and profound constitutional questions. Standing as it does only on brute power and Pentagon policy, it must be repudiated as a usurpation dangerous to the civil liberties on which free men are dependent. For, as Senator Sam Ervin has said, "this claim of an inherent executive branch power of investigation and surveillance on the basis of people's beliefs and attitudes may be more of a threat to our internal security than any enemies beyond our borders." Privacy and Government Investigations, 1971 U. Ill. L.F. 137, 153.

II

The claim that respondents have no standing to challenge the Army's surveillance of them and the other members of the class they seek to represent is too transparent for serious argument. The surveillance of the Army over the civilian sector — a part of society hitherto immune from its control — is a serious charge. It is alleged that the Army maintains files on the membership, ideology, programs, and practices of virtually every activist political group in the country, including groups such as the Southern Christian Leadership Conference, Clergy and Laymen United Against the War in Vietnam, the American Civil Liberties Union, Women's Strike for Peace, and the National Association for the Advancement of Colored People. The Army uses undercover agents to infiltrate these civilian groups and to reach into confidential files of students and other groups. The Army moves as a secret group among civilian audiences, using cameras and electronic ears for surveillance. The data it collects are distributed to civilian officials in state, federal, and local governments and to each military intelligence unit and troop command under the Army's jurisdiction (both here and abroad); and these data are stored in one or more data banks.

Those are the allegations; and the charge is that the purpose and effect of the system of surveillance is to harass and intimidate the respondents and to deter them from exercising their rights of political expression, protest, and dissent "by invading their privacy, damaging their reputations, adversely affecting their employment and their opportunities for employment, and in other ways." Their fear is that "permanent reports of their activities will be maintained in the Army's data bank, and their 'profiles' will appear in the so-called 'Blacklist' and that all of this information will be released to numerous federal and state agencies upon request."

Judge Wilkey, speaking for the Court of Appeals, properly inferred that this Army surveillance "exercises a present inhibiting effect on their full expression and utilization of their First Amendment rights." 444 F.2d 947, 954. That is the test. The "deterrent effect" on First Amendment rights by government oversight marks an unconstitutional intrusion, *Lamont v. Postmaster General,* 381 U.S. 301, 307. Or, as stated by Mr. Justice Brennan, "inhibition as well as prohibition against the exercise of precious First Amendment rights is a power denied to government." *Id.* at 309. . . .

The present controversy is not a remote, imaginary conflict. Respondents were targets of the Army's surveillance. First, the surveillance was not casual but massive and comprehensive. Second, the intelligence reports were regularly and widely circulated and were exchanged with reports of the FBI, state and municipal police departments, and the CIA. Third, the Army's surveillance was not collecting material in public records but staking out teams of agents, infiltrating undercover agents, creating command posts inside meetings, posing as press photographers and newsmen, posing as TV newsmen, posing as students, and shadowing public figures.

Finally, we know from the hearings conducted by Senator Ervin that the Army has misused or abused its reporting functions. Thus, Senator Ervin concluded that reports of the Army have been "taken from the Intelligence Command's highly inaccurate civil disturbance teletype and filed in Army dossiers on persons who have held, or were being considered for, security clearances, thus contaminating what are supposed to be investigative reports with unverified gossip and rumor. This practice directly jeopardized the employment and employment opportunities of persons seeking sensitive positions with the federal government or defense industry."[10]

Surveillance of civilians is none of the Army's constitutional business and Congress has not undertaken to entrust it with any such function. . . .

[Dissenting opinion of Mr. Justice BRENNAN, with whom Mr. Justice STEWART and Mr. Justice MARSHALL join, omitted.]

Notes and Questions

1. *Military vs. Non-Military Intelligence.* Is the domestic collection of intelligence by the military different in any legally significant way from collection by, say, the FBI? Can you say how?

2. *Grounds for Dismissal.* The *Laird* Court decided that the plaintiffs' claim was nonjusticiable because they could not demonstrate standing to sue, which would have required a showing of "actual present or immediately threatened injury." What might the plaintiffs have done to show the requisite personal injury? Could they have obtained the proof they needed through discovery? Through a request for DOD records under FOIA or the Privacy Act?

The *Laird* Court ruled that the plaintiffs' complaints about "the very existence of the Army's data-gathering system" and their "[a]llegation of a subjective 'chill' are not an adequate substitute for a claim of specific present objective harm or a threat of specific future harm." 408 U.S. at 13-14. Instead they claimed that they *might* be injured if information collected by the military in the future were misused in some way. Do you think Vietnam War protesters' fears of reprisal by government agencies were justified? See *supra* pp. 514-519

---

10. Hearings on Federal Data Banks, Computers and The Bill of Rights, before the Subcommittee on Constitutional Rights of the Senate Committee on the Judiciary, 92d Cong., 1st Sess. (1971).

3. Relevance of the Posse Comitatus Act? According to the *Laird* majority, the Army was "essentially a police force" when it collected domestic intelligence, ostensibly in planning for a response to civil unrest. Did the Army's surveillance program therefore run afoul of the Posse Comitatus Act? Why do you suppose the Court did not even mention the Act?

If the Court had addressed the Posse Comitatus Act, would any of its constitutional or statutory exceptions have applied? The Court cited the predecessor to 10 U.S.C. §251, one provision of the Insurrection Act, as authority for the deployment of military forces to help control rioting in several American cities in 1967 and 1968. But that authority was not invoked by the President for the Army's surveillance program, which extended over a number of years. Would any provision of the Insurrection Act have supported that program?

What about 10 U.S.C. §271, *supra*? It directs DOD to give "civilian law enforcement officials any information collected during the normal course of military training or operations that may be relevant to a violation of any Federal or State law," and it declares that the "needs of civilian law enforcement officials for information shall, to the maximum extent practicable, be taken into account in the planning and execution of military training or operations." *Id.* §271(a), (b). In light of this provision, are there any meaningful statutory constraints on military intelligence collection?

4. Post-Vietnam Reforms. In 1976, the Church Committee responded to the abuses outlined in *Laird* by proposing a "precisely drawn legislative charter" that would, *inter alia,* "limit military investigations to activities in the civilian community which are necessary and pertinent to the military mission, and which cannot feasibly be accomplished by civilian agencies." *Church Committee Report, supra,* bk. II, at 310-311. The committee apparently believed that military intelligence units could make no unique contributions to the domestic security efforts of the FBI, local law enforcement, and other civilian agencies. Its proposal also may have reflected concern about conducting domestic intelligence collection under a military chain of command, whose priority is completion of its military mission, rather than under the Attorney General, whose priority is law enforcement.

Congress did not enact the charter suggested by the Church Committee, but it did pass the Privacy Act in 1974, 5 U.S.C. §552a (2018), and the Foreign Intelligence Surveillance Act (FISA), 50 U.S.C. §§1801-1885c, analyzed in Chapters 21 and 22. Both measures limit the collection, retention, and sharing of information about how individuals exercise rights guaranteed by the First Amendment, as well as information not relevant to the mission of an agency. But as we saw earlier, serious doubts exist about the efficacy of these laws in safeguarding personal privacy.

Defense Department rules now limit the domestic collection and use of personal information. For example, DOD Dir. 5200.27, *Acquisition of Information Concerning Persons and Organizations Not Affiliated with the Department of Defense* (Jan. 7, 1980), includes the following restrictions:

> 5.2. No information shall be acquired about a person or organization solely because of lawful advocacy of measures in opposition to Government policy. . . .
>
> 5.5. There shall be no covert or otherwise deceptive surveillance or penetration of civilian organizations unless specifically authorized by the Secretary of Defense, or his designee. . . .

> 5.7. No computerized data banks shall be maintained relating to individuals or organizations not affiliated with the Department of Defense, unless authorized by the Secretary of Defense, or his designee. . . .
>
> 6.3. Access to information obtained under the provisions of this Directive shall be restricted to Governmental Agencies that require such information in the execution of their duties. . . .

See also DOD Dir. 5240.01, *DOD Intelligence Activities* (Aug. 27, 2007, with Change 2 Mar. 22, 2019). Moreover, according to DOD, "Defense Intelligence Components are not authorized to and will not engage in any intelligence activity, including dissemination to the White House, for the purpose of affecting the political process in the United States." DOD Man. 5240.01, *Procedures Governing the Conduct of DOD Intelligence Activities* 9 (Aug. 8, 2016).

Do the statutes and DOD rules outlined here effectively address the concerns expressed by the Church Committee and by the dissenters in *Laird*? Are additional reforms needed? If so, can you say what they are and what form they should take?

C. THE MILITARY'S ROLE IN RESPONDING TO DOMESTIC EMERGENCIES

Even before September 11, it was assumed that, for practical reasons, the military would be prominently involved in responding to substantial terrorist attacks at home, as well as to great natural disasters. Several qualities recommend it for such a role. No other agency of government has as much equipment, training, and experience in the use of force as the Defense Department does (although some worry that such force may not be sufficiently refined for use at home). No other agency has such a durable communications system. And no other agency, especially if the National Guard is counted among its forces, is so widely dispersed around the country in places where its services may be urgently needed.

1. Leading or Supporting Role?

The Homeland Security Act of 2002 directs the Administrator of FEMA to "lead the Nation's efforts to prepare for, protect against, respond to, recover from, and mitigate against the risk of natural disasters, acts of terrorism, and other man-made disasters, including catastrophic incidents." 6 U.S.C. §313(b)(2)(A) (2018). Current plans generally call for use of the armed forces in a domestic crisis upon "a request for DoD assistance from civil authorities or qualifying entities or [when] authorized by the President or Secretary of Defense." DOD Dir. No. 3025.18, *Defense Support of Civil Authorities (DSCA)* 3 (Dec. 29, 2010, with Change 2 Mar. 19, 2018). Troops providing that assistance nevertheless always operate under the military chain of command in coordination with civilian authorities. *Id.* at 6.

The Defense Department's own rules have long described its powers in the midst of a great domestic crisis as subordinate. For example, a 2015 manual declares, "The Department of Defense (DOD) leads homeland defense and is supported by the other federal agencies. In turn, the DOD supports the nation's homeland security effort, which is led by the Department of Homeland Security (DHS)." Dep't of

Defense, Air Land Sea Application Center, *Multi-Service Tactics, Techniques, and Procedures for Defense Support of Civil Authorities (DSCA)*, at 1 (Sept. 2015).

The distinction between homeland defense and homeland security may not always be easy, however. According to a 2013 DOD policy document, "[d]efending the homeland neither begins nor ends at U.S. borders.... The homeland is a functioning theater of operations, where DoD regularly performs a wide range of defense and civil support activities." Dep't of Defense, *Strategy for Homeland Defense and Defense Support of Civil Authorities* (Feb. 2013). The Defense Department also describes homeland defense as "a Constitutional exception" to the Posse Comitatus Act. Dep't of Defense, *Homeland Defense* (Jt. Pub. 3-27) (Apr. 10, 2018), at I-6. Moreover, it maintains, military operations conducted as homeland defense are not law enforcement activities, and thus are "not subject to the restriction of the PCA." *Id.* DOD protocols for homeland defense and homeland security are significantly different, but in the midst of a crisis there may be considerable confusion about which protocols to follow.

The Defense Department expects to play a lead role in at least two circumstances. According to DOD's internal rules, military commanders have "Immediate Response Authority" to act, in response to a request from civil officials, to "save lives, prevent human suffering, or mitigate great property damage within the United States" when "time does not permit approval from higher authority," DOD Dir. No. 3025.18, *supra*, at 5. They also may exercise "Emergency Authority" to "quell large-scale, unexpected civil disturbances... in extraordinary emergency circumstances where prior authorization by the President is impossible and duly constituted local authorities are unable to control the situation," and when such action is "necessary to prevent significant loss of life or wanton destruction of property and... to restore governmental function and public order." *Id.* at 6.

The military is necessarily in charge, of course, when martial law is declared.

2. Organizing for a Response

A "sense of Congress" provision in the Homeland Security Act of 2002 notes that existing laws, including the Insurrection Act and the Stafford Act, "grant the President broad powers that may be invoked in the event of domestic emergencies, including an attack against the Nation using weapons of mass destruction, and these laws specifically authorize the President to use the Armed Forces to help restore public order." 6 U.S.C. §466(a)(5) (2018).

In 2002, the Defense Department's newly-established Northern Command (NORTHCOM) assumed responsibility for DOD's homeland defense efforts and for provision of military support to civil authorities. *See generally U.S. Northern Command* (n.d.), *at* http://www.northcom.mil. NORTHCOM directs military responses to all kinds of threats, from terrorism to hurricanes, working closely with DHS. In a crisis, regular Army, National Guard, or Reserve personnel may be assigned to operate under NORTHCOM direction, depending on the scope of the mission and the nature of the situation.

The National Guard, with some 450,000 personnel, has a special role to play in the response to a terrorist attack. The nearly 5,000 Army and Air National Guard units scattered across the country have essentially the same relevant training and equipment as active-duty military elements, and they have extensive experience in firefighting, rescue, evacuation, and cleanup after storms and floods. Unless and until they are federalized by the President's order, however, Guard forces operate under the command of state governors, and so escape the strictures of the Posse Comitatus Act. Thus, there may be an incentive to delay placing these forces under federal command in order to preserve the maximum flexibility in their use.

Guard troops available to respond in a homeland security emergency include: (1) some 70 specialized WMD Civil Support Teams of 22 persons each, at least one in each state, who are ready on a moment's notice to deploy to the scene of a chemical or biological weapons attack; (2) 17 regional CBRN (chemical, biological, radiological, and nuclear weapons) teams, each including some 200 specially trained and equipped personnel; and (3) ten 570-member Homeland Response Forces, one for each of FEMA's ten geographical regions, to provide support for the CBRN units. In the event of a very large CBRN incident, perhaps involving simultaneous WMD attacks in different locations, DOD might also send in its brigade-size Defense CBRN Response Force, consisting of 5,200 individuals with special training and equipment, operating under NORTHCOM command.

Several developments in the wake of 9/11 point to an expanding domestic role for the military in intelligence collection. The Department of Homeland Security's Office of Intelligence & Analysis (I&A) receives, analyzes, and disseminates data about possible domestic terrorist threats from government and private sources, including the military's intelligence components. The National Counterterrorism Center (NCTC), located within the Office of the Director of National Intelligence, performs many of the same functions. Military intelligence personnel work in both of these agencies, where they become both suppliers and recipients of personal information, some of which may have no clear relevance to the Pentagon's homeland defense mission. And in 2002, NORTHCOM began receiving and "fusing" intelligence and law enforcement information from various sources, then redistributing it widely to federal, state, and local agencies.

3. New Rules After 9/11?

Six weeks after the terrorist attacks of 9/11, a 37-page Office of Legal Counsel (OLC) opinion described the domestic role of the military in these very expansive terms:

> [T]he President has ample constitutional and statutory authority to deploy the military against international or foreign terrorists operating within the United States. We further believe that the use of such military force generally is consistent with constitutional standards, and that it need not follow the exact procedures that govern law enforcement operations. [Memorandum for Alberto R. Gonzales, Counsel to the President, and William J. Haynes II, General Counsel, Dep't of Defense, from John C. Yoo, Deputy Ass't Att'y General, and Robert J. Delahunty, Special Counsel, Off. of Legal Counsel, *Re: Authority for Use of Military Force to Combat Terrorist Activities Within the United States* (Oct. 23, 2001), *available at* http://www.usdoj.gov/opa/documents/memomilitaryforcecombatus10232001.pdf.]

The opinion was not released to the public when it was written, and the extent of its influence on military planning and policy is unknown.

Seven years later, the Yoo/Delahunty memorandum was repudiated in substantial part by another OLC opinion. Memorandum for the Files from Steven G. Bradbury, Principal Deputy Ass't Att'y General, *October 23, 2001 OLC Opinion*

Addressing the Domestic Use of Military Force to Combat Terrorist Activities (Oct. 6, 2008), *available at* http://www.fas.org/irp/agency/doj/olc/caution.pdf. The new opinion urged "caution" in relying on the earlier one, describing several of its provisions as "either incorrect or highly questionable":

> The [2001] memorandum concludes . . . that the Fourth Amendment would not apply to domestic military operations, designed to deter and prevent further terrorist attacks. This conclusion does not reflect the current views of this Office. The Fourth Amendment is fully applicable to domestic military operations, though the application of the Fourth Amendment's essential "reasonableness" requirement to particular circumstances will be sensitive to the exigencies of military actions. . . .
>
> . . . [T]he memorandum also contains certain broad statements . . . suggesting that First Amendment speech and press rights and other guarantees of individual liberty under the Constitution would potentially be subordinated to overriding military necessities. These statements, too, were unnecessary to the opinion, are overbroad and general, and are not sufficiently grounded in the particular circumstances of a concrete scenario, and therefore cannot be viewed as authoritative.
>
> The memorandum concludes . . . that the domestic deployment of the Armed Forces by the President to prevent and deter terrorism would fundamentally serve a military purpose rather than a law enforcement purpose, and therefore the Posse Comitatus Act, 18 U.S.C. §1385 (2000), would not apply to such operations. Although the "military purpose" doctrine is a well-established limitation on the applicability of the Posse Comitatus Act, the broad conclusion . . . is far too general and divorced from specific facts and circumstances to be useful as an authoritative precedent of OLC.
>
> The memorandum treats the Authorization for Use of Military Force ("AUMF"), enacted by Congress in the immediate wake of 9/11, Pub. L. No. 107-40, 115 Stat. 224 (Sept. 18, 2001), as a statutory exception to the Posse Comitatus Act's restriction on the use of the military for domestic law enforcement. The better view, however, is that a reasonable and necessary use of military force taken under the authority of the AUMF would be a military action, potentially subject to the established "military purpose" doctrine, rather than a law enforcement action.
>
> The memorandum reasons . . . that in the aftermath of the 9/11 attacks, the Insurrection Act, 10 U.S.C. §333 (2000), would provide general authority for the President to deploy the military domestically to prevent and deter future terrorist attacks; whereas, consistent with the longstanding interpretation of the Executive Branch, any particular application of the Insurrection Act to authorize the use of the military for law enforcement purposes would require the presence of an actual obstruction of the execution of federal law or a breakdown in the ability of state authorities to protect federal rights. [Bradbury memorandum, at 1-2.]

Neither the Yoo/Delahunty nor the Bradbury memorandum was made public until March 2, 2009, after the Obama administration took office.

4. New Domestic Uses for the Military?

In 2018, President Donald J. Trump ordered the Secretary of Defense to "support the Department of Homeland Security in securing the southern border," and to request the use of National Guard troops to help "stop the flow of deadly drugs and other contraband, gang members and other criminals, and illegal aliens." Presidential Memorandum for the Sec. of Defense, the Att'y General, and the Sec. of Homeland Security, *Securing the Southern Border of the United States* (Apr. 4, 2018).

National Guard forces may be deployed pursuant to 32 U.S.C. §502(f)(2)(A) (2018), which provides that a member of the National Guard may be ordered to support "operations or missions undertaken by the member's unit at the request of the President or Secretary of Defense." Those serving in this special "Title 32 status" remain under the control of their state governors, and thus are not regarded as federal military personnel subject to the Posse Comitatus Act, even though they may receive federal pay and benefits. When Defense Secretary James Mattis requested Guard personnel to report for duty at the border to "support the men and women of law enforcement defending our nation's sovereignty and protecting the American people," DOD News, *National Guard Troops Deploy to Southern U.S. Border*, Apr. 7, 2018, some state governors complied, while others refused. Some subsequently withdrew state troops in protest of Trump administration immigration policies.

Subsequently, after Congress refused repeated requests from President Trump for funding to build a Border Wall stretching from Brownsville to San Diego, the President began sending about 5,900 active-duty U.S. troops to the southern border in October 2018, just before mid-term elections, to help stanch the flow of migrants. The following month, he signed a directive authorizing the troops to perform "military protective activities," including "a show or use of force (including lethal force, where necessary), crowd control, temporary detention, and cursory search" to protect border agents. *See* James LaPorta, *Donald Trump Signs Authorization for Border Troops Using Lethal Force as Migrant Caravan Approaches, Document Reveals*, Newsweek, Nov. 21, 2018.

Questioned about the legality of the deployment, Secretary Mattis responded that "they're not even carrying guns, so just relax. . . . Don't worry about it, OK?" *See* William Banks, *Legal Analysis of "Cabinet Memo" on the Military's Role at Southern Border*, Just Security, Nov. 26, 2018. One statute authorizes military personnel to provide limited support for counterdrug activities or to counter transnational organized crime, including the monitoring of traffic within 25 miles of the U.S. border, and the construction of roads and fences, but not to participate directly in searches, seizures, arrests, or similar activities. 10 U.S.C. §284. Otherwise, active duty military forces "do not appear to have a direct legislative mandate to protect or patrol the border or to engage in immigration enforcement." Jennifer K. Elsea, *The President's Authority to Use the National Guard or the Armed Forces to Secure the Border* 3 (Cong. Res. Serv. LSB10121), Apr. 19, 2018.

By mid-2019, some 6,600 National Guard and active-duty troops were deployed along the border. Their activities reportedly were largely confined to stringing concertina wire and creating other barriers, transporting Immigration and Customs Enforcement personnel, conducting surveillance, and caring for Border Patrol horses. They were also stationed inside at least one detention facility for undocumented immigrants, assigned to "monitor" adults and children confined there. Courtney Kube & Carol E. Lee, *Active-Duty U.S. Troops Are Now Just Feet Away from Migrants in Texas*, NBC News, July 25, 2019.

Notes and Questions

1. *How the Military Can Help.* Review carefully the plague scenario set forth *supra* p. 1161. What useful role could military forces have played in responding to the notional bioterrorist attack?

If military forces are deployed in such an emergency, who should make the decisions about when and how to use them? Do you agree that agencies other than DOD should play the lead role in responding whenever possible?

2. *Need for New Rules?* Suppose the Yoo/Delahunty OLC opinion accurately stated the law after 9/11 — that domestic military counterterrorism operations would not be constrained by the First and Fourth Amendments, and that the AUMF could be read as a statutory exception to the Posse Comitatus Act. (Note that the 2008 Bradbury memo does not altogether dismiss this possibility.) What, if any, limits would then exist on the domestic employment of military forces? Are new rules needed to provide or clarify limits?

3. *Cooperation Between DOD and Other Agencies.* Based on the brief description of authorities and plans set out in this chapter and the preceding one, how would you rate the chances for a strong, efficient collaboration between the Departments of Defense and Justice in responding to a terrorist attack? What about between DOD and FEMA?

4. *Troops on the Border.* Are there limits under the Posse Comitatus Act on the activities of troops deployed at the U.S. southern border? *See* Banks, *Legal Analysis, supra*; Scott R. Anderson, *The Constitutional Crisis Already at the Border*, Lawfare, Jan. 22, 2019; Mark Nevitt, *Update: The Military, the Mexican Border and Posse Comitatus*, Just Security, Nov. 6, 2018. What tasks might Title 32 Guard forces perform that active-duty federalized Guards could not?

Is there any legal limit to duties that could be assigned to troops at the border if the President invoked the Insurrection Act? Can you guess why he had not done so as of late 2019?

D. MARTIAL LAW: WHEN PLANNING FAILS

If, in the event of an actual or threatened terrorist attack, or a large natural disaster, the execution of federal emergency plans fails to restore order, or if such plans are perceived as inadequate, martial law might be invoked as the option of last resort. Such a drastic step might seem advisable because of the military's extensive, coherent organization, its tradition of discipline, its robust communications systems, and its training in the use of force. Martial law could be declared by the President as Commander in Chief of U.S. armed forces, by a state governor as head of an unfederalized National Guard, or by a military officer in the field. Without specific guidance from higher authority, military leaders would then be governed only by rules fashioned by them to fit the situation. The content of the rules and the duration of their enforcement would, by definition, be impossible to predict. So, necessarily, would be the effect on Americans' civil liberties.

In the middle of the eighteenth century, Blackstone described martial law as

> temporary excrescences bred out of the distemper of the state, and not any part of the permanent and perpetual laws of the kingdom. For martial law, which is built upon no settled principles, but is entirely arbitrary in its decisions, is . . . in truth and reality no law, but something indulged rather than allowed as a law. [2 William Blackstone, *Commentaries* *413.]

A century later, in a Civil War–era case, the Supreme Court, in dicta, described the circumstances under which martial law might be invoked.

Ex parte Milligan

United States Supreme Court, 1866
71 U.S. (4 Wall.) 2

[Another part of the decision is set forth *supra* p. 830.]

Mr. Justice DAVIS delivered the opinion of the court. . . . When peace prevails, and the authority of the government is undisputed, there is no difficulty of preserving the safeguards of liberty; for the ordinary modes of trial are never neglected, and no one wishes it otherwise; but if society is disturbed by civil commotion — if the passions of men are aroused and the restraints of law weakened, if not disregarded — these safeguards need, and should receive, the watchful care of those intrusted with the guardianship of the Constitution and laws. In no other way can we transmit to posterity unimpaired the blessings of liberty, consecrated by the sacrifices of the Revolution.

It is claimed that martial law covers with its broad mantle the proceedings of this military commission. The proposition is this: that in a time of war the commander of an armed force (if in his opinion the exigencies of the country demand it, and of which he is to judge), has the power, within the lines of the military district, to suspend all civil rights and their remedies, and subject citizens as well as soldiers to the *rule* of his will; and in the exercise of his lawful authority cannot be restrained, except by his superior officer or the President of the United States.

If this position is sound to the extent claimed, then when war exists, foreign or domestic, and the country is subdivided into military departments for mere convenience, the commander of one of them can, if he chooses, within his limits, on the plea of necessity, with the approval of the Executive, substitute military force for and to the exclusion of the laws, and punish all persons, as he thinks right and proper, without fixed or certain rules.

The statement of this proposition shows its importance; for, if true, republican government is a failure, and there is an end of liberty regulated by law. Martial law, established on such a basis, destroys every guarantee of the Constitution, and effectually renders the "military independent of and superior to the civil power" — the attempt to do which by the King of Great Britain was deemed by our fathers such an offence, that they assigned it to the world as one of the causes which impelled them to declare their independence. Civil liberty and this kind of martial law cannot endure together; the antagonism is irreconcilable; and, in the conflict, one or the other must perish. . . .

It will be borne in mind that this is not a question of the power to proclaim martial law, when war exists in a community and the courts and civil authorities are overthrown. Nor is it a question what rule a military commander, at the head of his army, can impose on states in rebellion to cripple their resources and quell the insurrection. The jurisdiction claimed is much more extensive. The necessities of the service, during the late Rebellion, required that the loyal states should be placed within the limits of certain military districts and commanders appointed in them; and, it is urged, that this, in a military sense, constituted them the theatre of military operations; and, as in this case, Indiana had been and was again threatened with invasion by the enemy, the occasion was furnished to establish martial law. The conclusion does not follow from the premises. If armies were collected in Indiana, they were to be employed in another locality, where the laws were obstructed and the national authority disputed. On *her* soil there was no hostile foot; if once invaded, that invasion was at an end, and with it all pretext for martial law. Martial law cannot arise from a *threatened* invasion. The necessity must be actual and present; the invasion real, such as effectually closes the courts and deposes the civil administration.

It is difficult to see how the *safety* for the country required martial law in Indiana. If any of her citizens were plotting treason, the power of arrest could secure them, until the government was prepared for their trial, when the courts were open and ready to try them. It was as easy to protect witnesses before a civil as a military tribunal; and as there could be no wish to convict, except on sufficient legal evidence, surely an ordained and established court was better able to judge of this than a military tribunal composed of gentlemen not trained to the profession of the law.

It follows, from what has been said on this subject, that there are occasions when martial rule can be properly applied. If, in foreign invasion or civil war, the courts are actually closed, and it is impossible to administer criminal justice according to law, *then*, on the theatre of active military operations, where war really prevails, there is a necessity to furnish a substitute for the civil authority, thus overthrown, to preserve the safety of the army and society; and as no power is left but the military, it is allowed to govern by martial rule until the laws can have their free course. As necessity creates the rule, so it limits its duration; for, if this government is continued *after* the courts are reinstated, it is a gross usurpation of power. Martial rule can never exist where the courts are open, and in the proper and unobstructed exercise of their jurisdiction. It is also confined to the locality of actual war. Because, during the late Rebellion it could have been enforced in Virginia, where the national authority was overturned and the courts driven out, it does not follow that it should obtain in Indiana, where that authority was never disputed, and justice was always administered. And so in the case of a foreign invasion, martial rule may become a necessity in one state, when, in another, it would be "mere lawless violence." . . .

Notes and Questions

1. Judicial Treatment of Martial Law. In an earlier case growing out of a rebellion in Rhode Island, the Court indicated that

> a State may use its military power to put down an armed insurrection, too strong to be controlled by the civil authority. The power is essential to the existence of every government, essential to the preservation of order and free institutions, and is as necessary to the States of this Union as to any other government. [*Luther v. Borden*, 48 U.S. (7 How.) 1, 44-45 (1849).]

In litigation arising in New Orleans, after that city had been captured by the Union Army in 1862 and placed under martial law, the Court declared that "[m]artial law is the law of military necessity in the actual presence of war." *United States v. Diekelman*, 92 U.S. 520, 526 (1876). And in his concurring opinion in *Youngstown Sheet & Tube Co.*

v. Sawyer (*Steel Seizure Case*), 343 U.S. 579 (1952), Justice Jackson was careful to exclude from his discussion of emergency powers based on necessity, "as in a very limited category by itself, the establishment of martial law." *Id.* at 650 n.19 (Jackson, J., concurring).

The governor of Hawaii declared martial law immediately after the Japanese attack on Pearl Harbor, as he was authorized to do by the Hawaii Organic Act, ch. 339, §67, 31 Stat. 141, 153 (1900). Testing a military tribunal's power to try civilians for ordinary criminal offenses, the Supreme Court observed that "the term 'martial law' carries no precise meaning. The Constitution does not refer to 'martial law' at all and no Act of Congress has defined the term. It has been employed in various ways by different people and at different times." *Duncan v. Kahanamoku,* 327 U.S. 304, 315 (1946). Then, struggling to avoid describing the limits of executive or legislative power, the Court found that in using the term "martial law" Congress had not intended to authorize the supplanting of courts by military tribunals, at least in the circumstances in Hawaii after Pearl Harbor.

2. Standby Martial Law? In June 1955, the government conducted a massive civil defense exercise to practice responses to a Soviet nuclear attack. To almost everyone's surprise, President Eisenhower hypothetically declared nationwide martial law, suspended the writ of habeas corpus, and authorized military commanders to stop the functioning of local courts. His action was widely criticized as unnecessary and improper. *See, e.g.,* Robert S. Rankin & Winfried R. Dallmayr, *Freedom and Emergency Powers in the Cold War* 56-60 (1964). Nevertheless, throughout much of the Cold War the government had in place a comprehensive secret plan, called "Plan D," for responding to the threat of a nuclear attack. One element of that plan, Presidential Emergency Action Directive No. 21, apparently included a draft executive order declaring martial law.

In 1987, the *Miami Herald* reported that Lt. Col. Oliver North (remembered now for his role in the Iran-Contra Affair) and FEMA had drafted a new emergency plan calling for suspension of the Constitution, imposition of martial law, appointment of military commanders to run state and local governments, and detention of dissidents and Central American refugees. Alfonso Chardy, *Reagan Advisors Ran "Secret" Government,* Miami Herald, July 5, 1987; *see also* Jules Lobel, *Emergency Power and the Decline of Liberalism,* 98 Yale L.J. 1385, 1420 (1989) (noting that North denied drawing up such a plan).

Do you think the President should carry a draft order declaring martial law with her at all times? If so, do you think the terms of the order and criteria for its execution, or at least the fact of its existence, should be publicized?

3. Conditions for Martial Law. One of us has argued that the insurrection statutes, 10 U.S.C. §§251-255, effectively delegate to the President the power to impose martial law. Vladeck, *supra* p. 1193, at 152-153. If Congress has so conferred this power on the President, it has done no more to clarify the circumstances under which the power might be exercised.

The Supreme Court in *Ex parte Milligan* did not have to discuss martial law to decide the case before it. But its dicta have long been regarded as setting forth conditions for the declaration of martial law. Can you describe reasons for each criterion based on practical considerations and on concerns for the preservation of representative civilian government?

For many years, a Defense Department regulation described circumstances that would justify the invocation of martial law this way:

> Martial law depends for its justification upon public necessity. Necessity gives rise to its creation; necessity justifies its exercise; and necessity limits its duration. The extent of the military force used and the actual measures taken, consequently, will depend upon the actual threat to order and public safety which exists at the time. In most instances the decision to impose martial law is made by the President. . . . However, the decision to impose martial law may be made by the local commander on the spot, if the circumstances demand immediate action, and time and available communications facilities do not permit obtaining prior approval from higher authority. [32 C.F.R. §501.4 (2007).]

The regulation was inexplicably removed in 2008 and not replaced with another that expressly addresses martial law. DOD's current rules and regulations for martial law, if any, are not publicly known.

Do the criteria in either *Ex parte Milligan* or the former DOD regulation allow you to predict when martial law might properly be declared? Would it be possible, or wise, to try to develop more specific guidelines? Could you draft the guidelines?

4. Planning to Avoid Martial Law. As a practical matter, do you think any statutory or regulatory prescriptions could deter the President or military officials from declaring martial law in the wake of a terrorist attack involving a weapon of mass destruction, or in the aftermath of a great natural disaster? Can you think of any way to limit the resort to martial law in such a crisis?

THE MILITARY'S DOMESTIC ROLE: SUMMARY OF BASIC PRINCIPLES

- From the earliest days of the Republic, Americans have sought to avoid military involvement in civilian affairs whenever possible, a concern reflected in the Declaration of Independence, the Commander in Chief Clause, and the Third and Fifth Amendments. Nevertheless, military forces have occasionally proved invaluable when civil authorities were unable to keep the peace or recover from natural disasters.
- The Posse Comitatus Act generally bars military participation in civilian law enforcement, with certain statutory or constitutional exceptions.
- Military actions may violate the Posse Comitatus Act if they are regulatory, proscriptive, or compulsory in nature, or if the military role in law enforcement is direct, active, or pervasive. These criteria are reflected in Defense Department rules but may be difficult to apply in practice.
- Compliance with the Posse Comitatus Act is a measure of reasonableness under the Fourth Amendment.
- The Insurrection Act gives the President very broad authority to order the deployment of National Guard or regular military forces to keep the peace

or enforce the law, while also providing political accountability by requiring a presidential proclamation.

- Massive civil rights violations by Army surveillance of civilians during the Vietnam War era were somewhat ambiguously addressed by statutory and regulatory reforms.

- Since 9/11, the military's role in homeland security has increased substantially, blurring the line between defense and homeland security. It has thus become increasingly difficult to distinguish among its domestic activities as law enforcement, peacekeeping, war fighting, or counterintelligence.

- Criteria for invoking martial law are uncertain, and the content of martial law is by definition unknowable.

PART IX

OBTAINING AND PROTECTING NATIONAL SECURITY INFORMATION

Safeguarding National Security Information

As citizens, we can only make rational decisions about our destinies — indeed, can only hope to be in control of our own futures — if we have access to information about the government to which we collectively submit. In 1966, the authors of the Freedom of Information Act (FOIA) observed that "[a] democratic society requires an informed, intelligent electorate, and the intelligence of the electorate varies as the quantity and quality of its information varies." H.R. Rep. No. 89-1497, at 12 (1966). Put more bluntly, as one federal circuit court wrote in 2002, "Democracies die behind closed doors." *Detroit Free Press v. Ashcroft*, 303 F.3d 681, 683 (6th Cir. 2002).

Of course, there are circumstances when it is in the public interest not to disclose some activities of the government. Among the most compelling are those involving national security and foreign relations. In this democracy, we have struck a bargain with ourselves to surrender some knowledge — and with it the power that knowledge gives — to our elected representatives, with the understanding that they will use that knowledge to keep us safe.

Yet the terms of that bargain have always been controversial and are the subject of constant renegotiation. In this chapter, we begin by examining some of the most controversial elements of that dynamic bargain, then review basic guidelines for withholding government information from public view when national security is implicated. We then consider restrictions on access to government secrets — security clearances — and criminal prosecution of leakers under the Espionage Act.

A. BALANCING SECRECY, SECURITY, AND SELF-DETERMINATION

1. Elements of the Bargain

One expert identifies three distinct categories of government secrecy:

> The first, "genuine national security secrecy," works to protect information that would pose an identifiable threat to the security of the nation by compromising its defense or the conduct of its foreign relations. Such information could include design details of weapons of mass destruction and other advanced military or intelligence technologies, current military operational plans, identities of intelligence sources, confidential diplomatic initiatives, and similarly sensitive matters. Protection of such information is not controversial. . . .
>
> A second category that often masks itself as genuine national security secrecy, however, is actually something quite different. . . . It reflects that natural tendency of bureaucracies . . . to hoard information. Whether out of convenience or a dim suspicion that disclosure is intrinsically riskier than non-disclosure, government agencies always seem to err on the side of secrecy even when there is no obvious advantage to doing so. . . .
>
> The third category of secrecy, "political secrecy," uses classification authority for political advantage. . . . It exploits the generally accepted legitimacy of genuine national security interests in order to advance a self-serving agenda, to evade controversy, or to thwart accountability. In extreme cases, political secrecy conceals violations of law and threatens the integrity of the political process itself. [Steven Aftergood, *Reducing Government Secrecy: Finding What Works,* 27 Yale L. & Pol'y Rev. 399, 402-403 (2009).]

Our concern here is with protecting the first category of secrets without leaving government officials entirely unaccountable to Congress or the people. Regarding the second and third categories of secrets, our goal is (according to almost everyone) to eliminate them. But agreement on how to pursue these goals has proven elusive.

We assume that the government has secrets (e.g., U.S. covert agents in Russia), although we don't know exactly what those secrets are. Suppose, however, that members of the public are "unaware of a secret's existence; they are in the dark about the fact that they are being kept in the dark." David E. Pozen, *Deep Secrecy,* 62 Stan. L. Rev. 257, 260 (2010). According to Pozen, this category of secrets is suggested in an oft-quoted remark by former Defense Secretary Donald Rumsfeld: "[A]s we know, there are known knowns; there are things we know we know. We also know there are known unknowns; that is to say we know there are some things we do not know. But there are also unknown unknowns — the ones we don't know we don't know." *Id.* at 257 (quoting Department of Defense News Briefing (Feb. 12, 2002), *available at* https://archive.defense.gov/Transcripts/Transcript.aspx?TranscriptID=2636). Such secrets might, in Pozen's view, pose an especially serious threat to democracy.

Hardly anyone argues that the government keeps too *few* secrets. A government body concerned with protection of sensitive information concluded recently that "present practices for classification and declassification of national security information are outmoded, unsustainable and keep too much information from the public." Pub. Interest Declassification Bd. *Transforming the Security Classification System* 1 (2012), *available at* https://www.archives.gov/declassification/pidb/recommendations. Justice Potter Stewart expressed a similar sentiment in his concurring opinion in the *Pentagon Papers* case: "[W]hen everything is classified, then nothing is classified, and the system becomes one to be disregarded by the cynical or the careless, and to be manipulated by those intent on self-protection or self-promotion." *N.Y. Times Co. v. United States,* 403 U.S. 713, 729 (1971) (Stewart, J., concurring).

2. Balancing Secrecy and Transparency

According to one scholar, "Under-enforced and often unenforceable laws and regulations, bureaucratic inertia and resistance, and the push and pull of an advanced democracy with vibrant civil institutions render both transparency and secrecy implausible." Mark Fenster, *The Implausibility of Secrecy*, 65 Hastings L.J. 309, 315 (2014). Reflecting the difficulty, there has been a recurring shift back and forth between the two, as one presidential administration has succeeded another. These shifts may be a reaction to world events as much as a reflection of differing political ideologies. For example, a George W. Bush administration official wrote that, given the possibility of further attacks after 9/11, "federal agencies are concerned with the need to protect critical systems, facilities, stockpiles, and other assets from security breaches and harm . . . [and] the protection of any agency information that could enable someone to succeed in causing the feared harm." Memorandum for Heads of All Federal Departments and Agencies from John Ashcroft, Att'y General, *The Freedom of Information Act*, Oct. 15, 2001. By contrast, on his first full day in office, President Barack Obama declared a "commit[ment] to creating an unprecedented level of openness in Government. We will work together to ensure the public trust and establish a system of transparency, public participation, and collaboration. Openness will strengthen our democracy and promote efficiency and effectiveness in Government." Memorandum from Barack Obama for Heads of Executive Departments and Agencies, *Transparency and Open Government*, Jan. 21, 2009.

The shifting balance is also reflected in part in a succession of statutes, executive orders, and agency regulations setting forth rules for classification and protection of national security information. *See* Jennifer K. Elsea, *The Protection of Classified Information: The Legal Framework* (Cong. Res. Serv. RS21900), May 18, 2017. The most important examples appear below.

B. CLASSIFICATION OF NATIONAL SECURITY INFORMATION

Executive Order No. 13,526, Classified National Security Information

75 Fed. Reg. 707 (Dec. 29, 2009)

This order prescribes a uniform system for classifying, safeguarding, and declassifying national security information, including information relating to defense against transnational terrorism. . . .

PART 1 — ORIGINAL CLASSIFICATION

Section 1.1. Classification Standards

(a) Information may be originally classified under the terms of this order only if all of the following conditions are met:

(1) an original classification authority is classifying the information;

(2) the information is owned by, produced by or for, or is under the control of the United States Government;

(3) the information falls within one or more of the categories of information listed in section 1.4 of this order; and

(4) the original classification authority determines that the unauthorized disclosure of the information reasonably could be expected to result in damage to the national security, which includes defense against transnational terrorism, and the original classification authority is able to identify or describe the damage.

(b) If there is significant doubt about the need to classify information, it shall not be classified. . . .

(c) Classified information shall not be declassified automatically as a result of any unauthorized disclosure of identical or similar information. . . .

Sec. 1.2. Classification Levels

(a) Information may be classified at one of the following three levels:

(1) "Top Secret" shall be applied to information, the unauthorized disclosure of which reasonably could be expected to cause exceptionally grave damage to the national security that the original classification authority is able to identify or describe.

(2) "Secret" shall be applied to information, the unauthorized disclosure of which reasonably could be expected to cause serious damage to the national security that the original classification authority is able to identify or describe.

(3) "Confidential" shall be applied to information, the unauthorized disclosure of which reasonably could be expected to cause damage to the national security that the original classification authority is able to identify or describe. . . .

(c) If there is significant doubt about the appropriate level of classification, it shall be classified at the lower level.

Sec. 1.3. Classification Authority

(a) The authority to classify information originally may be exercised only by:

(1) the President and the Vice President;

(2) agency heads and officials designated by the President; and

(3) United States Government officials delegated this authority. . . .

Sec. 1.4. Classification Categories

Information shall not be considered for classification unless its unauthorized disclosure could reasonably be expected to cause identifiable or describable damage to the national security in accordance with section 1.2 of this order, and it pertains to one or more of the following:

(a) military plans, weapons systems, or operations;

(b) foreign government information;

(c) intelligence activities (including covert action), intelligence sources or methods, or cryptology;

(d) foreign relations or foreign activities of the United States, including confidential sources;

(e) scientific, technological, or economic matters relating to the national security;

(f) United States Government programs for safeguarding nuclear materials or facilities;

(g) vulnerabilities or capabilities of systems, installations, infrastructures, projects, plans, or protection services relating to the national security; or

(h) the development, production, or use of weapons of mass destruction.

Sec. 1.5. Duration of Classification

(a) At the time of original classification, the original classification authority shall establish a specific date or event for declassification. . . . Upon reaching the date or event, the information shall be automatically declassified. Except for information that should clearly and demonstrably be expected to reveal the identity of a confidential human source or a human intelligence source or key design concepts of weapons of mass destruction, the date or event shall not exceed the time frame established in paragraph (b) of this section.

(b) If the original classification authority cannot determine an earlier specific date or event for declassification, information shall be marked for declassification 10 years from the date of the original decision, unless the original classification authority otherwise determines that the sensitivity of the information requires that it be marked for declassification for up to 25 years from the date of the original decision. . . .

Sec. 1.6. Identification and Markings

(a) At the time of original classification, the following shall be indicated in a manner that is immediately apparent:

(1) one of the three classification levels defined in section 1.2 of this order;

(2) the identity, by name and position, or by personal identifier, of the original classification authority;

(3) the agency and office of origin, if not otherwise evident;

(4) declassification instructions . . . ; and

(5) a concise reason for classification that, at a minimum, cites the applicable classification categories in section 1.4 of this order. . . .

Sec. 1.7. Classification Prohibitions and Limitations

(a) In no case shall information be classified, continue to be maintained as classified, or fail to be declassified in order to:

(1) conceal violations of law, inefficiency, or administrative error;

(2) prevent embarrassment to a person, organization, or agency; . . .

(b) Basic scientific research information not clearly related to the national security shall not be classified. . . .

PART 3 — DECLASSIFICATION AND DOWNGRADING

Sec. 3.1. Authority for Declassification

(a) Information shall be declassified as soon as it no longer meets the standards for classification under this order. . . .

(d) It is presumed that information that continues to meet the classification requirements under this order requires continued protection. In some exceptional cases, however, the need to protect such information may be outweighed by the public interest in disclosure of the information, and in these cases the information should be declassified. . . .

Sec. 3.3. Automatic Declassification

(a) Subject to paragraphs (b)-(d) and (g)-(j) of this section, all classified records that (1) are more than 25 years old and (2) have been determined to have permanent historical value under title 44, United States Code, shall be automatically declassified whether or not the records have been reviewed. . . .

(b) An agency head may exempt from automatic declassification under paragraph (a) of this section specific information, the release of which should clearly and demonstrably be expected to:

(1) reveal the identity of a confidential human source, a human intelligence source, a relationship with an intelligence or security service of a foreign government or international organization, or a nonhuman intelligence source; or impair the effectiveness of an intelligence method currently in use, available for use, or under development;

(2) reveal information that would assist in the development, production, or use of weapons of mass destruction;

(3) reveal information that would impair U.S. cryptologic systems or activities;

(4) reveal information that would impair the application of state-of-the-art technology within a U.S. weapon system;

(5) reveal formally named or numbered U.S. military war plans that remain in effect, or reveal operational or tactical elements of prior plans that are contained in such active plans;

(6) reveal information, including foreign government information, that would cause serious harm to relations between the United States and a foreign government, or to ongoing diplomatic activities of the United States;

(7) reveal information that would impair the current ability of United States Government officials to protect the President, Vice President, and other protectees for whom protection services, in the interest of the national security, are authorized;

(8) reveal information that would seriously impair current national security emergency preparedness plans or reveal current vulnerabilities of systems, installations, or infrastructures relating to the national security; or

(9) violate a statute, treaty, or international agreement that does not permit the automatic or unilateral declassification of information at 25 years. . . .

Sec. 3.5. Mandatory Declassification Review

(a) Except as provided in paragraph (b) of this section, all information classified under this order or predecessor orders shall be subject to a review for declassification by the originating agency if:

(1) the request for a review [most often under the Freedom of Information Act] describes the document or material containing the information with

sufficient specificity to enable the agency to locate it with a reasonable amount of effort. . . .

(b) Information originated by the incumbent President or the incumbent Vice President . . . or other entities within the Executive Office of the President that solely advise and assist the incumbent President is exempted from the provisions of paragraph (a) of this section. . . .

PART 4 — SAFEGUARDING

Sec. 4.1. General Restrictions on Access

(a) A person may have access to classified information provided that:

(1) a favorable determination of eligibility for access has been made by an agency head or the agency head's designee;

(2) the person has signed an approved nondisclosure agreement; and

(3) the person has a need-to-know the information. . . .

PART 6 — GENERAL PROVISIONS

Sec. 6.1. Definitions

For purposes of this order: . . .

(l) "Damage to the national security" means harm to the national defense or foreign relations of the United States from the unauthorized disclosure of information, taking into consideration such aspects of the information as the sensitivity, value, utility, and provenance of that information. . . .

Notes and Questions

1. *Who Can Classify?* According to the 2009 executive order, information may be classified only by an original classification authority, §1.1(a)(1), including the President and Vice President, department heads and others designated by the President, and "officials delegated this authority." §1.3(a). At the end of FY2018, there were 1,674 original classification authorities. Information Security Oversight Office (ISOO), *2018 Report to the President* 4 (Aug. 16, 2019). In practice, however, tens of thousands of agency employees apply classification markings to records every day. Who do you think should be authorized — or is needed — to create new government secrets? Should contractors ever be given this authority?

2. *Classification Standards.* What is the threshold standard for original classification of particular information? How does it differ by classification level?

If you were an agency official, would the executive order provide enough guidance to enable you to determine when information should be classified and at what level? *See* Steven Aftergood, *An Inquiry into the Dynamics of Government Secrecy*, 48 Harv. C.R.-C.L. L. Rev. 511, 513 (2013) (definitions of "damage" and "national security" "grant all but unlimited discretion to classification officials"). Could a federal judge apply these criteria with confidence in any case, or is deference to agency professionals a practical necessity? Can you suggest alternative or additional language that would be more helpful? Should Congress supply clearer guidance?

3. Categories of Classifiable Information. What categories of information can be classified? Obviously, information about a weapons system could qualify. What about information on interest rates set by the Federal Reserve? Highway construction standards generated by the Federal Highway Administration? What about information on bribery of government contracting officials in the development of a weapons system?

4. Duration. According to the executive order, "[n]o information may remain classified indefinitely." §1.5(d). Each document classified must be marked with a date for its automatic declassification not more than 25 years hence, unless its disclosure would "clearly and demonstrably be expected to reveal the identity of a confidential human source or a human intelligence source or key design concepts of weapons of mass destruction." §1.5(a). The order also requires the automatic declassification of records determined to have "permanent historical value" after 25 years, although an agency head may exempt such records from release if they present any of the risks described in §3.3(b). In exceptional circumstances, however, a record may be withheld for more than 75 years! §3.3(h)(3). In one remarkable case in 2003, the FBI was able to deny a history professor access to files on Gerhard Eisler and Clinton Jencks, suspected Communists investigated by the Bureau in 1947 and 1953, respectively. *See Schrecker v. U.S. Dep't of Justice,* 349 F.3d 657 (D.C. Cir. 2003). What are the implications for a representative democracy of keeping information about government actions secret for so long?

Of more than 83 million pages of materials reviewed for declassification in FY2017, almost all were part of the automatic declassification process, and more than 46 million pages were declassified. Information Security Oversight Office (ISOO), *2017 Report to the President* 14 (May 31, 2018). In its 2018 report, ISOO apparently discontinued its practice of disclosing numbers of pages classified and declassified each year.

5. Sources and Limits of Presidential Secrecy Power. Each President's classification order declares that the President is relying not upon any specific statutory provision, but rather upon "the authority vested in me by the Constitution and statutes, and as President of the United States."

Does the Commander in Chief Clause of Article II support the President's claim of inherent secrecy authority? In *Department of the Navy v. Egan,* 484 U.S. 518 (1988), the Supreme Court suggested in a widely quoted dictum that the President's "authority to classify and control access to information bearing on national security . . . flows primarily from this constitutional investment of power in the President and exists quite apart from any explicit congressional grant." *Id.* at 527. If the authority mentioned is not found in the Constitution's text, is it nevertheless a fair or even necessary inference?

Is the President authorized to ignore a congressional mandate to release information to the public if she believes that doing so could jeopardize national security? In another part of the *Egan* decision, the Court observed that "*unless Congress specifically has provided otherwise,* courts traditionally have been reluctant to intrude upon the authority of the Executive in military and national security affairs." *Id.* at 530 (emphasis added). At least since the Atomic Energy Act of 1954, 42 U.S.C. §§2011 to 2296b-7 (2018), Congress has claimed some authority over the substantive criteria for national security classification. And in the Freedom of Information Act (FOIA) and other open government laws, analyzed in the next chapter, Congress has required disclosure to the public of much information that might otherwise be kept secret.

6. *Controlled Unclassified Information.* During the George W. Bush administration, agency officials created a variety of new labels for records that didn't qualify for classification under the relevant executive order, but that they believed should be withheld from public disclosure. This practice, derisively referred to by some as "pseudo-classification," was widely criticized for its lack of uniform labeling or standards, absence of limits on personnel entitled to affix the labels, and lack of time limits. *See* Genevieve Knezo, *"Sensitive but Unclassified" Information and Other Controls: Policy and Options for Scientific and Technical Information* (Cong. Res. Serv. RL33303), Dec. 29, 2006. President Obama issued an order for safeguarding records bearing the single label "controlled unclassified information (CUI)." Exec. Order No. 13,556, *Controlled Unclassified Information,* 75 Fed. Reg. 68,675 (Nov. 4, 2010). Use of the CUI designation is to be "consistent with":

> (1) applicable law, including protections of confidentiality and privacy rights;
> (2) the statutory authority of the heads of agencies, including authorities related to the protection of information provided by the private sector to the Federal Government; and
> (3) applicable Government-wide standards and guidelines issued by the National Institute of Standards and Technology, and applicable policies established by the Office of Management and Budget. [*Id.* §6(a).]

Labeling a document CUI, however, does not exempt it from the statutory disclosure requirements in the Freedom of Information Act and other open government laws. By the end of FY2017, the majority of agencies still had not developed uniform standards and practices for dealing with CUI. *2017 Report, supra,* at 35-40; *see also A Bumpy Road for Controlled Unclassified Info,* Secrecy News, Oct. 30, 2017.

C. RESTRICTING ACCESS TO SENSITIVE INFORMATION: SECURITY CLEARANCES

Executive Order No. 13,526 does not discuss security clearances as such, but it does condition access to classified information on a favorable determination of eligibility, and it authorizes agency heads and officials to establish controls on the use and storage of such information. §4.1.

A "uniform Federal personnel security program" was established by Executive Order No. 12,968, *Access to Classified Information,* 60 Fed. Reg. 40245 (Aug. 2, 1995). The order sets out detailed procedures and criteria for vetting applicants for security clearances at different levels of access to classified information. A federal employee or government contractor may be granted a security clearance with the approval of a sponsoring federal agency following a background investigation of her character and trustworthiness. Most investigations are conducted by the National Background Investigations Bureau, part of the Office of Personnel Management. The applicant also must sign an appropriate nondisclosure agreement. After receiving a clearance, the individual is subject to continuing monitoring and evaluation. To gain access to particular classified materials, a clearance holder must demonstrate a "need to know" the information contained in those materials. *See generally* Michelle D. Christensen, *Security Clearance Process: Answers to Frequently Asked Questions* (Cong. Res. Serv. R43216), Oct. 7, 2016; Off. of the Dir. of Nat'l Intelligence, *Intelligence Community Directive 703: Protection of Classified National Intelligence, Including Sensitive Compartmented Information* (June 21, 2013).

Congress has given the Director of National Intelligence the job of establishing "uniform standards and procedures for the grant of access to sensitive compartmented information [SCI] to any officer or employee of any agency or department of the United States and to employees of contractors of those agencies or departments." 50 U.S.C. §3024(j)(1) (2018). *See* Off. of the Dir. of Nat'l Intelligence, *Intelligence Community Directive 704, Personnel Security Standards and Procedures Governing Eligibility for Access to Sensitive Compartmented Information* (June 20, 2018). SCI is a subset of national security intelligence that requires special protection, because it may concern or be derived from intelligence sources, methods, or analytical processes.

Security clearances are not required for the President, Vice President, members of Congress, Supreme Court Justices, or other constitutional officers. Exec. Order No. 13,467, *Reforming Processes Related to Suitability for Government Employment, Fitness for Contractor Employees, and Eligibility for Access to Classified National Security Information,* 73 Fed. Reg. 38,103 (June 30, 2008), further indicates that the personnel security program described in Exec. Order No. 12,968, *supra,* does not apply to the President's and Vice President's employees and domestic policy staff.

In 2019, President Trump reportedly directed that his son-in-law, Jared Kushner, be given a top-secret security clearance, overruling objections from members of his own White House personnel security office and intelligence officials, who expressed concerns about foreign influence, private business interests, and Kushner's personal conduct. *See* Maggie Haberman et al., *Trump Ordered Officials to Give Jared Kushner a Security Clearance,* N.Y. Times, Feb. 28, 2019. Other White House staffers, including the President's daughter Ivanka, were also reported to have received security clearances over the objections of career officials. Does the President have the authority to independently grant clearances? Could Congress restrict any such authority by statute?

1. Nondisclosure Agreements

Classified Information Nondisclosure Agreement (SF 312)

(Rev. 7-2013)
available at http://www.fas.org/sgp/othergov/intel/sf312.pdf

An Agreement Between ______________________ and the United States
(*Name — Printed or Typed*)

1. Intending to be legally bound, I hereby accept the obligations contained in this Agreement in consideration of my being granted access to classified information. As used in this Agreement, classified information is marked or unmarked classified

information, including oral communications, that is classified under the standards of Executive Order 13526, or under any other Executive order or statute that prohibits the unauthorized disclosure of information in the interest of national security; and unclassified information that meets the standards for classification and is in the process of a classification determination. . . .

3. I have been advised that the unauthorized disclosure, unauthorized retention, or negligent handling of classified information by me could cause damage or irreparable injury to the United States or could be used to advantage by a foreign nation. I hereby agree that I will never divulge classified information to anyone unless: (a) I have officially verified that the recipient has been properly authorized by the United States Government to receive it; or (b) I have been given prior written notice of authorization from the United States Government Department or Agency . . . responsible for the classification of information or last granting me a security clearance that such disclosure is permitted. . . .

4. I have been advised that any breach of this Agreement may result in the termination of any security clearances I hold; removal from any position of special confidence and trust requiring such clearances; or termination of my employment. . . . In addition, I have been advised that any unauthorized disclosure of classified information by me may constitute a violation, or violations, of United States criminal laws. . . .

5. I hereby assign to the United States Government all royalties, remunerations, and emoluments that have resulted, will result or may result from any disclosure, publication, or revelation of classified information not consistent with the terms of this Agreement.

6. I understand that the United States Government may seek any remedy available to it to enforce this Agreement including, but not limited to, application for a court order prohibiting disclosure of information in breach of this Agreement.

7. I understand that all information to which I have access or may obtain access by signing this Agreement is now and will remain the property of the United States Government. . . .

8. Unless and until I am released in writing by an authorized representative of the United States Government, I understand that all conditions and obligations imposed upon me by this Agreement apply during the time I am granted access to classified information, and at all times thereafter. . . .

Sensitive Compartmented Information Nondisclosure Agreement (SF 4414)

(Rev. 12-2013)
available at http://www.fas.org/sgp/othergov/intel/sf4414.pdf

4. (U) In consideration of being granted access to SCI [Sensitive Compartmented Information] . . . I hereby agree to submit for security review by the Department or Agency that last authorized my access to such information or material any writing or other preparation in any form, including a work of fiction, that contains or purports to contain any SCI or description of activities that produce or relate to SCI or that I have reason to believe are derived from SCI, that I contemplate disclosing to any person not authorized to have access to SCI or that I have prepared for public

disclosure. I understand and agree that my obligation to submit such preparations for review applies during the course of my access to SCI and thereafter. . . .

5. (U) I understand that the purpose of the review described in paragraph 4 is to give the United States a reasonable opportunity to determine whether the preparation submitted . . . sets forth any SCI. . . . [T]he Department or Agency to which I have made a submission will act upon it, coordinating with the Intelligence Community when appropriate, and make a response to me within a reasonable time, not to exceed 30 working days from date of receipt. . . .

Notes and Questions

1. Scope of Prepublication Review. Although SF 312 makes no reference to prepublication review, as a practical matter its obligation not to disclose classified information may include such a requirement. Many intelligence community agencies have policies that expressly require such review.

Prepublication review guidelines cover everything from newspaper columns and letters to the editor, to blogs, to works of fiction. They may also address the special risk of inadvertent oral disclosures. *See, e.g.*, 28 C.F.R. §17.18(g) (2019) (Department of Justice). Should an agency review speeches or writings on any subject? The CIA reviews only works that relate to "intelligence, foreign relations, or CIA employment or contract matters," but not material that concerns "cooking, stamp collecting, sports, fraternal organizations, and so forth." Cent. Intelligence Agency, *Agency Prepublication Review of Certain Material Prepared for Public Dissemination* (AR 13-10), ¶2(b)(3) (June 25, 2011), *available at* https://assets.documentcloud.org/documents/5767103/AR-13-10-Agency-Prepublication-Review-of-Certain.pdf.

Some agencies require prepublication review for the lifetime of a former employee. In one case the court held that a former Department of Energy employee had no First Amendment right to publish even classified information obtained by him *outside the scope of his employment.* His nondisclosure agreement covered it all. *Stillman v. Cent. Intelligence Agency*, 319 F.3d 546, 548 (D.C. Cir. 2003). Should the government be able to control the speech or publications of persons for so long? If so, why?

If you signed one of the secrecy agreements set out above, would you know when you were obligated to seek government approval before speaking or writing anything? In early 2019, five former military and intelligence officials filed suit challenging the entire prepublication review system on First and Fifth Amendment grounds. *Edgar v. Coats*, No. 8:19-cv-00985-GJH (D. Md. filed Apr. 2, 2019); Charlie Savage, *Former Officials File Suit over the Lifelong Limits on the Words They Write*, N.Y. Times, Apr. 3, 2019.

2. Curbing Media Contacts. One way government information is revealed to the public is through lower-level agency officials' statements to the media. In the national security community, these open communications have always been discouraged. Augmenting the prepublication review process described above, Off. of the Dir. of Nat'l Intelligence, *Intelligence Community Directive 119: Media Contacts* (Oct. 31, 2017), provides that "[w]ithin the IC, only the head or deputy head of an IC element, the designated public affairs official, and other persons designated in agency policy or authorized by that public affairs official are authorized to have contact with the media" about "intelligence-related information," and other IC employees "must obtain authorization" for such contacts. *See also Instruction 80.04, ODNI Pre-publication Review of Information to Be Publicly Released* (Apr. 8, 2014). The directive does not distinguish between classified and unclassified data. Can you guess what kinds of information are covered by each? Does the directive violate the First Amendment rights of IC employees?

3. Costs of Prepublication Review? Two knowledgeable observers argue that damage to First Amendment values from the current system of prepublication review is "pervasive but nearly invisible to the public. In an era characterized by endless war and a bloated secrecy bureaucracy, the restrictions on commentary and criticism about government policies and practices pose an intolerable cost to our democracy." Jack Goldsmith & Oona A. Hathaway, Opinion, *The Government's Prepublication Review Process Is Broken*, Wash. Post, Dec. 25, 2015. The current system, they say, "results in the non-publication, or excessively delayed publication, of a great deal of potential writing related to the government that has nothing to do with classified information." It "risks the politicization of intelligence and encourages the application of subjective standards for authors depending on seniority, political affiliations and views." Oona Hathaway & Jack Goldsmith, *Path Dependence and the Prepublication Review Process*, Just Security, Dec. 28, 2015. Just as important, they assert, the prepublication review process has a chilling effect that "leads authors simply not to write on certain topics at all." Jack Goldsmith & Oona Hathaway, *The Scope of the Prepublication Review Problem, and What to Do About It*, Just Security, Dec. 30, 2015.

What might be done to address both potential government abuses and unwarranted self-censorship? *See* Christopher E. Bailey, *Reform of the Intelligence Community Prepublication Review Process: Balancing First Amendment Rights and National Security Interests*, 5 J. Nat'l Security L. & Pol'y 203 (2017) (suggesting improvements in the prepublication review process); *New Pre-Publication Review Policy Is Coming*, Secrecy News, Dec. 12, 2018.

2. Enforcing Prepublication Review

Reading *United States v. Marchetti*

This was an action to enjoin publication of writings by a former employee of the CIA, Victor Marchetti. The defendant, as a condition of his employment, signed an agreement promising (1) not to reveal classified information or information relating to intelligence matters, and (2) to obtain the Agency's approval before publishing anything relating to the CIA or its activities. But he failed to submit the manuscripts of certain works to the CIA for prepublication review.

- Why do you suppose Marchetti failed to submit his writings for prepublication review?
- How did the court balance the defendant's First Amendment right of free expression against the interest of national security? Against the public's right to be informed about the workings of government?

- How did the court assess the risk to national security posed by publication without CIA approval? How important, if at all, was the classification of the information?
- What are the Agency's obligations in reviewing a submitted manuscript?

United States v. Marchetti

United States Court of Appeals, Fourth Circuit, 1972
466 F.2d 1309

HAYNSWORTH, C.J. . . . After his resignation [from the CIA, Victor] Marchetti published a novel, entitled *The Rope Dancer,* concerning an agency called the "National Intelligence Agency." Marchetti has also published an article in the April 3, 1972 issue of the magazine, *The Nation* . . . criticiz[ing] some policies and practices of the Agency. In March, 1972, Marchetti submitted to *Esquire* magazine and to six other publishers an article in which he reports some of his experiences as an agent. According to the United States, this article contains classified information concerning intelligence sources, methods and operations. . . . He has submitted to a publishing house an outline of a book he proposes to write about his intelligence experiences. . . .

[Relying on Marchetti's secrecy agreements, the District Court ordered him not to release to any person or corporation any writing, fictional or nonfictional, relating to the Agency or to intelligence without prior authorization from the CIA.]

We readily agree with Marchetti that the First Amendment limits the extent to which the United States, contractually or otherwise, may impose secrecy requirements upon its employees and enforce them with a system of prior censorship. It precludes such restraints with respect to information which is unclassified or officially disclosed, but we are here concerned with secret information touching upon the national defense and the conduct of foreign affairs, acquired by Marchetti while in a position of trust and confidence and contractually bound to respect it. . . .

Gathering intelligence information and the other activities of the Agency, including clandestine affairs against other nations, are all within the President's constitutional responsibility for the security of the Nation as the Chief Executive and as Commander in Chief of our Armed forces. Const., art. II, §2. Citizens have the right to criticize the conduct of our foreign affairs, but the Government also has the right and the duty to strive for internal secrecy about the conduct of governmental affairs in areas in which disclosure may reasonably be thought to be inconsistent with the national interest.

The Supreme Court recognized the need for secrecy in government in *United States v. Curtiss-Wright Export Corp.*, 229 U.S. 304, 320 where it said that the President

> "has his confidential sources of information. He has his agents in the form of diplomatic, consular and other officials. Secrecy in respect of information gathered by them may be highly necessary, and the premature disclosure of it productive of harmful results." . . .

Congress has imposed on the Director of Central Intelligence the responsibility for protecting intelligence sources and methods. [That duty has since been given to the Director of National Intelligence. 50 U.S.C. §3024(i)(1).] In attempting to comply with this duty, the Agency requires its employees as a condition of employment to sign a secrecy agreement, and such agreements are entirely appropriate to a program in implementation of the congressional direction of secrecy. Marchetti, of course, could have refused to sign, but then he would not have been employed, and he would not have been given access to the classified information he may now want to broadcast. . . .

. . . One may speculate that ordinary criminal sanctions might suffice to prevent unauthorized disclosure of such information, but the risk of harm from disclosure is so great and maintenance of the confidentiality of the information so necessary that greater and more positive assurance is warranted. Some prior restraints in some circumstances are approvable of course. See *Freedman v. Maryland,* 380 U.S. 51 [(1964)].

. . . Marchetti by accepting employment with the CIA and by signing a secrecy agreement did not surrender his First Amendment right of free speech. The agreement is enforceable only because it is not a violation of those rights. . . .

Thus Marchetti retains the right to speak and write about the CIA and its operations, and to criticize it as any other citizen may, but he may not disclose classified information obtained by him during the course of his employment which is not already in the public domain.

Because we are dealing with a prior restraint upon speech, we think that the CIA must act promptly to approve or disapprove any material which may be submitted to it by Marchetti. Undue delay would impair the reasonableness of the restraint. . . . We should think that, in all events, the maximum period for responding after the submission of material for approval should not exceed thirty days.

Furthermore, since First Amendment rights are involved, we think Marchetti would be entitled to judicial review of any action by the CIA disapproving publication of the material. . . . Because of the sensitivity of the area and confidentiality of the relationship in which the information was obtained, however, we find no reason to impose the burden of obtaining judicial review upon the CIA. It ought to be on Marchetti. . . .

Generally, therefore, we approve the injunctive order issued by the District Court. The case will be remanded, however, for the purpose of revising the order to limit its reach to classified information and for the conduct of such further proceedings as may be necessary if Marchetti contends that the CIA wrongfully withheld approval of the publication of any information under the standards we have laid down.

Affirmed and remanded.

[The opinion of CRAVEN, J., concurring, is omitted.]

Notes and Questions

1. *First Amendment Rights?* In *New York Times v. United States* (*The Pentagon Papers Case*), 403 U.S. 713, 714 (1971) (per curiam), *infra* p. 1303, the Supreme Court noted that "[a]ny system of prior restraints of expression comes to this Court bearing a heavy presumption against its constitutional validity." How did the court in the principal case find that the restrictions on Marchetti's right to publish overcame this heavy

presumption? Did Marchetti waive his First Amendment rights? Can such constitutional protections be waived just as, for example, an accused may waive a right to a jury trial?

In another case involving a former CIA agent, the Supreme Court declared that "even in the absence of an express agreement . . . the CIA could have acted to protect substantial government interests by imposing reasonable restrictions on employee activities that in other contexts might be protected by the First Amendment." *Snepp v. United States,* 444 U.S. 507, 509 n.3 (1980). What is the importance of the agreement, if any?

2. *The Importance of Classification.* In *Stillman v. Central Intelligence Agency,* 319 F.3d 546, 548 (D.C. Cir. 2003), the court declared, "If the Government classified the information properly, then [the employee] simply has no first amendment right to publish it." Conversely, the *Marchetti* court noted that the First Amendment precludes secrecy requirements for employees and enforcement with a system of prior censorship "with respect to information which is unclassified or officially disclosed." 466 F.2d at 1313. But why should classification or official disclosure mark the limits of a government employee's freedom of expression?

Two critics propose a different standard — "writings that might reasonably contain or be derived from classified information" — that they say would accommodate the interests of "both the reviewed and the reviewer, though the standard is still unclear and still susceptible to abuse by the government without the significant review and independent oversight." Oona Hathaway & Jack Goldsmith, *Path Dependence and the Prepublication Review Process,* Just Security, Dec. 28, 2015. Can you describe advantages and disadvantages of such an alternative standard?

In *Snepp v. United States, supra,* the Supreme Court imposed penalties for violation of a prepublication agreement even though the former CIA agent's book concededly divulged no classified information.

> Whether Snepp violated his trust does not depend upon whether his book actually contained classified information. The Government does not deny — as a general principle — Snepp's right to publish unclassified information. . . . The Government simply claims that, in light of the special trust reposed in him and the agreement that he signed, Snepp should have given the CIA an opportunity to determine whether the material he proposed to publish would compromise classified information or sources. . . .
>
> . . . [A] former intelligence agent's publication of unreviewed material relating to intelligence activities can be detrimental to vital national interests even if the published information is unclassified. When a former agent relies on his own judgment about what information is detrimental, he may reveal information that the CIA — with its broader understanding of what may expose classified information and confidential sources — could have identified as harmful. [444 U.S. at 511-512.]

Is the Supreme Court's refusal to distinguish between classified and unclassified material based on the language of either nondisclosure agreement set out above? If not, can its refusal be squared with the earlier ruling in *Marchetti*?

3. *Timing the Agency Review.* The *Marchetti* court observed that the CIA should complete its review of any written material submitted to it within 30 days. Department of Justice guidelines require a substantive response to a review request within 30

working days, with priority for material that the author wishes to publish on an expedited basis, such as speeches or newspaper articles. Administrative appeals must be processed within 15 working days. Authors who are dissatisfied with the administrative decision may seek judicial relief or, upon 30 days' notice, may seek an injunction against the government. 28 C.F.R. §17.18(i) (2019). Why is time for agency review so limited? Should the same time limits apply to, say, a letter to the editor or an op-ed article concerning a current news story?

Unfortunately, agencies sometimes fail to abide by their own timetables. After an employee of the Los Alamos National Laboratory, Danny Stillman, submitted his manuscript, *Inside China's Nuclear Weapons Program*, to the Department of Energy and other agencies for prepublication review, he waited nine months to learn that DOE, DOD, and CIA would approve none of it. *See Stillman v. Cent. Intelligence Agency*, 517 F. Supp. 2d 32, 35 (D.D.C. 2007). Two weeks after he sued to dislodge the manuscript, however, the government released 85 percent of it.

4. Judicial Review. The *Marchetti* court emphasized that an agency decision to prohibit publication is subject to judicial review. In *McGehee v. Casey*, 718 F.2d 1137 (D.C. Cir. 1983), the court noted that an author seeking prepublication approval had "a strong first amendment interest in ensuring that CIA censorship of his article results from a *proper* classification of the censored portions." *Id.* at 1148 (emphasis in original). Accordingly, it concluded that "reviewing courts should conduct a *de novo* review of the classification decision, while giving deference to reasoned and detailed CIA explanations of that classification decision." *Id.* But can you rehearse arguments that a court's role in such cases should be more limited?

Courts do sometimes support former agency employees. Applying the standard in *McGehee* and ruling mostly against the agency, one court described the case before it as "a sad and discouraging tale about the determined efforts of the FBI to censor various portions of a 500-page manuscript, written by a former long-time FBI agent, severely criticizing the FBI's conduct of the investigation of a money laundering scheme." *Wright v. Fed. Bureau of Investigation*, 613 F. Supp. 2d 13, 15 (D.D.C. 2009).

5. Remedies for Breach. What remedies other than injunction might the court have ordered in *Marchetti*? In *Snepp v. United States*, *supra*, the Supreme Court approved the imposition of a constructive trust on all royalties from a book written by a former CIA agent and published without the agreed agency review in advance. Thus, the author forfeited all royalties from his work. The Court remarked:

> The Government could not pursue the [remedy of damages alone] without losing the benefit of the bargain it seeks to enforce. Proof of the tortious conduct necessary to sustain an award of punitive damages might force the Government to disclose some of the very confidences that Snepp promised to protect. The trial of such a suit, before a jury if the defendant so elects, would subject the CIA and its officials to probing discovery into the Agency's highly confidential affairs. Rarely would the Government run this risk. . . .
>
> A constructive trust, on the other hand, protects both the Government and the former agent from unwarranted risks. . . . If the agent publishes unreviewed material in violation of his fiduciary and contractual obligation, the trust remedy simply requires him to disgorge the benefits of his faithlessness. Since the remedy is swift and sure, it is tailored to deter those who would place sensitive information at risk. And since the remedy reaches only funds attributable to the breach, it cannot saddle the former agent with exemplary damages out of all proportion to his gain. [444 U.S. at 514-515.]

More recently, the government sued former intelligence contractor Edward Snowden for breach of his prepublication review agreement, seeking forfeiture of all royalties from his memoir, *Permanent Record* (2019). *See* Charlie Savage, *U.S. Sues for Royalties from Snowden's Memoir,* N.Y. Times, Sept. 18, 2019. If deterrence of future breaches is an objective, can you think of other remedies that might provide a greater disincentive?

In 2012, a Navy SEAL involved in the killing of Osama bin Laden, writing under the pen name Mark Owen, published a best-selling account of that action entitled *No Easy Day.* Upon the advice of his attorney, he failed to submit the manuscript for review in advance to the Defense Department. DOD sued him for breach of his non-disclosure agreements, and for violating a "debriefing agreement" that assigned to the government "all royalties [that] may result from . . . publication or revelation of classified information" in violation of his earlier agreements. It did not, however, specifically allege any disclosure of classified information. After the Justice Department opened investigations into the author's possible violation of the Espionage Act, the suit was settled when the author agreed to forfeit all of his royalties — more than $6.6 million. The author then sued his attorney for malpractice. *See Bissonnette v. Podlaski,* No. 15-334 (N.D. Ind. June 6, 2018).

A different deterrent threat, criminal prosecution under the Espionage Act, is considered below.

D. CRIMINAL PROSECUTION OF LEAKERS: THE ESPIONAGE ACT

Every presidential administration worries about unauthorized "leaks" — either intentional or inadvertent disclosures of government secrets by present or past employees or contractors. The concern is that such disclosures may chill the candor of executive branch communications, warp the development of sound policies by exposing them prematurely, undermine the discipline of good decision making, or perhaps injure national security by sharing classified information with our enemies.

Nevertheless, unauthorized leaks of national security information have long played a key role in informing the public about illegal or morally questionable government activities, and in prompting reforms. One scholar has described the paradox this way:

> Ours is a polity saturated with, vexed by, and dependent upon leaks. The Bay of Pigs, the Pentagon Papers, warrantless wiretapping by the National Security Agency at home, targeted killings by the Central Intelligence Agency abroad: the contours of these and countless other government activities have emerged over the years through anonymous disclosures of confidential information to the press. Across the ideological spectrum, many Americans believe both that leaking "is a problem of major proportions" and that "our particular form of government wouldn't work without it." [David E. Pozen, *The Leaky Leviathan: Why the Government Condemns and Condones Unlawful Disclosures of Information,* 127 Harv. L. Rev. 512, 513-514 (2013) (citations omitted).]

The difficulty comes in striking the right balance between necessary secrecy in a dangerous world and the need for an informed citizenry in a democracy. Congress has sought to strike that balance in the Espionage Act.

Espionage and Censorship

18 U.S.C. §§793-798 (2018)

§793. GATHERING, TRANSMITTING, OR LOSING DEFENSE INFORMATION

(a) Whoever, for the purpose of obtaining information respecting the national defense with intent or reason to believe that the information is to be used to the injury of the United States, or to the advantage of any foreign nation, goes upon, enters, flies over, or otherwise obtains information concerning [any defense facility or property]; or

(b) Whoever, for the purpose aforesaid, and with like intent or reason to believe, copies, takes, makes, or obtains, or attempts to copy, take, make, or obtain, any sketch, photograph, photographic negative, blueprint, plan, map, model, instrument, appliance, document, writing, or note of anything connected with the national defense; or

(c) Whoever, for the purpose aforesaid, receives or obtains or agrees or attempts to receive or obtain from any person, or from any source whatever, any document [or tangible thing, such as a code book] connected with the national defense, knowing or having reason to believe, at the time he receives or obtains, or agrees or attempts to receive or obtain it, that it has been or will be obtained, taken, made, or disposed of by any person contrary to the provisions of this chapter; or

(d) Whoever, lawfully having possession of, access to, control over, or being entrusted with any document [or tangible thing] relating to the national defense, or information relating to the national defense which information the possessor has reason to believe could be used to the injury of the United States or to the advantage of any foreign nation, willfully communicates, delivers, transmits or causes to be communicated, delivered, or transmitted or attempts to communicate, deliver, transmit or cause to be communicated, delivered or transmitted the same to any person not entitled to receive it, or willfully retains the same and fails to deliver it on demand to the officer or employee of the United States entitled to receive it; or...

(e) [Substantially identical to §793(d), except that it provides punishment for one having "unauthorized" possession of sensitive materials.]

(f) [Punishes the loss of such materials through gross negligence or the failure to report their loss, theft, or destruction.]

Shall be fined under this title or imprisoned not more than ten years, or both.

(g) If two or more persons conspire to violate any of the foregoing provisions of this section, and one or more of such persons do any act to effect the object of the conspiracy, each of the parties to such conspiracy shall be subject to the punishment provided for the offense which is the object of such conspiracy....

§794. GATHERING OR DELIVERING DEFENSE INFORMATION TO AID FOREIGN GOVERNMENT

(a) Whoever, with intent or reason to believe that it is to be used to the injury of the United States or to the advantage of a foreign nation, communicates, delivers, or transmits, or attempts to communicate, deliver, or transmit, to any foreign government, or to any faction or party or military or naval force within a foreign country . . . or to any representative, officer, agent, employee, subject, or citizen thereof, either directly or indirectly, any document, writing, code book, signal book, sketch, photograph, photographic negative, blueprint, plan, map, model, note, instrument, appliance, or information relating to the national defense, shall be punished by death or by imprisonment. . . .

[Sections 795-797 criminalize the disclosure of several specific categories of national security information, including photographs or sketches of defense installations.]

§798. DISCLOSURE OF CLASSIFIED INFORMATION

(a) Whoever knowingly and willfully communicates, furnishes, transmits, or otherwise makes available to an unauthorized person, or publishes, or uses in any manner prejudicial to the safety or interest of the United States or for the benefit of any foreign government to the detriment of the United States any classified information —

(1) concerning the nature, preparation, or use of any code, cipher, or cryptographic system of the United States or any foreign government; or

(2) concerning the design, construction, use, maintenance, or repair of any device, apparatus, or appliance used or prepared or planned for use by the United States or any foreign government for cryptographic or communication intelligence purposes; or

(3) concerning the communication intelligence activities of the United States or any foreign government; or

(4) obtained by the processes of communication intelligence from the communications of any foreign government, knowing the same to have been obtained by such processes —

Shall be fined under this title or imprisoned. . . .

(b) As used in subsection (a) of this section — . . .

The term "communication intelligence" means all procedures and methods used in the interception of communications and the obtaining of information from such communications by other than the intended recipients; . . .

Public Money, Property, or Records

18 U.S.C. §641 (2018)

Whoever embezzles, steals, purloins, or knowingly converts to his use or the use of another, or without authority, sells, conveys or disposes of any record, voucher, money, or thing of value of the United States or of any department or agency thereof; or

Whoever receives, conceals, or retains the same with intent to convert it to his use or gain, knowing it to have been embezzled, stolen, purloined or converted —

Shall be fined under this title or imprisoned. . . .

Before the administration of President George W. Bush, only two government employees had ever been criminally charged for leaking classified information to the press, and only one of them was successfully prosecuted. And only in the last few years have charges ever been brought against individuals outside the government for their involvement in leaks of classified information when their purpose was not to jeopardize national security. The following case is one of those.

Reading *United States v. Rosen*

An Espionage Act prosecution was mounted against two lobbyists who obtained leaked classified information, then shared that information with others not entitled to receive it, including members of the media. The defendants argued that the prosecution violated their rights under the First and Fifth Amendments. As you review the following decision, consider these questions:

- How can either a leaker or the recipient of leaked information know that they may be criminally liable under the Espionage Act?
- What is the importance of classification in Espionage Act prosecutions?
- What different First Amendment values are implicated by the criminal prosecution of leakers, and how can these values be reconciled with the imperative of national security?
- Do journalists who receive leaked national defense information enjoy greater First Amendment protections than government employees responsible for the leaks?
- What, if any, is the significance of a leaker's motive in revealing government secrets?

United States v. Rosen

United States District Court, Eastern District of Virginia, 2006
445 F. Supp. 2d 602, *as amended*, 2006 WL 5049154

Ellis, District Judge. In this Espionage Act prosecution, defendants Steven Rosen and Keith Weissman have been charged in Count I of a superseding indictment with conspiring to transmit information relating to the national defense[1] to those not entitled to receive it, in violation of 18 U.S.C. §793(g). Defendants, by pretrial motion, attack the constitutionality of §793 in three ways. First, they argue that the statute, as applied to them, is unconstitutionally vague in violation of the Due Process Clause of the Fifth Amendment. Second, they argue that the statute, as applied to them, abridges their First Amendment right to free speech and their First Amendment right to petition the government. Third, defendants assert the First Amendment rights of others by attacking the statute as facially overbroad. In the alternative, defendants urge the Court to avoid these constitutional issues by interpreting the statute as

1. The phrase "information relating to the national defense" will sometimes be referred to herein as NDI.

applying only to the transmission of tangible items, *i.e.*, documents, tapes, discs, maps and the like. . . .

I.

During the period of the conspiracy alleged in Count I, defendants Rosen and Weissman were employed by the American Israel Public Affairs Committee (AIPAC) in Washington, D.C. AIPAC is a pro-Israel organization that lobbies the United States executive and legislative branches on issues of interest to Israel, especially U.S. foreign policy with respect to the Middle East. Rosen was AIPAC's Director of Foreign Policy Issues. . . . Rosen did not have a security clearance during the period of the alleged conspiracy. . . . Defendant Weissman was AIPAC's Senior Middle East Analyst. . . . Alleged co-conspirator Lawrence Franklin worked on the Iran desk in the Office of the Secretary of the Department of Defense (DOD) and held a top secret security clearance during the alleged conspiracy.[3]

In general, the superseding indictment alleges that in furtherance of their lobbying activities, defendants (i) cultivated relationships with government officials with access to sensitive U.S. government information, including NDI, (ii) obtained the information from these officials, and (iii) transmitted the information to persons not otherwise entitled to receive it, including members of the media, foreign policy analysts, and officials of a foreign government.

The government's recitation of the acts constituting the conspiracy begins on April 13, 1999, when Rosen told an unnamed foreign official (FO-1) that he had "picked up an extremely sensitive piece of intelligence" which he described as "codeword protected intelligence." Rosen proceeded to relate this piece of intelligence, which concerned terrorist activities in Central Asia, to the foreign official. . . . The superseding indictment alleges further that Weissman's role in the conspiracy became apparent on June 11, 1999, when Weissman told the same foreign official that he had learned of a "secret FBI, classified FBI report" relating to the Khobar Towers bombing from three different sources, including an official of the United States government. Later that day, Weissman told FO-1 that he had interested a member of the media in the report. . . .

In August 2002, Rosen was introduced to Franklin through a contact at the DOD. Rosen, Weissman, Franklin and another DOD employee finally met nearly six months later, on February 12, 2003. At this meeting, Franklin disclosed to Rosen and Weissman information relating to a classified draft internal United States government policy document concerning a certain Middle Eastern country. . . . Rosen met with FO-2 and discussed the same draft internal policy document that Franklin had discussed with Rosen and Weissman. . . .

[The court went on to describe in some detail other instances in which Rosen and Weissman allegedly knowingly received classified information and passed it on to other AIPAC employees, foreign officials, and journalists. It then ruled that §793 applies to information transmitted in oral, as well as tangible, form.]

---

3. On October 5, 2005, Franklin pled guilty to one count of conspiracy to communicate national defense information to one not entitled to receive it, in violation of 18 U.S.C. §§793(d) and (g), and to one count of conspiracy to communicate classified information to an agent of a foreign government in violation of 50 U.S.C. §783 [transmission of classified information by a government employee to a foreign government agent] and 18 U.S.C. §371 [conspiracy to commit an offense against the United States].

IV.

Defendants' first constitutional challenge to the statute is based on the principle that the Due Process clause of the Fifth Amendment prohibits punishment pursuant to a statute so vague that "men of common intelligence must necessarily guess at its meaning and differ as to its application." *United States v. Lanier*, 520 U.S. 259, 266 (1997) (quoting *Connally v. General Constr. Co.*, 269 U.S. 385, 391 (1926)). Specifically, defendants allege that, as applied to them, both §§793(d) and (e) are fatally vague with respect to determining: (1) the content of information covered by the phrase "information relating to the national defense," and (2) the individuals "not entitled to receive" that information. . . .

A. . . .

. . . [T]he phrase "information relating to the national defense," while potentially quite broad, is limited and clarified by the requirements that the information be a government secret, *i.e.*, that it is closely held by the government, and that the information is the type which, if disclosed, could threaten the national security of the United States. So cabined, the phrase "information relating to the national defense" avoids fatal vagueness and passes Due Process muster; given these two limitations the phrase provides fair notice of what it encompasses and is also an adequate safeguard against arbitrary enforcement.

B.

Defendants also argue that they lacked constitutionally adequate notice as to who was "entitled to receive" the national defense information, especially given the fact that the information was transmitted orally and therefore possessed no markings of "SECRET," "CONFIDENTIAL" or other indicia typical of classified material. . . .

. . . [W]hile the language of the statute, by itself, may lack precision, the gloss of judicial precedent has clarified that the statute incorporates the executive branch's classification regulations, which provide the requisite constitutional clarity.

C. . . .

. . . [T]he statute's "willfulness" requirement obligates the government to prove that the defendants knew that disclosing the NDI could threaten the nation's security, and that it was illegal, but it leaves open the possibility that defendants could be convicted for these acts despite some salutary motive. For example, if a person transmitted classified *documents* relating to the national defense to a member of the media despite knowing that such an act was a violation of the statute, he could be convicted for "willfully" committing the prohibited acts even if he viewed the disclosure as an act of patriotism. By contrast, the "reason to believe" scienter requirement that accompanies disclosures of *information*, requires the government to demonstrate the likelihood of defendant's bad faith purpose to either harm the United States or to aid a foreign government. . . .

. . . To the extent that oral transmission of information relating to the national defense makes it more difficult for defendants to know whether they are violating the statute, the statute is not thereby rendered unconstitutionally vague[,] because the statute permits conviction only of those who "willfully" commit the prohibited acts and do so with bad faith. So construed, both phrases pass Fifth Amendment muster; they are not unconstitutionally vague as applied to these defendants.

D....

Defendants argue that the present prosecution represents a novel construction of the statute which they could not have anticipated because "leaks" of classified information by non-governmental persons have never been prosecuted under this statute. The statute's plain language rebuts this argument. It is clear from this plain language that defendants' conduct, as alleged in the superseding indictment is within the sweep of the statute....

Also unsuccessful is defendants' claim that past applications of the statute fail to provide fair warning that the statute could be applied to the facts alleged in the superseding indictment. [*United States v. Morison,* 844 F.2d 1057 (4th Cir. 1988),] itself rebuts this claim. Notably, in *Morison* the Fourth Circuit considered the very similar argument that the statute was intended to apply only to classic espionage cases and therefore did not apply to Morison's "leak" to a news publication. In rejecting this argument, the Fourth Circuit noted the rarity of prosecutions under §793(e), but stated

> that the rarity of prosecution under the statutes does not indicate that the statutes were not to be enforced as written. We think in any event, the rarity of use of the statute as a basis for prosecution is at best a questionable basis for nullifying the clear language of the statute, and we think the revision of 1950 and its reenactment of section 793(d) demonstrate that Congress did not consider such statute meaningless or intend that the statute and its prohibitions were to be abandoned.

Morison, 844 F.2d at 1067. The Fourth Circuit's reasoning in rejecting Morison's challenge is equally applicable to the defendants here, and therefore, for the same reasons, defendants' vagueness challenge based on the novelty of this prosecution fails as well.

V.

The defendants' next constitutional challenge rests on the First Amendment's guarantees of free speech and the right to petition the government for grievances.... Defendants' First Amendment challenge exposes the inherent tension between the government transparency so essential to a democratic society and the government's equally compelling need to protect from disclosure information that could be used by those who wish this nation harm. In addressing this tension, it is important to bear in mind that the question to be resolved here is not whether §793 is the optimal resolution of this tension, but whether Congress, in passing this statute, has struck a balance between these competing interests that falls within the range of constitutionally permissible outcomes.

As an initial matter, it is necessary to confront the government's proposed categorical rule that espionage statutes cannot implicate the First Amendment. This contention overreaches. In the broadest terms, the conduct at issue — collecting information about United States' foreign policy and discussing that information with government officials (both United States and foreign), journalists, and other participants in the foreign policy establishment — is at the core of the First Amendment's guarantees. *See Mills v. Alabama,* 384 U.S. 214, 218 (1966) ("[T]here is practically universal agreement that a major purpose of [the First] Amendment was to protect the free discussion of governmental affairs."). And, even under a more precise description of the conduct — the passing of government secrets relating to the national defense to those not entitled to receive them in an attempt to influence United States foreign policy — the application of §793 to the defendants is unquestionably still deserving of First Amendment scrutiny. . . .

Given that the application of the statute to these defendants warrants First Amendment scrutiny, the question then becomes whether Congress may nonetheless penalize the conduct alleged in the superseding indictment, for while the invocation of "national security" does not free Congress from the restraints of the First Amendment, it is equally well established that the invocation of the First Amendment does not "provide immunity for every possible use of language," *Frohwerk v. U.S.*, 249 U.S. 204, 206 (1919), and that "the societal value of speech must, on occasion, be subordinated to other values and considerations." *Dennis v. United States,* 341 U.S. 494, 503 (1951). As Justice Frankfurter aptly put it in *Dennis*:

> The demands of free speech in a democratic society as well as the interest in national security are better served by a candid and informed weighing of the competing interests, within the confines of the judicial process, than by announcing dogmas too inflexible for the non-Euclidian problems to be solved.

Dennis, 341 U.S. at 524-25 (Frankfurter, J., concurring). Thus, to determine, on any given occasion, whether the government's interest prevails over the First Amendment, courts must begin with "an assessment of the competing societal interests" at stake, *Morison,* 844 F.2d at 1082, and proceed to the "delicate and difficult task" of weighing those interests "to determine whether the resulting restriction on freedom can be tolerated." *United States v. Robel,* 389 U.S. 258, 264 (1967).

As already noted, the defendants' First Amendment interests at stake in this prosecution, and those of the third parties raised by defendants, are significant and implicate the core values the First Amendment was designed to protect. The collection and discussion of information about the conduct of government by defendants and others in the body politic is indispensable to the healthy functioning of a representative government, for "[a]s James Madison put it in 1822: 'A popular Government, without popular information, or a means of acquiring it, is but a Prologue to a Farce or a Tragedy; or, perhaps both.'" *Morison,* 844 F.2d at 1081 (Wilkinson, J., concurring) (quoting 9 Writings of James Madison 103 (G. Hunt ed., 1910)). This is especially so in the context of foreign policy because, as Justice Stewart observed in the Pentagon Papers case:

> In the absence of the government checks and balances present in other areas of our national life, the only effective restraint upon executive policy and power in the areas of national defense and international affairs may lie in an enlightened citizenry — in an informed and critical public opinion which alone can here protect the values of democratic government.

New York Times v. United States, 403 U.S. 713, 728 (1971) (Stewart J., concurring). . . .

But importantly, the defendants here are not accused merely of disclosing government secrets, they are accused of disclosing NDI, *i.e.*, government secrets the disclosure of which could threaten the security of the nation. And, however vital an informed public may be, it is well established that disclosure of certain information may be restricted in service of the nation's security, for "[i]t is 'obvious and unarguable' that no governmental interest is more compelling than the security of the Nation." *Haig v. Agee,* 453 U.S. 280, 307 (1981). And, as the Supreme Court has repeatedly noted, one aspect of the government's paramount interest in protecting the nation's security is the government's "compelling interest in protecting both the secrecy of information important to our national security and the appearance of confidentiality so essential to the effective operation of our foreign intelligence service." [*Snepp v. United States,* 444 U.S. 507 (1980),] at 509 n.3. Thus, the right to free speech and the value of an informed citizenry [are] not absolute and must yield to the government's legitimate efforts to ensure "the environment of physical security which a functioning democracy requires." *Morison,* 844 F.2d at 1082. This point is best expressed in the Supreme Court's pithy phrase that "while the Constitution protects against the invasion of individual rights, it is not a suicide pact." [*Aptheker v. Secretary of State,* 378 U.S. 500 (1964),] at 509.

Of course, the abstract proposition that the rights protected by the First Amendment must at times yield to the need for national security does not address the concrete issue of whether the §793, as applied here, violates the First Amendment. This determination depends on whether §793 is narrowly drawn to apply only to those instances in which the government's need for secrecy is legitimate, or whether it is too indiscriminate in its sweep, seeking in effect, to excise the cancer of espionage with a chainsaw instead of a scalpel. In this respect, the first clause of §793(e) implicates only the defendants' right to disclose, willfully, information the government has sought to keep confidential due to the potential harm its disclosure poses to the national security in situations in which the defendants have reason to believe that such disclosure could be used to injure the United States or aid a foreign government. Likewise, §793(d), which defendants are charged with conspiring to violate, implicates the same interests, but is limited to those people — generally government employees or contractors — with authorized possession of the information. Thus, it seems fair to say that §793, taken together with its judicial glosses, is more the result of a legislative scalpel and not a chainsaw. This, however, does not end the analysis.

As defendants correctly argue, the analysis of the First Amendment interests implicated by §§793(d) and (e) depends on the relationship to the government of the person whose First Amendment rights are implicated. In this respect, there are two classes of people roughly correlating to those subject to prosecution under §793(d) and those subject to prosecution under §793(e). The first class consists of persons who have access to the information by virtue of their official position. These people are most often government employees or military personnel with access to classified information, or defense contractors with access to classified information, and are often bound by contractual agreements whereby they agree not to disclose classified information. As such, they are in a position of trust with the government. The second class of persons are those who have no employment or contractual relationship with the government, and therefore have not exploited a relationship of trust to obtain the national defense information they are charged with disclosing, but instead generally obtained the information from one who has violated such a trust.

There can be little doubt, as defendants readily concede, that the Constitution permits the government to prosecute the first class of persons for the disclosure of information relating to the national defense when that person knew that the information is the type which could be used to threaten the nation's security, and that person acted in bad faith, *i.e.*, with reason to believe the disclosure could harm the United States or aid a foreign government. Indeed, the relevant precedent teaches that the Constitution permits even more drastic restraints on the free speech rights of this class of persons. [Here the court reviewed the holdings in *Marchetti* and *Snepp*.] . . .

. . . For this reason, the government may constitutionally punish government employees like Franklin for the willful disclosure of national defense information, and if the government proves the defendants conspired with Franklin in his commission of that offense, they may be subject to prosecution, as well. 18 U.S.C. §793(g).

But the analysis must go beyond this because the defendants are also charged with conspiring to violate §793(e) for their own disclosures of NDI to those not entitled to receive it. In this regard, they belong in the second class of those subject to prosecution under §793 — namely, those who have not violated a position of trust with the government to obtain and disclose information, but have obtained the information from one who has. The defendants argue that unlike Morison, Marchetti or Snepp, they did not agree to restrain their speech as part of their employment, and accordingly their First Amendment interests are more robust. . . .

One possible implication . . . is that a special relationship with the government is necessary before the government may constitutionally punish the disclosure of information relating to the national defense. Seizing upon this possible implication, defendants here contend that the First Amendment bars Congress from punishing those persons, like defendants, without a special relationship to the government for the disclosure of NDI. In essence, their position is that once a government secret has been leaked to the general public and the first line of defense thereby breached, the government has no recourse but to sit back and watch as the threat to the national security caused by the first disclosure multiplies with every subsequent disclosure. This position cannot be sustained. Although the question whether the government's interest in preserving its national defense secrets is sufficient to trump the First Amendment rights of those not in a position of trust with the government is a more difficult question, and although the authority addressing this issue is sparse, both common sense and the relevant precedent point persuasively to the conclusion that the government can punish those outside of the government for the unauthorized receipt and deliberate retransmission of information relating to the national defense.

Of course, in some instances the government's interest is so compelling, and the defendant's purpose so patently unrelated to the values of the First Amendment, that a constitutional challenge is easily dismissed. The obvious example is the unauthorized disclosure of troop movements or military technology to hostile foreign powers by non-governmental persons, conduct typically prosecuted under §794. But this is not such a case; the government has not charged the defendants under §794(a). . . . Congress's attempt to provide for the nation's security by extending punishment for the disclosure of national security secrets beyond the first category of persons within its trust to the general populace is a reasonable, and therefore constitutional[,] exercise of its power. . . .

. . . [E]ven when a person is charged with the transmission of intangible "information" the person had "reason to believe could be used to the injury of the United States," the application of the statute without the requirement that disclosure of the information be potentially harmful to the United States would subject non-governmental employees to prosecution for the innocent, albeit negligent, disclosure of information relating to the national defense. Punishing defendants engaged in public debate for unwittingly harming a legitimate government interest is inconsistent with the Supreme Court's First Amendment jurisprudence. Limiting the set of information relating to the national defense to that information which the defendant *knows,* if disclosed, is potentially harmful to the United States, by virtue of the statute's willfulness requirement, avoids this problem. Thus, for these reasons, information relating to the national defense, whether tangible or intangible, must necessarily be information which if disclosed, is potentially harmful to the United States, and the defendant must know that disclosure of the information is potentially harmful to the United States. The alternative construction simply is not sustainable. So limited, the statute does not violate the defendants' First Amendment guarantee of free speech.

For essentially the same reasons, §793, as applied to these defendants, does not violate the defendants' First Amendment right to petition the government for grievances. The Supreme Court has stated that "[t]he right to petition is cut from the same cloth as the other guarantees of [the First] Amendment, and is an assurance of a particular expression of freedom." *McDonald v. Smith,* 472 U.S. 479, 482 (1985). Indeed, "this right is implicit in 'the very idea of government, republican in form.'" *Id.*. . . For this reason, defendants contend that §793 cannot constitutionally be applied to their alleged conduct.

This argument suffers the same fatal flaws as defendants' argument under the First Amendment's free speech guarantee. Like the First Amendment's guarantee of free speech, the right to petition the government for grievances is not absolute, and may be validly regulated. *See California Motor Transport v. Trucking Unlimited,* 404 U.S. 508, 514-15 (1972) ("First Amendment rights may not be used as the means or pretext for achieving 'substantive evils'"). . . .

[The court then rejected the defendants' challenge based on the overbreadth doctrine.]

VII.

In the end, it must be said that this is a hard case, and not solely because the parties' positions and arguments are both substantial and complex. It is also a hard case because it requires an evaluation of whether Congress has violated our Constitution's most sacred values, enshrined in the First and the Fifth Amendment[s], when it passed legislation in furtherance of our nation's security. The conclusion here is that the balance struck by §793 between these competing interests is constitutionally permissible because (1) it limits the breadth of the term "related to the national defense" to matters closely held by the government for the legitimate reason that their disclosure could threaten our collective security; and (2) it imposes rigorous scienter requirements as a condition for finding criminal liability. . . .

Notes and Questions

1. Espionage Act Prosecutions of Non-Spies. The decision in *Rosen* draws heavily from an earlier one in *United States v. Morison,* 604 F. Supp. 655 (D. Md.), *aff'd,* 844

F.2d 1057 (4th Cir. 1985). *Morison* marked the first successful prosecution under the Espionage Act of a person not accused of being a spy. Samuel Loring Morison was a Navy intelligence analyst who sold classified satellite photographs of a Soviet nuclear-powered aircraft carrier under construction to *Jane's Defence Weekly,* and who was apprehended with other classified materials. He raised, unsuccessfully, the same defenses of vagueness and overbreadth that the defendants in *Rosen* did. His case was widely viewed as a warning to government employees that unauthorized leaks, regardless of motive, would be vigorously prosecuted. Whether or to what extent it has had a chilling effect on individuals who might have used classified documents to inform the public generally, to air what they regarded as unwise policy choices, or even to publicize government misbehavior or mismanagement, is unknown.

Unauthorized leaks have in fact continued, and leakers have occasionally been identified, fired, and even criminally prosecuted. In one such case a former NSA senior executive released information, first to the Defense Department's Inspector General and to Congress, and then to a journalist, about financial waste, bureaucratic dysfunction, and possible illegal activities at the agency. *United States v. Drake,* 818 F. Supp. 2d 909 (D. Md. 2011). Other insider defendants include a former CIA officer who named an undercover agent allegedly engaged in waterboarding, *United States v. Kiriakou,* 898 F. Supp. 2d 921 (E.D. Va. 2012); a State Department contractor who told a reporter about North Korea's military capabilities, *United States v. Kim,* 808 F. Supp. 2d 44 (D.D.C. 2011); a CIA officer who allegedly disclosed details of Iran's nuclear weapons program to a *New York Times* reporter, *United States v. Sterling,* 724 F.3d 482 (4th Cir. 2013); and a former CIA and DIA operative who sold secrets to China, *United States v. Mallory,* No. 1:17-CR-154, 2018 WL 3587718 (E.D. Va. July 26, 2018).

The government has gone to considerable lengths to learn the identities of leakers or at least to deter additional leaks by bringing journalists before grand juries under threat of contempt to force the disclosure of their sources. In one case a reporter was jailed for 85 days for refusing to cooperate. *See* Don Van Natta Jr., Adam Liptak & Clifford J. Levy, *The Miller Case: A Notebook, a Cause, a Jail Cell and a Deal,* N.Y. Times, Oct. 16, 2005. And in the *Kim* case, *supra,* the government named the reporter who received the leak — Fox News's James Rosen — as an unindicted co-conspirator. *See* Ann E. Marimow, *A Rare Look into a Justice Department Leak Probe,* Wash. Post, May 19, 2013.

What really got the attention of the media in the *Rosen* case was the fact that the defendants were neither spies nor government employees; in this sense, the prosecution was unprecedented. While the *Rosen* defendants were not members of the media, as downstream recipients of unauthorized leaks they stood in the same position as a newspaper or TV network or its reporters. If they could be convicted of violating the Espionage Act, so presumably could any member of the press who received sensitive national security information from unnamed government sources, even if that information were not subsequently published. The threat to the media's ability to inform the American electorate about government activities, and to the ability of citizens to hold government accountable, was clear.

Reportedly because of pretrial rulings in the *Rosen* case on the admissibility of classified evidence or the requirement of proof that the defendants knew that their distribution of information would harm the United States, but also perhaps in part because of the implications for representative democracy, or because of the intense public interest in the case, the government dropped all charges in 2009, ending this dramatic chapter in the history of Espionage Act prosecutions — albeit without any formal resolution of whether and to what extent the Espionage Act could be used against leak recipients. *See* Neil A. Lewis & David Johnston, *U.S. Moves to End Secrets Case Against Israel Lobbyists,* N.Y. Times, May 2, 2009.

2. Adequate Warning to Potential Leakers? Responding to defendants' claim that §793 is void for vagueness, in violation of the Due Process Clause of the Fifth Amendment, the *Rosen* court concluded that "its language and history provided adequate warning to these defendants that the statute proscribed the alleged conduct." 445 F. Supp. 2d at 628. Do you agree? Do you think the defendants fairly claimed surprise because, with only two exceptions, the Espionage Act had never been applied except in "classic espionage cases"? If you had done what the *Rosen* defendants did, would you have been concerned about potential criminal liability?

3. "National Defense Information." The *Rosen* court attached particular importance to the fact that the information delivered to the defendants was NDI. Are you clear on the meaning of that term? In *United States v. Heine,* 151 F.2d 813, 815 (2d Cir. 1945), Judge Learned Hand, referring to the term "national defense" in an earlier version of the Espionage Act, wrote, "It seems plain that the section cannot cover information about all those activities which become tributary to 'the national defense' in time of war; for in modern war there are none which do not." Indeed, what information, secret or not, fails to qualify as NDI? How did the *Rosen* court determine that the term could withstand a Fifth Amendment challenge for vagueness? Might any doubts about the meaning of the term NDI be resolved by reference to the statutory language that leaked data "could be used to the injury of the United States or to the advantage of any foreign country"?

4. The Significance of Classification. In *Morison,* as in *Rosen,* the defendant argued that the phrase "not entitled to receive" was vague and overbroad when applied to a case not involving a "subversive purpose." The *Morison* court concluded that "authorization to possess documents and entitlement to receive them may be determined by reference to the classification system. . . ." 604 F. Supp. at 661.

By contrast, the *Rosen* court concluded that

> although evidence that the information was classified is neither strictly necessary nor always sufficient to obtain a prosecution under §793, the classification of the information by the executive branch is highly probative of whether the information at issue is "information relating to the national defense" and whether the person to whom they disclosed the information was "entitled to receive" the information. [445 F. Supp. 2d at 623.]

Then, in an opinion issued three years after the one set out above, the court declared that "evidence that information is classified does not, by itself, establish that the information is NDI; evidence that information is classified is, at most, evidence that the government intended that the designated information be closely held." *United States v. Rosen,* 599 F. Supp. 2d 690, 695 (E.D. Va. 2009). Moreover, "the government's classification decision is inadmissible hearsay on the [question of] whether unauthorized disclosure might potentially damage the United States or aid an enemy of the United States." *Id.*

There is evidence that Congress never intended to reach leaks to the press when it passed the Espionage Act in 1917. Harold Edgar & Benno L. Schmidt Jr., *The Espionage Statutes and Publication of Defense Information*, 73 Colum. L. Rev. 929, 946 (1973). Since that time, Congress has consistently refused to provide criminal sanctions for violations of classification restrictions generally. And on the few occasions when Congress has adopted prohibitions against disclosure of classified information as such, it has almost always opted for narrow restrictions. *See generally* Stephen P. Mulligan & Jennifer K. Elsea, *Criminal Prohibitions on Leaks and Other Disclosures of Classified Defense Information* (Cong. Res. Serv. R41404), Mar. 7, 2017.

One provision of the law does prohibit the disclosure of *any* classified material, whether or not it is "related to the national defense," but only to certain individuals. That provision is 50 U.S.C. §783(a) (2018), which in pertinent part states:

> It shall be unlawful for any . . . employee of the United States . . . to communicate in any manner or by any means, to any other person whom such . . . employee knows or has reason to believe to be an agent . . . of any foreign government, any information of a kind which shall have been classified by the President [or by the President's delegates] as affecting the security of the United States, knowing or having reason to know that such information has been so classified. . . .

See Scarbeck v. United States, 317 F.2d 546, 558 (D.C. Cir. 1963).

One might assume from this history that §793 was not meant to cover all disclosures of classified information. Still, notwithstanding the statement of the *Rosen* court above, one commentator notes that "[c]ourts have read the 'not entitled to receive it' language in light of the classification system," and, given the "breadth and malleability of the remaining statutory requirements, the bare fact that information is classified typically will be enough to bring it within the statute's protections." Heidi Kitrosser, *Leak Prosecutions and the First Amendment: New Developments and a Closer Look at the Feasibility of Protecting Leakers*, 56 Wm. & Mary L. Rev. 1221, 1232 (2015). Considering the massive overclassification of data and the attendant tradition of judicial deference, should it be enough?

5. First Amendment "Core Values." The *Rosen* court undertook the "delicate and difficult task" of weighing First Amendment rights of free expression and association — and the associated right of the public to gain information about the workings of government — against the need to prevent the disclosure of some information in the interest of national security. The answer turned, the court said, on "whether §793 is narrowly drawn to apply only to those instances in which the government's need for secrecy is legitimate, or whether it is too indiscriminate in its sweep, seeking in effect, to excise the cancer of espionage with a chainsaw instead of a scalpel." Do you agree with the court's finding about Congress's choice of tools?

Do First Amendment rights even exist with respect to sensitive information that would not have been obtained but for the leaker's employment? One of us suggested that the Supreme Court had, for a time, "adopted an effectively categorical rule that the First Amendment does not protect public employee speech 'that owes its existence to a public employee's professional responsibilities.'" Stephen I. Vladeck, *The Espionage Act and National Security Whistleblowing After Garcetti*, 57 Am. U. L. Rev. 1531, 1534-1535 (2008) (quoting *Garcetti v. Ceballos*, 547 U.S. 410, 421 (2006)). But in *Lane v. Franks*, 573 U.S. 228 (2014), the Court clarified *Garcetti*, explaining that "the mere fact that a citizen's speech concerns information acquired by virtue of his public employment does not transform that speech into employee — rather than citizen — speech." *Id.* at 240. Instead, "[t]he critical question under *Garcetti* is whether the speech at issue is itself ordinarily within the scope of an employee's duties, not whether it merely concerns those duties." *Id.* How would you apply that distinction to speech relating to classified information to which the speaker had access only by dint of her official duties?

6. *Insiders vs. Outsiders.* The defendants in *Rosen* argued that the First Amendment applies differently to persons "without a special relationship to the government." The court agreed that "the Constitution permits even more drastic restraints on the free speech rights" of insiders. 445 F. Supp. 2d at 635. But it went on to decide that "both common sense and the relevant precedent point persuasively to the conclusion that the government can punish those outside of the government for the unauthorized receipt and deliberate retransmission of information relating to the national defense." *Id.* at 637.

What are the broad implications of this bifurcated First Amendment analysis for representative democracy? One is that the "First Amendment's promise" of communications to enable the public to oversee and check government "would be empty indeed if its protections did not extend to information that the President wishes to keep secret," including "information from government insiders, who alone are structurally situated to reveal it." Heidi Kitrosser, *Free Speech Aboard the Leaky Ship of State: Calibrating First Amendment Protections for Leakers of Classified Information*, 6 J. Nat'l Security L. & Pol'y 409, 424 (2013). Another is that in future cases courts will ignore the case-by-case fact-finding for outsiders practiced in *Rosen*, leaving reporters and publishers exposed (or feeling exposed) for the first time to prosecution under the Espionage Act for publicizing government corruption. How could the "First Amendment's promise" be kept without unduly jeopardizing national security?

At the end of its opinion, the *Rosen* court concluded that "the time is ripe for Congress to engage in a thorough review and revision" of the Espionage Act. How could the statute be amended to address both constitutional and practical concerns it raises?

7. *Does Motive Matter?* Insiders who leak do so from a variety of motives, among them a desire to influence public debate of important issues or to expose government wrongdoing. But is a leaker's motive relevant in enforcing the Espionage Act? If so, what practical problems can you imagine in establishing motive?

Samuel Morison claimed that he disclosed classified information in order to reveal the progress of a Soviet naval buildup. The government charged that his motives were more selfish — money and ambition. 844 F.2d at 1062. The *Rosen* defendants claimed that their purpose was to further the goals of their employer, AIPAC, and that they had no intent to injure the United States. Quoting §793(d), the *Rosen* court concluded that motive was irrelevant in the disclosure of a "*document* relating to the national defense," but that the government must show bad faith to secure a conviction for disclosure of "*information* relating to the national defense which information the possessor has reason to believe could be used to the injury of the United States or to the advantage of any foreign nation." What is the purpose of this statutory distinction? Can you readily distinguish between "document" and "information"?

Should ignorance or negligence play a role in determining guilt? *See* Margaret B. Kwoka, *Leaking and Legitimacy*, 48 U.C. Davis L. Rev. 1387 (2015) (distinguishing "deluge leaks" by Bradley (now Chelsea) Manning and Edward Snowden from targeted leaks intended to expose corrupt government practices).

One scholar points out that "the perceived intent of those who disclose national security information without authorization plays an important role in whether they are labeled as heroes or traitors." Mary-Rose Papandrea, *National Security Information Disclosures and the Role of Intent*, 56 Wm. & Mary L. Rev. 1381, 1382 (2015). But should a leaker escape criminal liability if she did not *actually* intend to jeopardize national security, or if she believed that any risk was outweighed by the value of her disclosure to public discourse? Professor Papandrea asserts that while "strict liability for the unauthorized collection and dissemination of all defense-related information might be the safest way to protect our nation's security, such an approach would be inconsistent with our basic commitment to an informed democracy." *Id.* Can you argue that the First Amendment requires consideration of a leaker's intent?

If a leaker's motive is to call attention to unlawful government activity, she may be protected to some degree by whistleblower protection laws, which generally bar retaliation against government employees for disclosing information that they reasonably believe to show

> (i) any violation of any law, rule, or regulation, or
>
> (ii) gross mismanagement, a gross waste of funds, an abuse of authority, or a substantial and specific danger to public health or safety,
>
> if such disclosure is not specifically prohibited by law and if such information is not specifically required by Executive order to be kept secret in the interest of national defense or the conduct of foreign affairs. . . . [Whistleblower Protection Act, 5 U.S.C. §2302(b)(8)(A) (2018).]

See also the more restrictive provisions of the Military Whistleblower Protection Act, 10 U.S.C. §1034 (2018) (barring retaliation for a servicemember's report to a member of Congress or an agency Inspector General), and the Intelligence Community Whistleblower Protection Act, 5 U.S.C. app. 3 §8H (2018) (authorizing reporting to an agency IG). *See* Mary-Rose Papandrea, *Lapdogs, Watchdogs, and Scapegoats: The Press and National Security Information*, 83 Ind. L.J. 233, 246-248 (2008); PEN American Center, *Secret Sources: Whistleblowers, National Security, and Free Expression* (2015). But these measures offer only limited protection from negative personnel actions, such as firing or demotion, and not from criminal prosecution.

8. Is Leaking Theft? Might 18 U.S.C. §641, *supra*, which provides remedies for the common law crimes of larceny, embezzlement, and conversion of government property, be equally applicable to the unauthorized dissemination of information? The *Morison* court apparently thought so, holding that "information" fit within the meaning of the statutory term "a thing of value," which value could be measured by the payment Morison received. Moreover, said the court, the First Amendment may not be used "either to enable the governmental employee to excuse his act of theft or to excuse him, as in *Snepp* and *Marchetti*, from his contractual obligation." 844 F.2d at 1077. In the process, the Fourth Circuit court rejected the argument that the criminal statute should be read narrowly to encompass only the common law tort of conversion — which requires that the legitimate owner be *deprived* of possession (and would therefore not recognize as conversion the theft of copies, as in *Morison*).

9. The Biggest Leaks Ever? One of the most consequential leaks in the nation's history came in 1971 with the delivery to the *New York Times* and other newspapers of a 7,000-page top-secret history of the Vietnam War, the *Pentagon Papers,* by a former DOD employee, Daniel Ellsberg. See *infra* p. 1299. Publication of the document, which revealed decades of government lying about U.S. military involvement in Southeast Asia, had a profound impact on the course of the war, just as Ellsberg intended, and it created an enduring mistrust of government among the American public. Ellsberg was charged with violating part of the Espionage Act, 18 U.S.C. §793, theft of government property, and conspiracy, among other charges. But the charges were dismissed with prejudice when it came to light that White House operatives had burgled his psychiatrist's office in an effort to discredit him, and that the FBI had illegally wiretapped his phone. *See United States v. Russo,* No. 9373-CD (C.D. Cal. filed Dec. 29, 1971), *dismissed* (C.D. Cal. May 11, 1973); *see also* Martin Arnold, *Pentagon Papers Charges Are Dismissed; Judge Byrne Frees Ellsberg and Russo, Assails "Improper Government Conduct,"* N.Y. Times, May 12, 1973; *Text of Ruling by Judge in Ellsberg Case,* N.Y. Times, May 12, 1973.

In 2010, Army PFC Bradley (now Chelsea) Manning, utilizing a security loophole, was able to download 75,000 classified military incident reports and intelligence documents about U.S. combat activities in Afghanistan, 400,000 government documents relating to the war in Iraq, and another 250,000 confidential State Department diplomatic cables, then transfer them to *WikiLeaks,* which published them on the Internet. These releases, which Manning said were based on her concern for the "morality" of U.S. military efforts in Iraq and Afghanistan, not any desire to harm the United States, undoubtedly endangered Afghan lives, exposed intelligence sources and methods, and strained critical alliances. *See* Charlie Savage, *Gates Assails WikiLeaks over Release of Reports,* N.Y. Times, July 30, 2010; Scott Shane & Andrew W. Lehren, *Leaked Cables Offer a Raw Look Inside U.S. Diplomacy,* N.Y. Times, Nov. 29, 2010. Manning was charged with violating the Espionage Act, as applied through the Uniform Code of Military Justice, and an array of other offenses. Manning pleaded guilty to some of the charges in advance of trial, and was acquitted of the most serious charge (aiding the enemy) at trial. She was sentenced to a 35-year prison term based on both her plea and the charges upon which she was convicted at trial, but her sentence was commuted by President Obama to a total of seven years' confinement.

In 2013, Edward Snowden, a disaffected employee of an NSA contractor with a top-secret security clearance, fled the United States with a trove of classified information about the NSA's electronic intelligence programs. The programs had already become extremely controversial, but many details were unknown to the public. Snowden released some of the information to reporters for *The Guardian,* the *Washington Post,* and other newspapers, and each paper published at least some of the leaked material online. He said he was motivated to reveal "the federation of secret law, unequal pardon and irresistible executive powers that rule the world that I love." Barton Gellman & Jerry Markon, *Edward Snowden Says Motive Behind Leaks Was to Expose "Surveillance State,"* Wash. Post, June 10, 2013. Then-DNI James Clapper called Snowden's leaks "potentially the most massive and most damaging theft of intelligence information in our history." Andrea Peterson, *A Year After*

Snowden Revelations, Government Surveillance Reform Still a Work in Progress, Wash. Post, June 5, 2014. Snowden was charged with violating Sections 793(d) and 798(a)(3) of the Espionage Act, and with theft of government property, but at this writing in late 2019 he was residing in Moscow, out of the reach of U.S. extradition.

Finally, Julian Assange, founder and leader of *WikiLeaks*, was indicted in May 2019 for an array of offenses, including violations of various provisions of the Espionage Act. Among other things, he was charged with knowingly obtaining damaging national defense information and then communicating that information "to all the world by publishing [it] on the Internet," the first time the government had ever prosecuted an act of publication under the Espionage Act. *See* Superseding Indictment at 32, *United States v. Assange*, Crim. No. 1:18-cr-111 (CMH) (E.D. Va. May 23, 2019). After holing up in the Ecuadorian embassy in London for several years to avoid arrest, Assange was being held in a British jail at this writing, awaiting extradition to the United States.

If you were assigned to defend any of these four individuals — Ellsberg, Manning, Snowden, or Assange — how would you organize their defense?

E. "AUTHORIZED" LEAKS

Some leaks of classified information to the media are in fact authorized. Examples include

> [the] disclosure of this country's development of Multiple Independently Targeted Reentry Vehicles and the release of information about North Vietnamese forces operating in South Vietnam, including the identity of units, their strength and the routes they took to reach their operating areas. These . . . were the result of high level executive decisions that disclosure was in the public interest, to counter popular and congressional pressure for more missiles, in the first instance, and, in the second instance, to bolster domestic support for our own military effort in South Vietnam. They are instances of declassification by official public disclosure. [*Alfred A. Knopf, Inc. v. Colby*, 509 F.2d 1362, 1369 (4th Cir. 1975).]

According to one commentator, an authorized leak, which may or may not be publicly acknowledged, is frequently the result of "a planned strategy by a government official to advance or promote a particular policy, sabotage the plans or policies of rival agencies or political parties, discredit opponents, float a public opinion trial balloon, or expose corruption or illegal activities. . . . [T]he executive branch does not want to end all leaks; it simply wants to end the leaks that it does not like." Mary-Rose Papandrea, *The Publication of National Security Information in the Digital Age*, 5 J. Nat'l Security L. & Pol'y 119, 121 (2011).

Two examples of unacknowledged leaks came in 2003. Stressing one of the central rationales for the U.S. invasion of Iraq that year, President George W. Bush declared in his State of the Union address that "[t]he British Government has learned that Saddam Hussein recently sought significant quantities of uranium from Africa." 1 Pub. Papers 82, 88 (Jan. 28, 2003). But former ambassador Joseph C. Wilson IV, who earlier had been sent by the CIA to investigate claims that Iraq was seeking to purchase nuclear weapons materials in Niger, wrote in an op-ed article that the claims were "highly doubtful" and based on documents that were "probably forged," and that he had conveyed his findings to the CIA. "[S]ome of the intelligence related to

Iraq's nuclear weapons program," he concluded, "was twisted to exaggerate the Iraqi threat." *What I Didn't Find in Africa,* N.Y. Times, July 6, 2003.

In an effort to counter Wilson's assertions, the President and Vice President reportedly instructed the Vice President's Chief of Staff, I. Lewis "Scooter" Libby to covertly release portions of the then-classified 2002 *National Intelligence Estimate,* which contained language supporting Administration claims. Libby was said to have been advised that the President's instruction "amounted to declassification of the document," and he did as he was told. *See* David Johnston & David E. Sanger, *Cheney's Aide Says President Approved Leak,* N.Y. Times, Apr. 7, 2006.

Libby also disclosed to reporters for *Newsweek,* the *New York Times,* and perhaps others that Wilson was married to an undercover CIA operative, Valerie Plame. This leak allegedly was intended to discredit Wilson's account by suggesting that his trip to Niger was a junket arranged by his wife that resulted from nepotism. Libby was given this information by Vice President Cheney. *See* Murray Waas, *Bush Directed Cheney to Counter War Critic,* Nat'l J., July 3, 2006. The story was broken on July 14, 2003, by syndicated columnist Robert D. Novak, who said he got the information from Karl Rove, the President's deputy chief of staff, and others. *See* David Johnston, *Novak Told Prosecutor His Sources in Leak Case,* N.Y. Times, July 12, 2006.

Disclosure of the name of a CIA operative can be a felony under certain circumstances. The Intelligence Identities Protection Act, 50 U.S.C. §§3121-3126 (2018), provides in part:

> Whoever, having or having had authorized access to classified information that identifies a covert agent, intentionally discloses any information identifying such covert agent to any individual not authorized to receive classified information, knowing that the information disclosed so identifies such covert agent and that the United States is taking affirmative measures to conceal such covert agent's intelligence relationship to the United States, shall be fined . . . or imprisoned. . . . [*Id.* §3121(a).]

See Jennifer K. Elsea, *Intelligence Identities Protection Act* (Cong. Res. Serv. RS21636), Apr. 10, 2013.

After the publication of Plame's name, a special prosecutor was named to look into the case. Two years later, Libby was charged and convicted in a jury trial, not with violation of the Intelligence Identities Protection Act, but on four felony counts of making false statements, perjury, and obstruction of justice. His sentence of 30 months in prison was then commuted by President Bush in 2007, and he was pardoned by President Trump in 2018. Can you guess why Libby was not charged with a violation of the Intelligence Identities Protection Act? Why he was later pardoned?

Wilson and Plame subsequently filed suit for damages against Cheney, Rove, Libby, and Deputy Secretary of State Richard Armitage, alleging violations of First and Fifth Amendment rights. The court found that "special factors" counseled against creating a *Bivens* remedy for any constitutional violations: (1) the Privacy Act (*infra* p. 1273) provided a "comprehensive remedial scheme," even though that statute exempts members of the Offices of the President and Vice President from liability; and (2) litigation of the case would "inevitably require judicial intrusion into matters of national security and sensitive intelligence information." *Wilson v. Libby,* 535 F.3d 697, 704-711 (D.C. Cir. 2008).

More recently, President Donald Trump reportedly shared extremely sensitive intelligence with Russian officials during an Oval Office meeting, violating an agreement with an ally that furnished the information, and possibly jeopardizing a critical source within the Islamic State. The information, which was withheld from the public at the government's insistence, was said to concern a terrorist threat related to laptop computers on airplanes, as well as U.S. countermeasures. *See* Greg Miller & Greg Jaffe, *Trump Revealed Highly Classified Information to Russian Foreign Minister and Ambassador*, Wash. Post, May 15, 2017. A dispute immediately arose about whether the President had acted illegally. *Compare* Matt Zapotosky, *No, Trump Did Not Break the Law in Talking Classified Details with the Russians*, Wash. Post, May 16, 2017, *with* Elizabeth Goitein, *Don't Be So Quick to Call Those Disclosures "Legal,"* Just Security, May 17, 2017.

SAFEGUARDING NATIONAL SECURITY INFORMATION: SUMMARY OF BASIC PRINCIPLES

- Balancing secrecy and transparency in our representative democracy has always been difficult and controversial. The need to hold government officials accountable and encourage participation in government must be weighed against serious threats to national security from the disclosure of certain kinds of information.

- Standards for classification of government information are set forth in executive orders issued by a succession of Presidents, dictating levels of classification, classification authorities, the kinds of information that may be classified, the duration of classification, grounds for declassification, and other details.

- The President's independent constitutional basis for protecting national security information from disclosure is uncertain, as is Congress's authority to regulate his handling of such information.

- Every government employee who signs a secrecy agreement as a condition of employment surrenders some First Amendment freedom of expression. The precise extent of that surrender is, however, unknown.

- The government's ability to stop or to punish, either civilly or criminally, an employee's disclosure of national security information may depend on whether that information is properly classified.

- The Espionage Act and related criminal sanctions apply to government employees who leak sensitive information for purposes unrelated to espionage. They may apply as well to non-government recipients of leaked information, including perhaps members of the media.

- Thus far, no court has ruled that a leaker's motive matters, even if she is not engaged in espionage, and even if her purpose is to expose illegal government activity.

- Several lower courts have held that the language of the Espionage Act is not unconstitutionally vague — that it provides fair warning to potential violators — and that it does not infringe unduly on a leaker's First Amendment right of free expression.

- Every administration engages in "authorized" leaking, sometimes for purely political purposes. The monitoring or curtailment of such leaks has proven nearly impossible.

40

Access to National Security Information

> Knowledge will forever govern ignorance, and a people who mean to be their own governors, must arm themselves with the power knowledge gives. A popular government without popular information or the means of acquiring it, is but a prologue to a farce or a tragedy or perhaps both.
>
> *James Madison*
> Letter to W.T. Barry
> August 4, 1822

In the last chapter we examined the bargain that we have struck with ourselves to balance secrecy and knowledge, security and self-determination. Congress has played a key role in implementing that bargain by passing legislation that makes some executive branch information about national security available to the public. Courts have recognized additional grounds for access to information from all three branches of government in the common law and the Constitution. Congress also seeks information from the Executive that it says is needed to discharge its duties under Article I. In this chapter we review each of these processes for obtaining, or for preventing access to, "popular information" for a "popular government."

A. THE FREEDOM OF INFORMATION ACT

It would be difficult to overstate the importance of the Freedom of Information Act and its statutory analogues. The Justice Department calls FOIA "the law that keeps citizens in the know about their government." FOIA.gov, *What Is FOIA?* (n.d.), *at* https://www.foia.gov/about.html. Passed in 1966, it opened a window into the operation of the executive branch, transformed the way the government conducts its business, and gave the American people a renewed sense of self-determination. It has special relevance in the national security field, about which information has always been most closely held. In fact, much of the information in this book was obtained through, or otherwise derives from, FOIA requests.

A Citizen's Guide on Using the Freedom of Information Act and the Privacy Act of 1974 to Request Government Records

House Committee on Government Reform,
H.R. Rep. No. 109-226, at 3 (2005)

The Freedom of Information Act (FOIA) establishes a presumption that records in the possession of agencies and departments of the executive branch of the U.S. Government are accessible to the people. This was not always the approach to Federal information disclosure policy. Before enactment of FOIA in 1966, the burden was on the individual to establish a right to examine these government records. There were no statutory guidelines or procedures to help a person seeking information. There were no judicial remedies for those denied access.

With the passage of FOIA, the burden of proof shifted from the individual to the government. Those seeking information are no longer required to show a need for information. Instead, the "need to know" standard has been replaced by a "right to know" doctrine. The government now has to justify the need for secrecy.

FOIA sets standards for determining which records must be disclosed and which records may be withheld. The law also provides administrative and judicial remedies for those denied access to records. Above all, the statute requires federal agencies to provide the fullest possible disclosure of information to the public — although what disclosure is "possible" is, not surprisingly, a matter of ongoing (if not endless) debate.

1. The Statutory Text

Freedom of Information Act

5 U.S.C. §552 (2018)

§552. PUBLIC INFORMATION; AGENCY RULES, OPINIONS, ORDERS, RECORDS, AND PROCEEDINGS

(a) Each agency shall make available to the public information as follows: . . .

(2) Each agency, in accordance with published rules, shall make available for public inspection in an electronic format —

(A) final opinions, including concurring and dissenting opinions, as well as orders, made in the adjudication of cases;

(B) those statements of policy and interpretations which have been adopted by the agency and are not published in the Federal Register; . . .

(3) (A) . . . [E]ach agency, upon any request for records which (i) reasonably describes such records and (ii) is made in accordance with published rules stating the time, place, fees (if any), and procedures to be followed, shall make the records promptly available to any person. . . .

(C) In responding under this paragraph to a request for records, an agency shall make reasonable efforts to search for the records in electronic form or format. . . .

(4) (A) (i) . . . [E]ach agency shall promulgate regulations, pursuant to notice and receipt of public comment, specifying the schedule of fees applicable to the processing of requests under this section . . . .

(ii) Such agency regulations shall provide that —

(II) fees shall be limited to reasonable standard charges for document duplication when records are not sought for commercial use and the request is made by an educational or noncommercial scientific institution, whose purpose is scholarly or scientific research; or a representative of the news media; . . .

In this clause, the term "a representative of the news media" means any person or entity that gathers information of potential interest to a segment of the public, uses its editorial skills to turn the raw materials into a distinct work, and distributes that work to an audience. In this clause, the term "news" means information that is about current events or that would be of current interest to the public. . . .

(iii) Documents shall be furnished without any charge or at a charge reduced below the fees established under clause (ii) if disclosure of the information is in the public interest because it is likely to contribute significantly to public understanding of the operations or activities of the government and is not primarily in the commercial interest of the requester. . . .

(B) On complaint, the district court of the United States in the district in which the complainant resides, or has his principal place of business, or in which the agency records are situated, or in the District of Columbia, has jurisdiction to enjoin the agency from withholding agency records and to order the production of any agency records improperly withheld from the complainant. In such a case the court shall determine the matter de novo, and may examine the contents of such agency records in camera to determine whether such records or any part thereof shall be withheld under any of the exemptions set forth in subsection (b) of this section, and the burden is on the agency to sustain its action. . . .

(8) (A) An agency shall —

(i) withhold information under this section only if —

(I) the agency reasonably foresees that disclosure would harm an interest protected by an exemption described in subsection (b); or

(II) disclosure is prohibited by law; and

(ii) (I) consider whether partial disclosure of information is possible whenever the agency determines that a full disclosure of a requested record is not possible; and

(II) take reasonable steps necessary to segregate and release nonexempt information. . . .

(b) This section does not apply to matters that are —

(1) (A) specifically authorized under criteria established by an Executive order to be kept secret in the interest of national defense or foreign policy and (B) are in fact properly classified pursuant to such Executive order; . . .

(3) specifically exempted from disclosure by statute (other than section 552b of this title), if that statute —

(A) (i) requires that the matters be withheld from the public in such a manner as to leave no discretion on the issue; or

(ii) establishes particular criteria for withholding or refers to particular types of matters to be withheld; . . .

(5) inter-agency or intra-agency memorandums or letters that would not be available by law to a party other than an agency in litigation with the agency. . . .

Any reasonably segregable portion of a record shall be provided to any person requesting such record after deletion of the portions which are exempt under this subsection. . . .

(c) . . . (3) Whenever a request is made which involves access to records maintained by the Federal Bureau of Investigation pertaining to foreign intelligence or counterintelligence, or international terrorism, and the existence of the records is classified information as provided in subsection (b) (1), the Bureau may, as long as the existence of the records remains classified information, treat the records as not subject to the requirements of this section. . . .

(f) For purposes of this section, the term —

(1) "agency" . . . includes any executive department, military department, Government corporation, Government controlled corporation, or other establishment in the executive branch of the Government (including the Executive Office of the President), or any independent regulatory agency; . . .

Insight into the meaning of the statutory text is provided by Dep't of Justice, Off. of Information Pol'y, *Department of Justice Guide to the Freedom of Information Act* (Oct. 7, 2019), https://www.justice.gov/oip/doj-guide-freedom-information-act-0. The *Guide,* updated periodically, includes an analysis of important judicial opinions construing and applying FOIA.

Notes and Questions

1. Codifying the Balance. The Supreme Court has recognized that in enacting FOIA "Congress sought 'to reach a workable balance between the right of the public to know and the need of the Government'" to protect sensitive information. *John Doe Agency v. John Doe Corp.*, 493 U.S. 146, 152 (1989) (quoting H.R. Rep. No. 89-1497, at 6 (1966)). Do you think FOIA achieves a proper balance between public participation in government and legitimate needs for government secrecy? Does it strike the right balance between the political branches concerning control over sensitive information? Should Congress provide the Executive with greater flexibility to deal with emerging threats and changes in technology? If so, how could it do that?

2. Balancing Costs and Benefits. Can you say how exposure of agency records to public view, or at least the prospect of such exposure, might affect the way the government conducts its business? If your answer is that exposure of agency records makes the government process more costly in some ways, do you think the benefits from a better informed electorate outweigh the increased expense?

3. "Any Request." Although §552(a)(3) provides that an agency must respond to "any request," it was suggested early on that a requester should demonstrate some good reason for wanting particular information. It now seems well settled in principle that it is not necessary for a requester to make any showing of purpose or relevancy. *See Nat'l Archives & Records Admin. v. Favish,* 541 U.S. 157, 172 (2004) ("[A]s a general rule, when documents are within FOIA's disclosure provisions, citizens should not be required to explain why they seek the information."). Do you suppose that a court might nevertheless be more reluctant to order the release of records if it knew that the requester's intention was to compromise U.S. foreign policy? Should it matter that the release most likely would not have the intended effect? How would you incorporate any concern you have about motive into the statute?

FOIA was amended in 2002 to bar requests from foreign governments, international governmental organizations, or their representatives for records held by elements of the intelligence community. 5 U.S.C. §552(a)(3)(E). This change was reportedly intended to prevent access to intelligence agency records by states that support terrorism. Can you think of any other reasons to adopt such a restriction?

4. "Agency." What is an "agency" for FOIA purposes? *See* FOIA §552(f)(1). In *Rushforth v. Council of Economic Advisers,* 762 F.2d 1038, 1040-1043 (D.C. Cir. 1985), the court held that records of a government entity lacking "independent authority" to take "direct action," and whose "sole function is to advise and assist the President," need not be disclosed under FOIA. In *Armstrong v. Exec. Off. of the President,* 90 F.3d 553 (D.C. Cir. 1996), the court determined that the National Security Council (NSC) is not an "agency" within the meaning of FOIA because the NSC staff exercises "no substantial authority either to make or to implement policy" and no "significant non-advisory function." *Id.* at 561, 565. Similarly, courts have ruled that the Office of the White House Counsel, the Council of Economic Advisors, and the Vice President and his staff are not agencies for this purpose. Can you square the judicial definitions of "agency" with the statutory one?

5. "Agency Records." Do you understand what is included in the term "agency records"? In the words of one court, "For requested materials to qualify as 'agency records,' two requirements must be satisfied: (i) an agency must 'either create or obtain' the requested materials, and (ii) the agency must be in control of the requested materials at the time the FOIA request is made." *Grand Central P'ship, Inc. v. Cuomo,* 166 F.3d 473, 479 (2d Cir. 1999) (citations omitted). Thus, materials in agency files have been ruled exempt on grounds that they were not covered by FOIA when they were created, *Kissinger v. Reporters Comm. for Freedom of the Press,* 445 U.S. 136 (1980) (exempting notes in State Department files of the Secretary's telephone conversations while he was National Security Adviser), or because Congress (which is not an "agency" for FOIA purposes) had not given up control of the materials, *Goland v. Cent. Intelligence Agency,* 607 F.2d 339 (D.C. Cir. 1978) (exempting transcript of secret congressional hearing in CIA files). In a more recent case, the court, citing *Goland,* ruled that the Senate Select Committee on Intelligence's full report on the CIA's "enhanced interrogation" program, see *supra* p. 974, was not subject to FOIA because, even though it was in the possession of the CIA, it was still controlled by Congress. *Am. Civil Liberties Union v. Cent. Intelligence Agency,* 823 F.3d 655 (D.C. Cir. 2016).

6. "Reasonably" Described. FOIA §552(a)(3) requires an agency to make available records "reasonably" described by the requester. A description is sufficient if it enables a professional employee of the agency who is familiar with the subject area of the request to locate the record with a reasonable amount of effort. *Truitt v. Dep't of State,* 897 F.2d 540 (D.C. Cir. 1990). An agency is "not obliged to look beyond the four corners of the request for leads to the location of responsive documents," but it must "pursue a lead it cannot in good faith ignore, i.e., a lead that is both clear and certain." *Kowalczyk v. Dep't of Justice,* 73 F.3d 386, 389 (D.C. Cir. 1996). Since a requester usually will not have seen any responsive documents (or even know whether they exist) and will have no way to guess their location, what can she do to improve her chances of getting what she wants?

7. Economic Barriers and Incentives. In general, FOIA requesters may be charged for direct costs to search for and review requested records, plus duplication costs. These charges must be limited to standard duplication costs, however, if the requester is "an educational or noncommercial scientific institution, whose purpose is scholarly or scientific research; or a representative of the news media." 5 U.S.C. §552(a)(4)(A)(ii)(II). In *Nat'l Security Archive v. U.S. Dep't of Defense,* 880 F.2d 1381, 1387-1388 (D.C. Cir. 1989), for example, the court rejected, as "contrary to the manifest purpose of [FOIA] . . . and common sense," DOD's effort to charge "commercial" fees to a not-for-profit organization that compiles government data for scholars, news media, and government researchers.

All charges may be waived "if disclosure is in the public interest because it is likely to contribute significantly to public understanding of the operations or activities of the government and is not primarily in the commercial interest of the requester." 5 U.S.C. §552(a)(4)(A)(iii). *See Cause of Action v. Fed. Trade Comm'n,* 799 F.3d 1108, 1115 (D.C. Cir. 2015) (reciting these requirements).

If litigation is instituted to obtain a record, under §552(a)(4)(B), the court may award attorney's fees and costs when a requester has "substantially prevailed," that is, if she obtains relief through a judicial order, an enforceable agreement, a consent decree, or a voluntary or unilateral change in position by the agency. §552(a)(4)(E). Many otherwise unsuccessful FOIA requesters have discovered that merely filing suit can have a remarkable laxative effect in speeding the release of records. For example, in *Miller v. U.S. Dep't of State,* 779 F.2d 1378, 1388 (8th Cir. 1985), the requester initially received only seven documents from the agency. Another 56 were released when he filed suit, 72 more when he demanded a pretrial conference, and a total of 232 additional documents before the district court's decision in the case, even though the agency repeatedly insisted that it had already sent all responsive records. Nevertheless, a number of courts have denied fee awards unless a "causal nexus" can be shown between the litigation and the release. *See, e.g., First Amendment Coalition v. U.S. Dep't of Justice,* 878 F.3d 1119 (9th Cir. 2017).

8. Access in the Digital Age. In keeping with advances in technology, FOIA now requires agencies to search electronic databases and to furnish requested records in electronic form if requested. §552(a)(3)(B), (C). In the interest of efficiency, as well as to improve transparency, it also calls for frequently requested materials to be indexed and posted in electronic "reading rooms" maintained by all agencies. §552(a)(2)(D). And the 2019 OPEN Government Data Act, Pub. L. No. 115-435, §§201-202, 132 Stat. 5529, 5534, calls on all agencies to publish catalogues of data they hold that are available for public release, and to furnish those data in a machine-readable and open format under open licenses. Can you think of other ways to use technology to improve public access to agency records?

2. Litigating FOIA Requests

Reading *ACLU v. U.S. Dep't of Defense*

The ACLU filed a FOIA request with the CIA and the Defense Department for records relating to their use of "enhanced interrogation" techniques, some of which constituted torture, against terrorist suspects in their custody. When portions of the relevant documents were withheld, the ACLU sued, asking the court to conduct a de novo, in camera review of the documents, and arguing that because of voluntary public disclosures they were no longer properly classified. Consider these questions:

- What standards guide a court in conducting a "de novo" review of an agency's decision to withhold requested records?
- Why did the court act so deferentially toward the two agencies, refusing even to inspect the withheld documents?
- When may an exemption be denied on the ground that a requested record is already public?
- Does the court's decision reflect the balance struck by Congress between secrecy and self-determination when it passed FOIA?

American Civil Liberties Union v. United States Department of Defense

United States Court of Appeals, District of Columbia Circuit, 2011
628 F.3d 612

Sentelle, Chief Judge: Appellants, the American Civil Liberties Union and the American Civil Liberties Foundation (jointly "ACLU"), submitted Freedom of Information Act ("FOIA") requests to the Department of Defense and the Central Intelligence Agency ("CIA") seeking documents related to fourteen "high value" detainees held at the U.S. Naval Base in Guantanamo Bay, Cuba. In response, the government released redacted versions of the requested documents, from which specific information relating to the capture, detention, and interrogation of the detainees had been withheld. The government defended the redactions as justified by FOIA exemptions 1 and 3, which permit the government to withhold information related to "intelligence sources and methods." . . .

I. BACKGROUND

Since January of 2002, the United States has operated a detention facility at the United States Naval Base at Guantanamo Bay, Cuba, for detainees captured in the war on terror. In a September 2006 speech, President Bush revealed that fourteen "suspected terrorist leaders and operatives" had been held and questioned outside of the United States in a separate program operated by the CIA. Remarks on the War on Terror, 42 Weekly Comp. Pres. Doc. 1569, 1570 (Sept. 6, 2006). In his speech, the President announced that this program had been discontinued and that the fourteen detainees were being transferred to Guantanamo Bay. *Id.* at 1573-74. After their transfer, these so-called "high value" detainees received hearings before Combatant Status Review Tribunals ("CSRTs").

Although the Department of Defense had publicly posted redacted transcripts of the detainees' CSRT proceedings, the ACLU submitted Freedom of Information Act requests to the Department seeking full CSRT transcripts of the 14 detainees and all records provided to the CSRTs by or on behalf of the detainees. In response to the request, the government identified and released [eight unclassified CSRT transcripts, six redacted CSRT transcripts, and unclassified or redacted statements of several detainees]. From the redacted documents, the CIA withheld all information relating to the capture, detention, and interrogation of the "high value" detainees.

The ACLU filed the present action in the district court challenging the government's withholdings. The government stood by its withholdings and filed affidavits in support of its position. The government principally relied on the affidavit of Wendy Hilton, the Associate Information Review Officer of the National Clandestine Service of the CIA, to justify the redactions as information protected by FOIA exemptions 1 and 3. . . .

II. FOIA EXEMPTIONS 1 AND 3

. . . [E]xemption 1 permits the government to withhold information "specifically authorized under ceriteria established by an Executive order to be kept secret in the interest of national defense or foreign policy" if that information has been "properly classified pursuant to such Executive order." 5 U.S.C. §552(b)(1). In this case, the government argues that the redacted information was properly classified under Executive Order 12,958, which "prescribes a uniform system for classifying, safeguarding, and declassifying national security information." Exec. Order No. 12,958.[1] Specifically, the government asserts that the information it withheld was classified as "intelligence sources or methods" pursuant to section 1.4(c) of Executive Order 12,958.

. . . The government relies on the National Security Act of 1947 to justify withholding the redacted information under exemption 3. We have previously held that the National Security Act, which also authorizes the Executive to withhold "intelligence sources and methods" from public disclosure, 50 U.S.C. [§3024(i)(1)], qualifies as an exemption statute under exemption 3. *Larson v. Dep't of State,* 565 F.3d 857, 865 (D.C. Cir. 2009); *Fitzgibbon v. C.I.A.,* 911 F.2d 755, 761 (D.C. Cir. 1990).

An agency withholding responsive documents from a FOIA release bears the burden of proving the applicability of claimed exemptions. Typically it does so by affidavit. We review the district court's decision on the adequacy of the agency's showing *de*

1. Executive Order 12,598 and all amendments thereto have since been superseded by Executive Order 13,526, 75 Fed. Reg. 707 (Dec. 29, 2009) [*supra* p. 1219].

novo. Larson, 565 F.3d at 862; *Wolf v. C.I.A.*, 473 F.3d 370, 374 (D.C. Cir. 2007). Because courts "lack the expertise necessary to second-guess such agency opinions in the typical national security FOIA case," *Krikorian v. Dep't of State*, 984 F.2d 461, 464 (D.C. Cir. 1993), we "must accord substantial weight to an agency's affidavit concerning the details of the classified status of the disputed record." *Wolf*, 473 F.3d at 374 (quotations omitted). If an agency's affidavit describes the justifications for withholding the information with specific detail, demonstrates that the information withheld logically falls within the claimed exemption, and is not contradicted by contrary evidence in the record or by evidence of the agency's bad faith, then summary judgment is warranted on the basis of the affidavit alone. *Larson*, 565 F.3d at 862; *Wolf*, 473 F.3d at 374. Moreover, a reviewing court "must take into account . . . that any affidavit or other agency statement of threatened harm to national security will always be speculative to some extent, in the sense that it describes a potential future harm." *Wolf*, 473 F.3d at 374. "Ultimately, an agency's justification for invoking a FOIA exemption is sufficient if it appears 'logical' or 'plausible.'" *Larson*, 565 F.3d at 862 (quoting *Wolf*, 473 F.3d at 374-75).

A.

The ACLU first claims that the withheld information is not exempt from FOIA because it has already been declassified and is available to the public. The ACLU points to three sets of declassified and released government documents that the ACLU believes contain the same information that the CIA has withheld from the requested CSRT documents: the OLC memoranda [see *supra* p. 986 n.8], the CIA Inspector General's report [see *supra* p. 1001 n.16], and a CIA "Background Paper" released with the CIA Inspector General's report. The ACLU also argues that a fourth document, the leaked Red Cross report [see *supra* p. 1001 n.15], although not an official government disclosure, contains the same information and is available to the public.

In its affidavit, the CIA asserts that despite the declassification and disclosure of some government documents, the specific operational details of the capture, detention, and interrogation of the "high value" detainees remain classified. The affidavit states that the declassified documents contain "descriptions of the enhanced interrogation techniques *in the abstract*" that are "of a qualitatively different nature than the conditions of confinement and interrogation techniques *as applied* described in the CSRT transcripts and detainee written statements." The affidavit also asserts that the documents ". . . do not reveal the level of detail described in the [CSRT] transcripts and statements." The CIA also argues that under our opinion in *Fitzgibbon*, the leaked Red Cross report is irrelevant because it does not qualify as an official and documented disclosure by the government. *See* 911 F.2d at 765.

If the government has officially acknowledged information, a FOIA plaintiff may compel disclosure of that information even over an agency's otherwise valid exemption claim. *Wolf*, 473 F.3d at 378. For information to qualify as "officially acknowledged," it must satisfy three criteria: (1) the information requested must be as specific as the information previously released; (2) the information requested must match the information previously disclosed; and (3) the information requested must already have been made public through an official and documented disclosure. *Wolf*, 473 F.3d at 378. As we further explained in *Wolf*, "[p]rior disclosure of similar information does not suffice; instead, the *specific* information sought by the plaintiff must already be in the public domain by official disclosure. This insistence on exactitude recognizes the Government's vital interest in information relating to national security and foreign affairs." 473 F.3d at 378 (citations and quotation omitted).

. . . According the agency's affidavit the substantial weight it is due regarding the details of the classified status of the disputed record, *see Wolf*, 473 F.3d at 374, we agree with the district court's conclusion that the information withheld by the government "is specific and particular to each detainee and would reveal far more about the CIA's interrogation process than the previously released records." *A.C.L.U.*, 664 F. Supp. 2d at 77.

As the ACLU readily admits, the Red Cross report was not released pursuant to a government declassification process, but was instead leaked to a journalist. We note at the outset that the Red Cross report is not a government document, and we are hard pressed to understand the ACLU's contention that the release of a nongovernment document by a nonofficial source can constitute a disclosure affecting the applicability of the FOIA exemptions. . . .

Neither the official government disclosures of the OLC memoranda and CIA reports nor the unofficial publication of the Red Cross report are sufficient to qualify the information withheld from the CSRT documents as "officially acknowledged." Therefore, despite the ACLU's claim that the information is already widely available to the public, we conclude that FOIA exemptions 1 and 3 validly apply. . . .

D.

. . . [I]n addition to arguing that the information withheld from the requested documents does not qualify for FOIA exemptions 1 and 3 as "intelligence sources or methods," the ACLU also argues the government cannot withhold the information under exemption 1 because public release of the information would not damage national security.[3] . . .

. . . Executive Order 12,958, which authorizes the classification of "intelligence sources or methods," requires as a prerequisite to classification that disclosure of the information to be classified "reasonably could be expected to result in damage to the national security" and that the government must be "able to identify or describe the damage." Exec. Order No. 12,958 §1.1(a)(4). Thus, the "intelligence sources or methods" withheld by the government are properly classified under Executive Order 12,958, and therefore exempt from disclosure under exemption 1, only if the CIA can establish that public disclosure of the withheld information will harm national security. *See* 5 U.S.C. §552(a)(4)(B) (placing the burden on the agency to sustain its action under FOIA).

Because "[t]he assessment of harm to intelligence sources, methods and operations is entrusted to the Director of Central Intelligence, not to the courts," *Fitzgibbon*, 911 F.2d at 766, the government's burden is a light one. "[I]n the FOIA context, we have consistently deferred to executive affidavits predicting harm to national security, and have found it unwise to undertake searching judicial review." *Ctr. for Nat'l Sec. Studies v. U.S. Dep't of Justice*, 331 F.3d 918, 927 (D.C. Cir. 2003). The CIA's arguments need only be both "plausible" and "logical" to justify the invocation of a FOIA exemption in the national security context. *See Wolf*, 473 F.3d at 374-75.

In this case the CIA identified five reasons why the disclosure of the withheld information might harm national security. Specifically, the CIA affidavit asserted that

3. . . . [T]he government need prevail on only one exemption; it need not satisfy both.

public release of the information would potentially damage national security by: (1) revealing the CIA's needs, priorities, and capabilities; (2) degrading the CIA's ability to effectively question terrorist detainees; (3) providing terrorists with insight into the CIA's interrogation techniques, strategies, and methods; (4) damaging the CIA's relations with foreign governments; and (5) providing al Qaeda with material for propaganda. . . .

. . . According substantial weight and deference to the CIA's affidavit, *see Wolf*, 473 F.3d at 374, we conclude that it is both plausible and logical that the disclosure of information regarding the capture, detention, and interrogation of detainees would degrade the CIA's ability to carry out its mission. Having concluded that the CIA's arguments are both "plausible" and "logical," and finding no evidence in the record to support the opposite conclusion, no further investigation is required.

. . . Because the release of the information withheld by the CIA "reasonably could be expected to result in damage to the national security," we conclude that the information may be withheld under FOIA exemption 1.

E.

. . . The CIA affidavit described, in general terms but on a document-by-document basis, the information withheld from each responsive document. . . .

In the CIA affidavit, Hilton declared that she had personally reviewed the redacted information and affirmed that it was currently and properly classified. . . .

Based on the strength of the CIA affidavit, we hold that the government properly invoked FOIA exemptions 1 and 3. The CIA explained with sufficient detail why the withheld information qualifies as "intelligence sources or methods" and adequately described the potential harm to national security that could result from the information's public disclosure. Nothing in the CIA's affidavit is contradicted by the record and we find no evidence of bad faith by the government. We conclude that summary judgment was warranted on the basis of the CIA's affidavit alone.

III. *IN CAMERA* REVIEW

Finally, we consider the ACLU's argument that the district court erred by failing to perform *in camera* review of the redacted information. This court reviews a district court's decision whether to conduct *in camera* review of FOIA documents for abuse of discretion. *Larson*, 565 F.3d at 869. Although Congress provided district courts the option to conduct *in camera* review under FOIA, the statute does not compel the exercise of that option. *Larson*, 565 F.3d at 869. "Congress intended to impose no mandates upon the trial court, but instead leave the decision of whether to conduct *in camera* inspection to the broad discretion of the trial judge." *Center for Auto Safety v. E.P.A.*, 731 F.2d 16, 20 (D.C. Cir. 1984). "If the agency's affidavits 'provide specific information sufficient to place the documents within the exemption category, if this information is not contradicted in the record, and if there is no evidence in the record of agency bad faith, then summary judgment is appropriate without *in camera* review of the documents.'" *Larson*, 565 F.3d at 870 (quoting *Hayden v. N.S.A.*, 608 F.2d 1381, 1387 (D.C. Cir. 1979)). "When the agency meets its burden by means of affidavits, *in camera* review is neither necessary nor appropriate." *Hayden*, 608 F.2d at 1387. *In camera* inspection is particularly a last resort in national security situations like this case — a court should not resort to it routinely on the theory that "it can't hurt." *Larson*, 565 F.3d at 870.

The ACLU claims that *in camera* review of the withheld information is appropriate in this case because there is evidence of bad faith by the CIA. *See Spirko v. U.S. Postal Service*, 147 F.3d 992, 996 (D.C. Cir. 1998) (stating that "*in camera* inspection may be particularly appropriate when . . . there is evidence of bad faith on the part of the agency"). . . .

The ACLU's claim that the government acted in bad faith is meritless. None of the information originally redacted but later disclosed after the documents were reprocessed demonstrates that the CIA improperly withheld information. . . . The government's later decision to declassify [certain records] does not prove that they were originally improperly withheld or that the government acted in bad faith. To the contrary, we find that the government demonstrated good faith by voluntarily reprocessing the documents after the President declassified the OLC memoranda and the CIA Inspector General's report. As in previous FOIA cases, we decline to penalize a government agency for voluntarily reevaluating and revising its FOIA withholdings.

. . . The district court did not abuse its discretion by granting the government's motion for summary judgment without conducting *in camera* review.

IV. CONCLUSION

We affirm the district court's grant of summary judgment for the Department of Defense and CIA. We agree that the specific details of the "high value" detainees' capture, detention, and interrogation are exempt from FOIA disclosure under exemptions 1 and 3. The district court acted within its broad discretion when it declined to perform *in camera* review.

So ordered.

Notes and Questions

1. Standard of Review in Exemption 1 Cases. In 1974 Congress amended FOIA to provide that courts should conduct a de novo review, possibly in camera, of agency withholding claims, with the burden falling on the agency to justify its actions. The legislative history shows that Congress expected judges to "accord substantial weight to detailed agency affidavits and take into account that the executive had 'unique insights into what adverse affects [sic] might occur as a result of public disclosure of a particular classified record.'" *Ray v. Turner*, 587 F.2d 1187, 1194 (D.C. Cir. 1978) (citation omitted). But it debated and rejected a proposal that in national security cases courts should be limited to determining whether there was a "reasonable basis" for withholding a record. *Id.* Why do you think Congress wanted courts to play a larger role in these cases?

In spite of this history, courts today almost always apply the "reasonable basis" standard of review rejected by Congress in 1974. The court in *ACLU v. DOD* described the government's burden in justifying its withholding as "a light one." It went on to explain that "'we have consistently deferred to executive affidavits predicting harm to national security, and have found it unwise to undertake searching judicial review'" (citation omitted). 628 F.3d at 624. The court said it was applying the "substantial weight" test, but it concluded that it only needed to find that the agency's determination was "plausible" or "logical." Can you guess why there is a tendency toward greater judicial deference to executive secrecy claims in such cases? *See Ctr. for Nat'l Security Studs. v. U.S. Dep't of Justice*, 331 F.3d 918, 926-927 (D.C. Cir. 2003) (cataloging reasons for deference, and calling national security "a uniquely executive purview").

Could Exemption 1 be more clearly drawn to eliminate any confusion about this point? Can you suggest amending language?

2. *Vaughn Affidavit.* In *ACLU v. DOD,* as in other Exemption 1 cases, the government submitted affidavits from agency personnel to support its arguments to the court. These *Vaughn* affidavits (so-named for the court's decision in *Vaughn v. Rosen,* 484 F.2d 820 (D.C. Cir. 1973)) list withheld documents (in what is often described as a "*Vaughn* index") and explain the basis for withholding each one. Without revealing the sensitive information itself, they are supposed to represent a practical alternative to the particular burden courts face in inspecting numerous or voluminous contested documents. At the same time they are intended to give requesters some idea about what is being withheld, so they can play an adversarial role in the review process. *Ray,* 587 F.2d at 1203-1206. The explanation in the public affidavit must be as complete as possible without compromising the sensitive information. *See, e.g., Halpern v. Fed. Bureau of Investigation,* 181 F.3d 279, 285 (2d Cir. 1999) (rejecting a *Vaughn* affidavit as inadequate: although affiant "wrote much, she said little").

Do you think the government's affidavits in *ACLU v. DOD,* as described by the court, offered either a plausible or logical explanation for withholding, or were they merely conclusory? Can you find in the court's opinion a test for how much the government must reveal?

Courts are sometimes asked to rely on ex parte government affidavits, *Hayden v. Nat'l Security Agency/Cent. Security Serv.,* 608 F.2d 1381 (D.C. Cir. 1979), or even secret testimony from government witnesses, *Pollard v. Fed. Bureau of Investigation,* 705 F.2d 1151 (9th Cir. 1983). If they do so, is any meaningful adversary testing possible? Must the court play "devil's advocate" and rehearse the arguments for the requester? In *Arieff v. U.S. Dep't of the Navy,* 712 F.2d 1462, 1470-1471 (D.C. Cir. 1983), the court said government affidavits should be considered ex parte and in camera only "where absolutely necessary."

3. *In Camera Inspection.* In order to make a de novo determination that a record is properly withheld, a court may examine that record in camera. 5 U.S.C. §552(a)(4)(B). FOIA's in camera review provision is "discretionary by its terms," however. *Nat'l Labor Relations Bd. v. Robbins Tire & Rubber Co.,* 437 U.S. 214, 224 (1978). "When an agency meets its burden through affidavits, *in camera* review is neither necessary nor appropriate, and *in camera* inspection is particularly a last resort in national security situations." *Mobley v. Cent. Intelligence Agency,* 806 F.3d 568, 588 (D.C. Cir. 2015). But should the court in *ACLU v. DOD* have concluded that the district court did not abuse its discretion in refusing to review the disputed records in camera without itself inspecting the records?

4. *The "Glomar" Principle.* Some agency records are so sensitive that disclosure of their very existence could injure national security. Executive Order No. 13,526

repeats this caution in §3.6(a). The *Glomar* principle is named for the *Hughes Glomar Explorer*, a ship used by the CIA secretly in 1974 to raise a stricken Soviet submarine from the deep ocean floor. *See Phillippi v. Cent. Intelligence Agency*, 546 F.2d 1009 (D.C. Cir. 1976) (upholding refusal to confirm or deny existence of relevant records). In *Hudson River Sloop Clearwater v. Department of the Navy*, 891 F.2d 414 (2d Cir. 1989), the principle allowed the Navy to conceal from a FOIA requester the possible presence of nuclear weapons on ships based in New York Harbor. More recent cases upholding invocation of the Glomar principle include *Freedom Watch v. Nat'l Security Agency*, 783 F.3d 1340 (D.C. Cir. 2015) (records concerning leak of information about cyber attacks on Iran's nuclear facilities); and *James Madison Project v. Dep't of Justice*, 302 F. Supp. 3d 12 (D.D.C. 2018) (synopsis of alleged "Dossier" on Donald Trump prepared by Christopher Steele).

The *Glomar* principle is related to the "mosaic" theory, which has seen increasing use since 9/11. It is invoked to withhold bits and pieces of unclassified information that might, according to the theory, be aggregated by an enemy to reveal some important secret. For example, in *Ctr. for Nat'l Security Studies v. U.S. Dep't of Justice*, 331 F.3d 918 (D.C. Cir. 2003), the court declared that "[a] complete list of names informing terrorists of every suspect detained by the government at any point during the September 11 investigation" could "allow terrorists to better evade the ongoing investigation and more easily formulate or revise counter-efforts." *Id.* at 928. Can you see a potential for abuse with this theory?

This photographic record of an historic 1970 meeting in the White House was obtained through a FOIA request by the National Security Archive from the National Archives and Records Administration. Courtesy of the National Security Archive.

5. Belated Classification. Exemption 1 permits withholding of materials that "are in fact properly classified" under the relevant executive order. But may the government classify materials that were previously in the public domain after a FOIA request for those materials has been filed, then invoke Exemption 1 as a basis for nondisclosure? The most recent executive order says yes. Exec. Order No. 13,526, §1.7(d). Courts have also permitted this practice. *See, e.g., Mobley v. Cent. Intelligence Agency*, 806 F.3d 568, 584-585 (D.C. Cir. 2015); *Milner v. Dep't of the Navy*, 562 U.S. 562, 580-581 (2011). Does the procedural part of the classification requirement thus have any practical significance?

6. *Bad Faith.* As the *ACLU* court noted, evidence of agency bad faith in processing a FOIA request may trigger a more thorough judicial review of the requester's complaint. FOIA §552(a)(4)(F) also requires consideration of disciplinary action against agency personnel who act arbitrarily or capriciously in withholding information. Plaintiffs in the principal case argued that the government's delayed disclosure of certain records was evidence of bad faith in processing their request. The court found, however, that the belated declassification instead showed good faith.

Agencies do sometimes seem to act in bad faith. In *McGehee v. Cent. Intelligence Agency*, 697 F.2d 1095 (D.C. Cir. 1983), for example, the agency immediately conducted a search that revealed materials relevant to a FOIA request, then waited two and a half years to respond to the requester, after suit was filed in federal court. The agency also searched for records on only one narrow topic requested ("People's Temple") and ignored others ("Jonestown" and "Jim Jones") that were obviously related and relevant to the request. *Id.* at 1098-1100. On rehearing, the court nevertheless decided that the agency had not acted in bad faith. 711 F.2d 1076 (D.C. Cir. 1983).

7. *Waiver of Exemptions.* The *ACLU* court noted that "[i]f the government has officially acknowledged information, a FOIA plaintiff may compel disclosure of that information even over an agency's otherwise valid exemption claim." 628 F.3d at 620. The court then went on to declare that "[p]rior disclosure of similar information does not suffice; instead, the *specific* information sought by the plaintiff must already be in the public domain by official disclosure." *Id.* at 621. Other courts have ruled, however, that exemption may sometimes be denied if there has been only an unofficial or a partial prior release.

Thus, when the President, Attorney General, and CIA Director publicly described aspects of a classified OLC opinion later withheld from a FOIA requester, and a DOJ "white paper" containing similar legal analysis was officially released, the court found various exemptions unavailable. *N.Y. Times Co. v. U.S. Dep't of Justice*, 756 F.3d 100 (2d Cir. 2014). "Voluntary disclosures of all or part of a document may waive an otherwise valid FOIA exemption," the court concluded. *Id.* at 114. The court explained that "the substantial overlap in the legal analyses in the two documents fully establishes that the Government may no longer validly claim that the legal analysis in the [OLC] Memorandum is a secret." *Id.* at 116. But in a follow-on ruling, the court upheld exemptions for operational details in the OLC opinion about the targeted killing of a U.S. citizen, Anwar al-Aulaki. *N.Y. Times Co. v. U.S. Dep't of Justice*, 806 F.3d 682 (2d Cir. 2015).

One of us has written that "in the long term, [the Second Circuit's rulings] will disincentivize *any* disclosure of secret legal rationales, lest even fairly limited disclosures empower FOIA-based arguments such as those upon which the Court of Appeals seized. . . ." Steve Vladeck, *The Second Circuit and the Vices of Selective Disclosure,*

Just Security, Apr. 22, 2014. Indeed, in response to the Second Circuit's 2014 ruling, the White House Counsel "swiftly issued instructions to the Obama legal team: throttle back the legal policy speeches, and no more white papers." Charlie Savage, *Power Wars: Inside Obama's Post-9/11 Presidency* 471 (2015).

Is there any way to read FOIA to avoid discouraging at least selective voluntary disclosure of classified documents without officially declassifying them? The court in *Johnson v. Central Intelligence Agency*, 309 F. Supp. 3d 33 (S.D.N.Y. 2018), *aff'd*, 771 F. App'x 108 (2d Cir. June 28, 2019) (mem.), ruled that classified information in e-mails sent by the CIA to reporters for three newspapers, but not published by them, had not been "publicly disclosed," and therefore was still subject to withholding from a FOIA requester under Exemptions 1 and 3. According to the CIA, this was a "selective disclosure of information . . . to certain journalists in the hope of avoiding misreporting that might disclose intelligence sources and methods," and not "an official and documented disclosure." *Id.* at 36. And in *N.Y. Times Co. v. Cent. Intelligence Agency*, 314 F. Supp. 3d 519 (S.D.N.Y. 2018), the court held that public statements by President Trump appearing to confirm a covert CIA program to arm and train Syrian rebels did not prevent the CIA from making a *Glomar* response to a FOIA request for records about the program. "[A]bsent an unequivocal statement of declassification from the President or exceptional circumstances that are not present here," the Court said, it would "not infer whether the President's statements have the legal effect of declassifying information." *Id.* at 528.

8. Exemption 3. FOIA Exemption 3, often invoked in conjunction with Exemption 1, protects records that are "specifically exempted from disclosure" by a statute that either "requires that the matters be withheld from the public in such a manner as to leave no discretion on the issue" or "establishes particular criteria for withholding or refers to particular types of matters to be withheld." 5 U.S.C. §552(b)(3). The leading case is *Cent. Intelligence Agency v. Sims*, 471 U.S. 159 (1985), in which the Supreme Court applied Exemption 3 to permit withholding of information under the provision of the National Security Act of 1947 that requires the protection of "intelligence sources and methods from unauthorized disclosure," currently 50 U.S.C. §3024(i)(1). Based on its reading of "the express intention of Congress [and] the practical necessities of modern intelligence gathering," 471 U.S. at 169, the Court found plenary power in the CIA Director to protect *all* intelligence sources from disclosure, not merely those "who supplied the Agency with information unattainable without guaranteeing confidentiality." *Id.* at 174. "If potentially valuable intelligence sources come to think that the Agency will be unable to maintain the confidentiality of its relationship to them," the Court concluded, "many could well refuse to supply information to the Agency in the first place." *Id.* at 175.

Despite the apparent clarity of FOIA in this regard, however, the determination of which statutes qualify as Exemption 3 statutes, and whether particular records are protected by them, has provoked extensive litigation. So also has the question of agency deference in making those determinations. *See, e.g., Church of Scientology Int'l v. Dep't of Justice*, 30 F.3d 224, 235 (1st Cir. 1994) ("[A]gency decisions to withhold materials under Exemption 3 are entitled to some deference.").

9. Exemption 5. FOIA Exemption 5 does not, by its terms, address issues of national security. But requests for information about national defense and foreign policy are often frustrated by its application. The Supreme Court has interpreted this "somewhat Delphic provision" as "incorporat[ing] the privileges which the Government enjoys under the relevant statutory and case law in the pretrial discovery context." *U.S. Dep't of Justice v. Julian,* 486 U.S. 1, 11 (1988). The general purpose of Exemption 5 is to withhold "from a member of the public documents which a private party could not discover in litigation with the agency." *Nat'l Labor Rel. Bd. v. Sears, Roebuck & Co.,* 421 U.S. 132, 148 (1975).

The most important of these discovery privileges for our purposes is the "executive privilege," one aspect of which prevents the release of predecisional communications that might impair the consultative functions of government. For example, in *Russell v. Department of the Air Force,* 682 F.2d 1045 (D.C. Cir. 1982), the court decided that portions of a draft Air Force study of the use of the herbicide Agent Orange in Vietnam need not be disclosed to a veterans' organization or a college student writing an honors thesis.

> Exemption (b)(5) shields from the mandatory disclosure requirements of the FOIA the deliberative process that precedes most decisions of government agencies. Thus, the exemption protects not only communications which are themselves deliberative in nature, but all communications which, if revealed, would expose to public view the deliberative process of an agency. [*Id.* at 1047.]

The court suggested that any record may, in a sense, be deemed "antecedent to future . . . decisions." *Id.* at 1049 n.1. If it is true, as Antonio maintained in Shakespeare's *The Tempest,* that what's past is also prologue, will a requester ever succeed in obtaining any agency record if the agency chooses not to release it?

Concerning the characterization of a communication as "inter-agency or intra-agency," the Supreme Court has ruled that a document prepared for an agency by a truly independent outside consultant may be protected by the exemption, but that advice from an outside entity that has some interest in the agency's decision will not be. *Dep't of the Interior v. Klamath Water Users Protective Ass'n,* 532 U.S. 1 (2001). The decision could affect the availability of information about agency contacts with, say, defense contractors or public interest groups.

The Justice Department's Office of Legal Counsel has come to play an especially important role in contemporary national security law. Nevertheless, while OLC opinions are regarded as providing controlling legal advice to executive agencies, those opinions may be difficult to obtain. For example, in *Electronic Frontier Fdn. v. U.S. Dep't of Justice,* 739 F.3d 1 (D.C. Cir. 2014), the Court of Appeals applied Exemption 5 to a secret OLC opinion that the FBI had requested with regard to the legality of so-called "exigent letters" — correspondence with telephone companies requesting records "in cases in which FBI officials had not certified that the records were part of an authorized national security investigation, as required for a bona fide national security letter." *Id.* at 4. Although agencies are required under FOIA to disclose "working law," the court concluded, the opinion "did not explain and apply established policy. The OLC Opinion instead amounts to advice offered by OLC for consideration by officials of the FBI," *id.* at 8, and is therefore protected from disclosure by Exemption 5.

10. Categorical Exclusions. In 1984, Congress passed the CIA Information Act, 50 U.S.C. §3141 (2018), exempting most of the CIA's "operational" files — those that describe foreign intelligence and counterintelligence activities — from even the search and review requirements of FOIA. In effect, the very existence of relevant records may be shielded from public view, just as with the *Glomar* principle described above. Judicial review is available for complaints that records were improperly placed in excluded operational files, but only based on the requester's "personal knowledge or other admissible evidence." *Id.* §3141(f)(3).

Congress has also amended FOIA to provide that the FBI need not reveal the existence of classified records pertaining to "foreign intelligence or counterintelligence, or international terrorism." 5 U.S.C. §552(c)(3). Other categorical exclusions apply to operational files of the National Geospatial-Intelligence Agency, NSA, and National Reconnaissance Office.

Can you see how these various exclusions provide greater secrecy for agency records than any of the FOIA exemptions or even the *Glomar* principle?

B. OTHER OPEN GOVERNMENT LAWS

1. The Presidential Records Act

The Presidential Records Act of 1978 (PRA), 44 U.S.C. §§2201-2209 (2018), was passed in the wake of the Watergate scandal, when it was feared that President Nixon or his staff might destroy records that could prove embarrassing or even incriminating. The Act requires the President to "assure that the activities, deliberations, decisions, and policies that reflect the performance of his constitutional, statutory, or other official or ceremonial duties are adequately documented and that such records are preserved and maintained as Presidential records." *Id.* §2203(a). At the end of the President's term the documents are to be turned over to the Archivist of the United States, who is to make them "available to the public as rapidly and completely as possible." *Id.* §2203(g)(1). However, the outgoing President may require that documents falling into categories roughly paralleling the FOIA exemptions be withheld for up to 12 years. *Id.* §2204(a). Thereafter, public access is controlled by FOIA, except that Exemption 5 is not applicable. *Id.* §2204(c)(1).

On January 19, 1989, the final day of the Reagan presidency, the National Security Archive and other plaintiffs filed suit to enjoin the destruction of documents contained in White House electronic communications systems on grounds that they were entitled to protection under the PRA and the Federal Records Act, 44 U.S.C. §§2101-2120, 2501-2506, 2901-2911, 3101-3107, 3301-3314 (2018), the latter setting out requirements for the preservation and disposal of "agency" records. The court held that the PRA impliedly precludes judicial review of the President's creation, management, and disposal of records covered by that Act. *Armstrong v. Bush*, 924 F.2d 282 (D.C. Cir. 1991).

Twelve years after President Reagan left office, when the National Archives and Records Administration announced the impending release of some 68,000 pages of previously undisclosed "confidential communications" of the Reagan presidency, President George W. Bush ordered the release delayed to give him time to decide whether to invoke what he called "a constitutionally based privilege." Critics accused Bush of seeking to withhold information that might prove embarrassing to his father, who served as Reagan's Vice President, or to several members of his own administration who also held important positions under President Reagan. When a coalition of historians and organizations filed suit to compel the release of withheld documents, the court ruled against the President. *Am. Historical Ass'n v. Nat'l Archives & Records Admin.*, 516 F. Supp. 2d 90 (D.D.C. 2007). Congress then amended the PRA in 2014 to allow an incumbent President to block the release of records created by her predecessor. Pub. L. No. 113-187, §2(a)(1), 128 Stat. 2003, 2003-2005 (adding new 44 U.S.C. §2208).

The 2014 amendments also address the conduct of official business using non-official electronic messaging accounts, like Twitter, WhatsApp, or Gmail, by the President, Vice President, their staffs, or personnel of the Executive Office of the President or Vice President. *Id.* §2(e), 128 Stat. at 2006-2007 (adding new 44 U.S.C. §2209). Any presidential or vice presidential record sent from such an account must also be sent to an official messaging account, thereby making it subject to the same rules that govern preservation and disclosure of other government records. The amendments do not differentiate between messages sent from nominally "official" accounts (such as @POTUS) and nominally "unofficial" accounts (such as @realdonaldtrump). *See Knight First Amend. Inst. at Columbia Univ. v. Trump*, 928 F.3d 226 (2d Cir. 2019) (holding that the President's tweets from the @realdonaldtrump account are "official records" for purposes of the Presidential Records Act).

In 2017, two public interest organizations sued to require the preservation of official presidential communications sent by messaging apps that automatically delete text messages after they are sent or read. But in *Citizens for Responsibility and Ethics in Washington v. Trump*, 924 F.3d 602 (D.C. Cir. 2019), the court ruled for the President, declaring that "courts have no jurisdiction to review the President's 'day-to-day operations.'" *Id.* at 609 (citation omitted). Accordingly, it concluded, while not "all decisions made pursuant to the PRA are immune from judicial review," the statute is meant to "keep in equipoise important competing political and constitutional concerns," thus "preclud[ing] judicial review of the President's recordkeeping practices and decisions." *Id.* at 608-609 (citing its earlier decision in *Armstrong, supra*). Can you reconcile this conclusion with the statutory language quoted above?

2. The Privacy Act

The Privacy Act of 1974, 5 U.S.C. §552a (2018), was adopted in the wake of revelations that the government compiled secret dossiers on thousands of Americans during the Vietnam War. See *supra* p. 514. Its purpose is

> to prevent the kind of illegal, unwise, overbroad investigation and record surveillance of law-abiding citizens produced in recent years from actions of some over-zealous investigators, and the curiosity of some government administrators, or the wrongful disclosure and use, in some cases, of personal files held by Federal agencies. . . . It is to prevent the secret gathering of information on people or the creation of secret information systems or data banks on Americans . . . . [S. Rep. No. 93-1183, at 1 (1974), *reprinted in* 1974 U.S.C.C.A.N. 6916, 6916-6917.]

The Act accomplishes this purpose in five basic ways:

> It requires agencies to publicly report the existence of all systems of records maintained on individuals. It requires that the information contained in these record systems be accurate,

> complete, relevant, and up-to-date. It provides procedures whereby individuals can inspect and correct inaccuracies in almost all Federal files about themselves. It specifies that information about an individual gathered for one purpose not be used for another without the individual's consent. And, finally, it requires agencies to keep an accurate accounting of the disclosure of records and, with certain exceptions, to make these disclosures available to the subject of the record. In addition, the [Act] provides sanctions to enforce these provisions. [H. Comm. on Government Operations, *A Citizen's Guide on How to Use the Freedom of Information Act and the Privacy Act in Requesting Government Documents*, H.R. Rep. No. 95-793, at 16 (1977).]

By offering access to information about the requester, the Privacy Act may furnish an alternate route to disclosure of national security information. Privacy Act provisions for access to agency records and for judicial relief generally follow the pattern established in FOIA, including its exemptions.

The Act also creates a private cause of action for damages if an agency violation results in "an adverse effect on an individual." 5 U.S.C. §552a(g)(1)(D). In one recent case, for example, Jill Kelley sued the FBI and DOD for allegedly collecting personal information improperly about her, then sharing some of that information with the media. She claimed harm from the unwelcome exposure, which came in the midst of a scandal involving General David Petraeus, then Director of the CIA. *See Kelley v. Fed. Bureau of Investigation*, 67 F. Supp. 3d 240 (D.D.C. 2014).

3. Open Meetings Laws

The Government in the Sunshine Act, 5 U.S.C. §552b (2018), and the Federal Advisory Committee Act (FACA), 5 U.S.C. app. 2 §§1-16 (2018), are designed to open up the government decision-making process by giving members of the public an opportunity to attend and perhaps participate in the meetings of deliberative bodies. Each act contains exemptions analogous to those found in FOIA, permitting meetings to be closed or their transcripts to be withheld. Public access to such meetings may improve the quality of decision making or may stifle creative debate about grave matters of state, depending on one's point of view. What do you suppose are the implications of these two statutes for government decision making that affects national security?

C. NON-STATUTORY RIGHTS OF ACCESS

1. Common Law Right to Know

Long before the enactment of FOIA, courts recognized the existence of a common law right entitling members of the public to information about the government. That right "predates the Constitution itself." *United States v. Mitchell*, 551 F.2d 1252, 1260 (D.C. Cir. 1976).

> In England, the right was narrowly circumscribed, and only a limited number of persons enjoyed it. But the American courts tended to view any limitation as "repugnant to the spirit of our democratic institutions," and therefore granted all taxpayers and citizens

> access to public records. It was the courts' view that "no sound reason (could be) advanced for depriving a citizen of his right; for it is evident that the exercise thereof... will serve as a check upon dishonest public officials, and will in many respects conduce to the betterment of the public service." [*Id.* at 1257 (citations omitted).]

In the words of the Supreme Court, "The interest necessary to support the issuance of a writ compelling access has been found, for example, in the citizen's desire to keep a watchful eye on the workings of public agencies, and in a newspaper publisher's intention to publish information concerning the operation of government." *Nixon v. Warner Commc'ns, Inc.*, 435 U.S. 589, 597-598 (1978).

Unlike FOIA and the other open government statutes, which apply only to federal agencies, the common law right provides access to judicial and legislative information, as well. *See, e.g.*, *Schwartz v. U.S. Dep't of Justice*, 435 F. Supp. 1203 (D.D.C. 1977), *aff'd*, 595 F.2d 888 (D.C. Cir. 1979) (congressional records); *Nixon, supra* (evidence in a criminal trial); and *Hagestad v. Tragesser*, 49 F.3d 1430 (9th Cir. 1995) (records in civil litigation). Yet the common law right applies only to "public" information. According to one court, a "public record" is "a government document created and kept for the purpose of memorializing or recording an official action, decision, statement, or other matter of legal significance, broadly conceived." *Wash. Legal Found. v. U.S. Sentencing Comm'n*, 89 F.3d 897, 905 (D.C. Cir. 1996).

Might some information relating to national security nevertheless be withheld because it is regarded as "non-public"? In *In re Motion for Release of Court Records*, 526 F. Supp. 2d 484 (FISA Ct. 2007), the Foreign Intelligence Surveillance Court refused to disclose court orders and government pleadings regarding a top-secret NSA surveillance program.

> In the FISA context, there is an unquestioned tradition of secrecy, based on the vitally important need to protect national security. See *Haig v. Agee*, 453 U.S. 280, 307 (1981) (there is no governmental interest more compelling than the security of the nation). The requested records are being maintained under a comprehensive statutory scheme designed to protect FISC records from routine public disclosure. Thus, the statute [FISA], and the Security Procedures adopted thereunder, "occupy this field and would supercede the common law right [of access] even if one existed." *United States v. Gonzales*, 150 F.3d 1246, 1263 (10th Cir. 1998). [526 F. Supp. 2d at 490-491.]

In a similar vein, the court in *Ctr. for Nat'l Security Studies v. U.S. Dep't of Justice*, 331 F.3d 918 (D.C. Cir. 2003), decided that in FOIA, "Congress has provided a carefully calibrated statutory scheme, balancing the benefits and harms of disclosure. That scheme preempts any preexisting common law right." *Id.* at 936-937.

2. Constitutional Right to Know

The First Amendment to the U.S. Constitution provides, "Congress shall make no law... abridging the freedom of speech, or of the press...." While neither a public nor a press right of access to government information is apparent in this language, Professor Emerson argued that

> [t]he public, as sovereign, must have all information available in order to instruct its servants, the government. As a general proposition, if democracy is to work, there can be

> no holding back of information; otherwise, ultimate decisionmaking by the people, to whom that function is committed, becomes impossible. Whether or not such a guarantee of the right to know is the sole purpose of the first amendment, it is surely a main element of that provision and should be recognized as such. [Thomas I. Emerson, *Legal Foundations of the Right to Know,* 1976 Wash. U. L.Q. 1, 14.]

Yet the Supreme Court declared in a 1978 jail access case that "[n]either the First Amendment nor the Fourteenth Amendment mandates a right of access to government information or sources of information within the government's control." *Houchins v. KQED, Inc.*, 438 U.S. 1, 15 (1978). Concerning the media in particular, the Court remarked earlier that "the First Amendment does not guarantee the press a constitutional right of special access to information not available to the public generally." *Branzburg v. Hayes,* 408 U.S. 665, 684 (1972).

In 1980, however, the Court recognized a press right to attend criminal trials. *Richmond Newspapers, Inc. v. Virginia,* 448 U.S. 555 (1980). In a similar case two years later, the Court observed that "the First Amendment serves to ensure that the individual citizen can effectively participate in and contribute to our republican system of self-government." *Globe Newspapers v. Superior Court,* 457 U.S. 596, 604 (1982). Then, in a case involving records of a criminal proceeding, the Supreme Court explained that public access to "governmental processes" will be granted (1) when "there is a tradition of accessibility" — that is, when "the place and process have historically been open to the press and general public," (2) when "public access plays a significant positive role in the functioning of the particular process" — for example, in the selection of jurors to enhance fairness and inspire public confidence, and (3) when there is no "overriding interest based on findings that closure is essential to preserve higher values and is narrowly tailored to serve that interest." *Press-Enterprise Co. v. Superior Court* (*Press-Enterprise II*), 478 U.S. 1, 8, 9 (1986) (citation omitted).

Despite the broad language in *Press-Enterprise II,* there is considerable uncertainty about the scope of the First Amendment right of access — what kinds of judicial records are included, and whether it applies to non-judicial records or activities — and the Supreme Court has not addressed the issue again. *Compare WPIX, Inc. v. League of Women Voters,* 595 F. Supp. 1484, 1489 (S.D.N.Y. 1984) ("Under the first amendment, press organizations have a limited right of access to newsworthy events . . . ."), *with Foto USA, Inc. v. Bd. of Regents,* 141 F.3d 1032, 1035 (11th Cir. 1998) ("There is no First Amendment right of access to public information."). Some courts have recognized a broader right of access but applied the *Press-Enterprise* criteria to limit that access concerning non-judicial records and proceedings. *See, e.g., PG Pub. Co. v. Aichele,* 705 F.3d 91 (3d Cir. 2013).

Against this background, lower courts have addressed the scope and applicability of a First Amendment right of access in several cases implicating national security.

Reading *Dhiab v. Trump*

In this case several media sought access to videos in court records of the force-feeding of a Guantánamo prisoner who was on a hunger strike. They asserted rights based in the First Amendment and common law. The government argued that release of the videos, classified as "Secret," would jeopardize national security. As you review the court's decision, consider these questions:

- Is the First Amendment right of access different in civil and criminal cases? Can you say how and why?
- How did the court conclude that access cases implicating national security should be treated differently from others?
- How important to the outcome in this case was the "tradition of accessibility" required by *Press-Enterprise II*?
- Is the media's right of access to court records, if any, different from that of the public? Should it be?
- Media intervenors asserted both a First Amendment and a common law right of access to court records. How are the two rights different?

Dhiab v. Trump

United States Court of Appeals, District of Columbia Circuit, 2017
852 F.3d 1087

Before: ROGERS, Circuit Judge, and WILLIAMS and RANDOLPH, Senior Circuit Judges.

RANDOLPH, Senior Circuit Judge: The government's appeal, and the intervenors' cross-appeal, are from the district court's orders releasing video recordings made at the United States Naval Base, Guantanamo Bay, Cuba. The recordings are of military personnel removing a detainee from his cell, transporting him to a medical unit, and force-feeding him to keep him alive while he was on a hunger strike.

The government classified these recordings as "SECRET" because disclosing them could damage the national security. The district court decided that under the Constitution the public has a right to view the recordings because the detainee's attorney filed some of them under seal, at which point the recordings became part of the court's record. The government's appeal is on the ground that the public has no such constitutional right....

I.

The case began when Abu Wa'el (Jihad) Dhiab filed a petition for a writ of habeas corpus to prevent the government from force-feeding him....

... [Subsequently], Dhiab moved again for a preliminary injunction, this time challenging particular government force-feeding practices.... [T]he district court ordered the government to provide Dhiab's attorney, who had been given a security clearance, copies of the video recordings, the existence of which the government had disclosed. After the government complied with the order, to which it objected, Dhiab's attorney filed some of the recordings under seal.

The government recorded Dhiab's removal from his cell and his force-feeding in order to train military guards about how to handle detainees in such circumstances. In classifying each recording as "SECRET," we shall assume that the government complied with Executive Order No. 13,526, 75 Fed. Reg. 707 (Dec. 29, 2009)....

Press organizations — sixteen of them — sought to intervene in Dhiab's habeas case and asked the district court to unseal the recordings Dhiab's attorney had filed.

Their motion asserted that under the First Amendment, and common law, the public had a right to see these recordings because the recordings had become part of the record of Dhiab's habeas corpus proceeding. . . .

II.

The intervenors' claim that the Constitution requires this national security information, properly classified as "SECRET," to be divulged to the world because a lawyer representing a Guantanamo detainee filed some of the recordings under seal in his client's now-moot habeas corpus action is untenable. It is important to bear in mind that the Constitution gives "the President as head of the Executive Branch and as Commander in Chief" the "authority to classify and control access to information bearing on national security. . . ." [*Dep't of Navy v. Egan*, 484 U.S. 518, 527-28 (1988),] at 527. . . .

Yet the intervenors insist that under the First Amendment, classified information submitted under seal in a judicial proceeding becomes fair game for a judicial disclosure order, such as the one the district court issued in this case. Neither the First Amendment nor any other provision of the Constitution stands for such a principle.

The intervenors rely heavily on *Press-Enterprise Co. v. Superior Court,* 478 U.S. 1, 8-9 (1986). This *Press-Enterprise II* decision will not bear the weight they place on it. The Supreme Court framed the question in *Press-Enterprise II* this way: whether the public had "a First Amendment right of access to the transcript of a preliminary hearing growing out of a criminal prosecution." *Id.* at 3. The Court put the question in terms of the public's right because the "First Amendment generally grants the press no right to information about a trial superior to that of the general public." *Nixon v. Warner Commc'ns, Inc.*, 435 U.S. 589 (1978).

Press-Enterprise II discovered a constitutional right in the public, although it was a qualified one: such proceedings may be sealed but only if "specific, on the record findings are made demonstrating that 'closure is essential to preserve higher values and is narrowly tailored to serve that interest.'" 478 U.S. at 13-14. . . .

Press-Enterprise II is not comparable to this case. Two differences are immediately apparent. When the Court wrote of the importance of public access to evidentiary proceedings it could not possibly have had in mind classified national security information. The case came up from a California state court. . . . The sealed record in *Press-Enterprise II* consisted of testimony and exhibits relating to murder charges, not classified material. *Id.* at 4.

The second difference is just as obvious. Unlike Dhiab's case, which was civil in nature,[8] the underlying action in *Press-Enterprise II* was a criminal prosecution. When it comes to classified national security information the Supreme Court has decided that the distinction makes a difference. *See United States v. Reynolds,* 345 U.S. 1, 12 (1953). In criminal cases, the government initiates the prosecution. Access and disclosure rights in criminal cases "do not endanger the government's paramount interest in national security. The government's interest can be protected by dismissal of the prosecution or less drastic concessions by the government in a criminal case." Bruce E. Fein, *Access to Classified Information: Constitutional and Statutory Dimensions,* 26 Wm.

8. *See, e.g., Fay v. Noia,* 372 U.S. 391, 423 (1963), deciding that the writ of habeas corpus is a "civil remedy for the enforcement of the right to personal liberty" not "a stage of" a criminal proceeding.

& Mary L. Rev. 805, 828 (1985). Matters are quite different in civil cases: "the Government is not the moving party, but is a defendant. . . ." *Reynolds*, 345 U.S. at 12. For this reason, the Court in *Reynolds* held that the rationale behind access to national security information in criminal cases had "no application in a civil forum." *Id.*[10] . . .

There are additional reasons why *Press-Enterprise II* does not apply to this case. To reach its result, the Supreme Court recounted the English tradition of public criminal trials, beginning — the Court wrote — before the Norman conquest. *Press-Enterprise II*, 478 U.S. at 8. Although the Court did not say as much, the idea apparently was that the Framers of the First Amendment must have had this history in the back of their collective minds. . . .

In habeas corpus cases, there is no tradition of public access comparable to that recounted in *Press-Enterprise II* with respect to criminal trials. Habeas corpus proceedings do not involve juries. Since the beginning they have been decided by judges. Early English courts were in session for only a few months each year. Paul D. Halliday, Habeas Corpus: From England to Empire 355 n.79 (2010). Yet from the fifteenth to eighteenth century, English courts regularly adjudicated habeas petitions between sessions. *Id.* at 56-57. At such times the English judges required jailers to make their returns to the writ to the judge's private chambers or to the judge's home. *Id.* at 54. The judge then made his habeas decision in private. *Id.* Between 1500 and 1800, about one-fifth of the writs the judges of England issued required the jailer make the return to chambers. *Id.* Although English judges more frequently requested returns to chambers during the vacations, the practice also occurred during terms of court. *Id.* The Habeas Corpus Act of 1679, which Blackstone described as the bulwark of English liberties, 1 William Blackstone, Commentaries on the Laws of England 133 (1765), expressly authorized the courts to issue writs of habeas corpus during vacations, thus continuing this longstanding practice. 31 Car. 2 c. 2.

Of course in this country, proceedings in open court are the norm, although there are well-established exceptions. *See, e.g., In re Motions of Dow Jones & Co.*, 142 F.3d [496, 502-05 (D.C. Cir. 1998)]. But of importance here is not just the absence of any "unbroken, uncontradicted history" of public attendance at habeas corpus proceedings in eighteenth-century England. *Richmond Newspapers*, 448 U.S. [555, 573 (1980)] (Burger, C.J., plurality opinion). More significant is that from the beginning of the republic to the present day, there is no tradition of publicizing secret national security information involved in civil cases, or for that matter, in criminal cases. The tradition is exactly the opposite.[15] . . .

Add to *United States v. Reynolds*, already mentioned, the case of *Totten v. United States*, 92 U.S. 105 (1875). Both of these civil cases are well-known instances in the long history of protecting national security secrets of the United States. *Reynolds* held that in a suit against the government, the plaintiff had no right to discover military or state secrets; the privilege against revealing such information was, the Court wrote, "well established." 345 U.S. at 6-7. . . .

---

10. We also have recognized the difference between criminal and civil proceedings: "Neither the Supreme Court nor this Court has applied the [First Amendment right of access] outside the context of criminal judicial proceedings or the transcripts of such proceedings." *Ctr. for Nat'l Sec. Studies v. U.S. Dep't of Justice*, 331 F.3d 918, 935 (D.C. Cir. 2003).

15. *See, e.g., McGehee v. Casey*, 718 F.2d 1137, 1147 (D.C. Cir. 1983): "As a general rule, citizens have no first amendment right of access to traditionally nonpublic government information. . . ."

In *Boumediene v. Bush,* the case establishing the right of Guantanamo detainees to bring habeas actions, the Court thought the unique proceedings it was authorizing might risk "widespread dissemination of classified information." 553 U.S. 723, 796 (2008). To guard against this the Court wrote that the government "has a legitimate interest in protecting sources and methods of intelligence gathering; and we expect that the District Court will use its discretion to accommodate this interest to the greatest extent possible." *Boumediene,* 553 U.S. at 796.

To that end, Guantanamo habeas proceedings have been litigated under orders designed to protect classified information. *See, e.g., In re Guantanamo Bay Detainee Litig.,* 577 F. Supp. 2d 143 (D.D.C. 2008). These protective orders require not only that classified information be maintained under seal, but also that counsel (with a security clearance) not disclose classified information at any hearing or proceeding. *Id.* at 150, 153. The government informs us that Guantanamo habeas cases routinely involve closed sessions to protect classified information from the public eye. Dhiab's case is no exception: in his habeas proceedings, the district court held an evidentiary hearing from which the public was excluded. *Id.* at 21.

As against this, the intervenors are unable to cite a single case in which a court — other than the district court here — found that the First Amendment compelled public disclosure of properly classified national security information in a habeas proceeding, or in any other type of civil proceeding.

Press-Enterprise II spoke of a need to take into account "experience and logic" in determining whether the First Amendment required a record of a judicial proceeding to be released to the world. 478 U.S. at 9. The "experience" in habeas corpus cases and in cases involving classified documents have already been discussed.

As to "logic," it is important to remember that logic does not give starting points. First principles do. For this case the starting point was established at the Founding. The preamble to the Constitution gives equal billing to the national defense and "the Blessings of Liberty." U.S. Const. pmbl. As the Supreme Court stated, there is no higher value than the security of the nation, a value the Court deemed a "compelling interest." *Haig v. Agee,* 453 U.S. 280, 307 (1981) (internal quotation omitted).

Press-Enterprise II therefore does not apply to this case and neither the intervenors nor the public at large have a right under the First Amendment to receive properly classified national security information filed in court during the pendency of Dhiab's petition for a writ of habeas corpus.

III.

Even if the intervenors had a qualified First Amendment right of access to the Dhiab recordings, we would still reverse the district court's decision. The court's ruling that the government failed to show a "substantial probability" of harm to a higher value was clear error. *Press-Enterprise II,* 478 U.S. at 14 (internal quotation omitted).

The government identified multiple ways in which unsealing these recordings would likely impair national security. Two of these risks — detainees triggering forcible encounters and developing countermeasures — together and individually, were enough to prevent these recordings from becoming public. The government's declarations explained that the recordings would enable detainees, assisted by outside militants, to develop countermeasures to the guards' cell-extraction and enteral-feeding techniques. . . .

. . . Information gleaned from the recordings could reach current detainees, who communicate with family members and other outside persons and have some access to outside media. Militants could also use the recordings to train fighters the government may capture and detain in the future. When detainees resist what are already hazardous procedures for the guards, this could further endanger government personnel at Guantanamo. Guards have been kicked, grabbed, punched, knocked down, bitten, and sprayed with bodily fluids. The government's interest in ensuring safe and secure military operations clearly overcomes any qualified First Amendment right of access. . . .

The government also explained in detail the risk that extremists would use the recordings to incite violence against American troops abroad and as propaganda to recruit fighters. The recordings are "particularly subject to use" because they depict "a forcible interaction between . . . personnel and the detainees." Declaration of Rear Admiral Sinclair M. Harris, ¶12. Images are more provocative than written or verbal descriptions. Extremists have used Guantanamo Bay imagery in their propaganda and in carrying out attacks on Americans. *Id.* ¶¶8,10. For example, the Islamic State beheaded American journalists wearing orange jumpsuits commonly associated with Guantanamo Bay detainees. *Id.* ¶8. In his forced final statement before his execution, Steven Sotloff, one of the journalists, was forced to mention the continued operation of Guantanamo as a reason why he was about to be murdered. *Id.* . . .

The district court did not reach the intervenors' common-law claim because it ruled in their favor on the basis of the First Amendment. *Dhiab*, 70 F. Supp. 3d at 492 n.2; *see Nixon v. Warner Commc'ns, Inc.*, 435 U.S. at 598-99. The law of this circuit is that the need to "guard against risks to national security interests" overcomes a common-law claim for access. *United States v. Hubbard*, 650 F.2d 293, 315-16 (D.C. Cir. 1980). Because keeping the recordings sealed is narrowly tailored to protect the government's compelling interest in guarding national security, intervenors cannot prevail on their common-law claim. . . .

Reversed.

Rogers, Circuit Judge, concurring in part and concurring in the judgment. . . . I would apply the experience and logic analysis of *Press-Enterprise Co. v. Superior Court*, 478 U.S. 1, 8-9 (1986) ("*Press-Enterprise II*"), and so my conclusion about when the government's interest in protecting information classified as SECRET will outweigh the public's First Amendment interest is more tentative than Judge Randolph's. At the same time, I tend to be less tentative than my colleagues about the nature of the historical background and the level of generality properly used in the analysis. . . .

Although neither the Supreme Court nor this court has applied the qualified First Amendment right of access to judicial civil proceedings, in *Press-Enterprise II*, the Supreme Court explained that the access right extends to any judicial proceeding where there is a "tradition of accessibility" and "public access plays a significant positive role in the functioning of the particular process in question." 478 U.S. at 8. The First Amendment guarantees the "rights to speak and to publish concerning what takes place at a trial." *Richmond Newspapers, Inc. v. Virginia*, 448 U.S. 555, 576-77 (1980). The then-Chief Justice stated that "[w]hether the public has a right to attend trials of civil cases is a question not raised by this case, but we note that historically both civil and criminal trials have been presumptively open." *Id.* at 580 n.17. By its terms, the experience and logic test does not limit the right of access to criminal proceedings. Every circuit to consider the issue has concluded that the qualified First Amendment right of public access applies to civil as well as criminal proceedings. . . .

The Supreme Court has not required there be a history of absolute accessibility to satisfy the "experience" prong; a "*near* uniform practice of state and federal courts" suffices. *Press-Enterprise II,* 478 U.S. at 10 (emphasis added). There can be "gaps." . . . Nonetheless, in relying on English history from the 16th to 18th centuries, my colleagues appear unpersuaded, surprisingly, that the overwhelming practice of open habeas corpus proceedings — at least 80% — establishes a sufficient tradition of accessibility. . . . [T]here was a well-settled expectation that habeas proceedings would be open to the public when the courts were in session. . . .

The qualified First Amendment right of access fits well with the privilege of habeas corpus, which was originally "one of the few safeguards of liberty specified in [the] Constitution." [*Boumediene v. Bush,* 553 U.S. 723 (2008),] at 739. Because criminal trials and habeas proceedings are designed to protect against abuses of Executive power and guard individual liberty, why would the First Amendment right of access apply differently in the two proceedings? . . . The qualified right of public access plays a significant positive role in criminal proceedings by ensuring that "standards of fairness are being observed." *Press-Enterprise Co. v. Superior Court,* 464 U.S. 501, 508 (1984). In habeas proceedings, the absence of a jury, "long recognized as an inestimable safeguard against the corrupt or overzealous prosecutor and against the complaint, biased or eccentric judge[,] makes the importance of public access . . . significant." *Press-Enterprise II,* 478 U.S. at 12-13. Also, "[t]o the extent the First Amendment embraces a right of access to criminal trials, it is to ensure that th[e] constitutionally protected discussion of governmental affairs is an informed one." *Globe Newspaper Co. v. Superior Court,* 457 U.S. 596, 604-05 (1982) (internal quotation marks omitted). Because the writ of habeas corpus is an important part of our Constitution and a "vital instrument for the protection of individual liberty," *Boumediene,* 553 U.S. at 743, the public's qualified right to informed discussion about its government would apply no less in these proceedings.

Nor is there reason to conclude that when the Supreme Court articulated the experience and logic test, "it could not possibly have had in mind classified national security information." Op. at —— (Randolph, J.). The Court's test protects against threats to our nation's security by prohibiting disclosure when it will cause a "substantial probability" of harm to an "overriding interest." *Press-Enterprise II,* 478 U.S. at 7, 14. The . . . Court is well aware that First Amendment rights will often clash with national security concerns, *see, e.g., Dennis et al. v. United States,* 341 U.S. 494 (1951). Yet the Court crafted a test where the threshold First Amendment question is whether "the particular process in question" passes the experience and logic test, *Press-Enterprise II,* 478 U.S. at 8, not whether the records submitted in that proceeding contain classified information. Because the test accounts for the protection of national security information, the presence of such information in a judicial proceeding does not crowd out the decades-old and flexible approach set forth in *Press-Enterprise II.*

[The opinion of WILLIAMS, Senior Circuit Judge, concurring in part and concurring in the judgment, is omitted.]

Notes and Questions

1. Common Law vs. First Amendment Right. Comparing the common law and First Amendment rights of access, one court declared,

> Although the two rights of access are not coterminous, courts have employed much the same type of screen in evaluating their applicability to particular claims. This overlap is understandable because the jurisprudence discussing the First Amendment right of access to criminal proceedings has been derived in large measure from the jurisprudence that has shaped the common-law right of access. [*In re Providence Journal Co.*, 293 F.3d 1, 10 (1st Cir. 2002).]

Another court has concluded, however, that "[t]he common law does not afford as much substantive protection to the interests of the press and the public as does the First Amendment." *Rushford v. New Yorker Magazine, Inc.*, 846 F.2d 249, 253 (4th Cir. 1988). While there is a presumption of access to judicial records at common law that may be overcome only by a showing of "some significant interest that outweighs the presumption," said the court, "[u]nder the First Amendment... the denial of access must be necessitated by a compelling government interest and narrowly tailored to serve that interest." *Id.* (citing *Press-Enterprise Co. v. Superior Court* (*Press-Enterprise I*), 464 U.S. 501 (1984)).

According to the *Dhiab* court, "the need to 'guard against risks to national security interests' overcomes a common-law claim for access," because that need was both "compelling" and "narrowly tailored." 852 F.3d at 1098 (citation omitted). Do you see a difference in its analyses of common law and First Amendment rights? Can you predict when, if ever, the First Amendment will provide access in a case implicating national security when the common law right will not?

2. Press vs. Public Rights of Access. Judge Randolph, echoing earlier Supreme Court statements, wrote that the "First Amendment generally grants the press no right to information about a trial superior to that of the general public." 852 F.3d at 1091 (citations omitted). But can you argue that in a democracy the press should have a superior right, because the media play a uniquely critical "positive role in the functioning of the particular process" of informing the public, and that that role is "essential to preserve higher values" — quoting criteria from *Press-Enterprise II*? Can you think of a case in which the distinction would make a difference?

3. Civil vs. Criminal Cases. Neither Judge Rogers nor Judge Williams joined in Part II of Judge Randolph's opinion — wherein he concluded that there is no qualified First Amendment right of public access to habeas proceedings, including (but presumably not limited to) the Guantánamo detainee litigation, thus leaving that issue at least nominally open within the D.C. Circuit. *See* Steve Vladeck, *The D.C. Circuit Gives Short Shrift to Public Access to Guantánamo Proceedings*, Just Security, Apr. 10, 2017. Judge Rogers rejected the distinction between civil and criminal cases, arguing in part that both "criminal trials and habeas proceedings are designed to protect against abuses of Executive power and guard individual liberty." 852 F.3d at 1102 (Rogers, J., concurring in part and concurring in the judgment). Who do you believe was right? Can you think of other reasons for recognizing equal rights in the two kinds of cases more generally?

4. Deference in National Security Cases — The "Logic" Test. Judge Randolph also distinguished *Press-Enterprise II* in part on the ground that the earlier case did not, like the case before it, concern national security. Logic and "first principles," the court suggested, might preclude recognition of a First Amendment right of access in such cases. But would even the more detailed analysis of "the functioning of the particular process," "higher values," and narrow tailoring dictated by *Press-Enterprise II* yield a different result?

In *North Jersey Media Group v. Ashcroft,* 308 F.3d 198 (3d Cir. 2002), for example, the court denied access to closed deportation hearings before immigration courts involving individuals whom the Attorney General believed might have knowledge of or involvement in the 9/11 terrorist attacks. Applying the "logic" test from *Press-Enterprise II,* it ruled that while public access would "'promote informed discussion' among the citizenry," *id.* at 217, it would also threaten national security. The court accepted government assurances that open hearings would reveal intelligence sources and methods and inform terrorists' efforts to mount new attacks. "We are quite hesitant to conduct a judicial inquiry into the credibility of these security concerns," the court said, "as national security is an area where courts have traditionally extended great deference to Executive expertise.... To the extent that the Attorney General's national security concerns seem credible, we will not lightly second-guess them." *Id.* at 219.

> We are keenly aware of the dangers presented by deference to the executive branch when constitutional liberties are at stake, especially in times of national crisis, when those liberties are likely in greatest jeopardy. On balance, however, we are unable to conclude that openness plays a positive role in special interest deportation hearings at a time when our nation is faced with threats of such profound and unknown dimension. [*Id.* at 220.]

At about the same moment, a different case on identical facts came out the other way. *Detroit Free Press v. Ashcroft,* 303 F.3d 681 (6th Cir. 2002). "By the simple assertion of 'national security,'" the court observed, "the Government seeks a process where it may, without review, designate certain classes of cases as 'special interest cases' and, behind closed doors, adjudicate the merits of these cases to deprive non-citizens of their fundamental liberty interests." *Id.* at 710. Rejecting the government's argument, the court indicated that it was prepared to evaluate security threats on a case-by-case basis to determine whether closure is warranted. Moreover, said the court, "[p]ublic access undoubtedly enhances the quality of deportation proceedings." *Id.* at 703. Striking a different balance between secrecy and security, the court declared,

> In our democracy, based on checks and balances, neither the Bill of Rights nor the judiciary can second-guess government's choices. The only safeguard on this extraordinary governmental power is the public, deputizing the press as the guardians of their liberty. "An informed public is the most potent of all restraints upon misgovernment[.]"...
>
> ... Democracies die behind closed doors. [*Id.* at 683 (citations omitted).]

The differences between the two Court of Appeals decisions remain unresolved, as the Supreme Court denied certiorari in *North Jersey Media Group v. Ashcroft,* 538 U.S.

1056 (2003) (mem.). Do you think courts should be more or less deferential than in other national security cases when assessing a claimed First Amendment right?

In *Dhiab,* the court and the media seeking release of court records assumed that those records were properly classified. But if doubts had been raised about classification, should the court have conducted a de novo review of the disputed records in camera, as in FOIA cases? Or would the court have been justified in relying on the fact of classification in determining their sensitivity?

5. *Tradition of Accessibility — The "Experience" Test.* Judge Randolph found no "tradition of public access" in habeas proceedings like the one in which the media sought court records, nor any such tradition regarding secret national security information. Judge Rogers disagreed, pointing out that 80 percent of habeas cases historically have been open to the public. Why is a tradition of public access important in determining the existence of a First Amendment right in a given case?

6. *Access to Terrorism Trials.* During the criminal prosecution of Zacarias Moussaoui for his involvement in the September 11 terrorist attacks, see *supra* p. 1108, a consortium of media companies asserted common law and First Amendment rights of access to sealed records of pleadings, discovery materials, and oral arguments that included some information classified as top secret. In *United States v. Moussaoui,* 65 F. App'x 881, 887-888 (4th Cir. 2003), the court determined that the "interest of the public in the flow of information is protected by our exercising independent judgment concerning redactions" of materials from the records. *Id.* at 888. As for access to appellate proceedings, the court ordered bifurcated hearings. Arguments not involving the discussion of classified information would be open to the public, while others would be conducted in a sealed courtroom, followed by the prompt release of a redacted transcript. *Id.* at 890.

Media access to military commission proceedings at the Guantánamo Bay Naval Base has been uneven and controversial. A provision of the Military Commissions Act of 2009 gives a military judge authority to close military commission proceedings to the public (and the press) when she finds it necessary to "protect information the disclosure of which could reasonably be expected to cause damage to the national security." 10 U.S.C. §949d(c)(2)(A) (2018). Some proceedings have been closed. Reporters have been allowed to view others via a live video feed to press galleries at Guantánamo and Fort Meade, Maryland, but with a 40-second delay that allows sensitive information to be deleted. Court filings and rulings, as well as transcripts of public proceedings, are published online within 15 days, with classified material redacted. Do you think these arrangements fairly satisfy any First Amendment right of access?

7. *Access to the Battlefield.* For more than two centuries the press enjoyed virtually unrestricted access to America's battlefields, with no apparent breaches of security. Television coverage of the Vietnam War, however, was blamed (or credited) for turning public opinion against U.S. military involvement in Southeast Asia, especially after the Tet offensive in 1968.

That all changed with the U.S. invasion of Grenada in 1983, when reporters were barred from that small Caribbean island until the fighting was long over. The media were also excluded from Panama when U.S. military forces invaded that nation in 1989.

Press access was severely restricted during the 1990-1991 Persian Gulf conflict, as well, out of concern, the Pentagon declared, that with satellite uplink TV broadcasts and instant Internet reporting, "news media [are] able to broadcast reports instantaneously to the world, including the enemy." Dep't of Def., *Conduct of the Persian Gulf War: Final Report to Congress* (PB92-163674), at S-2 (Apr. 1992). "[R]eporters might not realize the sensitivity of certain information and might inadvertently divulge details of military plans, capabilities, operations, or vulnerabilities that would jeopardize the outcome of an operation or the safety of U.S. or other Coalition forces." *Id.* at S-4. A severely limited number of media representatives were allowed into Kuwait, but they had to be accompanied at all times by military escorts, whom reporters viewed as attempting to control rather than facilitate news coverage. Many news stories dispatched from the front were delayed — sometimes for days — at the military press center in Dhahran. Meanwhile, the Pentagon conducted its own carefully orchestrated public relations campaign, with daily press briefings and film footage of precision bombing raids. *See* John R. MacArthur, *Second Front: Censorship and Propaganda in the Gulf War* (1992); Marianne D. Short & Jodene Pope, *History and Scope of the Press' Right of Access to Foreign Battlefields,* 41 Naval L. Rev. 1, 8 (1993).

These restrictions on media access were challenged on First Amendment grounds. The court, ruling after a cease-fire had been signed with Saddam Hussein, declined to grant declaratory relief, calling the issue "highly abstract," and leaving a decision until another conflict when "a full record is available." *Nation Mag. v. U.S. Dep't of Def.*, 762 F. Supp. 1558, 1572 (S.D.N.Y. 1991).

Media coverage of U.S. military operations in Afghanistan after 9/11 was initially even more restricted than in the Persian Gulf War. *See* Carol Morello, *Tight Control Marks Coverage of Afghan War,* Wash. Post, Dec. 7, 2001. The small number of reporters allowed into Afghanistan were

> not permitted to accompany troops . . . , were prohibited from reporting much of what they saw, were diverted toward feature stories such as church services and promotion ceremonies, were not allowed to speak to [most] senior commanders, and were barred from reporting details even after they were leaked — and announced — by the Pentagon. [*Id.*]

The court in *Flynt v. Rumsfeld,* 355 F.3d 697 (D.C. Cir. 2004), found no First Amendment–based media right to be embedded with troops, but concluded that even if such a right existed, the Pentagon controls were reasonable "time, place, and manner restrictions."

The Pentagon dramatically revised its rules for press access to the battlefield during the 2003 invasion of Iraq. It "embedded" some 775 print and broadcast journalists into a number of military units, although only about 50 or 60 had "front row seats" for combat. *See* Dep't of Defense, *Public Affairs Guidance on Embedding Media* (Feb. 10, 2003). In return for access, reporters had to follow broad guidelines about what could be covered and what could not. Unit commanders could "impose temporary restrictions on electronic transmissions for operational security reasons," and reporters had to "seek approval to use electronic devices in a combat/hostile environment." *Id.* ¶2.C.4. Disputes about coverage of particular events were left to be worked out between reporters and unit commanders. *Id.* ¶6. Commanders were to "ensure that media are provided with every opportunity to observe actual combat operations," but reporters could be given "escorts." *Id.* ¶¶3.F., 3.G. There was no general review process for media products, as there was during the 1991 Persian Gulf War, but embargoes could be imposed "to protect operational security." *Id.* ¶¶3.R., 4.E.

Do you think it is important for the public (and Congress) to be able to receive current information about military operations from nongovernment sources? If you believe that there is a First Amendment-based right of battlefield access for the media, do Pentagon restrictions (in the form of conditions for access) impermissibly infringe that right?

8. The Case That Didn't Exist. In what may (or may not) be a common occurrence, a federal district court and court of appeals conducted secret hearings and issued secret rulings in a habeas corpus case that appeared on no public record. *M.K.B. v. Warden,* 540 U.S. 1213 (2004) (mem.), concerned an Algerian waiter in South Florida who was detained by immigration authorities and questioned by the FBI. The case was discovered by a reporter only because of an appeals court clerk's docketing error. Despite arguments by news organizations that the First Amendment and common law right of access required unsealing the records, the Supreme Court refused, without comment, to grant certiorari, following submission of a sealed brief by the Solicitor General. Thus, the government's theory of the case, like the fate of the detainee, is completely unknown, although we might assume that it included the arguments made earlier in *North Jersey Media.* The story is reported in Linda Greenhouse, *News Groups Seek to Open Secret Case,* N.Y. Times, Jan. 5, 2004; Dan Christensen, *Plea for Openness,* Miami Daily Bus. Rev., Nov. 5, 2003. Other cases totally or partially "off the record" are described in *"Sealed v. Sealed": How Courts Confront State Secrets,* Secrecy News, June 29, 2006; Julia Preston, *Judge Issues Secret Ruling in Case of 2 at Mosque,* N.Y. Times, Mar. 11, 2006. *See* Meliah Thomas, *The First Amendment Right of Access to Docket Sheets,* 94 Cal. L. Rev. 1537 (2006).

D. CONGRESS'S RIGHT OF ACCESS

It is hardly surprising that the two political branches of government sometimes compete with each other. That competition is nowhere keener than in the quest for — or the protection of — information about national security. Recall that President Washington resisted efforts by the House of Representatives to learn details about the negotiation of the Jay Treaty of 1795. See *supra* p. pp. 32, 35. As this is written more than two centuries later, the White House's refusal to comply with subpoenas for testimony and documents sought by a majority in the House of Representatives has led, in part, to the impeachment of President Donald J. Trump. In this part of the chapter we explore constitutional, statutory, and practical dimensions of this competition for information, noting carefully the part that courts play as referee.

Reading *McGrain v. Daugherty*

In the course of investigating the administration of the Department of Justice, a Senate select committee issued a subpoena to compel the testimony of a private witness. When the witness refused to comply, the committee ordered his arrest. After his arrest, he brought a petition for habeas corpus, challenging, *inter alia,* the Senate's constitutional authority to investigate. In reviewing the following decision, consider the following questions:

- What is the source of Congress's power to investigate and compel testimony?
- If Congress has the "power to secure needed information," what sort of information is "needed," and who is entitled to say that it is?
- May Congress investigate even before specific legislation has been proposed? May it use its investigative power to conduct oversight of the implementation of existing legislation?
- Why is it important for Congress to be able to compel the production of information "in aid of the legislative function"?
- What safeguards exist against Congress's abuse of its investigative power?

McGrain v. Daugherty

United States Supreme Court, 1927
273 U.S. 135

Mr. Justice VAN DEVANTER delivered the opinion of the court.... The first of the principal questions — the one which the witness particularly presses on our attention — is... whether the Senate — or the House of Representatives — both being on the same plane in this regard — has power, through its own process, to compel a private individual to appear before it or one of its committees and give testimony needed to enable it efficiently to exercise a legislative function belonging to it under the Constitution.

The Constitution provides for a Congress consisting of a Senate and House of Representatives and invests it with "all legislative powers" granted to the United States, and with power "to make all laws which shall be necessary and proper" for carrying into execution these powers and "all other powers" vested by the Constitution in the United States or in any department or officer thereof. Article 1, §§1, 8. Other provisions show that, while bills can become laws only after being considered and passed by both houses of Congress, each house is to be distinct from the other, to have its own officers and rules, and to exercise its legislative function independently. Article 1, §§2, 3, 5, 7. But there is no provision expressly investing either house with power to make investigations and exact testimony, to the end that it may exercise its legislative function advisedly and effectively. So the question arises whether this power is so far incidental to the legislative function as to be implied.

In actual legislative practice, power to secure needed information by such means has long been treated as an attribute of the power to legislate. It was so regarded in the British Parliament and in the Colonial legislatures before the American Revolution; and a like view has prevailed and been carried into effect in both houses of Congress and in most of the state Legislatures.

This power was both asserted and exerted by the House of Representatives in 1792, when it appointed a select committee to inquire into the St. Clair expedition and authorized the committee to send for necessary persons, papers and records. Mr. Madison, who had taken an important part in framing the Constitution only five years before, and four of his associates in that work, were members of the House of Representatives at the time, and all voted for the inquiry. 3 Cong. Ann. 494. Other exertions of the power by the House of Representatives, as also by the Senate, are shown in the citations already made. Among those by the Senate, the inquiry ordered in 1859 respecting the raid by John Brown and his adherents on the armory and arsenal of the United States at Harper's Ferry is of special significance. The resolution directing the inquiry authorized the committee to send for persons and papers, to inquire into the facts pertaining to the raid and the means by which it was organized and supported, and to report what legislation, if any, was necessary to preserve the peace of the country and protect the public property. . . .

We are of opinion that the power of inquiry — with process to enforce it — is an essential and appropriate auxiliary to the legislative function. It was so regarded and employed in American Legislatures before the Constitution was framed and ratified. Both houses of Congress took this view of it early in their history — the House of Representatives with the approving votes of Mr. Madison and other members whose service in the convention which framed the Constitution gives special significance to their action — and both houses have employed the power accordingly up to the present time. The acts of 1798 and 1857, judged by their comprehensive terms, were intended to recognize the existence of this power in both houses and to enable them to employ it "more effectually" than before. So, when their practice in the matter is appraised according to the circumstances in which it was begun and to those in which it has been continued, it falls nothing short of a practical construction, long continued, of the constitutional provisions respecting their powers, and therefore should be taken as fixing the meaning of those provisions, if otherwise doubtful.

We are further of opinion that the provisions are not of doubtful meaning, but, as was held by this Court in the cases we have reviewed, are intended to be effectively exercised, and therefore to carry with them such auxiliary powers as are necessary and appropriate to that end. While the power to exact information in aid of the legislative function was not involved in those cases, the rule of interpretation applied there is applicable here. A legislative body cannot legislate wisely or effectively in the absence of information respecting the conditions which the legislation is intended to affect or change; and where the legislative body does not itself possess the requisite information — which not infrequently is true — recourse must be had to others who do possess it. Experience has taught that mere requests for such information often are unavailing, and also that information which is volunteered is not always accurate or complete; so some means of compulsion are essential to obtain what is needed. All this was true before and when the Constitution was framed and adopted. In that period the power of inquiry — with enforcing process — was regarded and employed as a necessary and appropriate attribute of the power to legislate — indeed, was treated as inhering in it. Thus there is ample warrant for thinking, as we do, that the constitutional provisions which commit the legislative function to the two houses are intended to include this attribute to the end that the function may be effectively exercised.

The contention is earnestly made on behalf of the witness that this power of inquiry, if sustained, may be abusively and oppressively exerted. If this be so, it affords no ground for denying the power. The same contention might be directed against the power to legislate, and of course would be unavailing. We must assume, for present purposes, that neither house will be disposed to exert the power beyond its proper bounds, or without due regard to the rights of witnesses. But if, contrary to this assumption, controlling limitations or restrictions are disregarded, the decisions in

Kilbourn v. Thompson [103 U.S. 168 (1881)] and *Marshall v. Gordon* [243 U.S. 521 (1917)] point to admissible measures of relief. And it is a necessary deduction from the decisions in *Kilbourn v. Thompson* and *In re Chapman* [166 U.S. 661 (1897)] that a witness rightfully may refuse to answer where the bounds of the power are exceeded or the questions are not pertinent to the matter under inquiry.

We come now to the question whether it sufficiently appears that the purpose for which the witness's testimony was sought was to obtain information in aid of the legislative function. The court below answered the question in the negative and put its decision largely on this ground. . . .

It is quite true that the resolution directing the investigation does not in terms avow that it is intended to be in aid of legislation; but it does show that the subject to be investigated was the administration of the Department of Justice — whether its functions were being properly discharged or were being neglected or misdirected, and particularly whether the Attorney General and his assistants were performing or neglecting their duties in respect of the institution and prosecution of proceedings to punish crimes and enforce appropriate remedies against the wrongdoers — specific instances of alleged neglect being recited. Plainly the subject was one on which legislation could be had and would be materially aided by the information which the investigation was calculated to elicit. This becomes manifest when it is reflected that the functions of the Department of Justice, the powers and duties of the Attorney General and the duties of his assistants are all subject to regulation by congressional legislation, and that the department is maintained and its activities are carried on under such appropriations as in the judgment of Congress are needed from year to year.

The only legitimate object the Senate could have in ordering the investigation was to aid it in legislating; and we think the subject-matter was such that the presumption should be indulged that this was the real object. An express avowal of the object would have been better; but in view of the particular subject-matter was not indispensable. . . .

We conclude that the investigation was ordered for a legitimate object; that the witness wrongfully refused to appear and testify before the committee and was lawfully attached; that the Senate is entitled to have him give testimony pertinent to the inquiry, either at its bar or before the committee; and that the district court erred in discharging him from custody under the attachment. . . .

Mr. Justice STONE did not participate in the consideration or decision of the case.

Notes and Questions

1. *Authority for Congressional Investigations?* Where did the *McGrain* Court find authority for Congress to conduct investigations? The Supreme Court has described the power of the Congress to investigate as "inherent in the legislative process." *Watkins v. United States*, 354 U.S. 178, 187 (1957). In addition to the theories discussed in *McGrain*, a lower court has suggested in dictum that "Congress's power to monitor executive actions is implicit in the appropriations power." *United States v. Am. Tel. & Tel. Co.*, 551 F.2d 384, 394 (D.C. Cir. 1976). Once Congress is determined to possess the power to investigate, does it really matter what the source of that power is?

2. The Scope of Congress's Investigative Power. Does *McGrain* suggest any limitations or conditions on Congress's investigative power? Thirty years after *McGrain*, the Court described that power as "broad. It encompasses inquiries concerning the administration of existing laws as well as proposed or possibly needed statutes." *Watkins, supra,* 354 U.S. at 187. More recently, the Court indicated that "the scope of [Congress's] power of inquiry . . . is as penetrating and far-reaching as the potential power to enact and appropriate under the Constitution." *Eastland v. U.S. Servicemen's Fund,* 421 U.S. 491, 504 n.15 (1975).

In fact, the truism that "the power of Congress . . . to investigate" is "co-extensive with [its] power to legislate," *Quinn v. United States,* 349 U.S. 155, 160 (1955), actually understates the investigatory power, because that power includes "inquiries concerning the administration of existing laws [oversight], . . . and surveys of defects in our social, economic, or political system for the purpose of enabling Congress to remedy them" as well as "probes into departments of the Federal Government to expose corruption, inefficiency or waste." *Watkins,* 354 U.S. at 187. *See generally Trump v. Mazars USA, LLP,* 940 F.3d 710, 718-723 (D.C. Cir.), *cert. granted,* 140 S. Ct. 770 (2019). Thus, in one case involving the Navy, a lower court asserted that "[t]here is no doubt that Congress constitutionally can act, without recourse to the full legislative procedure of bicameral passage and presentment, to investigate the conduct of executive officials and others outside the legislative branch; . . . and to influence the executive through the 'illuminating power of investigation.'" *Lear Siegler, Inc. Energy Prods. Div. v. Lehman,* 842 F.2d 1102, 1109 (9th Cir. 1988) (dictum) (quoting *Ameron, Inc. v. U.S. Army Corps of Eng'rs,* 809 F.2d 979, 992 (3d Cir. 1986)). If Congress is entitled not only to oversee the execution of laws it passes, but also to gather information for legislation it might enact in the future, are there any meaningful limits to its subpoena power?

3. House Resolutions of Inquiry. Although *McGrain* involved a subpoena to a private witness, an alternative procedure in the House is a resolution of inquiry, "a simple resolution making a direct request or demand of the President or the head of an executive department to furnish the House of Representatives with specific factual information in the possession of the executive branch." Christopher M. Davis, *House Resolutions of Inquiry* 1 (Cong. Res. Serv. RL31909), June 17, 2009.

Such resolutions have left broad discretion in the executive concerning what information it must produce, however. In 1952, for example, the House passed a resolution of inquiry directing the Secretary of State to transmit "full and complete information" regarding any agreements entered into by President Truman and Prime Minister Winston Churchill regarding the deployment of U.S. armed forces beyond the continental limits of the United States or in armed conflict on foreign soil. But even its sponsors said in debate, "we cannot by this resolution make the Executive answer. . . . All we can do, if we pass this resolution, is to say to the Secretary of State and the Department of State: 'Please try again. That answer you sent down was not very good.'" *Id.* at 8 (quoting 98 Stat. 1205, 1208 (1952)). Nevertheless, such resolutions were sought often during the Vietnam War to request copies of the Pentagon Papers, information about U.S. covert operations in Laos, and information on military operations in Cambodia, among other matters. *Id.* at 15-18. Even when such resolutions have failed, however, "a substantial amount of information has usually [been] released to Congress." *Id.* at 22.

4. Executive Privilege. "Executive privilege" refers to a group of executive branch justifications for resisting disclosure of information to the public or the other branches. One justification is that the information is a state secret, disclosure of which would jeopardize the nation's security. See *supra* pp. 154-164. Another justification is that the information consists of intrabranch deliberative communications, whose exposure would chill the candor and usefulness of such communications. *See United States v. Nixon*, 418 U.S. 683, 705 (1974) ("Human experience teaches that those who expect public dissemination of their remarks may well temper candor with a concern for appearances and for their own interest to the detriment of the decision making process."). A third asserted by the President is simply to preserve the confidentiality of presidential communications. *See generally* Mark J. Rozell, *Executive Privilege: Presidential Power, Secrecy, and Accountability* (3d ed. 2010).

Executive privilege was invoked by the George W. Bush administration in 2007 to resist compliance with subpoenas from Senate and House committees investigating what some believed were politically motivated firings of a number of U.S. Attorneys. *See* Letter from Fred F. Fielding, Counsel to the President, to Senator Patrick J. Leahy and Representative John Conyers (Aug. 20, 2007). Subsequently, when the Senate Judiciary Committee issued subpoenas for documents relating to the secret NSA warrantless electronic surveillance program — the Terrorist Surveillance Program — the White House simply refused to comply, declaring that the documents requested were "potentially subject to claims of executive privilege." *See* Riley T. Keenan, Note, *Executive Privilege as Constitutional Common Law: Establishing Ground Rules in Political-Branch Information Disputes*, 101 Cornell L. Rev. 223 (2015). Other, more recent assertions of privilege are described below.

5. Enforcing Congress's Subpoena Power. Usually, but not always, conflicts between Congress and the executive branch about information are resolved by negotiation. *See* Louis Fisher, *Invoking Executive Privilege: Navigating Ticklish Political Waters*, 8 Wm. & Mary Bill Rts. J. 583 (2000). But when any person — private citizen or government official — fails to comply with a congressional subpoena for testimony or documents, she may be found in contempt of Congress. Congress then has three options: (a) it may exercise its own constitutional power to detain that person for as long as she refuses to cooperate; (b) it may invoke statutory authority to certify a citation for criminal contempt to the U.S. Attorney, whose duty it is to refer the matter to a grand jury; or (c) it may ask a federal court to declare the validity of the subpoena and/or to order compliance. Each of these three approaches presents legal and practical problems. *See generally* Todd Garvey, *Congressional Subpoenas: Enforcing Executive Branch Compliance* (Cong. Res. Serv. R45653), Mar. 27, 2019 (examining the historical development and procedures for each type of contempt proceeding).

a. *Congress's Inherent Power to Compel. McGrain v. Daugherty* arose from Congress's assertion of its inherent constitutional power to punish for contempt: "[T]he power of inquiry — with process to enforce it — is an essential and appropriate auxiliary to the legislative function.... [S]ome means of compulsion are essential to obtain what is needed." 273 U.S. at 174-175. The recalcitrant person may be taken into custody and confined by the Sergeant-at-Arms until she cooperates or until Congress adjourns. The inherent power is thus most useful as a means of coercion, rather than punishment. It has not been employed since 1935, however, presumably because it is relatively unwieldy and inefficient, compared to the two other contempt remedies outlined below. In a future case it might nevertheless be preferred, since it does not depend on the assistance of either of the other two branches.

b. *Criminal Liability for Contempt of Congress.* Congress has enacted legislation to punish a contemnor for non-compliance, rather than to obtain the information sought, although a threat of prosecution surely provides an incentive for cooperation.

Refusal of Witness to Testify or Produce Papers

2 U.S.C. §192 (2018)

Every person who having been summoned as a witness by the authority of either House of Congress to give testimony or to produce papers upon any matter under inquiry before either House, or any joint committee . . . or any committee of either House of Congress, willfully makes default, or who, having appeared, refuses to answer any question pertinent to the question under inquiry, shall be deemed guilty of a misdemeanor, punishable by a fine of not more than $1,000 nor less than $100 and imprisonment in a common jail for not less than one month nor more than twelve months.

Referral to a U.S. attorney for prosecution is prescribed by 2 U.S.C. §194 (2018).

If the person in contempt is an executive branch employee, criminal prosecution may not be a practical option. For example, in 1982, after EPA Administrator Anne Gorsuch was cited for contempt by the House for refusing to comply with a congressional subpoena, the Justice Department not only refused to go before the grand jury but sued the House, seeking a declaratory judgment that she need not comply. The suit was dismissed as premature, because claims of executive privilege could be raised as a defense to a contempt trial, which would be necessary only if the branches could not strike a deal. *United States v. U.S. House of Representatives,* 556 F. Supp. 150 (D.D.C. 1983). Ultimately, the political branches did reach a compromise.

c. *Civil Enforcement in Court.* Congress may ask a court to intervene either by declaring that a subpoena is valid or by ordering an uncooperative individual to comply. If the individual defies such a judicial order, she may then be held in contempt of court, with resulting sanctions designed to coerce compliance. A statutory civil enforcement procedure, applicable only to the Senate, was enacted in 1978, although it does not apply to federal officers and employees acting in their official capacity. 2 U.S.C. §§288b(b) and 288d (2018), and 28 U.S.C. §1365 (2018).

In 2008, the House Judiciary Committee won a declaratory judgment that former White House Counsel Harriet Miers and White House Chief of Staff Joshua Bolton were obliged to comply with subpoenas to testify and deliver documents about the forced resignations of seven U.S. Attorneys. *Comm. on the Judiciary, U.S. House of Representatives v. Miers,* 558 F. Supp. 2d 53 (D.D.C. 2008). In a lengthy opinion, the court found that a claim of "absolute immunity from compelled congressional process for senior presidential aides is without any support in the case law." *Id.* at 56. Executive privilege might be invoked, however, "in response to any specific questions posed by the Committee," *id.* at 105, and the aides might refuse to answer when "national security or foreign affairs form the basis for the Executive's assertion of privilege." *Id.* at

106. Then, noting that the case was one "of potentially great significance for the balance of power between the Legislative and Executive Branches," the D.C. Circuit ordered a stay of the proceedings on the ground that before the case could be resolved on the merits, the 110th Congress would expire, as would the subpoenas. *Comm. on the Judiciary of the U.S. House of Representatives v. Miers,* 542 F.3d 909 (D.C. Cir. 2008) (per curiam). The case was subsequently dismissed after the new Congress convened. No. 08-5357, 2009 WL 3568649 (D.C. Cir. Oct. 14, 2009) (mem.).

More recently, the Justice Department announced that it would not seek a grand jury indictment of the Attorney General for contempt when he refused, citing executive privilege, to comply with a House committee's subpoena for records of a failed operation to interdict gun running on the Mexican border. The court rejected DOJ arguments that judicial intervention would somehow threaten the separation of powers: "[N]either the Constitution nor prudential considerations require judges to stand on the sidelines." *Comm. on Oversight & Gov't Reform v. Holder,* 979 F. Supp. 2d 1, 4 (D.D.C. 2013). It also denied a blanket assertion that the deliberative process privilege covered all of the documents in dispute, but held that it would rule on applicability of the privilege to individual documents. *Comm. on Oversight & Gov't Reform v. Holder,* No. 12-1332, 2014 WL 12662665 (D.D.C. Aug. 20, 2014). Then, after the "sum and substance" of withheld documents were revealed in a DOJ Inspector General's report, the court ordered their delivery to the committee. *Comm. on Oversight & Gov't Reform v. Lynch,* 156 F. Supp. 3d 101, 106 (D.D.C. 2016).

6. Congress's Last Resort? If the Justice Department will not prosecute a contempt of Congress citation against an executive branch official, and a court will not order the Executive to turn over subpoenaed material, what recourse does Congress have? Its ultimate weapon may be impeachment of the President and his removal from office, on grounds that his obstruction of Congress's inquiry is a high crime or misdemeanor. *See, e.g.,* H.R. Rep. No. 93-1305, at 4 (1974) (recommending an article of impeachment against Richard Nixon for his failure to comply with subpoenas issued by the House Committee on the Judiciary during its Watergate investigation). Collecting information about other possible grounds for impeachment, however, may be difficult.

In 2019, several committees of the House of Representatives launched investigations into various activities of President Donald J. Trump. The House Committee on Oversight and Reform subpoenaed eight years of the President's financial records from the accounting firm Mazars USA, asserting that it needed the information to consider reforming ethics and disclosure laws, and to monitor the President's compliance with the Foreign Emoluments Clause. None of the information sought concerned the President's performance of any official duties (and thus none was subject to a claim of executive privilege). The President immediately filed suit to quash the committee's subpoena on grounds that its investigation had no relation to any possible current or future legislation, and, even more broadly, that Congress lacked the authority to investigate a sitting President's possible conflicts of interest or violations of law. *Trump v. Comm. on Oversight & Reform of the U.S. House of Representatives,* 380 F. Supp. 3d 76 (D.D.C. 2019).[1]

---

1. The President's lawyers have also argued that state criminal prosecutors lack such authority. Candidate Trump had notoriously declared during his campaign that "I could stand in the middle of 5th

Citing *McGrain* repeatedly, the court rejected the President's claims, finding that the subpoena had "facially valid legislative purposes," *id.* at 83, and concluding that "[i]f there is some discernable legislative purpose, courts shall not impede Congress's investigative actions." *Id.* at 92. The court went on to declare that

> a congressional investigation into "illegal conduct before and during [the President's] tenure in office" fits comfortably within the broad scope of Congress's investigative powers. At a minimum, such an investigation is justified based on Congress's . . . power "to inquire into and publicize corruption." It is simply not fathomable that a Constitution that grants Congress the power to remove a President for reasons including criminal behavior would deny Congress the power to investigate him for unlawful conduct — past or present — even without formally opening an impeachment inquiry. [*Id.* at 95 (citations omitted).]

See Marty Lederman, *Can Congress Investigate Whether the President Has Conflicts of Interest, Is Compromised by Russia, or Has Violated the Law?*, Balkinization, July 29, 2019 (examining the gravity and historical uniqueness of the President's claim).

On appeal, the D.C. Circuit agreed, but finding ample evidence that the committee's purpose was legislative, not prosecutorial, that the subject of its investigation was one on which legislation might properly be had, and that the particular records sought were "reasonably relevant to remedial legislation." *Trump v. Mazars USA, LLP*, 940 F.3d 710, 740 (D.C. Cir. 2019). The court went on to observe that "Congress has, at various points throughout our history, debated and decided when it wishes to shift from legislating to impeaching. Where legislation may be had . . . the Constitution assigns that decision to Congress." *Id.* at 737. The Supreme Court granted a stay of the lower court rulings, then granted certiorari, *Trump v. Mazars USA, LLP*, 140 S. Ct. 660 (2019) (mem.), and the matter was pending as this book went to press.

Are you now prepared to say what purposes are constitutionally appropriate for a congressional inquiry, and what purposes are not? If you think purpose matters, how carefully should courts inquire into the purpose of a committee investigation? Does *McGrain* help to answer these questions?

In August 2019, the House Judiciary Committee asked a court to enforce its subpoena of former White House Counsel Donald F. McGahn II to testify and produce documents related to Special Counsel Robert Mueller's investigation into the 2016 presidential election. As in the *Miers* case, *supra*, the President asserted absolute testimonial immunity for his immediate advisors, and he ordered McGahn not to appear. Recalling its earlier holding in *Miers*, the court concluded that the President's "claim to unreviewable absolute testimonial immunity on separation-of-powers grounds — essentially, that the Constitution's scheme countenances unassailable Executive branch authority — is baseless, and as such, cannot be sustained." *Comm. on the Judiciary, U.S. House of Representatives v. McGahn*, No. 19-cv-2379, 2019 WL 6312011, at *3

Avenue and shoot somebody, okay, and I wouldn't lose voters, okay." *Trump's Lawyer Argues President Can't Be Prosecuted for Shooting Someone on Fifth Avenue*, 4 New York, Oct. 23, 2019, https://www.nbcnewyork.com/news/local/trump-fifth-avenue-shooting-no-prosecution/1994970/. In a challenge to a state grand jury subpoena to the President's accountants for his financial and tax records, his lawyer argued that "[t]he President cannot be 'subject to the criminal process' while he is in office." Citing candidate Trump's declaration, the court then asked his lawyer during oral argument, "What's your view on the 5th Avenue example? Local authorities couldn't investigate? They couldn't do anything about it . . . while [he's] in office?" Answer: "No." The court asked again, "*Nothing* could be done? That's your position?" Answer: "That is correct." *Id.* The court held that "temporary presidential immunity" did not bar enforcement of the subpoena. *Trump v. Vance*, 941 F.3d 631 (2d Cir.), *cert. granted*, 140 S. Ct. 659 (2019).

(D.D.C. Nov. 25, 2019). "Nor does it make any difference whether the aides in question are privy to national security matters, or work solely on domestic issues." *Id.* at *45. The Constitution does not give the President the power, the court ruled, to "kneecap House investigations of Executive branch operations by demanding that his senior-level aides breach their legal duty to respond to compelled congressional process." *Id.* at *15. The decision was immediately appealed by McGahn and the ruling on appeal was pending at this writing.

One potent weapon in the President's arsenal in such cases is time. In December 2019, when this was written, the presidential election of 2020 was less than one year away. As House committees sought court orders to enforce subpoenas for information related to possible articles of impeachment, the White House employed various delaying tactics to try to avoid compelled disclosures that might hurt the President's reelection prospects — protracted negotiations for release of testimony or records, pleas for extended briefing and discovery, and last-minute appeals from adverse lower court rulings. Efforts to obtain expedited appeals met with mixed success.

Forty-five years earlier, the Watergate Special Prosecutor employed a rare procedure to bring a case to the Supreme Court as soon as an appeal had been filed in the court of appeals "upon a showing that the case is of such imperative public importance as to justify deviation from normal appellate practice and to require immediate determination in this Court." S. Ct. R. 11; *see also* 28 U.S.C. §2101(e). The Court issued an expedited writ of certiorari "before judgment," and ultimately ordered compliance with the prosecutor's subpoena for incriminating Oval Office tapes — 39 days after granting review and 16 days after hearing argument. *United States v. Nixon*, 418 U.S. 683 (1974). If you were counsel to a House committee, would you recommend such a short-cut to the Supreme Court?

ACCESS TO NATIONAL SECURITY INFORMATION: SUMMARY OF BASIC PRINCIPLES

- When it was enacted in 1966, FOIA opened a window into the operation of the executive branch, transformed the way the government conducts its business, and gave the American people a renewed sense of self-determination.

- Among the most significant issues in FOIA litigation in the national security field are the definitions of "agency" and "agency records." Not all records in the possession of agencies necessarily qualify as "agency records" subject to disclosure.

- The ability of an agency to withhold requested records under Exemption 1 turns entirely on whether the records are properly classified (both procedurally and substantively). Courts tend to defer broadly to agencies when this exemption is invoked.

- Other statutes allow members of the public and the media to obtain information in the government's possession, and impose constraints on the government's ability to withhold (or destroy) certain information, including the

Presidential Records Act, the Privacy Act, the Government in the Sunshine Act, and the Federal Advisory Committee Act.

- The common law provides a right of access to government records of all three branches, at least where that right has not been preempted by statute. This right presumptively applies to all public records, although the strength of the presumption remains unclear, as does the definition of precisely what records are public.
- An overlapping press and public right of access to government places, activities, and records is based in the First Amendment. The Supreme Court has held that the right applies to criminal trials and related documents. Lower courts have applied it to a variety of other types of government information.
- Availability of the First Amendment right of access to national security information is uncertain, although in a given case the answer may turn on the history of access to such information, the public or other interests in exposing it, the gravity of the perceived security risk, a court's view of its own competence to decide, and perhaps other factors.
- Congress has an implied right to investigate pursuant to its lawmaking function. It may exercise that right before legislation is introduced, as well as to oversee the execution of laws already enacted.
- Congress may compel testimony or the production of documents by issuance of subpoenas, and refusals are punishable by criminal sanctions, by Congress itself, or by criminal contempt.

41

Censorship

Sometimes information that the government would prefer to keep secret nevertheless gets out — through leaks, espionage, or inadvertence. At least some of that information might, if widely disseminated, jeopardize national security or damage U.S. foreign relations. In this chapter we explore the power of the federal government to censor — to stop the further exposure of information to which members of the public (most particularly the press) have already gained access.

A. FUNDAMENTALS OF CENSORSHIP: THE *PENTAGON PAPERS* CASE

In 1971, a former Defense Department employee named Daniel Ellsberg surreptitiously provided members of the press with unauthorized copies of a Defense Department study titled *United States-Vietnam Relations 1945-1967.* Ellsberg was one of the principal authors of the Vietnam War history, which was commissioned by then-Defense Secretary Robert McNamara. Each of the 7,000 pages of analysis and documents was stamped Secret, Top Secret, or Top Secret-Sensitive. *See* Daniel Ellsberg, *Secrets: A Memoir of Vietnam and the Pentagon Papers* (2002).

The decision to publish the "Pentagon Papers," as they came to be called, and thus to precipitate the most important modern case involving government censorship, was heralded on the front page of the Sunday *New York Times* on June 13, 1971, in a story by Neil Sheehan, *Vietnam Archive: Pentagon Study Traces 3 Decades of Growing U.S. Involvement.* There it was revealed that American involvement in the Vietnam War did not begin with an attack on American ships in the Gulf of Tonkin, as the government had led the public to believe, but with large-scale shipments of military equipment to the French by the Truman and Eisenhower administrations as far back as 1950. In 1954, U.S. personnel began engaging in sabotage and terror warfare against North Vietnam. The study also reported on U.S. complicity in the overthrow and perhaps in the assassination of South Vietnamese President Ngo Dinh Diem in 1963, on planning for a wider war in the months before the Tonkin Gulf incident in August 1964, and on the careful cultivation of public opinion for support of an expanded conflict. It disclosed that the government deliberately misled the public and Congress for years about the nature and extent of U.S. involvement in Southeast Asia.[1] The publication of these documents had a profound effect on the growing antiwar movement, and, many believe, it seriously eroded people's trust in the government.

Excerpts from the study, along with analyses by several *New York Times* reporters, were published in a series of daily installments. Following the second installment, Attorney General John Mitchell sent a telegram to the *Times* (reproduced on the following page) containing a thinly veiled threat of prosecution under the Espionage Act.[2] The telegram was based on the premise that the publication of *any* classified material was a *per se* violation of the criminal law, no matter what the reports actually contained (and independent of the motive of the publisher). The *Times* rejected the Attorney General's demand that it halt publication.

The next day, Tuesday, June 15, 1971, the government sued for a temporary restraining order, supported solely by an affidavit from an assistant attorney general declaring that he had "reviewed" the 47-volume study, that the study was classified "top secret-sensitive," and that its publication would prejudice the defense interests of the United States and result in "irreparable injury" to the national defense. The court granted the restraining order on the ground that it needed a more thorough briefing, and that any temporary harm to the *Times* was far outweighed by the "irreparable harm" that could be done to the interests of the United States.

At a hearing three days later, on Friday, June 18, the Espionage Act was mentioned merely as implicitly supporting the primary argument that the government has "inherent power" to protect the public interest in such matters, citing *In re Debs*, 158 U.S. 564 (1895) (noted *supra* p. 77). The government also asserted that the mere fact that the study was classified raised a presumption that its release would injure national security, and that the court should intervene to stop publication. The court rejected the presumption argument. Then, when the government failed to describe any specific risk from the disclosure of any particular document, the court ruled that publication could continue, but subject to a stay by the Second Circuit. *United States v. N.Y. Times Co.*, 328 F. Supp. 324, 331 (S.D.N.Y. 1971).

When the Wednesday, June 16, issue of the *Times* appeared without a fourth installment of the *Pentagon Papers*, Daniel Ellsberg supplied the *Washington Post* with substantial portions of the study, and two days later the *Post* picked up where the *Times* had left off. The same day, Judge Gerhard A. Gesell in Washington denied a temporary restraining order, and the government immediately appealed to the D.C. Circuit, which reversed Judge Gesell by a vote of 2-1 a few hours later. *United States v. Wash. Post Co.*, 446 F.2d 1322 (D.C. Cir. 1971) (per curiam). But it directed Judge Gesell to hold an evidentiary hearing on the government's request for a preliminary injunction and reach a decision by 5:00 P.M. the following Monday afternoon, June 21.

Meanwhile, in New York, the government obtained an extension of the stay of the district court ruling in favor of the *Times*, pending further review by the Second Circuit on Monday. In other words, both newspapers now had received favorable trial court rulings, but both still were restrained from publication.

---

1. The unabridged *Times* series was republished in book form: Neil Sheehan et al., *The Pentagon Papers* (1971).

2. This copy of the original telegram was furnished by Floyd Abrams, Esq., of Cahill, Gordon & Reindel.

NY K TIMES NY

X

NY K TIMES NY

ARTHUR OCHSSULZBERGER

PRESIDENT AND PUBLISHER

THE NEW YORK TIMES

NEW YORK, NEW YORK

1971 JUN 14 PM 8: 34

I HAVE BEEN ADVISED BYTHE SECRETARYOF DEFENSE THAT THE MATERIAL PUBLISHED IN THE NEW YORK TIMES ON JUNE L3, 14, 1971

CAPTIONED "KEY TEXTS FROM PENTAGON'S VIETNAM STUDY" CONTAINS INFORMATION RELATING TO THE NATIONAL DEFENSE OF THE UNITED STATES AND BEARS A TOP SECRET CLASSIFICATION.

AS, SUCH, PUBLICATION OF THIS INFORMATION IS DIRECTLY PROHIBITED BY THE PROVISIONS OF THE ESPIONAGE LAW, TITLE 18, UNITED STATES CODE, SECTION 793.

MOREOVER, FURTHER PUBLICATION OF INFORMATION OF THIS CHARACTER WILL CAUSEIREXXX IRREPARABLE INJURY TO THE DEFENSE INTERESTS OF THE UNITED STATES.

ACCORDINGLY, I RESPECTFULLY REQUEST THAT YOU PUBLISH NO FURTHER INFORMATION OF THIS CHARACTER AND ADVISE ME THAT YOU HAVE MADE ARRANGEMENTS FOR THE RETURN OF THESE DOCUMENTS TO THE DEPARTMENT OF DEFENSE.

JOHN N. MITCHELL

ATTORNEY GENERAL

Following a secret hearing on Monday, Judge Gesell ruled for the newspaper in an oral opinion in which he concluded that the government had failed to show

> that there will be a definite break in diplomatic relations, that there will be an armed attack on the United States, that there will be an armed attack on an ally, that there will be a war, that there will be a compromise of military or defense plans, a compromise of intelligence operations, or a compromise of scientific and technological materials. [Sanford Ungar, *The Papers & The Papers: An Account of the Legal and Political Battle over the Pentagon Papers* 173 (1989).]

Then on Wednesday, June 23, the D.C. Circuit sitting en banc ruled 7-2 in favor of the *Post*, finding that "the government's proof, judged by the standard suggested in *Near v. Minnesota*... does not justify an injunction." *United States v. Wash. Post Co.*, 446 F.2d 1327, 1328 (D.C. Cir. 1971) (en banc) (per curiam). The most often quoted dictum in *Near*, 283 U.S. 697 (1931), is

> limitation [on publication] has been recognized only in exceptional cases. "When a nation is at war many things that might be said in time of peace are such a hindrance to its effort that their utterance will not be endured so long as men fight and that no court could regard them as protected by any constitutional right." *Schenck v. United States*, 249 U.S. 47, 52. No one would question but that a government might prevent actual obstruction to its recruiting service or the publication of the sailing dates of transports or the number and location of troops. [283 U.S. at 716.]

Also on Wednesday, June 23, the Second Circuit, also sitting en banc, ruled 5-3 in favor of the government. *United States v. N.Y. Times Co.*, 444 F.2d 544 (2d Cir. 1971) (en banc) (per curiam).

The next day, Thursday, June 24, the *New York Times* sought a writ of certiorari from the Supreme Court, and the government sought Supreme Court review of the D.C. Circuit's judgment. On June 25, five Justices voted to grant review in the consolidated cases on an expedited basis. These five also voted to extend restraint pending the Supreme Court's resolution. The case was set for oral argument the very next day, Saturday, June 26, and the Supreme Court issued the following decision four days later, on Wednesday, June 30, 1971 — one of the fastest decisions from the inception of lower-court litigation in the Court's history.

Reading the *Pentagon Papers* Case

In reviewing the decision in this landmark case, consider these questions:

- What did a majority of the Justices actually agree on? Why did the Justices write eight separate concurring and dissenting opinions, in addition to the decision per curiam?
- How did the authors of the concurring opinions differ in their reasons for upholding the decision of the Court?
- How did the Court evaluate and weigh the risks that publication would harm national security? What was the effect of secret pleadings on the outcome of this case?

New York Times Co. v. United States

United States Supreme Court, 1971
403 U.S. 713

Per Curiam. We granted certiorari in these cases in which the United States seeks to enjoin the New York Times and the Washington Post from publishing the contents of a classified study entitled "History of U.S. Decision-Making Process on Vietnam Policy." . . .

"Any system of prior restraints of expression comes to this Court bearing a heavy presumption against its constitutional validity." *Bantam Books, Inc. v. Sullivan,* 372 U.S. 58, 70 (1963); see also *Near v. Minnesota,* 283 U.S. 697 (1931). The Government "thus carries a heavy burden of showing justification for the imposition of such a restraint." *Organization for a Better Austin v. Keefe,* 402 U.S. 415, 419 (1971). The District Court for the Southern District of New York in the *New York Times* case and the District Court for the District of Columbia and the Court of Appeals for the District of Columbia Circuit in the *Washington Post* case held that the Government had not met that burden. We agree.

The judgment of the Court of Appeals for the District of Columbia Circuit is therefore affirmed. The order of the Court of Appeals for the Second Circuit is reversed. . . . The stays entered June 25, 1971, by the Court are vacated. The judgments shall issue forthwith.

So ordered.

Mr. Justice Black, with whom Mr. Justice Douglas joins, concurring. . . . [E]very moment's continuance of the injunctions against these newspapers amounts to a flagrant, indefensible, and continuing violation of the First Amendment. . . .

In the First Amendment the Founding Fathers gave the free press the protection it must have to fulfill its essential role in our democracy. The press was to serve the governed, not the governors. The Government's power to censor the press was abolished so that the press would remain forever free to censure the Government. The press was protected so that it could bare the secrets of government and inform the people. Only a free and unrestrained press can effectively expose deception in government. And paramount among the responsibilities of a free press is the duty to prevent any part of the government from deceiving the people and sending them off to distant lands to die of foreign fevers and foreign shot and shell. In my view, far from deserving condemnation for their courageous reporting, the New York Times, the Washington Post, and other newspapers should be commended for serving the purpose that the Founding Fathers saw so clearly. In revealing the workings of government that led to the Vietnam war, the newspapers nobly did precisely that which the Founders hoped and trusted they would do.

The Government's case here is based on premises entirely different from those that guided the Framers of the First Amendment. . . . And the Government argues in its brief that in spite of the First Amendment, "[t]he authority of the Executive Department to protect the nation against publication of information whose disclosure would endanger the national security stems from two interrelated sources: the constitutional power of the President over the conduct of foreign affairs and his authority as Commander-in-Chief."

. . . To find that the President has "inherent power" to halt the publication of news by resort to the courts would wipe out the First Amendment and destroy the fundamental liberty and security of the very people the Government hopes to make "secure." . . .

The word "security" is a broad, vague generality whose contours should not be invoked to abrogate the fundamental law embodied in the First Amendment. The guarding of military and diplomatic secrets at the expense of informed representative government provides no real security for our Republic. The Framers of the First Amendment, fully aware of both the need to defend a new nation and the abuses of the English and Colonial governments, sought to give this new society strength and security by providing that freedom of speech, press, religion, and assembly should not be abridged. . . .

Mr. Justice DOUGLAS, with whom Mr. Justice BLACK joins, concurring. . . . The power to wage war is "the power to wage war successfully." See *Hirabayashi v. United States*, 320 U.S. 81, 93. But the war power stems from a declaration of war. . . . Nowhere are presidential wars authorized. We need not decide therefore what leveling effect the war power of Congress might have. . . .

. . . It is common knowledge that the First Amendment was adopted against the widespread use of the common law of seditious libel to punish the dissemination of material that is embarrassing to the powers-that-be. . . . The present cases will, I think, go down in history as the most dramatic illustration of that principle. A debate of large proportions goes on in the Nation over our posture in Vietnam. That debate antedated the disclosure of the contents of the present documents. The latter are highly relevant to the debate in progress.

Secrecy in government is fundamentally anti-democratic. . . .

Mr. Justice BRENNAN, concurring. . . . The relative novelty of the questions presented, the necessary haste with which decisions were reached, the magnitude of the interests asserted, and the fact that all the parties have concentrated their arguments upon the question whether permanent restraints were proper may have justified at least some of the restraints heretofore imposed in these cases. Certainly it is difficult to fault the several courts below for seeking to assure that the issues here involved were preserved for ultimate review by this Court. But even if it be assumed that some of the interim restraints were proper in the two cases before us, that assumption has no bearing upon the propriety of similar judicial action in the future. . . . [T]he First Amendment stands as an absolute bar to the imposition of judicial restraints in circumstances of the kind presented by these cases.

. . . [T]he First Amendment tolerates absolutely no prior judicial restraints of the press predicated upon surmise or conjecture that untoward consequences may result.* Our cases, it is true, have indicated that there is a single, extremely narrow class of cases in which the First Amendment's ban on prior judicial restraint may be overridden. Our cases have thus far indicated that such cases may arise only when the Nation "is at war," *Schenck v. United States*, 249 U.S. 47, 52 (1919), during

---

* *Freedman v. Maryland*, 380 U.S. 51 (1965), and similar cases regarding temporary restraints of allegedly obscene materials are not in point. For those cases rest upon the proposition that "obscenity is not protected by the freedoms of speech and press." *Roth v. United States*, 354 U.S. 476, 481 (1957). Here there is no question but that the material sought to be suppressed is within the protection of the First Amendment. . . .

which times "[n]o one would question but that a government might prevent actual obstruction to its recruiting service or the publication of the sailing dates of transports or the number and location of troops." *Near v. Minnesota,* 283 U.S. 697, 716 (1931). Even if the present world situation were assumed to be tantamount to a time of war, or if the power of presently available armaments would justify even in peacetime the suppression of information that would set in motion a nuclear holocaust, in neither of these actions has the Government presented or even alleged that publication of items from or based upon the material at issue would cause the happening of an event of that nature.... [O]nly governmental allegation and proof that publication must inevitably, directly, and immediately cause the occurrence of an event kindred to imperiling the safety of a transport already at sea can support even the issuance of an interim restraining order. In no event may mere conclusions be sufficient: for if the Executive Branch seeks judicial aid in preventing publication, it must inevitably submit the basis upon which that aid is sought to scrutiny by the judiciary. And therefore, every restraint issued in this case, whatever its form, has violated the First Amendment—and not less so because that restraint was justified as necessary to afford the courts an opportunity to examine the claim more thoroughly. Unless and until the Government has clearly made out its case, the First Amendment commands that no injunction may issue.

Mr. Justice STEWART, with whom Mr. Justice WHITE joins, concurring. In the governmental structure created by our Constitution, the Executive is endowed with enormous power in the two related areas of national defense and international relations. This power, largely unchecked by the Legislative and Judicial branches, has been pressed to the very hilt since the advent of the nuclear missile age....

In the absence of the governmental checks and balances present in other areas of our national life, the only effective restraint upon executive policy and power in the areas of national defense and international affairs may lie in an enlightened citizenry.... For this reason, it is perhaps here that a press that is alert, aware, and free most vitally serves the basic purpose of the First Amendment. For without an informed and free press there cannot be an enlightened people.

Yet it is elementary that the successful conduct of international diplomacy and the maintenance of an effective national defense require both confidentiality and secrecy. Other nations can hardly deal with this Nation in an atmosphere of mutual trust unless they can be assured that their confidences will be kept. And within our own executive departments, the development of considered and intelligent international policies would be impossible if those charged with their formulation could not communicate with each other freely, frankly, and in confidence. In the area of basic national defense the frequent need for absolute secrecy is, of course, self-evident.

I think there can be but one answer to this dilemma if dilemma it be. The responsibility must be where the power is. If the Constitution gives the Executive a large degree of unshared power in the conduct of foreign affairs and the maintenance of our national defense, then under the Constitution the Executive must have the largely unshared duty to determine and preserve the degree of internal security necessary to exercise that power successfully. It is an awesome responsibility, requiring judgment and wisdom of a high order. I should suppose that moral, political, and practical considerations would dictate that a very first principle of that wisdom would be an insistence upon avoiding secrecy for its own sake. For when everything is classified, then nothing is classified, and the system becomes one to be disregarded by the cynical or the careless, and to be manipulated by those intent on self-protection or self-promotion....

This is not to say that Congress and the courts have no role to play. Undoubtedly Congress has the power to enact specific and appropriate criminal laws to protect government property and preserve government secrets. Congress has passed such laws, and several of them are of very colorable relevance to the apparent circumstances of these cases. And if a criminal prosecution is instituted, it will be the responsibility of the courts to decide the applicability of the criminal law under which the charge is brought. Moreover, if Congress should pass a specific law authorizing civil proceedings in this field, the courts would likewise have the duty to decide the constitutionality of such a law as well as its applicability to the facts proved.

But in the cases before us we are asked neither to construe specific regulations nor to apply specific laws.... I am convinced that the Executive is correct with respect to some of the documents involved. But I cannot say that disclosure of any of them will surely result in direct, immediate, and irreparable damage to our Nation or its people....

Mr. Justice White, with whom Mr. Justice Stewart joins, concurring.... I do not say that in no circumstances would the First Amendment permit an injunction against publishing information about government plans or operations. Nor, after examining the materials the Government characterizes as the most sensitive and destructive, can I deny that revelation of these documents will do substantial damage to public interests. Indeed, I am confident that their disclosure will have that result. But I nevertheless agree that the United States has not satisfied the very heavy burden that it must meet to warrant an injunction against publication in these cases, at least in the absence of express and appropriately limited congressional authorization for prior restraints in circumstances such as these.

The Government's position is simply stated: The responsibility of the Executive for the conduct of the foreign affairs and for the security of the Nation is so basic that the President is entitled to an injunction against publication of a newspaper story whenever he can convince a court that the information to be revealed threatens "grave and irreparable" injury to the public interest; and the injunction should issue whether or not the material to be published is classified, whether or not publication would be lawful under relevant criminal statutes enacted by Congress, and regardless of the circumstances by which the newspaper came into possession of the information.

At least in the absence of legislation by Congress, based on its own investigations and findings, I am quite unable to agree that the inherent powers of the Executive and the courts reach so far as to authorize remedies having such sweeping potential for inhibiting publications by the press. Much of the difficulty inheres in the "grave and irreparable danger" standard suggested by the United States. If the United States were to have judgment under such a standard in these cases, our decision would be of little guidance to other courts in other cases, for the material at issue here would not be available from the Court's opinion or from public records, nor would it be published by the press. Indeed, even today where we hold that the United States has not met its burden, the material remains sealed in court records and it is properly not discussed in today's opinions....

The Criminal Code contains numerous provisions potentially relevant to these cases. . . . [Justice White devotes five pages to a discussion of the criminal provisions.]

. . . I am not, of course, saying that either of these newspapers has yet committed a crime or that either would commit a crime if it published all the material now in its possession. That matter must await resolution in the context of a criminal proceeding if one is instituted by the United States. In that event, the issue of guilt or innocence would be determined by procedures and standards quite different from those that have purported to govern these injunctive proceedings.

[The concurring opinion of MARSHALL, J., and the dissenting opinion of BURGER, C.J., are omitted.]

Mr. Justice HARLAN, with whom THE CHIEF JUSTICE and Mr. Justice BLACKMUN join, dissenting. . . . Due regard for the extraordinarily important and difficult questions involved in these litigations should have led the Court to shun such a precipitate timetable. . . .

Forced as I am to reach the merits of these cases, I dissent from the opinion and judgments of the Court. . . .

. . . It is plain to me that the scope of the judicial function in passing upon the activities of the Executive Branch of the Government in the field of foreign affairs is very narrowly restricted. This view is, I think, dictated by the concept of separation of powers upon which our constitutional system rests. . . .

The power to evaluate the "pernicious influence" of premature disclosure is not, however, lodged in the Executive alone. I agree that, in performance of its duty to protect the values of the First Amendment against political pressures, the judiciary must review the initial Executive determination to the point of satisfying itself that the subject matter of the dispute does lie within the proper compass of the President's foreign relations power. Constitutional considerations forbid "a complete abandonment of judicial control." Cf. *United States v. Reynolds*, 345 U.S. 1, 8 (1953). Moreover, the judiciary may properly insist that the determination that disclosure of the subject matter would irreparably impair the national security be made by the head of the Executive Department concerned — here the Secretary of State or the Secretary of Defense — after actual personal consideration by that officer. This safeguard is required in the analogous area of executive claims of privilege for secrets of state.

But in my judgment the judiciary may not properly go beyond these two inquiries and redetermine for itself the probable impact of disclosure on the national security. . . .

Even if there is some room for the judiciary to override the executive determination, it is plain that the scope of review must be exceedingly narrow. I can see no indication in the opinions of either the District Court or the Court of Appeals in the *Post* litigation that the conclusions of the Executive were given even the deference owing to an administrative agency, much less that owing to a co-equal branch of the Government operating within the field of its constitutional prerogative. . . .

Pending further hearings in each case conducted under the appropriate ground rules, I would continue the restraints on publication. I cannot believe that the doctrine prohibiting prior restraints reaches to the point of preventing courts from maintaining the status quo long enough to act responsibly in matters of such national importance as those involved here.

Mr. Justice BLACKMUN, dissenting.... [I] would remand these cases to be developed expeditiously, of course, but on a schedule permitting the orderly presentation of evidence from both sides, with the use of discovery, if necessary, as authorized by the rules, and with the preparation of briefs, oral argument, and court opinions of a quality better than has been seen to this point....

I strongly urge, and sincerely hope, that these two newspapers will be fully aware of their ultimate responsibilities to the United States of America. Judge Wilkey, dissenting in the District of Columbia case, after a review of only the affidavits before his court (the basic papers had not then been made available by either party), concluded that there were a number of examples of documents that... if published, "could clearly result in great harm to the nation," and he defined "harm" to mean "the death of soldiers, the destruction of alliances, the greatly increased difficulty of negotiation with our enemies, the inability of our diplomats to negotiate...." I, for one, have now been able to give at least some cursory study not only to the affidavits, but to the material itself. I regret to say that from this examination I fear that Judge Wilkey's statements have possible foundation. I therefore share his concern. I hope that damage has not already been done. If, however, damage has been done, and if, with the Court's action today, these newspapers proceed to publish the critical documents and there results therefrom [the aforementioned harm] to which list I might add the factors of prolongation of the war and of further delay in the freeing of United States prisoners, then the Nation's people will know where the responsibility for these sad consequences rests.

Notes and Questions

1. The Holding. The per curiam decision in the *Pentagon Papers* case is spare: prior restraint of expression bears a heavy presumption of unconstitutionality. The government did not discharge the burden of overcoming it.

How did Justice Black, concurring, view prior restraints differently from all the other Justices? When would Justice Brennan have stopped the presses? How did Justice Stewart describe the role of the press in America? What would Justice White have required before granting any injunction to halt publication?

The decision was reached within six days from the date of filing and four days after arguments were heard. There simply was too little time to circulate opinions in order to form majority and minority positions. Instead, each Justice wrote an opinion, and except for a concurrence here and there, no single opinion mustered the support of enough Justices to become the majority opinion. Six Justices, however, could agree on the common denominator expressed in the per curiam opinion, so that opinion became the opinion for the Court. One important question the limited per curiam opinion poses is: what is the precedential value of this case?

After the remand by the three-judge D.C. Circuit panel, Judge Gesell complained that he was uncomfortable in the role of censor, particularly without standards to guide him. *See* Ungar, *supra*, at 173. Can you say what kinds of evidence would meet the government's burden in a given case, what kinds of public interests will be protected against publication, or how to weigh the competing public interests? Do the concurring opinions provide useful guidance?

2. The Secret Pleadings. The opinions reveal almost nothing about the contents of the *Pentagon Papers* or about the government's efforts to discharge its "heavy burden of showing justification" for a prior restraint. We know that none of the judges or Justices reviewed all of the 7,000-page history. Following the district court's continuation of its temporary restraining order in New York, Defense Department and intelligence officials identified what they thought were the most sensitive parts of the document. Those portions were then described in classified appendices to pleadings in the courts of appeals and in a secret brief in the Supreme Court.[3]

The government, the Court, and apparently the *New York Times* were all unaware that Daniel Ellsberg had withheld from the *Times* four volumes of the study devoted to ongoing diplomatic negotiations. Those four volumes headed the list of items the release of which the government felt would injure national interests. They were later published separately. *The Secret Diplomacy of the Vietnam War: The Negotiating Volumes of the Pentagon Papers* (George C. Herring ed., 1983). How, if at all, should this failure of knowledge have affected the government's burden of proof? Should it affect our reliance on a newspaper's independent determination of what information can be safely released to the public?

No specific examples of threatened injuries were provided to any of the courts. And there was no assertion that publication would "inevitably" result in harm, as Justice Brennan would have required. According to Professor Sims, the government probably established that the nature and magnitude of the threatened injury were constitutionally adequate to justify a prior restraint, and that the injury would likely result from disclosure. But it failed to show that the feared harm would be a "direct" and "immediate" consequence of publication. John Cary Sims, *Triangulating the Boundaries of the Pentagon Papers*, 2 Wm. & Mary Bill Rts. J. 341, 404-415 (1993). The Solicitor General who argued the case for the government later declared, "I have never seen any trace of a threat to the national security from the publication." Erwin N. Griswold, Opinion, *Secrets Not Worth Keeping: The Courts and Classified Information*, Wash. Post, Feb. 15, 1989.

3. Justiciability. Did the *Pentagon Papers* Court implicitly determine what the public needs to know in order to make a reasoned expression of its political will? Or did the Court confine its inquiry to whether the dissemination of certain information was likely to imperil the national security? Are the two questions related? Is any court properly equipped to deal with either question? *See* Louis Henkin, *The Right to Know and the Duty to Withhold: The Case of the Pentagon Papers*, 120 U. Pa. L. Rev. 271, 278-279 (1971) (suggesting no). Is the judiciary entitled under the Constitution to make such a determination?

4. Balancing Freedom and Death. During oral argument, Justice Stewart addressed this question to *New York Times* counsel Alexander Bickel:

> Let us assume that when the members of the Court go back and open up this sealed record we find something there that absolutely convinces us that its disclosure would result in the

---

3. The secret pleadings, along with streaming audio and transcripts of taped White House conversations between President Nixon and his advisors about the Pentagon Papers, arguments in the Supreme Court, and a trove of related materials, may be found in National Security Archive, *The Pentagon Papers: Secrets, Lies and Audiotapes* (n.d.), *at* http://www.gwu.edu/~nsarchiv/NSAEBB/NSAEBB48/briefs.html.

sentencing to death of a hundred young men whose only offense had been that they were 19 years old and had low draft numbers. What should we do?

Professor Bickel reluctantly conceded that such material should not be published. William R. Glendon, lawyer for the *Washington Post,* tried to brush the question aside by responding that the hypothetical was not the case before the Court. William R. Glendon, *Fifteen Days in June That Shook the First Amendment: A First Person Account of the Pentagon Papers Case,* 65 N.Y. St. B.J. 24, 26 (1993). How would you have answered? How do you suppose Justice Black would have responded to Justice Stewart?

5. *Who Really Won?* Did the press *really* win the *Pentagon Papers* case? Some think the press's lawyers yielded too much ground and actually emerged with a balancing test where previously there had been an absolute rule against prior restraint. The *New York Times*'s lawyer, Alexander Bickel, recognized that something had been lost:

> [L]aw can never make us as secure as we are when we do not need it. Those freedoms which are neither challenged nor defined are the most secure. . . . Before June 15, 1971, through the troubles of 1798, through one civil and two world wars, . . . there had never been an effort by the federal government to censor a newspaper. . . . That spell was broken, and in a sense freedom was thus diminished. . . .
>
> . . . We extend the legal reality of freedom at some cost in its limitless appearance. [Alexander M. Bickel, *The "Uninhibited, Robust, and Wide-Open" First Amendment,* 54 Comment. 60, 61 (Nov. 1972).]

If you had represented either the newspapers or the government, how would you have advised them about the potential for an adverse ruling in the Supreme Court, and about the legal consequences of such a ruling?

6. *Press Self-Censorship.* If you had been an editor of the *Times,* would you have read the leaked Pentagon study in consideration of its publication? Or would you have returned it to the government unread?

What criteria would you have used in deciding whether to go forward with publication, despite the classification stamps on the document? Would you have consulted with the government before deciding? Would you have asked for legal advice? Would your advice as the *Times*'s lawyer have been influenced by the threat of criminal prosecution?

Anthony Lewis recounts the following history from a 1966 speech by Clifton Daniel, then the *Times*'s managing editor.

> *The Times* had a story for the paper of April 7, 1961, saying that the United States was training an army of Cuban exiles to attack Fidel Castro and that an invasion was imminent. The publisher then, Orvil Dryfoos, was "gravely troubled by the security implications. He could envision failure for the invasion, and he could see *The New York Times* being blamed for a bloody fiasco." After discussion, the story was given less prominent play and mention of the imminence of the invasion deleted. The Bay of Pigs invasion occurred 10 days later. Despite the downplaying of that story, President Kennedy scolded *The Times.* At one newspaper association meeting he suggested that editors, in addition to asking whether a story was news, start asking: "Is it in the interest of national security?" But privately he told a *Times* editor, "If you had printed more about the operation you would have saved us from

a colossal mistake." On Sept. 13, 1962, in a conversation with Orvil Dryfoos at the White House, Kennedy remarked, "I wish you had run everything on Cuba." [Anthony Lewis, The Constitution and the Press 41 (1974) (unpublished course materials, Harvard Law School).]

In the case of the *Pentagon Papers*, the *New York Times* opted not to print portions of the history that were identified in an off-the-record briefing and in in camera court proceedings as most potentially damaging. Whitney North Seymour Jr., *Press Paranoia — Delusions of Persecution in the Pentagon Papers Case*, 66 N.Y. St. B.J. 10, 11 (1994).

Other examples of media self-censorship — decisions by editors not to publish, or to withhold parts of a story, or to delay publication — abound. The *New York Times* was excoriated by officials in the George W. Bush administration for publishing a story about a long-running, top-secret, warrantless electronic surveillance program. James Risen & Eric Lichtblau, *Bush Lets U.S. Spy on Callers Without Courts*, N.Y. Times, Dec. 16, 2005. See *supra* p. 642. The *Times* revealed, however, that it had delayed publication of the story for more than a year, to give the government an opportunity to demonstrate that public release of the information would harm national security (which had the effect of pushing the program's disclosure to the far side of the 2004 elections). *Id.*

In 2006, several newspapers published stories about secret government monitoring of international banking transfers. Following scathing criticism from officials, editors of the *Los Angeles Times* and *New York Times* described an elaborate process for deciding whether to publish. There is "no magic formula, no neat metric," they wrote, for measuring either the public interest in a story or the danger its publication might pose to the nation. But, they insisted, the responsibility to decide is "not one we can surrender to the government." Dean Baquet & Bill Keller, *When Do We Publish a Secret?*, N.Y. Times, July 1, 2006. More recently, media outlets have delayed publication of stories about CIA efforts to sabotage an Iranian nuclear weapons program, Matt Apuzzo, *Rice Testifies on Urging The Times to Not Run Article*, N.Y. Times, Jan. 16, 2015; about deteriorating security in Afghanistan, Howard Kurtz, *At Pentagon's Request, Post Delayed Story on General's Afghanistan Report*, Wash. Post, Sept. 23, 2009; and about prisoner exchange and hostage negotiations. *See* Sydney Ember, *News Media Cite Reasons for Holding Iran Story*, N.Y. Times, Jan. 18, 2016.

What is the effect of a self-imposed delay in publication on the ability of citizens to hold government officials accountable for their actions? How, if at all, should the perhaps uneven tradition of self-regulation by the media affect the judiciary's willingness to impose its own prior or subsequent review of a decision to publish?

7. The Extreme Case: The Progressive. Eight years after Justice Brennan's opinion in the *Pentagon Papers* case speculated about "the suppression of information that would set in motion a nuclear holocaust," *The Progressive* magazine sought to publish an article by Howard Morland titled "The H-Bomb Secret: How We Got It, Why We're Telling It," purportedly containing a number of details, with illustrations, about the design of a thermonuclear weapon. The Energy Department concluded that the Morland piece violated §§2014(y) and 2274 of the Atomic Energy Act of 1946, 42 U.S.C. §§2011-2296b-7 (2018), which prohibit the disclosure of any information concerning the "design, manufacture, or utilization of atomic weapons."

When the government sought an injunction against publication of the article, the court apparently felt that the gravity of the risk of harm outweighed the First Amendment interests at stake:

> What is involved here is information dealing with the most destructive weapon in the history of mankind, information of sufficient destructive potential to nullify the right to free speech and to endanger the right to life itself. . . .
>
> A mistake in ruling against The Progressive will seriously infringe cherished First Amendment rights. . . . It will curtail defendants' First Amendment rights in a drastic and substantial fashion. It will infringe upon our right to know and to be informed as well.
>
> A mistake in ruling against the United States could pave the way for thermonuclear annihilation for us all. In that event, our right to life is extinguished and the right to publish becomes moot. [*United States v. The Progressive, Inc.*, 467 F. Supp. 990, 995-996 (W.D. Wis. 1979).]

The government later withdrew from an appeal to the Seventh Circuit when similar information appeared in another publication, and the case was dismissed. *United States v. Progressive, Inc.*, 610 F.2d 819 (7th Cir. 1979) (unpublished table decision). The article was then published in *The Progressive*, Nov. 1979, at 14.

According to one observer,

> the trial court in fact succumbed to the danger that the *New York Times* test was designed to prevent. Instead of requiring that the government meet its heavy burden of proof with clear and convincing evidence, the court weighed the interests on both sides. It balanced the gravity of the risk, posited to be death from nuclear annihilation, against the importance to the public of knowing the specific details of hydrogen bomb manufacture. With the issue thus presented, the result was a foregone conclusion. [Mary M. Cheh, *The Progressive Case and the Atomic Energy Act: Waking to the Dangers of Government Information Controls*, 48 Geo. Wash. L. Rev. 163, 200 (1980).]

Is that what the court did? If you had been on the bench when this case was presented, how would you have ruled?

8. Pentagon Papers Redux? In 2019, the *Washington Post* used the Freedom of Information Act to obtain and publish a 2,000-page history of U.S. involvement in Afghanistan after 9/11, created by the Office of the Special Inspector General for Afghanistan Reconstruction. *See* Craig Whitlock, Leslie Shapiro & Armand Emamdjomeh, *The Afghanistan Papers: A Secret History of the War*, Wash. Post, Dec. 9, 2019. The document was said to reveal "a secret, unvarnished history of the conflict and offer new insights into how three presidential administrations have failed for nearly two decades to deliver on their promises to end the war." *Id.* It included descriptions of "explicit efforts by the U.S. government to deliberately mislead the public," in which "officials issued rosy pronouncements they knew to be false and hid unmistakable evidence the war had become unwinnable." *Id.*

Comparisons to the *Pentagon Papers* were inevitable. *See, e.g.*, Gillian Brockell, *"Modern-Day Pentagon Papers": Comparing the Afghanistan Papers to Blockbuster Vietnam War Study*, Wash. Post, Dec. 9, 2019. The *Post* did not have to rely on a leak to obtain the history, however, although its existence became known only from a tip. The newspaper's FOIA request was denied when the government invoked the "deliberative process" privilege under Exemption 5, and it required three years of litigation to dislodge even a portion of the requested records, some of which were heavily redacted.

Do you think the availability of FOIA and other open government laws has changed the way courts should apply the First Amendment to limit publication of leaked government information? Why or why not?

B. *WIKILEAKS*: THE NEW *NEW YORK TIMES*?

In recent years, members of the public have begun to rely ever more heavily on Internet sources for news, rather than on traditional print media. This change offers advantages, but also risks. Information can travel around the world instantaneously, sometimes portraying events as they happen. The benefits to representative democracy are obvious. At the same time, however, the new electronic media provide an unprecedented opportunity to quickly and irretrievably distribute information that could be harmful to national security.

A spectacular example came in 2010, when *WikiLeaks.org* posted on its website hundreds of thousands of classified military and intelligence reports from the wars in Afghanistan and Iraq, and confidential State Department cables. *See* C.J. Chivers et al., *The War Logs; The Afghan Struggle: A Secret Archive*, N.Y. Times, July 26, 2010; *The Iraq Archive: The Strands of a War*, N.Y. Times, Oct. 23, 2010; Scott Shane & Andrew W. Lehren, *Leaked Cables Offer a Raw Look Inside U.S. Diplomacy*, N.Y. Times, Nov. 29, 2010. All of the released materials are believed to have been provided to *WikiLeaks* by a low-level Army intelligence analyst who gained access to them because of a security loophole. See *supra* p. 1250. Their electronic publication raised a host of new questions about the scope of the Espionage Act, First Amendment press freedoms, and the public's right to know.

Notes and Questions

1. *Stopping the WikiLeaks Leaks? WikiLeaks.org* has no official headquarters, and its computer servers are located around the world. Its founder and director, Julian Assange, is an Australian citizen. U.S. government information held by *WikiLeaks* and not yet posted to its website purportedly is held by an unknown number of individuals in several countries. These facts present both practical and legal obstacles to preventing further releases that might be harmful to U.S. national security. Can you point to other legally significant facts that distinguish the controversy surrounding the *WikiLeaks* releases from the controversy over publication of the *Pentagon Papers* in 1971? Ignoring for the moment questions about extraterritorial jurisdiction and enforcement, and without knowing more about the contents of documents yet to be released, can you say whether a U.S. court would be likely to enjoin such releases based on the precedent set in the *Pentagon Papers* case?

2. *Applying the First Amendment to WikiLeaks. WikiLeaks* declares that it "specializes in the analysis and publication of large datasets of censored or otherwise restricted official materials involving war, spying and corruption. It has so far published more than 10 million documents and associated analyses." Wikileaks, *What Is WikiLeaks*

(Nov. 3, 2015), https://wikileaks.org/What-is-Wikileaks.html. Does it qualify as "press" for purposes of the First Amendment? If not, would its First Amendment protections, if any, be fewer than those held by, say, the *New York Times*?

Does the First Amendment afford any protection for the press abroad, or for that matter for anyone outside the United States seeking freedom of expression? If so, does it apply the same way abroad that it does domestically? Does it matter for this purpose that neither *WikiLeaks* nor Assange is a U.S. citizen or organization? See generally Chapter 7. Should the answer be affected by the fact that data released by *WikiLeaks* anywhere in the world are instantly available in the United States, as well as worldwide?

3. Compounding a Felony? The *New York Times* and other newspapers published many of the documents posted by *WikiLeaks* on the Internet. A number of the documents were classified. Why do you suppose the *Times* wanted to reproduce materials that had already been publicly released? *See A Note to Readers: The Decision to Publish Diplomatic Documents,* N.Y. Times, Nov. 29, 2010 (asserting that "the documents serve an important public interest, illuminating the goals, successes, compromises and frustrations of American diplomacy in a way that other accounts cannot match," and explaining that the *Times* had "taken care to exclude . . . information that would endanger confidential informants or compromise national security"). Why did the government make no effort to stop republication? Whatever you concluded about the right of the *Times* to make its own decision about whether to publish the *Pentagon Papers,* do you think this case is different? If so, why?

C. PUBLICATION AS A CRIME?

Recall that in his June 14, 1971, telegram to the *New York Times,* Attorney General Mitchell asserted that publication of the Pentagon study was "directly prohibited by the provisions of the Espionage Law." In the government's motion the next day for an injunction against the *Times,* it sought to halt what it said was a violation of 18 U.S.C. §793(e) (2018), *supra* p. 1235, which applies to persons having "unauthorized possession" of documents or information relating to the national defense. The court responded this way:

> It will be noted that the word "publication" does not appear in [§793(e)]. The Government contends that the word "communicates" covers the publication by a newspaper of the material interdicted by the subsection. A careful reading of the section would indicate that this is truly an espionage section where what is prohibited is the secret or clandestine communication to a person not entitled to receive it where the possessor has reason to believe that it may be used to the injury of the United States or the advantage of any foreign nation. This conclusion is fortified by the circumstance that in other sections of [the Act] there is specific reference to publication. The distinction is sharply made in Section 794 entitled "Gathering or delivering defense information to aid foreign government." Subsection (a) deals with peace-time communication of documents, writings, code books, etc. relating to national defense. It does not use the word "publication." Subsection (b) on the other hand which deals with "in time of war" does punish anyone who "publishes" specific information "with respect to the movement, numbers, description, condition, or disposition of any of the Armed Forces, ships, [etc.]. . . ."

> Similarly, in Section 797 one who publishes photographs, sketches, etc. of vital military and naval installations or equipment is subject to punishment. . . . [F]inally, in Section 798 which deals with "Disclosure of Classified Information" there is a specific prohibition against one who "publishes" any classified information. This classified information is limited to the nature, preparation, or use of any code, cipher, or cryptographic system . . . for . . . communications intelligence purposes. . . .
>
> . . . The Government does not contend, nor do the facts indicate, that the publication of the documents in question would disclose the types of classified information specifically prohibited by the Congress. [*United States v. N.Y. Times Co.*, 328 F. Supp. 324, 328-329 (S.D.N.Y. 1971).]

Before *United States v. Rosen*, 445 F. Supp. 2d 602 (E.D. Va. 2006) (*supra* p. 1237), no reported case involved an Espionage Act prosecution of a third party — including a journalist or a media outlet who received leaked national security information. That case came close, however. It involved the prosecution of two lobbyists who received classified information from a DOD employee and passed it on to others outside the government. Although the case was ultimately dismissed, the court upheld the indictment of the lobbyists for conspiring with a DOD employee to violate §793(d), which concerns the communication of defense-related documents or information by persons "lawfully having possession" of it, as well as for conspiring to violate §793(e). While the *Rosen* lobbyists were not journalists, and the organization that employed them was not the press, they were, like many members of the media, third-party recipients of national security secrets.

The *Rosen* court expressed the belief that the result in the *Pentagon Papers* case more than three decades earlier might have been different if the government had sought to prosecute the newspapers under §793(e):

> Of the six Justices concurring in the result three — Justices Stewart, White and Marshall — explicitly acknowledged the possibility of a prosecution of the newspapers under §793(e). And, with the exception of Justice Black, . . . the opinions of the other concurring justices arguably support, or at least do not contradict, the view that the application of §793(e) to the instant facts would be constitutional. [445 F. Supp. 2d at 638.]

Then, saying that it felt bound by the concurring opinions in the 1971 case, the *Rosen* court concluded that "Congress's attempt to provide for the nation's security by extending punishment for the disclosure of national security secrets beyond the first category of persons within its trust [government employees and contractors] to the general populace is a reasonable, and therefore constitutional exercise of its power." *Id.* at 639. The "general populace" presumably could include the media.

More recently, President Donald Trump has repeatedly described the media (or at least some media) as "the enemy of the people." *See, e.g.*, Brett Samuels, *Trump Ramps Up Rhetoric on Media, Calls Press "The Enemy of the People,"* The Hill, Apr. 5, 2019. He declared at a February 16, 2017 press conference, "I've actually called the Justice Department to look into the leaks. Those are criminal leaks."

But while numerous leakers were criminally prosecuted in recent years, no publisher of leaked information was ever charged with violating the Espionage Act until 2019, when *Wikileaks* founder Julian Assange was indicted for doing so. Superseding Indictment, *United States v. Assange*, Crim. No. 1:18-cr-111 (CMH) (E.D. Va. May 23, 2019). The move was immediately decried by some who worried that it would establish a precedent for future criminal prosecutions of national security journalism.

According to one critic, "The indictment should be understood as a frontal attack on press freedom." *See* Charlie Savage, *Assange Indicted over Leak as U.S. Expands Charges*, N.Y. Times, May 24, 2019; Gabriel Schoenfeld, *Indictment of Assange for Espionage Directly Threatens Press Freedoms*, Just Security, May 23, 2019. But a Justice Department official declared that Assange was "no journalist," and that in any case "[n]o responsible actor, journalist or otherwise, would purposefully publish the names of individuals he or she knew to be confidential human sources in a war zone, exposing them to the gravest of dangers." Savage, *supra*.

Many of the issues raised here are examined in Stephen P. Mulligan & Jennifer K. Elsea, *Criminal Prohibitions on Leaks and Other Disclosures of Classified Defense Information* (Cong. Res. Serv. R41404), Mar. 7, 2017.

Notes and Questions

1. Criminal State of Mind. Sections 793(d) and 793(e), part of the Espionage Act, both require the government to prove that a defendant had "reason to believe" that information improperly communicated "could be used to the injury of the United States or to the advantage of any foreign nation." In the *Rosen* case, *supra*, the court noted that to convict the *recipient* of a leak (as opposed to the leaker himself), the information "must necessarily be information which if disclosed, is potentially harmful to the United States, and the defendant must *know* that disclosure of the information is potentially harmful to the United States." 445 F. Supp. 2d at 641 (emphasis added). Can you imagine that the *New York Times*, its editors, or its reporters *intended* to injure the United States? Do you think they had reason to believe that published excerpts of the *Pentagon Papers would* be used to injure the United States? That those excerpts *could* be so used?

In 2005, when the *New York Times* broke the story about the NSA's secret warrantless electronic surveillance program, there were calls for criminal prosecution of the *Times* and its staff. *See, e.g.*, Peter Baker, *Surveillance Disclosure Denounced*, Wash. Post, June 27, 2006. Would either §793(d) or §793(e) have supported a conviction? *See* Stephen I. Vladeck, *Inchoate Liability and the Espionage Act: The Statutory Framework and the Freedom of the Press*, 1 Harv. L. & Pol'y Rev. 219 (2007) (examining the indeterminacy of the law concerning a defendant's state of mind).

Do you think Julian Assange had "reason to believe" that *Wikileaks*' publication of hundreds of thousands of classified documents would injure the United States?

2. Statutes That Expressly Criminalize Publication. Several provisions of the federal criminal code expressly criminalize the publication of specific kinds of classified information. Why do you suppose Congress has not forbidden the publication of classified information generally?

In 18 U.S.C. §798(a)(3) (2018), the Espionage Act expressly prohibits the knowing and willful publication of "any classified information . . . concerning the communication intelligence activities of the United States." Might the *New York Times* and its reporters have been criminally liable under that section for their dramatic 2005 story about the NSA's warrantless electronic surveillance program? Might the *Washington Post* and other papers have been prosecuted under the same section for publishing classified NSA documents leaked by Edward Snowden in 2013? Why do suppose that neither newspaper was criminally charged?

3. Enemy of the Press? Strictly speaking, Julian Assange is neither a journalist nor "the press," at least in conventional terms. Yet his actions were as damaging to U.S. security as if the data posted on the Internet by *Wikileaks* had been published in the *New York Times.* Whether or not you regard Assange as a journalist, does his alleged criminal involvement in obtaining the leaked information overcome any protection otherwise afforded him by the First Amendment in publishing it? Do you agree that Assange's indictment poses a threat to the First Amendment's guarantee of freedom of the press? Can you think of other ways to try to abate the threat he poses to national security?

4. Enemy of the People? The President may use whatever language he chooses to publicly criticize his critics, including the media, so long as his speech does not itself constitute criminal behavior. But many worry that President Trump's attacks on those providing unflattering press coverage, including threats of criminal prosecution, may constitute an informal form of censorship, with a chilling effect on reporters, editors, and publishers, leaving the electorate less well informed. And fomenting mistrust of the media, they argue, may erode public confidence in democratic self-government. Do their worries describe a legal problem, a political one, or both? Is there a solution?

D. SHOOTING THE MESSENGER'S MESSENGER?

Threatening criminal prosecution of a newspaper and its reporters is only one way to discourage publication of information that the government wants to keep secret. Another is to cut off the flow of that information by unmasking and prosecuting the reporters' sources. For example, when a *Washington Post* reporter wrote that the CIA operated a network of secret prisons for terrorism suspects in Eastern Europe and elsewhere, Dana Priest, *CIA Holds Terror Suspects in Secret Prisons,* Wash. Post, Nov. 2, 2005 (a story for which she was awarded a Pulitzer Prize), the CIA asked the Justice Department to open a criminal investigation to determine the sources of Ms. Priest's information. David Johnston & Carl Hulse, *C.I.A. Asks Criminal Inquiry over Secret-Prison Article,* N.Y. Times, Nov. 9, 2005. And when *New York Times* reporter Judith Miller refused to disclose to a grand jury her source of information about the Bush administration's leak of a CIA covert operative's name (see *supra* p. 1252), she was jailed for contempt for 85 days. *See In re Grand Jury Subpoena, Judith Miller,* 438 F.3d 1141 (D.C. Cir. 2006); *see also* Don Van Natta Jr., Adam Liptak & Clifford J. Levy, *The Miller Case: A Notebook, a Cause, a Jail Cell and a Deal,* N.Y. Times, Oct. 16, 2005.

Forty-eight states and the District of Columbia have recognized a "reporter's privilege" to keep her sources secret, either based on common law or codified by statute. But a corresponding federal privilege has never been clearly recognized, and Congress has not passed legislation to protect reporters' sources from compelled disclosure.

Reading *United States v. Sterling*

Jeffrey Sterling was a CIA case officer with a top secret security clearance, assigned to a highly classified program intended to impede Iran's efforts to acquire or develop nuclear weapons. After unsuccessfully suing the CIA for employment discrimination, Sterling "threatened to go to the press," although it is unclear whether he was referring to the program or his lawsuits. He then called *New York Times* reporter James Risen and e-mailed him on multiple occasions. Risen subsequently published a book, *State of War: The Secret History of the CIA and the Bush Administration* (2006), which included classified information about the Iran program on which Sterling worked.

Sterling was indicted on six counts of unauthorized retention and communication of national defense information in violation of Sections 793(d) and 793(e) of the Espionage Act. When the government subpoenaed Risen to testify about the identity of his sources, Risen moved to quash the subpoena, asserting that he was protected from such compelled testimony by the First Amendment or, in the alternative, by a federal common law reporter's privilege.

- How did the court know that Risen got the information for his book from Sterling?
- Why did Risen fail in his assertion of a First Amendment–based privilege to protect his news sources from disclosure?
- Why was the court unwilling to recognize a common law reporter's privilege?
- How important, in balancing Risen's duty to testify against the public's need to be informed by an independent press, was the fact that the subject matter of the investigation concerned national security?

United States v. Sterling

United States Court of Appeals, Fourth Circuit, July 19, 2013
724 F.3d 482, *cert. denied*, 572 U.S. 1149 (2014)

Traxler, Chief Judge, writing for the court on [the First Amendment and reporter's privilege claims]:

II. THE REPORTER'S PRIVILEGE CLAIM . . .

B. The First Amendment Claim

1.

There is no First Amendment testimonial privilege, absolute or qualified, that protects a reporter from being compelled to testify by the prosecution or the defense in criminal proceedings about criminal conduct that the reporter personally witnessed or participated in, absent a showing of bad faith, harassment, or other such non-legitimate motive, even though the reporter promised confidentiality to his source. In *Branzburg v. Hayes,* 408 U.S. 665 (1972), the Supreme Court "in no uncertain terms rejected the existence of such a privilege." *In re Grand Jury Subpoena, Judith Miller,* 438 F.3d 1141, 1146 (D.C. Cir. 2006).

Like Risen, the *Branzburg* reporters were subpoenaed to testify regarding their personal knowledge of criminal activity. One reporter was subpoenaed to testify regarding his observations of persons synthesizing hashish and smoking marijuana; two others were subpoenaed to testify regarding their observations of suspected criminal activities of the Black Panther Party. All resisted on the ground that they possessed a qualified privilege against being "forced either to appear or to testify before a grand jury or at trial."...

... [T]he Court proceeded to unequivocally reject [their claim]. Noting "the longstanding principle that the public... has a right to every man's evidence, except for those persons protected by a constitutional, common-law, or statutory privilege," *id.* at 688, the Court held as follows:

> Until now the only testimonial privilege for unofficial witnesses that is rooted in the Federal Constitution is the Fifth Amendment privilege against compelled self-incrimination. We are asked to create another by interpreting the First Amendment to grant newsmen a testimonial privilege that other citizens do not enjoy. *This we decline to do.*

Id. at 689-90 (emphasis added).

The First Amendment claim in *Branzburg* was grounded in the same argument offered by Risen — that the absence of such a qualified privilege would chill the future newsgathering abilities of the press, to the detriment of the free flow of information to the public. And the *Branzburg* claim, too, was supported by affidavits and amicus curiae memoranda from journalists claiming that their news sources and news reporting would be adversely impacted if reporters were required to testify about confidential relationships. However, the *Branzburg* Court rejected that rationale as inappropriate in criminal proceedings:

> The preference for anonymity of... confidential informants *involved in actual criminal conduct* is presumably a product of their desire to escape criminal prosecution, [but] this preference, while understandable, is hardly deserving of constitutional protection. It would be frivolous to assert — and no one does in these cases — that the First Amendment, in the interest of securing news or otherwise, confers a license on either the reporter or his news sources to violate valid criminal laws. Although stealing documents or private wiretapping could provide newsworthy information, neither reporter nor source is immune from conviction for such conduct, whatever the impact on the flow of news. Neither is immune, on First Amendment grounds, from testifying against the other, before the grand jury or at a criminal trial.

Id. at 691 (emphasis added)....

Although the Court soundly rejected a First Amendment privilege in criminal proceedings, the Court did observe, in the concluding paragraph of its analysis, that the press would not be wholly without protection:

> [N]ews gathering is not without its First Amendment protections, and grand jury investigations if *instituted or conducted other than in good faith,* would pose wholly different issues for resolution under the First Amendment. *Official harassment of the press undertaken not for purposes of law enforcement but to disrupt a reporter's relationship with his news sources would have no justification.*

Id. at 707-08 (majority opinion) (emphasis added). This is the holding of *Branzburg,* and the Supreme Court has never varied from it....

... The *Branzburg* Court considered the arguments we consider today, balanced the respective interests of the press and the public in newsgathering and in prosecuting crimes, and held that, so long as the subpoena is issued in good faith and is based on a legitimate need of law enforcement, the government need not make any special showing to obtain evidence of criminal conduct from a reporter in a criminal proceeding. The reporter must appear and give testimony just as every other citizen must. We are not at liberty to conclude otherwise....

3.

Like the *Branzburg* reporters, Risen has "direct information ... concerning the commission of serious crimes." *Branzburg,* 408 U.S. at 709. Indeed, he can provide the *only* first-hand account of the commission of a most serious crime indicted by the grand jury — the illegal disclosure of classified, national security information by one who was entrusted by our government to protect national security, but who is charged with having endangered it instead. The subpoena for Risen's testimony was not issued in bad faith or for the purposes of harassment....

... The only constitutional, testimonial privilege that Risen was entitled to invoke was the Fifth Amendment privilege against self-incrimination, but he has been granted immunity from prosecution for his potential exposure to criminal liability....

III. THE COMMON-LAW PRIVILEGE CLAIM

Risen next argues that, even if *Branzburg* prohibits our recognition of a First Amendment privilege, we should recognize a qualified, federal common-law reporter's privilege protecting confidential sources. We decline to do so.

A.

In the course of rejecting the First Amendment claim in *Branzburg,* the Supreme Court also plainly observed that the common law recognized no such testimonial privilege:

> It is thus not surprising that the great weight of authority is that newsmen are not exempt from the normal duty of appearing before a grand jury and answering questions relevant to a criminal investigation. At common law, courts consistently refused to recognize the existence of any privilege authorizing a newsman to refuse to reveal confidential information to a grand jury.

Branzburg, 408 U.S. at 685; *see also Judith Miller,* 438 F.3d at 1154 (Sentelle, J., concurring) (*Branzburg* is "as dispositive of the question of common law privilege as it is of a First Amendment privilege")....

C.

Even if we were at liberty to reconsider the existence of a common-law reporter's privilege under Rule 501, we would decline to do so.

... New or expanded privileges "may be recognized 'only to the very limited extent that permitting a refusal to testify or excluding relevant evidence has a public good transcending the normally predominant principle of utilizing all rational means for ascertaining truth.'" [*United States v. Dunford,* 148 F.3d 385 (4th Cir. 1998),] at 391.

Risen contends that the public and private [interests] recognizing a reporter's privilege "are surely as significant [as the] public interest at stake in patient and psychotherapist communication." But we see several critical distinctions.

1.

First, unlike in the case of the spousal, attorney-client, and psychotherapist-patient privileges that have been recognized, the reporter-source privilege does not share the same relational privacy interests or ultimate goal. The recognized privileges promote the public's interest in full and frank communications between persons in special relationships by protecting the confidentiality of their private communications. A reporter's privilege might also promote free and full discussion between a reporter and his source, but Risen does not seek to protect from public disclosure the "confidential communications" made to him. Risen *published* information conveyed to him by his source or sources. His primary goal is to protect the *identity* of the person or persons who communicated with him because their communications violated federal, criminal laws. . . .

We are admonished that refusal to provide a [common law or] First Amendment reporter's privilege will undermine the freedom of the press to collect and disseminate news. But this is not the lesson history teaches us. As noted previously, the common law recognized no such privilege, and the constitutional argument was not even asserted until 1958. From the beginning of our country the press has operated without constitutional protection for press informants, and the press has flourished. The existing constitutional rules have not been a serious obstacle to either the development or retention of confidential news sources by the press. . . .

[Separate opinions of Chief Judge TRAXLER and of GREGORY, Circuit Judge, concurring and dissenting on various issues, are omitted].

Notes and Questions

1. The Relevance of Risen's Source? The *Sterling* court concluded that Risen had "direct information . . . concerning the commission of serious crimes." The court apparently presumed that the only way Risen could have received classified information to include in his book was to get it from an unauthorized leaker. But might Risen have gotten the information some other way? And should it have mattered whether Risen knew or didn't know that the information was properly classified?

In the end, Sterling was convicted without Risen's testimony, and Risen was not forced to reveal his sources. *See* Matt Apuzzo, *Ex-C.I.A. Officer Sentenced in Leak Case Tied to Times Reporter,* N.Y. Times, May 11, 2015.

2. A First Amendment Reporter's Privilege? In a dissenting opinion in *Sterling,* Judge Gregory wrote,

> The protection of confidential sources is "necessary to ensure a free and vital press, without which an open and democratic society would be impossible to maintain." *Ashcraft v. Conoco, Inc.,* 218 F.3d 282, 287 (4th Cir. 2000). If reporters are compelled to divulge

> their confidential sources, "the free flow of newsworthy information would be restrained and the public's understanding of important issues and events would be hampered in ways inconsistent with a healthy republic." *Id.*
>
> Yet if a free press is a necessary condition of a vibrant democracy, it nevertheless has its limits. "[T]he reporter's privilege . . . is not absolute and will be overcome whenever society's need for the confidential information in question outweighs the intrusion on the reporter's First Amendment interests." *Ashcraft,* 218 F.3d at 287. [724 F.3d at 521 (Gregory, J., dissenting).]

Judge Gregory went on to describe the *Branzburg* precedent for denying the existence of a reporter's privilege as "about as clear as mud." *Id.* at 523. He based his assessment in part on Justice Powell's "enigmatic concurring opinion" in the 1972 Supreme Court case, in which Powell

> emphasized "the limited nature of the Court's holding," and endorsed a balancing test, according to which "if the newsman is called upon to give information bearing only a remote and tenuous relationship to the subject of the investigation," then courts should consider the applicability of the reporter's privilege on a "case-by-case basis" by "the striking of a proper balance between freedom of the press and the obligation of all citizens to give relevant testimony with respect to criminal conduct." [408 U.S.] at 709-10 (Powell, J., concurring). [724 F.3d at 522-523 (Gregory, J., dissenting).]

Several lower courts have, since *Branzburg,* recognized a qualified reporter's privilege. Among these are *United States v. Caporale,* 806 F.2d 1487 (11th Cir. 1986) (applying the reporter's privilege in a criminal case); *United States v. Burke,* 700 F.2d 70 (2d Cir. 1983) (recognizing a qualified privilege in criminal cases); *Zerilli v. Smith,* 656 F.2d 705 (D.C. Cir. 1981) (applying the reporter's privilege in a civil case); and *Silkwood v. Kerr-McGee Corp.,* 563 F.2d 433, 437 (10th Cir. 1977) (asserting that asserted that the existence of a qualified reporter's privilege was "no longer in doubt").

How did the *Sterling* majority know that the government was acting in "good faith," and not to "disrupt a reporter's relationship with his news sources," or more broadly to discourage reliance on inside sources by making an example of Mr. Risen? How did the court balance the reporter's privilege (and interests of the press and public) against the government's interests in a criminal prosecution?

3. A Federal Common Law Reporter's Privilege? Based on its reading of *Branzburg,* the *Sterling* majority emphatically denied the existence of a common law reporter's privilege. Was its ruling on this point consistent with what you know about the functioning of common law in American jurisprudence?

4. A Statutory Reporter's Privilege? Because, in practical terms, government efforts to discover reporters' sources threaten freedom of the press as surely as prior restraints on publication, every state but two (Hawaii and Wyoming) has by judicial decision or statute recognized a reporter's "shield" law to limit such efforts. Congress has repeatedly considered but failed to enact federal shield legislation, however. *See* Kathleen Ann Ruane, *Journalists' Privilege: Overview of the Law and Legislation in the 113th Congress* (Cong. Res. Serv. RL34193), Jan. 19, 2011. For example, the Free Flow of Information Act of 2009, H.R. 985, 111th Cong. (2010), passed by the House but not the Senate, would have created a privilege for any "person who regularly gathers, prepares, collects, photographs, records, writes, edits, reports, or publishes news or information that concerns local, national, or international events or other matters of public interest for dissemination to the public" commercially. Such a person could not have been forced by courts or executive agencies to furnish information that could reasonably have been expected to reveal the identity of a source, unless

> (A) disclosure of the identity of such a source is necessary to prevent, or to identify any perpetrator of, an act of terrorism against the United States or its allies or other significant and specified harm to national security with the objective to prevent such harm;
>
> (B) disclosure of the identity of such a source is necessary to prevent imminent death or significant bodily harm with the objective to prevent such death or harm, respectively; . . .
>
> (D) (i) disclosure of the identity of such a source is essential to identify in a criminal investigation or prosecution a person who without authorization disclosed properly classified information and who at the time of such disclosure had authorized access to such information; and
>
> (ii) such unauthorized disclosure has caused or will cause significant and articulable harm to the national security. [*Id.* §2(a)(3).]

Would this measure have prevented the threat of punishment of James Risen for contempt? Do you think it struck the right balance between national security and the right of the press to keep the public informed? Why do you suppose even so modest a protection for journalists has been so difficult to enact?

Not everyone thinks a shield law is a good idea. *See, e.g.*, William H. Freivogel, *Publishing National Security Secrets: The Case for "Benign Indeterminacy,"* 3 J. Nat'l Security L. & Pol'y 95, 97 (2009) (arguing that "the press — and by extension the public — is better served by a continuation of the state of uncertainty than by brightline rules"). Can you fashion criteria for a statutory reporter's privilege that would strike the right balance between security and democracy?

CENSORSHIP: SUMMARY OF BASIC PRINCIPLES

- A vibrant democracy depends on a well-informed electorate, and the media play a critical role in providing the needed information.
- Once government information has gotten into the hands of parties outside the government, even classified information received via an unauthorized leak, any government effort to prevent its publication bears a "heavy presumption" against its validity under the First Amendment.
- Precisely what is required to overcome that presumption is unclear, however, except perhaps in a case involving an immediate, obvious threat to national security or human life.
- Increasing reliance on the Internet and the proliferation of news outlets around the world have vastly complicated efforts to stop the publication of leaked data.

- Criminal liability of the media and journalists for publishing leaked or classified information generally is unclear and untested.
- Court decisions vary on the availability of federal testimonial privilege to protect reporters from the compelled disclosure of their sources. That availability may depend on the potential danger to national security, a balance between freedom of the press and the obligation of all citizens to testify about criminal matters, or perhaps other factors.

Appendix

Constitution of the United States

We the People of the United States, in Order to form a more perfect Union, establish Justice, insure domestic Tranquility, provide for the common defence, promote the general Welfare, and secure the Blessings of Liberty to ourselves and our Posterity, do ordain and establish this Constitution for the United States of America.

Article I

Section 1. All legislative Powers herein granted shall be vested in a Congress of the United States, which shall consist of a Senate and House of Representatives.

Section 2. The House of Representatives shall be composed of Members chosen every second Year by the People of the several States, and the Electors in each State shall have the Qualifications requisite for Electors of the most numerous Branch of the State Legislature....

The House of Representatives shall chuse their Speaker and other Officers; and shall have the sole Power of Impeachment.

Section 3. The Senate of the United States shall be composed of two Senators from each State, [chosen by the Legislature thereof,][1] for six Years; and each Senator shall have one Vote....

The Senate shall have the sole Power to try all Impeachments. When sitting for that Purpose, they shall be on Oath or Affirmation. When the President of the United States is tried, the Chief Justice shall preside: And no Person shall be convicted without the Concurrence of two thirds of the Members present.

Judgment in Cases of Impeachment shall not extend further than to removal from Office, and disqualification to hold and enjoy any Office of honor, Trust or Profit under the United States: but the Party convicted shall nevertheless be liable and subject to Indictment, Trial, Judgment and Punishment, according to Law.

---

1. Changed by the Seventeenth Amendment to read "elected by the people thereof."

Section 4. The Times, Places and Manner of holding Elections for Senators and Representatives, shall be prescribed in each State by the Legislature thereof; but the Congress may at any time by Law make or alter such Regulations, except as to the Places of chusing Senators.

The Congress shall assemble at least once in every Year, and such Meeting shall [be on the first Monday in December,][2] unless they shall by Law appoint a different Day.

Section 5.. . . Each House shall keep a Journal of its Proceedings, and from time to time publish the same, excepting such Parts as may in their Judgment require Secrecy; and the Yeas and Nays of the Members of either House on any question shall, at the Desire of one fifth of those Present, be entered on the Journal. . . .

Section 6. The Senators and Representatives shall receive a Compensation for their Services, to be ascertained by Law, and paid out of the Treasury of the United States. They shall in all Cases, except Treason, Felony and Breach of the Peace, be privileged from Arrest during their Attendance at the Session of their respective Houses, and in going to and returning from the same; and for any Speech or Debate in either House, they shall not be questioned in any other Place.

. . . [N]o Person holding any Office under the United States, shall be a Member of either House during his Continuance in Office.

Section 7. All Bills for raising Revenue shall originate in the House of Representatives; but the Senate may propose or concur with amendments as on other Bills.

Every Bill which shall have passed the House of Representatives and the Senate, shall, before it becomes a Law, be presented to the President of the United States; If he approve he shall sign it, but if not he shall return it, with his Objections to that House in which it shall have originated, who shall enter the Objections at large on their Journal, and proceed to reconsider it. If after such Reconsideration two thirds of that House shall agree to pass the Bill, it shall be sent, together with the Objections, to the other House, by which it shall likewise be reconsidered, and if approved by two thirds of that House, it shall become a Law. . . . If any Bill shall not be returned by the President within ten Days (Sundays excepted) after it shall have been presented to him, the Same shall be a Law, in like Manner as if he had signed it, unless the Congress by their Adjournment prevent its Return, in which Case it shall not be a Law.

Every Order, Resolution, or Vote to which the Concurrence of the Senate and House of Representatives may be necessary (except on a question of Adjournment) shall be presented to the President of the United States; and before the Same shall take Effect, shall be approved by him, or being disapproved by him, shall be repassed by two thirds of the Senate and House of Representatives, according to the Rules and Limitations prescribed in the Case of a Bill.

Section 8. [1] The Congress shall have Power To lay and collect Taxes, Duties, Imposts and Excises, to pay the Debts and provide for the common Defence and

---

2. Changed by section 2 of the Twentieth Amendment to read "begin at noon on the 3d day of January."

general Welfare of the United States; but all Duties, Imposts and Excises shall be uniform throughout the United States;

[2] To borrow Money on the credit of the United States;

[3] To regulate Commerce with foreign Nations, and among the several States, and with the Indian Tribes;

[4] To establish an uniform Rule of Naturalization . . . ;

[9] To constitute Tribunals inferior to the supreme Court;

[10] To define and punish Piracies and Felonies committed on the high Seas, and Offences against the Law of Nations;

[11] To declare War, grant Letters of Marque and Reprisal, and make Rules concerning Captures on Land and Water;

[12] To raise and support Armies, but no Appropriation of Money to that Use shall be for a longer Term than two Years;

[13] To provide and maintain a Navy;

[14] To make Rules for the Government and Regulation of the land and naval Forces;

[15] To provide for calling forth the Militia to execute the Laws of the Union, suppress Insurrections and repel Invasions;

[16] To provide for organizing, arming, and disciplining, the Militia, and for governing such Part of them as may be employed in the Service of the United States, reserving to the States respectively, the Appointment of the Officers, and the Authority of training the Militia according to the discipline prescribed by Congress; . . .

[18] To make all Laws which shall be necessary and proper for carrying into Execution the foregoing Powers, and all other Powers vested by this Constitution in the Government of the United States, or in any Department or Officer thereof.

Section 9. . . . [2] The Privilege of the Writ of Habeas Corpus shall not be suspended, unless when in Cases of Rebellion or Invasion the public Safety may require it. . . .

[3] No Bill of Attainder or ex post facto Law shall be passed. . . .

[7] No Money shall be drawn from the Treasury, but in Consequence of Appropriations made by Law; and a regular Statement and Account of the Receipts and Expenditures of all public Money shall be published from time to time.

[8] No Title of Nobility shall be granted by the United States: And no Person holding any Office of Profit or Trust under them, shall, without the Consent of the Congress, accept of any present, Emolument, Office, or Title, of any kind whatever, from any King, Prince, or foreign State.

Section 10. [1] No State shall enter into any Treaty, Alliance, or Confederation; grant Letters of Marque and Reprisal; coin Money; emit Bills of Credit; make any Thing but gold and silver Coin a Tender in Payment of Debts; pass any Bill of Attainder, ex post facto Law, or Law impairing the Obligation of Contracts, or grant any Title of Nobility. . . .

[3] No State shall, without the Consent of Congress, lay any Duty of Tonnage, keep Troops, or Ships of War in time of Peace, enter into any Agreement or Compact with another State, or with a foreign Power, or engage in War, unless actually invaded, or in such imminent Danger as will not admit of delay.

Article II

Section 1. The executive Power shall be vested in a President of the United States of America. He shall hold his Office during the Term of four Years, and, together with the Vice President, chosen for the same Term, be elected, as follows . . .

Before he enter on the Execution of his Office, he shall take the following Oath or Affirmation: — "I do solemnly swear (or affirm) that I will faithfully execute the Office of President of the United States, and will to the best of my Ability, preserve, protect and defend the Constitution of the United States."

Section 2. The President shall be Commander in Chief of the Army and Navy of the United States, and of the Militia of the several States, when called into the actual Service of the United States; he may require the Opinion, in writing, of the principal Officer in each of the executive Departments, upon any Subject relating to the Duties of their respective Offices, and he shall have Power to grant Reprieves and Pardons for Offences against the United States, except in Cases of Impeachment.

He shall have Power, by and with the Advice and Consent of the Senate, to make Treaties, provided two thirds of the Senators present concur; and he shall nominate, and by and with the Advice and Consent of the Senate, shall appoint Ambassadors, other public Ministers and Consuls, Judges of the supreme Court, and all other Officers of the United States, whose Appointments are not herein otherwise provided for, and which shall be established by Law: but the Congress may by Law vest the Appointment of such inferior Officers, as they think proper, in the President alone, in the Courts of Law, or in the Heads of Departments. . . .

Section 3. He shall from time to time give to the Congress Information of the State of the Union, and recommend to their Consideration such Measures as he shall judge necessary and expedient; he may, on extraordinary Occasions, convene both Houses, or either of them, and in Case of Disagreement between them, with Respect to the Time of Adjournment, he may adjourn them to such Time as he shall think proper; he shall receive Ambassadors and other public Ministers; he shall take Care that the Laws be faithfully executed, and shall Commission all the Officers of the United States.

Section 4. The President, Vice President and all civil Officers of the United States, shall be removed from Office on Impeachment for, and Conviction of, Treason, Bribery, or other high Crimes and Misdemeanors.

Article III

Section 1. The judicial Power of the United States, shall be vested in one supreme Court, and in such inferior Courts as the Congress may from time to time ordain and establish. The Judges, both of the supreme and inferior Courts, shall hold their Offices during good Behaviour, and shall, at stated Times, receive for their Services, a Compensation, which shall not be diminished during their Continuance in Office.

Section 2. The judicial Power shall extend to all Cases, in Law and Equity, arising under this Constitution, the Laws of the United States, and Treaties made, or which shall be made, under their Authority; — to all Cases affecting Ambassadors, other public Ministers and Consuls; — to all Cases of admiralty and maritime Jurisdiction; — to Controversies to which the United States shall be a Party; — to Controversies between two or more States; — [between a State and Citizens of another State; —] between Citizens of different States, — between Citizens of the same State claiming Lands under Grants of different States, [and between a State, or the Citizens thereof, and foreign States, Citizens or Subjects.][3]

In all Cases affecting Ambassadors, other public Ministers and Consuls, and those in which a State shall be Party, the supreme Court shall have original Jurisdiction. In all the other Cases before mentioned, the supreme Court shall have appellate Jurisdiction, both as to Law and Fact, with such Exceptions, and under such Regulations as the Congress shall make....

Section 3. Treason against the United States, shall consist only in levying War against them, or in adhering to their Enemies, giving them Aid and Comfort. No Person shall be convicted of Treason unless on the Testimony of two Witnesses to the same overt Act, or on Confession in open Court.

The Congress shall have Power to declare the Punishment of Treason, but no Attainder of Treason shall work Corruption of Blood, or Forfeiture except during the Life of the Person attainted.

Article IV . . .

Section 4. The United States shall guarantee to every State in this Union a Republican Form of Government, and shall protect each of them against Invasion; and on Application of the Legislature, or of the Executive (when the Legislature cannot be convened) against domestic Violence....

Article VI

... This Constitution, and the Laws of the United States which shall be made in Pursuance thereof; and all Treaties made, or which shall be made, under the Authority of the United States, shall be the supreme Law of the Land; and the Judges in every State shall be bound thereby, any Thing in the Constitution or Laws of any State to the Contrary notwithstanding.

The Senators and Representatives before mentioned, and the Members of the several State Legislatures, and all executive and judicial Officers, both of the United States and of the several States, shall be bound by Oath or Affirmation, to support this Constitution; . . .

---

3. The bracketed material in this section is changed by the Eleventh Amendment.

AMENDMENTS TO THE CONSTITUTION OF THE UNITED STATES OF AMERICA

Amendment I

Congress shall make no law respecting an establishment of religion, or prohibiting the free exercise thereof; or abridging the freedom of speech, or of the press, or the right of the people peaceably to assemble, and to petition the Government for a redress of grievances.

Amendment II

A well regulated Militia, being necessary to the security of a free State, the right of the people to keep and bear Arms, shall not be infringed.

Amendment III

No Soldier shall, in time of peace be quartered in any house, without the consent of the Owner, nor in time of war, but in a manner to be prescribed by law.

Amendment IV

The right of the people to be secure in their persons, houses, papers, and effects, against unreasonable searches and seizures, shall not be violated, and no Warrants shall issue, but upon probable cause, supported by Oath or affirmation, and particularly describing the place to be searched, and the persons or things to be seized.

Amendment V

No person shall be held to answer for a capital, or otherwise infamous crime, unless on a presentment or indictment of a Grand Jury, except in cases arising in the land or naval forces, or in the Militia, when in actual service in time of War or public danger; nor shall any person be subject for the same offence to be twice put in jeopardy of life or limb, nor shall be compelled in any criminal case to be a witness against himself, nor be deprived of life, liberty, or property, without due process of law; nor shall private property be taken for public use without just compensation.

Amendment VI

In all criminal prosecutions, the accused shall enjoy the right to a speedy and public trial, by an impartial jury of the State and district wherein the crime shall have been committed; which district shall have been previously ascertained by law, and to be informed of the nature and cause of the accusation; to be confronted with the witnesses against him; to have compulsory process for obtaining witnesses in his favor, and to have the assistance of counsel for his defence....

Amendment VIII

Excessive bail shall not be required, nor excessive fines imposed, nor cruel and unusual punishments inflicted.

Amendment IX

The enumeration in the Constitution of certain rights shall not be construed to deny or disparage others retained by the people.

Amendment X

The powers not delegated to the United States by the Constitution, nor prohibited by it to the States, are reserved to the States respectively, or to the people....

Amendment XIV

Section 1. All persons born or naturalized in the United States and subject to the jurisdiction thereof, are citizens of the United States and of the State wherein they reside. No State shall make or enforce any law which shall abridge the privileges or immunities of citizens of the United States; nor shall any State deprive any person of life, liberty, or property, without due process of law; nor deny to any person within its jurisdiction the equal protection of the laws....

TABLE OF CASES

Principal cases are set in italics. Cases cited in the authors' text, notes, and questions are set in Roman type.

INDEX